Street by Street

GREATER LONDON

Ist edition May 2001

© Automobile Association Developments Limited 2001

Published by AA Publishing (a trading name of Automobile Association Developments Limited, whose registered office is Norfolk House, Priestley Road, Basingstoke, Hampshire, RG24 9NY. Registered number 1878835).

Mapping produced by the Cartographic Department of The Automobile Association.

IA CIP Catalogue record for this book is available from the British Library.

Printed by Jarrold and Sons Ltd, Norwich.

The contents of this atlas are believed to be correct at the time of the latest revision. However, the publishers cannot be held responsible for loss occasioned to any person acting or refraining from action as a result of any material in this atlas, nor for any errors, omissions or changes in such material. The publishers would welcome information to correct any errors or omissions and to keep this atlas up to date. Please write to Publishing, The Automobile Association, Fanum House, Basing View, Basingstoke, Hampshire, RG21 4EA.

Ref: GS040

Key to map pages — ii-iii

Key to map symbols — iv-1

Enlarged scale pages — 2-19

Street by Street — 20-285

Index – town & villages — 286-288

Index – streets — 289-385

Index – featured places — 386-410

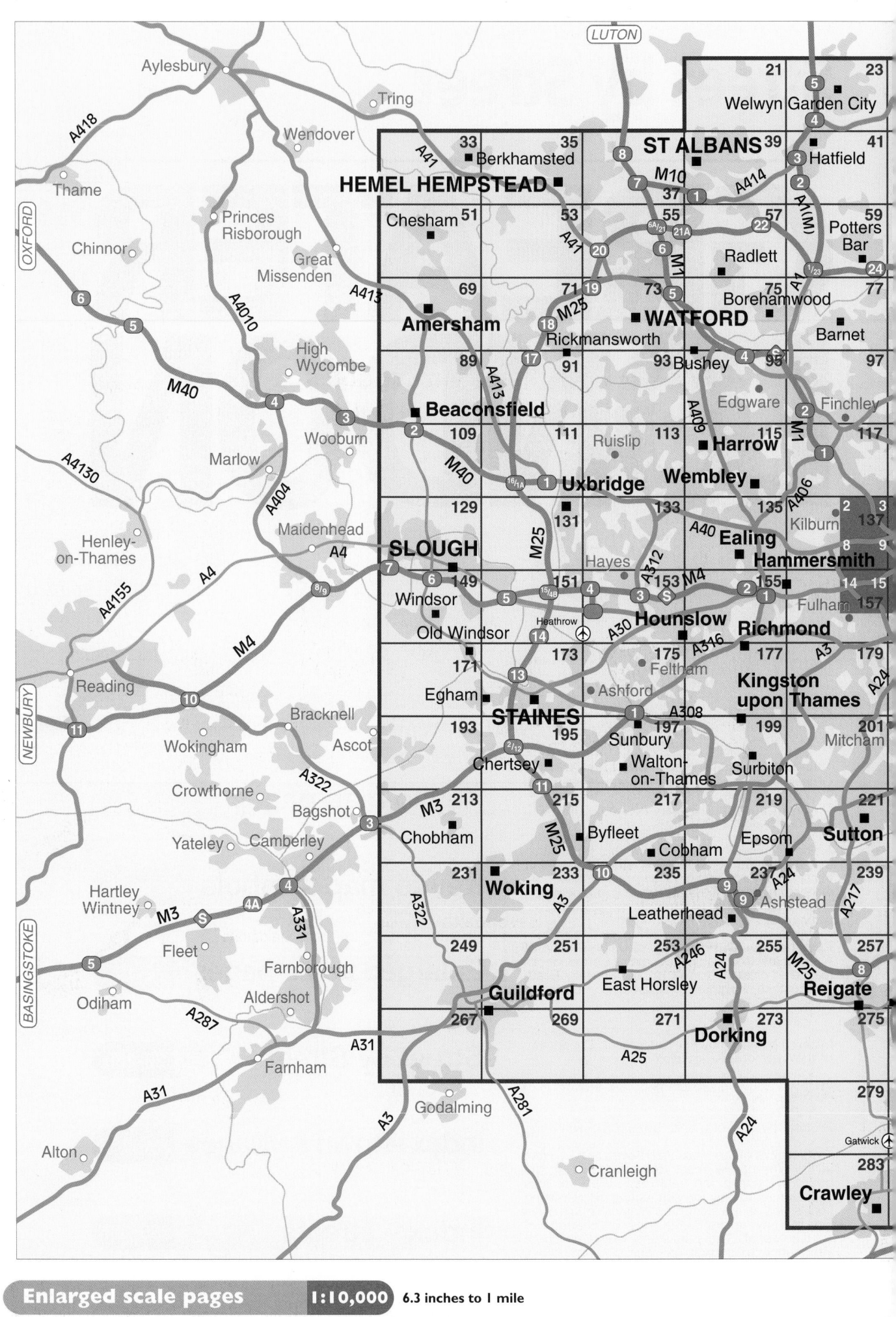

LUTON

Aylesbury

A418

Tring

Wendover

OXFORD

Thame

A41

33   Berkhamsted   35

HEMEL HEMPSTEAD

8   ST ALBANS   39

M10   7   A414   3   Hatfield

Chinnor

Princes
Risborough

Chesham   51   53   55   57   Potters   59
A41   6A/21   21A   22   Bar

Great
Missenden

A413   20   6   M1   Radlett

6   High
Wycombe

M40   69   71   19   73   Borehamwood   75   77
M25   A413   18   WATFORD   4   95

5   A4010   Amersham   Rickmansworth   Edgware   Barnet

4   89   17   91   93   Bushey   97

3   Wooburn   A409   Finchley

A4130   Marlow   2   109   111   Ruislip   113   Harrow   115   M1   117

Henley-
on-Thames   A404   Maidenhead   M40   16/1A   1   Uxbridge   Wembley   A406

A4155   A4   129   M25   133   Ealing   135   137

SLOUGH   131   A40   Kilburn

A4   7   149   6   151   4   153 M4   155   14   15
5   15/4B   3   S   2   1   157

M4   Windsor   Hayes   A312   Fulham

Reading   Old Windsor   14   Heathrow   A30   Hounslow   Richmond   A3

NEWBURY   10   13   171   173   175   Feltham   177   179
Egham   Ashford   A316   Kingston
upon Thames   A24

Bracknell   193   195   1   A308   199   201
Ascot   STAINES   197   Mitcham

11   Wokingham   A322   2/12   Sunbury   Surbiton

Crowthorne   Chertsey   Walton-
on-Thames   Epsom

Bagshot   3   11   M3   213   215   217   219   221
Yateley   Camberley   M25   Byfleet   Cobham   Sutton

A331   4   231   233   10   235   237   A24   239
M3   S   Woking   A3   9   Ashstead   A217

Hartley
Wintney   4A   Leatherhead   9

Fleet   A322   249   251   253   255   257
A246   A24   M25   8

5   Odiham   Farnborough   East Horsley   Reigate

Aldershot   Guildford   267   269   271   273   Dorking   275
A287   A25

Farnham   A31   279

A31   Godalming   A281   A24   Gatwick

Alton   A3   283

Cranleigh   Crawley

0   1/4   miles   1/2   3/4

0   1/4   1/2   kilometres   3/4   1   1 1/4

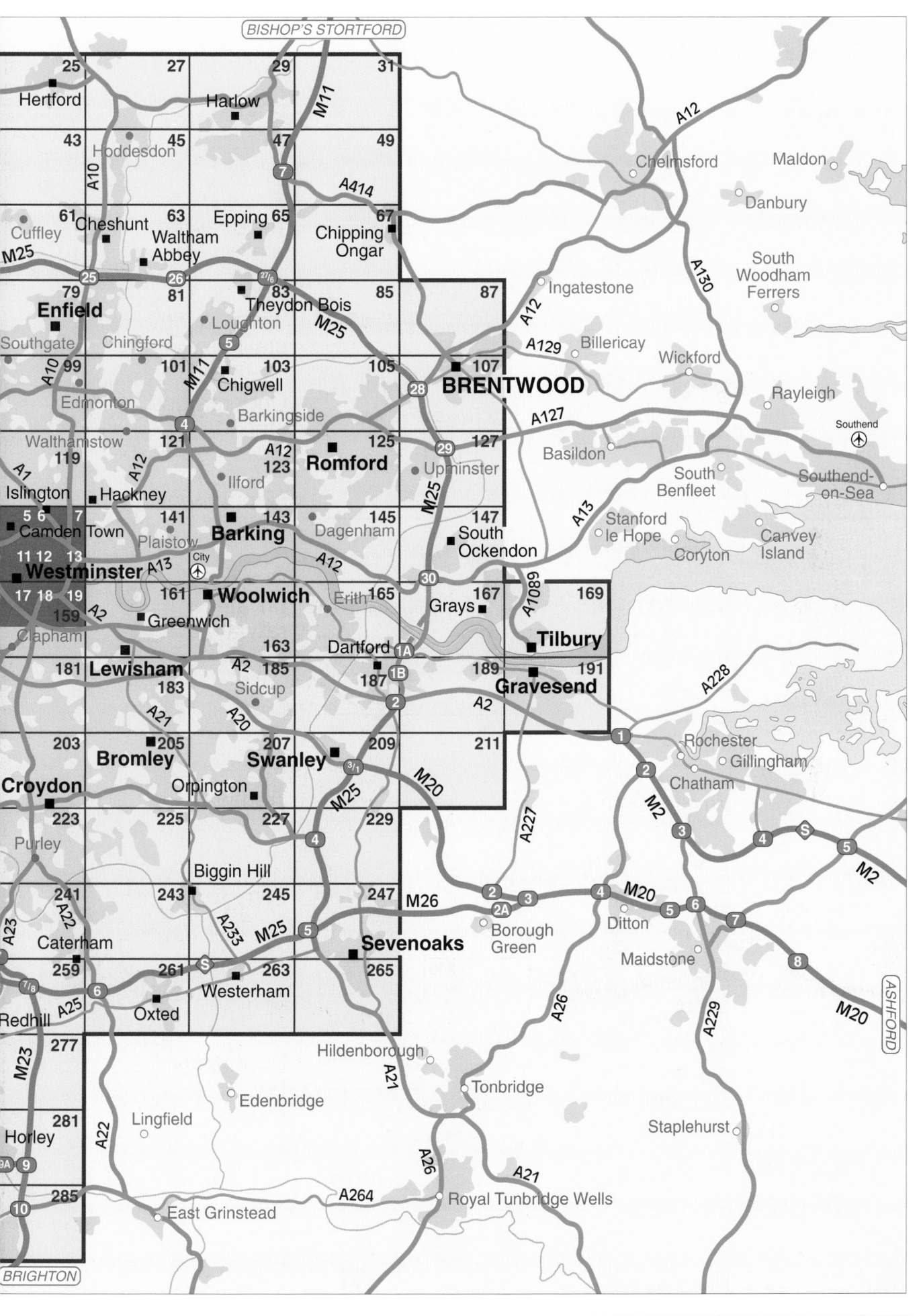

BISHOP'S STORTFORD

25 Hertford
27
29 Harlow
31
M11

A12

43
Hoddesdon
A10
45
47
7
49
A414

Chelmsford
Maldon
Danbury

A130

61 Cheshunt
Cuffley
63 Waltham Abbey
65 Epping
67 Chipping Ongar
M25

South Woodham Ferrers

25
26
27/6
83 Theydon Bois
85
87 Ingatestone
A12

79 Enfield
Southgate
81
Loughton
M25
A12
A129 Billericay
Wickford
Rayleigh

99 Edmonton
A10
101 Chigwell
M11
103
Barkingside
105
28 BRENTWOOD
107
A127
Basildon
Southend

119 Islington
A1
Walthamstow
121
A12
123 Romford
Ilford
125
Upminster
29
127
M25
South Benfleet
A13
Stanford le Hope
Coryton
Canvey Island
Southend-on-Sea

5 6 7 Camden Town
11 12 13 Westminster
A13
Plaistow
141 Barking
Dagenham
143
145
147 South Ockendon
30
A1089

17 18 19
159
A2
Greenwich
161 Woolwich
Erith
165
Grays
167
169
Tilbury

Clapham
163
Dartford
1A
187
1B
189
191 Gravesend
A228

181 Lewisham
183 Sidcup
A21
185
A2
2
A2
1
Rochester
Gillingham
Chatham
2
M2

203 Bromley
Croydon
205 Orpington
A20
207 Swanley
M25
209
3/1
M20
211
A227
3
4
S
5
M2

223 Purley
225
227
4
229
M26
2
2A
3
4
M20
Ditton
5
6
7
8
M20

241 Caterham
A22
243 Biggin Hill
A233
245
M25
247
Borough Green
Maidstone
A26
A229

259 Redhill
7/8
6
261 S
Oxted
263 Westerham
5
265 Sevenoaks
Hildenborough
A26
A21
Staplehurst
A229

M23
277
A22
Lingfield
Edenbridge
A21 Tonbridge

281 Horley
9A 9
285 East Grinstead
A264
A26
Royal Tunbridge Wells

10
BRIGHTON

3.2 inches to 1 mile   **Scale of main map pages** 1:20,000

0   1/2   miles   1   1 1/2
0   1/2   1   kilometres   1 1/2   2   2 1/2

Junction 9	Motorway & junction		P+🚐	Park & Ride
Services	Motorway service area		🚌	Bus/coach station
	Primary road single/dual carriageway			Railway & main railway station
Services	Primary road service area			Railway & minor railway station
	A road single/dual carriageway		⊖	Underground station
	B road single/dual carriageway		⊖	Light railway & station
	Other road single/dual carriageway		++++++++++++	Preserved private railway
	Restricted road		LC	Level crossing
	Private road		•—•—•—•—	Tramway
← ←	One way street		------------	Ferry route
	Pedestrian street		··············	Airport runway
=========	Track/ footpath		-·-·-·-·-·-	Boundaries- borough/ district
	Road under construction		ᚇᚇᚇᚇᚇᚇ	Mounds
[------]	Road tunnel		**93**	Page continuation 1:20,000
P	Parking		**7**	Page continuation to enlarged scale 1:10,000

River/canal
lake, pier

Toilet with
disabled facilities

Aqueduct,
lock, weir

Petrol station

465
Winter Hill

Peak (with
height in
metres)

PH

Public house

Beach

PO

Post Office

Coniferous
woodland

Public library

Broadleaved
woodland

i

Tourist
Information
Centre

Mixed
woodland

Castle

Park

Historic house/
building

Cemetery

Wakehurst
Place NT

National Trust
property

Built-up
area

M

Museum/
art gallery

Featured building

✝

Church/chapel

City wall

Country park

A&E

Accient &
Emergency
hospital

Theatre/
performing arts

Toilet

Cinema

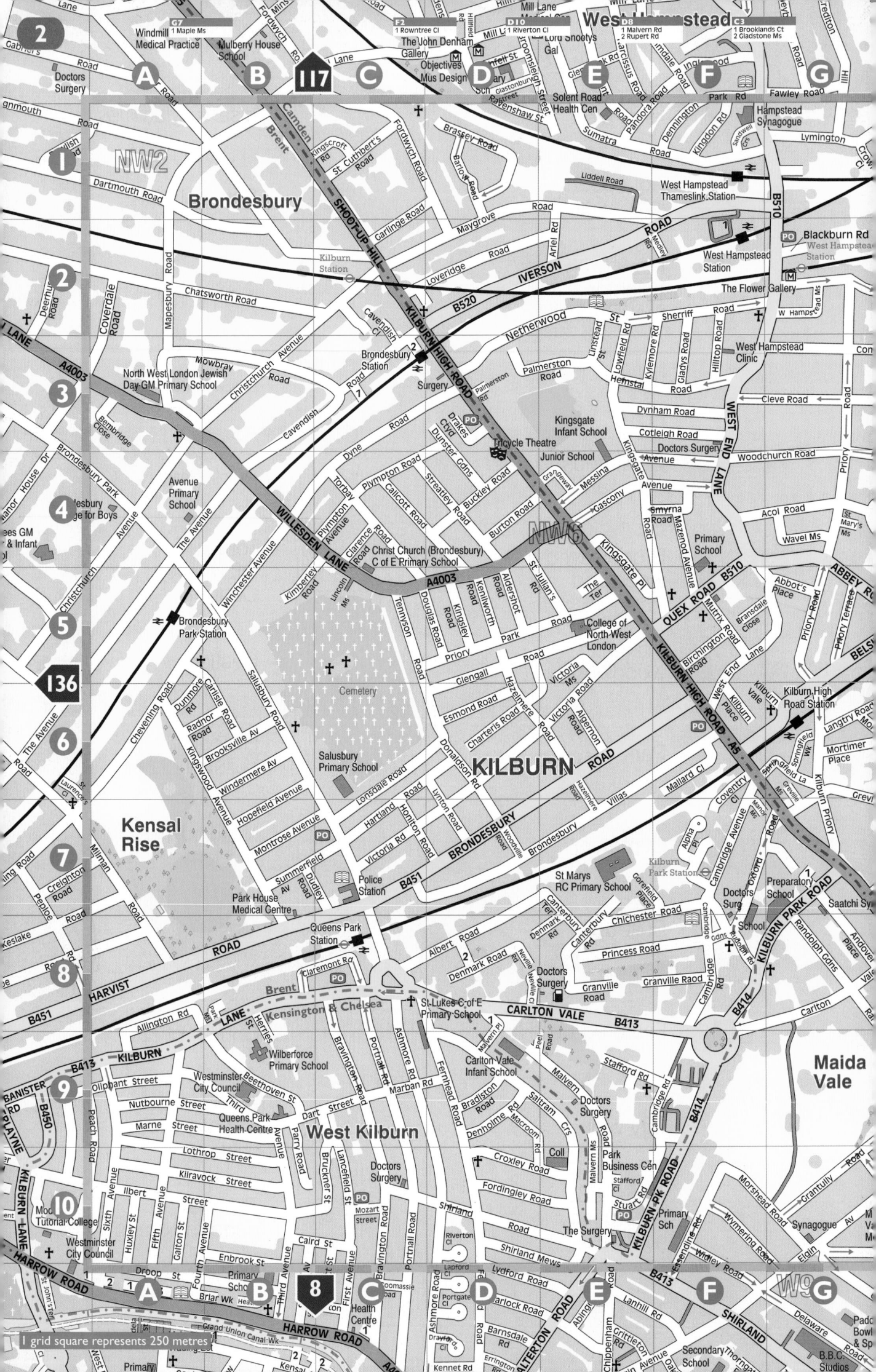

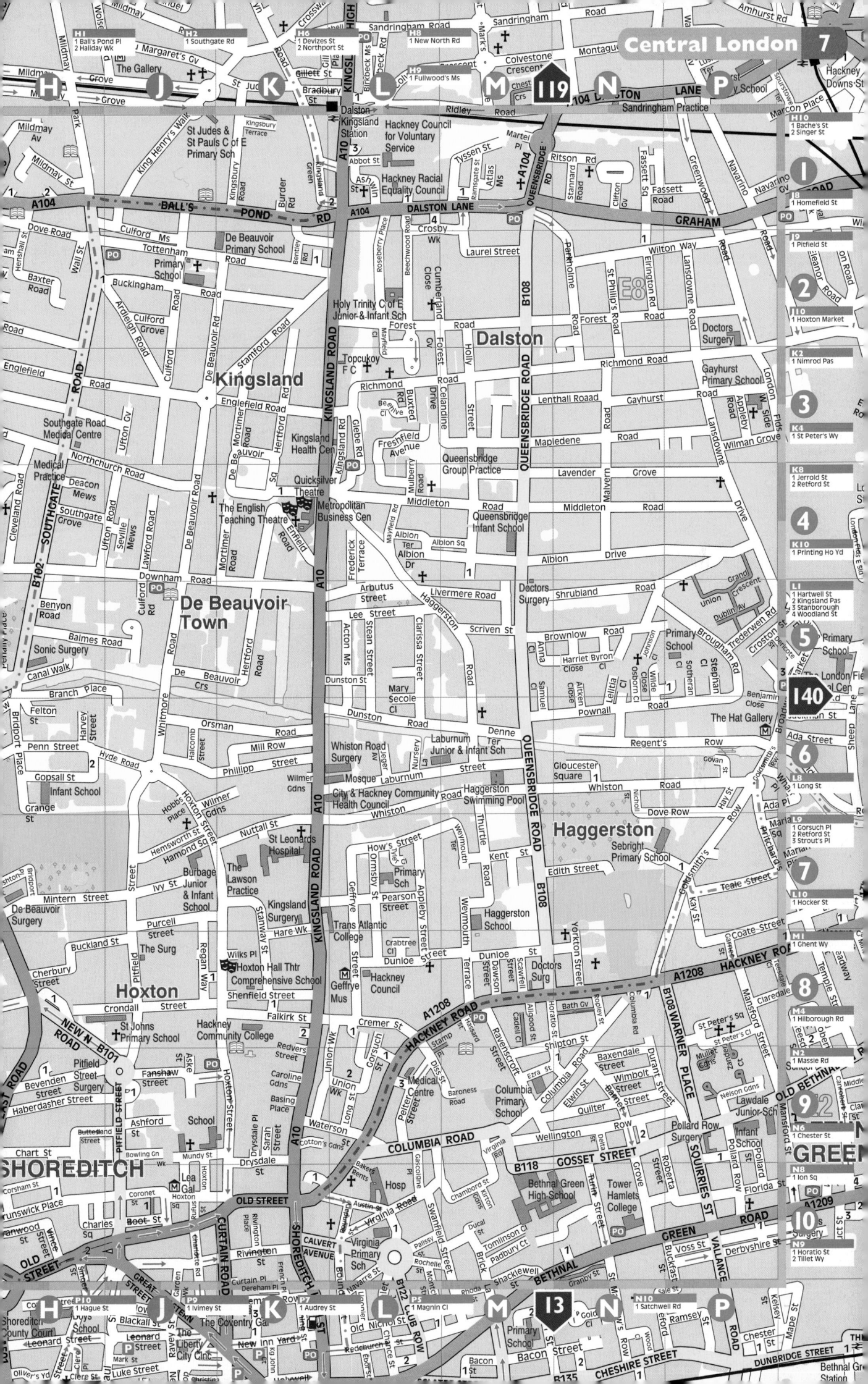

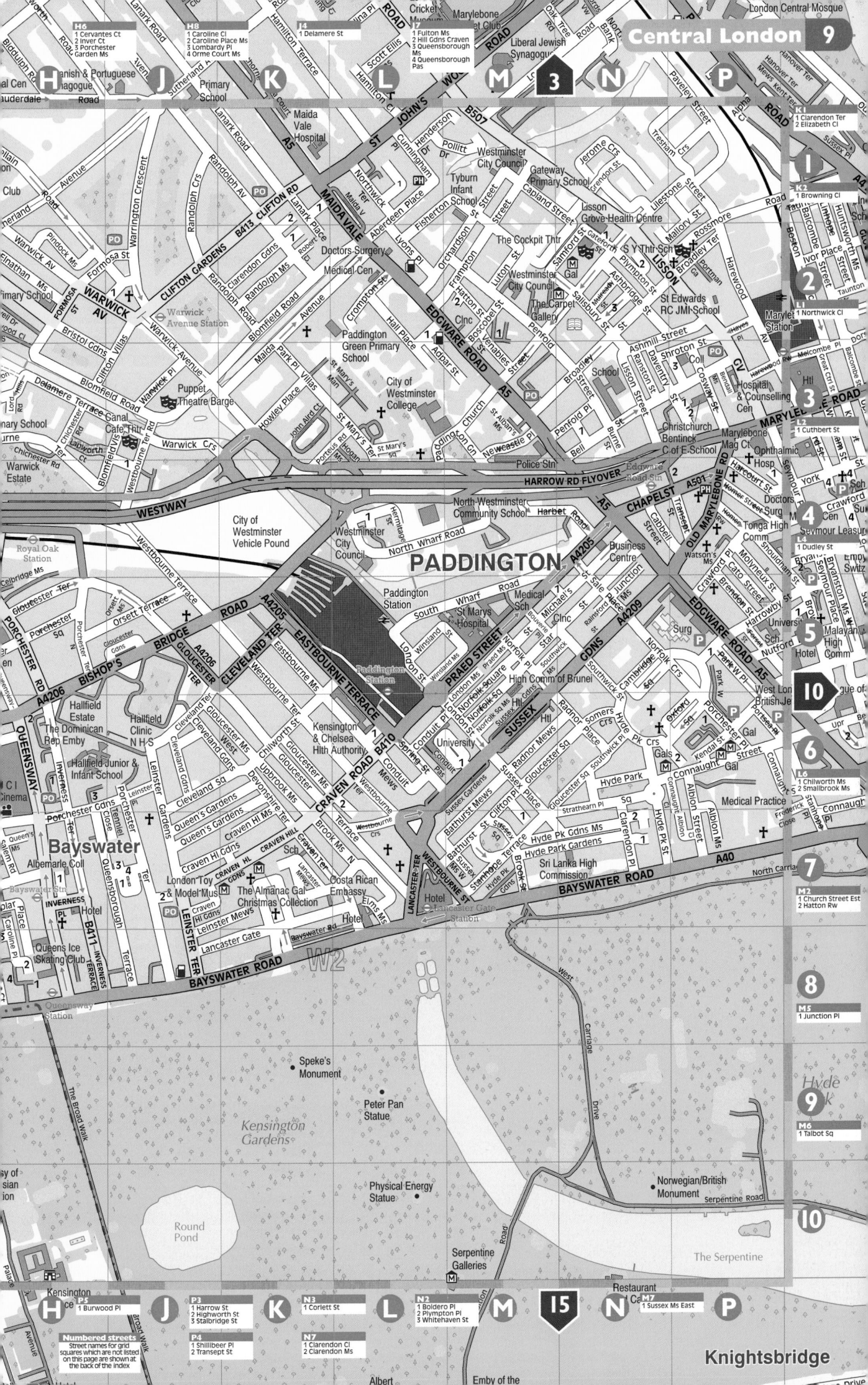

Knightsbridge

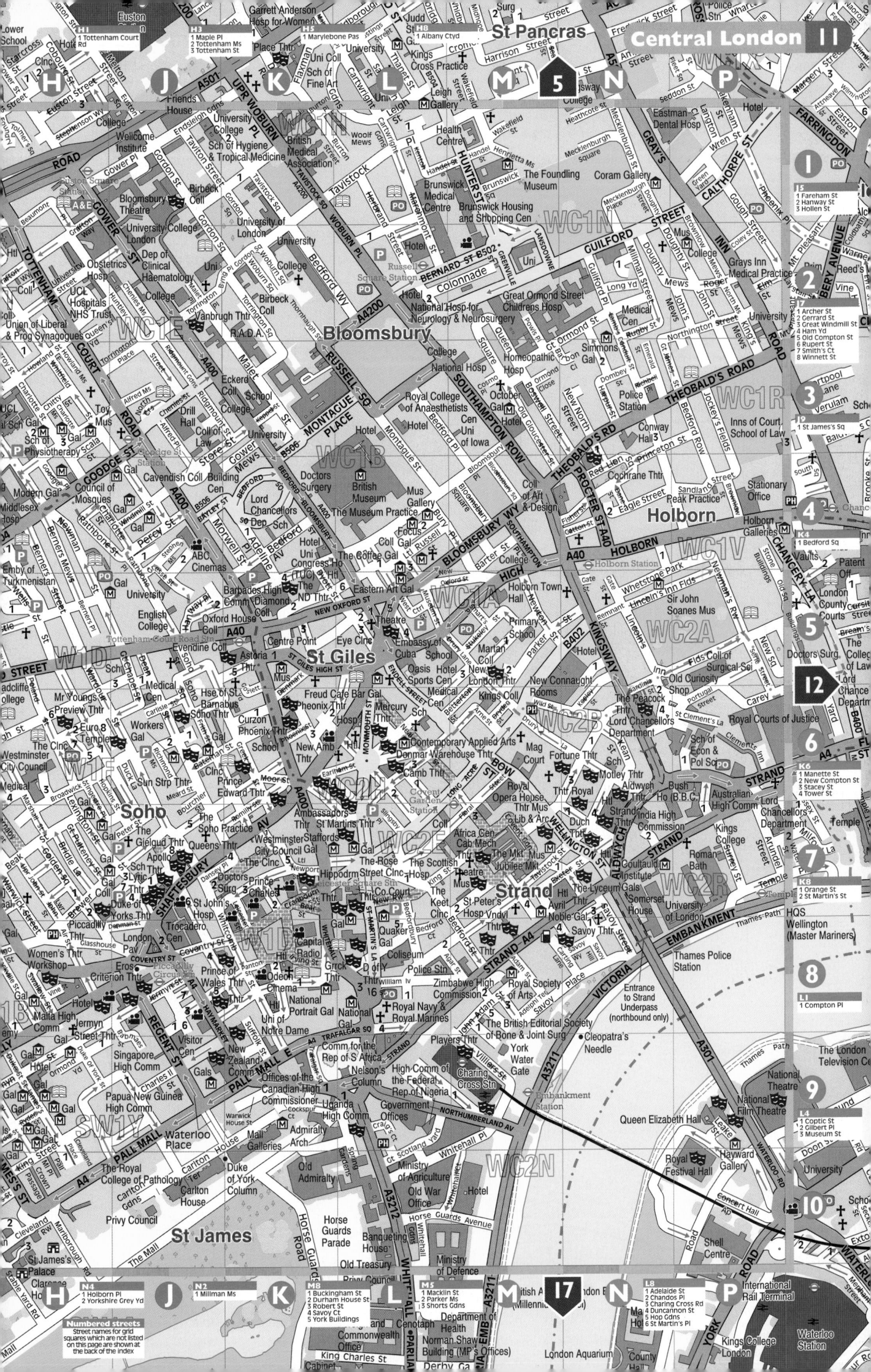

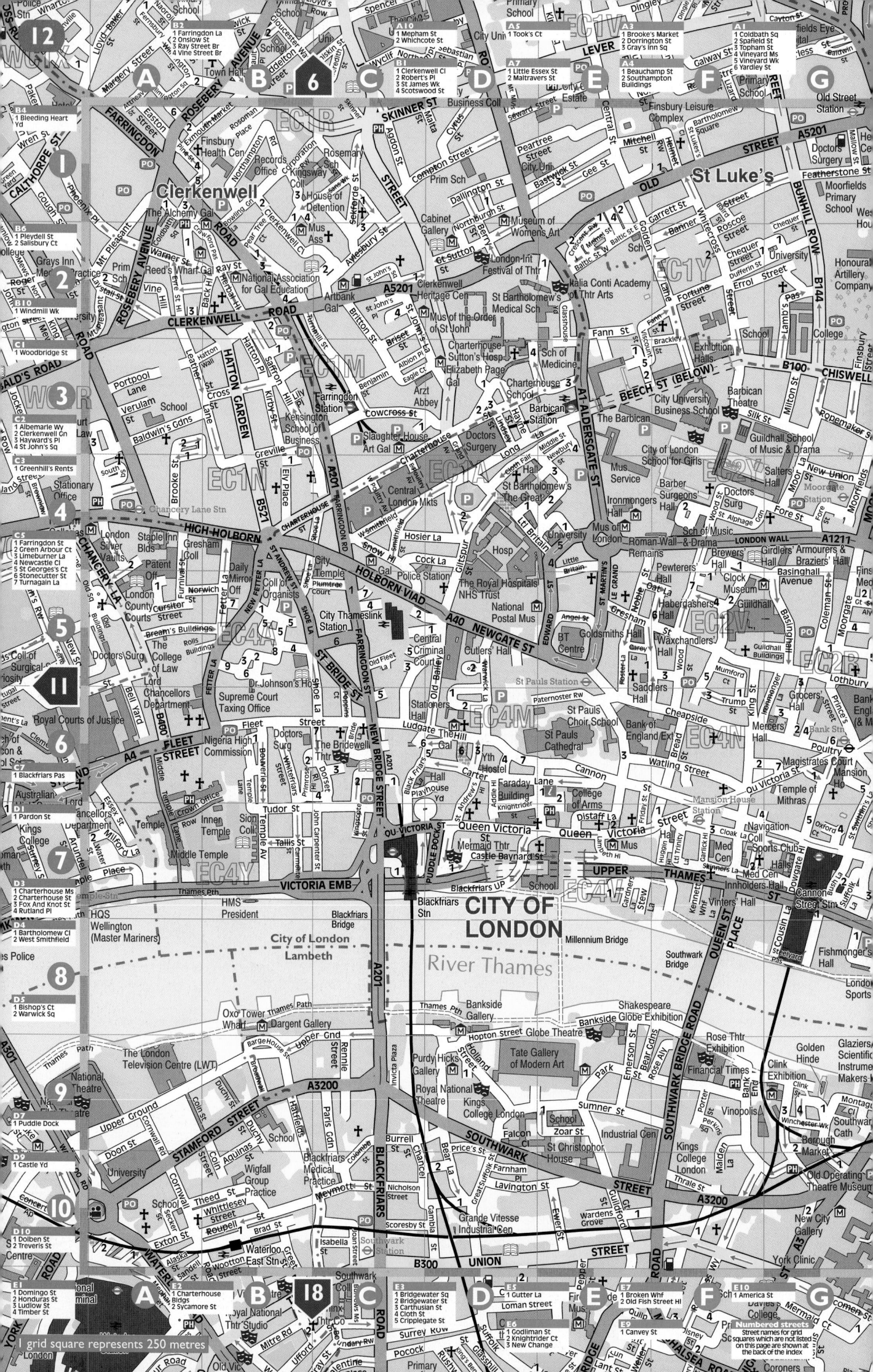

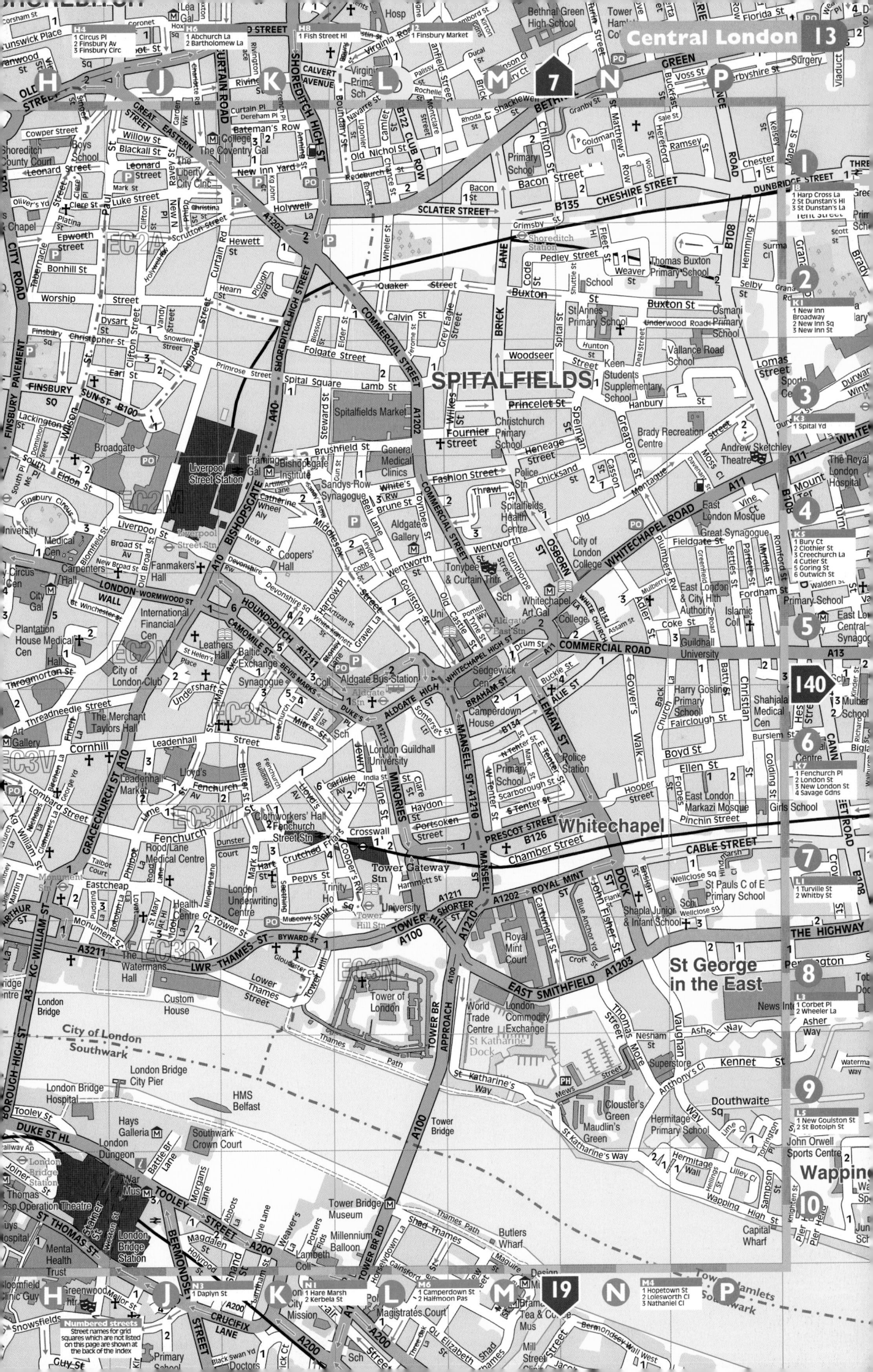

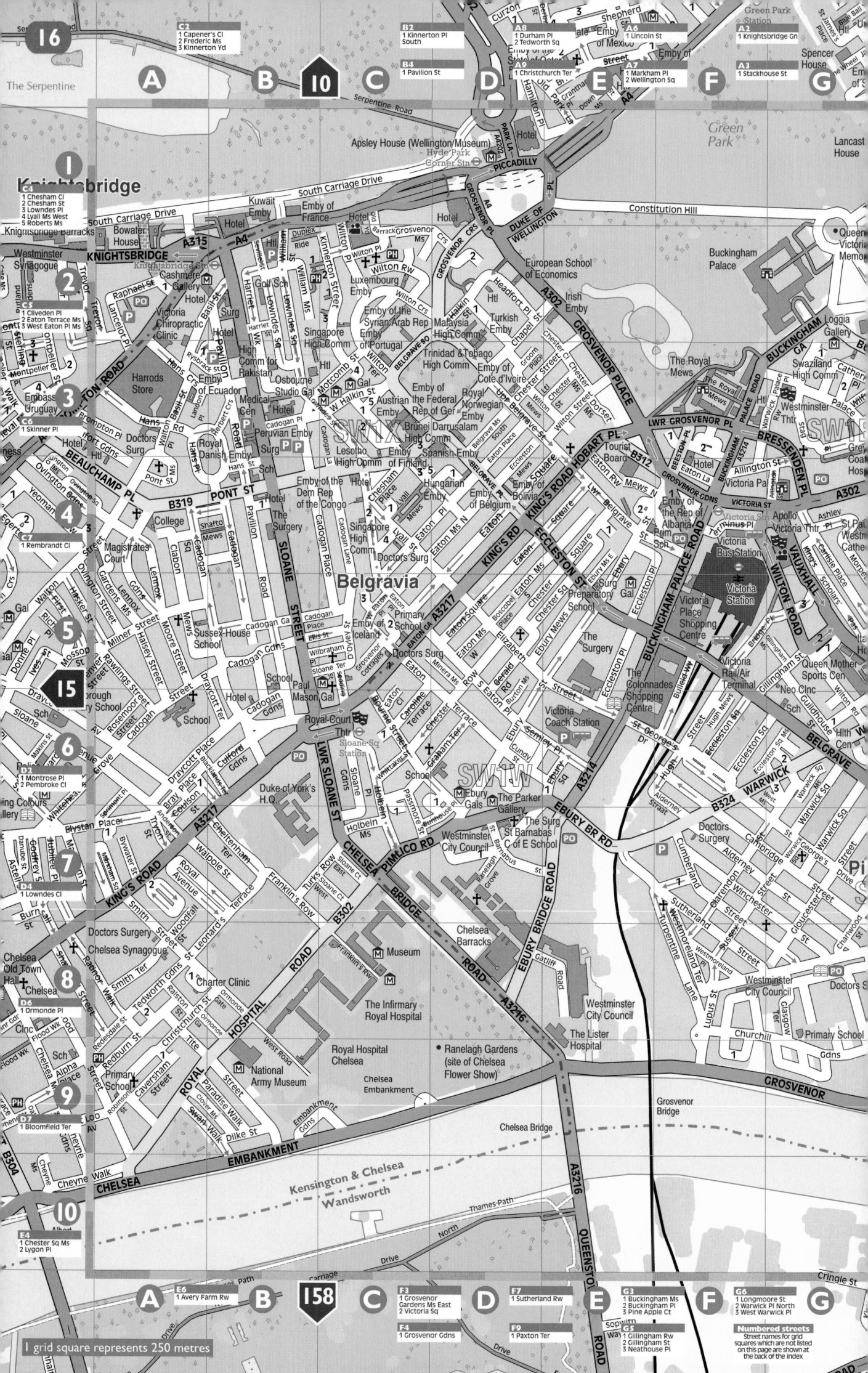

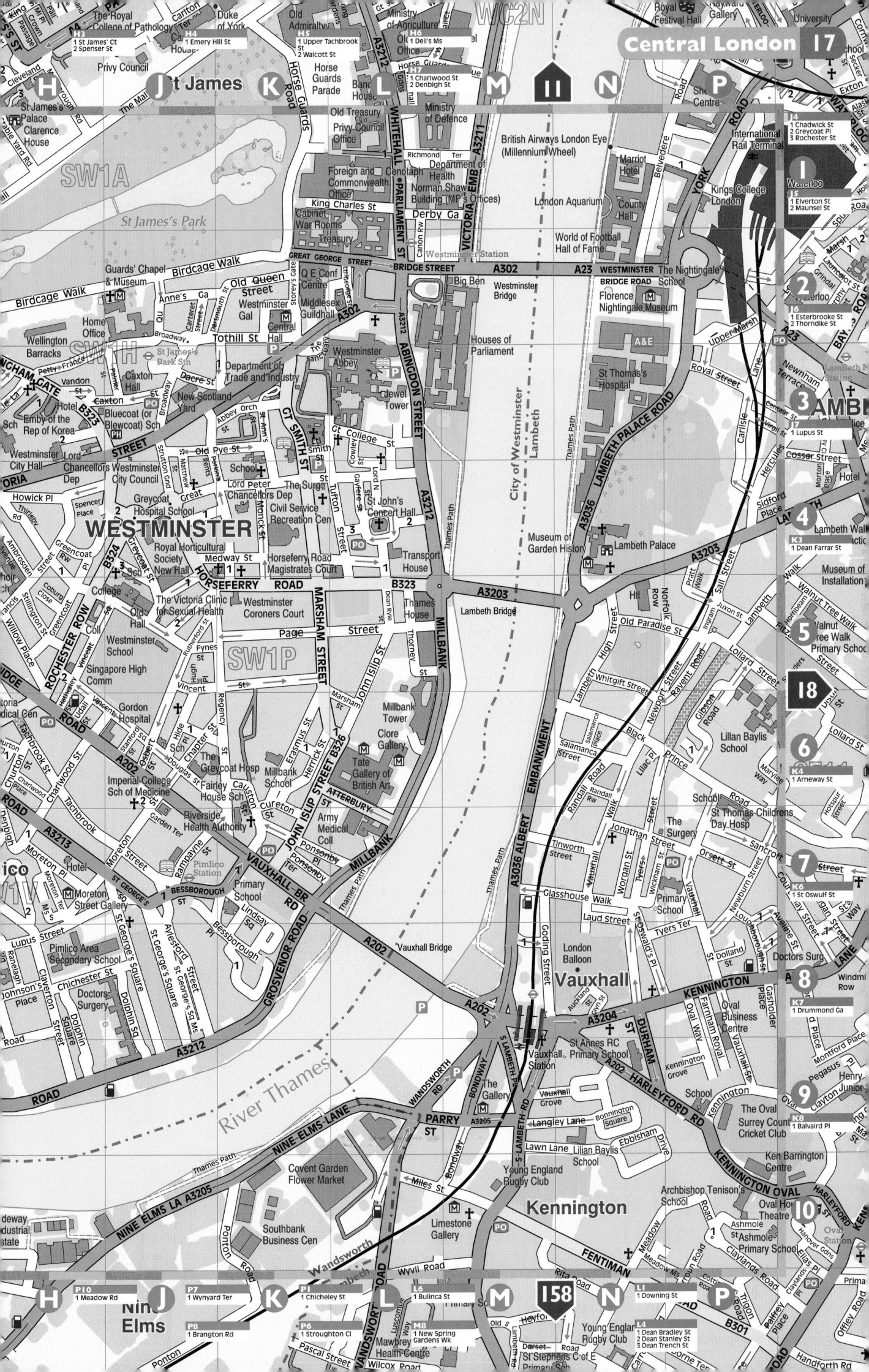

H9
1 Spencer Pl

H10
1 St Leonard's Ct

J2
1 Abbot John Ms
2 Canons Fld
3 East Mt

J3
1 Granary Cl
2 St Helen's Cl

K4
1 Housden Cl
2 Smallwood Cl

Delaport

H J K L M N P

I
2
3 aterend
4
5
22
6
7
8
9
10

Codicote Road

Lea Valley Walk

Sheepcote
Lane

Lea Valley Walk

River Lea or Lee

Lea Valley Walk

Waterend Lane

Cromer-
Hyde

Rose Lane

B653

Garden Ct

CODICOTE ROAD

CORY-WRIGHT

WAY

B653

MARFORD ROAD

Marford Road

B653

Marford Road

mpstead

Ash Gv

Kingfisher Cl

HIGH ST

STATION RD

Mount Rd

Meads La

East La
Doctors Surg

St Thomas Pl

Brockett Vw

Necton Road

Bury Green

High Meads

Church St

St Helen's School

Four Limes

Garrard Way

Offas Way

Tudor Rd

Battleview

Marford Road

Chalkdell Farm

Brewhouse Hill

Lattimore Rd

Barton Rd

WICK

THE HILL

Maltings Dr

Butterfield

Caesars Road

Saxon

Nurseries Rd

Conquerors Hl

Road

Beech Hyde Lane

Hill Fort

mwell

High Ash Rd

Lane

Road

Middle & Infant School

Wright
Dyke Rd

Davy's Cl

Vale Court

Beech

Dyke Lane

Beech Hyde Farm

Marford Road

Nomansland

B651

Nomansland Common

Nomansland Farm

Ferrers Lane

Coleman Green Lane

Tower

Darblay Cl

Hill Lane

Coleman Green

Hammonds Farm

Hammonds Lane

Symondshyde Farm

Symondshyde Great Wood

Hammonds La

Langley

B651

Grove

Snatchill

Lyndon Md

Sandridge JMI School

Woodcockhill

AL4

Fairfold's Farm

Coopers Green Lane

Sandridge

Jersey La

St Leonards Crs

House Lane

Sutton's Farm

Astwick

University of Hertfordshire

Froghter Way

H J K L M 39 N P

Cooper's Green

Wendover Cl

Pirton Cl

Cromwell Close

Nashe's Farm

House Lane

Green Lane

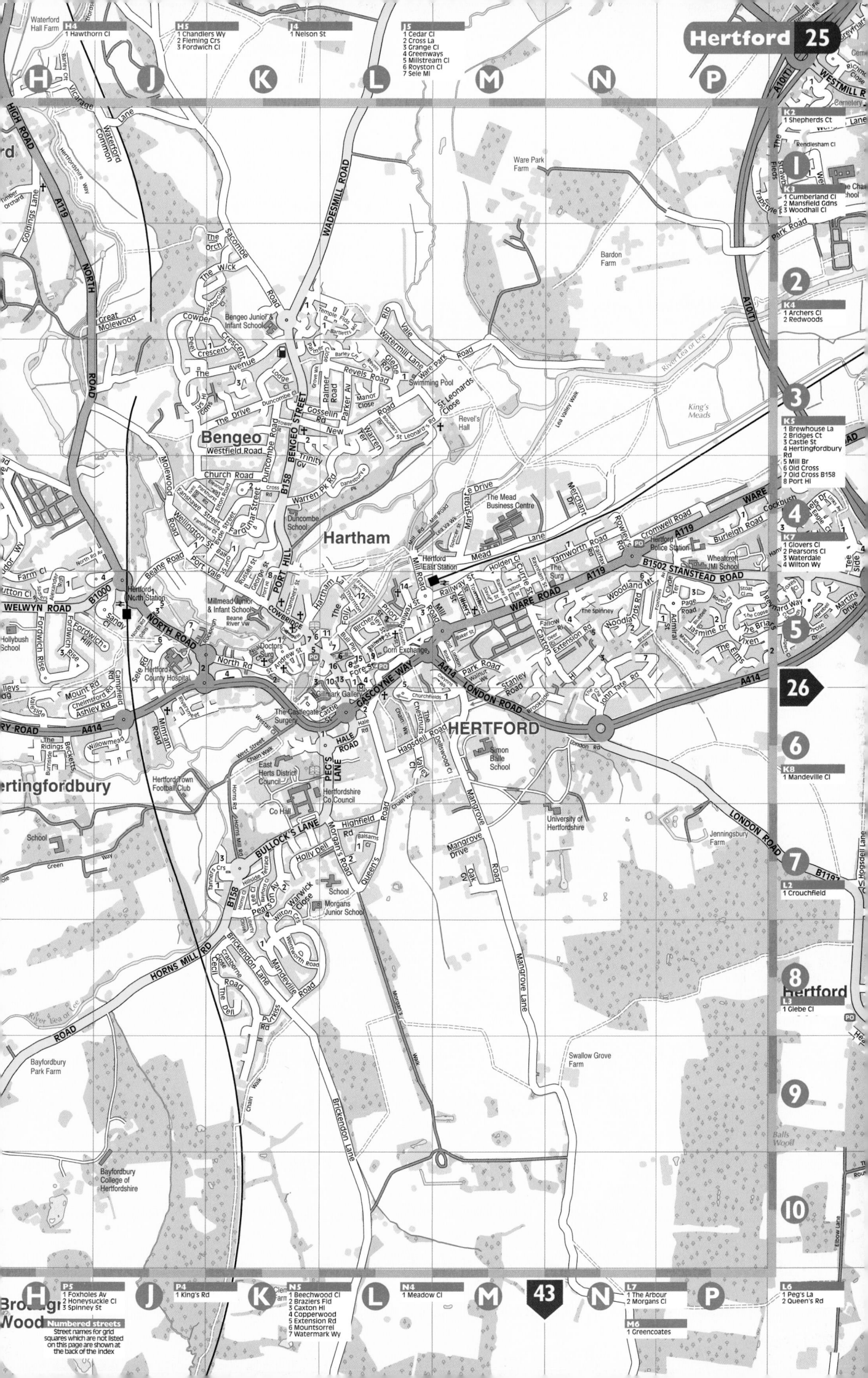

Hertford 25

1 grid square represents 500 metres

A   B   C   D   E   F   G

E3
1 Water End Rd

B5
1 Paxton Rd

A6
1 Cedar Wy

A5
1 Cambridge Ter
2 Ivy House La
3 Little Bridge Rd
4 Manor St

A4
1 Hill Ct

Frithsden Gardens

1

2

3

4

5

33

6

7

8

9

10

Frithsden

Vineyard

Nettleden Road

Potten End

Berkhamsted Golf Club

Vicarage Road

Vicarage Gdns

Homefield

Browns Spring

Water End Road

Olivers

The Back

School

The Front

The Common

PO

Common Gdns

The Common

Rambling Wy

Rambling Way

Hempstead Lane

Haresfoot Senior School

Little Heath

Little Heath Farm

Fields End

Castle Hill Av

Castle (Remains)

Berkhamsted Station Club

Lower Kings Road

Gutteridge Farm

Bullbeggars Lane

Little Heath Lane

Pouchen End Lane

Mill Street

Service Practice

Berkhamsted Sch

STREET

Manor Street

PO

Old Mill Gdns

Bank Mill

Ellesmere Road

George Street

Ivy House Lane

Meadway

LONDON ROAD

Bank

Mill Lane

Bankmill Bridge

River Bulbourne

Little Heath Lane

Pouchen End

Curtis Way

Holly Dr

Hillside Gdns

Hall Park

Hall Park Hill

Hall Park Gate

Fieldway

Upper Hall Park

Gardener Rd

Broadway Farm

Pix Farm Lane

Ashlyns School

The Thomas Coram Middle School

Ashlyns Hall

Long Green

Swing Gate Lane

A41(T)

A41(T)

Sandpit Green

Bottom Farm

Lower Farm

Bourne Gutter

Sugar

Sharpes Lane

Grand Union Canal Wk

Hotel

LONDON ROAD   A4251

Bourne End La

Upper Bourne End Lane

Bourne End

Stoney La

Vale Farm

Golf Course

A41(T)

Westbrook Hay Preparatory School

Westbrook H

Upper Bourne End Lane

B4505

BOX

A   B   52   C   D   E   F   G

Spencer's

A4
1 Nicholas Wy
2 Tannsmore Cl
3 Triton Wy

A3
1 Callisto Ct
2 Ganymede Pl
3 Pentland

A2
1 Cwmbran Ct
2 Kilbride Ct
3 Peterlee Ct
4 Sherwood Pl
5 Welwyn Ct

A1
1 Clyde Sq
2 Great Palmers
3 Mersey Pl
4 Robin Hood Meadow

A B C D E F G

A5
1 Coral Gdns
2 Hammer La
3 Rice Cl

A6
1 The Queen's Sq
2 Sawyers Wy
3 Sheepcote Rd

A7
1 St Albans Rd
2 Wadley Cl

A8
1 Bennetts End Cl

A9
1 Sunrise Crs

B1
Roa 1 The Dart
2 Denham Cl
3 Frome Sq

B4
1 Sainfoin End
2 Winds End Cl

B5
1 Saracens Head
2 Southernwood Cl

B7
1 Grange Cl
2 Haddon Cl
3 Mariner Wy
4 Marston Cl
5 Sandmere Cl

B9
1 Hill Common

C5
1 Duxons Turn
2 Wellswood Cl

C7
1 Tile Kiln Cl

C8
1 Grasmere Cl
2 St Michaels Av
3 Stornoway
4 Thorncroft

Cupid Green

Redbourn Road

Highfield

HP2

Adeyfield

HEMEL HEMPSTEAD

Leverstock Green

Westwick Row

Bennetts End

Pimlico

Nash

D5
1 Hales Park Cl
2 Romany Ct
3 Welkin Gn
4 Wood End Cl

D6
1 Chartridge Wy
2 Pelham Ct

D7
1 Church Rd
2 Coniston Cl
3 Cumberlow Pl
4 Gravely Ct
5 Hartsbourne Wy
6 Ryecroft Cl

E6
1 St Margarets Wy

E7
1 Badger Cft
2 Trinity Ms

E8
1 Woodfield Gdns

D4
1 Grovelands Retail Park

A B C D E F G

Numbered streets
Street names for grid squares which are not listed on this page are shown on the back of the index

1 grid square represents 500 metres

H J K L M **31** N P

Cobbler's
Pieces

1

Blackcat

Envilles
Farm

2

Robins
Acre

Watery Lane

✝ **Little
Laver**

Red House

High Laver
Grange

America
Farm

Little Laver Road

3

L
F

**High
Laver**

✝

Poppin
House

Moreton
Mill

Newhouse

4

Greens

5

Start
Farm

Mill Lane

Crispins

Ashlings
Cottages

Embleys
Farm

6

Maltings
Hill

Scotts
Farm

Fyfield Road

Little Laver Road

Wind Hill

Maltings Hill

Nether
Hall

Penny
Farm

Harlow Road

The Hoppitt

Moreton C of E
Primary School

PO

✝

Church Road

Gould Close

Moreton Road

Bridge End

Moreton

Upper
Hall

Cripsey Brook

Moreton Road

7

Harriets
Farm

**Pedlars
End**

Pedlars

Bovinger
Lodge

New
Farm

Newhouse
Lane

Gainsthorpe Road

Bridge Road

Moreton Road

Cross Lees
Farm

8

Wood
Farm

Bundish
Hall

9

Moreton Road

Stony Lane

Hobban's
Farm

Bobbingworth Mill Road

Bobbingworth

✝

Stony Lane

er

A414
EPPING ROAD

**Lower
Bobbingworth
Green**

Blake
Hall

10
Shelley
✝ Church Lane

ONGAR

ROAD B184

Newgate Street

1 Maynard Pl

A B 42 C D New Park Road E F G

Newgate Street Village

1

Justice Hill

2 Great Wood Grimes Brook Tolmers

Carbone Hill Chain Walk

3 THE RIDGEWAY The Ridgeway The Ridgeway Home Wood Brookside Crescent Homewood Avenue
B157 Bradgate Farm Close Wood Vw Hill Leys Thruan Lane

Well Wood Hanyards Lane Hill Rise Tolmers Road CUFFL

4 Orchard Close Foxes Lane Starling Lane The Meadway B157 EAST RIDGEWAY Acorn Lane Oak Lane Sopers Road

Vineyards Road Cranfield Crescent Bacons Drive PLOUGH HILL Health Centre Cuffley Station

5 B156 JUDGE'S HILL Northaw C of E School STATION ROAD

59

6 Church Lane Vicarage Close Northaw NORTHAW Park Road Kingswell Ride Kingsway Cuffley School

PO ROAD WEST B156 Colesdale

Park Farm Wells Farm

7 Hook Wood Colesdale Farm Chain Walk Chain Walk

Cattlegate Road

8 Barvin Park Woodgate Avenue Oakmead Drive Cattlegate Farm

9 Coopers Lane Road

Hertfordshire County Enfield

10 New Cottage Farm Holly Hill Farm Crews Hill Station Cattlegate Road Crews Hill

Crews Hill Golf Club

A B 78 C D E F G

A1005 WAY

H8
1 Hereward Cl

H9
1 Church St
2 Darby Dr
3 Greenyard
4 Mile Cl

H10
1 Fountain Pl
2 King George Rd
3 Milton Ct
4 Paradise Rd
5 Rue De St Lawrence
6 Silver St

J9
1 Margaret Cl
2 Pasfield
3 St Pauls Wy
4 Takeley Cl

J8
1 Willinghall Cl

I10
1 Cypress Cl
2 Joyce Ct
3 Larsen Dr

K8
1 Brookside
2 Galleyhill Rd
3 Old Oaks
4 Smeaton Cl

K9
1 The Granaries
2 Windsor Wd

K10
1 Downlands
2 Patmore Rd

L9
1 Poplar Shaw

M9
1 Bromefield Ct
2 Stanford Ct
3 Sudicamps Ct
4 Tillingham Ct
5 Webster Cl
6 Wormley Ct
7 Wormyngford Ct
8 Wrangley Ct

M10
1 Hawk Cl
2 Lamplighters Cl

Nazeing Long Green

Nazeing Gate

Claverhambury

Aimes Green

EN9

Holyfield

WALTHAM ABBEY

Upshire

Wood Green

Nazeing Parish Council

Harold's Park Farm

Maynards Farm

Fernhall Farm

Deerpark Wood

Breach Barns

Wadlies Park

Pick Hill Farm

64

45

81

HOLYFIELD ROAD B194

CROOKED MILE B194

MARSH HILL B194

Waltham Road

Claverhambury Road

Galleyhill Road

HONEY LANE A121

FARM HILL ROAD A121

SEWARDSTONE ROAD A121

WOODRIDE

Cobbinsend Road

HONEY LANE A121

M25

Shelley

N2
1 Betjeman Wy
2 Kimpton's Cl

N3
1 Aukingford Gdns
2 Aukingford Gn

N5
1 Kilnfield

N6
1 Parkland Wy

P5
1 Jacksons Cl

Lower
Jobbingworth
Green

H J K L M **49** N P

Church Lane

Bobbingworth Mill

A414 EPPING ROAD

B184

Blake Hall Road

Water End Farm

Bilsdens Farm

Perrills

A414

Lane

Penson's

EPPING ROAD

Brookfields

Moreton Road

Shortlands Avenue

Cripsey Avenue

Acres Avenue

St Peter's Avenue

Shelley Close

Coles Close

FYFIELD ROAD

Ongar War Memorial Hospital

Clare Mews

Ongar Leisure Centre

Queensway

Springfield Close

Shelley County Primary School

Essex County Council

High Road Ongar (Chelm

CHELMSFORD ROAD

Greensted House

Penson's Lane

Greensted Road

Road

Greensted Green

Epping Forest Railway

Mark's Avenue

Barron's Close

Bowes Drive

Great Lawn

Great Stony School

Mayflower Way

St Johns

Churchill Close

Onslow Gardens

Cemetery

Love Lane

Ongar & District Sports Club

Ongar Parish Council

Three Fo

Essex Way

Essex Way

Greensted

Log Church

Essex Way

A128

Ongar Health Centre

Banson's Lane

Shakletons

Peter's Way

Way

Fairbank Close

Millbank Avenue

Glebe Road

Fairfield Road

Rodney Road

Greensted Road

Turner's

PO

Castle Street

HIGH STREET

Stanley

Place

CHIPPING ONGAR

Lodge Farm

The Borough

Stanley

Green

COPPERS HILL A128

The Elms

Cloverley Road

Long Fields

Clatterford End

Toot Hill Road

Mutton Row

Chipping Ongar Primary School

Woodland Way

Landview Gardens

St James' Avenue

Head Walk

Kettlebury Way

Sandon Place

Marden Ash

Marden Ash House

STANFORD RIVERS ROAD

Hallsfo

Stondon

BRENTW

ROAD

Coleman's Farm

Clark's Farm

Three Forests Way

Gray's Farm

Stewarts

A113

Great Colemans

Langford Bridge

Langford Bridge Farm

School Road

Mutton Row

Three Forests Way

Three Forests Way

Stanford Rivers

Old Rectory Road

Church Road

Bridge Farm

ROMFORD ROAD

A113

Littlebury Hall

Park Wood

The Old Rectory

LONDON ROAD

Field Colemans

Little End

Kelvedon Hall

H J K L M **85** N P

Three Forests Way

Murrells Farm

Traceys Farm

River Roding

Germains

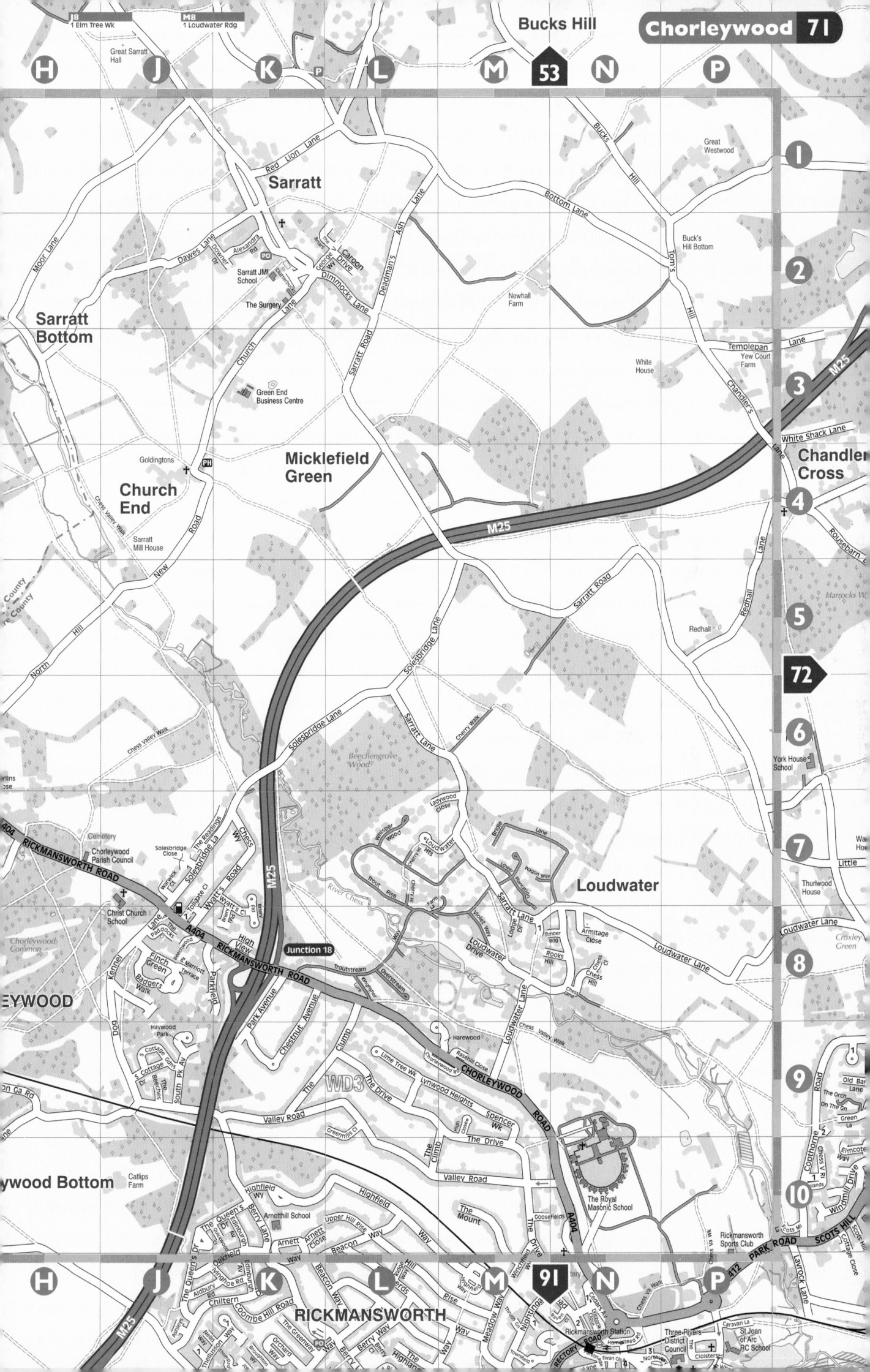

84

Grid references and street index

78

A New Cottage Farm
B9 1 Balmore Crs
60 B
A10 1 Mansfield Av
A9 1 Daneland 2 Heddon Rd
D
A8 1 Cheriton Cl
E
A7 1 Osborne Cl 2 The Paddocks
F
G Cattlegate Road Crews Hill Station Crews Hill Crews Hill Golf Club

1 **C10** 1 Monkfrith Av 2 Tavistock Pl

THE RIDGEWAY A1005

2 **D9** 1 Belgrave Cl 2 Catherine Ct 3 Conisbee Ct

Botany Bay
THE RIDGEWAY
East Lodge Lane
Botany Bay Cricket Club

3 **D10** 1 St Johns Cl

London Loop

4 **E8** 1 South Lodge Crs

Hotel A111 Cockfosters Road Ferny   Hill   Hadley Road
London Loop Hadley Road Hotel High Oaks Oak Avenue Ridge

5

77 EN4

6 **E10** 1 Fairlawn Cl

University of Middlesex

Trent Country Park
Bournwell Close
Fairgreen
Coombehurst Close
Snakes Lane

7 **F8** 1 Bewcastle Gdns 2 Clifton Gdns 3 Corby Crs 4 Woodend Gdns

Games   Road
Cockfosters Sports Ground
Southgate Compton Cricket Club
Trent Park Cemetery
Grafton Road
Trentwood Side
Elmer Close
Merryhills Clinic
Merryhills Primary School
Bincote Rd

8 **F9** 1 Fothergill Dr 2 Lower Kenwood Av 3 Macleod Rd 4 Moynihan Dr 5 Simpson Cl 6 South Lodge Dr 7 Tarnbank

Cockfosters Station
Enfield & Haringey Hlth Authority
Primary School
A111
A110 ENFIELD RD
Lowther   Drive
Merryhills Drive
Glenbrook
Roundhill Dr
Rushey Hill
Silverdale
Lindal Crescent

9 **G4** 1 Aragon Cl 2 Roundhedge Wy 3 William Covell Cl

Cockfosters
Belmont   Avenue
Heddon Court Avenue
Preston Gardens
Leys Gdns
Westpole
Avenue
Southgate School
Sussex   Way
Oakwood Medical Cen
Oakwood Station
Prince George
Doctors Surgery
Chaseville Park Road
Eversley Primary School
Chasevillet Clinic
Pennington Dr
Tresilian Av
Highlands Av
Newsholme Dr

10

CAT   HILL   A110
East Barnet Grammar School
Oakland CP School
Saracens Rugby Football Club
Bramley School
Homestead Paddock
Ashmead
Priory Close
Reservoir Road
Addison Av
Stafford Cl
Tregenna Cl
Doctors Surgery
Merrivale
Sheringham Avenue
Oakwood
The Fairway
Cowper Gardens
Linden Close
Oakwood Close
Hillel School
Dalrymple Cl
Oakwood Park Rd
Park View

Primary School
St M C of E
BARNET RD CAT HILL
Bohun Grove
Oak Hill College
Canon Mohan Close
Southgate Surgery
De Bohun Av
Nursery Rd
Sir Thomas Lipton Memorial
Cowper Gardens
Salcombe Preparatory School
Mayfair
Springbank
The Birches
Holly Hill
Willow Walk
Brookdale

A
B **98** Monkfrith Primary School
C
D **G8** 1 Chadwick Av 2 Cotswold Gn 1 Anderson Cl 2 Banting Dr 3 Buchanan Cl 4 Corfield Rd 5 Macleod Rd
E
F **G10** 1 Meadowbank
G

1 grid square represents 500 metres

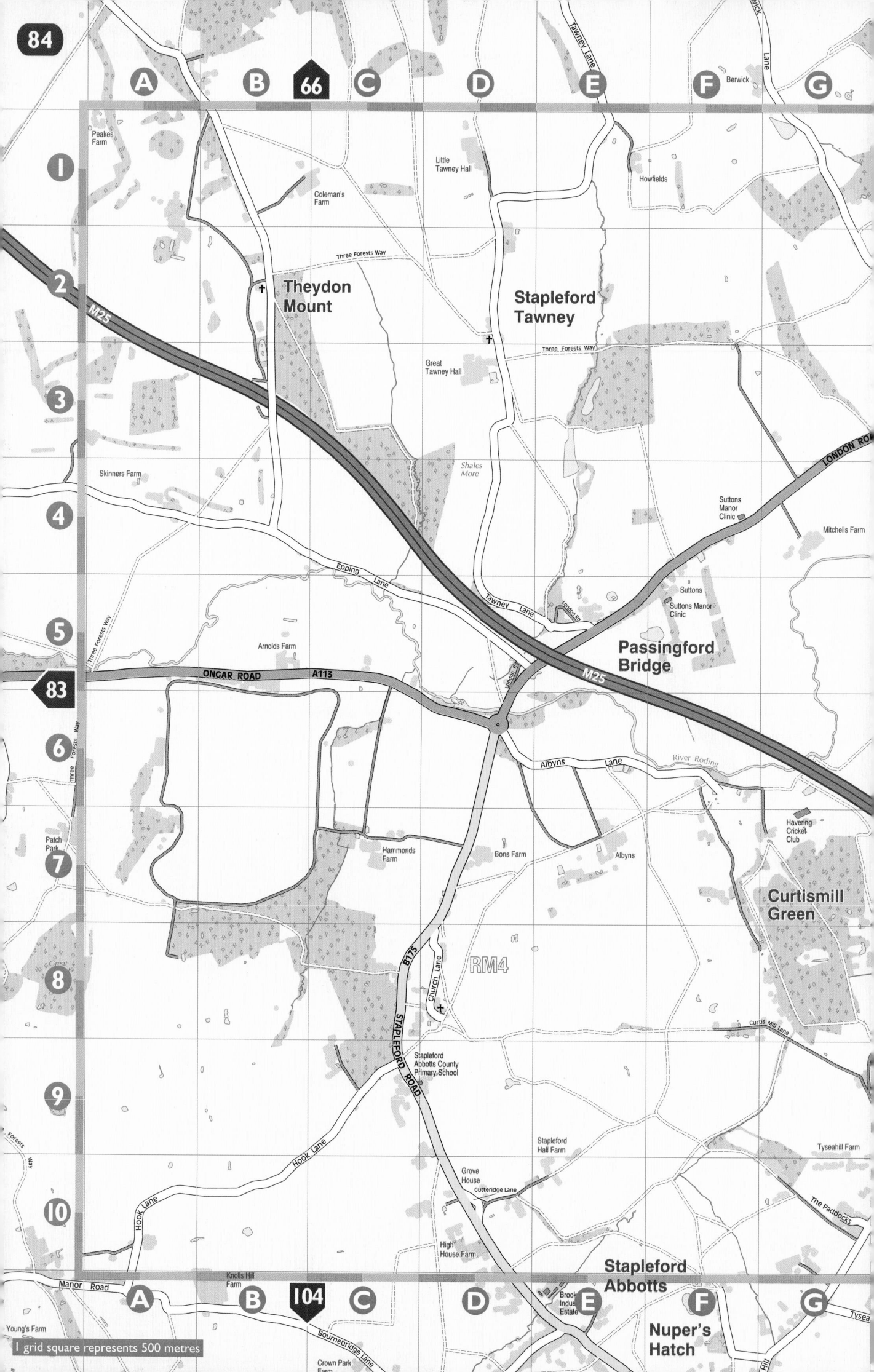

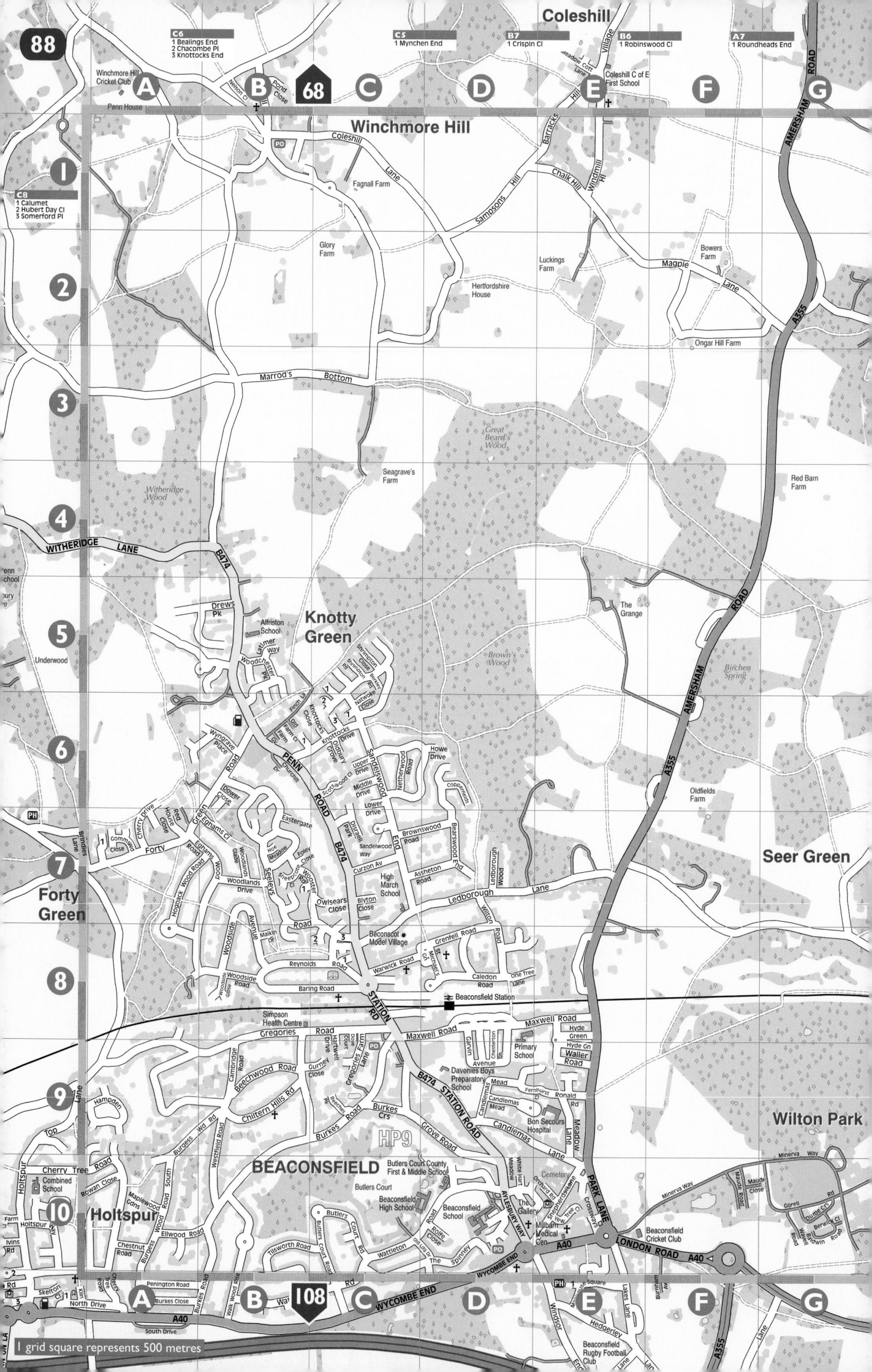

H1
1 Rushdene Rd

H2
1 Mayfield Gdns
2 Wingway

H3
1 Crown St
2 Regency Ct

H4
1 King Edward Rd
2 The Mount
3 Rose Va
4 White Lyons Rd

H6
1 Hampden Crs
2 Pompadour Cl

H7
1 Ashbeam Cl
2 Birchwood Cl
3 Burnell Wk
4 Canterbury Wy
5 Flemings
6 Meadsway
7 Wilmot Gn

J3
1 Alfred Rd

J6
1 Blackthorn Wy

L1
1 Margaret Av

L4
1 The Limes
2 Maple Cl
3 Oaktree Cl
4 Rowan Gn East
5 Rowan Gn West

M4
1 The Broad Wk (North)
2 Grangewood Cl
3 Norman Crs
4 Wingfield Cl

M5
1 The Broadwalk (South)

P2
1 Challacombe Cl

P7
1 Meadows Cl

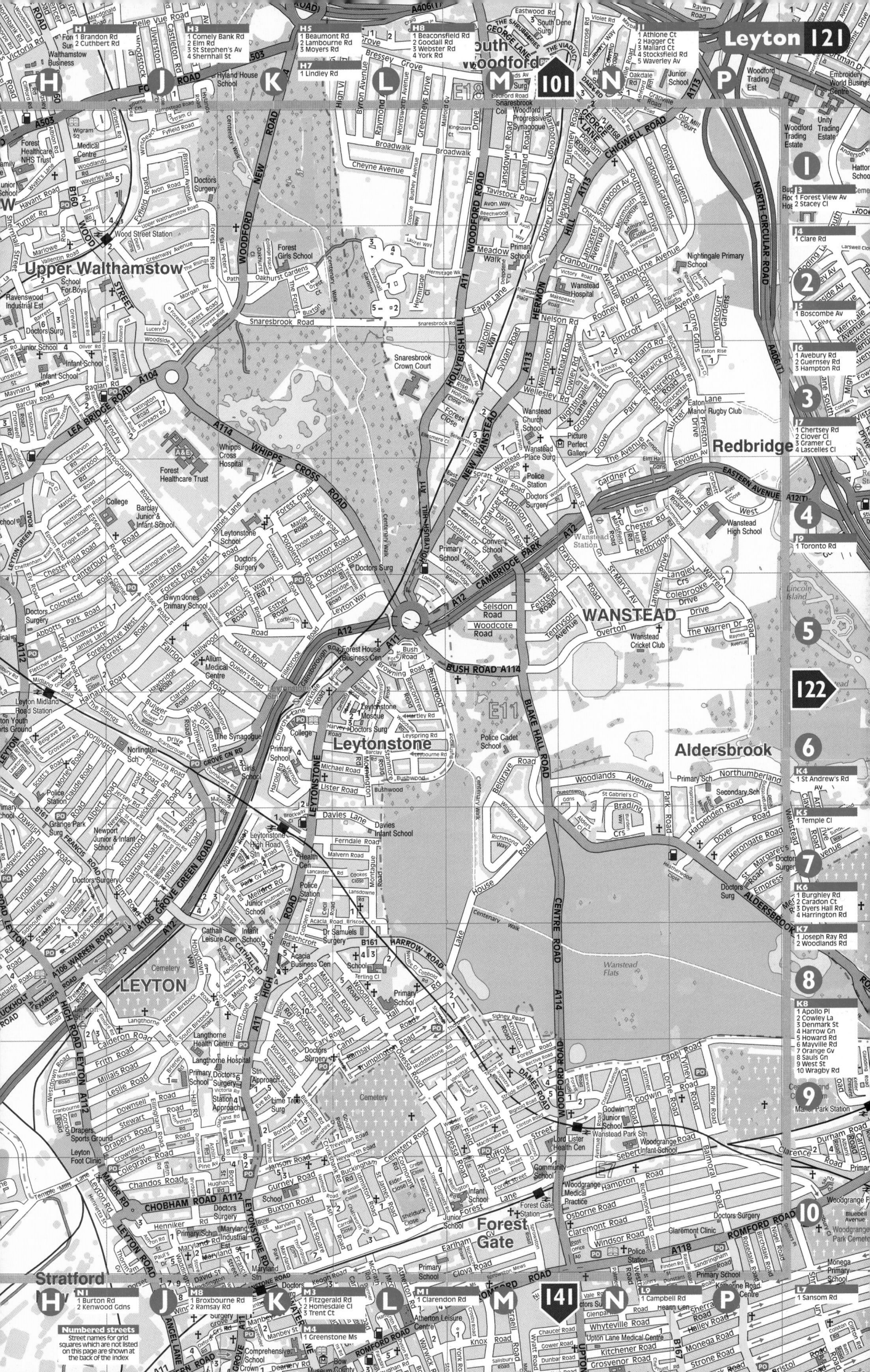

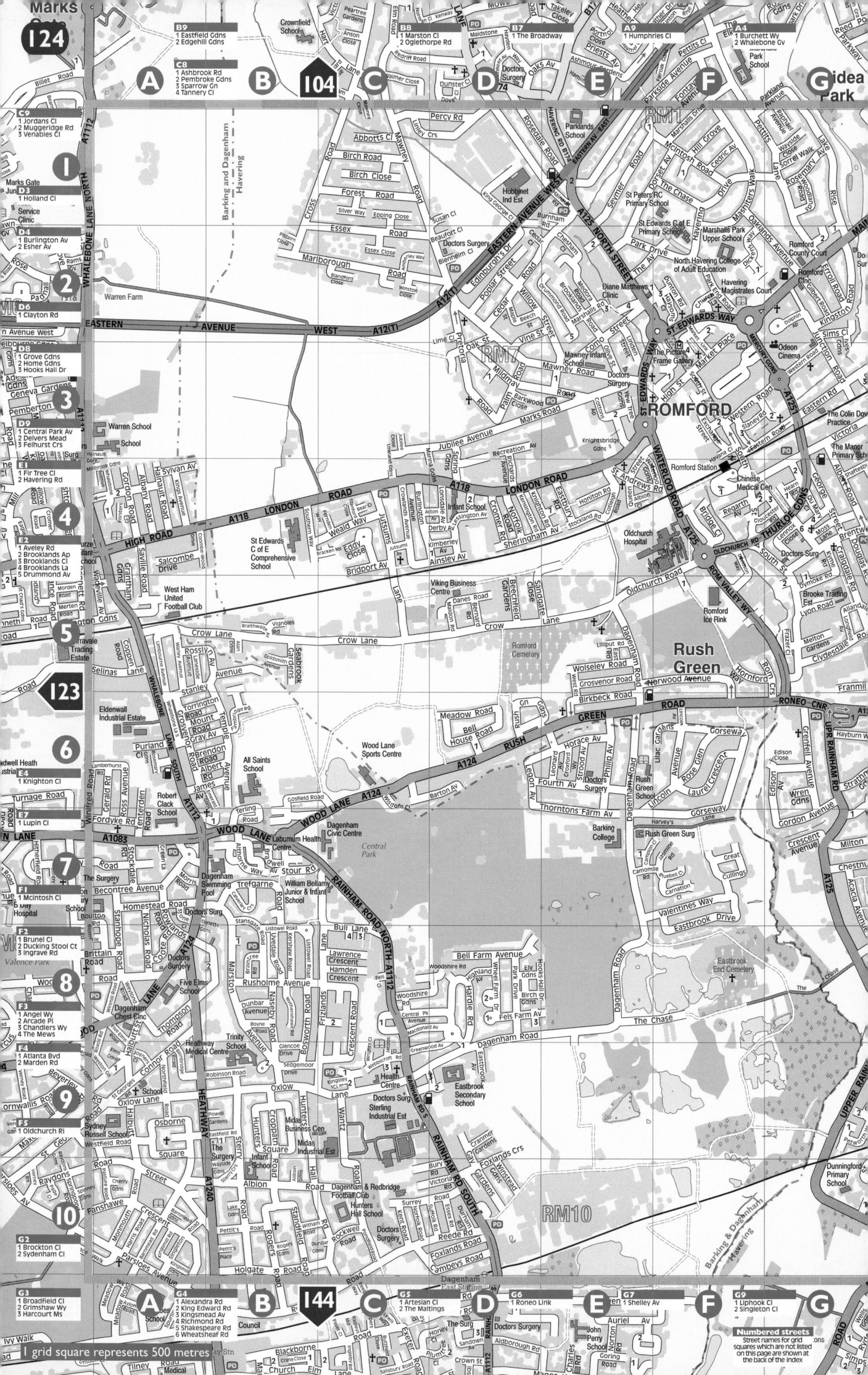

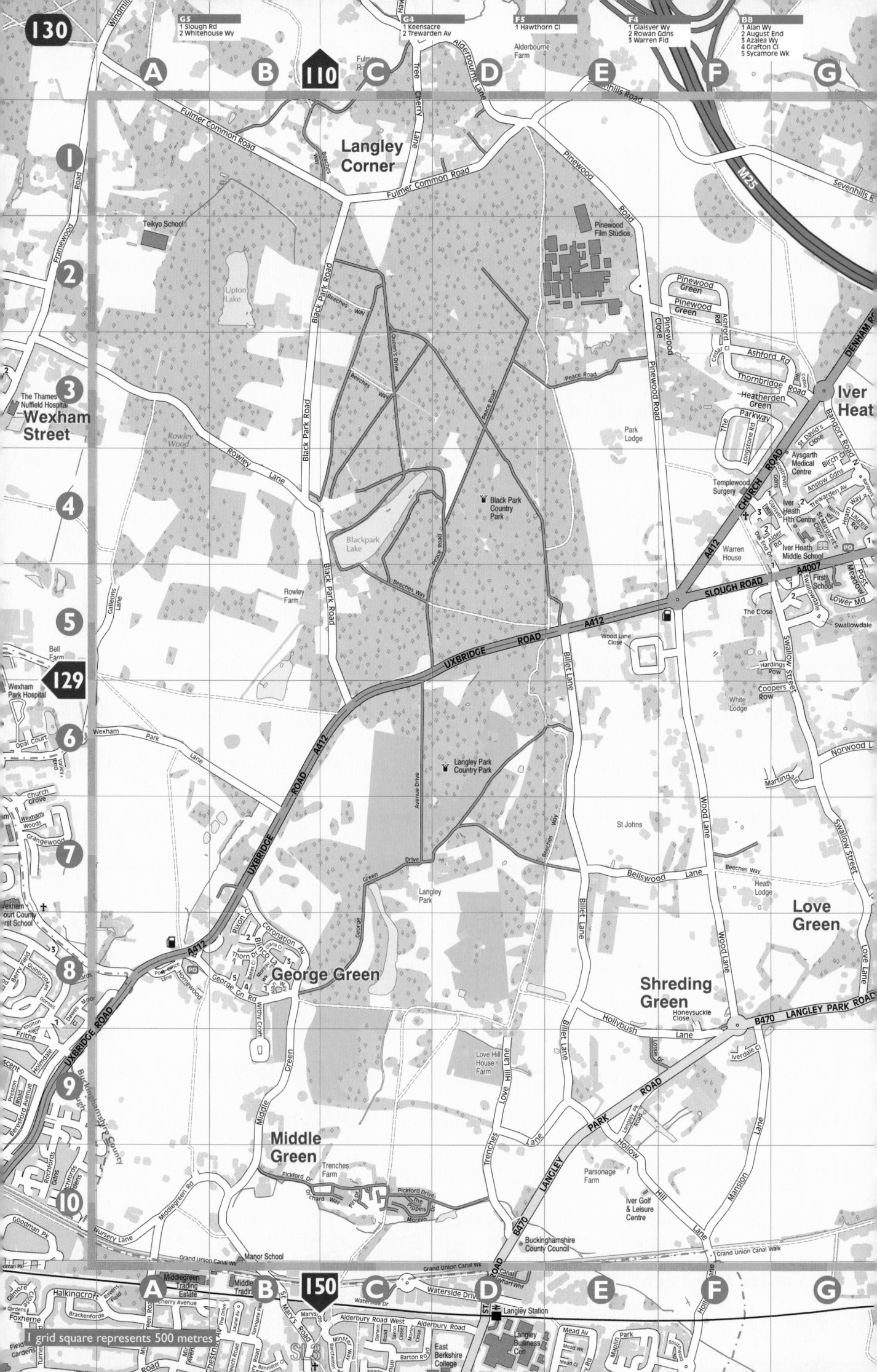

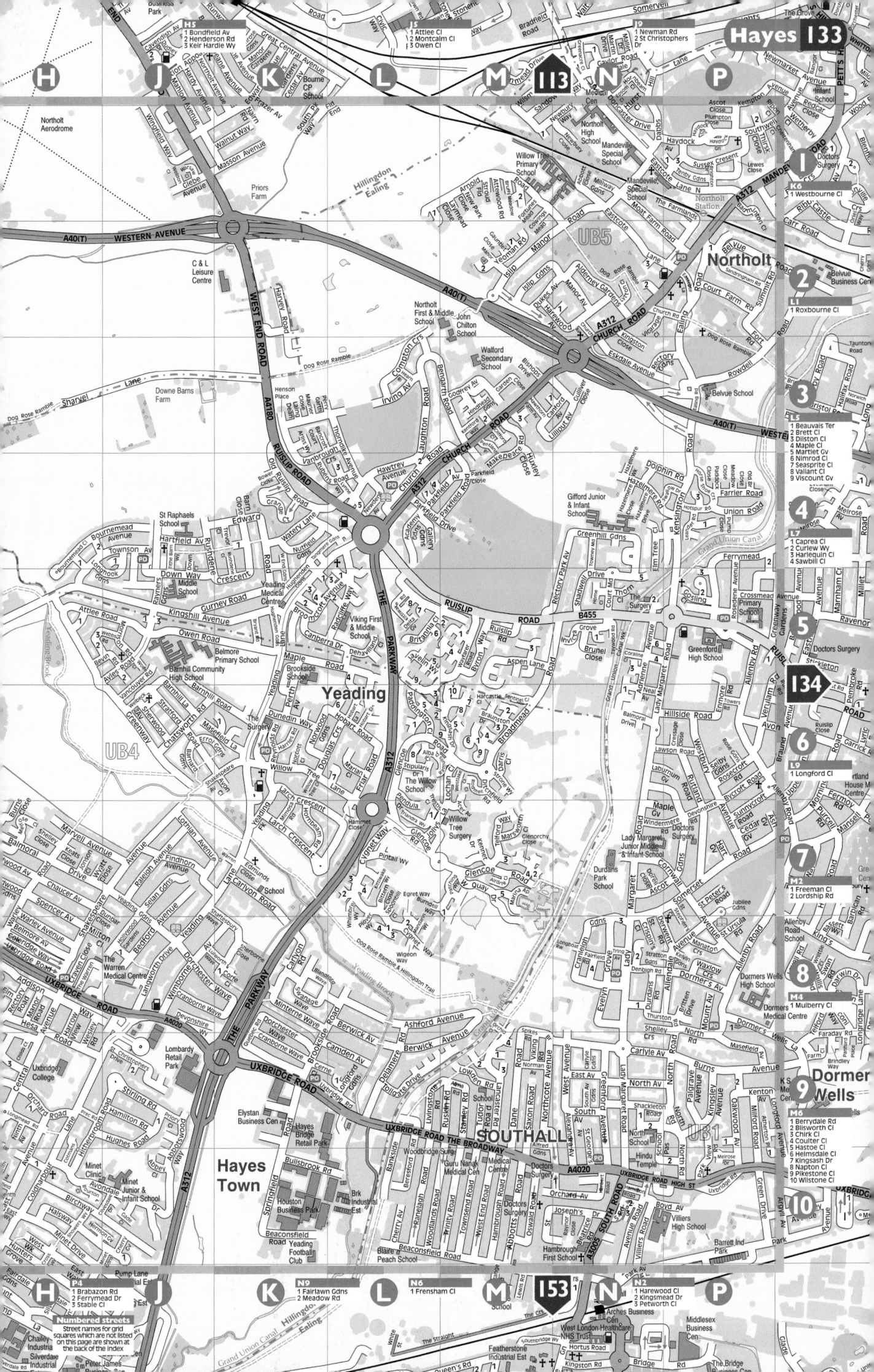

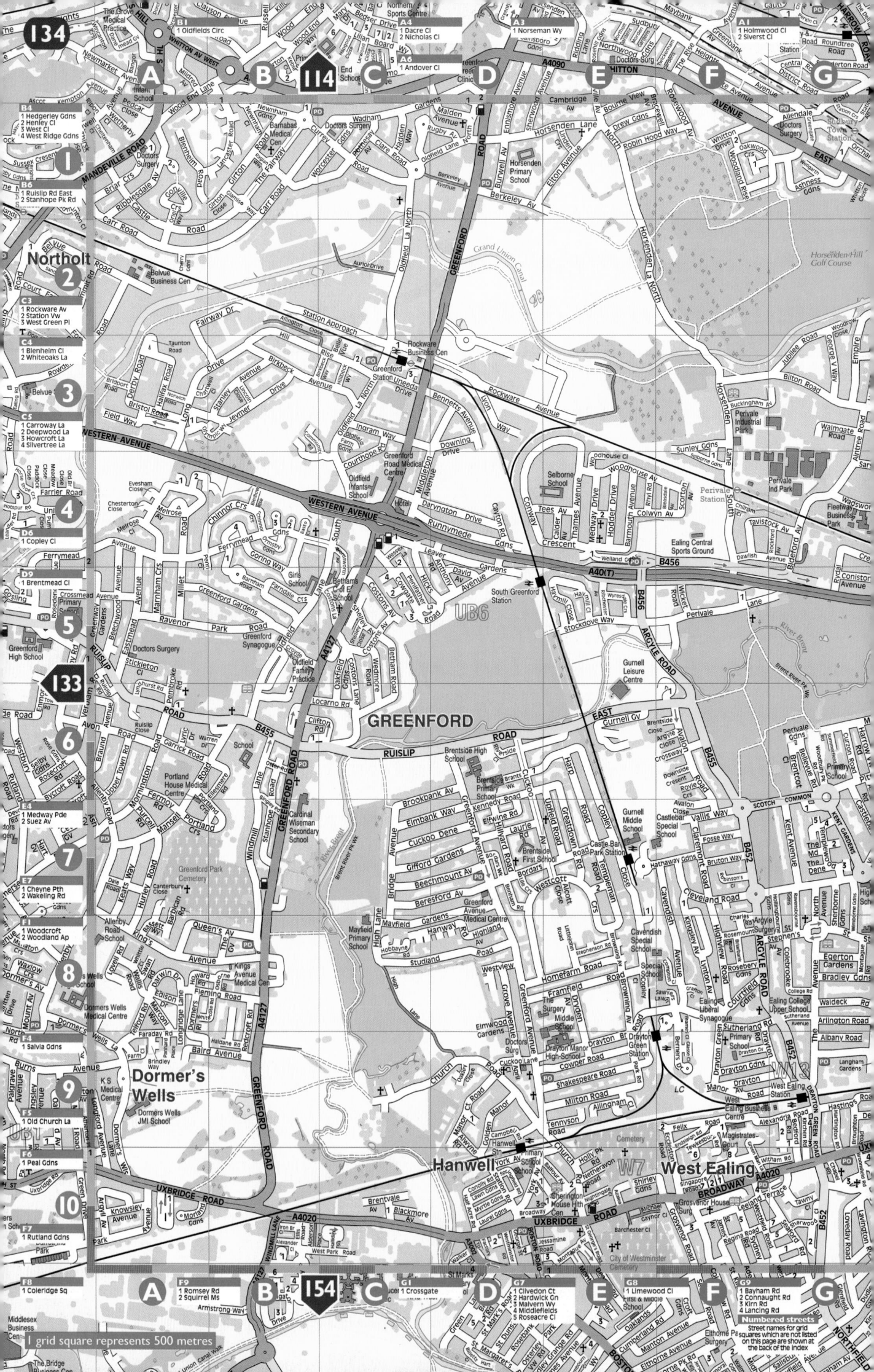

H | J | K | L | M | 119 | N | P

H1
1 Crane Gv
2 Digswell St
3 Epping Pl
4 Highbury Stn Rd
5 Westbourne Rd

DALSTON LANE
A1207 GRAHAM ROAD

ISLINGTON

Canonbury

Kingsland

Dalston

De Beauvoir Town

Haggerston

Hoxton

Pentonville

BETHNAL GREEN

FINSBURY

SHOREDITCH

140

Clerkenwell

St Luke's

BETHNAL

SCLATER STREET

SPITALFIELD

1 Blackfriars Ct
2 Blackfriars Pas
3 Blackfriars U/P
4 Castle Baynard St
5 Carpenter St
6 Kingscote St
7 Knightrider St
8 Puddle Dock
9 Queen Victoria St
10 White Lion Hl

1 Alwyne Pl
2 Ashby Gv
3 Douglas Rd
4 Hedingham Cl
5 Northampton St
6 Queensbury St

CITY

1 Arlington Sq
2 Basire St
3 Canon St
4 Pickering St
5 Rector St
6 Ridgewell Cl
7 Raynor Pl
8 Rydon St
9 St Paul St
10 St Philip's Wy

St George in the East

opping

COMMERCIAL ROAD

LONDON

River Thames

BERMONDSEY

The Borough

L4
1 Avebury St
2 Baring St
3 Devizes St
4 Orange St
5 Hullbridge Ms
6 Imber St
7 Northport St
8 Wilton Vls

L3
1 Bracklyn St
2 Bridport Pl
3 Cherbury St
4 Clunbury St
5 New North Rd

N1
1 Crowland Ter
2 Southgate Gv

1 Addle St
2 Albion Wy
3 Aldermanbury
4 Bartholomew Cl
5 Brackley St
6 Bridgewater St
7 Bridgewater Sq
8 Carthusian St
9 Cripplegate St
10 Glasshouse Yd
11 Kinghorn St
12 Little Britain
13 Middle St
14 Monkwell Sq
15 Montague St
16 Newbury St
17 St Alphage Gdn

146

E8
1 Frances Gdns
2 Fullarton Crs

E9
1 Fusedale Wy
2 Groves Cl

F7
1 Derry Av
2 Deveron Gdns

F8
1 Dale Cl
2 Dent Cl
3 Dunkellin Gv
4 Dunning Cl
5 Faymore Gdns
6 Jack Evans Ct

G6
1 Aire Dr

145

G7
1 Araglen Av
2 Bovey Wy

G8
1 Avon Gn
2 Bingham Cl
3 Brock Gn
4 Galey Gn

G9
1 Cander Wy
2 Chanlock Pth
3 Clayburn Gdns

C10
1 Broome Pl

126

B10
1 Alfred Rd
2 Buchanan Cl
3 Hanford Rd
4 The Rowans

B9
1 St Paul's Cl
2 St Paul's Pl
3 Tyne Gdns

B8
1 Shannon Wy
2 Swale Cl

166

AVELEY

RM15

Junction 30

1 grid square represents 500 metres

H4
1 Peartree Cl

H5
1 Benyon Pth
2 Bradd Cl
3 Copper Beech Rd
4 Tamarisk Rd
5 Tyssen Pl
6 Whitebeam Dr

H6
1 Quince Tree Cl
2 Tamarisk Rd

H8
1 Elwick Rd
2 Foxglove Rd
3 Verbena Cl

H9
1 Broxburn Dr
2 Colne Cl
3 Stifford Rd

J5
1 Cherry Tree Dr

J6
1 Cedar Ri
2 Laburnum Gv
3 Maple Dr
4 Nordmann Pl
5 Redwood Cha

K5
1 Rosewood Cl

K6
1 Lavender Cl
2 Medlar Dr

M9
1 Silverwood Cl
2 Stifford Clays Rd

M10
1 Hogarth Rd
2 Simmons Pl
3 Westland Vw

N9
1 Kingsman Dr
2 Prince Philip Av

N10
1 The Pines
2 St Annes Cl

White Post Fa

Ockendon Road

North Road

B186

Havering Thurrock

Fen Farm

Corner Farm

Home Farm

Stone Hall

Cheelson Road
Wilsman Road
Nelson Road

South Ockendon Hall

Benyon CP School
Peartree Surgery

Dorsett Fen

Mar Dyke

Hoblet

Rosemary Cl
Nicholas Cl
Cliff Pl
Church Crs
Birch Crs

Larkspur Cl
Lime
Hazel Dr
Birch Crescent
Ash Wk
Hornbeam Cha
Sniper Dr

Viola Cl
Brandon
Groves
Rowan
Holl
Magnolia Cl

Celandine Cl
Avenue
Birch Cl
Mar Rd
Holly Drive
Medlar Drive
Poplar Cl

Mayflower Medical Centre
Aveley Garth Cl
Nursery
Sycamore Way
Laurel
Mollands
Lane
Mollands Ct
Mollands La

Tamarisk Rd
B186
Orchard

SOUTH OCKENDON

Medebridge Road

Mar Dyke

Orchard
Moss Rd
B186

Oaklands Drive

Buckles Lane

SOUTH ROAD

Green Lane

Green Lane

Springfield

Stifford Clays Road

Stifford Clays Farm

William Edwards GM School

Blackshots

Fairfield Av
Ashley Gardens

South Rd
Cruick

Chelmer Dr
Cruick Av

Cullen Square

Stifford Hill

Back Lane
Pilgrims La

Stifford

Ardale Sch

Clockhouse Lane

North Stifford

Hotel

High

Marian Close

Cuckoo Lane

A1012

A13(T)

Stifford Clays Road

Clays Road

Prince
Crammavill Street
Jennings
Grantham
Hogarth Road
Bradshaw
Fleethall
Phillip
Gourney Gv
Whitmore
Avenue
Oakway
Blackthorn Rd
Elmway
Meadow Rd
Fairway
The Firs
Leasway

Stifford Clays County Junior School

Stifford Clays Health Cen

Pallins Way
Goddard Road
Crammavill Street
Thorley
Harty
Crawford
Fieldway
Farrow Gdns

Long Lane

Denholm CP School

Victoria Road
Windsor Avenue
Chestnut Avenue
Cobham
Harvey
Crowstone
Victoria Path

Highfield Gardens

Laird Avenue

Broadview Avenue

Blackshots Leisure Centre

B186
A13(T)
ARTERIAL ROAD NORTH STIFF
A1012
1306
167

Dudley Close
Calshot Cl
Bark Burr Road
Drake
Lenthall
Advice
Conrad Close

H7 1 Myrtle Cl

J7 1 Ingleside

L7 1 The Square

N1 1 Caroline Cl 2 Catherines Cl 3 Hatton Gv

H · J · K · L · M · **131** · N · P

N2 1 Rickard Cl 2 Wren Dr

1

N4 1 Verbena Cl

2

N5 1 Wilton Cl

3

N7 1 Northwood Rd

4

P1 1 Classon Cl 2 Swains Cl

5

152

6

P3 1 Great Benty

7

8 London Heathrow Airport

9

10

Thorney

West Drayton

Harmondsworth

Longford

Poyle

Junction 15/4b

M25

M4

Junction 14

173

H · J · K · L · M · **173** · N · P

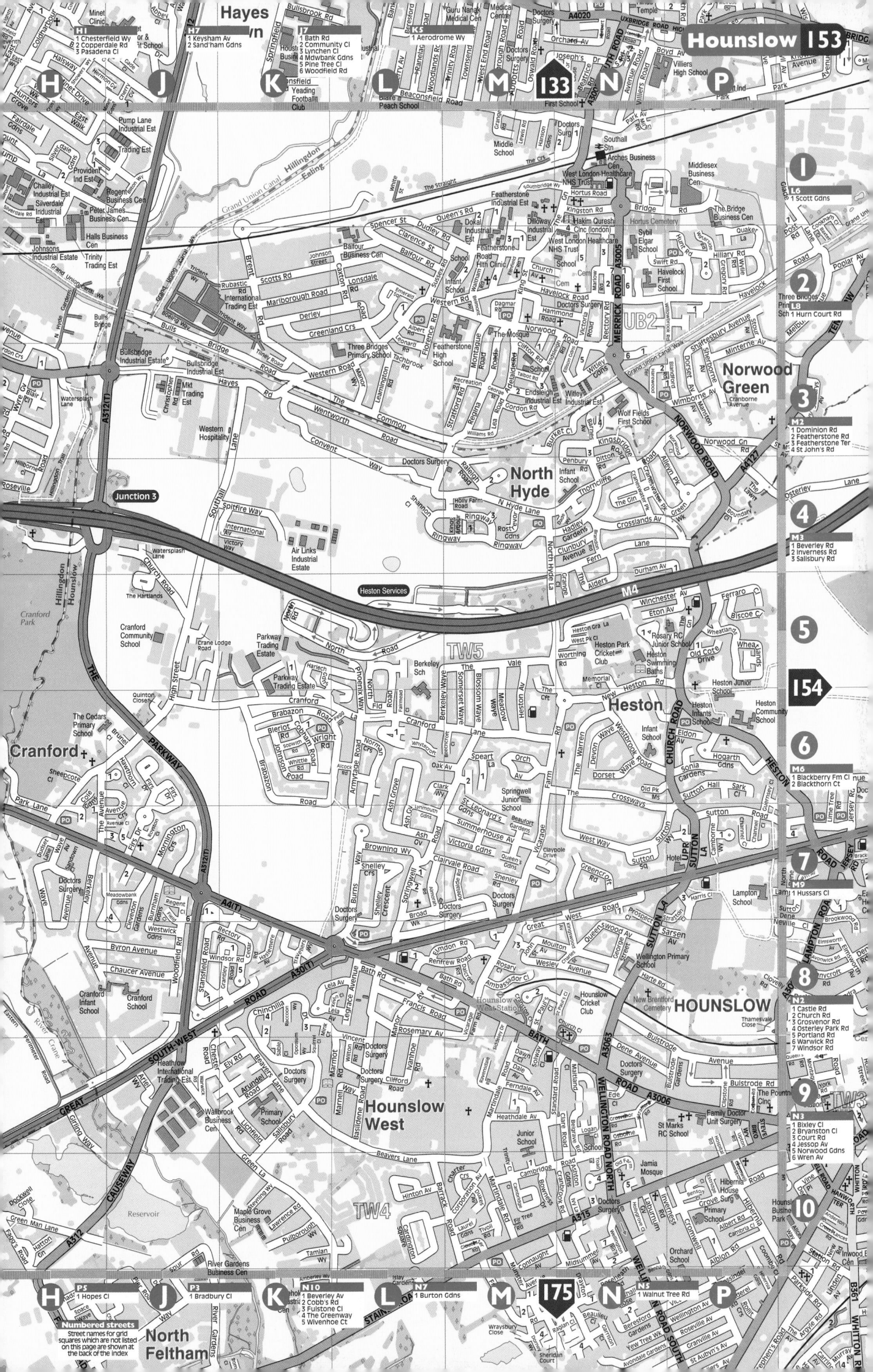

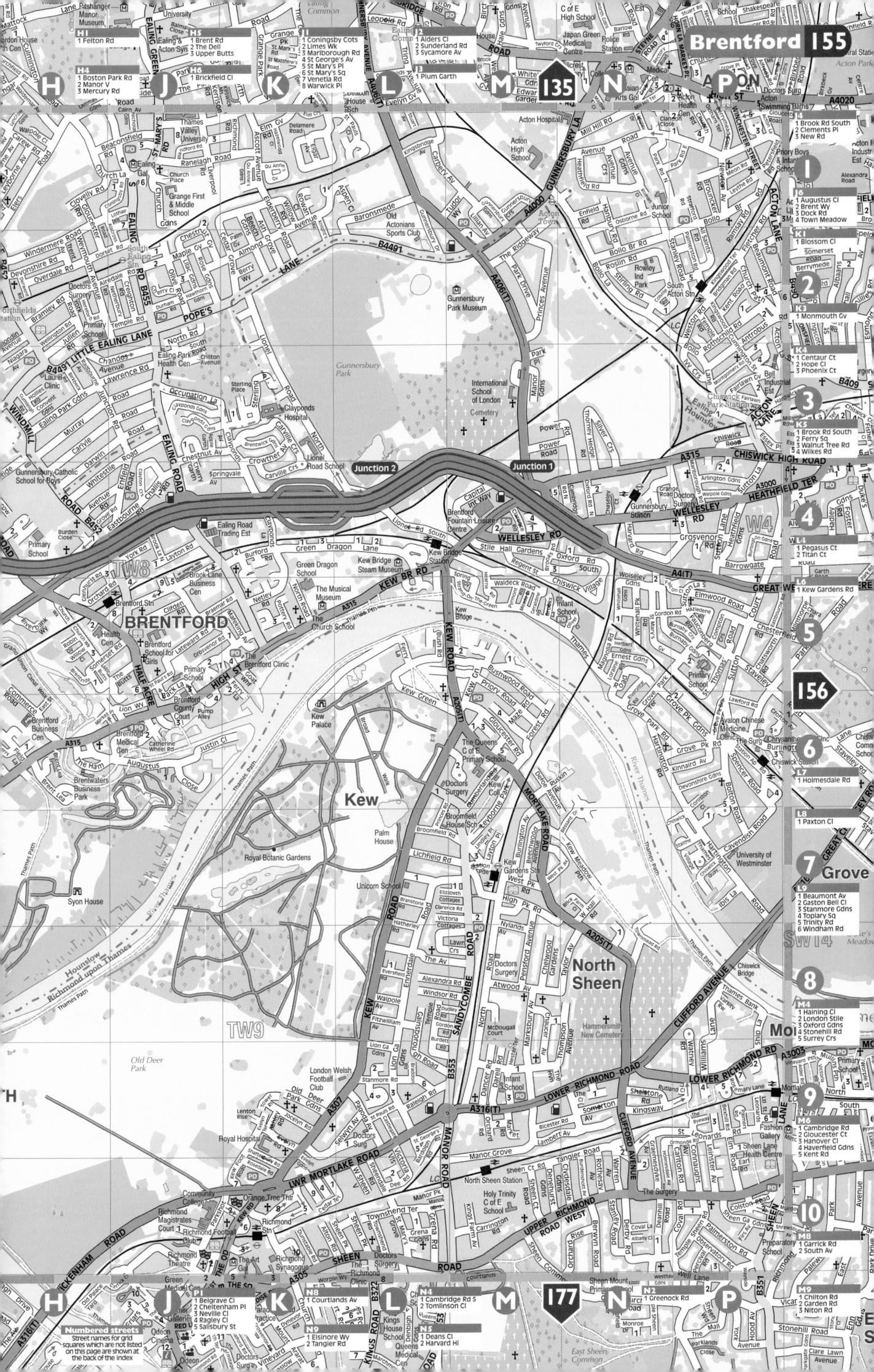

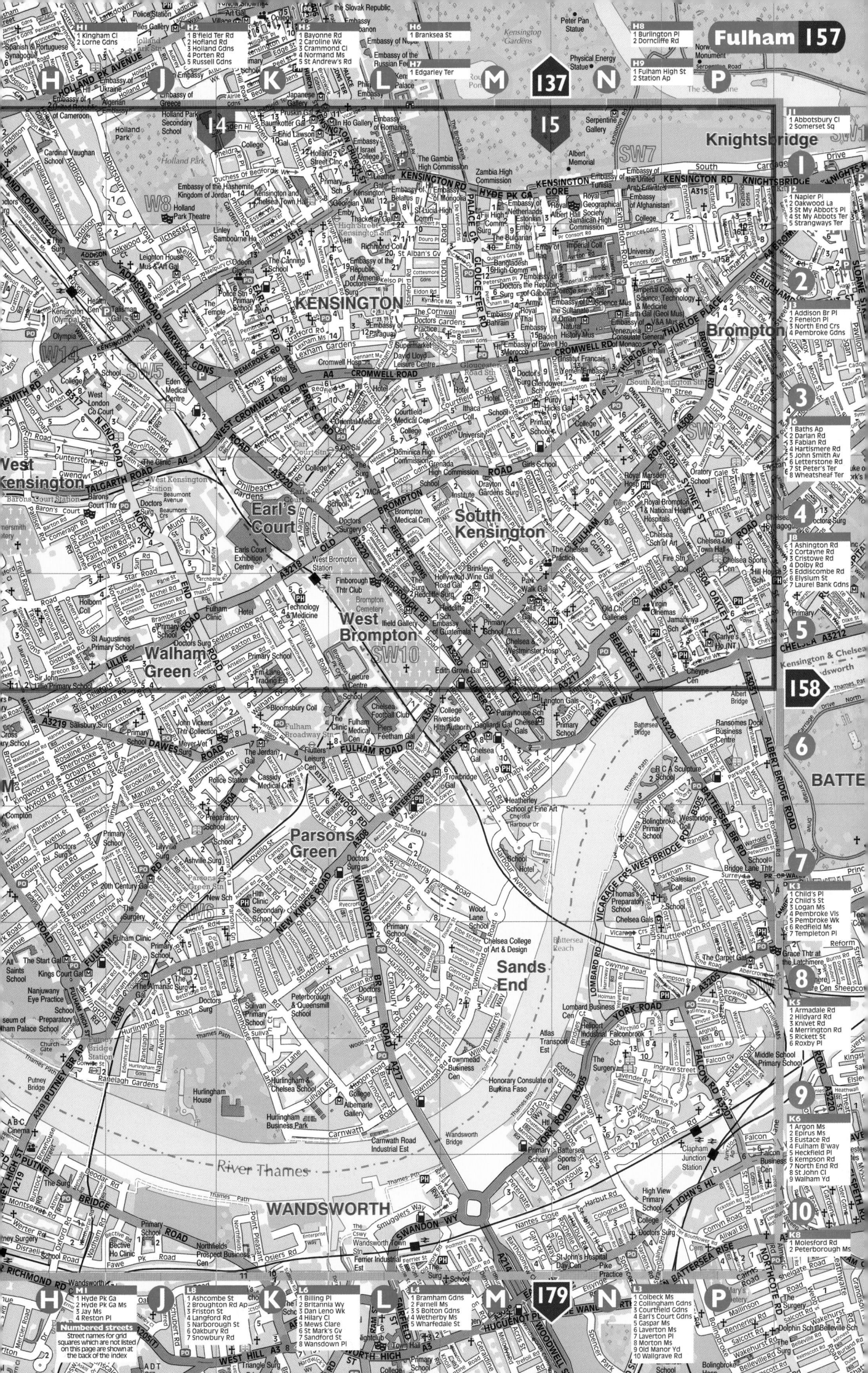

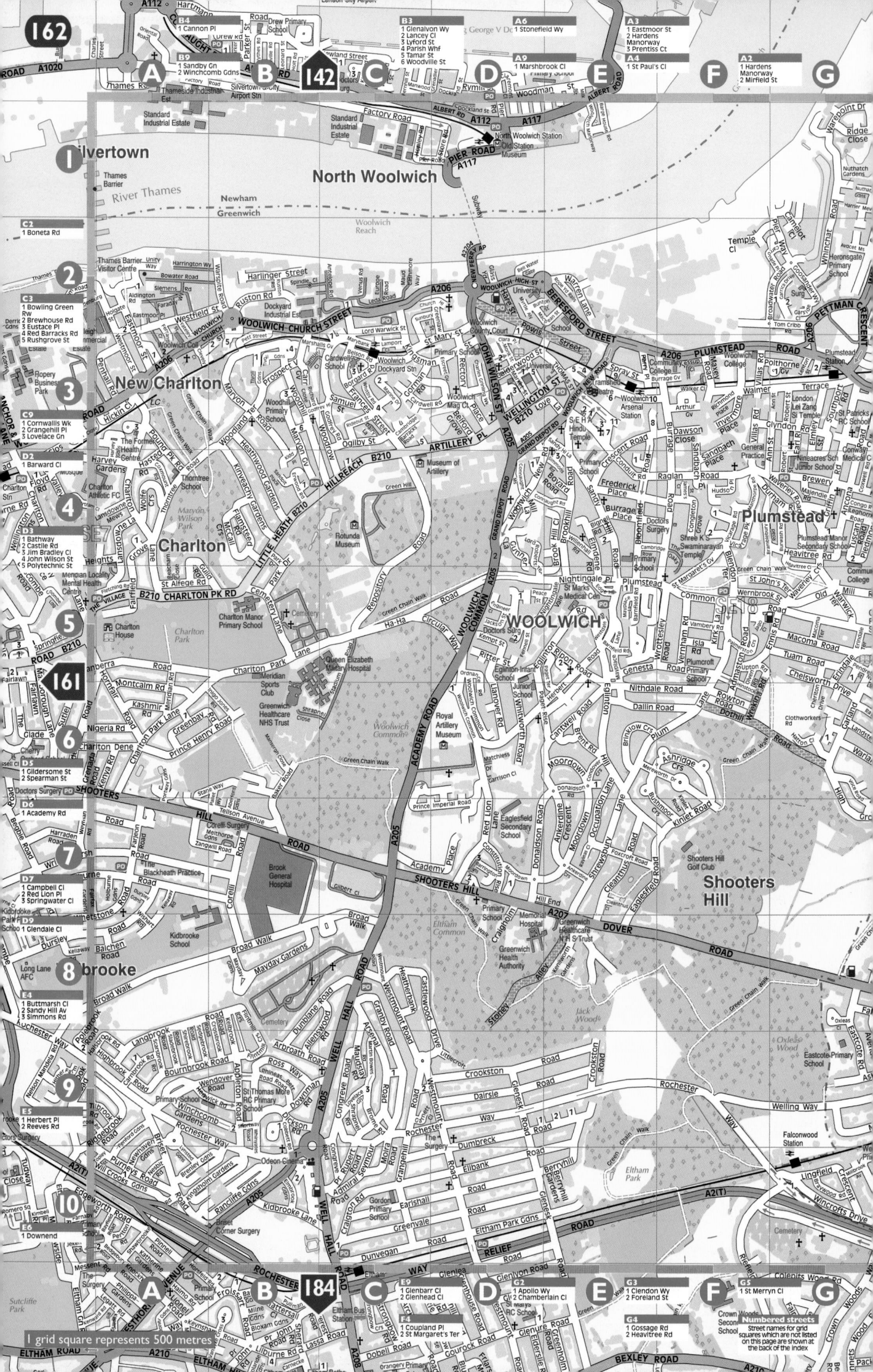

Coldharbour

Purfleet

Slade Green

Barnes Cray

Temple Hill

Crayford

K3
1 Hazelwood

L2
1 Pinewood Cl

M3
1 Queen Elizabeth Av
2 Strathmore

H **J** **K** **L** **M** **N** **P**

Walton's Hall Road

Docking
Marshes

Holford Road

Northumberland Road

Essex Gdns

East

Buckingham Hill Road

Linford

Tilbury Road

PO

Stafford Close

Lower Crescent

Somerset Road

Meadow Cl

Muckingford

Becksland

LC

Severn

Solway

Colne

Doctors
Surgery

Alexandra Way

Queen Elizabeth Avenue

Waldon

Pure

Hayle

Coronation

Clyde

Avenue

Half Drive

East
Tilbury
Station

Beechcroft

Brindles

Steming Av

King George

V Avenue

Thomas Bata Av

Princess Margaret Road

Severn

2

Tweed

Frome

Arun

Muckingford Road

Bata
Medical Centre

Queen Mary
Av

Trent

East Tilbury
Surgery

PO

Bata Av

Coronation

Princess Av

Gloucester Av

Farm
Road

Doctors
Surgery

Anchor Lane

Low Street Lane

**West
Tilbury**

**Low
Street**

Church Road

Road

LC

LC

Love Lane

Shaw Road

RM18

LC

Buckland

Station Road

Bowaters
Farm

**East
Tilbury**

Unley

Princess Margaret Road

Gordon
Close

West
Tilbury
Marshes

East
Tilbury
Marshes

Coalhouse
Point

1
2
3
4
5
6
7
8
9
10

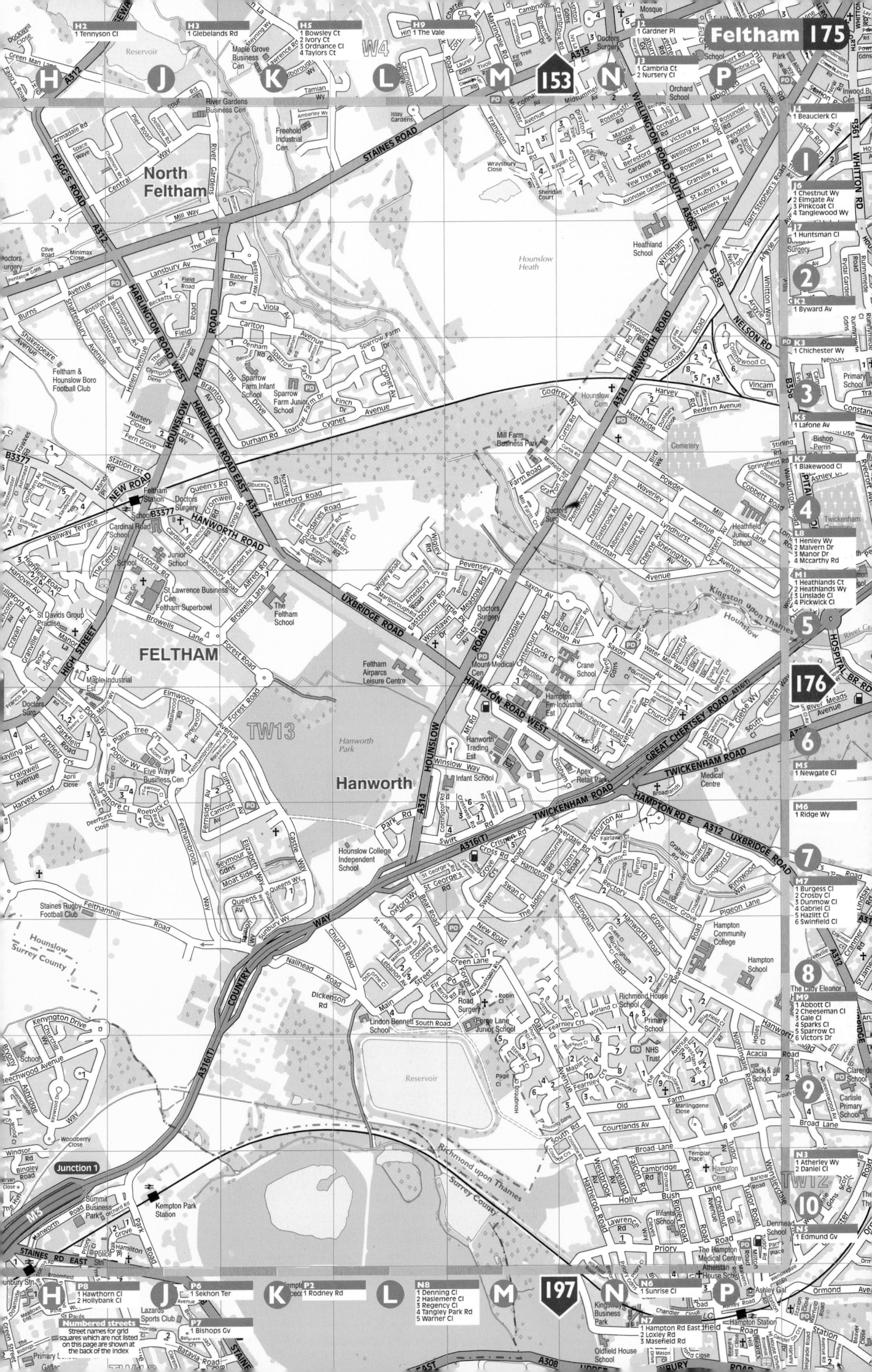

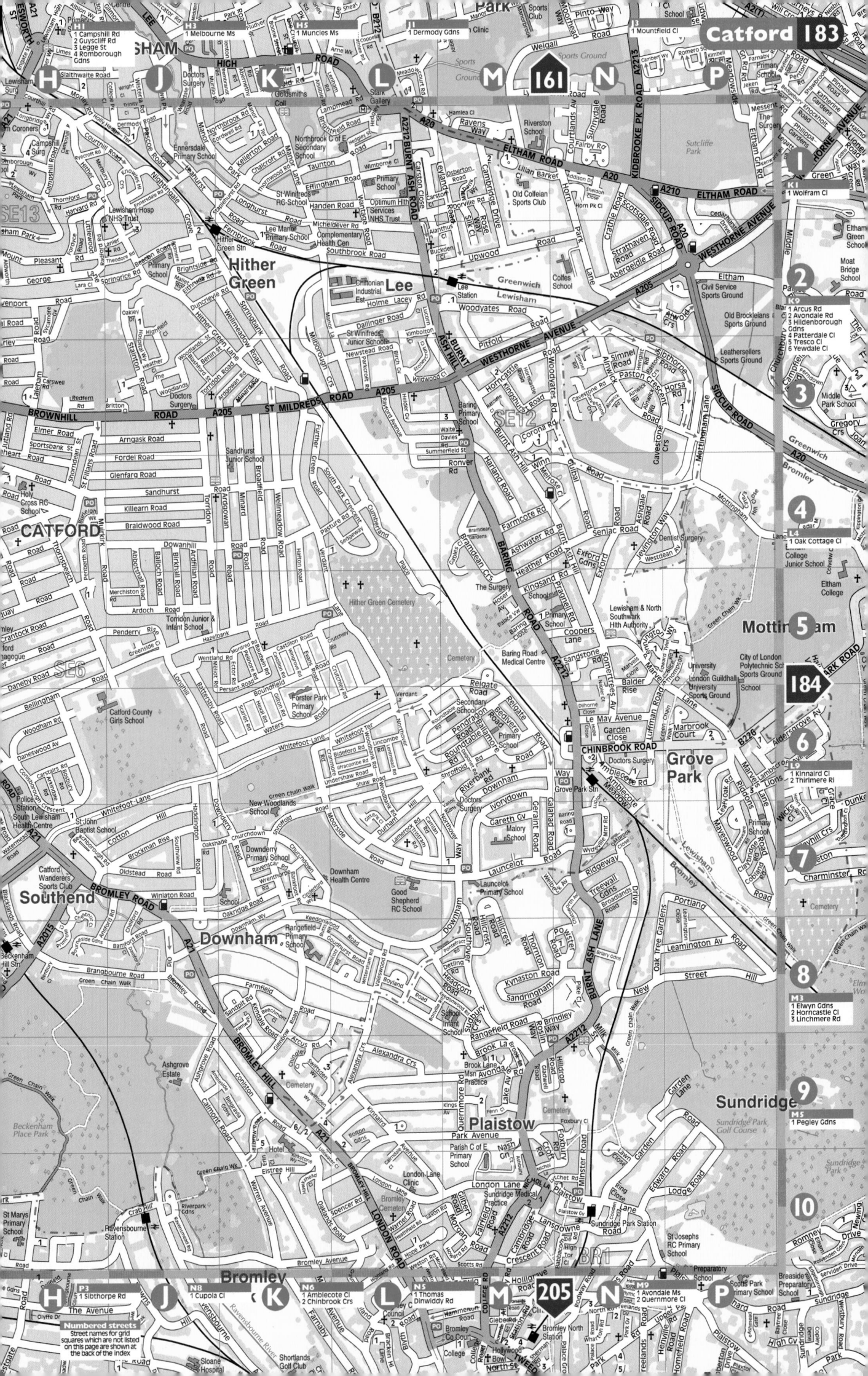

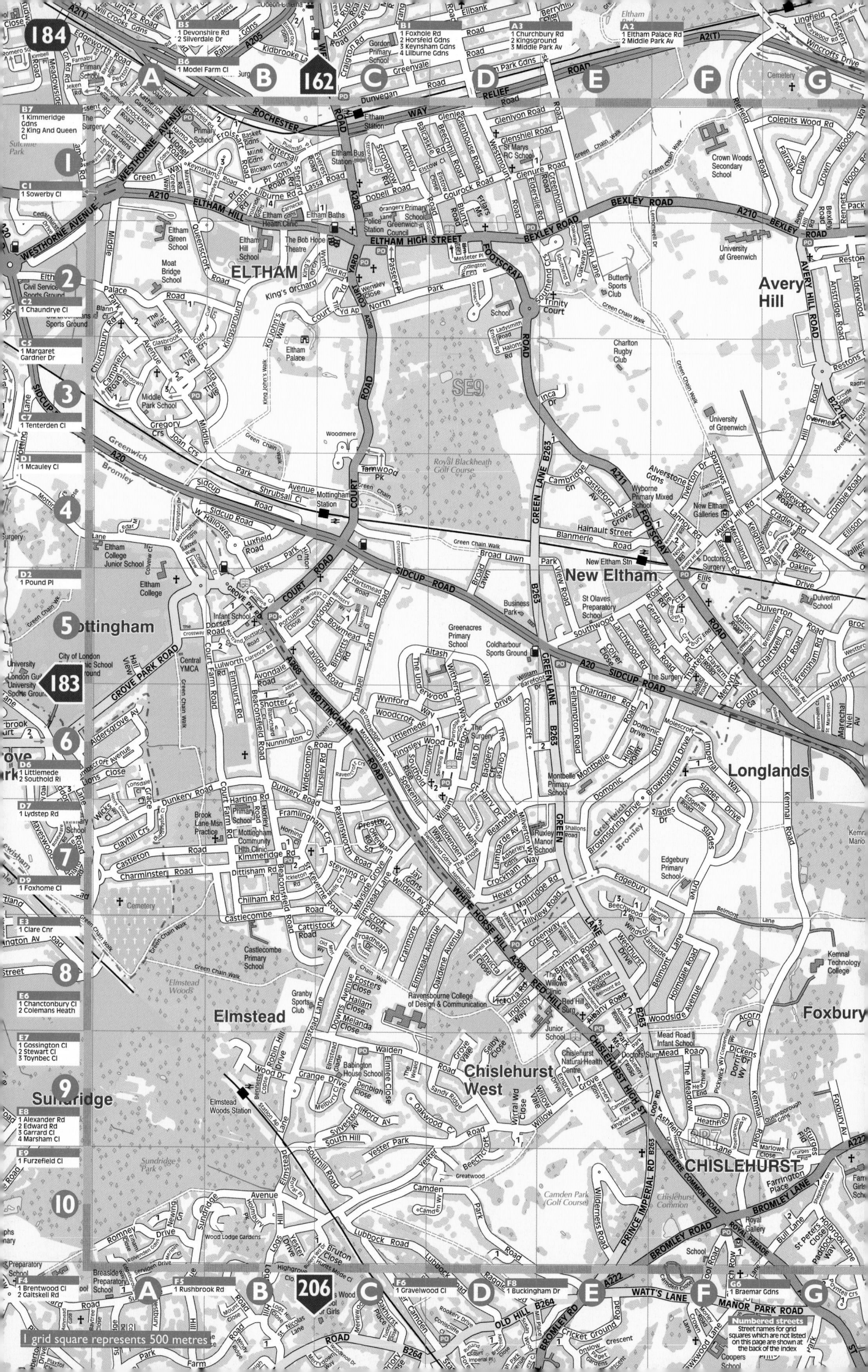

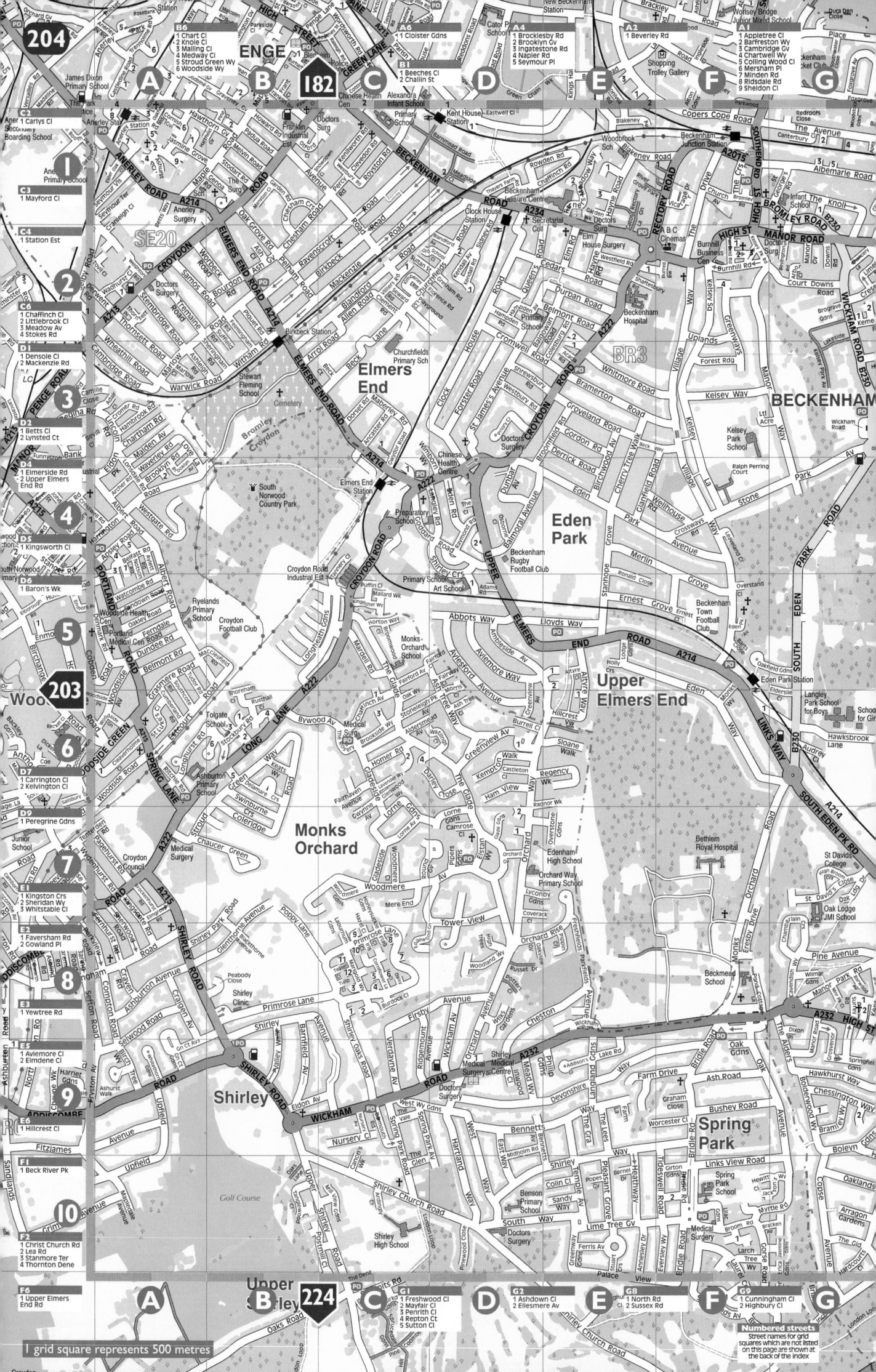

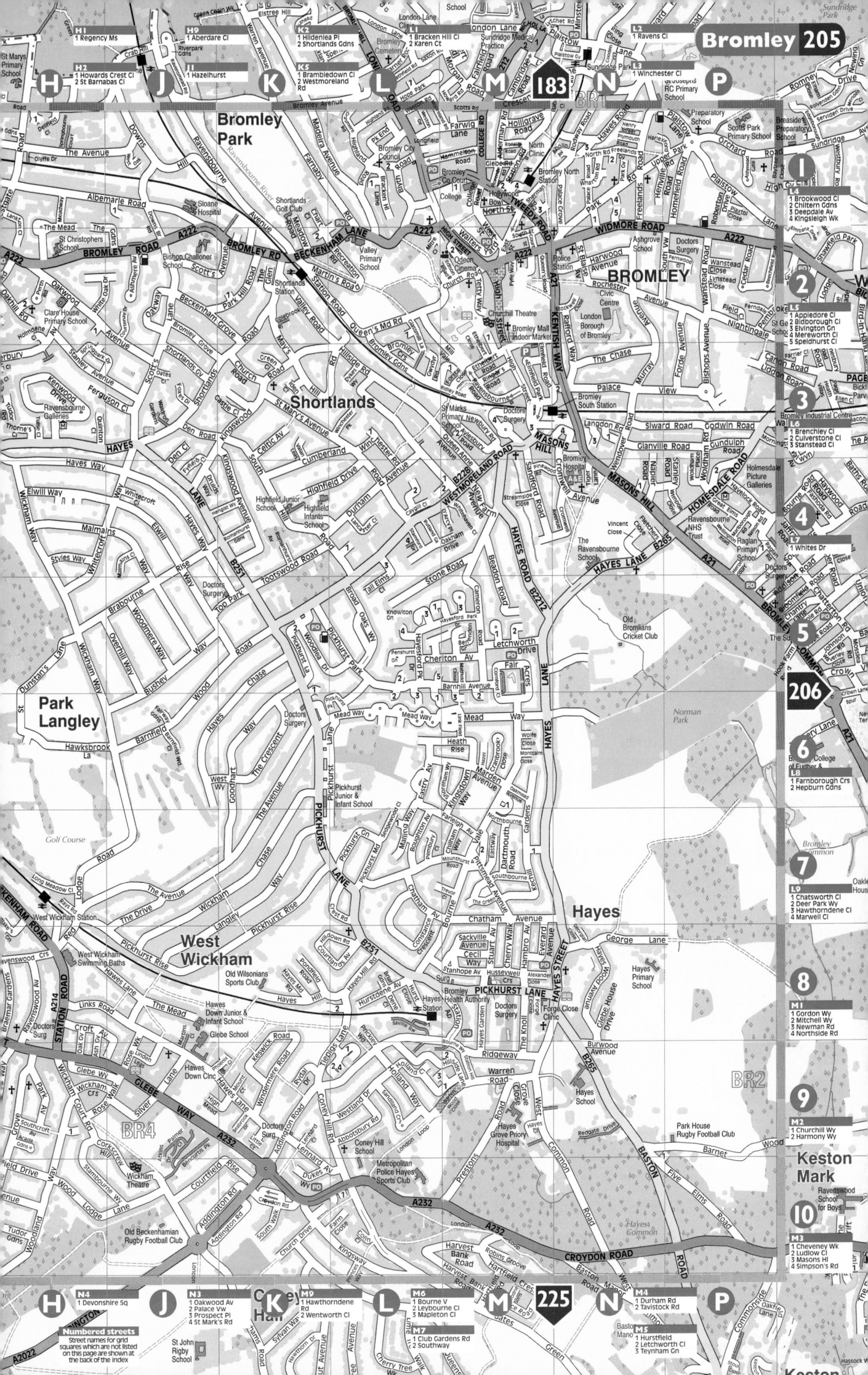

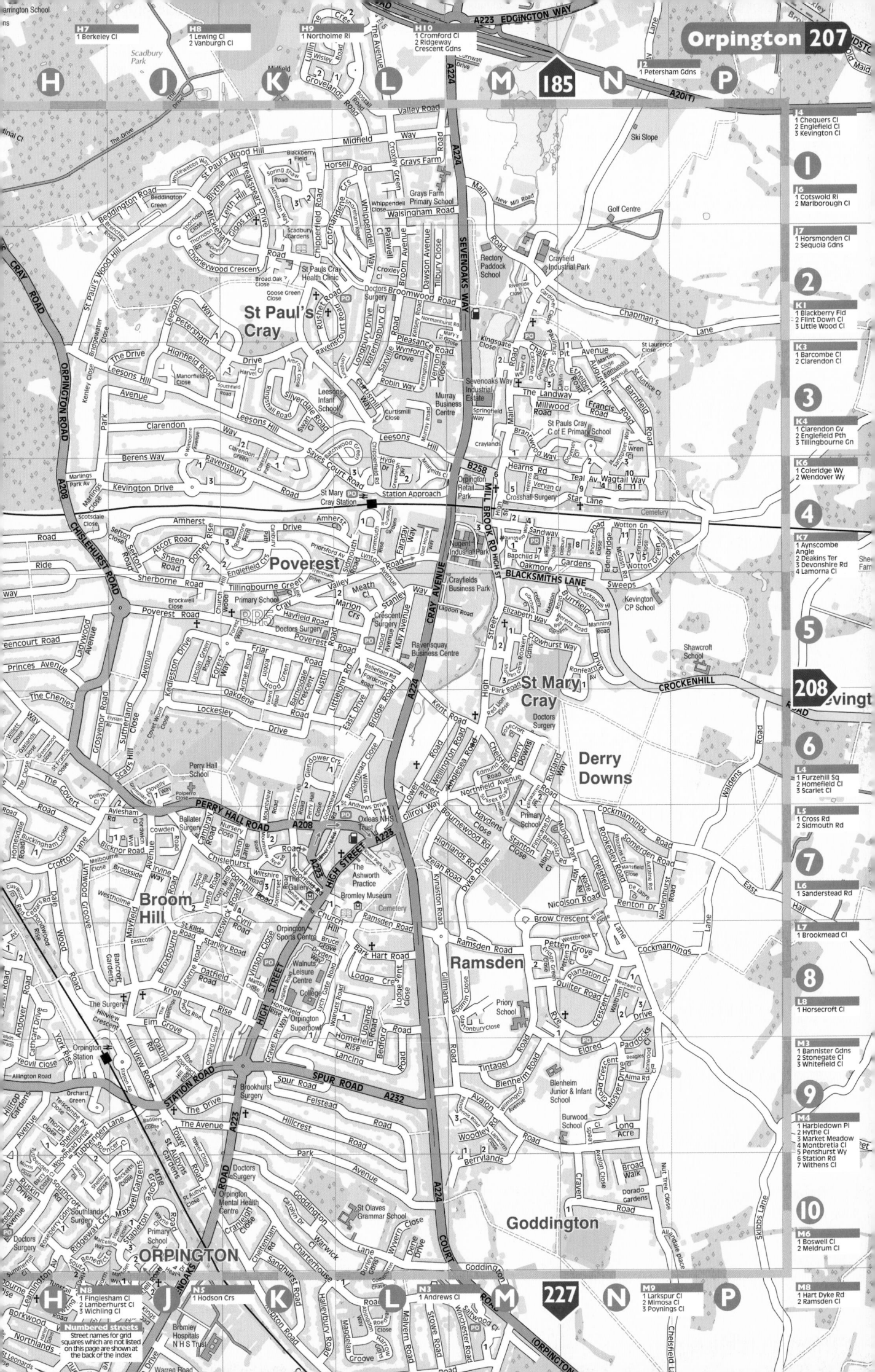

208

A **B**  **186** **C** **D** **E** **F** **G**

207

228

E1
1 Aspen Cl

D7
1 Barnfield Cl

D6
1 Sounds Lodge

D4
1 Wood End

D2
1 Nursery Cl

E2
1 Greenside
2 The Orchard
3 Pear Tree Cl
4 St Lukes Cl

E3
1 Westharold

E4
1 Apple Orch
2 Edwards Gdns
3 Ellis Waterton Cl
4 Leewood Pl
5 Southern Pl

E5
1 Heather End

E6
1 West View Rd

F2
1 Heath Cl
2 Maple Cl
3 Strawberry Flds
4 Whitecroft

F3
1 London Rd
2 Pemberton Gdns
3 Ruxton Ct

F4
1 Greenacre Cl
2 Lila Pl
3 Station Rd

F5
1 Hazel End
2 Leyhill Cl
3 Overmead

G2
1 Woodgers Gv
2 Woodlands Cl
3 Woodlands Ri

G3
1 Downsview Cl
2 The Grove
3 Old Farm Gdns

G4
1 Bevan Pl
2 Pine Cl
3 St Georges Rd
4 Springfield Av

Hockenden

White Oak

Kevingtown

Crockenhill

Wested

I grid square represents 500 metres

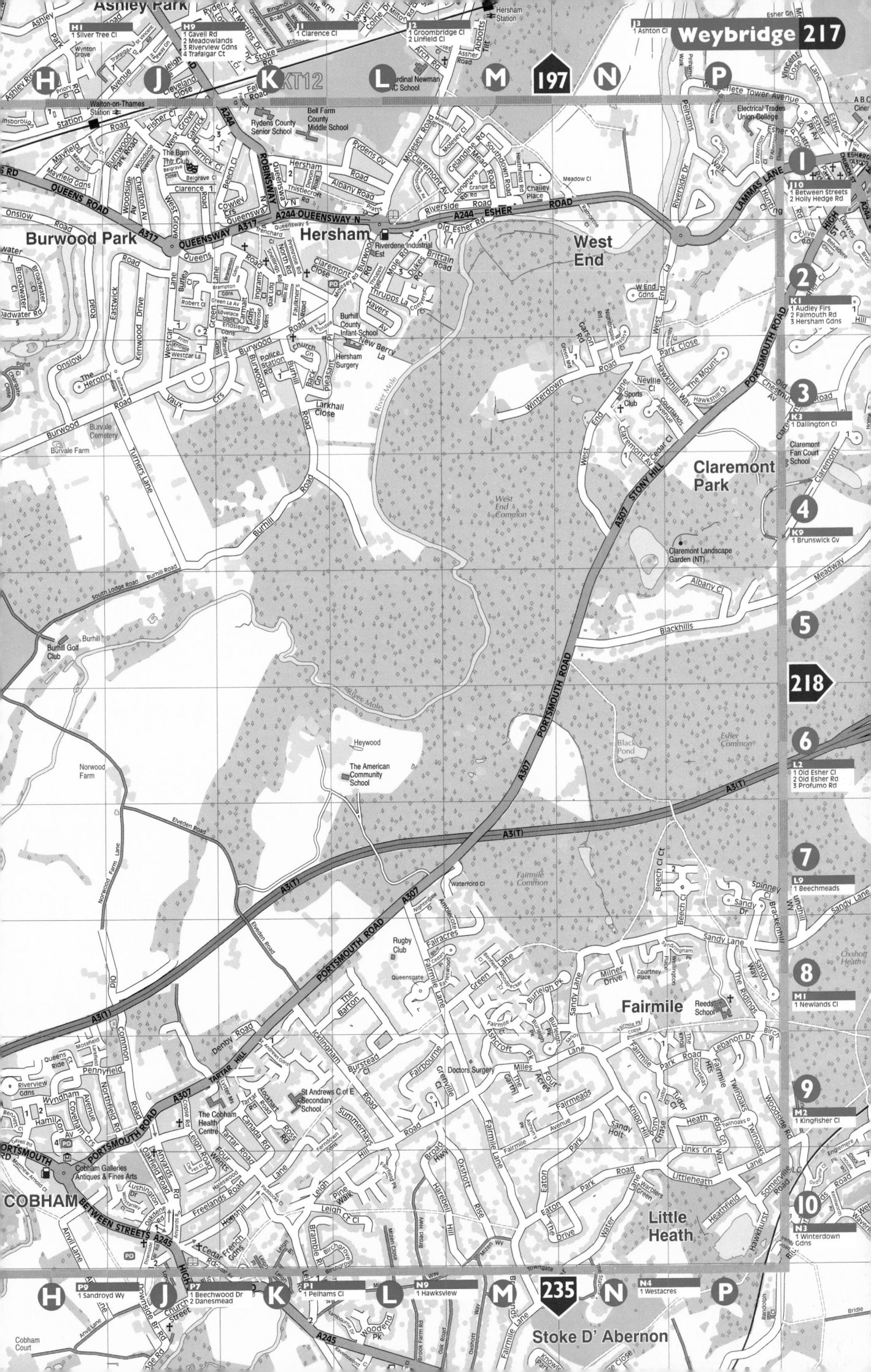

H2
1 Gibson Cl
2 Tedder Cl

H3
1 Hubbard Dr

J1
1 Bramham Gdns
2 Hook Rd
3 St Paul's Cl

J2
1 Babbacombe Cl
2 Hatherleigh Cl
3 Trewenna Dr

K1
1 Merritt Gdns

K2
1 Coutts Av

L1
1 Fleetwood Cl
2 Harrow Cl
3 York Wy

199

K4
1 Lara Cl
2 Lindsay Cl
3 Wetherby Wy

L2
1 Melford Cl

L3
1 Clippesby Cl

M2
1 Finlays Cl

220

M3
1 Kelvin Cl

K5
1 Galen Cl
2 Nell Gwynne Cl

M8
1 Nightingale Cl

Hook

Chessington

Barwell

Chessington World
of Adventures

Horton Country
Park

Horton Park Farm

West Park Farm

Horton Hospital

Epsom Ewell
& St Helliers
NHS Trust

Surrey Heartlands
NHS Trust

KT19

Rushett
Farm

Epsom
Common

The Forest

The Wells

EPSOM

H
P8
1 Oak Leaf Cl

J
P2
1 Cyclamen Wy

P6
1 Parkhurst
2 Tichmarsh

K
P1
1 Bourne Wy
2 Cherwell Ct
3 Fairway Cl

L

M
237

N3
1 Orchard Cl

N2
1 Devon Wy
2 Iris Rd
3 Pemberley Cl
4 Ruxley Ms

P

Numbered streets
Street names for grid
squares which are not listed
on this page are shown at
the back of the index

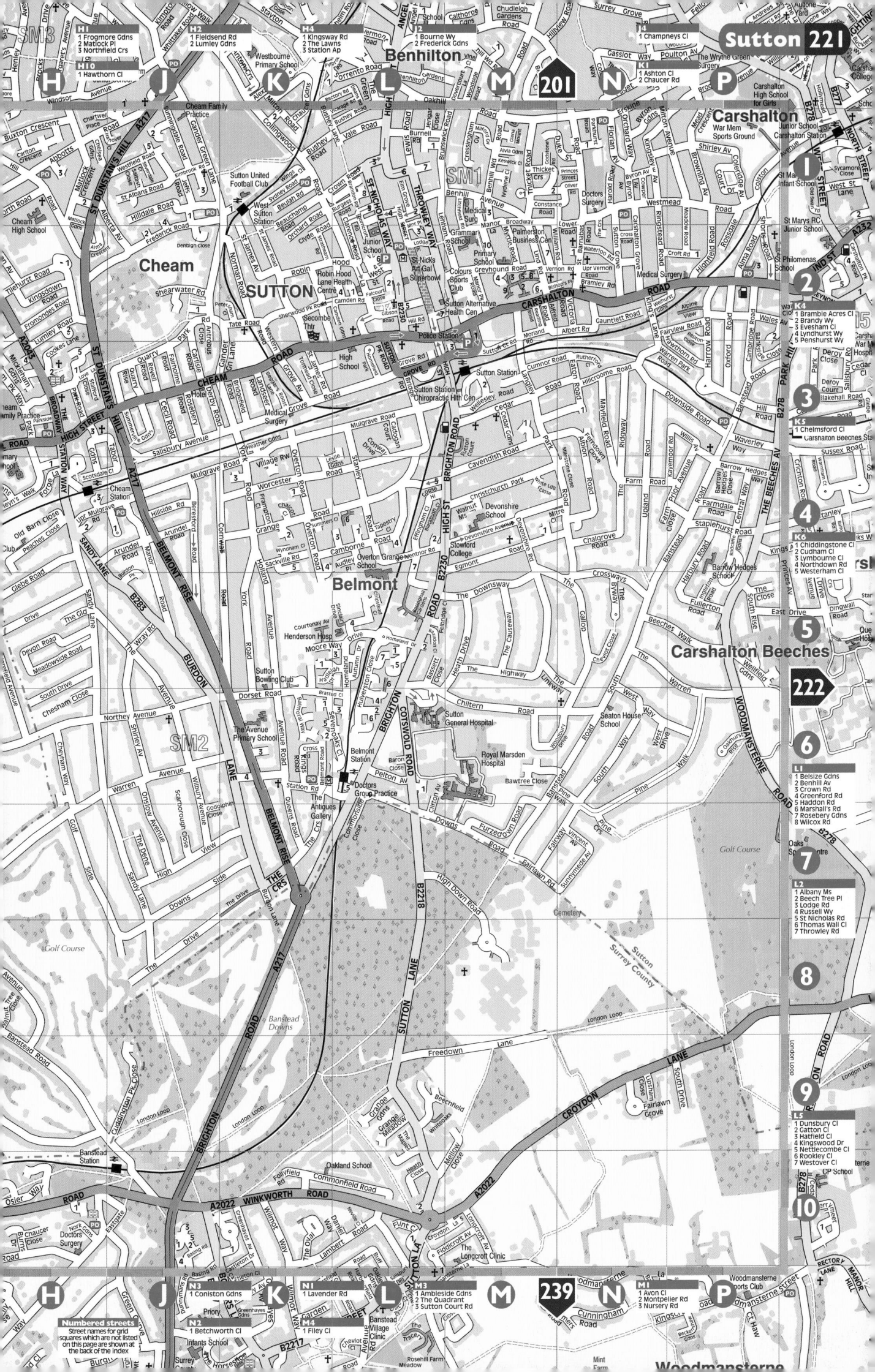

Mark

Ravenswood
School for Boys

F1
1 Beeken Dene
2 Brickfield Farm
Gdns
3 Greenacres Cl
4 Hunter's Gv
5 Romsey Cl
6 Shurlock Dr
7 Sumner Cl

A   **B**   206   **C**   **D**   **E**   **F**   **G**

CROFTON

E1
1 Ashtree Cl
2 Bassetts Cl
3 Harlands Gv
4 Paddock Cl
5 Tugmutton Cl

D1
1 Claremont Cl

A2
1 Colliers Wd

Locksbottom

Edward
Ash Gallery

Darrick Wood
Swimming Pool

Darrick Wood
Junior &
Primary School

School for Girls

1

F2
1 Crabbs Croft Cl
2 Ladycroft Gdns
3 Starts Hill Av

Keston

Keston C of E
Primary School

Bromley Hospitals
N H S Trust

The Birches

Farnborough

FARNBOROUGH WAY A21

HIGH STREET

Farnborough
Primary School

2

G1
1 Beechcroft Cl
2 Topcliffe Dr
3 Walmer Cl

Heathfield
College

Church

3

G2
1 Saphora Cl

Holwood

Shire Lane

The Larches

High Elms
Country
Park

Shire Lane

4

Church Road

Downe Road

Shire Lane

Lower Hook
Farm

North End
Farm

High Elms
Golf Course

Holwood
Farm

Farthing Street

5

225

Orange Court
Lane

North End Lane

High Elms Road

6

The
Rookery

Rookery Road

Mill
Lane

Gorringes

Cuckoo Wood

PH

Leaves Green

Standard Road

Downe
Primary
School

7

Leaves Green
Crescent

Cemetery

Butchers
Yard

Downe

High Street

Hazelwood

Hazel
Wood

8

Milking Lane

Green Hill

West Hill

Cudham Road

Snag

Keith Park
Crescent

Down
House

Hang Grove Hill

9

Biggin Hill
Airport

Hostye Farm

Mace

10

Luxted

Luxted Road

Bird House Lane

Cudham Lane North

Cemetery

Biggin Hill
Business
Park

Airport
Industrial
Estate

A   **B**   244   **C**   **D**   **E**   **F**   **G**

Cudham

1 grid square represents 500 metres

Costains
Farm

Charles
Darwin

Westend
Common

West **d**

F2
1 Daffodil Dr
2 Yellowcress Dr

F1
1 Cobbetts Farm
2 Coombe Manor
3 Marigold Dr
4 Nasturtium Dr
5 Primrose Dr
6 Strawberry Rl

C9
1 West Heath

A B **212** C D E F G

Lucas Green

Lucas Green Road
Priest Lane

Ford Road

School Lane
Cedar Grove
Church Lane
Greyfriars Walk
Cobbett's Walk
King's Cl
Inns Rd
Lower Rd
Freesia Dr
Rose Dr
Eder Rd
Angelica Rd

Bisley

Furze Farm

Shaftesbury Road
Corteslor Close
Arthus Way
South Road
Marie Cone Rd
Hawthorn Way
Port Way
Queens Cl
Elm Gv
Snowdrop Way
Wilcot Cl
PO
GUILDFORD
Pilgrims Way
Clews
Oakwood Court

ROAD

Bisley
Common

Miles Green

Chatton Row

Queens Road

Limecroft Road
Ivydene
Chobham Road
A322

Bisley
Ranges

Staffordlake

Stafford Lake
Stafford
Grindstone Crs
Oak
Oakwood Gardens
Rapsley Lane
The Spur
Sparvell Road

BAGSHOT ROAD

Water Lane
Echo Road
Bisley Camp
King's Avenue
Queens Road

Sheets Heath

Benwell Road

Sheet's Heath Lane
The Ridgeway
Riverside Close
Connaught Crs

Brookwood

Brookwood Bridge

Brookwood County Primary School
Heath Drive
Lockswood

Cow Moor

Pirbright Camp
Greenwood Road
Alexander Barracks
Army Training Regiment
North Dr
Beech
Beech Cv
Billesden Road
Coopers Hill
South Drive
Brunswick Drive
Slade Road
Mainstone
Herons Way
Manor Way
Heather Way
Plovers Rl
Cobbetts Rd
Brunswick

Union St
Prince St
St George
abeth Barracks
Brunswick Road
rzon dge
B3012

Basingstoke Canal

Connaught Close
PO
CONNAUGHT
Church Close
Brookwood Station
ROAD
Pine Avenue
Long Avenue
Military Cemetery
Western Avenue
Eastern Avenue

A324

B3012 **GOLE ROAD**
Stanley Pool
Mazamboni Farm
Stanley Hill
Goal Farm Golf Club
Vapery Lane
Pirbright Common
Porter Cl
Dawney Hill
Dawney's Hill
Stanley Rd

Cemetery Pales
Brookwood Cemetery

B3405
Grange Road
SCHOOL LANE
Pirbright County First & Middle School
Knowl Hill School
The Gardens
Doctors Surgery
Av. De Cagny
A324
St Barnabas Av

Church Lane
Thompsons Close
Gibb's Acre
PO

A324

GUILDFORD ROAD

Pirbright

Rapley's Field
Colter's Field
White's Farm

Mill Lane
Pirbright Lodge
Rowe Lane
Chapel Lane
Duchies

A B **248** C D E **A324** F **GUILDFORD** G **B3032 ROAD**

Bullswater Common Road
Bullswater Common

1 2 3 4 5 6 7 8 9 10

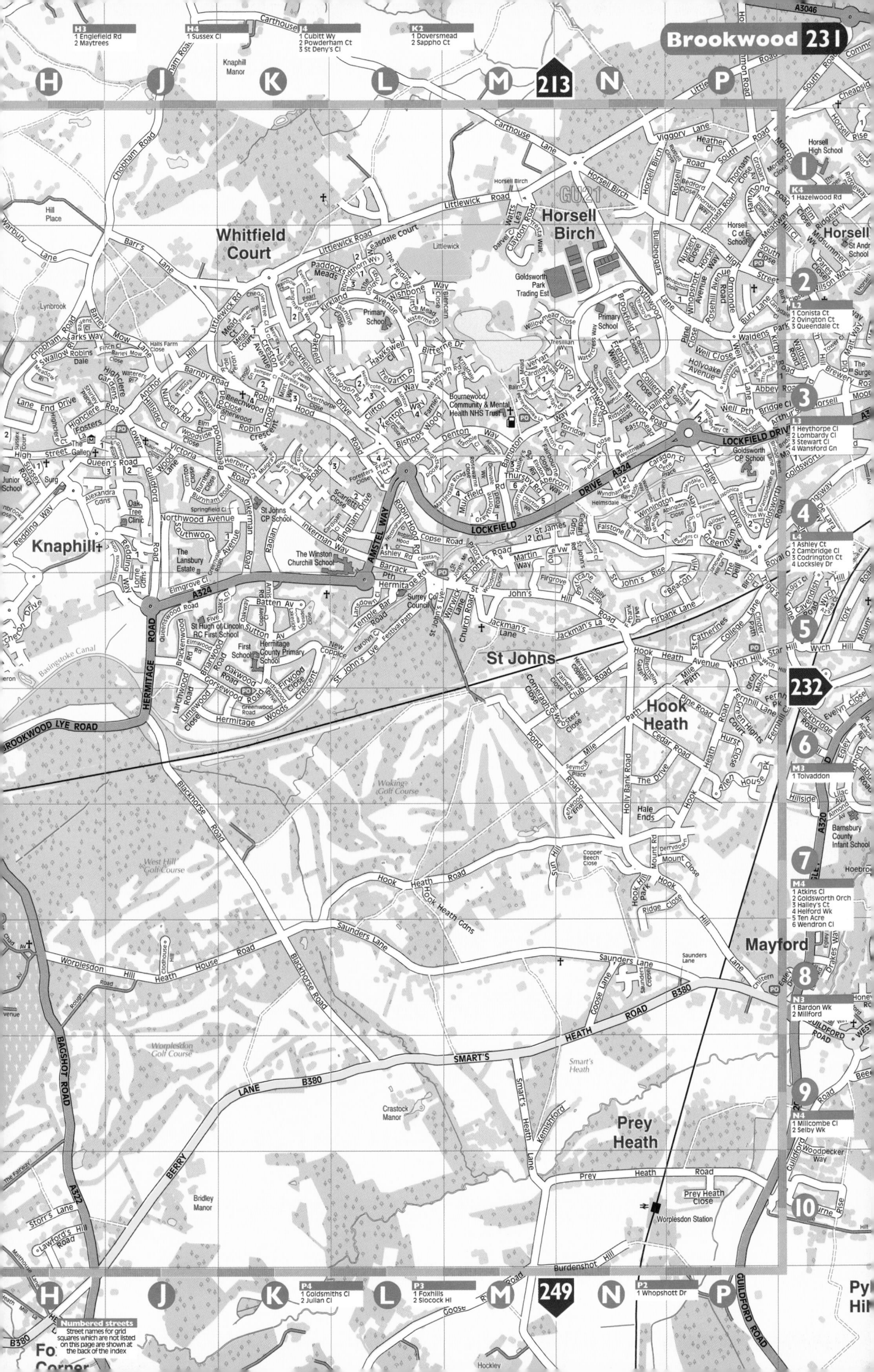

A B 216 C D E F G

I

Wisley

M25

2

Wisley Lane

3

Wisley Common

Semaphore Tower

Junction 10

Ockham Common

Chatley Farm

Pointers Road

M25

Poynters

4

Royal Horticultural Society's Gardens Wisley

PORTSMOUTH ROAD

A3(M)

Bolder Mere

Hatchford Park

Elm Corner

Elm Lane

Hatch Lane

Cold Norton Farm

5

A3(M)

233

Old Lane

6

Bridge End

Hatch Lane

Ockham Lane

Upton Farm

Martyr's Green

May's Green

Church End

7

B2039

Alms Heath

School Lane

Stumps Grove

Ockham

Ockham Park

Guileshill Lane

8

Guileshill Farm

OCKHAM ROAD NORTH B2039

Blackmoor Farm

Slade Farm

Whitehill Lane

9

Ryde Farm

Ridley Lane

Bachelor's Lane

Green Lane

Waterloo Farm

The Drift

The Forest

10

Bachelors

Long Reach

Green Lane

Northcote Crs

The Raleigh School

Glenesk House Preparatory School

Horsley Station

Parkside Cl

Parkside Pl

Hooke Road

Forest Road

Forest Close

The Ridings

Nightingale Road

A B 252 C D E F G

Green Lane West

Manor

Edwin Rd

1 grid square represents 500 metres

226

A   B   C   D   E   F   G

Luxted

C4
1 Rosecroft Cl

B
1 Blackthorn Rd

Cemetery

Cudham

Biggin Hill Business Park

Airport Industrial Estate

Surex Swimming Pools

Costains Farm

Charles Darwin School

Cudham School

Berry's Green

New Barn Farm

Biggin Hill Junior School

Doctors Surgery

The Rings Police Station

Aperfield

South Street

Southwood

Bombers Farm

Cudham Grange

Grays Road

Silversted Lane

Grays Farm

243

Tatsfield

Hawley's Corner

Bromley Kent County

Tatsfield Primary School

New Surgery

Betsom's Hill

Hill Park

Hill School

TN16

Betsoms Farm

Pilgrim House

Clarks Lane Farm

Tatsfield Court Farm

Chestnut Avenue

The Avenue

WESTERHAM HILL

Gaysham Farm

Pilgrims Farm

A233 LONDON ROAD

Force Green

Westerham Wood

A   B   C   D   E   F   G

262

Clacket Lane Service Area

Court Lodge

Churchill School

1 grid square represents 500 metres

L3
1 Crossways

L4
1 The Crossroads

N1
1 Bennetts Farm Pl
2 Childs Hall Dr
3 Longmeadow

P2
1 Brodrick Gv

H   J   K   L   M   235   N   P

Effingham
Cricket Club

Lower
Farm

Hinterland
House

Thornet
Wood

Little
Bookham

KT23

Greatlee
Wood

Sole Farm Avenue

Fairlawn

The Park

Junior School

Fetcham Vill
Surgery

I

P3
1 Mayfield Gn

Fairfield Medical
Centre

Effingham Common Road

Leewood
Way

St Lawrence
CP School

PH

Orestan
Farm

Orestan   Lane

Middle Farm Pl

Church   Lane

Chapel

Effingham
Place

Howard of
Effingham School

Manor House
School

Water Lane

Cemetery

Preston Cross
Hotel & Country Club

The Grange

Swanns
Meadow

Hawkwood
Rise

Hawkwood
Dell

GUILDFORD   ROAD   A246

West Down

Beales   Road

Foxwarren

2

Great
Book

3

The Surgery

Yew Tree Wk

PO

Effingham

St Teresas
Preparatory School

Browns La

The St

A246

Mount
Pleasant

Lingens
Cl

Norwood
Close

Norwood

Meadway

Links Wy

Rectory   Lane

Manorhouse   Lane

Guildford
Road

Orchard
Gdns

4

Goldstone
Farm

Chester
Road

Calvert   Road

Salmons   Road

Effingham
Golf Club

Beech   Cl

Strathcona   Avenue

Woodlands   Road

Polesden

5

254

Dirtham Lane

A246

Park

Horsley

Rowbarns

Warren
Farm

High Barn   Road

Beech   Avenue

High Barn

6

Polesden
Lacey (NT)

7

Yewtree
Farm

Oldlands
Wood

Critten   Lane

Effingham Hill
Farm

8

Ranmore
Common

Crocknorth

St Teresas
School

9

Pigden
Cottage

Dogkennel Green

10

Dunley Hill
Farm

High Barn   Road

North Downs Way

Landbarn
Farm

H   J   K   L   M   271   N   P

Oaken
Grove

254

236

253

272

A B C D E F G

Hill

Street

Great Bookham

Fetcham Downs

Norbury Park

Druids Grove

Micklehar

Box Hill School

Swanworth Lane

Fr

Goldstone Farm

Polesden

Phoenice Farm

Crabtree Cottage

Crabtree Lane

Crabtree Lane

Chapel Farm

Camilla Drive

Polesden Lacey (NT)

Bagden Farm

Chapel Lane

Chapel Lane

Westhumble

Box Hill & Westhumble Station

Westhumble St

Yewtree Farm

Tanner's Hatch

Ashcombe Wood

North Downs Way

Denbies Wine Estate

Ranmore Common

Ranmore Common

Ranmore Common Road

Ranmore Common Road

North Downs Way

Denbies

Ranmore Road

Ranmore Road

North Downs Way

Ashcombe Road

St Martins C of E School

Dorking West Station

Station Road

The Dorking Business Park

1 grid square represents 500 metres

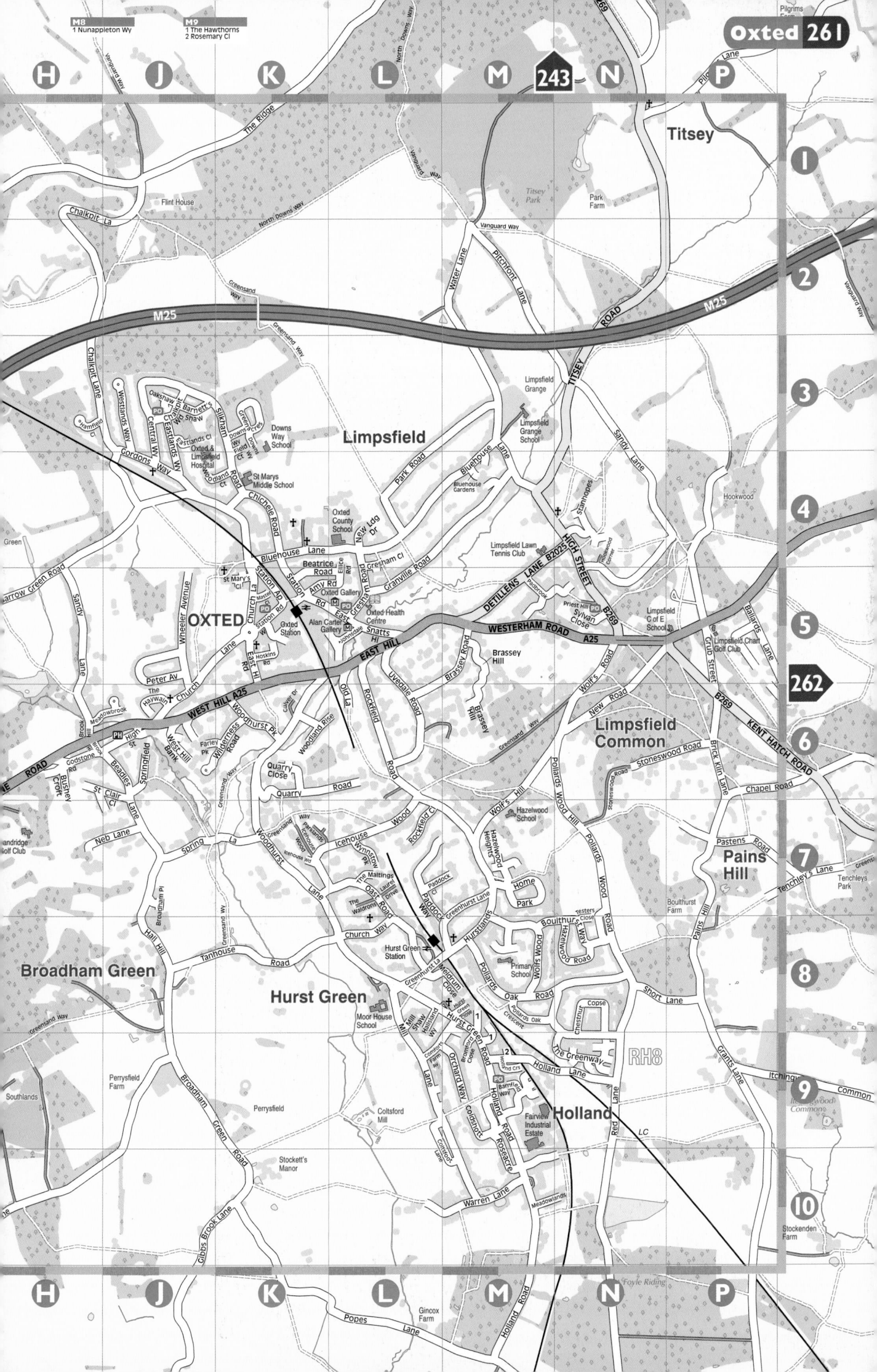

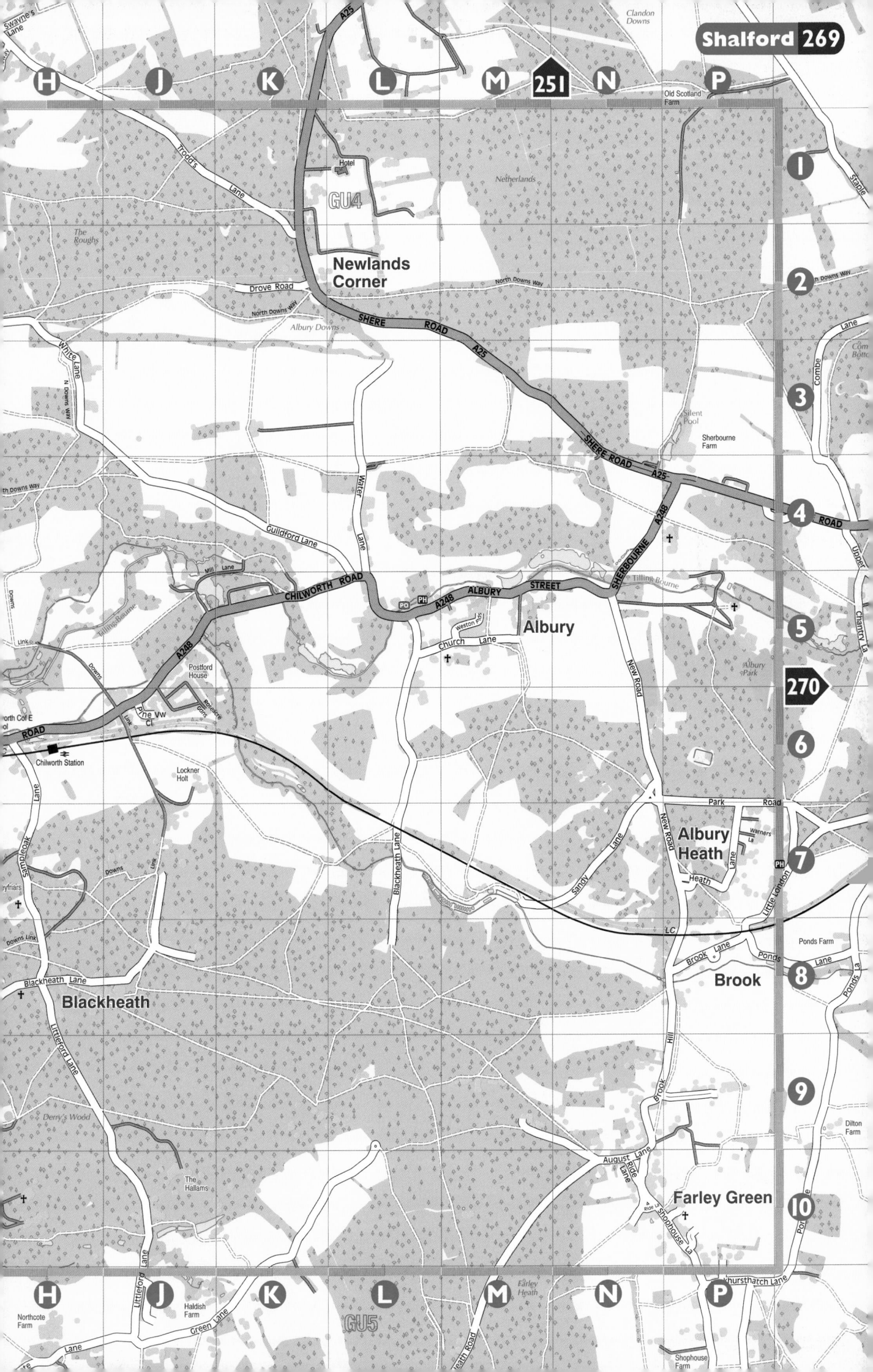

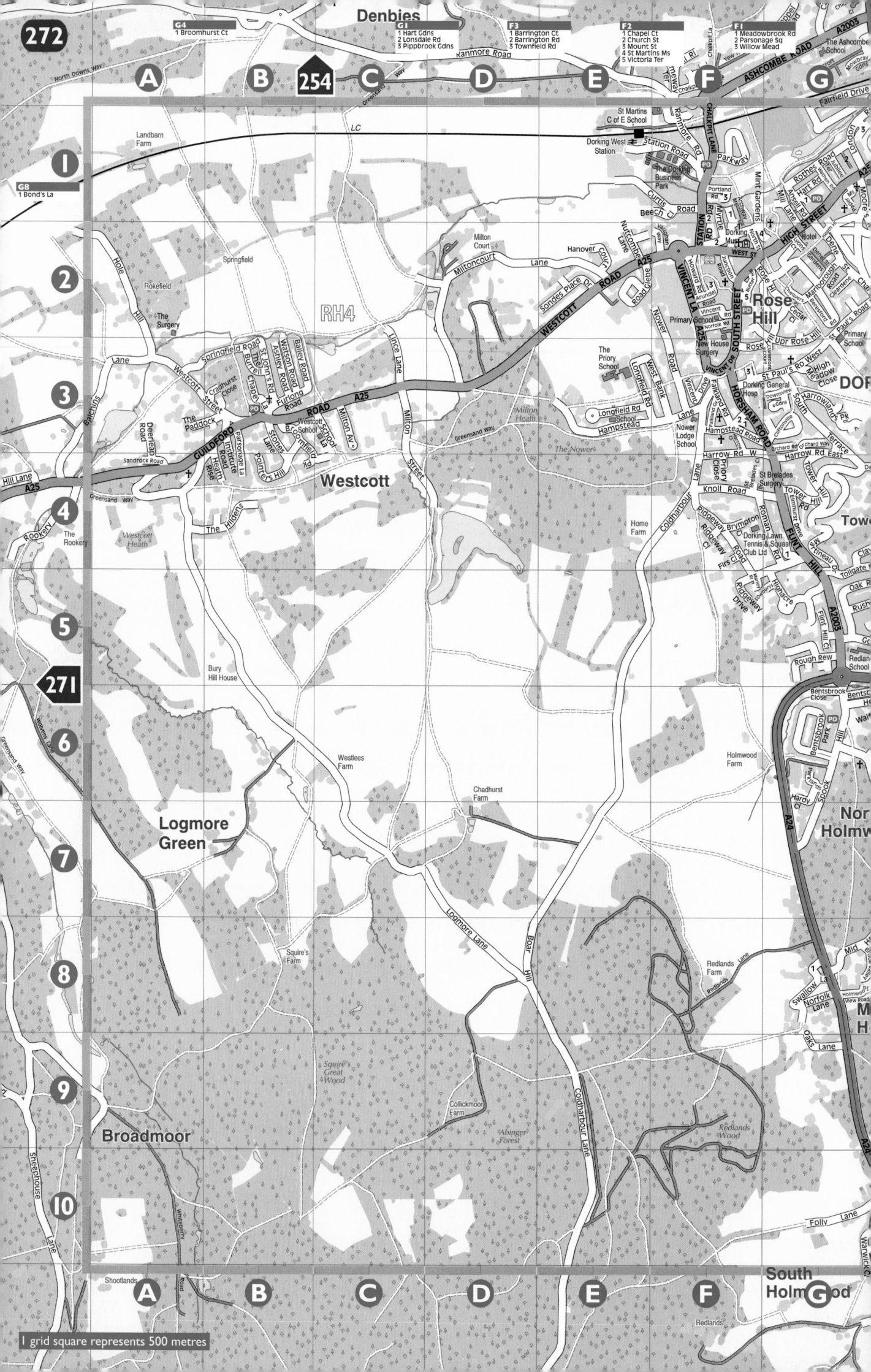

282

Newhouse Farm

278

Charlwood

Russ Hill

G9
1 Coniston Cl
2 Kittiwake Cl
3 Langdale Rd
4 Sandpiper Cl
5 Woodcroft Rd

G8
1 Abbotsfield Rd
2 Fulmar Cl
3 Hunstanton Cl
4 Moor Park Crs
5 The Orchards
6 Prestwick Cl
7 Puffin Rd
8 Troon Cl

Upper Prestwood Farm

Ivyhouse Farm

Sussex Border Path

Oaklands Park

Prestwood Lane

Lower Prestwood Farm

Orltons

Jordans

Partridge Lane

Chaffold's Farm

Surrey County
West Sussex County

Orltons Lane

Ifieldwood

The Mount

The Mount

Langhurst

Rusper Road

Sussex Border Path

Highams

Capel Road

Newdigate Road

Hillybarn Road

Ifield Wood

Bonwycks Place

Chowles

East Street

Burnt House Lane

Langhurst Lane

Rusper Road

Sussex Border Path

Rusper

School

PO

Normans

COOKS Md

Steeres Road

Ashmore La

Horsham

Pucks Croft

Faygate Lane

Cobnor

Lambs Green

Stumbleholm Farm

St Andrews Road

Hoylake Close

Birkdale Drive

Fairway

Fairway

Baldhorns Park

River Mole

Axmas Farm

Lambs Green Road

Rusper Court House

Wimland Road

Kilnwood End

Kilnwood

Coombers Farm

Carylls

Kilnwood Lane

Faygate Lane

Wimlands Lane

Carylls Lea

HORSHAM RD

Chetwood Road

1 grid square represents 500 metres

Place	Page	Grid
Abbey Mead	195	L6
Abbey Wood	163	L3
Abbots Langley	54	F8
Abbotswood	250	C8
Abinger Common	271	L9
Abinger Hammer	270	F6
Abridge	83	M7
Acton	135	P10
Acton Green	156	A3
Addington	224	F3
Addiscombe	203	N8
Addlestone	215	M2
Addlestonemoor	195	M9
Adeyfield	36	B6
Aimes Green	63	L4
Albury	269	M5
Albury Heath	269	P7
Aldborough Hatch	123	H2
Aldenham	73	P3
Aldersbrook	121	P6
Alperton	135	K3
Amersham	69	J4
Amersham Common	69	H5
Amersham Old Town	68	E6
Amersham on the Hill	68	G3
Amwell	21	H4
Anerley	203	P2
Anthonys	214	D8
Aperfield	244	C3
Apsley	35	N10
Ardleigh Green	125	K1
Ardley End	31	J2
Arkley	76	E9
Artington	267	N5
Asheridge	50	C2
Ashford	174	A8
Ashford Common	174	E9
Ashley Green	33	L10
Ashley Park	197	H10
Ashtead	237	K4
Austenwood	109	N1
Aveley	146	C9
Avery Hill	184	F2
Ayot Green	22	C3
Ayres End	20	E6
Badgers Mount	228	C5
Baker's Wood	111	H6
Balham	180	A3
Bandonhill	222	E2
Banstead	239	K2
Barking	142	C2
Barkingside	122	E1
Barnehurst	164	E9
Barnes	156	E7
Barnes Cray	165	J10
Barnet	77	J10
Barnet Gate	76	B10
Barnsbury	5	N3
Barwell	219	H4
Batchworth	92	A3
Batchworth Heath	92	B5
Batlers Green	74	E4
Battersea	158	A6
Bayford	42	G4
Bayley's Hill	264	F7
Bayswater	9	H7
Beaconsfield	88	B10
Bean	188	G6
Beaumont	171	N4
Beckenham	204	G3
Beckton	142	C8
Becontree	123	N10
Beddington	202	F9
Beddington Corner	202	B7
Bedford Park	156	C2
Bedmond	54	F3
Belgravia	16	C5
Bell Bar	41	K10
Bell Common	64	G8
Bellfields	249	P7
Bell Green	182	E6
Bellingdon	32	E10
Bellingham	182	F7
Belmont	94	F10
Belmont	221	K5
Belsize	53	H8
Belvedere	164	C4
Bengeo	25	J3
Benhilton	201	L10
Bennetts End	36	A9
Bentley	86	D7
Bentley Heath	77	J1
Berkhamsted	33	M5
Bermondsey	19	N2
Bernards Heath	38	C4
Berrylands	199	L6
Berry's Green	244	D2
Bessels Green	246	E10
Betchworth	255	P9
Bethnal Green	140	A5
Betsham	189	L7
Bewbush	283	J10
Bexley	163	M10
Bexleyheath	164	A10
Bickley	206	B2
Biggin	168	F5
Biggin Hill	243	N3
Binscombe	267	H9
Birch Green	24	D7
Birchwood	40	E2
Bishopsgate	171	L7
Bisley	230	G2
Blackbrook	273	K7
Black Corner	284	E1
Blackfen	185	J2
Blackheath	161	L8
Blackheath	269	H8
Blackheath Park	161	M10
Blacknest	193	H3
Blackwall	141	J9
Bletchingley	259	L10
Bloomsbury	11	K2
Bobbingworth	49	L9
Borehamwood	75	K7
The Borough	18	F2
Botany Bay	78	E2
Botley	51	M6
Bourne End	34	F8
Boveney	148	B5
Bovingdon	52	E3
Bovingdon Green	52	C5
Bovinger	48	C10
Bow	140	F4
Bow Common	140	F7
Bowes Park	98	F7
Bowmans	186	G3
Box Hill	255	M8
Boxmoor	35	L8
Brands Hill	150	E6
Brasted	245	N10
Brasted Chart	263	L4
Brays Grove	47	K2
Brentford	155	J5
Brentford End	154	G5
Brewer Street	259	K7
Brickendon	43	K5
Bricket Wood	55	M7
Brick Hill	213	H1
Bridge End	234	C6
Brimsdown	80	D6
Britwell	128	B7
Brixton	159	H10
Broad Colney	57	J4
Broadfield	267	P7
Broadford	203	J7
Broadgreen Wood	43	H1
Broadgreen Green	261	H8
Bradley Common	46	A6
Broadmoor	272	A9
Broadoak End	24	G3
Brockham	273	M1
Brockham Park	273	P5
Brockley	182	E1
Bromley	140	G5
Bromley	205	N2
Bromley Common	206	A6
Bromley Park	205	K1
Brompton	15	N4
Brondesbury	2	A1
Brondesbury Park	136	G3
Brook	269	P8
Brook Green	156	F2
Brooklands	216	A5
Brookmans Park	59	H2
Brook Place	212	G7
Brook Street	106	D5
Brookwood	230	F6
Broomhall	192	F7
Broom Hill	207	J7
Broxbourne	44	F6
Brunswick Park	98	B4
Buckhurst Hill	101	P4
Buckland	256	D9
Bucks Hill	53	M10
Bullen's Green	40	B8
Bulls Cross	79	P2
Bulstrode	53	H4
Bumble's Green	45	M10
Bunce Common	274	A7
Burgh Heath	238	G5
Burnham	128	B4
Burntcommon	251	J1
Burnt Oak	96	A8
Burpham	250	D6
Burrowhill	213	L5
Burrows Cross	270	C7
Burstow	281	H8
Burwood Park	217	H2
Bury Green	62	A7
Bushbury	273	M5
Bushey	94	B1
Bushey Heath	94	D1
Bushey Mead	200	G3
Bush Hill Park	79	M10
Bushy Hill	250	E8
Butlers Cross	89	L5
Byfleet	215	N9
Caldecote Hill	94	E1
Camberwell	159	N7
Camden Town	4	D4
Campions	30	A6
The Camp	38	F8
Canary Wharf	140	G10
Cannon Hill	200	G4
Canonbury	6	F3
Canons Park	95	K8
Carpenders Park	93	N3
Carshalton	221	P1
Carshalton Beeches	221	P5
Carshalton on the Hill	222	A4
Cartbridge	232	E8
Carter's Green	30	F9
Castle Green	143	M3
Castle Green	213	J9
Caterham	241	M9
Catford	183	H4
Chadwell Heath	123	N3
Chadwell St Mary	168	C2
Chaldon	241	J10
Chalfont Common	90	C5
Chalfont Grove	89	N7
Chalfont St Giles	89	L3
Chalfont St Peter	90	D8
Chalk	191	K4
Chalvey	149	H1
Chandler's Cross	72	A5
Charlton	162	A4
Charlton	196	D2
Charlwood	279	J8
Chartridge	50	B4
The Chart	263	L6
Chase Cross	104	F7
Chattern Hill	174	C7
Chaulden	34	G7
Cheam	221	J2
Cheapside	192	D2
Chelsea	15	M8
Chelsfield	227	P2
Chelsham	242	F3
Chenies	70	F4
Chertsey	195	K7
Chertsey Meads	195	P8
Chesham	51	H7
Chesham Bois	69	H2
Cheshunt	62	A6
Chessington	219	K3
Chessmount	51	K8
Chevening	246	A5
Chigwell	102	E3
Chigwell Row	103	L3
Childerditch	127	L2
Childsbridge	247	N5
Child's Hill	117	H7
Childwick Bury	20	B10
Childwick Green	20	A9
Chilworth	268	F6
Chingford	101	H3
Chingford Green	101	H2
Chingford Hatch	101	K5
Chipperfield	53	L7
Chipping Barnet	77	H8
Chipstead	240	B5
Chipstead	246	D8
Chislehurst	184	F10
Chislehurst West	184	D9
Chiswell Green	55	N1
Chiswick	156	C3
Chobham	213	J6
Cholesbury	32	B7
Chorleywood	70	G8
Chorleywood Bottom	70	G10
Chorleywood West	70	D9
Christmaspie	266	A1
Church End	71	J4
Church End	97	K10
Church End	136	C2
Church End	234	A7
Churchgate	62	A5
Churchgate Street	30	A1
Church Langley	47	N1
Church Town	260	B7
Cippenham	128	C10
City of London	12	D7
Clapham	158	C8
Clapham Park	180	A3
Clapton Park	120	E9
Claremont Park	217	P4
Clatterford End	67	J6
Claverhambury	63	N3
Claygate	218	E3
Clayhall	102	C10
Clay Hill	79	K3
Clement Street	187	L9
Clerkenwell	12	A1
Clewer Green	148	D9
Clewer New Town	148	F8
Clewer Village	148	F6
Clock House	222	D10
Cobham	217	H10
Cockfosters	77	P9
Codmore	51	K6
Coldblow	186	D5
Coldblow	186	G7
Coldharbour	165	H3
Cole Green	24	B7
Coleman Green	21	M6
Cole Park	176	F2
Coleshill	68	E10
Coles Meads	258	A7
Colham Green	132	A6
Colindale	116	B1
College Park	104	D9
Collier Row	104	D9
Colliers Hatch	66	D6
Collier's Wood	179	N10
Colnbrook	150	F7
Colney Hatch	98	A7
Colney Heath	39	P8
Colney Street	56	D6
Commonwood	53	K10
Compton	266	F6
Coney Hall	225	K1
Coombe	178	B10
Coopersale Common	65	N5
Coopersale Street	65	M7
Cooper's Green	39	N1
Cooper's Hill	172	A6
Copse Hill	178	D10
Copthall Green	64	A9
Copthorne	285	J2
Corbets Tey	126	A10
Cottenham Park	200	E1
Coulsdon	240	F2
Counters End	35	K6
Cowley	131	M6
Cowley Peachy	131	M8
Coxtie Green	86	C9
Cranbourne	170	A5
Cranbrook	122	D5
Cranford	153	H6
Cranham	126	D5
Cranley Gardens	118	B2
Crawley	283	P8
Crawley Down	285	M3
Crayford	187	H1
Creekmouth	143	H7
Crews Hill	79	J1
Cricklewood	116	G9
Crockenhill	208	E7
Crockham Hill	262	F9
Crofton	206	G9
Cromer-Hyde	21	P6
Crooked Billet	178	E9
Cross Keys	264	C3
Crouch End	118	D4
Crow Green	86	F7
Croxley Green	72	B9
Croydon	203	L10
Cubitt Town	161	H3
Cudham	244	C1
Cudworth	278	B7
Cuffley	60	G4
Cupid Green	36	C2
Curtismill Green	84	G7
Custom House	142	B9
Dagenham	144	C2
Dalston	7	M2
Dancers Hill	76	F1
Darenth	188	B8
Dartford	187	K3
Dartmouth Park	118	B7
Datchet	149	N7
Datchet Common	149	P8
Dawesgreen	274	B6
Deacons Hill	75	M10
Dean Bottom	210	G3
Debden Green	82	F4
De Beauvoir Town	7	J5
Dedworth	148	C7
Deepdene	273	J2
Denbies	254	C10
Denham	111	K7
Denham Green	111	H4
Denton	191	M3
Deptford	160	E5
Derry Downs	207	N6
Digswell Park	22	G1
Digswell Water	23	K1
Doddinghurst	86	G3
Dollis Hill	136	E8
Donkey Town	212	C9
Dorking	272	G3
Dormer's Wells	134	A9
Dorney	148	A2
Doversgreen	275	L4
Downe	226	C7
Downham	183	J8
Down Park	285	P4
Downside	235	J5
Dryhill	246	C10
Ducks Island	96	A1
Dudden Hill	116	D10
Dudswell	33	J1
Dulwich	181	N5
Dulwich Village	181	M3
Dunton Green	246	F5
Ealing	135	N9
Earl's Court	14	E6
Earlsfield	179	M4
Earlswood	276	A2
East Acton	136	B9
East Barnet	97	N1
East Bedfont	174	C3
East Burnham	128	E3
Eastbury	92	G5
East Clandon	251	P7
Eastcote	113	J5
Eastcote Village	62	A5
East Dulwich	181	P1
Eastend	28	B10
East End Green	24	D9
East Ewell	220	G6
East Finchley	117	N1
East Ham	142	B4
East Horsley	252	E3
East Molesey	198	B5
East Sheen	178	A1
East Tilbury	169	M6
Eastwick	28	E7
Eden Park	204	E4
Edgware	95	N5
Edmonton	99	N5
Effingham	253	L3
Egham	172	D9
Egham Hythe	172	G9
Egham Wick	171	L10
Egypt	108	G9
Ellenbrook	40	A3
Elm Corner	234	B5
Elmers End	204	C3
Elm Park	125	J10
Elmstead	184	B8
Elstree	75	K10
Eltham	184	M4
Emerson Park	125	M4
Enfield	79	K8
Enfield Highway	80	B6
Enfield Lock	80	E3
Enfield Town	79	L7
Enfield Wash	80	D4
Englefield Green	171	N10
Epping	65	K6
Epping Green	42	E8
Epping Green	46	D10
Epping Upland	64	F2
Epsom	219	P10
Erith	164	G4
Esher	218	B1
Essendon	42	A3
Eton	149	H5
Eton Wick	148	E3
Ewell	220	E7
Eynsford	209	M9
Fair Cross	143	J10
Fairlands	249	J7
Fairlop	103	H9
Fairmile	217	N8
Falconwood	163	H10
Farleigh	224	E10
Farleigh Court	224	F10
Farley Green	269	P10
Farnborough	226	E2
Farncombe	267	J9
Farnham Common	129	J1
Farnham Park	129	H3
Farnham Royal	129	H4
Farningham	209	P7
Fawkham Green	210	C10
Felden	35	K10
Feltham	175	J5
Felthamhill	174	E1
Fernhill	280	F8
Fetcham	236	C9
Ficklesshole	225	K10
Fiddlers Hamlet	65	M8
Field Common	197	N7
Fields End	34	G5
Finchley	97	K9
Finsbury	6	K9
Finsbury Park	118	G7
Flamstead End	62	A4
Flaunden	52	D8
Fleet Downs	188	A5
Fleetville	38	F6
Fletcher's Green	265	L10
Flexford	248	C10
The Folly	20	G1
Foots Cray	185	L9
Force Green	245	H10
Forestdale	224	D5
Forest Gate	121	M10
Forest Hill	182	C4
Fortis Green	118	B2
Forty Hill	79	N5
Foster Street	48	A2
Foxbury	184	C4
Fox Corner	249	H1
Fox Hatch	86	E4
Fredley	254	G5
Freezy Water	80	D2
French Street	263	J6
Friday Hill	101	J4
Friday Street	271	J9
Friern Barnet	97	N6
Frithsden	34	D1
Froghole	262	G8
Frogmore	56	D4
The Frythe	22	D1
Fulham	156	G6
Fullwell Cross	102	C9
Fulmer	110	A9
Furnace Green	284	B9
Furzedown	180	C7
Gadbrook	274	A2
Gadebridge	35	J4
Gallows Corner	105	L9
Gants Hill	122	C4
Ganwick Corner	77	L1
Garston	73	K1
Gatton	258	A4
George Green	130	B8
Gerrards Cross	109	J5
Gidea Park	104	G10
Giggshill	198	F7
Gilston	28	G6
Gilston Park	28	G5
Cilwell Park	81	H7
Givons Grove	255	J1
Globe Town	140	C5
Goathurst Common	264	C6
Goddington	207	M10
Godstone	260	A7
Goff's Oak	61	K4
Golders Green	117	H4
Gomshall	270	C6
Goodley Stock	262	G6
Goodmayes	123	L7
Goose Green	44	C2
Gorhambury	37	K5
Gospel Oak	118	B10
Gossops Green	283	L8
Grange Hill	102	G3
Grange Park	79	H9
Gravel Hill	90	C7
Gravesend	190	F2
Grays	167	M6
Great Amwell	26	D6
Great Bookham	254	A2
Great Hivings	50	F4
Greatness	247	L6
Great Parndon	46	E3
Great Warley	106	F9
Green End	35	J7
Greenford	134	C6
Greenhill	114	A3
Greenhithe	188	G1
Greensted	67	K4
Greensted Green	67	J4
Green Street	75	J3
Green Street Green	188	F9
Green Street Green	227	H4
Greenwich	161	J4
Grovehill	35	N2
Grove Park	156	A7
Grove Park	183	P6
The Grove	72	B9
Grubb Street	210	G1
Guildford	267	N2
Guildford Park	267	M1
Hackbridge	202	C6
Hackney	140	B1
Hackney Wick	140	F1
Hacton	125	M10
Hadley	77	K7
Hadley Wood	77	N4
Haggerston	7	H1
Hailey	26	E9
Hainault	103	J8
Haldens	23	K1
Hale End	101	J7
Hall Grove	23	L7
Halls Green	45	P3
Halstead	228	C5
Ham	177	J6
Hammerfield	35	L5
Hammersmith	156	E3
Hamm Moor	215	N1
Hammond Street	61	K2
Hampstead	117	L3
Hampstead Garden Suburb	117	L1
Hampton	198	A1
Hampton Hill	176	B7
Hampton Wick	198	G1
Hamsey Green	242	B1
Handside	22	E6
Hanging Bank	264	D6
Hanwell	134	D10
Hanworth	175	L6
Harefield	91	M10
Harefield Grove	91	K8
Hare Street	46	E2
Harlesden	136	B4
Harlington	152	D5
Harlow	46	C1
Harmondsworth	151	M3
Harold Hill	105	M6
Harold Park	106	A7
Harold Wood	105	P7
Harpenden Common	20	A4
Harringay	119	H3
Harrow	114	C4
Harrow on the Hill	114	D6
Harrow Weald	94	B3
Hartham	25	L4
Hartley	211	L5
Hartley Green	211	K5
Hastingwood	48	A5
Hatch End	93	M8
Hatfield	40	C5
Hatfield Garden Village	40	B1
Hatfield Hyde	23	J8
Hatton	152	F10
Havering-atte-Bower	104	G4
Hawk's Hill	236	E10
Hawley	187	M8
Hayes	132	C3
Hayes	205	N7
Hayes End	132	E6
Hayes Town	133	K10
Hazelwood	226	F7
Headley	255	P2
Headstone	114	A2
Heath End	32	F7
Heath Park	125	J3
Heath Side	186	G5
Hedgerley	109	J6
Hedgerley Green	109	L5
Hedgerley Hill	109	K7
Hemel Hempstead	35	P6
Hendon	116	E3
Herne Hill	181	M2
Heronsgate	90	G1
Hersham	217	K2
Hertford	25	M6
Hertford Heath	26	A4
Hertingfordbury	25	H6
Heston	153	N6
Hextable	187	H10
Higham Hill	100	D10
Highams Park	100	G8
High Barnet	76	F7
High Beach	81	N5
Highbury	119	J9
High Cross	74	C2
Higher Denham	110	F5
Highfield	35	N4
Highgate	118	C5
High Laver	49	J3
The High	28	F10
Highwood Hill	96	C3
High Wych	29	L7
Hill End	91	J7
Hillingdon	132	B3
Hillingdon Heath	132	C7
Hill Park	244	E9
Hilltop	51	J5
Hinchley Wood	198	E10
Hither Green	183	K2
Hobbs Cross	30	B10
Hobbs Cross	83	N2
Hockenden	208	C3
Hoddesdon	44	D4
Hoe	270	D4
Hogpits Bottom	52	E8
Holborn	11	N4
Holders Hill	96	C9
Holland	261	M9
Hollybush Hill	129	N1
Holmethorpe	258	C8

Holtspur ... 88 A10
Holyfield ... 63 H4
Holywell ... 72 F10
Homerton ... 140 C1
Honor Oak ... 182 C2
Honor Oak Park ... 182 D2
Hook ... 219 K2
Hook End ... 87 H1
Hook Green ... 186 G7
Hook Green ... 189 L9
Hook Heath ... 231 N6
Hookwood ... 279 M5
Hooley ... 240 B8
Horley ... 280 C2
Hornchurch ... 125 L7
Horne ... 281 N2
Hornsey ... 118 F2
Hornsey Vale ... 118 G3
Horns Green ... 245 H3
Horsell ... 232 A2
Horsell Birch ... 231 M1
Horseman Side ... 85 M8
Horton ... 150 D9
Horton Kirby ... 210 C4
Hosey Hill ... 263 H4
Hounslow ... 153 P8
Hounslow West ... 153 L9
Housham Tye ... 30 E9
How Wood ... 56 B3
Hoxton ... 7 J8
Hubbard's Hill ... 265 J6
Hulberry ... 209 J9
Hunsdon ... 27 P2
Hunsdonbury ... 27 P5
Hunton Bridge ... 54 C9
Hurst Green ... 261 K8
Hurst Park ... 198 B2
Hurtmore ... 266 F10
Hutton ... 87 P10
Hutton Mount ... 107 N2
Hyde Heath ... 50 B10
Hyde Heath ... 68 C1
The Hyde ... 116 C3
Hythe End ... 172 E6
Ickenham ... 112 B8
Ide Hill ... 263 P7
Ifield ... 283 K5
Ifield Green ... 283 K4
Ifieldwood ... 282 G4
Ilford ... 122 D8
Irons Bottom ... 275 K8
Isle of Dogs ... 160 G3
Isleworth ... 154 C9
Islington ... 6 A5
Istead Rise ... 190 B10
Iver ... 131 J8
Iver Heath ... 130 G3
Ivy Chimneys ... 65 H8
Jack's Hatch ... 46 E7
Jacobs Well ... 249 P5
Jordans ... 89 L8
Katherines ... 46 B4
Kelvedon Hatch ... 86 C3
Kemsing ... 247 N3
Kenley ... 241 L2
Kennington ... 17 M10
Kensal Green ... 136 F5
Kensal Rise ... 2 A7
Kensal Town ... 8 A2
Kensington ... 14 G4
Kentish Town ... 4 F1
Kenton ... 115 H3
Keston ... 226 A1
Keston Mark ... 206 A10
Kevingtown ... 208 A6
Kew ... 155 L6
Keysers Estate ... 44 G7
Kidbrooke ... 161 P8
Kilburn ... 2 D6
Kingfield ... 232 B6
Kingsbury ... 115 N4
Kings Farm ... 190 F6
Kingsland ... 7 J3
Kings Langley ... 53 P4
Kingsmoor ... 46 F6
Kingston upon Thames ... 199 L3
Kingston Vale ... 178 A8
Kingswood ... 55 J10
Kingswood ... 239 J9
Kippington ... 265 H2
Kitt's End ... 77 H4
Knaphill ... 231 H4
Knightsbridge ... 15 P1
Knight's Hill ... 181 K4
Knockhall ... 188 G1
Knockholt ... 245 K3
Knotty Green ... 88 B5
Knowle Green ... 173 L8
Knowle Hill ... 193 N7
Ladywell ... 160 F10
Lake End ... 148 A1
Lakeside ... 166 F3
Laleham ... 195 M3
Lambeth ... 18 A3
Lambourne ... 83 N8
Lambourne End ... 103 M1
Lambs Green ... 282 C7
Lampton ... 154 A7
Lane End ... 188 C8
Langley ... 150 C2
Langleybury ... 54 C10
Langley Corner ... 130 C1
Langley Green ... 283 L3
Langley Vale ... 238 A6
Latimer ... 70 B3
Latton Bush ... 47 K5
Layters Green ... 89 N9
Lea Bridge ... 120 C8
Leasey Bridge ... 20 E2
Leatherhead ... 236 D7
Leavesden Green ... 54 G10
Leaves Green ... 226 A7
Lee ... 183 L2
Leigh ... 274 D7
Lemsford ... 22 C6
Lessness Heath ... 164 C5
Letchmore Heath ... 74 D5
Lett's Green ... 245 J2
Letty Green ... 24 B9
Leverstock Green ... 36 D7
Lewisham ... 161 H10
Ley Hill ... 51 N6
Leyton ... 121 J6
Leytonstone ... 121 L6
Lightwater ... 212 B7
Limehouse ... 140 E8
Limpsfield ... 261 L3
Limpsfield Chart ... 262 C7
Limpsfield Common ... 261 N6
Linford ... 169 J1

Lippitts Hill ... 81 L6
Lisson Grove ... 10 B3
Little Berkhamstead ... 42 B5
Little Bookham ... 253 M1
Little Chalfont ... 69 N6
Little End ... 67 M10
Littlefield Common ... 248 G5
Little Heath ... 34 D4
Little Heath ... 59 L5
Little Heath ... 123 M2
Little Heath ... 217 N10
Little Ilford ... 122 D10
Little Laver ... 49 N1
Little Missenden ... 68 A3
Little Parndon ... 28 E10
Little Stanmore ... 95 L9
Little Thurrock ... 167 P3
Littleton ... 196 C3
Littleton ... 267 M6
Littleton Common ... 174 C10
Little Warley ... 107 L10
Little Woodcote ... 222 B7
Littleworth Common ... 108 C8
Lockesbottom ... 206 E10
Logmore Green ... 272 A7
London Colney ... 57 H2
Longcross ... 193 N10
Long Ditton ... 198 G8
Longfield ... 211 L3
Longford ... 151 M7
Longford ... 246 E6
Longlands ... 184 F6
Loudwater ... 71 N7
Loughton ... 82 C8
Love Green ... 130 G7
Lower Ashtead ... 237 H5
Lower Bobbingworth Green ... 49 J10
Lower Bois ... 51 H10
Lower Clapton ... 120 B9
Lower Edmonton ... 99 M3
Lower Feltham ... 174 F6
Lower Green ... 198 A9
Lower Halliford ... 196 E7
Lower Holloway ... 118 G10
Lower Kingswood ... 257 K2
Lower Nazeing ... 45 J9
Lower Place ... 135 P4
Lower Sheering ... 30 B2
Lower Sydenham ... 182 C7
Lower Woodside ... 41 J8
Lowfield Heath ... 280 A10
Low Street ... 169 J5
Loxford ... 122 F10
Loyter's Green ... 30 G10
Lucas End ... 61 K3
Lucas Green ... 230 C1
Luxted ... 226 D10
Lye Green ... 51 L4
Magdalen Laver ... 48 E4
Maida Vale ... 2 G9
Maidenbower ... 284 D9
Maitland Park ... 4 A1
Malden Rushett ... 218 G8
Manor Park ... 122 B9
Manor Park ... 129 H6
Manor Royal ... 283 P3
Mantles Green ... 68 F4
Manwood Green ... 31 M6
Maple Cross ... 90 G5
Marden Ash ... 67 N6
Margery ... 257 K5
Mark Hall North ... 29 K8
Mark Hall South ... 29 K9
Marks Gate ... 103 P10
Marshalswick ... 38 F3
Marshmoor ... 40 G8
Martyr's Green ... 234 F6
Marylebone ... 10 C4
Matching ... 31 H7
Matching Green ... 31 L8
Matching Tye ... 30 G10
Maybury ... 232 E3
Mayfair ... 10 E8
Mayford ... 231 P8
Maypole ... 186 F4
Maypole ... 228 A3
May's Green ... 234 G6
Mead Vale ... 275 M3
Meath Green ... 279 N2
Meriden ... 73 M2
Merrow ... 250 F9
Merry Hill ... 94 A2
Merstham ... 258 C4
Merton ... 201 L1
Merton Park ... 201 J2
Micklefield Green ... 71 K4
Mickleham ... 254 C4
Middle Green ... 130 B9
Mid Holmwood ... 272 G8
Mile End ... 140 D6
Miles Green ... 230 E3
Mill End ... 91 J2
Mill Green ... 41 H1
Mill Hill ... 96 D6
Mill Meads ... 141 J4
Millwall ... 160 F2
Milton ... 190 G2
Mimbridge ... 213 N9
Mitcham ... 202 C3
Mogador ... 256 C5
Moneyhill ... 91 L2
Monken Hadley ... 77 H6
Monks Orchard ... 204 B7
Moorhouse Bank ... 262 D4
Moor Park ... 92 B5
Morden ... 201 K4
Morden Park ... 201 H6
Moreton ... 49 K7
Mortlake ... 155 N9
Motspur Park ... 200 D6
Mottingham ... 183 P5
Mount End ... 66 A4
Mount Hermon ... 232 C5
Mount Pleasant ... 91 L9
Mugswell ... 257 L1
Muswell Hill ... 98 B10
Naldersood ... 274 F10
Nash ... 225 M1
Nash Mills ... 54 B1
Nast Hyde ... 40 A5
Navestock Heath ... 85 K6
Navestock Side ... 86 B6
Nazeing ... 45 N8
Nazeing Gate ... 63 P1
Nazeing Long Green ... 45 M1
Nazeing Mead ... 45 J2
Neasden ... 116 A9
Netteswell ... 29 H10
New Addington ... 225 J4
New Ash Green ... 211 M9

New Barn ... 211 N2
New Barnet ... 77 L9
New Beckenham ... 182 D9
Newbury Park ... 122 G4
New Charlton ... 162 A3
New Cross ... 160 D8
New Cross Gate ... 160 D7
New Denham ... 131 K1
New Eltham ... 184 E5
Newgate Street ... 42 F10
New Greens ... 38 B1
New Haw ... 215 M4
New House ... 190 B5
Newington ... 18 B4
Newlands Corner ... 269 L2
Newman's End ... 30 G6
New Malden ... 200 C3
New Southgate ... 98 D5
Newtown ... 51 H5
New Town ... 187 N2
Newyears Green ... 112 B5
Nine Elms ... 158 E6
Noah's Arks ... 247 P5
Noak Hill ... 105 M3
Noel Park ... 99 J10
Nomansland ... 21 H5
Norbiton ... 199 L2
Norbury ... 203 J2
Nork ... 221 H10
Nork ... 238 G2
North Acton ... 135 P6
Northaw ... 60 B6
North Cheam ... 200 G10
Northchurch ... 33 J3
North Cray ... 186 B6
North End ... 117 M6
North End ... 164 G7
North Feltham ... 175 J1
North Finchley ... 97 M7
Northfleet ... 189 P1
Northfleet Green ... 189 P8
Northgate ... 284 A5
North Harrow ... 113 N4
North Hillingdon ... 132 C2
North Holmwood ... 272 C7
North Hyde ... 153 M4
North Kensington ... 136 G7
North Looe ... 220 F9
North Ockendon ... 126 G10
Northolt ... 133 P2
North Sheen ... 155 N8
North Stifford ... 147 K9
Northumberland Heath ... 164 D6
North Watford ... 73 J5
North Weald Bassett ... 66 A2
North Wembley ... 114 G6
Northwood ... 92 D9
Northwood Hills ... 92 E10
North Woolwich ... 162 B1
Norwood Green ... 153 P3
Norwood Hill ... 279 H4
Norwood New Town ... 181 L9
Notting Hill ... 8 B7
Nunhead ... 160 B10
Nuper's Hatch ... 104 F1
Nutfield ... 258 G10
Oakhurst ... 265 P9
Oakleigh Park ... 97 N3
Oakwood ... 78 E10
Oatlands Park ... 216 F1
Ockham ... 234 B8
Old Bexley ... 186 B3
Old Coulsdon ... 241 J6
Old Ford ... 140 D3
Old Harlow ... 29 M7
Old Hatfield ... 40 G3
Old Malden ... 200 A7
Old Oak Common ... 136 C6
Old Windsor ... 171 L3
Old Woking ... 232 E6
Onslow Village ... 267 K2
Orchard Leigh ... 51 N3
Orpington ... 207 J10
Orsett Heath ... 168 C1
Osidge ... 98 D3
Osterley ... 154 B6
Otford ... 247 H3
Ottershaw ... 214 F2
Otterspool ... 73 N3
Outwood ... 277 K9
Oxhey ... 73 L10
Oxlease ... 40 E5
Oxshott ... 218 B9
Oxted ... 261 J5
Pachesham Park ... 236 F2
Paddington ... 9 L4
Pains Hill ... 261 P7
Palmers Green ... 98 F4
Panshanger ... 23 K4
Park Barn ... 249 K9
Parkgate ... 278 A3
Park Langley ... 205 H6
Park Royal ... 135 M5
Park Street ... 56 B2
Parrock Farm ... 190 G6
Parsons Green ... 157 K7
Passingford Bridge ... 84 E5
Passmores ... 46 G4
Patchetts Green ... 74 B5
Peartree ... 23 H6
Peartree Green ... 87 J3
Peasemarsh ... 267 P8
Peckham ... 160 A8
Pedlars End ... 49 J7
Pednor Bottom ... 50 B5
Pednormead End ... 50 B8
Penge ... 182 B10
Penn ... 88 A8
Pentonville ... 5 P7
Perivale ... 135 H3
Perry Street ... 190 C3
Petersham ... 177 K4
Petts Wood ... 206 G4
Piccotts End ... 35 M2
Piercing Hill ... 82 G1
Pilgrims Hatch ... 86 G8
Pimlico ... 16 G7
Pimlico ... 36 F10
Pinnacles ... 46 D1
Pinner ... 113 L2
Pinner Green ... 93 K10
Pinnerwood Park ... 93 K8
Pirbright ... 230 E9
Pitch Place ... 249 L5
Pixham ... 255 H9
Plaistow ... 141 L4
Plaistow ... 183 M9
Plashet ... 142 A1
Plumstead ... 162 F4
Plumstead Common ... 163 J5

Ponders End ... 80 B9
Pond Park ... 50 C5
Poplar ... 140 F9
Potten End ... 34 D3
Potter's Bar ... 59 N9
Potters Crouch ... 37 L10
Potter Street ... 47 N3
Pouchen End ... 34 G7
Pound Hill ... 284 D5
Poverest ... 207 K4
Povey Cross ... 279 N6
Poyle ... 151 H7
Pratt's Bottom ... 227 L6
Presdales ... 26 D4
Preston ... 115 J6
Prey Heath ... 231 N9
Primrose Hill ... 4 D6
Puddledock ... 186 E9
Puddledock ... 263 K9
Pudds Cross ... 52 B4
Purfleet ... 165 P5
Purley ... 223 H8
Putney ... 178 C1
Putney Heath ... 178 F3
Putney Vale ... 178 D6
Puttenham ... 266 A4
Pyle Hill ... 250 A1
Pyrford ... 233 J1
Pyrford Green ... 233 L3
Pyrford Village ... 233 H4
Queensbury ... 115 K1
Radlett ... 56 D10
Radlett ... 75 H1
Rainham ... 145 J5
Ramsden ... 207 M8
Ranmore Common ... 254 B9
Ratcliff ... 140 D9
Rayners Lane ... 113 N6
Raynes Park ... 200 F3
Redbridge ... 121 P3
Redhill ... 258 B8
Regent's Park ... 4 F8
Reigate ... 257 J10
Reigate Hill ... 257 J8
Richings Park ... 151 H2
Richmond ... 177 K1
Richmond Hill ... 177 K2
Rickmansworth ... 91 K1
Ridge ... 58 C10
Ridge Green ... 276 F3
The Ridgeway ... 60 C3
Ripley ... 233 J1
Rise Park ... 104 F9
The Rise ... 192 D6
Riverhead ... 246 E8
Riverview Park ... 191 K7
Roe Green ... 40 D4
Roehampton ... 178 C1
Roestock ... 40 A9
Romford ... 124 E3
Romney Street ... 229 N8
The Rookery ... 93 H1
Rosedale ... 61 N4
Rosehill ... 201 L8
Rose Hill ... 272 F2
Rosherville ... 190 C1
Rotherhithe ... 160 C2
Round Bush ... 74 C4
Roundshaw ... 222 G3
Rowley Green ... 76 C7
Row Town ... 215 J3
Roxeth ... 114 B7
Roydon ... 27 N10
Roydon Hamlet ... 45 P5
Rucklers Lane ... 53 P2
Ruislip ... 112 F4
Ruislip Common ... 112 E2
Ruislip Gardens ... 112 F8
Ruislip Manor ... 113 H7
Rush Green ... 26 B5
Rush Green ... 124 F5
Rushmore Hill ... 227 M9
Russell Hill ... 222 G6
Russ Hill ... 278 F10
Ruxley ... 185 P9
Rydens ... 197 K9
Rydeshill ... 249 J8
The Ryde ... 40 F1
Rye Meads ... 27 J10
Rye Park ... 44 G2
Sabine's Green ... 85 L6
St Albans ... 38 E4
St George in the East ... 13 P8
St George's Hill ... 216 D5
St Giles ... 11 K5
St Helier ... 201 M8
St James ... 11 J10
St Johns ... 160 F8
St Johns ... 231 M5
St John's ... 247 H8
St John's Wood ... 3 K6
St Julians ... 38 B10
St Luke's ... 12 F1
St Margarets ... 26 F7
St Margarets ... 177 H2
St Mary Cray ... 207 M5
St Pancras ... 5 M10
St Paul's Cray ... 207 K2
St Stephens ... 37 P8
St Vincent's Hamlet ... 105 P2
Salfords ... 276 C8
Salt Hill ... 129 J10
Sanderstead ... 223 N8
Sandridge ... 21 H10
Sands End ... 157 M8
Sarratt ... 71 K1
Sarratt Bottom ... 71 H2
Sawbridgeworth ... 29 L1
Scotswood ... 192 C8
Seal ... 247 P7
Seer Green ... 88 G7
Seething Wells ... 198 C6
Selhurst ... 203 L5
Selsdon ... 224 B6
Send ... 232 F10
Send Grove ... 250 E2
Send Marsh ... 233 J2
Seven Kings ... 123 H6
Sevenoaks ... 247 L10
Sevenoaks Common ... 265 H5
Sevenoaks Weald ... 265 H8
Sewardstone ... 81 J6
Sewardstonebury ... 81 K9
Shacklewell ... 119 P9
Shacklford ... 266 C10
Shadwell ... 140 E4
Shadford ... 268 C2
Sheering ... 30 E3
Sheerwater ... 214 F9
Sheets Heath ... 230 E5

Shelley ... 49 P10
Shellwood Cross ... 274 B9
Shenfield ... 107 K1
Shenley ... 57 L10
Shenleybury ... 57 J7
Shepherd's Bush ... 136 E10
Shepperton ... 196 B6
Shepperton Green ... 196 B6
Shere ... 270 B4
Sherrardspark ... 22 B4
Shipley Bridge ... 280 G9
Shirley ... 204 B9
Shooters Hill ... 162 F7
Shootersway ... 33 K5
Shoreditch ... 7 H10
Shoreham ... 228 F7
Shorne ... 191 P8
Shorne Ridgeway ... 191 N10
Shortlands ... 205 K3
Shreding Green ... 130 E8
Shrubs Hill ... 193 H6
Sidcup ... 185 L7
Sidlow ... 275 L7
Silvertown ... 161 P1
Singlewell ... 190 F9
Sipson ... 152 A4
Slade Green ... 165 H8
Sleapshyde ... 39 P7
Slough ... 128 G8
Slough ... 149 P1
Slyfield ... 250 A7
Smallfield ... 281 H5
Smallford ... 39 N5
Smug Oak ... 56 A6
Soho ... 11 J7
Somers Town ... 5 J8
Sopwell ... 38 D9
Southall ... 133 M9
South Beddington ... 222 E3
Southborough ... 206 C6
South Bromley ... 141 J4
South Croydon ... 223 K3
South Darenth ... 210 C1
South Earlswood ... 275 P5
Southend ... 183 H7
South Field ... 148 F4
Southfields ... 179 K4
Southfleet ... 189 N9
Southgate ... 98 F2
South Hackney ... 140 B2
South Hampstead ... 3 L3
South Harefield ... 111 N2
South Harrow ... 114 A8
South Hatfield ... 40 F7
South Hornchurch ... 144 E3
South Kensington ... 15 J6
South Lambeth ... 158 F6
South Merstham ... 258 E6
South Mimms ... 58 E8
South Norwood ... 203 L3
South Nutfield ... 276 F2
South Ockendon ... 147 H6
South Oxhey ... 93 J4
South Park ... 275 H3
South Ruislip ... 113 L9
South Stifford ... 167 J4
South Street ... 244 C5
South Tottenham ... 119 M3
South Weald ... 106 D3
South Wimbledon ... 179 M8
South Woodford ... 101 M10
Speed Gate ... 210 E9
Spital ... 148 G10
Spitalbrook ... 44 F5
Spitalfields ... 13 L3
Spring Grove ... 154 C7
Spring Park ... 204 F9
Staines ... 173 J7
Staines Green ... 24 D7
Stamford Hill ... 119 N5
Stanborough ... 22 C8
Stanford Rivers ... 67 K9
Stanmore ... 94 G6
Stanstead Abbots ... 27 K7
Stanwell ... 173 M2
Stanwell Moor ... 173 K2
Stapleford Abbotts ... 84 E10
Stapleford Tawney ... 84 D2
Stepney ... 140 B7
Stewards ... 47 H6
Steward's Green ... 65 L8
Stockwell ... 158 F9
Stoke D'Abernon ... 235 N1
Stoke Green ... 129 M6
Stoke Newington ... 119 N7
Stoke Poges ... 129 L4
Stone ... 188 E1
Stonebridge ... 135 P2
Stonebridge ... 273 J5
Stonehill ... 214 B3
Stonehill Green ... 186 D9
Stoneleigh ... 220 C2
Stonewood ... 189 J6
Stoughton ... 249 N7
Strand ... 11 M7
Stratford ... 141 H2
Stratford Marsh ... 140 G3
Stratford New Town ... 141 H1
Strawberry Hill ... 176 D6
Streatham ... 180 F8
Streatham Hill ... 180 F4
Streatham Park ... 180 C7
Streatham Vale ... 180 C10
Stroude ... 194 C2
Stroud Green ... 119 H4
Sudbury ... 114 E10
Summerstown ... 179 N5
Sumners ... 46 D5
Sunbury ... 197 H3
Sunbury Common ... 174 G10
Sundridge ... 183 P9
Sundridge ... 246 A10
Sunningdale ... 192 C5
Sunninghill ... 192 C5
Sunnymeads ... 150 B10
Surbiton ... 199 J8
Sutton ... 150 F4
Sutton ... 221 K2
Sutton Abinger ... 271 J9
Sutton at Hone ... 187 P10
Sutton Green ... 250 C1
Swallows Cross ... 87 L3
Swanley ... 209 H3
Swanley Bar ... 59 L4
Swanley Village ... 209 H2
Swanscombe ... 189 J2
The Swillett ... 90 F1
Tadworth ... 238 F8
Tandridge ... 260 F4

Tatling End … 110 E6
Tatsfield … 244 A6
Teddington … 176 C9
Temple Fields … 29 K7
Temple Hill … 165 L10
Temple Mills … 120 G10
Thames Ditton … 198 F7
Thamesmead … 143 J10
Theydon Bois … 82 C3
Theydon Garnon … 83 M2
Theydon Mount … 84 B2
Thong … 191 K9
Thorney … 151 L1
Thornton Heath … 202 F5
Thornwood Common … 65 L1
Thorpe … 194 F3
Thorpe Green … 194 D4
Thorpe Lea … 172 F10
Three Bridges … 284 A6
Three Households … 89 L4
Threshers Bush … 48 B2
Tilbury … 168 D7
Tilegate Green … 48 E3
Tilgate … 283 N10
Timberden Bottom … 228 F6
Tinsley Green … 284 D1
Titsey … 261 P1
Tittenhurst … 193 H3
Tokyngton … 135 N1
Tolmers … 60 F2
Tolworth … 199 M8
Toot Hill … 66 C6
Tooting Graveney … 179 N8
Tottenham … 99 M10
Tottenham Hale … 119 N1
Totteridge … 97 H1
Tower Hill … 53 J5
Tower Hill … 272 G4
Townsend … 38 A4
Toy's Hill … 263 M8
Trumps Green … 194 A6
Tufnell Park … 118 D9
Tulse Hill … 181 J4
Turners Hill … 285 P9
Turnford … 62 C1
Twickenham … 176 D3
Twitton … 246 F2
Two Waters … 35 M9
Tye Green … 46 G3

Tylers Causeway … 42 C8
Tyler's Green … 48 E10
Tyler's Green … 260 A6
Tyler's Hill … 51 M7
Tyrell's Wood … 237 L10
Tyttenhanger … 39 K9
Underhill … 77 K10
Underriver … 265 P6
Upminster … 126 B7
Upper Clapton … 119 P6
Upper Edmonton … 99 P5
Upper Elmers End … 204 E5
Upper Halliford … 196 E4
Upper Holloway … 118 D7
Upper Norwood … 203 L1
Upper Shirley … 224 B1
Upper Sydenham … 181 P7
Upper Tooting … 179 P6
Upper Walthamstow … 121 H2
Upshire … 63 P8
Upton … 141 N2
Upton … 149 M2
Upton Lea … 129 M8
Upton Park … 141 P3
Uxbridge … 131 M3
Uxbridge Moor … 131 L3
Vale of Health … 117 N8
Valley End … 212 F2
Vauxhall … 17 M8
Venus Hill … 52 E7
The Village … 170 G6
Virginia Water … 193 P3
Waddon … 202 C9
Wallend … 142 D3
Wallington … 222 C2
Waltham Abbey … 63 J8
Waltham Cross … 62 B9
Walthamstow … 120 F1
Walton-on-Thames … 197 H8
Walton on the Hill … 238 C10
Walworth … 18 F8
Wanborough … 266 A3
Wandle Park … 203 H9
Wandsworth … 157 K10
Wanstead … 121 N5
Wapping … 140 A10
Ware … 26 E1
Warley … 106 G6
Warlingham … 242 C4

Warners End … 35 H5
Warwick Wold … 259 H5
Wasp Green … 277 K10
Waterdale … 55 K6
Waterend … 22 A3
Water End … 58 F2
Waterford … 24 C1
Waterhales … 85 L10
Waterside … 51 J9
Watford … 73 H5
Watford Heath … 93 M1
Watton's Green … 85 J10
Wealdstone … 114 F1
Weatherhill … 281 H3
Welham Green … 40 E9
Well End … 75 P4
Well Hill … 228 C2
Welling … 163 L9
The Wells … 219 L10
Welsh Harp … 116 A6
Welwyn Garden City … 23 L3
Wembley … 115 H10
Wembley Park … 115 M8
Wennington … 145 M9
West Acton … 135 M8
West Barnes … 200 F5
West Bedfont … 174 A3
Westbourne Green … 8 D2
West Brompton … 14 C9
Westbrook Hay … 34 F10
West Byfleet … 215 L9
West Clandon … 251 L5
Westcott … 272 C4
West Court … 191 H5
West Drayton … 151 N2
West Dulwich … 181 L5
Wested Fm … 208 F7
West End … 41 N4
West End … 212 E10
West End … 217 N2
Westerham … 262 G3
West Ewell … 220 B4
Westfield … 232 C8
West Green … 119 K1
West Green … 283 M6
West Hampstead … 117 K10
West Harrow … 114 B5
West Heath … 117 L7

West Heath … 163 N5
West Hendon … 116 D5
West Hill … 179 H3
West Horndon … 127 P4
West Horsley … 252 C4
Westhumble … 254 F7
West Hyde … 91 H8
West Kensington … 156 G4
West Kilburn … 2 B9
Westminster … 17 H4
West Molesey … 197 N4
West Norwood … 181 K7
Weston Green … 198 D8
West Ruislip … 112 D6
West Thurrock … 166 F4
West Tilbury … 169 H5
West Watford … 73 H9
West Wickham … 205 J8
Westwick Row … 36 F7
Westwood … 189 H10
West Yoke … 211 J10
Wexham Street … 129 P3
Weybridge … 216 B1
Wheathampstead … 20 C2
Whelpley Hill … 52 A2
Whetstone … 97 L3
Whippendell Botton … 53 M6
Whitebushes … 276 C5
Whitechapel … 13 M7
Whiteley Village … 216 G5
White Oak … 208 F2
Whitfield Court … 231 J2
Whitley Row … 264 C5
Whitton … 176 B2
Whyteleafe … 241 N4
Widmore … 206 C2
Wigginton Bottom … 32 D1
Wildernesse … 247 M8
Wildhill … 41 M7
Willesden … 136 D1
Willesden Green … 136 E2
Willey Green … 248 C7
Willowbank … 111 M10
Wilmington … 187 J7
Wilton Park … 88 C9
Wimbledon … 179 H8
Winchmore Hill … 88 C1
Winchmore Hill … 99 J2
Windlesham … 212 A3

Windsor … 149 J7
Wisley … 233 P1
Woking … 232 B4
Woldingham … 242 F9
Woldingham Garden Village … 268 F10
Wonersh … 249 M8
Woodbridge Hill … 91 P5
Woodcock Hill … 91 H8
Woodcote … 222 F7
Woodcote … 238 C5
Woodcote Green … 222 C6
Wood End … 132 F6
Wood End … 170 B9
Wood End Green … 132 F7
Woodford … 101 N7
Woodford Bridge … 102 C8
Woodford Green … 101 M8
Woodford Wells … 101 N4
Wood Green … 63 P10
Wood Green … 99 H9
Woodhall … 23 H7
Woodham … 215 K6
Woodhatch … 275 K3
Woodlands … 154 C9
Woodmansterne … 239 M5
Woodrow … 68 B8
Woodside … 41 K7
Woodside … 55 J8
Woodside … 65 N1
Woodside … 170 A7
Woodside … 203 P6
Woodside Park … 97 K5
Wood Street Village … 248 E9
Woollensbrook … 26 C3
Woolwich … 162 D5
Worcester Park … 200 E9
World's End … 79 H8
Wormley … 44 D10
Wormleybury … 44 A9
Wormley West End … 43 P8
Worplesdon … 249 J3
Worth … 284 J8
Wotton … 271 M5
Wray Common … 257 M5
Wraysbury … 172 B3
The Wrythe … 201 P9
Yeading … 133 K6
Yiewsley … 131 P9

USING THE STREET INDEX

Street names are listed alphabetically. Each street name is followed by its postal town or area locality, the Postcode District, the page number, and the reference to the square in which the name is found.

Example: **Abbeville Ms** *CLAP* SW4................................ **158** E10 [1]

Some entries are followed by a number in a blue box. This number indicates the location of the street within the referenced grid square. The full street name is listed at the side of the map page.

GENERAL ABBREVIATIONS

ACC ... ACCESS	CTYD ... COURTYARD	HLS ... HILLS	MWY ... MOTORWAY	SE ... SOUTH EAST
ALY ... ALLEY	CUTT ... CUTTINGS	HO ... HOUSE	N ... NORTH	SER ... SERVICE AREA
AP ... APPROACH	CV ... COVE	HOL ... HOLLOW	NE ... NORTH EAST	SH ... SHORE
AR ... ARCADE	CYN ... CANYON	HOSP ... HOSPITAL	NW ... NORTH WEST	SHOP ... SHOPPING
ASS ... ASSOCIATION	DEPT ... DEPARTMENT	HRB ... HARBOUR	O/P ... OVERPASS	SKWY ... SKYWAY
AV ... AVENUE	DL ... DALE	HTH ... HEATH	OFF ... OFFICE	SMT ... SUMMIT
BCH ... BEACH	DM ... DAM	HTS ... HEIGHTS	ORCH ... ORCHARD	SOC ... SOCIETY
BLDS ... BUILDINGS	DR ... DRIVE	HVN ... HAVEN	OV ... OVAL	SP ... SPUR
BND ... BEND	DRO ... DROVE	HWY ... HIGHWAY	PAL ... PALACE	SPR ... SPRING
BNK ... BANK	DRY ... DRIVEWAY	IMP ... IMPERIAL	PAS ... PASSAGE	SQ ... SQUARE
BR ... BRIDGE	DWGS ... DWELLINGS	IN ... INLET	PAV ... PAVILION	ST ... STREET
BRK ... BROOK	E ... EAST	IND EST ... INDUSTRIAL ESTATE	PDE ... PARADE	STN ... STATION
BTM ... BOTTOM	EMB ... EMBANKMENT	INF ... INFIRMARY	PH ... PUBLIC HOUSE	STR ... STREAM
BUS ... BUSINESS	EMBY ... EMBASSY	INFO ... INFORMATION	PK ... PARK	STRD ... STRAND
BVD ... BOULEVARD	ESP ... ESPLANADE	INT ... INTERCHANGE	PKWY ... PARKWAY	SW ... SOUTH WEST
BY ... BYPASS	EST ... ESTATE	IS ... ISLAND	PL ... PLACE	TDG ... TRADING
CATH ... CATHEDRAL	EX ... EXCHANGE	JCT ... JUNCTION	PLN ... PLAIN	TER ... TERRACE
CEM ... CEMETERY	EXPY ... EXPRESSWAY	JTY ... JETTY	PLNS ... PLAINS	THWY ... THROUGHWAY
CEN ... CENTRE	EXT ... EXTENSION	KG ... KING	PLZ ... PLAZA	TNL ... TUNNEL
CFT ... CROFT	F/O ... FLYOVER	KNL ... KNOLL	POL ... POLICE STATION	TOLL ... TOLLWAY
CH ... CHURCH	FC ... FOOTBALL CLUB	L ... LAKE	PR ... PRINCE	TPK ... TURNPIKE
CHA ... CHASE	FK ... FORK	LA ... LANE	PREC ... PRECINCT	TR ... TRACK
CHYD ... CHURCHYARD	FLD ... FIELD	LDG ... LODGE	PREP ... PREPARATORY	TRL ... TRAIL
CIR ... CIRCLE	FLDS ... FIELDS	LGT ... LIGHT	PRIM ... PRIMARY	TWR ... TOWER
CIRC ... CIRCUS	FLS ... FALLS	LK ... LOCK	PROM ... PROMENADE	U/P ... UNDERPASS
CL ... CLOSE	FLS ... FLATS	LKS ... LAKES	PRS ... PRINCESS	UNI ... UNIVERSITY
CLFS ... CLIFFS	FM ... FARM	LNDG ... LANDING	PRT ... PORT	UPR ... UPPER
CMP ... CAMP	FT ... FORT	LTL ... LITTLE	PT ... POINT	V ... VALE
CNR ... CORNER	FWY ... FREEWAY	LWR ... LOWER	PTH ... PATH	VIAD ... VIADUCT
CO ... COUNTY	FY ... FERRY	MAG ... MAGISTRATE	PZ ... PIAZZA	VIL ... VILLA
COLL ... COLLEGE	GA ... GATE	MAN ... MANSIONS	QD ... QUADRANT	VIS ... VISTA
COM ... COMMON	GAL ... GALLERY	MD ... MEAD	QU ... QUEEN	VLG ... VILLAGE
COMM ... COMMISSION	GDN ... GARDEN	MDW ... MEADOWS	QY ... QUAY	VLS ... VILLAS
CON ... CONVENT	GDNS ... GARDENS	MEM ... MEMORIAL	R ... RIVER	VW ... VIEW
COT ... COTTAGE	GLD ... GLADE	MKT ... MARKET	RBT ... ROUNDABOUT	W ... WEST
COTS ... COTTAGES	GLN ... GLEN	MKTS ... MARKETS	RD ... ROAD	WD ... WOOD
CP ... CAPE	GN ... GREEN	ML ... MALL	RDG ... RIDGE	WHF ... WHARF
CPS ... COPSE	GND ... GROUND	ML ... MILL	REP ... REPUBLIC	WK ... WALK
CR ... CREEK	GRA ... GRANGE	MNR ... MANOR	RES ... RESERVOIR	WKS ... WALKS
CREM ... CREMATORIUM	GRG ... GARAGE	MS ... MEWS	RFC ... RUGBY FOOTBALL CLUB	WLS ... WELLS
CRS ... CRESCENT	GT ... GREAT	MSN ... MISSION	RI ... RISE	WY ... WAY
CSWY ... CAUSEWAY	GTWY ... GATEWAY	MT ... MOUNT	RP ... RAMP	YD ... YARD
CT ... COURT	GV ... GROVE	MTN ... MOUNTAIN	RW ... ROW	YHA ... YOUTH HOSTEL
CTRL ... CENTRAL	HGR ... HIGHER	MTS ... MOUNTAINS		
CTS ... COURTS	HL ... HILL	MUS ... MUSEUM		

POSTCODE TOWNS AND AREA ABBREVIATIONS

ABLGY ... Abbots Langley	BERM/RHTH ... Bermondsey/Rotherhithe	BTFD ... Brentford	CHESW ... Cheshunt west	DAGW ... Dagenham west
ABR/ST ... Abridge/Stapleford Abbotts	BETH ... Bethnal Green	BTSEA ... Battersea	CHIG ... Chigwell	DART ... Dartford
ABYW ... Abbey Wood	BF/WBF ... Byfleet/West Byfleet	BUSH ... Bushey	CHING ... Chingford	DEN/HRF ... Denham/Harefield
ACT ... Acton	BFN/LL ... Blackfen/Longlands	BXLY ... Bexley	CHOB/PIR ... Chobham/Pirbright	DEPT ... Deptford
ADL/WDHM ... Addlestone/Woodham	BFOR ... Bracknell Forest/Windlesham	BXLYHN ... Bexleyheath north	CHONG ... Chipping Ongar	DORK ... Dorking
ALP/SUD ... Alperton/Sudbury	BGR/WK ... Borough Green/West Kingsdown	BXLYHS ... Bexleyheath south	CHSGTN ... Chessington	DTCH/LGLY ... Datchet/Langley
AMS ... Amersham	BGVA ... Belgravia	CAMTN ... Camden Town	CHST ... Chislehurst	DUL ... Dulwich
AMSS ... Amersham south	BH/WHM ... Biggin Hill/Westerham	CAN/RD ... Canning Town/Royal Docks	CHSWK ... Chiswick	E/WMO/HCT ... East & West Molesey/
ARCH ... Archway	BKHH ... Buckhurst Hill	CANST ... Cannon Street station	CITYW ... City of London west	Hampton Court
ASC ... Ascot	BKHTH/KID ... Blackheath/Kidbrooke	CAR ... Carshalton	CLAP ... Clapham	EA ... Ealing
ASHF ... Ashford (Surrey)	BLKFR ... Blackfriars	CAT ... Catford	CLAY ... Clayhall	EBAR ... East Barnet
ASHTD ... Ashtead	BMLY ... Bromley	CAVSQ/HST ... Cavendish Square/	CLKNW ... Clerkenwell	EBED/NFELT ... East Bedfont/North Feltham
BAGS ... Bagshot	BMSBY ... Bloomsbury	Harley Street	CLPT ... Clapton	ECT ... Earl's Court
BAL ... Balham	BNSTD ... Banstead	CDALE/KGS ... Colindale/Kingsbury	CMBW ... Camberwell	ED ... Edmonton
BANK ... Bank	BORE ... Borehamwood	CDW/CHF ... Chadwell St Mary/	COB ... Cobham	EDEN ... Edenbridge
BAR ... Barnet	BOW ... Bow	Chafford Hundred	CONDST ... Conduit Street	EDGW ... Edgware
BARB ... Barbican	BRKHM/BTCW ... Brockham/Betchworth	CEND/HSY/TPKLN ... Crouch End/Hornsey/	COUL/CHIP ... Coulsdon/Chipstead	EDUL ... East Dulwich
BARK ... Barking	BRKMPK ... Brookmans Park	Turnpike Lane	COVGDN ... Covent Garden	EFNCH ... East Finchley
BARK/HLT ... Barkingside/Hainault	BRKMPK ... Brookmans Park	CFSP/GDCR ... Chalfont St Peter/	CRAWE ... Crawley east	EGH ... Egham
BARN ... Barnes	BROCKY ... Brockley	Gerrards Cross	CRAWW ... Crawley west	EHAM ... East Ham
BAY/PAD ... Bayswater/Paddington	BROX ... Broxbourne	CHARL ... Charlton	CRICK ... Cricklewood	EHSLY ... East Horsley
BCTR ... Becontree	BRW ... Brentwood	CHCR ... Charing Cross	CROY/NA ... Croydon/New Addington	ELTH/MOT ... Eltham/Mottingham
BEAC ... Beaconsfield	BRWN ... Brentwood north	CHDH ... Chadwell Heath	CRW ... Collier Row	EMB ... Embankment
BECK ... Beckenham	BRXN/ST ... Brixton north/Stockwell	CHEAM ... Cheam	CSHM ... Chesham	EMPK ... Emerson Park
BELMT ... Belmont	BRXS/STRHM ... Brixton south/	CHEL ... Chelsea	CSTG ... Chalfont St Giles	EN ... Enfield
BELV ... Belvedere	Streatham Hill	CHERT ... Chertsey	CTHM ... Caterham	ENC/FH ... Enfield Chase/Forty Hill
BERK ... Berkhamsted	BRYLDS ... Berrylands	CHES/WCR ... Cheshunt/Waltham Cross	DAGE ... Dagenham east	EPP ... Epping

289

EPSOM .... Epsom
ERITH .... Erith
ERITHM .... Erith Marshes
ESH/CLAY .... Esher/Claygate
EW .... Ewell
EYN .... Eynsford
FARR .... Farringdon
FBAR/BDGN .... Friern Barnet/Bounds Green
FELT .... Feltham
FENCHST .... Fenchurch Street
FITZ .... Fitzrovia
FLKWH .... Flackwell Heath
FLST/FETLN .... Fleet Street/Fetter Lane
FNCH .... Finchley
FSBYE .... Finsbury east
FSBYPK .... Finsbury Park
FSBYW .... Finsbury west
FSTGT .... Forest Gate
FSTH .... Forest Hill
FUL/PGN .... Fulham/Parsons Green
GDMY/SEVK .... Goodmayes/Seven Kings
GDST .... Godstone
GFD/PVL .... Greenford/Perivale
GINN .... Gray's Inn
GLDGN .... Golders Green
GNTH/NBYPK .... Gants Hill/Newbury Park
GNWCH .... Greenwich
GPK .... Gidea Park
GRAYS .... Grays
GRH .... Greenhithe
GSTN .... Garston
GT/LBKH .... Great Bookham/Little Bookham
GTDUN .... Great Dunmow
GTPST .... Great Portland Street
GU .... Guildford
GUW .... Guildford west
GVE .... Gravesend east
GVW .... Gravesend west
GWRST .... Gower Street
HACK .... Hackney
HAMP .... Hampstead
HARH .... Harold Hill
HARP .... Harpenden
HART .... Hartley
HAT .... Hatfield
HAYES .... Hayes
HBRY .... Highbury
HCH .... Hornchurch
HCIRC .... Holborn Circus
HDN .... Hendon
HDTCH .... Houndsditch
HERT/BAY .... Hertford/Bayford
HERT/WAS .... Hertford/Watton at Stone
HEST .... Heston
HGDN/ICK .... Hillingdon/Ickenham
HGT .... Highgate
HHNE .... Hemel Hempstead northeast
HHOL .... High Holborn
HHS/BOV .... Hemel Hempstead south/Bovingdon
HHW .... Hemel Hempstead west
HLW .... Harlow
HLWE .... Harlow east
HLWS .... Harlow south
HLWW/ROY .... Harlow west/Roydon
HMSMTH .... Hammersmith
HNHL .... Herne Hill
HNWL .... Hanwell
HOD .... Hoddesdon
HOL/ALD .... Holborn/Aldwych
HOLWY .... Holloway
HOM .... Homerton
HOR/WEW .... Horton/West Ewell
HORL .... Horley
HORS .... Horsham
HPTN .... Hampton
HRW .... Harrow
HSLW .... Hounslow
HSLWW .... Hounslow west
HTHAIR .... Heathrow Airport
HYS/HAR .... Hayes/Harlington
IL .... Ilford
ING .... Ingatestone
IS .... Islington
ISLW .... Isleworth
IVER .... Iver
KENS .... Kensington
KGLGY .... Kings Langley
KIL/WHAMP .... Kilburn/West Hampstead
KTBR .... Knightsbridge
KTN/HRWW/WS .... Kenton/Harrow Weald/Wealdstone
KTTN .... Kentish Town
KUT .... Kingston upon Thames
KUTN/CMB .... Kingston upon Thames north/Coombe
KWD/TDW/WH .... Kingswood/Tadworth/Walton on the Hill
LBTH .... Lambeth
LEE/GVPK .... Lee/Grove Park
LEW .... Lewisham
LEY .... Leyton
LHD/OX .... Leatherhead/Oxshott
LING .... Lingfield
LINN .... Lincoln's Inn
LOTH .... Lothbury
LOU .... Loughton
LSQ/SEVD .... Leicester Square/Seven Dials
LTWR .... Lightwater
LVPST .... Liverpool Street
MANHO .... Mansion House
MBLAR .... Marble Arch
MDHD .... Maidenhead
MEO .... Meopham
MFD/CHID .... Milford/Chiddingfold
MHST .... Marylebone High Street
MLHL .... Mill Hill
MNPK .... Manor Park
MON .... Monument
MORT/ESHN .... Mortlake/East Sheen
MRDN .... Morden
MTCM .... Mitcham
MUSWH .... Muswell Hill
MV/WKIL .... Maida Vale/West Kilburn
MYFR/PICC .... Mayfair/Piccadilly
MYFR/PKLN .... Mayfair/Park Lane
NFNCH/WDSPK .... North Finchley/Woodside Park
NKENS .... North Kensington
NOXST/BSQ .... New Oxford Street/Bloomsbury Square
NRWD .... Norwood
NTGHL .... Notting Hill
NTHLT .... Northolt
NTHWD .... Northwood
NWCR .... New Cross
NWDGN .... Norwood Green
NWMAL .... New Malden
OBST .... Old Broad Street
ORP .... Orpington
OXHEY .... Oxhey
OXSTW .... Oxford Street west
OXTED .... Oxted
PECK .... Peckham
PEND .... Ponders End
PGE/AN .... Penge/Anerley
PIM .... Pimlico
PIN .... Pinner
PLMGR .... Palmers Green
PLSTW .... Plaistow
POP/IOD .... Poplar/Isle of Dogs
POTB/CUF .... Potters Bar/Cuffley
PUR .... Purfleet
PUR/KEN .... Purley/Kenley
PUT/ROE .... Putney/Roehampton
RAD .... Radlett
RAIN .... Rainham (Gt Lon)
RBRW/HUT .... Rural Brentwood/Hutton
RBSF .... Rural Bishop's Stortford
RCH/KEW .... Richmond/Kew
RCHPK/HAM .... Richmond Park/Ham
RDART .... Rural Dartford
RDKG .... Rural Dorking
REDBR .... Redbridge
REDH .... Redhill
REGST .... Regent Street
REIG .... Reigate
RGODL .... Rural Godalming
RGUE .... Rural Guildford east
RGUW .... Rural Guildford west
RKW/CH/CXG .... Rickmansworth/Chorleywood/Croxley Green
ROM .... Romford
ROMW/RG .... Romford west/Rush Green
RPLY/SEND .... Ripley/Send
RSEV .... Rural Sevenoaks
RSLP .... Ruislip
RSQ .... Russell Square
RTON .... Rural Tonbridge
RYLN/HDSTN .... Rayners Lane/Headstone
RYNPK .... Raynes Park
SBW .... Sawbridgeworth
SCUP .... Sidcup
SDTCH .... Shoreditch
SEV .... Sevenoaks
SEVS/STOTM .... Seven Sisters/South Tottenham
SHB .... Shepherd's Bush
SHGR .... Shamley Green
SHPTN .... Shepperton
SKENS .... South Kensington
SL .... Slough
SLN .... Slough north
SNWD .... South Norwood
SOCK/AV .... South Ockendon/Aveley
SOHO/CST .... Soho/Carnaby Street
SOHO/SHAV .... Soho/Shaftesbury Avenue
SRTFD .... Stratford
STA .... Staines
STAL .... St Albans
STALE/WH .... St Albans east/Wheathampstead
STALW/RED .... St Albans west/Redbourn
STALW/RED .... St Albans west/Redbourn
STAN .... Stanmore
STBT .... St Bart's
STHGT/OAK .... Southgate/Oakwood
STHL .... Southall
STHWK .... Southwark
STJS .... St James's
STJSPK .... St James's Park
STJWD .... St John's Wood
STKPK .... Stockley Park
STLK .... St Luke's
STMC/STPC .... St Mary Cray/St Paul's Cray
STNW/STAM .... Stoke Newington/Stamford Hill
STP .... St Paul's
STPAN .... St Pancras
STRHM/NOR .... Streatham/Norbury
STWL/WRAY .... Stanwell/Wraysbury
SUN .... Sunbury
SURB .... Surbiton
SUT .... Sutton
SWCM .... Swanscombe
SWFD .... South Woodford
SWLY .... Swanley
SYD .... Sydenham
TEDD .... Teddington
THDIT .... Thames Ditton
THHTH .... Thornton Heath
THMD .... Thamesmead
TIL .... Tilbury
TOOT .... Tooting
TOTM .... Tottenham
TPL/STR .... Temple/Strand
TRDG/WHET .... Totteridge/Whetstone
TRING .... Tring
TWK .... Twickenham
TWRH .... Tower Hill
UED .... Upper Edmonton
UPMR .... Upminster
UX/CGN .... Uxbridge/Colham Green
VW .... Virginia Water
VX/NE .... Vauxhall/Nine Elms
WAB .... Waltham Abbey
WALTH .... Walthamstow
WALW .... Walworth
WAN .... Wanstead
WAND/EARL .... Wandsworth/Earlsfield
WANTN .... Watford north
WAP .... Wapping
WARE .... Ware
WARL .... Warlingham
WAT .... Watford
WATW .... Watford west
WBLY .... Wembley
WBPTN .... West Brompton
WCHMH .... Winchmore Hill
WCHPL .... Whitechapel
WDGN .... Wood Green
WDR/YW .... West Drayton/Yiewsley
WDSR .... Windsor
WEA .... West Ealing
WELL .... Welling
WEST .... Westminster
WESTW .... Westminster west
WEY .... Weybridge
WFD .... Woodford
WGCE .... Welwyn Garden City east
WGCW .... Welwyn Garden City west
WHALL .... Whitehall
WHTN .... Whitton
WIM/MER .... Wimbledon/Merton
WKENS .... West Kensington
WLGTN .... Wallington
WLSDN .... Willesden
WLYN .... Welwyn
WNWD .... West Norwood
WOKN/KNAP .... Woking north/Knaphill
WOKS/MYFD .... Woking south/Mayford
WOOL/PLUM .... Woolwich/Plumstead
WOT/HER .... Walton-on-Thames/Hersham
WPK .... Worcester Park
WTHK .... West Thurrock
WWKM .... West Wickham
YEAD .... Yeading

Index - streets

10th - Add

10th Av *KWD/TDW/WH* KT20 .... 257 H2
11th Av *KWD/TDW/WH* KT20 .... 257 H1
12th Av *KWD/TDW/WH* KT20 .... 257 H2
13th Av *KWD/TDW/WH* KT20 .... 257 H2
14th Av *KWD/TDW/WH* KT20 .... 257 H2
15th Av *KWD/TDW/WH* KT20 .... 257 J2
16th Av *KWD/TDW/WH* KT20 .... 257 H1
1st Av *KWD/TDW/WH* KT20 .... 257 H1
2nd Av *KWD/TDW/WH* KT20 .... 257 H1
3rd Av *KWD/TDW/WH* KT20 .... 257 H1
4th Av *KWD/TDW/WH* KT20 .... 257 H1
5th Av *KWD/TDW/WH* KT20 .... 257 H1
6th Av *KWD/TDW/WH* KT20 .... 257 H1
7th Av *KWD/TDW/WH* KT20 .... 257 H1
8th Av *KWD/TDW/WH* KT20 .... 257 H2
9th Av *KWD/TDW/WH* KT20 .... 257 H1

A

Abbess Cl *BRXS/STRHM* SW2 .... 181 J4
Abbeville Ms *CLAP* SW4 .... 158 E10
Abbeville Rd *CEND/HSY/T* N8 .... 118 E2
CLAP SW4 .... 180 D2
Abbey Av *ALP/SUD* HA0 .... 135 K4
STALW/RED AL3 .... 37 P9
Abbey Cl *HYS/HAR* UB3 .... 133 J10
NTHLT UB5 .... 133 N5
PIN HA5 .... 113 J1
ROM RM1 .... 125 H4
SL SL1 .... 128 D9
WOKS/MYFD GU22 .... 233 H2
Abbey Ct *WAB* EN9 .... 62 G10
Abbey Crs *BELV* DA17 .... 164 B3
Abbey Dale Cl *HLWE* CM17 .... 47 M2
Abbeydale Rd *ALP/SUD* HA0 .... 135 L3
Abbey Dr *ABLGY* WD5 .... 55 H8
STA TW18 .... 195 M4
TOOT SW17 .... 180 B8
Abbeyfield Rd *BERM/RHTH* SE16 .... 160 B3
Abbeyfields Cl *WLSDN* NW10 .... 135 M5
Abbey Gdns *CHERT* KT16 .... 195 K6
HMSMTH W6 .... 14 A10
STJWD NW8 .... 3 J8
Abbey Gn *CHERT* KT16 .... 195 K6
Abbey Gv *ABYW* SE2 .... 163 L3
Abbeyhill Rd *BFN/LL* DA15 .... 185 M4
Abbey La *BECK* BR3 .... 182 F10
SRTFD E15 .... 141 H4
Abbey Mill End *STALW/RED* AL3 .... 38 B7
Abbey Mill La *STALW/RED* AL3 .... 38 B7
Abbey Orchard St *WEST* SW1P 17 K3
Abbey Pk *BECK* BR3 .... 182 F10
Abbey Park La *SL* SL1 .... 108 D7
Abbey Rd *BARK* IG11 .... 142 E2
BELV DA17 .... 163 N3
BXLYHS DA6 .... 163 P10
CHERT KT16 .... 195 L7
CHES/WCR EN8 .... 62 D10
CROY/NA CR0 .... 203 J10
EN EN1 .... 79 M9
GNTH/NBYPK IG2 .... 122 G3
GRH DA9 .... 189 H1
GVE DA12 .... 191 H4
KIL/WHAMP NW6 .... 2 G5
SAND/SEL CR2 .... 224 C6
SHPTN TW17 .... 196 B8
SRTFD E15 .... 141 J4
VW GU25 .... 194 A5
WIM/MER SW19 .... 179 M10
WOKN/KNAP GU21 .... 231 P3
Abbey St *PLSTW* E13 .... 141 M6
STHWK SE1 .... 19 L3
Abbey Ter *ABYW* SE2 .... 163 M2
Abbey Vw *MLHL* NW7 .... 96 C4
RAD WD7 .... 74 E1
Abbeyview *WAB* EN9 .... 62 G9
Abbey View Rd *STALW/RED* AL3 .... 38 B6
Abbey Wk *E/WMO/HCT* KT8 .... 198 A3
Abbey Wd *ASC* SL5 .... 192 F7
Abbey Wood La *RAIN* RM13 .... 145 L4
Abbey Wood Rd *ABYW* SE2 .... 163 L3
Abbot Cl *BF/WBF* KT14 .... 215 N6
RSLP HA4 .... 113 L8
STA TW18 .... 173 N10
Abbot John Ms *STALE/WH* AL4 .... 21 J2
Abbot Rd *GU* GU1 .... 268 A2
Abbots Av *STAL* AL1 .... 38 D9
Abbots Av West *STAL* AL1 .... 38 C9
Abbotsbury Cl *SRTFD* E15 .... 141 H4
WKENS W14 .... 14 C2
Abbotsbury Gdns *PIN* HA5 .... 113 K4
Abbotsbury Ms *PECK* SE15 .... 160 B9
Abbotsbury Rd *MRDN* SM4 .... 201 L4
NTGHL W11 .... 14 B1
WWKM BR4 .... 205 L9
Abbots Cl *BRWN* CM15 .... 107 M2
GUW GU2 .... 267 K3
RAIN RM13 .... 145 K4
STMC/STPC BR5 .... 206 F8
Abbots Dr *RYLN/HDSTN* HA2 .... 113 P7
VW GU25 .... 193 P4
Abbotsfield Rd *CRAWW* RH11 .... 282 G8
Abbotsford Av *SEVS/STOTM* N15 .... 119 K2
Abbotsford Cl
WOKS/MYFD GU22 .... 232 D3
Abbotsford Gdns *WFD* IG8 .... 101 M8
Abbotsford Rd *GDMY/SEVK* IG3 .... 123 K7
Abbots Gdns *EFNCH* N2 .... 117 N2
Abbots Gn *CROY/NA* CR0 .... 224 C3
Abbotshade Rd
BERM/RHTH SE16 .... 140 C10
Abbotshall Av *STHGT/OAK* N14 .... 98 D4
Abbotshall Rd *CAT* SE6 .... 183 J4
Abbots La *PUR/KEN* CR8 .... 241 K1
STHWK SE1 .... 13 K10
Abbotsleigh Cl *BELMT* SM2 .... 221 L4
Abbotsleigh Rd
STRHM/NOR SW16 .... 180 D7
Abbotsmede Cl *TWK* TW1 .... 176 E5
Abbots Pk *BRXS/STRHM* SW2 .... 181 H4
STAL AL1 .... 38 E8
Abbot's Pl *KIL/WHAMP* NW6 .... 2 G5
Abbots Ri *KGLGY* WD4 .... 54 A3
Abbots Rd *ABLGY* WD5 .... 54 D7
EDGW HA8 .... 96 A8
EHAM E6 .... 142 A3
Abbots Ter *CEND/HSY/T* N8 .... 118 F4
Abbotstone Rd *PUT/ROE* SW15 .... 156 F9
Abbot St *HACK* E8 .... 7 L1
Abbots Vw *KGLGY* WD4 .... 54 A3
Abbots Wk *CTHM* CR3 .... 242 A8
WDSR SL4 .... 148 D8
Abbots Wy *BECK* BR3 .... 204 D5
GU GU1 .... 250 G9
Abbotsweld *HLWS* CM18 .... 46 G4
Abbotswell Rd *BROCKY* SE4 .... 182 E1
Abbotswood *GU* GU1 .... 250 C8
Abbotswood Cl *BELV* DA17 .... 163 P2
GU GU1 .... 250 C7
Abbotswood Dr *WEY* KT13 .... 216 E6
Abbotswood Gdns *CLAY* IG5 .... 122 C1
Abbotswood Rd *EDUL* SE22 .... 159 M10
STRHM/NOR SW16 .... 180 E6
Abbotswood Wy *HYS/HAR* UB3 .... 133 J10
Abbott Av *RYNPK* SW20 .... 200 G2
Abbott Cl *HPTN* TW12 .... 175 M9
NTHLT UB5 .... 133 N1
Abbott Rd *POP/IOD* E14 .... 141 H7
Abbotts Cl *ROMW/RG* RM7 .... 124 C1
SWLY BR8 .... 209 H4
THMD SE28 .... 143 M9
UX/CGN UB8 .... 131 N7
Abbotts Crs *CHING* E4 .... 101 J5
ENC/FH EN2 .... 79 J6
Abbotts Dr *ALP/SUD* HA0 .... 114 G7
WAB EN9 .... 63 M10
Abbotts Park Rd *LEY* E10 .... 121 H5
Abbotts Ri *REDH* RH1 .... 258 B8
WARE SG12 .... 27 J7
Abbotts Rd *BAR* EN5 .... 77 L8
CHEAM SM3 .... 221 H1
MTCM CR4 .... 202 D4
STHL UB1 .... 133 M10
Abbotts Tilt *WOT/HER* KT12 .... 197 M10
Abbotts V *CSHM* HP5 .... 51 H4
Abbott's Wk *BXLYHN* DA7 .... 163 N6
Abbotts Wy *SL* SL1 .... 128 C10
WARE SG12 .... 27 J7
Abbs Cross Gdns *HCH* RM12 .... 125 K6
Abbs Cross La *HCH* RM12 .... 125 K8
Abchurch La *MANHO* EC4N 13 H6
Abdale La *BRKMPK* AL9 .... 58 E3
Abdale Rd *SHB* W12 .... 136 E10
Abel Cl *HHNE* HP2 .... 36 B6
Abelia Cl *CHOB/PIR* GU24 .... 212 D9
Abenberg Wy *RBRW/HUT* CM13 .... 107 M3
Aberavon Rd *BOW* E3 .... 140 D5
Abercairn Rd *STRHM/NOR* SW16 .... 180 D10
Aberconway Rd *MRDN* SM4 .... 201 L3
Abercorn Cl *MLHL* NW7 .... 97 H8
SAND/SEL CR2 .... 224 C8
STJWD NW8 .... 3 J8
Abercorn Crs *RYLN/HDSTN* HA2 .... 114 A6
Abercorn Gdns *CHDH* RM6 .... 123 L4
KTN/HRWW/W HA3 .... 115 J5
Abercorn Gv *RSLP* HA4 .... 112 E2
Abercorn Pl *STJWD* NW8 .... 3 J9
Abercorn Rd *MLHL* NW7 .... 97 H8
STAN HA7 .... 95 H8
Abercorn Wy *STHWK* SE1 .... 19 N7
WOKN/KNAP GU21 .... 231 M4
Abercrombie Dr *EN* EN1 .... 79 P5
Abercrombie St *BTSEA* SW11 .... 157 P8
Abercrombie Wy
HLWW/ROY CM19 .... 46 F3
Aberdale Gdns *POTB/CUF* EN6 .... 59 J9
Aberdare Cl *WWKM* BR4 .... 205 H9
Aberdare Gdns *KIL/WHAMP* NW6 .... 3 H4
MLHL NW7 .... 96 G8
Aberdare Rd *PEND* EN3 .... 80 B8
Aberdeen Av *SL* SL1 .... 128 F9
Aberdeen La *HBRY* N5 .... 119 J10
Aberdeen Pk *HBRY* N5 .... 119 J10
Aberdeen Pl *STJWD* NW8 .... 9 L2
Aberdeen Rd *CROY/NA* CR0 .... 223 K1
HBRY N5 .... 119 K9
KTN/HRWW/W HA3 .... 94 E10
UED N18 .... 99 P6
UED N18 .... 100 A6
WLSDN NW10 .... 116 C10
Aberdeen Ter *BKHTH/KID* SE3 .... 161 J8
Aberdour Rd *BCTR* RM8 .... 123 L8
Aberdour St *STHWK* SE1 .... 19 J5
Aberfeldy St *POP/IOD* E14 .... 141 H8
POP/IOD E14 .... 141 H8
Aberford Gdns
WOOL/PLUM SE18 .... 162 B7
Aberford Rd *BORE* WD6 .... 75 M6
Aberfoyle Rd *STRHM/NOR* SW16 .... 180 E9
Abergeldie Rd *LEE/GVPK* SE12 .... 183 N2
Abernethy Rd *LEW* SE13 .... 161 K10
Abersham Rd *HACK* E8 .... 119 N10
Abery St *WOOL/PLUM* SE18 .... 163 H3
Abingdon Cl *CAMTN* NW1 .... 5 J2
HGDN/ICK UB10 .... 132 A3
WIM/MER SW19 .... 179 M9
WOKN/KNAP GU21 .... 231 N4
Abingdon Pl *POTB/CUF* EN6 .... 59 L8
Abingdon Rd *FNCH* N3 .... 97 M10
KENS W8 .... 14 F4
STRHM/NOR SW16 .... 202 F1
Abingdon St *WEST* SW1P 17 L2
Abingdon Vls *KENS* W8 .... 14 E4
Abingdon Wy *ORP* BR6 .... 227 L1
Abinger Av *BELMT* SM2 .... 220 F5
Abinger Cl *BMLY* BR1 .... 206 B3
GDMY/SEVK IG3 .... 123 K9
RDKG RH5 .... 273 H6
WLGTN SM6 .... 222 F2
Abinger Common Rd *RDKG* RH5 .... 271 M10
Abinger Dr *REDH* RH1 .... 276 A10
Abinger Gdns *ISLW* TW7 .... 154 D9
Abinger Gv *DEPT* SE8 .... 160 E5
Abinger La *RDKG* RH5 .... 271 L8
Abinger Ms *MV/WKIL* W9 .... 8 E1
Abinger Rd *CHSWK* W4 .... 156 C2
REDH RH1 .... 275 P3
Abinger Wy *RGUE* GU4 .... 250 E5
Ablett St *BERM/RHTH* SE16 .... 160 B4
Aboyne Dr *RYNPK* SW20 .... 200 D2
Aboyne Rd *TOOT* SW17 .... 179 N6
WLSDN NW10 .... 116 B8
Abridge Cl *CHES/WCR* EN8 .... 80 C1
Abridge Gdns *CRW* RM5 .... 104 B7
Abridge Rd *CHIG* IG7 .... 83 H10
EPP CM16 .... 83 K3
Abridge Wy *BARK* IG11 .... 143 L4
Abyssinia Cl *BTSEA* SW11 .... 157 P10
Abyssinia Rd *BTSEA* SW11 .... 157 P10
Acacia Av *ALP/SUD* HA0 .... 115 K10
BTFD TW8 .... 154 G6
HCH RM12 .... 124 G7
HYS/HAR UB3 .... 132 G8
RSLP HA4 .... 113 H6
SHPTN TW17 .... 196 B5
STWL/WRAY TW19 .... 150 B10
TOTM N17 .... 99 L8
WDR/YW UB7 .... 132 A9
WOKS/MYFD GU22 .... 232 A6
Acacia Cl *ADL/WDHM* KT15 .... 215 J6
CHESW EN7 .... 61 M3
DEPT SE8 .... 160 D3
KTN/HRWW/W HA3 .... 94 D7
STMC/STPC BR5 .... 206 G5
Acacia Dr *ADL/WDHM* KT15 .... 215 J7
CHEAM SM3 .... 201 J8
EW KT17 .... 220 G10
UPMR RM14 .... 125 P9
Acacia Gdns *STJWD* NW8 .... 3 M7
UPMR RM14 .... 126 E5
WWKM BR4 .... 205 H9
Acacia Gv *BERK* HP4 .... 33 N6
DUL SE21 .... 181 L5
NWMAL KT3 .... 200 B3
Acacia Ms *WDR/YW* UB7 .... 151 N5
Acacia Pl *STJWD* NW8 .... 3 M7
Acacia Rd *ACT* W3 .... 135 P9
BECK BR3 .... 204 E3
DART DA1 .... 187 K4
ENC/FH EN2 .... 79 L5
GRH DA9 .... 188 D2
GU GU1 .... 250 A10
HPTN TW12 .... 175 P9
MTCM CR4 .... 202 B2
STA TW18 .... 173 L8
STJWD NW8 .... 3 M7
STRHM/NOR SW16 .... 202 F1
WALTH E17 .... 120 D4
WAN E11 .... 121 K7
WDGN N22 .... 99 H9
Acacia St *HAT* AL10 .... 40 D7
Acacia Wk *HARP* AL5 .... 20 C5
Acacia Wy *BFN/LL* DA15 .... 185 J3
Academy Gdns *CROY/NA* CR0 .... 203 N8
NTHLT UB5 .... 133 L4
Academy Pl *WOOL/PLUM* SE18 .... 162 C7
Academy Rd *WOOL/PLUM* SE18 .... 162 D6
Acanthus Dr *STHWK* SE1 .... 19 P7
Acanthus Rd *BTSEA* SW11 .... 158 B9
Accommodation La
WDR/YW UB7 .... 151 M5
Accommodation Rd *CHERT* KT16 .... 194 A10
GLDGN NW11 .... 117 J5
Acer Av *RAIN* RM13 .... 145 L5
YEAD UB4 .... 133 M6
Acer Dr *CHOB/PIR* GU24 .... 212 E9
Acer Rd *BH/WHM* TN16 .... 244 A2
Acers *LCOL/BKTW* AL2 .... 56 B4
Acfold Rd *FUL/PGN* SW6 .... 157 L7
Achilles Cl *HHNE* HP2 .... 36 A4
STHWK SE1 .... 19 P7
Achilles Rd *KIL/WHAMP* NW6 .... 117 K10
Achilles St *NWCR* SE14 .... 160 D6
Acklam Rd *NKENS* W10 .... 8 C4
Acklington Dr *CDALE/KGS* NW9 .... 96 B9
Ackmar Rd *FUL/PGN* SW6 .... 157 K7
Ackroyd Dr *BOW* E3 .... 140 E7
Ackroyd Rd *FSTH* SE23 .... 182 C3
Acland Cl *WOOL/PLUM* SE18 .... 162 G6
Acland Crs *CMBW* SE5 .... 159 L10
Acland Rd *CRICK* NW2 .... 136 E1
Acme Rd *WATN* WD24 .... 73 H4
Acol Crs *RSLP* HA4 .... 113 J10
Acol Rd *KIL/WHAMP* NW6 .... 2 F4
Acorn Cl *CHING* E4 .... 100 G6
CHST BR7 .... 184 F8
ENC/FH EN2 .... 79 H5
HORL RH6 .... 280 D3
HPTN TW12 .... 176 A9
STAN HA7 .... 94 G8
Acorn Gdns *ACT* W3 .... 136 A7
NRWD SE19 .... 203 N1
Acorn Gv *HYS/HAR* UB3 .... 152 G6
KWD/TDW/WH KT20 .... 239 J10
RSLP HA4 .... 112 G9
Acorn La *POTB/CUF* EN6 .... 60 F5
Acorn Pl *WATN* WD24 .... 73 H3
Acorn Rd *HHS/BOV* HP3 .... 36 B7
The Acorns *HORL* RH6 .... 281 J4
SEV TN13 .... 247 H9
Acorn St *WARE* SG12 .... 28 A4
Acorns Wy *ESH/CLAY* KT10 .... 218 B2
Acorn Wy *FSTH* SE23 .... 182 C6
ORP BR6 .... 226 E1
Acre Dr *EDUL* SE22 .... 159 P10
Acrefield Rd *CFSP/GDCR* SL9 .... 110 A1
Acre La *BRXS/STRHM* SW2 .... 158 G10
CAR SM5 .... 222 B1
Acre Pas *WDSR* SL4 .... 149 J7
Acre Rd *DAGE* RM10 .... 144 D2
KUTN/CMB KT2 .... 199 K1
WIM/MER SW19 .... 179 N9
Acres Av *CHONG* CM5 .... 67 N2
Acres End *AMSS* HP7 .... 69 K5
Acres Gdns *KWD/TDW/WH* KT20 .... 238 F5
Acre Wy *NTHWD* HA6 .... 92 G9
Acre Wy *HHNE* HP2 .... 35 P7
Acrewood Wy *STALE/WH* AL4 .... 39 L6
Acris St *WAND/EARL* SW18 .... 179 M1
Acton Cl *CHES/WCR* EN8 .... 62 D7
ED N9 .... 99 P3
Acton La *ACT* W3 .... 155 P1
CHSWK W4 .... 155 P2
Acton Ms *HACK* E8 .... 7 L5
Acton St *FSBYW* WC1X 5 N10
Acuba Rd *WAND/EARL* SW18 .... 179 L5
Ada Ct *MV/WKIL* W9 .... 3 K10
Ada Gdns *POP/IOD* E14 .... 141 J8
SRTFD E15 .... 141 L3
Adair Cl *SNWD* SE25 .... 204 A3
Adair Rd *NKENS* W10 .... 8 B2
Adam & Eve Ms *KENS* W8 .... 14 F3
Adam Cl *SL* SL1 .... 128 F10
Adam Rd *CHING* E4 .... 100 E7
Adams Cl *BRYLDS* KT5 .... 199 L6
FNCH N3 .... 97 K8
WBLY HA9 .... 115 N7
Adams Ct *CHOB/PIR* GU24 .... 230 B6
Adamsfield *CHESW* EN7 .... 61 N2
Adams House *HLW* CM20 .... 28 G10
Adams Ms *WDGN* N22 .... 98 G8
Adamson Rd *CAN/RD* E16 .... 141 M8
HAMP NW3 .... 3 M3
Adamsrill Cl *WCHMH* N21 .... 79 L10
Adamsrill Rd *SYD* SE26 .... 182 C7
Adams Rd *BECK* BR3 .... 204 D5
TOTM N17 .... 99 L10
Adam's Rw *MYFR/PKLN* W1K 10 D8
Adams Sq *BXLYHN* DA7 .... 163 P9
Adam St *TPL/STR* WC2R 11 M8
Adams Wy *SNWD* SE25 .... 203 N6
Ada Pl *BETH* E2 .... 7 P6
BETH E2 .... 140 A3
Ada Rd *ALP/SUD* HA0 .... 115 J8
CMBW SE5 .... 159 M6
Ada St *HACK* E8 .... 140 A3
Adderley Gdns *ELTH/MOT* SE9 .... 184 D7
Adderley Gv *BTSEA* SW11 .... 180 B1
Adderley Rd *KTN/HRWW/W* HA3 .... 94 E9
Adderley St *POP/IOD* E14 .... 141 H8
Addington Cl *WDSR* SL4 .... 148 F9
Addington Dr *NFNCH/WDSP* N12 .... 97 N7
Addington Gv *SYD* SE26 .... 182 D7

Addington Rd BOW E3 140 F5
CAN/RD E16 141 K6
CROY/NA CR0 203 H8
FSBYPK N4 119 H4
SAND/SEL CR2 223 P7
Addington Sq CMBW SE5 159 K6
Addington Village Rd
CROY/NA CR0 224 E3
Addis Cl PEND EN3 80 C5
Addiscombe Av CROY/NA CR0 203 P7
Addiscombe Cl
KTN/HRWW/W HA3 115 H3
Addiscombe Court Rd
CROY/NA CR0 203 M8
Addiscombe Gv CROY/NA CR0 203 L9
Addiscombe Rd CROY/NA CR0 203 M9
WATW WD18 73 J8
Addison Av HSLW TW3 154 B7
NTGHL W11 8 A9
STHGT/OAK N14 78 C10
Addison Bridge Pl WKENS W14 14 C5
Addison Cl CTHM CR3 241 L8
IVER SL0 131 H9
NTHWD HA6 93 H9
STMC/STPC BR5 206 F6
Addison Crs WKENS W14 14 B3
Addison Dr LEE/GVPK SE12 183 N1
Addison Gdns BRYLDS KT5 199 L4
GRAYS RM17 167 P3
WKENS W14 156 G2
Addison Gv CHSWK W4 156 B2
Addison Pl NTGHL W11 8 A10
Addison Rd BARK/HLT IG6 102 F9
CSHM HP5 51 H5
CTHM CR3 241 L7
GU GU1 268 C2
HAYES BR2 206 A5
PEND EN3 80 B5
SNWD SE25 203 P4
TEDD TW11 176 G9
WALTH E17 120 C3
WAN E11 121 M4
WKENS W14 14 B2
Addison's Cl CROY/NA CR0 204 E9
Addison Wy GLDGN NW11 117 J2
HYS/HAR UB3 133 H8
NTHWD HA6 92 G9
Addle Hl BLKFR EC4V 12 D7
Addlestone Moor
ADL/WDHM KT15 195 M9
Addlestone Pk ADL/WDHM KT15 215 L2
Addlestone Rd
ADL/WDHM KT15 215 P1
Addle St CITYW EC2V 12 F5
Adecroft Wy E/WMO/HCT KT8 198 B3
Adela Av NWMAL KT3 200 E5
Adelaide Av BROCKY SE4 160 F10
Adelaide Cl CRAWW RH11 283 N4
EN EN1 79 M4
SL SL1 148 F1
STAN HA7 94 F5
Adelaide Ct HNWL W7 154 E1
Adelaide Gdns CHDH RM6 123 P3
Adelaide Gv SHB W12 136 D10
Adelaide Pl WEY KT13 216 E1
Adelaide Rd ASHF TW15 173 N8
CHST BR7 184 E8
HAMP NW3 3 N3
HEST TW5 153 M7
IL IG1 122 E7
LEY E10 121 H8
NWDGN UB2 153 M3
RCH/KEW TW9 155 L10
SURB KT6 199 K5
TEDD TW11 176 E9
TIL RM18 168 C7
WAND/EARL SW18 179 K1
WDSR SL4 149 L7
WEA W13 154 F1
WOT/HER KT12 197 H10
Adelaide Sq WDSR SL4 149 J8
Adelaide St CHCR WC2N 11 L8
STALW/RED AL3 38 C5
Adela St NKENS W10 8 A1
Adelina Gv WCHPL E1 140 B7
Adelina Ms BAL SW12 180 E4
Adeline Pl RSQ WC1B 11 K4
Adeliza Cl BARK IG11 142 F2
Adelphi Cl CRAWE RH10 284 E9
Adelphi Crs HCH RM12 125 H7
YEAD UB4 132 F5
Adelphi Gdns SL SL1 149 K1
Adelphi Rd EW KT17 220 A9
Adelphi Ter CHCR WC2N 11 M8
Adelphi Wy YEAD UB4 132 G5
Adeney Cl HMSMTH W6 156 G5
Aden Gv STNW/STAM N16 119 L9
Adenmore Rd CAT SE6 182 F3
Aden Rd IL IG1 122 E5
PEND EN3 80 D8
Adeyfield Gdns HHNE HP2 36 A5
Adeyfield Rd HHNE HP2 36 A6
Adhara Rd NTHWD HA6 92 G6
Adie Rd HMSMTH W6 156 F2
Adine Rd PLSTW E13 141 M6
Adlers La RDKG RH5 254 F7
Adler St WCHPL E1 13 N5
Adley St CLPT E5 120 D10
Adlington Cl UED N18 99 L6
Admaston Rd WOOL/PLUM SE18 162 F6
Admiral Cl STMC/STPC BR5 207 N4
Admiral Ms NKENS W10 136 G6
Admiral Rd CRAWW RH11 283 K10
Admirals Cl STALE/WH AL4 40 B9
SWFD E18 121 N2
Admirals Ct GU GU1 250 E9
Admiral Seymour Rd
ELTH/MOT SE9 162 C10
Admiral's Ga GNWCH SE10 160 G7
Admiral St DEPT SE8 160 F7
HERT/BAY SG13 25 P5
Admirals Wk GRH DA9 188 G1
HAMP NW3 117 M8
HOD EN11 44 F5
STAL AL1 38 F8
Admirals Wy POP/IOD E14 160 G1
Admiralty Rd TEDD TW11 176 E10
Admiral Wk MV/WKIL W9 8 F3
Admiral Wy BERK HP4 33 L3
Adnams Wk RAIN RM13 145 H1
Adolf St CAT SE6 182 F7
Adolphus Rd FSBYPK N4 119 J7
Adolphus St DEPT SE8 160 E6
Adomar Rd BCTR RM8 123 N8
Adpar St BAY/PAD W2 9 L3
Adrian Cl DEN/HRF UB9 91 N9
Adrian Rd ABLGY WD5 54 F7
Adrienne Av STHL UB1 133 N6
Adstock Wy GRAYS RM17 167 L3
Advance Rd WNWD SE27 181 K7
Advent Wy UED N18 100 C6
Advice Av CDH/CHF RM16 167 M1
Adys Rd PECK SE15 159 N9
Aerodrome Rd CDALE/KGS NW9 96 C10
Aerodrome Wy HEST TW5 153 K5
Affleck St IS N1 5 P8
Afghan Rd BTSEA SW11 157 P8
Afton Dr SOCK/AV RM15 146 G8
Agamemnon Rd
KIL/WHAMP NW6 117 J10
Agar Cl SURB KT6 199 L9
Agar Gv CAMTN NW1 5 K3
Agar Pl CAMTN NW1 5 H4
Agars Pl DTCH/LGLY SL3 149 M5
Agar St CHCR WC2N 11 L8
Agate Cl CAN/RD E16 142 A8
Agate Rd HMSMTH W6 156 F2
Agates La ASHTD KT21 237 J4
Agatha Cl WAP E1W 140 A10
Agaton Rd ELTH/MOT SE9 184 F5
Agave Rd CRICK NW2 116 F9
Agdon St FSBYE EC1V 12 C1
Agincourt Pl ASC SL5 192 B3
Agincourt Rd HAMP NW3 118 A9
Agister Rd CHIG IG7 103 K6
Agnes Av IL IG1 122 D9
Agnes Cl EHAM E6 142 D9
Agnesfield Cl NFNCH/WDSP N12 97 P7
Agnes Gdns BCTR RM8 123 N9
Agnes Rd ACT W3 156 C1
Agnes St POP/IOD E14 140 E8
Agnew Rd FSTH SE23 182 D3
Agraria Rd GUW GU2 267 N1
Agricola Pl EN EN1 79 N9
Aidan Cl DAGW RM9 123 P9
Ailsa Av TWK TW1 176 F1
Ailsa Cl CRAWW RH11 283 L10
Ailsa Rd TWK TW1 176 G1
Ailsa St POP/IOD E14 141 H7
Ainger Rd HAMP NW3 4 B4
Ainsdale Cl ORP BR6 206 G8
Ainsdale Crs PIN HA5 113 P1
Ainsdale Dr STHWK SE1 19 N8
Ainsdale Rd EA W5 135 J6
OXHEY WD19 93 K4
Ainsdale Wy WOKN/KNAP GU21 231 M3
Ainsley Av ROMW/RG RM7 124 D4
Ainsley Cl ED N9 99 M2
Ainsley St BETH E2 140 A5
Ainslie Wood Crs CHING E4 100 G6
Ainslie Wood Gdns CHING E4 100 G5
Ainslie Wood Rd CHING E4 100 F6
Ainsworth Cl CMBW SE5 159 M8
CRICK NW2 116 D8
Ainsworth Rd CROY/NA CR0 203 J9
HOM E9 140 B2
Aintree Av EHAM E6 142 B3
Aintree Cl DTCH/LGLY SL3 151 H7
GVE DA12 190 E6
UX/CGN UB8 132 C8
Aintree Crs BARK/HLT IG6 102 F10
Aintree Gv UPMR RM14 125 N8
Aintree Rd CRAWE RH10 284 B9
GFD/PVL UB6 134 G4
Aintree St FUL/PGN SW6 157 H6
Airdrie Cl YEAD UB4 133 M7
Airedale Av CHSWK W4 156 C4
Airedale Av South CHSWK W4 156 C4
Airedale Cl RDART DA2 188 B4
Airedale Rd BAL SW12 180 A3
EA W5 155 H2
Aire Dr SOCK/AV RM15 146 G6
Airfield Wy HCH RM12 145 J1
Airlie Gdns IL IG1 122 E6
KENS W8 8 E10
Airport Wy HORL RH6 280 B7
STWL/WRAY TW19 151 K10
Air St REGST W1B 11 H8
Aisgill Av ECT SW5 14 D8
Aisher Rd THMD SE28 143 M9
Aisher Wy SEV TN13 246 F7
Aislibie Rd LEW SE13 161 K10
Aiten Pl HMSMTH W6 156 D3
Aitken Cl HACK E8 7 N5
MTCM CR4 202 A7
Aitken Rd BAR EN5 76 F9
CAT SE6 182 G5
Ajax Av CDALE/KGS NW9 116 B1
SL SL1 128 G9
Ajax Rd KIL/WHAMP NW6 117 J9
Akabusi Cl SNWD SE25 203 P6
Akehurst Cl CRAWE RH10 285 H2
Akehurst St PUT/ROE SW15 178 D2
Akeman Cl STALW/RED AL3 37 N8
Akenside Rd HAMP NW3 117 N10
Akerman Rd CMBW SE5 159 J7
SURB KT6 199 H6
Alabama St WOOL/PLUM SE18 162 G6
Alacross Rd EA W5 155 H1
Alamein Cl BROX EN10 44 C6
Alamein Gdns RDART DA2 188 C3
Alamein Rd SWCM DA10 189 J2
Alanbrooke GVE DA12 190 F3
Alanbrooke Cl WOKN/KNAP GU21 231 H4
Alan Cl DART DA1 165 K10
Alandale Dr PIN HA5 93 J9
Alan Dr BAR EN5 77 H10
Alan Gdns ROMW/RG RM7 124 B5
Alan Hocken Wy SRTFD E15 141 K4
Alan Rd WIM/MER SW19 179 H8
Alanthus Cl LEE/GVPK SE12 183 L2
Alan Wy DTCH/LGLY SL3 130 B8
Alaska St STHWK SE1 12 A10
Alba Cl YEAD UB4 133 L6
Albacore Crs LEW SE13 182 G2
Alba Gdns GLDGN NW11 117 H4
Albain Crs ASHF TW15 173 P5
Alban Av STALW/RED AL3 38 C4
Alban Crs BORE WD6 75 N5
EYN DA4 209 P8
Albans Vw GSTN WD25 55 J9
Albany Cl BUSH WD23 74 C10
BXLY DA5 185 M3
ESH/CLAY KT10 217 P5
HGDN/ICK UB10 112 B10
MORT/ESHN SW14 155 N10
SEVS/STOTM N15 119 J2
Albany Ct EPP CM16 65 J6
Albany Ctyd MYFR/PICC W1J 11 H8
Albany Crs EDGW HA8 95 M8
ESH/CLAY KT10 218 D3
Albany Ga CSHM HP5 50 G6
Albany Ms KUTN/CMB KT2 177 J9
KUTN/CMB KT2 177 J9
SUT SM1 221 L2
WALW SE17 18 F10
Albany Pk DTCH/LGLY SL3 150 G6
Albany Park Av PEND EN3 80 B5
Albany Park Rd KUTN/CMB KT2 177 J9
LHD/OX KT22 236 F5
Albany Pl BTFD TW8 155 J5
EGH TW20 172 E7
HOLWY N7 119 H9
Albany Rd BELV DA17 164 A5
BRWN CM15 86 G10
BTFD TW8 155 J5
BXLY DA5 185 M3
CHDH RM6 124 A4
CHST BR7 184 E8
CMBW SE5 19 J9
CRAWW RH11 283 M7
FSBYPK N4 118 G4
HCH RM12 125 H6
LEY E10 120 F5
MNPK E12 122 A9
NWMAL KT3 200 A4
PEND EN3 80 C3
RCHPK/HAM TW10 177 L1
TIL RM18 168 D7
UED N18 100 A6
WALTH E17 120 D4
WDSR SL4 149 H8
WEA W13 134 G9
WIM/MER SW19 179 L8
WOT/HER KT12 217 L1
The Albanys REIG RH2 257 K7
Albany St CAMTN NW1 4 F9
The Albany KUTN/CMB KT2 177 J9
Albany Vw BKHH IG9 101 M2
Alba Pl NTGHL W11 8 C5
Albatross Gdns SAND/SEL CR2 224 C7
Albatross St WOOL/PLUM SE18 163 H6
Albemarle Ap GNTH/NBYPK IG2 122 E4
Albemarle Av CHES/WCR EN8 62 B4
POTB/CUF EN6 59 L9
WHTN TW2 175 N4
Albemarle Cl GRAYS RM17 167 M1
Albemarle Gdns
GNTH/NBYPK IG2 122 E4
NWMAL KT3 200 A4
Albemarle Pk STAN HA7 95 H6
Albemarle Rd BECK BR3 204 G1
EBAR EN4 97 P1
Albemarle St CONDST W1S 10 G8
Albemarle Wy FARR EC1M 12 C2
Alberon Gdns GLDGN NW11 117 J2
Alberta Av SUT SM1 221 H1
Alberta Dr HORL RH6 281 H4
Alberta Rd BXLYHN DA7 164 D7
EN EN1 79 N10
Alberta St WALW SE17 18 D7
Albert Av CHERT KT16 195 K3
CHING E4 100 F5
VX/NE SW8 158 G6
Albert Br BTSEA SW11 157 P6
Albert Bridge Rd BTSEA SW11 157 P6
Albert Carr Gdns STRHM/NOR SW16 180 F8
Albert Cl CDH/CHF RM16 167 P2
HOM E9 140 A3
WDGN N22 98 E9
Albert Crs CHING E4 100 F5
Albert Dr WIM/MER SW19 179 H5
WOKN/KNAP GU21 214 F10
Albert Emb LBTH SE11 17 M7
Albert Gdns HLWE CM17 47 N2
WCHPL E1 140 C8
Albert Gv RYNPK SW20 200 G1
Albertine Cl EW KT17 238 E2
Albert Ms KENS W8 15 J3
Albert Murray Cl GVE DA12 190 F3
Albert Pl FNCH N3 97 K9
KENS W8 15 H2
WDSR SL4 148 F4
Albert Rd ADL/WDHM KT15 195 N10
ASHF TW15 174 A8
ASHTD KT21 237 L4
BCTR RM8 124 A6
BELV DA17 164 A4
BKHH IG9 102 A3
BXLY DA5 186 B2
CAN/RD E16 162 D1
CSHM HP5 51 H7
EA W5 134 G6
EBAR EN4 77 M8
EGH TW20 172 A9
ELTH/MOT SE9 184 B6
EW KT17 220 C9
FSBYPK N4 118 G6
HAYES BR2 206 A5
HDN NW4 116 G2
HORL RH6 280 B4
HPTN TW12 176 B8
HSLW TW3 153 P10
HYS/HAR UB3 152 F2
IL IG1 122 F8
KIL/WHAMP NW6 2 D8
KUT KT1 199 L2
MLHL NW7 96 C6
MTCM CR4 202 A3
NWDGN UB2 153 L2
NWMAL KT3 200 C4
ORP BR6 227 K2
PGE/AN SE20 182 C10
RCHPK/HAM TW10 177 K1
RDART DA2 187 K6
REDH RH1 258 D5
ROM RM1 124 G4
RYLN/HDSTN HA2 114 B1
SEVS/STOTM N15 119 M4
SNWD SE25 204 A4
STMC/STPC BR5 207 L6
SUT SM1 221 N2
SWCM DA10 189 L2
SWFD E18 121 N1
TEDD TW11 176 E9
TWK TW1 176 E4
WALTH E17 120 F3
WAN E11 121 H7
WARL CR6 242 D3
WDGN N22 98 E9
WDR/YW UB7 131 P10
WDSR SL4 149 K10
Albert Rd North REIG RH2 257 J9
WAT WD17 73 J6
Albert Rd South WAT WD17 73 J7
Albert Sq SRTFD E15 121 K10
VX/NE SW8 158 G6
Albert St BRW CM14 107 H6
CAMTN NW1 4 F6
NFNCH/WDSP N12 97 M6
SL SL1 149 K2
STAL AL1 38 C7
WDSR SL4 148 G7
Albert Ter CAMTN NW1 4 C5
Albert Terrace Ms CAMTN NW1 4 C5
Albion Av MUSWH N10 98 B9
VX/NE SW8 158 E8
Albion Cl BAY/PAD W2 9 P7
CRAWE RH10 284 E8
ROMW/RG RM7 124 E4
SLN SL2 129 M10
Albion Crs CSTG HP8 89 N4
Albion Dr HACK E8 7 L4
Albion Gdns HMSMTH W6 156 E3
Albion Gv STNW/STAM N16 119 M9
Albion Hl HHNE HP2 35 N7
LOU IG10 81 P9
Albion Ms BAY/PAD W2 9 P6
IS N1 6 A4
Albion Pk LOU IG10 82 A9
Albion Pl FARR EC1M 12 C3
HMSMTH W6 156 E3
Albion Rd BELMT SM2 221 N3
BXLYHS DA6 164 A10
CSTG HP8 89 N3
DAGE RM10 124 B10
GVE DA12 190 F3
HSLW TW3 153 P10
HYS/HAR UB3 132 F7
KUTN/CMB KT2 199 P1
REIG RH2 275 M1
STAL AL1 38 E6
STNW/STAM N16 119 L10
TOTM N17 99 N10
WALTH E17 121 H1
WHTN TW2 176 D4
Albion Sq HACK E8 7 L4
Albion St BAY/PAD W2 9 P6
BERM/RHTH SE16 160 B1
CROY/NA CR0 203 J8
Albion Ter GVE DA12 190 F2
HACK E8 7 L4
Albion Villas Rd FSTH SE23 182 B6
Albion Wy LEW SE13 161 H10
STBT EC1A 12 E4
WBLY HA9 115 M8
Albion Yd IS N1 5 M8
Albrighton Rd CMBW SE5 159 M9
CMBW SE5 159 M9
Albuhera Cl ENC/FH EN2 79 H5
Albury Av BELMT SM2 220 F5
BXLYHN DA7 163 P8
ISLW TW7 154 E6
Albury Cl CHERT KT16 193 M10
HPTN TW12 175 P9
Albury Dr PIN HA5 93 K9
Albury Grove Rd CHES/WCR EN8 62 C6
Albury Keep HORL RH6 280 C3
Albury Ms MNPK E12 121 P6
Albury Ride CHES/WCR EN8 62 C7
Albury Rd CHSGTN KT9 219 K2
GU GU1 268 C1
REDH RH1 258 D5
WOT/HER KT12 216 F3
Albury St DEPT SE8 160 F5
SHGR GU5 269 M5
Albury Wk CHES/WCR EN8 62 B6
Albyfield BMLY BR1 206 C3
Albyn Rd DEPT SE8 160 F7
Albyns La ABR/ST RM4 84 E6
Alcester Crs CLPT E5 120 A7
Alcester Rd WLGTN SM6 222 C1
Alcock Cl WLGTN SM6 222 E4
Alcock Rd HEST TW5 153 L6
Alcocks Cl KWD/TDW/WH KT20 239 H6
Alcocks La KWD/TDW/WH KT20 239 H6
Alconbury WGCE AL7 23 P5
Alconbury Rd CLPT E5 119 P7
Alcorn Cl CHEAM SM3 201 K9
Alcott Cl HNWL W7 134 E7
Aldborough Rd DAGE RM10 144 D1
UPMR RM14 125 N7
Aldborough Rd North
GNTH/NBYPK IG2 123 J3
Aldborough Rd South
GDMY/SEVK IG3 123 H6
Aldborough Sp SL SL1 129 K8
Aldbourne Rd ACT W3 136 C10
SL SL1 128 A7
Aldbridge St WALW SE17 19 K7
Aldbury Av WBLY HA9 135 N2
Aldbury Cl GSTN WD25 73 L2
STALE/WH AL4 39 H1
Aldbury Gv WGCE AL7 23 L5
Aldbury Ms WCHMH N21 99 L1
Aldbury Rd RKW/CH/CXG WD3 91 J1
Aldebert Ter VX/NE SW8 158 G6
Aldeburgh Pl WFD IG8 101 M5
Aldeburgh St GNWCH SE10 161 M4
Alden Av SRTFD E15 141 L5
Aldenham Av RAD WD7 74 F3
Aldenham Dr UX/CGN UB8 132 C6
Aldenham Gv RAD WD7 56 G10
Aldenham Rd BUSH WD23 73 N8
GSTN WD25 74 E6
OXHEY WD19 73 L10
RAD WD7 74 F1
Aldenham St CAMTN NW1 5 H8
Aldenholme WEY KT13 216 F3
Aldensley Rd HMSMTH W6 156 E2
Alden Vw WDSR SL4 148 C7
Alder Av UPMR RM14 125 N9
Alderbourne La DTCH/LGLY SL3 110 A9
Alderbrook Rd BAL SW12 180 C2
Alderbury Rd BARN SW13 156 D5
DTCH/LGLY SL3 150 C1
Alderbury Rd West
DTCH/LGLY SL3 150 C1
Alder Cl EGH TW20 172 B8
HOD EN11 44 G1
LCOL/BKTW AL2 56 A4
SL SL1 128 E10
Aldercombe La CTHM CR3 259 M3
Alder Dr SOCK/AV RM15 147 H6
Alder Gv CRICK NW2 116 D7
Alderley Ct BERK HP4 33 N6
Alderman Av BARK IG11 143 K5
Aldermanbury CITYW EC2V 12 F5
Aldermanbury Sq CITYW EC2V 12 F4
Alderman Cl BRKMPK AL9 40 F10
Alderman's Hl PLMGR N13 98 F5
Aldermary Rd BMLY BR1 205 M1
Aldermoor Rd CAT SE6 182 E6
Alderney Av HEST TW5 154 A6
Alderney Gdns NTHLT UB5 133 N2
Alderney Rd ERITH DA8 165 H6
WCHPL E1 140 C6
Alderney St PIM SW1V 16 F7
Alder Rd DEN/HRF UB9 131 L1
IVER SL0 130 F4
MORT/ESHN SW14 156 A9
SCUP DA14 185 H6
Alders Av WFD IG8 101 K7
Aldersbrook Av EN EN1 79 M6
Aldersbrook Dr KUTN/CMB KT2 177 L9
Aldersbrook La MNPK E12 122 C8
Aldersbrook Rd MNPK E12 121 P7
Alders Cl EA W5 155 J2
EDGW HA8 95 P6
WAN E11 121 N7
Aldersey Gdns BARK IG11 142 G1
Aldersey Rd GU GU1 250 C10
Aldersford Cl BROCKY SE4 160 C10
Aldersgate St STBT EC1A 12 E3
Aldersgrove E/WMO/HCT KT8 198 C5
Aldersgrove Av LEE/GVPK SE12 183 P6
Aldershot Rd CHOB/PIR GU24 248 D2
GUW GU2 249 N8
KIL/WHAMP NW6 2 D5
RGUW GU3 248 D6
Alderside Wk EGH TW20 172 A8
Aldersmead Av CROY/NA CR0 204 C6
Aldersmead Rd BECK BR3 182 D10
Alderson Pl STHL UB1 134 B10
Alderson St NKENS W10 8 B1
Alders Rd EDGW HA8 95 P6
REIG RH2 257 L8
Alderstead La REDH RH1 258 E1
The Alders BF/WBF KT14 215 M8
FELT TW13 175 M8
NWDGN UB2 153 N5
WCHMH N21 79 H10
WWKM BR4 204 G8
Alders Wk SBW CM21 29 P1
Alderton Cl BRWN CM15 86 G9
LOU IG10 82 D8
WLSDN NW10 116 A7
Alderton Crs HDN NW4 116 E3
Alderton Hall La LOU IG10 82 D8
Alderton Hl LOU IG10 82 C9
Alderton Ri LOU IG10 82 D8
Alderton Rd CROY/NA CR0 203 N7
HNHL SE24 159 K9
Alderton Wy HDN NW4 116 E3
LOU IG10 82 C9
Alderville Rd FUL/PGN SW6 157 J8
Alder Wk GSTN WD25 73 J1
Alder Wy SWLY BR8 208 E2
Alderwick Dr HSLW TW3 154 C9
Alderwood Cl CTHM CR3 259 M1
Alderwood Dr ABR/ST RM4 83 L7
Alderwood Rd ELTH/MOT SE9 184 G2
Aldford St MYFR/PKLN W1K 10 C9
Aldgate FENCHST EC3M 13 K6
Aldgate High St TWRH EC3N 13 L6
Aldin Av North SL SL1 149 M1
Aldin Av South SL SL1 149 M1
Aldine St SHB W12 156 F1
Aldingbourne Cl CRAWW RH11 283 J6
Aldingham Gdns HCH RM12 125 H10
Aldington Cl CHDH RM6 123 M5
Aldington Rd WOOL/PLUM SE18 162 A2
Aldis Ms TOOT SW17 179 P8
Aldis St TOOT SW17 179 P8
Aldock WGCE AL7 23 K7
Aldred Rd KIL/WHAMP NW6 117 K10
Aldren Rd TOOT SW17 179 M6
Aldrich Crs CROY/NA CR0 225 H5
Aldriche Wy CHING E4 101 H7
Aldrich Gdns CHEAM SM3 201 J10
Aldrich Ter WAND/EARL SW18 179 M5
Aldridge Av EDGW HA8 95 N4
PEND EN3 80 F4
RSLP HA4 113 L7
STAN HA7 95 K9
Aldridge Ri NWMAL KT3 200 B7
Aldridge Rd SLN SL2 128 F6
Aldridge Road Vls NTGHL W11 8 D4
Aldridge Wk STHGT/OAK N14 98 F1
Aldrington Rd STRHM/NOR SW16 180 D8
Aldsworth Cl MV/WKIL W9 8 G2
Aldwick STAL AL1 38 F8
Aldwickbury Crs HARP AL5 20 C2
Aldwick Cl CHST BR7 184 G6
Aldwick Rd CROY/NA CR0 202 G10
HARP AL5 20 D3
Aldworth Gv LEW SE13 183 H2
Aldworth Rd SRTFD E15 141 K2
Aldwych TPL/STR WC2R 11 N7
Aldwych Av BARK/HLT IG6 122 F2
Aldwych Cl HCH RM12 125 H7
Aldykes HAT AL10 40 C4
Alers Rd BXLYHS DA6 185 N1
Alesia Cl WDGN N22 98 F8
Alestan Beck Rd CAN/RD E16 142 A8
Alexander Av WLSDN NW10 136 E2
Alexander Cl BFN/LL DA15 185 H1
EBAR EN4 77 N8
HAYES BR2 205 M8
STHL UB1 134 B10
WHTN TW2 176 D5
Alexander Evans Ms FSTH SE23 182 C5
Alexander Godley Cl ASHTD KT21 237 L5
Alexander La BRWN CM15 87 M9
Alexander Ms BAY/PAD W2 8 G5
Alexander Pl SKENS SW7 15 N5
Alexander Rd ARCH N19 118 F8
CHST BR7 184 E8
COUL/CHIP CR5 240 C1
EGH TW20 172 E8
GRH DA9 189 H1
HERT/WAS SG14 25 H5
LCOL/BKTW AL2 57 H1
REIG RH2 275 K3
WELL DA16 163 N8
Alexander Sq CHEL SW3 15 N5
Alexander St BAY/PAD W2 8 F5
CSHM HP5 51 H6
Alexanders Wk CTHM CR3 259 N2
Alexandra Av BTSEA SW11 158 B7
RYLN/HDSTN HA2 113 N6
STHL UB1 133 N9
SUT SM1 201 K10
WARL CR6 242 E3
WDGN N22 98 E9
Alexandra Cl ASHF TW15 174 E10
CDH/CHF RM16 168 E1
RYLN/HDSTN HA2 114 A8
STA TW18 173 N9
SWLY BR8 208 F2
WOT/HER KT12 197 H9
Alexandra Cottages NWCR SE14 160 E7
Alexandra Ct ASHF TW15 174 E9
Alexandra Crs BMLY BR1 183 L9
Alexandra Dr BRYLDS KT5 199 M7
NRWD SE19 181 M8
Alexandra Gdns CAR SM5 222 B5
HSLW TW3 154 A8
MUSWH N10 118 C2
WOKN/KNAP GU21 231 H4
Alexandra Gv FSBYPK N4 119 J6
NFNCH/WDSP N12 97 L6
Alexandra Ms EFNCH N2 118 A1
WAT WD17 73 H6
Alexandra Palace Wy
CEND/HSY/T N8 118 D2
Alexandra Park Rd MUSWH N10 98 C10
WDGN N22 98 D9
Alexandra Pl CROY/NA CR0 203 M8
GU GU1 268 C2
SNWD SE25 203 L5
STJWD NW8 3 K5
Alexandra Rd ADL/WDHM KT15 215 N1
ASHF TW15 174 E10
BH/WHM TN16 243 N5
BORE WD6 76 A4
BTFD TW8 155 J5
CEND/HSY/T N8 119 H1
CHDH RM6 123 N4
CHSWK W4 156 A1
CROY/NA CR0 203 M8
ED N9 100 A1
EGH TW20 171 P9
EHAM E6 142 D5
ERITH DA8 164 G5
EW KT17 220 C9
GVE DA12 191 H3
HDN NW4 116 G2
HHNE HP2 35 N6
HSLW TW3 154 A8
KGLGY WD4 53 K6
KUTN/CMB KT2 177 M10
LEY E10 121 H8
MORT/ESHN SW14 156 A9
MUSWH N10 98 C9
PEND EN3 80 C8
RAIN RM13 144 G3
RCH/KEW TW9 155 L8
RKW/CH/CXG WD3 71 K2
ROM RM1 124 G4
SEVS/STOTM N15 119 L3
SL SL1 149 J2
STAL AL1 38 D6
STJWD NW8 3 K5
SWFD E18 121 N1
SYD SE26 182 C9
THDIT KT7 198 E5
TIL RM18 168 C8
TWK TW1 177 H2
UX/CGN UB8 131 N4
WALTH E17 120 E4
WARL CR6 242 D3
WAT WD17 73 H6
WDSR SL4 149 J8
WIM/MER SW19 179 P10
Alexandra Sq MRDN SM4 201 K5
Alexandra St CAN/RD E16 141 M7
NWCR SE14 160 D6
Alexandra Ter GU GU1 268 B1
Alexandra Wy CHES/WCR EN8 62 E10
TIL RM18 169 L3
Alexandria Rd WEA W13 134 F9
Alexis St BERM/RHTH SE16 19 N5
Alfearn Rd CLPT E5 120 B9
Alford Cl RGUE GU4 250 C7
Alford Gn CROY/NA CR0 225 J3
Alford Pl IS N1 6 F8
Alford Rd ERITH DA8 164 D4
Alfoxton Av SEVS/STOTM N15 119 J2
Alfreda St BTSEA SW11 158 C7
Alfred Cl CHSWK W4 156 A3
CRAWE RH10 284 F8
Alfred Gdns STHL UB1 133 M9
Alfred Ms FITZ W1T 11 J3
Alfred Pl FITZ W1T 11 J3
GVW DA11 190 C4
Alfred Rd ACT W3 135 P10
BAY/PAD W2 8 F3
BELV DA17 164 A4
BKHH IG9 102 A3
BRW CM14 107 J3
FELT TW13 175 K5
FSTGT E7 121 L10
GVW DA11 190 E5
KUT KT1 199 K3
RDART DA2 187 N7
SNWD SE25 203 P5
SOCK/AV RM15 146 B10
SUT SM1 221 M2
Alfred's Gdns BARK IG11 143 H4
Alfred St BOW E3 140 E5
GRAYS RM17 167 P5
Alfred's Wy
(East Ham & Barking By-pass)
BARK IG11 142 G4

Alfreton Cl WIM/MER SW19 — 178 G6
Alfreton BRYLDS KT5 — 199 L6
Alfriston Av CROY/NA CR0 — 202 F7
  RYLN/HDSTN HA2 — 113 J4
Alfriston Cl BRYLDS KT5 — 199 L6
Alfriston Rd BTSEA SW11 — 180 A5
Algar Cl STAN HA7 — 94 E6
Algar Rd ISLW TW7 — 154 E6
Algarve Rd WAND/EARL SW18 — 179 L4
Algernon Rd HDN NW4 — 116 D4
  KIL/WHAMP NW6 — 2 E1
  LEW SE13 — 160 G10
Algers Cl LOU IG10 — 82 A9
Algers Rd LOU IG10 — 82 A9
Alghers Md LOU IG10 — 82 A9
Algiers Rd LEW SE13 — 160 F10
Alguin Ct STAN HA7 — 95 H8
Alibon Gdns DAGE RM10 — 124 B10
Alice La BOW E3 — 140 E3
  SL SL1 — 128 A6
Alice Ms TEDD TW11 — 176 E8
Alice St STHWK SE1 — 19 J4
Alice Thompson Cl LEE/GVPK SE12 — 183 P5
Alice Walker Cl HNHL SE24 — 159 J10
Alice Wy HSLW TW3 — 154 A10
Alicia Av CRAWE RH10 — 284 C6
  KTN/HRWW/W HA3 — 114 G2
Alicia Cl KTN/HRWW/W HA3 — 115 H2
Alicia Gdns KTN/HRWW/W HA3 — 114 G2
Alie St WCHPL E1 — 13 M6
Alington Crs CDALE/KGS NW9 — 115 P6
Alington Gv WLGTN SM6 — 222 F4
Alison Cl CROY/NA CR0 — 204 C8
  EHAM E6 — 142 H7
  WOKN/KNAP GU21 — 232 B1
Aliwal Rd BTSEA SW11 — 157 P10
Alkerden La GRH DA9 — 189 N2
Alkerden Rd CHSWK W4 — 156 B4
Alkham Rd STNW/STAM N16 — 119 N7
Allan Barclay Cl STNW/STAM N16 — 119 N4
Allan Cl NWMAL KT3 — 200 A5
Allandale HHNE HP2 — 35 N4
  STALW/RED AL3 — 38 A9
Allandale Av FNCH N3 — 117 H1
Allandale Crs POTB/CUF EN6 — 59 H8
Allandale Pl ORP BR6 — 207 N10
Allandale Rd EMPK RM11 — 124 G5
  PEND EN3 — 80 D9
Allan Wy ACT W3 — 135 P7
  STMC/STPC BR5 — 207 M7
Allard Cl CHESW EN7 — 61 K1
  STMC/STPC BR5 — 207 N10
Allard Crs BUSH WD23 — 94 B3
Allard Wy BROX EN10 — 44 D7
Allbrook Cl TEDD TW11 — 176 D8
  EBED/NFELT TW14 — 174 G4
Allcroft Rd KTTN NW5 — 4 D1
Alldicks Rd HHS/BOV HP3 — 36 A9
Allenby Av SAND/SEL CR2 — 223 K5
Allenby Cl GFD/PVL UB6 — 133 P5
Allenby Crs GRAYS RM17 — 167 N4
Allenby Dr EMPK RM11 — 125 M6
Allenby Rd BH/WHM TN16 — 244 B3
  FSTH SE23 — 182 D6
  GFD/PVL UB6 — 133 P8
Allen Cl MTCM CR4 — 202 C1
  RAD WD7 — 57 K8
  STALE/WH AL4 — 21 J4
  SUN TW16 — 197 J1
Allen Ct HAT AL10 — 40 E6
Allendale Av STHL UB1 — 133 P8
Allendale Cl CMBW SE5 — 159
  RDART DA2 — 188 C4
  SYD SE26 — 182 C9
Allendale Rd GFD/PVL UB6 — 133 G1
Allen Edwards Dr VX/NE SW8 — 158 H7
Allen House Pk WOKS/MYFD GU22 — 231 P6
Allen Rd BECK BR3 — 204 C2
  BOW E3 — 140 E4
  CROY/NA CR0 — 202 G7
  GT/LBKH KT23 — 254 A2
  RAIN RM13 — 145 K5
  STNW/STAM N16 — 119 M9
  SUN TW16 — 197 J1
Allens Rd PEND EN3 — 80 B9
Allensword Rd ELTH/MOT SE9 — 162 H10
Allerds Rd SLN SL2 — 28 E3
Allerford Rd CAT SE6 — 182 C7
Allerton Cl BORE WD6 — 75 L4
Allerton Rd BORE WD6 — 75 K4
  STNW/STAM N16 — 118 F10
Allestree Rd FUL/PGN SW6 — 157 H5
Alleyn Crs DUL SE21 — 181 L5
Alleyndale Rd BCTR RM8 — 123 M7
Alleyn Pk DUL SE21 — 181 L5
  NWDGN UB2 — 153 N4
Alleyn Rd DUL SE21 — 181 L5
Allfarthing La WAND/EARL SW18 — 179 N2
Allgood Cl MRDN SM4 — 200 G6
Allgood St BETH E2 — 7 M8
All Hallows Av CHOB/PIR GU24 — 230 G8
Allhallows La CANST EC4R — 12 C7
Allhallows Rd EHAM E6 — 142 H8
All Hallows Rd TOTM N17 — 99 M9
Alliance Cl ALP/SUD HA0 — 115 J9
  WOOL/PLUM SE18 — 145 K5
Alliance Rd ACT W3 — 135 N6
  PLSTW E13 — 141 N4
  WOOL/PLUM SE18 — 145 L5
Allingham Cl HNWL W7 — 134 D7
Allingham Rd REIG RH2 — 275 K3
Allingham St IS N1 — 6 E7
Allington Av SHPTN TW17 — 99 M7
  TOTM N17 — 99 M7
Allington Cl GFD/PVL UB6 — 134 D2
  WIM/MER SW19 — 178 C8
Allington Rd HDN NW4 — 116 E3
  NKENS W10 — 2 A9
  ORP BR6 — 207 H8
  RYLN/HDSTN HA2 — 114 F4
Allington St WESTW SW1E — 16 F4
Allison Cl GNWCH SE10 — 161 H7
  WAB EN9 — 63 H9
Allison Gv DUL SE21 — 181 M4
Allison Rd ACT W3 — 135 P8
  CEND/HSY/T N8 — 119 H3
Allitsen Rd STJWD NW8 — 3 H11
Allmains Cl WAB EN9 — 63 N1
Allnutts Rd EPP CM16 — 65 K9
Allnutt Wy CLAP SW4 — 180 E1
Alloa Rd DEPT SE8 — 160 C4
  GDMY/SEVK IG3 — 123 L7
Allonby Dr RSLP HA4 — 112 C5
Allonby Gdns WBLY HA9 — 115 H6
Allotment La SEV TN13 — 247 R5
Alloway Cl WOKN/KNAP GU21 — 231 N4
Alloway Rd BOW E3 — 140 D5
All Saints Cl BRWN CM15 — 86 G2
  CHIG IG7 — 103 L4
  ED N9 — 99 N3
  SWCM DA10 — 189 L1
Allsaints Crs GSTN WD25 — 55 L5
All Saints Dr BKHTH/KID SE3 — 161 L8
  SAND/SEL CR2 — 223 K6
All Saints La RKW/CH/CXG WD3 — 72 K10
All Saints Ms KTN/HRWW/W HA3 — 94 D7
All Saints Pas WAND/EARL SW18 — 179 K1
All Saints' Rd ACT W3 — 155 P1
  GVW DA11 — 190 C4
  LTWR GU18 — 212 B6
  WBLY W11 — 8 C5
  SUT SM1 — 201 L4
  WIM/MER SW19 — 179 M10
All Saints St IS N1 — 5 N7

Allsop Pl CAMTN NW1 — 10 B2
All Souls Av CHOB/PIR GU24 — 230 G7
  WLSDN NW10 — 136 G4
All Souls' Pl REGST W1B — 10 F4
Allum Gv KWD/TDW/WH KT20 — 238 E7
Allum La BORE WD6 — 75 K9
Allum Wy TRDG/WHET N20 — 97 M2
Allwood Cl SYD SE26 — 182 C10
Allwood Rd CHESW EN7 — 61 N3
Allyington Wy CRAWE RH10 — 284 D10
Allyn Cl STA TW18 — 173 J9
  HCH RM12 — 125 M8
Almack Rd CLPT E5 — 120 B9
Alma Cl WOKN/KNAP GU21 — 231 K3
Alma Crs SUT SM1 — 221 H2
Alma Cut STAL AL1 — 38 C7
Alma Gv STHWK SE1 — 19 M6
Alma Pl NRWD SE19 — 181 N10
  THHTH CR7 — 204 H5
  WLSDN NW10 — 136 E5
Alma Rd BERK HP4 — 33 K3
  CAR SM5 — 221 P2
  CSHM HP5 — 41 H5
  ESH/CLAY KT10 — 198 D3
  MUSWH N10 — 98 B3
  PEND EN3 — 80 D9
  REIG RH2 — 257 L9
  SCUP DA14 — 185 K6
  STAL AL1 — 38 D6
  STHL UB1 — 133 M9
  STMC/STPC BR5 — 207 N9
  SWCM DA10 — 189 N1
  WAND/EARL SW18 — 148 G10
  WDSR SL4 — 148 A3
  WDSR SL4 — 149 H8
Alma Rw KTN/HRWW/W HA3 — 94 C9
Alma Sq STJWD NW8 — 3 H3
Alma St KTTN NW5 — 4 C2
  SRTFD E15 — 141 J1
Alma Ter BORE WD6 — 6 D3
  WAND/EARL SW18 — 179 N5
Almeida St IS N1 — 6 D3
Almeric Rd BTSEA SW11 — 158 A10
Almer Rd RYNPK SW20 — 178 D10
Almington St FSBYPK N4 — 118 G6
Almners Rd CHERT KT16 — 194 F6
Almond Av CAR SM5 — 202 A9
  EA W5 — 155 K2
  HGDN/ICK UB10 — 112 C8
  WDR/YW UB7 — 152 B2
  WOKS/MYFD GU22 — 232 A3
Almond Cl CDH/CHF RM16 — 168 D2
  CRAWW RH11 — 283 K8
  ECH TW20 — 171 N9
  GU GU1 — 250 A6
  HAYES BR2 — 206 D7
  HYS/HAR UB3 — 132 F9
  RSLP HA4 — 113 H2
  SHPTN TW17 — 196 D2
  WDSR SL4 — 148 G8
Almond Dr SWLY BR8 — 208 E3
Almond Gv BTFD TW8 — 154 G6
Almond Rd BERM/RHTH SE16 — 160 A3
  HOR/WEW KT19 — 220 A1
  RDART DA2 — 188 B3
  SL SL1 — 128 A5
  TOTM N17 — 99 P8
Almonds Av BKHH IG9 — 101 M3
The Almonds STAL AL1 — 38 C10
Almond Wy BORE WD6 — 75 N8
  HAYES BR2 — 206 D7
  MTCM CR4 — 202 F7
  RYLN/HDSTN HA2 — 94 B10
Almons Wy SLN SL2 — 129 N5
Almorah Rd HEST TW5 — 153 L7
  IS N1 — 6 G4
Alms Heath RPLY/SEND GU23 — 234 A3
Almshouse La CHSGTN KT9 — 219 H5
  EN EN1 — 80 A4
Alnwick Gv MRDN SM4 — 201 L4
Alnwick Rd CAN/RD E16 — 141 P8
  LEE/GVPK SE12 — 183 N5
Alperton La ALP/SUD HA0 — 135 J5
Alperton St NKENS W10 — 8 B1
Alphabet Gdns CAR SM5 — 201 N6
Alpha Cl CAMTN NW1 — 9 P1
Alpha Gv POP/IOD E14 — 160 F1
Alpha Pl CHEL SW3 — 15 P9
  KIL/WHAMP NW6 — 2 E7
Alpha Rd BRYLDS KT5 — 199 P9
  CHING E4 — 100 F4
  CHOB/PIR GU24 — 213 L6
  CRAWW RH11 — 283 M7
  CROY/NA CR0 — 203 N1
  HGDN/ICK UB10 — 132 C6
  HPTN TW12 — 176 C8
  NWCR SE14 — 160 F2
  UED N18 — 99 P7
  WOKS/MYFD GU22 — 232 E2
Alpha St PECK SE15 — 159 P8
Alpha St North SL SL1 — 149 L2
Alpha St South SL SL1 — 149 L2
Alpha Wy EGH TW20 — 194 F7
Alphea Cl WIM/MER SW19 — 179 P10
Alpine Cl CROY/NA CR0 — 203 M10
  REDH RH1 — 258 D7
  WOT/HER KT12 — 197 H7
Alpine Vw SUT SM1 — 221 P2
Alpine Wk BUSH WD23 — 94 D3
Alpine Wy EHAM E6 — 142 H7
Alresford Rd GUW GU2 — 267 M1
  WLSDN NW10 — 136 A2
Alric Av NWMAL KT3 — 200 B3
  WLSDN NW10 — 136 H1
Alroy Rd FSBYPK N4 — 119 H5
Alsace Rd WALW SE17 — 19 J7
Alscot Rd BERM/RHTH SE16 — 19 L6
Alscot Wy STHWK SE1 — 19 L5
Alsike Rd BXLYHN DA7 — 165 N2
Alsom Av HOR/WEW KT19 — 220 C1
Alsop Cl LCOL/BKTW AL2 — 57 K4
Alston Cl THDIT KT7 — 198 G7
Alston Rd BAR EN5 — 77 H7
  HHW HP1 — 35 K7
  TOOT SW17 — 180 G7
  UED N18 — 100 A6
Altair Cl UED N18 — 99 N7
Altair Wy NTHWD HA6 — 92 H6
Altash Wy ELTH/MOT SE9 — 184 C5
Altenburg Gdns BTSEA SW11 — 158 A10
Alterton Cl WOKN/KNAP GU21 — 231 M3
Alt Gv WIM/MER SW19 — 179 J10
Altham Gv HLW CM20 — 29 H9
Althea St FUL/PGN SW6 — 157 L8
Althorne Gdns SWFD E18 — 121 L2
Althorne Rd REDH RH1 — 276 B2
Althorne Wy DAGE RM10 — 124 B7
Althorp Cl TRDG/WHET N20 — 96
Althorpe Rd HRW HA1 — 114 C3
Althorp Rd TOOT SW17 — 180 C3
Altmore Av EHAM E6 — 142 G2
Alton Av STAN HA7 — 94 G8
Alton Cl BXLY DA5 — 185 H6
  ISLW TW7 — 135 L8 (154 A8)
Alton Gdns BECK BR3 — 183 K2
  WHTN TW2 — 176 C3
Alton Rd CROY/NA CR0 — 203 H10
  PUT/ROE SW15 — 178 D2

  RCH/KEW TW9 — 155 K10
  TOTM N17 — 119 L1
Alton St POP/IOD E14 — 160 B10
Altwood Cl HARP AL5 — 20 C2
Altwood Cl SL SL1 — 128 D7
Altyre Cl BECK BR3 — 204 E5
Altyre Rd CROY/NA CR0 — 203 L6
Altyre Wy BECK BR3 — 204 E5
Aluric Cl CDH/CHF RM16 — 168 C6
Alvanley Gdns KIL/WHAMP NW6 — 117 L10
Alva Wy OXHEY WD19 — 93 L7
Alverstoke Rd HARH RM3 — 105 M8
Alverstone Av EBAR EN4 — 97 N1
  WAND/EARL SW18 — 179 K5
Alverstone Gdns ELTH/MOT SE9 — 184 E4
Alverstone Rd CRICK NW2 — 136 F2
  MNPK E12 — 122 D9
  NWMAL KT3 — 200 C4
  WBLY HA9 — 115 L6
Alverston Gdns SNWD SE25 — 203 H5
Alverton St DEPT SE8 — 160 L4
Alvey St WALW SE17 — 19 J7
Alvia Gdns SUT SM1 — 221 P2
Alwin Pl WATW WD18 — 72 F8
Alwold Crs LEE/GVPK SE12 — 183 P5
Alwyn Av CHSWK W4 — 156 A4
Alwyne Av BRWN CM15 — 87 L10
  CROY/NA CR0 — 224 G4
Alwyne La IS N1 — 6 D1
Alwyne Pl IS N1 — 6 E2
Alwyne Rd HNWL W7 — 134 D9
  IS N1 — 6 E1
  WIM/MER SW19 — 179 J9
Alwyne Sq IS N1 — 6 E1
Alwyne Vls IS N1 — 6 D1
Alwyn Gdns ACT W3 — 135 N8
Alwyns Cl CHERT KT16 — 195 K6
Alwyns La CHERT KT16 — 195 J6
Alyngton BERK HP4 — 33 J1
Alyth Gdns GLDGN NW11 — 117 J4
Alzey Gdns HARP AL5 — 20 C3
Amalgamated Dr BTFD TW8 — 154 G5
Amanda Cl CHIG IG7 — 103 J6
Amanda Ct DTCH/LGLY SL3 — 150 A2
Amar Ct WOOL/PLUM SE18 — 163 J4
Amardeep Ct WOOL/PLUM SE18 — 163 J4
Ambassador Cl HSLW TW3 — 153 M8
Ambassador Gdns EHAM E6 — 142 G7
Ambassador Sq POP/IOD E14 — 160 C8
Amber Av WALTH E17 — 100 D9
Ambercroft Wy COUL/CHIP CR5 — 241 J5
Amberden Av FNCH N3 — 117 K1
Ambergate St WALW SE17 — 18 C7
Amber Gv CRICK NW2 — 116 G6
Amberley Cl CRAWE RH10 — 284 D7
  HARP AL5 — 20 A1
  ORP BR6 — 227 J2
  PIN HA5 — 113 N1
  RPLY/SEND GU23 — 251 J1
Amberley Ct SCUP DA14 — 185 M8
Amberley Dr ADL/WDHM KT15 — 215 J6
Amberley Gdns EN EN1 — 80 A8
  HOR/WEW KT19 — 220 C1
Amberley Gv CROY/NA CR0 — 203 N7
  SYD SE26 — 182 A7
Amberley Rd ABYW SE2 — 165 N5
  BKHH IG9 — 101 P2
  EN EN1 — 79 N10
  LEY E10 — 120 F5
  MV/WKIL W9 — 8 F3
  PLMGR N13 — 98 G3
  SLN SL2 — 128 D7
Amberley Wy HGDN/ICK UB10 — 131 P4
  HSLWW TW4 — 175 K1
  MRDN SM4 — 201 J7
  ROMW/RG RM7 — 124 C2
  UX/CGN UB8 — 131 K5
Amberside Cl ISLW TW7 — 176 C2
Amberwood Cl WLGTN SM6 — 223 J4
Amberwood Ri NWMAL KT3 — 200 B6
Amblecote COB KT11 — 217 L7
Amblecote Cl LEE/GVPK SE12 — 183 N6
Amblecote Meadow LEE/GVPK SE12 — 183 N6
Amblecote Rd LEE/GVPK SE12 — 183 N6
Ambleside BMLY BR1 — 183 J9
  EPP CM16 — 65 K7
Ambleside Av BECK BR3 — 204 D5
  HCH RM12 — 125 N4
  STRHM/NOR SW16 — 180 E7
  WOT/HER KT12 — 197 K8
Ambleside Cl CRAWW RH11 — 282 C8
  LEY E10 — 120 C5
  REDH RH1 — 276 C5
Ambleside Crs PEND EN3 — 80 C7
Ambleside Dr EBED/NFELT TW14 — 174 G4
Ambleside Gdns BELMT SM2 — 221 M3
  REDBR IG4 — 122 B2
  SAND/SEL CR2 — 224 E5
  WBLY HA9 — 115 J3
Ambleside Rd BXLYHN DA7 — 164 G2
  WLSDN NW10 — 136 C2
Ambleside Wy EGH TW20 — 172 G10
Ambrey Wy WLGTN SM6 — 222 G6
Ambrook Rd BELV DA17 — 164 G2
Ambrosden Av WEST SW1P — 17 H4
Ambrose Av GLDGN NW11 — 117 J4
Ambrose Cl DART DA1 — 164 G10
  ORP BR6 — 207 H8
  WHTN TW2 — 176 C4
Ambrose St BERM/RHTH SE16 — 160 A3
Ambrose Wk BOW E3 — 140 A1
Amelia St WALW SE17 — 18 D7
Amen Cnr STP EC4M — 12 D6
Amen Ct STP EC4M — 12 D6
Amerden Wy SL SL1 — 148 F1
America Sq TWRH EC3N — 13 L3
America St STHWK SE1 — 12 E10
Amerland Rd WAND/EARL SW18 — 179 J2
Amersham Av UED N18 — 99 L7
Amersham Ct HARH RM3 — 105 N7
Amersham Gv NWCR SE14 — 160 E6
Amersham Pl AMSS HP7 — 69 P5
Amersham Rd AMS HP6 — 68 G1
  AMS HP6 — 70 A5
  BEAC HP9 — 88 D3
  CFSP/GDCR SL9 — 70 A4
  CROY/NA CR0 — 203 L6
  CSTG HP8 — 69 N10
  HARH RM3 — 105 M7
  NWCR SE14 — 160 F6
  RKW/CH/CXG WD3 — 70 G5
Amersham Wk HARH RM3 — 105 N7
Amersham Wy AMS HP6 — 70 B5
Amery Gdns GPK RM2 — 105 L2
  WLSDN NW10 — 136 E3
Amery Rd HRW HA1 — 114 F7
Amesbury WAB EN9 — 63 H8
Amesbury Av BRXS/STRHM SW2 — 180 F3
Amesbury Cl WPK KT4 — 200 H7
Amesbury Dr CHING E4 — 80 B10
Amesbury Rd BMLY BR1 — 206 A3
  DAGW RM9 — 143 P7
  EPP CM16 — 65 J7
  FELT TW13 — 175 P8
Ames Rd SWCM DA10 — 189 K2
Amethyst Rd WAN E11 — 121 P2
Amey Dr GT/LBKH KT23 — 236 B10
Amherst Av WEA W13 — 135 H5

Amherst Cl STMC/STPC BR5 — 207 K4
Amherst Dr STMC/STPC BR5 — 207 J4
Amherst Hl SEV TN13 — 246 F8
Amherst Pk SEV TN13 — 247 J8
  WEA W13 — 135 H8
Amherst Rd STNW/STAM N16 — 119 N5
  WEA W13 — 135 H5
Amhurst Gdns ISLW TW7 — 154 E7
Amhurst Pk STNW/STAM N16 — 119 M5
Amhurst Rd HACK E8 — 119 P10
Amhurst Ter HACK E8 — 119 P9
Amidas Gdns BCTR RM8 — 123 L9
Amiel St WCHPL E1 — 140 B6
Amies St BTSEA SW11 — 158 A10
Amis Av ADL/WDHM KT15 — 215 K7
  HOR/WEW KT19 — 219 M3
Amis Rd WOKN/KNAP GU21 — 231 K5
Amity Gv RYNPK SW20 — 200 F1
Amity Rd SRTFD E15 — 141 L2
Ammer Rd BTSEA SW11 — 180 B2
Amor Rd HMSMTH W6 — 156 F2
Amott Rd PECK SE15 — 159 P9
Ampere Wy CROY/NA CR0 — 202 F7
Ampleforth Cl ORP BR6 — 227 M1
Ampleforth Rd ABYW SE2 — 163 L1
Ampton St FSBYW WC1X — 5 M9
Amroth Cl FSTH SE23 — 182 A4
Amstel Wy WOKN/KNAP GU21 — 231 L4
Amsterdam Rd POP/IOD E14 — 161 H2
Amwell Cl GSTN WD25 — 73 M1
  WCHMH N21 — 79 L9
Amwell Common WGCE AL7 — 23 L6
Amwell End WARE SG12 — 26 C3
Amwell La STALE/WH AL4 — 20 G4
  WARE SG12 — 26 G3
Amwell St CLKNW EC1R — 6 A9
  HOD EN11 — 44 F3
Amyand Cottages TWK TW1 — 176 G2
Amyand Park Gdns TWK TW1 — 176 G3
Amyand Park Rd TWK TW1 — 176 G3
Amy Cl WLGTN SM6 — 222 F4
Amy La CSHM HP5 — 50 G4
Amy Rd OXTED RH8 — 261 K5
Amyruth Rd BROCKY SE4 — 182 F1
Amy Warne Cl EHAM E6 — 142 B7
Ancaster Cr NWMAL KT3 — 200 D6
Ancaster Rd BECK BR3 — 204 C3
Ancaster St WOOL/PLUM SE18 — 163 L5
Anchorage Cl WIM/MER SW19 — 179 K8
Anchor and Hope La CHARL SE7 — 161 N1
Anchor Bvd GRH DA9 — 166 B10
Anchor Dr RAIN RM13 — 145 J5
Anchor Hl WOKN/KNAP GU21 — 231 J3
Anchor La HHW HP1 — 35 L7
Anchor Ms BERM/RHTH SE16 — 160 A3
Anchor Yd FSBYE EC1V — 12 F1
Ancill Cl HMSMTH W6 — 156 G5
Ancona Rd WLSDN NW10 — 136 C4
  WOOL/PLUM SE18 — 163 L4
Andalus Rd BRXN/ST SW9 — 158 F9
Andace Park Gdns BMLY BR1 — 184 C5
Ander Cl ALP/SUD HA0 — 115 J9
Andermans WDSR SL4 — 148 C2
Anderson Av GUW GU2 — 249 N6
Anderson Cl ACT W3 — 136 A8
  DEN/HRF UB9 — 91 K9
  HOR/WEW KT19 — 219 M3
  WCHMH N21 — 78 G9
Anderson Dr ASHF TW15 — 174 F7
  RAD WD7 — 57 M9
  WEY KT13 — 196 E10
Anderson's Pl HSLW TW3 — 154 A10
Anderson St CHEL SW3 — 16 A7
Anderson Wy BELV DA17 — 164 C1
Andover Av CAN/RD E16 — 142 A8
Andover Cl EBED/NFELT TW14 — 134 C4
  GFD/PVL UB6 — 134 A6
  HOR/WEW KT19 — 220 A5
  UX/CGN UB8 — 131 L4
Andover Pl KIL/WHAMP NW6 — 2 C8
Andover Rd HOLWY N7 — 118 C7
  ORP BR6 — 207 H8
  WHTN TW2 — 176 C4
Andre St HACK E8 — 119 P10
Andrea Av CDH/CHF RM16 — 167 L1
Andrew Borde St LSQ/SEVD WC2H — 11 K5
Andrew Cl BARK/HLT IG6 — 102 C7
  DART DA1 — 186 E1
Andrewes Gdns EHAM E6 — 142 B8
Andrew Hill La SLN SL2 — 109 H6
Andrew Pl VX/NE SW8 — 158 E7
Andrews Cl BKHH IG9 — 101 P5
  EW KT17 — 220 C10
  HHNE HP2 — 35 N4
  HRW HA1 — 114 D6
  STMC/STPC BR5 — 207 N1
  WPK KT4 — 200 G7
Andrewsfield WGCE AL7 — 23 M5
Andrew's La CHESW EN7 — 61 M4
Andrews Rd HACK E8 — 140 A3
Andrew St POP/IOD E14 — 141 H8
Andromeda Cl CRAWW RH11 — 283 H3
Andwell Cl ABYW SE2 — 163 L1
Anelle Ri HHS/BOV HP3 — 36 A10
Anerley Gv NRWD SE19 — 181 N10
Anerley Hl NRWD SE19 — 181 N9
Anerley Pk PGE/AN SE20 — 182 A10
Anerley Park Rd PGE/AN SE20 — 182 A10
Anerley Rd NRWD SE19 — 181 P10
  PGE/AN SE20 — 204 A1
Anerley Station Rd PGE/AN SE20 — 204 A1
Anerley V NRWD SE19 — 181 N10
Anfield Cl BAL SW12 — 180 D3
Angas Ct WEY KT13 — 216 F5
Angel Cl HMSMTH W6 — 126 F3
Angel Wy ROM RM1 — 124 F3
Angerstein La BKHTH/KID SE3 — 161 L6
Angle Cl HGDN/ICK UB10 — 132 B3
Anglefield Rd BERK HP4 — 33 M5
Angle Gn DAGW RM9 — 123 J6
Angles Rd STRHM/NOR SW16 — 180 F7
Anglesey Rd OXHEY WD19 — 93 K6
  PEND EN3 — 80 A8
Anglesmede Crs PIN HA5 — 113 P1
Anglesmede Wy PIN HA5 — 113 N1
Anglia Cl TOTM N17 — 100 A8
Anglian Cl WATN WD24 — 73 K6
Anglian Rd WAN E11 — 121 J8
Anglo Rd BOW E3 — 140 E4
Angus Cl CHSGTN KT9 — 219 M2
Angus Dr RSLP HA4 — 113 K9
Angus Gdns CDALE/KGS NW9 — 96 A9
Angus Rd PLSTW E13 — 141 P5
Angus St NWCR SE14 — 160 G6
Anhalt Rd BTSEA SW11 — 15 P10
Ankerdine Crs WOOL/PLUM SE18 — 162 E7
Anlaby Rd TEDD TW11 — 176 D8
Anley Rd HMSMTH W6 — 156 D5
Anmersh Gv STAN HA7 — 95 J9
Annabel Cl POP/IOD E14 — 140 G8
Anna Cl HACK E8 — 7 M5
Annalee Gdns SOCK/AV RM15 — 146 G2
Annalee Rd SOCK/AV RM15 — 146 F1
Annandale Gv HGDN/ICK UB10 — 112 G3
Annandale Rd BFN/LL DA15 — 185 H3
  CHSWK W4 — 156 B3
  CROY/NA CR0 — 203 P9
  GNWCH SE10 — 161 L4
  GUW GU2 — 267 N2
Anna Neagle Cl FSTGT E7 — 121 M9
Annan Wy ROM RM1 — 104 G2
Anne Boleyn's Wk BELMT SM2 — 220 G4
  KUTN/CMB KT2 — 177 K8
Anne of Cleves Rd DART DA1 — 187 L1
Annesley Av CDALE/KGS NW9 — 116 B1
Annesley Cl WLSDN NW10 — 116 D8
Annesley Dr CROY/NA CR0 — 204 E10
Annesley Rd BKHTH/KID SE3 — 161 N1
Anne's Wk CTHM CR3 — 241 M6
Annett Cl SHPTN TW17 — 196 F4
Annette Cl KTN/HRWW/W HA3 — 94 D10
  HOLWY N7 — 118 C9
  HOLWY N7 — 118 C9
Annett Rd WOT/HER KT12 — 197 H7
Anne Wy BARK/HLT IG6 — 102 F7
Annie Besant Cl BOW E3 — 140 E3
Annie Brookes Cl STA TW18 — 172 G6
Anningsley Pk CHERT KT16 — 214 E6
Anning St SDTCH EC2A — 13 K1
Annington Rd EFNCH N2 — 118 A1
Annisdowne Cl SHGR GU5 — 270 G8
Annis Rd HOM E9 — 140 D1
Ann La WBPTN SW10 — 157 N6
Ann Moss Wy BERM/RHTH SE16 — 160 B2
Ann St WOOL/PLUM SE18 — 162 G3
Annsworthy Av THHTH CR7 — 203 L3
Ansar Gdns WALTH E17 — 120 E3
Anscuff Rd SLN SL2 — 128 F5
Ansdell Rd PECK SE15 — 160 B8
Ansdell St KENS W8 — 15 H3
Ansdell Ter KENS W8 — 15 H3
Ansell Gv CAR SM5 — 202 A8
Ansell Rd DORK RH4 — 272 C1
  TOOT SW17 — 179 P6
Anselm Cl CROY/NA CR0 — 203 N10
Anselm Rd FUL/PGN SW6 — 14 E10
  PIN HA5 — 93 N8
Ansford Rd BMLY BR1 — 183 H8
Ansleigh Pl NTGHL W11 — 136 C9
Ansley Cl SAND/SEL CR2 — 224 A10
Anslow Gdns IVER SL0 — 130 C4
Anson Cl HHW HP1 — 52 C3
  PUR/KEN CR8 — 241 L6
  ROMW/RG RM7 — 104 C10
  STAL AL1 — 38 C8
  STALE/WH AL4 — 21 H10
Anson Rd CRICK NW2 — 116 E10
  HOLWY N7 — 117 P7
Anson Wk NTHWD HA6 — 92 D5
Anstead Dr RAIN RM13 — 145 H4
Anstey Rd PECK SE15 — 159 P9
Anstice Cl CHSWK W4 — 156 B6
Anstridge Rd ELTH/MOT SE9 — 184 C2
Antelope Av CDH/CHF RM16 — 167 M2
Antelope Rd WOOL/PLUM SE18 — 162 C2
Anthony Cl OXHEY WD19 — 93 L2
  SEV TN13 — 246 F7
Anthony Rd BORE WD6 — 75 K6
  GFD/PVL UB6 — 134 D4
  SNWD SE25 — 203 P6
  WELL DA16 — 163 K7
Anthony's Cl WAP E1W — 13 N9
Anthonys La SWLY BR8 — 209 H1
Anthony St WCHPL E1 — 140 A8
Anthony Wy SL SL1 — 128 C9
  WHTN TW2 — 176 B7
Antill Rd BOW E3 — 140 D5
  SEVS/STOTM N15 — 119 P2
Antill Ter WCHPL E1 — 140 C8
Antlands La HORL RH6 — 280 C10
Antlands La East HORL RH6 — 280 F10
Antlands La West HORL RH6 — 280 F10
Antlers Hl CHING E4 — 80 G9
Anton Crs SUT SM1 — 201 K10
Antoneys Cl PIN HA5 — 93 L10
Antonine Ga STALW/RED AL3 — 37 P7
Anton Rd SOCK/AV RM15 — 146 G2
Anton St HACK E8 — 119 P10
Antrim Gv HAMP NW3 — 4 A1
Antrim Rd HAMP NW3 — 4 A1
Antrobus Cl SUT SM1 — 221 J2
Antrobus Rd CHSWK W4 — 155 P3
Anvil Cl HHS/BOV HP3 — 52 E4
  STRHM/NOR SW16 — 180 D10
Anvil La COB KT11 — 217 H10
Anvil Rd SUN TW16 — 197 H3
Anyards Rd COB KT11 — 217 J10
Apeldoorn Dr WLGTN SM6 — 222 F5
Aperdele Rd LHD/OX KT22 — 234 C6
Aperfield Rd BH/WHM TN16 — 244 B3
  ERITH DA8 — 164 C5
Apers Av WOKS/MYFD GU22 — 232 C2
Apex Cl BECK BR3 — 204 C3
  WEY KT13 — 196 E10
Apley Rd REIG RH2 — 275 K3
Aplin Wy ISLW TW7 — 154 D7
Apollo Av BMLY BR1 — 205 N1
  NTHWD HA6 — 93 H6
Apollo Cl HCH RM12 — 125 J7
Apollo Pl WAN E11 — 121 K8
  WBPTN SW10 — 157 N6
Apollo Wy HHNE HP2 — 35 N4
  WOOL/PLUM SE18 — 162 G2
Apothecary St BLKFR EC4V — 12 C6
Appach Rd BRXS/STRHM SW2 — 181 H1
Appleby Cl CHING E4 — 101 H2
  SEVS/STOTM N15 — 119 L5
  WHTN TW2 — 176 B6
Appleby Dr HARH RM3 — 105 K6
Appleby Gdns EBED/NFELT TW14 — 174 G4
Appleby Rd CAN/RD E16 — 141 M8
  HACK E8 — 7 P3
Appleby St BETH E2 — 7 L6
  CHESW EN7 — 61 M2
Applecroft BERK HP4 — 33 K3
  LCOL/BKTW AL2 — 56 G2
Applecroft Rd WCCW AL8 — 22 E5
Appledore Av BXLYHN DA7 — 164 D7
  RSLP HA4 — 113 J8
Appledore Cl EDGW HA8 — 95 M9
  HARH RM3 — 105 K9
  HAYES BR2 — 205 L5

TOOT SW17 180 A5 1
Appledore Crs BFN/LL DA15 185 H6
Applefield AMSS HP7 69 P5
CRAWE RH10 283 P6
Appleford Rd NKENS W10 8 B2
Appleford's Cl HOD EN11 44 E1 1
Apple Garth BTFD TW8 155 J3
RGODL GU7 267 H10 1
Applegarth ESH/CLAY KT10 218 E2
Applegarth Av GUW GU2 249 J10
Applegarth Dr DART DA1 187 M5
GNTH/NBYPK IG2 123 J2
Applegarth Rd THMD SE28 143 L10
WKENS W14 156 G2 1
Apple Ga BRW CM14 86 E9
Apple Gv CHSGTN KT9 219 K1
EN EN1 79 M7
Apple Orch SWLY BR8 208 E4 1
The Apple Orch HHNE HP2 36 A4
Apple Rd WAN E11 121 K8
Appleshaw Cl GVW DA11 190 D8 1
Appleton Cl AMSS HP7 69 N6
HLWW/ROY CM19 46 F2
Appleton Dr RDART DA2 187 J6
Appleton Gdns NWMAL KT3 200 D6
Appleton Rd ELTH/MOT SE9 162 B9
LOU IG10 82 E7
Appleton Wy HCH RM12 125 L6
Apple Tree Av WDR/YW UB7 132 A8
Apple Tree Cl GT/LBKH KT23 236 B10
Appletree Cl PGE/AN SE20 204 A1 1
Appletree Ct RGUE GU4 250 G8 1
Apple Tree Crs BRWN CM15 87 H4
Appletree Gdns EBAR EN4 77 P8
Appletree La DTCH/LGLY SL3 149 P2
Appletree Wk CSHM HP5 51 J10 1
GSTN WD25 73 J1
Apple Tree Yd STJS SW1Y 11 H9 1
Applewood Cl CRICK NW2 116 E8
TRDG/WHET N20 97 P2
Appold St ERITH DA8 164 G5
LVPST EC2M 13 J3 1
SDTCH EC2A 13 J3
Apprentice Wy CLPT E5 120 A9 1
Approach La MLHL NW7 97 H6 1
NFNCH/WDSP N12 97 H6
Approach Rd ASHF TW15 174 D9
BAR EN5 77 N8 1
BETH E2 140 B4
E/WMO/HCT KT8 197 P5
PUR/KEN CR8 223 J8
RYNPK SW20 200 F3
STAL AL1 38 D7 1
WARL CR6 243 N8
The Approach ACT W3 136 A8
EN EN1 80 A6 1
HDN NW4 116 G3 1
ORP BR6 207 J9
POTB/CUF EN6 59 J8 1
UPMR RM14 126 A8
Appspond La LCOL/BKTW AL2 37 K10
Aprey Gdns HDN NW4 116 F2
April Cl ASHTD KT21 237 L4
FELT TW13 175 H6
HNWL W7 134 D9
ORP BR6 227 J2
April Gln FSTH SE23 182 C6
April St STNW/STAM N16 119 N9
Aprilwood Cl ADL/WDHM KT15 215 J7
Apsley Cl HRW HA1 114 B3
Apsley Rd NWMAL KT3 199 P3
SNWD SE25 204 A4
Apsley Wy CRICK NW2 116 D7
Aquarius Wy NTHWD HA6 93 H6
Aquila Cl ASHTD KT21 237 K7
Aquila St STJWD NW8 3 M7 1
Aquinas St STHWK SE1 12 B10
Arabella Dr PUT/ROE SW15 156 B10
Arabia Cl CHING E4 101 H1
Arabin Rd BROCKY SE4 160 D10
Araglen Av SOCK/AV RM15 146 G7 1
Aragon Av EW KT17 220 E5
THDIT KT7 198 E5
Aragon Cl CROY/NA CR0 225 K6
ENC/FH EN2 78 G4 1
HAYES BR2 206 C8
HHNE HP2 36 D1
SUN TW16 174 G10
Aragon Dr BARK/HLT IG6 102 F8
RSLP HA4 113 L6 1
Aragon Rd KUTN/CMB KT2 177 K8
MRDN SM4 200 G7
Aran Cl HARP AL5 20 C5
Arandora Crs CHDH RM6 123 L5
Arbery Rd BOW E3 140 D5
Arbor Cl BECK BR3 204 G2
Arborfield Cl BRXS/STRHM SW2 180 G4
SL SL1 149 K2
Arbor Rd CHING E4 101 J4
Arbour Cl BRW CM14 107 J6
LHD/OX KT22 236 E9 1
Arbour Rd PEND EN3 80 C8
Arbour Sq WCHPL E1 140 C8 2
The Arbour HERT/BAY SG13 25 L7 1
Arbour Vw AMSS HP7 69 N5
Arbour Wy HCH RM12 125 J10
Arbroath Gn OXHEY WD19 93 H4
Arbroath Rd ELTH/MOT SE9 162 B9
Arbrook Cl STMC/STPC BR5 207 K3
Arbrook La ESH/CLAY KT10 218 B3
Arbuthnot La BXLY DA5 185 P2
Arbuthnot Rd NWCR SE14 160 C8
Arbutus Cl REIG RH2 275 M2
Arbutus Rd REIG RH2 275 M2
Arbutus St HACK E8 7 L5
Arcade Pl ROM RM1 124 F3 2
Arcadia Av FNCH N3 97 K9
Arcadia Cl CAR SM5 222 B1 1
Arcadian Av BXLY DA5 185 P2
Arcadian Cl BXLY DA5 185 P2
Arcadian Gdns WDGN N22 99 H8
Arcadian Rd BXLY DA5 185 P3
Arcadia St POP/IOD E14 140 F8
Arcany Rd SOCK/AV RM15 146 G6
Archangel St BERM/RHTH SE16 160 C1
Archates Av CDH/CHF RM16 167 M2
Archbishop's Pl
BRXS/STRHM SW2 180 G2
Archdale Ct SHB W12 136 E10 1
Archdale Pl NWMAL KT3 199 N3
Archdale Rd EDUL SE22 181 N1
Archel Rd WKENS W14 14 C9
Archer Cl KGLGY WD4 54 A5
KUTN/CMB KT2 177 K10
Archer Rd SNWD SE25 204 A4
STMC/STPC BR5 207 K6
Archers EPP CM16 46 E6 1
Archers Cl HERT/WAS SG14 25 K4 1
Archers Dr PEND EN3 80 B6 1
Archers Flds STAL AL1 38 E4
Archers Green La WLYN AL6 23 N3
Archer Sq DEPT SE8 160 D5 1
Archers Ride WGCE AL7 23 L7
Archer St SOHO/SHAV W1D 11 J7 1
Archer Wy SWLY BR8 208 G3
Archery Cl KTN/HRWW/W HA3 114 E1
Archery Rd ELTH/MOT SE9 184 C1
The Arches RYLN/HDSTN HA2 114 A7
Archfield WGCE AL7 23 H2 1
Archibald Ms MYFR/PICC W1J 10 D8
Archibald Rd HARH RM3 105 P9
HOLWY N7 118 E9
Arch Rd WOT/HER KT12 197 L10
Arch St STHWK SE1 18 E4
Archway HARH RM3 105 J7
Archway Cl NKENS W10 136 G7 1
WIM/MER SW19 179 L7 1
WLGTN SM6 202 F10 1
Archway Ms DORK RH4 272 F1
Archway Rd ARCH N19 118 D6
HGT N6 118 A3
Archway St BARN SW13 156 B9
Arcola St HACK E8 119 N10
Arctic St KTTN NW5 118 C10 1
Arcturus Rd CRAWW RH11 283 H9
Arcus Rd BMLY BR1 183 K9 1
Ardbeg Rd HNHL SE24 181 L2
Arden Cl BUSH WD23 94 E1
HHS/BOV HP3 52 D4
HRW HA1 114 C8
REIG RH2 275 L4
Arden Court Gdns EFNCH N2 117 N5 1
Arden Crs DAGW RM9 143 N2
POP/IOD E14 160 F3
Arden Gv HARP AL5 20 A2
ORP BR6 226 E1
Arden Mhor PIN HA5 113 J2
Arden Rd CRAWE RH10 284 A9
FNCH N3 117 J1
WEA W13 135 H9
Ardens Wy STALE/WH AL4 39 J4
Ardent Cl SNWD SE25 203 M3
Ardesley Wd WEY KT13 216 F1 1
Ardfern Av STRHM/NOR SW16 203 H3
Ardfillan Rd CAT SE6 183 J4
Ardilaun Rd HBRY N5 119 K9 1
Ardingly Cl CRAWW RH11 283 L5
CROY/NA CR0 204 C10
Ardleigh Cl EMPK RM11 125 L1
Ardleigh Ct BRWN CM15 107 L1
Ardleigh Gdns CHEAM SM3 201 K8
Ardleigh Green Rd EMPK RM11 125 L3
Ardleigh Rd IS N1 7 J2
WALTH E17 100 E9
Ardleigh Ter WALTH E17 100 E9 1
Ardley Cl FSTH SE23 182 D6
WLSDN NW10 116 B8
Ardley Crs RBSF CM22 31 J1
Ardlui Rd WNWD SE27 181 K5
Ardmay Gdns SURB KT6 199 K4 1
SURB KT6 199 K5 1
Ardmere Rd LEW SE13 183 J2
Ardmore Av GUW GU2 249 N8
Ardmore La BKHH IG9 101 N2
Ardmore Rd SOCK/AV RM15 146 G6
Ardmore Wy GUW GU2 249 N8
Ardoch Rd CAT SE6 183 J5
Ardra Rd ED N9 100 C4
Ardrossan Cl SLN SL2 129 H6 1
Ardrossan Gdns WPK KT4 200 D10
Ardross Av NTHWD HA6 92 F6
Ardshiel Cl PUT/ROE SW15 156 G9 1
Ardshiel Dr REDH RH1 275 P2 1
Ardwell Av BARK/HLT IG6 122 F3
Ardwell Rd BRXS/STRHM SW2 180 F5
Ardwick Rd CRICK NW2 117 K9
Arethusa Wy CHOB/PIR GU24 230 E2
Argall Av LEY E10 120 C5
Argenta Wy WLSDN NW10 135 N2 1
Argent Cl EGH TW20 172 F9
Argent St GRAYS RM17 167 N6
WTHK RM20 167 K5
Argent Wy CHESW EN7 61 L3
Argles Cl GRH DA9 188 F1
Argon Ms FUL/PGN SW6 157 K6 1
Argon Rd UED N18 100 C6
Argosy Gdns STA TW18 173 J9
Argosy La STWL/WRAY TW19 173 N3
Argus Cl ROMW/RG RM7 104 C9
Argus Wk CRAWW RH11 283 K10
Argus Wy NTHLT UB5 133 M5 1
Argyle Av HSLW TW3 175 P2
WHTN TW2 175 P2
Argyle Cl WEA W13 134 F6
Argyle Gdns UPMR RM14 126 C8
Argyle Pl HMSMTH W6 156 E3 1
Argyle Rd BAR EN5 76 F8
CAN/RD E16 141 N8
GFD/PVL UB6 134 E5
HSLW TW3 176 A1
IL IG1 122 D7
NFNCH/WDSP N12 97 K6
RYLN/HDSTN HA2 114 A4
SEV TN13 265 J1
SRTFD E15 121 K9
TOTM N17 99 P9
UED N18 99 P5
WCHPL E1 140 C6
WEA W13 134 F7
Argyle Sq STPAN WC1H 5 M9
Argyle St STPAN WC1H 5 M10
Argyle Wy STHWK SE1 19 P8
Argyll Av SL SL1 128 F9
STHL UB1 134 A10
Argyll Cl BRXN/ST SW9 158 G9
Argyll Gdns EDGW HA8 95 N10 1
Argyll Rd GRAYS RM17 167 M4
HHNE HP2 35 P1
KENS W8 14 E2
Argyll St REGST W1B 10 G6
Arica Rd BROCKY SE4 160 D10
Ariel Cl GVE DA12 191 J7
Ariel Rd KIL/WHAMP NW6 2 E2
Ariel Wy HSLWW TW4 153 J9
SHB W12 136 F10
Arisdale Av SOCK/AV RM15 146 G5
Aristotle Rd CLAP SW4 158 E9
Ark Av CDH/CHF RM16 167 M2
Arkell Gv STRHM/NOR SW16 181 J10
Arkindale Rd CAT SE6 183 H6
Arkley Crs WALTH E17 120 E3 2
Arkley Dr BAR EN5 76 D8
Arkley La BAR EN5 76 D7
Arkley Rd HHNE HP2 36 C1
WALTH E17 120 E3 3
Arkley Vw BAR EN5 76 E8
Arklow Rd NWCR SE14 160 E5
Arkwright Rd DTCH/LGLY SL3 151 H8
HAMP NW3 117 M10
SAND/SEL CR2 223 N6
TIL RM18 168 D8
Arkwrights HLW CM20 29 J10
Arlesford Rd BRXN/ST SW9 158 F9
Arlingford Rd
BRXS/STRHM SW2 181 H1 1
Arlington NFNCH/WDSP N12 97 K4
Arlington Av IS N1 6 F6
Arlington Cl BFN/LL DA15 185 H3
SUT SM1 201 K9 1
TWK TW1 177 H1 1
Arlington Ct HYS/HAR UB3 152 E4
Arlington Crs CHES/WCR EN8 62 D10
Arlington Dr CAR SM5 202 A9
RSLP HA4 112 E4
Arlington Gdns CHSWK W4 155 P4
HARH RM3 105 M9
IL IG1 122 C5
Arlington Ldg WEY KT13 216 C1 1
Arlington Rd ASHF TW15 174 A8
CAMTN NW1 4 F6
RCHPK/HAM TW10 177 J5
STHGT/OAK N14 98 C3
SURB KT6 199 J6
TEDD TW11 176 E7
TWK TW1 177 H2
WEA W13 134 G8
WFD IG8 101 N8 1
Arlington Sq IS N1 6 F6
Arlington St MYFR/PICC W1J 10 G9
Arlington Wy CLKNW EC1R 6 B9
Arliss Wy NTHLT UB5 133 K3
Arlow Rd WCHMH N21 99 H2
Armadale Cl WALTH E17 120 A2
Armadale Rd EBED/NFELT TW14 175 H1
WOKN/KNAP GU21 231 M3
Armada St DEPT SE8 160 F5 1
Armada Wy EHAM E6 142 F8
Armagh Rd BOW E3 140 E3
Armand Cl WAT WD17 72 G4
Armfield Cl E/WMO/HCT KT8 197 N5
Armfield Crs MTCM CR4 202 A2
Armfield Rd ENC/FH EN2 79 L5
Arminger Rd SHB W12 136 E10
Armitage Cl RKW/CH/CXG WD3 71 N8
Armitage Ct ASC SL5 192 B6
Armitage Rd GLDGN NW11 117 H6
GNWCH SE10 161 L3
Armor Rd PUR RM19 166 C3
Armour Cl HOLWY N7 5 N2
Armoury Dr GVE DA12 190 F3
Armoury Rd DEPT SE8 160 G8
Armoury Wy WAND/EARL SW18 179 K1
Armstead Wk DAGE RM10 144 B2
Armstrong Av WFD IG8 101 K7
Armstrong Cl BCTR RM8 123 N5 1
BMLY BR1 206 B3 1
EHAM E6 142 C8
LCOL/BKTW AL2 57 K3 1
RSEV TN14 246 C1
RSLP HA4 113 H4
WOT/HER KT12 197 H6 1
Armstrong Crs EBAR EN4 77 N7
Armstrong Gdns RAD WD7 57 K8 1
Armstrong Rd ACT W3 136 C10
EGH TW20 171 P9
FELT TW13 175 M8
Armstrong Wy STHL UB1 154 A1
Armytage Rd HEST TW5 153 L6
Arnal Crs WAND/EARL SW18 179 H3
Arndale Wy EGH TW20 172 D8
Arne Cl CRAWW RH11 283 J10
Arne Gv HORL RH6 279 P2
ORP BR6 207 J10
Arne St LSQ/SEVD WC2H 11 M6
Arnett Cl RKW/CH/CXG WD3 71 K10
Arnett Sq CHING E4 100 E7
Arnett Wy RKW/CH/CXG WD3 71 K10
Arne Wk BKHTH/KID SE3 161 L10
Arneways Av CHDH RM6 123 N2
Arneway St WEST SW1P 17 K4 1
Arnewood Cl LHD/OX KT22 218 A10 1
PUT/ROE SW15 178 D4
Arney's La MTCM CR4 202 B6 1
Arnfield Cl CRAWW RH11 283 H8 1
Arngask Rd CAT SE6 183 J3
Arnheim Pl POP/IOD E14 160 F2
Arnhem Av SOCK/AV RM15 146 B10
Arnhem Dr CROY/NA CR0 225 J7
Arnison Rd E/WMO/HCT KT8 198 C4
Arnold Av East PEND EN3 80 E4 1
Arnold Cl KTN/HRWW/W HA3 115 L5
Arnold Crs ISLW TW7 176 C1
Arnold Dr CHSGTN KT9 219 J3
Arnold Gdns PLMGR N13 99 J6
Arnold Pl TIL RM18 168 F7
Arnold Rd BOW E3 140 F5
DAGW RM9 144 A2
GVE DA12 190 F5
NTHLT UB5 133 M1
STA TW18 173 M10
TOOT SW17 180 A10
TOTM N17 119 N1
WOKN/KNAP GU21 232 E2
Arnolds Av RBRW/HUT CM13 87 P9
Arnolds Cl RBRW/HUT CM13 87 P9
Arnolds La RDART DA2 187 P9
Arnos Gv STHGT/OAK N14 98 E5
Arnos Rd FBAR/BDGN N11 98 D6
Arnott Cl CHSWK W4 156 A3
THMD SE28 143 M10
Arnould Av CMBW SE5 159 L10
Arnsberg Wy BXLYHN DA7 164 B10
BXLYHS DA6 164 A10 1
Arnside Gdns WBLY HA9 115 J6
Arnside Rd BXLYHN DA7 164 B7
Arnside St WALW SE17 18 F9
Arnulf St CAT SE6 182 G7
Arnull's Rd STRHM/NOR SW16 181 J9
Arodene Rd BRXS/STRHM SW2 180 G2
Arosa Rd TWK TW1 177 J2
Arragon Gdns STRHM/NOR SW16 180 F10
WWKM BR4 204 G10
Arragon Rd EHAM E6 142 A3
TWK TW1 176 F4 1
WAND/EARL SW18 179 K4
Arragon Wk BF/WBF KT14 216 A9
Arran Cl CRAWW RH11 283 L10
ERITH DA8 164 E5
HHS/BOV HP3 36 D8
WLGTN SM6 222 D1
Arran Dr MNPK E12 122 A6
STAN HA7 95 H5
Arran Ms EA W5 135 L10
Arran Rd CAT SE6 182 G5
Arran Wk IS N1 6 E3
Arran Wy ESH/CLAY KT10 198 A9
Arras Av MRDN SM4 201 M5
Arretine Cl STALW/RED AL3 37 N8
Arreton Md WOKN/KNAP GU21 214 B10
Arrol Rd BECK BR3 204 B3
Arrow Rd BOW E3 140 G5
Arrowsmith Rd CHIG IG7 103 J6
Arsenal Rd ELTH/MOT SE9 162 C8
Artel Cft CRAWE RH10 284 A7
Artemis Cl GVE DA12 191 H3
Arterberry Rd RYNPK SW20 178 F10
Arterial Av RAIN RM13 145 K6
Arterial Road North Stifford
CDH/CHF RM16 167 K1
Arterial Road Purfleet
PUR RM19 166 B3
Arterial Road West Thurrock
WTHK RM20 166 E2
Artesian Cl ROM RM1 124 G5 1
WLSDN NW10 136 A2
Artesian Gv BAR EN5 77 M8
Artesian Rd NTGHL W11 8 E6
Arthingworth St SRTFD E15 141 K3
Arthurdon Rd LEW SE13 182 F1
Arthur Gv WOOL/PLUM SE18 162 F3
Arthur Rd BH/WHM TN16 243 P1
CHDH RM6 123 M5
CRAWW RH11 283 H7
ED N9 99 N3
EHAM E6 142 C4
HOLWY N7 118 G9
KUTN/CMB KT2 177 M10 1
NWMAL KT3 200 E5
SL SL1 149 J1
STAL AL1 38 G6
WDSR SL4 149 H7
WIM/MER SW19 179 J7
Arthur's Bridge Rd
WOKN/KNAP GU21 231 P3
Arthur St BUSH WD23 73 L7
CANST EC4R 13 H8
ERITH DA8 164 G6
GRAYS RM17 167 P5
GVW DA11 190 D3
Artichoke Hl WAP E1W 140 A9 1
Artichoke Pl CMBW SE5 159 L7 1
Artillery Cl GNTH/NBYPK IG2 122 G4 1
Artillery La LVPST EC2M 13 K4
Artillery Pl WOOL/PLUM SE18 162 C4
Artillery Rw GVE DA12 190 F3
Artillery Ter GU GU1 250 A10
Artington Cl ORP BR6 226 F1
Artington Wk GUW GU2 267 P3
Artisan Crs STALW/RED AL3 38 B5
Artizan St WCHPL E1 13 K5
Arun TIL RM18 169 M3
Arundel Av EW KT17 220 E6
MRDN SM4 201 J4
SAND/SEL CR2 223 P6
Arundel Cl BTSEA SW11 179 P1 1
BXLY DA5 186 A2 1
CHES/WCR EN8 62 A4
CRAWE RH10 284 D7
CROY/NA CR0 203 J10 1
HHNE HP2 36 C5
HPTN TW12 176 A8
SRTFD E15 121 K9
Arundel Ct DTCH/LGLY SL3 150 A3
Arundel Dr BORE WD6 75 P8
ORP BR6 227 L2
RYLN/HDSTN HA2 113 N9
WFD IG8 101 M8
Arundel Gdns EDGW HA8 96 A8 1
GDMY/SEVK IG3 123 K7
NTGHL W11 8 C7
WCHMH N21 99 H2
Arundel Gv STALW/RED AL3 38 C2 1
STNW/STAM N16 119 M10
Arundell Rd ABLGY WD5 55 H8
Arundel Pl IS N1 6 A2
Arundel Rd BELMT SM2 221 J4
CROY/NA CR0 203 L6
DART DA1 165 K10
DORK RH4 272 F2
EBAR EN4 77 P7
HARH RM3 105 N8
HSLWW TW4 153 K9
KUT KT1 199 N2
UX/CGN UB8 131 L4
Arundel Sq HOLWY N7 6 A2
Arundel St TPL/STR WC2R 11 P7
Arundel Ter BARN SW13 156 E5
Arvon Rd HBRY N5 119 H10
Asbaston Ter IL IG1 142 F1 1
Ascalon St VX/NE SW8 158 D6
Ascension Rd CRW RM5 104 D7
Ascham Dr CHING E4 100 G8
Ascham End WALTH E17 100 D9 1
Ascham St KTTN NW5 118 D10 1
Aschurch Rd CROY/NA CR0 203 N7
Ascot Cl BARK/HLT IG6 103 H7
BORE WD6 75 M9
NTHLT UB5 113 P10
Ascot Gdns HCH RM12 125 M9
PEND EN3 80 B3
STHL UB1 133 N7
Ascot Ms WLGTN SM6 222 D5 1
Ascot Rd ASHF TW15 174 B4
EHAM E6 142 C5
GVW DA11 190 E6
SEVS/STOTM N15 119 L3
STMC/STPC BR5 207 J4
TOOT SW17 180 B9
UED N18 99 P5
WATW WD18 72 F9
Ascots La BRKMPK AL9 23 H10
Ascott Av EA W5 155 K1
Ashbeam Cl RBRW/HUT CM13 107 H7 1
Ashborurne Sq NTHWD HA6 92 F7 1
Ashbourne Av BXLYHN DA7 163 P6
GLDGN NW11 117 J3
RYLN/HDSTN HA2 114 C7 1
SWFD E18 121 N2
TRDG/WHET N20 98 A3
Ashbourne Cl COUL/CHIP CR5 240 D4 1
EA W5 135 M7
NFNCH/WDSP N12 97 L5
Ashbourne Ct STALE/WH AL4 39 H8 1
Ashbourne Gv CHSWK W4 156 B4
EDUL SE22 181 N1
MLHL NW7 96 A6 1
Ashbourne Ri ORP BR6 226 G1
Ashbourne Rd BROX EN10 44 E7 1
EA W5 135 L6
HARH RM3 105 K5
MTCM CR4 180 B9
Ashbourne Ter
WIM/MER SW19 179 K10 1
Ashbourne Wy GLDGN NW11 117 J3 1
Ashbridge Rd WAN E11 121 K5
Ashbridge St STJWD NW8 9 N2
Ashbrook Rd ARCH N19 118 E6
DAGE RM10 124 C8 1
WDSR SL4 171 N3
Ashburn Gdns SKENS SW7 15 J5
Ashburnham Av HRW HA1 114 E5
Ashburnham Cl EFNCH N2 117 N2 1
OXHEY WD19 93 H4 1
Ashburnham Dr OXHEY WD19 93 H4
Ashburnham Gdns HRW HA1 114 E4 1
UPMR RM14 126 A6
Ashburnham Gv GNWCH SE10 160 G6
Ashburnham Pk ESH/CLAY KT10 218 B1
Ashburnham Pl GNWCH SE10 160 G6
Ashburnham Retreat
GNWCH SE10 160 G6 1
Ashburnham Rd BELV DA17 164 D3
CRAWE RH10 284 B9
RCHPK/HAM TW10 176 G6
WBPTN SW10 157 M6 1
WLSDN NW10 136 F5
Ashburn Pl SKENS SW7 15 J5
Ashburton Av CROY/NA CR0 204 A8
GDMY/SEVK IG3 123 J9
Ashburton Cl CROY/NA CR0 203 P9 1
Ashburton Gdns CROY/NA CR0 203 P9 2
Ashburton Gv HOLWY N7 119 H9
Ashburton Rd CAN/RD E16 141 M8 1
CROY/NA CR0 203 P9
RSLP HA4 113 H7
Ashbury Cl HAT AL10 40 B4 1
Ashbury Ct BMLY BR1 183 M10
Ashbury Crs RGUE GU4 250 F8
Ashbury Dr HGDN/ICK UB10 112 C7
Ashbury Gdns CHDH RM6 123 N3
Ashbury Pl WIM/MER SW19 179 M9 2
Ashbury Rd BTSEA SW11 158 A9
Ashby Av CHSGTN KT9 219 M3
Ashby Cl EMPK RM11 125 P6 1
Ashby Gdns STAL AL1 38 C10
Ashby Gv IS N1 6 F3 1
Ashby Ms BROCKY SE4 160 E9
Ashby Rd BERK HP4 33 J2
BROCKY SE4 160 E8
SEVS/STOTM N15 119 P3
WATN WD24 73 H4
Ashby St FSBYE EC1V 6 D10
Ashby Wk CROY/NA CR0 203 K6 1
Ashby Wy WDR/YW UB7 152 B6
Ashchurch Gv SHB W12 156 D1
Ashchurch Park Vls SHB W12 156 D2
Ashchurch Ter SHB W12 156 C2
Ash Cl ABLGY WD5 54 E8
BRKMPK AL9 59 K1
BRWN CM15 86 E9
CAR SM5 202 A9
DEN/HRF UB9 91 N9
DTCH/LGLY SL3 150 E2
EDGW HA8 95 P5
GSTN WD25 73 J1
KWD/TDW/WH KT20 255 P7
NWMAL KT3 200 A2
PGE/AN SE20 204 B2
REDH RH1 258 D6
ROMW/RG RM7 104 C8
SCUP DA14 185 L6
STAN HA7 94 F7
STMC/STPC BR5 206 G5
SWLY BR8 208 D2
WOKS/MYFD GU22 232 B6
WOKS/MYFD GU22 233 K1
Ashcombe WGCW AL8 23 H1 1
Ashcombe Av SURB KT6 199 J7
Ashcombe Gdns EDGW HA8 95 M5
Ashcombe Pk CRICK NW2 116 B8
Ashcombe Rd CAR SM5 222 B3
DORK RH4 254 F10
REDH RH1 258 D3
WIM/MER SW19 179 K8
Ashcombe Sq NWMAL KT3 199 P3 1
Ashcombe St FUL/PGN SW6 157 L8 1
Ashcombe Ter
KWD/TDW/WH KT20 238 E6
Ash Copse LCOL/BKTW AL2 55 N7
Ash Ct HOR/WEW KT19 219 P1
Ashcroft PIN HA5 93 P7
RGUE GU4 268 B7
Ashcroft Av BFN/LL DA15 185 K2
Ashcroft Cl HARP AL5 20 D3
Ashcroft Ct SL SL1 128 A4
Ashcroft Crs BFN/LL DA15 185 K2
Ashcroft Dr DEN/HRF UB9 111 J4
Ashcroft Pk COB KT11 217 M8
Ashcroft Ri COUL/CHIP CR5 240 F2
Ashcroft Rd BOW E3 140 D5
CHSGTN KT9 199 L10
Ashdale GT/LBKH KT23 254 B2
Ashdale Cl STWL/WRAY TW19 173 P5
WHTN TW2 176 A3
Ashdale Gv STAN HA7 94 E7
Ashdale Rd LEE/GVPK SE12 183 N4
Ashdales STAL AL1 38 C10
Ashdene PIN HA5 113 K1
Ashdene Cl ASHF TW15 174 D10 1
Ashdon Cl RBRW/HUT CM13 87 P10
SOCK/AV RM15 146 G8
WFD IG8 101 N7
Ashdown Cl BECK BR3 204 G2 1
BXLY DA5 186 D3
REIG RH2 275 L4 1
Ashdown Crs CHES/WCR EN8 62 D4
KTTN NW5 118 B10 1
Ashdown Dr BORE WD6 75 L6
Ashdown Gdns SAND/SEL CR2 242 A1
Ashdown Pl THDIT KT7 198 F6
Ashdown Rd BUSH WD23 73 L7
EW KT17 220 C9
HGDN/ICK UB10 132 B5
KUT KT1 199 K2
PEND EN3 80 B6 2
REIG RH2 275 L4
WLSDN NW10 136 B3
Ashdown Wk ROMW/RG RM7 104 C9
Ashdown Wy AMS HP6 69 J3
TOOT SW17 180 B5
Ash Dr HAT AL10 40 D7
REDH RH1 276 B2
Ashendene Rd CHESW EN7 61 J1
HERT/BAY SG13 42 G4
Ashenden Rd CLPT E5 120 D10
GUW GU2 249 L10
Ashenden Wk SLN SL2 109 J9
Ashen Dr DART DA1 187 H2
Ashen Gv WIM/MER SW19 179 K6
Ashen V SAND/SEL CR2 224 C5
Asheridge Rd CSHM HP5 50 E4
Asher Loftus Wy FBAR/BDGN N11 98 A7
Asher Wy WAP E1W 140 A9
Ashfield Av BUSH WD23 74 A10
FELT TW13 175 J4
Ashfield Cl BECK BR3 182 F10
RCHPK/HAM TW10 177 K4
Ashfield La CHST BR7 184 F9
Ashfield Rd ACT W3 136 C10
CSHM HP5 51 J5
FSBYPK N4 119 K4
STHGT/OAK N14 98 D4
Ashfields GSTN WD25 72 G1 1
LOU IG10 82 C6
Ashfield St WCHPL E1 140 A7
Ashford Av ASHF TW15 174 C9
BRW CM14 106 G4
CEND/HSY/T N8 118 F2
YEAD UB4 133 L8
Ashford Cl ASHF TW15 173 P7 1
WALTH E17 120 E4 1
Ashford Crs ASHF TW15 173 P6
PEND EN3 80 B6
Ashford Gdns COB KT11 235 L2 1
Ashford Gn OXHEY WD19 93 L6 1
Ashford La MDHD SL6 148 A1
Ashford Rd CRICK NW2 116 C9
EHAM E6 142 C1
FELT TW13 174 E7
IVER SL0 130 F3
SHPTN TW17 174 D10
STA TW18 173 N10
SWFD E18 101 N10
Ashford St IS N1 7 J9
Ash Gn DEN/HRF UB9 131 L1
Ash Gv ALP/SUD HA0 114 F9
AMS HP6 68 F2
CRICK NW2 116 G9
DEN/HRF UB9 91 N9
EA W5 155 K1
EBED/NFELT TW14 174 F4
EN EN1 99 M1
GUW GU2 249 M10
HACK E8 140 A3 3
HEST TW5 153 L7
HHS/BOV HP3 36 A10
HYS/HAR UB3 132 E9
PGE/AN SE20 204 B2
PLMGR N13 99 K4
SLN SL2 129 L2 1
STA TW18 173 M9
STALE/WH AL4 21 H2
STHL UB1 133 P7
WDR/YW UB7 132 A9
WWKM BR4 205 H9
Ashgrove Rd ASHF TW15 174 D8
BMLY BR1 183 J9
GDMY/SEVK IG3 123 J6
SEV TN13 265 H3
Ash Groves SBW CM21 30 B1
Ash Hill Cl BUSH WD23 94 A2
Ash Hill Dr PIN HA5 113 K1
Ashingdon Cl CHING E4 101 H4 1
Ashington Rd FUL/PGN SW6 157 J8 1
Ash Keys CRAWE RH10 283 P8
Ashlake Rd STRHM/NOR SW16 180 F7
Ashland Pl MHST W1U 10 C3 1
Ash La WDSR SL4 148 C8
Ashlar Pl WOOL/PLUM SE18 162 E3 3
Ashlea Rd CFSP/GDCR SL9 90 B10
Ashleigh Av EGH TW20 172 F10
Ashleigh Cl HORL RH6 280 A4
Ashleigh Gdns SUT SM1 201 L9
UPMR RM14 126 C8
Ashleigh Rd MORT/ESHN SW14 156 B9
PGE/AN SE20 204 A3
Ashley Av BARK/HLT IG6 102 E10
EPSOM KT18 220 A9
MRDN SM4 201 K5 1
Ashley Cl GT/LBKH KT23 253 N1
HDN NW4 96 F10
HHS/BOV HP3 36 A8
PIN HA5 93 J10
SEV TN13 247 J10
WEY KT13 196 F8
WGCW AL8 22 F3
Ashley Ct WOKN/KNAP GU21 231 L4 1
Ashley Crs BTSEA SW11 158 B9
WDGN N22 99 H10 1
Ashley Dr BNSTD SM7 221 K10 1
BORE WD6 75 P9
ISLW TW7 154 D5
WHTN TW2 176 A4
WOT/HER KT12 197 H10
Ashley Gdns CDH/CHF RM16 147 P10

ORP BR6 .... 227 H2
PLMGR N13 .... 99 K5
RCHPK/HAM TW10 .... 177 J6
WBLY HA9 .... 115 K7
Ashley Green Rd CSHM HP5 .... 51 J3
Ashley La CROY/NA CR0 .... 204 F1
MDN NW4 .... 96 F10
MLHL NW7 .... 96 F8
Ashley Park Av WOT/HER KT12 .... 196 G8
Ashley Park Crs WOT/HER KT12 .... 196 G8
Ashley Park Rd WOT/HER KT12 .... 197 H8
Ashley PI WEST SW1P 16 C4
Ashley Ri WOT/HER KT12 .... 197 H10
Ashley Rd ARCH N19 .... 118 F6
CHING E4 .... 100 F6
DORK RH4 .... 272 B3
EPSOM KT18 .... 238 C3
EW KT17 .... 220 A9
FSTGT E7 .... 141 J2 ⊡
HERT/WAS SG14 .... 25 H6
HPTN TW12 .... 197 H5
PEND EN3 .... 80 B6 ⊡
RCH/KEW TW9 .... 155 K9
SEV TN13 .... 247 J10
STAL AL1 .... 39 H6
THDIT KT7 .... 190 B6
THHTH CR7 .... 202 G4
TOTM N17 .... 119 P7 ⊡
UX/CGN UB8 .... 131 L4
WIM/MER SW19 .... 179 L9
WOKN/KNAP GU21 .... 231 L9
WOT/HER KT12 .... 216 C1
Ashleys RKW/CH/CXG WD3 .... 91 J1
Ashley Wy CHOB/PIR GU24 .... 212 C9
Ashling Rd CROY/NA CR0 .... 203 P8
Ashlin Rd SRTFD E15 .... 121 J9
Ashlone Rd PUT/ROE SW15 .... 156 C8 ⊡
Ashlyn Cl BUSH WD23 .... 73 M8
Ashlyn Gv EMPK RM11 .... 125 L1
Ashlyns Ct BERK HP4 .... 33 N6 ⊡
Ashlyn's Pk COB KT11 .... 217 M9
Ashlyns La CHONG CM5 .... 48 G7
Ashlyns Rd BERK HP4 .... 33 N6
EPP CM16 .... 65 J6 ⊡
Ashlyns Wy CHSGTN KT9 .... 219 J3
Ashmead STHGT/OAK N14 .... 78 D9
Ash Mead Dr DEN/HRF UB9 .... 111 K7
Ashmead Ga BMLY BR1 .... 205 P1
Ashmead La DEN/HRF UB9 .... 111 K7
Ashmead Rd DEPT SE8 .... 160 F8
EBED/NFELT TW14 .... 175 H4
Ashmere Av BECK BR3 .... 205 J2
Ashmere Cl CHEAM SM3 .... 220 C2
Ashmere Gv BRXS/STRHM SW2 .... 158 F10 ⊡
Ash Ms EPSOM KT18 .... 220 B9 ⊡
Ashmill St CAMTN NW1 .... 9 N3
Ashmole St VX/NE SW8 .... 17 P10
Ashmore Gdns GVW DA11 .... 190 A6 ⊡
HHS/BOV HP3 .... 36 C7
Ashmore Cl WELL DA16 .... 162 G9
Ashmore La HAYES BR2 .... 225 P7
Ashmore Rd MV/WKIL W9 .... 2 C8
Ashmount Rd HGT N6 .... 118 D5
SEVS/STOTM N15 .... 119 N3 ⊡
Ashmour Gdns ROM RM1 .... 104 E10
Ashness Gdns GFD/PVL UB6 .... 114 G1
Ashness Rd BTSEA SW11 .... 180 A1
Ashotts La CSHM HP5 .... 50 A1
Ash Platt Rd BGR/WK TN15 .... 247 N1
Ashridge Cl HHS/BOV HP3 .... 52 D4
KTN/HRWW/W HA3 .... 115 H4
Ashridge Crs WOOL/PLUM SE18 .... 162 F1
OXHEY WD19 .... 93 K6
Ashridge Gdns PIN HA5 .... 113 M2
PLMGR N13 .... 98 F6
Ashridge La CSHM HP5 .... 52 A7
Ashridge Ri BERK HP4 .... 33 L4
Ashridge Wy MRDN SM4 .... 201 J4
SUN TW16 .... 175 H9
Ash Rd BH/WHM TN16 .... 262 G1
CHOB/PIR GU24 .... 248 F2
CRAWE RH10 .... 284 B5
CROY/NA CR0 .... 204 F9
DART DA1 .... 187 L4
GVE DA12 .... 190 F7
HART DA3 .... 211 K10
MRDN SM4 .... 201 H7
ORP BR6 .... 227 N4
RDART DA2 .... 187 N7
SHPTN TW17 .... 196 B4
SRTFD E15 .... 121 K10
WOKS/MYFD GU22 .... 232 A6
Ash Rw HAYES BR2 .... 206 D6
Ashtead Rd CLPT E5 .... 119 P5
Ashtead Woods Rd ASHTD KT21 .... 237 H3
Ashton Cl SUT SM1 .... 221 K1 ⊡
WOT/HER KT12 .... 217 J3 ⊡
Ashton Gdns CHDH RM6 .... 123 P4
HSLWW TW4 .... 153 N10
Ashton Rd HARH RM3 .... 105 L8
PEND EN3 .... 80 D2
SRTFD E15 .... 121 H7
WOKN/KNAP GU21 .... 231 L3
Ashton St POP/IOD E14 .... 141 H9
Ashtree Av MTCM CR4 .... 201 N2
Ash Tree Cl CROY/NA CR0 .... 204 D6
SURB KT6 .... 199 K8
Ashtree Cl ORP BR6 .... 226 E1 ⊡
Ash Tree Dell CDALE/KGS NW9 .... 115 C9
Ash Tree Fld HLW CM20 .... 28 D9
Ash Tree Rd WATN WD24 .... 73 J2
Ashtree Wy HHW HP1 .... 35 K7
Ashurst Cl DART DA1 .... 164 C10
NTHWD HA6 .... 92 F8 ⊡
PGE/AN SE20 .... 204 A1
PUR/KEN CR8 .... 241 L1 ⊡
Ashurst Dr BARK/HLT IG6 .... 122 F3
CRAWE RH10 .... 284 E7
GNTH/NBYPK IG2 .... 122 E4
KWD/TDW/WH KT20 .... 255 N6
SHPTN TW17 .... 195 P5
Ashurst Rd EBAR EN4 .... 78 A4
KWD/TDW/WH KT20 .... 238 E7
NFNCH/WDSP N12 .... 97 P6
Ashurst Wk CROY/NA CR0 .... 204 D5
Ash V RKW/CH/CXG WD3 .... 90 G6
Ashvale Dr UPMR RM14 .... 126 D7
Ashvale Gdns CRW RM5 .... 104 E6
UPMR RM14 .... 126 D7
Ashvale Rd TOOT SW17 .... 180 A8
Ashview Cl ASHF TW15 .... 173 P9 ⊡
Ashview Gdns ASHF TW15 .... 173 P9
Ashville Rd WAN E11 .... 121 J7
Ash Wk ALP/SUD HA0 .... 115 H3
SOCK/AV RM15 .... 147 J5
Ashwater Rd LEE/GVPK SE12 .... 183 M4
Ashwell Pk HARP AL5 .... 20 C2
Ashwells Rd BRWN CM15 .... 86 E7
Ashwells St STALW/RED AL3 .... 38 C5 ⊡
Ashwells Wy CSTG HP8 .... 89 P3
Ashwin St HACK E8 .... 7 L1
Ashwood WARL CR6 .... 242 F4
Ashwood Av RAIN RM13 .... 145 J5
UX/CGN UB8 .... 132 A6
Ashwood Gdns CROY/NA CR0 .... 224 C3 ⊡
HYS/HAR UB3 .... 152 C3 ⊡
Ashwood Pk LHD/OX KT22 .... 236 B9 ⊡
WOKS/MYFD GU22 .... 232 D4 ⊡
Ashwood Rd CHING E4 .... 101 N9
POTB/CUF EN6 .... 59 L4
WOKS/MYFD GU22 .... 232 C4 ⊡
Ashworth Cl CMBW SE5 .... 159 L8 ⊡

Ashworth PI HLWE CM17 .... 47 N1
Ashworth Rd MV/WKIL W9 .... 3 H9
Askern Cl BXLYHS DA6 .... 163 N10
Aske St IS N1 .... 7 J6
Askew Crs SHB W12 .... 156 C1 ⊡
Askew Rd NTHWD HA6 .... 92 E5
SHB W12 .... 156 C1
Askews Farm RM GRAYS RM17 .... 167 K4
Askham Rd SHB W12 .... 136 D10
Askill Dr PUT/ROE SW15 .... 179 H1
Askwith Rd RAIN RM13 .... 144 E4
Asland Rd SRTFD E15 .... 141 K3 ⊡
Aslett St WAND/EARL SW18 .... 179 L3
Asmara Rd CRICK NW2 .... 117 H10
Asmar Cl COUL/CHIP CR5 .... 240 F7 ⊡
Asmuns Hl GLDGN NW11 .... 117 K3
Asmuns Pl GLDGN NW11 .... 117 J3
Asolando Dr WALW SE17 .... 18 F6 ⊡
Aspasia Cl STAL AL1 .... 38 C7
Aspdin Rd GVW DA11 .... 190 A6
Aspen Cl COB KT11 .... 235 M2
EA W5 .... 155 L1
ORP BR6 .... 227 K2
RGUE GU4 .... 250 C2
SL SL1 .... 128 G7
STA TW18 .... 173 J6
SWLY BR8 .... 208 E1 ⊡
WDR/YW UB7 .... 132 A10
Aspen Copse BMLY BR1 .... 206 C2
Aspen Dr ALP/SUD HA0 .... 114 F8
Aspen Gdns MTCM CR4 .... 202 B5
Aspen Gn ERITH DA8 .... 164 A2
Aspen Gv UPMR RM14 .... 125 P9
Aspen La NTHLT UB5 .... 133 M5
Aspenlea Rd HMSMTH W6 .... 156 G5
Aspen Park Dr GSTN WD25 .... 73 J1
Aspen V CTHM CR3 .... 241 N4
Aspen Wy EW KT17 .... 220 G10 ⊡
FELT TW13 .... 175 J4
PEND EN3 .... 80 C1
WCCE AL7 .... 23 M6 ⊡
Aspern Gv HAMP NW3 .... 117 P10 ⊡
Aspfield Rw HHW HP1 .... 35 L4
Aspinall Rd BROCKY SE4 .... 160 C9
NWCR SE14 .... 160 C9 ⊡
Aspinden Rd BERM/RHTH SE16 .... 160 A5
Aspley Rd WAND/EARL SW18 .... 179 L1
Asplins Rd TOTM N17 .... 99 P9
Asprey Gv CTHM CR3 .... 241 P10 ⊡
Asquith Cl BCTR RM8 .... 123 M6 ⊡
Assam St WCHPL E1 .... 13 N5
Assata Ms IS N1 .... 6 D1 ⊡
Assembly Pas WCHPL E1 .... 140 E7
Assembly Wk CAR SM5 .... 201 P7 ⊡
Assher Rd WOT/HER KT12 .... 197 M10
Assheton Rd BEAC HP9 .... 88 C7
Ass House La KTN/HRWW/W HA3 .... 94 A5
Astall Cl KTN/HRWW/W HA3 .... 94 C10
Astbury Rd PECK SE15 .... 160 B7
Astell St CHEL SW3 .... 15 P7
The Asters CHESW E7 .... 61 L4
Asthall Gdns BARK/HLT IG6 .... 122 F2 ⊡
Astleham Wy SHPTN TW17 .... 195 P3 ⊡
Astle St BTSEA SW11 .... 158 B8
Astley GRAYS RM17 .... 167 L5
Astley Av CRICK NW2 .... 116 F10
Astley Rd HHW HP1 .... 35 M6
Aston Av KTN/HRWW/W HA3 .... 115 H5
Aston Cl ASHTD KT21 .... 237 H4
BUSH WD23 .... 74 B10
SCUP DA14 .... 185 K6
WATN WD24 .... 73 K6 ⊡
Aston Gn HEST TW5 .... 153 K8 ⊡
Aston Md WDSR SL4 .... 148 D7
Aston Rd EA W5 .... 135 J8 ⊡
ESH/CLAY KT10 .... 218 D2
RYNPK SW20 .... 200 F2
Astons Rd NTHWD HA6 .... 92 D4
Aston St WCHPL E1 .... 140 D8
Astonville St WAND/EARL SW18 .... 179 J4
Aston Wy EPSOM KT18 .... 238 C2
POTB/CUF EN6 .... 59 N8
Astor Av ROMW/RG RM7 .... 124 C4
Astor Cl ADL/WDHM KT15 .... 215 N1
KUTN/CMB KT2 .... 177 N9
Astoria Wk BRXN/ST SW9 .... 159 H9 ⊡
Astra Cl RAIN RM13 .... 145 J1 ⊡
Astra Dr GVE DA12 .... 191 H4
Astrop Ms HMSMTH W6 .... 156 F2
Astrop Ter HMSMTH W6 .... 156 F1 ⊡
Astwick Av HAT AL10 .... 11 H5
Astwood Ms SKENS SW7 .... 15 H5
Asylum Rd PECK SE15 .... 160 A6
Atalanta Cl PUR/KEN CR8 .... 223 H6
Atalanta St FUL/PGN SW6 .... 156 G7
Atbara Rd TEDD TW11 .... 176 G9
Atcham Rd HSLW TW3 .... 154 B10 ⊡
Atcost Rd BARK IG11 .... 143 K7
Atfield Gv BFOR GU20 .... 212 C3
Atheldene Rd WAND/EARL SW18 .... 179 L4
Athelney St CAT SE6 .... 182 F6
Athelstan Cl CRAWE RH10 .... 284 F7
HARH RM3 .... 105 N9
Athelstane Gv BOW E3 .... 140 E4
Athelstane Ms FSBYPK N4 .... 119 H6 ⊡
Athelstan Rd HARH RM3 .... 105 N9 ⊡
HHS/BOV HP3 .... 35 P9
KUT KT1 .... 199 L4
Athelstan Wk North WCCE AL7 .... 23 H6 ⊡
Athelstan Wk South WCCE AL7 .... 22 G6 ⊡
Athelstan Wy STMC/STPC BR5 .... 207 K1
Athelstone Rd KTN/HRWW/W HA3 .... 94 C10
Athena Cl KUT KT1 .... 199 L3
RYLN/HDSTN HA2 .... 114 C7 ⊡
Athenaeum Pl MUSWH N10 .... 98 A2
Athenaeum Rd TRDG/WHET N20 .... 97 M2
Athena Pl NTHWD HA6 .... 92 C9
Athenlay Rd PECK SE15 .... 182 C1
Atherden Rd CLPT E5 .... 120 B9
Atherfield Rd REDH RH1 .... 275 M3
Atherfold Rd BRXN/ST SW9 .... 158 F9
Atherley Wy HSLWW TW4 .... 175 N3 ⊡
Atherstone Ms SKENS SW7 .... 15 H5
Atherton Cl STWL/WRAY TW19 .... 173 N2 ⊡
Atherton Dr WIM/MER SW19 .... 178 G7
Atherton Gdns CDH/CHF RM16 .... 168 G3 ⊡
Atherton Hts ALP/SUD HA0 .... 135 H1 ⊡
Atherton Ms FSTGT E7 .... 141 M1
Atherton Rd BARN SW13 .... 156 D6
CLAY IG5 .... 102 B2
FSTGT E7 .... 121 L10
Atherton St BTSEA SW11 .... 158 A8 ⊡
Athlone ESH/CLAY KT10 .... 218 D3 ⊡
Athlone Cl CLPT E5 .... 120 A10 ⊡
RAD WD7 .... 74 C2 ⊡
Athlone Ct WALTH E17 .... 121 J1 ⊡
Athlone Rd BRXS/STRHM SW2 .... 180 G3
Athlone St KTTN NW5 .... 4 D1
Athlon Rd ALP/SUD HA0 .... 135 L5
Athol Cl PIN HA5 .... 93 J9
Athole Gdns EN EN1 .... 79 M9
Athol Gdns PIN HA5 .... 93 J9
Atholl Rd GDMY/SEVK IG3 .... 123 K5
Athol Rd ERITH DA8 .... 164 C10
Athol Sq POP/IOD E14 .... 141 H8 ⊡
Athol Wy HGDN/ICK UB10 .... 132 B5
Atkins Dr WWKM BR4 .... 205 J1
Atkinson Cl ORP BR6 .... 227 K2 ⊡
Atkinson Rd CAN/RD E16 .... 141 P7
CRAWE RH10 .... 284 D9 ⊡
Atkins Rd BAL SW12 .... 180 D1
CLAP SW4 .... 180 E3

LEY E10 .... 120 G4 ⊡
Atlanta Bvd ROM RM1 .... 124 F4 ⊡
Atlantic Rd BRXN/ST SW9 .... 159 H10
Atlas Gdns CHARL SE7 .... 161 P5
Atlas Ms HACK E8 .... 7 M1
Atlas Rd DART DA1 .... 141 M4
PLSTW E13 .... 141 M4
WBLY HA9 .... 115 P9
WLSDN NW10 .... 136 B5
Atley Rd BOW E3 .... 140 F3
Atlip Rd ALP/SUD HA0 .... 135 K3
Atney Rd PUT/ROE SW15 .... 157 H10
Atria Rd NTHWD HA6 .... 93 H6
Attenborough Cl OXHEY WD19 .... 93 M4 ⊡
Atterbury Cl BH/WHM TN16 .... 262 G2
Atterbury Rd FSBYPK N4 .... 119 J4 ⊡
Atterbury St WEST SW1P 17 K6
Attewood Av CRICK NW2 .... 116 B8
Attewood Rd NTHLT UB5 .... 133 M1
Attfield Cl TRDG/WHET N20 .... 97 N3
Attimore Cl WGCW AL8 .... 22 E6
Attimore Rd WGCW AL8 .... 22 E6
Attle Cl HGDN/ICK UB10 .... 132 B4
Attlee Cl CROY/NA CR0 .... 203 K6
YEAD UB4 .... 133 J5 ⊡
Attlee Ct GRAYS RM17 .... 167 L6
Attlee Dr DART DA1 .... 187 P1
Attlee Rd THMD SE28 .... 143 L9
YEAD UB4 .... 133 H5
Attneave St FSBYW WC1X 12 A1
Atwell Rd PECK SE15 .... 159 P8 ⊡
Atwood GT/LBKH KT23 .... 235 M10
Atwood Av RCH/KEW TW9 .... 155 M8
Atwood Rd HMSMTH W6 .... 156 E3
Aubert Pk HBRY N5 .... 119 H9
Aubert Rd HBRY N5 .... 119 J9
Aubrey Av LCOL/BKTW AL2 .... 57 H2
Aubrey Pl STJWD NW8 .... 3 J8
Aubrey Rd CEND/HSY/T N8 .... 118 F3 ⊡
KENS W8 .... 8 D10
WALTH E17 .... 120 F1
Aubreys Rd HHW HP1 .... 35 H7
Aubrey Wk KENS W8 .... 8 D10
Aubrietia Cl HARH RM3 .... 105 M9 ⊡
Auburn Cl NWCR SE14 .... 160 D6
Aubyn Hl WNWD SE27 .... 181 K7
Aubyn Sq PUT/ROE SW15 .... 156 D10
Auckland Av RAIN RM13 .... 144 C5 ⊡
Auckland Cl CRAWW RH11 .... 283 N4 ⊡
EN EN1 .... 80 A3
NRWD SE19 .... 203 N1
TIL RM18 .... 168 D8
Auckland Hl WNWD SE27 .... 181 K7
Auckland Rd NRWD SE19 .... 203 N1
BTSEA SW11 .... 157 P10
CHST BR7 .... 241 M8
EPP CM16 .... 82 G2
IL IG1 .... 122 E6
KUT KT1 .... 199 L4
LEY E10 .... 120 G8
NRWD SE19 .... 203 N1
POTB/CUF EN6 .... 58 G8
Aucklands Gdns NRWD SE19 .... 203 M1
Auckland St LBTH SE11 .... 17 N8
Audleigh PI CHIG IG7 .... 102 D7
Audley Cl ADL/WDHM KT15 .... 215 L2
BORE WD6 .... 75 M7
MUSWH N10 .... 98 C3
Audley Ct PIN HA5 .... 93 K10
SWFD E18 .... 121 L2 ⊡
Audley Dr CAN/RD E16 .... 141 N10
SAND/SEL CR2 .... 242 B1
Audley Firs WOT/HER KT12 .... 217 K1 ⊡
Audley Gdns GDMY/SEVK IG3 .... 123 J7
LOU IG10 .... 82 G7
WAB EN9 .... 63 H10
Audley PI BELMT SM2 .... 221 L4
Audley Rd EA W5 .... 135 L7
ENC/FH EN2 .... 79 J6
HDN NW4 .... 116 D4
RCHPK/HAM TW10 .... 177 L2 ⊡
Audrey Cl BECK BR3 .... 204 G6
Audrey Gdns ALP/SUD HA0 .... 114 G7
Audrey Rd IL IG1 .... 122 E8
Audrey St BETH E2 .... 7 P7 ⊡
Audric Cl KUTN/CMB KT2 .... 199 M1 ⊡
Audwick Cl CHES/WCR EN8 .... 62 C4
Augurs La PLSTW E13 .... 141 M5 ⊡
Augusta Cl E/WMO/HCT KT8 .... 197 N3 ⊡
Augusta Rd WHTN TW2 .... 176 B5
August End DTCH/LGLY SL3 .... 130 B8 ⊡
Augustine Cl DTCH/LGLY SL3 .... 151 N9
Augustine Rd KTN/HRWW/W HA3 .... 94 A9
STMC/STPC BR5 .... 207 N3
August La SHGR GU5 .... 269 N10
Augustus Cl BTFD TW8 .... 155 J6 ⊡
HMSMTH W6 .... 156 E1 ⊡
STALW/RED AL3 .... 37 P8
Augustus Rd WIM/MER SW19 .... 179 H4
Augustus St CAMTN NW1 .... 4 F8
Aukingford Gdns CHONG CM5 .... 67 N3 ⊡
Aukingford Gn CHONG CM5 .... 67 N3 ⊡
Aultone Wy CAR SM5 .... 202 A10
SUT SM1 .... 201 L9
Aurelia Gdns THHTH CR7 .... 202 C5
Aurelia Rd CROY/NA CR0 .... 202 G5
Auriel Av DAGE RM10 .... 144 E1
Auriga Ms STNW/STAM N16 .... 119 L10 ⊡
Auriol Cl WPK KT4 .... 200 B10
Auriol Dr GFD/PVL UB6 .... 134 C2
HGDN/ICK UB10 .... 132 C1 ⊡
Auriol Park Rd WPK KT4 .... 200 B10
Auriol Rd WKENS W14 .... 14 G5
Aurum Cl HORL RH6 .... 280 C5 ⊡
Austell Gdns MLHL NW7 .... 96 B4
Austen Cl GRH DA9 .... 189 H2 ⊡
LOU IG10 .... 82 G7 ⊡
THMD SE28 .... 143 L10
TIL RM18 .... 168 B8 ⊡
Austen Rd ERITH DA8 .... 164 C6
GU GU1 .... 268 C1
RYLN/HDSTN HA2 .... 114 A7
Austenway CFSP/GDCR SL9 .... 110 G1
Austenwood Cl CFSP/GDCR SL9 .... 89 P10
Austenwood La CFSP/GDCR SL9 .... 110 F1
Austin Av HAYES BR2 .... 206 B6
Austin Cl CAT SE6 .... 182 D5
COUL/CHIP CR5 .... 241 J5
Austin Friars OBST EC2N .... 13 H5 ⊡
Austin Friars Sq OBST EC2N .... 13 H5 ⊡
Austin Rd BTSEA SW11 .... 158 A7
GVW DA11 .... 190 C4
HYS/HAR UB3 .... 152 C1
STMC/STPC BR5 .... 207 K6
Austin's La HGDN/ICK UB10 .... 112 C9
Austins Md HHS/BOV HP3 .... 35 N5
Austin St BETH E2 .... 7 L6
Austral Cl BFN/LL DA15 .... 185 J6
Austral Dr EMPK RM11 .... 125 L3
Australia Rd SHB W12 .... 136 N9
SL SL1 .... 149 N1
Austral St LBTH SE11 .... 18 C5
Austyn Gdns BRYLDS KT5 .... 199 N3 ⊡
Autumn Cl EN EN1 .... 80 A6
SL SL1 .... 128 E10
WIM/MER SW19 .... 179 M9
Autumn Dr BELMT SM2 .... 221 L6
Autumn Glades HHS/BOV HP3 .... 36 D8
Autumn Gv WCCE AL7 .... 23 L7 ⊡
Autumn St BOW E3 .... 140 E9
Avalon Cl ENC/FH EN2 .... 79 H6
GSTN WD25 .... 55 M8
ORP BR6 .... 207 N9

RYNPK SW20 .... 201 N1
WEA W13 .... 134 F7
Avalon Rd FUL/PGN SW6 .... 157 P7
ORP BR6 .... 207 M9
WEA W13 .... 134 F6
Avard Gdns ORP BR6 .... 226 E1
Avarn Rd TOOT SW17 .... 180 A3
Avebury SL SL1 .... 128 F10
Avebury Rd ORP BR6 .... 206 G10
WAN E11 .... 121 J6 ⊡
WIM/MER SW19 .... 201 J1
Avebury St IS N1 .... 6 G6
Aveley By-pass SOCK/AV RM15 .... 146 B9
Aveley Cl ERITH DA8 .... 164 C5 ⊡
Aveley Rd ROM RM1 .... 124 C2 ⊡
UPMR RM14 .... 146 A2
Aveline St LBTH SE11 .... 17 P7 ⊡
Aveling Cl CRAWE RH10 .... 284 D9 ⊡
PUR/KEN CR8 .... 222 C9
Aveling Park Rd WALTH E17 .... 100 F10
Avelon Rd CRW RM5 .... 104 E7
RAIN RM13 .... 145 H3
Avenell Rd FSBYPK N4 .... 119 J8
Avening Rd WAND/EARL SW18 .... 179 K3 ⊡
Avening Ter WAND/EARL SW18 .... 179 K2
Avenue Ap KGLGY WD4 .... 54 B6
Avenue Cl ADL/WDHM KT15 .... 195 P10 ⊡
HEST TW5 .... 153 J7
KWD/TDW/WH KT20 .... 238 E10
STHGT/OAK N14 .... 78 D10
WDR/YW UB7 .... 151 N2
Avenue Crs ACT W3 .... 155 H7
HEST TW5 .... 153 J6 ⊡
HORL RH6 .... 280 D5
MORT/ESHN SW14 .... 156 B9
TEDD TW11 .... 176 E10
Avenue De Cagny CHOB/PIR GU24 .... 230 E8
Avenue Dr DTCH/LGLY SL3 .... 130 C7
HEST TW5 .... 153 J6 ⊡
HORL RH6 .... 280 D5
MORT/ESHN SW14 .... 156 B9
TEDD TW11 .... 176 E10
Avenue La GRH DA9 .... 189 H2
Avenue Ms MUSWH N10 .... 118 C1
Avenue One ADL/WDHM KT15 .... 215 P1 ⊡
Avenue Park Rd WNWD SE27 .... 181 J5
Avenue Ri BUSH WD23 .... 73 P6
Avenue Rd ACT W3 .... 155 N1
BELMT SM2 .... 221 K6
BH/WHM TN16 .... 244 B6
BNSTD SM7 .... 239 L1
BRW CM14 .... 107 H5
BTFD TW8 .... 155 H4
BXLYHS DA6 .... 163 P9
COB KT11 .... 235 L2
CTHM CR3 .... 241 L8
EPP CM16 .... 82 G2
EPSOM KT18 .... 220 A10
ERITH DA8 .... 164 D6
FELT TW13 .... 174 D6
FSTGT E7 .... 121 N10
GDMY/SEVK IG3 .... 123 L5
HAMP NW3 .... 3 J5
HARH RM3 .... 105 N8
HGT N6 .... 118 D5
HOD EN11 .... 45 J5
HPTN TW12 .... 198 A1
ISLW TW7 .... 154 D7
KUT KT1 .... 199 K5
NFNCH/WDSP N12 .... 97 M5
NWMAL KT3 .... 200 B3
PGE/AN SE20 .... 204 B1
PIN HA5 .... 113 M1
RYNPK SW20 .... 200 E2
SEV TN13 .... 247 K10
SEVS/STOTM N15 .... 119 J3
SNWD SE25 .... 203 P2
STA TW18 .... 172 G8
STAL AL1 .... 38 D5 ⊡
STHGT/OAK N14 .... 78 D10
STHL UB1 .... 133 N10
STJWD NW8 .... 3 H2
STJWD NW8 .... 3 M4
STRHM/NOR SW16 .... 202 E2
TEDD TW11 .... 176 F10
WFD IG8 .... 101 P7
WLGTN SM6 .... 222 C4
Avenue South BRYLDS KT5 .... 199 L7
OXHEY WD19 .... 73 M10 ⊡
The Avenue ADL/WDHM KT15 .... 215 P1
AMSS HP7 .... 69 H4
BAR EN5 .... 77 J6
BECK BR3 .... 204 G1
BELMT SM2 .... 221 K6
BH/WHM TN16 .... 244 C8
BMLY BR1 .... 206 A3
BRYLDS KT5 .... 199 L6
BTSEA SW11 .... 180 B1
BUSH WD23 .... 73 N8
BXLY DA5 .... 185 K3
BXLY DA5 .... 185 K3
CAR SM5 .... 222 B4
CEND/HSY/T N8 .... 119 H1 ⊡
CHING E4 .... 101 J7
CHOB/PIR GU24 .... 213 L5
CHSWK W4 .... 156 B2
COUL/CHIP CR5 .... 240 E1
CROY/NA CR0 .... 203 M3
CTHM CR3 .... 241 P5
DTCH/LGLY SL3 .... 149 N2
EGH TW20 .... 172 E7
ESH/CLAY KT10 .... 218 D3
EW KT17 .... 220 F4
FBAR/BDGN N11 .... 98 E3 ⊡
GNWCH SE10 .... 161 J5
GVW DA11 .... 190 D4
HCH RM12 .... 125 J7
HERT/WAS SG14 .... 25 J3
HEST TW5 .... 153 H7
HGDN/ICK UB10 .... 112 B8
HHW HP1 .... 35 H5
HOD EN11 .... 44 E5
HORL RH6 .... 280 A5
HPTN TW12 .... 175 N9
HSLW TW3 .... 176 A1
KIL/WHAMP NW6 .... 136 G2
KTN/HRWW/W HA3 .... 94 E9
KWD/TDW/WH KT20 .... 238 E8
LHD/OX KT22 .... 218 E8
LOU IG10 .... 82 C7
MUSWH N10 .... 98 D10
NTHWD HA6 .... 92 D9
ORP BR6 .... 207 J9
PIN HA5 .... 93 N4
PIN HA5 .... 113 N4
POTB/CUF EN6 .... 59 J4
RAD WD7 .... 56 F10
RBRW/HUT CM13 .... 107 K7
RCH/KEW TW9 .... 155 N8
RDKG RH5 .... 255 M10
REDH RH1 .... 276 F5
RGUE GU4 .... 249 K3
RGUW GU3 .... 267 N6
ROM RM1 .... 124 C2
SLN SL2 .... 108 G9
STA TW18 .... 195 L1
STMC/STPC BR5 .... 185 L10
STWL/WRAY TW19 .... 150 A9
SUN TW16 .... 195 J1
TOTM N17 .... 99 M10
TWK TW1 .... 177 H1
UX/CGN UB8 .... 131 N6 ⊡
WAB EN9 .... 63 P1
WAN E11 .... 121 J1
WAT WD17 .... 73 H6
WBLY HA9 .... 115 L7

WDSR SL4 .... 171 N1
WEA W13 .... 134 C9
WPK KT4 .... 200 C9
WPK KT4 .... 200 D5 J7
Avenue Three ADL/WDHM KT15 .... 195 P10
Avenue Two ADL/WDHM KT15 .... 215 P1
Averil Ct SL SL1 .... 128 B8
Averil Gv STRHM/NOR SW16 .... 181 J9
Averill St HMSMTH W6 .... 156 G5
Avernons Rd E/WMO/HCT KT8 .... 198 A4
Avern Rd PLSTW E13 .... 141 M7
Avery Farm Rw BGVA SW1W .... 16 E6 ⊡
Avery Gdns GNTH/NBYPK IG2 .... 122 C3
Avery Hill Rd ELTH/MOT SE9 .... 184 G2
Avery Rw MYFR/PKLN W1K 10 E7
Avey La LOU IG10 .... 81 L3
Avia Cl HHS/BOV HP3 .... 35 N10
Avial Cl CAN/RD E16 .... 141 L7
Aviary Cl WOKS/MYFD GU22 .... 233 J1
Aviemore Cl BECK BR3 .... 204 E5 ⊡
Aviemore Wy BECK BR3 .... 204 D5
Avignon Rd BROCKY SE4 .... 160 C9
Avington Cl GU GU1 .... 250 B10
Avington Gv PGE/AN SE20 .... 192 B10
Avington Wy PECK SE15 .... 159 N6 ⊡
Avior Dr NTHWD HA6 .... 92 C5
Avis Sq WCHPL E1 .... 140 C8
Avoca Rd TOOT SW17 .... 180 B7
Avocet Ms THMD SE28 .... 162 G2
Avon Cl ADL/WDHM KT15 .... 215 K3
GSTN WD25 .... 55 K10
GVE DA12 .... 190 C5
SL SL1 .... 128 D9
SUT SM1 .... 221 M1 ⊡
WPK KT4 .... 200 D9
YEAD UB4 .... 133 K6
Avondale Av CRICK NW2 .... 116 B8
EBAR EN4 .... 98 A2
ESH/CLAY KT10 .... 198 F10
NFNCH/WDSP N12 .... 97 L6
STA TW18 .... 173 J10
WOT/HER KT12 .... 197 J8
Avondale Cl HORL RH6 .... 280 A2
LOU IG10 .... 102 C1
WOT/HER KT12 .... 217 K2
Avondale Ct WFD IG8 .... 101 N9
Avondale Crs PEND EN3 .... 80 C1
REDBR IG4 .... 122 A3
Avondale Dr HYS/HAR UB3 .... 133 H10
LOU IG10 .... 82 C10
Avondale Gdns HSLWW TW4 .... 175 N1
Avondale Ms BMLY BR1 .... 183 M9 ⊡
Avondale Park Gdns NTCHL W11 .... 8 A8 ⊡
Avondale Park Rd NTCHL W11 .... 8 A7
Avondale Ri PECK SE15 .... 159 N9
Avondale Rd ASHF TW15 .... 173 N6
BMLY BR1 .... 183 K9 ⊡
CAN/RD E16 .... 141 K7
ELTH/MOT SE9 .... 184 B5
FNCH N3 .... 97 M9
KTN/HRWW/W HA3 .... 114 E1
MORT/ESHN SW14 .... 156 A9
PLMGR N13 .... 99 H3
SAND/SEL CR2 .... 223 K3
SEVS/STOTM N15 .... 119 J3
WALL DA16 .... 163 M8
WELL DA16 .... 163 M8
WIM/MER SW19 .... 179 L8
Avondale Sq STHWK SE1 .... 19 L8
Avon Gn SOCK/AV RM15 .... 146 G3 ⊡
Avonley Rd NWCR SE14 .... 160 B6
Avonmore Av GU GU1 .... 250 C9
Avonmore Pl WKENS W14 .... 14 B5 ⊡
Avonmore Rd WKENS W14 .... 14 B5
Avonmouth Rd DART DA1 .... 187 L3
Avonmouth St STHWK SE1 .... 18 E3 ⊡
Avon Rd BROCKY SE4 .... 160 F9
GFD/PVL UB6 .... 133 P6
SUN TW16 .... 174 G10
UPMR RM14 .... 126 B4
WALTH E17 .... 121 J1
Avon Sq HHNE HP2 .... 36 A1
Avonstowe Cl ORP BR6 .... 206 F10
Avontar Rd SOCK/AV RM15 .... 146 G6
Avon Wk CRAWW RH11 .... 283 J8
Avonwick Rd HSLW TW3 .... 154 A8
Avril Wy CHING E4 .... 101 H6
Avro Wy WEY KT13 .... 215 P7
WLGTN SM6 .... 222 F4
Awlfield Av TOTM N17 .... 99 J9
Awliscombe Rd WELL DA16 .... 163 J8
Axcombe Av EDGW HA8 .... 95 N9
Axe St BARK IG11 .... 142 F3
Axholme Av EDGW HA8 .... 95 M9
Axminster Crs WELL DA16 .... 163 M7
Axminster Rd HOLWY N7 .... 118 E7
Axtaine Rd STMC/STPC BR5 .... 207 N2
Axtane Cl EYN DA4 .... 210 B2 ⊡
Aybrook St MHST W1U 10 C3
Aycliff Ct KUT KT1 .... 199 M2 ⊡
Aycliffe Cl BMLY BR1 .... 206 C4
Aycliffe Dr HHNE HP2 .... 35 P2
Aycliffe Rd BORE WD6 .... 75 L5
SHB W12 .... 136 C10
Ayebridges Av EGH TW20 .... 172 F10
Ayelands HART DA3 .... 211 K9 ⊡
Ayelands La HART DA3 .... 211 K10
Aylands Cl WBLY HA9 .... 115 K7
Aylands Rd PEND EN3 .... 80 C2
Aylesbury Cl FSTGT E7 .... 141 L1 ⊡
Aylesbury Crs SL SL1 .... 129 J8
Aylesbury End BEAC HP9 .... 88 D10
Aylesbury Rd HAYES BR2 .... 205 H3
WALW SE17 .... 19 H8
WLSDN NW10 .... 116 A8
Aylesford Av BECK BR3 .... 204 D5
Aylesford St PIM SW1V 17 J7
Aylesham Cl MLHL NW7 .... 96 D8 ⊡
Aylesham Rd ORP BR6 .... 207 H1
Ayles Rd YEAD UB4 .... 133 J3
Aylestone Av KIL/WHAMP NW6 .... 136 G2
Aylesworth Av SLN SL2 .... 128 C5 ⊡
Aylesworth Sp WDSR SL4 .... 171 K3 ⊡
Aylets Fld HLWS CM18 .... 47 H4
Aylett Rd ISLW TW7 .... 154 D8
SNWD SE25 .... 204 A14
UPMR RM14 .... 126 B7 ⊡
Ayley Cft EN EN1 .... 79 P7
Aylmer Cl STAN HA7 .... 94 F5
Aylmer Dr STAN HA7 .... 94 F5
Aylmer Pde BCTR RM8 .... 123 P8
EFNCH N2 .... 117 H2
SHB W12 .... 156 B1
WAN E11 .... 121 L5
Ayloffe Rd DAGW RM9 .... 144 A4
Ayloffs Cl EMPK RM11 .... 125 M3 ⊡
Ayloff's Wk EMPK RM11 .... 125 M3
Aylsham Dr HGDN/ICK UB10 .... 112 D7
Aylsham La HARH RM3 .... 105 K5
Aylsham Rd HOD EN11 .... 45 H4
Aylward Gdns CSHM HP5 .... 50 F6
Aylward Rd FSTH SE23 .... 182 C5
RYNPK SW20 .... 201 J2
Aylwards Ri STAN HA7 .... 94 F5
Aylward St WCHPL E1 .... 140 C7 ⊡
WCHPL E1 .... 140 D8 ⊡
Aylwyn Est STHWK SE1 .... 19 L3
Aymer Cl STA TW18 .... 195 H1
Aymer Dr STA TW18 .... 195 H1
Aynhoe Rd WKENS W14 .... 156 C2 ⊡
Aynho St WATW WD18 .... 73 J9
Aynscombe Angle ORP BR6 .... 207 K7 ⊡
Aynsley Gdns HLWE CM17 .... 47 N1

Ayot Gn WGCW AL8 .... 22 C2
Ayot Little Green La WLYN AL6 .... 22 C2
Ayres Cl PLSTW E13 .... 141 M5
Ayres Crs WLSDN NW10 .... 136 A2
Ayres End La HARP AL5 .... 20 D5
Ayres St STHWK SE1 .... 18 F1
Ayr Gn ROM RM1 .... 104 F9
Ayron Rd SOCK/AV RM15 .... 146 G6
Ayrsome Rd STNW/STAM N16 .... 119 M8
Ayr Wy ROM RM1 .... 104 F9
Aysgarth Ct HARP AL5 .... 20 A3
Aysgarth Rd DUL SE21 .... 181 L2
Aytoun Pl BRXN/ST SW9 .... 158 C8
Aytoun Rd BRXN/ST SW9 .... 158 C8
Azalea Cl HNWL W7 .... 134 E10
IL IG1 .... 122 E10
Azalea Ct WOKS/MYFD GU22 .... 232 A5
Azalea Dr SWLY BR8 .... 208 E4
Azalea Wk PIN HA5 .... 113 J4
Azalea Wy DTCH/LGLY SL3 .... 130 B8
Azania Ms KTTN NW5 .... 4 E1
Azenby Rd PECK SE15 .... 159 N8
Azof St GNWCH SE10 .... 161 K3

B

Baalbec Rd HBRY N5 .... 119 J10
Baas Hl BROX EN10 .... 44 C7
Baas Hill Cl BROX EN10 .... 44 D7
Baas La BROX EN10 .... 44 D7
Babbacombe Cl CHSGTN KT9 .... 219 J2
Babbacombe Gdns REDBR IG4 .... 122 B2
Babbacombe Rd BMLY BR1 .... 205 N1
Baber Dr EBED/NFELT TW14 .... 175 K2
Babington Ri WBLY HA9 .... 135 M1
Babington Rd BCTR RM8 .... 123 M10
HCH RM12 .... 125 J6
HDN NW4 .... 116 E2
STRHM/NOR SW16 .... 180 E7
Babmaes St STJS SW1Y 11 J8
Babylon La KWD/TDW/WH KT20 .... 257 L3
Bachelor's La RPLY/SEND GU23 .... 234 B10
Bache's St IS N1 .... 7 H10
Back Church La WCHPL E1 .... 13 N6
Back Gn WOT/HER KT12 .... 217 K3
Back Hl CLKNW EC1R 12 B2
Back La BGR/WK TN15 .... 247 P10
BTFD TW8 .... 155 J6
BXLY DA5 .... 186 B3
CDH/CHF RM16 .... 147 H10
CEND/HSY/T N8 .... 118 F3
CHDH RM6 .... 123 P5
EDGW HA8 .... 95 P9
GSTN WD25 .... 74 D5
HAMP NW3 .... 117 M9
PUR RM19 .... 166 D3
RBSF CM22 .... 30 D3
RCHPK/HAM TW10 .... 177 H5
RGUE GU4 .... 251 N7
RSEV TN14 .... 264 C4
SEV TN13 .... 246 E10
WAB EN9 .... 45 P9
WLYN AL6 .... 23 P1
Backley Gdns SNWD SE25 .... 203 P6
Back Rd SCUP DA14 .... 185 K7
TEDD TW11 .... 176 D10
The Backs CSHM HP5 .... 51 H7
The Back BERK HP4 .... 34 E2
Bacon Gv STHWK SE1 .... 19 L5
Bacon La CDALE/KGS NW9 .... 115 N2
EDGW HA8 .... 95 M9
Bacon Link CRW RM5 .... 104 C7
Bacons Dr POTB/CUF EN6 .... 60 F4
Bacon's La HGT N6 .... 118 B6
Baconsmead DEN/HRF UB9 .... 111 K7
Bacon St BETH E2 .... 13 M1
WCHPL E1 .... 13 M1
Bacton St BETH E2 .... 140 B5
Badburgham Ct WAB EN9 .... 63 L9
Baddow Cl DAGE RM10 .... 144 B3
WFD IG8 .... 102 A7
Baden Cl STA TW18 .... 173 K10
Baden Dr HORL RH6 .... 279 P3
Baden Powell Cl DAGW RM9 .... 143 P3
SURB KT6 .... 199 L9
Baden Powell Rd SEV TN13 .... 246 F8
Baden Rd CEND/HSY/T N8 .... 118 E2
GUW GU2 .... 249 M8
IL IG1 .... 122 E10
Bader Cl PUR/KEN CR8 .... 241 L1
WGCE AL7 .... 23 M5
Bader Gdns SL SL1 .... 148 F1
Bader Wk GVW DA11 .... 190 B6
Bader Wy RAIN RM13 .... 145 H1
Badger Cl FELT TW13 .... 175 J6
GUW GU2 .... 249 N7
HSLWW TW4 .... 153 K8
Badger Cft HHNE HP2 .... 36 E7
Badgers Cl ASHF TW15 .... 174 A8
BORE WD6 .... 75 L6
ENC/FH EN2 .... 79 J7
HERT/BAY SG13 .... 26 A5
HRW HA1 .... 114 C4
HYS/HAR UB3 .... 132 F10
RGODL GU7 .... 267 J9
WOKN/KNAP GU21 .... 231 P4
Badgers Copse ORP BR6 .... 207 J9
WPK KT4 .... 200 C9
Badgers Cft BROX EN10 .... 44 D7
ELTH/MOT SE9 .... 184 D6
TRDG/WHET N20 .... 97 H1
Badgers Hl VW GU25 .... 193 P5
Badgers La WARL CR6 .... 242 B5
Badgers Mt CDH/CHF RM16 .... 168 C1
Badgers Ri RSEV TN14 .... 228 B6
Badgers Rd RSEV TN14 .... 228 C6
Badgers Wk CTHM CR3 .... 241 N4
NWMAL KT3 .... 200 B2
PUR/KEN CR8 .... 222 D7
RKW/CH/CXG WD3 .... 71 J8
Badgers Wd CTHM CR3 .... 259 K1
SLN SL2 .... 109 H10
Badger Wy HAT AL10 .... 40 E6
Badingham Dr LHD/OX KT22 .... 236 D9
Badlis Rd WALTH E17 .... 100 F10
Badlow Cl ERITH DA8 .... 164 F6
Badminton Cl BORE WD6 .... 75 M6
HRW HA1 .... 114 D2
NTHLT UB5 .... 133 P1
Badminton Ms CAN/RD E16 .... 141 M10
Badminton Pl BROX EN10 .... 44 D6
Badminton Rd BAL SW12 .... 180 B2
Badsworth Rd CMBW SE5 .... 159 K6
Bagley Cl WDR/YW UB7 .... 151 P1
Bagley's La FUL/PGN SW6 .... 157 L7
Bagleys Spring CHDH RM6 .... 123 P2
Bagot Cl ASHTD KT21 .... 237 L2
Bagshot Rd ASC SL5 .... 192 A8
CHOB/PIR GU24 .... 212 C7
EGH TW20 .... 171 P10
EN EN1 .... 79 N10
WOKN/KNAP GU21 .... 230 G5
Bagshot St WALW SE17 .... 19 K8
Bahram Rd HOR/WEW KT19 .... 220 A6
Baigents La BFOR GU20 .... 212 C3
Baildon St DEPT SE8 .... 160 E6
Bailes La RGUW GU3 .... 248 C9
Bailey Cl PUR RM19 .... 166 C3
WDGN N22 .... 98 E9
WDSR SL4 .... 148 F8
Bailey Pl SYD SE26 .... 182 B9
Bailey Rd DORK RH4 .... 272 B3
Baillie Cl RAIN RM13 .... 145 J6
Baillie Rd GU GU1 .... 268 C1
Bainbridge Cl KUTN/CMB KT2 .... 177 K8
Bainbridge Rd DAGW RM9 .... 124 A9
Bainbridge St NOXST/BSQ WC1A 11 K5
Baines Cl SAND/SEL CR2 .... 223 L2
Bainton Md WOKN/KNAP GU21 .... 231 M3
Baird Av GFD/PVL UB6 .... 134 A9
Baird Cl BUSH WD23 .... 74 A10
CDALE/KGS NW9 .... 115 P4
CRAWE RH10 .... 284 B4
SL SL1 .... 148 G1
Baird Dr RGUW GU3 .... 248 G9
Baird Gdns NRWD SE19 .... 181 M7
Baird Rd EN EN1 .... 80 A7
Baird St STLK EC1Y 12 F1
Bairstow Cl BORE WD6 .... 75 K5
Baizdon Rd BKHTH/KID SE3 .... 161 K8
Bakeham La EGH TW20 .... 171 P10
Bakehouse Rd HORL RH6 .... 280 A2
Baker Cl CRAWE RH10 .... 283 N9
Baker Hill Cl GVW DA11 .... 190 C7
Baker La MTCM CR4 .... 202 B1
Baker Ms ORP BR6 .... 227 J3
Baker Rd WLSDN NW10 .... 136 B3
WOOL/PLUM SE18 .... 162 B7
Bakers Av LEY E10 .... 120 G4
Bakers End RYNPK SW20 .... 201 H2
Bakers Gdns CAR SM5 .... 201 P9
Bakers Gv WGCE AL7 .... 23 M4
Bakers Hl BAR EN5 .... 77 L6
CLPT E5 .... 120 B6
Bakers La EPP CM16 .... 65 J6
Bakers Md GDST RH9 .... 260 B6
Bakers Meadow BRWN CM15 .... 87 H3
Baker's Ms MHST W1U 10 C5
Bakers Rents BETH E2 .... 7 L10
Bakers Rd CHESW EN7 .... 62 A6
UX/CGN UB8 .... 131 N2
Baker's Rw CLKNW EC1R 12 A2
SRTFD E15 .... 141 K4
Baker St CAMTN NW1 .... 10 B2
EN EN1 .... 79 L6
HERT/BAY SG13 .... 25 M5
MHST W1U 10 C4
POTB/CUF EN6 .... 59 J9
WEY KT13 .... 216 B1
Bakers Wd DEN/HRF UB9 .... 110 G6
Bakery Cl HLWW/ROY CM19 .... 45 P1
Bakewell Dr NWMAL KT3 .... 200 B2
Balaams La STHGT/OAK N14 .... 98 E3
Balaam St PLSTW E13 .... 141 M5
Balaclava Rd STHWK SE1 .... 19 M6
SURB KT6 .... 199 H7
Balcary Gdns BERK HP4 .... 33 K6
Balcaskie Rd ELTH/MOT SE9 .... 184 C1
Balchen Rd BKHTH/KID SE3 .... 162 A8
Balchier Rd EDUL SE22 .... 182 A2
Balchins La DORK RH4 .... 271 P3
Balcombe Cl BXLYHS DA6 .... 163 N10
Balcombe Gdns HORL RH6 .... 280 D5
Balcombe Rd CRAWE RH10 .... 284 E6
HORL RH6 .... 280 C3
Balcombe St CAMTN NW1 .... 10 A1
Balcon Wy BORE WD6 .... 75 P5
Balcorne St HOM E9 .... 140 B2
Balder Ri LEE/GVPK SE12 .... 183 N5
Balderton St MYFR/PKLN W1K 10 D6
Baldocks Rd EPP CM16 .... 83 H1
Baldock St BOW E3 .... 140 G4
WARE SG12 .... 26 C1
Baldock Wy BORE WD6 .... 75 L5
Baldry Gdns STRHM/NOR SW16 .... 180 F9
Baldwin Cl CRAWE RH10 .... 284 D10
Baldwin Crs CMBW SE5 .... 159 K7
RGUE GU4 .... 250 F8
Baldwin Rd BEAC HP9 .... 88 G10
SL SL1 .... 128 B5
Baldwins WGCE AL7 .... 23 L5
Baldwin's Gdns FSBYW WC1X 12 A3
Baldwin's Hl LOU IG10 .... 82 C5
Baldwins La RKW/CH/CXG WD3 .... 72 B8
Baldwin's Shore WDSR SL4 .... 149 J5
Baldwin St FSBYE EC1V 6 G10
Baldwin Ter IS N1 .... 6 E7
Baldwyn Gdns ACT W3 .... 135 P9
Baldwyn's Pk BXLY DA5 .... 186 E5
Baldwyn's Rd BXLY DA5 .... 186 E5
Balfern Gv CHSWK W4 .... 156 B4
Balfern St BTSEA SW11 .... 157 P8
Balfe St IS N1 .... 5 M8
Balfont Cl SAND/SEL CR2 .... 223 P9
Balfour Av HNWL W7 .... 134 E10
WOKS/MYFD GU22 .... 232 B8
Balfour Gv TRDG/WHET N20 .... 98 A4
Balfour Ms ED N9 .... 99 P4
MYFR/PKLN W1K 10 D9
Balfour Pl MYFR/PKLN W1K 10 D8
Balfour Rd ACT W3 .... 135 P7
CAR SM5 .... 222 A4
GRAYS RM17 .... 167 P3
HAYES BR2 .... 206 A5
HBRY N5 .... 119 K9
HRW HA1 .... 114 C3
HSLW TW3 .... 154 A9
IL IG1 .... 122 E7
NWDGN UB2 .... 153 L2
SNWD SE25 .... 203 P4
WEA W13 .... 154 G1
WEY KT13 .... 216 A1
WIM/MER SW19 .... 179 L10
Balfour St HERT/WAS SG14 .... 25 K4
STHWK SE1 .... 18 G5
Balgonie Rd CHING E4 .... 101 J2
Balgores Crs GPK RM2 .... 125 J1
Balgores La GPK RM2 .... 125 J2
Balgores Sq GPK RM2 .... 125 J2
Balgowan Cl NWMAL KT3 .... 200 B4
Balgowan Rd BECK BR3 .... 204 D3
Balgowan St WOOL/PLUM SE18 .... 163 J3
Balham Gv BAL SW12 .... 180 B3
Balham High Rd BAL SW12 .... 180 C4
Balham Hl BAL SW12 .... 180 C3
Balham New Rd BAL SW12 .... 180 C3
Balham Park Rd TOOT SW17 .... 180 A4
Balham Rd ED N9 .... 99 P3
Balham Station Rd BAL SW12 .... 180 B4
Balladier Wk POP/IOD E14 .... 140 G7
Ballamore Rd BMLY BR1 .... 183 M6
Ballance Rd HOM E9 .... 140 C1
Ballands North LHD/OX KT22 .... 236 D8
The Ballands' South
LHD/OX KT22 .... 236 D9
Ballantine St
WAND/EARL SW18 .... 157 M10
Ballantyne Dr
KWD/TDW/WH KT20 .... 239 J7
Ballard Cl KUTN/CMB KT2 .... 178 A10
Ballard Gn WDSR SL4 .... 148 D6
Ballards Cl DAGE RM10 .... 144 C3
Ballards Farm Rd SAND/SEL CR2 .... 223 P3
Ballards Gn KWD/TDW/WH KT20 .... 239 H5
Ballards La FNCH N3 .... 97 L8
OXTED RH8 .... 261 P5
Ballards Ri SAND/SEL CR2 .... 223 P3
Ballards Rd CRICK NW2 .... 116 D7
DAGE RM10 .... 144 C3
Ballast Quay GNWCH SE10 .... 161 J4
Ballater Cl OXHEY WD19 .... 93 J5
Ballater Rd CLAP SW4 .... 158 F10
SAND/SEL CR2 .... 223 N2
Ballencrieff Rd ASC SL5 .... 192 E7
Ballina St FSTH SE23 .... 182 C3
Ballingdon Rd BTSEA SW11 .... 180 B2
Ballinger Ct BERK HP4 .... 33 M6
Balliol Av CHING E4 .... 101 J5
Balliol Cl CRAWE RH10 .... 284 E4
Balliol Rd NKENS W10 .... 136 F8
TOTM N17 .... 99 M9
WELL DA16 .... 163 L8
Balloch Rd CAT SE6 .... 183 J4
Ballogie Av WLSDN NW10 .... 116 B9
Ball's Pond Pl IS N1 .... 7 H1
Ball's Pond Rd IS N1 .... 7 J1
Balmain Cl EA W5 .... 135 J10
Balmer Rd BOW E3 .... 140 E4
Balmes Rd IS N1 .... 7 H5
Balmoral Av BECK BR3 .... 204 D4
FBAR/BDGN N11 .... 98 B7
Balmoral Cl CHES/WCR EN8 .... 62 C10
LCOL/BKTW AL2 .... 56 B4
SL SL1 .... 128 D8
Balmoral Crs E/WMO/HCT KT8 .... 197 P3
Balmoral Dr BORE WD6 .... 76 A8
STHL UB1 .... 133 N6
WOKS/MYFD GU22 .... 232 F2
YEAD UB4 .... 132 F6
Balmoral Gdns BXLY DA5 .... 186 A3
HNWL W7 .... 154 F2
SAND/SEL CR2 .... 223 L6
WDSR SL4 .... 149 J9
Balmoral Gv HOLWY N7 .... 5 N2
Balmoral Ms SHB W12 .... 156 C2
Balmoral Rd BRWN CM15 .... 86 G10
CRICK NW2 .... 136 E1
EYN DA4 .... 187 P10
FSTGT E7 .... 121 P9
GPK RM2 .... 125 J2
GSTN WD25 .... 55 H8
HCH RM12 .... 125 L8
KUT KT1 .... 199 L4
LEY E10 .... 120 G7
PEND EN3 .... 80 C2
RYLN/HDSTN HA2 .... 113 P9
WATN WD24 .... 73 K4
WPK KT4 .... 200 E10
Balmoral Wy BELMT SM2 .... 221 K6
Balmore Crs EBAR EN4 .... 78 B9
Balmore St KTTN NW5 .... 118 C7
Balmuir Gdns PUT/ROE SW15 .... 156 F10
Balnacraig Av WLSDN NW10 .... 116 B9
Balquhain Cl ASHTD KT21 .... 237 J3
Balsams Cl HERT/BAY SG13 .... 25 L7
Baltic Cl WIM/MER SW19 .... 179 N10
Baltic St East STLK EC1Y 12 E2
Baltic St West FARR EC1M 12 E2
Baltimore Pl WELL DA16 .... 163 J8
Balvaird Pl PIM SW1V 17 K8
Balvernie Gv WAND/EARL SW18 .... 179 J3
Bamborough Gdns SHB W12 .... 156 F1
Bamford Av ALP/SUD HA0 .... 135 L3
Bamford Rd BMLY BR1 .... 183 J8
Bamford Wy CRW RM5 .... 104 C6
Bampfylde Cl WLGTN SM6 .... 202 D10
Bampton Dr MLHL NW7 .... 96 D8
Bampton Rd FSTH SE23 .... 182 C6
HARH RM3 .... 105 M8
Bampton Wy WOKN/KNAP GU21 .... 231 M4
Banavie Gdns BECK BR3 .... 204 G1
Banbury Av SL SL1 .... 128 E7
Banbury Cl ENC/FH EN2 .... 79 J5
Banbury Rd HOM E9 .... 140 C2
WALTH E17 .... 100 D8
Banbury St BTSEA SW11 .... 157 P8
WATW WD18 .... 73 J9
Banbury Vls MEO DA13 .... 189 L9
Banchory Rd BKHTH/KID SE3 .... 161 N6
Banckside HART DA3 .... 211 K4
Bancroft Av EFNCH N2 .... 117 P3
Bancroft Cl ASHF TW15 .... 174 B8
Bancroft Ct NTHLT UB5 .... 133 K3
REIG RH2 .... 257 L10
Bancroft Gdns
KTN/HRWW/W HA3 .... 94 B9
ORP BR6 .... 207 J8
Bancroft Rd CRAWE RH10 .... 284 E8
KTN/HRWW/W HA3 .... 94 B10
REIG RH2 .... 257 K10
WCHPL E1 .... 140 C5
Banders Ri GU GU1 .... 250 F9
Band La EGH TW20 .... 172 C8
Bandon Ri WLGTN SM6 .... 222 E3
Banes Down WAB EN9 .... 45 K8
Bangalore St PUT/ROE SW15 .... 156 F9
Bangor Cl NTHLT UB5 .... 114 A10
Bangors Cl IVER SL0 .... 131 J8
Bangors Rd North IVER SL0 .... 130 G3
Bangors Rd South IVER SL0 .... 131 H6
Banim St HMSMTH W6 .... 156 E2
Banister Rd WLSDN NW10 .... 136 G5
Bank Av MTCM CR4 .... 201 N2
Bank End STHWK SE1 .... 12 F9
Bankfoot GRAYS RM17 .... 167 L3
Bankfoot Rd BMLY BR1 .... 183 K7
Bank Gn CSHM HP5 .... 32 B9
Bankhurst Rd CAT SE6 .... 182 E3
Bank La BGR/WK TN15 .... 265 P8
CRAWE RH10 .... 283 N7
KUTN/CMB KT2 .... 177 K10
PUT/ROE SW15 .... 178 B1
Bank Ml BERK HP4 .... 34 B5
Bankmill Br BERK HP4 .... 34 C6
Bank Mill La BERK HP4 .... 34 B6
Banksia Rd UED N18 .... 100 B6
Bankside ENC/FH EN2 .... 79 J5
GVW DA11 .... 189 P2
SAND/SEL CR2 .... 223 N3
SEV TN13 .... 246 E7
STHL UB1 .... 133 L10
STHWK SE1 .... 12 E8
WOKN/KNAP GU21 .... 231 N4
Bankside Av NTHLT UB5 .... 133 H4
Bankside Cl BH/WHM TN16 .... 243 P4
CAR SM5 .... 221 P2
ISLW TW7 .... 154 E10
RDART DA2 .... 186 E7
Bankside Dr THDIT KT7 .... 198 G9
Bankside Rd IL IG1 .... 122 F10
Banks La BXLYHS DA6 .... 164 A10
EHSLY KT24 .... 235 J8
EPP CM16 .... 83 L3
Banks Rd BORE WD6 .... 75 P6
CRAWE RH10 .... 284 D8
Banks Sp SL SL1 .... 148 G1
Banks St GVE DA12 .... 190 E2
Banks Wy GU GU1 .... 250 C7
The Bank HGT N6 .... 118 C5
Banktón Rd BRXS/STRHM SW2 .... 159 H10
Bankwell Rd LEW SE13 .... 161 K10
Bank Willow RCHPK/HAM TW10 .... 176 G6
Bann Cl SOCK/AV RM15 .... 146 G9
Banner Cl PUR RM19 .... 166 C3
Banner St STLK EC1Y 12 F2
Banning St GNWCH SE10 .... 161 K4
Bannister Cl BRXS/STRHM SW2 .... 181 H4
DTCH/LGLY SL3 .... 150 B1
NTHLT UB5 .... 114 C10
Bannister Dr RBRW/HUT CM13 .... 87 P10
Bannister Gdns
STMC/STPC BR5 .... 207 M3
Bannister's Rd GUW GU2 .... 267 L2
Bannockburn Rd
WOOL/PLUM SE18 .... 163 H3
Banson's La CHONG CM5 .... 67 P4
Bansons Wy CHONG CM5 .... 67 P4
Banstead Gdns ED N9 .... 99 L4
Banstead Rd BELMT SM2 .... 221 N4
BNSTD SM7 .... 221 H9
CAR SM5 .... 221 P5
CTHM CR3 .... 241 L8
EW KT17 .... 220 E6
PUR/KEN CR8 .... 223 H7
Banstead Rd South BELMT SM2 .... 221 M6
Banstead St PECK SE15 .... 160 B9
Banstead Wy WLGTN SM6 .... 222 F2
Banstock Rd EDGW HA8 .... 95 P7
Banting Dr WCHMH N21 .... 78 G9
Banton Cl EN EN1 .... 80 A6
Bantry St CMBW SE5 .... 159 L6
Banwell Rd BXLY DA5 .... 185 N2
Banyard Rd BERM/RHTH SE16 .... 160 A2
Banyards EMPK RM11 .... 125 M2
Bapchild Pl STMC/STPC BR5 .... 207 M4
Baptist Gdns HAMP NW3 .... 4 C1
Barbara Cl SHPTN TW17 .... 196 C5
Barbauld Rd STNW/STAM N16 .... 119 M8
Barbel Cl CHES/WCR EN8 .... 62 F10
Barber Cl WCHMH N21 .... 99 H1
Barberry Cl HARH RM3 .... 105 L8
Barberry Rd HHW HP1 .... 35 K6
Barbers Rd SRTFD E15 .... 140 G4
Barbican Rd GFD/PVL UB6 .... 134 A8
Barb Ms HMSMTH W6 .... 156 F2
Barbon Cl BMSBY WC1N 11 M3
Barbot Cl ED N9 .... 99 N4
Barchard St WAND/EARL SW18 .... 179 L1
Barchester Cl HNWL W7 .... 134 E10
Barchester Rd DTCH/LGLY SL3 .... 150 C1
KTN/HRWW/W HA3 .... 94 C9
Barchester St POP/IOD E14 .... 140 G7
Barclay Cl GT/LBKH KT23 .... 236 A9
HERT/BAY SG13 .... 26 A7
WATW WD18 .... 73 H10
Barclay Ct HOD EN11 .... 44 F4
Barclay Ov WFD IG8 .... 101 M5
Barclay Rd CROY/NA CR0 .... 203 L10
FUL/PGN SW6 .... 157 K6
PLSTW E13 .... 141 P6
UED N18 .... 99 L7
WALTH E17 .... 121 H3
WAN E11 .... 121 L6
Barclay Wy WTHK RM20 .... 166 E4
Barcombe Av BRXS/STRHM SW2 .... 180 F5
Barcombe Cl CHST BR7 .... 207 K3
Barden Cl DEN/HRF UB9 .... 91 M9
Barden St WOOL/PLUM SE18 .... 163 H6
Bardeswell Cl BRW CM14 .... 107 H3
Bardfield Av CHDH RM6 .... 123 N1
Bardney Rd MRDN SM4 .... 201 L4
Bardolph Av CROY/NA CR0 .... 224 E5
Bardolph Rd HOLWY N7 .... 118 F9
RCH/KEW TW9 .... 155 L10
Bardon Wk WOKN/KNAP GU21 .... 231 N3
Bard Rd NKENS W10 .... 136 G9
Bards Cnr HHW HP1 .... 35 L5
Bardsey Pl WCHPL E1 .... 140 B7
Bardsley Cl CROY/NA CR0 .... 203 N10
Bardsley La BRXS/STRHM SW2 .... 159 H10
GNWCH SE10 .... 161 H5
Bardwell Rd STAL AL1 .... 38 C7
Barfett St NKENS W10 .... 8 C1
Barfield EYN DA4 .... 210 A1
Barfield Av TRDG/WHET N20 .... 98 A3
Barfield Rd BMLY BR1 .... 206 D3
WAN E11 .... 121 L6
Barfields LOU IG10 .... 82 D8
REDH RH1 .... 259 J9
Barford Cl HDN NW4 .... 96 D10
Barford St IS N1 .... 6 B6
Barforth Rd PECK SE15 .... 160 A9
Barfreston Wy PGE/AN SE20 .... 204 A1
Bargate Cl NWMAL KT3 .... 200 D7
WOOL/PLUM SE18 .... 163 J4
Barge House Rd CAN/RD E16 .... 162 E1
Barge House St STHWK SE1 .... 12 B9
Bargery Rd CAT SE6 .... 182 G4
Bargrove Av HHW HP1 .... 35 K7
Bargrove Cl PGE/AN SE20 .... 181 P10
Bargrove Crs CAT SE6 .... 182 E5
Barham Av BORE WD6 .... 75 L7
Barham Cl ALP/SUD HA0 .... 134 G1
CHST BR7 .... 184 E8
GVE DA12 .... 191 J4
HAYES BR2 .... 206 B8
ROMW/RG RM7 .... 104 C10
WEY KT13 .... 216 D1
Barham Ct ALP/SUD HA0 .... 135 H1
Barham Rd CHST BR7 .... 184 E8
CROY/NA CR0 .... 223 K1
DART DA1 .... 187 P3
RYNPK SW20 .... 178 D10
Baring Cl LEE/GVPK SE12 .... 183 M5
Baring Rd BEAC HP9 .... 88 B8
BMLY BR1 .... 183 N7
CROY/NA CR0 .... 203 P8
EBAR EN4 .... 77 N7
LEE/GVPK SE12 .... 183 M4
Baring St IS N1 .... 6 G6
Barington Ct RBRW/HUT CM13 .... 87 P10
Bark Burr Rd CDH/CHF RM16 .... 167 L1
Barker Dr CAMTN NW1 .... 5 H4
Barker Rd CHERT KT16 .... 195 H7
Barkham Rd TOTM N17 .... 99 L8
Bark Hart Rd ORP BR6 .... 207 L8
Barking Rd CAN/RD E16 .... 141 L7
EHAM E6 .... 142 C3
PLSTW E13 .... 141 N6
POP/IOD E14 .... 141 K8
Bark Pl BAY/PAD W2 .... 8 G7
Barkston Gdns ECT SW5 .... 14 G6
Barkwood Cl ROMW/RG RM7 .... 124 D3
Barkworth Rd BERM/RHTH SE16 .... 160 A4
Barlborough St NWCR SE14 .... 160 C6
Barlby Gdns NKENS W10 .... 136 G6
Barlby Rd NKENS W10 .... 136 F7
Barlee Crs UX/CGN UB8 .... 131 M7
Barle Gdns SOCK/AV RM15 .... 146 G8
Barley Cl BUSH WD23 .... 74 A9
CRAWW RH11 .... 283 N8
RBSF CM22 .... 31 M1
Barleycorn Wy EMPK RM11 .... 125 N4
Barley Cft HERT/WAS SG14 .... 25 L3
HHNE HP2 .... 36 D6
HLWS CM18 .... 46 G5
Barleycroft Gn WGCW AL8 .... 22 F5
Barleycroft Rd WGCW AL8 .... 22 F6
Barley Fld BRWN CM15 .... 86 E3
Barley La GDMY/SEVK IG3 .... 123 K4
Barley Mow Cl WOKN/KNAP GU21 .... 231 J3
Barley Mow Ct
BRKHM/BTCW RH3 .... 255 P10
Barley Mow La STALE/WH AL4 .... 39 K9
WOKN/KNAP GU21 .... 231 H2
Barley Mow Pas CHSWK W4 .... 156 A4
Barley Mow Rd EGH TW20 .... 171 P8
Barley Mow Wy SHPTN TW17 .... 196 B4
Barley Ponds Cl WARE SG12 .... 26 E2
Barley Ponds Rd WARE SG12 .... 26 E2
Barlings Rd HARP AL5 .... 20 A6
Barlow Cl WLGTN SM6 .... 222 F3
Barlow Pl MYFR/PICC W1J 10 F8
Barlow Rd ACT W3 .... 135 N10
CRAWW RH11 .... 283 H10
CRICK NW2 .... 2 D1
HPTN TW12 .... 175 P10
Barlow St WALW SE17 .... 19 H5
Barlow Wy DAGW RM9 .... 144 E8
RAIN RM13 .... 144 F8
Barmeston Rd CAT SE6 .... 182 G5
Barmor Cl RYLN/HDSTN HA2 .... 94 A10
Barmouth Av GFD/PVL UB6 .... 134 E4
Barmouth Rd CROY/NA CR0 .... 204 C9
WAND/EARL SW18 .... 179 M2
Barnabas Rd HOM E9 .... 140 C1
Barnaby Cl RYLN/HDSTN HA2 .... 114 B7
Barnaby Pl SKENS SW7 .... 15 L6
Barnaby Wy CHIG IG7 .... 102 D4
Barnacre Cl UX/CGN UB8 .... 131 N8
Barnacres Rd HHS/BOV HP3 .... 36 A10
Barnard Acres WAB EN9 .... 45 K9
Barnard Cl CHST BR7 .... 206 G1
SUN TW16 .... 175 J10
WLGTN SM6 .... 222 E4
Barnard Gdns NWMAL KT3 .... 200 D4
YEAD UB4 .... 133 J6
Barnard Gn WGCE AL7 .... 23 J6
Barnard Hl MUSWH N10 .... 98 C10
Barnard Ms BTSEA SW11 .... 157 P10
Barnardo Dr BARK/HLT IG6 .... 122 F2
Barnardo St WCHPL E1 .... 140 C8
Barnard Rd BTSEA SW11 .... 157 P10
EN EN1 .... 80 A6
MTCM CR4 .... 202 B3
WARL CR6 .... 242 G5
Barnards Pl SAND/SEL CR2 .... 223 J5
Barnard Wy HHS/BOV HP3 .... 35 P7
Barnato Cl BF/WBF KT14 .... 215 P8
Barnby Rd WOKN/KNAP GU21 .... 231 J3
Barnby St CAMTN NW1 .... 5 H8
SRTFD E15 .... 141 K3
Barn Cl ASHF TW15 .... 174 C8
BNSTD SM7 .... 239 N1
HHS/BOV HP3 .... 36 A9
NTHLT UB5 .... 133 K4
RAD WD7 .... 74 F1
SLN SL2 .... 108 G9
WGCW AL8 .... 22 F5
Barn Ct CRAWE RH10 .... 285 M3
Barn Crs PUR/KEN CR8 .... 223 L9
STAN HA7 .... 95 H7
Barncroft Cl LOU IG10 .... 82 D9
UX/CGN UB8 .... 132 C7
Barncroft Gn LOU IG10 .... 82 D9
Barncroft Rd BERK HP4 .... 33 L6
LOU IG10 .... 82 D9
Barncroft Wy STAL AL1 .... 38 F7
Barndicott WGCE AL7 .... 23 M5
Barnehurst Av BXLYHN DA7 .... 164 D7
Barnehurst Cl ERITH DA8 .... 164 D7
Barnehurst Rd BXLYHN DA7 .... 164 D8
Barn End Dr RDART DA2 .... 187 K7
Barn End La SWLY BR8 .... 187 K9
Barnes Av BARN SW13 .... 156 D6
CSHM HP5 .... 51 H6
NWDGN UB2 .... 153 N3
Barnes Br CHSWK W4 .... 156 B8
Barnes Cl MNPK E12 .... 122 A9
Barnes Cray Rd DART DA1 .... 165 H10
Barnesdale Crs STMC/STPC BR5 .... 207 K6
Barnes End NWMAL KT3 .... 200 D5
Barnes High St BARN SW13 .... 156 C8
Barnes La KGLGY WD4 .... 53 M4
Barnes Ri KGLGY WD4 .... 54 A3
Barnes Rd IL IG1 .... 122 F10
RGODL GU7 .... 267 K9
UED N18 .... 100 B5
Barnes St POP/IOD E14 .... 140 D8
Barnes Ter DEPT SE8 .... 160 E4
Barnes Wallis Dr WEY KT13 .... 215 P7
Barnes Wy IVER SL0 .... 131 J9
Barnet By-pass BORE WD6 .... 76 B9
Barnet Dr HAYES BR2 .... 206 B9
Barnet Gate La BAR EN5 .... 76 C10
Barnet Gv BETH E2 .... 7 N9
Barnet Hl BAR EN5 .... 77 J8
Barnet La BORE WD6 .... 75 L10
TRDG/WHET N20 .... 97 J2
Barnet Rd EBAR EN4 .... 77 K3
LCOL/BKTW AL2 .... 57 L4
MLHL NW7 .... 76 B10
POTB/CUF EN6 .... 59 M9
POTB/CUF EN6 .... 59 M10
Barnett Cl ERITH DA8 .... 164 G8
LHD/OX KT22 .... 236 G5
SHGR GU5 .... 268 F9
Barnett La SHGR GU5 .... 268 E10
Barnett Rw RGUE GU4 .... 250 A5
Barnett's Shaw OXTED RH8 .... 261 J3
Barnett St WCHPL E1 .... 140 A8
Barnett Wood La ASHTD KT21 .... 237 H4
Barnet Wy
(Barnet By-pass) MLHL NW7 .... 96 A1
Barnet Wood Rd HAYES BR2 .... 205 N10
Barney Cl CHARL SE7 .... 161 P4
Barn Fld BNSTD SM7 .... 221 L10
Barnfield EPP CM16 .... 65 K4
GVW DA11 .... 190 D5
HHS/BOV HP3 .... 36 A9
IVER SL0 .... 131 H8
NWMAL KT3 .... 200 B6
SL SL1 .... 128 C10
Barnfield Av CROY/NA CR0 .... 204 B8
KUTN/CMB KT2 .... 177 J7
MTCM CR4 .... 202 C4
Barnfield Cl COUL/CHIP CR5 .... 241 K5
CRH DA9 .... 188 E2
HOD EN11 .... 44 F1
SWLY BR8 .... 208 D7
WAB EN9 .... 45 L8
Barnfield Ct HARP AL5 .... 20 B3
Barnfield Crs RSEV TN14 .... 247 M3
Barnfield Gdns KUTN/CMB KT2 .... 177 K8
Barnfield Rd BELV DA17 .... 164 A5
BH/WHM TN16 .... 244 A6
CRAWE RH10 .... 283 N6
EA W5 .... 135 H6
EDGW HA8 .... 95 P9
HARP AL5 .... 20 B3
SAND/SEL CR2 .... 223 M5
SEV TN13 .... 246 E9
STALE/WH AL4 .... 39 H4
STMC/STPC BR5 .... 207 N3
WGCE AL7 .... 23 H7
WOOL/PLUM SE18 .... 162 E5
Barnfield Wy OXTED RH8 .... 261 M9
Barnfield Wood Cl BECK BR3 .... 205 J6
Barnfield Wood Rd BECK BR3 .... 205 J6
Barnham Rd GFD/PVL UB6 .... 134 B5
Barnham St STHWK SE1 .... 19 K1
Barn Hl HLWW/ROY CM19 .... 45 N5
Barnhill PIN HA5 .... 113 K3
Barn Hl WBLY HA9 .... 115 N7
Barnhill Av HAYES BR2 .... 205 M5
Barnhill La YEAD UB4 .... 133 J5
Barnhill Rd WBLY HA9 .... 115 P8
YEAD UB4 .... 133 J6
Barnhurst Pth OXHEY WD19 .... 93 K6
Barningham Wy CDALE/KGS NW9 .... 115 P6
Barn Lea RKW/CH/CXG WD3 .... 91 K2
Barnlea Cl FELT TW13 .... 175 M5
Barn Md BRWN CM15 .... 87 H2
Barnmead CHOB/PIR GU24 .... 213 L6
Barn Md HLWS CM18 .... 46 G3
Barnmead Gdns DAGW RM9 .... 124 A10
Barn Meadow La GT/LBKH KT23 .... 235 N10
Barnmead Rd BECK BR3 .... 204 D1
DAGW RM9 .... 124 A10
Barn Ri WBLY HA9 .... 115 M6
Barn Rd ADL/WDHM KT15 .... 215 L5
Barnsbury Cl NWMAL KT3 .... 199 P4
Barnsbury Crs BRYLDS KT5 .... 199 P8
Barnsbury Gv HOLWY N7 .... 5 P3
Barnsbury La BRYLDS KT5 .... 199 N9
Barnsbury Pk IS N1 .... 6 A3
Barnsbury Rd IS N1 .... 6 A7
Barnsbury Sq IS N1 .... 6 A4
Barnsbury St IS N1 .... 6 B4
Barnsbury Ter IS N1 .... 6 A4
Barns Ct EPP CM16 .... 46 E6
Barnscroft RYNPK SW20 .... 200 E3
Barnsdale Av POP/IOD E14 .... 160 G3
Barnsdale Cl BORE WD6 .... 75 L5
Barnsdale Rd MV/WKIL W9 .... 8 D1
Barnsfield Pl UX/CGN UB8 .... 131 M3
Barnsford Crs CHOB/PIR GU24 .... 212 F8
Barnside Ct WGCW AL8 .... 22 F5
Barnsley Rd HARH RM3 .... 105 N8
Barnsley St WCHPL E1 .... 140 A6
Barnstaple La LEW SE13 .... 161 H10
Barnstaple Rd HARH RM3 .... 105 K6
RSLP HA4 .... 113 K8

Barnston Wy *RBRW/HUT* CM13 ..... 87 P9 🔢
Barn St *STNW/STAM* N16 ..... 119 M7 🔢
Barnsway *KGLGY* WD4 ..... 53 F9
Barnway *EGH* TW20 ..... 171 P8
Barn Wy *WBLY* HA9 ..... 115 M6
Barnwell Rd *BRXS/STRHM* SW2 ..... 181 H1
DART DA1 ..... 165 N9
MV/WKIL W9 ..... 8 C2
RGUW GU3 ..... 249 K8
RSLP HA4 ..... 112 E7
Barnwood Cl *CRAWE* RH10 ..... 284 D6
Barnwood Ct *GUW* GU2 ..... 249 K8
Barnwood Rd *GUW* GU2 ..... 249 K9
The Barnyard
KWD/TDW/WH KT20 ..... 238 D10
Baron Cl *BELMT* SM2 ..... 221 L6
FBAR/BDGN N11 ..... 98 B6
Baroness Rd *BETH* E2 ..... 7 M9
Baronet Gv *TOTM* N17 ..... 99 P9 🔢
Baronet Rd *TOTM* N17 ..... 99 P9
Baron Gdns *BARK/HLT* IG6 ..... 122 F1
Baron Gv *MTCM* CR4 ..... 201 P4
Baron Rd *BCTR* RM8 ..... 123 N6
Baron's Ct *WKENS* W14 ..... 14 E1
Baronsfield Rd *TWK* TW1 ..... 176 C2 🔢
Baron Cl *EBAR* EN4 ..... 77 P10 🔢
Baron's Hurst *EPSOM* KT18 ..... 237 P2
Barons Md *HRW* HA1 ..... 114 D2
Baronsmead Rd *BARN* SW13 ..... 156 D7 🔢
Baronsmede *EA* W5 ..... 155 L1
Baronsmere Rd *EFNCH* N2 ..... 117 P2
Barons Pl *STHWK* SE1 ..... 18 B2
Barons Rw *HARP* AL5 ..... 20 C4
The Barons *TWK* TW1 ..... 176 C2
Baron St *IS* N1 ..... 6 A8
Barons Wk *CROY/NA* CR0 ..... 204 D6 🔢
Barons Wy *EGH* TW20 ..... 172 C9
REIG RH2 ..... 275 K4
Barque Ms *DEPT* SE8 ..... 160 F5 🔢
Barrack La *WDSR* SL4 ..... 149 J7 🔢
Barrack Pth *WOKN/KNAP* GU21 ..... 231 L4
Barrack Rd *GUW* GU2 ..... 249 M8
HSLWW TW4 ..... 153 L10
Barrack Rw *GVW* DA11 ..... 190 D2 🔢
Barracks Hl *AMSS* HP7 ..... 88 E1
Barra Cl *HHS/BOV* HP3 ..... 36 C9
Barra Hall Rd *HYS/HAR* UB3 ..... 132 F5
Barrards Wy *BEAC* HP9 ..... 89 H7
Barratt Av *WDGN* N22 ..... 98 G10
Barratt Wy *KTN/HRWW/W* HA3 ..... 114 C1
Barrenger Rd *MUSWH* N10 ..... 98 A9
Barrens Brae *WOKS/MYFD* GU22 ..... 232 D4
Barrens Pk *WOKS/MYFD* GU22 ..... 232 D4
Barrens Rd *GT/LBKH* KT23 ..... 254 B1
WALTH E17 ..... 121 H2
Barrett's Green Rd *WLSDN* NW10 ..... 135 P4
Barrett's Gv *STNW/STAM* N16 ..... 119 M10
Barretts Rd *SEV* TN13 ..... 246 E6
Barrett St *MBLAR* W1H 10 D6
MHST W1U 10 D6
Barrhill Rd *BRXS/STRHM* SW2 ..... 180 F5 🔢
Barricane *WOKN/KNAP* GU21 ..... 231 N5
Barrie Cl *COUL/CHIP* CR5 ..... 240 C7
Barriedale *NWCR* SE14 ..... 160 D7
Barringer Sq *TOOT* SW17 ..... 180 B7 🔢
Barrington Cl *CLAY* IG5 ..... 102 C9
Barrington Ct *DORK* RH4 ..... 272 F3 🔢
Barrington Dr *DEN/HRF* UB9 ..... 91 K8
Barrington Gn *LOU* IG10 ..... 82 F8
Barrington Ldg *WEY* KT13 ..... 216 D2 🔢
Barrington Rd *BRXN/ST* SW9 ..... 159 J9
CEND/HSY/T N8 ..... 118 C3
CHEAM SM3 ..... 201 K8
CRAWE RH10 ..... 283 N9
DORK RH4 ..... 272 F3 🔢
LOU IG10 ..... 82 F8
MNPK E12 ..... 123 N2
PUR/KEN CR8 ..... 222 D8
WELL DA16 ..... 148 C1
Barrington Vls *WOOL/PLUM* SE18... 162 D7
Barron's Cl *CHMS* CM5 ..... 67 N3
Barrow Av *CAR* SM5 ..... 222 A7
Barrow Cl *WCHMH* N21 ..... 99 J4
Barrowdene Cl *PIN* HA5 ..... 93 M10 🔢
Barrowell Gn *WCHMH* N21 ..... 99 J3
Barrowfield Cl *ED* N9 ..... 100 A4
Barrowgate Rd *CHSWK* W4 ..... 155 P4
Barrow Hedges Cl *CAR* SM5 ..... 221 P4
Barrow Hedges Wy *CAR* SM5 ..... 221 P4
Barrow Hl *WPK* KT4 ..... 200 B9
Barrow Hill Cl *WPK* KT4 ..... 200 B9 🔢
Barrow La *CHESW* EN7 ..... 61 N7
Barrow Point Av *PIN* HA5 ..... 93 M10
Barrow Point La *PIN* HA5 ..... 93 M10
Barrow Rd *CROY/NA* CR0 ..... 223 H2
STRHM/NOR SW16 ..... 180 E9
Barrows Rd *HLWW/ROY* CM19 ..... 46 C1
Barr Rd *GVE* DA12 ..... 191 J3
POTB/CUF EN6 ..... 59 M9
Barr's La *WOKN/KNAP* GU21 ..... 231 J2
Barr's Rd *MDHD* SL6 ..... 128 A8
WLSDN NW10 ..... 136 A2 🔢
Barry Av *BXLYHN* DA7 ..... 163 P6
SEVS/STOTM N15 ..... 119 N4 🔢
WDSR SL4 ..... 148 G2
Barry Cl *CDH/CHF* RM16 ..... 168 D2
CRAWE RH10 ..... 283 P10
LCOL/BKTW AL2 ..... 56 A1
ORP BR6 ..... 207 H10
Barry Rd *EDUL* SE22 ..... 181 P2
EHAM E6 ..... 142 B8
WLSDN NW10 ..... 135 P2
Barset Rd *PECK* SE15 ..... 160 B9 🔢
Barsons Cl *PGE/AN* SE20 ..... 182 B10
The Bars *GU* GU1 ..... 268 A1
Barston Rd *WNWD* SE27 ..... 181 K5
Barstow Crs *BRXS/STRHM* SW2 ..... 180 G4
Bartel Cl *HHS/BOV* HP3 ..... 36 E6
Bartelotts Rd *SLN* SL2 ..... 128 C6
Barter St *NOXST/BSQ* WC1A 11 M4
Bartholomew Cl *STBT* EC1A ..... 12 E4 🔢
STBT EC1A ..... 12 E4 🔢
WAND/EARL SW18 ..... 157 M10 🔢
Bartholomew Dr *HARH* RM3 ..... 105 L10
Bartholomew La *OBST* EC2N ..... 13 H6 🔢
Bartholomew Rd *KTTN* NW5 ..... 4 G3
Bartholomew Sq *FSBYE* EC1V ..... 12 F1 🔢
Bartholomew St *STHWK* SE1 ..... 19 H4
Bartholomew Vls *KTTN* NW5 ..... 4 G3
Bartholomew Wy *SWLY* BR8 ..... 208 F3
Barth Rd *WOOL/PLUM* SE18 ..... 163 H3
Bartle Av *EHAM* E6 ..... 142 B4
Bartlett Cl *POP/IOD* E14 ..... 140 F8
Bartlett Ct *FLST/FETLN* EC4A ..... 12 B5 🔢
Bartlett Rd *BH/WHM* TN16 ..... 262 F2 🔢
GVW DA11 ..... 190 E6 🔢
Bartlett St *SAND/SEL* CR2 ..... 223 L2 🔢
Bartlow Gdns *CRW* RM5 ..... 104 D3
Barton Av *DAGE* RM10 ..... 124 D6
Barton Cl *ADL/WDHM* KT15 ..... 215 K3
BXLYHS DA6 ..... 185 P1
CHIG IG7 ..... 102 F3
HDN NW4 ..... 116 D3
PECK SE15 ..... 160 A3 🔢
SHPTN TW17 ..... 196 C6
Barton Gn *NWMAL* KT3 ..... 200 A2
Barton Mdw *BARK/HLT* IG6 ..... 122 E2
Barton Rd *DTCH/LGLY* SL3 ..... 150 C1
EYN DA4 ..... 210 A1
HCH RM12 ..... 125 H6
HMSMTH W6 ..... 14 A8
SCUP DA14 ..... 185 P9
SHCR GU5 ..... 268 D10

STALE/WH AL4 ..... 21 H3
The Bartons *BORE* WD6 ..... 75 J10 🔢
The Barton *COB* KT11 ..... 217 L8
Barton Wy *BORE* WD6 ..... 75 M6
RKW/CH/CXG WD3 ..... 72 C9
Bartram Cl *UX/CGN* UB8 ..... 132 C6 🔢
Bartram Rd *BROCKY* SE4 ..... 182 A1
Bartrams La *EBAR* EN4 ..... 77 M4
Bartrip St *HOM* E9 ..... 140 D1 🔢
Barts Cl *BECK* BR3 ..... 204 F5
Barward Ct *WOOL/PLUM* SE18 ..... 162 D2 🔢
Barwick Rd *FSTGT* E7 ..... 121 N9
Barwood Av *WWKM* BR4 ..... 204 G8
Basden Gv *FELT* TW13 ..... 175 P5
Basedale Rd *DAGW* RM9 ..... 143 J4
Baseing Cl *EHAM* E6 ..... 142 D9
Basford Wy *WDSR* SL4 ..... 148 C9
Bashford Wy *CRAWE* RH10 ..... 284 E5
Bashley Rd *WLSDN* NW10 ..... 136 A6
Basil Av *EHAM* E6 ..... 142 B5
Basildene Rd *HSLWW* TW4 ..... 153 L9
Basildon Av *CLAY* IG5 ..... 102 D9
Basildon Cl *BELMT* SM2 ..... 221 L5
WATW WD18 ..... 72 D10
Basildon Rd *ABYW* SE2 ..... 163 K3
Basildon Sq *HHNE* HP2 ..... 36 A1
Basildon Wy *CRAWW* RH11 ..... 283 H10
WNWD SE27 ..... 181 K8
Basilon Rd *BXLYHN* DA7 ..... 163 P8
Basil St *CHEL* SW3 ..... 16 A2
Basing Ct *THDIT* KT7 ..... 198 E7 🔢
Basingdon Wy *CMBW* SE5 ..... 159 L10 🔢
Basing Dr *BXLY* DA5 ..... 186 A2
Basingfield Rd *THDIT* KT7 ..... 198 E7
Basinghall Av *CITYW* EC2V ..... 12 G5 🔢
Basinghall Gdns *BELMT* SM2 ..... 221 L5
Basinghall St *CITYW* EC2V ..... 12 G5 🔢
Basing Hl *GLDGN* NW11 ..... 117 J6
WBLY HA9 ..... 115 L7
Basing Pl *BETH* E2 ..... 7 K9
Basing Rd *BNSTD* SM7 ..... 221 J10
BNSTD SM7 ..... 239 J1
RKW/CH/CXG WD3 ..... 91 J2
Basing Wy *FNCH* N3 ..... 117 K1
THDIT KT7 ..... 198 E7
Basire St *IS* N1 ..... 6 F3
Baskerville Gdns *WLSDN* NW10 ..... 116 B9 🔢
Baskerville Rd *WAND/EARL* SW18 ..... 179 J3
Basket Gdns *ELTH/MOT* SE9 ..... 184 B1
Baslow Cl *KTN/HRWW/W* HA3 ..... 94 C9
Baslow Wk *CLPT* E5 ..... 120 C9 🔢
Basnett Rd *BTSEA* SW11 ..... 158 B9 🔢
Bassano St *EDUL* SE22 ..... 181 N1
Bassant Rd *WOOL/PLUM* SE18 ..... 163 J5
Bassein Park Rd *SHB* W12 ..... 156 E1
Basset Cl *ADL/WDHM* KT15 ..... 215 L6
Bassett Cl *BELMT* SM2 ..... 221 L5
Bassett Gdns *EPP* CM16 ..... 66 C2
ISLW TW7 ..... 154 B6
Bassett Rd *CRAWE* RH10 ..... 284 E10
NKENS W10 ..... 136 C8
UX/CGN UB8 ..... 131 M2 🔢
WOKS/MYFD GU22 ..... 232 F2 🔢
Bassetts Cl *ORP* BR6 ..... 226 E2 🔢
Bassett St *KTTN* NW5 ..... 4 C1
Bassetts Wy *ORP* BR6 ..... 226 E1
Bassett Wy *GFD/PVL* UB6 ..... 134 A6
Bassil Rd *HHS/BOV* HP3 ..... 35 N7
Bassingbourne Cl *BROX* EN10 ..... 44 E6 🔢
Bassingburn Wk *WCCE* AL7 ..... 23 J4
Bassingham Rd *ALP/SUD* HA0 ..... 135 J1
WAND/EARL SW18 ..... 179 M3
Basswood Cl *PECK* SE15 ..... 160 A9 🔢
Bastable Av *BARK* IG11 ..... 143 K4
Bastion Rd *ABYW* SE2 ..... 163 K4
Baston Manor Rd *WWKM* BR4 ..... 205 N10
Baston Rd *HAYES* BR2 ..... 205 N9
Bastwick St *FSBYE* EC1V 12 D1
Basuto Rd *FUL/PGN* SW6 ..... 157 K7
Bata Av *TIL* RM18 ..... 169 L4
Batavia Cl *SUN* TW16 ..... 197 J3
Batavia Rd *NWCR* SE14 ..... 160 D6 🔢
SUN TW16 ..... 197 H3
Batchelor St *IS* N1 ..... 6 B7
Batchelors Wy *AMSS* HP7 ..... 69 J5
CSHM HP5 ..... 50 G5
Batchwood Dr *STALW/RED* AL3 ..... 38 B3 🔢
Batchwood Gdns *STALW/RED* AL3 ..... 38 C3 🔢
Batchwood Rd *STMC/STPC* BR5 ..... 207 K4
Batchwood Vw *STALW/RED* AL3 ..... 38 C3 🔢
Batchworth Hill London Rd
RKW/CH/CXG WD3 ..... 91 P3
Batchworth La *NTHWD* HA6 ..... 92 D6
Bateman Cl *BARK* IG11 ..... 142 F1 🔢
Bateman Rd *CHING* E4 ..... 100 F7
RKW/CH/CXG WD3 ..... 72 B10
Batemans Ct *CRAWE* RH10 ..... 284 B10
Bateman's Rw *SDTCH* EC2A 13 K1
Bateman St *SOHO/SHAV* W1D 11 J6
Bateson Wy *WOKN/KNAP* GU21 ..... 214 F10
Bates Cl *DTCH/LGLY* SL3 ..... 130 B8
Bates Crs *CROY/NA* CR0 ..... 223 H3
STRHM/NOR SW16 ..... 180 D10
Bate St *POP/IOD* E14 ..... 140 E9 🔢
Bates Wk *ADL/WDHM* KT15 ..... 215 M3
Batford Cl *WGCE* AL7 ..... 23 L6 🔢
Bath Cl *PECK* SE15 ..... 160 A6
Bathgate Rd *WIM/MER* SW19 ..... 178 C6 🔢
Bath Gv *BETH* E2 ..... 7 N8
Bath House Rd *CROY/NA* CR0 ..... 202 F8 🔢
Bath Pas *KUT* KT1 ..... 199 J2 🔢
Bath Rd *CHSWK* W4 ..... 156 B3
DART DA1 ..... 187 J3
DTCH/LGLY SL3 ..... 151 H7
FSTGT E7 ..... 142 A1
HEST TW5 ..... 153 J7 🔢
HSLWW TW4 ..... 153 L8
HTHAIR TW6 ..... 152 C7
SL SL1 ..... 128 C9
SL SL1 ..... 129 H10 🔢
WOKS/MYFD GU22 ..... 232 F2
Baths Ap *FUL/PGN* SW6 ..... 157 J6 🔢
Baths Rd *BMLY* BR1 ..... 206 A4
Bath St *FSBYE* EC1V 6 F10
GVW DA11 ..... 190 E2 🔢
Bath Ter *STHWK* SE1 ..... 18 E4
Bathurst Av *WIM/MER* SW19 ..... 201 L1 🔢
Bathurst Cl *IVER* SL0 ..... 151 J1
Bathurst Gdns *WLSDN* NW10 ..... 136 C1
Bathurst Ms *BAY/PAD* W2 ..... 9 M7
Bathurst Rd *HHNE* HP2 ..... 35 N7
IL IG1 ..... 122 E6
Bathurst St *BAY/PAD* W2 ..... 9 M7
Bathurst Wk *IVER* SL0 ..... 151 H1
Bathway *WOOL/PLUM* SE18 ..... 162 D3 🔢
Batley Cl *MTCM* CR4 ..... 202 A7
Batley Pl *STNW/STAM* N16 ..... 119 N8 🔢
Batley Rd *STNW/STAM* N16 ..... 119 N8 🔢
Batman Cl *SHB* W12 ..... 136 F9 🔢
Baton Cl *PUR* RM19 ..... 166 F5
Batoum Gdns *HMSMTH* W6 ..... 156 F2
Batson St *SHB* W12 ..... 156 F2
Batsworth Rd *MTCM* CR4 ..... 201 N3
Batten Av *WOKN/KNAP* GU21 ..... 231 K5
Batten Cl *EHAM* E6 ..... 142 A2
Battenburg Wk *NRWD* SE19 ..... 181 J7 🔢
Batterdale *BRKMPK* AL9 ..... 43 J2
Battersby Rd *CAT* SE6 ..... 183 J5
Battersea Br *BTSEA* SW11 ..... 157 P7
Battersea Bridge Rd *BTSEA* SW11.. 157 P6
Battersea Church Rd
BTSEA SW11 ..... 157 N7
Battersea High St *BTSEA* SW11 ..... 157 N7
Battersea Park Rd *BTSEA* SW11 ..... 158 B7
VX/NE SW8 ..... 158 C6

Battersea Ri *BTSEA* SW11 ..... 179 P1
Battery Rd *THMD* SE28 ..... 163 H1
Battishill St *IS* N1 ..... 6 C4
Battlebridge La *REDH* RH1 ..... 258 C6
Battle Bridge La *STHWK* SE1 ..... 13 J10
Battle Cl *WIM/MER* SW19 ..... 179 M9 🔢
Battledean Rd *HBRY* N5 ..... 119 J10
Battle Rd *ERITH* DA8 ..... 164 D3
Battlers Green Dr *RAD* WD7 ..... 74 D3
Battleview *STALE/WH* AL4 ..... 21 K3
Batts Hl *REDH* RH1 ..... 257 N8
Batty St *WCHPL* E1 ..... 13 P3
Baudwin Rd *CAT* SE6 ..... 183 K5
Baugh Rd *SCUP* DA14 ..... 185 M8
The Baulk *WAND/EARL* SW18 ..... 179 K3
Bavant Rd *STRHM/NOR* SW16 ..... 202 A2
Bavaria Rd *ARCH* N19 ..... 118 E1
Bavent Rd *CMBW* SE5 ..... 159 K8
Bawdale Rd *EDUL* SE22 ..... 181 N1
Bawdsey Av *GNTH/NBYPK* IG2 ..... 123 J2
Bawtree Cl *BELMT* SM2 ..... 221 M6
Bawtree Rd *NWCR* SE14 ..... 160 D9
UX/CGN UB8 ..... 131 L2
Bawtry Rd *TRDG/WHET* N20 ..... 98 A4
Baxendale *TRDG/WHET* N20 ..... 97 N4
Baxendale St *BETH* E2 ..... 7 N9
Baxter Av *REDH* RH1 ..... 257 P10
HGDN/ICK UB10 ..... 132 C5
NWDGN UB2 ..... 154 A2
Baxter Cl *CAN/RD* E16 ..... 141 P8
GRH DA9 ..... 188 G2
Bayards *WARL* CR6 ..... 242 B4
Bay Cl *HORL* RH6 ..... 279 P11 🔢
Baycroft Cl *PIN* HA5 ..... 113 K1 🔢
Bayeux *KWD/TDW/WH* KT20 ..... 258 C8
Bayfield Rd *ELTH/MOT* SE9 ..... 162 A10
HORL RH6 ..... 279 P3 🔢
Bayford Cl *HERT/BAY* SG13 ..... 25 K7
HHNE HP2 ..... 35 P5
Bayford Gn *HERT/BAY* SG13 ..... 43 H3
Bayford La *HERT/BAY* SG13 ..... 42 G1
Bayford Rd *WLSDN* NW10 ..... 136 G5 🔢
Bayford St *HACK* E8 ..... 140 A2 🔢
Bayham Pl *CAMTN* NW1 ..... 4 G6
MRDN SM4 ..... 201 L4
SEV TN13 ..... 247 K9
WEA W13 ..... 134 C9 🔢
Bayham Rd *CHSWK* W4 ..... 156 A2 🔢
MRDN SM4 ..... 201 L4
SEV TN13 ..... 247 K9
WEA W13 ..... 134 C9 🔢
Bayham St *CAMTN* NW1 ..... 5 H4
Bayhorne La *HORL* RH6 ..... 280 D6
Bayhurst Dr *NTHWD* HA6 ..... 92 C7
Bayleaf Cl *HPTN* TW12 ..... 176 C8
Bayley's Hl *RSEV* TN14 ..... 264 F8
Bayley St *FITZ* W1T 11 J4
Baylie Ct *HHNE* HP2 ..... 35 P5
Baylie La *HHNE* HP2 ..... 35 P5
Baylis Rd *STHWK* SE1 ..... 18 A3
Bayliss Av *THMD* SE28 ..... 141 M6 🔢
Bayliss Cl *STHGT/OAK* N14 ..... 78 F2
Bayly Rd *DART* DA1 ..... 187 P2
Bay Manor La *WTHK* RM20 ..... 166 E5
Baymans Wd *BRWN* CM15 ..... 107 K3
Bayne Cl *EHAM* E6 ..... 142 C8
Bayne Hl *BEAC* HP9 ..... 89 J8
Baynes Cl *EN* EN1 ..... 79 P5
Baynes Ms *HAMP* NW3 ..... 3 M1 🔢
Baynes St *CAMTN* NW1 ..... 5 H4
Baynham Cl *BXLY* DA5 ..... 186 A2 🔢
Bayonne Rd *HMSMTH* W6 ..... 14 A10
Bay Rd *BFN/LL* DA15 ..... 185 J4
Baytree Cl *BFN/LL* DA15 ..... 185 J4
BMLY BR1 ..... 206 A1
Bay Tree Cl *CHESW* EN7 ..... 61 N3 🔢
LCOL/BKTW AL2 ..... 56 B3
Bay Tree Ct *SL* SL1 ..... 128 B5 🔢
Baytree Rd *BRXS/STRHM* SW2 ..... 158 G10
Bay Tree Wk *WAT* WD17 ..... 72 G4
Baywood Sq *CHIG* IG7 ..... 103 L5
Bazalgette Cl *NWMAL* KT3 ..... 199 P5
Bazalgette Gdns *NWMAL* KT3 ..... 200 A5
Bazely St *POP/IOD* E14 ..... 141 H9
Bazile Rd *WCHMH* N21 ..... 79 H10
Beacham Cl *CHARL* SE7 ..... 162 A5
Beachborough Rd *BMLY* BR1 ..... 183 H7
Beachcroft Rd *WAN* E11 ..... 121 K8
Beach Gv *FELT* TW13 ..... 175 N5
Beachy Rd *BOW* E3 ..... 140 F7
Beacon Cl *BNSTD* SM7 ..... 238 G2
CFSP/GDCR SL9 ..... 90 B8
UX/CGN UB8 ..... 111 N10
Beacon Dr *RDART* DA2 ..... 189 H6
Beaconfield Av *EPP* CM16 ..... 65 J5
Beaconfield Rd *CAMTN* NW1 ..... 4 A4
Beaconfields *SEV* TN13 ..... 264 G2
Beaconfield Wy *EPP* CM16 ..... 65 K5 🔢
Beacon Hl *BRW* CM14 ..... 86 A3
Beacon Ri *SEV* TN13 ..... 265 H2
Beacon Rd *ERITH* DA8 ..... 165 J6
HTHAIR TW6 ..... 174 B2
LEW SE13 ..... 183 J2
WARE SG13 ..... 26 F1 🔢
Beaconsfield *BKHTH/KID* SE3 ..... 161 M5 🔢
CHSWK W4 ..... 155 P2 🔢
Beaconsfield Common La
SLN SL2 ..... 109 H5
Beaconsfield Pl *EW* KT17 ..... 220 B8 🔢
Beaconsfield Rd *BKHTH/KID* SE3 ..... 161 M5
BMLY BR1 ..... 206 A3
BRYLDS KT5 ..... 199 L7
BXLY DA5 ..... 186 G4
CAN/RD E16 ..... 141 J4
CHSWK W4 ..... 156 A2
CROY/NA CR0 ..... 203 L6
EA W5 ..... 155 K1
ED N9 ..... 100 B4
ELTH/MOT SE9 ..... 184 B6
EPSOM KT18 ..... 238 A5
ESH/CLAY KT10 ..... 218 A4
FBAR/BDGN N11 ..... 98 B5
HYS/HAR UB3 ..... 133 K10
LEY E10 ..... 121 H8 🔢
NWMAL KT3 ..... 202 B1 🔢
PEND EN3 ..... 80 C3
SEVS/STOTM N15 ..... 119 H2
SLN SL2 ..... 129 H1
STAL AL1 ..... 39 H6 🔢
TRDG/WHET N20 ..... 98 A4
TWK TW1 ..... 176 F3
WALTH E17 ..... 120 E5
WALW SE17 ..... 18 G8 🔢
WLSDN NW10 ..... 136 A1
WOKS/MYFD GU22 ..... 232 F2
Beaconsfield Wk *FUL/PGN* SW6 ..... 157 J7 🔢
The Beacons *LOU* IG10 ..... 81 M3
Beacontree Av *WALTH* E17 ..... 101 N4
Beacontree Rd *WAN* E11 ..... 121 L5

Beacon Wy *BNSTD* SM7 ..... 238 G2
RKW/CH/CXG WD3 ..... 91 L1
Beadles La *OXTED* RH8 ..... 261 J6
Beadlow Rd *MRDN* SM4 ..... 201 N6 🔢
Beadman Pl *WNWD* SE27 ..... 181 J7 🔢
Beadman St *WNWD* SE27 ..... 181 J7 🔢
Beadnell Rd *FSTH* SE23 ..... 182 C4
Beadon Rd *HAYES* BR2 ..... 205 M4
HMSMTH W6 ..... 156 F3 🔢
Beads Hall La *BRWN* CM15 ..... 86 G8
Beaford Gv *RYNPK* SW20 ..... 201 H3
Beagle Cl *FELT* TW13 ..... 175 J7
RAD WD7 ..... 74 E3
Beagles Cl *STMC/STPC* BR5 ..... 207 N9
Beak St *REGST* W1B 11 H7
Beal Cl *WELL* DA16 ..... 148 C2 🔢
Beale Cl *PLMCR* N13 ..... 99 K8
Beale Pl *BOW* E3 ..... 140 E4 🔢
Beale Rd *BOW* E3 ..... 140 E2
Beales La *WEY* KT13 ..... 196 C10
Beales Rd *GT/LBKH* KT23 ..... 254 A3
Bealings End *BEAC* HP9 ..... 88 C6 🔢
Beam Av *DAGE* RM10 ..... 144 D7
Beaminster Gdns *BARK/HLT* IG6 ..... 122 D7
Beamish Cl *EPP* CM16 ..... 66 D1
Beamish Dr *BUSH* WD23 ..... 94 B2
Beamish Rd *ED* N9 ..... 99 P2
STMC/STPC BR5 ..... 207 M7
Beamway *DAGE* RM10 ..... 144 G7
Beane River Vw *HERT/WAS* SG14 ... 25 K5
Beane Rd *HERT/WAS* SG14 ..... 25 J5
Bean La *RDART* DA2 ..... 188 C3
Bean Rd *BXLYHS* DA6 ..... 163 N10
GRH DA9 ..... 188 G2
Beanshaw *ELTH/MOT* SE9 ..... 184 E9
Beansland Gv *CHDH* RM6 ..... 103 P10
Beara Cl *ROMW/RG* RM7 ..... 124 C4
Beard Rd *RCHPK/HAM* TW10 ..... 177 L8 🔢
Beardell St *NRWD* SE19 ..... 181 N9
Beardsfield *PLSTW* E13 ..... 141 M4 🔢
Beard's Hl *HPTN* TW12 ..... 197 P1
Beards Hill Cl *HPTN* TW12 ..... 197 P1
Beardsley Wy *ACT* W3 ..... 156 A1 🔢
Beardsfield Rd *KUTN/CMB* KT2 ..... 177 K10
Bear Gdns *STHWK* SE1 ..... 12 E9
Bearing Cl *CHIG* IG7 ..... 103 K5
Bearing Wy *CHIG* IG7 ..... 103 K5
Bear La *STHWK* SE1 ..... 12 E9
Bear Rd *FELT* TW13 ..... 175 L7
Bears Den *KWD/TDW/WH* KT20 ..... 239 J8
Bearstead Ri *BROCKY* SE4 ..... 182 C4
Bear St *LSQ/SEVD* WC2H 11 K7
Bearswood End *BEAC* HP9 ..... 88 D7
POTB/CUF EN6 ..... 59 N7
Beasant House *WATN* WD24 ..... 73 J6 🔢
Beasley's Ait *SUN* TW16 ..... 196 G6
Beasley's Ait La *SUN* TW16 ..... 196 G6
Beaton Cl *PECK* SE15 ..... 160 G10
Beatrice Av *STRHM/NOR* SW16 ..... 202 C3
WBLY HA9 ..... 115 K10
Beatrice Cl *PIN* HA5 ..... 113 H2
PLSTW E13 ..... 141 M6 🔢
Beatrice Gdns *GVW* DA11 ..... 190 A8
Beatrice Pl *KENS* W8 ..... 14 C3 🔢
Beatrice Rd *ED* N9 ..... 100 B1
FSBYPK N4 ..... 119 H5
OXTED RH8 ..... 261 K4
RCHPK/HAM TW10 ..... 177 L1 🔢
STHL UB1 ..... 133 N10
STHWK SE1 ..... 19 P6
WALTH E17 ..... 120 F3
Beattie Cl *EBED/NFELT* TW14 ..... 174 G4
GT/LBKH KT23 ..... 235 N10
Beattock Ri *MUSWH* N10 ..... 118 C2 🔢
Beatty Av *GU* GU1 ..... 250 D9
Beatty Rd *CHES/WCR* EN8 ..... 62 A1
STAN HA7 ..... 95 H7
STNW/STAM N16 ..... 119 M9
Beatty St *CAMTN* NW1 ..... 4 G7 🔢
Beattyville Gdns *BARK/HLT* IG6 ..... 122 D2
Beauchamp Gdns
RKW/CH/CXG WD3 ..... 91 K2 🔢
Beauchamp Pl *BORE* WD6 ..... 75 N3 🔢
CHEL SW3 ..... 15 P3
Beauchamp Rd *BTSEA* SW11 ..... 157 P10
E/WMO/HCT KT8 ..... 198 A5
FSTGT E7 ..... 141 N2
SUT SM1 ..... 221 K2
TWK TW1 ..... 176 F5
Beauchamp St *HCIRC* EC1N ..... 12 A4 🔢
Beauchamp Ter *PUT/ROE* SW15 ..... 156 F9 🔢
Beauclare Cl *ASHTD* KT21 ..... 237 J7 🔢
Beauclerc Rd *HMSMTH* W6 ..... 156 E2
Beauclerk Cl *FELT* TW13 ..... 175 J4 🔢
Beaufort *EHAM* E6 ..... 142 D7
Beaufort Av *KTN/HRWW/W* HA3 ..... 114 F2
Beaufort Cl *CDH/CHF* RM16 ..... 167 L2
CHING E4 ..... 100 C7
EA W5 ..... 135 L7
EPP CM16 ..... 66 B3
PUT/ROE SW15 ..... 178 F4
REIG RH2 ..... 257 J9
ROMW/RG RM7 ..... 124 D2
WOKS/MYFD GU22 ..... 232 F2
Beaufort Dr *GLDGN* NW11 ..... 117 K2
HDN NW4 ..... 116 F4
HEST TW5 ..... 153 M7
IL IG1 ..... 122 D6
STRHM/NOR SW16 ..... 180 G10
Beaufort Rd *EA* W5 ..... 135 L7
KUT KT1 ..... 199 K4
RCHPK/HAM TW10 ..... 177 H7
REIG RH2 ..... 257 J9
RSLP HA4 ..... 112 E7 🔢
TWK TW1 ..... 177 H5
WOKS/MYFD GU22 ..... 232 F2
Beauforts *EGH* TW20 ..... 171 P8
Beaufort St *CHEL* SW3 ..... 15 P5
Beaufort Wy *EW* KT17 ..... 220 D8
Beaufoy Rd *TOTM* N17 ..... 99 M8 🔢
Beaufoy Wk *LBTH* SE11 ..... 17 M7
Beaulieu Cl *CAN/RD* E16 ..... 141 N10 🔢
CDALE/KGS NW9 ..... 116 B2
DTCH/LGLY SL3 ..... 149 P8 🔢
DTCH/LGLY SL3 ..... 149 K7 🔢
HSLWW TW4 ..... 175 N1
MTCM CR4 ..... 202 B1 🔢
OXHEY WD19 ..... 93 K2 🔢
TWK TW1 ..... 177 J2 🔢
Beaulieu Dr *PIN* HA5 ..... 113 L4
WAB EN9 ..... 62 C9
Beaulieu Gdns *WCHMH* N21 ..... 99 K1
Beaulieu Pl *CHSWK* W4 ..... 155 P2 🔢
Beauly Wy *ROM* RM1 ..... 104 F9
Beaumont Av *ALP/SUD* HA0 ..... 115 H10
RCHPK/HAM TW9 ..... 155 U9 🔢
RYLN/HDSTN HA2 ..... 114 A4
STAL AL1 ..... 38 G5
WKENS W14 ..... 14 C7
Beaumont Cl *CRAWW* RH11 ..... 283 H10 🔢
GPK RM2 ..... 105 K10
Beaumont Crs *RAIN* RM13 ..... 145 H1 🔢
WKENS W14 ..... 14 C7
Beaumont Dr *ASHF* TW15 ..... 174 E8 🔢
GVW DA11 ..... 190 B3
Beaumont Gdns
RBRW/HUT CM13 ..... 87 P10 🔢
Beaumont Ga *RAD* WD7 ..... 74 F1
Beaumont Gv *WCHPL* E1 ..... 140 C10
Beaumont Ms *CAVSQ/HST* W1G ..... 10 D3 🔢

Beaumont Park Dr
HLWW/ROY CM19 ..... 45 N1
Beaumont Pl *BAR* EN5 ..... 77 J5
FITZ W1T 11 H1
ISLW TW7 ..... 176 E1
Beaumont Ri *ARCH* N19 ..... 118 E6
Beaumont Rd *BROX* EN10 ..... 43 N10
CHSWK W4 ..... 155 P2
GVW DA11 ..... 190 B3
LEY E10 ..... 120 G5 🔢
LEY E10 ..... 120 G5 🔢
LEY E10 ..... 121 H5 🔢
NRWD SE19 ..... 181 K9
PLSTW E13 ..... 141 N5
PUR/KEN CR8 ..... 223 H8
SL SL1 ..... 129 J7
STMC/STPC BR5 ..... 206 C8
WDSR SL4 ..... 149 H8 🔢
WIM/MER SW19 ..... 179 H3
Beaumonts *REDH* RH1 ..... 276 A8 🔢
Beaumont Sq *WCHPL* E1 ..... 140 C7
Beaumont St *MHST* W1U 10 D3
Beaumont Vw *CHESW* EN7 ..... 61 L2 🔢
Beauvais Ter *NTHLT* UB5 ..... 133 L5 🔢
Beauval Rd *EDUL* SE22 ..... 181 N2
Beaverbank Rd *ELTH/MOT* SE9 ..... 184 G4
Beaver Cl *HPTN* TW12 ..... 198 A1
PGE/AN SE20 ..... 181 P10 🔢
Beavers Cl *GUW* GU2 ..... 249 K9 🔢
Beavers La *HSLWW* TW4 ..... 153 K9
Beaverwood Rd *CHST* BR7 ..... 185 H6
Beavor La *HMSMTH* W6 ..... 156 D3
Beazley Cl *WARE* SG12 ..... 26 D1 🔢
Bebbington Rd
WOOL/PLUM SE18 ..... 163 H3 🔢
Beblets Cl *ORP* BR6 ..... 227 J3
Beccles St *POP/IOD* E14 ..... 140 E8
Bec Cl *RSLP* HA4 ..... 113 L8
Beck Cl *LEW* SE13 ..... 160 G7
Beck Ct *BECK* BR3 ..... 204 C3
Beckenham Gdns *ED* N9 ..... 99 M4
Beckenham Gv *HAYES* BR2 ..... 205 J2
Beckenham Hill Rd *BECK* BR3 ..... 182 G9
Beckenham La *HAYES* BR2 ..... 205 K2
Beckenham Place Pk *BECK* BR3 ..... 182 G10
Beckenham Rd *BECK* BR3 ..... 204 C1
WWKM BR4 ..... 204 G5
Beckenshaw Gdns *BNSTD* SM7 ..... 239 P1
Becket Av *EHAM* E6 ..... 142 D5
Becket Cl *RBRW/HUT* CM13 ..... 107 H7
SNWD SE25 ..... 203 P6
Becket Fold *HRW* HA1 ..... 114 E3 🔢
Beckets Sq *BERK* HP4 ..... 33 M3 🔢
Becket St *STHWK* SE1 ..... 18 G3
Becket Av *FUL/PGN* SW6 ..... 241 J1 🔢
Becket Cl *BXLY* DA17 ..... 163 P2 🔢
STRHM/NOR SW16 ..... 202 A2
WLSDN NW10 ..... 136 A1 🔢
Beckett La *CRAWW* RH11 ..... 283 N4
Becketts *HERT/WAS* SG14 ..... 25 H6
Becketts Cl *EBED/NFELT* TW14 ..... 175 J2
ORP BR6 ..... 207 J10
Becketts Pl *KUT* KT1 ..... 199 J1
Beckett Wk *BECK* BR3 ..... 182 D9
Beckford Dr *STMC/STPC* BR5 ..... 206 C7
Beckford Pl *WALW* SE17 ..... 18 F8 🔢
Beckford Rd *CROY/NA* CR0 ..... 203 N6
Beckingham Rd *GUW* GU2 ..... 249 M9
Beck La *BECK* BR3 ..... 204 C3
Beckley Cl *GVE* DA12 ..... 191 L5 🔢
Becklow Rd *SHB* W12 ..... 156 C1
Beckman Cl *RSEV* TN14 ..... 246 D1
Beck River Pk *BECK* BR3 ..... 204 F1 🔢
Beck Rd *HACK* E8 ..... 140 A3
Beckton Rd *CAN/RD* E16 ..... 141 J6
Beck Wy *BECK* BR3 ..... 204 E3
Beckway Rd *STRHM/NOR* SW16 ..... 202 E2
Beckway St *WALW* SE17 ..... 19 H6
Beckwith Rd *HNHL* SE24 ..... 181 L2
Beclands Rd *TOOT* SW17 ..... 180 B9
Becmead Av *KTN/HRWW/W* HA3 ..... 114 D1
STRHM/NOR SW16 ..... 180 E7
Becondale Rd *NRWD* SE19 ..... 181 M8
Becontree Av *BCTR* RM8 ..... 123 N7
Bective Rd *FSTGT* E7 ..... 121 M9
PUT/ROE SW15 ..... 157 J10
Becton Pl *ERITH* DA8 ..... 164 C6
Bedale Cl *CRAWW* RH11 ..... 283 M9
Bedale Rd *ENC/FH* EN2 ..... 79 K4 🔢
HARH RM3 ..... 105 P6
Bedale St *STHWK* SE1 ..... 12 G10 🔢
Beddington Farm Rd
CROY/NA CR0 ..... 202 F8
Beddington Gdns *CAR* SM5 ..... 222 B3
WLGTN SM6 ..... 222 C3
Beddington Gn *STMC/STPC* BR5 ..... 207 J1
Beddington Gv *WLGTN* SM6 ..... 222 E4
Beddington La *CROY/NA* CR0 ..... 202 D6
MTCM CR4 ..... 202 D6
Beddington Rd *GDMY/SEVK* IG3 ..... 123 J5
STMC/STPC BR5 ..... 207 H1
Beddlestead La *WARL* CR6 ..... 243 L4
Bede Cl *PIN* HA5 ..... 93 L9 🔢
Bedens Rd *SCUP* DA14 ..... 185 P9
Bede Rd *CHDH* RM6 ..... 123 M4
Bedfont Cl *EBED/NFELT* TW14 ..... 174 D2
MTCM CR4 ..... 202 B2
Bedfont Ct *STWL/WRAY* TW19 ..... 151 N2
Bedfont Green Cl
EBED/NFELT TW14 ..... 174 D4
Bedfont La *EBED/NFELT* TW14 ..... 174 C3
FELT TW13 ..... 174 C3
STWL/WRAY TW19 ..... 174 A2
Bedford Av *AMS* HP6 ..... 69 P5
BAR EN5 ..... 77 J9
SL SL1 ..... 128 F8
YEAD UB4 ..... 133 J8
Bedfordbury *CHCR* WC2N 11 K7
Bedford Cl *CHSWK* W4 ..... 156 B5 🔢
MUSWH N10 ..... 98 B8
RKW/CH/CXG WD3 ..... 70 E4
WOKN/KNAP GU21 ..... 231 P1
Bedford Ct *CHCR* WC2N 11 L8
Bedford Crs *PEND* EN3 ..... 80 D1
Bedford Dr *SLN* SL2 ..... 108 G10
Bedford Gdns *HCH* RM12 ..... 125 K4
KENS W8 ..... 14 B1
Bedford Hl *BAL* SW12 ..... 180 C5
Bedford La *ASC* SL5 ..... 192 G5
Bedford Pk *CROY/NA* CR0 ..... 203 K8
Bedford Park Rd *STAL* AL1 ..... 38 G6
Bedford Pl *CROY/NA* CR0 ..... 203 L8
RSQ WC1B 11 L3
Bedford Rd *BFN/LL* DA15 ..... 185 H6
CEND/HSY/T N8 ..... 118 C4
CHSWK W4 ..... 156 A1
CLAP SW4 ..... 158 F10
DART DA1 ..... 187 P3
ED N9 ..... 100 A1
EFNCH N2 ..... 117 J2
EHAM E6 ..... 142 D3
GRAYS RM17 ..... 167 N4
GU GU1 ..... 267 P1
GVW DA11 ..... 190 C5
HRW HA1 ..... 114 C4
IL IG1 ..... 122 B8
MLHL NW7 ..... 96 F4
NTHWD HA6 ..... 92 B5
ORP BR6 ..... 207 L9
RSLP HA4 ..... 112 G6
SEVS/STOTM N15 ..... 119 J3
STAL AL1 ..... 38 G7

SWFD E18... 101 M10
WALTH E17... 100 F10
WDGN N22... 98 F9
WEA W13... 134 C9
WHTN TW2... 176 C6
WPK KT4... 200 F9
Bedford Rw FSBYW WC1X... 11 P3
Bedford Sq BERK HP4... 11 K4
Bedford St BERK HP4... 34 M8
COVGDN WC2E... 11 L7
WATN WD24... 73 J5
Bedford Wy STPAN WC1H... 11 K2
Bedgebury Gdns
WIM/MER SW19... 179 H5
Bedgebury Rd ELTH/MOT SE9... 162 A10
Bedivere Rd BMLY BR1... 183 M6
Bedlow Wy CROY/NA CR0... 222 C1
Bedmond La ABLGY WD5... 55 H3
STALW/RED AL3... 37 N8
Bedmond Rd ABLGY WD5... 54 C3
HHS/BOV HP3... 36 E8
Bedonwell Rd BELV DA17... 163 P5
BXLYHN DA7... 164 A5
Bedser Cl THHTH CR7... 203 K3
WOKN/KNAP GU21... 232 D2
Bedser Dr NTHLT UB5... 114 C10
Bedster Gdns E/WMO/HCT KT8... 198 A2
Bedwardine Rd NRWD SE19... 181 M10
Bedwell Av BERK HP4... 42 B4
HERT/BAY SG13... 42 B2
Bedwell Cl WGCE AL7... 23 H6
Bedwell Rd BELV DA17... 164 B4
TOTM N17... 99 H9
Beeby Rd CAN/RD E16... 141 N7
Beech Av ACT W3... 136 B10
BFN/LL DA15... 185 K3
BH/WHM TN16... 244 A5
BKHH IG9... 101 N5
BTFD TW8... 154 G6
EHSLY KT24... 253 L6
ENC/FH EN2... 79 H1
RAD WD7... 56 F9
RBRW/HUT CM13... 107 L4
RSLP HA4... 113 J6
SAND/SEL CR2... 223 L7
SWLY BR8... 208 G4
TRDG/WHET N20... 97 P2
UPMR RM14... 126 A8
Beech Bottom STALW/RED AL3... 38 C3
Beech Cl ASHF TW15... 174 B8
BF/WBF KT14... 215 P8
CAR SM5... 202 A9
COB KT11... 217 P8
DEPT SE8... 160 E5
DORK RH4... 272 E1
ED N9... 79 P10
EHSLY KT24... 253 L4
HARP AL5... 20 B6
HAT AL10... 40 D5
HCH RM12... 125 J8
LOU IG10... 82 E7
PUT/ROE SW15... 178 D3
RYNPK SW20... 178 F9
STWL/WRAY TW19... 173 N3
SUN TW16... 197 L2
WDR/YW UB7... 152 B2
WOT/HER KT12... 217 K1
Beech Close Ct COB KT11... 217 N7
SAND/SEL CR2... 223 M2
Beech Ct BERK HP4... 34 A4
STALW/WH AL4... 21 J4
Beechcroft ASHTD KT21... 237 L5
BERK HP4... 33 P6
CHST BR7... 184 D10
Beechcroft Av BXLYHN DA7... 164 E7
GLDGN NW11... 117 J5
NWMAL KT3... 199 P1
PUR/KEN CR8... 241 L1
RKW/CH/CXG WD3... 72 D10
RYLN/HDSTN HA2... 113 P5
STHL UB1... 133 N10
TIL RM18... 169 K3
Beechcroft Cl ASC SL5... 192 C4
HEST TW5... 153 M6
ORP BR6... 226 G1
STRHM/NOR SW16... 180 C8
Beechcroft Dr RGUW GU3... 267 J3
Beechcroft Gdns WBLY HA9... 115 L8
Beechcroft Rd BUSH WD23... 73 M9
CHSGTN KT9... 199 L10
CSHM HP5... 50 F6
MORT/ESHN SW14... 155 P9
ORP BR6... 226 G1
SWFD E18... 101 N10
TOOT SW17... 160 A6
Beechdale WCHMH N21... 98 G3
Beechdale Rd BRXS/STRHM SW2... 180 A2
Beech Dell HAYES BR2... 226 C1
Beechdene KWD/TDW/WH KT20... 238 E8
Beech Dr BERK HP4... 33 P6
BORE WD6... 75 L6
EFNCH N2... 98 A10
KWD/TDW/WH KT20... 239 J8
REIG RH2... 257 N10
RPLY/SEND GU23... 233 J10
SBW CM21... 29 M3
Beechen Cliff Wy ISLW TW7... 154 E7
Beechengrove PIN HA5... 113 N1
Beechen Gv WAT WD17... 73 J7
Beechenlea La SWLY BR8... 209 H4
Beechen Pl FSTH SE23... 182 B5
The Beeches BAR SM5... 221 P4
Beeches Cl KWD/TDW/WH KT20... 239 K9
PGE/AN SE20... 182 F3
Beeches Crs CRAWE RH10... 283 P9
Beeches Dr SLN SL2... 108 G3
Beeches Pk BEAC HP9... 88 C3
Beeches Rd CHEAM SM3... 201 H8
SLN SL2... 108 G10
TOOT SW17... 179 P6
The Beeches BNSTD SM7... 239 L2
BRW CM14... 106 G4
LCOL/BKTW AL2... 56 C3
LHD/OX KT22... 236 D10
RKW/CH/CXG WD3... 71 J9
TIL RM18... 168 G5
Beeches Wk CAR SM5... 221 N6
Beechey Cl CRAWE RH10... 285 J2
Beechey Wy DTCH/LGLY SL3... 110 B10
SLN SL1... 128 A5
Beeches Wd KWD/TDW/WH KT20... 239 K8
Beechey Cl CRAWE RH10... 285 J2
Beech Farm Dr STALW/WH AL4... 21 J6
Beech Farm Rd WARL CR6... 243 J6
Beechfield BNSTD SM7... 26 F9
HOD EN11... 40 A7
KGLGY WD4... 54 A6
SBW CM21... 29 L6
Beechfield Gdns ROMW/RG RM7... 124 D5
Beechfield Rd BMLY BR1... 205 P2
CAT SE6... 182 A4
ERITH DA8... 164 F6
FSBYPK N4... 119 K4
HHW HP1... 35 L1
WARE SG12... 26 E1
WGCE AL7... 23 H1
Beechfield Wk WAB EN9... 81 J1
Beech Gdns CRAWE RH10... 285 P6
DAGE RM10... 144 C2
EA W5... 155 K1
WOKN/KNAP GU21... 232 B1
Beech Gv ADL/WDHM KT15... 215 L1
AMSS HP7... 69 H5
BARK/HLT IG6... 103 H7
CHOB/PIR GU24... 230 B6
CTHM CR3... 259 L2
EPSOM KT18... 238 C1
GT/LBKH KT23... 253 P5
GUW GU2... 249 L10
MTCM CR4... 202 E5
NWMAL KT3... 200 A3
SOCK/AV RM15... 166 B1
Beech Hall Crs CHING E4... 101 J8
Beech Hall Rd CHING E4... 101 H8
Beech Hl EBAR EN4... 77 N4
WOKS/MYFD GU22... 232 A9
Beech Hill Av EBAR EN4... 77 N5
Beech Hill Gdns WAB EN9... 81 N3
Beech Hill Rd ASC SL5... 192 D6
Beechhill Rd ELTH/MOT SE9... 184 D1
Beech Holme CRAWE RH10... 285 P6
Beech Holt LHD/OX KT22... 237 H8
Beech House La STALW/WH AL4... 21 L4
Beech House Rd CROY/NA CR0... 203 L10
Beech Hyde La STALW/WH AL4... 21 L4
Beechlands CI HART DA3... 211 M5
Beech La BEAC HP9... 89 K8
GUW GU2... 267 P3
Beechlawn GU GU1... 268 C1
Beechmeads COB KT11... 217 L9
Beechmont Av VW GU25... 194 A6
Beechmont CI BMLY BR1... 183 K8
Beechmont Rd SEV TN13... 265 J5
Beechmore Gdns CHEAM SM3... 200 C9
Beechmore Rd BTSEA SW11... 158 A7
Beechmount Av HNWL W7... 134 C2
Beecholme KWD/TDW/WH KT20... 202 C1
Beecholme Av MTCM CR4... 202 C1
Beechpark Wy WAT WD17... 72 F3
Beech Pl EPP CM16... 65 J7
STALW/RED AL3... 38 C3
Beech Rd BH/WHM TN16... 243 P8
DART DA1... 187 L4
DTCH/LGLY SL3... 150 B1
EBED/NFELT TW14... 174 F3
EPSOM KT18... 238 C1
FBAR/BDGN N11... 98 F1
ORP BR6... 227 K4
REDH RH1... 258 D2
REIG RH2... 257 K7
SEV TN13... 265 J1
STALW/RED AL3... 38 D3
STRHM/NOR SW16... 202 F2
WATN WD24... 73 H3
WEY KT13... 216 E1
Beechrow KUTN/CMB KT2... 177 K7
Beechside CRAWE RH10... 283 P6
Beech St ROMW/RG RM7... 124 D2
Beech Street (below) STBT EC1A... 12 D1
Beechtree Av EGH TW20... 171 N9
Beech Tree Cl IS N1... 5 P1
STAN HA7... 95 H6
Beech Tree Gld CHING E4... 101 L2
Beech Tree La STA TW18... 195 L2
Beechtree La STALW/RED AL3... 37 J8
Beech Tree Pl SUT SM1... 221 L2
Beechvale CI NFNCH/WDSP N12... 97 P5
Beech Wk DART DA1... 165 H10
EW KT17... 220 D4
MLHL NW7... 96 A7
Beech Wy EW KT17... 238 C1
FELT TW13... 175 P6
Beechway BXLY DA5... 185 N2
Beechway GU GU1... 250 E9
Beech Wy WLSDN NW10... 136 A2
Beechwaye Gdns RYLN/HDSTN HA2... 114 A8
Beechwood Av AMS HP6... 69 P4
COUL/CHIP CR5... 240 C1
FNCH N3... 117 J1
GFD/PVL UB6... 134 A5
HHS/HAR UB3... 132 E9
KWD/TDW/WH KT20... 239 K7
ORP BR6... 227 H3
POTB/CUF EN6... 59 L9
RCH/KEW TW9... 155 M7
RKW/CH/CXG WD3... 70 E8
RSLP HA4... 112 G1
RYLN/HDSTN HA2... 114 A8
STA TW18... 173 L9
STAL AL1... 38 C4
SUN TW16... 175 H9
THHTH CR7... 203 J4
UX/CGN UB8... 132 A8
WEY KT13... 216 F1
Beechwood CI AMS HP6... 69 P5
CHESW EN7... 61 M2
HERT/BAY SG13... 25 N5
MLHL NW7... 96 B6
SURB KT6... 199 H7
WEY KT13... 216 F1
WOKN/KNAP GU21... 231 K3
Beechwood Ct BXLYHN DA7... 163 N9
Beechwood Dr COB KT11... 217 P7
HAYES BR2... 226 A1
WFD IG8... 101 L6
Beechwood Gdns CLAY IG5... 122 C3
CTHM CR3... 241 P8
RAIN RM13... 145 J7
RYLN/HDSTN HA2... 114 A8
SL SL1... 149 K1
Beechwood Gv ACT W3... 136 B9
Beechwood La WARL CR6... 242 C5
Beechwood Mnr WEY KT13... 216 F1
Beechwood Ms ED N9... 99 P8
Beechwood Pk HHS/BOV HP3... 35 J10
LHD/OX KT22... 237 H8
RKW/CH/CXG WD3... 71 J9
SWFD E18... 101 L10
Beechwood Ri CHST BR7... 184 E7
WATN WD24... 73 J2
Beechwood Rd BEAC HP9... 88 B9
CEND/HSY/T N8... 118 E2
CTHM CR3... 241 P8
HACK E8... 7 L2
SAND/SEL CR2... 223 M5
SLN SL2... 129 J2
VW GU25... 193 N7
WOKN/KNAP GU21... 231 K4
Beechwood Vls REDH RH1... 276 B10
Beechworth CI HAMP NW3... 117 J7
Beechy Lees Rd RSEV TN14... 247 L3
Beecot La WOT/HER KT12... 197 K9
Beecroft Rd BROCKY SE4... 182 D1
Beehive Cha BRWN CM15... 87 J1
Beehive CI BORE WD6... 75 J10
HACK E8... 7 L3
HGDN/ICK UB10... 132 A2
Beehive Gn WGCE AL7... 23 K7
Beehive La REDBR IG4... 122 C3
WGCE AL7... 23 K8
Beehive Ring Rd CRAWE RH10... 284 C1
Beehive Rd CHESW EN7... 61 J4
STA TW18... 173 J8
Beehive Wy REIG RH2... 275 L4
Beeken Dene ORP BR6... 226 F10
Beel CI AMSS HP7... 69 P5
Beeleigh Rd MRDN SM4... 201 L4
Beesfield La EYN DA4... 209 P8
Beeston CI OXHEY WD19... 93 L5
Beeston Dr CHES/WCR EN8... 62 C3
Beeston PI BGVA SW1W... 16 F4
Beeston Wy EBED/NFELT TW14... 175 K2
Beethoven Rd BORE WD6... 95 H1
Beethoven St NKENS W10... 2 D9
Beeton CI PIN HA5... 93 P8
Begbie Rd BKHTH/KID SE3... 161 P7
Beggars Bush La WATW WD18... 72 A6
Beggarshouse La HORL RH6... 278 F7
Beggars La BH/WHM TN16... 262 G1
CHOB/PIR GU24... 213 H7
SHGR GU5... 270 F4
Beggar's Roost La SUT SM1... 221 K3
Begonia CI EHAM E6... 142 B7
Begonia PI HPTN TW12... 175 P9
Behenna CI CRAWW RH11... 283 H8
Beira St BAL SW12... 180 C3
Bekesbourne St POP/IOD E14... 140 B8
Belcher Rd HOD EN11... 44 F2
Belchers La WAB EN9... 45 P10
Belcroft CI BMLY BR1... 183 L10
Beldam Bridge Rd
CHOB/PIR GU24... 212 F9
Beldam Haw RSEV TN14... 228 B7
Beldham Gdns E/WMO/HCT KT8... 198 A3
Belfairs Dr CHDH RM6... 123 M5
Belfast Av SL SL1... 129 H8
Belfast Rd SNWD SE25... 204 A4
STNW/STAM N16... 119 N1
Belfont Wk HOLWY N7... 5 L1
Belford Gv WOOL/PLUM SE18... 162 D2
Belford Rd BORE WD6... 75 J10
Belfort Rd PECK SE15... 160 B1
Belfry Av DEN/HRF UB9... 91 K9
Belgrade Rd HPTN TW12... 198 A1
STNW/STAM N16... 119 M9
Belgrave Av GPK RM2... 125 K1
WOTN...
Belgrave CI ACT W3... 155 P1
MLHL NW7... 96 A6
STALW/WH AL4... 39 H2
STHGT/OAK N14... 98 D9
STMC/STPC BR5... 207 M4
WOT/HER KT12... 217 J1
Belgrave Crs SUN TW16... 197 J1
Belgrave Gdns STHGT/OAK N14... 78 E9
STJWD NW8... 3 H6
Belgrave Mnr WOKS/MYFD GU22... 232 B9
Belgrave Ms KTBR SW1X... 16 D3
Belgrave Ms South KTBR SW1X... 16 C3
Belgrave Ms West KTBR SW1X... 16 C3
Belgrave PI KTBR SW1X... 16 D4
Belgrave Rd BARN SW13... 156 C6
HSLWW TW4... 153 N9
IL IG1... 122 D7
LEY E10... 121 H6
MTCM CR4... 201 N3
PIM SW1V... 16 G6
PLSTW E13... 141 P6
SL SL1... 129 K9
SNWD SE25... 203 N4
SUN TW16... 197 J1
WALTH E17... 121 K6
Belgrave Sq KTBR SW1X... 16 C3
Belgrave St WCHPL E1... 140 C7
Belgrave Wk MTCM CR4... 201 N3
Belgravia CI BAR EN5... 77 J2
Belgravia Gdns BMLY BR1... 183 K5
Belgravia Ms KUT KT1... 199 J4
Belgrove St CAMTN NW1... 5 J4
Belham Rd KGLGY WD4... 54 A4
Belinda Rd BRXN/ST SW9... 159 J9
Belitha Vls IS N1... 5 L5
Bellamy CI ECT SW5... 14 D8
EDGW HA8... 95 P4
HGDN/ICK UB10... 112 B8
WAT WD17... 73 H5
Bellamy Dr STAN HA7... 94 G9
Bellamy Rd CHES/WCR EN8... 62 D5
CHING E4... 100 G7
ENC/FH EN2... 79 L6
Bellamy St BAL SW12... 180 C3
Bellasis Av BRXS/STRHM SW2... 180 A3
Bell Av HARH RM3... 105 J9
WDR/YW UB7... 152 A2
Bell Bridge Rd CHERT KT16... 195 J3
Bell CI ABLGY WD5... 54 C3
GRH DA9... 188 C1
PIN HA5... 113 K1
SLN SL2... 129 N7
Bellclose Rd WDR/YW UB7... 151 P1
Bell Common EPP CM16... 64 G7
Bell Crs COUL/CHIP CR5... 240 C7
Bell Dr WAND/EARL SW18... 179 H3
Belle Vue GFD/PVL UB6... 134 C3
Belle Vue CI STA TW18... 195 K10
Belle Vue La BUSH WD23... 94 C2
Bellevue Pk THHTH CR7... 203 K3
Belle Vue PI SL SL1... 149 L2
Bellevue Rd BARN SW13... 156 D10
Belle Vue Rd CRW RM5... 104 D7
Bellevue Rd EMPK RM11... 125 N6
FBAR/BDGN N11... 98 B5
KUT KT1... 199 K3
Belle Vue Rd ORP BR6... 226 D6
Belle Vue Rd TOOT SW17... 180 A3
Belle Vue Rd WALTH E17... 101 K1
WARE SG12... 26 E2
Bellevue Rd WEA W13... 134 G2
Belle Vue St TOOT SW17... 179 M6
Bellfield CROY/NA CR0... 203 H8
Bellfield Av KTN/HRWW/W HA3... 94 C7
Bellfield Gdns HLWE CM17... 47 M2
Bellfields Rd GU GU1... 250 A8
Bell Gdns STMC/STPC BR5... 207 M5
Bellgate Ms KTTN NW5... 118 C9
Bell Gn SYD SE26... 182 D7
Bell Green La SYD SE26... 182 E8
Bellhouse La BRW CM14... 86 D9
Bell House Rd ROMW/RG RM7... 124 D4
Bellina Ms KTTN NW5... 118 C9
Bellingdon Rd CSHM HP5... 50 D5
Bellingham Gn CAT SE6... 182 B8
Bellingham Rd CAT SE6... 183 J6
Bell La ABLGY WD5... 55 H5
BERK HP4... 33 K4
BRKMPK AL9... 41 K10
BROX EN10... 44 D7
CAN/RD E16... 141 M10
HDN NW4... 116 C2
HERT/WAS SG14... 25 L5
HOD EN11... 44 F1
LCOL/BKTW AL2... 57 K10
LHD/OX KT22... 236 C9
PEND EN3... 79 L1
TWK TW1... 176 F4
WCHPL E1... 13 L4
WDSR SL4... 148 C5
Bell Lane CI LHD/OX KT22... 236 C9
Bellman Av GVE DA12... 191 H4
Bellmarsh Rd ADL/WDHM KT15... 215 L3
Bell Mdw NRWD SE19... 181 M7
Bell Meadow GDST RH9... 260 B8
Bellmount Wood Av WAT WD17... 72 F5
Belloc CI CRAWE RH10... 284 C6
Bello CI BRXS/STRHM SW2... 181 J4
Bellot St GNWCH SE10... 161 L4
Bellring CI BELV DA17... 164 E5
Bell Rd E/WMO/HCT KT8... 198 D2
ENC/FH EN2... 79 J1
HSLW TW3... 154 A9
Bells Al FUL/PGN SW6... 157 L8
Bells Gdn PECK SE15... 159 M6
Bells Hill BAR EN5... 76 B6
Bells Hill Gn SLN SL2... 129 M1
Bells La DTCH/LGLY SL3... 150 A3
Bell St BAY/PAD... 9 N3
REIG RH2... 257 K10
SBW CM21... 29 P1
Bellswood La IVER SL0... 130 C3
Belltrees Gv STRHM/NOR SW16... 180 C8
Bell Vw STALE/WH AL4... 39 J6
WDSR SL4... 148 E8
Bell Water Ga WOOL/PLUM SE18... 162 D2
Bellwether La REDH RH1... 277 J9
Bellwood Rd PECK SE15... 160 C10
Bell Yd LINN WC2A... 12 A6
Belmont SLN SL2... 128 E7
Belmont Av ALP/SUD HA0... 135 L3
EBAR EN4... 78 A9
ED N9... 99 P2
GUW GU2... 249 L7
NWDGN UB2... 153 M2
NWMAL KT3... 200 D5
PLMGR N13... 98 F6
TOTM N17... 119 K1
UPMR RM14... 125 N7
WELL DA16... 163 H8
Belmont CI CHING E4... 101 K6
CLAP SW4... 158 D9
EBAR EN4... 78 A9
TRDG/WHET N20... 97 L2
UX/CGN UB8... 131 N1
WFD IG8... 101 N5
Belmont Gv CHSWK W4... 156 A3
LEW SE13... 161 J9
Belmont Hl LEW SE13... 161 J9
STAL AL1... 38 C7
Belmont La CHST BR7... 184 F7
STAN HA7... 95 H8
Belmont Pk LEW SE13... 161 J10
Belmont Park CI LEW SE13... 161 K10
Belmont Park Rd LEY E10... 120 E4
Belmont Ri BELMT SM2... 221 J4
Belmont Rd BECK BR3... 204 D2
BELMT SM2... 221 K6
BUSH WD23... 73 M8
CHST BR7... 184 E8
CLAP SW4... 158 D9
CSHM HP5... 50 G5
ERITH DA8... 164 B10
GRAYS RM17... 191 L4
HCH RM12... 125 J3
HHS/BOV HP3... 35 P9
IL IG1... 122 F8
KTN/HRWW/W HA3... 114 E1
LHD/OX KT22... 236 F8
REIG RH2... 275 M1
SEVS/STOTM N15... 119 K2
SNWD SE25... 204 A3
UX/CGN UB8... 131 N2
WHTN TW2... 176 C5
WLGTN SM6... 222 D2
Belmont St CAMTN NW1... 4 D3
Belmont Ter CHSWK W4... 156 A3
Belmor BORE WD6... 75 M9
Belmore Av WOKS/MYFD GU22... 232 G2
YEAD UB4... 133 H8
Beloe CI BARN SW13... 156 D10
Belsham St HOM E9... 140 B1
Belsize Av HAMP NW3... 3 N1
PLMGR N13... 98 G7
WEA W13... 154 G2
Belsize CI HHS/BOV HP3... 36 B7
STALW/WH AL4... 39 H1
Belsize Court Garages
HAMP NW3... 117 N10
Belsize Crs HAMP NW3... 117 N10
Belsize Gdns SUT SM1... 221 L1
Belsize Gv HAMP NW3... 3 P1
Belsize La HAMP NW3... 3 M1
Belsize Ms HAMP NW3... 3 M1
Belsize Pk HAMP NW3... 3 M1
Belsize Park Gdns HAMP NW3... 3 N1
Belsize Park Ms HAMP NW3... 3 M1
Belsize PI HAMP NW3... 117 N10
Belsize Rd HHS/BOV HP3... 36 B7
KIL/WHAMP NW6... 3 K4
KTN/HRWW/W HA3... 94 C8
Belsize Sq HAMP NW3... 3 M2
Belsize Ter HAMP NW3... 3 M1
Belson Rd WOOL/PLUM SE18... 162 C8
Beltana Dr GVE DA12... 191 H7
Belthorn Crs BAL SW12... 180 D3
Beltinge Rd HARH RM3... 105 M1
Beltona Gdns CHES/WCR EN8... 62 C1
Belton Rd BERK HP4... 33 M4
CRICK NW2... 136 D1
FSTGT E7... 141 K7
SCUP DA14... 185 K7
TOTM N17... 119 J1
WAN E11... 121 K9
Belton Wy BOW E3... 140 F7
Beltran Rd FUL/PGN SW6... 157 L8
Beltwood Rd BELV DA17... 164 D3
Belvedere Av CLAY IG5... 102 E10
WIM/MER SW19... 179 H6
Belvedere Buildings STHWK SE1... 18 D2
Belvedere CI ESH/CLAY KT10... 218 A2
GUW GU2... 249 N8
GVE DA12... 190 F4
TEDD TW11... 176 D8
WEY KT13... 216 B2
Belvedere Dr WIM/MER SW19... 179 H6
Belvedere Gdns E/WMO/HCT KT8... 197 N5
LCOL/BKTW AL2... 55 N3
Belvedere Gv WIM/MER SW19... 179 H6
Belvedere Ms PECK SE15... 160 B9
Belvedere Rd BH/WHM TN16... 244 E4
BRW CM14... 106 E4
BXLYHN DA7... 164 A9
HNWL W7... 154 D2
LEY E10... 120 D6
NRWD SE19... 181 N10
STHWK SE1... 17 L9
THMD SE28... 143 H10
Belvedere Sq WIM/MER SW19... 179 H6
Belvedere Strd CDALE/KGS NW9... 96 C10
Belvedere Wy
KTN/HRWW/W HA3... 115 K4
Belvoir CI ELTH/MOT SE9... 184 C4
Belvoir Rd EDUL SE22... 181 P3
Belvue CI NTHLT UB5... 133 P2
Belvue Rd NTHLT UB5... 133 P2
Bembridge CI KIL/WHAMP NW6... 2 A3
Bembridge Gdns RSLP HA4... 112 C7
Bemerton St IS N1... 5 N5
Bemish Rd PUT/ROE SW15... 156 G9
Bempton Dr RSLP HA4... 113 J7
Bemsted Rd WALTH E17... 120 E1
Benares Rd WOOL/PLUM SE18... 163 J3
Benbow CI STAL AL1... 38 C6
Benbow St DEPT SE8... 160 F5
Benbow Wy UX/CGN UB8... 131 M7
Benbrick Rd GUW GU2... 267 M1
Benbury CI BMLY BR1... 183 J5
The Bence EGH TW20... 194 C3
Bench Fld SAND/SEL CR2... 223 N2
Bench Manor Crs
CFSP/GDCR SL9... 89 P10
Bencombe Rd PUR/KEN CR8... 223 H10
Bencroft CHESW EN7... 61 J2
Bencroft Rd
STRHM/NOR SW16... 180 D10
Bencurtis Pk WWKM BR4... 205 J10
Bendall Ms CAMTN NW1... 9 P1
Bendemeer Rd PUT/ROE SW15... 156 G9
Bendish Rd EHAM E6... 142 B2
Bendmore Av ABYW SE2... 163 K4
Bendon Va WAND/EARL SW18... 179 L3
Bendysh Rd BUSH WD23... 73 M7
Benedict Dr EBED/NFELT TW14... 174 F3
Benedict Rd BRXN/ST SW9... 158 G9
MTCM CR4... 201 P3
Benedict Wy EFNCH N2... 117 M1
Benedict Whf MTCM CR4... 201 P3
Benenden Gn HAYES BR2... 205 M5
Benen-stock Rd
STWL/WRAY TW19... 173 N1
Benets Rd EMPK RM11... 125 P6
Benett Gdns STRHM/NOR SW16... 202 F2
Benfleet CI COB KT11... 217 M8
SUT SM1... 201 M10
Benford Rd HOD EN11... 44 E5
Bengal Rd IL IG1... 122 E9
Bengarth Dr KTN/HRWW/W HA3... 94 C10
Bengarth Rd NTHLT UB5... 133 L3
Bengeo Gdns CHDH RM6... 123 M5
Bengeworth Rd HRW HA1... 114 G7
Ben Hale CI STAN HA7... 94 F6
Benham CI BTSEA SW11... 157 N9
CHSGTN KT9... 219 H3
COUL/CHIP CR5... 241 J4
CSHM HP5... 50 G6
Benham Gdns HSLWW TW4... 175 N1
Benham Rd HNWL W7... 134 D7
Benhams PI HORL RH6... 280 B2
Benhill Av SUT SM1... 221 L1
Benhill Rd CMBW SE5... 159 L6
SUT SM1... 201 M4
Benhill Wood Rd SUT SM1... 201 M10
Benhilton Gdns SUT SM1... 201 L1
Benhurst Av HCH RM12... 125 J9
Benhurst CI SAND/SEL CR2... 224 C5
Benhurst Gdns SAND/SEL CR2... 224 B6
Benhurst La STRHM/NOR SW16... 181 H8
Benin St LEW SE13... 183 J3
Benjafield CI UED N18... 100 A5
Benjamin CI CRAWE RH10... 284 E2
EMPK RM11... 125 H4
HACK E8... 7 P6
Benjamin St FARR EC1M... 12 C3
Ben Jonson Rd WCHPL E1... 140 D7
Benledi St POP/IOD E14... 141 J8
Benling St SHB W12... 136 E9
Benner La CHOB/PIR GU24... 212 E1
Bennerley Rd BTSEA SW11... 179 P1
Bennet CI KUT KT1... 199 H1
Bennetsfield Rd STKPK UB11... 132 C10
Bennett CI BRKMPK AL9... 23 J9
COB KT11... 217 H9
NTHWD HA6... 92 C8
WELL DA16... 163 K8
Bennett Gv LEW SE13... 160 G7
Bennett Pk BKHTH/KID SE3... 161 L9
CHDH RM6... 123 P4
PLSTW E13... 141 P6
Bennetts CSHM HP5... 51 J6
Bennetts Av CROY/NA CR0... 204 D9
GFD/PVL UB6... 134 D3
Bennett's Castle La BCTR RM8... 123 M4
Bennetts CI MTCM CR4... 202 C1
SL SL1... 128 F7
STALE/WH AL4... 40 A9
TOTM N17... 99 N7
Bennetts Copse CHST BR7... 184 B9
Bennetts End CI HHS/BOV HP3... 36 A8
Bennetts End Rd HHS/BOV HP3... 36 A7
Bennetts Farm PI
GT/LBKH KT23... 253 L5
Bennett St CHSWK W4... 156 B5
WHALL SW1A... 10 G9
Bennetts Wy CROY/NA CR0... 204 D9
Bennett Wy RDART DA2... 188 C2
RGUE GU4... 251 K5
Benning CI WDSR SL4... 148 C9
Benningholme Rd EDGW HA8... 96 B7
Bennington Rd TOTM N17... 99 H9
WFD IG8... 101 K8
Bennions CI HCH RM12... 145 L1
Bennison Dr HARH RM3... 105 L10
Benn St HOM E9... 140 D1
Benrek CI BARK/HLT IG6... 102 F8
Bensbury CI PUT/ROE SW15... 178 F3
Bensham CI THHTH CR7... 203 K4
Bensham Gv THHTH CR7... 203 J7
Bensham La CROY/NA CR0... 203 J7
THHTH CR7... 203 J5
Bensham Manor Rd THHTH CR7... 203 K4
Benskin Rd WATW WD18... 73 J8
Benskins La ABR/ST RM4... 105 L2
Benson Av PLSTW E13... 141 P4
Benson CI HSLW TW3... 153 P10
SLN SL2... 129 M10
UX/CGN UB8... 131 P7
Benson Quay WAP E1W... 140 E9
Benson Rd CROY/NA CR0... 203 H10
FSTH SE23... 182 B4
GRAYS RM17... 167 N5
Benthall Gdns PUR/KEN CR8... 241 K2
Bentham Av WOKN/KNAP GU21... 214 F10
Bentham Rd HOM E9... 140 C1
THMD SE28... 143 J9
Ben Tillet CI BARK IG11... 143 L1
CAN/RD E16... 142 C10
Bentinck CI CFSP/GDCR SL9... 110 A3
Bentinck Ms MHST W1U... 10 D5
Bentinck Rd WDR/YW UB7... 131 N10
Bentinck St MHST W1U... 10 D5
Bentley CI HART DA3... 211 P3
Bentley Dr GNTH/NBYPK IG2... 122 F4
HLWE CM17... 47 M2
WEY KT13... 216 B5
Bentley Heath La BAR EN5... 77 H1
Bentley Ms WCHMH N21... 79 L10
Bentley Pk SL SL1... 128 C4
Bentley Rd HERT/WAS SG14... 24 F4
IS N1... 7 K2
SL SL1... 128 C4
Bentley's Meadow BGR/WK TN15... 247 L5
Bentley Wy STAN HA7... 94 F6
WFD IG8... 101 M4
Benton Rd IL IG1... 122 G9
OXHEY WD19... 93 H7
Benton's La WNWD SE27... 181 K7
Benton's Ri WNWD SE27... 181 L8
Bentry CI BCTR RM8... 123 P7
Bentry Rd BCTR RM8... 123 P7
Bentsbrook CI RDKG RH5... 272 G6
Bentsbrook Pk RDKG RH5... 272 G6
Bentsbrook Rd RDKG RH5... 272 G6
Bentsley CI STALE/WH AL4... 38 G2
Bentworth Rd SHB W12... 136 E8
Benwell Ct SUN TW16... 197 N1
Benwell Rd HOLWY N7... 119 H9
Benwick CI BERM/RHTH SE16... 160 A3
Benworth St BOW E3... 140 E5
Benyon Pth SOCK/AV RM15... 147 H5
Benyon Rd IS N1... 7 H5
Beomonds Rw CHERT KT16... 195 K7
Berberis CI GU GU1... 249 P8
Berberis Wk WDR/YW UB7... 151 P3
Berber Rd BTSEA SW11... 180 A1
Berceau Wk WAT WD17... 72 G2
Bercta Rd ELTH/MOT SE9... 184 F6
Berecroft HLWS CM18... 46 G6
Beredens La RBRW/HUT CM13... 106 E10
Berefield HHNE HP2... 35 P1
Berens Rd STMC/STPC BR5... 207 M5
WLSDN NW10... 136 G5
Berens Wy CHST BR7... 207 J4

Beresford Av ALP/SUD HA0 ...... 135 M3
BRYLDS KT5 ...... 199 N8
HNWL W7 ...... 134 C7
SLN SL2 ...... 129 P9
TRDG/WHET N20 ...... 98 A3
TWK TW1 ...... 177 H2
Beresford Dr BMLY BR1 ......
WFD IG8 ...... 101 P5
Beresford Gdns CHDH RM6 ...... 123 P3
EN N1 ...... 79 M8
HSLWW TW4 ...... 175 M5
Beresford Rd BELMT SM2 ...... 221 J4
CEND/HSY/T N8 ...... 119 M3
CHING E4 ...... 101 K2
DORK RH4 ...... 272 C4
EFNCH N2 ...... 117 P1
GVW DA11 ...... 190 B3
HBRY N5 ...... 119 L10
HRW HA1 ...... 114 C3
KUTN/CMB KT2 ...... 199 L1
NWMAL KT3 ...... 199 G8
RKW/CH/CXG WD3 ...... 91 J2
STAL AL1 ...... 39 H7
STHL UB1 ...... 133 L10
WALTH E17 ...... 100 J9
Beresford St WOOL/PLUM SE18 ...... 162 F2
Beresford Ter HBRY N5 ...... 119 K10
Bere St WAP E1W 140 C9
Berestede Rd HMSMTH W6 ...... 156 C4
Bergenia Ct CHOB/PIR GU24 ...... 212 D9
Berger Cl STMC/STPC BR5 ...... 206 C6
Berger Rd HOM E9 ...... 140 C1
Berghem Ms WKENS W14 ...... 156 G2
Bergholt Av REDBR IG4 ...... 122 B3
Bergholt Crs STNW/STAM N16 ...... 119 M5
Bergholt Ms CAMTN NW1 ...... 5 H4
Bericot Wy WGCE AL7 ...... 23 M5
Bering Wk CAN/RD E16 ...... 142 A9
Berisford Ms WAND/EARL SW18 ...... 179 M2
Berkeley Av CLAY IG5 ...... 102 D10
CRW RM5 ...... 104 D8
CSHM HP5 ...... 50 D8
GFD/PVL UB6 ...... 134 D1
HEST TW5 ...... 153 H7
WELL DA16 ...... 163 N7
Berkeley Cl ABLGY WD5 ...... 54 G8
BORE WD6 ...... 75 M9
CSHM HP5 ...... 50 F6
KUTN/CMB KT2 ...... 177 K10
ORP BR6 ...... 207 H7
POTB/CUF EN6 ...... 59 M
RSLP HA4 ...... 113 H8
STWL/WRAY TW19 ...... 172 C3
UPMR RM14 ......
WARE SG12 ...... 26 B1
Berkeley Ct WEY KT13 ...... 196 E9
WLGTN SM6 ...... 202 D10
Berkeley Crs DART DA1 ...... 187 N4
EBAR EN4 ...... 77 N9
Berkeley Dr E/WMO/HCT KT8 ...... 197 N3
EMPK RM11 ...... 125 P4
WDSR SL4 ...... 170 A4
Berkeley Gdns BF/WBF KT14 ...... 215 J10
ESH/CLAY KT10 ...... 218 F4
WCHMH N21 ...... 99 L1
WOT/HER KT12 ...... 196 C7
Berkeley Ms MBLAR W1H 10 B5
SUN TW16 ...... 197 K5
Berkeley Pl EPSOM KT18 ...... 238 A1
WIM/MER SW19 ...... 178 C9
Berkeley Rd BARN SW13 ...... 156 D7
CDALE/KGS NW9 ...... 115 M2
CEND/HSY/T N8 ...... 118 E3
HGDN/ICK UB10 ...... 132 D2
MNPK E12 ...... 122 B10
SEVS/STOTM N15 ...... 119 L4
Berkeley Sq MYFR/PICC W1J 10 F7
The Berkeleys LHD/OX KT22 ...... 236 D10
Berkeley St MYFR/PICC W1J 10 F7
Berkeley Waye HEST TW5 ...... 153 M6
Berkhampstead Rd BELV DA17 ...... 146 B4
CSHM HP5 ...... 51 H6
Berkhamsted Av WBLY HA9 ...... 135 L1
Berkhamsted La HERT/BAY SG13 ...... 42 C5
Berkhamsted Rd HHW HP1 ...... 34 C4
Berkley Av CHES/WCR EN8 ...... 62 C10
Berkley Cl STALE/WH AL4 ...... 39 H2
Berkley Ct GU GU1 ...... 250 B10
Berkley Gv CAMTN NW1 ...... 4 C4
Berkley Rd BEAC HP9 ...... 88 C5
CAMTN NW1 ...... 4 B4
GVE DA12 ...... 190 E2
Berks Hl RKW/CH/CXG WD3 ...... 70 C9
Berkshire Av SL SL1 ...... 128 C8
Berkshire Cl CTHM CR3 ...... 241 L8
Berkshire Gdns PLMGR N13 ...... 99 H2
UED N18 ...... 100 A6
Berkshire Rd HOM E9 ...... 140 E1
Berkshire Wy EMPK RM11 ...... 125 P3
MTCM CR4 ...... 202 F4
Bermans Wy WLSDN NW10 ...... 116 B9
Bermer Rd WATN WD24 ...... 73 K5
Bermondsey Sq STHWK SE1 ...... 13 J10
Bermondsey Wall East
BERM/RHTH SE16 ...... 19 P2
Bermondsey Wall West
BERM/RHTH SE16 ...... 19 N1
Bermuda Rd TIL RM18 ...... 168 D8
Bernal Cl THMD SE28 ...... 143 N9
Bernard Ashley Dr CHARL SE7 ...... 161 N4
Bernard Av WEA W13 ...... 154 G2
Bernard Cassidy St CAN/RD E16 ...... 141 L7
Bernard Cl BARK/HLT IG6 ...... 102 C7
Bernard Gdns WIM/MER SW19 ...... 179 J5
Bernard Gv WAB EN9 ...... 62 C9
Bernard Rd ROMW/RG RM7 ...... 124 D5
SEVS/STOTM N15 ...... 119 N3
WLGTN SM6 ...... 222 E1
Bernard St BMSBY WC1N 11 L2
GVE DA12 ...... 190 E2
STALW/RED AL3 ...... 38 C5
Bernays Cl STAN HA7 ...... 95 H7
Bernay's Gv BRXN/ST SW9 ...... 158 G10
Bernel Dr CROY/NA CR0 ...... 204 E10
Berne Rd THHTH CR7 ...... 203 J5
Berners Cl SL SL1 ...... 128 D9
Berners Dr STAL AL1 ...... 38 C9
WEA W13 ...... 134 F4
Berners Ms FITZ W1T 11 H4
Berners Pl FITZ W1T 11 H5
Berners Rd IS N1 ...... 6 C1
UED N18 ...... 99 H9
Berners St FITZ W1T 11 H4
Berney Rd CROY/NA CR0 ...... 203 L7
Bernice Cl RAIN RM13 ...... 145 K6
Bernville Wy KTN/HRWW/WS HA3 ...... 114 E1
Bernwell Rd CHING E4 ...... 101 K4
Berridge Gn EDGW HA8 ...... 95 M8
Berridge Rd NRWD SE19 ...... 181 L8
The Berries STALE/WH AL4 ...... 38 F2
Berriman Rd HOLWY N7 ...... 118 C2
Berrington Dr EHSLY KT24 ...... 234 C10
Berry Av WATN WD24 ...... 73 J4
Berrybank Cl CHING E4 ...... 101 H3
Berry Cl HCH RM12 ...... 125 L10
RKW/CH/CXG WD3 ...... 91 L1
WLSDN NW10 ...... 136 B2
Berrydale Rd YEAD UB4 ...... 133 M6
Berry Fld SLN SL2 ...... 128 F8
Berryfield Cl BMLY BR1 ...... 206 B1
WALTH E17 ...... 120 C2
Berry Field Pk AMS HP6 ...... 68 G3
Berrygrove La GSTN WD25 ...... 73 P5
Berry Grove La BUSH WD23 ...... 73 M4

Berryhill ELTH/MOT SE9 ...... 162 E10
Berryhill Gdns ELTH/MOT SE9 ...... 162 E10
Berrylands BRYLDS KT5 ...... 199 M5
Berrylands BRYLDS KT5 ...... 199 M5
Berrylands Rd BRYLDS KT5 ...... 199 M5
Berryman Cl BCTR RM8 ...... 123 M8
Berryman's La SYD SE26 ...... 182 C7
Berry Meade ASHTD KT21 ...... 237 L3
Berrymead HHNE HP2 ...... 36 A4
Berrymead Gdns ACT W3 ...... 135 P10
Berrymede Rd CHSWK W4 ...... 156 A2
Berry Pl FSBYE EC1V 6 D10
Berryscroft Rd STA TW18 ...... 173 M10
Berry's Green Rd BH/WHM TN16 ...... 244 B6
Berry's Hl BH/WHM TN16 ...... 244 E1
Berry's La BF/WBF KT14 ...... 215 N7
Berry Wy EA W5 ...... 155 K2
RKW/CH/CXG WD3 ...... 91 L1
Bersham La GRAYS RM17 ...... 167 J3
Bertal Rd TOOT SW17 ...... 180 C7
Berther Rd EMPK RM11 ...... 125 M5
Berthon St DEPT SE8 ...... 160 F6
Bertie Rd SYD SE26 ...... 182 C7
WLSDN NW10 ...... 119 J9
Bertram Rd EN EN1 ...... 79 P8
HDN NW4 ...... 116 D4
KUTN/CMB KT2 ...... 177 M10
Bertram St KTTN NW5 ...... 94 E7
Bertrand St LEW SE13 ...... 160 C8
Bertrand Wy THMD SE28 ...... 143 J9
Bert Rd THHTH CR7 ...... 203 K5
Bert Wy EN EN1 ...... 79 N8
Berwick Av SL SL1 ...... 128 C9
YEAD UB4 ...... 133 L9
Berwick Cl BEAC HP9 ...... 88 G10
CHES/WCR EN8 ...... 62 F10
STAN HA7 ...... 94 E7
Berwick Crs BFN/LL DA15 ...... 185 J7
Berwick La CHONG CM5 ...... 66 F9
Berwick Pond Cl RAIN RM13 ...... 145 L4
Berwick Pond Rd RAIN RM13 ...... 145 M4
UPMR RM14 ...... 145 N1
Berwick Rd BORE WD6 ...... 75 L4
CAN/RD E16 ...... 141 N8
RAIN RM13 ...... 145 N4
WDGN N22 ...... 99 J9
WELL DA16 ...... 163 L7
Berwick St SOHO/CST W1F 11 H6
Berwick Wy RSEV TN14 ...... 247 J5
Berwyn Av HSLW TW3 ...... 154 A7
Berwyn Rd HNHL SE24 ...... 181 J4
RCHPK/HAM TW10 ...... 155 N10
Beryl Av EHAM E6 ...... 142 B7
Beryl Rd HMSMTH W6 ...... 156 G4
Berystede KUTN/CMB KT2 ...... 177 N10
Besant Wy WLSDN NW10 ...... 115 P10
Besley St STRHM/NOR SW16 ...... 180 D9
Bessant Dr RCH/KEW TW9 ...... 155 N7
Bessborough Pl PIM SW1V 17 J8
Bessborough Rd HRW HA1 ...... 114 C6
PUT/ROE SW15 ...... 178 D4
Bessborough St PIM SW1V 17 J7
Bessels Green Rd SEV TN13 ...... 246 B10
Bessels Meadow SEV TN13 ...... 246 B10
Bessemer Rd CMBW SE5 ...... 159 K8
WGCE AL7 ...... 23 J1
WGCW AL8 ...... 23 H1
Bessie Lansbury Cl EHAM E6 ...... 142 D8
Bessingby Rd RSLP HA4 ...... 113 H7
Besson St NWCR SE14 ...... 160 C7
Bessy St BETH E2 ...... 140 B5
Bestobell Rd SL SL1 ...... 129 H8
Bestwood St DEPT SE8 ...... 160 C3
Beswick Ms HAMP NW3 ...... 3 H1
Betam Rd HYS/HAR UB3 ...... 152 E1
Beta Rd CHOB/PIR GU24 ...... 213 L6
WOKS/MYFD GU22 ...... 232 E2
Beta Wy EGH TW20 ...... 194 F1
Betchworth Cl SUT SM1 ...... 221 N2
Betchworth Rd GDMY/SEVK IG3 ...... 123 H7
Betchworth Wy CROY/NA CR0 ...... 223 H5
Betenson Av SEV TN13 ...... 246 C8
Betham Rd GFD/PVL UB6 ...... 134 C5
Bethany Waye
EBED/NFELT TW14 ...... 174 F3
Bethecar Rd HRW HA1 ...... 114 D3
Bethell Av CAN/RD E16 ...... 141 L6
IL IG1 ...... 122 D5
Bethel Rd SEV TN13 ...... 247 K9
WELL DA16 ...... 163 M9
Bethersden Cl BECK BR3 ...... 182 E10
Bethnal Green Rd BETH E2 ...... 13 M1
Bethune Av FBAR/BDGN N11 ...... 98 A5
Bethune Cl CRAWW RH10 ...... 284 E8
Bethune Rd STNW/STAM N16 ...... 119 M1
WLSDN NW10 ...... 136 A6
Bethwin Rd CMBW SE5 ...... 159 J6
Betjeman Cl CHESW EN7 ...... 61 P4
COUL/CHIP CR5 ...... 240 G3
RYLN/HDSTN HA2 ...... 113 P2
Betjeman Wy CHONG CM5 ...... 35 L4
Betley Ct WOT/HER KT12 ...... 197 J8
Betony Cl CROY/NA CR0 ...... 204 C8
Betoyne Av CHING E4 ...... 101 K5
Betsham Rd ERITH DA8 ...... 164 G6
MEO DA13 ...... 189 J8
SWCM DA10 ...... 189 J8
Betstyle Rd FBAR/BDGN N11 ...... 98 C5
Betterton Dr SCUP DA14 ...... 185 P5
Betterton Rd RAIN RM13 ...... 144 F4
Betterton St LSQ/SEVD WC2H 11 L6
Bettles Cl UX/CGN UB8 ...... 131 M4
Bettons Pk SRTFD E15 ...... 141 K3
Bettridge Rd FUL/PGN SW6 ...... 157 J8
Betts Cl BECK BR3 ...... 204 D2
Betts La WAB EN9 ...... 45 P7
Betts Rd CAN/RD E16 ...... 141 N8
Betts St WCHPL E1 ...... 140 A9
Betts Wy CRAWW RH11 ...... 283 N3
PGE/AN SE20 ...... 204 A2
THDIT KT7 ...... 210 G8
Betula Cl PUR/KEN CR8 ...... 223 K5
Between Streets COB KT11 ...... 217 J10
Beulah Cl EDGW HA8 ...... 95 L4
Beulah Crs THHTH CR7 ...... 203 K2
Beulah Gv CROY/NA CR0 ...... 203 K6
Beulah Hl NRWD SE19 ...... 181 L10
Beulah Pk EPP CM16 ......
HCH RM12 ...... 125 K8
SUT SM1 ...... 221 K1
THHTH CR7 ...... 203 K3
WALTH E17 ...... 120 C3
WIM/MER SW19 ...... 179 J8
Beulah Wk CTHM CR3 ...... 242 D6
Beult Rd DART DA1 ...... 165 H9
Bevan Av BARK IG11 ...... 143 K2
Bevan Cl HHS/BOV HP3 ...... 35 N8
Bevan Ct CROY/NA CR0 ...... 223 H2
Bevan House Watn WD24 ...... 73 L6
Bevan Pl SWLY BR8 ...... 208 C4
Bevan Rd ABYW SE2 ...... 163 L4
EBAR EN4 ...... 78 A3
Bevans Cl GRH DA9 ...... 189 H2
Bevan St IS N1 ...... 6 F1
Bevan Wy HCH RM12 ...... 125 N8

Bev Callender Cl VX/NE SW8 ...... 158 C9
Bevenden St IS N1 ...... 7 H3
Beverley Av BFN/LL DA15 ...... 185 J7
HSLWW TW4 ...... 153 N10
RYNPK SW20 ...... 200 C1
Beverley Cl ADL/WDHM KT15 ...... 215 N1
BARN SW13 ...... 156 D8
BTSEA SW11 ...... 157 N10
CHSGTN KT9 ...... 219 H4
EMPK RM11 ...... 125 N5
EW KT17 ...... 220 F7
WCHMH N21 ...... 99 L1
WEY KT13 ...... 196 F9
Beverley Ct BROCKY SE4 ...... 160 E9
Beverley Crs WFD IG8 ...... 101 H9
Beverley Dr EDGW HA8 ...... 115 N1
Beverley Gdns BARN SW13 ...... 156 C9
CHESW EN7 ...... 61 N7
EMPK RM11 ...... 125 M5
GLDGN NW11 ...... 117 H4
STALE/WH AL4 ...... 39 L2
STAN HA7 ...... 94 F9
WBLY HA9 ...... 115 M8
WGCE AL7 ...... 23 M5
WPK KT4 ...... 200 D8
Beverley Hts REIG RH2 ...... 257 L8
Beverley La KUTN/CMB KT2 ...... 178 B10
Beverley Ms CRAWW RH10 ...... 284 E8
Beverley Rd BARN SW13 ...... 156 C9
BXLYHN DA7 ...... 164 D8
CHING E4 ...... 101 J7
CHSWK W4 ...... 156 A4
CTHM CR3 ...... 241 M3
DAGW RM9 ...... 123 P5
EHAM E6 ...... 141 H8
HAYES BR2 ...... 206 A5
KUT KT1 ...... 199 H1
MTCM CR4 ...... 202 E4
NWDGN UB2 ...... 153 M3
NWMAL KT3 ...... 200 D4
PGE/AN SE20 ...... 204 A2
RSLP HA4 ...... 113 H4
SUN TW16 ...... 196 C1
WPK KT4 ...... 200 F9
Beverley Wy NWMAL KT3 ...... 200 C1
NWMAL KT3 ......
Beverley Wy (Kingston By Pass)
NWMAL KT3 ...... 200 C1
Beverly CL BROX EN10 ...... 44 D7
Beversbrook Rd ARCH N19 ...... 118 C8
Beverstone Rd
BRXS/STRHM SW2 ...... 180 G1
THHTH CR7 ...... 203 H4
Bevill Cl SNWD SE25 ...... 203 P3
Bevin Cl BERM/RHTH SE16 ...... 140 D10
NKENS W10 ...... 8 B3
Bevington Rd BECK BR3 ...... 204 G2
NKENS W10 ...... 8 B3
Bevington St BERM/RHTH SE16 ...... 19 P2
Bevin Rd YEAD UB4 ...... 133 J3
Bevin Sq TOOT SW17 ...... 180 A6
Bevin Wy FSBYW WC1X 6 A8
Bevis Cl RDART DA2 ...... 188 B3
Bevis Marks HDTCH EC3A 13 K5
Bewbush Dr CRAWW RH11 ...... 283 J10
Bewcastle Gdns ENC/FH EN2 ...... 78 F8
Bewdley Cl HARP AL5 ...... 20 C5
Bewdley St IS N1 ...... 6 A1
Bewick Ms PECK SE15 ...... 159 K1
Bewick St VX/NE SW8 ...... 158 C8
Bewley Cl CHES/WCR EN8 ...... 62 C7
Bewley St WCHPL E1 ...... 140 A9
Bewlys Rd WNWD SE27 ...... 181 J8
Bexhill Cl FELT TW13 ...... 175 M5
Bexhill Dr GRAYS RM17 ...... 167 K5
Bexhill Rd BROCKY SE4 ...... 182 E1
FBAR/BDGN N11 ...... 98 E6
MORT/ESHN SW14 ...... 155 M6
Bexley Cl DART DA1 ...... 186 F1
Bexley Gdns CHDH RM6 ...... 123 M6
ED N9 ...... 99 L4
Bexley High St BXLY DA5 ...... 186 A2
Bexley La DART DA1 ...... 186 F1
SCUP DA14 ...... 185 M7
Bexley Rd ELTH/MOT SE9 ...... 184 C1
ERITH DA8 ...... 164 G4
Beyers Gdns HOD EN11 ...... 26 F10
Beyers Prospect HOD EN11 ...... 26 F10
Beyers Ride HOD EN11 ...... 26 F9
Beynon Rd CAR SM5 ...... 222 A2
Bianca Rd PECK SE15 ...... 19 M10
Bibsworth Rd FNCH N3 ...... 97 J10
Bibury Cl PECK SE15 ...... 19 K10
Bicester Rd RCH/KEW TW9 ...... 155 N9
Bickenhall St MBLAR W1H 10 B3
Bickersteth Rd TOOT SW17 ...... 180 A9
Bickerton Rd KTTN NW5 ...... 118 A6
Bickley Crs BMLY BR1 ...... 206 A2
Bickley Park Rd BMLY BR1 ...... 206 A2
Bickley Rd BMLY BR1 ...... 206 A1
LEY E10 ...... 120 E6
Bickley St TOOT SW17 ...... 179 G5
Bicknell Rd CMBW SE5 ...... 159 K9
Bickney Wy LHD/OX KT22 ...... 236 E9
Bicknoller Cl BELMT SM2 ...... 221 L6
Bicknoller Rd EN EN1 ...... 79 N5
Bicknor Rd ORP BR6 ...... 207 H7
Bidborough Cl HAYES BR2 ...... 205 L5
Bidborough St STPAN WC1H 5 L8
Biddenden Wy ELTH/MOT SE9 ...... 184 D7
Biddenham Turn CDTN WD25 ...... 73 K1
Bidder St CAN/RD E16 ...... 141 K7
Biddestone Rd HOLWY N7 ...... 118 E1
Biddles Cl SL SL1 ...... 128 D10
Biddulph Rd MV/WKIL W9 ...... 3 H10
SAND/SEL CR2 ...... 223 K5
Bideford Av GFD/PVL UB6 ...... 134 G2
Bideford Cl EDGW HA8 ...... 115 N5
FELT TW13 ...... 175 M6
HARH RM3 ...... 105 H2
Bideford Gdns EN EN1 ...... 99 M1
Bideford Rd BMLY BR1 ...... 183 M7
PEND EN3 ...... 80 E5
RSLP HA4 ...... 113 H5
WELL DA16 ...... 163 L6
Bideford Sp SLN SL2 ...... 128 G5
Bidhams Crs KWD/TDW/WH KT20 ...... 238 G5
Bidwell Gdns FBAR/BDGN N11 ...... 98 D9
Bidwell St PECK SE15 ...... 160 A7
The Bield REIG RH2 ...... 275 K2
Big Common La REDH RH1 ...... 278 C9
Bigbury Cl SRTFD E15 ...... 141 H3
Biggerstaff Rd SRTFD E15 ...... 141 H10
Biggerstaff St FSBYPK N4 ...... 119 H7
Biggin Av MTCM CR4 ...... 202 A4
Biggin Cl CRAWW RH11 ...... 283 M9
Biggin Hl STRHM/NOR SW16 ...... 181 H10
Biggin La GRAYS RM17 ...... 168 D5
Biggin Wy NRWD SE19 ...... 181 J10
Bigginwood Rd
STRHM/NOR SW16 ...... 181 J10
Bigg's Rw PUT/ROE SW15 ...... 157 H10
Bigland St WCHPL E1 ...... 140 A8
Bignell Rd WOOL/PLUM SE18 ...... 162 L4
Bignells Cnr POTB/CUF EN6 ...... 58 D7
Bignold Rd FSTGT E7 ...... 121 M9
Bigwood Rd GLDGN NW11 ...... 117 L4
Biko Cl UX/CGN UB8 ...... 131 M8
Bilberry Cl CRAWW RH11 ...... 283 L10
Bilsdean Rd CHOB/PIR GU24 ...... 211 P9
Billet Cl CHDH RM6 ...... 123 K1
DTCH/LGLY SL3 ...... 150 B7
Billet La BERK HP4 ...... 33 M4
Billet Rd CHDH RM6 ...... 123 L1
ROMW/RG RM7 ...... 123 M1
WALTH E17 ...... 100 C10
Billets Hart Cl HNWL W7 ...... 135 N6
Bill Hamling Cl ELTH/MOT SE9 ...... 184 D1
Billingford Cl BROCKY SE4 ...... 160 C10

Billing Pl WBPTN SW10 ...... 157 L6
Billing Rd WBPTN SW10 ...... 157 L6
Billings HART DA3 ...... 211 L6
Billington Rd NWCR SE14 ...... 160 C6
Billinton Dr CRAWE RH10 ...... 284 C7
Billiter Sq FENCHST EC3M 13 K6
Billiter St FENCHST EC3M 13 K6
Billockby Cl CHSGTN KT9 ...... 219 L3
Billson St POP/IOD E14 ...... 161 H3
Billy Lows La POTB/CUF EN6 ...... 59 L7
Bilton Rd GFD/PVL UB6 ...... 134 C3
Bilton Wy HYS/HAR UB3 ...... 153 J1
PEND EN3 ...... 80 E5
Bina Gdns ECT SW5 ...... 16 G6
Bincote Rd ENC/FH EN2 ...... 78 C7
Binden Rd SHB W12 ...... 156 C2
Binfield Rd BF/WBF KT14 ...... 215 P8
SAND/SEL CR2 ...... 223 N2
VX/NE SW8 ...... 158 F7
Bingfield St IS N1 ...... 5 N5
Bingham Cl SOCK/AV RM15 ...... 146 C8
Bingham Dr STA TW18 ...... 173 N10
Bingham Pl MHST W1U 10 C2
Bingham Rd CROY/NA CR0 ...... 203 P8
Bingham St IS N1 ...... 6 G1
Bingley Rd CAN/RD E16 ...... 141 P8
GFD/PVL UB6 ...... 134 B6
HOD EN11 ...... 45 H3
SUN TW16 ...... 175 H10
Binney Ct CRAWE RH10 ...... 284 F4
Binney St MYFR/PKLN W1K 10 D7
Binns Rd CHSWK W4 ...... 156 B4
Binscombe CROY/NA CR0 ...... 204 A9
Binscombe Crs RGODL GU7 ...... 267 K10
Binscombe La RGODL GU7 ...... 267 J9
Binsey Wk ABYW SE2 ...... 163 M1
Binstead Cl YEAD UB4 ...... 133 M7
Binstead Ct CRAWW RH11 ...... 283 L5
YEAD UB4 ...... 133 M7
Binyon Crs STAN HA7 ...... 94 E6
Birbetts Rd ELTH/MOT SE9 ...... 184 E6
Birchall La HERT/WAS SG14 ...... 23 P7
Birchall Wd WGCE AL7 ...... 23 M6
Birchanger Rd SNWD SE25 ...... 203 P5
Birch Av CTHM CR3 ...... 259 K1
PLMGR N13 ...... 99 K4
WDR/YW UB7 ...... 132 A8
Birch Cir RGODL GU7 ...... 267 L8
Birch Cl ADL/WDHM KT15 ...... 215 L1
AMS HP6 ...... 69 K3
BKHH IG9 ...... 102 A4
BTFD TW8 ...... 154 G6
CAN/RD E16 ...... 141 K7
EYN DA4 ...... 209 L10
HART DA3 ...... 211 P2
HSLW TW3 ...... 154 C9
IVER SL0 ...... 130 G4
ROMW/RG RM7 ...... 124 C1
RPLY/SEND GU23 ...... 251 J1
SEV TN13 ...... 247 J9
SOCK/AV RM15 ...... 147 J6
TEDD TW11 ...... 176 F8
WOKS/MYFD GU22 ...... 231 P5
Birch Copse LCOL/BKTW AL2 ...... 55 M6
Birch Crs EMPK RM11 ...... 125 M2
HGDN/ICK UB10 ...... 132 A3
SOCK/AV RM15 ...... 147 J5
Birchcroft Cl CTHM CR3 ...... 259 K1
Birchdale CFSP/GDCR SL9 ...... 110 A6
Birchdale Cl BF/WBF KT14 ...... 215 M7
Birchdale Gdns CHDH RM6 ...... 123 N5
Birchdale Rd FSTGT E7 ...... 121 P10
Birchdene Dr THMD SE28 ...... 143 K10
Birch Dr HAT AL10 ...... 40 D5
RKW/CH/CXG WD3 ...... 90 D5
Birchen Cl CDALE/KGS NW9 ...... 116 A7
Birchend Cl SAND/SEL CR2 ...... 223 L3
Birchen Gv CDALE/KGS NW9 ...... 116 A7
Birchen La BANK EC3V 13 H6
Bircherley Ct HERT/WAS SG14 ...... 25 L5
Bircherley St HERT/WAS SG14 ...... 25 L5
Birches Cl EPSOM KT18 ...... 238 E1
MTCM CR4 ...... 202 A3
PIN HA5 ...... 113 M3
The Birches BUSH WD23 ...... 74 B9
CHARL SE7 ...... 161 N5
CRAWE RH10 ...... 284 B6
EHSLY KT24 ...... 252 F2
EPP CM16 ...... 66 C2
HHS/BOV HP3 ...... 35 J9
ORP BR6 ...... 226 D9
RBRW/HUT CM13 ...... 107 K4
STHGT/OAK N14 ...... 78 G10
SWLY BR8 ...... 208 F2
WOKS/MYFD GU22 ...... 232 C4
Birchfield Cl ADL/WDHM KT15 ...... 215 L1
COUL/CHIP CR5 ...... 240 G2
Birchfield Gv EW KT17 ...... 220 F6
Birchfield Rd CHES/WCR EN8 ...... 62 A5
Birchfields GU GU1 ...... 271 N6
Birch Gdns AMSS HP7 ...... 69 K5
DAGE RM10 ...... 124 E2
Birch Gv ACT W3 ...... 135 M10
CHOB/PIR GU24 ...... 212 C8
HHS/BOV HP3 ...... 52 E9
PUR/KEN CR8 ...... 222 F7
SHPTN TW17 ...... 196 F2
SL SL1 ...... 128 G7
WAN E11 ...... 120 E6
WDSR SL4 ...... 148 C7
WELL DA16 ...... 163 K10
WOKS/MYFD GU22 ...... 232 G1
Birch Hl CROY/NA CR0 ...... 224 C2
Birchin Cl SEV TN13 ...... 247 P9
Birchington Cl BXLYHN DA7 ...... 164 C7
Birchington Rd BRYLDS KT5 ...... 199 J6
CEND/HSY/T N8 ...... 118 E4
KIL/WHAMP NW6 ...... 2 F5
Birchin La BANK EC3V 13 H6
Birch La CHOB/PIR GU24 ...... 212 C8
HHS/BOV HP3 ...... 52 E9
PUR/KEN CR8 ...... 222 F7
Birchlands Av BAL SW12 ...... 180 A3
Birch Lea CRAWE RH10 ...... 284 B4
Birch Leys HHNE HP2 ...... 36 D1
Birch Md HAYES BR2 ...... 206 D9
Birchmead WAT WD17 ...... 72 C4
Birchmead Av PIN HA5 ...... 95 G1
Birchmead Cl STALW/RED AL3 ...... 38 C3
Birchmere Rw BKHTH/KID SE3 ...... 161 J1
Birchmore Wk HBRY N5 ...... 118 J2
Birch Pk KTN/HRWW/WS HA3 ...... 94 B8
Birch Platt CHOB/PIR GU24 ...... 212 D2
Birch Rd FELT TW13 ...... 176 A2
ROMW/RG RM7 ...... 124 C1
Birch Rw HAYES BR2 ...... 206 D7
Birch Tree Av WWKM BR4 ...... 205 J4
Birch Tree Gv CSHM HP5 ...... 51 N6
Birch Tree Wk WAT WD17 ...... 72 C3
Birch Tree Wy CROY/NA CR0 ...... 204 A9
Birch V COB KT11 ...... 217 P9
Birch Wk MTCM CR4 ...... 202 C1
Birchway HYS/HAR UB3 ...... 133 J8
Birchway REDH RH1 ...... 276 C2
Birch Wy WARL CR6 ...... 242 D4
Birchwood HAT AL10 ...... 40 D5
HYS/HAR UB3 ...... 133 H10
Birchwood Av BECK BR3 ...... 204 E4
CAR SM5 ...... 202 B10
HAT AL10 ...... 40 D2
MUSWH N10 ...... 98 B2
SCUP DA14 ...... 185 L6
Birchwood Cl CRAWE RH10 ...... 284 D2
HAT AL10 ...... 40 D2
HORL RH6 ...... 280 D12
MRDN SM4 ...... 201 L4
RBRW/HUT CM13 ...... 107 H7
Birchwood Ct EDGW HA8 ...... 95 P10
Birchwood Dr BF/WBF KT14 ...... 215 K8
HAMP NW3 ...... 117 L8
LTWR GU18 ...... 212 B6
RDART DA2 ...... 186 F7
Birchwood Gv HPTN TW12 ...... 176 A9
Birchwood La CTHM CR3 ...... 259 J1
RSEV TN14 ...... 246 A1
Birchwood Park Av SWLY BR8 ...... 208 A4
RDART DA2 ...... 186 F7
STMC/STPC BR5 ...... 206 G4
TOOT SW17 ...... 180 D8
Birchwood Rd LCOL/BKTW AL2 ...... 56 A4
Birdbrook Cl DAGE RM10 ...... 144 D2
Birdbrook Rd BKHTH/KID SE3 ...... 161 P9
Birdcage Wk STSPK SW1H 17 H2
Birdcroft Rd WGCW AL8 ...... 22 G6
Birdham Cl BMLY BR1 ...... 206 B5
CRAWW RH11 ...... 283 L5
Bird House La ORP BR6 ...... 226 D10
Birdhurst Av SAND/SEL CR2 ...... 223 L1
Birdhurst Gdns SAND/SEL CR2 ...... 223 L1
Birdhurst Ri SAND/SEL CR2 ...... 223 M2
Birdhurst Rd SAND/SEL CR2 ...... 223 M2
WAND/EARL SW18 ...... 157 M10
WIM/MER SW19 ...... 179 P9
Birdie Wy HERT/BAY SG13 ...... 26 A1
Bird In Bush Rd PECK SE15 ...... 159 P6
Bird-in-hand La BMLY BR1 ...... 206 A2
Bird-in-hand Pas FSTH SE23 ...... 182 B5
Bird La RBRW/HUT CM13 ...... 107 H10
UPMR RM14 ...... 126 C3
Birdlip Cl PECK SE15 ...... 19 J10
Birds Cl WGCE AL7 ...... 23 L7
Birds Farm Av ROMW/RG RM7 ...... 104 C3
Birdsfield La HOM E9 ...... 140 E3
Birds Hill Dr LHD/OX KT22 ...... 218 C9
Birds Hill Ri LHD/OX KT22 ...... 218 C8
Birds Hill Rd LHD/OX KT22 ...... 218 C8
Bird St MHST W1U 10 D6
Birdsworth Dr WOKN/KNAP GU21 ...... 231 K5
Bird Wk WHTN TW2 ...... 175 N4
Birdwood Cl SAND/SEL CR2 ...... 224 B7
TEDD TW11 ...... 176 D7
Birkbeck Av ACT W3 ...... 135 P9
GFD/PVL UB6 ...... 134 B3
Birkbeck Gv ACT W3 ...... 156 A1
Birkbeck Hl DUL SE21 ...... 181 J5
Birkbeck Ms HACK E8 ...... 119 N10
Birkbeck Pl DUL SE21 ...... 181 J4
Birkbeck Rd ACT W3 ...... 136 A10
BECK BR3 ...... 204 A2
CEND/HSY/T N8 ...... 118 F2
EA W5 ...... 155 H3
ENC/FH EN2 ...... 79 J4
CNTH/NBYPK IG2 ...... 122 D3
HACK E8 ...... 119 N10
MLHL NW7 ...... 96 C6
NFNCH/WDSP N12 ...... 97 M6
ROMW/RG RM7 ...... 124 E6
SCUP DA14 ...... 185 K6
TOTM N17 ...... 99 N9
WIM/MER SW19 ...... 179 L8
Birkbeck St BETH E2 ...... 140 A5
Birkbeck Wy GFD/PVL UB6 ...... 134 C3
Birkdale Av HARH RM3 ...... 105 P8
PIN HA5 ...... 113 H2
Birkdale Cl ORP BR6 ...... 206 G7
Birkdale Dr CRAWW RH11 ...... 282 G8
Birkdale Gdns CROY/NA CR0 ...... 224 C5
OXHEY WD19 ...... 93 L4
Birkdale Rd ABYW SE2 ...... 163 K3
EA W5 ...... 135 K6
Birkenhead Av KUTN/CMB KT2 ...... 199 L2
Birkenhead St IS N1 ...... 5 M7
Birkett Wy CSTG HP8 ...... 70 A7
Birkhall Rd CAT SE6 ...... 183 J4
Birkheads Rd REIG RH2 ...... 257 K9
Birklands La STAL AL1 ...... 38 G10
Birkwood Cl BAL SW12 ...... 180 E3
Birley Rd SL SL1 ...... 129 J8
TRDG/WHET N20 ...... 97 M3
Birley St BTSEA SW11 ...... 158 B8
Birling Rd ERITH DA8 ...... 164 E6
Birnam Rd HOLWY N7 ...... 118 D2
Birnham Rd RPLY/SEND GU23 ...... 233 K10
Birse Crs WLSDN NW10 ...... 116 B9
Birstal Gn OXHEY WD19 ...... 93 L5
Birstall Rd SEVS/STOTM N15 ...... 119 M3
Biscay Rd HMSMTH W6 ...... 156 G4
Biscoe Cl HEST TW5 ...... 153 P5
Biscoe Wy LEW SE13 ...... 161 E9
Bisenden Rd CROY/NA CR0 ...... 203 M9
Bisham Cl CRAWE RH10 ...... 284 E10
MTCM CR4 ...... 202 A7
Bisham Gdns HGT N6 ...... 118 A6
Bishop Butts Cl ORP BR6 ...... 207 J10
Bishop Cl RCHPK/HAM TW10 ...... 177 J6
Bishop Duppas Pk SHPTN TW17 ...... 196 F2
Bishop Fox Wy E/WMO/HCT KT8 ...... 197 N4
Bishop Ken Rd KTN/HRWW/WS HA3 ...... 94 E10
Bishop King's Rd WKENS W14 ...... 14 G5
Bishops Av BORE WD6 ...... 75 L9
CHDH RM6 ...... 123 M4
FUL/PGN SW6 ...... 156 G8
NTHWD HA6 ...... 92 F5
PLSTW E13 ...... 141 N3
The Bishops Av EFNCH N2 ...... 117 H2
Bishop's Bridge Rd BAY/PAD W2 ...... 9 H5
Bishops Cl BAR EN5 ...... 76 C10
CHSWK W4 ...... 155 P4
COUL/CHIP CR5 ...... 241 H4
ELTH/MOT SE9 ...... 184 F5
EN EN1 ...... 80 A4
HAT AL10 ...... 40 G4
HGDN/ICK UB10 ...... 132 B4
STALE/WH AL4 ...... 38 F2
SUT SM1 ...... 201 L10
WALTH E17 ...... 120 C2
Bishops Ct GRH DA9 ...... 188 D1
STP EC4M 12 D5
Bishops Dr EBED/NFELT TW14 ...... 174 A2
NTHLT UB5 ...... 133 M3
Bishops Farm Cl WDSR SL4 ...... 148 A8
Bishopsfield HLWS CM18 ...... 46 G4
Bishopsford Rd MRDN SM4 ...... 201 M7
Bishopsgate LVPST EC2M 13 J4
Bishopsgate Rd WDSR SL4 ...... 171 M6
Bishops Gn BFOR GU20 ...... 212 B3
EFNCH N2 ...... 117 N4
HPTN TW12 ...... 175 P7
Bishop's Hall KUT KT1 ...... 199 J2
Bishop's Hall Rd BRWN CM15 ...... 86 G10
Bishops Hl WOT/HER KT12 ...... 197 H7
Bishopsmead CMBW SE5 ...... 159 K6
HOR/WEW KT19 ...... 220 A6
Bishopsmead Cl EHSLY KT24 ...... 252 C6
Bishopsmead Dr EHSLY KT24 ...... 252 C6
Bishops Orch SLN SL2 ...... 128 C5
Bishop's Pk FUL/PGN SW6 ...... 156 G8
Bishops Park Rd FUL/PGN SW6 ...... 156 G8
STRHM/NOR SW16 ...... 202 F1
Bishop's Pl SUT SM1 ...... 221 M2

Bishops Ri HAT AL10 40 C8
Bishop's Rd CROY/NA CR0 203 J7
HGT N6 118 B4
HNWL W7 154 D1
SL SL1 149 M1
UX/CGN UB8 132 D8
Bishop's Ter LBTH SE11 18 B5
Bishopsthorpe Rd SYD SE26 182 B7
Bishop St IS N1 6 E5
Bishops Wk BRWN CM15 107 L3
CHST BR7 206 F1
CROY/NA CR0 224 C2
Bishop's Wy BETH E2 140 B4
EGH TW20 172 G9
Bishops Wd WOKN/KNAP GU21 231 L3
Bishopswood Rd HGT N6 118 A5
Bishop Wy WLSDN NW10 136 B2 1
Biskra WAT WD17 73 H5
Bisley Cl CHES/WCR EN8 62 C9
WPK KT4 200 F8
Bispham Rd WLSDN NW10 135 L5
Bisson Rd SRTFD E15 141 H4
Bistern Av WALTH E17 121 J1
Bitmead Cl CRAWW RH11 283 H8 4
Bittacy Cl MLHL NW7 96 G7
Bittacy Hl MLHL NW7 96 G7
Bittacy Park Av MLHL NW7 96 G7
Bittacy Ri MLHL NW7 96 G7
Bittacy Rd MLHL NW7 96 G7
Bittams La CHERT KT16 214 G1
Bittern Cl CHESW EN7 61 J1
CRAWW RH11 282 G8
YEAD UB4 133 L7
Bitterne Dr WOKN/KNAP GU21 231 L3
Bittern St STHWK SE1 18 E2
The Bittoms KUT KT1 199 J3
Bixley Cl NWDGN UB2 153 N3 1
Black Acre Cl AMSS HP7 69 K5
Blackacre Rd EPP CM16 83 H3
Blackall St SDTCH EC2A 13 J1
Blackberry Cl GU GU1 249 N7
SHPTN TW17 196 F4 2
Blackberry Farm Cl HEST TW5 153 M6 1
Blackberry Fld STMC/STPC BR5 207 K1 1
Blackbird Hl WBLY HA9 115 P7
Blackbirds La GSTN WD25 56 B10
Blackborne Rd DAGE RM10 144 B1
Blackborough Cl REIG RH2 257 M10
Blackborough Rd REDH RH1 257 N10 1
REIG RH2 257 N10
Black Boy La SEVS/STOTM N15 119 K3
Black Boy Wd LCOL/BKTW AL2 55 P6
Blackbridge Rd
WOKS/MYFD GU22 232 A6
Blackbrook La HAYES BR2 206 D5
Blackbrook Rd RDKG RH5 273 K7
Blackburne's Ms MYFR/PKLN W1K 10 C7
Blackburn Rd KIL/WHAMP NW6 2 G2
The Blackburn GT/LBKH KT23 235 N10 1
Blackbury Cl POTB/CUF EN6 59 M7 1
Blackbush Av CHDH RM6 123 N3
Blackbush Cl BELMT SM2 221 L4
Blackbush Spring HLW CM20 29 K10
Blackcap Cl CRAWW RH11 283 M9 2
Black Cut STAL AL1 38 D7 2
Blackdale CHESW EN7 61 P3
Black Ditch Rd WAB EN9 81 H2
Black Ditch Wy WAB EN9 80 G2
Black Dog Wk CRAWE RH10 283 P5 1
Blackdown Av
WOKS/MYFD GU22 233 H1
Blackdown Cl EFNCH N2 97 M10
WOKS/MYFD GU22 232 F2
Black Eagle Cl BH/WHM TN16 262 F3
Blackenham Rd TOOT SW17 180 A7
Blackett Cl EGH TW20 195 H2
Blackett Rd CRAWE RH10 284 D8
Blackett St PUT/ROE SW15 156 G9
Blacketts Wood Dr
RKW/CH/CXG WD3 70 E8
Black Fan Cl ENC/FH EN2 79 K5
Black Fan Rd WGCE AL7 23 J4 1
WGCE AL7 23 M6
Blackfen Rd BFN/LL DA15 185 J1
Blackfold Rd CRAWE RH10 284 B8 2
Blackford Cl SAND/SEL CR2 223 J5
Blackford Rd OXHEY WD19 93 L6
Blackfriars Br EMB EC4Y 12 C7
Black Friars La BLKFR EC4V 12 C6
Blackfriars Pas BLKFR EC4V 12 C7 1
Blackfriars Rd STHWK SE1 12 C9
Blackfriars U/P BLKFR EC4V 12 D7
Blackhall La BGR/WK TN15 247 M9
Blackheath CRAWE RH10 284 E5
Blackheath Av GNWCH SE10 161 J6
Blackheath Gv BKHTH/KID SE3 161 L8
SHGR GU5 268 E9
Blackheath Hl GNWCH SE10 161 H7
Blackheath La SHGR GU5 268 F9
Blackheath Ri LEW SE13 161 H8
Blackheath Rd GNWCH SE10 160 G7
Blackheath V BKHTH/KID SE3 161 K8
Blackhills ESH/CLAY KT10 217 N5
Black Horse Av CSHM HP5 51 J9
Black Horse Cl WDSR SL4 148 C8 1
Black Horse Ct STHWK SE1 19 H4 1
Blackhorse Crs AMS HP6 69 K4
Blackhorse La CROY/NA CR0 203 P7
EPP CM16 66 E1
POTB/CUF EN6 58 B6
REIG RH2 257 L5
WALTH E17 100 C10
Blackhorse Rd DEPT SE8 160 D5
Black Horse Rd SCUP DA14 185 K7 1
Blackhorse Rd WALTH E17 120 D3
WOKS/MYFD GU22 231 J6
Blacklands Dr YEAD UB4 132 D6
Blacklands Meadow REDH RH1 258 F9
Blacklands Rd CAT SE6 183 H7
Blacklands Ter CHEL SW3 16 A6
Blackley Cl WAT WD17 72 G3
Black Lion Ct HLWE CM17 29 M7 1
Black Lion Hl RAD WD7 57 K8
Black Lion La HMSMTH W6 156 D3
Blackmans Cl DART DA1 187 K4 1
Blackman's La WARL CR6 225 K10
Blackmead SEV TN13 246 F7
Blackmoor La WATW WD18 72 E9
Blackmore Av STHL UB1 134 C10
Blackmore Ct WAB EN9 63 M9
Blackmore Crs
WOKN/KNAP GU21 214 F10
Blackmore Rd BKHH IG9 102 B1 1
BRWN CM15 86 G1
GRAYS RM17 167 P4 1
Blackmore's Gv TEDD TW11 176 F9 1
Blackmore Wy UX/CGN UB8 131 N1 1
Blackness La HAYES BR2 226 A5
WOKS/MYFD GU22 232 B5
Blacknest Rd ASC SL5 193 J3
Black Park Rd DTCH/LGLY SL3 130 C4
Blackpond La SLN SL2 128 G3
Blackpool Gdns YEAD UB4 132 F6 1
Blackpool Rd PECK SE15 160 A8
Black Prince Cl BF/WBF KT14 216 A10
Black Prince Rd LBTH SE11 17 N6
Black Rod Cl HYS/HAR UB3 152 G2 1
Blackshaw Rd TOOT SW17 179 N8
Blackshots La CDH/CHF RM16 147 P9
Blacksmith Cl ASHTD KT21 237 L5 1
CHDH RM6 123 M4
Blacksmith La RGUE GU4 268 F5
Blacksmith Rw DTCH/LGLY SL3 150 D3 1
Black Smiths Cl WARE SG12 26 F4 1
Blacksmiths Hl SAND/SEL CR2 224 A9
Blacksmiths La CHERT KT16 195 K7 2
DEN/HRF UB9 110 G7
RAIN RM13 144 G3
STA TW18 195 M3 1
STALW/RED AL3 38 A6 1
STMC/STPC BR5 207 M5
Blacksmiths Wy SBW CM21 29 L2 1
Black's Rd HMSMTH W6 156 F4
Blackstock Rd FSBYPK N4 119 J7
Blackstone Cl REIG RH2 275 P1
Blackstone Hl REDH RH1 257 P10
Blackstone Rd CRICK NW2 116 F10
Blackstroud La East LTWR GU18 212 C7
Blackstroud La West LTWR GU18 212 C7
Black Swan Yd STHWK SE1 19 J1
Blackthorn Av WDR/YW UB7 152 B3
Blackthorn Cl CRAWW RH11 283 M5
GSTN WD25 55 J8
REIG RH2 275 M2
STALE/WH AL4 39 H3
Blackthorn Ct HEST TW5 153 M6 2
Blackthorn Dell DTCH/LGLY SL3 149 P2
Blackthorn Dr LTWR GU18 212 A8
Blackthorne Av CROY/NA CR0 204 B8
Blackthorne Cl HAT AL10 40 C7 1
Blackthorne Crs DTCH/LGLY SL3 151 H8
Blackthorne Dr CHING E4 101 J5
Blackthorne Rd DTCH/LGLY SL3 151 H9
GT/LBKH KT23 254 B2
Blackthorn Gv BXLYHN DA7 163 P9
Blackthorn Rd BH/WHM TN16 244 B2 1
CDH/CHF RM16 147 N10
REIG RH2 275 M2
WGCE AL7 23 K6
Blackthorn St BOW E3 140 F6
Blackthorn Wy BRW CM14 107 J6 1
Blackwall La GNWCH SE10 161 K2
Blackwall Tunnel Northern Ap
BOW E3 140 G5
Blackwall Wy POP/IOD E14 141 H9
Blackwater Cl RAIN RM13 144 E7
Blackwater La CRAWE RH10 284 D8
HHS/BOV HP3 36 F9
Blackwater St EDUL SE22 181 N1
Blackwell Av GUW GU2 249 J10
Blackwell Cl CLPT E5 120 D9
KTN/HRWW/W HA3 94 C8
Blackwell Dr OXHEY WD19 73 K10
Blackwell Gdns EDGW HA8 95 M5
Blackwellhall La CSHM HP5 51 P7
Blackwell Hall La CSHM HP5 51 P9
Blackwell Rd KGLGY WD4 54 B5
Blackwood Cl BF/WBF KT14 215 M8
Blackwood St WALW SE17 18 G7
Bladen Cl WEY KT13 216 E3
Blades Cl LHD/OX KT22 237 J6
Bladindon Dr BXLY DA5 185 N3
Bladon Cl GU GU1 250 D9
Bladon Gdns RYLN/HDSTN HA2 114 A4
Blagden's La STHGT/OAK N14 98 E3
Blagdon Rd LEW SE13 182 G2
NWMAL KT3 200 C4
Blagdon Wk TEDD TW11 177 H9 1
Blagrove Rd NKENS W10 8 B4
Blair Av CDALE/KGS NW9 116 B5
ESH/CLAY KT10 198 B9
Blair Cl BFN/LL DA15 185 H1
HYS/HAR UB3 153 H3
Blairderry Rd BRXS/STRHM SW2 180 F5
Blair Dr SEV TN13 247 J9
Blairhead Dr OXHEY WD19 93 J4
Blair Rd SL SL1 129 K10
Blair St POP/IOD E14 141 H8
Blake Av BARK IG11 143 H3
Blake Cl CAR SM5 201 P8
RAIN RM13 144 G3
STAL AL1 38 F9
WELL DA16 163 H7
Blakeden Dr ESH/CLAY KT10 218 E4
Blake Gdns DART DA1 165 N10
FUL/PGN SW6 157 K7
Blakehall Rd CAR SM5 222 A3
Blake Hall Rd CHONG CM5 67 H2
WAN E11 121 M6
Blakemere Rd WGCW AL8 22 G3
Blakemore Rd
STRHM/NOR SW16 180 F6 1
THHTH CR7 202 G5
Blakemore Wy BELV DA17 163 P2 2
Blakeney Av BECK BR3 204 E1
Blakeney Cl HOR/WEW KT19 220 A7
TRDG/WHET N20 97 M2
Blakeney Rd BECK BR3 204 E1
Blake Rd CAN/RD E16 141 L6
CROY/NA CR0 203 M9
FBAR/BDGN N11 98 D8
MTCM CR4 201 P3 2
Blaker Rd SRTFD E15 141 H3
Blakes Av NWMAL KT3 200 C5
Blakes Cl NKENS W10 136 F7
Blake's Gn WWKM BR4 205 H7
Blakes La NWMAL KT3 200 C5
RGUE GU4 252 A7
Blakesley Av EA W5 135 H8
Blake's Rd PECK SE15 159 M6
Blakes Ter NWMAL KT3 200 D5
Blakesware Gdns WCHMH N21 99 L1
Blakewood Cl FELT TW13 175 K7 1
Blanchard Cl ELTH/MOT SE9 184 B6
Blanchards Hl RGUE GU4 250 B3
Blanch Cl PECK SE15 160 B6
Blanchedowne CMBW SE5 159 L10
Blanche La POTB/CUF EN6 58 C10
Blanche St CAN/RD E16 141 L6
Blanchland Rd MRDN SM4 201 L5
Blanchman's Rd WARL CR6 242 D4
Blandfield Rd BAL SW12 180 B2
Blandford Av BECK BR3 204 D2
WHTN TW2 176 A4
Blandford Cl CROY/NA CR0 202 F10 2
DTCH/LGLY SL3 150 A2
EFNCH N2 117 M3
ROMW/RG RM7 124 C2
WOKS/MYFD GU22 232 E3
Blandford Crs CHING E4 101 H1
Blandford Rd BECK BR3 204 C2
CHSWK W4 156 B2
EA W5 155 J1
NWDGN UB2 153 P3
STAL AL1 38 F5
TEDD TW11 176 C8
Blandford Rd North
DTCH/LGLY SL3 150 A2
Blandford Rd South
DTCH/LGLY SL3 150 A3 1
Blandford St MHST W1U 10 B5
Blandford Waye YEAD UB4 133 K8
Bland St ELTH/MOT SE9 162 A10 1
Blaney Crs EHAM E6 142 E5
Blanford Rd REIG RH2 275 M1
Blanks La HORL RH6 278 D4
Blanmerle Rd ELTH/MOT SE9 184 E4
Blann Cl ELTH/MOT SE9 184 A2
Blantyre St WBPTN SW10 157 N6
Blashford St LEW SE13 183 J3
Blattner Cl BORE WD6 75 K8
Blawith Rd HRW HA1 114 D2
Blaydon Cl RSLP HA4 112 F5
Blaydon Wk TOTM N17 100 A8
Blays Cl EGH TW20 171 P9
Blay's La EGH TW20 171 N9
Bleak Hill La WOOL/PLUM SE18 163 J5
Blean Gv PGE/AN SE20 182 B10
Bleasdale Av GFD/PVL UB6 134 F4
Blechynden St NTGHL W11 136 G9 1
Bledlow Cl THMD SE28 143 M9
Bledlow Ri GFD/PVL UB6 134 B4
Bleeding Heart Yd HCIRC EC1N 12 B4 1
Blegborough Rd
STRHM/NOR SW16 180 D9
Blencarn Cl WOKN/KNAP GU21 231 M2
Blendon Dr BXLY DA5 185 N2
Blendon Rd BXLY DA5 185 N2
Blendon Ter WOOL/PLUM SE18 162 F4
Blenheim Av GNTH/NBYPK IG2 122 D4
Blenheim Cl BF/WBF KT14 215 J9
CRAWE RH10 284 E4 2
DART DA1 187 K2
GFD/PVL UB6 134 C4 1
OXHEY WD19 93 K1
ROMW/RG RM7 124 D2
RYNPK SW20 200 F3
SBW CM21 29 L3
UPMR RM14 126 D6 1
WCHMH N21 99 K2
WLGTN SM6 222 D4 1
Blenheim Ct BFN/LL DA15 184 G6
WFD IG8 101 N8 2
WGCE AL7 23 J4
Blenheim Crs NTGHL W11 8 A7
RSLP HA4 112 E7
SAND/SEL CR2 223 K4
Blenheim Dr WELL DA16 163 J7
Blenheim Gdns
BRXS/STRHM SW2 180 G2
CRICK NW2 116 F10
KUTN/CMB KT2 177 N10
SAND/SEL CR2 223 P8
SOCK/AV RM15 146 A10
WBLY HA9 115 K8
WLGTN SM6 222 D3
WOKS/MYFD GU22 231 N5
Blenheim Gv GVE DA12 190 F3 2
PECK SE15 159 P8
Blenheim Park Rd SAND/SEL CR2 223 K5
Blenheim Pas STJWD NW8 3 J7 1
Blenheim Rd BAR EN5 76 G7
BFN/LL DA15 185 M4
BRWN CM15 86 F10
CHSWK W4 156 B2
DART DA1 187 K2
DTCH/LGLY SL3 150 A3
EHAM E6 142 A5
FSTGT E7 121 K9
HAYES BR2 206 B4
HOR/WEW KT19 220 A7
NTHLT UB5 134 A1
ORP BR6 207 M9
PGE/AN SE20 182 B10 1
RYLN/HDSTN HA2 114 A4
RYNPK SW20 200 F3
STAL AL1 38 E5
STJWD NW8 3 K7
SUT SM1 201 K10
WALTH E17 120 C1
Blenheim St MYFR/PKLN W1K 10 E6 1
Blenheim Ter STJWD NW8 3 J7
Blenheim Wy EPP CM16 66 B3
ISLW TW7 154 F7
Blenhiem Rd GSTN WD25 55 H9
Blenkarne Rd BTSEA SW11 180 A2
Blenkin Cl STALW/RED AL3 38 B2
Bleriot Rd HEST TW5 153 K6
Blessbury Rd EDGW HA8 95 P9
Blessington Rd LEW SE13 161 J10
Blessing Wy BARK IG11 143 M4
Bletchingley Cl REDH RH1 258 D5
Bletchingley Rd GDST RH9 259 P7
REDH RH1 258 D5
Bletchingly Cl THHTH CR7 203 J4
Bletchley St IS N1 6 F8
Bletchmore Cl HYS/HAR UB3 152 E4
Bletsoe Wk IS N1 6 F7
Bligh Cl CRAWE RH10 284 A9
Bligh Rd GVW DA11 190 D2
Bligh's Rd SEV TN13 265 J1
Blincoe Cl WIM/MER SW19 178 G5
Blinco La DTCH/LGLY SL3 130 B8
Blindley Rd CRAWE RH10 284 E4 3
Blindman's La CHES/WCR EN8 62 C6
Blissett St GNWCH SE10 161 H7
Blisworth Cl YEAD UB4 133 M6 2
Blithbury Rd DAGW RM9 143 L1
Blithdale Rd ABYW SE2 163 K3
Blithfield St KENS W8 14 G4
Blockhouse Rd GRAYS RM17 167 P5 1
Blockley Rd ALP/SUD HA0 114 G7
Bloemfontein Av SHB W12 136 E10
Bloemfontein Rd SHB W12 136 E9
Blomfield Rd BAY/PAD W2 9 H3
Blomfield St LVPST EC2M 13 H4
Blomfield Vls BAY/PAD W2 9 H4
Blomville Rd BCTR RM8 123 P7
Blondell Cl WDR/YW UB7 151 N5
Blondel St BTSEA SW11 158 B8
Blondin Av EA W5 155 H3
Blondin St BOW E3 140 F4
Bloomfield Cl WOKN/KNAP GU21 231 K4
Bloomfield Crs GNTH/NBYPK IG2 122 E4
Bloomfield Pl MYFR/PKLN W1K 10 F7 1
Bloomfield Rd CHESW EN7 61 K1 1
HAYES BR2 206 A5
HGT N6 118 B4
KUT KT1 199 K4
WOOL/PLUM SE18 162 E4
Bloomfield Ter BGVA SW1W 16 D7 1
Bloom Gv WNWD SE27 181 J6 1
Bloomhall Rd NRWD SE19 181 L8
Bloom Park Rd FUL/PGN SW6 157 J6
Bloomsbury Cl EA W5 135 L9
HOR/WEW KT19 220 A6
Bloomsbury Pl NOXST/BSQ WC1A 11 M4
Bloomsbury Sq NOXST/BSQ WC1A 11 M4
Bloomsbury St NOXST/BSQ WC1A 11 L5 1
RSQ WC1B 11 K4
Bloomsbury Wy
NOXST/BSQ WC1A 11 L4
Blore Cl VX/NE SW8 158 E7 1
Blossom Cl DAGW RM9 144 A3
EA W5 155 K1 1
SAND/SEL CR2 223 N2
Blossom La ENC/FH EN2 79 K5
Blossom St WCHPL E1 13 K3
Blossom Wy HGDN/ICK UB10 132 A2
WDR/YW UB7 152 B3
Blossom Waye HEST TW5 153 M5
Blount St POP/IOD E14 140 D8 2
Bloxam Gdns ELTH/MOT SE9 184 B1
Bloxhall Rd LEY E10 120 E6
Bloxham Crs HPTN TW12 197 N1
Bloxworth Cl WLGTN SM6 202 D10
Blucher Rd CMBW SE5 159 K6
Blucher St CSHM HP5 50 G7 1
Blue Anchor La BERM/RHTH SE16 19 P5
TIL RM18 169 H3
Blue Anchor Yd WCHPL E1 13 N7
Blue Ball La EGH TW20 172 C8 1
Blue Ball Yd WHALL SW1A 10 G10
Blue Barn Wy WEY KT13 216 B7
Bluebell Av FSTGT E7 122 A10
MNPK E12 122 B10
Bluebell Cl CRAWW RH11 283 L10 2
HERT/BAY SG13 25 P5
HHW HP1 35 H7 1
MTCM CR4 202 C8 1
ORP BR6 206 F9
ROMW/RG RM7 124 F7
SYD SE26 181 N7
Bluebell Ct WOKS/MYFD GU22 232 A5 1
Bluebell Dr ABLGY WD5 54 G3
CHESW EN7 61 L4
Bluebell La EHSLY KT24 252 F5 1
Bluebell Ri LTWR GU18 212 A7 1
Bluebell Wy IL IG1 142 E1
Blueberry Cl STALW/RED AL3 38 C2 2
WFD IG8 101 M7 1
Blueberry Gdns COUL/CHIP CR5 240 G2
Blueberry La RSEV TN14 245 M2
Bluebridge Av BRKMPK AL9 59 H3
Blue Bridge Rd BRKMPK AL9 59 H3
Blue Cedars BNSTD SM7 220 G10
Blue Cedars Pl COB KT11 217 L8
Bluecoats Av HERT/WAS SG14 25 L5 3
Bluecoat Yd WARE SG12 26 C2 1
Bluefield Cl HPTN TW12 175 P8
Bluegates EW KT17 220 D4
Bluehouse Gdns OXTED RH8 261 M4
Bluehouse Hill Hemel
Hempstead Rd STALW/RED AL3 37 P7
Bluehouse La OXTED RH8 261 K4
Bluehouse Rd CHING E4 101 K4
Bluemans EPP CM16 48 E10
Bluemans End EPP CM16 48 E10
Bluett Rd LCOL/BKTW AL2 57 J3
Bluewater Pkwy GRH DA9 188 E3
Blumfield Crs SL SL1 128 C7
Blundel La COB KT11 218 A10
Blundell Av HORL RH6 280 A4
Blundell Cl STALW/RED AL3 38 C2
Blundell Rd EDGW HA8 96 B8 1
Blundell St HOLWY N7 5 M3
Blunden Cl BCTR RM8 123 M6 2
Blunden Dr DTCH/LGLY SL3 150 E3
Blunesfield POTB/CUF EN6 59 N7 1
Blunt Rd CROY/NA CR0 223 L2 3
Blunts Av WDR/YW UB7 152 B6
Blunts La LCOL/BKTW AL2 37 L10
Blunts Rd ELTH/MOT SE9 184 D1
Blurton Rd CLPT E5 120 C9
Blyth Cl BORE WD6 75 L5
TWK TW1 176 E2 1
Blythe Cl FSTH SE23 182 E3
IVER SL0 131 J8
Blythe Hl FSTH SE23 182 E3
STMC/STPC BR5 207 J1
Blythe Hill La FSTH SE23 182 E3
Blythe Rd HOD EN11 45 J5
WKENS W14 156 G2
Blythe V FSTH SE23 182 E4
Blyth Rd BMLY BR1 205 L1
HYS/HAR UB3 152 F1
THMD SE28 143 M9
WALTH E17 120 E5
Blythswood Rd GDMY/SEVK IG3 123 K6
Blyth Wk UPMR RM14 126 D5
Blythway WGCE AL7 23 J2 1
Blythwood Rd FSBYPK N4 118 F5
PIN HA5 93 L9
Blyton Cl BEAC HP9 88 C7
Boadicea St IS N1 5 N6
Boakes Meadow RSEV TN14 228 G7
Boardman Av CHING E4 80 G9
Boardman Cl BAR EN5 77 H9
Board School Rd
WOKN/KNAP GU21 232 C2
Boardwalk Pl POP/IOD E14 141 H10
Boar Hl RDKG RH5 272 D8
Boarlands Cl SL SL1 128 E9 1
Boathouse Wk PECK SE15 159 N6 1
Boat Lifter Wy BERM/RHTH SE16 160 D3
Bob Anker Cl PLSTW E13 141 M5 1
Bobbin Cl CLAP SW4 158 D9 1
Bobbingworth Ml CHONG CM5 49 H10
Bob Marley Wy HNHL SE24 159 H10
Bockhampton Rd
KUTN/CMB KT2 177 L10
Bocking St HACK E8 140 A3
Boddicott Cl WIM/MER SW19 179 H5
Bodell Cl CDH/CHF RM16 167 N1
Bodiam Cl CRAWE RH10 284 D7
EN EN1 79 L6
Bodiam Rd STRHM/NOR SW16 202 E1
Bodle Av SWCM DA10 189 K2
Bodley Cl EPP CM16 65 J6
NWMAL KT3 200 B5
Bodley Rd NWMAL KT3 200 B6
Bodmin Av SL SL1 128 F7
Bodmin Cl RYLN/HDSTN HA2 113 N8
STMC/STPC BR5 207 M8
Bodmin Gv MRDN SM4 201 L4
Bodmin St WAND/EARL SW18 179 K4
Bodnant Gdns RYNPK SW20 200 D3
Bodney Rd CLPT E5 120 A10
Bodwell Cl HHW HP1 35 K5 1
Boeing Wy NWDGN UB2 153 J2
Boelyn Dr RSLP HA4 113 L7
Bognor Gdns OXHEY WD19 93 K6 1
Bognor Rd WELL DA16 163 N7
Bohemia HHNE HP2 35 P5
Bohemia Pl HACK E8 140 B1
Bohun Gv EBAR EN4 77 P10
Boileau Rd BARN SW13 156 D6
EA W5 135 L8
Bois Av AMS HP6 68 G2
Bois Hall Rd ADL/WDHM KT15 215 N2
Bois Hl CSHM HP5 51 J10
Bois Moor Rd CSHM HP5 51 H10
Boissy Cl STALE/WH AL4 39 K7
Bolden St DEPT SE8 160 G8
Boldero Pl STJWD NW8 9 N2 1
Bolderwood Wy WWKM BR4 204 G9
Bolding House La
CHOB/PIR GU24 212 E9
Boldmere Rd PIN HA5 113 K5
Boleyn Av EN EN1 80 A5
EW KT17 220 D6
Boleyn Cl CDH/CHF RM16 167 L2 1
CRAWE RH10 284 E10
HHNE HP2 36 D1
STA TW18 173 H8 1
Boleyn Ct BKHH IG9 101 M2
BROX EN10 44 D7
WALTH E17 120 F2 1
Boleyn Dr E/WMO/HCT KT8 197 N3
STAL AL1 38 C8
Boleyn Gdns DAGE RM10 144 D2 3
RBRW/HUT CM13 107 M4
WWKM BR4 204 G9
Boleyn Rd EHAM E6 142 A4
FSTGT E7 141 M2
RSEV TN14 247 M3
STNW/STAM N16 119 M10
Boleyn Wk LHD/OX KT22 236 E6
Boleyn Wy BAR EN5 77 M7
BARK/HLT IG6 102 F7
SWCM DA10 189 K3
Bolina Rd BERM/RHTH SE16 160 B4
Bolingbroke Gv BTSEA SW11 179 P1
Bolingbroke Rd WKENS W14 156 G2
Bolingbroke Wk BTSEA SW11 157 N7 1
Bolingbroke Wy HYS/HAR UB3 132 E10
Bolingbrook STALE/WH AL4 38 F2 2
Bollo La ACT W3 155 N2
CHSWK W4 155 P3
Bolney Ct CRAWW RH11 283 J10
Bolney St VX/NE SW8 158 G6
Bolsover Gv REDH RH1 258 F5
Bolsover St GTPST W1W 10 F2
Bolstead Rd MTCM CR4 202 C1 2
Bolters La BNSTD SM7 239 J1
Bolters Rd HORL RH6 280 B2
Bolters Rd South HORL RH6 280 A2
Bolton Av WDSR SL4 149 J9
Bolton Cl CHSGTN KT9 219 J3
Bolton Crs CMBW SE5 18 B10
WDSR SL4 149 H9
Bolton Gdns BMLY BR1 183 L9
ECT SW5 15 H7
TEDD TW11 176 F9
WLSDN NW10 136 G4
Bolton Gardens Ms WBPTN SW10 15 H7
Bolton Rd CHSGTN KT9 219 J3
CHSWK W4 155 P6
FSTGT E7 141 L1
HRW HA1 114 B2
KIL/WHAMP NW6 3 H6
UED N18 99 N6
WDSR SL4 149 H9
WLSDN NW10 136 B3 1
Boltons Cl WOKS/MYFD GU22 233 K1
Bolton's La WDR/YW UB7 152 D6
WOKS/MYFD GU22 233 K2
The Boltons ALP/SUD HA0 114 E9 1
WBPTN SW10 15 J7
Bolton St MYFR/PICC W1J 10 F9
Bombay St BERM/RHTH SE16 160 A3
Bombers La BH/WHM TN16 244 G6
Bomer Cl WDR/YW UB7 152 B6
Bomore Rd NTGHL W11 8 A7
Bonar Pl CHST BR7 184 B10
Bonar Rd PECK SE15 159 P6
Bonaventure Ct GVE DA12 191 J7
Bonchester Cl CHST BR7 184 D10 1
Bonchurch Cl BELMT SM2 221 L4 2
Bonchurch Rd NKENS W10 8 A3 1
WEA W13 134 G10 1
Bond Cl RSEV TN14 245 N1
WDR/YW UB7 132 A8
Bondfield Av YEAD UB4 133 H5 1
Bond Gdns WLGTN SM6 222 D1
Bond Rd MTCM CR4 202 A2
SURB KT6 199 L9
WARL CR6 242 C4
Bond's La RDKG RH5 272 G8 1
Bond St EA W5 135 J9
EGH TW20 171 N9
GRAYS RM17 167 P5
SRTFD E15 121 K10
Bondway VX/NE SW8 17 M10
Bonehurst Rd HORL RH6 276 B10
Bone Mill La GDST RH9 260 D10
Bones La HORL RH6 281 P3
Boneta Rd WOOL/PLUM SE18 162 C2 1
Bonfield Rd LEW SE13 161 H10
Bonham Gdns BCTR RM8 123 N7 1
Bonham Rd BCTR RM8 123 N7
BRXS/STRHM SW2 180 G1
Bonheur Rd CHSWK W4 156 A1 2
Bonhill St SDTCH EC2A 13 H2
Boniface Gdns KTN/HRWW/W HA3 94 A8
Boniface Rd HGDN/ICK UB10 112 C8
Boniface Wk KTN/HRWW/W HA3 94 A8
Bonington Rd HCH RM12 125 L10 2
Bonks Hl SBW CM21 29 N2
Bonner Hill Rd KUT KT1 199 L3
Bonner Rd BETH E2 140 B4
Bonners Cl WOKS/MYFD GU22 232 C8
Bonnersfield Cl HRW HA1 114 F4 1
Bonnersfield La HRW HA1 114 E4
Bonner St BETH E2 140 C5 1
Bonner Wk CDH/CHF RM16 167 L2 2
Bonnetts La CRAWW RH11 283 K2
Bonneville Gdns CLAP SW4 180 D2
Bonney Gv CHESW EN7 61 P6
Bonney Wy SWLY BR8 208 F2
Bonningtons RBRW/HUT CM13 107 N4
Bonnington Sq VX/NE SW8 17 N9
Bonnys Rd REIG RH2 256 G10
Bonny St CAMTN NW1 4 G4
Bonser Rd TWK TW1 176 E5
Bonsey Cl WOKS/MYFD GU22 232 B7
Bonsey La WOKS/MYFD GU22 232 B7
Bonsey's La CHOB/PIR GU24 214 B5
Bonsor Dr KWD/TDW/WH KT20 239 H8
Bonsor St CMBW SE5 159 M6
Bonville Gdns HDN NW4 116 D2 1
Bonville Rd BMLY BR1 183 L8
Booker Rd UED N18 99 P6 2
Bookham Ct GT/LBKH KT23 235 N9 1
Bookham Gv GT/LBKH KT23 254 A2 1
Bookham Rd COB KT11 235 L6
Boones Rd LEW SE13 161 K10
Boone St LEW SE13 161 K10
Boord St GNWCH SE10 161 K2
Boothby Rd ARCH N19 118 E7
Booth Cl THMD SE28 143 L10 1
Booth Dr STA TW18 173 N9
Booth Rd CDALE/KGS NW9 96 A9
CRAWW RH11 283 H10
CROY/NA CR0 203 J9 2
Booths Cl BRKMPK AL9 40 G10
Boot St IS N1 7 J10
Bordars Rd HNWL W7 134 D7
Bordars Wk HNWL W7 134 D7
Borden Av WCHMH N21 79 L10
Border Cha CRAWE RH10 285 H3
Border Crs SYD SE26 182 A8
Border Gdns CROY/NA CR0 224 G1
Border Ga MTCM CR4 201 P1
Border Rd SYD SE26 182 A8
Borderside SLN SL2 129 M8
Border's La LOU IG10 82 D8
Bordesley Rd MRDN SM4 201 L4 2
Bordon Wk PUT/ROE SW15 178 D3 1
Boreham Av CAN/RD E16 141 M8
Boreham Rd WDGN N22 99 K9
Borers Arms Rd CRAWE RH10 285 J1
Borgard Rd WOOL/PLUM SE18 162 C3
Borkwood Pk ORP BR6 227 J1
Borkwood Wy ORP BR6 227 H1
Borland Cl GRH DA9 188 F1 1
Borland Rd PECK SE15 160 B10
TEDD TW11 176 G9
Bornedene POTB/CUF EN6 59 H7
Borneo St PUT/ROE SW15 156 F9
Borough High St STHWK SE1 12 G10 2
Borough Hl CROY/NA CR0 203 J10
Borough Rd BH/WHM TN16 244 A7
ISLW TW7 154 D7
KUTN/CMB KT2 199 M1
MTCM CR4 201 P2
STHWK SE1 18 C3
The Borough CHONG CM5 67 N5
RDKG RH5 273 M1
Borough Wy POTB/CUF EN6 59 H8
Borrell Cl BROX EN10 44 D6
Borrett Cl WALW SE17 18 E8
Borrodaile Rd WAND/EARL SW18 179 L2
Borrowdale Av
KTN/HRWW/W HA3 94 F10
Borrowdale Cl CRAWW RH11 283 L9 1
EGH TW20 172 E10 1
REDBR IG4 122 B2 1
SAND/SEL CR2 223 N9 1
Borrowdale Dr SAND/SEL CR2 223 N8
Borthwick Ms SRTFD E15 121 K9 2
Borthwick Rd CDALE/KGS NW9 116 C4 1
SRTFD E15 121 K9
Borthwick St DEPT SE8 160 F4
Borwick Av WALTH E17 120 E1 1
Bosanquet Cl UX/CGN UB8 131 N7
Bosanquet Rd HOD EN11 45 H1 1
Bosbury Rd CAT SE6 183 H6
Boscastle Rd KTTN NW5 118 C8
Boscobel Pl BGVA SW1W 16 D5
Boscobel St BAY/PAD W2 9 M3
Boscombe Av EMPK RM11 125 L5
GRAYS RM17 168 A3
WAN E11 121 J5 1
Boscombe Cl CLPT E5 120 D10
EGH TW20 194 F1 1
Boscombe Rd SHB W12 156 D1
TOOT SW17 180 B9
WIM/MER SW19 201 K1
WPK KT4 200 F8
Bosgrove CHING E4 101 H2
Bosham Rd CRAWE RH10 284 D10 3
Boshers Gdns EGH TW20 172 C9
Bosman Dr BFOR GU20 192 A10

Boss St STHWK SE1 19 L1
Bostall Hl ABYW SE2 163 L4
Bostall La ABYW SE2 163 L3
Bostall Manorway ABYW SE2 163 L3
Bostall Park Av BXLYHN DA7 163 P6
Bostall Rd STMC/STPC BR5 185 L10
Boston Gdns BTFD TW8 154 F3
　CHSWK W4 156 B5
Boston Gv RSLP HA4 112 D4
　SL SL1 129 H8
Boston Manor Rd BTFD TW8 154 F3
Boston Park Rd BTFD TW8 155 H4
Boston Pl CAMTN NW1 10 A2
Boston Rd CROY/NA CR0 202 G6
　EDGW HA8 95 P8
　EHAM E6 142 B5
　HNWL W7 154 E1
Bostonthorpe Rd HNWL W7 154 F3
Boston V HNWL W7 154 D1
Bosville Dr SEV TN13 247 H9
Bosville Rd SEV TN13 247 H9
Boswell Cl RAD WD7 57 K8
　STMC/STPC BR5 207 H8
Boswell Rd CRAWE RH10 283 P10
　THHTH CR7 203 K4
Boswell St BMSBY WC1N 11 M3
Boswick La BERK HP4 33 J1
Bosworth Cl WALTH E17 100 E9
Bosworth Crs HARH RM3 105 K7
Bosworth Rd BAR EN5 77 K7
　DAGE RM10 124 D9
　FBAR/BDGN N11 98 E7
　NKENS W10 8 B2
Botany Bay La CHST BR7 206 F2
Botany Cl EBAR EN4 77 P8
Botany Wy PUR RM19 166 A4
Boteley Cl CHING E4 101 J3
Botham Cl EDGW HA8 95 P8
Botha Rd PLSTW E13 141 N7
Bothwell Cl CAN/RD E16 141 M7
Bothwell Rd CROY/NA CR0 225 H6
Bothwell St FUL/PGN SW6 156 L5
Botley La CSHM HP5 51 M6
Botley Rd CSHM HP5 51 N6
　HHNE HP2 36 B1
Botolph La MON EC3R 13 J8
Botsford Rd RYNPK SW20 201 H2
Bottom Harrow Rd VW GU25 194 C6
Bottom La KGLGY WD4 71 M1
Bott Rd RDART DA2 187 N1
Bott's Ms BAY/PAD W2 8 F6
Botwell Common Rd HYS/HAR UB3 132 E9
Botwell Crs HYS/HAR UB3 132 F8
Botwell La HYS/HAR UB3 152 G1
Boucher Cl TEDD TW11 176 B8
Boughton Av HAYES BR2 205 L1
Boughton Hall Av RPLY/SEND GU23 251 H1
Boughton Rd THMD SE28 163 H2
Boughton Wy AMHS HP6 69 P5
Boulcott St WCHPL E1 140 C8
The Boulevard CRAWE RH10 283 N7
　WATW WD18 72 G9
　WCCE AL7 23 J3
Boulmer Rd UX/CGN UB8 131 M5
Boulogne Rd CROY/NA CR0 203 K6
Boulter Gdns RAIN RM13 145 H1
Boulters Cl SL SL1 148 F1
Boulthurst Wy OXTED RH8 261 M8
Boulton Rd BCTR RM8 123 P7
Boultwood Rd EHAM E6 142 C8
Bounces La ED N9 100 A3
Bounces Rd ED N9 100 A3
The Bounce HHNE HP2 35 N4
Boundaries Rd BAL SW12 180 L5
　FELT TW13 175 K4
Boundary Av WALTH E17 120 E5
Boundary Cl BAR EN5 77 J5
　CDMY/SEVK IG3 123 H9
　KUT KT1 199 P3
　NWDGN UB2 153 P4
　PLSTW E13 141 P4
Boundary Dr HERT/WAS SG14 25 L3
Boundary La PLSTW E13 142 A5
　WALW SE17 18 F10
　WCCE AL7 23 H9
Boundary Ms STJWD NW8 3 K5
Boundary Rd ASHF TW15 173 M8
　BARK IG11 142 G3
　BFN/LL DA15 185 H1
　CRAWE RH10 283 P6
　ED N9 80 B10
　PIN HA5 113 L4
　PLSTW E13 141 P4
　ROM RM1 125 H4
　STAL AL1 38 D7
　STJWD NW8 3 J6
　UPMR RM14 125 P9
　WALTH E17 120 E5
　WDGN N22 99 K10
　WIM/MER SW19 179 N9
　WLGTN SM6 222 D2
　WOKN/KNAP GU21 232 D2
Boundary Rd East ADL/WDHM KT15 215 L5
Boundary Rd North ADL/WDHM KT15 215 L5
Boundary Rd West ADL/WDHM KT15 215 L5
Boundary Rw STHWK SE1 18 C1
Boundary St BETH E2 7 L10
　ERITH DA8 164 G6
Boundary Wy CROY/NA CR0 224 F2
　GSTN WD25 55 K8
　HHNE HP2 36 D4
　WOKN/KNAP GU21 232 D2
Boundfield Rd CAT SE6 183 K6
Bounds Green Rd FBAR/BDGN N11 98 E7
　WDGN N22 98 F8
Bourchier St SOHO/CST W1F 11 J7
Bourdon Pl MYFR/PKLN W1K 10 F7
Bourdon Rd PGE/AN SE20 204 B2
Bourdon St MYFR/PKLN W1K 10 E8
Bourke Cl CLAP SW4 180 F2
　WLSDN NW10 136 B1
Bourke Hl COUL/CHIP CR5 240 A4
Bourlet Cl FITZ W1T 10 G4
Bourn Av EBAR EN4 77 N9
　SEVS/STOTM N15 119 J2
　UX/CGN UB8 131 J10
Bourne Av CHERT KT16 195 K3
　HYS/HAR UB3 152 F2
　RSLP HA4 113 A10
　STHGT/OAK N14 98 F3
　WDSR SL4 149 H10
Bournebridge La ABR/ST RM4 104 C1
Bourne Cl BF/WBF KT14 215 L10
　BROX EN10 44 E6
　RGUE GU4 268 G6
　WARE SG12 26 C5
Bourne Ct RSLP HA4 113 J10
Bourne Dr MTCM CR4 202 N2
Bourne End EMPK RM11 125 N2
Bourne End La HHW HP1 34 F8
Bourne End Rd NTHWD HA6 92 F5
Bournefield Rd CTHM CR3 241 P4
Bourne Gdns CHING E4 100 G5
Bourne Gv ASHTD KT21 237 J6
Bournehall Av BUSH WD23 73 P9
Bournehall La BUSH WD23 73 P10
Bournehall Rd BUSH WD23 73 P10
Bourne Hl PLMGR N13 98 G3
Bourne La CTHM CR3 241 L7
Bourne Md BXLY DA5 186 D1

Bournemead Av NTHLT UB5 133 H4
Bournemead Cl NTHLT UB5 133 H5
Bourne Meadow ECH TW20 194 B10
Bournemouth Cl PECK SE15 159 P8
Bournemouth Rd PECK SE15 159 P8
　WIM/MER SW19 201 K1
Bourne Park Cl PUR/KEN CR8 241 M2
Bourne Rd ADL/WDHM KT15 215 L5
　BERK HP4 33 L4
　BUSH WD23 73 P9
　BXLY DA5 186 C3
　CEND/HSY/T N8 118 F4
　FSTGT E7 121 L8
　GVE DA12 191 J5
　REDH RH1 258 D6
　RGODL GU7 267 L9
　SL SL1 149 H1
　VW GU25 193 M7
Bourneside VW GU25 193 M7
Bourneside Crs STHGT/OAK N14 98 E2
Bourneside Gdns CAT SE6 183 H8
Bourneside Rd ADL/WDHM KT15 215 N2
Bourne St BCVA SW1W 16
　CROY/NA CR0 203 J9
Bourne Ter BAY/PAD W2 8 G3
The Bourne HHW HP1 52 D3
　STHGT/OAK N14 98 F2
　WARE SG12 26 C1
Bourne V HAYES BR2 205 M6
Bournevale Rd STRHM/NOR SW16 180 F7
　PUR/KEN CR8 241 L1
Bourne Wy ADL/WDHM KT15 215 M2
　HAYES BR2 205 M9
　HOR/WEW KT19 219 P1
　SUT SM1 221 J2
　SWLY BR8 208 D3
　WOKS/MYFD GU22 232 A8
Bournewood Rd STMC/STPC BR5 207 L7
　WOOL/PLUM SE18 163 K6
Bournville Rd CAT SE6 182 F3
Bournwell Cl EBAR EN4 78 A7
Bourton Cl HYS/HAR UB3 133 H10
Bousfield Rd NWCR SE14 160 C8
Bousley Ri CHERT KT16 214 G4
Boutflower Rd BTSEA SW11 157 P10
Bouverie Gdns KTN/HRWW/W HA3 115 J4
　PUR/KEN CR8 222 F10
Bouverie Ms STNW/STAM N16 119 M7
Bouverie Pl BAY/PAD W2 9 M5
　HRW HA1 114 A3
　STNW/STAM N16 119 M7
Bouverie St EMB EC4Y 12 B6
Bouverie Wy DTCH/LGLY SL3 150 A3
Bouvier Rd PEND EN3 80 B4
Boveney Cl SL SL1 148 D3
Boveney New Rd WDSR SL4 148 B3
Boveney Rd FSTH SE23 182 C3
　WDSR SL4 148 B3
Boveney Wood Cl SL SL1 108 C8
Bovey Rd SOCK/AV RM15 146 G7
Bovill Rd FSTH SE23 182 C3
Bovingdon Av WBLY HA9 135 M1
Bovingdon Crs GSTN WD25 55 L10
Bovingdon Green La HHS/BOV HP3 52 C4
Bovingdon La CDALE/KGS NW9 96 B9
Bovingdon Rd FUL/PGN SW6 157 L7
Bow Arrow La DART DA1 187 P4
　RDART DA2 188 A2
Bowater Cl CDALE/KGS NW9 116 A3
　CLAP SW4 180 F2
Bowater Pl BKHTH/KID SE3 161 N6
Bowater Rdg WEY KT13 216 E9
Bowater Rd CRAWE RH10 284 D10
　WOOL/PLUM SE18 162 A2
Bow Br STALW/RED AL3 37 M3
Bow Common La BOW E3 140 E6
Bowden Cl EBED/NFELT TW14 174 F4
Bowden Dr EMPK RM11 125 M6
Bowden Rd ASC SL5 192 B5
Bowden St LBTH SE11 18 A9
Bowditch DEPT SE8 160 E4
Bowdon Rd LEY E10 120 F5
Bowen Dr DUL SE21 181 M6
Bowen Rd HRW HA1 114 B5
Bowen St POP/IOD E14 140 C8
Bower Av GNWCH SE10 161 K7
Bower Cl CRW RM5 104 B8
　NTHLT UB5 133 K4
Bowerdean St FUL/PGN SW6 157 L7
Bower Farm Rd ABR/ST RM4 104 C1
Bower Hl EPP CM16 65 K8
Bower Hill Cl REDH RH1 276 E1
Bower Hill La REDH RH1 276 E1
Bower La EYN DA4 209 M10
Bowerman Av NWCR SE14 160 D5
Bowerman Rd CDH/CHF RM16 168 D3
Bower Rd SWLY BR8 187 H10
Bowers Av GVW DA11 190 D9
Bowers Cl RGUE GU4 250 D6
Bowers Farm Dr RGUE GU4 250 D6
Bowers Rd RSEV TN14 228 G2
Bower St WCHPL E1 140 C8
Bower V EPP CM16 65 K8
Bower Wy SL SL1 128 D9
Bowes Cl BFN/LL DA15 185 L2
Bowes Dr CHONG CM5 67 N3
Bowes Lyon Ms STALW/RED AL3 38 C6
Bowes Rd ACT W3 136 D3
　BCTR RM8 123 M9
　FBAR/BDGN N11 98 C6
　STA TW18 173 H9
　WOT/HER KT12 197 J9
Bowes Rd (North Circular Rd) PLMGR N13 98 F6
Bowes Wd HART DA3 211 L10
Bowfell Rd HMSMTH W6 156 F5
Bowford Av BXLYHN DA7 165 P7
Bowgate STAL AL1 38 D5
Bowhay RBRW/HUT CM13 107 N3
Bowhill Cl BRXN/ST SW9 159 H6
Bowie Cl CLAP SW4 180 F6
Bowland Rd CLAP SW4 158 L10
　WFD IG8 101 P7
Bow La FNCH N3 97 M8
Bowler's Orch CSTG HP8 89 M8
Bowles Gn EN EN1 80 A2
Bowley Cl NRWD SE19 181 N9
Bowley La NRWD SE19 181 N8
Bowley St POP/IOD E14 140 E9
Bowling Cl HARP AL5 118
Bowling Green Cl PUT/ROE SW15 178 E3
Bowling Green Ct WBLY HA9 115 L7
Bowling Green La CLKNW EC1R 12 B?
Bowling Green Pl STHWK SE1 18 G1
Bowling Green Rd CHOB/PIR GU24 213 K5
Bowling Green Rw WOOL/PLUM SE18 162 C5
Bowling Green St LBTH SE11 18 A9
Bowling Green Wk IS N1 7 J9
Bowls Cl STAN HA7 94 G6
Bowman Av CAN/RD E16 141 L9
Bowman Ms WAND/EARL SW18 179 J5
Bowmans Cl POTB/CUF EN6 59 N8
　SL SL1 128 A3
　WEA W13 134 G1
Bowmans Ct HHNE HP2 35 N4
Bowmans Lea FSTH SE23 182 B5

Bowman's Meadow WLGTN SM6 202 C10
Bowman's Ms HOLWY N7 118 F8
Bowman's Pl HOLWY N7 118 F8
Bowmead ELTH/MOT SE9 184 C5
Bowmont Cl RBRW/HUT CM13 87 N10
Bown Cl TIL RM18 168 B8
Bowness Crs PUT/ROE SW15 178 B8
Bowness Dr HSLWW TW4 153 M10
Bowness Rd BXLYHN DA7 164 C8
　CAT SE6 183 M10
Bowness Wy HCH RM12 125 H10
Bowood Rd BTSEA SW11 158 B10
　PEND EN3 80 C6
Bowring Gn OXHEY WD19 93 K6
Bow Rd BOW E3 140 A8
Bowrons Av ALP/SUD HA0 135 J2
Bowry Dr STWL/WRAY TW19 172 C2
Bowsley Ct FELT TW13 175 H5
The Bowsprit COB KT11 235 K1
　SRTFD E15 121 K10
Bowyer Cl EHAM E6 142 C7
Bowyer Crs DEN/HRF UB9 111 J4
Bowyer Dr SL SL1 128 D9
Bowyer Pl CMBW SE5 159 K6
Bowyers HHNE HP2 35 M4
Bowyers Cl ASHTD KT21 237 L4
Bowzell Rd RSEV TN14 264 C9
Boxall Rd DUL SE21 181 M2
Boxfield Rd ALT7 23 L8
Boxford Cl SAND/SEL CR2 224 C8
Boxgrove Av GU GU1 250 D8
Boxgrove La GU GU1 250 D9
Boxgrove Rd ABYW SE2 163 K2
　GU GU1 250 D9
Boxhill HHNE HP2 35 M3
Boxhill Rd DORK RH4 255 K8
　KWD/TDW/WH KT20 255 L8
Boxhill Wy BRKHM/BTCW RH3 273 N4
Box La BARK IG11 143 L4
　HHW HP1 52 G1
　HOD EN11 44 D2
Boxley Rd MRDN SM4 201 N4
Boxley St CAN/RD E16 141 N10
Boxmoor Rd CRW RM5 104 D6
　KTN/HRWW/W HA3 114 G2
Box Ridge Av PUR/KEN CR8 222 C6
Boxted Cl BKHH IG9 102 B2
Boxtree La KTN/HRWW/W HA3 94 B9
Boxtree Rd KTN/HRWW/W HA3 94 C8
Boxwell Rd BERK HP4 33 N5
Boxwood Cl WDR/YW UB7 152 A1
Boxwood Wy WARL CR6 242 C3
Boxworth Gv IS N1 5 P5
Boyard Rd WOOL/PLUM SE18 162 E4
Boyce Cl BORE WD6 75 K5
Boyce Wy PLSTW E13 141 M6
Boycroft Av CDALE/KGS NW9 115 N4
Boyd Av STHL UB1 133 N10
Boyd Cl KUTN/CMB KT2 177 M10
Boydell Ct STJWD NW8 3 L4
Boyd Rd WIM/MER SW19 179 N9
Boyd St WCHPL E1 13 N6
Boyfield St STHWK SE1 18 D2
Boyland Rd BMLY BR1 183 L2
Boyle Av STAN HA7 94 F7
Boyle Farm Rd THDIT KT7 198 F6
Boyne Av HDN NW4 116 C2
Boyne Rd DAGE RM10 124 B8
　LEW SE13 161 J9
Boyne Terrace Ms NTGHL W11 8 C9
Boyson Rd WALW SE17 18 F9
Boyton Cl CEND/HSY/T N8 118 F1
　WCHPL E1 140 D6
Boyton Rd CEND/HSY/T N8 118 F1
Brabant Rd WDGN N22 98 G10
Brabazon Av WLGTN SM6 222 F5
Brabazon Rd HEST TW5 153 K6
　NTHLT UB5 133 P4
Brabazon St POP/IOD E14 140 A8
Brabourne Cl NRWD SE19 181 M8
Brabourne Crs BXLYHN DA7 164 A5
Brabourne Ri BECK BR3 205 A5
Brabourn Gv PECK SE15 160 B8
Brace Cl CHESW EN7 61 J1
Bracewell Av GFD/PVL UB6 114 C10
Bracewell Rd NKENS W10 136 F7
Bracewood Gdns CROY/NA CR0 203 N10
Bracey St ARCH N19 118 F7
Bracken Av BAL SW12 180 B2
　CROY/NA CR0 204 F10
Brackenbridge Dr RSLP HA4 113 L8
Brackenbury Gdns HMSMTH W6 156 E2
Brackenbury Rd EFNCH N2 117 M1
　HMSMTH W6 156 E2
Bracken Cl CRAWE RH10 283 P5
　EHAM E6 142 C7
　GT/LBKH KT23 235 N10
　HSLWW TW4 175 P3
　LOU IG10 82 E5
　SUN TW16 174 G9
　WOKS/MYFD GU22 232 C4
Bracken Dr CHIG IG7 102 C7
Bracken End ISLW TW7 176 C1
Brackenforde DTCH/LGLY SL3 149 P1
Bracken Gdns BARN SW13 156 D8
Bracken Hl BERK HP4 34 B4
Brackenhill COB KT11 217 P7
Bracken Hill Cl BMLY BR1 205 L1
Bracken Hill La BMLY BR1 205 L1
Brackenlea RGODL GU7 267 J10
Bracken Ms ROMW/RG RM7 124 B5
Brackens Dr BRW CM14 107 J6
Brackenside ED N9 99 H1
The Brackens ED N9 99 H1
　HHNE HP2 35 N5
　ORP BR6 227 K2
The Bracken CHING E4 101 L3
Bracken Wy CHOB/PIR GU24 213 L6
　RGUW GU3 249 K8
Brackenwood SUN TW16 197 H1
Brackenwood Rd WOKN/KNAP GU21 231 J5
Brackley WEY KT13 216 E2
Brackley Cl WLGTN SM6 222 F4
Brackley Rd BECK BR3 182 E10
　CHSWK W4 156 B3
Brackley Sq WFD IG8 102 A8
Brackley St BARB EC2Y 12 F1
Brackley Ter CHSWK W4 156 B3
Bracklyn St IS N1 6 G7
Bracknell Cl WDGN N22 99 H9
Bracknell Gdns HAMP NW3 117 H1
Bracknell Pl HHNE HP2 36 A2
Bracknell Wy HAMP NW3 117 H1
Bracondale ESH/CLAY KT10 218 B2
Bracondale Av ABYW SE2 163 K3
Bradbery RKW/CH/CXG WD3 50 G6
Bradbourne Park Rd SEV TN13 247 H9
Bradbourne Rd BXLY DA5 186 B3

GRAYS RM17 167 N5
　SEV TN13 247 J8
Bradbourne St FUL/PGN SW6 157 K8
Bradbourne Vale Rd SEV TN13 246 G8
Bradbury Cl BORE WD6 75 N5
　NWDGN UB2 153 P3
Bradbury Rd CRAWE RH10 284 D10
Bradbury St STNW/STAM N16 119 M10
Bradd Cl SOCK/AV RM15 147 K5
Braddock Cl ISLW TW7 154 E10
Braddon Rd RCH/KEW TW9 155 N6
Braddyll St GNWCH SE10 161 K4
Bradenham Av WELL DA16 163 K10
Bradenham Rd KTN/HRWW/W HA3 114 G2
　YEAD UB4 132 F5
Bradenhurst Cl CTHM CR3 259 N2
Braden St MV/WKIL W9 8 G1
Bradfield Cl GU GU1 250 D7
　WOKS/MYFD GU22 232 B4
Bradfield Dr BARK IG11 123 K10
Bradfield Rd CAN/RD E16 161 M1
　RSLP HA4 113 M10
Bradford Cl HAYES BR2 206 C8
　SYD SE26 182 A7
　UED N18 99 H7
Bradford Dr HOR/WEW KT19 220 C3
Bradford Rd ACT W3 156 B1
　IL IG1 122 G6
　RKW/CH/CXG WD3 90 F1
　SL SL1 128 F8
Bradgate POTB/CUF EN6 60 E3
Bradgate Cl POTB/CUF EN6 60 E4
Bradgate Rd CAT SE6 182 C2
Brading Crs WAN E11 121 N1
Brading Rd BRXS/STRHM SW2 180 A2
　CROY/NA CR0 202 G6
Brading Ter SHB W12 156 D2
Bradiston Rd MV/WKIL W9 2 D9
Bradleigh Av GRAYS RM17 167 P3
Bradley Cl HOLWY N7 5 M2
Bradley Gdns WEA W13 134 G3
Bradley La DORK RH4 254 C8
Bradley Rd NRWD SE19 181 K9
　PEND EN3 80 D4
　SL SL1 129 J9
　WDGN N22 98 G10
Bradley Stone Rd EHAM E6 142 C7
Bradmead VX/NE SW8 158 D6
Bradmore Gn BRKMPK AL9 59 H4
Bradmore La BRKMPK AL9 58 G2
Bradmore Park Rd HMSMTH W6 156 E2
Bradmore Wy BRKMPK AL9 59 H2
　COUL/CHIP CR5 240 D1
Bradshaw Cl WDSR SL4 148 D7
　WIM/MER SW19 179 K8
Bradshaw Rd CDH/CHF RM16 147 M10
　WATN WD24 75 K5
Bradshaws HAT AL10 40 C8
Bradshaws Cl SNWD SE25 203 P3
Bradstock Rd EW KT17 220 C2
　HOM E9 140 C1
Brad St STHWK SE1 12 B10
Bradwell Av DAGE RM10 124 B7
Bradwell Cl HCH RM12 145 J1
　SWFD E18 120 C2
Bradwell Gn RBRW/HUT CM13 87 P10
Bradwell Ms UED N18 99 P5
Bradwell Rd BKHH IG9 102 B2
Brady Av LOU IG10 82 F6
Bradymead EHAM E6 142 D8
Brady St WCHPL E1 140 A6
Braemar ALP/SUD HA0 135 J2
Braemar Av ALP/SUD HA0 135 J2
　BXLYHN DA7 164 D10
　SAND/SEL CR2 223 K6
　THHTH CR7 203 H3
　WDGN N22 98 F9
　WIM/MER SW19 179 K5
　WLSDN NW10 118 A8
Braemar Gdns BFN/LL DA15 184 G6
　CDALE/KGS NW9 96 A9
　EMPK RM11 125 P4
　SL SL1 148 F1
　WWKM BR4 205 H8
Braemar Rd BTFD TW8 141 M6
　PLSTW E13 141 M6
　SEVS/STOTM N15 119 M3
　WPK KT4 200 F10
Braeside ADL/WDHM KT15 215 L7
　BECK BR3 182 E7
Braeside Av SEV TN13 246 G10
　WIM/MER SW19 201 H1
Braeside Cl PIN HA5 93 P8
　SEV TN13 246 F9
Braeside Crs BXLYHN DA7 164 D10
Braeside Rd STRHM/NOR SW16 180 C1
Braes Md REDH RH1 276 F1
Braes St IS N1 6 C1
Braesyde Cl BELV DA17 163 K11
Brafferton Rd CROY/NA CR0 223 K3
Braganza St WALW SE17 18 C10
Bragg Rd TEDD TW11 176 D10
Bragmans La RKW/CH/CXG WD3 52 G9
Braham St WCHPL E1 13 M6
Braid Av ACT W3 136 B8
Braid Cl FELT TW13 175 N5
The Braid CSHM HP5 51 K6
Braidwood Rd CAT SE6 183 J4
Brailsford Cl WIM/MER SW19 179 P10
Brailsford Rd BRXS/STRHM SW2 181 H2
Brain Cl HAT AL10 40 E1
Brainton Av EBED/NFELT TW14 175 J3
Braintree Av REDBR IG4 122 B3
Braintree Rd DAGE RM10 124 B6
　RSLP HA4 113 J9
Braintree St BETH E2 140 B5
Brair Bank CAR SM5 222 B5
Braithwaite Av ROMW/RG RM7 124 B5
Braithwaite Gdns STAN HA7 95 H9
Braithwaite Rd PEND EN3 80 G4
Brakefield Rd MEO DA13 189 N9
Brakey Hl REDH RH1 259 M10
Brakynbery BERK HP4 33 K2
Brallings La CFSP/GDCR SL9 90 D5
Bramall Cl FSTGT E7 121 L10
Bramber Cl CRAWE RH10 283 P5
Bramber Ct SL SL1 128 F10
Bramber Rd NFNCH/WDSP N12 97 P6
　WKENS W14 14 C9
Bramble Acres Cl BELMT SM2 221 K4
Bramble Banks CAR SM5 222 B5
Bramblebury Rd WOOL/PLUM SE18 162 G4
Bramble Cl CFSP/GDCR SL9 90 B7
　CRAWE RH10 285 J2
　CROY/NA CR0 224 F1
　GSTN WD25 55 H10
　REDH RH1 276 B2
　RGUW GU3 249 K8
　SEVS/STOTM N15 119 P2
　STAN HA7 95 J8
　UX/CGN UB8 132 A7
Bramble Cft ERITH DA8 164 C7
Brambledene Cl WOKN/KNAP GU21 231 N4
Brambledown STA TW18 195 L1
Brambledown Cl HAYES BR2 205 K5
Brambledown Rd CAR SM5 222 B4
　SAND/SEL CR2 223 N4
Bramblefield Cl HART DA3 211 J3
Bramble Gdns SHB W12 136 C9
Bramble La AMSS HP7 69 L5
　HPTN TW12 175 N9

SEV TN13 265 J4
UPMR RM14 146 B3
Bramble Md CSTG HP8 89 M4
Bramble Ri COB KT11 217 K10
　HLW CM20 28 F10
Bramble Rd HAT AL10 39 P5
Brambles Cl BTFD TW8 154 G6
　CTHM CR3 241 M8
Brambles Farm Dr UX/CGN UB8 132 B5
The Brambles CHES/WCR EN8 62 C7
　CHIG IG7 102 F7
　RGODL GU7 267 J10
　STAL AL1 38 C3
　WDR/YW UB7 151 N4
Brambletye Park Rd REDH RH1 276 A2
Bramble Wk CRAWE RH10 276 A2
Bramble Wk EPSOM KT18 219 N10
Bramble Wy RPLY/SEND GU23 233 J10
Bramblewood REIG RH2 258 C5
Bramblewood Cl CAR SM5 201 N10
Brambling Cl BUSH WD23 73 N8
Brambling Ri HHNE HP2 35 P3
The Bramblings CHING E4 101 J5
Bramcote Av MTCM CR4 202 A4
Bramcote Gv BERM/RHTH SE16 160 B4
Bramcote Rd PUT/ROE SW15 156 G10
Bramdean Crs LEE/GVPK SE12 183 M4
Bramdean Gdns LEE/GVPK SE12 183 M4
Bramerton Rd BECK BR3 204 E3
Bramerton St CHEL SW3 15 N9
Bramfield GSTN WD25 55 M10
Bramfield Rd BTSEA SW11 179 P2
　HERT/WAS SG14 24 F5
Bramford Rd WAND/EARL SW18 157 M10
Bramham Gdns CHSGTN KT9 219 J1
　ECT SW5 14 G2
Bramhope La CHARL SE7 161 N5
Bramlands Cl BTSEA SW11 157 P9
Bramleas WATW WD18 72 C9
Bramley Cl COUL/CHIP CR5 240 D1
　SHPTN TW17 196 F5
Bramley Ct GSTN WD25 55 J8
　VX/NE SW8
Bramley Gdns OXHEY WD19 93 K7
Bramley Hl SAND/SEL CR2 223 K1
Bramley Ldg ALP/SUD HA0 115 J9
Bramley Pl DART DA1 165 H10
Bramley Rd BELMT SM2 220 G5
　EA W5 155 H2
　NKENS W10 136 G9
　STHGT/OAK N14 78 C9
　SUT SM1 221 N2
Bramley Shaw WAB EN9 63 L9
Bramley Wk ASHTD KT21 237 L3
　HSLWW TW4 175 N1
　STALE/WH AL4 39 H7
　WWKM BR4 204 C9
Brammas Cl SL SL1 149 H2
Brampton Cl CHESW EN7 61 P4
　CLPT E5 120 A7
Brampton Gdns WOT/HER KT12 217 J2
Brampton Gv HDN NW4 116 F2
　KTN/HRWW/W HA3 114 F2
　WBLY HA9 115 M6
Brampton La HDN NW4 116 F2
Brampton Park Rd WDGN N22 119 H3
Brampton Rd BXLYHN DA7 163 N9
　CDALE/KGS NW9 115 M2
　CROY/NA CR0 203 N7
　EHAM E6 142 A6
　FSBYPK N4 119 K3
　HGDN/ICK UB10 132 C4
　OXHEY WD19 93 H4
　STAL AL1 38 F5
Brampton Ter BORE WD6 75 M4
Bramshaw Gdns OXHEY WD19 93 L6
Bramshaw Ri NWMAL KT3 200 B4
Bramshaw Rd HOM E9 140 C1
Bramshill Gdns KTTN NW5 118 C2
Bramshill Rd WLSDN NW10 136 B4
Bramshot Av CHARL SE7 161 N5
Bramston Cl BARK/HLT IG6 103 J7
Bramston Rd WLSDN NW10 136 D2
　TOOT SW17 180 A7
Bramwell Cl SUN TW16 197 L2
Brancaster Dr MLHL NW7 96 D3
Brancaster La PUR/KEN CR8 223 L1
Brancaster Rd GNTH/NBYPK IG2 122 G4
　STRHM/NOR SW16 180 F6
Branch Cl HAT AL10 40 F2
Branch Pl IS N1 7 H1
Branch Rd BARK/HLT IG6 103 L6
　LCOL/BKTW AL2 56 C3
　POP/IOD E14 140 D9
　STALW/RED AL3 37 M3
Branch St PECK SE15 159 N6
Brancker Rd KTN/HRWW/W HA3 115 J1
Brancroft Wy PEND EN3 80 D5
Brandesbury Sq WFD IG8 103 H6
Brandlehow Rd PUT/ROE SW15 157 J10
Brandon Cl CHESW EN7 61 M2
　CRAWE RH10 284 E9
Brandon Groves Av SOCK/AV RM15 147 H5
Brandon Ms BARB EC2Y 12
Brandon Rd DART DA1 187 P3
　HOLWY N7 5 L9
　NWDGN UB2 153 N4
　SUT SM1 221 L1
　WALTH E17 121 H1
Brandon St GVW DA11 190 D3
　WALW SE17 18 F6
Brandram Rd LEW SE13 161 K9
Brandreth Rd EHAM E6 142 C8
　TOOT SW17 180 C5
The Brandries WLGTN SM6 202 F10
Brands Hatch Rd BGR/WK TN15 210 F10
Brandsland REIG RH2 275 L4
Brands Rd DTCH/LGLY SL3 150 E5
Brand St GNWCH SE10 161 H6
Brandville Gdns BARK/HLT IG6 122 C4
Brandville Rd WDR/YW UB7 151 P1
Brandy Wy BELMT SM2 221 K4
Branfil Rd UPMR RM14 126 A7
Brangbourne Rd BMLY BR1 183 H8
Brangton Rd LBTH SE11 17 M9
Brangwyn Crs WIM/MER SW19 201 N2
Branksea St FUL/PGN SW6 157 H6
Branksome Av UED N18 99 N7
Branksome Cl HHNE HP2 36 A5
　WOT/HER KT12 197 L5
Branksome Rd BRXS/STRHM SW2 180 L1
　WIM/MER SW19 201 K3
Branksome Wy KTN/HRWW/W HA3 115 L3
　NWMAL KT3 199 N2
Bransby Rd CHSGTN KT9 219 K4
Branscombe Gdns WCHMH N21 99 H7
Branscombe St LEW SE13 160 G9
Bransdale Cl KIL/WHAMP NW6 2 E1

Bransell Cl SWLY BR8 .... 208 D6
Bransgrove Rd EDGW HA8 .... 95 L9
Branston Crs STMC/STPC BR5 .... 206 G8
Branstone Rd RCH/KEW TW9 .... 155 L7
Branton Rd GRH DA9 .... 188 E2
Brantridge Rd CRAWE RH10 .... 284 A9
Brants Wk HNWL W7 .... 134 D6
Brantwood Av ERITH DA8 .... 164 D6
ISLW TW7 .... 154 F10
Brantwood Cl WALTH E17 .... 120 C1
Brantwood Dr BF/WBF KT14 .... 215 J9
Brantwood Gdns BF/WBF KT14 .... 215 J9
ENC/FH EN2 .... 78 F8
REDBR IG4 .... 122 B3
Brantwood Rd BXLYHN DA7 .... 164 C8
HNHL SE24 .... 181 K1
SAND/SEL CR2 .... 223 K5
TOTM N17 .... 99 P7
Brantwood Wy STMC/STPC BR5 .... 207 M3
Brasher Cl NTHLT UB5 .... 114 C10
Brasted Cl EBED/NFELT TW14 .... 175 H4
Brassey Hl ESH/CLAY KT10 .... 261 M5
Brassey Rd CRICK NW2 .... 2 D1
OXTED RH8 .... 261 M5
Brassey Sq BTSEA SW11 .... 158 B9
Brassie Av ACT W3 .... 136 B8
Brasted Cl BELMT SM2 .... 221 K6
BXLYHS DA6 .... 185 N1
SYD SE26 .... 182 B7
Brasted Hl RSEV TN14 .... 245 K7
Brasted Hl Rd BH/WHM TN16 .... 245 M8
Brasted La RSEV TN14 .... 245 J6
Brasted Rd BH/WHM TN16 .... 263 H2
ERITH DA8 .... 164 F6
Brathway Rd WAND/EARL SW18 .... 179 L3
Bratley St WCHPL E1 .... 13 N2
Brattle Wd SEV TN13 .... 265 K5
Braund Av GFD/PVL UB6 .... 134 A6
Braundton Av BFN/LL DA15 .... 185 J4
Braunston Dr YEAD UB4 .... 133 M6
Bravington Cl SHPTN TW17 .... 196 A5
Bravington Pl MV/WKIL W9 .... 8 C1
Bravington Rd MV/WKIL W9 .... 2 C0
Braxfield Rd BROCKY SE4 .... 160 D10
Braxted Pk STRHM/NOR SW16 .... 180 C9
Brayard's Rd PECK SE15 .... 160 A8
Braybourne Cl UX/CGN UB8 .... 131 M1
Braybourne Dr ISLW TW7 .... 154 E6
Braybrooke Gdns NRWD SE19 .... 181 M10
Braybrook St SHB W12 .... 136 C7
Brayburne Av VX/NE SW8 .... 158 D8
Bray Cl BORE WD6 .... 75 P5
CRAWE RH10 .... 284 E3
Braycourt Av WOT/HER KT12 .... 197 K2
Bray Crs BERM/RHTH SE16 .... 160 C1
Braydon Rd STNW/STAM N16 .... 119 N6
Bray Dr CAN/RD E16 .... 141 L9
Brayfield Ter IS N1 .... 6 A4
Bray Gdns WOKS/MYFD GU22 .... 233 H2
Bray Pl CHEL SW3 .... 16 J7
Bray Rd COB KT11 .... 235 M2
GUW GU2 .... 267 N1
MLHL NW7 .... 96 C7
Brays Cl ABWS HP6 .... 68 A1
Brays Green La AMS HP6 .... 68 A1
Brays La AMS HP6 .... 50 B10
Brays Md HLWS CM18 .... 47 J3
Brays Meadow AMS HP6 .... 68 B1
Brayton Gdns ENC/FH EN2 .... 78 B8
Braywood Av EGH TW20 .... 172 C9
Braywood Rd ELTH/MOT SE9 .... 162 G10
Braziers End CSHM HP5 .... 32 B7
Braziers Fld HERT/BAY SG13 .... 25 N5
Breach La DAGW RM9 .... 144 B5
Breach Rd WTHK RM20 .... 166 E5
Bread And Cheese La BROX EN10 .... 43 M10
Breadcroft La HARP AL5 .... 20 A1
Bread St BLKFR EC4V 12 F7
STP EC4M 12 F6
Breakfield COUL/CHIP CR5 .... 240 F2
Breakmead WGCE AL7 .... 23 L7
Breakneck Hl GRH DA9 .... 188 G1
Breakspear Av STAL AL1 .... 38 E7
Breakspear Ct ABLGY WD5 .... 54 G6
Breakspear Rd ABLGY WD5 .... 54 F7
Breakspeare Rd North
DEN/HRF UB9 .... 111 N1
Breakspear Rd South
HGDN/ICK UB10 .... 112 A8
Breakspears Dr STMC/STPC BR5 .... 207 K1
Breakspears Ms BROCKY SE4 .... 160 E9
Breakspears Rd BROCKY SE4 .... 160 E9
Breakspear Wy HHNE HP2 .... 36 A1
Breaks Rd HAT AL10 .... 40 E3
Bream Cl WALTH E17 .... 120 A1
Bream Gdns EHAM E6 .... 142 D5
Breamore Cl PUT/ROE SW15 .... 178 D4
Breamore Rd GDMY/SEVK IG3 .... 123 J7
Bream's Buildings LINN WC2A 12 A5
Bream St BOW E3 .... 140 F2
Breamwater Gdns
RCHPK/HAM TW10 .... 176 G6
Brearley Cl EDGW HA8 .... 95 P8
HGDN/ICK UB10 .... 131 P1
Breasley Cl PUT/ROE SW15 .... 156 F10
Brechin Pl SKENS SW7 .... 15 K7
Brecken Cl STALE/WH AL4 .... 38 F2
Brecknock Rd ARCH N19 .... 118 D9
HOLWY N7 .... 5 K1
Brecon Cl MTCM CR4 .... 202 C4
WPK KT4 .... 200 F9
Brecon Rd HMSMTH W6 .... 14 A10
PEND EN3 .... 80 B8
Brede Cl EHAM E6 .... 142 D5
Bredgar Rd ARCH N19 .... 118 D7
Bredhurst Cl PGE/AN SE20 .... 182 B9
Bredon Rd CROY/NA CR0 .... 203 N1
Bredune PUR/KEN CR8 .... 241 L1
Bredward Cl SL1 SL1 .... 128 A5
Breer St FUL/PGN SW6 .... 157 L9
Breezehurst Dr CRAWW RH11 .... 283 J10
Breezer's Hl WAP E1W 13 P8
Brember Rd RYLN/HDSTN HA2 .... 14 B7
Bremer Ms WALTH E17 .... 120 C2
Bremer Rd STA TW18 .... 173 K6
Bremner Av HORL RH6 .... 280 D4
Bremner Rd SWLY BR8 .... 209 H4
Bremner Rd SKENS SW7 .... 15 K3
Brenchley Av GVW DA11 .... 190 B4
Brenchley Cl CHST BR7 .... 206 D1
HAYES BR2 .... 205 L6
Brenchley Gdns FSTH SE23 .... 182 B2
Brenchley Rd STMC/STPC BR5 .... 207 H1
Brendans Cl EMPK RM11 .... 125 M6
Brenda Rd TOOT SW17 .... 180 A5
Brende Gdns E/WMO/HCT KT8 .... 198 A4
Brendon Av WLSDN NW10 .... 116 G3
Brendon Cl BXLYHN DA7 .... 164 F7
ESH/CLAY KT10 .... 218 B3
HYS/HAR UB3 .... 152 D6
Brendon Dr ESH/CLAY KT10 .... 218 B3
Brendon Gdns GNTH/NBYPK IG2 .... 123 H3
RYLN/HDSTN HA2 .... 114 A10
Brendon Ov EFNCH N2 .... 97 N10
Brendon Rd BCTR RM8 .... 124 A6
CHST BR7 .... 205 P4
Brendon St MBLAR W1H 9 P5
Brendon Wy EN EN1 .... 99 N1
Brenley Cl MTCM CR4 .... 202 B3
Brenley Gdns ELTH/MOT SE9 .... 162 A10
Brennan Rd TIL RM18 .... 168 B4
Brent Cl BXLY DA5 .... 185 P4
RDART DA2 .... 188 B4
Brentcot Cl WEA W13 .... 134 G6

Brent Crs WLSDN NW10 .... 135 L4
Brent Cross F/O HDN NW4 .... 116 A4
Brentfield WLSDN NW10 .... 135 N2
Brentfield Rd DART DA1 .... 187 P4
WLSDN NW10 .... 136 A1
Brent Cl YEAD UB4 .... 133 L6
Brent Gn HDN NW4 .... 116 F3
Brentham Wy EA W5 .... 135 J6
Brenthouse Rd HACK E8 .... 140 A2
Brenthurst Rd WLSDN NW10 .... 136 C1
Brentlands Dr DART DA1 .... 187 P4
Brent La DART DA1 .... 187 N3
Brent Lea BTFD TW8 .... 155 H6
Brentmead Cl HNWL W7 .... 134 D9
Brentmead Gdns WLSDN NW10 .... 135 L4
Brentmoor Rd CHOB/PIR GU24 .... 212 B9
Brenton St POP/IOD E14 .... 140 D8
Brent Park Rd CDALE/KGS NW9 .... 116 D6
Brent Pl BAR EN5 .... 77 K9
Brent River Park Wk HNWL W7 .... 134 C5
WEA W13 .... 134 G5
Brent Rd BTFD TW8 .... 155 H5
CAN/RD E16 .... 141 M8
NWDGN UB2 .... 153 K2
SAND/SEL CR2 .... 224 A5
WOOL/PLUM SE18 .... 162 G6
Brentside BTFD TW8 .... 155 H5
Brentside Cl WEA W13 .... 134 G6
Brent St HDN NW4 .... 116 G3
Brent Ter CRICK NW2 .... 116 F6
The Brent DART DA1 .... 188 A3
Brentvale Av ALP/SUD HA0 .... 135 L3
STHL UB1 .... 134 C10
Brent View Rd CDALE/KGS NW9 .... 116 D4
Brentwick Gdns BTFD TW8 .... 155 K3
Brentwood Cl ELTH/MOT SE9 .... 184 F4
Brentwood Pl BRWN CM15 .... 107 J2
Brentwood Rd CDH/CHF RM16 .... 168 A5
CHONG CM5 .... 67 P7
GPK RM2 .... 125 K3
RBRW/HUT CM13 .... 107 N6
ROM RM1 .... 124 D5
Brereton Rd TOTM N17 .... 99 N8
Bressenden Pl WESTW SW1E 16 J1
Bressey Av EN EN1 .... 79 P5
Bressey Gv SWFD E18 .... 101 L10
Bretlands Rd CHERT KT16 .... 195 H9
Brett Cl NTHLT UB5 .... 133 L5
STNW/STAM N16 .... 119 M7
Brettell St WALW SE17 .... 19 H8
Brettenham Av WALTH E17 .... 100 F9
WALTH E17 .... 100 F10
Brett Gdns DAGW RM9 .... 143 P2
Brettgrave HOR/WEW KT19 .... 219 P6
Brettingham Cl CRAWW RH11 .... 283 H10
Brett Pas HACK E8 .... 120 A10
Brett Rd BAR EN5 .... 75 H5
HACK E8 .... 120 A10
Brevet Cl PUR RM19 .... 166 C3
Brewer Rd CRAWE RH10 .... 283 N9
Brewers Fld RDART DA2 .... 187 K7
Brewer St REDH RH1 .... 259 K7
REGST W1B 11 H7
Brewery Cl ALP/SUD HA0 .... 114 C10
Brewery Cl BF/WBF KT14 .... 215 P9
Brewery Rd HAYES BR2 .... 206 B8
HOD EN11 .... 44 F3
HOLWY N7 .... 5 L2
WOKN/KNAP GU21 .... 232 A3
WOOL/PLUM SE18 .... 162 G4
Brewhouse La STALE/WH AL4 .... 21 H3
Brewhouse La HERT/WAS SG14 .... 25 K5
WAP E1W 140 A10
Brew House Rd
BRKHM/BTCW RH3 .... 273 N4
Brewhouse Rd
WOOL/PLUM SE18 .... 162 C3
Brewhouse St PUT/ROE SW15 .... 157 H10
Brewhouse Wk
BERM/RHTH SE16 .... 140 D10
Brewhouse Yd GVE DA12 .... 190 E2
Brewood Rd BCTR RM8 .... 143 L1
Brewster Gdns NKENS W10 .... 136 K9
Brewster Rd LEY E10 .... 120 G6
Brian Av SAND/SEL CR2 .... 223 M8
Brian Cl HCH RM12 .... 125 J9
Briane Rd HOR/WEW KT19 .... 219 P6
Brian Rd CHDH RM6 .... 123 M3
Briants Cl PIN HA5 .... 93 M9
Briant St NWCR SE14 .... 160 C7
Briar Av STRHM/NOR SW16 .... 180 C10
Briarbank Rd WEA W13 .... 134 F8
Briarcliff HHW HP1 .... 35 H5
Briar Cl BERK HP4 .... 34 D2
BF/WBF KT14 .... 215 L7
BKHH IG9 .... 102 A5
CHES/WCR EN8 .... 62 A3
CRAWW RH11 .... 283 M4
EFNCH N2 .... 97 H10
HPTN TW12 .... 175 N8
ISLW TW7 .... 154 E1
MDHB SL6 .... 128 A3
PLMGR N13 .... 99 K4
Briar Crs NTHLT UB5 .... 134 A1
Briardale Gdns HAMP NW3 .... 117 K8
Briarfield Av FNCH N3 .... 97 L3
Briar Gdns HAYES BR2 .... 205 L8
Briar Gv SAND/SEL CR2 .... 223 P9
Briar Hl PUR/KEN CR8 .... 222 F7
Briar La CAR SM5 .... 222 B5
CROY/NA CR0 .... 224 C1
Briarleas Gdns UPMR RM14 .... 126 D5
Briarley Cl BROX EN10 .... 44 E4
Briar Rd BXLY DA5 .... 186 E6
CRICK NW2 .... 116 F9
GSTN WD25 .... 55 H10
HARH RM3 .... 105 K8
KTN/HRWW/W HA3 .... 115 M8
RPLY/SEND GU23 .... 232 E10
SHPTN TW17 .... 196 A5
STALE/WH AL4 .... 39 H3
STRHM/NOR SW16 .... 202 F3
WHTN TW2 .... 176 D4
Briars Cl HAT AL10 .... 40 D4
Briars Ct LHD/OX KT22 .... 218 C10
Briars La HAT AL10 .... 40 D4
The Briars CHES/WCR EN8 .... 62 D7
DTCH/LGLY SL3 .... 150 G4
HERT/BAY SG13 .... 25 P5
HLWS CM18 .... 47 H3
RKW/CH/CXG WD3 .... 71 K2
STWL/WRAY TW19 .... 173 K1
Briars Wk HARH RM3 .... 105 M10
Briars Wy HAT DA3 .... 211 M3
Briarswood Cl CRAWE RH10 .... 284 G5
Briarswood Wy ORP BR6 .... 227 J2
Briar Wk BF/WBF KT14 .... 215 K8
EDGW HA8 .... 96 D3
NKENS W10 .... 138 E10
PUT/ROE SW15 .... 156 E10
Briar Wy BERK HP4 .... 34 D2
RGUE GU4 .... 250 E6
SLN SL2 .... 130 A1
WDR/YW UB7 .... 152 B1
Briarwood BRWN CM15 .... 86 A3
Briarwood Cl
CDALE/KGS NW9 .... 115 P2

Briarwood Dr NTHWD HA6 .... 93 H10
Briarwood Rd CLAP SW4 .... 180 E1
_EW_ KT17 .... 220 E5
WOKN/KNAP GU21 .... 231 J5
Briary Cl EDGW HA8 .... 95 N10
HAMP NW3 .... 3 N3
Briary Ct SCUP DA14 .... 185 L8
Briary Gdns BMLY BR1 .... 183 N8
Briary La N9 .... 99 N4
Brickcroft BROX EN10 .... 62 D2
Brickenden La HERT/BAY SG13 .... 25 K8
Bricket Rd STAL AL1 .... 38 C7
Brickett Cl RSLP HA4 .... 112 D3
Brick Farm Cl RCH/KEW TW9 .... 155 N7
Brickfield HAT AL10 .... 40 D7
Brickfield Av HHS/BOV HP3 .... 36 C7
Brickfield Cottages
WOOL/PLUM SE18 .... 163 J6
Brickfield La BAR EN5 .... 76 C10
HYS/HAR UB3 .... 152 E5
Brickfield Rd BOW E3 .... 140 G6
EPP CM16 .... 65 N5
REDH RH1 .... 277 P6
THHTH CR7 .... 203 J10
WIM/MER SW19 .... 179 L7
Brickfields RYLN/HDSTN HA2 .... 114 C7
The Brickfields WARE SG12 .... 26 A1
Brickfields Wy WDR/YW UB7 .... 152 A2
Brick Kiln Cl BUSH WD23 .... 73 M10
Brick Kiln La OXTED RH8 .... 261 P6
Brick Knoll Pk STALE/WH AL4 .... 39 H7
Brick La BETH E2 .... 7 M10
_EN_ EN1 .... 80 A6
PEND EN3 .... 80 B6
STAN HA7 .... 95 J8
WCHPL E1 .... 13 M2
Brickmakers La HHS/BOV HP3 .... 36 C7
Brick St MYFR/PICC W1J 10 G10
Brickwall Cl WCCW AL8 .... 22 D3
Brickwall La RSLP HA4 .... 112 F6
Brickwood Cl SYD SE26 .... 182 A6
Brickwood Rd CROY/NA CR0 .... 203 M9
Brickyard La RDKG RH5 .... 271 L7
Brideake Cl CRAWW RH11 .... 283 K10
Bride La EMB EC4Y 12 C6
Bride St HOLWY N7 .... 5 P2
Bridewain St STHWK SE1 .... 19 L3
Bridewell Pl BLKFR EC4V 12 C6
WAP E1W 140 A10
Bridford Ms REGST W1B 10 F3
Bridge Ap CAMTN NW1 .... 4 C3
Bridge Cl BF/WBF KT14 .... 216 B2
_EN_ EN1 .... 80 A5
GRH DA9 .... 166 C9
NKENS W10 .... 136 G8
RBRW/HUT CM13 .... 107 K4
ROM RM1 .... 124 F4
_SL1_ SL1 .... 128 E6
STA TW18 .... 173 H7
WOKN/KNAP GU21 .... 231 P3
WOT/HER KT12 .... 196 F7
Bridge Dr PLMGR N13 .... 98 C5
Bridge End WALTH E17 .... 101 H9
Bridgefield Cl BNSTD SM7 .... 238 F1
Bridgefield Rd SUT SM1 .... 221 K3
Bridgefields WGCE AL7 .... 23 J4
Bridge Foot WARE SG12 .... 26 C2
Bridge Gdns ASHF TW15 .... 174 D10
E/WMO/HCT KT8 .... 198 C4
Bridge Ga WCHMH N21 .... 99 K1
Bridgeham Cl WEY KT13 .... 216 B2
Bridgeham Wy HORL RH6 .... 281 J5
Bridge Hl EPP CM16 .... 65 J9
Bridgehill Cl GUW GU2 .... 249 M8
Bridge House Quay
POP/IOD E14 .... 141 H10
Bridgeland Rd CAN/RD E16 .... 141 K8
Bridgelands CRAWE RH10 .... 284 C2
Bridge La BTSEA SW11 .... 157 P7
GLDGN NW11 .... 117 H3
_VW_ GU25 .... 194 B6
Bridgeman Dr WDSR SL4 .... 148 B9
Bridgeman Rd IS N1 .... 5 P4
TEDD TW11 .... 176 F9
Bridgeman St STJWD NW8 .... 3 N4
Bridge Mdw NWCR SE14 .... 160 C5
Bridge Ms WOKN/KNAP GU21 .... 232 A3
Bridgend Rd EN EN1 .... 80 B1
Bridgenhall Rd EN EN1 .... 79 N1
Bridgen Rd BXLY DA5 .... 185 P3
Bridge Pl AMS HP6 .... 69 K4
CROY/NA CR0 .... 203 L8
PIM SW1V 16 F5
WAT WD17 .... 73 H4
Bridge Rd ASC SL5 .... 192 C5
BECK BR3 .... 182 C3
BELMT SM2 .... 221 L3
BXLYHN DA7 .... 163 P9
CHERT KT16 .... 195 L1
CHONG CM5 .... 49 K7
CHSGTN KT9 .... 219 K2
COB KT11 .... 235 J1
E/WMO/HCT KT8 .... 198 D4
_ED_ N9 .... 99 P4
EHAM E6 .... 142 C2
ERITH DA8 .... 164 C7
_EW_ KT17 .... 220 C8
GRAYS RM17 .... 167 K5
HSLW TW3 .... 154 C9
KGLGY WD4 .... 54 D9
LEY E10 .... 120 C5
NWDGN UB2 .... 153 N1
RAIN RM13 .... 145 H6
SRTFD E15 .... 141 J3
STMC/STPC BR5 .... 207 L6
TWK TW1 .... 176 G2
WBLY HA9 .... 115 M8
WDGN N22 .... 98 F4
WEY KT13 .... 216 A1
WGCE AL7 .... 23 H4
WGCW AL8 .... 22 F4
WLGTN SM6 .... 222 C2
WLSDN NW10 .... 136 B1
Bridge Rd East WGCE AL7 .... 23 J4
Bridge Rw CROY/NA CR0 .... 203 L8
Bridges Ct BTSEA SW11 .... 157 N9
Bridges Dr DART DA1 .... 188 A1
Bridges La CROY/NA CR0 .... 222 F1
Bridges Rd STAN HA7 .... 94 F5
Bridge St BERK HP4 .... 34 C3
CHSWK W4 .... 156 A3
DTCH/LGLY SL3 .... 150 G4
_GU_ GU1 .... 267 P5
HHW HP1 .... 35 M7
LHD/OX KT22 .... 236 F8
PIN HA5 .... 113 L4
STHL UB1 .... 134 B9
TWK TW1 .... 177 H2
WEST SW1P 17 H2
WOT/HER KT12 .... 196 C8
Bridge Ter SRTFD E15 .... 141 J2
The Bridge KTN/HRWW/W HA3 .... 114 E1
Bridgetown Cl NRWD SE19 .... 181 M8
Bridge Vw ASC SL5 .... 192 C7
Bridgeview HMSMTH W6 .... 156 F4
Bridgewater Cl CHST BR7 .... 207 H4
Bridgewater Ct DTCH/LGLY SL3 .... 150 D4

Bridgewater Gdns EDGW HA8 .... 95 L10
Bridgewater Hl BERK HP4 .... 33 L2
Bridgewater Rd BERK HP4 .... 33 N3
RSLP HA4 .... 113 H9
SRTFD E15 .... 141 H3
WEY KT13 .... 216 E3
Bridgewater Sq BARB EC2Y 12 E3
Bridgewater St BARB EC2Y 12 E3
Bridgewater Ter WDSR SL4 .... 149 J6
Bridgewater Wy BUSH WD23 .... 74 A10
WDSR SL4 .... 149 J7
Bridgeway ALP/SUD HA0 .... 135 K2
BARK IG11 .... 143 J2
Bridgeway St CAMTN NW1 .... 4 D3
Bridgewood Cl PGE/AN SE20 .... 182 A10
Bridgewood Rd
STRHM/NOR SW16 .... 180 D10
WPK KT4 .... 220 D1
Bridgford St WAND/EARL SW18 .... 179 M6
Bridgman Rd CHSWK W4 .... 155 P2
Bridgwater Rd HARH RM3 .... 105 K6
Bridgwater Wk HARH RM3 .... 105 L6
Bridle Cl HOD EN11 .... 45 J1
HOR/WEW KT19 .... 219 P1
KUT KT1 .... 199 J4
PEND EN3 .... 80 E3
STALW/RED AL3 .... 38 D4
SUN TW16 .... 197 H3
Bridle La COB KT11 .... 236 A1
RKW/CH/CXG WD3 .... 71 M7
SOHO/CST W1F 11 H7
TWK TW1 .... 176 G2
Bridle Pth CROY/NA CR0 .... 202 F10
WAT WD17 .... 73 J6
The Bridle Pth EW KT17 .... 220 F6
WFD IG8 .... 101 K8
Bridlepath Wy
EBED/NFELT TW14 .... 174 F3
Bridle Rd CROY/NA CR0 .... 204 F10
ESH/CLAY KT10 .... 218 C3
_EW_ KT17 .... 220 D5
PIN HA5 .... 113 K4
The Bridle Rd PUR/KEN CR8 .... 222 F6
Bridle Wy BERK HP4 .... 33 M3
CRAWE RH10 .... 284 E6
CROY/NA CR0 .... 224 F2
HOD EN11 .... 26 F10
ORP BR6 .... 226 F1
WARE SG12 .... 26 F5
Bridle Wy (North) HOD EN11 .... 26 F9
Bridle Wy (South) HOD EN11 .... 26 F10
The Bridle Wy WLGTN SM6 .... 222 D1
Bridlington Cl BH/WHM TN16 .... 243 N5
Bridlington Rd ED N9 .... 100 H3
OXHEY WD19 .... 93 L4
Bridlington Sp SL1 SL1 .... 148 G2
Bridport Av ROMW/RG RM7 .... 124 C4
Bridport Pl IS N1 .... 7 H7
Bridport Rd NTHLT UB5 .... 134 A3
THHTH CR7 .... 203 H3
UED N18 .... 99 M6
Bridport Wy SLN SL2 .... 128 G6
Bridstow Pl BAY/PAD W2 .... 8 F5
Brief St CMBW SE5 .... 159 J7
Brier Lea KWD/TDW/WH KT20 .... 257 J2
Brierley Av ED N9 .... 100 B2
Brierley Cl EMPK RM11 .... 125 K4
SNWD SE25 .... 203 P4
Brierley Rd BAL SW12 .... 180 D5
WAN E11 .... 121 J9
Brierly Cl GUW GU2 .... 249 M8
Brierly Gdns BETH E2 .... 140 B4
Brier Rd KWD/TDW/WH KT20 .... 238 E5
Briery Fld RKW/CH/CXG WD3 .... 71 K8
Briery Wy AMS HP6 .... 69 K3
HHNE HP2 .... 36 B4
Brigade Cl RYLN/HDSTN HA2 .... 114 C7
Brigade St BKHTH/KID SE3 .... 161 L8
Brigadier Av ENC/FH EN2 .... 79 K4
Brigadier Hl ENC/FH EN2 .... 79 K3
Briggeford Cl CLPT E5 .... 119 P7
Briggs Cl MTCM CR4 .... 202 C1
Bright Cl BELV DA17 .... 163 N3
Brightfield Rd LEW SE13 .... 183 K1
Bright Hl GU GU1 .... 268 A2
Brightlands CGW DA11 .... 190 B7
Brightlands Rd REIG RH2 .... 257 M8
Brightling Rd BROCKY SE4 .... 182 C1
Brightlingsea Pl POP/IOD E14 .... 140 E9
Brightman Rd WAND/EARL SW18 .... 179 M4
Brighton Av WALTH E17 .... 120 E3
Brighton Cl ADL/WDHM KT15 .... 215 M2
HGDN/ICK UB10 .... 132 C2
Brighton Dr NTHLT UB5 .... 133 P1
Brighton Rd ADL/WDHM KT15 .... 215 M1
BELMT SM2 .... 221 L6
BNSTD SM7 .... 221 J10
COUL/CHIP CR5 .... 240 D4
CRAWW RH11 .... 283 N10
EFNCH N2 .... 97 M10
EHAM E6 .... 142 D5
HORL RH6 .... 280 D6
KWD/TDW/WH KT20 .... 257 J2
PUR/KEN CR8 .... 222 F10
REDH RH1 .... 258 A10
REDH RH1 .... 276 B8
SAND/SEL CR2 .... 223 K5
STNW/STAM N16 .... 119 M9
SURB KT6 .... 199 H6
WATN WD24 .... 73 H4
Brighton Sp SLN SL2 .... 128 G6
Brighton Ter BRXN/ST SW9 .... 158 C10
Brights Av RAIN RM13 .... 145 J6
Brightside Av STA TW18 .... 173 M10
Brightside Rd LEW SE13 .... 183 J10
The Brightside PEND EN3 .... 80 C5
Bright St POP/IOD E14 .... 140 G8
Brightview Cl LCOL/BKTW AL2 .... 55 M5
Brightwell Cl CROY/NA CR0 .... 203 M3
Brightwell Crs TOOT SW17 .... 180 A8
Brightwell Rd WATW WD18 .... 73 H9
Brig Ms DEPT SE8 .... 160 F5
Brigstock Rd BELV DA17 .... 164 C3
COUL/CHIP CR5 .... 240 C1
THHTH CR7 .... 203 J5
Brill Pl CAMTN NW1 .... 5 K8
Brimfield Rd PUR RM19 .... 166 C3
Brim Hl EFNCH N2 .... 117 M2
Brimpsfield Cl ABYW SE2 .... 163 L2
Brimsdown Av PEND EN3 .... 80 D5
Brimshot Cl CHOB/PIR GU24 .... 213 K5
Brimstone Cl ORP BR6 .... 227 N4
Brimstone Wy BERK HP4 .... 33 J3
Brindle Ga BFN/LL DA15 .... 185 H4
Brindles EMPK RM11 .... 125 M4
Brindles RBRW/HUT CM13 .... 107 K3
The Brindles BNSTD SM7 .... 239 J7
Brindley Cl BXLYHN DA7 .... 164 C9
GFD/PVL UB6 .... 135 N2
Brindley St NWCR SE14 .... 160 E7
Brindley Wy BMLY BR1 .... 183 M8
STHL UB1 .... 134 B6
Brindwood Rd CHING E4 .... 100 F4
Brinkburn Cl ABYW SE2 .... 163 K3
EDGW HA8 .... 96 A6
Brinkburn Gdns EDGW HA8 .... 115 N1
Brinkley Rd WPK KT4 .... 200 E9
Brinklow Ct STAL AL1 .... 38 A9
Brinklow Crs WOOL/PLUM SE18 .... 162 G6
Brinkworth Rd CLAY IG5 .... 122 B1
Brinley Cl CHES/WCR EN8 .... 62 C7

Brinsdale Rd HDN NW4 .... 116 G1
Brinsley Rd KTN/HRWW/W HA3 .... 94 C10
Brinsley St WCHPL E1 .... 140 E1
Brinsmead LCOL/BKTW AL2 .... 56 C3
Brinsmead Rd HARH RM3 .... 105 P10
Brinsworth Cl WHTN TW2 .... 176 C4
Brion Pl POP/IOD E14 .... 141 J1
Brisbane Av WIM/MER SW19 .... 201 L1
Brisbane Cl CRAWW RH11 .... 283 N4
Brisbane Rd IL IG1 .... 122 F5
LEY E10 .... 120 C7
Brisbane St CMBW SE5 .... 159 L6
Briscoe Cl HOD EN11 .... 44 E1
WAN E11 .... 121 L7
Briscoe Rd HOD EN11 .... 44 E1
RAIN RM13 .... 145 K4
WIM/MER SW19 .... 179 N8
Briset Rd ELTH/MOT SE9 .... 162 A9
Briset St FARR EC1M 12 C3
Briset Wy HOLWY N7 .... 118 C7
Brisson Cl ESH/CLAY KT10 .... 217 N3
Bristol Cl CRAWE RH10 .... 284 E3
STWL/WRAY TW19 .... 173 P2
Bristol Gdns MV/WKIL W9 .... 9 H1
Bristol Park Rd WALTH E17 .... 120 D2
Bristol Rd FSTGT E7 .... 141 J5
GFD/PVL UB6 .... 134 A3
GVE DA12 .... 190 G6
MRDN SM4 .... 201 M5
Bristol Wy SL1 SL1 .... 129 L10
Briston Gv CEND/HSY/T N8 .... 118 F4
Bristow Rd BXLYHN DA7 .... 163 P7
CROY/NA CR0 .... 222 F1
HSLW TW3 .... 154 A3
NRWD SE19 .... 181 M8
Britannia Cl CLAP SW4 .... 158 E10
NTHLT UB5 .... 133 L3
Britannia Dr GVE DA12 .... 191 J3
Britannia Ga CAN/RD E16 .... 141 M10
Britannia Rd BRW CM14 .... 107 N5
BRYLDS KT5 .... 199 L7
CHES/WCR EN8 .... 62 E10
CSHM HP5 .... 51 H5
FUL/PGN SW6 .... 15 L3
_IL_ IG1 .... 122 E8
NFNCH/WDSP N12 .... 97 M4
POP/IOD E14 .... 160 F3
Britannia Rw IS N1 .... 6 D5
Britannia Wk IS N1 .... 6 G9
Britannia Wy FUL/PGN SW6 .... 157 L6
STWL/WRAY TW19 .... 173 N3
WLSDN NW10 .... 135 N6
British Gv CHSWK W4 .... 156 C4
British Grove Pas CHSWK W4 .... 156 C4
British Legion Rd CHING E4 .... 101 L3
British St BOW E3 .... 140 E5
Briton Cl SAND/SEL CR2 .... 223 M7
Briton Crs SAND/SEL CR2 .... 223 M6
Briton Hill Rd SAND/SEL CR2 .... 223 M6
Brittain Rd BCTR RM8 .... 123 P1
WOT/HER KT12 .... 217 L2
Brittains La SEV TN13 .... 246 G10
Britten Cl BORE WD6 .... 75 P1
CRAWW RH11 .... 283 J10
GLDGN NW11 .... 117 L6
Britten Dr STHL UB1 .... 133 P8
Brittens Cl GUW GU2 .... 249 M5
Britten St CHEL SW3 .... 15 N8
Britton Av STALW/RED AL3 .... 38 C6
Britton Cl CAT SE6 .... 183 J3
Britton St FARR EC1M 12 C2
Britwell Rd SL1 SL1 .... 128 B5
Brixham Crs RSLP HA4 .... 113 H6
Brixham Gdns GDMY/SEVK IG3 .... 123 H10
Brixham Rd WELL DA16 .... 163 N1
Brixham St CAN/RD E16 .... 142 C10
Brixton Hl BRXS/STRHM SW2 .... 180 G2
Brixton Hill Pl
BRXS/STRHM SW2 .... 180 F3
Brixton Ov BRXN/ST SW9 .... 159 H10
LBTH SE11 .... 18 A10
Brixton Rd WATN WD24 .... 73 J5
Brixton Station Rd BRXN/ST SW9 .... 159 H9
Brixton Water La
BRXS/STRHM SW2 .... 180 G1
Broad Acre LCOL/BKTW AL2 .... 55 M6
Broadacre STA TW18 .... 173 K8
Broadacre Cl HGDN/ICK UB10 .... 112 C8
Broadacres GUW GU2 .... 249 M8
Broad Acres HAT AL10 .... 40 C1
RGODL GU7 .... 267 K9
Broadbent St MYFR/PKLN W1K 10 E7
Broad Bridge Cl BKHTH/KID SE3 .... 161 M6
Broadbridge La HORL RH6 .... 281 H5
Broad Cl WOT/HER KT12 .... 197 L10
Broadcoombe SAND/SEL CR2 .... 224 C4
Broad Ct WCCE AL7 .... 23 H6
Broadcroft HHW HP1 .... 35 H4
Broadcroft Av STAN HA7 .... 95 L9
Broadcroft Rd STMC/STPC BR5 .... 206 G2
Broad Ditch Rd MEO DA13 .... 189 P10
Broadfield HLW CM20 .... 29 H10
Broadfield Cl CRICK NW2 .... 116 F8
KWD/TDW/WH KT20 .... 238 F6
ROM RM1 .... 124 G3
Broadfield Ct BUSH WD23 .... 94 D3
Broadfield Dr CRAWW RH11 .... 283 L10
Broadfield La HOLWY N7 .... 5 L4
Broadfield Pl WGCW AL8 .... 22 E6
Broadfield Rd CAT SE6 .... 183 N6
HHNE HP2 .... 36 A6
SHGR GU5 .... 270 E8
Broadfields CHESW EN7 .... 61 J5
E/WMO/HCT KT8 .... 198 C4
PIN HA5 .... 94 A10
RYLN/HDSTN HA2 .... 94 A10
SBW CM21 .... 29 L2
Broadfields Av EDGW HA8 .... 95 N5
WCHMH N21 .... 99 H1
Broadfields Hts EDGW HA8 .... 95 N5
Broadfields La WATW WD19 .... 93 J2
Broadfield Sq EN EN1 .... 80 A7
Broadfields Wy WLSDN NW10 .... 116 C10
Broadfield Wy BKHH IG9 .... 101 P7
Broadford La CHOB/PIR GU24 .... 213 H8
Broadford Pk RGUE GU4 .... 268 A7
Broadgate WAB EN9 .... 63 L9
Broadgates Rd
WAND/EARL SW18 .... 179 M6
Broad Gn HERT/BAY SG13 .... 42 G5
Broad Green Av CROY/NA CR0 .... 203 J3
Broad Green Wd HERT/BAY SG13 .... 42 G5
Broadham Green Rd OXTED RH8 .... 261 L4
Broadhead Strd CDALE/KGS NW9 .... 96 C10
Broadheath Dr CHST BR7 .... 184 C4
Broad Hwy COB KT11 .... 217 L10
Broadhinton Rd CLAP SW4 .... 158 C9
Broadhurst AV EDGW HA8 .... 95 N5
Broadhurst Av GDMY/SEVK IG3 .... 123 J9
Broadhurst Cl KIL/WHAMP NW6 .... 3 J1
Broadhurst Gdns KIL/WHAMP NW6 .... 3 H1
REIG RH2 .... 275 L3
RSLP HA4 .... 113 K7
Broadlake Cl LCOL/BKTW AL2 .... 57 J3
Broadlands FELT TW13 .... 175 N6
GRAYS RM17 .... 167 L4
HORL RH6 .... 280 D3
Broadlands Av CSHM HP5 .... 51 H6
PEND EN3 .... 80 A2
SHPTN TW17 .... 196 D6
STRHM/NOR SW16 .... 180 A3

Broadlands Cl HGT N6........118 B5
PEND EN3........80 B7
STRHM/NOR SW16........180 F5
Broadlands Dr ASC SL5........192 B7
WARL CR6........242 A5
Broadlands Rd BMLY BR1........183 N7
HGT N6........118 A5
Broadlands Wy NWMAL KT3........200 C6
Broad La HPTN TW12........175 N10
RDART DA2........187 J7
RDKG RH5........278 A2
Broad Lawn ELTH/MOT SE9........184 D4
Broadlawns Ct KTN/HRWW/W HA3........94 E9
Broadleaf Gv WLYN AL6........22 E2
Broadley Gn BFOR GU20........212 C4
Broadley Rd HLWW/ROY CM19........46 C5
Broadley St STJWD NW8........9 N3
Broadley Ter CAMTN NW1........9 N2
Broadmark Rd SLN SL2........129 N9
Broadmead ASHTD KT21........237 K4
CAT SE6........182 F6
HORL RH6........280 D3
Broadmead Av WPK KT4........200 D7
Broadmead Cl HPTN TW12........175 P9
PIN HA5........93 M8
Broad Meadow BRWN CM15........86 E4
Broadmead Rd WFD IG8........101 M7
YEAD UB4........133 M6
Broadmeads RPLY/SEND GU23........232 E8
WARE SG12........26 C2
Broad Oak SLN SL2........129 H6
SUN TW16........174 F9
WFD IG8........101 N6
Broadoak Av PEND EN3........80 C1
Broadoak Cl RDART DA2........187 P9
Broad Oak Cl CHING E4........100 H6
STMC/STPC BR5........207 K2
Broad Oak Ct SLN SL2........129 H6
Broadoak Rd ERITH DA8........164 E6
Broadoaks EPP CM16........65 J8
Broad Oaks SURB KT6........199 N8
Broadoaks Crs BF/WBF KT14........215 L10
Broad Oaks Wy HAYES BR2........205 L5
Broad Platts DTCH/LGLY SL3........150 A3
Broad Rd SWCM DA10........189 K2
Broadstone Pl MHST W1U........10 C4
Broadstone Rd HARP AL5........20 B5
ERITH DA8........164
Broad St CHOB/PIR GU24........212 C8
CSHM HP5........50 F2
DAGE RM10........144 B2
HHNE HP2........35 N6
RCUW GU3........249 J8
TEDD TW11........176 E9
Broad Street Av LVPST EC2M........13 J4
Broadstrood LOU IG10........82 D4
Broadview WBLY HA9........115 M4
Broadview Av CDH/CHF RM16........168 A1
Broadview Rd CSHM HP5........50 G3
STRHM/NOR SW16........180 C10
Broadwalk SWFD E18........121 L1
Broad Wk BGR/WK TN15........265 M4
BKHTH/KID SE3........161 P8
COUL/CHIP CR5........240 B8
CTHM CR3........241 N8
HEST TW5........153 L7
KWD/TDW/WH KT20........238 F5
ORP BR6........207 N10
RCH/KEW TW9........99 H2
WCHMH N21........99 H2
WOOL/PLUM SE18........162 G8
Broadwalk La GLDGN NW11........117 J5
The Broad Walk (North) RBRW/HUT CM13........107 M4
The Broadwalk (South) RBRW/HUT CM13........107 M5
The Broad Wk KENS W8........9 H9
Broadwall STHWK SE1........12 B1
Broadwater BERK HP4........33 P4
POTB/CUF EN6........59 P6
Broadwater Cl STWL/WRAY TW19........172 B2
WOKN/KNAP GU21........214 G8
WOT/HER KT12........217 H2
Broadwater Crs WGCE AL7........22 G2
Broadwater Gdns DEN/HRF UB9........111 L2
ORP BR6........226 E1
Broadwater La DEN/HRF UB9........111 L2
Broadwater Ri GU GU1........268 D1
Broadwater Rd TOOT SW17........99 M10
TOTM N17........99 M10
WGCE AL7........23 H6
WGCW AL8........22 G5
WOOL/PLUM SE18........162 G2
Broadwater Rd North WOT/HER KT12........217 H2
Broadwater Rd South WOT/HER KT12........217 H2
Broadway AMSS HP7........68 G6
BARK IG11........142 F3
BXLYHS DA6........163 P10
GPK RM2........125 H1
GRAYS RM17........167 P5
HNWL W7........134 D10
RAIN RM13........145 H6
SRTFD E15........141 J2
STJSPK SW1H........17 J3
SURB KT6........199 N8
SUT SM1........221 M1
TIL RM18........170 A4
WDSR SL4........170 A4
WOKN/KNAP GU21........230 C5
Broadway Av CROY/NA CR0........203 L5
HLWE CM17........29 L7
TWK TW1........176 G2
Broadway Cl AMSS HP7........68 G6
SAND/SEL CR2........224 A10
WFD IG8........101 N7
Broadway Gdns MTCM CR4........201 P4
Broadway Market HACK E8........140 A3
Broadway Ms STNW/STAM N16........119 N5
Broadway Rd CHOB/PIR GU24........212 C9
The Broadway ADL/WDHM KT15........215 K6
BCTR RM8........124 B7
BRKMPK AL9........40 F4
CDALE/KGS NW9........116 C4
CEND/HSY/T N8........118 F4
CHEAM SM3........221 H3
CRAWE RH10........283 N7
CSHM HP5........51 H7
EA W5........135 J9
HCH RM12........125 H4
KTN/HRWW/W HA3........94 D10
LOU IG10........82 A3
MLHL NW7........96 B6
PIN HA5........51 H6
PLSTW E13........141 M4
STA TW18........195 M3
STAN HA7........95 H1
THDIT KT7........198 D8
WAT WD17........73 K1
WFD IG8........101 N7
WIM/MER SW19........179 J9
WOKN/KNAP GU21........232 C3
Broadwick St SOHO/CST W1F........11 H6
Broadwood CVW DA11........190 E8
Broadwood Av RSLP HA4........112 F4
Brocas Cl HAMP NW3........3 P3
Brocas St WDSR SL4........149 J2
Brockdene Dr HAYES BR2........226 A1
Brockdish Av BARK IG11........123 J10
Brockenhurst E/WMO/HCT KT8........147 K8
Brockenhurst Av WPK KT4........200 B8
Brockenhurst Cl WOKN/KNAP GU21........214 C10
Brockenhurst Gdns IL IG1........122 F10

MLHL NW7........96 B6
Brockenhurst Rd ASC SL5........192 A5
CROY/NA CR0........204 A7
Brockenhurst Wy STRHM/NOR SW16........202 E2
Brocket Cl CHIG IG7........103 J5
Brocket Rd HOD EN11........44 F3
WGCW AL8........22 C7
Brockett Cl WGCW AL8........22 C5
Brockett Rd CDH/CHF RM16........168 E2
Brocket Vw STALE/WH AL4........21 J3
Brocket Wy CHIG IG7........103 H6
Brock Gn SOCK/AV RM15........146 C8
Brockham Cl WIM/MER SW19........179 J5
Brockham Crs CROY/NA CR0........223 J7
Brockham Dr BRXS/STRHM SW2........180 G3
GNTH/NBYPK IG2........122 F4
Brockham Hill Pk KWD/TDW/WH KT20........255 P7
Brockhamhurst Rd BRKHM/BTCW RH3........273 N7
Brockham La BRKHM/BTCW RH3........255 M10
Brockham St STHWK SE1........18 F3
Brockhurst Cl STAN HA7........94 E7
Brockhurst Rd CSHM HP5........51 H5
Brockill Crs BROCKY SE4........160 D10
Brocklebank Rd CHARL SE7........161 N3
WAND/EARL SW18........179 M3
Brocklehurst St NWCR SE14........160 C6
Brocklesbury Cl WATN SE20........46 F5
Brocklesby Rd SNWD SE25........204 A4
Brockles Md HLWW/ROY CM19........46 C5
Brockley Av EDGW HA8........95 K4
Brockley Cl STAN HA7........95 K5
Brockley Combe WEY KT13........216 E2
Brockley Crs CRW RM5........104 D8
Brockley Cross BROCKY SE4........160 D9
Brockley Gv BROCKY SE4........182 E1
RBRW/HUT CM13........107 M2
Brockley Hall Rd BROCKY SE4........182 D2
Brockley Hl STAN HA7........95 H3
Brockley Ms BROCKY SE4........182 D1
Brockley Pk FSTH SE23........182 D3
Brockley Ri FSTH SE23........182 D3
Brockleyside STAN HA7........95 K5
Brockley Vw FSTH SE23........182 D3
Brockley Vw FSTH SE23........182 C1
Brock Pl BOW E3........140 A2
Brock Rd CRAWW RH11........283 L4
PLSTW E13........141 N7
Brocks Dr CHEAM SM3........201 H10
RGUW GU3........249 H6
Brockshot Cl BTFD TW8........155 J5
Brocksparkwood RBRW/HUT CM13........107 N4
Brock St PECK SE15........160 B9
Brockswood La WGCW AL8........22 A4
Brockton Cl ROM RM1........124 C2
Brock Wy VW GU25........193 P5
Brockway Cl GU GU1........250 E9
WAN E11........121 K7
Brockwell Cl STMC/STPC BR5........207 J5
Brockwell Park Gdns HNHL SE24........181 J3
Brockworth Cl PECK SE15........19 J10
Brodewater Rd BORE WD6........75 N6
Brodia Rd STNW/STAM N16........119 M8
Brodie Rd CHING E4........101 H2
ENC/FH EN2........79 K4
GU GU1........268 D4
Brodie St STHWK SE1........19 M7
Brodlove La WAP E1W........140 G8
Brodrick Gv ABYW SE2........163 L3
GT/LBKH KT23........253 P2
Brograve Gdns BECK BR3........204 C2
Broke Ct RGUE GU4........250 F7
Broke Farm Dr ORP BR6........227 M5
Broken Furlong WDSR SL4........148 G4
Broken Gate La DEN/HRF UB9........110 F6
Broken Whf BLKFR EC4V........12 E7
Brokes Crs REIG RH2........257 K8
Brokesley St BOW E3........140 E6
Brokes Rd REIG RH2........257 K8
Bromar Rd CMBW SE5........159 M9
Bromefield STAN HA7........95 H9
Bromehead St WCHPL E1........140 B8
Bromell's Rd CLAP SW4........158 D10
Brome Rd ELTH/MOT SE9........162 C9
Bromet Cl WAT WD17........72 C4
Bromfelde Rd CLAP SW4........158 E9
Bromfield St IS N1........6 B7
Bromford Cl OXTED RH8........261 M9
Bromhall Rd DAGW RM9........143 L1
Bromhedge ELTH/MOT SE9........184 C6
Bromholm Rd ABYW SE2........163 L2
Bromleigh Cl CHES/WCR EN8........62 D4
Bromley GRAYS RM17........167 L5
Bromley Av BMLY BR1........183 K10
Bromley Common HAYES BR2........206 B7
Bromley Crs HAYES BR2........205 L3
RSLP HA4........112 G9
Bromley Gdns HAYES BR2........205 L2
Bromley Gv HAYES BR2........205 J2
Bromley Hall Rd POP/IOD E14........141 N1
Bromley High St BOW E3........140 C5
Bromley La CHST BR7........184 F10
Bromley Pk BMLY BR1........183 K9
Bromley Rd BECK BR3........204 G1
CAT SE6........182 G5
CHST BR7........206 E1
HAYES BR2........205 K2
LEY E10........120 C4
TOTM N17........99 N9
UED N18........99 L1
WALTH E17........100 F10
Bromley St WCHPL E1........140 C7
Brompton Cl HSLWW TW4........175 N3
Brompton Dr ERITH DA8........165 J6
Brompton Gv EFNCH N2........117 F2
Brompton Park Crs FUL/PGN SW6........14 F1
Brompton Pl CHEL SW3........15 P3
Brompton Rd CHEL SW3........15 N5
Brompton Sq CHEL SW3........15 N4
Bromwich Av HGT N6........118 A7
Bromyard Av ACT W3........136 D10
Bromycroft Rd SLN SL2........128 F5
Brondesbury Pk CRICK NW2........136 F2
KIL/WHAMP NW6........136 G2
Brondesbury Vls KIL/WHAMP NW6........2 D7
Bronsart Rd FUL/PGN SW6........157 H6
Bronson Rd RYNPK SW20........200 G3
Bronte Cl ERITH DA8........164 C6
FSTGT E7........121 N10
GNTH/NBYPK IG2........122 D3
TIL RM18........168 F8
Bronte Gv DART DA1........165 N10
Bronte Vw GVE DA12........190 F4
Bronti Cl WALW SE17........18 F7
Bronze Age Wy BELV DA17........164 D2
Bronze St DEPT SE8........160 F6
Brook Av DAGE RM10........144 C2
EDGW HA8........95 N7
WBLY HA9........115 M8

SL SL1........128 D8
UED N18........100 A5
Brookdale FBAR/BDGN N11........98 D5
Brookdale Av UPMR RM14........125 P6
Brookdale Cl UPMR RM14........126 A8
Brookdale Rd BXLY DA5........185 P2
CAT SE6........182 G1
LEW SE13........182 G2
WALTH E17........120 F1
Brookdene Av OXHEY WD19........93 J1
Brookdene Dr NTHWD HA6........92 C6
Brookdene Rd WOOL/PLUM SE18........163 H3
Brook Dr RAD WD7........112 F4
RSLP HA4........112 F4
RYLN/HDSTN HA2........114 B2
STHWK SE1........18 B4
SUN TW16........174 F9
Brooke Av RYLN/HDSTN HA2........114 B8
Brooke Cl BUSH WD23........94 B1
Brooke Dr GVE DA12........191 L4
Brookehowse Rd CAT SE6........182 G6
Brook End SBW CM21........29 N1
Brookend Rd BFN/LL DA15........185 H4
Brooker Rd WAB EN9........63 H10
Brookers Cl ASHTD KT21........237 H3
Brooke St HCIRC EC1N........12 A4
Brooke Wy BUSH WD23........94 B1
Brook Farm Rd COB KT11........235 L1
Brookfield EPP CM16........65 M1
RGODL GU7........267 M9
RSEV TN14........247 N3
WOKN/KNAP GU21........231 N2
Brookfield Av EA W5........135 J6
MLHL NW7........96 E7
SUT SM1........201 P10
WALTH E17........121 K1
Brookfield Cl CHERT KT16........214 C3
MLHL NW7........96 E7
RBRW/HUT CM13........87 P10
REDH RH1........276 B6
Brookfield Crs KTN/HRWW/W HA3........115 K3
MLHL NW7........96 E7
Brookfield Gdns CHES/WCR EN8........62 C3
ESH/CLAY KT10........218 E3
Brookfield La East CHES/WCR EN8........62 A4
Brookfield La West CHES/WCR EN8........62 B3
Brookfield Pk KTTN NW5........118 C8
Brookfield Pth CHING E4........101 J7
Brookfields EN3........80 C8
PEND EN3........80 C8
SBW CM21........29 N1
Brookfields Av MTCM CR4........201 P5
Brook Gdns BARN SW13........156 C9
CHING E4........100 G3
KUTN/CMB KT2........199 P1
Brook Gn HMSMTH W6........156 F2
Brook Hl OXTED RH8........261 H6
SHGR GU5........269 N6
Brookhill Cl CRAWE RH10........285 H2
EBAR EN4........77 P9
Brookhill Rd CRAWE RH10........285 H3
WOOL/PLUM SE18........162 E4
Brookhouse Gdns CHING E4........101 K5
Brookhurst Rd ADL/WDHM KT15........215 L3
Brooking Rd FSTGT E7........121 M10
Brookland Garth GLDGN NW11........117 L2
Brookland Hl GLDGN NW11........117 K2
Brookland Ri GLDGN NW11........117 K2
Brooklands DART DA1........187 M4
Brooklands Ap ROMW/RG RM7........124 D2
Brooklands Av BFN/LL DA15........184 G5
WAND/EARL SW18........179 L5
Brooklands Cl COB KT11........235 M1
ROMW/RG RM7........124 D2
SUN TW16........196 F1
Brooklands Ct KIL/WHAMP NW6........2 C3
WCHMH N21........79 L9
Brooklands Dr GFD/PVL UB6........135 J3
Brooklands Gdns EMPK RM11........125 K3
POTB/CUF EN6........59 J4
Brooklands La ROMW/RG RM7........124 D2
WEY KT13........216 A3
Brooklands Pk BKHTH/KID SE3........161 M9
Brooklands Pl ROMW/RG RM7........124 D2
THDIT KT7........198 F8
WEY KT13........216 A3
Brooklands Wy REDH RH1........257 P8
Brook La BERK HP4........33 N4
BKHTH/KID SE3........161 N8
BMLY BR1........183 M9
BRWN CM15........87 H3
BXLY DA5........185 N2
CHOB/PIR GU24........213 J7
RPLY/SEND GU23........233 H4
SBW CM21........29 N2
SHGR GU5........269 P8
Brookland Fld HLWS CM18........47 L4
Brook La North BTFD TW8........155 J5
Brooklea Cl CDALE/KGS NW9........96 E1
Brookleys CHOB/PIR GU24........213 L6
Brooklyn Av LOU IG10........82 G9
Brooklyn Cl CAR SM5........201 P9
WOKN/KNAP GU21........232 B5
Brooklyn Gv SNWD SE25........204 A4
Brooklyn Rd HAYES BR2........206 A3
SNWD SE25........204 A4
WOKN/KNAP GU21........232 B4
Brooklyn Wy WDR/YW UB7........151 N2
Brookmans Av BRKMPK AL9........59 J2
Brookmans Cl CDH/CHF RM16........147 P10
Brook Md HOR/WEW KT19........220 B3
Brookmead MTCM CR4........202 D6
Brookmead Av HAYES BR2........206 C1
Brook Meadow CHIG IG7........103 H1
Brook Meadow Cl WFD IG8........101 K7
Brookmead Rd CROY/NA CR0........202 D6
Brookmead Wy ORP BR6........207 L6
Brook Ms North BAY/PAD W2........9 K7
Brookmill Cl OXHEY WD19........93 J1
Brookmill Rd DEPT SE8........160 ...
Brook Park Cl WCHMH N21........79 J10
Brook Pth LOU IG10........82 B9
Brook Pl BAR EN5........77 N6
Brook Ri CHIG IG7........102 G4
Brook Rd BKHH IG9........101 M3
BORE WD6........75 P1
BRW CM14........106 E4
CEND/HSY/T N8........118 F2
CHES/WCR EN8........62 E10
CRICK NW2........117 K8
EPP CM16........65 H9
GNTH/NBYPK IG2........122 E4
GPK RM2........104 G10
GVW DA11........191 H7
LOU IG10........82 B9
REDH RH1........275 N6
RYNPK SW20........200 E4
SURB KT6........199 K9

SWLY BR8........208 E3
THHTH CR7........203 K4
TWK TW1........176 P2
Brook Rd South BTFD TW8........155 J4
BTFD TW8........155 K5
Brooks Av EHAM E6........155 K5
Brooksbank St HOM E9........140 C1
Brooksby Ms IS N1........6 A4
Brooksby St IS N1........6 A4
Brooksby's Wk HOM E9........120 C10
Brooks Cl WEY KT13........216 B6
Brookscroft Rd WALTH E17........100 C9
Brooksfield WGCE AL7........23 L4
Brookshill KTN/HRWW/W HA3........94 C6
Brookshill Av KTN/HRWW/W HA3........94 C6
Brookshill Dr KTN/HRWW/W HA3........94 C6
Brookside BARK/HLT IG6........102 F7
CAR SM5........222 B2
CHERT KT16........195 H7
CRAWE RH10........284 A6
CRAWE RH10........285 H2
DTCH/LGLY SL3........150 F6
EBAR EN4........77 P10
EMPK RM11........125 M3
HAT AL10........40 E4
HERT/BAY SG13........25 M6
HGDN/ICK UB10........132 A2
HLWW/ROY CM19........46 C4
HOD EN11........44 F3
ORP BR6........207 J7
POTB/CUF EN6........58 D8
RGUE GU4........250 A5
WAB EN9........63 K8
WCHMH N21........78 G10
Brookside Av ASHF TW15........173 M8
STWL/WRAY TW19........150 A9
Brookside Cl BAR EN5........76 G10
FELT TW13........175 H6
KTN/HRWW/W HA3........115 J3
RSLP HA4........113 M9
Brookside Crs POTB/CUF EN6........60 F3
WPK KT4........200 D8
Brookside Gdns EN EN1........80 A5
Brookside Rd ED N9........118 H4
GLDGN NW11........117 H4
MEO DA13........190 C10
OXHEY WD19........93 J1
UED N18........100 A5
YEAD UB4........133 K9
Brookside South EBAR EN4........98 A1
Brookside Wy CROY/NA CR0........204 C6
Brooks La CHSWK W4........155 M5
Brooks Rd CHSWK W4........155 M5
PLSTW E13........141 M3
Brook St BAY/PAD W2........9 M7
BELV DA17........164 C4
BRW CM14........106 D5
KUT KT1........199 K2
MYFR/PKLN W1K........10 E7
WDSR SL4........149 J8
Brooksville Av KIL/WHAMP NW6........2 B6
Brookswood RGUE GU4........268 C3
Brook Va RDKG RH5........272 G8
Brookview CRAWE RH10........284 D8
Brookview Rd STRHM/NOR SW16........180 D8
Brookville Rd FUL/PGN SW6........157 J6
Brook Wk EDGW HA8........96 A7
Brook Wy CHIG IG7........102 D4
LHD/OX KT22........236 F7
Brookway BKHTH/KID SE3........161 M9
RAIN RM13........145 J7
Brookwood HORL RH6........280 C3
Brookwood Av BARN SW13........156 C9
Brookwood Br WOKN/KNAP GU21........230 ...
Brookwood Cl HAYES BR2........205 L4
Brookwood Lye Rd WOKS/MYFD GU22........230 G6
Brookwood Rd HSLW TW3........154 A8
WAND/EARL SW18........179 J4
Broom Av STMC/STPC BR5........207 L2
Broom Bank WARL CR6........243 H5
Broom Cl CHESW EN7........61 P3
ESH/CLAY KT10........218 A2
HAT AL10........40 C7
HAYES BR2........206 B6
TEDD TW11........177 J10
Broomcroft Dr WOKS/MYFD GU22........232 G1
Broome Cl EPSOM KT18........256 A2
Broome Pl SOCK/AV RM15........146 C10
Broome Rd HPTN TW12........197 N1
Broomer Pl CHES/WCR EN8........62 B1
Broome Wy CMBW SE5........159 L6
Broomfield GUW GU2........249 K8
HLW CM20........29 L8
LCOL/BKTW AL2........56 B3
SUN TW16........197 H1
WALTH E17........120 E5
Broomfield Av BROX EN10........62 D2
LOU IG10........82 C10
PLMGR N13........98 F6
RCH/KEW TW9........155 L7
SEV TN13........246 E7
SWCM DA10........189 K2
WLSDN NW10........136 A2
Broomfield Cl CRW RM5........104 E7
RGUW GU3........249 K8
WOKS/MYFD GU22........232 G2
Broomfield Ct WEY KT13........216 B5
Broomfield Dr ASC SL5........192 C6
Broomfield La PLMGR N13........98 G6
Broomfield Pl WEA W13........134 G10
Broomfield Ride LHD/OX KT22........218 C8
Broomfield Rd ADL/WDHM KT15........214 ...
BECK BR3........204 D3
BRYLDS KT5........199 L8
BXLYHS DA6........186 B1
CHDH RM6........123 N5
PLMGR N13........98 F6
RCH/KEW TW9........155 L7
SEV TN13........246 E7
SWCM DA10........189 K2
WEA W13........134 G10
Broomfield St POP/IOD E14........140 F10
Broom Gdns CROY/NA CR0........204 F10
Broom Gv WAT WD17........73 H4
Broomgrove Gdns EDGW HA8........95 M4
Broomgrove Rd BRXN/ST SW9........158 B8
Broom Hall LHD/OX KT22........218 B10
Broomhall End WOKN/KNAP GU21........232 B2
Broomhall La ASC SL5........192 E6
WOKN/KNAP GU21........232 B2
Broomhall Rd SAND/SEL CR2........223 L5
WOKN/KNAP GU21........232 B2
Broom HI HHW HP1........35 H7
SLN SL2........129 M2
Broomhill Rd BXLYHS DA6........186 B1
DART DA1........187 J2
GDMY/SEVK IG3........123 K1
ORP BR6........207 L1
WAND/EARL SW18........179 L4
WFD IG8........101 M7
Broomhills ESH/CLAY KT10........218 A2
HART DA3........211 K5
Broomhouse La FUL/PGN SW6........157 K8
Broomhouse Rd FUL/PGN SW6........157 K8
Broomlands La OXTED RH8........262 B5
Broomleys STALE/WH AL4........39 H3
Broomloan La SUT SM1........201 K9
Broom Md BXLYHS DA6........186 B2

Broom Pk KUT KT1........177 J10
TEDD TW11........177 J10
Broom Rd CROY/NA CR0........204 F10
TEDD TW11........176 G8
Brooms Cl WGCW AL8........22 G2
Broomsleigh St KIL/WHAMP NW6........117 J10
Broomstick Hall Rd WAB EN9........63 K9
Broomstick La CSHM HP5........51 M6
Broom Water TEDD TW11........177 K8
Broom Water West TEDD TW11........177 K8
Broom Wy WEY KT13........216 E1
Broomwood Cl BXLY DA5........186 C5
CROY/NA CR0........204 C5
Broomwood Gdns BRWN CM15........86 F10
Broomwood Rd BTSEA SW11........179 P2
STMC/STPC BR5........207 L2
Broseley Gdns HARH RM3........105 M5
Broseley Gv SYD SE26........182 D8
Broseley Rd HARH RM3........105 M5
Broster Gdns SNWD SE25........203 N3
Brougham Rd ACT W3........135 P8
HACK E8........139 P3
Brougham St BTSEA SW11........158 B8
Broughinge Rd BORE WD6........75 N6
Broughton Av FNCH N3........117 H1
RCHPK/HAM TW10........176 H1
Broughton Dr BRXN/ST SW9........159 J10
Broughton Gdns HGT N6........118 D4
Broughton Rd FUL/PGN SW6........157 L8
ORP BR6........206 G9
THHTH CR7........203 H6
WEA W13........134 G9
Broughton Road Ap FUL/PGN SW6........157 L8
Broughton St VX/NE SW8........158 B8
Broughton Wy RKW/CH/CXG WD3........91 K3
Brouncker Rd ACT W3........155 P1
Brow Cl STMC/STPC BR5........207 N7
Brow Crs STMC/STPC BR5........207 M8
Browells La FELT TW13........175 K5
Brown Cl WLGTN SM6........222 E4
Browne Rd BRW CM14........106 G2
Brownfields WGCE AL7........23 J4
Brownfield St POP/IOD E14........140 G8
Browngraves Rd HYS/HAR UB3........152 D6
Brown Hart Gdns MYFR/PKLN W1K........10 D7
Brownhill Rd CAT SE6........183 H3
Browning Av HNWL W7........134 E1
SUT SM1........221 P1
WPK KT4........200 E6
Browning Cl CRAWE RH10........284 D6
HPTN TW12........175 N7
MV/WKIL W9........9 K2
WALTH E17........121 L1
WELL DA16........163 H7
Browning Rd DART DA1........165 N10
ENC/FH EN2........79 L4
HARP AL5........20 B1
LHD/OX KT22........254 C1
MNPK E12........142 C1
WAN E11........121 L5
Browning St WALW SE17........18 F7
Browning Wy HEST TW5........153 L7
Brownlea Gdns GDMY/SEVK IG3........123 K1
Brownlow Ms FSBYW WC1X........11 P1
Brownlow Rd BERK HP4........33 P4
BORE WD6........75 M8
CROY/NA CR0........223 M1
FBAR/BDGN N11........98 F2
FNCH N3........97 L8
FSTGT E7........121 M9
HACK E8........7 M5
REDH RH1........257 P10
WEA W13........134 F10
WLSDN NW10........136 B2
Brownlow St GINN WC1R........11 P4
Brownrigg Rd ASHF TW15........174 B7
Brown Rd GVE DA12........191 H5
Browns HI REDH RH1........277 L7
Browns La EHSLY KT24........253 L3
Brownspring Dr ELTH/MOT SE9........184 E6
Brown's Rd BRYLDS KT5........199 L7
WALTH E17........120 F1
Browns Spring BERK HP4........34 F2
Brown St MBLAR W1H........10 A5
Brownswell Rd EFNCH N2........97 N10
Brownswood Rd FSBYPK N4........119 K4
The Brow CSTG HP8........90 A4
GSTN WD25........55 J9
REDH RH1........276 B5
Broxash Rd BTSEA SW11........180 A1
Broxbourne Av WAN E11........121 N2
Broxbourne House BOW E3........140 E1
Broxbourne Rd FSTGT E7........121 M8
ORP BR6........207 J1
Broxburn Dr SOCK/AV RM15........146 G8
SOCK/AV RM15........147 H9
Broxhill Rd ABR/ST RM4........105 H4
Broxholm Rd WNWD SE27........181 H6
Brox La ADL/WDHM KT15........214 G5
Brox Rd CHERT KT16........214 F4
Broxted Rd CAT SE6........182 E5
Broxwood Wy STJWD NW8........3 L5
Bruce Av HCH RM12........125 K7
SHPTN TW17........196 D6
Bruce Castle Rd TOTM N17........99 H9
Bruce Cl BF/WBF KT14........215 N9
NKENS W10........136 C6
SL SL1........128 F10
WELL DA16........163 L7
Bruce Dr SAND/SEL CR2........224 C5
Bruce Gdns WCHMH N21........98 A4
Bruce Gv ORP BR6........207 K8
TOTM N17........99 N10
WATN N22........73 J4
Bruce Rd BAR EN5........77 H7
BOW E3........140 G5
KTN/HRWW/W HA3........94 D10
MTCM CR4........180 B10
SNWD SE25........203 L4
WLSDN NW10........136 A2
Bruces Wharf Rd GRAYS RM17........167 M5
Bruce Wy CHES/WCR EN8........62 C9
Bruckner St NKENS W10........2 C10
Brudenell WDSR SL4........148 E9
Brudenell Rd TOOT SW17........180 E5
Bruffs Meadow NTHLT UB5........133 M1
Brumana Cl WEY KT13........216 C3
Brumfield Rd HOR/WEW KT19........219 P3
Brunel Cl HEST TW5........153 J6
NRWD SE19........181 N9
NTHLT UB5........133 N5
ROM RM1........124 F2
TIL RM18........168 E8
Brunel Ct WLSDN NW10........136 D5
Brunel Pl CRAWE RH10........283 P7
Brunel Rd ACT W3........136 B7
BERM/RHTH SE16........140 B10
WALTH E17........120 C1
WFD IG8........102 C6
Brunel St CAN/RD E16........141 L8
Brunel Wk HSLWW TW4........175 D3
TOTM N17........99 N7
Brunel Wy SL SL1........129 L10
Bruner St WCHPL E1........13 N4
Brunner Cl GLDGN NW11........117 L3
Brunner Ct CHERT KT16........214 F2
Brunner Rd EA W5........135 J1
WALTH E17........120 E3
Bruno Pl KTN/HRWW/W HA3........115 P7
Brunswick Av FBAR/BDGN N11........98 A3
UPMR RM14........126 D5
Brunswick Cl BXLYHS DA6........163 N10
CRAWE RH10........284 B9
PIN HA5........113 M4

THDIT KT7 198 E8 1
WHTN TW2 176 C6
WOT/HER KT12 197 K9
Brunswick Ct STHWK SE1 19 K2
Brunswick Crs FBAR/BDGN N11 98 B4
Brunswick Dr CHOB/PIR GU24 230 C6
Brunswick Gdns BARK/HLT IG6 102 F8
EA W5 135 K5
KENS W8 8 F10
Brunswick Gv COB KT11 217 K9 1
FBAR/BDGN N11 98 B4
Brunswick Ms MBLAR W1H 10 B5 1
STRHM/NOR SW16 180 E9 1
Brunswick Pk CMBW SE5 159 L7
Brunswick Park Gdns
FBAR/BDGN N11 98 B3
Brunswick Park Rd
FBAR/BDGN N11 98 C5 1
Brunswick Pl IS N1 7 H10
NRWD SE19 181 P10 3
Brunswick Quay
BERM/RHTH SE16 160 C2
Brunswick Rd BXLYHS DA6 163 N10
CHOB/PIR GU24 230 C7
EA W5 135 J6
KUTN/CMB KT2 199 M1
LEY E10 121 H6
SEVS/STOTM N15 119 M2 1
SEVS/STOTM N15 119 M3 2
SUT SM1 221 L1
WAB EN9 80 F4
Brunswick Sq BMSBY WC1N 11 M1
Brunswick St WALTH E17 121 H3
Brunswick Vls CMBW SE5 159 M7 1
Brunswick Wk GVE DA12 190 G2 1
Brunswick Wy FBAR/BDGN N11 98 C5
Brunton Pl POP/IOD E14 140 D8 5
Brushfield St WCHPL E1 13 K3
Brushrise WATN WD24 73 H2
Brushwood Dr RKW/CH/CXG WD3 70 F8
Brushwood Rd CSHM HP5 51 J5
Brussels Rd BTSEA SW11 157 N10
Bruton Cl CHST BR7 184 C10
Bruton La MYFR/PICC W1J 10 F8
Bruton Pl MYFR/PKLN W1K 10 F8
Bruton Rd MRDN SM4 201 M4
Bruton St MYFR/PICC W1J 10 F8
Bruton Wy WEA W13 134 F7
Bryan Av WLSDN NW10 136 E2
Bryan Cl SUN TW16 175 H10
Bryan Rd BERM/RHTH SE16 160 E1
Bryanston Av WHTN TW2 176 A4
Bryanston Cl NWDGN UB2 153 N3 2
Bryanstone Av GUW GU2 249 L6
Bryanstone Cl GUW GU2 249 L7
Bryanstone Gv GUW GU2 249 L6
Bryanstone Rd CEND/HSY/T N8 118 E4 1
CHES/WCR EN8 62 E10
Bryanston Ms East MBLAR W1H 10 A4
Bryanston Ms West MBLAR W1H 10 A4
Bryanston Pl MBLAR W1H 10 A4
Bryanston Rd TIL RM18 168 F8
Bryanston Sq MBLAR W1H 10 A5
Bryanston St MBLAR W1H 10 A6
Bryant Av HARH RM3 105 L10
SLN SL2 129 J7
Bryant Cl BAR EN5 77 J9
Bryant Rd NTHLT UB5 133 K5
Bryant St SRTFD E15 141 J2 1
Bryantwood Rd HOLWY N7 119 H10
Brycedale Crs STHGT/OAK N14 98 E5
Bryce Rd BCTR RM8 123 M9
Bryden Cl SYD SE26 182 D8
Brydges Rd SRTFD E15 121 J10
Bryer Pl WDSR SL4 148 C9
Brymay Cl BOW E3 140 F4
Brympton Cl DORK RH4 272 F4
Brynford Cl WOKN/KNAP GU21 232 B1 1
Brynmaer Rd BTSEA SW11 158 A7
Bryn-y-mawr Rd EN EN1 79 P8
Bryony Cl UX/CGN UB8 132 A7
Bryony Rd GU GU1 250 E7
SHB W12 136 D9
Bryony Wy SUN TW16 175 H9
Bubblestone Rd RSEV TN14 247 J2
Buccleuch Rd DTCH/LGLY SL3 149 M6
Buchanan Cl SOCK/AV RM15 146 B10 2
WCHMH N21 78 G9 3
Buchanan Ct BORE WD6 75 P6 1
Buchanan Gdns WLSDN NW10 136 E4
Buchan Cl UX/CGN UB8 131 M5 1
Buchan Rd PECK SE15 160 B9
Bucharest Rd WAND/EARL SW18 179 M3
Buckden Cl LEE/GVPK SE12 183 L2
Buckettsland La BORE WD6 76 A4
Buckfast Rd MRDN SM4 201 L4
Buckfast St BETH E2 7 P10
Buckham Thorns Rd
BH/WHM TN16 262 F2
Buckhold Rd WAND/EARL SW18 179 K2
Buckhurst Av CAR SM5 201 P8
Buckhurst Cl REDH RH1 257 P8
Buckhurst La ASC SL5 192 F3
SEV TN13 265 K1
Buckhurst Rd ASC SL5 192 E2
BH/WHM TN16 244 E6
Buckhurst St WCHPL E1 140 A6
Buckhurst Wy BKHH IG9 102 A4
Buckingham Av E/WMO/HCT KT8 198 A2
EBED/NFELT TW14 175 J2
GFD/PVL UB6 134 F3
SL SL1 128 F8
THHTH CR7 203 H1
TRDG/WHET N20 97 M1
WELL DA16 163 H10
Buckingham Av East SL SL1 129 H8
Buckingham Cl EA W5 135 H7
EMPK RM11 125 L3 1
EN EN1 79 M6
GU GU1 250 C9
HPTN TW12 175 N8
STMC/STPC BR5 207 H7
Buckingham Dr CHST BR7 184 F8 1
Buckingham Gdns SL SL1 149 L1 1
STAN HA7 95 K8
THHTH CR7 203 H2 1
Buckingham Ga HORL RH6 280 D7
WESTW SW1E 16 G3
Buckingham Gv
HGDN/ICK UB10 132 B4 1
Buckingham La FSTH SE23 182 D3 1
Buckingham Ms WESTW SW1E 16 G3 1
WLSDN NW10 136 C4
Buckingham Palace Rd PIM SW1V 16 E5
WESTW SW1E 16 F4
Buckingham Pl WESTW SW1E 16 G3 2
Buckingham Rd BORE WD6 76 A8
EDGW HA8 95 L8
FELT TW13 175 N7
FSTGT E7 121 L10
GVW DA11 190 A3 1
HRW HA1 114 C3
IL IG1 122 G7
IS N1 7 J2
KUT KT1 199 L4
LEY E10 120 G8
MTCM CR4 202 F5 1
RCHPK/HAM TW10 177 J5
RDKG RH5 273 H10
SWFD E18 101 L9
WAN E11 121 N2
WATN WD24 73 K3 1
WDGN N22 98 F9 1
WLSDN NW10 136 C4
Buckingham St CHCR WC2N 11 M8 1
Buckingham Wy WLGTN SM6 222 D5
Buckland Av DTCH/LGLY SL3 149 N2
Buckland Crs HAMP NW3 3 L3
WDSR SL4 148 E7
Buckland La BRKHM/BTCW RH3 256 D6
Buckland Ri PIN HA5 93 K9
Buckland Rd BELMT SM2 220 F6
CHSGTN KT9 219 L2
KWD/TDW/WH KT20 257 J5
LEY E10 121 H7
ORP BR6 227 H1
REIG RH2 256 G9
Bucklands Rd TEDD TW11 177 H9
Buckland St IS N1 7 H8
Buckland Wk MRDN SM4 201 M4 1
Buckland Wy WPK KT4 200 F8
Buck La CDALE/KGS NW9 116 A3
Buckleigh Av RYNPK SW20 201 J3
Buckleigh Rd STRHM/NOR SW16 180 E9
Buckleigh Wy NRWD SE19 181 N10 1
Bucklersbury MANHO EC4N 12 G6 1
Bucklers Cl BROX EN10 44 E8
Bucklers Ct BRW CM14 107 H6
Bucklers' Wy CAR SM5 202 A10
Buckles La SOCK/AV RM15 147 H7
Buckle St WCHPL E1 13 M5
Buckles Wy BNSTD SM7 239 H2
Buckley Cl DART DA1 164 G8
Buckley Pl CRAWE RH10 285 P5
Buckley Rd KIL/WHAMP NW6 2 D4
Buckmans Rd CRAWW RH11 283 N7
Buckmaster Rd BTSEA SW11 157 P10 4
Bucknalls Cl GSTN WD25 55 M8
Bucknalls Dr LCOL/BKTW AL2 55 N7
Bucknalls La GSTN WD25 55 M8
Bucknall St LSQ/SEVD WC2H 11 L5 2
Buckner Rd BRXS/STRHM SW2 158 G10
Bucknills Cl EPSOM KT18 219 N10
Buckrell Rd CHING E4 101 J3
Bucks Aly HERT/BAY SG13 42 E5
Bucks Av OXHEY WD19 93 M1
Bucks Cl BF/WBF KT14 215 L10
Bucks Cross Rd GVW DA11 190 C6
ORP BR6 227 P2
Bucks Hl KGLGY WD4 53 M9
Buckstone Cl FSTH SE23 182 B2
Buckstone Rd UED N18 99 P6 3
Buck St CAMTN NW1 4 F5
Buckswood Dr CRAWW RH11 283 K9
Buckters Rents
BERM/RHTH SE16 140 D10
Buckthorne Rd BROCKY SE4 182 D2
Buckton Rd BORE WD6 75 L4
Budd Cl NFNCH/WDSP N12 97 L5 1
Buddcroft WGCE AL7 23 L4 1
Buddings Cir WBLY HA9 115 P8 1
Budebury Rd STA TW18 173 J8
Budge La MTCM CR4 202 A7 2
Budgen Cl CRAWE RH10 284 E4
Budgen Dr REDH RH1 258 B7
Budgin's Hl ORP BR6 227 L8
Budleigh Crs WELL DA16 163 M7
Budoch Dr GDMY/SEVK IG3 123 K7
Buer Rd FUL/PGN SW6 157 H8
Buff Av BNSTD SM7 221 L10
Buffers La LHD/OX KT22 236 F5
Bug Hl WARL CR6 242 C6
Bugsby's Wy GNWCH SE10 161 L3
Bulbourne Cl BERK HP4 33 L3 1
HHW HP1 35 K7
Bulganak Rd THHTH CR7 203 K4 1
Bulinca St WEST SW1P 17 L6 1
Bulkeley Av WDSR SL4 148 G9
Bulkeley Cl EGH TW20 171 P8
Bullace Cl HHW HP1 35 K5 2
Bullace Rw CMBW SE5 159 L7 2
Bull Aly WELL DA16 163 L9
Bullar Cl PECK SE15 159 P6
Bullard Rd TEDD TW11 176 E9 2
Bullards Pl BETH E2 140 C5 2
Bullbaiters La AMS HP6 50 A10
Bullbanks Rd BELV DA17 164 D3
Bullbeggars La BERK HP4 34 D5
GDST RH9 260 B8
WOKN/KNAP GU21 231 N2
Bull Cl CDH/CHF RM16 167 L1 1
Bulleid Wy PIM SW1V 16 F6
Bullen's Green La STALE/WH AL4 40 B9
Bullen St BTSEA SW11 157 P8
Buller Rd BARK IG11 143 H2
THHTH CR7 203 L3
TOTM N17 99 P10
WDGN N22 99 H10
WLSDN NW10 136 G5
Bullers Cl SCUP DA14 185 P8
Bullers Wood Dr CHST BR7 206 B1
Bullescroft Rd EDGW HA8 95 M4
Bullfinch Cl HORL RH6 279 P3 1
SEV TN13 246 E8
Bullfinch Dene SEV TN13 246 E8
Bullfinch La SEV TN13 246 F8
Bullfinch Rd SAND/SEL CR2 224 C6
Bullhead Rd BORE WD6 75 P6
Bull Hl LHD/OX KT22 236 F7
Bullivant Cl GRH DA9 188 F1
Bullivant St POP/IOD E14 141 H9 1
Bull La CFSP/GDCR SL9 110 A2
CHST BR7 184 G10 1
DAGE RM10 124 C8
RGUE GU4 250 C2
STALE/WH AL4 20 F5
UED N18 99 M6
Bullock's La HERT/BAY SG13 25 K7
Bull Pln HERT/WAS SG14 25 L5
Bull Rd HARP AL5 20 A3
SRTFD E15 141 L4
Bullrush Cl CROY/NA CR0 203 M6 1
HAT AL10 40 E5
Bullrush Gv UX/CGN UB8 131 M6
Bulls Aly MORT/ESHN SW14 156 A9 1
Bull's Br HYS/HAR UB3 153 H2
Bulls Bridge Rd NWDGN UB2 153 J2
Bullsbrook Rd HYS/HAR UB3 133 K10
Bull's Cross ENC/FH EN2 79 P2
Bulls Cross Ride CHESW EN7 61 P10
Bullsland Gdns RKW/CH/CXG WD3 70 E10
Bullsland La RKW/CH/CXG WD3 70 E10
Bulls La BRKMPK AL9 41 H10
Bullsmoor Cl CHES/WCR EN8 80 B1 1
Bullsmoor Gdns CHES/WCR EN8 80 A1 1
Bullsmoor La EN EN1 80 A1
PEND EN3 80 C1
Bullsmoor Ride CHES/WCR EN8 80 B1
Bullsmoor Wy CHES/WCR EN8 80 A1
Bull Stag Gn BRKMPK AL9 40 F2
Bullswater Common Rd
CHOB/PIR GU24 248 F1
Bullwell Crs CHES/WCR EN8 62 D5
Bull Yd PECK SE15 159 P7
Bulmer Gdns KTN/HRWW/W HA3 115 J5
Bulmer Ms NTGHL W11 8 E9
Bulstrode Av HSLW TW3 153 N9
Bulstrode Cl KGLGY WD4 53 H5
Bulstrode Gdns HSLW TW3 153 P9
Bulstrode La KGLGY WD4 53 H5
Bulstrode Pl MHST W1U 10 D4 1
Bulstrode Rd HSLW TW3 153 P9
Bulstrode St MHST W1U 10 D5 2
Bulstrode Wy CFSP/GDCR SL9 110 A3
Bulwer Court Rd WAN E11 121 J6
Bulwer Gdns BAR EN5 77 M8 1
Bulwer Rd BAR EN5 77 L8
UED N18 99 M5
WAN E11 121 J6
Bulwer St SHB W12 136 F10
Bumbles Green La WAB EN9 63 N1
Bunbury Wy EW KT17 238 E2
Bunby Rd SLN SL2 129 L2
Bunce Common Rd REIG RH2 274 A7
Bunce Dr CTHM CR3 241 L9
Buncefield La HHNE HP2 36 D3
Bunces Cl WDSR SL4 148 G4
Bunces La WFD IG8 101 L8
Bundy's Wy STA TW18 173 J9
Bungalow Rd SNWD SE25 203 M4
The Bungalows
STRHM/NOR SW16 180 C10 1
Bunhill Rw STLK EC1Y 12 G1
Bunhouse Pl BGVA SW1W 16 C7
Bunkers Hl SCUP DA14 186 A6
Bunkers La HHS/BOV HP3 36 C10
Bunning Wy HOLWY N7 5 M3
Bunnsfield WGCE AL7 23 M4
Bunn's La MLHL NW7 96 B7
Bunsen St BOW E3 140 D4 1
Bunten Meade SL SL1 128 G10 1
Bunting Cl ED N9 100 C2 1
MTCM CR4 202 A5
Bunton St WOOL/PLUM SE18 162 D2
Bunyan Cl CRAWW RH11 283 H10
Bunyan Rd WALTH E17 120 D1
Bunyard Dr WOKN/KNAP GU21 214 F10
Burbage Cl CHES/WCR EN8 62 D7
STHWK SE1 18 G4
Burbage Rd HNHL SE24 181 L2
Burbeach Cl CRAWW RH11 283 L10 3
Burberry Cl NWMAL KT3 200 B2
Burbidge Rd SHPTN TW17 196 B4 2
Burbridge Wy TOTM N17 99 P10 1
Burcham St POP/IOD E14 140 G8
Burcharbro Rd ABYW SE2 163 N5
Burchell Ct BUSH WD23 94 B1 2
Burchell Rd LEY E10 120 G6
PECK SE15 160 A7 2
Burchets Hollow SHGR GU5 270 E10
Burchetts Wy SHPTN TW17 196 C6
Burchett Wy CHDH RM6 124 A4 1
Burchwall Cl CRW RM5 104 D8
Burcote Rd WAND/EARL SW18 179 N4
Burcott Gdns ADL/WDHM KT15 215 N3
Burcott Rd PUR/KEN CR8 223 H10
Burden Cl BTFD TW8 155 H4
Burdenshot Hl RGUW GU3 249 M1
Burdenshott Av
RCHPK/HAM TW10 155 N10
Burdenshott Rd RGUW GU3 249 M1
Burden Wy GUW GU2 249 N5
WAN E11 121 N7
Burder Rd IS N1 7 K1
Burdett Av GVE DA12 191 P7
RYNPK SW20 200 D1
Burdett Cl CRAWE RH10 284 E8 3
HNWL W7 134 E10 1
SCUP DA14 185 P8
Burdett Rd BOW E3 140 E6
CROY/NA CR0 203 L6
RCH/KEW TW9 155 L8
Burdetts Rd DAGW RM9 144 A3
Burdock Cl CROY/NA CR0 204 C8
LTWR GU18 212 A7
Burdock Rd TOTM N17 119 P1 2
Burdon La BELMT SM2 221 J5
Burdon Pk BELMT SM2 221 J5
Bure TIL RM18 169 M2
Burfield Cl HAT AL10 40 D2 1
TOOT SW17 179 M7
Burfield Dr WARL CR6 242 B5
Burfield Rd RKW/CH/CXG WD3 70 E9
WDSR SL4 171 M3
Burford Cl BARK/HLT IG6 122 F2
BCTR RM8 123 M8
HGDN/ICK UB10 111 P9
Burford Gdns HOD EN11 44 G2
PLMGR N13 98 G4
SL SL1 128 B7 1
Burford La EW KT17 220 F7
Burford Rd BMLY BR1 206 B4
BTFD TW8 155 K4
CAT SE6 182 E5
EHAM E6 142 B5
SRTFD E15 141 J2
SUT SM1 201 K9
WPK KT4 200 D7
Burford St HOD EN11 44 F3
Burford Wy CROY/NA CR0 225 H4
Burgate Cl DART DA1 164 G9
Burges Cl EMPK RM11 125 N4
Burges Gv BARN SW13 156 E6 1
Burges Rd EHAM E6 142 D2
STA TW18 173 K9
Burgess Av CDALE/KGS NW9 116 A4
Burgess Cl FELT TW13 175 M7 1
Burgess Rd SRTFD E15 121 K9
SUT SM1 221 L1
Burgess St POP/IOD E14 140 F7
Burgess Wood Rd BEAC HP9 88 A10
Burgess Wood Rd South
BEAC HP9 88 A10
Burge St STHWK SE1 19 H4
Burgett Rd SL SL1 148 G2
Burgh Cl CRAWE RH10 284 E4
Burghfield EW KT17 238 C1
Burghfield Rd MEO DA13 190 C10
Burgh Heath Rd EW KT17 238 C1
Burghill Rd SYD SE26 182 C7
Burghley Av BORE WD6 75 P9
NWMAL KT3 200 A1
Burghley Hall Cl
WIM/MER SW19 179 H4 1
Burghley Pl MTCM CR4 202 A5 1
Burghley Rd CDH/CHF RM16 167 H2
CEND/HSY/T N8 119 H1
KTTN NW5 118 C9
WAN E11 121 K6 1
WIM/MER SW19 178 G7
Burgh Mt BNSTD SM7 239 J1
Burgh St IS N1 6 D7
Burgh Wd BNSTD SM7 239 H1
Burgos Cl CROY/NA CR0 223 H3
Burgos Gv GNWCH SE10 160 G7 1
Burgoyne Rd BRXN/ST SW9 158 G9 2
FSBYPK N4 119 J4
SNWD SE25 203 N4
SUN TW16 174 G9
Burgundy Cft WGCE AL7 23 J7 1
Burham Cl PGE/AN SE20 182 B10
Burhill Gv PIN HA5 93 M10 2
Burhill Rd WOT/HER KT12 217 K3
Burke Cl PUT/ROE SW15 156 B10
Burkes Cl BEAC HP9 108 A1
Burkes Crs BEAC HP9 88 C9
Burkes Rd BEAC HP9 88 C9
Burke St CAN/RD E16 141 L8 1
Burket Cl NWDGN UB2 153 M3
Burland Rd BRWN CM15 107 J2
BTSEA SW11 180 A1
CRW RM5 104 D7
Burlands CRAWW RH11 283 K4
Burlea Cl WOT/HER KT12 217 J2
Burleigh Av BFN/LL DA15 185 J1
WLGTN SM6 202 B10
Burleigh Cl ADL/WDHM KT15 215 L2
Burleigh Gdns ASHF TW15 174 D8
STHGT/OAK N14 98 D2
WOKN/KNAP GU21 232 C3 1
Burleigh Md BRKMPK AL9 40 F2
Burleigh Pk COB KT11 217 M8
Burleigh Pl PUT/ROE SW15 178 G1 1
Burleigh Rd ADL/WDHM KT15 215 L1
CHEAM SM3 201 H8
CHES/WCR EN8 62 D8 1
EN EN1 79 M8
HERT/BAY SG13 25 P4
HGDN/ICK UB10 132 C3
HHS/BOV HP3 36 D7
STAL AL1 38 G6
Burleigh St COVGDN WC2E 11 M7 1
Burleigh Wk CAT SE6 183 H4
Burleigh Wy ENC/FH EN2 79 L7 1
POTB/CUF EN6 60 F6
Burley Cl CHING E4 100 F6 1
STRHM/NOR SW16 202 E2
Burley Hl HLWE CM17 47 N2
Burley Rd CAN/RD E16 141 P8
Burleys Rd CRAWE RH10 284 E7
Burlingham Cl RGUE GU4 250 G8 2
Burlings La RSEV TN14 245 J3
Burlington Av RCH/KEW TW9 155 M7
ROMW/RG RM7 124 D4 1
SL SL1 149 K1
Burlington Cl EBED/NFELT TW14 174 E3
EHAM E6 142 B8 1
ORP BR6 206 E9
Burlington Gdns ACT W3 135 P10
CHDH RM6 123 P5
CHSWK W4 155 P4
MYFR/PICC W1J 10 G8 1
Burlington La CHSWK W4 155 P6
Burlington Ms ACT W3 135 P10
Burlington Pl FUL/PGN SW6 157 H8 1
PIN HA5 113 J1
REIG RH2 257 K10
WFD IG8 101 M4
Burlington Ri EBAR EN4 97 P2
Burlington Rd CHSWK W4 155 P4 3
ENC/FH EN2 79 L5
FUL/PGN SW6 157 H8
ISLW TW7 154 C7
MUSWH N10 118 B1
NWMAL KT3 200 C4
SL SL1 128 A7
THHTH CR7 203 K2
TOTM N17 99 P9 2
Burman Cl RDART DA2 188 B3
Burma Rd CHOB/PIR GU24 193 L9
STNW/STAM N16 119 L9
Burmester Rd TOOT SW17 179 M6
Burnaby Crs CHSWK W4 155 N5
Burnaby Gdns CHSWK W4 155 N5
Burnaby Rd GVW DA11 190 B3
Burnaby St WBPTN SW10 157 M6
Burnbrae Cl FNCH N3 97 L7
Burnbury Rd BAL SW12 180 D4
Burn Cl ADL/WDHM KT15 215 N1 2
LHD/OX KT22 236 B1
Burncroft Av PEND EN3 80 B6 4
PEND EN3 80 C6 1
Burndell Wy YEAD UB4 133 L7
Burnell Av RCHPK/HAM TW10 177 H8
WELL DA16 163 K8
Burnell Gdns STAN HA7 95 J10
Burnell Rd SUT SM1 221 L1
Burnell Wk RBRW/HUT CM13 107 H7 3
Burnels Av EHAM E6 142 D5
Burness Cl UX/CGN UB8 131 N4 1
Burne St CAMTN NW1 9 N3
Burnet Av GU GU1 250 E7
Burnet Cl CHOB/PIR GU24 212 D9
HHS/BOV HP3 35 P7
Burnet Gv HOR/WEW KT19 219 P9
Burnett Pk HLWW/ROY CM19 46 E6 2
Burnett Rd ERITH DA8 165 L5
Burnett Sq HERT/WAS SG14 24 G4
Burnetts Rd WDSR SL4 148 D7
Burney Av BRYLDS KT5 199 L5
Burney Cl GT/LBKH KT23 254 B1
Burney Dr LOU IG10 82 F7
Burney Rd RDKG RH5 254 F7
Burney St GNWCH SE10 161 H6
Burnfoot Av FUL/PGN SW6 157 H7
Burnham Av BEAC HP9 108 F1
HGDN/ICK UB10 112 D9
Burnham Cl ENC/FH EN2 79 M4
KTN/HRWW/W HA3 114 F2
MLHL NW7 96 D8 3
STHWK SE1 19 M6
WDSR SL4 148 C8
WOKN/KNAP GU21 231 J4
Burnham Crs DART DA1 165 K10
WAN E11 121 P2 1
Burnham Dr REIG RH2 257 K9
WPK KT4 200 G9
Burnham Gdns CROY/NA CR0 203 N7 2
HEST TW5 153 J7
HYS/HAR UB3 152 E2
Burnham La SL SL1 128 C7
Burnham Rd BEAC HP9 108 D4
CHING E4 100 E6
DART DA1 187 L1
MRDN SM4 201 L5
ROMW/RG RM7 124 D1
SCUP DA14 185 P5
STAL AL1 38 F6
WOKN/KNAP GU21 231 J4
Burnhams Rd GT/LBKH KT23 235 M10
Burnham St BETH E2 140 B5 4
KUTN/CMB KT2 199 M1 2
Burnham Wy SYD SE26 182 E8
WEA W13 154 G3
Burnhill Rd BECK BR3 204 F2
Burnley Cl OXHEY WD19 93 K6
Burnley Rd BRXN/ST SW9 158 G8
WLSDN NW10 116 C10
WTHK RM20 166 E7
Burnsall Pl HARP AL5 20 B5
Burnsall St CHEL SW3 15 P7
Burns Av BFN/LL DA15 185 L2
CHDH RM6 123 M5
EBED/NFELT TW14 175 H2
STHL UB1 133 P9
Burns Cl ERITH DA8 164 G7
TOOT SW17 179 N9 1
WELL DA16 163 J7
YEAD UB4 133 H7
Burns Dr BNSTD SM7 221 H10
HHNE HP2 36 C1
Burnside ASHTD KT21 237 L4 1
HERT/WAS SG14 25 H6
HOD EN11 44 E3
SBW CM21 29 N1
STAL AL1 38 G8
Burnside Av CHING E4 100 E7
Burnside Cl BAR EN5 77 K7
BERM/RHTH SE16 140 C10 2
TWK TW1 176 F2
Burnside Crs ALP/SUD HA0 135 J3
Burnside Rd BCTR RM8 123 M7
Burns Pl TIL RM18 168 E7
Burns Rd ALP/SUD HA0 135 K4
BTSEA SW11 158 A8
CRAWE RH10 284 D5
WEA W13 154 G1 1
WLSDN NW10 136 C3
Burns Wy HEST TW5 153 L7
Burnt Ash Hl LEE/GVPK SE12 183 L2
Burnt Ash La BMLY BR1 183 N8
Burnt Ash Rd LEE/GVPK SE12 183 L2 1
Burntcommon Cl
RPLY/SEND GU23 251 J1 1
Burntcommon La
RPLY/SEND GU23 251 K1
Burntfarm Ride CHESW EN7 61 J8
Burnt House La HORS RH12 282 C6
RDART DA2 187 M7
Burnthwaite Rd FUL/PGN SW6 157 J6
Burntmill Cl HLW CM20 28 F8 1
Burntmill La HLW CM20 28 F8
Burnt Oak Broadway EDGW HA8 95 N8
Burnt Oak Flds EDGW HA8 95 P9
Burnt Oak La BFN/LL DA15 185 K2
Burnt Pollard La CHOB/PIR GU24 212 D6
Burntwood Av EMPK RM11 125 L4
Burntwood Cl CTHM CR3 241 P7
WAND/EARL SW18 179 P4 1
Burntwood Grange Rd
WAND/EARL SW18 179 N4
Burntwood Gv SEV TN13 265 J3
Burntwood La CTHM CR3 241 P7
Burntwood Rd SEV TN13 265 J4
Burntwood Vw NRWD SE19 181 N8 1
Burnway EMPK RM11 125 M5
Burnwood Park Rd
WOT/HER KT12 217 J1
Buross St WCHPL E1 140 A8 4
Burpham La RGUE GU4 250 D5
Burrage Gv WOOL/PLUM SE18 162 E3
Burrage Pl WOOL/PLUM SE18 162 E4
Burrage Rd WOOL/PLUM SE18 162 F3
Burrard Rd CAN/RD E16 141 M8
KIL/WHAMP NW6 117 K10
Burr Cl BXLYHN DA7 164 A9
LCOL/BKTW AL2 57 K3
Burrell Cl CROY/NA CR0 204 D6
EDGW HA8 95 N3
Burrell Rw BECK BR3 204 F2
Burrell St STHWK SE1 12 C9
The Burrell DORK RH4 272 B3
Burrfield Dr STMC/STPC BR5 207 N5
Burr Hill La CHOB/PIR GU24 213 K5
Burritt Rd KUT KT1 199 M2
Burroughs Gdns HDN NW4 116 E2 2
The Burroughs HDN NW4 116 E2
Burroway Rd DTCH/LGLY SL3 150 E2
Burrowfield WGCE AL7 22 G7
Burrow Gn CHIG IG7 103 J6
Burrow Hill Gn CHOB/PIR GU24 213 J5
Burrow Rd CHIG IG7 103 K6
CMBW SE5 159 M10
Burrows Cl GT/LBKH KT23 235 N10
GUW GU2 249 L9
Burrows Hill Cl STWL/WRAY TW19 151 L10
Burrows La SHGR GU5 270 D6
Burrows Ms STHWK SE1 18 C1
Burrows Rd WLSDN NW10 136 F5
Burr Rd WAND/EARL SW18 179 K4
Bursar St STHWK SE1 13 J10 1
Bursdon Cl BFN/LL DA15 185 J5
Burses Wy RBRW/HUT CM13 107 N1
Bursland Rd PEND EN3 80 C8
Burslem Av BARK/HLT IG6 103 K7
Burslem St WCHPL E1 13 P6
Burstead Cl COB KT11 217 L9
Burstock Rd PUT/ROE SW15 157 H10
Burston Dr LCOL/BKTW AL2 56 B4
Burston Rd PUT/ROE SW15 178 G1
Burstow Rd RYNPK SW20 201 H1
Burtenshaw Rd THDIT KT7 198 F7
Burtley Cl FSBYPK N4 119 K6
Burton Av WATW WD18 73 H8
Burton Cl CHSGTN KT9 219 J4
HORL RH6 280 B5 1
Burton Gdns HEST TW5 153 N7 1
Burton Gv WALW SE17 18 G8
Burtonhole Cl MLHL NW7 96 G5
Burtonhole La MLHL NW7 96 G6
NFNCH/WDSP N12 97 H5
Burton La CHESW EN7 61 M4
Burton Ms BGVA SW1W 16 D6
Burton Pl STPAN WC1H 11 K1
Burton Rd BRXN/ST SW9 159 H8 1
KIL/WHAMP NW6 2 D4
KUTN/CMB KT2 177 K10
LOU IG10 82 F8
SWFD E18 121 N1 1
Burtons Ct SRTFD E15 141 J2 2
Burton's La CSTG HP8 70 B8
RKW/CH/CXG WD3 70 C9
Burton's Rd HPTN TW12 176 A7
Burton St STPAN WC1H 11 K1
Burton's Wy CSTG HP8 69 P6
Burton Wy WDSR SL4 148 D9
Burt Rd CAN/RD E16 141 P10
Burtwell La WNWD SE27 181 L7
Burwash Cl STMC/STPC BR5 207 M5 1
Burwash Rd CRAWE RH10 284 B8 4
WOOL/PLUM SE18 162 G4
Burway Crs CHERT KT16 195 K4
Burwell Av GFD/PVL UB6 134 D1
Burwell Cl WCHPL E1 140 A8 6
Burwell Rd LEY E10 120 D6
Burwood Av HAYES BR2 205 N9
PIN HA5 113 K3
PUR/KEN CR8 223 J10
Burwood Cl GU GU1 250 F9
REIG RH2 257 N10
SURB KT6 199 M8
WOT/HER KT12 217 K3
Burwood Gdns RAIN RM13 144 G5 2
Burwood Pl BAY/PAD W2 9 P5 1
Burwood Rd WEY KT13 216 E4
WOT/HER KT12 216 G4
Bury Av RSLP HA4 112 D4
YEAD UB4 132 F4
Bury Cl BERM/RHTH SE16 140 C10 3
WOKN/KNAP GU21 232 A2
Bury Ct HDTCH EC3A 13 K5 1
Burycroft WGCW AL8 23 H2
Burydell La LCOL/BKTW AL2 56 C3
Bury Farm AMSS HP7 69 H6
Bury Flds GUW GU2 267 P2
Bury Gn HHW HP1 35 M5 1
STALE/WH AL4 21 H3
Bury Green Rd CHESW EN7 61 P7
Bury Gv MRDN SM4 201 L5
Bury Hl HHW HP1 35 M5
Bury Hill Cl HHW HP1 35 M5
Bury Holme BROX EN10 44 E9
Bury La EPP CM16 64 G6
RKW/CH/CXG WD3 91 N2
WOKN/KNAP GU21 231 P2
Bury Mdw RKW/CH/CXG WD3 91 N2
Bury Pl NOXST/BSQ WC1A 11 L4
Bury Ri HHS/BOV HP3 52 G1
Bury Rd CHING E4 81 J8
DAGE RM10 124 D10
EPP CM16 65 H7
HAT AL10 40 F3
HHW HP1 35 M5
HLWE CM17 29 M7
WDGN N22 119 H1
Bury St ED N9 99 P2 1
GUW GU2 267 P2
HDTCH EC3A 13 K6 3
RSLP HA4 112 E4
STJS SW1Y 10 G9
Bury St West ED N9 99 N1 1
Bury Wk CHEL SW3 15 N6
Burywick HARP AL5 20 A6
Busby Pl KTTN NW5 5 J1
Busch Cl ISLW TW7 154 G7
Bushbarns CHESW EN7 61 P5
Bushberry Rd HOM E9 140 D1
Bushbury La BRKHM/BTCW RH3 273 M5
Bushby Av BROX EN10 44 E8
Bush Cl ADL/WDHM KT15 215 M2 1
GNTH/NBYPK IG2 122 G3
Bush Cottages
WAND/EARL SW18 179 K1 3
Bushell Cl BRXS/STRHM SW2 180 G5
Bushell Gn BUSH WD23 94 C3 1
Bushell St WAP E1W 13 P10 1
Bushell Wy CHST BR7 184 D8
Bush Elms Rd EMPK RM11 125 H5
Bushetts Gv REIG RH2 258 C5
Bushey Av STMC/STPC BR5 206 G7
SWFD E18 121 L1
Bushey Cl CHING E4 101 H4
HGDN/ICK UB10 112 B7
PUR/KEN CR8 241 N2
WGCE AL7 23 L6 3

Bushey Cft HLWS CM18 ... 47 H3
OXTED RH8 ... 261 H6
Bushey Gn WCCE AL8 ... 23 L6
Bushey Grove Rd BUSH WD23 ... 73 L8
Bushey Hall Dr BUSH WD23 ... 73 M8
Bushey Hall Rd BUSH WD23 ... 73 M8
Bushey Hill Rd CMBW SE5 ... 159 N7
Bushey La SUT SM1 ... 201 K10
Bushey Ley WCCE AL7 ... 23 L6
Busheymill Br BUSH WD23 ... 73 M3
Bushey Mill Crs WATN WD24 ... 73 K3
Bushey Mill La BUSH WD23 ... 73 N6
WATN WD24 ... 73 L5
Bushey Rd CROY/NA CR0 ... 204 F9
HGDN/ICK UB10 ... 112 B7
HYS/HAR UB3 ... 152 F1
PLSTW E13 ... 141 P4
RYNPK SW20 ... 200 D9
SEVS/STOTM N15 ... 119 M4
SUT SM1 ... 221 K1
Bushey Wy BECK BR3 ... 205 P6
Bushfield CI EDGW HA8 ... 95 N3
Bushfield Crs EDGW HA8 ... 95 N3
Bushfield Dr REDH RH1 ... 276 B5
Bushfield Rd HHS/BOV HP3 ... 52 F1
Bushfields LOU IG10 ... 82 D9
Bush Gv CDALE/KGS NW9 ... 115 P5
STAN HA7 ... 95 J9
Bushgrove Rd BCTR RM8 ... 123 N8
Bush Hall La BRKMPK AL9 ... 40 G1
Bush HI WCHMH N21 ... 99 K1
Bush Hill Rd KTN/HRWW/W HA3 ... 115 L4
WCHMH N21 ... 79 L10
Bush La CANST EC4R ... 12 G7
RPLY/SEND GU23 ... 232 E12
Bushmead CI SEVS/STOTM N15 ... 119 N2
Bushmoor Crs WOOL/PLUM SE18 ... 162 E6
Bushnell Rd TOOT SW17 ... 180 C5
Bush Rd BERM/RTHS SE16 ... 160 C6
BKHH IG9 ... 102 A5
HACK E8 ... 140 A5
RCH/KEW TW9 ... 155 L5
SHPTN TW17 ... 196 A5
WAN E11 ... 121 L5
Bushway BCTR RM8 ... 123 N9
Bushwood WAN E11 ... 121 L5
Bushwood CI BRKMPK AL9 ... 40 E1
Bushwood Dr STHWK SE1 ... 19 M6
Bushwood Rd RCH/KEW TW9 ... 155 M5
Bushy Hill Dr GU GU1 ... 250 F9
Bushy Park Gdns HPTN TW12 ... 176 F12
Bushy Park Rd TEDD TW11 ... 176 G10
Bushy Rd GT/LBKH KT23 ... 236 A8
TEDD TW11 ... 176 G10
Bushy Shaw ASHTD KT21 ... 237 H3
Buslins La CSHM HP5 ... 50 D4
Butcher Rw POP/IOD E14 ... 140 C5
Butchers La BGR/WK TN15 ... 211 J9
Butchers Rd CAN/RD E16 ... 141 M8
Butchers Yd ORP BR6 ... 226 D7
Bute Av RCHPK/HAM TW10 ... 177 K5
Bute Gdns HMSMTH W6 ... 222 D1
WLGTN SM6 ... 222 D1
Bute Gdns West WLGTN SM6 ... 222 D1
Bute Rd BARK/HLT IG6 ... 122 F2
CROY/NA CR0 ... 203 H8
WLGTN SM6 ... 222 D1
Bute St SKENS SW7 ... 15 L5
Butler Av HRW HA1 ... 114 C5
Butler Rd BCTR RM8 ... 123 L9
HRW HA1 ... 114 B5
WLSDN NW10 ... 136 C2
Butlers CI AMS HP6 ... 68 F3
WDSR SL4 ... 148 C8
Butlers Court Rd BEAC HP9 ... 88 C10
Butlers Dene Rd CTHM CR3 ... 242 E6
Butlers Dr CHING E4 ... 81 H4
Butlers HI EHSLY KT24 ... 252 C6
Butler St BETH E2 ... 140 C5
BETH E2 ... 140 B5
HGDN/ICK UB10 ... 132 C6
Buttercross La EPP CM16 ... 65 K6
Buttercup CI HARH RM3 ... 105 L9
Buttercup CI STWL/WRAY TW19 ... 173 N4
Butterfield CI TOTM N17 ... 99 K7
TWK TW1 ... 176 E2
Butterfield La STAL AL1 ... 38 D10
Butterfield Rd STALE/WH AL4 ... 21 H4
Butterfields WALTH E17 ... 121 H3
Butterfield Sq EHAM E6 ... 142 C8
Butterfly Av DART DA1 ... 187 N5
Butterfly La BORE WD6 ... 74 F7
ELTH/MOT SE9 ... 184 E2
Butterfly Wk WARL CR6 ... 242 B6
Butter HI DORK RH4 ... 272 F2
WLGTN SM6 ... 222 B10
Butteridges CI DAGW RM9 ... 144 A3
Buttermere Av SL SL1 ... 128 C3
Buttermere CI EBED/NFELT TW14 ... 174 G4
MRDN SM4 ... 200 C6
STAL AL1 ... 38 G7
STHWK SE1 ... 19 L5
Buttermere Dr PUT/ROE SW15 ... 179 J8
Buttermere Gdns PUR/KEN CR8 ... 223 L9
Buttermere Rd STMC/STPC BR5 ... 207 N4
Buttermere Wy EGH TW20 ... 172 E10
Buttersweet Rd SBW CM21 ... 29 P2
Butterwick GSTN WD25 ... 73
HMSMTH W6 ... 156 F3
Butterworth Gdns WFD IG8 ... 101 M6
Buttesland St IS N1 ... 7 H9
Buttfield Rd LCOL/BKTW AL2
Butt Field CI DAGE RM10 ... 144 C1
Buttlehide RKW/CH/CXG WD3 ... 90 G1
Buttmarsh CI WOOL/PLUM SE18 ... 162 E4
Buttondene Crs BROX EN10 ... 44 D10
Button Rd CDH/CHF RM16 ... 167 L3
Button St SWLY BR8 ... 209 N4
Buttsbury Rd IL IG1 ... 122 F10
Butts CI CRAWW RH11 ... 283 J7
Butts Crs FELT TW13 ... 175 P6
Butts End HHW HP1 ... 35 H5
Butts Green Rd EMPK RM11 ... 125 L4
Buttsmead NTHWD HA6 ... 92 D8
Butts Piece NTHLT UB5 ... 133 J4
Butts Rd BMLY BR1 ... 183 K8
WOKN/KNAP GU21 ... 231 K5
The Butts BROX EN10 ... 48 D10
BTFD TW8 ... 155 J5
RSEV TN14 ... 247 J3
Buxted Rd EDUL SE22 ... 159 M10
HACK E8 ... 7 L3
NFNCH/WDSP N12 ... 97 P6
Buxton CI CTHM CR3 ... 241 M7
Buxton Dr NWMAL KT3 ... 200 A2
WAN E11 ... 121 K2
Buxton Crs CHEAM SM3 ... 221 H1
Buxton Dr NWMAL KT3 ... 200 A2
WAN E11 ... 121 K2
Buxton La CTHM CR3 ... 241 M7
Buxton Pth OXHEY WD19 ... 93 K4
Buxton Rd ARCH N19 ... 118 D8
ASHF TW15 ... 173 N8
CDH/CHF RM16 ... 168 B1
CHING E4 ... 101 J1
CRICK NW2 ... 136 E2
EHAM E6 ... 142 B5
EPP CM16 ... 83 H2
ERITH DA8 ... 164 E6
GNTH/NBYPK IG2 ... 123 H4
MORT/ESHN SW14 ... 156 B9
SRTFD E15 ... 121 K10
THHTH CR7 ... 203 J5
WAB EN9 ... 63 M8
WALTH E17 ... 120 D2

Buxton St WCHPL E1 ... 13 M2
Byam St FUL/PGN SW6 ... 157 M8
Byards Cft STRHM/NOR SW16 ... 202 E1
Bybend CI SLN SL2 ... 128 C3
Bychurch End TEDD TW11 ... 176 E8
Bycroft Rd STHL UB1 ... 133 P7
Bycroft St PGE/AN SE20 ... 182 C10
Bycullah Av ENC/FH EN2 ... 79 J7
Bycullah Rd ENC/FH EN2 ... 79 J7
Byde St HERT/WAS SG14 ... 25 K4
Byefield CI BERM/RTHS SE16 ... 160 D1
Byelands CI BERM/RTHS SE16 ... 140 C10
Byerley Wy CRAWE RH10 ... 284 F6
Byers CI POTB/CUF EN6 ... 59 M10
The Bye ACT W3 ... 136 B8
Byewaters WATW WD18 ... 72 E10
Bye Ways WHTN TW2 ... 176 A6
The Byeways BRYLDS KT5 ... 199 M5
The Byeway MORT/ESHN SW14 ... 155 P9
RKW/CH/CXG WD3 ... 91 P3
Byfeld Gdns BARN SW13 ... 156 C7
Byfield WCCW AL8 ... 23 H2
Byfield CI BERM/RTHS SE16 ... 160 D1
Byfield Rd ISLW TW7 ... 154 F9
Byfleet Rd ADL/WDHM KT15 ... 215 N6
COB KT11 ... 216 C8
Byford CI SRTFD E15 ... 141 K7
Bygrove Rd WIM/MER SW19 ... 179 N9
Bygrove St POP/IOD E14 ... 140 G8
Byland CI ABYW SE2 ... 163 L2
WCHMH N21 ... 98 G1
Bylands WOKS/MYFD GU22 ... 232 D4
Byne Rd CAR SM5 ... 201 P9
SYD SE26 ... 182 B9
Bynes Rd SAND/SEL CR2 ... 223 L4
Byng Dr POTB/CUF EN6 ... 59 K7
Bynghams HLWW/ROY CM19 ... 46 C3
Byng PI GWRST WC1E ... 11 K2
Byng Rd BAR EN5 ... 76 C7
Byng St POP/IOD E14 ... 160 F1
Bynon Av BXLYHN DA7 ... 163 P9
Byrd Rd CRAWW RH11 ... 283 J10
Byre Rd STHCT/OAK N14 ... 78 B10
Byrne Rd BAL SW12 ... 180 C4
Byron Av BORE WD6 ... 75 M9
CDALE/KGS NW9 ... 115 N2
COUL/CHIP CR5 ... 240 F1
HSLWW TW4 ... 153 J8
MNPK E12 ... 142 B1
NWMAL KT3 ... 200 D5
SUT SM1 ... 221 N1
SWFD E18 ... 101 L10
WATN WD24 ... 73 L3
Byron Av East SUT SM1 ... 221 N1
Byron CI CRAWE RH10 ... 284 C6
HACK E8 ... 7 N5
HPTN TW12 ... 175 P7
THMD SE28 ... 143 M10
WOKN/KNAP GU21 ... 231 K5
WOT/HER KT12 ... 197 N8
Byron Ct ENC/FH EN2 ... 79 J6
ERITH DA8 ... 164 C6
Byron Dr ERITH DA8 ... 164 C6
EFNCH N2 ... 117 N4
TIL RM18 ... 168 F7
Byron Gdns SUT SM1 ... 221 N1
TIL RM18 ... 168 F7
Byron Hill Rd RYLN/HDSTN HA2 ... 114 C3
Byron Ms HAMP NW3 ... 117 N10
Byron PI LHD/OX KT22 ... 236 G3
Byron Rd ACT W3 ... 135 L10
ADL/WDHM KT15 ... 215 N1
ALP/SUD HA0 ... 115 N7
CRICK NW2 ... 116 E7
DART DA1 ... 186 A10
HRW HA1 ... 114 D4
KTN/HRWW/W HA3 ... 114 E10
LEY E10 ... 120 C6
MLHL NW7 ... 96 D6
SAND/SEL CR2 ... 224 A5
WALTH E17 ... 120 F1
Byron St POP/IOD E14 ... 141 H8
Byron Wy HARH RM3 ... 105 K9
NTHLT UB5 ... 133 M5
WDR/YW UB7 ... 152 A3
YEAD UB4 ... 132 F6
Bysouth CI CLAY IG5 ... 102 A9
By the Wd OXHEY WD19 ... 93 L3
Bythorn St CLAP SW4 ... 158 G9
Byton Rd TOOT SW17 ... 180 A9
Byttom HI RDKG RH5 ... 255 H9
Byward Av EBED/NFELT TW14 ... 175 K2
Byward St MON EC3R ... 13 L4
Bywater PI BERM/RTHS SE16 ... 140 D10
Bywater St CHEL SW3 ... 16 A7
Byways BERK ... 34 B4
The Byways BELMT SM2 ... 221 N5
The Byway BELMT SM2 ... 221 N5
POTB/CUF EN6 ... 59 K7
Bywell PI GTPST W1W ... 10 G4
Bywood Av CROY/NA CR0 ... 204 B6
Bywood CI PUR/KEN CR8 ... 241 J1

C

Cabbell PI ADL/WDHM KT15 ... 215 M1
Cabbell St CAMTN NW1 ... 9 N4
Cabell Rd GUW GU2 ... 249 K9
Cabinet Wy CHING E4 ... 100 E7
Cable PI GNWCH SE10 ... 161 H7
Cables CI BELV DA17 ... 164 D2
Cable St WCHPL E1 ... 140 A9
Cabot Sq POP/IOD E14 ... 140 G8
Cabot Wy EHAM E6 ... 142 A3
Cabrera Av VW GU25 ... 194 A5
Cabrera CI VW GU25 ... 195 P5
Cabul Rd BTSEA SW11 ... 157 N8
Caburn Hts CRAWW RH11 ... 283 M9
Cacket's La RSEV TN14 ... 244 G1
The Cackstones CRAWE RH10 ... 284 E6
Cactus CI CMBW SE5 ... 159 M8
Cadbury CI ISLW TW7 ... 154 F7
Cadbury Rd SUN TW16 ... 174 F10
Cadbury Wy BERM/RTHS SE16 ... 19 M4
Caddington CI EBAR EN4 ... 77 P9
Caddington Rd CRICK NW2 ... 116 E1
Caddis CI STAN HA7 ... 94 E8
Caddy CI EGH TW20 ... 172 D8
Cade La SEV TN13 ... 265 K4
Cadell CI BETH E2 ... 7 M8
Cade Rd GNWCH SE10 ... 161 J7
Cader Rd WAND/EARL SW18 ... 179 M2
Cadet Dr STHWK SE1 ... 19 M7
Cadet PI GNWCH SE10 ... 161 H4
Cadiz Rd DAGE RM10 ... 144 D2
Cadiz St WALW SE17 ... 18 F10
Cadley Ter FSTH SE23 ... 162 G5
Cadlocks HI RSEV TN14 ... 228 A4
Cadman CI BRXN/ST SW9 ... 159 J6
Cadmer CI NWMAL KT3 ... 200 B4
Cadmore La CHES/WCR EN8 ... 62 C4
Cadmus CI CLAP SW4 ... 158 C3
Cadnam CI RDKG RH5 ... 188 C3
Cadogan CI BECK BR3 ... 182 G9
HOM E9 ... 140 E2
RYLN/HDSTN HA2 ... 114 A8
TEDD TW11 ... 176 D8
Cadogan Ct BELMT SM2 ... 221 L3
Cadogan Gdns CHEL SW3 ... 16 B6
FNCH N3 ... 97 L9
SWFD E18 ... 101 K1
WCHMH N21 ... 79 H9
Cadogan Ga KTBR SW1X ... 16 B6
Cadogan La KTBR SW1X ... 16 C4
Cadogan PI KTBR SW1X ... 16 B4
Cadogan Rd SURB KT6 ... 199 J5

Cadogan Sq KTBR SW1X ... 16 A4
Cadogan St CHEL SW3 ... 16 A6
Cadogan Ter HOM E9 ... 140 E1
Cadoxton Av SEVS/STOTM N15 ... 119 N4
Cadwallon Rd ELTH/MOT SE9 ... 184 E5
Caedmon Rd HOLWY N7 ... 118 C9
Caenshill Rd WEY KT13 ... 216 B4
Caenswood HI WEY KT13 ... 216 B6
Caenwood CI WEY KT13 ... 216 B3
Caen Wood Rd ASHTD KT21 ... 237 H4
Caerleon CI SCUP DA14 ... 185 M8
Caernarvon CI EMPK RM11 ... 125 P6
HHNE HP2 ... 35 N6
MTCM CR4 ... 202 F3
Caernarvon Dr CLAY IG5 ... 102 D9
Caesars Rd STALE/WH AL4 ... 21 J3
Caesars Wk MTCM CR4 ... 202 A5
Caesar's Wy SHPTN TW17 ... 196 E6
Caffins CI CRAWE RH10 ... 283 P5
Cage Pond Rd RAD WD7 ... 57 M9
Cages Wood Dr SLN SL2 ... 108 C9
Cahill CI STLK EC1Y ... 12 F2
Cahir St POP/IOD E14 ... 160 G3
Caillard Rd BF/WBF KT14 ... 215 N7
Cain's La EBED/NFELT TW14 ... 174 C1
Caird St NKENS W10 ... 2 B10
Cairn Av EA W5 ... 135 J10
Cairndale CI BMLY BR1 ... 183 L10
Cairnfield Av CRICK NW2 ... 116 B8
Cairns Av WFD IG8 ... 102 C7
Cairns CI DART DA1 ... 187 L1
Cairns Rd BTSEA SW11 ... 179 N1
Cairn Wy STAN HA7 ... 94 E7
Cairo New Rd CROY/NA CR0 ... 203 J9
Cairo Rd WALTH E17 ... 120 F2
Caishowe Rd BORE WD6 ... 75 N5
Caister CI HHS/BOV HP3 ... 35 P7
Caister Park Rd SRTFD E15 ... 141 L3
Caistor Rd BAL SW12 ... 180 C3
Caithness Dr EPSOM KT18 ... 220 A10
Caithness Gdns BFN/LL DA15 ... 185 J2
Caithness Rd MTCM CR4 ... 180 C10
WKENS W14 ... 156 G2
Calabria Rd HBRY N5 ... 6 D1
Calais St CMBW SE5 ... 159 J7
Calbourne Av HCH RM12 ... 125 J10
Calbourne Rd BAL SW12 ... 180 A2
Calbroke Rd SLN SL2 ... 128 E5
Calcott CI BRW CM14 ... 106 G2
Calcutta Rd TIL RM18 ... 168 G8
Caldbeck WAB EN9 ... 63 J10
Caldecot Av CHESW EN7 ... 61 N5
Caldecote Gdns BUSH WD23 ... 74 D10
Caldecote La BUSH WD23 ... 94 E1
Caldecott Wy CLPT E5 ... 120 C8
Caldecot Wy BROX EN10 ... 44 E8
Calder Av BRKMPK AL9 ... 59 L2
Calder Ct DTCH/LGLY SL3 ... 150 C4
Calder Gdns EDGW HA8 ... 115 M1
Calderon PI NKENS W10 ... 2 A1
EN EN1 ... 79 P6
Calderon Rd WAN E11 ... 121 H9
Caldervale Rd CLAP SW4 ... 180 E1
Calder CI DTCH/LGLY SL3 ... 151 J9
Calderdale CI CRAWW RH11 ... 283 L9
Calder Rd MRDN SM4 ... 201 M5
Calderwood St WOOL/PLUM SE18 ... 162 D3
Caldicott WOOL/PLUM SE18 ... 162 D3
PGE/AN SE20 ... 204 A1
Caldwell Rd OXHEY WD19 ... 93 L5
Caldwell St BRXN/ST SW9 ... 158 G6
Caldy Rd BELV DA17 ... 164 C2
Caldy Wk IS N1 ... 6 D1
Caledonian CI GDMY/SEVK IG3 ... 123 L6
Caledonian Rd HOLWY N7 ... 118 C9
IS N1 ... 5 N4
Caledonian Wy HORL RH6 ... 280 C8
Caledonia Rd STWL/WRAY TW19 ... 173 P4
Caledonia St IS N1 ... 5 M8
Caledon PI GU GU1 ... 250 D7
Caledon Rd BEAC HP9 ... 88 D8
EHAM E6 ... 142 C3
WLGTN SM6 ... 222 B1

Camberwell Gn CMBW SE5 ... 159 L7
Camberwell Gv CMBW SE5 ... 159 L7
Camberwell La RSEV TN14 ... 264 A7
Camberwell New Rd CMBW SE5 ... 159 J6
Camberwell Rd CMBW SE5 ... 18 F10
Camberwell Station Rd CMBW SE5 ... 159 K7
Cambeys Rd DAGE RM10 ... 124 D10
Camborne Av HARH RM3 ... 105 M8
WEA W13 ... 154 C1
Camborne CI WEY KT13 ... 216 B3
Camborne Rd BELMT SM2 ... 221 K4
CROY/NA CR0 ... 203 P7
MRDN SM4 ... 200 C5
SCUP DA14 ... 185 M6
WAND/EARL SW18 ... 179 K3
WELL DA16 ... 163 H8
Camborne Rd South HARH RM3 ... 105 M8
Cambourne Av ED N9 ... 100 C1
Cambourne Ms NTCHL W11 ... 8 A6
Cambray Rd BAL SW12 ... 180 C3
ORP BR6 ... 207 J2
Cambria CI BFN/LL DA15 ... 184 C4
HSLW TW3 ... 154 C1
Cambria Ct EBED/NFELT TW14 ... 175 J3
Cambria Crs GVE DA12 ... 191 H7
Cambria Gdns STWL/WRAY TW19 ... 173 P5
Cambrian Av GNTH/NBYPK IG2 ... 123 H3
Cambrian CI WNWD SE27 ... 181 J6
Cambrian Gv GRVDA11 ... 190 D3
Cambrian Rd LEY E10 ... 120 C5
RCHPK/HAM TW10 ... 177 L5
Cambria Rd CMBW SE5 ... 159 K9
Cambria St FUL/PGN SW6 ... 157 L6
Cambridge Av CFD/PVL UB6 ... 114 C10
KIL/WHAMP NW6 ... 2 F1
NWMAL KT3 ... 200 C1
RYNPK SW20 ... 200 E1
SL SL1 ... 128 A4
SL SL1 ... 128 F8
WELL DA16 ... 163 J10
Cambridge Barracks Rd WOOL/PLUM SE18 ... 162 C3
Cambridge CI CHES/WCR EN8 ... 62 B7
HSLWW TW4 ... 153 M10
RYNPK SW20 ... 200 E1
WDGN N22 ... 99 H9
WDR/YW UB7 ... 151 N5
WLSDN NW10 ... 115 P3
WOKN/KNAP GU21 ... 231 L4
Cambridge Crs BETH E2 ... 140 A4
TEDD TW11 ... 176 F8
Cambridge Dr LEE/GVPK SE12 ... 183 M1
POTB/CUF EN6 ... 59 H7
RSLP HA4 ... 113 K7
Cambridge Gdns CDH/CHF RM16 ... 168 D3
EN EN1 ... 79 P6
KIL/WHAMP NW6 ... 2 F1
MUSWH N10 ... 98 B9
NKENS W10 ... 8 B5
TOTM N17 ... 99 L8
WCHMH N21 ... 99 L1
Cambridge Ga CAMTN NW1 ... 4 E10
Cambridge Gate Ms CAMTN NW1 ... 4 F10
Cambridge Gn ELTH/MOT SE9 ... 184 E4
Cambridge Gv HMSMTH W6 ... 156 E3
PGE/AN SE20 ... 204 A1
Cambridge Grove Rd KUT KT1 ... 199 M2
Cambridge Heath Rd BETH E2 ... 140 A5
WAN E11 ... 121 M5
Cambridge Park Rd WAN E11 ... 121 M5
Cambridge Pas HOM E9 ... 140 B2
Cambridge PI KENS W8 ... 15 H2
Cambridge Rd ASHF TW15 ... 174 D10
BARK IG11 ... 142 F2
BARN SW13 ... 156 C8
BEAC HP9 ... 88 B7
BMLY BR1 ... 183 M10
BTSEA SW11 ... 158 A7
CAR SM5 ... 221 P3
CHING E4 ... 101 J2
E/WMO/HCT KT8 ... 197 N4
GDMY/SEVK IG3 ... 123 H6
HLW CM20 ... 29 M5
HNWL W7 ... 154 E1
HPTN TW12 ... 175 N10
HSLWW TW4 ... 153 M10
KIL/WHAMP NW6 ... 2 F3
KUT KT1 ... 199 M2
MTCM CR4 ... 202 D3
NWMAL KT3 ... 200 C1
RCH/KEW TW9 ... 155 M6
RYLN/HDSTN HA2 ... 113 P3
RYNPK SW20 ... 200 E1
SCUP DA14 ... 185 M7
SNWD SE25 ... 203 P3
STAL AL1 ... 38 G7
STHL UB1 ... 133 N10
TEDD TW11 ... 176 F7
TWK TW1 ... 177 J7
UX/CGN UB8 ... 131 N1
WAN E11 ... 121 M4
WATW WD18 ... 73 K8
WOT/HER KT12 ... 197 K5
Cambridge Rd North CHSWK W4 ... 155 N4
Cambridge Rd South CHSWK W4 ... 155 N4
Cambridge Rw WOOL/PLUM SE18 ... 162 G4
Cambridge Sq BAY/PAD W2 ... 9 N5
Cambridge St PIM SW1V ... 16 F7
Cambridge Ter CAMTN NW1 ... 4 E10
BERK HP4 ... 34 A5
Cambridge Terrace Ms CAMTN NW1 ... 4 F10
Cambstone CI YEAD UB4 ... 133 M7
Cambus CI YEAD UB4 ... 133 M7
Cambus Rd CAN/RD E16 ... 141 M7
Camdale Rd WOOL/PLUM SE18 ... 163 J5
YEAD UB4 ... 133 K9
Camden CI CDH/CHF RM16 ... 168 D3
CHST BR7 ... 206 F1
GVW DA11 ... 189 P4
Camden Gdns CAMTN NW1 ... 4 F4
SUT SM1 ... 221 L4
THHTH CR7 ... 204 A7
Camden Gv CHST BR7 ... 184 F4
Camden High St CAMTN NW1 ... 4 C2
Camden Hill Rd NRWD SE19 ... 181 M4
Camdenhurst St POP/IOD E14 ... 140 D8
Camden Lock PI CAMTN NW1 ... 4 C1
Camden Ms CAMTN NW1 ... 4 F2
Camden Pk CHST BR7 ... 184 G10
Camden Pas IS N1 ... 6 C7
Camden Rd BXLY DA5 ... 186 A4
CAMTN NW1 ... 4 C1
CAR SM5 ... 222 A1
CDH/CHF RM16 ... 167 K2
HOLWY N7 ... 118 F9
SEV TN13 ... 265 K9
SUT SM1 ... 221 L4
WALTH E17 ... 120 F2
WAN E11 ... 121 N4
Camden Rw BKHTH/KID SE3 ... 161 K3
CAMTN NW1 ... 4 F2
Camden Sq CAMTN NW1 ... 4 F1
Camden St CAMTN NW1 ... 4 E1
Camden Wk IS N1 ... 6 C6
Camden Wy CHST BR7 ... 184 G10
THHTH CR7 ... 203 M8
Camel Gv KUTN/CMB KT2 ... 176 C6
Camelia CI HARH RM3 ... 105 M9
Camellia Ct HARH RM3 ... 105 M9

Camellia Ct CHOB/PIR GU24 ... 212 E9
Camellia PI WHTN TW2 ... 176 A3
Camelot CI BH/WHM TN16 ... 243 P2
WIM/MER SW19 ... 179 J7
WOOL/PLUM SE18 ... 162 G1
Camel Rd CAN/RD E16 ... 142 A10
Camera PI WBPTN SW10 ... 15 L10
Cameron CI BRW CM14 ... 107 H5
BXLY DA5 ... 186 E6
TRDG/WHET N20 ... 97 P3
Cameron Dr CHES/WCR EN8 ... 62 C10
Cameron Rd CAT SE6 ... 182 E5
CROY/NA CR0 ... 203 J6
CSHM HP5 ... 51 H6
GDMY/SEVK IG3 ... 123 H6
HAYES BR2 ... 205 M6
Camfield WCCE AL7 ... 23 J9
Cam Gn SOCK/AV RM15 ... 146 G8
Camilla CI GT/LBKH KT23 ... 254 A1
SUN TW16 ... 174 C9
Camilla Dr RDKG RH5 ... 254 F6
Camilla Rd BERM/RTHS SE16 ... 160 A3
Camille CI SNWD SE25 ... 203 P3
Camlan Rd BMLY BR1 ... 183 L1
Camlet St BETH E2 ... 13 L1
Camlet Wy EBAR EN4 ... 77 K6
STALW/RED AL3 ... 38 A5
Camley St CAMTN NW1 ... 5 J4
Camm Av WDSR SL4 ... 148 D9
Camm Gdns KUT KT1 ... 199 L2
THDIT KT7 ... 198 D7
Camomile Av MTCM CR4 ... 202 A1
Camomile St HDTCH EC3A ... 13 K5
LVPST EC2M ... 13 J5
Camomile Wy WDR/YW UB7 ... 131 P8
Camomile Rd ROMW/RG RM7 ... 124 C7
Campana Rd FUL/PGN SW6 ... 157 K7
Campbell Av BARK/HLT IG6 ... 122 F2
WOKS/MYFD GU22 ... 232 C7
Campbell CI HLWE CM17 ... 47 L2
ROM RM1 ... 104 F7
RSLP HA4 ... 113 H4
STRHM/NOR SW16 ... 180 E7
WHTN TW2 ... 176 C4
WOOL/PLUM SE18 ... 162 D7
Campbell Cft EDGW HA8 ... 95 M6
Campbell Rd BOW E3 ... 140 F5
CRAWE RH10 ... 284 D9
CROY/NA CR0 ... 203 J7
CTHM CR3 ... 241 L7
EHAM E6 ... 142 B3
FSTGT E7 ... 121 L9
GVW DA11 ... 190 C4
HNWL W7 ... 134 D9
TOTM N17 ... 99 N9
WALTH E17 ... 120 E2
WEY KT13 ... 216 B4
WHTN TW2 ... 176 C5
Campdale Rd ARCH N19 ... 118 C8
Campden Crs ALP/SUD HA0 ... 114 C8
BCTR RM8 ... 123 L9
Campden Gv KENS W8 ... 14 F1
Campden HI KENS W8 ... 14 E1
Campden Hill Gdns KENS W8 ... 8 E10
Campden Hill PI KENS W8 ... 8 D9
Campden Hill Rd KENS W8 ... 14 F1
Campden Hill Sq KENS W8 ... 8 D9
Campden House CI KENS W8 ... 14 F1
Campden Rd HGDN/ICK UB10 ... 112 A8
SAND/SEL CR2 ... 223 N2
Campden St KENS W8 ... 8 E10
Campen CI WIM/MER SW19 ... 179 H5
Camp End Rd WEY KT13 ... 216 C8
Camperdown St WCHPL E1 ... 13 M6
Campfield Rd ELTH/MOT SE9 ... 184 A3
HERT/WAS SG14 ... 24
STAL AL1 ... 38 F6
Camphill Ct BF/WBF KT14 ... 215 K8
Camphill Rd BF/WBF KT14 ... 215 K8
Campine CI CHES/WCR EN8 ... 62 C4
Campion CI DEN/HRF UB9 ... 131 K8
EHAM E6 ... 142 C9
GSTN WD25 ... 55 H9
GVW DA11 ... 190 B7
KTN/HRWW/W HA3 ... 115 L4
ROMW/RG RM7 ... 124 C7
SAND/SEL CR2 ... 223 M1
UX/CGN UB8 ... 132 A7
Campion Dr KWD/TDW/WH KT20 ... 238 E6
Campion Gdns WFD IG8 ... 101 M6
Campion PI THMD SE28 ... 143 L10
Campion Rd HHW HP1 ... 35 H7
ISLW TW7 ... 154 E7
PUT/ROE SW15 ... 156 F10
Campions LOU IG10 ... 82 D4
Campions Ct BERK HP4 ... 33 M6
The Campions BORE WD6 ... 75 L4
Campion Wy EDGW HA8 ... 95 P5
Cample La SOCK/AV RM15 ... 146 F9
Camplin Rd KTN/HRWW/W HA3 ... 115 K3
Camplin St NWCR SE14 ... 160 C6
Camp Rd CFSP/GDCR SL9 ... 110 A5
CTHM CR3 ... 242 D7
STAL AL1 ... 38 E7
Campsbourne Rd CEND/HSY/T N8 ... 118 F1
The Campsbourne CEND/HSY/T N8 ... 118 F2
Campsey Rd DAGW RM9 ... 143 L2
Campshill Rd LEW SE13 ... 183 H1
Campshill PI LEW SE13 ... 183 H1
Campus Rd WALTH E17 ... 120 C4
The Campus WCCW AL8 ... 22 G4
Camp Vw WIM/MER SW19 ... 178 G4
Camp View Rd STAL AL1 ... 38 G7
Cam Rd SRTFD E15 ... 141 J9
Camrose Av EDGW HA8 ... 95 K10
ERITH DA8 ... 164 C5
FELT TW13 ... 175 J7
STAN HA7 ... 95 K10
Camrose CI CROY/NA CR0 ... 204 D7
MRDN SM4 ... 201 K4
Camrose St ABYW SE2 ... 163 K4
Canada Av REDH RH1 ... 276 B4
UED N18 ... 99 K7
Canada Crs ACT W3 ... 135 P7
Canada Dr REDH RH1 ... 276 B4
Canada Farm Rd EYN DA4 ... 210 G5
Canada La BROX EN10 ... 62 D1
Canada Rd ACT W3 ... 135 N7
BF/WBF KT14 ... 215 N7
COB KT11 ... 217 K9
ERITH DA8 ... 165 J10
SL SL1 ... 149 N1
The Canadas BROX EN10 ... 62 D1
Canada St BERM/RTHS SE16 ... 160 C1
Canada Wy SHB W12 ... 136 E9
Canadian Av CAT SE6 ... 182 G4
Canal Ap DEPT SE8 ... 160 D5
Canal Basin GVE DA12 ... 190 G2
Canal CI NKENS W10 ... 136 G6
Canal Gv PECK SE15 ... 159 P9
Canal Rd GVE DA12 ... 190 C2
WCHPL E1 ... 140 D6
Canal St CMBW SE5 ... 18 G10
Canal Wk CROY/NA CR0 ... 203 H6
IS N1 ... 7 H3
Canal Wy NKENS W10 ... 136 D3
Canberra CI CRAWW RH11 ... 283 N4
DAGE RM10 ... 144 E2
HCH RM12 ... 125 K9
HDN NW4 ... 116 D1
STALW/RED AL3 ... 38 G2
Canberra Crs DAGE RM10 ... 144 E2

Canberra Dr *NTHLT* UB5 .... 133 K5
Canberra Rd *ABYW* SE2 .... 163 N5
  CHARL SE7 .... 161 L5
  EHAM E6 .... 142 C3 🔒
Canberra Sq *TIL* RM18 .... 168 D8 🔒
Canbury Av *KUTN/CMB* KT2 .... 199 L1
Canbury Ms *SYD* SE26 .... 181 N6 🔒
Canbury Park Rd *KUTN/CMB* KT2 .... 199 K1
Canbury Pth *STMC/STPC* BR5 .... 207 K4
Cancell Rd *BRXN/ST* SW9 .... 159 H7
Candahar Rd *BTSEA* SW11 .... 157 P8
Canderfield Rd *HHS/BOV* HP3 .... 36 B9
Candlemas La *BEAC* HP9 .... 88 D9
Candlemas Md *BEAC* HP9 .... 88 D9
Candler Ms *TWK* TW1 .... 176 F3 🔒
Candler St *SEVS/STOTM* N15 .... 119 M4 🔒
Candover Rd *WDR/YW* UB7 .... 151 N6
Candover St *GTPST* W1W .... 10 C4 🔒
Candy Cft *GT/LBKH* KT23 .... 254 A2 🔒
Candy St *BOW* E3 .... 140 E5
Cane HI *HARH* RM3 .... 105 L10
Canes La *HLWE* CM17 .... 47 P8
Canewden CI *WOKS/MYFD* GU22 .... 232 B5 🔒
Caney Ms *CRICK* NW2 .... 116 C2 🔒
Canfield Dr *HHA4* 113 J10
Canfield Gdns *KIL/WHAMP* NW6 .... 3 H3
Canfield PI *KIL/WHAMP* NW6 .... 3 J2
Canfield Rd *RAIN* RM13 .... 144 C3
  WFD IG8 .... 102 B8
Canford Av *NTHLT* UB5 .... 133 K1
Canford CI *ENC/FH* EN2 .... 79 H6
Canford Dr *ADL/WDHM* KT15 .... 195 L9
Canford Gdns *NWMAL* KT3 .... 200 B6 🔒
Canford PI *TEDD* TW11 .... 177 H9 🔒
Canford Rd *BTSEA* SW11 .... 158 B10
Cangelis CI *HHW* HP1 .... 35 K8
Canham Rd *CHSWK* W4 .... 156 B1
  SNWD SE25 .... 203 M3
Can Hatch *KWD/TDW/WH* KT20 .... 239 H4
Canmore Gdns
  STRHM/NOR SW16 .... 180 D10
Cann Hall Rd *FSTGT* E7 .... 121 L9
Canning Crs *WDGN* N22 .... 98 G9
Canning Cross *CMBW* SE5 .... 159 M8 🔒
Canning PI *KENS* W8 .... 15 J3
Canning Rd *CROY/NA* CR0 .... 203 N9
  FSBYPK N4 .... 119 K3 🔒
  KTN/HRWW/W HA3 .... 114 D1
  SRTFD E15 .... 141 K4
  WALTH E17 .... 120 D2
Cannington Rd *DAGW* RM9 .... 143 M1
Cannizaro Rd *WIM/MER* SW19 .... 178 F9
Cannonbury Av *PIN* HA5 .... 113 L4
Cannon CI *HPTN* TW12 .... 176 A9
  RYNPK SW20 .... 200 F5
Cannon Crs *CHOB/PIR* GU24 .... 213 K7
Cannon Dr *POP/IOD* E14 .... 140 F9
Cannon Gv *LHD/OX* KT22 .... 236 D8
Cannon HI *KIL/WHAMP* NW6 .... 117 L10
  STHGT/OAK N14 .... 98 E1 🔒
Cannon Hill La *MRDN* SM4 .... 200 A8
Cannon La *HAMP* NW3 .... 117 N8 🔒
  PIN HA5 .... 113 M5
Cannon Ms *WAB* EN9 .... 62 G9
Cannon Mill Av *CHSH* HP5 .... 51 J9
Cannon PI *CHARL* SE7 .... 162 B4 🔒
  HAMP NW3 .... 117 M8
Cannon Rd *BXLYHN* DA7 .... 163 P7
  STHGT/OAK N14 .... 98 F4
  WATW WD18 .... 73 K9 🔒
Cannon Side *LHD/OX* KT22 .... 236 D8
Cannons Meadow *WLYN* AL6 .... 23 P2
Cannon St *STALW/RED* AL3 .... 38 C5
  STP EC4M 12 E6
Cannon Street Rd *WCHPL* E1 .... 140 A8
Cannon Wy *E/WMO/HCT* KT8 .... 197 P4
  LHD/OX KT22 .... 236 D7
Canon Beck Rd
  BERM/RHTH SE16 .... 160 B1 🔒
Canonbie Rd *FSTH* SE23 .... 182 B3
Canonbury Crs *IS* N1 .... 6 F3
Canonbury Gv *IS* N1 .... 6 E3
Canonbury La *IS* N1 .... 6 C3
Canonbury Pk North *IS* N1 .... 6 E2
Canonbury Pk South *IS* N1 .... 6 E2
Canonbury PI *IS* N1 .... 6 D2
Canonbury Rd *ENC/FH* EN2 .... 79 M5
  IS N1 .... 6 D3
Canonbury Sq *IS* N1 .... 6 D3
Canonbury St *IS* N1 .... 6 E3
Canonbury Vls *IS* N1 .... 6 D3
Canon Mohan CI *EBAR* EN4 .... 78 B10
Canon Murnane Rd *STHWK* SE1 .... 19 L4
Canon Rd *BMLY* BR1 .... 205 P3
Canon Rw *WHALL* SW1A 17 L2
Canons Brook *HLWW/ROY* CM19 .... 46 D7
Canons CI *EDGW* HA8 .... 95 L7
  EFNCH N2 .... 117 N5
  RAD WD7 .... 74 G1
  REIG RH2 .... 257 J9
Canons Dr *EDGW* HA8 .... 95 K7
Canons Fld *STALE/WH* AL4 .... 21 J2 🔒
Canons Ga *CHES/WCR* EN8 .... 62 E3
  HLW CM20 .... 28 D7
Canonsleigh Rd *DAGW* RM9 .... 143 L2
Canons La *KWD/TDW/WH* KT20 .... 239 H5
Canonsleigh Rd *WARE* SG12 .... 26 B1
Canon St *IS* N1 .... 6 E6
Canon's Wk *CROY/NA* CR0 .... 204 C10
Canopus Wy *NTHWD* HA6 .... 93 M1
  STWL/WRAY TW19 .... 173 P3
Canrobert St *BETH* E2 .... 140 A2 🔒
  BETH E2 .... 140 A5 🔒
Cantelowes Rd *CAMTN* NW1 .... 5 K2
Canterbury Av *BFN/LL* DA15 .... 185 M5
  IL IG1 .... 122 A9
  SLN SL3 .... 129 H6
  UPMR RM14 .... 126 E8
Canterbury CI *AMSS* HP7 .... 69 K5
  BECK BR3 .... 204 G1
  CHIG IG7 .... 103 J4
  DART DA1 .... 188 A3
  EHAM E6 .... 142 C8 🔒
  GFD/PVL UB6 .... 134 A7
  NTHWD HA6 .... 92 A7
Canterbury Crs *BRXN/ST* SW9 .... 159 H9
Canterbury Gv *WNWD* SE27 .... 181 H6
Canterbury Rd *BORE* WD6 .... 75 M6
  CROY/NA CR0 .... 202 G5
  FELT TW13 .... 175 M4
  GUW GU2 .... 249 L8
  GVE GU3 .... 190 F5 🔒
  HRW HA1 .... 114 A3
  KIL/WHAMP NW6 .... 1 E8
  LEY E10 .... 121 H5
  MRDN SM4 .... 201 M6
  RYLN/HDSTN HA2 .... 114 A3
  WAT WD17 .... 73 J6 🔒
Canterbury Ter *KIL/WHAMP* NW6 .... 2 E7
Canterbury Wy *DART* DA1 .... 166 B10
  RBRW/HUT CM13 .... 107 H7 🔒
  RKW/CH/CXG WD3 .... 72 D7
  WTHK RM20 .... 166 G6
The Canter *CRAWE* RH10 .... 284 F6
Cantley Gdns *GNTH/NBYPK* IG2 .... 122 F4
  NRWD SE19 .... 203 N1
Cantley Rd *HNWL* W7 .... 154 F2
Canton St *POP/IOD* E14 .... 140 E8
Cantrell Rd *BOW* E3 .... 140 F6
Canvey CI *CRAWW* RH11 .... 283 M10 🔒
Canvey St *STHWK* SE1 .... 12 E9 🔒

Cape CI *BARK* IG11 .... 142 E2
Capel Av *WLGTN* SM6 .... 222 G2
Capel CI *HAYES* BR2 .... 206 B8
  TRDG/WHET N20 .... 97 M4
Capel Crs *STAN* HA7 .... 95 H1 🔒
  PIN HA5 .... 113 N2
Capel La *CRAWW* RH11 .... 283 J6
Capella Rd *NTHWD* HA6 .... 92 B6
Capel Pl *RKW/CH/CXG* WD3 .... 70 G9
Capel Rd *RKW/CH/CXG* WD3 .... 70 G9
  EBAR EN4 .... 78 C2
  EN EN1 .... 80 A2
  FSTGT E7 .... 121 N9
  OXHEY WD19 .... 73 L10
Capel Wk *WAT* WD17 .... 73 L10
Capenure Wk *WAT* WD17 .... 54 G8
Capener's CI *KTBR* SW1X .... 16 C2 🔒
Cape Rd *SEVS/STOTM* N15 .... 119 P1 🔒
  STAL AL1 .... 38 G6
Capital Interchange Wy *CHSWK* W4 .... 155 M4
Capital Interchange Wy *CHSWK* W4 .... 155 M4
Capitol Wy *CDALE/KGS* NW9 .... 115 P1
Capland St *STJWD* NW8 .... 9 H1
Caple Rd *WLSDN* NW10 .... 136 C4 🔒
Capon CI *BRW* CM14 .... 106 G2
Caponfield *WGCE* AL7 .... 23 J7
Capper St *STPAN* WC1E 11 J1
Caprea CI *YEAD* UB4 .... 133 L7 🔒
Capricorn CI *CRAWW* RH11 .... 283 H9
Capri Rd *CROY/NA* CR0 .... 203 N9
Capsey Rd *CRAWW* RH11 .... 283 H8
Capstan CI *CHDH* RM6 .... 123 L4
Capstan Ct *DEN/HRF* UB9 .... 166 B10 🔒
Capstan Ride *ENC/FH* EN2 .... 79 H6 🔒
Capstan Rd *DEPT* SE8 .... 160 F5 🔒
Capstan Sq *POP/IOD* E14 .... 161 N1 🔒
Capstans Whf *WOKN/KNAP* GU21 .... 231 L4 🔒
Capstan Wy *BERM/RHTH* SE16 .... 140 D10
Capstone Rd *BMLY* BR1 .... 183 M7 🔒
Captain Cook CI *CSTG* HP8 .... 89 M5
Captain Ct *DEN/HRF* UB9 .... 166 B10 🔒
Captains CI *CSHM* HP5 .... 50 F7 🔒
Captains Wk *BERK* HP4 .... 34 A6
Capthorne Av *RYLN/HDSTN* HA2 .... 113 M6
Capuchin CI *STAN* HA7 .... 94 G7
Capulet Ms *CAN/RD* E16 .... 141 M10
Capworth St *LEY* E10 .... 120 F6
Caractacus Cottage Vw
  WATW WD18 .... 93 H1
Caractacus Gn *WATW* WD18 .... 72 C10
Caradoc CI *BAY/PAD* W2 .... 8 B6
Caradoc St *GNWCH* SE10 .... 161 K4
Caradon CI *WOKN/KNAP* GU21 .... 231 N4
Caradon Ct *WAN* E11 .... 121 K6 🔒
Caravan La *RKW/CH/CXG* WD3 .... 91 P1
The Caravan Site *SOCK/AV* RM15 .... 166 C2
Caravel CI *CDH/CHF* RM16 .... 167 L2
Caravel Ms *DEPT* SE8 .... 160 F5 🔒
Caraway CI *PLSTW* E13 .... 141 N7
Caraway PI *GUW* GU2 .... 249 M5 🔒
  WLGTN SM6 .... 202 C10 🔒
Carberry Rd *NRWD* SE19 .... 181 M9
Carbery Av *ACT* W3 .... 155 L1
Carbery La *ASC* SL5 .... 192 A3
Carbis CI *CHING* E4 .... 101 J2 🔒
Carbone HI *POTB/CUF* EN6 .... 60 E2
Carburton St *GTPST* W1W 10 E1
Cardamom CI *GUW* GU2 .... 249 M6
Carde St *PECK* SE15 .... 160 A9
Cardiff Rd *ENC/FH* EN1 .... 80 A3
  HCH RM12 .... 145 K1
  HNWL W7 .... 154 F2
  PEND EN3 .... 80 A8
  WATW WD18 .... 73 J10
Cardiff St *WOOL/PLUM* SE18 .... 163 N10
Cardiff Wy *ABLGY* WD5 .... 55 H8
Cardigan CI *SL* SL1 .... 128 E9
  WOKN/KNAP GU21 .... 231 K4
Cardigan Gdns *GDMY/SEVK* IG3 .... 123 K7
Cardigan Rd *BARN* SW13 .... 156 D8
  BOW E3 .... 140 E4
  RCHPK/HAM TW10 .... 177 K2
  WIM/MER SW19 .... 179 M9
Cardigan St *LBTH* SE11 .... 18 A7
Cardigan Ter *SYD* SE26 .... 182 B6 🔒
Cardinal Av *BORE* WD6 .... 75 P1
  KUTN/CMB KT2 .... 177 K8
  MRDN SM4 .... 201 H6 🔒
Cardinal Bourne St *STHWK* SE1 .... 19 H4 🔒
Cardinal CI *CHESW* EN7 .... 61 N2 🔒
  CHST BR7 .... 206 C1
  EDGW HA8 .... 96 A8
  MRDN SM4 .... 201 H6 🔒
  WPK KT4 .... 200 D1
Cardinal Crs *NWMAL* KT3 .... 199 P2
Cardinal Dr *BARK/HLT* IG6 .... 102 F7 🔒
  WOT/HER KT12 .... 197 L8
Cardinal Gv *STALW/RED* AL3 .... 38 A8
Cardinal Rd *FELT* TW13 .... 175 J4
  RSLP HA4 .... 113 L6
Cardinal's Wk *HPTN* TW12 .... 176 B10
  MDHD SL6 .... 128 B8
  SUN TW16 .... 174 F9 🔒
Cardinals Wy *ARCH* N19 .... 118 C9
Cardinal Wy *KTN/HRWW/W* HA3 .... 114 D1 🔒
  RAIN RM13 .... 145 K4
Cardingham *WOKN/KNAP* GU21 .... 231 N5
Cardington Sq *HSLWW* TW4 .... 153 L10
Cardington St *CAMTN* NW1 .... 5 H9
Cardozo Rd *HOLWY* N7 .... 118 F10
Cardrew Av *NFNCH/WDSP* N12 .... 97 H3
Cardross St *HMSMTH* W6 .... 156 E2
Cardwell Crs *ASC* SL5 .... 192 B5
Cardwell Rd *HOLWY* N7 .... 118 F9 🔒
  WOOL/PLUM SE18 .... 162 C3
Cardwells Keep *GUW* GU2 .... 249 M7 🔒
Carey Rd *HNWL* W7 .... 35 L7
Carew CI *COUL/CHIP* CR5 .... 241 J5
  HOLWY N7 .... 118 D7
Carew Rd *ASHF* TW15 .... 174 D9
  MTCM CR4 .... 202 B2
  NTHWD HA6 .... 92 F7
  THHTH CR7 .... 203 J3
  TOTM N17 .... 99 P10
  WEA W13 .... 155 H1
  WLGTN SM6 .... 222 D5
Carew St *CMBW* SE5 .... 159 K8
Carew Wy *OXHEY* WD19 .... 93 N4
  STMC/STPC BR5 .... 207 N3
Carey Gdns *VX/NE* SW8 .... 158 D7
Carey La *CITYW* EC2V 12 E5
Carey PI *PIM* SW1V 17 H7
Careys Cft *BERK* HP4 .... 33 L2
Carey's Fld *SEV* TN13 .... 246 F6 🔒
Carey's Wd *HORL* RH6 .... 281 J4
Carey Wy *WBLY* HA9 .... 115 N9
Carfax PI *CLAP* SW4 .... 36 B8
Carfax Rd *HCH* RM12 .... 124 G9
  HYS/HAR UB3 .... 153 H4
Carfree CI *IS* N1 .... 6 B3 🔒
Cargill Rd *WAND/EARL* SW18 .... 179 M4
Cargo Forecourt Rd *HORL* RH6 .... 279 N6
Cargo Rd *HORL* RH6 .... 279 N6
Cargreen Rd *SNWD* SE25 .... 203 N4
Carholme Rd *FSTH* SE23 .... 182 B4
Carisbrook CI *EN* EN1 .... 79 N1
Carisbrooke Av *BXLY* DA5 .... 185 N4
  WATN WD24 .... 73 L1
Carisbrooke CI *EMPK* RM11 .... 125 P6 🔒
  STAN HA7 .... 95 J10
Carisbrooke Rd *BRWN* CM15 .... 86 C10
  HARP AL5 .... 20 B1

  HAYES BR2 .... 205 P4 🔒
  MTCM CR4 .... 202 F4
  WALTH E17 .... 120 D3 🔒
Carisbrook Rd *LCOL/BKTW* AL2 .... 56 A2
Carleton Av *WLGTN* SM6 .... 222 E5
Carleton CI *ESH/CLAY* KT10 .... 198 C1
Carleton PI *EYN* DA4 .... 210 B4
Carleton Rd *CHES/WCR* EN8 .... 62 C5
  DART DA1 .... 187 P3
  HOLWY N7 .... 118 E10
Carlile CI *BOW* E3 .... 140 E4
Carlina Gdns *WFD* IG8 .... 101 N6
Carlingford Rd *HAMP* NW3 .... 117 N9 🔒
  MRDN SM4 .... 200 G6
  SEVS/STOTM N15 .... 119 J1
Carlisle Av *ACT* W3 .... 136 B8
  STALW/RED AL3 .... 38 B6
  TWRH EC3N 13 K6
Carlisle CI *KUTN/CMB* KT2 .... 199 M1 🔒
  KTN/HRWW/W HA3 .... 115 J5
Carlisle Gdns *IL* IG1 .... 122 A4 🔒
  KTN/HRWW/W HA3 .... 115 J5
Carlisle PI *FBAR/BDGN* N11 .... 98 C5
  WEST SW1P 16 F4
Carlisle Rd *CDALE/KGS* NW9 .... 115 P1
  DART DA1 .... 187 P2
  FSBYPK N4 .... 119 H6
  HPTN TW12 .... 176 A10
  KIL/WHAMP NW6 .... 2 B3 🔒
  LEY E10 .... 120 F6
  ROM RM1 .... 124 G3
  SL SL1 .... 221 J9
  SUT SM1 .... 221 J3
Carlisle St *SOHO/CST* W1F 11 J6
Carlisle Wy *TOOT* SW17 .... 180 B8 🔒
Carlos PI *MYFR/PKLN* W1K 10 B7
Carlow St *CAMTN* NW1 .... 4 C1
Carlton Av *EBED/NFELT* TW14 .... 175 J2
  GRH DA9 .... 188 D2
  HYS/HAR UB3 .... 152 F3
  KTN/HRWW/W HA3 .... 114 G3
  SAND/SEL CR2 .... 223 L4
  STHGT/OAK N14 .... 78 E9
Carlton Av East *WBLY* HA9 .... 115 J7
Carlton Av West *ALP/SUD* HA0 .... 115 J7
Carlton CI *BORE* WD6 .... 76 A8 🔒
  CHSGTN KT9 .... 219 J3
  EDGW HA8 .... 95 M6
  UPMR RM14 .... 117 K7
  WOKS/MYFD GU22 .... 211 P8 🔒
Carlton Crs *CHEAM* SM3 .... 221 H1
Carlton Dr *BARK/HLT* IG6 .... 122 C1
  PUT/ROE SW15 .... 178 G1
Carlton Gdns *EA* W5 .... 135 H8
  STJS SW1Y 11 J10
Carlton Gn *REDH* RH1 .... 258 A4 🔒
Carlton HI *STJWD* NW8 .... 3 H3
Carlton House Ter *STJS* SW1Y 11 J10
Carlton Park Av *RYNPK* SW20 .... 200 F5
Carlton Rd *CDH/CHF* RM16 .... 168 C5
  CHSWK W4 .... 156 A1
  EA W5 .... 135 H9
  ERITH DA8 .... 149 K5
  FBAR/BDGN N11 .... 98 A5
  FSBYPK N4 .... 119 H5
  GPK RM2 .... 125 H3
  MNPK E12 .... 141 L1
  MORT/ESHN SW14 .... 155 P9
  NWMAL KT3 .... 200 D10
  REDH RH1 .... 257 N6
  SAND/SEL CR2 .... 223 L4
  SCUP DA14 .... 185 J8
  SLN SL2 .... 129 H3
  SUN TW16 .... 174 C10
  WALTH E17 .... 100 D9
  WAN E11 .... 121 L6
  WELL DA16 .... 163 L9
  WOKN/KNAP GU21 .... 214 D10
  WOT/HER KT12 .... 197 J7
Carlton Sq *WCHPL* E1 .... 140 C6 🔒
Carlton St *STJS* SW1Y .... 11 J8 🔒
Carlton Ter *SYD* SE26 .... 182 B6 🔒
  WAN E11 .... 121 N3 🔒
Carlton Tye *HORL* RH6 .... 280 E4
Carlton V *KIL/WHAMP* NW6 .... 2 E1
Carlwell St *TOOT* SW17 .... 179 P8
Carlyle Av *BMLY* BR1 .... 206 A3 🔒
  STHL UB1 .... 133 N6
Carlyle CI *E/WMO/HCT* KT8 .... 198 A1
  EFNCH N2 .... 117 M4
  WLSDN NW10 .... 136 A3
Carlyle Gdns *STHL* UB1 .... 133 N6
Carlyle PI *PUT/ROE* SW15 .... 157 J10
Carlyle Rd *CROY/NA* CR0 .... 203 P9
  EA W5 .... 155 H5
  MNPK E12 .... 122 B9
  STA TW18 .... 173 J10
  THMD SE28 .... 143 J9
Carlyle Sq *CHEL* SW3 .... 15 M8
Carlyon CI *RYLN/HDSTN* HA2 .... 113 N9
  ALP/SUD HA0 .... 135 K5
Carlyon Rd *ALP/SUD* HA0 .... 135 K4
  YEAD UB4 .... 133 J4
Carlys CI *BECK* BR3 .... 204 C2 🔒
Carmalt Gdns *PUT/ROE* SW15 .... 156 F10
  WOT/HER KT12 .... 217 K2
Carmarthen Rd *SL* SL1 .... 129 K8
Carpenter St *MYFR/PKLN* W1K 10 B7
Carpenters CI *EBAR* EN4 .... 78 E6
Carpenters Ms *HOLWY* N7 .... 118 D1
Carpenter's PI *CLAP* SW4 .... 158 G10
Carpenters Rd *EN* EN1 .... 80 B2
  SRTFD E15 .... 140 G2
Carpenters Wood Dr
  RKW/CH/CXG WD3 .... 70 E8
Carpenter Wy *POTB/CUF* EN6 .... 59 M9
Carr Gv *WOOL/PLUM* SE18 .... 162 B5
Carriage Dr North *BTSEA* SW11 .... 158 A6
Carriage Dr South *BTSEA* SW11 .... 158 A7
Carriage Dr West *BTSEA* SW11 .... 158 A7
Carriage Ms *IL* IG1 .... 122 F7
The Carriageway *RSEV* TN14 .... 245 N10
Carrick CI *ISLW* TW7 .... 154 F7 🔒
Carrick Dr *BARK/HLT* IG6 .... 102 F9 🔒
  SEV TN13 .... 247 J9
Carrick Ga *ESH/CLAY* KT10 .... 198 B10
Carrick Ms *DEPT* SE8 .... 160 F5 🔒
Carrill Wy *BELV* DA17 .... 148 E4
Carrington Av *BAR* EN5 .... 76 D9
  HSLW TW3 .... 176 A1
Carrington CI *BAR* EN5 .... 76 A1
  CROY/NA CR0 .... 204 D7 🔒
  REDH RH1 .... 258 A5 🔒
Carrington Gdns *FSTGT* E7 .... 121 M9 🔒
Carrington Rd *DART* DA1 .... 187 N2
  RCHPK/HAM TW10 .... 155 M10
  SL SL1 .... 129 K9
Carrington Sq
  KTN/HRWW/W HA3 .... 94 B8 🔒
Carrington St *MYFR/PICC* W1J .... 10 E10 🔒
Carrol CI *KTTN* NW5 .... 118 C9
Carroll CI *SRTFD* E15 .... 121 L10
Carroll HI *LOU* IG10 .... 82 C7
Carronade PI *WOOL/PLUM* SE18 .... 162 G6
Carroun Rd *VX/NE* SW8 .... 158 G6
Carroway La *GFD/PVL* UB6 .... 134 C5 🔒
Carrow Rd *DAGW* RM9 .... 143 L2
  WOT/HER KT12 .... 197 L10 🔒
Carr Rd *NTHLT* UB5 .... 134 A2
  WALTH E17 .... 100 E10
Carrs La *WCHMH* N21 .... 79 L9
Carshalton Gv *SUT* SM1 .... 222 A2
Carshalton Park Rd *CAR* SM5 .... 222 A2 🔒
Carshalton PI *CAR* SM5 .... 222 C1
Carshalton Rd *BNSTD* SM7 .... 222 A9
  MTCM CR4 .... 202 B5
  SUT SM1 .... 221 M2
Carsington Gdns *DART* DA1 .... 187 L5
Carslake Rd *PUT/ROE* SW15 .... 178 F2
Carson Rd *CAN/RD* E16 .... 141 M7
  DUL SE21 .... 181 K5
  EBAR EN4 .... 78 A8
Carstairs Rd *CAT* SE6 .... 183 L1
Carston CI *LEE/GVPK* SE12 .... 183 L1
Carswell CI *REDBR* IG4 .... 121 K5
Carswell Rd *CAT* SE6 .... 183 L1
Cartbridge CI *RPLY/SEND* GU23 .... 232 E9 🔒
Cartel CI *PUR* RM19 .... 166 C3
Carter CI *CRW* RM5 .... 104 C5
  WLGTN SM6 .... 222 E4
Carter Dr *CRW* RM5 .... 104 C5
Carteret Rd *SFT/JSPK* SW1H 17 J2
Carteret Wy *DEPT* SE8 .... 160 D3
Carterhatch La *EN* EN1 .... 79 N5
  PEND EN3 .... 80 D6
Carterhatch Rd *PEND* EN3 .... 80 B5
Carter La *BLKFR* EC4V 12 D6
Carter PI *WALW* SE17 .... 18 F8
Carter Rd *CRAWE* RH10 .... 284 C11
  PLSTW E13 .... 141 N3
  WIM/MER SW19 .... 179 N9
Cartersfield Rd *WAB* EN9 .... 63 H10
Carters Hill CI *ELTH/MOT* SE9 .... 183 P4
Carters La *EPP* CM16 .... 46 E10
  WOKS/MYFD GU22 .... 232 F6
Carters Md *HLWE* CM17 .... 47 L2
Cartersmead CI *HORL* RH6 .... 280 C3 🔒
Carter St *WALW* SE17 .... 18 E9
Carter's Yd *WAND/EARL* SW18 .... 179 K1 🔒
Carthew Rd *HMSMTH* W6 .... 156 E1
Carthew Vls *HMSMTH* W6 .... 156 E1
Carthouse La *WOKN/KNAP* GU21 .... 213 K10
Carthusian St *FARR* EC1M .... 12 E3 🔒
Carting La *TPL/STR* WC2R .... 11 M8 🔒
Cart La *CHING* E4 .... 101 K2
Cartmel CI *REDH* RH1 .... 257 P9
  TOTM N17 .... 100 A8 🔒
Cartmel Ct *NTHLT* UB5 .... 133 M1 🔒
Cartmel Gdns *MRDN* SM4 .... 201 M6 🔒
Cartmel Rd *BXLYHN* DA7 .... 164 B7
Cartwright Gdns *STPAN* WC1H 5 K10
Cartwright St *TWRH* EC3N 13 M7
Cartwright Wy *BARN* SW13 .... 156 E6
Carve Ley *WGCE* AL7 .... 23 L5
Carver CI *EA* W5 .... 135 J2 🔒
Carver Rd *HNHL* SE24 .... 181 L1
Carville Crs *BTFD* TW8 .... 155 K3
Cary Rd *WAN* E11 .... 121 K6
Carysfort Rd *CEND/HSY/T* N8 .... 118 E3
  STNW/STAM N16 .... 119 J3
Cary Wk *RAD* WD7 .... 58 G10
Cascade Av *MUSWH* N10 .... 118 D2
Cascade CI *STMC/STPC* BR5 .... 207 M3
Cascade Rd *BKHH* IG9 .... 102 A3
Cascades *CROY/NA* CR0 .... 223 N7
Caselden CI *ADL/WDHM* KT15 .... 215 M2 🔒
Casella Rd *NWCR* SE14 .... 160 G5
Casewick Rd *WNWD* SE27 .... 181 H8
Casimir Rd *CLPT* E5 .... 120 A8
Casino Av *HNHL* SE24 .... 181 K1
Caspian Strret *CMBW* SE5 .... 159 L6
Caspian Wk *CAN/RD* E16 .... 142 A8
Cassandra CI *NTHLT* UB5 .... 114 C10 🔒
Cassandra Ga *CHES/WCR* EN8 .... 62 E3
Casselden Rd *WLSDN* NW10 .... 137 A2
Cassidy Rd *FUL/PGN* SW6 .... 157 K5
Cassilda Rd *ABYW* SE2 .... 148 A4
Cassilis Rd *TWK* TW1 .... 176 G2
Cassiobridge Rd *WATW* WD18 .... 72 B7 🔒
Cassiobury Av *EBED/NFELT* TW14 .... 153 J10
Cassiobury Dr *WATW* WD17 .... 72 C5
Cassiobury Park Av *WATW* WD18 .... 72 A7
Cassiobury Rd *WALTH* E17 .... 120 C3
Cassio Rd *WATW* WD18 .... 73 J8
Cassland Rd *HOM* E9 .... 140 C2 🔒
  THHTH CR7 .... 203 L1
Cassocks Sq *WIM/MER* SW19 .... 157 N9 🔒
Casson St *WCHPL* E1 .... 13 N4
Casstine CI *SWLY* BR8 .... 208 C1
Castellain Rd *MV/WKIL* W9 .... 8 E1
Castellan Av *GPK* RM2 .... 125 J1
Castellane CI *STAN* HA7 .... 94 E8 🔒
Castello Av *PUT/ROE* SW15 .... 178 F1
Castell Rd *LOU* IG10 .... 83 M1
Castelnau *BARN* SW13 .... 156 E5
Casterbridge Rd *BKHTH/KID* SE3 .... 161 M9
Casterton St *HACK* E8 .... 140 A1 🔒
Castile Rd *WOOL/PLUM* SE18 .... 162 D3 🔒
Castillon Rd *CAT* SE6 .... 183 K5

Castlands Rd *CAT* SE6 .... 182 E5
Castle Av *CHING* E4 .... 101 E4
  DTCH/LGLY SL3 .... 149 M5
  EW KT17 .... 220 D5
  RAIN RM13 .... 144 F2
  WDR/YW UB7 .... 131 P5
Castlebar HI *WEA* W13 .... 134 G7
Castlebar Ms *EA* W5 .... 134 G7
Castlebar Pk *EA* W5 .... 134 G7
Castlebar Rd *WEA* W13 .... 135 H8
Castle Baynard St *BLKFR* EC4V 12 D7
Castle CI *BUSH* WD23 .... 74 A10
  HARH RM3 .... 105 K4
  HAYES BR2 .... 205 P1
  HOD EN11 .... 27 H10
  REDH RH1 .... 259 K9
  REIG RH2 .... 275 L4 🔒
  RSEV TN14 .... 247 M8
  WIM/MER SW19 .... 178 G6
Castlecombe Dr *WIM/MER* SW19 .... 178 B8
Castlecombe Rd *ELTH/MOT* SE9 .... 184 B8
Castle Ct *SYD* SE26 .... 182 D7 🔒
Castle Dr *HORL* RH6 .... 280 C8
  REDBR IG4 .... 122 B4 🔒
  REIG RH2 .... 275 L4
  RSEV TN14 .... 247 M8
Castle Farm Rd *RSEV* TN14 .... 228 C5
Castlefield Rd *REIG* RH2 .... 257 K9
Castleford Av *ELTH/MOT* SE9 .... 184 E4
Castleford CI *UED* N18 .... 99 N7 🔒
Castle Gdns *DORK* RH4 .... 255 L10
Castlegate *RCH/KEW* TW9 .... 155 L9
Castle Gn *WEY* KT13 .... 196 F10
Castle Grove Rd *CHOB/PIR* GU24 .... 213 K8
Castlehaven Rd *CAMTN* NW1 .... 4 C1
Castle HI *BERK* HP4 .... 33 P5
  GU GU1 .... 268 A2
  HART DA3 .... 211 J5
  WDSR SL4 .... 149 J7
Castle Hill Av *BERK* HP4 .... 33 P4
  CROY/NA CR0 .... 224 C5
Castle Hill CI *BERK* HP4 .... 33 N4
Castle Hill Rd *EGH* TW20 .... 171 N7
  WESTW SW1E 16 C3
Castleleigh Ct *ENC/FH* EN2 .... 79 L9
Castlemaine Av *EW* KT17 .... 220 E5
  SAND/SEL CR2 .... 223 N2
Castle Md *HHW* HP1 .... 35 L8
Castle Ms *CAMTN* NW1 .... 4 E2
  NFNCH/WDSP N12 .... 97 H6
Castlereagh St *MBLAR* W1H .... 10 A5 🔒
Castle Ri *STALE/WH* AL4 .... 20 D1
Castle Rw *CAMTN* NW1 .... 4 F7
  COUL/CHIP CR5 .... 239 P5
  DAGW RM9 .... 143 L3
  EPSOM KT18 .... 237 N1
  EYN DA4 .... 229 J3
  GRAYS RM17 .... 167 K5
  HOD EN11 .... 26 C10
  ISLW TW7 .... 154 E8
  NFNCH/WDSP N12 .... 97 H6
  NTHLT UB5 .... 134 A1
  NWDGN UB2 .... 153 N2 🔒
  PEND EN3 .... 80 D5
  STAL AL1 .... 38 G6
  SWCM DA10 .... 189 L2
  WEY KT13 .... 196 F10
  WOKN/KNAP GU21 .... 214 D10
Castle Sq *REDH* RH1 .... 259 K9
Castle St *BERK* HP4 .... 33 P5
  CHONG CM5 .... 67 P5
  EHAM E6 .... 141 P4
  GRH DA9 .... 169 N7
  GU GU1 .... 268 A2
  HERT/BAY SG13 .... 25 L6
  HERT/WAS SG14 .... 25 K5 🔒
  KUT KT1 .... 199 K2 🔒
  SL SL1 .... 149 J2 🔒
  SWCM DA10 .... 189 L2
  WEY KT13 .... 196 F10
Castleton Av *BXLYHN* DA7 .... 164 E7 🔒
  WBLY HA9 .... 115 K9
Castleton CI *BNSTD* SM7 .... 239 K1
  CROY/NA CR0 .... 204 D6
Castleton Dr *BNSTD* SM7 .... 239 K1
Castleton Gdns *GDMY/SEVK* IG3 .... 123 K6
  LEE/GVPK SE12 .... 184 A1
  MTCM CR4 .... 202 E4
  RSLP HA4 .... 113 L6
  WALTH E17 .... 101 H10
Castletown Rd *WKENS* W14 .... 14 B8
Castleview CI *FSBYPK* N4 .... 122 B4
Castle View Gdns *IL* IG1 .... 122 B4
Castle View Rd *DTCH/LGLY* SL3 .... 149 K7
  WEY KT13 .... 216 C1 🔒
Castle Wy *EW* KT17 .... 220 D6
  FELT TW13 .... 175 K7
  WIM/MER SW19 .... 178 F6
Castlewood Dr *ELTH/MOT* SE9 .... 162 G3
Castlewood Rd *EBAR* EN4 .... 77 N7
  SEVS/STOTM N15 .... 119 N4
Castor La *POP/IOD* E14 .... 140 G9
Catalina Av *CDH/CHF* RM16 .... 167 L1
Catalina Rd *HTHAIR* TW6 .... 152 B9
Cater Gdns *GUW* GU2 .... 249 K8
Caterham By-pass *CTHM* CR3 .... 242 A9
Caterham CI *CHOB/PIR* GU24 .... 230 D7
Caterham Ct *WAB* EN9 .... 63 L10
Caterham Dr *COUL/CHIP* CR5 .... 241 K5
Caterham Rd *LEW* SE13 .... 161 N9
Catesby St *WALW* SE17 .... 19 H6
Catford Broadway *CAT* SE6 .... 182 G6
Catford HI *CAT* SE6 .... 182 D3
Catford Rd *CAT* SE6 .... 182 E4
Cathall Rd *WAN* E11 .... 121 K6
Catham CI *STAL* AL1 .... 38 G8
Catharine CI *CDH/CHF* RM16 .... 167 L1
Cathay St *BERM/RHTH* SE16 .... 160 A6
Cathcart Dr *ORP* BR6 .... 207 H9
Cathcart HI *KTTN* NW5 .... 118 D4
Cathcart Rd *WBPTN* SW10 .... 15 J9
Cathcart St *KTTN* NW5 .... 4 E1
Cathedral CI *GUW* GU2 .... 267 J1
Cathedral St *STHWK* SE1 .... 12 G9 🔒
Cathedral Vw *GUW* GU2 .... 249 L10
Catherall Rd *HBRY* N5 .... 119 K5
  BRWN CM15 .... 86 F9 🔒
  HHNE HP2 .... 9 A8
Catherine Ct *STHGT/OAK* N14 .... 78 D9 🔒
  RCH/KEW TW9 .... 155 K10 🔒
  SUN TW16 .... 174 C10
Catherine Gdns *HSLW* TW3 .... 154 C10
Catherine PI *WESTW* SW1E 16 G3
Catherine Rd *GPK* RM2 .... 125 J2
  PEND EN3 .... 80 G3
  SURB KT6 .... 199 J3
Catherines CI *WDR/YW* UB7 .... 151 N1 🔒
Catherine St *HOL/ALD* WC2B .... 11 N7 🔒
  STALW/RED AL3 .... 38 C5
Catherine Wheel Aly *LVPST* EC2M 13 K4
Catherine Wheel Rd *BTFD* TW8 .... 155 L6
Catherine Wheel Yd *WHALL* SW1A .... 10 G10 🔒
Cat HI *EBAR* EN4 .... 78 A9
Cathles Rd *BAL* SW12 .... 180 C2
Cathnor Rd *SHB* W12 .... 156 G1
Catisfield Rd *PEND* EN3 .... 81 H1
Catkin CI *HHW* HP1 .... 35 L5
Catlin Crs *SHPTN* TW17 .... 195 N5
Catlin Gdns *GDST* RH9 .... 260 A3

Catling Cl FSTH SE23 ... 182 B6
Catlin's La PIN HA5 ... 113 J1
Catlin St BERM/RHTH SE16 ... 19 P8
HHS/BOV HP3 ... 35 L9
Cator Crs CROY/NA CR0 ... 225 K7
Cator La BECK BR3 ... 204 E2
Cator Rd CAR SM5 ... 222 A2
SYD SE26 ... 182 C4
Cator St PECK SE15 ... 19 L10
Catsdell Bottom HHS/BOV HP3 ... 36 C9
Catsey La BUSH WD23 ... 94 B1
Catsey Wd BUSH WD23 ... 94 B1
Catterick Cl FBAR/BDGN N11 ... 98 B3
Catterick Wd BUSH ... 75 L5
Cattistock Rd POTB/CUF EN6 ... 60 E7
Cattlegate Rd POTB/CUF EN6 ... 60 G7
Cattlegate Road Crews Hl
  ENC/FH EN2 ... 60 G10
Cattley Cl BAR EN5 ... 77 H8
Catlins Cl CHESW EN7 ... 61 M5
Catton St RSQ WC1B ... 11 M5
Catsdell HHNE HP2 ... 35 P4
Caulfield Rd EHAM E6 ... 142 C2
  PECK SE15 ... 160 A8
Causeway La WARE SG12 ... 153 J10
Causeway Br SOCK/AV RM15 ... 166 D2
Causeway Cl POTB/CUF EN6 ... 59 N7
The Causeway BELMT SM2 ... 221 M5
  CAR SM5 ... 202 B10
  CHSGTN KT9 ... 219 L6
  EFNCH N2 ... 117 N2
  ESH/CLAY KT10 ... 218 C4
  POTB/CUF EN6 ... 59 M7
  STA TW18 ... 172 F7
  TEDD TW11 ... 176 B8
  WAND/EARL SW18 ... 157 L10
  WIM/MER SW19 ... 178 F8
Causeyware Rd ED N9 ... 100 A1
Causton Rd HGT N6 ... 118 C5
Causton St WEST SW1P ... 17 K6
Cautherly La WARE SG12 ... 26 E6
Cautley Av CLAP SW4 ... 180 D1
Cavalier Cl CHDH RM6 ... 142 C2
Cavalier Ct BERK HP4 ... 33 P5
Cavalier Gdns HYS/HAR UB3 ... 132 E8
Cavalry Crs WDSR SL4 ... 148 G9
Cavalry Gdns PUT/ROE SW15 ... 179 J1
Cavan Dr STALW/RED AL3 ... 38 C1
Cavaye Pl WBPTN SW10 ... 15 K8
Cavell Crs DART DA1 ... 165 H10
Cavell Dr ENC/FH EN2 ... 79 H6
Cavell Rd CHESW EN7 ... 61 N3
  TOTM N17 ... 99 H8
Cavell St WCHPL E1 ... 140 E7
Cavell Wy CRAWE RH10 ... 284 D1
  ERITH DA8 ... 164 C1
  FNCH N3 ... 97 K10
  NTHLT UB5 ... 114 C9
  NWMAL KT3 ... 200 E5
  RAIN RM13 ... 145 J1
  RSLP HA4 ... 113 J10
  SEV TN13 ... 247 H8
  STJWD NW8 ... 3 M8
  WEA W13 ... 134 F7
  WELL DA16 ... 163 J9
  WFD IG8 ... 101 N8
Cavendish Cl AMS HP6 ... 69 N5
  KIL/WHAMP NW6 ... 2 C1
  STJWD NW8 ... 3 M9
  SUN TW16 ... 174 C9
  UED N18 ... 100 A6
  YEAD UB4 ... 132 F7
Cavendish Ct SUN TW16 ... 174 C9
Cavendish Crs BORE WD6 ... 75 M8
  RAIN RM13 ... 145 J1
Cavendish Dr EDGW HA8 ... 95 M7
  ESH/CLAY KT10 ... 218 D2
  WAN E11 ... 121 J6
Cavendish Gdns BARK IG11 ... 123 J10
  CHDH RM6 ... 123 P3
  IL IG1 ... 122 F6
  REDH RH1 ... 258 B9
Cavendish Meads ASC SL5 ... 192 C6
Cavendish Ms North REGST W1B ... 10 F1
Cavendish Ms South GTPST W1W ... 10 F4
Cavendish Pl CAVSQ/HST W1G ... 10 E5
  MHST W1U ... 10 E5
Cavendish Rd BAL SW12 ... 180 D3
  BAR EN5 ... 76 F7
  BELMT SM2 ... 221 M4
  CHING E4 ... 100 G8
  CHSWK W4 ... 155 P9
  CLAP SW4 ... 180 C2
  CROY/NA CR0 ... 203 J4
  CSHM HP5 ... 51 J8
  FSBYPK N4 ... 119 J4
  KIL/WHAMP NW6 ... 2 B3
  NWMAL KT3 ... 200 D8
  REDH RH1 ... 258 B10
  STAL AL1 ... 38 E6
  SUN TW16 ... 174 C9
  UED N18 ... 100 A6
  WEY KT13 ... 216 C5
  WIM/MER SW19 ... 179 P10
  WOKS/MYFD GU22 ... 232 A5
Cavendish Sq CAVSQ/HST W1G ... 10 F5
Cavendish St IS N1 ... 6 G4
Cavendish Wy HAT AL10 ... 40 C4
  WWKM BR4 ... 204 C7
Cavenham Cl WOKS/MYFD GU22 ... 232 B5
Cavenham Gdns EMPK RM11 ... 125 K3
  IL IG1 ... 122 G8
Caverleigh Wy WPK KT4 ... 200 D8
Caverleigh Gdns
  KTN/HRWW/W HA3 ... 115 J5
Cave Rd PLSTW E13 ... 141 N4
  RCHPK/HAM TW10 ... 177 H7
Caversham Av CHEAM SM3 ... 201 H9
  PLMGR N13 ... 99 H4
Caversham Rd KTTN NW5 ... 4 D1
  KUT KT1 ... 199 L2
  SEVS/STOTM N15 ... 119 K2
Caversham St CHEL SW3 ... 16 A9
Caverswall St SHB W12 ... 138 D7
Cawcott Dr WDSR SL4 ... 148 D7
Cawdor Av SOCK/AV RM15 ... 146 F9
Cawdor Crs HNWL W7 ... 154 F3
Cawnpore St NRWD SE19 ... 181 M8
Cawsey Wy WOKN/KNAP GU21 ... 232 B3
Caxton Cl CRAWE RH10 ... 283 N10
  HART DA3 ... 211 L4
Caxton Dr UX/CGN UB8 ... 131 M4
  UX/CGN UB8 ... 131 N4
Caxton Gv BOW E3 ... 140 F5
Caxton Hl HERT/BAY SG13 ... 25 N5
Caxton La OXTED RH8 ... 262 D4
Caxton Ri REDH RH1 ... 258 A9
Caxton Rd HOD EN11 ... 26 F1
  NWDGN UB2 ... 153 L2
  SHB W12 ... 136 G10
  WDGN N22 ... 98 G10
  WIM/MER SW19 ... 179 N8
Caxton St STJSPK SW1H ... 17 H3
Caxton St North CAN/RD E16 ... 141 L8
Caxton Wy WATW WD18 ... 92 G4
Caygill Cl HAYES BR2 ... 205 L4
Cayton Rd GFD/PVL UB6 ... 134 D2
Cayton St FSBYE EC1V ... 6 C10
Cazenove Rd STNW/STAM N16 ... 119 N7
  WALTH E17 ... 100 F9
Cearn Wy COUL/CHIP CR5 ... 240 G1

Cecil Av BARK IG11 ... 142 G2
  CDH/CHF RM16 ... 167 L1
  EMPK RM11 ... 125 M1
  EN EN1 ... 79 N8
  WBLY HA9 ... 115 L10
Cecil Cl ASHF TW15 ... 174 D7
  CHSGTN KT9 ... 219 J3
Cecil Ct BAR EN5 ... 76 G7
  HLWS CM18 ... 46 F4
Cecil Crs HAT AL10 ... 40 F4
Cecile Pk CEND/HSY/T N8 ... 118 F4
Cecilia Cl EFNCH N2 ... 117 M1
Cecilia Rd HACK E8 ... 119 N10
Cecil Pk PIN HA5 ... 113 M2
Cecil Pl MTCM CR4 ... 202 A5
Cecil Rd ACT W3 ... 135 P7
  ASHF TW15 ... 174 D10
  CDALE/KGS NW9 ... 116 A1
  CHDH RM6 ... 123 N5
  CHES/WCR EN8 ... 62 C5
  CROY/NA CR0 ... 202 F6
  ENC/FH EN2 ... 79 L8
  GVW DA11 ... 190 C4
  HSLW TW3 ... 154 B9
  HOD EN11 ... 45 H1
  IL IG1 ... 122 E9
  IVER SL0 ... 131 H5
  KTN/HRWW/W HA3 ... 114 D1
  MUSWH N10 ... 98 C10
  PLSTW E13 ... 141 M4
  POTB/CUF EN6 ... 59 P6
  STAL AL1 ... 38 E6
  STHGT/OAK N14 ... 99 H1
  SUT SM1 ... 221 J3
  WALTH E17 ... 100 F5
  WAN E11 ... 121 K7
  WIM/MER SW19 ... 179 L10
  WLSDN NW10 ... 136 B5
Cecil St WATN WD24 ... 73 J4
Cecil Wy HAYES BR2 ... 205 M8
  SLN SL2 ... 128 E6
Cedar Av BFN/LL DA15 ... 185 K3
  CDH RM1 ... 123 P5
  CHES/WCR EN8 ... 62 C5
  CROY/NA CR0 ... 217 J10
  EBAR EN4 ... 97 P1
  GVE DA12 ... 190 F7
  HYS/HAR UB3 ... 133 H8
  PEND EN3 ... 80 B5
  RSLP HA4 ... 113 K10
  UPMR RM14 ... 125 P3
  WDR/YW UB7 ... 132 A10
  WHTN TW2 ... 176 A2
Cedar Cl BKHH IG9 ... 102 A3
  CAR SM5 ... 222 A3
  CRAWW RH11 ... 283 M4
  DORK RH4 ... 272 C2
  DUL SE21 ... 181 K4
  ESH/CLAY KT10 ... 217 M4
  EW KT17 ... 220 C10
  HAYES BR2 ... 206 B10
  IVER SL0 ... 130 F3
  KUTN/CMB KT2 ... 178 A7
  POTB/CUF EN6 ... 59 K6
  REIG RH2 ... 275 N1
  ROMW/RG RM7 ... 124 D2
  SBW CM21 ... 29 P7
  STA TW18 ... 195 M3
  SWLY BR8 ... 208 D2
  WARE SG12 ... 26 C3
  WARL CR6 ... 242 F4
Cedar Copse BMLY BR1 ... 206 C2
Cedar Ct ADL/WDHM KT15 ... 215 M1
  ELTW20 ... 172 D7
  STALE/WH AL4 ... 39 J4
  WIM/MER SW19 ... 178 F8
Cedar Crs HAYES BR2 ... 206 B10
Cedarcroft Rd CHSGTN KT9 ... 219 L1
Cedar Dr ASC SL5 ... 192 D7
  EFNCH N2 ... 117 P2
  EYN DA4 ... 210 A2
  LHD/OX KT22 ... 236 D9
  LOU IG10 ... 82 E6
  PIN HA5 ... 93 P7
Cedar Gdns BELMT SM2 ... 221 M3
  UPMR RM14 ... 126 B9
  WOKN/KNAP GU21 ... 231 N4
Cedar Gn HOD EN11 ... 44 F4
Cedar Gv AMSS HP7 ... 69 J5
  BXLY DA5 ... 185 N3
  CHOB/PIR GU24 ... 230 F1
  CSHM HP5 ... 32 C3
  EA W5 ... 155 J2
  STHL UB1 ... 133 P7
  WEY KT13 ... 216 D1
Cedar Hts RCHPK/HAM TW10 ... 177 K4
Cedar Hl EPP CM16 ... 237 P1
Cedarhurst Dr ELTH/MOT SE9 ... 183 P1
Cedar Lawn Av BAR EN5 ... 77 H9
Cedar Mt ELTH/MOT SE9 ... 184 F4
Cedarne Rd FUL/PGN SW6 ... 139 M4
Cedar Park Gdns CHDH RM6 ... 123 N5
Cedar Park Rd ENC/FH EN2 ... 79 K4
Cedar Pl CHARL SE7 ... 142 B4
  STHGT/OAK N14 ... 98 B1
Cedar Ri STHGT/OAK N14 ... 98 B1
Cedar Rd BELMT SM2 ... 221 M3
  BERK HP4 ... 34 A6
  BMLY BR1 ... 205 P2
  CDH/CHF RM16 ... 168 D2
  COB KT11 ... 217 L10
  CRICK NW2 ...
  CROY/NA CR0 ... 203 M9
  DART DA1 ... 187 L4
  E/WMO/HCT KT8 ... 198 A2
  EBED/NFELT TW14 ... 174 E4
  ENC/FH EN2 ... 79 J4
  ERITH DA8 ... 165 H7
  HAT AL10 ... 40 F4
  HEST TW5 ... 153 K8
  OXHEY WD19 ... 73 K10
  ROMW/RG RM7 ... 124 D2
  TEDD TW11 ... 176 B8
  TOTM N17 ... 99 N8
  WAT WD17 ...
  WOKS/MYFD GU22 ... 231 N6

Cedar Ter RCH/KEW TW9 ... 155 K10
Cedar Terrace Rd SEV TN13 ... 247 K9
Cedar Tree Gv WNWD SE27 ... 181 J8
Cedarville Gdns
  STRHM/NOR SW16 ... 180 G9
Cedar Wk ESH/CLAY KT10 ... 218 D3
  HHS/BOV HP3 ... 35 N8
  KWD/TDW/WH KT20 ... 239 J7
  PUR/KEN CR8 ... 241 K2
Cedar Wy BERK HP4 ... 34 A6
  CAMTN NW1 ...
  DTCH/LGLY SL3 ... 150 B3
  GU GU1 ... 249 P7
  SUN TW16 ... 174 F10
Cedar Wood Dr GSTN WD25 ... 73 J1
Cedric Av ROM RM1 ... 124 F1
Cedric Rd ELTH/MOT SE9 ... 184 F6
Celadon Cl PEND EN3 ... 80 D7
Celandine Cl POP/IOD E14 ... 140 F7
  SOCK/AV RM15 ... 147 H6
Celandine Dr HACK E8 ... 7 M3
  THMD SE28 ... 143 L10
Celandine Rd WOT/HER KT12 ... 217 M1
Celandine Wy SRTFD E15 ... 141 K5
Celbridge Ms BAY/PAD W2 ... 9 H5
Celedon Cl CDH/CHF RM16 ... 167 K1
Celestial Gdns LEW SE13 ... 161 J10
Celia Crs ASHF TW15 ... 173 N9
Celia Rd ARCH N19 ... 118 D9
Cell Barnes Cl STAL AL1 ... 38 C8
Cell Barnes La STAL AL1 ... 38 C9
Cell Farm Av WDSR SL4 ... 171 N1
Celtic Av HAYES BR2 ... 205 K3
Celtic Rd BF/WBF KT14 ... 215 P10
Celtic St POP/IOD E14 ... 140 G4
Cement Block Cottages
  GRAYS RM17 ... 167 P4
Cemetery Hl HHW HP1 ... 35 M7
Cemetery La CHARL SE7 ... 162 B5
  SHPTN TW17 ... 196 C7
Cemetery Pales CHOB/PIR GU24 ... 230 F8
Cemetery Rd ABYW SE2 ... 163 L5
  FSTGT E7 ... 121 L10
  TOTM N17 ... 99 H8
Cemmaes Court Rd HHW HP1 ... 35 M5
Cemmaes Meadow HHW HP1 ... 35 M6
Cenacle Cl HAMP NW3 ... 117 K8
Centaur Ct BTFD TW8 ... 155 K4
Centaur St STHWK SE1 ... 17 M2
Centenary Wk EPP CM16 ... 81 N10
  LOU IG10 ... 81 N10
  WALTH E17 ... 121 M6
  WAN E11 ... 121 M6
  WFD IG8 ... 101 K7
Central Av CHES/WCR EN8 ... 62 D9
  E/WMO/HCT KT8 ... 197 N5
  ED N9 ... 99 M4
  EFNCH N2 ... 97 N10
  EN EN1 ... 80 E5
  GVE DA12 ... 190 E5
  HSLW TW3 ... 154 B10
  HYS/HAR UB3 ... 132 G10
  PIN HA5 ... 113 N4
  SOCK/AV RM15 ... 166 B9
  TIL RM18 ... 168 D7
  WAN E11 ... 121 J7
  WELL DA16 ... 163 K8
  WLGTN SM6 ... 222 F3
  WTHK RM20 ... 166 E4
Central Dr HCH RM12 ... 125 M8
  SL SL1 ... 128 E9
  STAL AL1 ... 39 H5
  WGCE AL7 ... 23 L4
Central Hl NRWD SE19 ... 181 K8
Central Pde CROY/NA CR0 ... 225 K6
  HRW HA1 ... 114 E3
Central Park Av DAGE RM10 ... 124 D9
Central Park Rd EHAM E6 ... 142 B4
Central Pl ALP/SUD HA0 ... 114 G10
  DART DA1 ... 187 M1
  HLW CM20 ... 29 M1
  MRDN SM4 ... 201 L5
  WPK KT4 ... 200 G1
Central Rd E/WMO/HCT KT8 ... 197 N4
  GLDGN NW11 ... 117 K4
  MRDN SM4 ... 201 M6
  WPK KT4 ... 200 F1
Central Sq E/WMO/HCT KT8 ... 197 N4
  GLDGN NW11 ... 117 K4
  WBLY HA9 ...
Central St FSBYE EC1V ... 6 E8
Central Wy CAR SM5 ... 221 P4
  EBED/NFELT TW14 ... 175 J1
  NTHWD HA6 ... 92 F8
  OXTED RH8 ... 261 J5
  THMD SE28 ... 143 L9
  WLSDN NW10 ... 135 L2
Centre Av ACT W3 ... 137 A10
  EFNCH N2 ... 97 P10
  EPP CM16 ... 65 J8
Centre Common Rd CHST BR7 ... 184 F10
Centre Dr EPP CM16 ... 65 J8
Centre Gn EPP CM16 ... 65 J8
Centre Rd DAGE RM10 ... 144 D3
  HART DA3 ... 211 K10
  WAN E11 ... 121 M7
Centre St BETH E2 ... 140 A4
The Centre FELT TW13 ... 175 H5
Centre Wy ED N9 ... 100 B3
  WAB EN9 ... 81 H1
Centurion Cl HOLWY N7 ... 5 N3
Centurion La BOW E3 ... 140 E4
Centurion Wy ERITH DA18 ... 164 A2
  PUR RM19 ... 165 N5
Century Rd EGH TW20 ... 172 F8
  HOD EN11 ... 44 F2
  WALTH E17 ... 120 D1
  WARE SG12 ... 26 C1
Cephas Av WCHPL E1 ... 140 E6
Cephas St WCHPL E1 ... 140 E6
Ceres Rd WOOL/PLUM SE18 ... 143 J3
Cerise Rd PECK SE15 ... 159 N7
Cerne Cl YEAD UB4 ... 133 K9
Cerne Rd GVE DA12 ... 191 M6
  MRDN SM4 ... 201 M6
Cerotus Pl CHERT KT16 ... 195 J7
Cervantes Ct BAY/PAD W2 ... 9 H6
  NTHWD HA6 ... 92 G3
Cervia Wy GVE DA12 ... 191 J6
Cestreham Crs CSHM HP5 ... 51 J5
Ceylon Rd WKENS W14 ... 14 A4
Chace Av POTB/CUF EN6 ... 59 N8
Chacombe Pl BEAC HP9 ... 88 C6
Chadacre Av CLAY IG5 ... 122 C1
Chadacre Rd EW KT17 ... 220 E2
Chadbourn St POP/IOD E14 ... 140 G7
Chadd Dr BMLY BR1 ... 206 B3
Chadfields TIL RM18 ... 168 D6
Chadhurst Cl RDKG RH5 ... 273 J5
Chadville Gdns CHDH RM6 ... 123 N3
Chadway BCTR RM8 ... 123 N3
Chadwell WARE SG12 ... 26 B3
Chadwell Av CHDH RM6 ... 123 J6
  CHES/WCR EN8 ... 62 B4
Chadwell By-pass GRAYS RM17 ... 168 D4
Chadwell Heath La CHDH RM6 ... 123 J2
Chadwell Hi CDH/CHF RM16 ... 168 E4
Chadwell Ri WARE SG12 ... 26 C1
Chadwell Rd GRAYS RM17 ... 167 P3
Chadwell St CLKNW EC1R ... 6 A7
Chadwick Av CHING E4 ... 101 N1
  WCHMH N21 ...
  WIM/MER SW19 ... 179 K9
Chadwick Cl GVW DA11 ... 190 B5
  PUT/ROE SW15 ...
  TEDD TW11 ... 176 B3
Chadwick Dr HARH RM3 ... 105 L10
Chadwick Rd CMBW SE5 ... 159 N4
  IL IG1 ... 122 E8
  PECK SE15 ... 159 L2
  WAN E11 ... 121 K1
  WLSDN NW10 ... 136 C3

Chadwick St WEST SW1P ... 17 J4
Chadwin Rd PLSTW E13 ... 141 N4
Chadworth Wy ESH/CLAY KT10 ... 218 C2
Chaffers Md ASHTD KT21 ... 250 F8
Chaffinch Av CROY/NA CR0 ... 204 C6
Chaffinch Cl CRAWW RH11 ... 283 N5
  CROY/NA CR0 ... 204 C6
  ED N9 ... 100 C2
  SURB KT6 ... 199 M10
Chaffinches Gn HHS/BOV HP3 ... 36 B10
Chaffinch La WATW WD18 ... 92 G1
Chaffinch Rd BECK BR3 ... 204 D1
Chafford Wy HORL RH6 ... 279 P3
  CHDH RM6 ... 123 M2
Chagford St CAMTN NW1 ... 10 A2
Chailey Av EN EN1 ... 79 N6
Chailey Cl CRAWW RH11 ... 283 K10
  HEST TW5 ... 153 L7
Chailey Pl WOT/HER KT12 ... 217 M1
Chailey St CLPT E5 ... 120 B3
Chain Wk
  ENC/FH EN2 ... 61 K6
  HERT/BAY SG13 ... 42 E1
  HERT/WAS SG14 ... 24 B1
Chalcombe Rd ABYW SE2 ... 163 L2
Chalcot Cl BELMT SM2 ... 221 K4
Chalcot Crs CAMTN NW1 ... 4 B5
Chalcot Gdns HAMP NW3 ... 4 A1
Chalcot Ms STRHM/NOR SW16 ... 180 F6
Chalcot Rd CAMTN NW1 ... 4 C3
Chalcot Sq CAMTN NW1 ... 4 C4
Chalcott Gdns SURB KT6 ... 199 H8
Chalcroft Rd LEW SE13 ... 183 K1
Chaldon Cl REDH RH1 ... 275 P2
Chaldon Common Rd CTHM CR3 ... 241 K10
Chaldon Rd CTHM CR3 ... 241 L9
  FUL/PGN SW6 ... 157 H6
Chaldon Wy COUL/CHIP CR5 ... 240 F5
Chale Rd BRXS/STRHM SW2 ... 180 F2
Chalet Cl BERK HP4 ... 33 L5
  RDART DA2 ... 188 E7
Chalfont Av WBLY HA9 ... 136 C4
Chalfont Cl HHNE HP2 ... 36 C1
Chalfont Gn ED N9 ... 99 P4
Chalfont La RKW/CH/CXG WD3 ... 90 E4
  RKW/CH/CXG WD3 ... 90 E4
Chalfont Rd CFSP/GDCR SL9 ... 90 E4
  ED N9 ... 99 N10
  HYS/HAR UB3 ... 153 H1
  SNWD SE25 ...
Chalfont Station Rd AMSS HP7 ... 69 P6
Chalfont Wy WEA W13 ... 154 C2
Chalford Cl E/WMO/HCT KT8 ... 197 P4
Chalforde Gdns GPK RM2 ... 125 J2
Chalford Rd DUL SE21 ... 181 L7
Chalford Wk WFD IG8 ... 102 A2
Chalgrove WGCE AL7 ... 23 N4
Chalgrove Av MRDN SM4 ... 201 K5
Chalgrove Crs CLAY IG5 ... 121 N1
Chalgrove Gdns FNCH N3 ... 116 B10
Chalgrove Rd BELMT SM2 ... 221 N4
  HOM E9 ... 140 B1
  TOTM N17 ...
Chalice Cl WLGTN SM6 ... 222 E3
Chalice Wy GRH DA9 ... 188 D1
Chalk Dl WGCE AL7 ... 23 L4
Chalkdell Flds STAL AL1 ... 38 D3
Chalkdell Hl HHNE HP2 ... 35 P6
Chalkenden Cl PGE/AN SE20 ... 182 A10
Chalk Farm Rd CAMTN NW1 ... 4 C3
Chalk Hl AMSS HP7 ... 50 C5
  OXHEY WD19 ... 73 M10
Chalkhill Rd WBLY HA9 ... 115 P7
Chalklands WBLY HA9 ... 115 P8
Chalk La ASHTD KT21 ... 237 M5
  EBAR EN4 ... 78 A7
  EHSLY KT24 ... 252 G7
  EPSOM KT18 ... 238 B2
  HLWE CM17 ... 30 B9
  MFD/CHID GU8 ... 266 C9
Chalkley Cl MTCM CR4 ... 202 A2
Chalk Paddock EPSOM KT18 ... 238 A1
Chalk Pit Av STMC/STPC BR5 ... 207 M3
Chalkpit La DORK RH4 ... 273 H5
  OXTED RH8 ... 261 H3
Chalk Pit La SL SL1 ... 128 A3
Chalk Pit Rd ASHTD KT21 ... 237 P5
  BNSTD SM7 ... 239 K8
  SUT SM1 ... 221 M2
Chalkpit Ter DORK RH4 ... 254 F10
Chalkpit Wd OXTED RH8 ... 261 J3
Chalk Rd GVE DA12 ... 191 K4
  PLSTW E13 ... 141 N7
Chalkstone Cl WELL DA16 ... 163 K7
Chalkways RSEV TN14 ... 247 N4
Chalkwell Park Av EN EN1 ... 79 M8
Chalky Bank GVW DA11 ... 190 D7
Chalky La CHSGTN KT9 ... 219 J5
Challacombe Cl
  RBRW/HUT CM13 ... 107 P2
Challenge Cl GVE DA12 ... 191 J7
Challenge Ct LHD/OX KT22 ... 236 C5
Challenge Rd ASHF TW15 ... 174 D6
Challice Wy BRXS/STRHM SW2 ... 180 A6
Challinor HLWE CM17 ... 47 P1
Challin St PGE/AN SE20 ... 204 B3
Challis Rd BTFD TW8 ... 137 K8
Challock Cl BH/WHM TN16 ... 243 P2
Challoner Cl EFNCH N2 ... 97 M10
Challoner Crs WKENS W14 ... 14 C8
Challoners Cl E/WMO/HCT KT8 ... 198 C4
Challoners ... WKENS W14 ... 14 C7
Chalmers Ct HORL RH6 ... 279 H9
Chalmers Rd ASHF TW15 ... 174 C7
  BNSTD SM7 ...
Chalmers Rd East ASHF TW15 ... 174 C7
Chalmers Wy EBED/NFELT TW14 ... 175 K1
Chalsey Rd BROCKY SE4 ... 160 E10
Chalton Dr EFNCH N2 ... 117 M4
Chalton Rd CAMTN NW1 ... 5 J2
  SL SL1 ... 148 G2
Chalvey Pk SL SL1 ... 148 G2
Chalvey Rd East SL SL1 ... 149 H1
Chalvey Rd West SL SL1 ... 149 H1
Chamberlain Cl HLWE CM17 ... 47 M3
  WOOL/PLUM SE18 ... 162 G2
Chamberlain Crs WWKM BR4 ... 204 C8
Chamberlain La PIN HA5 ... 113 H2
Chamberlain Pl WALTH E17 ... 120 D1
Chamberlain Rd ED N9 ... 97 M10
  WEA W13 ... 154 F1
Chamberlain St CAMTN NW1 ... 4 B1
  SURB KT6 ... 199 K7
Chamberlayne Rd WLSDN NW10 ... 136 E2
Chambersbury La HHS/BOV HP3 ... 36 C10
  HHS/BOV HP3 ... 54 B1
Chambers Cl GRH DA9 ... 188 B4
Chambers Gdns EFNCH N2 ... 97 M9
Chambers La WLSDN NW10 ... 136 E2
Chambers Rd HOLWY N7 ... 118 F9
Chambers St BERM/RHTH SE16 ... 19 N9
  HERT/WAS SG14 ... 25 K5
Chamber St WCHPL E1 ... 19 L1
Chambon Pl HMSMTH W6 ... 156 D3
Chambord St BETH E2 ... 7 M10
Champion Crs SYD SE26 ... 182 G7
Champion Gv CMBW SE5 ... 159 K8
Champion Hl CMBW SE5 ... 159 L9
Champion Pk CMBW SE5 ... 159 L9
Champion Rd SYD SE26 ... 182 G7

UPMR RM14 ... 126 A7
Champions Cl BORE WD6 ... 75 N3
Champions Wy HOD EN11 ... 26 F10
Champness Cl WNWD SE27 ... 181 L7
Champneys Cl BELMT SM2 ... 221 J4
Chance Cl CDH/CHF RM16 ... 167 L2
Chancellor Gdns SAND/SEL CR2 ... 223 L3
Chancellor Gv DUL SE21 ... 181 K5
Chancellor Pl CDALE/KGS NW9 ... 96 C1
Chancellors ... AMSS HP7 ... 68 A8
Chancellor's Rd HMSMTH W6 ... 156 F4
Chancellor's St HMSMTH W6 ... 156 F4
Chancelot Rd ABYW SE2 ... 163 L3
Chancel St STHWK SE1 ... 12 C9
Chancery Cl STALE/WH AL4 ... 39 J1
Chancery La BECK BR3 ... 204 G2
  LINN WC2A ... 11 M4
Chance St BETH E2 ... 7 L9
Chanctonbury Cha REDH RH1 ... 276 C1
Chanctonbury Cl ELTH/MOT SE9 ... 184 F5
Chanctonbury Dr ASC SL5 ... 192 D10
Chanctonbury Gdns BELMT SM2 ... 221 L5
Chanctonbury Wy CRAWW RH11 ... 283 M9
  NFNCH/WDSP N12 ... 97 K5
Chandler Av CAN/RD E16 ... 141 K8
Chandler Cl CRAWW RH11 ... 283 N9
  HPTN TW12 ... 197 N1
Chandler Rd LOU IG10 ... 65 P9
Chandlers Cl EBED/NFELT TW14 ... 174 G3
Chandlers Dr ERITH DA8 ... 164 A5
Chandler's La RKW/CH/CXG WD3 ... 71 P3
Chandlers Ms POP/IOD E14 ... 160 F1
Chandlers Rd STALE/WH AL4 ... 39 H3
Chandler St WAP E1W ... 140 D10
Chandlers Wk BRWN CM15 ... 86 D3
Chandlers Wy HERT/WAS SG14 ... 25 H5
  ROM RM1 ... 124 F3
Chandler Wy PECK SE15 ... 159 N6
Chandos Av EA W5 ... 155 H3
  STHGT/OAK N14 ... 98 D4
  TRDG/WHET N20 ... 97 N2
  WALTH E17 ... 100 F10
Chandos Cl AMS HP6 ... 69 N4
  BKHH IG9 ... 101 N3
Chandos Crs EDGW HA8 ... 95 L8
Chandos Pl CHCR WC2N ... 11 L8
Chandos Rd BORE WD6 ... 75 L6
  CRICK NW2 ... 116 F10
  EFNCH N2 ... 97 N10
  HRW HA1 ... 114 B3
  PIN HA5 ... 113 K5
  SRTFD E15 ... 121 J10
  STA TW18 ... 172 G8
  TOTM N17 ... 99 M10
  WLSDN NW10 ... 136 B6
Chandos St CAVSQ/HST W1G ... 10 F4
Chandos Wy GLDGN NW11 ... 117 L6
Chanlock Pth SOCK/AV RM15 ... 146 G3
Channel Cl HEST TW5 ... 153 P7
Channelsea Rd SRTFD E15 ... 141 J3
Channing Cl EMPK RM11 ... 125 N5
Channings WOKN/KNAP GU21 ... 231 N1
Chanton Dr BELMT SM2 ... 220 F6
Chantress Cl DAGE RM10 ... 144 D3
Chantrey Cl ASHTD KT21 ... 237 H5
  SCUP DA14 ... 185 P8
Chantry Cl BRXN/ST SW9 ... 158 A2
  CRAWE RH10 ... 283 P10
Chantry Hurst EPSOM KT18 ... 238 A1
Chantry La HAT AL10 ... 40 E4
  HAYES BR2 ... 206 A3
  LCOL/BKTW AL2 ...
  SHGR GU5 ... 270 A5
Chantry Pl RYLN/HDSTN HA2 ... 94 A9
Chantry Rd CHERT KT16 ... 195 L8
  CHSGTN KT9 ... 219 L2
  KTN/HRWW/W HA3 ... 94 A9
  RGUE GU4 ... 268 E2
The Chantry HLW CM20 ... 29 K8
  UX/CGN UB8 ... 132 A5
Chantry View Rd GU GU1 ... 268 A3
  RGUE GU4 ... 268 B3
Chantry Wy MTCM CR4 ... 201 N3
  RAIN RM13 ... 144 E4
Chant Sq SRTFD E15 ... 141 J2
Chant St SRTFD E15 ... 141 J2
Chapel Av ADL/WDHM KT15 ... 215 L1
  CHOB/PIR GU24 ... 230 G7
Chapel Cl DART DA1 ... 186 F1
  GSTN WD25 ... 54 C10
  STAL AL1 ... 38 C9
  WTHK RM20 ... 166 C8
Chapel Cottages HHNE HP2 ... 35 N5
Chapel Ct DORK RH4 ... 272 F2
  EFNCH N2 ... 117 P1
Chapel Crofts BERK HP4 ... 33 K3
Chapel End HOD EN11 ... 44 F4
Chapel Farm Rd ELTH/MOT SE9 ... 184 F4
Chapel Flds HLWE CM17 ... 47 M3
Chapelfields WARE SG12 ... 27 J6
Chapel Gn PUR/KEN CR8 ... 223 M8
Chapel Gv ADL/WDHM KT15 ... 215 L1
  KWD/TDW/WH KT20 ... 238 F5
Chapel Hl DART DA1 ... 186 F1
  EFNCH N2 ... 97 P10
  EHSLY KT24 ... 253 L3
Chapelhouse Cl GUW GU2 ... 249 K10
Chapel House St POP/IOD E14 ... 160 G4
Chapel La CHIG IG7 ... 103 J4
  CHOB/PIR GU24 ... 230 F7
  CRAWE RH10 ... 283 N1
  DORK RH4 ... 273 J3
  GT/LBKH KT23 ... 254 B4
  HERT/WAS SG14 ... 25 H3
  HLWE CM17 ... 47 M3
  PIN HA5 ... 113 L2
  SLN SL2 ... 129 N2
  UX/CGN UB8 ... 132 B8
Chapel Market IS N1 ... 6 A7
Chapel Park Rd ADL/WDHM KT15 ... 215 L1
Chapel Pl CAVSQ/HST W1G ... 10 E5
  IS N1 ... 6 A7
  TOTM N17 ... 99 N8
Chapel Rd BXLYHN DA7 ... 164 B10
  EPP CM16 ... 65 J2
  HORL RH6 ... 279 H8
  HSLW TW3 ... 154 A9
  IL IG1 ... 122 D8
  KWD/TDW/WH KT20 ... 238 F10
  OXTED RH8 ... 261 P6
  REDH RH1 ... 258 A10
  TWK TW1 ... 176 C3
  WARL CR6 ... 242 F4
  WEA W13 ... 134 G10
  WNWD SE27 ... 181 J7
Chapel Rw DEN/HRF UB9 ... 91 M9
Chapel Side BAY/PAD W2 ... 8 F7
Chapels Cl SL SL1 ... 128 D10
Chapel Sq VW GU25 ... 194 B8
Chapel St BAY/PAD W2 ... 9 M2
  BERK HP4 ... 33 P5
  ENC/FH EN2 ... 79 K7
  GU GU1 ... 268 A2
  HHNE HP2 ... 35 N5
  KTBR SW1X ... 16 D3

SL SL1 149 L1
WOKN/KNAP GU21 232 C3
Chapel Vw SAND/SEL CR2 224 B4
Chapel Wy ABLGY WD5 54 G3
KWD/TDW/WH KT20 238 F5
Chapel Wd HART DA3 211 K9
Chapel Wood Rd HART DA3 211 K9
Chaplaincy Gdns EMPK RM11 125 M6
Chaplemount Rd WFD IG8 102 C7
Chaplin Crs SUN TW16 174 F9
Chaplin Rd ALP/SUD HA0 135 H1
CRICK NW2 136 D1
SRTFD E15 141 K4
TOTM N17 119 N1
Chapman Cl WDR/YW UB7 152 A2
Chapman Crs KTN/HRWW/W HA3 115 K3
Chapman Rd BELV DA17 164 B4
CROY/NA CR0 203 H8
HOM E9 140 E1
Chapmans Crs CSHM HP5 50 F5
Chapman's La STMC/STPC BR5 207 N2
SWLY BR8 208 B2
Chapmans Rd RSEV TN14 245 P10
Chapman St WCHPL E1 140 A9
Chapmans Yd WAT WD17 73 K8
Chapone Pl SOHO/SHAV W1D 11 J6
Chapter Cl HGDN/ICK UB10 132 A2
Chapter Ms WDSR SL4 149 J6
Chapter Rd CRICK NW2 116 E10
WALW SE17 18 D8
Chapter St WEST SW1P 17 J6
Chapter Wy HPTN TW12 175 P7
Chara Pl CHSWK W4 156 A5
Charcroft Gdns PEND EN3 80 C8
Chardin Rd CHSWK W4 156 B3
Chardins Cl HHW HP1 35 J5
Chardmore Rd STNW/STAM N16 119 P6
Chardwell Cl EHAM E6 142 B8
Charecroft Wy WKENS W14 156 G1
Charford Rd CAN/RD E16 141 M7
Chargate Cl WOT/HER KT12 216 G3
Chargeable La PLSTW E13 141 M6
Chargeable St CAN/RD E16 141 L6
Charing Cl ORP BR6 227 J1
Charing Cross CHCR WC2N 11 L9
Charing Cross Rd
LSQ/SEVD WC2H 11 L8
SOHO/SHAV W1D 11 K6
Charlbert St STJWD NW8 3 N7
Charlbury Av STAN HA7 95 J6
Charlbury Cl HARH RM3 105 K7
Charlbury Crs HARH RM3 105 K7
Charlbury Gdns GDMY/SEVK IG3 123 J7
Charlbury Gv EA W5 135 H8
Charlbury Rd HGDN/ICK UB10 112 A9
Charldane Rd ELTH/MOT SE9 184 E6
Charlecote Gv SYD SE26 182 A6
Charlecote Rd BCTR RM8 123 P8
Charlemont Rd EHAM E6 142 C5
Charles Barry Cl CLAP SW4 158 D9
Charles Cl SCUP DA14 185 L7
Charles Coveney Rd PECK SE15 159 N7
Charles Crs HRW HA1 114 C5
Charlesfield LEE/GVPK SE12 183 P6
Charlesfield Rd HORL RH6 280 A3
Charles Flemwell Ms
CAN/RD E16 141 M10
Charles Grinling Wk
WOOL/PLUM SE18 162 D3
Charles II St STJS SW1Y 11 J9
Charles La STJWD NW8 3 N8
Charles Pl CAMTN NW1 5 H10
Charles Rd CHDH RM6 123 N5
DAGE RM10 144 E1
FSTGT E7 141 P2
RSEV TN14 228 C6
STA TW18 173 N9
WEA W13 134 F8
WIM/MER SW19 201 K1
Charles Sevright Dr MLHL NW7 96 G6
Charles Sq IS N1 7 H10
Charles St BARN SW13 156 B9
BERK HP4 33 N5
CAN/RD E16 141 P10
CHERT KT16 195 J8
CROY/NA CR0 203 K10
EN EN1 79 N9
EPP CM16 65 K8
GRAYS RM17 167 N5
GRH DA9 188 E1
HHW HP1 35 M7
HSLW TW3 153 N8
MYFR/PICC W1J 10 E9
UX/CGN UB8 132 C6
WDSR SL4 149 H7
Charleston Cl FELT TW13 175 H6
Charleston Ct CRAWE RH10 284 C10
Charleston St WALW SE17 18 F6
Charlesworth Cl HHS/BOV HP3 35 N8
Charleville Circ SYD SE26 182 A8
Charleville Rd WKENS W14 14 B8
Charlieville Rd ERITH DA8 164 D6
Charlmont Rd TOOT SW17 179 P9
Charlock Wy GU GU1 250 E8
WATW WD18 72 G10
Charlotte Cl BXLYHS DA6 185 P1
STALE/WH AL4 39 K6
Charlotte Despard Av
BTSEA SW11 158 B7
Charlotte Gdns CRW RM5 104 C7
Charlotte Gv HORL RH6 281 H3
Charlotte Ms FITZ W1T 11 H3
NKENS W10 136 G8
Charlotte Park Av BMLY BR1 206 B3
Charlotte Pl WTHK RM20 166 G5
Charlotte Rd BARN SW13 156 C7
IS N1 7 J10
WLGTN SM6 222 D3
Charlotte Rw CLAP SW4 158 D9
Charlotte St FITZ W1T 11 H3
Charlotte Ter IS N1 5 P6
Charlow Cl FUL/PGN SW6 157 M8
Charlton WDSR SL4 148 B8
Charlton Av WOT/HER KT12 217 J1
Charlton Church La CHARL SE7 161 P4
Charlton Cl HGDN/ICK UB10 112 C7
HOD EN11 44 F3
SL SL1 148 G1
Charlton Crs BARK IG11 143 J4
Charlton Dene CHARL SE7 161 P6
Charlton Dr BH/WHM TN16 244 A3
Charlton Gdns COUL/CHIP CR5 240 D4
Charlton Kings WEY KT13 196 F10
Charlton King's Rd KTTN NW5 118 E10
Charlton La CHARL SE7 162 A4
SHPTN TW17 196 F4
Charlton Mead La HOD EN11 45 H4
Charlton Park La CHARL SE7 162 A6
Charlton Park Rd CHARL SE7 162 A5
Charlton Pl IS N1 6 C7
Charlton Rd BKHTH/KID SE3 161 M6
CHARL SE7 161 P5
ED N9 100 C2
KTN/HRWW/W HA3 115 J2
SHPTN TW17 196 D2
WBLY HA9 115 L6
WLSDN NW10 136 B3
Charlton St WTHK RM20 167 J5
Charlton Wy BKHTH/KID SE3 161 K7
HOD EN11 44 F4
Charlwood Cl GT/LBKH KT23 236 A10
KTN/HRWW/W HA3 94 D7
Charlwood Dr LHD/OX KT22 236 C1
Charlwood La RDKG RH5 278 D10
Charlwood Pl PIM SW1V 17 H6
Charlwood Rd CRAWW RH11 283 J3
HORL RH6 279 M7
PUT/ROE SW15 156 G10
Charlwood St PIM SW1V 17 H7
Charlwood Ter PUT/ROE SW15 156 G10
Charlwood Wk CRAWW RH11 283 L4
Charman Rd REDH RH1 257 P10
Charm Cl HORL RH6 279 P3
Charmian Av STAN HA7 115 J1
Charminster Av WIM/MER SW19 201 K2
Charminster Rd LEE/GVPK SE12 184 A7
WPK KT4 200 G8
Charmouth Ct STAL AL1 38 F3
Charmouth Rd STAL AL1 38 F4
WELL DA16 163 M7
Charmwood La ORP BR6 227 L6
The Charne RSEV TN14 247 H3
Charnock SWLY BR8 208 F4
Charnock Rd CLPT E5 120 A8
Charnwood ASC SL5 192 E6
Charnwood Av WIM/MER SW19 201 K2
Charnwood Cl NWMAL KT3 200 B4
Charnwood Dr SWFD E18 121 N1
Charnwood Gdns POP/IOD E14 160 F3
Charnwood Pl TRDG/WHET N20 97 M4
Charnwood Rd EN EN1 80 A2
HGDN/ICK UB10 132 B4
SNWD SE25 203 L5
Charnwood St CLPT E5 120 A7
Charrington Rd CROY/NA CR0 203 K9
Charrington St CAMTN NW1 5 J7
Charsley Cl AMS HP6 69 P5
Charsley Rd CAT SE6 182 G5
Charta Rd EGH TW20 172 F8
Chart Cl CROY/NA CR0 204 B6
HAYES BR2 205 K1
MTCM CR4 202 A4
RDKG RH5 273 H4
Chart Downs RDKG RH5 273 H4
Charter Av GNTH/NBYPK IG2 122 G6
Charter Cl SL SL1 149 L2
Charter Crs HSLWW TW4 153 M10
Charter Dr BXLY DA5 185 P3
Charterhouse Av ALP/SUD HA0 115 H10
Charterhouse Bldgs FARR EC1M 12 E2
Charterhouse Dr SEV TN13 247 H9
Charterhouse Ms FARR EC1M 12 D3
Charterhouse Rd ORP BR6 207 K10
Charterhouse St FARR EC1M 12 D3
HCIRC EC1N 12 B4
Charteris Rd FSBYPK N4 118 G6
KIL/WHAMP NW6 2 D6
WFD IG8 101 N7
Charter Pl UX/CGN UB8 131 N2
Charter Rd KUT KT1 199 N3
SL SL1 128 D9
The Charter Rd WFD IG8 101 K7
Charters Cl NRWD SE19 181 M8
Charters Cross HLWS CM18 46 G4
Charters La ASC SL5 192 C5
Charter Sq KUT KT1 199 N2
Charters Rd ASC SL5 192 E7
Charters Wy ASC SL5 192 E7
Charter Wy GLDGN NW11 117 J2
STHGT/OAK N14 78 D10
Chartfield Av PUT/ROE SW15 178 E1
Chartfield Rd REIG RH2 275 M1
Chartfield Sq PUT/ROE SW15 178 G1
Chart Gdns RDKG RH5 273 H5
Chartham Gv WNWD SE27 181 J6
Chartham Rd SNWD SE25 204 A3
Chart La BH/WHM TN16 263 M1
DORK RH4 272 G2
REIG RH2 257 L10
Chart La South RDKG RH5 273 J4
Chartley Av CRICK NW2 116 B8
STAN HA7 94 E7
Charton Cl BELV DA17 164 A5
Chartridge Cl BAR EN5 76 D9
BUSH WD23 74 B10
Chartridge Grange Dr CSHM HP5 50 C3
Chartridge La CSHM HP5 50 C4
Chartridge Wy HHNE HP2 36 D6
Chart St IS N1 7 H9
Chart Vw BGR/WK TN15 247 P3
Chartway BGR/WK TN15 247 K10
REIG RH2 257 L10
Chartwell Cl CHST BR7 184 G5
GFD/PVL UB6 134 A3
WAB EN9 63 K9
Chartwell Dr ORP BR6 226 G2
Chartwell Pl CHEAM SM3 221 H1
EPSOM KT18 220 B10
RYLN/HDSTN HA2 114 C7
Chartwell Rd NTHWD HA6 92 G7
Chartwell Wy PGE/AN SE20 204 A1
Charville La HGDN/ICK UB10 132 D5
Charville La West
HGDN/ICK UB10 132 C5
Charwood Cl RAD WD7 57 K9
Chasden Rd HHW HP1 35 J3
Chase Cl AMSS HP7 68 F9
Chase Ct RYNPK SW20 201 H2
Chase Court Gdns ENC/FH EN2 79 K7
Chase Cross Rd CRW RM5 104 D8
Chase End HOR/WEW KT19 220 A8
Chasefield Cl GU GU1 250 D7
Chasefield Rd TOOT SW17 180 A7
Chase Gdns CHING E4 100 F5
WHTN TW2 176 C2
Chase Gn ENC/FH EN2 79 K7
Chase Green Av ENC/FH EN2 79 J6
Chase Hl ENC/FH EN2 79 K7
Chase House Gdns EMPK RM11 125 N3
Chase La BARK/HLT IG6 122 G3
CHIG IG7 103 K4
Chaseley Ct CHSWK W4 155 N4
Chaseley Dr SAND/SEL CR2 223 L6
Chaseley St POP/IOD E14 140 D8
Chasemore Cl MTCM CR4 202 A7
Chasemore Gdns CROY/NA CR0 223 H2
Chase Ridings ENC/FH EN2 79 H6
Chase Rd ACT W3 136 A6
BRW CM14 107 H4
HOR/WEW KT19 220 A8
STHGT/OAK N14 78 D9
Chase Side ENC/FH EN2 79 K6
STHGT/OAK N14 78 B9
Chase Side Av ENC/FH EN2 79 K6
Chaseside Av RYNPK SW20 201 H1
Chaseside Cl ROM RM1 104 F7
Chase Side Crs ENC/FH EN2 79 L5
Chaseside Gdns CHERT KT16 195 L7
Chase Sq GVE DA12 190 E2
The Chase ASHTD KT21 237 H4
BMLY BR1 205 N3
BRW CM14 106 G5
BXLYHN DA7 164 C9
CHESW EN7 61 J4
CHIG IG7 102 E5
CLAP SW4 158 C9
COUL/CHIP CR5 222 D10
CRAWE RH10 284 B8
CSHM HP5 50 G5
DAGE RM10 124 G8
EDGW HA8 95 N9
EHSLY KT24 252 G2
GUW GU2 249 M10
GUW GU2 267 M1
HERT/BAY SG13 25 N6
HGDN/ICK UB10 112 B10
HHNE HP2 35 P7
KWD/TDW/WH KT20 239 M7
LHD/OX KT22 236 B1
LOU IG10 101 P1
MNPK E12 122 A9
ORP BR6 227 K7
PIN HA5 113 K4
RAD WD7 74 E1
RBRW/HUT CM13 107 P6
REIG RH2 257 N10
REIG RH2 275 N1
ROM RM1 124 F1
RSEV TN14 247 M2
STAN HA7 94 F7
STRHM/NOR SW16 180 G10
SUN TW16 197 J1
UPMR RM14 126 D8
WARE SG12 26 F5
WATW WD18 72 F8
WLGTN SM6 222 F2
WTHK RM20 167 J5
Chaseville Park Rd WCHMH N21 78 F9
Chase Wy STHGT/OAK N14 98 C2
Chaseways SBW CM21 29 L3
Chasewood Av ENC/FH EN2 79 J6
Chastilian Rd DART DA1 187 H3
Chatelet Cl HORL RH6 280 C3
Chatfield SLN SL2 128 F7
Chatfield Ct CTHM CR3 241 L8
Chatfield Dr RGUE GU4 250 F8
Chatfield Rd BTSEA SW11 157 M9
CROY/NA CR0 203 J8
Chatfields CRAWW RH11 283 L9
Chatham Av HAYES BR2 205 L7
Chatham Cl CHEAM SM3 201 J7
GLDGN NW11 117 K3
Chatham Hill Rd RSEV TN14 247 K7
Chatham Pl HOM E9 140 B1
Chatham Rd BTSEA SW11 180 A2
KUTN/CMB KT2 199 M2
SWFD E18 101 L10
WALTH E17 120 D1
Chatham St WALW SE17 18 G5
Chatsfield EW KT17 220 D6
Chatsfield Pl EA W5 135 K8
Chatsworth Av BFN/LL DA15 185 K4
BMLY BR1 183 N8
HDN NW4 96 F10
RYNPK SW20 201 H1
WBLY HA9 115 L10
Chatsworth Cl BORE WD6 75 M7
HDN NW4 96 F10
WWKM BR4 205 L9
Chatsworth Crs HSLW TW3 154 C10
Chatsworth Dr EN EN1 99 P1
Chatsworth Gdns ACT W3 135 N9
NWMAL KT3 200 C5
RYLN/HDSTN HA2 114 A6
Chatsworth Pl LHD/OX KT22 218 C8
MTCM CR4 202 A3
TEDD TW11 176 F7
Chatsworth Ri EA W5 135 L6
Chatsworth Rd CHEAM SM3 220 G2
CHSWK W4 155 P5
CLPT E5 120 B8
CRICK NW2 136 G1
CROY/NA CR0 223 L1
DART DA1 165 K10
EA W5 135 L6
FSTGT E7 121 L10
YEAD UB4 133 J6
Chatteris Av HARH RM3 105 K7
Chattern Hl ASHF TW15 174 C7
Chattern Rd ASHF TW15 174 D7
Chatterton Rd FSBYPK N4 119 J8
HAYES BR2 206 A5
Chatton Rw CHOB/PIR GU24 230 F3
Chatto Rd BTSEA SW11 180 A1
Chaucer Av HSLWW TW4 153 J8
RCH/KEW TW9 155 M8
WEY KT13 216 B4
YEAD UB4 133 H7
Chaucer Cl BERK HP4 33 L4
BNSTD SM7 221 H10
FBAR/BDGN N11 98 D6
TIL RM18 168 F8
WDSR SL4 149 J9
Chaucer Dr STHWK SE1 19 M6
Chaucer Gdns SUT SM1 221 K1
Chaucer Gn CROY/NA CR0 204 A7
Chaucer Pk DART DA1 187 N3
Chaucer Rd ACT W3 135 P10
ASHF TW15 173 P7
BFN/LL DA15 185 M4
CRAWE RH10 284 C5
FSTGT E7 141 M1
GVW DA11 190 A6
HARH RM3 105 J8
HNHL SE24 181 J1
SUT SM1 221 K1
WALTH E17 101 H9
WAN E11 121 M4
WELL DA16 163 J7
Chaucer Wy ADL/WDHM KT15 215 K3
DART DA1 165 P10
HOD EN11 26 F9
Chaulden House Gdns HHW HP1 35 J8
Chaulden La HHW HP1 35 H8
Chaulden Ter HHW HP1 35 J7
Chauncey Cl ED N9 99 P4
Chauncy Av POTB/CUF EN6 59 M9
Chaundrye Cl ELTH/MOT SE9 184 C2
Chauntler Rd CAN/RD E16 141 N9
Chave Rd DART DA1 187 M6
Chaworth Cl CHERT KT16 214 F3
Chaworth Rd CHERT KT16 214 F3
Cheam Cl KWD/TDW/WH KT20 238 E7
Cheam Common Rd WPK KT4 200 E9
Cheam Park Wy CHEAM SM3 220 G3
Cheam Rd BELMT SM2 220 G5
EW KT17 220 D6
SUT SM1 221 J3
Cheam St PECK SE15 160 A9
Cheapside CITYW EC2V 12 F6
PLMGR N13 99 K5
WOKN/KNAP GU21 214 A10
Cheapside La DEN/HRF UB9 111 J7
Cheapside Rd ASC SL5 192 B3
Chedburgh WGCE AL7 23 N4
Cheddar Waye YEAD UB4 133 J8
Cheddington Rd UED N18 99 M5
Cheelson Rd SOCK/AV RM15 147 H4
Cheeseman Cl HPTN TW12 175 M9
Cheffins Rd HOD EN11 26 E10
Chelford Rd BMLY BR1 183 J8
Chelmer Crs BARK IG11 143 L4
Chelmer Dr SOCK/AV RM15 147 H9
Chelmer Rd CDH/CHF RM16 168 D4
HOM E9 120 C10
UPMR RM14 126 C4
Chelmsford Av CRW RM5 104 E8
Chelmsford Cl BELMT SM2 221 K5
EHAM E6 142 C8
HMSMTH W6 156 G5
Chelmsford Dr UPMR RM14 125 N8
Chelmsford Gdns IL IG1 122 B5
Chelmsford Rd BRWN CM15 87 P7
HERT/WAS SG14 25 H6
RBSF CM22 31 J1
STHGT/OAK N14 98 D1
SWFD E18 101 L9
WALTH E17 120 F4
WAN E11 121 J6
Chelmsford Sq WLSDN NW10 136 F3
Chelsea Br CHEL SW3 16 D9
Chelsea Bridge Rd BGVA SW1W 16 C7
Chelsea Cl HPTN TW12 176 B9
WLSDN NW10 136 A3
WPK KT4 200 D7
Chelsea Emb CHEL SW3 16 C9
Chelsea Flds HOD EN11 26 G9
Chelsea Gdns CHEAM SM3 221 H1
HLWE CM17 47 P2
Chelsea Harbour Dr
WBPTN SW10 157 M7
Chelsea Manor Gdns CHEL SW3 15 N9
Chelsea Manor St CHEL SW3 15 P9
Chelsea Park Gdns CHEL SW3 15 L9
WBPTN SW10 15 L9
Chelsea Sq CHEL SW3 15 M8
Chelsfield Av ED N9 100 C1
Chelsfield Gdns SYD SE26 182 B6
Chelsfield Hl ORP BR6 227 M5
Chelsfield La ORP BR6 227 N1
ORP BR6 228 B4
RSEV TN14 228 D5
STMC/STPC BR5 207 N7
Chelsfield Rd STMC/STPC BR5 207 M6
Chelsham Common Rd
WARL CR6 242 F2
Chelsham Court Rd WARL CR6 243 J4
Chelsham Rd CLAP SW4 158 E9
SAND/SEL CR2 223 L4
WARL CR6 242 E3
Chelsing Ri HHNE HP2 36 D7
Chelston Rd RSLP HA4 113 H7
Chelsworth Dr HARH RM3 105 M9
WOOL/PLUM SE18 162 G5
Cheltenham Av TWK TW1 176 F3
Cheltenham Cl GVE DA12 190 F8
NTHLT UB5 134 A1
NWMAL KT3 199 P3
Cheltenham Gdns EHAM E6 142 B4
LOU IG10 82 B10
Cheltenham Pl ACT W3 155 P1
KTN/HRWW/W HA3 115 K2
Cheltenham Rd LEY E10 121 H4
ORP BR6 207 K10
PECK SE15 160 B10
Cheltenham Ter CHEL SW3 16 B7
Chelverton Rd PUT/ROE SW15 156 G10
Chelveston WGCE AL7 23 N4
Chelwood Av HAT AL10 40 D2
Chelwood Cl CHING E4 80 G10
CRAWE RH10 284 A9
EW KT17 220 C8
NTHWD HA6 92 D8
Chelwood Gdns RCH/KEW TW9 155 M8
Chenappa Cl PLSTW E13 141 M5
Chenduit Wy STAN HA7 94 E6
Cheney Rd CAMTN NW1 5 L8
Cheney Rw WALTH E17 100 E9
Cheneys Rd WAN E11 121 K8
Cheney St PIN HA5 113 K2
Chenies Av AMS HP6 70 A5
Chenies Ct HHNE HP2 36 C1
Chenies Ms GWRST WC1E 11 J2
Chenies Pl CAMTN NW1 5 K7
Chenies Rd RKW/CH/CXG WD3 70 G6
Chenies St GWRST WC1E 11 J3
The Chenies ORP BR6 207 H6
RDART DA2 186 F7
Chenies Wy WATW WD18 92 F1
Cheniston Cl BF/WBF KT14 215 K9
Cheniston Gdns KENS W8 14 F3
Chennells HAT AL10 40 C5
The Chennies HARP AL5 20 B4
Chepstow Av HCH RM12 125 M8
Chepstow Cl CRAWE RH10 284 F7
PUT/ROE SW15 179 H1
Chepstow Crs GDMY/SEVK IG3 123 H4
NTGHL W11 8 E7
Chepstow Gdns STHL UB1 133 N8
Chepstow Pl BAY/PAD W2 8 F6
Chepstow Ri CROY/NA CR0 203 M10
Chepstow Rd BAY/PAD W2 8 F5
CROY/NA CR0 203 M10
HNWL W7 154 F2
Chepstow Vls NTGHL W11 8 D7
Chequers BKHH IG9 101 N2
BRKMPK AL9 40 G1
WGCE AL7 22 G7
Chequers Cl CDALE/KGS NW9 116 B1
HORL RH6 280 B3
KWD/TDW/WH KT20 256 D1
STMC/STPC BR5 207 J4
Chequers Dr HORL RH6 280 B3
Chequers Fld WGCE AL7 22 G8
Chequers La DAGW RM9 144 A6
GSTN WD25 55 J6
KWD/TDW/WH KT20 256 D1
Chequers Orch IVER SL0 131 J8
Chequers Pl DORK RH4 272 G2
Chequers Rd ABR/ST RM4 105 M3
LOU IG10 82 D9
Chequer St STAL AL1 38 C6
STLK EC1Y 12 F2
Chequers Wy PLMGR N13 99 K6
Chequer Tree Cl
WOKN/KNAP GU21 231 K2
Cherbury Cl THMD SE28 143 N8
Cherbury St IS N1 7 H8
Cherimoya Gdns
E/WMO/HCT KT8 198 A3
Cherington Rd HNWL W7 134 E10
Cheriton Av CLAY IG5 102 D10
HAYES BR2 205 M5
Cheriton Cl EA W5 135 H7
EBAR EN4 78 A8
STALE/WH AL4 39 J2
Cheriton Ct WOT/HER KT12 197 K8
Cheriton Dr WOOL/PLUM SE18 162 G6
Cheriton Sq TOOT SW17 180 B5
Cherkley Hl RDKG RH5 255 H2
The Cherries SLN SL2 129 P8
Cherry Acre CFSP/GDCR SL9 90 A5
Cherry Av DTCH/LGLY SL3 150 A1
RBRW/HUT CM13 107 L4
STHL UB1 133 L10
SWLY BR8 208 E3
Cherry Blossom Cl PLMGR N13 99 J6
Cherry Cl CAR SM5 202 A9
EA W5 155 J2
EW KT17 220 G10
MRDN SM4 201 H4
RSLP HA4 112 G8
Cherrycot Ri ORP BR6 226 F1
Cherry Crs BTFD TW8 154 G6
Cherry Cft WGCW AL8 22 G1
Cherry Croft Gdns PIN HA5 93 N8
Cherrydale WATW WD18 72 G8
Cherrydown Av CHING E4 100 E4
Cherrydown Cl CHING E4 100 E4
Cherrydown Rd SCUP DA14 185 N5
Cherrydown Wk
ROMW/RG RM7 104 C10
Cherry Dr BEAC HP9 88 A7
Cherry Gdns DAGW RM9 124 A10
NTHLT UB5 134 A2
Cherry Garden St
BERM/RHTH SE16 160 A1
Cherry Garth BTFD TW8 155 J4
Cherry Green Cl REDH RH1 276 C2
Cherry Gv HYS/HAR UB3 133 J10
UX/CGN UB8 132 D7
Cherry Hl BAR EN5 77 L10
KTN/HRWW/W HA3 94 D7
LCOL/BKTW AL2 55 P1
RKW/CH/CXG WD3 71 L7
Cherry Hill Gdns CROY/NA CR0 222 G1
Cherry Hollow ABLGY WD5 54 G7
Cherry La AMSS HP7 68 F6
CRAWW RH11 283 M4
WDR/YW UB7 152 A3
Cherry Orch AMS HP6 69 K3
ASHTD KT21 237 N4
CHARL SE7 161 P5
HHW HP1 35 J4
SLN SL2 129 N2
STA TW18 173 K8
WDR/YW UB7 151 P1
Cherry Orchard Cl
STMC/STPC BR5 207 M5
Cherry Orchard Gdns
E/WMO/HCT KT8 197 N3
Cherry Orchard Rd CROY/NA CR0 203 L8
E/WMO/HCT KT8 197 P3
HAYES BR2 206 B9
Cherry Ri CSTG HP8 90 A3
Cherry Rd PEND EN3 80 B4
Cherry St ROMW/RG RM7 124 E3
WOKN/KNAP GU21 232 B4
Cherry Tree Av GUW GU2 249 L10
LCOL/BKTW AL2 57 J2
STA TW18 173 L9
WDR/YW UB7 132 A8
Cherry Tree Cl ALP/SUD HA0 114 F9
CRAWE RH10 284 E5
RAIN RM13 145 H4
Cherry Tree Ct COUL/CHIP CR5 240 G4
Cherry Tree Dr SOCK/AV RM15 147 J5
STRHM/NOR SW16 180 F6
Cherry Tree Gn HERT/WAS SG14 24 G3
SAND/SEL CR2 224 A10
Cherry Tree Hl EFNCH N2 117 P3
Cherry Tree La DTCH/LGLY SL3 110 C10
HHNE HP2 36 D3
RAIN RM13 144 F5
RDART DA2 186 G6
RGODL GU7 267 J9
RKW/CH/CXG WD3 90 F2
STALE/WH AL4 20 F1
Cherrytree La CFSP/GDCR SL9 90 A10
HHNE HP2 36 D1
IVER SL0 131 K3
Cherry Tree Ri BKHH IG9 102 A5
Cherry Tree Rd BEAC HP9 108 A1
EFNCH N2 118 A2
HOD EN11 44 F2
SLN SL2 128 G2
SRTFD E15 121 K10
WATN WD24 73 J2
Cherry Trees HART DA3 211 L6
Cherry Tree Wk BECK BR3 204 E4
CSHM HP5 51 J5
WWKM BR4 225 L1
Cherry Tree Wy STAN HA7 94 G7
Cherry Wk CDH/CHF RM16 168 D2
HAYES BR2 205 M8
RAIN RM13 144 G4
RKW/CH/CXG WD3 71 M6
Cherry Wy DTCH/LGLY SL3 150 F9
HAT AL10 40 D7
HOR/WEW KT19 220 A3
SHPTN TW17 196 E4
Cherrywood Av EGH TW20 171 N10
Cherrywood Cl BEAC HP9 89 J6
BOW E3 140 D5
KUTN/CMB KT2 177 M10
Cherrywood Dr GVW DA11 190 B7
PUT/ROE SW15 178 G1
Cherrywood La MRDN SM4 201 H4
Chertsey Bridge Rd CHERT KT16 195 N7
Chertsey Cl PUR/KEN CR8 241 J1
Chertsey Crs CROY/NA CR0 225 H6
Chertsey Dr CHEAM SM3 201 H9
Chertsey La STA TW18 173 H8
Chertsey Rd ADL/WDHM KT15 195 M10
ASHF TW15 174 E10
BF/WBF KT14 215 N7
BFOR GU20 212 D3
CHOB/PIR GU24 213 M6
IL IG1 122 G9
SHPTN TW17 195 P7
SUN TW16 174 F9
TWK TW1 176 F2
WAN E11 121 J7
WHTN TW2 176 B4
WOKN/KNAP GU21 214 D9
Chertsey St TOOT SW17 180 B8
Chertsey Wk CHERT KT16 195 K7
Chervil Cl FELT TW13 175 H6
Chervil Ms THMD SE28 143 L10
Cherwell Cl DTCH/LGLY SL3 150 E5
RKW/CH/CXG WD3 72 B9
Cherwell Ct HOR/WEW KT19 219 P1
Cherwell Gv SOCK/AV RM15 146 G9
Cherwell Wk CRAWW RH11 283 J8
Cherwell Wy RSLP HA4 112 D4
Cheryls Cl FUL/PGN SW6 157 L7
Cheselden Rd GU GU1 268 B1
Cheseman St SYD SE26 182 A6
Chesfield Rd KUTN/CMB KT2 177 K10
Chesham Av HAYES BR2 206 E6
Chesham Cl BELMT SM2 221 H6
KTBR SW1X 16 C4
ROMW/RG RM7 124 E2
Chesham Crs PGE/AN SE20 204 B1
Chesham La CFSP/GDCR SL9 90 B5
Chesham Ms GU GU1 268 B1
KTBR SW1X 16 C3
Chesham Pl KTBR SW1X 16 C3
Chesham Rd AMS HP6 69 H3
BERK HP4 33 P6
CSHM HP5 32 D10
CSHM HP5 33 L9
GU GU1 268 C1
HHS/BOV HP3 52 B4
KUTN/CMB KT2 199 M1
PGE/AN SE20 204 B2
TRING HP23 32 C1
Chesham St KTBR SW1X 16 C4
WLSDN NW10 116 A8
Chesham Ter WEA W13 154 G1
Chesham Wy WATW WD18 72 F10
Cheshire Cl CHERT KT16 214 G3
EMPK RM11 125 P3
MTCM CR4 202 F3
WALTH E17 100 G9
Cheshire Gdns CHSGTN KT9 219 J3
Cheshire Rd WDGN N22 98 G8
Cheshire St BETH E2 13 N1
Chesholm Rd STNW/STAM N16 119 M8
Cheshunt Rd BELV DA17 164 B4
FSTGT E7 141 N1
Cheshunt Wash CHES/WCR EN8 62 D3
Chesilton Rd FUL/PGN SW6 157 J7
Chesil Wy YEAD UB4 132 G5
Chesley Gdns EHAM E6 142 A4
Chesney Crs CROY/NA CR0 225 H4
Chesney St BTSEA SW11 158 B7
Chesnut Av North WALTH E17 121 J2
Chesnut Gv TOTM N17 119 P1
TOTM N17 119 P1
TOTM N17 119 N1
Chesnut Rd TOTM N17 119 P1
Chessbury Rd CSHM HP5 50 F8
Chess Cl CSHM HP5 70 A2
RKW/CH/CXG WD3 71 N8
Chessfield Pk AMS HP6 70 B5
Chess Hl RKW/CH/CXG WD3 71 N8
Chessholme Rd ASHF TW15 174 D9
Chessington Av BXLYHN DA7 163 P6
FNCH N3 117 H1
Chessington Cl HOR/WEW KT19 219 P3
Chessington Ct PIN HA5 113 N2
Chessington Hall Gdns
CHSGTN KT9 219 J4
Chessington Hill Pk CHSGTN KT9 219 M3
Chessington Rd CHSGTN KT9 219 M3
HOR/WEW KT19 219 N3
Chessington Wy WWKM BR4 204 G9
Chess La RKW/CH/CXG WD3 71 N8
Chessmount Ri CSHM HP5 51 J9
Chesson Rd WKENS W14 14 C9
Chess Vale Ri RKW/CH/CXG WD3 72 A10
Chess Valley Wk CSHM HP5 69 L1
Chess Wy RKW/CH/CXG WD3 71 K7

HORL RH6............ 280 F9
KGLGY WD4............ 54 B6
KTN/HRWW/W HA3............ 94 E9
LOU IG10............ 82 C7
OXTED RH8............ 261 J6
PIN HA5............ 113 M1
POTB/CUF EN6............ 60 L4
PUR RM19............ 165 P4
RAIN RM13............ 145 L8
RBRW/HUT CM13............ 127 H4
RBSF CM22............ 30 E3
REDH RH1............ 259 L9
RGUW GU3............ 249 K3
RKW/CH/CXG WD3............ 71 K3
RKW/CH/CXG WD3............ 91 K2
ROM RM1............ 124 F2
RPLY/SEND GU23............ 250 E2
SHGR GU5............ 269 L5
SHGR GU5............ 270 B5
SLN SL2............ 129 N6
SLN SL2............ 129 L6
STALE/WH AL4............ 59 N8
TEDD TW11............ 176 E8
THDIT KT7............ 198 E6
TOTM N17............ 99 M9
TWK TW1............ 176 F4
UPMR RM14............ 126 C10
WALTH E17............ 121 H2
WAN E11............ 121 K6
WARL CR6............ 242 C3
WARL CR6............ 243 J1
WDSR SL4............ 149 J7
WEA W13............ 155 H1
WEY KT13............ 216 B1
WIM/MER SW19............ 201 K2
WLGTN SM6............ 202 E10

Church Lane Av *COUL/CHIP* CR5............ 240 C8
Church Lane Dr *COUL/CHIP* CR5............ 240 C8
Church Langley Wy *HLWE* CM17............ 47 M1
Churchley Rd *SYD* SE26............ 182 A7
Church Leys *HLWS* CM18............ 47 J2
Church Manor Wy *ABYW* SE2............ 163 K3
Church Manorway *ERITH* DA8............ 164 D2
Church Md *HLWW/ROY* CM19............ 27 N10
Churchmead Cl *EBAR* EN4............ 77 P10
Church Meadow *SURB* KT6............ 199 H9
Churchmead Rd *WLSDN* NW10............ 136 D1
Church Ms *ADL/WDHM* KT15............ 215 H1
Churchmore Rd
    STRHM/NOR SW16............ 202 D1
Church Mt *EFNCH* N2............ 117 N3
Church Pth *CHSWK* W4............ 155 P2
    CROY/NA CR0............ 203 N9
    GRH DA9............ 188 E2
    GVW DA13............ 189 P2
    MTCM CR4............ 201 P3
    RYNPK SW20............ 201 J2
    WAN E11............ 121 M3
    WIM/MER SW19............ 201 J2
Church Pl *EA* W5............ 155 J1
    MTCM CR4............ 201 P3
Church Ri *CHSGTN* KT9............ 219 L3
    FSTH SE23............ 182 C4
Church Rd *ABR/ST* RM4............ 85 L5
    ABR/ST RM4............ 105 L2
    ACT W3............ 155 P1
    ADL/WDHM KT15............ 192 F10
    ASC SL5............ 192 F10
    ASHF TW15............ 174 A7
    ASHTD KT21............ 237 J4
    BARK IG11............ 142 F1
    BARN SW13............ 156 D8
    BEAC HP9............ 89 J7
    BERK HP4............ 34 E3
    BF/WBF KT14............ 215 P9
    BFOR GU20............ 212 A3
    BGR/WK TN15............ 247 N7
    BH/WHM TN16............ 244 A3
    BH/WHM TN16............ 245 L10
    BRW CM14............ 86 B3
    BXLYHN DA7............ 164 A8
    CHEAM SM3............ 221 H3
    CHOB/PIR GU24............ 212 E8
    CHONG CM5............ 49 K7
    CHONG CM5............ 67 L9
    CRAWE RH10............ 284 F7
    CRAWE RH10............ 285 J2
    CROY/NA CR0............ 203 K10
    CROY/NA CR0............ 223 K1
    CTHM CR3............ 241 N4
    CTHM CR3............ 242 C7
    DEN/HRF UB9............ 111 M1
    E/WMO/HCT KT8............ 198 C4
    EFNCH N2............ 97 N9
    EGH TW20............ 172 D8
    ERITH DA8............ 164 D4
    ESH/CLAY KT10............ 218 C3
    EW KT17............ 220 B8
    EYN DA4............ 187 P9
    FELT TW13............ 175 K8
    GNTH/NBYPK IG2............ 123 H4
    GRH DA9............ 188 D1
    GT/LBKH KT23............ 235 N9
    GU GU1............ 268 A1
    GVE DA12............ 190 F9
    HARH RM3............ 105 P8
    HART DA3............ 211 L5
    HAYES BR2............ 205 K3
    HAYES BR2............ 226 A4
    HDN NW4............ 116 B2
    HERT/BAY SG13............ 42 D5
    HERT/WAS SG14............ 25 J4
    HEST TW5............ 153 J4
    HEST TW5............ 153 P6
    HHS/BOV HP3............ 36 D7
    HLWE CM17............ 47 M4
    HNWL W7............ 134 F4
    HOR/WEW KT19............ 220 A4
    HORL RH6............ 279 P10
    HORL RH6............ 280 A5
    HORL RH6............ 281 H8
    HORL RH6............ 281 P8
    HYS/HAR UB3............ 132 G10
    ISLW TW7............ 154 C7
    IVER SL0............ 130 F4
    KUT KT1............ 199 L2
    LEY E10............ 120 F6
    LHD/OX KT22............ 236 G8
    LOU IG10............ 81 M7
    MNPK E12............ 122 C10
    MTCM CR4............ 201 N2
    NRWD SE19............ 181 M10
    NTHLT UB5............ 133 N2
    NWDGN UB2............ 153 N2
    ORP BR6............ 226 F2
    ORP BR6............ 227 N3
    PEND EN3............ 80 B10
    POTB/CUF EN6............ 59 L6
    PUR/KEN CR8............ 222 F6
    PUR/KEN CR8............ 241 L1
    RCHPK/HAM TW10............ 177 K7
    RCHPK/HAM TW10............ 177 K7
    REDH RH1............ 275 P4
    REIG RH2............ 275 K2
    RSEV TN14............ 263 P2
    RSEV TN14............ 265 K3
    SCUP DA14............ 185 K7
    SHPTN TW17............ 196 C7
    SLN SL2............ 129 H5
    STAN HA7............ 94 G6
    SURB KT6............ 199 L2
    SWCM DA10............ 189 L2
    SWLY BR8............ 208 E7
    SWLY BR8............ 209 L1
    TEDD TW11............ 176 D7

TIL RM18............ 168 B7
TIL RM18............ 169 H5
TOTM N17............ 99 N8
UX/CGN UB8............ 131 N6
WALTH E17............ 100 D10
WARL CR6............ 242 C5
WAT WD17............ 73 H5
WDR/YW UB7............ 151 N1
WDSR SL4............ 171 N1
WELL DA16............ 163 K8
WGCW AL8............ 22 G5
WIM/MER SW19............ 179 H8
WLGTN SM6............ 202 D10
WLSDN NW10............ 136 B3
WOKN/KNAP GU21............ 231 M5
WOKN/KNAP GU21............ 232 A2
WPK KT4............ 200 B8

Church Rd South *EFNCH* N2............ 97 N10
Church Rw *CHST* BR7............ 206 F1
    HAMP NW3............ 117 M9
    WAND/EARL SW18............ 179 K1
Church Row Ms *CHST* BR7............ 184 F10
Church Side *EPSOM* KT18............ 219 N9
Churchside Cl *BH/WHM* TN16............ 243 P4
Church Sq *SHPTN* TW17............ 196 C7
Church St *AMSS* HP7............ 68 C6
    BAY/PAD W2............ 9 M3
    BGR/WK TN15............ 247 P6
    BRKHM/BTCW RH3............ 274 B1
    BRKMPK AL9............ 40 F3
    BRKMPK AL9............ 41 P3
    CHSWK W4............ 156 B5
    COB KT11............ 235 J1
    CRAWW RH11............ 283 N7
    CROY/NA CR0............ 203 J10
    CSHM HP5............ 50 G7
    DAGE RM10............ 144 C2
    DORK RH4............ 272 F2
    ED N9............ 99 M2
    EHSLY KT24............ 253 L3
    ENC/FH EN2............ 79 K7
    EPSOM KT18............ 220 B9
    ESH/CLAY KT10............ 218 A1
    EW KT17............ 220 D5
    GRAYS RM17............ 167 P5
    GVW DA11............ 190 G2
    HERT/WAS SG14............ 25 L5
    HHNE HP2............ 35 N4
    HHS/BOV HP3............ 52 E3
    HPTN TW12............ 198 B1
    HSLW TW3............ 176 B1
    ISLW TW7............ 154 C9
    KUT KT1............ 199 J2
    LHD/OX KT22............ 236 C8
    MEO DA13............ 189 M8
    REIG RH2............ 257 L10
    RKW/CH/CXG WD3............ 91 P2
    RSEV TN14............ 228 G7
    SBW CM21............ 29 P1
    SL SL1............ 128 B6
    SL SL1............ 149 L2
    SL SL1............ 149 H1
    SRTFD E15............ 141 K3
    STA TW18............ 172 C7
    STALE/WH AL4............ 21 J3
    STALL/RED AL3............ 38 C1
    SUN TW16............ 197 H3
    TWK TW1............ 176 F4
    WAB EN9............ 63 H9
    WARE SG12............ 26 C2
    WATW WD18............ 73 K8
    WDSR SL4............ 149 J7
    WEY KT13............ 216 B1
    WOKS/MYFD GU22............ 232 F7
    WOT/HER KT12............ 197 H8

Church St East
    WOKN/KNAP GU21............ 232 C3
Church Street Est *STJWD* NW8............ 9 M2
Church St North *SRTFD* E15............ 141 K3
Church St West
    WOKN/KNAP GU21............ 232 B3
Church Ter *HDN* NW4............ 116 C1
    LEW SE13............ 161 K9
    RCHPK/HAM TW10............ 177 J1
    FSTH SE23............ 182 B5
Church Vw *EFNCH* N2............ 98 A10
    SOCK/AV RM15............ 166 B1
    UPMR RM14............ 126 A7
Church View Cl *HORL* RH6............ 280 A5
Churchview Rd *WHTN* TW2............ 176 C4
Church Wk *BTFD* TW8............ 155 H5
    BUSH WD23............ 73 P10
    CDALE/KGS NW9............ 116 A7
    CRICK NW2............ 117 J8
    CTHM CR3............ 241 P10
    DART DA1............ 187 L6
    GVE DA12............ 190 G3
    HORL RH6............ 280 A5
    HYS/HAR UB3............ 132 F8
    LHD/OX KT22............ 236 G8
    REIG RH2............ 257 L10
    REIG RH2............ 257 M10
    RYNPK SW20............ 200 F3
    SBW CM21............ 30 A1
    STNW/STAM N16............ 119 J2
    STRHM/NOR SW16............ 202 D2
    WEY KT13............ 196 B10
    WOT/HER KT12............ 197 H6
Churchway *CAMTN* NW1............ 5 K10
    SAND/SEL CR2............ 223 N6
    TRDG/WHET N20............ 97 P4
Church Wy *OXTED* RH8............ 261 L8

Cissbury Rd *SEVS/STOTM* N15............ 119 L3
Citizen Rd *HOLWY* N7............ 119 H8
City Gdn *EDGW* HA8............ 95 M7
City Garden Rw *IS* N1............ 6 D1
City Rd *FSBYE* EC1V............ 6 G2
    STLK EC1Y............ 13 H2
Civic Sq *TIL* RM18............ 168 D8
Civic Wy *BARK/HLT* IG6............ 122 F2
    RSLP HA4............ 113 L10
Clabon Ms *KTBR* SW1X............ 16 A4
Clacket La *BH/WHM* TN16............ 244 B10
    BH/WHM TN16............ 262 C3
Clack St *BERM/RHTH* SE16............ 160 B1
Clacton Rd *TOTM* N17............ 119 N1
    WALTH E17............ 120 D4
Claigmar Gdns *FNCH* N3............ 97 L9
Claire Cl *RBRW/HUT* CM13............ 107 M5
Claire Ct *NFNCH/WDSP* N12............ 97 M4
Claire Gdns *STAN* HA7............ 95 H4
Clairvale *EMPK* RM11............ 125 M5
Clairvale Rd *HEST* TW5............ 153 L7
Clairview Rd *TOOT* SW17............ 180 C8
Clairville Gdns *HNWL* W7............ 134 D10
Clammas Wy *UX/CGN* UB8............ 131 M7
Clamp HI *KTN/HRWW/W* HA3............ 94 F8
Clancarty Rd *FUL/PGN* SW6............ 157 K8
Clandon Av *EGH* TW20............ 172 F10
Clandon Cl *ACT* W3............ 155 N1
    EW KT17............ 220 C3
Clandon Gdns *FNCH* N3............ 117 K1
Clandon Rd *GDMY/SEVK* IG3............ 123 H7
    GU GU1............ 268 D5
    RPLY/SEND GU23............ 251 K2
Clandon St *DEPT* SE8............ 160 F8
Clanricarde Gdns *BAY/PAD* W2............ 8 F1
Clapgate Rd *BUSH* WD23............ 74 A10

Clapham Common North Side
    CLAP SW4............ 158 C10
Clapham Common South Side
    CLAP SW4............ 180 C2
Clapham Common West Side
    BTSEA SW11............ 180 B1
Clapham High St *CLAP* SW4............ 158 E10
Clapham Manor St *CLAP* SW4............ 158 D9
Clapham Park Rd *CLAP* SW4............ 158 D10
Clapham Rd *BRXN/ST* SW9............ 158 F8
Clapham Rd South *IS* N1............ 6 C2
Clapton Common *CLPT* E5............ 119 P5
    STNW/STAM N16............ 119 P5
Clapton Sq *CLPT* E5............ 120 B10
Clapton Ter *STNW/STAM* N16............ 119 P5
Clapton Wy *CLPT* E5............ 119 P9
Clara Pl *WOOL/PLUM* SE18............ 162 D3
Clare Cl *BF/WBF* KT14............ 215 K9
    BORE WD6............ 75 L10
    CRAWE RH10............ 284 D4
    EFNCH N2............ 117 M1
Clare Cnr *ELTH/MOT* SE9............ 184 E3
    NTHWD HA6............ 92 F6
Clare Ct *CTHM* CR3............ 242 F9
    NTHWD HA6............ 92 F6
Clare Crs *LHD/OX* KT22............ 236 F4
Claredale *WOKS/MYFD* GU22............ 232 B5
Claredale St *BETH* E2............ 7 P8
Clare Dr *SLN* SL2............ 108 C9
Clare Gdns *BARK* IG11............ 143 J1
    EGH TW20............ 172 D8
    FSTGT E7............ 121 M9
Clare HI *ESH/CLAY* KT10............ 218 A2
Clare Hill *ESH/CLAY* KT10............ 218 A2
Clare La *IS* N1............ 6 F4
Clare Lawn Av *MORT/ESHN* SW14............ 178 A1
Clare Ms *CHONG* CM5............ 67 P2
Claremont *CHESW* EN7............ 61 N5
    IS N1............ 6 A8
    LCOL/BKTW AL2............ 55 P7
Claremont Av *ESH/CLAY* KT10............ 217 N3
    KTN/HRWW/W HA3............ 115 K3
    NWMAL KT3............ 200 E5
    SUN TW16............ 197 J1
    WOKS/MYFD GU22............ 232 B5
Claremont Cl *BRXS/STRHM* SW2............ 180 C4
    CAN/RD E16............ 142 D10
    CDH/CHF RM16............ 167 P2
    ORP BR6............ 226 D11
    SAND/SEL CR2............ 224 A10
    WOT/HER KT12............ 217 K2
Claremont Ct *DORK* RH4............ 272 C3
    RKW/CH/CXG WD3............ 72 D9
Claremont Dr *ESH/CLAY* KT10............ 218 A4
    SHPTN TW17............ 196 C6
    WOKS/MYFD GU22............ 232 B5
Claremont End *ESH/CLAY* KT10............ 218 A3
Claremont Gdns *GDMY/SEVK* IG3............ 123 H7
    SURB KT6............ 199 K4
    UPMR RM14............ 126 C6
Claremont Gv *CHSWK* W4............ 156 B5
    WFD IG8............ 101 P7
Claremont Park Rd
    ESH/CLAY KT10............ 218 A2
Claremont Pk *FNCH* N3............ 97 H9
Claremont Rd *BF/WBF* KT14............ 215 K8
    BMLY BR1............ 206 B4
    CRICK NW2............ 116 F5
    CROY/NA CR0............ 203 P8
    EBAR EN4............ 77 M4
    EMPK RM11............ 125 H4
    ESH/CLAY KT10............ 218 A4
    FSTGT E7............ 121 N10
    HGT N6............ 118 C5
    KTN/HRWW/W HA3............ 94 D10
    MV/WKIL W9............ 2 B8
    REDH RH1............ 258 B7
    STA TW18............ 172 G8
    SURB KT6............ 199 K5
    SWLY BR8............ 206 F10
    TEDD TW11............ 176 E8
    TWK TW1............ 176 G3
    WALTH E17............ 100 D10
    WAN E11............ 121 J8
    WDSR SL4............ 149 H8
    WEA W13............ 134 F7
Claremont Sq *IS* N1............ 6 A6
Claremont St *GNWCH* SE10............ 160 G5
    UED N18............ 99 P7
Claremount Wy *CRICK* NW2............ 116 F6
Claremount Cl *EPSOM* KT18............ 238 F3
Claremount Rd *EPSOM* KT18............ 238 F3
Clarence Av *CLAP* SW4............ 180 C2
    HAYES BR2............ 206 B4
    IL IG1............ 122 C4
    NWMAL KT3............ 199 P2
    UPMR RM14............ 125 P7
Clarence Cl *BUSH* WD23............ 94 B1
    WOT/HER KT12............ 217 K1
Clarence Crs *CLAP* SW4............ 180 C2
    SCUP DA14............ 185 L6
    WDSR SL4............ 149 H7
Clarence Dr *EGH* TW20............ 171 P7
    PUT/ROE SW15............ 178 C2
Clarence Ms *CLPT* E5............ 120 C1
    GVE DA12............ ...
Clarence Rd *BERK* HP4............ 33 P5
    BH/WHM TN16............ 244 D4
    BMLY BR1............ 206 B5
    BRWN CM15............ 86 C10
    BXLYHS DA6............ 163 P10
    CAN/RD E16............ 141 K6
    CHSWK W4............ 155 M4

CLPT E5............ 120 A9
CROY/NA CR0............ 203 L7
ELTH/MOT SE9............ 184 B5
GRAYS RM17............ 167 N5
KIL/WHAMP NW6............ 2 C4
PEND EN3............ 80 B9
RCH/KEW TW9............ 155 L7
REDH RH1............ 275 N3
SCUP DA14............ 185 L6
SEVS/STOTM N15............ 119 K3
STAL AL1............ 38 F6
SUT SM1............ 221 L1
TEDD TW11............ 176 E8
WALTH E17............ 100 C10
WDGN N22............ 98 C10
WDSR SL4............ 148 G2
WIM/MER SW19............ 179 L9
WLGTN SM6............ 222 C2
WOT/HER KT12............ 217 J1
Clarence Rw *GVE* DA12............ 190 E3
Clarence St *EGH* TW20............ 172 C9
    KUT KT1............ 199 J2
    NWDGN UB2............ 153 L2
    RCH/KEW TW9............ 155 K10
    STA TW18............ 173 H7
Clarence Ter *CAMTN* NW1............ 10 B1
    HSLW TW3............ 154 A10
Clarence Wk *CLAP* SW4............ 158 F8
    REDH RH1............ 275 N3
Clarence Wy *CAMTN* NW1............ 4 E3
    HORL RH6............ 280 E4
Clarendon Cl *BAY/PAD* W2............ 9 N7
    HHNE HP2............ 35 P5
Clarendon Ct *SLN* SL2............ 129 N9
Clarendon Crs *WHTN* TW2............ 176 C6
Clarendon Dr *PUT/ROE* SW15............ 156 F10
Clarendon Gdns *HDN* NW4............ 116 D1
    IL IG1............ 122 C6
    MV/WKIL W9............ 9 K2
    RDART DA2............ 188 C4
    WBLY HA9............ 115 K9
Clarendon Ga *CHERT* KT16............ 214 G3
Clarendon Gn *STMC/STPC* BR5............ 207 J3
Clarendon Gv *MTCM* CR4............ 202 A3
    STMC/STPC BR5............ 207 K4
Clarendon Ms *BAY/PAD* W2............ 9 N7
    BORE WD6............ 75 M7
Clarendon Pth *STMC/STPC* BR5............ 207 K4
Clarendon Pl *BAY/PAD* W2............ 9 N7
    RDART DA2............ 186 B8
Clarendon Ri *LEW* SE13............ 161 K9
Clarendon Rd *ASHF* TW15............ 174 A7
    BORE WD6............ 75 M7
    CEND/HSY/T N8............ 118 C2
    CHES/WCR EN8............ 62 C5
    CROY/NA CR0............ 203 J9
    EA W5............ 135 K5
    GVE DA12............ 190 F2
    HRW HA1............ 114 D4
    HYS/HAR UB3............ 152 G1
    LEY E10............ 120 C4
    NTGHL W11............ 8 A7
    REDH RH1............ 258 A9
    SEV TN13............ 247 H10
    SEVS/STOTM N15............ 119 J2
    SWFD E18............ 121 M1
    UED N18............ 99 P7
    WAN E11............ 121 J6
    WAT WD17............ 73 J7
    WDGN N22............ 98 C10
    WIM/MER SW19............ 179 P10
    WLSDN NW10............ 136 D2
Clarendon St *PIM* SW1V............ 16 F7
Clarendon Ter *MV/WKIL* W9............ 9 K1
Clarendon Wy *CHST* BR7............ 207 J3
    PIM SW1V............ 16 F7
    STMC/STPC BR5............ 207 J3
Clarens St *CAT* SE6............ 182 E1
Clare Pk *AMSS* HP7............ 69 K6
Clare Rd *HSLWW* TW4............ 153 N9
    MDHD SL6............ 128 B8
    NTHLT UB5............ 134 C1
    NWCR SE14............ 160 E8
    STWL/WRAY TW19............ 173 N4
    WAN E11............ 121 J6
    WLSDN NW10............ 136 D2
The Clares *CTHM* CR3............ 241 P10
Clare St *BETH* E2............ 140 A4
Claret Gdns *SNWD* SE25............ 203 M4
Clareville Rd *CTHM* CR3............ 241 P10
    STMC/STPC BR5............ 206 F9
Clareville St *SKENS* SW7............ 15 K6
Clare Wy *BXLYHN* DA7............ 163 P7
    SEV TN13............ 265 K4
Clare Wd *LHD/OX* KT22............ 236 F4
Clarges Ms *MYFR/PICC* W1J............ 10 C7
Clarges St *MYFR/PICC* W1J............ 10 D7
Claribel Rd *BRXN/ST* SW9............ 159 J8
Claridge St *HACK* E8............ 7 L5
Clarissa Rd *CHDH* RM6............ 123 N6
Clarissa St *HACK* E8............ 7 L5
Clarkbourne Dr *GRAYS* RM17............ 168 A5
Clark Cl *ERITH* DA8............ 165 H7
Clarks Av *WPK* KT4............ 200 G8
Clarkes Dr *WDR/YW* UB7............ 131 P8
Clarkes Green Rd *BGR/WK* TN15............ 229 P7
Clarkes Ms *CAVSQ/HST* W1G............ 10 D3
Clarke's Rd *HART* N1............ 40 E3
Clarke Wy *GSTN* WD25............ 73 H1
Clarkfield *RKW/CH/CXG* WD3............ 91 K2
Clarkhill *HLWS* CM18............ 47 H5
Clarks La *EPP* CM16............ 65 J7
    RSEV TN14............ 228 A8
    WARL CR6............ 243 N9
Clarks Md *BUSH* WD23............ 94 B1
Clarkson Rd *CAN/RD* E16............ 141 K9
Clarkson St *BETH* E2............ 140 A5
Clark's Rd *IL* IG1............ 122 G7
Clark Wy *HEST* TW5............ 153 L6
Clarnico La *SRTFD* E15............ 140 G7
Clasford Rd *CHDH* RM6............ ...
Classon Cl *WDR/YW* UB7............ 151 P1
Clatterbury Rd *SEV* TN13............ 265 H4
Claude Rd *LEY* E10............ 121 H6
    PECK SE15............ 160 A8
    PLSTW E13............ 141 N1
Claude St *POP/IOD* E14............ 160 F3
Claudian Pl *STALW/RED* AL3............ 37 P8
Claudian Wy *CDH/CHF* RM16............ 168 E2
Claudia Pl *WIM/MER* SW19............ 179 H4
Claughton Rd *PLSTW* E13............ 141 P4
Clauson Av *NTHLT* UB5............ 133 L5
Clavell St *GNWCH* SE10............ 161 H5
Claverdale Rd *BRXS/STRHM* SW2............ 180 C3
Claverhambury Rd *WAB* EN9............ 63 H5
Clavering Av *BARN* SW13............ 156 F5
Clavering Cl *TWK* TW1............ 176 F7
Clavering Rd *MNPK* E12............ 122 A4
Clavering Wy *RBRW/HUT* CM13............ 87 P10
Claverley Gv *FNCH* N3............ 97 K9
Claverley Vls *FNCH* N3............ 97 L8
Claverton St *PIM* SW1V............ 17 H5
Clave St *WAP* E1W............ 140 B10
Claxton Gv *HMSMTH* W6............ 156 G4
Clay Acre *CSHM* HP5............ 51 H6
Clay Av *MTCM* CR4............ 202 C2
Claybank Gv *LEW* SE13............ 161 H9
Claybridge Rd *LEE/GVPK* SE12............ 183 P7
Claybrook Cl *EFNCH* N2............ 117 N1
Claybrook Rd *HMSMTH* W6............ 157 H5
Claybury *BUSH* WD23............ 94 A1
Claybury Rd *WFD* IG8............ 102 B8
Claycroft *WGCE* AL7............ 23 L4
Claydon Dr *CROY/NA* CR0............ 222 F1

Claydon End *CFSP/GDCR* SL9............ 110 B1
Claydon La *CFSP/GDCR* SL9............ 110 B1
Claydon Rd *WOKN/KNAP* GU21............ 231 M2
Claydown Ms
    WOOL/PLUM SE18............ 162 D4
Claygate Cl *HCH* RM12............ 125 H9
Claygate Crs *CROY/NA* CR0............ 225 N5
Claygate La *THDIT* KT7............ 198 F8
Claygate Lodge Cl
    ESH/CLAY KT10............ 218 D4
Claygate Rd *DORK* RH4............ 272 G4
    WEA W13............ 155 J2
Clayhall Av *CLAY* IG5............ 102 D10
Clay Hall La *CRAWE* RH10............ 285 K11
Clayhall La *REIG* RH2............ 275 H5
    WDSR SL4............ 171 L1
Clayhanger *RGUE* GU4............ 250 F8
Clay HI *ENC/FH* EN2............ 79 K3
Clayhill Cl *REIG* RH2............ 274 F7
Clayhill Crs *LEE/GVPK* SE12............ 184 A7
Clayhill Rd *REIG* RH2............ 274 C8
Claylands Pl *VX/NE* SW8............ 159 H6
Claylands Rd *VX/NE* SW8............ 17 P10
Clay La *BUSH* WD23............ 94 D1
    EPSOM KT18............ 238 D1
    REDH RH1............ 276 D1
    RGUE GU4............ 250 A4
Claymore *HHNE* HP2............ 35 P3
Claymore Cl *MRDN* SM4............ 201 K7
Claypole Dr *SRTFD* E15............ 141 H4
Claypits Av *BTFD* TW8............ 155 K3
Claypole Rd *SRTFD* E15............ 140 F4
Clayponds Av *BTFD* TW8............ 155 K3
Clayponds Gdns *BTFD* TW8............ 155 J4
    EA W5............ 155 J3
Clayponds La *BTFD* TW8............ 155 K4
Clayside *CHIG* IG7............ 102 G7
Clay's La *LOU* IG10............ 82 D9
Clays Lane Cl *SRTFD* E15............ 120 G10
    SRTFD E15............ 120 G10
Clay St *MHST* W1U............ 10 B4
Clayton Av *ALP/SUD* HA0............ 135 K2
    UPMR RM14............ 126 A10
Clayton Cl *EHAM* E6............ 142 C8
Clayton Crs *BTFD* TW8............ 155 J4
Clayton Croft Rd *RDART* DA2............ 187 H5
Clayton Dr *GUW* GU3............ 249 L7
Clayton Fld *CDALE/KGS* NW9............ 96 B9
Clayton HI *CRAWW* RH11............ 283 N6
Clayton Md *GDST* RH9............ 260 A6
Clayton Ms *GNWCH* SE10............ 161 J7
Clayton Rd *CHSGTN* KT9............ 219 H1
    EW KT17............ 220 B9
    HYS/HAR UB3............ 152 F1
    ISLW TW7............ 154 A9
    PECK SE15............ 159 P7
    ROMW/RG RM7............ 124 D6
Clayton St *LBTH* SE11............ 18 A4
Clayton Wk *AMSS* HP7............ 69 P5
Clayton Wy *UX/CGN* UB8............ 131 N6
Clay Tye Rd *UPMR* RM14............ 127 H8
Clay Wood Cl *ORP* BR6............ 207 H7
Claywood La *RDART* DA2............ 189 J6
Clayworth Cl *BFN/LL* DA15............ 185 L2
Cleall Av *WAB* EN9............ 63 H10
Cleanthus Cl *WOOL/PLUM* SE18............ 162 F7
Cleanthus Rd *WOOL/PLUM* SE18............ 162 E7
Clearbrook Wy *WCHPL* E1............ 140 B8
Cleardene *DORK* RH4............ 272 G2
Cleardown *WOKS/MYFD* GU22............ 232 E4
Cleares Pasture *SL* SL1............ 128 A5
The Clears *REIG* RH2............ 257 H6
Clearwater Pl *SURB* KT6............ 199 H6
Clearwater Ter *WKENS* W14............ 156 G1
Clearwell Dr *MV/WKIL* W9............ 8 G2
Cleave Av *HYS/HAR* UB3............ 152 F3
    ORP BR6............ 227 H3
Cleaveland Rd *SURB* KT6............ 199 J5
Cleave Prior *COUL/CHIP* CR5............ 259 P5
Cleaverholme Cl *SNWD* SE25............ 204 A4
Cleaver Sq *LBTH* SE11............ 18 B7
Cleaver St *LBTH* SE11............ 18 B7
The Cleave *HARP* AL5............ 20 C2
Cleeve HI *FSTH* SE23............ 182 A4
Cleeve Park Gdns *SCUP* DA14............ 185 L5
Cleeve Rd *LHD/OX* KT22............ 256 F6
The Cleeve *GU* GU1............ 250 D10
Clegg St *PLSTW* E13............ 141 M1
    WAP E1W............ 140 A10
Cleland Pth *LOU* IG10............ 82 G5
Clematis Cl *HARH* RM3............ 105 K8
Clematis Gdns *WFD* IG8............ 101 M6
Clematis St *SHB* W12............ 136 C9
Clemence Rd *DAGE* RM10............ 144 D3
Clemence St *POP/IOD* E14............ 140 E7
Clement Av *CLAP* SW4............ 158 E10
Clement Cl *CHSWK* W4............ 156 A3
    KIL/WHAMP NW6............ 136 F2
    PUR/KEN CR8............ 241 J2
Clement Gdns *HYS/HAR* UB3............ 152 F3
Clementhorpe Rd *DAGW* RM9............ 143 M9
Clementina Rd *LEY* E10............ 120 E6
Clementine Cl *WEA* W13............ 154 G1
Clement Rd *BECK* BR3............ 204 C2
    CHES/WCR EN8............ 62 D3
    WIM/MER SW19............ 179 H8
Clements Av *CAN/RD* E16............ 141 M9
Clements Cl *SL* SL1............ 149 N1
Clements Inn *LINN* WC2A............ 11 J3
Clements La *IL* IG1............ 122 E8
    MANHO EC4N............ 13 H7
Clements Md *LHD/OX* KT22............ 256 F5
Clement's Rd *BTFD* TW8............ 155 L4
Clement's Rd *BERM/RHTH* SE16............ 19 P4
Clements Rd *EHAM* E6............ 142 C2
    IL IG1............ 122 E8
    RKW/CH/CXG WD3............ 91 P6
    WOT/HER KT12............ 197 J9
Clements St *SWLY* BR8............ ...
Clement Wy *HCH* RM12............ 125 N8
Clenches Farm Rd *SEV* TN13............ 265 H2
Clennam St *STHWK* SE1............ 18 F1
Clensham La *SUT* SM1............ 201 K9
Clenston Ms *MBLAR* W1H............ 10 A5
Clephane Rd *IS* N1............ 6 F1
Clere Pl *SDTCH* EC2A............ 13 H1
Clere St *SDTCH* EC2A............ 13 H1
Clerkenwell Cl *CLKNW* EC1R............ 12 C2
Clerkenwell Gn *CLKNW* EC1R............ 12 C2
Clerkenwell Rd *CLKNW* EC1R............ 12 A2
Clerks Cft *REDH* RH1............ 259 L9
Clerks Piece *LOU* IG10............ ...
Cleton St *SWLY* BR8............ ...
Clevedon *WEY* KT13............ 216 C2
Clevedon Gdns *HEST* TW5............ 153 J8
    HYS/HAR UB3............ 152 F3
Clevedon Rd *KUT* KT1............ 199 M2
    PGE/AN SE20............ 204 C1
    TWK TW1............ 177 J2
Clevehurst Cl *SLN* SL2............ 129 L1
Cleveland Av *CHSWK* W4............ 156 C3
    HPTN TW12............ 175 N10
Cleveland Cl *WOT/HER* KT12............ 197 J10
Cleveland Crs *BORE* WD6............ 75 P9
Cleveland Dr *STA* TW18............ 195 L2
Cleveland Gdns *BARN* SW13............ 156 B8
    BAY/PAD W2............ 8 F4
    CRICK NW2............ 117 K3
    FSBYPK N4............ 119 K3
    WPK KT4............ 200 B9
Cleveland Ms *FITZ* W1T............ 10 G3
Cleveland Park Av *WALTH* E17............ 120 F2
Cleveland Park Crs *WALTH* E17............ 120 F2

Cleveland Pl STJS SW1Y 11 H9
Cleveland Ri MRDN SM4 .... 201 H7
Cleveland Rd BARN SW13 .... 156 C8
CHSWK W4 .... 155 P2
ED N9 .... 100 A1
HHNE HP2 .... 36 C4
IL IG1 .... 122 E8
IS N1 .... 7 H4
ISLW TW7 .... 154 F10
NWMAL KT3 .... 200 B4
SWFD E18 .... 121 M1
UX/CGN UB8 .... 131 N5
WEA W13 .... 134 F7
WELL DA16 .... 163 J8
WPK KT4 .... 200 B9
Cleveland Rw WHALL SW1A 11 H10
Cleveland Sq BAY/PAD W2 .... 9 J6
Cleveland St CAMTN NW1 .... 10 F2
Cleveland Ter BAY/PAD W2 .... 9 H5
Cleveland Wy WCHPL E1 .... 140 B6
Cleveley Crs EA W5 .... 135 K4
Cleveleys Rd CLPT E5 .... 120 A8
Clevely Cl CHARL SE7 .... 162 A1
Cleve Rd KIL/WHAMP NW6 .... 2 F3
SCUP DA14 .... 185 N6
Cleves Av BRW CM14 .... 106 C2
EW KT17 .... 220 E5
Cleves Cl COB KT11 .... 214 F8
Cleves Crs CROY/NA CRO 225 F7
Cleves Rd EHAM E6 .... 142 A3
HHNE HP2 .... 36 C1
RCHPK/HAM TW10 .... 177 H6
RSEV TN14 .... 247 M3
Cleves Wk BARK/HLT IG6 .... 102 F8
RSLP HA4 .... 113 L6
SUN TW16 .... 174 C9
Cleves Wy WEY KT13 .... 196 F10
Clewer Av WDSR SL4 .... 148 F8
Clewer Court Rd WDSR SL4 .... 148 C6
Clewer Crs KTN/HRWW/W HA3 .... 94 C3
Clewer Hill Rd WDSR SL4 .... 148 D8
Clewer New Town WDSR SL4 .... 148 D8
Clewer Pk WDSR SL4 .... 148 F6
Clews La CHOB/PIR GU24 .... 230 F2
Clifden Rd BTFD TW8 .... 155 J5
CLPT E5 .... 120 B10
TWK TW1 .... 176 E4
Cliff End PUR/KEN CR8 .... 223 J8
Cliffe Rd SAND/SEL CR2 .... 223 L2
Clifford Av CHST BR7 .... 184 C9
CLAY IG5 .... 102 C9
MORT/ESHN SW14 .... 155 P8
RCH/KEW TW9 .... 155 N9
WLGTN SM6 .... 222 D1
Clifford Cl NTHLT UB5 .... 133 M3
PLSTW E13 .... 141 M5
Clifford Dr BRXN/ST SW9 .... 159 J10
Clifford Gdns WLSDN NW10 .... 136 F4
Clifford Gv ASHF TW15 .... 174 F2
Clifford Manor Rd RGUE GU4 .... 268 A4
Clifford Rd ALP/SUD HAO 135 J3
BAR EN5 .... 77 L7
CAN/RD E16 .... 141 L6
CDH/CHF RM16 .... 167 L1
ED N9 .... 80 B10
HSLWW TW4 .... 153 L9
RCHPK/HAM TW10 .... 177 J5
SNWD SE25 .... 203 P4
WALTH E17 .... 101 H10
Clifford St CONDST W1S 10 E7
Clifford Wy WLSDN NW10 .... 116 C9
Cliff Pl SOCK/AV RM15 .... 147 H5
Cliff Reach GRH DA9 .... 188 D2
Cliff Rd HOLWY N7 .... 5 K1
Cliff Ter DEPT SE8 .... 160 F8
Cliffview Rd LEW SE13 .... 160 F9
Cliff Vls HOLWY N7 .... 5 K1
Cliff Wk CAN/RD E16 .... 141 H5
Clifton Av BELMT SM2 .... 221 L7
FELT TW13 .... 175 K6
FNCH N3 .... 97 J9
KTN/HRWW/W HA3 .... 94 G10
SHB W12 .... 156 C1
WALTH E17 .... 120 G2
WBLY HA9 .... 135 L1
Clifton Cl ADL/WDHM KT15 .... 195 N10
CHES/WCR EN8 .... 62 D5
CTHM CR3 .... 241 L9
ORP BR6 .... 226 F7
Clifton Ct PECK SE15 .... 160 A6
Clifton Gdns CHSWK W4 .... 156 A3
ENC/FH EN2 .... 78 F8
HGDN/ICK UB10 .... 132 C4
MV/WKIL W9 .... 9 J2
SEVS/STOTM N15 .... 119 N4
Clifton Gv GVW DA11 .... 190 B3
HACK E8 .... 7 H1
Clifton Hatch HLWS CM18 .... 47 K4
Clifton Hi KIL/WHAMP NW6 .... 3 H7
STJWD NW8 .... 3 J6
Clifton Lawns AMS HP6 .... 69 H1
Clifton Marine Pde GVW DA11 .... 190 D2
Clifton Ms SNWD SE25 .... 203 M4
Clifton Park Av RYNPK SW20 .... 200 F2
Clifton Pl BAY/PAD W2 .... 9 M7
BERM/RHTH SE16 .... 160 A1
BNSTD SM7 .... 239 K1
Clifton Ri NWCR SE14 .... 160 D6
WDSR SL4 .... 148 C7
Clifton Rd AMS HP6 .... 68 C1
CAN/RD E16 .... 141 K7
CEND/HSY/T N8 .... 118 D2
COUL/CHIP CR5 .... 240 C1
CRAWE RM11 .... 125 H4
EMPK RM11 .... 125 M2
FNCH N3 .... 97 M4
FSTGT E7 .... 142 A1
GFD/PVL UB6 .... 134 D2
GNTH/NBYPK IG2 .... 122 G4
GVW DA11 .... 190 D2
HTHAIR TW6 .... 152 C10
ISLW TW7 .... 154 B7
KTN/HRWW/W HA3 .... 115 L3
KUTN/CMB KT2 .... 199 L1
LOU IG10 .... 82 B8
MV/WKIL W9 .... 9 K1
NWDGN UB2 .... 153 M3
SCUP DA14 .... 185 H7
SL SL1 .... 149 M1
SNWD SE25 .... 203 M4
TEDD TW11 .... 176 D7
WATW WD18 .... 73 J9
WDGN N22 .... 98 D9
WELL DA16 .... 163 M9
WIM/MER SW19 .... 178 C8
WLSDN NW10 .... 136 G4
Clifton's La REIG RH2 .... 256 C9
Clifton St SDTCH EC2A 13 J1
STAL AL1 .... 38 D5
Clifton Ter FSBYPK N4 .... 119 H1
Clifton Vls MV/WKIL W9 .... 9 H3
Cliftonville DORK RH4 .... 272 C6
Clifton Wy ALP/SUD HAO 135 K3
BORE WD6 .... 75 M5
PECK SE15 .... 160 B6
WOKN/KNAP GU21 .... 231 J1
The Climb RKW/CH/CXG WD3 .... 71 H4
Climping Rd CRAWW RH11 .... 283 L5
Cline Rd FBAR/BDGN N11 .... 98 D7
GU GU1 .... 268 C2
Clink St STHWK SE1 .... 12 G8
Clinton Av E/WMO/HCT KT8 .... 198 B4
WELL DA16 .... 163 H10
Clinton Cl WOKN/KNAP GU21 .... 231 J4
Clinton Crs BARK/HLT IG6 .... 103 H7

Clinton End HHNE HP2 .... 36 D5
Clinton Rd BOW E3 .... 140 D9
FSTGT E7 .... 121 M9
LHD/OX KT22 .... 237 H9
SEVS/STOTM N15 .... 119 L2
Clipper Bvd GRH DA9 .... 166 D10
Clipper Bvd West GRH DA9 .... 166 C9
Clipper Cl BERM/RHTH SE16 .... 160 C1
Clipper Crs GVE DA12 .... 191 J7
Clippesby Cl CHSGTN KT9 .... 219 L3
Clipstone Ms GTPST W1W 10 C3
Clipstone Rd HSLW TW3 .... 153 P9
Clipstone St GTPST W1W 10 F3
Clissold Crs STNW/STAM N16 .... 119 L9
Clissold Rd STNW/STAM N16 .... 119 L8
Clitheroe Av RYLN/HDSTN HA2 .... 113 P6
Clitheroe Gdns OXHEY WD19 .... 93 L4
Clitheroe Rd BRXN/ST SW9 .... 158 F8
CRW RM5 .... 104 D6
Clitherow Av HNWL W7 .... 154 F2
Clitherow Gdns CRAWE RH10 .... 283 P8
Clitherow Rd BTFD TW8 .... 154 C4
Clitterhouse Crs CRICK NW2 .... 116 F6
Clitterhouse Rd CRICK NW2 .... 116 F6
Clive Av DART DA1 .... 186 C2
UED N18 .... 99 P7
Clive Cl POTB/CUF EN6 .... 59 J1
Clive Ct SL SL1 .... 149 J1
Cliveden Cl BRWN CM15 .... 107 L1
NFNCH/WDSP N12 .... 97 M5
SHPTN TW17 .... 196 D6
Cliveden Pl BGVA SW1W 16 C5
Cliveden Rd WIM/MER SW19 .... 201 J1
Clivedon Ct WEA W13 .... 134 G7
Clivedon Rd CHING E4 .... 101 K6
Clive Pde NTHWD HA6 ....
Clive Rd BELV DA17 .... 164 B3
DUL SE21 .... 181 L6
EBED/NFELT TW14 .... 175 H2
EN EN1 .... 79 P8
ESH/CLAY KT10 .... 218 A1
GPK RM2 .... 125 J3
GVW DA11 .... 190 D2
RBRW/HUT CM13 .... 107 H8
TWK TW1 .... 176 E7
WIM/MER SW19 .... 179 P9
Clivesdale Dr HYS/HAR UB3 .... 133 H10
Clive Wy CRAWE RH10 .... 284 D7
EN EN1 .... 79 P8
WATN WD24 .... 73 K5
Cloak La BLKFR EC4V 12 F7
Clockhouse Av BARK IG11 .... 142 E3
Clock House Cl BF/WBF KT14 .... 216 A8
Clockhouse Cl WIM/MER SW19 .... 178 F6
Clockhouse La ASHF TW15 .... 174 C6
CDH/CHF RM16 .... 147 J10
CRW RM5 .... 104 B9
Clockhouse La East EGH TW20 .... 172 E10
Clockhouse La West EGH TW20 .... 172 D10
Clock House Md COB KT11 .... 218 A10
Clock House Pl PUT/ROE SW15 .... 179 H1
Clock House Rd BECK BR3 .... 204 D3
Clock Tower Rd ISLW TW7 .... 154 E9
Clodhouse Hi WOKS/MYFD GU22 .... 231 J8
Cloister Cl RAIN RM13 .... 111 M6
TEDD TW11 .... 176 G8
Cloister Gdns EDGW HA8 .... 95 P6
SNWD SE25 .... 204 A6
Cloister Garth BERK HP4 .... 33 P5
STAL AL1 .... 38 D10
Cloister Rd ACT W3 .... 135 P7
CRICK NW2 .... 117 J1
Cloisters Av HAYES BR2 .... 206 C5
The Cloisters RKW/CH/CXG WD3 .... 91 P1
WGCW AL8 .... 22 C5
WOKS/MYFD GU22 .... 232 E7
Clonard Wy PIN HA5 .... 93 P7
Clonbrock Rd STNW/STAM N16 .... 119 M9
Cloncurry St FUL/PGN SW6 .... 156 C8
Clonmel Cl CHSGTN KT9 .... 114 C6
Clonmel Rd FUL/PGN SW6 .... 157 J6
HPTN TW12 .... 176 C7
Clonmel Wy SL SL1 .... 128 A5
Clonmore St WAND/EARL SW18 .... 179 A5
Cloonmore Av ORP BR6 .... 227 J2
Clorane Gdns HAMP NW3 .... 92 D7
Closemead Cl NTHWD HA6 .... 92 C7
The Close ALP/SUD HAO 135 K1
BECK BR3 .... 204 D4
BF/WBF KT14 .... 215 K9
BRKHM/BTCW RH3 .... 273 N6
BRKMPK AL9 .... 59 H2
BRW CM14 .... 107 J2
BUSH WD23 .... 74 A10
BXLY DA5 .... 186 B2
CAR SM5 .... 221 P5
CDH/CHF RM16 .... 167 N1
CHDH RM6 .... 201 J1
CHEAM SM3 .... 201 H10
CHING E4 .... 101 H8
EBAR EN4 .... 78 A10
GNTH/NBYPK IG2 .... 123 H4
HART DA3 .... 211 N2
HGDN/ICK UB10 .... 131 P2
HGDN/ICK UB10 .... 132 B3
HORL RH6 .... 280 D6
ISLW TW7 .... 154 B7
IVER SL0 .... 130 F5
MTCM CR4 .... 202 A4
NWMAL KT3 .... 199 P2
PIN HA5 .... 113 K5
PIN HA5 .... 113 N5
POTB/CUF EN6 .... 59 K8
PUR/KEN CR8 .... 222 E8
RAD WD7 .... 56 E9
RCH/KEW TW9 .... 155 N9
RDART DA2 .... 187 K6
REIG RH2 .... 275 L1
RKW/CH/CXG WD3 .... 90 B7
SCUP DA14 .... 185 L6
SEV TN13 .... 246 F10
SHGR GU5 .... 268 C10
SL SL1 .... 128 C9
STAL AL1 .... 38 B9
STHGT/OAK N14 .... 153 N10
STMC/STPC BR5 .... 207 H6
SURB KT6 .... 199 K7
VW GU25 .... 194 A5
WARE SG12 .... 26 D2
WBLY HA9 .... 115 P9
WOKS/MYFD GU22 .... 232 E3
Cloth Fair STBT EC1A 12 D4
Clothier St HDTCH EC3A 13 K5
Cloth St STBT EC1A 12 E3
Clothworkers Rd
  WOOL/PLUM SE18 .... 162 G6
Cloudberry Rd HARH RM3 .... 105 L7
Cloudesdale Rd TOOT SW17 .... 180 D3
Cloudesley Pl IS N1 .... 6 B6
Cloudesley Rd BXLYHN DA7 .... 164 A2
ERITH DA8 .... 164 G2
IS N1 .... 6 A6
Cloudesley Sq IS N1 .... 6 B5
Cloudesley St IS N1 .... 6 B6
Clouston Cl WLGTN SM6 .... 222 F2
Clova Rd FSTGT E7 .... 141 M1
Clove Crs POP/IOD E14 .... 141 P4
Clovelly Av CDALE/KGS NW9 .... 116 C2
HGDN/ICK UB10 .... 112 D9
WARL CR6 .... 242 A4
Clovelly Cl HGDN/ICK UB10 .... 112 D9
PIN HA5 .... 113 J1
Clovelly Gdns EN EN1 .... 99 M1
ROMW/RG RM7 .... 104 C9
Clovelly Rd BXLYHN DA7 .... 163 P5

CEND/HSY/T N8 .... 118 E2
CHSWK W4 .... 156 A1
HSLW TW3 .... 153 P6
WEA W13 .... 155 H1
Clovelly Wy ORP BR6 .... 207 J6
RYLN/HDSTN HA2 .... 113 N8
Clover Cl WAN E11 .... 121 J7
Clover Ct WOKS/MYFD GU22 .... 232 A4
Cloverdale Gdns BFN/LL DA15 .... 185 J2
Cloverfield WGCE AL7 .... 23 J2
Cloverfields HORL RH6 .... 280 C3
The Clover Fld BUSH WD23 .... 73 N10
Clover Hl COUL/CHIP CR5 .... 240 C7
Cloverland HAT AL10 .... 40 C7
Cloverlands CRAWE RH10 .... 284 A5
Clover Leas EPP CM16 .... 65 J5
Clover Ley RGODL GU7 .... 267 J5
Cloverley Rd CHONG CM5 .... 67 P6
Clover Ms CHEL SW3 .... 16 A9
Clover Rd GUW GU2 .... 249 K9
The Clovers GVW DA11 .... 35 L5
Clover Wy HNWL W7 .... 281 K4
HORL RH6 .... 281 K4
MTCM CR4 .... 202 B8
Clove St PLSTW E13 .... 141 M6
Clowders Rd CAT SE6 .... 182 E6
Clowser Cl SUT SM1 .... 221 M2
Cloyster Wd EDGW HA8 .... 95 J3
Club Gardens Rd HAYES BR2 .... 205 M7
Club Rw BETH E2 .... 7 L10
Clump Av KWD/TDW/WH KT20 .... 255 P7
The Clump RKW/CH/CXG WD3 .... 71 K9
Clunas Gdns GPK RM2 .... 125 L1
Clunbury Av NWDGN UB2 .... 153 M4
Cluny Ms ECT SW5 .... 14 E6
Cluny Pl STHWK SE1 .... 13 K2
Clutterbucks RKW/CH/CXG WD3 .... 71 K2
Clutton St POP/IOD E14 .... 140 G7
Clydach Rd EN EN1 .... 79 N7
Clyde Av SAND/SEL CR2 .... 242 A1
Clyde Circ SEVS/STOTM N15 .... 119 M2
Clyde Cl REDH RH1 .... 258 B9
Clyde Crs UPMR RM14 .... 126 A9
Clyde Fl LEY E10 .... 120 C5
Clyde Rd CROY/NA CRO 203 N9
HOD EN11 .... 45 J5
SEVS/STOTM N15 .... 119 M2
STWL/WRAY TW19 .... 173 N4
SUT SM1 .... 221 K2
WDGN N22 .... 98 B9
WLGTN SM6 .... 222 D2
Clydesdale PEND EN3 .... 80 C8
Clydesdale Av
  KTN/HRWW/W HA3 .... 115 J1
ISLW TW7 .... 154 F9
Clydesdale Cl BORE WD6 .... 76 A9
ISLW TW7 .... 154 F9
Clydesdale Gdns
  RCHPK/HAM TW10 .... 155 N10
Clydesdale Rd EMPK RM11 .... 124 C5
NTCHL W11 .... 8 C5
Clyde Sq HHNE HP2 .... 36 A1
Clyde St DEPT SE8 .... 160 L5
Clyde Ter FSTH SE23 .... 182 B5
HERT/BAY SG13 .... 25 P5
Clyde V FSTH SE23 .... 182 B5
Clyde Wy ROM RM1 .... 104 F9
Clydon Cl ERITH DA8 .... 164 F5
Clyfford Rd RSLP HA4 .... 112 G9
Clyfton Cl BROX EN10 .... 44 E9
Clymping Dene
  EBED/NFELT TW14 .... 175 J3
Clyston Rd WATW WD18 .... 72 G10
Clyston St VX/NE SW8 .... 195 H1
Clyve Wy STA TW18 .... 195 H1
Coach And Horses Yd
  CONDST W1S 10 G7
Coach House La HBRY N5 .... 119 J9
WIM/MER SW19 .... 178 C7
Coachlads Av GUW GU2 .... 249 L10
Coach Rd BRKHM/BTCW RH3 .... 273 N2
CHERT KT16 .... 214 F3
RDKG RH5 .... 255 K10
Coalbrook Av
  WOKN/KNAP GU21 .... 231 N2
Coalecroft Rd PUT/ROE SW15 .... 156 F10
Coalport Cl HLWE CM17 .... 47 M2
Coast Hi RDKG RH5 .... 271 N4
Coast Hill La DORK RH4 .... 271 P4
Coates Dell GSTN WD25 .... 55 M9
Coates Hill Rd BMLY BR1 .... 185 J9
Coates Rd BORE WD6 .... 95 J1
Coate St BETH E2 .... 7 P8
Coates Wy GSTN WD25 .... 55 N9
Cobb Cl DTCH/LGLY SL3 .... 150 A7
Cobbett Cl CRAWE RH10 .... 284 D5
PEND EN3 .... 80 D3
Cobbett Rd ELTH/MOT SE9 .... 162 B9
GUW GU2 .... 249 L10
WHTN TW2 .... 175 P4
Cobbetts Av REDBR IG4 .... 122 A3
Cobbetts Cl WOKN/KNAP GU21 .... 231 N2
Cobbetts Farm CHOB/PIR GU24 .... 230 F1
Cobbetts Hi WEY KT13 .... 216 C4
Cobbett St VX/NE SW8 .... 158 C6
Cobbetts Wk CHOB/PIR GU24 .... 230 F1
Cobb Gn GSTN WD25 .... 55 J8
Cobbin's Br EPP CM16 .... 64 G3
Cobbinsend Rd WAB EN9 .... 64 A5
The Cobbins WAB EN9 .... 63 K8
Cobbins Wy HLWE CM17 .... 29 P7
Cobble La IS N1 .... 6 C2
Cobble Ms FSBYPK N4 .... 119 K8
Cobblers Cl SLN SL2 .... 128 A3
Cobbler's Wk TEDD TW11 .... 176 D10
Cobbles Crs CRAWE RH10 .... 283 P6
The Cobbles BRWN CM15 .... 107 K3
UPMR RM14 ....
Cobblestone Pl CROY/NA CRO 2 E3
Cobbold Ms SHB W12 .... 156 C1
Cobbold Rd SHB W12 .... 156 C1
WAN E11 .... 121 K1
WLSDN NW10 .... 136 F1
Cobb Rd BERK HP4 .... 33 L5
Cobb St WCHPL E1 .... 13 L5
Cobb's Rd HSLWW TW4 .... 153 N10
Cobden Cl UX/CGN UB8 .... 131 M3
Cobden Hi RAD WD7 .... 74 G2
Cobden Ms SYD SE26 .... 182 A8
Cobden Rd ORP BR6 .... 226 G1
SEV TN13 .... 247 K9
SNWD SE25 .... 203 P5
Cob Dr GVE DA12 .... 191 P6
Cobham CDH/CHF RM16 .... 167 N1
Cobham Av NWMAL KT3 .... 200 E5
Cobham Cl BFN/LL DA15 .... 185 L2
BTSEA SW11 .... 179 P2
EDGW HA8 .... 95 N10
HAYES BR2 .... 206 B7
SL SL1 .... 128 E10
WLGTN SM6 .... 222 F5
Cobham Park Rd COB KT11 .... 235 P4
Cobham Pl BXLYHS DA6 .... 185 N1
Cobham Rd COB KT11 .... 235 P4
CDHV/SEVK IG3 .... 123 H7
HEST TW5 .... 153 K6
KUT KT1 .... 199 M2
WALTH E17 .... 101 H1
WARE SG12 .... 26 E1
WDGN N22 .... 98 E10
Cobham St GVW DA11 .... 190 D3
Cobham Wy CRAWE RH10 .... 284 C1
EHSLY KT24 .... 252 F1

Cobill Cl EMPK RM11 .... 125 K2
Cobland Rd LEE/GVPK SE12 .... 183 P7
Cobmead HAT AL10 .... 40 C2
Cobnor Cl CRAWW RH11 .... 283 J9
Coborn Rd BOW E3 .... 140 E5
Coborn St BOW E3 .... 140 E5
Cobourg Rd CMBW SE5 .... 19 L9
Cobourg St CAMTN NW1 .... 5 H10
Cobs Wy ADL/WDHM KT15 .... 215 M6
Coburg Cl WEST SW1P 17 H5
Coburg Crs BRXS/STRHM SW2 .... 180 G4
Coburg Gdns CLAY IG5 .... 102 G3
Coburg Rd WDGN N22 .... 98 G10
Cob Wk CRAWW RH11 .... 283 P8
Cochrane Cl STJWD NW8 .... 3 M8
Cochrane Ms STJWD NW8 .... 3 M8
Cochrane Pl BFOR GU20 .... 212 C2
Cochrane Rd WIM/MER SW19 .... 179 H10
Cochrane St STJWD NW8 .... 3 M8
Cockbush Av HAT AL10 .... 25 P4
Cockerell Rd WALTH E17 .... 120 D5
Cockerhurst Rd RSEV TN14 .... 228 F5
Cocker Rd EN EN1 .... 78 A4
Cockett Rd DTCH/LGLY SL3 .... 150 B2
Cockfosters Rd EBAR EN4 .... 78 A4
Cock La BROX EN10 .... 44 B5
LHD/OX KT22 .... 236 B3
STBT EC1A 12 C4
Cockle Wy RAD WD7 .... 57 K9
Cockmannings La
  STMC/STPC BR5 .... 207 N8
Cockmannings Rd
  STMC/STPC BR5 .... 207 N7
Cockrobin La HLW CM20 .... 28 D4
Cocks Crs NWMAL KT3 .... 200 C4
Cockshot Hi REIG RH2 .... 275 L2
Cockshot Rd REIG RH2 .... 275 L3
Cockspur Ct STJS SW1Y 11 K9
Cockspur St STJS SW1Y 11 K9
Cocksure La SCUP DA14 .... 186 B7
Code Wk CHPL E1 .... 13 M2
Codham Hall La
  RBRW/HUT CM13 .... 126 G3
Codicote Dr GSTN WD25 .... 55 L10
Codicote Rd STALE/WH AL4 .... 21 L1
WLYN AL6 .... 21 L1
Codicote Rw HHNE HP2 .... 36 B1
Codling Cl WAP E1W 13 P9
Codling Wy ALP/SUD HAO 115 J9
Codmore Crs CSHM HP5 .... 51 K6
Codmore Wood Rd CSHM HP5 .... 51 P9
Codrington Ct
  WOKN/KNAP GU21 .... 231 L4
Codrington Crs GVE DA12 .... 190 F8
Codrington Gdns GVE DA12 .... 190 F8
Codrington Hl FSTH SE23 .... 182 D3
Codrington Ms NTCHL W11 .... 8 B6
Cody Cl KTN/HRWW/W HA3 .... 115 J1
WLGTN SM6 .... 222 E4
Cody Rd CAN/RD E16 .... 141 J6
Coe Av SNWD SE25 .... 203 P6
Coe's Aly BAR EN5 .... 148 C1
Cofers Cir WBLY HA9 .... 115 N10
Coffey St DEPT SE8 .... 160 K8
Coftards SLN SL2 .... 129 P8
Cogan Av WALTH E17 .... 100 D9
Cogdells Cl CSHM HP5 .... 50 A3
Cogdells La CSHM HP5 .... 50 A3
Cohen Cl CHES/WCR EN8 .... 62 D8
Coin St STHWK SE1 .... 12 A9
Coity Rd KTTN NW5 .... 4 D1
Cokers La BRXS/STRHM SW2 .... 181 K4
Coke St WCHPL E1 .... 13 N5
Colbeck Ms ECT SW5 .... 14 E5
Colbeck Rd HRW HA1 .... 114 B5
Colberg Pl STNW/STAM N16 .... 119 M5
Colborne Wy WPK KT4 .... 200 F10
Colbrook Av HYS/HAR UB3 .... 152 E2
Colbrook Cl HYS/HAR UB3 .... 152 E2
Colburn Av CTHM CR3 .... 241 N10
PIN HA5 .... 93 M7
Colburn Crs GU GU1 .... 250 D7
Colburn Wy SUT SM1 .... 201 N10
Colby Rd NRWD SE19 .... 181 M8
WOT/HER KT12 .... 197 H8
Colchester Dr PIN HA5 .... 113 L3
Colchester Rd EDGW HA8 .... 95 P3
HARH RM3 .... 105 M8
LEY E10 .... 121 H5
NTHWD HA6 .... 93 H10
WALTH E17 .... 120 F4
Colchester St WCHPL E1 .... 13 M5
Colcokes Rd BNSTD SM7 .... 239 K2
Cold Arbor Rd SEV TN13 .... 246 E10
Coldbath Sq CLKNW EC1R 12 A1
Coldbath St LEW SE13 .... 160 G8
Cold Blow Crs BXLY DA5 .... 186 E4
Coldblow La NWCR SE14 .... 160 C6
Coldershaw Rd WEA W13 .... 154 F1
Coldfall Av MUSWH N10 .... 98 A10
Coldharbour La BRXN/ST SW9 .... 180 A1
BUSH WD23 .... 74 A10
CHOB/PIR GU24 .... 212 A7
DORK RH4 .... 272 F4
EGH TW20 .... 172 E7
HYS/HAR UB3 .... 152 C1
PUR/KEN CR8 .... 223 H2
RAIN RM13 .... 145 H2
RDKG RH5 .... 272 E9
REDH RH1 .... 259 N10
WOKS/MYFD GU22 .... 233 J1
Coldharbour Pl CMBW SE5 .... 159 L8
Coldharbour Rd BF/WBF KT14 .... 215 J10
CROY/NA CRO 223 H2
GUW GU2 .... 250 A5
HLWW/ROY CM19 .... 46 D2
WOKS/MYFD GU22 .... 233 J1
Coldharbour Wy CROY/NA CRO 223 H2
Coldmoreham Yd AMSS HP7 .... 68 F5
Coldstream Gdns
  WAND/EARL SW18 .... 179 J2
Cole Av CDH/CHF RM16 .... 168 A3
Colebeck Ms IS N1 .... 6 D2
Colebert Av WCHPL E1 .... 140 E6
Colebrook CHERT KT16 .... 214 G4
Colebrook Av WAND/EARL SW18 .... 179 M1
Colebrooke Dr WAN E11 .... 121 N1
Colebrooke Rd REDH RH1 .... 257 P9
Colebrooke Rw IS N1 .... 6 C6
Colebrook Gdns LOU IG10 .... 82 E6
Colebrook Ho POP/IOD E14 .... 141 H8
Colebrook La LOU IG10 .... 82 E6
Colebrook Ri HAYES BR2 .... 205 K2
Colebrook Rd STRHM/NOR SW16 .... 201 P2
Colebrook Wy FBAR/BDGN N11 .... 98 C6
Cole Cl THMD SE28 .... 145 H10
Coledale Dr STAN HA7 .... 95 H9
Coleford Rd WAND/EARL SW18 .... 179 M1
Cole Gdns HEST TW5 .... 153 H6
Colegrave Rd SRTFD E15 .... 121 J10
Colegrove Rd PECK SE15 .... 19 N10
Coleherne Ms WBPTN SW10 .... 14 C8
Coleherne Rd WBPTN SW10 .... 14 C8
Colehill La FUL/PGN SW6 .... 157 H7
Colekitchen La SHGR GU5 .... 270 E2
Coleman Flds IS N1 .... 6 F3
Coleman Green La STALE/WH AL4 .... 21 L6
Coleman Rd BELV DA17 .... 164 B2
CMBW SE5 .... 159 M4

Colemans Heath ELTH/MOT SE9 .... 184 E6
Coleman's La WAB EN9 .... 63 J2
Coleman St LOTH EC2R 12 G5
Colenorton Crs WDSR SL4 .... 148 D3
Colenso Rd CLPT E5 .... 120 B9
GNTH/NBYPK IG2 .... 123 H6
Cole Park Gdns TWK TW1 .... 176 F2
Cole Park Rd TWK TW1 .... 176 F2
Colepits Wood Rd ELTH/MOT SE9 .... 163 L5
Coleraine Rd BKHTH/KID SE3 .... 161 L5
CEND/HSY/T N8 .... 119 H1
Coleridge Av MNPK E12 .... 142 B1
SUT SM1 .... 221 P1
Coleridge Cl CHESW EN7 .... 61 N3
VX/NE SW8 .... 158 C8
Coleridge Crs DTCH/LGLY SL3 .... 151 H7
Coleridge Rd ASHF TW15 .... 118 C4 (sic)
CEND/HSY/T N8 .... 118 C2
CROY/NA CRO 204 B7
DART DA1 .... 165 P10
FSBYPK N4 .... 119 H7
HARH RM3 .... 105 J8
NFNCH/WDSP N12 .... 97 M6
TIL RM18 .... 168 F8
WALTH E17 .... 120 G2
Coleridge Sq WEA W13 .... 134 F8
Coleridge Wk GLDGN NW11 .... 117 K2
RBRW/HUT CM13 .... 107 H5
Coleridge Wy ORP BR6 .... 207 K6
WDR/YW UB7 .... 152 A3
YEAD UB4 .... 133 H8
Cole Rd TWK TW1 .... 176 F2
WAT WD17 .... 73 H4
Colesburg Rd BECK BR3 .... 204 E5
Coles Cl CHONG CM5 .... 67 P2
Coles Crs RYLN/HDSTN HA2 .... 114 A7
Colescroft Hl PUR/KEN CR8 .... 241 H1
Colesdale POTB/CUF EN6 .... 60 F6
Coles Gn BUSH WD23 .... 94 B2
LOU IG10 .... 82 E5
Coles Green Rd CRICK NW2 .... 116 D6
Coles Hl HHW HW7 .... 35 K4
Coleshill La AMSS HP7 .... 88 C1
Coleshill Rd TEDD TW11 .... 176 D9
Coles La BH/WHM TN16 .... 245 M9
Colesmead Rd REDH RH1 .... 258 A7
Colestown St BTSEA SW11 .... 157 P8
Cole St STHWK SE1 .... 18 F2
Coleswood Rd HARP AL5 .... 20 B4
Colet Cl PLMGR N13 .... 99 J7
Colet Gdns WKENS W14 .... 156 C4
Colets Orch RSEV TN14 .... 247 J2
Coley Av WOKS/MYFD GU22 .... 232 D4
Coley St FSBYW WC1X 11 P2
Colfe Rd FSTH SE23 .... 182 B1
Colgate Cl CRAWW RH11 .... 283 L5
Colgrove WGCW AL8 .... 22 F6
Colham Av WDR/YW UB7 .... 131 P10
Colham Green Rd UX/CGN UB8 .... 132 B7
Colham Mill Rd WDR/YW UB7 .... 151 N1
Colina Ms SEVS/STOTM N15 .... 119 J2
Colina Rd CEND/HSY/T N8 .... 119 J3
Colin Chapman Wy HART DA3 .... 210 E10
Colin Cl CDALE/KGS NW9 .... 116 B2
CROY/NA CRO 204 E10
RDART DA2 .... 188 A2
WWKM BR4 .... 205 L10
Colin Crs CDALE/KGS NW9 .... 116 C3
Colindale Av CDALE/KGS NW9 .... 96 B3
STAL AL1 .... 38 B8
Colindeep Gdns HDN NW4 .... 116 D3
Colindeep La CDALE/KGS NW9 .... 116 C2
Colinette Rd PUT/ROE SW15 .... 156 F10
Colin Gdns CDALE/KGS NW9 .... 116 C3
Colin Park Rd CDALE/KGS NW9 .... 116 B1
WLSDN NW10 .... 136 D1
Colinton Rd BCTR RM8 .... 123 L7
Colin Wy SL SL1 .... 148 G2
Coliston Rd WAND/EARL SW18 .... 179 K3
Collamore Av WAND/EARL SW18 .... 179 M1
Collapit Cl RYLN/HDSTN HA2 .... 114 A4
Collard Av LOU IG10 .... 82 F6
Collard Pl CAMTN NW1 .... 4 E3
College Ap GNWCH SE10 .... 161 H5
College Av EGH TW20 .... 172 E9
EW KT17 .... 220 C10
GRAYS RM17 .... 167 N3
KTN/HRWW/W HA3 .... 94 D9
SL SL1 .... 149 K2
College Cl ADL/WDHM KT15 .... 195 N10
KTN/HRWW/W HA3 .... 94 D8
UED N18 .... 99 N6
WARE SG12 .... 26 C3
WHTN TW2 .... 176 C4
College Ct CHES/WCR EN8 .... 62 B6
CHSWK W4 ....
HAMP NW3 .... 3 K2
KIL/WHAMP NW6 2
REDH RH1 .... 258 B7
WDSR SL4 .... 148 G2
College Cross IS N1 .... 6 B1
College Gdns CHING E4 .... 100 G10
ENC/FH EN2 .... 79 L3
NWMAL KT3 .... 200 C5
REDBR IG4 .... 122 B3
TOOT SW17 .... 179 P5
UED N18 .... 99 N6
College Gn NRWD SE19 .... 181 M10
College Gv CAMTN NW1 .... 5 J6
College Hl CANST EC4R 12 F7
College Hill Rd KTN/HRWW/W HA3 .... 94 D6
College La HAT AL10 .... 40 C4
WOKS/MYFD GU22 .... 231 P5
College Ms IS N1 .... 6 B6
College Park Cl LEW SE13 .... 161 J10
College Pl CAMTN NW1 .... 5 H5
STALW/RED AL3 38
WALTH E17 .... 121 K2
College Rd ABLGY WD5 .... 55 J7
BMLY BR1 .... 183 M10
CHES/WCR EN8 .... 62 C6
CHESW EN7 .... 62 A7
CRAWE RH10 .... 283 P6
CROY/NA CRO 3 G7
DUL SE21 .... 181 M3
ENC/FH EN2 .... 79 L3
EW KT17 .... 220 C10
GRAYS RM17 .... 167 P3
GU GU1 .... 268 A1
GVW DA11 .... 189 N1
HERT/BAY SG13 .... 26 A3
HOD EN11 .... 44 E1
HRW HA1 .... 114 D4
ISLW TW7 .... 154 E7
LEY E10 .... 120 B6
NRWD SE19 .... 181 N9
SL SL1 .... 128 E10
STAL AL1 .... 38 D6
SWLY BR8 .... 186 F10
TOTM N17 .... 99 N7
WBLY HA9 .... 115 J6
WCHMH N21 .... 99 H9
WEA W13 .... 134 G8
WIM/MER SW19 .... 179 N9
WOKS/MYFD GU22 .... 232 G2
College Sq HLW CM20 .... 46 G1
College St STALW/RED AL3 .... 38 C6
College Ter FNCH N3 .... 97 J10
College Vw ELTH/MOT SE9 .... 184 A4
College Wy ASHF TW15 .... 174 A7
NTHWD HA6 .... 92 G7
WGCW AL8 .... 22 G4

Collendean La HORL RH6 ... 279 J3
Collens Fld CHOB/PIR GU24 ... 230 D10
Collens Rd HARP AL5 ... 20 A6
Collent St HOM E9 ... 140 B1 回
Coller Crs RDART DA2 ... 188 D8
Collet Cl CHES/WCR EN8 ... 62 C4
Collett Rd SEVS/STOTM N15 ... 119 N3
Collett Rd BERM/RHTH SE16 ... 19 P4
  HHW HP1 ... 35 M6
  WARE SG12 ... 26 C1
Colley Hill La SLN SL2 ... 109 L8
Colley Land RKW/CH/CXG WD3 ... 70 C8
Colley Manor Dr REIG RH2 ... 256 D9
Colley Wy REIG RH2 ... 257 H7
Collier Cl EHAM E6 ... 142 E9 回
  HOR/WEW KT19 ... 219 M3
Collier Rd EDGW HA8 ... 95 M10
Collier Row CRAWE RH10 ... 283 N10
Collier Row La CRW RM5 ... 104 C9
Collier Row Rd CRW RM5 ... 104 B9
  ROMW/RG RM7 ... 104 A9
Colliers CTHM CR3 ... 259 P1
Colliers St IS N1 ... 5 N8
Colliers Water La THHTH CR7 ... 203 H5
Colliers Wd HAYES BR2 ... 226 A2 回
Collier Wy RGUE GU4 ... 250 C4
Collindale Av BFN/LL DA15 ... 185 K4
  CDALE/KGS NW9 ... 116 A1
  ERITH DA8 ... 164 C5
Collingbourne Rd SHB W12 ... 136 E10
Collingham Gdns ECT SW5 ... 15 H6
Collingham Pl ECT SW5 ... 14 E6
Collingham Rd ECT SW5 ... 15 H5
Collings Cl WDGN N22 ... 98 G7
Collington Cl GVW DA11 ... 190 B3 回
Collington St GNWCH SE10 ... 161 J4 回
Collingtree Rd SYD SE26 ... 182 B7
Collingwood Av BRYLDS KT5 ... 199 P8
  MUSWH N10 ... 98 B1
Collingwood Cl HORL RH6 ... 280 C5 回
  HSLWW TW4 ... 175 H3
Colling Wood Cl PGE/AN SE20 ... 204 A1 回
Collingwood Crs GU GU1 ... 250 D9
Collingwood Rd LCOL/BKTW AL2 ... 57 J1 回
  MTCM CR4 ... 201 P2
  SEVS/STOTM N15 ... 119 M2
  SUT SM1 ... 221 L1
  UX/CGN UB8 ... 132 C6
Collingwood St WCHPL E1 ... 140 A6
Collins Av STAN HA7 ... 95 K10
Collins Dr RSLP HA4 ... 113 K7
Collins Meadow HLWW/ROY CM19 ... 46 C1
Collinson St STHWK SE1 ... 18 E2
Collins Rd CRAWW RH11 ... 283 H9
  HBRY N5 ... 119 K9
Collins St BKHTH/KID SE3 ... 161 K8
Collinswood Rd SLN SL2 ... 108 G7
Collinwood Av PEND EN3 ... 80 B7
Collinwood Gdns GNTH/NBYPK IG2 ... 122 C3
Coll's Rd PECK SE15 ... 160 B7
Collum Green Rd SLN SL2 ... 109 K8
Collyer Av CROY/NA CR0 ... 222 F1
Collyer Pl PECK SE15 ... 159 P7 回
Collyer Rd CROY/NA CR0 ... 222 F1 回
  LCOL/BKTW AL2 ... 57 J3
Colman Cl EPSOM KT18 ... 238 C7
Colman Rd CAN/RD E16 ... 141 P7
Colmans Hl SHGR GU5 ... 270 E10
Colman Wy REDH RH1 ... 263 H9
Colmar Cl WCHPL E1 ... 140 C6 回
Colmer Pl KTN/HRWW/W HA3 ... 94 C8 回
Colmer Rd STRHM/NOR SW16 ... 180 F10
Colmore Rd PEND EN3 ... 80 B8
Colnbrook By-pass
  DTCH/LGLY SL3 ... 150 E5 回
  WDR/YW UB7 ... 151 L6
Colnbrook Cl LCOL/BKTW AL2 ... 57 K3 回
Colnbrook St STHWK SE1 ... 18 C4
Colndale Rd DTCH/LGLY SL3 ... 151 H8 回
Colne TIL RM18 ... 169 M2
Colne Av OXHEY WD19 ... 73 J10
  RKW/CH/CXG WD3 ... 91 K3
  WDR/YW UB7 ... 151 M1
Colne Bank STWL/WRAY TW19 ... 150 F9
Colne Cl HOR/NEW KT19 ... 219 P1 回
  SOCK/AV RM15 ... 147 H9 回
Colne Dr HARH RM3 ... 105 N7
  WOT/HER KT12 ... 197 L10
Colne Gdns LCOL/BKTW AL2 ... 57 K3
Colne Md RKW/CH/CXG WD3 ... 91 K3
Colne Orch IVER SL0 ... 131 J8
Colne Rd CLPT E5 ... 120 C9
  WCHMH N21 ... 99 L1
  WHTN TW2 ... 176 D4
Colne St PLSTW E13 ... 141 M1
Colne Va UPMR RM14 ... 126 C1
Colne Valley Trail
  HGDN/ICK UB10 ... 111 M8
  RKW/CH/CXG WD3 ... 91 K3
  STWL/WRAY TW19 ... 173 H4
Colne Wy HHNE HP2 ... 35 H7
Colney Hatch La FBAR/BDGN N11 ... 98 A7
  MUSWH N10 ... 98 B3
Colney Heath La STALE/WH AL4 ... 39 K7
Colney Rd DART DA1 ... 187 N2
Cologne Rd BTSEA SW11 ... 157 N10
Colombo Rd IL IG1 ... 122 F6
Colombo St STHWK SE1 ... 12 C10
Colomb St GNWCH SE10 ... 161 K4 回
Colonel's La CHERT KT16 ... 195 K6
Colonels Wk ENC/FH EN2 ... 79 J6
Colonial Av WHTN TW2 ... 176 B2
Colonial Dr CHSWK W4 ... 155 P3 回
Colonial Rd EBED/NFELT TW14 ... 174 F3
  SL SL1 ... 149 N1
Colonial Wy WATN WD24 ... 73 K5
The Colonnade CHES/BOV HP3 ... 62 C4 回
Colonsay HHS/BOV HP3 ... 36 B5
Colonsay Rd CRAWW RH11 ... 283 L10
Colson Pth LOU IG10 ... 82 D9
Colson Rd CROY/NA CR0 ... 203 L9
  LOU IG10 ... 82 D9
Colson Wy STRHM/NOR SW16 ... 180 D7
Colsterworth Rd
  SEVS/STOTM N15 ... 119 N2 回
Colston Av CAR SM5 ... 221 P1
Colston Crs CHESW EN7 ... 61 J3
Colston Rd FSTGT E7 ... 142 A1
  MORT/ESHN SW14 ... 155 P10
Coltash Rd CRAWE RH10 ... 284 B8
Colthurst Crs FSBYPK N4 ... 119 J1
Coltishall Rd HCH RM12 ... 145 K1
Coltness Crs ABYW SE2 ... 163 L4 回
Colton Gdns TOTM N17 ... 119 K1
Colton Rd HRW HA1 ... 114 C5 回
Coltsfoot WCCE AL7 ... 23 L7
Coltsfoot Ct GRAYS RM17 ... 168 A5
Coltsfoot Dr GU GU1 ... 250 E7
  WDR/YW UB7 ... 131 P8 回
Coltsfoot Pth HARH RM3 ... 105 L8
The Coltsfoot HHW HP1 ... 35 H7
Coltstead HART DA3 ... 211 K9 回
Columbia Av EDGW HA8 ... 95 N10
  RSLP HA4 ... 113 K5
  WPK KT4 ... 200 C9
Columbia Rd BETH E2 ... 7 M9
  PLSTW E13 ... 141 L6 回
Columbia Wharf Rd GRAYS RM17 ... 167 M5

Columbine Av EHAM E6 ... 142 B7
  SAND/SEL CR2 ... 223 J4
Columbine Wy HARH RM3 ... 105 M9
Columbus Gdns NTHWD HA6 ... 93 H7 回
Colveiw Ct ELTH/MOT SE9 ... 184 A5
Colvers HLWE CM17 ... 31 K9
Colvestone Crs HACK E8 ... 8 B1
Colville Gdns LTWR GU18 ... 212 A1 回
  NTCHL W11 ... 8 C5
Colville Houses NTGHL W11 ... 8 C5
Colville Ms NTCHL W11 ... 8 C6
Colville Rd ACT W3 ... 155 N10
  ED N9 ... 100 A2
  NTGHL W11 ... 8 C5
  WALTH E17 ... 100 D10
  WAN E11 ... 121 H8
Colville Sq NTGHL W11 ... 8 C5
Colville Ter NTCHL W11 ... 8 C5
Colvin Cl SYD SE26 ... 182 B8
Colvin Gdns BARK/HLT IG6 ... 102 F3
  CHES/WCR EN8 ... 80 C1
  CHING E4 ... 101 H4
  SWFD E18 ... 101 N2
Colvin Rd EHAM E6 ... 142 B2
  THHTH CR7 ... 203 H5
Colwall Gdns WFD IG8 ... 101 MK9 回
Colwell Rd EDUL SE22 ... 181 N1
Colwick Cl HGT N6 ... 118 C5
Colwith Rd HMSMTH W6 ... 156 F5
Colwood Gdns WIM/MER SW19 ... 179 N10
Colworth Gv WALW SE17 ... 18 F6 回
Colworth Rd CROY/NA CR0 ... 203 P8
  WAN E11 ... 121 K4
Colwyn Av GFD/PVL UB6 ... 134 C4
Colwyn Cl CRAWW RH11 ... 283 H9
  STRHM/NOR SW16 ... 180 C8
Colwyn Crs HSLW TW3 ... 154 B7 回
Colwyn Rd CRICK NW2 ... 116 E8 回
Colyer Cl ELTH/MOT SE9 ... 184 E5
Colyer Rd GVW DA11 ... 190 A5
Colyers Cl ERITH DA8 ... 164 E7
Colyers La ERITH DA8 ... 164 D7
Colyton Cl ALP/SUD HA0 ... 135 H1 回
  WELL DA16 ... 163 H7
  WOKN/KNAP GU21 ... 231 P4
Colyton Rd EDUL SE22 ... 182 A1
Colyton Wy UED N18 ... 99 P6
Combe Av BKHTH/KID SE3 ... 161 L6
Combe Bank Dr RSEV TN14 ... 245 P9
Combedale Rd GNWCH SE10 ... 161 M4
Combe La EHSLY KT24 ... 270 C1
  SHGR GU5 ... 270 A3
  WOT/HER KT12 ... 216 C5
Combemartin Rd WAND/EARL SW18 ... 179 H3
Comber Cl CRICK NW2 ... 116 D8
Comber Gv CMBW SE5 ... 159 K6
Combermere Cl WDSR SL4 ... 148 B2 回
Combermere Rd BRXN/ST SW9 ... 158 G3 回
  MRDN SM4 ... 201 M5
Combe Rd RGODL GU7 ... 267 K9
  WATW WD18 ... 72 G10
Comberton Rd CLPT E5 ... 120 A7 回
Combeside WOOL/PLUM SE18 ... 163 A6
Combes Rd DAGW RM9 ... 144 A2
Combe St HHW HP1 ... 35 M6 回
Combwell Crs ABYW SE2 ... 163 K2
Comely Bank Rd WALTH E17 ... 121 H3 回
Comeragh Cl WOKS/MYFD GU22 ... 231 M5
Comeragh Rd WKENS W14 ... 14 B8
Comerford Rd BROCKY SE4 ... 160 D10
Comet Cl GSTN WD25 ... 54 C10
  MNPK E12 ... 122 A9
  PUR RM19 ... 165 P3
Comet Pl DEPT SE8 ... 160 L6 回
Comet Rd HAT AL10 ... 40 C4
  STWL/WRAY TW19 ... 173 H4
Comet St DEPT SE8 ... 160 F6 回
Comet Wy HAT AL10 ... 40 C4
Comforts Farm Av OXTED RH8 ... 261 L9
Comfrey Ct GRAYS RM17 ... 168 A3
Coniers Wy RGUE GU4 ... 250 E7
Comfrere Rd BTFD TW8 ... 155 H5
  WDGN N22 ... 98 G9
Commerce Rd CROY/NA CR0 ... 202 G10
Commercial Pl GVE DA12 ... 190 F2
Commercial Rd GU GU1 ... 268 A4
  POP/IOD E14 ... 140 D8
  STA TW18 ... 173 K9
  UED N18 ... 99 M6
  WCHPL E1 ... 13 M5 回
Commercial St WCHPL E1 ... 13 L2
Commercial Wy WLSDN NW10 ... 135 N4
  WOKN/KNAP GU21 ... 232 C3
Commerell Pl GNWCH SE10 ... 161 L4 回
Commerell St GNWCH SE10 ... 161 L4
Commodore St WCHPL E1 ... 140 C7 回
Common Cl WOKN/KNAP GU21 ... 214 A10
Commondale PUT/ROE SW15 ... 156 F3
Commonfield Rd BNSTD SM7 ... 221 K10
Commonfields CHOB/PIR GU24 ... 212 E9
  HLW CM20 ... 29 H10
Common Gdns BERK HP4 ... 34 E3
Common Gate Rd
  RKW/CH/CXG WD3 ... 70 G9
Common La ADL/WDHM KT15 ... 215 M5
  ESH/CLAY KT10 ... 218 F4
  GSTN WD25 ... 74 A4
  KGLGY WD4 ... 54 A4
  RDART DA2 ... 187 H5
  SL SL1 ... 108 C3
  WDSR SL4 ... 149 H4
Common Rd BARN SW13 ... 156 D9
  DTCH/LGLY SL3 ... 150 D3
  ESH/CLAY KT10 ... 218 F3
  RBRW/HUT CM13 ... 107 P6
  REDH RH1 ... 276 A2
  RKW/CH/CXG WD3 ... 70 G8
  STAN HA7 ... 94 C4
  WAB EN9 ... 46 B7
  WDSR SL4 ... 148 C3
Common Side EPSOM KT18 ... 237 M1
Commonside GT/LBKH KT23 ... 235 P8
  HAYES BR2 ... 225 P7
Commonside East MTCM CR4 ... 202 D4 回
Commonside Rd HLWS CM18 ... 47 J5
Commons La HHNE HP2 ... 35 P5
The Commons WCCE AL7 ... 23 K8
The Common BERK HP4 ... 34 C3
  EA W5 ... 135 K10
  HAT AL10 ... 40 C3
  KGLGY WD4 ... 54 A4
  NWDGN UB2 ... 153 L3
  STAN HA7 ... 94 C3
Commonwealth Av
  HYS/HAR UB3 ... 133 J8
  SHB W12 ... 136 E9 回
Commonwealth Rd CTHM CR3 ... 241 M9 回
  TOTM N17 ... 99 P8
Commonwealth Wy ABYW SE2 ... 163 Q4
Community Cl HGDN/ICK UB10 ... 111 J10
  HEST TW5 ... 153 J7 回
Community Rd GFD/PVL UB6 ... 134 B3
  SRTFD E15 ... 121 J10 回
Como Rd FSTH SE23 ... 182 D5
Como St ROMW/RG RM7 ... 124 E3
Compass Hl RCHPK/HAM TW10 ... 177 J9 回
Compayne Gdns KIL/WHAMP NW6 ... 2 C1 回
Comper Cl CRAWW RH11 ... 283 H8 回
Compton Av CROY/NA CR0 ... 225 N10 回
  EHAM E6 ... 142 A4 回
  GPK RM2 ... 125 J1
  HGT N6 ... 117 P5

IS N1 ... 6 C2
  RBRW/HUT CM13 ... 107 P2
Compton Cl CRICK NW2 ... 116 C8
  EDGW HA8 ... 95 P8 回
  ESH/CLAY KT10 ... 218 B4
  WEA W13 ... 134 F8
Compton Crs CHSGTN KT9 ... 219 K3
  CHSWK W4 ... 155 K5
  NTHLT UB5 ... 133 L3
  TOTM N17 ... 99 K8
Compton Gdns LCOL/BKTW AL2 ... 56 A2
Compton Pl ERITH DA8 ... 164 A2
  OXHEY WD19 ... 93 M5
  STPAN WC1H ... 11 L1
Compton Ri PIN HA5 ... 113 M8
Compton Rd CROY/NA CR0 ... 204 A8
  HYS/HAR UB3 ... 132 F9
  IS N1 ... 6 C2
  WIM/MER SW19 ... 179 J7
  WLSDN NW10 ... 136 G3
Compton St FSBYE EC1V ... 12 C1
Compton Ter IS N1 ... 6 C2
Comredy Cl ENC/FH EN2 ... 79 J5
Comus Pl WALW SE17 ... 19 J6
Comyn Rd BTSEA SW11 ... 157 P10
Comyns Cl CAN/RD E16 ... 141 L7
Comyns Rd DAGW RM9 ... 144 B2
The Comyns BUSH WD23 ... 94 B2 回
Conaways Cl EW KT17 ... 220 D6
Concanon Rd BRXS/STRHM SW2 ... 158 G10
Concert Hall Ap STHWK SE1 ... 11 P10
Concord Cl NTHLT UB5 ... 133 H5 回
Concorde Cl HSLW TW3 ... 154 A8 回
  UX/CGN UB8 ... 131 P4 回
Concorde Dr EHAM E6 ... 142 C7
  HHNE HP2 ... 35 N2 回
Concord Rd ACT W3 ... 135 N6
  PEND EN3 ... 80 B9
Condell Rd VX/NE SW8 ... 158 D7
Conder St POP/IOD E14 ... 140 D8 回
Condor Rd STA TW18 ... 195 M3
Condover Crs WOOL/PLUM SE18 ... 162 G6 回
Condray Pl BTSEA SW11 ... 157 N10
Conduit La DTCH/LGLY SL3 ... 150 B4
  HOD EN11 ... 44 F3
  SAND/SEL CR2 ... 223 P2
  UED N18 ... 100 B6
Conduit La East HOD EN11 ... 44 G3
Conduit Ms BAY/PAD W2 ... 9 L6
Conduit Pas BAY/PAD W2 ... 9 L6
Conduit Pl BAY/PAD W2 ... 9 L6
Conduit Rd WOOL/PLUM SE18 ... 162 L4
Conduit St CONDST W1S ... 10 C7
Conduit Wy WLSDN NW10 ... 135 P2
The Conduit REDH RH1 ... 259 L5
Conewood St HBRY N5 ... 119 J8
Coney Acre DUL SE21 ... 181 K4 回
Coneyberry REDH RH1 ... 275 M4
Coney Burrows CHING E4 ... 101 K3 回
Coneybury REDH RH1 ... 259 M9
Coneybury Cl WARL CR6 ... 242 A5
Coney Cl CRAWW RH11 ... 283 L5
  HAT AL10 ... 40 E6 回
Coneydale WCCW AL8 ... 22 C3
Coney Gv UX/CGN UB8 ... 132 A5
Coney Hill Rd WWKM BR4 ... 204 K9
Conference Cl CHING E4 ... 101 K3 回
Conference Rd ABYW SE2 ... 163 M3 回
Conford Dr RGUE GU4 ... 268 B7
Congleton Gv WOOL/PLUM SE18 ... 162 F4
Congo Rd WOOL/PLUM SE18 ... 162 G4
Congress Rd ABYW SE2 ... 163 M3
Congreve Rd ELTH/MOT SE9 ... 162 C9
  WAB EN9 ... 63 K9
Congreve St WALW SE17 ... 19 J6
Conical Cnr ENC/FH EN2 ... 79 K6
Conifer Av CRW RM5 ... 104 C6 回
Conifer Cl CHESW EN7 ... 61 N5
  ORP BR6 ... 226 G1
  REIG RH2 ... 259 H6
Conifer Dr BRW CM14 ... 104 G4
Conifer Gdns EN EN1 ... 79 N10
  STRHM/NOR SW16 ... 180 G6
  SUT SM1 ... 201 L9 回
Conifer La EGH TW20 ... 172 F8
Conifers WEY KT13 ... 216 F1 回
Conifers Cl TEDD TW11 ... 177 N10 回
Conifer Wy ALP/SUD HA0 ... 115 N8
  HYS/HAR UB3 ... 133 J9 回
  SWLY BR8 ... 208 B1
Coniger Rd FUL/PGN SW6 ... 157 K8
Coningesby Dr WAT WD17 ... 72 B1
Coningham Ms SHB W12 ... 136 D10 回
Coningham Rd SHB W12 ... 156 E1
Coningsby Bank STAL AL1 ... 38 B10
Coningsby Cottages EA W5 ... 155 J1 回
Coningsby Dr POTB/CUF EN6 ... 59 N9
Coningsby Gdns CHING E4 ... 100 G7
Coningsby Rd EA W5 ... 155 H1
  FSBYPK N4 ... 119 J3 回
  SAND/SEL CR2 ... 223 K5
Conington Rd LEW SE13 ... 160 G8
Conisbee Ct STHGT/OAK N14 ... 78 D9 回
Conisborough Crs CAT SE6 ... 183 H7 回
Coniscliffe Cl CHST BR7 ... 206 F1 回
Coniscliffe Rd PLMGR N13 ... 99 N1
Conista Ct WOKN/KNAP GU21 ... 231 L2 回
Coniston Av BARK IG11 ... 143 H2 回
  GFD/PVL UB6 ... 134 C6
  UPMR RM14 ... 126 B9
  WELL DA16 ... 163 P9
Coniston Cl BARN SW13 ... 156 C6 回
  BXLYHN DA7 ... 164 D7
  CHSWK W4 ... 155 P7
  CRAWW RH11 ... 282 G9 回
  DART DA1 ... 187 J4
  ERITH DA8 ... 164 D7
  HHS/BOV HP3 ... 36 D7 回
  MRDN SM4 ... 200 G6
Coniston Crescent SL SL1 ... 128 B7
Conistone Wy HOLWY N7 ... 5 M3
Coniston Gdns BELMT SM2 ... 221 N5 回
  CDALE/KGS NW9 ... 116 A3
  ED N9 ... 100 B2
  PIN HA5 ... 113 H2
  REDBR IG4 ... 121 N2
  WBLY HA9 ... 115 H5
Coniston Rd BMLY BR1 ... 183 N5
  BXLYHN DA7 ... 164 D7
  COUL/CHIP CR5 ... 240 D2
  KGLGY WD4 ... 54 A4
  MUSWH N10 ... 98 C10
  TOTM N17 ... 99 P7
  WHTN TW2 ... 176 A2
  WOKS/MYFD GU22 ... 232 C6
Coniston Cl CHSGTN KT9 ... 199 K10 回
  EGH TW20 ... 172 E10 回
  HCH RM12 ... 145 J8
  REDH RH1 ... 259 P9
Coniston Bank NWMAL KT3 ... 200 B4 回
Coniston Cl CRAWW RH11 ... 283 M1 回
  EDGW HA8 ... 95 M4
  HSLW TW3 ... 153 P10
Coniston Cnr WCHMH N21 ... 99 J2

EN EN1 ... 79 M6
  HSLWW TW4 ... 175 H1
  LOU IG10 ... 82 A8
  MORT/ESHN SW14 ... 155 P9
Connaught Br CAN/RD E16 ... 142 A10
Connaught Cl BAY/PAD W2 ... 9 J2
  EN EN1 ... 79 M6 回
  HHNE HP2 ... 36 B4
  SUT SM1 ... 201 N9 回
  UX/CGN UB8 ... 132 D7 回
Connaught Crs CHOB/PIR GU24 ... 230 E6
Connaught Dr GLDGN NW11 ... 117 K2
  WEY KT13 ... 216 A7 回
Connaught Gdns BERK HP4 ... 33 L2 回
  CRAWH RH11 ... 283 N5 回
  MRDN SM4 ... 201 N5
  MUSWH N10 ... 118 C3
  PLMGR N13 ... 99 J8
Connaught Hl LOU IG10 ... 82 A7
Connaught La IL IG1 ... 122 F6
Connaught Ms BAY/PAD W2 ... 9 P6
  WOOL/PLUM SE18 ... 162 D4
Connaught Pl BAY/PAD W2 ... 10 A2
Connaught Rd BAR EN5 ... 76 C10
  CAN/RD E16 ... 141 P9
  CHING E4 ... 101 L1 回
  CHOB/PIR GU24 ... 230 E6
  FSBYPK N4 ... 119 H5
  HARP AL5 ... 20 A1 回
  HCH RM12 ... 125 L3
  HPTN TW12 ... 176 C8
  IL IG1 ... 122 G7
  KTN/HRWW/W HA3 ... 94 E9
  NWMAL KT3 ... 200 B4
  RCHPK/HAM TW10 ... 177 M7
  SL SL1 ... 149 N1 回
  STALW/RED AL3 ... 38 B4
  SUT SM1 ... 201 N9
  WALTH E17 ... 120 F3 回
  WAN E11 ... 121 J6
  WEA W13 ... 134 G9 回
  WLSDN NW10 ... 136 B3 回
  WOOL/PLUM SE18 ... 162 D4
Connaught Sq BAY/PAD W2 ... 9 P6
Connaught St BAY/PAD W2 ... 9 P6
Connaught Wy PLMGR N13 ... 99 J5
Connell Crs EA W5 ... 135 L6
Connemara Cl BORE WD6 ... 76 A10 回
Connington Crs CHING E4 ... 101 M1
Connop Rd PEND EN3 ... 80 C4
Connor Rd DAGW RM9 ... 124 A9
Connor St HOM E9 ... 140 C5 回
Conolly Rd HNWL W7 ... 134 D10
Conquerors HI STALE/WH AL4 ... 21 K3
Conquest Rd ADL/WDHM KT15 ... 215 K2
Conrad Cl CDH/CHF RM16 ... 167 N1
Conrad Dr WPK KT4 ... 200 F8
Conrad Gdns CDH/CHF RM16 ... 167 M1
Consfield Av NWMAL KT3 ... 200 D2
Consort Cl BRW CM14 ... 107 H6
  FBAR/BDGN N11 ... 98 A6
Consort Ms ISLW TW7 ... 176 C2
Consort Rd PECK SE15 ... 160 A8 回
Consort Wy HORL RH6 ... 280 B6
Consort Wy East HORL RH6 ... 280 C5
Cons St STHWK SE1 ... 18 E1 回
Constable Cl GLDGN NW11 ... 117 L4
  YEAD UB4 ... 132 D4 回
Constable Crs SEVS/STOTM N15 ... 119 P3
Constable Gdns EDGW HA8 ... 96 B6
  ISLW TW7 ... 176 C1
Constable Ms BCTR RM8 ... 123 L10 回
Constable Rd CROY/NA CR0 ... 203 J7
  EN EN1 ... 79 N10
  SUT SM1 ... 221 M1
  WHTN TW2 ... 176 A3
Constance St CAN/RD E16 ... 142 B10 回
Constantine Rd HAMP NW3 ... 3 P4 回
Constitution Hl GVE DA12 ... 190 F4
  WHALL SW1A ... 16 E1
  WOKS/MYFD GU22 ... 232 B4
Constitution Ri WOOL/PLUM SE18 ... 162 D7
Content St WALW SE17 ... 18 F6
Contessa Cl ORP BR6 ... 227 H2
Control Tower Rd HTHAIR TW6 ... 152 B9
Convent Cl BECK BR3 ... 183 H10
  WDSR SL4 ... 148 F8
Convent Gdns EA W5 ... 155 K3
  NTCHL W11 ... 8 C6
Convent Hl NRWD SE19 ... 181 K9
Convent Rd ASHF TW15 ... 174 C2
  WDSR SL4 ... 148 F8
Convent Wy NWDGN UB2 ... 153 K3
Conway Cl RAIN RM13 ... 145 H2 回
  STAN HA7 ... 94 F7 回
Conway Crs CHDH RM6 ... 123 M5
  GFD/PVL UB6 ... 134 D4
Conway Dr ASHF TW15 ... 174 D10
  BELMT SM2 ... 221 L3
  HYS/HAR UB3 ... 152 D2
Conway Gdns ENC/FH EN2 ... 79 M4
  GRAYS RM17 ... 167 N6
  MTCM CR4 ... 202 A4
  WBLY HA9 ... 115 H5
Conway Gv ACT W3 ... 115 K5
Conway Ms FITZ W1T ... 10 G2 回
Conway Rd CRICK NW2 ... 116 F7
  FELT TW13 ... 175 L8
  HSLWW TW4 ... 175 H3
  MDHD SL6 ... 128 A8
  RYNPK SW20 ... 200 F1 回
  SEVS/STOTM N15 ... 119 K3 回
  STHGT/OAK N14 ... 98 H4
  WOOL/PLUM SE18 ... 162 G4 回
Conway St FITZ W1T ... 10 G3 回
Conybeare HAMP NW3 ... 3 P4 回
Conybury Cl WAB EN9 ... 63 M8
Conyers HLW CM20 ... 28 F9
Conyers Cl WOT/HER KT12 ... 217 L2
Conyer's Rd STRHM/NOR SW16 ... 180 L2
Conyer St BOW E3 ... 140 D4 回
Conyers Wy LOU IG10 ... 82 G7
Cooden Cl BMLY BR1 ... 183 N10
Cookes Cl WAN E11 ... 121 L7
Cookes La CHEAM SM3 ... 221 H3
Cookham Cl NWDGN UB2 ... 154 A2
Cookham Dene Cl CHST BR7 ... 206 G3
Cookham Rd SWLY BR8 ... 208 B1
Cookhill Rd ABYW SE2 ... 163 L1
Cook's Cl CRW RM5 ... 104 E4
Cooks Ferry Rbt UED N18 ... 100 D6
Cook's Hole Rd ENC/FH EN2 ... 79 J4
Cooks Md BUSH WD23 ... 74 A10
  HORS RH12 ... 282 A6
Cooksons Gv ERIT*/ DA8 ... 164 C6
Cook's Rd SRTFD E15 ... 140 G2
  WALW SE17 ... 18 C9 回
Cooks Spinney HLW CM20 ... 29 K9
Cooks Vennel HHW HP1 ... 35 L4 回
Cook's Wy HAT AL10 ... 40 C6
Coolfin Rd CAN/RD E16 ... 141 M8
Coolgardie Av CHIG IG7 ... 102 A4 回
  CHING E4 ... 101 N4
Coolgardie Rd ASHF TW15 ... 174 C10 回
Coolhurst Rd CEND/HSY/T N8 ... 118 C4
Cool Oak Br CDALE/KGS NW9 ... 116 C5
Cool Oak La CDALE/KGS NW9 ... 116 C5
Coomassie Rd MV/WKIL W9 ... 137 N3 回
Coombe Av CROY/NA CR0 ... 223 N4
  RSEV TN14 ... 247 H5
Coombe Bank NWMAL KT3 ... 200 F4 回
Coombe Cl CRAWW RH11 ... 283 N11 回
  EDGW HA8 ... 95 H4
  HSLW TW3 ... 153 P10 回

Coombe Crs HPTN TW12 ... 175 M10
Coombe Dr ADL/WDHM KT15 ... 215 J3
  RSLP HA4 ... 113 J6
Coombe End KUTN/CMB KT2 ... 178 A10
Coombefield Cl NWMAL KT3 ... 200 B5 回
Coombe Gdns BERK HP4 ... 33 L4
  NWMAL KT3 ... 200 D3
  RYNPK SW20 ... 200 B3
Coombe Hill Ct WDSR SL4 ... 148 C10
Coombe Hill Gld KUTN/CMB KT2 ... 178 B10
Coombe Hill Rd KUTN/CMB KT2 ... 178 B10
  RKW/CH/CXG WD3 ... 91 K1
Coombe House Cha NWMAL KT3 ... 200 A1 回
Coombehurst Cl EBAR EN4 ... 78 A1
Coombelands La
  ADL/WDHM KT15 ... 215 K3
Coombe La CROY/NA CR0 ... 224 A2
  RGUW GU3 ... 249 H4
Coombe La West KUTN/CMB KT2 ... 199 P3
  NWMAL KT3 ... 178 B10
Coombe Lea BMLY BR1 ... 206 B3
Coombe Ldg CHARL SE7 ... 161 P4
Coombe Mnr CHOB/PIR GU24 ... 230 F1 回
Coombe Neville KUTN/CMB KT2 ... 177 P8
Coombe Pk KUTN/CMB KT2 ... 177 P8
Coombe Ridings KUTN/CMB KT2 ... 177 P5
Coombe Ri BRW CM14 ... 107 L2 回
  KUTN/CMB KT2 ... 199 P1
Coombe Rd BUSH WD23 ... 94 B3
  CHSWK W4 ... 156 B4
  CROY/NA CR0 ... 223 N4
  GVE DA12 ... 190 F5
  HARH RM3 ... 125 N1
  HPTN TW12 ... 175 M9
  KUTN/CMB KT2 ... 199 M1
  NWMAL KT3 ... 200 B3
  RSEV TN14 ... 247 K5
  SAND/SEL CR2 ... 223 M1
  SYD SE26 ... 182 A3
  WDGN N22 ... 99 H10 回
  WEA W13 ... 154 G2 回
  WLSDN NW10 ... 116 A8
Coombes Rd DAGW RM9 ... 144 A4
  LCOL/BKTW AL2 ... 57 H2
The Coombe BRKHM/BTCW RH3 ... 256 A7
Coombe V CFSP/GDCR SL9 ... 110 B6
Coombe Wd HF/WBF KT14 ... 216 A8 回
Coombe-wood Dr CHDH RM6 ... 124 A4
Coombe Wood Hl PUR/KEN CR8 ... 223 N4 回
Coombe Wood Rd
  KUTN/CMB KT2 ... 177 P8
Coombfield Dr RDART DA2 ... 188 C7
Coombs St IS N1 ... 6 D8
Coomer Pl FUL/PGN SW6 ... 14 E4
Cooperage Cl TOTM N17 ... 99 N7
Cooper Av WALTH E17 ... 101 K3
Cooper Cl GRH DA9 ... 188 D1
  HORL RH6 ... 281 H4
Cooper Crs CAR SM5 ... 202 A10
Cooper Rd BFOR GU20 ... 212 C3
  CRICK NW2 ... 116 D10
  CROY/NA CR0 ... 223 H2
  GU GU1 ... 268 B2
  HDN NW4 ... 116 G4 回
Cooper Rw CRAWE RH10 ... 283 N10
Coopersale Common EPP CM16 ... 65 N3
Coopersale La EPP CM16 ... 83 K3
Coopersale Rd HOM E9 ... 120 C10
Coopers Cl CHIG IG7 ... 103 L3
  DAGE RM10 ... 144 C1
  EYN DA4 ... 210 B1
  STA TW18 ... 173 H8 回
  WCHPL E1 ... 140 B6
Coopers Crs BORE WD6 ... 75 P5
Coopers Green La HAT AL10 ... 21 P10
  STALE/WH AL4 ... 39 L3
  WCCW AL8 ... 22 C9
Cooper Shaw Rd TIL RM18 ... 168 G6
Coopers HI CHONG CM5 ... 67 P3
Coopers Hill Dr CHOB/PIR GU24 ... 230 B6
Cooper's Hill La EGH TW20 ... 171 P6
Cooper's Hill Rd REDH RH1 ... 258 C5
Coopers La LEE/GVPK SE12 ... 183 N5
  LEY E10 ... 120 G6
  POTB/CUF EN6 ... 59 P5
Cooper's Lane Rd POTB/CUF EN6 ... 60 B9
Cooper's Rd GVW DA11 ... 190 B4
  POTB/CUF EN6 ... 59 M8
  STHWK SE1 ... 19 M8
Coopers Rw IVER SL0 ... 130 F6
  TWRH EC3N ... 13 L7
Cooper St CAN/RD E16 ... 141 L7 回
Cooper's Yd NRWD SE19 ... 181 M9
Cooper Wy SL SL1 ... 148 G2
Coote Rd BCTR RM8 ... 124 A8
  BXLYHN DA7 ... 164 A7
Copeland Dr POP/IOD E14 ... 160 F3 回
Copeland Rd LEY E10 ... 120 G3
  PECK SE15 ... 159 P8
Copeman Cl SYD SE26 ... 182 D3
Copenhagen Pl POP/IOD E14 ... 140 L8 回
Copenhagen St IS N1 ... 5 P2
Copenhagen Wy WOT/HER KT12 ... 197 J10 回
Cope Pl KENS W8 ... 14 E4
Copers Cope Rd BECK BR3 ... 182 E4
Cope St BERM/RHTH SE16 ... 160 C3 回
Copland Av ALP/SUD HA0 ... 115 N10
Copland Cl ALP/SUD HA0 ... 115 H10
Copland Ms ALP/SUD HA0 ... 135 K1 回
Copland Rd ALP/SUD HA0 ... 135 K1
Copleigh Dr KWD/TDW/WH KT20 ... 259 H6
Copleston Rd PECK SE15 ... 159 N9
Copley Cl CMBW SE5 ... 159 K9 回
  HNWL W7 ... 134 D6 回
  REDH RH1 ... 257 P8
  WOKN/KNAP GU21 ... 231 K3 回
Copley Dene BMLY BR1 ... 206 A1
Copley Pk STRHM/NOR SW16 ... 180 A3
Copley Rd STAN HA7 ... 95 K4
Copley Wy KWD/TDW/WH KT20 ... 238 G6
Copmans Wick RKW/CH/CXG WD3 ... 70 C9
Coppard Gdns CHSGTN KT9 ... 219 H5
Coppelia Rd BKHTH/KID SE3 ... 161 L10
Coppen Rd BCTR RM8 ... 124 A5
Copperas St DEPT SE8 ... 160 G5
Copper Beech Cl CLAY IG5 ... 102 A1 回
  GVE DA12 ... 190 G3 回
  STMC/STPC BR5 ... 207 H5 回
  WDSR SL4 ... 148 C7 回
  WOKS/MYFD GU22 ... 231 N7 回
Copper Beeches HARP AL5 ... 20 F5 回
Copper Beech Rd SOCK/AV RM15 ... 147 H5 回
Copper Cl NRWD SE19 ... 181 N10 回
Copperdale Rd CHIC IG7 ... 102 C7 回
Copperfield Av UX/CGN UB8 ... 132 B6
Copperfield Cl GVE DA12 ... 191 K4
  PUR/KEN CR8 ... 223 K7 回
Copperfield Dr
  SEVS/STOTM N15 ... 119 N2 回
Copperfield Gdns BRW CM14 ... 106 G2 回
Copperfield Ri ADL/WDHM KT15 ... 215 G2 回
Copperfield Rd BOW E3 ... 140 G6
  THMD SE28 ... 143 M8
Copperfields BEAC HP9 ... 88 D6 回
  BGR/WK TN15 ... 231 K7
  LHD/OX KT22 ... 236 B8 回
  WCCE AL7 ... 23 L7
Copperfield St STHWK SE1 ... 18 D1 回
Copperfield Wy CHST BR7 ... 185 M3 回
  PIN HA5 ... 113 N2 回
Copperkins Gv AMS HP6 ... 68 G2 回

Coppermead Cl CRICK NW2 ...... 116 F8
Copper Mill Dr ISLW TW7 ...... 154 E8
Coppermill La RKW/CH/CXG WD3 .. 95 M7
Coppermill La TOOT SW17 ...... 179 M7
Coppermill La WALTH E17 ...... 121 J5
Coppermill Rd STWL/WRAY TW19 172 E2
Copper Rdg CFSP/GDCR SL9 .... 25 N5
Coppetts Cl NFNCH/WDSP N12 ... 98 A3
Coppetts Rd MUSWH N10 ...... 98 A9
Coppice Cl GUW GU2 ...... 249 J8
  HAT AL10 ...... 40 C8
  KTN/HRWW/W HA3 ...... 94 E7
  RSLP HA4 ...... 112 E4
  RYNPK SW20 ...... 200 F3
Coppice Dr PUT/ROE SW15 ...... 178 D2
  STWL/WRAY TW19 ...... 172 A3
Coppice La REIG RH2 257
Coppice Pth CHIG IG7 ...... 103 L5
Coppice Rw EPP CM16 ...... 82 G3
The Coppice ASHF TW15 ...... 174 C9
  ENC/FH EN2 ...... 79 J8
  HHNE HP2 ...... 36 C5
  OXHEY WD19 ...... 73 K10
  WDR/YW UB7 ...... 131 P8
Coppice Wk CRAWE RH10 ...... 284 B6
  TRDG/WHET N20 ...... 97 K4
Coppice Wy SLN SL2 ...... 109 J7
  SWFD E18 ...... 121 L2
Coppies Gv FBAR/BDGN N11 .... 98 C5
Copping Cl CROY/NA CR0 ...... 223 M1
The Coppings HOD EN11 ...... 26 F10
Coppins Cl BERK HP4 ...... 33 K5
Coppins La IVER SL0 ...... 131 J7
The Coppins KTN/HRWW/W HA3 .. 94 D7
Coppock Cl BTSEA SW11 ...... 157 P8
Coppsfield E/WMO/HCT KT8 .. 197 P3
Copse Av WBAR BR4 ...... 204 C10
Copse Bank BGR/WK TN15 ...... 247 N6
Copse Cl CHARL SE7 ...... 161 N5
  NTHWD HA6 ...... 92 D9
  RGUE GU4 ...... 268 F6
  SL SL1 ...... 128 E10
  WDR/YW UB7 ...... 151 N2
Copse Crs CRAWW RH11 ...... 283 M6
Copse Edge Av EW KT17 ...... 199 C3
Copse Gld SURB KT6 ...... 199 J8
Copse HI BELMT SM2 ...... 221 L6
  HLWW/ROY CM19 ...... 46 E4
  PUR/KEN CR8 ...... 222 F9
  RYNPK SW20 ...... 200 D1
Copse Hill HHS/BOV HP3 ...... 52 A1
Copse La BEAC HP9 ...... 89 K8
  HORL RH6 280
Copsem Dr ESH/CLAY KT10 ...... 218 A5
Copsem La ESH/CLAY KT10 ...... 218 B5
  LHD/OX KT22 ...... 218 B7
Copsem Wy ESH/CLAY KT10 ..... 218 B5
Copsen Wd OXTED KT22 ...... 218 B7
Copse Rd COB KT11 ...... 217 J9
  REIG RH2 ...... 275 N2
  WOKN/KNAP GU21 ...... 231 L4
Copse Side HART DA3 ...... 211 K3
  RGODL GU7 ...... 267 J9
The Copse AMSS HP7 ...... 69 H4
  CHING E4 ...... 101 L2
  CTHM CR3 ...... 259 P2
  GT/LBKH KT23 ...... 236 A9
  HERT/BAY SG13 ...... 25 P5
  HHW HP1 ...... 35 H4
  REDH RH1 ...... 276 F2
Copse Vw SAND/SEL CR2 ...... 224 C5
Copse Wy IVER SL0 ...... 130 C3
Copsewood Av WATN WD24 ...... 73 J5
Copse Wood Wy NTHWD HA6 .. 92 D9
Copshall Cl HLWS CM18 ...... 47 H5
Copsleigh Av REDH RH1 ...... 276 B6
Copsleigh Cl REDH RH1 ...... 276 B6
Copsleigh Wy REDH RH1 ...... 276 B6
Coptefold Dr BELV DA17 ...... 163 N2
Coptfold Rd BRW CM14 ...... 107 H3
Copthall Av LOTH EC2R 13 H5
Copthall Cl CFSP/GDCR SL9 .... 90 C8
Copthall Cnr CFSP/GDCR SL9 .. 90 B8
Copthall Dr MLHL NW7 ...... 96 D8
Copthall Gdns MLHL NW7 ...... 96 C8
  TWK TW1 ...... 176 F4
Copthall La CFSP/GDCR SL9 .... 90 B8
Copthall Rd East HGDN/ICK UB10 .. 112 B7
Copthall Rd West
  HGDN/ICK UB10 ...... 112 B7
Copthall Wy ADL/WDHM KT15 .. 215 J6
Copt Hill La PUR/KEN CR8 ...... 223 L9
Copthorne Av BAL SW12 ...... 180 C3
  BARK/HLT IG6 ...... 102 E4
  BROX EN10 ...... 44 E6
  HAYES BR2 ...... 206 C9
Copthorne Bank CRAWE RH10 .. 285 J3
  HORL RH6 280
Copthorne Cl RKW/CH/CXG WD3 .. 72 A9
  SHPTN TW17 ...... 196 B6
Copthorne Common Rd
  CRAWE RH10 ...... 285 J3
Copthorne Dr LTWR QU18 ...... 212 A6
Copthorne Gdns EMPK RM11 .. 125 P3
Copthorne Ms WHS/HAR UB3 .. 152 F3
Copthorne Ri PUR/KEN CR8 .... 223 L9
Copthorne Rd CRAWE RH10 .... 284 C6
  LHD/OX KT22 ...... 236 C6
  RKW/CH/CXG WD3 ...... 72 A10
Copthorne Wy CRAWE RH10 .. 284 A10
Coptic St NOXST/BSQ WC1A ... 11 L4
Copwood Cl NFNCH/WDSP N12.. 98 F9
Coral Cl CHDH RM6 ...... 123 N1
Coral Gdns HHNE HP2 ...... 36 A5
Coraline Cl STHL UB1 ...... 133 N9
Corals Md WGCW AL7 ...... 22 C6
Coral St STHWK SE1 ...... 18 B2
Coram Cl BERK HP4 ...... 33 P6
Coram St BMSBY WC1N 11 L2
Coran Cl ED N9 ...... 100 C1
Corans BRWN CM15 ...... 86 C10
Corban Rd HSLW TW3 ...... 153 P9
Corbar Cl EBAR EN4 ...... 77 N4
Corbet Cl MTCM CR4 ...... 202 B8
Corbet Pl WCHPL E1 ...... 13 L3
Corbet Rd EW KT17 ...... 220 B7
Corbets Av UPMR RM14 ...... 126 A10
Corbets Tey UPMR RM14 ...... 126 A9
Corbett Cl CROY/NA CR0 ...... 223 N7
Corbett Gv FBAR/BDGN N11 .... 98 A3
Corbett Rd WALTH E17 ...... 101 J3
  WAN E11 ...... 121 P4
Corbett's La BERM/RHTH SE16 .. 142 F10
Corbicum WAN E11 ...... 121 K5
Corbin's La RYLN/HDSTN HA2 .. 114 A3
Corbridge Crs BETH E2 ...... 140 A8
Corby Cl EGH TW20 ...... 171 P9
  LCOL/BKTW AL2 ...... 55 P7
Corby Crs ENC/FH EN2 ...... 78 E4
Corby Dr EGH TW20 ...... 171 P9
Corbylands Rd BFN/LL DA15 .. 185 H3
Corbyn St FSBYPK N4 ...... 118 F6
Corby Rd WLSDN NW10 ...... 135 P4
Cordelia Cl HNHL SE24 ...... 159 J10
Cordelia Gdns STWL/WRAY TW19 173 P3
Cordelia Rd STWL/WRAY TW19 173 P3
Cordelia St POP/IOD E14 ...... 140 G8
Corderoy Pl CHERT KT16 ...... 195 H6

Cordrey Gdns COUL/CHIP CR5 .. 240 F1
Cordwell Rd LEW SE13 ...... 183 J1
Corelli Rd BKHTH/KID SE3 .... 162 B3
Corfe Cl ASHTD KT21 ...... 237 H4
  HHS/BOV HP3 ...... 35 P7
  YEAD UB4 ...... 133 K8
Corfe Gdns SL SL1 ...... 128 F9
Corfield Rd WCHMH N21 ...... 78 G9
Corfield St BETH E2 ...... 140 A6
Corfton Rd EA W5 ...... 135 K8
Coriander Av POP/IOD E14 .... 141 N1
Coriander Crs GUW GU2 ...... 249 N5
Cories Cl BCTR RM8 ...... 123 N7
Corinium Cl WBLY HA9 ...... 115 L9
Corinium Ga STALW/RED AL3 .. 37 P8
Corinne Rd ARCH N19 ...... 118 C9
Corinthian Manorway ERITH DA8.. 164 E3
Corinthian Rd ERITH DA8 .... 164 E3
Corkran Rd SURB KT6 ...... 199 J7
Cork St CONDST W1S 10 C8
Cork Tree Wy CHING E4 ...... 100 D6
Corkscrew Hi WWKM BR4 ...... 205 H9
Corkett St SCAMTN NW1 ...... 9 N3
Cormongers La REDH RH1 .... 258 C9
Cormont Rd CMBW SE5 ...... 159 J7
Cormorant Cl WALTH E17 ...... 100 C9
Cormorant Rd FSTGT E7 ...... 121 L10
Cornbury Rd EDGW HA8 ...... 95 J8
Corncroft HAT AL10 ...... 40 E2
Cornelia St HOLWY N7 ...... 5 P2
Cornell Cl SCUP DA14 ...... 185 P9
Cornell Wy CRW RM5 ...... 104 C6
Corner Farm Cl KWD/TDW/WH KT20.. 238 F5
Cornerfield HAT AL10 ...... 40 E1
Corner Gn BKHTH/KID SE3 ..... 161 M8
Corner Hall HHS/BOV HP3 ...... 35 N8
Corner Hall Av HHS/BOV HP3 .. 35 N8
Corner Mead CDALE/KGS NW9 .. 96 C8
Corner Meadow HLWS CM18 ... 47 P3
Corners WGCE AL7 ...... 23 K4
Corney Reach Wy CHSWK W4 .. 156 B6
Corney Rd CHSWK W4 ...... 156 B5
Cornfield Cl UX/CGN UB8 ...... 131 N4
Cornfield Crs BERK HP4 ...... 33 J2
Cornfield Rd BUSH WD23 ...... 74 A8
  REIG RH2 ...... 275 M1
Cornfields HHW HP1 ...... 35 L7
  RGODL GU7 ...... 267 L9
Cornflower La CROY/NA CR0 .... 204 C9
Cornflower Ter EDUL SE22 .... 182 A2
Cornflower Wy HARH RM3 ..... 105 M9
Cornford Cl HAYES BR2 ...... 205 M5
Cornford Gv BAL SW12 ...... 180 C5
Cornhill BANK EC3V 13 H6
Cornhill Dr ADL/WDHM KT15 .. 195 J6
Cornhill Dr PEND EN3 ...... 80 D3
Cornish Gv PGE/AN SE20 ...... 204 A1
Corn Md WGCW AL8 ...... 22 F7
Corn Mill Dr ORP BR6 ...... 207 J7
Cornmill La LEW SE13 ...... 160 G9
Cornmow Dr WLSDN NW10 .... 116 C10
Cornshaw Rd BCTR RM8 ...... 123 N6
Cornsland BRW CM14 ...... 107 J4
Cornthwaite Rd CLPT E5 ...... 120 B8
Cornwall Av BETH E2 ...... 140 B5
  BF/WBF KT14 ...... 216 A10
  ESH/CLAY KT10 ...... 218 E4
  FNCH N3 ...... 97 K8
  SLN SL2 ...... 129 H6
  STHL UB1 ...... 133 N7
  WDGN N22 ...... 98 D9
  WELL DA16 ...... 163 H9
Cornwall Cl BARK IG11 ...... 143 J1
  CHES/WCR EN8 ...... 62 D9
  EMPK RM11 ...... 125 P2
  WDSR SL4 ...... 148 D4
Cornwall Crs NTGHL W11 ...... 8 A1
Cornwall Dr STMC/STPC BR5 .. 185 M10
Cornwall Gdns SKENS SW7 .... 15 J4
  WLSDN NW10 ...... 136 E10
Cornwall Gv CHSWK W4 ...... 156 B4
Cornwallis Av BFN/LL DA15 ... 184 C5
  ED N9 ...... 100 A3
Cornwallis Cl CTHM CR3 ...... 241 K8
  ERITH DA8 ...... 164 G5
Cornwallis Gv ED N9 ...... 100 A3
Cornwallis Rd ARCH N19 ...... 118 F7
  DAGW RM9 ...... 123 P9
  ED N9 ...... 100 A3
  WALTH E17 ...... 120 C2
Cornwallis Sq ARCH N19 ...... 118 F7
Cornwallis Wk ELTH/MOT SE9 .. 162 C9
Cornwall Ms South SKENS SW7 .. 15 J4
Cornwall Ms West SKENS SW7 .. 15 H4
Cornwall Rd BELMT SM2 ...... 221 J4
  BRWN CM15 ...... 86 C9
  CROY/NA CR0 ...... 203 J9
  DART DA1 ...... 165 N9
  FSBYPK N4 ...... 119 H5
  HARP AL5 ...... 20 A1
  HRW HA1 ...... 114 C5
  PIN HA5 ...... 93 N8
  RSLP HA4 ...... 112 C7
  SEVS/STOTM N15 ...... 119 L3
  STAL AL1 ...... 12 A10
  STHWK SE1 ...... 12 A10
  UED N18 ...... 99 P6
  UX/CGN UB8 ...... 131 N1
Cornwall St WCHPL E1 ...... 140 E9
Cornwall Terrace Ms CAMTN NW1 .. 10 B2
Cornwall Wy STA TW18 ...... 173 H8
Corn Wy WAN E11 ...... 121 J8
Cornwell Av DA12 ...... 190 F6
Cornwell Rd WDSR SL4 ...... 171 M2
Cornwood Cl EFNCH N2 ...... 117 N3
Cornwood Dr WCHPL E1 ...... 140 E8
Cornworthy Rd BCTR RM8 ..... 123 M10
Corona Rd LEE/GVPK SE12 .... 183 M4
Coronation Av BARK/HLT IG6 .. 122 F2
  BXLY DA5 ...... 185 N2
Coronation Dr HCH RM12 ...... 125 J10
Coronation Hi EPP CM16 ...... 65 J6
Coronation Rd HYS/HAR UB3 .. 152 C3
  PLSTW E13 ...... 141 P5
  WARE SG12 ...... 26 C1
  WLSDN NW10 ...... 136 C5
Coronet St IS N1 ...... 7 J10
The Coronet HORL RH6 ...... 280 D6
Corporation Av HSLWW TW4 .. 153 M10
Corporation Rw CLKNW EC1R .. 12 B1
Corporation St HOLWY N7 .... 118 F10
  SRTFD E15 ...... 141 K4
Corrance Rd BRXS/STRHM SW2.. 158 A10
Corran Wy SOCK/AV RM15 .... 146 G9
Corri Av STHGT/OAK N14 ...... 98 E5
Corrib Dr SUT SM1 ...... 221 P2
Corrie Gdns VW GU25 ...... 193 P7
Corrie Rd ADL/WDHM KT15 ... 215 N1
  WOKS/MYFD GU22 ...... 232 E6
Corrigan Av COUL/CHIP CR5 .. 240 B1
Corringham Ct STAL AL1 ...... 38 E5
Corringham Rd GLDGN NW11 .. 117 K5
  WBLY HA9 ...... 116 C9
Corringway EA W5 ...... 135 M2
  GLDGN NW11 ...... 117 K5
Corsair Cl STWL/WRAY TW19 .. 173 P3
Corsair Rd STWL/WRAY TW19 .. 173 P3
Corscombe Cl KUTN/CMB KT2 .. 177 J6
Corsehill St STRHM/NOR SW16 .. 180 D9
Corsham St IS N1 ...... 7 H10

Corsica St HBRY N5 ...... 6 D1
Cortayne Rd FUL/PGN SW6 .... 157 J8
Cortina Dr DAGW RM9 ...... 144 D5
Cortis Rd PUT/ROE SW15 ...... 178 F4
Cortis Ter PUT/ROE SW15 ...... 178 E1
Corunna Rd VX/NE SW8 ...... 158 D7
Corunna Ter VX/NE SW8 ...... 158 D7
Corve La SOCK/AV RM15 ...... 146 G9
Corwell Gdns UX/CGN UB8 .... 132 D8
Corwell La UX/CGN UB8 ...... 132 D8
Cory Dr RBRW/HUT CM15 ...... 107 N1
Cory-wright Wy STALE/WH AL4.. 21 N1
Cosbycote Av HNHL SE24 ...... 181 K1
Cosdach Av WLGTN SM6 ...... 222 G1
Cosedge Crs CROY/NA CR0 .... 223 J7
Cosgrove Cl WCHMH N21 ...... 99 K3
  YEAD UB4 ...... 133 L6
Cosmo Pl RSQ WC1B 11 M5
Cosmur Cl SHB W12 ...... 156 C2
Cossall Wk PECK SE15 ...... 159 K7
Cosser St STHWK SE1 ...... 18 A3
Costa St PECK SE15 ...... 159 P8
Costead Manor Rd BRW CM14 .. 106 C3
Costells Meadow BH/WHM TN16 .. 242 C2
Costons Av GFD/PVL UB6 ...... 134 C5
Costons La GFD/PVL UB6 ...... 134 C5
Cosway St POP/IOD E14 ...... 140 F8
Cotall St POP/IOD E14 ...... 140 F8
Coteford Cl LOU IG10 ...... 82 E6
  PIN HA5 ...... 113 H5
Coteford St TOOT SW17 ...... 180 A7
Cotelands CROY/NA CR0 ...... 203 M10
Cotesbach Rd CLPT E5 ...... 120 B8
Cotesmore Gdns BCTR RM8 ... 123 N6
Cotesmore Rd HHW HP1 ...... 35 H7
Cotford Rd THHTH CR7 ...... 203 K4
Cotham St WALW SE17 ...... 18 F6
Cotherstone Rd
  BRXS/STRHM SW2 ...... 180 A3
  CDH/CHF RM16 ...... 167 L2
Cotland Acres REDH RH1 ...... 275 P2
  REDH RH1 ...... 275 N2
Cotmandene Crs STMC/STPC BR5.. 207 L2
Cotman Gdns EDGW HA8 ...... 95 M10
Cotmans Cl HYS/HAR UB3 ..... 133 H10
Coton Rd WELL DA16 ...... 163 K9
Cotsford Av NWMAL KT3 ...... 199 P5
Cotswold Av BUSH WD23 ...... 74 B10
Cotswold Cl BXLYHN DA7 ...... 164 F7
  CRAWW RH11 ...... 283 L7
  ESH/CLAY KT10 ...... 198 F7
  KUTN/CMB KT2 ...... 177 P9
  SL SL1 ...... 148 G2
  STA TW18 ...... 173 K8
  STALE/WH AL4 ...... 39 H1
  UX/CGN UB8 ...... 131 M3
Cotswold Gdns CRICK NW2 .... 116 C7
  GNTH/NBYPK IG2 ...... 122 C5
Cotswold Ga CRICK NW2 ...... 117 H6
Cotswold Gn ENC/FH EN2 ..... 78 C8
Cotswold Ri ORP BR6 ...... 207 J6
Cotswold Rd BELMT SM2 ...... 221 L6
  GVW DA11 ...... 191 M9
  HARH RM3 ...... 105 N10
  HPTN TW12 ...... 175 P9
Cotswolds HAT AL10 ...... 40 D6
Cotswold St WNWD SE27 ...... 181 J7
Cotswold Wy ENC/FH EN2 ..... 78 G7
  WPK KT4 ...... 200 F9
Cottage Av HAYES BR2 ...... 206 B8
Cottage Cl CHERT KT16 ...... 214 F5
  RKW/CH/CXG WD3 ...... 72 A10
  RSLP HA4 ...... 112 G6
  WAT WD17 ...... 72 G6
Cottage Farm Wy EGH TW20 .. 194 F3
Cottage Field Cl SCUP DA14 .. 185 M4
Cottage Gdns CHES/WCR EN8 .. 62 B5
Cottage Gn CMBW SE5 ...... 159 M6
Cottage Gv BRXN/ST SW9 ..... 158 F9
  CLAP SW4 ...... 158 F9
  SURB KT6 ...... 199 J2
Cottage Park Rd SLN SL2 ...... 109 J7
Cottage Pl CRAWE RH10 ...... 285 M2
  SKENS SW7 ...... 15 N3
Cottage Rd HOR/WEW KT19 ... 220 A4
Cottages Crs SEV TN13 ...... 246 F6
Cottage St POP/IOD E14 ...... 140 G9
Cottenham Dr CDALE/KGS NW9.. 116 C1
  VX/NE SW8 ...... 158 C6
Cottenham Park Rd
  RYNPK SW20 ...... 200 D1
Cottenham Rd WALTH E17 ..... 120 E10
Cotterells HHS/BOV HP3 ...... 35 M8
Cotterells Hi HHW HP1 ...... 35 M6
Cotterill Rd SURB KT6 ...... 199 L9
Cottesbrooke Cl DTCH/LGLY SL3 .. 150 D6
Cottesbrook St NWCR SE14 ... 160 D6
Cottesloe Cl CHOB/PIR GU24 .. 230 E2
Cottesmore Av CLAY IG5 ...... 102 C10
Cottesmore Gdns KENS W8 ... 15 H3
Cottimore Av WOT/HER KT12 .. 197 J8
Cottimore Crs WOT/HER KT12 .. 197 J7
Cottimore La WOT/HER KT12 .. 197 K8
Cottimore Ter WOT/HER KT12 .. 197 J7
Cottingham Cha HLWS CM18 .. 113 H8
Cottingham Rd PGE/AN SE20 .. 182 C10
  VX/NE SW8 ...... 158 C6
Cottington Rd FELT TW13 ..... 175 L7
Cottington St LBTH SE11 ...... 18 B7
Cotton Av ACT W3 ...... 136 A8
Cotton Cl DAGW RM9 ...... 143 M2
Cotton Dr HERT/BAY SG13 .... 26 A4
Cotton Fld HAT AL10 ...... 40 E2
Cottongrass Cl CROY/NA CR0 .. 204 C8
Cotton Hi BMLY BR1 ...... 183 J1
Cotton La GRH DA9 ...... 188 B1
Cottonmill Crs STAL AL1 ...... 38 C7
Cottonmill La STAL AL1 ...... 38 C7
Cotton Rd POTB/CUF EN6 ..... 59 M7
Cotton Rw BTSEA SW11 ...... 157 N9
Cottons Ap ROMW/RG RM7 ... 124 C3
Cotton's Gdns BETH E2 ...... 7 K9
Cotton St POP/IOD E14 ...... 141 N9
Cotts Wood Dr RGUE GU4 .... 250 D5
Couchmore Av CLAY IG5 ...... 102 C10
  ESH/CLAY KT10 ...... 198 D10
Coulgate St BROCKY SE4 ...... 160 D9

Country Wy FELT TW13 ...... 175 K8
  CHST BR7 ...... 184 F6
  TRDG/WHET N20 ...... 77 L10
County Ga CMBW SE5 ...... 159 K7
County Oak La CRAWW RH11 .. 283 N10
County Oak Wy CRAWW RH11 .. 283 M10
County Rd EHAM E6 ...... 142 E7
  THHTH CR7 ...... 203 J2
County St STHWK SE1 ...... 18 F4
Coupland Pl WOOL/PLUM SE18 .. 162 F4
Courage Cl EMPK RM11 ...... 125 K4
Courcy Rd CEND/HSY/T N8 .... 119 H1
Courier Rd DAGW RM9 ...... 144 D6
Courland Gv VX/NE SW8 ...... 158 D7
Courland Rd ADL/WDHM KT15 .. 195 L10
Courland St VX/NE SW8 ...... 158 D7
Coursers Rd STALE/WH AL4 ... 57 M3
The Course ELTH/MOT SE9 .... 184 D6
Court Av BELV DA17 ...... 164 A4
  COUL/CHIP CR5 ...... 241 H4
  HARH RM3 ...... 105 P8
Court Bushes Rd CTHM CR3 ... 241 P5
Court Cl FELT TW13 ...... 176 A6
  KTN/HRWW/W HA3 ...... 115 J1
Court Close Av FELT TW13 .... 176 A6
Court Crs CHSGTN KT9 ...... 219 J3
  SL SL1 ...... 129 J8
  SWLY BR8 ...... 208 F4
Court Downs Rd BECK BR3 .... 204 C2
Court Dr CROY/NA CR0 ...... 222 G1
  HGDN/ICK UB10 ...... 132 A3
  STAN HA7 ...... 95 K5
  SUT SM1 ...... 221 P1
Court Farm Av HOR/WEW KT19 .. 220 A2
Court Farm Rd ELTH/MOT SE9 .. 184 C5
  NTHLT UB5 ...... 133 P2
  WARL CR6 ...... 241 P4
Courtfield Av HRW HA1 ...... 114 E5
Courtfield Cl BROX EN10 ...... 44 A3
Courtfield Crs HRW HA1 ...... 114 E5
Courtfield Gdns DEN/HRF UB9 .. 111 K8
  ECT SW5 ...... 15 H6
  RSLP HA4 ...... 112 G7
  WEA W13 ...... 134 F3
Courtfield Ms SKENS SW7 ..... 15 J6
Courtfield Ri WWKM BR4 ...... 205 J10
Courtfield Rd ASHF TW15 ..... 174 C9
  SKENS SW7 ...... 15 J6
Courtfields HARP AL5 ...... 20 C2
Court Gdns HOLWY N7 ...... 6 B2
Court Haw BNSTD SM7 ...... 239 P7
Court HI COUL/CHIP CR5 ...... 239 P4
  SAND/SEL CR2 ...... 223 M8
Courthill Rd LEW SE13 ...... 161 H10
Courthope Rd GFD/PVL UB6 .. 134 C4
  HAMP NW3 ...... 118 A9
  WIM/MER SW19 ...... 179 H8
Courthope Vls WIM/MER SW19 .. 179 H10
Court House Rd FNCH N3 ..... 97 L7
Courtland Av CHING E4 ...... 102 C7
  IL IG1 ...... 122 C7
  MLHL NW7 ...... 96 A4
  STRHM/NOR SW16 ...... 180 G10
Courtland Dr CHIG IG7 ...... 102 F4
Courtland Gv THMD SE28 ..... 143 N9
Courtland Rd EHAM E6 ...... 142 B3
Courtlands RCHPK/HAM TW10 .. 177 M1
Courtlands Av DTCH/LGLY SL3 .. 150 A3
  ESH/CLAY KT10 ...... 217 N3
  HAYES BR2 ...... 205 K8
  HPTN TW12 ...... 175 K9
  LEE/GVPK SE12 ...... 183 N1
  RCH/KEW TW9 ...... 155 N8
Courtlands Cl RSLP HA4 ...... 112 G5
  SAND/SEL CR2 ...... 223 N6
  WATN WD24 ...... 72 F1
Courtlands Crs BNSTD SM7 .... 239 K6
Courtlands Dr HOR/WEW KT19 .. 220 B3
  WAT WD17 ...... 72 F2
Courtlands Rd BRYLDS KT5 .... 199 M7
Court La DUL SE21 ...... 181 N3
  HOR/WEW KT19 ...... 219 P9
  IVER SL0 ...... 131 K10
  SL SL1 ...... 128 C5
Court Lane Gdns DUL SE21 ... 181 M3
Courtleas COB KT11 ...... 217 N8
Courtleet Dr BXLYHN DA7 ..... 185 M4
Courtleigh GLDGN NW11 ...... 117 K2
Courtman Rd TOTM N17 ...... 99 K8
Court Md NTHLT UB5 ...... 133 N5
Courtmead Cl HNHL SE24 ..... 181 K2
Courtnell St BAY/PAD W2 ..... 8 B1
Courtney Cl POB KT11 ...... 217 N8
Courtney Crs CAR SM5 ...... 222 A4
Courtney Pl COB KT11 ...... 217 N8
  CROY/NA CR0 ...... 203 H10
  HOLWY N7 ...... 119 H10
Courtney Rd CDH/CHF RM16 .. 168 F1
  CROY/NA CR0 ...... 203 H10
  HTHAIR TW6 ...... 152 B9
  WIM/MER SW19 ...... 179 P10
Courtney Wy HTHAIR TW6 .... 152 B9
Court Rd BNSTD SM7 ...... 239 K1
  BROCKY SE4 160
  CTHM CR3 ...... 241 L9
  ELTH/MOT SE9 ...... 184 C4
  GDST RH9 ...... 260 B7
  HGDN/ICK UB10 ...... 112 C10
  NWDGN UB2 ...... 153 N3
  RDART DA2 ...... 188 D8
  SNWD SE25 ...... 203 N2
Court Wy ACT W3 ...... 135 P7
  BARK/HLT IG6 ...... 122 B2
  CDALE/KGS NW9 ...... 95 L9
  HARH RM3 ...... 105 M10
  WHTN TW2 ...... 176 B3
The Courtyard WDHN WD19 ... 93 M3
Court Wood La CROY/NA CR0 .. 224 F10
Court Yd ELTH/MOT SE9 ...... 184 B2
The Courtyard BF/WBF KT14 .. 215 K8
  IS N1 ...... 5 P3
  STALE/WH AL4 ...... 39 H7
Cousin La CANST EC4R 12 G8
Cousins Cl WDR/YW UB7 ...... 131 P9
Couthurst Rd BKHTH/KID SE3 .. 161 N5
Coutts Av CHSGTN KT9 ...... 219 K2
Coval Gdns MORT/ESHN SW14 .. 155 N10
Coval La MORT/ESHN SW14 ... 155 N10
Coval Rd MORT/ESHN SW14 .. 155 P10

Coveham Crs COB KT11 ...... 217 J9
Covelees Wall EHAM E6 ...... 142 D8
Covenbrook RBRW/HUT CM13 .. 107 M4
Covent Gdn COVGDN WC2E 11 M7
Coventry Cl EHAM E6 ...... 142 C8
  KIL/WHAMP NW6 ...... 2 F7
Coventry Rd BETH E2 ...... 140 A6
  IL IG1 ...... 122 E6
  SNWD SE25 ...... 203 P4
  WCHPL E1 ...... 140 A6
Coventry St MYFR/PICC W1J ... 11 J8
Coverack Cl CROY/NA CR0 .... 204 D7
  STHGT/OAK N14 ...... 78 D10
Coverdale Gdns CROY/NA CR0 .. 203 N10
Coverdale Rd CRICK NW2 ..... 2 A2
  FBAR/BDGN N11 ...... 98 B7
  SHB W12 ...... 136 E10
The Coverdales BARK IG11 .... 142 C4
Coverley Gv SLN SL2 ...... 128 D6
  WCHPL E1 ...... 136 E10
Covert Cl BERK HP4 ...... 33 J9
  CRAWE RH10 ...... 285 P6
Coverton Rd TOOT SW17 ...... 179 P7
Coverts Rd ESH/CLAY KT10 ... 218 E4
The Coverts RBRW/HUT CM13 .. 107 M2
  NTHWD HA6 ...... 92 D9
  ORP BR6 ...... 207 H6
Covert Wy EBAR EN4 ...... 77 M6
Covet Wood Cl STMC/STPC BR5 .. 207 J6
Covey Cl WIM/MER SW19 ..... 201 L2
The Covey CRAWE RH10 ...... 284 E5
Covington Gdns
  STRHM/NOR SW16 ...... 181 J10
Covington Wy
  STRHM/NOR SW16 ...... 181 J10
Cowbridge HERT/WAS SG14 ... 25 L3
Cowbridge La BARK IG11 ...... 142 C1
Cowbridge Rd
  KTN/HRWW/W HA3 ...... 115 L2
Cowcross St FARR EC1M 12 C3
Cowden Rd ORP BR6 ...... 207 J7
Cowden St CAT SE6 ...... 182 F5
Cowdray Cl CRAWE RH10 ..... 284 D8
Cowdray Rd HGDN/ICK UB10 .. 132 D3
Cowdray Wy HCH RM12 ...... 125 H9
Cowdrey Cl EN EN1 ...... 79 M6
Cowdrey Ct DART DA1 ...... 187 J3
Cowdrey Rd WIM/MER SW19 .. 179 L9
Cowen Av RYLN/HDSTN HA2 .. 114 C7
Cowfold Cl CRAWW RH11 ..... 283 J10
Cowgate Rd GFD/PVL UB6 .... 134 C5
Cowick Rd TOOT SW17 ...... 180 A7
Cowings Md NTHLT UB5 ...... 133 M2
Cow La BUSH WD23 ...... 73 P10
  GSTN WD25 ...... 73 K2
Cow Leaze EHAM E6 ...... 142 C4
Cowleaze Rd KUTN/CMB KT2 .. 199 K1
Cowles CHESW EN7 ...... 61 N3
Cowley Av DARTT DA1 187
  GRH DA9 ...... 188 E1
Cowley Cl SAND/SEL CR2 ..... 224 B5
Cowley Crs UX/CGN UB8 ...... 131 M7
  WOT/HER KT12 ...... 217 K1
Cowley HI BORE WD6 ...... 75 P2
Cowley La CHERT KT16 ...... 195 J7
  WAN E11 ...... 121 K8
Cowley Mill Rd UX/CGN UB8 .. 131 L4
Cowley Rd HDN NW4 ...... 116 F3
  MORT/ESHN SW14 ...... 156 D9
  UX/CGN UB8 ...... 131 M5
  UX/CGN UB8 ...... 131 M5
  UX/CGN UB8 ...... 131 M4
  WAN E11 ...... 121 N3
Cowley St WEST SW1P 17 L4
Cowling Cl NTGHL W11 ...... 8 A8
Cowlins HLWE CM17 ...... 29 N7
Coworth Cl ASC SL5 ...... 192 G5
Coworth Rd ASC SL5 ...... 192 F5
Cowper Av EHAM E6 ...... 142 B2
  SUT SM1 ...... 221 N1
  TIL RM18 ...... 168 E7
Cowper Cl CHERT KT16 ...... 195 J6
  HAYES BR2 ...... 206 A4
  WELL DA16 ...... 185 K1
Cowper Ct WATN WD24 ...... 73 H3
Cowper Crs HERT/WAS SG14 .. 25 J2
Cowper Gdns STHGT/OAK N14 .. 98
  WLGTN SM6 ...... 222 D5
Cowper Rd ACT W3 ...... 136 A10
  BELV DA17 ...... 164 A3
  BERK HP4 ...... 33 N5
  CSHM HP5 ...... 50 C5
  HARP AL5 ...... 20 A2
  HAYES BR2 ...... 206 A4
  HHW HP1 ...... 35 L7
  HNWL W7 ...... 134 F2
  RAIN RM13 ...... 145 H6
  RCHPK/HAM TW10 ...... 177 L8
  SLN SL2 ...... 128 F6
  STHGT/OAK N14 ...... 98 C12
  STNW/STAM N16 ...... 119 M9
  UED N18 ...... 99 P6
  WCCE AL7 ...... 23 J7
  WIM/MER SW19 ...... 179 M9
Cowper St STLK EC1Y 13 H1
Cowshot Crs CHOB/PIR GU24 .. 230 C6
Cowslip Cl HGDN/ICK UB10 ... 113 K6
Cowslip La RDKG RH5 ...... 254 F4
Cowslip Rd SWFD E18 ...... 101 N10
Cowthorpe Rd VX/NE SW8 .... 158 E7
Cox Cl RAD WD7 ...... 57 K8
Coxdean KWD/TDW/WH KT20 .. 238 F5
Coxe Pl KTN/HRWW/W HA3 ... 114 F2
Cox La CHSGTN KT9 ...... 219 L1
  HOR/WEW KT19 ...... 219 N2
Coxley Ri PUR/KEN CR8 ...... 223 K9
Coxmount Rd CHARL SE7 ..... 162 A4
Cox's Wk DUL SE21 182
Coxson Wy STHWK SE1 ...... 19 L2
Coxtie Green Rd BRW CM14 .. 85 P10
Coxwell Rd NRWD SE19 ...... 181 M10
  WOOL/PLUM SE18 ...... 162 G4
Cozens La East BROX EN10 ... 44 D8
Cozens La West BROX EN10 .. 44 D8
Cozens Rd WARE SG12 ...... 26 E1
Crabbe Crs CSHM HP5 ...... 51 J5
Crabbet Rd CRAWE RH10 ..... 285 P5
Crabbs Croft Cl ORP BR6 ..... 226 F2
Crab HI BECK BR3 ...... 183 J10
Crab Hill La REDH RH1 ...... 276 G4
Crab La GSTN WD25 ...... 56 A10
Crabtree Av ALP/SUD HA0 .... 135 K4
  CHDH RM6 ...... 123 N2
Crabtree Cl BETH E2 ...... 7 L8
  BUSH WD23 ...... 74 A8
  GT/LBKH KT23 ...... 254 B2
  HHS/BOV HP3 ...... 35 N8
Crabtree Dr LHD/OX KT22 ..... 237 H10
Crabtree La FUL/PGN SW6 .... 156 G6
  GT/LBKH KT23 ...... 254 B2
  HARP AL5 ...... 20 B3
  HHS/BOV HP3 ...... 35 N8
  LHD/OX KT22 ...... 255 P2
  RDKG RH5 ...... 254 E6
Crabtree Manorway North
  BELV DA17 ...... 164 D1

312 Cra - Cro

Crabtree Manorway South
BELV DA17 164 D1
Crabtree Rd CRAWW RH11 283 M6
EGH TW20 194 F2
Crackley Meadow HHNE HP2 36 C1 3
Craddock Rd EN EN1 79 N7
Craddocks Av ASHTD KT21 237 L2
Craddock St KTTN NW5 4 C2
Cradhurst Cl DORK RH4 272 B3
Cradley Rd ELTH/MOT SE9 184 G4
Cragg Av RAD WD7 74 E2
Craigans CRAWW RH11 283 K7
Craigavon Rd HHNE HP2 36 A2
Craigdale Rd ROM RM1 124 G4
Craigen Av CROY/NA CR0 204 A8
Craigerne Rd BKHTH/KID SE3 161 N6
Craig Gdns SWFD E18 101 L10
Craigholm WOOL/PLUM SE18 162 D8
Craiglands STALE/WH AL4 39 J2
Craig Mt RAD WD7 74 G1
Craigmuir Pk ALP/SUD HA0 135 L3
Craignair Rd BRXS/STRHM SW2 180 G3
Craignish Av STRHM/NOR SW16 202 G2
Craig Park Rd UED N18 100 A6 4
Craig Rd RCHPK/HAM TW10 177 H7
UX/CGN UB8 132 C8
Craig's Ct WHALL SW1A 11 L9
Craigs Wk CHES/WCR EN8 62 C4
Craigton Rd ELTH/MOT SE9 162 C10
Craigweil Av RAD WD7 74 G1
Craigweil Cl STAN HA7 95 J6
Craigweil Dr STAN HA7 95 J6
Craigwell Av FELT TW13 175 H6
Craigwell Cl STA TW18 195 H1
Crail Rw WALW SE17 19 H6
Crakell Rd REIG RH2 275 M1
Cramer St MHST W1U 10 D4
Crammavill St CDH/CHF RM16 147 M10
Crammond Cl HMSMTH W6 14 A9 1
Crampshaw La ASHTD KT21 237 L6
Crampton Rd PGE/AN SE20 182 B9
Crampton's Rd RSEV TN14 247 J6
Crampton St WALW SE17 18 E7
Cranberry Cl NTHLT UB5 133 L4 1
Cranberry La CAN/RD E16 141 K6 1
Cranborne Av NWDGN UB2 153 P3
SURB KT6 199 M10
Cranborne Cl HERT/BAY SG13 25 K8
POTB/CUF EN6 59 H7
Cranborne Crs POTB/CUF EN6 59 H7
Cranborne Gdns UPMR RM14 126 A7
WGCE AL7 23 J6 1
Cranborne Rd BARK IG11 142 G3
CHES/WCR EN8 62 C8 1
HAT AL10 40 E3
HOD EN11 44 G2
POTB/CUF EN6 59 H6
Cranborne Wk CRAWE RH10 284 A9 1
Cranborne Waye YEAD UB4 133 K9
Cranbourne Av WAN E11 121 N2
WDSR SL4 148 E8
Cranbourne Cl HORL RH6 280 C2 1
SL SL1 129 H10 2
STRHM/NOR SW16 202 F3 2
Cranbourne Dr HARP AL5 20 B5
HOD EN11 26 G9
PIN HA5 113 L3
Cranbourne Gdns BARK/HLT IG6 122 F1
GLDGN NW11 117 J3 2
Cranbourne Rd MNPK E12 122 B10 1
MUSWH N10 98 C10
NTHWD HA6 112 G1
SL SL1 129 H10
SRTFD E15 121 H9
Cranbourn St LSQ/SEVD WC2H 11 K7
Cranbrook Cl HAYES BR2 205 M6
Cranbrook Dr ESH/CLAY KT10 198 B8
GPK RM2 125 J2
STALE/WH AL4 39 K6
WHTN TW2 176 A4 1
Cranbrook Ms WALTH E17 120 E3
Cranbrook Pk WDGN N22 99 H9
Cranbrook Ri IL IG1 122 C4
Cranbrook Rd BARK/HLT IG6 122 E2
BXLYHN DA7 164 A7
CHSWK W4 156 B4
DEPT SE8 160 F7 1
EBAR EN4 77 N10
HSLWW TW4 153 N10
IL IG1 122 D5
THHTH CR7 203 K2
WIM/MER SW19 179 H10
Cranbrook St BETH E2 140 C4 1
Cranbury Rd FUL/PGN SW6 157 L8
Crane Av ACT W3 135 P9 1
ISLW TW7 176 F1
Cranebrook WHTN TW2 176 B5 1
Crane Cl DAGE RM10 144 B1
Cranefield Dr GSTN WD25 55 M8
Craneford Cl WHTN TW2 176 E3
Craneford Wy WHTN TW2 176 D3
Crane Gdns HYS/HAR UB3 152 G3
Crane Gv HOLWY N7 6 B1
Crane Lodge Rd HEST TW5 153 J5
Crane Md BERM/RHTH SE16 160 C3
WARE SG12 26 D3
Crane Park Rd WHTN TW2 176 A5
Crane Rd STWL/WRAY TW19 174 B2
WHTN TW2 176 D4
Cranes Dr BRYLDS KT5 199 K4
Cranes Pk SURB KT6 199 K4
Cranes Park Av SURB KT6 199 K4
Cranes Park Crs BRYLDS KT5 199 L4
Crane St PECK SE15 159 N7 2
Craneswater HYS/HAR UB3 152 G6
Craneswater Pk NWDGN UB2 153 N4
Cranes Wy BORE WD6 75 P9
Crane Wy WHTN TW2 176 B3
Cranfield Crs POTB/CUF EN6 60 F5
Cranfield Dr CDALE/KGS NW9 96 B8
Cranfield Rd BROCKY SE4 160 E9
Cranfield Rd East CAR SM5 222 B5
Cranfield Rd West CAR SM5 222 A5 1
Cranford Av PLMGR N13 98 F6
STWL/WRAY TW19 173 P3
Cranford Cl PUR/KEN CR8 223 K9 1
RYNPK SW20 200 E1 1
STWL/WRAY TW19 173 P3 1
Cranford Dr HYS/HAR UB3 152 G3
Cranford La HEST TW5 153 L6
HTHAIR TW6 152 G9
HYS/HAR UB3 152 E5
Cranford Park Rd HYS/HAR UB3 152 G3 2
Cranford Ri ESH/CLAY KT10 218 B2
Cranford Rd DART DA1 187 M4
Cranford St WAP E1W 140 C9 2
Cranford Wy CEND/HSY/T N8 118 G3
Cranham Gdns UPMR RM14 126 E5
Cranham Rd EMPK RM11 125 J4
Cranhurst Rd CRICK NW2 116 F10
Cranleigh Cl BXLY DA5 186 C2 1
CHESW EN7 61 P4
ORP BR6 207 K10
PGE/AN SE20 204 A2
SAND/SEL CR2 223 P8
Cranleigh Dr SWLY BR8 208 F4
Cranleigh Gdns BARK IG11 142 G2
KTN/HRWW/W HA3 115 K3
KUTN/CMB KT2 177 L9
LOU IG10 82 C10 1
SAND/SEL CR2 223 P8
SNWD SE25 203 M3 1
STHL UB1 133 N8
SUT SM1 201 L9
WCHMH N21 79 H9
Cranleigh Ms BTSEA SW11 157 P8
Cranleigh Rd ESH/CLAY KT10 198 B8
FELT TW13 174 G7
SEVS/STOTM N15 119 K3
SHGR GU5 268 F10
WIM/MER SW19 201 K3
Cranleigh St CAMTN NW1 5 H8
Cranley Cl GU GU1 250 D10
Cranley Dr GNTH/NBYPK IG2 122 F5
RSLP HA4 112 G7
Cranley Gdns CHEL SW3 15 L7
MUSWH N10 118 C2
PLMGR N13 98 G4
SKENS SW7 15 K7
WLGTN SM6 222 D4
Cranley Ms SKENS SW7 15 K7
Cranley Pl SKENS SW7 15 L6
Cranley Rd GNTH/NBYPK IG2 122 F4
GU GU1 250 C10
PLSTW E13 141 N7 1
WOT/HER KT12 216 G3
Cranmer Av WEA W13 154 G2
Cranmer Cl MRDN SM4 200 G6
POTB/CUF EN6 59 M6
RSLP HA4 113 L6 2
STAN HA7 95 H8
WARL CR6 242 D3
WEY KT13 216 B4
Cranmer Ct HPTN TW12 176 A8
Cranmer Farm Cl MTCM CR4 202 A4 1
Cranmer Gdns DAGE RM10 124 D9
WARL CR6 242 D3
Cranmer Rd BRXN/ST SW9 159 H6
CROY/NA CR0 203 J10
EDGW HA8 95 N4
FSTGT E7 121 N9
HPTN TW12 176 A8
HYS/HAR UB3 132 E8
KUTN/CMB KT2 177 K8
MTCM CR4 202 A4
SEV TN13 246 F9
Cranmer Ter TOOT SW17 179 N8
Cranmore La EHSLY KT24 252 C5
Cranmore Rd BMLY BR1 183 K6
CHST BR7 184 C8
Cranston Cl HGDN/ICK UB10 112 D7
HSLW TW3 153 M8
REIG RH2 275 L1
Cranston Gdns CHING E4 100 G7
Cranston Park Av UPMR RM14 126 B9
Cranston Rd FSTH SE23 182 D4
Cranstoun Cl RGUW GU3 249 L6
Cranswick Rd BERM/RHTH SE16 160 A4
Crantock Rd CAT SE6 183 H5
Cranwell Cl BOW E3 140 G6
Cranwell Gv SHPTN TW17 196 A4
Cranwich Av WCHMH N21 99 L1
Cranwich Rd STNW/STAM N16 119 M5
Cranwood St FSBYE EC1V 7 H10
Cranworth Crs CHING E4 101 J2 3
Cranworth Gdns BRXN/ST SW9 159 H7
Craster Rd BRXS/STRHM SW2 180 G3
Crathie Rd LEE/GVPK SE12 183 N2
Cravan Av FELT TW13 175 H5
Cravells Rd HARP AL5 20 B5
Craven Av WEA W13 135 H9
Craven Cl YEAD UB4 133 H8
Craven Gdns BARK IG11 143 H4
BARK/HLT IG6 102 G10
CRW RM5 104 B6
HARH RM3 106 B7
WIM/MER SW19 179 L8
Craven Hl BAY/PAD W2 9 K7
Craven Hill Gdns BAY/PAD W2 9 J7
Craven Hill Ms BAY/PAD W2 9 K7
Craven Ms BTSEA SW11 158 B9 3
Craven Pk WLSDN NW10 136 B3 4
Craven Park Ms WLSDN NW10 136 B2
Craven Park Rd STNW/STAM N16 119 N4
WLSDN NW10 136 B3
Craven Rd BAY/PAD W2 9 K7
CRAWE RH10 284 C8
CROY/NA CR0 204 A8
KUTN/CMB KT2 199 L1
ORP BR6 207 N10
WEA W13 135 H9
WLSDN NW10 136 A3 1
The Cravens HORL RH6 281 H4
Craven St CHCR WC2N 11 M9 1
Craven Ter BAY/PAD W2 9 K7
Craven Wk CLPT E5 119 P5
Crawford Av ALP/SUD HA0 115 J10
CDH/CHF RM16 147 N10
Crawford Cl ISLW TW7 154 D8
Crawford Gdns GFD/PVL UB6 133 N5 2
PLMGR N13 99 J4
Crawford Pas CLKNW EC1R 12 A2
Crawford Pl BAY/PAD W2 9 P5
Crawford Rd CMBW SE5 159 K8
HAT AL10 40 D2
Crawfords SWLY BR8 186 F10
Crawford St MBLAR W1H 10 A4
Crawley Av CRAWE RH10 283 P5
CRAWW RH11 283 L10
Crawley Dr HHNE HP2 36 A2
Crawley La CRAWE RH10 284 D6
Crawley Rd EN EN1 99 M1
LEY E10 120 G6
WDGN N22 99 K10
Crawley's La TRING HP23 32 D2
Craword Compton Cl HCH RM12 145 K1 1
Crawshaw Rd CHERT KT16 214 G3
Crawshay Cl SEV TN13 247 H9
Crawters Cl CRAWE RH10 284 A6 1
Crawthew Gv EDUL SE22 159 N10
Cray Av ASHTD KT21 237 K2
STMC/STPC BR5 207 L5
Craybrooke Rd SCUP DA14 185 L7
Crayburne MEO DA13 189 L8
Craybury End ELTH/MOT SE9 184 F5
Cray Cl DART DA1 187 H1
Craydene Rd ERITH DA8 164 G7
Crayford High St DART DA1 164 F10
Crayford Rd DART DA1 186 G1
HOLWY N7 118 F9
Crayford Wy DART DA1 165 H10
Crayke Hl CHSGTN KT9 219 K4
Craylands STMC/STPC BR5 207 M3
Craylands La SWCM DA10 189 J1
Craylands Sq SWCM DA10 189 J1 1
Crayle St SLN SL2 128 F5
Cray Rd BELV DA17 164 B5
SCUP DA14 185 M9
SWLY BR8 208 D6
Cray Valley Rd STMC/STPC BR5 207 K5
Crealock Gv WFD IG8 101 L6
Crealock St WAND/EARL SW18 179 L2
Creasey Cl HCH RM12 125 J7
Crebor St EDUL SE22 181 P2
Credenhall Dr HAYES BR2 206 C8 1
Credenhill St STRHM/NOR SW16 180 D9
Crediton Hl KIL/WHAMP NW6 117 L10 1
Crediton Rd WLSDN NW10 136 G3
Crediton Wy ESH/CLAY KT10 218 F2
Credon Rd BERM/RHTH SE16 160 A4
PLSTW E13 141 P4
Credo Wy WTHK RM20 166 G5
Creechurch La HDTCH EC3A 13 K5 3
Creechurch Pl HDTCH EC3A 13 K6 4
Creed La BLKFR EC4V 12 D6 3
Creek Rd BARK IG11 143 J5
DEPT SE8 160 F5
E/WMO/HCT KT8 198 D4
GNWCH SE10 161 H5
Creekside DEPT SE8 160 F6
RAIN RM13 144 G6 1
The Creek GVW DA11 189 N1
SUN TW16 197 H5
Creeland Gv CAT SE6 182 E4 1
Cree's Meadow BFOR GU20 212 C4 1
Cree Wy ROM RM1 104 F8
Crefeld Cl FUL/PGN SW6 14 A10
Creffield Rd ACT W3 135 M9
Creighton Av EFNCH N2 98 A10
EHAM E6 142 A4
STAL AL1 38 C10
Creighton Rd EA W5 155 J2
KIL/WHAMP NW6 136 G4
TOTM N17 99 M8
Creigton Av EFNCH N2 117 P1
Cremer St BETH E2 7 L8
Cremorne Gdns HOR/WEW KT19 220 A5 2
Cremorne Rd GVW DA11 190 C3 1
WBPTN SW10 157 M6 2
Crescent Av GRAYS RM17 168 A4
HCH RM12 124 G7
Crescent Dr BRWN CM15 107 K2
STMC/STPC BR5 206 F6
Crescent East EBAR EN4 77 M4
Crescent Gdns RSLP HA4 113 J5
SWLY BR8 208 D2
WIM/MER SW19 179 K6
Crescent Gv CLAP SW4 158 D10
MTCM CR4 201 P4
Crescent La CLAP SW4 180 E1
Crescent Pl CHEL SW3 15 N5
Crescent Ri EBAR EN4 77 P9 1
WDGN N22 98 E9
Crescent Rd BECK BR3 204 G2
BFN/LL DA15 185 J6
BMLY BR1 183 M10
BRW CM14 106 G5
CEND/HSY/T N8 118 E4
CHING E4 101 K1
CTHM CR3 241 P10
DAGE RM10 124 C9
EBAR EN4 77 N8
ED N9 99 P2
ENC/FH EN2 79 J8
ERITH DA8 164 G5
FBAR/BDGN N11 98 A5
FNCH N3 97 J9
HHNE HP2 35 N6
KUTN/CMB KT2 177 M10
LEY E10 120 G7
PLSTW E13 141 M3 1
REDH RH1 259 K9
REIG RH2 275 K2
RYNPK SW20 200 G1
SEVS/STOTM N15 119 J1 1
SHPTN TW17 196 D5
SOCK/AV RM15 166 B1 1
SWFD E18 101 P9
WDGN N22 98 E9
WOOL/PLUM SE18 162 E4
Crescent Rw STLK EC1Y 12 E2
Crescent St IS N1 5 P3
The Crescent ABLGY WD5 54 G6
ACT W3 136 B8
ALP/SUD HA0 114 G7
ASHF TW15 174 A8
BAR EN5 77 L7
BARN SW13 156 C8
BECK BR3 204 F1
BELMT SM2 221 K7
BXLY DA5 185 M3
CHERT KT16 195 K3 2
CRICK NW2 116 E8
CTHM CR3 242 F9
E/WMO/HCT KT8 197 N4
EGH TW20 172 B9
EPP CM16 65 J8
EPSOM KT18 219 M10
FBAR/BDGN N11 98 A5
GNTH/NBYPK IG2 122 D4 1
GRH DA9 189 H2
GSTN WD25 74 A4
GUW GU2 249 M9
GVW DA11 190 C5
HART DA3 211 K3
HLWE CM17 29 M5
HORL RH6 280 B6
HYS/HAR UB3 152 D6
LCOL/BKTW AL2 55 P6
LHD/OX KT22 236 G8
LOU IG10 82 A10
NWDGN UB2 153 M1
NWMAL KT3 199 P2
REIG RH2 257 L10
RKW/CH/CXG WD3 72 C10
RYLN/HDSTN HA2 114 B6
SCUP DA14 185 J7
SEV TN13 247 L8
SHPTN TW17 196 G7
SL SL1 149 K1
SNWD SE25 203 L6
STHL UB1 153 N1 1
SURB KT6 199 K5
SUT SM1 221 N2
UPMR RM14 126 D5
WALTH E17 120 D3 3
WAT WD17 73 K8 4
WEY KT13 196 B10
WIM/MER SW19 179 K6
WWKM BR4 205 K6
Crescent Vw LOU IG10 82 A10
Crescent Wk SOCK/AV RM15 166 B1
Crescent Wy BROCKY SE4 160 F9
HORL RH6 280 B6
Crescentway NFNCH/WDSP N12 97 P7
Crescent Wy ORP BR6 227 H2
SOCK/AV RM15 146 C10
STRHM/NOR SW16 180 G10
Crescent West EBAR EN4 77 M4
Crescent Wood Rd DUL SE21 181 P6
Cresford Rd FUL/PGN SW6 157 L7
Crespigny Rd HDN NW4 116 E4
Cressage Cl STHL UB1 133 P6
Cressall Cl LHD/OX KT22 236 G6
Cressall Md LHD/OX KT22 236 G6
Cress End RKW/CH/CXG WD3 91 K2
Cresset Cl WARE SG12 27 H8
Cresset Rd HOM E9 140 B1
Cresset St CLAP SW4 158 E9
Cressfield Cl KTTN NW5 118 B10
Cressida Rd ARCH N19 118 D6
Cressingham Gv SUT SM1 221 M1
Cressingham Rd EDGW HA8 96 A8
LEW SE13 161 H9
Cressington Cl
STNW/STAM N16 119 M10 2
Cress Rd SL SL1 148 G1
Cresswell Gdns ECT SW5 15 J7 1
Cresswell Pk BKHTH/KID SE3 161 L9 1
Cresswell Pl ECT SW5 15 J7
Cresswell Rd CSHM HP5 51 J10
FELT TW13 175 M6
SNWD SE25 203 P4
TWK TW1 177 J2
Cresswell Wy WCHMH N21 99 H1
Cressy Ct HMSMTH W6 156 E2 2
Cressy Pl WCHPL E1 140 B7
Cressy Rd HAMP NW3 118 A9 1
Cresta Dr ADL/WDHM KT15 215 J6
Crest Av GRAYS RM17 167 N6
Crestbrook Av PLMGR N13 99 J4
Crest Cl RSEV TN14 228 C7 1
Crest Dr PEND EN3 80 B4
Crestfield St CAMTN NW1 5 M9
Crest Gdns RSLP HA4 113 K8
Crest Hl SHGR GU5 270 F8
Cresthill Av GRAYS RM17 167 P4
Creston Av WOKN/KNAP GU21 231 K3
Creston Wy WPK KT4 200 G8
Crest Pk HHNE HP2 36 D5
Crest Rd CRICK NW2 116 D7
HAYES BR2 205 L7
SAND/SEL CR2 224 A4
The Crest BRYLDS KT5 199 M5
CHESW EN7 61 J3
HDN NW4 116 F3
PLMGR N13 99 H5
SBW CM21 29 N1
Crest Vw GRH DA9 166 F10 1
PIN HA5 113 L2
Crest View Dr STMC/STPC BR5 206 E5
Crestway PUT/ROE SW15 178 D2
Crestwood Wy HSLWW TW4 175 N1 3
Creswick Ct WGCE AL7 22 G6 2
Creswick Rd ACT W3 135 N9
Creswick Wk GLDGN NW11 117 J2
Crete Hall Rd GVW DA11 190 A2
Crew Curve BERK HP4 33 L2
Crewdson Rd BRXN/ST SW9 158 G6
HORL RH6 280 C4
Crewe Pl WLSDN NW10 136 C5 1
Crewe's Av WARL CR6 242 B2
Crewe's Cl WARL CR6 242 B2
Crewe's La WARL CR6 242 C2
Crews St POP/IOD E14 160 F3 3
Crewys Rd CRICK NW2 117 J7
PECK SE15 160 A8
Crib St WARE SG12 26 C1
Crichton Av WLGTN SM6 222 E2
Crichton Rd CAR SM5 222 A4
Crichton St VX/NE SW8 158 D8 1
Cricketers Arms Rd ENC/FH EN2 79 K6 2
Cricketers Cl CHSGTN KT9 219 J2
ERITH DA8 164 F4
STAL AL1 38 D5
STHGT/OAK N14 98 D1
Cricketers La BFOR GU20 212 C2
Cricketers Wk SYD SE26 182 B8 1
Cricketfield Rd CLPT E5 120 A9
Cricket Field Rd UX/CGN UB8 131 N3
Cricketfield Rd WDR/YW UB7 151 M3
Cricket Gn MTCM CR4 202 A3
Cricket Ground Rd CHST BR7 206 E1
Cricket Hl REDH RH1 276 G2
Cricket La BECK BR3 182 D9
Cricket Vw WEY KT13 216 C2 1
Cricket Wy WEY KT13 196 F9
Cricklade Av BRXS/STRHM SW2 180 F5
HARH RM3 105 L7
Cricklewood Broadway
CRICK NW2 116 F8
Cricklewood La CRICK NW2 117 H9
Cridland St SRTFD E15 141 L3 2
Crieff Rd WAND/EARL SW18 179 M2
Criffel Av BRXS/STRHM SW2 180 E5
Crimp Hl EGH TW20 171 M5
WDSR SL4 171 L3
Crimscott St STHWK SE1 19 K4
Crinan St IS N1 5 M7
Cringle St VX/NE SW8 158 D6
Cripplegate St BARB EC2Y 12 E3 5
Cripsey Av CHONG CM5 67 N2
Crispen Rd FELT TW13 175 M7
Crispian Cl WLSDN NW10 116 B9 3
Crispin Cl BEAC HP9 88 B7 1
Crispin Crs WLGTN SM6 202 E10
Crispin Rd EDGW HA8 95 P7
Crispin St WCHPL E1 13 L4 1
Crispin Wy SLN SL2 109 J9
Crisp Rd HMSMTH W6 156 F4
Criss Gv CFSP/GDCR SL9 89 P10
Cristowe Rd FUL/PGN SW6 157 J8 3
Criterion Ms ARCH N19 118 E7 1
Critten La RDKG RH5 253 L8
Crlcketers Ms WAND/EARL SW18 179 L1 2
Crockenhill Hl STMC/STPC BR5 207 N5
Crockenhill La SWLY BR8 209 H7
Crockenhill Rd STMC/STPC BR5 207 N6
Crockerton Rd TOOT SW17 180 A5
Crockford Cl ADL/WDHM KT15 215 M1 3
Crockford Park Rd
ADL/WDHM KT15 215 M2
Crockham Cl CRAWW RH11 283 M9 3
Crockham Wy ELTH/MOT SE9 184 D7
Crocknorth Rd EHSLY KT24 252 G8
Crocus Cl CROY/NA CR0 204 C8 6
Crocus Fld BAR EN5 77 J10
Croffets KWD/TDW/WH KT20 238 G7
Croft Av DORK RH4 254 G10
WWKM BR4 205 H8
Croft Cl BELV DA17 164 A4
CHST BR7 184 C8
HGDN/ICK UB10 132 B2
HYS/HAR UB3 152 D6
KGLGY WD4 53 K6
MLHL NW7 96 B4
Croftdown Rd KTTN NW5 118 B8
Croft End Rd KGLGY WD4 53 K6
Crofters WDSR SL4 171 M2
Crofters Cl ISLW TW7 176 C1
Crofters Rd NTHWD HA6 92 F5
Crofters Wy CAMTN NW1 5 J5
Croft Fld HAT AL10 40 D4 1
KGLGY WD4 53 K6
Croft Gdns HNWL W7 154 F1
RSLP HA4 112 F6
Crofthill Rd SLN SL2 128 G6
Croft La KGLGY WD4 53 K6
Croftleigh Av PUR/KEN CR8 241 H2
Croft Lodge Cl WFD IG8 101 N7
Croft Meadow KGLGY WD4 53 K6
Croft Ms NFNCH/WDSP N12 97 M4
Crofton ASHTD KT21 237 K4
Crofton Av BXLY DA5 185 N3
CHSWK W4 155 P6
ORP BR6 206 F9
WOT/HER KT12 197 K10
Crofton Cl CHERT KT16 214 F4
Crofton Gate Wy BROCKY SE4 182 D1
Crofton Gv CHING E4 101 J5
Crofton La STMC/STPC BR5 206 G8
Crofton Park Rd BROCKY SE4 182 E2
Crofton Rd CDH/CHF RM16 168 B1
CMBW SE5 159 M7
ORP BR6 206 D10
PLSTW E13 141 N6
Crofton Wy BAR EN5 77 L10 1
ENC/FH EN2 79 H6
Croft Rd BH/WHM TN16 262 E2
BMLY BR1 183 M9
CFSP/GDCR SL9 90 B10
CTHM CR3 242 E8
PEND EN3 80 D5
STRHM/NOR SW16 181 H10
SUT SM1 221 N2
WARE SG12 26 B1
WIM/MER SW19 179 M10
Crofts Pth HHS/BOV HP3 36 C8
Crofts Rd HRW HA1 114 F4
The Crofts HHS/BOV HP3 36 C7
SHPTN TW17 196 F4
Croft St DEPT SE8 160 D3
WCHPL E1 13 N8
The Croft ALP/SUD HA0 115 H10
BAR EN5 77 H8
BROX EN10 44 D9
CHING E4 101 K3
CRAWW RH11 283 K7
EA W5 135 K7
HEST TW5 153 M6
LCOL/BKTW AL2 55 P1
LOU IG10 82 D6
RSLP HA4 113 K9
SWLY BR8 208 D3
WGCE AL7 23 J8
WLSDN NW10 136 C4
Croft Wy BFN/LL DA15 185 H6
RCHPK/HAM TW10 176 G6
SEV TN13 264 G1
Croftwell HARP AL5 20 E3
Crogsland Rd CAMTN NW1 4 C3
Croham Cl SAND/SEL CR2 223 M3 1
Croham Manor Rd
SAND/SEL CR2 223 M4
Croham Mt SAND/SEL CR2 223 M4
Croham Park Av SAND/SEL CR2 223 N2
Croham Valley Rd SAND/SEL CR2 223 P3
Croindene Rd
STRHM/NOR SW16 202 F1 1
Cromartie Rd ARCH N19 118 E5
Cromarty Rd EDGW HA8 95 N3 1
Crombie Cl REDBR IG4 122 C3 1
Crombie Ms BTSEA SW11 157 P8 4
Crombie Rd BFN/LL DA15 184 G4
Cromer Cl UX/CGN UB8 132 D8
Cromer Rd BAR EN5 77 M8
CHDH RM6 123 P4
EMPK RM11 125 L5
HTHAIR TW6 152 B9
LEY E10 121 J5
ROMW/RG RM7 124 D4
SNWD SE25 204 A3
TOOT SW17 180 B9
TOTM N17 99 P10 2
WATN WD24 73 K4 2
Cromer St STPAN WC1H 5 M10
Cromer Villas Rd
WAND/EARL SW18 179 J2
Cromford Cl ORP BR6 207 H10 1
Cromford Rd PUT/ROE SW15 179 J1
Cromford Wy NWMAL KT3 200 A1
Cromlix Cl CHST BR7 206 E2
Crompton Flds CRAWE RH10 283 P4
Crompton St BAY/PAD W2 9 L2
Crompton Wy CRAWE RH10 283 P5
Cromwell Av CHESW EN7 62 A6
HAYES BR2 205 N3
HGT N6 118 C6
HMSMTH W6 156 E4
NWMAL KT3 200 C5
Cromwell Cl CSTG HP8 89 P4
EFNCH N2 117 N2 2
STALE/WH AL4 39 J1
WOT/HER KT12 197 J8
Cromwell Ct ALP/SUD HA0 135 K4 1
Cromwell Crs ECT SW5 14 E5
Cromwell Dr SL SL1 129 K8
Cromwell Gv CTHM CR3 241 K7
HMSMTH W6 156 F2
Cromwell Ms SKENS SW7 15 M5 1
Cromwell Pl ACT W3 135 P10 1
HGT N6 118 C6 1
MORT/ESHN SW14 155 P9 2
SKENS SW7 15 M5 2
Cromwell Rd ALP/SUD HA0 135 J4
ASC SL5 192 A4
BECK BR3 204 D2
BORE WD6 75 K5
BRW CM14 106 G5
BRXN/ST SW9 159 J7
CROY/NA CR0 203 L7
CTHM CR3 241 K7
FELT TW13 175 J4
FNCH N3 97 M10
FSTGT E7 141 P2
GRAYS RM17 167 M3
HERT/BAY SG13 25 N4
HSLW TW3 153 P10
HYS/HAR UB3 132 E8
KUTN/CMB KT2 199 L1 1
MUSWH N10 98 B8
REDH RH1 258 A10 1
SKENS SW7 15 L5
TEDD TW11 176 F9
WALTH E17 121 H3
WARE SG12 26 E2
WIM/MER SW19 179 K8
WPK KT4 200 A10
Cromwell St HSLW TW3 153 P10
Crondace Rd FUL/PGN SW6 157 K7
Crondall St IS N1 7 H8
Cronin St PECK SE15 159 N6
Cronks Hl REIG RH2 275 M1
Cronks Hill Cl REDH RH1 275 N2 2
Cronks Hill Rd REIG RH2 275 N2
Crooked Billet Rbt CHING E4 100 G8
Crooked La GVE DA12 190 E2
Crooked Mile WAB EN9 63 H6
Crooked Usage FNCH N3 117 H1
Crooked Wy WAB EN9 45 K8
Crooke Rd DEPT SE8 160 D4
Crookham Rd FUL/PGN SW6 157 J7
Crookhams WGCE AL7 23 K3
Crook Log BXLYHN DA7 163 N9
Crookston Rd ELTH/MOT SE9 162 E9
Croombs Rd CAN/RD E16 141 P7
Croom's Hl GNWCH SE10 161 J6
Croom's Hill Gv GNWCH SE10 161 H6
Crop Common HAT AL10 40 E2
Cropley St IS N1 6 G7
Croppath Rd DAGE RM10 124 B9
Cropthorne Ct MV/WKIL W9 3 K10
Crosby Cl BEAC HP9 108 E1 1
FELT TW13 175 M7 2
STALE/WH AL4 39 H9
Crosby Rd DAGE RM10 144 C4
FSTGT E7 141 M1
Crosby Rw STHWK SE1 18 G2
Crosby Wk HACK E8 7 L2
Crosier Rd HGDN/ICK UB10 112 D9
Crosier Wy RSLP HA4 112 F8
Crossacres WOKS/MYFD GU22 233 H2
Crossbow Rd CHIG IG7 103 J6
Crossbrook HAT AL10 40 B5
Crossbrook Rd BKHTH/KID SE3 162 B8
Crossbrook St CHES/WCR EN8 62 C6 1
Cross Deep TWK TW1 176 E6
Cross Deep Gdns TWK TW1 176 E5
Crossett Gn HHS/BOV HP3 36 D8 1
Crossfell Rd HHS/BOV HP3 36 C8
Crossfield Cl BERK HP4 33 L5
Crossfield Pl WEY KT13 216 C4
Crossfield Rd HAMP NW3 3 M2
HOD EN11 44 G1
TOTM N17 119 K1 1
Crossfields STALW/RED AL3 38 A9
Crossfield St DEPT SE8 160 F6 1
Crossford St BRXN/ST SW9 158 G8
Crossgate EDGW HA8 95 M4
GFD/PVL UB6 134 G1 1
Crossing Rd EPP CM16 65 K8
Cross Keys CRAWW RH11 283 N7
Cross Keys Cl MHST W1U 10 D4 2
Cross Lances Rd HSLW TW3 154 A10
Crossland Rd REDH RH1 258 B10
THHTH CR7 203 J6
Crosslands CHERT KT16 195 H10
Crosslands Av EA W5 135 L10
NWDGN UB2 153 N4
Crosslands Rd HOR/WEW KT19 220 A3
Cross La BEAC HP9 108 E1
BXLY DA5 186 A3
CEND/HSY/T N8 118 G1
CHERT KT16 214 E3
HARP AL5 20 B6
HERT/WAS SG14 25 J5 2
HORL RH6 281 K7
Cross La East GVE DA12 190 E5
Cross Lanes CFSP/GDCR SL9 90 C6
GU GU1 250 C10
Cross Lanes Cl CFSP/GDCR SL9 90 C6 1
Cross La West GVW DA11 190 E5
Crosslet St WALW SE17 19 H6 1
Crosslet V GNWCH SE10 160 G7
Crossley Cl BH/WHM TN16 244 A1

Crossley St *HOLWY* N7 6 A1
Crossmead *ELTH/MOT* SE9 184 C4
OXHEY WD19 73 J10
Crossmead Av *GFD/PVL* UB6 133 P5
Cross Meadow *CSHM* HP5 50 E5
Crossness Rd *BARK* IG11 143 J5
Cross Oak *WDSR* SL4 148 F8
Cross Oak La *REDH* RH1 276 D10
Cross Oak Rd *BERK* HP4 33 M6
Crossoaks La *BORE* WD6 76 A1
POTB/CUF EN6 58 B10
The Crosspath *RAD* WD7 74 F1
Cross Rd *ASC* SL5 192 E8
BELMT SM2 221 K6
BUSH WD23 73 M10
CHDH RM6 123 M5
CHES/WCR EN8 62 D9 1
CMBW SE5 159 M8
CROY/NA CR0 203 L8
DART DA1 187 K2
EN EN1 79 N8
FBAR/BDGN N11 98 C6
FELT TW13 175 M7
GVW DA11 190 C2
HAYES BR2 206 B9
HERT/WAS SG14 25 K4
HRW HA1 114 C2
KTN/HRWW/W HA3 94 F10
KUTN/CMB KT2 177 L10
KWD/TDW/WH KT20 238 F8
PUR/KEN CR8 223 J9
RDART DA2 187 N7
ROMW/RG RM7 124 B1
RYLN/HDSTN HA2 113 P8
SCUP DA14 185 L7 1
STMC/STPC BR5 207 L5 1
SUT SM1 221 N2
WDGN N22 99 H7
WEY KT13 196 E10 2
WFD IG8 102 C7
WIM/MER SW19 179 K10
Cross Roads *LOU* IG10 81 N6
The Crossroads *EHSLY* KT24 253 L4 1
Cross St *BARN* SW13 156 B8
ERITH DA8 164 F5
HPTN TW12 176 B8
IS N1 6 D5
STALW/RED AL3 38 C6
UED N18 99 P6 5
WARE SG12 26 D2
WAT WD17 73 K7
Crossthwaite Av *HNHL* SE24 159 L10
Crosswall *TWRH* EC3N 13 L7
Cross Wy *HYS/HAR* UB3 153 H1
Crossway *BCTR* RM8 123 M8
CDALE/KGS NW9 116 C2
CSHM HP5 51 K6
EN EN1 99 M1
NFNCH/WDSP N12 97 N7
NWMAL KT3 200 F4
PIN HA5 93 J10
RSLP HA4 113 K9
STMC/STPC BR5 206 G4
STNW/STAM N16 119 M10
THMD SE28 143 M8
WEA W13 134 F6
WGCW AL8 22 E1
WOT/HER KT12 197 J9
Crossways *BEAC* HP9 88 E10
BELMT SM2 221 N5
BERK HP4 33 L6
BH/WHM TN16 243 P6
BRWN CM15 87 M10
CRAWE RH10 284 B6
EGH TW20 172 G9
EHSLY KT24 253 L3 1
GPK RM2 125 J1
HHS/BOV HP3 36 C6
SAND/SEL CR2 224 E4
SUN TW16 196 G1
Crossways Bvd *GRH* DA9 188 D1
Crossways Cl *CRAWE* RH10 284 A6
Crossways La *REIG* RH2 257 M4
Crossways Rd *BECK* BR3 204 F4
MTCM CR4 202 C3
The Crossways *COUL/CHIP* CR5 240 G5
HEST TW5 153 N6
REDH RH1 258 C5
WBLY HA9 115 M7
The Crossway *ELTH/MOT* SE9 184 A5
The Cross Wy *KTN/HRWW/W* HA3 94 D10
The Crossway *WDGN* N22 99 J8
Crosswell Cl *SHPTN* TW17 196 D2 1
Crosthwaite Wy *SL* SL1 128 C7
Croston St *HACK* E8 7 P5
Crosts La *WDGN* N22 99 H8
Crothall Cl *PLMGR* N13 98 G4
Crouch Av *BARK* IG11 143 L4
Crouch Cl *BECK* BR3 182 F9 1
Crouch Cft *ELTH/MOT* SE9 184 D6
Crouch End Hl *ARCH* N19 118 E5
Crouchfield *HERT/WAS* SG14 25 L2 1
HHW HP1 35 L7
Crouch Hall Rd *CEND/HSY/T* N8 118 E4
Crouch Hl *ARCH* N19 118 F5
Crouch La *CHESW* EN7 61 K3
Crouchmans Cl *DUL* SE21 181 N6
Crouch Oak La *ADL/WDHM* KT15 215 M1
Crouch Rd *GRAYS* RM17 168 D4
WLSDN NW10 136 A2
Crouch Va *UPMR* RM14 126 D5
Crowborough Cl *WARL* CR6 242 D4 1
Crowborough Dr *WARL* CR6 242 D4
Crowborough Pth *OXHEY* WD19 93 L5 1
Crowborough Rd *TOOT* SW17 180 B8
Crowden Wy *THMD* SE28 143 M9
Crowder St *WCHPL* E1 140 A9
Crow Dr *RSEV* TN14 246 D1
Crowfoot Cl *HOM* E9 120 E10 1
Crow Green La *BRWN* CM15 86 F9
Crow Green Rd *BRWN* CM15 86 E9
Crowhurst Cl *BRXN/ST* SW9 159 H8
CRAWE RH10 284 F7
Crowhurst Md *GDST* RH9 260 B6 1
Crowhurst Wy *STMC/STPC* BR5 207 M5
Crowland Av *HYS/HAR* UB3 152 F3
Crowland Gdns *STHGT/OAK* N14 98 F1
Crowland Rd *SEVS/STOTM* N15 119 N3
THHTH CR7 203 L4 1
Crowlands Av *ROMW/RG* RM7 124 C4
Crowland Ter *IS* N1 6 G3
Crowland Wk *MRDN* SM4 201 L6
Crow La *ROMW/RG* RM7 124 A5
ROMW/RG RM7 124 D5
Crowley Crs *CROY/NA* CR0 223 H2
Crown Cl *BOW* E3 140 F3
DTCH/LGLY SL3 150 F6
HYS/HAR UB3 152 G1
KIL/WHAMP NW6 2 G1
MLHL NW7 96 C3
ORP BR6 227 K1
RBSF CM22 30 D3
WOT/HER KT12 197 K7
Crown Dl *NRWD* SE19 181 K9
Crowndale Rd *CAMTN* NW1 5 H7
Crownfield *BROX* EN10 44 F7
Crownfield Av *GNTH/NBYPK* IG2 123 H3
Crownfield Rd *SRTFD* E15 121 J10
Crownfields *SEV* TN13 265 J1
Crown Ga *HLW* CM20 46 G1
Crown Gn *GVE* DA12 191 P8 1
Crown Hts *GU* GU1 268 B3
Crown Hl *WAB* EN9 64 C9
Crown Hill Ct *ASC* SL5 192 A5
Crownhill Rd *WFD* IG8 102 B8
WLSDN NW10 136 C3
Crown La *CHST* BR7 206 F1
GVE DA12 191 P7
HAYES BR2 206 A5
MRDN SM4 201 K3
SLN SL2 128 G2
STHGT/OAK N14 98 D2
STRHM/NOR SW16 181 H8
VW GU25 194 A6
WIM/MER SW19 201 K3
Crown Lane Sp *HAYES* BR2 206 A6
Crown Meadow *DTCH/LGLY* SL3 150 E6
Crown Office Rw *EMB* EC4Y 12 A7
Crown Pas *STJS* SW1Y 11 H10
Crown Pl *KTTN* NW5 4 F1
Crown Ri *CHERT* KT16 195 J8
GSTN WD25 55 K10
Crown Rd *BARK/HLT* IG6 122 G2
BORE WD6 75 M5
BRW CM14 86 C5
EN EN1 79 P7
GRAYS RM17 167 M5
MUSWH N10 98 B8
NWMAL KT3 199 P1
ORP BR6 227 K2
RSEV TN14 228 G6
RSLP HA4 113 L10
SUT SM1 221 L1 3
TWK TW1 176 G2
VW GU25 193 P6
WIM/MER SW19 201 K4
Crownstone Rd
BRXS/STRHM SW2 181 H1
Crown St *ACT* W3 135 N10
BRW CM14 107 H3 1
CMBW SE5 159 K6
DAGE RM10 144 D1
EGH TW20 172 D8
RYLN/HDSTN HA2 114 C6
Crown Ter *RCH/KEW* TW9 155 L10 2
Crowntree Cl *ISLW* TW7 154 E5
Crown Wk *WBLY* HA9 115 L8
Crown Wy *WDR/YW* UB7 132 A10
Crown Woods Wy *ELTH/MOT* SE9 184 G1
Crown Yd *HSLW* TW3 154 B9 1
Crow Piece La *SLN* SL2 128 E2
Crowshott Av *STAN* HA7 95 H10
Crows Rd *BARK* IG11 142 E1
EPP CM16 65 J6
SRTFD E15 141 J5
Crowstone Rd *CDH/CHF* RM16 167 P1
Crowther Av *BTFD* TW8 155 K4
Crowther Rd *SNWD* SE25 203 P4
Crowthorne Cl *WAND/EARL* SW18 179 J3
Crowthorne Rd *NKENS* W10 136 G8
Croxdale Rd *BORE* WD6 75 L6
Croxden Cl *EDGW* HA8 115 M1 1
Croxden Wk *MRDN* SM4 201 M6 1
Croxford Gdns *WDGN* N22 99 J8
Croxford Wy *ROMW/RG* RM7 124 E6
Croxley Cl *STMC/STPC* BR5 207 L2
Croxley Gn *STMC/STPC* BR5 207 L1
Croxley Rd *MV/WKIL* W9 2 D10
Croxley Vw *WATW* WD18 72 F10
Croxted Cl *DUL* SE21 181 K3
Croxted Rd *DUL* SE21 181 L5 1
Croyde Av *GFD/PVL* UB6 134 B5
HYS/HAR UB3 152 F3
Croyde Cl *ELTH/MOT* SE9 184 G3
Croydonbarn La *GDST* RH9 281 P3
The Croydon F/O *CROY/NA* CR0 223 J1
Croydon Gv *CROY/NA* CR0 203 J8 1
Croydon La *BNSTD* SM7 221 N9
Croydon La South *BNSTD* SM7 221 L10
Croydon Rd *BECK* BR3 204 D3
BH/WHM TN16 262 E2
CROY/NA CR0 204 C5
CROY/NA CR0 222 F1
CTHM CR3 241 P8
MTCM CR4 202 C5
PGE/AN SE20 204 A2
PLSTW E13 141 M6
REIG RH2 257 M9
WARL CR6 243 J8
WLGTN SM6 202 E10 1
WWKM BR4 205 K10
Croyland Rd *ED* N9 99 P2
Croylands Dr *SURB* KT6 199 K7
Croysdale Av *SUN* TW16 197 H3
Crozier Dr *SAND/SEL* CR2 224 A6
Crozier Ter *HOM* E9 120 C10 1
Crucible Cl *CHDH* RM6 123 L4
Crucifix La *STHWK* SE1 19 J1
Cruden Rd *GVE* DA12 191 J6
Cruden St *IS* N1 6 D6
Cruick Av *SOCK/AV* RM15 147 H8
Cruickshank St *FSBYW* WC1X 6 A9
Cruikshank Rd *SRTFD* E15 121 K9
Crummock Cl *SL* SL1 128 B8 1
Crummock Gdns
CDALE/KGS NW9 116 B3
Crumpsall St *ABYW* SE2 163 M3
Crundale Av *CDALE/KGS* NW9 115 M3
Crunden Rd *SAND/SEL* CR2 223 L4
Crusader Cl *PUR* RM19 165 P3
Crusader Gdns *CROY/NA* CR0 203 M10 1
Crusader Wy *WATW* WD18 72 G10
Crusoe Ms *STNW/STAM* N16 119 L7
Crusoe Rd *ERITH* DA8 164 E4
MTCM CR4 180 A10
Crutched Friars *MON* EC3R 13 K7
Crutchfield La *HORL* RH6 279 K1
WOT/HER KT12 197 J8 1
Crutchley Rd *CAT* SE6 183 K5
Crystal Av *HCH* RM12 125 M9
Crystal Palace *NRWD* SE19 181 P9 1
Crystal Palace Pde *NRWD* SE19 181 N9
Crystal Palace Park Rd
NRWD SE19 181 P8
Crystal Palace Rd *EDUL* SE22 181 N2
Crystal Ter *NRWD* SE19 181 L9
Crystal Wy *BCTR* RM8 123 M6
HRW HA1 114 E3
Cuba Dr *PEND* EN3 80 B6
Cuba St *POP/IOD* E14 160 F1
Cubitt Sq *STHL* UB1 134 B10 1
Cubitt St *CROY/NA* CR0 222 G2
FSBYW WC1X 5 P10
Cubitt Ter *CLAP* SW4 158 D9
Cubitt Wy *WOKN/KNAP* GU21 231 J4 1
Cublands *HERT/BAY* SG13 26 A5
Cuckfield Cl *CRAWW* RH11 283 J10
Cuckmans Dr *LCOL/BKTW* AL2 55 P1
Cuckmere Crs *CRAWW* RH11 283 J8
Cuckoo Av *HNWL* W7 134 D6
Cuckoo Dene *HNWL* W7 134 C7
Cuckoo Hall La *ED* N9 100 B1
Cuckoo Hl *PIN* HA5 113 K1
Cuckoo Hill Dr *PIN* HA5 113 K1
Cuckoo Hill Rd *PIN* HA5 113 L2
Cuckoo La *CDH/CHF* RM16 147 L10
CHOB/PIR GU24 212 C9
HNWL W7 134 D9
Cuckoo V *CHOB/PIR* GU24 212 C9
Cucumber La *BRKMPK* AL9 42 A7
Cuda's Cl *HOR/WEW* KT19 220 C1
Cuddington Av *WPK* KT4 200 C10
Cuddington Cl
KWD/TDW/WH KT20 238 F6
Cuddington Gld *HOR/WEW* KT19 219 M8
Cuddington Park Cl *BNSTD* SM7 221 J9
Cuddington Wy *BELMT* SM2 220 G8
Cudham Cl *BELMT* SM2 221 K6 2
Cudham Dr *CROY/NA* CR0 224 G6
Cudham La North *RSEV* TN14 226 F10
Cudham La South *RSEV* TN14 244 F1
Cudham Park Rd *RSEV* TN14 227 H6
Cudham Rd *BH/WHM* TN16 244 B5
ORP BR6 226 D7
Cudham St *CAT* SE6 183 H3
Cudworth La *RDKG* RH5 278 A7
Cudworth St *WCHPL* E1 140 A6
Cuff Crs *ELTH/MOT* SE9 184 A3
Cuffley Av *GSTN* WD25 55 L10
Cuffley Ct *HHNE* HP2 36 D1
Cuffley Hl *CHESW* EN7 61 J5
Cugley Rd *RDART* DA2 188 B3
Culcroft *HART* DA3 211 L4
Culford Gdns *CHEL* SW3 16 B6
Culford Gv *IS* N1 7 J2
Culford Ms *IS* N1 7 J1
Culford Rd *CDH/CHF* RM16 167 P1
IS N1 7 J5
Culgaith Gdns *ENC/FH* EN2 78 F8
Cullen Sq *SOCK/AV* RM15 147 H9
Cullen Wy *WLSDN* NW10 135 P6 1
Cullera Cl *NTHWD* HA6 92 G7
Cullerne Cl *EW* KT17 220 C6
Cullesden Rd *PUR/KEN* CR8 241 J1
Culling Rd *BERM/RHTH* SE16 160 B2
Cullings Ct *WAB* EN9 63 L9
Cullington Cl *KTN/HRWW/W* HA3 114 F2
Cullingworth Rd *WLSDN* NW10 116 D10
Culloden Cl *STHWK* SE1 19 P8
Culloden Rd *ENC/FH* EN2 79 J6
Culloden St *POP/IOD* E14 141 H8 5
Cull's Rd *RGUW* GU3 248 A10
Cullum St *FENCHST* EC3M 13 J7 1
Culmington Rd *SAND/SEL* CR2 223 K4
WEA W13 135 H10
Culmore Rd *PECK* SE15 160 A6
Culmstock Rd *BTSEA* SW11 180 B1
Culpepper Cl *CHIG* IG7 102 E7
Culross Cl *SEVS/STOTM* N15 119 K2
Culross St *MYFR/PKLN* W1K 10 C8
Culsac Rd *SURB* KT6 199 K9
Culverden Rd *BAL* SW12 180 D6
OXHEY WD19 93 J4
Culver Dr *OXTED* RH8 261 K6
Culver Gv *STAN* HA7 95 H10
Culverhay *ASHTD* KT21 237 K2
Culverhouse Gdns
STRHM/NOR SW16 180 G7
Culverlands Cl *STAN* HA7 94 G5 1
Culverley Rd *CAT* SE6 182 G4
Culver Rd *STAL* AL1 38 D5
Culvers Av *CAR* SM5 202 A9
Culvers Cft *BEAC* HP9 89 H7 1
Culvers Retreat *CAR* SM5 202 A8
Culverstone Cl *HAYES* BR2 205 L6 2
Culvers Wy *CAR* SM5 202 A9
Culvert La *UX/CGN* UB8 131 L4
Culvert Pl *BTSEA* SW11 158 B8
Culvert Rd *BTSEA* SW11 158 B8 1
SEVS/STOTM N15 119 M3
Culvey Cl *HART* DA3 211 K5
Culworth St *STJWD* NW8 3 N8
Cumberland Av *GUW* GU2 249 M5
GVE DA12 190 F3 4
HCH RM12 125 M8 1
SLN SL2 129 H6
WELL DA16 163 H9
WLSDN NW10 135 N5
Cumberland Cl *AMSS* HP7 69 N5 1
BARK/HLT IG6 102 F9 1
HACK E8 7 L2
HERT/WAS SG14 25 K3 1
HHS/BOV HP3 36 F10
HOR/WEW KT19 220 B6
RYNPK SW20 178 G10 1
TWK TW1 176 G2 5
Cumberland Dr *BXLYHN* DA7 163 P6
CHSGTN KT9 199 K10
DART DA1 187 N3
ESH/CLAY KT10 198 F9
Cumberland Gdns *FSBYW* WC1X 5 P9
HDN NW4 97 H10 1
Cumberland Ga *BAY/PAD* W2 10 A7
MBLAR W1H 10 A7
Cumberland Market *CAMTN* NW1 4 F10 2
Cumberland Pk *ACT* W3 135 P9
Cumberland Pl *CAMTN* NW1 4 E9 1
CAT SE6 183 L4
SUN TW16 197 H4
Cumberland Rd *ACT* W3 135 P9
ASHF TW15 173 N6
BARN SW13 156 C7
CDALE/KGS NW9 115 L1 1
ED N9 100 B2
HAYES BR2 205 K4
HNWL W7 154 E1
HRW HA1 114 A3
MNPK E12 122 A9 2
PLSTW E13 141 N7
RCH/KEW TW9 155 M7
SNWD SE25 204 A6
WALTH E17 100 D10 2
WDGN N22 98 G10
Cumberlands *PUR/KEN* CR8 241 L1
Cumberland St *PIM* SW1V 16 F7
STA TW18 172 G8 1
Cumberland Ter *CAMTN* NW1 4 E8
Cumberland Terrace Ms
CAMTN NW1 4 E8 1
Cumberlow Av *SNWD* SE25 203 P3
Cumberlow Pl *HHS/BOV* HP3 36 D7 3
Cumbernauld Gdns *SUN* TW16 174 G8 1
Cumberton Rd *TOTM* N17 99 L9
Cumbrae Cl *SLN* SL2 129 M10 1
Cumbrae Gdns *SURB* KT6 199 J8 1
Cumbrian Av *BXLYHN* DA7 164 F8
Cumbrian Gdns *CRICK* NW2 116 G7
Cumbrian Wy *UX/CGN* UB8 131 N3
Cumley Rd *CHONG* CM5 66 F6
Cummings Hall La *ABR/ST* RM4 105 K4
Cumming St *IS* N1 5 P8
Cumnor Gdns *EW* KT17 220 D3
Cumnor Ri *PUR/KEN* CR8 241 K3 1
Cumnor Rd *BELMT* SM2 221 M3
Cunard Crs *WCHMH* N21 79 L10
Cunard Rd *WLSDN* NW10 136 A5
Cundalls Rd *WARE* SG12 26 D1
Cundy Rd *CAN/RD* E16 141 P8
Cundy St *BGVA* SW1W 16 D6
Cunliffe Cl *EPSOM* KT18 237 N10
Cunliffe Rd *HOR/WEW* KT19 220 C1
Cunliffe St *STRHM/NOR* SW16 180 D9
Cunningham Av *GU* GU1 250 D9
PEND EN3 80 D2
STAL AL1 38 E8
Cunningham Cl *CHDH* RM6 123 M3 1
WWKM BR4 204 G9 1
Cunningham Hill Rd *STAL* AL1 38 E8
Cunningham Pk *HRW* HA1 114 C3
Cunningham Pl *STJWD* NW8 9 L1
Cunningham Ri *EPP* CM16 66 E1 1
Cunningham Rd *BNSTD* SM7 239 N1
CHES/WCR EN8 62 D3
SEVS/STOTM N15 119 P2 2
Cunnington St *CHSWK* W4 155 P2
Cupar Rd *BTSEA* SW11 158 B7 4
Cupola Cl *BMLY* BR1 183 N8 1
Cureton St *WEST* SW1P 17 K7
Curfew Bell Rd *CHERT* KT16 195 J7
Curlew Cl *BERK* HP4 33 P6
SAND/SEL CR2 224 C7
THMD SE28 143 N9
Curlew Gdns *RGUE* GU4 250 G8
The Curlews *GVE* DA12 190 G5
Curlew St *STHWK* SE1 19 M1
Curlew Wy *YEAD* UB4 133 L7 2
Curling Cl *COUL/CHIP* CR5 240 G6
Curling La *GRAYS* RM17 167 L4
Curling V *GUW* GU2 267 M2
Curnick's La *WNWD* SE27 181 K7 2
Curran Av *BFN/LL* DA15 185 J1
WLGTN SM6 202 B10
Curran Cl *UX/CGN* UB8 131 M6
Currey Rd *NTHLT* UB5 134 B1
Curricle St *ACT* W3 136 B10 1
Currie Hill Cl *WIM/MER* SW19 179 J7
Curriers La *SL* SL1 108 C10
Currie St *HERT/BAY* SG13 25 M4
Curry Ri *MLHL* NW7 96 G7
Cursitor St *FLST/FETLN* EC4A 12 A5
Curtain Pl *SDTCH* EC2A 13 K1
Curtain Rd *IS* N1 7 K10
SDTCH EC2A 13 J2
Curteys *HLWE* CM17 29 N6
Curthwaite Gdns *ENC/FH* EN2 78 E8
Curtis Cl *RKW/CH/CXG* WD3 91 K2
Curtis Dr *ACT* W3 136 A8 2
Curtis Field Rd
STRHM/NOR SW16 180 G7
Curtis La *ALP/SUD* HA0 135 K1
Curtismill Cl *STMC/STPC* BR5 207 L3
Curtis Mill La *ABR/ST* RM4 84 F8
Curtismill Wy *STMC/STPC* BR5 207 L3
Curtis Rd *DORK* RH4 272 E1
EMPK RM11 125 N6
HHS/BOV HP3 36 E7
HOR/WEW KT19 219 P1
HSLWW TW4 175 N3
Curtis St *STHWK* SE1 19 L5
Curtis Wy *BERK* HP4 34 A6
Curvan Cl *EW* KT17 220 C6 1
The Curve *SHB* W12 136 D9
Curwen Av *FSTGT* E7 121 N9 1
Curwen Rd *SHB* W12 156 D1
Curzon Av *BEAC* HP9 88 C7
PEND EN3 80 C9
STAN HA7 94 F9
Curzon Cl *ORP* BR6 226 G1
WEY KT13 216 B1 3
Curzon Crs *BARK* IG11 143 J5
WLSDN NW10 136 B2
Curzon Dr *GRAYS* RM17 167 P6
Curzon Pl *MYFR/PKLN* W1K 10 D10 1
PIN HA5 113 K3
Curzon Rd *EA* W5 134 G6
MUSWH N10 98 C10
THHTH CR7 203 H6
WEY KT13 216 B1
Curzon St *MYFR/PICC* W1J 10 F9
MYFR/PKLN W1K 10 D10
Cusack Cl *TWK* TW1 176 E7 1
Cussons Cl *CHESW* EN7 61 P5
Cutcombe Rd *CMBW* SE5 159 K8
Cuthberga Cl *BARK* IG11 142 F2 2
Cuthbert Cl *CHESW* EN7 61 N5 2
Cuthbert Gdns *SNWD* SE25 203 M3
Cuthbert Rd *CROY/NA* CR0 203 J9
UED N18 99 P6 6
WALTH E17 121 H1 2
Cuthbert St *BAY/PAD* W2 9 L2 1
Cutler St *HDTCH* EC3A 13 K5 4
Cutmore Dr *STALE/WH* AL4 39 N8
Cutmore St *GVW* DA11 190 E3
The Cut *STHWK* SE1 18 B1
Cuttinglye La *CRAWE* RH10 285 P4
Cuttsfield Ter *HHW* HP1 35 J7
Cutty Sark Ct *GRH* DA9 188 F1 2
Cuxton Cl *BXLYHS* DA6 185 P1
Cwmbran Ct *HHNE* HP2 36 A2 1
Cyclamen Cl *HPTN* TW12 175 P9 2
Cyclamen Rd *SWLY* BR8 208 E4
Cyclamen Wy *HOR/WEW* KT19 219 P2 1
Cygnet Av *EBED/NFELT* TW14 175 K3
Cygnet Cl *BORE* WD6 75 P5 1
NTHWD HA6 92 D8
WLSDN NW10 116 A10 1
The Cygnets *FELT* TW13 175 M7
STA TW18 173 J8 2
Cygnet St *WCHPL* E1 13 M1 1
Cygnet Vw *WTHK* RM20 166 E2
Cygnet Wy *YEAD* UB4 133 L8
Cynthia St *IS* N1 5 P8
Cypress Av *ENC/FH* EN2 79 H1
WGCE AL7 23 M6
WHTN TW2 176 B3
Cypress Cl *WAB* EN9 63 J10 1
Cypress Gdns *BROCKY* SE4 182 D1 1
Cypress Gv *BARK/HLT* IG6 103 H7
Cypress Rd *GU* GU1 249 P8
KTN/HRWW/W HA3 94 C10
SNWD SE25 203 M2
Cypress Tree Cl *BFN/LL* DA15 185 J4
Cypress Wk *EGH* TW20 171 N9
GSTN WD25 73 J1 1
Cypress Wy *EW* KT17 220 G10
Cyprians Av *CHOB/PIR* GU24 230 G7
Cyprus Av *FNCH* N3 97 H10
Cyprus Cl *FSBYPK* N4 119 J4 2
Cyprus Gdns *FNCH* N3 97 H10
Cyprus Pl *BETH* E2 140 B4 2
EHAM E6 142 D9
Cyprus Rd *ED* N9 99 N3
FNCH N3 97 J10
Cyprus St *BETH* E2 140 B4
Cyrena Rd *EDUL* SE22 181 N2
Cyril Rd *BXLYHN* DA7 163 P8
ORP BR6 207 K7
Cyrils Wy *STAL* AL1 38 C9
Cyrus St *FSBYE* EC1V 12 D1
Czar St *DEPT* SE8 160 F5

D

Dabbling Cl *ERITH* DA8 165 J6 1
Dabbs Hill La *NTHLT* UB5 133 N1
D'abernon Cl *ESH/CLAY* KT10 217 P1
D'abernon Dr *COB* KT11 235 M2
Dabin Crs *GNWCH* SE10 161 H7
Dacca St *DEPT* SE8 160 E5
Dace Rd *BOW* E3 140 F3
Dacorum Wy *HHW* HP1 35 M6
Dacre Av *CLAY* IG5 102 D10
SOCK/AV RM15 146 C10
Dacre Cl *CHIG* IG7 102 F5 1
GFD/PVL UB6 134 A4 1
Dacre Crs *SOCK/AV* RM15 146 C10
Dacre Gdns *BORE* WD6 76 A9
CHIG IG7 102 F5
Dacre Pk *LEW* SE13 161 K9
Dacre Pl *LEW* SE13 161 K9
Dacre Rd *CROY/NA* CR0 202 F7
PLSTW E13 141 N3
WAN E11 121 L6 2
Dacres Rd *FSTH* SE23 182 C6
Dacre St *STJSPK* SW1H 17 J3
Dade Wy *NWDGN* UB2 153 N4
Daerwood Cl *HAYES* BR2 206 C8
Daffodil Av *BRWN* CM15 86 G9
Daffodil Cl *CROY/NA* CR0 204 C8 7
HPTN TW12 175 P9 3
Daffodil Dr *CHOB/PIR* GU24 230 F2 1
Daffodil Gdns *IL* IG1 122 E10
Daffodil St *SHB* W12 136 C9
Dafforne Rd *TOOT* SW17 180 A6
Dagden Rd *RGUE* GU4 268 B6
Dagenham Av *DAGW* RM9 143 P3
Dagenham Rd *DAGE* RM10 124 D9
LEY E10 120 E6 1
RAIN RM13 144 E2
ROMW/RG RM7 124 E5
Dagger La *BORE* WD6 74 F10
Daggs Dell Rd *HHW* HP1 35 H4
Dagley La *RGUE* GU4 268 A6
Dagmar Av *WBLY* HA9 115 L9
Dagmar Gdns *WLSDN* NW10 136 G4
Dagmar Rd *CMBW* SE5 159 M7
DAGE RM10 144 D2
FSBYPK N4 119 H5
KUTN/CMB KT2 199 L1
NWDGN UB2 153 M2
SEVS/STOTM N15 119 L2 2
SNWD SE25 203 M4
WDGN N22 98 E9
WDSR SL4 149 J8
Dagmar Ter *IS* N1 6 D5
Dagnall Crs *UX/CGN* UB8 131 M7
Dagnall Pk *SNWD* SE25 203 M5
Dagnall Rd *SNWD* SE25 203 M5
Dagnall St *BTSEA* SW11 158 A8
Dagnam Park Cl *HARH* RM3 105 P6
Dagnam Park Dr *HARH* RM3 105 M6
Dagnam Park Gdns *HARH* RM3 105 P7 1
Dagnam Park Sq *HARH* RM3 106 A7 1
Dagnan Rd *BAL* SW12 180 C3
Dagonet Rd *BMLY* BR1 183 M6
Dagwood La *BRWN* CM15 86 G4
Dahlia Cl *CHESW* EN7 61 K1
Dahlia Dr *SWLY* BR8 208 G2
Dahlia Gdns *IL* IG1 142 E1
MTCM CR4 202 E4
Dahlia Rd *ABYW* SE2 163 L4
Dahomey Rd *STRHM/NOR* SW16 180 D9
Daiglen Dr *SOCK/AV* RM15 146 F9
Daimler Wy *WLGTN* SM6 222 F4
Daines Cl *MNPK* E12 122 C8
SOCK/AV RM15 146 F6
Dainford Cl *BMLY* BR1 183 J8
Daintry Cl *KTN/HRWW/W* HA3 114 F2
Dairsie Rd *ELTH/MOT* SE9 162 D9
Dairy Cl *BMLY* BR1 183 N10 1
EYN DA4 188 A10
THHTH CR7 203 K2 2
Dairyfields *CRAWW* RH11 283 K8 2
Dairyglen Av *CHES/WCR* EN8 62 C7
Dairy La *EDEN* TN8 262 E10
WOOL/PLUM SE18 162 C3
Dairyman Cl *CRICK* NW2 116 G9 1
Dairymans Wk *RGUE* GU4 250 E5
Daisy Cl *CROY/NA* CR0 204 C8
Daisy La *FUL/PGN* SW6 157 K9
Daisy Rd *SWFD* E18 101 N10
Dakota Gdns *EHAM* E6 142 B6
Dalberg Rd *BRXS/STRHM* SW2 181 H1
Dalberg Wy *ABYW* SE2 163 N2
Dalby Rd *WAND/EARL* SW18 157 M10
Dalbys Crs *TOTM* N17 99 M7
Dalby St *KTTN* NW5 4 E2
Dalcross Rd *HEST* TW5 153 M8
Dale Av *EDGW* HA8 95 L9
HSLWW TW4 153 M9
Dalebury Rd *TOOT* SW17 180 A5
Dale Cl *ADL/WDHM* KT15 215 L2
ASC SL5 192 F5
BAR EN5 77 L10
BKHTH/KID SE3 161 M9 1
DART DA1 186 G2
PIN HA5 93 J9
SOCK/AV RM15 146 F8 1
Dale Ct *SBW* CM21 29 N2 1
Dale Dr *YEAD* UB4 132 G6
Dale Gdns *WFD* IG8 101 N5
Dalegarth Gdns *PUR/KEN* CR8 223 L9
Dale Green Rd *FBAR/BDGN* N11 98 C4
Dale Gv *NFNCH/WDSP* N12 97 M6
Daleham Av *EGH* TW20 172 D9
Daleham Dr *UX/CGN* UB8 132 C8
Daleham Gdns *HAMP* NW3 117 N10
Dale Lodge Rd *ASC* SL5 192 F5
Dale Park Av *CAR* SM5 202 A9
Dale Park Rd *NRWD* SE19 203 K1
Dale Rd *DART* DA1 186 G2
GFD/PVL UB6 134 A7
KTTN NW5 118 B10 2
MEO DA13 189 M7
PUR/KEN CR8 223 H8
SUN TW16 174 G10 1
SUT SM1 221 J1 1
SWLY BR8 208 D3
WALW SE17 18 D10
WOT/HER KT12 196 G7
Dale Rw *NTGHL* W11 8 B6 2
Dale Side *CFSP/GDCR* SL9 110 B6
Daleside *ORP* BR6 227 K2
Daleside Cl *ORP* BR6 227 K3
Daleside Dr *POTB/CUF* EN6 59 J8
Daleside Gdns *CHIG* IG7 102 F4
Daleside Rd *HOR/WEW* KT19 220 A3
TOOT SW17 180 C8
Dales Rd *BORE* WD6 76 A9
Dale St *CHSWK* W4 156 B4
The Dale *HAYES* BR2 226 A1
WAB EN9 63 K10
Dale Vw *EPSOM* KT18 237 N9
ERITH DA8 165 H8
WOKN/KNAP GU21 231 M4
Dale View Av *CHING* E4 101 H3
Dale View Crs *CHING* E4 101 H4
Dale View Gdns *CHING* E4 101 J4
Daleview Rd *SEVS/STOTM* N15 119 M4
Dalewood *HARP* AL5 20 C2 1
WGCE AL7 23 N6
Dalewood Cl *EMPK* RM11 125 M5 2
Dalewood Gdns *CRAWE* RH10 284 A5
WPK KT4 200 E9 2
Dale Wood Rd *ORP* BR6 207 H7
Daley St *HOM* E9 140 C1 4
Daley Thompson Wy
VX/NE SW8 158 C9 1
Dalgarno Gdns *NKENS* W10 136 F7
Dalgarno Wy *NKENS* W10 136 F6
Dalkeith Gv *STAN* HA7 95 J6
Dalkeith Rd *DUL* SE21 181 K4
HARP AL5 20 B1
IL IG1 122 F8
Dallas Rd *CHEAM* SM3 221 H3 3
EA W5 135 L7
HDN NW4 116 D5
SYD SE26 182 A7
Dallas Ter *HYS/HAR* UB3 152 G2
Dallega Cl *HYS/HAR* UB3 132 D9
Dallinger Rd *LEE/GVPK* SE12 183 L2
Dalling Rd *HMSMTH* W6 156 E2
Dallington Cl *WOT/HER* KT12 217 K3 1
Dallington St *FSBYE* EC1V 12 D1
Dallin Rd *BXLYHS* DA6 163 N10
WOOL/PLUM SE18 162 E6
Dalmain Rd *FSTH* SE23 182 C4
Dalmally Rd *CROY/NA* CR0 203 N7
Dalmeny Av *HOLWY* N7 118 E9
STRHM/NOR SW16 203 H2
Dalmeny Cl *ALP/SUD* HA0 135 H1
Dalmeny Crs *HSLW* TW3 154 C10 1
Dalmeny Rd *ARCH* N19 118 E8
BAR EN5 77 M10
CAR SM5 222 B4
ERITH DA8 164 C7
WPK KT4 200 E10
Dalmore Av *ESH/CLAY* KT10 218 E3
Dalmore Rd *DUL* SE21 181 K5
Dalroy Cl *SOCK/AV* RM15 146 F8
Dalrymple Cl *STHGT/OAK* N14 78 E10
Dalrymple Rd *BROCKY* SE4 160 D10
Dalston Gdns *STAN* HA7 95 K9
Dalston La *HACK* E8 7 L1
Dalton Av *MTCM* CR4 201 P2
Dalton Cl *ORP* BR6 207 H10
YEAD UB4 132 E6 1
Daltons Rd *SWLY* BR8 208 D9
Dalton St *STALW/RED* AL3 38 C5
WNWD SE27 181 J5
Dalton Wy *WAT* WD17 73 L10
Dalwood St *CMBW* SE5 159 M7
Dalyell Rd *BRXN/ST* SW9 158 G9

Damask Cl CHOB/PIR GU24 ... 212 D9
Damask Crs CAN/RD E16 ... 141 K6
Damask Gn HHW HP1 ... 35 H7
Damer Ter WBPTN SW10 ... 157 M6
Dames Rd FSTGT E7 ... 121 M9
Dame St IS N1 ... 6 E7
Damien St WCHPL E1 ... 140 A7
Damigos Rd GVE DA12 ... 191 J4
Damon Cl SCUP DA14 ... 185 L6
Damsel Ct BERM/RHTH SE16 ... 19 P2
Damson Gv SL SL1 ... 149 H1
Damsonwood Rd NWDGN UB2 ... 153 P2
Danbrook Rd STRHM/NOR SW16 ... 202 F1
Danbury Cl BRW CM14 ... 86 E9
CHDH RM6 ... 123 N1
Danbury Crs SOCK/AV RM15 ... 146 G8
Danbury Ms CAR SM5 ... 222 C10
Danbury Rd LOU IG10 ... 82 B10
RAIN RM13 ... 144 G3
Danbury Wy WFD IG8 ... 101 P2
Danby St PECK SE15 ... 159 N9
Dancer Rd FUL/PGN SW6 ... 157 J7
RCH/KEW TW9 ... 155 M9
Dancers Hill Rd BAR ... 76 G2
Dando Crs BKHTH/KID SE3 ... 161 N9
Dandridge Cl DTCH/LGLY SL3 ... 150 A3
GNWCH SE10 ... 161 L4
Danebury CROY/NA CR0 ... 204 C6
Danebury Av PUT/ROE SW15 ... 178 C3
Daneby Rd CAT SE6 ... 183 H6
Dane Cl AMSS HP7 ... 69 L7
BXLY DA5 ... 186 B3
ORP BR6 ... 226 G2
Dane Ct WOKS/MYFD GU22 ... 233 J1
Danecourt Gdns CROY/NA CR0 ... 203 N10
Danecroft Rd HNHL SE24 ... 181 K1
Danehurst Cl EGH TW20 ... 172 B9
Danehurst Gdns REDBR IG4 ... 122 B3
Danehurst Rd FUL/PGN SW6 ... 157 H7
Daneland EBAR EN4 ... 78 A9
Danemead HOD EN11 ... 26 F10
Danemead Gv NTHLT UB5 ... 114 A10
Danemere St PUT/ROE SW15 ... 156 F9
Dane Pl BOW E3 ... 140 E4
Dane Rd ASHF TW15 ... 174 D9
IL IG1 ... 122 F10
SEV TN13 ... 246 F3
STHL UB1 ... 133 M9
UED N18 ... 100 B5
WARL CR6 ... 242 C3
WEA W13 ... 135 H9
WIM/MER SW19 ... 201 M1
Danesbury Pk HERT/WAS SG14 ... 25 L4
Danesbury Rd FELT TW13 ... 175 J4
Danes Cl GVW DA11 ... 189 P6
Danescombe LEE/GVPK SE12 ... 183 M4
Danescourt Crs SUT SM1 ... 201 M9
Danescroft Av HDN NW4 ... 116 C3
Danescroft Gdns HDN NW4 ... 116 C3
Danesdale Rd HOM E9 ... 140 D1
Danesfield RPLY/SEND GU23 ... 233 J9
Danesfield Cl WOT/HER KT12 ... 197 J3
Danes Ga HRW HA1 ... 114 D1
Danes Hl WOKS/MYFD GU22 ... 232 E4
Daneshill Cl REDH RH1 ... 257 P9
Daneshill La REDH RH1 ... 257 P9
Danesmead COB KT11 ... 217 P7
Danes Rd ROMW/RG RM7 ... 124 D5
The Danes LCOL/BKTW AL2 ... 56 B4
Dane St GINN WC1R ... 11 L4
Danes Wy BRWN CM15 ... 86 E9
LHD/OX KT22 ... 218 C10
Daneswood Av CAT SE6 ... 183 H6
Daneswood Cl WEY KT13 ... 216 C2
Danethorpe Rd ALP/SUD HA0 ... 135 J1
Danetree Cl HOR/WEW KT19 ... 219 P4
Danetree Rd HOR/WEW KT19 ... 219 P4
Danette Gdns DAGE RM10 ... 124 A7
Daneville Rd CMBW SE5 ... 159 L7
Dangan Rd WAN E11 ... 121 M4
Daniel Bolt Cl POP/IOD E14 ... 140 G7
Daniel Cl CDH/CHF RM16 ... 167 K1
CDH/CHF RM16 ... 168 E2
HSLWW TW4 ... 175 N3
UED N18 ... 100 B5
WIM/MER SW19 ... 179 P9
Daniel Gdns PECK SE15 ... 159 N6
Daniells WGCE AL7 ... 23 K4
Daniell Wy CROY/NA CR0 ... 202 G8
Daniel Pl HDN NW4 ... 116 E4
Daniel Rd ACT W3 ... 135 V4
Daniels La WARL CR6 ... 242 E2
Daniel's Rd PECK SE15 ... 160 B9
Daniel Wy BNSTD SM7 ... 221 K10
Dan Leno Wk FUL/PGN SW6 ... 157 L6
Danses Cl RGUE GU4 ... 250 G8
Dansey Pl SOHO/SHAV W1D ... 11 J7
Dansington Rd WELL DA16 ... 163 K10
Danson Crs WELL DA16 ... 163 L9
Danson La WELL DA16 ... 163 M9
Danson Md WELL DA16 ... 163 M9
Danson Rd BXLYHS DA6 ... 185 N1
Danson U/P BFN/LL DA15 ... 185 M2
Dante Rd LBTH SE11 ... 18 C5
Danube St CHEL SW3 ... 15 P7
Danvers Rd CEND/HSY/T N8 ... 118 E2
Danvers St CHEL SW3 ... 15 M10
Danvers Wy CTHM CR3 ... 241 K9
Danziger Wy BORE WD6 ... 75 P5
Dapdune Rd GU GU1 ... 250 A10
Daphne Gdns CHING E4 ... 101 H4
Daphne St WAND/EARL SW18 ... 179 M1
Daplyn St WCHPL E1 ... 13 N3
D'arblay St SOHO/CST W1F ... 11 H6
Darby Cl CTHM CR3 ... 241 K8
Darby Crs SUN TW16 ... 197 K2
Darby Dr WAB EN9 ... 63 H9
Darby Gdns SUN TW16 ... 197 K2
Darcy Av WLGTN SM6 ... 222 D1
Darcy Cl CHES/WCR EN8 ... 62 D7
COUL/CHIP CR5 ... 241 J5
RBRW/HUT CM13 ... 107 N1
TRDG/WHET N20 ... 97 N3
D'arcy Dr KTN/HRWW/W HA3 ... 115 J2
HAYES BR2 ... 205 M4
D'arcy Gdns DAGW RM9 ... 144 A3
KTN/HRWW/W HA3 ... 115 K3
Darcy Pl ASHTD KT21 ... 237 L5
CHEAM SM3 ... 220 G1
ISLW TW7 ... 154 F7
STRHM/NOR SW16 ... 202 F3
Darell Rd RCH/KEW TW9 ... 155 N9
Darent Cl SEV TN13 ... 246 D8
Darenth Dr GVE DA12 ... 191 L4
Darenth Gdns BH/WHM TN16 ... 262 G2
Darenth Hl RDART DA2 ... 188 A3
Darenth La SEV TN13 ... 246 F7
SOCK/AV RM15 ... 146 F8
Darenth Park Av RDART DA2 ... 188 C5
Darenth Rd DART DA1 ... 187 N4
STNW/STAM N16 ... 119 N5
WELL DA16 ... 163 H7
Darenth Rd South RDART DA2 ... 188 A3
Darenth Wy HORL RH6 ... 280 A2
RSEV TN14 ... 229 H7
Darenth Wood Rd RDART DA2 ... 188 D4
Darent Valley Pth DART DA1 ... 165 L7
EYN DA4 ... 210 A3
RSEV TN14 ... 247 H1
SEV TN13 ... 246 C7
Darfield Rd BROCKY SE4 ... 182 E1

GU GU1 ... 250 D7
Darfield Wy NKENS W10 ... 136 G9
Darfur St PUT/ROE SW15 ... 156 G9
Dargate Cl NRWD SE19 ... 181 N10
Darien Rd BTSEA SW11 ... 157 N9
Darkes La POTB/CUF EN6 ... 59 K8
Dark La BRW CM14 ... 106 F8
CHESW EN7 ... 61 P7
HARP AL5 ... 20 C4
RGUW UB5 ... 266 A5
Darlan Rd FUL/PGN SW6 ... 157 J6
Darlaston Rd WIM/MER SW19 ... 178 G10
Darley Cl ADL/WDHM KT15 ... 215 M2
CROY/NA CR0 ... 204 C6
Darleydale CRAWW RH11 ... 283 M10
Darley Dr NWMAL KT3 ... 200 A12
Darley Gdns MRDN SM4 ... 201 M6
Darley Rd BTSEA SW11 ... 180 A2
ED N9 ... 99 N2
Darling Rd BROCKY SE4 ... 160 F9
Darling Rw WCHPL E1 ... 140 A6
Darlington Ct BERM CM15 ... 86 F10
Darlington Gdns HARH RM3 ... 105 L6
Darlington Rd WNWD SE27 ... 181 J8
Darlton Cl DART DA1 ... 164 C8
Darmaine Cl SAND/SEL CR2 ... 223 K4
Darndale Cl WALTH E17 ... 100 E10
Darnets Fld RSEV TN14 ... 246 C3
Darnicle Hl CHESW EN7 ... 61 H1
Darnley Pk WEY KT13 ... 196 C10
GVW DA11 ... 190 D2
HACK E8 ... 140 A1
WFD IG8 ... 101 M9
Darnley Ter NTGHL W11 ... 136 U10
Darns Hl SWLY BR8 ... 208 D7
Darrell Cl DTCH/LGLY SL3 ... 150 C3
Darrell Rd EDUL SE22 ... 181 P1
Darren Cl FSBYPK N4 ... 118 C5
Darrick Wood Rd ORP BR6 ... 206 C9
Darrington Rd BORE WD6 ... 75 K5
Darris Cl YEAD UB4 ... 133 M6
Darsley Dr VX/NE SW8 ... 158 E7
Dart Cl DTCH/LGLY SL3 ... 150 E5
UPMR RM14 ... 126 C4
Dartfields HARH RM3 ... 105 L7
Dartford Av ED N9 ... 80 B10
Dartford Rd BXLY DA5 ... 186 D4
DART DA1 ... 187 H2
EYN DA4 ... 209 N6
SEV TN13 ... 247 K10
Dartford St WALW SE17 ... 18 F9
Dart Gn SOCK/AV RM15 ... 146 G8
Dartmoor Wk POP/IOD E14 ... 160 F3
Dartmouth Av WOKN/KNAP GU21 ... 214 F10
Dartmouth Cl NTGHL W11 ... 8 D5
Dartmouth Gv GNWCH SE10 ... 161 H7
Dartmouth Hl GNWCH SE10 ... 161 H7
Dartmouth Park Av KTTN NW5 ... 118 C6
Dartmouth Park Hl ARCH N19 ... 118 C6
KTTN NW5 ... 118 C6
Dartmouth Park Rd KTTN NW5 ... 118 C8
FSTH SE23 ... 182 B5
Dartmouth Pl CHSWK W4 ... 156 B5
FSTH SE23 ... 182 B5
Dartmouth Rd CRICK NW2 ... 2 A1
HAYES BR2 ... 205 M7
HDN NW4 ... 116 D4
RSLP HA4 ... 113 H8
SYD SE26 ... 182 A6
Dartmouth Rw LEW SE13 ... 161 H8
Dartmouth St STJSPK SW1H ... 17 J2
Dartmouth Ter GNWCH SE10 ... 161 J7
Dartnell Av BF/WBF KT14 ... 215 M8
Dartnell Cl BF/WBF KT14 ... 215 L8
Dartnell Crs BF/WBF KT14 ... 215 M7
Dartnell Park Rd BF/WBF KT14 ... 215 L8
Dartnell Pl BF/WBF KT14 ... 215 L8
Dartnell Rd CROY/NA CR0 ... 205 L8
Dart St NKENS W10 ... 2 B9
The Dart HHNE HP2 ... 36 B1
Dartview Cl GRAYS RM17 ... 168 B3
Darvel Cl WOKN/KNAP GU21 ... 231 M2
Darvell Dr CSHM HP5 ... 50 C1
Darville Rd STNW/STAM N16 ... 119 N8
Darvill's La SL SL1 ... 149 L1
Darwell Cl EHAM E6 ... 142 D4
Darwin Av FBAR/BDGN N11 ... 98 C4
ORP BR6 ... 226 G2
STALW/RED AL3 ... 38 D2
Darwin Dr GFD/PVL UB6 ... 134 A8
Darwin Gdns OXHEY WD19 ... 93 K6
Darwin Rd BTFD TW8 ... 155 H4
DTCH/LGLY SL3 ... 150 C1
TIL RM18 ... 168 C7
WDGN N22 ... 99 J9
WELL DA16 ... 163 J9
Darwin St WALW SE17 ... 19 H5
Daryngton Dr GFD/PVL UB6 ... 134 C4
GU GU1 ... 251 P5
The Dashes HLW CM20 ... 29 H10
Dashwood Cl BF/WBF KT14 ... 215 M8
BXLYHS DA6 ... 186 B1
DTCH/LGLY SL3 ... 149 P3
Dashwood Rd CEND/HSY/T N8 ... 118 G4
GVW DA11 ... 190 D4
Dassett Rd WNWD SE27 ... 181 J8
Datchelor Pl CMBW SE5 ... 159 L7
Datchet Pl DTCH/LGLY SL3 ... 149 N7
Datchet Rd CAT SE6 ... 182 E6
DTCH/LGLY SL3 ... 150 C9
WDSR SL4 ... 149 J9
Datchworth Turn HHNE HP2 ... 36 D6
Date St WALW SE17 ... 18 G8
Daubeney Gdns TOTM N17 ... 99 K8
Daubeney Rd CLPT E5 ... 120 D10
TOTM N17 ... 99 K8
Dault Rd WAND/EARL SW18 ... 179 M2
Davenant Rd ARCH N19 ... 118 C2
Davenant St WCHPL E1 ... 13 P4
Davenham Av NTHWD HA6 ... 92 C5
Davenport Rd HLWE CM17 ... 47 P2
Davenport Cl TEDD TW11 ... 176 F9
Davenport Rd LEW SE13 ... 182 G2
SCUP DA14 ... 185 N5
Daventer Dr STAN HA7 ... 94 F8
Daventry Av WALTH E17 ... 120 F4
Daventry Cl DTCH/LGLY SL3 ... 151 J2
Daventry Gdns HARH RM3 ... 105 K6
Daventry Rd HARH RM3 ... 105 K6
Daventry St CAMTN NW1 ... 9 N3
Davern Cl GNWCH SE10 ... 161 L3
Davey Cl HOLWY N7 ... 5 P2
Davey Rd HOM E9 ... 140 F2
Davey St PECK SE15 ... 19 M10
David Av GFD/PVL UB6 ... 134 D5
David Cl HYS/HAR UB3 ... 152 A5
David Dr HARH RM3 ... 105 P7
Davidge St STHWK SE1 ... 18 C2
David Rd BCTR RM8 ... 123 P7
DTCH/LGLY SL3 ... 151 J2
Davidson Gdns VX/NE SW8 ... 158 F6
Davidson Rd CROY/NA CR0 ... 203 M8
Davidson Wy ROMW/RG RM7 ... 124 F4
David's Rd FSTH SE23 ... 182 B4
David St SRTFD E15 ... 141 J1
David Twigg Cl KUTN/CMB KT2 ... 199 K1
Davies Cl RAIN RM13 ... 145 K5
Davies La WAN E11 ... 121 K7
Davies Ms MYFR/PKLN W1K ... 10 C7

Davies St HERT/BAY SG13 ... 25 M5
MYFR/PKLN W1K ... 10 E7
Davies Wk ISLW TW7 ... 154 C7
Davington Gdns BCTR RM8 ... 123 L10
Davington Rd BCTR RM8 ... 143 L1
Davinia Cl WFD IG8 ... 102 C3
Davis Av GVW DA11 ... 190 B6
Davis Cl SEV TN13 ... 247 K8
Davison Cl CHES/WCR EN8 ... 62 C4
Davison Dr CHES/WCR EN8 ... 62 C4
Davis Rd ACT W3 ... 136 C10
CDH/CHF RM16 ... 167 L2
CHSGTN KT9 ... 219 M1
SOCK/AV RM15 ... 146 C10
WEY KT13 ... 216 A6
Davis St PLSTW E13 ... 141 N4
Davisville Rd SHB W12 ... 156 D1
Davos Cl WOKS/MYFD GU22 ... 232 B5
Davy Cl STALE/WH AL4 ... 21 K4
Davy's Pl GVE DA12 ... 191 H9
Dawell Dr BH/WHM TN16 ... 243 P3
Dawes Av HCH RM12 ... 125 L8
ISLW TW7 ... 176 F1
Dawes Cl CSHM HP5 ... 50 C8
GRH DA9 ... 188 E1
HGDN/ICK UB10 ... 131 P4
Dawes East Rd SL SL1 ... 128 B6
Dawes La RKW/CH/CXG WD3 ... 71 J2
Dawes Moor Cl SL SL1 ... 129 P8
Dawes Rd FUL/PGN SW6 ... 157 J6
HGDN/ICK UB10 ... 131 P4
Dawes St WALW SE17 ... 19 H7
Dawley WGCE AL7 ... 23 J2
Dawley Av UX/CGN UB8 ... 132 C7
Dawley Ct HMEL HP2 ... 36 A2
Dawley Gn SOCK/AV RM15 ... 146 F8
Dawley Pde UX/CGN UB8 ... 132 D9
Dawley Ride DTCH/LGLY SL3 ... 151 H7
Dawlish Av HYS/HAR UB3 ... 152 F5
PLMGR N13 ... 98 F5
WAND/EARL SW18 ... 179 L5
Dawlish Dr GDMY/SEVK IG3 ... 123 J9
PIN HA5 ... 113 M3
RSLP HA4 ... 113 H7
Dawlish Rd CRICK NW2 ... 136 C1
LEY E10 ... 121 H7
TOTM N17 ... 119 P7
Dawnay Gdns WAND/EARL SW18 ... 179 N5
Dawnay Rd GT/LBKH KT23 ... 254 E7
WAND/EARL SW18 ... 179 M5
Dawn Cl HSLWW TW4 ... 153 M9
Dawn Crs SRTFD E15 ... 141 J3
Dawnay Hl CHOB/PIR GU24 ... 230 D7
Dawneys Rd CHOB/PIR GU24 ... 230 D8
Dawn Redwood Cl DTCH/LGLY SL3 ... 150 D9
Dawpool Rd CRICK NW2 ... 116 C10
Daws Hl CHING E4 ... 81 H7
Daws La MLHL NW7 ... 96 C6
Dawson Av BARK IG11 ... 143 J2
STMC/STPC BR5 ... 207 L2
Dawson Cl HYS/HAR UB3 ... 132 E7
WDSR SL4 ... 148 F8
WOOL/PLUM SE18 ... 162 F3
Dawson Dr RAIN RM13 ... 145 J2
SWLY BR8 ... 186 F10
Dawson Gdns BARK IG11 ... 143 J2
Dawson Pl BAY/PAD W2 ... 8 E7
Dawson Rd BF/WBF KT14 ... 215 N7
CRICK NW2 ... 116 F10
KUT KT1 ... 199 L3
Dawson St BETH E2 ... 7 M8
Dawson Ter ED N9 ... 100 B1
Daybrook Rd WIM/MER SW19 ... 201 L2
Dayemead WGCE AL7 ... 23 L8
Daylesford Av PUT/ROE SW15 ... 156 D10
Daylop Dr CHIG IG7 ... 103 L4
Daymer Gdns PIN HA5 ... 113 K2
Daymerslea Rdg LHD/OX KT22 ... 237 H7
Day's Acre SAND/SEL CR2 ... 223 N6
Daysbrook Rd BRXS/STRHM SW2 ... 180 G4
Days Cl HAT AL10 ... 40 C4
Dayseys Hl REDH RH1 ... 277 H9
Days La BFN/LL DA15 ... 185 H3
BRWN CM15 ... 86 E9
Days Md HAT AL10 ... 40 C4
Dayspring GUW GU2 ... 249 N6
Dayton Dr ERITH DA8 ... 165 L4
Dayton Gv PECK SE15 ... 160 B7
Deacon Cl COB KT11 ... 235 J5
CTHM CR3 ... 241 K9
PUR/KEN CR8 ... 222 F5
STAL AL1 ... 38 C10
Deacon Fld GUW GU2 ... 249 M9
Deacon Ms IS N1 ... 7 H4
Deacon Rd CRICK NW2 ... 136 D1
KUTN/CMB KT2 ... 199 L1
Deacons Cl BORE WD6 ... 75 M8
PIN HA5 ... 93 J10
Deacons Hts BORE WD6 ... 75 M10
Deacons Cl OXHEY WD19 ... 73 K10
Deacon's Hill Rd BORE WD6 ... 75 L9
Deacons Leas ORP BR6 ... 226 G1
Deacons Wk HPTN TW12 ... 175 P7
Deacon Wy WALW SE17 ... 18 E6
WFD IG8 ... 102 G8
Deadhearn La CSTG HP8 ... 90 B2
Deadman's Ash La RKW/CH/CXG WD3 ... 71 L2
Deakin Cl WATW WD18 ... 33 P7
Deakins Ter ORP BR6 ... 207 K7
Deal Av DTCH/LGLY SL3 ... 150 B2
Deal Porters Wy BERM/RHTH SE16 ... 160 B2
Deal Rd TOOT SW17 ... 180 B9
Deal St WCHPL E1 ... 13 N3
Deal St POP/IOD E14 ... 141 M8
Dealtree Cl BRWN CM15 ... 86 C3
Dealtry Rd PUT/ROE SW15 ... 156 F10
Deanacre Cl CFSP/GDCR SL9 ... 90 B7
Dean Bradley St WEST SW1P ... 17 L4
Dean Cl HGDN/ICK UB10 ... 132 A2
WDSR SL4 ... 148 C9
WOKS/MYFD GU22 ... 233 H2
Dean Ct ALP/SUD HA0 ... 114 G8
Deancroft Rd CFSP/GDCR SL9 ... 90 B7
Deancross St WCHPL E1 ... 140 B8
Dean Dr STAN HA7 ... 95 K10
Deane Av RSLP HA4 ... 113 J10
Deane Croft Rd PIN HA5 ... 113 K4
Deanery Cl EFNCH N2 ... 117 P2
Deanery Ms MYFR/PKLN W1K ... 10 D9
Deanery Rd EDEN TN8 ... 262 F10
SRTFD E15 ... 141 L1
Deanery St MYFR/PKLN W1K ... 10 D9
Dean Farrar St STJSPK SW1H ... 17 K3
Dean Gdns WALTH E17 ... 121 J2
Deanhill Rd MORT/ESHN SW14 ... 155 N10
REDH RH1 ... 240 D10
Deanoak La REIG RH2 ... 274 D10
Dean Rd CRICK NW2 ... 136 C1
CROY/NA CR0 ... 223 L1
HPTN TW12 ... 175 P8
HSLW TW3 ... 176 A1
THMD SE28 ... 143 K9
Dean Ryle St WEST SW1P ... 17 L5
Deansbrook Cl EDGW HA8 ... 95 P8
Deansbrook Rd EDGW HA8 ... 95 N10
Deans Buildings WALW SE17 ... 19 H6
Deans Cl ABLGY WD5 ... 54 B8
AMS HP6 ... 35 A7
CHSWK W4 ... 155 N5

CROY/NA CR0 ... 203 N10
EDGW HA8 ... 95 P7
KWD/TDW/WH KT20 ... 238 C10
SLN SL2 ... 129 N3
Deans Ct BFOR GU20 ... 212 C3
BLKFR EC4V ... 12 D6
Deanscroft Av CDALE/KGS NW9 ... 115 P7
PLMGR N13 ... 99 J7
Deansfield CTHM CR3 ... 259 N1
Dean's Gdns STALE/WH AL4 ... 38 F2
Dean's Gate Cl FSTH SE23 ... 182 C6
Dean's La EDGW HA8 ... 95 P7
KWD/TDW/WH KT20 ... 256 E1
REDH RH1 ... 259 H9
Dean's Ms CAVSQ/HST W1G ... 10 F5
Deans Rd BRW CM14 ... 106 C4
HNWL W7 ... 154 E1
REDH RH1 ... 258 D6
SUT SM1 ... 201 L10
Dean Stanley St WEST SW1P ... 17 L4
Dean St FSTGT E7 ... 121 P10
SOHO/FST W1F ... 11 J5
Deans Wk COUL/CHIP CR5 ... 241 H4
Deansway ED N9 ... 99 M4
Deansway CSHM HP5 ... 50 G5
EFNCH N2 ... 117 N2
Dean Trench St WEST SW1P ... 17 L4
Dean Wy CSTG HP8 ... 89 M4
Dearne Cl STAN HA7 ... 94 F6
De'arn Gdns MTCM CR4 ... 201 P3
Dearsley Rd EN EN1 ... 79 P7
Deason St SRTFD E15 ... 141 H3
Debden Cl KUTN/CMB KT2 ... 177 J8
WFD IG8 ... 102 A8
Debden La LOU IG10 ... 82 E4
Debden Rd LOU IG10 ... 82 E4
De Beauvoir Crs IS N1 ... 7 J5
De Beauvoir Rd IS N1 ... 7 J4
De Beauvoir Sq IS N1 ... 7 K4
Debenham Rd CHESW EN7 ... 62 A3
Debnams Rd BERM/RHTH SE16 ... 160 B3
De Bohun Av STHGT/OAK N14 ... 78 C10
Deborah Cl ISLW TW7 ... 154 D7
Debrabant Cl ERITH DA8 ... 164 E5
De Broome Rd FELT TW13 ... 175 K4
De Burgh Pk BNSTD SM7 ... 239 L2
Deburgh Rd WIM/MER SW19 ... 179 M10
Decies Wy SLN SL2 ... 129 M3
Decima St STHWK SE1 ... 19 J3
Deck Cl BERM/RHTH SE16 ... 140 C10
Decoy Av GLDGN NW11 ... 117 H3
De Crespigny Pk CMBW SE5 ... 159 L8
Dedisham Cl CRAWE RH10 ... 284 B3
Dedswell Dr RGUE GU4 ... 251 K5
Dedworth Dr WDSR SL4 ... 148 B5
Dedworth Rd WDSR SL4 ... 148 E8
Dee Cl UPMR RM14 ... 126 C4
Deeley Rd VX/NE SW8 ... 158 E7
Deena Cl EA W5 ... 135 L8
SL SL1 ... 128 D9
Deep Acres AMS HP6 ... 35 H2
Deepdale WIM/MER SW19 ... 178 G7
Deepdale Av HAYES BR2 ... 205 L4
Deepdale Cl FBAR/BDGN N11 ... 98 B7
Deepdene POTB/CUF EN6 ... 58 G7
Deepdene Av CROY/NA CR0 ... 203 N10
RDKG RH5 ... 273 H2
Deepdene Ct WCHMH N21 ... 79 J10
Deepdene Dr RDKG RH5 ... 273 H1
Deepdene Gdns BRXS/STRHM SW2 ... 180 G3
DORK RH4 ... 272 G3
Deepdene Park Rd RDKG RH5 ... 273 H1
Deepdene Pth LOU IG10 ... 82 E4
Deepdene Rd HNHL SE24 ... 159 V10
LOU IG10 ... 82 D8
WELL DA16 ... 163 K9
Deepdene Wd DORK RH4 ... 255 H10
Deepdene Wd RDKG RH5 ... 273 J2
Deep Fld DTCH/LGLY SL3 ... 149 N6
Deepfields HORL RH6 ... 280 A2
Deepfield Wy COUL/CHIP CR5 ... 240 F2
Deeprose Cl GUW GU2 ... 249 N6
Deepwell Cl ISLW TW7 ... 154 F7
Deepwood La GFD/PVL UB6 ... 134 C5
Deerbarn Rd GUW GU2 ... 249 N9
Deerbrook Rd BRXS/STRHM SW2 ... 181 J10
Deerdale Rd HNHL SE24 ... 159 H10
Deere Av RAIN RM13 ... 145 H1
Deerfield Cl WARE SG12 ... 26 C1
Deerhurst Cl FELT TW13 ... 175 J1
HART DA3 ... 211 P3
Deerhurst Crs HPTN TW12 ... 176 B3
Deerhurst Rd KIL/WHAMP NW6 ... 136 G2
STRHM/NOR SW16 ... 180 G8
Deerings Dr PIN HA5 ... 113 H3
Deerings Rd REIG RH2 ... 257 L10
Deerleap Gv CHING E4 ... 80 C9
Deerleap La RSEV TN14 ... 227 N9
Deerleap Rd DORK RH4 ... 272 A3
Dee Rd RCH/KEW TW9 ... 155 L10
Deer Pk HLWW/ROY CM19 ... 46 D4
Deer Park Gdns MTCM CR4 ... 201 N4
Deer Park Rd WIM/MER SW19 ... 201 L2
Deer Park Wy WWKM BR4 ... 205 L9
Deers Farm Cl RPLY/SEND GU23 ... 233 J7
Deerswood Av HAT AL10 ... 40 E6
Deerswood Cl CRAWW RH11 ... 283 L6
CTHM CR3 ... 241 P10
Deerswood Rd CRAWW RH11 ... 283 L6
Deeside Rd TOOT SW17 ... 179 N6
The Dee HHNE HP2 ... 36 A1
Dees Hall La POTB/CUF EN6 ... 58 B9
De Vere Wy HOR/WEW KT19 ... 220 B6
Defiant Wy WLGTN SM6 ... 222 G7
Defoe Av RCH/KEW TW9 ... 155 M6
Defoe Cl WIM/MER SW19 ... 179 P9
Defoe Pde CDH/CHF RM16 ... 168 E2
Defoe Rd BERM/RHTH SE16 ... 160 E1
STNW/STAM N16 ... 119 M7
Defoe Wy CRW RM5 ... 104 B7
De Frene Rd SYD SE26 ... 182 C7
Dehar Crs CDALE/KGS NW9 ... 116 C5
De Havilland Cl HAT AL10 ... 40 C3
De Havilland Ct RAD WD7 ... 57 K2
De Havilland Dr WEY KT13 ... 215 J10
De Havilland Rd EDGW HA8 ... 96 N10
HEST TW5 ... 153 N6
WLGTN SM6 ... 222 F14
De Havilland Wy ABLGY WD5 ... 54 G8
STWL/WRAY TW19 ... 173 N2
Deimos Dr HHNE HP2 ... 36 B3
Dekker Rd DUL SE21 ... 181 M2
Delabole Rd REDH RH1 ... 258 F5
Delacourt Rd BKHTH/KID SE3 ... 161 N6
Delafield Rd CHARL SE7 ... 161 K3
GRAYS RM17 ... 168 A4
Delaford Cl IVER SLO ... 131 K8
Delaford Rd BERM/RHTH SE16 ... 160 B4
Delaford St FUL/PGN SW6 ... 157 H5
Delagarde Rd BH/WHM TN16 ... 262 G4
Delahay Ri BERK HP4 ... 33 N3
Delamare Crs CROY/NA CR0 ... 204 D4
Delamare Rd CHES/WCR EN8 ... 62 C5
Delamere Gdns MLHL NW7 ... 96 A7

Delamere Rd BORE WD6 ... 75 N5
EA W5 ... 135 K10
REIG RH2 ... 275 L4
RYNPK SW20 ... 200 G1
YEAD UB4 ... 133 L9
Delamere St BAY/PAD W2 ... 9 J4
Delamere Ter BAY/PAD W2 ... 9 H3
Delancey St CAMTN NW1 ... 4 F6
Delaporte Cl EW KT17 ... 220 B8
De Lara Wy WOKN/KNAP GU21 ... 232 A4
Delargy Cl CDH/CHF RM16 ... 168 E2
De Laune St WALW SE17 ... 18 C8
Delaware Rd MV/WKIL W9 ... 8 G1
Delawyk Crs HNHL SE24 ... 181 L2
Delcombe Av WPK KT4 ... 200 G9
Delderfield ASHTD KT21 ... 237 J6
Delfont Cl CRAWE RH10 ... 284 E3
Delhi Cl IS N1 ... 99 N1
Delhi Rd EN EN1 ... 99 N5
Delhi St IS N1 ... 5 M6
Delia St WAND/EARL SW18 ... 179 L3
Delius Cl BORE WD6 ... 75 H10
Dellbow Rd EBED/NFELT TW14 ... 174 A7
Dell Cl LHD/OX KT22 ... 236 C9
RDKG RH5 ... 255 H3
SLN SL2 ... 109 H10
SRTFD E15 ... 141 J3
WFD IG8 ... 101 N4
WLGTN SM6 ... 222 E1
Dellcott Cl WGCW AL8 ... 22 E4
Dellcut Rd HHNE HP2 ... 36 B4
Dell Farm Rd RSLP HA4 ... 112 E3
Dellfield BERK HP4 ... 33 M3
CSHM HP5 ... 50 F5
STAL AL1 ... 38 F7
Dellfield Av BERK HP4 ... 33 N3
Dellfield Cl BECK BR3 ... 205 H1
RAD WD7 ... 74 D1
WAT WD17 ... 73 H6
Dellfield Crs UX/CGN UB8 ... 131 M6
Dell La EW KT17 ... 220 D2
Dell Lees BEAC HP9 ... 89 H7
Dellmeadow ABLGY WD5 ... 54 F6
Dell Meadow HHS/BOV HP3 ... 35 P10
Dellors Cl BAR EN5 ... 76 C9
Dellow Cl GNTH/NBYPK IG2 ... 122 G5
Dellow St WCHPL E1 ... 140 V4
Dell Rd BERK HP4 ... 33 J2
EW KT17 ... 220 D3
GRAYS RM17 ... 167 N3
PEND EN3 ... 80 B4
WATN WD24 ... 73 H3
WDR/YW UB7 ... 152 A2
Dells Cl CHING E4 ... 100 G1
Dellside DEN/HRF UB9 ... 111 M3
Dell Side WATN WD24 ... 73 H3
Dell's Ms PIM SW1V ... 17 H6
Dellsome La BRKMPK AL9 ... 40 E9
STALE/WH AL4 ... 40 B9
The Dells HHS/BOV HP3 ... 36 C7
Dellswood Cl HERT/BAY SG13 ... 25 M6
Dells Wood Cl HOD EN11 ... 26 E10
The Dell ABYW SE2 ... 163 K4
ALP/SUD HA0 ... 114 C10
BRW CM14 ... 106 G7
BTFD TW8 ... 155 H5
BXLY DA5 ... 186 F4
CFSP/GDCR SL9 ... 90 B7
EBED/NFELT TW14 ... 175 J3
HERT/BAY SG13 ... 25 K8
HORL RH6 ... 279 P8
KWD/TDW/WH KT20 ... 238 F7
NRWD SE19 ... 203 N1
NTHWD HA6 ... 92 F3
PIN HA5 ... 93 L10
RAD WD7 ... 74 F2
STAL AL1 ... 38 F4
WFD IG8 ... 101 N4
WOKN/KNAP GU21 ... 231 P5
Dell Wk NWMAL KT3 ... 200 B2
Dell Wy WEA W13 ... 135 H8
Dellwood RKW/CH/CXG WD3 ... 91 L2
Dellwood Gdns CLAY IG5 ... 122 D1
Delmar Av HHNE HP2 ... 36 F7
Delmeade Rd CSHM HP5 ... 50 C5
Delmey Cl CROY/NA CR0 ... 203 N10
Deloraine St DEPT SE8 ... 160 F7
Delorme St HMSMTH W6 ... 156 G5
Delta Cl CHOB/PIR GU24 ... 213 L6
WPK KT4 ... 200 B10
Delta Dr HORL RH6 ... 280 B6
Delta Gain OXHEY WD19 ... 93 L3
Delta Gv NTHLT UB5 ... 133 L5
Delta Rd CHOB/PIR GU24 ... 213 L6
WOKN/KNAP GU21 ... 232 D1
WPK KT4 ... 200 B10
Delta St BETH E2 ... 7 N9
De Luci Rd ERITH DA8 ... 164 D4
De Lucy St ABYW SE2 ... 163 L3
Delvers Md DAGE RM10 ... 124 D9
Delverton Rd WALW SE17 ... 18 D7
Delves KWD/TDW/WH KT20 ... 238 G2
De Mandeville Ga EN EN1 ... 79 N7
Demesne Rd WLGTN SM6 ... 222 F1
Demeta Cl WBLY HA9 ... 115 P8

De Montfort STRHM/NOR SW16 ... 180 E5
De Morgan Rd FUL/PGN SW6 ... 157 M8
Dempster Rd WAND/EARL SW18 ... 179 M1
Denberry Dr SCUP DA14 ... 185 L6
Denbigh Cl CHST BR7 ... 184 C9
EMPK RM11 ... 125 N7
HHS/BOV HP3 ... 35 P7
NTGHL W11 ... 8 D7
STHL UB1 ... 133 N8
SUT SM1 ... 221 J2
WLSDN NW10 ... 136 B2
Denbigh Dr WDR/YW UB7 ... 152 D1
Denbigh Gdns RCHPK/HAM TW10 ... 177 L1
Denbigh Pl PIM SW1V ... 16 G7
Denbigh Rd EHAM E6 ... 142 A5
HSLW TW3 ... 154 A8
NTGHL W11 ... 8 D7
STHL UB1 ... 133 N8
WEA W13 ... 134 G9
Denbigh St PIM SW1V ... 17 H7
Denbigh Ter NTGHL W11 ... 8 D7
Denbridge Rd BMLY BR1 ... 206 C2
Denby Gra HLWE CM17 ... 47 P5
Denby Rd COB KT11 ... 217 J9
Den Cl BECK BR3 ... 205 A4
Dendridge Cl EN EN1 ... 80 B3
Dendy St BAL SW12 ... 180 B4
Dene Av BFN/LL DA15 ... 185 H4
HSLW TW3 ... 154 D5
Dene Cl BROCKY SE4 ... 160 D9
COUL/CHIP CR5 ... 239 P5
HAYES BR2 ... 205 L8
HORL RH6 ... 286 P2
RDART DA2 ... 187 K2
WPK KT4 ... 200 C9
Denecroft Gdns GRAYS RM17 ... 168 A4
Dene Gdns STAN HA7 ... 95 M4
THDIT KT7 ... 208 B1
Dene Holm Rd GVW DA11 ... 190 A6
Denehurst Gdns ACT W3 ... 135 N10
HDN NW4 ... 116 F4

RCHPK/HAM TW10 ..... 155 M10
WFD IG8 ..... 101 N5
WHTN TW2 ..... 176 B9
Dene Pth SOCK/AV RM15 ..... 146 F8
Dene Rd ASHTD KT21 ..... 237 L5
BKHH IG9 ..... 102 A3
DART DA1 ..... 187 N3
GU GU1 ..... 268 B9
NTHWD HA6 ..... 92 D7
TRDG/WHET N20 ..... 98 A2
Dene St DORK RH4 ..... 272 G2
Dene Street Gdns DORK RH4 ..... 272 G2
The Dene BELMT SM2 ..... 221 J1
CROY/NA CR0 ..... 224 C1
SEV TN13 ..... 265 J2
WBLY HA9 ..... 115 K9
WEA W13 ..... 134 D4
WOT/HER KT12 ..... 197 N5
Dene Tye CRAWE RH10 ..... 284 D3
Dene Wk HART DA3 ..... 211 K3
Denewood BAR EN5 ..... 77 M9
Denewood Cl WAT WD17 ..... 72 G3
Denewood Rd HGT N6 ..... 117 N6
Denfield DORK RH4 ..... 272 G4
Dengil Crs KTTN NW5 ..... 118 B10 ⊡
Denham Av DEN/HRF UB9 ..... 111 J7
Denham Cl DEN/HRF UB9 ..... 111 K8 ⊡
HHNE HP2 ..... 36 B1 ⊡
Denham Court Dr DEN/HRF UB9 ..... 111 L8
Denham Ct MTCM CR4 ..... 202 A4
Denham Dr GNTH/NBYPK IG2 ..... 122 F4
Denham Green Cl DEN/HRF UB9 ..... 111 K5
Denham Green La DEN/HRF UB9 ..... 111 K5
Denham La CFSP/GDCR SL9 ..... 90 C7
Denham Rd DEN/HRF UB9 ..... 111 J10
EBED/NFELT TW14 ..... 175 K3
EGH TW20 ..... 172 D7
EW KT17 ..... 220 D3
IVER SL0 ..... 130 C3
TRDG/WHET N20 ..... 98 A2
Denham Wk BARK IG11 ..... 143 N5
BORE WD6 ..... 75 P5
DEN/HRF UB9 ..... 111 J10
Denham Wy (North Orbital Rd)
RKW/CH/CXG WD3 ..... 91 H8
Denholme Rd MV/WKIL W9 ..... 2 D9
Denholm Gdns RGUE GU4 ..... 250 D7 ⊡
Denison Cl EFNCH N2 ..... 117 M1
Denison Rd EA W5 ..... 135 H6
FELT TW13 ..... 175 H7
WIM/MER SW19 ..... 179 N9
Deniston Av BXLY DA5 ..... 185 N4
WCHMH N21 ..... 99 H1
Denleigh Gdns THDIT KT7 ..... 198 D6 ⊡
WCHMH N21 ..... 99 H1
Denly Wy LTWR GU18 ..... 212 B6
Denman Dr ASHF TW15 ..... 174 J7
ESH/CLAY KT10 ..... 218 F2 ⊡
GLDGN NW11 ..... 117 K3
Denman Rd PECK SE15 ..... 159 H4
Denmans CRAWE RH10 ..... 284 E6 ⊡
Denman St REGST W1B 11 H8
Denmark Av WIM/MER SW19 ..... 179 H10
Denmark Gdns CAR SM5 ..... 202 A10
Denmark Gv IS N1 ..... 6 C1
Denmark Hl CMBW SE5 ..... 159 L7
HNHL SE24 ..... 159 L10
Denmark Hill Dr CDALE/KGS NW9 ..... 116 C2
Denmark Rd BMLY BR1 ..... 184 D5
CAR SM5 ..... 202 A10
CEND/HSY/T N8 ..... 118 G2
CMBW SE5 ..... 159 K7
GU GU1 ..... 268 B9
KIL/WHAMP NW6 ..... 2 D8
KUT1 KT1 ..... 199 K3
SNWD SE25 ..... 203 P5
WEA W13 ..... 134 C9
WHTN TW2 ..... 176 C9
WIM/MER SW19 ..... 178 G9
Denmark St LSQ/SEVD WC2H 11 K6
PLSTW E13 ..... 141 N7 ⊡
TOTM N17 ..... 100 H9
WAN E11 ..... 121 K8 ⊡
WAT WD17 ..... 73 J6
Denmead Rd CROY/NA CR0 ..... 203 J8 ⊡
Denmead Rd CROY/NA CR0 ..... 203 J8 ⊡
Dennan Rd SURB KT6 ..... 199 L8
Denne Rd CRAWE RH11 ..... 283 N8
Denner Rd CHING E4 ..... 100 F3
Dene Ter HACK E8 ..... 7 M6
Dennett Rd CROY/NA CR0 ..... 203 H7
Dennett's Gv NWCR SE14 ..... 160 C8
Dennett'sland Rd EDEN TN8 ..... 262 F10
Dennett's Rd NWCR SE14 ..... 160 B7
Denning Av CROY/NA CR0 ..... 223 H1
Denning Cl HPTN TW12 ..... 175 N8 ⊡
STJWD NW8 ..... 3 K9
Denning Rd HAMP NW3 ..... 117 N9
Dennington Park Rd
KIL/WHAMP NW6 ..... 2 F1
The Denningtons WPK KT4 ..... 200 B9 ⊡
Dennis Av WBLY HA9 ..... 115 L10 ⊡
Dennis Cl REDH RH1 ..... 257 P8
Dennises La UPMR RM14 ..... 146 E2
Dennis Gdns STAN HA7 ..... 95 H4
Dennis La STAN HA7 ..... 94 G5
Dennis Park Crs RYNPK SW20 ..... 201 H1
Dennis Reeve Cl MTCM CR4 ..... 202 A1
Dennis Rd E/WMO/HCT KT8 ..... 198 A1
GVW DA11 ..... 190 D6
UPMR RM14 ..... 146 F5
Dennis Wy CLAP SW4 ..... 158 E9
SL SL1 ..... 128 C9
Denny Av WAB EN9 ..... 63 J10
Denny Crs LBTH SE11 ..... 18 E7
Denny Ga CHES/WCR EN8 ..... 62 E5
Denny Rd DTCH/LGLY SL3 ..... 150 C3 ⊡
ED N9 ..... 100 A3
Denny's La BERK HP4 ..... 33 L7
Denny St LBTH SE11 ..... 18 B7
Den Rd HAYES BR2 ..... 205 J3
Densham Rd SRTFD E15 ..... 141 K3
Densley Cl WGCW AL8 ..... 22 F3
Densole Cl BECK BR3 ..... 204 D1 ⊡
Densworth Gv ED N9 ..... 100 B3
Dent Cl SOCK/AV RM15 ..... 146 F8 ⊡
Denton Cl BAR EN5 ..... 76 B9
REDH RH1 ..... 276 F5
Denton Court Rd GVE DA12 ..... 191 H4
Denton Gv WOT/HER KT12 ..... 197 N8
Denton Rd BXLY DA5 ..... 186 F4
CEND/HSY/T N8 ..... 118 G3
DART DA1 ..... 186 F3
TWK TW1 ..... 177 J2
UED N18 ..... 99 M3
WELL DA16 ..... 167 H3
Denton St GVE DA12 ..... 191 H4
WAND/EARL SW18 ..... 179 L2
Denton Wy CLPT E5 ..... 120 C8
WOKN/KNAP GU21 ..... 231 M3
Dents Gv KWD/TDW/WH KT20 ..... 257 H10
Dents Rd BTSEA SW11 ..... 180 A3
Denvale Wk WOKN/KNAP GU21 ..... 231 M4
Denver Cl ORP BR6 ..... 207 H6
Denver Rd DART DA1 ..... 187 H1
STNW/STAM N16 ..... 119 P5
Denyer St CHEL SW3 ..... 15 P5
Denziloe Av HGDN/ICK UB10 ..... 132 C5
Denzil Rd GUW GU2 ..... 267 H5
NWDGN UB2 ..... 133 N1
Deodar Rd PUT/ROE SW15 ..... 157 H10
Deodora Cl TRDG/WHET N20 ..... 97 P4 ⊡
Depot Ap CRICK NW2 ..... 116 B2
Depot Rd CRAWW RH11 ..... 283 N4

EW KT17 ..... 220 B9
HSLW TW3 ..... 154 C9
Depot St CMBW SE5 ..... 18 G10
Deptford Br GNWCH SE10 ..... 160 F7 ⊡
Deptford Broadway DEPT SE8 ..... 160 F7 ⊡
Deptford Gn DEPT SE8 ..... 160 F5 ⊡
Deptford High St DEPT SE8 ..... 160 F5
Deptford St DEPT SE8 ..... 160 E5 ⊡
De Quincey Rd TOTM N17 ..... 99 J9
Derby Arms Rd EPSOM KT18 ..... 238 C5
Derby Av KTN/HRWW/W HA3 ..... 94 G9
NFNCH/WDSP N12 ..... 97 H6
ROMW/RG RM7 ..... 124 C4
UPMR RM14 ..... 125 J8
Derby Cl EPSOM KT18 ..... 238 C5
Derby Ga WHALL SW1A 17 L1
Derby Hl FSTH SE23 ..... 182 B5
Derby Hill Crs FSTH SE23 ..... 182 B5
Derby Rd BRYLDS KT5 ..... 199 M8
CROY/NA CR0 ..... 203 J9
FSTGT E7 ..... 142 A2
GFD/PVL UB6 ..... 134 A3
GUW GU2 ..... 249 L10
HOD EN11 ..... 45 J3
HOM E9 ..... 140 C3 ⊡
HSLW TW3 ..... 154 A10
MORT/ESHN SW14 ..... 155 N10
PEND EN3 ..... 80 A9
SUT SM1 ..... 221 J3
SWFD E18 ..... 101 L9
UED N18 ..... 100 B6
UX/CGN UB8 ..... 131 M4
WAT WD17 ..... 73 K8 ⊡
WIM/MER SW19 ..... 179 K10 ⊡
Derby Road Br GRAYS RM17 ..... 167 N4
Derbyshire St BETH E2 ..... 7 P10
Derby Stables Rd EPSOM KT18 ..... 238 B3
Derby St MYFR/PICC W1J 10 D10
Dereham Pl SDTCH EC2A 13 K1
Dereham Rd BARK IG11 ..... 143 J1
Derek Av HOR/WEW KT19 ..... 219 M3
WBLY HA9 ..... 135 N2
WLGTN SM6 ..... 202 C10
Derek Cl HOR/WEW KT19 ..... 219 J3
Derek Walcott Cl HNHL SE24 ..... 181 J1 ⊡
Derham Gdns UPMR RM14 ..... 126 B8
Dericote St HACK E8 ..... 7 N3
Deri Av RAIN RM13 ..... 145 J6
Deri Dene Cl STWL/WRAY TW19 ..... 173 P2 ⊡
Derifall Cl EHAM E6 ..... 142 C7 ⊡
Dering Pl CROY/NA CR0 ..... 223 K1
Dering Rd CROY/NA CR0 ..... 223 K1
Dering St CONDST W1S 10 D6
Dering Wy GVE DA12 ..... 191 J4
Derinton Rd TOOT SW17 ..... 180 B7
Derley Rd NWDGN UB2 ..... 153 K2
Dermody Gdns LEW SE13 ..... 183 J1 ⊡
Dermody Rd LEW SE13 ..... 183 J1
Deronda Rd BRXS/STRHM SW2 ..... 181 J4
Deroy Cl CAR SM5 ..... 222 A3
Deroy Ct CAR SM5 ..... 222 A3
Derrick Av SAND/SEL CR2 ..... 223 K6
Derrick Gdns CHARL SE7 ..... 161 P2
Derrick Rd BECK BR3 ..... 204 B3
Derry Av SOCK/AV RM15 ..... 146 F7 ⊡
Derrydown WOKS/MYFD GU22 ..... 231 N9
Derry Downs STMC/STPC BR5 ..... 207 N6
Derry Rd WLGTN SM6 ..... 202 F10
Derry St KENS W8 ..... 14 C2
Dersingham Av MNPK E12 ..... 122 G2
Dersingham Rd CRICK NW2 ..... 117 H8
Derwent Av CDALE/KGS NW9 ..... 116 B5 ⊡
EBAR EN4 ..... 98 A2
HGDN/ICK UB10 ..... 112 B7
MLHL NW7 ..... 96 A1
PIN HA5 ..... 93 M7
PUT/ROE SW15 ..... 178 B7
UED N18 ..... 99 J9
Derwent Cl ADL/WDHM KT15 ..... 215 N2
AMSS HP7 ..... 69 N5
CRAWW RH11 ..... 283 J8 ⊡
DART DA1 ..... 187 J4
EBED/NFELT TW14 ..... 174 A1
ESH/CLAY KT10 ..... 218 D3
Derwent Crs BXLYHN DA7 ..... 164 B8 ⊡
NFNCH/WDSP N12 ..... 97 H4
STAN HA7 ..... 95 H10
Derwent Dr PUR/KEN CR8 ..... 223 L10
SL SL1 ..... 128 B7
STMC/STPC BR5 ..... 206 C7
YEAD UB4 ..... 132 F7
Derwent Gdns REDBR IG4 ..... 122 B2
WBLY HA9 ..... 115 H5
Derwent Gv EDUL SE22 ..... 159 N10
Derwent Pde SOCK/AV RM15 ..... 146 F8
Derwent Ri CDALE/KGS NW9 ..... 116 B3
Derwent Rd EA W5 ..... 155 H2
EGH TW20 ..... 172 E9
HHS/BOV HP3 ..... 36 D7
LTWR GU18 ..... 212 A9
MRDN SM4 ..... 200 D6
PGE/AN SE20 ..... 203 P2
PLMGR N13 ..... 98 G5
STHL UB1 ..... 133 N1
WHTN TW2 ..... 176 A2
Derwent St GNWCH SE10 ..... 161 K4
Derwentwater Rd ACT W3 ..... 135 P10
Derwent Wy HCH RM12 ..... 125 J10 ⊡
De Salis Rd HGDN/ICK UB10 ..... 132 D6 ⊡
Desborough Cl HERT/WAS SG14 ..... 25 K2 ⊡
SHPTN TW17 ..... 196 B7
Desenfans Rd DUL SE21 ..... 181 M2
Desford Rd CAN/RD E16 ..... 141 K6
Desford Wy ASHF TW15 ..... 174 A5
Desmond Rd WATN WD24 ..... 72 C2
Desmond St NWCR SE14 ..... 160 D5 ⊡
Despard Rd ARCH N19 ..... 118 D6
De Tany Ct STAL AL1 ..... 38 C7
Detillens La OXTED RH8 ..... 261 M5
Detling Cl HCH RM12 ..... 125 K10 ⊡
Detling Rd BMLY BR1 ..... 183 N8
ERITH DA8 ..... 168 E6
GVW DA11 ..... 190 A6
Detmold Rd CLPT E5 ..... 120 A6
Deva Cl STALW/RED AL3 ..... 37 P3
Devalls Cl EHAM E6 ..... 142 D9
Devana End CAR SM5 ..... 202 A10
Devas Rd RYNPK SW20 ..... 200 F1
Devas St BOW E3 ..... 140 G6 ⊡
Devema Cl CHST BR7 ..... 206 D1 ⊡
Devenay Rd SRTFD E15 ..... 141 J7
Devenish La ASC SL5 ..... 192 C3
Devenish Rd ABYW SE2 ..... 163 K1
ASC SL5 ..... 192 C6
De Vere Wk WAT WD17 ..... 72 F6
Deverills Wy DTCH/LGLY SL3 ..... 150 F3
Deveron Gdns SOCK/AV RM15 ..... 146 F7 ⊡
Deveron Wy ROM RM1 ..... 104 D4
Devey Cl KUTN/CMB KT2 ..... 178 C10
Devil's La EGH TW20 ..... 172 F9
Devitt Cl ASHTD KT21 ..... 237 M2 ⊡
Devizes St IS N1 ..... 7 H6 ⊡
Devoil Cl RGUE GU4 ..... 250 E4
Devoke Wy WOT/HER KT12 ..... 197 N7
Devon Av TWK TW1 ..... 176 B4
Devon Bank GUW GU2 ..... 267 P3
Devon Cl BKHH IG9 ..... 101 N5
GFD/PVL UB6 ..... 135 H3

PUR/KEN CR8 ..... 241 N2 ⊡
TOTM N17 ..... 119 N1
Devon Ct STAL AL1 ..... 38 D7 ⊡
Devon Crs REIG RH2 ..... 275 J4
Devoncroft Gdns TWK TW1 ..... 176 F3 ⊡
Devon Gdns FSBYPK N4 ..... 119 J4 ⊡
Devonia Gdns UED N18 ..... 99 J7
Devonia Rd IS N1 ..... 6 C3
Devonport Gdns IL IG1 ..... 122 C4
Devonport Ms SHB W12 ..... 136 E10
Devonport Rd SHB W12 ..... 136 E10
Devonport St WCHPL E1 ..... 140 C8 ⊡
WCHPL E1 ..... 140 D8
Devon Ri EFNCH N2 ..... 117 N2
Devon Rd BARK IG11 ..... 143 H5
BELMT SM2 ..... 221 H5
EYN DA4 ..... 210 A1
REDH RH1 ..... 258 D6
WATN WD24 ..... 73 L5
WOKN/KNAP GU21 ..... 214 F10
Devons Rd BOW E3 ..... 140 C1
Devonshire Av AMS HP6 ..... 68 A3
BELMT SM2 ..... 221 M4
DART DA1 ..... 187 J4
WOKN/KNAP GU21 ..... 231 P7
Devonshire Cl CAVSQ/HST W1G 10 C1
SRTFD E15 ..... 121 K9
Devonshire Crs MLHL NW7 ..... 96 E4
Devonshire Dr GNWCH SE10 ..... 160 G6 ⊡
SURB KT6 ..... 199 J8
Devonshire Gdns CHSWK W4 ..... 155 P6
SLN/COR SS17 ..... 169 K2
TOTM N17 ..... 99 J1
WCHMH N21 ..... 99 J1
Devonshire Gn CHSWK W4 ..... 155 P6
Devonshire Gv PECK SE15 ..... 160 A5
Devonshire Hill La TOTM N17 ..... 99 K7
Devonshire Ms South
CAVSQ/HST W1G 10 C1
Devonshire Ms West
CAVSQ/HST W1G 10 D2
Devonshire Pl CAVSQ/HST W1G 10 C2
CRICK NW2 ..... 117 K8 ⊡
KENS W8 ..... 14 G4 ⊡
Devonshire Place Ms MHST W1U 10 C1
Devonshire Rd BELMT SM2 ..... 221 M4
BXLYHS DA6 ..... 165 P10
CAR SM5 ..... 222 B1 ⊡
CDH/CHF RM16 ..... 167 K3
CHSWK W4 ..... 156 B5 ⊡
CRICK NW2 ..... 117 K8
ED N9 ..... 100 G2
ELTH/MOT SE9 ..... 184 B5 ⊡
FELT TW13 ..... 175 M6
FSTH SE23 ..... 182 C5 ⊡
GNTH/NBYPK IG2 ..... 122 G5
GVW DA11 ..... 190 E4
HARP AL5 ..... 20 A1 ⊡
HCH RM12 ..... 125 J4
HRW HA1 ..... 114 C4
MLHL NW7 ..... 96 F5
ORP BR6 ..... 207 K7 ⊡
PLMGR N13 ..... 98 G5
STHL UB1 ..... 133 P7
TOTM N17 ..... 99 J1
WALTH E17 ..... 120 F4
WEA W13 ..... 155 H2
WEY KT13 ..... 216 B1 ⊡
WIM/MER SW19 ..... 179 P10
Devonshire Rw LVPST EC2M 13 L4
Devonshire Rw Ms
LVPST EC2M 13 K4
Devonshire Sq HAYES BR2 ..... 205 N4 ⊡
LVPST EC2M 13 L4
Devonshire St CAVSQ/HST W1G 10 D3
CHSWK W4 ..... 156 B4
Devonshire Ter BAY/PAD W2 ..... 9 K6
YEAD UB4 ..... 133 J8
Devons Rd BOW E3 ..... 140 F7
Devon St PECK SE15 ..... 160 A5
Devon Wy CHSGTN KT9 ..... 219 H1
HGDN/ICK UB10 ..... 132 A4
HOR/WEW KT19 ..... 219 N2 ⊡
Devon Waye HEST TW5 ..... 151 N9
De Walden St CAVSQ/HST W1G ..... 10 D4 ⊡
Dewar Cl CRAWW RH11 ..... 283 H8 ⊡
Dewar St PECK SE15 ..... 159 P9
Dewberry Gdns EHAM E6 ..... 142 B7
Dewberry St POP/IOD E14 ..... 141 H7 ⊡
Dewey Rd DAGE RM10 ..... 145 H5
IS N1 ..... 6 A1
Dewey St TOOT SW17 ..... 180 A8
Dewgrass Gv CHES/WCR EN8 ..... 80 C1 ⊡
Dewhurst Rd CHES/WCR EN8 ..... 62 B5
HMSMTH W6 ..... 156 G2
Dewlands CDST RH9 ..... 260 B7
Dewlands Av DART DA2 ..... 188 A3
Dewsbury Cl PIN HA5 ..... 113 M4 ⊡
Dewsbury Gdns HARH RM3 ..... 105 L7 ⊡
WPK KT4 ..... 200 D10 ⊡
Dewsbury Rd HARH RM3 ..... 105 M7 ⊡
WLSDN NW10 ..... 116 D10
Dexter Cl GRAYS RM17 ..... 167 M2
STAL AL1 ..... 38 F7
Dexter Rd BAR EN5 ..... 76 B9
DEN/HRF UB9 ..... 91 M10
Deyncourt Gdns UPMR RM14 ..... 126 B7
Deyncourt Rd TOTM N17 ..... 99 J8
Deyncourt Gdns WAN E11 ..... 121 P2
D'eynsford Rd CMBW SE5 ..... 159 J7
Dial Cl GRH DA9 ..... 189 H1
Diamedes Av STWL/WRAY TW19 ..... 173 N3 ⊡
Diameter Rd STMC/STPC BR5 ..... 206 E7
Diamond Cl BCTR RM8 ..... 123 M6 ⊡
CDH/CHF RM16 ..... 167 L2
Diamond Rd RSLP HA4 ..... 113 L9
SL SL1 ..... 149 N1
WATN WD24 ..... 73 H4
Diamond St PECK SE15 ..... 159 M6
Diamond Ter GNWCH SE10 ..... 161 H7
Diana Cl CDH/CHF RM16 ..... 167 L2 ⊡
DEPT SE8 ..... 160 E5 ⊡
DTCH/LGLY SL3 ..... 130 C4
SWFD E18 ..... 101 N9
Diana Gdns SURB KT6 ..... 199 J5
Diana Pl CAMTN NW1 ..... 10 F1
Diana Rd WALTH E17 ..... 120 C1
Dianne Wy EBAR EN4 ..... 77 P8 ⊡
Dianthus Cl ABYW SE2 ..... 163 L4 ⊡
CHERT KT16 ..... 195 H7 ⊡
Dianthus Ct WOKS/MYFD GU22 ..... 232 A4
Diban Av HCH RM12 ..... 125 J9
Dibden La RSEV TN14 ..... 264 F5
Dibden St IS N1 ..... 6 E5
Dibdin Cl SUT SM1 ..... 201 N10
Dibdin Rd SUT SM1 ..... 201 N10
Diceland Rd BNSTD SM7 ..... 239 J2
Dicey Av CRICK NW2 ..... 116 F10
Dickens Av DART DA1 ..... 169 P10
FNCH N3 ..... 97 M9
TIL RM18 ..... 168 E7
UX/CGN UB8 ..... 132 C6
Dickens Cl ERITH DA8 ..... 167 N3
HART DA3 ..... 211 K5
HYS/HAR UB3 ..... 152 F3 ⊡
RCHPK/HAM TW10 ..... 177 K5
STALW/RED AL3 ..... 38 C5
Dickens Dr ADL/WDHM KT15 ..... 215 N5 ⊡
CHST BR7 ..... 185 K3
Dickens La UED N18 ..... 99 M6
Dickenson Rd CEND/HSY/T N8 ..... 118 F5
FELT TW13 ..... 175 H7
Dickenson's La SNWD SE25 ..... 203 P6
Dickenson's Pl SNWD SE25 ..... 203 P6 ⊡
Dickens Ri CHIG IG7 ..... 102 D4
Dickens Rd CRAWE RH10 ..... 283 N10
EHAM E6 ..... 141 N2
GVE DA12 ..... 191 H4
Dickens Sq STHWK SE1 ..... 18 F3 ⊡

Dickens St VX/NE SW8 ..... 158 C8
Dickens Wy ROM RM1 ..... 124 F2
Dickerage Hl NWMAL KT3 ..... 199 P2
Dickerage La NWMAL KT3 ..... 199 P2
Dickerage Rd KUT1 KT1 ..... 199 P1
NWMAL KT3 ..... 199 P2 ⊡
Dickins Cl CHESW EN7 ..... 62 B10
Dickinson Av RKW/CH/CXG WD3 ..... 72 B10
Dickinson Sq RKW/CH/CXG WD3 ..... 72 C10
Dickson CHESW EN7 ..... 61 N3
Dickson Fold PIN HA5 ..... 113 L2
Dickson Rd ELTH/MOT SE9 ..... 162 B9
Dick Turpin Wy
EBED/NFELT TW14 ..... 152 G10
Didsbury Cl EHAM E6 ..... 142 C3 ⊡
Digby Crs FSBYPK N4 ..... 119 K7
Digby Gdns DAGE RM10 ..... 144 B3
Digby Pl CROY/NA CR0 ..... 203 N10
Digby Rd BARK IG11 ..... 143 J2
HOM E9 ..... 140 C1
Digby St BETH E2 ..... 140 B5 ⊡
Digby Wy BF/WBF KT14 ..... 216 A8 ⊡
Dig Dag Hl CHESW EN7 ..... 61 N3
Digdens Ri EPSOM KT18 ..... 237 P1
Diggon St WCHPL E1 ..... 140 C8 ⊡
Dighton Rd WAND/EARL SW18 ..... 179 M1
Dignum St IS N1 ..... 6 A7 ⊡
Digswell Cl BORE WD6 ..... 75 M4
Digswell Hl WLYN AL6 ..... 22 D2
Digswell La WGCE AL7 ..... 23 J1
Digswell Ri WGCW AL8 ..... 22 C1
Digswell Rd WGCW AL8 ..... 22 D1
HOLWY N7 ..... 6 B1
Dilhorne Cl LEE/GVPK SE12 ..... 183 N6
Dilke St CHEL SW3 ..... 16 B1
Dillwyn Cl SYD SE26 ..... 182 D7
Dilston Cl NTHLT UB5 ..... 133 L5 ⊡
Dilston Rd LHD/OX KT22 ..... 236 F5
Dilton Gdns PUT/ROE SW15 ..... 178 D4
Dimes Pl HMSMTH W6 ..... 156 E3 ⊡
Dimmock Dr GFD/PVL UB6 ..... 114 C10
Dimmocks La RKW/CH/CXG WD3 ..... 71 K2
Dimond Cl FSTGT E7 ..... 121 P4
Dimsdale Dr CDALE/KGS NW9 ..... 115 P6
EN EN1 ..... 99 P1
Dimsdale St HERT/WAS SG14 ..... 25 K5
Dimson Crs BOW E3 ..... 140 F5 ⊡
Dinant Link Rd HOD EN11 ..... 44 F2
Dingle Cl BAR EN5 ..... 76 C10
Dingle Gdns POP/IOD E14 ..... 140 F9 ⊡
Dingle Rd ASHF TW15 ..... 174 C8
The Dingle CRAWW RH11 ..... 283 L7
HGDN/ICK UB10 ..... 132 C5 ⊡
Dingley La STRHM/NOR SW16 ..... 180 E5
Dingley Pl FSBYE EC1V 6 E10
Dingley Rd FSBYE EC1V 6 D10
Dingwall Av CROY/NA CR0 ..... 203 K9
Dingwall Gdns GLDGN NW11 ..... 117 K4
Dingwall Rd CAR SM5 ..... 222 A5
CROY/NA CR0 ..... 203 L5
WAND/EARL SW18 ..... 179 M3
Dinmont St BETH E2 ..... 140 A4 ⊡
Dinmore HHS/BOV HP3 ..... 52 C4
Dinsdale Cl WOKS/MYFD GU22 ..... 232 C4
Dinsdale Gdns BAR EN5 ..... 77 L9
SNWD SE25 ..... 203 M4
Dinsdale Rd BKHTH/KID SE3 ..... 161 L5
Dinsmore Rd BAL SW12 ..... 180 C3
Dinton Rd KUTN/CMB KT2 ..... 177 L10
WIM/MER SW19 ..... 179 N9
Diploma Av EFNCH N2 ..... 117 P2 ⊡
Dippers Cl BGR/WK TN15 ..... 247 N5
Dirdene Cl EW KT17 ..... 220 C8 ⊡
Dirdene Gdns EW KT17 ..... 220 C8 ⊡
Dirdene Gv EW KT17 ..... 220 C8 ⊡
Dirleton Rd SRTFD E15 ..... 141 L3
Dirtham La EHSLY KT24 ..... 253 J5
Disbrowe Rd HMSMTH W6 ..... 157 H4
Dishforth La CDALE/KGS NW9 ..... 96 B9
Disney Pl STHWK SE1 ..... 18 F1
Disney St STHWK SE1 ..... 18 F1
Dison Cl PEND EN3 ..... 80 C5 ⊡
Disraeli Cl THMD SE28 ..... 143 L10
Disraeli Ct DTCH/LGLY SL3 ..... 150 E5 ⊡
Disraeli Pk BEAC HP9 ..... 88 C7
Disraeli Rd EA W5 ..... 135 J10
FSTGT E7 ..... 141 M1
PUT/ROE SW15 ..... 157 H10
WLSDN NW10 ..... 135 P4
Diss St BETH E2 ..... 7 L9
Distaff La BLKFR EC4V 12 E7
Distillery La HMSMTH W6 ..... 156 F4
Distillery Rd HMSMTH W6 ..... 156 G4
Distin St LBTH SE11 ..... 18 A6
District Rd GFD/PVL UB6 ..... 114 C10
Ditchburn St POP/IOD E14 ..... 141 H9 ⊡
Ditches La COUL/CHIP CR5 ..... 240 E3
Ditchfield Rd HOD EN11 ..... 26 F10
YEAD UB4 ..... 133 M6
Ditchling Hl CRAWW RH11 ..... 283 M10
Dittisham Rd ELTH/MOT SE9 ..... 184 F7
Ditton Cl THDIT KT7 ..... 198 F7
Dittoncroft Cl CROY/NA CR0 ..... 223 M1 ⊡
Ditton Grange Cl SURB KT6 ..... 199 J8
Ditton Grange Dr SURB KT6 ..... 199 J8
Ditton Hl SURB KT6 ..... 199 J8
Ditton Hill Rd SURB KT6 ..... 199 J8
Ditton Lawn THDIT KT7 ..... 198 F8
Ditton Park Rd DTCH/LGLY SL3 ..... 150 B9
Ditton Reach THDIT KT7 ..... 198 G6
Ditton Rd BXLYHS DA6 ..... 185 N1
DTCH/LGLY SL3 ..... 150 A7
NWDGN UB2 ..... 153 N4
SURB KT6 ..... 199 K8
Divot Pl HERT/BAY SG13 ..... 26 A1 ⊡
Dixon Cl EHAM E6 ..... 142 C8
Dixon Dr WEY KT13 ..... 216 A6
Dixon Pl WWKM BR4 ..... 204 A10
Dixon Rd NWCR SE14 ..... 160 D7
SNWD SE25 ..... 203 M3
Dixons Hill Cl BRKMPK AL9 ..... 58 C1
Dixons Hill Rd BRKMPK AL9 ..... 44 F9
Dobbin Cl KTN/HRWW/W HA3 ..... 95 M3
Dobbins Pl CRAWW RH11 ..... 283 H8 ⊡
Dobb's Weir Rd HOD EN11 ..... 45 J4
Dobell Rd ELTH/MOT SE9 ..... 184 C1
Dobree Av WLSDN NW10 ..... 136 E2
Dobson Cl KIL/WHAMP NW6 ..... 3 L4
Dobson Rd CRAWW RH11 ..... 283 N4
GVE DA12 ..... 191 H4
Dock Approach Rd GRAYS RM17 ..... 168 B4
Dockers Tanner Rd
POP/IOD E14 ..... 160 F3 ⊡
Dockett Eddy La SHPTN TW17 ..... 196 A7
Dockhead STHWK SE1 ..... 19 M2
Dock Hill Av BERM/RHTH SE16 ..... 160 C1
Dockland St CAN/RD E16 ..... 142 D10
Dockley Rd BERM/RHTH SE16 ..... 19 N4
Dock Rd BTFD TW8 ..... 154 J6 ⊡
CAN/RD E16 ..... 141 N10
GRAYS RM17 ..... 168 A5
TIL RM18 ..... 168 B7
Dockside Rd CAN/RD E16 ..... 142 E8
Dockwell Cl EBED/NFELT TW14 ..... 153 H10
Doctors Cl SYD SE26 ..... 182 B8
Doctor's Commons Rd BERK HP4 ..... 33 N4
Doctors La CTHM CR3 ..... 241 H10
Doddbrooke Rd WNWD SE27 ..... 181 H1
Doddington Gv WALW SE17 ..... 18 C9
Doddington Pl WALW SE17 ..... 18 C9 ⊡
Dodds Crs BF/WBF KT14 ..... 215 L10
Doddsfield Rd SLN SL2 ..... 149 K2
Dodd's La BF/WBF KT14 ..... 215 K10
CSTG HP8 ..... 89 N3

HHNE HP2 ..... 35 M1
Dodds Pk BRKHM/BTCW RH3 ..... 273 N2
Dodsley Pl ED N9 ..... 100 B4 ⊡
Dodson St STHWK SE1 ..... 18 B2
Dod St POP/IOD E14 ..... 140 E8
Dodwood WGCE AL7 ..... 23 L6
Doebury Wk WOOL/PLUM SE18 ..... 163 K5 ⊡
Doel Cl WIM/MER SW19 ..... 179 M10
Doggett Rd CAT SE6 ..... 182 E1
Doggetts Ct EBAR EN4 ..... 77 P9
Doggetts Farm Rd DEN/HRF UB9 ..... 90 C4
Doggetts Wy STAL AL1 ..... 38 B8
Doggetts Wood Cl CSTG HP8 ..... 69 N7
Doggetts Wood La CSTG HP8 ..... 69 N7
Doghurst Av WDR/YW UB7 ..... 152 C6
Doghurst Dr WDR/YW UB7 ..... 152 C6 ⊡
Doghurst La COUL/CHIP CR5 ..... 240 G5
Dog Kennel Hill EDUL SE22 ..... 159 M9
Dog Kennel La HAT AL10 ..... 40 D3
RKW/CH/CXG WD3 ..... 71 J9
Dog La WLSDN NW10 ..... 116 B9
Dognell Gn WGCW AL8 ..... 22 E4
Dog Rose Ramble YEAD UB4 ..... 133 H3
Dog Rose Ramble & Hillingdon Trail
YEAD UB4 ..... 132 G3
Dogwood Cl CVW DA11 ..... 190 C7
Doherty Rd PLSTW E13 ..... 141 M6
Dolben St STHWK SE1 ..... 12 D10 ⊡
Dolby Rd FUL/PGN SW6 ..... 157 J8 ⊡
Dollis Valley Green Wk FNCH N3 ..... 97 H10
GLDGN NW11 ..... 117 H2
Dolland St LBTH SE11 ..... 17 P8
Dollis Cl CRAWE RH10 ..... 284 D8 ⊡
Dollis Ms FNCH N3 ..... 97 J9
Dollis Av FNCH N3 ..... 97 H9
Dollis Hill Av CRICK NW2 ..... 116 E8
Dollis Hill La CRICK NW2 ..... 116 C9
Dollis Pk FNCH N3 ..... 97 J9
Dollis Rd FNCH N3 ..... 97 H9
Dollis Valley Green Wk
TRDG/WHET N20 ..... 77 L10
Dollis Valley Wy BAR EN5 ..... 77 J9
Dolman Rd CHSWK W4 ..... 156 A3
Dolman St CLAP SW4 ..... 158 G10
Dolphin Ap ROM RM1 ..... 124 C2
Dolphin Cl BERM/RHTH SE16 ..... 160 C2
SURB KT6 ..... 199 J6
THMD SE28 ..... 143 M8
Dolphin Ct SL SL1 ..... 149 N1
Dolphin Cl SLN SL2 ..... 173 K6 ⊡
Dolphin Ct North
STWL/WRAY TW19 ..... 173 K6 ⊡
Dolphin La POP/IOD E14 ..... 140 G9 ⊡
Dolphin Rd NTHLT UB5 ..... 133 N4
SL SL1 ..... 149 N1
Dolphin Sq PIM SW1V 17 J8
Dolphin St KUT1 KT1 ..... 199 K1 ⊡
Dombey St BMSBY WC1N 11 N3
Dome Hl CTHM CR3 ..... 259 M3
Dome Hill Pk SYD SE26 ..... 181 N7
Dome Hill Peak CTHM CR3 ..... 259 M2
Domett Cl CMBW SE5 ..... 159 L10 ⊡
Dome Wy REDH RH1 ..... 258 A9
Domingo St FSBYE EC1V 12 E1
Dominica Cl EHAM E6 ..... 142 A4 ⊡
Dominion Dr CRW RM5 ..... 104 C7
Dominion Pde HRW HA1 ..... 114 E3 ⊡
Dominion Rd CROY/NA CR0 ..... 203 N1
NWDGN UB2 ..... 153 M2
Dominion St LVPST EC2M 13 H5
Dominion Wy RAIN RM13 ..... 144 G5
Domonic Dr ELTH/MOT SE9 ..... 184 E6
Domville Cl TRDG/WHET N20 ..... 97 H1
Donald Dr CHDH RM6 ..... 123 M3
Donald Rd CROY/NA CR0 ..... 202 G6
PLSTW E13 ..... 141 N3
Donaldson Rd KIL/WHAMP NW6 ..... 2 D6
WOOL/PLUM SE18 ..... 162 D7
Donald Woods Gdns BRYLDS KT5 ..... 199 N8
Doncaster Dr NTHLT UB5 ..... 113 N10
Doncaster Gdns FSBYPK N4 ..... 119 K4 ⊡
NTHLT UB5 ..... 113 N10 ⊡
Doncaster Gn OXHEY WD19 ..... 93 K6 ⊡
Doncaster Rd ED N9 ..... 100 A1 ⊡
Doncaster Wy UPMR RM14 ..... 125 N8
Donegal St IS N1 ..... 5 P8
Doneraile St FUL/PGN SW6 ..... 156 G7
Dongola Rd PLSTW E13 ..... 141 N5
Dongola Rd West PLSTW E13 ..... 141 N5 ⊡
Donington Av BARK/HLT IG6 ..... 122 F3
Donkey Aly EDUL SE22 ..... 181 P3
Donkey La EN EN1 ..... 79 P6
EBAR EN4 ..... 210 A9
HORL RH6 ..... 280 E8 ⊡
RDKG RH5 ..... 271 J9
Donnafields CHOB/PIR GU24 ..... 230 F2
Donnay Cl CFSP/GDCR SL9 ..... 110 A4
Donne Cl CRAWE RH10 ..... 284 C5
Donnefield Av EDGW HA8 ..... 95 K7
Donne Gdns WOKS/MYFD GU22 ..... 233 H1
Donne Pl CHEL SW3 ..... 15 P5
MTCM CR4 ..... 202 C4
Donne Rd BCTR RM8 ..... 123 M7
Donnington Ct CRAWW RH11 ..... 283 J10 ⊡
Donnington Rd
KTN/HRWW/W HA3 ..... 115 J3
WLSDN NW10 ..... 136 E3 ⊡
WPK KT4 ..... 200 D9
Donnybrook Rd
STRHM/NOR SW16 ..... 180 D10
Donovan Av MUSWH N10 ..... 98 C10
Donovan Cl HOR/WEW KT19 ..... 220 A6
Don Phelan Cl CMBW SE5 ..... 159 L7
Don Wy ROM RM1 ..... 104 F8
Doods Park Rd REIG RH2 ..... 257 M9
Doods Rd REIG RH2 ..... 257 N9
Doone Cl TEDD TW11 ..... 176 F9 ⊡
Doon St STHWK SE1 ..... 12 A1
Dorado Gdns ORP BR6 ..... 207 N10
Doral Wy CAR SM5 ..... 222 A2 ⊡
Dorando Cl SHB W12 ..... 136 E9 ⊡
Doran Dr REIG RH2 ..... 257 N10
Doran Gv WOOL/PLUM SE18 ..... 163 H6
Doran Rd WIM/MER SW19 ..... 179 K8
Dora Rd POP/IOD E14 ..... 140 G8
Dora St POP/IOD E14 ..... 140 E8
Dorchester Av BXLY DA5 ..... 185 N4
HOD EN11 ..... 44 F1
PLMGR N13 ..... 99 K5
RYLN/HDSTN HA2 ..... 114 A3
Dorchester Cl DART DA1 ..... 187 N3
NTHLT UB5 ..... 114 A10
STMC/STPC BR5 ..... 185 L10 ⊡
Dorchester Ct CRICK NW2 ..... 181 K1
STHGT/OAK N14 ..... 98 B1
WOKS/MYFD GU22 ..... 232 D2
Dorchester Dr EBED/NFELT TW14 ..... 174 F1
HNHL SE24 ..... 181 K1
Dorchester Gdns CHING E4 ..... 100 F5 ⊡
GLDGN NW11 ..... 117 K2 ⊡
Dorchester Gv CHSWK W4 ..... 156 B5
Dorchester Ms TWK TW1 ..... 177 H3 ⊡
Dorchester Rd GVE DA12 ..... 190 G6
MRDN SM4 ..... 201 L7
NTHLT UB5 ..... 114 A10
WEY KT13 ..... 196 C10
WPK KT4 ..... 200 F8
Dorchester Wy
KTN/HRWW/W HA3 ..... 115 L4
Dorchester Waye YEAD UB4 ..... 133 K8
Dorcis Av BXLYHN DA7 ..... 163 P8
Dordrecht Rd ACT W3 ..... 136 E6
Dore Av MNPK E12 ..... 122 G10
Doreen Av CDALE/KGS NW9 ..... 116 A6
Dore Gdns MRDN SM4 ..... 201 L7 ⊡
Dorell Cl STHL UB1 ..... 133 N7
Dorian Ct WARL CR6 ..... 242 A5 ⊡

Dorian Dr ASC SL5 .... 192 D1
Dorian Rd HCH RM12 .... 125 H6
Doria Rd FUL/PGN SW6 .... 157 J8
Doric Dr KWD/TDW/WH KT20 .... 239 D6
Doric Wy CAMTN 5 J9
Dorien Rd RYNPK SW20 .... 200 G2
Dorin Ct WOKS/MYFD GU22 .... 233 H1
Doris Av BXLYHN DA7 .... 164 D7
Doris Rd ASHF TW15 .... 174 L9
  FSTGT E7 .... 141 M2
Dorking Ct DEPT SE8 .... 160 E5
  WPK KT4 .... 200 C9
Dorking Ri RM3 .... 105 L5
Dorking Rd EPSOM KT18 .... 237 N1
  GT/LBKH KT23 .... 254 L5
  HARH RM3 .... 105 L5
  KWD/TDW/WH KT20 .... 256 C2
  LHD/OX KT22 .... 236 C8
  RGUE GU4 .... 268 G6
Dorking Wk HARH RM3 .... 105 L5
Dorkins Wy UPMR RM14 .... 126 D5
Dorlcote Rd WAND/EARL SW18 .... 179 N5
Dorling Dr EW KT17 .... 220 C8
Dorly Cl SHPTN TW17 .... 196 F4
Dorman Pl ED N9 .... 99 P5
Dormans CRAWW RH11 .... 283 K8
Dormans Cl NTHWD HA6 .... 92 B8
Dorman Wy STJWD NW8 .... 2 L1
Dormay St WAND/EARL SW18 .... 179 L1
Dormer Cl BAR EN5 .... 76 G9
  SRTFD E15 .... 141 L1
Dormer's Av STHL UB1 .... 133 P8
Dormers Cl RGODL GU7 .... 267 J10
Dormers Ri GFD/PVL UB6 .... 134 A8
Dormer's Wells La STHL UB1 .... 133 P8
Dormywood RSLP HA4 .... 112 C3
Dornberg Cl BKHTH/KID SE3 .... 161 M6
Dornberg Rd BKHTH/KID SE3 .... 161 N6
Dorncliffe Rd FUL/PGN SW6 .... 157 H8
Dornels SLN SL2 .... 129 P8
Dorney Gv WEY KT13 .... 196 C9
Dorney Hl North BEAC HP9 .... 108 A4
Dorney Hl South BEAC HP9 .... 108 F5
Dorney Ri STMC/STPC BR5 .... 207 J4
Dorney Wy HSLWW TW4 .... 175 M1
Dorney Wood Rd SL SL1 .... 108 B8
Dornfell St KIL/WHAMP NW6 .... 117 J10
Dornford Gdns COUL/CHIP CR5 .... 241 K5
Dornton Rd SAND/SEL CR2 .... 223 M2
  TOOT SW17 .... 180 C5
Dorothy Av ALP/SUD HA0 .... 135 K2
Dorothy Evans Cl BXLYHN DA7 .... 164 C10
Dorothy Gdns BCTR RM8 .... 123 L9
Dorothy Rd BTSEA SW11 .... 158 A9
Dorrien's Cft BERK HP4 .... 33 L2
Dorrington Gdns HCH RM12 .... 125 L6
Dorrington St HCIRC EC1N 12 A3
Dorrit Crs RGUE GU3 .... 249 K8
Dorrit St STHWK SE1 .... 18 F1
Dorrofield Cl RKW/CH/CXG WD3 .... 72 D9
Dors Cl CDALE/KGS NW9 .... 116 A6
Dorset Av NWDGN UB2 .... 153 P3
  ROM RM1 .... 124 L1
  WELL DA16 .... 163 J10
  YEAD UB4 .... 132 F5
Dorset Buildings EMB EC4Y 12 C6
Dorset Cl BERK HP4 .... 33 L4
  CAMTN NW1 .... 3 M7
  YEAD UB4 .... 132 F5
Dorset Dr EDGW HA8 .... 95 L7
  WOKS/MYFD GU22 .... 232 E3
Dorset Gdns STRHM/NOR SW16 .... 202 G4
Dorset Ms FNCH N3 .... 97 K9
  KTBR SW1X 16 E3
Dorset Pl SRTFD E15 .... 141 L1
Dorset Ri EMB EC4Y 12 C6
Dorset Rd ASHF TW15 .... 173 N6
  BECK BR3 .... 204 C3
  BELMT SM2 .... 221 K6
  EA W5 .... 155 H2
  ELTH/MOT SE9 .... 184 B5
  HRW HA1 .... 114 B4
  MTCM CR4 .... 201 P2
  SEVS/STOTM N15 .... 119 L2
  VX/NE SW8 .... 158 G6
  WDGN N22 .... 98 F9
  WDSR SL4 .... 149 H8
  WIM/MER SW19 .... 201 K1
Dorset Sq CAMTN NW1 .... 10 A2
Dorset St MHST W1U 10 A2
Dorset Wy BF/WBF KT14 .... 215 N7
  HGDN/ICK UB10 .... 132 A4
  WHTN TW2 .... 176 B4
Dorset Waye HEST TW5 .... 153 N6
Dorton Wy RPLY/SEND GU23 .... 233 L2
Dorville Crs HMSMTH W6 .... 156 L2
Dorville Rd LEE/GVPK SE12 .... 183 M1
Dothill Rd WOOL/PLUM SE18 .... 162 F6
Douai Gv HPTN TW12 .... 198 B1
Doubleday Rd LOU IG10 .... 82 F7
Doughty Ms BMSBY WC1N 11 N2
Doughty St BMSBY WC1N 11 N1
Douglas Av ALP/SUD HA0 .... 135 K2
  HARH RM3 .... 105 M10
  NWMAL KT3 .... 200 H4
  WALTH E17 .... 100 F9
  WATW WD24 .... 73 L3
Douglas Cl CDH/CHF RM16 .... 167 K2
  RGUE GU4 .... 250 A4
  STAN HA7 .... 94 F6
  WLGTN SM6 .... 222 F3
Douglas Ct CTHM CR3 .... 241 K8
Douglas Crs YEAD UB4 .... 133 K6
Douglas Dr CROY/NA CR0 .... 204 F10
Douglas Gdns BERK HP4 .... 33 M4
Douglas La STWL/WRAY TW19 .... 172 C1
Douglas Ms BNSTD SM7 .... 239 J2
  CRICK NW2 .... 117 H8
Douglas Pl POP/IOD E14 .... 117 H8
Douglas Rd ADL/WDHM KT15 .... 195 L10
  CAN/RD E16 .... 141 M7
  CHING E4 .... 101 K1
  ESH/CLAY KT10 .... 198 A9
  GDMY/SEVK IG3 .... 123 K5
  HSLW TW3 .... 154 A9
  IS N1 .... 6 E3
  KIL/WHAMP NW6 .... 2 C1
  KUT KT1 .... 199 N2
  REIG RH2 .... 257 K9
  ROM RM1 .... 124 C4
  SLN SL2 .... 129 J7
  STWL/WRAY TW19 .... 173 N2
  SURB KT6 .... 199 L9
  WDGN N22 .... 99 H9
  WELL DA16 .... 163 L7
Douglas Rd North IS N1 .... 6 F1
Douglas Rd South IS N1 .... 6 F2
Douglas St WEST SW1P 17 J6
Douglas Ter WALTH E17 .... 100 E9
  WGCE AL7 .... 23 M5
Doug Siddons Ct GRAYS RM17 .... 167 P5
Doulton Cl HLWE CM17 .... 47 P2
Doulton Ms HAMP NW3 .... 3 H1
Dounesforth Gdns WAND/EARL SW18 .... 179 L4
Douro Pl KENS W8 .... 15 H3
Douro St BOW E3 .... 140 A1
Douthwaite Sq WAP E1W 13 M7
Dove Ap EHAM E6 .... 142 B7
Dove Cl CRAWW RH11 .... 283 N5
  SAND/SEL CR2 .... 224 C7
  YEAD UB4 .... 133 L6
Dovecot Cl PIN HA5 .... 113 K3

Dovecote Cl WEY KT13 .... 196 C10
Dove Ct BEAC HP9 .... 88 C8
  HAT AL10 .... 40 D6
  LOTH EC2R 12 G6
Dovedale Av CLAY IG5 .... 102 D10
  KTN/HRWW/W HA3 .... 115 H4
Dovedale Cl DEN/HRF UB9 .... 91 M10
  GU GU1 .... 250 D7
  WELL DA16 .... 163 K7
Dovedale Crs CRAWW RH11 .... 283 L9
Dovedale Ri MTCM CR4 .... 180 A10
Dovedale Rd EDUL SE22 .... 182 A1
  RDART DA2 .... 188 B4
Dovedon Cl STHGT/OAK N14 .... 98 F3
Dove House Gdns SLN SL2 .... 128 D5
Dovehouse Cft HLW CM20 .... 29 K9
Dove House Md BARK IG11 .... 142 C4
Dovehouse St CHEL SW3 .... 15 M8
Dove La POTB/CUF EN6 .... 59 L10
Dove Ms ECT SW5 .... 15 J6
Doveney Cl STMC/STPC BR5 .... 207 N4
Dove Pk PIN HA5 .... 93 N8
  RKW/CH/CXG WD3 .... 70 F2
Dover Cl ROMW/RG RM7 .... 104 D10
Dovercourt Av THHTH CR7 .... 203 H4
Dovercourt Gdns STAN HA7 .... 95 K6
Dovercourt La SUT SM1 .... 201 M10
Dovercourt Rd EDUL SE22 .... 181 N2
Doverfield CHESW EN7 .... 61 K5
Doverfield Rd BRXS/STRHM SW2 .... 180 F2
  RGUE GU4 .... 250 D7
Dover Gdns CAR SM5 .... 202 A10
Dover House Rd PUT/ROE SW15 .... 156 D10
Doveridge Gdns PLMGR N13 .... 99 J5
Dove Rd IS N1 .... 7 H1
Dover Rw BETH E2 .... 7 N7
Dover Park Dr PUT/ROE SW15 .... 178 E2
Dover Patrol BKHTH/KID SE3 .... 161 N8
Dover Rd ED N9 .... 100 B3
  GVW DA11 .... 190 A3
  MNPK E12 .... 121 P7
  NRWD SE19 .... 181 L10
  SL SL1 .... 128 C8
  WOOL/PLUM SE18 .... 162 A8
Dover Rd East GVW DA11 .... 190 B3
Dovers Green Rd REIG RH2 .... 275 L4
Doversmead WOKN/KNAP GU21 .... 231 K2
Dover St MYFR/PICC W1J 10 F8
Dover Wy RKW/CH/CXG WD3 .... 72 D8
Doves Cl HAYES BR2 .... 206 B9
Doves Yd IS N1 .... 6 A6
Doveton Rd SAND/SEL CR2 .... 223 L2
Doveton St WCHPL E1 .... 140 B6
Dowanhill Rd CAT SE6 .... 183 J4
Dowdeswell Cl PUT/ROE SW15 .... 156 B10
Dowding Cl RAIN RM13 .... 145 J2
Dowding Rd BH/WHM TN16 .... 244 A1
  HGDN/ICK UB10 .... 132 A2
Dower Av WLGTN SM6 .... 222 C5
Dower Cl BEAC HP9 .... 88 B6
Dower Pk WDSR SL4 .... 148 D10
Dower Wk CRAWW RH11 .... 283 K8
Dowgate Hi CANST EC4R 12 G7
Dowlands La HORL RH6 .... 281 L5
Dowlans Cl GT/LBKH KT23 .... 253 P3
Dowlans Rd GT/LBKH KT23 .... 254 A3
Dowlas St CMBW SE5 .... 159 N6
Dowlerville Rd ORP BR6 .... 227 J3
Dowling Ct HHS/BOV HP3 .... 35 N9
Dowman Cl WIM/MER SW19 .... 179 L10
The Downage NW4 .... 96 F10
Downalong BUSH WD23 .... 94 C2
Downbank BXLYHN DA7 .... 164 E7
Down Barns Rd RSLP HA4 .... 113 L4
Down Cl NTHLT UB5 .... 133 J5
Downderry Rd BMLY BR1 .... 183 J7
Downe Av RSEV TN14 .... 226 F10
Downe Cl HORL RH6 .... 279 P2
  WELL DA16 .... 163 M6
Downedge STALW/RED AL3 .... 38 A5
Downend WOOL/PLUM SE18 .... 162 E6
Downer Dr RKW/CH/CXG WD3 .... 71 J2
Downer Meadow RGODL GU7 .... 267 K9
  MTCM CR4 .... 202 A2
  RSEV TN14 .... 226 F10
Downer's Cottages CLAP SW4 .... 158 D7
Downes Cl TWK TW1 .... 176 C2
Downes Ct WCHMH N21 .... 99 H2
Downes Rd STALE/WH AL4 .... 33 G2
Downfield WPK KT4 .... 200 D8
Downfield Cl HERT/BAY SG13 .... 26 B7
  MV/WKIL W9 .... 8 G2
Downfield Rd CHES/WCR EN8 .... 62 D7
  HERT/BAY SG13 .... 26 B7
Downfields WCCW AL8 .... 22 E7
Down Green La STALE/WH AL4 .... 20 C4
Down Hall Rd KUTN/CMB KT2 .... 199 J1
Downhall Rd RBSF CM22 .... 31 J5
Downham Cl CRW RM5 .... 104 B8
Downham Rd IS N1 .... 7 J1
Downham Wy BMLY BR1 .... 183 K8
Downhills Park Rd TOTM N17 .... 119 K1
Downhills Av TOTM N17 .... 119 L1
Downhills Wy TOTM N17 .... 99 K10
Downhurst Av MLHL NW7 .... 96 A7
Downing Av GUW GU2 .... 267 L1
Downing Cl RYLN/HDSTN HA2 .... 114 B1
Downing Dr GFD/PVL UB6 .... 134 D3
Downing Rd DAGW RM9 .... 144 A2
Downings EHAM E6 .... 142 D8
Downing St WHALL SW1A 17 L1
Downings Wd RKW/CH/CXG WD3 .... 90 C6
Downland Cl COUL/CHIP CR5 .... 222 C10
  EPSOM KT18 .... 238 C4
  TRDG/WHET N20 .... 97 M2
Downland Dr CRAWW RH11 .... 283 M9
Downland Gdns EPSOM KT18 .... 238 C4
Downland Pl CRAWW RH11 .... 283 M9
Downlands WAB EN9 .... 63 K10
Downlands Rd PUR/KEN CR8 .... 222 F9
Downlands Wy EPSOM KT18 .... 238 C4
Down La RGUW GU3 .... 266 G4
Downleys Cl ELTH/MOT SE9 .... 184 B5
Down Pl HMSMTH W6 .... 156 F3
Down Rd GU GU1 .... 250 E10
  TEDD TW11 .... 176 G9
Downs Av CHST BR7 .... 184 H2
  DART DA1 .... 187 P3
  EPSOM KT18 .... 238 C4
  PIN HA5 .... 113 N4
Downs Bridge Rd BECK BR3 .... 205 J1
Downs Court Rd PUR/KEN CR8 .... 223 K9
Downsell Rd WAN E11 .... 121 J6
Downsfield Rd WALTH E17 .... 120 D4
Downshall Av GDMY/SEVK IG3 .... 123 H4
Downs Hi BECK BR3 .... 205 J1
Downs Hill Rd EPSOM KT18 .... 238 B10
Downshire HI HAMP NW3 .... 117 N9
Downside EPSOM KT18 .... 220 C10
  HHNE HP2 .... 35 P3
  SUN TW16 .... 197 H1
  TWK TW1 .... 176 C2
Downside Bridge Rd COB KT11 .... 217 J10
Downside Cl WIM/MER SW19 .... 179 N9
Downside Common COB KT11 .... 235 J4
Downside Common Rd
  COB KT11 .... 235 K4
Downside Crs HAMP NW3 .... 117 N9
  WEA W13 .... 134 F6
Downside Orch
  WOKS/MYFD GU22 .... 232 D3

Downside Rd BELMT SM2 .... 221 N3
  COB KT11 .... 235 J4
  RGUE GU4 .... 268 E1
Downsland Dr BRW CM14 .... 107 H4
Downs La CLPT E5 .... 120 A9
  HAT AL10 .... 40 D6
  LHD/OX KT22 .... 236 C9
Downs Link RGUE GU4 .... 269 H5
  SHGR GU5 .... 268 C9
Downs Park Rd HACK E8 .... 119 P10
Downs Rd BECK BR3 .... 204 G2
  BELMT SM2 .... 221 L7
  CLPT E5 .... 119 P9
  COUL/CHIP CR5 .... 240 E4
  DTCH/LGLY SL3 .... 150 A1
  EN EN1 .... 79 M8
  EPSOM KT18 .... 237 P6
  MEO DA13 .... 190 A8
  PUR/KEN CR8 .... 223 J7
  RDKG RH5 .... 255 H4
  THHTH CR7 .... 203 K1
Downs Side BELMT SM2 .... 221 J7
The Downs HAT AL10 .... 40 D6
  HLW CM20 .... 47 H1
  LHD/OX KT22 .... 254 G1
  RYNPK SW20 .... 178 G10
Down St E/WMO/HCT KT8 .... 197 P5
  MYFR/PICC W1J 16 E1
Down Street Ms MYFR/PICC W1J 16 E1
Downs Va HART DA3 .... 211 K4
Downs Vw DORK RH4 .... 255 H10
  ISLW TW7 .... 154 F7
  KWD/TDW/WH KT20 .... 238 C7
Downsview Av WOKS/MYFD GU22 .... 232 C7
Downsview Cl COB KT11 .... 235 J5
  ORP BR6 .... 227 M6
Downsview Gdns SWLY BR8 .... 208 G3
  DORK RH4 .... 272 G3
  NRWD SE19 .... 181 K10
Downs View Rd GT/LBKH KT23 .... 254 B3
Downsview Rd NRWD SE19 .... 181 K10
  SEV TN13 .... 264 G1
Downs Wy EPSOM KT18 .... 238 C2
  GT/LBKH KT23 .... 254 B2
  KWD/TDW/WH KT20 .... 238 E7
  OXTED RH8 .... 261 K3
Downsway CTHM CR3 .... 241 N2
  GU GU1 .... 250 G10
  ORP BR6 .... 227 H2
  SAND/SEL CR2 .... 223 M7
Downsway Cl KWD/TDW/WH KT20 .... 238 D7
The Downsway BELMT SM2 .... 221 M5
Downs Wd EPSOM KT18 .... 238 E3
Downswood REDH RH1 .... 257 N8
Downton Av BRXS/STRHM SW2 .... 180 C5
Downtown Rd BERM/RHTH SE16 .... 160 D1
Downway NFNCH/WDSP N12 .... 97 P8
Down Wy NTHLT UB5 .... 133 J5
Dowrey St IS N1 .... 6 A5
Dowry Wk WAT WD17 .... 72 G4
Dowsett Rd TOTM N17 .... 99 P10
Dowson Cl CMBW SE5 .... 159 L10
Doyce St STHWK SE1 .... 18 E1
Doyle Cl ERITH DA8 .... 164 F7
Doyle Gdns WLSDN NW10 .... 136 E3
Doyle Rd SNWD SE25 .... 203 P4
D'oyley St KTBR SW1X 16 C5
Doynton St KTTN NW5 .... 118 C7
Draco St WALW SE17 .... 18 E9
Dragonfly Cl PLSTW E13 .... 141 N5
Dragon La WEY KT13 .... 216 B6
Dragon Rd NKENS W10 .... 135 P6
Dragor Rd WLSDN NW10 .... 135 P6
Drake Av CTHM CR3 .... 241 K8
  DTCH/LGLY SL3 .... 150 A3
  STA TW18 .... 173 J8
Drake Cl BERM/RHTH SE16 .... 160 C1
  BRW CM14 .... 107 J6
Drake Crs THMD SE28 .... 143 M8
Drakefell Rd NWCR SE14 .... 160 C8
Drakefield Rd TOOT SW17 .... 180 B6
Drake Ms RAIN RM13 .... 145 H2
Drake Rd BROCKY SE4 .... 160 F9
  CDH/CHF RM16 .... 167 K1
  CHSGTN KT9 .... 219 M2
  CRAWE RH10 .... 283 P10
  CROY/NA CR0 .... 202 G7
  HORL RH6 .... 279 P4
  MTCM CR4 .... 202 B6
  RYLN/HDSTN HA2 .... 113 N7
Drakes Cl CHES/WCR EN8 .... 62 C4
  ESH/CLAY KT10 .... 217 L2
Drakes Ctyd KIL/WHAMP NW6 .... 2 D5
Drakes Dr NTHWD HA6 .... 92 C9
  STAL AL1 .... 38 G9
Drake's Rd AMSS HP7 .... 69 J5
Drakes Ter ENC/FH EN2 .... 79 L5
Drakes Wy HAT AL10 .... 40 E6
  WOKS/MYFD GU22 .... 232 A9
Drakewood Rd
  STRHM/NOR SW16 .... 180 E10
Draper Cl BELV DA17 .... 164 A3
Drapers Rd ENC/FH EN2 .... 79 J6
  SRTFD E15 .... 121 H9
  TOTM N17 .... 119 N1
Drappers Wy BERM/RHTH SE16 .... 19 P5
Drawell Cl WOOL/PLUM SE18 .... 163 H4
Drax Av RYNPK SW20 .... 178 D10
Draxmont WIM/MER SW19 .... 179 H9
Draycot Rd SURB KT6 .... 199 M8
Draycott Av CHEL SW3 .... 15 N6
  KTN/HRWW/W HA3 .... 114 G4
Draycott Cl CMBW SE5 .... 16 A6
  KTN/HRWW/W HA3 .... 7 K7
Draycott Pl CHEL SW3 .... 16 A5
Draycott Ter CHEL SW3 .... 16 A5
Drayford Cl MV/WKIL W9 .... 8 D1
Draymans Wy ISLW TW7 .... 154 F9
Drayson Ms KENS W8 .... 14 F2
Drayton Av LOU IG10 .... 82 C10
  ORP BR6 .... 206 E9
  POTB/CUF EN6 .... 59 H4
  WEA W13 .... 136 F9
Drayton Bridge Rd HNWL W7 .... 134 F4
Drayton Cl HSLWW TW4 .... 175 N1
  IL IG1 .... 122 G6
  LHD/OX KT22 .... 236 C9
Drayton Gdns WBPTN SW10 .... 15 K7
  WCHMH N21 .... 99 J1
  WDR/YW UB7 .... 151 N1
  WEA W13 .... 136 F9
Drayton Gn WEA W13 .... 136 F9
Drayton Green Rd WEA W13 .... 134 G9
Drayton Gv WEA W13 .... 136 F9
Drayton Rd BORE WD6 .... 75 M4
  CROY/NA CR0 .... 203 J9
  TOTM N17 .... 99 H10
  WAN E11 .... 121 J6
  WEA W13 .... 134 F9
  WLSDN NW10 .... 136 C3
Dreadnought St GNWCH SE10 .... 161 N4
Drenon Sq HYS/HAR UB3 .... 132 C9
Dresden Cl HAMP NW3 .... 3 H1
Dresden Rd ARCH N19 .... 118 D2
Dresden Wy WEY KT13 .... 216 D2
Dressington Av BROCKY SE4 .... 182 F2
Drew Av MLHL NW7 .... 97 H2
Drew Gdns GFD/PVL UB6 .... 134 C1
Drew Pl CTHM CR3 .... 241 L9
Drew Rd CAN/RD E16 .... 142 B10
Drews Pk BEAC HP9 .... 88 B5
Drewstead Rd STRHM/NOR SW16 .... 180 E5
The Drey CFSP/GDCR SL9 .... 90 B6
Driffield Rd BOW E3 .... 140 D4

The Drift COB KT11 .... 234 F10
  HAYES BR2 .... 206 A10
Drift Wy DTCH/LGLY SL3 .... 150 F2
The Driftway BNSTD SM7 .... 238 F1
  HHNE HP2 .... 36 A6
  LHD/OX KT22 .... 237 H9
  MTCM CR4 .... 202 B1
Drill Hall Rd CHERT KT16 .... 195 K7
Drinkwater Rd
  RYLN/HDSTN HA2 .... 114 A7
Drive Rd COUL/CHIP CR5 .... 240 G6
The Drive ACT W3 .... 135 P8
  AMSS HP7 .... 69 J4
  ASHF TW15 .... 174 E10
  BAR EN5 .... 77 M10
  BAR EN5 .... 77 H7
  BARK IG11 .... 143 J2
  BECK BR3 .... 204 F2
  BELMT SM2 .... 221 J8
  BKHH IG9 .... 101 P1
  BNSTD SM7 .... 239 H3
  BRKMPK AL9 .... 59 K1
  BXLY DA5 .... 185 N3
  CFSP/GDCR SL9 .... 90 B8
  CHESW EN7 .... 61 J4
  CHESW EN7 .... 62 A4
  CHING E4 .... 101 J1
  CHST BR7 .... 207 J1
  COB KT11 .... 217 M10
  COUL/CHIP CR5 .... 222 F10
  CRAWE RH10 .... 285 K2
  CRW RM5 .... 104 E9
  DTCH/LGLY SL3 .... 149 N7
  DTCH/LGLY SL3 .... 150 B1
  EBED/NFELT TW14 .... 175 K3
  EDGW HA8 .... 95 M6
  ENC/FH EN2 .... 79 L5
  ERITH DA8 .... 164 C6
  ESH/CLAY KT10 .... 198 B8
  FBAR/BDGN N11 .... 98 D7
  FNCH N3 .... 97 K8
  GLDGN NW11 .... 117 H5
  GUW GU2 .... 249 L10
  GUW GU2 .... 267 L2
  GVE DA12 .... 190 G7
  HARH RM3 .... 105 M9
  HART DA3 .... 211 N3
  HGDN/ICK UB10 .... 111 P8
  HGT N6 .... 118 A3
  HLW CM20 .... 29 H10
  HOD EN11 .... 44 F1
  HOLWY N7 .... 5 N2
  HOR/WEW KT19 .... 220 C3
  HORL RH6 .... 280 C5
  HSLW TW3 .... 154 C8
  IL IG1 .... 122 B4
  KUTN/CMB KT2 .... 177 P10
  LCOL/BKTW AL2 .... 56 F1
  LHD/OX KT22 .... 236 D8
  LHD/OX KT22 .... 237 M10
  LHD/OX KT22 .... 237 K9
  LOU IG10 .... 82 B7
  MRDN SM4 .... 201 M5
  NTHWD HA6 .... 92 F9
  ORP BR6 .... 207 J9
  POTB/CUF EN6 .... 59 J9
  RAD WD7 .... 56 F10
  RBRW/HUT CM13 .... 107 H7
  RGUW GU3 .... 266 A4
  RKW/CH/CXG WD3 .... 71 J3
  RYLN/HDSTN HA2 .... 113 P5
  RYNPK SW20 .... 178 F10
  SBW CM21 .... 29 P1
  SCUP DA14 .... 185 L6
  SEV TN13 .... 247 J10
  STWL/WRAY TW19 .... 172 A1
  SWFD E18 .... 121 M1
  THHTH CR7 .... 203 L4
  WALTH E17 .... 120 G1
  WAT WD17 .... 72 F3
  WBLY HA9 .... 115 P7
  WLGTN SM6 .... 222 F6
  WOKS/MYFD GU22 .... 231 N6
  WWKM BR4 .... 205 P5
The Driveway POTB/CUF EN6 .... 60 F4
Dr Johnson Av TOOT SW17 .... 180 C6
Drodges Cl SHGR GU5 .... 268 C9
Droitwich Cl SYD SE26 .... 181 P6
Dromey Gdns KTN/HRWW/W HA3 .... 94 F8
Dromore Rd PUT/ROE SW15 .... 178 G2
Dronfield Gdns BCTR RM8 .... 123 M10
Droop St NKENS W10 .... 8 A1
Drop La LCOL/BKTW AL2 .... 56 A7
Dropmore Rd SL SL1 .... 128 A4
Drove Rd RGUE GU4 .... 269 K2
Drovers Pl PECK SE15 .... 160 A6
Drovers Rd SAND/SEL CR2 .... 223 L2
Drovers Wy HAT AL10 .... 40 C1
  STALW/RED AL3 .... 38 C6
The Drove MEO DA13 .... 190 B10
Druce Rd DUL SE21 .... 181 M2
Drudgeon Wy RDART DA2 .... 188 G4
Druid's Cl ASHTD KT21 .... 237 L6
Druid St STHWK SE1 .... 19 L1
Druids Wy HAYES BR2 .... 205 J4
Drumaline Rdg WPK KT4 .... 200 B9
Drummond Av ROMW/RG RM7 .... 124 E2
Drummond Cl ERITH DA8 .... 164 F7
Drummond Crs CAMTN NW1 .... 5 J9
Drummond Dr KTN/HRWW/W HA3 .... 94 F8
Drummond Ga PIM SW1V 17 K7
Drummond Rd BERM/RHTH SE16 .... 160 A2
  CRAWW RH11 .... 283 H8
  CROY/NA CR0 .... 203 K9
  GU GU1 .... 250 A10
  ROMW/RG RM7 .... 124 D2
  WAN E11 .... 121 M1
Drummonds Pl RCH/KEW TW9 .... 155 K10
The Drummonds EPP CM16 .... 65 K6
Drummond St CAMTN NW1 .... 10 G1
Drum St WCHPL E1 .... 13 M5
Drury Cl CRAWE RH10 .... 284 E12
Drury Crs CROY/NA CR0 .... 203 H9
Drury La HHOL WC1V 11 M3
  HOL/ALD WC2B 11 M6
  WARE SG12 .... 28 A2
Drury Rd HRW HA1 .... 114 B4
Drury Wy WLSDN NW10 .... 116 A10
Dryad St PUT/ROE SW15 .... 156 G9
Dry Arch Rd ASC SL5 .... 192 D7
Dryburgh Gdns CDALE/KGS NW9 .... 115 H4
Dryburgh Rd PUT/ROE SW15 .... 156 G8
Drycroft WGCE AL7 .... 23 H9
Drydell La CSHM HP5 .... 50 F7
Dryden Av HNWL W7 .... 134 F4
Dryden Cl BARK/HLT IG6 .... 103 J7
  KTN/HRWW/W HA3 .... 94 F8
  WIM/MER SW19 .... 179 M9
  WOOL/PLUM SE18 .... 163 J7
Dryden Pl TIL RM18 .... 168 A7
Dryden Rd EN EN1 .... 79 M10
  KTN/HRWW/W HA3 .... 94 F3
  WELL DA16 .... 147 P9
  WIM/MER SW19 .... 179 M9
  WOOL/PLUM SE18 .... 163 J7
Dryden Wy ORP BR6 .... 207 N3
Dryfield Cl WLSDN NW10 .... 135 P1
Dryfield Rd EDGW HA8 .... 95 P7
Dryhill La RSEV TN14 .... 246 C9
Dryhill Rd BELV DA17 .... 164 E5
Dryland Av ORP BR6 .... 227 J3
Drylands Rd CEND/HSY/T N8 .... 118 F5
Drynham Pk WEY KT13 .... 196 F10
Drysdale Av CHING E4 .... 80 C10
Drysdale Cl NTHWD HA6 .... 92 F8
Drysdale Pl BETH E2 .... 7 K9
Drysdale St IS N1 .... 7 K10

Duarte Pl CDH/CHF RM16 .... 167 L2
Dublin Av HACK E8 .... 7 P5
Dubrae Cl STALW/RED AL3 .... 37 P8
Du Burstow Ter HNWL W7 .... 154 D1
Ducal St BETH E2 .... 7 M10
Du Cane Rd SHB W12 .... 136 E8
Duchess Cl FBAR/BDGN N11 .... 98 C6
  SUT SM1 .... 10 F3
Duchess Ms REGST W1B 10 F3
Duchess of Bedford's Wk KENS W8 .... 14 D2
Duchess St REGST W1B 10 F3
  STHWK SE1 .... 128 D10
Duchess' Wk BCR/WK TN15 .... 265 M1
Duchy Rd EBAR EN4 .... 77 N4
Duchy St STHWK SE1 .... 12 B9
Ducie St CLAP SW4 .... 158 F10
Duckett Rd FSBYPK N4 .... 119 J4
Ducketts Md HLWW/ROY CM19 .... 27 L6
Ducketts Rd DART DA1 .... 186 G1
Duckett St WCHPL E1 .... 140 C7
Duck La EPP CM16 .... 65 M2
  SOHO/CST W1F 11 J6
Duck Lees La PEND EN3 .... 80 D8
Duckling La SBW CM21 .... 29 P1
Ducks Hill Rd NTHWD HA6 .... 92 B10
  NTHWD HA6 .... 92 C8
Du Cros Dr STAN HA7 .... 95 J7
Du Cros Rd ACT W3 .... 136 D10
Dudbrook Rd BRW CM14 .... 106 A2
Dudden Hill La WLSDN NW10 .... 116 C9
Duddington Cl ELTH/MOT SE9 .... 184 A7
Dudely Rd GVW DA11 .... 190 B3
Dudley Av CHES/WCR EN8 .... 62 C8
  KTN/HRWW/W HA3 .... 115 H1
Dudley Cl CDH/CHF RM16 .... 167 K1
  RSLP HA4 .... 113 J10
Dudley Dr MRDN SM4 .... 201 H8
Dudley Gdns RYLN/HDSTN HA2 .... 114 C6
  WEA W13 .... 154 G1
Dudley Gv EPSOM KT18 .... 219 P10
Dudley Rd ASHF TW15 .... 174 A8
  EBED/NFELT TW14 .... 174 E4
  FNCH N3 .... 97 L11
  HARH RM3 .... 105 L7
  IL IG1 .... 122 E9
  KIL/WHAMP NW6 .... 2 A2
  KUT KT1 .... 199 L3
  NWDGN UB2 .... 152 A1
  RCH/KEW TW9 .... 155 L5
  RYLN/HDSTN HA2 .... 114 B7
  WALTH E17 .... 100 F10
  WIM/MER SW19 .... 179 K9
  WOT/HER KT12 .... 197 N6
Dudley St BAY/PAD W2 .... 9 L4
Dudlington Rd CLPT E5 .... 120 B7
Dudmaston Ms CHEL SW3 .... 15 M7
Dudsbury Rd DART DA1 .... 187 J2
Dudset La HEST TW5 .... 153 H7
Dudswell La BERK HP4 .... 33 M1
Dufferin Av STLK EC1Y 12 G2
Dufferin St STLK EC1Y 12 F2
Duffield Cl CDH/CHF RM16 .... 167 L2
  HRW HA1 .... 114 E3
Duffield Dr SEVS/STOTM N15 .... 119 N2
Duffield La STLK SL2 .... 129 L2
Duffield Pk SLN SL2 .... 129 L5
Duffins Orch CHERT KT16 .... 214 F4
Duffy's Pl SOHO/CST W1F 11 H6
Dugdale Hill La POTB/CUF EN6 .... 59 H9
Dugdales RKW/CH/CXG WD3 .... 72 B9

Duke Humphrey Rd
  BKHTH/KID SE3 .... 161 K7
Duke of Cambridge Cl
  WHTN TW2 .... 176 C2
Duke of Edinburgh Rd SUT SM1 .... 201 N10
Duke of Wellington Pl
  WHALL SW1A 16 D2
Duke of York St STJS SW1Y 11 H9
Duke Rd BARK/HLT IG6 .... 122 C2
  CHSWK W4 .... 156 A4
Dukes Av CDH/CHF RM16 .... 156 A4
  CHSWK W4 .... 156 A4
  EDGW HA8 .... 95 L7
  EPP CM16 .... 83 H1
  FNCH N3 .... 97 C9
  HRW HA1 .... 114 D2
  HSLWW TW4 .... 153 M10
  MUSWH N10 .... 117 H1
  NTHLT UB5 .... 133 M2
  NWMAL KT3 .... 200 B9
  PIN HA5 .... 113 N4
  RCHPK/HAM TW10 .... 177 H7
Dukes Cl ASHF TW15 .... 174 D7
  CFSP/GDCR SL9 .... 110 A6
  EPP CM16 .... 66 C3
  HPTN TW12 .... 175 N7
Duke's Ct Dr RDKG RH5 .... 278 A9
  RGODL GU7 .... 266 G10
  SLN SL2 .... 108 F10
Dukes HI CTHM CR3 .... 242 D6
Dukes Kiln Dr CFSP/GDCR SL9 .... 109 P7
Duke's La ASC SL5 .... 192 C1
  KENS W8 .... 14 G1
Duke's Ms MHST W1U 10 C5
  MUSWH N10 .... 118 C1
Dukes Orch BXLY DA5 .... 186 D4
Duke's Pl HDTCH EC3A 13 L6
  RKW/CH/CXG WD3 .... 72 B9
  RDKG RH5 .... 273 J5
Dukes Rd ACT W3 .... 135 M6
  EHAM E6 .... 142 D3
  STPAN WC1H 5 K10
  WOT/HER KT12 .... 217 L2
Dukesthorpe Rd SYD SE26 .... 182 C7
Dukes St HOD EN11 .... 44 F2
  MBLAR W1H 10 D5
  RCH/KEW TW9 .... 177 J1
  SUT SM1 .... 221 M1
  WAT WD17 .... 73 K7
  WDSR SL4 .... 149 H7
  WOKN/KNAP GU21 .... 232 C3
Duke Street HI STHWK SE1 .... 13 H9
Duke Street St James's
  MYFR/PICC W1J 11 H9
Dukes Va CFSP/GDCR SL9 .... 109 N7
Dukes Wd Av CFSP/GDCR SL9 .... 109 N7
Dukes Wood Dr CFSP/GDCR SL9 .... 109 P6
Dukes's Yd MYFR/PKLN W1K 10 D7
Dulas St FSBYPK N4 .... 118 G6
Dulford St NTCHL W11 .... 8 A7
Dulka Rd BTSEA SW11 .... 180 L1
Dulverton Rd ELTH/MOT SE9 .... 184 F5
  HARH RM3 .... 105 L7
  RSLP HA4 .... 113 H7
  SAND/SEL CR2 .... 224 B5
Dulwich Common BDS SE21 .... 181 N3
The Dulwich Oaks DUL SE21 .... 181 N6
Dulwich Rd HNHL SE24 .... 181 H1
Dulwich Village DUL SE21 .... 181 N1
Dulwich Wd Av NRWD SE19 .... 181 J7
Dulwich Wd Pk NRWD SE19 .... 181 J6
Dumbarton Av CHES/WCR EN8 .... 62 C10
Dumbarton Rd BRXS/STRHM SW2 .... 180 G1
Dumbleton Cl KUT KT1 .... 199 N1
Dumbreck Rd ELTH/MOT SE9 .... 162 D10
Dumfries Cl OXHEY WD19 .... 93 H4
Dumont Rd STNW/STAM N16 .... 119 M8
Dumpton Pl CAMTN NW1 .... 4 C4
Dumville Dr GDST RH9 .... 260 D1

Dunally Pk *SHPTN* TW17 196 E7
Dunbar Av *BECK* BR3 204 D4
DAGE RM10 124 B8
STRHM/NOR SW16 203 H2
Dunbar Cl *SLN* SL2 129 M9
YEAD UB4 133 H7
Dunbar Ct *WOT/HER* KT12 197 K9
Dunbar Gdns *DAGE* RM10 124 B10
Dunbar Rd *FSTGT* E7 141 M1
NWMAL KT3 199 P4
WDGN N22 99 H9
Dunbar St *WNWD* SE27 181 K6
Dunblane Rd *ELTH/MOT* SE9 162 B9
Dunboe Pl *SHPTN* TW17 196 D7
Dunboyne Rd *HAMP* NW3 118 A10
Dunbridge St *BETH* E2 13 P1
Duncan Cl *BAR* EN5 77 M8
WGCE AL7 23 H6
Duncan Dr *GU* GU1 250 D9
Duncan Gdns *STA* TW18 173 K9
Duncan Gv *ACT* W3 136 B8
Duncannon Crs *WDSR* SL4 148 C9
Duncannon St *CHCR* WC2N 11 L8
Duncan Rd *HACK* E8 140 A3
KWD/TDW/WH KT20 239 H5
RCH/KEW TW9 155 K10
Duncan St *IS* N1 6 C7
Duncan Ter *IS* N1 6 C8
Duncan Wy *BUSH* WD23 73 N6
Dunch St *WCHPL* E1 140 A8
Duncombe Cl *AMS* HP6 69 K4
HERT/WAS SG14 25 K3
Duncombe Hl *FSTH* SE23 182 D3
Duncombe Rd *ARCH* N19 118 E6
BERK HP4 33 K3
HERT/WAS SG14 25 K4
Duncrievie Rd *LEW* SE13 183 J2
Duncroft *WDSR* SL4 148 E9
WOOL/PLUM SE18 163 H6
Duncroft Cl *REIG* RH2 257 J10
Dundalk Rd *BROCKY* SE4 160 D9
Dundas Gdns *E/WMO/HCT* KT8 198 A3
Dundas Rd *PECK* SE15 160 B8
Dundee Rd *PLSTW* E13 141 N4
SL SL1 128 E8
SNWD SE25 204 A5
Dundee St *WAP* E1W 140 A10
Dundee Wy *PEND* EN3 80 D7
Dundela Gdns *WPK* KT4 220 E1
Dundonald Cl *EHAM* E6 142 B8
Dundonald Rd *WIM/MER* SW19 179 J10
WLSDN NW10 136 G3
Dundrey Crs *REDH* RH1 258 F5
Dunedin Dr *CTHM* CR3 259 M1
Dunedin Rd *IL* IG1 122 F6
LEY E10 120 G8
RAIN RM13 144 G5
Dunedin Wy *YEAD* UB4 133 K6
Dunelm Gv *WNWD* SE27 181 K7
Dunelm St *WCHPL* E1 140 C8
Dunfee Wy *BF/WBF* KT14 215 P8
Dunfield Rd *CAT* SE6 182 G8
Dunford Rd *HOLWY* N7 118 G9
Dungarvan Av *PUT/ROE* SW15 156 D10
Dungates La *BRKHM/BTCW* RH3 256 D9
Dunheved Cl *THHTH* CR7 203 H6
Dunheved Rd North *THHTH* CR7 203 H6
Dunheved Rd South *THHTH* CR7 203 H6
Dunheved Rd West *THHTH* CR7 203 H6
Dunholme Gn *ED* N9 99 N4
Dunholme La *ED* N9 99 N4
Dunholme Rd *ED* N9 99 N4
Dunkeld Rd *BCTR* RM8 123 L7
SNWD SE25 203 L4
Dunkellin Gv *SOCK/AV* RM15 146 F8
Dunkellin Wy *SOCK/AV* RM15 146 F8
Dunkery Rd *ELTH/MOT* SE9 184 A7
Dunkin Rd *DART* DA1 165 P10
Dunkirk Cl *GVE* DA12 190 F8
Dunkirk St *WNWD* SE27 181 K7
Dunlace Rd *CLPT* E5 120 B10
Dunleary Cl *HSLWW* TW4 175 N3
Dunley Dr *CROY/NA* CR0 225 H3
Dunlin Cl *REDH* RH1 275 P5
Dunlin Ri *RGUE* GU4 250 G8
Dunlin Rd *HHNE* HP2 35 P1
Dunloe Av *TOTM* N17 119 L1
Dunloe St *BETH* E2 7 L8
Dunlop Pl *BERM/RHTH* SE16 19 M4
Dunlop Rd *TIL* RM18 168 C7
Dunmail Dr *PUR/KEN* CR8 223 M9
Dunmore *GUW* GU2 249 J9
Dunmore Rd *KIL/WHAMP* NW6 2 A6
RYNPK SW20 200 F1
Dunmow Cl *CHDH* RM6 123 M3
FELT TW13 175 M7
LOU IG10 82 B10
Dunmow Dr *RAIN* RM13 144 G3
Dunmow Rd *SRTFD* E15 121 J9
Dunnets *WOKN/KNAP* GU21 231 K3
Dunning Cl *SOCK/AV* RM15 146 F8
Dunningford Cl *HCH* RM12 124 G10
Dunnings La *RBRW/HUT* CM13 127 N7
Dunn Md *CDALE/KGS* NW9 96 C8
Dunnock Cl *BORE* WD6 75 M8
ED N9 100 C2
Dunnock Rd *EHAM* E6 142 B8
Dunn St *HACK* E8 119 N10
Dunny La *KGLGY* WD4 53 J8
RKW/CH/CXG WD3 53 J9
Dunnymans Rd *BNSTD* SM7 239 J1
Dunollie Pl *KTTN* NW5 118 D10
Dunollie Rd *KTTN* NW5 118 D10
Dunoon Rd *FSTH* SE23 182 B3
Dunottar Cl *REIG* RH2 275 N2
Dunraven Av *REDH* RH1 276 C8
Dunraven Dr *ENC/FH* EN2 79 H6
Dunraven Rd *SHB* W12 136 D10
Dunraven St *MYFR/PKLN* W1K 10 B7
Dunsany Rd *HMSMTH* W6 156 G2
Dunsbury Cl *BELMT* SM2 221 L5
Dunsdon Av *GUW* GU2 267 N1
Dunsfold Cl *CRAWW* RH11 283 K8
Dunsfold Ri *COUL/CHIP* CR5 222 E9
Dunsfold Wy *CROY/NA* CR0 225 H4
Dunsmore Cl *BUSH* WD23 74 C10
YEAD UB4 133 L6
Dunsmore Rd *WOT/HER* KT12 197 J5
Dunsmore Wy *BUSH* WD23 74 B10
Dunsmure Rd *STNW/STAM* N16 119 M6
Dunspring La *CLAY* IG5 102 E10
Dunstable Ms *CAVSQ/HST* W1G 10 D3
Dunstable Rd *E/WMO/HCT* KT8 197 N4
HARH RM3 105 L7
RCH/KEW TW9 155 K10
Dunstall Rd *RYNPK* SW20 178 E9
Dunstalls *HLWW/ROY* CM19 46 D5
Dunstall Wy *E/WMO/HCT* KT8 198 A3
Dunstan Cl *EFNCH* N2 117 M1
Dunstan Rd *COUL/CHIP* CR5 240 E3
GLDGN NW11 117 J6
Dunstan's Gv *EDUL* SE22 182 A2
Dunstan's Rd *EDUL* SE22 181 P3
Dunster Av *MRDN* SM4 200 G8
Dunster Cl *BAR* EN5 76 G8
DEN/HRF UB9 91 L9
ROMW/RG RM7 104 D10
Dunster Ct *FENCHST* EC3M 13 J7
Dunster Crs *UPMR* RM14 125 P7
Dunster Dr *CDALE/KGS* NW9 115 P6
Dunster Gdns *KIL/WHAMP* NW6 2 D3
SL SL1 128 F9
Dunsters Md *WGCE* AL7 23 K7
Dunster Wy *RYLN/HDSTN* HA2 113 M8
Dunston Rd *HACK* E8 7 L6
Dunston St *HACK* E8 7 K5
Dunton Cl *SURB* KT6 199 K8
Dunton Rd *LEY* E10 120 G5
ROM RM1 124 F2
STHWK SE1 19 L6
Duntshill Rd *WAND/EARL* SW18 179 L4
Dunvegan Cl *E/WMO/HCT* KT8 198 A4
Dunvegan Rd *ELTH/MOT* SE9 162 C10
Dunwich Rd *BXLYHN* DA7 164 A7
Dunworth Ms *NTGHL* W11 8 C6
Duplex Ride *KTBR* SW1X 16 B2
Dupont Rd *RYNPK* SW20 200 G2
Dupont St *POP/IOD* E14 140 D7
Duppas Av *CROY/NA* CR0 223 J1
Duppas Cl *SHPTN* TW17 196 E5
Duppas Hill Rd *CROY/NA* CR0 223 H1
Duppas Hill Ter *CROY/NA* CR0 203 J10
Duppas Rd *CROY/NA* CR0 203 H10
Dupre Cl *SL* SL1 148 D1
Dupree Rd *CHARL* SE7 161 N4
Dura Den Cl *BECK* BR3 182 G10
Durand Gdns *BRXN/ST* SW9 158 G7
Durand Wy *WLSDN* NW10 135 P2
Durant Rd *SWLY* BR8 187 H9
Durants Park Av *PEND* EN3 80 C8
Durants Rd *PEND* EN3 80 B8
Durant St *BETH* E2 7 N9
Durban Gdns *DAGE* RM10 144 D2
Durban Rd *BECK* BR3 204 E2
GNTH/NBYPK IG2 123 H6
SRTFD E15 141 K5
TOTM N17 99 M7
WALTH E17 100 E9
WNWD SE27 181 K7
Durban Rd East *WATW* WD18 73 H8
Durban Rd West *WATW* WD18 73 H8
Durbin Rd *CHSGTN* KT9 219 K1
Durdans Rd *STHL* UB1 133 N8
Durell Gdns *DAGW* RM9 123 N10
Durell Rd *DAGW* RM9 123 N10
Durfold Dr *REIG* RH2 257 M10
Durford Crs *PUT/ROE* SW15 178 D4
Durham Av *GPK* RM2 125 K2
HAYES BR2 205 L4
HEST TW5 153 N5
SL SL1 128 F8
WFD IG8 102 A6
Durham Cl *GUW* GU2 249 L8
SBW CM21 29 M2
WARE SG12 26 G6
Durham Hl *BMLY* BR1 183 L7
Durham House St *CHCR* WC2N 11 M8
Durham Pl *CHEL* SW3 16 A8
Durham Ri *WOOL/PLUM* SE18 162 F4
Durham Rd *CAN/RD* E16 141 K6
DAGE RM10 124 D10
EA W5 155 J2
EBED/NFELT TW14 175 K3
ED N9 100 B2
EFNCH N2 117 P1
HAYES BR2 205 M4
HOLWY N7 118 G7
HRW HA1 114 A3
MNPK E12 122 A9
RYNPK SW20 200 E1
SCUP DA14 185 L8
Durham Rw *WCHPL* E1 140 D7
Durham St *LBTH* SE11 17 N8
Durham Ter *BAY/PAD* W2 8 G5
Duriun Wy *ERITH* DA8 165 J6
Durleston Park Dr *GT/LBKH* KT23 254 B1
Durley Av *PIN* HA5 113 M4
Durley Gdns *ORP* BR6 227 L1
Durley Rd *STNW/STAM* N16 119 M5
Durlston Rd *CLPT* E5 119 P7
KUTN/CMB KT2 177 K9
Durndale La *GVW* DA11 190 B7
Durnell Wy *LOU* IG10 82 D7
Durnford St *SEVS/STOTM* N15 119 M3
Durning Rd *NRWD* SE19 181 L8
Durnsford Av *WAND/EARL* SW18 179 K5
Durnsford Rd *FBAR/BDGN* N11 98 E9
WAND/EARL SW18 179 K5
WIM/MER SW19 179 K6
Durpe Crs *BEAC* HP9 88 G10
Durrants Cl *RAIN* RM13 145 K4
Durrants Dr *RKW/CH/CXG* WD3 72 D7
Durrants Hill Rd *HHS/BOV* HP3 35 N9
Durrants La *BERK* HP4 33 L4
Durrants Rd *BERK* HP4 33 L4
Durrant Wy *ORP* BR6 226 G2
SWCM DA10 189 K3
Durrell Rd *FUL/PGN* SW6 157 H7
Durrell Wy *SHPTN* TW17 196 E6
Durrington Av *RYNPK* SW20 178 F10
Durrington Park Rd *RYNPK* SW20 200 F1
Durrington Rd *CLPT* E5 120 D9
Dursley Cl *BKHTH/KID* SE3 161 P8
Dursley Gdns *BKHTH/KID* SE3 162 A7
Dursley Rd *BKHTH/KID* SE3 161 P8
Durward St *WCHPL* E1 13 P3
WCHPL E1 140 A7
Durweston Ms *MHST* W1U 10 B3
Dury Falls Cl *EMPK* RM11 125 N6
Dury Rd *BAR* EN5 77 J5
Dutch Barn Cl *STWL/WRAY* TW19 173 N2
Dutch Gdns *KUTN/CMB* KT2 177 N9
Dutch Yd *WAND/EARL* SW18 179 K1
Duthie St *POP/IOD* E14 141 H9
Dutton St *GNWCH* SE10 161 H7
Dutton Wy *IVER* SL0 131 H8
Duxford Cl *HCH* RM12 145 J1
Duxhurst La *HORL* RH6 275 L10
Duxons Turn *HHNE* HP2 36 C5
Dwight Rd *WATW* WD18 92 E1
Dye House La *BOW* E3 140 F3
Dyer's Fld *HORL* RH6 281 J4
Dyers Hall Rd *WAN* E11 121 K6
WAN E11 121 K6
Dyer's La *PUT/ROE* SW15 156 E9
Dyers Wy *HARH* RM3 105 H8
Dyke Dr *STMC/STPC* BR5 207 M7
Dyke La *STALE/WH* AL4 21 K4
Dykes Wy *HAYES* BR2 205 L3
Dykewood Cl *BXLY* DA5 186 E6
Dylan Cl *BORE* WD6 95 J1
Dylan Rd *BELV* DA17 164 B2
Dylways *CMBW* SE5 159 L10
Dymchurch Cl *CLAY* IG5 102 D10
ORP BR6 227 H1
Dymock St *FUL/PGN* SW6 157 L9
Dymoke Gn *STALE/WH* AL4 38 F3
Dymoke Rd *ROM* RM1 124 G5
Dymokes Wy *HOD* EN11 26 F10
Dyneley Rd *LEE/GVPK* SE12 183 P6
Dyne Rd *KIL/WHAMP* NW6 2 C4
Dynes Rd *RSEV* TN14 247 M3
Dynevor Pl *RGUW* GU3 249 H6
Dynevor Rd *RCHPK/HAM* TW10 177 K1
STNW/STAM N16 119 M8
Dynham Rd *KIL/WHAMP* NW6 2 E3
Dyott St *NOXST/BSQ* WC1A 11 L5
RSQ WC1B 11 K4
Dyrham La *BAR* EN5 76 D2
Dysart Av *KUTN/CMB* KT2 177 H8
Dysart St *SDTCH* EC2A 13 H2
Dyson Cl *WDSR* SL4 148 G9
Dyson Ct *ALP/SUD* HA0 114 F9
Dyson Rd *FSTGT* E7 141 L1
WAN E11 121 K4
Dysons Cl *CHES/WCR* EN8 62 C9
Dyson's Rd *UED* N18 100 A6
Dytchleys Rd *BRW* CM14 85 N8

E

Eade Rd *FSBYPK* N4 119 K5
Eagans Cl *EFNCH* N2 117 N1
Eagle Av *CHDH* RM6 123 P4
Eagle Cl *PEND* EN3 80 B8
RAIN RM13 145 J1
WAB EN9 63 M10
WLGTN SM6 222 F3
Eagle Ct *FARR* EC1M 12 C3
HERT/BAY SG13 26 A4
Eagle Dr *CDALE/KGS* NW9 96 B10
Eagle Hl *NRWD* SE19 181 L9
Eagle La *BRWN* CM15 86 D3
WAN E11 121 M2
Eagle Pl *WBPTN* SW10 15 K7
Eagle Rd *ALP/SUD* HA0 135 J2
GU GU1 268 A1
Eagles Dr *BH/WHM* TN16 244 A4
Eaglesfield Rd *WOOL/PLUM* SE18 162 F7
Eagles Rd *GRH* DA9 166 G10
Eagle St *GINN* WC1R 11 N4
Eagle Ter *WFD* IG8 101 N8
Eagle Wy *GVW* DA11 189 M1
HAT AL10 40 D6
RBRW/HUT CM13 107 H7
Eagle Wharf Rd *IS* N1 6 F7
Ealdham Sq *ELTH/MOT* SE9 162 A10
Ealing Cl *BORE* WD6 76 A5
Ealing Gn *EA* W5 135 J10
Ealing Park Gdns *EA* W5 155 H3
Ealing Rd *ALP/SUD* HA0 135 K1
BTFD TW8 155 J3
NTHLT UB5 133 P2
Ealing Village *EA* W5 135 K8
Eamont Cl *RSLP* HA4 112 C5
Eamont St *STJWD* NW8 3 N7
Eardemont Cl *DART* DA1 164 G10
Eardley Crs *ECT* SW5 14 F7
Eardley Rd *BELV* DA17 164 B4
SEV TN13 247 J10
STRHM/NOR SW16 180 D9
Earl Cl *FBAR/BDGN* N11 98 C6
Earldom Rd *PUT/ROE* SW15 156 F10
Earle Gdns *KUTN/CMB* KT2 177 K10
Earleswood *COB* KT11 217 L8
Earleydene *ASC* SL5 192 A8
Earlham Gv *FSTGT* E7 121 L10
WDGN N22 98 G8
Earlham St *LSQ/SEVD* WC2H 11 K6
Earl Ri *WOOL/PLUM* SE18 162 G4
Earl Rd *GVW* DA11 190 B5
MORT/ESHN SW14 155 P10
Earlsbrook Rd *REDH* RH1 276 A2
Earl's Court Gdns *ECT* SW5 14 G6
Earl's Court Rd *ECT* SW5 14 F6
KENS W8 14 E4
Earl's Court Sq *ECT* SW5 14 G7
Earls Crs *HRW* HA1 114 D2
Earlsferry Wy *IS* N1 5 M4
Earlsfield Rd *WAND/EARL* SW18 179 M4
Earlshall Rd *ELTH/MOT* SE9 162 C10
Earls La *POTB/CUF* EN6 58 B8
SL SL1 128 E10
Earlsmead *RYLN/HDSTN* HA2 113 N9
Earlsmead Rd *SEVS/STOTM* N15 119 N3
WLSDN NW10 136 E5
Earl's Pth *LOU* IG10 81 P7
Earls Ter *KENS* W8 14 E4
Earlsthorpe Ms *BAL* SW12 180 B2
Earlsthorpe Rd *SYD* SE26 182 C7
Earlstoke St *FSBYE* EC1V 6 C9
Earlston Gv *HOM* E9 140 A3
Earl St *SDTCH* EC2A 13 J3
WAT WD17 73 K7
Earls Wk *BCTR* RM8 123 L9
KENS W8 14 E4
Earlswood Av *THHTH* CR7 203 H5
Earlswood Gdns *CLAY* IG5 122 D1
Earlswood Rd *REDH* RH1 276 A2
Earlswood St *GNWCH* SE10 161 K4
Early Commons *CRAWE* RH10 284 A6
CRAWE RH10 284 A6
Early Ms *CAMTN* NW1 4 F5
Earnshaw St *LSQ/SEVD* WC2H 11 K5
Earsby St *WKENS* W14 14 B5
Easby Crs *MRDN* SM4 201 L6
Easebourne Rd *BCTR* RM8 123 M10
Easedale Dr *HCH* RM12 125 J10
Easington Pl *GU* GU1 268 C1
Easington Wy *SOCK/AV* RM15 146 F7
East Acton La *ACT* W3 136 B9
East Arbour St *WCHPL* E1 140 C8
East Av *CROY/NA* CR0 222 G2
HYS/HAR UB3 152 G1
MNPK E12 142 B2
STHL UB1 133 N9
WALTH E17 120 G2
East Bank *STNW/STAM* N16 119 M5
Eastbank Rd *HPTN* TW12 176 B8
East Barnet Rd *BAR* EN5 77 M8
EBAR EN4 77 N9
Eastbourne Av *ACT* W3 136 A8
Eastbourne Gdns
MORT/ESHN SW14 155 P9
Eastbourne Ms *BAY/PAD* W2 9 K5
Eastbourne Rd *BTFD* TW8 155 J4
CHSWK W4 155 P5
EHAM E6 142 D5
FELT TW13 175 L5
GDST RH9 260 B8
SEVS/STOTM N15 119 M4
SL SL1 128 F8
SRTFD E15 141 K3
TOOT SW17 180 B9
Eastbourne Ter *BAY/PAD* W2 9 K5
Eastbournia Av *ED* N9 100 A4
Eastbridge *SLN* SL2 149 N1
Eastbrook Av *DAGE* RM10 124 D9
ED N9 100 B1
Eastbrook Cl *WOKN/KNAP* GU21 232 D2
Eastbrook Dr *DAGE* RM10 124 F8
Eastbrook Rd *BKHTH/KID* SE3 161 N7
WAB EN9 63 K9
Eastbrook Wy *HHNE* HP2 35 P6
East Burnham La *SLN* SL2 128 F3
East Burrowfield *WGCE* AL7 22 G7
Eastbury Av *BARK* IG11 143 H3
EN EN1 79 M5
NTHWD HA6 92 F6
Eastbury Ct *STAL* AL1 38 E5
Eastbury Gv *CHSWK* W4 156 B4
Eastbury La *RGUW* GU3 266 F6
Eastbury Rd *EHAM* E6 142 D6
KUTN/CMB KT2 177 K10
NTHWD HA6 92 F7
OXHEY WD19 93 K1
ROMW/RG RM7 124 E4
STMC/STPC BR5 206 G6
Eastbury Sq *BARK* IG11 143 J3
Eastbury Ter *WCHPL* E1 140 C6
Eastcastle St *GTPST* W1W 10 G5
Eastcheap *BANK* EC3V 13 H7
FENCHST EC3M 13 H7
East Churchfield Rd *ACT* W3 136 A10
Eastchurch Rd *HTHAIR* TW6 152 F9
East Cl *EA* W5 135 M6
EBAR EN4 78 B8
GFD/PVL UB6 134 B4
LCOL/BKTW AL2 56 A1
RAIN RM13 145 J6
Eastcombe Av *CHARL* SE7 161 N5
East Common *CFSP/GDCR* SL9 110 B4
Eastcote *ORP* BR6 207 J8
Eastcote Av *E/WMO/HCT* KT8 197 N5
GFD/PVL UB6 114 F10
RYLN/HDSTN HA2 114 A7
Eastcote Dr *HARP* AL5 20 C5
Eastcote La *NTHLT* UB5 133 N1
RYLN/HDSTN HA2 113 N9
Eastcote La North *NTHLT* UB5 133 N1
Eastcote Rd *PIN* HA5 113 L3
RSLP HA4 112 F5
RYLN/HDSTN HA2 114 B8
WELL DA16 162 G8
Eastcote St *BRXN/ST* SW9 158 G8
Eastcote Vw *PIN* HA5 113 K2
East Ct *ALP/SUD* HA0 115 H7
East Crs *EN* EN1 79 M9
TRDG/WHET N20 98 A5
Eastcroft *SLN* SL2 128 G6
Eastcroft Rd *HOR/WEW* KT19 220 B4
East Cross Route *HOM* E9 140 E1
Eastdean Av *EPSOM* KT18 219 N9
East Dene Dr *HARH* RM3 105 L6
Eastdown Pk *LEW* SE13 161 J10
East Dr *CAR* SM5 221 P5
GSTN WD25 73 J2
NTHWD HA6 92 F3
SBW CM21 29 P2
STMC/STPC BR5 207 L6
VW GU25 193 N6
East Dulwich Gv *EDUL* SE22 181 M1
East Dulwich Rd *EDUL* SE22 159 N10
East End Rd *EFNCH* N2 117 M1
FNCH N3 117 L1
East End Wy *PIN* HA5 113 M1
East Entrance *DAGE* RM10 144 C4
Eastergate *BEAC* HP9 88 B7
Eastern Av *CHDH* RM6 123 N2
CHERT KT16 195 K3
CHES/WCR EN8 62 E9
CHOB/PIR GU24 230 G7
GNTH/NBYPK IG2 123 J3
PIN HA5 113 L5
REDBR IG4 122 A4
SOCK/AV RM15 166 B1
WAN E11 121 P4
WTHK RM20 166 E4
Eastern Av East *GPK* RM2 104 G9
ROM RM1 124 E1
Eastern Av West *CHDH* RM6 123 P2
ROMW/RG RM7 124 D2
Eastern Perimeter Rd
HTHAIR TW6 152 G9
Eastern Rd *BROCKY* SE4 160 F10
EFNCH N2 118 A1
GRAYS RM17 168 A3
PLSTW E13 141 N4
ROM RM1 124 G3
WALTH E17 121 H3
WDGN N22 98 F9
Eastern Vw *BH/WHM* TN16 243 P3
Easternville Gdns
GNTH/NBYPK IG2 122 F4
Eastern Wy *ERITH* DA18 164 B1
GRAYS RM17 167 M5
THMD SE28 163 K1
East Ferry Rd *POP/IOD* E14 161 H2
Eastfield Av *WATN* WD24 73 L5
Eastfield Cl *SL* SL1 149 M2
Eastfield Ct *STALE/WH* AL4 39 J3
Eastfield Gdns *DAGE* RM10 124 B9
Eastfield Rd *BRW* CM14 107 J3
CEND/HSY/T N8 118 F1
CHES/WCR EN8 62 E8
DAGE RM10 124 B9
PEND EN3 80 C4
REDH RH1 276 C1
WALTH E17 120 F2
Eastfields *PIN* HA5 113 K3
Eastfields Rd *ACT* W3 135 P7
MTCM CR4 202 B2
East Flexford La *RGUW* GU3 266 E3
East Flint *HHW* HP1 35 H5
East Gdns *WIM/MER* SW19 179 P9
WOKS/MYFD GU22 232 F3
Eastgate *BNSTD* SM7 221 J10
East Ga *HLW* CM20 28 G10
Eastgate Cl *THMD* SE28 143 N8
Eastglade *NTHWD* HA6 92 F6
PIN HA5 113 N1
East Hall La *RAIN* RM13 145 L8
East Hall Rd *STMC/STPC* BR5 207 P7
Eastham Cl *BAR* EN5 77 J9
East Ham Crs *RBRW/HUT* CM13 107 M5
East Ham Manor Wy *EHAM* E6 142 D8
East Harding St
FLST/FETLN EC4A 12 B5
East Heath Rd *HAMP* NW3 117 N8
East Hl *BH/WHM* TN16 243 N4
DART DA1 187 N3
EYN DA4 210 C1
OXTED RH8 261 L5
SAND/SEL CR2 223 M6
WAND/EARL SW18 179 M1
WBLY HA9 115 M7
WOKS/MYFD GU22 232 F2
East Hill Dr *DART* DA1 187 N3
East Hill La *CRAWE* RH10 281 L9
East Hill Rd *OXTED* RH8 261 L5
Eastholm *GLDGN* NW11 117 L2
East Holme *ERITH* DA8 164 E7
Eastholme *HYS/HAR* UB3 133 H10
East Kent Av *GVW* DA11 189 P2
Eastlake Rd *CMBW* SE5 159 J8
Eastlands Cl *OXTED* RH8 261 J3
Eastlands Crs *EDUL* SE22 181 N2
Eastlands Wy *OXTED* RH8 261 J3
East La *ABLGY* WD5 55 H4
ALP/SUD HA0 115 H8
EHSLY KT24 252 D2
GSTN WD25 55 J6
KUT KT1 199 J3
STALE/WH AL4 21 J2
Eastlea Av *GSTN* WD25 73 M3
Eastlea Ms *CAN/RD* E16 141 K6
Eastleigh Av *RYLN/HDSTN* HA2 114 A7
Eastleigh Cl *BELMT* SM2 221 L4
CRICK NW2 116 B8
Eastleigh Rd *BXLYHN* DA7 164 D8
WALTH E17 100 E10
Eastleigh Wy *EBED/NFELT* TW14 175 H4
East Lodge La *ENC/FH* EN2 78 E2
Eastman Rd *ACT* W3 156 A1
Eastman Wy *HHNE* HP2 36 B3
East Md *RSLP* HA4 113 L8
WGCE AL7 23 L8
Eastmead *WOKN/KNAP* GU21 231 N3
Eastmead Av *GFD/PVL* UB6 134 A5
Eastmead Cl *BMLY* BR1 206 B2
East Meads *GUW* GU2 267 L1
Eastmearn Rd *DUL* SE21 181 K5
East Milton Rd *GVE* DA12 190 E5
East Mimms *HHNE* HP2 35 P5
Eastmont Rd *ESH/CLAY* KT10 198 E9
Eastmoor Pk *HARP* AL5 20 B5
Eastmoor Pl *WOOL/PLUM* SE18 162 A2
Eastmoor St *CHARL* SE7 162 A3
East Mt *STALE/WH* AL4 21 H1
East Mount St *WCHPL* E1 140 A7
Eastney Rd *CROY/NA* CR0 203 J8
Eastney St *GNWCH* SE10 161 J4
Eastnor *HHS/BOV* HP3 52 D4
Eastnor Rd *ELTH/MOT* SE9 184 F4
REIG RH2 275 J2
Easton Gdns *BORE* WD6 76 B8
Easton St *FSBYW* WC1X 12 A1
Eastor *WGCE* AL7 23 K8
East Pk *CRAWW* RH11 283 N8
HLWE CM17 29 M8
SBW CM21 29 P2
East Park Cl *CHDH* RM6 123 N3
East Pl *WNWD* SE27 181 K7
East Poultry Av *FARR* EC1M 12 C4
East Rp *HTHAIR* TW6 152 C7
East Ridgeway *POTB/CUF* EN6 60 E4
East Rd *CHDH* RM6 123 P3
EBAR EN4 98 B2
EBED/NFELT TW14 174 E3
EDGW HA8 95 N9
EFNCH N2 97 P9
HLW CM20 29 L7
IS N1 6 G10
KUTN/CMB KT2 199 K1
PEND EN3 80 B4
REIG RH2 257 J9
ROMW/RG RM7 124 E5
SRTFD E15 141 M3
WDR/YW UB7 152 A3
WELL DA16 163 L8
WEY KT13 216 E4
WIM/MER SW19 179 M9
East Rochester Wy *BFN/LL* DA15 185 H1
DART DA1 186 E3
East Rw *NKENS* W10 8 B2
WAN E11 121 M4
Eastry Av *HAYES* BR2 205 L6
Eastry Rd *ERITH* DA8 164 B6
East Shalford La *RGUE* GU4 268 C5
East Sheen Av *MORT/ESHN* SW14 178 A1
Eastside Rd *GLDGN* NW11 117 J2
East Smithfield *WAP* E1W 13 M8
East Stanley Gn *DTCH/LGLY* SL3 150 C3
East St *BARK* IG11 142 F2
BMLY BR1 205 M2
BTFD TW8 155 H6
BXLYHN DA7 164 B10
CSHM HP5 50 G8
EW KT17 220 B8
GT/LBKH KT23 254 A1
HHNE HP2 35 N6
HORS RH12 282 B6
WALW SE17 19 H7
WARE SG12 26 C2
WTHK RM20 167 K5
East Surrey Gv *PECK* SE15 159 N6
East Tenter St *WCHPL* E1 13 M6
East Ter *GVE* DA12 190 F2
East Thurrock Rd *GRAYS* RM17 167 N5
East Tilbury Rd *SLH/COR* SS17 169 K1
East Towers *PIN* HA5 113 L4
East Vw *BAR* EN5 77 J6
BRKMPK AL9 42 A3
CHING E4 101 H6
Eastview Av *WOOL/PLUM* SE18 163 H6
Eastville Av *GLDGN* NW11 117 J3
East Wk *EBAR* EN4 98 B2
HYS/HAR UB3 153 H1
REIG RH2 257 L10
East Wy *CROY/NA* CR0 204 D9
Eastway *GUW* GU2 249 L10
HAYES BR2 205 M7
HOR/WEW KT19 219 P8
East Wy *HYS/HAR* UB3 133 H10
Eastway *MRDN* SM4 200 G5
East Wy *RSLP* HA4 113 H6
Eastway *SRTFD* E15 120 F10
East Wy *WAB* EN9 81 J1
Eastway *WAN* E11 121 N3
WLGTN SM6 222 D1
Eastwell Cl *BECK* BR3 204 D1
Eastwick Crs *RKW/CH/CXG* WD3 91 J3
Eastwick Dr *GT/LBKH* KT23 236 A10
Eastwick Hall La *HLW* CM20 28 D5
Eastwick Park Av *GT/LBKH* KT23 236 A10
Eastwick Rd *GT/LBKH* KT23 254 A1
HLW CM20 28 E7
WOT/HER KT12 217 J3
Eastwick Rw *HHNE* HP2 36 B7
Eastwood *CRAWE* RH10 284 A7
Eastwood Cl *SWFD* E18 101 M10 1
TOTM N17 100 A8 2
Eastwood Dr *RAIN* RM13 145 J8
Eastwood Rd *GDMY/SEVK* IG3 123 K5
MUSWH N10 98 B10
SHGR GU5 268 C10
SWFD E18 101 M10
Eastwood St *STRHM/NOR* SW16 180 D9
Eastworth Rd *CHERT* KT16 195 J8
Eatington Rd *LEY* E10 121 J3
Eaton Cl *BGVA* SW1W 16 C6
STAN HA7 94 G5 2
Eaton Dr *BRXN/ST* SW9 159 J10 4
CRW RM5 104 C8
KUTN/CMB KT2 177 M10
Eaton Gdns *DAGW* RM9 143 P2
Eaton Ga *BGVA* SW1W 16 D5
NTHWD HA6 92 D7
Eaton La *BGVA* SW1W 16 F4
Eaton Ms North *KTBR* SW1X 16 D4
Eaton Ms South *BGVA* SW1W 16 D5
Eaton Ms West *BGVA* SW1W 16 D5
Eaton Pk *COB* KT11 217 M10
Eaton Park Rd *COB* KT11 217 M10
PLMGR N13 99 H3
Eaton Pl *KTBR* SW1X 16 C4
Eaton Ri *EA* W5 135 H7
WAN E11 121 P3
Eaton Rd *BELMT* SM2 221 N3
EN EN1 79 M7
HDN NW4 116 F3
HHNE HP2 36 C3
HSLW TW3 154 C10
SCUP DA14 185 N5
STAL AL1 38 G6
UPMR RM14 126 D7
Eaton Rw *BGVA* SW1W 16 E3
Eatons Md *CHING* E4 100 F3
Eaton Sq *BGVA* SW1W 16 D4
Eaton Ter *BGVA* SW1W 16 C5
Eaton Terrace Ms *KTBR* SW1X 16 C5
Eatonville Rd *TOOT* SW17 180 A5
Eatonville Vls *TOOT* SW17 180 A5
Ebba's Wy *EPSOM* KT18 237 N1
Ebberns Rd *HHS/BOV* HP3 35 P9
Ebbisham Dr *VX/NE* SW8 17 N9
Ebbisham La *KWD/TDW/WH* KT20 238 C7
Ebbisham Rd *EPSOM* KT18 219 N10
WPK KT4 200 F9
Ebbsfleet Rd *CRICK* NW2 117 H10
Ebdon Wy *BKHTH/KID* SE3 161 N9
Ebenezer St *IS* N1 6 G10
Ebenezer Wk *MTCM* CR4 202 D1
Ebley Cl *PECK* SE15 19 L10
Ebner St *WAND/EARL* SW18 179 L1
Ebor St *BETH* E2 13 L1
Ebrington Rd *KTN/HRWW/W* HA3 115 H4
Ebsworth St *FSTH* SE23 182 C3
Eburne Rd *HOLWY* N7 118 F8
Ebury Ap *RKW/CH/CXG* WD3 91 N2
Ebury Bridge Rd *BGVA* SW1W 16 D8
Ebury Cl *HAYES* BR2 206 B10
NTHWD HA6 92 D6
Ebury Ms *BGVA* SW1W 16 D5
Ebury Ms East *BGVA* SW1W 16 E5
Ebury Rd *RKW/CH/CXG* WD3 91 N2
WAT WD17 73 L7
Ebury Sq *BGVA* SW1W 16 E6
Ebury St *BGVA* SW1W 16 D6
Ecclesbourne Cl *PLMGR* N13 99 H6
Ecclesbourne Gdns *PLMGR* N13 99 H6
Ecclesbourne Rd *IS* N1 6 F4
THHTH CR7 203 K5
Eccleshill *RDKG* RH5 273 H6
Eccles Rd *BTSEA* SW11 158 A10
Eccleston Cl *EBAR* EN4 77 P9
ORP BR6 206 G8
Eccleston Crs *CHDH* RM6 123 L5
Ecclestone Ct *ALP/SUD* HA0 115 K10
Ecclestone Ms *ALP/SUD* HA0 115 K10
Ecclestone Pl *WBLY* HA9 115 L10
Eccleston Ms *KTBR* SW1X 16 D4
Eccleston Pl *BGVA* SW1W 16 E6

Eccleston Rd HNWL W7 — 134 F9
Eccleston Sq PIM SW1V — 16 F6
Eccleston Square Ms PIM SW1V — 16 F6
Eccleston St BCVA SW1W — 16 G4
Echelforde Dr ASHF TW15 — 174 B7
Echo Ct GVE DA12 — 190 F15
Echo Hts CHING E4 — 100 G2
Echo Pit Rd RGUE GU4 — 268 B4
Eckford St IS N1 — 6 A7
Eckstein Rd BTSEA SW11 — 157 P10
Ecob CI RGUW GU3 — 249 L6
Ecton Rd ADL/WDHM KT15 — 215 L1
Ector Rd CAT SE6 — 183 K5
Edans Ct SHB W12 — 156 C1
Edbrooke Rd MV/WKIL W9 — 8 E2
Eddiscombe Rd FUL/PGN SW6 — 157 J8
Eddy CI ROMW/RG RM7 — 124 C4
Eddystone Rd BROCKY SE4 — 182 D11
Eddy St BERK HP4 — 33 M4
Ede CI HSLWW TW4 — 153 N9
Edenbridge CI STMC/STPC BR5 — 207 N5
Edenbridge Rd EN EN1 — 79 N10
  HOM E9 — 140 C2
Eden CI ALP/SUD HA0 — 135 J3
  ALP/SUD HA0 — 135 J3
  BXLY DA5 — 186 E2
  DTCH/LGLY SL3 — 150 D4
  KENS W8 — 14 F5
Edencourt Rd STRHM/NOR SW16 — 180 C9
Edencroft SHGR GU5 — 268 D10
Edendale Rd BXLYHN DA7 — 164 G1
Edenfield Gdns WPK KT4 — 200 C10
Eden Gn SOCK/AV RM15 — 146 C7
Eden Gv HOLWY N7 — 118 G10
Eden Grove Rd BF/WBF KT14 — 215 P9
Edenhall CI HHNE HP2 — 36 F7
Edenhall Rd HARH RM3 — 105 K6
Edenham Wy NKENS W10 — 8 C3
Edenhurst Av FUL/PGN SW6 — 157 J9
Eden Park Av BECK BR3 — 204 E4
Eden PI GVE DA12 — 190 E3
Eden Rd BECK BR3 — 204 D4
  BXLY DA5 — 186 D7
  CRAWW RH11 — 283 J9
  CROY/NA CR0 — 223 L1
  WALTH E17 — 120 G3
  WNWD SE27 — 181 J8
Edenside Rd GT/LBKH KT23 — 235 N10
Edensor Rd CHSWK W4 — 156 B6
Eden St KUT KT1 — 199 K2
Edenvale Rd MTCM CR4 — 180 B10
Edenvale St FUL/PGN SW6 — 157 L8
Eden Wy BECK BR3 — 204 F5
  WARL CR6 — 242 D4
Ederline Av STRHM/NOR SW16 — 202 C3
Edgar CI CRAWE RH10 — 284 F8
  SWLY BR8 — 208 C5
Edgar Kail Wy CMBW SE5 — 159 M9
Edgar Rd BH/WHM TN16 — 244 A4
  BOW E3 — 140 A5
  HSLWW TW4 — 175 N5
  RSEV TN14 — 247 M3
  SAND/SEL CR2 — 223 L6
  WDR/YW UB7 — 131 P9
Edgars Ct WGCE AL7 — 23 H6
Edgbaston Dr RAD WD7 — 57 K8
Edgeborough Wy BMLY BR1 — 206 A1
Edgebury CHST BR7 — 184 E7
Edge CI WEY KT13 — 216 B4
Edgecombe CI KUTN/CMB KT2 — 178 A10
Edgecoombe SAND/SEL CR2 — 224 C5
Edgecote CI ACT W3 — 135 P10
Edgefield Av BARK IG11 — 143 J2
Edgefield CI DART DA1 — 188 A4
  REDH RH1 — 276 B5
Edge Hill WIM/MER SW19 — 178 G10
  WOOL/PLUM SE18 — 162 E15
Edge Hill Av GLDGN NW11 — 117 K2
Edgehill Ct WOT/HER KT12 — 197 K8
Edgehill Gdns DAGE RM10 — 124 B9
Edgehill Rd CHST BR7 — 184 E4
  MTCM CR4 — 202 C2
  PUR/KEN CR8 — 223 H6
  WEA W13 — 135 H8
Edge St KENS W8 — 8 F9
Edgewood Dr ORP BR6 — 227 J2
Edgewood Gn CROY/NA CR0 — 204 C8
Edgeworth Av HDN NW4 — 116 C3
Edgeworth CI CTHM CR3 — 241 P4
  ELTH/MOT SE9 — 161 P10
Edgington Rd STRHM/NOR SW16 — 180 D12
Edgington Wy SCUP DA14 — 185 M10
Edgware Gdns EDGW HA8 — 95 M6
  EDGW HA8 — 95 L2
Edgware Rd BAY/PAD W2 — 9 L2
  CDALE/KGS NW9 — 115 P1
  CRICK NW2 — 116 F1
Edgware Road Burnt Oak Broadway EDGW HA8 — 95 N8
Edgware Road High St EDGW HA8 — 95 N8
Edgware Road the Hyde CDALE/KGS NW9 — 116 B2
  EDGW HA8 — 95 P10
Edgware Way (Watford By-pass) EDGW HA8 — 95 M5
Edinburgh Av RKW/CH/CXG WD3 — 71 K10
  SL SL1 — 128 F8
Edinburgh CI BETH E2 — 140 B4
  HGDN/ICK UB10 — 112 C9
Edinburgh Crs CHES/WCR EN8 — 62 C9
Edinburgh Dr CSTN WD25 — 55 H8
  HGDN/ICK UB10 — 112 C9
  STA TW18 — 173 N9
Edinburgh Gdns WDSR SL4 — 149 J8
Edinburgh Ms TIL RM18 — 168 E8
Edinburgh Rd HNWL W7 — 154 E1
  PLSTW E13 — 141 N4
  SUT SM1 — 201 M9
  UED N18 — 99 P6
  WALTH E17 — 120 F3
Edinburgh's Dr ROMW/RG RM7 — 124 D2
Edinburgh Wy HLW CM20 — 29 L7
  HLWE CM17 — 29 M6
Edington Rd ABYW SE2 — 163 L2
  PEND EN3 — 80 B6
Edison Av HCH RM12 — 124 C6
Edison CI HCH RM12 — 124 C6
  STALE/WH AL4 — 39 H7
Edison Dr CFD/PVL UB6 — 134 A8
  WOOL/PLUM SE18 — 163 H6
Edison Gv WOOL/PLUM SE18 — 163 H6
Edison Rd CEND/HSY/T N8 — 118 C4
  HAYES BR2 — 205 M2
  PEND EN3 — 80 E6
  WELL DA16 — 163 J7
Edis St CAMTN NW1 — 4 C5
Edith Gdns BRYLDS KT5 — 199 N7
Edith Gv WBPTN SW10 — 15 K10
Edithna St BRXN/ST SW9 — 158 F9
Edith Rd CHDH RM6 — 123 N5
  EHAM E6 — 142 A2
  FBAR/BDGN N11 — 98 E8
  ORP BR6 — 227 K2
  SNWD SE25 — 203 L5
  SRTFD E15 — 121 J10
  WIM/MER SW19 — 179 L9

WKENS W14 — 14 B6
Edith Rw FUL/PGN SW6 — 157 L7
Edith St BETH E2 — 7 M7
Edith Ter WBPTN SW10 — 157 N6
Edith Vis WKENS W14 — 14 C6
Edison CI WALTH E17 — 120 F3
Edlyn CI BERK HP4 — 33 L4
Edmeston CI HOM E9 — 140 D1
Edmund Beaufort Dr STALW/RED AL3 — 38 C4
Edmund Gv FELT TW13 — 175 N5
Edmund Rd CDH/CHF RM16 — 167 J1
  MTCM CR4 — 201 P3
  RAIN RM13 — 144 F5
  STMC/STPC BR5 — 207 M6
  WELL DA16 — 163 K9
Edmunds Av STMC/STPC BR5 — 207 N5
Edmunds CI YEAD UB4 — 133 K7
Edmund St CMBW SE5 — 159 L6
Edmunds Wk HDN NW4 — 117 P2
Edmunds Wy SLN SL2 — 129 N8
Edna Rd RYNPK SW20 — 200 G3
Edna St BTSEA SW11 — 157 P7
Edrick Rd EDGW HA8 — 95 P7
Edrick Wk EDGW HA8 — 95 P7
Edric Rd NWCR SE14 — 160 C6
Edridge CI BUSH WD23 — 74 B9
  HCH RM12 — 125 L10
Edridge Rd CROY/NA CR0 — 203 K10
Edulf Rd BUSH WD23 — 74 E4
Edward Amey CI GSTN WD25 — 73 K2
Edward Av CHING E4 — 100 G6
  MRDN SM4 — 201 N5
Edward CI ABLGY WD5 — 54 G8
  ED N9 — 99 N1
  GPK RM2 — 125 K1
  HPTN TW12 — 176 B8
  STAL AL1 — 38 E7
Edward Ct CAN/RD E16 — 141 M7
  HHS/BOV HP3 — 35 N10
  STA TW18 — 173 M9
  WAB EN9 — 63 J9
Edwardes Sq KENS W8 — 14 E4
Edwards Gv EBAR EN4 — 77 N3
Edward Ii Av BF/WBF KT14 — 216 A10
Edward Ms CAMTN NW1 — 4 F9
Edward PI DEPT SE8 — 160 E5
Edward Rd BFOR GU20 — 212 C3
  BH/WHM TN16 — 244 B4
  BMLY BR1 — 183 N10
  CHDH RM6 — 123 P4
  CHST BR7 — 184 E8
  COUL/CHIP CR5 — 240 E1
  CROY/NA CR0 — 203 M7
  EBAR EN4 — 77 N9
  EBED/NFELT TW14 — 174 E1
  HPTN TW12 — 176 B8
  NTHLT UB5 — 133 K4
  PGE/AN SE20 — 182 C10
  RYLN/HDSTN HA2 — 114 B1
  WALTH E17 — 120 C2
Edward's Av RSLP HA4 — 113 K10
Edward's CI WPK KT4 — 200 C9
Edward's Cottages IS N1 — 6 C2
Edward's Ct SL SL1 — 149 K1
Edwards Gdns SWLY BR8 — 208 E4
Edward's La STNW/STAM N16 — 119 L7
Edwards Ms IS N1 — 6 B3
  MBLAR W1H — 10 C1
Edward Sq IS N1 — 5 N6
Edwards Rd BELV DA17 — 164 B3
Edward St DEPT SE8 — 160 E6
  NWCR SE14 — 160 E6
  PLSTW E13 — 141 M6
  SBTF EC1A — 12 E5
Edward Temme Av SRTFD E15 — 141 L2
Edward Tyler Rd LEE/GVPK SE12 — 183 N5
Edwina Gdns REDBR IG4 — 122 B3
Edwin Av EHAM E6 — 142 D4
Edwin CI BXLYHN DA7 — 164 A5
  EHSLY KT24 — 252 F1
  RAIN RM13 — 144 C5
Edwin Petty PI RDART DA2 — 188 B3
Edwin Rd EDGW HA8 — 96 A7
  EHSLY KT24 — 252 D1
  RDART DA2 — 187 J6
  WHTN TW2 — 176 D4
Edwin's Md HOM E9 — 120 D9
Edwin St CAN/RD E16 — 141 M7
  GVE DA12 — 190 E3
  WCHPL E1 — 140 B6
Edwyn CI BAR EN5 — 76 F9
Effie PI FUL/PGN SW6 — 157 K6
Effie Rd FUL/PGN SW6 — 157 K6
Effingham CI BELMT SM2 — 221 L4
Effingham Common Rd EHSLY KT24 — 253 K1
Effingham La CRAWE RH10 — 281 M10
Effingham PI EHSLY KT24 — 253 L3
Effingham Rd CEND/HSY/T N8 — 119 H5
  CROY/NA CR0 — 202 C7
  HORL RH6 — 281 K9
  LEW SE13 — 183 K1
  REIG RH2 — 275 J1
  SURB KT6 — 198 C2
Effort St TOOT SW17 — 179 H8
Effra Pde BRXS/STRHM SW2 — 158 F4
Effra Rd WIM/MER SW19 — 179 L8
Egan Wy HYS/HAR UB3 — 132 F9
Egbert St CAMTN NW1 — 4 C5
Egbury Dr BRYLDS KT5 — 199 N8
Egerton Crs CHEL SW3 — 15 N5
Egerton Dr GNWCH SE10 — 160 G7
Egerton Gdns CHEL SW3 — 15 N4
  GDMY/SEVK IG3 — 123 J8
  HDN NW4 — 116 E2
  WEA W13 — 134 G8
  WLSDN NW10 — 136 F3
Egerton Gardens Ms CHEL SW3 — 15 P4
Egerton PI CHEL SW3 — 15 P4
  WEY KT13 — 216 D3
Egerton Rd ALP/SUD HA0 — 135 L2
  BERK HP4 — 33 M3
  CLPT E5 — 119 N5
  GUW GU2 — 249 L10
  NWMAL KT3 — 200 C4
  SLN SL2 — 128 D6
  SNWD SE25 — 203 M3
  WEY KT13 — 216 D3
  WHTN TW2 — 176 D3
Egerton Ter CHEL SW3 — 15 P4
Egg Hall EPP CM16 — 65 K5
Egham By-pass EGH TW20 — 172 A9
Egham CI CHEAM SM3 — 201 H9
Egham Crs CHEAM SM3 — 200 C10
Egham HI EGH TW20 — 172 A9
Egham Rd PLSTW E13 — 141 N1
Eghams CI BEAC HP9 — 44 A2
Eghams Wood Rd BEAC HP9 — 88 A7
Eglantine La EYN DA4 — 210 A6
Eglantine Rd WAND/EARL SW18 — 179 M1
Egleston Rd MRDN SM4 — 201 L6
Egley Dr WOKS/MYFD GU22 — 232 A6
Egley Rd WOKS/MYFD GU22 — 232 A6
Eglington Ct WALW SE17 — [—]
Eglington Rd CHING E4 — 101 J1
Eglinton HI WOOL/PLUM SE18 — 162 G5
Eglinton Rd SWCM DA10 — 189 L2
  WOOL/PLUM SE18 — 162 G5
Eglise Rd WARL CR6 — 242 D6
Egliston Ms PUT/ROE SW15 — 156 F9
Egliston Rd PUT/ROE SW15 — 156 F9
Egmont Av SURB KT6 — 199 L8

Egmont Park Rd KWD/TDW/WH KT20 — 256 F6
Egmont Rd BELMT SM2 — 221 M4
  NWMAL KT3 — 200 C4
  SURB KT6 — 199 L8
  WOT/HER KT12 — 197 J7
Egmont St NWCR SE14 — 160 C6
Egremont Gdns SL SL1 — 128 F10
Egremont Rd WNWD SE27 — 181 H6
Egret Wy YEAD UB4 — 133 L7
Egypt La SLN SL2 — 108 G8
Eight Acres SL SL1 — 128 B8
Eighteenth Rd MTCM CR4 — 202 F4
Eighth Av HYS/HAR UB3 — 133 H10
  MNPK E12 — 122 C9
Eileen Rd SNWD SE25 — 203 L5
Eindoven CI MTCM CR4 — 202 B8
Eisenhower Dr EHAM E6 — 142 B7
Elaine Gv KTTN NW5 — 118 B10
Elam CI CMBW SE5 — 159 J8
Elam St CMBW SE5 — 159 J8
Eland Rd BTSEA SW11 — 158 A9
  CROY/NA CR0 — 203 J10
Elan Rd SOCK/AV RM15 — 146 F7
Elberon Av CROY/NA CR0 — 202 D8
Elbe St FUL/PGN SW6 — 157 N8
Elbow La HERT/BAY SG13 — 26 A10
Elbury Dr CAN/RD E16 — 141 M8
Elcho St BTSEA SW11 — 157 P6
Elcot Av PECK SE15 — 160 A6
Elder Av CEND/HSY/T N8 — 118 F3
Elderbeck CI CHESW EN7 — 61 P4
Elderberry Rd EA W5 — 155 N1
Elderberry Wy GSTN WD25 — 73 J1
Elder CI BFN/LL DA15 — 185 J6
  GU GU1 — 250 D7
  WDR/YW UB7 — 131 P9
Elder Ct BUSH WD23 — 94 D3
Elderfield HLWE CM17 — 29 N7
Elderfield Rd CLPT E5 — 120 C9
  SLN SL2 — 129 L1
Elderfield Wk WAN E11 — 121 N3
Elderflower Wy SRTFD E15 — 141 K2
Elder Oak CI PGE/AN SE20 — 204 A1
Elder Rd CHOB/PIR GU24 — 230 F1
  WNWD SE27 — 181 K8
Eldersley CI REDH RH1 — 258 A3
Eldersley Gdns REDH RH1 — 258 A3
Elderslie CI BECK BR3 — 204 F6
Elderslie Rd ELTH/MOT SE9 — 184 D1
Elder St WCHPL E1 — 13 L5
Elderton Rd SYD SE26 — 182 D7
Eldertree PI MTCM CR4 — 202 C1
Eldertree Wy MTCM CR4 — 202 C1
Elder Wk IS N1 — 6 D5
Elder Wy RAIN RM13 — 145 L5
  RDKG RH5 — 273 H6
Eldon Av BORE WD6 — 75 M6
  CROY/NA CR0 — 204 B9
  HEST TW5 — 153 P6
Eldon Gv HAMP NW3 — 117 N10
Eldon Pk SNWD SE25 — 204 A4
Eldon Rd CTHM CR3 — 241 L7
  ED N9 — 100 B2
  HOD EN11 — 45 J5
  KENS W8 — 15 H4
  WALTH E17 — 120 E2
  WDGN N22 — 99 J9
Eldon St LVPST EC2M — 13 H4
Eldon Wy WLSDN NW10 — 135 N4
Eldred Dr STMC/STPC BR5 — 207 N8
Eldred Gdns UPMR RM14 — 126 D5
Eldredge CI EBED/NFELT TW14 — 175 H4
Eleanor Av HOR/WEW KT19 — 220 A6
  STALW/RED AL3 — 38 C4
Eleanor CI TOTM N17 — 119 N1
  NWCR SE14 — 96 C5
Eleanor Crs MLHL NW7 — 96 C5
Eleanor Cross Rd CHES/WCR EN8 — 62 D10
Eleanor Gdns BAR EN5 — 76 C9
  DAGW RM9 — 143 M2
Eleanor Gv BARN SW13 — 156 A8
  HGDN/ICK UB10 — 112 C9
Eleanor Rd CFSP/GDCR SL9 — 89 P9
  CHES/WCR EN8 — 62 D9
  FBAR/BDGN N11 — 98 E12
  HACK E8 — 140 A1
  HERT/WAS SG14 — 25 K4
  SRTFD E15 — 141 L1
Eleanor St BOW E3 — 140 A2
Eleanor Wy BRW CM14 — 107 J6
  CHES/WCR EN8 — 62 E10
Electric Av BRXN/ST SW9 — 159 H10
Electric La BRXN/ST SW9 — 159 H10
Elephant La BERM/RHTH SE16 — 160 B1
Elephant Rd WALW SE17 — 18 D15
Elers Rd HYS/HAR UB3 — 152 D5
  WEA W13 — 155 H1
Eleven Acre Ri LOU IG10 — 82 C7
Eley Rd UED N18 — 100 C6
Elfindale Rd HNHL SE24 — 181 H1
Elfin Gv TEDD TW11 — 176 E8
Elford CI ELTH/MOT SE9 — 161 P10
Elfort Rd HBRY N5 — 119 H9
Elfrida Crs CAT SE6 — 182 F7
Elfrida Rd WATW WD18 — 73 K9
Elf Rw WAP E1W — 140 E9
Elfwine Rd HNWL W7 — 134 D1
Elgal CI ORP BR6 — 226 E7
Elgar Av BRYLDS KT5 — 199 N8
  EA W5 — 155 K1
  STRHM/NOR SW16 — 202 A3
  WLSDN NW10 — 136 A1
Elgar CI BKHH IG9 — 102 A3
  BORE WD6 — 95 H1
  DEPT SE8 — 160 F6
  HGDN/ICK UB10 — 112 B7
  PLSTW E13 — 141 P4
Elgar Gdns TIL RM18 — 168 E8
Elgar St BERM/RHTH SE16 — 160 F7
Elgin Av ASHF TW15 — 174 A9
  HARH RM3 — 106 A8
  KTN/HRWW/W HA3 — 94 G10
  MV/WKIL W9 — 8 E2
Elgin Crs CTHM CR3 — 241 P8
  HTHAIR TW6 — 152 F8
  NTGHL W11 — 8 B7
Elgin Gdns GU GU1 — 250 D9
Elginmeads South MV/WKIL W9 — 3 H9
Elgin Ms NTGHL W11 — 8 B6
Elgin Ms North MV/WKIL W9 — 3 H9
Elgin Rd BROX EN10 — 44 E10
  CROY/NA CR0 — 204 B9
  GDMY/SEVK IG3 — 123 H1
  SUT SM1 — 201 M10
  WDGN N22 — 98 D10
  WLGTN SM6 — 223 J4
Elgiva La CSHM HP5 — 50 C7
Elham CI BMLY BR1 — 184 A10
Elia Ms IS N1 — 6 C8
Elias PI LBTH SE11 — 18 A10
Elia St IS N1 — 6 C8
Elibank Rd ELTH/MOT SE9 — 162 D10
Elim Est STHWK SE1 — 19 H3
Elim Wy PLSTW E13 — 141 L9
Eliot Bank FSTH SE23 — 182 A5
Eliot Dr RYLN/HDSTN HA2 — 114 A7
Eliot Gdns PUT/ROE SW15 — 156 D10
Eliot HI BKHTH/KID SE3 — 161 H6
Eliot Pk LEW SE13 — 161 J6

Eliot PI BKHTH/KID SE3 — 161 K8
Eliot Rd DAGW RM9 — 123 N9
  DART DA1 — 188 A1
Eliot V BKHTH/KID SE3 — 161 J8
Elizabethan Wy CRAWE RH10 — 284 D8
Elizabeth Av AMS HP6 — 69 P5
  ENC/FH EN2 — 79 J7
  IL IG1 — 122 G7
  IS N1 — 6 F4
  STA TW18 — 173 M8
Elizabeth CI BAR EN5 — 76 C7
  MV/WKIL W9 — 9 K1
  RGODL GU7 — 267 K10
  ROMW/RG RM7 — 104 C9
  SUT SM1 — 221 J1
  WAB EN9 — 45 J9
  WCCE AL7 — 23 M5
Elizabeth Clyde CI SEVS/STOTM N15 — 119 M2
Elizabeth Cottages RCH/KEW TW9 — 155 L7
Elizabeth Ct HORL RH6 — 280 B4
  STALE/WH AL4 — 39 J3
Elizabeth Dr EPP CM16 — 83 H2
Elizabeth Gdns ACT W3 — 136 C10
  ASC SL5 — 192 A5
  STAN HA7 — 95 H7
  SUN TW16 — 197 K3
Elizabeth Ms HAMP NW3 — 3 J2
Elizabeth PI SEVS/STOTM N15 — 119 L2
Elizabeth Ride ED N9 — 100 A1
Elizabeth Rd BRWN CM15 — 86 G10
  CDH/CHF RM16 — 167 L2
  EHAM E6 — 142 A3
  RAIN RM13 — 145 J7
  RGODL GU7 — 267 K10
  SEVS/STOTM N15 — 119 M3
Elizabeth Sq POP/IOD E14 — 140 D9
Elizabeth St BGVA SW1W — 16 G5
  GRH DA9 — 189 D1
Elizabeth Wy FELT TW13 — 175 K7
  HLW CM20 — 28 D9
  HLWW/ROY CM19 — 46 C2
  NRWD SE19 — 181 L10
  SLN SL2 — 129 L3
  STMC/STPC BR5 — 207 M5
Elkington Rd PLSTW E13 — 141 N6
Elkins Gdns RGUE GU4 — 250 D7
Elkins Rd SLN SL2 — 109 K7
Elkstone Rd NKENS W10 — 8 C3
The Elkins ROM RM1 — 104 F10
Elladine Rd HMSMTH W6 — [—]
Ella Ms HAMP NW3 — 118 A10
Ellanby Crs UED N18 — 100 A6
Elland Rd PECK SE15 — 160 B10
  WOT/HER KT12 — 197 L9
Ella Rd CEND/HSY/T N8 — 118 F7
Ellement CI PIN HA5 — 113 L3
Ellenborough PI PUT/ROE SW15 — 156 D10
Ellenborough Rd SCUP DA14 — 185 N9
  WDGN N22 — 99 K9
Ellenbrook CI WATN WD24 — 73 K5
Ellenbrook Crs HAT AL10 — 40 A4
Ellenbrook La HAT AL10 — 40 B5
Ellen CI BMLY BR1 — 206 A3
  HHNE HP2 — 36 A5
Ellen Ct ED N9 — 100 B3
Ellen St WCHPL E1 — 13 P6
Ellen Webb Dr KTN/HRWW/W HA3 — 114 D1
Elleray Rd TEDD TW11 — 176 B9
Ellerby St FUL/PGN SW6 — 156 G7
Ellerdale Rd HAMP NW3 — 117 M10
Ellerdale St LEW SE13 — 160 G13
Ellerdine Rd HSLW TW3 — 154 B10
Ellerker Gdns RCHPK/HAM TW10 — 177 K2
Ellerman Av WHTN TW2 — 175 J4
Ellerman Rd TIL RM18 — 168 C8
Ellerslie Rd SHB W12 — 136 G10
Ellerslie Sq BRXS/STRHM SW2 — 181 M2
Ellerton Gdns DAGW RM9 — 143 M2
Ellerton Rd BARN SW13 — 156 D7
  DAGW RM9 — 143 M2
  RYNPK SW20 — 178 D10
  SURB KT6 — 199 L8
  WAND/EARL SW18 — 179 N4
Ellery Rd NRWD SE19 — 181 L10
Ellery St PECK SE15 — 160 A8
Elles Av GU GU1 — 250 E10
Ellesborough CI OXHEY WD19 — 93 K6
Ellesmere Av BECK BR3 — 204 G2
  MLHL NW7 — 96 A4
Ellesmere CI RSLP HA4 — 112 D5
  WAN E11 — 121 L3
Ellesmere Dr SAND/SEL CR2 — 224 A10
Ellesmere Gdns REDBR IG4 — 122 B3
Ellesmere Gv BAR EN5 — 77 J3
Ellesmere Rd BERK HP4 — 34 A5
  BOW E3 — 140 D4
  CFD/PVL UB6 — 134 B8
  TWK TW1 — 177 H2
  WEY KT13 — 216 F5
  WLSDN NW10 — 116 D10
Ellesmere St POP/IOD E14 — 140 G8
Ellice Rd OXTED RH8 — 261 L5
Ellies Ms ASHF TW15 — 173 N5
Elliman Av SL SL1 — 129 K9
Ellingfort Rd HACK E8 — 140 A2
Ellingham CI HHNE HP2 — 36 A5
  HHNE HP2 — 36 A5
Ellingham Rd CHSGTN KT9 — 219 J5
  SHB W12 — 156 D1
  WAN E11 — 121 J9
Ellington Rd FELT TW13 — 174 G7
  HSLW TW3 — 154 A8
  MUSWH N10 — 118 C2
Ellington St HOLWY N7 — 6 A1
Ellington Wy EPSOM KT18 — 238 E3
Elliot CI CRAWE RH10 — 284 D8
  SRTFD E15 — 141 K2
  WBLY HA9 — 115 L4
Elliot Rd HDN NW4 — 116 K4
  RSLP HA4 — 113 J7
Elliott Av RSLP HA4 — 113 J7
Elliott CI WCCE AL7 — 23 M1
Elliott Gdns HARH RM3 — 105 J9
  SHPTN TW17 — 196 B4
Elliott Rd BRXN/ST SW9 — 159 J6
  CHSWK W4 — 156 B3
  HAYES BR2 — 206 A4
  STAN HA7 — 94 F7
  THHTH CR7 — 203 J1
Elliotts La BH/WHM TN16 — 245 M10
Elliott's PI IS N1 — 6 C6
Elliott's Rw LBTH SE11 — 18 D5
Ellis Av CFSP/GDCR SL9 — 90 C9
  GUW GU2 — 267 L2
  RAIN RM13 — 145 H7
  SL SL1 — 149 K1
Ellis CI COUL/CHIP CR5 — 240 F6
  ELTH/MOT SE9 — 184 F5
Elliscombe Rd CHARL SE7 — 161 K4
Ellis Farm CI WOKS/MYFD GU22 — 232 A9
Ellisfield Dr PUT/ROE SW15 — 178 C5
Ellison CI WDSR SL4 — 148 C9
Ellison Gdns NWDGN UB2 — 153 N3
Ellison Rd BARN SW13 — 156 C8
  BFN/LL DA15 — 184 G4
  STRHM/NOR SW16 — 180 E10
Ellis Rd COUL/CHIP CR5 — 240 G6
  MTCM CR4 — 202 A8
  STHL UB1 — 134 B3
Ellis St KTBR SW1X — 16 B5

Ellis Waterton CI SWLY BR8 — 208 E4
Ellis Wy DART DA1 — 187 N5
Elliswick Rd HARP AL5 — 20 A1
Ellman Rd CRAWW RH11 — 283 J9
Ellmore CI HARH RM3 — 105 J9
Ellora Rd STRHM/NOR SW16 — 180 E8
Ellison CI RGUW GU3 — 284 D9
Ellsworth St BETH E2 — 140 A5
Ellwood Gdns GSTN WD25 — 55 J3
Ellwood Rd BEAC HP9 — 88 A3
Elmar Gn SLN SL2 — 128 F5
Elmar Rd SEVS/STOTM N15 — 119 L2
Elm Av EA W5 — 135 K10
  OXHEY WD19 — 93 M4
  RSLP HA4 — 113 H6
  UPMR RM14 — 126 A8
Elmbank WCHMH N21 — 98 F1
Elmbank Av BAR EN5 — 75 N6
  EGH TW20 — 171 N10
  GU GU1 — 267 M1
Elm Bank Dr BMLY BR1 — 206 A2
Elm Bank Gdns BARN SW13 — 156 A8
Elmbank Wy HNWL W7 — 134 C7
Elmbourne Dr BELV DA17 — 164 C3
Elmbourne Rd TOOT SW17 — 180 C6
Elmbridge HLWE CM17 — 30 A8
Elmbridge Av BRYLDS KT5 — 199 P6
Elmbridge CI RSLP HA4 — 113 H4
Elmbridge Dr RSLP HA4 — 113 H4
Elmbridge La WOKS/MYFD GU22 — 232 G3
Elmbridge Rd BARK/HLT IG6 — 103 K7
Elmbrook CI SUN TW16 — 197 L3
Elmbrook Gdns ELTH/MOT SE9 — 162 B10
Elmbrook Rd SUT SM1 — 221 J1
Elm CI AMS HP6 — 69 H4
  BKHH IG9 — 102 A3
  BRYLDS KT5 — 199 P7
  CAR SM5 — 202 A8
  DART DA1 — 187 K4
  EPP CM16 — 46 E1
  HDN NW4 — 116 G3
  HYS/HAR UB3 — 133 H6
  KWD/TDW/WH KT20 — 256 G8
  LHD/OX KT22 — 256 C8
  ROMW/RG RM7 — 104 C9
  RYLN/HDSTN HA2 — 114 A4
  RYNPK SW20 — 200 F6
  SAND/SEL CR2 — 223 L3
  SLN SL2 — 129 L1
  STWL/WRAY TW19 — 173 N4
  WAB EN9 — 63 J9
  WAN E11 — 121 N4
  WARL CR6 — 242 C5
  WHTN TW2 — 176 A5
  WOKN/KNAP GU21 — 232 A1
Elmcote Wy RKW/CH/CXG WD3 — 72 A10
Elm Cft WOKN/KNAP GU21 — 231 J3
Elmcourt Rd WNWD SE27 — 181 J5
Elm Crs EA W5 — 155 K1
  KUTN/CMB KT2 — 199 K1
Elmcroft CEND/HSY/T N8 — 118 G3
Elm Cft DTCH/LGLY SL3 — 149 P7
Elmcroft Av BFN/LL DA15 — 185 J5
  ED N9 — 80 A10
  GLDGN NW11 — 117 L5
  WAN E11 — 121 N1
Elmcroft CI CHSGTN KT9 — 199 K10
  EA W5 — 135 J8
  EBED/NFELT TW14 — 174 G2
Elmcroft Crs GLDGN NW11 — 116 G5
  RYLN/HDSTN HA2 — 113 P1
Elmcroft Dr ASHF TW15 — 174 B10
  CHSGTN KT9 — 199 K10
Elmcroft Gdns CDALE/KGS NW9 — 115 N3
Elmcroft Rd ORP BR6 — 207 K7
Elmcroft St CLPT E5 — 120 E2
Elmdale Rd PLMGR N13 — 98 G6
Elmdene BRYLDS KT5 — 199 P8
Elmdene Av EMPK RM11 — 125 L2
Elmdene CI BECK BR3 — 204 E5
Elmdene Rd WOOL/PLUM SE18 — 162 E4
Elmdon Rd HEST TW5 — 153 J7
  HTHAIR TW6 — 152 G7
  SOCK/AV RM15 — 146 F7
Elm Dr CHES/WCR EN8 — 62 D6
  CHOB/PIR GU24 — 213 L6
  HAT AL10 — 40 D5
  LHD/OX KT22 — 236 G8
  RYLN/HDSTN HA2 — 114 A4
  STALE/WH AL4 — 39 H6
  SUN TW16 — 197 K2
  SWLY BR8 — 208 E2
  WDSR SL4 — 170 A4
Elmer Av ABR/ST RM4 — 104 F4
Elmer CI ENC/FH EN2 — 78 G7
  RAIN RM13 — 145 H2
Elmer Gdns EDGW HA8 — 95 N6
  ISLW TW7 — 154 C9
  RAIN RM13 — 145 H2
Elmer Ms LHD/OX KT22 — 236 F9
Elmer Rd CAT SE6 — 183 H5
Elmers Av SURB KT6 — 199 K5
Elmer's Dr TEDD TW11 — 176 G9
Elmers End Rd BECK BR3 — 204 B3
  PGE/AN SE20 — 204 B3
Elmerside Rd BECK BR3 — 204 D4
Elmers Rd CROY/NA CR0 — 203 P7
Elmfield GT/LBKH KT23 — 235 P9
Elmfield Av CEND/HSY/T N8 — 118 F3
  MTCM CR4 — 202 B1
  TEDD TW11 — 176 B8
Elmfield CI GVW DA11 — 190 A1
  HRW HA1 — 114 D7
  POTB/CUF EN6 — 59 H3
  RSEV TN14 — 265 J9
Elmfield Pk BMLY BR1 — 205 M3
Elmfield Rd BMLY BR1 — 205 M3
  CHING E4 — 101 N1
  EFNCH N2 — 117 N1
  NWDGN UB2 — 152 G2
  POTB/CUF EN6 — 59 H3
  TOOT SW17 — 180 C5
  WALTH E17 — 120 C4
Elmfield Wy MV/WKIL W9 — 8 E3
  SAND/SEL CR2 — 223 N5
Elm Gdns EFNCH N2 — 117 H2
  ENC/FH EN2 — 79 L4
  EPP CM16 — 66 C2
  ESH/CLAY KT10 — 218 E3
  KWD/TDW/WH KT20 — 238 E15
  MTCM CR4 — 202 G4
  WCCW AL8 — 22 C3
Elmgate Av FELT TW13 — 175 J6
Elmgate Gdns EDGW HA8 — 95 P6
Elm Gn ACT W3 — 136 B8
  HHW HP1 — 35 L1
Elmgreen CI SRTFD E15 — 141 K3
Elm Gv BERK HP4 — 33 P5
  CEND/HSY/T N8 — 118 F4
  CHOB/PIR GU24 — 230 F2
  CRICK NW2 — 116 C2
  EPSOM KT18 — 238 A6
  ERITH DA8 — 164 G6
  HACK E8 — 7 N1
  HAYES BR2 — 205 P1
  KUTN/CMB KT2 — 177 N7
  ORP BR6 — 207 N14
  PECK SE15 — 159 H9
  RYLN/HDSTN HA2 — 113 P5
  SUT SM1 — 221 N3
  WATN WD24 — 73 H3
  WDR/YW UB7 — 132 A2
  WOKN/KNAP GU21 — 231 J3
Elm Grove Pde WLGTN SM6 — 202 B4

Elm Grove Rd BARN SW13 ... 156 D7
COB KT11 ... 235 L2
Elmgrove Rd CROY/NA CR0 ... 204 A7
Elm Grove Rd EA W5 ... 155 K1
Elmgrove Rd HRW HA1 ... 114 E3
WEY KT13 ... 216 B1
Elm Hall Gdns WAN E11 ... 121 N4
Elm Hatch PIN HA5 ... 93 N8
Elmhurst BELV DA17 ... 163 P5
Elmhurst Av EFNCH N2 ... 117 N1
MTCM CR4 ... 180 B10
Elmhurst Dr DORK RH4 ... 272 C4
EMPK RM11 ... 125 K5
SWFD E18 ... 101 N10
Elmhurst Rd DTCH/LGLY SL3 ... 150 D2
ELTH/MOT SE9 ... 184 N2
FSTGT E7 ... 141 N2
PEND EN3 ... 80 B3
TOTM N17 ... 99 M10
Elmhurst St CLAP SW4 ... 158 E10
Elmhurst Wy LOU IG10 ... 102 C1
Elmington Cl BXLY DA5 ... 186 E3
Elmira St LEW SE13 ... 160 G9
RPLY/SEND GU23 ... 234 A3
Elm Lawn Cl UX/CGN UB8 ... 131 P2
Elmlee Cl CHST BR7 ... 184 C9
Elmley St WOOL/PLUM SE18 ... 162 C9
Elmore Cl ALP/SUD HA0 ... 135 K4
Elmore Rd COUL/CHIP CR5 ... 240 A7
LEY E10 ... 121 H8
PEND EN3 ... 80 B3
Elmores LOU IG10 ... 82 D7
Elmore St IS N1 ... 6 G3
Elm Pk ASC SL5 ... 192 D8
BRXS/STRHM SW2 ... 180 A5
STAN HA7 ... 94 G6
Elm Park Av HCH RM12 ... 125 J6
SEVS/STOTM N15 ... 119 N3
Elm Park Gdns CHEL SW3 ... 15 L8
HDN NW4 ... 116 C3
WBPTN SW10 ... 15 L8
Elmpark Gdns SAND/SEL CR2 ... 224 B6
Elm Park La CHEL SW3 ... 15 L9
Elm Park Rd CHEL SW3 ... 15 L8
FNCH N3 ... 97 J8
LEY E10 ... 120 D6
PIN HA5 ... 113 L1
SNWD SE25 ... 203 N3
WCHMH N21 ... 99 K1
Elm Pl SKENS SW7 ... 15 L7
Elm Rd BAR EN5 ... 77 J8
BECK BR3 ... 204 E2
BH/WHM TN16 ... 263 H1
CHSGTN KT9 ... 219 K1
DART DA1 ... 187 L4
EBED/NFELT TW14 ... 174 A1
ERITH DA8 ... 165 H7
ESH/CLAY KT10 ... 218 A3
EW KT17 ... 220 C3
FSTGT E7 ... 141 L1
GRAYS RM17 ... 167 P5
GRH DA9 ... 188 D2
GVE DA12 ... 190 F6
KUTN/CMB KT2 ... 177 L10
KUTN/CMB KT2 ... 199 L1
LHD/OX KT22 ... 236 G8
MORT/ESHN SW14 ... 155 P9
MTCM CR4 ... 202 B8
NWMAL KT3 ... 200 A3
ORP BR6 ... 227 K4
PUR/KEN CR8 ... 223 J9
REDH RH1 ... 257 P10
RGODL GU7 ... 267 L9
ROMW/RG RM7 ... 104 C10
SCUP DA14 ... 185 K7
SOCK/AV RM15 ... 146 C10
THHTH CR7 ... 203 K4
WALTH E17 ... 121 H3
WAN E11 ... 121 J7
WARL CR6 ... 242 C3
WBLY HA9 ... 115 K10
WDGN N22 ... 99 J9
WDSR SL4 ... 148 C9
WOKN/KNAP GU21 ... 232 A4
Elm Rd West MRDN SM4 ... 201 J7
Elm Rw HAMP NW3 ... 117 M8
Elmroyd Av POTB/CUF EN6 ... 59 J9
Elmroyd Cl POTB/CUF EN6 ... 59 J9
Elms Av HDN NW4 ... 116 C3
MUSWH N10 ... 118 C1
Elmscott Gdns WCHMH N21 ... 79 K10
Elmscott Rd BMLY BR1 ... 183 K8
Elms Ct ALP/SUD HA0 ... 114 E9
Elms Crs CLAP SW4 ... 180 D2
Elmscroft Gdns POTB/CUF EN6 ... 59 J8
Elmsdale Rd WALTH E17 ... 120 D7
Elms Farm Rd HCH RM12 ... 125 K10
Elms Gdns ALP/SUD HA0 ... 114 F9
DAGW RM9 ... 124 A9
Elmshaw Rd PUT/ROE SW15 ... 178 D1
Elmshorn EW KT17 ... 238 F2
Elmshott La SL1 SL1 ... 135 M8
Elmside Rd WBLY HA9 ... 115 M8
Elms La ALP/SUD HA0 ... 114 F9
Elmsleigh Av KTN/HRWW/W HA3 ... 114 G2
Elmsleigh Rd STA TW18 ... 173 J8
WHTN TW2 ... 176 B3
Elmslie Cl EPSOM KT18 ... 219 P10
WFD IG8 ... 102 C3
Elms Ms BAY/PAD W2 ... 9 L7
Elms Park Av ALP/SUD HA0 ... 114 F9
Elms Rd CFSP/GDCR SL9 ... 90 B8
CLAP SW4 ... 180 D1
KTN/HRWW/W HA3 ... 94 D8
WARE SG12 ... 26 F1
Elmstead Av CHST BR7 ... 184 C8
WBLY HA9 ... 115 K6
Elmstead Cl HOR/WEW KT19 ... 220 B2
TRDG/WHET N20 ... 97 K3
Elmstead Gdns WPK KT4 ... 200 D10
Elmstead Gld CHST BR7 ... 184 C8
Elmstead La CHST BR7 ... 184 B10
Elmstead Rd BF/WBF KT14 ... 215 K9
ERITH DA8 ... 164 F7
GDMY/SEVK IG3 ... 123 H7
Elmsted Crs WELL DA16 ... 163 M5
The Elms BARN SW13 ... 156 C9
CHONG CM5 ... 67 P6
HERT/BAY SG13 ... 25 P5
Elmstone Rd FUL/PGN SW6 ... 157 K6
Elm St FSBYW WC1X ... 11 L2
Elmsway ASHF TW15 ... 174 A8
Elmswood GT/LBKH KT23 ... 235 N10
Elmsworth Av HSLW TW3 ... 154 A8
Elm Ter CRICK NW2 ... 117 K8
ELTH/MOT SE9 ... 184 C1
KTN/HRWW/W HA3 ... 94 D8
WTHK RM20 ... 166 G5
Elmton Wy STNW/STAM N16 ... 119 P8
Elmtree Av BRWN CM15 ... 86 A9
Elm Tree Av ESH/CLAY KT10 ... 198 C7
Elm Tree Cl ASHF TW15 ... 174 A8
CHERT KT16 ... 195 H9
NTHLT UB5 ... 133 N5
STJWD NW8 ... 3 L9
Elmtree Cl BF/WBF KT14 ... 215 P9
Elmtree Hl CSHM HP5 ... 50 G6
Elmtree Rd STJWD NW8 ... 3 L10
Elm Tree Rd TEDD TW11 ... 176 D8
Elm Tree Rw RKW/CH/CXG WD3 ... 71 J8
Elm Wk GPK RM2 ... 125 H1
HAMP NW3 ... 117 K7
ORP BR6 ... 206 G10
RAD WD7 ... 74 E2
RYNPK SW20 ... 200 F4
Elmway CDH/CHF RM16 ... 147 P9

Elm Wy BRW CM14 ... 106 F4
FBAR/BDGN N11 ... 98 B7
HOR/WEW KT19 ... 220 A2
RKW/CH/CXG WD3 ... 91 L2
WLSDN NW10 ... 116 B9
WPK KT4 ... 200 F10
Elmwood SBW CM21 ... 30 A2
WGCW AL8 ... 22 C6
Elmwood Av BORE WD6 ... 75 N8
FELT TW13 ... 175 J6
KTN/HRWW/W HA3 ... 114 F3
PLMGR N13 ... 98 F6
Elmwood Cl EW KT17 ... 220 D4
WLGTN SM6 ... 202 C9
Elmwood Ct ASHTD KT21 ... 237 J3
Elmwood Crs CDALE/KGS NW9 ... 115 D2
EW KT17 ... 220 D4
Elmwood Dr BXLY DA5 ... 185 P3
EW KT17 ... 220 D4
Elmwood Gdns HNWL W7 ... 134 D6
Elmwood Pk CHSWK W4 ... 155 P5
Elmwood Rd CHSWK W4 ... 155 P5
CROY/NA CR0 ... 203 J7
HNHL SE24 ... 181 L1
MTCM CR4 ... 202 A3
REDH RH1 ... 258 B6
SLN SL2 ... 129 N9
WOKN/KNAP GU21 ... 231 J5
Elmworth Gv DUL SE21 ... 181 L5
Elnathan Ms MV/WKIL W9 ... 9 H2
Elphinstone Rd WALTH E17 ... 100 H10
Elphinstone St HBRY N5 ... 119 J9
Elrick Cl ERITH DA8 ... 164 F5
Elrington Rd HACK E8 ... 7 N2
WFD IG8 ... 101 M6
Elruge Cl WDR/YW UB7 ... 151 N2
Elsa Rd WELL DA16 ... 163 M8
Elsa St WCHPL E1 ... 140 D7
Elsdale St HOM E9 ... 140 B1
Elsden Ms BETH E2 ... 140 B4
Elsden Rd TOTM N17 ... 99 M9
Elsenham Rd WOKN/KNAP GU21 ... 231 N4
Elsenham Rd MNPK E12 ... 122 C10
Elsenham St WIM/MER SW19 ... 179 J4
Elsham Rd WAN E11 ... 121 K8
WKENS W14 ... 14 A1
Elsiedene Rd WCHMH N21 ... 99 K1
Elsie Lane Ct BAY/PAD W2 ... 8 H2
Elsiemaud Rd BROCKY SE4 ... 182 L1
Elsie Rd EDUL SE22 ... 159 N10
Elsinge Rd EN EN1 ... 80 A2
Elsinore Av STWL/WRAY TW19 ... 173 P3
Elsinore Gdns CRICK NW2 ... 117 H8
Elsinore Rd FSTH SE23 ... 182 L4
Elsinore Wy RCH/KEW TW9 ... 155 N9
Elsley Rd BTSEA SW11 ... 158 G10
Elspeth Rd ALP/SUD HA0 ... 115 A10
BTSEA SW11 ... 158 A10
Elsrick Av MRDN SM4 ... 201 K5
Elstan Wy CROY/NA CR0 ... 204 A3
Elsted Cl CRAWW RH11 ... 285 L5
Elsted St WALW SE17 ... 19 H6
Elstow Cl ELTH/MOT SE9 ... 184 C1
RSLP HA4 ... 77 J4
Elstow Gdns DAGW RM9 ... 143 P3
Elstow Rd DAGW RM9 ... 143 P2
Elstree Gdns BELV DA17 ... 163 P3
ED N9 ... 100 A2
IL IG1 ... 122 F10
Elstree Hl BMLY BR1 ... 183 H10
Elstree Hl North BORE WD6 ... 75 J9
Elstree Hl South BORE WD6 ... 95 J1
Elstree Rd BORE WD6 ... 74 F10
BUSH WD23 ... 94 C2
STAN HA7 ... 94 E1
Elstree Wy BORE WD6 ... 75 P6
Elswick Rd LEW SE13 ... 160 G9
Elswick St FUL/PGN SW6 ... 157 N8
Elsworth Cl EBED/NFELT TW14 ... 174 F4
Elsworthy THDIT KT7 ... 198 D6
Elsworthy Ri HAMP NW3 ... 3 P4
Elsworthy Rd HAMP NW3 ... 3 N5
Elsworthy Ter HAMP NW3 ... 3 P4
Eltham Av SL1 SL1 ... 128 D10
Eltham Green Road Rd
ELTH/MOT SE9 ... 183 P1
Eltham Green Rd ELTH/MOT SE9 ... 161 P10
Eltham High St ELTH/MOT SE9 ... 184 C2
Eltham Hl ELTH/MOT SE9 ... 184 A1
Eltham Palace Rd
ELTH/MOT SE9 ... 184 A2
Eltham Park Gdns ELTH/MOT SE9 ... 162 D10
Eltham Rd ELTH/MOT SE9 ... 183 P1
Elthiron Rd FUL/PGN SW6 ... 157 K7
Elthorne Av HNWL W7 ... 154 E2
Elthorne Ct FELT TW13 ... 175 K4
Elthorne Park Rd HNWL W7 ... 154 E2
Elthorne Rd ARCH N19 ... 118 C7
CDALE/KGS NW9 ... 116 A5
UX/CGN UB8 ... 131 N4
Elthorne Wy CDALE/KGS NW9 ... 116 A4
Elthruda Rd LEW SE13 ... 183 J2
Eltisley Rd IL IG1 ... 122 E9
Elton Av ALP/SUD HA0 ... 114 F3
BAR EN5 ... 77 J9
GFD/PVL UB6 ... 134 E1
Elton Cl STNW/STAM N16 ... 119 M10
Elton Pl STNW/STAM N16 ... 119 M10
Elton Rd HERT/WAS SG14 ... 25 K4
KUTN/CMB KT2 ... 199 L1
PUR/KEN CR8 ... 222 D8
Eltringham St
WAND/EARL SW18 ... 157 M10
Elvaston Ms SKENS SW7 ... 15 K4
Elvaston Pl SKENS SW7 ... 15 J4
Elveden Cl WOKS/MYFD GU22 ... 233 L3
Elveden Pl WLSDN NW10 ... 135 M4
Elveden Rd COB KT11 ... 217 J7
WLSDN NW10 ... 135 M4
Elvendon Rd FBAR/BDGN N11 ... 98 B7
Elverson Rd DEPT SE8 ... 160 G8
Elverton St WEST SW1P ... 17 J5
Elver Av EMPK RM11 ... 125 K4
Elvington Gn HAYES BR2 ... 205 L5
Elvington La CDALE/KGS NW9 ... 96 B9
Elvino Rd SYD SE26 ... 182 D6
Elvis Rd CRICK NW2 ... 136 F1
Elwell Cl EGH TW20 ... 172 D9
Elwick Rd SOCK/AV RM15 ... 147 H8
Elwill Wy BECK BR3 ... 205 J4
Elwin St BETH E2 ... 7 N9
Elwood St HLWE CM17 ... 47 P2
Elworthy HBRY N5 ... 119 J8
Elwyn Gdns LEE/GVPK SE12 ... 183 M3
Ely Cl AL SL SL1 ... 129 L1
Ely Cl AMSS HP7 ... 69 K5
ERITH DA8 ... 164 C3
HAT AL10 ... 40 C3
NWMAL KT3 ... 200 C2
WOKN/KNAP GU21 ... 231 H3
Ely Cottages VX/NE SW8 ... 158 G6
Ely Gdns BORE WD6 ... 76 A9
DAGE RM10 ... 124 D9
Elyne Rd FSBYPK N4 ... 119 J6
Ely Pl HCIRC EC1N ... 12 B4
Ely Rd CROY/NA CR0 ... 203 L5
HSLWW TW4 ... 153 K9
HTHAIR TW6 ... 152 D8
LEY E10 ... 121 H4
STAL AL1 ... 38 C7
Elysian Av STMC/STPC BR5 ... 207 H6
Elysium Pl FUL/PGN SW6 ... 157 J8
Elysium St FUL/PGN SW6 ... 157 J8
Elystan Cl WLGTN SM6 ... 222 D5
Elystan Pl CHEL SW3 ... 15 N7
Elystan St CHEL SW3 ... 15 M6
Elystan Wk IS N1 ... 6 A1
Emanuel Av ACT W3 ... 135 P8

Embankment PUT/ROE SW15 ... 156 G9
Embankment Gdns CHEL SW3 ... 16 B9
The Embankment
STWL/WRAY TW19 ... 171 P3
TWK TW1 ... 176 F4
Embassey Ct SCUP DA14 ... 185 L6
Emba St BERM/RHTH SE16 ... 19 P2
Ember Cl ADL/WDHM KT15 ... 215 N10
STMC/STPC BR5 ... 206 F7
Embercourt Rd THDIT KT7 ... 198 A6
Ember Farm Av E/WMO/HCT KT8 ... 198 C6
Ember Farm Wy
E/WMO/HCT KT8 ... 198 C5
Ember Gdns ESH/CLAY KT10 ... 198 D7
Ember La ESH/CLAY KT10 ... 198 C8
Ember Rd DTCH/LGLY SL3 ... 150 E2
Emberson Wy EPP CM16 ... 66 C2
Embleton Rd LEW SE13 ... 160 G10
OXHEY WD19 ... 93 H4
Embry Cl STAN HA7 ... 94 F5
Embry Dr STAN HA7 ... 94 F6
Embry Wy STAN HA7 ... 94 F6
Emden Cl WDR/YW UB7 ... 152 B1
Emden St FUL/PGN SW6 ... 157 L7
Emerald Cl CAN/RD E16 ... 142 B8
Emerald Ct SL SL1 ... 149 K1
Emerald Gdns BCTR RM8 ... 124 B6
Emerald Sq NWDGN UB2 ... 153 L2
Emerald St BMSBY WC1N ... 11 M3
Emerson Dr EMPK RM11 ... 125 L5
Emerson Gdns
KTN/HRWW/W HA3 ... 115 L4
Emersons Av SWLY BR8 ... 186 G10
Emerson Rd STHWK SE1 ... 12 E9
Emerton Cl BXLYHS DA6 ... 163 P10
Emerton Rd LHD/OX KT22 ... 236 B6
Emerton Garden BERK HP4 ... 33 K2
Emery Hill St WEST SW1P ... 17 H4
Emery St STHWK SE1 ... 18 B3
Emes Rd ERITH DA8 ... 165 K1
Emilia Cl PEND EN3 ... 80 A1
Emily Pl HOLWY N7 ... 119 H9
Emily St CAN/RD E16 ... 141 L8
Emlyn La LHD/OX KT22 ... 236 F8
REDH RH1 ... 276 B2
SHB W12 ... 156 B1
Emmanuel Cl GUW GU2 ... 249 N2
Emmanuel Rd BAL SW12 ... 180 D4
NTHWD HA6 ... 92 G8
Emma's Crs WARE SG12 ... 26 C7
Emma St BETH E2 ... 140 A4
Emmaus Wy CHIG IG7 ... 102 D6
Emmetts Cl WOKN/KNAP GU21 ... 232 A3
Emmetts Rd BH/WHM TN16 ... 263 H6
Emmitt Cl RAD WD7 ... 57 K9
Emmott Av BARK/HLT IG6 ... 122 F5
Emmott Cl WCHPL E1 ... 140 G6
Empire Ct BERK HP4 ... 33 L2
Emperor's Ga SKENS SW7 ... 15 J5
Empire Av UED N18 ... 99 K9
Empire Rd GFD/PVL UB6 ... 135 K4
Empire Vls REDH RH1 ... 276 B10
Empire Wy WBLY HA9 ... 115 L9
Empire Wharf Rd POP/IOD E14 ... 161 J3
Empress Av CHING E4 ... 100 F8
IL IG1 ... 122 C7
MNPK E12 ... 121 P7
WFD IG8 ... 101 L8
Empress Dr CHST BR7 ... 184 E9
Empress Pl ECT SW5 ... 14 E8
Empress St WALW SE17 ... 18 F9
Empson St BOW E3 ... 140 G6
Emsworth Cl CRAWE RH10 ... 284 D10
ED N9 ... 100 B2
Emsworth Rd BARK/HLT IG6 ... 102 E10
Emsworth St BRXS/STRHM SW2 ... 180 A5
Emu Rd VX/NE SW8 ... 158 C8
Enborne Gn SOCK/AV RM15 ... 146 F7
Enbrook St NKENS W10 ... 2 B10
Endale Cl CAR SM5 ... 202 A9
Endeavour Rd CHES/WCR EN8 ... 62 A9
Endeavour Wy BARK IG11 ... 143 K4
CROY/NA CR0 ... 202 E4
WIM/MER SW19 ... 179 L7
Endell St LSQ/SEVD WC2H ... 11 L5
Enderby St GNWCH SE10 ... 161 K4
Enderley Rd KTN/HRWW/W HA3 ... 94 D9
Endersby Rd BAR EN5 ... 76 F7
Endersleigh Gdns HDN NW4 ... 116 D2
Endlebury Rd CHING E4 ... 101 H3
Endlesham Rd BAL SW12 ... 180 B3
Endsleigh Cl SAND/SEL CR2 ... 224 B6
Endsleigh Gdns IL IG1 ... 122 C6
STPAN WC1H ... 11 J1
SURB KT6 ... 199 H6
WOT/HER KT12 ... 217 K2
Endsleigh Pl STPAN WC1H ... 11 K1
Endsleigh Rd NWDGN UB2 ... 153 N3
REDH RH1 ... 258 D5
Endsleigh St STPAN WC1H ... 11 K1
Endway BRYLDS KT5 ... 199 M7
Endwell Rd BROCKY SE4 ... 160 B8
Endymion Ct HAT AL10 ... 40 F3
Endymion Ms HAT AL10 ... 40 F3
Endymion Rd BRXS/STRHM SW2 ... 180 G3
FSBYPK N4 ... 119 J3
HAT AL10 ... 40 F3
Enfield Cl UX/CGN UB8 ... 131 N4
Enfield Rd ACT W3 ... 155 N1
BTFD TW8 ... 155 A4
EBAR EN4 ... 78 E8
HTHAIR TW6 ... 152 B7
IS N1 ... 7 K4
Enford St MBLAR W1H ... 10 A3
Engadine Cl CROY/NA CR0 ... 203 N10
Engadine St WAND/EARL SW18 ... 179 J4
Engate St LEW SE13 ... 161 H10
Engayne Gdns UPMR RM14 ... 126 A6
Engel Pk MLHL NW7 ... 97 H6
Engineer Cl WOOL/PLUM SE18 ... 162 D5
Engineers Wy WBLY HA9 ... 115 M9
England's La HAMP NW3 ... 4 A1
LOU IG10 ... 82 D6
Englefield Cl CROY/NA CR0 ... 203 K6
EGH TW20 ... 171 P9
ENC/FH EN2 ... 79 H6
STMC/STPC BR5 ... 207 J4
Englefield Crs STMC/STPC BR5 ... 207 K4
Englefield Pth STMC/STPC BR5 ... 207 K4
Englefield Rd IS N1 ... 7 H3
WOKN/KNAP GU21 ... 231 H3
Engleheart Dr EBED/NFELT TW14 ... 174 B1
Engleheart Rd CAT SE6 ... 182 G3
Englehurst ECH TW20 ... 171 P9
HARP AL5 ... 20 C2
Englemere Pk COB KT11 ... 218 A10
Englewood Rd CLAP SW4 ... 180 C2
Engliff La WOKS/MYFD GU22 ... 233 A10
English Gdns STWL/WRAY TW19 ... 150 A10
English St BOW E3 ... 140 E6
Enid Cl LCOL/BKTW AL2 ... 55 L7
Enid St STHWK SE1 ... 19 M3
Enmore Av SNWD SE25 ... 203 P5
Enmore Gdns MORT/ESHN SW14 ... 178 A1
Enmore Rd PUT/ROE SW15 ... 156 G10
SNWD SE25 ... 203 P5
STHL UB1 ... 133 P6
Ennerdale Av HCH RM12 ... 125 H5
STAN HA7 ... 115 H1
Ennerdale Cl CRAWW RH11 ... 283 L9

EBED/NFELT TW14 ... 174 G4
STAL AL1 ... 38 C2
SUT SM1 ... 221 J1
Ennerdale Dr CDALE/KGS NW9 ... 116 B7
Ennerdale Gdns WBLY HA9 ... 115 H6
RCH/KEW TW9 ... 155 L8
Ennersdale Rd LEW SE13 ... 183 J1
Ennis Cl HARP AL5 ... 20 C5
Ennis Rd FSBYPK N4 ... 119 H6
WOOL/PLUM SE18 ... 162 G5
Ensign Cl PUR/KEN CR8 ... 223 L10
STWL/WRAY TW19 ... 173 N4
Ensign Dr PLMGR N13 ... 99 K4
Ensign St WCHPL E1 ... 13 N1
Enslin Rd ELTH/MOT SE9 ... 184 D2
Ensor Ms SKENS SW7 ... 15 L7
Enstone Rd HGDN/ICK UB10 ... 112 A8
Enterdent Rd GDST RH9 ... 260 B10
Enterprise Cl CROY/NA CR0 ... 203 H8
Enterprise Rw
SEVS/STOTM N15 ... 119 N3
Enterprise Wy TEDD TW11 ... 176 B8
WAND/EARL SW18 ... 157 K10
WLSDN NW10 ... 136 C5
Enterprize Wy DEPT SE8 ... 160 E3
Eothen Cl CTHM CR3 ... 241 P10
Epirus Ms FUL/PGN SW6 ... 157 K6
Epirus Rd FUL/PGN SW6 ... 157 K6
Epping Cl POP/IOD E14 ... 160 F5
ROMW/RG RM7 ... 124 C1
Epping Gn HHNE HP2 ... 36 C1
Epping La ABR/ST RM4 ... 83 L6
Epping New Rd BKHH IG9 ... 101 N1
LOU IG10 ... 82 A4
Epping Pl HOLWY N7 ... 6 B2
Epping Rd CHONG CM5 ... 48 G10
EPP CM16 ... 46 E10
EPP CM16 ... 65 N4
EPP CM16 ... 66 B6
LOU IG10 ... 82 C1
WAB EN9 ... 46 C6
Epping Wk CRAWE RH10 ... 284 A9
Epping Wy CHING E4 ... 80 G10
Epple Rd FUL/PGN SW6 ... 157 J7
Epsom Cl BXLYHS DA7 ... 164 C9
NTHLT UB5 ... 113 N10
Epsom La North
KWD/TDW/WH KT20 ... 238 E5
Epsom La South
KWD/TDW/WH KT20 ... 238 F7
Epsom Rd ASHTD KT21 ... 237 L4
CRAWE RH10 ... 284 B9
CROY/NA CR0 ... 223 H1
EHSLY KT24 ... 252 E5
EW KT17 ... 220 C7
GDMY/SEVK IG3 ... 123 J4
GU GU1 ... 268 C1
LEY E10 ... 121 H4
LHD/OX KT22 ... 236 G7
MRDN SM4 ... 201 J7
RGUE GU4 ... 250 D9
RGUE GU4 ... 251 N7
Epsom Wy HCH RM12 ... 125 H9
Epstein Rd THMD SE28 ... 143 L10
Epworth Rd ISLW TW7 ... 154 C6
Epworth St SDTCH EC2A ... 13 H2
Erasmus St WEST SW1P ... 17 J7
Ercorwald St ACT W3 ... 136 C8
Eresby Dr BECK BR3 ... 204 F8
Erica Cl CHOB/PIR GU24 ... 212 D9
SL SL1 ... 128 D9
Erica Ct WOKS/MYFD GU22 ... 232 A12
Erica St SHB W12 ... 136 D9
Erica Wy CRAWE RH10 ... 284 G2
Eric Clarke La BARK IG11 ... 142 F6
Ericcson Cl WAND/EARL SW18 ... 179 K1
Eric Rd CHDH RM6 ... 123 N5
FSTGT E7 ... 121 M9
WLSDN NW10 ... 136 C1
Eric St BOW E3 ... 140 E6
Eridge Cl CRAWE RH10 ... 284 D10
Eridge Green Cl STMC/STPC BR5 ... 207 M8
Eridge Rd CHSWK W4 ... 156 A2
Erin Cl BMLY BR1 ... 183 K10
Erindale WOOL/PLUM SE18 ... 162 C6
Erindale Ter WOOL/PLUM SE18 ... 162 C6
Eriswell Crs WOT/HER KT12 ... 216 G3
Eriswell Rd WOT/HER KT12 ... 216 G4
Erith Ct PUR RM19 ... 165 P3
Erith Crs CRW RM5 ... 104 E1
Erith High St ERITH DA8 ... 164 F1
Erith Rd BELV DA17 ... 164 C4
BXLYHS DA7 ... 164 C3
Erkenwald Cl CHERT KT16 ... 195 H6
Erlanger Rd NWCR SE14 ... 160 C2
Erlesmere Gdns HNWL W7 ... 154 C2
Ermine Cl CHESW EN7 ... 62 A2
HSLWW TW4 ... 153 K8
STALW/RED AL3 ... 37 P7
Ermine Rd LEW SE13 ... 160 G10
SEVS/STOTM N15 ... 119 N4
Ermine Side EN EN1 ... 79 N4
Ermington Rd ELTH/MOT SE9 ... 184 F5
Ermyn Cl LHD/OX KT22 ... 237 J7
Ermyn Wy LHD/OX KT22 ... 237 J7
Ernald Av EHAM E6 ... 142 B4
Ernan Cl SOCK/AV RM15 ... 146 F7
Ernan Rd SOCK/AV RM15 ... 146 F7
Erncroft Wy TWK TW1 ... 176 B2
Ernest Av WNWD SE27 ... 181 J7
Ernest Cl BECK BR3 ... 204 F5
Ernest Gdns CHSWK W4 ... 155 N5
Ernest Gv BECK BR3 ... 204 E5
Ernest Rd EMPK RM11 ... 125 M4
KUT KT1 ... 199 N2
Ernest Sq KUT KT1 ... 199 N2
Ernle Rd RYNPK SW20 ... 178 E10
Ernshaw Pl PUT/ROE SW15 ... 179 H1
Erpingham Rd PUT/ROE SW15 ... 156 G9
Erridge Rd WIM/MER SW19 ... 201 K2
Erriff Dr SOCK/AV RM15 ... 146 F7
Errington Rd MV/WKIL W9 ... 8 G1
Errington Dr WDSR SL4 ... 148 F3
Errol Gdns NWMAL KT3 ... 200 E4
YEAD UB4 ... 133 J6
Erroll Rd ROM RM1 ... 105 L2
Errol St STLK EC1Y ... 12 F2
Erskine Cl SUT SM1 ... 201 P10
Erskine Crs TOTM N17 ... 120 A2
Erskine Hl GLDGN NW11 ... 117 H2
Erskine Ms HAMP NW3 ... 4 A1
Erskine Rd HAMP NW3 ... 3 P1
SUT SM1 ... 221 P1
WALTH E17 ... 120 C2
Erwood Rd CHARL SE7 ... 162 B4
Esam Wy STRHM/NOR SW16 ... 181 N8
Escombe Dr GUW GU2 ... 249 N5
Escot Rd SUN TW16 ... 174 F10
Escott Pl CHERT KT16 ... 214 F3
Escot Wy BAR EN5 ... 76 F7
Escreet Gv WOOL/PLUM SE18 ... 162 D4

Esdaile Gdns UPMR RM14 ... 126 C5
Esdaile La HOD EN11 ... 44 H4
Esher Av CHEAM SM3 ... 200 G10
ROMW/RG RM7 ... 124 D4
WOT/HER KT12 ... 197 H7
Esher Cl BXLY DA5 ... 185 P4
ESH/CLAY KT10 ... 218 A2
Esher Crs HTHAIR TW6 ... 152 C8
Esher Gn ESH/CLAY KT10 ... 218 A1
Esher Green Dr ESH/CLAY KT10 ... 197 P10
Esher Ms MTCM CR4 ... 202 B3
Esher Park Av ESH/CLAY KT10 ... 218 B2
Esher Place Av ESH/CLAY KT10 ... 217 P1
Esher Rd GDMY/SEVK IG3 ... 123 K8
WOT/HER KT12 ... 217 M1
Eskdale LCOL/BKTW AL2 ... 57 L3
Eskdale Av CSHM HP5 ... 51 J6
NTHLT UB5 ... 133 N5
Eskdale Cl RDART DA2 ... 187 M5
WBLY HA9 ... 115 J7
Eskdale Gdns PUR/KEN CR8 ... 223 L10
Eskdale Rd BXLYHS DA7 ... 164 B8
IVER SL0 ... 131 L4
Eskley Gdns SOCK/AV RM15 ... 146 F7
Eskmont Rdg NRWD SE19 ... 181 M10
Esk Rd PLSTW E13 ... 141 N6
Esk Wy ROM RM1 ... 104 F8
Esmar Crs CDALE/KGS NW9 ... 116 D5
Esmeralda Rd STHWK SE1 ... 19 P6
Esmond Cl RAIN RM13 ... 145 J2
Esmond Rd CHSWK W4 ... 156 A2
KIL/WHAMP NW6 ... 2 D6
Esmond St PUT/ROE SW15 ... 157 H10
Esparto St WAND/EARL SW18 ... 157 L3
Essendene Cl CTHM CR3 ... 241 M9
Essendene Rd CTHM CR3 ... 241 M9
Essenden Rd BELV DA17 ... 164 B4
SAND/SEL CR2 ... 223 M4
Essendine Rd MV/WKIL W9 ... 8 F1
Essendon Gdns WCCE AL7 ... 23 J5
Essendon Hl BRKMPK AL9 ... 41 P5
Essex Av ISLW TW7 ... 154 D9
SL SL1 ... 129 H7
Essex Cl ADL/WDHM KT15 ... 215 M1
MRDN SM4 ... 200 G3
ROMW/RG RM7 ... 124 C2
RSLP HA4 ... 113 L6
WALTH E17 ... 120 C4
Essex Ct BARN SW13 ... 156 C8
Essex Gdns EMPK RM11 ... 125 J4
FSBYPK N4 ... 119 J4
SLH/COR SS17 ... 169 K1
Essex Gv NRWD SE19 ... 181 L9
Essex La ABLGY WD5 ... 54 E9
Essex Pk FNCH N3 ... 97 L7
Essex Park Ms ACT W3 ... 136 B10
Essex Pl CHSWK W4 ... 155 P3
Essex Place Sq CHSWK W4 ... 156 A3
Essex Rd ACT W3 ... 135 P9
BARK IG11 ... 142 C2
BORE WD6 ... 76 A3
CHDH RM6 ... 123 M6
CHING E4 ... 101 K2
CHSWK W4 ... 156 A3
CSHM HP5 ... 51 H5
DAGE RM10 ... 124 D10
DART DA1 ... 187 L3
ENC/FH EN2 ... 79 L8
GVW DA11 ... 190 D4
HART DA3 ... 211 J2
HOD EN11 ... 44 G3
IS N1 ... 6 F4
LEY E10 ... 121 H4
ROMW/RG RM7 ... 124 C2
SWFD E18 ... 101 N10
WALTH E17 ... 120 D4
WAT WD17 ... 73 H5
WLSDN NW10 ... 136 B2
WTHK RM20 ... 166 F5
Essex Rd South WAN E11 ... 121 J5
Essex St FSTGT E7 ... 121 M10
STAL AL1 ... 38 D5
TPL/STR WC2R ... 12 A6
Essex Vls KENS W8 ... 14 E2
Essex Wy CHONG CM5 ... 66 G5
EPP CM16 ... 66 G5
RBRW/HUT CM13 ... 107 K8
Essian St WCHPL E1 ... 140 D7
Essoldo Wy EDGW HA8 ... 115 L1
Estate Wy LEY E10 ... 120 E6
Estcourt Rd FUL/PGN SW6 ... 157 J5
SNWD SE25 ... 204 A6
WAT WD17 ... 73 K4
Estella Av NWMAL KT3 ... 200 G4
Estelle Rd HAMP NW3 ... 118 A9
Este Rd BTSEA SW11 ... 157 P9
Estfeld Cl HOD EN11 ... 26 G10
Esther Cl WCHMH N21 ... 99 H1
Esther Rd WAN E11 ... 121 K5
Estoria Cl BRXS/STRHM SW2 ... 181 H3
Estreham Rd STRHM/NOR SW16 ... 181 P10
Estridge Cl HSLW TW3 ... 153 P10
Estuary Cl BARK IG11 ... 143 L3
Eswyn Rd TOOT SW17 ... 180 A7
Etchingham Park Rd FNCH N3 ... 97 L7
Etchingham Rd SRTFD E15 ... 121 H10
Etfield Gv SCUP DA14 ... 185 L6
Ethelbert Cl HAYES BR2 ... 205 M2
Ethelbert Gdns GNTH/NBYPK IG2 ... 122 C3
Ethelbert Rd BMLY BR1 ... 205 M3
ERITH DA8 ... 164 D5
RYNPK SW20 ... 200 C1
STMC/STPC BR5 ... 207 N3
Ethelbert St BAL SW12 ... 180 C4
Ethelberga Rd HARH RM3 ... 105 N9
Etheldene Av MUSWH N10 ... 118 C2
Ethelden Rd SHB W12 ... 136 E10
Ethelred Cl WGCE AL7 ... 23 J6
Ethel Rd ASHF TW15 ... 173 P9
CAN/RD E16 ... 18 F6
Etheridge Rd CRICK NW2 ... 116 F5
LOU IG10 ... 82 F7
Etherley Rd SEVS/STOTM N15 ... 119 K3
Etherow St EDUL SE22 ... 181 P2
Etherstone Rd
STRHM/NOR SW16 ... 180 A5
Ethnard Rd PECK SE15 ... 160 A5
Ethorpe Crs CFSP/GDCR SL9 ... 110 B3
Ethronvi Rd BXLYHN DA7 ... 163 P9
Etloe Rd LEY E10 ... 120 F7
Eton Av ALP/SUD HA0 ... 115 H9
EBAR EN4 ... 77 N2
HAMP NW3 ... 3 M3
HEST TW5 ... 153 N5
NFNCH/WDSP N12 ... 97 M8
NWMAL KT3 ... 200 A5
Eton Cl DTCH/LGLY SL3 ... 149 M3
WAND/EARL SW18 ... 179 L3
Eton College Rd HAMP NW3 ... 4 A1
Eton Ct ALP/SUD HA0 ... 115 H9
STA TW18 ... 173 J8
WDSR SL4 ... 149 G3
Eton Garages HAMP NW3 ... 3 P1
Eton Gv CDALE/KGS NW9 ... 115 M1
LEW SE13 ... 161 K9
Eton Rd DTCH/LGLY SL3 ... 149 M5
HAMP NW3 ... 4 A1
HYS/HAR UB3 ... 152 C9
ORP BR6 ... 227 L4
Eton Sq WDSR SL4 ... 149 G3
Eton St RCHPK/HAM TW10 ... 177 J1
Eton Vls HAMP NW3 ... 4 A1
Eton Wy DART DA1 ... 165 K10

Eton Wick Rd WDSR SL4 ... 148 E4
Etta St DEPT SE8 ... 160 D5
Etton Cl HCH RM12 ... 125 M4
Etton Rd HSLW TW3 ... 176 B1
Ettrick St POP/IOD E14 ... 141 J8
Etwell Pl BRYLDS KT5 ... 199 J8
Euclid Wy WTHK RM20 ... 166 E3
Eugene Cl GPK RM2 ... 125 K2
Eugenia Rd BERM/RHTH SE16 ... 160 B4
Eunice Gv CSHM HP5 ... 51 J9
Eureka Rd KUT KT1 ... 199 M2
Europa Park Rd GU GU1 ... 249 P9
Europa Pl FSBYE EC1V ... 6 E10
Europa Rd HHNE HP2 ... 36 A3
Europe Rd WOOL/PLUM SE18 ... 162 C2
Eustace Pl WOOL/PLUM SE18 ... 162 C3
Eustace Rd CHDH RM6 ... 123 N5
　EHAM E6 ... 142 B5
　FUL/PGN SW6 ... 157 K6
　RGUE GU4 ... 250 G8
Euston Av WATW WD18 ... 72 G9
Euston Rd CAMTN NW1 ... 10 G1
　CROY/NA CR0 ... 203 H8
Euston Sq CAMTN NW1 ... 5 J10
Euston St CAMTN NW1 ... 11 H1
Evandale Rd BRXN/ST SW9 ... 159 H4
Evangelist Rd KTTN NW5 ... 118 C9
Evans Av GSTN WD25 ... 72 G1
Evans Cl CRAWE RH10 ... 284 E8
　GRH DA9 ... 188 F1
　RKW/CH/CXG WD3 ... 72 B9
Evansdale RAIN RM13 ... 144 G5
Evans Gv FELT TW13 ... 175 P5
　STALE/WH AL4 ... 39 H2
Evans Rd CAT SE6 ... 183 K5
Evanston Av CHING E4 ... 101 H8
Evanston Gdns REDBR IG4 ... 122 B4
Eva Rd CHDH RM6 ... 123 M5
Evelina Rd PECK SE15 ... 160 B9
　PGE/AN SE20 ... 182 B10
Eveline Rd MTCM CR4 ... 202 A1
　RSLP HA4 ... 112 C5
Evelyn Av CDALE/KGS NW9 ... 116 A2
　RSLP HA4 ... 112 C5
Evelyn Cl WHTN TW2 ... 176 A3
　WOKS/MYFD GU22 ... 232 A6
Evelyn Crs SUN TW16 ... 196 C1
Evelyn Denington Rd EHAM E6 ... 142 B6
Evelyn Dr PIN HA5 ... 93 L8
Evelyn Gdns GDST RH9 ... 260 D6
　RCH/KEW TW9 ... 155 K10
　WBPTN SW10 ... 15 L10
Evelyn Gv EA W5 ... 135 L10
　STHL UB1 ... 133 N8
Evelyn Rd CAN/RD E16 ... 141 M10
　CHSWK W4 ... 156 A1
　EBAR EN4 ... 78 A4
　RCH/KEW TW9 ... 155 K9
　RCHPK/HAM TW10 ... 177 H6
　RSEV TN14 ... 247 L2
　WALTH E17 ... 121 H2
　WIM/MER SW19 ... 179 L8
Evelyns Cl UX/CGN UB8 ... 132 B8
Evelyn Sharp Cl GPK RM2 ... 125 L1
Evelyn St DEPT SE8 ... 160 E5
Evelyn Ter RCH/KEW TW9 ... 155 K9
Evelyn Wk IS N1 ... 6 G8
Evelyn Wy COB KT11 ... 235 N2
　SUN TW16 ... 196 C1
　WLGTN SM6 ... 222 E1
Evensyde WATW WD18 ... 72 D10
Evenwood Cl PUT/ROE SW15 ... 179 H1
Everard Av HAYES BR2 ... 205 M8
　SL SL1 ... 149 K1
Everard Cl STAL AL1 ... 38 C8
Everard Wy WBLY HA9 ... 115 K8
Everatt Cl WAND/EARL SW18 ... 179 J2
Everdon Rd BARN SW13 ... 156 D5
Everest Cl GVW DA11 ... 190 B6
Everest Ct WOKN/KNAP GU21 ... 231 K2
Everest Pl POP/IOD E14 ... 141 H7
　SWLY BR8 ... 208 E4
Everest Rd ELTH/MOT SE9 ... 184 B1
　STWL/WRAY TW19 ... 173 N3
Everett Cl BUSH WD23 ... 94 D2
　CHESW EN7 ... 61 K1
　PIN HA5 ... 112 C1
Everglade BH/WHM TN16 ... 244 A4
Everglade Cl HART DA3 ... 211 L4
Everglade Strd CDALE/KGS NW9 ... 96 C9
Evergreen Oak Av WDSR SL4 ... 149 N8
Evergreen Wk HHS/BOV HP3 ... 35 P8
Evergreen Wy HYS/HAR UB3 ... 132 F9
　STWL/WRAY TW19 ... 173 N3
Evering Rd CLPT E5 ... 119 J7
　STNW/STAM N16 ... 119 N8
Everington Rd MUSWH N10 ... 98 A10
Everington St HMSMTH W6 ... 156 C5
Everitt Rd WLSDN NW10 ... 136 A5
Everlands Cl WOKS/MYFD GU22 ... 232 B4
Everlasting La STALW/RED AL3 ... 38 B4
Everleigh St FSBYPK N4 ... 118 G6
Eve Rd ISLW TW7 ... 154 F10
　SRTFD E15 ... 121 K10
　TOTM N17 ... 119 M1
　WOKN/KNAP GU21 ... 232 E1
Eversfield Gdns EDGW HA8 ... 96 B8
Eversfield Rd RCH/KEW TW9 ... 155 L8
　REIG RH2 ... 257
Evershot St CAMTN NW1 ... 5 H8
Evershot Rd FSBYPK N4 ... 118 G6
Eversleigh Gdns UPMR RM14 ... 126 C6
Eversleigh Rd BAR EN5 ... 77 M9
　BTSEA SW11 ... 158 A9
　EHAM E6 ... 142 A4
　FNCH N3 ... 97 J8
Eversley Av BXLYHN DA7 ... 164 F8
　WBLY HA9 ... 115 M7
Eversley Cl WCHMH N21 ... 78 G10
　ISLW TW7 ... 154 C7
Eversley Crs ISLW TW7 ... 154 C7
　RSLP HA4 ... 112 F7
　WCHMH N21 ... 78 G10
Eversley Cross BXLYHN DA7 ... 164 F8
Eversley Mt WCHMH N21 ... 78 G10
Eversley Pk WIM/MER SW19 ... 178 E8
Eversley Park Rd WCHMH N21 ... 78 G10
Eversley Rd BRYLDS KT5 ... 199 L6
　CHARL SE7 ... 161 N5
　NRWD SE19 ... 181 L10
Eversley Wy CROY/NA CR0 ... 204 F10
　EGH TW20 ... 194 F2
Everthorpe Rd PECK SE15 ... 159 N9
Everton Buildings CAMTN NW1 ... 4 G10
Everton Dr STAN HA7 ... 115 L1
Everton Rd CROY/NA CR0 ... 203 N1
Evesham Av WALTH E17 ... 100 F10
Evesham Cl BELMT SM2 ... 221 K4
　GFD/PVL UB6 ... 134 A4
　REIG RH2 ... 257
Evesham Gn MRDN SM4 ... 201 L6
Evesham Rd FBAR/BDGN N11 ... 98 D6
　GVE DA12 ... 190 G5
　MRDN SM4 ... 201 L6
　REIG RH2 ... 257
　SRTFD E15 ... 141 L2
Evesham Rd North REIG RH2 ... 257 J9
Evesham St NTCHL W11 ... 136 C9
Evesham Wk BRXN/ST SW9 ... 159 H9
　CMBW SE5 ... 159 L9
Evesham Wy BTSEA SW11 ... 158 D9
　CLAY IG5 ... 122 D1
Evreham Rd IVER SL0 ... 131 H3
Evry Rd SCUP DA14 ... 185 M9
Ewald Rd FUL/PGN SW6 ... 157
Ewanrigg Ter WFD IG8 ... 101 P6
Ewan Rd HARH RM3 ... 105 L10
Ewart Gv WDGN N22 ... 99 H9

Ewart Pl BOW E3 ... 140 E4
Ewart St FSTH SE23 ... 182
Ewe Cl HOLWY N7 ... 5 M1
Ewelands HORL RH6 ... 280 D3
Ewell By-pass EW KT17 ... 220 D4
Ewell Court Av HOR/WEW KT19 ... 220 B2
Ewell Downs Rd EW KT17 ... 220 D7
Ewell House Gv EW KT17 ... 220 C6
Ewellhurst Rd CLAY IG5 ... 102 B10
Ewell Park Gdns EW KT17 ... 220 D4
Ewell Park Wy EW KT17 ... 220 D3
Ewell Rd CHEAM SM3 ... 220 G3
　SURB KT6 ... 199 L6
　THDIT KT7 ... 198 D7
Ewelme Rd FSTH SE23 ... 182 B4
Ewen Crs BRXS/STRHM SW2 ... 181 H3
Ewer St STHWK SE1 ... 12 E10
Ewhurst Av SAND/SEL CR2 ... 223 N6
Ewhurst Cl BELMT SM2 ... 220 F5
　CRAWW RH11 ... 283 M7
Ewhurst Rd CRAWW RH11 ... 283 L7
Ewood La RDKG RH5 ... 278 A5
Exbury Rd CAT SE6 ... 182 F5
Excalibur Cl CRAWW RH11 ... 283 H8
Excelsior Cl KUT KT1 ... 199 M2
Exchange Rd ASC SL5 ... 192 B5
　CRAWE RH10 ... 283 P7
　WATW WD18 ... 73 J8
Exchange St ROM RM1 ... 124 F3
Exeforde Av ASHF TW15 ... 174 B7
Exeter Cl EHAM E6 ... 142 C6
　WATN WD24 ... 73 K6
Exeter Gdns IL IG1 ... 122 C6
Exeter Rd CAN/RD E16 ... 141 M7
　CRICK NW2 ... 117 H10
　CROY/NA CR0 ... 203 M7
　DAGE RM10 ... 144 C1
　ED N9 ... 100 B3
　FELT TW13 ... 175 N6
　GVE DA12 ... 190 G6
　HTHAIR TW6 ... 152 F2
　PEND EN3 ... 80 C7
　RYLN/HDSTN HA2 ... 113 M7
　STHGT/OAK N14 ... 98 C2
　WALTH E17 ... 120 F5
　WELL DA16 ... 163 M7
Exeter St COVGDN WC2E ... 11 M7
Exeter Wy HTHAIR TW6 ... 152 F8
　NWCR SE14 ... 160 E6
Exford Gdns LEE/GVPK SE12 ... 183 N4
Exford Rd LEE/GVPK SE12 ... 183 N5
Exhibition Rd BAY/PAD W2 ... 15 M1
　SKENS SW7 ... 15 M5
Exit Rd EFNCH N2 ... 97 N10
Exmoor Cl BARK/HLT IG6 ... 102 F4
Exmoor St NKENS W10 ... 136 G6
Exmouth Market CLKNW EC1R ... 12 A1
Exmouth Ms CAMTN NW1 ... 5 H10
Exmouth Pl HACK E8 ... 140 A2
Exmouth Rd GRAYS RM17 ... 167 N5
　RSLP HA4 ... 113 K8
　WALTH E17 ... 120 E3
　WELL DA16 ... 163 M7
　YEAD UB4 ... 132 F5
Exmouth St WCHPL E1 ... 140 B8
Exning Rd CAN/RD E16 ... 141 L6
Exon St WALW SE17 ... 19 J6
Explorer Av STWL/WRAY TW19 ... 173 P4
Explorer Dr WATW WD18 ... 72 G10
Express Dr GDMY/SEVK IG3 ... 123 L6
Extension Rd HERT/BAY SG13 ... 25 N5
Exton Crs WLSDN NW10 ... 135 P2
Exton Gdns BCTR RM8 ... 123 N10
Exton St STHWK SE1 ... 12 A10
Eyhurst Av HCH RM12 ... 125 H8
Eyhurst Cl CRICK NW2 ... 116 D7
　KWD/TDW/WH KT20 ... 239 J10
Eyhurst Sp KWD/TDW/WH KT20 ... 239 J10
Eylewood Rd WNWD SE27 ... 181 N8
Eynella Rd DUL SE21 ... 181 N3
Eynham Rd SHB W12 ... 136 F8
Eynsford Cl STMC/STPC BR5 ... 206 F7
Eynsford Crs SCUP DA14 ... 185 M4
Eynsford Ri EYN DA4 ... 229 L1
Eynsford Rd EYN DA4 ... 209 N8
　GDMY/SEVK IG3 ... 123 H7
　GRH DA9 ... 189 H1
　SWLY BR8 ... 208 F6
Eynsham Dr ABYW SE2 ... 163 L2
Eynswood Dr SCUP DA14 ... 185 L8
Eyot Gdns HMSMTH W6 ... 156 C4
Eyre Cl GPK RM2 ... 125 J2
Eyre Street HI CLKNW EC1R ... 12 A1
Eyston Dr WEY KT13 ... 216 B6
Eythorne Rd BRXN/ST SW9 ... 159 H4
Eywood Rd STAL AL1 ... 38 B4
Ezra St BETH E2 ... 7 M9

F

Faber Gdns HDN NW4 ... 116 D3
Fabian Rd FUL/PGN SW6 ... 157 J6
Fabian St EHAM E6 ... 142 C6
Fackenden La BGR/WK TN15 ... 229 P9
Factory La CROY/NA CR0 ... 203 H9
　TOTM N17 ... 99 N10
Factory Pl POP/IOD E14 ... 160 G4
Factory Rd CAN/RD E16 ... 142 A10
　GVW DA11 ... 189 P2
Factory Yd HNWL W7 ... 134 D10
Faesten Wy BXLY DA5 ... 186 F6
Faggots Cl RAD WD7 ... 75 H1
Faggotters La HLWE CM17 ... 30 F10
Faggs Rd EBED/NFELT TW14 ... 152 C10
　EBED/NFELT TW14 ... 153 H10
Fagus Av RAIN RM13 ... 145 L5
Faints Cl CHESW EN7 ... 61 M5
Fairacre HHS/BOV HP3 ... 36 A10
　NWMAL KT3 ... 200 B3
Fairacres COB KT11 ... 217
Fair Acres HAYES BR2 ... 205 M5
Fairacres KWD/TDW/WH KT20 ... 238
　RSLP HA4 ... 112 G5
Fairacres Cl POTB/CUF EN6 ... 59 J9
Fairbairn Gn BRXN/ST SW9 ... 159
Fairbank Av ORP BR6 ... 206
Fairbank Cl CHONG CM5 ... 67 N5
Fairbanks Rd TOTM N17 ... 119 P1
Fairborne Wy GUW GU2 ... 249 N7
Fairbourne COB KT11 ... 217
Fairbourne Cl WOKN/KNAP GU21 ... 231
Fairbourne La CTHM CR3 ... 241
Fairbridge Rd ARCH N19 ... 118
Fairbrook Cl PLMGR N13 ... 99
Fairburn Cl BORE WD6 ... 75
Fairby La HART DA3 ... 211
Fairby Rd LEE/GVPK SE12 ... 183
Fairchild Cl BTSEA SW11 ... 157
Fairchildes Av CROY/NA CR0 ... 225
Fairchildes Rd WARL CR6 ... 243
Fairchild Pl SDTCH EC2A ... 13 K2
Fairchild St SDTCH EC2A ... 13 K2
Fair Cl BUSH WD23 ... 94 A1
Fairclough St WCHPL E1 ... 13
Faircroft SL SL2 ... 128
Faircross Av BARK IG11 ... 142
　CRW RM5 ... 104
Faircross Wy STAL AL1 ... 38
Fairdale Gdns HYS/HAR UB3 ... 156
　PUT/ROE SW15 ... 156
Fairdene Rd COUL/CHIP CR5 ... 240
Fairey Av HYS/HAR UB3 ... 152
Fairfax Av EW KT17 ... 220
　REDH RH1 ... 258

　WLSDN NW10 ... 136 B4
Fairfax Cl WOT/HER KT12 ... 197 J8
Fairfax Gdns BKHTH/KID SE3 ... 161 P2
　WPK KT4 ... 220 F1
Fairfax Pl KIL/WHAMP NW6 ... 3 K3
Fairfax Rd CEND/HSY/T N8 ... 119 H2
　CHSWK W4 ... 156 B2
　GRAYS RM17 ... 167 N4
　HERT/BAY SG13 ... 25 N4
　KIL/WHAMP NW6 ... 3 K3
　TEDD TW11 ... 176 F10
　TIL RM18 ... 168 C7
　WOKS/MYFD GU22 ... 232 E6
Fairfax Wy MUSWH N10 ... 98 B8
Fairfield GVE DA12 ... 191 H8
Fairfield Ap STWL/WRAY TW19 ... 172 A2
　DTCH/LGLY SL3 ... 149 P6
　EDGW HA8 ... 95 N7
　HDN NW4 ... 116 A4
　HORL RH6 ... 280 B6
　OXHEY WD19 ... 93 K4
　RSLP HA4 ... 112 D5
　STA TW18 ... 173 J7
　UPMR RM14 ... 126 B8
　WHTN TW2 ... 176 A3
Fairfield Cl BFN/LL DA15 ... 185 J2
　BGR/WK TN15 ... 247 P4
　GT/LBKH KT23 ... 254 A1
　HARP AL5 ... 20 C2
　HCH RM12 ... 125 H6
　HOR/WEW KT19 ... 220 B2
　NFNCH/WDSP N12 ... 97 M5
　PEND EN3 ... 80 D8
　RAD WD7 ... 74 D3
Fairfield Crs EDGW HA8 ... 95 N7
Fairfield Dr BROX EN10 ... 44 E10
　DORK RH4 ... 254 G10
　GFD/PVL UB6 ... 135 H3
　RYLN/HDSTN HA2 ... 114 B1
　WAND/EARL SW18 ... 179 L1
Fairfield East KUT KT1 ... 199 K2
Fairfield Gdns CEND/HSY/T N8 ... 118 F3
Fairfield Gv CHARL SE7 ... 162 A5
Fairfield La CHOB/PIR GU24 ... 212 E8
　SLN SL2 ... 128 G4
Fairfield North KUT KT1 ... 199 K2
Fairfield Pk COB KT11 ... 217 L10
Fairfield Pth CROY/NA CR0 ... 203 L10
Fairfield Pl KUT KT1 ... 199 K3
Fairfield Rd BECK BR3 ... 204 F2
　BMLY BR1 ... 183 M10
　BOW E3 ... 140 F4
　BRW CM14 ... 107 H4
　BXLYHN DA7 ... 164 A8
　CEND/HSY/T N8 ... 118 F3
　CHONG CM5 ... 67 N5
　CROY/NA CR0 ... 203 L10
　EPP CM16 ... 65 L5
　HOD EN11 ... 44 F1
　IL IG1 ... 142 E1
　KUT KT1 ... 199 K2
　LHD/OX KT22 ... 236 E7
　SL SL1 ... 128 B5
　STHL UB1 ... 133 N8
　STMC/STPC BR5 ... 206 G7
　STWL/WRAY TW19 ... 172 A2
　UED N18 ... 99 P5
　UX/CGN UB8 ... 131 N1
　WALTH E17 ... 100 D10
　WDR/YW UB7 ... 131 P10
Fairfield St WAND/EARL SW18 ... 179 L1
Fairfields CDALE/KGS NW9 ... 115 P3
Fairfields Cl CDALE/KGS NW9 ... 115 P3
Fairfield South KUT KT1 ... 199 K3
Fairfield Wy BAR EN5 ... 77 K9
　COUL/CHIP CR5 ... 222 E10
　HOR/WEW KT19 ... 220 B2
Fairfield West KUT KT1 ... 199 K2
Fairfolds GSTN WD25 ... 73 M1
Fairfoot Rd BOW E3 ... 140 F6
Fairford Av BXLYHN DA7 ... 164 D7
　CROY/NA CR0 ... 204 C5
Fairford Cl BF/WBF KT14 ... 215 J9
　CROY/NA CR0 ... 204 C5
　HARH RM3 ... 105 A7
　REIG RH2 ... 257 M8
Fairford Gdns WPK KT4 ... 200 C10
Fairford Wy HARH RM3 ... 106 A2
Fairgreen EBAR EN4 ... 78 A4
Fairgreen Rd THHTH CR7 ... 203 J5
Fairham Av SOCK/AV RM15 ... 146 F9
Fairhaven EGH TW20 ... 172 C8
Fairhaven Av CROY/NA CR0 ... 204 C6
Fairhaven Crs OXHEY WD19 ... 93 H4
Fairhaven Rd REDH RH1 ... 258 B6
Fairhazel Gdns KIL/WHAMP NW6 ... 3 J3
Fairhill HHS/BOV HP3 ... 36 A10
Fairholme EBED/NFELT TW14 ... 174 E3
Fairholme Av GPK RM2 ... 125 H3
Fairholme Cl HDN NW4 ... 117 H3
　YEAD UB4 ... 132 G6
Fairholme Gdns FNCH N3 ... 117 H1
　UPMR RM14 ... 126 B8
Fairholme Rd ASHF TW15 ... 173 P8
　CROY/NA CR0 ... 203 J5
　HRW HA1 ... 114 D3
　IL IG1 ... 122 C5
　SUT SM1 ... 221 J5
　WKENS W14 ... 14 C8
Fairholt Rd STNW/STAM N16 ... 119 L8
Fairkytes Av EMPK RM11 ... 125 K6
Fairland Rd SRTFD E15 ... 141 L1
Fairlands Av BKHH IG9 ... 101 M3
　RGUW GU3 ... 249 H6
　SUT SM1 ... 201 K9
　THHTH CR7 ... 202 G4
Fairlands Rd RGUW GU3 ... 249 H5
Fair La COUL/CHIP CR5 ... 257 K1
Fairlawn CHARL SE7 ... 161 P6
　GT/LBKH KT23 ... 235 N10
Fairlawn Av BXLYHN DA7 ... 164 G2
　CHSWK W4 ... 155 P3
　EFNCH N2 ... 117 P2
　WELL DA16 ... 163 N8
Fairlawn Cl ESH/CLAY KT10 ... 218 E3
　FELT TW13 ... 175 N7
　KUTN/CMB KT2 ... 177 P9
　STHGT/OAK N14 ... 78 C10
Fairlawn Dr REDH RH1 ... 275 P2
　WFD IG8 ... 101 M8
Fairlawn Gdns STHL UB1 ... 133 N9
Fairlawn Gv BNSTD SM7 ... 221 N9
　CHSWK W4 ... 155 P3
Fairlawn Pk SYD SE26 ... 182 B8
　WDSR SL4 ... 148 D10
　WOKN/KNAP GU21 ... 214 B10
Fairlawn Rd BELMT SM2 ... 221 M8
　WIM/MER SW19 ... 179 J10
Fairlawns ADL/WDHM KT15 ... 215 J7
　HORL RH6 ... 280 C5
　SUN TW16 ... 197 H3
　TWK TW1 ... 177 J2
　WAT WD17 ... 72 G5
Fairlawns Cl EMPK RM11 ... 125 N5
　STHWK SE1 ... 12 D7
Fairlea Pl EA W5 ... 135 H7
Fair Leas CSHM HP5 ... 50 F5
Fairley House CHSW EN7 ... 62 A4
Fairlie Gdns FSTH SE23 ... 182 B3
Fairlie Rd SL SL1 ... 128 F8
Fairlight Av CHING E4 ... 101
　WDSR SL4 ... 149 J8
　WFD IG8 ... 101 M8

　WLSDN NW10 ... 136 B4
Fairlight Cl CHING E4 ... 101 J3
　WPK KT4 ... 220 F1
Fairlight Cross HART DA3 ... 211 N3
Fairlight Dr UX/CGN UB8 ... 131 N1
Fairlight Rd TOOT SW17 ... 179 N7
Fairlop Cl HCH RM12 ... 145 J1
Fairlop Gdns BARK/HLT IG6 ... 102 F8
Fairlop Rd BARK/HLT IG6 ... 102 F10
　WAN E11 ... 121 J3
Fairmark Dr HGDN/ICK UB10 ... 132 B1
Fairmead BMLY BR1 ... 206 C4
　BRYLDS KT5 ... 199 N8
　WOKN/KNAP GU21 ... 231 P4
Fairmead Av HARP AL5 ... 20 B3
Fairmead Cl BMLY BR1 ... 206 C4
　HEST TW5 ... 153 L6
　NWMAL KT3 ... 200 A3
Fairmead Crs EDGW HA8 ... 95 P5
Fairmead Gdns REDBR IG4 ... 122 A3
Fairmead Rd CROY/NA CR0 ... 202 G7
　HOLWY N7 ... 118 F8
　LOU IG10 ... 81 N8
Fairmeads COB KT11 ... 217 M9
　LOU IG10 ... 82 E6
Fairmile Av COB KT11 ... 217 M10
　STRHM/NOR SW16 ... 180 D8
Fairmile Ct COB KT11 ... 217 M8
Fairmile Hts COB KT11 ... 217 P9
Fairmile La COB KT11 ... 217 L8
Fairmile Park Copse COB KT11 ... 217 N8
Fairmile Park Rd COB KT11 ... 217 N9
Fairmont Cl BELV DA17 ... 164 A4
Fair Oak Cl LHD/OX KT22 ... 218 C7
Fairoak Cl BRXS/STRHM SW2 ... 180 G2
　STMC/STPC BR5 ... 206 E7
　PUR/KEN CR8 ... 241 J1
Fairoak Dr ELTH/MOT SE9 ... 184 G1
Fairoak Gdns ROM RM1 ... 104 F10
Fairoak La LHD/OX KT22 ... 218 D7
Fairoaks Gv PEND EN3 ... 80 C3
Fairseat Cl BUSH WD23 ... 94 D3
Fairs Rd LHD/OX KT22 ... 236 F5
Fairstone Ct HORL RH6 ... 280 C3
Fair St HSLW TW3 ... 154 B9
　STHWK SE1 ... 19 K1
Fairthorn Rd CHARL SE7 ... 161 M4
Fairtrough Rd ORP BR6 ... 227 L9
Fairview ERITH DA8 ... 164 G6
　POTB/CUF EN6 ... 59 L6
Fair Vw POTB/CUF EN6 ... 59 L6
Fairview Av ALP/SUD HA0 ... 135 J1
　RAIN RM13 ... 145 L4
　WOKS/MYFD GU22 ... 232 C4
Fairview Cl CHIG IG7 ... 103 H5
　WOKS/MYFD GU22 ... 232 B4
Fairview Ct CHIG IG7 ... 103 H5
Fairview Dr CHIG IG7 ... 103 H6
　ORP BR6 ... 226 C1
　SHPTN TW17 ... 196 A5
　WAT WD17 ... 72 F2
Fairview Gdns WFD IG8 ... 101 N9
Fairview Pl BRXS/STRHM SW2 ... 180 G3
Fairview Rd CHIG IG7 ... 103 H5
　ENC/FH EN2 ... 79 H5
　EW KT17 ... 220 C7
　MEO DA13 ... 190 A10
　SEVS/STOTM N15 ... 119 N3
　SLN SL2 ... 128 E6
　STRHM/NOR SW16 ... 202 G1
　SUT SM1 ... 221 N2
Fairview Wy EDGW HA8 ... 95 M5
Fairwater Av WELL DA16 ... 163 K10
Fairwater Dr ADL/WDHM KT15 ... 215 N5
Fairway BXLYHN DA6 ... 185 J5
　CAR SM5 ... 221 M7
　CDH/CHF RM16 ... 147 N10
　CHERT KT16 ... 195 L8
　CRAWE RH10 ... 285 J3
　CRAWW RH11 ... 282 C8
　GU GU1 ... 250 G10
　HHS/BOV HP3 ... 36 A10
　RYNPK SW20 ... 200 F3
　SBW CM21 ... 30 A1
　STMC/STPC BR5 ... 206 C3
　WARE SG12 ... 26 B3
　WFD IG8 ... 101 P6
Fairway Av BORE WD6 ... 75 N6
　CDALE/KGS NW9 ... 115 P2
　WDR/YW UB7 ... 131 M10
Fairway Cl CRAWE RH10 ... 285 H3
　CROY/NA CR0 ... 204 D5
　GLDGN NW11 ... 117 M6
　HOR/WEW KT19 ... 219 P1
　LCOL/BKTW AL2 ... 56 B3
　WOKS/MYFD GU22 ... 231 N5
Fairway Dr GFD/PVL UB6 ... 134 A2
　RDART DA2 ... 188 A3
　THMD SE28 ... 143 N8
Fairway Gdns BECK BR3 ... 205 J6
　IL IG1 ... 122 F10
Fairways ASHF TW15 ... 174 B9
　CHES/WCR EN8 ... 62 C2
　PUR/KEN CR8 ... 241 K3
　STAN HA7 ... 95 K10
　TEDD TW11 ... 177 J10
The Fairways REDH RH1 ... 275 N5
The Fairway ABLGY WD5 ... 54 E8
　ACT W3 ... 136 B8
　ALP/SUD HA0 ... 114 C7
　BAR EN5 ... 77 L10
　BMLY BR1 ... 206 C5
　CHOB/PIR GU24 ... 231 H10
　E/WMO/HCT KT8 ... 198 A3
　GVW DA11 ... 190 A3
　HGDN/ICK UB10 ... 132 A5
　HLWS CM18 ... 47 J4
　LHD/OX KT22 ... 236 F4
　MLHL NW7 ... 96 A4
　NTHLT UB5 ... 134 B1
　NTHWD HA6 ... 92 A3
　NWMAL KT3 ... 200 A1
　PLMGR N13 ... 99 K4
　RGUW GU3 ... 249 H6
　SL SL1 ... 128 B5
　STHGT/OAK N14 ... 78 C10
　UPMR RM14 ... 126 B5
　WEY KT13 ... 216 B7
Fairweather Cl SEVS/STOTM N15 ... 119 M2
Fairweather Rd STNW/STAM N16 ... 119 P4
Fairwell Rd EHSLY KT24 ... 252 D8
Fairwyn Rd SYD SE26 ... 182 D6
Fakenham Cl MLHL NW7 ... 96 D8
　NTHLT UB5 ... 133 N4
Fakruddin St WCHPL E1 ... 13 P2
Falaise EGH TW20 ... 172 B8
Falcon Av BMLY BR1 ... 206 B3
　GRAYS RM17 ... 167 N6
Falcon Cl CHSWK W4 ... 155 N5
　CRAWW RH11 ... 283 N5
　DART DA1 ... 187 N1
　HAT AL10 ... 40 D6
　NTHWD HA6 ... 92 B7
　SBW CM21 ... 29 M2
　STHWK SE1 ... 18 F1
　WAT WD17 ... 72 C10
Falcon Crs PEND EN3 ... 80 D7
Falconer Rd BARK/HLT IG6 ... 103 H2
　BUSH WD23 ... 93 P10
Falconers Pk SBW CM21 ... 29 N2
Falconhurst LHD/OX KT22 ... 236 C1
Falcon La BTSEA SW11 ... 157 P9
Falcon Ms GVW DA11 ... 190 B4

Falcon Rdg BERK HP4 ... 33 P6
Falcon Rd BTSEA SW11 ... 157 P9
　GU GU1 ... 250 A10
　HPTN TW12 ... 175 N10
　PEND EN3 ... 80
Falcons Cl BH/WHM TN16 ... 244 A3
Falcon St PLSTW E13 ... 141 M4
Falcon Ter BTSEA SW11 ... 157 P9
Falcon Wy CDALE/KGS NW9 ... 96 K3
　GSTN WD25 ... 55 M10
　KTN/HRWW/W HA3 ... 115 K3
　SUN TW16 ... 196 F2
　WAN E11 ... 121 M2
　WGCE AL7 ... 23 H3
Falconwood EGH TW20 ... 172 B8
　EHSLY KT24 ... 234 C10
Falcon Wd LHD/OX KT22 ... 236 B6
Falconwood Av WELL DA16 ... 163 J8
Falconwood Pde WELL DA16 ... 163 H10
Falconwood Rd CROY/NA CR0 ... 224 C5
Falcourt Cl SUT SM1 ... 221 M7
Falkirk Cl EMPK RM11 ... 125 P6
Falkirk Gdns OXHEY WD19 ... 93 L6
Falkirk St IS N1 ... 7 K8
Falkland Av FBAR/BDGN N11 ... 98 B8
　FNCH N3 ... 97 K8
Falkland Gv DORK RH4 ... 272 F5
Falkland Park Av SNWD SE25 ... 203 M3
Falkland Rd BAR EN5 ... 77 H6
　CEND/HSY/T N8 ... 119 H2
　DORK RH4 ... 272 F3
　KTTN NW5 ... 118 D10
Falling La WDR/YW UB7 ... 131 P9
Falloden Wy GLDGN NW11 ... 117 K2
Fallow Cl CHIG IG7 ... 103 J6
Fallowfield RDART DA2 ... 188 G6
　STAN HA7 ... 94 F4
　WGCE AL7 ... 23 J7
Fallowfield Cl DEN/HRF UB9 ... 91 M9
Fallowfield Ct STAN HA7 ... 94 F4
Fallow Flds LOU IG10 ... 102 A1
Fallowfield Dr NFNCH/WDSP N12 ... 97
Fallowfield Wy HORL RH6 ... 280 C3
Fallow Ri HERT/BAY SG13 ... 25 M5
Fallows Cl EFNCH N2 ... 97 H10
Falsbrook Rd STRHM/NOR SW16 ... 180 P2
Falman Cl ED N9 ... 99
Falmer Cl CRAWW RH11 ... 283 N3
Falmer Rd EN EN1 ... 79 M8
　SEVS/STOTM N15 ... 119 K3
　WALTH E17 ... 120 C1
Falmouth Av CHING E4 ... 101 A6
Falmouth Cl LEE/GVPK SE12 ... 183 L1
Falmouth Gdns REDBR IG4 ... 122 A2
Falmouth Rd SL SL1 ... 128 F8
　STHWK SE1 ... 18 F4
　WOT/HER KT12 ... 217 K1
Falstaff Gdns STAL AL1 ... 38
Falstone WOKN/KNAP GU21 ... 231 N4
Fambridge Cl SYD SE26 ... 182 G7
Fambridge Rd BCTR RM8 ... 124 B6
Famet Av PUR/KEN CR8 ... 223 K9
Famet Cl PUR/KEN CR8 ... 223 K9
Famet Wk PUR/KEN CR8 ... 223 K9
Fane St WKENS W14 ... 14 D9
Fanhams Rd WARE SG12 ... 26 D1
Fann St FARR EC1M ... 12 E2
　STLK EC1Y ... 12 E2
Fanshawe Ct HERT/WAS SG14 ... 25 J4
Fanshawe Av BARK IG11 ... 142 F1
Fanshawe Crs DAGW RM9 ... 123 P10
　EMPK RM11 ... 125 L4
　WARE SG12 ... 26 A1
Fanshawe Rd CDH/CHF RM16 ... 168 D2
　RCHPK/HAM TW10 ... 177 H7
Fanshaws La HERT/BAY SG13 ... 43 K4
Fanshaw St IS N1 ... 7 J9
Fanthorpe St PUT/ROE SW15 ... 156 G9
Faraday Av SCUP DA14 ... 185 L5
Faraday Cl HOLWY N7 ... 5 M1
　SLN SL2 ... 128 G7
　WATW WD18 ... 72 E10
Faraday Rd ACT W3 ... 135 P4
　CRAWE RH10 ... 284 A3
　E/WMO/HCT KT8 ... 197 P4
　GFD/PVL UB6 ... 134 A3
　NKENS W10 ... 136 A3
　SLN SL2 ... 128 G7
　SRTFD E15 ... 141 L1
　WELL DA16 ... 163 K9
　WIM/MER SW19 ... 179 K3
Faraday Wy STMC/STPC BR5 ... 207 H4
　WOOL/PLUM SE18 ... 162 A2
Fareham Rd EBED/NFELT TW14 ... 175 K3
Fareham St SOHO/CST W1F ... 11 J5
Farewell Pl MTCM CR4 ... 201 N1
Farfield Av HARH RM3 ... 105 P3
　HAYES BR2 ... 206 E6
Faringdon Av HARH RM3 ... 105 P3
Faringdon Rd SRTFD E15 ... 141 K2
Faringford Cl POTB/CUF EN6 ... 59 N7
Faris Barn Dr ADL/WDHM KT15 ... 215 J7
Faris La ADL/WDHM KT15 ... 215 J7
Farjeon Rd BKHTH/KID SE3 ... 162 A3
Farland Rd HHNE HP2 ... 36 B6
Farleigh Av HAYES BR2 ... 205 L2
Farleigh Court Rd WARL CR6 ... 224 E10
Farleigh Dean Crs CROY/NA CR0 ... 224 C7
Farleigh Pl STNW/STAM N16 ... 119 N9
Farleigh Rd ADL/WDHM KT15 ... 215 K2
　STNW/STAM N16 ... 119 N9
　WARL CR6 ... 242 E3
Farleton Cl WEY KT13 ... 216 E3
Farleycroft BH/WHM TN16 ... 262 E3
Farley Dr GDMY/SEVK IG3 ... 123 H6
Farley La BH/WHM TN16 ... 262 C5
Farley Nursery BH/WHM TN16 ... 262 C6
Farley Pk OXTED RH8 ... 261 J3
Farley Rd CAT SE6 ... 183
Farleys Cl EHSLY KT24 ... 252
Farlington Pl PUT/ROE SW15 ... 178 E3
Farlow Cl GVW DA11 ... 190 C6
Farlow Rd PUT/ROE SW15 ... 156 G9
Farlton Rd WAND/EARL SW18 ... 179 L3
Farm Av ALP/SUD HA0 ... 135 H1
　CRICK NW2 ... 116 A10
　RYLN/HDSTN HA2 ... 113 P10
　STRHM/NOR SW16 ... 180 F7
　SWLY BR8 ... 208 A3
Farmborough Cl HRW HA1 ... 114 C5
Farm Cl AMS HP6 ... 70 A3
　ASC SL5 ... 192 B5
　BAR EN5 ... 76 B7
　BELMT SM2 ... 221 N4
　BF/WBF KT14 ... 216 A6
　BKHH IG9 ... 101 P4
　BORE WD6 ... 75 N4
　CHERT KT16 ... 194 D6
　CHES/WCR EN8 ... 62 B6
　CRAWE RH10 ... 284 A6
　DAGE RM10 ... 144 D2
　EHSLY KT24 ... 252 G4
　HERT/WAS SG14 ... 25 H5
　HGDN/ICK UB10 ... 132 C8
　LHD/OX KT22 ... 216 G10
　POTB/CUF EN6 ... 60 E2
　RBRW/HUT CM13 ... 107 P4
　RGUW GU3 ... 249 H5
　SHPTN TW17 ... 196 B7
　STA TW18 ... 173 H4
　STHL UB1 ... 134 A6

WGCW AL8 22 F5
WLGTN SM6 222 D6
WWKM BR4 205 L10
Farmcote Rd LEE/GVPK SE12 183 M4
Farm Crs SLN SL2 129 N7
Farmcroft GVW DA11 190 D5
Farmdale Rd CAR SM5 221 P4
GNWCH SE10 161 M4
Farm Dr CROY/NA CR0 204 E9
PUR/KEN CR8 222 E8
WDSR SL4 171 N2
Farm End CHING E4 81 K9
Farmer Ct WAB EN9 63 M9
Farmer Rd LEY E10 120 G6
Farmers Cl GSTN WD25 55 J9
Farmers Rd CMBW SE5 159 J6
STA TW18 173 H8 2
Farmer St KENS W8 8 E9
Farmfield Rd BMLY BR1 183 K8
Farm Flds SAND/SEL CR2 223 N7
Farm Gv BEAC HP9 88 B6
Farm Hill Rd WAB EN9 63 J10
Farm Holt HART DA3 211 L8
Farmhouse Cl BROX EN10 62 E1 1
WOKS/MYFD GU22 232 G1 1
Farmhouse La HHNE HP2 36 B4
Farmhouse Rd
STRHM/NOR SW16 180 D10
Farmilo Rd WALTH E17 120 F5
Farmington Av SUT SM1 201 N10
Farmlands ENC/FH EN2 79 H5
PIN HA5 113 H2
The Farmlands NTHLT UB5 133 N1
Farmland Wk CHST BR7 184 E8
Farm La ADL/WDHM KT15 215 K3
ASHTD KT21 237 N4
BEAC HP9 89 J9
CROY/NA CR0 204 E9
EHSLY KT24 252 G4
FUL/PGN SW6 14 F10
PUR/KEN CR8 222 D6
RKW/CH/CXG WD3 71 L7
RPLY/SEND GU23 232 F9
STHGT/OAK N14 78 B10
WTHK RM20 167 K5
Farmleigh STHGT/OAK N14 98 D1
Farmleigh Cl CRAWE RH10 284 D5 1
Farmleigh Gv WOT/HER KT12 216 G2
Farm Pl BERK HP4 33 L4 1
DART DA1 165 H10
KENS W8 8 E9
Farm Rd BELMT SM2 221 N4
CDH/CHF RM16 168 C1
EDGW HA8 95 P6
ESH/CLAY KT10 197 P8
HSLWW TW4 175 M4
MRDN SM4 201 L5
NTHWD HA6 92 D6
RAIN RM13 145 K5
RKW/CH/CXG WD3 70 D8
RSEV TN14 247 K6
STA TW18 173 L9
STAL AL1 38 G5
TIL RM18 169 M3
WARL CR6 242 D5
WCHMH N21 99 K2
WOKS/MYFD GU22 232 E6
Farmstead Rd CAT SE6 182 G7
KTN/HRWW/W HA3 94 C9
Farm St MYFR/PICC W1J 10 E8
Farm V BXLY DA5 186 C2
Farmview COB KT11 235 L2
Farmway BCTR RM8 123 M9
Farm Wy BKHH IG9 101 P5
BUSH WD23 74 A8
HCH RM12 125 J9
NTHWD HA6 92 F5
STWL/WRAY TW19 173 J2
WPK KT4 200 F10
Farm Yd WDSR SL4 149 J6
Farnaby Dr SEV TN13 264 G2
Farnaby Rd BMLY BR1 205 K1
ELTH/MOT SE9 161 P10
Farnan Av WALTH E17 100 F10
Farnan Rd STRHM/NOR SW16 180 F8
Farnborough Av SAND/SEL CR2 224 D4
WALTH E17 120 D1 2
Farnborough Cl WBLY HA9 115 N7 1
Farnborough Common ORP BR6 206 C10
Farnborough Crs HAYES BR2 205 L8 1
SAND/SEL CR2 224 D5
Farnborough Hl ORP BR6 226 G2
Farnborough Wy ORP BR6 227 H3
Farnburn Av SL SL1 128 G7
Farncombe Hl RGODL GU7 267 J10
Farncombe St BERM/RHTH SE16 19 P2
RGODL GU7 267 K10
Farndale Av PLMGR N13 99 J4
Farndale Crs GFD/PVL UB6 134 B5
Farnell Ms ECT SW5 14 G7
Farnell Rd ISLW TW7 154 C9
STA TW18 173 K6
Farnes Dr GPK RM2 105 K10
Farnham Cl HHS/BOV HP3 52 D4
SBW CM21 29 M2
TRDG/WHET N20 97 M1
Farnham Gdns RYNPK SW20 200 E2 1
Farnham La SLN SL2 128 E4
Farnham Park La SLN SL2 129 H2
Farnham Pl STHWK SE1 12 D10
Farnham Rd GDMY/SEVK IG3 123 J4
GUW GU2 267 J3
HARH RM3 105 L6
SL SL1 129 H10 3
WELL DA16 163 M8
Farnham Royal LBTH SE11 17 P8
Farningham Crs CTHM CR3 241 P9
Farningham Hill Rd SWLY BR8 209 K5
Farningham Rd CTHM CR3 241 P9
TOTM N17 99 P8
Farnley WOKN/KNAP GU21 231 L3
Farnley Rd CHING E4 101 K1
THHTH CR7 203 L4
Farnol Rd DART DA1 187 P1 1
Faro Cl BMLY BR1 206 D2
Faroe Rd WKENS W14 156 G2
Farorna Wk ENC/FH EN2 79 H5
Farquhar Rd NRWD SE19 181 N8
WIM/MER SW19 179 K6 1
Farquharson Rd CROY/NA CR0 203 K8
Farquhar St HERT/WAS SG14 25 K4
Farraline Rd WATW WD18 73 J9 3
Farrance Rd CHDH RM6 123 P4
Farrance St POP/IOD E14 140 F8
Farrans Ct KTN/HRWW/W HA3 114 G1
Farrant Av WDGN N22 99 H10
Farrant Cl ORP BR6 227 K4 1
Farrant Wy BORE WD6 75 K5 1
Farr Av BARK IG11 143 K4
Farren Rd FSTH SE23 182 D5
Farrer Ms CEND/HSY/T N8 118 D2 1
Farrer Rd CEND/HSY/T N8 118 D2
KTN/HRWW/W HA3 115 K3
Farriday Cl STALW/RED AL3 38 D2
Farrier Cl BMLY BR1 206 A3
UX/CGN UB8 132 B8
Farrier Rd NTHLT UB5 133 P4
Farriers WARE SG12 26 F5
Farriers Cl EW KT17 220 B8 3
GVE DA12 191 J4 2
Farriers End BROX EN10 62 E2 1
Farriers Rd EW KT17 220 B7
Farrier St CAMTN NW1 4 F3
Farriers Wy BORE WD6 76 A10
Farringdon La CLKNW EC1R 12 B2 1
Farringdon Rd FARR EC1M 12 C4
FSBYW WC1X 12 A1
HCIRC EC1N 12 C4
Farringdon St FLST/FETLN EC4A 12 C5 1
Farringford Cl LCOL/BKTW AL2 55 P2
Farrington Av STMC/STPC BR5 207 L3
Farrington Pl CHST BR7 184 G10
Farrins Rents
BERM/RHTH SE16 140 D10 2
Farrow Gdns CDH/CHF RM16 147 N10
Farrow La PECK SE15 160 B6
Farrow Pl BERM/RHTH SE16 160 D2
Farr Rd ENC/FH EN2 79 L5
Farthingale La WAB EN9 63 M10
Farthing Aly STHWK SE1 19 N2 1
Farthing Flds WAP E1W 140 A10 3
Farthing Green La SLN SL2 129 M4
Farthings WOKN/KNAP GU21 231 K2
Farthings Cl CHING E4 101 K4
PIN HA5 113 J4
The Farthings HHW HP1 35 L6 1
Farthing St ORP BR6 226 C4
Farwell Rd SCUP DA14 185 L7
Farwig La BMLY BR1 205 M1
Fashion St WCHPL E1 13 L4
Fashoda Rd HAYES BR2 206 A4
Fassett Rd HACK E8 7 N1
KUT KT1 199 K4
Fassett Sq HACK E8 7 N1
Fauconberg Rd CHSWK W4 155 P5
Faulkner Cl BCTR RM8 123 N5
Faulkner's Rd WOT/HER KT12 217 K2
Faulkner St NWCR SE14 160 B7 1
Fauna Cl CHDH RM6 123 M4
Faunce St WALW SE17 18 C8
Favart Rd FUL/PGN SW6 157 K7
Faverolle Gn CHES/WCR EN8 62 C4 1
Faversham Av CHING E4 101 K2
WCHMH N21 79 L10
Faversham Cl CHIG IG7 103 L3
Faversham Rd BECK BR3 204 E2 1
CAT SE6 182 E3
MRDN SM4 201 L6
Fawcett Cl BTSEA SW11 157 N8
STRHM/NOR SW16 181 H7 1
Fawcett Rd CROY/NA CR0 203 J10
WDSR SL4 148 G7
WLSDN NW10 136 C2
Fawcett St WBPTN SW10 15 J9
Fawcus Cl ESH/CLAY KT10 218 D3
Fawe Park Rd PUT/ROE SW15 157 J10
Fawe St POP/IOD E14 140 G7
Fawkes Av DART DA1 187 N5
Fawkham Av HART DA3 211 P3 2
Fawkham Green Rd HART DA3 210 G10
Fawkham Rd HART DA3 211 J4
Fawley Rd KIL/WHAMP NW6 117 L10
Fawnbrake Av HNHL SE24 181 J1
Fawn Ct BRKMPK AL9 40 F2
Fawn Rd CHIG IG7 103 J6
PLSTW E13 141 P4
Fawns Manor Rd
EBED/NFELT TW14 174 E4
Fawood Av WLSDN NW10 136 A2
Fawsley Cl DTCH/LGLY SL3 151 H6
Faygate Crs BXLYHS DA6 186 B1
Faygate La HORS RH12 282 B6
Faygate Rd BRXS/STRHM SW2 180 G5
Fay Gn ABLGY WD5 54 E9
Fayland Av STRHM/NOR SW16 180 D8
Faymore Gdns SOCK/AV RM15 146 F8 1
Feacey Down HHW HP1 35 K4
Fearn Cl EHSLY KT24 252 F5
Fearney Md RKW/CH/CXG WD3 91 K2
Fearnley Crs HPTN TW12 175 M8
Fearnley Rd WGCW AL8 22 F6
Fearnley St WATW WD18 73 J8 1
WATW WD18 73 J8 1
Fearon St GNWCH SE10 161 M4
Featherbed La CROY/NA CR0 224 G6
HHS/BOV HP3 35 M10
Feather Dell HAT AL10 40 C4
Feathers La STWL/WRAY TW19 172 D5
Feathers Pl GNWCH SE10 161 J5
Featherstone Av FSTH SE23 182 B5 1
Featherstone Gdns BORE WD6 76 A8
Featherstone Rd MLHL NW7 96 E7
NWDGN UB2 153 M2 1
Featherstone St STLK EC1Y 12 G1
Featherstone Ter NWDGN UB2 153 M2 1
Featley Rd BRXN/ST SW9 159 J9
Federal Rd GFD/PVL UB6 135 H4
Federal Wy WATN WD24 73 K5 2
Federation Rd ABYW SE2 163 M3
Fee Farm Rd ESH/CLAY KT10 218 E4
Feenan Hwy TIL RM18 168 E6
Felbridge Av CRAWE RH10 284 E6
STAN HA7 94 F9
Felbridge Cl BELMT SM2 221 L5
STRHM/NOR SW16 181 H7
Felbrigge Rd GDMY/SEVK IG3 123 J7
Felcott Cl WOT/HER KT12 197 K10
Felcott Rd WOT/HER KT12 197 K10
Felday Rd LEW SE13 182 G2
RDKG RH5 270 G6
Felden Cl GSTN WD25 55 L10
Felden Dr HHS/BOV HP3 35 K10
Felden La HHS/BOV HP3 35 K9
Felden St FUL/PGN SW6 157 J7
Feldman Cl STNW/STAM N16 119 P6 1
Feldon Cl PIN HA5 93 M8
Felgate Ms HMSMTH W6 156 E3 3
Felhampton Rd ELTH/MOT SE9 184 E6
Felhurst Crs DAGE RM10 124 D9 3
Felipe Rd CDH/CHF RM16 168 E3
Felix Av CEND/HSY/T N8 118 F4
Felix Dr RGUE GU4 251 K4
Felix La SHPTN TW17 196 G6
Felix Rd HNWL W7 134 F9
WOT/HER KT12 197 H6
Felixstowe Rd ABYW SE2 163 L2
ED N9 99 P4
TOTM N17 119 N1 1
UED N18 99 P5
WLSDN NW10 136 E5 1
Felix St BETH E2 140 A4 1
Felland Wy REDH RH1 275 N4
Fellbrigg Rd EDUL SE22 181 N1
Fellbrigg St WCHPL E1 140 A6 1
Fellbrook RCHPK/HAM TW10 176 G6
Fellmongers Yd CROY/NA CR0 203 K10
Fellowes Cl YEAD UB4 133 L6 1
Fellowes La STALE/WH AL4 40 A9
Fellowes Rd CAR SM5 201 P10
Fellow Gn CHOB/PIR GU24 212 E9
Fellow Green Rd CHOB/PIR GU24 212 E9
Fellows Rd HAMP NW3 3 M3
Fell Rd CROY/NA CR0 203 K10
Felltram Wy CHARL SE7 161 M4
Felmersham Cl CLAP SW4 158 F10 2
Felmingham Rd PGE/AN SE20 204 B2
Felmongers HLW CM20 29 L9
Felsberg Rd BRXS/STRHM SW2 180 F3
Fels Cl DAGE RM10 124 C8
Fels Farm Av DAGE RM10 124 D8
Felsham Rd PUT/ROE SW15 156 F9
Felspar Cl WOOL/PLUM SE18 163 J4 3
Felstead Av CLAY IG5 102 D9
Felstead Cl RBRW/HUT CM13 87 P10 1
Felstead Rd CHES/WCR EN8 62 D8
CRW RM5 104 D7
HOM E9 140 F1 1
HOR/WEW KT19 220 A7
LOU IG10 102 B1
ORP BR6 207 K9
WAN E11 121 M5
Felstead St HOM E9 140 E1
Felsted Rd CAN/RD E16 142 A8
Feltham Av E/WMO/HCT KT8 198 D4
Felthambrook Wy FELT TW13 175 J6
Feltham Hill Rd ASHF TW15 174 B8
Felthamhill Rd FELT TW13 175 H7
Feltham Rd ASHF TW15 174 C7
MTCM CR4 202 A2
REDH RH1 276 A5
Felton Cl BORE WD6 75 K4 2
BROX EN10 62 E1 2
STMC/STPC BR5 206 E6
Felton Lea SCUP DA14 185 J8
Felton Rd BARK IG11 143 H4
WEA W13 155 H1 1
Felton St IS N1 7 H6
Fencepiece Rd BARK/HLT IG6 102 F7
CHIG IG7 102 F7
Fenchurch Av FENCHST EC3M 13 J6
Fenchurch Buildings
FENCHST EC3M 13 K6
Fenchurch Pl FENCHST EC3M 13 K7 1
Fenchurch Rd CRAWE RH10 284 C9
Fenchurch St FENCHST EC3M 13 J7
Fen Cl BRWN CM15 87 P8
Fendall Rd HOR/WEW KT19 219 P2
Fendall St STHWK SE1 19 K4
Fendt Cl CAN/RD E16 141 L8 4
Fendyke Rd ABYW SE2 163 N3
Fenelon Pl WKENS W14 14 D6
Fengates Rd REDH RH1 257 P10
Fen Gv BFN/LL DA15 185 J2
Fenham Rd PECK SE15 159 P6
Fen La UPMR RM14 127 J10
UPMR RM14 127 N10
Fenman Ct TOTM N17 100 A9 1
Fenman Gdns GDMY/SEVK IG3 123 L6
Fenn Cl BMLY BR1 183 M9
Fennel Cl CAN/RD E16 141 K6 4
CROY/NA CR0 204 C8 3
GU GU1 250 E7
Fennel Crs CRAWW RH11 283 L10
Fennells HLWW/ROY CM19 46 E6
Fennells Md HOR/WEW KT19 220 C5
Fennell St WOOL/PLUM SE18 162 D5
Fenner Cl BERM/RHTH SE16 160 A3 3
Fenner Rd CDH/CHF RM16 167 H2
Fenner Sq BTSEA SW11 157 N9 2
The Fennings AMS HP6 69 J2
Fenning St STHWK SE1 19 J1 1
Fennscombe Ct CHOB/PIR GU24 212 D9
Fenns La CHOB/PIR GU24 212 D9
Fenn St HOM E9 120 C10
Fenn's Wy WOKN/KNAP GU21 232 B1
Fennycroft Rd HHW HP1 35 J3
Fensomes Aly HHNE HP2 35 N5 3
Fensom's Cl HHNE HP2 35 N5 4
Fenstanton Av NFNCH/WDSP N12 97 N6
Fen St CAN/RD E16 141 L9 3
Fens Wy SWLY BR8 187 H9
Fentiman Rd VX/NE SW8 17 N10
Fentiman Wy EMPK RM11 125 M6
Fenton Av STA TW18 173 M9
Fenton Cl BRXN/ST SW9 158 G8 3
CHST BR7 184 C8
REDH RH1 258 B10
Fenton Gra HLWE CM17 47 M2
Fenton Rd REDH RH1 258 B10
TOTM N17 99 K8
Fenton's Av PLSTW E13 141 N5
Fenton St WCHPL E1 140 A8
Fentum Rd GUW GU2 249 M8
Fenwick Cl WOKN/KNAP GU21 231 N4
Fenwick Gv PECK SE15 159 P9 1
Fenwick Pl BRXN/ST SW9 158 F9 2
SAND/SEL CR2 223 J4 1
Fenwick Rd PECK SE15 159 P9
Ferdinand Pl CAMTN NW1 4 D3
Ferdinand St CAMTN NW1 4 D3
Ferguson Av BRYLDS KT5 199 L5
GPK RM2 105 K10
GVE DA12 190 F7
Ferguson Cl BECK BR3 205 H3
Ferguson Ct GPK RM2 105 L10
Ferguson Dr ACT W3 136 A8 3
Ferguson's Cl POP/IOD E14 160 F3
Fergus Rd HBRY N5 119 J10 1
Fermandy La CRAWE RH10 285 P4
Ferme Park Rd CEND/HSY/T N8 118 F3
Fermor Rd FSTH SE23 182 D4
Fermoy Rd GFD/PVL UB6 134 A6
MV/WKIL W9 8 C2
Fern Av MTCM CR4 202 E4
Fernbank BKHH IG9 101 N2
Fernbank Av ALP/SUD HA0 114 E9
HCH RM12 125 K9
WOT/HER KT12 197 M7
Fernbank Ms CLAP SW4 180 C2
Fernbank Rd ADL/WDHM KT15 215 K2
Fernbrook Av BFN/LL DA15 184 G1
Fernbrook Dr RYLN/HDSTN HA2 114 D4
Fernbrook Rd LEW SE13 183 K2
Ferncliff Rd HACK E8 119 P10
Fern Cl BROX EN10 44 E9 1
ERITH DA8 165 J7
WARL CR6 242 D4
Ferncroft Av HAMP NW3 117 K8
NFNCH/WDSP N12 97 P7
RSLP HA4 113 K7
Ferndale BMLY BR1 205 P2
GUW GU2 249 K8
Ferndale Av CHERT KT16 195 K10
HSLWW TW4 153 M9
WALTH E17 121 J3
Ferndale Cl BXLYHN DA7 163 P7
Ferndale Crs UX/CGN UB8 131 M5
Ferndale Rd ASHF TW15 173 N8
BNSTD SM7 239 J2
CLAP SW4 158 F10
CRW RM5 104 D10
FSTGT E7 141 N2
GVE DA12 190 D3
PEND EN3 80 D3
SEVS/STOTM N15 119 N4
SNWD SE25 204 A5
WAN E11 121 L7
WOKN/KNAP GU21 232 C2
Ferndale St EHAM E6 142 E9
Ferndale Ter HRW HA1 114 E2 1
Ferndale Wy ORP BR6 226 G2
Ferndell Av BXLY DA5 186 E6
Fern Dells HAT AL10 40 C5
Ferndene LCOL/BKTW AL2 55 N2
Ferndene Rd HNHL SE24 159 K10
Fernden Wy ROMW/RG RM7 124 C4
Ferndown CRAWE RH10 284 E3
EMPK RM11 125 P4
HORL RH6 280 B2 1
NTHWD HA6 113 H1
Ferndown Av ORP BR6 206 G8 2
Ferndown Cl BELMT SM2 221 N3
GU GU1 268 D1
PIN HA5 93 M8
Ferndown Gdns COB KT11 217 K10
Ferndown Rd ELTH/MOT SE9 184 A3
OXHEY WD19 93 K4
Fern Dr HHS/BOV HP3 35 P7
MDHD SL6 128 A3
Fernecroft STAL AL1 38 B9
The Fernery STA TW18 173 H8 3
Fernes Cl UX/CGN UB8 131 M8
Ferney Ct BF/WBF KT14 215 N8
Ferney Meade Wy ISLW TW7 154 F8 1
Ferney Rd EBAR EN4 98 B1
Fern Gv EBED/NFELT TW14 175 J3
WGCW AL8 22 G1
Fernhall Dr REDBR IG4 122 A3
Fernhall La WAB EN9 64 A7
Fernham Rd THHTH CR7 203 K3
Fernhead Rd MV/WKIL W9 2 D9
Fernheath Wy RDART DA2 186 E8
Fernhill HLWS CM18 47 H5
LHD/OX KT22 218 C10
Fernhill Cl WOKS/MYFD GU22 231 P6
Fernhill Ct WALTH E17 101 J10 1
Fernhill Gdns KUTN/CMB KT2 177 J8
Fern Hill La HLWS CM18 47 J5
Fernhill La WOKS/MYFD GU22 231 P6
Fernhill Pk WOKS/MYFD GU22 231 P6
Fernhill Rd HORL RH6 280 E8
Fernhills ABLGY WD5 54 E10
Fernhill St CAN/RD E16 142 C10
Fernholme Rd PECK SE15 182 C1
Fernhurst Cl BEAC HP9 88 D9
CRAWW RH11 283 L5
Fernhurst Gdns EDGW HA8 95 M7
Fernhurst Rd ASHF TW15 174 D7
CROY/NA CR0 203 P7
FUL/PGN SW6 157 H7
Fernihough Cl WEY KT13 216 B7 1
Fernlands Cl CHERT KT16 195 H10
Fern La NWDGN UB2 153 N4
Fernlea GT/LBKH KT23 236 A10
Fernlea Rd BAL SW12 180 C4
MTCM CR4 202 B2
Fernleigh Cl CROY/NA CR0 223 H1 1
WOT/HER KT12 197 J10
Fernleigh Ct RYLN/HDSTN HA2 94 A10
WBLY HA9 115 K6
Fernleigh Rd WCHMH N21 99 H3
Fernleys STALE/WH AL4 39 H3
Fernsbury St FSBYW WC1X 6 A10
Ferns Cl PEND EN3 80 D2 1
SAND/SEL CR2 224 A6
Fernshaw Rd WBPTN SW10 15 J10
Fernside BKHH IG9 101 N2
Fernside Av FELT TW13 175 J7
MLHL NW7 96 A4
Fernside La SEV TN13 265 K5
Fernside Rd BAL SW12 180 A4
Fernsleigh Cl CFSP/GDCR SL9 90 B7 2
Ferns Rd SRTFD E15 141 K1
Fern St BOW E3 140 F6
Fernthorpe Rd
STRHM/NOR SW16 180 D9
Ferntower Rd HBRY N5 119 L10
Fern Towers CTHM CR3 259 P1
Fernville La HHNE HP2 35 N6
Fern Wk ASHF TW15 173 N8
Fern Wy GSTN WD25 73 J1
Fernways IL IG1 122 E8
Fernwood CROY/NA CR0 224 D5
Fernwood Av ALP/SUD HA0 135 H1
STRHM/NOR SW16 180 E7
Fernwood Cl BMLY BR1 205 P2
Fernwood Crs TRDG/WHET N20 98 A4
Ferny Hl EBAR EN4 78 A4
Feroners Cl CRAWE RH10 284 B9 2
Ferranti Cl WOOL/PLUM SE18 162 A2
Ferraro Cl HEST TW5 153 P5
Ferrers Av WDR/YW UB7 151 N1
WLGTN SM6 222 E1
Ferrers Cl SL SL1 128 D10
Ferrers La STALE/WH AL4 20 F6
STALE/WH AL4 21 J6
Ferrers Rd STRHM/NOR SW16 180 E8
Ferrestone Rd CEND/HSY/T N8 118 G2 1
Ferriby Cl IS N1 6 A3
Ferrier St WAND/EARL SW18 157 L10
Ferriers Wy KWD/TDW/WH KT20 238 F5
Ferring Cl RYLN/HDSTN HA2 114 B6
Ferrings DUL SE21 181 M5
Ferris Av CROY/NA CR0 204 E10
Ferris Rd EDUL SE22 159 P10
Ferron Rd CLPT E5 120 A8 1
Ferro Rd RAIN RM13 145 H6
Ferry Av STA TW18 173 H10
Ferryhills Cl OXHEY WD19 93 K4
Ferry La BARN SW13 156 C5
BTFD TW8 155 K5
CHERT KT16 195 K6
GUW GU2 267 P4
RAIN RM13 144 F8
RCH/KEW TW9 155 L5
SHPTN TW17 196 B8
STA TW18 195 M3
STWL/WRAY TW19 172 E5
TOTM N17 120 A2
Ferrymead Av GFD/PVL UB6 133 P4
Ferrymead Dr GFD/PVL UB6 133 P4 2
Ferrymead Gdns GFD/PVL UB6 134 B4
Ferrymoor RCHPK/HAM TW10 176 G6 1
Ferry Rd BARN SW13 156 D6
E/WMO/HCT KT8 197 P3 2
TEDD TW11 176 G8
THDIT KT7 198 G6
TIL RM18 168 D8
TWK TW1 176 G4
Ferry Sq BTFD TW8 155 K5 2
Ferry St POP/IOD E14 161 H4
Feryby Rd CDH/CHF RM16 168 E2
Fesants Cft HLW CM20 29 L8
Festing Rd PUT/ROE SW15 156 G9
Festival Cl BXLY DA5 185 N4
ERITH DA8 164 G6
HGDN/ICK UB10 132 C3
Fetcham Common La
LHD/OX KT22 236 A7 1
Fetcham Park Dr LHD/OX KT22 236 D9
Fetherstone Cl POTB/CUF EN6 59 N9 1
Fetter La FLST/FETLN EC4A 12 B5
Ffinch St DEPT SE8 160 F6 2
Fiddicroft Av BNSTD SM7 239 L1 1
Fiddle Bridge La HAT AL10 40 C3
Fiddlers Cl GRH DA9 166 G10
Fidler Pl BUSH WD23 74 A10 3
Field Cl ABR/ST RM4 83 L7
BKHH IG9 101 P4
BMLY BR1 205 P2
CHING E4 100 G7 2
CHSGTN KT9 219 H2
CSHM HP5 51 K4
E/WMO/HCT KT8 198 A5 1
HARP AL5 20 C4
HGDN/ICK UB10 112 B7
HSLWW TW4 153 J7
HYS/HAR UB3 152 D6
RGUE GU4 250 G8
RSLP HA4 112 D6 1
SAND/SEL CR2 224 A10
STALE/WH AL4 38 F2
Fieldcommon La WOT/HER KT12 197 M8
Field Ct OXTED RH8 261 K4
Field End CHOB/PIR GU24 212 E9
COUL/CHIP CR5 222 E10
RSLP HA4 133 K1
Fieldend TEDD TW11 176 E7
Field End Cl OXHEY WD19 93 M1 1
Field End Rd PIN HA5 113 J3
RSLP HA4 113 K5
Fieldend Rd STRHM/NOR SW16 202 D1
Fielders Cl EN EN1 79 M8 1
RYLN/HDSTN HA2 114 B6
Fielders Gn GU GU1 250 D10 1
Fielders Wy RAD WD7 57 K9
Fieldfare Rd THMD SE28 143 M9
Fieldfares LCOL/BKTW AL2 57 J3
Field Gdns CHONG CM5 67 M10
Fieldgate St WCHPL E1 13 P4
Fieldhouse Cl SWFD E18 101 N9
Fieldhouse Rd BAL SW12 180 D4
Field Hurst DTCH/LGLY SL3 150 C3
Fieldhurst Cl ADL/WDHM KT15 215 L2
Fielding Av TIL RM18 168 E7
WHTN TW2 176 B6
Fielding Gdns DTCH/LGLY SL3 149 P1
Fielding Rd WKENS W14 156 G2 3
Fieldings Rd CHES/WCR EN8 62 E5
The Fieldings FSTH SE23 182 B4
HORL RH6 280 C3
WOKN/KNAP GU21 231 L2
Fielding St WALW SE17 18 E9
Fielding Wy RBRW/HUT CM13 87 P10 4
Field Kiln BRWN CM15 87 J1
Field La BTFD TW8 155 H6
RGODL GU7 267 L10
TEDD TW11 176 F8
Field Md CDALE/KGS NW9 96 B8
Field Pl NWMAL KT3 200 C6 1
Field Rd DEN/HRF UB9 111 H9
EBED/NFELT TW14 175 J2
FSTGT E7 121 M9
HHNE HP2 36 B7
HMSMTH W6 14 A8
OXHEY WD19 73 M10
SOCK/AV RM15 146 B10
TOTM N17 119 L1
Fields End La HHW HP1 34 G4
Fieldsend Rd CHEAM SM3 221 H2 1
Fieldside Cl ORP BR6 226 F1
Fields Park Crs CHDH RM6 123 N3
Field St FSBYW WC1X 5 N9
Field Vw BAR EN5 76 E8
EGH TW20 172 F8
FELT TW13 174 E7
Fieldview HORL RH6 280 C3 1
WAND/EARL SW18 179 N4
Field View Ri LCOL/BKTW AL2 55 M5
Field View Rd POTB/CUF EN6 59 K9
Field Wk HORL RH6 281 K3
Field Wy AMSS HP7 68 G7
CFSP/GDCR SL9 90 A8
CROY/NA CR0 224 G4
GFD/PVL UB6 134 A3
HHW HP1 52 D3
HOD EN11 26 G9
RKW/CH/CXG WD3 91 L2
RPLY/SEND GU23 251 J1
RSLP HA4 112 D6
UX/CGN UB8 131 N6
WLSDN NW10 135 P2
Fieldway BCTR RM8 123 L9
BERK HP4 34 B7
CDH/CHF RM16 147 M10
STMC/STPC BR5 206 G6
WARE SG12 26 G7
Fieldway Crs HOLWY N7 119 H10
Fiennes Cl BCTR RM8 123 M6
Fiennes Wy SEV TN13 265 K3
Fiesta Dr DAGW RM9 144 D5 2
Fifehead Cl ASHF TW15 173 P9
Fife Rd CAN/RD E16 141 M7
KUT KT1 199 K2 2
MORT/ESHN SW14 177 P1
WDGN N22 99 J8
Fife Ter IS N1 5 P7
Fife Wy GT/LBKH KT23 253 P1
Fifield Pth FSTH SE23 182 C6
Fifth Av GSTN WD25 73 L1
MNPK E12 122 C9
NKENS W10 2 A10
WTHK RM20 166 F5
Fifth Avenue Allende Av
HLW CM20 28 G10
Fifth Cross Rd WHTN TW2 176 C5
Fifth Wy WBLY HA9 115 N9
Figge's Rd MTCM CR4 180 B10
Figtree Hl HHNE HP2 35 N5
Filbert Crs CRAWW RH11 283 K7
Filborough Wy GVE DA12 191 L4
Filby Rd CHSGTN KT9 219 L3
Filey Av STNW/STAM N16 119 P6
Filey Cl BELMT SM2 221 M4 1
BH/WHM TN16 243 N5
CRAWW RH11 283 J9
Filey Sp SL SL1 148 G1 1
Filey Waye RSLP HA4 113 H7
Fillebrook Av EN EN1 79 M6
Fillebrook Rd WAN E11 121 K5
Filmer La RSEV TN14 247 M7
Filmer Rd FUL/PGN SW6 157 J7
WDSR SL4 148 C8
Filston La RSEV TN14 228 F9
Finborough Rd TOOT SW17 180 A10
WBPTN SW10 15 H9
Finchale Rd ABYW SE2 163 K2
Fincham Cl HGDN/ICK UB10 112 D8 3
Finch Av WNWD SE27 181 L7
Finch Cl BAR EN5 77 K9
HAT AL10 40 D6
WOKN/KNAP GU21 231 H3
Finchdale HHW HP1 35 K6
Finch Dr EBED/NFELT TW14 175 L3
Finches Ri GU GU1 250 E8
The Finches HERT/BAY SG13 26 A5 1
Finch Gn RKW/CH/CXG WD3 71 J8
Finchingfield Av WFD IG8 101 P8
The Finchingfields BRWN CM15 86 D3 1
Finch La BANK EC3V 13 H6
BEAC HP9 88 B6
BUSH WD23 73 P9
Finchley Cl DART DA1 187 P2
Finchley La HDN NW4 116 G2
Finchley Pk NFNCH/WDSP N12 97 M5
Finchley Pl STJWD NW8 3 L7 1
Finchley Rd GLDGN NW11 117 J3 3
GRAYS RM17 167 N5
HAMP NW3 117 K7
KIL/WHAMP NW6 3 K2
STJWD NW8 3 L6
Finchley Wy FNCH N3 97 K7
Finch Ms PECK SE15 159 N7 3
Finchmoor HLWS CM18 46 G4
Finch Rd BERK HP4 33 M5
GU GU1 250 A10 3
Finden Rd FSTGT E7 121 N10
Findhorn Av YEAD UB4 133 J7
Findhorn St POP/IOD E14 141 H8
Findlay Dr RGUW GU3 249 L6
Findon Cl RYLN/HDSTN HA2 114 A8 3
WAND/EARL SW18 179 K2
Findon Gdns RAIN RM13 145 H7
Findon Rd CRAWW RH11 283 L5
ED N9 100 A2
SHB W12 156 D1
Fine Bush La DEN/HRF UB9 112 C4
Fingal St GNWCH SE10 161 L4
Finglesham Cl STMC/STPC BR5 207 N8 1
Finians Cl HGDN/ICK UB10 132 A2 1
Finland Rd BROCKY SE4 160 D9
Finland St BERM/RHTH SE16 160 D2
Finlay Gdns ADL/WDHM KT15 215 M1
Finlays Cl CHSGTN KT9 219 M2 1
Finlay St FUL/PGN SW6 156 G7
Finnart Cl WEY KT13 216 D1 1
Finney Dr BFOR GU20 212 C3
Finnis St BETH E2 140 A5
Finnymore Rd DAGW RM9 143 P2
Finsbury Av LVPST EC2M 13 H4 2
Finsbury Circ LVPST EC2M 13 H4 2
Finsbury Cottages WDGN N22 98 F8 2
Finsbury Market SDTCH EC2A 13 J3 2
SDTCH EC2A 13 J2 1
Finsbury Park Av FSBYPK N4 119 K4
Finsbury Park Rd FSBYPK N4 119 J8 2
Finsbury Pavement SDTCH EC2A 13 H3
Finsbury Rd WDGN N22 98 G9 1
Finsbury Sq SDTCH EC2A 13 H2
Finsbury St STLK EC1Y 12 G3
Finsbury Wy BXLY DA5 186 A2
Finsen Rd HNHL SE24 159 K10
Finstock Rd NKENS W10 136 G8
Finucane Dr STMC/STPC BR5 207 M7
Finucane Gdns RAIN RM13 145 H1
Finucane Ri BUSH WD23 94 B3
Finway Rd HHNE HP2 36 C2

Fiona Cl GT/LBKH KT23 ..... 235 P10
Firbank Rd EDW E16 ..... 142 A7
  ENC/FH EN2 ..... 79 K8
Firbank Dr OXHEY WD19 ..... 93 M1
Firbank La WOKN/KNAP GU21 ..... 231 N5
Firbank Pl EGH TW20 ..... 171 N9
Firbank Rd CRW RM5 ..... 104 C6
  PECK SE15 ..... 160 A8
  STALW/RED AL3 ..... 38 E2
Fir Cl WOT/HER KT12 ..... 197 H7
Fircroft Cl SLN SL2 ..... 129 N1
  WOKS/MYFD GU22 ..... 232 C4
Fircroft Gdns HRW HA1 ..... 114 D8
Fircroft Rd CHSGTN KT9 ..... 219 L1
  TOOT SW17 ..... 180 A6
Firdene BRYLDS KT5 ..... 199 P8
Fir Dene ORP BR6 ..... 206 C10
Fireball HI ASC SL5 ..... 192 C7
Firebell Ms SURB KT6 ..... 199 K6
Firecrest Cl HART DA3 ..... 211 N3
Firecrest Dr HAMP NW3 ..... 117 L8
Firefly Gdns EHAM E6 ..... 142 B6
Firfield Rd ADL/WDHM KT15 ..... 215 K1
Fir Grange Av WEY KT13 ..... 216 C2
Firgrove WOKN/KNAP GU21 ..... 231 M5
Firham Park Av HARH RM3 ..... 105 P8
Firhill Rd CAT SE6 ..... 182 F6
Firlands HORL RH6 ..... 280 C3
  WEY KT13 ..... 216 F3
Firle Cl CRAWE RH10 ..... 283 P5
Firmingers Rd ORP BR6 ..... 228 C2
Firmin Rd DART DA1 ..... 187 K1
Fir Pk CHEAM SM3 ..... 201 J8
Fir Rd CHEAM SM3 ..... 201 J8
  FELT TW13 ..... 175 L8
Firs Av FBAR/BDGN N11 ..... 98 B7
  MORT/ESHN SW14 ..... 155 N3
  MUSWH N10 ..... 118 B1
  WDSR SL4 ..... 148 A5
Firsby Av CROY/NA CR0 ..... 204 C8
Firsby Rd STNW/STAM N16 ..... 119 N6
Firs Cl DORK RH4 ..... 272 F4
  ESH/CLAY KT10 ..... 218 D3
  FSTH SE23 ..... 182 C3
  HAT AL10 ..... 40 E5
  MTCM CR4 ..... 202 C2
Firscroft PLMGR N13 ..... 99 K4
Firsdene Cl CHERT KT16 ..... 214 C8
Firs Dr DTCH/LGLY SL3 ..... 130 C10
  HEST TW5 ..... 153 L6
  LOU IG10 ..... 82 D5
Firsgrove Crs BRW CM14 ..... 106 C3
Firside Gv BFN/LL DA15 ..... 185 J4
Firs La PLMGR N13 ..... 99 K4
  POTB/CUF EN6 ..... 59 L9
  WCHMH N21 ..... 99 K1
Firs Park Av WCHMH N21 ..... 99 L2
Firs Park Gdns WCHMH N21 ..... 99 L2
Firs Rd PUR/KEN CR8 ..... 241 J1
First Av ACT W3 ..... 136 C10
  ADL/WDHM KT15 ..... 215 L5
  AMSS HP7 ..... 69 H6
  BXLYHN DA7 ..... 163 M6
  CHDH RM6 ..... 123 M3
  DAGE RM10 ..... 144 C4
  E/WMO/HCT KT8 ..... 197 N4
  EN EN1 ..... 79 N9
  GSTN WD25 ..... 73 K1
  GVW DA11 ..... 190 B4
  HDN NW4 ..... 116 F2
  HOR/WEW KT19 ..... 220 B5
  HYS/HAR UB3 ..... 132 C10
  MNPK E12 ..... 122 B9
  MORT/ESHN SW14 ..... 156 B8
  NKENS W10 ..... 8 C1
  PLSTW E13 ..... 141 M5
  UED N18 ..... 100 B5
  WALTH E17 ..... 120 F3
  WBLY HA9 ..... 115 J7
  WOT/HER KT12 ..... 197 J6
  WTHK RM20 ..... 166 F5
First Avenue Mandela Av
  HLW CM20 ..... 28 G10
  HLWE CM17 ..... 29 L8
First Cl E/WMO/HCT KT8 ..... 198 B4
First Crs SL SL1 ..... 129 H7
First Cross Rd WHTN TW2 ..... 176 D5
The Firs BRWN CM15 ..... 86 F10
  BXLY DA5 ..... 186 E4
  CDH/CHF RM16 ..... 147 P10
  CHESW EN7 ..... 61 M2
  EA W5 ..... 135 J7
  RGUW GU3 ..... 267 N4
  STAL AL1 ..... 38 G10
  TRDG/WHET N20 ..... 97 N2
  WGCW AL8 ..... 22 F1
First St CHEL SW3 ..... 15 N5
Firstway RYNPK SW20 ..... 200 F2
First Wy WBLY HA9 ..... 115 N9
Firs Wk NTHWD HA6 ..... 92 E7
  WFD IG8 ..... 101 M6
Firsway GUW GU2 ..... 249 L9
Firswood Av HOR/WEW KT19 ..... 220 B2
Firth Gdns FUL/PGN SW6 ..... 157 H7
Firtree Av MTCM CR4 ..... 202 B2
Fir Tree Av SLN SL2 ..... 129 L6
  WDR/YW UB7 ..... 152 B2
Fir Tree Cl CRAWW RH11 ..... 283 L4
  EA W5 ..... 135 K8
  ESH/CLAY KT10 ..... 218 B2
  EW KT17 ..... 238 F1
  HHS/BOV HP3 ..... 9 N9
  HOR/WEW KT19 ..... 220 C1
  LHD/OX KT22 ..... 237 H9
  ORP BR6 ..... 227 J3
  ROM RM1 ..... 124 E1
  STRHM/NOR SW16 ..... 180 A8
Fir Tree Ct BORE 75 J3
Fir Tree Gdns CROY/NA CR0 ..... 224 F1
Fir Tree Gv CAR SM5 ..... 222 A4
Fir Tree HI RKW/CH/CXG WD3 ..... 72 B3
Fir Tree Rd BNSTD SM7 ..... 220 G10
  EW KT17 ..... 238 E2
  GU GU1 ..... 249 P7
  HSLWW TW4 ..... 155 M10
  LHD/OX KT22 ..... 237 H9
Fir Trees ABR/ST RM4 ..... 83 L7
Fir Trees Cl BERM/RHTH SE16 ..... 140 D10
Fir Tree Wk EN EN1 ..... 79 M7
  REIG RH2 ..... 257 N10
Fir Wk EW EW17 ..... 220 G3
Firwood Av STALE/WH AL4 ..... 39 K6
Firwood Cl WOKN/KNAP GU21 ..... 231 K6
Firwood Rd VW GU25 ..... 193 K6
Fisher Cl CRAWE RH10 ..... 283 P9
  CROY/NA CR0 ..... 203 N4
  GFD/PVL UB6 ..... 133 P5
  KGLGY WD4 ..... 54 B5
  WOT/HER KT12 ..... 217 J1
Fisherdene ESH/CLAY KT10 ..... 218 F4
Fisherman Cl
  RCHPK/HAM TW10 ..... 177 H7
Fishermans Dr BERM/RHTH SE16.. 160 C1
Fishermen's HI GVW DA11 ..... 189 N1
Fisher Rd KTN/HRWW/WS HA3 .. 94 E10
Fishers Cl CHES/WCR EN8.. 62 F10
  WALTH E17 ..... 160 C7
Fisher's La CHSWK W4 ..... 156 A3
Fisher St CAN/RD E16 ..... 141 M7
  RSQ WC1B 11 L2
Fishers Wy BELV DA17 ..... 144 D10
Fishers Wd ASC SL5 ..... 193 H8
Fisherton St STJWD NW8 ..... 9 L2

Fishery Rd HHW HP1 ..... 35 K8
Fishguard Sp SL SL1 ..... 149 N1
Fishponds Rd HAYES BR2 ..... 226 A2
  TOOT SW17 ..... 179 P7
Fishpool St STALW/RED AL3 ..... 38 B6
Fish Street HI MON EC3R 13 H7
  MON EC3R 13 H8
Fisons Cl CAN/RD E16 ..... 141 M10
Fitchet Cl CRAWW RH11 ..... 285 L5
Fitzalan Rd ESH/CLAY KT10 ..... 218 D4
  FNCH N3 ..... 97 J1
Fitzalan St LBTH SE11 ..... 17 P5
Fitzgeorge Av WKENS W14 ..... 136 F8
Fitzgerald Av MORT/ESHN SW14 ..... 200 B1
Fitzgerald Rd
  MORT/ESHN SW14 ..... 156 A2
  THDIT KT7 ..... 198 F6
  WAN E11 ..... 121 M3
Fitzhardinge St MBLAR W1H 10 C3
Fitzhugh Gv WAND/EARL SW18 ..... 179 M1
Fitzilian Av HARH RM3 ..... 105 N9
Fitzjames Av RCH/KEW TW9 ..... 155 J8
  WKENS W14 ..... 14 B6
Fitzjohn Av BAR EN5 ..... 77 H9
Fitzjohn Cl RGUE GU4 ..... 250 F7
Fitzjohn's Av HAMP NW3 ..... 117 N10
Fitzmaurice Pl MYFR/PICC W1J 10 F9
Fitzneal St ACT W3 ..... 136 C8
Fitzrobert Pl EGH TW20 ..... 172 D9
Fitzroy Cl HGT N6 ..... 118 A6
Fitzroy Crs CHSWK W4 ..... 156 A6
Fitzroy Gdns NRWD SE19 ..... 181 M10
Fitzroy Ms GTPST W1W 10 F2
Fitzroy Pk HGT N6 ..... 118 A6
Fitzroy Rd CAMTN NW1 ..... 4 C5
Fitzroy Sq FITZ W1T 10 G2
Fitzroy St CAMTN NW1 ..... 10 G2
  FITZ W1T 10 G3
Fitzstephen Rd BCTR RM8 ..... 123 L10
Fitzwarren Gdns ARCH N19 ..... 118 D6
Fitzwilliam Av RCH/KEW TW9 ..... 155 L5
Fitzwilliam Ms CAN/RD E16 ..... 141 M10
Fitzwilliam Rd CLAP SW4 ..... 158 D10
Fitzwilliams Ct HLWE CM17 ..... 29 P7
Fitz Wygram Cl HPTN TW12 ..... 176 B8
Five Acre CDALE/KGS NW9 ..... 96 C10
Five Acres CRAWE RH10 ..... 285 P5
  CSHM HP5 ..... 51 J9
  HLWS CM18 ..... 47 H4
  KGLGY WD4 ..... 54 A5
  LCOL/BKTW AL2 ..... 57 J7
Five Acres La LCOL/BKTW AL2.. 56 N5
Five Elms Rd DAGW RM9 ..... 124 A8
  HAYES BR2 ..... 205 P10
Five Fields Cl OXHEY WD19 ..... 93 N3
Five Oaks WOKN/KNAP GU21 ..... 231 J5
Five Oaks La CHIG IG7 ..... 103 P7
Five Ways Jct HDN NW4 ..... 96 F9
Fiveways BRXN/ST SW9 ..... 159 N8
Five Wents SWLY BR8 ..... 209 H2
Fladbury Rd SEVS/STOTM N15 .. 119 L2
Fladgate Rd WAN E11 ..... 121 K4
Flag Cl CROY/NA CR0 ..... 204 C8
Flagstaff Cl WAB EN9 ..... 62 C8
Flagstaff Rd WAB EN9 ..... 62 C8
The Flags HHNE HP2 ..... 36 C6
Flag Wk PIN HA5 ..... 113 H4
Flambard Rd HRW HA1 ..... 114 F4
Flamborough Cl BH/WHM TN16 .. 243 N5
Flamborough Rd RSLP HA4 ..... 113 H8
Flamborough Sp SL SL1 ..... 148 C1
Flamborough St POP/IOD E14 .. 140 D8
Flamingo Wk RAIN RM13 ..... 148 F5
Flamstead End Rd CHES/WCR EN8.. 62 A4
Flamstead Gdns DAGW RM9 ..... 143 M2
Flamstead Rd DAGW RM9 ..... 143 M2
Flamstead Av WBLY HA9 ..... 135 M4
Flamsted Rd CHARL SE7 ..... 162 B4
Flanchford Rd REIG RH2 ..... 256 C10
  SHB W12 ..... 156 C2
Flanders Crs TOOT SW17 ..... 180 A10
Flanders Rd CHSWK W4 ..... 156 B3
  EHAM E6 ..... 142 C4
Flanders Wy HOM E9 ..... 140 C1
Flank St WCHPL E1 ..... 13 N7
Flash La ENC/FH EN2 ..... 79 K3
Flask Wk HAMP NW3 ..... 117 M9
Flatfield Rd HHS/BOV HP3 ..... 36 B8
Flaunden Bottom CSHM HP5 ..... 52 C10
Flaunden HI HHS/BOV HP3 ..... 52 C9
Flaunden La HHS/BOV HP3 ..... 52 E8
  RKW/CH/CXG WD3 ..... 52 E8
Flavell Ms GNWCH SE10 ..... 161 K4
Flavian Cl STALW/RED AL3 ..... 37 N8
Flaxen Cl CHING E4 ..... 100 G4
Flaxen Rd CHING E4 ..... 100 G4
Flaxley Rd MRDN SM4 ..... 201 L6
Flaxman Rd CMBW SE5 ..... 159 J8
Flaxman Ter STPAN WC1H 5 K10
Flaxton Rd WOOL/PLUM SE18 .. 162 G10
Flecker Cl STAN HA7 ..... 94 E6
Fleece Dr UED N18 ..... 99 P5
Fleece Rd SURB KT6 ..... 199 H8
Fleece Wk HOLWY N7 ..... 5 M1
Fleeming Cl WALTH E17 ..... 100 E10
Fleeming Rd WALTH E17 ..... 100 E10
Fleet Av RDART DA2 ..... 188 B4
  UPMR RM14 ..... 126 C4
Fleet Cl E/WMO/HCT KT8 ..... 197 N5
  RSLP HA4 ..... 112 D4
  UPMR RM14 ..... 126 C4
Fleethall Gv CDH/CHF RM16 ..... 147 M10
Fleet Rd GVW DA11 ..... 189 P6
  HAMP NW3 ..... 117 P10
  RDART DA2 ..... 188 B4
Fleetside E/WMO/HCT KT8 ..... 197 N5
Fleet Sq FSBYW WC1X 5 N10
Fleet St EMB EC4Y 12 B6
Fleet Street HI BETH E2 ..... 13 N2
Fleetway EGH TW20 ..... 194 F3
Fleetwood Cl CAN/RD E16 ..... 142 A7
  CHSGTN KT9 ..... 219 J4
  CROY/NA CR0 ..... 203 N10
  CSTG N9 ..... 89 M5
  KWD/TDW/WH KT20 ..... 238 G7
Fleetwood Ct BF/WBF KT14 ..... 215 K9
  STWL/WRAY TW19 ..... 151 N3
Fleetwood Rd CRICK NW2 ..... 117 K1
  KUTN/CMB KT1 ..... 200 C3
  WLSDN NW10 ..... 116 D9
Fleetwood Sq STNW/STAM N16 ..... 199 H3
Fleetwood St STNW/STAM N16 .. 119 M7
Fleetwood Wy OXHEY WD19 ..... 93 K5
Fleming Cl CHESW EN7 ..... 61 P2
Fleming Ct CROY/NA CR0 ..... 223 H2
  HERT/WAS SG14 ..... 25 H3
Fleming Gdns HARH RM3 ..... 105 L10
  TIL RM18 ..... 168 F7
Fleming Md WIM/MER SW19 ..... 179 M10
Fleming Rd CDH/CHF RM16 ..... 167 H3
  GFD/PVL UB6 ..... 134 A2
  WALW SE17 ..... 18 D7
Flemings RBRW/HUT CM13 ..... 107 H7
Fleming Wy CRAWE RH10 ..... 283 P3
  ISLW TW7 ..... 154 E4
  THMD SE28 ..... 143 N9
Flemish Flds CHERT KT16 ..... 195 K7
Flempton Rd LEY E10 ..... 120 D6
Fletcher Cl CHERT KT16 ..... 214 C3
  CHIG IG7 ..... 103 K3
  EHAM E6 ..... 142 E9
Fletcher La LEY E10 ..... 121 H5
Fletcher Rd CHERT KT16 ..... 214 C3
  CHIG IG7 ..... 103 K3
  CHSWK W4 ..... 155 P1

Fletchers Cl HAYES BR2 ..... 205 N4
Fletcher St WCHPL E1 ..... 13 P6
Fletcher Wy HHNE HP2 ..... 35 M4
Fletching Rd CHARL SE7 ..... 162 A5
  CLPT E5 ..... 120 E2
Fletton Rd FBAR/BDGN N11 ..... 98 F8
Fleur De Lis St WCHPL E1 ..... 13 L2
Flexford Rd RGUW GU3 ..... 266 A1
Flexley Wd WGCE AL7 ..... 23 J2
Flex Meadow HLWW/ROY CM19 .. 46 B2
Flexmere Rd TOTM N17 ..... 99 L9
Flimwell Cl BMLY BR1 ..... 183 K8
Flinders Cl STAL AL1 ..... 38 F8
Flint Cl BNSTD SM7 ..... 221 L10
  CRAWE RH10 ..... 284 C10
  GT/LBKH KT23 ..... 254 B2
  ORP BR6 ..... 227 J3
  REDH RH1 ..... 258 A5
Flint Down Cl STMC/STPC BR5 .. 207 K1
Flint HI DORK RH4 ..... 272 C5
Flint Hill Cl DORK RH4 ..... 272 C5
Flintlock Cl STWL/WRAY TW19 .. 151 K10
Flintmill Crs BKHTH/KID SE3 ..... 162 B8
  ELTH/MOT SE9 ..... 162 B8
Flinton St WALW SE17 ..... 19 K7
  WTHK RM20 ..... 166 C5
Flint Wy STALW/RED AL3 ..... 38 B2
Flitcroft St LSQ/SEVD WC2H
Flock Mill Pl WAND/EARL SW18 .. 179 L4
Flockton St BERM/RHTH SE16 .. 19 N1
  BERM/RHTH SE16 ..... 19 N2
Flodden Rd CMBW SE5 ..... 159 K7
Flood La TWK TW1 ..... 176 F4
Flood St CHEL SW3 ..... 15 P9
Flood Wk CHEL SW3 ..... 15 P9
Flora Cl POP/IOD E14 ..... 140 G8
Flora Gdns CHDH RM6 ..... 123 M4
  CROY/NA CR0 ..... 225 H7
Flora Gv STAL AL1 ..... 38 E7
Floral Dr LCOL/BKTW AL2 ..... 57 J2
Floral St COVGDN WC2E 11 M7
Flora St BELV DA17 ..... 164 A4
Florence Av ADL/WDHM KT15 .. 215 K7
  ENC/FH EN2 ..... 79 K7
  MRDN SM4 ..... 201 M5
Florence Cl GSTN WD25 ..... 73 H1
  HCH RM12 ..... 125 M7
  HLWE CM17 ..... 47 M3
  WOT/HER KT12 ..... 197 J7
  WTHK RM20 ..... 167 K5
Florence Crt WAN E11 ..... 121 N2
Florence Dr ENC/FH EN2 ..... 79 K7
Florence Gdns CHSWK W4 ..... 155 P5
  STA TW18 ..... 173 L10
Florence Rd ABYW SE2 ..... 153 M2
  BECK BR3 ..... 204 C2
  BMLY BR1 ..... 205 M1
  CHSWK W4 ..... 156 A2
  EA W5 ..... 135 K9
  EHAM E6 ..... 141 P3
  FELT TW13 ..... 175 J4
  FSBYPK N4 ..... 118 G5
  KUTN/CMB KT2 ..... 177 L10
  NWCR SE14 ..... 160 E7
  NWDGN UB2 ..... 153 L3
  PLSTW E13 ..... 141 M4
  SAND/SEL CR2 ..... 223 L5
  WIM/MER SW19 ..... 179 L9
  WOT/HER KT12 ..... 197 J7
Florence Ter NWCR SE14 ..... 160 E7
Florence Wy BAL SW12 ..... 179 J1
Florfield Rd HACK E8 ..... 140 A1
Florian Av SUT SM1 ..... 221 N1
Florian Rd PUT/ROE SW15 ..... 157 H10
Florida Cl BUSH WD23 ..... 94 C3
Florida Rd RGUE GU4 ..... 268 B6
  THHTH CR7 ..... 203 J1
Florida St BETH E2 ..... 7 P10
  BETH E2 ..... 140 A5
Florin Cl UED N18 ..... 99 M5
Floriston Av HGDN/ICK UB10 .. 132 D2
Floriston Cl STAN HA7 ..... 94 G9
Floriston Gdns STAN HA7 ..... 94 G9
Floss St PUT/ROE SW15 ..... 156 F8
Flower Crs CHERT KT16 ..... 214 E3
Flowerfield RSEV TN14 ..... 246 G3
Flowerhill Wy MEO DA13 ..... 190 B10
Flower La GDST RH9 ..... 260 C5
  MLHL NW7 ..... 96 C6
Flowers Ms ARCH N19 ..... 118 D7
Flower Wk GUW GU2 ..... 267 P3
Floyd Rd CHARL SE7 ..... 161 P4
Floyds La WOKS/MYFD GU22 .. 233 K2
Fludyer St LEW SE13 ..... 161 K10
Flux's La EPP CM16 ..... 65 K9
The Flyers Wy BH/WHM TN16 .. 262 C4
Fold Cft HLW CM20 ..... 28 D10
Foley Cl BEAC HP9 ..... 88 B7
Foley Ms ESH/CLAY KT10 ..... 218 D3
Foley Rd BH/WHM TN16 ..... 244 A4
  ESH/CLAY KT10 ..... 218 D4
Foley St GTPST W1W 10 E3
Folgate St WCHPL E1 ..... 13 K3
Foliot St ACT W3 ..... 136 C8
Folkes La UPMR RM14 ..... 126 E3
Folkestone Ct DTCH/LGLY SL3 .. 150 A7
Folkestone Rd EHAM E6 ..... 142 G1
  UED N18 ..... 99 P5
  WALTH E17 ..... 120 C2
Folkingham La CDALE/KGS NW9 .. 96 B9
Folkington Cnr NFNCH/WDSP N12.. 97 H2
Follet Dr ABLGY WD5 ..... 54 C7
Follett Dr ABLGY WD5 ..... 54 C7
Follett St POP/IOD E14 ..... 141 N9
Folly Cl RAD WD7 ..... 74 E2
Folly Av STALW/RED AL3 ..... 38 B5
Folly Flds STALE/WH AL4 ..... 20 C1
Folly La RDKG RH5 ..... 272 G10
  STALW/RED AL3 ..... 38 B5
  WALTH E17 ..... 100 D9
Folly Pathway RAD WD7 ..... 74 E1
Folly Vw WARE SG12 ..... 26 C6
Folly Wall POP/IOD E14 ..... 161 H1
Fontaine Rd STRHM/NOR SW16 .. 180 C9
Fontayne Av CHIG IG7 ..... 102 F5
  RAIN RM13 ..... 144 F2
  ROM RM1 ..... 104 F10
Fontenoy Rd TOOT SW17 ..... 180 C5
Fonteyne Gdns WFD IG8 ..... 102 A10
Fonthill Cl NRWD SE19
Fonthill Ms FSBYPK N4 ..... 119 H7
Fonthill Rd FSBYPK N4 ..... 118 G7
Font Hills EFNCH N2 ..... 97 H10
Fontley Wy PUT/ROE SW15 ..... 178 D3
Fontmell Cl ASHF TW15 ..... 174 B8
  STALW/RED AL3 ..... 38 B1
Fontmell Pk ASHF TW15 ..... 174 B8
Fontwell Cl KTN/HRWW/WS HA3.. 94 B8
  NTHLT UB5 ..... 133 M7
Fontwell Dr HAYES BR2 ..... 206 D2
Fontwell Park Gdns HCH RM12 .. 125 M9
Fontwell Rd CRAWE RH10 ..... 284 D10
Foord Cl RDART DA2 ..... 188 D3
Football La HRW HA1 ..... 114 F6
Footbury Hill Rd ORP BR6 ..... 207 H2
The Footpath PUT/ROE SW15 .. 178 D1
Foots Cray High St SCUP DA14 .. 185 M3
Foots Cray La BXLY DA5 ..... 185 M4
Footscray Rd ELTH/MOT SE9 .. 184 D2
Forbes Av POTB/CUF EN6 ..... 59 N4
Forbes Cl CRICK NW2 ..... 116 D8

HCH RM12 ..... 125 J6
Forbes St WCHPL E1 ..... 13 P6
Forbes Wy RSLP HA4 ..... 113 J7
Forburg Rd STNW/STAM N16 .. 119 P6
Force Green La BH/WHM TN16 .. 244 G10
Fordbridge Rd ASHF TW15 ..... 173 P9
  SHPTN TW17 ..... 196 F6
  SUN TW16 ..... 197 H5
Ford Cl ASHF TW15 ..... 173 P9
  BUSH WD23 ..... 74 B8
  HRW HA1 ..... 114 C5
  RAIN RM13 ..... 144 G2
  SHPTN TW17 ..... 196 B4
  THHTH CR7 ..... 203 J6
Fordcroft Rd STMC/STPC BR5 .. 207 L5
Forde Av BMLY BR1 ..... 205 P3
Ford End CAT SE6 ..... 183 J4
  DEN/HRF UB9 ..... 111 J7
  WFD IG8 ..... 101 N7
Fordham Cl EMPK RM11 ..... 125 P5
Fordham Rd EBAR EN4 ..... 77 N7
  STNW/STAM N16 ..... 119 P6
Fordham St WCHPL E1 ..... 13 P4
Fordhook Av ACT W3 ..... 135 L3
Fordingbridge Cl CHERT KT16 .. 195 L8
Fordingley Rd MV/WKIL W9 ..... 2 D10
Fordington Rd HGT N6 ..... 118 A2
Ford La IVER SL0 ..... 131 K8
  RAIN RM13 ..... 144 G2
Fordmill Rd CAT SE6 ..... 182 F5
Ford Rd ASHF TW15 ..... 174 A7
  BOW E3 ..... 140 D4
  CHOB/PIR GU24 ..... 213 H6
  CHOB/PIR GU24 ..... 230 E1
  DAGE RM10 ..... 144 C4
  DAGW RM9 ..... 144 A2
  GVW DA11 ..... 189 L10
  WOKS/MYFD GU22 ..... 232 E6
Ford's Gv WCHMH N21 ..... 99 K2
Fords Park Rd CAN/RD E16 ..... 141 M8
Ford Sq WCHPL E1 ..... 140 A7
  CAN/RD E16 ..... 141 L8
Ford St BOW E3 ..... 140 D3
  CAN/RD E16 ..... 141 L8
Fordwater Rd CHERT KT16 ..... 195 L8
Fordwich Cl HERT/WAS SG14 .. 25 H5
  ORP BR6 ..... 207 J7
Fordwich HI HERT/WAS SG14 .. 25 H5
Fordwich Rd WGCW AL8 ..... 22 F6
Fordwych Rd CRICK NW2 ..... 117 H10
Fordyce Cl EMPK RM11 ..... 125 P5
Fordyce Rd LEW SE13 ..... 183 H2
Fordyke Rd BCTR RM8 ..... 123 P7
Forbury Av SBW CM21 ..... 30 A1
The Forebury SBW CM21 ..... 30 A1
Forefield LCOL/BKTW AL2 ..... 57 H3
Foreland Ct HDN NW4 ..... 97 H9
Foreland St WOOL/PLUM SE18 .. 162 G3
Forelands Wy CSHM HP5 ..... 51 H3
Foremark Cl BARK/HLT IG6 ..... 103 J6
Foreshore DEPT SE8 ..... 160 L5
Forest Ap CHING E4 ..... 101 K1
  WFD IG8 ..... 101 J4
Forest Av CHIC IG7 ..... 102 F6
  CHING E4 ..... 101 K1
  HHS/BOV HP3 ..... 35 N3
Forest Cl CHST BR7 ..... 206 D1
  EHSLY KT24 ..... 252 G1
  WAB EN9 ..... 81 N3
  WAN E11 ..... 121 N1
  WFD IG8 ..... 101 N5
  WOKS/MYFD GU22 ..... 232 C1
Forest Ct CHING E4 ..... 101 L2
  EPP CM16 ..... 64 C9
  FSTGT E7 ..... 121 P2
Forest Crs ASHTD KT21 ..... 237 M2
Forestdale STHGT/OAK N14 ..... 98 F5
Forest Dr EPP CM16 ..... 83 H2
  HAYES BR2 ..... 206 B10
  KWD/TDW/WH KT20 ..... 239 K7
  MNPK E12 ..... 122 A8
  SUN TW16 ..... 174 G10
  WFD IG8 ..... 101 J4
Forest Dr East WAN E11 ..... 121 J3
Forest Dr West WAN E11 ..... 121 H3
Forest Edge BKHH IG9 ..... 101 P4
Forester Rd CRAWE RH10 ..... 283 P9
  PECK SE15 ..... 160 A10
Foresters Cl CHESW EN7 ..... 61 M3
  WLGTN SM6 ..... 222 E4
  WOKN/KNAP GU21 ..... 231 L4
Foresters Dr WALTH E17 ..... 121 J2
  WLGTN SM6 ..... 222 E4
Forestfield CRAWE RH10 ..... 284 F6
Forest Gdns TOTM N17 ..... 99 N10
Forest Ga CDALE/KGS NW9 ..... 116 E2
  EPP CM16 ..... 65 P3
  WAN E11 ..... 121 K4
Forest Gv HACK E8 ..... 7 K1
Forest Hill Rd EDUL SE22 ..... 182 A2
Forest La CHIG IG7 ..... 102 F6
  EHSLY KT24 ..... 234 G10
  FSTGT E7 ..... 121 N10
Forest Mount Rd WFD IG8 ..... 101 J7
Fore St BARB EC2Y 12 G4
  BRKMPK AL9 ..... 40 F7
  ED N9 ..... 99 P5
  HERT/WAS SG14 ..... 25 H5
  HLWE CM17 ..... 29 M7
  PIN HA5 ..... 113 H3
Forest Rdg BECK BR3 ..... 204 F3
  HAYES BR2 ..... 226 B1
Forest Ri WALTH E17 ..... 121 J1
Forest Rd BARK/HLT IG6 ..... 103 L1
  CHEAM SM3 ..... 201 N8
  CHES/WCR EN8 ..... 62 C5
  ED N9 ..... 100 C4
  EHSLY KT24 ..... 255 H9
  ERITH DA8 ..... 165 H7
  FELT TW13 ..... 175 K6
  FSTGT E7 ..... 121 M2
  GSTN WD25 ..... 55 J9
  HACK E8 ..... 7 N2
  LOU IG10 ..... 82 A6
  PEND EN3 ..... 80 D2
  RCH/KEW TW9 ..... 155 N9
  ROMW/RG RM7 ..... 124 C1
  WALTH E17 ..... 121 L3
  WAN E11 ..... 121 L3
  WDSR SL4 ..... 148 C3
  WFD IG8 ..... 101 M4
  WOKS/MYFD GU22 ..... 232 C1
Forest Side CHING E4 ..... 101 L1
  EPP CM16 ..... 64 C9
  FSTGT E7 ..... 121 N2
  KUTN/CMB KT4 ..... 200 B10
The Forest WALTH E17 ..... 121 K2
Forest Vw CHING E4 ..... 81 J10
  CRAWE RH10 ..... 284 A10
  WAN E11 ..... 121 L5
Forest View Av LEY E10 ..... 121 J5
Forest View Rd MNPK E12 ..... 122 B7
  WALTH E17 ..... 121 L1
Forest Wy ASHTD KT21 ..... 237 M3
  BFN/LL DA15 ..... 167 C10
  HLWE CM17 ..... 30 C10
  HLWE CM17 ..... 47 L1
  LOU IG10 ..... 82 D7
  WAB EN9 ..... 64 D1
  WFD IG8 ..... 101 L3

Forge Cl HAYES BR2 ..... 205 M8
  KGLGY WD4 ..... 53 K7
Forge Dr ESH/CLAY KT10 ..... 218 F4
  SLN SL2 ..... 129 H1
Forge End WOKN/KNAP GU21 .. 232 B3
Forgefield BH/WHM TN16 ..... 244 A2
Forge La BELMT SM2 ..... 221 M4
  CRAWE RH10 ..... 284 B6
  EYN DA4 ..... 210 B4
  FELT TW13 ..... 175 M8
  GVE DA12 ..... 191 J5
  GVE DA12 ..... 191 N5
  NTHWD HA6 ..... 92 D6
  SUN TW16 ..... 197 H4
Forge Rd CRAWE RH10 ..... 284 B6
Forge Wy RSEV TN14 ..... 228 G7
Forge Wd CRAWE RH10 ..... 284 E2
Forman Pl STNW/STAM N16 ..... 119 N9
Formby Av KTN/HRWW/W HA3.. 115 H1
Formby Cl DTCH/LGLY SL3 ..... 150 F3
Formosa St MV/WKIL W9 ..... 9 H2
Formunt Cl CAN/RD E16 ..... 141 L7
Forres Cl HOD EN11 ..... 44 F1
Forres Gdns GLDGN NW11 ..... 117 K4
Forrester Pth SYD SE26 ..... 182 B7
Forresters Dr WCCE AL7 ..... 23 M6
Forris Av HYS/HAR UB3 ..... 132 C10
Forset St MBLAR W1H 9 P5
Forstal Cl HAYES BR2 ..... 205 M3
Forsters Cl CHDH RM6 ..... 124 A4
Forster Rd BECK BR3 ..... 204 D3
  BRXS/STRHM SW2 ..... 180 F3
  TOTM N17 ..... 117 K1
  WALTH E17 ..... 120 D4
Forsters Cl CHDH RM6 ..... 124 A4
Forston St IS N1 ..... 6 F7
Forsyte Crs NRWD SE19 ..... 203 M1
Forsyth Gdns WALW SE17 ..... 18 D10
Forsythia Cl IL IG1 ..... 122 C10
Forsyth Pl EN EN1 ..... 79 M9
Forsyth Rd WOKN/KNAP GU21.. 214 F10
Forterie Gdns GDMY/SEVK IG3.. 123 K3
Fortescue Av WHTN TW2 ..... 176 B6
Fortescue Rd EDGW HA8 ..... 96 D4
  WEY KT13 ..... 216 A1
  WIM/MER SW19 ..... 179 N10
Fortess Gv KTTN NW5 ..... 118 C10
Fortess Rd KTTN NW5 ..... 118 C10
Fortess Wk KTTN NW5 ..... 118 C10
Forthbridge Rd BTSEA SW11 .. 158 D10
Forth Rd UPMR RM14 ..... 126 C4
Fortin Cl SOCK/AV RM15 ..... 146 F2
Fortin Wy SOCK/AV RM15 ..... 146 F2
Fortis Cl CAN/RD E16 ..... 141 P8
Fortis Grn EFNCH N2 ..... 118 A1
Fortis Green Av EFNCH N2 ..... 118 B1
Fortis Green Rd MUSWH N10 .. 118 B1
Fort La REIG RH2 ..... 257 L6
Fortnam Rd ARCH N19 ..... 118 C7
Fortnums Acre STAN HA7 ..... 94 E7
Fort Rd GU GU1 ..... 268 B3
  KWD/TDW/WH KT20 ..... 255 H7
  NTHLT UB5 ..... 133 P2
  RSEV TN14 ..... 246 D1
  STHWK SE1 ..... 19 M6
  TIL RM18 ..... 168 G10
Fortrose Gdns BRXS/STRHM SW2.. 180 F4
Fortrye Cl GVW DA11 ..... 190 B5
Fort St CAN/RD E16 ..... 141 N10
  WCHPL E1 ..... 13 K4
Fortunegate Rd WLSDN NW10 .. 136 B3
Fortune Green Rd
  KIL/WHAMP NW6 ..... 117 K10
Fortunes Mead NTHLT UB5 ..... 133 M1
The Fortunes HLWS CM18 ..... 47 J3
Fortune St STLK EC1Y 12 F2
Fortune Wy WLSDN NW10 ..... 136 D5
Forty Acre La CAN/RD E16 ..... 141 M6
Forty Av WBLY HA9 ..... 115 L8
Forty Cl WBLY HA9 ..... 115 L8
Fortyfoot Rd LHD/OX KT22 ..... 237 J8
Forty Green Rd BEAC HP9 ..... 88 A7
Forty HI EN EN1 ..... 79 N3
Forty La WBLY HA9 ..... 115 N7
Forumside EDGW HA8 ..... 96 A7
The Forum E/WMO/HCT KT8 ..... 198 A4
Forum Wy EDGW HA8 ..... 96 A7
Forval Cl MTCM CR4 ..... 202 A4
Forward Dr KTN/HRWW/W HA3 .. 114 E2
Foscote Ms MV/WKIL W9 ..... 8 F2
Foscote Rd HDN NW4 ..... 116 E3
Foskett Rd FUL/PGN SW6 ..... 157 J8
Foss Av CROY/NA CR0 ..... 223 H2
Fossdene Rd CHARL SE7 ..... 161 N4
Fossdyke Cl YEAD UB4 ..... 133 M4
Fosse Wy BF/WBF KT14 ..... 215 J9
  WEA W13 ..... 134 F7
Fossil Rd LEW SE13 ..... 161 J2
Fossington Rd BELV DA17 ..... 163 N3
Foss Rd TOOT SW17 ..... 179 N7
Fossway BCTR RM8 ..... 123 M7
Foster Av WDSR SL4 ..... 148 C9
Fosterdown GDST RH9 ..... 260 A5
Foster La CITYW EC2V 12 E5
Foster Rd ACT W3 ..... 136 B9
  CHSWK W4 ..... 156 A4
  HHW HP1 ..... 35 L8
  PLSTW E13 ..... 141 M4
Fosters Cl CHST BR7 ..... 184 C8
  SWFD E18 ..... 101 N9
Fosters Gv BFOR GU20 ..... 212 A1
Fosters La WOKN/KNAP GU21 .. 231 H3
Fosters Pth SLN SL2 ..... 128 E6
Foster St HDN NW4 ..... 116 F2
  HLWE CM17 ..... 48 A3
Fothergill Cl PLSTW E13 ..... 141 M2
Fothergill Dr WCHMH N21 ..... 78 F10
Fotheringham Rd EN EN1 ..... 79 N8
Fotherley Rd RKW/CH/CXG WD3 .. 91 J3
Fotherley Rd RKW/CH/CXG WD3 .. 91 J3
Foubert's Pl SOHO/CST W1F 10 F6
Foulden Rd STNW/STAM N16 .. 119 N9
Foulden Ter STNW/STAM N16 .. 119 N9
Foulis Ter SKENS SW7 ..... 15 L6
Foulser Rd TOOT SW17 ..... 180 A6
Foulsham Rd THHTH CR7 ..... 203 K8
Founders Gdns NRWD SE19 .. 181 K10
Founders Rd HOD EN11 ..... 44 D1
Foundry Cl BERM/RHTH SE16 .. 140 D10
Foundry La DTCH/LGLY SL3 ..... 150 F9
Foundry Ms CAMTN NW1 ..... 11 H1
Fountain Cl UX/CGN UB8 ..... 132 D7
Fountain Dr CAR SM5 ..... 222 A4
  NRWD SE19 ..... 181 H7
Fountain Farm HLWS CM18 ..... 47 J3
Fountain Gdns WDSR SL4 ..... 149 H9
Fountain Pl BRXN/ST SW9 ..... 159 H7
  WAB EN9 ..... 63 H10
Fountain Rd REDH RH1 ..... 275 P2
  THHTH CR7 ..... 203 K2
  TOOT SW17 ..... 179 N8
Fountains Av FELT TW13 ..... 175 N6
Fountains Cl CRAWW RH11 ..... 283 K9
  FELT TW13 ..... 175 N5
Fountains Crs STHGT/OAK N14 .. 98 F1
Fountain Wk GVW DA11 ..... 191 P7
Fountayne Rd SEVS/STOTM N15.. 119 P2
  STNW/STAM N16 ..... 119 P7
Fount St VX/NE SW8 ..... 17 P7
Four Acres COB KT11 ..... 217 N9
  GU GU1 ..... 250 F8
Fouracres PEND EN3 ..... 80 D5

Four Acres WGCE AL7 ... 23 H7
Fouracres Dr HHS/BOV HP3 ... 36 A8
The Four Acres SBW CM21 ... 30 B1
Fouracres Wk HHS/BOV HP3 ... 36 A8
Fourland Wk EDGW HA8 ... 95 P7
Four Limes STALE/WH AL4 ... 21 J3
Fournier St WCHPL E1 ... 13 M5
Four Seasons Crs CHEAM SM3 ... 201 J9
Fourth Av GSTN WD25 ... 73 L1
HLW CM20 ... 28 F10
HLWW/ROY CM19 ... 46 D1
HYS/HAR UB3 ... 132 G10
MNPK E12 ... 122 C9
NKENS W10 ... 8 A1
ROMW/RG RM7 ... 124 D6
WTHK RM20 ... 166 F5
Fourth Dr COUL/CHIP CR5 ... 240 E2
Fourth Wy WBLY HA9 ... 115 N9
The Four Tubs BUSH WD23 ... 94 C1
Four Wents COB KT11 ... 217 J9
The Four Wents CHING E4 ... 101 J3
Fovant St HARP AL5 ... 20 B5
Fowler Cl BTSEA SW11 ... 157 N9
CRAWE RH10 ... 284 D9
SCUP DA14 ... 185 P9
Fowler Rd BARK/HLT IG6 ... 103 M6
FSTGT E7 ... 121 N9
IS N1 ... 6 D5
Fowlers Md CHOB/PIR GU24 ... 213 K5
Fowler's Wk EA W5 ... 135 J6
Fownes St BTSEA SW11 ... 157 N9
Foxacre CTHM CR3 ... 241 M8
Foxberry Rd BROCKY SE4 ... 160 D10
Foxborough Cl DTCH/LGLY SL3 ... 150 D4
Foxborough Gdns BROCKY SE4 ... 182 F2
Foxborough Hill Rd SHGR GU5 ... 268 B9
Foxbourne Rd TOOT SW17 ... 180 B5
Fox Burrow Rd CHIG IG7 ... 103 N5
Foxbury Av CHST BR7 ... 184 C9
Foxbury Cl BMLY BR1 ... 183 N9
ORP BR6 ... 227 K2
Foxbury Dr ORP BR6 ... 227 K3
Foxbury Rd BMLY BR1 ... 183 N9
Fox Cl BORE WD6 ... 75 J10
BUSH WD23 ... 74 A9
CAN/RD E16 ... 141 M7
CRAWW RH11 ... 283 K6
CRW RM5 ... 104 C6
ORP BR6 ... 227 K2
WCHPL E1 ... 140 B6
WEY KT13 ... 216 E2
WOKS/MYFD GU22 ... 232 G1
Fox Covert LHD/OX KT22 ... 236 C10
Fox Covert Cl ASC SL5 ... 192 B5
Foxcroft STAL AL1 ... 38 F8
Foxcroft Rd WOOL/PLUM SE18 ... 162 E7
Foxdell NTHWD HA6 ... 92 E7
Foxdells HERT/WAS SG14 ... 24 D8
Foxdell Wy CFSP/GDCR SL9 ... 90 B6
Foxearth Cl BH/WHM TN16 ... 244 B4
Foxearth Rd SAND/SEL CR2 ... 224 B5
Foxearth Sp SAND/SEL CR2 ... 224 B5
Foxes Cl HERT/BAY SG13 ... 25 P5
Foxes Dale BKHTH/KID SE3 ... 161 M9
HAYES BR2 ... 205 J3
Foxes Dr CHESW EN7 ... 61 N5
Foxes Gn CDH/CHF RM16 ... 168 D1
Foxes La POTB/CUF EN6 ... 60 F4
Foxes Pth RGUE GU4 ... 250 C2
Foxfield Cl NTHWD HA6 ... 92 E7
Foxfield Rd ORP BR6 ... 206 G9
Foxglove Cl HAT AL10 ... 40 E5
STHL UB1 ... 133 M9
STWL/WRAY TW19 ... 173 M4
Foxglove Dr WAN E11 ... 121 P2
Foxglove Gdns PUR/KEN CR8 ... 222 F7
RGUE GU4 ... 250 F8
Foxglove La CHSGTN KT9 ... 219 M1
Foxglove Rd SOCK/AV RM15 ... 147 H8
The Foxgloves HHW HP1 ... 35 H7
Foxglove St ACT W3 ... 136 C9
Foxglove Wy MTCM CR4 ... 202 B7
Foxgrove PLMGR N13 ... 98 F4
Fox Gv WOT/HER KT12 ... 197 J7
Foxgrove Av BECK BR3 ... 182 G10
Foxgrove Dr WOKN/KNAP GU21 ... 231 N3
Foxgrove Pth OXHEY WD19 ... 93 L6
Foxgrove Rd BECK BR3 ... 182 G10
Foxhall Rd UPMR RM14 ... 126 B10
Foxham Rd ARCH N19 ... 118 E8
Foxhanger Gdns WOKS/MYFD GU22 ... 232 D3
Fox Hatch BRWN CM15 ... 86 D4
Foxherne DTCH/LGLY SL3 ... 149 P1
Fox HI NRWD SE19 ... 181 N10
Foxhill WATN WD24 ... 73 H2
Fox Hill Gdns NRWD SE19 ... 181 M10
Foxhills WOKN/KNAP GU21 ... 231 P3
Foxhills Cl CHERT KT16 ... 214 E3
Fox Hills Rd CHERT KT16 ... 214 D2
Fox Hole Rd ELTH/MOT SE9 ... 184 B1
Foxholes WEY KT13 ... 216 E2
Foxholes Rd HERT/BAY SG13 ... 25 P5
Fox Hollow Cl WOOL/PLUM SE18 ... 163 H4
Foxhollow Dr SLN SL2 ... 109 H10
Fox Hollow Dr BXLYHN DA16 ... 163 N9
Foxhollows HAT AL10 ... 40 E2
Foxholt Gdns WLSDN NW10 ... 135 P2
Fox Home Cl CHST BR7 ... 184 D9
Foxlake Rd BF/WBF KT14 ... 216 A8
Foxlands Cl GSTN WD25 ... 54 C10
Foxlands Crs DAGE RM10 ... 124 D10
Foxlands Rd DAGE RM10 ... 124 D10
Fox La EA W5 ... 135 K7
GT/LBKH KT23 ... 235 N10
HAYES BR2 ... 225 N2
PLMGR N13 ... 98 G3
Fox La North CHERT KT16 ... 195 J7
Fox La South CHERT KT16 ... 195 J8
Foxlees ALP/SUD HA0 ... 114 F9
Foxley Cl REDH RH1 ... 276 B5
Foxley Gdns PUR/KEN CR8 ... 223 J9
Foxley Hill Rd PUR/KEN CR8 ... 223 H8
Foxley La PUR/KEN CR8 ... 222 F6
Foxley Rd CMBW SE5 ... 158 G6
PUR/KEN CR8 ... 241 J1
THHTH CR7 ... 203 J6
Foxleys OXHEY WD19 ... 93 M4
Fox Manor Wy WTHK RM20 ... 166 C5
Foxmead Cl ENC/FH EN2 ... 78 G2
Foxmore St BTSEA SW11 ... 158 A7
Foxoak HI WEY KT13 ... 216 E3
Foxon Cl CTHM CR3 ... 241 M7
Foxon La CTHM CR3 ... 241 L7
Foxon Lane Gdns CTHM CR3 ... 241 M7
Fox Rd CAN/RD E16 ... 141 M7
DTCH/LGLY SL3 ... 150 A3
Fox's La BRKMPK AL9 ... 41 H10
Foxton Gv MTCM CR4 ... 201 N2
Foxton Rd HOD EN11 ... 44 E3
WTHK RM20 ... 167 J3
Foxwarren ESH/CLAY KT10 ... 218 E5
Foxwell St BROCKY SE4 ... 160 D9
Foxwood Cl FELT TW13 ... 175 J6
MLHL NW7 ... 96 B5
Foxwood Green Cl EN EN1 ... 79 M10
Foxwood Gv CVW GU11 ... 227 N6
Foxwood Rd BKHTH/KID SE3 ... 161 L10
RDART DA2 ... 188 G6
Foxwood Wy HART DA3 ... 211 P2

Foyle Dr SOCK/AV RM15 ... 146 F7
Foyle Rd BKHTH/KID SE3 ... 161 L5
TOTM N17 ... 99 P9
Frailey Cl WOKS/MYFD GU22 ... 232 E2
Frailey HI WOKS/MYFD GU22 ... 232 E2
Framewood Rd DTCH/LGLY SL3 ... 129 P2
Framfield Cl CRAWW RH11 ... 285 K5
NFNCH/WDSP N12 ... 97 K5
Framfield Rd HBRY N5 ... 119 J10
HNWL W7 ... 134 E8
MTCM CR4 ... 180 A6
Framlingham Crs ELTH/MOT SE9 ... 184 B7
Frampton Cl BELMT SM2 ... 221 K4
Frampton Park Rd HOM E9 ... 140 E1
Frampton Rd EPP CM16 ... 65 K4
HSLWW TW4 ... 175 M1
POTB/CUF EN6 ... 59 M6
Frampton St HERT/WAS SG14 ... 25 L5
STJWD NW8 ... 9 J3
Francemary Rd LEW SE13 ... 182 F1
Frances Gdns SOCK/AV RM15 ... 146 E8
Frances Rd CHING E4 ... 100 F7
WDSR SL4 ... 149 H9
Frances St CSHM HP5 ... 51 H6
WOOL/PLUM SE18 ... 162 C3
Franche Court Rd TOOT SW17 ... 179 M6
Franchise St CSHM HP5 ... 51 H6
Francis Av BXLYHN DA7 ... 164 B8
FELT TW13 ... 175 H6
IL IG1 ... 122 C2
STALW/RED AL3 ... 38 C3
Francis Barber Cl STRHM/NOR SW16 ... 180 G7
Franciscan Rd TOOT SW17 ... 180 B7
Francis Chichester Cl ASC SL5 ... 192 A5
Francis Chichester Wy BTSEA SW11 ... 158 B7
Francis Cl HOR/WEW KT19 ... 220 A1
SHPTN TW17 ... 196 B4
Francisco Cl CDH/CHF RM16 ... 167 H2
Francis Gv WIM/MER SW19 ... 179 J9
Francis Rd CROY/NA CR0 ... 203 J7
CTHM CR3 ... 241 M8
DART DA1 ... 187 L1
EFNCH N2 ... 118 A2
GFD/PVL UB6 ... 135 H4
HRW HA1 ... 114 F3
HSLWW TW4 ... 155 L8
LEY E10 ... 139 H4
PIN HA5 ... 113 N3
STMC/STPC BR5 ... 207 N3
WAN E11 ... 121 J8
WARE SG12 ... 26 C1
WATW WD18 ... 73 J8
WLGTN SM6 ... 222 D3
Francis St SRTFD E15 ... 121 K10
WEST SW1P ... 17 H5
Francis Ter ARCH N19 ... 118 D5
Francis Wy SL SL1 ... 128 C9
Francklyn Gdns EDGW HA8 ... 95 M4
Francombe Gdns ROM RM1 ... 125 H4
Franconia Rd CLAP SW4 ... 180 D1
Frank Burton Cl CHARL SE7 ... 161 N4
Frank Dixon Cl DUL SE21 ... 181 M3
Frank Dixon Wy DUL SE21 ... 181 M4
Frankfurt Rd HNHL SE24 ... 181 K1
Frankham St DEPT SE8 ... 160 F6
Frankland Cl BERM/RTH SE16 ... 160 A2
WFD IG8 ... 101 P6
Frankland Rd CHING E4 ... 100 F6
RKW/CH/CXG WD3 ... 92 B1
Franklin Av CHESW EN7 ... 61 P6
SLN SL2 ... 128 C3
Franklin Cl KUT KT1 ... 199 M3
LEW SE13 ... 160 F10
STALE/WH AL4 ... 40 B8
TRDG/WHET N20 ... 97 M1
WNWD SE27 ... 181 J6
Franklin Crs MTCM CR4 ... 202 D4
Franklin Rd BXLYHN DA7 ... 163 P7
CRAWE RH10 ... 284 D8
GVE DA12 ... 190 G8
HCH RM12 ... 145 K1
PGE/AN SE20 ... 182 B10
WAT WD17 ... 73 J6
WOT/HER KT12 ... 197 H6
Franklins Ms RYLN/HDSTN HA2 ... 114 B7
Franklin Sq WKENS W14 ... 14 D8
Franklin's Rw CHEL SW3 ... 16 B7
Franklin St BOW E3 ... 140 C5
SEVS/STOTM N15 ... 119 M4
Franklin Wy CROY/NA CR0 ... 202 F8
Franklyn Crs WDSR SL4 ... 148 C9
Franklyn Gdns BARK/HLT IG6 ... 102 C7
Franklyn Rd WLSDN NW10 ... 136 C2
WOT/HER KT12 ... 197 J6
Frank Martin Ct CHESW EN7 ... 61 P6
Franks Av NWMAL KT3 ... 199 P4
Franksfield SHGR GU5 ... 270 F10
Franks La EYN DA4 ... 210 A3
Franks Rd GUW GU2 ... 249 M7
Frank Sutton Wy SL SL1 ... 129 J9
Franks Wood Av STMC/STPC BR5 ... 206 A5
Franlaw Crs PLMGR N13 ... 99 K5
Franmil Rd EMPK RM11 ... 124 F4
Fransfield Gv SYD SE26 ... 181 J6
Frant Cl PGE/AN SE20 ... 182 G10
Franthorne Wy CAT SE6 ... 182 G5
Frant Rd THHTH CR7 ... 203 J5
Fraser Cl BXLY DA5 ... 186 D4
CHES/WCR EN8 ... 62 D4
Fraser Rd CHES/WCR EN8 ... 62 D4
ED N9 ... 100 A4
ERITH DA8 ... 164 D4
GFD/PVL UB6 ... 135 H3
LEY E10 ... 139 L6
WALTH E17 ... 120 D3
Fraser St CHSWK W4 ... 156 B4
Frating Crs WFD IG8 ... 101 N7
Frays Av WDR/YW UB7 ... 151 N1
Frays Cl WDR/YW UB7 ... 151 N2
Frayslea UX/CGN UB8 ... 131 N4
Fray's Waye UX/CGN UB8 ... 131 M3
Frazer Av RSLP HA4 ... 113 K10
Frazer Cl ROMW/RG RM7 ... 124 D5
Frazier St STHWK SE1 ... 18 A2
Frean St BERM/RTH SE16 ... 19 N3
Freda Corbett Cl PECK SE15 ... 159 P6
Frederica Rd CHING E4 ... 101 J1
Frederica St HOLWY N7 ... 9 N3
Frederick Crs BRXN/ST SW9 ... 159 J6
PEND EN3 ... 80 B6
Frederick Gdns SUT SM1 ... 221 J4
Frederick Pl WOOL/PLUM SE18 ... 162 K4
Frederick Rd RAIN RM13 ... 144 E4
SUT SM1 ... 221 J2
WALW SE17 ... 18 D8
Frederick Sanger Rd GUW GU2 ... 267 J1
Frederick's Pl LOTH EC2R ... 12 G6
NFNCH/WDSP N12 ... 97 M5
Frederick Sq POP/IOD E14 ... 140 D9
Frederick St FSBYW WC1X ... 11 J6
Frederic Ms KTBR SW1X ... 16 C2
Frederick Ter HACK E8 ... 7 L4
Fredora Av YEAD UB4 ... 132 B1
Freeborne Gdns RAIN RM13 ... 145 H1
Freedom Cl WALTH E17 ... 120 C2
Freedom St BTSEA SW11 ... 158 A8
Freedown La BELMT SM2 ... 221 N10
Freegrove Rd HOLWY N7 ... 118 F10
Freeland Pk HDN NW4 ... 97 H10
Freeland Rd EA W5 ... 135 L9
Freelands Av SAND/SEL CR2 ... 224 C6

Freelands Gv BMLY BR1 ... 205 N1
Freelands Rd BMLY BR1 ... 205 N1
COB KT11 ... 217 J10
Freeland Wy ERITH DA8 ... 165 H7
Freeling St IS N1 ... 5 N4
Freeman Cl NTHLT UB5 ... 133 M2
SHPTN TW17 ... 196 C4
Freeman Ct CSHM HP5 ... 51 H6
Freeman Dr E/WMO/HCT KT8 ... 197 N4
Freeman Rd GVE DA12 ... 191 H6
MRDN SM4 ... 201 N5
Freemans Cl SLN SL2 ... 129 L1
Freemans La HYS/HAR UB3 ... 132 F9
Freemantle Av PEND EN3 ... 80 C9
Freemantle St WALW SE17 ... 19 J7
Freeman Wy EMPK RM11 ... 125 J4
Freemasons Rd CAN/RD E16 ... 141 N8
CROY/NA CR0 ... 203 M8
Free Prae Rd CHERT KT16 ... 195 K8
Freesia Cl ORP BR6 ... 227 J2
Freesia Dr CHOB/PIR GU24 ... 230 F2
Freethorpe Cl NRWD SE19 ... 203 M1
Freezeland Wy HGDN/ICK UB10 ... 132 L2
Fremantle Rd BARK/HLT IG6 ... 102 L10
BELV DA17 ... 164 B3
Fremont St HOM E9 ... 140 D3
HOME E9 ... 140 B3
Frenchaye ADL/WDHM KT15 ... 215 P4
Frenches Rd REDH RH1 ... 258 G2
The Frenches REDH RH1 ... 258 B8
French Gdns COB KT11 ... 217 K10
French Horn La HAT AL10 ... 40 E3
French Ordinary Ct TWRH EC3N ... 13 K4
French Pl SDTCH EC2A ... 7 K10
French Rw STAL AL1 ... 38 C6
French St SUN TW16 ... 197 K2
Frenchum Gdns SL SL1 ... 128 D10
Frendsbury Rd BROCKY SE4 ... 160 D10
Frensham CHESW EN7 ... 61 N3
Frensham Cl STHL UB1 ... 133 N6
Frensham Dr CROY/NA CR0 ... 225 H4
PUT/ROE SW15 ... 178 D6
Frensham Rd BFN/LL DA15 ... 184 G5
PUR/KEN CR8 ... 223 J10
Frensham St PECK SE15 ... 19 P10
Frensham Wk FUL HA ... 109 H10
Frensham Wy EW KT17 ... 238 F2
Frere St BTSEA SW11 ... 157 P8
Freshborough Ct GU GU1 ... 268 C3
Freshfield Av HACK E8 ... 7 L3
Freshfield Cl CRAWE RH10 ... 284 D8
LEW SE13 ... 161 J10
Freshfield Dr STHGT/OAK N14 ... 98 C1
Freshfields CROY/NA CR0 ... 204 E7
Freshfields Av UPMR RM14 ... 126 A10
Freshford St TOOT SW17 ... 179 M6
Freshmount Gdns HOR/WEW KT19 ... 219 N7
Freshwater Cl TOOT SW17 ... 180 B9
Freshwater Rd BCTR RM8 ... 123 N6
TOOT SW17 ... 180 B9
Freshwaters HLW CM20 ... 29 H10
Freshwell Av CHDH RM6 ... 123 M2
Fresh Wharf Rd BARK IG11 ... 142 E3
Freshwood Cl BECK BR3 ... 204 G1
Freshwood Wy WLGTN SM6 ... 222 D5
Freston Gdns EBAR EN4 ... 78 B9
Freston Pk FNCH N3 ... 97 H10
Freston Rd NKENS W10 ... 136 G9
Freta Rd BXLYHS DA6 ... 186 A1
Fretherne Rd WGCW AL8 ... 22 C5
Frewin Rd WAND/EARL SW18 ... 179 N4
Friar Ms WNWD SE27 ... 181 J6
Friar Rd STMC/STPC BR5 ... 207 K5
YEAD UB4 ... 133 L6
Friar's Av BRWN CM15 ... 107 M1
PUT/ROE SW15 ... 178 C6
TRDG/WHET N20 ... 97 P4
Friar's Cl BRWN CM15 ... 107 M1
CHING E4 ... 101 H4
NTHLT UB5 ... 133 K5
Friarscroft BROX EN10 ... 44 F6
Friars Cft RGUE GU4 ... 250 F7
Friars Fld BERK HP4 ... 33 K2
Friars Gdns ACT W3 ... 136 A8
Friar's Ga GUW GU2 ... 267 M2
Friars Gate Cl WFD IG8 ... 101 M5
Friars La RBSF CM22 ... 31 J1
RCH/KEW TW9 ... 177 J1
Friars Md POP/IOD E14 ... 161 H2
Friars Ms ELTH/MOT SE9 ... 184 D1
Friars Orch LHD/OX KT22 ... 236 C7
Friars Place La ACT W3 ... 136 A9
Friars Ri WOKS/MYFD GU22 ... 232 D4
Friar's Rd EHAM E6 ... 142 A3
VW GU25 ... 194 A4
Friars Rookery CRAWE RH10 ... 283 P7
Friars Stile Rd RCHPK/HAM TW10 ... 177 K2
Friars Wk ABYW SE2 ... 163 N5
STHGT/OAK N14 ... 98 C1
Friars Wy ACT W3 ... 136 A8
BUSH WD23 ... 73 N5
CHERT KT16 ... 195 K6
KGLGY WD4 ... 54 B6
Friary Br GU GU1 ... 267 P2
Friary Cl NFNCH/WDSP N12 ... 97 P5
Friary Est PECK SE15 ... 159 J6
Friary La WFD IG8 ... 101 K9
Friary Park Ct ACT W3 ... 135 P8
Friary Pas GU GU1 ... 267 P2
Friary Rd ACT W3 ... 135 P8
ASC SL5 ... 192 A6
NFNCH/WDSP N12 ... 97 N5
PECK SE15 ... 159 J6
STWL/WRAY TW19 ... 171 P2
Friary St GU GU1 ... 268 A1
The Friary STWL/WRAY TW19 ... 171 P2
Friary Wy CRAWW RH11 ... 283 P8
NFNCH/WDSP N12 ... 97 P5
Friday HI CHING E4 ... 101 K4
Friday HI East CHING E4 ... 101 L4
Friday HI West CHING E4 ... 101 K3
Friday Rd ERITH DA8 ... 164 A4
MTCM CR4 ... 180 A10
Friday St BLKFR EC4V ... 12 E7
Friday Street Rd RDKG RH5 ... 271 M9
Frideswide Pl KTTN NW5 ... 118 C10
Friendly Pl LEW SE13 ... 160 F7
Friendly St DEPT SE8 ... 160 F8
Friendly Street Ms DEPT SE8 ... 160 F9
Friends Av CHES/WCR EN8 ... 62 D3
Friends' Rd CROY/NA CR0 ... 203 L10
PUR/KEN CR8 ... 223 J8
Friend St FSBYE EC1V ... 6 C9
Friern Barnet La TRDG/WHET N20 ... 97 J3
Friern Barnet Rd FBAR/BDGN N11 ... 98 B5
Friern Mount Dr TRDG/WHET N20 ... 97 M1
Friern Pk NFNCH/WDSP N12 ... 97 M5
Friern Rd EDUL SE22 ... 181 P2
Friern Watch Av NFNCH/WDSP N12 ... 97 N5
Frigate Ms DEPT SE8 ... 160 F5
Frimley Av EMPK RM11 ... 125 H4
WIM/MER SW19 ... 179 N5
Frimley Cl CROY/NA CR0 ... 225 H4
WIM/MER SW19 ... 179 H5
Frimley Ct SCUP DA14 ... 185 M4
Frimley Crs CROY/NA CR0 ... 225 H4
Frimley Gdns MTCM CR4 ... 202 B1
Frimley Rd CHSGTN KT9 ... 219 J3
GDMY/SEVK IG3 ... 123 H4

Frimley Wy WCHPL E1 ... 140 C6
Fringewood Cl NTHWD HA6 ... 92 C9
Frinstead Cl STMC/STPC BR5 ... 207 N4
Frinsted Rd ERITH DA8 ... 164 E6
Frinton Cl OXHEY WD19 ... 93 J3
Frinton Dr WFD IG8 ... 101 J8
Frinton Ms IL IG1 ... 122 D4
Frinton Rd CRW RM5 ... 104 B8
EHAM E6 ... 141 J2
SCUP DA14 ... 185 P5
SEVS/STOTM N15 ... 119 M4
TOOT SW17 ... 180 B7
Friston St FUL/PGN SW6 ... 157 L8
Friston Wk CRAWW RH11 ... 283 H6
Friswell Pl BXLYHN DA7 ... 164 B9
Fritham Cl NWMAL KT3 ... 200 B6
Frith Ct MLHL NW7 ... 97 H8
The Frithe SLN SL2 ... 129 H8
Frith La MLHL NW7 ... 97 J7
Frith Rd CROY/NA CR0 ... 203 K9
WAN E11 ... 121 K9
Frithsden Copse BERK HP4 ... 34 C1
Friths Dr REIG RH2 ... 257 L7
Frith St SOHO/SHAV W1D ... 11 J5
Frithville Gdns SHB W12 ... 136 F10
Frithwald Rd CHERT KT16 ... 195 J7
Frithwood Av NTHWD HA6 ... 92 C7
Fritlands Cl DAGE RM10 ... 124 C8
Frobisher Cl BUSH WD23 ... 73 P10
PIN HA5 ... 113 L5
PUR/KEN CR8 ... 241 K3
Frobisher Crs STWL/WRAY TW19 ... 173 P3
Frobisher Gdns GU GU1 ... 250 D9
Frobisher Rd CEND/HSY/T N8 ... 119 H3
EHAM E6 ... 142 C8
ERITH DA8 ... 165 H6
STAL AL1 ... 39 H8
Frobisher Wy GRH DA9 ... 166 G10
HAT AL10 ... 40 A1
Frog Grove La RGUW GU3 ... 248 E6
Froggy La DEN/HRF UB9 ... 110 C8
Froghole La EDEN TN8 ... 263 H8
Frog La DAGW RM9 ... 144 E7
RGUE GU4 ... 250 B1
Frogley Rd EDUL SE22 ... 159 N10
Frogmoor La RKW/CH/CXG WD3 ... 91 N3
Frogmore LCOL/BKTW AL2 ... 56 D7
WAND/EARL SW18 ... 179 K1
Frogmore Av YEAD UB4 ... 132 F6
Frogmore Cl CHEAM SM3 ... 200 G10
SL SL1 ... 148 F1
Frogmore Dr WDSR SL4 ... 149 K7
Frogmore Gdns CHEAM SM3 ... 221 H1
YEAD UB4 ... 132 F5
Frognal HAMP NW3 ... 117 M10
Frognal Av HRW HA1 ... 114 E2
SCUP DA14 ... 185 K9
Frognal Cl HAMP NW3 ... 117 M10
Frognal Gdns HAMP NW3 ... 117 M9
Frognal La HAMP NW3 ... 117 L10
Frognal Pl SCUP DA14 ... 185 K8
Frognal Ri HAMP NW3 ... 117 M8
Frognal Wy HAMP NW3 ... 117 M9
Frog St BRWN CM15 ... 86 D5
Froissart Rd ELTH/MOT SE9 ... 184 B1
Frome TIL RM18 ... 119 ...
Frome Rd SEVS/STOTM N15 ... 119 J1
Frome Sq HHNE HP2 ... 36 B1
Frome St IS N1 ... 6 E7
Fromondes Rd CHEAM SM3 ... 221 H4
Fromow Gdns BFOR GU20 ... 212 C3
Front La UPMR RM14 ... 126 D7
The Front BERK HP4 ... 34 E2
Froude St VX/NE SW8 ... 158 C8
Frowick Cl BRKMPK AL9 ... 40 E9
Frowyke Crs POTB/CUF EN6 ... 58 D9
Fruen Rd EBED/NFELT TW14 ... 174 A3
Fryatt Rd TOTM N17 ... 99 J8
Fry Cl CRW RM5 ... 104 B6
Fryent Cl KTN/HRWW/W HA3 ... 115 H4
Fryent Crs CDALE/KGS NW9 ... 116 B4
Fryent Flds CDALE/KGS NW9 ... 116 B4
Fryent Gv CDALE/KGS NW9 ... 116 B4
Fryent Wy CDALE/KGS NW9 ... 115 M3
Fryer Cl CSHM HP5 ... 51 J9
Fryern Wd CTHM CR3 ... 241 K10
Frymley Vw WDSR SL4 ... 148 C7
Fry Rd EHAM E6 ... 141 J5
WLSDN NW10 ... 136 E1
Fryston Av COUL/CHIP CR5 ... 240 C1
CROY/NA CR0 ... 203 P9
Fryth Md RAD WD7 ... 38 A5
Fuchsia Cl ABYW SE2 ... 163 L4
Fuchsia Wy CHOB/PIR GU24 ... 212 D9
Fulbeck Dr CDALE/KGS NW9 ... 96 B9
Fulbeck Wy RYLN/HDSTN HA2 ... 94 B10
Fulbourne Cl REDH RH1 ... 257 P9
Fulbourne Rd WALTH E17 ... 101 H9
Fulbourne St WCHPL E1 ... 140 E7
Fulbrook La SOCK/AV RM15 ... 146 E9
Fulbrook Ms ELTH/MOT SE9 ... 184 D1
Fulbrook Rd ARCH N19 ... 118 C4
Fulford Gv OXHEY WD19 ... 93 J3
Fulford Rd CTHM CR3 ... 241 L7
HOR/WEW KT19 ... 220 A4
Fulford St BERM/RTH SE16 ... 160 A1
Fulham Broadway FUL/PGN SW6 ... 157 K6
Fulham Cl UX/CGN UB8 ... 132 D6
Fulham High St FUL/PGN SW6 ... 157 H9
Fulham Palace Rd FUL/PGN SW6 ... 156 G6
Fulham Park Gdns FUL/PGN SW6 ... 157 J8
Fulham Park Rd FUL/PGN SW6 ... 157 J8
Fulham Rd WBPTN SW10 ... 15 K9
Fullarton Crs SOCK/AV RM15 ... 146 E9
Fullbrook Av ADL/WDHM KT15 ... 215 K9
Fullbrooks Av WPK KT4 ... 200 C8
Fuller Cl ORP BR6 ... 227 L4
Fuller Gdns WATN WD24 ... 73 J3
Fuller Rd BCTR RM8 ... 123 M8
WATN WD24 ... 73 J3
Fullers Av SURB KT6 ... 199 L10
WFD IG8 ... 101 P8
Fullers Cl CRW RM5 ... 104 D8
CSHM HP5 ... 50 G8
WAB EN9 ... 63 J4
Fullers Hill CSHM HP5 ... 50 G8
BH/WHM TN16 ... 262 G2
Fullers Md HLWE CM17 ... 47 M2
Fuller St HDN NW4 ... 116 G1
Fuller's Rd SWFD E18 ... 101 L9
Fuller St BETH E2 ... 140 ...
Fullers Wy North SURB KT6 ... 199 L10
Fullers Wy South CHSGTN KT9 ... 219 K1
Fuller's Wd CROY/NA CR0 ... 224 E5
Fullers Wood La REDH RH1 ... 258 D10
Fullerton Cl BF/WBF KT14 ... 216 A10
Fullerton Dr BF/WBF KT14 ... 215 P10
CAR SM5 ... 221 P5
CROY/NA CR0 ... 203 P9
WAND/EARL SW18 ... 179 N1
Fullerton Wy BF/WBF KT14 ... 215 P10
Fuller Wy HYS/HAR UB3 ... 152 G4
RKW/CH/CXG WD3 ... 72 G7
Fullmer Wy ADL/WDHM KT15 ... 215 J6
Fullwell Av CLAY IG5 ... 102 F9
Fullwood's Ms IS N1 ... 7 H9
Fulmar Cl CRAWW RH11 ... 282 D5
Fulmar Ct SURB KT6 ... 199 L6
Fulmar Rd HCH RM12 ... 144 B10
Fulmead St FUL/PGN SW6 ... 157 L7
Fulmer Cl HPTN TW12 ... 175 H8
Fulmer Common Rd DTCH/LGLY SL3 ... 130 A1
Fulmer Dr CFSP/GDCR SL9 ... 110 B8

Fulmer La CFSP/GDCR SL9 ... 110 C8
Fulmer Rd CAN/RD E16 ... 142 A7
DTCH/LGLY SL3 ... 110 B9
Fulmer Wy CFSP/GDCR SL9 ... 110 B8
WEA W13 ... 154 C2
Fulready Rd LEY E10 ... 121 J3
Fulstone Cl HSLWW TW4 ... 153 N10
Fulthorp Rd BKHTH/KID SE3 ... 161 L8
Fulton Ms BAY/PAD W2 ... 9 J7
Fulton Rd WBLY HA9 ... 115 N8
Fulvens GROUS ... 270 F9
Fulwell Park Av WHTN TW2 ... 176 B5
Fulwell Rd HPTN TW12 ... 176 C7
Fulwich Rd DART DA1 ... 187 N2
Fulwood Av ALP/SUD HA0 ... 135 L4
Fulwood Gdns TWK TW1 ... 176 E2
Fulwood Wk WIM/MER SW19 ... 179 H4
Furber St HMSMTH W6 ... 156 E2
Furham Fld PIN HA5 ... 93 P8
Furley Rd PECK SE15 ... 159 P6
Furlong Cl MTCM CR4 ... 202 C8
Furlong Rd DORK RH4 ... 272 B3
HOLWY N7 ... 6 B1
Furlongs HHW HP1 ... 35 K5
Furlong Wy WARE SG12 ... 26 E4
The Furlough WOKS/MYFD GU22 ... 232 D3
Furmage St WAND/EARL SW18 ... 179 L3
Furnace Dr CRAWE RH10 ... 284 B9
Furnace Farm Rd CRAWE RH10 ... 284 B9
Furnace Pde CRAWE RH10 ... 284 B9
Furnace Pl CRAWE RH10 ... 284 B9
Furneaux Av WNWD SE27 ... 181 J8
Furner Cl DART DA1 ... 164 G9
Furness WDSR SL4 ... 148 B9
Furness Cl CDH/CHF RM16 ... 168 E4
Furness Rd FUL/PGN SW6 ... 157 L8
MRDN SM4 ... 201 L6
RYLN/HDSTN HA2 ... 114 A5
WLSDN NW10 ... 136 D4
Furness Wy HCH RM12 ... 125 H10
Furnival Av SLN SL2 ... 128 C7
Furnival Cl VW GU25 ... 194 A6
Furnival St FLST/FETLN EC4A ... 12 A2
Furrow La HOM E9 ... 120 B10
Furrows Pl CTHM CR3 ... 241 N9
The Furrows WOT/HER KT12 ... 197 K9
Fursby Av FNCH N3 ... 97 K7
Furse Av STALE/WH AL4 ... 22 B1
Further Acre CDALE/KGS NW9 ... 96 C10
Furtherfield ABLGY WD5 ... 54 F8
Furtherfield Cl CROY/NA CR0 ... 203 H6
Further Green Rd CAT SE6 ... 183 K3
Furtherground HHNE HP2 ... 35 P7
Furzebank ASC SL5 ... 192 C4
Furze Cl OXHEY WD19 ... 93 K6
REDH RH1 ... 258 A9
Furzedown Cl EGH TW20 ... 172 B9
Furzedown Dr TOOT SW17 ... 180 C8
Furzedown Rd BELMT SM2 ... 221 M7
TOOT SW17 ... 180 C8
Furze Farm Cl CHDH RM6 ... 103 P10
Furzefield CRAWW RH11 ... 285 L6
Furze Fld LHD/OX KT22 ... 218 C9
Furzefield Cl CHST BR7 ... 184 E9
Furzefield Rd REIG RH2 ... 275 M2
Furzeglade BKHTH/KID SE3 ... 181 N5
REIG RH2 ... 275 M2
WGCE AL7 ... 23 H6
Furzeground Wy STKPK UB11 ... 132 D10
Furze Gv KWD/TDW/WH KT20 ... 239 J7
Furzeham Rd WDR/YW UB7 ... 151 P1
Furze Hi KWD/TDW/WH KT20 ... 239 J7
PUR/KEN CR8 ... 222 F7
Furzehill REDH RH1 ... 257 P9
Furzehill Rd BORE WD6 ... 75 P4
Furzehill Sq STMC/STPC BR5 ... 207 L4
Furze La PUR/KEN CR8 ... 222 F7
RGODL GU7 ... 267 L9
Furzen Cl SLN SL2 ... 128 F5
Furzen Crs HAT AL10 ... 40 C7
Furze Rd ADL/WDHM KT15 ... 215 J3
HHW HP1 ... 35 H7
THHTH CR7 ... 203 K3
Furze St BOW E3 ... 140 F7
Furze Vw RKW/CH/CXG WD3 ... 70 F10
Furzewood SUN TW16 ... 197 H1
Fusedale Wy SOCK/AV RM15 ... 146 D8
Fuzzens Wk WDSR SL4 ... 148 D8
Fydlers Cl ASC SL5 ... 170 A9
Fyfe Wy BMLY BR1 ... 205 M2
Fyfield Cl BECK BR3 ... 205 J4
Fyfield Dr SOCK/AV RM15 ... 146 E9
Fyfield Rd BRXN/ST SW9 ... 159 H9
CHONG CM5 ... 49 N6
CHONG CM5 ... 67 P2
EN EN1 ... 79 M7
RAIN RM13 ... 144 C3
WALTH E17 ... 121 J1
WFD IG8 ... 101 P8
Fynes St WEST SW1P ... 17 J5

G

Gabion Av PUR RM19 ... 166 C3
Gable Cl ABLGY WD5 ... 54 F8
DART DA1 ... 187 H1
PIN HA5 ... 93 P8
Gable Ct SYD SE26 ... 182 A7
Gables Av ASHF TW15 ... 174 A8
BORE WD6 ... 75 L7
Gables Cl CFSP/GDCR SL9 ... 90 B5
CMBW SE5 ... 159 M7
DTCH/LGLY SL3 ... 149 M5
LEE/GVE SE12 ... 183 M4
WOKS/MYFD GU22 ... 232 C6
The Gables BNSTD SM7 ... 239 J3
HART DA3 ... 211 P2
LHD/OX KT22 ... 218 B8
WBLY HA9 ... 115 L8
WEY KT13 ... 216 D2
Gabriel Cl CRW RM5 ... 104 D8
FELT TW13 ... 175 M7
Gabriel Gdns GVE DA12 ... 191 H8
Gabrielle Cl WBLY HA9 ... 115 L8
Gabrielspring Rd EYN DA4 ... 210 C9
Gabriel Spring Rd (East) EYN DA4 ... 210 D9
Gabriel St FSTH SE23 ... 182 C3
Gabrook Rd BRKHM/BTCW RH3 ... 274 A5
Gad Cl PLSTW E13 ... 141 K1
Gaddesden Av WBLY HA9 ... 135 L1
Gaddesden Crs GSTN WD25 ... 55 L10
Gaddesden Gv WGCE AL7 ... 23 L5
Gade Bank RKW/CH/CXG WD3 ... 72 F5
Gadebridge La HHW HP1 ... 35 M4
Gadebridge Rd HHW HP1 ... 35 L3
Gade Cl HHW HP1 ... 35 J3
HYS/HAR UB3 ... 133 J10
WATW WD18 ... 72 F8
Gadesden Rd HOR/WEW KT19 ... 219 P3
Gade Valley Cl KGLGY WD4 ... 54 B4
Gade View Rd HHS/BOV HP3 ... 35 N10
Gadsbury Cl CDALE/KGS NW9 ... 116 C4
Gadsden Cl UPMR RM14 ... 126 D4
Gadswell Cl GSTN WD25 ... 73 M2
Gadwall Cl CAN/RD E16 ... 141 N8
Gage Rd CAN/RD E16 ... 141 K7
Gainford St IS N1 ... 6 A1
Gainsboro Gdns GFD/PVL UB6 ... 114 D9
Gainsborough Av DART DA1 ... 187 K1
MNPK E12 ... 122 D10
STAL AL1 ... 38 D1

TIL RM18... 168 D7
Gainsborough Cl BECK BR3... 182 F10
ESH/CLAY KT10... 198 D8
Gainsborough Ct SHB W12... 156 F1
WOT/HER KT12... 217 H1
Gainsborough Dr GVW DA11... 190 A6
SAND/SEL CR2... 223 P9
Gainsborough Gdns EDGW HA8... 95 L10
GLDGN NW11... 117 J5
HAMP NW3... 117 N8
ISLW TW7... 176 C1
Gainsborough Rd BCTR RM8... 123 J9
CHSWK W4... 156 C3
HOR/WEW KT19... 219 P6
NFNCH/WDSP N12... 97 L6
NWMAL KT3... 200 A6
RAIN RM13... 145 H3
RCH/KEW TW9... 155 L8
SRTFD E15... 141 K5
WAN E11... 121 K5
WFD IG8... 102 B7
YEAD UB4... 132 D4
Gainsborough Sq BXLYHN DA7... 163 N9
Gainsford Rd WALTH E17... 120 E4
Gainsford St STHWK SE1... 13 L10
Gainsthorpe Rd CHONG CM5... 49 L9
Gainswood WOCE AL7... 23 H6
Gairloch Rd CMBW SE5... 143 H3
Gaisford St KTTN NW5... 4 C1
Gaist Av CTHM CR3... 242 A8
Gaitskell Rd ELTH/MOT SE9... 184 F4
Galahad Cl SL SL1... 148 F1
Galahad Rd BMLY BR1... 183 M6
CRAWW RH11... 283 H7
Galata Rd BARN SW13... 156 D6
Galatea Sq PECK SE15... 160 A9
Galbraith St POP/IOD E14... 161 H2
Galdana Av BAR EN5... 77 M7
Galeborough Av WFD IG8... 101 J8
Gale Cl HPTN TW12... 175 M9
MTCM CR4... 201 N3
Gale Crs BNSTD SM7... 239 K3
Galena Rd HMSMTH W6... 156 E3
Galen Cl HOR/WEW KT19... 219 M7
Galesbury Rd WAND/EARL SW18... 179 M2
Gales Cl RGUE GU4... 250 C7
Gales Dr CRAWE RH10... 284 A7
Gales Pl CRAWE RH10... 284 A7
Gale St BOW E3... 140 F7
CHEL SW3... 15 N7
DAGW RM9... 143 N1
Gales Wy WFD IG8... 102 B8
Galey Gn SOCK/AV RM15... 146 G8
Galgate Cl WIM/MER SW19... 179 H4
Gallants Farm Rd EBAR EN4... 97 P1
Galleon Bvd GRH DA9... 166 C10
Galleon Cl BERM/RHTH SE16... 160 F2
ERITH DA8... 164 E3
Galleons La DTCH/LGLY SL3... 130 A5
Galleons Rd CAN/RD E16... 142 G5
Gallery Gdns NTHLT UB5... 133 L4
Gallery Rd DUL SE21... 181 L4
Galley Gn HERT/BAY SG13... 26 F9
Galley Hl HHW HP1... 35 K4
Galley Hill Rd SWCM DA10... 189 L1
Galleyhill Rd WAB EN9... 63 K8
Galley La BAR EN5... 76 D4
Galleymead Rd DTCH/LGLY SL3... 151 J7
Galleywall Rd BERM/RHTH SE16... 160 A3
Galleywood Crs CRW RM5... 104 F2
Galliard Crs ED N9... 99 P1
Galliard Rd ED N9... 99 P1
Gallia Rd HBRY N5... 119 J10
Gallions Cl BARK IG11... 143 K5
Gallions Rd CAN/RD E16... 142 C4
CHARL SE7... 161 N3
Gallions View Rd THMD SE28... 163 H1
Gallon Cl CHARL SE7... 161 P3
The Gallop BELMT SM2... 221 N5
SAND/SEL CR2... 223 M6
Gallosson Rd WOOL/PLUM SE18... 163 H3
Galloway Cha SLN SL2... 129 M9
Galloway Cl BROX EN10... 62 C1
Galloway Pth CROY/NA CRO... 223 L1
Galloway Rd SHB W12... 136 D10
Gallows Hl KGLGY WD4... 54 D7
Gallows Hill La ABLGY WD5... 54 D8
Gallus Cl WCHMH N21... 78 C10
Gallus Sq BKHTH/KID SE3... 161 N3
Gallys Rd WDSR SL4... 148 C7
Galpin's Rd THHTH CR7... 202 F4
Galsworthy Av CHDH RM6... 123 L5
Galsworthy Cl THMD SE28... 143 L10
Galsworthy Rd CHERT KT16... 195 K7
CRICK NW2... 117 H9
KUTN/CMB KT2... 199 N1
TIL RM18... 168 F7
Galton Rd ASC SL5... 192 E6
Galton St NKENS W10... 2 A10
Galva Cl EBAR EN4... 78 D1
Galveston Rd PUT/ROE SW15... 179 J1
Galvin Rd SL SL1... 129 H9
Galway St VX/NE SW8... 6 F10
Gambetta St VX/NE SW8... 158 C8
Gambia St STHWK SE1... 12 D10
Gambles La RPLY/SEND GU23... 251 M1
Gamble Rd TOOT SW17... 179 P7
Games Rd EBAR EN4... 77 P7
Gamlen Rd PUT/ROE SW15... 156 G10
Gammon Cl HHS/BOV HP3... 56 B7
Gammons La WATN WD24... 75 H5
Gamuel Cl WALTH E17... 120 F4
Gander Green Crs HPTN TW12... 197 P1
Gander Green La CHEAM SM3... 201 H9
SUT SM1... 221 K3
Ganders Ash GSTN WD25... 55 H9
Gandhi Cl WALTH E17... 120 F4
Gandhi Ct WATN WD24... 73 L6
Gangers Hl GDST RH9... 260 E5
Ganghill GU GU1... 250 D8
Gant Ct WAB EN9... 63 L10
Ganton Cl SOHO/CST W1F... 11 H6
Ganton Wk OXHEY WD19... 93 M5
Gantshill Crs GNTH/NBYPK IG2... 122 D3
Ganymede Pl HHNE HP2... 36 A3
Gap Rd WIM/MER SW19... 179 K3
Garage Rd ACT W3... 135 M8
Garbrand Wk EW KT17... 220 C5
Garbutt Pl MHST W1U... 10 D3
Garbutt Rd UPMR RM14... 126 B7
Garden Av BXLYHN DA7... 165 H8
HAT AL10... 40 D8
MTCM CR4... 180 C10
Garden Cl ADL/WDHM KT15... 215 N1
ASHF TW15... 174 D9
BAR EN5... 76 E4
BNSTD SM7... 239 K1
CHING E4... 100 F4
HPTN TW12... 175 M8
LEE/GVPK SE12... 183 N6
LHD/OX KT22... 237 H10
NTHLT UB5... 133 M3
PUT/ROE SW15... 178 E3
RSLP HA4... 112 F4
STAL AL1... 38 G5
WAT WD17... 72 G6
WLGTN SM6... 222 F2
Garden Ct STALE/WH AL4... 21 J2
Garden End HMS HP6... 69 K3
Gardeners Cl FBAR/BDGN N11... 98 B3
Gardeners Rd CROY/NA CRO... 203 J8
Gardener's Wk GT/LBKH KT23... 254 A2
Garden Field La BAR EN5... 34 C7
Gardenia Ct CHOB/PIR GU24... 212 E9
Gardenia Rd EN EN1... 79 M10
Gardenia Wy WFD IG8... 101 M6
Garden La BMLY BR1... 183 P9

BRXS/STRHM SW2... 180 G4
Garden Pl RDART DA2... 187 L6
Garden Reach CSTG HP8... 70 A7
Garden Rd ABLGY WD5... 54 F7
BMLY BR1... 184 B1
PGE/AN SE20... 204 B1
RCH/KEW TW9... 155 M9
SEV TN13... 247 L8
STJWD NW8... 3 K9
WOT/HER KT12... 197 J6
Garden Rw GVW DA11... 190 C6
STHWK SE1... 18 C4
The Gardens BECK BR3... 205 H2
BRKMPK AL9... 59 H5
BRWN CM15... 86 C2
CHOB/PIR GU24... 230 E8
EBED/NFELT TW14... 174 L2
EDUL SE22... 159 P10
ESH/CLAY KT10... 217 P1
HGDN/ICK UB10... 111 P7
HRW HA1... 114 B9
PIN HA5... 113 N4
WAT WD17... 72 G6
Garden Ter PIM SW1V... 17 J7
Garden Terrace Rd HLWE CM17... 29 M7
Garden Wk BECK BR3... 204 E1
COUL/CHIP CR5... 240 C9
SDTCH EC2A... 13 J1
Garden Wy LOU IG10... 82 D4
WLSDN NW10... 135 P1
Gardiner Av CRICK NW2... 116 F10
Gardiner Cl BCTR RM8... 123 N9
PEND EN3... 80 C10
STMC/STPC BR5... 207 M2
The Gardiners HLWE CM17... 47 L2
Gardner Cl WAN E11... 121 N4
Gardner La CRAWE RH10... 285 P5
Gardner Pl EBED/NFELT TW14... 175 J2
Gardner Rd GU GU1... 249 P10
PLSTW E13... 141 N6
Gardners La BLKFR EC4V... 12 E7
Gardnor Rd HAMP NW3... 117 N9
Gard St FSBYE EC1V... 6 D9
Garendon Gdns MRDN SM4... 201 L7
Garendon Rd MRDN SM4... 201 L7
Gareth Cl WPK KT4... 201 M9
Gareth Dr ED N9... 100 D1
Gareth Gv BMLY BR1... 183 M7
Garfield Rd ADL/WDHM KT15... 215 M1
ADL/WDHM KT15... 215 M2
BTSEA SW11... 158 D9
CHING E4... 101 J2
PEND EN3... 80 B8
PLSTW E13... 141 L6
TWK TW1... 176 F4
WIM/MER SW19... 179 M9
Garford St POP/IOD E14... 140 F9
Garibaldi Rd REDH RH1... 276 A1
Garibaldi St WOOL/PLUM SE18... 163 H3
Garland Cl CHES/WCR EN8... 62 D7
HHNE HP2... 35 N5
Garland Rd STAN HA7... 95 K9
WARE SG12... 26 J1
WOOL/PLUM SE18... 162 G6
Garlands La LHD/OX KT22... 236 G7
REDH RH1... 258 A10
Garland Wy CTHM CR3... 241 L6
EMPK RM11... 125 M2
Garlichill Rd EPSOM KT18... 238 E3
Garlick Hl BLKFR EC4V... 12 F7
Garlies Rd FSTH SE23... 182 D6
Garlinge Rd KIL/WHAMP NW6... 2 C1
Garman Cl UED N18... 99 L6
Garman Rd TOTM N17... 100 B7
Garnault Ms CLKNW EC1R... 6 B10
Garnault Pl CLKNW EC1R... 6 B10
Garnault Rd EN EN1... 79 N4
Garner Dr BROX EN10... 62 D2
Garner Rd WALTH E17... 101 H9
Garners Cl CFSP/GDCR SL9... 90 B7
Garners End CFSP/GDCR SL9... 90 B7
Garners Rd CFSP/GDCR SL9... 90 B7
Garner St BETH E2... 7 L1
Garnet Rd SL SL1... 148 F1
THHTH CR7... 203 K4
WLSDN NW10... 136 B1
Garnet St WAP E1W... 140 B9
Garnett Cl ELTH/MOT SE9... 162 C9
WATN WD24... 73 L3
Garnett Dr LCOL/BKTW AL2... 5 N5
Garnett Rd HAMP NW3... 118 A10
Garnham St STNW/STAM N16... 119 N7
Garnies Cl PECK SE15... 159 N6
Garnon Md EPP CM16... 65 N4
Garrad's Rd STRHM/NOR SW16... 180 E6
Garrard Cl BXLYHN DA7... 164 B9
CHST BR7... 184 E8
SLN SL2... 128 D6
Garrard Wy STALE/WH AL4... 21 J3
Garratt Cl CROY/NA CRO... 222 F1
Garratt La WAND/EARL SW18... 179 L3
Garratt Rd EDGW HA8... 95 M8
Garratts La BNSTD SM7... 239 J2
Garratts Rd BUSH WD23... 94 B1
Garratt Ter TOOT SW17... 179 P7
Garrett Cl ACT W3... 136 A7
CRAWE RH10... 284 D9
CSHM HP5... 51 H9
Garrick Av GLDGN NW11... 117 H4
Garrick Cl BTSEA SW11... 157 M10
EA W5... 135 K6
RCH/KEW TW9... 177 H1
STA TW18... 173 K10
WOT/HER KT12... 217 J10
Garrick Crs CROY/NA CRO... 203 M9
Garrick Dr HDN NW4... 96 A10
WOOL/PLUM SE18... 162 G2
Garrick Gdns E/WMO/HCT KT8... 197 P3
Garrick Pk HDN NW4... 96 C10
Garrick Rd CDALE/KGS NW9... 116 C4
GFD/PVL UB6... 134 A6
RCH/KEW TW9... 155 M8
Garrick St COVGDN WC2E... 11 J7
GVW DA11... 190 E2
Garrick Wy HDN NW4... 116 C2
Garrison Cl HSLWW TW4... 175 N1
WOOL/PLUM SE18... 162 G6
Garrolds Cl SWLY BR8... 208 E2
The Garrones CRAWE RH10... 284 F6
Garron La SOCK/AV RM15... 146 E8
Garrow HART SL3... 211 N3
Garry Cl ROM RM1... 104 F3
Garry Wy ROM RM1... 104 F3
Garsdale Cl FBAR/BDGN N11... 98 B7
Garside Cl HPTN TW12... 176 A10
WOOL/PLUM SE18... 162 G2
Garsmouth Wy GSTN WD25... 73 L2
Garson Gv CSHM HP5... 50 F5
Garson La STWL/WRAY TW19... 172 A3
Garson Rd ESH/CLAY KT10... 217 H2
Garston Crs GSTN WD25... 55 K10
Garston Dr GSTN WD25... 55 L10
Garston La GSTN WD25... 55 L10
PUR/KEN CR8... 241 L1
The Garstons GT/LBKH KT23... 253 N2
Garth Cl KUTN/CMB KT2... 177 L8
MRDN SM4... 201 J7
RSLP HA4... 113 L6
Garthland Dr BAR EN5... 76 B9
Garthorne Rd FSTH SE23... 182 C3
Garth Rd CHSWK W4... 156 A4
CRICK NW2... 117 J7
KUTN/CMB KT2... 177 L8

MRDN SM4... 200 G8
SEV TN13... 265 K4
SOCK/AV RM15... 147 H6
Garthside RCHPK/HAM TW10... 177 K8
The Garth ABLGY WD5... 54 E9
COB KT11... 217 M9
HPTN TW12... 175 M9
KTN/HRWW/W HA3... 115 L4
Garthway NFNCH/WDSP N12... 97 P7
Gartlet Rd WAT WD17... 73 J7
Gartmoor Gdns WIM/MER SW19... 179 J4
Garton Cl CRAWW RH11... 283 H8
Garton Pl WAND/EARL SW18... 179 J4
Gartons Cl PEND EN3... 80 B9
Gartons Wy BTSEA SW11... 157 M9
Garvary Rd CAN/RD E16... 141 N8
Garvin Av BEAC HP9... 88 D8
Garvock Dr SEV TN13... 265 H2
Garway Rd BAY/PAD W2... 8 C6
Gascoigne Gdns WFD IG8... 101 K8
Gascoigne Pl BETH E2... 7 L9
Gascoigne Rd BARK IG11... 142 F3
CROY/NA CRO... 225 N4
WEY KT13... 196 C10
Gascon's Gv SLN SL2... 128 C6
Gascoyne Av KIL/WHAMP NW6... 2 E4
Gascoyne Cl HARH RM3... 105 J3
Gascoyne Dr DART DA1... 164 C9
Gascoyne Rd HOM E9... 140 C2
Gascoyne Wy HERT/BAY SG13... 25 K3
Gaselee St POP/IOD E14... 141 N9
Gasholder Pl LBTH SE11... 17 P8
Gaskarth Rd BAL SW12... 180 C2
EDGW HA8... 95 N4
Gaskell Rd HGT N6... 118 A4
Gaskell St CLAP SW4... 158 F8
Gaskin St IS N1... 6 C1
Gaspar Cl ECT SW5... 15 M5
Gaspar Ms ECT SW5... 15 H5
Gassiot Rd TOOT SW17... 180 A10
Gassiot Wy SUT SM1... 201 N10
Gasson Rd SWCM DA10... 189 K1
Gasson Wood Rd CRAWW RH11... 283 H9
Gastein Rd HMSMTH W6... 156 G5
Gaston Bell Cl RCH/KEW TW9... 155 L9
Gaston Bridge Rd SHPTN TW17... 196 F5
Gaston Rd MTCM CR4... 202 B3
Gaston Wy SHPTN TW17... 196 F4
Gataker St BERM/RHTH SE16... 160 A2
Gatcombe Ms EA W5... 135 L4
Gatcombe Rd ARCH N19... 118 C9
CAN/RD E16... 160 D1
Gate Cl BORE WD6... 75 P5
Gatecroft HHS/BOV HP3... 36 A8
Gate End NTHWD HA6... 93 H8
Gateforth St STJWD NW8... 9 N2
Gatehill Rd NTHWD HA6... 92 D8
Gatehope Dr SOCK/AV RM15... 146 E8
Gatehouse Cl KUTN/CMB KT2... 177 P10
Gateley Rd BRXN/ST SW9... 158 G9
Gate Ms SKENS SW7... 15 P2
Gater Dr ENC/FH EN2... 79 L5
Gatesborough St SDTCH EC2A... 7 J9
Gatesden Rd LHD/OX KT22... 236 B9
Gates Green Rd WWKM BR4... 205 M1
Gateshead Rd BORE WD6... 75 M1
Gateside Rd TOOT SW17... 180 A6
Gatestone Rd NRWD SE19... 181 M8
Gate St HHOL WC1V... 11 N5
HOL/ALD WC2B... 11 N5
Gateway WALW SE17... 18 F9
Gateway Ar IS N1... 6 C7
Gateway Ms HACK E8... 119 N10
Gateway Rd LEY E10... 139 N2
Gateways GU GU1... 268 C3
The Gateways CHESW EC1Y... 61 L4
The Gateway WOKN/KNAP GU21... 214 E10
Gatewick Cl SL SL1... 129 K10
Gatfield Gv FELT TW13... 175 P5
Gathorne Rd WDGN N22... 99 H10
Gathorne St BETH E2... 140 C4
Gatley Av HOR/WEW KT19... 219 N2
Gatley Dr GU GU1... 250 C9
Gatliff Rd BGVA SW1W... 16 E8
Gatling Rd ABYW SE2... 163 K4
Gatting Cl EDGW HA8... 95 P8
Gatting Wy HGDN/ICK UB10... 131 P3
Gatton Bottom REIG RH2... 258 A4
Gatton Cl BELMT SM2... 221 L5
SUT SM1... 221 L5
Gatton Park Rd REDH RH1... 257 N7
Gatton Rd REIG RH2... 257 N7
TOOT SW17... 179 P7
Gattons Wy SCUP DA14... 186 A8
Gatward Cl WCHMH N21... 79 J10
Gatward Gn ED N9... 99 M3
Gatwick Rd CRAWE RH10... 284 D3
GVE DA12... 190 E5
HORL RH6... 284 B1
WAND/EARL SW18... 179 J3
Gatwick Wy HORL RH6... 280 A2
Gauden Cl CLAP SW4... 158 G9
Gauden Rd CLAP SW4... 158 G9
Gaumont Ap WATW WD18... 73 J7
Gauntlet Cl NTHLT UB5... 133 J4
Gauntlet Crs PUR/KEN CR8... 241 L5
Gauntlett Ct ALP/SUD HA0... 114 F10
Gauntlett Rd SUT SM1... 222 B4
Gaunt St STHWK SE1... 18 E2
Gautrey Rd PECK SE15... 160 B8
Gavell Rd COB KT11... 217 H9
Gavel St WALW SE17... 19 H5
Gavenny Pth SOCK/AV RM15... 146 E8
Gaverick Ms POP/IOD E14... 160 F3
Gaveston Cl BF/WBF KT14... 216 A3
Gaveston Dr BERK HP4... 33 N3
Gavestone Crs LEE/GVPK SE12... 183 N3
Gavestone Rd LEE/GVPK SE12... 183 N3
Gaveston Rd LHD/OX KT22... 236 F6
Gavina Cl MRDN SM4... 201 P5
Gaviots Cl CFSP/GDCR SL9... 110 C6
Gaviots Gn CFSP/GDCR SL9... 110 B6
Gaviots Wy CFSP/GDCR SL9... 110 B5
Gawber St BETH E2... 140 D5
Gawdrey Cl CSHM HP5... 51 J9
Gawsworth Cl SRTFD E15... 121 L10
Gawthorne Av MLHL NW7... 97 H6
Gay Cl CRICK NW2... 116 E10
Gaydon La CDALE/KGS NW9... 95 N9
Gayfere Rd CLAY IG5... 122 C1
Gayfere St WEST SW1P... 17 J4
Gayford Rd SHB W12... 156 C1
Gay Gdns DAGE RM10... 124 E1
Gayhouse La REDH RH1... 277 M10
Gayhurst St HACK E8... 7 M1
Gayler Cl REDH RH1... 259 N10
Gaylor Rd NTHLT UB5... 113 N10
TIL RM18... 168 B7
Gaynes Ct UPMR RM14... 125 M5
Gaynesford Rd CAR SM5... 222 A4
FSTH SE23... 182 C5
Gaynes Hill Rd WFD IG8... 102 F8
Gaynes Park Rd UPMR RM14... 125 M7
Gaynes Rd UPMR RM14... 126 A5
Gay Rd SRTFD E15... 141 J4
Gaysham Av GNTH/NBYPK IG2... 122 C3
Gayton Cl AMS HP6... 69 K1
Gayton Crs HAMP NW3... 117 N8
Gayton Rd HAMP NW3... 117 N9
HRW HA1... 114 E6
WOOL/PLUM SE18... 162 D5
Gayville Rd BTSEA SW11... 180 A1
Gaywood Av CHES/WCR EN8... 62 C6
Gaywood Cl BRXS/STRHM SW2... 180 A6
Gaywood Rd ASHTD KT21... 237 L4
WALTH E17... 120 F1

Gaywood St STHWK SE1... 18 D4
Gaza St WALW SE17... 18 D8
Gazelle Gld GVE DA12... 191 J8
Geariesville Gdns BARK/HLT IG6... 122 E2
Geary Cl HORL RH6... 281 J6
Geary Dr BRW CM14... 87 J3
Geary Rd WLSDN NW10... 116 D10
Geary St HOLWY N7... 118 C10
Geddes Pl BXLYHN DA7... 164 B10
Geddes Rd BUSH WD23... 74 B8
Geddings Rd HOD EN11... 44 C3
Gedeney Rd TOTM N17... 99 K9
Gedling Pl STHWK SE1... 19 L3
Gee Red SRTFD E15... 141 L3
Gee St FSBYE EC1V... 12 E1
Geffrye St BETH E2... 7 L7
Geisthorp Ct WAB EN9... 63 M9
Geldart Rd PECK SE15... 160 A6
Geldeston Rd CLPT E5... 119 P7
Gellatly Rd NWCR SE14... 160 B8
Gemini Cl CRAWW RH11... 282 C9
General Gordon Pl WOOL/PLUM SE18... 162 E3
The Generals Wk PEND EN3... 80 D3
General Wolfe Rd GNWCH SE10... 161 J7
Genesis Cl STWL/WRAY TW19... 174 A4
Genesta Gld GVE DA12... 191 K8
Genesta Rd WOOL/PLUM SE18... 162 G5
Geneva Cl SHPTN TW17... 196 F2
Geneva Dr HNHL SE24... 159 H10
Geneva Gdns CHDH RM6... 123 P5
Geneva Rd KUT KT1... 199 K4
THHTH CR7... 203 K5
Genever Cl CHING E4... 100 F5
Genoa Av PUT/ROE SW15... 178 F1
Genoa Rd PGE/AN SE20... 204 B3
Genotin Rd ENC/FH EN2... 79 L7
Gentleman's Rw ENC/FH EN2... 79 K7
Genyn Rd GUW GU2... 267 L5
Geoffrey Av HARH RM3... 105 P3
Geoffrey Cl CMBW SE5... 159 K8
Geoffrey Gdns EHAM E6... 142 B4
Geoffrey Rd BROCKY SE4... 160 B9
George Avey Cft EPP CM16... 66 C2
George Beard Rd DEPT SE8... 160 E8
George Crs MUSWH N10... 98 B8
George Gange Wy KTN/HRWW/W HA3... 114 D1
George Green Dr DTCH/LGLY SL3... 130 C8
George Green Rd DTCH/LGLY SL3... 130 C8
George Groves Rd PGE/AN SE20... 203 P1
George La HAYES BR2... 205 N8
LEW SE13... 183 H2
SWFD E18... 121 N1
George Mathers Rd LBTH SE11... 18 C5
George Ms CAMTN NW1... 4 G10
George Rd CHING E4... 100 F7
GU GU1... 250 A10
KUTN/CMB KT2... 177 N10
NWMAL KT3... 200 C4
George Rw BERM/RHTH SE16... 19 N2
Georges Cl STMC/STPC BR5... 207 M3
Georges Dr BRWN CM15... 86 C2
Georges Md BORE WD6... 75 J10
Georges Rd BH/WHM TN16... 244 A6
HOLWY N7... 118 G10
Georges Ter CTHM CR3... 241 L8
George St BARK IG11... 142 F7
BERK HP4... 34 A5
CAN/RD E16... 141 L8
CROY/NA CRO... 203 K9
CSHM HP5... 51 H9
GRAYS RM17... 167 M5
HERT/WAS SG14... 25 K5
HHNE HP2... 35 N5
HNWL W7... 134 D10
HSLW TW3... 153 N8
MBLAR W1H... 10 B5
MHST W1U... 10 C5
NWDGN UB2... 153 N3
RCHPK/HAM TW10... 177 J1
ROM RM1... 124 G4
STA TW18... 173 J7
STALW/RED AL3... 38 C6
UX/CGN UB8... 131 N2
WATW WD18... 73 K8
George's Wood Rd BRK/MPK AL9... 59 K2
Georgetown Cl NRWD SE19... 181 L8
Georgette Pl GNWCH SE10... 161 H6
George V Av PIN HA5... 113 P2
George V Wy GFD/PVL UB6... 134 G2
RKW/CH/CXG WD3... 71 K2
George Wk WARE SG12... 26 C2
George Wyver Cl WIM/MER SW19... 179 H3
George Yd BANK EC3V... 13 H6
MYFR/PKLN W1K... 10 D7
Georgia Rd NWMAL KT3... 199 P4
THHTH CR7... 203 J1
Georgiana St CAMTN NW1... 4 G5
Georgian Cl CRAWE RH10... 284 G5
HAYES BR2... 205 N8
STA TW18... 173 L7
STAN HA7... 94 F8
Georgian Ct WBLY HA9... 114 C7
Georgian Wy RYLN/HDSTN HA2... 114 C7
Georgina Gdns BETH E2... 7 M9
Geraint Rd BMLY BR1... 183 M6
Geraldine Rd CHSWK W4... 155 M5
WAND/EARL SW18... 179 N4
Geraldine St LBTH SE11... 18 C4
Gerald Rd BCTR RM8... 124 A7
BGVA SW1W... 16 D5
CAN/RD E16... 141 J4
GVE DA12... 191 H3
Gerald's Gv BNSTD SM7... 220 G10
Gerard Av HSLWW TW4... 175 P4
Gerard Gdns RAIN RM13... 144 F4
Gerard Rd BARN SW13... 156 C4
HRW HA1... 114 F4
Gerards Cl BERM/RHTH SE16... 160 B5
Gerda Rd ELTH/MOT SE9... 184 E6
Gerdview Dr RDART DA2... 187 K7
Germains Cl CSHM HP5... 50 G8
Germain St CSHM HP5... 50 F8
Germander Dr CHOB/PIR GU24... 230 F2
Germander Wy SRTFD E15... 141 K5
Gernon Cl RAIN RM13... 145 J4
Gernon Rd BOW E3... 139 K7
Geron Wy CRICK NW2... 116 E7
Gerpins La UPMR RM14... 145 K4
Gerrard Crs BRW CM14... 107 H4
Gerrard Gdns PIN HA5... 113 H3
Gerrard Pl SOHO/SHAV W1D... 11 K7
Gerrard Rd IS N1... 6 D4
Gerrards Cl STHGT/OAK N14... 78 D9
Gerrards Cross Rd SLN SL2... 129 M1
Gerrards Md BNSTD SM7... 239 J7
Gerrard St SOHO/SHAV W1D... 11 J7
Gerridge St STHWK SE1... 18 C2
Gertrude Rd BELV DA17... 164 B3
Gertrude St WBPTN SW10... 15 K10
Gervaise Cl SL SL1... 128 E10
Gervase Cl WBLY HA9... 115 P8
Gervase Rd EDGW HA8... 95 P9
Gervase St PECK SE15... 160 B6
Gew's Cnr CHES/WCR EN8... 62 C5
Ghent St CAT SE6... 183 N5
Ghent Wy HACK E8... 7 M1
Ghilbert Wy BERK HP4... 33 M5
Giant Arches Rd HNHL SE24... 181 K3
Giant Tree Hl BUSH WD23... 94 C3
Gibb Cft HLWS CM18... 47 H5

Gibbfield Cl CHDH RM6... 123 P7
Gibbon Rd SRTFD E15... 141 H2
ACT W3... 136 B9
PECK SE15... 160 B8
KUTN/CMB KT2... 191 L10
Gibbons Cl BORE WD6... 75 K5
CRAWE RH10... 284 D10
STALE/WH AL4... 21 H10
Gibbons Rd WLSDN NW10... 136 G2
Gibbon Wk PUT/ROE SW15... 156 D10
Gibb's Acre CHOB/PIR GU24... 230 E9
Gibbs Av NRWD SE19... 181 L9
Gibbs Brook La OXTED RH8... 261 J10
Gibbs Cl CHES/WCR EN8... 62 C5
NRWD SE19... 181 L8
Gibbs Couch OXHEY WD19... 93 L4
Gibbs Gn EDGW HA8... 95 P5
Gibbs Rd UED N18... 100 B5
Gibbs Sq NRWD SE19... 181 L8
Gibraltar Cl RBRW/HUT CM13... 107 H7
Gibraltar Crs HOR/WEW KT19... 220 C6
Gibson Cl BCTR RM8... 123 M6
CHSGTN KT9... 219 H2
EPP CM16... 66 C1
GVW DA11... 190 C5
ISLW TW7... 175 H7
WCHPL E1... 140 B6
Gibson Ct DTCH/LGLY SL3... 150 C4
Gibson Gdns STNW/STAM N16... 119 N7
Gibson Pl STWL/WRAY TW19... 173 M2
Gibson Rd BCTR RM8... 123 M6
HGDN/ICK UB10... 112 A9
LBTH SE11... 17 P6
SUT SM1... 221 L2
Gibson Sq IS N1... 6 B1
Gibson St GNWCH SE10... 161 K4
Gidd Hl COUL/CHIP CR5... 240 D5
Gidea Av GPK RM2... 125 H1
Gidea Cl GPK RM2... 125 H1
Gideon Cl BELV DA17... 164 C3
Gideon Rd BTSEA SW11... 158 A9
Giesbach Rd ARCH N19... 118 C7
Giffard Rd UED N18... 99 P4
Giffard Wy GUW GU2... 249 M7
Giffin St DEPT SE8... 160 F6
Gifford Gdns HNWL W7... 133 P5
Giffordside GRAYS RM17... 168 C4
Gifford St IS N1... 5 M4
Gift La SRTFD E15... 141 K3
Giggs Hl STMC/STPC BR5... 207 J2
Giggs Hill Gdns THDIT KT7... 198 B5
Giggs Hill Rd THDIT KT7... 198 B5
Gilbert Cl SWCM DA10... 189 J2
WOOL/PLUM SE18... 162 G2
Gilbert Gv EDGW HA8... 95 P9
Gilbert Pl NOXST/BSQ WC1A... 11 J3
Gilbert Rd BELV DA17... 164 A2
BMLY BR1... 183 M10
CDH/CHF RM16... 167 H2
DEN/HRF UB9... 91 N10
LBTH SE11... 18 B6
PIN HA5... 113 L2
ROM RM1... 124 G2
WIM/MER SW19... 179 M9
Gilbert St HSLW TW3... 154 B9
MYFR/PKLN W1K... 10 D6
PEND EN3... 80 B5
SRTFD E15... 121 K9
Gilbey Cl HGDN/ICK UB10... 112 C9
Gilbey Rd TOOT SW17... 179 P7
Gilbeys Yd CAMTN NW1... 4 D1
Gilbourne Rd WOOL/PLUM SE18... 163 J5
Gilda Av PEND EN3... 80 D3
Gilda Crs STNW/STAM N16... 119 P6
Gildea Cl PIN HA5... 93 P8
Gildea St REGST W1B... 10 F3
Gilden Cl HLWE CM17... 29 P7
Gildenhill Rd SWLY BR8... 187 K10
Gilden Wy HLWE CM17... 29 N6
HLWS CM18... 29 N1
Gildersome St WOOL/PLUM SE18... 162 G7
Giles Cl RAIN RM13... 145 L4
STALE/WH AL4... 21 H10
Giles Coppice NRWD SE19... 181 N7
Giles Travers Cl EGH TW20... 194 G8
Gilfrid Cl UX/CGN UB8... 132 C8
Gilham's Av BNSTD SM7... 220 G8
Gilkes Crs DUL SE21... 181 M2
EDUL SE22... 181 M2
Gilkes Pl DUL SE21... 181 M2
Gillam Wy RAIN RM13... 145 H1
Gillan Gn BUSH WD23... 94 B3
Gillards Ms WALTH E17... 120 F2
Gillards Wy WALTH E17... 120 F2
Gill Av CAN/RD E16... 141 M8
Gill Cl WATW WD18... 72 E5
Gill Crs GVW DA11... 190 D6
Gillender St BOW E3... 140 E2
Gillespie Rd FSBYPK N4... 119 H4
Gillett Av EHAM E6... 142 F2
Gillett Pl STNW/STAM N16... 119 N10
Gillett Rd THHTH CR7... 203 L4
Gillett St STNW/STAM N16... 119 N10
Gillham Ter TOTM N17... 99 P7
Gilliam Gv PUR/KEN CR8... 223 H8
Gillian Crs GPK RM2... 105 H10
Gillian Park Rd CHEAM SM3... 201 J8
Gillian St LEW SE13... 183 K4
Gilliat Dr RGUE GU4... 250 C7
Gilliat Rd SL SL1... 129 K9
Gilliat's Gn RKW/CH/CXG WD3... 70 B3
Gilliatt Cl IVER SL0... 131 H8
Gillingham Ms PIM SW1V... 16 F5
Gillingham Rd CRICK NW2... 117 H8
Gillingham Rw PIM SW1V... 16 G5
Gillingham St PIM SW1V... 16 F5
Gillman Dr SRTFD E15... 141 K3
Gillman's Rd STMC/STPC BR5... 207 L8
Gills Hl RAD WD7... 74 F3
Gills Hill La RAD WD7... 74 E3
Gills Hollow RAD WD7... 74 E3
Gill's Rd EYN DA4... 210 D10
Gill St POP/IOD E14... 140 G9
Gillum Cl EBAR EN4... 98 A2
Gilmais GT/LBKH KT23... 254 C4
Gilmore Crs WDSR SL4... 148 C9
Gilmore Rd LEW SE13... 183 K2
Gilmour Cl ENC/FH EN2... 79 P7
Gilpin Av MORT/ESHN SW14... 156 A10
Gilpin Cl MTCM CR4... 201 P2
WHTN TW2... 176 A3
Gilpin Gn HARP AL5... 20 D1
Gilpin Crs UED N18... 99 N6
WHTN TW2... 176 A3
Gilpin Rd CLPT E5... 120 D10
WARE SG12... 26 C2
Gilpin's Gallop WARE SG12... 26 G2
Gilpin's Ride BERK HP4... 34 B4
Gilpin Wy HYS/HAR UB3... 152 L6
Gilroy Cl RAIN RM13... 144 C10
Gilroy Wy STMC/STPC BR5... 207 L2
Gilsland WAB EN9... 81 K1
Gilsland Rd THHTH CR7... 203 L4
Gilson Ct STWL/WRAY TW19... 171 P3
Gilstead Rd FUL/PGN SW6... 157 L8
Gilston Rd WBPTN SW10... 15 K8
Gilton Rd CAT SE6... 183 H5
Giltspur St STBT EC1A... 12 D5
Gilwell Cl CHING E4... 80 G10
Gilwell La CHING E4... 81 J4
Gimcrack Hl LHD/OX KT22... 236 G10
Ginhams Rd CRAWW RH11... 283 J7
Gippeswyck Cl PIN HA5... 93 L9

Gipsy Hl NRWD SE19 181 M8
Gipsy La BARN SW13 156 D9
GRAYS RM17 167 P5
Gipsy Rd WELL DA16 163 N8
WNWD SE27 181 L7
Gipsy Road Gdns WNWD SE27 181 K7
Giralda Cl CAN/RD E16 142 A7
Giraud St POP/IOD E14 140 G8
Girdlers Rd HMSMTH W6 156 G3
Girdwood Rd WAND/EARL SW18 179 H3 2
Girling Wy EBED/NFELT TW14 153 H9
Gironde Rd FUL/PGN SW6 157 J6
Girtin Rd BUSH WD23 74 A9
Girton Av CDALE/KGS NW9 115 M1
Girton Cl NTHLT UB5 134 B1
Girton Ct CHES/WCR EN8 62 D6
Girton Gdns CROY/NA CR0 204 F10
Girton Rd NTHLT UB5 134 B1
SYD SE26 182 C8
Girton Wy RKW/CH/CXG WD3 72 D9
Gisborne Gdns RAIN RM13 144 G5 4
Gisbourne Cl WLGTN SM6 202 E10 2
Gisburne Wy WATN WD24 73 H3
Gisburn Rd CEND/HSY/T N8 118 G2
Gittens Cl BMLY BR1 183 L7
Glacier Wy ALP/SUD HA0 135 J4
Gladbeck Wy ENC/FH EN2 79 K8
WCHMH N21 79 J8
Gladden Ct HLWS CM18 47 H5 1
Gladding Rd CHESW EN7 61 J1
MNPK E12 122 A9
Glade Cl SURB KT6 199 J9 1
Glade Gdns CROY/NA CR0 204 D7
Glade La NWDGN UB2 154 A1
Gladeside CROY/NA CR0 204 C6
STALE/WH AL4 39 J3
WCHMH N21 98 G1
Gladesmore Rd SEVS/STOTM N15 119 N4
Glade Sp KWD/TDW/WH KT20 239 L7
The Glades GVE DA12 190 G9
HHW HP1 35 H5
The Glade ASC SL5 192 B5
BELMT SM2 221 H5
BF/WBF KT14 215 H9
BMLY BR1 206 A2
CFSP/GDCR SL9 110 A6
CHARL SE7 161 P6
CLAY IG5 102 C9
COUL/CHIP CR5 241 H5
CRAWE RH10 284 B9
CROY/NA CR0 204 C5
ENC/FH EN2 79 H7
EW KT17 220 D3
KWD/TDW/WH KT20 239 L7
LHD/OX KT22 235 P8
RBRW/HUT CM13 107 M2
SEV TN13 247 J9
STA TW18 173 L10
UPMR RM14 126 B10
WCHMH N21 78 G10
WFD IG8 101 N4
WGCW AL8 22 F3 1
WWKM BR4 204 G10
The Gladeway WAB EN9 63 J9
Gladiator St FSTH SE23 182 D2
Glading Ter STNW/STAM N16 119 N8 3
Gladioli Cl HPTN TW12 175 P9 4
Gladsdale Dr PIN HA5 113 H2
Gladsmuir Cl WOT/HER KT12 197 K9
Gladsmuir Rd ARCH N19 118 D6
BAR EN5 77 H6
Gladstone Av EBED/NFELT TW14 175 H2
MNPK E12 142 B2
WDGN N22 99 J10
WHTN TW2 176 C3
Gladstone Gdns HSLW TW3 154 B7 2
Gladstone Ms KIL/WHAMP NW6 2 C3 2
PGE/AN SE20 182 B10 2
WDGN N22 99 H10 3
Gladstone Park Gdns CRICK NW2 116 E8
Gladstone Rd ASHTD KT21 237 J4
BKHH IG9 101 P2
CHSWK W4 156 A2 5
CROY/NA CR0 203 L7 2
CSHM HP5 51 H7
DART DA1 187 N2
HOD EN11 44 G2
KUT KT1 199 M3
NWDGN UB2 153 M1 1
ORP BR6 226 F2
SURB KT6 199 J9
WARE SG12 26 B1
WAT WD17 73 K7
WIM/MER SW19 179 K10 3
Gladstone St STHWK SE1 18 C3
Gladstone Ter VX/NE SW8 158 C7 2
Gladstone Wy
KTN/HRWW/W HA3 114 D1 2
SL SL1 148 F1
Gladwell Rd BMLY BR1 183 M9
CEND/HSY/T N8 118 G4
Gladwyn Rd PUT/ROE SW15 156 G9
Gladys Rd KIL/WHAMP NW6 2 F3
Glaisyer Wy IVER SL0 130 F4 1
Glamis Cl CHESW EN7 61 P5
Glamis Crs HYS/HAR UB3 152 D2
Glamis Dr EMPK RM11 125 M6
Glamis Pl WAP E1W 140 B9
Glamis Rd WAP E1W 140 B9
Glamis Wy NTHLT UB5 134 B1
Glamorgan Cl MTCM CR4 202 F3 3
Glamorgan Rd KUT KT1 177 H10
Glanfield Rd BECK BR3 204 E4
Glanleam Rd STAN HA7 95 J5
Glanmead BRWN CM15 107 K2
Glanmor Rd SLN SL2 129 N9
Glanthams Rd BRWN CM15 107 L3
The Glanty EGH TW20 172 F7
Glanville Dr EMPK RM11 125 N6
Glanville Rd BRXS/STRHM SW2 180 F1
HAYES BR2 205 N3
Glasbrook Av WHTN TW2 175 N4
Glasbrook Rd ELTH/MOT SE9 184 A3
Glaserton Rd STNW/STAM N16 119 M5
Glasford St TOOT SW17 180 A9
Glasgow Rd PLSTW E13 141 N4
SL SL1 128 F8 5
UED N18 100 A6 6
Glasgow Ter PIM SW1V 16 G8
Glasse Cl WEA W13 134 F9
Glasshill St STHWK SE1 18 D1
Glasshouse Flds WAP E1W 140 C9 3
Glasshouse St REGST W1B 11 H8
Glasshouse Wk LBTH SE11 17 M7
Glasshouse Yd STBT EC1A 12 E2
Glasslyn Rd CEND/HSY/T N8 118 E3
Glassmill La HAYES BR2 205 L2
Glass St BETH E2 140 A6 5
Glass Yd WOOL/PLUM SE18 162 D2
Glastonbury Av WFD IG8 102 A8
Glastonbury Cl STMC/STPC BR5 207 M8
Glastonbury Rd ED N9 99 P2 3
MRDN SM4 201 K7 1
MRDN SM4 201 K6 1
Glastonbury St
KIL/WHAMP NW6 117 J10 3
Glaucus St BOW E3 140 G7
Glazbury Rd WKENS W14 14 B7
Glazebrook Cl DUL SE21 181 L5
Glazebrook Rd TEDD TW11 176 E10
Glaziers La RGUW GU3 248 A8
Gleave Cl STAL AL1 38 G5
Glebe Av ENC/FH EN2 79 J7
HGDN/ICK UB10 112 C8
KTN/HRWW/W HA3 115 K1
MTCM CR4 201 P2
RSLP HA4 133 J1
WFD IG8 101 M7
Glebe Cl BRKMPK AL9 42 A3 1
CFSP/GDCR SL9 90 A9
CRAWE RH10 283 N6
GT/LBKH KT23 253 P2
HERT/WAS SG14 25 L3 1
HGDN/ICK UB10 112 D9
HHS/BOV HP3 35 P9
LTWR GU18 212 B6
SAND/SEL CR2 223 N8
Glebe Cottages BRKMPK AL9 42 A3
RGUE GU4 251 L8
Glebe Ct STAN HA7 95 H6
Glebe Crs HDN NW4 116 F2 3
KTN/HRWW/W HA3 115 K1
The Glebefield SEV TN13 246 G9
Glebe Gdns BF/WBF KT14 215 N10
NWMAL KT3 200 B7
Glebe House Dr HAYES BR2 205 N8
Glebe Hyrst SAND/SEL CR2 223 N8
Glebeland Gdns SHPTN TW17 196 D6
Glebelands CHIG IG7 103 L4
CRAWE RH10 285 P5
DART DA1 164 G10
E/WMO/HCT KT8 198 A5
ESH/CLAY KT10 218 E5
HLW CM20 29 J8
Glebelands Av GNTH/NBYPK IG2 122 G5
SWFD E18 101 M10
Glebelands Rd
EBED/NFELT TW14 175 H3 1
Glebe La KTN/HRWW/W HA3 115 K2
RDKG RH5 271 L9
SEV TN13 265 J2
Glebe Pth MTCM CR4 202 A3
Glebe Pl CHEL SW3 15 N9
EYN DA4 210 B4
Glebe Rd ASHTD KT21 237 J4
BARN SW13 156 D8
BELMT SM2 221 H5
BMLY BR1 205 M1
CAR SM5 222 A3
CEND/HSY/T N8 118 G2
CFSP/GDCR SL9 89 P9
CHONG CM5 67 N5
COUL/CHIP CR5 240 B10
DAGE RM10 144 C1 1
DORK RH4 272 E2
EGH TW20 172 F9
FNCH N3 97 M9
GVW DA11 190 C4
HACK E8 7 L3
HERT/WAS SG14 25 L3
RAIN RM13 145 J5
RSEV TN14 265 J8
STA TW18 173 L8
STAN HA7 95 H6
UX/CGN UB8 131 M4
WARL CR6 242 C3
WDSR SL4 171 N1
WLSDN NW10 136 D1
Glebe Side TWK TW1 176 E2
Glebe St CHSWK W4 156 A4
Glebe Ter BOW E3 140 G5 3
The Glebe BKHTH/KID SE3 161 K9
CHST BR7 206 F1
CRAWE RH10 285 J2
GSTN WD25 55 K9
HORL RH6 280 A4 1
KGLGY WD4 54 B5 2
REIG RH2 274 D7
WDR/YW UB7 151 P3
WPK KT4 200 C8
Glebe Wy AMS HP6 69 J2
EMPK RM11 125 M5
ERITH DA8 164 F5
FELT TW13 175 P6
SAND/SEL CR2 223 N8
Glebeway WFD IG8 101 P6
Glebe Wy WWKM BR4 205 H9
Gledhow Gdns ECT SW5 15 J6
Gledhow Wd
KWD/TDW/WH KT20 239 L8
Gledstanes Rd WKENS W14 14 B8
Gledwood Av YEAD UB4 133 H7
Gledwood Crs YEAD UB4 132 G7
Gledwood Dr YEAD UB4 132 G7
Gledwood Gdns YEAD UB4 133 H7
Gleed Av BUSH WD23 94 C3
Gleeson Dr ORP BR6 227 J2
Glegg Pl PUT/ROE SW15 156 G10 2
Glemsford Dr HARP AL5 20 C1
Glenaffric Av POP/IOD E14 161 J3 2
Glen Albyn Rd WIM/MER SW19 178 G5
Glenalla Rd RSLP HA4 112 G5
Glenalmond Rd
KTN/HRWW/W HA3 115 K2
Glenalvon Wy CHARL SE7 162 B3 1
Glena Mt SUT SM1 221 M1
Glenarm Rd CLPT E5 120 B9
Glen Av ASHF TW15 174 B7
Glenavon Cl ESH/CLAY KT10 218 F3
Glenavon Gdns DTCH/LGLY SL3 149 P3
Glenavon Rd SRTFD E15 141 K2
Glenbarr Cl ELTH/MOT SE9 162 E9 1
Glenbow Rd BMLY BR1 183 K9
Glenbrook North ENC/FH EN2 78 G8
Glenbrook Rd
KIL/WHAMP NW6 117 K10 1
Glenbrook South ENC/FH EN2 78 G8
Glenbuck Rd SURB KT6 199 J6
Glenburnie Rd TOOT SW17 180 A6
Glencairn Dr EA W5 134 G6
Glencairne Cl CAN/RD E16 142 A7 3
Glencairn Rd STRHM/NOR SW16 180 F10
Glen Cl KWD/TDW/WH KT20 239 H9
SHPTN TW17 196 B4
Glencoe Av GNTH/NBYPK IG2 123 H5
Glencoe Dr DAGE RM10 124 B9
Glencoe Rd BUSH WD23 73 P10
WEY KT13 196 B10 1
YEAD UB4 133 L7
Glencorse Gn OXHEY WD19 93 L5 2
Glen Crs WFD IG8 101 N7
Glendale HHW HP1 35 L6
SWLY BR8 208 G5
Glendale Av CHDH RM6 123 M5
EDGW HA8 95 L5
WDGN N22 99 H8
Glendale Cl BRWN CM15 107 K2
ELTH/MOT SE9 162 D9 1
WOKN/KNAP GU21 231 P4
Glendale Dr RGUE GU4 250 F6
Glendale Gdns WBLY HA9 115 J6
Glen Dale Ms BECK BR3 204 G1
Glendale Ri PUR/KEN CR8 241 J1
Glendale Rd ERITH DA8 164 D3
GVW DA11 190 B7
Glendale Wy THMD SE28 143 M10
Glendall St CLAP SW4 158 G10 1
Glendarvon St PUT/ROE SW15 156 G9
Glendene Av EHSLY KT24 252 F2
Glendish Rd TOTM N17 99 P9
Glendor Gdns MLHL NW7 96 A5
Glendower Crs ORP BR6 207 K6
Glendower Gdns
MORT/ESHN SW14 156 A9 4
Glendower Pl SKENS SW7 15 L5
Glendower Rd CHING E4 101 J2 4
MORT/ESHN SW14 156 A9 5
Glendown Rd ABYW SE2 163 K4
Glendun Rd ACT W3 136 B9
Gleneagle Ms
STRHM/NOR SW16 180 E8 1
Gleneagle Rd STRHM/NOR SW16 180 E8 2
Gleneagles STAN HA7 94 G7
Gleneagles Cl HARH RM3 105 N8 3
HTHAIR TW6 173 M1
ORP BR6 206 G8
OXHEY WD19 93 L6 3
Gleneldon Ms
STRHM/NOR SW16 180 F7 1
Gleneldon Rd STRHM/NOR SW16 180 F7
Glenelg Rd BRXS/STRHM SW2 180 F1
Glenesk Rd ELTH/MOT SE9 162 D9
Glenester Cl HOD EN11 26 F10
Glen Faba Rd HLWW/ROY CM19 45 L3
Glenfarg Rd CAT SE6 183 J4
Glenferrie Rd STAL AL1 38 F6
Glenfield Cl BRKHM/BTCW RH3 273 N3
Glenfield Ct HERT/WAS SG14 24 G4 1
Glenfield Crs RSLP HA4 112 E5
Glenfield Rd ASHF TW15 174 C9
BAL SW12 180 D4
BNSTD SM7 239 L1
BRKHM/BTCW RH3 273 N4
WEA W13 154 G1
Glenfinlas Wy CMBW SE5 159 J6
Glenforth St GNWCH SE10 161 L3
Glengall Br POP/IOD E14 160 G2
Glengall Gv POP/IOD E14 160 G2
Glengall Pl STAL AL1 38 D9 2
Glengall Rd BXLYHN DA7 163 P9
EDGW HA8 95 N4
KIL/WHAMP NW6 2 D6
PECK SE15 19 M9
WFD IG8 101 N7
Glengall Ter PECK SE15 19 M9
Glen Gdns CROY/NA CR0 203 H10
Glengarnock Av POP/IOD E14 161 H3
Glengarry Rd EDUL SE22 159 M10
Glenham Dr GNTH/NBYPK IG2 122 E3
Glenhaven Av BORE WD6 75 M7
Glen Hazel BRWN CM15 87 J1 1
Glenhead Cl ELTH/MOT SE9 162 E9 2
Glenheadon Cl LHD/OX KT22 237 J9
Glenheadon Ri LHD/OX KT22 237 J9
Glenhill Cl FNCH N3 97 K10
Glenhouse Rd ELTH/MOT SE9 184 D1
Glenhurst Av BXLY DA5 186 A4
KTTN NW5 118 B9
RSLP HA4 112 D5
Glenhurst Ri NRWD SE19 181 K10
Glenhurst Rd BTFD TW8 155 H5
NFNCH/WDSP N12 97 N5
Glenilla Rd HAMP NW3 3 N1
Glenister Park Rd
STRHM/NOR SW16 180 E10
Glenister Rd CSHM HP5 51 H4
GNWCH SE10 161 L4
Glenlea Rd ELTH/MOT SE9 184 D1
Glenloch Rd HAMP NW3 3 N1
PEND EN3 80 B6
Glenluge Rd BKHTH/KID SE3 161 M5
Glenlyn Av STAL AL1 38 G7 2
Glenlyon Rd ELTH/MOT SE9 184 D1
Glenmere Av MLHL NW7 96 D8
Glenmore Cl ADL/WDHM KT15 195 L10
Glenmore Rd HAMP NW3 3 N1
WELL DA16 163 J7
Glenmore Wy BARK IG11 143 K5
Glenn Av PUR/KEN CR8 223 J7
Glennie Rd WNWD SE27 181 H6
Glenny Rd BARK IG11 142 F1
Glenorchy Cl YEAD UB4 133 M7
Glenparke Rd FSTGT E7 141 N1
Glen Ri WFD IG8 101 N7
Glen Rd CHSGTN KT9 199 K10
PLSTW E13 141 P6
WALTH E17 120 E3 5
Glenrosa Gdns GVE DA12 191 J8
Glenrosa St FUL/PGN SW6 157 M8
Glenroy St SHB W12 136 F8 2
Glensdale Rd BROCKY SE4 160 E9
Glenshiel Rd ELTH/MOT SE9 184 D1
Glenside CHIG IG7 102 E7
Glentanner Wy TOOT SW17 179 N6 1
Glen Ter POP/IOD E14 161 H1
Glentham Gdns BARN SW13 156 E4
Glentham Rd BARN SW13 156 D5
The Glen ADL/WDHM KT15 215 J2
CROY/NA CR0 204 C10
DTCH/LGLY SL3 149 P3
ENC/FH EN2 79 J8
HAYES BR2 205 K2
HHNE HP2 36 B1
NTHWD HA6 92 E8
NWDGN UB2 153 N4
ORP BR6 206 C10
PIN HA5 113 M5
PIN HA5 113 J3
RAIN RM13 145 K6
WBLY HA9 115 J9
Glenthorne Av CROY/NA CR0 204 B8
Glenthorne Cl CHEAM SM3 201 K8
Glenthorne Gdns BARK/HLT IG6 122 D1
CHEAM SM3 201 K8
Glenthorne Rd FBAR/BDGN N11 98 A6
HMSMTH W6 156 F3 4
KUT KT1 199 L4 1
WALTH E17 120 D3
Glenthorpe Rd MRDN SM4 200 G5
Glenton Cl ROM RM1 104 F8
Glenton Rd LEW SE13 161 K10
Glenton Wy ROM RM1 104 F8
Glentrammon Av ORP BR6 227 J3
Glentrammon Cl ORP BR6 227 J3
Glentrammon Gdns ORP BR6 227 J3
Glentrammon Rd ORP BR6 227 J3
Glentworth Pl SL SL1 129 H10
Glentworth St CAMTN NW1 10 B2
Glenure Rd ELTH/MOT SE9 184 D1
Glenview ABYW SE2 163 N5
Glen Vw GVE DA12 190 F4
Glenview Cl CRAWE RH10 284 A5
Glen View Rd BMLY BR1 206 A2
Glenview Rd HHW HP1 35 L6
Glenville Av ENC/FH EN2 79 K4
Glenville Gv DEPT SE8 160 E6 3
Glenville Rd KUTN/CMB KT2 199 M1
Glen Wy WAT WD17 72 F4
Glenwood BROX EN10 44 E5
RDKG RH5 273 H4
WGCE AL7 23 M6 3
Glenwood Av CDALE/KGS NW9 116 B6
RAIN RM13 145 H6
Glenwood Cl HRW HA1 114 E3
Glenwood Dr GPK RM2 125 H3
Glenwood Gdns
GNTH/NBYPK IG2 122 D3
Glenwood Gv CDALE/KGS NW9 115 P6
Glenwood Rd CAT SE6 182 E4
EW KT17 220 D3
HSLW TW3 154 C9
MLHL NW7 96 B4
SEVS/STOTM N15 119 J3
Glenwood Wy CROY/NA CR0 204 C6
Glenworth Av POP/IOD E14 161 J3 3
Glevum Cl STALW/RED AL3 37 N8
Gliddon Rd WKENS W14 14 A7
Glimpsing Gn ERITHM DA18 163 P2
Glisson Rd HGDN/ICK UB10 132 B4
Gload Crs STMC/STPC BR5 207 N9
Globe Cl HARP AL5 20 B2
Globe Pond Rd
BERM/RHTH SE16 140 D10 4
Globe Rd BETH E2 140 B5
EMPK RM11 125 H4
FSTGT E7 121 L10 3
WFD IG8 101 P7
Globe St STHWK SE1 18 G2
Globe Ter BETH E2 140 B5 9
Glory Md DORK RH4 273 H5
Glossop Rd SAND/SEL CR2 223 L5
Gloster Rd NWMAL KT3 200 B4 3
WOKS/MYFD GU22 232 D6
Gloucester Av BFN/LL DA15 185 H5
CAMTN NW1 4 C4
CDH/CHF RM16 167 P1 1
CHES/WCR EN8 62 D9
EMPK RM11 125 P3
SL SL1 129 H7
TIL RM18 169 M4
WELL DA16 185 J1
Gloucester Circ GNWCH SE10 161 H6 1
Gloucester Cl THDIT KT7 198 F8 3
WLSDN NW10 136 A2
Gloucester Ct MON EC3R 13 K8
RCH/KEW TW9 155 M6 2
Gloucester Crs CAMTN NW1 4 E5
STA TW18 173 N9
Gloucester Dr FSBYPK N4 119 J7
GLDGN NW11 117 K2
STWL/WRAY TW19 172 F6
Gloucester Gdns BAY/PAD W2 9 H5
EBAR EN4 78 B8
GLDGN NW11 117 J5
IL IG1 122 B5
SUT SM1 201 L9
Gloucester Ga CAMTN NW1 4 E7
Gloucester Gate Ms CAMTN NW1 4 E7
Gloucester Gv EDGW HA8 96 A9
Gloucester Ms BAY/PAD W2 9 K6
Gloucester Ms West BAY/PAD W2 9 J6
Gloucester Pl CAMTN NW1 10 A2
MHST W1U 10 B4
WDSR SL4 149 J8
Gloucester Place Ms MBLAR W1H 10 B4
Gloucester Rd ACT W3 155 P1
BAR EN5 77 L9
BELV DA17 164 A4 2
BRWN CM15 86 G9
CROY/NA CR0 203 L7
DART DA1 187 J2
EA W5 155 H1
ENC/FH EN2 79 K4
FELT TW13 175 K4
GUW GU2 249 L8
GVE DA12 190 F7
HPTN TW12 176 A10
HSLWW TW4 153 M10
KUT KT1 199 M2
LEY E10 120 F5
MNPK E12 122 C8
RCH/KEW TW9 155 M6
REDH RH1 258 A9
ROM RM1 124 F4
RYLN/HDSTN HA2 114 A3
SKENS SW7 15 J3
TEDD TW11 176 D8
TOTM N17 99 L10
UED N18 99 N6
WALTH E17 100 C10
WAN E11 121 N3
WHTN TW2 176 B4
Gloucester Sq BAY/PAD W2 9 M6
BETH E2 7 N6
Gloucester St PIM SW1V 16 G8
Gloucester Ter BAY/PAD W2 9 H5
Gloucester Wk KENS W8 14 F1
Gloucester Wy CLKNW EC1R 6 B10
Glover Cl ABYW SE2 163 M3
CHESW EN7 61 N3 2
Glover Dr UED N18 100 B7
Glover Rd PIN HA5 113 L4
Glovers Cl HERT/BAY SG13 25 K7 1
Glovers Fld BRWN CM15 86 E3
Glovers Gv RSLP HA4 112 C5
Glovers La HLWE CM17 47 P6
Glover's Rd HORL RH6 278 G8
REIG RH2 275 L1
Gloxinia Rd MEO DA13 189 N9
Glycena Rd BTSEA SW11 158 A9
Glyn Av EBAR EN4 77 N8
Glyn Cl EW KT17 220 D5
SNWD SE25 203 M2
Glyn Davies Cl SEV TN13 246 F6
Glyndebourne Pk ORP BR6 206 E10
Glynde Ms CHEL SW3 15 P4 3
Glynde Rd BXLYHN DA7 163 P9
Glynde St BROCKY SE4 182 E2
Glyndon Rd WOOL/PLUM SE18 162 F3
Glyn Dr SCUP DA14 185 L7
Glynfield Rd WLSDN NW10 136 B2
Glynne Rd WDGN N22 99 H10 4
Glyn Rd CLPT E5 120 C9
PEND EN3 80 B8 1
WPK KT4 200 G9
Glyn St LBTH SE11 17 N8
Glynswood CFSP/GDCR SL9 90 C8
Goat La EN EN1 79 N4
Goat Rd MTCM CR4 202 B7
Goatsfield Rd BH/WHM TN16 243 P6
Goatswood La ABR/ST RM4 105 J1
Goat Whf BTFD TW8 155 K5
Gobions Av CRW RM5 104 E8
Goblins Gn WGCE AL7 22 G6
Godalming Av WLGTN SM6 222 F2
Godalming Rd POP/IOD E14 140 G7 6
Godbold Rd SRTFD E15 141 K6
Goddard Cl CRAWE RH10 284 C10
SHPTN TW17 196 A3 1
Goddard Pl ARCH N19 118 D8
Goddard Rd BECK BR3 204 C4
CDH/CHF RM16 147 M10
Goddards Cl HERT/BAY SG13 42 D5
Goddington Cha ORP BR6 227 L1
Goddington La ORP BR6 207 M10
Godfrey Av NTHLT UB5 133 M3
WHTN TW2 176 C3
Godfrey Hl WOOL/PLUM SE18 162 B3
Godfrey Rd WOOL/PLUM SE18 162 C3
Godfrey St CHEL SW3 15 P7
SRTFD E15 141 H4
Godfrey Wy HSLWW TW4 175 M3
Goding St LBTH SE11 17 M8
Godley Rd BF/WBF KT14 216 A9
WAND/EARL SW18 179 N4
Godliman St BLKFR EC4V 12 E6 1
Godman Rd CDH/CHF RM16 168 E2
PECK SE15 160 A8 3
Godolphin Cl BELMT SM2 221 J7
PLMGR N13 99 J7 1
Godolphin Pl ACT W3 136 A9 1
Godolphin Rd BEAC HP9 89 H7 2
SHB W12 136 E10
SL SL1 129 J9
WEY KT13 216 E3
Godric Crs CROY/NA CR0 225 J5 1
Godson Rd CROY/NA CR0 203 H10
Godstone Green Rd GDST RH9 260 A7
Godstone Hl GDST RH9 260 B6
Godstone Rd CTHM CR3 241 P10
GDST RH9 260 G7
OXTED RH8 261 H6
PUR/KEN CR8 241 M1
REDH RH1 259 M9
SUT SM1 221 M1
TWK TW1 176 F2
Godstow Rd ABYW SE2 163 M1
Godwin Cl CHING E4 81 H4
HOR/WEW KT19 219 P3
IS N1 6 F7
Godwin Rd FSTGT E7 121 N9
HAYES BR2 205 P3
Goffers Rd BKHTH/KID SE3 161 K7
Goffs Cl CRAWW RH11 283 M8
Goffs Crs CHESW EN7 61 K5
Goff's La CHESW EN7 61 N5
CRAWW RH11 283 L7
Goff's Oak Av CHESW EN7 61 J4
Goffs Park Rd CRAWW RH11 283 M8
Goffs Rd ASHF TW15 174 E9
Gogmore Farm Cl CHERT KT16 195 H7
Gogmore La CHERT KT16 195 K7 6
Goidel Cl WLGTN SM6 222 E1 1
Golborne Gdns NKENS W10 8 B2
Golborne Ms NKENS W10 8 B3 1
Golborne Rd NKENS W10 8 B3
Goldace GRAYS RM17 167 L5 2
Golda Cl BAR EN5 76 G10
Goldbeaters Gv EDGW HA8 96 B8 2
Goldcliff Cl MRDN SM4 201 K7
Gold Cl BROX EN10 44 D6
Goldcrest Cl CAN/RD E16 142 A7 4
HORL RH6 279 N3
THMD SE28 143 M9
Goldcrest Wy BUSH WD23 94 B2
CROY/NA CR0 225 J5
PUR/KEN CR8 222 E6
Goldcroft HHS/BOV HP3 36 B8
Golden Crs HYS/HAR UB3 132 F10
Golden Dell WGCE AL7 23 J9
Golden La STLK EC1Y 12 E1
Golden Mnr HNWL W7 134 D9
Golden Oak Cl SLN SL2 129 H1 1
Golden Plover Cl CAN/RD E16 141 M8
Golden Sq SOHO/CST W1F 11 H7
Golders Cl EDGW HA8 95 N6
Golders Gdns GLDGN NW11 117 H5
Golders Green Crs GLDGN NW11 117 J5
Golders Manor Dr GLDGN NW11 116 G4
Golders Park Cl GLDGN NW11 117 K6
Golders Ri HDN NW4 116 G3 4
Golders Wy GLDGN NW11 117 J5
Goldfinch Cl CRAWW RH11 283 N5
ORP BR6 227 K2
Goldfinch Gdns RGUE GU4 250 G9
Goldfinch Rd SAND/SEL CR2 224 D6
THMD SE28 162 G2
Goldfinch Wy BORE WD6 75 M8 3
Goldhawk Ms SHB W12 156 E1 2
Goldhawk Rd HMSMTH W6 156 C3
SHB W12 156 E2
Goldhaze Cl WFD IG8 102 A8 2
Gold Hl EDGW HA8 96 A7 1
Gold Hl East CFSP/GDCR SL9 90 A10
Gold Hl North CFSP/GDCR SL9 89 P9
Gold Hl West CFSP/GDCR SL9 89 P9
Goldhurst Ter KIL/WHAMP NW6 3 H4
Golding Cl CRAWE RH10 284 D8 3
Goldingham Av LOU IG10 82 F6
Golding Rd SEV TN13 247 K8
Goldings Crs HAT AL10 40 E3
Golding's Hl LOU IG10 82 C4
Goldings La HERT/WAS SG14 25 H2
Goldings Ri LOU IG10 82 D5
Goldings Rd LOU IG10 82 D5
The Goldings WOKN/KNAP GU21 231 L2
Golding St WCHPL E1 13 P6
Goldington Cl HOD EN11 26 E10 1
Goldington Crs CAMTN NW1 5 J7
Goldington St CAMTN NW1 5 J7
Goldman Cl BETH E2 13 N1
Goldney Rd MV/WKIL W9 8 E2
Goldrill Dr FBAR/BDGN N11 98 B3
Goldrings Rd LHD/OX KT22 218 B9
Goldsboro' Rd VX/NE SW8 158 E7
Goldsborough Crs CHING E4 101 H3 3
Goldsdown Cl PEND EN3 80 D6
Goldsdown Rd PEND EN3 80 C6
Goldsel Rd SWLY BR8 208 F4
Goldsmid St WOOL/PLUM SE18 163 H4
Goldsmith GRAYS RM17 167 L5 3
Goldsmith Av ACT W3 136 A9
CDALE/KGS NW9 116 B3
MNPK E12 142 B1
ROMW/RG RM7 124 B5
Goldsmith Cl RYLN/HDSTN HA2 113 P6
Goldsmith La CDALE/KGS NW9 115 P2
Goldsmith Rd ACT W3 136 A10
FBAR/BDGN N11 98 A6
LEY E10 120 G6
PECK SE15 159 P7
WALTH E17 100 C10
Goldsmiths Cl
WOKN/KNAP GU21 231 P4 1
Goldsmith's Rw BETH E2 7 P7
Goldsmith St CITYW EC2V 12 F5 3
Goldstone Cl WARE SG12 26 C1 3
Goldsworth Orch
WOKN/KNAP GU21 231 M4 2
Goldsworth Rd
WOKN/KNAP GU21 231 P4
Goldsworthy Gdns
BERM/RHTH SE16 160 B4 2
Goldsworthy Wy SL SL1 128 B8
Goldwell Rd THHTH CR7 202 G4
Goldwing Cl CAN/RD E16 141 M8
Gole Rd CHOB/PIR GU24 230 C7
Golf Cl BUSH WD23 73 L7
STAN HA7 95 H8
STRHM/NOR SW16 203 H1
WOKS/MYFD GU22 215 H10
Golf Club Dr KUTN/CMB KT2 178 A10
Golf Club Rd BRKMPK AL9 59 K2
WEY KT13 216 C6
WOKS/MYFD GU22 231 M6
Golfe Rd IL IG1 122 G8
Golf Links Av GVW DA11 190 E8
Golf Ride ENC/FH EN2 79 H1
Golf Rd BMLY BR1 206 D3
EA W5 135 L8 1
PUR/KEN CR8 241 L4
Golf Side BELMT SM2 221 H7
WHTN TW2 176 C6 1
Golf Side Cl NWMAL KT3 200 B2
Golfside Cl TRDG/WHET N20 97 P4
Gollogly Ter CHARL SE7 161 P4
Gombards STALW/RED AL3 38 C5 2
Gomer Gdns TEDD TW11 176 F9 3
Gomer Pl TEDD TW11 176 F9
Gomm Rd BERM/RHTH SE16 160 B2
Gomms Wood Cl BEAC HP9 88 A7
Gomshall Av WLGTN SM6 222 F2
Gomshall Gdns PUR/KEN CR8 241 M1
Gomshall La SHGR GU5 270 B5
Gomshall Rd BELMT SM2 220 F6 3
EW KT17 220 F6
Gondar Gdns CRICK NW2 117 J10
Gonson St DEPT SE8 160 G5 1
Gonston Cl WIM/MER SW19 179 H5 2
Gonville Av RKW/CH/CXG WD3 72 C10
Gonville Crs NTHLT UB5 134 A1
Gonville Rd THHTH CR7 202 G5
Gonville St FUL/PGN SW6 157 H9
Goodall Rd WAN E11 121 H8 2
Gooden Ct HRW HA1 114 D8
Goodenough Cl COUL/CHIP CR5 241 H6
Goodenough Rd WIM/MER SW19 179 J10
Goodenough Wy COUL/CHIP CR5 240 G6
Goodge Pl FITZ W1T 11 H4
Goodge St FITZ W1T 11 H4
Goodhall St WLSDN NW10 136 C5
Goodhart Wy WWKM BR4 205 K6
Goodhew Rd SNWD SE25 203 P6
Gooding Cl NWMAL KT3 199 P4
Goodinge Rd HOLWY N7 5 L1
Goodlake Ct DEN/HRF UB9 111 J5 1
Goodley Stock Rd EDEN TN8 262 E5
Goodman Crs BRXS/STRHM SW2 180 E5 1
BRXS/STRHM SW2 180 F5 3
Goodman Pk SLN SL2 129 P10
Goodman Rd LEY E10 121 H5
Goodmans Ct ALP/SUD HA0 115 J9
Goodman's Stile WCHPL E1 13 N5 1
Goodman's Yd WCHPL E1 13 M7 1
Goodmayes Av GDMY/SEVK IG3 123 K6

Goodmayes La GDMY/SEVK IG3.... 123 K9
Goodmayes Rd GDMY/SEVK IG3.... 123 K9
Goodmead Rd ORP BR6... 207 K7
Goodrich Cl GSTN WD25... 73 H1
Goodson Rd WLSDN NW10... 136 B2
Goods Wy CAMTN NW1... 5 L7
Goodway Gdns POP/IOD E14... 143 J8
Goodwin Cl BERM/RHTH SE16... 19 M4
CRAWW RH11... 283 H10
MTCM CR4... 201 N3
Goodwin Ct CHES/WCR EN8... 62 D4
Goodwin Dr SCUP DA14... 185 N5
Goodwin Gdns CROY/NA CR0... 223 J8
SAND/SEL CR2... 223 J3
Goodwin Rd CROY/NA CR0... 223 J2
ED N9... 100 B2
SHB W12... 156 D1
SLN SL2... 128 E5
Goodwin St FSBYPK N4... 119 H7
Goodwood Av HCH RM12... 125 M8
PEND EN3... 80 B3
WATN WD24... 72 F1
Goodwood Cl CRAWE RH10... 284 B10
HOD EN11... 44 G2
MRDN SM4... 201 K4
Goodwood Crs GVE DA12... 190 F9
Goodwood Dr NTHLT UB5... 133 P1
Goodwood Rd NWCR SE14... 160 D6
REDH RH1... 258 A8
Goodwyn Av MLHL NW7... 96 B6
Goodwyns Rd DORK RH4... 272 G5
Goodwyn's v MUSWH N10... 98 B9
Goodyers Av RAD WD7... 56 E9
Goodyers Gdns HDN NW4... 116 G3
Goosander Wy
WOOL/PLUM SE18... 162 G2
Goose Acre CSHM HP5... 51 M6
Gooseacre La KTN/HRWW/W HA3.. 115 J3
Goosecroft HHW HP1... 35 G5
Goosefields HHW HP1... 71 M10
Goose Gn SHGR GU5... 270 C9
SLN SL2... 128 C4
Goose Green Cl STMC/STPC BR5... 207 K2
Goose La WOKS/MYFD GU22... 231 N8
Gooseley La EHAM E6... 142 D5
Goose Rye Rd RGUW GU3... 248 A3
Gooshays Dr HARH RM3... 105 M7
Gooshays Gdns HARH RM3... 105 M7
Goossens Cl SUT SM1... 221 M2
Gophir La CANST EC4R... 12 C7
Gopsall St IS N1... 7 H6
Goral Md RKW/CH/CXG WD3... 91 N2
Gordon Av CHING E4... 101 K7
HCH RM12... 124 C6
MORT/ESHN SW14... 156 B10
PUR/KEN CR8... 223 K6
STAN HA7... 94 E7
TWK TW1... 176 F1
Gordonbrock Rd BROCKY SE4... 182 F1
STA TW18... 173 L9
STAL AL1... 38 G7
TIL RM18... 169 N6
WALTH E17... 120 F4
Gordon Crs CROY/NA CR0... 203 M8
HYS/HAR UB3... 153 H3
Gordondale Rd WIM/MER SW19... 179 K5
Gordon Dr CHERT KT16... 195 H10
SHPTN TW17... 196 E6
Gordon Gdns EDGW HA8... 95 N10
Gordon Gv CMBW SE5... 159 J8
Gordon Hl ENC/FH EN2... 79 K5
Gordon House Rd KTTN NW5... 118 B9
Gordon Pl GVE DA12... 190 F2
KENS W8... 14 F1
Gordon Rd ASHF TW15... 173 P6
BARK IG11... 143 H3
BECK BR3... 204 E3
BELV DA17... 164 D3
BFN/LL DA15... 185 H1
BRWN CM15... 107 M2
BRYLDS KT5... 199 L2
CAR SM5... 222 A3
CDH/CHF RM16... 168 B1
CHDH RM6... 124 A4
CHES/WCR EN8... 62 F10
CHING E4... 101 K1
CHSWK W4... 155 N5
CSHM HP5... 51 L8
CTHM CR3... 241 L7
DART DA1... 187 L3
EA W5... 135 H9
ED N9... 100 A3
ENC/FH EN2... 79 L5
ESH/CLAY KT10... 218 C4
FBAR/BDGN N11... 98 E8
FNCH N3... 97 J8
GVW DA11... 190 B3
HSLW TW3... 154 B10
IL IG1... 122 G8
KTN/HRWW/W HA3... 114 D1
KUTN/CMB KT2... 199 L1
NWDGN UB2... 153 M3
PECK SE15... 160 A8
RCH/KEW TW9... 155 L8
REDH RH1... 258 B7
SEV TN13... 265 J1
SHPTN TW17... 196 E6
SRTFD E15... 121 H9
SWFD E18... 101 N1
WAN E11... 121 M4
WDR/YW UB7... 131 P9
WDSR SL4... 148 A3
Gordon Sq STPAN WC1H... 11 K1
Gordon St PLSTW E13... 141 M5
STPAN WC1H... 11 J1
Gordons Wk HARP AL5... 20 B3
Gordons Wd RGUE RH8... 261 J4
Gordon Wy BAR EN5... 77 J3
BMLY BR1... 205 M1
Gorefield Pl KIL/WHAMP NW6... 2 E7
Gore Hl AMSS HP7... 68 G8
Gorelands La CSTG HP8... 90 B3
Gorell Rd BEAC HP9... 88 C10
Gore Rd HOM E9... 140 B3
RDART DA2... 188 C5
RYNPK SW20... 200 F2
SL SL1... 128 A5
Goresbrook Rd DAGW RM9... 143 J1
Gore St SKENS SW7... 15 K3
Gorham Dr STAL AL1... 38 D7
Gorham Pl NTGHL W11... 8 A8
Goring Cl CRW RM5... 104 D9
Goring Gdns BCTR RM8... 123 M9
Goring Rd DAGE RM10... 144 E1
FBAR/BDGN N11... 98 F7
STA TW18... 172 G8
Goring St HDTCH EC3A... 13 K5
Goring Wy GFD/PVL UB6... 134 B4
Gorle Cl GSTN WD25... 55 H10
Gorleston Rd SEVS/STOTM N15.. 119 L3
Gorleston St WKENS W14... 14 B5
Gorling Cl CRAWW RH11... 283 H8
Gorman Rd WOOL/PLUM SE18.. 162 C3
Gorringe Av EDUL SE22... 210 C2
Gorringe Park Av MTCM CR4... 180 A10
Gorse Cl CRAWE RH10... 285 J1
HAT AL10... 40 C7
KWD/TDW/WH KT20... 238 E6
Gorse Cnr STAL/WRED AL3... 38 C4
Gorse Ct RGUE GU4... 250 F8
Gorse Dr HORL RH6... 281 E6
Gorse Hill La VW GU25... 194 A4
Gorse Hill Rd VW GU25... 194 A4
Gorselands HARP AL5... 20 B4
Gorselands Cl BF/WBF KT14... 215 M7
Gorse La CHOB/PIR GU24... 213 L4
Gorse Meade SL SL1... 128 G10
Gorse Ri TOOT SW17... 180 B8
Gorse Rd CROY/NA CR0... 204 F10
STMC/STPC BR5... 208 B9
Gorse Wk WDR/YW UB7... 131 P8
Gorse Wy HART DA3... 211 L5
Gorseway ROMW/RG RM7... 124 F2
Gorse Wood Rd HART DA3... 211 L5
Gorsewood Rd
WOKN/KNAP GU21... 231 J5
Gorst Rd BTSEA SW11... 180 A2
WLSDN NW10... 136 A6
Gorsuch Pl BETH E2... 7 L9
Gorsuch St BETH E2... 7 L9
Gosberton Rd BAL SW12... 180 A4
Gosbury Hl CHSGTN KT9... 219 K1
Gosden Cl CRAWE RH10... 284 B8
SHGR GU5... 268 C9
Gosden Hill Rd RGUE GU4... 250 F6
Gosden La CHOB/PIR GU24... 212 D4
Gosfield Rd BCTR RM8... 124 B6
HOR/WEW KT19... 220 A8
Gosfield St GTPST W1W... 10 F3
Gosford Gdns REDBR IG4... 122 C3
Gosforth La OXHEY WD19... 93 H4
Gosforth Pth OXHEY WD19... 93 H4
Goshawk Gdns YEAD UB4... 132 F5
Goslar Wy WDSR SL4... 148 G8
Goslett Yd SOHO/SHAV W1D... 11 K5
Gosling Cl GFD/PVL UB6... 133 P5
Gosling Gdns DTCH/LGLY SL3... 150 B2
Gosling Rd DTCH/LGLY SL3... 150 B2
Gosling Wy BRXN/ST SW9... 159 H4
Gospatrick Rd TOTM N17... 99 K9
Gospel Oak Wk WALTH E17... 99 P7
Gosport Rd WALTH E17... 120 E3
Gosport Rd WALTH E17... 145 K1
Gossage Rd HGDN/ICK UB10... 132 A2
WOOL/PLUM SE18... 162 G4
The Gossamers GSTN WD25... 73 M1
Gosselin Rd HERT/WAS SG14... 25 K3
Gosset St BETH E2... 7 N10
Goss Hl SWLY BR8... 187 K9
Gosshill Rd CHST BR7... 206 D2
Gossington Cl CHST BR7... 184 E7
Cossoms Ryde BERK HP4... 33 M4
Cossops Dr CRAWW RH11... 283 K3
Gossops Green La CRAWW RH11.. 283 K3
Costerwood St DEPT SE8... 160 D5
Gostling Rd WHTN TW2... 175 P4
Goston Gdns THHTH CR7... 203 H3
Goswell Hl WDSR SL4... 149 J7
Goswell Rd FSBYE EC1V... 6 D9
WDSR SL4... 149 J7
Gothic Cl DART DA1... 187 L6
Gothic Ct HYS/HAR UB3... 152 E5
Gothic Rd WHTN TW2... 176 C5
Gottfried Ms KTTN NW5... 118 D9
Goudhurst Cl CRAWE RH10... 284 F7
Goudhurst Rd BMLY BR1... 183 K8
Gouge Av GVW DA11... 190 B4
Gough Rd EN EN1... 80 A6
FSTGT E7... 121 L9
Gough St FSBYW WC1X... 11 P1
Gould Cl BRKMPK AL9... 40 E10
CHONG CM5... 49 K7
Gould Ct RGUE GU4... 250 G8
Goulden Gdns THHTH CR7... 203 K8
Gould Rd EBED/NFELT TW14... 174 F3
WHTN TW2... 176 D4
Gould's Gn UX/CGN UB8... 132 C8
Goulston St HACK E8... 120 A10
Goulton Rd CLPT E5... 120 A10
Gourley Pl SEVS/STOTM N15.... 119 M3
Gourley St SEVS/STOTM N15.... 119 M3
Gourney Gv CDH/CHF RM16... 147 N9
Gourock Rd ELTH/MOT SE9... 184 D1
Govan St BETH E2... 7 P6
Government Rw PEND EN3... 80 F3
Govett Av SHPTN TW17... 196 D5
Govett Gv BFOR GU20... 212 C2
Govier Cl SRTFD E15... 141 K2
Gowan Av FUL/PGN SW6... 157 H7
Gowan Rd WLSDN NW10... 136 G2
Gowar Fld POTB/CUF EN6... 58 D2
Gower Cl BAL SW12... 180 D2
Gower Ms GWRST WC1E... 11 K4
Gower Pl STPAN WC1H... 11 H1
Gower St FSTGT E7... 141 M1
HORL RH6... 279 P4
ISLW TW7... 154 E5
WEY KT13... 216 E3
Gowers La COCH/CHF RM16... 168 C1
The Gowers AMS HP6... 69 K3
HLW CM20... 29 K9
Gower St GWRST WC1E... 11 H1
Gower's Wk WCHPL E1... 13 N5
Gowland Pl BECK BR3... 204 E2
Gowlett Rd PECK SE15... 159 P9
Gowrie Rd BTSEA SW11... 158 B9
Graburn Wy E/WMO/HCT KT8... 198 C3
Grace Av BXLYHN DA7... 164 A4
RAD WD7... 57 K9
Gracechurch St BANK EC3V... 13 H7
Grace Cl BARK/HLT IG6... 103 J7
BORE WD6... 76 A5
EDGW HA8... 96 B5
ELTH/MOT SE9... 184 A6
Grace Ct SL SL1... 129 H10
Gracedale Rd TOOT SW17... 180 C6
Gracefield Gdns
STRHM/NOR SW16... 180 A5
Grace Pl BOW E3... 140 A9
Grace Rd CROY/NA CR0... 203 K6
Grace's Ms CMBW SE5... 159 L8
Grace's Rd CMBW SE5... 159 M8
Grace St BOW E3... 140 C9
Gracious La SEV TN13... 265 H6
Gracious Lane End RSEV TN14... 264 G6
Gracious Pond Rd
CHOB/PIR GU24... 213 L4
The Gradient SYD SE26... 181 P7
Graeme En EN1... 79 M6
Graemesdyke Av
MORT/ESHN SW14... 155 N9
Graemes Dyke Rd BERK HP4... 33 M6
Graffham Cl CRAWW RH11... 283 L5
Grafton Cl BF/WBF KT14... 215 M9
DTCH/LGLY SL3... 130 B8
HSLWW TW4... 175 M4
STALE/WH AL4... 39 J7
WEA W13... 134 F4
WPK KT4... 200 B10
Grafton Crs CAMTN NW1... 4 E2
Grafton Gdns BCTR RM8... 123 P7
FSBYPK N4... 119 K4
Grafton Ms FITZ W1T... 10 F2
Grafton Park Rd WPK KT4... 200 B9
Grafton Pl CAMTN NW1... 5 J9
Grafton Rd ACT W3... 135 K4
CROY/NA CR0... 203 H8
ENC/FH EN2... 78 D7
HRW HA1... 114 B3
KTTN NW5... 118 B10
NWMAL KT3... 200 B4
WPK KT4... 200 A10
Grafton Sq CLAP SW4... 158 D9
Grafton St MYFR/PICC W1J... 10 D8
Grafton Ter KTTN NW5... 118 A10
FITZ W1T... 11 H2
Grafton Wy E/WMO/HCT KT8... 197 N4
FITZ W1T... 11 H1
GTPST W1W... 10 G3
Grafton Yd KTTN NW5... 4 F2
Graham Av BROX EN10... 44 D6
MTCM CR4... 202 B1
WEA W13... 154 G1
Graham Cl CROY/NA CR0... 204 F9
RBRW/HUT CM13... 87 P9
Graham Gdns SURB KT6... 199 K8
Graham Park Wy MLHL NW7... 96 C8
Graham Rd BFOR GU20... 212 B3
BXLYHN DA7... 164 D3
CHSWK W4... 156 A2
HACK E8... 7 N1
HDN NW4... 116 E4
HPTN TW12... 175 P7
KTN/HRWW/W HA3... 114 D1
MTCM CR4... 202 B1
PLSTW E13... 141 M6
PUR/KEN CR8... 223 H9
SEVS/STOTM N15... 119 J1
WIM/MER SW19... 179 J10
Graham St IS N1... 6 D7
Graham Ter BGVA SW1W... 16 C5
Grainger Cl NTHLT UB5... 114 B10
Grainger Rd ISLW TW7... 154 E8
WDGN N22... 99 K9
Gramer Cl WAN E11... 121 J7
Grampian Cl HYS/HAR UB3... 152 E6
ORP BR6... 207 J6
Grampian Gdns CRICK NW2... 117 H6
Grampian Wy DTCH/LGLY SL3... 150 D4
Granada St TOOT SW17... 180 A1
Granard Av PUT/ROE SW15... 178 L1
Granard Rd BAL SW12... 180 A3
The Granaries WAB EN9... 63 K3
Granary Cl ED N9... 100 B1
HORL RH6... 280 B2
STALE/WH AL4... 21 J3
Granary La HARP AL5... 20 A2
Granary Rd WCHPL E1... 140 A6
Granary St CAMTN NW1... 5 J6
Granby Av HARP AL5... 20 B1
Granby Park Rd CHESW CR7... 61 N4
Granby Rd ELTH/MOT SE9... 162 G4
GVW DA11... 190 A2
Granby St BETH E2... 13 M1
Granby Ter CAMTN NW1... 4 C8
Grand Av BRYLDS KT5... 199 N6
FARR EC1M... 12 D3
MUSWH N10... 118 B2
WBLY HA9... 115 M10
Grand Avenue East WBLY HA9... 116 A10
Grand Depot Rd WOOL/PLUM SE18.. 162 D4
Grand Dr RYNPK SW20... 200 F3
STHL UB1... 154 B1
Granden Rd STRHM/NOR SW16.. 202 F2
Grandfield Av WAT WD17... 72 C4
Grandison Rd BTSEA SW11... 180 A1
WPK KT4... 200 F9
Grand Stand Rd EPSOM KT18... 238 C3
Grand Union Canal Wk
BAY/PAD W2... 8 F3
BERK HP4... 33 K2
DEN/HRF UB9... 111 L1
DTCH/LGLY SL3... 130 A10
HNWL W7... 154 D2
HNWL W7... 153 P3
NKENS W10... 8 A1
NWDGN UB2... 153 J2
RKW/CH/CXG WD3... 91 K5
SLN SL2... 129 N10
STHL UB1... 133 N6
STKPK UB11... 152 C1
WLSDN NW10... 135 N4
Grand Union Crs HACK E8... 7 P5
Grand View Av BH/WHM TN16.. 243 P3
Granfield St BTSEA SW11... 157 N7
Grange Av EBAR EN4... 97 P2
KTN/HRWW/W HA3... 94 G10
NFNCH/WDSP N12... 97 M6
SNWD SE25... 203 M2
TRDG/WHET N20... 97 J1
WHTN TW2... 176 D5
Grangecliffe Gdns SNWD SE25.. 203 M3
Grange Cl BFN/LL DA15... 185 K6
BH/WHM TN16... 262 G2
CFSP/GDCR SL9... 90 B9
CRAWE RH10... 284 B5
E/WMO/HCT KT8... 198 A4
GUW GU2... 249 N6
HERT/WAS SG14... 25 J3
HYS/HAR UB3... 132 F7
LHD/OX KT22... 237 J2
NWDGN UB2... 153 N2
RBRW/HUT CM13... 107 P6
REDH RH2... 259 J4
STWL/WRAY TW19... 172 B2
WAT WD17... 73 H5
WFD IG8... 101 P3
Grange Ct NTHLT UB5... 133 K4
WAB EN9... 63 H10
WOT/HER KT12... 197 N9
Grange Court Rd HARP AL5... 20 B5
Grangecourt Rd
STNW/STAM N16... 119 M6
Grange Crs CHIG IG7... 102 C6
RDART DA2... 188 A2
THMD SE28... 143 M8
Grangedale Cl NTHWD HA6... 92 F9
Grange Dr CHST BR7... 184 B9
ORP BR6... 227 M5
REDH RH1... 258 C4
WOKN/KNAP GU21... 232 B1
Grange End HORL RH6... 281 H4
Grange Farm Cl
RYLN/HDSTN HA2... 114 B7
Grange Flds CFSP/GDCR SL9... 90 B9
Grangefields Rd RGUE GU4... 250 E4
Grange Gdns BNSTD SM7... 221 L8
HAMP NW3... 117 L8
PIN HA5... 113 N2
SLN SL2... 109 J10
SNWD SE25... 203 M2
STHGT/OAK N14... 98 E2
WARE SG12... 26 D3
Grange Gv IS N1... 6 E1
Grange Hl SNWD SE25... 203 M2
SNWD SE25... 203 M2
Grangehill Pl ELTH/MOT SE9... 162 G9
Grangehill Rd ELTH/MOT SE9... 162 G10
Grange La DUL SE21... 181 N10
GSTN WD25... 74 C5
HART DA3... 211 N7
HLWW/ROY CM19... 45 P7
Grange Meadow BNSTD SM7... 221 L9
Grangemill Rd CAT SE6... 182 B7
Grangemill Wy CAT SE6... 182 A7
Grangemount LHD/OX KT22... 237 J2
Grange Pk WCHMH N21... 79 J10
WOKN/KNAP GU21... 214 C10
Grange Park Av WCHMH N21... 79 J9
Grange Park Pl RYNPK SW20... 178 G10
Grange Park Rd LEY E10... 120 C6
THHTH CR7... 203 L4
Grange Pl STA TW18... 195 M2
Grange Rd ADL/WDHM KT15... 215 M6
BELMT SM2... 221 M9
BELV DA17... 164 E3
BORE WD6... 75 J3
BUSH WD23... 73 M9
CFSP/GDCR SL9... 90 A9
CHOB/PIR GU24... 230 G4
CHSGTN KT9... 219 K1
CHSWK W4... 155 M4

CRAWE RH10... 285 P6
CTHM CR3... 259 P1
E/WMO/HCT KT8... 198 A4
EA W5... 135 J10
EDGW HA8... 96 A7
EGH TW20... 172 C8
GRAYS RM17... 167 N5
GVW DA11... 190 D3
HARH RM3... 105 J7
HCT N6... 118 B4
HRW HA1... 114 F4
HYS/HAR UB3... 132 F6
IL IG1... 122 F9
KUT KT1... 199 K3
LEY E10... 120 F6
LHD/OX KT22... 237 J6
ORP BR6... 206 F9
ORP BR6... 207 L5
PLSTW E13... 141 L5
RGUW GU3... 249 N5
SAND/SEL CR2... 223 J6
SEV TN13... 265 K3
SNWD SE25... 203 L3
SOCK/AV RM15... 168 B10
STHWK SE1... 19 K4
STHWK SE1... 19 N3
TOTM N17... 99 P7
WALTH E17... 120 D3
WLSDN NW10... 136 E1
WOKN/KNAP GU21... 232 B1
WOT/HER KT12... 217 N1
Grange St IS N1... 7 H6
STALW/RED AL3... 38 C5
The Grange ALP/SUD HA0... 135 M2
CHOB/PIR GU24... 213 K6
CROY/NA CR0... 204 C3
EYN DA4... 210 C1
HOR/WEW KT19... 220 A1
STHWK SE1... 19 L3
WDSR SL4... 171 N1
WIM/MER SW19... 178 G9
WOT/HER KT12... 197 J9
Grange V BELMT SM2... 221 L4
Grangeview Rd TRDG/WHET N20.. 97 M2
Grange Wk STHWK SE1... 19 K3
Grange Wy ERITH DA8... 165 J6
HART DA3... 211 L6
Grangeway HORL RH6... 281 H4
Grange Wy IVER SL0... 131 J2
KIL/WHAMP NW6... 2 G4
NFNCH/WDSP N12... 97 L5
WFD IG8... 101 P5
Grangeway Gdns REDBR IG4... 122 B5
Grangeways Cl GVW DA11... 190 C7
The Grangeway WCHMH N21... 79 J10
Grangewood BXLY DA5... 186 A4
DTCH/LGLY SL3... 129 P7
POTB/CUF EN6... 59 L6
Grangewood Av CDH/CHF RM16.. 168 B2
RAIN RM13... 145 K2
Grangewood Cl PIN HA5... 113 H3
RBRW/HUT CM13... 107 M4
Grangewood Dr SUN TW16... 196 E9
Grangewood La BECK BR3... 182 E9
Grange Yd STHWK SE1... 19 L4
Granham Gdns ED N9... 100 C2
Granite St WOOL/PLUM SE18... 163 J4
Granleigh Rd WAN E11... 121 K7
Gransden Av HACK E8... 140 C2
Gransden Rd SHB W12... 156 C1
Grant Av SL SL1... 129 K8
Grantbridge St IS N1... 6 D7
Grantchester Cl HRW HA1... 114 E8
Grant Cl SHPTN TW17... 196 C6
STHGT/OAK N14... 98 D7
Grant Gdns HARP AL5... 20 A1
Grantham Cl EDGW HA8... 95 M4
WARE SG12... 26 D1
Grantham Gdns CHDH RM6... 124 A4
Grantham Pl MYFR/PICC W1J... 10 E10
Grantham Rd BRXN/ST SW9... 158 F9
CHSWK W4... 156 B6
MNPK E12... 122 D8
Grantham Wy CDH/CHF RM16... 147 N10
Grantley Cl RGUE GU4... 268 F7
Grantley Gdns GUW GU2... 249 N6
Grantley Rd GUW GU2... 249 N6
HSLWW TW4... 153 K8
Grantley St WCHPL E1... 140 C5
Grantock Rd WALTH E17... 101 J9
Granton Av HCH RM11... 125 N7
Granton Rd GDMY/SEVK IG3... 123 K6
SCUP DA14... 185 L10
STRHM/NOR SW16... 202 E4
Grant Rd BTSEA SW11... 157 P9
CROY/NA CR0... 203 N8
KTN/HRWW/W HA3... 114 D1
Grants Cl MLHL NW7... 96 F6
Grants La OXTED RH8... 261 P9
Grant St IS N1... 6 A7
PLSTW E13... 141 M5
Grantully Rd MV/WKIL W9... 2 C10
Grant Wk ASC SL5... 192 D8
Grant Wy ISLW TW7... 154 F5
Grantwood Cl REDH RH1... 276 B5
Granville Av ED N9... 100 E4
FELT TW13... 175 H7
HSLWW TW4... 175 P1
Granville Cl BF/WBF KT14... 216 A9
CROY/NA CR0... 203 M9
WEY KT13... 216 D3
Granville Dene HHS/BOV HP3... 52 D3
Granville Gdns ACT W3... 135 L10
HOD EN11... 44 E3
STRHM/NOR SW16... 202 A1
Granville Gv LEW SE13... 161 L9
Granville Ms SCUP DA14... 185 K7
Granville Pl LEW SE13... 161 K9
PIN HA5... 113 J1
Granville Rd BAR EN5... 76 B4
BH/WHM TN16... 262 F7
CRICK NW2... 117 J7
EPP CM16... 65 L5
FSBYPK N4... 118 G4
GVW DA11... 190 C3
HGDN/ICK UB10... 132 C1
HYS/HAR UB3... 152 D1
IL IG1... 122 C5
KIL/WHAMP NW6... 2 E1
LEY E10... 120 G4
NFNCH/WDSP N12... 97 H6
OXTED RH8... 261 L10
PLMGR N13... 98 G7
SCUP DA14... 185 K7
SEV TN13... 247 L10
STAL AL1... 38 E6
SWFD E18... 101 N10
WATW WD18... 73 H3
WDGN N22... 99 J9
WELL DA16... 165 J10
WEY KT13... 216 D4
WIM/MER SW19... 179 K10
WOKS/MYFD GU22... 232 C6
Granville Sq PECK SE15... 159 P5
Granville St FSBYW WC1X... 5 P9
Grape St LSQ/SEVD WC2H... 11 L5
Grasdene Rd WOOL/PLUM SE18.. 163 P3
Grasholm Wy DTCH/LGLY SL3... 150 D1
Grasmere Av ACT W3... 135 P9
HARP AL5... 20 A2
HSLW TW3... 176 A2

WBLY HA9... 115 J3
WIM/MER SW19... 201 K3
Grasmere Cl EBED/NFELT TW14.. 173 P1
EGH TW20... 172 E10
GSTN WD25... 55 J8
GU GU1... 250 E9
HHS/BOV HP3... 36 C8
LOU IG10... 82 C6
Grasmere Ct WDGN N22... 98 G7
Grasmere Gdns
KTN/HRWW/W HA3... 94 F10
ORP BR6... 206 E10
REDBR IG4... 122 B3
Grasmere Rd BMLY BR1... 205 L3
BXLYHN DA7... 164 D7
LTWR GU18... 212 A6
MUSWH N10... 98 B7
ORP BR6... 206 E10
PLSTW E13... 141 M4
PUR/KEN CR8... 223 J7
SNWD SE25... 203 N5
STAL AL1... 38 A5
STRHM/NOR SW16... 181 P7
TOTM N17... 99 P7
Grasmere Wy BF/WBF KT14... 216 A8
Grassingham End CFSP/GDCR SL9.. 90 B8
Grassingham Rd CFSP/GDCR SL9.. 90 B8
Grassington Cl FBAR/BDGN N11.. 98 B6
LCOL/BKTW AL2... 55 P6
Grassington Rd SCUP DA14... 185 K7
Grasslands HORL RH6... 281 H4
Grassmere HORL RH6... 280 C3
Grassmere Rd EMPK RM11... 125 N2
FSTH SE23... 182 A5
WLGTN SM6... 222 D8
Grass Pk FNCH N3... 97 J9
Grass Warren WLYN AL6... 23 K7
Grassway WLGTN SM6... 222 D1
Grassy Cl HHW HP1... 35 K5
Grassy La SEV TN13... 265 J3
Grasvenor Av BAR EN5... 77 K10
Gratton Dr WDSR SL4... 148 D10
Gratton Rd WKENS W14... 14 B5
Grattons Dr CRAWE RH10... 284 D4
Gravel Cl CHIG IG7... 103 K3
Graveley Av BORE WD6... 75 P4
Graveley Rd SHB W12... 23 L6
Gravel Hl BXLYHS DA6... 164 C10
CFSP/GDCR SL9... 90 A7
CROY/NA CR0... 224 C3
FNCH N3... 97 H9
LHD/OX KT22... 236 G7
UX/CGN UB8... 111 N10
Gravel Hill Cl BXLY DA6... 186 C5
BXLYHS DA6... 186 C5
Gravelhill Ter HHW HP1... 35 K7
Gravel La CHIG IG7... 83 K10
HHW HP1... 35 K6
WCHPL E1... 13 L5
Gravelly Hl REDH RH1... 259 N6
Gravel Pth BERK HP4... 34 A5
Gravel Pits La SHGR GU5... 270 D5
Gravel Pit Wy ORP BR6... 207 K9
Gravel Rd DART DA1... 188 B2
HAYES BR2... 206 B9
WHTN TW2... 176 D4
Gravelwood Cl CHST BR7... 184 F6
Gravelly Ct HHS/BOV HP3... 36 D7
Graveney Gv PGE/AN SE20... 182 B10
Graveney Rd CRAWE RH10... 284 D8
TOOT SW17... 179 P7
Gravesend Rd GVE DA12... 191 P7
SHB W12... 136 D9
Gravetts La RGUW GU3... 249 K7
Gravetye Cl CRAWE RH10... 284 B9
Gray Av BCTR RM8... 124 A6
Gray Gdns RAIN RM13... 145 H1
Gray's Gdns RAIN RM13... 145 H1
Grayburn Cl CSTG HP8... 89 M3
Gray Gdns RAIN RM13... 145 H1
Grayham Crs NWMAL KT3... 200 A4
Grayham Rd NWMAL KT3... 200 A4
Grayland Cl BMLY BR1... 206 A1
Graylands WOKN/KNAP GU21... 231 P5
Grayling Cl CAN/RD E16... 141 K1
Grayling Rd STNW/STAM N16... 119 L9
The Graylings ABLGY WD5... 54 F9
Gray Pl CHERT KT16... 214 G3
Grayscroft Rd STRHM/NOR SW16.. 180 E10
Grays End Cl CDH/CHF RM16... 167 M2
Grays Farm Rd STMC/STPC BR5.. 207 L1
Graysfield WCGE AL7... 23 K8
Grayshott Rd BTSEA SW11... 158 B9
Gray's Inn Rd FSBYW WC1X... 5 M9
Gray's Inn Sq GINN WC1R... 12 A3
Grays La ASHF TW15... 174 C7
ASHTD... 237 L5
Grays Park Rd SLN SL2... 129 L10
Grays Pl SLN SL2... 129 L10
Grays Rd BH/WHM TN16... 244 D7
HGDN/ICK UB10... 131 P2
RGODL GU7... 267 L10
SL SL1... 129 L10
Gray St STHWK SE1... 18 C1
Grays Wk CSHM HP5... 50 C4
Grays Wd HORL RH6... 280 E3
Grayswood Gdns RYNPK SW20... 200 E2
Gray's Yd MHST W1U... 10 A4
Graywood Ct NFNCH/WDSP N12.. 97 M8
Grazebrook Rd STNW/STAM N16.. 119 L7
Grazeley Cl BXLYHS DA6... 186 D1
The Grazings HHNE HP2... 36 A4
Greasy Cl ABLGY WD5... 54 C7
Great Benty WDR/YW UB7... 151 P3
Great Braitch La HAT AL10... 22 A9
Great Brays WLSDN CM18... 47 K2
Great Break WCGE AL7... 23 J7
Great Brownings DUL SE21... 181 P3
Great Bushey Dr TRDG/WHET N20.. 97 J2
Great Cambridge Jct PLMGR N13.. 99 H6
Great Cambridge Rd BROX EN10.. 62 D2
CHES/WCR EN8... 62 D1
UED N18... 99 L6
Great Castle St REGST W1B... 10 C5
Great Central Av RSLP HA4... 113 K10
Great Central St CAMTN NW1... 10 A3
Great Central Wy WBLY HA9... 115 P10
WLSDN NW10... 116 B10
Great Chapel St SOHO/CST W1F... 11 J5
Great Chertsey Rd CHSWK W4... 156 A7
FELT TW13... 175 N6
Great Church La HMSMTH W6... 156 G4
Great College St WEST SW1P... 17 L3
Great Conduit WCGE AL7... 23 M4
Great Cross Av GNWCH SE10... 161 K6
Great Cullings ROMW/RG RM7... 124 F7
Great Cumberland Ms
MBLAR W1H... 10 A6
Great Cumberland Pl MBLAR W1H.. 10 A5
Great Dell WCGW AL8... 22 G3
Great Dover St STHWK SE1... 18 G3
Greatdown Rd HNWL W7... 134 E7
Great Eastern Rd BRW CM14... 107 H5
SRTFD E15... 141 J7
Great Eastern St SDTCH EC2A... 7 J10
Great Elms Rd HAYES BR2... 205 P4
HHS/BOV HP3... 36 A10
Great Elshams BNSTD SM7... 239 M6
Great Fld CDALE/KGS NW9... 96 B9
Greatfield Av EHAM E6... 142 C4
Greatfield Cl LEW SE13... 160 F10
Greatfields Dr UX/CGN UB8... 132 B7
Greatfields Rd BARK IG11... 142 G3
Greatford Dr GU GU1... 250 G10
Great Fox Meadow BRWN CM15.. 86 E3
Great Galley Cl BARK IG11... 143 L5
Great Ganett WCGE AL7... 23 J4
Great Gardens Rd EMPK RM11... 125 J4
Great George St STJSPK SW1H... 17 J2

Great Goodwin Dr GU GU1 ..... 250 E8
Great Gregories La EPP CM16 ..... 65 H9
Great Gv BUSH WD23 ..... 74 A8
Great Groves CHESW EN7 ..... 61 N4
Great Guildford St STHWK SE1 ..... 12 E10
Greatham Rd BUSH WD23 ..... 73 L7
  CRAWE RH10 ..... 284 D10
Great Harry Dr ELTH/MOT SE9 ..... 184 D6
Great Heart HHNE HP2 ..... 35 P4
Great Heath HAT AL10 ..... 40 E1
Great Hivings CSHM HP5 ..... 50 F3
Great James St BMSBY WC1N 11 N3
Great Lawn CHONG CM5 ..... 67 P5
Great Ley WCCE AL7 ..... 23 H7
Great Leylands HLWS CM18 ..... 47 K2
Great Marlborough St
  SOHO/CST W1F 10 G6
Great Maze Pond STHWK SE1 ..... 13 H10
Great Meadow BROX EN10 ..... 44 F8
Great Molewood HERT/WAS SG14 ..... 25 J2
Great Nelmes Cha EMPK RM11 ..... 125 N3
Greatness La FLST/FETLN EC4A 12 B5
Greatness Rd RSEV TN14 ..... 247 K7
Great New St FLST/FETLN EC4A 12 B5
Great North Rd BRKMPK AL9 ..... 22 E10
  EFNCH N2 ..... 117 P2
  HAT AL10 ..... 40 F1
  WGCW AL8 ..... 22 E9
Great North Wy (Barnet By-Pass)
  HDN NW4 ..... 116 G1
Great Oaks CHIG IG7 ..... 102 F5
  RBRW/HUT CM13 ..... 87 N10
Great Oaks Pk RGUE GU4 ..... 250 C6
Greatorex St WCHPL E1 ..... 13 N5
Great Ormond St BMSBY WC1N 11 N8
Great Owl Rd CHIG IG7 ..... 102 D4
Great Palmers HHNE HP2 ..... 36 A1
Great Pk KGLGY WD4 ..... 54 B6
Great Percy St FSBYW WC1X 5 P7
Great Peter St WEST SW1P 17 J4
Great Plumtree HLW CM20 ..... 29 J9
Great Portland St GTPST W1W 10 F2
Great Pulteney St SOHO/CST W1F 11 H7
Great Quarry GU GU1 ..... 268 A3
Great Queen St DART DA1 ..... 187 N2
  HOL/ALD WC2B 11 N5
Great Rd HHNE HP2 ..... 36 A5
Great Ropers La BRW CM14 ..... 106 F7
Great Russell St RSQ WC1B 11 K5
Great St Helen's HDTCH EC3A 13 J5
Great Scotland Yd WHALL SW1A 11 L1
Great Slades POTB/CUF EN6 ..... 59 J9
Great Smith St WEST SW1P 17 K3
Great Spilmans EDUL SE22 ..... 181 M1
Great Strd CDALE/KGS NW9 ..... 96 C10
Great Sturgess Rd HHW HP1 ..... 35 J6
Great Suffolk St STHWK SE1 ..... 12 D10
Great Sutton St FSBYE EC1V 12 D2
Great Swan Aly LOTH EC2R 12 G5
Great Tattenhams EPSOM KT18 ..... 238 F4
Great Thrift STMC/STPC BR5 ..... 206 F4
Great Till Rd RSEV TN14 ..... 246 F2
Great Titchfield St GTPST W1W 10 F2
Great Tower St MON EC3R 13 J7
Great Trinity La BLKFR EC4V 12 F7
Great Warley St
  RBRW/HUT CM13 ..... 106 F9
Great Western Rd NTGHL W11 ..... 8 D4
Great West Rd CHSWK W4 ..... 155 P5
  HEST TW5 ..... 153 M8
  HMSMTH W6 ..... 156 E4
  ISLW TW7 ..... 154 D6
Great West Road Chiswick
  CHSWK W4 ..... 156 C5
Great West Road Ellesmere Rd
  CHSWK W4 ..... 155 P5
Great West Road Hogarth La
  CHSWK W4 ..... 156 A5
Great Whites Rd HHS/BOV HP3 ..... 36 A8
Great Winchester St OBST EC2N 13 H5
Great Windmill St
  MYFR/PICC W1J 11 J8
  SOHO/SHAV W1D 11 J7
Greatwood CHST BR7 ..... 184 D10
Greatwood Cl CHERT KT16 ..... 214 F5
Great Woodcote Dr
  PUR/KEN CR8 ..... 222 E6
Great Woodcote Pk
  PUR/KEN CR8 ..... 222 F6
Greaves Cl BARK IG11 ..... 142 G2
Greaves Pl TOOT SW17 ..... 179 J7
Grebe Av YEAD UB4 ..... 133 L8
Grebe Cl FSTGT E7 ..... 121 L10
  WALTH E17 ..... 100 D8
Grebe Crest WTHK RM20 ..... 166 F3
Grecian Crs NRWD SE19 ..... 181 J9
Greding Wk RBRW/HUT CM13 ..... 107 N3
Greek St SOHO/SHAV W1D 11 K6
Greenacre WDSR SL4 ..... 148 N3
Greenacre Cl BAR EN5 ..... 77 J4
  NTHLT UB5 ..... 113 N10
  SWLY BR8 ..... 208 F4
Greenacre Ct EGH TW20 ..... 171 P9
Greenacre Pl WLGTN SM6 ..... 202 C9
Green Acres CROY/NA CR0 ..... 203 N10
  WGCE AL7 ..... 23 J8
Greenacres BUSH WD23 ..... 94 C3
  CRAWE RH10 ..... 284 C8
  ELTH/MOT SE9 ..... 184 E1
  EPP CM16 ..... 65 J4
  GT/LBKH KT23 ..... 235 P10
  HHS/BOV HP3 ..... 36 A8
  OXTED RH8 ..... 261 K3
Greenacres Av HGDN/ICK UB10 ..... 112 A8
Greenacres Cl ORP BR6 ..... 226 F1
  RAIN RM13 ..... 145 N5
Greenacres Dr STAN HA7 ..... 94 G8
Greenacres Gv BERM/RHTH SE16 ..... 160 C1
Greenacre Sq STHGT/OAK N14 ..... 98 E4
Greenall Cl CHES/WCR EN8 ..... 62 D5
Green Arbour Ct STP EC4M 12 C5
Green Av MLHL NW7 ..... 96 A1
  WEA W13 ..... 154 G2
Greenaway Gdns HAMP NW3 ..... 117 L9
Greenbank CHESW EN7 ..... 62 A4
Greenbank Cl CHING E4 ..... 101 L3
  HARH RM3 ..... 105 L4
Greenbank Crs HDN NW4 ..... 117 H2
Greenbank Rd WAT WD17 ..... 72 E2
Greenbanks DART DA1 ..... 187 M5
  UPMR RM14 ..... 126 D7
Greenbay Rd CHARL SE7 ..... 162 A6
Greenberry St STJWD NW8 ..... 3 N8
Greenbrook Av EBAR EN4 ..... 77 N5
Greenbury Cl RKW/CH/CXG WD3 ..... 70 F7
Green Chain Wk BECK BR3 ..... 183 H10
  BMLY BR1 ..... 183 J10
  CHARL SE7 ..... 162 A4
  ELTH/MOT SE9 ..... 184 E1
  SYD SE26 ..... 182 C9
  THMD SE28 ..... 143 M9
Green Cl BRKMPK AL9 ..... 59 J7
  CAR SM5 ..... 202 A9
  CDALE/KGS NW9 ..... 115 P4
  CHES/WCR EN8 ..... 62 D8
  EFNCH N2 ..... 117 M5
  EPP CM16 ..... 46 E10
  FELT TW13 ..... 175 M8
  HAYES BR2 ..... 205 K3
Greencoates HERT/BAY SG13 ..... 25 M6
Greencoat Pl WEST SW1P 17 H5
Greencoat Rw WEST SW1P 17 H4
Green Common La FLKWH HP10 ..... 108 C5

Green Court Av CROY/NA CR0 ..... 204 A9
Greencourt Av EDGW HA8 ..... 95 M9
Greencourt Gdns CROY/NA CR0 ..... 204 A9
Greencourt Rd STMC/STPC BR5 ..... 207 H5
Green Court Rd SWLY BR8 ..... 208 E5
Greencroft GU GU1 ..... 250 E10
Greencroft Av RSLP HA4 ..... 113 K7
Greencroft Cl EHAM E6 ..... 89 K8
  KIL/WHAMP NW6 ..... 3 J3
Greencroft Gdns EN EN1 ..... 79 M7
  KIL/WHAMP NW6 ..... 2 G1
Greencroft Rd HEST TW5 ..... 153 N7
Green Curve BNSTD SM7 ..... 239 L1
Green Dl EDUL SE22 ..... 181 M1
Greendale Ms SLN SL2 ..... 129 M9
Green Dell Wy HHS/BOV HP3 ..... 36 C5
Green Dene EHSLY KT24 ..... 252 E9
Green Dragon La BTFD TW8 ..... 155 K4
  WCHMH N21 ..... 78 D9
Green Dr RPLY/SEND GU23 ..... 233 J9
  STHL UB1 ..... 133 P10
Green East Rd BEAC HP9 ..... 89 K8
Greene Fielde End STA TW18 ..... 173 N10
Greene Field Rd BERK HP4 ..... 33 P5
Green End CHSGTN KT9 ..... 219 J1
  WCHMH N21 ..... 99 J3
Green End Gdns HHW HP1 ..... 35 K7
Green End La HHW HP1 ..... 35 J6
Greenend Rd CHSWK W4 ..... 156 B1
Green End Rd HHW HP1 ..... 35 K7
Greenes Ct BERK HP4 ..... 33 P4
Greene Wk BERK HP4 ..... 34 A6
Green Farm Cl ORP BR6 ..... 227 J2
Green Farm La GVE DA12 ..... 191 P6
Greenfern Av SL SL1 ..... 128 B8
Greenfield BRKMPK AL9 ..... 40 G1
  WGCW AL8 ..... 22 C2
Greenfield Av BRYLDS KT5 ..... 199 N7
  OXHEY WD19 ..... 73 M3
Greenfield Dr EFNCH N2 ..... 118 A3
Greenfield End CFSP/GDCR SL9 ..... 90 C8
Greenfield Gdns CRICK NW2 ..... 117 H7
  DAGW RM9 ..... 143 M3
  STMC/STPC BR5 ..... 206 F3
Greenfield Link COUL/CHIP CR5 ..... 240 F1
Greenfield Rd DAGW RM9 ..... 143 M3
  RDART DA2 ..... 186 E8
  SEVS/STOTM N15 ..... 119 H1
  WCHPL E1 ..... 13 P4
Greenfields LOU IG10 ..... 82 D8
  STHL UB1 ..... 133 P8
Greenfields Cl HORL RH6 ..... 279 P2
Greenfields Rd HORL RH6 ..... 279 P2
Greenfield St WAB EN9 ..... 63 H10
Greenfield Wy RYLN/HDSTN HA2 ..... 114 A1
Greenford Av HNWL W7 ..... 134 D6
  STHL UB1 ..... 133 N9
Greenford Gdns GFD/PVL UB6 ..... 134 A5
Greenford Rd GFD/PVL UB6 ..... 114 D10
  GFD/PVL UB6 ..... 134 B9
  SUT SM1 ..... 221 L1
Green Gdns ORP BR6 ..... 226 F2
Greengate GFD/PVL UB6 ..... 134 G1
Greengate St PLSTW E13 ..... 141 N4
Green Gld EPP CM16 ..... 83 H3
Greenhalgh Wk EFNCH N2 ..... 117 M2
Greenham Cl STHWK SE1 ..... 18 A1
Greenham Crs CHING E4 ..... 100 E7
Greenham Rd MUSWH N10 ..... 98 B10
Greenham Wk WOKN/KNAP GU21 ..... 231 P4
Greenhayes Av BNSTD SM7 ..... 221 K10
Greenhayes Cl REIG RH2 ..... 257 M10
Greenhayes Gdns BNSTD SM7 ..... 239 K1
Green Heights Ct
  WOKS/MYFD GU22 ..... 231 P6
Greenheys Cl NTHWD HA6 ..... 92 F9
Greenheys Dr SWFD E18 ..... 121 L1
Greenheys Pl WOKS/MYFD GU22 ..... 232 C4
Green Hl ORP BR6 ..... 226 B8
  WOOL/PLUM SE18 ..... 162 G4
Greenhill BKHH IG9 ..... 101 P2
  HAMP NW3 ..... 117 N9
  SUT SM1 ..... 201 N9
  WBLY HA9 ..... 115 N7
Greenhill Av CTHM CR3 ..... 242 A7
Greenhill Crs WATW WD18 ..... 72 F10
Greenhill Gdns NTHLT UB5 ..... 133 N4
  RGUE GU4 ..... 250 F8
Greenhill La WARL CR6 ..... 242 D3
Greenhill Pk BAR EN5 ..... 77 M9
  WLSDN NW10 ..... 136 B3
Greenhill Rd GVW DA11 ..... 190 C5
  HRW HA1 ..... 114 D4
  RSEV TN14 ..... 247 K1
  WLSDN NW10 ..... 136 B3
Greenhills HLW CM20 ..... 47 H1
Greenhills Cl RKW/CH/CXG WD3 ..... 71 J8
Greenhill's Rents FARR EC1M 12 C3
Greenhill Ter NTHLT UB5 ..... 133 N4
  WOOL/PLUM SE18 ..... 146 F10
Greenhill Wy HRW HA1 ..... 114 D4
  WBLY HA9 ..... 115 N7
Greenhithe Cl ELTH/MOT SE9 ..... 185 H3
Greenholm Rd ELTH/MOT SE9 ..... 184 E1
Green Hundred Rd PECK SE15 ..... 19 F10
Greenhurst La OXTED RH8 ..... 261 L8
Greenhurst Rd WNWD SE27 ..... 181 H8
Greening St ABYW SE2 ..... 163 M3
Greenland Crs NWDGN UB2 ..... 153 K2
Greenland Ms DEPT SE8 ..... 160 C4
Greenland Pl CAMTN NW1 ..... 4 F5
Greenland Quay
  BERM/RHTH SE16 ..... 160 C3
Greenland Rd BAR EN5 ..... 76 F10
  CAMTN NW1 ..... 4 G5
Greenlands CHERT KT16 ..... 194 F10
  HOR/WEW KT19 ..... 219 N2
Greenlands Rd STA TW18 ..... 173 K2
  WEY KT13 ..... 196 C10
Greenland St CAMTN NW1 ..... 4 F5
Green La AMS HP6 ..... 69 J1
  ASC SL5 ..... 192 D1
  ASHTD KT21 ..... 237 H3
  BCTR RM8 ..... 124 A7
  BF/WBF KT14 ..... 216 A8
  BROX EN10 ..... 44 C9
  BRW CM14 ..... 86 C5
  BRW CM14 ..... 106 F2
  BRWN CM15 ..... 87 H10
  CDH/CHF RM16 ..... 147 P7
  CHERT KT16 ..... 195 H4
  CHIG IG7 ..... 103 H4
  CHSGTN KT9 ..... 219 K5
  COB KT11 ..... 217 L6
  CRAWE RH10 ..... 283 P5
  CRAWE RH10 ..... 284 E7
  CSHM HP5 ..... 285 N1
  CTHM CR3 ..... 241 K9
  DTCH/LGLY SL3 ..... 149 N7
  E/WMO/HCT KT8 ..... 198 A5
  EDGW HA8 ..... 95 L5
  EGH TW20 ..... 172 E7
  EGH TW20 ..... 194 F2
  EHSLY KT24 ..... 234 C10
  ELTH/MOT SE9 ..... 184 E1
  FELT TW13 ..... 175 M8
  GU GU1 ..... 250 D10
  HDN NW4 ..... 116 G3
  HHNE HP2 ..... 36 E4
  HHS/BOV HP3 ..... 52 D4
  HLWE CM17 ..... 48 C2
  HNWL W7 ..... 154 D1
  HORL RH6 ..... 280 C3
  HSLWW TW4 ..... 153 K10
  IL IG1 ..... 122 D1

RKW/CH/CXG WD3 ..... 72 A10
SCUP DA14 ..... 185 N8
SEV TN13 ..... 247 L8
SL SL1 ..... 149 J1
SRTFD E15 ..... 141 L1
STHGT/OAK N14 ..... 98 E3
STMC/STPC BR5 ..... 185 L10
STWL/WRAY TW19 ..... 172 B2
SUT SM1 ..... 201 L10
TOTM N17 ..... 99 J4
WAN E11 ..... 121 K4
WCHMH N21 ..... 99 H4
WDR/YW UB7 ..... 151 N2
WELL DA16 ..... 163 H10
WHTN TW2 ..... 176 D4
Green Tiles La DEN/HRF UB9 ..... 111 J4
Green Trees EPP CM16 ..... 65 K7
Green U WALYHS DA6 ..... 185 M1
  EA W5 ..... 135 L8
  WGCE AL7 ..... 23 K6
Greenvale Rd ELTH/MOT SE9 ..... 162 C10
  WOKN/KNAP GU21 ..... 231 J3
Green Verges STAN HA7 ..... 95 J8
Greenview Av BECK BR3 ..... 204 D6
  CROY/NA CR0 ..... 204 D6
Green View Cl HHS/BOV HP3 ..... 52 D5
Green Wk CHONG CM5 ..... 67 N6
  CRAWE RH10 ..... 283 P5
  DART DA1 ..... 164 G10
  HDN NW4 ..... 116 G2
  RSLP HA4 ..... 112 C6
  STHWK SE1 ..... 19 J4
  WFD IG8 ..... 102 B7
The Green Wk CHING E4 ..... 101 J2
Green Wy ELTH/MOT SE9 ..... 184 A1
  HART DA3 ..... 211 K5
  HAYES BR2 ..... 206 B6
  REDH RH1 ..... 257 P8
  SL SL1 ..... 128 A4
  SUN TW16 ..... 197 H4
Greenway BCTR RM8 ..... 123 M7
  BERK HP4 ..... 33 N5
  BH/WHM TN16 ..... 243 P6
  CHST BR7 ..... 184 D8
  CSHM HP5 ..... 50 G4
  GT/LBKH KT23 ..... 236 A9
  HARH RM3 ..... 106 A7
  HARP AL5 ..... 20 C3
  HLWW/ROY CM19 ..... 46 B1
  KTN/HRWW/W HA3 ..... 115 K3
  PIN HA5 ..... 93 J10
  RBRW/HUT CM13 ..... 107 M1
  RYNPK SW20 ..... 200 F4
  STHGT/OAK N14 ..... 98 F3
  TRDG/WHET N20 ..... 97 K3
  WLGTN SM6 ..... 222 D1
  YEAD UB4 ..... 133 J6
Greenway Av WALTH E17 ..... 121 J2
Greenway Cl BF/WBF KT14 ..... 215 K9
  CDALE/KGS NW9 ..... 96 A10
  FBAR/BDGN N11 ..... 98 B7
  FSBYPK N4 ..... 119 K7
  TRDG/WHET N20 ..... 97 K3
Greenway Ct IL IG1 ..... 122 C6
Greenway Dr STA TW18 ..... 194 A5
Greenway Gdns CDALE/KGS NW9 ..... 95 P10
  CROY/NA CR0 ..... 204 E10
  GFD/PVL UB6 ..... 133 P5
Green Way Gdns
  KTN/HRWW/W HA3 ..... 94 D10
Greenways ABLGY WD5 ..... 54 E7
  BECK BR3 ..... 204 F2
  CHESW EN7 ..... 61 J5
  EGH TW20 ..... 172 B9
  ESH/CLAY KT10 ..... 218 D1
  HERT/WAS SG14 ..... 25 J5
  KWD/TDW/WH KT20 ..... 256 D1
Greenways Dr ASC SL5 ..... 192 D8
The Greenway CDALE/KGS NW9 ..... 96 A10
The Greenway KTN/HRWW/W HA3 ..... 94 D10
  CFSP/GDCR SL9 ..... 110 A1
  EPSOM KT18 ..... 219 M10
  HGDN/ICK UB10 ..... 112 C7
  HSLWW TW4 ..... 153 N10
  OXTED RH8 ..... 261 M9
  PEND EN3 ..... 80 C1
  PIN HA5 ..... 113 N4
  POTB/CUF EN6 ..... 59 K9
  RKW/CH/CXG WD3 ..... 91 K1
  SL SL1 ..... 128 C10
  UX/CGN UB8 ..... 131 N4
Greenwell Cl GDST RH9 ..... 260 A6
Greenwell St GTPST W1W 10 F2
Greenwich Church St
  GNWCH SE10 ..... 161 H5
Greenwich Crs EHAM E6 ..... 142 B7
Greenwich High Rd GNWCH SE10 ..... 160 G6
Greenwich Park St GNWCH SE10 ..... 161 H5
Greenwich South St
  GNWCH SE10 ..... 160 G7
Greenwich Vw POP/IOD E14 ..... 160 G2
Greenwood Av CHESW EN7 ..... 62 A4
  DAGE RM10 ..... 124 C4
  PEND EN3 ..... 80 D5
Greenwood Cl ADL/WDHM KT15 ..... 215 J7
  BFN/LL DA15 ..... 185 K5
  CHESW EN7 ..... 62 A7
  MRDN SM4 ..... 201 H4
  RAD WD7 ..... 57 K8
  STMC/STPC BR5 ..... 207 P3
  THDIT KT7 ..... 197 N7
Greenwood Dr CHING E4 ..... 101 J6
  GSTN WD25 ..... 55 J10
  REDH RH1 ..... 276 B5
Greenwood Gdns BARK/HLT IG6 ..... 102 F8
  CTHM CR3 ..... 259 P1
  PLMGR N13 ..... 99 J4
  RAD WD7 ..... 57 K9
Greenwood La HPTN TW12 ..... 176 A8
Greenwood Pk KUTN/CMB KT2 ..... 178 B10
Greenwood Pl KTTN NW5 ..... 118 C10
Greenwood Rd BXLY DA5 ..... 186 E2
  CHIG IG7 ..... 103 L5
  CHOB/PIR GU24 ..... 230 A7
  CROY/NA CR0 ..... 203 J7
  HACK E8 ..... 7 J1
  ISLW TW7 ..... 154 E9
  MTCM CR4 ..... 202 E3
  PLSTW E13 ..... 141 L4
  THDIT KT7 ..... 198 F8
  WOKN/KNAP GU21 ..... 231 K6
The Greenwood GU GU1 ..... 250 D10
Green Wrythe Crs CAR SM5 ..... 201 P8
Green Wrythe La CAR SM5 ..... 201 P8
  MRDN SM4 ..... 201 N6
Green Yd FSBYW WC1X 11 P1
Greenyard WAB EN9 ..... 63 H9
Greer Rd KTN/HRWW/W HA3 ..... 94 D10
Grees St STHWK SE1 ..... 12 D10
Greg Cl LEY E10 ..... 121 H4
Gregories Farm La BEAC HP9 ..... 88 B3
Gregories Rd BEAC HP9 ..... 88 B3
Gregor Ms BKHTH/KID SE3 ..... 161 M10
Gregory Av POTB/CUF EN6 ..... 59 M9
Gregory Crs ELTH/MOT SE9 ..... 184 A10
Gregory Dr WDSR SL4 ..... 171 J10
Gregory Pl KENS W8 ..... 14 C1
Gregory Rd CHDH RM6 ..... 123 N2
  NWDGN UB2 ..... 153 H2
  SLN SL2 ..... 109 J7
Gregson Cl BORE WD6 ..... 75 D4
Greig Cl CEND/HSY/T N8 ..... 118 F3
Grenaby Av CROY/NA CR0 ..... 203 L7
Grenaby Rd CROY/NA CR0 ..... 203 L7

Grenada Rd CHARL SE7 ..... 161 P6
Grenade St POP/IOD E14 ..... 140 C9
Grenadier St STALE/WH AL4 ..... 39 H7
Grenadier St CAN/RD E16 ..... 142 D10
Grenadine Cl CHESW EN7 ..... 61 N3
Grena Gdns RCH/KEW TW9 ..... 155 L10
Grena Rd RCH/KEW TW9 ..... 155 L10
Grendon Cl HORL RH6 ..... 280 A2
Grendon Gdns WBLY HA9 ..... 115 M7
Grendon St STJWD NW8 ..... 9 N1
Grenfell Av HORL RH6 ..... 124 C6
Grenfell Cl BORE WD6 ..... 75 P5
Grenfell Gdns KTN/HRWW/W HA3 ..... 115 N5
Grenfell Rd BEAC HP9 ..... 88 D2
  NTGHL W11 ..... 136 C9
  TOOT SW17 ..... 180 A9
Grennell Cl SUT SM1 ..... 201 N9
Grennell Rd SUT SM1 ..... 201 N9
Grenoble Gdns PLMGR N13 ..... 99 H7
Grenside Rd WEY KT13 ..... 196 C10
Grenville Av BROX EN10 ..... 44 E7
Grenville Cl BRYLDS KT5 ..... 199 P8
  CHES/WCR EN8 ..... 62 C8
  COB KT11 ..... 217 L10
  FNCH N3 ..... 97 J9
  SL SL1 ..... 128 A4
Grenville Gdns WFD IG8 ..... 101 P8
Grenville Ms HPTN TW12 ..... 176 A8
Grenville Pl MLHL NW7 ..... 96 A6
  SKENS SW7 ..... 15 J5
Grenville Rd ARCH N19 ..... 118 F6
  CROY/NA CR0 ..... 225 H6
Grenville St BMSBY WC1N 11 M2
Gresford Cl STALE/WH AL4 ..... 39 L4
  TRDG/WHET N20 ..... 98 A5
Gresham Av HART DA3 ..... 211 L5
  WARL CR6 ..... 242 D4
Gresham Cl BXLY DA5 ..... 185 P2
  ENC/FH EN2 ..... 79 K7
  OXTED RH8 ..... 261 L5
Gresham Ct BERK HP4 ..... 33 N6
  BRW CM14 ..... 107 H4
Gresham Dr CHDH RM6 ..... 123 J3
Gresham Gdns CRICK NW2 ..... 117 H6
Gresham Rd BECK BR3 ..... 204 D2
  BRW CM14 ..... 107 H4
  BRXN/ST SW9 ..... 159 H9
  CAN/RD E16 ..... 141 N8
  EDGW HA8 ..... 95 L7
  EHAM E6 ..... 142 C4
  HEST TW5 ..... 154 B7
  HGDN/ICK UB10 ..... 132 B4
  HPTN TW12 ..... 175 P9
  OXTED RH8 ..... 261 L5
  SL SL1 ..... 128 F8
  SNWD SE25 ..... 203 P4
  STA TW18 ..... 173 J8
  WLSDN NW10 ..... 116 A10
Gresham St CITYW EC2V 12 E5
Gresham Wk CRAWE RH10 ..... 283 P10
Gresham Wy WIM/MER SW19 ..... 179 K6
Gresley Cl SEVS/STOTM N15 ..... 119 L2
  WALTH E17 ..... 120 D4
  WGCW AL8 ..... 23 H4
Gresley Rd ARCH N19 ..... 118 D3
Gressenhall Rd
  WAND/EARL SW18 ..... 179 J3
Gresse St FITZ W1T 11 J3
Gresswell Cl SCUP DA14 ..... 186 K6
Creswell St FUL/PGN SW6 ..... 156 G6
Greta Bank EHSLY KT24 ..... 252 D2
Gretton Rd TOTM N17 ..... 99 N8
Greville Av SAND/SEL CR2 ..... 224 C6
Greville Cl ASHTD KT21 ..... 237 K5
  BRKMPK AL9 ..... 40 C10
  GUW GU2 ..... 249 K10
  TWK TW1 ..... 176 C3
Greville Ct GT/LBKH KT23 ..... 254 A1
Greville Ms KIL/WHAMP NW6 ..... 2 C6
Greville Park Av ASHTD KT21 ..... 237 K4
Greville Park Rd ASHTD KT21 ..... 237 K4
Greville Rd KIL/WHAMP NW6 ..... 2 C6
  RCHPK/HAM TW10 ..... 177 J2
  WALTH E17 ..... 121 H2
Greville St HCIRC EC1N 12 B4
Grey Alders EW KE17 ..... 220 F10
Greycaine Rd WATN WD24 ..... 73 L3
Grey Cl ENC/FH EN2 ..... 117 M4
Greycoat Pl WEST SW1P 17 J4
Greycoat St WEST SW1P 17 J4
Greycot Rd BECK BR3 ..... 182 F8
Grey Eagle St WCHPL E1 ..... 13 M3
Greyfell Cl STAN HA7 ..... 94 C6
Greyfields Cl PUR/KEN CR8 ..... 223 J9
Greyfriars RBRW/HUT CM13 ..... 107 N1
Greyfriars Dr ASC SL5 ..... 192 A6
  CHOB/PIR GU24 ..... 230 F1
Greyfriars La RPLY/SEND GU23 ..... 233 K10
Greygoose Pk HLWW/ROY CM19 ..... 46 A3
Greyhound Hl HDN NW4 ..... 116 C1
Greyhound La CDH/CHF RM16 ..... 168 D1
  POTB/CUF EN6 ..... 58 G9
  STRHM/NOR SW16 ..... 180 F9
Greyhound Rd HMSMTH W6 ..... 156 G4
  SUT SM1 ..... 221 M2
  TOTM N17 ..... 119 N1
  WLSDN NW10 ..... 136 E5
Greyhound Slip CRAWE RH10 ..... 284 E6
Greyhound Ter
  STRHM/NOR SW16 ..... 202 D1
Greyhound Wy DART DA1 ..... 186 F1
Greys Park Cl HAYES BR2 ..... 225 P2
Greystead Rd FSTH SE23 ..... 182 B3
Greystoke Av PIN HA5 ..... 113 P1
Greystoke Dr RSLP HA4 ..... 112 C5
Greystoke Gdns EA W5 ..... 135 K6
  ENC/FH EN2 ..... 78 E8
Greystoke Cl SL SL1 ..... 128 C8
Greystone Cl SAND/SEL CR2 ..... 224 B7
Greystone Gdns BARK/HLT IG6 ..... 102 F10
  KTN/HRWW/W HA3 ..... 115 H4
Greystone Pk RSEV TN14 ..... 263 P9
Greystones Cl REDH RH1 ..... 275 N2
  RSEV TN14 ..... 247 N3
Greystones Dr REIG RH2 ..... 257 N8
Greyswood Av UPMR RM14 ..... 180 C9
Greythorne Rd
  WOKN/KNAP GU21 ..... 231 M4
Grey Towers Av EMPK RM11 ..... 125 L6
Grey Towers Gdns EMPK RM11 ..... 125 K5
Grice Av BH/WHM TN16 ..... 225 N9
Gridiron Pl UPMR RM14 ..... 126 A7
Grieve Cl CRAWW RH11 ..... 283 H10

Grieves Rd GVW DA11 ..... 190 C6
Griffin Av UPMR RM14 ..... 126 D4
Griffin Cl SL SL1 ..... 149 K1
  WLSDN NW10 ..... 116 F10
Griffin Manor Wy THMD SE28 ..... 162 C2
Griffin Rd TOTM N17 ..... 99 M10
  WOOL/PLUM SE18 ..... 162 C4
Griffins Cl WCHMH N21 ..... 99 N1
The Griffins CDH/CHF RM16 ..... 167 N1
Griffin Wk GRH DA9 ..... 188 E3
Griffin Wy GT/LBKH KT23 ..... 253 P2
  SUN TW16 ..... 197 H2
Griffith Cl CHDH RM6 ..... 123 M6
Griffiths Cl WPK KT4 ..... 201 H1
Griffiths Rd WIM/MER SW19 ..... 179 K10
Griffiths Wy STALW AL1 ..... 38 D3
Grifon Rd CDH/CHF RM16 ..... 167 N2
Grogan Cl HPTN TW12 ..... 175 H8
Grogan Cl HPTN TW12 ..... 175 J8
Grooms Dr PIN HA5 ..... 112 G2
Grosmont Rd WOOL/PLUM SE18 ..... 162 C6
Grosse Wy PUT/ROE SW15 ..... 176 E4

Grimsdyke Rd PIN HA5 — 93 M8
Grimshaw Wy ROM RM1 — 124 C3
Grimston Rd FUL/PGN SW6 — 157 J8
  STAL AL1 — 38 E6
  STAL AL1 — 38 E7
Grimthorpe Cl STALW/RED AL3 — 38 B3
Grimwade Av CROY/NA CR0 — 203 P10
Grimwood Rd TWK TW1 — 176 B3
Grindall Cl CROY/NA CR0 — 223 J1
Grindal St STHWK SE1 — 18 A2
Grindcobbe St STAL AL1 — 38 C9
Grindleford Av FBAR/BDGN N11 — 98 A3
Grindley Gdns CROY/NA CR0 — 203 N6
Grindstone Crs
  WOKN/KNAP GU21 — 230 A8
Grinling Pl DEPT SE8 — 160 F5
Grinstead Rd DEPT SE8 — 160 D4
Grisedale Cl CRAWW RH11 — 283 M9
  PUR/KEN CR8 — 223 N10
Grisedale Gdns PUR/KEN CR8 — 223 M10
Grisle Cl ED N9 — 100 A5
Grittleton Av WBLY HA9 — 135 N1
Grittleton Rd MV/WKIL W9 — 8 E1
Grobars Av WOKN/KNAP GU21 — 231 P1
Grocers' Hall Ct LOTH EC2R — 12 G6
Groombridge Cl WELL DA16 — 185 K1
  WOT/HER KT12 — 217 J2
Groombridge Rd HOM E9 — 140 C2
Groom Crs WAND/EARL SW18 — 179 N3
Groomfield Cl TOOT SW17 — 180 B7
Groom Pl KTBR SW1X — 16 C3
Groom Rd BROX EN10 — 62 E2
Grooms Cottages CSHM HP5 — 51 N6
Grooms Dr PIN HA5 — 113 H3
The Grooms CRAWE RH10 — 284 E5
Grosmont Rd WOOL/PLUM SE18 — 163 J4
Grosse Wy PUT/ROE SW15 — 178 D3
Grosvenor Av CAR SM5 — 222 A3
  HBRY N5 — 119 K10
  MORT/ESHN SW14 — 156 B9
  RYLN/HDSTN HA2 — 114 A3
  YEAD UB4 — 132 G4
Grosvenor Br PIM SW1V — 16 F4
  CRICK NW2 — 136 F1
  EHAM E6 — 142 A5
  GLDGN NW11 — 117 J4
  KUTN/CMB KT2 — 177 J9
  MORT/ESHN SW14 — 156 B9
  MUSWH N10 — 118 D1
  STHGT/OAK N14 — 78 A9
  UPMR RM14 — 126 C7
  WFD IG8 — 101 N7
  WLGTN SM6 — 222 D4
Grosvenor Gardens Ms East
  BGVA SW1W — 16 F3
Grosvenor Hl WIM/MER SW19 — 179 H9
Grosvenor Pk CMBW SE5 — 18 E10
Grosvenor Park Rd WALTH E17 — 120 G3
Grosvenor Pl WBLY HA9 — 136 D1
  WEY KT13 — 196 E10
Grosvenor Ri East WALTH E17 — 120 G3
Grosvenor Rd BCTR RM8 — 124 A6
  BELV DA17 — 164 A5
  BORE WD6 — 75 M7
  BROX EN10 — 44 E8
  BTFD TW8 — 155 J5
  BXLYHS DA6 — 185 N1
  CHOB/PIR GU24 — 213 J4
  CHSWK W4 — 155 P4
  ED N9 — 100 A2
  EHAM E6 — 142 A3
  EPSOM KT18 — 238 E5
  FNCH N3 — 97 J8
  FSTGT E7 — 141 N1
  HNWL W7 — 134 F10
  HSLWW TW4 — 153 N9
  IL IG1 — 122 F8
  LEY E10 — 121 H6
  MUSWH N10 — 98 C9
  NTHWD HA6 — 92 G6
  NWDGN UB2 — 153 N2
  PIM SW1V — 16 F9
  RCHPK/HAM TW10 — 177 K1
  ROMW/RG RM7 — 124 C5
  SNWD SE25 — 203 P4
  STA TW18 — 173 K10
  STAL AL1 — 38 D7
  STMC/STPC BR5 — 207 H6
  TWK TW1 — 176 F3
  WAN E11 — 121 N3
  WAT WD17 — 73 K8
  WLGTN SM6 — 222 D4
  WWKM BR4 — 204 C9
Grosvenor Sq MYFR/PKLN W1K — 10 D7
Grosvenor St MYFR/PKLN W1K — 10 D7
Grosvenor Ter CMBW SE5 — 18 E10
  HHW HP1 — 35 K7
Grosvenor V RSLP HA4 — 112 C7
Grosvenor Wy CLPT E5 — 120 B7
Grosvenor Wharf Rd
  POP/IOD E14 — 161 J3
Grote's Buildings
  BKHTH/KID SE3 — 161 K8
Grote's Pl BKHTH/KID SE3 — 161 K8
Groton Rd WAND/EARL SW18 — 179 L5
Grotto Ct STHWK SE1 — 18 E1
Grotto Rd TWK TW1 — 176 E5
  WEY KT13 — 216 D1
Grovebury Cl ERITH DA8 — 164 E5
Grovebury Ct DART DA1 — 56 D7
Grovebury Gdns LCOL/BKTW AL2 — 56 F2
Grovebury Rd THMD SE28 — 163 L1
Grove Cl FSTH SE23 — 182 C4
  HAYES BR2 — 205 M9
  HGDN/ICK UB10 — 112 B10
  KUT KT1 — 177 H3
  SL SL1 — 149 M2
  WDSR SL4 — 171 N3
Grove Ct E/WMO/HCT KT8 — 198 C5
  ECH TW20 — 172 D8
  WAB EN9 — 62 C1
Grove Crs CDALE/KGS NW9 — 115 P2
  FELT TW13 — 175 M7
  KUT KT1 — 199 K3
  RKW/CH/CXG WD3 — 72 B8
  SWFD E18 — 101 L10
  WOT/HER KT12 — 197 J7
Grove Crescent Rd SRTFD E15 — 141 J1
Grovedale Cl CHESW EN7 — 61 N6
Grovedale Rd ARCH N19 — 118 E7
Grove End KTTN NW5 — 118 C9
  SWFD E18 — 101 L10
Grove End La ESH/CLAY KT10 — 198 C8
Grove End Rd STJWD NW8 — 3 L8
Grove Farm Pk NTHWD HA6 — 92 E6
Grove Gdns DAGE RM10 — 124 D8

  HDN NW4 — 116 D2
  PEND EN3 — 80 C5
  STJWD NW8 — 3 P10
  TEDD TW11 — 176 F7
Grove Green Rd WAN E11 — 121 J6
Grove Hall Rd BUSH WD23 — 73 M8
Grove Heath La RPLY/SEND GU23 — 233 M10
Grove Heath North
  RPLY/SEND GU23 — 233 L8
Groveherst Rd DART DA1 — 165 N9
Grove Hl CFSP/GDCR SL9 — 89 P8
  HRW HA1 — 114 D5
Grove Hill Rd CMBW SE5 — 159 M9
  HRW HA1 — 114 E5
Grovehill Rd REDH RH1 — 257 P7
Grove House Rd
  CEND/HSY/T N8 — 118 F2
Groveland Av STRHM/NOR SW16 — 180 G1
Groveland Rd BECK BR3 — 204 E3
Grovelands E/WMO/HCT KT8 — 197 P4
  HHNE HP2 — 36 D4
  LCOL/BKTW AL2 — 56 A3
Grovelands Cl CMBW SE5 — 159 M8
  RYLN/HDSTN HA2 — 114 A8
Grovelands Rd PLMGR N13 — 98 G5
  PUR/KEN CR8 — 222 G8
  SEVS/STOTM N15 — 119 P4
  STMC/STPC BR5 — 185 K10
Grovelands Wy GRAYS RM17 — 167 L4
Groveland Wy NWMAL KT3 — 199 P5
Grove La CFSP/GDCR SL9 — 89 J4
  CHIC IG7 — 103 J4
  CMBW SE5 — 159 L7
  COUL/CHIP CR5 — 240 C1
  CSHM HP5 — 51 N3
  EPP CM16 — 65 K6
  KUT KT1 — 199 K4
  UX/CGN UB8 — 132 A6
Grove Lea HAT AL10 — 40 D7
Groveley Rd SUN TW16 — 174 G6
Grove Md HAT AL10 — 40 C4
Grove Meadow WGCE AL7 — 23 M5
Grove Ms HMSMTH W6 — 156 F2
Grove Mill La RKW/CH/CXG WD3 — 72 D4
Grove Pk CDALE/KGS NW9 — 115 P2
  CMBW SE5 — 159 M8
  WAN E11 — 121 N3
Grove Park Av CHING E4 — 100 G8
Grove Park Gdns CHSWK W4 — 155 N6
Grove Park Rd CHSWK W4 — 155 N6
  ELTH/MOT SE9 — 184 B5
  RAIN RM13 — 145 H3
  SEVS/STOTM N15 — 119 M2
Grove Park Ter CHSWK W4 — 155 N6
Grove Pl ACT W3 — 135 P10
  BAL SW12 — 180 C2
  BRKMPK AL9 — 40 F10
  WEY KT13 — 216 D2
Grover Cl HHNE HP2 — 35 N5
Grove Rd ACT W3 — 135 P10
  AMS HP6 — 69 J3
  ASHTD KT21 — 237 L4
  BARN SW13 — 156 C8
  BEAC HP9 — 88 D9
  BELMT SM2 — 221 K5
  BELV DA17 — 164 A5
  BGR/WK TN15 — 247 P8
  BH/WHM TN16 — 243 P6
  BORE WD6 — 75 M5
  BOW E3 — 140 D4
  BTFD TW8 — 155 H4
  BXLYHN DA7 — 164 D10
  CHDH RM6 — 123 M5
  CHERT KT16 — 195 J6
  CHING E4 — 101 H4
  CRICK NW2 — 136 F1
  E/WMO/HCT KT8 — 198 C4
  EA W5 — 135 J9
  EBAR EN4 — 77 P7
  EDGW HA8 — 95 M7
  EPSOM KT18 — 220 B9
  FBAR/BDGN N11 — 98 C10
  GRAYS RM17 — 167 P5
  GU GU1 — 250 F10
  GVW DA11 — 189 N1
  HARP AL5 — 20 C4
  HHW HP1 — 35 K8
  HOM E9 — 140 C3
  HORL RH6 — 279 P3
  HSLW TW3 — 153 P10
  ISLW TW7 — 154 D7
  LEY E10 — 120 C3
  MTCM CR4 — 202 C4
  NFNCH/WDSP N12 — 97 N6
  NTHWD HA6 — 92 E4
  PIN HA5 — 113 N3
  RCHPK/HAM TW10 — 177 L2
  RKW/CH/CXG WD3 — 91 K3
  RSEV TN14 — 247 K7
  SEVS/STOTM N15 — 119 K7
  SHPTN TW17 — 196 D6
  SL SL1 — 128 D2
  STAL AL1 — 38 C7
  SURB KT6 — 199 J5
  SUT SM1 — 221 L3
  SWFD E18 — 101 L10
  UX/CGN UB8 — 131 N2
  WAN E11 — 121 L5
  WARE SG12 — 26 E1
  WDSR SL4 — 149 A8
  WHTN TW2 — 176 C6
  WIM/MER SW19 — 179 M10
  WOKN/KNAP GU21 — 232 C2
Grove Rd West PEND EN3 — 80 B3
Grover Rd OXHEY WD19 — 89 H9
Groves Cl SOCK/AV RM15 — 146 E9
Groveside GT/LBKH KT23 — 253 P5
Groveside Cl ACT W3 — 135 M8
  CAR SM5 — 201 P9
  GT/LBKH KT23 — 253 P5
Groveside Rd CHING E4 — 101 K4
Grovestile Waye
  EBED/NFELT TW14 — 174 A3
Grove St BERM/RHTH SE16 — 160 E3
  UED N18 — 99 N1
Grove Ter KTTN NW5 — 118 B8
  TEDD TW11 — 176 F6
The Grove ADL/WDHM KT15 — 215 L2
  AMS HP6 — 69 J1
  BH/WHM TN16 — 244 A8
  BRKMPK AL9 — 59 K3
  BRW CM14 — 106 C5
  BXLYHS DA6 — 163 N10
  CDALE/KGS NW9 — 116 A3
  CEND/HSY/T N8 — 118 E3
  COUL/CHIP CR5 — 240 E1
  CRAWW RH11 — 283 M7
  CSHM HP5 — 70 A2
  CTHM CR3 — 241 J7
  EA W5 — 135 J10
  EDGW HA8 — 95 N5
  ECH TW20 — 172 D8
  ENC/FH EN2 — 79 H6
  EW KT17 — 220 B9
  FNCH N3 — 97 K8
  FSBYPK N4 — 138 E1
  GFD/PVL UB6 — 134 B9
  GLDGN NW11 — 117 H5
  GVE DA12 — 190 E3
  HGT N6 — 118 B6
  HORL RH6 — 280 C5
  ISLW TW7 — 154 D7
  PLMGR N13 — 99 H5

  POTB/CUF EN6 — 59 M8
  RAD WD7 — 56 F10
  SCUP DA14 — 185 P7
  SL SL1 — 149 M1
  SRTFD E15 — 141 K2
  SWCM DA10 — 189 K1
  SWLY BR8 — 208 G3
  TEDD TW11 — 176 F7
  UPMR RM14 — 125 P9
  WOKN/KNAP GU21 — 232 C2
  WOT/HER KT12 — 197 J7
  WWKM BR4 — 205 H10
Grove V CHST BR7 — 184 D9
  EDUL SE22 — 159 M10
Grove Wk HERT/WAS SG14 — 25 K3
Groveway BCTR RM8 — 123 N3
  BRXN/ST SW9 — 158 C7
Grove Wy ESH/CLAY KT10 — 198 B8
  RKW/CH/CXG WD3 — 70 G8
  UX/CGN UB8 — 131 N2
  WBLY HA9 — 136 C2
Grovewood Cl RKW/CH/CXG WD3 — 70 E9
Grove Wood Hl COUL/CHIP CR5 — 222 E10
Grovewood Pl WFD IG8 — 102 E10
Grubbs La BRKMPK AL9 — 41 L8
Grub St OXTED RH8 — 261 P5
Grummant Rd PECK SE15 — 159 N7
Gruneisen Rd FNCH N3 — 97 L8
Guardian Cl HCH RM12 — 125 J7
Guards Ct ASC SL5 — 192 C7
Guardsman Cl BRW CM14 — 107 J6
Guards Rd WDSR SL4 — 148 B8
Gubbins La HARH RM3 — 105 N9
Gubyon Av HNHL SE24 — 181 K1
Guernsey Cl HEST TW5 — 153 P7
  RGUE GU4 — 250 D5
Guernsey Farm Dr
  WOKN/KNAP GU21 — 232 A1
Guernsey Gv HNHL SE24 — 181 K3
Guernsey Rd IS N1 — 6 F2
  WAN E11 — 121 J6
Guessens Gv WGCW AL8 — 22 E5
Guessens Rd WGCW AL8 — 22 F5
Guessens Wk WGCW AL8 — 22 F4
Guibal Rd LEE/GVPK SE12 — 183 N4
Guildables La OXTED RH8 — 262 B10
Guildcroft GU GU1 — 250 D10
Guildersfield Rd
  STRHM/NOR SW16 — 180 F10
Guildford Av FELT TW13 — 175 H5
Guildford Business Park Rd
  GU GU1 — 249 N9
Guildford Gv GNWCH SE10 — 160 G9
Guildford La SHGR GU5 — 269 K4
Guildford Park Av GUW GU2 — 267 N5
Guildford Park Rd GUW GU2 — 267 N5
Guildford Rd CHERT KT16 — 194 G10
  CHERT KT16 — 195 J8
  CHOB/PIR GU24 — 212 C10
  CROY/NA CR0 — 203 L6
  DORK RH4 — 272 A4
  EHAM E6 — 142 A3
  GDMY/SEVK IG3 — 123 H7
  GT/LBKH KT23 — 253 N4
  HARH RM3 — 105 M4
  LHD/OX KT22 — 236 F8
  RDKG RH5 — 271 H6
  RGUE GU4 — 249 P1
  RGUW GU3 — 249 L5
  STAL AL1 — 38 G7
  VX/NE SW8 — 158 F7
  WALTH E17 — 101 H9
  WOKS/MYFD GU22 — 232 A8
Guildford St CHERT KT16 — 195 K7
  STA TW18 — 173 K9
Guildford Wy WLGTN SM6 — 222 F4
Guildhall Buildings CITYW EC2V — 12 F5
Guildhouse St PIM SW1V — 16 G6
Guildown Av GUW GU2 — 267 N5
  NFNCH/WDSP N12 — 97 L3
Guildown Rd GUW GU2 — 267 N5
Guild Rd CHARL SE7 — 162 A4
  ERITH DA8 — 164 G6
Guildsway WALTH E17 — 100 E9
Guileshill La RPLY/SEND GU23 — 233 P8
Guilford Av BRYLDS KT5 — 199 J5
Guilford Pl BMSBY WC1N — 11 L2
The Guilfords HLWE CM17 — 29 N6
Guilford St BMSBY WC1N — 11 L2
Guilsborough Cl WLSDN NW10 — 136 B2
Guinery Gv HHS/BOV HP3 — 36 A10
Guinevere Gdns CHES/WCR EN8 — 62 D6
Guinevere Rd CRAWW RH11 — 283 H7
Guinness Cl HOM E9 — 140 D2
  HYS/HAR UB3 — 152 E2
Guinness Sq STHWK SE1 — 19 J3
Guion Rd FUL/PGN SW6 — 157 J8
Gulland Cl BUSH WD23 — 74 B9
Gullbrook HHW HP1 — 35 K6
Gull Cl WLGTN SM6 — 222 F4
Gullet Wood Rd GSTN WD25 — 73 H1
Gulliver Cl NTHLT UB5 — 133 N3
Gulliver Rd BFN/LL DA15 — 184 G5
Gulliver St BERM/RHTH SE16 — 160 E2
The Gulphs HERT/BAY SG13 — 25 L5
Gumbrells Cl RGUW GU3 — 249 H6
Gumleigh Rd EA W5 — 155 H3
Gumley Gdns ISLW TW7 — 154 F9
Gumley Rd WTHK RM20 — 167 J5
Gumping Rd STMC/STPC BR5 — 206 F9
Gundulph Rd HAYES BR2 — 205 H3
Gunfleet Cl GVE DA12 — 190 D3
Gun Hl TIL RM18 — 168 G5
Gunmakers La HOM E9 — 139 M10
Gunnell Cl SNWD SE25 — 203 N6
Gunner La WOOL/PLUM SE18 — 162 G4
Gunners Gv CHING E4 — 101 H4
Gunners Rd WAND/EARL SW18 — 179 N5
Gunning Cl CRAWW RH11 — 283 K10
Gunning Rd GRAYS RM17 — 167 P8
  WOOL/PLUM SE18 — 163 H3
Gunn Rd SWCM DA10 — 189 K2
Gun St WCHPL E1 — 13 L4
Gunter Gv EDGW HA8 — 96 D7
  WBPTN SW10 — 15 J10
Gunterstone Rd WKENS W14 — 14 A4
Gunthorpe St WCHPL E1 — 13 M4
Gunton Rd CLPT E5 — 120 A8
  TOOT SW17 — 180 B9
Gunwhale Cl BERM/RHTH SE16 — 140 C10
Gurdon Rd CHARL SE7 — 161 N4
Gurnard Cl WDR/YW UB7 — 131 N9
Gurnell Gv WEA W13 — 134 E4
Gurnells Rd BEAC HP9 — 89 H6
Gurney Cl BARK IG11 — 142 E1
  BEAC HP9 — 88 D9
  SRTFD E15 — 121 K10
  WALTH E17 — 101 G9
Gurney Court Rd STAL AL1 — 38 G3
Gurney Crs CROY/NA CR0 — 202 G3
Gurney Dr EFNCH N2 — 117 N2
Gurney Rd CAR SM5 — 222 D3
  FUL/PGN SW6 — 157 M9
  NTHLT UB5 — 133 J3
  SRTFD E15 — 121 K10
Gurney's Cl REDH RH1 — 276 A1
Guthrie St CHEL SW3 — 15 N7
Gutteridge La ABR/ST RM4 — 84 D10

Gutter La CITYW EC2V — 12 E5
Guyatt Gdns MTCM CR4 — 202 B2
Guy Barnett Gv BKHTH/KID SE3 — 161 M9
Guy Rd WLGTN SM6 — 202 E10
Guyscliff Rd LEW SE13 — 183 H1
Guysfield Cl RAIN RM13 — 145 H3
Guysfield Dr RAIN RM13 — 145 J3
Guy St STHWK SE1 — 19 H1
Gwalior Rd PUT/ROE SW15 — 156 G9
Gwendolen Av PUT/ROE SW15 — 178 G1
Gwendolen Cl PUT/ROE SW15 — 178 G1
Gwendwr Rd WKENS W14 — 14 B3
Gwent Cl GSTN WD25 — 55 L10
Gwillim Cl BFN/LL DA15 — 185 K2
Gwydor Rd BECK BR3 — 204 C4
Gwydyr Rd HAYES BR2 — 205 L3
Gwyn Cl FUL/PGN SW6 — 157 N6
Gwynne Av CROY/NA CR0 — 204 C7
Gwynne Cl WDSR SL4 — 148 D7
Gwynne Park Av WFD IG8 — 102 G3
Gwynne Rd BTSEA SW11 — 157 N8
Gwynne Vaughan Av GUW GU2 — 249 M6
Gwynne Whf CHSWK W4 — 156 C5
Gwyn Rd GVW DA11 — 189 P5
Gwynns Wk HERT/BAY SG13 — 25 M5
Gylcote Cl HNHL SE24 — 159 L10
Gyles Pk STAN HA7 — 95 H9
Gyllyngdune Gdns
  GDMY/SEVK IG3 — 123 J8
Gypsy Cl WARE SG12 — 26 E7
Gypsy La BRKMPK AL9 — 23 J10
  GSTN WD25 — 72 E1
  SLN SL2 — 109 K9
  WARE SG12 — 26 E7

H

Haarlem Rd HMSMTH W6 — 156 G2
Haberdasher St IS N1 — 7 H9
Habgood Rd LOU IG10 — 82 B7
Haccombe Rd WIM/MER SW19 — 179 P1
Hackbridge Park Gdns CAR SM5 — 202 B9
Hackbridge Rd CAR SM5 — 202 B9
Hacketts La WOKS/MYFD GU22 — 215 J10
Hackford Rd BRXN/ST SW9 — 158 B7
Hackford Wk BRXN/ST SW9 — 158 C7
Hackforth Cl BAR EN5 — 76 A6
Hackhurst La RDKG RH5 — 270 G5
Hackington Crs BECK BR3 — 182 F9
Hackney Cl BORE WD6 — 76 A9
Hackney Rd BETH E2 — 7 L9
Hacton Dr HCH RM12 — 125 M9
Hacton La HCH RM12 — 125 M10
  UPMR RM14 — 125 N10
Hadden Rd THMD SE28 — 163 N2
Hadden Wy NTHLT UB5 — 134 C1
Haddestoke Ga BROX EN10 — 62 E2
Haddington Rd BMLY BR1 — 183 M9
Haddon Cl BORE WD6 — 75 M6
  EN EN1 — 79 D10
  HHS/BOV HP3 — 36 B7
  NWMAL KT3 — 200 C5
  WEY KT13 — 216 E1
Haddon Gv BFN/LL DA15 — 185 K3
Haddon Rd RKW/CH/CXG WD3 — 70 E9
  STMC/STPC BR5 — 207 M5
  SUT SM1 — 221 L1
Haddo St GNWCH SE10 — 160 G5
Hadfield Rd STWL/WRAY TW19 — 173 N2
Hadland Cl HHW HP1 — 52 D2
Hadleigh Cl RYNPK SW20 — 201 J2
  WCHPL E1 — 20 D5
Hadleigh Ct BROX EN10 — 44 E8
  HARP AL5 — 20 D5
Hadleigh Dr BELMT SM2 — 221 K5
Hadleigh Rd ED N9 — 100 A1
Hadleigh St BETH E2 — 140 B6
Hadley Cl BORE WD6 — 75 L9
  WCHMH N21 — 79 H6
Hadley Gdns CHSWK W4 — 156 A4
  NWDGN UB2 — 153 M4
Hadley Gra HLWE CM17 — 47 N3
Hadley Gn BAR EN5 — 77 H3
Hadley Green Rd BAR EN5 — 77 J6
Hadley Gn West BAR EN5 — 77 H6
Hadley Gv BAR EN5 — 77 H5
Hadley Highstone BAR EN5 — 77 H3
Hadley Pl WEY KT13 — 216 B9
Hadley Rdg BAR EN5 — 77 J5
Hadley Rd BAR EN5 — 77 L7
  BELV DA17 — 164 A3
  EBAR EN4 — 78 E4
  ENC/FH EN2 — 78 E4
  MTCM CR4 — 202 E4
Hadley St KTTN NW5 — 4 C2
Hadley Wy WCHMH N21 — 79 H10
Hadley Wood Ri PUR/KEN CR8 — 241 J1
Hadley Wood Rd BAR EN5 — 77 M6
Hadlow Ct SL SL1 — 129 H10
Hadlow Rd SCUP DA14 — 186 B6
  WELL DA16 — 163 M6
Hadlow Wy MEO DA13 — 190 B10
Hadrian Cl STWL/WRAY TW19 — 173 N3
  STWL/WRAY TW19 — 173 P3
Hadrian's Ride EN EN1 — 79 N9
Hadrian St GNWCH SE10 — 161 K4
Hadrian Wy STWL/WRAY TW19 — 173 P3
Hadyn Park Rd SHB W12 — 158 A10
Hafer Rd BTSEA SW11 — 158 A10
Hafton Rd CAT SE6 — 183 K4
Hagden La WATW WD18 — 72 D3
Haggard Rd TWK TW1 — 176 C5
Hagger Ct WALTH E17 — 121 J1
Haggerston Rd BORE WD6 — 75 J4
  HACK E8 — 7 L5
Hagsdell Rd HERT/BAY SG13 — 25 L6
Hague St BETH E2 — 7 P10
Ha-ha Rd WOOL/PLUM SE18 — 162 G5
Haig Cl STAL AL1 — 38 G7
Haig Dr SL SL1 — 148 G1
Haig Gdns GVE DA12 — 190 F3
Haigh Crs REDH RH1 — 276 C2
Haig Rd BH/WHM TN16 — 244 B3
  CDH/CHF RM6 — 168 C7
  STAN HA7 — 95 H6
  UX/CGN UB8 — 132 C7
Haig Rd East PLSTW E13 — 141 P5
Haig Rd West PLSTW E13 — 141 P5
Haigville Gdns BARK/HLT IG6 — 122 C2
Hailes Cl WIM/MER SW19 — 179 M9
Hailey Av HOD EN11 — 26 C10
Haileybury Av EN EN1 — 79 N10
Haileybury Rd ORP BR6 — 227 L3
Hailey La HOD EN11 — 26 C10
Hailey Rd ERITH DA8 — 164 B1
Hailsham Av BRXS/STRHM SW2 — 180 A5
Hailsham Cl HARH RM3 — 105 K6
  SURB KT6 — 199 J7
Hailsham Dr HRW HA1 — 114 C1
Hailsham Rd HARH RM3 — 105 K6
  TOOT SW17 — 180 B9
Haimo Rd ELTH/MOT SE9 — 184 A1
Hainault Gore CHDH RM6 — 123 N1
Hainault Gv CHIG IG7 — 102 F9
Hainault Rd CHDH RM6 — 123 J1
  CHIG IG7 — 102 E3
  ROMW/RG RM7 — 124 E3
  WAN E11 — 121 P3
Hainault St ELTH/MOT SE9 — 184 D4
  IL IG1 — 123 H8
Haines Ct WEY KT13 — 216 F4
Haines Wk MRDN SM4 — 201 L7
Hainford Cl PECK SE15 — 160 C10

Haining Cl CHSWK W4 — 155 M4
Hainthorpe Rd WNWD SE27 — 181 J6
Hainton Cl WCHPL E1 — 140 A8
Halbutt St DAGW RM9 — 124 A9
Halcomb St IS N1 — 7 J2
Halcot Av BXLYHS DA6 — 186 C1
Halcrow St WCHPL E1 — 140 A7
Halcyon Wy EMPK RM11 — 125 N6
Haldane Cl MUSWH N10 — 98 C8
Haldane Gdns GVW DA11 — 189 M1
Haldane Pl WAND/EARL SW18 — 179 L4
Haldane Rd EHAM E6 — 142 A3
  FUL/PGN SW6 — 157 J6
  GFD/PVL UB6 — 134 B9
  THMD SE28 — 143 N9
Haldan Rd CHING E4 — 101 H7
Haldens WGCE AL7 — 23 J2
Haldon Rd WAND/EARL SW18 — 179 J1
Halebourne La CHOB/PIR GU24 — 212 F6
Hale Cl CHING E4 — 101 H4
  EDGW HA8 — 95 P6
  ORP BR6 — 226 F1
Hale Dr EDGW HA8 — 95 P7
  MLHL NW7 — 96 A7
Hale End HARH RM3 — 105 J7
Hale End Cl RSLP HA4 — 113 H4
Hale End Rd CHING E4 — 101 J7
  WALTH E17 — 101 J7
  WFD IG8 — 101 J8
Hale Ends WOKS/MYFD GU22 — 231 N7
Halefield Rd TOTM N17 — 99 P9
Hale Gdns ACT W3 — 135 M10
  SEVS/STOTM N15 — 119 P2
Hale Grove Gdns MLHL NW7 — 96 A5
Hale La EDGW HA8 — 95 P6
  MLHL NW7 — 96 A6
  RSEV TN14 — 246 G3
Hale Oak Rd RSEV TN14 — 265 H10
Hale Pit Rd GT/LBKH KT23 — 254 B2
Hale Rd EHAM E6 — 142 B6
  HERT/BAY SG13 — 25 L6
  TOTM N17 — 119 P1
Hales Oak GT/LBKH KT23 — 254 B2
Halesowen Rd MRDN SM4 — 201 L7
Hales Pk HHNE HP2 — 36 D5
Hales Park Cl HHNE HP2 — 36 D5
Hales St DEPT SE8 — 160 L6
Hale St POP/IOD E14 — 160 B2
  STA TW18 — 173 H7
Haleswood COB KT11 — 217 J10
Haleswood Rd HHNE HP2 — 36 B5
Halesworth Cl HARH RM3 — 105 M7
Halesworth Rd HARH RM3 — 105 M7
  LEW SE13 — 160 G9
The Hale CHING E4 — 101 J8
  SEVS/STOTM N15 — 119 P1
  TOTM N17 — 119 P1
Half Acre BTFD TW8 — 155 J5
Halfacre Hl CFSP/GDCR SL9 — 90 C9
Half Acre Ms BTFD TW8 — 155 J5
Half Acre Rd HNWL W7 — 134 D10
Halfhide La CHES/WCR EN8 — 62 C1
Halfhides WAB EN9 — 63 J9
Half Moon Crs IS N1 — 5 P7
Half Moon La EPP CM16 — 65 J7
Half Moon Meadow HHNE HP2 — 36 D1
Halfmoon Pas WCHPL E1 — 13 M6
Half Moon St MYFR/PICC W1J — 10 F10
  HGDN/ICK UB10 — 112 B10
  RCHPK/HAM TW10 — 177 K1
  WALTH E17 — 121 J3
Halfpenny Cl RGUE GU4 — 268 G6
Halfpenny La ASC SL5 — 192 F7
  RGUE GU4 — 268 F3
Halfway Ct RAIN RM19 — 165 P3
Halfway Gn WOT/HER KT12 — 197 J10
Halfway St BFN/LL DA15 — 185 H4
Haliburton Rd TWK TW1 — 176 F1
Haliday Wk IS N1 — 7 H1
Halidon Ri HARH RM3 — 106 A7
Halifax Cl CRAWE RH10 — 284 F4
  GFD/PVL UB6 — 134 A3
  RKW/CH/CXG WD3 — 90 F1
Halifax St SYD SE26 — 182 A6
Halifield Dr BELV DA17 — 163 P2
Haling Gv SAND/SEL CR2 — 223 J5
Haling Park Gdns SAND/SEL CR2 — 223 J4
Haling Park Rd SAND/SEL CR2 — 223 J3
Haling Rd SAND/SEL CR2 — 223 L5
Halings La DEN/HRF UB9 — 110 G2
Halkingcroft DTCH/LGLY SL3 — 149 P1
Halkin Ms KTBR SW1X — 16 C3
Halkin Pl KTBR SW1X — 16 C3
Halkin St KTBR SW1X — 16 D2
Hallam Cl BRWN CM15 — 86 G3
  CHST BR7 — 184 C8
  WATN WD24 — 73 K6
Hallam Gdns PIN HA5 — 93 M8
Hallam Rd BARN SW13 — 156 D8
  SEVS/STOTM N15 — 119 J2
Hallam St GTPST W1W — 10 F3
Halland Cl CRAWE RH10 — 284 B6
Hall Av SOCK/AV RM15 — 146 B10
Hall Cl EA W5 — 135 K7
  RGODL GU7 — 267 K10
  RKW/CH/CXG WD3 — 91 K2
Hall Ct DTCH/LGLY SL3 — 149 N6
  TEDD TW11 — 176 E8
Hall Crs SOCK/AV RM15 — 146 B10
Hall Dene Cl GU GU1 — 250 F9
Hall Dr DEN/HRF UB9 — 91 M9
  SYD SE26 — 182 B8
Halley Rd FSTGT E7 — 141 P1
Halley's Ap WOKN/KNAP GU21 — 231 M4
Halley's Ct WOKN/KNAP GU21 — 231 M4
Halleys Rdg HERT/WAS SG14 — 25 H6
Halley St POP/IOD E14 — 140 D7
Halley's Wk ADL/WDHM KT15 — 215 M4
Hall Farm Cl STAN HA7 — 94 G5
Hall Farm Dr WHTN TW2 — 176 C3
Hallford Wy DART DA1 — 187 K2
Hall Gdns CHING E4 — 100 E5
  STALE/WH AL4 — 40 A9
Hall Ga STJWD NW8 — 3 K10
Hall Gv WGCE AL7 — 23 L4
Hall Heath Cl STAL AL1 — 38 G4
Hall Hill OXTED RH8 — 261 J8
The Halliards WOT/HER KT12 — 197 H6
Halliday Cl RAD WD7 — 134 C10
Halliday Sq STHL UB1 — 134 C10
Hallford Cl SHPTN TW17 — 196 F3
Hallford Ct SHPTN TW17 — 197 H4
  SUN TW16 — 197 H4
Halliford St IS N1 — 6 G1
Halling Hl HLW CM20 — 29 J10
Hallington Cl WOKN/KNAP GU21 — 231 N3
Halliwell Rd BRXS/STRHM SW2 — 180 A1
Halliwick Rd MUSWH N10 — 97 P8
Hall La BRWN CM15 — 87 L10
  CHING E4 — 100 G6
  HARH RM3 — 106 B10
  HDN NW4 — 96 D10
  HYS/HAR UB3 — 152 A3
  UPMR RM14 — 126 B3
Hall Meadow SL SL1 — 128 B4
Hallmead Rd SUT SM1 — 201 L10
Hallmores BROX EN10 — 44 F5
Hallowell Av CROY/NA CR0 — 222 F1
Hallowell Cl MTCM CR4 — 202 B3
Hallowell Rd NTHWD HA6 — 93 H4
Hallowes Crs OXHEY WD19 — 89 N3
Hallowfield Wy MTCM CR4 — 201 N3
Hall Pk BERK HP4 — 34 B5
Hall Park Ga BERK HP4 — 34 B6

Hall Park HI *BERK* HP4 .... 34 B7
Hall Park Rd *UPMR* RM14 .... 126 B10
Hall PI *BAY/PAD* W2 .... 9 J2
  WOKN/KNAP GU21 .... 232 D2
Hall Place Crs *BXLY* DA5 .... 186 D1
Hall Place Dr *WEY* KT13 .... 216 F2
Hall Place Gdns *STAL* AL1 .... 38 D5
Hall Rd *CHDH* RM6 .... 123 M4
  DART DA1 .... 165 N10
  EHAM E6 .... 142 C3
  GPK RM2 .... 125 J1
  GVW RM2 .... 189 P6
  ISLW TW7 .... 176 C1
  MV/WKIL W9 .... 3 K10
  SHGR GU5 .... 268 C10
  SOCK/AV RM15 .... 166 B1
  WAN E11 .... 121 J9
  WLGTN SM6 .... 222 C5
Halls Farm CI *WOKN/KNAP* GU21 .... 231 J3
Hallside Rd *EN* EN1 .... 79 N4
Hallsland Wy *OXTED* RH8 .... 261 L9
Hall St *FSBYE* EC1V 6 D9
  NFNCH/WDSP N12 .... 97 M6
Hallsville Rd *CAN/RD* E16 .... 141 J9
Hallswelle Rd *HLWW/ROY* NW11 .... 117 J3
Hall Ter *SOCK/AV* RM15 .... 166 C1
The Hall *BKHTH/KID* SE3 .... 161 M9
Hall Vw *ELTH/MOT* SE9 .... 184 A5
Hallwood Crs *EHAM* E6 .... 142 C7
Hallywell Crs *EHAM* E6 .... 142 C7
Halons Rd *ELTH/MOT* SE9 .... 184 D3
Halpin PI *WALW* SE17 .... 19 H6
Halsbrook Rd *BKHTH/KID* SE3 .... 161 P9
Halsbury CI *STAN* HA7 .... 94 G6
Halsbury Rd *SHB* W12 .... 156 E10
Halsbury Rd East *NTHLT* UB5 .... 114 B9
Halsbury Rd West *NTHLT* UB5 .... 114 A10
Halse Dr *SLN* SL2 .... 108 C10
Halsend *HYS/HAR* UB3 .... 133 J10
Halsey Dr *HHW* HP1 .... 35 J4
Halsey Pk *LCOL/BKTW* AL2 .... 57 L3
Halsey Pk *WATW* WD24 .... 73 J4
Halsey Rd *WATW* WD18 .... 73 J7
Halsey St *CHEL* SW3 .... 16 A5
Halsham Crs *BARK* IG11 .... 143 J1
Halsmere Rd *CMBW* SE5 .... 159 J7
Halstead CI *CROY/NA* CR0 .... 203 K10
Halstead Gdns *WCHMH* N21 .... 99 J2
Halstead HI *CHESW* EN7 .... 61 M6
Halstead La *RSEV* TN14 .... 245 P1
Halstead Rd *EN* EN1 .... 79 M8
  ERITH DA8 .... 164 F7
  WAN E11 .... 121 N3
  WCHMH N21 .... 99 J2
Halstead Wy *RBRW/HUT* CM13 .... 81 N10
Halstow Rd *GNWCH* SE10 .... 161 M4
  WLSDN NW10 .... 136 C5
Halsway *HYS/HAR* UB3 .... 133 H10
Halt Dr *TIL* RM18 .... 169 K3
Halter CI *BORE* WD6 .... 76 A9
Halton Cross St *IS* N1 .... 6 D5
Halton PI *IS* N1 .... 6 E5
Halton Rd *CDH/CHF* RM16 .... 168 C2
  IS N1 .... 6 D4
Halt Robin Rd *BELV* DA17 .... 164 B3
Haltside *HAT* AL10 .... 40 A5
Halwick CI *HHW* HP1 .... 35 L7
Hambalt Rd *CLAP* SW4 .... 180 D1
Hamberlins La *BERK* HP4 .... 32 G2
Hamble CI *RSLP* HA4 .... 112 F7
  WOKN/KNAP GU21 .... 231 M3
Hambledon CI *UX/CGN* UB8 .... 132 C6
Hambledon Gdns *SNWD* SE25 .... 203 N3
Hambledon PI *EPSOM* KT18 .... 237 P2
Hambledon PI *DUL* SE21 .... 181 N4
  GT/LBKH KT23 .... 285 P9
Hambledon Rd *CTHM* CR3 .... 241 L9
  WAND/EARL SW18 .... 179 J3
Hambledon V *EPSOM* KT18 .... 237 P2
Hambledown Rd
  ELTH/MOT SE9 .... 185 H3
Hamble St *FUL/PGN* SW6 .... 157 L9
Hambleton CI *WPK* KT4 .... 200 F9
Hambleton HI *CRAWW* RH11 .... 283 N6
Hamblings CI *RAD* WD7 .... 57 J9
Hambro Av *HAYES* BR2 .... 205 M8
Hambrook Rd *SNWD* SE25 .... 204 A3
Hambro Rd *BRW* CM14 .... 107 J3
  STRHM/NOR SW16 .... 180 E9
Hambrough Rd *STHL* UB1 .... 133 M10
Hamburgh Ct *CHES/WCR* EN8 .... 62 C4

OXHEY WD19 .... 93 J4
SL SL1 .... 128 F8
SRTFD E15 .... 141 K5
STAL AL1 .... 38 F5
STHL UB1 .... 133 N10
THHTH CR7 .... 203 L3
UX/CGN UB8 .... 131 N6
WALTH E17 .... 100 D10
WHTN TW2 .... 176 D4
WIM/MER SW19 .... 179 L10
WLSDN NW10 .... 116 D10
WNWD SE27 .... 181 L7
Hamilton Road Ms
  WIM/MER SW19 .... 179 L10
Hamilton St *DEPT* SE8 .... 160 F6
  WATW WD18 .... 73 K7
Hamilton Ter *STJWD* NW8 .... 3 J8
  PLMGR N13 .... 97 J5
  WLGTN SM6 .... 222 C5
Ham La *EGH* TW20 .... 171 N7
  WDSR SL4 .... 149 P10
Hamlea CI *BKHTH/KID* SE3 .... 183 M1
  LEW SE13 .... 161 K10
Hamlet CI *CRW* RM5 .... 104 B8
  LEW SE13 .... 161 K10
Hamlet Gdns *HMSMTH* W6 .... 156 D3
Hamlet HI *HLWW/ROY* CM19 .... 45 P5
Hamlet Rd *CRW* RM5 .... 104 B8
  NRWD SE19 .... 181 N10
Hamlet Sq *CRICK* NW2 .... 117 H8
Hamlets Wy *BOW* E3 .... 140 E6
The Hamlet *BERK* HP4 .... 34 D2
Hamlet Wy *STHWK* SE1 .... 19 J2
Hamlin Crs *PIN* HA5 .... 113 K3
Hamlin Rd *SEV* TN13 .... 246 F7
Hamlyn CI *EDGW* HA8 .... 95 K4
Hamlyn Gdns *NRWD* SE19 .... 181 M10
Hammarskjold Rd *HLW* CM20 .... 28 F10
Hammelton Rd *BMLY* BR1 .... 205 M1
Hammerfield Dr *RDKG* RH5 .... 270 C7
Hammer La *HHNE* HP2 .... 36 A5
Hammers Ga *LCOL/BKTW* AL2 .... 55 P2
Hammers La *MLHL* NW7 .... 96 D5
Hammersmith Bridge Rd
  BARN SW13 .... 156 E5
  HMSMTH W6 .... 156 F4
Hammersmith Broadway
  HMSMTH W6 .... 156 F3
Hammersmith F/O *HMSMTH* W6 .... 156 F4
Hammersmith Gv *HMSMTH* W6 .... 156 F3
Hammet CI *YEAD* UB4 .... 133 L7
Hammett St *TWRH* EC3N 13 L7
Hamm Moor La *ADL/WDHM* KT15 .... 215 P7
Hammond Av *MTCM* CR4 .... 202 C2
Hammond CI *CHESW* EN7 .... 61 N1
  HPTN TW12 .... 174 G10
  NTHLT UB5 .... 114 C10
  WOKN/KNAP GU21 .... 231 N2
Hammond End *SLN* SL2 .... 108 C9
Hammond Rd *EN* EN1 .... 80 A7
  WOKN/KNAP GU21 .... 231 P1
Hammonds CI *BCTR* RM8 .... 123 M8
Hammonds La *HAT* AL10 .... 21 N8
  RBRW/HUT CM13 .... 106 C7
  STALE/WH AL4 .... 44 G6
Hammond St *KTTN* NW5 .... 4 G1
Hammondstreet Rd *CHESW* EN7 .... 61 M2
Hammond Wy *LTWR* GU18 .... 212 A6
Hamond CI *SAND/SEL* CR2 .... 223 J5
Hamonde CI *EDGW* HA8 .... 95 N3
Hamond Sq *IS* N1 .... 7 J2
Ham Park Rd *FSTGT* E7 .... 141 M4
Hampden Av *BECK* BR3 .... 204 D2
Hampden CI *CRAWE* RH10 .... 284 F4
  CSHM HP5 .... 50 F6
  SLN SL2 .... 129 M5
  CHESW EN7 .... 62 A7
Hampden Crs *BRW* CM14 .... 107 H6
Hampden Gurney St
  BAY/PAD W2 .... 10 A2
  WARE SG12 .... 26 E2
Hampden HI *BEAC* HP9 .... 88 A9
Hampden Hill CI *WARE* SG12 .... 26 E1
Hampden La *TOTM* N17 .... 99 N9
Hampden PI *LCOL/BKTW* AL2 .... 56 D5
Hampden Rd *ARCH* N19 .... 118 E7
  BECK BR3 .... 204 D2
  CEND/HSY/T N8 .... 119 H2
  DTCH/LGLY SL3 .... 150 C2
  GRAYS RM17 .... 167 N4
  KTN/HRWW/W HA3 .... 94 B9
  KUT/HW KT1 .... 199 M3
  MUSWH N10 .... 98 B4
  TOTM N17 .... 99 P9
Hampden Sq *STHCT/OAK* N14 .... 98 C7
  WAT WD17 .... 72 F2
Hampshire Av *SL* SL1 .... 129 H7
Hampshire CI *UED* N18 .... 100 A4
Hampshire Hog La *HMSMTH* W6 .... 156 E3
Hampshire Rd *EMPK* RM11 .... 125 P2
  WDGN N22 .... 98 D3
Hampshire St *KTTN* NW5 .... 5 J1
  KTTN NW5 .... 118 C10
Hampson Wy *VX/NE* SW8 .... 158 G7
Hampstead CI *THMD* SE28 .... 143 L10
Hampstead Gdns *GLDGN* NW11 .... 117 K4
Hampstead Ga *HAMP* NW3 .... 117 M10
Hampstead Gn *HAMP* NW3 .... 117 M10
Hampstead Hill Gdns
  HAMP NW3 .... 117 P9
Hampstead La *DORK* RH4 .... 272 E3
  HGT N6 .... 118 A5
Hampstead Rd *CAMTN* NW1 .... 4 G8
  DORK RH4 .... 272 F3
Hampstead Sq *HAMP* NW3 .... 117 M9
Hampton CI *FBAR/BDGN* N11 .... 98 B6
  RYNPK SW20 .... 178 F10
Hampton Ct *IS* N1 .... 6 C2
Hampton Court Av
  E/WMO/HCT KT8 .... 198 D5
Hampton Court Rd
  E/WMO/HCT KT8 .... 198 F3
  HPTN TW12 .... 198 C2
Hampton Court Wy
  E/WMO/HCT KT8 .... 198 D4
  ESH/CLAY KT10 .... 198 D4
  THDIT KT7 .... 198 D2
Hampton Crs *GVE* DA12 .... 191 H5
Hampton Gdns *SBW* CM21 .... 29 L4
Hampton Gv *EW* KT17 .... 220 E5
Hampton La *FELT* TW13 .... 175 M7
Hampton Ri *KTN/HRWW/W* HA3 .... 115 K4
Hampton Rd *CHING* E4 .... 100 G6
  CROY/NA CR0 .... 203 K6
  FSTGT E7 .... 121 N10
  HPTN TW12 .... 176 C8
  IL IG1 .... 122 F9
  REDH RH1 .... 276 A5
  WAN E11 .... 121 J6
  WHTN TW2 .... 176 B3
  WPK KT4 .... 200 D1
Hampton Rd East *FELT* TW13 .... 175 N7
Hampton Rd West *FELT* TW13 .... 175 K4
Hampton St *WALW* SE17 .... 18 F6
Ham Ridings *RCHPK/HAM* TW10 .... 177 L8
Hamsey Green Gdns *WARL* CR6 .... 242 A2
Hamsey Wy *SAND/SEL* CR2 .... 242 A1
Ham Shades CI *BFN/LL* DA15 .... 185 J6
Hamstel Rd *HLW* CM20 .... 28 E9
Ham St *RCHPK/HAM* TW10 .... 177 H5
The Ham *BTFD* TW8 .... 155 H6
Ham Vw *CROY/NA* CR0 .... 204 D6

Ham Yd *SOHO/SHAV* W1D 11 J7
Hanameel St *CAN/RD* E16 .... 141 N10
Hanbury CI *CHES/WCR* EN8 .... 62 C1
  HDN NW4 .... 116 F1
  WARE SG12 .... 26 F1
Hanbury Dr *BR/WHM* TN16 .... 225 N9
  WCHMH N21 .... 78 G8
Hanbury Rd *ACT* W3 .... 155 N1
  CRAWW RH11 .... 283 H8
  TOTM N17 .... 100 A10
Hanbury St *WCHPL* E1 .... 13 N3
Hancock Ct *BORE* WD6 .... 75 P3
Hancock Rd *BOW* E3 .... 141 H5
  NRWD SE19 .... 181 L9
Hancocks Mt *ASC* SL5 .... 192 C6
Hancroft Rd *HHS/BOV* HP3 .... 36 A4
Handa CI *HHS/BOV* HP3 .... 36 C9
Handcroft Rd *CROY/NA* CR0 .... 203 J8
Handel CI *EDGW* HA8 .... 95 M8
Handel Crs *TIL* RM18 .... 168 D6
Handel PI *WLSDN* NW10 .... 136 A1
Handel St *BMSBY* WC1N 11 L1
Handel Wy *EDGW* HA8 .... 95 M8
Handen Rd *LEW* SE13 .... 183 K1
Handforth Rd *BRXN/ST* SW9 .... 159 H6
  IL IG1 .... 122 E8
Hand La *SBW* CM21 .... 29 M2
Handley Rd *HOM* E9 .... 140 E2
Handowe CI *HDN* NW4 .... 116 D2
Handside CI *WGCW* AL8 .... 22 F5
  WPK KT4 .... 200 C8
Handside Gn *WGCW* AL8 .... 22 F4
Handside La *WGCW* AL8 .... 22 F6
Handsworth Av *CHING* E4 .... 101 J7
Handsworth CI *OXHEY* WD19 .... 93 H4
Handsworth Rd *TOTM* N17 .... 119 L1
Handtrough Wy *BARK* IG11 .... 142 E4
Hanford CI *WAND/EARL* SW18 .... 179 K4
Hanford Rd *SOCK/AV* RM15 .... 146 B10
Hangar Dr *DEN/HRF* UB9 .... 91 H2
Hangar Ruding *OXHEY* WD19 .... 93 N1
Hangar View Wy *ACT* W3 .... 155 J7
Hanger La *EA* W5 .... 135 M6
Hanger HI *WEY* KT13 .... 216 C2
Hanger La *EA* W5 .... 135 L9
Hanger La (North Circular Rd)
  EA W5 .... 135 K5
Hanger Vale La *EA* W5 .... 135 L4
Hang Grove HI *ORP* BR6 .... 226 E9
Hanging Hill La *RBRW/HUT* CM13 .... 107 P10
Haning Hill La *RBRW/HUT* CM13 .... 87 P10
Hankey PI *STHWK* SE1 .... 19 J2
Hankins La *MLHL* NW7 .... 96 B3
Hanley CI *WDSR* SL4 .... 148 C7
Hanley Gdns *FSBYPK* N4 .... 118 C6
Hanley PI *BECK* BR3 .... 182 F2
Hanley Rd *FSBYPK* N4 .... 118 F6
Hannah CI *BECK* BR3 .... 204 F3
Hannan Ct *WLSDN* NW10 .... 115 P9
Hannards Wy *CHIG* IG7 .... 103 L6
Hannell Rd *FUL/PGN* SW6 .... 157 H6
Hannen Rd *WNWD* SE27 .... 181 J6
Hannay La *ARCH* N19 .... 118 C5
Hannibal Rd *STWL/WRAY* TW19 .... 173 P3
  WCHPL E1 .... 140 B7
Hannibal Wy *CROY/NA* CR0 .... 222 G2
Hannington Rd *CLAP* SW4 .... 158 C9
Hanover Av *CAN/RD* E16 .... 141 M10
  FELT TW13 .... 175 L4
Hanover Cir *HYS/HAR* UB3 .... 132 D8
Hanover CI *CHEAM* SM3 .... 221 H1
  CRAWE RH10 .... 284 A9
  EGH TW20 .... 171 N9
  RCH/KEW TW9 .... 155 M6
  REDH RH1 .... 258 D4
  SL SL1 .... 149 M2
  WDSR SL4 .... 148 E7
Hanover Ct *DORK* RH4 .... 272 E2
  WOKS/MYFD GU22 .... 232 G5
Hanover Dr *CHST* BR7 .... 184 F7
Hanover Gdns *BARK/HLT* IG6 .... 102 F8
  LBTH SE11 .... 18 A10
Hanover Gn *HHW* HP1 .... 35 K8
Hanover Pk *PECK* SE15 .... 159 P7
Hanover Rd *SEVS/STOTM* N15 .... 119 L2
  WIM/MER SW19 .... 179 M10
  WLSDN NW10 .... 136 F2
Hanover St *CONDST* W1S 10 F6
  CROY/NA CR0 .... 203 J10
Hanover Ter *CAMTN* NW1 .... 3 P10
Hanover Terrace Ms *CAMTN* NW1 .... 3 N10
  WEY KT13 .... 196 G10
Hanover Wy *BXLYHN* DA7 .... 163 N9
  WDSR SL4 .... 148 E8
Hanover Yd *IS* N1 .... 6 D7
Hansard Ms *WKENS* W14 .... 156 G1
Hansart Wy *ENC/FH* EN2 .... 79 H5
Hans Crs *CHEL* SW3 .... 16 A3
Hanselin CI *STAN* HA7 .... 94 E6
Hansells Md *HLWW/ROY* CM19 .... 45 M1
Hansen Dr *WCHMH* N21 .... 78 G10
Hanshaw Dr *EDGW* HA8 .... 96 A9
Hansler Gv *E/WMO/HCT* KT8 .... 198 C5
Hansler Rd *EDUL* SE22 .... 181 N1
Hansol Rd *BXLYHS* DA6 .... 185 P1
Hanson CI *BAL* SW12 .... 180 C3
  BECK BR3 .... 182 G1
  GU GU1 .... 250 F5
  MORT/ESHN SW14 .... 155 P9
  WDR/YW UB7 .... 152 A2
Hanson Dr *LOU* IG10 .... 82 F6
Hanson Gdns *STHL* UB1 .... 153 M1
Hanson St *GTPST* W1W 10 G3
Hans PI *KTBR* SW1X 16 A3
Hans Rd *CHEL* SW3 .... 16 A3
Hans St *KTBR* SW1X 16 B4
Hanway PI *SOHO/SHAV* W1D 11 J4
Hanway Rd *HNWL* W7 .... 134 C8
Hanway St *FITZ* W1T 11 J5
Hanworth *CHERT* KT16 .... 195 J8
Hanworth Rd *FELT* TW13 .... 175 J4
  HPTN TW12 .... 175 N7
  HSLW TW3 .... 154 A9
  HSLW TW4 .... 175 N3
  REDH RH1 .... 276 A3
  SUN TW16 .... 175 L10
Hanworth Ter *HSLW* TW3 .... 154 A10
Hanyards La *POTB/CUF* EN6 .... 60 A2
Hapgood CI *NTHLT* UB5 .... 114 C10
Harben Rd *KIL/WHAMP* NW6 .... 3 K3
Harberson Rd *BAL* SW12 .... 180 C1
  SRTFD E15 .... 141 L3
Harbert Gdns *LCOL/BKTW* AL2 .... 56 A1
Harberton Rd *ARCH* N19 .... 118 C6
Harberts Rd *HLWW/ROY* CM19 .... 46 E2
Harbet Rd *BAY/PAD* W2 .... 9 M4
  UED N18 .... 100 G5
Harbex CI *BXLY* DA5 .... 186 G4
Harbinger Rd *POP/IOD* E14 .... 160 G3
Harbledown PI *STMC/STPC* BR5 .... 207 K7
Harbledown Rd *FUL/PGN* SW6 .... 157 K7
  SAND/SEL CR2 .... 223 P7
Harbord CI *CMBW* SE5 .... 159 L8
Harbord St *FUL/PGN* SW6 .... 156 G6
Harborne CI *OXHEY* WD19 .... 93 K6
Harborough Av *BFN/LL* DA15 .... 185 J5
Harborough Rd
  STRHM/NOR SW16 .... 180 A6
Harbour Av *WBPTN* SW10 .... 157 N9
Harbourer CI *BARK/HLT* IG6 .... 103 L6
Harbourer Rd *BARK/HLT* IG6 .... 103 M6
Harbourfield Rd *BNSTD* SM7 .... 239 L6
Harbour Rd *CMBW* SE5 .... 159 K9
Harbridge Av *PUT/ROE* SW15 .... 178 E1
Harbury Rd *CAR* SM5 .... 221 P5
Harbut Rd *BTSEA* SW11 .... 157 N10

Harcamlow Wy *WARE* SG12 .... 27 M3
Harcastle CI *YEAD* UB4 .... 133 M6
Harcombe Rd *STNW/STAM* N16 .... 119 M8
Harcourt *STWL/WRAY* TW19 .... 172 B2
Harcourt Av *BFN/LL* DA15 .... 185 M2
  EDGW HA8 .... 95 P4
  MNPK E12 .... 122 C9
  WLGTN SM6 .... 222 C1
Harcourt CI *EGH* TW20 .... 172 F9
  ISLW TW7 .... 154 F9
Harcourt Fld *WLGTN* SM6 .... 222 C1
Harcourt Ms *GPK* RM2 .... 124 C3
Harcourt Rd *BROCKY* SE4 .... 160 E10
  BUSH WD23 .... 74 B9
  BXLYHS DA6 .... 163 P10
  SRTFD E15 .... 141 L4
  THHTH CR7 .... 202 G6
  WDGN N22 .... 98 E9
  WDSR SL4 .... 148 D7
  WIM/MER SW19 .... 179 K10
  WLGTN SM6 .... 222 C1
Harcourt St *CAMTN* NW1 .... 9 P4
Harcourt Ter *WBPTN* SW10 .... 15 H8
Hardcastle CI *SNWD* SE25 .... 203 P6
Hardcourts CI *WWKM* BR4 .... 224 C1
Hardel Wk *BRXS/STRHM* SW2 .... 181 J3
Harden Rd *GVW* DA11 .... 190 C5
Hardens Manorway *CHARL* SE7 .... 162 A2
  WOOL/PLUM SE18 .... 162 A2
Harders Rd *PECK* SE15 .... 160 A8
Hardess St *HNHL* SE24 .... 159 K9
Hardham CI *CRAWW* RH11 .... 283 H5
Hardie CI *WLSDN* NW10 .... 116 A10
Hardie Rd *DAGE* RM10 .... 124 D8
Harding CI *CROY/NA* CR0 .... 203 N10
  CSTN WD25 .... 59 L1
  KUTN/CMB KT2 .... 199 L1
  WALW SE17 .... 18 G9
Hardinge Rd *UED* N18 .... 99 M7
  WLSDN NW10 .... 136 F1
Hardinge St *WCHPL* E1 .... 140 B8
  WCHPL E1 .... 140 B8
Harding Rd *BXLYHN* DA7 .... 164 A8
  CDH/CHF RM16 .... 168 D2
  CSHM HP5 .... 51 J6
  EPSOM KT18 .... 238 B5
Hardings *WGCE* AL7 .... 23 M4
Hardings Rw *IVER* SL0 .... 130 F5
Hardley Crs *EMPK* RM11 .... 125 L2
Hardman Rd *CHARL* SE7 .... 161 N4
  KUTN/CMB KT2 .... 199 K2
Hardwick CI *LHD/OX* KT22 .... 236 B1
  STAN HA7 .... 95 H6
Hardwick Crs *DART* DA1 .... 188 A2
Hardwicke Av *HEST* TW5 .... 153 P7
Hardwicke Ms *FSBYW* WC1X 5 P10
Hardwicke PI *LCOL/BKTW* AL2 .... 57 J3
Hardwicke Rd *CHSWK* W4 .... 155 P3
  PLMGR N13 .... 98 F7
  RCHPK/HAM TW10 .... 177 H7
  REIG RH2 .... 257 K7
Hardwicke St *BARK* IG11 .... 142 F3
Hardwick Gn *WEA* W13 .... 134 G7
Hardwick La *CHERT* KT16 .... 194 F7
Hardwick Rd *REDH* RH1 .... 275 N2
Hardwicks Wy
  WAND/EARL SW18 .... 179 K1
Hardwidge St *STHWK* SE1 .... 19 J1
Hardy Av *CAN/RD* E16 .... 141 M10
  GVW DA11 .... 190 B5
  RSLP HA4 .... 113 J10
Hardy CI *BAR* EN5 .... 77 H9
  BERM/RHTH SE16 .... 160 C1
  CRAWE RH10 .... 284 D6
  HORL RH6 .... 279 P4
  PIN HA5 .... 113 L5
  RDKG RH5 .... 272 G6
Hardy Gv *DART* DA1 .... 165 P10
Hardy Pas *WDGN* N22 .... 98 G9
Hardy Rd *BKHTH/KID* SE3 .... 161 L5
  HHNE HP2 .... 36 A5
  WIM/MER SW19 .... 179 L10
Hardy Wy *ENC/FH* EN2 .... 79 H5
Hare and Billet Rd
  BKHTH/KID SE3 .... 161 J7
Harebell CI *HERT/BAY* SG13 .... 26 A5
Harebell Dr *EHAM* E6 .... 142 D7
Harebell HI *COB* KT11 .... 217 L10
Harebell Wy *HARH* RM3 .... 105 L8
The Harebreaks *WATN* WD24 .... 73 J3
Harecourt Rd *IS* N1 .... 6 E1
Hare Crs *GSTN* WD25 .... 59 H3
Harecroft *DORK* RH4 .... 273 H5
  GT/LBKH KT23 .... 236 A9
Haredale Rd *HNHL* SE24 .... 159 K10
Haredon CI *FSTH* SE23 .... 182 B3
Harefield *ESH/CLAY* KT10 .... 198 D10
  HLW CM20 .... 29 K10
Harefield Av *BELMT* SM2 .... 221 H5
Harefield CI *ENC/FH* EN2 .... 79 H5
Harefield Ms *BROCKY* SE4 .... 160 E9
Harefield PI *STALE/WH* AL4 .... 39 J3
Harefield Rd *BROCKY* SE4 .... 160 E9
  CEND/HSY/T N8 .... 118 E3
  RKW/CH/CXG WD3 .... 91 H3
  SCUP DA14 .... 185 N5
  STRHM/NOR SW16 .... 180 C10
  UX/CGN UB8 .... 131 N1
Hare Hall La *GPK* RM2 .... 125 J2
Harehatch La *SLN* SL2 .... 108 F6
Hare HI *ADL/WDHM* KT15 .... 215 J3
Hare Hill CI *WOKS/MYFD* GU22 .... 233 K1
Harelands CI *WOKN/KNAP* GU21 .... 231 J5
Hare La *CRAWW* RH11 .... 283 L4
  ESH/CLAY KT10 .... 218 D3
  HAT AL10 .... 40 E6
Hare Marsh *BETH* E2 .... 13 N1
Harendon *KWD/TDW/WH* KT20 .... 249 J4
Harepark CI *HHW* HP1 .... 35 J5
Hare Rw *BETH* E2 .... 140 A3
Hares Bank *CROY/NA* CR0 .... 225 J6
Haresfield Rd *DAGE* RM10 .... 144 B1
Harestone Dr *CTHM* CR3 .... 241 N10
Harestone HI *CTHM* CR3 .... 259 N2
Harestone La *CTHM* CR3 .... 259 M1
Harestone Valley Rd *CTHM* CR3 .... 259 N1
Hare St *HLWW/ROY* CM19 .... 46 E1
  WOOL/PLUM SE18 .... 162 D2
Hare Street Springs
  HLWW/ROY CM19 .... 46 F1
Hare Wk *IS* N1 .... 7 K8
Harewood *RKW/CH/CXG* WD3 .... 71 M9
Harewood Av *CAMTN* NW1 .... 9 P2
  NTHLT UB5 .... 133 M2
Harewood CI *CRAWE* RH10 .... 284 B4
  NTHLT UB5 .... 133 N2
  REIG RH2 .... 257 M8
Harewood Dr *CLAY* IG5 .... 102 C10
Harewood Gdns *SAND/SEL* CR2 .... 242 F7
Harewood HI *EPP* CM16 .... 83 H1
Harewood PI *CONDST* W1S 10 F6
  SL SL1 .... 149 M2
Harewood Rd *BRWN* CM15 .... 86 G10
  ISLW TW7 .... 154 F9
  OXHEY WD19 .... 93 J3
  RGUE GU4 .... 250 F7
  SAND/SEL CR2 .... 223 M3
  WIM/MER SW19 .... 179 P9
Harewood Ter *NWDGN* UB2 .... 153 M3
Harfield Gdns *CMBW* SE5 .... 159 L5
Harfield Rd *SUN* TW16 .... 197 L2
Harford CI *CHING* E4 .... 101 H4
Harford Dr *WAT* WD17 .... 72 E4

Harford Rd *CHING* E4 .... 100 G1
Harford St *WCHPL* E1 .... 140 D6
Harford Wk *EFNCH* N2 .... 117 N2
Harfst Wy *SWLY* BR8 .... 208 D1
Hargood CI *KTN/HRWW/W* HA3 .... 115 K4
Hargood Rd *BKHTH/KID* SE3 .... 161 P7
Hargrave Pk *KTTN* NW5 .... 118 A7
Hargrave PI *KTTN* NW5 .... 118 A8
Hargrave Rd *ARCH* N19 .... 118 D7
Hargreaves Av *CHESW* EN7 .... 62 A7
Hargreaves CI *CHESW* EN7 .... 62 A7
Hargwyne St *BRXN/ST* SW9 .... 158 G9
Haringey Pk *CEND/HSY/T* N8 .... 118 F4
Haringey Rd *CEND/HSY/T* N8 .... 118 F2
Harington PI *REIG* RH2 .... 257 K8
Harkett CI *KTN/HRWW/W* HA3 .... 94 E10
Harkness CI *EW* KT17 .... 238 F2
  HARH RM3 .... 105 N6
Harkness Rd *BARK* SL SL1 .... 128 A7
Harland Av *BFN/LL* DA15 .... 184 G6
  CROY/NA CR0 .... 203 N10
Harland CI *WIM/MER* SW19 .... 201 L3
Harland Rd *LEE/GVPK* SE12 .... 183 M4
Harlands Gv *ORP* BR6 .... 226 E10
Harlech Gdns *HEST* TW5 .... 153 K5
  PIN HA5 .... 113 K7
Harlech Rd *ABLGY* WD5 .... 55 H7
  STHGT/OAK N14 .... 98 F7
Harlequin Av *BTFD* TW8 .... 154 F5
  YEAD UB4 .... 133 L7
Harlequin CI *ISLW* TW7 .... 176 D1
Harlequin Rd *TEDD* TW11 .... 176 G10
Harlescott Rd *PECK* SE15 .... 160 C10
Harlesden Gdns *WLSDN* NW10 .... 136 C3
Harlesden Rd *HARH* RM3 .... 105 N7
  STAL AL1 .... 38 F6
  WLSDN NW10 .... 136 D3
Harley CI *ALP/SUD* HA0 .... 135 J1
Harley Ct *STALE/WH* AL4 .... 39 J2
Harley Crs *HRW* HA1 .... 114 C2
Harleyford *BMLY* BR1 .... 205 N1
Harleyford Rd *LBTH* SE11 .... 17 N9
Harleyford St *LBTH* SE11 .... 18 A10
Harley Gdns *ORP* BR6 .... 227 H1
  WBPTN SW10 .... 15 K8
Harley Gv *BOW* E3 .... 140 E5
Harley PI *CAVSQ/HST* W1G 10 E4
Harley Rd *HAMP* NW3 .... 3 M4
  HRW HA1 .... 114 C2
  WLSDN NW10 .... 136 B4
Harley St *CAVSQ/HST* W1G 10 E3
Harlinger St *WOOL/PLUM* SE18 .... 162 B2
The Harlings *HERT/BAY* SG13 .... 26 B9
Harlington CI *HYS/HAR* UB3 .... 152 D6
Harlington High St *HYS/HAR* UB3 .... 152 E4
Harlington Rd *BXLYHN* DA7 .... 163 P9
  UX/CGN UB8 .... 132 C7
Harlington Rd East
  EBED/NFELT TW14 .... 175 J3
Harlington Rd West
  EBED/NFELT TW14 .... 175 J2
Harlow Common *HLWE* CM17 .... 47 N4
Harlow Ct *HHNE* HP2 .... 36 B3
Harlow Gdns *CRW* RM5 .... 104 D7
Harlow Rd *CHONG* CM5 .... 49 K6
  HLWE CM17 .... 30 C4
  HLWW/ROY CM19 .... 27 P10
  PLMGR N13 .... 99 L4
  RAIN RM13 .... 144 G3
  SBW CM21 .... 29 M3
Harlyn Dr *PIN* HA5 .... 113 J1
Harman Av *GVW* DA11 .... 190 E8
  WFD IG8 .... 101 L8
Harman CI *CHING* E4 .... 101 J5
  CRICK NW2 .... 117 H8
Harman Dr *BFN/LL* DA15 .... 185 J2
  CRICK NW2 .... 117 H8
Harman PI *PUR/KEN* CR8 .... 223 J7
Harman Rd *EN* EN1 .... 79 N4
Harmer Rd *SWCM* DA10 .... 189 L2
Harmer St *GVE* DA12 .... 190 F2
Harmondsworth La
  WDR/YW UB7 .... 151 P7
Harmondsworth Rd
  WDR/YW UB7 .... 151 P2
Harmony CI *GLDGN* NW11 .... 117 H3
  HAT AL10 .... 40 D3
  WLGTN SM6 .... 222 F5
Harmony Wy *HAYES* BR2 .... 205 M2
  HDN NW4 .... 116 F2
Harmood Gv *CAMTN* NW1 .... 4 E3
Harmood St *CAMTN* NW1 .... 4 E2
Harms Gv *RGUE* GU4 .... 250 F2
Harmsworth St *WALW* SE17 .... 18 C8
Harmsworth Wy *TRDG/WHET* N20 .... 97 H10
Harness Rd *THMD* SE28 .... 163 K1
Harness Wy *STALE/WH* AL4 .... 39 J3
Harold Av *BELV* DA17 .... 164 A4
  HYS/HAR UB3 .... 152 C2
Harold Court Rd *HARH* RM3 .... 106 A7
Harold Crs *WAB* EN9 .... 63 H8
Harold Rd *CHING* E4 .... 101 H4
  CRAWE RH10 .... 284 F4
  NRWD SE19 .... 181 L10
  PLSTW E13 .... 141 L10
  RDART DA2 .... 187 M5
  SEVS/STOTM N15 .... 119 N3
  SUT SM1 .... 221 N1
  WAN E11 .... 121 K6
  WFD IG8 .... 101 M9
  WLSDN NW10 .... 136 A5
Haroldslea *HORL* RH6 .... 280 F5
Haroldslea CI *HORL* RH6 .... 280 D6
Haroldslea Dr *HORL* RH6 .... 280 E6
Harolds Rd *HLWW/ROY* CM19 .... 46 C2
Haroldstone Rd *WALTH* E17 .... 120 C3
Harold Vw *HARH* RM3 .... 105 N10
Harp Cross La *MON* EC3R 13 J8
Harpenden Rd *HARP* AL5 .... 20 A4
  MNPK E12 .... 121 P7
  STALW/RED AL3 .... 20 B7
  WNWD SE27 .... 181 J5
Harper CI *STHCT/OAK* N14 .... 78 D9
Harper La *RAD* WD7 .... 56 F7
Harper Rd *EHAM* E6 .... 142 C8
  STHWK SE1 .... 18 F3
Harpers La *BRWN* CM15 .... 87 J3
Harpesford Av *VW* GU25 .... 193 P5
Harp Island CI *WLSDN* NW10 .... 116 A10
Harpley Sq *WCHPL* E1 .... 140 C6
Harpour Rd *BARK* IG11 .... 142 F1
Harp Rd *HNWL* W7 .... 134 F4
Harpsden St *BTSEA* SW11 .... 158 B7
Harpsfield Broadway *HAT* AL10 .... 40 C3
Harps Oak La *REDH* RH1 .... 258 A4
Harptree Wy *STAL* AL1 .... 38 E4
Harpurs *KWD/TDW/WH* KT20 .... 238 G7
Harpur St *BMSBY* WC1N 11 L3
Harraden Rd *BKHTH/KID* SE3 .... 161 P7
Harrap Cha *GRAYS* RM17 .... 145 J3
Harrier CI *RAIN* RM13 .... 145 H10
Harrier Ms *THMD* SE28 .... 162 G1
Harriers CI *EA* W5 .... 135 K9
Harrier Rd *WAB* EN9 .... 63 M10
Harrier Wy *EHAM* E6 .... 142 C7
Harries CI *CSHM* HP5 .... 50 C8
Harriescourt *WAB* EN9 .... 63 M8
Harriet CI *HACK* E8 .... 7 N3
Harriet Gdns *CROY/NA* CR0 .... 203 P9
Harriet St *KTBR* SW1X 16 A2
Harriet Wk *KTBR* SW1X 16 A2
Harriet Walker Wy
  RKW/CH/CXG WD3 .... 91 J1

Harriet Wy BUSH WD23 ... 94 C1
Harringay Gdns CEND/HSY/T N8 .. 119 J2
SEVS/STOTM N15 ... 119 J2
Harrington Cl CROY/NA CR0 ... 202 F9
REIG RH2 ... 274 D7
WDSR SL4 ... 148 E10
WLSDN NW10 ... 116 A8
Harrington Gdns SKENS SW7 ... 15 J6
Harrington Hl CLPT E5 ... 120 A6
Harrington Rd SKENS SW7 ... 15 L5
SNWD SE25 ... 203 P4
WAN E11 ... 121 K6
Harrington Sq CAMTN NW1 ... 4 C1
Harrington St CAMTN NW1 ... 4 C9
Harrington Wy
WOOL/PLUM SE18 ... 162 A2
Harriott Cl GNWCH SE10 ... 161 L3
Harriotts Cl ASHTD KT21 ... 237 J6
LHD/OX KT22 ... 237 J6
Harriotts La ASHTD KT21 ... 237 H5
Harris Cl CRAWW RH11 ... 283 L10
ENC/FH EN2 ... 79 J5
GVW DA11 ... 190 B6
HEST TW5 ... 153 P7
Harris La RAD WD7 ... 57 M10
Harrison Cl NTHWD HA6 ... 92 D7
REIG RH2 ... 275 L1
TRDG/WHET N20 ... 97 P2
Harrison Ct SHPTN TW17 ... 196 C5
Harrison Dr EPP CM16 ... 66 C2
Harrison Rd DAGE RM10 ... 144 C1
Harrison's Ri CROY/NA CR0 ... 203 J10
Harrison St STPAN WC1H ... 5 M10
Harrisons Whf PUR RM19 ... 165 P4
Harrison Wk CHES/WCR EN8 ... 62 C6
Harrison Wy SEV TN13 ... 247 H8
SL SL1 ... 128 C10
Harris Rd BXLYHN DA7 ... 163 P10
DAGW RM9 ... 124 A10
GSTN WD25 ... 73 H1
Harris's La WARE SG12 ... 26 B2
Harris St CMBW SE5 ... 159 L6
WALTH E17 ... 120 E5
Harris Wy SUN TW16 ... 196 F1
Harrogate Ct DTCH/LGLY SL3 .. 150 D4
Harrogate Rd OXHEY WD19 ... 93 K4
Harrold Rd BCTR RM8 ... 123 L10
Harrow Av EN EN1 ... 79 N10
Harroway Rd BTSEA SW11 ... 157 N8
Harrowby Gdns GVW DA11 ... 190 B5
Harrowby St MBLAR W1H ... 9 G7
Harrowdene Cl ALP/SUD HA0 ... 115 J9
CHSGTN KT9 ... 219 J4
DORK RH4 ... 272 F5
Harrowdene Ct HARH RM3 ... 105 J8
Harrowdene Gdns TEDD TW11 .. 176 P10
Harrowdene Rd ALP/SUD HA0 .. 115 J9
Harrow Dr ED N9 ... 99 N2
EMPK RM11 ... 125 K6
Harrowes Meade EDGW HA8 ... 95 M4
Harrow Fields Gdns HRW HA1... 114 D8
Harrow Gdns ORP BR6 ... 227 L1
WARL CR6 ... 242 E2
Harrowgate Rd HOM E9 ... 140 D1
Harrow Gn WAN E11 ... 121 K8
WAN E11 ... 121 K8
Harrowlands Pk DORK RH4 ... 272 G3
Harrow La POP/IOD E14 ... 141 H9
RCODL GU7 ... 267 K10
Harrow Manor Wy ABYW SE2... 163 M2
THMD SE28 ... 143 M10
Harrow Pk HRW HA1 ... 114 D7
Harrow Pl WCHPL E1 ... 13 K5
Harrow Rd ASHF TW15 ... 174 B4
CAR SM5 ... 221 P3
DTCH/LGLY SL3 ... 150 C2
IL IG1 ... 122 F9
RSEV TN14 ... 245 P1
WAN E11 ... 121 L8
WARL CR6 ... 242 E11
WBLY HA9 ... 115 L10
WLSDN NW10 ... 136 G5
Harrow Rd East DORK RH4 ... 272 G4
Harrow Road F/O BAY/PAD W2 ... 9 M4
Harrow Rd West DORK RH4 ... 272 F4
Harrowsley Ct HORL RH6 ... 280 C3
Harrow St CAMTN NW1 ... 9 P3
Harrow Vw HGDN/ICK UB10... 132 D5
HYS/HAR UB3 ... 133 H9
RYLN/HDSTN HA2 ... 114 C1
Harrow View Rd EA W5 ... 134 C6
Harrow Wy OXHEY WD19 ... 93 M4
SHPTN TW17 ... 196 D2
Harrow Weald Pk
KTN/HRWW/W HA3 ... 94 C7
Harston Dr PEND EN3 ... 80 F4
Hart Cl REDH RH1 ... 259 N9
Hart Crs CHIG IG7 ... 103 J6
Hart Dyke Rd STMC/STPC BR5.. 207 M8
SWLY BR8 ... 208 B3
Harte Rd HSLW TW3 ... 153 N8
NTHLT UB5 ... 133 J4
Hartfield Av BORE WD6 ... 75 M8
Hartfield Cl BORE WD6 ... 75 M8
Hartfield Crs WIM/MER SW19... 179 J10
WWKM BR4 ... 205 M10
Hartfield Gv PGE/AN SE20 ... 204 A1
Hartfield Pl GVW DA11 ... 190 A3
Hartfield Rd CHSGTN KT9 ... 219 J2
WIM/MER SW19 ... 179 J10
WWKM BR4 ... 225 M1
Hartfield Ter BOW E3 ... 140 F4
Hartford Av KTN/HRWW/W HA3 .. 114 F1
Hartforde Rd BORE WD6 ... 75 M6
Hartford Rd BXLY DA5 ... 186 B2
HOR/WEW KT19 ... 219 M8
Hart Gdns DORK RH4 ... 272 C1
Hart Gv ACT W3 ... 135 P1
STHL UB1 ... 133 P7
Harthall La KGLGY WD4 ... 54 C4
Hartham Cl HOLWY N7 ... 118 F10
ISLW TW7 ... 154 F7
Hartham La HERT/WAS SG14 ... 25 K5
Hartham Rd HOLWY N7 ... 118 F10
ISLW TW7 ... 154 E7
TOTM N17 ... 99 N10
Harting Ct CRAWW RH11 ... 283 J10
Harting Rd ELTH/MOT SE9 ... 184 D1
ORP BR6 ... 226 F2
Hartington Cl HRW HA1 ... 114 D9
ORP BR6 ... 226 F7
Hartington Rd CAN/RD E16 ... 141 N8
CHSWK W4 ... 155 N6
NWDGN UB2 ... 153 M1
TWK TW1 ... 176 C3
VX/NE SW8 ... 158 F7
WALTH E17 ... 120 D4
WEA W13 ... 134 G9
Hartismere Rd FUL/PGN SW6... 139 J6
Hartlake Rd HOM E9 ... 140 C1
Hartland Cl ADL/WDHM KT15... 195 M3
EDGW HA8 ... 95 M3
SL SL1 ... 129 J10
WCHMH N21 ... 79 L10
Hartland Dr EDGW HA8 ... 95 M3
RSLP HA4 ... 113 J8
Hartland Rd ADL/WDHM KT15... 215 K4
CAMTN NW1 ... 4 C1
CHES/WCR EN8 ... 62 C5
EPP CM16 ... 65 K7
FBAR/BDGN N11 ... 98 A6
HCH RM12 ... 125 H7
HPTN TW12 ... 176 A7
ISLW TW7 ... 154 F7
KIL/WHAMP NW6 ... 2 C7
MRDN SM4 ... 201 K7

SRTFD E15 ... 141 L2
Hartland Cl BXLY DA5 ... 186 A2
The Hartlands HEST TW5 ... 153 J5
Hartland Wy CROY/NA CR0 ... 204 D9
MRDN SM4 ... 201 J7
Hartley Av EHAM E6 ... 142 B3
MLHL NW7 ... 96 C6
Hartley Bottom Rd HART DA3 .. 211 N8
Hartley Cl BMLY BR1 ... 206 C2
DTCH/LGLY SL3 ... 129 P3
MLHL NW7 ... 96 C6
Hartley Copse WDSR SL4 ... 171 M2
Hartley Down COUL/CHIP CR5 .. 240 C1
Hartley Farm PUR/KEN CR8 ... 240 C1
Hartley Hl HART DA3 ... 211 M8
PUR/KEN CR8 ... 240 C1
Hartley Old Rd PUR/KEN CR8 ... 240 C1
CROY/NA CR0 ... 203 K7
HART DA3 ... 211 K2
WAN E11 ... 121 L6
WELL DA16 ... 163 M6
Hartley St BETH E2 ... 140 B5
Hartley Wy PUR/KEN CR8 ... 240 C1
Hartmann Rd CAN/RD E16 ... 142 A10
Hartmoor Ms PEND EN3 ... 80 C3
Hartnoll St HOLWY N7 ... 118 G10
Harton Cl BMLY BR1 ... 206 A1
Harton Rd ED N9 ... 100 A3
Hart Rd BF/WBF KT14 ... 215 P9
DORK RH4 ... 272 C1
HLWE CM17 ... 29 M6
STAL AL1 ... 58 C7
Hartsbourne Av BUSH WD23 ... 94 B3
Hartsbourne Rd BUSH WD23 ... 94 C3
Hartsbourne Wy BUSH WD23... 36 D7
Harts Cl BUSH WD23 ... 73 P6
Harts Gdns GUW GU2 ... 249 J9
Harts Gv WFD IG8 ... 101 M6
Hart Shaw HART DA3 ... 211 N2
Hartshill GUW GU2 ... 249 J9
Hartshill Rd HGDN/ICK UB10 .. 132 B3
Hartshill Rd GVW DA11 ... 190 C5
Hartshorn Gdns EHAM E6 ... 142 B3
Hartsland Rd SEV TN13 ... 247 K9
Harts La BARK IG11 ... 142 C1
NWCR SE14 ... 160 D6
Hartslock Dr ABYW SE2 ... 163 N1
Hartsmead Rd ELTH/MOT SE9 .. 184 C5
Hartspiece Rd REDH RH1 ... 276 B2
Hartspring La GSTN WD25 ... 74 A5
Hart St BRW CM14 ... 107 H3
MON EC3R ... 13 K7
Hartsway PEND EN3 ... 80 A8
Hartswood Av REIG RH2 ... 275 K4
Hartswood Cl BRW CM14 ... 107 H3
Hartswood Gn BUSH WD23 ... 94 C3
Hartswood Rd BRW CM14 ... 107 H3
SHB W12 ... 156 C1
Hartsworth Cl PLSTW E13 ... 141 L4
Hartville Rd WOOL/PLUM SE18 .. 163 H3
Hartwell Cl BRXS/STRHM SW2 .. 158 F10
Hartwell Dr BEAC HP9 ... 88 C3
Hartwell St HACK E8 ... 7 L1
Harty Cl CDH/CHF RM16 ... 147 N10
Harvard Hl CHSWK W4 ... 155 N5
Harvard Rd CHSWK W4 ... 155 N5
ISLW TW7 ... 154 A7
LEW SE13 ... 183 H1
Harvel Cl CHST BR7 ... 207 K3
Harvel Crs ABYW SE2 ... 163 N4
Harvest Bank AMS HP6 ... 50 B10
Harvest Bank Rd WWKM BR4 .. 205 M10
Harvest Ct STALE/WH AL4 ... 39 H2
Harvest End GSTN WD25 ... 73 L2
Harvester Rd HOR/WEW KT19 .. 220 A6
Harvesters Cl ISLW TW7 ... 176 F1
Harvest La LOU IG10 ... 102 A1
THDIT KT7 ... 198 F6
Harvest Md HAT AL10 ... 40 E3
Harvest Rd BUSH WD23 ... 74 A8
CRAWE RH10 ... 284 D9
EGH TW20 ... 172 A8
FELT TW13 ... 175 H7
Harvestside HORL RH6 ... 280 D3
Harvest Wy SWLY BR8 ... 208 A7
Harvey CDH/CHF RM16 ... 167 N1
Harveyfields WAB EN9 ... 63 H10
Harvey Gdns CHARL SE7 ... 161 P4
LOU IG10 ... 82 E7
Harvey Rd CEND/HSY/T N8 ... 118 G3
CMBW SE5 ... 159 L7
DTCH/LGLY SL3 ... 150 E2
GU GU1 ... 268 B2
HGDN/ICK UB10 ... 132 B4
HSLWW TW4 ... 175 H3
IL IG1 ... 122 E10
LCOL/BKTW AL2 ... 57 H2
NTHLT UB5 ... 133 K2
RKW/CH/CXG WD3 ... 72 B10
WAN E11 ... 121 K6
WOT/HER KT12 ... 197 H7
Harvey's La ROMW/RG RM7 ... 124 F7
Harvey St IS N1 ... 7 H6
Harvill Rd SCUP DA14 ... 185 N8
Harvil Rd DEN/HRF UB9 ... 111 M2
Harwater Dr LOU IG10 ... 82 C6
Harwell Cl RSLP HA4 ... 112 E6
Harwich Rd SCUP DA14 ... 128 F8
Harwood Av BMLY BR1 ... 205 N8
EMPK RM11 ... 125 M1
MTCM CR4 ... 201 P3
Harwood Cl ALP/SUD HA0 ... 115 J9
NFNCH/WDSP N12 ... 97 P7
WGCW AL8 ... 23 H1
WLYN AL6 ... 23 H2
Harwood Dr HGDN/ICK UB10 .. 132 A3
Harwood Gdns WDSR SL4 ... 171 N3
Harwood Hall La UPMR RM14 .. 146 A1
Harwood Ms FUL/PGN SW6 ... 139 L6
Harwood Pk REDH RH1 ... 276 B9
Harwood Rd FUL/PGN SW6 ... 157 K6
Harwoods Rd WATW WD18 ... 73 L5
Harwood Ter FUL/PGN SW6 ... 157 L7
Hasedines Rd HHW HP1 ... 35 L5
Haselbury Rd UED N18 ... 99 M5
Haseldine Mdw HAT AL10 ... 40 E3
Haseldine Rd LCOL/BKTW AL2 .. 57 J2
Haselrigge Rd CLAP SW4 ... 158 F10
Haseltine Rd SYD SE26 ... 182 E7
Haselwood Dr ENC/FH EN2 ... 79 J8
Haskard Rd DAGW RM9 ... 123 N9
Hasker St CHEL SW3 ... 15 P5
Haslam Av CHEAM SM3 ... 201 H8
Haslam Cl HGDN/ICK UB10 ... 112 D7
IS N1 ... 6 B3
Haslemere Av EBAR EN4 ... 98 A2
HDN NW4 ... 116 C4
HEST TW5 ... 153 K8
HNWL W7 ... 154 F2
MTCM CR4 ... 201 N2
WAND/EARL SW18 ... 179 L5
Haslemere Cl HPTN TW12 ... 175 P7
WLGTN SM6 ... 222 F2
Haslemere Gdns FNCH N3 ... 117 J1
Haslemere Rd BXLYHN DA7 ... 164 B1
CEND/HSY/T N8 ... 118 F5
GDMY/SEVK IG3 ... 123 J2
THHTH CR7 ... 203 J3
WCHMH N21 ... 99 J3
WDSR SL4 ... 148 F7
Hasler Cl THMD SE28 ... 143 L9
Haslett Av East CRAWE RH10... 284 A7
Haslett Av West CRAWE RH10 .. 283 N8
CRAWW RH11 ... 283 N7

Haslett Rd SHPTN TW17 ... 196 F2
Haslewood Av HOD EN11 ... 44 F7
Hasluck Gdns BAR EN5 ... 77 M10
Hassard St BETH E2 ... 7 M8
Hassendean Rd BKHTH/KID SE3 .. 161 N5
Hassett Rd HOM E9 ... 140 C1
Hassocks Cl SYD SE26 ... 182 A6
Hassocks Ct CRAWW RH11 ... 283 J10
Hassocks Rd STRHM/NOR SW16 .. 202 E1
Hassock Wd HAYES BR2 ... 226 A1
Hassop Rd CRICK NW2 ... 116 C9
Hasted Cl ERH DA8 ... 189 H2
Hasted Rd CHARL SE7 ... 162 A4
Hastings Av BARK/HLT IG6 ... 122 F2
Hastings Cl BAR EN5 ... 77 M8
GPK RM2 ... 125 J3
HAYES BR2 ... 206 B8
TOTM N17 ... 119 L1
WEA W13 ... 134 G9
Hastings Dr SURB KT6 ... 199 H6
Hastings Rd CRAWE RH10 ... 284 C7
CROY/NA CR0 ... 203 N8
FBAR/BDGN N11 ... 98 D6
GPK RM2 ... 125 J3
HAYES BR2 ... 206 B8
TOTM N17 ... 119 L1
WEA W13 ... 134 G9
Hastings St STPAN WC1H ... 5 L10
Hastingwood Rd HLWE CM17 ... 47 P6
Hastoe Cl YEAD UB4 ... 133 M6
Hatcham Park Ms NWCR SE14 .. 160 C7
Hatcham Park Rd NWCR SE14 .. 160 C7
Hatcham Rd PECK SE15 ... 160 C5
Hatchard Rd ARCH N19 ... 118 E10
Hatch Cl ADL/WDHM KT15 ... 195 L10
Hatchcroft HDN NW4 ... 116 E1
Hatch End BFOR GU20 ... 212 B3
Hatch End Rd KWD/TDW/WH KT20 .. 238 C6
Hatchett Rd EBED/NFELT TW14 .. 174 D4
Hatchgate HORL RH6 ... 280 A5
Hatchgate Gdns SL SL1 ... 128 C5
Hatch Gv CHDH RM6 ... 123 P2
Hatch La CHING E4 ... 101 J5
REDH RH1 ... 276 C7
RPLY/SEND GU23 ... 234 C10
WDR/YW UB7 ... 151 N6
WDSR SL4 ... 148 F9
Hatch Rd RCHPK/HAM TW10 ... 177 L8
Hatch Rd STRHM/NOR SW16 ... 202 F2
Hatch Side CHIG IG7 ... 102 D6
The Hatch PEND EN3 ... 80 C5
WDSR SL4 ... 148 B6
Hatchwoods WFD IG8 ... 101 L5
Hatcliffe Cl BKHTH/KID SE3 ... 161 L9
Hatcliffe St GNWCH SE10 ... 161 L4
Hatfield Av HOD EN11 ... 40 C1
Hatfield Rd BARK/HLT IG6 ... 122 E1
BELMT SM2 ... 221 L5
BF/WBF KT14 ... 215 L8
HCH RM12 ... 125 L10
MTCM CR4 ... 201 N4
Hatfield Crs HHNE HP2 ... 36 A2
Hatfield Rd ASHTD KT21 ... 237 L7
BRKMPK AL9 ... 23 P10
CHSWK W4 ... 156 A1
HNWL W7 ... 134 F10
POTB/CUF EN6 ... 59 M7
SL SL1 ... 149 M1
SRTFD E15 ... 121 K10
STAL AL1 ... 38 C6
STALE/WH AL4 ... 39 H6
WATN WD24 ... 73 J5
Hatfields LOU IG10 ... 82 E7
STHWK SE1 ... 12 B9
Hathaway Cl HAYES BR2 ... 206 C8
RSLP HA4 ... 112 G9
STAN HA7 ... 94 F6
Hathaway Ct STALE/WH AL4 ... 39 K6
Hathaway Crs MNPK E12 ... 142 C1
Hathaway Gdns CHDH RM6 ... 123 N3
WEA W13 ... 134 E7
Hathaway Rd CROY/NA CR0 ... 203 J7
GRAYS RM17 ... 167 N2
Hatherleigh Cl CHSGTN KT9 ... 219 J2
MRDN SM4 ... 201 K4
Hatherleigh Gdns POTB/CUF EN6 .. 59 N8
Hatherleigh Rd RSLP HA4 ... 113 H7
Hatherleigh Wy HARH RM3 ... 105 L9
Hatherley Crs SCUP DA14 ... 185 K5
Hatherley Gdns CEND/HSY/T N8 .. 118 F4
EHAM E6 ... 142 A5
Hatherley Gv BAY/PAD W2 ... 8 C5
Hatherley Rd RCH/KEW TW9 ... 155 L7
SCUP DA14 ... 185 K5
WALTH E17 ... 120 C2
Hatherley St WEST SW1P ... 17 H6
Hathern Gdns ELTH/MOT SE9 .. 184 D1
Hatherop Rd HPTN TW12 ... 175 N10
Hathersage Ct IS N1 ... 6 G1
Hathersham La HORL RH6 ... 280 C1
Hatherwood ASHTD KT21 ... 237 J6
Hathorne Cl PECK SE15 ... 160 A4
Hathway St PECK SE15 ... 160 C8
Hatley Av BARK/HLT IG6 ... 122 F2
Hatley Cl FBAR/BDGN N11 ... 98 A6
Hatley Rd HOLWY N7 ... 118 D2
Hatteraick St BERM/RHTH SE16 .. 160 B1
Hattersfield Cl BELV DA17 ... 164 A3
Hatters La WATW WD18 ... 72 F9
Hatton Av SLN SL2 ... 129 J6
Hatton Cl CDH/CHF RM16 ... 167 J2
GVW DA11 ... 190 B6
WOOL/PLUM SE18 ... 162 G6
Hatton Gdn HCIRC EC1N ... 12 B3
Hatton Gdns MTCM CR4 ... 202 A5
Hatton Gn EBED/NFELT TW14 .. 174 A3
Hatton Gv WDR/YW UB7 ... 151 N1
Hatton Hl BFOR GU20 ... 212 B2
Hatton Pl HCIRC EC1N ... 12 B2
Hatton Rd CHES/WCR EN8 ... 62 C5
CROY/NA CR0 ... 203 H8
EBED/NFELT TW14 ... 174 D3
HTHAIR TW6 ... 152 G10
Hatton Rw STJWD NW8 ... 9 M2
Hatton St STJWD NW8 ... 9 M2
Hatton Wall HCIRC EC1N ... 12 A3
Havana Cl ROM RM1 ... 124 D4
Havana Rd WIM/MER SW19 ... 179 K5
Havannah St POP/IOD E14 ... 160 E1
Havant Rd WALTH E17 ... 121 H1
Havelock Pl HRW HA1 ... 114 D4
Havelock Rd BELV DA17 ... 164 A3
CROY/NA CR0 ... 203 N9
DART DA1 ... 187 J3
GVW DA11 ... 190 C4
HAYES BR2 ... 206 B8
KGLGY WD4 ... 54 C8
KTN/HRWW/W HA3 ... 114 D1
NWDGN UB2 ... 153 M2
TOTM N17 ... 99 P10
WIM/MER SW19 ... 179 M8
Havelock St IL IG1 ... 122 D10
IS N1 ... 5 M1
Havelock Ter VX/NE SW8 ... 158 C5
Havelock Wk FSTH SE23 ... 182 B4
Haven Cl ELTH/MOT SE9 ... 184 C1
HAT AL10 ... 40 C3
SCUP DA14 ... 185 M9
SWLY BR8 ... 208 G2
WIM/MER SW19 ... 178 G6
YEAD UB4 ... 132 F7
Havenfield KGLGY WD4 ... 53 L7
Haven Gdns CRAWE RH10 ... 285 P4
Havengore Av GVE DA12 ... 191 H3
Haven Gn EA W5 ... 135 K4

Havenhurst Ri ENC/FH EN2 ... 79 H6
Haven La EA W5 ... 135 K8
Haven Pl CDH/CHF RM16 ... 167 P1
Haven Rd ASHF TW15 ... 174 C7
Haven St CAMTN NW1 ... 4 E1
The Haven GRAYS RM17 ... 168 C4
RCH/KEW TW9 ... 155 M9
SUN TW16 ... 175 H10
Havenwood WBLY HA9 ... 115 N8
Havercroft Cl STAL AL1 ... 38 B8
Haverfield Gdns RCH/KEW TW9 .. 155 M6
Haverfield Rd BOW E3 ... 140 C5
Haverford Wy EDGW HA8 ... 95 L9
Havergal Av SL SL1 ... 128 C10
Havering Dr ROM RM1 ... 124 F2
Havering Gdns CHDH RM6 ... 123 M3
Havering Rd CRW RM5 ... 104 E10
ROM RM1 ... 124 F2
Havering St WCHPL E1 ... 140 C8
Havering Wy BARK IG11 ... 143 L5
Havers Av WOT/HER KT12 ... 217 L2
Haversham Cl CRAWE RH10 ... 284 A7
TWK TW1 ... 177 J2
Haverstock Hl HAMP NW3 ... 3 P1
Haverstock Rd KTTN NW5 ... 118 B10
Haverstock St IS N1 ... 6 D8
Haverthwaite Rd ORP BR6 ... 206 C10
Havil St CMBW SE5 ... 159 L6
Havisham Pl STRHM/NOR SW16 .. 181 J9
Hawarden Gv HNHL SE24 ... 181 K3
Hawarden Hl CRICK NW2 ... 116 D8
Hawarden Rd CTHM CR3 ... 241 K7
WALTH E17 ... 120 C2
Haward Rd HOD EN11 ... 45 H1
Hawbridge Rd WAN E11 ... 121 J6
Hawes Cl NTHWD HA6 ... 92 G8
Hawes La WAB EN9 ... 81 H4
WWKM BR4 ... 205 H8
Hawes Rd BMLY BR1 ... 205 N1
KWD/TDW/WH KT20 ... 238 C6
UED N18 ... 100 A7
Hawes St IS N1 ... 6 D4
Haweswater Dr GSTN WD25 ... 55 K10
Hawfield Bank ORP BR6 ... 207 N10
Hawfield Gdns LCOL/BKTW AL2 .. 56 C2
Hawgood St BOW E3 ... 140 F7
Hawk Cl WAB EN9 ... 63 H10
Hawkdene CHING E4 ... 80 G10
Hawkenbury HLWW/ROY CM19 .. 46 D3
Hawke Park Rd WDGN N22 ... 119 J1
Hawke Rd BERM/RHTH SE16 ... 160 C10
Hawke Rd NRWD SE19 ... 181 L9
Hawkesbury Rd PUT/ROE SW15 .. 178 E1
Hawkes Cl GRAYS RM17 ... 167 N5
Hawkesfield Rd FSTH SE23 ... 182 B5
Hawkesley Cl TWK TW1 ... 176 F7
Hawkesmoor Rd CRAWW RH11 .. 283 H9
Hawkes Pl SEV TN13 ... 265 H3
Hawkes Rd EBED/NFELT TW14 .. 175 H3
MTCM CR4 ... 201 P1
Hawkesworth Cl NTHWD HA6 .. 92 F8
Hawkewood Rd SUN TW16 ... 197 J3
Hawkhirst Rd PUR/KEN CR8 ... 241 L2
Hawkhurst COB KT11 ... 217 P10
Hawkhurst Gdns CRW RM5 ... 104 E2
Hawkhurst Rd STRHM/NOR SW16 .. 180 E10
Hawkhurst Wk CRAWE RH10 .. 284 C9
Hawkhurst Wy NWMAL KT3 ... 200 A5
WWKM BR4 ... 204 D9
Hawkinge Wy HCH RM12 ... 55 K1
Hawkins Av GVE DA12 ... 190 F7
Hawkins Cl BORE WD6 ... 75 P6
EDGW HA8 ... 96 A6
HRW HA1 ... 114 C5
Hawkins Rd CRAWE RH10 ... 283 P9
TEDD TW11 ... 176 G9
Hawkins Wy CAT SE6 ... 182 F8
Hawkley Gdns WNWD SE27 ... 181 J5
Hawkridge Cl CHDH RM6 ... 123 M4
Hawksbrook La BECK BR3 ... 204 C6
Hawkshead La BRKMPK AL9 ... 59 H4
Hawkshead Rd CHSWK W4 ... 156 B1
WLSDN NW10 ... 136 C2
Hawks Hl EPP CM16 ... 66 B3
LHD/OX KT22 ... 236 E5
Hawkshill Cl ESH/CLAY KT10 ... 217 P3
Hawks Hill Cl LHD/OX KT22 ... 236 E9
Hawks Hill Ct LHD/OX KT22 ... 236 E9
Hawkshill Dr HHW HP1 ... 35 H9
Hawkshill Rd SLN SL2 ... 128 F5
Hawkshill Wy ESH/CLAY KT10 .. 217 N3
Hawkslade Rd PECK SE15 ... 182 C1
Hawksley Rd STNW/STAM N16 .. 119 M8
Hawksmead Cl PEND EN3 ... 80 C1
Hawksmoor RAD WD7 ... 57 M9
Hawksmoor Cl EHAM E6 ... 142 B3
WOOL/PLUM SE18 ... 163 H4
Hawksmoor Ms WCHPL E1 ... 140 A9
Hawksmoor St HMSMTH W6 ... 156 G5
Hawksmouth CHING E4 ... 100 C1
Hawks Rd KUT KT1 ... 199 L2
Hawkstone Rd BERM/RHTH SE16 .. 160 B3
Hawksview COB KT11 ... 217 N3
Hawksway STA TW18 ... 173 H6
Hawkswell Cl WOKN/KNAP GU21 .. 231 L3
Hawkswood La CDH/LGLY SL3 .. 110 C10
Hawkwood Crs CHING E4 ... 80 G10
Hawkwood Dell GT/LBKH KT23 .. 253 P2
Hawkwood La CHST BR7 ... 206 F1
Hawkwood Mt CLPT E5 ... 120 A6
Hawkwood Ri GT/LBKH KT23 .. 253 P2
Hawlands Dr PIN HA5 ... 113 M5
Hawley Cl HPTN TW12 ... 175 N9
Hawley Crs CAMTN NW1 ... 4 D1
DART DA1 ... 187 M5
UED N18 ... 100 C4
Hawley Ms CAMTN NW1 ... 4 C1
Hawley Rd CAMTN NW1 ... 4 D1
DART DA1 ... 187 M5
UED N18 ... 100 C4
Hawley St CAMTN NW1 ... 4 D1
Haworth Rd CRAWE RH10 ... 284 D8
Hawth Av CRAWE RH10 ... 284 B7
Hawth Cl CRAWE RH10 ... 284 A7
Hawthorn Av BELV DA17 ... 164 A3
RAIN RM13 ... 145 J6
RBRW/HUT CM13 ... 107 L4
THHTH CR7 ... 203 J1
WCHMH N21 ... 99 H2
Hawthorn Centre HRW HA1 ... 114 E2
Hawthorn Cl ABLGY WD5 ... 54 C8
BNSTD SM7 ... 221 H6
CRAWW RH11 ... 283 M4
GVE DA12 ... 190 E7
HARP AL5 ... 20 C1
HEST TW5 ... 153 J6
HPTN TW12 ... 175 P8
IVER SL0 ... 130 F5
REDH RH1 ... 276 B5
STMC/STPC BR5 ... 206 B5
WAT WD17 ... 72 C4
WOKS/MYFD GU22 ... 232 B6
Hawthorn Crs SAND/SEL CR2 ... 224 B7
Hawthornden Cl
NFNCH/WDSP N12 ... 97 P7
Hawthorndene Cl HAYES BR2 .. 205 L9
Hawthorndene Rd HAYES BR2 .. 205 M9
Hawthorn Dr DEN/HRF UB9 ... 131 M1
RYLN/HDSTN HA2 ... 113 P4

WWKM BR4 ... 225 K1
Hawthorne Av BH/WHM TN16 .. 244 A1
CAR SM5 ... 222 B4
CHESW EN7 ... 62 A6
HRW HA1 ... 114 F4
MTCM CR4 ... 201 J2
RSLP HA4 ... 113 J4
SL SL3 ... 150 A5
Hawthorne Cl BMLY BR1 ... 206 C3
CHESW EN7 ... 62 A7
IS N1 ... 7 H1
SUT SM1 ... 209 P10
WDR/YW UB7 ... 151 N3
Hawthorne Ct WDSR SL4 ... 170 A4
WDR/YW UB7 ... 152 A1
Hawthorne Gv CDALE/KGS NW9 .. 115 P5
Hawthorne Pl EW KT17 ... 220 B8
Hawthorne Rd BMLY BR1 ... 206 C3
EGH TW20 ... 172 F8
RAD WD7 ... 56 F10
UED N18 ... 99 N7
WALTH E17 ... 120 F1
Hawthornes HAT AL10 ... 40 C6
Hawthornes Wy ED N9 ... 99 N3
RGUE GU4 ... 250 E6
Hawthorn Farm Av NTHLT UB5 .. 133 M3
Hawthorn Gdns EA W5 ... 155 J2
Hawthorn Gv ENC/FH EN2 ... 79 L4
PGE/AN SE20 ... 204 A1
Hawthorn Hatch BTFD TW8 ... 135 K8
Hawthorn La HHW HP1 ... 35 J5
SLN SL2 ... 128 E2
Hawthorn Ms HDN NW4 ... 97 H9
Hawthorn Pl ERITH DA8 ... 164 D4
HYS/HAR UB3 ... 132 G9
Hawthorn Rd BKHH IG9 ... 101 P5
CEND/HSY/T N8 ... 118 F1
DART DA1 ... 187 L5
HOD EN11 ... 44 D1
RPLY/SEND GU23 ... 233 J10
SUT SM1 ... 221 N2
WLGTN SM6 ... 222 C4
WLSDN NW10 ... 136 D2
WOKS/MYFD GU22 ... 232 A6
Hawthorns HART DA3 ... 211 L4
HLWS CM18 ... 47 J5
WFD IG8 ... 101 M4
WGCW AL8 ... 22 G3
The Hawthorns BERK HP4 ... 33 M4
CSTG HP8 ... 69 P6
DTCH/LGLY SL3 ... 151 J7
EW KT17 ... 220 C3
HHS/BOV HP3 ... 35 J10
OXTED RH8 ... 261 M9
RKW/CH/CXG WD3 ... 90 G6
Hawthorn Ter NKENS W10 ... 8 A1
Hawthorn Wk NKENS W10 ... 8 A1
Hawthorn Wy ADL/WDHM KT15 .. 215 L6
CHOB/PIR GU24 ... 230 F2
CSHM HP5 ... 51 J5
LCOL/BKTW AL2 ... 37 P10
REDH RH1 ... 276 C2
SHPTN TW17 ... 196 E4
Hawtrees RAD WD7 ... 74 F1
Hawtrey Av NTHLT UB5 ... 133 L4
Hawtrey Cl SL SL1 ... 149 N1
Hawtrey Dr RSLP HA4 ... 113 H5
Hawtrey Rd HAMP NW3 ... 3 N4
Haxted Rd BMLY BR1 ... 205 N1
Haybourn Md HHW HP1 ... 35 L3
Hayburn Wy HCH RM12 ... 124 C6
Hay Cl BORE WD6 ... 75 P6
SRTFD E15 ... 141 K2
Haycroft Cl PUR/KEN CR8 ... 241 N7
Haycroft Gdns WLSDN NW10 .. 136 D3
Haycroft Rd BRXS/STRHM SW2 .. 180 F1
SURB KT6 ... 199 J3
Hay Currie St POP/IOD E14 ... 140 G8
Hayday Rd CAN/RD E16 ... 141 M7
Haydens Cl STMC/STPC BR5 ... 207 M7
Hayden's Pl NTGHL W11 ... 8 C2
Haydens Rd HLWW/ROY CM19 .. 46 F1
Haydn Av PUR/KEN CR8 ... 241 H1
Haydock Av NTHLT UB5 ... 133 P1
Haydock Cl HCH RM12 ... 125 N9
Haydock Gn NTHLT UB5 ... 133 P1
Haydon Cl CDALE/KGS NW9 ... 115 P2
EN EN1 ... 79 P9
RYLN/HDSTN HA2 ... 114 A4
Haydon Dr PIN HA5 ... 113 H2
Haydon Park Rd WIM/MER SW19 .. 179 K6
Haydon Pl GU GU1 ... 268 A1
Haydon Rd BCTR RM8 ... 123 M7
OXHEY WD19 ... 73 H10
Haydon's Rd WIM/MER SW19 .. 179 M9
Haydon St TWRH EC3N ... 13 L7
Haydon Wy BTSEA SW11 ... 157 M10
Hayes Barton WOKS/MYFD GU22 .. 232 G5
Hayes Cha WWKM BR4 ... 205 J6
Hayes Cl HAYES BR2 ... 205 M9
Hayes Crs CHEAM SM3 ... 220 G1
GLDGN NW11 ... 117 J3
Hayes Dr RAIN RM13 ... 145 J2
Hayes End Dr YEAD UB4 ... 132 E2
Hayes End Rd YEAD UB4 ... 132 E2
Hayesford Park Dr HAYES BR2 .. 205 L5
Hayes Gdn HAYES BR2 ... 205 M9
Hayes Hl HAYES BR2 ... 205 J6
Hayes Hill Rd HAYES BR2 ... 205 K6
Hayes La BECK BR3 ... 205 H4
HAYES BR2 ... 205 L4
PUR/KEN CR8 ... 241 J2
Hayes Mead Rd HAYES BR2 ... 205 K6
Hayes Pl CAMTN NW1 ... 9 P2
Hayes Rd HAYES BR2 ... 205 M4
NWDGN UB2 ... 153 J3
RDART DA2 ... 188 D3
Hayes St HAYES BR2 ... 205 M8
The Hayes EPSOM KT18 ... 238 A5
Hayes Wk HORL RH6 ... 281 H1
Hayes Wy BECK BR3 ... 205 H4
Hayes Wood Av HAYES BR2 ... 205 M8
Hayfield Cl BUSH WD23 ... 74 B5
Hayfield Pas WCHPL E1 ... 140 B6
Hayfield Rd STMC/STPC BR5 ... 207 K3
Hayfields HORL RH6 ... 280 D3
Haygarth Pl WIM/MER SW19 ... 178 G8
Haygreen Cl KUTN/CMB KT2 ... 177 N9
Hay Green La BRWN CM15 ... 87 J1
Hay Hl MYFR/PICC W1J ... 10 E8
Hayland Cl CDALE/KGS NW9 ... 116 A2
Hay La CDALE/KGS NW9 ... 116 A2
DTCH/LGLY SL3 ... 110 A9
Hayle TIL RM18 ... 169 M2
Hayles St LBTH SE11 ... 18 C5
Hayling Av FELT TW13 ... 175 H6
Hayling Cl OXHEY WD19 ... 92 G4
Hayman Crs YEAD UB4 ... 132 E4
Haymarket STJS SW1Y ... 11 J8
Haymeads WGCW AL8 ... 23 H2
Haymeads Dr ESH/CLAY KT10 .. 218 B3
Haymer Gdns WPK KT4 ... 200 D10
Haymerle Rd PECK SE15 ... 19 N9
Haymill Cl GFD/PVL UB6 ... 134 C5
Haymill Rd SLN SL2 ... 128 C6
Hayne Rd BECK BR3 ... 204 G1
Haynes Cl DTCH/LGLY SL3 ... 150 C4
FBAR/BDGN N11 ... 98 A4
LEW SE13 ... 161 K9
RPLY/SEND GU23 ... 233 J10
TOTM N17 ... 100 A3
WCCE AL7 ... 23 M6
Haynes La NRWD SE19 ... 181 M9

Haynes Md BERK HP4 ... 33 M3
Haynes Rd ALP/SUD HA0 ... 135 K2
EMPK RM11 ... 125 L3
GVW DA11 ... 190 C6
Hayne St STBT EC1A ... 12 D3
Haynt Wk RYNPK SW20 ... 201 H3
Hayse Hl WDSR SL4 ... 148 C7
Haysleigh Gdns PGE/AN SE20 ... 203 P2
Hay's Ms MYFR/PICC W1J ... 10 E8
Haysoms Cl ROM RM1 ... 124 F2
Haystall Cl YEAD UB4 ... 132 F4
Hay St BETH E2 ... 7 P6
Hays Wk BELMT SM2 ... 220 G6
Hayter Rd BRXS/STRHM SW2 ... 180 F1
The Haywain OXTED RH8 ... 261 J6
Hayward Cl DART DA1 ... 186 E1
WIM/MER SW19 ... 179 L10
Hayward Gdns PUT/ROE SW15 ... 178 F2
Hayward Rd THDIT KT7 ... 198 E8
TRDG/WHET N20 ... 97 M3
Haywards CRAWE RH10 ... 284 E4
Haywards Cl CHDH RM6 ... 123 M3
Haywards WDSR SL4 ... 148 E4
Hayward's Pl CLKNW EC1R ... 12 C2
Haywood Cl PIN HA5 ... 93 L10
Haywood Pk RKW/CH/CXG WD3 ... 71 J9
Haywood Ri ORP BR6 ... 227 H2
Haywoods Dr HHW HP1 ... 35 J9
Haywoods Ct WAB EN9 ... 63 L10
Hazel Av GU GU1 ... 249 P6
WDR/YW UB7 ... 152 B2
Hazel Bank BRYLDS KT5 ... 199 P8
Hazelbank Rd CAT SE6 ... 183 J5
CHERT KT16 ... 195 M7
Hazelbourne Rd BAL SW12 ... 180 C2
Hazelbrouck Gdns BARK/HLT IG6 ... 102 C3
Hazelbury Av ABLGY WD5 ... 54 D8
Hazelbury Cl WIM/MER SW19 ... 201 M1
Hazelbury Gn ED N18 ... 99 M4
Hazelbury La ED N9 ... 99 M4
Hazel Cl BTFD TW8 ... 154 C6
CHESW ... 61 M2
CRAWW RH11 ... 283 N4
CROY/NA CR0 ... 204 C7
EGH TW20 ... 171 N9
HCH RM12 ... 125 J8
MTCM CR4 ... 202 E4
PLMGR N13 ... 99 L4
REIG RH2 ... 275 M2
WHTN TW2 ... 176 B5
Hazelcroft PIN HA5 ... 93 P7
Hazelcroft Cl PUR/KEN CR8 ... 241 L1
Hazeldean Rd WLSDN NW10 ... 136 A2
Hazeldell Link HHW HP1 ... 35 H7
Hazeldell Rd HHW HP1 ... 35 H7
Hazeldene ADL/WDHM KT15 ... 215 M2
CHES/WCR EN8 ... 62 D8
Hazeldene Ct PUR/KEN CR8 ... 241 L1
Hazeldene Dr PIN HA5 ... 113 K1
Hazeldene Gdns HGDN/ICK UB10 ... 132 D3
Hazeldene Rd BCTR RM8 ... 123 L7
WELL DA16 ... 163 M8
Hazeldon Rd BROCKY SE4 ... 182 C1
Hazel Dr ERITH DA8 ... 165 H7
RPLY/SEND GU23 ... 251 J1
SOCK/AV RM15 ... 147 H5
Hazeleigh RBRW/HUT CM13 ... 107 N4
Hazeleigh Gdns WFD IG8 ... 102 B6
Hazel End SWLY BR8 ... 208 F5
Hazel Gdns CDH/CHF RM16 ... 168 B2
EDGW HA8 ... 96 B7
Hazelgreen Cl WCHMH N21 ... 99 J2
Hazel Gv ALP/SUD HA0 ... 135 K3
CHDH RM6 ... 123 P1
EN EN1 ... 79 P10
GSTN WD25 ... 73 J7
HAT AL10 ... 40 C7
ORP BR6 ... 206 E9
STA TW18 ... 173 L9
SYD SE26 ... 182 C7
WGCE AL7 ... 23 L4
Hazelhurst BECK BR3 ... 205 J1
HORL RH6 ... 280 D3
Hazelhurst Cl RGUE GU4 ... 250 C5
Hazelhurst Dr CRAWE RH10 ... 284 F7
Hazelhurst Rd SL SL1 ... 128 B4
TOOT SW17 ... 179 M7
Hazell Crs ROMW/RG RM7 ... 104 C9
Hazell Pk AMSS HP7 ... 69 H5
Hazelleville Rd ARCH N19 ... 118 C5
Hazel Md SLN SL2 ... 129 L1
Hazel Md BAR EN5 ... 76 E9
Hazelmere Av NTHLT UB5 ... 133 N4
Hazelmere Cl EBED/NFELT TW14 ... 174 C2
LHD/OX KT22 ... 236 C5
NTHLT UB5 ... 133 N4
Hazelmere Dr NTHLT UB5 ... 133 N4
Hazelmere Gdns EMPK RM11 ... 125 J3
NTHLT UB5 ... 133 N4
SLN SL2 ... 129 N10
STALE/WH AL4 ... 39 H3
STMC/STPC BR5 ... 206 F4
Hazelmere Wk NTHLT UB5 ... 133 N4
Hazelmere Wy HAYES BR2 ... 205 M6
Hazel Ri EMPK RM11 ... 125 K4
Hazel Rd BERK HP4 ... 34 A6
BF/WBF KT14 ... 215 K10
DART DA1 ... 187 L5
ERITH DA8 ... 165 H7
LCOL/BKTW AL2 ... 56 A4
REIG RH2 ... 275 M2
SRTFD E15 ... 121 K10
WLSDN NW10 ... 136 E5
The Hazels WLYN AL6 ... 23 P7
Hazeltree La NTHLT UB5 ... 133 M5
Hazel Tree Rd WATN WD24 ... 73 J8
Hazel Wk HAYES BR2 ... 206 D6
Hazel Wy CHING E4 ... 100 E7
COUL/CHIP CR5 ... 240 A5
LHD/OX KT22 ... 236 B8
Hazelwick Av CRAWE RH10 ... 284 B5
Hazelwick Mill La CRAWE RH10 ... 284 B5
Hazelwick Rd CRAWE RH10 ... 284 B6
Hazelwood CRAWW RH11 ... 283 K7
TIL RM18 ... 169 K3
Hazelwood Av MRDN SM4 ... 201 L4
Hazelwood Cl CLPT E5 ... 120 D8
CRAWW RH10 ... 285 N5
CSHM HP5 ... 51 J5
EA W5 ... 155 K1
RYLN/HDSTN HA2 ... 114 A2
Hazelwood Ct SURB KT6 ... 199 K6
Hazelwood Crs PLMGR N13 ... 99 H2
Hazelwood Dr PIN HA5 ... 93 H10
STALE/WH AL4 ... 39 H10
Hazelwood Gdns BRWN CM15 ... 86 F10
Hazelwood Gv SAND/SEL CR2 ... 224 A10
Hazelwood Hts OXTED RH8 ... 261 M7
Hazelwood La ABLGY WD5 ... 54 E8
COUL/CHIP CR5 ... 240 A5
PLMGR N13 ... 99 H2
Hazelwood Park Cl BARK/HLT IG6 ... 103 H6
Hazelwood Rd EN EN1 ... 79 N10
OXTED RH8 ... 261 N8
RKW/CH/CXG WD3 ... 72 D10
RSEV TN14 ... 226 G8
WALTH E17 ... 120 C3
WOKN/KNAP GU21 ... 231 K4
Hazlebury Rd FUL/PGN SW6 ... 157 L8
Hazledean Rd CROY/NA CR0 ... 203 L10
Hazledene Rd CHSWK W4 ... 155 P5
Hazlemere Gdns WPK KT4 ... 200 E8
Hazlewell Rd PUT/ROE SW15 ... 178 F1
Hazlewood Crs NKENS W10 ... 8 B2
Hazlitt Cl FELT TW13 ... 175 M7

Hazlitt Rd WKENS W14 ... 14 A4
Hazon Wy HOR/WEW KT19 ... 220 A4
Heacham Av HGDN/ICK UB10 ... 112 D8
Headcorn Rd BMLY BR1 ... 183 L8
THHTH CR7 ... 202 C4
TOTM N17 ... 99 N8
Headfort Pl KTBR SW1X ... 16 D2
Headingley Cl CHESW EN7 ... 61 N2
RAD WD7 ... 57 K8
Headington Rd WAND/EARL SW18 ... 179 M4
Headlam Rd CLAP SW4 ... 180 E2
Headlam St WCHPL E1 ... 140 A6
Headley Ap IL IG1 ... 122 D3
Headley Av WLGTN SM6 ... 222 G2
Headley Cha CHSGTN KT9 ... 219 M3
CRAWE RH10 ... 284 E3
Headley Common Rd EPSOM KT18 ... 256 A3
Headley Dr CROY/NA CR0 ... 225 H4
GNTH/NBYPK IG2 ... 122 C4
KWD/TDW/WH KT20 ... 238 E5
Headley Gv KWD/TDW/WH KT20 ... 238 E6
KWD/TDW/WH KT20 ... 256 A4
Headley Heath Ap KWD/TDW/WH KT20 ... 255 N6
Headley Rd ASHTD KT21 ... 237 P4
EPSOM KT18 ... 237 P6
LHD/OX KT22 ... 237 H8
RDKG RH5 ... 255 H5
Headstone Dr HRW HA1 ... 114 D1
KTN/HRWW/W HA3 ... 114 D1
Headstone Gdns RYLN/HDSTN HA2 ... 114 A2
Headstone La KTN/HRWW/W HA3 ... 94 A10
RYLN/HDSTN HA2 ... 94 A10
Headstone Rd HRW HA1 ... 114 D2
Head St WCHPL E1 ... 140 C8
WCHPL E1 ... 140 C8
Headway Cl RCHPK/HAM TW10 ... 177 H7
The Headway EW KT17 ... 220 C5
Heald St NWCR SE14 ... 160 E7
Healey Rd WATW WD18 ... 72 G10
Healey St CAMTN NW1 ... 4 E2
Healy Dr ORP BR6 ... 207 J10
Heard's La BRWN CM15 ... 87 L7
Hearne Rd CHSWK W4 ... 155 M4
Hearne's Cl BEAC HP9 ... 89 J6
Hearn Ri NTHLT UB5 ... 133 L3
Hearn Rd ROM RM1 ... 124 C4
Hearn's Buildings WALW SE17 ... 19 H6
Hearns Cl STMC/STPC BR5 ... 207 N4
Hearns Rd STMC/STPC BR5 ... 207 N4
Hearn St SDTCH EC2A ... 13 K2
Hearnville Rd BAL SW12 ... 180 B4
Heatham Pk WHTN TW2 ... 176 E3
Heath Av BXLYHN DA7 ... 163 N5
STALW/RED AL3 ... 38 E2
Heathbourne Rd BUSH WD23 ... 94 E2
STAN HA7 ... 94 E2
Heathbridge WEY KT13 ... 216 B4
Heath Brow HAMP NW3 ... 117 M8
HHW HP1 ... 35 M8
Heath Cl BNSTD SM7 ... 221 L10
EA W5 ... 135 L6
GLDGN NW11 ... 117 L5
GPK RM2 ... 125 H1
HARP AL5 ... 20 A4
HHW HP1 ... 35 M7
HYS/HAR UB3 ... 152 E6
POTB/CUF EN6 ... 59 L6
STMC/STPC BR5 ... 207 N6
STWL/WRAY TW19 ... 173 M2
SWLY BR8 ... 208 F2
VW GU25 ... 194 A4
Heathclose Av DART DA1 ... 187 J3
Heathclose Rd DART DA1 ... 187 H4
Heathcote KWD/TDW/WH KT20 ... 238 G8
Heathcote Av CLAY IG5 ... 102 C10
HAT AL10 ... 40 D2
Heathcote Gdns HLWE CM17 ... 47 P1
Heathcote Gv CHING E4 ... 101 N4
Heathcote Rd EPSOM KT18 ... 220 A10
TWK TW1 ... 176 C2
Heathcote St BMSBY WC1N ... 11 N1
Heathcote Wy WDR/YW UB7 ... 131 N10
Heathcroft EA W5 ... 135 L6
Heathcroft Av SUN TW16 ... 174 G10
Heathdale Av HSLWW TW4 ... 153 M9
Heathdene KWD/TDW/WH KT20 ... 239 H5
Heathdene Dr BELV DA17 ... 164 C3
Heathdene Rd STRHM/NOR SW16 ... 180 G10
WLGTN SM6 ... 222 C4
Heathdown Rd WOKS/MYFD GU22 ... 232 G1
Heath Dr BELMT SM2 ... 221 M5
CHOB/PIR GU24 ... 230 F1
EPP CM16 ... 83 H1
GPK RM2 ... 125 H1
KWD/TDW/WH KT20 ... 256 D1
POTB/CUF EN6 ... 59 K6
RPLY/SEND GU23 ... 232 G9
RYNPK SW20 ... 200 F4
Heathedge FSTH SE23 ... 182 A5
Heathend Rd BXLY DA5 ... 186 F4
Heatherbank CHST BR7 ... 206 D2
ELTH/MOT SE9 ... 162 C10
Heatherbank Cl DART DA1 ... 186 F2
Heather Cl ABLGY WD5 ... 55 H8
ADL/WDHM KT15 ... 215 L6
BRWN CM15 ... 86 G9
CRAWE RH10 ... 285 J3
EHAM E6 ... 142 D4
GUW GU2 ... 249 N8
HPTN TW12 ... 197 N1
ISLW TW7 ... 176 C1
KWD/TDW/WH KT20 ... 239 H8
LEW SE13 ... 183 J3
REDH RH1 ... 258 C7
ROM RM1 ... 104 F2
UX/CGN UB8 ... 132 A7
VX/NE SW8 ... 158 G4
WOKN/KNAP GU21 ... 231 P1
Heatherdale Cl KUTN/CMB KT2 ... 177 M10
Heatherdeane EHSLY KT24 ... 252 E1
Heatherdene Cl FNCH N3 ... 97 M8
MTCM CR4 ... 201 N4
Heatherden Gn IVER SL0 ... 130 F3
Heather Dr ASC SL5 ... 192 G7
DART DA1 ... 187 H3
ENC/FH EN2 ... 79 J6
ROM RM1 ... 104 E10
Heather Gln ROM RM1 ... 104 E10
Heatherlands HORL RH6 ... 280 D3
SUN TW16 ... 175 H9
Heather La WDR/YW UB7 ... 131 J8
Heatherley Dr CLAY IG5 ... 122 C1
Heather Park Dr ALP/SUD HA0 ... 135 M2
Heather Pl ESH/CLAY KT10 ... 218 A1
Heather Ri BUSH WD23 ... 73 N6
Heather Rd CHING E4 ... 100 F6
CRICK NW2 ... 116 C1
LEE/GVPK SE12 ... 183 M5
WGCW AL8 ... 23 L4
Heatherset Cl ESH/CLAY KT10 ... 218 B2
Heatherset Gdns STRHM/NOR SW16 ... 180 G10
Heatherside Dr VW GU25 ... 193 M6
Heatherside Gdns SLN SL2 ... 109 J8
Heatherside Rd HOR/WEW KT19 ... 220 A4

SCUP DA14 ... 185 M6
Heathers Land RDKG RH5 ... 273 H5
The Heathers STWL/WRAY TW19 ... 174 A3
Heatherton Pk EPSOM KT18 ...
Heathervale Rd ADL/WDHM KT15 ... 215 L6
Heather Wk CHOB/PIR GU24 ... 230 C7
EDGW HA8 ... 95 N6
HORL RH6 ... 281 K4
NKENS W10 ... 8
Heather Wy CHOB/PIR GU24 ... 213 K4
POTB/CUF EN6 ... 59 J8
ROM RM1 ... 104 E9
SAND/SEL CR2 ... 224 C5
STAN HA7 ... 94 E7
Heatherwood Cl MNPK E12 ... 121 N7
Heatherwood Dr YEAD UB4 ... 132 A5
Heath Farm La STALW/RED AL3 ... 38 D4
Heathfield CHING E4 ... 101 H4
CHST BR7 ... 184 F9
COB KT11 ... 217 P10
CRAWE RH10 ... 284 E4
Heathfield Av ASC SL5 ... 192 D5
WAND/EARL SW18 ... 179 N3
Heathfield Cl CAN/RD E16 ... 142 A7
HAYES BR2 ... 225 P2
POTB/CUF EN6 ... 59 L6
WOKS/MYFD GU22 ... 232 D4
Heathfield Dr MTCM CR4 ... 201 P1
REDH RH1 ... 275 P5
WIM/MER SW19 ... 179 P10
Heathfield Gdns CHSWK W4 ... 155 P4
GLDGN NW11 ... 116 G4
WAND/EARL SW18 ... 179 N2
Heathfield La CHST BR7 ... 184 F9
Heathfield North WHTN TW2 ... 176 B3
Heathfield Park CRICK NW2 ... 136 F1
Heathfield Park Dr CHDH RM6 ... 123 L3
Heathfield Ri RSLP HA4 ... 112 D5
Heathfield Rd ACT W3 ... 155 N1
BMLY BR1 ... 183 L10
BUSH WD23 ... 94 A3
BXLYHS DA6 ... 164 A10
CROY/NA CR0 ... 223 L2
HAYES BR2 ... 225 P2
SEV TN13 ... 246 G8
WAND/EARL SW18 ... 179 M2
WOKS/MYFD GU22 ... 232 D4
WOT/HER KT12 ... 217 M1
Heathfield South WHTN TW2 ... 176 C3
Heathfield Sq WAND/EARL SW18 ... 179 N3
Heathfield Ter CHSWK W4 ... 155 H5
WOOL/PLUM SE18 ... 143 P10
Heathfield V SAND/SEL CR2 ... 224 C5
Heath Gdns TWK TW1 ... 176 B4
Heathgate GLDGN NW11 ... 117 L4
HERT/BAY SG13 ... 26 A8
Heath Gv PGE/AN SE20 ... 182 B10
SUN TW16 ... 174 G10
Heathhurst Rd SAND/SEL CR2 ... 223 P6
Heathland Rd STNW/STAM N16 ... 119 M6
Heathlands KWD/TDW/WH KT20 ... 238 G8
Heathlands Cl SUN TW16 ... 197 H2
TWK TW1 ... 176 E5
WOKN/KNAP GU21 ... 214 B10
Heathlands Dr STALW/RED AL3 ... 38 D4
Heathlands Ri DART DA1 ... 187 J3
Heathlands Wy HSLWW TW4 ... 175 M1
Heath La BKHTH/KID SE3 ... 161 J8
DART DA1 ... 187 J4
HERT/BAY SG13 ... 26 B9
HHW HP1 ... 35 M8
SHGR GU5 ... 269 P7
Heathlee Rd BKHTH/KID SE3 ... 161 L10
DART DA1 ... 186 F2
Heathley End CHST BR7 ... 184 F9
Heathman's Rd FUL/PGN SW6 ... 157 K7
Heath Md WIM/MER SW19 ... 178 G6
Heath Mill La RGUW GU3 ... 249 H1
Heathpark Dr BAGS GU20 ... 212 D3
Heath Park Dr BMLY BR1 ... 206 F3
Heath Park Rd GPK RM2 ... 125 H3
Heath Ridge Gn COB KT11 ... 217 P9
Heath Ri DORK RH4 ... 272 B4
HAYES BR2 ... 205 M6
PUT/ROE SW15 ... 178 G2
Heathrise RPLY/SEND GU23 ... 233 L9
Heath Ri VW GU25 ... 194 A4
Heath Rd AMS HP6 ... 50 B10
BXLY DA5 ... 187 H5
CDH/CHF RM16 ... 168 E6
CHDH RM6 ... 123 N5
CTHM CR3 ... 241 L9
DART DA1 ... 186 G2
HGDN/ICK UB10 ... 132 D6
HRW HA1 ... 114 D5
HSLW TW3 ... 154 B10
LHD/OX KT22 ... 218 B8
OXHEY WD19 ... 93 L1
POTB/CUF EN6 ... 59 L6
STAL AL1 ... 38 G5
THHTH CR7 ... 203 K3
TWK TW1 ... 176 B4
VX/NE SW8 ... 158 C8
WEY KT13 ... 216 B2
WOKN/KNAP GU21 ... 232 C1
Heathrow SHGR GU5 ... 269 L7
Heathrow Cl WDR/YW UB7 ... 151 L7
Heath's Cl EN EN1 ... 79 L6
Heathside ESH/CLAY KT10 ... 198 D10
HAMP NW3 ... 117 N9
HSLWW TW4 ... 175 N3
STALE/WH AL4 ... 39 N9
STALW/RED AL3 ... 38 D4
Heath Side STMC/STPC BR5 ... 206 F8
Heathside WEY KT13 ... 216 C2
Heathside Av BXLYHN DA7 ... 163 P8
Heathside Cl ESH/CLAY KT10 ... 198 D10
Heathside Ct KWD/TDW/WH KT20 ... 238 E9
Heathside Crs WOKS/MYFD GU22 ... 232 C3
Heathside Gdns WOKS/MYFD GU22 ... 232 D3
Heathside Park Rd WOKS/MYFD GU22 ... 232 C4
Heathside Pl KWD/TDW/WH KT20 ... 238 E9
Heathside Rd NTHWD HA6 ... 92 E5
WOKS/MYFD GU22 ... 232 C4
Heathstan Rd SHB W12 ... 136 D8
Heath St HAMP NW3 ... 117 M8
The Heath CTHM CR3 ... 241 K10
HNWL W7 ... 154 D1
RAD WD7 ...
Heath Vw EFNCH N2 ... 117 M2
EHSLY KT24 ... 252 C1
Heathview Av DART DA1 ... 186 F2
Heathview Crs DART DA1 ... 187 H3
Heath View Dr ABYW SE2 ... 163 N5
Heath View Gdns CDH/CHF RM16 ... 167 P4
Heath View Rd CDH/CHF RM16 ... 167 P1
Heathville Rd ARCH N19 ... 118 F5
Heath Vls WOOL/PLUM SE18 ... 163 H4
Heathwall St BTSEA SW11 ... 158 A9
Heath Wy ERITH DA8 ... 165 M7
IVER SL0 ... 130 D4
Heathway BKHTH/KID SE3 ... 161 M6
CROY/NA CR0 ... 204 E10
CTHM CR3 ... 259 K1
DAGW RM9 ... 124 C5
EHSLY KT24 ... 234 G10
WFD IG8 ... 101 P5

SWLY BR8 ... 208 D2
Heathwood Gdns CHARL SE7 ... 162 B3
Heathwood Wk BXLY DA5 ... 186 F4
Heaton Av HARH RM3 ... 105 J8
Heaton Cl CHING E4 ... 101 H4
HARH RM3 ... 105 K8
Heaton Grange Rd GPK RM2 ... 104 G9
Heaton Rd MTCM CR4 ... 180 B10
PECK SE15 ... 160 A9
Heaton Wy HARH RM3 ... 105 J8
Heaver Rd BTSEA SW11 ... 157 N9
Heavitree Cl WOOL/PLUM SE18 ... 143 G4
Heavitree Rd WOOL/PLUM SE18 ... 162 G4
Heay Flds WCCE AL7 ... 23 M4
Hebden Ter TOTM N17 ... 99 M7
Hebdon Rd TOOT SW17 ... 179 P6
Heber Rd CRICK NW2 ... 116 G10
EDUL SE22 ... 181 N2
Hebron Rd HMSMTH W6 ... 156 E2
Hecham Cl WALTH E17 ... 100 D10
Heckfield Pl FUL/PGN SW6 ... 157 K6
Heckford St WAP E1W ... 140 G9
Hector St WOOL/PLUM SE18 ... 163 H3
Heddington Gv HOLWY N7 ... 118 G10
Heddon Cl ISLW TW7 ... 154 F10
Heddon Court Av EBAR EN4 ... 78 A9
Heddon Rd EBAR EN4 ... 78 A9
Heddon St CONDST W1S ... 10 C8
Hedgebrooms WCCE AL7 ... 23 M4
Hedge Hl ENC/FH EN2 ... 79 J5
Hedge La PLMGR N13 ... 99 K5
Hedgemans Rd DAGW RM9 ... 143 N2
Hedgemans Wy DAGW RM9 ... 143 P1
Hedge Place Rd GRH DA9 ... 188 D2
Hedgerley GFD/PVL UB6 ... 134 B4
Hedgerley Gdns GFD/PVL UB6 ... 134 B4
Hedgerley Hl BEAC HP9 ... 108 E1
Hedgerley La BEAC HP9 ... 108 E1
SLN SL2 ... 109 K4
Hedgerow CFSP/GDCR SL9 ... 90 A2
Hedge Rw HHW HP1 ... 35 K8
Hedgerows SBW CM21 ... 30 A1
The Hedgerows GVW DA11 ... 190 B5
Hedger's Gv HOM E9 ... 140 D1
Hedger St LBTH SE11 ... 18 C5
Hedges Cl HAT AL10 ... 40 E5
Hedgeside BRKMPK AL9 ... 34 D2
Hedgeway GUW GU2 ... 267 M2
Hedgewood Gdns CLAY IG5 ... 122 D2
Hedgley St LEE/GVPK SE12 ... 183 L1
Hedingham Cl IS N1 ... 6 E4
Hedingham Rd BCTR RM8 ... 123 L10
EMPK RM11 ... 125 P6
Hedley Av WTHK RM20 ... 167 N6
Hedley Rd HSLWW TW4 ... 175 P3
STAL AL1 ... 38 G6
Hedley Rw HBRY N5 ... 119 L10
Heenan Cl BARK IG11 ... 142 F1
Heene Rd ENC/FH EN2 ... 79 L6
Heidegger Crs BARN SW13 ... 156 E6
Heigham Rd EHAM E6 ... 142 A2
Heighams RBRW/HUT CM19 ... 46 C4
Heighton Gdns CROY/NA CR0 ... 223 J2
Heights Cl BNSTD SM7 ... 239 H2
RYNPK SW20 ... 178 E10
The Heights CHARL SE7 ... 161 P4
LOU IG10 ... 82 C6
NTHLT UB5 ... 113 P10
WAB EN9 ... 63 N1
Heiron St WALW SE17 ... 18 D10
Helby Rd CLAP SW4 ... 180 D2
Helder Gv LEE/GVPK SE12 ... 183 L3
Helder St SAND/SEL CR2 ... 223 L3
Heldmann Cl ISLW TW7 ... 154 C10
Helena Cl EBAR EN4 ... 77 N4
Helena Pl HOM E9 ... 140 A3
Helena Rd EA W5 ... 135 J7
PLSTW E13 ... 141 J1
WALTH E17 ... 120 F3
WDSR SL4 ... 149 J8
WLSDN NW10 ... 116 K10
Helena Sq POP/IOD E14 ... 140 D9
Helen Av EBED/NFELT TW14 ... 175 J3
Helen Cl DART DA1 ... 187 J3
E/WMO/HCT KT8 ... 198 A4
EFNCH N2 ... 117 M1
Helen Rd EMPK RM11 ... 125 L1
Helens Ga CHES/WCR EN8 ... 62 E2
Helenslea Av GLDGN NW11 ... 117 J6
Helen's Pl BETH E2 ... 140 B5
Helen St WOOL/PLUM SE18 ... 162 E3
Helford Cl RSLP HA4 ... 112 D7
Helford Wk WOKN/KNAP GU21 ... 231 M4
Helford Wy UPMR RM14 ... 126 C4
Helgiford Gdns SUN TW16 ... 174 F10
Helions Rd HLWW/ROY CM19 ... 46 C1
Helix Gdns BRXS/STRHM SW2 ... 180 G3
Helix Rd BRXS/STRHM SW2 ... 180 G3
Helleborine GRAYS RM17 ... 167 L4
Hellings St WAP E1W ... 13 P10
Helme Cl WIM/MER SW19 ... 179 J3
Helmet Rw FSBYE EC1V ... 12 F1
Helmsdale WOKN/KNAP GU21 ... 231 N4
Helmsdale Cl ROM RM1 ... 104 F8
YEAD UB4 ... 133 M6
Helmsdale Rd ROM RM1 ... 104 F8
STRHM/NOR SW16 ... 202 D1
Helmsley Pl HACK E8 ... 140 A2
Helmsley St HACK E8 ... 140 A2
Helsinki Sq BERM/RHTH SE16 ... 160 E2
Helston Cl PIN HA5 ... 93 N8
Helston Gv HHNE HP2 ... 35 P1
Helston La WDSR SL4 ... 148 G7
Helston Pl ABLGY WD5 ... 54 G8
Helvellyn Cl EGH TW20 ... 172 F10
Helvetia St CAT SE6 ... 182 B5
Hemans St VX/NE SW8 ... 158 E6
Hemel Hempstead Rd HHS/BOV HP3 ... 36 F8
STALW/RED AL3 ... 37 J8
Hemery Rd GFD/PVL UB6 ... 133 P2
Heming Rd EDGW HA8 ... 96 C2
Hemingford Cl NFNCH/WDSPK N12 ... 98 A6
Hemingford Rd CHEAM SM3 ... 220 B10
IS N1 ... 5 P5
WAT WD17 ... 72 F2
Hemington Av FBAR/BDGN N11 ... 98 A6
Hemlock Cl KWD/TDW/WH KT20 ... 259 H10
Hemlock Rd SHB W12 ... 136 C9
Hemmen La HYS/HAR UB3 ... 132 C9
Hemming Cl HPTN TW12 ... 197 P1
Hemmings Cl SCUP DA14 ... 185 L5
The Hemmings BERK HP4 ... 33 L2
Hemming St WCHPL E1 ... 13 P2
Hemming Wy GSTN WD25 ... 73 H1
Hemmingway Cl KTTN NW5 ... 118 B9
Hemnall St EPP CM16 ... 83 M1
Hempshaw Av BNSTD SM7 ... 240 A2
Hempson Av DTCH/LGLY SL3 ... 149 P2
Hempstall WCCE AL7 ... 23 L7
Hempstead Cl BKHH IG9 ... 101 M5
Hempstead La BERK HP4 ... 34 F7
Hempstead Rd HHS/BOV HP3 ... 54 A3
WALTH E17 ... 102 E10
WAT WD17 ... 72 D2
Hemsby Rd CHSGTN KT9 ... 219 N5
Hemstal Rd KIL/WHAMP NW6 ... 2 E1
Hemsted Rd ERITH DA8 ... 164 C1
Hemswell Dr CDALE/KGS NW9 ... 96 B9
Hemsworth St IS N1 ... 7 J7
Henbit Cl KWD/TDW/WH KT20 ... 238 E5
Henbury Wy OXHEY WD19 ... 93 L2
Henchley Dene RGUE GU4 ... 250 C7
Henchman St SHB W12 ... 136 C8
Hendale Av HDN NW4 ... 116 G1

Hencroft St South SL SL1 ... 149 L2
Hendale Av HDN NW4 ... 116 G1
Henderson Av GUW GU2 ... 249 N5
Henderson Cl STALW/RED AL3 ... 38 D2
WLSDN NW10 ... 135 P1
Henderson Dr DART DA1 ... 165 P10
STJWD NW8 ... 9 L1
Henderson Pl ABLGY WD5 ... 54 G5
Henderson Rd BH/WHM TN16 ... 225 P8
CROY/NA CR0 ... 203 L6
ED N9 ... 100 A2
FSTGT E7 ... 141 P1
WAND/EARL SW18 ... 179 P3
YEAD UB4 ... 133 H5
Hendersons Cl NTHLT RM12 ... 125 J7
Hendham Rd TOOT SW17 ... 179 M5
Hendon Av FNCH N3 ... 97 H9
Hendon Gdns CRW RM5 ... 104 D7
Hendon La FNCH N3 ... 117 H1
Hendon Park Rw GLDGN NW11 ... 117 J4
Hendon Rd ED N9 ... 99 P3
Hendon Wy CRICK NW2 ... 117 H6
HDN NW4 ... 116 F4
STWL/WRAY TW19 ... 173 N1
Hendon Wood La MLHL NW7 ... 96 D1
Hendren Cl NTHLT UB5 ... 114 C10
Hendre Rd STHWK SE1 ... 19 K6
Hendrick Av BAL SW12 ... 180 C5
Heneage Crs CROY/NA CR0 ... 225 H6
Heneage La HDTCH EC3A ... 13 M4
Heneage St WCHPL E1 ... 13 N4
Henfield Cl ARCH N19 ... 118 D6
BXLY DA5 ... 186 B2
Henfield Rd WIM/MER SW19 ... 201 J4
Henfold La RDKG RH5 ... 273 K10
Hengelo Gdns MTCM CR4 ... 201 N4
Hengist Rd ERITH DA8 ... 164 D6
LEE/GVPK SE12 ... 183 N3
Hengist Wy HAYES BR2 ... 205 J4
Hengrave Rd FSTH SE23 ... 182 B3
Hengrove Ct BXLY DA5 ... 185 P4
Hengrove Crs ASHF TW15 ... 173 N6
Henley Av CHEAM SM3 ... 201 H10
Henley Bank GUW GU2 ... 267 M4
Henley Cl CRAWE RH10 ... 284 E10
GFD/PVL UB6 ... 134 B4
ISLW TW7 ... 154 E7
Henley Ct WOKS/MYFD GU22 ... 232 D6
PIN HA5 ... 113 J1
Henley Deane GVW DA11 ... 190 B7
Henley Dr BERM/RHTH SE16 ... 19 M5
KUTN/CMB KT2 ... 178 A7
Henley Ga CHOB/PIR GU24 ... 248 B3
Henley Rd CAN/RD E16 ... 162 C1
IL IG1 ... 122 F9
SL SL1 ... 128 D8
UED N18 ... 99 M5
WLSDN NW10 ... 136 F3
Henley St BTSEA SW11 ... 158 B8
Henley Wy FELT TW13 ... 175 L8
Hennel Cl FSTH SE23 ... 182 B6
Hennessy Ct WOKN/KNAP GU21 ... 214 F9
Henniker Gdns EHAM E6 ... 142 A5
Henniker Ms CHEL SW3 ... 15 J8
Henniker Rd SRTFD E15 ... 121 J10
Henningham Rd TOTM N17 ... 99 L8
Henning St BTSEA SW11 ... 157 P7
Henrietta Ms BMSBY WC1N ... 11 M1
Henrietta Pl CAVSQ/HST W1G ... 10 E5
Henrietta St COVGDN WC2E ... 11 M7
SRTFD E15 ... 121 H10
Henriques St WCHPL E1 ... 13 P5
Henry Cooper Wy LEE/GVPK SE12 ... 184 A6
Henry Darlot Dr MLHL NW7 ... 97 H6
Henry Doulton Dr TOOT SW17 ... 180 B7
Henry Jackson Rd PUT/ROE SW15 ... 156 G9
Henry Peters Dr TEDD TW11 ... 176 B8
Henry Rd EBAR EN4 ... 77 N9
EHAM E6 ... 142 B4
FSBYPK N4 ... 119 K6
SL SL1 ... 149 J1
Henry's Av WFD IG8 ... 101 L6
Henrys Grant STAL AL1 ... 38 D7
Henryson Rd BROCKY SE4 ... 182 A7
Henry St BMLY BR1 ... 205 N1
GRAYS RM17 ... 167 P5
HHS/BOV HP3 ... 35 N10
Hensford Gdns SYD SE26 ... 182 B2
Henshall St IS N1 ... 7 H2
Henshaw Cl CRAWW RH11 ... 283 J9
Henshawe Rd BCTR RM8 ... 123 N8
Henshaw St WALW SE17 ... 18 G5
Henslowe Rd EDUL SE22 ... 181 P1
Henslow Wy WOKN/KNAP GU21 ... 214 G10
Henson Av CRICK NW2 ... 116 F10
Henson Cl ORP BR6 ... 206 B9
Henson Pl NTHLT UB5 ... 133 K3
Henson Rd CRAWE RH10 ... 284 C6
Henstridge Pl STJWD NW8 ... 3 N7
Hensworth Rd ASHF TW15 ... 173 N9
Henty Cl BTSEA SW11 ... 157 P7
CRAWW RH11 ... 283 H10
Henty Wk PUT/ROE SW15 ... 178 A2
Henville Rd BMLY BR1 ... 205 N1
Henwick Rd ELTH/MOT SE9 ... 162 A9
Henwood Side WFD IG8 ... 102 C7
Hepburn Gdns HAYES BR2 ... 205 L8
Hepple Cl ISLW TW7 ... 155 J9
Hepscott Rd HOM E9 ... 140 F2
Hepworth Gdns BARK IG11 ... 123 K10
Hepworth Rd STRHM/NOR SW16 ... 180 F10
Hepworth Wy WOT/HER KT12 ... 196 G8
Herald Gdns WLGTN SM6 ... 202 C10
Herald St BETH E2 ... 140 A2
Herbal Hl CLKNW EC1R ... 12 B2
Herbert Crs KTBR SW1X ... 16 B3
WOKN/KNAP GU21 ... 231 K4
Herbert Gdns CHDH RM6 ... 123 N4
CHSWK W4 ... 155 N5
WLSDN NW10 ... 136 E4
Herbert Pl WOOL/PLUM SE18 ... 162 G6
Herbert Rd BXLYHN DA7 ... 163 P8
CDALE/KGS NW9 ... 116 D4
EMPK RM11 ... 125 M5
FBAR/BDGN N11 ... 98 F8
GDMY/SEVK IG3 ... 123 H7
HAYES BR2 ... 206 A5
KUT KT1 ... 199 L8
MNPK E12 ... 141 L1
SEVS/STOTM N15 ... 119 N3
STHL UB1 ... 133 N10
SWCM DA10 ... 189 L2
SWLY BR8 ... 187 J9
WALTH E17 ... 120 C7
WIM/MER SW19 ... 179 J10
WOOL/PLUM SE18 ... 162 G6
Herberts Hole CSHM HP5 ... 50 F9
Herbert St HHNE HP2 ... 35 N5
KTTN NW5 ... 4 C1
PLSTW E13 ... 141 M4
Herbrand St BMSBY WC1N ... 11 L2
Hercies Rd HGDN/ICK UB10 ... 132 A1
Hercules Pl HOLWY N7 ... 118 E6
HOLWY N7 ... 118 E6
Hercules Rd STHWK SE1 ... 17 N3
Hercules St HOLWY N7 ... 118 E6
Hereford Av EBAR EN4 ... 98 A2
Hereford Cl EPSOM KT18 ... 220 A10
GUW GU2 ... 249 J1
STA TW18 ... 195 J1
Hereford Copse WOKS/MYFD GU22 ... 231 N5

Hereford Gdns *IL* IG1 122 B5
PIN HA5 113 M3
WHTN TW2 176 B4 1
Hereford Ms *BAY/PAD* W2 8 F5
Hereford Pl *NWCR* SE14 160 E6 4
Hereford Retreat *PECK* SE15 159 P6 2
Hereford Rd *ACT* W3 135 P9
BAY/PAD W2 8 F6
EA W5 155 H2
FELT TW13 175 K4
WAN E11 121 N3
Hereford Sq *SKENS* SW7 15 K6 1
Hereford St *BETH* E2 13 N1
Hereford Wy *CHSGTN* KT9 219 H2
Herent Dr *CLAY* IG5 122 C1
Hereward Av *PUR/KEN* CR8 223 H6
Hereward Cl *WAB* EN9 63 H8 1
Hereward Gdns *PLMGR* N13 99 H6
Hereward Gn *LOU* IG10 82 F5 1
Hereward Rd *TOOT* SW17 179 P7
Herga Ct *WAT* WD17 73 H6
Herga Rd *KTN/HRWW/W* HA3 114 E2
Herington Gv *RBRW/HUT* CM13 107 M1
Heriot Av *CHING* E4 100 F3
Heriot Rd *CHERT* KT16 195 K7
HDN NW4 116 F3
Heriots Cl *STAN* HA7 94 F5
Heritage Cl *UX/CGN* UB8 131 M6
Heritage Hl *HAYES* BR2 225 P2
Heritage Lawn *HORL* RH6 280 D3
Heritage Vw *HRW* HA1 114 E8
Herkomer Cl *BUSH* WD23 74 A10 4
Herkomer Rd *BUSH* WD23 73 P9
Herlwyn Av *RSLP* HA4 112 F8
Herlwyn Gdns *TOOT* SW17 180 A7
Herm Cl *ISLW* TW7 154 B6
Hermes St *IS* N1 6 A8 1
Hermes Wy *WLGTN* SM6 222 E4
Hermiston Av *CEND/HSY/T* N8 118 F3
Hermitage Cl *DTCH/LGLY* SL3 149 P2
ENC/FH EN2 79 J6 2
ESH/CLAY KT10 218 F3
SHPTN TW17 196 B4
SWFD E18 121 L2
Hermitage Ct *POTB/CUF* EN6 59 M9 2
Hermitage Gdns *HAMP* NW3 117 K8
NRWD SE19 181 K10 3
Hermitage La *CRICK* NW2 117 K8
CROY/NA CR0 203 N7
STRHM/NOR SW16 180 G10 2
WDSR SL4 148 F9
Hermitage Rd *FSBYPK* N4 119 K5
NRWD SE19 181 L9
PUR/KEN CR8 241 K2
WOKN/KNAP GU21 231 J5
Hermitage St *BAY/PAD* W2 9 L4
The Hermitage *BARN* SW13 156 C7 1
FSTH SE23 182 B4
RCHPK/HAM TW10 177 K1
UX/CGN UB8 131 N1 3
Hermitage Wk *SWFD* E18 121 L2
Hermitage Wall *WAP* E1W 13 P10
Hermitage Wy *STAN* HA7 94 F9
Hermitage Woods Crs
WOKN/KNAP GU21 231 J6
Hermit Rd *CAN/RD* E16 141 L6
Hermits Rd *CRAWE* RH10 284 A5
Hermit St *FSBYE* EC1V 6 C9
Hermon Gv *HYS/HAR* UB3 133 H10
Hermon Hl *WAN* E11 121 M2
Herndon Cl *EGH* TW20 172 D7
Herndon Rd *WAND/EARL* SW18 179 M1
Herne Cl *WLSDN* NW10 116 A10 3
Herne Hl *HNHL* SE24 181 K1
Herne Hill Rd *HNHL* SE24 159 K9
Herne Ms *UED* N18 99 P5
Herne Pl *HNHL* SE24 181 J2
Herne Rd *BUSH* WD23 74 A10
SURB KT6 199 J9
Herneshaw *HAT* AL10 40 C6 2
Herns La *WGCE* AL7 23 L5
Herns Wy *WGCE* AL7 23 K3
Heron Cl *BKHH* IG9 101 M2
CRAWW RH11 283 M5 1
GUW GU2 249 N7
HHS/BOV HP3 54 A1
RKW/CH/CXG WD3 91 N3
SBW CM21 29 N2
UX/CGN UB8 131 N1
WALTH E17 100 E10
WLSDN NW10 136 B1 1
Heron Ct *HAYES* BR2 205 P4
Heron Crs *SCUP* DA14 185 H7
Heron Dl *ADL/WDHM* KT15 215 N2
Herondale *SAND/SEL* CR2 224 C5 1
Herondale Av *WAND/EARL* SW18 179 N4
Heron Dr *DTCH/LGLY* SL3 150 E3
FSBYPK N4 119 K7
WARE SG12 27 H8
Heronfield *EGH* TW20 171 N9 2
POTB/CUF EN6 59 M6
Heron Flight Av *RAIN* RM13 145 J2 3
Herongate Rd *CHES/WCR* EN8 62 C3
MNPK E12 121 P7
SWLY BR8 186 F9
Heron Hl *BELV* DA17 164 A3
Heron Ms *IL* IG1 122 E7
Heron Quays *POP/IOD* E14 140 F10
Heron Rd *CROY/NA* CR0 203 M8 2
HNHL SE24 159 K10
TWK TW1 154 F10
The Heronry *WOT/HER* KT12 217 H3
Herons Cl *CRAWE* RH10 281 P10
Heronscourt *LTWR* GU18 212 B7
Heronscroft *LTWR* GU18 212 B7
Herons Cft *WEY* KT13 216 D3
Herons Elm *BERK* HP4 33 K2
Heronsforde *WEA* W13 135 H8 1
Heronsgate *EDGW* HA8 95 M6
Heronsgate Rd *RKW/CH/CXG* WD3 70 E10
Herons Lea *CRAWE* RH10 281 P10
Heronslea *GSTN* WD25 73 K2
Heronslea Dr *STAN* HA7 95 K6
Herons Pl *ISLW* TW7 154 G9
Herons Ri *EBAR* EN4 77 P8
Herons Wy *CHOB/PIR* GU24 230 C7
Herons Wd *HLW* CM20 28 E9
Herons Wood Ct *HORL* RH6 280 C3 11
Heronswood Pl *WGCE* AL7 23 K6 1
Heronswood Rd *WGCE* AL7 23 J5
Heron Wk *NTHWD* HA6 92 F5
Heron Wy *HAT* AL10 40 D6
Heronway *RBRW/HUT* CM13 107 N2
Heron Wy *UPMR* RM14 126 D6
WTHK RM20 166 G4
Herrick Cl *CRAWE* RH10 284 D5
Herrick Rd *FSBYPK* N4 119 K8
Herrick St *WEST* SW1P 17 K6
Herries St *NKENS* W10 2 B8
Herringham Rd *CHARL* SE7 161 P2
Herrings La *BFOR* GU20 212 C3
Herrongate Cl *EN* EN1 79 M6
Hersant Cl *WLSDN* NW10 136 D3
Herschell Rd *FSTH* SE23 182 C3
Herschel Park Dr *SL* SL1 149 L1
Herschel St *SL* SL1 149 L1
Hersham Cl *PUT/ROE* SW15 178 D3
Hersham Gdns *WOT/HER* KT12 217 K1 3
Hersham Rd *WOT/HER* KT12 217 K1
Hertford Av *MORT/ESHN* SW14 178 A1
Hertford Cl *EBAR* EN4 77 N7
Hertford Rd *BARK* IG11 142 E2
BRKMPK AL9 23 L10
EBAR EN4 77 M7
ED N9 100 A2
EFNCH N2 117 P1
GNTH/NBYPK IG2 123 H4
HOD EN11 44 D1
IS N1 7 K5
PEND EN3 80 C1
PEND EN3 80 B4 1
PEND EN3 80 B6 7
WARE SG12 26 E7
WGCE AL7 23 K2
WLYN AL6 24 A1
Hertford Road High St
PEND EN3 80 B8 2
Hertfordshire Wy *HERT/WAS* SG14 25 H1
Hertford St *MYFR/PICC* W1J 10 E10 2
MYFR/PKLN W1K 10 E10 2
Hertford Wy *MTCM* CR4 202 F4 2
Hertingfordbury Rd
HERT/WAS SG14 24 F7
HERT/WAS SG14 25 K5 4
Hertslet Rd *HOLWY* N7 118 G8
Hervey Cl *FNCH* N3 97 K9
Hervey Park Rd *WALTH* E17 120 D2
Hervines Ct *AMS* HP6 69 H3
Hervines Rd *AMS* HP6 68 G3
Hesa Rd *HYS/HAR* UB3 133 H8
Hesewall Cl *VX/NE* SW8 158 D8
Hesiers Hl *WARL* CR6 243 K3
Hesiers Rd *WARL* CR6 243 K2
Hesketh Av *RDART* DA2 188 A4
Hesketh Pl *NTGHL* W11 8 A8
Hesketh Rd *FSTGT* E7 121 M8
Heslop Rd *BAL* SW12 180 A4
Hesper Ms *ECT* SW5 14 G7
Hesperus Crs *POP/IOD* E14 160 G3
Hessel Rd *WEA* W13 154 F1
Hessel St *WCHPL* E1 140 A8 8
Hesselyn Dr *RAIN* RM13 145 J2 4
Hessle Gv *EW* KT17 220 C7
Hestercombe Av *FUL/PGN* SW6 157 H8
Hesterman Wy *CROY/NA* CR0 202 F8
Hester Rd *BTSEA* SW11 157 P6
UED N18 99 P6
Hester Ter *RCH/KEW* TW9 155 M9
Heston Av *HEST* TW5 153 M6
Heston Grange La *HEST* TW5 153 N5
Heston Rd *HEST* TW5 153 P6
REDH RH1 276 A5
Heston St *DEPT* SE8 160 E7
Heswell Gn *OXHEY* WD19 93 H4 3
Hetchleys *HHW* HP1 35 K3
Hetherington Cl *SLN* SL2 128 E5
Hetherington Rd *CLAP* SW4 158 F10 3
SHPTN TW17 196 D2
Hetherington Wy
HGDN/ICK UB10 111 P9 1
Hethersett Cl *REIG* RH2 257 M7
Hetley Rd *SHB* W12 136 E10
Heton Gdns *HDN* NW4 116 D2 3
Heusden Wy *CFSP/GDCR* SL9 110 C6
Hevelius Cl *GNWCH* SE10 161 L4 3
Hever Court Rd *GVE* DA12 190 F9
Hever Cft *ELTH/MOT* SE9 184 D7
Hever Gdns *BMLY* BR1 206 D2
Heverham Rd *WOOL/PLUM* SE18 163 H3
Hevers Av *HORL* RH6 280 A3
Heversham Rd *BXLYHN* DA7 164 B8
Hewens Rd *HGDN/ICK* UB10 132 D5
Hewer St *NKENS* W10 136 G7
Hewers Wy *KWD/TDW/WH* KT20 238 E6
Hewett Cl *STAN* HA7 94 G5 3
Hewett Pl *SWLY* BR8 208 E4
Hewett St *SDTCH* EC2A 13 K2
Hewish Rd *UED* N18 99 M5
Hewison St *BOW* E3 140 E4
Hewitt Av *WDGN* N22 99 J10
Hewitt Cl *CROY/NA* CR0 204 F10
STALE/WH AL4 21 J4
Hewitt Rd *CEND/HSY/T* N8 119 H3
Hewitts Rd *ORP* BR6 228 A4
Hewlett Rd *BOW* E3 140 D4
The Hexagon *HGT* N6 118 A6
Hexal Rd *CAT* SE6 183 K6
Hexham Cl *CRAWE* RH10 284 F7
Hexham Gdns *ISLW* TW7 154 F6
Hexham Rd *BAR* EN5 77 L8
MRDN SM4 201 L8
WNWD SE27 181 K5
Hextalls La *REDH* RH1 259 L4
Heybourne Rd *TOTM* N17 100 A8
Heybridge Av *STRHM/NOR* SW16 180 G9
Heybridge Ct *HERT/WAS* SG14 24 G4 2
Heybridge Dr *BARK/HLT* IG6 122 G1
Heybridge Wy *LEY* E10 120 D5
Heydons Cl *STALW/RED* AL3 38 C4
Heyford Av *RYNPK* SW20 201 J3
VX/NE SW8 158 F6
Heyford Rd *MTCM* CR4 201 P2
RAD WD7 74 E3
Heyford Wy *HAT* AL10 40 F2
Heygate St *WALW* SE17 18 E6
Heymede *LHD/OX* KT22 237 H9
Heynes Rd *BCTR* RM8 123 M9
Heysham Dr *OXHEY* WD19 93 K6
Heysham La *HAMP* NW3 117 L8
Heysham Rd *SEVS/STOTM* N15 119 L4
Heythorpe Cl *WOKN/KNAP* GU21 231 L3 1
Heythorp St *WAND/EARL* SW18 179 J4
Heythrop Dr *HGDN/ICK* UB10 112 A9
Heywood Av *CDALE/KGS* NW9 96 B9
Heyworth Rd *CLPT* E5 120 A9
FSTGT E7 121 L10
Hibbert Av *WATN* WD24 73 L4
Hibbert Rd *KTN/HRWW/W* HA3 94 E10
WALTH E17 120 E5
Hibbert St *BTSEA* SW11 157 N9 5
Hibberts Wy *CFSP/GDCR* SL9 110 B1
Hibbs Cl *SWLY* BR8 208 E2
Hibernia Dr *GVE* DA12 191 J6
Hibernia Gdns *HSLW* TW3 175 P1
Hibernia Rd *HSLW* TW3 153 P10
Hichisson Rd *PECK* SE15 182 B1
Hickin Cl *CHARL* SE7 162 A3
Hickin St *POP/IOD* E14 161 H2 3
Hickling Rd *IL* IG1 122 E10
Hickman Av *CHING* E4 101 H7
Hickman Cl *BROX* EN10 44 D6 1
CAN/RD E16 142 A7 6
Hickman Rd *CHDH* RM6 123 M5
Hickmans Cl *GDST* RH9 260 B8
Hicks Av *GFD/PVL* UB6 134 C5
Hicks Cl *BTSEA* SW11 157 P9
Hicks St *DEPT* SE8 160 D4
Hidalgo Ct *HHNE* HP2 36 A4
Hidcote Cl *WOKS/MYFD* GU22 232 E2
Hidcote Gdns *RYNPK* SW20 200 E3 1
The Hideaway *ABLGY* WD5 54 G7 1
Hide Pl *WEST* SW1P 17 J6
Hide Rd *HRW* HA1 114 C2
The Hides *HLW* CM20 28 G10
Highacre *DORK* RH4 272 G5
High Acres *ABLGY* WD5 54 E8
Higham Hill Rd *WALTH* E17 120 D1
Higham Md *CSHM* HP5 51 H6
Higham Pl *WALTH* E17 120 D1 3
Higham Rd *CSHM* HP5 51 H6
TOTM N17 119 L1
WFD IG8 101 M7
Highams Hl *CRAWW* RH11 283 J8
Highams La *CHOB/PIR* GU24 212 F3
Higham Station Av *CHING* E4 100 G7
Higham St *WALTH* E17 120 D1
Higham Vw *EPP* CM16 66 C2
High Ash Cl *TIL* RM18 169 K2
High Ash Rd *STALE/WH* AL4 21 H4
Highbanks Cl *WELL* DA16 163 K6
Highbanks Rd *PIN* HA5 94 A7
Highbank Wy *CEND/HSY/T* N8 119 H4 2
High Barn Rd *EHSLY* KT24 253 L5
Highbarns *HHS/BOV* HP3 54 B1
Highbarrow Rd *CROY/NA* CR0 203 N8
High Beech *SAND/SEL* CR2 223 M4
High Beeches *CFSP/GDCR* SL9 110 A6
EW KT17 220 G10
ORP BR6 227 K3
SCUP DA14 185 P8
High Beeches Cl *PUR/KEN* CR8 222 E6 2
High Beech Rd *LOU* IG10 82 B8
High Bois La *AMS* HP6 69 J1
Highbridge Rd *BARK* IG11 142 E3
Highbridge St *WAB* EN9 62 G9
Highbrook Rd *BKHTH/KID* SE3 162 A9
High Broom Crs *WWKM* BR4 204 G7
Highbury Av *HOD* EN11 44 F1
THHTH CR7 203 H2
Highbury Cl *NWMAL* KT3 199 P4
WWKM BR4 204 G9 2
Highbury Crs *HBRY* N5 119 J10
Highbury Gdns *IL* IG1 123 H7
Highbury Gra *HBRY* N5 119 J9
Highbury Gv *HBRY* N5 119 J10
Highbury Hl *HBRY* N5 119 J9
Highbury New Pk *HBRY* N5 6 D1
Highbury Pk *HBRY* N5 119 J9 3
Highbury Pl *HBRY* N5 6 C1
Highbury Qd *HBRY* N5 119 K8
Highbury Rd *WIM/MER* SW19 179 H8
Highbury Station Rd *IS* N1 6 B2
Highbury Ter *HBRY* N5 119 J10
Highbury Terrace Ms *HBRY* N5 119 J10
High Canons *BORE* WD6 75 P3
High Cedar Dr *RYNPK* SW20 178 E10
Highclere *ASC* SL5 192 C5
GU GU1 250 D7
Highclere Cl *PUR/KEN* CR8 241 K1
Highclere Ct *WOKN/KNAP* GU21 231 H3
Highclere Dr *HHS/BOV* HP3 36 C10
Highclere Gdns
WOKN/KNAP GU21 231 H3
Highclere Rd *NWMAL* KT3 200 A3
WOKN/KNAP GU21 231 H3
Highclere St *SYD* SE26 182 D7
Highcliffe Dr *PUT/ROE* SW15 178 C2
Highcliffe Gdns *REDBR* IG4 122 B3
High Cl *RKW/CH/CXG* WD3 71 M9
Highcombe *CHARL* SE7 161 N5
High Coombe Pl *KUTN/CMB* KT2 178 A10
High Coppice *AMSS* HP7 69 H5
Highcotts La *RGUE* GU4 251 K2
Highcroft *CDALE/KGS* NW9 116 B3
Highcroft Av *ALP/SUD* HA0 135 L2
Highcroft Ct *GT/LBKH* KT23 235 P9 1
Highcroft Gdns *GLDGN* NW11 117 J4 2
Highcroft Rd *ARCH* N19 118 F5
HHS/BOV HP3 53 K1
High Cross *GSTN* WD25 74 C3
Highcross Rd *MEO* DA13 189 J9
High Cross Rd *SEVS/STOTM* N15 119 P1 7
Highdaun Dr *STRHM/NOR* SW16 202 G4
High Dells *HAT* AL10 40 C5
Highdown *WPK* KT4 200 B9
Highdown Ct *CRAWE* RH10 284 C10
High Down Rd *BELMT* SM2 221 L7
Highdown Rd *PUT/ROE* SW15 178 E2
High Dr *CTHM* CR3 242 E8
LHD/OX KT22 218 C10
NWMAL KT3 199 P1
High Elms *CHIG* IG7 103 H5
UPMR RM14 126 D6
WFD IG8 101 M6 5
High Elms Cl *NTHWD* HA6 92 D7
High Elms La *GSTN* WD25 55 J7
High Elms Rd *ORP* BR6 226 F5
Higher Dr *BNSTD* SM7 220 G9
EHSLY KT24 252 F3
PUR/KEN CR8 223 H9
Higher Gn *EW* KT17 220 D9
Highfield *BNSTD* SM7 239 P3
HLWS CM18 47 K2
KGLGY WD4 53 P4
OXHEY WD19 93 N4 1
RGUE GU4 268 C8
Highfield Av *CDALE/KGS* NW9 115 P3
ERITH DA8 164 C5 2
GFD/PVL UB6 114 D10
GLDGN NW11 116 G5
HARP AL5 20 B3
ORP BR6 227 J3
PIN HA5 113 N3
WBLY HA9 115 K8
Highfield Cl *AMS* HP6 69 J3
CDALE/KGS NW9 115 P3 1
CRW RM5 104 D7
LEW SE13 183 J2
LHD/OX KT22 218 C7
NTHWD HA6 92 F9
SURB KT6 199 H8
WDGN N22 99 H9
Highfield Ct *STHGT/OAK* N14 78 D10
Highfield Crs *HCH* RM12 125 N7
NTHWD HA6 92 F9
Highfield Dr *BROX* EN10 44 D7
HAYES BR2 205 K4
HGDN/ICK UB10 111 P8
HOR/WEW KT19 220 C4
WWKM BR4 204 G10
Highfield Gdns *CDH/CHF* RM16 168 A1
GLDGN NW11 117 H4
Highfield Gn *EPP* CM16 65 H7
Highfield Hl *NRWD* SE19 181 L10
Highfield La *HHNE* HP2 36 A4
STALE/WH AL4 39 H8
Highfield Link *CRW* RM5 104 D7
Highfield Pl *EPP* CM16 65 H7
Highfield Rd *ACT* W3 135 N7
BERK HP4 34 A6
BF/WBF KT14 215 K9
BH/WHM TN16 243 P3
BMLY BR1 206 C4
BRYLDS KT5 199 P7
BUSH WD23 73 M9
BXLYHS DA6 186 A1
CHERT KT16 195 K8 1
CHESW EN7 61 M2
CRW RM5 104 D7
CSHM HP5 50 G5 3
CTHM CR3 241 P8
DART DA1 187 L3
EGH TW20 172 A9
FELT TW13 175 H4
GLDGN NW11 117 H4 2
HCH RM12 125 N7
HERT/BAY SG13 25 L7
ISLW TW7 154 E7
NTHWD HA6 92 F9
PUR/KEN CR8 222 G6
RSEV TN14 247 M2
STALE/WH AL4 20 G10
STMC/STPC BR5 207 J3
SUN TW16 196 G5
SUT SM1 221 P2
WCHMH N21 99 J3
WDSR SL4 148 E9 1
WFD IG8 102 B8
WOT/HER KT12 197 H8
Highfield Rd South *DART* DA1 187 L3
High Flds *ASC* SL5 192 E5
Highfields *ASHTD* KT21 237 J5
EHSLY KT24 252 G4
LHD/OX KT22 236 C10
POTB/CUF EN6 60 F4
RAD WD7 74 E1 1
Highfields Gv *HGT* N6 118 B6
Highfield Wy *POTB/CUF* EN6 59 L7
RKW/CH/CXG WD3 71 L10
High Firs *RAD* WD7 74 E1
SWLY BR8 208 F4
High Firs Crs *HARP* AL5 20 C3
High Foleys *ESH/CLAY* KT10 218 G4 1
High Garth *ESH/CLAY* KT10 218 B3
Highgate Av *HGT* N6 118 C5
Highgate Cl *HGT* N6 118 B5
Highgate Gv *SBW* CM21 29 N1 1
Highgate High St *HGT* N6 118 B6
Highgate Hl *ARCH* N19 118 C6
Highgate Rd *KTTN* NW5 118 B8
Highgate West Hl *HGT* N6 118 B7
High Gv *BMLY* BR1 205 P1
WGCW AL8 22 E4
WOOL/PLUM SE18 162 G6
Highgrove Cl *CHST* BR7 206 B1
FBAR/BDGN N11 98 B6
Highgrove Ms *CAR* SM5 202 A10 1
Highgrove Rd *BCTR* RM8 123 M10
Highgrove Wy *RSLP* HA4 113 H4
High Hill Ferry *CLPT* E5 120 A6
High Holborn *HCIRC* EC1N 12 A4
HHOL WC1V 11 M5
High House La *CDH/CHF* RM16 168 G2
Highland Av *BRW* CM14 107 H2
DAGE RM10 124 D8
HNWL W7 134 D8
LOU IG10 82 C10
Highland Cft *BECK* BR3 182 G8
Highland Dr *BUSH* WD23 94 A1
HHS/BOV HP3 36 C6
Highland Pk *FELT* TW13 174 G7
Highland Rd *AMSS* HP7 69 J5
BMLY BR1 205 L1
BXLYHS DA6 164 B10 1
NRWD SE19 181 M9
NTHWD HA6 93 H10
PUR/KEN CR8 223 H10
RSEV TN14 228 C7
WAB EN9 45 K8
Highlands *BRKMPK* AL9 40 F1 1
OXHEY WD19 93 K2
Highlands Av *ACT* W3 135 P9
LHD/OX KT22 237 H8
WCHMH N21 78 G9
Highlands Cl *CFSP/GDCR* SL9 90 C8
HSLW TW3 154 A7 1
LHD/OX KT22 236 G8 1
Highlands End *CFSP/GDCR* SL9 90 C8 2
Highlands Gdns *IL* IG1 122 B6
Highlands Hl *SWLY* BR8 209 H2
Highlands La *CFSP/GDCR* SL9 90 C7
WOKS/MYFD GU22 232 B7
Highlands Pk *BGR/WK* TN15 247 M7
LHD/OX KT22 237 J9
Highlands Rd *BAR* EN5 77 K8
BEAC HP9 89 H6
LHD/OX KT22 237 H8
REDH RH1 257 N9
STMC/STPC BR5 207 L7
The Highlands *EDGW* HA8 95 N10
EHSLY KT24 252 F1
POTB/CUF EN6 59 M6 1
RKW/CH/CXG WD3 91 L1
SLN SL2 109 H9
High La *CTHM* CR3 242 E5
HNWL W7 134 C8
RBSF CM22 30 F5
WARL CR6 242 E4
Highlea Cl *CDALE/KGS* NW9 96 B9
High Level Dr *SYD* SE26 181 P7
Highlever Rd *NKENS* W10 136 F7
High Md *CHIG* IG7 102 F3
HRW HA1 114 D3
WWKM BR4 205 J9
Highmead *WOOL/PLUM* SE18 163 J6
Highmead Crs *ALP/SUD* HA0 135 L2
High Meadow Cl *DORK* RH4 272 G3
PIN HA5 113 K2 2
High Meadow Crs
CDALE/KGS NW9 116 A3 1
High Meadow Pl *CHERT* KT16 195 J6 1
High Mdw *CHIG* IG7 102 G6
High Meads *STALE/WH* AL4 21 H3
High Meads Rd *CAN/RD* E16 142 A8
Highmoor *AMSS* HP7 69 J5
Highmore Rd *BKHTH/KID* SE3 161 K6
High Oak Rd *WARE* SG12 26 C1
High Oaks *CRAWW* RH11 283 L9
ENC/FH EN2 78 G4
STALW/RED AL3 38 B1
High Oaks Rd *WGCW* AL8 22 E4
Highover Pk *AMSS* HP7 69 H6
High Park Av *EHSLY* KT24 252 G2
High Park Rd *RCH/KEW* TW9 155 M7
High Pastures *RBSF* CM22 30 D3
High Pth *WIM/MER* SW19 201 L1
High Path Rd *GU* GU1 250 F10
High Pewley *GU* GU1 268 B2
High Pine Cl *WEY* KT13 216 D2
High Pines *WARL* CR6 242 B5
High Point *ELTH/MOT* SE9 184 E6
Highpoint *WEY* KT13 216 B2
High Rdg *POTB/CUF* EN6 60 F3
Highridge Cl *EPSOM* KT18 238 B1 2
High Ridge Cl *HHS/BOV* HP3 53 N1
High Ridge Rd *HHS/BOV* HP3 53 N1
High Rd *BF/WBF* KT14 215 P8
BKHH IG9 101 N3
BRKMPK AL9 41 P4
BROX EN10 44 E6
BUSH WD23 94 C2
CDH/CHF RM16 147 K10
CHDH RM6 124 A4
CHIG IG7 102 E4
COUL/CHIP CR5 239 P10
EFNCH N2 97 N10
EPP CM16 47 L10
EPP CM16 48 E10
EPP CM16 64 F9
EPP CM16 66 C3
FBAR/BDGN N11 98 C6
FNCH N3 97 M9
GDMY/SEVK IG3 123 K6
GSTN WD25 54 G10
IL IG1 122 E8
KTN/HRWW/W HA3 94 D9 1
LEY E10 120 G4
NFNCH/WDSP N12 97 M4 1
RDART DA2 187 K6
SEVS/STOTM N15 119 N3
TOTM N17 99 N10
TRDG/WHET N20 97 M1
UX/CGN UB8 131 M7
WBLY HA9 115 K10
High Road Broxbourne
BROX EN10 44 E7
High Road Eastcote *PIN* HA5 113 K2
High Road Great North Rd
EFNCH N2 97 N10
High Road Ickenham
HGDN/ICK UB10 112 D7
High Road Leytonstone
WAN E11 121 K8
High Road Turnford *BROX* EN10 62 D2
High Road Woodford Gn
SWFD E18 101 M9
WFD IG8 101 M5
High Road Wormley *BROX* EN10 44 E10
Highshore Rd *PECK* SE15 159 N8 2
High Silver *LOU* IG10 82 A8
High Standing *CTHM* CR3 259 K1
Highstead Crs *ERITH* DA8 164 F7
Highstone Av *WAN* E11 121 M4
High St *ABLGY* WD5 54 G3
ACT W3 135 P10
ADL/WDHM KT15 215 L1
AMSS HP7 68 F6
ASC SL5 192 F5
ASC SL5 192 C5
BAR EN5 77 J8
BARK/HLT IG6 102 F10
BECK BR3 204 F2
BERK HP4 33 K2
BGR/WK TN15 247 P3
BH/WHM TN16 245 M10
BH/WHM TN16 262 F3
BMLY BR1 205 M3
BNSTD SM7 239 K1
BORE WD6 75 J10
BROX EN10 62 D1
BRW CM14 107 H3
BTFD TW8 155 L5
BUSH WD23 73 P10
CAR SM5 222 A2
CEND/HSY/T N8 118 F2
CFSP/GDCR SL9 90 B9
CHEAM SM3 221 H3
CHES/WCR EN8 62 D10
CHOB/PIR GU24 212 D8
CHOB/PIR GU24 213 K7
CHONG CM5 67 P5
COB KT11 217 J10
CRAWW RH11 283 N7 1
CROY/NA CR0 203 K10
CSHM HP5 50 G7
CTHM CR3 241 M9
DART DA1 187 M2
DEN/HRF UB9 91 M10
DORK RH4 272 G2
DTCH/LGLY SL3 149 N7
DTCH/LGLY SL3 150 D3
DTCH/LGLY SL3 150 F6
E/WMO/HCT KT8 197 P4
EA W5 135 J9
EGH TW20 172 C8
EMPK RM11 125 L6
EPP CM16 65 J7
ESH/CLAY KT10 218 E3
ESH/CLAY KT10 218 A1
EW KT17 220 C6
EYN DA4 209 N6
FELT TW13 174 G6
GDST RH9 260 B7
GRAYS RM17 167 M4
GRH DA9 166 G10
GT/LBKH KT23 254 A1
GU GU1 268 A2
GUW GU2 267 P2
GVE DA12 190 E2
GVW DA11 189 N2
HEST TW5 153 J6
HHNE HP2 35 M5
HHS/BOV HP3 52 D3
HLWE CM17 29 M7
HLWW/ROY CM19 27 N10
HOD EN11 44 F3
HORL RH6 280 C4
HPTN TW12 198 A1
HRW HA1 114 D7
HSLW TW3 154 A9
HYS/HAR UB3 152 E5
IVER SL0 131 J8
KGLGY WD4 54 B5
KTN/HRWW/W HA3 94 D10
KUT KT1 199 J2
KWD/TDW/WH KT20 238 F9
LCOL/BKTW AL2 57 H1
LHD/OX KT22 218 C9
LHD/OX KT22 236 G8
MLHL NW7 96 E6
NTHWD HA6 92 G9
NWMAL KT3 200 B4
ORP BR6 207 K7
ORP BR6 226 D7
ORP BR6 226 F2
OXTED RH8 261 J6
OXTED RH8 261 N4
PGE/AN SE20 182 B10
PIN HA5 113 M1
POTB/CUF EN6 59 M8
PUR/KEN CR8 223 H7
RDART DA2 188 G6
REDH RH1 258 C4
REDH RH1 258 A9
REDH RH1 258 A10 2
REDH RH1 258 G10
REDH RH1 259 L9
REIG RH2 257 K10
RKW/CH/CXG WD3 91 N2
ROM RM1 124 F3
RPLY/SEND GU23 233 M7
RSEV TN14 228 G6
RSEV TN14 247 H2
RSLP HA4 112 F5
SCUP DA14 185 K7
SEV TN13 246 D8
SEV TN13 265 K1
SHPTN TW17 196 D6 3
SL SL1 128 B5
SL SL1 149 L1
SNWD SE25 203 N4
SOCK/AV RM15 146 B10
SRTFD E15 141 J2
STA TW18 173 J7
STAL AL1 38 C6
STALE/WH AL4 20 G10
STALE/WH AL4 21 J2
STALE/WH AL4 39 N8
STMC/STPC BR5 207 M6
STWL/WRAY TW19 172 B2
STWL/WRAY TW19 173 N2
SUT SM1 221 L1
SWCM DA10 189 L1
SWLY BR8 208 F3
TEDD TW11 176 F8
THDIT KT7 198 F6
THHTH CR7 203 K4
UX/CGN UB8 131 M6
UX/CGN UB8 131 M2
WAN E11 121 N4
WARE SG12 26 C2
WARE SG12 27 H7
WARE SG12 28 A2
WAT WD17 73 J7
WATW WD18 73 J7
WBLY HA9 115 L9
WDR/YW UB7 131 P10
WDR/YW UB7 151 N5
WDSR SL4 149 J5
WEY KT13 216 B1
WHTN TW2 176 B3
WIM/MER SW19 178 G8
WOKN/KNAP GU21 231 H4
WOKN/KNAP GU21 231 P2
WOKN/KNAP GU21 232 C3
WOKS/MYFD GU22 232 D7
WOT/HER KT12 197 H8
WWKM BR4 204 G8
High Street Collier's Wd
WIM/MER SW19 179 N10
High Street Gn *HHNE* HP2 36 B4
High Street Harlesden
WLSDN NW10 136 C4 2
High Street Ms *WIM/MER* SW19 179 H8
High St North *EHAM* E6 142 B3
MNPK E12 122 B9
High St South *EHAM* E6 142 C4
The High St *CRAWW* RH11 283 N7
High Tor Cl *BMLY* BR1 183 N10
High Tree Cl *ADL/WDHM* KT15 215 K2 1
High Trees *BRXS/STRHM* SW2 181 H4
CROY/NA CR0 204 D8
EBAR EN4 77 P9
High Trees Cl *CTHM* CR3 241 N8
High Trees Rd *REIG* RH2 275 N1

Highview CTHM CR3 ...... 241 M10
High Vw BELMT SM2 ...... 221 J7
CSTG HP8 ...... 90 A3
HAT AL10 ...... 40 C6
PIN HA5 ...... 113 K2
RKW/CH/CXG WD3 ...... 71 K8
SHGR GU5. ...... 270 D5
WATW WD18 ...... 72 G10
Highview Av EDGW HA8. ...... 95 P5
High View Av GRAYS RM17 ...... 167 P4
WLGTN SM6 ...... 222 G2
High View Cl LOU IG10 ...... 81 P9
SNWD SE25 ...... 203 N2
Highview Cl POTB/CUF EN6 ...... 59 N9
Highview Crs RBRW/HUT CM13. ...... 87 P10
High View Gdns GRAYS RM17 ...... 167 P4
Highview Gdns EDGW HA8. ...... 95 P6
FBAR/BDGN N11 ...... 98 D2
FNCH N3. ...... 117 H1
POTB/CUF EN6 ...... 59 M9
STALE/WH AL4. ...... 39 H1
UPMR RM14. ...... 126 A7
High View Rd GUW GU2 ...... 267 J3
NRWD SE19 ...... 181 L9
SWFD E18 ...... 101 L10
Highview Rd SCUP DA14 ...... 185 L7
WEA W13. ...... 134 F8
Highwayman's Rdg BFOR GU20 ...... 212 A1
The Highway BELMT SM2 ...... 221 N5
ORP BR6 ...... 227 L2
STAN HA7 ...... 94 E9
High Wickfield WGCE AL7 ...... 23 M6
Highwold COUL/CHIP CR5 ...... 240 B4
Highwood Av BUSH WD23 ...... 75 N5
NFNCH/WDSP N12 ...... 97 N5
Highwood Cl BRW CM14. ...... 106 G1
ORP BR6 ...... 206 F9
PUR/KEN CR8 ...... 241 K3
Highwood Dr ORP BR6 ...... 206 F9
Highwood Gdns CLAY IG5. ...... 122 C3
Highwood Gv MLHL NW7 ...... 96 A6
Highwoodhall La HHS/BOV HP3 ...... 8 E10
Highwood La LOU IG10 ...... 82 D10
Highwood Rd ARCH N19 ...... 118 F8
High Wood Rd HOD EN11 ...... 26 E10
Highwoods CTHM CR3 ...... 259 M1
LHD/OX KT22 ...... 237 H7
High Worple RYLN/HDSTN HA2 ...... 113 M5
Highworth Rd FBAR/BDGN N11 ...... 98 E2
Highworth St CAMTN NW1 ...... 9 P3
High Wych La SBW CM21 ...... 29 K1
High Wych Rd HLW CM20 ...... 29 H5
SBW CM21 ...... 29 N2
Hilary Av MTCM CR4 ...... 202 B3
Hilary Cl FUL/PGN SW6 ...... 157 L6
HCH RM12 ...... 125 L10
Hilary Rd ACT W3 ...... 156 C9
SHB W12 ...... 136 C8
Hilbert Rd CHEAM SM3 ...... 220 C1
Hilborough Cl WIM/MER SW19 ...... 178 M10
Hilborough Rd HACK E8 ...... 7 M4
Hilborough Wy ORP BR6 ...... 226 C2
Hilbury HAT AL10 ...... 40 C5
Hilda May Av SWLY BR8 ...... 208 F3
Hilda Rd CAN/RD E16 ...... 141 K6
EHAM E6. ...... 142 A2
Hilda Vale Rd ORP BR6 ...... 226 D1
Hildenborough Gdns BMLY BR1 ...... 183 K9
Hilden Dr ERITH DA8 ...... 165 J8
Hildenlea Pl HAYES BR2 ...... 205 K2
The Hildens DORK RH4 ...... 272 B4
The Hilders ASHTD KT21 ...... 237 N3
Hildreth St BAL SW12 ...... 180 C4
Hildyard Rd FUL/PGN SW6 ...... 14 F9
Hiley Rd WLSDN NW10 ...... 136 F5
Hilfield La GSTN WD25 ...... 74 A5
Hilgay GU GU1 ...... 250 C10
Hilgay Cl GU GU1 ...... 250 C10
Hiliary Gdns STAN HA7 ...... 95 H10
Hiljon Crs CFSP/GDCR SL9 ...... 90 B8
Hilars Heath Rd COUL/CHIP CR5 ...... 240 F1
Hillary Av GVW GU1 ...... 190 B6
Hillary Crs WOT/HER KT12 ...... 197 K8
Hillary Ri BAR EN5 ...... 77 K8
Hillary Rd DTCH/LGLY SL3. ...... 157 J7
HHNE HP2 ...... 36 B5
NWDGN UB2 ...... 153 P2
Hill Av AMS HP6 ...... 69 H4
Hillbarn SAND/SEL CR2 ...... 223 M7
Hillbeck Cl PECK SE15 ...... 160 B6
Hillbrook Cl GYD/PVL UB6 ...... 134 C3
Hillborne Cl HYS/HAR UB3 ...... 153 H4
Hillbrook Gdns WEY KT13 ...... 216 B4
Hillbrook Rd TOOT SW17 ...... 180 A6
Hill Brow BMLY BR1 ...... 206 A1
DART DA1 ...... 188 C2
Hillbrow NWMAL KT3. ...... 200 D3
Hillbrow Cl BXLY DA5. ...... 186 E7
RGUW GU3 ...... 248 C10
Hillbrow Rd BMLY BR1 ...... 183 K10
ESH/CLAY KT10 ...... 218 A1
Hill Bunker's BELV DA17 ...... 164 B3
Hill Burgess CRICK NW2 ...... 117 K9
Hillbury Av KTN/HRWW/W HA3 ...... 114 G3
Hillbury Cl AMS HP6. ...... 69 H4
WARL CR6 ...... 242 A4
Hillbury Gdns WARL CR6 ...... 242 B4
Hillbury Rd TOOT SW17 ...... 180 C6
WARL CR6 ...... 241 P3
Hill Cl BAR EN5 ...... 76 F9
CHST BR7 ...... 184 E8
CRICK NW2 ...... 116 E8
GLDGN NW11 ...... 117 K4
HRW HA1 ...... 114 D8
MEO DA15 ...... 199 B10
PUR/KEN CR8 ...... 223 K8
STAN HA7 ...... 94 C5
WOKN/KNAP GU21 ...... 232 A2
Hill Common HHS/BOV HP3 ...... 36 B9
Hillcote Av STRHM/NOR SW16 ...... 181 H10
Hill Ct BERK HP4 ...... 34 A4
Hillcourt Av NFNCH/WDSP N12 ...... 97 L7
Hillcourt Rd EDUL SE22 ...... 182 A2
Hill Crs BRYLDS KT5 ...... 199 L5
BXLY DA5. ...... 186 D4
EMPK RM11 ...... 125 K4
HRW HA1 ...... 114 F8
TRDG/WHET N20 ...... 97 L3
WPK KT4 ...... 200 F9
Hill Crest BFN/LL DA15. ...... 185 K3
POTB/CUF EN6 ...... 59 N10
SEV TN13 ...... 247 H8
Hillcrest HAT AL10 ...... 40 E1
HGT N6 ...... 118 B5
WCHMH N21 ...... 99 J1
Hillcrest Av CHERT KT16 ...... 195 H10
EDGW HA8 ...... 94 N5
GLDGN NW11 ...... 117 K3
PIN HA5 ...... 113 L2
WTHK RM20 ...... 166 F5
Hillcrest Cl BECK BR3 ...... 204 E6
CRAWE RH10 ...... 284 C4
EPSOM KT18 ...... 238 C1
SYD SE26 ...... 181 P7
Hillcrest Dr GRH DA9 ...... 188 F1
Hill Crest Gdns CRICK NW2 ...... 116 D8
Hillcrest Gdns ESH/CLAY KT10 ...... 198 E10
HDN NW4 ...... 117 H2
Hill Crest Rd CHONG CM5 ...... 66 F6
Hillcrest Rd ACT W3 ...... 135 M10
BH/WHM TN16 ...... 244 A2
BMLY BR1 ...... 183 M7
CTHM CR3 ...... 241 N3

DART DA1 ...... 186 F3
EA W5. ...... 135 K2
EMPK RM11 ...... 125 H5
GUW GU2 ...... 249 L9
LOU IG10. ...... 82 A10
ORP BR6 ...... 207 K9
PUR/KEN CR8 ...... 222 G6
RAD WD7 ...... 57 M9
SWFD E18. ...... 101 L10
WALTH E17. ...... 101 J10
Hillcrest Vw BECK BR3 ...... 204 E6
Hillcrest Wy EPP CM16 ...... 65 K9
Hillcroft LOU IG10. ...... 82 D6
Hillcroft Av PIN HA5 ...... 113 N4
PUR/KEN CR8 ...... 222 D9
Hillcroft Crs EA W5 ...... 135 J8
OXHEY WD19 ...... 93 J2
RSLP HA4 ...... 113 L8
WBLY HA9 ...... 115 L9
Hillcroft Rd CSHM HP5 ...... 51 J5
EHAM E6 ...... 142 E7
Hillcroome Rd BELMT SM2 ...... 221 N3
Hillcross Av MRDN SM4 ...... 201 H6
Hilldale Rd SUT SM1 ...... 221 J1
Hilldeane Rd PUR/KEN CR8 ...... 223 H6
Hilldene Av HARH RM3 ...... 105 K7
Hilldene Cl HARH RM3 ...... 105 L6
Hilldown Rd HAYES BR2 ...... 205 K8
HHW HP1 ...... 35 K4
STRHM/NOR SW16 ...... 180 F10
Hill Dr CDALE/KGS NW9 ...... 115 P6
STRHM/NOR SW16 ...... 202 D3
Hilldrop Crs HOLWY N7 ...... 118 E10
Hilldrop La HOLWY N7 ...... 118 E10
Hilldrop Rd BMLY BR1 ...... 183 N9
HOLWY N7 ...... 118 E10
Hill Dyke Rd STALE/WH AL4 ...... 21 J4
Hill End ORP BR6 ...... 207 J3
WOOL/PLUM SE18 ...... 162 D7
Hill End La STAL AL1. ...... 38 D9
STALE/WH AL4 ...... 39 H9
Hill End Rd DEN/HRF UB9 ...... 91 L7
Hillersdon SLN SL2 ...... 129 N7
Hillersdon Av BARN SW13 ...... 156 D8
EDGW HA8 ...... 95 L6
Hillery Cl WALW SE17 ...... 19 H6
Hill Farm Av WATW WD25 ...... 75 M5
Hill Farm Cl CSTG HP8 ...... 89 L2
Hill Farm Rd CFSP/GDCR SL9 ...... 90 B8
CSHM HP5 ...... 51 J10
NKENS W10 ...... 136 F7
Hillfield HAT AL10 ...... 40 E1
Hillfield Av ALP/SUD HA0 ...... 135 K2
CDALE/KGS NW9 ...... 116 B3
CEND/HSY/T N8 ...... 118 C2
MRDN SM4 ...... 201 P6
Hillfield Cl GU GU1 ...... 250 F8
REDH RH1 ...... 258 B10
RYLN/HDSTN HA2 ...... 114 B2
Hillfield Ct HHNE HP2 ...... 9 H2
Hillfield La South BUSH WD23 ...... 74 D10
Hillfield Pk WCHMH N21. ...... 99 H3
Hillfield Park Ms MUSWH N10 ...... 118 C2
Hillfield Rd CFSP/GDCR SL9 ...... 90 B8
CRICK NW2 ...... 117 J10
HHNE HP2 ...... 35 N6
Hill Field Rd HPTN TW12 ...... 175 N10
Hillfield Rd KIL/WHAMP NW6 ...... 117 J10
REDH RH1 ...... 258 B10
SEV TN13 ...... 246 F6
Hillfield Sq CFSP/GDCR SL9 ...... 90 B8
Hillfoot Av CRW RM5 ...... 104 D9
Hillfoot Rd CRW RM5 ...... 104 D9
Hillford Pl REDH RH1 ...... 259 K8
Hill Gardens Craven BAY/PAD W2 ...... 9 J7
Hillgate Pl BAL SW12 ...... 180 C2
KENS W8 ...... 8 E9
Hillgate St KENS W8 ...... 8 E9
Hill Gv FELT TW13 ...... 175 N5
ROM RM1 ...... 124 F1
Hillhampton AMS HP6 ...... 69 G3
Hillhouse WAB EN9 ...... 63 J9
Hill House Av STAN HA7 ...... 94 E8
Hill House Cl CRAWE RH10 ...... 285 P9
WCHMH N21 ...... 99 H1
Hill House Dr HPTN TW12 ...... 197 P1
Hill House Rd RDART SW14 ...... 188 B3
STRHM/NOR SW16 ...... 180 G8
Hillhurst Gdns CTHM CR3 ...... 241 M6
Hilliard Rd NTHWD HA6 ...... 92 D9
Hilliard's Ct WAP E1W 140 D10
Hilliards Rd UX/CGN UB8 ...... 131 N8
Hillier Cl BAR EN5 ...... 77 L10
Hillier Gdns CROY/NA CR0 ...... 223 H2
Hillier Pl CHSGTN KT9 ...... 219 J3
Hillier Rd BTSEA SW11 ...... 180 A2
GU GU1 ...... 250 D10
Hilliers Av UX/CGN UB8 ...... 132 B5
Hillier's La CROY/NA CR0. ...... 202 F10
Hillingdale BH/WHM TN16 ...... 243 N4
Hillingdon Av SEV TN13 ...... 247 K7
STWL/WRAY TW19 ...... 173 P4
Hillingdon Hl HGDN/ICK UB10 ...... 131 P5
UX/CGN UB8 ...... 132 A5
Hillingdon Ri SEV TN13 ...... 247 L8
Hillingdon Rd BXLYHN DA7. ...... 164 D9
GSTN WD25 ...... 55 H10
GVW DA11 ...... 190 E5
HGDN/ICK UB10. ...... 131 P3
Hillingdon St WALW SE17 ...... 18 D10
Hillingdon Trail DEN/HRF UB9 ...... 111 N1
HYS/HAR UB3 ...... 153 H4
Hill La KWD/TDW/WH KT20 ...... 239 H7
RSLP HA4 ...... 112 D6
Hill Ley HAT AL10 ...... 40 C4
Hill Leys POTB/CUF EN6 ...... 60 F4
Hillman Cl EMPK RM11 ...... 125 L1
Hillman St HACK E8 ...... 140 E1
Hillmarton Rd HOLWY N7 ...... 118 E10
Hill Md BERK HP4 ...... 33 M6
Hillmead CRAWW RH11 ...... 283 J12
Hillmead Dr BRXN/ST SW9 ...... 159 J10
Hillmont Rd ESH/CLAY KT10 ...... 198 D10
Hillmore Gv SYD SE26 ...... 182 C8
Hill Pl CRAWW RH11 ...... 283 M8
SLN SL2 ...... 128 C2
Hillreach WOOL/PLUM SE18 ...... 162 C4
DORK RH4 ...... 272 A4
Hill Ri DTCH/LGLY SL3 ...... 150 D5
Hill Rd ED N9 ...... 120 E4
ESH/CLAY KT10 ...... 198 G9
GFD/PVL UB6 ...... 134 B3
GLDGN NW11 ...... 117 J2
POTB/CUF EN6 ...... 59 N10
RCHPK/HAM TW10 ...... 177 J7
RDART DA2 ...... 188 C3
RKW/CH/CXG WD3 ...... 91 L1
RSLP HA4 ...... 112 D6
UPMR RM14 ...... 125 P2
Hillrise Av WATN WD24 ...... 73 L4
Hill Rise Crs CFSP/GDCR SL9 ...... 90 B10
Hillrise Rd ARCH N19 ...... 118 F5
CRW RM5 ...... 104 D7
Hill Rd BRW CM14. ...... 106 F4
CAR SM5 ...... 221 P4
DART DA1 ...... 187 M5
EPP CM16 ...... 65 J6
GT/LBKH KT23 ...... 236 A8
HRW HA1 ...... 114 F7
MTCM CR4 ...... 202 C1
MUSWH N10 ...... 96 E7
NTHWD HA6 ...... 92 E7
PIN HA5 ...... 113 M4

PUR/KEN CR8 ...... 222 G8
STJWD NW8 ...... 3 L1
SUT SM1. ...... 221 L2
Hillsboro Rd EDUL SE22 ...... 181 M1
Hillsborough Gn OXHEY WD19 ...... 93 H4
Hill's Chace BRW CM14. ...... 107 H5
Hillsgrove Cl WELL DA16 ...... 163 M6
Hill Shaw HARF DA3. ...... 211 L6
Hillside BNSTD SM7 ...... 239 H1
CDALE/KGS NW9 ...... 116 A2
CSHM HP5 ...... 51 J5
DEN/HRF UB9 ...... 50 F4
EYN DA4. ...... 209 N7
GRAYS RM17 ...... 168 A3
HAT AL10 ...... 40 D4
HLWE CM17 ...... 47 M3
HOD EN11 ...... 44 E2
RDART DA2 ...... 188 D2
SL SL1. ...... 149 K1
VW GU25 ...... 195 M8
WARE SG12. ...... 26 C3
WGCE AL7 ...... 23 M4
WIM/MER SW19 ...... 178 C9
WLSDN NW10 ...... 136 A3
WOKS/MYFD GU22 ...... 232 A6
Hillside Av BORE WD6 ...... 75 P7
CHES/WCR EN8 ...... 62 C7
FBAR/BDGN N11 ...... 98 A7
GVE DA12 ...... 190 C5
PUR/KEN CR8 ...... 223 J9
WBLY HA9 ...... 115 L9
WFD IG8 ...... 101 P6
WOKN/KNAP GU21 ...... 231 J3
Hillside Cl ABLGY WD5. ...... 54 F8
BNSTD SM7 ...... 239 H2
CFSP/GDCR SL9 ...... 90 B7
CRAWW RH11 ...... 283 J13
CSTG HP8 ...... 89 M3
MRDN SM4 ...... 201 H4
MV/WKIL W9 ...... 3 M1
RDKG RH5 ...... 273 M1
WFD IG8 ...... 101 P6
WOKN/KNAP GU21 ...... 231 J3
Hillside Crs CHES/WCR EN8 ...... 62 C7
ENC/FH EN2 ...... 79 L4
NTHWD HA6 ...... 93 H9
OXHEY WD19 ...... 73 M10
RYLN/HDSTN HA2 ...... 114 C7
WARE SG12 ...... 26 C7
Hillside Dr EDGW HA8 ...... 95 M7
GVE DA12 ...... 190 C5
Hillside Gdns ADL/WDHM KT15 ...... 215 J2
BAR EN5 ...... 77 H8
BERK HP4. ...... 34 A4
BRKHM/BTCW RH3 ...... 255 M10
EDGW HA8 ...... 95 L5
HGT N6 ...... 118 B4
KTN/HRWW/W HA3 ...... 115 J1
NTHWD HA6 ...... 93 H8
WLGTN SM6 ...... 240 C6
Hillside Gv MLHL NW7 ...... 96 D8
STHGT/OAK N14 ...... 98 E1
Hillside La HAYES BR2 ...... 205 N6
WARE SG12 ...... 12 E8
Hillside Pk ASC SL5. ...... 192 E6
Hillside Ri NTHWD HA6 ...... 93 J8
Hillside Rd ASHTD KT21 ...... 237 L3
BELMT SM2 ...... 221 J4
BH/WHM TN16 ...... 244 B5
BRXS/STRHM SW2 ...... 180 C5
BUSH WD23 ...... 73 M9
COUL/CHIP CR5 ...... 240 F4
CROY/NA CR0 ...... 223 J2
CTHM CR3 ...... 241 P4
DART DA1 ...... 187 H2
EA W5. ...... 135 K2
EW KT17 ...... 125 D9
HAYES BR2 ...... 205 L3
NTHWD HA6 ...... 93 J8
PIN HA5 ...... 93 J8
RAD WD7 ...... 74 G1
RKW/CH/CXG WD3 ...... 70 F9
RSEV TN14 ...... 265 J8
SEV TN13 ...... 247 L9
SEVS/STOTM N15 ...... 119 N4
STAL AL1. ...... 38 D5
STHL UB1 ...... 133 P6
STNW/STAM N16 ...... 119 M8
Hillside Ter HERT/BAY SG13 ...... 25 K7
The Hillside ORP BR6 ...... 227 L5
Hillside Wk BRW CM14 ...... 106 F4
Hillside Wy RGODL GU7 ...... 267 J10
Hills La NTHWD HA6 ...... 92 E8
Hillsleigh Rd KENS W8 ...... 8 D9
Hillsmead Wy SAND/SEL CR2 ...... 223 P9
Hill Pl SOHO/CST W1F 10 C6
Hillspur Cl GUW GU2 ...... 249 L5
Hillspur Rd GUW GU2 ...... 249 L5
Hill's Rd BKHH IG9 ...... 101 N2
Hillstowe St CLPT E5 ...... 120 E9
Hill St MYFR/PICC W1J. 10 B9
STALW/RED AL3. ...... 39 K7
Hillswood Dr CHERT KT16 ...... 214 F1
The Hill AMSS HP7 ...... 68 B10
Hilltop Cl ASC SL5. ...... 192 D2
CHESW EN7 ...... 60 C3
LHD/OX KT22 ...... 237 H9
RGUW GU3 ...... 249 L6
Hilltop Gdns DART DA1 ...... 187 N1
ORP BR6. ...... 207 P9
Hilltop La CTHM CR3 ...... 259 H8
Hilltop Rd BERK HP4. ...... 34 A4
CTHM CR3 ...... 241 M3
KGLGY WD4 ...... 53 L6
KIL/WHAMP NW6 ...... 2 F3
REIG RH2 ...... 275 L2
WTHK RM20 ...... 166 F5
Hill Top Vw WFD IG8 ...... 102 C7
Hilltop Wk CTHM CR3 ...... 242 F6
Hilltop Wy STAN HA7 ...... 95 H7
Hill Tree Cl SBW CM21 ...... 29 N2
Hillview CTHM CR3 ...... 241 N3
RYNPK SW20 ...... 178 E10
Hillview Av EMPK RM11 ...... 125 K4
KTN/HRWW/W HA3 ...... 115 K3
Hill View Cl KWD/TDW/WH KT20 ...... 238 F7
PUR/KEN CR8 ...... 223 J7
Hill View Crs GUW GU2 ...... 249 L8
IL IG1 ...... 122 B10
Hillview Crs ORP BR6 ...... 207 P9
Hillview Dr REDH RH1 ...... 276 B1
Hill View Dr WELL DA16 ...... 163 N9
Hill View Gdns CDALE/KGS NW9 ...... 116 C2
Hillview Gdns CHES/WCR EN8 ...... 62 D3
HDN NW4 ...... 116 C2
PIN HA5 ...... 113 P1
Hill View Rd ESH/CLAY KT10 ...... 198 G9
HART DA3. ...... 211 N3
ORP BR6. ...... 207 P9
STWL/WRAY TW19. ...... 172 A2
TWK TW1 ...... 176 C7
WOKS/MYFD GU22 ...... 232 D5
Hillview Rd CHST BR7 ...... 184 E2
MLHL NW7 ...... 96 E6
PIN HA5 ...... 93 N8

SUT SM1. ...... 201 M10
Hill Wy AMSS HP7 ...... 68 A7
HGT N6 ...... 118 B7
Hillway CDALE/KGS NW9 ...... 116 B6
HGT N6 ...... 118 B7
Hill Waye CFSP/GDCR SL9 ...... 110 C4
Hillwood Cl RBRW/HUT CM13 ...... 107 N2
Hillwood Gv RBRW/HUT CM13. ...... 107 N2
Hillworth Rd BRXS/STRHM SW2 ...... 181 N3
Hillyard Rd HNWL W7 ...... 134 D7
Hillyard St BRXN/ST SW9 ...... 159 H7
Hillyfield Rd RSEV TN14 ...... 247 K1
Hilly Fld HLWS CM18 ...... 47 K3
Hillyfield WALTH E17 ...... 100 D10
Hillyfields LOU IG10 ...... 82 B3
Hilly Flds WGCE AL7 ...... 23 M4
Hilly Fields Crs BROCKY SE4 ...... 160 F10
Hilmay Dr HHW HP1 ...... 35 L7
Hilperton Rd SL SL1 ...... 149 K1
Hilsea St CLPT E5 ...... 120 B9
Hilton Av NFNCH/WDSP N12 ...... 97 N6
Hilton Cl UX/CGN UB8 ...... 131 L4
Hilton Wy SAND/SEL CR2 ...... 242 A1
Himalayan Wy WATW WD18 ...... 72 G10
Himley Rd TOOT SW17 ...... 179 P8
Hinchley Cl ESH/CLAY KT10 ...... 198 E10
Hinchley Dr ESH/CLAY KT10 ...... 198 E10
Hinchley Wy ESH/CLAY KT10 ...... 198 F10
Hinckley Rd EDUL SE22 ...... 159 P10
Hind Cl CHIG IG7 ...... 103 J6
Hind Crs ERITH DA8 ...... 164 D6
Hinde Ms MHST W1U 10 D5
Hinds Rd HRW HA1 ...... 114 E3
Hinde St MHST W1U 10 D5
Hind Gv POP/IOD E14 ...... 140 F8
Hindhead Cl CRAWW RH11 ...... 283 M9
UX/CGN UB8 ...... 132 C7
Hindhead Gdns NTHLT UB5 ...... 133 H5
Hindhead Gn OXHEY WD19 ...... 93 K6
Hindhead Wy WLGTN SM6 ...... 222 F2
Hindmans Rd EDUL SE22 ...... 181 P1
Hindmans Wy DAGW RM9 ...... 144 A5
Hindmarsh Cl WCHPL E1 ...... 13 P7
Hindrey Rd CLPT E5. ...... 120 A10
Hindsley's Pl FSTH SE23 ...... 182 B5
Hinkler Rd KTN/HRWW/W HA3 ...... 115 J1
Hinkley Cl DEN/HRF UB9 ...... 111 M2
Hinksey Cl DTCH/LGLY SL3 ...... 150 E2
Hinstock Rd WOOL/PLUM SE18 ...... 162 F6
Hinton Av HSLWW TW4 ...... 153 L10
Hinton Cl ELTH/MOT SE9 ...... 184 B4
Hinton Rd BRXN/ST SW9 ...... 159 J9
HNHL SE24 ...... 159 K9
SL SL1. ...... 128 D9
UED N18 ...... 99 M5
UX/CGN UB8 ...... 131 M3
WLGTN SM6 ...... 240 D1
Hipley St WOKS/MYFD GU22 ...... 232 E6
Hippodrome Pl NTGHL W11 ...... 8 A8
Hitcham Rd LEY E10 ...... 120 E5
Hitchcock Cl SHPTN TW17 ...... 196 A3
Hitchen Hatch La SEV TN13 ...... 247 H6
Hitchens Cl HHW HP1 ...... 35 J5
Hitchin Cl HARH RM3 ...... 105 K5
Hitchings Wy REIG RH2 ...... 275 K4
Hitherbaulk WGCE AL7 ...... 22 G7
Hitherbroom Rd HYS/HAR UB3 ...... 133 J8
Hitherbury Cl GUW GU2 ...... 267 P3
Hither Farm Rd BKHTH/KID SE3 ...... 161 P9
Hitherfield Rd BCTR RM8 ...... 123 P9
STRHM/NOR SW16 ...... 180 G5
Hither Green La LEW SE13 ...... 183 H1
Hither Meadow CFSP/GDCR SL9 ...... 90 B10
Hithermoor Rd
STWL/WRAY TW19. ...... 173 K2
Hitherway WGCW AL8 ...... 23 G1
Hitherwell Dr KTN/HRWW/W HA3 ...... 94 C9
Hitherwood Cl HCH RM12 ...... 125 J7
REDH RH1 ...... 257 P8
Hitherwood Dr DUL SE21 ...... 181 J3
Hive Cl BUSH WD23 ...... 94 C3
Hive La GVW DA11 ...... 189 N1
Hive Rd BUSH WD23 ...... 94 C3
Hiving's Hl CSHM HP5 ...... 50 F4
Hivings Pk CSHM HP5 ...... 50 G4
Hoadly Rd STRHM/NOR SW16 ...... 180 E6
Hobart Cl TRDG/WHET N20 ...... 97 P3
YEAD UB4 ...... 133 L6
Hobart Gdns THHTH CR7 ...... 203 L3
Hobart La YEAD UB4 ...... 133 L6
Hobart Pl BGVA SW1W 16 E4
RCHPK/HAM TW10 ...... 177 L7
Hobart Rd DAGW RM9 ...... 123 N9
TIL RM18. ...... 168 D7
WPK KT4. ...... 200 E10
YEAD UB4 ...... 133 L6
Hobayne Rd HNWL W7 ...... 134 C8
Hobbes Wk PUT/ROE SW15 ...... 178 E10
Hobbs Cl BF/WBF KT14 ...... 215 L9
CHES/WCR EN8 ...... 62 C5
STALE/WH AL4 ...... 39 K7
Hobbs Cross Rd EPP CM16. ...... 65 M10
HLWE CM17 ...... 30 A8
Hobbs Gn EFNCH N2 ...... 117 M1
Hobbs Hill Rd HHS/BOV HP3 ...... 35 P10
Hobbs Pl IS N1 ...... 7 J6
Hobbs Rd WNWD SE27 ...... 181 K7
Hobbs Wy WGCW AL8 ...... 22 F6
Hobday St POP/IOD E14 ...... 140 G8
Hoblands End CHST BR7 ...... 185 H9
Hobletts Rd HHNE HP2 ...... 36 A5
Hobsons Pl WCHPL E1 ...... 13 N1
Hobtoe Rd HLW CM20 ...... 28 D10
Hobury St WBPTN SW10 ...... 15 C10
Hockenden La SWLY BR8 ...... 208 B3
Hocken Md CRAWE RH10 ...... 284 E5
Hockering Gdns
WOKS/MYFD GU22 ...... 232 E4
Hockering Rd WOKS/MYFD GU22 ...... 232 D4
Hocker St BETH E2 ...... 7 L10
Hockford Cl RGUW GU3 ...... 248 D3
Hocklands WGCE AL7 ...... 23 N6
Hockley Av EHAM E6. ...... 142 A1
Hockley Dr GPK RM2 ...... 105 J10
Hockley La SLN SL2 ...... 129 N2
Hockley Ms BARK IG11 ...... 142 G2
Hocroft Av CRICK NW2 ...... 117 J8
Hocroft Rd CRICK NW2 ...... 117 J8
Hocroft Wk CRICK NW2 ...... 117 J8
Hodder Dr GFD/PVL UB6 ...... 134 C4
Hoddesdon Rd BELV DA17 ...... 164 B3
WARE SG12. ...... 26 C3
Hodds Wood Rd CSHM HP5 ...... 51 H9
Hodford Rd GLDGN NW11 ...... 117 H4
Hodge Wy WATW WD18 ...... 73 H10
Hodgemoor Vw CSTG HP8 ...... 89 M4
Hodges Wy WATW WD18 ...... 73 H10
Hodgkin Cl THMD SE28 ...... 143 N9
Hodgson Gdns GU GU1 ...... 250 D7
Hodings Rd HLW CM20 ...... 28 C10
Hodson Cl RYLN/HDSTN HA2 ...... 113 N8
Hodson Crs STMC/STPC BR5 ...... 207 N5
Hoebrook Cl WOKS/MYFD GU22 ...... 232 A7
Hoe La ABR/ST RM4. ...... 83 L7
EN EN1. ...... 80 A4
PEND EN3 ...... 81 H3
SHGR GU5. ...... 270 F9
WAB EN9 ...... 64 A5
WARE SG12. ...... 26 E3
Hoe Meadow BEAC HP9 ...... 88 F3
Hoestock Rd SBW CM21 ...... 29 N1
Hoe St WALTH E17 ...... 120 D4
The Hoe OXHEY WD19 ...... 93 L3
Hogan Ms BAY/PAD W2 ...... 9 J1
Hogarth Av ASHF TW15 ...... 174 D2
BRW CM14 ...... 107 K4

Hogarth Cl CAN/RD E16 ...... 142 A7
EA W5. ...... 135 K7
SL SL1. ...... 128 D9
Hogarth Crs CROY/NA CR0 ...... 203 K7
WIM/MER SW19 ...... 201 N1
Hogarth Gdns HEST TW5 ...... 153 P6
Hogarth Hl GLDGN NW11 ...... 117 J2
Hogarth Reach LOU IG10 ...... 82 B8
Hogarth Rd BCTR RM8 ...... 123 L10
CDH/CHF RM16 ...... 147 N10
CRAWE RH10 ...... 284 A10
ECT SW5. ...... 14 G6
EDCW HA8 ...... 95 N7
Hogarth Wy HPTN TW12 ...... 198 B1
Hopback Wood Rd BEAC HP9 ...... 88 A2
Hogfair La SL SL1 ...... 128 B6
Hogg End La STALW/RED AL3 ...... 37 H4
Hogg La BORE WD6 ...... 74 F8
CDH/CHF RM16 ...... 167 M2
GRAYS RM17 ...... 167 M3
Hog Hill Rd CRW RM5 ...... 104 A8
Hog La CSHM HP5 ...... 32 D8
MEO DA15 ...... 190 A6
Hogpits Bottom HHS/BOV HP3 ...... 52 D8
Hogscross La COUL/CHIP CR5 ...... 240 A8
Hogsdell La HERT/BAY SG13 ...... 26 A7
Hogshill La COB KT11 ...... 217 K10
Hogsmill Wy HOR/WEW KT19 ...... 219 P2
Hogtrough Hl BH/WHM TN16 ...... 245 K8
Hogtrough La OXTED RH8 ...... 260 G4
REDH RH1 ...... 276 E1
Holbeach Gdns BFN/LL DA15. ...... 183 H2
Holbeach Rd CAT SE6 ...... 182 F3
Holbeck La CHESW EN7 ...... 61 N2
Holbeck Rw PECK SE15. ...... 159 P6
Holbein Ga NTHWD HA6 ...... 92 F6
Holbein Ms BGVA SW1W 16 C5
Holbein Pl BGVA SW1W 16 C5
Holberton Gdns WLSDN NW10 ...... 136 B5
Holborn Cl STALE/WH AL4 ...... 39 J1
Holborn Pl LINN WC2A 11 L4
Holborn Rd PLSTW E13 ...... 141 N7
Holborn Viad STBT EC1A. 12 C5
Holborn Wy MTCM CR4 ...... 202 A2
Holbreck Pl WOKS/MYFD GU22 ...... 232 C4
Holbrook Cl EN EN1. ...... 79 N5
Holbrook La CHST BR7 ...... 184 G10
Holbrook Meadow EGH TW20 ...... 172 F9
Holbrook Rd SRTFD E15 ...... 141 L4
Holbrook Wy HAYES BR2 ...... 206 C6
Holburne Cl BKHTH/KID SE3. ...... 161 P7
Holburne Gdns BKHTH/KID SE3 ...... 162 A7
Holburne Rd BKHTH/KID SE3 ...... 161 P7
Holcombe Cl BH/WHM TN16 ...... 262 C6
Holcombe Hl MLHL NW7 ...... 96 D4
Holcombe Rd TOTM N17 ...... 119 N1
Holcombe St HMSMTH W6 ...... 156 E3
Holcon Ct REDH RH1 ...... 258 B7
Holcote Cl BELV DA17 ...... 163 P2
Holcroft Rd HOM E9 ...... 140 B2
Holdbrook Wy HARH RM3 ...... 105 N10
Holden Av CDALE/KGS NW9 ...... 115 P6
NFNCH/WDSP N12 ...... 97 L6
Holdenby Rd BROCKY SE4 ...... 182 D1
Holden Cl BCTR RM8 ...... 123 L8
HERT/BAY SG13 ...... 25 M4
Holden Gdns BRW CM14. ...... 107 J6
Holden Rd NFNCH/WDSP N12 ...... 97 L5
Holden St BTSEA SW11 ...... 158 B8
Holden Wy UPMR RM14 ...... 126 C6
Holdernesse Rd ISLWW TW7 ...... 154 F7
TOOT SW17. ...... 180 A6
Holderness Wy WNWD SE27 ...... 181 J8
Holder Rd CRAWE RH10 ...... 284 C10
Holders Hill Av HDN NW4 ...... 116 C1
Holder Cl Dr HDN NW4 ...... 96 G10
Holders Hill Gdns HDN NW4 ...... 96 G9
Holders Hill Rd HDN NW4 ...... 96 G9
The Holdings BRKMPK AL9. ...... 40 G2
Holecroft WAB EN9 ...... 63 K10
Hole In DORK RH4 ...... 272 A2
Holford Rd CDH/CHF RM16 ...... 169 H2
GU GU1 ...... 250 F10
HAMP NW3 ...... 117 M8
TIL RM18. ...... 168 G3
Holford Av WC1X 6 A9
Holgate Av BTSEA SW11 ...... 157 N9
Holgate Rd DAGE RM10 ...... 124 B10
Holgate St CHARL SE7 ...... 162 A2
RYNPK SW20 ...... 200 C1
Holland Cl BAR EN5 ...... 97 N1
HAYES BR2 ...... 205 L9
ROMW/RG RM7 ...... 124 D3
STAN HA7 ...... 94 G6
Holland Crs OXTED RH8 ...... 261 M9
Holland Dr FSTH SE23 ...... 182 D6
Holland Gdns EGH TW20 ...... 195 J2
GSTN WD25 ...... 73 K1
WKENS W14 ...... 8 C9
Holland Gv BRXN/ST SW9 ...... 159 H6
Holland La OXTED RH8 ...... 261 M9
Holland Pk NTGHL W11 ...... 8 B10
Holland Park Av NTGHL W11 ...... 8 B10
IL IG1 ...... 123 H3
KENS W8 ...... 8 C9
NTGHL W11 ...... 8 A10
WKENS W14 ...... 8 A10
Holland Park Gdns WKENS W14 ...... 8 A10
Holland Park Ms NTGHL W11 ...... 8 C10
Holland Park Rd WKENS W14 ...... 14 G1
Holland Rd ALP/SUD HA0 ...... 135 K2
EHAM E6. ...... 142 C3
OXTED RH8 ...... 261 M9
SNWD SE25 ...... 203 P5
SRTFD E15 ...... 141 K5
WKENS W14 ...... 8 A10
WLSDN NW10 ...... 136 D3
Hollands Cl GVW DA11 ...... 191 P8
Holland's Cft WARE SG12 ...... 28 A3
The Hollands WPK KT4 ...... 200 E9
Holland St KENS W8 ...... 8 E1
STHWK SE1. ...... 12 E10
Holland Villas Rd WKENS W14 ...... 8 A1
Holland Wk STAN HA7 ...... 94 F4
Holland Wy HAYES BR2 ...... 205 L9
Hollar Rd STNW/STAM N16 ...... 119 N2
Hollen St SOHO/CST W1F 11 J5
Holles Cl HPTN TW12 ...... 175 P9
Holles St CAVSQ/HST W1G 10 E1
Holley Rd ACT W3 ...... 156 N1
Hollickwood Av
NFNCH/WDSP N12 ...... 98 A7
Holliday Sq BTSEA SW11 ...... 157 N9
Holliday St BERK HP4 ...... 34 A5
Holliday Wy DAGE RM10 ...... 144 C3
Holliers Wy HAT AL10 ...... 40 D4
Hollies Av BF/WBF KT14 ...... 215 J9
BFN/LL DA15. ...... 185 J5
TWK TW1 ...... 176 D3
Hollies Cl STRHM/NOR SW16 ...... 181 H9
SWFD E18 ...... 102 E2
Hollies End MLHL NW7 ...... 96 E6
Hollies Rd EA W5 ...... 155 H3
The Hollies GVE DA12 ...... 190 A7
HART DA3. ...... 211 P3
HHS/BOV HP3. ...... 52 D5
KTN/HRWW/W HA3 ...... 114 F2
RKW/CH/CXG WD3 ...... 90 A5
Hollies Wy POTB/CUF EN6 ...... 59 M7
Holligrave Rd BMLY BR1 ...... 205 M1
Hollin Ct CRAWW RH11 ...... 283 P4

Hollingbourne Av BXLYHN DA7 164 A7
Hollingbourne Gdns WEA W13 134 G7
Hollingbourne Rd HNHL SE24 181 K1
Hollingsworth Rd SAND/SEL CR2 224 A3
Hollington Crs NWMAL KT3 200 C6
Hollington Rd EHAM E6 142 C5
TOTM N17 99 P10
Hollingworth Cl
E/WMO/HCT KT8 197 N4 2
Hollingworth Rd STMC/STPC BR5 206 E7
Hollingworth Wy
BH/WHM TN16 262 G2 3
Hollis Pl GRAYS RM17 167 M2
Hollman Gdns STRHM/NOR SW16 181 J9
Holloway Cl WDR/YW UB7 151 P4
Holloway Dr VW GU25 194 B4
Holloway Hl CHERT KT16 194 F10
Holloway La RKW/CH/CXG WD3 70 E4
Holloway Rd ARCH N19 118 E7
EHAM E6 142 C5
WAN E11 121 J8 4
Holloways La BRKMPK AL9 40 G9
Holloway St HSLW TW3 154 A9
Hollow Cl GUW GU2 267 N1 1
Hollowfield Av GRAYS RM17 168 A3
Hollow Hill La DTCH/LGLY SL3 150 F1
IVER SL0 130 E9
Hollow La RDKG RH5 271 L7
VW GU25 193 P3
The Hollow CRAWW RH11 283 J8
WFD IG8 101 L5 2
Hollow Wy CSHM HP5 50 D6
Hollow Way La AMS HP6 69 K1
Holly Av ADL/WDHM KT15 215 K6
STAN HA7 95 K10
WOT/HER KT12 197 L8
Hollybank CHOB/PIR GU24 212 E9 2
Hollybank Cl HPTN TW12 175 P8 2
Hollybank Rd BF/WBF KT14 215 K10
Holly Bank Rd WOKS/MYFD GU22 231 N7
Hollybrake Cl CHST BR7 184 G10 2
Hollybush Av LCOL/BKTW AL2 37 P10
Hollybush Cl BERK HP4 34 G2
OXHEY WD19 93 K1 1
SEV TN13 247 K10
WAN E11 121 M3
Hollybush Gdns BETH E2 140 A5 8
Hollybush Hl SLN SL2 129 N2
WAN E11 121 L4
Hollybush La AMS HP6 69 J3
BRKMPK AL9 23 J9
DEN/HRF UB9 110 F7 1
HHW HP1 35 J5
Holly Bush La HPTN TW12 175 N10
Hollybush La IVER SL0 130 E8
ORP BR6 228 B3
Holly Bush La SEV TN13 247 K10 1
Hollybush La WGCE AL7 23 H8
Hollybush Pl BETH E2 140 A5 9
Hollybush Rd CRAWE RH10 283 P6
CSHM HP5 50 F3 1
GVE DA12 190 F5
KUTN/CMB KT2 177 K8
Hollybush St PLSTW E13 141 N5
Holly Bush V HAMP NW3 117 M9 3
Hollybush Wy CHESW EN7 61 P4
Holly Cl BKHH IG9 102 A4
CHERT KT16 193 M10
CRAWE RH10 284 B5
EGH TW20 171 N9
FELT TW13 175 M8
HAT AL10 40 C5
SLN SL2 109 H9
WLSDN NW10 136 B2
WOKN/KNAP GU21 231 N5
Hollycombe EGH TW20 172 A7
Holly Crs BECK BR3 204 E5
WDSR SL4 148 C8
WFD IG8 101 J8
Holly Cft HERT/WAS SG14 24 G4
Hollycroft Av HAMP NW3 117 K8
WBLY HA9 115 K7
Hollycroft Cl SAND/SEL CR2 223 M2
WDR/YW UB7 152 B5
Hollycroft Gdns WDR/YW UB7 152 B5
Hollycross Rd WARE SG12 26 E3
Hollydale Dr HAYES BR2 206 C10
Hollydale Rd PECK SE15 160 B8
Holly Dell HERT/BAY SG13 25 K7
Hollydown Wy WAN E11 121 J8
Holly Dr BERK HP4 34 A6
CHING E4 100 G1
POTB/CUF EN6 59 L9
SOCK/AV RM15 147 J6
WDSR SL4 171 K1
Holly Farm Rd NWDGN UB2 153 M4
Hollyfield HAT AL10 40 D7
Holly Fld HLWW/ROY CM19 46 F4
Hollyfield Av FBAR/BDGN N11 98 A6
Hollyfield Rd BRYLDS KT5 199 L7
Hollyfields BROX EN10 62 D2
Holly Gdns WDR/YW UB7 152 A1
Hollygrove BUSH WD23 94 C1
Holly Gv CDALE/KGS NW9 115 P5
PECK SE15 159 P8
PIN HA5 93 M9
Hollygrove Cl HSLWW TW4 153 N10
Holly Hedge Rd COB KT11 217 J10 2
Holly Hedges La HHS/BOV HP3 52 F6
Holly Hedge Ter LEW SE13 183 H1
Holly Hl HAMP NW3 117 M9
WCHMH N21 78 G10
Holly Hill Dr BNSTD SM7 239 K3
Holly Hill Rd BELV DA17 164 C4
Holly Hock CHOB/PIR GU24 230 F1
Holly Hough KWD/TDW/WH KT20 255 N6
Holly La BNSTD SM7 239 N4
RGUW GU3 249 J5
Holly La East BNSTD SM7 239 L2
Holly La West BNSTD SM7 239 L3
Holly Lea RGUE GU4 250 A4
Holly Lodge Gdns HGT N6 118 B7
Hollymead CAR SM5 202 A10
Hollymead Rd COUL/CHIP CR5 240 B4
Holly Ms WBPTN SW10 15 K8
Hollymoor La HOR/WEW KT19 220 A6
Holly Mt HAMP NW3 117 M9 4
Hollymount Cl GNWCH SE10 161 H7 3
Holly Pk FNCH N3 117 J1
FSBYPK N4 118 G5 1
Holly Park Gdns FNCH N3 117 K1
Holly Park Rd FBAR/BDGN N11 98 B6
HNWL W7 134 E10
Holly Rd CHSWK W4 156 A3 6
DART DA1 187 L4
HPTN TW12 176 B9
HSLW TW3 154 A10
ORP BR6 227 K4
PEND EN3 80 C2
REIG RH2 275 L2
TWK TW1 176 F4
Holly St HACK E8 7 M2
Hollytree Av SWLY BR8 208 F2
Hollytree Cl CFSP/GDCR SL9 90 B6 1
CSHM HP5 51 N7 1
WIM/MER SW19 178 G4
Holly Tree Ct HHNE HP2 36 C6
Holly Tree Rd CTHM CR3 241 M8
Hollyview Cl HDN NW4 116 D4 2
Holly Wk HAMP NW3 117 M9
HARP AL5 20 C2
WDSR SL4 170 D7
WGCW AL8 22 F1
Holly Wy MTCM CR4 202 E4
Hollywood Gdns YEAD UB4 133 J8
Hollywood Ms WBPTN SW10 15 J9 1
Hollywood Rd CHING E4 100 D6 2
WBPTN SW10 15 J9
Hollywood Wy ERITH DA8 165 J7
WFD IG8 101 J8
Holman Rd BTSEA SW11 157 N8
HOR/WEW KT19 219 P2
Holmbank Dr SHPTN TW17 196 F4
Holmbridge Gdns PEND EN3 80 C8
Holmbrook Dr HDN NW4 116 G3
Holmbury Cl BUSH WD23 94 D3 2
CRAWW RH11 283 M9
Holmbury Ct WIM/MER SW19 179 P10 2
Holmbury Dr RDKG RH5 273 H5
Holmbury Gdns HYS/HAR UB3 132 G10 1
Holmbury Pk CHST BR7 184 B10
Holmbury Vw CLPT E5 120 A6
Holmbush Rd PUT/ROE SW15 179 H2
Holm Cl ADL/WDHM KT15 215 H8
Holmcote Gdns HBRY N5 119 K10 2
Holmcroft CRAWE RH10 283 P8
KWD/TDW/WH KT20 256 E1
Holmcroft Wy HAYES BR2 206 C5
Holmdale SLN SL2 129 P9
Holmdale Cl BORE WD6 75 L6 3
Holmdale Gdns HDN NW4 116 G3
Holmdale Rd CHST BR7 184 F8
KIL/WHAMP NW6 117 K10
Holmdale Ter SEVS/STOTM N15 119 M4 4
Holmdene Av HNHL SE24 181 K1
MLHL NW7 96 D7
RYLN/HDSTN HA2 114 A1
Holmdene Cl BECK BR3 205 H2
Holmdene Ct BMLY BR1 206 B3 3
Holmead Rd FUL/PGN SW6 157 L6
Holme Cl CHES/WCR EN8 62 D7 3
HAT AL10 40 C1
Holme Lacey Rd LEE/GVPK SE12 183 L2
Holme Lea GSTN WD25 55 K10
Holme Pk BORE WD6 75 L6 4
Holme Rd EHAM E6 142 B3
EMPK RM11 125 P6
HAT AL10 40 C1
Holmes Av MLHL NW7 97 H6 3
WALTH E17 120 E1
Holmes Cl ASC SL5 192 B6
WOKS/MYFD GU22 232 C7
Holmesdale CHES/WCR EN8 80 B1
Holmesdale Av
MORT/ESHN SW14 155 N9
Holmesdale Cl GU GU1 250 E9 1
SNWD SE25 203 N3 2
Holmesdale Hl EYN DA4 210 C1
Holmesdale Rd CROY/NA CR0 203 L5
EYN DA4 210 B1
HGT N6 118 C5
RCH/KEW TW9 155 L7 1
RDKG RH5 272 G6
REDH RH1 276 G2
REIG RH2 257 L9
SNWD SE25 203 M4
TEDD TW11 177 H10
WELL DA16 163 N8
Holmesley Rd BROCKY SE4 182 D2
Holmes Meadow EPP CM16 46 E7 1
Holmes Rd KTTN NW5 4 E1
TWK TW1 176 E5
WIM/MER SW19 179 M10
Holmes Ter STHWK SE1 18 A1
Holmethorpe Av REDH RH1 258 C7
Holme Wy STAN HA7 94 E7
Holmewood Gdns
BRXS/STRHM SW2 180 G3
Holmewood Rd
BRXS/STRHM SW2 180 F3
SNWD SE25 203 M3
Holmfield Av HDN NW4 116 G3
Holm Gv HGDN/ICK UB10 132 B2
Holmhurst Rd BELV DA17 164 C4
Holmlea Rd DTCH/LGLY SL3 150 A7
Holmlea Wk DTCH/LGLY SL3 149 P7
Holmleigh Av DART DA1 165 K10
Holmleigh Rd STNW/STAM N16 119 M6
Holm Oak Cl WAND/EARL SW18 179 J2 2
Holmsdale Cl IVER SL0 131 J8
Holmsdale Gv BXLYHN DA7 164 F8
Holmshaw Cl SYD SE26 182 D7
Holmshill La BORE WD6 76 C3
Holmside Ri OXHEY WD19 93 J4
Holmside Rd BAL SW12 180 B2
Holmsley Cl NWMAL KT3 200 C6
Holmstall Av EDGW HA8 95 P10
Holmwood Av BRWN CM15 87 M9
SAND/SEL CR2 223 N9
Holmwood Cl ADL/WDHM KT15 215 K2 2
BELMT SM2 220 G5
EHSLY KT24 252 F4
NTHLT UB5 134 A1 1
RYLN/HDSTN HA2 114 B1
Holmwood Gdns FNCH N3 97 K10
WLGTN SM6 222 C3
Holmwood Gv MLHL NW7 96 A6
Holmwood Rd BELMT SM2 220 F5
CHSGTN KT9 219 K2
GDMY/SEVK IG3 123 H7
PEND EN3 80 C2
Holmwood View Rd RDKG RH5 272 G8
Holne Cha EFNCH N2 117 M4
MRDN SM4 201 K6
Holness Rd SRTFD E15 141 L1
Holroyd Rd ESH/CLAY KT10 218 E5 1
PUT/ROE SW15 156 F10
Holstein Av WEY KT13 216 B1
Holstock Rd IL IG1 122 F7
Holsworth Cl RYLN/HDSTN HA2 114 B3 1
Holsworthy Wy CHSGTN KT9 219 H2
Holt Cl BORE WD6 75 L8
CHIG IG7 103 J6
MUSWH N10 118 B2
THMD SE28 143 L9
Holton St WCHPL E1 140 C6 7
Holt Rd ALP/SUD HA0 114 G8
CAN/RD E16 142 B10
Holtsmere Cl GSTN WD25 73 K1
The Holt BARK/HLT IG6 102 F7
HHNE HP2 35 P7
WGCE AL7 23 N6
WLGTN SM6 222 D1
Holt Wy CHIG IG7 103 J6
Holtwhite Av ENC/FH EN2 79 K6
Holtwhite's Hl ENC/FH EN2 79 J5
Holtwood Rd LHD/OX KT22 218 B9
Holwell Hyde WGCE AL7 23 M6 7
Holwell Hyde La BRKMPK AL9 23 M9
Holwell La BRKMPK AL9 23 P10
Holwell Pl PIN HA5 113 M2
Holwell Rd WGCE AL7 23 H6
Holwood Cl WOT/HER KT12 197 K9
Holwood Park Av ORP BR6 226 C1
Holwood Pl CLAP SW4 158 E10 4
Holybourne Av PUT/ROE SW15 178 D3
Holy Cross Hl BROX EN10 43 P9
Holyfield Rd WAB EN9 63 H5
Holyhead Cl BOW E3 140 F5
Holyoake Av WOKN/KNAP GU21 231 P3
Holyoake Ct BERM/RHTH SE16 160 E1 2
Holyoake Crs WOKN/KNAP GU21 231 P3
Holyoake Ter SEV TN13 247 H10
Holyoake Wk EA W5 135 H6
EFNCH N2 117 M1
Holyoak Rd LBTH SE11 18 C5
Holyport Rd FUL/PGN SW6 156 F6
Holyrood Av RYLN/HDSTN HA2 113 M9
Holyrood Crs STAL AL1 38 C10
Holyrood Gdns CDH/CHF RM16 168 F3
EDGW HA8 95 N10
Holyrood Rd BAR EN5 77 M10
Holyrood St STHWK SE1 13 J10
Holywell Cl BKHTH/KID SE3 161 M5 2
STWL/WRAY TW19 173 P4
Holywell Hl STAL AL1 38 C7
Holywell La SDTCH EC2A 13 K1
Holywell Rd WATW WD18 73 H9
Holywell Rw SDTCH EC2A 13 J2
Holywell Wy STWL/WRAY TW19 173 P4
Home Cl BROX EN10 44 E10
CAR SM5 202 A9
CRAWE RH10 284 D5
HLW CM20 47 J1
LHD/OX KT22 236 C7
NTHLT UB5 133 N5
VW GU25 194 A6
Homecroft Gdns LOU IG10 82 E8
Homecroft Rd SYD SE26 182 B8
WDGN N22 99 J9
Homedean Rd SEV TN13 246 D8
Home Farm Cl
BRKHM/BTCW RH3 274 B1
CHERT KT16 214 D4
EPSOM KT18 238 G3
ESH/CLAY KT10 218 A3
SHPTN TW17 196 F4
THDIT KT7 198 E7
Home Farm Gdns WOT/HER KT12 197 K9
Home Farm Rd BERK HP4 33 J2 2
Homefarm Rd HNWL W7 134 D8
Home Farm Rd RBRW/HUT CM13 107 K9
RKW/CH/CXG WD3 92 B5
Home Farm Wy DTCH/LGLY SL3 129 P3 2
Homefield BERK HP4 34 E2
HHS/BOV HP3 52 E4
WAB EN9 63 M8
Homefield Av GNTH/NBYPK IG2 123 H3
Homefield Cl ADL/WDHM KT15 215 H8
EPP CM16 65 K5
HORL RH6 280 C3 12
LHD/OX KT22 237 H7
STMC/STPC BR5 207 L4 2
SWLY BR8 208 G3
WLSDN NW10 135 P1 2
YEAD UB4 133 L6 7
Homefield Gdns EFNCH N2 117 N1
KWD/TDW/WH KT20 238 F6
WIM/MER SW19 201 M2
Homefield Pk SUT SM1 221 L3
Homefield Ri ORP BR6 207 K8
Homefield Rd ALP/SUD HA0 114 F9
BMLY BR1 205 P1
BUSH WD23 73 P9
CHSWK W4 156 C3
COUL/CHIP CR5 241 J6
EDGW HA8 96 A7
HHNE HP2 36 B6
RAD WD7 74 E3
RKW/CH/CXG WD3 70 G8
SEV TN13 246 F8
WARE SG12 26 D1
WARL CR6 242 B5
WIM/MER SW19 178 G9 1
WOT/HER KT12 197 N7
Homefield St IS N1 7 J8 1
Home Gdns DAGE RM10 124 D8 2
DART DA1 187 M2
Home Hl SWLY BR8 186 G10
Homeland Dr BELMT SM2 221 L5
Homelands LHD/OX KT22 237 H7
Homelands Dr NRWD SE19 181 M10
Home Lea ORP BR6 227 J2
Homeleigh Ct CHES/WCR EN8 62 A6 1
Homeleigh Rd PECK SE15 182 C1
Home Ley WGCE AL7 23 H5 1
Home Md STAN HA7 95 H9 1
Home Mead Cl GVE DA12 190 E3
Home Meadow BNSTD SM7 239 K2
SLN SL2 129 H4 1
WGCE AL7 23 J5 1
Homemead Rd CROY/NA CR0 202 D6 3
HAYES BR2 206 C5
Home Pk OXTED RH8 261 M7
Home Park Mill Link Rd
KGLGY WD4 54 C7
Home Park Rd WIM/MER SW19 179 J7
Home Park Wk KUT KT1 199 J4 2
Homer Cl BXLYHN DA7 164 D7
Homer Dr POP/IOD E14 160 F3
Homerfield WGCW AL8 22 F5
Home Rd BTSEA SW11 157 P8
Homer Rd CROY/NA CR0 204 C6
HOM E9 140 D1
Homer Rw CAMTN NW1 9 P4
Homersham Rd KUT KT1 199 M2
Homers Rd WDSR SL4 148 C7
Homer St CAMTN NW1 9 P4
Homerswood La WLYN AL6 22 D1
Homerton Gv HOM E9 120 C10
Homerton High St HOM E9 120 C10
Homerton Rd HOM E9 120 E10
Homerton Rw HOM E9 120 B10
Homerton Ter HOM E9 140 B1 4
Homesdale Cl WAN E11 121 M3 2
Homesdale Rd CTHM CR3 241 L9
HAYES BR2 205 P4
ORP BR6 207 H7
Homesfield GLDGN NW11 117 K3 1
Homestall GUW GU2 249 J10
Homestall Rd EDUL SE22 182 B1
Homestead Cl LCOL/BKTW AL2 56 B3
Homestead Gdns
ESH/CLAY KT10 218 D2 1
Homestead La WGCE AL7 23 J8
Homestead Paddock
STHGT/OAK N14 78 C9
Homestead Pk CRICK NW2 116 C8
Homestead Rd BCTR RM8 124 A7
CTHM CR3 241 L9
FUL/PGN SW6 157 J6
HAT AL10 40 E2
ORP BR6 227 L4
RKW/CH/CXG WD3 91 N1
STA TW18 173 L9
The Homestead DART DA1 187 K2
Homestead Wy CROY/NA CR0 225 H7
Homewaters Av SUN TW16 196 G1
Homeway HARH RM3 106 A7
Home Wy RKW/CH/CXG WD3 91 J2
Homewillow Cl WCHMH N21 79 J10 1
Homewood DTCH/LGLY SL3 130 A8
Homewood Av POTB/CUF EN6 60 F3
Homewood Cl HPTN TW12 175 N9 4
Homewood Crs CHST BR7 185 H9
Homewood La POTB/CUF EN6 60 D3
Homewood Rd STAL AL1 38 G3
Honduras St FSBYE EC1V 12 E1 2
Honeybourne Rd
KIL/WHAMP NW6 117 L10 2
Honeybourne Wy
STMC/STPC BR5 206 F8
Honey Brook WAB EN9 63 K9
Honeybrook Rd BAL SW12 180 D3
Honey Cl BRWN CM15 87 J1
DAGE RM10 144 D1
Honeycrock La REDH RH1 276 B7
Honeycroft LOU IG10 82 D8
WGCW AL8 22 F6 3
Honeycroft Dr STALE/WH AL4 39 H9
Honeycroft Hl HGDN/ICK UB10 131 P2
Honeycross Rd HHW HP1 35 H7
Honeyden Rd SCUP DA14 185 P9
Honey Hl HGDN/ICK UB10 132 A2
Honey La CHES/WCR EN8 62 E10
WAB EN9 63 L10
Honeyman Cl CRICK NW2 136 C2
KIL/WHAMP NW6 136 G2
Honeymeade HLW CM20 29 M4
Honeypot Cl KTN/HRWW/W HA3 115 L2 1
Honeypot La BRW CM14 106 F3
CDALE/KGS NW9 115 L2 2
KTN/HRWW/W HA3 115 L1
STAN HA7 115 K1
Honeypots Rd WOKS/MYFD GU22 232 A8
Honeysett Rd TOTM N17 99 N10 1
Honeysuckle Bottom
EHSLY KT24 252 F10
Honeysuckle Cl BRWN CM15 86 G9
HARH RM3 105 L7 3
HERT/BAY SG13 25 P5 2
HORL RH6 280 D3
IVER SL0 130 F8
STHL UB1 133 M9 2
Honeysuckle Fld CSHM HP5 51 H5
Honeysuckle Gdns CROY/NA CR0 204 C7
HAT AL10 40 E5
Honeysuckle La CRAWW RH11 283 M4
Honeywell Rd BTSEA SW11 179 P2
Honeywood Cl POTB/CUF EN6 59 N9
Honeywood Rd ISLW TW7 154 F10 2
WLSDN NW10 136 C4 3
Honeywood Wk CAR SM5 222 A1 2
Honister Cl STAN HA7 94 G9
Honister Gdns STAN HA7 94 G8
Honister Hts PUR/KEN CR8 223 L10
Honister Pl STAN HA7 94 G9
Honiton Rd KIL/WHAMP NW6 2 C7
ROMW/RG RM7 124 E4
WELL DA16 163 J8
Honley Rd CAT SE6 182 G3
Honnor Rd STA TW18 173 N10
Honor Oak Ri FSTH SE23 182 B2
Honor Oak Rd FSTH SE23 182 B4
Hood Av MORT/ESHN SW14 177 P1
STHGT/OAK N14 78 C10
STMC/STPC BR5 207 L5
Hoodcote Gdns WCHMH N21 99 J1
Hood Rd RAIN RM13 144 F3
RYNPK SW20 178 C10
Hood Wk ROMW/RG RM7 104 C9
Hook End Rd BRWN CM15 86 G1
Hooke Rd EHSLY KT24 252 G1
Hooker's Rd WALTH E17 120 C1
Hook Farm Rd HAYES BR2 206 A5
Hook Fld HLWS CM18 47 H3
Hookfield HOR/WEW KT19 219 P9
Hookfields GVW DA11 190 B6
Hook Ga EN EN1 80 A3
Hook Green La RDART DA2 186 G6
Hook Green Rd MEO DA13 189 L10
Hook Heath Av
WOKS/MYFD GU22 231 N5
Hook Heath Gdns
WOKS/MYFD GU22 231 L7
Hook Heath Rd
WOKS/MYFD GU22 231 P7
Hook Hl SAND/SEL CR2 223 M6
Hook Hill La WOKS/MYFD GU22 231 N7
Hook Hill Pk WOKS/MYFD GU22 231 N7
Hooking Gn RYLN/HDSTN HA2 114 A3 1
Hook La ABR/ST RM4 84 A10
CHOB/PIR GU24 212 B9
POTB/CUF EN6 60 A8
RGUW GU3 266 C7
SHGR GU5 270 C7
WELL DA16 163 J10
Hook Mill La CHOB/PIR GU24 212 C5
Hook Ri North SURB KT6 199 L10
Hook Ri South CHSGTN KT9 199 L10
Hook Rd CHSGTN KT9 219 J1 2
HOR/WEW KT19 219 P6
SURB KT6 199 K9
Hooks Hall Dr DAGE RM10 124 D8 3
Hookstone La CHOB/PIR GU24 212 E7
Hookstone Wy WFD IG8 102 A8
The Hook BAR EN5 77 N10
Hook Underpass (Kingston By-pass)
SURB KT6 199 J10
Hook Wk EDGW HA8 95 P7
Hookwood Cnr OXTED RH8 261 N4
Hookwood Rd ORP BR6 227 M7
Hooley La REDH RH1 276 A1
Hooper Rd CAN/RD E16 141 M8
Hooper's Ms ACT W3 135 P10 3
Hooper St WCHPL E1 13 N6
Hoop La GLDGN NW11 117 J5
The Hoo HLWE CM17 29 M6
Hope Cl BTFD TW8 155 K4 2
CHDH RM6 123 N2
IS N1 6 F1
LEE/GVPK SE12 183 N6
SUT SM1 221 M2 4
Hopedale Rd CHARL SE7 161 N5
Hopefield Av KIL/WHAMP NW6 2 B7
Hope Gn GSTN WD25 55 H9
Hope Pk BMLY BR1 183 L10
Hope Rd SWCM DA10 189 L2
Hopes Cl HEST TW5 153 P5 1
Hope St BTSEA SW11 157 N9
Hopetown St WCHPL E1 13 M4 1
Hopewell Dr GVE DA12 191 J8
Hopewell St CMBW SE5 159 L6
Hopfield Av BF/WBF KT14 215 P8
Hopgarden La SEV TN13 265 H4
Hop Gdns CHCR WC2N 11 L8 5
Hopgood St SHB W12 136 F10 1
Hopground Cl STAL AL1 38 F8
Hopkins Cl GPK RM2 125 K1
MUSWH N10 98 B8 2
Hopkins Crs STALE/WH AL4 20 G10
Hopkins St SOHO/CST W1F 11 H6
Hopkins Yd STAL AL1 38 D7 5
Hoppers Rd WCHMH N21 99 H3
Hoppett Rd CHING E4 101 K4
The Hoppety
KWD/TDW/WH KT20 238 G8
Hopping La IS N1 6 D2
Hoppingwood Av NWMAL KT3 200 B3
The Hoppitt CHONG CM5 49 K6
Hoppner Rd YEAD UB4 132 E4
Hopton Gdns NWMAL KT3 200 D6
Hopton Rd STRHM/NOR SW16 180 F8
Hopton St STHWK SE1 12 D9
Hopwood Cl TOOT SW17 179 M6 2
Hopwood Rd WALW SE17 19 H9
Horace Av ROMW/RG RM7 124 E6
Horace Rd BARK/HLT IG6 122 F1
FSTGT E7 121 N9 2
KUT KT1 199 L3
Horatio Pl POP/IOD E14 161 H1
Horatio St BETH E2 7 N9 1
Horatius Wy CROY/NA CR0 222 G3
Horbeam Cl BORE WD6 75 M5 3
Horbury Crs NTGHL W11 8 E8
Horbury Ms NTGHL W11 8 D8
Horder Rd FUL/PGN SW6 157 H7
Hordle Gdns STAL AL1 38 E7
Hordle Prom North PECK SE15 159 N6 4
Horksley Gdns
RBRW/HUT CM13 87 P10 5
Horley Cl BXLYHS DA6 186 B1 1
Horley Lodge La REDH RH1 276 A9
Horley Rd ELTH/MOT SE9 184 B7
HORL RH6 279 K8
REDH RH1 276 A5
Horley Rw HORL RH6 280 A3
Hormead Rd NKENS W10 8 C2
Hornbeam Av UPMR RM14 125 P9
Hornbeam Cha SOCK/AV RM15 147 J5
Hornbeam Cl EPP CM16 83 H3
IL IG1 122 G10
LBTH SE11 18 A5
NTHLT UB5 113 N10
RBRW/HUT CM13 107 N4
Hornbeam Crs BTFD TW8 154 G6
Hornbeam Gdns
DTCH/LGLY SL3 149 M2 2
Hornbeam Gv CHING E4 101 K4
Hornbeam La BRKMPK AL9 41 P7
CHING E4 81 K9
Hornbeam Rd BKHH IG9 102 A4
EPP CM16 82 G3 1
GU GU1 249 P7
REIG RH2 275 M3
YEAD UB4 133 K7
Hornbeams LCOL/BKTW AL2 55 N6
Hornbeams Av EN EN1 80 B1
Hornbeams Ri FBAR/BDGN N11 98 B7 1
The Hornbeams HLW CM20 28 F9
Hornbeam Wy CHESW EN7 61 N5
HAYES BR2 206 D6
Hornbill Cl UX/CGN UB8 131 N8
Hornbuckle Cl
RYLN/HDSTN HA2 114 C7 5
Hornby Cl HAMP NW3 3 M3
Horncastle Cl LEE/GVPK SE12 183 M3 2
Horncastle Rd LEE/GVPK SE12 183 M3
Hornchurch Cl KUTN/CMB KT2 177 J8 2
Hornchurch Hl CTHM CR3 241 N3
Hornchurch Rd EMPK RM11 125 J6
HCH RM12 125 H6
Horndean Cl CRAWE RH10 284 E3 1
PUT/ROE SW15 178 D4 2
Horndon Cl CRW RM5 104 D9
Horndon Gn CRW RM5 104 D9
Horndon Rd CRW RM5 104 D9
Hornecourt Hl GDST RH9 277 N10
Horner La MTCM CR4 201 N2 1
Horne Rd SHPTN TW17 196 A4
The Hornets WATW WD18 73 J8 2
Horne Wy PUT/ROE SW15 156 F8
Hornfair Rd CHARL SE7 162 A5
Hornford Wy ROMW/RG RM7 124 F5
Hornhatch RGUE GU4 268 E7
Hornhatch Cl RGUE GU4 268 E6 1
Hornhatch La RGUE GU4 268 D6
Hornhill Rd RKW/CH/CXG WD3 90 F6
Horniman Dr FSTH SE23 182 A4
Horning Cl ELTH/MOT SE9 184 B7
Horn La ACT W3 135 P10
GNWCH SE10 161 M4 1
WFD IG8 101 M7
Hornminster Gln EMPK RM11 125 P7 1
Horn Park Cl LEE/GVPK SE12 183 N1
Horn Park La LEE/GVPK SE12 183 N1
Horns Cl HERT/BAY SG13 25 K7
Horns End Pl PIN HA5 113 K2
Hornsey La ARCH N19 118 D5
Hornsey Lane Gdns HGT N6 118 D5
Hornsey Park Rd
CEND/HSY/T N8 118 G1
Hornsey Ri ARCH N19 118 E5
Hornsey Rise Gdns ARCH N19 118 E5
Hornsey Rd ARCH N19 118 F6
Hornsey St HOLWY N7 118 G10 4
Hornsfield WGCE AL7 23 M4
Hornshay St PECK SE15 160 B5
Horns Mill Rd HERT/BAY SG13 25 J8
Horns Rd BARK/HLT IG6 122 F3
HERT/BAY SG13 25 K6
Hornton Pl KENS W8 14 F2
Hornton St KENS W8 14 F1
Horn Yd GVE DA12 190 E2 8
Horsa Rd ERITH DA8 164 D6
LEE/GVPK SE12 183 P3
Horsebridges Cl DAGW RM9 143 P3 2
Horsecroft BNSTD SM7 239 J3 1
Horsecroft Cl ORP BR6 207 L8 1
Horsecroft Rd EDGW HA8 96 A8
HHW HP1 35 K8
HLWW/ROY CM19 46 B2
Horse Fair KUT KT1 199 J2
Horseferry Pl GNWCH SE10 161 H5 5
Horseferry Rd POP/IOD E14 140 D9
WEST SW1P 17 J4
Horse Guards Av WHALL SW1A 11 L10
Horse Guards Rd WHALL SW1A 11 K10
Horse Hl CSHM HP5 52 A8
HORL RH6 279 L3
Horse Leaze EHAM E6 142 E8
Horselers HHS/BOV HP3 36 B9
Horsell Birch WOKN/KNAP GU21 231 M1
Horsell Common Rd
WOKN/KNAP GU21 213 P10
Horsell Ct CHERT KT16 195 L7
Horsell Moor WOKN/KNAP GU21 232 A3
Horsell Pk WOKN/KNAP GU21 232 A2
Horsell Park Cl
WOKN/KNAP GU21 232 A3
Horsell Ri WOKN/KNAP GU21 232 A1
Horsell Rise Cl WOKN/KNAP GU21 232 A1
Horsell Rd HBRY N5 119 H10 3
STMC/STPC BR5 207 K1
Horsell V WOKN/KNAP GU21 232 B1
Horsell Wy WOKN/KNAP GU21 231 P2
Horselydown La STHWK SE1 19 L1
Horsemans Dr LCOL/BKTW AL2 55 P2
Horseman Side BRW CM14 85 L10
Horsemoor Cl DTCH/LGLY SL3 150 D3 2
Horsenden Av GFD/PVL UB6 114 D10
Horsenden Crs GFD/PVL UB6 114 E10
Horsenden La North
GFD/PVL UB6 134 D1
Horsenden La South
GFD/PVL UB6 134 F3
Horseshoe Cl CRAWE RH10 284 F6 2
CRICK NW2 116 E7
POP/IOD E14 161 H4 2
Horse Shoe Crs NTHLT UB5 133 P4
Horseshoe Dr UX/CGN UB8 132 B8
Horseshoe Hl SL SL1 108 B9
WAB EN9 63 P9
Horseshoe La ENC/FH EN2 79 K7 4
GSTN WD25 55 J8
TRDG/WHET N20 96 G2
Horseshoe La West GU GU1 250 E9
Horseshoe Rdg WEY KT13 216 D7
The Horseshoe BNSTD SM7 239 J1
COUL/CHIP CR5 222 E9
HHS/BOV HP3 36 D8
Horse Yd IS N1 6 D5
Horsfeld Gdns ELTH/MOT SE9 184 B1 2
Horsfeld Rd ELTH/MOT SE9 184 A1
Horsfield Cl RDART DA2 188 B3 2
Horsford Rd BRXS/STRHM SW2 180 G1
Horsham Av NFNCH/WDSP N12 97 P6
Horsham Rd BXLYHS DA6 186 A2
CRAWW RH11 283 M8
DORK RH4 272 F3
EBED/NFELT TW14 174 D2
SHGR GU5 268 B8
SHGR GU5 270 G8
Horshoe La East GU GU1 250 E9
Horsley Cl HOR/WEW KT19 220 A9
Horsley Dr CROY/NA CR0 225 H4
KUTN/CMB KT2 177 J8 3
Horsley Rd BMLY BR1 205 N1 3
CHING E4 101 H3
COB KT11 235 J5
Horsleys RKW/CH/CXG WD3 90 G6
Horsley St WALW SE17 18 G9
Horsman St CMBW SE5 18 F10
Horsmonden Cl ORP BR6 207 J7 1
Horsmonden Rd BROCKY SE4 182 E1
Hortensia Rd WBPTN SW10 15 J10
Horticultural Pl CHSWK W4 156 A4 2
Horton Av CRICK NW2 117 H9
Horton Bridge Rd WDR/YW UB7 132 A10
Horton Cl WDR/YW UB7 132 A10
Horton Gdns HOR/WEW KT19 219 P7
Horton Hl HOR/WEW KT19 219 P7
Horton La HOR/WEW KT19 219 M7
Horton Pl BH/WHM TN16 262 G2
Horton Rd DTCH/LGLY SL3 149 P7

DTCH/LGLY SL3 ... 150 E7
EYN DA4 ... 210 B3
HACK E8 ... 140 A1
STWL/WRAY TW19 ... 151 K10
WDR/YW UB7 ... 131 P10
Horton St LEW SE13 ... 160 C9
Hortons Wy BH/WHM TN16 ... 262 G2
Horton Wy CROY/NA CR0 ... 204 C5
EYN DA4 ... 209 N1
Hortus Rd NWDGN UB2 ... 153 N1
Horvath Cl WEY KT13 ... 216 E1
Hosack Rd BAL SW12 ... 180 A5
Hoselands Vw HART DA3 ... 211 K4
Hoser Av LEE/GVPK SE12 ... 183 M5
Hosey Common La
 BH/WHM TN16 ... 263 H5
Hosey Common Rd
 BH/WHM TN16 ... 263 H5
Hosey HI BH/WHM TN16 ... 263 H3
Hosier La STBT EC1A ... 12 C4
Hoskin's Cl CAN/RD E16 ... 141 P8
 HYS/HAR UB3 ... 152 G3
Hoskins Rd OXTED RH8 ... 261 K5
Hoskins St GNWCH SE10 ... 161 J4
Hospital Bridge Rd WHTN TW2 ... 176 A4
Hospital La CSHM HP5 ... 51 H8
Hospital Rd HSLW TW3 ... 153 P9
 SEV TN13 ... 247 K7
Hospital Wy LEW SE13 ... 183 J2
Hotham Cl E/WMO/HCT KT8 ... 197 P3
 EYN DA4 ... 187 P10
 SWLY BR8 ... 209 J1
Hotham Rd PUT/ROE SW15 ... 156 F9
 WIM/MER SW19 ... 179 M10
Hotham St SRTFD E15 ... 141 K3
Hothfield Pl BERM/RHTH SE16 ... 160 B2
Hotspur Rd NTHLT UB5 ... 133 P4
Hotspur St LBTH SE11 ... 18 A7
Hottsfield HART DA3 ... 211 K3
Houblon Rd RCHPK/HAM TW10 ... 177 K1
Houblons HI EPP CM16 ... 65 N7
Houghton Cl HOL/ALD WC2B ... 11 P6
Houghton Rd CRAWE RH10 ... 284 D10
 SEVS/STOTM N15 ... 119 N2
Houlder Crs CROY/NA CR0 ... 223 J3
Hound House Rd SHGR GU5 ... 270 B7
Houndsden Rd WCHMH N21 ... 78 G10
Houndsditch HDTCH EC3A ... 13 L6
Houndsfield Rd ED N9 ... 100 A1
Hounslow Av HSLW TW3 ... 176 A1
Hounslow Gdns HSLW TW3 ... 176
 FELT TW13 ... 175 L6
 HSLW TW3 ... 176 A2
 WHTN TW2 ... 176 B2
Housden Cl STALE/WH AL4 ... 21 K4
Housefield Wy STALE/WH AL4 ... 39 H9
House La STALE/WH AL4 ... 21 H10
Housewood End HHW HP1 ... 35 L3
Houston Rd FSTH SE23 ... 182 D5
Hove Av WALTH E17 ... 167 M5
Hove Cl GRAYS RM17 ... 167 M5
 RBRW/HUT CM13 ... 116 G10
Hoveden Rd CRICK NW2 ... 116 C10
Hove Gdns SUT SM1 ... 201 L8
Hoveton Rd THMD SE28 ... 143 M8
Howard Agne Cl HHW HP1 ... 52 D3
Howard Av BXLY DA5 ... 185 M4
 EW KT17 ... 220 D6
 SLN1 ... 129 J7
Howard Cl ACT W3 ... 135 N6
 ASHTD KT21 ... 237 L4
 BUSH WD23 ... 94 D1
 CRICK NW2 ... 117 H9
 EHSLY KT24 ... 252 E1
 FBAR/BDGN N11 ... 98 B3
 HPTN TW12 ... 176 B10
 KWD/TDW/WH KT20 ... 256 F10
 LHD/OX KT22 ... 237 H9
 STALE/WH AL4 ... 39 H9
 SUN TW16 ... 174 G9
 WAB EN9 ... 63 J10
 WATN WD24 ... 73 H3
Howard Dr BORE WD6 ... 76 A8
Howard Gdns GU GU1 ... 250 D9
Howard Rdg RGUE GU4 ... 250 D6
Howard Rd BARK IG11 ... 142 G3
 BEAC HP9 ... 89 H6
 BMLY BR1 ... 183 M10
 BRYLDS KT5 ... 199 L8
 CDH/CHF NW6 ... 167 H2
 COUL/CHIP CR5 ... 240 D1
 CRICK NW2 ... 116 G9
 CSHM HP5 ... 50 C4
 DART DA1 ... 187 P2
 DORK RH4 ... 272 F2
 EHAM E6 ... 142 C4
 EHSLY KT24 ... 235 H8
 GFD/PVL UB6 ... 134 B3
 GT/LBKH KT23 ... 254 A3
 IL IG1 ... 122 C6
 ISLW TW7 ... 154 E9
 NWMAL KT3 ... 200 B3
 PGE/AN SE20 ... 204 B1
 SEVS/STOTM N15 ... 119 M4
 SNWD SE25 ... 203 P5
 STNW/STAM N16 ... 119 L9
 UPMR RM14 ... 126 B7
 WALTH E17 ... 120 P1
 WAN E11 ... 121 K8
Howards Cl PIN HA5 ... 93 J10
 WOKS/MYFD GU22 ... 232 D6
Howards Crest Cl BECK BR3 ... 205 H2
Howards Dr HHW HP1 ... 35 J3
Howardsgate WGC AL8 ... 22 C5
Howards La ADL/WDHM KT15 ... 215 H3
 PUT/ROE SW15 ... 156 F10
Howard's Rd PLSTW E13 ... 141 K1
 WOKS/MYFD GU22 ... 232 C6
Howards Thicket CFSP/GDCR SL9 ... 109 H7
Howard St THDIT KT7 ... 198 C9
Howards Wood Dr
 CFSP/GDCR SL9 ... 110 A7
Howard Wk EFNCH N2 ... 117 M2
Howard Wy BAR EN5 ... 76 C9
 HLW CM20 ... 29 J8
Howarth Rd ABYW SE2 ... 163 K4
Howberry Cl EDGW HA8 ... 95 J3
Howberry Rd EDGW HA8 ... 95 J3
 THHTH CR7 ... 203 L1
Howbury La ERITH DA8 ... 165 H8
Howbury Rd DART DA1 ... 165 H8
 PECK SE15 ... 160 B9
Howcroft Crs FNCH N3 ... 97 L7
Howcroft La GFD/PVL UB6 ... 134 C5
Howden Cl THMD SE28 ... 143 M9
Howden Rd SNWD SE25 ... 203 N9
Howden St PECK SE15 ... 159 P9
Howe Cl RAD WD7 ... 57 K8
 ROMW/RG RM7 ... 104 B9
Howe Dell HAT AL10 ... 40 C4
Howe Dr BEAC HP9 ... 88 D6
 CTHM CR3 ... 241 L8
Howell Cl CHDH RM6 ... 123 N3
Howell Hill Cl EW KT17 ... 220 F7
Howell Hill Gv EW KT17 ... 220 F7
Howell Wk WALW SE17 ... 18 F6
Howes Cl FNCH N3 ... 97 H6
Howfield Gn HOD EN11 ... 26 E10
Howfield Pl MORT/ESHN SW14 ... 156 A4
Howick Pl WEST SW1P ... 17 H4
Howicks Gn WGCE AL7 ... 23 K8
Howie St BTSEA SW11 ... 157 P6
Howitt Rd HAMP NW3 ... 3 P1

Howitts Cl ESH/CLAY KT10 ... 217 P3
Howland Garth STAL AL1 ... 38 B10
Howland Ms East FITZ W1T ... 11 H3
Howlands WGCE AL7 ... 23 K8
Howland St FITZ W1T ... 11 H3
Howletts La RSLP HA4 ... 112 D4
Howletts Rd HNHL SE24 ... 181 K2
Howley Pl BAY/PAD W2 ... 9 K3
Howley Rd CROY/NA CR0 ... 203 J10
Howsman Rd BARN SW13 ... 156 D5
Hows Md EPP CM16 ... 48 E10
Hows St BETH E2 ... 7 L7
Howton Pl BUSH WD23 ... 94 C2
How Wd LCOL/BKTW AL2 ... 56 A4
Hoxton Market IS N1 ... 7 J10
Hoxton Sq IS N1 ... 7 J10
Hoxton St IS N1 ... 7 J6
Hoylake Cl CRAWW RH11 ... 282 C8
Hoylake Crs HGDN/ICK UB10 ... 112 B6
Hoylake Gdns HARH RM3 ... 105 P8
 MTCM CR4 ... 202 D3
 OXHEY WD19 ... 93 L5
 RSLP HA4 ... 113 J6
Hoylake Rd ACT W3 ... 136 B8
Hoyle Rd TOOT SW17 ... 179 P8
Hoy St CAN/RD E16 ... 141 L8
Hubbard Dr CHSGTN KT9 ... 219 H3
Hubbard Rd WNWD SE27 ... 181 L7
Hubbards Cha EMPK RM11 ... 125 P3
Hubbards Rd EMPK RM11 ... 125 P3
Hubbard's HI SEV TN13 ... 265 J7
Hubbards Rd RKW/CH/CXG WD3 ... 70 G9
Hubbard St SRTFD E15 ... 141 K3
Hubert Day Cl BEAC HP9 ... 88 C3
Hubert Gv BRXN/ST SW9 ... 158 F3
Hubert Rd BRW CM14 ... 106 C4
 DTCH/LGLY SL3 ... 150 A2
 EHAM E6 ... 142 A5
 RAIN RM13 ... 144 D5
Hucknall St HARH RM3 ... 105 N7
Huddart St BOW E3 ... 140 E7
Huddleston Rd REDH RH1 ... 258 E4
Huddlestone Rd CRICK NW2 ... 136 E1
 FSTGT E7 ... 121 L9
Hudson Cl STAL AL1 ... 38 B9
 WATN WD24 ... 72 C2
Hudson Pl WOOL/PLUM SE18 ... 162 F4
 CRAWE RH10 ... 283 P9
 HYS/HAR UB3 ... 152 F5
Hudson Rd BXLYHN DA7 ... 164 A8
 CRAWE RH10 ... 283 P9
 HYS/HAR UB3 ... 152 F5
Huggin HI BLKFR EC4V ... 12 F7
Huggins La BRKMPK AL9 ... 40 A8
Huggins Pl BRXS/STRHM SW2 ... 180 G4
Hughan Rd SRTFD E15 ... 121 J10
Hughenden Av
 KTN/HRWW/W HA3 ... 114 C3
Hughenden Gdns NTHLT UB5 ... 133 K5
Hughenden Rd SL SL1 ... 129 J8
 STALE/WH AL4 ... 38 G3
 WPK KT4 ... 200 D7
Hughes Rd ASHF TW15 ... 174 D10
 CDH/CHF RM16 ... 168 D2
 HYS/HAR UB3 ... 133 J9
Hughes Wk CROY/NA CR0 ... 203 K7
Hugh Dalton Av FUL/PGN SW6 ... 14 C10
Hugh Gaitskell Cl FUL/PGN SW6 ... 14 C10
Hugh Ms PIM SW1V ... 16 F6
Hugh Pl WEST SW1P ... 17 J5
Hugh St PIM SW1V ... 16 F6
Hugo Gdns RAIN RM13 ... 144 C1
Hugo Rd ARCH N19 ... 118 D9
Huguenot Pl WAND/EARL SW18 ... 179 M1
Hullbridge Ms IS N1 ... 6 G2
Hull Cl BERM/RHTH SE16 ... 140 C10
 SL SL1 ... 149 H1
Hullets La BRWN CM15 ... 86 E8
Hull Gv HLWM CM17 ... 31 L9
Hull Pl HLWW/ROY CM19 ... 46 D7
Hull St FSBYE EC1V ... 6 E10
Hulse Av BARK IG11 ... 142 C1
 ROMW/RG RM7 ... 104 C9
Hulsewood Cl RDART DA2 ... 187 H4
Hulton Cl LHD/OX KT22 ... 237 H10
Hulverston Cl BELMT SM2 ... 221 L6
Humber Av SOCK/AV RM15 ... 146 E8
Humber Dr NKENS W10 ... 136 G6
Humber Rd BKHTH/KID SE3 ... 161 N5
 CRICK NW2 ... 116 E7
 DART DA1 ... 187 L1
Humberstone Rd PLSTW E13 ... 141 P5
Humber Wy DTCH/LGLY SL3 ... 150 D3
Humbolt Cl GUW GU2 ... 249 K10
Humbolt Rd HMSMTH W6 ... 14 A10
Hume Cl TIL RM18 ... 168 D9
Humes Av HNWL W7 ... 154 F2
Hume Wy RSLP HA4 ... 113 H4
Hummer Rd EGH TW20 ... 172 D9
Humphrey Cl CLAY IG5 ... 102 C9
 LHD/OX KT22 ... 236 B7
Humphrey St STHWK SE1 ... 19 L7
Humphries Cl DAGW RM9 ... 124 A9
Hundred Acre CDALE/KGS NW9 ... 96 C10
Hundred Acres La AMSS HP7 ... 69 J6
Hungerford Av SLN SL2 ... 129 K7
Hungerford Rd HOLWY N7 ... 118 F10
Hungerford St WCHPL E1 ... 140 A8
Hungry Hill La RPLY/SEND GU23 ... 251 M2
Hunsdon WGCE AL7 ... 23 N1
Hunsdon Cl DAGW RM9 ... 143 P1
Hunsdon Dr SEV TN13 ... 247 J9
Hunsdon Rd NWCR SE14 ... 160 C1
 WARE SG12 ... 27 K7
Hunslett St BETH E2 ... 140 B4
Hunstanton Cl CRAWW RH11 ... 282 C8
 DTCH/LGLY SL3 ... 150 F6
Hunston Rd MRDN SM4 ... 201 L8
Hunt Cl STALE/WH AL4 ... 39 J3
Hunter Av BRWN CM15 ... 87 M10
Hunter Cl BAL SW12 ... 180 A4
 BORE WD6 ... 75 N7
 POTB/CUF EN6 ... 59 L9
 STHWK SE1 ... 19 K4
Hunters Cl BXLY DA5 ... 186 F6
 CSHM HP5 ... 50 F6
 HHS/BOV HP3 ... 35 P8
 HOR/WEW KT19 ... 219 P9
Hunters Gv RCH/KEW TW9 ... 177 J1
Huntersfield Cl REIG RH2 ... 257 N5
Hunter's Gv CRW RM5 ... 104 C6
 HYS/HAR UB3 ... 133 H10
 KTN/HRWW/W HA3 ... 115 H2
 ORP BR6 ... 226 F1
Hunters Hall Rd DAGE RM10 ... 124 B2
Hunters HI RSLP HA4 ... 113 K6
Hunter's La GSTN WD25 ... 54 G10
Hunters Meadow NRWD SE19 ... 181 M7

Hunters Oak HHNE HP2 ... 36 C1
Hunters Pk BERK HP4 ... 35 N1
Hunters Reach CHESW EN7 ... 61 N5
Hunters Ride LCOL/BKTW AL2 ... 55 P7
Hunters Rd CHSGTN KT9 ... 199 K10
 IL IG1 ... 122 C10
Hunters Sq DAGE RM10 ... 124 B2
Hunter St BMSBY WC1N ... 11 M1
Hunters Wk RSEV TN14 ... 227 P10
Hunters Wy CROY/NA CR0 ... 223 M1
 ENC/FH EN2 ... 79 H5
 SL SL1 ... 148 D1
 WGCE AL7 ... 23 H8
Hunting Cl ESH/CLAY KT10 ... 217 P3
Huntingdon Cl BROX EN10 ... 44 D10
 MTCM CR4 ... 202 F3
 WPK KT4 ... 200 F10
Huntingdon Gdns CHSWK W4 ... 155 P6
Huntingdon Rd ED N9 ... 100 B2
 EFNCH N2 ... 117 J1
 REDH RH1 ... 258 A10
 WOKN/KNAP GU21 ... 231 K3
Huntingdon St CAN/RD E16 ... 141 L8
 IS N1 ... 5 P3
Huntingfield CROY/NA CR0 ... 224 E4
Huntingfield Wy EGH TW20 ... 172 G10
Hunting Ga HHNE HP2 ... 35 P2
Hunting Gate Cl ENC/FH EN2 ... 79 H7
Hunting Gate Dr CHSGTN KT9 ... 219 K4
Hunting Gate Ms WHTN TW2 ... 176 D4
Huntland Cl RAIN RM13 ... 145 J7
Huntley Av GVW DA11 ... 189 N2
Huntley Cl STWL/WRAY WC1E ... 11 K1
Huntley Wy RYNPK SW20 ... 200 D2
Huntly Dr FNCH N3 ... 97 K1
Hunton Bridge HI KGLGY WD4 ... 54 D9
Hunton St WCHPL E1 ... 13 N1
 NWDGN UB2 ... 153 P7
Hunts Cl GUW GU2 ... 249 J9
Hunt's La SRTFD E15 ... 141 H4
Huntsman Cl FELT TW13 ... 175 J7
Huntsman Rd BARK/HLT IG6 ... 103 L7
Huntsmans Cl WARL CR6 ... 242 B5
Huntsmans Dr UPMR RM14 ... 126 B10
Huntsman St WALW SE17 ... 19 J6
Hunts Md PEND EN3 ... 80 C7
Hunts Mede Cl CHST BR7 ... 184 C10
Huntsmoor Rd HOR/WEW KT19 ... 220 A2
Huntsmore Rd UPMR RM14 ... 126 F3
Hunts Slip Rd DUL SE21 ... 181 M6
Hunt St NTGHL W11 ... 136 G10
Huntsworth Ms CAMTN NW1 ... 10 A1
Hurley Cl WOT/HER KT12 ... 197 J9
Hurley Gdns RGUE GU4 ... 250 D2
Hurley Rd GFD/PVL UB6 ... 134 A7
Hurlfield RDART DA2 ... 187 K6
Hurlford WOKN/KNAP GU21 ... 231 M3
Hurlingham Gdns FUL/PGN SW6 ... 157 J9
Hurlingham Rd CDH/CHF RM16 ... 168 C6
 FUL/PGN SW6 ... 157 J9
Hurlingham Sq FUL/PGN SW6 ... 157 J9
Hurlock St HBRY N5 ... 119 J8
Hurlstone Rd SNWD SE25 ... 203 L5
Hurn Court Rd HEST TW5 ... 153 L8
Hurnford Cl SAND/SEL CR2 ... 224 A1
Huron Cl ORP BR6 ... 227 J3
Huron Rd TOOT SW17 ... 180 B5
Hurren Cl BKHTH/KID SE3 ... 161 N5
Hurricane Wy EPP CM16 ... 66 A3
 CSTN WD25 ... 55 H8
Hurry Cl SRTFD E15 ... 141 K2
Hursley Rd CHIG IG7 ... 103 J6
Hurst Av CHING E4 ... 100 F4
 HGT N6 ... 118 C4
Hurst Cl CHING E4 ... 100 E1
 CHSGTN KT9 ... 219 N2
 CRAWW RH11 ... 283 J10
 EPSOM KT18 ... 237 P10
 GLDGN NW11 ... 117 L4
 HAYES BR2 ... 205 L8
 NTHLT UB5 ... 133 N5
 WGCE AL7 ... 23 M6
 WOKS/MYFD GU22 ... 231 P5
Hurstcourt Rd CHEAM SM3 ... 201 L8
Hurst Dr CHES/WCR EN8 ... 62 C10
 KWD/TDW/WH KT20 ... 256 D2
Hurst Farm Rd RSEV TN14 ... 265 P10
Hurstfield HAYES BR2 ... 205 M5
Hurstfield Crs YEAD UB4 ... 132 F7
Hurstfield Dr MDHD SL6 ... 128 A8
Hurstfield Rd GLDGN NW11 ... 117 L4
Hurstmere Cha GLDGN NW11 ... 117 L4
Hurstmere Cl GU GU1 ... 268 C2
Hurtmore Rd RGODL GU7 ... 266 C5
Hurtwood Rd WOT/HER KT12 ... 197 N3
Huson Cl HAMP NW3 ... 3 N3
Hussars Cl HSLWW TW4 ... 153 M9
Husseywell Crs HAYES BR2 ... 205 M8
Hutchinson's Rd
 CROY/NA CR0 ... 225 H7
Hutchings St POP/IOD E14 ... 160 F1
Hutchings Wk GLDGN NW11 ... 117 L2
Hutchins Cl HCH RM12 ... 125 M8
 SRTFD E15 ... 141 H2
Hutchinson Ter WBLY HA9 ... 115 J8

Hutchins Rd THMD SE28 ... 143 K9
Hutchins Wy HORL RH6 ... 280 A2
Hutton Cl BFOR GU20 ... 212 C10
 HERT/WAS SG14 ... 25 H5
 NTHLT UB5 ... 114 C10
 WFD IG8 ... 101 N7
Hutton Ga RBRW/HUT CM13 ... 107 L4
Hutton Gv NFNCH/WDSP N12 ... 97 L5
Hutton La KTN/HRWW/W HA3 ... 94 B3
Hutton Rd BRWN CM15 ... 107 L1
Hutton St EMB EC4Y ... 12 C6
Hutton Wk KTN/HRWW/W HA3 ... 94 B9
Huxbear St BROCKY SE4 ... 182 C1
Huxley Cl NTHLT UB5 ... 133 M4
 RGODL GU7 ... 267 J10
Huxley Dr CHDH RM6 ... 123 L5
Huxley Pl PLMGR N13 ... 99 J5
Huxley Rd LEY E10 ... 121 N1
 UED N18 ... 99 L5
 WELL DA16 ... 163 J9
Huxley St NKENS W10 ... 2 A10
Hyacinth Cl HPTN TW12 ... 175 P9
Hyacinth Dr HGDN/ICK UB10 ... 131 P2
Hyacinth Rd PUT/ROE SW15 ... 178 D2
Hycliffe Gdns CHIG IG7 ... 102 F5
Hyde Av POTB/CUF EN6 ... 59 L9
Hyde Cl BAR EN5 ... 77 J7
 PLSTW E13 ... 141 M4
Hyde Crs CDALE/KGS NW9 ... 116 B3
Hyde Dr STMC/STPC BR5 ... 207 L4
Hyde Estate Rd CDALE/KGS NW9 ... 116 C3
Hydefield Cl ED N9 ... 99 J3
Hydefield Ct ED N9 ... 99 M3
Hyde Gn BEAC HP9 ... 88 B3
Hyde La BTSEA SW11 ... 157 P7
 HHS/BOV HP3 ... 52 D3
 KGLGY WD4 ... 54 C3
 LCOL/BKTW AL2 ... 56 D4
Hyde Mdw HHS/BOV HP3 ... 52 D3
Hyde Park Crs BAY/PAD W2 ... 9 M3
Hyde Park Gdns BAY/PAD W2 ... 9 K2
Hyde Park Gardens Ms
 BAY/PAD W2 ... 9 M7
Hyde Park Ga KENS SW7 ... 15 J2
 SKENS SW7 ... 15 K2
Hyde Park Gate Ms SKENS SW7 ... 15 K2
Hyde Park Sq BAY/PAD W2 ... 9 M6
Hyde Park St BAY/PAD W2 ... 9 M6
Hyderabad Wy SRTFD E15 ... 141 K2
Hyde Rd BXLYHN DA7 ... 164 A8
 IS N1 ... 7 H6
 RCHPK/HAM TW10 ... 177 L1
 SAND/SEL CR2 ... 223 N9
 WAT WD17 ... 73 H7
Hyder Rd CDH/CHF RM16 ... 168 E3
Hydeside Gdns ED N9 ... 99 N3
Hyde's Pl IS N1 ... 6 C3
Hyde St DEPT SE8 ... 160 F5
Hyde Ter ASHF TW15 ... 174 F9
The Hyde CDALE/KGS NW9 ... 116 B3
 WARE SG12 ... 26 A1
Hydethorpe Av ED N9 ... 99 N3
Hydethorpe Rd BAL SW12 ... 180 D4
Hyde V GNWCH SE10 ... 161 H6
Hyde Va GNWCH SE10 ... 161 H6
Hyde Wk MRDN SM4 ... 201 K7
Hyde Wy ED N9 ... 99 N3
 HYS/HAR UB3 ... 152 C3
 WGCE AL7 ... 23 L8
Hyland Cl EMPK RM11 ... 125 J5
Hylands Cl CRAWE RH10 ... 284 B8
 EPSOM KT18 ... 237 P1
Hylands Ms EPSOM KT18 ... 237 P1
Hylands Rd EPSOM KT18 ... 237 P1
 WALTH E17 ... 101 J10
Hyland Wy EMPK RM11 ... 125 J5
Hylle Cl WDSR SL4 ... 148 G7
Hylton St WOOL/PLUM SE18 ... 163 J3
Hyndewood FSTH SE23 ... 182 A10
Hyndman Rd PECK SE15 ... 160 A5
Hyndman St PECK SE15 ... 160 A5
Hynton Rd BCTR RM8 ... 123 M7
Hyperion Ct CRAWW RH11 ... 283 P9
Hyperion Pl HOR/WEW KT19 ... 220 A5
Hyrons Cl AMS HP6 ... 69 A5
Hyrons La AMS HP6 ... 69 A5
 AMSS HP7 ... 69 A5
Hyson Rd BERM/RHTH SE16 ... 160 A4
Hythe Av BXLYHN DA7 ... 163 P6
Hythe Cl STMC/STPC BR5 ... 207 N4
 UED N18 ... 99 P5
Hythe End Rd STWL/WRAY TW19 ... 172 B10
Hythe Field Av EGH TW20 ... 172 F9
Hythe Park Rd EGH TW20 ... 172 F8
Hythe Rd STA TW18 ... 172 C8
 THHTH CR7 ... 203 L2
 WLSDN NW10 ... 136 C5
Hythe St DART DA1 ... 187 M1
The Hythe STA TW18 ... 173 H8
Hyver HI MLHL NW7 ... 76 A10

I

Ibbetson Pth LOU IG10 ... 82 E7
Ibbotson Av CAN/RD E16 ... 141 L8
Iberian Av WLGTN SM6 ... 222 F4
Ibis La CHSWK W4 ... 155 P7
Ibis Wy YEAD UB4 ... 133 L8
Ibscott Cl DAGE RM10 ... 144 D1
Ibsley Gdns PUT/ROE SW15 ... 178 D4
Ibsley Wy EBAR EN4 ... 77 P9
Icehouse Wd OXTED RH8 ... 261 N10
Iceland Rd BOW E3 ... 140 F3
Ickburgh Rd CLPT E5 ... 120 A8
Ickenham Cl RSLP HA4 ... 112 E7
Ickenham Rd HGDN/ICK UB10 ... 112 D7
 RSLP HA4 ... 112 E6
Ickleton Rd ELTH/MOT SE9 ... 184 C7
Icklingham Rd COB KT11 ... 217 K8
Icknield Dr CNTH/NBYPK IG2 ... 122 E3
Ickworth Park Rd WALTH E17 ... 120 D2
Ida Rd SEVS/STOTM N15 ... 119 L3
Ida St POP/IOD E14 ... 141 N9
Ide Hill Rd RSEV TN14 ... 264 A8
Iden Cl HAYES BR2 ... 205 N5
Idlecombe Rd TOOT SW17 ... 180 D3
Idleigh Court Rd HART DA3 ... 211 N9
Idmiston Rd FSTGT E7 ... 121 L10
 WNWD SE27 ... 181 K6
 WPK KT4 ... 200 D7
Idmiston Sq WPK KT4 ... 200 C7
Idol La MON EC3R ... 13 L5
Idonia St DEPT SE8 ... 160 E6
Iffley Cl UX/CGN UB8 ... 131 N2
Iffley Rd HMSMTH W6 ... 156 F2
Ifield Av CRAWW RH11 ... 283 M6
Ifield Cl REDH RH1 ... 283 M6
Ifield Dr CRAWW RH11 ... 283 K6
Ifield Gn CRAWW RH11 ... 283 K5
Ifield Rd CRAWW RH11 ... 283 M7
 HORL RH6 ... 279 P10
 WBPTN SW10 ... 15 H9
Ifield St CRAWW RH11 ... 283 L6
Ifold Rd REDH RH1 ... 276 D2
Ightham Rd ERITH DA8 ... 164 B6
Ilbert St NKENS W10 ... 2 A10

Ilchester Gdns BAY/PAD W2 ... 8 G7
Ilchester Pl WKENS W14 ... 14 D3
Ilchester Rd BCTR RM8 ... 123 L10
Ildersly Gv DUL SE21 ... 181 L5
Ilderton Rd BERM/RHTH SE16 ... 160 B5
Ilex Cl EGH TW20 ... 171 N10
 SUN TW16 ... 197 K2
Ilex Rd WLSDN NW10 ... 136 C1
Ilex Wy STRHM/NOR SW16 ... 181 H8
Ilford HI IL IG1 ... 122 D8
Ilford La IL IG1 ... 122 D8
Iliffe St WALW SE17 ... 18 D7
Iliffe Yd WALW SE17 ... 18 D7
Ilkley Cl NRWD SE19 ... 181 L9
Ilkley Rd CAN/RD E16 ... 141 P7
 OXHEY WD19 ... 93 L6
Illingworth WDSR SL4 ... 148 A5
Illingworth Cl MTCM CR4 ... 201 N3
Illingworth Wy EN EN1 ... 79 M9
Ilmington Rd KTN/HRWW/W HA3 ... 115 J4
Ilminster Gdns BTSEA SW11 ... 157 P10
Imber Cl STHGT/OAK N14 ... 98 D1
Imber Gv ESH/CLAY KT10 ... 198 C8
Imber Park Rd ESH/CLAY KT10 ... 198 C8
Imber St IS N1 ... 6 G6
Imperial Cl RYLN/HDSTN HA2 ... 113 P6
Imperial College Rd SKENS SW7 ... 15 M3
Imperial Ct WDSR SL4 ... 148 F9
Imperial Dr GVE DA12 ... 191 J8
 RYLN/HDSTN HA2 ... 113 P6
Imperial Pl CHST BR7 ... 206 D1
Imperial Rd EBED/NFELT TW14 ... 174 F3
 FUL/PGN SW6 ... 157 L2
 WDGN N22 ... 98 F8
 WDSR SL4 ... 148 F9
Imperial Sq FUL/PGN SW6 ... 157 L7
Imperial St BOW E3 ... 141 M4
Imperial Wy CHST BR7 ... 184 F6
 CROY/NA CR0 ... 222 G3
 KTN/HRWW/W HA3 ... 115 K4
 WATN WD24 ... 73 K5
Inca Dr ELTH/MOT SE9 ... 184 E3
Ince Rd WOT/HER KT12 ... 216 F2
Inchmery Rd CAT SE6 ... 182 G5
Inchwood CROY/NA CR0 ... 224 C1
Indells HAT AL10 ... 40 C5
Independents Rd
 BKHTH/KID SE3 ... 161 L9
Inderwick Rd CEND/HSY/T N8 ... 118 C4
Indescon Ct POP/IOD E14 ... 160 L1
India Rd SL SL1 ... 149 N1
India St TWRH EC3N ... 13 L4
India Wy SHB W12 ... 136 E9
Indigo Ms STNW/STAM N16 ... 119 L8
Indus Rd CHARL SE7 ... 161 P6
Ingal Rd PLSTW E13 ... 141 M6
Ingate Pl VX/NE SW8 ... 158 C2
Ingatestone Rd MNPK E12 ... 121 P6
 SNWD SE25 ... 204 A4
 WFD IG8 ... 101 N8
Ingelow Rd VX/NE SW8 ... 158 C8
Ingels Md EPP CM16 ... 65 J5
Ingersoll Rd PEND EN3 ... 80 B4
 SHB W12 ... 136 E10
Ingestre Pl SOHO/SHAV W1F ... 11 H6
Ingestre Rd FSTGT E7 ... 121 M9
 KTTN NW5 ... 118 C9
Ingham Cl SAND/SEL CR2 ... 224 C5
Ingham Rd KIL/WHAMP NW6 ... 117 K9
 SAND/SEL CR2 ... 224 B5
Inglebert St CLKNW EC1R ... 6 A9
Ingleboro Dr PUR/KEN CR8 ... 223 L9
Ingleborough St BRXN/ST SW9 ... 159 H8
Ingleby Dr HRW HA1 ... 114 C8
Ingleby Gdns CHIG IG7 ... 103 L4
Ingleby Rd CDH/CHF RM16 ... 168 E2
 DAGE RM10 ... 144 C1
 IL IG1 ... 122 B6
Ingleby Wy CHST BR7 ... 184 D8
 WLGTN SM6 ... 222 E5
Ingle Cl PIN HA5 ... 113 N1
Ingledew Rd WOOL/PLUM SE18 ... 163 L6
Inglefield POTB/CUF EN6 ... 59 K6
Ingleglen EMPK RM11 ... 125 P5
 SLN SL2 ... 108 G10
Inglehurst Gdns REDBR IG4 ... 122 C3
Inglemere Rd FSTH SE23 ... 182 C6
 TOOT SW17 ... 180 A10
Ingleside DTCH/LGLY SL3 ... 150 B5
Ingleside Cl BECK BR3 ... 182 F10
Ingleside Gv BKHTH/KID SE3 ... 161 J5
Inglethorpe St FUL/PGN SW6 ... 156 G7
Ingleton Av WELL DA16 ... 185 K1
Ingleton Rd CAR SM5 ... 221 P5
 UED N18 ... 99 P5
Ingleton St BRXN/ST SW9 ... 159 H8
Ingleway NFNCH/WDSP N12 ... 97 N7
Inglewood CHERT KT16 ... 195 J10
 WOKN/KNAP GU21 ... 231 N4
Inglewood Cl BARK/HLT IG6 ... 103 J7
 HCH RM12 ... 125 L9
 POP/IOD E14 ... 160 F3
Inglewood Copse BMLY BR1 ... 206 B2
Inglewood Rd BXLYHN DA7 ... 164 E10
 KIL/WHAMP NW6 ... 117 K10
Inglis Rd CROY/NA CR0 ... 203 N8
 EA W5 ... 135 L9
Inglis St CMBW SE5 ... 159 J7
Ingoldsby Rd GVE DA12 ... 191 H4
Ingram Av EFNCH N2 ... 117 M5
Ingram Cl LBTH SE11 ... 17 P5
 STAN HA7 ... 95 H6
Ingram Rd DART DA1 ... 187 M4
 EFNCH N2 ... 117 M2
 GRAYS RM17 ... 167 P3
 THHTH CR7 ... 203 K1
Ingrams Cl WOT/HER KT12 ... 217 L4
Ingram Wy GFD/PVL UB6 ... 134 C3
Ingrave Rd BRW CM14 ... 107 K4
 ROM RM1 ... 124 F2
Ingrave St BTSEA SW11 ... 157 N9
Ingrebourne Gdns UPMR RM14 ... 125 J6
Ingrebourne Rd RAIN RM13 ... 145 J6
Ingress St CHSWK W4 ... 156 B4
Ingreway HARH RM3 ... 106 A7
Inholms La RDKG RH5 ... 273 H6
Inigo Jones Rd CHARL SE7 ... 162 A6
Inkerman Rd KTTN NW5 ... 4 C5
 STAL AL1 ... 38 D7
 WOKN/KNAP GU21 ... 231 K4
Inkerman Ter CSHM HP5 ... 51 H9
Inks Green CHING E4 ... 101 H6
Inkwell Cl NFNCH/WDSP N12 ... 97 H4
Inman Rd WAND/EARL SW18 ... 179 M3
 WLSDN NW10 ... 136 B3
Inmans Rw WFD IG8 ... 101 M5
Inner Cir CAMTN NW1 ... 4 C10
Inner Park Rd WIM/MER SW19 ... 178 C3
Innes Cl RYNPK SW20 ... 201 H2
 WAND/EARL SW18 ... 179 K3
Innes Ct HHS/BOV HP3 ... 35 N8
Innes Gdns PUT/ROE SW15 ... 178 E2
Innes Rd CROY/NA CR0 ... 203 K10
Inniskilling Rd PLSTW E13 ... 141 P7
Innovation Cl ALP/SUD HA0 ... 135 K3
Inskip Cl LEY E10 ... 120 C2
Inskip Dr EMPK RM11 ... 125 M6
Inskip Rd BCTR RM8 ... 123 N6
Institute Pl HACK E8 ... 120 A10

Institute Rd DORK RH4 .... 272 B3
EPP CM16 .... 65 N5
Instone Rd DART DA1 .... 187 L3
International Av HEST TW5 .... 153 K4
Inver Ct BAY/PAD W2 .... 9 H6
Inveresk Gdns WPK KT4 .... 200 C10
Inverforth Cl HAMP NW3 .... 117 M7
Inverforth Rd FBAR/BDGN N11 .... 98 C6
Inverine Rd CHARL SE7 .... 161 N4
Invermore Pl WOOL/PLUM SE18 .... 162 F5
Inverness Av EN EN1 .... 79 N5
Inverness Dr BARK/HLT IG6 .... 103 H7
Inverness Gdns KENS W8 .... 8 C10
Inverness Ms BAY/PAD W2 .... 9 H7
Inverness Pl BAY/PAD W2 .... 9 H7
Inverness Rd HSLW TW3 .... 153 N10
NWDGN UB2 .... 153 M3
UED N18 .... 106 A6
WPK KT4 .... 200 C8
Inverness St CAMTN NW1 .... 4 E5
Inverness Ter BAY/PAD W2 .... 9 H6
Invicta Cl CHST BR7 .... 184 D8
EBED/NFELT TW14 .... 174 G4
Invicta Gv NTHLT UB5 .... 133 N5
Invicta Plaza STHWK SE1 .... 12 D1
Invicta Rd BKHTH/KID SE3 .... 161 N6
RDART DA2 .... 188 A2
Inville Rd WALW SE17 .... 19 H8
Inwood Av COUL/CHIP CR5 .... 241 H6
HSLW TW3 .... 154 B9
Inwood Rd HSLW TW3 .... 154 B10
Inworth St BTSEA SW11 .... 157 P8
Iona Cl CAT SE6 .... 182 C7
CRAWW RH11 .... 283 C10
Iona Crs SL SL1 .... 128 D8
Ion Sq BETH E2 .... 7 N8
Ipswich Rd SL SL1 .... 128 D8
TOOT SW17 .... 180 B9
Ireland Cl EHAM E6 .... 142 C7
Ireland Pl WDGN N22 .... 98 H3
Irene Rd COB KT11 .... 217 P10
FUL/PGN SW6 .... 157 K7
ORP BR6 .... 207 J7
Ireton Av ESH/CLAY KT10 .... 196 C9
Ireton Cl MUSWH N10 .... 98 B8
Ireton Pl GRAYS RM17 .... 167 M3
Ireton St BOW E3 .... 140 F6
Iris Av BXLY DA5 .... 185 P2
Iris Cl BRWN CM15 .... 86 C9
CROY/NA CR0 .... 204 C8
EHAM E6 .... 142 B7
SURB KT6 .... 199 L7
Iris Crs BXLYHN DA7 .... 164 A10
Iris Rd CHOB/PIR GU24 .... 230 F1
HOR/WEW KT19 .... 219 N2
Iris Wy CHING E4 .... 100 G9
Irkdale Av EN EN1 .... 79 N5
Iron Bridge Cl STHL UB1 .... 134 B10
WLSDN NW10 .... 116 B10
Iron Bridge Rd North
WDR/YW UB7 .... 152 B1
Iron Bridge Rd South
WDR/YW UB7 .... 152 B1
Iron Dr HERT/BAY SG13 .... 26 A4
Iron Mill La DART DA1 .... 164 G10
Iron Mill Pl DART DA1 .... 164 G10
WAND/EARL SW18 .... 179 L2
Iron Mill Rd WAND/EARL SW18 .... 179 L2
Ironmonger La CITYW EC2V 12 G6
Ironmonger Rw FSBYE EC1V 6 F10
Irons Bottom Rd REIG RH2 .... 275 J9
Ironside Cl BERM/RHTH SE16 .... 160 C1
Irons Wy CRW RM5 .... 104 D4
Irvine Av KTN/HRWW/W HA3 .... 114 F1
Irvine Cl TRDG/WHET N20 .... 97 P3
Irvine Gdns SOCK/AV RM15 .... 146 E8
Irvine Pl VW GU25 .... 194 B5
Irvine Wy ORP BR6 .... 207 J7
Irving Av NTHLT UB5 .... 133 L3
Irving Gv BRXN/ST SW9 .... 158 A4
Irving Rd WKENS W14 .... 156 G2
Irving St LSQ/SEVD WC2H 11 L8
Irving Wk CRAWE RH10 .... 283 P10
Irving Wy SWLY BR8 .... 208 E2
Irwin Av WOOL/PLUM SE18 .... 163 H6
Irwin Cl HGDN/ICK UB10 .... 112 B8
Irwin Gdns WLSDN NW10 .... 136 E3
Irwin Rd GUW GU2 .... 267 M1
Isabel Ga CHES/WCR EN8 .... 62 D1
Isabella Cl STHGT/OAK N14 .... 98 D1
Isabella Dr ORP BR6 .... 226 F1
Isabella Rd HOM E9 .... 120 B10
Isabella St STHWK SE1 .... 12 C10
Isabelle Cl CHESW EN7 .... 61 L3
Isabel St BRXN/ST SW9 .... 158 G7
Isambard Ms POP/IOD E14 .... 161 H7
Isambard Pl BERM/RHTH SE16 .... 160 B1
Isbells Dr REIG RH2 .... 275 L2
Isenburg Wy HHNE HP2 .... 35 N1
Isham Rd STRHM/NOR SW16 .... 202 A1
Isis Cl PUT/ROE SW15 .... 158 F10
Isis Dr UPMR RM14 .... 126 D4
Isis St WAND/EARL SW18 .... 179 M5
Island Cl STA TW18 .... 173 H7
Island Farm Av E/WMO/HCT KT8 .. 197 H5
Island Farm Rd E/WMO/HCT KT8 .. 197 N5
Island Rd MTCM CR4 .... 180 A10
Isla Rd WOOL/PLUM SE18 .... 162 F5
Islay Gdns HSLWW TW4 .... 175 L1
Isledon Rd HOLWY N7 .... 119 H8
Islehurst Cl CHST BR7 .... 206 D1
Islington Gn IS N1 .... 6 C6
Islington High St IS N1 .... 6 C7
Islington Park Ms IS N1 .... 6 C3
Islington Park St IS N1 .... 6 B3
Islip Gdns EDGW HA8 .... 96 F6
NTHLT UB5 .... 133 M2
Islip Manor Rd NTHLT UB5 .... 133 M2
Islip St KTTN NW5 .... 118 D10
Ismailia Rd FSTGT E7 .... 141 M4
Isom Cl PLSTW E13 .... 141 N5
Istead Ri MEO DA13 .... 190 C10
Itchingwood Common Rd
OXTED RH8 .... 261 P9
Ivanhoe Cl CRAWW RH11 .... 283 N7
UX/CGN UB8 .... 131 N7
Ivanhoe Dr KTN/HRWW/W HA3 .. 94 C10
Ivanhoe Rd CMBW SE5 .... 159 N9
HSLWW TW4 .... 153 L9
Ivatt Pl WKENS W14 .... 157 J3
Ivatt Wy SEVS/STOTM N15 .... 119 J1
Iveagh Av WLSDN NW10 .... 135 M4
Iveagh Cl HOM E9 .... 140 C3
NTHWD HA6 .... —
WLSDN NW10 .... 135 M4
Iveagh Rd GUW GU2 .... 267 M1
Ivedon Rd WELL DA16 .... 163 M8
Ive Farm Cl LEY E10 .... 120 F7
Ive Farm La LEY E10 .... 120 F7
Iveley Rd CLAP SW4 .... 158 A8
Iverdale Cl IVER SL0 .... 130 F9
Ivere Dr BAR EN5 .... 77 L10
Iverhurst Cl BXLYHS DA6 .... 185 H1
Iver La IVER SL0 .... 131 L7
Iverna Ct KENS W8 .... 14 C1
Iverna Gdns EBED/NFELT TW14 .. 174 B1
KENS W8 .... 14 C1
Iverson Rd KIL/WHAMP NW6 .... 2 A1
Ivers Wy CROY/NA CR0 .... 224 G1
Ives Gdns ROM RM1 .... 124 G2
Ives Rd DAGE RM10 E16 .... 141 K7
DTCH/LGLY SL3 .... 150 D2
HERT/WAS SG14 .... 25 J4
Ives St CHEL SW3 .... 15 N3

Ivimey St BETH E2 .... 7 P9
Ivinghoe Cl EN EN1 .... 79 N6
GSTN WD25 .... 73 L1
STALE/WH AL4 .... 39 H1
Ivinghoe Rd BCTR RM8 .... 123 L10
BUSH WD23 .... 74 C10
RKW/CH/CXG WD3 .... 91 J1
Ivor Cl GU GU1 .... 268 C1
Ivor Gv ELTH/MOT SE9 .... 184 E4
Ivor Pl CAMTN NW1 .... 10 A2
Ivor St CAMTN NW1 .... 4 G4
Ivory Cl FELT TW13 .... 175 H5
HHS/BOV HP3 .... 35 P9
Ivorydown BMLY BR1 .... 183 M7
Ivory Sq BTSEA SW11 .... 158 C10
Ivorywk CRAWW RH11 .... 283 H10
Ivy Bower Cl GRH DA9 .... 188 C1
Ivybridge BROX EN10 .... 44 F5
Ivybridge Cl TWK TW1 .... 156 F2
UX/CGN UB8 .... 131 P5
Ivy Church La STHWK SE1 .... 19 L7
Ivy Cl DART DA1 .... 187 P2
GVE DA12 .... 190 F7
PIN HA5 .... 113 K5
RYLN/HDSTN HA2 .... 113 N9
SUN TW16 .... 197 K2
Ivy Crs CHSWK W4 .... 155 P3
SL SL1 .... 128 E9
Ivydale Rd CAR SM5 .... 202 A9
PECK SE15 .... 160 C9
Ivyday Gv STRHM/NOR SW16 .... 180 C6
Ivydene WOKN/KNAP GU21 .... 230 G4
WOT/HER KT12 .... 197 N5
Ivydene Cl REDH RH1 .... 276 C5
SUT SM1 .... 221 N4
Ivy Gdns CEND/HSY/T N8 .... 118 F4
MTCM CR4 .... 202 E3
SEV TN13 .... 246 E3
Ivyhouse Rd DAGW RM9 .... 143 N1
HGDN/ICK UB10 .... 112 C8
Ivy La HSLWW TW4 .... 153 N10
RSEV TN14 .... 245 P2
WOKS/MYFD GU22 .... 232 E4
Ivy Lea RKW/CH/CXG WD3 .... 91 K2
Ivy Lodge La HARH RM3 .... 106 B10
Ivy Mill Cl GDST RH9 .... 260 B10
Ivy Mill La GDST RH9 .... 260 B10
Ivymount Rd WNWD SE27 .... 181 H6
Ivy Rd BROCKY SE4 .... 161 M8
CAN/RD E16 .... 141 M8
CRICK NW2 .... 116 F9
HSLW TW3 .... 154 A10
LEY E10 .... 120 F4
STHGT/OAK N14 .... 98 D1
SURB KT6 .... 199 M8
TOOT SW17 .... 179 P8
Ivy St IS N1 .... 7 J7
Ivy Ter HOD EN11 .... 45 H1
Ivy Wk DAGW RM9 .... 143 P1
Ixworth Pl CHEL SW3 .... 15 N5
Izane Rd BXLYHS DA6 .... 164 A10

J

Jacaranda Cl NWMAL KT3 .... 200 B3
Jackass La GDST RH9 .... 260 E7
HAYES BR2 .... 225 N3
Jack Clow Rd SRTFD E15 .... 141 K4
Jack Cornwell St MNPK E12 .... 122 D9
Jackdaw Cl CRAWW RH11 .... 283 M5
Jackdaws WGCE AL7 .... 23 M5
Jacketts Fld ABLGY WD5 .... 54 G7
Jack Evans Ct SOCK/AV RM15 .. 146 F8
Jack Jones Wy DAGW RM9 .... —
Jack Rd HA .... —
Jackman Ms WLSDN NW10 .... 116 B3
Jackman's La WOKN/KNAP GU21 .. 231 M5
Jackman St HACK E8 .... 140 A3
Jacks La DEN/HRF UB9 .... 91 H9
Jackson Cl EMPK RM11 .... 125 N2
EPSOM KT18 .... 220 A10
GRH DA9 .... 188 C1
HOM E9 .... 140 C2
Jackson Rd BARK IG11 .... 142 C3
EBAR EN4 .... 77 P10
HAYES BR2 .... 206 C8
HGDN/ICK UB10 .... 131 P2
HOLWY N7 .... 118 C9
Jacksons Cl CHONG CM5 .... 67 P5
Jacksons Dr CHESW EN7 .... 61 P4
Jackson's La HGT N6 .... 118 B5
Jackson's Pl CROY/NA CR0 .... 203 M8
Jackson's Wy WOOL/PLUM SE18 .. 162 D5
Jackson's Wy CROY/NA CR0 .... 204 F10
Jack Stevens Cl HLWE CM17 .... 47 M3
Jack Walker Ct HBRY N5 .... 119 J3
Jacob Cl WDSR SL4 .... 148 D7
Jacobean Cl CRAWE RH10 .... 284 D8
Jacobs Av HARH RM3 .... 105 M10
Jacobs Cl DAGE RM10 .... 124 C9
Jacob St STHWK SE1 .... 19 M1
Jacob's Well Ms MHST W1U 10 D5
Jacob Well Rd RGUE GU4 .... 250 A5
Jacqueline Cl NTHLT UB5 .... 133 M1
Jade Cl BCTR RM8 .... 123 M6
CAN/RD E16 .... 142 A8
CRICK NW2 .... 116 C5
Jaffe Rd IL IG1 .... 122 F6
Jaffray Rd HAYES BR2 .... 206 A4
Jaggard Wy BAL SW12 .... 180 A3
Jagger Cl RDART DA2 .... 188 B3
Jago Cl WOOL/PLUM SE18 .... 162 D5
Jail La BH/WHM TN16 .... 244 A4
Jamaica Rd BERM/RHTH SE16 .. 160 A2
STHWK SE1 .... 19 M2
THHTH CR7 .... 203 J6
Jamaica St WCHPL E1 .... 140 F7
CRICK NW2 .... 116 F10
Jamaica Cl BUSH WD23 .... 73 M9
Jambala Bridge Rd SYD SE26 .. GPK RM2 .... 125 J3
James Av BCTR RM8 .... 124 A6
PLSTW E13 .... 141 M4
James Gdns WDGN N22 .... 99 K8
James Joyes Wk HNHL SE24 .. 159 J10
James La WAN E11 .... 121 H5
James Martin Cl DEN/HRF UB9 .. 111 K4
Jameson St KENS W8 .... 8 C9
James Pl TOTM N17 .... 99 N8
James Rd DART DA1 .... 187 H3
RGUW GU3 .... 267 P2
James St BARK IG11 .... 142 F7
COVGDN WC2E 11 M7
EN EN1 .... 79 N9
EPP CM16 .... 65 J4
HSLW TW3 .... 154 C9
MHST W1U 10 D6
WDSR SL4 .... 149 J7
Jamestown Rd CAMTN NW1 .. 4 E5
Jamestown Wy POP/IOD E14 .. 141 P9
James Watt Wy CRAWE RH10 .. 284 B1
ERITH DA8 .... 164 G5
Jannagar Cl STA TW18 .... 173 H9
Jane Cl HHNE HP2 .... 35 N1
Janet St POP/IOD E14 .... 160 F2
Janeway Pl BERM/RHTH SE16 .. 160 A1
Janeway St BERM/RHTH SE16 .. 19 P3
Janmead RBRW/HUT CM13 .. 107 N1
Janoway Hill La
WOKN/KNAP GU21 .... 231 P5
Janson Cl SRTFD E15 .... 121 K10
WLSDN NW10 .... 116 A8
Janson Rd SRTFD E15 .... 121 K10

Jansons Rd SEVS/STOTM N15 .. 119 M1
Japan Crs FSBYPK N4 .... 118 G6
Japan Rd CHDH RM6 .... 123 N4
Japonica Cl WOKN/KNAP GU21 .. 231 P4
Jardine Rd WAP E1W 140 G9
Jarman Cl HHS/BOV HP3 .... 35 P8
Jarrett Cl BRXS/STRHM SW2 .. 181 J4
Jarrow Cl MRDN SM4 .... 201 L5
Jarrow Rd BERM/RHTH SE16 .. 160 A4
CHDH RM6 .... 123 M4
TOTM N17 .... 120 A2
Jarrow Wy HOM E9 .... 120 D9
Jarvis Cleys CHESW EN7 .... 61 N2
Jarvis Cl BAR EN5 .... 76 C7
SAND/SEL CR2 .... 223 L6
Jarvis Rd SED22 .... 159 M10
Jarvis Wy HARH RM3 .... 105 M10
Jasmin Cl NTHWD HA6 .... 92 G9
Jasmine Cl HAYES BR2 .... 206 E9
IL IG1 .... 122 E10
REDH RH1 .... 276 B5
STHL UB1 .... 133 M9
WOKN/KNAP GU21 .... 231 L2
Jasmine Ct LEE/GVPK SE12 .. 183 M2
Jasmine Dr HERT/BAY SG13 .. 25 P5
Jasmine Gdns CROY/NA CR0 .. 204 G10
HAT AL10 .... 40 C2
RYLN/HDSTN HA2 .... 113 P7
Jasmine Gv PGE/AN SE20 .... 204 A1
Jasmine Rd ROM/RG RM7 .... 124 E1
Jasmine Ter WDR/YW UB7 .... 152 B1
Jasmin Rd HOR/WEW KT19 .... 219 N3
Jasmin Wy HHW HP1 .... 35 H5
Jason Cl REDH RH1 .... 275 P5
WEY KT13 .... 216 D2
Jasons Cl BRW CM14 .... 106 C5
Jasons Dr RGUE GU4 .... 250 F7
Jason Wk ELTH/MOT SE9 .... 184 D7
Jasper Cl PEND EN3 .... 80 A4
Jasper Rd CAN/RD E16 .... 142 A8
NRWD SE19 .... 181 N7
Javelin Wy NTHLT UB5 .... 133 L5
Jay Av ADL/WDHM KT15 .... 195 N10
Jaycroft ENC/FH EN2 .... 79 H5
Jay Gdns CHST BR7 .... 184 C7
Jay Ms SKENS SW7 .... 15 K2
Jebb Av BRXS/STRHM SW2 .. 180 F2
Jebb St BOW E3 .... 140 F4
Jedburgh Rd PLSTW E13 .... 141 P5
Jedburgh St BTSEA SW11 .... 158 B10
Jeddo Rd SHB W12 .... 156 C1
Jefferson Cl DTCH/LGLY SL3 .. 150 D3
GNTH/NBYPK IG2 .... 122 E3
WEA W13 .... 154 G2
Jeffrey's Pl CAMTN NW1 .... 4 G3
Jeffrey's Rd CLAP SW4 .... 158 F3
PEND EN3 .... 80 B3
Jeffrey's St CAMTN NW1 .... 4 F3
Jeffries Rd EHSLY KT24 .... 252 C7
Jeffs Cl HPTN TW12 .... 176 A3
Jeffs Rd SUT SM1 .... 221 J1
Jeger Av BETH E2 .... 7 L6
Jeken Rd ELTH/MOT SE9 .... 161 P10
Jelf Rd BRXS/STRHM SW2 .. 181 H1
Jellicoe Av GVE DA12 .... 190 F6
Jellicoe Cl SL SL1 .... 148 G1
Jellicoe Gdns STAN HA7 .... 94 E7
Jellicoe Rd TOTM N17 .... 99 L8
WATW WD18 .... 73 H10
Jemmett Cl KUTN/CMB KT2 .. 199 N1
Jengar Cl SUT SM1 .... 221 L3
Jenkins Av LCOL/BKTW AL2 .. 55 M6
Jenkins La BARK IG11 .... 142 E4
Jenkins Rd PLSTW E13 .... 141 N6
Jenner Av ACT W3 .... 136 A7
Jenner Dr CHOB/PIR GU24 .. 212 F9
Jenner Rd CRAWE RH10 .... 284 A2
GU GU1 .... 268 E1
STNW/STAM N16 .... 119 N7
Jennery La SL SL1 .... 128 B5
Jennett Rd CROY/NA CR0 .... 203 H10
Jennifer Rd BMLY BR1 .... 183 L6
Jenningham Dr CDH/CHF RM16 .. 147 M10
Jenningtree Rd BELV DA17 .. 164 D3
Jenningtree Wy BELV DA17 .. 164 D1
Jenny Hammond Cl WAN E11 .. 121 L8
Jenson Wy NRWD SE19 .... 181 N10
Jenton Av BXLYHN DA7 .... 164 A1
Jephson Rd FSTGT E7 .... 141 P2
Jephson St CMBW SE5 .... 159 L7
Jephtha Rd WAND/EARL SW18 .. 179 K2
Jeppo's La MTCM CR4 .... 202 A1
Jerdan Pl FUL/PGN SW6 .... 157 K6
Jeremiah St POP/IOD E14 .... 140 G8
Jeremy's Gn UED N18 .... 100 A5
Jermyn Av CLAY IG5 .... 102 E10
Jermyn St STJS SW1Y 10 G9
Jerningham Av CLAY IG5 .... 102 E10
Jerningham Rd NWCR SE14 .. 160 D8
Jerome Crs STJWD NW8 .... 9 N1
Jerome Dr STALW/RED AL3 .. 37 P4
Jerome St WCHPL E1 .... 13 L1
Jerrard St LEW SE13 .... 160 G9
Jerrold St IS N1 .... 7 K8
Jersey Av KTN/HRWW/W HA3 .. 94 G10
Jersey Cl CHERT KT16 .... 195 J10
HOD EN11 .... 44 F2
RGUE GU4 .... 250 E5
Jersey Dr STMC/STPC BR5 .. 201 P2
Jersey La STAL AL1 .... 38 C4
STALE/WH AL4 .... 21 H10
Jersey Rd CAN/RD E16 .... 141 P7
HEST TW5 .... 154 A1
HNWL W7 .... 154 F1
IL IG1 .... 122 C9
IS N1 .... 6 F2
ISLW TW7 .... 154 B6
RAIN RM13 .... 145 H2
TOOT SW17 .... 180 C10
WAN E11 .... 121 N2
Jersey St BETH E2 .... 140 A5
Jervis Av PEND EN3 .... 80 D1
Jerviston Gdns
STRHM/NOR SW16 .... 181 H9
Jesmond Av WBLY HA9 .... 135 L1
Jesmond Cl MTCM CR4 .... 202 C3
Jesmond Rd CROY/NA CR0 .. 203 N7
Jessam Av CLPT E5 .... 120 A3
Jessamine Pl RDART DA2 .... 188 B3
Jessamine Rd HNWL W7 .... 134 D10
Jessamy Rd WEY KT13 .... 196 B5
Jesse Dr LOU IG10 .... 82 F6
Jesse Rd LEY E10 .... 121 H6
Jessett Cl ERITH DA8 .... 164 L3
Jessica Rd WAND/EARL SW18 .. 179 M2
Jessiman Ter SHPTN TW17 .. 196 A5
Jessops Wy MTCM CR4 .... 202 D6
Jessop Sq POP/IOD E14 .... 141 M3
Jessup Cl WOOL/PLUM SE18 .. 162 A6
Jevington Wy LEE/GVPK SE12 .. 183 L5
Jewel Rd WALTH E17 .... 101 H10
Jewels HI WARL CR6 .... 225 M8
Jewry St TWRH EC3N 13 L6
Jews Rw WAND/EARL SW18 .. 157 P10
Jews Wk SYD SE26 .... 182 A7
Jeymer Av CRICK NW2 .... 116 G3
Jeymer Dr GFD/PVL UB6 .... 134 B1

Jeypore Rd WAND/EARL SW18 .. 179 M3
Jillian Cl HPTN TW12 .... 175 P10
Jim Bradley Cl
WOOL/PLUM SE18 .... 162 D3
The Jinnings WGCE AL7 .... 23 N7
Joan Crs ELTH/MOT SE9 .... 184 A3
Joan Gdns BCTR RM8 .... 123 P7
Joan Rd BCTR RM8 .... 123 P7
Joan St STHWK SE1 .... 12 C2
Jocelyn Rd RCH/KEW TW9 .. 155 K9
Jocelyns HLWE CM17 .... 29 M7
Jocelyn St PECK SE15 .... 159 P7
Jocketts HI HHW HP1 .... 35 J7
Jocketts Rd HHW HP1 .... 35 J7
Jockey's Flds FSBYW WC1X .. 11 P3
Jodane St DEPT SE8 .... 160 E3
Jodrell Cl ISLW TW7 .... 154 F7
Jodrell Rd HOM E9 .... 140 E3
Jodrell Wy WTHK RM20 .... 166 E4
Joel St HAYES BR2 .... —
PIN HA5 .... 113 H1
Johanna St STHWK SE1 .... 18 A2
John Adam St CHCR WC2N .. 11 M9
John Aird Ct BAY/PAD W2 .. 9 K3
John Archer Wy
WAND/EARL SW18 .... 179 N2
John Ashby Cl BRXS/STRHM SW2 .. 180 F2
John Austin Cl KUTN/CMB KT2 .. 199 L1
John Bradshaw Rd
STHGT/OAK N14 .... 98 E2
John Burns Dr BARK IG11 .... 143 H3
Johnby Cl PEND EN3 .... 80 D3
John Campbell Rd
STNW/STAM N16 .... 119 M10
John Carpenter St EMB EC4Y .. 12 C7
John Cobb Rd WEY KT13 .... 216 B4
John Eliot Cl WAB EN9 .... 45 K8
John Felton Rd BERM/RHTH SE16 .. 19 N2
John Fisher St WCHPL E1 .... 13 N7
John Gooch Dr ENC/FH EN2 .. 79 J5
John Islip St WEST SW1P 17 L7
John Lamb Ct KTN/HRWW/W HA3 .. 94 D3
John Maurice Cl WALW SE17 .. 18 G5
John Parker Sq BTSEA SW11 .. 157 N7
John Penn St LEW SE13 .... 160 G7
John Perrin Pl
KTN/HRWW/W HA3 .... 115 K5
John Prince's St CAVSQ/HST W1G .. 10 F5
John Roll Wy BERM/RHTH SE16 .. 19 P3
John Ruskin St CMBW SE5 .. 159 J6
John Russell Cl GUW GU2 .. 267 M2
John's Av HDN NW4 .... 116 F2
John's Cl ASHF TW15 .... 174 D7
HART DA3 .... 211 L5
Johnsdale OXTED RH8 .... 261 L5
John Silkin La DEPT SE8 .... 160 C4
Johns La MRDN SM4 .... 201 M5
John's Ms BMSBY WC1N 11 N2
John Smith Av FUL/PGN SW6 .. 157 J6
Johnson Cl HHS/BOV HP3 .. 35 P8
Johnson Rd CROY/NA CR0 .. 203 L7
HAYES BR2 .... 206 A5
HEST TW5 .... 153 K6
Johnsons Cl CAR SM5 .... 202 A10
Johnsons Dr HPTN TW12 .... 198 B1
Johnson's Pl PIM SW1V 17 H8
Johnson St NWDGN UB2 .... 153 K2
WCHPL E1 .... 140 F9
Johnsons Wy GRH DA9 .... 189 J1
WLSDN NW10 .... 135 N6
Johnson Wk CRAWE RH10 .... 283 N10
John Spencer Sq IS N1 .... 6 D2
John's Rd BH/WHM TN16 .... 244 A6
John's Ter CROY/NA CR0 .... 203 M8
The Johns CHONG CM5 .... 67 P3
Johnston Cl BRXN/ST SW9 .. 158 A3
Johnstone Rd EHAM E6 .... 142 C5
Johnston Rd WFD IG8 .... 101 M6
Johnston Wk GUW GU2 .... 249 M6
John St BMSBY WC1N 11 N2
EN EN1 .... 79 N9
GRAYS RM17 .... 167 P5
HSLW TW3 .... 153 M8
SNWD SE25 .... 203 P4
SRTFD E15 .... 141 L3
Johns Wk CTHM CR3 .... 241 P5
John Tate Rd HERT/BAY SG13 .. 25 N6
John Taylor Ct SL SL1 .... 129 H10
John Williams Cl PECK SE15 .. 160 C5
John Wilson St
WOOL/PLUM SE18 .... 162 D3
John Wooley Cl LEW SE13 .. 161 K10
Joiners Arms Yd CMBW SE5 .. 159 L7
Joiners Cl CFSP/GDCR SL9 .. 90 B9
Joiners La CFSP/GDCR SL9 .. 90 B9
Joiners St STHWK SE1 .... 13 H10
Joiners Wy CFSP/GDCR SL9 .. 90 B8
Joint Rd EFNCH N2 .... 97 P9
Joinville Pl ADL/WDHM KT15 .. 215 N1
Jolesfield CRAWW RH11 .... 283 J10
Jolliffe Rd REDH RH1 .... 258 D2
Jollys La YEAD UB4 .... 133 L2
Jonathan St LBTH SE11 .... 17 N7
Jones Rd CHESW EN7 .... 61 N2
PLSTW E13 .... 141 N6
Jones Wy SLN SL2 .... 109 J7
Jonquil Cl WGCE AL7 .... 23 L7
Jonson Cl MTCM CR4 .... 202 C4
YEAD UB4 .... 133 H7
Jordan Cl GFD/PVL UB6 .... 134 C3
Jordans Cl CRAWW RH11 .... 283 N5
DAGE RM10 .... 124 C9
Jordans Crs CRAWW RH11 .... 283 N4
Jordans La BEAC HP9 .... 88 A1
Jordans Ms WHTN TW2 .... 176 D5
Jordans Rd RKW/CH/CXG WD3 .. 91 K1
Jordans Wy BEAC HP9 .... 89 C7
LCOL/BKTW AL2 .... 55 M6
RAIN RM13 .... 145 L2
Josephine Av BRXS/STRHM SW2 .. 180 C1
KWD/TDW/WH KT20 .... 257 J7
Josephine Cl KWD/TDW/WH KT20 .. 257 J7
Joseph Locke Wy ESH/CLAY KT10 .. 197 P9
Joseph Powell Cl BAL SW12 .. 180 D2
Joseph Ray Rd WAN E11 .... 121 K7
Joseph Russell Cl GU GU1 .. 250 A9
Joseph St BOW E3 .... 140 E7
Joshua St POP/IOD E14 .... 141 M8
Joslin Rd PUR RM19 .... 166 B4
Joslyn Cl PEND EN3 .... 80 F4
Joubert St BTSEA SW11 .... 158 A1
Journeys End SLN SL2 .... 129 K7
Jowett St PECK SE15 .... 159 N6
Joyce Av UED N18 .... 100 A6
Joyce Green La DART DA1 .. 165 L2
Joyce Page Cl CHARL SE7 .. 162 D6
Joyce Wk BRXS/STRHM SW2 .. 180 C5
Joydens Wood La BXLY DA5 .. 186 E7
Joydon Dr CHDH RM6 .... 123 J4
Joyners Cl DAGW RM9 .... 124 B7
Joy Rd GVE DA12 .... 190 F8
Jubilee Av CHING E4 .... 101 P1
LCOL/BKTW AL2 .... 57 J2
ROMW/RG RM7 .... 124 D3
WARE SG12 .... 26 E1
WHTN TW2 .... 176 B4

Jubilee Cl CDALE/KGS NW9 .... 116 A4
GRH DA9 .... 189 H2
PIN HA5 .... 93 K10
ROMW/RG RM7 .... 124 C3
STWL/WRAY TW19 .... 173 N5
Jubilee Crs ADL/WDHM KT15 .. 215 N2
ED N9 .... 99 P2
GPK RM2 .... 191 H5
Jubilee Gv RSLP HA4 .... 113 L9
Jubilee Gdns STHL UB1 .... 133 P7
ORP BR6 .... 228 B3
WATN WD24 .... 73 H4
Jubilee Pl BGR/WK TN15 .... 247 L6
CHEAM SM3 .... 220 G4
GFD/PVL UB6 .... 134 C3
ORP BR6 .... 228 B3
WATN WD24 .... 73 H4
Jubilee Rd CHEAM SM3 .... 220 G4
GFD/PVL UB6 .... 134 C3
ORP BR6 .... 228 B3
WATN WD24 .... 73 H4
Jubilee St WCHPL E1 .... 140 G8
Jubilee Ter BRKHM/BTCW RH3 .. 273 P4
DORK RH4 .... 272 C1
Jubilee Wk CRAWE RH10 .... 284 B7
Jubilee Wy CHSGTN KT9 .... 199 N10
EBED/NFELT TW14 .... 175 H4
SCUP DA14 .... 185 K5
WIM/MER SW19 .... 201 L1
Judd St CAMTN NW1 .... 5 J9
Jude St CAN/RD E16 .... 141 L8
Judeth Gdns GVE DA12 .... 191 H8
Judge Heath La UX/CGN UB8 .. 132 D8
Judge's HI POTB/CUF EN6 .. 60 A5
Judge St WATN WD24 .... 73 J4
Judges' Wk HAMP NW3 .... 117 M8
Judith Av CRW RM5 .... 104 C7
Juer St BTSEA SW11 .... 157 P6
Juglans Rd ORP BR6 .... 207 K8
Julia Gdns BARK IG11 .... 143 N4
Juliana Cl EFNCH N2 .... 117 M1
Julian Av ACT W3 .... 135 P9
Julian Cl BAR EN5 .... 77 L7
WOKN/KNAP GU21 .... 231 P4
Julian HI HRW HA1 .... 114 D7
WEY KT13 .... 216 B4
Julian Pl POP/IOD E14 .... 160 G4
Julian Rd ORP BR6 .... 227 K3
Julians Cl SEV TN13 .... 265 H3
Julians Wy SEV TN13 .... 265 H3
Juliette Rd PLSTW E13 .... 141 L4
Juliette Wy PUR RM19 .... 145 N1
Junction Ap BTSEA SW11 .... 157 P10
LEW SE13 .... 161 H9
Junction Ms BAY/PAD W2 .. 9 N5
Junction Pl BAY/PAD W2 .. 9 M5
Junction Rd ARCH N19 .... 118 D8
ASHF TW15 .... 174 D8
BRW CM14 .... 107 H5
DART DA1 .... 187 L2
DORK RH4 .... 272 F2
EA W5 .... 155 H3
ED N9 .... 99 P2
LTWR GU18 .... 212 A6
PLSTW E13 .... 141 N3
ROM RM1 .... 124 G2
SAND/SEL CR2 .... 223 L3
TOTM N17 .... 119 P5
Junction Rd East CHDH RM6 .. 123 P5
Junction Rd West CHDH RM6 .. 123 P5
June Cl COUL/CHIP CR5 .... 222 C10
June La REDH RH1 .... 276 C7
Junewood Cl ADL/WDHM KT15 .. 215 J7
Juniper Av LCOL/BKTW AL2 .. 55 P8
Juniper Cl BAR EN5 .... 76 C9
BH/WHM TN16 .... 244 B3
BROX EN10 .... 62 E1
CHSGTN KT9 .... 219 L3
GU GU1 .... 249 N5
REIG RH2 .... 275 M2
Juniper Ct CHDH RM6 .... 123 L4
REIG RH2 .... 275 M2
Juniper Ga RKW/CH/CXG WD3 .. 91 H5
Juniper Gv WAT WD17 .... 73 H4
Juniper La EHAM E6 .... 142 B7
IL IG1 .... 122 E9
REIG RH2 .... 275 M2
Juniper Rd CRAWW RH11 .... 283 M4
IL IG1 .... 122 E9
REIG RH2 .... 275 M2
Juniper St WCHPL E1 .... 140 G9
Juniper Wk HARH RM3 .... 105 M9
HYS/HAR UB3 .... 132 E9
Juno Wy NWCR SE14 .... 160 C5
Jupiter Dr HHNE HP2 .... 36 A4
Jupp Rd SRTFD E15 .... 141 J2
Jupp Rd West SRTFD E15 .. 141 H3
Jura Cl CRAWW RH11 .... 283 L10
Jury St GVE DA12 .... 190 E2
Justice Wk CHEL SW3 .... 15 N10
Justin Cl BTFD TW8 .... 155 J6
Justin Rd CHING E4 .... 100 C1
Jute La PEND EN3 .... 80 E2
Jutland Pl EGH TW20 .... 172 F8
Jutland Rd CAT SE6 .... 183 H3
PLSTW E13 .... 141 M5
Jutsums Av ROMW/RG RM7 .. 124 C4
Jutsums La ROMW/RG RM7 .. 124 C4
Juxon Cl CRAWW RH11 .... 283 J9
RYLN/HDSTN HA2 .... 94 A3
Juxon St LBTH SE11 .... 17 P5

K

Kaduna Cl PIN HA5 .... 113 J3
Kale Rd ERITHM DA18 .... 163 N1
Kambala Rd BTSEA SW11 .... 157 N9
Kandlewood RBRW/HUT CM13 .. 107 N1
Kangley Bridge Rd SYD SE26 .. 182 E8
Kaplan Dr WCHMH N21 .... 78 G9
Karen Cl BRWN CM15 .... 107 H4
RAIN RM13 .... 144 F4
Karen Ct BMLY BR1 .... 205 L1
Karenza Ct WBLY HA9 .... 115 H5
Karina Cl CHIG IG7 .... 103 H6
Kashgar Rd WOOL/PLUM SE18 .. 163 J4
Kashmir Cl ADL/WDHM KT15 .. 215 N1
Kashmir Rd CHARL SE7 .... 162 A6
Kassala Rd BTSEA SW11 .... 158 A7
Katescroft WGCE AL7 .... 23 H9
Katharine St CROY/NA CR0 .. 203 K10
Katherine Cl ADL/WDHM KT15 .. 215 N1
BERM/RHTH SE16 .... 140 C10
Katherine Gdns BARK/HLT IG6 .. 102 F8
ELTH/MOT SE9 .... 162 A10
Katherine Pl ABLGY WD5 .... 55 H8
Katherine Rd EHAM E6 .... 142 A2
KWD/TDW/WH KT20 .... 257 K9
TWK TW1 .... 156 C3
Katherine Sq NTGHL W11 .... 8 A9
Kathleen Av ACT W3 .... 135 P7
ALP/SUD HA0 .... 135 K2
Kathleen Rd BTSEA SW11 .... 158 A9
Katrine Sq HHNE HP2 .... 35 N1
Kavanaghs Rd BRW CM14 .... 106 T4
Kavanaghs Ter BRW CM14 .... 106 C4
Kay Av ADL/WDHM KT15 .... 195 P10
Kaye Don Wy WEY KT13 .... 216 B6
Kayemoor Rd BELMT SM2 .. 221 P4
Kay Rd BRXN/ST SW9 .... 158 F8
Kay St BETH E2 .... 7 P7
SRTFD E15 .... 141 J2
WELL DA16 .... 163 P2
Kaywood Cl DTCH/LGLY SL3 .. 149 P2
Kean St HOL/ALD WC2B 11 N6

Kearton Cl PUR/KEN CR8 241 K3
Keary Rd SWCM DA2 189 L3
Keatley Gn CHING E4 E4
Keats Av HARH RM3 105 J8
  REDH RH1 258 E8
Keats Cl CHIG IG7 102 F7
  PEND EN3 80 C1
  STHWK SE1 19 L6
  WAN E11 121 H4
  WIM/MER SW19 179 N9
  YEAD UB4 133 H7
Keats Gdns TIL RM18 168 E8
Keats Gv HAMP NW3 117 P9
Keats La WDSR SL4 149 J5
Keats Rd BELV DA17 164 D2
  WELL DA16 163 H7
Keats Wy CROY/NA CR0 204 B6
  GFD/PVL UB6 134 A7
  WDR/YW UB7 152 A3
Keble Cl CRAWE RH10 284 E4
  NTHLT UB5 114 B10
  WPK KT4 200 C8
Keble Pl BARN SW13 156 E5
Keble St TOOT SW17 179 M7
Keble Ter ABLGY WD5 54 C8
Kechill Gdns HAYES BR2 205 M7
Kedleston Dr STMC/STPC BR5 207 L4
Kedleston Wk BETH E2 140 C10
Keedonwood Rd BMLY BR1 183 K7
Keel Cl BARK IG11 143 M4
  BERM/RHTH SE16 140 C10
Keel Dr SL SL1 128 G10
Keele Cl WATN WD24 73 K6
Keeler Cl WDSR SL4 148 D9
Keeley Rd CROY/NA CR0 203 D9
Keeley St HOL/ALD WC2B 11 N6
Keeling Rd ELTH/MOT SE9 184 A1
Keely Cl EBAR EN4 77 P9
Keensacre IVER SL0 130 G4
Keens Cl STRHM/NOR SW16 180 E8
Keens Park Rd RGUW GU3 249 L6
Keens Rd CROY/NA CR0 223 K1
Keen's Yd IS N1 6 E1
Keep La RGUE GU4 250 G7
The Keep BKHTH/KID SE3 161 M8
  KUTN/CMB KT2 177 L9
Keeton's Rd BERM/RHTH SE16 160 A2
Keevil Dr WIM/MER SW19 178 G3
Keighley Cl HOLWY N7 118 F9
Keightley Dr ELTH/MOT SE9 184 H4
Keilder Cl HGDN/ICK UB10 132 B4
Keildon Rd BTSEA SW11 158 A10
Keir Hardie Wy BARK IG11 143 K2
  YEAD UB4 133 H5
Keith Av EYN DA4 188 A9
Keith Connor Cl VX/NE SW8 158 C9
Keith Gv SHB W12 156 D1
Keith Park Crs BH/WHM TN16 225 J8
Keith Park Rd HGDN/ICK UB10 132 A4
Keith Rd BARK IG11 142 G4
  HYS/HAR UB3 133 F2
  WALTH E17 100 F1
Keiths Rd HHS/BOV HP3 36 H1
Keith Wy EMPK RM11 125 M5
Kelbrook Rd BKHTH/KID SE3 162 B8
Kelbys WGCE AL7 23 M4
Kelceda Cl CRICK NW2 116 F10
Kelf Gv HYS/HAR UB3 133 G2
Kelfield Gdns NKENS W10 136 G8
Kelland Rd PLSTW E13 141 M6
Kellaway Rd BKHTH/KID SE3 161 P8
Keller Cresent MNPK E12 122 A9
Kellerton Rd LEW SE13 183 K1
Kellett Rd BRXS/STRHM SW2 159 H10
Kelling Gdns CROY/NA CR0 203 J1
Kellino St TOOT SW17 180 A7
Kellner Rd THMD SE28 163 J1
Kell St STHWK SE1 18 D3
Kelly Cl BORE WD6 76 A6
  SHPTN TW17 196 F2
  WLSDN NW10 116 H2
Kelly Ct CAMTN NW1 4 F7
Kelly Rd MLHL NW7 97 H7
Kelly St CAMTN NW1 4 B1
Kelly Wy CHDH RM6 123 P3
Kelman Cl CHES/WCR EN8 62 C7
  CLAP SW4 158 E8
Kelmore Gv EDUL SE22 159 F10
Kelmscott Cl WALTH E17 100 F1
  WATW WD18 73 H10
Kelmscott Crs WATW WD18 73 H5
Kelmscott Gdns SHB W12 156 D2
Kelmscott Rd BTSEA SW11 179 P1
Kelpatrick Rd SL SL1 128 C8
Kelross Rd HBRY N5 119 J9
Kelsall Cl BKHTH/KID SE3 161 N8
Kelsey Cl BECK BR3 204 F3
Kelsey Park Av BECK BR3 204 F2
Kelsey Park Rd BECK BR3 204 F2
Kelsey Rd STMC/STPC BR5 207 L2
Kelsey Sq BECK BR3 204 F2
Kelsey St BETH E2 13 P1
Kelsey Wy BECK BR3 204 E3
Kelshall GSTN WD25 73 M2
Kelsie Wy BARK/HLT IG6 103 N1
Kelso Cl CRAWE RH10 284 F6
Kelso Dr GVE DA12 191 J7
Kelso Pl KENS W8 14 G3
Kelso Rd CAR SM5 201 M7
Kelston Rd BARK/HLT IG6 102 E10
Kelvedon Av WOT/HER KT12 216 F4
Kelvedon Cl KUTN/CMB KT2 177 M9
Kelvedon Gn BRWN CM15 86 E3
Kelvedon Hall La BRW CM14 86 G3
Kelvedon Rd FUL/PGN SW6 157 J6
Kelvedon Wy WFD IG8 102 C7
Kelvin Av LHD/OX KT22 236 E6
  PLMGR N13 98 G2
Kelvinbrook E/WMO/HCT KT8 198 A3
Kelvin Cl HOR/WEW KT19 219 M3
Kelvin Crs KTN/HRWW/W HA3 94 D8
Kelvin Dr TWK TW1 177 M2
Kelvin Gdns CROY/NA CR0 202 F7
  STHL UB1 114 A5
Kelvin Gv SURB KT6 199 K10
  SYD SE26 182 A10
Kelvington Cl CROY/NA CR0 204 D7
Kelvington Rd PECK SE15 182 C4
Kelvin La CRAWE RH10 284 A3
Kelvin Pde ORP BR6 207 H8
Kelvin Rd HBRY N5 119 J9
  TIL RM18 168 D8
  WELL DA16 163 K9
Kelvin Wy CRAWE RH10 284 A3
Kember St IS N1 5 N4
Kemble Cl POTB/CUF EN6 59 J9
  WEY KT13 216 E1
Kemble Dr HAYES BR2 206 B10
Kemble Rd CROY/NA CR0 203 J10
  FSTH SE23 182 C4
  TOTM N17 99 P9
Kembleside Rd BH/WHM TN16 243 P4
Kemble St HOL/ALD WC2B 11 N6
Kemerton Rd BECK BR3 183 M5
  CMBW SE5 159 K9
  CROY/NA CR0 203 N7
Kemey's St HOM E9 120 D10
Kemishford WOKS/MYFD GU22 231 M9
Kemnal Rd CHST BR7 184 F10
Kempe Cl DTCH/LGLY SL3 150 B1
  STAI AL1 38 B10

Kempe Rd EN EN1 80 A2
  KIL/WHAMP NW6 136 G4
Kemp Gdns CROY/NA CR0 203 K6
Kemplay Rd HAMP NW3 117 N9
Kemp Pl BUSH WD23 73 P10
Kempsford Gdns ECT SW5 14 F8
Kempsford Rd LBTH SE11 18 B6
Kempshott Rd STRHM/NOR SW16 180 F10
Kempson Rd FUL/PGN SW6 157 K6
Kempthorne Rd DEPT SE8 160 E3
Kempton Av HCH RM12 125 N9
  NTHLT UB5 133 P1
  SUN TW16 197 J1
Kempton Cl ERITH DA8 164 D5
  HGDN/ICK UB10 112 D9
Kempton Ct SUN TW16 197 J1
Kempton Rd EHAM E6 142 C7
  HPTN TW12 197 N2
Kempton Wk CROY/NA CR0 204 D6
Kempt St WOOL/PLUM SE18 162 D5
Kemsing Cl BXLY DA5 185 P3
  THHTH CR7 202 F8
Kemsing Rd GNWCH SE10 161 M4
Kemsley Cha SLN SL2 129 J3
  GVW RM20 190 C7
Kemsley Rd BH/WHM TN16 244 A5
Kenbury Cl HGDN/ICK UB10 112 B8
Kenbury St CMBW SE5 159 K8
Kenchester Cl VX/NE SW8 158 C6
Kendal Av ACT W3 135 M7
  BARK IG11 143 H3
  EPP CM16 65 K6
  UED N18 99 L5
Kendal Cl CMBW SE5 159 J6
  EBED/NFELT TW14 174 G4
  REDH RH1 257 N9
  SLN SL2 129 M9
  WFD IG8 101 L3
  YEAD UB4 132 F4
Kendal Ct ACT W3 135 M7
Kendal Cft HCH RM12 125 H10
Kendal Dr SLN SL2 129 M9
Kendale CDH/CHF RM16 168 E2
  HHS/BOV HP3 36 C7
Kendale Rd BMLY BR1 183 K4
Kendal Gdns SUT SM1 201 M9
  UED N18 99 L5
Kendall Av BECK BR3 204 D2
  SAND/SEL CR2 223 L5
Kendall Av South SAND/SEL CR2 223 K6
Kendall Ct WGCE AL7 23 J7
  ISLW TW7 154 F8
Kendall Pl MHST W1U 10 C3
Kendall Rd BECK BR3 204 D2
  ISLW TW7 154 F8
Kendalmere Cl MUSWH N10 98 C9
Kendal Pl PUT/ROE SW15 179 J1
Kendals Cl RAD WD7 74 D2
Kendal St BAY/PAD W2 9 P6
Kender St NWCR SE14 160 E10
Kendon Cl WAN E11 121 N1
Kendor Av HOR/WEW KT19 219 P7
Kendra Hall Rd SAND/SEL CR2 223 J4
Kendrey Gdns WHTN TW2 176 D2
Kendrick Ms SKENS SW7 15 L6
Kendrick Pl SKENS SW7 15 L6
Kenelm Cl HRW HA1 114 F8
Kenerne Dr BAR EN5 77 H9
Kenford Cl GSTN WD25 55 J8
Kenilford Rd BAL SW12 180 C3
Kenilworth Av COB KT11 218 A10
  HARH RM3 106 A6
  RYLN/HDSTN HA2 113 N9
  WALTH E17 100 F10
  WIM/MER SW19 179 L4
Kenilworth Cl BNSTD SM7 239 L2
  HHS/BOV HP3 35 P7
  SL SL1 149 L2
Kenilworth Ct WAT WD17 73 H5
Kenilworth Crs EN EN1 79 M5
Kenilworth Dr BORE WD6 75 P7
  RKW/CH/CXG WD3 72 C8
  WOT/HER KT12 197 L10
Kenilworth Gdns GDMY/SEVK IG3 123 J7
  HCH RM12 125 K8
  LOU IG10 82 C10
  OXHEY WD19 93 K6
  STA TW18 173 M8
  STHL UB1 133 N5
  WOOL/PLUM SE18 162 E8
  YEAD UB4 132 G7
Kenilworth Rd ASHF TW15 173 N6
  BOW E3 140 D4
  EA W5 135 K10
  EDGW HA8 95 P3
  EW KT17 220 D3
  KIL/WHAMP NW6 2 D5
  PGE/AN SE20 204 C1
  STMC/STPC BR5 206 F6
Kenley Av CDALE/KGS NW9 96 B3
Kenley Cl BXLY DA5 185 P5
  CHST BR7 207 H3
  EBAR EN4 77 P8
Kenley Gdns HCH RM12 125 N7
  THHTH CR7 203 J4
Kenley La PUR/KEN CR8 223 K10
Kenley Rd KUT KT1 199 L2
  TWK TW1 176 F2
  WIM/MER SW19 201 K3
Kenley Wk CHEAM SM3 220 B4
  NTGHL W11 8 D2
Kenlor Rd TOOT SW17 179 N8
Kenmare Dr MTCM CR4 180 A10
Kenmare Gdns PLMGR N13 99 K5
Kenmare Rd THHTH CR7 203 J4
Kenmere Gdns ALP/SUD HA0 135 M3
Kenmere Rd WELL DA16 163 M8
Kenmont Gdns WLSDN NW10 136 E5
Kenmore Av KTN/HRWW/W HA3 95 J10
Kenmore Crs YEAD UB4 132 G5
Kenmore Gdns EDGW HA8 95 N10
Kenmore Rd KTN/HRWW/W HA3 115 J1
  PUR/KEN CR8 223 J10
Kennacraig Cl CAN/RD E16 160 A3
Kennard Rd FBAR/BDGN N11 48 A1
  SRTFD E15 141 J2
Kennard St BTSEA SW11 158 A7
  CAN/RD E16 142 C10
Kenneally WDSR SL4 148 A3
Kennedy Av HOD EN11 44 E3
  PEND EN3 80 B10
Kennedy Cl CHES/WCR EN8 62 C7
  MTCM CR4 202 B1
  MTCM CR4 202 B2
  PIN HA5 93 N2
  PLSTW E13 141 M4
  SLN SL2 129 H1
  STMC/STPC BR5 206 H2
Kennedy Gdns SEVT TN13 247 K9
Kennedy Rd BARK IG11 143 H9
  HNWL W7 134 D7
Kennel Cl LT/LBKH KT23 256 B10
Kennel La BFOR GU20 212 B2
  HORL RH6 276 N9
  LHD/OX KT22 236 B9
Kennel Wood Crs CROY/NA CR0 204 D7
Kennelwood La HAT AL10 40 G1
Kennet Cl BTSEA SW11 157 N10
  CRAWW RH11 283 J8

UPMR RM14 126 D4
Kennet Dr YEAD UB4 133 M7
Kenneth Av IL IG1 122 E9
Kenneth Crs CRICK NW2 116 F10
Kenneth Gdns STAN HA7 94 F7
Kenneth Moor Rd IL IG1 122 E9
Kenneth Rd BNSTD SM7 239 N1
  CHDH RM6 123 P5
Kennet Rd DTCH/LGLY SL3 150 E2
  ISLW TW7 154 C6
  MV/WKIL W9 8 D1
Kennet St WAP E1W 13 P9
Kennett Ct DTCH/LGLY SL3 150 E2
Kennett Rd DTCH/LGLY SL3 150 E2
Kennett Wharf La BLKFR EC4V 12 F7
Kenninghall Rd CLPT E5 120 A8
  UED N18 100 A4
Kenning St BERM/RHTH SE16 160 B7
Kennings Wy LBTH SE11 18 B7
Kennington Gv LBTH SE11 17 P9
Kennington La LBTH SE11 17 P8
Kennington Ov LBTH SE11 17 P9
Kennington Park Gdns LBTH SE11 18 C3
Kennington Park Pl WALW SE17 18 A10
Kennington Park Rd LBTH SE11 18 A10
Kennington Rd LBTH SE11 18 A7
Kennylands Rd BARK/HLT IG6 103 K8
Kenny Rd MLHL NW7 97 P4
Kenrick Pl MHST W1U 10 C3
Kenrick Sq REDH RH1 259 M10
Kensal Rd NKENS W10 136 G8
Kensington Av MNPK E12 142 C5
  THHTH CR7 202 H1
  WATW WD18 72 D5
Kensington Church Ct KENS W8 14 C2
Kensington Church St KENS W8 14 C2
Kensington Church Wk KENS W8 14 C2
Kensington Ct KENS W8 15 H2
Kensington Court Ms KENS W8 15 H2
Kensington Court Pl KENS W8 15 H3
Kensington Dr WFD IG8 102 A10
Kensington Gdns IL IG1 122 C6
Kensington Gdns Sq BAY/PAD W2 8 G6
Kensington Ga SKENS SW7 15 J3
Kensington Gore SKENS SW7 15 L2
Kensington High St KENS W8 14 E3
Kensington Palace Gdns KENS W8 8 C8
Kensington Park Gdns NTGHL W11 8 C8
Kensington Park Ms NTGHL W11 8 C6
Kensington Park Rd NTGHL W11 8 C6
Kensington Pl KENS W8 8 C8
Kensington Rd BRWN CM15 86 F10
  KENS W8 15 H2
  NTHLT UB5 133 P4
  ROMW/RG RM7 124 D4
  SKENS SW7 15 N2
Kensington Sq KENS W8 14 G2
Kensington Ter SAND/SEL CR2 223 L4
Kensington Wy BORE WD6 76 A3
Kent Av DAGW RM9 144 B6
  SL SL1 129 H7
  WEA W13 135 G2
  WELL DA16 163 M7
Kent Cl BORE WD6 76 A3
  MTCM CR4 202 F4
  ORP BR6 227 H3
  STA TW18 173 N9
  UX/CGN UB8 113 H9
Kent Dr EBAR EN4 78 B8
  HCH RM12 125 J7
  TEDD TW11 176 D8
Kentford Wy NTHLT UB5 133 M3
Kent Gdns RSLP HA4 113 H4
  WEA W13 135 G2
Kent Gate Wy CROY/NA CR0 224 E3
Kent Hatch Rd OXTED RH8 261 P6
Kent House La BECK BR3 182 D9
Kent House Rd BECK BR3 182 C10
Kentish La BRKMPK AL9 41 M10
Kentish Rd BELV DA17 164 B3
Kentish Town Rd CAMTN NW1 4 F4
  KTTN NW5 4 C1
Kentish Wy BMLY BR1 205 N2
Kentmere Rd WOOL/PLUM SE18 163 M4
Kenton Av HRW HA1 114 E5
  STHL UB1 133 P9
  SUN TW16 197 L2
Kenton Gdns KTN/HRWW/W HA3 115 H2
  STAL AL1 38 E7
Kenton Park Av KTN/HRWW/W HA3 115 J2
Kenton Park Cl KTN/HRWW/W HA3 115 H2
Kenton Park Crs KTN/HRWW/W HA3 115 J2
Kenton Park Rd KTN/HRWW/W HA3 115 H2
Kenton Rd HOM E9 140 C1
  KTN/HRWW/W HA3 115 K3
Kenton St STPAN WC1H 11 J1
Kenton Wy WOKN/KNAP GU21 231 L3
  YEAD UB4 132 F5
Kent Rd BFOR GU20 212 C2
  CHSWK W4 155 P7
  DAGE RM10 124 C10
  DART DA1 187 L2
  E/WMO/HCT KT8 198 B4
  GRAYS RM17 167 P9
  GVW RM20 190 D4
  HART DA3 211 J2
  RCH/KEW TW9 155 N6
  STMC/STPC BR5 207 M5
  WCHMH N21 99 J2
  WOKS/MYFD GU22 232 E2
  WWKM BR4 204 G8
Kents Av HHS/BOV HP3 35 N10
Kents La EPP CM16 48 E7
Kent St BETH E2 7 M7
  PLSTW E13 141 N5
Kent Ter CAMTN NW1 3 P10
Kent Vw SOCK/AV RM15 166 B1
Kent View Gdns GDMY/SEVK IG3 123 H7
Kent Wy SURB KT6 199 K10
Kentwode Gn BARN SW13 156 D6
Kenwyns Ri REDH RH1 276 C1
Kenver Av NFNCH/WDSP N12 97 H4
Kenward Rd ELTH/MOT SE9 183 P1
Kenway RAIN RM13 145 L5
  ROMW/RG RM7 104 D10
Ken Wy WBLY HA9 115 P2
Kenway Rd ECT SW5 14 G6
Kenwood Av NFNCH/WDSP N14 85 H10
Kenwood Cl HAMP NW3 117 M4
  WDR/YW UB7 152 B6
Kenwood Dr BECK BR3 205 H1
  RKW/CH/CXG WD3 91 K4
  WOT/HER KT12 217 J3
Kenwood Gdns CLAY IG5 122 D2
  SWFD E18 121 N1
Kenwood Pk WEY KT13 216 E3
Kenwood Rdg PUR/KEN CR8 241 J3
Kenworth Cl CHES/WCR EN8 62 C9
Kenworthy Rd HOM E9 120 D10
Kenwyn Dr CRICK NW2 115 M1
Kenwyn Rd CLAP SW4 158 A10
  DART DA1 187 L1
  RYNPK SW20 200 F1
Kenya Rd CHARL SE7 162 A6
Kenynton Dr SUN TW16 175 H8

Kenyngton Pl KTN/HRWW/W HA3 115 H3
Kenyons EHSLY KT24 252 C4
Kenyon St FUL/PGN SW6 156 G7
Keogh Rd SRTFD E15 141 K6
Kepler Rd CLAP SW4 158 F10
Keppel Rd DAGW RM9 123 P9
  DORK RH4 254 G10
  EHAM E6 142 C2
Keppel Sp WDSR SL4 171 N3
Keppel St GWRST WC1E 11 K3
  WDSR SL4 149 J8
Kerbela St BETH E2 13 N1
Kerbey St POP/IOD E14 140 G7
Kerdistone Cl POTB/CUF EN6 59 L6
Kerfield Crs CMBW SE5 159 L7
Kerfield Pl CMBW SE5 159 L7
Kerria Wy CHOB/PIR GU24 212 D9
Kerri Cl BAR EN5 76 F8
Kerril Cft HLW CM20 28 D10
Kerrill Av COUL/CHIP CR5 241 H5
Kerrison Pl EA W5 135 J10
Kerrison Rd BTSEA SW11 157 N9
  CAN/RD E16 141 J3
  EA W5 135 J10
  SRTFD E15 141 J3
Kerry Av PUR RM19 165 N1
  STAN HA7 95 H5
Kerry Cl CAN/RD E16 141 N8
  PLMGR N13 98 D2
  UPMR RM14 126 E5
Kerry Ct STAN HA7 95 J5
Kerry Dr UPMR RM14 126 E5
Kerry Pth NWCR SE14 160 E5
Kerry Rd NWCR SE14 160 E5
Kerry Ter WOKN/KNAP GU21 232 E2
Kersey Dr SAND/SEL CR2 224 B8
Kersey Gdns HARH RM3 105 M8
  ELTH/MOT SE9 184 C10
Kersfield Rd PUT/ROE SW15 178 G2
Kershaw Cl CDH/CHF RM16 167 H2
  EMPK RM11 125 L5
Kershaw Rd DAGE RM10 124 B8
Kersley Ms BTSEA SW11 158 A7
Kersley Rd STNW/STAM N16 119 M8
Kersley St BTSEA SW11 158 A8
Kerstin Cl HYS/HAR UB3 133 C9
Kerswell Cl SEVS/STOTM N15 119 M3
Kerwick Cl HOLWY N7 5 M3
Keslake Rd KIL/WHAMP NW6 136 C5
Kessock Cl WALTH E17 120 A3
Kesters Rd CSHM HP5 51 J8
Kesteven Cl BARK/HLT IG6 103 J7
Keston Av ADL/WDHM KT15 215 K7
  COUL/CHIP CR5 241 H5
  HAYES BR2 225 P2
Keston Cl UED N18 99 L4
  WELL DA16 163 M6
Keston Gdns HAYES BR2 225 P1
Keston Ms WAT WD17 73 J6
Keston Park Cl HAYES BR2 226 C1
Keston Rd PECK SE15 159 P9
  THHTH CR7 202 G6
  TOTM N17 119 L1
Kestrel Av EHAM E6 142 B7
  HNHL SE24 181 J1
  STA TW18 173 J6
Kestrel Cl BARK/HLT IG6 103 M5
  BERK HP4 33 J2
  CDALE/KGS NW9 96 B10
  CRAWW RH11 283 E5
  CSTN WD25 55 M10
  KUTN/CMB KT2 177 J7
  RAIN RM13 145 J2
  RGUE GU4 250 G8
  WLSDN NW10 116 A10
Kestrel Gn HAT AL10 40 D5
Kestrel Ho WAB EN9 63 M10
The Kestrels LCOL/BKTW AL2 55 M7
Kestrel Wy CROY/NA CR0 225 J5
  WGCE AL7 23 J3
Keswick Av EMPK RM11 125 L6
  KUTN/CMB KT2 178 B5
  SHPTN TW17 196 F5
  WIM/MER SW19 201 K2
Keswick Cl CRAWW RH11 282 C9
  STAL AL1 38 E1
  SUT SM1 201 M1
Keswick Ct SLN SL2 129 L9
  PEND EN3 80 B2
Keswick Dr LTWR GU18 212 A7
Keswick Gdns REDBR IG4 122 B3
  RSLP HA4 113 H3
  WBLY HA9 115 K10
Keswick Ms EA W5 135 K10
Keswick Rd BXLYHN DA7 164 B8
  ECH TW20 172 C10
  GT/LBKH KT23 254 B1
  ORP BR6 207 J8
  PUT/ROE SW15 179 H1
  WHTN TW2 176 B2
  WWKM BR4 205 K9
Kettering Rd HARH RM3 105 M8
  PEND EN3 80 C3
Kettering St STRHM/NOR SW16 180 C3
Kettlebaston Rd LEY E10 120 E6
Kettlewell Cl FBAR/BDGN N11 98 B7
  WOKN/KNAP GU21 232 B1
Kettlewell Ct SWLY BR8 209 P2
Kettlewell Hl WOKN/KNAP GU21 232 B1
Kevan Dr RPLY/SEND GU23 251 H1
Kevelioc Rd TOTM N17 99 K9
Kevin Cl HSLWW TW4 153 L8
Kevington Cl STMC/STPC BR5 207 L1
Kevington Dr CHST BR7 207 L2
Kew Br RCH/KEW TW9 155 N5
Kew Bridge Rd BTFD TW8 155 L5
Kew Crs CHEAM SM3 201 J10
Kewferry Dr NTHWD HA6 92 D7
Kewferry Rd NTHWD HA6 92 D7
Kew Foot Rd RCH/KEW TW9 155 L6
Kew Gardens Rd RCH/KEW TW9 155 L7
Kew Gn RCH/KEW TW9 155 K10
Kew Meadow Pth RCH/KEW TW9 155 K10
Kew Rd RCH/KEW TW9 155 K10
Key Cl WCHPL E1 140 C3
Keyes Rd CRICK NW2 116 C3
Keyfield Ter STAL AL1 38 C7
Keymer Cl BH/WHM TN16 243 P2
Keymer Rd BRXS/STRHM SW2 180 B5
  CRAWW RH11 283 N5
Keynes Cl EFNCH N2 118 B2
Keynsham Av WFD IG8 101 K6
Keynsham Gdns ELTH/MOT SE9 184 B5
Keynsham Rd ELTH/MOT SE9 184 A4
  MRDN SM4 201 A1
Keynton Cl HERT/WAS SG14 23 N1
Keyse Rd STHWK SE1 19 L4
Keysers Rd BROX EN10 44 F2
Keysham Av HEST TW5 153 H7
Keystone Crs IS N1 5 H8
Keywood Dr SUN TW16 175 H9
Keyworth Cl CLPT E5 120 D3
Keyworth St STHWK SE1 18 E4
Kezia St DEPT SE8 160 D7
Khama Rd TOOT SW17 179 P7
Khartoum Rd IL IG1 122 B4
  PLSTW E13 141 L5
  TOOT SW17 179 N7
Khyber Rd BTSEA SW11 158 F9
Kibes La WARE SG12 26 C1
Kibworth St VX/NE SW8 158 G6
Kidborough Down GT/LBKH KT23 253 P3
Kidborough Rd CRAWW RH11 283 H7
Kidbrooke Gdns BKHTH/KID SE3 161 K2
Kidbrooke Gv BKHTH/KID SE3 161 M1
Kidbrooke La ELTH/MOT SE9 162 B10

Kidbrooke Park Cl
  BKHTH/KID SE3 161 N7
Kidbrooke Park Rd
  BKHTH/KID SE3 161 P9
  ELTH/MOT SE9 183 N1
Kidderminster Rd CROY/NA CR0 203 J8
  SLN SL2 128 F5
Kidderpore Av HAMP NW3 117 K9
Kidderpore Gdns HAMP NW3 117 K9
Kidd Pl CHARL SE7 162 B4
Kidlington Wy CDALE/KGS NW9 96 B10
Kidworth Cl HORL RH6 280 A2
Kielder Cl BARK/HLT IG6 103 J7
Kier Pk ASC SL5 192 B3
Kilberry Cl ISLW TW7 154 C7
Kilbride Ct HHNE HP2 36 A2
Kilburn High Rd KIL/WHAMP 2 C2
Kilburn La NKENS W10 2 C1
Kilburn Park Rd KIL/WHAMP NW6 2 C5
Kilburn Priory KIL/WHAMP NW6 2 F3
Kilburn Priory KIL/WHAMP NW6 2 F5
Kilburn Sq KIL/WHAMP NW6 2 F2
Kilby Cl GSTN WD25 73 L1
Kilcorral Cl EW KT17 220 D10
Kildare Cl RSLP HA4 113 K6
Kildare Gdns BAY/PAD W2 8 F5
Kildare Rd CAN/RD E16 141 N8
Kildare Ter BAY/PAD W2 8 F5
Kildoran Rd CLAP SW4 180 F1
Kildowan Rd GDMY/SEVK IG3 123 K6
Kilfillan Gdns BERK HP4 33 M6
Kilgour Rd FSTH SE23 182 D2
Kilkie St FUL/PGN SW6 157 M8
Killarney Rd WAND/EARL SW18 179 M2
Killearn Rd CAT SE6 183 J4
Killester Gdns WPK KT4 220 E1
Killewarren Wy STMC/STPC BR5 207 N1
Killick Cl SEV TN13 246 P9
Killick St IS N1 5 N7
Killieser Av BRXS/STRHM SW2 179 P1
Killip Cl CAN/RD E16 141 L8
Killowen Av NTHLT UB5 114 B10
Killowen Rd HOM E9 140 C2
Killyon Rd VX/NE SW8 158 D8
Kilmaine Rd FUL/PGN SW6 157 H6
Kilmarnock Gdns BCTR RM8 123 M8
Kilmarnock Rd OXHEY WD19 93 L5
Kilmarsh Rd HMSMTH W6 156 F3
Kilmartin Av STRHM/NOR SW16 201 P1
Kilmartin Rd GDMY/SEVK IG3 123 K7
Kilmartin Wy HCH RM12 125 J7
Kilmington Cl RBRW/HUT CM13 107 N3
Kilmington Rd BARN SW13 156 D5
Kilmiston Av SHPTN TW17 196 D6
Kilmorey Gdns TWK TW1 176 G1
Kilmorey Rd TWK TW1 154 G10
Kilmorie Rd FSTH SE23 182 D4
Kiln Av AMS HP6 69 P4
Kiln Cl HYS/HAR UB3 152 E5
Kilncroft HHS/BOV HP3 36 G8
Kildown CVE DA12 191 J9
Kilner St POP/IOD E14 140 F7
Kilnfield CHONG CM5 67 N5
  WGCE AL7 23 J3
Kiln Gnd HHS/BOV HP3 36 B8
Kiln House Cl WARE SG12 26 D1
Kiln La ASC SL5 170 A9
  ASC SL5 192 F5
  BRKHM/BTCW RH3 255 P10
  CSHM HP5 51 N7
  EW KT17 220 B7
  HLWE CM17 47 N2
  HORL RH6 280 A2
  RPLY/SEND GU23 233 L10
  SLN SL2 109 H6
Kilnmead CRAWE RH10 283 P6
Kilnmead Cl CRAWE RH10 283 P6
Kiln Mdw RGUW GU3 249 H6
Kiln Ms TOOT SW17 179 N8
Kiln Pl KTTN NW5 118 B9
Kiln Rd EPP CM16 66 A1
Kilnside ESH/CLAY KT10 218 F4
Kiln Wy GRAYS RM17 167 L4
  NTHWD HA6 92 F7
Kilnwood CRAWE RH10 283 P6
Kilnwood La HORS RH12 282 D10
Kilpatrick Wy YEAD UB4 133 M7
Kilravock St NKENS W10 2 A10
Kilross Rd EBED/NFELT TW14 174 E4
Kilrue La WOT/HER KT12 216 C1
Kilrush Ter WOKN/KNAP GU21 232 D2
Kilsha Rd WOT/HER KT12 197 J6
Kilsmore La CHES/WCR EN8 62 C4
Kilvinton Dr ENC/FH EN2 79 L4
Kilworth Av BRWN CM15 87 M10
Kilworth Cl WGCE AL7 23 M7
Kimbell Gdns FUL/PGN SW6 157 H7
Kimbell Pl ELTH/MOT SE9 161 P10
Kimber Cl WDSR SL4 148 F9
Kimber Ct RGUE GU4 250 G8
Kimberley Av EHAM E6 142 B2
  GNTH/NBYPK IG2 122 C5
  ROMW/RG RM7 124 C5
Kimberley Cl DTCH/LGLY SL3 150 C3
  HORL RH6 279 P4
Kimberley Dr SCUP DA14 185 N5
Kimberley Gdns EN EN1 79 N7
  FSBYPK N4 119 J3
Kimberley Pl PUR/KEN CR8 223 H7
Kimberley Ride COB KT11 218 A3
Kimberley Rd BECK BR3 204 C5
  BRXN/ST SW9 158 F8
  CAN/RD E16 141 L6
  CHING E4 101 K2
  CRAWE RH10 284 C6
  CROY/NA CR0 203 J6
  KIL/WHAMP NW6 2 B5
  STALW/RED AL3 38 B5
  TOTM N17 99 P10
  UED N18 100 A7
  WALTH E17 100 P10
  WAN E11 121 K2
Kimber Rd WAND/EARL SW18 179 L3
Kimbers Dr SL SL1 128 C5
Kimble Cl WATW WD18 72 F10
Kimble Crs BUSH WD23 94 B1
Kimble Rd TOOT SW17 179 N9
Kimbolton Cl LEE/GVPK SE12 183 L2
Kimbolton Gn BORE WD6 75 P8
Kimmeridge Gdns
  ELTH/MOT SE9 184 B7
Kimmeridge Rd ELTH/MOT SE9 184 B8
Kimps Wy HHS/BOV HP3 36 B9
Kimpton Av BRWN CM15 106 C1
Kimpton Cl HHNE HP2 36 C1
Kimpton Pl CSTN WD25 55 L10
Kimpton Rd CHEAM SM3 201 J10
  CMBW SE5 159 L7
Kimpton's Cl CHONG CM5 67 N2
  POTB/CUF EN6 58 G9
Kimptons Md POTB/CUF EN6 58 G9
Kinburn Dr EGH TW20 172 B8
Kinburn St BERM/RHTH SE16 160 C1
Kincaid Rd PECK SE15 160 A6
Kinch Gv WBLY HA9 115 L5
Kincraig Dr SEV TN13 247 M9
Kinder Cl THMD SE28 143 M9
Kinderscout HHS/BOV HP3 36 B9
Kindersley Wy ABLGY WD5 50 C6
Kinfauns Av EMPK RM11 125 K4
Kinfauns Rd BRXS/STRHM SW2 181 J3
  GDMY/SEVK IG3 123 N1
Kingaby Gdns RAIN RM13 145 H2

King Alfred Av CAT SE6 .... 182 F6
King Alfred Rd HARH RM3 .... 105 N10
King And Queen Cl
  ELTH/MOT SE9 .... 184 B7⑪
King And Queen St WALW SE17 .... 18 F7
King Arthur Cl PECK SE15 .... 160 B6⑪
King Arthur Ct CHES/WCR EN8 .... 62 D7
King Charles Crs BRYLDS KT5 ..... 199 L7
King Charles Rd BRYLDS KT5 ...... 199 L6
  RAD WD7 .... 57 K8
King Charles St WHALL SW1A 17 K1
King Charles Wk
  WIM/MER SW19 .... 179 H4⑪
King Croft Rd HARP AL5 .... 20 C4
Kingcup Cl CROY/NA CR0 .... 204 C8⑪
Kingcup Dr CHOB/PIR GU24 .... 230 F7
King David La WCHPL E1 .... 140 B9⑪
Kingdon Rd KIL/WHAMP NW6 ...... 2 F1
King Edward Av DART DA1 .... 187 L2
  RAIN RM13 .... 145 L4
King Edward Dr CDH/CHF RM16 ... 168 B2
  GRAYS RM17 .... 168 B2
  SURB KT6 .... 199 K10
King Edward Rd BAR EN5 .... 77 K8
  BRW CM14 .... 107 H4⑪
  CHES/WCR EN8 .... 62 D9
  GRH DA9 .... 166 F10
  LEY E10 .... 121 H6
  OXHEY WD19 .... 73 M10
  RAD WD7 .... 57 L9
  ROM RM1 .... 124 G4⑪
  WALTH E17 .... 120 D1
King Edward's Gdns ACT W3 .... 135 M10
King Edward's Gv TEDD TW11 ..... 176 G9
King Edward's Rd BARK IG11 ...... 142 G3
  ED N9 .... 100 A1
  HACK E8 .... 140 A3
  PEND EN3 .... 80 C8
  RSLP HA4 .... 112 E6
  WARE SG12 .... 26 D1
King Edward St HHS/BOV HP3 ..... 35 N10
  SL1 SL1 .... 149 J1
King Edward Vii Av WDSR SL4 ..... 149 K6
King Edward Wk STHWK SE1 .... 18 B4
Kingfield Cl WOKS/MYFD GU22 .... 232 C6
Kingfield Dr WOKS/MYFD GU22 ... 232 C6
Kingfield Gdns
  WOKS/MYFD GU22 .... 232 C6
Kingfield Rd EA W5 .... 135 J6
  WOKS/MYFD GU22 .... 232 C6
Kingfisher Cl CRAWE RH10 .... 284 B4⑪
  NTHWD HA6 .... 92 C9
  RBRW/HUT CM13 .... 107 M1
  STALE/WH AL4 .... 21 J2
  STMC/STPC BR5 .... 207 N4⑪
  THMD SE28 .... 143 M9
  WARE SG12 .... 27 H8⑪
  WOT/HER KT12 .... 217 M2⑪
Kingfisher Dr HHS/BOV HP3 .... 54 A1
  RCHPK/HAM TW10 .... 177 H1
  REDH RH1 .... 258 F2
  RGUE GU4 .... 250 F8
  STA TW18 .... 173 J7
Kingfisher Gdns SAND/SEL CR2 ... 224 C6
Kingfisher Lure RKW/CH/CXG WD3 71 L8
Kingfisher St UPMR RM14 .... 126 E6
Kingfisher St EHAM E6 .... 142 E7
Kingfisher Wy CROY/NA CR0 ...... 204 C5
  WLSDN NW10 .... 116 A10⑪
King Gdns CROY/NA CR0 .... 223 J2⑪
King Garth Ms FSTH SE23 .... 182 B5
King George Av BUSH WD23 ...... 74 A10
  CAN/RD E16 .... 142 A8
  GNTH/NBYPK IG2 .... 122 G4
  WOT/HER KT12 .... 197 L8
King George Cl ROMW/RG RM7 ... 124 D1
  SUN TW16 .... 174 F8⑪
  WARE SG12 .... 26 D1
King George Rd WAB EN9 .... 63 H10⑪
  WARE SG12 .... 26 D1
King Georges Av WATW WD18 .... 72 F9
King George's Dr
  ADL/WDHM KT15 .... 215 K6
King George Sq
  RCHPK/HAM TW10 .... 177 L2
King George's Rd BRWN CM15 ... 86 G10
King George St GNWCH SE10 ..... 161 H6
King George VI Av MTCM CR4 ..... 202 A4
  TIL RM18 .... 169 L3
Kingham Cl WAND/EARL SW18 ... 179 M3
  WCHMH N21 .... 99 J2
Kingham Cl WAND/EARL SW18 ... 179 M3
King Harolds Wy BXLYHN DA7 .... 163 N6
King Harry La STALW/RED AL3 .... 37 P7
King Harry St HHNE HP2 .... 35 N6
King Henry Ms ORP BR6 .... 227 J2
King Henry's Dr CROY/NA CR0 .... 225 H5
King Henry's Ms PEND EN3 .... 80 F3⑪
King Henry's Rd HAMP NW3 .... 3 M7
  KUT KT1 .... 199 N3
King Henry St STNW/STAM N16 .. 7 M1⑪
King Henry's Wk IS N1 .... 7 J1
Kinghorn St STBT EC1A 12 E4⑪
King James Av POTB/CUF EN6 .... 60 F5
King James St STHWK SE1 .... 18 D2
King John Ct SDTCH EC2A 13 K1
King John Cl STWL/WRAY TW19 .. 171 P2
King John St WCHPL E1 .... 140 C7
King John's Wk ELTH/MOT SE9 ... 184 B3
Kinglake Cl WALW SE17 .... 19 J8
Kingly St REGST W1B 10 G6
Kingsand Rd LEE/GVPK SE12 ..... 183 M5
King's Arbour NWDGN UB2 .... 153 M4⑪
King's Arms Yd LOTH EC2R 12 G5⑪
Kingsash Dr YEAD UB4 .... 133 M6⑪
Kings Av BAL SW12 .... 180 L4
  BF/WBF KT14 .... 215 N8
  BMLY BR1 .... 183 M9
  CAR SM5 .... 221 P4
  CHDH RM6 .... 124 A4
  CHOB/PIR GU24 .... 230 C5
  CLAP SW4 .... 180 F2
  EA W5 .... 135 J8
  GFD/PVL UB6 .... 134 A8
  HHS/BOV HP3 .... 36 A10
  HSLW TW3 .... 154 A7⑪
  MUSWH N10 .... 114 B1
  NWMAL KT3 .... 200 C4
  REDH RH1 .... 275 P2
  SUN TW16 .... 174 C8
  WATW WD18 .... 73 N8
  WCHMH N21 .... 99 J2
  WFD IG8 .... 101 P5
King's Bench St STHWK SE1 ...... 18 D1
Kingsbridge Av EA W5 .... 155 L1
Kingsbridge Ct POP/IOD E14 ..... 160 F2⑪
Kingsbridge Rd BARK IG11 .... 142 G4
  HARH RM3 .... 105 M7⑪
  MRDN SM4 .... 200 D7
  NKENS W10 .... 136 F8
  NWDGN UB2 .... 153 N10
  WOT/HER KT12 .... 197 J7⑪
Kingsbrook LHD/OX KT22 .... 236 F4
Kingsbury Crs STA TW18 .... 172 G7
Kingsbury Dr WDSR SL4 .... 171 M3
Kingsbury Rd CDALE/KGS NW9 .. 45 J3
  IS N1 .... 7 K1
  STNW/STAM N16 .... 119 M10⑪
Kingsbury Ter IS N1 .... 7 K1
King's Cha BRW CM14 .... 107 H4
  E/WMO/HCT KT8 .... 198 B3
Kingsclere Cl PUT/ROE SW15 .... 178 D3⑪
Kingscliffe Gdns WIM/MER SW19 179 H6⑪
Kings Cl CSTG HP8 .... 90 A3
  DART DA1 .... 164 F10
  HDN NW4 .... 116 D2
  KGLGY WD4 .... 53 L7
  LEY E10 .... 120 C2

NTHWD HA6 .... 92 G7
STA TW18 .... 173 N10⑪
THDIT KT7 .... 198 F6
WATW WD18 .... 73 K8⑪
WOT/HER KT12 .... 197 J8⑪
King's College Rd HAMP NW3 .... 3 N3
  RSLP HA4 .... 112 C4
Kingscote Hl CRAWW RH11 ...... 283 L9
Kingscote Rd CHSWK W4 .... 156 A2
  CROY/NA CR0 .... 204 A7
  NWMAL KT3 .... 200 A3
Kingscote St EMB EC4Y 12 C7
Kings Ct KWD/TDW/WH KT20 .... 238 F3⑪
  PLSTW E13 .... 141 N3
  STHWK SE1 .... 18 D1⑪
Kingscourt Rd STRHM/NOR SW16 180 E6
King's Crs FSBYPK N4 .... 119 K8
Kingscroft WGCE AL7 .... 25 L4⑪
Kingscroft Rd BNSTD SM7 .... 239 N1
  CRICK NW2 .... 2 C1
  LHD/OX KT22 .... 236 G6
King's Cross Br FSBYW WC1X ... 5 M8
King's Cross Rd FSBYW WC1X .. 5 N8⑪
King's Cross Rd FSBYW WC1X .. 5 P9
Kingsdale Gdns NTGHL W11 ..... 136 G10⑪
Kingsdale Rd BERK HP4 .... 33 M6
  PGE/AN SE20 .... 182 C10⑪
  WOOL/PLUM SE18 .... 163 J5
Kingsdene KWD/TDW/WH KT20 .. 238 E7
Kingsdon La HLWE CM17 .... 47 M2
Kingsdown Av ACT W3 .... 136 B9⑪
  SAND/SEL CR2 .... 223 K5
  WEA W13 .... 154 G1
Kingsdown Cl GVE DA12 .... 191 J4⑪
  NTGHL W11 .... 136 G6
Kingsdowne Rd SURB KT6 .... 199 K7
Kingsdown Rd ARCH N19 .... 118 F1
  CHEAM SM3 .... 221 H2
  EW KT17 .... 220 D9
  WAN E11 .... 121 K8
Kingsdown Wy HAYES BR2 .... 205 M6
Kings Dr BRYLDS KT5 .... 199 M7
  EDGW HA8 .... 95 L5
  GVE DA12 .... 190 E6
  THDIT KT7 .... 198 G6
  WBLY HA9 .... 115 N7
The Kings Dr WOT/HER KT12 .... 216 C5
Kingsend RSLP HA4 .... 112 F6
Kings Farm Av
  RCHPK/HAM TW10 .... 155 M10
Kings Farm Rd RKW/CH/CXG WD3 70 C10
Kingsfield HOD EN11 .... 44 F1
  WDSR SL4 .... 148 C7⑪
Kingsfield Av RYLN/HDSTN HA2 . 114 A3
Kingsfield Ct OXHEY WD19 .... 73 L10
Kingsfield Dr HRW HA1 .... 114 C5⑪
  OXHEY WD19 .... 93 L1
Kingsfield Wy PEND EN3 .... 80 C1⑪
Kingsford Av WLGTN SM6 .... 222 F4
Kingsford St KTTN NW5 .... 118 A10⑪
Kingsford Wy EHAM E6 .... 142 C7
Kings Gdns IG1 IG1 .... 122 G6
  UPMR RM14 .... 126 E6
Kingsgate WBLY HA9 .... 115 P8
Kingsgate Av FNCH N3 .... 117 K1
Kingsgate Cl BXLYHN DA7 .... 163 P7
  STMC/STPC BR5 .... 207 M2
Kingsgate Pl KIL/WHAMP NW6 ... 2 E3
Kingsgate Rd KIL/WHAMP NW6 .. 2 E3
  KUT KT1 .... 199 K1

STALE/WH AL4 .... 39 J3
WOKN/KNAP GU21 .... 232 D2⑪
Kingsmead Av CDALE/KGS NW9 . 116 A3
  ED N9 .... 100 A2
  MTCM CR4 .... 202 D3
  ROM RM1 .... 124 G4⑪
  SUN TW16 .... 197 K3
  SURB KT6 .... 199 M9
  WPK KT4 .... 200 E10
Kingsmead Cl BFN/LL DA15 ...... 185 N5
  HLWW/ROY CM19 .... 45 N2
  HOR/WEW KT19 .... 220 A4
  TEDD TW11 .... 176 D9
Kings Meadow KGLGY WD4 ...... 54 B4
Kings Mead Pk ESH/CLAY KT10 . 218 D4
Kingsmead Rd BRXS/STRHM SW2 181 H5
Kingsmere Cl PUT/ROE SW15 .... 156 G9⑪
Kingsmere Pk CDALE/KGS NW9 . 115 P6
Kingsmere Rd WIM/MER SW19 .. 178 G5⑪
King's Ms BMSBY WC1N 11 P2
Kingsmill La HAT AL10 .... 40 E6⑪
Kingsmill Gdns DAGW RM9 ...... 124 A10⑪
Kings Mill La REDH RH1 .... 276 E4
Kingsmill Ter STJWD NW8 .... 3 M7
Kingsmoor Rd HLWW/ROY CM19 46 A7
Kingsnympton Pk
  KUTN/CMB KT2 .... 177 N10⑪
King's Orch ELTH/MOT SE9 .... 184 D4
King's Paddock HPTN TW12 ...... 198 D1⑪
Kingspark Ct SWFD E18 .... 121 M1
Kings Pl BKHH IG9 .... 101 P3⑪
  CHSWK W4 .... 155 P4⑪
  STHWK SE1 .... 18 E2⑪
Kings Sq FSBYE EC1V 6 E10
Kingsridge Gdns DART DA1 ...... 187 L2
Kings Rd ADL/WDHM KT15 ...... 215 L6
  ASC SL5 .... 192 C5
  BAR EN5 .... 76 F7
  BARK IG11 .... 142 F2⑪
  BELMT SM2 .... 221 L5⑪
  BERK HP4 .... 33 N6
  BGVA SW1W 16 D4
  BH/WHM TN16 .... 243 P3
  BRW CM14 .... 107 H4
  CHES/WCR EN8 .... 62 D10
  CHING E4 .... 101 J2
  CHOB/PIR GU24 .... 212 F10
  EA W5 .... 135 J7
  EGH TW20 .... 172 D7
  EHAM E6 .... 141 P3
  FELT TW13 .... 175 K4
  FUL/PGN SW6 .... 157 N6
  HERT/BAY SG13 .... 25 P4⑪
  HORL RH6 .... 280 B4
  KUTN/CMB KT2 .... 199 K1
  LCOL/BKTW AL2 .... 57 H2
  MORT/ESHN SW14 .... 156 A3
  MTCM CR4 .... 202 B3
  ORP BR6 .... 227 J1
  RCHPK/HAM TW10 .... 156 G6
  RGUE GU4 .... 268 B6⑪
  ROM RM1 .... 125 H5
  RYLN/HDSTN HA2 .... 113 N7
  SHGR GU5 .... 268 C4⑪
  SL SL1 .... 149 K2
  SNWD SE25 .... 203 P3
  STALW/RED AL3 .... 38 A5
  SURB KT6 .... 199 J8
  TEDD TW11 .... 176 C8
  TOTM N17 .... 99 N9
  TWK TW1 .... 176 C2⑪
  UED N18 .... 99 P6⑪
  UX/CGN UB8 .... 131 N4
  WAN E11 .... 121 K5
  WBPTN SW10 .... 15 L10
  WDGN N22 .... 98 G9
  WDR/YW UB7 .... 152 A1
  WDSR SL4 .... 149 J10
  WIM/MER SW19 .... 179 K9
  WOKN/KNAP GU21 .... 231 P2
  WOT/HER KT12 .... 197 J9
King's Scholars' Pas WEST SW1P 16 C4
Kings's Gv RGUE GU4 .... 250 A10⑪
King Stable St WDSR SL4 .... 149 J6
King Stairs Cl BERM/RHTH SE16 160 A1
King's Ter CAMTN NW1 .... 4 C6
Kingston Av CHEAM SM3 .... 201 H10
  EBED/NFELT TW14 .... 174 A2
  EHSLY KT24 .... 252 F2
  LHD/OX KT22 .... 236 F2⑪
  WDR/YW UB7 .... 132 A9
Kingston By-pass BRYLDS KT5 .. 199 P5
  CHSGTN KT9 .... 199 L10
  ESH/CLAY KT10 .... 198 D10
Kingston Cl CHDH RM6 .... 123 P1⑪
  NTHLT UB5 .... 133 N2⑪
Kingston Crs ASHF TW15 .... 173 M8
  BECK BR3 .... 204 E1⑪
Kingston Gdns CROY/NA CR0 .... 202 F10
Kingston Hall Rd KUT KT1 .... 199 J3
Kingston Hi KUTN/CMB KT2 ...... 199 M1
Kingston Hill Av CHDH RM6 ...... 123 P1
Kingston Hill Pl KUTN/CMB KT2 . 177 P7⑪
Kingston House Gdns
  LHD/OX KT22 .... 236 G2⑪
Kingston La EHSLY KT24 .... 252 B3
  TEDD TW11 .... 176 D9⑪
  UX/CGN UB8 .... 131 N7⑪
  WDR/YW UB7 .... 152 A1
Kingston Ldg NWMAL KT3 .... 200 D4⑪
Kingston Ri ADL/WDHM KT15 ... 215 K6
Kingston Rd ASHF TW15 .... 173 K8
  BRYLDS KT5 .... 199 N9
  EBAR EN4 .... 77 N9
  ED N9 .... 99 P3
  EW KT17 .... 220 B2
  HOR/WEW KT19 .... 220 B2
  IL IG1 .... 122 F9
  LHD/OX KT22 .... 236 F4
  NWDGN UB2 .... 153 N3
  NWMAL KT3 .... 200 A4
  PUT/ROE SW15 .... 178 A4
  ROM RM1 .... 124 G2
  RYNPK SW20 .... 201 H2
  SHPTN TW17 .... 174 A7
  STA TW18 .... 173 K7
  WIM/MER SW19 .... 201 K1
Kingston Sq NRWD SE19 .... 181 L8
Kingston V St CAMTN NW15 ..... 4 C5
Kingstown St CAMTN NW1 .... 4 C5
King St CHERT KT16 .... 195 K8
  CHSWK W4 .... 156 A3
  CITYW EC2V 12 F6
  COVGDN WC2E 11 L7
  CSHM HP5 .... 64 F2
  EFNCH N2 .... 97 N10⑪
  GVE DA12 .... 190 E2
  NWDGN UB2 .... 153 M2
  PLSTW E13 .... 141 M6
  RCH/KEW TW9 .... 156 D10
  TOTM N17 .... 99 N10
  TWK TW1 .... 176 F4
  WATW WD18 .... 73 K8
Kingswater Pl BTSEA SW11 ...... 157 P6⑪
Kings Wy CROY/NA CR0 .... 222 G2
Kingsway ECT SW5 .... ⑪ A4⑪
  HRW HA1 .... 114 D2
Kingsway CFSP/GDCR SL9 .... 110 B1
  HOL/ALD WC2B 11 N5
  HYS/HAR UB3 .... 132 D7

MORT/ESHN SW14 .... 155 N9
NWMAL KT3 .... 200 F4
PEND EN3 .... 80 A9
POTB/CUF EN6 .... 60 F6
SLN SL2 .... 128 G1
STMC/STPC BR5 .... 206 C5
STWL/WRAY TW19 .... 173 N4
WBLY HA9 .... 115 K9
WOKN/KNAP GU21 .... 232 A4
WWKM BR4 .... 205 L10
Kingsway Av SAND/SEL CR2 .... 224 B5
  WOKN/KNAP GU21 .... 232 A4
Kingsway Crs RYLN/HDSTN HA2 114 B2
Kingsway North Orbital Rd
  GSTN WD25 .... 55 J10
Kingsway Rd CHEAM SM3 .... 221 H4⑪
Kingsway Ter WEY KT13 .... 216 B4
The Kingsway EW KT17 .... 220 C6
Kingswear Rd KTTN NW5 .... 118 C2
  RSLP HA4 .... 113 H7
Kingswell Ride POTB/CUF EN6 .. 60 F6
Kingswick Cl ASC SL5 .... 192 D4
Kingswick Dr ASC SL5 .... 192 D4
Kingswood Av BELV DA17 .... 164 A3
  HAYES BR2 .... 205 K3
  HEST TW5 .... 153 N6
  HPTN TW12 .... 176 B9⑪
  KIL/WHAMP NW6 .... 2 A6
  SAND/SEL CR2 .... 242 A1
  SWLY BR8 .... 208 G4
  THHTH CR7 .... 203 H5
Kingswood Cl DART DA1 .... 187 A2
  EGH TW20 .... 172 A7
  EN EN1 .... 79 N9⑪
  GU GU1 .... 250 F9⑪
  NWMAL KT3 .... 200 C6
  ORP BR6 .... 206 G7⑪
  SURB KT6 .... 199 K7⑪
  TRDG/WHET N20 .... 77 M10
  WEY KT13 .... 216 C4
Kingswood Creek
  STWL/WRAY TW19 .... 172 A1
Kingswood Dr BELMT SM2 .... 221 L5⑪
  CAR SM5 .... 202 A8
  NRWD SE19 .... 181 M7
Kingswood La WARL CR6 .... 242 B1
Kingswood Pk FNCH N3 .... 97 J9⑪
Kingswood Pl LEW SE13 .... 161 K10⑪
Kingswood Ri EGH TW20 .... 172 A8
Kingswood Rd BRXS/STRHM SW2 180 F2
  CHSWK W4 .... 155 P2
  GDMY/SEVK IG3 .... 123 K6
  GSTN WD25 .... 55 J10
  HAYES BR2 .... 205 K3
  KWD/TDW/WH KT20 .... 238 C7
  PGE/AN SE20 .... 182 B9
  SEV TN13 .... 246 F7
  WIM/MER SW19 .... 201 J1
Kingswood Ter CHSWK W4 .... 155 P2⑪
  WLGTN SM6 .... 222 F2⑪
Kingsworth Cl BECK BR3 .... 204 D5⑪
Kingsworthy Cl KUT KT1 .... 199 L3⑪
Kingthorpe Rd WLSDN NW10 .... 136 N4⑪
Kingwell Rd EBAR EN4 .... 77 N4
King William La GNWCH SE10 ... 161 K4⑪
King William St CANST EC4R 13 H7
King William Wk GNWCH SE10 .. 161 H5⑪
Kingwood Av HPTN TW12 .... 176 B9⑪
Kingwood Rd FUL/PGN SW6 ..... 157 H6
Kinlet Rd WOOL/PLUM SE18 ..... 162 F6
Kinloch Cl CDALE/KGS NW9 ..... 116 B5
Kinloch St HOLWY N7 .... 118 G2⑪
Kinloss Ct FNCH N3 .... 117 J1
Kinloss Gdns CAR SM5 .... 201 M7
Kinloss Rd CAR SM5 .... 201 M7
Kinnaird Av BMLY BR1 .... 183 J2⑪
  CHSWK W4 .... 155 P6
Kinnaird Cl BMLY BR1 .... 183 J2⑪
  SL SL1 .... 128 B8⑪
Kinnaird Wy WFD IG8 .... 102 C7
Kinnear Rd SHB W12 .... 156 C1
Kinnersley Ms REIG RH2 .... 275 K5
Kinnerton Pl South KTBR SW1X . 16 B2⑪
Kinnerton Pl St KTBR SW1X 16 B2⑪
Kinnerton Yd KTBR SW1X 16 C2⑪
Kinnoul Rd HMSMTH W6 .... 14 A1
Kinross Av WPK KT4 .... 200 D9
Kinross Cl KTN/HRWW/W HA3 .. 115 L3
  SUN TW16 .... 174 C8
Kinross Dr SUN TW16 .... 174 C8
Kinsale Rd PECK SE15 .... 159 P9
Kintyre Cl STRHM/NOR SW16 ... 202 A2
Kinveachy Gdns CHARL SE7 ..... 162 B4
Kipings KWD/TDW/WH KT20 .... 238 G8
Kipling Av TIL RM18 .... 168 E7
Kipling Cl CRAWE RH10 .... 284 D5⑪
Kipling Dr TOOT SW17 .... 179 N9⑪
Kipling Rd BXLYHN DA7 .... 163 P7
  DART DA1 .... 188 A1⑪
Kipling St STHWK SE1 .... 19 H2
Kipling Ter HARP AL5 .... 20 A2
Kipling Wy HARP AL5 .... 20 A2
Kippings Cl SEV TN13 .... 246 C10
Kippington Dr ELTH/MOT SE9 ... 184 A4
Kippington Rd SEV TN13 .... 265 H1⑪
Kirby Cl BARK/HLT IG6 .... 105 P6
  HARH RM3 .... 105 P6
  HOR/WEW KT19 .... 220 C2
  LOU IG10 .... 102 B7⑪
  NTHWD HA6 .... 92 C7
Kirby Gv STHWK SE1 .... 19 J1
Kirby Rd RDART DA2 .... 188 B3
  WOKN/KNAP GU21 .... 231 P2
Kirby St HCIRC EC1N 12 B3
Kirchen Rd WEA W13 .... 134 G9
Kirdford Cl CRAWW RH11 .... 283 K5
Kirkcaldy Gn OXHEY WD19 ...... 93 K4⑪
Kirkdale SYD SE26 .... 182 A5
Kirkdale Rd WAN E11 .... 121 K6
Kirkefields GUW GU2 .... 249 M7⑪
Kirkfield Cl WEA W13 .... 134 G10⑪
Kirkham Rd EHAM E6 .... 142 B4
Kirkham St WOOL/PLUM SE18 .. 163 H5
Kirkland Av CLAY IG5 .... 102 D10
  WOKN/KNAP GU21 .... 231 K2
Kirkland Cl BFN/LL DA15 .... 185 H1
Kirklands WGCW AL8 .... 23 H1
Kirk La WOOL/PLUM SE18 .... 162 F6
Kirklees Rd BCTR RM8 .... 123 M10⑪
  THHTH CR7 .... 203 K2
Kirkley Rd WIM/MER SW19 ...... 201 K1
Kirkly Cl SAND/SEL CR2 .... 223 M5
Kirkmichael Rd POP/IOD E14 ... 141 N8⑪
Kirk Ri SUT SM1 .... 209 K9
Kirk Rd WALTH E17 .... 120 D1
Kirkside Rd BKHTH/KID SE3 ..... 161 N5
Kirk's Pl POP/IOD E14 .... 140 K7⑪
Kirkstall Av TOTM N17 .... 119 L2
Kirkstall Gdns BRXS/STRHM SW2 180 E4
Kirkstall Rd BRXS/STRHM SW2 . 180 D4
Kirksted Rd MRDN SM4 .... 201 L8
Kirkstone NWCR SE14 .... 161 H3⑪
Kirkton Rd SEVS/STOTM N15 ... 119 J1
Kirkwall Pl BETH E2 .... 140 B5⑪
Kirkwall Sp SL1 .... 128 C7
Kirkwood Rd PECK SE15 .... 160 A8
Kirn Rd WEA W13 .... 134 G9⑪
Kirrane Cl NWMAL KT3 .... 200 D4
Kirtle Rd CSHM HP5 .... 51 H7
Kirtley Rd SYD SE26 .... 182 B2
Kirtling St VX/NE SW8 .... 158 D6
Kirton Cl CHSWK W4 .... 156 A3⑪
  HCH RM12 .... 145 K1
Kirton Gdns BETH E2 .... 7 M10
Kirton Rd PLSTW E13 .... 141 N1
Kirton Wk EDGW HA8 .... 95 H3
Kitcat Ter BOW E3 .... 140 F5

Kitchener Av GVE DA12 .... 190 F7
Kitchener Cl STAL AL1 .... 38 F7
Kitchener Rd EFNCH N2 .... 117 J1
  FSTGT E7 .... 141 N1
  THHTH CR7 .... 203 L3
  TOTM N17 .... 119 M1
  WALTH E17 .... 100 G9
Kite Fld BERK HP4 .... 33 K2
Kites Cl CRAWW RH11 .... 283 M7
Kithurst Cl CRAWW RH11 .... 283 N9⑪
Kitley Gdns NRWD SE19 .... 203 N1
Kitsbury Rd BERK HP4 .... 33 N5
Kitsbury Ter BERK HP4 .... 33 N5
Kitsmead CRAWE RH10 .... 285 J4
Kitson Rd BARN SW13 .... 156 C7
  CMBW SE5 .... 158 G8
Kitson Wy HLW CM20 .... 28 F10⑪
Kitswell Wy RAD WD7 .... 56 G9
Kittiwake Cl CRAWW RH11 .... 282 C9⑪
  SAND/SEL CR2 .... 224 D6
Kittiwake Rd NTHLT UB5 .... 153 J2
Kittiwake Wy YEAD UB4 .... 133 M6⑪
Kitto Rd NWCR SE14 .... 160 C5
Kitt's End Rd BAR EN5 .... 77 N5
Kiver Rd ARCH N19 .... 118 F7
Klea Av BAL SW12 .... 180 D2
Knapdale Cl FSTH SE23 .... 182 A5
Knapmill Rd CAT SE6 .... 182 F5
Knapmill Wy CAT SE6 .... 182 F5
Knapp Cl WLSDN NW10 .... 136 B1
Knapp Rd ASHF TW15 .... 174 A7⑪
  BOW E3 .... 140 F2⑪
Knapton Ms TOOT SW17 .... 180 B9⑪
Knaresborough Dr
  WAND/EARL SW18 .... 179 L4
Knaresborough Pl ECT SW5 ..... 14 G5
Knatchbull Rd CMBW SE5 .... 159 J8
  WLSDN NW10 .... 136 A3⑪
Knave Wood Rd RSEV TN14 ..... 247 M3
Knebworth Av WALTH E17 .... 100 F9
Knebworth Pth BORE WD6 .... 76 M8⑪
Knebworth Rd
  STNW/STAM N16 .... 119 M9⑪
Knee Hl ABYW SE2 .... 163 M3
Knee Hill Crs ABYW SE2 .... 163 M3
Knella Gn WGCE AL7 .... 23 K5
Knella Rd WGCE AL7 .... 23 K5
Kneller Gdns ISLW TW7 .... 176 C2
Kneller Rd BROCKY SE4 .... 160 D10
  NWMAL KT3 .... 200 B3
  WHTN TW2 .... 176 B2
Knepp Cl CRAWE RH10 .... 285 H8
Knighten St WAP E1W 140 A10⑪
Knightland Rd CLPT E5 .... 120 A7
Knighton Cl CRAWE RH10 .... 284 C1⑪
  ROMW/RG RM7 .... 124 E4⑪
  SAND/SEL CR2 .... 223 J7
  WFD IG8 .... 101 N5
Knighton Dr WFD IG8 .... 101 N5
Knighton La BKHH IG9 .... 101 N3⑪
Knighton Park Rd SYD SE26 ..... 181 M8
Knighton Rd FSTGT E7 .... 121 M8
  REDH RH1 .... 276 B2
  ROMW/RG RM7 .... 124 D4
  RSEV TN14 .... 246 F8
Knighton-way La DEN/HRF UB9 . 111 L10
Knightrider Ct BLKFR EC4V 12 E6⑪
Knightrider St BLKFR EC4V 12 D7
Knight's Av EA W5 .... 155 K1
Knightsbridge KTBR SW1X 16 B3
  SKENS SW7 .... 15 P2
Knightsbridge Crs STA TW18 .... 173 J8
Knightsbridge Gdns
  ROMW/RG RM7 .... 124 D4
Knightsbridge Gn KTBR SW1X .. 16 A2⑪
  WDSR SL4 .... 148 C7
Knights Cl ECH TW20 .... 172 G9⑪
  WDSR SL4 .... 148 C7
Knights Cft HART DA3 .... 211 L10
Knightsfield WGCW AL8 .... 22 G1
Knight's Hl WNWD SE27 .... 181 J4
Knight's Hill Sq WNWD SE27 .... 181 J7⑪
Knight's La ED N9 .... 99 P4⑪
Knights Manor Wy DART DA1 ... 187 N2
Knights Orch HHW HP1 .... 35 K3
Knights Pk KUT KT1 .... 199 K3
Knights Pl REDH RH1 .... 258 B9⑪
  WDSR SL4 .... 149 H9⑪
Knights Rdg ORP BR6 .... 227 L2⑪
Knights Rd CAN/RD E16 .... 141 M10
  STAN HA7 .... 95 H5
Knights Wk BARK/HLT IG6 .... 102 K7
  RBRW/HUT CM13 .... 107 M5
Knightswood WOKN/KNAP GU21 231 L3
Knightswood Cl EDGW HA8 ...... 95 P3⑪
Knightswood Crs NWMAL KT3 .. 200 B6
Knipp Hl COB KT11 .... 217 P9
Knivet Rd FUL/PGN SW6 .... 14 C10
Knobfield SHGR GU5 .... 270 G9
Knobs Hill Rd SRTFD E15 .... 140 G3
Knockhall Cha GRH DA9 .... 189 H1
Knockhall Rd GRH DA9 .... 189 H1
Knockholt Rd ELTH/MOT SE9 ... 184 A1
  RSEV TN14 .... 228 A10
Knole Cl CRAWE RH10 .... 284 E6⑪
  CROY/NA CR0 .... 204 B6⑪
Knole La BGR/WK TN15 .... 265 K2
Knole Rd DART DA1 .... 187 H3
  SEV TN13 .... 247 L2
The Knole ELTH/MOT SE9 .... 184 D7
  MEO DA13 .... 190 B10
Knole Wy BGR/WK TN15 .... 265 K4
Knoll Crs NTHWD HA6 .... 92 F10
Knoll Dr STHGT/OAK N14 .... 98 D7
Knolles Crs BRKMPK AL9 .... 40 E10
Knollmead BRYLDS KT5 .... 199 P8
Knoll Park Rd CHERT KT16 ...... 195 J8⑪
Knoll Ri ORP BR6 .... 207 J8
Knoll Rd BXLY DA5 .... 186 B3
  DORK RH4 .... 272 F4
  SCUP DA14 .... 186 E1
  WAND/EARL SW18 .... 179 M1
Knolls Cl WPK KT4 .... 200 F10
The Knolls EW KT17 .... 238 F2
The Knoll BECK BR3 .... 204 G1
  CHERT KT16 .... 195 J8
  COB KT11 .... 217 P9
  HAYES BR2 .... 205 M9
  HERT/BAY SG13 .... 26 A4
  LHD/OX KT22 .... 237 L7
  WEA W13 .... 135 J7
Knolly's Cl WNWD SE27 .... 181 H6⑪
Knolly's Rd STRHM/NOR SW16 . 181 H6
Knolton Wy SLN SL2 .... 129 N8
Knottisford St BETH E2 .... 140 C5⑪
Knottocks Cl BEAC HP9 .... 88 B6
Knottocks Dr BEAC HP9 .... 88 C6
Knottocks End BEAC HP9 .... 88 C6
Knotts Green Rd LEY E10 .... 121 H4
Knotts Pl SEV TN13 .... 247 H10
Knowle Av BXLYHN DA7 .... 163 P6
Knowle Cl BRXN/ST SW9 .... 159 H9⑪
  CRAWE RH10 .... 285 J2
Knowle Dr CRAWE RH10 .... 285 J2
  HARP AL5 .... 20 C4
Knowle Gdns BF/WBF KT14 ..... 215 J9⑪
Knowle Gn STA TW18 .... 173 K8
Knowle Gv VW GU25 .... 195 P7
Knowle Grove Cl VW GU25 ...... 195 P7
Knowle Hl VW GU25 .... 195 N7
Knowle Pk COB KT11 .... 235 M1
Knowle Park Av STA TW18 .... 173 L8
Knowle Rd HAYES BR2 .... 206 B9⑪
  WHTN TW2 .... 176 D4⑪

Knowles Cl WDR/YW UB7 131 P10
Knowles Ct HRW HA1 114 E4
Knowles Hill Crs LEW SE13 183 J1
The Knowle HOD EN11 44 F4
Knowlton Gn HAYES BR2 205 L5
Knowsley Av STHL UB1 134 A10
Knowsley Rd BTSEA SW11 158 A4
Knox Rd FSTGT E7 141 M1
  GUW GU2 249 N6
Knox St MBLAR W1H 10 A3
Knoyle St NWCR SE14 160 D5
Knutsford Av WATN WD24 73 L4
Kohat Rd WIM/MER SW19 179 L8
Koh-i-noor Av BUSH WD23 73 P10
Koonowla Cl BH/WHM TN16 244 A5
Kooringa WARL CR6 242 A5
Korda Cl SHPTN TW17 196 A3
Kossuth St GNWCH SE10 161 K4
Kramer Ms ECT SW5 14 F8
Kuala Gdns STRHM/NOR SW16 202 B1
Kydbrook Cl STMC/STPC BR5 206 F2
Kylemore Cl EHAM E6 142 A4
Kylemore Rd KIL/WHAMP NW6 2 E1
Kymberley Rd HRW HA1 114 C4
Kyme Rd ROM RM1 124 C4
  HNWL W7 135 K4
Kynance Av STAN HA7 95 H9
Kynance Gdns STAN HA7 95 H9
Kynance Ms KENS W8 15 H4
Kynance Pl KENS W8 15 J4
Kynaston Av KTN/HRWW/W HA3 94 C6
  THHTH CR7 203 K5
Kynaston Cl KTN/HRWW/W HA3 94 C6
Kynaston Crs THHTH CR7 203 K5
Kynaston Rd BMLY BR1 183 M8
  ENC/FH EN2 79 L5
  STMC/STPC BR5 207 L2
  STNW/STAM N16 119 M8
  THHTH CR7 203 K5
Kynaston Wd KTN/HRWW/W HA3 94 C6
Kynersley Cl CAR SM5 202 A10
Kynoch Rd UED N18 100 C1
Kyrle Rd BTSEA SW11 180 B2
Kytes Dr GSTN WD25 55 L9
Kyverdale Rd STNW/STAM N16 119 N5

L

Laburnham Cl UPMR RM14 126 F5
Laburnham Gdns UPMR RM14 126 F5
Laburnum Av DART DA1 187 K4
  ED N9 99 M3
  HCH RM12 125 H7
  SUT SM1 201 P10
  SWLY BR8 208 B3
  TOTM N17 99 L8
  WDR/YW UB7 132 A9
Laburnum Cl CHES/WCR EN8 62 C1
  CHING E4 100 E7
  GU GU1 249 N6
Laburnum Ct STAN HA7 95 H5
Laburnum Crs SUN TW16 197 L1
Laburnum Gdns CROY/NA CR0 204 C5
Laburnum Gv CDALE/KGS NW9 115 P5
  DTCH/LGLY SL3 150 D5
  GVW DA11 190 A3
  HSLW TW3 153 N10
  LCOL/BKTW AL2 55 P1
  NWMAL KT3 200 A1
  SOCK/AV RM15 147 J6
  STHL UB1 133 N6
  WCHMH N21 99 K3
Laburnum Pl EGH TW20 171 N9
Laburnum Rd CHERT KT16 195 K8
  EPP CM16 65 M5
  EPSOM KT18 220 A10
  HOD EN11 44 C1
  HYS/HAR UB3 152 C5
  MTCM CR4 180 A10
  WIM/MER SW19 179 M10
  WOKS/MYFD GU22 232 A6
Laburnum Wy HAYES BR2 206 D7
  STWL/WRAY TW19 174 A4
Lacebark Cl BFN/LL DA15 185 J3
Lacey Av COUL/CHIP CR5 241 H6
Lacey Cl ED N9 99 P3
  EGH TW20 172 C10
Lacey Dr BCTR RM8 123 M8
  COUL/CHIP CR5 241 H6
  EDGW HA8 95 K5
  HPTN TW12 197 N1
Lackford Rd COUL/CHIP CR5 240 F6
Lackington St SDTCH EC2A 13 H3
Lackmore Rd EN EN1 80 B1
Lacock Cl WIM/MER SW19 179 N4
Lacon Rd EDUL SE22 159 P10
Lacy Gn COUL/CHIP CR5 241 H6
Lacy Rd PUT/ROE SW15 156 G10
Ladas Rd WNWD SE27 181 M5
Ladbroke Crs NTGHL W11 8 B6
Ladbroke Gdns NTGHL W11 8 C7
Ladbroke Gv NKENS W10 8 A4
  REDH RH1 258 B9
Ladbroke Ms NTGHL W11 8 B9
Ladbroke Rd EN EN1 79 N10
  EPSOM KT18 220 A10
  HORL RH6 280 D8
  NTGHL W11 8 D9
  REDH RH1 258 B9
Ladbroke Sq NTGHL W11 8 D8
Ladbroke Ter NTGHL W11 8 D8
Ladbroke Wk NTGHL W11 8 D9
Ladbrook Cl PIN HA5 113 N10
Ladbrooke Crs SCUP DA14 185 N6
Ladbrooke Dr POTB/CUF EN6 59 K8
Ladbrooke Rd SL SL1 149 K8
Ladbrook Rd SNWD SE25 203 L3
Ladderstile Ride RCHPK/HAM TW10 177 N8
Ladderswood Wy FBAR/BDGN N11 98 D6
Ladds Wy SWLY BR8 208 E4
Ladies Gv STALW/RED AL3 38 C4
Lady Booth Rd KUT KT1 8 L8
Ladycroft Gdns ORP BR6 226 F2
Ladycroft Rd LEW SE13 160 C9
Ladycroft Wk STAN HA7 95 M8
Ladycroft Wy ORP BR6 226 F2
Ladygate La RSLP HA4 112 D4
Lady Gv WGCE AL7 23 H9
Ladygrove Dr RGUE GU4 250 E5
Lady Hay WGCW AL8 22 C9
Lady Margaret Rd ARCH N19 118 D7
  ASC SL5 192 G5
  CRAWW RH11 283 K6
  KTTN NW5 118 D10
  STHL UB1 133 N6
Ladymead GU GU1 249 P9
Ladymead Cl CRAWE RH10 284 D10
Ladymeadow HHS/BOV HP3 53 N3
Ladymount WLGTN SM6 222 E1
Lady's Cl WATW WD18 73 H9
Ladysmith Av EHAM E6 142 A2
  GNTH/NBYPK IG2 122 G5
Ladysmith Rd CAN/RD E16 141 H4
  ELTH/MOT SE9 184 D2
  EN EN1 79 N6
  KTN/HRWW/W HA3 94 D10
  STALW/RED AL3 38 C5
  TOTM N17 99 P10
  UED N18 100 A6
Lady Somerset Rd KTTN NW5 118 C9
Ladythorpe Cl ADL/WDHM KT15 215 L5
Ladywalk RKW/CH/CXG WD3 31 H6
Ladywell Prospect SBW CM21 30 A2
Ladywell Rd LEW SE13 182 F1
Ladywell St SRTFD E15 141 L8
Ladywood Av STMC/STPC BR5 207 H5
Ladywood Rd RKW/CH/CXG WD3 71 L7
  SURB KT6 199 M8
Ladywood Rd HERT SG14 24 C5
  RDART DA2 188 D8
  SURB KT6 199 M8
Lafone Av FELT TW13 175 K5
Lafone St STHWK SE1 19 L1
Lagado Ms BERM/RHTH SE16 140 C10
Lagger Cl CSTG HP8 46 B1
The Lagger CSTG HP8 46 B1
Laglands Cl REIG RH2 257 M8
Lagonda Av BARK/HLT IG6 103 J7
Lagonda Wy DART DA1 165 N10
Laidlaw Dr WCHMH N21 78 G9
Laing Cl CHIG IG7 102 C7
Laing Dean NTHLT UB5 133 K3
Laings Av MTCM CR4 202 A2
Lainlock Pl HSLW TW3 154 A7
Lainson St WAND/EARL SW18 179 K3
Lairdale Cl DUL SE21 181 K4
Laird Av CDH/CHF RM16 168 A1
Laitwood Rd BAL SW12 180 C4
Lake Av BMLY BR1 145 L4
  RAIN RM13 145 L4
  SL SL1 129 J9
Lake Cl BF/WBF KT14 215 M8
  WIM/MER SW19 179 K4
Lake Dr BUSH WD23 94 B3
Lake End Rd MDHD SL6 128 A4
  WDSR SL4 148 A2
Lakefield Rd WDGN N22 99 J10
Lakefields Cl RAIN RM13 145 L4
Lake Gdns DAGE RM10 124 D10
  RCHPK/HAM TW10 176 G6
  WLGTN SM6 202 C10
Lakehall Gdns THHTH CR7 203 J5
Lakehall Rd THHTH CR7 203 J5
Lake House Rd WAN E11 121 H6
Lakehurst Rd HOR/WEW KT19 220 B2
Lakeland Cl CHIG IG7 103 L5
  KTN/HRWW/W HA3 94 C7
Lake La HORL RH6 280 D2
Lakenheath STHGT/OAK N14 78 G4
Lake Ri ROM RM1 124 C1
  WTHK RM20 166 F3
Lake Rd CHDH RM6 123 N6
  CROY/NA CR0 204 E9
  DAGW RM9 144 C5
  VW GU25 193 N4
  WAB EN9 45 K7
  WIM/MER SW19 179 J8
Lakers Ri BNSTD SM7 239 P2
Lakes Cl RGUE GU4 268 E6
Lakeside BECK BR3 184 G3
  ENC/FH EN2 78 E8
  HOR/WEW KT19 220 B3
  RAIN RM13 145 M4
  REDH RH1 258 B8
  WEA W13 135 H8
  WEY KT13 196 F9
  WLGTN SM6 222 C1
Lakeside Av BFN/LL DA15 185 M1
  CHIG IG7 103 J5
  RSLP HA4 112 D2
  SNWD SE25 203 P2
  THMD SE28 143 K10
Lakeside Crs BRW CM14 107 J4
  EBAR EN4 78 A10
Lakeside Dr ESH/CLAY KT10 218 B3
  HAYES BR2 206 B10
  TOTM N17 99 P8
  WOKN/KNAP GU21 232 B2
Lakeside Gra WEY KT13 196 D10
Lakeside Pl LCOL/BKTW AL2 57 J4
Lakeside Rd CHES/WCR EN8 62 D1
  DTCH/LGLY SL3 151 J6
  PLMGR N13 98 G5
  WKENS W14 156 G2
Lakeswood Rd STMC/STPC BR5 206 E6
The Lake BUSH WD23 94 C2
Lakeview Rd WELL DA16 184 G4
  WNWD SE27 181 H8
Lakis Cl HAMP NW3 117 M9
Laleham Av MLHL NW7 96 A4
Laleham Cl STA TW18 195 L1
Laleham Rd CAT SE6 183 H3
  SHPTN TW17 195 H4
  STA TW18 173 J9
Lalor St FUL/PGN SW6 157 H8
Lambarde Av ELTH/MOT SE9 184 D7
Lambarde Dr SEV TN13 247 H9
Lambarde Rd SEV TN13 247 H9
Lambardes HART DA3 211 L10
Lamb Cl GSTN WD25 55 K10
  HAT AL10 40 E5
  TIL RM18 168 F3
Lamberhurst Cl STMC/STPC BR5 207 N8
Lamberhurst Rd BCTR RM8 123 P6
  WNWD SE27 181 H7
Lambert Av DTCH/LGLY SL3 150 B2
  RCH/KEW TW9 155 M9
Lambert Cl BH/WHM TN16 244 A4
Lambert Ct BUSH WD23 73 L8
Lambert Rd BNSTD SM7 239 K10
  BRXS/STRHM SW2 180 F1
  CAN/RD E16 141 M8
  NFNCH/WDSP N12 97 H6
Lambert's Pl CROY/NA CR0 203 J7
Lambert St IS N1 6 A1
Lambert Wy NFNCH/WDSP N12 97 H5
Lambeth Bridge WEST SW1P 17 L5
Lambeth High St STHWK SE1 17 N6
Lambeth Hill BLKFR EC4V 12 E7
Lambeth Palace Rd STHWK SE1 17 N4
Lambeth Rd CROY/NA CR0 203 H7
  STHWK SE1 18 A4
Lamble St KTTN NW5 118 B9
Lambley Rd DAGW RM9 143 L6
Lambly Hl VW GU25 194 B3
Lambolle Pl HAMP NW3 3 M2
Lambolle Rd HAMP NW3 3 M2
Lambourn Cha RAD WD7 74 E2
Lambourn Cl HNWL W7 154 A1
  SAND/SEL CR2 241 L7
Lambourne Av WIM/MER SW19 179 J4
Lambourne Cl CHIG IG7 103 L4
Lambourne Crs CHIG IG7 103 L4
  WOKN/KNAP GU21 214 G9
Lambourne Dr COB KT11 235 K1
Lambourne Gdns BARK IG11 143 J2
  CHING E4 100 F3
  EN EN1 79 N6
  HCH RM12 125 L7
Lambourne Gv KUT KT1 9 L7
Lambourne Pl BKHTH/KID SE3 161 K2
Lambourne Rd BARK IG11 143 H2
  CHIG IG7 103 J5
  GDMY/SEVK IG3 123 H1
Lamb Wk STHWK SE1 19 J2
Lambrook Ter FUL/PGN SW6 157 H7
Lambs Conduit St BMSBY WC1N 11 L2
Lambscroft Av LEE/GVPK SE12 183 P6
Lambscroft Wy CFSP/GDCR SL9 90 B10
Lambs Green Rd HORS RH12 282 D10
Lamb's La North RAIN RM13 145 L4
Lamb's La South RAIN RM13 145 L4
Lamb's Pas STLK EC1Y 12 G2
Lambton Av CHES/WCR EN8 62 C5
Lambton Pl NTGHL W11 8 D6
Lambton Rd ARCH N19 118 F6
  RYNPK SW20 200 F2
Lamb Wk STHWK SE1 19 J2
Lamerock Rd BMLY BR1 183 L1
Lamerton Rd BARK/HLT IG6 122 G2
Lamerton St DEPT SE8 160 F5
Lamford Cl TOTM N17 99 L7
Lamington St HMSMTH W6 156 E8
Lamlash St LBTH SE11 18 C5
Lammas Av MTCM CR4 202 B2
Lammas Cl STA TW18 173 H6
Lammas Ct WDSR SL4 149 H6
Lammas La ESH/CLAY KT10 217 P1
Lammasmead BROX EN10 44 E9
Lammas Park Gdns EA W5 135 H10
Lammas Rd HOM E9 140 C2
  LEY E10 120 F7
  RCHPK/HAM TW10 176 G6
  WATW WD18 73 K9
Lammermoor Rd BAL SW12 180 C4
Lamont Rd WBPTN SW10 15 K10
Lamorbey Cl BFN/LL DA15 185 J7
Lamorna Av GVE DA12 190 G6
Lamorna Cl ORP BR6 207 K7
  RAD WD7 56 C10
  WALTH E17 101 H10
Lamorna Gv STAN HA7 95 M9
Lampard Gv STNW/STAM N16 119 N6
Lampeter Cl WOKS/MYFD GU22 232 B2
Lampits HOD EN11 44 C3
Lamplighter Cl WCHPL E1 140 B6
Lamplighters Cl DART DA1 187 N2
  WAB EN9 63 M10
Lampmead Rd LEE/GVPK SE12 183 K1
Lamport Cl WOOL/PLUM SE18 162 C3
Lampton Av HEST TW5 153 P7
Lampton House Cl WIM/MER SW19 178 G7
Lampton Park Rd HSLW TW3 154 A8
Lampton Rd HSLW TW3 154 A8
Lamsey Rd HHS/BOV HP3 35 N8
Lamson Rd RAIN RM13 144 C7
Lanacre Av CDALE/KGS NW9 96 B9
Lanark Cl EA W5 135 H7
Lanark Pl MV/WKIL W9 9 K1
Lanark Rd MV/WKIL W9 3 H8
Lanata Wk YEAD UB4 132 F4
Lanbury Rd PECK SE15 160 C10
Lancaster Av BARK IG11 143 H2
  MTCM CR4 202 A3
  SL SL2 129 H6
  WAN E11 121 N2
  WIM/MER SW19 179 H6
  WNWD SE27 181 J5
Lancaster Cl BRW CM15 86 F9
  CDALE/KGS NW9 96 C8
  CRAWE RH10 284 E4
  EGH TW20 172 A8
  HAYES BR2 205 L4
  STWL/WRAY TW19 173 P2
  TOTM N17 99 P8
  WOKN/KNAP GU21 232 B2
Lancaster Ct BAY/PAD W2 9 M2
  FUL/PGN SW6 157 L8
  WFD IG8 101 P7
Lancaster Dr HAMP NW3 3 N2
  HHW HP1 52 C3
  LOU IG10 82 B10
  POP/IOD E14 141 N10
Lancaster Gdns KUTN/CMB KT2 177 J8
  WIM/MER SW19 179 H6
Lancaster Ga BAY/PAD W2 9 M3
Lancaster Gv HAMP NW3 3 M2
Lancaster Ms BAY/PAD W2 9 M3
  RCHPK/HAM TW10 177 K2
  WAND/EARL SW18 179 L1
Lancaster Pk RCHPK/HAM TW10 177 K1
Lancaster Pl TWK TW1 178 G8
  WIM/MER SW19 178 G8
Lancaster Rd EBAR EN4 77 N9
  ENC/FH EN2 79 L5
  EPP CM16 66 F7
  FBAR/BDGN N11 98 E7
  FSBYPK N4 119 H5
  FSTGT E7 141 M2
  NTGHL W11 8 A1
  NTHLT UB5 134 B1
  RYLN/HDSTN HA2 113 P3
  SNWD SE25 203 L1
  STAL AL1 38 E4
  STHL UB1 133 N6
  UED N18 99 N6
  WALTH E17 100 G1
  WAN E11 121 K7
  WIM/MER SW19 179 H6
  WLSDN NW10 116 C10
Lancaster Stables HAMP NW3 3 P2
Lancaster St STHWK SE1 18 C2
Lancaster Ter BAY/PAD W2 9 L7
Lancaster Wy ABLGY WD5 54 G7
Lancefield St MV/WKIL W9 2 C10
Lancell St STNW/STAM N16 119 M7
Lancelot Av ALP/SUD HA0 115 J9
Lancelot Cl CRAWW RH11 283 H7
Lancelot Crs ALP/SUD HA0 115 J9
Lancelot Gdns EBAR EN4 98 B1
Lancelot Pl SKENS SW7 16 A2
Lancelot Rd ALP/SUD HA0 115 J10
  BARK/HLT IG6 103 H7
  WELL DA16 163 H4
Lance Rd HRW HA1 114 B5
Lancey Cl CHARL SE7 162 B3
Lanchester Rd HGT N6 118 B5
Lancing Cl CRAWW RH11 283 K4
Lancing Gdns ED N9 100 G3
Lancing Rd CROY/NA CR0 202 G3
  FELT TW13 174 G5
  GNTH/NBYPK IG2 122 G5
  HARH RM3 105 L8
  ORP BR6 207 L5
  WEA W13 135 L7
Lancing St CAMTN NW1 5 J10
Lancresse Cl UX/CGN UB8 131 N1
Lancresse Ct IS N1 7 H1
Landale Gdns DART DA1 187 K4
Landau Wy BROX EN10 62 G2
  ERITH DA8 165 L4
Landcroft Rd EDUL SE22 181 N2
Landells Rd EDUL SE22 181 N2
Landen Pk HORL RH6 279 P2
Lander Rd GRAYS RM17 168 A4
Landford Rd PUT/ROE SW15 156 F9
Landgrove Rd WIM/MER SW19 179 K5
Landmann Wy NWCR SE14 160 C5
Landmead Rd CHES/WCR EN8 62 D1
Landon Pl KTBR SW1X 16 A3
Landons Cl POP/IOD E14 141 N10
Landon Wy ASHF TW15 174 C9
Landor Rd BRXN/ST SW9 158 F9
Landor Wk SHB W12 156 D1
Landra Gdns WCHMH N21 79 J10
Landridge Rd FUL/PGN SW6 157 J8
Landrock Rd CEND/HSY/T N8 118 F6
Landscape Rd WARL CR6 242 A5
  WFD IG8 101 N8
Landseer Av GVW DA11 190 A6
  WIM/MER SW19 201 N1
Landseer Cl EDGW HA8 95 M10
  WIM/MER SW19 201 N1
Landseer Rd ARCH N19 118 F8
  EN EN1 79 P6
  NWMAL KT3 200 A7
  SUT SM1 221 K3
Lands' End BORE WD6 75 J10
Landstead Rd WOOL/PLUM SE18 162 G6
Landview Gdns CHONG CM5 67 N6
Landway BGR/WK TN15 247 N6
The Landway BGR/WK TN15 247 N6
  STMC/STPC BR5 207 M3
Lane Cl ADL/WDHM KT15 215 L5
  CRICK NW2 116 G1
Lane End BERK HP4 33 L5
  EPSOM KT18 219 N10
  HAT AL10 40 C7
  HLWE CM17 47 P2
Lane End Dr WOKN/KNAP GU21 231 H3
Lane Gdns BUSH WD23 94 D2
Lanercost Gdns STHGT/OAK N14 78 F10
Lanercost Rd BRXS/STRHM SW2 181 H5
  CRAWW RH11 283 K6
Lanes Av GVW DA11 190 C6
Laneside CHST BR7 185 H1
  EDGW HA8 95 P6
Laneside Av BCTR RM8 123 L2
The Lane BKHTH/KID SE3 161 M9
  CHERT KT16 195 K3
  VW GU25 194 B3
Lanfranc Rd BOW E3 140 D4
Lanfrey Pl WKENS W14 157 J1
Langafel Cl HART DA3 211 K2
Langaller La LHD/OX KT22 236 A7
Langbourne Av HGT N6 118 A7
Langbourne Wy ESH/CLAY KT10 218 E5
Langbrook Rd BKHTH/KID SE3 162 D4
Lang Cl GT/LBKH KT23 236 A9
Langcroft Cl CAR SM5 202 A10
Langdale Av HARP AL5 20 C1
  MTCM CR4 202 A3
Langdale Cl BCTR RM8 123 M6
  MORT/ESHN SW14 155 N10
  ORP BR6 206 E10
  WALW SE17 18 E9
  WOKN/KNAP GU21 231 P2
Langdale Crs BXLYHN DA7 164 B7
Langdale Dr YEAD UB4 132 F4
  PEND EN3 80 C1
Langdale Gdns HCH RM12 125 H10
Langdale Pde MTCM CR4 202 A3
Langdale Rd CRAWW RH11 282 C9
  GNWCH SE10 161 H6
  THHTH CR7 203 H4
Langdon Ct WLSDN NW10 136 B3
Langdon Crs EHAM E6 142 D4
Langdon Dr CDALE/KGS NW9 115 P6
Langdon Park Rd HGT N6 118 C6
Langdon Pl MORT/ESHN SW14 155 P9
Langdon Rd EHAM E6 142 A7
  HAYES BR2 205 N3
  MRDN SM4 201 M5
Langdon Shaw SCUP DA14 185 J8
Langdon Wk MRDN SM4 201 M5
Langfield Cl WAB EN9 45 K8
Langford Cl HACK E8 119 P10
  SEVS/STOTM N15 119 M4
  STJWD NW8 3 H3
Langford Crs EBAR EN4 78 A4
Langford Pl SCUP DA14 185 K6
  STJWD NW8 3 H3
Langford Rd EBAR EN4 78 A4
  FUL/PGN SW6 157 L8
  WFD IG8 101 J7
Langfords BKHH IG9 102 A3
Langham Cl STALE/WH AL4 39 H1
  SEVS/STOTM N15 119 K2
Langham Dene PUR/KEN CR8 241 J1
Langham Dr GDMY/SEVK IG3 123 L4
Langham Gdns ALP/SUD HA0 115 J6
  EDGW HA8 95 P8
  RCHPK/HAM TW10 176 G6
  WCHMH N21 79 H4
  WEA W13 135 J5
Langham House Cl RCHPK/HAM TW10 176 G6
Langham Pl CAVSQ/HST W1G 10 F4
  CHSWK W4 156 B5
  EGH TW20 172 C8
  SEVS/STOTM N15 119 J1
Langham Rd EDGW HA8 95 P7
  RYNPK SW20 200 F1
  SEVS/STOTM N15 119 K2
  TEDD TW11 176 D2
Langham St GTPST W1W 10 E2
  REGST W1B 10 F4
Langhedge Cl UED N18 99 N7
Langhedge La UED N18 99 N7
Langholm Cl BAL SW12 180 E3
Langholme BUSH WD23 94 B2
Langhorn Dr WHTN TW2 176 D3
Langhorne Rd DAGE RM10 144 B5
Langhurst Cl HORS RH12 282 A2
Langland Ct NTHWD HA6 92 D8
Langland Crs STAN HA7 95 N8
Langland Dr PIN HA5 93 M8
Langland Gdns CROY/NA CR0 204 E9
  HAMP NW3 117 J10
Langlands Dr RDART DA2 188 D6
Langlands Ri HOR/WEW KT19 219 P9
Langler Rd WLSDN NW10 136 F4
Langley Av HHS/BOV HP3 35 P9
  RSLP HA4 113 J1
  SURB KT6 200 F1
  WPK KT4 200 F10
Langley Broom DTCH/LGLY SL3 150 C4
Langleybury La KGLGY WD4 54 C10
Langley Cl EPSOM KT18 238 C8
  GU GU1 250 A8
  HARH RM3 105 L8
Langley Crs DAGW RM9 143 N6
  EDGW HA8 95 M2
  HYS/HAR UB3 153 H6
  KGLGY WD4 54 B6
  STALW/RED AL3 38 C5
  WAN E11 121 N5
Langley Dr ACT W3 156 A1
  BRW CM14 106 F4
  WAN E11 121 N5
Langley Gdns DAGW RM9 143 L7
  STMC/STPC BR5 207 H3
Langley Gv NWMAL KT3 200 C1
  STALE/WH AL4 39 H1
Langley Hl KGLGY WD4 54 A5
Langley Hill Cl KGLGY WD4 54 B5
Langley La ABLGY WD5 54 C7
  CRAWW RH11 283 K5
  VX/NE SW8 17 M9
Langley Lodge La KGLGY WD4 53 P7
Langley Oaks Av SAND/SEL CR2 223 P6
Langley Pde CRAWW RH11 283 K4
Langley Pk EDGW HA8 96 B7
Langley Park Rd BELMT SM2 221 M8
  IVER SL0 130 G8
Langley Pl CRAWW RH11 283 M4
Langley Rd ABLGY WD5 54 F7
  BECK BR3 204 C2
  DTCH/LGLY SL3 149 P2
  ISLW TW7 154 E8
  KGLGY WD4 53 L6
  SAND/SEL CR2 224 C5
  STA TW18 173 J9
  SURB KT6 199 K7
  WAT WD17 72 C5
  WELL DA16 163 M5
  WIM/MER SW19 201 N1
Langley Rw BAR EN5 77 J5
Langley St LSQ/SEVD WC2H 11 L6
Langley Vale Rd EPSOM KT18 238 A4
Langley Wk CRAWW RH11 283 L4
Langley Wy WAT WD17 72 C5
  WWKM BR4 205 J8
Langmans Wy WOKN/KNAP GU21 231 H2
Langmead Dr BUSH WD23 94 D2
Langmead St WNWD SE27 181 K7
Langport Ct WOT/HER KT12 197 K8
Langridge Ms HPTN TW12 175 N9
Langroyd Rd TOOT SW17 180 A5
Langshott HORL RH6 280 E2
Langshott Cl ADL/WDHM KT15 215 H7
Langshott La HORL RH6 280 D3
Langside Av PUT/ROE SW15 156 D10
Langside Crs STHGT/OAK N14 98 E4
Langstone Cl CRAWE RH10 284 D10
Langton Hughes Cl HNHL SE24 159 J10
Lang St WCHPL E1 140 B6
Langthorn Ct LOTH EC2R 13 H5
Langthorne Rd GRAYS RM17 168 ...
Langthorne Rd WAN E11 121 J4
Langthorne St FUL/PGN SW6 156 G6
Langton Av EHAM E6 142 D5
  EW KT17 220 C7
  TRDG/WHET N20 97 M1
Langton Cl ADL/WDHM KT15 215 L5
  FSBYW WC1X 5 P10
  SL SL1 128 C10
  WOKN/KNAP GU21 231 L3
Langton Gv NTHWD HA6 92 B5
Langton Ri EDUL SE22 182 A3
Langton Rd BRXN/ST SW9 159 J6
  CRICK NW2 116 F8
  E/WMO/HCT KT8 198 B5
  HOD EN11 44 E5
  KTN/HRWW/W HA3 94 B8
Langton's Meadow SLN SL2 129 H1
Langton St WBPTN SW10 15 K10
Langton Wy BKHTH/KID SE3 161 M6
  CDH/CHF RM16 168 F5
  CROY/NA CR0 223 M1
  EGH TW20 172 F9
Langtry Pl FUL/PGN SW6 133 L4
Langtry Rd KIL/WHAMP NW6 2 B1
  NTHLT UB5 133 H6
Langtry Wk KIL/WHAMP NW6 2 E1
Langwood Cha TEDD TW11 177 H9
Langwood Gdns WAT WD17 73 H5
Langworth Cl RDART DA2 187 L6
Langworth Dr YEAD UB4 133 J2
Lanhill Rd MV/WKIL W9 2 D1
Lanier Rd LEW SE13 183 H2
Lanigan Dr HSLW TW3 176 A3
Lankers Dr RYLN/HDSTN HA2 113 N1
Lankton Cl BECK BR3 205 H1
Lannock Rd HYS/HAR UB3 132 G10
Lannoy Rd ELTH/MOT SE9 184 F4
Lanrick Copse BERK HP4 34 A1
Lanrick Rd POP/IOD E14 141 P8
Lanridge Rd ABYW SE2 163 N2
Lansbury Av BARK IG11 143 K2
  CHDH RM6 123 P3
  EBED/NFELT TW14 175 J2
  UED N18 99 L6
Lansbury Cl WLSDN NW10 115 P10
Lansbury Crs DART DA1 187 P1
Lansbury Dr YEAD UB4 132 G5
Lansbury Gdns POP/IOD E14 141 P8
  PEND EN3 80 C5
Lansbury Wy UED N18 99 M6
Lansdell Rd MTCM CR4 202 B2
Lansdown GU GU1 249 M5
Lansdown Cl WOKN/KNAP GU21 231 L5
  WOT/HER KT12 197 K8
Lansdowne Av BXLYHN DA7 163 M6
  ORP BR6 206 E8
  SL SL1 129 K10
Lansdowne Cl BRYLDS KT5 199 N3
  RYNPK SW20 178 G10
  TWK TW1 176 E4
  WAT WD19 72 F4
Lansdowne Crs NTGHL W11 8 B8
Lansdowne Gdns VX/NE SW8 158 F7
Lansdowne Gv WLSDN NW10 116 B9
Lansdowne Hl WNWD SE27 181 J4
Lansdowne La CHARL SE7 162 A4
Lansdowne Ms CHARL SE7 162 A4
  NTGHL W11 8 C10
Lansdowne Pl NRWD SE19 181 N10
  STHWK SE1 19 H3
Lansdowne Ri NTGHL W11 8 B9
Lansdowne Rd BMLY BR1 183 M10
  CHING E4 100 K9
  CROY/NA CR0 203 K9
  CSHM HP5 35 H5
  FNCH N3 97 H5
  GDMY/SEVK IG3 123 J6
  HACK E8 7 K2
  HOR/WEW KT19 219 P4
  HSLW TW3 154 A9
  MUSWH N10 98 D10
  NTGHL W11 8 B8
  PUR/KEN CR8 223 H8
  SEV TN13 247 L6
  STA TW18 173 L10
  STAN HA7 95 J4
  SWFD E18 101 M1
  TOTM N17 99 P1
  UX/CGN UB8 131 J4
  WALTH E17 120 F1
  WAN E11 121 L2
Lansdowne Sq GVW DA11 190 C2
Lansdowne Ter BMSBY WC1N 11 M2
Lansdowne Wk NTGHL W11 8 C9
Lansdowne Wy VX/NE SW8 158 F7
Lansdowne Wood Cl WNWD SE27 181 J6
Lansdown Rd CFSP/GDCR SL9 90 A9
  FSTGT E7 141 P2
  GVW DA11 190 C4
  SCUP DA14 185 L6
  TIL RM18 168 G8
Lansfield Av UED N18 99 P5
Lanson Cl ALP/SUD HA0 115 J10
  PUT/ROE SW15 156 F10
Lanterns Ct POP/IOD E14 160 G1
Lant St STHWK SE1 18 E1
Lanvanor Rd PECK SE15 160 A8
Lapford Cl MV/WKIL W9 8 D1
Lapis Cl GVE DA12 196 C4
La Plata Gv BRW CM14 106 C4

Lapse Wood Wk *DUL* SE21 .... 182 A4
Lapstone Gdns
  KTN/HRWW/W HA3 .... 115 H4
Lapwing CI *CROY/NA* CR0 .... 224 D6
  ERITH DA8 .... 165 J6 🗄
  HHNE HP2 .... 35 P2
Lapwing Gv *RGUE* GU4 .... 250 G8
Lapwings *HART* DA3 .... 211 H3
Lapwing Wy *ABLGY* WD5 .... 55 H7 🗄
  YEAD UB4 .... 133 L8 🗄
Lapworth CI *ORP* BR6 .... 217 M3
Lapworth Ct *BAY/PAD* W2 .... 9 J1
Lara CI *CHSGTN* KT9 .... 219 K4 🗄
  LEW SE13 .... 183 H2
Larbert Rd *STRHM/NOR* SW16 ... 202 D1
Larby PI *EW* KT17 .... 220 B6
Larch Av *ACT* W3 .... 136 B10
  ASC SL5 .... 192 D5
  GU GU1 .... 249 P8
  LCOL/BKTW AL2 .... 55 M6
Larch CI *SWS12* 180 C5
  CHESW EN7 .... 61 M3 🗄
  DEPT SE8 .... 160 E5 🗄
  FBAR/BDGN N11 .... 98 B7
  KWD/TDW/WH KT20 .... 239 M7
  REIG RH2 .... 275 M2
  SLN SL2 .... 128 C7
  WARL CR6 .... 242 D5
Larch Crs *HOR/WEW* KT19 ...... 219 N3
  YEAD UB4 .... 133 J7
Larch Dene *ORP* BR6 .... 206 D9
Larches Av *EN* EN1 .... 80 B1
  MORT/ESHN SW14 .... 156 A10 🗄
The Larches *BERK* HP4 .... 33 J4
  BUSH WD23 .... 73 M9
  HGDN/ICK UB10 .... 132 C4
  PLMGR N13 .... 99 K4
  STALE/WH AL4 .... 39 J2
  WOKN/KNAP GU21 .... 232 J2
Larch Gv *BFN/LL* DA15 .... 185 J4
Larch Rd *CRICK* NW2 .... 116 F9
  DART DA1 .... 187 L4
  LEY E10 .... 120 F7 🗄
Larch Tree Wy *CROY/NA* CR0 .... 204 F10
Larch Wy *HAYES* BR2 .... 206 D7
Larchwood Av *CRW* RM5 .... 104 C7
Larchwood CI *BNSTD* SM7 ...... 239 H2
  CRW RM5 .... 104 D7
Larchwood Dr *ECH* TW20 .... 171 N9
Larchwood Gdns *BRWN* CM15 .... 86 F10
Larchwood Rd *ELTH/MOT* SE9 .. 184 E5
  HHNE HP2 .... 36 M4
  WOKN/KNAP GU21 .... 231 J6
Larcombe CI *CROY/NA* CR0 ...... 223 N1
Larcom St *WALW* SE17 .... 18 F6
Larden Rd *ACT* W3 .... 156 B1
Largewood Av *SURB* KT6 .... 199 M9
Larissa St *WALW* SE17 .... 19 H6 🗄
Lark Av *STA* TW18 .... 173 J6
Larkbere Rd *SYD* SE26 .... 182 D7
Larken CI *BUSH* WD23 .... 94 B7
Larken Dr *BUSH* WD23 .... 94 B2
Larkfield Av *KTN/HRWW/W* HA3 ... 114 C1
Larkfield CI *HAYES* BR2 .... 227 K8 🗄
Larkfield Rd *RCH/KEW* TW9 .... 155 K10 🗄
  SCUP DA14 .... 185 J4
  SEV TN13 .... 246 E9
Larkfields *GVW* DA11 .... 190 B6
Larkhall CI *WOT/HER* KT12 .... 217 K3
Larkhall La *CLAP* SW4 .... 158 F9
Larkhall Ri *CLAP* SW4 .... 158 D9
Larkham CI *FELT* TW13 .... 174 F6 🗄
Larkin CI *COUL/CHIP* CR5 ...... 240 G3
  RBRW/HUT CM13 .... 107 P1
Larkings La *DTCH/LGLY* SL3 .... 129 N3 🗄
Larkins Rd *HORL* RH6 .... 279 N8
Lark Ri *CRAWW* RH11 .... 283 M5
  EHSLY KT24 .... 252 F7
  HAT AL10 .... 40 D6
Lark Rw *BETH* E2 .... 140 B3 🗄
Larksfield *EGH* TW20 .... 171 N10
Larks Fld *HART* DA3 .... 211 L4
Larksfield *HORL* RH6 .... 280 C3 🗄
Larkshall Crs *CHING* E4 .... 101 H5
Larkshall Rd *CHING* E4 .... 101 J7
Larkspur CI *CDALE/KGS* NW9 ... 115 N3
  HHW HP1 .... 35 L1
  ORP BR6 .... 207 M9 🗄
  RSLP HA4 .... 112 C5
  SOCK/AV RM15 .... 147 H5
  TOTM N17 .... 100 A5
Larkspur Gv *EDGW* HA8 .... 95 P5
Larkspur Wy *HOR/WEW* KT19 .... 219 P2
  RDKG RH5 .... 273 J5
Larks Rdg *LCOL/BKTW* AL2 ...... 55 J2
Larks Ri *CSHM* HP5 .... 51 J9
Larks Wy *WOKN/KNAP* GU21 ... 231 H2
Larkswood CI *ERITH* DA8 .... 165 H4
Larkswood Ri *PIN* HA5 .... 113 K2
  STALE/WH AL4 .... 39 H1
Larkswood Rd *CHING* E4 .... 100 F5
Lark Wy *CAR* SM5 .... 201 P7
Larkway CI *CDALE/KGS* NW9 ... 116 A2
Larkwell La *HART* DA3 .... 211 L4
Larmans Rd *PEND* EN3 .... 80 B2 🗄
Larnach Rd *HMSMTH* W6 .... 156 C1
Larne Rd *RSLP* HA4 .... 112 C5
Larner Rd *ERITH* DA8 .... 164 F6
La Roche CI *DTCH/LGLY* SL3 .... 149 P2 🗄
Larpent Av *PUT/ROE* SW15 ...... 178 V1
Larsen Dr *WAB* EN9 .... 63 J10 🗄
Larwood CI *NTHLT* UB5 .... 114 C10
Lascelles Av *HRW* HA1 .... 114 C5
Lascelles CI *BRWN* CM15 .... 86 C9
  WAN E11 .... 121 J7
Lascelles Rd *DTCH/LGLY* SL3 .. 149 N2
Lascott's Rd *WDGN* N22 .... 98 G7
Lashmere *CRAWE* RH10 .... 285 J1
Lassa Rd *ELTH/MOT* SE9 .... 184 B1
Lassell St *GNWCH* SE10 .... 161 J4
Lasswade Rd *CHERT* KT16 ...... 195 J7
Latchett Rd *SWFD* E18 .... 101 N9
Latchford PI *CHIG* IG7 .... 23 L5
Latchingdon Gdns *WFD* IG8 .... 102 B7 🗄
Latchmere CI *RCHPK/HAM* TW10 . 177 K8
Latchmere La *KUTN/CMB* KT2 ... 177 K8
Latchmere Rd *BTSEA* SW11 .... 158 A10 🗄
  KUTN/CMB KT2 .... 177 K9
Latchmere St *BTSEA* SW11 .... 158 A10 🗄
Latchmoor Av *CFSP/GDCR* SL9 . 110 A2
Latchmoor Gv *CFSP/GDCR* SL9 .. 110 A2
Latchmoor Wy *CFSP/GDCR* SL9 . 110 A2
Lateward Rd *BTFD* TW8 .... 155 J5
Latham CI *BH/WHM* TN16 .... 243 P7
  EHAM E6 .... 142 B4
Latham Rd *BXLYHS* DA6 .... 186 A1
  TWK TW1 .... 176 E3
Latham's Wy *CROY/NA* CR0 .... 202 G4
Lathkill CI *EN* EN1 .... 99 H4
Lathom Rd *EHAM* E6 .... 142 C1
Latimer *AMS* HP6 .... 142 C3
Latimer CI *AMS* HP6 .... 69 P5
  CRAWW RH11 .... 283 N4
  HHNE HP2 .... 36 C1
  PIN HA5 .... 93 K9
  WATW WD18 .... 48 B2
  WOKS/MYFD GU22 .... 232 E4
  WPK KT4 .... 220 E1
Latimer Dr *HCH* RM12 .... 125 L8
Latimer Gdns *PIN* HA5 .... 93 K9
  WCCE AL7 .... 23 L5
Latimer PI *NKENS* W10 .... 136 F8 🗄
Latimer Rd *AMS* HP6 .... 70 C4
  BAR EN5 .... 77 L7

Latimer Rd *CROY/NA* CR0 .... 204 C6
  CSHM HP5 .... 51 K10
  FSTGT E7 .... 121 N9
  NKENS W10 .... 136 F8
  SEVS/STOTM N15 .... 119 M4 🗄
  TEDD TW11 .... 176 E8 🗄
  WIM/MER SW19 .... 179 L9
Latimer Wy *BEAC* HP9 .... 88 B5
Latium CI *STAL* AL1 .... 38 C7
Latona Dr *GVE* DA12 .... 191 J8
Latona Rd *PECK* SE15 .... 139 H6
La Tourne Gdns *ORP* BR6 ...... 206 F10 🗄
Lattimer PI *CHSWK* W4 .... 156 B6 🗄
Lattimore Rd *STAL* AL1 .... 38 D7
  STALE/WH AL4 .... 21 H3
Latton CI *ESH/CLAY* KT10 ...... 218 A1
  WOT/HER KT12 .... 197 N1
Latton Gn *HLWS* CM18 .... 47 L6
Latton Hall CI *HLW* CM20 .... 29 K10
Latton Hall Rd *HLWS* CM18 ...... 47 L1
Latton House *HLWS* CM18 .... 47 L4
Latton St *HLW* CM20 .... 47 L1
  HLWE CM17 .... 47 L2
Laud Dr *CRAWE* RH10 .... 284 E8
Lauder CI *NTHLT* UB5 .... 133 L4 🗄
Lauderdale Dr *RCHPK/HAM* TW10 . 177 J6
Lauderdale Rd *ABLGY* WD5 ...... 54 D9
  MV/WKIL W9 .... 3 H10
Laud St *CROY/NA* CR0 .... 203 K10
  LBTH SE11 .... 17 N7
Laughton Rd *NTHLT* UB5 .... 133 M7
Launcelot Rd *BMLY* BR1 .... 183 M7
Launcelot St *STHWK* SE1 .... 18 A2
Launceston CI *HARH* RM3 .... 105 K9
Launceston Gdns *GFD/PVL* UB6 . 135 H3
Launceston PI *KENS* W8 .... 15 J3
Launceston Rd *GFD/PVL* UB6 .. 135 H3
Launch St *POP/IOD* E14 .... 161 K2
Launder's La *RAIN* RM13 .... 145 N7
Laundry La *WAB* EN9 .... 63 L1
Laundry Rd *GU* GU1 .... 267 P1
  HMSMTH W6 .... 14 A10
Laura CI *EN* EN1 .... 79 M9
  WAN E11 .... 121 P3
Lauradale Rd *EFNCH* N2 .... 118 A2
Laura Dr *SWLY* BR8 .... 187 H10
Laura PI *CLPT* E5 .... 120 B9
Laureate Wy *HHW* HP1 .... 35 L4
Laurel Av *DTCH/LGLY* SL3 ...... 150 B1
  EGH TW20 .... 171 N8
  GVE DA12 .... 190 F5
  POTB/CUF EN6 .... 59 J8
  TWK TW1 .... 176 A4
Laurel Bank *HHS/BOV* HP3 .... 35 J9
Laurel Bank Gdns *FUL/PGN* SW6 . 157 J8 🗄
Laurel Bank Rd *ENC/FH* EN2 .... 79 K5
Laurel CI *BARK/HLT* IG6 .... 102 F7
  CRAWE 284 B10
  DART DA1 .... 187 K4
  DTCH/LGLY SL3 .... 150 B1
  HHNE HP2 .... 36 A5
  RBRW/HUT CM13 .... 87 N9
  SCUP DA14 .... 185 K6
  TOOT SW17 .... 180 C8
Laurel Ct *AMS* HP6 .... 69 J2
Laurel Crs *CROY/NA* CR0 .... 204 F10
  ROMW/RG RM7 .... 124 F6
  WOKN/KNAP GU21 .... 214 F9
Laureldene *RGUW* GU3 .... 248 A10
Laurel Dr *OXTED* RH8 .... 261 L7
  SOCK/AV RM15 .... 147 J6
  WCHMH N21 .... 99 H1
Laurel Flds *POTB/CUF* EN6 ...... 59 J7
Laurel Gdns *CHING* E4 .... 100 U1 🗄
  HNWL W7 .... 134 D10
  HSLWW TW4 .... 153 M10
  MLHL NW7 .... 96 A4
Laurel Gv *PGE/AN* SE20 .... 182 A10
  SYD SE26 .... 182 C8
Laurel La *WDR/YW* UB7 .... 151 P3
Laurel Pk *KTN/HRWW/W* HA3 .... 94 F3
Laurel Rd *BARN* SW13 .... 156 D8
  CFSP/GDCR SL9 .... 90 A9
  HPTN TW12 .... 175 N10
  RYNPK SW20 .... 200 E1
  STAL AL1 .... 38 E6
Laurels CI *STALW/RED* AL3 ...... 38 A3
Laurels Rd *IVER* SL0 .... 130 G4
The Laurels *BERK* HP4 .... 34 E3
  BNSTD SM7 .... 239 J3 🗄
  CHESW EN7 .... 61 M5
  COB KT11 .... 235 M1 🗄
  HART DA3 .... 211 P3
Laurel St *HACK* E8 .... 7 M2
Laurel Vw *NFNCH/WDSP* N12 .... 97 L4
  NFNCH/WDSP N12 .... 97 K4
  SWFD E18 .... 101 N1
Laurence Ms *SHB* W12 .... 156 D1 🗄
Laurence Pountney La
  CANST EC4R 12 G8
Laurence Pountney HI
  CANST EC4R .... 12 G7 🗄
Laurie Gv *NWCR* SE14 .... 160 D7
Laurie Rd *HNWL* W7 .... 134 D7
Laurier Rd *CROY/NA* CR0 .... 203 N7
  KTTN NW5 .... 118 C3
Lauries CI *HHW* HP1 .... 34 E8
Laurimel CI *STAN* HA7 .... 94 G7 🗄
Laurino PI *BUSH* WD23 .... 94 B3
Lawrie Park Av *SYD* SE26 ...... 182 A8
Lawrie Park Crs *SYD* SE26 ...... 182 A8
Lawrie Park Gdns *SYD* SE26 .... 182 A8
Lawrie Park Rd *SYD* SE26 ...... 182 B8
Lausanne Rd *GEND/HSY/T* N8 .. 119 H2
  PECK SE15 .... 160 B7
Lauser Rd *STWL/WRAY* TW19 .. 173 M3
Laustan CI *GU* GU1 .... 250 F10
Lavant CI *CRAWW* RH11 .... 283 J9
Lavender Av *BRWN* CM15 .... 86 C9
  CDALE/KGS NW9 .... 115 N9
  MTCM CR4 .... 201 P1
  WPK KT4 .... 200 F10
Lavender CI *CAR* SM5 .... 222 B1
  CHEL SW3 .... 15 M10
  CHESW EN7 .... 61 K3 🗄
  COUL/CHIP CR5 .... 240 D5 🗄
  CTHM CR3 .... 259 K1
  HARH RM3 .... 106 B6
  HLW CM20 .... 29 M4
  REDH RH1 .... 299 J6
  SOCK/AV RM15 .... 147 K6 🗄
Lavender Gdns *BTSEA* SW11 .... 158 A10 🗄
  ENC/FH EN2 .... 79 K5
  KTN/HRWW/W HA3 .... 94 D1 🗄
Lavender Gv *HACK* E8 .... 7 N4
  MTCM CR4 .... 201 P1
Lavender HI *BTSEA* SW11 ...... 158 A10 🗄
  ENC/FH EN2 .... 79 K5
  SWLY BR8 .... 208 B3 🗄
Lavender PI *IL* IG1 .... 122 C10
Lavender Ri *WDR/YW* UB7 ...... 152 B1
Lavender Rd *BERM/RHTH* SE16 . 140 D1
  BTSEA SW11 .... 157 N9
  CAR SM5 .... 222 B2
  CROY/NA CR0 .... 202 G6
  ENC/FH EN2 .... 79 L5
  HOR/WEW KT19 .... 219 N1
  SUT SM1 .... 221 N1 🗄
  UX/CGN UB8 .... 132 A7
  WOKS/MYFD GU22 .... 232 E2 🗄
Lavender Sweep *BTSEA* SW11 .. 158 A10 🗄
Lavender Ter *BTSEA* SW11 ...... 157 P9 🗄

Lavender V *WLGTN* SM6 .... 222 E3
Lavender Vw *CROY/NA* CR0 ...... 204 C6
Lavengro Rd *WNWD* SE27 ...... 181 K5
Lavenham Rd *WAND/EARL* SW18 . 179 J5
Lavernock Rd *BXLYHN* DA7 .... 164 B8
Laverock La *RDART* DA2 ...... 164 C10
Laverock Rd *STNW/STAM* N16 .. 119 M8
Laverstoke Gdns *PUT/ROE* SW15 . 178 C3
Laverton PI *ECT* SW5 .... 15 H6
Lavidge Rd *ELTH/MOT* SE9 .... 184 B5
Lavina Gv *IS* N1 .... 5 J1
Lavington CI *CRAWW* RH11 ...... 283 J9
Lavington Rd *CROY/NA* CR0 .... 202 G10
  WEA W13 .... 134 G10
Lavington St *STHWK* SE1 .... 12 D10
Lavinia Av *GSTN* WD25 .... 55 L10
Lavinia Rd *DART* DA1 .... 187 N2
Lavrock La *RKW/CH/CXG* WD3 .... 92 A1
Lawbrook La *SHGR* GU5 .... 270 D9
Lawdons Gdns *CROY/NA* CR0 .. 223 J1 🗄
Lawdon Gdns *CROY/NA* CR0 .... 223 J1 🗄
Lawford Av *RKW/CH/CXG* WD3 .. 70 F10
Lawford CI *HCH* RM12 .... 125 M3 🗄
  RKW/CH/CXG WD3 .... 70 F10
  WLGTN SM6 .... 222 F5
Lawford Gdns *DART* DA1 .... 187 K1
  PUR/KEN CR8 .... 241 K2
Lawford Rd *CHSWK* W4 .... 155 P6 🗄
  IS N1 .... 7 J4
  KTTN NW5 .... 4 G2
Lawley Rd *STHGT/OAK* N14 .... 98 C1
Lawley St *CLPT* E5 .... 120 B9 🗄
Lawn Av *WDR/YW* UB7 .... 151 M1
Lawn CI *BMLY* BR1 .... 183 N10
  DTCH/LGLY SL3 .... 149 P6
  EN EN1 .... 99 N1
  NWMAL KT3 .... 200 B9
  RSLP HA4 .... 112 G8
  SWLY BR8 .... 208 D3
Lawn Crs *RCH/KEW* TW9 .... 155 M8
Lawn Farm Gv *CHDH* RM6 .... 104 A3
Lawn Gdns *HNWL* W7 .... 134 D10
Lawn House CI *POP/IOD* E14 ...... 161 H1
Lawn La *HHS/BOV* HP3 .... 35 M8
  VX/NE SW8 .... 17 M9
Lawn Pk *SEV* TN13 .... 265 J3
Lawn Rd *BECK* BR3 .... 182 E10
  GUW GU2 .... 267 P3
  UX/CGN UB8 .... 131 M2
Lawns Crs *GRAYS* RM17 .... 168 A5
The Lawns Dr *BROX* EN10 .... 44 B8
The Lawns *BELMT* SM2 .... 221 H4 🗄
  CHING E4 .... 100 F6
  HHW HP1 .... 35 H5
  NRWD SE19 .... 203 L1
  PIN HA5 .... 94 A8
  RAD WD7 .... 57 K9 🗄
  SCUP DA14 .... 185 L7 🗄
  STALW/RED AL3 .... 38 B5 🗄
Lawns Wy *CRW* RM5 .... 104 D8
Lawn Ter *BKHTH/KID* SE3 ...... 161 L9
The Lawn *NWDGN* UB2 .... 153 J3
Lawn V *PIN* HA5 .... 93 L10
Lawrance Gdns *CHES/WCR* EN8 . 62 C4
Lawrence Av *MLHL* NW7 .... 96 B5
  MNPK E12 .... 123 D9
  PLMGR N13 .... 99 J5 🗄
  WALTH E17 .... 100 C9
  WARE SG12 .... 27 H7
Lawrence CI *HERT/WAS* SG14 .... 24 F4
Lawrence Ct *MLHL* NW7 .... 96 B5 🗄
Lawrence Dr *HGDN/ICK* UB10 .... 112 D9
Lawrence Gdns *STNW/STAM* N16 . 119 M6
  TIL RM18 .... 168 G6
Lawrence HI *CHING* E4 .... 101 H1
Lawrence Hill Gdns *DART* DA1 .. 187 K2 🗄
Lawrence Hill Rd *DART* DA1 .... 187 K2
Lawrence La *BRKHM/BTCW* RH3 . 256 G1
  CITYW EC2V 12 F6
Lawrence Moorings *SBW* CM21 .. 30 A2
Lawrence Rd *EA* W5 .... 155 J3
  EHAM E6 .... 142 B3
  ERITH DA8 .... 164 C6
  GPK RM2 .... 125 J3
  HPTN TW12 .... 175 N10
  HSLWW TW4 .... 153 K10
  PIN HA5 .... 113 J2
  PLSTW E13 .... 141 K8 🗄
  RCHPK/HAM TW10 .... 177 H8
  SNWD SE25 .... 203 N4
  UED N18 .... 100 A5 🗄
  WWKM BR4 .... 225 M1
  YEAD UB4 .... 132 D4
Lawrence St *CAN/RD* E16 .... 141 J7 🗄
  CHEL SW3 .... 15 N10
  MLHL NW7 .... 96 C5
Lawrence Wy *SL* SL1 .... 128 B7
  WLSDN NW10 .... 117 H6
Lawrence Yd *SEVS/STOTM* N15 . 119 M2 🗄
Lawrie Park Av *SYD* SE26 ...... 182 A8
Lawrie Park Crs *SYD* SE26 ...... 182 A8
Lawrie Park Gdns *SYD* SE26 .... 182 A8
Lawrie Park Rd *SYD* SE26 ...... 182 B8
Laws CI *CRAWW* RH11 .... 283 H9
Lawson CI *CAN/RD* E16 .... 141 P8 🗄
  WIM/MER SW19 .... 178 G6 🗄
Lawson Gdns *DART* DA1 .... 187 L1
  PIN HA5 .... 113 J1
Lawson Rd *DART* DA1 .... 165 L10 🗄
  PEND EN3 .... 80 B5
  STHL UB1 .... 133 K4
Lawson Wy *ASC* SL5 .... 192 G6
Law St *STHWK* SE1 .... 19 H3
Lawton Rd *BOW* E3 .... 140 D5
  EBAR EN4 .... 77 N7
  LEY E10 .... 121 H6
Laxcon CI *WLSDN* NW10 .... 116 A10
Laxey Rd *ORP* BR6 .... 227 J3
Laxley CI *CMBW* SE5 .... 159 J6
Laxton Gdns *REDH* RH1 .... 258 F6 🗄
Laxton PI *CAMTN* NW1 .... 10 F1 🗄
Layard Rd *BERM/RHTH* SE16 .... 159 P3
  THHTH CR7 .... 203 L2 🗄
Lay Brook *STALE/WH* AL4 .... 38 F2 🗄
Laybrook *STALE/WH* AL4 .... 38 F2 🗄
Layburn Crs *DTCH/LGLY* SL3 .... 150 E5
Laycock St *IS* N1 .... 6 D2
Layer Gdns *ACT* W3 .... 135 M9
Layfield CI *HDN* NW4 .... 116 C5
Layfield Crs *HDN* NW4 .... 116 C6
Layfield Rd *HDN* NW4 .... 116 C5
Layhams Rd *HAYES* BR2 .... 225 M4
  WWKM BR4 .... 225 N1
Layhill *HHNE* HP2 .... 35 N1
Laymarsh CI *BELV* DA17 .... 141 L7 🗄
Laymead CI *NTHLT* UB5 .... 133 J3
Laystall St *FSBYW* WC1X 12 A2
Layters Av *CFSP/GDCR* SL9 ...... 89 P10
Layter's End *CFSP/GDCR* SL9 .... 89 P10
Layter's Green La *CFSP/GDCR* SL9 . 89 M10 🗄
Layters Wy *CFSP/GDCR* SL9 .... 110 A1
Layton Ct *WEY* KT13 .... 216 C1 🗄
Layton Crs *CROY/NA* CR0 .... 223 H2
Layton PI *RCH/KEW* TW9 .... 155 N7
Layton Rd *BTFD* TW8 .... 155 J5

  HSLW TW3 .... 154 A10
  IS N1 .... 6 B7
Laytons La *SUN* TW16 .... 196 C6
Layzell Wk *ELTH/MOT* SE9 ...... 184 A4
Leabank CI *HRW* HA1 .... 114 D8 🗄
Leabank Sq *HOM* E9 .... 140 F1 🗄
Leabank Vw *SEVS/STOTM* N15 .. 119 P4 🗄
Leabourne Rd *STNW/STAM* N16 . 119 P4 🗄
Lea Bridge Rd *CLPT* E5 .... 120 C7
Lea Bushes *GSTN* WD25 .... 71 M8
Leach Gv *LHD/OX* KT22 .... 237 H10
Lea CI *BUSH* WD23 .... 74 A9 🗄
  CRAWW RH11 .... 283 J8
Lea Crs *RSLP* HA4 .... 112 C9
Leacroft *ASC* SL5 .... 192 F5
  STA TW18 .... 173 L8
Leacroft Av *BAL* SW12 .... 180 A3
Leacroft CI *PUR/KEN* CR8 ...... 241 K1
  STA TW18 .... 173 L7
  WDR/YW UB7 .... 131 P9
Leacroft Rd *IVER* SL0 .... 130 C9
Leadale Av *CHING* E4 .... 100 F3
Leadale Rd *SEVS/STOTM* N15 .. 119 P6
Leadbeaters CI *FBAR/BDGN* N11 . 98 A6 🗄
Leadenhall PI *FENCHST* EC3M .. 13 J6 🗄
Leadenhall St *BANK* EC3V 13 J6
Leaf CI *STRHM/NOR* SW16 ...... 181 H8
Leafield CI *STRHM/NOR* SW16 .. 181 J9
  WOKN/KNAP GU21 .... 231 N4
Leafield La *SCUP* DA14 .... 186 A7
  SUT SM1 .... 201 K9
Leaford Crs *WATN* WD24 .... 72 C3
Leaforis Rd *CHESW* EN7 .... 61 P4
Leafy Gv *HAYES* BR2 .... 225 P8
Leafy Oak Rd *LEE/GVPK* SE12 .. 183 P7
Leafy Wy *CROY/NA* CR0 .... 203 P6
Lea Gdns *WBLY* HA9 .... 115 L10
Lea Hall Rd *LEY* E10 .... 120 F6
Leaholme Gdns *SL* SL1 .... 128 B7
Leaholme Waye *RSLP* HA4 ...... 112 C3
Leahurst Rd *LEW* SE13 .... 183 K2 🗄
Leake St *STHWK* SE1 .... 11 P9
Lealand Rd *SEVS/STOTM* N15 .. 119 P6
Leamington Av *BMLY* BR1 .... 183 P8
  MRDN SM4 .... 201 J4
  ORP BR6 .... 227 H1
  WALTH E17 .... 120 F3 🗄
Leamington CI *BMLY* BR1 .... 183 P7
  HSLW TW3 .... 176 B1 🗄
Leamington Crs
  RYLN/HDSTN HA2 .... 113 M8
Leamington Gdns
  GDMY/SEVK IG3 .... 123 J7
Leamington Pk *ACT* W3 .... 136 A7 🗄
Leamington PI *YEAD* UB4 .... 132 G6
Leamington Rd *HARH* RM3 ...... 105 P6
  NWDGN UB2 .... 153 L3
Leamington Road VIs *NTGHL* W11 . 8 D4
Leamore St *HMSMTH* W6 .... 156 E3
Lea Mt *CHESW* EN7 .... 61 M4
Leamouth Rd *EHAM* E6 .... 142 B8
  POP/IOD E14 .... 141 P8
Leander Dr *GVE* DA12 .... 191 J7
Leander Gdns *GSTN* WD25 ...... 73 M3 🗄
Leander Rd *BRXS/STRHM* SW2 .. 180 G2
  NTHLT UB5 .... 133 L1
  THHTH CR7 .... 202 G4
Leapale La *GU* GU1 .... 268 A1
Leapale Rd *GU* GU1 .... 268 A1
Learner Dr *RYLN/HDSTN* HA2 .... 113 P7
Lea Rd *BECK* BR3 .... 204 F2 🗄
  CDH/CHF RM16 .... 168 D4
  ENC/FH EN2 .... 79 L5
  HOD EN11 .... 45 H1
  NWDGN UB2 .... 153 M3
  SEV TN13 .... 265 K3
  WAB EN9 .... 63 L1
  WATN WD24 .... 73 J4 🗄
Learoyd Gdns *EHAM* E6 .... 142 D9 🗄
Leas CI *CHSGTN* KT9 .... 219 L4
Leas DI *ELTH/MOT* SE9 .... 184 D6
Leas Dr *IVER* SL0 .... 131 H8
Leas Gn *CHST* BR7 .... 185 J3
Leaside *GT/LBKH* KT23 .... 235 P9
  HHNE HP2 .... 36 D7
Leaside Av *MUSWH* N10 .... 119 B1
Leaside Ct *HGDN/ICK* UB10 .... 132 C5 🗄
Leaside Rd *CLPT* E5 .... 120 E5
Leas La *WARL* CR6 .... 242 C4
Leasowes Rd *LEY* E10 .... 120 E6
Leas Rd *WARL* CR6 .... 242 C4
The Leas *BUSH* WD23 .... 73 H5
  HHS/BOV HP3 .... 36 B10
  UPMR RM14 .... 126 C5
Leasway *BRW* CM14 .... 107 J4
  CDH/CHF RM16 .... 147 P10
Leathart CI *HCH* RM12 .... 145 J2 🗄
The Lea *EGH* TW20 .... 172 C10
Leather CI *MTCM* CR4 .... 202 B2 🗄
Leatherbottle Gn *ERITH* DA18 .. 164 C5 🗄
Leatherdale St *WCHPL* E1 ...... 140 C5 🗄
Leatherhead by Pass Rd
  LHD/OX KT22 .... 236 G6
Leatherhead By-pass Rd
  LHD/OX KT22 .... 236 G6
Leatherhead CI *STNW/STAM* N16 . 119 M6
Leatherhead Rd *ASHTD* KT21 .. 237 J6
  CHSGTN KT9 .... 218 G10
  GT/LBKH KT23 .... 254 B2
  LHD/OX KT22 .... 218 G10
Leather La *EMPK* RM11 .... 125 L6
  HCIRC EC1N 12 A3
Leathermarket St *STHWK* SE1 .. 19 J2
Leathersale Rd *RYLN/HDSTN* HA2 . 114 A8
Leathwaite Rd *BTSEA* SW11 .... 158 A10
Leathwell Rd *DEPT* SE8 .... 160 E6
Lea V *DART* DA1 .... 164 G10
Lea Valley Rd *CHING* E4 .... 80 G10
Lea Valley Wk *BRKMPK* AL9 ...... 22 F9
  BRKMPK AL9 .... 24 A10
  BRKMPK AL9 .... 41 H1
  CLPT E5 .... 120 A5
  HERT/BAY SG13 .... 25 J6
  HERT/WAS SG14 .... 24 D3
  TOTM N17 .... 100 A10
  WAB EN9 .... 62 F2
  WARE SG12 .... 27 J2
Leaveland CI *BECK* BR3 .... 204 E3
Leaver Gdns *GFD/PVL* UB6 ...... 134 C4
Leavesden Rd *STAN* HA7 .... 94 F7
  WEY KT13 .... 216 C2 🗄
Leaves Green Crs *HAYES* BR2 .. 225 P9
Leaves Green Rd *HAYES* BR2 .. 226 A8
Leaview *WAB* EN9 .... 62 G4
Leazes Av *CTHM* CR3 .... 241 N7 🗄
Lebanon Av *FELT* TW13 .... 175 H4
Lebanon CI *WAT* WD17 .... 72 C2
Lebanon Dr *COB* KT11 .... 217 H9
Lebanon Gdns *BH/WHM* TN16 .. 244 A5 🗄
  WAND/EARL SW18 .... 179 K5
Lebanon Pk *TWK* TW1 .... 176 D6 🗄
Lebanon Rd *CROY/NA* CR0 ...... 204 B1 🗄
  WAND/EARL SW18 .... 179 K5
Lebrun Sq *BKHTH/KID* SE3 ...... 161 N10
Lechford Rd *HORL* RH6 .... 280 C4 🗄
Lechmere Ap *WFD* IG8 .... 102 A10

Lechmere Av *CHIG* IG7 .... 102 F5
Lechmere Rd *CRICK* NW2 .... 136 E1
Leckford Rd *WAND/EARL* SW18 . 179 M5
Leckwith Av *ABYW* SE2 .... 163 P5 🗄
Lecky St *SKENS* SW7 .... 15 L7
Leconfield Av *PUT/ROE* SW15 .. 156 C9 🗄
Leconfield Rd *HBRY* N5 .... 6 C9
Le Corte CI *KGLGY* WD4 .... 54 A5
Lectern La *STAL* AL1 .... 38 D10 🗄
Leda Av *PEND* EN3 .... 81 H5
Leda Rd *WOOL/PLUM* SE18 ...... 142 C2 🗄
Ledborough La *BEAC* HP9 .... 88 B5
Ledborough Wd *BEAC* HP9 ...... 88 B5
Ledbury Ms North *NTGHL* W11 .. 8 E1
Ledbury Ms West *NTGHL* W11 .. 8 E1 🗄
Ledbury Rd *CROY/NA* CR0 ...... 223 J4
  NTGHL W11 .... 8 D2
  REIG RH2 .... 257 K9 🗄
Ledbury St *PECK* SE15 .... 159 P6
Ledger CI *GU* GU1 .... 250 F9
Ledger Dr *ADL/WDHM* KT15 .... 215 J3 🗄
Ledger's Rd *SL* SL1 .... 128 A5
  WARL CR6 .... 242 G5
Ledrington Rd *NRWD* SE19 ...... 181 N9 🗄
Ledway Dr *WBLY* HA9 .... 115 L5
Leechcroft Av *BFN/LL* DA15 .... 185 J1
  SWLY BR8 .... 208 G3
Leechcroft La *LHD/OX* KT22 .... 255 P7
Lee Church St *LEW* SE13 .... 161 K10
Lee CI *HERT/BAY* SG13 .... 25 K7 🗄
  WALTH E17 .... 100 C9
Lee Conservancy Rd *HOM* E9 .. 120 E10 🗄
Leecroft Rd *BAR* EN5 .... 77 H9
Leeds CI *ORP* BR6 .... 207 N9
Leeds Rd *IL* IG1 .... 122 G6
  SL SL1 .... 129 K9
Leeds St *UED* N18 .... 99 P6
Leefe Wy *POTB/CUF* EN6 .... 59 N8
Lee Gardens Av *EMPK* RM11 .... 125 P6 🗄
Lee Gv *CHIG* IG7 .... 102 C2
Lee High Rd *LEW* SE13 .... 161 L10
Leeke St *FSBYW* WC1X 5 N9
Leeland Rd *WEA* W13 .... 134 F10 🗄
Leeland Wy *WLSDN* NW10 ...... 116 C9 🗄
Leeming Rd *BORE* WD6 .... 75 P1
Lee Navigation *CLPT* E5 .... 120 D9
Lee Pk *BKHTH/KID* SE3 .... 161 L10
Lee Park Wy *UED* N18 .... 100 C6
  EN EN1 .... 79 N10
  GFD/PVL UB6 .... 135 H3
  MLHL NW7 .... 96 C8
  WIM/MER SW19 .... 201 L1
Lees Av *NTHWD* HA6 .... 92 N9
Leeside *POTB/CUF* EN6 .... 59 N8
Leeside Crs *GLDGN* NW11 ...... 117 H4
Leeside Gdns *WDSR* SL4 .... 148 D3
Leeson HI *CHST* BR7 .... 207 H3
Leesons HI *CHST* BR7 .... 207 H3
Leesons Wy *STMC/STPC* BR5 .. 207 K5
Lees PI *MYFR/PKLN* W1K 10 C7
The Lees *CROY/NA* CR0 .... 204 E9
Lee St *HACK* E8 .... 7 L5
  HORL RH6 .... 279 P3
Lee Vw *ENC/FH* EN2 .... 79 J3
Leeward Gdns *WIM/MER* SW19 .. 179 H9
Leeway *DEPT* SE8 .... 160 E4
Leewood CI *LEE/GVPK* SE12 ...... 183 L2 🗄
Leewood Wy *EHSLY* KT24 .... 253 K3
Lefevre Wk *BOW* E3 .... 140 E3
Leffern Rd *SHB* W12 .... 156 D1
Lefroy Rd *SHB* W12 .... 156 C1
Legard Rd *HBRY* N5 .... 119 J8 🗄
Legatt Rd *ELTH/MOT* SE9 ...... 184 A1
Leggatt Rd *SRTFD* E15 .... 141 H4
Leggatts CI *WATN* WD24 .... 72 G2
Leggatts Ri *GSTN* WD25 .... 73 H1
Leggatts Wy *WATN* WD24 .... 73 J3
Leggatts Wood Av *WATN* WD24 . 73 J2
Legge St *LEW* SE13 .... 183 H1 🗄
Leggfield Ter *HHW* HP1 .... 35 J6 🗄
Leghorn Rd *WLSDN* NW10 ...... 136 D4
  WOOL/PLUM SE18 .... 162 G4
Legion CI *IS* N1 .... 6 B2
Legion Ter *BOW* E3 .... 140 E9 🗄
Legion Wy *NFNCH/WDSP* N12 ... 97 P8
Legon Av *ROMW/RG* RM7 .... 124 D6
Legra Av *HOD* EN11 .... 44 F3 🗄
Legrace Av *HSLWW* TW4 .... 153 L8
Leicester Av *MTCM* CR4 .... 202 F4 🗄
Leicester CI *WPK* KT4 .... 220 F1
Leicester Gdns *GDMY/SEVK* IG3 . 123 J4
Leicester PI *LSQ/SEVD* WC2H ... 11 K7 🗄
Leicester Rd *BAR* EN5 .... 77 M4
  CROY/NA CR0 .... 204 B8
  EFNCH N2 .... 117 P1
  TIL RM18 .... 131 N3
  WAN E11 .... 121 N3
  WLSDN NW10 .... 136 E1
Leicester Sq *SOHO/SHAV* W1D .. 11 K7
Leicester St *LSQ/SEVD* WC2H .. 11 K7 🗄
Leigham Court Rd
  STRHM/NOR SW16 .... 180 G6
Leigham Dr *ISLW* TW7 .... 154 D6 🗄
Leigham Vale *STRHM/NOR* SW16 . 181 H6
Leigh Av *REDBR* IG4 .... 122 A2
Leigh CI *ADL/WDHM* KT15 ...... 215 J4
  NWMAL KT3 .... 200 A3
Leigh Common *WGCE* AL7 ...... 23 J5
Leigh Ct *COB* WD6 .... 76 A6 🗄
  RYLN/HDSTN HA2 .... 114 D6 🗄
Leigh Court CI *COB* KT11 ...... 217 K10
Leigh Crs *CROY/NA* CR0 .... 224 C4
Leigh Dr *HARH* RM3 .... 105 L5
Leigh Gdns *WLSDN* NW10 .... 136 F4
Leigh Hill Rd *COB* KT11 .... 217 K10
Leigh Hunt Dr *STHGT/OAK* N14 . 98 C2
Leighlands *CRAWE* RH10 .... 284 D10
Leigh Orchard CI
  STRHM/NOR SW16 .... 180 G6 🗄
Leigh Pk *DTCH/LGLY* SL3 ...... 149 K6 🗄
Leigh PI *COB* KT11 .... 217 K10
  COB KT11 .... 235 K1
  DAGE RM10 .... 163 K8
  WELL DA16 .... 165 H8
Leigh Place Rd *GDST* RH9 ...... 280 G5
Leigh Place Rd *REIG* RH2 .... 274 D6
Leigh Rd *BRKHM/BTCW* RH3 .... 275 P6
  COB KT11 .... 217 J9
  EHAM E6 .... 142 D2
  GVW DA11 .... 190 E6
  HBRY N5 .... 118 E10
  HSLW TW3 .... 154 C10 🗄
  LEY E10 .... 121 H3
  SL SL1 .... 128 C5
Leigh Rodd *OXHEY* WD19 .... 93 M4
Leigh Sq *WDSR* SL4 .... 148 C8
Leigh St *STPAN* WC1H 11 L1
Leighton Av *MNPK* E12 .... 123 M9
  PIN HA5 .... 113 M1
Leighton Buzzard Rd *HHW* HP1 . 35 M4
Leighton CI *EDGW* HA8 .... 95 M10
Leighton Crs *KTTN* NW5 .... 118 D10 🗄
Leighton Gdns *SAND/SEL* CR2 .. 224 A9
  TIL RM18 .... 168 D6
  WLSDN NW10 .... 136 F4
Leighton Gv *KTTN* NW5 .... 118 D10 🗄
Leighton PI *KTTN* NW5 .... 118 D10 🗄
Leighton Rd *EN* EN1 .... 79 N10

KTN/HRWW/W HA3 .... 94 C10
KTTN NW5 .... 118 D10
WEA W13 .... 154 F1
Leighton Wy EPSOM KT18 .... 220 A10
Leila Parnell Pl CHARL SE7 .... 161 P5 ⬚
Leinster Av MORT/ESHN SW14 .... 155 P9
Leinster Gdns BAY/PAD W2 .... 9 J6
Leinster Ms BAY/PAD W2 .... 9 J6
Leinster Pl BAY/PAD W2 .... 9 J6
Leinster Pl MUSWH N10 .... 118 C2
Leinster Sq BAY/PAD W2 .... 8 F7
Leinster Ter BAY/PAD W2 .... 9 J6
Leiston Sp SL SL1 .... 129 K8
Leisure La BF/WBF KT14 .... 215 L8 ⬚
Leisure Wy NFNCH/WDSP N12 .... 97 N8
Leith CI CDALE/KGS NW9 .... 116 A6
SL SL1 .... 129 M10
Leithcote Gdns
   STRHM/NOR SW16 .... 180 G7
Leithcote Pth STRHM/NOR SW16 .... 180 G6
Leith HI STMC/STPC BR5 .... 207 K1
Leith Hill Rd RDKG RH5 .... 271 M10
Leith Park Rd GVW DA11 .... 190 E4
Leith Rd EW KT17 .... 220 B8
WDGN N22 .... 99 J9
Leith Vw RDKG RH5 .... 273 N6
Lela Av HSLWW TW4 .... 153 K8
Lelitia CI HACK E8 .... 7 N6
Leman St WCHPL E1 .... 13 M6
Lemark CI STAN HA7 .... 95 H7 ⬚
Le May Av LEE/GVPK SE12 .... 183 N6
Le May CI HORL RH6 .... 280 B3
Lemmon Rd GNWCH SE10 .... 161 K5 ⬚
Lemna Rd WAN E11 .... 121 K5
Lemon Field Dr WATDS WD25 .... 55 M9 ⬚
Lemonwell Dr ELTH/MOT SE9 .... 184 E1
Lemsford CI SEVS/STOTM N15 .... 180 D9
Lemsford Ct BORE WD6 .... 75 P8
Lemsford La WGCW AL8 .... 22 E6
Lemsford Rd HAT AL10 .... 40 D2 ⬚
STAL AL1 .... 38 E6
Lemsford Village WGCW AL8 .... 22 D6 ⬚
Lena Gdns HMSMTH W6 .... 156 F2
Lena Kennedy CI CHING E4 .... 101 H7
Lendal Ter CLAP SW4 .... 158 F9 ⬚
Lenelby Rd SURB KT6 .... 199 M8
Len Freeman Pl FUL/PGN SW6 .... 14 A8
Lenham Rd BXLYHN DA7 .... 164 A5
   LEW SE13 .... 161 L10
   SUT SM1 .... 221 L1
   THHTH CR7 .... 203 L1
Lenmore Av GRAYS RM17 .... 167 P2
Lennard Av WWKM BR4 .... 205 K6
Lennard CI WWKM BR4 .... 205 K6
Lennard Rd CROY/NA CR0 .... 203 K8
   HAYES BR2 .... 206 C8
   PGE/AN SE20 .... 182 C9
   SEV TN13 .... 246 F6
   SYD SE26 .... 182 B9
Lennon Rd CRICK NW2 .... 116 F10
Lennox Av GVW DA11 .... 190 D2
Lennox CI ROM RM1 .... 124 C4
Lennox Gdns CROY/NA CR0 .... 223 J1 ⬚
   IL IG1 .... 122 C6
   KTBR SW1X 16 A4
   WLSDN NW10 .... 116 C9
Lennox Gardens Ms CHEL SW3 .... 16 A5
Lennox Rd FSBYPK N4 .... 118 C2
   GVW DA11 .... 190 D2
   WALTH E17 .... 120 E4 ⬚
Lennox Rd East GVW DA11 .... 190 D3
Lenor CI BXLYHS DA6 .... 163 P10
Lensbury CI CHES/WCR EN8 .... 62 D4 ⬚
Lensbury Wy ABYW SE2 .... 163 N2
Lens Rd FSTGT E7 .... 141 P2
Lenten CI SHGR GU5 .... 270 C8
Lent Green La SL SL1 .... 128 A6
Lenthall Av GRAYS RM17 .... 167 M1
Lenthall Rd HACK E8 .... 7 M3
Lenthorp Rd GNWCH SE10 .... 161 L4 ⬚
Lentmead Rd BMLY BR1 .... 183 L6
Lenton Ri RCH/KEW TW9 .... 155 K9
Lenton St WOOL/PLUM SE18 .... 162 C3
Lent Rise Rd MDHD SL6 .... 128 A3
Leof Crs CAT SE6 .... 182 C8
Leominster Rd MRDN SM4 .... 201 M6
Leominster Wk MRDN SM4 .... 201 M6 ⬚
Leonard Av MRDN SM4 .... 201 M5
   ROMW/RG RM7 .... 124 F6
   RSEV TN14 .... 247 J1
   SWCM DA10 .... 189 K7 ⬚
Leonard Ct KENS W8 .... 14 E3 ⬚
Leonard Pl STNW/STAM N16 .... 119 M9 ⬚
Leonard Rd CHING E4 .... 100 T7
   ED N9 .... 99 P4 ⬚
   FSTGT E7 .... 121 M9
   MTCR CR4 .... 202 D1
   NWDGN UB2 .... 153 L2
Leonardslee Ct CRAWE RH10 .... 284 C10 ⬚
Leonard St CAN/RD E16 .... 142 B10
   SDTCH EC2A 13 J1
Leonard Wy BRW CM14 .... 106 D5
Leontine CI PECK SE15 .... 159 P6
Leopold Av WIM/MER SW19 .... 179 J3 ⬚
Leopold Ms HOM E9 .... 140 B3 ⬚
Leopold Rd CRAWW RH11 .... 283 N7
   EA W5 .... 135 L10
   EFNCH N2 .... 117 N1
   WALTH E17 .... 120 F3
   WIM/MER SW19 .... 179 J7
   WLSDN NW10 .... 118 G6
Leopold St BOW E3 .... 140 E7 ⬚
Leo St PECK SE15 .... 160 A6
Le Personne Rd CTHM CR3 .... 241 L8
Leppoc Rd CLAP SW4 .... 180 E1
Leret Wy LHD/OX KT22 .... 236 E7
Leroy St STHWK SE1 .... 19 J5
Lerwick Dr SL SL1 .... 129 K7
Lesbourne Rd REIG RH2 .... 275 L1
Lescombe CI FSTH SE23 .... 182 B3
Lescombe Rd FSTH SE23 .... 182 D6
Lesley CI BXLY DA5 .... 186 B3
   SWLY BR8 .... 208 E3
Leslie Gdns BELMT SM2 .... 221 K4
Leslie Gv CROY/NA CR0 .... 203 L8
Leslie Park Rd CROY/NA CR0 .... 203 M8
Leslie Rd CAN/RD E16 .... 141 N8
   CHOB/PIR GU24 .... 213 J6
   DORK RH4 .... 255 J10
   EFNCH N2 .... 117 N1
   WAN E11 .... 121 J9
Lesney Ct ERITH DA8 .... 164 E5
Lesney Park Rd ERITH DA8 .... 164 E5
Lessar Av CLAP SW4 .... 180 D1
Lessingham Av TOOT SW17 .... 180 A9
Lessing St FSTH SE23 .... 182 B3
Lessington Av ROMW/RG RM7 .... 124 D4
Lessness Av BXLYHN DA7 .... 147 L6
Lessness Pk BELV DA17 .... 164 A4
Lessness Rd MRDN SM4 .... 201 N6
   BELV DA17 .... 164 A3 ⬚
Lester Av SRTFD E15 .... 141 K6
Leston CI RAIN RM13 .... 145 J3 ⬚
Leswin Pl STNW/STAM N16 .... 119 N8 ⬚
Leswin Rd STNW/STAM N16 .... 119 N8 ⬚
Letchfield CSHM HP5 .... 51 N7
Letchford Gdns WLSDN NW10 .... 136 D5 ⬚
Letchford Ms WLSDN NW10 .... 136 D5 ⬚
Letchmore Rd RAD WD7 .... 74 F2
Letchworth Av
   EBED/NFELT TW14 .... 174 A3
Letchworth CI HAYES BR2 .... 205 L6 ⬚
   OXHEY WD19 .... 93 L6 ⬚
Letchworth Dr HAYES BR2 .... 205 M6
Letchworth St TOOT SW17 .... 180 A7
Letter Box La SEV TN13 .... 265 K5
Letterstone Rd FUL/PGN SW6 .... 157 J6 ⬚

Lettice St FUL/PGN SW6 .... 157 J8
Lett Rd SRTFD E15 .... 141 J2
Leucha Rd WALTH E17 .... 120 D3
Levana CI WIM/MER SW19 .... 179 H4 ⬚
Levehurst Wy CLAP SW4 .... 158 F9 ⬚
Leven CI CHES/WCR EN8 .... 62 C9 ⬚
   OXHEY WD19 .... 93 L6 ⬚
Levendale Rd FSTH SE23 .... 182 D5
Leven Dr CHES/WCR EN8 .... 62 C9
Leven Rd POP/IOD E14 .... 141 J8 ⬚
Leven Wy HHN HP2 .... 35 N2 ⬚
   HYS/HAR UB3 .... 132 F8
Leverett CI CRAWW RH11 .... 283 L5
   GSTN WD25 .... 55 H10
Leveret La CRAWW RH11 .... 283 L5
Leverett St CHEL SW3 .... 15 P5 ⬚
Leverholme Gdns ELTH/MOT SE9 .... 184 D7
Leverson St STRHM/NOR SW16 .... 180 D9
Lever Sq G/CHF RM16 .... 168 B7
Leverstock Green Rd HHNE HP2 .... 36 B5
   HHS/BOV HP3 .... 36 D7
Lever St FSBYE EC1V 6 E10
Leverton PI KTTN NW5 .... 118 C10 ⬚
Leverton St KTTN NW5 .... 118 D10
Leverton Wy WAB EN9 .... 63 H9
Leveson Rd CDH/CHF RM16 .... 168 E2
Levett Gdns GDMY/SEVK IG3 .... 123 J9
Levett Rd BARK IG11 .... 143 H1
   LHD/OX KT22 .... 236 G6
Levine Gdns BARK IG11 .... 143 N4
Levylsdene GU GU1 .... 250 G10
Lewes CI CRAWE RH10 .... 284 D7
   GRAYS RM17 .... 167 M5
   NTHLT UB5 .... 133 P1
Lewesdon CI WIM/MER SW19 .... 178 G4 ⬚
Lewes Rd BMLY BR1 .... 206 A2
   HARH RM3 .... 105 L5
   NFNCH/WDSP N12 .... 97 P6
Leweston PI STNW/STAM N16 .... 119 N5 ⬚
Lewes Wy RKW/CH/CXG WD3 .... 72 C8
Lewgars Av CDALE/KGS NW9 .... 115 P4
Lewin CI CFSP/GDCR SL9 .... 219 N10
   EPSOM KT18 .... 228 C9
Lewins Wy SL SL1 .... 129 J8
Lewins Wy SL WALTH E17 .... 100 F9
Lewis Av WALTH E17 .... 101 H10
Lewis CI ADL/WDHM KT15 .... 215 M1
   BRWN CM15 .... 107 L1
   DEN/HRF UB9 .... 91 M10
   STHGT/OAK N14 .... 98 D1
Lewis Crs WLSDN NW10 .... 116 A10
Lewis Gdns EFNCH N2 .... 97 N10
Lewis Gv LEW SE13 .... 161 H10
Lewisham HI LEW SE13 .... 161 H8
Lewisham Rd LEW SE13 .... 161 H8
Lewisham Wy BROCKY SE4 .... 160 E8
   NWCR SE14 .... 160 E7
Lewis La CFSP/GDCR SL9 .... 90 B3
Lewis St CAMTN NW1 .... 4 F3
Lewis Wy DAGE RM10 .... 144 C1
Lexden Dr CHDH RM6 .... 123 L9
Lexden Rd ACT W3 .... 135 N9
   MTCR CR4 .... 202 G4
Lexham Gdns AMS HP6 .... 69 H3
   KENS W8 .... 14 F5
Lexham Ms KENS W8 .... 14 F5
Lexington CI BORE WD6 .... 75 M7 ⬚
Lexington PI PUR/KEN CR8 .... 223 K6
Lexington St SOHO/CST W1F 11 H6
Lexington Wy BAR EN5 .... 76 C4
   UPMR RM14 .... 126 D4
Lexton Gdns BAL SW12 .... 180 E4
Leyborne Av WEA W13 .... 155 H1
Leyborne Pk RCH/KEW TW9 .... 155 M7
Leybourne CI BF/WBF KT14 .... 216 A9 ⬚
   HAYES BR2 .... 205 M6 ⬚
Leybourne Rd CAMTN NW1 .... 4 F4 ⬚
   CDALE/KGS NW9 .... 115 M3
   HCDN/ICK UB10 .... 132 D3
   WAN E11 .... 121 L6
Leybourne St CAMTN NW1 .... 4 E4 ⬚
Leyburn CI WALTH E17 .... 121 N2 ⬚
Leyburn Crs HARH RM3 .... 105 M8
Leyburn Gdns CROY/NA CR0 .... 203 M9
Leyburn Gv UED N18 .... 99 P9
Leyburn Rd HARH RM3 .... 105 M8
   UED N18 .... 99 P9
Leycester CI BFOR GU20 .... 212 A1
Leycroft CI ERITH DA8 .... 165 J7
Leycroft Wy HARP AL5 .... 20 D1
Leydenhatch La SWLY BR8 .... 208 E1
Leyden St WCHPL E1 .... 13 L4
Leyes Rd CAN/RD E16 .... 141 P9
Leyfield WPK KT4 .... 200 B9
Leyhill CI SWLY BR8 .... 208 F5 ⬚
Leyland Av EN EN1 .... 79 J4
   STAL AL1 .... 38 G2 ⬚
Leyland CI CHES/WCR EN8 .... 62 B4 ⬚
Leyland Rd LEE/GVPK SE12 .... 183 N1
Leylands La STWL/WRAY TW19 .... 151 L10
Leylang Rd NWCR SE14 .... 160 C6
Leys Av DAGE RM10 .... 144 D2 ⬚
Leys CI DAGE RM10 .... 144 D2 ⬚
   DEN/HRF UB9 .... 91 N9
   HRW HA1 .... 114 C2
Leysdown WGCE AL7 .... 23 N5 ⬚
Leysdown Av BXLYHN DA7 .... 164 D10
Leysfield Rd SHB W12 .... 156 D1 ⬚
Leys Gdns EBAR EN4 .... 78 B9
Leyspring Rd WAN E11 .... 121 L1
Leys Rd HHS/BOV HP3 .... 36 A8
   LHD/OX KT22 .... 218 C3
Leys Rd East PEND EN3 .... 80 D5 ⬚
The Leys AMS HP6 .... 68 G5 ⬚
Leys The EFNCH N2 .... 117 M2
   KTN/HRWW/W HA3 .... 115 L4 ⬚
   STALE/WH AL4 .... 39 H7 ⬚
Ley St IL IG1 .... 122 C6
Leyswood Dr GNTH/NBYPK IG2 .... 123 J3
Leythe Rd ACT W3 .... 155 P1
Leyton Cross Rd RDART DA2 .... 186 G6
Leyton Gra LEY E10 .... 120 F7
Leyton Green Rd LEY E10 .... 120 F4
Leyton Park Rd LEY E10 .... 120 F9
Leyton Rd SRTFD E15 .... 121 H10
   WIM/MER SW19 .... 179 M10
Leyton Wy WAN E11 .... 121 L2
Leywick St SRTFD E15 .... 141 K5 ⬚
Leywood CI AMSS HP7 .... 69 J3
Liardet St NWCR SE14 .... 160 D5
Liberia Rd HBRY N5 .... 6 D1
Liberty Av WIM/MER SW19 .... 179 N10
Liberty CI HERT/BAY SG13 .... 25 K7
Liberty Hall Rd ADL/WDHM KT15 .... 215 M1
Liberty La ADL/WDHM KT15 .... 215 L2
Liberty Ri ADL/WDHM KT15 .... 215 L3
Liberty St BRXN/ST SW9 .... 158 A7
Libra Rd BOW E3 .... 129 H1
   PLSTW E13 .... 141 M4
Library St STHWK SE1 .... 18 D2 ⬚
Lichfield CI EBAR EN4 .... 78 A7

Lichfield Gdns
   RCHPK/HAM TW10 .... 177 K1 ⬚
Lichfield Gv FNCH N3 .... 97 K9
Lichfield Rd BCTR RM8 .... 123 L9
   BOW E3 .... 140 D5
   CRICK NW2 .... 117 M9
   ED N9 .... 99 P3 ⬚
   EHAM E6 .... 142 A5
   HSLWW TW4 .... 153 K9
   NTHWD HA6 .... 113 H1
   RCH/KEW TW9 .... 155 L7
   WFD IG8 .... 101 K5
Lichfield Ter UPMR RM14 .... 126 D7 ⬚
   UPMR RM14 .... 126 E7 ⬚
Lichfield Wy BROX EN10 .... 44 E8 ⬚
   SAND/SEL CR2 .... 224 C6
Lidbury Rd MLHL NW7 .... 97 H1
Liddall Wy WDR/YW UB7 .... 132 A10
Liddell CI KTN/HRWW/W HA3 .... 115 J1
Liddell Gdns WLSDN NW10 .... 136 F4
Liddell Rd KIL/WHAMP NW6 .... 2 E1
Lidding Rd KTN/HRWW/W HA3 .... 115 J1
Liddington Hall Dr RGUW GU3 .... 249 K7
Liddington New Rd RGUW GU3 .... 249 K7
Liddington Rd SRTFD E15 .... 141 L3
Liddon Rd BMLY BR1 .... 205 P3
   PLSTW E13 .... 141 N5
Liden CI LEY E10 .... 120 E5
Lidfield Rd STNW/STAM N16 .... 119 L9 ⬚
Lidgate Rd PECK SE15 .... 159 N6 ⬚
Lidiard Rd WAND/EARL SW18 .... 179 M5
Lido Rd GU GU1 .... 250 A9
Lido Sq TOTM N17 .... 99 L10 ⬚
Lidsey CI CRAWE RH10 .... 284 D9
Lidstone CI WOKN/KNAP GU21 .... 231 N3
Lidyard Rd ARCH N19 .... 118 D6
Lieutenant Ellis Wy CHESW EN7 .... 61 N7
Liffler Rd WOOL/PLUM SE18 .... 163 H4
Lifford St PUT/ROE SW15 .... 156 G10
Lightcliffe Rd PLMGR N13 .... 99 H5
Lighterman Ms WCHPL E1 .... 140 C8 ⬚
Lighterman's Rd POP/IOD E14 .... 160 F1
Lightfoot Rd CEND/HSY/T N8 .... 117 H3
Lightwater Meadow LTWR GU18 .... 212 A7
Lightwater Rd LTWR GU18 .... 212 A7
Ligonier St BETH E2 .... 13 L1
Lilac Av EN EN1 .... 80 B2
   WOKN/KNAP GU22 .... 232 A6
Lilac CI BRW CM15 .... 86 C9
   CHESW EN7 .... 62 A7 ⬚
   CHING E4 .... 100 F7
   GU GU1 .... 249 P6
Lilac Gdns CROY/NA CR0 .... 204 F10
   EA W5 .... 155 J2
   HYS/HAR UB3 .... 132 A5
   ROMW/RG RM7 .... 124 F6
   SWLY BR8 .... 208 E3
Lilac PI LBTH SE11 .... 17 N6
   WDR/YW UB7 .... 132 A9
Lilac Rd HOD EN11 .... 44 G1
Lilac St SHB W12 .... 136 D9
Lila PI SWLY BR8 .... 208 F4 ⬚
Lilah Ms HAYES BR2 .... 205 H10
Liliburne Gdns ELTH/MOT SE9 .... 184 B1
Liliburne Rd ELTH/MOT SE9 .... 184 B1
Lile Crs HNWL W7 .... 134 D7
Lilestone St CAMTN NW1 .... 9 N1
Lilford Rd BRXN/ST SW9 .... 159 J8
Lilian Barker CI LEE/GVPK SE12 .... 183 M1
Lilian CI STNW/STAM N16 .... 119 M9
Lilian Crs BRWN/HUT CM13 .... 107 P3
Lilian Gdns WFD IG8 .... 101 K9
Lilian Rd MTCR CR4 .... 202 D1
Lillechurch Rd BCTR RM8 .... 143 J5
Lilleshall Rd MRDN SM4 .... 201 N6
Lilley CI BRW CM14 .... 106 E5
   WAP E1W 13 P6
Lilley Dr KWD/TDW/WH KT20 .... 239 L8
Lilley La MLHL NW7 .... 96 F1
Lilley Wy SL SL1 .... 128 D10 ⬚
Lillian Av ACT W3 .... 155 M1
Lillian Rd BARN SW13 .... 140 D5
Lilliard CI HOD EN11 .... 26 C1
Lillie Rd BH/WHM TN16 .... 244 A4
Lillieshall Rd CLAP SW4 .... 158 C9
Lillie Yd FUL/PGN SW6 .... 14 E9
Lilliput Av NTHLT UB5 .... 133 M1
Lilliput Rd ROMW/RG RM7 .... 124 E5
Lily La HNHE ⬚ SE24 .... 36 E2
Lily Gdns ALP/SUD HA0 .... 135 H4
Lily PI HCIRC EC1N 12 B3
Lily Rd LEY E10 .... 120 F4
Lilyville Rd FUL/PGN SW6 .... 157 J7
Limbourne Av BCTR RM8 .... 124 A5
Limbrick Rd HARP AL5 .... 20 D1
Limburg Rd BTSEA SW11 .... 157 P10
Lime Av GVW DA11 .... 190 A3
   RBRW/HUT CM13 .... 107 L6
   UPMR RM14 .... 125 P9
   WDR/YW UB7 .... 132 A9
   WDSR SL4 .... 149 L6
   WDSR SL4 .... 170 A6
Limeburner La STP EC4M .... 12 C5 ⬚
Limebush CI ADL/WDHM KT15 .... 215 M5 ⬚
Lime CI BKHH IG9 .... 102 A3
   BMLY BR1 .... 206 B4
   CRAWE RH10 .... 285 J4
   CRAWW RH11 .... 87 H4
   GU GU1 .... 249 N6
   HYS/HAR UB3 .... 132 A5
   NWMAL KT3 .... 200 A3
   ORP BR6 .... 206 G9
   RSLP HA4 .... 113 A4
   SHB W12 .... 156 F1
   TRDG/WHET N20 .... 97 H2
   TWK TW1 .... 176 A3
   WARL CR6 .... 242 E5
   WOKS/MYFD GU22 .... 232 A6
Lime Crs SUN TW16 .... 197 K2
Limecroft CI HOR/WEW KT19 .... 220 A5
Limecroft Rd WOKN/KNAP GU21 .... 230 C3
Limedene CI PIN HA5 .... 93 H3
Lime Gv ADL/WDHM KT15 .... 215 K1
   BARK/HLT IG6 .... 103 J1
   BFN/LL DA15 .... 185 J2
   BRWN CM15 .... 87 H4
   GU GU1 .... 249 N6
   HYS/HAR UB3 .... 132 A5
   NWMAL KT3 .... 200 A3
   ORP BR6 .... 206 G9
   RSLP HA4 .... 113 A4
   SHB W12 .... 156 F1
   STHGT/OAK N14 .... 78 D10
   THDIT KT7 .... 198 F7 ⬚
Lime Kiln Dr CHARL SE7 .... 161 N5 ⬚
Lime Meadow Av SAND/SEL CR2 .... 223 P9
Lime Pit La RSEV TN14 .... 246 D3 ⬚
Limerick CI BAL SW12 .... 180 D3 ⬚
Limerick Gdns UPMR RM14 .... 126 A5
Lime Rd SWLY BR8 .... 208 E3
Limerston St WBPTN SW10 .... 14 G9 ⬚
Limes Av BARN SW13 .... 156 C8

PGE/AN SE20 .... 182 A10 ⬚
WAN E11 .... 121 N2
The Limes Av FBAR/BDGN N11 .... 174 B8
Limes CI ASHF TW15 .... 202 A9 ⬚
   CAR SM5 .... 8 F3
Limes Ct HOD EN11 .... 44 F3 ⬚
Limesdale Gdns EDGW HA8 .... 114 D5
Limes Field Rd BARN SW13 .... 156 D10
Limesford Rd PECK SE15 .... 160 C10
Limes Gdns WAND/EARL SW18 .... 179 K2
Limes Gv LEW SE13 .... 161 H10
Limes Rd BECK BR3 .... 184 F5
   CHES/WCR EN8 .... 62 C8
   CROY/NA CR0 .... 203 L6
   EGH TW20 .... 172 C8
   WEY KT13 .... 216 B1
Limes Rw ORP BR6 .... 226 E2
   STAL/RED AL3 .... 38 C3
Limes Wk EA W5 .... 155 J1 ⬚
   PECK SE15 .... 160 C10
Lime Street Pas BANK EC3V .... 13 J6 ⬚
Lime Tree Av ESH/CLAY KT10 .... 188 F4
   THDIT KT7 .... 198 D8
Limetree CI BRXS/STRHM SW2 .... 180 G4 ⬚
Lime Tree Ct GT/LBKH KT23 .... 235 P10
Lime Tree Gv CROY/NA CR0 .... 204 E10
Limetree PI MTCR CR4 .... 202 C1 ⬚
Lime Tree PI STAL AL1 .... 38 D7 ⬚
Lime Tree Rd HEST TW5 .... 154 A7
Lime Tree Wk AMS HP6 .... 69 L5 ⬚
   BUSH WD23 .... 94 D2
   ENC/FH EN2 .... 79 K4
   RKW/CH/CXG WD3 .... 89 H8
   SEV TN13 .... 265 J1
   VW GU25 .... 194 B4
   WWKM BR4 .... 225 L1
Lime Wk DEN/HRF UB9 .... 111 M10 ⬚
   HHS/BOV HP3 .... 36 A10
Limeway Ter DORK RH4 .... 254 F10
Limewood CI WALTH E17 .... 120 E2
   WEA W13 .... 134 G8 ⬚
   WOKN/KNAP GU21 .... 231 J6
Limewood Rd ERITH DA8 .... 164 D6
Limpsfield Av THHTH CR7 .... 202 G5
   WIM/MER SW19 .... 178 C5
Limpsfield Rd SAND/SEL CR2 .... 224 A10
   WARL CR6 .... 242 F5
Linacre Rd CRICK NW2 .... 136 E1
Lince La RDKG RH4 .... 272 C2
Linces Wy WGCE AL7 .... 23 L7
Linchfield Rd DTCH/LGLY SL3 .... 149 P7
Linchmere PI CRAWW RH11 .... 283 H4
Linchmere Rd LEE/GVPK SE12 .... 183 M3 ⬚
Linclon CI ERITH DA8 .... 164 C8
   STHGT/OAK N14 .... 98 D4
   WHTN TW2 .... 176 B5
   WIM/MER SW19 .... 178 C6
Lincoln CI CRAWE RH10 .... 283 P10
   EMPK RM11 .... 124 G3
   GFD/PVL UB6 .... 134 B3
   RYLN/HDSTN HA2 .... 113 N3
   WGCE AL7 .... 23 M4
Lincoln Ct BERK HP4 .... 33 N5
   BORE WD6 .... 76 A1 ⬚
Lincoln Crs EN EN1 .... 79 M8
Lincoln Dr OXHEY WD19 .... 93 K4
   RKW/CH/CXG WD3 .... 72 C8
   WOKS/MYFD GU22 .... 233 H1
Lincoln Gdns IL IG1 .... 122 B5
Lincoln Green Rd
   STMC/STPC BR5 .... 207 J5
Lincoln Hatch La SL SL1 .... 128 B6
Lincoln Ms KIL/WHAMP NW6 .... 2 C5
Lincoln Pk AMSS HP7 .... 69 K5
Lincoln Rd ALP/SUD HA0 .... 90 P9
   CFSP/GDCR SL9 .... 90 B3
   DORK RH4 .... 255 H10
   EFNCH N2 .... 117 P1
   EN EN1 .... 79 M8
   ERITH DA8 .... 164 C8
   FELT TW13 .... 175 H6
   MTCR CR4 .... 202 F5 ⬚
   NTHWD HA6 .... 112 G9
   NWMAL KT3 .... 199 P3 ⬚
   PLSTW E13 .... 141 N6
   RYLN/HDSTN HA2 .... 113 N3
   SCUP DA14 .... 185 L8
   SNWD SE25 .... 204 A3
   SWFD E18 .... 101 L9
   WPK KT4 .... 200 E8
Lincoln's CI STALE/WH AL4 .... 39 H1
Lincolns Fld EPP CM16 .... 65 J5
Lincoln's Inn Flds LINN WC2A 11 N5
Lincolns La BRW CM14 .... 86 B10
The Lincolns MLHL NW7 .... 96 C4
Lincoln St CHEL SW3 .... 16 A6 ⬚
   WAN E11 .... 121 K7
Lincoln Wy EN EN1 .... 79 M8
   RKW/CH/CXG WD3 .... 72 C8
   SL SL1 .... 129 H9
   SUN TW16 .... 196 B9
Lincombe Rd BMLY BR1 .... 183 L6
Lindal Crs STHGT/OAK N14 .... 78 F9
Lindale CI VW GU25 .... 193 L4
The Lindales TOTM N17 .... 99 P7 ⬚
Lindal Rd BROCKY SE4 .... 182 L1
Lindbergh WGCE AL7 .... 23 M5 ⬚
Lindbergh Rd WLGTN SM6 .... 222 F6
Linden Av COUL/CHIP CR5 .... 240 C2
   DART DA1 .... 187 K4
   EN EN1 .... 79 P9 ⬚
   HSLW TW3 .... 176 A1
   RSLP HA4 .... 113 H6
   THHTH CR7 .... 203 J4
   WBLY HA9 .... 135 L10
   WLSDN NW10 .... 136 C4
Linden Cha SEV TN13 .... 247 K7
Linden CI ADL/WDHM KT15 .... 215 K7
   CHESW EN7 .... 62 B2
   CRAWE RH10 .... 284 B10
   KWD/TDW/WH KT20 .... 238 G6
   ORP BR6 .... 227 L2
   RSLP HA4 .... 113 H6
   SHB W12 .... 156 F1
   STHGT/OAK N14 .... 78 D10
   THDIT KT7 .... 198 F7 ⬚
Linden Ct ECH TW20 .... 171 N9 ⬚
   HARP AL5 .... 20 A3
   LHD/OX KT22 .... 236 G7
Linden Crs GFD/PVL UB6 .... 134 C1
   KUT KT1 .... 199 L2
   STAL AL1 .... 39 H1
   WFD IG8 .... 101 N2
Linden Gld HHW HP1 .... 35 L2 ⬚
Linden Gv CROY/NA CR0 .... 204 C10
   GLDGN NW11 .... 117 H5
   HORL RH6 .... 280 D1
   MLHL NW7 .... 96 B7
Linden Gv NWMAL KT3 .... 200 B1
   PECK SE15 .... 160 A4
   PGE/AN SE20 .... 182 D4
   NFNCH/WDSP N12 .... 97 M5

WOT/HER KT12 .... 196 G9
   GSTN WD25 .... 55 H9
Linden Lea EFNCH N2 .... 117 M3
   GSTN WD25 .... 55 H9
Linden Leas WWKM BR4 .... 205 J7
Linden Ms BAY/PAD W2 .... 8 F7
Linden Pit Pth LHD/OX KT22 .... 236 G7
Linden PI EW KT17 .... 220 B8 ⬚
   MTCR CR4 .... 201 P4
Linden Ri BRW CM14 .... 107 J8
Linden Rd FBAR/BDGN N11 .... 98 A3
   GU GU1 .... 250 A10
   HPTN TW12 .... 197 P1
   LHD/OX KT22 .... 236 G7
   MUSWH N10 .... 118 C2
   SEVS/STOTM N15 .... 119 K2
   WEY KT13 .... 216 D5
Lindens CI EHSLY KT24 .... 253 M6
Linden Sq SEV TN13 .... 246 F8 ⬚
The Lindens CHSWK W4 .... 155 P7 ⬚
   CRAWE RH10 .... 284 B10
   HHS/BOV HP3 .... 35 J3
   LHD/OX 82 C9
Linden St ROMW/RG RM7 .... 124 D2
Linden Wy RPLY/SEND GU23 .... 251 J1
   SHPTN TW17 .... 196 D5
   STHGT/OAK N14 .... 78 D10
   WLGTN SM6 .... 222 D6
   WOKS/MYFD GU22 .... 232 C7
Lindfield Gdns GU GU1 .... 250 C9
   HAMP NW3 .... 117 M10
Lindfield Rd CROY/NA CR0 .... 203 N6
   EA W5 .... 135 H6
   HARH RM3 .... 105 M6
Lindhill CI PEND EN3 .... 80 C6 ⬚
Lindisfarne CI GVE DA12 .... 191 H5 ⬚
Lindisfarne Md HOM E9 .... 120 D9
Lindisfarne Rd BCTR RM8 .... 123 M8
   RYNPK SW20 .... 178 D10
Lindley CI HRW HA1 .... 35 H7
Lindley Rd GDST RH9 .... 260 B6
   LEY E10 .... 121 H7 ⬚
   WOT/HER KT12 .... 197 M10
Lindley St WCHPL E1 .... 140 B7
Lindlings HHW HP1 .... 35 H7
Lindo CI CSHM HP5 .... 50 G6
Lindore Rd BTSEA SW11 .... 158 A10
Lindores Rd CAR SM5 .... 201 M7
Lindo St PECK SE15 .... 160 B8 ⬚
Lind Rd SUT SM1 .... 221 M2
Lindrop St FUL/PGN SW6 .... 157 N8
Lindsay CI CHSGTN KT9 .... 219 K4 ⬚
   HOR/WEW KT19 .... 219 P9
   STWL/WRAY TW19 .... 173 N2
Lindsay Dr KTN/HRWW/W HA3 .... 115 K4
   SHPTN TW17 .... 196 E6
Lindsay PI CHESW EN7 .... 62 A6 ⬚
Lindsay Rd ADL/WDHM KT15 .... 215 K7
   HPTN TW12 .... 176 A7
   WPK KT4 .... 200 E8
Lindsay Sq PIM SW1V 17 K7
Lindsell St GNWCH SE10 .... 161 H7
Lindsey CI BMLY BR1 .... 206 A3
   BRW CM14 .... 106 F5
   MTCR CR4 .... 202 F4 ⬚
Lindsey Gdns EBED/NFELT TW14 .... 173 L3
   DEN/HRF UB9 .... 111 K8
Lindsey Rd BCTR RM8 .... 123 M8
   DEN/HRF UB9 .... 111 K8
Lindsey St EPP CM16 .... 65 K5
   STBT EC1A 12 D3
Lindsey Wy EMPK RM11 .... 125 K3 ⬚
Lind St DEPT SE8 .... 160 G8
Lindum PI STALW/RED AL3 .... 37 N8
Lindum Rd TEDD TW11 .... 177 H10
Lindway WNWD SE27 .... 181 J8
Linfield CI HDN NW4 .... 116 F1
   WOT/HER KT12 .... 217 J2 ⬚
Linfields AMSS HP7 .... 69 P6
Linford CI HLWW/ROY CM19 .... 46 F3
Linford End HLWW/ROY CM19 .... 46 F3
Linford Rd CDH/CHF RM16 .... 168 F4
   WALTH E17 .... 121 H1
Linford St VX/NE SW8 .... 157 P8
Lingards Rd LEW SE13 .... 161 H10 ⬚
Lingey CI BFN/LL DA15 .... 185 J5
Lingfield Av BRYLDS KT5 .... 199 K4
   RDART DA2 .... 188 A3
   UPMR RM14 .... 125 N8
Lingfield CI EN EN1 .... 79 M10
   NTHWD HA6 .... 92 F10
Lingfield Crs ELTH/MOT SE9 .... 162 G10
Lingfield Dr CRAWE RH10 .... 284 F6
Lingfield Gdns COUL/CHIP CR5 .... 241 J5
   ED N9 .... 100 A1
Lingfield Rd GVE DA12 .... 190 G5
   WIM/MER SW19 .... 179 H7
   WPK KT4 .... 200 F10
Lingfield Wy WAT WD17 .... 72 G4
Lingham St BRXN/ST SW9 .... 158 F9
Lingholm Wy BAR EN5 .... 76 C9
Lingmere CI CHIG IG7 .... 102 F3
Lingmoor Dr GSTN WD25 .... 55 M4
Ling Rd CAN/RD E16 .... 141 M7
   ERITH DA8 .... 164 D5
Lingwell Rd TOOT SW17 .... 179 N6
Lingwood Gdns ISLW TW7 .... 154 D6
Lingwood Rd CLPT E5 .... 119 P5
Linhope St CAMTN NW1 .... 10 A1
Linington Av CSHM HP5 .... 51 N6
Link CI HAT AL10 .... 40 E4
Link Dr HAT AL10 .... 40 E4
Linkfield E/WMO/HCT KT8 .... 197 P3
Link Fld HAYES BR2 .... 205 M6
Linkfield WGCE AL7 .... 23 H9
Linklea CI CDALE/KGS NW9 .... 96 D6
Link La WLGTN SM6 .... 222 F6
Link Rd ADL/WDHM KT15 .... 215 P1 ⬚
   DAGW RM9 .... 149 C5
   DTCH/LGLY SL3 .... 149 P6
   EBED/NFELT TW14 .... 174 C3
   FBAR/BDGN N11 .... 98 B5
   MTCR CR4 .... 202 B8
   WATN WD24 .... 57 J5
Links Av GPK RM2 .... 105 J10
   HERT/BAY SG13 .... 26 A4
   MRDN SM4 .... 201 K4
Links Brow LHD/OX KT22 .... 236 D9
Links CI ASHTD KT21 .... 237 H3
Linkscroft Av ASHF TW15 .... 174 C9
Links Dr BORE WD6 .... 75 L8 ⬚
   RAD WD7 .... 56 F9
   TRDG/WHET N20 .... 97 K2
Linkside CHIG IG7 .... 102 F6
   NFNCH/WDSP N12 .... 97 K7
   NWMAL KT3 .... 200 B9
Linkside CI ENC/FH EN2 .... 78 C7
Linkside Gdns ENC/FH EN2 .... 78 C7
Links Rd ASHF TW15 .... 174 C9
   ACT W3 .... 135 M8
Links Rd ACT W3 .... 173 P8 ⬚
   ASHTD KT21 .... 237 H3
   CRICK NW2 .... 116 D10
   EW KT17 .... 220 D6
   SHGR GU5 .... 268 B10
   TOOT SW17 .... 180 B9
   WFD IG8 .... 101 M6
   WWKM BR4 .... 205 H8
Links Side ENC/FH EN2 .... 78 C7
The Links CHES/WCR EN8 .... 62 C2 ⬚
   WALTH E17 .... 120 D2 ⬚
   WOT/HER KT12 .... 197 H9

Link St HOM E9 140 B1
Links Vw DART DA1 187 K4
　FNCH N3 97 J8
　STALW/RED AL3 38 A4
Links View Av RDKG RH5 255 N10
Links View Cl STAN HA7 94 F7
Links View Rd CROY/NA CR0 204 F10
　HPTN TW12 176 B8
Links Wy BECK BR3 204 F6
　EHSLY KT24 253 M4
　NTHWD HA6 92 D9
　RKW/CH/CXG WD3 72 D7
Linksway HDN NW4 96 C10
　NTHWD HA6 92 E9
Linkswood Rd SL SL1 128 B4
The Link ACT W3 135 M4
　ALP/SUD HA0 115 H6
　CRAWW RH11 283 N7
　NTHLT UB5 113 N10
　PEND EN3 80 D5
　PIN HA5 113 K4
　SLN SL2 129 N8
　TEDD TW11 176 A4
Link Wy DEN/HRF UB9 111 K4
　EMPK RM11 125 M6
　HAYES BR2 206 B7
　RCHPK/HAM TW10 176 D5
　STA TW18 173 L9
Linkway BCTR RM8 123 M9
　FSBYPK N4 119 K5
　GUW GU2 249 L10
　PIN HA5 93 L9
　RYNPK SW20 200 E3
　WOKS/MYFD GU22 232 F3
Linkway Rd BRW CM14 106 E4
The Linkway BAR EN5 77 K10
　BELMT SM2 221 M5
Linley Cl FLT RM18 169 N6
Linley Crs ROMW/RG RM7 124 C1
Linley Rd TOTM N17 99 H10
Linnell Cl GLDGN NW11 117 L4
Linnell Dr GLDGN NW11 117 L4
Linnell Rd CMBW SE5 159 M8
　REDH RH1 276 B1
　UED N18 99 P6
Linnet Cl BUSH WD23 94 B2
　ED N9 100 C2
　SAND/SEL CR2 224 C6
　THMD SE28 143 M9
Linnet Gv RGUE GU4 250 G8
Linnet Ms BAL SW12 180 B3
Linnet Rd ABLGY WD5 55 H7
Linnett Cl CHING E4 101 H5
Linnet Wy PUR RM19 166 A4
Linom Rd BRXS/STRHM SW2 158 F10
Linscott Rd CLPT E5 120 B9
Linsdell Rd BARK IG11 142 F3
Linsey Cl HHS/BOV HP3 36 B10
Linsey St BERM/RHTH SE16 19 P4
Linslade Cl HSLWW TW4 175 M1
　PIN HA5 113 J1
Linslade Rd ORP BR6 227 K3
Linstead St KIL/WHAMP NW6 2 —
Linstead Wy WAND/EARL SW18 179 H1
Linster Gv BORE WD6 75 P9
Linthorpe Av ALP/SUD HA0 135 H1
Linthorpe Rd EBAR EN4 77 P7
　STNW/STAM N16 119 M5
Linton Cl CAR SM5 202 A7
　CHARL SE7 161 P4
　WELL DA16 163 K7
Linton Ct ROM RM1 104 F4
Linton Gdns EHAM E6 142 B8
Linton Gld CROY/NA CR0 224 D6
Linton Gv WNWD SE27 181 J8
Linton Rd BARK IG11 142 F2
Linton's La EW KT17 220 B8
Linton St IS N1 6 F6
Lintott Ct STWL/WRAY TW19 173 N2
Linver Rd FUL/PGN SW6 157 J8
Linwood SBW CM21 29 P1
Linwood Cl CMBW SE5 159 N8
Linwood Crs EN EN1 79 P5
Linwood Rd HARP AL5 20 B4
Linzee Rd CEND/HSY/T N8 118 F2
Lion Av TWK TW1 176 E4
Lion Cl SHPTN TW17 195 P3
Lion Ct BORE WD6 75 P5
Lionel Gdns ELTH/MOT SE9 184 A1
Lionel Ms NKENS W10 8 A3
Lionel Rd ELTH/MOT SE9 184 A1
Lionel Rd North BTFD TW8 155 K2
Lionel Rd South BTFD TW8 155 L4
Lion Gate Gdns RCH/KEW TW9 155 L9
Lion Green Rd COUL/CHIP CR5 240 E1
Lion La CRAWE RH10 285 P9
Lion Park Av CHSGTN KT9 219 M1
Lion Rd BXLYHS DA6 163 F10
　CROY/NA CR0 203 K5
　ED N9 99 P3
　EHAM E6 142 C7
　WHTN TW2 176 E4
Lions Cl LEE/GVPK SE12 183 P6
Lion Wy BTFD TW8 155 J6
Lion Wharf Rd ISLW TW7 154 C9
Liphook Cl HCH RM12 124 C9
Liphook Crs FSTH SE23 182 B3
Liphook Rd OXHEY WD19 93 K3
Lippitts HI LOU IG10 81 K6
Lipsham Cl BNSTD SM7 221 P4
Lisbon Av WHTN TW2 176 B5
Lisburne Rd HAMP NW3 118 J2
Lisford St PECK SE15 159 N10
Lisgar Ter WKENS W14 14 C1
Liskeard Cl BKHTH/KID SE3 161 M7
Lisle Cl GVE DA12 191 L5
　TOOT SW17 180 C7
Lisle Pl GRAYS RM17 167 M2
Lisle St SOHO/SHAV W1D 11 K7
Lismore HHS/BOV HP3 36 D8
Lismore Cl ISLW TW7 154 F8
Lismore Crs CRAWW RH11 283 L10
Lismore Pk SLN SL2 129 L8
Lismore Rd SAND/SEL CR2 223 M3
　TOTM N17 119 L1
Lismore Wk IS N1 6 F1
Lissenden Gdns KTTN NW5 118 B9
Lissoms Rd COUL/CHIP CR5 240 B4
Lisson Gv CAMTN NW1 9 N2
Lisson St CAMTN NW1 9 N2
Lister Av HARH RM3 105 L10
Lister Cl WIM/MER SW19 201 P1
Lister Gdns UED N18 99 K6
Lister Ms HOLWY N7 118 C9
Lister Rd FLT RM18 168 D8
　WAN E11 121 K6
Liston Rd CLAP SW4 158 F10
　TOTM N17 99 D9
Listowel Cl BRXN/ST SW9 159 H6
Listowel Rd DAGE RM10 124 B8
Listria Pk STNW/STAM N16 119 M7
Litcham Sp SL SL1 129 J3
Litchfield Av MRDN SM4 201 J7
　SRTFD E15 141 K1
Litchfield Gdns WLSDN NW10 136 D1
Litchfield Rd SUT SM1 221 M3
Litchfield Wy GLDGN NW11 117 M3
　GUW GU2 267 L2
Lithgow's Rd HTHAIR TW6 152 F10
Lithos Rd HAMP NW3 3 H1
Little Acre BECK BR3 204 F4
　STALW/RED AL3 38 C3
Little Acres WARE SG12 26 C3
Little Albany St CAMTN NW1 10 J1
Little Argyll St CONDST W1S 10 G6

Little Aston Rd HARH RM3 105 N8
Little Belhus Cl SOCK/AV RM15 146 F6
Little Benty WDR/YW UB7 151 N4
Little Birch Cl ADL/WDHM KT15 215 N5
Little Birches BFN/LL DA15 185 H5
The Little Boltons WBPTN SW10 15 H7
Little Bookham La GT/LBKH KT23 253 K2
Little Bornes DUL SE21 181 M7
Little Borough BRKHM/BTCW RH3 273 M1
Little Brays HLWS CM18 47 K3
Little Bridge Rd BERK HP4 34 G3
Little Britain STBT EC1A 12 E4
Littlebrook Av SL SL1 128 D7
Littlebrook Cl CROY/NA CR0 204 C6
Littlebrook Gdns CHES/WCR EN8 62 C6
Littlebrook Manor Wy DART DA1 187 P1
Little Brook Rd HLWW/ROY CM19 45 P1
Little Buntings WDSR SL4 148 E9
Little Burrow WCCE AL7 22 G7
Littlebury Ct BRWN CM15 86 E3
Littlebury Rd CLAP SW4 158 F9
Little Bury St ED N9 99 M1
Little Bushey La BUSH WD23 73 P7
Little Catherells HHW HP1 35 J4
Little Cattins HLWW/ROY CM19 46 C5
Little Cedars NFNCH/WDSP N12 97 M5
Little Chester St KTBR SW1X 16 B2
Little Common La REDH RH1 259 J8
Littlecote Cl WIM/MER SW19 178 G3
Littlecote Pl PIN HA5 93 N9
Little Ct WWKM BR4 205 K9
Littlecourt Rd SEV TN13 247 H10
Little Crabtree CRAWW RH11 283 M6
Little Cranmore La EHSLY KT24 252 C4
Littlecroft ELTH/MOT SE9 162 D9
　MEO DA13 190 B10
Littlecroft Rd EGH TW20 172 C8
Littledale ABYW SE2 163 K5
Little Dell WCCW AL8 22 C3
Little Dimocks BAL SW12 180 C5
Little Dorrit Ct STHWK SE1 18 F1
Littledown Rd SL SL1 129 L10
Little Dragons LOU IG10 82 A3
Little Ealing La EA W5 155 H3
Little Edward St CAMTN NW1 4 F9
Little Elms HYS/HAR UB3 152 L6
Little Essex St TPL/STR WC2R 12 A7
Little Ferry Rd TWK TW1 176 G4
Littlefield Cl ARCH N19 118 D9
　KUT KT1 199 K2
　RGUW GU3 249 J8
Littlefield Rd EDGW HA8 95 P8
Littlefield Wy RGUW GU3 249 H6
Littleford La RGUE GU4 250 F8
Little Friday Rd CHING E4 101 K3
Little Ganett WGCE AL7 23 L7
Little Gaynes Gdns UPMR RM14 126 A3
Little Gaynes La UPMR RM14 125 N9
Little Gearies BARK/HLT IG6 122 C2
Little George St WSWP SW1P 17 L2
Little Gerpins La UPMR RM14 145 N3
Little Graylings ABLGY WD5 54 F9
Little Greencroft CSHM HP5 50 F3
Little Green La CHERT KT16 195 H10
　RKW/CH/CXG WD3 72 A7
Little Green St KTTN NW5 118 C9
Little Gregories La EPP CM16 82 C1
Little Gv BUSH WD23 74 A8
Littlegrove EBAR EN4 77 P10
Little Grove Fld HLWW/ROY CM19 46 F1
Little Hardings WGCE AL7 23 M4
Little Hayes KGLGY WD4 54 B5
Little Heath CHARL SE7 162 B5
　CHDH RM6 123 L2
Little Heath La BERK HP4 34 F7
Littleheath La COB KT11 217 P10
Little Heath Rd BXLYHN DA7 164 A7
　CHOB/PIR GU24 213 K5
Littleheath Rd SAND/SEL CR2 224 A5
Little Hide GU GU1 250 E8
Little HI RKW/CH/CXG WD3 70 F10
Little Hivings CSHM HP5 50 F3
Little How Cft ABLGY WD5 54 D7
Little Ilford La MNPK E12 122 C9
Littlejohn Crs HNW HA1 114 F2
Littlejohn Rd HNWL W7 134 E8
　STMC/STPC BR5 207 K6
Little Julians HI SEV TN13 265 H3
Little Kiln RGODL GU7 267 K9
Little Lake WGCE AL7 23 L8
Little La HARP AL5 20 B5
Little Laver Rd CHONG CM5 49 N6
　HLWE CM17 31 M9
Little Ley WGCE AL7 23 H8
Little London SHGR GU5 269 P7
Little Marlborough St REGST W1B 10 G6
Little Martins BUSH WD23 74 A9
Littlemead ESH/CLAY KT10 218 C1
Little Md HAT AL10 40 E1
　WOKN/KNAP GU21 215 H8
Littlemede ELTH/MOT SE9 184 D6
Little Mimms HHNE HP2 35 N5
Littlemoor Rd IL IG1 122 C8
Littlemore Rd ABYW SE2 163 K1
Little Moreton Cl BF/WBF KT14 215 L8
Little Moss La PIN HA5 93 M10
Little Mundells WGCE AL7 23 J4
Little Newport St SOHO/SHAV W1D 11 K7
Little New St FLST/FETLN EC4A 12 B5
Little Orch ADL/WDHM KT15 215 K7
　WOKN/KNAP GU21 214 D10
Little Orchard Cl ABLGY WD5 54 D7
　PIN HA5 93 M10
Little Orchards EPSOM KT18 220 B10
Little Orchard Wy RGUE GU4 268 B8
Little Pk HHS/BOV HP3 52 D4
Little Park Dr FELT TW13 175 L5
Little Park Gdns ENC/FH EN2 79 L1
Little Piper's Cl CHESW EN7 61 J3
Little Platt GUW GU2 249 J9
Little Pluckett's Wy BKHH IG9 102 A2
Little Portland St REGST W1B 10 F5
Littleport Sp SL SL1 129 K8
Little Potters BUSH WD23 94 C1
Little Queens Rd TEDD TW11 176 D9
Little Queen St DART DA1 187 N3
Little Redlands BMLY BR1 206 B2
Little Reeves Av AMSS HP7 69 L5
Little Rdg WGCE AL7 23 K5
Little Rivers WCCE AL7 23 K4
Little Roke Av PUR/KEN CR8 223 J10
Little Roke Rd PUR/KEN CR8 223 K10
Little Rownings FSTH SE23 182 A5
Littlers Cl WIM/MER SW19 201 N1
Little Russell St NOXST/BSQ WC1A 11 L4
Little St James's St WHALL SW1A 10 G1
Little St Leonards MORT/ESHN SW14 155 P9
Little Shardeloes AMSS HP7 68 F6
Little Smith St WEST SW1P 17 K3
Little Spring CSHM HP5 50 G4
Littlestone Cl BECK BR3 182 F10
Little Strd CDALE/KGS NW9 96 D6
Little Stream Cl NTHWD HA6 92 F6
Little Sutton La DTCH/LGLY SL3 150 E4
Little Thistle WGCE AL7 23 M7
Little Thrift STMC/STPC BR5 206 F4

Little Titchfield St GTPST W1W 10 G4
Littleton Av CHING E4 101 L2
Littleton La REIG RH2 275 H2
　RGUW GU3 267 N6
　STA TW18 195 P5
Littleton Rd ASHF TW15 174 D10
　HRW HA1 114 F7
Littleton St WAND/EARL SW18 179 M5
Little Trinity La BCVPX EC4V 12 F7
Little Turners Ct RGODL GU7 267 K10
Little Wade WGCE AL7 23 J8
Little Warley Hall La RBRW/HUT CM13 127 K3
Little Warren Cl RGUE GU4 268 E3
Littlewick Rd WOKN/KNAP GU21 213 P10
Little Widbury WARE SG12 26 E2
Little Widbury La WARE SG12 26 E2
Little Windmill HI KGLGY WD4 53 H8
Littlewood LEW SE13 183 H1
Little Wd SEV TN13 247 K8
Little Wood Cl STMC/STPC BR5 207 K1
Littlewood Cl WEA W13 154 C2
Little Woodcote La CAR SM5 222 C8
Little Woodlands WDSR SL4 148 E9
Littleworth Av ESH/CLAY KT10 218 C2
Littleworth Common Rd ESH/CLAY KT10 198 C10
Littleworth La ESH/CLAY KT10 218 C1
Littleworth Pl ESH/CLAY KT10 218 C1
Littleworth Rd ESH/CLAY KT10 218 C2
Little Youngs WGCW AL8 22 F5
Litttt Halliards WOT/HER KT12 197 H6
Livermere Rd HACK E8 7 L5
Liverpool Gv WALW SE17 18 G8
Liverpool Rd CAN/RD E16 141 K7
　EA W5 155 J1
　HOLWY N7 6 A1
　KUTN/CMB KT2 177 M10
　LEY E10 121 H4
　SL SL1 128 C8
　STAL AL1 38 D6
　THHTH CR7 203 K3
　WATW WD18 73 J3
Liverpool St LVPST EC2M 13 J4
Livesey Cl KUT KT1 199 L3
Livesey Pl PECK SE15 19 P9
Livingstone Gdns GVE DA12 190 G8
Livingstone Rd BTSEA SW11 157 N9
　CRAWW RH10 285 P5
　CTHM CR3 241 L8
　GVE DA12 190 G8
　HSLW TW3 154 B10
　LEY E10 120 G4
　PLMGR N13 98 F7
　SRTFD E15 141 H3
　STHL UB1 133 L3
　THHTH CR7 203 L2
Livonia St SOHO/CST W1F 11 H6
Lizard St FSBYE EC1V 6 F10
Lizban St BKHTH/KID SE3 161 N6
Llanbury Cl CFSP/GDCR SL9 90 B8
Llanelly Rd CRICK NW2 117 J7
Llanover Rd WBLY HA9 115 J8
　WOOL/PLUM SE18 162 D6
Llanthony Rd MRDN SM4 201 N6
Llanvanor Rd CRICK NW2 117 J7
Llewellyn St BERM/RHTH SE16 19 P2
Lloyd Av COUL/CHIP CR5 222 B10
　STRHM/NOR SW16 202 F1
Lloyd Baker St FSBYW WC1X 5 L3
Lloyd Ct PIN HA5 113 L3
Lloyd Park Av CROY/NA CR0 223 N1
Lloyd Rd DAGW RM9 144 A1
　EHAM E6 142 C3
　WALTH E17 120 C2
　WPK KT4 200 F10
Lloyd's Av TWRH EC3N 13 K6
Lloyd's Pl BKHTH/KID SE3 161 K8
Lloyd Sq FSBYW WC1X 6 A9
Lloyd's Rw CLKNW EC1R 6 C9
Lloyd St FSBYW WC1X 6 A9
Lloyds Wy BECK BR3 204 D5
Lloyd Thomas Ct WDGN N22 98 C3
Lloyd Vls BROCKY SE4 160 F8
Lobelia Rd CHOB/PIR GU24 230 F1
Local Board Rd WAT WD17 73 K9
Locarno Rd ACT W3 135 P10
　GFD/PVL UB6 134 B6
Lochaber Rd LEW SE13 161 K10
Lochaline St HMSMTH W6 156 F5
Lochan Cl YEAD UB4 133 M6
Lochinvar Cl SL SL1 148 C3
Lochinvar St BAL SW12 180 C3
Lochmere Cl ERITH DA8 164 C5
Lochnagar St POP/IOD E14 141 H7
Lock Cha LEW SE13 161 K9
Lock Cl RAIN RM13 144 G1
Locke Gdns DTCH/LGLY SL3 149 P1
Locke Cl RAIN RM13 144 G1
Locke King Rd WEY KT13 216 B4
Locke-king Cl WEY KT13 216 B4
Lockers Park La HHW HP1 35 L8
Lockesley Dr STMC/STPC BR5 207 J6
Locket Rd KTN/HRWW/W HA3 94 E10
Lockets Cl WDSR SL4 148 B2
Lockfield Av PEND EN3 80 D6
Lockfield Dr WOKN/KNAP GU21 231 M4
Lockgate Cl HOM E9 120 E10
Lockhart Cl HOLWY N7 5 N1
　PEND EN3 80 D6
Lockhart St BOW E3 140 E6
Lockhurst St CLPT E5 120 C9
Lockington Rd VX/NE SW8 158 C7
Lock La WOKS/MYFD GU22 233 L2
Lockley Crs HAT AL10 40 E2
Lockmead Rd LEW SE13 161 H9
　SEVS/STOTM N15 119 P4
Lock Pth WDSR SL4 148 C5
Lock Rd GU GU1 250 A6
　RCHPK/HAM TW10 177 H7
Locksley Dr WOKN/KNAP GU21 231 L4
Locksley St POP/IOD E14 140 L7
Locksmeade Rd RCHPK/HAM TW10 176 D7
Lockswood CHOB/PIR GU24 230 C6
Lock Wk SYD SE26 182 C7
Lockwood Pth WOKN/KNAP GU21 214 G9
Lockwood Wy CHSGTN KT9 219 N2
　WALTH E17 100 C10
Lockyer Rd PUR RM19 166 B4
Lockyer St STHWK SE1 19 H2
Loddiges Rd HOM E9 120 G2
Loddon Sp SL SL1 129 K9
Loder Cl WOKN/KNAP GU21 214 G9
Loder St PECK SE15 160 B7
Lodge Av BCTR RM8 123 L10
　BORE WD6 75 P4
　CROY/NA CR0 202 G10
　DAGW RM9 143 L3
　DART DA1 187 K2
　GPK RM2 125 H3
　HRW HA1 96 A10
　KTN/HRWW/W HA3 115 H2
Lodge Cl CHIC IG7 103 L3
　COB KT11 235 N2
　CRAWW RH11 283 M7
　EDGW HA8 95 L7
　EGH TW20 172 A8

　EW KT17 220 F6
　HERT/WAS SG14 25 K3
　ISLW TW7 154 D7
　LHD/OX KT22 236 C5
　MTCM CR4 202 B8
　ORP BR6 207 L8
　RDKG RH5 273 H6
　SL SL1 149 H1
　UED N18 99 K6
　UX/CGN UB8 131 M6
Lodge Ct GVE DA12 191 P9
Lodge Crs CHES/WCR EN8 62 D10
　ORP BR6 207 L8
Lodge Dr BRKMPK AL9 40 G1
　PLMGR N13 99 H5
　RKW/CH/CXG WD3 71 M8
Lodge End RAD WD7 56 C10
　RKW/CH/CXG WD3 72 E8
Lodge Fld WGCE AL7 23 H7
Lodge Gdns BECK BR3 204 E5
Lodge Hall HLWS CM18 47 H5
Lodge HI PUR/KEN CR8 241 H1
　WELL DA16 163 L6
Lodgehill Park Cl RYLN/HDSTN HA2 114 A7
Lodge La BH/WHM TN16 262 F3
　BXLY DA5 185 N2
　CDH/CHF RM16 167 N1
　CROY/NA CR0 224 G4
　CRW RM5 104 B2
　CSTG HP8 70 C9
　GRAYS RM17 167 P2
　NFNCH/WDSP N12 97 M6
　RDKG RH5 273 H6
　REDH RH1 275 P8
　WAB EN9 81 J1
Lodge Pl SUT SM1 221 L2
Lodge Rd BMLY BR1 183 P10
　CROY/NA CR0 203 J6
　EPP CM16 64 D10
　HDN NW4 116 F2
　LHD/OX KT22 236 B8
　RKW/CH/CXG WD3 72 E8
　STJWD NW8 3 M10
　SUT SM1 221 L2
　WLGTN SM6 222 C2
Lodge Vls WFD IG8 101 L8
Lodge Wy ASHF TW15 173 P5
　SHPTN TW17 196 D2
　WDSR SL4 148 D9
Lodore Gdns CDALE/KGS NW9 116 B3
Lodore Gn HGDN/ICK UB10 111 P8
Lodore St POP/IOD E14 141 M8
Loewen Rd CDH/CHF RM16 168 D2
Lofthouse Pl CHSGTN KT9 219 H3
Loftie St BERM/RHTH SE16 19 P7
Lofting Rd IS N1 6 A4
Loftus Rd SHB W12 136 E10
Logan Cl HSLWW TW4 153 N9
　PEND EN3 80 C5
Logan Ms KENS W8 14 E5
Logan Pl KENS W8 14 E5
Logan Rd ED N9 100 A3
　WBLY HA9 115 K7
Logmore La DORK RH4 272 D7
Logs Hill CHST BR7 184 B10
Logs Hill Cl CHST BR7 206 B1
Lois Dr SHPTN TW17 196 C5
Lolesworth Cl WCHPL E1 13 M4
Lollards Cl AMS HP6 69 H3
Lollard St LBTH SE11 17 P5
Lollesworth La EHSLY KT24 252 D2
Loman Pth SOCK/AV RM15 146 E8
Loman St STHWK SE1 18 D1
Lomas Cl CROY/NA CR0 225 P4
Lomas St WCHPL E1 13 P3
Lombard Av GDMY/SEVK IG3 123 H6
　PEND EN3 80 B5
The Lombards EMPK RM11 125 N5
Lombard Rd BTSEA SW11 157 N9
　FBAR/BDGN N11 98 C2
　WIM/MER SW19 201 L2
Lombard St BANK EC3V 13 H6
Lombard Wall CHARL SE7 161 N7
Lombardy Cl WOKN/KNAP GU21 231 L3
Lombardy Dr BERK HP4 34 A6
Lombardy Pl BAY/PAD W2 9 H8
　WOKN/KNAP GU21 231 L3
Lomond Cl ALP/SUD HA0 135 L2
　SEVS/STOTM N15 119 M2
Lomond Gv CMBW SE5 159 L6
Lomond Gv CMBW HP2 35 N2
Loncin Mead Av ADL/WDHM KT15 215 M5
Loncroft Rd CMBW SE5 19 K9
Londesborough Rd STNW/STAM N16 119 M9
London Br CANST EC4R 13 H8
London Fds HACK E8 140 A2
London Fields East Side HACK E8 140 A2
London Fields West Side HACK E8 7 P3
London La BMLY BR1 183 L10
　HACK E8 140 A2
　SHGR GU5 270 B5
London Loop BNSTD SM7 221 J9
　BORE WD6 75 N10
　COUL/CHIP CR5 240 C5
　CROY/NA CR0 204 C10
　ENC/FH EN2 78 F3
　MLHL NW7 95 P1
　PUR/KEN CR8 241 M1
　SAND/SEL CR2 241 P1
London Ms BAY/PAD W2 9 M6
London Rd ABR/ST RM4 83 K7
　ASC SL5 192 B3
　BARK IG11 142 E2
　BEAC HP9 88 D1
　BERK HP4 34 E2
　BFOR GU20 192 B10
　BGR/WK TN15 265 N9
　BH/WHM TN16 244 P8
　BMLY BR1 183 L10
　BRW CM14 106 F4
　BUSH WD23 73 M10
　CHDH RM6 123 L3
　CHEAM SM3 201 —
　CHONG CM5 67 L10
　CRAWW RH11 283 J10
　CROY/NA CR0 203 J6
　CSTG HP8 89 P3
　CTHM CR3 241 L9
　DART DA1 186 F1
　DORK RH4 272 E3
　DTCH/LGLY SL3 149 P2
　EGH TW20 171 P10
　ENC/FH EN2 79 J1
　EPP CM16 47 L8
　EYN DA4 209 L4
　FSTH SE23 182 B4
　GRAYS RM17 167 K5
　GRH DA9 188 D2
　GU GU1 250 E7
　HERT/BAY SG13 25 P7
　HHS/BOV HP3 35 N9
　HHW HP1 34 G8
　HLWE CM17 29 M8
　HORL RH6 280 A6
　ISLW TW7 154 D8
　KUT KT1 199 K2
　MTCM CR4 202 A2
　PLSTW E13 141 M4

　RAD WD7 57 L9
　RDART DA2 188 B3
　REDH RH1 258 B9
　REIG RH2 257 K10
　RKW/CH/CXG WD3 91 D7
　ROMW/RG RM7 124 D4
　RPLY/SEND GU23 251 K2
　RSEV TN14 228 A3
　RYLN/HDSTN HA2 114 D7
　SBW CM21 29 P7
　SEV TN13 246 F6
　SOCK/AV RM15 165 P—
　STA TW18 173 J7
　STAL AL1 38 F9
　STHWK SE1 18 C3
　STRHM/NOR SW16 202 G2
　STWL/WRAY TW19 173 N5
　SWCM DA10 189 K1
　SWLY BR8 208 F3
　THHTH CR7 203 H6
　TIL RM18 168 E8
　TWK TW1 176 F3
　WARE SG12 26 B4
　WBLY HA9 115 K10
　WTHK RM20 167 J5
London Rd East AMSS HP7 69 M4
　CSTG HP8 69 L8
London Rd North COUL/CHIP CR5 240 C10
　REDH RH1 240 C10
London Road Purfleet PUR RM19 166 A3
London Rd South REDH RH1 258 C6
London Rd West AMSS HP7 69 M4
London Road West Thurrock WTHK RM20 166 G5
Londons Cl UPMR RM14 126 B10
London Stile CHSWK W4 155 M4
London St BAY/PAD W2 9 L6
　CHERT KT16 195 K7
　MON EC3R 13 K7
London Wall BARB EC2Y 12 F4
　OBST EC2N 13 H5
Loneacre BFOR GU20 212 D3
Lone Oak HORL RH6 281 H6
Lonesome La REIG RH2 275 M4
Long Acre COVGDN WC2E 11 L6
　CRAWE RH10 285 P5
　HLWE CM17 29 L7
　STMC/STPC BR5 207 N9
Longacre Pl CAR SM5 222 D3
Longacre Rd WALTH E17 101 J3
Longaford Wy RBRW/HUT CM13 107 P2
Long Arrotts HHW HP1 35 L4
Long Av CHOB/PIR GU24 230 F7
Long Banks HLWS CM18 46 G4
Long Barn Cl GSTN WD25 55 H8
Long Barn Rd RSEV TN14 265 H3
Longbeach Rd BTSEA SW11 158 A9
Longboat Rw STHL UB1 133 N6
Longbourne Wy CHERT KT16 195 J6
Longboyds COB KT11 235 J1
Longbridge Rd BARK IG11 142 G1
　BCTR RM8 123 K9
　HORL RH6 280 A6
Longbridge Wk HORL RH6 280 A6
Longbridge Wy LEW SE13 183 H1
　UX/CGN UB8 131 L4
Long Buftlers HARP AL5 20 D1
Longbury Cl STMC/STPC BR5 207 L2
Longbury Dr STMC/STPC BR5 207 L3
Longchamp Cl HORL RH6 280 D4
Long Chaulden HHW HP1 35 H3
Longcliffe Pth OXHEY WD19 93 H4
Long Cl SLN SL2 128 C2
Long Copse Cl GT/LBKH KT23 236 A9
Long Cft PUR RM19 165 P3
Longcroft ELTH/MOT SE9 184 D6
Longcroft Av BNSTD SM7 221 H10
Long Croft Dr CHES/WCR EN8 62 E10
Longcrofte Rd EDGW HA8 95 J8
Longcroft Gdns WGCW AL8 22 G6
Longcroft Gn WGCW AL8 22 G6
Longcroft La HHS/BOV HP3 52 F4
　WGCW AL8 22 G6
Longcroft Ri LOU IG10 82 E9
Long Croft Rd RKW/CH/CXG WD3 90 C6
Longcross Rd CHERT KT16 193 N10
Long Deacon Rd CHING E4 101 K2
Longdean Pk HHS/BOV HP3 36 B10
Longdon Wd HAYES BR2 226 B3
Longdown La North EW KT17 220 D9
Longdown La South EW KT17 238 D1
Longdown Rd CAT SE6 182 F7
　EW KT17 220 D10
　RGUE GU4 268 C3
Long Dr ACT W3 136 B8
　GFD/PVL UB6 134 A3
　RSLP HA4 113 K9
　SL SL1 128 B5
Long Dyke GU GU1 250 E8
Long Elms KTN/HRWW/W HA3 94 B9
Long Elms ABLGY WD5 54 E9
Long Elms Cl ABLGY WD5 54 E9
Long Fallow LCOL/BKTW AL2 58 B3
Longfellow Dr RBRW/HUT CM13 107 P1
Longfellow Rd BOW E3 140 D3
　WALTH E17 120 E4
　WPK KT4 —
Longfellow Wy STHWK SE1 19 M6
Longfield BMLY BR1 —
Long Fld CDALE/KGS NW9 96 B8
Longfield HHS/BOV HP3 36 C8
　HLWS CM18 47 K3
　LOU IG10 81 P9
　SLN SL2 109 J8
Longfield Av EA W5 135 H9
　EMPK RM11 124 G5
　HART —
　MLHL NW7 96 D8
　PEND EN3 80 B3
　WALTH E17 119 M8
　WBLY HA9 115 K6
　WLGTN SM6 202 B8
Longfield Crs KWD/TDW/WH KT20 238 F6
　SYD SE26 182 B6
Longfield Dr AMS HP6 68 G4
　MORT/ESHN SW14 155 N1
　WIM/MER SW19 201 P1
Longfield La CHESW EN7 61 N1
Longfield Rd CSHM HP5 50 A5
　DORK RH4 272 E3
　EA W5 135 H8
　HARP AL5 20 B4
Long Flds CHONG CM5 67 P6
Longford Av EBED/NFELT TW14 174 F2
　STHL UB1 133 P4
　STWL/WRAY TW19 173 P4
Longford Cl HPTN TW12 175 P5
　YEAD UB4 133 L9
Longford Ct HOR/WEW KT19 219 P1
Longford Gdns SUT SM1 201 N10
　YEAD UB4 133 L9
Longford St CAMTN NW1 10 D7
Longford Wy STWL/WRAY TW19 173 P4
Long Furlong Dr SLN SL2 128 C6
Long Gn CHIG IG7 103 M7
Long Gv GU GU3 —
Long Gv Rd RGODL GU7 267 K9
Long Gro BEAC HP9 88 B7
　HARH RM3 105 M10
Long Grove Rd HOR/WEW KT19 219 N10

Longhayes Av CHDH RM6...... 123 N1
Longheath Dr GT/LBKH KT23 ....235 M10
Longlands Gdns CROY/NA CRO... 204 B5
Longhedge St BTSEA SW11 .....158 B8
Long CI CTHM CR3..............242 D7
Longhill Rd CAT SE6...........183 J5
Longhook Gdns NTHLT UB5......133 H4
Longhope CI PECK SE15.........19 K10
Longhouse Rd CDH/CHF RM16....168 E2
Longhurst Rd CROY/NA CRO.....204 B6
 EHSLY KT24...................252 F5
 LEW SE13.....................183 J1
Long John HHS/BOV HP3.........36 A8
Longland Dr TRDG/WHET N20....97 J3
Longlands HHNE HP2............52 C7
Longlands Av COUL/CHIP CR5...222 C10
Longlands CI CHES/WCR EN8....62 C8
Longlands Park Crs BFN/LL DA15..185 H6
Longlands Rd BFN/LL DA15.....185 H6
 WGCE AL7.....................23 J7
Long La BXLYHN DA7............164 A8
 CDH/CHF RM16.................167 N1
 CROY/NA CRO..................204 B6
 EFNCH N2.....................117 M1
 FNCH N3......................97 M10
 HGDN/ICK UB10................112 C10
 HHS/BOV HP3..................52 C7
 RKW/CH/CXG WD3...............70 F10
 STBT EC1A....................12 D4
 STHWK SE1....................19 H2
 STWL/WRAY TW19...............174 A3
Longleat Rd EN EN1............79 M9
Longleat Wy EBED/NFELT TW14..174 D3
Longleigh La ABYW SE2.........163 N5
Long Ley HLW CM20.............47 J1
 WGCE AL7.....................23 M5
Longley Av ALP/SUD HA0........135 L5
Longley CI CROY/NA CRO........203 J7
 HRW HA1......................114 C3
 TOOT SW17....................179 P9
Long Leys CHING E4............100 G7
Longley St STHWK SE1..........19 N6
Longley Wy CRICK NW2..........116 F8
Long Lodge Dr WOT/HER KT12....197 K10
Long Mark Rd CAN/RD E16......142 A8
Longmarsh Vw EYN DA4..........210 A1
Long Md CDALE/KGS NW9.........96 C9
Longmead CHST BR7.............206 C2
 GU GU1.......................250 F10
 HAT AL10.....................40 E1
 WDSR SL4.....................148 D7
Longmead Dr SCUP DA14.........185 N5
Longmead La SL SL1............128 C2
Long Meadow CSHM HP5..........51 H8
Longmeadow GT/LBKH KT23......253 N12
Long Meadow RBRW/HUT CM13....107 P3
Longmeadow SEV TN13...........246 E7
Long Meadow CI BECK BR3......205 H7
Longmeadow Rd BFN/LL DA15....185 H4
 HOR/WEW KT19.................220 B6
Longmere Gdns
 KWD/TDW/WH KT20.............238 F5
Longmere Rd CRAWW RH11.......283 J7
Long Mimms HHNE HP2...........35 P5
Long Moor CHES/WCR EN8.......62 G2
Longmoore Av BAR EN5..........77 M10
Longmoore St PIM SW1V.........16 G6
Longmore Av BAR EN5...........77 M10
Longmore Gdns WGCE AL7........23 J5
Longmore Rd RKW/CH/CXG WD3...91 J5
Longmore Gdns WGCE AL7........23 J5
Longmore Rd WOT/HER KT12.....217 M1
Longnor Rd WCHPL E1...........140 C5
Long Pk AMS HP6...............69 H2
Long Pk CI AMS HP6............69 H2
Long Park Wy AMS HP6..........69 H2
Long Pond Rd BKHTH/KID SE3...161 K1
Longport CI BARK/HLT IG6.....103 K7
Long Reach EHSLY KT24.........234 C10
Long Reach Rd BARK IG11......143
Longreach Rd ERITH DA8.......165 J6
Long Readings La SLN SL2.....128 G5
Longridge Gv
 WOKS/MYFD GU22.............215 J10
Longridge Rd CRAWW RH11......228 F5
Longridge La STNW/STAM N16...119 J4
Longridge La GFD/PVL UB6.....134 A9
Longridge Rd ECT SW5.........14 C6
Long Ridings Av RBRW/HUT CM13..87 N9
Long Rd CLAP SW4..............158 D10
Longs CI WOKS/MYFD GU22......233 J1
Longsdon Wy CTHM CR3.........241 P10
Long Shaw LHD/OX KT22.........236 F5
Longshaw Rd CHING E4..........101 J4
Longshore DEPT SE8............160 E3
Longside CI EGH TW20..........194 F1
Long Spring STALW/RED AL4.....38 C2
Longspring WATN WD24.........73 J3
Longstaff Crs WAND/EARL SW18..179 J4
Longstaff Rd WAND/EARL SW18..179 K2
Longstone Av WLSDN NW10......138 C2
Longstone Rd IVER SLO.........150 C8
 TOOT SW17...................180 C8
Long St BETH E2...............7 L8
 WAB EN9.....................64 B6
Longthornton Rd
 STRHM/NOR SW16.............202 D2
Longton Av SYD SE26...........181 P7
Longton Gv SYD SE26...........182 A7
Longtown Rd HARH RM3..........105 K6
Long Vw BERK HP4..............33 M3
Longview Wy CRW RM5...........104 E9
Longville Rd LBTH SE11.........18 C5
Long Wk STCTC SE1.............70 B7
 KWD/TDW/WH KT20.............238 G5
 NWMAL KT3...................199 P3
 STHWK SE1...................19 K3
Longwalk Rd STKPK UB11.......132 C10
The Long Wk WDSR SL4..........171 J4
Long Wd HLWS CM18.............46 G6
Longwood CI UPMR RM14........126 B10
Long Wood Dr BECK BR3.........39 L7
Longwood Ct PUT/ROE SW15.....178 D2
Longwood Dr PUT/ROE SW15.....178 D2
Longwood Gdns CLAY IG5.......122 C2
Longwood La AMSS HP7..........69 J5
Longwood Rd HERT/WAS SG14....24 C1
 PUR/KEN CR8.................241 L2
Longwood Vw CRAWE RH10.......284 B10
Longworth CI THMD SE28.......143 N8
Long Yd BMSBY WC1N............11 L1
The Loning CDALE/KGS NW9.....116 C2
 PEND EN3....................80 B4
Lonsdale HHNE HP2.............35 P3
Lonsdale Av EHAM E6..........142 A6
 ROMW/RG RM7.................124 A4
 WBLY HA9....................115 K10
Lonsdale CI EHAM E6..........142 B6
 LEE/GVPK SE12...............184 A6
 UX/CGN UB8..................132 D8
Lonsdale Crs GNTH/NBYPK IG2..122 C7
 RDART DA2...................188 B5
Lonsdale Dr ENC/FH EN2.......78 E2
 STHGT/OAK N14...............78 F9
Lonsdale Dr North ENC/FH EN2..78 E2
Lonsdale Gdns
 STRHM/NOR SW16.............202 C4
Lonsdale Ms RCH/KEW TW9......155 M7
Lonsdale PI IS N1.............6 B4
Lonsdale Rd BARN SW13........156 C6
 BXLYHN DA7..................164 A8
 CHSWK W4....................156 C3
 DORK RH4....................272 C4
 KIL/WHAMP NW6...............2 D1
 NTGHL W11...................8 C3
 NWDGN UB2...................153 L2

SNWD SE25.....................204 A4
WAN E11.......................121 L5
WEY KT13......................216 B4
Lonsdale Sq IS N1.............6 B4
Loobert Rd SEVS/STOTM N15....119 M1
Looe Gdns BARK/HLT IG6.......122 F1
Loom La RAD WD7...............74 E3
Loom PI RAD WD7...............74 E2
Loop Rd CHST BR7.............184 F9
 EPSOM KT18..................237 P2
 WAB EN9.....................62 G8
 WOKS/MYFD GU22..............232 G6
Lopen Rd UED N18.............99 M5
Loppets Dr CRAWE RH10........284 B9
Loraine CI PEND EN3..........80 B9
Loraine Gdns ASHTD KT21......237 K3
Loraine Rd CHSWK W4..........155 N5
 HOLWY N7....................118 C9
Lord Av CLAY IG5.............122 C2
Lord Chancellor Wk
 KUTN/CMB KT2...............199 P1
Lord Chatham's Ride RSEV TN14..245 M1
Lord Hills Rd BAY/PAD W2.....9 H3
Lord Knyvett CI
 STWL/WRAY TW19.............173 N2
Lord Knyvetts Ct
 STWL/WRAY TW19.............173 P2
Lord Mayors Dr SLN SL2.......128 C8
Lord Napier PI HMSMTH W6.....156 D4
Lord North St WEST SW1P......17 L4
Lord Roberts Ter
 WOOL/PLUM SE18.............162 D4
Lordsbury Fld WLGTN SM6......222 D6
Lords CI DUL SE21............181 K5
 FELT TW13..................175 M5
 RAD WD7....................57 K8
Lordsgrove CI
 KWD/TDW/WH KT20............238 E6
Lordship Gv STNW/STAM N16....119 L7
Lordship La DUL SE21.........181 N2
 EDUL SE22..................181 K2
 TOTM N17...................99 K9
 WDGN N22...................99 J3
Lordship Pk STNW/STAM N16....119 L7
Lordship Park Ms
 STNW/STAM N16..............119 K7
Lordship PI CHEL SW3.........15 N10
Lordship Rd CHESW SW3........62 A6
 NTHLT UB5..................133 M2
 STNW/STAM N16..............119 L7
Lordship Ter STNW/STAM N16...119 L7
Lords St CAN/RD E16..........142 B10
 GVE DA12...................190 E3
 HOD EN11...................44 D3
 WAT WD17...................73 K7
Lords Vw STJWD NW8...........3 N10
Lords Wd WGCE AL7............23 M5
Lordswood Rd RDART DA2......188 D7
Lord Warwick St
 WOOL/PLUM SE18.............162 C2
Lorenzo St FSBYW WC1X........5 N9
Loretto Gdns KTN/HRWW/W HA3..115 K3
Lorian CI NFNCH/WDSP N12.....97 L5
Lorian Dr REIG RH2...........257 M9
Loriners CRAWE RH10..........283 N10
Loring Rd BERK HP4...........33 P6
 ISLW TW7...................154 E8
 TRDG/WHET N20..............97 P3
 WDSR SL4...................148 E7
Loris Rd HMSMTH W6...........159 H8
Lorn Ct BRXN/ST SW9..........159 H8
Lorne Av CROY/NA CRO.........204 C7
Lorne CI STJWD NW8...........3 N8
 WDSR SL4...................148 G2
Lorne Gdns CROY/NA CRO.......204 C7
 NTGHL W11..................14 A1
 WAN E11....................121 P2
 WOKN/KNAP GU21.............231 J5
Lorne Rd BRW CM14............118 C6
 FSBYPK N4..................119 H2
 FSTGT E7...................121 N9
 KTN/HRWW/W HA3.............94 E10
 RCHPK/HAM TW10.............177 L1
 WALTH E17..................120 F3
The Lorne GT/LBKH KT23.......253 P2
Lorn Rd BRXN/ST SW9..........158 G8
Lorraine Pk KTN/HRWW/W HA3..94 D8
Lorrimore Rd WALW SE17......18 D10
Lorrimore Sq WALW SE17......18 C10
Lorton CI GVE DA12...........191 H5
Loseberry Rd ESH/CLAY KT10..218 C5
Loseley Rd RGODL GU7.........267 K9
Losfield Rd WDSR SL4.........148 D5
Lossie Dr IVER SLO...........130 E9
Lothair Rd EA W5.............155 J1
Lothair Rd North FSBYPK N4...119 J4
Lothair Rd South FSBYPK N4...119 J5
Lothbury LOTH EC2R...........12 G5
Lothian Av YEAD UB4..........133 J7
Lothian CI ALP/SUD HA0.......114 A9
Lothian Rd BRXN/ST SW9.......159 J7
Lothian Wk KUTN/CMB/TDW/WH KT20..238 E8
Lothrop St NKENS W10.........2 A10
Lots Rd WBPTN SW10...........157 M6
Lotus Rd BH/WHM TN16.........244 C6
Loubet St TOOT SW17..........180 A9
Loudhams Rd AMSS HP7.........69 H5
Loudhams Wood La CSTG HP8....70 A6
Loudoun Av CLAY IG5..........122 C2
Loudoun Rd STJWD NW8.........3 K4
Loudwater CI SUN TW16........197 H4
Loudwater Dr RKW/CH/CXG WD3..71 M7
Loudwater Hts RKW/CH/CXG WD3..71 L7
Loudwater Rdg
 RKW/CH/CXG WD3............71 M8
Loudwater Rd SUN TW16........197 H4
Loughborough Pk HNHL SE24....159 J10
Loughborough St LBTH SE11....17 P7
Lough Rd HOLWY N7............5 P1
 HOLWY N7...................118 C10
Loughton La EPP CM16.........82 G3
Loughton Wy BKHH IG9.........102 A2
Louisa CI WCHPL E1...........140 C7
Louise Bennett CI HNHL SE24..159 J10
Louise Gdns RAIN RM13........144 F5
Louise Rd SRTFD E15..........141 K1
Louise Wk HHS/BOV HP3........52 B1
Louis Flds RGUW GU3..........249 H6
Louisville Rd TOOT SW17......180 B6
Louvaine Rd BTSEA SW11.......157 N10
Louvain Rd RDART DA2.........188 D3
Lovage Ap EHAM E6............142 B7
Lovat CI CRICK NW2...........116 C2
Lovatt Dr RKW/CH/CXG WD3.....72 A1
Lovat La FENCHST EC3M........13 J7
Lovatts RKW/CH/CXG WD3.......72 A5
Loveday Rd WEA W13...........130 G10
Love Green La IVER SLO.......130 F9
Lovegrove St STHWK SE1......159 M5
Lovegrove Wk POP/IOD E14....141 N10
Love Hill La DTCH/LGLY SL3..130 D9
Lovejoy La WDSR SL4..........148 C3
Lovekyn CI KUTN/CMB KT2......199 L3
Lovelace Av HAYES BR2........206 D6
Lovelace CI EHSLY KT24.......235 H4
Lovelace Dr WOKS/MYFD GU22..233 J2
Lovelace Gdns BARK IG11......123 K3
 SURB KT6...................199 J7
 WOT/HER KT12...............217 K2
Lovelace Gn ELTH/MOT SE9....162 C9
Lovelace Rd DUL SE21.........181 K5

Lovelands La CHOB/PIR GU24...213 H9
 KWD/TDW/WH KT20............257 L3
Love La ABLGY WD5............54 C6
 BXLY DA5...................186 B5
 CHEAM SM3..................201 H3
 CHONG CM5..................67 H5
 CITYW EC2V.................12 F5
 GDST RH9...................260 D8
 IVER SLO...................130 G8
 KGLGY WD4..................53 M7
 KWD/TDW/WH KT20............256 D2
 MRDN SM4...................201 K7
 MTCM CR4...................202 A1
 PIN HA5....................115 M1
 SNWD SE25..................204 A3
 SOCK/AV RM15...............166 B1
 SURB KT6...................199 J9
 TIL RM18...................169 N5
 TOTM N17...................99 N8
 WFD IG8....................102 G7
 WOOL/PLUM SE18.............162 D3
Lovel Av WELL DA16...........163 K8
Lovel CI HHW HP1.............35 K6
Lovel End CFSP/GDCR SL9......89 P8
Lovelinch CI PECK SE15......160 B5
Lovell PI BERM/RHTH SE16....160 D2
Lovell Rd EN EN1.............80 A1
 GFD/PVL UB6................134 A8
 RCHPK/HAM TW10.............177 H6
Lovell Wk RAIN RM13..........145 H1
Lovelock CI PUR/KEN CR8......241 K3
Lovel Rd CFSP/GDCR SL9......89 P8
Loveridge Rd KIL/WHAMP NW6...2 C1
Lovering Rd CHES/WCR EN8.....61 K1
Lover's La GRH DA9...........167 J10
Lovett Dr CAR SM5............201 M7
Lovett Rd DEN/HRF UB9........111 M1
Lovett Wy WLSDN NW10.........115 P10
Lovibonds Av ORP BR6.........206 E10
 WDR/YW UB7.................132 A8
Lowbell La LCOL/BKTW AL2.....57 J3
Lowbrook Rd IL IG1...........122 C9
Lowburys DORK RH4............272 F5
Low CI GRH DA9...............188 F1
Lowdell CI WDR/YW UB7........131 P9
Lowden Rd ED N9..............100 A2
 HNHL SE24..................159 J10
 STHL UB1...................133 M9
Lowe Av CAN/RD E16...........141 M7
Lowe CI CHIG IG7.............103 K6
Lowell St POP/IOD E14........140 D8
Lowen Rd RAIN RM13...........144 A4
Lower Addiscombe Rd
 CROY/NA CRO................203 J8
Lower Addison Gdns WKENS W14..14 A2
Lower Adeyfield Rd HHNE HP2..35 N5
Lower Barn HHS/BOV HP3.......36 A9
Lower Barn Rd PUR/KEN CR8...223 K8
Lower Bedfords Rd ROM RM1...105 H7
Lower Belgrave St BGVA SW1W..16 E4
Lower Boston Rd HNWL W7.....134 D10
Lower Bridge Rd REDH RH1....258 A10
Lower Britwell Rd SL SL1....128 C6
Lower Broad St DAGE RM10....144 B3
Lower Bury La EPP CM16......65 H7
Lower Camden CHST BR7.......206 C4
Lower Church St CROY/NA CRO..203 J9
Lower Cippenham La SL SL1...128 E10
Lower Clabdens WARE SG12....26 E1
Lower Clapton Rd CLPT E5....120 A9
Lower Common South
 PUT/ROE SW15..............156 F9
Lower Coombe St CROY/NA CRO..223 K1
Lower Ct HOR/WEW KT19.......220 A7
Lower Court Rd HOR/WEW KT19..219 P7
Lower Crs SLH/COR SW17......169 K2
Lower Cft SWLY BR8...........208 A4
Lower Dagnall St STAL/WD AL3..38 B6
Lower Derby Rd WAT WD17.....73 K8
Lower Downs Rd RYNPK SW20...200 D1
Lower Dunnymans BNSTD SM7...221 J10
Lower Edgeborough Rd GU GU1..268 C3
Lower Emms HHNE HP2..........36 D1
Lower Farm Rd EHSLY KT24....235 J10
Lowerfield WGCE AL7..........23 K6
Lower Gravel Rd HAYES BR2...206 B8
Lower Green Rd ESH/CLAY KT10..198 A9
Lower Grn West MTCM CR4......201 P3
Lower Grosvenor PI KTBR SW1X..16 E3
Lower Grove Rd
 RCHPK/HAM TW10............177 L2
Lower Guildford Rd
 WOKN/KNAP GU21............231 J3
Lower Hall CI CHING E4......100 D6
Lower Hampton Rd SUN TW16...197 J2
Lower Ham Rd KUTN/CMB KT1...197 L3
Lower Hatfield Rd HERT/BAY SG13..24 G10
Lower Higham Rd GVE DA12....191 J4
Lower High St WAT WD17......73 J2
Lower Hill Rd HOR/WEW KT19..219 N8
Lower Island Wy WAB E9......80 G1
Lower James St SOHO/CST W1F..11 H7
Lower John St SOHO/CST W1F..11 H7
Lower Kenwood Av
 STHGT/OAK N14.............78 F9
Lower Kings Rd BERK HP4.....33 P4
Lower Lea Crossing
 POP/IOD E14...............141 K9
Lower Lees Rd SLN SL2.......128 F5
Lower Luton Rd STALE/WH AL4..20 E1
Lower Maidstone Rd
 FBAR/BDGN N11.............98 D7
Lower Mardyke Av RAIN RM13..144 A2
Lower Marsh STHWK SE1.......18 A2
Lower Marsh La KUT KT1......199 L4
Lower Md IVER SLO...........130 C5
Lower Meadow CHES/WCR EN8...62 G3
 HLWS CM18.................47 H5
Lower Merton Ri HAMP NW3....3 N4
Lower Morden La MRDN SM4....201 H6
Lower Mortlake Rd
 RCH/KEW TW9...............155 K10
Lower Noke CI BRW CM14......105 M3
Lower Northfield BNSTD SM7..221 J10
Lower Paddock Rd OXHEY WD19..73 H10
Lower Park Rd BELV DA17.....164 B2
 BNSTD SM7.................239 P4
 FBAR/BDGN N11.............98 D6
 LOU IG10..................82 B6
Lower Paxton Rd STAL AL1....38 D7
Lower Pervers EHSLY KT24....254 F4
Lower Pillory Down CAR SM5..222 B9
Lower Plantation
 RKW/CH/CXG WD3............71 M7
Lower Queen's Rd BKHH IG9...102 B3
Lower Range Rd GVE DA12.....191 H3
Lower Richmond Rd
 MORT/ESHN SW14............155 N9
 PUT/ROE SW15..............156 F9
 RCH/KEW TW9...............155 N9
Lower Rd BELV DA17..........164 D3
 BERM/RHTH SE16............160 B1
 CFSP/GDCR SL9.............90 B7
 DEN/HRF UB9...............110 D5
 ERITH DA8.................164 D2
 GT/LBKH KT23..............253 M1
 GVE DA12..................191 P7
 HHS/BOV HP3...............54 A1
 LHD/OX KT22...............236 D1
 LOU IG10..................82 D5

PUR/KEN CR8..................223 J9
REIG RH2.....................275 N2
RKW/CH/CXG WD3...............70 C8
RYLN/HDSTN HA2...............114 C7
STMC/STPC BR5................207 L6
SUT SM1......................221 N2
SWLY BR8.....................187 J10
TIL RM18.....................168 D10
WARE SG12....................26 E5
Lower Sales HHW HP1..........35 J7
Lower Sandfields
 RPLY/SEND GU23.............232 C9
Lower Sawleywood
 BNSTD SM7..................221 J10
Lower Shott GT/LBKH KT23.....254 A2
Lower Sloane St BGVA SW1W....16 B6
Lower Station Rd DART DA1....186 F2
Lower Strd CDALE/KGS NW9.....96 C10
Lower Sunbury Rd HPTN TW12...197 N2
Lower Tail OXHEY WD19........93 M4
Lower Teddington Rd KUT KT1..199 J3
Lower Ter HAMP NW3...........1 M8
Lower Thames St MON EC3R....13 J8
Lower Tub BUSH WD23..........94 C1
Lower Village Rd ASC SL5....192 B5
Lower Wood Rd ESH/CLAY KT10..218 F3
Lower Yott HHNE HP2..........35 P7
Lowestoft CI CLPT E5........120 E9
Lowestoft Rd WATN WD24......73 J5
Loweswater CI GSTN WD25.....59 K9
 WBLY HA9..................115 J7
The Lowe CI IG7.............103 K6
Lowfield SBW CM21...........29 P2
Lowfield Heath Rd HORL RH6..279 J9
Lowfield La HOD EN11........44 F3
Lowfield Rd ACT W3..........135 P6
 KIL/WHAMP NW6.............2 E1
Lowfield St DART DA1........187 M3
Lowfield Wy HORL RH6........279 P10
Low Hall CI CHING E4........100 F1
Low Hall La WALTH E17.......120 B4
Low Hill Rd HLWW/ROY CM19...45 L3
Lowick Rd HRW HA1...........114 D2
Lowland Gdns ROMW/RG RM7....124 C3
Lowlands BRKMPK AL9.........40 F1
Lowlands HRW HA1............114 D5
 PIN HA5...................113 K5
 SOCK/AV RM15..............146 B10
 STWL/WRAY TW19............173 N1
Lowman Rd HOLWY N7..........118 C9
Lowndes Av CSHM HP5.........50 G6
Lowndes CI KTBR SW1X........16 D4
Lowndes PI KTBR SW1X........16 C4
Lowndes Sq KTBR SW1X........16 B3
Lowndes St KTBR SW1X........16 C3
Lowood St WCHPL E1..........140 A9
Lowry Crs MTCM CR4..........201 J7
Lowry Rd BCTR RM8...........123 L10
Lowshoe La ROMW/RG RM7......104 C9
Lowson Gv OXHEY WD19........93 M1
Low Street La TIL RM18......169 L4
Lowswood CI NTHWD HA6.......92 D9
Lowther CI BORE WD6.........75 L9
Lowther Dr ENC/FH EN2.......78 E3
Lowther HI FSTH SE23........182 D3
Lowther Rd BARN SW13........156 C7
 KUTN/CMB KT2..............199 L1
 STAN HA7..................100 D10
 WALTH E17.................100 D10
Lowth Rd CMBW SE5...........159 K8
Loxford Av EHAM E6..........141 K8
Loxford La IL IG1...........122 F10
Loxford Rd BARK IG11........142 E1
Loxford Wy CTHM CR3.........259 N1
Loxham Rd CHING E4..........100 C8
Loxham St STPAN WC1H........5 M10
Loxley CI SYD SE26..........182 C8
Loxley Rd BERK HP4..........33 K3
 HPTN TW12.................175 P3
 WAND/EARL SW18............179 P5
Loxton Rd FSTH SE23.........182 A2
Loxwood CI EBED/NFELT TW14..174 E4
 STMC/STPC BR5.............207 N9
Loxwood Rd TOTM N17.........119 M1
Lubbock Rd CHST BR7.........184 C10
Lubbock St NWCR SE14........160 A6
Lucan Dr STA TW18...........173 N10
Lucan PI CHEL SW3...........15 N6
Lucan Rd BAR EN5............77 H7
Lucas Av PLSTW E13..........122 A9
 RYLN/HDSTN HA2............113 P7
Lucas Gdns EFNCH N2.........97 H6
Lucas Green Rd CHOB/PIR GU24..230 C1
Lucas Rd GRAYS RM17.........167 K2
 PGE/AN SE20...............182 B9
Lucas St DEPT SE8...........160 F8
Lucerne CI PLMGR N13........99 F4
 WOKS/MYFD GU22............231 J7
Lucerne Dr CRAWE RH10.......284 E9
Lucerne Gv WALTH E17........121 J2
Lucerne Ms KENS W8..........8 F9
Lucerne Rd HBRY N5..........119 J8
 ORP BR6...................207 J8
 THHTH CR7.................203 J3
Lucerne Wy HARH RM3.........105 L7
Lucey Rd BERM/RHTH SE16.....19 N5
Lucey Wy BERM/RHTH SE16.....19 P5
Lucie Av ASHF TW15..........174 C9
Lucien Rd TOOT SW17.........180 B7
 WAND/EARL SW18............179 L1
Lucknow St WOOL/PLUM SE18...163 J1
Lucks HI HHW HP1............35 H6
Lucorn CI LEE/GVPK SE12.....183 L2
Lucton Ms LOU IG10..........101 P2
Luddenham Rd ERITH DA8......164 B6
Luddington Av VW GU25.......212 B1
Ludford CI CDALE/KGS NW9....96 B10
 CROY/NA CRO...............223 J1
Ludgate Broadway BLKFR EC4V..12 D6
Ludgate HI STP EC4M.........12 D6
Ludgate Sq BLKFR EC4V.......12 D6
Ludham CI THMD SE28.........143 M10
Ludlow CI HAYES BR2.........205 M3
 RYLN/HDSTN HA2............113 N10
Ludlow Md OXHEY WD19........93 J4
Ludlow PI GRAYS RM17........167 K2
Ludlow Rd EA W5.............135 H6
 FELT TW13.................175 J1
Ludlow St FSBYE EC1V........12 E1
Ludlow Wy EFNCH N2..........117 M2
 RKW/CH/CXG WD3............72 D1
Ludwick Wy WGCE AL7.........23 K5
Luffield Rd ABYW SE2........163 L2
Luffman Rd LEE/GVPK SE12....183 N5
Lugard Rd PECK SE15.........160 A8
Lugg Ap MNPK E12............122 D8
Luke St SDTCH EC2A..........13 J1
Lukin Crs CHING E4..........101 J4
Lukin St WCHPL E1...........140 C7
Lullarook CI BH/WHM TN16....243 P6
Lullingstone Av SWLY BR8....208 D3
Lullingstone CI BKHTH/KID SE3..161 L5
Lullingstone Crs STMC/STPC BR5..185 K10
Lullingstone Garth BORE WD6..75 P9
Lullingstone La EYN DA4.....209 H10
Lullington Garth BORE WD6...75 P9
 FBAR/BDGN N11.............97 P7
Lullington Rd DAGW RM9......143 P2
 PGE/AN SE20...............181 P10

Lulworth Av CHESW EN7.......61 J5
 HEST TW5..................154 A7
 WBLY HA9..................115 H5
Lulworth CI CRAWW RH11......283 K10
 RYLN/HDSTN HA2............113 N8
Lulworth Crs MTCM CR4.......201 P2
Lulworth Dr CRW RM5.........104 C5
 PIN HA5...................113 L5
Lulworth Gdns RYLN/HDSTN HA2..113 M7
Lulworth Rd ELTH/MOT SE9....184 B5
 PECK SE15.................160 A8
 WELL DA16.................164 A2
Lulworth Waye YEAD UB4......133 J8
Lumbards WGCE AL7...........23 J1
Lumley CI BELV DA17.........164 B5
Lumley Gdns CHEAM SM3.......221 H2
Lumley Rd CHEAM SM3.........221 H3
 HORL RH6..................280 B4
Lumley St MYFR/PKLN W1K.....10 D6
Lunar CI BH/WHM TN16........244 A2
Luna Rd THHTH CR7...........203 K3
Lundin Wk OXHEY WD19........93 L5
Lundy Dr HYS/HAR UB3........152 F3
Lunedale Rd RDART DA2.......188 B4
Lunghurst Rd CTHM CR3.......242 F7
Lunham Rd NRWD SE19.........181 M9
Lupin CI BRXS/STRHM SW2.....181 J5
 CROY/NA CRO...............204 C8
 ROMW/RG RM7...............124 E2
 WDR/YW UB7................
Luppits CI RBRW/HUT CM13....107 M2
Lupton CI LEE/GVPK SE12.....183 N7
Lupton St KTTN NW5..........118 D2
Lupus St PIM SW1V...........17 J7
Lurgan Av HMSMTH W6.........156 C5
Lurline Gdns BTSEA SW11.....158 F2
Luscombe Wy VX/NE SW8.......158 F6
Lushes Ct LOU IG10..........82 E9
Lushes Rd LOU IG10..........82 E9
Lushington Dr COB KT11......217 J10
Lushington Rd CAT SE6.......182 C8
 WLSDN NW10................136 K4
Lushington Ter HACK E8......119 P10
Lusted Hall La BH/WHM TN16..243 P6
Lusteds CI DORK RH4.........273 H5
Luther CI EDGW HA8..........96 D3
Luther King CI WALTH E17....120 D4
Luther King Rd HLW CM20.....46 F1
Luthers CI BRWN CM15........86 D3
Luton PI GNWCH SE10.........161 H6
Luton Rd PLSTW E13..........141 M6
 WALTH E17.................120 D1
Luton St STJWD NW8..........9 M2
Luttrell Av PUT/ROE SW15....178 F4
Lutwyche Rd FSTH SE23.......182 E5
Lutyens CI CRAWW RH11.......283 H9
Luxborough La CHIG IG7......102 C5
Luxborough St MHST W1U......10 C2
Luxemburg Gdns HMSMTH W6....156 G3
Luxfield Rd ELTH/MOT SE9....184 B4
Luxford PI SBW CM21.........30 A2
Luxford St BERM/RHTH SE16...160 C3
Luxmore St BROCKY SE4.......160 F2
Luxor St CMBW SE5...........159 J8
Luxted Rd ORP BR6...........226 D8
Lyall Av DUL SE21...........181 M7
Lyall Ms KTBR SW1X..........16 C4
Lyall Ms West KTBR SW1X.....16 C4
Lyall St KTBR SW1X..........16 C4
Lyal Rd BOW E3..............140 D4
Lycaste CI STAL AL1.........38 E7
Lycett PI SHB W12...........156 D1
Lych Ga GSTN WD25...........59 L9
Lych Gate Rd ORP BR6........207 L8
Lych Gate Wk HYS/HAR UB3....132 C9
Lych Wy WOKN/KNAP GU21......232 A2
Lyconby Gdns CROY/NA CRO....204 D7
Lycrome La CSHM HP5.........51 J4
Lycrome Rd CSHM HP5.........51 K4
Lydd CI BFN/LL DA15.........185 H6
Lydden Gv WAND/EARL SW18....179 L4
Lydden Rd WAND/EARL SW18....179 L4
Lydd Rd BXLYHN DA7..........164 B6
Lydeard Rd EHAM E6..........142 C2
Lydele CI WOKN/KNAP GU21....232 C1
Lydford Av SLN SL2..........129 J7
Lydford CI CRICK NW2........
 MV/WKIL W9................8 D1
Lydford Rd SEVS/STOTM N15...119 L3
 CRICK NW2.................
 MV/WKIL W9................8 D1
Lydhurst Av BRXS/STRHM SW2..180 A5
Lydia Ms BRKMPK AL9.........40 F1
Lydia Rd ERITH DA8..........164 G5
Lydney CI PECK SE15.........159 M6
 WIM/MER SW19..............178 G3
Lydon Rd CLAP SW4...........158 D9
Lydsey CI SLN SL2...........128 G2
Lydstep Rd CHST BR7.........184 D7
Lye Green Rd CSHM HP5.......51 K6
Lye La LCOL/BKTW AL2........55 P4
Lyell Rd WDSR SL4...........148 B9
The Lye KWD/TDW/WH KT20.....238 F5
Lyfield COB KT11............218 A10
Lyford Rd WAND/EARL SW18....179 L5
Lyford St CHARL SE7.........162 B3
Lygean Av WARE SG12.........26 D1
Lygon PI BGVA SW1W..........16 E4
Lyham CI CLAP SW4...........180 F1
Lyham Rd BRXS/STRHM SW2.....180 F1
Lyle CI MTCM CR4............202 B7
Lyle Pk SEV TN13............247 J9
Lyles La WGCW AL8...........23 H3
Lymbourne Rd BELMT SM2......221 K6
Lymden Gdns REIG RH2........275 J2
Lyme Av BERK HP4............33 J2
Lyme Farm Rd LEE/GVPK SE12..161 M10
Lyme Gv HOM E9..............
Lymer Av NRWD SE19..........181 N8
Lyme Regis Rd BNSTD SM7.....239 J8
Lyme Rd WELL DA16...........163 L7
Lymescote Gdns SUT SM1......201 K9
Lyme St CAMTN NW1...........4 G1
Lyminge CI SCUP DA14........185 J7
Lyminge Gdns WAND/EARL SW18..179 J4
Lymington Av WDGN N22.......99 H10
Lymington CI STRHM/NOR SW16..202 E2
 EHAM E6...................142 A7
Lymington Dr RSLP HA4.......112 A7
Lymington Gdns HOR/WEW KT19..220 C2
Lymington Rd BCTR RM8.......123 N8
 KIL/WHAMP NW6.............2 G1
Lynbridge Gdns PLMGR N13....99 J3
Lynbrook CI PECK SE15.......159 M6
 RAIN RM13.................144 A2
Lynceley Gra EPP CM16.......65 K5
Lynch CI UX/CGN UB8.........
Lynch Hill La SLN SL2.......128 D6
The Lynch HOD EN11..........44 C3
 UX/CGN UB8................131 M2
Lyncroft Av PIN HA5.........113 L3
Lyncroft Gdns EW KT17.......176 B1
 HSLW TW3..................155 H3
 KIL/WHAMP NW6.............2 E3
 WEA W13...................155 H1
Lyndale BRWN CM15...........86 E3
Lyndale Av CRICK NW2........117 J8
Lyndale CI BKHTH/KID SE3....161 J5
Lyndale Hampton Court Wy
 ESH/CLAY KT10.............198 D7
Lyndale Rd REDH RH1.........258 A7
Lynden Wy SWLY BR8..........208 D3
Lyndhurst Av BRYLDS KT5.....199 N8
 MLHL NW7..................96 B7
 NFNCH/WDSP N12............98 A7
 PIN HA5...................93 J9
 STHL UB1..................134 A10

344 Lyn - Man

STRHM/NOR SW16 202 E2
SUN TW16 197 H3
WHTN TW2 175 N4
Lyndhurst Cl *BXLYHN* DA7 164 C9
CRAWW RH11 283 N8
CROY/NA CR0 203 N10 5
HARP AL5 20 B1 1
ORP BR6 226 E1
WLSDN NW10 116 A8
WOKN/KNAP GU21 232 A1 2
Lyndhurst Dr *EMPK* RM11 125 K6
HARP AL5 20 B1
NWMAL KT3 200 B6
SEV TN13 246 F10
WAN E11 121 H5
Lyndhurst Gdns *BARK* IG11 143 H1
EN EN1 79 M8
FNCH N3 97 H9
GNTH/NBYPK IG2 122 G4
HAMP NW3 117 N10 3
PIN HA5 93 J9
Lyndhurst Gv *CMBW* SE5 159 M8
Lyndhurst Ri *CHIG* IG7 102 D5
Lyndhurst Rd *BXLYHN* DA7 164 C9
CHING E4 101 H8
COUL/CHIP CR5 240 B2
CSHM HP5 50 G4
GFD/PVL UB6 134 A6
HAMP NW3 117 N10
REIG RH2 275 K3
THHTH CR7 203 H4
UED N18 99 P5
WDGN N22 99 H7
Lyndhurst Sq *PECK* SE15 159 N7 3
Lyndhurst Ter *HAMP* NW3 117 N10 4
Lyndhurst Wy *BELMT* SM2 221 K4 4
CHERT KT16 195 H9 1
PECK SE15 159 N7
RBRW/HUT CM13 107 P2
Lyndon Av *BFN/LL* DA15 185 J1
PIN HA5 93 M7
WLGTN SM6 202 B10
Lyndon Md *STALE/WH* AL4 21 H9
Lyndon Rd *BELV* DA17 164 B3
Lyndon Yd *TOOT* SW17 179 L7
Lyndwood Dr *WDSR* SL4 171 M2
Lyne Cl *VW* GU25 194 C6
Lyne Crs *WALTH* E17 100 E9
Lyne Crossing Rd *CHERT* KT16 194 D6
Lynegrove Av *ASHF* TW15 174 D8
Lyneham Wk *CLPT* E5 120 D10 2
Lyne La *CHERT* KT16 194 D8
Lyne Rd *VW* GU25 194 A6
Lynette Av *CLAP* SW4 180 C2
Lyne Wy *HHW* HP1 35 J4
Lynford Cl *EDGW* HA8 95 P9
Lynford Gdns *EDGW* HA8 95 N4
GDMY/SEVK IG3 123 J7
Lynhurst Crs *HGDN/ICK* UB10 132 D2
Lynhurst Rd *HGDN/ICK* UB10 132 D2
Lynmere Rd *WELL* DA16 163 L8
Lynmouth Av *EN* EN1 79 N10
MRDN SM4 200 G7
Lynmouth Dr *RSLP* HA4 113 J7
Lynmouth Gdns *GFD/PVL* UB6 134 G3
HEST TW5 153 L7
Lynmouth Ri *STMC/STPC* BR5 207 L4
Lynmouth Rd *EFNCH* N2 118 A1
GFD/PVL UB6 134 G3
STNW/STAM N16 119 N6
WALTH E17 120 D4
WGCE AL7 23 J5
Lynn Cl *ASHF* TW15 174 E8
KTN/HRWW/W HA3 94 C10
Lynne Cl *ORP* BR6 227 J3 3
SAND/SEL CR2 224 B7
Lynnett Rd *BCTR* RM8 123 N7
Lynne Wk *ESH/CLAY* KT10 218 B2
Lynne Wy *NTHLT* UB5 133 L4
WLSDN NW10 136 B2
Lynn Rd *BAL* SW12 180 C3
GNTH/NBYPK IG2 122 G5
WAN E11 121 K7
Lynn St *ENC/FH* EN2 79 L5
Lynn Wk *REIG* RH2 275 L4
Lynross Cl *HARH* RM3 105 M10
Lynscott Wy *SAND/SEL* CR2 223 J5
Lynstead Cl *BMLY* BR1 205 P2
Lynsted Cl *BXLYHS* DA6 186 C1
Lynsted Ct *BECK* BR3 204 D2 2
Lynsted Gdns *ELTH/MOT* SE9 162 A10
Lynton Av *ACT* W3 135 P8
CDALE/KGS NW9 116 C2
NFNCH/WDSP N12 97 N5
ROMW/RG RM7 104 C9
STAL AL1 39 H8
STMC/STPC BR5 207 L4
WEA W13 134 F8
Lynton Cl *CHSGTN* KT9 219 K1
ISLW TW7 154 E10
WLSDN NW10 116 B10
Lynton Crs *GNTH/NBYPK* IG2 122 E4
Lynton Gdns *EN* EN1 99 M1
FBAR/BDGN N11 98 F7
Lynton Md *TRDG/WHET* N20 97 K4
Lynton Rd *ACT* W3 135 M9
CEND/HSY/T N8 118 E3
CHING E4 100 G6
CROY/NA CR0 203 H6
CSHM HP5 50 G4
GVW DA11 190 D4
KIL/WHAMP NW6 2 D6
NWMAL KT3 200 A5
RYLN/HDSTN HA2 113 M7
STHWK SE1 19 M6
Lynton Rd South *GVW* DA11 190 D4
Lynwood *GUW* GU2 267 N1
Lynwood Av *COUL/CHIP* CR5 240 C1
DTCH/LGLY SL3 150 A2
EGH TW20 172 B9
EW KT17 220 C10
Lynwood Cl *RYLN/HDSTN* HA2 113 M8
SWFD E18 101 P9
WOKN/KNAP GU21 214 G9
Lynwood Crs *ASC* SL5 192 D6
Lynwood Dr *CRW* RM5 104 C8
NTHWD HA6 92 F9
WPK KT4 200 D9
Lynwood Gdns *CROY/NA* CR0 222 G1
STHL UB1 133 N8 3
Lynwood Gv *ORP* BR6 207 H7
WCHMH N21 99 H2
Lynwood Hts *RKW/CH/CXG* WD3 71 L9
Lynwood Rd *EA* W5 135 J5
EW KT17 220 C10
REDH RH1 258 B8
THDIT KT7 198 E9
TOOT SW17 180 A6
Lynx Hl *EHSLY* KT24 252 G3
Lyon Meade *STAN* HA7 95 H9
Lyon Park Av *ALP/SUD* HA0 135 K1
Lyon Rd *HRW* HA1 114 E4
ROM RM1 124 G5
WIM/MER SW19 201 M1
WOT/HER KT12 197 M9
Lyons Ct *DORK* RH4 272 G2
Lyonsdene *KWD/TDW/WH* KT20 257 J3
Lyonsdown Av *BAR* EN5 77 M10
Lyonsdown Rd *BAR* EN5 77 M10
Lyons Dr *GUW* GU2 249 M5
Lyons Pl *STJWD* NW8 9 L2
Lyon St *IS* N1 5 N4
Lyons Wk *WKENS* W14 14 A5
Lyon Wy *GFD/PVL* UB6 134 D3
STALE/WH AL4 39 M6
Lyoth Rd *STMC/STPC* BR5 206 F9 1
Lyrical Wy *HHW* HP1 35 L4
Lyric Cl *CRAWE* RH10 284 E9
Lyric Dr *GFD/PVL* UB6 134 A6
Lyric Ms *SYD* SE26 182 B7
Lyric Rd *BARN* SW13 156 C7
Lysander Cl *HHW* HP1 52 C3
Lysander Gdns *SURB* KT6 199 L6 3
Lysander Gv *ARCH* N19 118 E6
Lysander Rd *CROY/NA* CR0 222 G3
RSLP HA4 112 E7
Lysander Wy *ABLGY* WD5 55 H8 4
ORP BR6 206 F10 2
WGCE AL7 23 N4 2
Lys Hill Gdns *HERT/WAS* SG14 25 J3
Lysias Rd *BAL* SW12 180 B2
Lysia St *FUL/PGN* SW6 156 G6
Lysons Wk *PUT/ROE* SW15 178 D1 2
Lyster Ms *COB* KT11 217 K9
Lytchet Rd *BMLY* BR1 183 M10
Lytchet Wy *PEND* EN3 80 B5
Lytchgate Cl *SAND/SEL* CR2 223 M4
Lytcott Dr *E/WMO/HCT* KT8 197 N3 2
Lytcott Gv *EDUL* SE22 181 N1
Lytham Av *OXHEY* WD19 93 L6
Lytham Gv *EA* W5 135 K5
Lytham St *WALW* SE17 18 G8
Lyttelton Rd *EFNCH* N2 117 N3 1
LEY E10 120 G8
Lyttleton Cl *HAMP* NW3 3 N4
Lyttleton Rd *CEND/HSY/T* N8 119 H1 4
Lytton Av *PEND* EN3 80 D4
PLMGR N13 99 H3
Lytton Cl *EFNCH* N2 117 N3 2
NTHLT UB5 133 N2
Lytton Dr *CRAWE* RH10 284 E6
Lytton Gdns *WGCW* AL8 22 G5
WLGTN SM6 222 E1
Lytton Gv *PUT/ROE* SW15 178 G1
Lytton Rd *BAR* EN5 77 M8
CDH/CHF RM16 168 D3
GPK RM2 125 J3
PIN HA5 93 M8
WAN E11 121 K5
WOKS/MYFD GU22 232 E2
Lyttons Wy *HOD* EN11 26 F10
Lyveden Rd *BKHTH/KID* SE3 161 N6
WIM/MER SW19 179 P9
Lywood Cl *KWD/TDW/WH* KT20 238 F8

M

Mabbotts *KWD/TDW/WH* KT20 238 G7 2
Mabbutt Cl *LCOL/BKTW* AL2 55 M6
Mabel Rd *SWLY* BR8 187 H9
Mabel St *WOKN/KNAP* GU21 232 A4
Maberley Crs *NRWD* SE19 181 P10
Maberley Rd *BECK* BR3 204 C3
NRWD SE19 203 N1
Mabey's Wk *SBW* CM21 29 L2
Mabledon Pl *CAMTN* NW1 5 K10
Mablethorpe Rd *FUL/PGN* SW6 157 H6
Mabley St *HOM* E9 120 D10
Macaret Cl *TRDG/WHET* N20 97 L1
Macarthur Cl *FSTGT* E7 141 M1
Macaulay Av *ESH/CLAY* KT10 198 D9
Macaulay Rd *CLAP* SW4 158 C9
CTHM CR3 241 M8
EHAM E6 142 A4
Macaulay Sq *CLAP* SW4 180 C1
Macbean St *WOOL/PLUM* SE18 162 D2
Macbeth St *HMSMTH* W6 156 E4
Macclesfield Rd *FSBYE* EC1V 6 E9
SNWD SE25 204 A5
Macclesfield St *SOHO/SHAV* W1D 11 K7 4
Macdonald Av *DAGE* RM10 124 C8
EMPK RM11 125 M2
Macdonald Cl *AMS* HP6 69 H1
Macdonald Rd *ARCH* N19 118 D7 2
FBAR/BDGN N11 98 A6
FSTGT E7 121 M9
WALTH E17 101 H10
Macdonald Wy *EMPK* RM11 125 M2 2
Macdonnell Gdns *GSTN* WD25 72 G1 2
Macduff Rd *BTSEA* SW11 158 B7
Mace Ctwy *CAN/RD* E16 141 M9
Mace La *RSEV* TN14 226 G9
Macer's La *BROX* EN10 44 E10
Mace St *BETH* E2 140 C4 3
BETH E2 140 C4 4
Macfarlane La *ISLW* TW7 154 E5
Macfarlane Rd *SHB* W12 136 F10
Mac Farren Pl *CAMTN* NW1 10 D2
Macgregor Rd *CAN/RD* E16 141 P7
Machell Rd *PECK* SE15 160 B9
Macintosh Cl *CHESW* EN7 61 L2 2
Mackay Rd *CLAP* SW4 158 C9 3
Mackennal St *STJWD* NW8 3 P8
Mackenzie Rd *BECK* BR3 204 D1 2
HOLWY N7 5 N1
Mackenzie Wy *GVE* DA12 190 G9
Mackeson Rd *HAMP* NW3 118 A9 2
Mackie Rd *BRXS/STRHM* SW2 181 H3
Mackies Hl *SHGR* GU5 270 E10
Mackintosh La *HOM* E9 120 C10 2
Macklin St *HOL/ALD* WC2B 11 M5 1
Macks Rd *BERM/RHTH* SE16 19 P5
Mackworth St *CAMTN* NW1 4 G9
Maclean Rd *FSTH* SE23 182 D2
Maclennan Av *RAIN* RM13 145 L5
Macleod Cl *GRAYS* RM17 168 A3 2
Macleod Rd *STHGT/OAK* N14 78 F9 3
WCHMH N21 78 G9 2
Macleod St *WALW* SE17 18 F8
Maclise Rd *WKENS* W14 14 A4
Macoma Rd *WOOL/PLUM* SE18 162 G5
Macoma Ter *WOOL/PLUM* SE18 162 G5
Maconochies Rd *POP/IOD* E14 160 G4 1
Macon Wy *UPMR* RM14 126 E4
Macquarie Wy *POP/IOD* E14 160 G3
Macroom Rd *MV/WKIL* W9 2 D9
Madan Rd *BH/WHM* TN16 262 G1
Mada Rd *ORP* BR6 206 E10
Maddams St *BOW* E3 140 G6
Madden Cl *SWCM* DA10 189 K2 1
Maddesfield Ct *RAD* WD7 57 K9 3
Maddison Cl *TEDD* TW11 176 E9
Maddocks Cl *SCUP* DA14 185 N9
Maddox La *GT/LBKH* KT23 235 M10
Maddox Pk *GT/LBKH* KT23 235 M9
Maddox Rd *HHNE* HP2 36 C6
HLW CM20 29 H10
Maddox St *MYFR/PKLN* W1K 10 F7
Madehurst Ct *CRAWW* RH11 283 J10 3
Madeira Av *BMLY* BR1 205 K1
Madeira Crs *BF/WBF* KT14 215 J9 3
Madeira Gv *WFD* IG8 101 P7 2
Madeira Rd *BF/WBF* KT14 215 J9
MTCM CR4 202 A4
PLMGR N13 99 J5
STRHM/NOR SW16 180 F8
WAN E11 121 J6
Madeira Wk *EPSOM* KT18 220 A10
REIG RH2 257 N9
Madeley Rd *EA* W5 135 K8
Madeline Gv *IL* IG1 122 G10
Madeline Rd *PGE/AN* SE20 181 P10
Madells *EPP* CM16 65 J7
Madge Gill Wy *EHAM* E6 142 B3
Madgeways Cl *WARE* SG12 26 E6 1
Madgeways La *WARE* SG12 26 E6
Madison Crs *WELL* DA16 163 M6
Madison Gdns *BXLYHN* DA7 163 M6
Madison Wy *SEV* TN13 246 G9
Madras Pl *HOLWY* N7 6 A1
Madras Rd *IL* IG1 122 E9
Madrid Rd *BARN* SW13 156 D7
GUW GU2 267 N1
Madron St *STHWK* SE1 19 K7
Maesmaur Rd *BH/WHM* TN16 244 A7
Mafeking Av *BTFD* TW8 155 K5
EHAM E6 142 A4
GNTH/NBYPK IG2 122 G5
Mafeking Rd *CAN/RD* E16 141 L6
EN EN1 79 N7
STWL/WRAY TW19 172 E5
TOTM N17 99 P10
Magazine Pl *LHD/OX* KT22 236 G8
Magazine Rd *CTHM* CR3 241 J8
Magdala Av *KTTN* NW5 118 D7
Magdala Rd *ISLW* TW7 154 F9
SAND/SEL CR2 223 L4 2
Magdalen Cl *BF/WBF* KT14 215 P10
Magdalen Crs *BF/WBF* KT14 215 P10
Magdalene Cl *CRAWE* RH10 284 D4 1
Magdalene Gdns *EHAM* E6 142 D6 2
Magdalene Rd *SHPTN* TW17 196 A3
Magdalen Rd *WAND/EARL* SW18 179 M4
Magdalen St *STHWK* SE1 13 J10 2
Magdelan Gv *ORP* BR6 227 L1
Magee St *LBTH* SE11 18 A9
Magna Carta La
STWL/WRAY TW19 172 A4
Magna Cl *HARP* AL5 20 C5
Magna Rd *EGH* TW20 171 N9
Magnaville Rd *BUSH* WD23 94 D1
Magnet Rd *WTHK* RM20 167 H5
Magnin Cl *HACK* E8 7 P5 1
Magnolia Av *ABLGY* WD5 54 G8
Magnolia Cl *HERT/BAY* SG13 25 P5
KUTN/CMB KT2 177 N9
LCOL/BKTW AL2 56 C2 1
LEY E10 120 F7 2
SOCK/AV RM15 147 K6
Magnolia Ct *KTN/HRWW/W* HA3 115 L5 1
Magnolia Dr *BH/WHM* TN16 244 A2
Magnolia Pl *CLAP* SW4 180 F1 1
Magnolia Rd *CHSWK* W4 155 N5
Magnolia St *WDR/YW* UB7 151 N3
Magnolia Wy *BRWN* CM15 86 G9
HOR/WEW KT19 219 P2
RDKG RH5 273 J5
Magnum Cl *RAIN* RM13 145 K6 3
Magpie Cl *COUL/CHIP* CR5 240 D4 2
EN EN1 79 P5
FSTGT E7 121 L10
Magpie Hall Cl *HAYES* BR2 206 B6
Magpie Hall La *HAYES* BR2 206 C5 1
Magpie Hall Rd *BUSH* WD23 94 D3
Magpie La *AMSS* HP7 88 F2
RBRW/HUT CM13 107 J10
Magpies *EPP* CM16 46 D10
Maguire Dr *RCHPK/HAM* TW10 177 H7
Maguire St *STHWK* SE1 19 M1
WAP E1W 13 M10
Mahlon Av *RSLP* HA4 113 J10
Mahogany Cl *BERM/RHTH* SE16 140 D10
Mahon Cl *EN* EN1 79 N5
Mahonia Cl *CHOB/PIR* GU24 212 E9 3
Maida Av *BAY/PAD* W2 9 K3
CHING E4 100 G1
Maida Rd *BELV* DA17 164 B2
Maida V *KIL/WHAMP* NW6 3 H8
MV/WKIL W9 9 K1
STJWD NW8 9 L1
Maida Vale Rd *DART* DA1 187 H2
Maida Wy *CHING* E4 100 G1
Maidenbower Dr *CRAWE* RH10 284 E9
Maidenbower La *CRAWE* RH10 284 D9 5
Maidenbower Pl *CRAWE* RH10 284 D9 6
Maiden Erlegh Av *BXLY* DA5 185 P4
Maidenhead Rd *WDSR* SL4 148 D6
Maidenhead St *HERT/WAS* SG14 25 L5 6
Maidenhead Yd *HERT/WAS* SG14 25 L5 7
Maiden La *CAMTN* NW1 5 K3
CRAWW RH11 283 M5
DART DA1 165 H9
STHWK SE1 12 F10
Maiden Rd *SRTFD* E15 141 K2
Maidenshaw Rd *HOR/WEW* KT19 220 A8
Maidenstone Hl *GNWCH* SE10 161 H7
Maidstone Av *CRW* RM5 104 D10
Maidstone Rd *FBAR/BDGN* N11 98 E7
GRAYS RM17 167 M5
SCUP DA14 186 A10
SWLY BR8 208 C1
Main Av *EN* EN1 79 N9
NTHWD HA6 92 D4
Main Dr *CFSP/GDCR* SL9 109 P3
IVER SL0 151 H2
Mainridge Rd *CHST* BR7 184 D7
Main Rd *BFN/LL* DA15 185 H6
BH/WHM TN16 225 P9
EDEN TN8 262 F10
EYN DA4 188 A9
EYN DA4 209 M6
GPK RM2 105 K10
HART DA3 211 K2
RDART DA2 211 H1
ROM RM1 124 G2
RSEV TN14 245 K4
RSEV TN14 245 P10
STMC/STPC BR5 207 M3
SWLY BR8 208 D6
SWLY BR8 208 G1
Main Road Gorse Hl *EYN* DA4 210 A8
Mainstone Crs *CHOB/PIR* GU24 230 C7
Mainstone Rd *CHOB/PIR* GU24 230 E2
Main St *ADL/WDHM* KT15 195 P10
FELT TW13 175 L8
Maise Webster Cl
STWL/WRAY TW19 173 N3 3
Maismore St *PECK* SE15 19 N10
Maitland Cl *BF/WBF* KT14 215 K9
GNWCH SE10 160 G6 3
HSLWW TW4 153 N9
WOT/HER KT12 197 M9
Maitland Park Rd *HAMP* NW3 4 B2
Maitland Park Vls *HAMP* NW3 4 B1
Maitland Rd *SRTFD* E15 141 L1 3
SYD SE26 182 C9
Maizecroft *HORL* RH6 280 D3 3
Maizey Ct *BRWN* CM15 86 F9
Majendie Rd *WOOL/PLUM* SE18 162 G4
Major Rd *BERM/RHTH* SE16 19 P3
SRTFD E15 121 J10 3
Major's Farm Rd *DTCH/LGLY* SL3 150 A6
Major's Hl *CRAWE* RH10 285 L9
Makepeace Av *HGT* N6 118 B7
Makepeace Rd *NTHLT* UB5 133 M4
WAN E11 121 M2
Makins St *CHEL* SW3 15 P6
Malabar St *POP/IOD* E14 160 F1
Malacca Farm *RGUE* GU4 251 L4
Malam Gdns *POP/IOD* E14 140 G9 3
Malan Cl *BH/WHM* TN16 244 B3
Malan Sq *RAIN* RM13 145 J1
Malborough Rd *WATW* WD18 73 J8
Malbrook Rd *PUT/ROE* SW15 156 E10
Malcolm Ct *STAN* HA7 95 H6
Malcolm Crs *HDN* NW4 116 D3
Malcolm Dr *SURB* KT6 199 J8
Malcolm Gdns *HORL* RH6 279 N6
Malcolm Pl *BETH* E2 140 B6
Malcolm Rd *COUL/CHIP* CR5 240 E1
HGDN/ICK UB10 112 A9
PGE/AN SE20 182 B10
SNWD SE25 203 P6
WCHPL E1 140 B6
WIM/MER SW19 179 H9
Malcolm Wy *WAN* E11 121 M3
Malden Av *NTHLT* UB5 134 D1
SNWD SE25 204 A4
Malden Crs *KTTN* NW5 4 D2
Malden Flds *BUSH* WD23 73 L9
Malden Green Av *WPK* KT4 200 C8
Malden Hl *NWMAL* KT3 200 C4
Malden Hill Gdns *NWMAL* KT3 200 C3
Malden Pk *NWMAL* KT3 200 C6
Malden Pl *KTTN* NW5 118 B10 4
Malden Rd *BORE* WD6 75 M7
CHEAM SM3 220 G1
KTTN NW5 118 A10
NWMAL KT3 200 C7
WAT WD17 73 H6 2
WPK KT4 200 C7
Malden Wy *NWMAL* KT3 200 C5 3
Malden Wy (Kingston By Pass)
NWMAL KT3 200 B6
Maldon Cl *CMBW* SE5 159 M9 2
IS N1 6 E5
Maldon Ct *HARP* AL5 20 A1 3
Maldon Rd *ACT* W3 135 P9
ED N9 99 N4
ROMW/RG RM7 124 D5
WLGTN SM6 222 C2
Maldon Wk *WFD* IG8 101 P7
Malet Cl *EGH* TW20 172 G9 2
Malet St *GWRST* WC1E 11 K3
Maley Av *WNWD* SE27 181 J5
Malford Gv *SWFD* E18 121 M1
Malfort Rd *CMBW* SE5 159 M9
Malham Cl *CRAWE* RH10 284 D10
Malham Rd *FSTH* SE23 182 C4
Malins Cl *BAR* EN5 76 F9 1
Malkin Dr *BEAC* HP9 88 B8
Mallams Ms *BRXN/ST* SW9 159 J9 1
Mallard Cl *BAR* EN5 77 N10 2
DART DA1 187 N1
HORL RH6 280 B2
HSLWW TW4 175 P3 4
KIL/WHAMP NW6 2 F6
REDH RH1 258 B7 1
UPMR RM14 126 E5 1
Mallard Ct *WALTH* E17 121 J1 3
Mallard Dr *SL* SL1 128 E9
Mallard Pl *TWK* TW1 176 F6
Mallard Rd *ABLGY* WD5 55 H7
SAND/SEL CR2 224 C6
Mallard's Reach *WEY* KT13 196 E9
Mallards Ri *HLWE* CM17 47 M1
Mallards Rd *WFD* IG8 101 N8
The Mallards *HHS/BOV* HP3 54 A1
STA TW18 195 L2
Mallard Wk *CROY/NA* CR0 204 C5
Mallard Wy *CDALE/KGS* NW9 115 P5
GSTN WD25 73 M2 1
NTHWD HA6 92 D8
RBRW/HUT CM13 107 M1
WLGTN SM6 222 D5
Mallet Dr *NTHLT* UB5 113 N10
Mallet Rd *LEW* SE13 183 J2
Malling Cl *CROY/NA* CR0 204 B6 3
Malling Gdns *MRDN* SM4 201 M6 4
Malling Wy *HAYES* BR2 205 L7
Mallinson Cl *HCH* RM12 125 K10 3
Mallinson Rd *BTSEA* SW11 179 P1
WLGTN SM6 202 E10
Mallion Ct *WAB* EN9 63 L9
Mallord St *CHEL* SW3 15 M9
Mallory Cl *BROCKY* SE4 160 D10
Mallory Gdns *EBAR* EN4 98 B1
Mallory St *CAMTN* NW1 9 P2
Mallow Cl *CROY/NA* CR0 204 C8 11
GVW DA11 190 B7 3
KWD/TDW/WH KT20 238 E5
Mallow Ct *GRAYS* RM17 168 A5
Mallow Crs *RGUE* GU4 250 E7
Mallow Md *MLHL* NW7 97 H8
Mallows Gn *HLWW/ROY* CM19 46 D6
The Mallows *HGDN/ICK* UB10 112 C8
Mallow St *FSBYE* EC1V 12 G1
Mall Rd *HMSMTH* W6 156 E4
The Mall *EA* W5 135 K9
HCH RM12 125 J6
KTN/HRWW/W HA3 115 L4
LCOL/BKTW AL2 56 B3
MORT/ESHN SW14 177 P1
STHGT/OAK N14 98 F4
SURB KT6 199 J5
WHALL SW1A 16 G1
Mallys Pl *EYN* DA4 210 B1 1
Malmains Cl *BECK* BR3 205 J5
Malmains Wy *BECK* BR3 205 H4
Malm Cl *RKW/CH/CXG* WD3 91 N3
Malmesbury Cl *PIN* HA5 113 H2
Malmesbury Rd *BOW* E3 140 E4
CAN/RD E16 141 K7
MRDN SM4 201 M7
SWFD E18 101 L9
Malmesbury Ter *CAN/RD* E16 141 L7 5
Malmes Cft *HHS/BOV* HP3 36 D8
Malmsdale *WGCW* AL8 22 G1
Malmstone Av *REDH* RH1 258 D4
Malpas Dr *PIN* HA5 113 L5
Malpas Rd *BROCKY* SE4 160 E8
CDH/CHF RM16 168 F2
DAGW RM9 143 N1
HACK E8 140 A1
SLN SL2 129 N9
Malta Rd *LEY* E10 120 F8
TIL RM18 168 C8
Malta St *FSBYE* EC1V 12 C1
Maltby Cl *ORP* BR6 207 K8
Maltby Dr *EN* EN1 80 A4
Maltby Rd *CHSGTN* KT9 219 M3
Maltby St *STHWK* SE1 19 L3
Malt Hl *EGH* TW20 172 B8
Malt House Cl *WDSR* SL4 171 N3
Malthouse Dr *FELT* TW13 175 L8
Malthouse La *CHOB/PIR* GU24 212 E8
GVE DA12 191 P8
RGUW GU3 231 H10
Malthouse Rd *CRAWE* RH10 283 N8
Malthouse Sq *BEAC* HP9 108 E1
Maltings Dr *STALE/WH* AL4 21 H4
Maltings Hl *CHONG* CM5 49 L6
Maltings La *EPP* CM16 65 K5 3
Maltings Pl *FUL/PGN* SW6 157 L7
The Maltings *BF/WBF* KT14 215 P9
KGLGY WD4 54 D9
ORP BR6 207 J8
OXTED RH8 261 L7
ROMW/RG RM7 124 C5 3
STA TW18 173 H7 1
STAL AL1 38 C6 4
Malting Wy *ISLW* TW7 154 E9
Maltmans La *CFSP/GDCR* SL9 109 P1
Malton Av *SL* SL1 128 G8
Malton Ms *NKENS* W10 8 A5 1
WOOL/PLUM SE18 163 H5 2
Malton Rd *NKENS* W10 8 A5
Malton St *WOOL/PLUM* SE18 163 H5
Maltravers St *TPL/STR* WC2R 12 A7 2
Malt St *STHWK* SE1 19 N9
Malus Cl *ADL/WDHM* KT15 215 J4
HHNE HP2 36 B6
Malus Dr *ADL/WDHM* KT15 215 J4
Malva Cl *WAND/EARL* SW18 179 L1
Malvern Av *BXLYHN* DA7 163 P6
CHING E4 101 J8
RYLN/HDSTN HA2 113 M8
Malvern Cl *CHERT* KT16 214 F3 2
HGDN/ICK UB10 112 B7
MTCM CR4 202 D3
NKENS W10 8 C4
STALE/WH AL4 38 G2
SURB KT6 199 K8
Malvern Dr *FELT* TW13 175 L8 2
GDMY/SEVK IG3 123 J9
WFD IG8 101 P6
Malvern Gdns *CRICK* NW2 117 H7
KTN/HRWW/W HA3 115 K2
LOU IG10 82 C10
Malvern Ms *KIL/WHAMP* NW6 2 E10
Malvern Pl *MV/WKIL* W9 2 D9
Malvern Rd *CEND/HSY/T* N8 118 G1
CRAWW RH11 283 M9
EHAM E6 142 B3 1
EMPK RM11 125 H4
GRAYS RM17 168 B3
HACK E8 7 N4
HPTN TW12 197 P1
HYS/HAR UB3 152 F6
KIL/WHAMP NW6 2 B8 1
ORP BR6 227 L1
PEND EN3 80 D3
SURB KT6 199 K9
THHTH CR7 203 H4
TOTM N17 119 P1 3
WAN E11 121 K7
Malvern Ter *ED* N9 99 N2 1
IS N1 6 A5
Malvern Wy *HHNE* HP2 35 P4
RKW/CH/CXG WD3 72 C9
WEA W13 134 G7 3
Malvina Av *GVE* DA12 190 E5
Malwood Rd *BAL* SW12 180 C2
Malyons Rd *LEW* SE13 182 G1
SWLY BR8 186 G10
Malyons Ter *BROCKY* SE4 182 G1
The Malyons *SHPTN* TW17 196 E6 3
Managers St *POP/IOD* E14 141 H10 2
Manan Cl *HHS/BOV* HP3 36 D8 2
Manaton Cl *PECK* SE15 160 A9
Manaton Crs *STHL* UB1 133 P8
Manbey Gv *SRTFD* E15 141 K1
Manbey Park Rd *SRTFD* E15 141 K1
Manbey Rd *SRTFD* E15 141 K1 2
Manbey St *SRTFD* E15 141 K1
Manbre Rd *HMSMTH* W6 156 F5
Manbrough Av *EHAM* E6 142 C5
Manchester Dr *NKENS* W10 8 A2
Manchester Gv *POP/IOD* E14 161 H4
Manchester Ms *MHST* W1U 10 C4 1
Manchester Rd *POP/IOD* E14 161 H4
SEVS/STOTM N15 119 L4 3
THHTH CR7 203 K3
Manchester Sq *MHST* W1U 10 D5 6
Manchester St *MHST* W1U 10 C4 2
Manchuria Rd *BTSEA* SW11 180 B2
Manciple St *STHWK* SE1 19 H2
Mandalay Rd *CLAP* SW4 180 D1
Mandarin Wy *YEAD* UB4 133 L8
Mandela Cl *WLSDN* NW10 135 P2
Mandela Pl *WATN* WD24 73 L6 4
Mandela Rd *CAN/RD* E16 141 M8
Mandela St *BRXN/ST* SW9 159 H6
CAMTN NW1 5 H5
Mandela Wy *STHWK* SE1 19 K5
Mandelyns *BERK* HP4 33 K2
Mandeville Cl *BKHTH/KID* SE3 161 L6 1
BROX EN10 44 E6
GUW GU2 249 M7
HERT/BAY SG13 25 K8 1
WAT WD17 72 G4
WIM/MER SW19 179 H10
Mandeville Dr *STAL* AL1 38 C9
SURB KT6 199 J8
Mandeville Pl *MHST* W1U 10 D5 7
Mandeville Ri *WGCW* AL8 22 G3
Mandeville Rd *HERT/BAY* SG13 25 K8
ISLW TW7 154 F8
NTHLT UB5 133 P1
PEND EN3 80 D3
POTB/CUF EN6 59 M8
SHPTN TW17 196 B5
STHGT/OAK N14 98 C3
Mandeville St *CLPT* E5 120 D8
Mandrake Rd *TOOT* SW17 180 A6
Mandrake Wy *SRTFD* E15 141 K2 3
Mandrell Rd *BRXS/STRHM* SW2 180 F1
Manette St *SOHO/SHAV* W1D 11 K6 1
Manfield Cl *SLN* SL2 128 F5
Manford Cl *CHIG* IG7 103 L5
Manford Cross *CHIG* IG7 103 K6
Manford Wy *CHIG* IG7 103 K6
Manfred Rd *PUT/ROE* SW15 179 J1
Manger Rd *HOLWY* N7 5 M1
Mangles Rd *RG* GU1 250 A8
Mangrove Dr *HERT/BAY* SG13 25 M7
Mangrove La *HERT/BAY* SG13 25 M8
Mangrove Rd *HERT/BAY* SG13 25 M6
Manilla St *POP/IOD* E14 160 F1
Manister Rd *ABYW* SE2 163 K2
Manland Av *HARP* AL5 20 B1
Manland Wy *HARP* AL5 20 B1
Manley Ct *STNW/STAM* N16 119 N8
Manley Rd *HHNE* HP2 35 P5 4
Manley St *CAMTN* NW1 4 C5
Manly Dixon Dr *PEND* EN3 80 D3
Mannamead *EPSOM* KT18 238 B5
Mannamead Cl *EPSOM* KT18 238 B5 1
Mann Cl *CROY/NA* CR0 203 K10
Mannicotts *WGCW* AL8 22 E3
Manningford Cl *FSBYE* EC1V 6 C9 2
Manning Gdns
KTN/HRWW/W HA3 115 J5
Manning Pl *RCHPK/HAM* TW10 177 L2 2
Manning Rd *DAGE* RM10 144 B2
STMC/STPC BR5 207 N5
WALTH E17 120 D3 6
Mannings Cl *CRAWE* RH10 284 E4
Manning St *SOCK/AV* RM15 146 B10
Manningtree Cl *WIM/MER* SW19 179 H4
Manningtree Rd *RSLP* HA4 113 J9
Manningtree St *WCHPL* E1 13 N5 2
Mannin Rd *CHDH* RM6 123 L5
Mannock Dr *LOU* IG10 82 F6
Mannock Rd *DART* DA1 165 N9 1
WDGN N22 119 J1
Mann's Cl *ISLW* TW7 176 E1
Manns Rd *EDGW* HA8 95 M7
Manoel Rd *WHTN* TW2 176 B5
Manor Av *BROCKY* SE4 160 E8
CTHM CR3 241 M10
EMPK RM11 125 K3
HHS/BOV HP3 35 N9 1
HSLWW TW4 153 L9
NTHLT UB5 133 N2
Manorbrook *BKHTH/KID* SE3 161 M10
Manor Cha *WEY* KT13 216 C2
Manor Cl *BAR* EN5 77 H8
BERK HP4 33 P5 4
CDALE/KGS NW9 115 N2
DAGE RM10 144 E1 1
DART DA1 164 E10
EHSLY KT24 252 F4
GVE DA12 191 L5 2
HAT AL10 40 C1
HERT/WAS SG14 25 L3
HORL RH6 280 A4
RDART DA2 187 H6
ROM RM1 125 H3
RSLP HA4 112 G6
SOCK/AV RM15 146 B10
THMD SE28 143 M8
WARL CR6 242 D3
WOKS/MYFD GU22 233 J2
WPK KT4 200 B8
Manor Cottages *NTHWD* HA6 92 G9 1
Manor Cottages Ap *EFNCH* N2 97 M10 3
Manor Ct *DEN/HRF* UB9 91 M10
EN EN1 80 A2
RAD WD7 74 E3
SL SL1 128 E10 2
WEY KT13 216 C1
Manor Court Rd *HNWL* W7 134 D9
Manor Crs *BEAC* HP9 89 J6

BF/WBF KT14 .... 216 A9
BRYLDS KT5 .... 199 M4
CHOB/PIR GU24 .... 250 C6
EMPK RM11 .... 125 K3
GUW GU2 .... 249 N8
Manorcrofts Rd *ECH* TW20 .. 172 D9
Manordene Cl *THDIT* KT7 ... 198 F8 🔢
Manordene Rd *THMD* SE28 .. 143 M8
Manor Dr *ADL/WDHM* KT15 .. 215 K6
AMS HP6 .... 68 G2
BRYLDS KT5 .... 199 M4
ESH/CLAY KT10 .... 198 E10
FELT TW13 .... 175 L8 🔢
HART DA3 .... 211 H4
HOR/WEW KT19 .... 220 B3
HORL RH6 .... 280 A4
LCOL/BKTW AL2 .... 55 P3
MLHL NW7 .... 96 A6
STHGT/OAK N14 .... 98 C1
SUN TW16 .... 197 H2
TRDG/WHET N20 .... 97 P4
WBLY HA9 .... 115 L9
Manor Dr North *NWMAL* KT3 200 M10
WPK KT4 .... 200 B8
The Manor Dr WPK KT4 ...... 200 B8
Manor Farm Av *SHPTN* TW17 196 C6
Manor Farm Cl *WDSR* SL4 .. 148 E9
Manor Farm Cottages *WDSR* SL4 171 M4
Manor Farm Dr *CHING* E4 ... 101 K4
Manor Farm La *ECH* TW20 .. 172 D8
Manor Farm Rd *ALP/SUD* HA0 135 J4
EN EN1 .... 80 A1
STRHM/NOR SW16 .... 203 H2 🔢
Manor Fld *GVE* DA12 .... 191 P8
Manorfields Cl *CHST* BR7 .. 207 J3
Manor Forstal *HART* DA3 ... 211 L10
Manor Gdns *ACT* W3 .... 155 M3
EHSLY KT24 .... 253 L4
GUW GU2 .... 249 N8
HOLWY N7 .... 118 F8
HPTN TW12 .... 176 A10
RCH/KEW TW9 .... 155 L10
RGODL GU7 .... 267 K10 🔢
RSLP HA4 .... 113 K10
RYNPK SW20 .... 201 J2
SAND/SEL CR2 .... 223 N3
SUN TW16 .... 197 H1
Manor Ga *NTHLT* UB5 ...... 133 M2
Manorgate Rd *KUTN/CMB* KT2 199 M1
Manor Green Rd *HOR/WEW* KT19 219 P8
Manor Gv *BECK* BR3 .... 204 G2
PECK SE15 .... 160 B5
RCH/KEW TW9 .... 155 M10
Manor Hall Av *HDN* NW4 ... 96 F10
Manor Hall Dr *HDN* NW4 ... 96 G10
Manor Hall Gdns *LEY* E10 .. 120 F6
Manor Hatch *HLWS* CM18 .. 47 K2
Manor Hatch Cl *HLWS* CM18 47 L2
Manor Hl *BNSTD* SM7 .... 240 A1
Manor House Dr ....
KIL/WHAMP NW6 .... 136 G2
NTHWD HA6 .... 2 F7
Manor House Gdns *ABLGY* WD5 54 E7
Manor House La *DTCH/LGLY* SL3 149 Y7
Manorhouse La *GT/LBKH* KT23 253 M2
Manor House Wy *ISLW* TW7 154 C9 🔢
Manor La *CFSP/GDCR* SL9 .. 110 A3
FELT TW13 .... 175 H5
HART DA3 .... 211 H7
HART DA3 .... 211 H6
HYS/HAR UB3 .... 152 E5
KWD/TDW/WH KT20 .... 257 K5
LEW SE13 .... 183 K1
SUN TW16 .... 197 H2
SUT SM1 .... 221 M2
Manor Lane Ter *LEW* SE13 .. 161 K10
Manor Leaze *ECH* TW20 .... 172 E8
Manor Ms *KIL/WHAMP* NW6 2 F7
Manor Mt *FSTH* SE23 .... 182 B4
Manor Pde *HAT* AL10 .... 40 C1 🔢
Manor Pk *CHST* BR7 .... 206 G2
LEW SE13 .... 183 J1
RCH/KEW TW9 .... 155 L10
STA TW18 .... 172 G6
Manor Park Cl *WWKM* BR4 .. 204 C8
Manor Park Crs *EDGW* HA8 95 M7
Manor Park Dr *RYLN/HDSTN* HA2 114 A1
Manor Park Gdns *EDGW* HA8 95 M6
Manor Park Rd *CHST* BR7 ... 206 F1
EFNCH N2 .... 117 M1
MNPK E12 .... 122 A9
SUT SM1 .... 221 M2
WLSDN NW10 .... 136 C3 🔢
WWKM BR4 .... 204 B8
Manor Pl *CHST* BR7 .... 206 G2
EBED/NFELT TW14 .... 175 H4
GT/LBKH KT23 .... 253 P2
MTCM CR4 .... 202 D3 🔢
STA TW18 .... 173 L8
SUT SM1 .... 221 L2
WALW SE17 .... 18 D8
Manor Rd *ABR/ST* RM4 ..... 103 N2
ASHF TW15 .... 174 A8
BAR EN5 .... 77 H8
BEAC HP9 .... 89 J4
BECK BR3 .... 204 F2
BELMT SM2 .... 221 J4
BFN/LL DA15 .... 185 J6
BH/WHM TN16 .... 244 B6
BXLY DA5 .... 186 C4
CAN/RD E16 .... 141 K7
CDH/RM6 .... 123 N4
CHIG IG7 .... 102 D7
CSHM HP5 .... 50 C5 🔢
DAGE RM10 .... 144 D1
DART DA1 .... 164 F10
E/WMO/HCT KT8 .... 198 C4
ENC/FH EN2 .... 79 L6
ERITH DA8 .... 164 C5
GRAYS RM17 .... 167 P5
GUW GU2 .... 249 N8
GVE DA12 .... 190 E2 🔢
HART DA3 .... 211 P5
HAT AL10 .... 40 C1
HLWE CM17 .... 29 M6
HOD EN11 .... 44 F7
HRW HA1 .... 114 F4
HYS/HAR UB3 .... 133 H8
LCOL/BKTW AL2 .... 57 H2
LEY E10 .... 120 F5
LOU IG10 .... 81 N5
LOU IG10 .... 81 N10
MTCM CR4 .... 202 D3 🔢
POTB/CUF EN6 .... 59 L9
RCH/KEW TW9 .... 155 L10
REDH RH1 .... 125 H3
REIC RH2 .... 257 J8
ROM RM1 .... 125 H3
RPLY/SEND GU23 .... 233 K10
RSEV TN14 .... 245 N10
RSLP HA4 .... 112 E6
RYNPK SW20 .... 201 J2
SNWD SE25 .... 203 P3
STAL AL1 .... 38 D5
STALE/WH AL4 .... 20 E1
STNW/STAM N16 .... 119 M6
SWCM DA10 .... 189 J2
TEDD TW11 .... 176 D8
TIL RM18 .... 168 D8
TOTM N17 .... 99 P9
WAB EN9 .... 63 J9
WALTH E17 .... 100 D10
WAT WD17 .... 73 H5
WDGN N22 .... 98 F7
WDSR SL4 .... 148 D3
WEA W13 .... 134 F9

WHTN TW2 .... 176 B5
WLGTN SM6 .... 222 C2 🔢
WOT/HER KT12 .... 196 G7
WTHK RM20 .... 167 H5
WWKM BR4 .... 204 C9
Manor Rd North *ESH/CLAY* KT10 198 E10
WLGTN SM6 .... 222 C1
Manor Rd South *ESH/CLAY* KT10 218 D1
Manor Royal *CRAWE* RH10 .. 283 P4
Manorside *BAR* EN5 .... 77 H8
Manor Sq *BCTR* RM8 .... 123 M7
Manor St *BERK* HP4 .... 34 A5 🔢
Manor V *BTFD* TW8 .... 155 H4 🔢
Manorville Rd *HHS/BOV* HP3 35 M10
Manor Wk *WEY* KT13 .... 216 C2
Manorway *EN* EN1 .... 99 M1
WFD IG8 .... 101 P6 🔢
Manor Wy *BECK* BR3 .... 204 F3
BKHTH/KID SE3 .... 161 M10
BNSTD SM7 .... 240 A2
BORE WD6 .... 75 P8
BRW CM14 .... 106 F4
BXLY DA5 .... 186 B4
BXLYHN DA7 .... 164 E9
CDALE/KGS NW9 .... 116 B2
CHING E4 .... 101 J5
CSHM HP5 .... 51 J6
ECH TW20 .... 172 C9
GRAYS RM17 .... 167 J5
GUW GU2 .... 267 K3
GVW DA11 .... 191 M9
HAYES BR2 .... 206 B6
LHD/OX KT22 .... 236 B2
MTCM CR4 .... 202 D3
NWDGN UB2 .... 153 L3
POTB/CUF EN6 .... 59 K6
PUR/KEN CR8 .... 222 F8
RAIN RM13 .... 144 F7
RKW/CH/CXG WD3 .... 72 B8
RSLP HA4 .... 112 F5
RYLN/HDSTN HA2 .... 114 A2
SAND/SEL CR2 .... 223 M3
STMC/STPC BR5 .... 206 F4
SWCM DA10 .... 167 K10
WOKS/MYFD GU22 .... 232 E6
WPK KT4 .... 200 B8
Manor Waye *UX/CGN* UB8 .. 131 N4
The Manor Wy *WLGTN* SM6 222 C1
Manor Wood Rd *PUR/KEN* CR8 222 F9
Manresa Rd *CHEL* SW3 ..... 15 M8
Mansard Beeches *TOOT* SW17 180 B8
Mansard Cl *HCH* RM12 ..... 125 H10
PIN HA5 .... 113 L1 🔢
Manscroft Rd *HHW* HP1 .... 35 L4
Manse Rd *HYS/HAR* UB3 ... 152 E3
Mansefield *CSHM* HP5 ..... 50 C4 🔢
Mansel Gv *WALTH* E17 ..... 100 F9
Mansell Cl *WDSR* SL4 .... 148 D8
Mansell Rd *ACT* W3 .... 136 A10
GFD/PVL UB6 .... 134 A7
Mansell Wy *CTHM* CR3 .... 241 L8
Mansel Rd *WIM/MER* SW19 179 H9
Mansergh Cl *WOOL/PLUM* SE18 162 B6
Manse Rd *STNW/STAM* N16 119 N8
Manser Rd *RAIN* RM13 ...... 144 F5
Manse Wy *SWLY* BR8 .... 209 H4
Mansfield *SBW* CM21 .... 29 K2
Mansfield Av *EBAR* EN4 .... 78 A10 🔢
RSLP HA4 .... 113 J6 🔢
SEVS/STOTM N15 .... 119 L2
Mansfield Cl *ED* N9 .... 79 P10
STMC/STPC BR5 .... 207 N7
YEAD UB4 .... 132 F6
Mansfield Dr *REDH* RH1 ... 258 E4
Mansfield Gdns *HCH* RM12 125 L7
HERT/WAS SG14 .... 25 K3 🔢
Mansfield Hl *CHING* E4 ..... 100 G2
Mansfield Ms *CAVSQ/HST* W1G 10 E4 🔢
Mansfield Pl *SAND/SEL* CR2 223 L3 🔢
Mansfield Rd *ACT* W3 .... 135 N6
CHSGTN KT9 .... 219 H2
HAMP NW3 .... 118 A10
IL IG1 .... 122 D7
SAND/SEL CR2 .... 223 L3
SWLY BR8 .... 186 F9
WALTH E17 .... 120 E2
WAN E11 .... 121 N4
Mansfield St *CAVSQ/HST* W1G 10 E4
Mansford St *BETH* E2 .... 7 P8
Manship Rd *MTCM* CR4 ..... 180 D10
Mansion House Pl *MANHO* EC4N 12 G6 🔢
Mansion La *BAR* EN5 .... 130 F10
Manson Ms *SKENS* SW7 .... 15 K5
Manson Pl *SKENS* SW7 ..... 15 L6
Manstead Gdns *CHDH* RM6 123 M5
RAIN RM13 .... 145 J8 🔢
Manston Av *NWDGN* UB2 .. 153 P3
Manston Cl *CHES/WCR* EN8 62 B6 🔢
PGE/AN SE20 .... 204 B1
Manstone Rd *CRICK* NW2 .. 117 N10
Manston Gv *KUTN/CMB* KT2 177 J8
Manston Rd *HLW* CM20 .... 47 N1
RGUE GU4 .... 250 D6
Manston Wy *HCH* RM12 .... 145 J1
Manthorpe Rd *WOOL/PLUM* SE18 162 B7
Mantilla Rd *TOOT* SW17 ... 180 B7
Mantle Rd *BROCKY* SE4 .... 160 B9
Mantlet Cl *STRHM/NOR* SW16 180 D10
Mantle Wy *SRTFD* E15 ...... 141 K2 🔢
Manton Av *HNWL* W7 .... 154 E1
Manton Cl *HYS/HAR* UB3 ... 133 H8
Manton Rd *ABYW* SE2 ...... 163 K3
Mantua St *BTSEA* SW11 .... 157 N9 🔢
Mantus Rd *WCHPL* E1 .... 140 B8
Manus Wy *TRDG/WHET* N20 97 M3
Manville Gdns *TOOT* SW17 180 C6 🔢
Manville Rd *TOOT* SW17 ... 180 B5
Manwood Rd *BROCKY* SE4 182 C2
Manwood St *CAN/RD* E16 .. 142 C10
Manygate La *SHPTN* TW17 .. 196 C6
Many Gates *BAL* SW12 ...... 180 C5
Maori Rd *GU* GU1 .... 268 C5
Mapesbury Rd *CRICK* NW2 .. 2 A2
Mape St *BETH* E2 .... 140 A2
Maple Av *ACT* W3 .... 136 B10
CHING E4 .... 100 F7
RYLN/HDSTN HA2 .... 114 A7
STALW/RED AL3 .... 38 B2
UPMR RM14 .... 126 A8
WDR/YW UB7 .... 131 P9 🔢
Maple Cl *BARK/HLT* IG6 .... 103 H6 🔢
BKHH IG9 .... 102 A4
BUSH WD23 .... 73 M6
CLAP SW4 .... 180 E2
CRAWW RH11 .... 284 M4
CTHM CR3 .... 241 N3 🔢
FNCH N3 .... 97 K7 🔢
HAT AL10 .... 40 D5 🔢
HCH RM12 .... 125 J8 🔢
HPTN TW12 .... 175 M10
MTCM CR4 .... 202 C1 🔢
RBRW/HUT CM13 .... 107 L4 🔢
RSLP HA4 .... 113 H4
STMC/STPC BR5 .... 206 G3
STNW/STAM N16 .... 119 P4 🔢
SWLY BR8 .... 208 F2 🔢
YEAD UB4 .... 133 L5 🔢
Maple Ct *ECH* TW20 .... 171 N9 🔢
NWMAL KT3 .... 200 A3 🔢
Maple Crs *BFN/LL* DA15 ... 185 K2
SLN SL2 .... 129 N3
Maplecroft Cl *EHAM* E6 .... 142 A8

Maplecroft La *WAB* EN9 ..... 45 K7
Mapledale Av *CROY/NA* CR0 204 A10
Mapledene Rd *HACK* E8 ..... 7 M3
Maple Dr *SOCK/AV* RM15 .. 147 J6 🔢
Maplefield *LCOL/BKTW* AL2 56 N7
Maple Gdns *ASHF* TW15 .... 173 P5 🔢
EDGW HA8 .... 96 B8
Maple Ga *LOU* IG10 .... 82 D6 🔢
Maple Gn *HHW* HP1 .... 35 L4
Maple Gv *BTFD* TW8 .... 154 G6
CDALE/KGS NW9 .... 115 P5
EA W5 .... 155 J2
GU GU1 .... 250 A8
STHL UB1 .... 133 N7
WAT WD17 .... 73 H5 🔢
WOKS/MYFD GU22 .... 232 B7
Maplehurst *LHD/OX* KT22 .. 236 C9
Maple Leaf Cl *ABLGY* WD5 .. 55 H8 🔢
Maple Leaf Dr *BFN/LL* DA15 185 J4
Mapleleafe Gdns *BARK/HLT* IG6 122 E1
Maple Leaf Sq ....
BERM/RHTH SE16 .... 160 C1 🔢
Maple Lodge Cl *RKW/CH/CXG* WD3 71 H5
Maple Ms *KIL/WHAMP* NW6 2 C1 🔢
STRHM/NOR SW16 .... 180 C8
Maple Pl *EW* KT17 .... 220 G10 🔢
FITZ W1T .... 11 H3 🔢
WDR/YW UB7 .... 131 P10
Maple Rd *ASHTD* KT21 ..... 237 J5
CTHM CR3 .... 241 N3
DART DA1 .... 187 N4
GRAYS RM17 .... 167 P5
GVE DA12 .... 190 F7
PGE/AN SE20 .... 204 A1
REDH RH1 .... 276 A4
RPLY/SEND GU23 .... 233 K10
SURB KT6 .... 199 K5
WAN E11 .... 121 K4
YEAD UB4 .... 133 K5
Maplescombe La *EYN* DA4 .. 209 P10
Maples Pl *WCHPL* E1 .... 140 A7 🔢
Maple Springs *WAB* EN9 .... 63 M9
Maplestead Rd ....
BRXS/STRHM SW2 .... 180 G3
DAGW RM9 .... 143 L3
The Maples *BNSTD* SM7 .... 240 A3
CHERT KT16 .... 214 E3
CHESW EN7 .... 61 M4
HART DA3 .... 211 N3 🔢
HLWW/ROY IG4 .... 48 G6
Maple St *FITZ* W1T 10 E3
ROMW/RG RM7 .... 124 D2
Maplethorpe Rd *THHTH* CR7 203 H2
Mapleton Cl *HAYES* BR2 ... 205 M6 🔢
Mapleton Crs *PEND* EN3 ... 80 B4
WAND/EARL SW18 .... 179 L2
Mapleton Rd *BH/WHM* TN16 263 H6
CHING E4 .... 101 H4
EN EN1 .... 80 A6
WAND/EARL SW18 .... 179 L2
Maple Wk *NKENS* W10 ...... 136 C6 🔢
Maple Wy *COUL/CHIP* CR5 240 C7
FELT TW13 .... 175 H6
Maplewood Gdns *BEAC* HP9 88 A10
Maplin Pk *DTCH/LGLY* SL3 150 E1
Maplin Rd *CAN/RD* E16 ..... 141 M8
Maplin St *BOW* E3 .... 140 E5
Maran Wy *ERITH* DA18 ...... 163 N2
Marban Rd *MV/WKIL* W9 .... 2 C9
Marbeck Cl *WDSR* SL4 ...... 147 P7
Marble Cl *ACT* W3 .... 135 N10
Marble Dr *CRICK* NW2 ...... 116 C6
Marble Hill Cl *TWK* TW1 ... 176 C3 🔢
Marble Hill Gdns *TWK* TW1 176 C3 🔢
Marbles Wy *KWD/TDW/WH* KT20 238 C5
Marbrook Ct *LEE/GVPK* SE12 183 P6
Marcellina Wy *ORP* BR6 .... 207 H10
Marcet Rd *DART* DA1 .... 187 K1
Marchant Rd *WAN* E11 ...... 121 K7
Marchant St *NWCR* SE14 ... 160 D5 🔢
Marchbank Rd *WKENS* W14 14 D8 🔢
Marchmant Cl *HCH* RM12 .. 125 K8 🔢
Marchmont Rd ....
RCHPK/HAM TW10 .... 177 L1 🔢
WLGTN SM6 .... 222 D5
Marchmont St *BMSBY* WC1N 11 L1
Marchside Cl *HEST* TW5 .... 153 L2 🔢
Marchwood Cl *CMBW* SE5 .. 159 M6 🔢
Marchwood Crs *EA* W5 ...... 135 H8
Marcia Ct *SL* SL1 .... 128 E10 🔢
Marcia Rd *STHWK* SE1 ...... 19 K6
Marcilly Rd *WAND/EARL* SW18 179 N1 🔢
Marconi Ct *GVW* DA11 ...... 190 A6
LEY E10 .... 120 F6
Marconi Wy *GFD/PVL* UB6 .. 134 A3
STALE/WH AL4 .... 39 J6
Marcon Pl *HACK* E8 .... 7 P1
Marco Rd *HMSMTH* W6 ..... 156 F2
Marcus Ct *WOKS/MYFD* GU22 232 C4 🔢
Marcuse Rd *CTHM* CR3 ..... 241 N9
Marcus Garvey Ms *EDUL* SE22 182 J2
Marcus Garvey Wy *HNHL* SE24 159 H10 🔢
Marcus Rd *DART* DA1 .... 187 H3
Marcus St *SRTFD* E15 .... 141 K3
WAND/EARL SW18 .... 179 L2 🔢
Mardale Dr *CDALE/KGS* NW9 116 A3
Mardell Rd *CROY/NA* CR0 .. 204 C5
Marden Av *HAYES* BR2 ...... 205 N6
Marden Crs *BXLY* DA5 .... 186 D1
CROY/NA CR0 .... 202 C6
Marden Rd *CROY/NA* CR0 .. 202 C6
ROM RM1 .... 124 F4 🔢
TOTM N17 .... 99 M10
The Mardens *CRAWW* RH11 283 M4
Marder Rd *WEA* W13 .... 154 F1
Mardyke Rd *HLW* CM20 ..... 29 K9
Marechal Niel Av *BFN/LL* DA15 184 G6
Mareschal Rd *GUW* GU2 .... 267 P2
Marescroft Rd *SLN* SL2 ..... 128 D6
Mare St *HACK* E8 .... 140 A3
Marfleet Cl *CAR* SM5 .... 201 P9 🔢
Marford Rd *STALE/WH* AL4 21 J3
WGCW AL8 .... 22 C6
Margaret Av *BRWN* CM15 .. 107 L1 🔢
CHING E4 .... 35 N2
STALW/RED AL3 .... 38 C10
Margaret Bondfield Av ....
BARK IG11 .... 143 K2
Margaret Dr *ABLGY* WD5 ... 54 G8 🔢
GPK RM2 .... 125 N9
POTB/CUF EN6 .... 59 M9
STA TW18 .... 173 N10
WAB EN9 .... 63 J9 🔢
Margaret Gardner Dr ....
ELTH/MOT SE9 .... 184 C5 🔢
Margaret Ingram Cl ....
FUL/PGN SW6 .... 15 C10
Margaret Lockwood Cl *KUT* KT1 199 L4 🔢
Margaret Rd *BXLY* DA5 ..... 185 N1 🔢
EBAR EN4 .... 77 N4
EPP CM16 .... 65 K5 🔢
GPK RM2 .... 125 J3
GU GU1 .... 267 P1 🔢
STNW/STAM N16 .... 119 M6
Margaret St *CTPST* W1W .... 10 C3 🔢
REGST W1B 10 C5
Margaretta Ter *CHEL* SW3 .. 15 M9 🔢
Margaretting Rd *MNPK* E12 121 P7 🔢
Margaret Wy *PUR/KEN* CR8 241 J5

REDBR IG4 .... 122 B4
Margate Rd *CLAP* SW4 ...... 180 F1
Margeholes *OXHEY* WD19 .. 257 H5
Margery Gv *KWD/TDW/WH* KT20 257 P5
Margery La *KWD/TDW/WH* KT20 257 P5
Margery Rd *BCTR* RM8 ...... 123 N8
Margery St *FSBYW* WC1X ... 5 L4
Maple Gdns *ASHF* TW15 .... 173 P5
Margherita Pl *WAB* EN9 ..... 63 L10
Margravine Gdns *HMSMTH* W6 156 G4
Margravine Rd *HMSMTH* W6 156 G5
Marham Gdns *MRDN* SM4 .. 201 M6 🔢
WAND/EARL SW18 .... 179 P4 🔢
Mariam Gdns *HCH* RM12 .... 125 N7
Marian Cl *BARK/HLT* IG6 ... 102 C2 🔢
CDH/CHF RM16 .... 147 N10
YEAD UB4 .... 133 L6
Marian Pl *BETH* E2 .... 140 A4
Marian Rd *STRHM/NOR* SW16 202 D1
Marian Sq *BETH* E2 .... 7 P7
Marian St *BETH* E2 .... 140 A4 🔢
Maria Ter *WCHPL* E1 .... 140 C7
Maria Theresa Cl *NWMAL* KT3 200 A5 🔢
Maricas Av *KTN/HRWW/W* HA3 94 C9
Mariette Wy *WLGTN* SM6 .. 222 F5
Marigold Cl *STHL* UB1 .... 133 M9 🔢
Marigold Ct *GU* GU1 .... 250 B7
Marigold Dr *CHOB/PIR* GU24 230 F1 🔢
Marigold Pl *HLWE* CM17 .... 29 L7 🔢
Marigold St *BERM/RHTH* SE16 160 A1
Marigold Wy *CROY/NA* CR0 204 C8
Marina Ap *YEAD* UB4 .... 133 M7
Marina Av *NWMAL* KT3 ...... 200 E6
Marina Cl *CHERT* KT16 ...... 195 L8
Marina Dr *DART* DA1 .... 187 P4
GVW DA11 .... 190 C3
WELL DA16 .... 163 H8
Marina Gdns *CHES/WCR* EN8 62 B6
ROMW/RG RM7 .... 124 C3
Marina Wy *IVER* SL0 .... 131 J9
SL SL1 .... 128 C9 🔢
TEDD TW11 .... 177 J10 🔢
Marine Ct *PUR* RM19 .... 168 C3
Marine Dr *WOOL/PLUM* SE18 162 C3 🔢
Marinefield Rd *FUL/PGN* SW6 157 K4 🔢
Mariner Gdns *RCHPK/HAM* TW10 176 G6
Mariners Dr *RGUW* GU3 ..... 248 A8 🔢
Mariners Ms *POP/IOD* E14 .. 161 J3
Mariner Wy *HHNE* HP2 ...... 36 B7 🔢
Marine St *BERM/RHTH* SE16 19 M3
Marion Av *SHPTN* TW17 ..... 196 C5
Marion Crs *STMC/STPC* BR5 207 L5
Marion Gv *WFD* IG8 .... 101 K6
Marion Rd *CRAWE* RH10 .... 284 C10
CROY/NA CR0 .... 203 K5
MLHL NW7 .... 96 D6
Marischal Rd *LEW* SE13 .... 161 J9
Marisco Cl *GVW* DA11 ...... 168 E3 🔢
Marish La *DEN/HRF* UB9 ... 110 F2
Maritime Cl *GRH* DA9 .... 188 C1
Maritime St *BOW* E3 .... 140 E6 🔢
Marius Rd *TOOT* SW17 ...... 180 B5
Marjoram Cl *GUW* GU2 ...... 249 M6 🔢
Marjorams Av *LOU* IG10 .... 82 D6
Marjorie Gv *BTSEA* SW11 .. 158 A10
Mark Av *CHING* E4 .... 80 G10
Mark Cl *BXLYHN* DA7 .... 163 P7
HAYES BR2 .... 226 B1
STHL UB1 .... 133 P10 🔢
Mark Dr *CFSP/GDCR* SL9 .. 90 A9
Markedge La *COUL/CHIP* CR5 240 A10
Markenfield Rd *GU* GU1 ..... 250 A10
Markenhorn *RGODL* GU7 ... 267 J10 🔢
Markeston Gn *OXHEY* WD19 93 L5 🔢
Market Field Rd *REDH* RH1 258 A9 🔢
Market La *DTCH/LGLY* SL3 .. 150 F2
EDGW HA8 .... 95 P9
Market Link *ROM* RM1 ...... 124 F2
Market Meadow ....
STMC/STPC BR5 .... 207 M4 🔢
Market Ms *MYFR/PICC* W1J 10 E10 🔢
Market Oak La *HHS/BOV* HP3 35 B10
Market Pl *ACT* W3 .... 135 P10
BTFD TW8 .... 155 H6
BXLYHS DA6 .... 164 B10
CFSP/GDCR SL9 .... 90 A9
DART DA1 .... 187 M3 🔢
EFNCH N2 .... 117 N1 🔢
HERT/WAS SG14 .... 25 L5 🔢
ROM RM1 .... 124 F3
SOHO/SHAV W1F 10 G5
STAL AL1 .... 38 C6
WATW WD18 .... 73 K8 🔢
Market Sq *BH/WHM* TN16 .. 262 F2
BMLY BR1 .... 205 M2
Market St *DART* DA1 .... 187 M3
EHAM E6 .... 142 C4
GU GU1 .... 268 C4
HERT/WAS SG14 .... 25 L5 🔢
HLWE CM17 .... 29 M7
WOOL/PLUM SE18 .... 73 J8
Market Wy *BH/WHM* TN16 .. 262 G2 🔢
Markfield Gdns *CHING* E4 .. 100 G1
Markfield Rd *CTHM* CR3 .... 260 A1
SEVS/STOTM N15 .... 119 P2
Mark Hall Moors *HLW* CM20 29 L1
Markham Pl *CHEL* SW3 ...... 16 A7 🔢
Markham Rd *CHESW* EN7 .. 61 K2 🔢
Markham Sq *CHEL* SW3 ..... 16 A7
Markham St *CHEL* SW3 ...... 15 P7
Markhole Cl *HPTN* TW12 ... 175 N10 🔢
Markhouse Av *WALTH* E17 .. 120 C1
Markhouse Rd *WALTH* E17 .. 120 D1
Mark La *GVE* DA12 .... 191 H3
MON EC3R 13 K7
Markmanor Av *WALTH* E17 .. 120 D5
Mark Oak La *LHD/OX* KT22 235 P7
Mark Rd *HHNE* HP2 .... 36 B4
WDGN N22 .... 99 J10
Mark's Av *CHONG* CM5 ...... 49 N3
Marksbury Av *RCH/KEW* TW9 155 N9
Marks Rd *ROMW/RG* RM7 .. 124 D3
WARL CR6 .... 242 D4
Marks Sq *GVW* DA11 .... 190 D5
Mark St *REIC* RH2 .... 257 L9 🔢
SDTCH EC2A 13 J1
SRTFD E15 .... 141 K2 🔢
Markville Gdns *CTHM* CR3 .. 259 P1
Mark Wy *RGODL* GU7 .... 266 D9
The Markway *SUN* TW16 .... 197 K2
Markwell Cl *SYD* SE26 .... 182 A7 🔢
Markwell Rd *EPP* CM16 ..... 46 E7
Markyate Rd *BCTR* RM8 ..... 123 L10
Marlands Rd *CLAY* IG5 ...... 103 P1
Marlborogh Av *ISLW* TW7 .. 154 G6
Marlborough Av *EDGW* HA8 95 N4
RSLP HA4 .... 112 D4
STHGT/OAK N14 .... 98 F7
Marlborough Cl *CDH/CHF* RM16 167 P1
ORP BR6 .... 207 J6 🔢
TRDG/WHET N20 .... 98 A4 🔢
UPMR RM14 .... 126 D6 🔢
WIM/MER SW19 .... 178 F9
WOT/HER KT12 .... 197 L10 🔢
Marlborough Crs *CHSWK* W4 156 A2
SEV TN13 .... 246 F10
Marlborough Dr *CLAY* IG5 .. 122 D1 🔢
WEY KT13 .... 196 D10

Marlborough Gdns ....
TRDG/WHET N20 .... 98 A4
UPMR RM14 .... 126 D6
Marlborough Ga *STAL* AL1 .. 38 D6
Marlborough Gv *STHWK* SE1 19 M8 🔢
Marlborough HI *HRW* HA1 .. 114 D2
STJWD NW8 .... 3 P5
Marlborough La *CHARL* SE7 161 P5
Marlborough Park Av ....
BFN/LL DA15 .... 185 K4
Marlborough Ri *HHNE* HP2 .. 35 P3
Marlborough Rd *ARCH* N19 118 F7
ASHF TW15 .... 173 P8
BCTR RM8 .... 123 M9
BRWN CM15 .... 86 F10
CHING E4 .... 100 C7
CHSWK W4 .... 155 P4
DART DA1 .... 187 K2 🔢
DORK RH4 .... 272 G2
DTCH/LGLY SL3 .... 42 A3
EA W5 .... 155 J1 🔢
ED N9 .... 99 N2
FELT TW13 .... 175 L5
FSTGT E7 .... 141 P2
HAYES BR2 .... 205 P4
HGDN/ICK UB10 .... 132 C6
HPTN TW12 .... 175 P9 🔢
NWDGN UB2 .... 153 K2
RCHPK/HAM TW10 .... 177 K2
ROMW/RG RM7 .... 124 B2
SAND/SEL CR2 .... 223 K4 🔢
SRTFD E15 .... 121 K9 🔢
STAL AL1 .... 38 D6 🔢
SUT SM1 .... 201 K10
SWFD E18 .... 121 M1
WDGN N22 .... 98 G8
WELL DA16 .... 163 N9
WHALL SW1A 11 H10
WIM/MER SW19 .... 179 P9
WOKN/KNAP GU21 .... 232 D2
Marlborough Yd *ARCH* N19 118 F7 🔢
The Marld *ASHTD* KT21 ..... 237 L4
Marle Gdns *WAB* EN9 .... 63 J7
Marler Rd *FSTH* SE23 .... 182 E4
Marlescroft Wy *LOU* IG10 .. 82 E9
Marley Av *BXLYHN* DA7 ..... 163 N5
GFD/PVL UB6 .... 133 P5 🔢
SEVS/STOTM N15 .... 119 J2
Marley Cl *BERK* HP4 .... 33 L4
SUN TW16 .... 174 F9 🔢
Marley Ri *DORK* RH4 .... 272 F5
Marley Rd *WGCE* AL7 .... 23 K7
Marlin Cl *BERK* HP4 .... 33 L4
SUN TW16 .... 174 F9 🔢
Marlin Copse *BERK* HP4 .... 33 M6 🔢
Marlingdene Cl *HPTN* TW12 175 P9
Marlings Cl *CHST* BR7 .... 207 H4
CTHM CR3 .... 241 M3
Marlings Park Av *CHST* BR7 207 H4
Marling Wy *GVE* DA12 ...... 191 H8
Marlins Cl *RKW/CH/CXG* WD3 71 H6
SUT SM1 .... 221 M2 🔢
Marlins Meadow *WATW* WD18 72 E10
Marlin Sq *ABLGY* WD5 ...... 54 G7
The Marlins *NTHWD* HA6 ... 72 E10
Marlins Turn *HHW* HP1 ...... 35 L3
Marloes Cl *ALP/SUD* HA0 .. 115 J9
Marloes Rd *KENS* W8 .... 14 G3
Marlow Av *PUR* RM19 .... 165 P3
Marlow Ct *PGE/AN* SE20 ... 204 A3
CRAWW RH11 .... 283 N6 🔢
Marlow Crs *TWK* TW1 .... 176 E2
Marlow Dr *CHEAM* SM3 ..... 200 G10
Marlowe Cl *BARK/HLT* IG6 .. 102 F9
CHST BR7 .... 184 G9
Marlowe Rd *WALTH* E17 .... 121 H2
Marlowes HHNE HP2 .... 35 N6
The Marlowes *DART* DA1 ... 164 E10
STJWD NW8 .... 3 L6
Marlow Wy *CROY/NA* CR0 .. 202 F9
Marlow Gdns *HYS/HAR* UB3 152 E3
Marlow Rd *EHAM* E6 .... 142 C5
NWDGN UB2 .... 132 C5
PGE/AN SE20 .... 204 A3
Marlow Wy *BERM/RHTH* SE16 160 C1
Marlpit Av *COUL/CHIP* CR5 240 F5
Marlpit La *COUL/CHIP* CR5 .. 240 E2
Marl Rd *WAND/EARL* SW18 157 L10
Marlton St *GNWCH* SE10 ... 161 L4 🔢
Marlwood Cl *BFN/LL* DA15 .. 185 H5
Marlyns Cl *RGUE* GU4 .... 250 D6
Marlyns Dr *RGUE* GU4 .... 250 D7
Marlyon Rd *BARK/HLT* IG6 .. 103 M6
Marmadon Rd *WOOL/PLUM* SE18 163 J3
Marmion Ap *CHING* E4 .... 100 F5 🔢
Marmion Av *CHING* E4 .... 100 E5
Marmion Cl *CHING* E4 .... 100 E5
Marmion Ms *BTSEA* SW11 .. 158 B9 🔢
Marmion Rd *BTSEA* SW11 .. 158 B10 🔢
Marmont Rd *PECK* SE15 .... 159 P7
Marmora Rd *EDUL* SE22 .... 182 B2
Marmot Rd *HSLWW* TW4 ... 153 L9
Marne Av *FBAR/BDGN* N11 98 C5
WELL DA16 .... 163 K9
Marnell Wy *HSLWW* TW4 ... 2 L9
Marne St *NKENS* W10 .... 2 D5
Marney Rd *BTSEA* SW11 .... 158 B10
Marneys Cl *EPSOM* KT18 .. 237 M1
Marnham Av *CRICK* NW2 ... 117 M9
Marnham Crs *GFD/PVL* UB6 134 A5
Marnham Pl *ADL/WDHM* KT15 215 M1
Marnham Ri *HHW* HP1 .... 35 K4 🔢
Marnock Rd *BROCKY* SE4 .. 182 K1
Maroon St *POP/IOD* E14 .... 140 D7 🔢
Maroons Wy *CAT* SE6 .... 182 G8
Marquess Rd *IS* N1 .... 6 G2
Marquess Rd North *IS* N1 .. 6 F2
Marquess Rd South *IS* N1 .. 6 F2
Marquis Cl *ALP/SUD* HA0 .. 135 L2
HARP AL5 .... 20 C1
Marquis La *HARP* AL5 .... 20 C1
Marquis Rd *CAMTN* NW1 ... 5 K2
FSBYPK N4 .... 118 G6
WDGN N22 .... 98 G7 🔢
Marrabon Cl *BFN/LL* DA15 .. 185 K4
Marrick Cl *PUT/ROE* SW15 156 D10
Marrilyne Av *PEND* EN3 ..... 80 E1
Marriott Rd *MUSWH* N10 ... 98 A9
Marriott Rd *EN* EN1 .... 80 A1
WIM/MER SW19 .... 178 G8
Marsala Rd *LEW* SE13 .... 160 G10
Marsden Cl *WGCW* AL8 ..... 22 E7 🔢
Marsden Gn *WGCW* AL8 .... 22 E6
Marsden Rd *ED* N9 .... 100 A3
PECK SE15 .... 159 N9
WGCW AL8 .... 22 E6
Marsden St *KTTN* NW5 ...... 4 C2
Marsden Wy *ORP* BR6 .... 227 J1
Marshall Av *STALW/RED* AL3 38 D3
Marshall Cl *FBAR/BDGN* N11 98 C5

HRW HA1 114 C5
HSLWW TW4 175 N1
SAND/SEL CR2 223 P9
WAND/EARL SW18 179 M2
Marshall Dr YEAD UB4 132 C12
Marshall Rd ADL/WDHM KT15 215 M5
Marshall Rd CRAWE RH10 284 D9
TOTM N17 99 L3
Marshalls Dr HOR/WEW KT19 219 P9
Marshalls Dr ROM RM1 124 F1
Marshalls Gv WOOL/PLUM SE18 142 A8
Marshalls Rd ROMW/RG RM7 124 C2
SUT SM1 221 L1
Marshall St SOHO/CST W1F 11 H7
Marshalls Wy STALE/WH AL4 20 C1
Marshal's Dr STAL AL1 38 F3
Marshalsea Rd STHWK SE1 18 F1
Marsham CI CHST BR7 184 E8
Marsham Ldg CFSP/GDCR SL9 110 C3
Marsham La CFSP/GDCR SL9 110 B4
Marsham St WEST SW1P 17 K5
Marsham Wy CFSP/GDCR SL9 110 B3
Marsh Av HOR/WEW KT19 220 B6
MTCM CR4 202 A2
Marshbrook CI BKHTH/KID SE3 162 A9
Marsh CI CHES/WCR EN8 62 E9
MLHL NW7 96 C4
Marshcroft Dr CHES/WCR EN8 62 F9
Marshe CI POTB/CUF EN6 59 N8
Marsh Farm Rd WHTN TW2 176 A4
Marshfield DTCH/LGLY SL3 112 B5
Marshfield St POP/IOD E14 161 H2
Marshfoot Rd GRAYS RM17 168 D2
Marshgate Dr HERT/BAY SG13 25 M4
Marshgate La SRTFD E15 140 B3
Marsh Green Rd DAGE RM10 144 B3
WAB EN9 63 K3
Marsh HI HOM E9 120 D10
Marsh La ADL/WDHM KT15 215 L1
HLWE CM17 29 P6
LEY E10 120 E7
MLHL NW7 96 B4
STAN HA7 95 H6
TOTM N17 100 A3
WARE SG12 26 D3
WARE SG12 27 J8
Marshside CI ED N9 100 D2
Marsh St DART DA1 65 P9
POP/IOD E14 160 G3
Marsh Wall POP/IOD E14 160 F1
Marsh Wy DAGW RM9 144 E6
Marshwood Rd LTWR GU18 212 C7
Marsland CI WALW SE17 18 D8
Marston HOR/WEW KT19 219 P7
Marston Av CHSGTN KT9 219 K3
DAGE RM10 124 B8
Marston CI CSHM HP5 50 F3
DAGE RM10 124 B8
HHS/BOV HP3 36 B7
KIL/WHAMP NW6 3 K3
Marston Ct WOT/HER KT12 197 K8
Marston Dr WARL CR6 242 D4
Marston Rd CLAY IG5 102 B10
HOD EN11 44 G2
TEDD TW11 176 G8
WOKN/KNAP GU21 231 N3
Marston Wy NRWD SE19 181 J10
Marsworth Av PIN HA5 93 L9
Marsworth CI WATW WD18 92 F11
YEAD UB4 133 M7
Martaban Rd STNW/STAM N16 119 N7
Martello St HACK E8 140 A2
Martell Rd DUL SE21 181 L6
Martel PI HACK E8 7 M1
Marten Ga STALE/WH AL4 38 C7
Marten Rd WALTH E17 100 F10
Martens Av BXLYHN DA7 164 D10
Martens CI BXLYHN DA7 164 D10
Martham CI THMD SE28 143 N9
Martha Rd SRTFD E15 141 K1
Martha St WCHPL E1 140 B8
Marthorne Crs KTN/HRWW/W HA3 94 C10
Martian Av HHNE HP2 36 A3
Martin Bowes Rd ELTH/MOT SE9 162 F2
Martin CI CRAWW RH11 283 N5
ED N9 100 C2
HAT AL10 40 D6
HCDN/ICK UB10 131 P4
SAND/SEL CR2 224 C7
WARL CR6 242 A2
WDSR SL4 148 B7
Martin Crs CROY/NA CR0 202 C4
Martindale IVER SL0 130 F6
MORT/ESHN SW14 177 P1
ORP BR6 227 K2
Martindale Av CAN/RD E16 141 M9
ORP BR6 227 K2
Martindale CI RGUE GU4 250 G8
Martindale Rd BAL SW12 180 C3
HHW HP1 35 J5
WOKN/KNAP GU21 231 L4
Martin Dene BXLYHS DA6 186 A1
Martin Dr NTHLT UB5 113 N10
RAIN RM13 145 J4
Martineau CI ESH/CLAY KT10 218 C1
Martineau Dr DORK RH4 272 C4
Martineau Rd HBRY N5 119 J9
Martineau St WCHPL E1 140 B9
Martinfield WGCE AL7 23 J4
Martin Gdns BCTR RM8 123 M9
Martingale CI RCHPK/HAM TW10 177 J9
Martin Gdns BCTR RM8 123 M9
Martin Gv MRDN SM4 201 K3
Martin La CANST EC4R 13 H7
Martin Ri BXLYHS DA6 186 A1
Martin Rd BCTR RM8 123 M9
GUW GU2 249 M8
RDART DA2 187 K6
SL SL1 149 K2
SOCK/AV RM15 146 C10
Martins CI GU GU1 250 F9
RAD WD7 74 D2
STMC/STPC BR5 207 N3
WWKM BR4 205 L8
Martins Dr CHES/WCR EN8 62 C4
HERT/BAY SG13 26 A5
Martins Mt BAR EN5 77 K8
Martin's Pln SLN SL2 129 L5
Martin's Rd HAYES BR2 205 K2
Martin's Shaw SEV TN13 246 D8
The Martins SEV TN13 182 A8
Martins Wk MUSWH N10 98 B3
Martinsyde WOKS/MYFD GU22 232 F3
Martin Wy RYNPK SW20 231 M4
WOKN/KNAP GU21 231 M4
Martlesham WGCE AL7 23 P5
Martlesham CI HCH RM12 125 K10
Martlet Gv NTHLT UB5 133 L5
Martley Dr IL IG1 122 E3
The Martlets CRAWE RH10 283 P7
Martock CI KTN/HRWW/W HA3 114 F2
Marton CI CAT SE6 182 F6
Marton Rd STNW/STAM N16 119 M8
Martyr CI STAL AL1 38 C10
Martyr Rd GU GU1 268 A1
Martyrs Av CRAWW RH11 283 N4
Martyrs La WOKN/KNAP GU21 214 E8
Marunden Gn SLN SL2 128 E5
Marvell Av YEAD UB4 133 H7
Marvell CI CRAWE RH10 284 D5
Marvels CI LEE/GVPK SE12 183 N5
Marvels La LEE/GVPK SE12 183 N5

Marville Rd FUL/PGN SW6 157 J6
Marvin St HACK E8 140 A1
Marwell BH/WHM TN16 262 A12
Marwell CI ROM RM1 124 F1
WWKM BR4 205 L9
Marwood CI KGLGY WD4 54 A5
WELL DA16 163 L9
Mary Adelaide CI
PUT/ROE SW15 178 B7
Mary Ann Buildings DEPT SE8 160 F5
Mary Av RYLN/HDSTN HA2 114 A7
Marybank WOOL/PLUM SE18 142 A8
Mary CI KTN/HRWW/W HA3 115 L2
Mary Datchelor CI CMBW SE5 159 L7
Mayfield CI BXLY DA5 186 F6
Marygold Wk AMS HP6 69 P5
Maryhill CI PUR/KEN CR8 241 K3
Maryland HAT AL10 40 D4
Maryland Pk SRTFD E15 121 K10
SRTFD E15 121 K10
Marylands Rd MV/WKIL W9 8 F2
Maryland Sq SRTFD E15 121 K10
Maryland St SRTFD E15 121 K10
Mary Lawrenson PI
BKHTH/KID SE3 161 L6
Marylebone High St MHST W1U 10 D3
Marylebone La MHST W1U 10 D5
Marylebone Ms CAVSQ/HST W1G 10 D4
Marylebone Pas GTPST W1W 11 H5
Marylebone Rd CAMTN NW1 10 B2
Marylee Wy LBTH SE11 17 P6
Maryon Gv CHARL SE7 162 B3
Maryon Ms CHARL SE7 117 P9
Maryon Rd CHARL SE7 162 B3
Mary Peters Dr WBLY HA9 114 C10
Mary PI NTGHL W11 8 A8
Mary Rd GU GU1 267 P1
Mary Rose CI HPTN TW12 197 P1
Mary Rose Gdns CHSGTN KT9 219 K1
Maryrose Wy TRDG/WHET N20 97 N2
Mary Secole CI HACK E8 7 L5
Mary's Ter TWK TW1 176 F3
Mary Ter CAMTN NW1 4 F6
Masbro' Rd WKENS W14 156 C2
Mascalls La BRW CM14 106 C5
Mascalls Rd CHARL SE7 106 C5
Mascotte Rd PUT/ROE SW15 156 G10
Mascotts CI CRICK NW2 116 E8
Masefield Av STAN HA7 94 E6
STHL UB1 133 P9
Masefield CI ERITH DA8 164 C7
HARH RM3 105 K3
Masefield Crs GPK RM2 105 K9
STHGT/OAK N14 78 D9
Masefield Dr UPMR RM14 126 B5
Masefield Gdns EHAM E6 142 D6
Masefield La YEAD UB4 133 J6
Masefield Rd CDH/CHF RM16 168 B1
CRAWW RH11 283 H10
DART DA1 188 A1
FELT TW13 175 N7
GVW DA11 190 A6
Masefield Vw ORP BR6 206 F10
Masefield Wy STWL/WRAY TW19 174 A4
Mashie Rd ACT W3 156 B7
Mashiters HI CRW RH5 104 E9
Mashiters Wk ROM RM1 124 F1
Maskell Rd TOOT SW17 179 M6
Maskelyne CI BTSEA SW11 157 P7
Mason CI BERM/RHTH SE16 19 P7
BORE WD6 76 A4
BXLYHN DA7 164 C9
HPTN TW12 197 H1
RYNPK SW20 200 G1
Mason Dr HARH RM3 105 M10
Masonic Hall Rd CHERT KT16 195 J6
Mason Rd CRAWE RH10 283 P9
WFD IG8 101 K5
Mason's Arms Ms CONDST W1S 10 F6
Mason's Av CROY/NA CR0 203 K10
KTN/HRWW/W HA3 114 E2
Mason's Bridge Rd REDH RH1 276 C5
WOOL/PLUM SE18 162 E3
Masons Paddock DORK RH4 254 F10
Mason's PI MTCM CR4 180 A6
Masons Rd EN EN1 80 A2
HHNE HP2 36 C5
SL SL1 128 D9
Mason St WALW SE17 19 H5
Mason Wy WAB EN9 63 K9
Massetts Rd HORL RH6 280 A5
Massey CI FBAR/BDGN N11 98 C5
Massie Rd HACK E8 7 N1
Massingberd Wy TOOT SW17 180 C7
Massinger St WALW SE17 19 J6
Massingham St WCHPL E1 140 C6
Masson Av RSLP HA4 133 K1
Master CI OXTED RH8 261 K5
Masterman Rd EHAM E6 142 D6
Masters Dr BERM/RHTH SE16 160 A4
Master's St WCHPL E1 140 C7
Masthead CI GRH DA9 166 B10
Mast House Ter POP/IOD E14 160 F3
Mastmaker Rd POP/IOD E14 160 F1
Maswell Park Crs HSLW TW3 175 J8
Maswell Park Rd HSLW TW3 176 A11
Matcham Rd WAN E11 121 K8
Matching Fld BRWN CM15 86 E3
Matching Rd HLWE CM17 30 C7
RBSF CM22 31 J2
Matchless Dr WOOL/PLUM SE18 162 G8
Matfield CI HAYES BR2 205 M6
Matfield Rd BELV DA17 164 B5
Matham Gv EDUL SE22 159 N10
Matham Rd E/WMO/HCT KT8 198 A5
Matheson Rd WKENS W14 14 C6
Mathews Av EHAM E6 142 D4
Mathews Park Av SRTFD E15 121 L1
Mathias CI EPSOM KT18 219 P9
Mathisen Wy DTCH/LGLY SL3 151 H7
Matilda CI NRWD SE19 181 L10
Matilda St IS N1 5 P6
Matlock CI BAR EN5 76 C5
HNHL SE24 158 G3
OXHEY WD19 93 K4
Matlock Gdns CHEAM SM3 221 H1
HCH RM12 125 M8
Matlock PI SUT SM1 221 H1
Matlock Rd CTHM CR3 241 M8
LEY E10 121 H4
Matlock St POP/IOD E14 140 D8
Matlock Wy NWMAL KT3 200 A1
Matthew Arnold CI COB KT11 214 G3
STA TW18 173 M9
Matthew CI NKENS W10 136 C6
Matthew Ct MTCM CR4 202 E5
Matthew's Gdns CROY/NA CR0 225 J7
Matthew's La STA TW18 173 J7
Matthews Rd NTHLT UB5 114 A5
Matthews St BTSEA SW11 158 A3
REIG RH2 275 K4
Matthey PI CRAWE RH10 284 E4
Matthias Rd STNW/STAM N16 119 M3
Mattingly Wy PECK SE15 159 N6
Mattison Rd FSBYPK N4 119 H4

Mattock La WEA W13 135 H10
Maud Cashmore Wy
WOOL/PLUM SE18 162 C2
Maude CI HNWL W7 88 F10
Maude Crs WATN WD24 73 J3
Maude Rd BEAC HP9 88 F10
CMBW SE5 159 M8
SWLY BR8 187 H9
WALTH E17 120 D3
Maudesville Cottages
HNWL W7 134 D10
Maude Ter WALTH E17 120 D2
Maud Gdns BARK IG11 143 J4
PLSTW E13 141 L4
Maud Rd LEY E10 121 H8
PLSTW E13 141 L3
Maudslay Rd ELTH/MOT SE9 162 C9
Maud St CAN/RD E16 141 L7
Mauleverer Rd
BRXS/STRHM SW2 180 F1
Maunder Rd HNWL W7 134 D10
Maunds Hatch HLWS CM18 46 G5
Maunsell Pk CRAWE RH10 284 C7
Maunsel St WEST SW1P 17 J5
Maurice Av CTHM CR3 241 L8
WDGN N22 99 J10
Maurice St SHB W12 136 E8
Maurier CI NTHLT UB5 133 K3
Mauritius Rd GNWCH SE10 161 K3
Maury Rd STNW/STAM N16 119 P7
Mavelstone Rd BMLY BR1 206 A1
Maverton Rd BOW E3 140 F11
Mavis Av HOR/WEW KT19 220 B2
Mavis CI HOR/WEW KT19 220 B2
Mavis Gv HCH RM12 125 M7
Mawbey PI STHWK SE1 19 M8
Mawbey Rd CHERT KT16 214 G3
STHWK SE1 19 M8
Mawbey St VX/NE SW8 158 F6
Mawney CI ROMW/RG RM7 104 C10
Mawney Rd ROMW/RG RM7 104 C10
Mawson CI RYNPK SW20 201 H2
Mawson La CHSWK W4 156 C5
Maxey Gdns DAGW RM9 123 P9
Maxey Rd DAGW RM9 123 P9
WOOL/PLUM SE18 162 F3
Maxfield CI TRDG/WHET N20 97 N1
Maxim Rd DART DA1 186 F1
ERITH DA8 164 F4
WCHMH N21 79 H10
Maxted Pk HRW HA1 114 D5
Maxted Rd HHNE HP2 36 C4
PECK SE15 159 N9
Maxwell CI CROY/NA CR0 202 F8
RKW/CH/CXG WD3 91 K3
Maxwell Dr BF/WBF KT14 215 M7
Maxwell Gdns ORP BR6 207 J5
Maxwell Ri OXHEY WD19 93 M1
Maxwell Rd ASHF TW15 174 D9
BEAC HP9 88 C3
BORE WD6 75 N7
FUL/PGN SW6 157 L6
NTHWD HA6 92 E8
STAL AL1 38 G7
WDR/YW UB7 151 P3
WELL DA16 163 K10
Maxwelton Av MLHL NW7 96 A6
Maxwelton CI MLHL NW7 96 A6
Mayall Rd HNHL SE24 181 J1
Maya Rd EFNCH N2 117 M2
Maybank Av ALP/SUD HA0 114 F9
HCH RM12 125 J10
SWFD E18 101 N10
Maybank Gdns PIN HA5 113 H3
Maybank Rd SWFD E18 101 P9
May Bate Av KUTN/CMB KT2 199 J1
Mayberry PI BRYLDS KT5 199 L7
Maybourne CI WOKS/MYFD GU22 232 A10
Maybrick Rd EMPK RM11 125 K3
Maybury Av CHES/WCR EN8 62 A4
WLSDN NW10 136 D2
Maybury CI KWD/TDW/WH KT20 239 H5
STMC/STPC BR5 206 E5
Maybury Gdns WLSDN NW10 136 D2
Maybury HI WOKS/MYFD GU22 232 E5
Maybury Rd BARK IG11 143 K4
WOKN/KNAP GU21 232 D2
Maybury St TOOT SW17 179 M5
Maybush Rd EMPK RM11 125 M5
Maychurch CI STAN HA7 95 J9
May CI CHSGTN KT9 219 L3
STALW/RED AL3 38 C4
Maycock Gv NTHWD HA6 92 G7
Maycroft PIN HA5 93 J10
Maycroft Av GRAYS RM17 168 A4
Maycroft Gdns GRAYS RM17 168 A4
Maycroft Rd CHESW EN7 61 M2
Maycross Av MRDN SM4 201 J4
Mayday Gdns BKHTH/KID SE3 162 E3
Mayday Rd THHTH CR7 202 C3
Mayell CI LHD/OX KT22 257 H9
Mayerne Rd ELTH/MOT SE9 184 A1
Mayesbrook Rd BARK IG11 143 J3
GDMY/SEVK IG3 123 K3
Mayes CI CRAWE RH10 284 D8
SWLY BR8 209 H4
WARL CR6 242 C4
Mayesford Rd CHDH RM6 123 M5
Mayes Rd CEND/HSY/T N8 119 H1
WDGN N22 98 G10
Mayeswood Rd LEE/GVPK SE12 183 P7
Mayfair Av CHDH RM6 123 N4
BXLYHN DA7 163 P7
IL IG1 122 C7
WHTN TW2 176 B3
WPK KT4 200 E10
WAN E11 121 K8
Mayfair CI BECK BR3 204 G1
SURB KT6 199 K8
Mayfair Gdns TOTM N17 99 K7
WFD IG8 101 M7
Mayfair PI MYFR/PICC W1J 10 F9
Mayfair Rd DART DA1 186 F1
Mayfair Ter STHGT/OAK N14 98 F1
Mayfare RKW/CH/CXG WD3 72 E7
Mayfield BXLYHN DA7 164 A9
CRAWE RH10 284 E7
CHSWK W4 156 B3
KTN/HRWW/W HA3 114 C3
NFNCH/WDSP N12 97 M5
ORP BR6 207 J1
STHGT/OAK N14 98 D3
WEA W13 154 G2
WFD IG8 101 M7
Mayfield Av ADL/WDHM KT15 215 L6
CHSWK W4 156 B3
Mayfield CI ADL/WDHM KT15 215 M6
CHSWK W4 156 B3
CLAP SW4 180 C1
HACK E8 7 L2
HGDN/ICK UB10 132 C5
HLWE CM17 30 A7
REDH RH1 276 B6
THDIT KT7 198 C3
WOT/HER KT12 217 H1

THHTH CR7 202 G4
Mayfield Dr PIN HA5 113 N2
Mayfield Gdns BRW CM14 106 G2
BRW CM14 107 H2
HDN NW4 116 C4
HNWL W7 134 C8
STA TW18 173 J10
WOT/HER KT12 217 H1
Mayfield Gn GT/LBKH KT23 253 P3
Mayfield Rd ACT W3 135 N9
BCTR RM8 123 M6
BELMT SM2 221 N3
BELV DA17 164 D3
BMLY BR1 206 B3
CEND/HSY/T N8 118 C4
CHING E4 101 J3
GVW DA11 190 C4
HACK E8 7 L4
PEND EN3 80 C6
PLSTW E13 141 L6
SAND/SEL CR2 223 L5
SHB W12 156 B1
WALTH E17 100 D10
WEY KT13 216 A2
WIM/MER SW19 201 J1
WOT/HER KT12 217 H1
Mayfields CDH/CHF RM16 167 P1
WBLY HA9 115 M7
Mayfields CI WBLY HA9 115 M7
Mayflower Av HHNE HP2 35 N6
Mayflower CI BERM/RHTH SE16 160 C3
CRAWE RH10 284 E8
HERT/WAS SG14 24 C7
RSLP HA4 112 D4
SOCK/AV RM15 147 H6
WAB EN9 45 K9
Mayflower Rd BRXN/ST SW9 158 F9
LCOL/BKTW AL2 56 A3
Mayflower St BERM/RHTH SE16 160 B1
Mayflower Wy CHONG CM5 67 P3
SLN SL2 109 H10
Mayfly CI PIN HA5 113 K5
STMC/STPC BR5 207 N4
Mayford CI BAL SW12 180 A3
BECK BR3 204 C3
WOKS/MYFD GU22 232 A8
Mayford Rd BAL SW12 180 A3
May Gdns BORE WD6 75 J10
GFD/PVL UB6 135 H4
Maygoods UX/CGN UB8 131 N7
Maygoods CI UX/CGN UB8 131 N7
Maygoods Gn UX/CGN UB8 131 N7
Maygoods St IS N1 5 P7
Maygreen Crs EMPK RM11 125 H2
Maygrove Rd KIL/WHAMP NW6 2 C2
Mayhall La AMS HP6 68 C1
Mayhew CI CHING E4 100 F4
Mayhill Rd BAR EN5 77 H10
CHARL SE7 161 N5
Mayhurst Av WOKS/MYFD GU22 232 E4
Mayhurst Crs WOKS/MYFD GU22 232 F2
Maylands Av HCH RM12 125 J9
HHNE HP2 36 C4
Maylands Dr SCUP DA14 185 N6
UX/CGN UB8 131 N1
Maylands Rd OXHEY WD19 93 K5
Maylands Wy HARH RM3 106 B7
Maylins Dr SBW CM21 29 N1
Maynard CI ERITH DA8 164 C6
FUL/PGN SW6 157 L6
SEVS/STOTM N15 119 M3
Maynard Dr STAL AL1 38 C9
Maynard PI POTB/CUF EN6 60 F5
Maynard Rd HHNE HP2 35 N7
WALTH E17 121 H1
Maynards EMPK RM11 125 M5
Maynard Wy STALW/RED AL3 37 N8
Maynooth Gdns MTCM CR4 202 A7
Mayo CI CHES/WCR EN8 62 B4
Mayo Gdns HHW HP1 35 L7
Mayola Rd CLPT E5 120 B9
Mayo Rd CROY/NA CR0 203 L5
WLSDN NW10 136 B1
WOT/HER KT12 197 H7
Mayow Rd SYD SE26 182 C7
CHESW EN7 62 A4
Mayplace Av DART DA1 165 H10
Mayplace CI BXLYHN DA7 164 D11
Mayplace La WOOL/PLUM SE18 162 G5
Mayplace Rd BXLYHN DA7 164 D10
Mayplace Rd East BXLYHN DA7 164 E11
Mayplace Rd West
BXLYHN DA7 164 B10
Maypole Crs BARK/HLT IG6 102 G8
ERITH DA8 165 L5
Maypole Dr CHIG IG7 103 K4
Maypole Rd GVE DA12 191 J4
ORP BR6 228 A3
May Rd CHING E4 100 F7
PLSTW E13 141 M4
RDART DA2 187 N7
WHTN TW2 176 C6
Mayroyd Av SURB KT6 199 M9
May's Buildings Ms
GNWCH SE10 161 J6
Mays CI WEY KT13 216 A6
Maysfield Rd RPLY/SEND GU23 232 G9
Mays Gv RPLY/SEND GU23 232 G9
May's Hill Rd HAYES BR2 205 K2
Mays La BAR EN5 96 E1
Maysoule Rd BTSEA SW11 157 N10
Mays Rd HPTN TW12 176 C8
May St WKENS W14 14 C8
Maythorne CI WATW WD18 72 F8
Maythorne Cottages LEW SE13 183 J2
Mayton St HOLWY N7 118 G8
Maytree CI EDGW HA8 95 P4
RAIN RM13 144 F2
Maytree Crs WATN WD24 72 G3
Maytree La STAN HA7 94 C7
Maytrees RAD WD7 74 F3
WOKN/KNAP GU21 231 H3
Mayville Est STNW/STAM N16 7 J1
Mayville Rd IL IG1 122 E10
WAN E11 121 K8
Maywater CI SAND/SEL CR2 223 L7
Maywin Dr EMPK RM11 125 N3
Maze HI GNWCH SE10 161 K5
STALE/WH AL4 39 H1
Mazenod Av KIL/WHAMP NW6 2 E10
Maze Rd RCH/KEW TW9 155 M6
Mcadam CI HOD EN11 44 F1
Mcadam Dr ENC/FH EN2 79 J6
Mcalmont Rdg RGODL GU7 267 J3
Mcauley CI ELTH/MOT SE9 184 D1
STHWK SE1 18 A3
Mc Auliffe Dr SLN SL2 110 D1
Mccall CI CLAP SW4 158 A5
Mc Call Crs CHARL SE7 162 B4
Mccarthy Rd FELT TW13 175 L8
Mccoid Wy STHWK SE1 18 E3
Mccrone Ms HAMP NW3 3 M1
Mccudden Rd DART DA1 165 N9
Mccullum Rd BOW E3 140 F11
Mcdermott CI BTSEA SW11 157 P9
Mcdermott Rd PECK SE15 159 J3
Mcdonald Ct HAT AL10 40 D2
HAT AL10 40 D7
Mcdonough CI CHSGTN KT9 219 K11
Mcdougall Ct RCH/KEW TW9 155 N8
Mcdowall CI CAN/RD E16 141 M7
Mcentee Av WALTH E17 100 D9
Mcewan Wy SRTFD E15 141 J3
Mcgrath Rd FSTGT E7 121 L10
Mcgregor Rd NTGHL W11 8 C5
Mcintosh CI ROM RM1 124 F1
WLGTN SM6 222 F4

Mcintosh Rd ROM RM1 124 F1
Mckay Rd RYNPK SW20 178 E10
Mc Kellar CI BUSH WD23 94 B3
Mc Kenzie Rd BROX EN10 44 F6
Mckerrell Rd PECK SE15 159 P7
Mcleod Rd ABYW SE2 163 M3
Mcmillan CI GVE DA12 190 F7
Mcmillan St DEPT SE8 160 F5
Mcneil Rd CMBW SE5 159 M8
Mcnicol Dr WLSDN NW10 135 P4
Mcrae La MTCM CR4 202 A7
Mead Av DTCH/LGLY SL3 150 F1
REDH RH1 276 B8
Mead Barn EPP CM16 83 M7
Mead CI CDH/CHF RM16 167 N1
DEN/HRF UB9 111 K7
DTCH/LGLY SL3 150 E1
EGH TW20 172 E9
GPK RM2 105 H10
KTN/HRWW/W HA3 94 C9
LOU IG10 82 G6
REDH RH1 258 D3
STWL/WRAY TW19 172 A4
SWLY BR8 209 H5
Mead Ct CDALE/KGS NW9 115 P3
EGH TW20 172 F9
WAB EN9 63 C10
WOKN/KNAP GU21 231 K3
Mead Crs CHING E4 101 H5
DART DA1 167 P3
CT/LBKH KT23 253 P1
SUT SM1 221 P1
Meadcroft Rd LBTH SE11 18 C10
WALW SE17 18 C10
Mead Dr COUL/CHIP CR5 222 F10
Meade CI CHSWK W4 155 M5
Mead End ASHTD KT21 237 L3
Meades La CSHM HP5 50 G8
Meadfield EDGW HA8 95 N3
Meadfield Av DTCH/LGLY SL3 150 D2
Meadfield Rd DTCH/LGLY SL3 150 D2
Meadfoot Rd STRHM/NOR SW16 180 D1
Meadgate Av WFD IG8 102 B6
Meadgate Rd HOD EN11 45 J6
Mead Gv CHDH RM6 123 N1
Mead House La YEAD UB4 132 C6
Meadhurst Rd CHERT KT16 195 L8
Meadlands Dr RCHPK/HAM TW10 177 J5
Mead La CHERT KT16 195 L8
HERT/BAY SG13 25 M4
Meadow Ap CRAWE RH10 285 H2
Meadow Av CROY/NA CR0 204 C6
Meadowbank BKHTH/KID SE3 161 L9
BRYLDS KT5 199 L6
Meadow Bank EHSLY KT24 252 G3
Meadowbank HAMP NW3 4 A4
KGLGY WD4 53 K6
OXHEY WD19 93 K1
WCHMH N21 78 C10
Meadowbank CI FUL/PGN SW6 156 F6
Meadowbank Gdns HEST TW5 153 J7
Meadowbank Rd
CDALE/KGS NW9 116 A5
LTWR GU18 212 B6
Meadowbanks BAR EN5 76 D9
Meadowbrook OXTED RH8 261 H6
Meadowbrook Rd DORK RH4 272 F1
Meadow CI BAR EN5 77 K7
BERK HP4 33 M7
BRKMPK AL9 40 G10
BXLYHS DA6 186 A1
CAT SE6 182 F9
CHING E4 100 G2
CHST BR7 184 E8
CRAWE RH10 285 H2
CSHM HP5 50 F3
ESH/CLAY KT10 198 E10
HERT/BAY SG13 25 N4
HOM E9 120 E10
HSLWW TW4 175 P9
LCOL/BKTW AL2 55 P6
NTHLT UB5 133 P4
PEND EN3 80 D5
PUR/KEN CR8 222 F9
RCHPK/HAM TW10 177 K4
RGODL GU7 267 K10
RSLP HA4 112 C2
RYNPK SW20 200 F6
SEV TN13 247 P9
SLH/COR SS17 169 K2
STALE/WH AL4 39 H5
WDSR SL4 147 N4
WOT/HER KT12 217 N1
Meadow Cott La AMSS HP7 68 D7
Meadow Dr EPSOM KT18 219 P9
STA TW18 173 H6

Meadowcourt Rd
BKHTH/KID SE3 161 L10
Meadowcroft BERK HP4 33 J2
BMLY BR1 206 C3
Meadowcroft BUSH WD23 74 A10
CFSP/GDCR SL9 90 A10
Meadow Cft HAT AL10 40 C4
Meadowcroft CI CRAWW RH11 283 H8
Meadowcroft Rd PLMGR N13 99 H3
Meadowcross WAB EN9 63 K10
Meadow Dell HAT AL10 40 C4
Meadow Dr AMS HP6 69 K3
HDN NW4 96 F10
MUSWH N10 98 B3
RPLY/SEND GU23 233 J9
Meadow Gdns EDGW HA8 95 P2
STA TW18 172 G8
Meadow Garth WLSDN NW10 135 P7
Meadow Gn WGCW AL8 22 D5
Meadow HI NWMAL KT3 200 C5
PUR/KEN CR8 222 G9
Meadow La BEAC HP9 236 B9
LHD/OX KT22 257 H7
WDSR SL4 148 G5
Meadowlands BGR/WK TN15 247 N6
COB KT11 217 H9
CRAWW RH11 283 M7
EMPK RM11 125 M5
OXTED RH8 261 N10
RGUE GU4 251 L6
Meadowlea CI WDR/YW UB7 151 N5
Meadow Ms VX/NE SW8 17 N10
Meadow PI VX/NE SW8 158 F6
CHSWK W4 156 C6
Meadow Ri COUL/CHIP CR5 222 D9
WOKN/KNAP GU21 231 H3
Meadow Rd ASHF TW15 174 A10
ASHTD KT21 237 K3
BARK IG11 143 K6
BERK HP4 33 N3
BORE WD6 75 N6
BUSH WD23 74 A7
CDH/CHF RM16 168 A1
DAGW RM9 144 A4
DTCH/LGLY SL3 150 B1
EPP CM16 65 J3
ESH/CLAY KT10 218 D2
FELT TW13 175 H5
GSTN WD25 51 H10
GVW DA11 190 D5
HAYES BR2 205 K1
LOU IG10 82 G6

PIN HA5 ....113 L2
RGUE GU4 ....250 D6
ROMW/RG RM7 ....124 D6
STHL UB1 ....133 N9
SUT SM1 ....221 P1
VW GU25 ....193 K5
VX/NE SW8 ....17 P10
WIM/MER SW19 ....179 N10
Meadow Road Cl BERK HP4 ....33 M3
Meadow Rw STHWK SE1 ....18 E4
Meadows Cl LEY E10 ....120 F7
  RBRW/HUT CM13 ....107 P7
Meadows End SUN TW16 ....197 H1
Meadowside BEAC HP9 ....89 L8
  DART DA1 ....187 M4
  ELTH/MOT SE9 ....161 P10
  GT/LBKH KT23 ....235 P9
  HORL RH6 ....280 C3
  TWK TW1 ....197 K9
  WOT/HER KT12 ....197 K9
Meadowside Leigh Cl WEY KT13 ....196 D10
The Meadows AMSS HP7 ....69 K5
  GUW GU2 ....267 P3
  ORP BR6 ....227 M3
  RBRW/HUT CM13 ....107 P7
  RSEV TN14 ....228 A9
  SBW CM21 ....30 B1
  WARL CR6 ....242 C3
Meadow Stile CROY/NA CRO 203 K10
Meadowsweet Cl CAN/RD E16 ....142 A7
  NWMAL KT3 ....200 F5
The Meadow CHST BR7 ....184 F9
  CRAWE RH10 ....285 H2
  HERT/BAY SG13 ....26 D9
  WGCE AL7 ....23 M5
Meadow Vw BFN/LL DA15 ....89 M4
  CSTC HP8 ....89 M4
  EPP CM16 ....65 K5
  HORL RH6 ....281 K4
  HRW HA1 ....114 D6
  STWL/WRAY TW19 ....173 J1
Meadowview Rd BXLY DA5 ....185 P2
  CAT SE6 ....182 F4
  HOR/WEW KT19 ....220 B5
  YEAD UB4 ....132 E6
Meadow Vw THHTH CR7 ....203 J5
Meadow Wk DAGW RM9 ....144 A1
  EW KT17 ....220 C4
  HARP AL5 ....20 B3
  HOR/WEW KT19 ....220 B3
  KWD/TDW/WH KT20 ....238 E10
  RDART DA2 ....187 K7
  SWFD E18 ....121 M2
  WLGTN SM6 ....202 C10
Meadow Wy ABLGY WD5 ....54 C3
  ADL/WDHM KT15 ....215 L1
  AMS HP6 ....68 B1
  CDALE/KGS NW9 ....102 F3
  CHIG IG7 ....102 F3
  CHOB/PIR GU24 ....212 E9
  CHSGTN KT9 ....219 K2
  EHSLY KT24 ....252 E1
  GT/LBKH KT23 ....236 A9
  HHS/BOV HP3 ....35 J9
  KGLGY WD4 ....54 B6
  KWD/TDW/WH KT20 ....239 H3
  ORP BR6 ....206 D10
  POTB/CUF EN6 ....59 K10
  RDART DA2 ....188 B3
  REIG RH2 ....275 L3
  RKW/CH/CXG WD3 ....91 M1
  RSLP HA4 ....113 J4
  SBW CM21 ....30 B2
  UPMR RM14 ....126 B8
  WBLY HA9 ....115 J9
  WDSR SL4 ....171 N2
Meadow Waye HEST TW5 ....153 M6
The Meadow Wy
  KTN/HRWW/W HA3 ....94 D9
Mead Pth TOOT SW17 ....179 N9
Mead Pl CROY/NA CRO 203 J8
  HOM E9 ....140 B1
  RKW/CH/CXG WD3 ....91 L2
Mead Plat WLSDN NW10 ....135 P7
Mead Rd CHST BR7 ....184 F9
  CRAWE RH10 ....284 A6
  CTHM CR3 ....241 N9
  DART DA1 ....187 L4
  EDGW HA8 ....95 M8
  GVW DA11 ....190 E5
  RAD WD7 ....57 N9
  RCHPK/HAM TW10 ....177 H6
  UX/CGN UB8 ....131 N1
  WOT/HER KT12 ....217 M1
Mead Rw STHWK SE1 ....18 A3
Meadside Cl BECK BR3 ....204 D1
Meads La GDMY/SEVK IG3 ....123 J5
  STALE/WH AL4 ....21 J2
Meads Rd GU GU1 ....250 E10
  PEND EN3 ....80 D5
  WDGN N22 ....99 J10
The Meads BERK HP4 ....33 L3
  CHEAM SM3 ....200 G10
  EDGW HA8 ....96 B7
  LCOL/BKTW AL2 ....55 N5
  UPMR RM14 ....126 D7
  UX/CGN UB8 ....131 P6
  WEY KT13 ....216 D3
Meadsway RBRW/HUT CM13 ....107 H7
The Mead ABR/ST RM4 ....83 L7
  ASHTD KT21 ....237 K5
  BECK BR3 ....205 H2
  CHES/WCR EN8 ....62 B5
  EFNCH N2 ....97 M10
  HART DA3 ....211 K9
  HGDN/ICK UB10 ....112 B7
  OXHEY WD19 ....93 M4
  WEA W13 ....134 G7
  WLGTN SM6 ....202 E3
  WWKM BR4 ....205 J8
Meadvale Rd CROY/NA CRO 203 N7
  EA W5 ....134 C6
Meadview Rd WARE SG12 ....26 B3
Mead Wk CHONG CM5 ....67 N6
  DTCH/LGLY SL3 ....150 L1
Mead Wy SL SL1 ....128 C7
  BUSH WD23 ....73 M6
  COUL/CHIP CR5 ....240 F4
  CROY/NA CRO 204 D9
  HAYES BR2 ....205 L6
  RGUE GU4 ....250 F5
  RSLP HA4 ....112 E5
Meadway ASHF TW15 ....174 B7
  BAR EN5 ....77 K8
  BECK BR3 ....205 H1
  BERK HP4 ....34 B5
  BRYLDS KT5 ....199 P8
  EHSLY KT24 ....253 M4
  ESH/CLAY KT10 ....218 A5
  GDMY/SEVK IG3 ....123 H9
  GLDGN NW11 ....105 H10
  GPK RM2 ....124 G1
  GRAYS RM17 ....168 A3
  HARP AL5 ....20 D4
  HOD EN11 ....44 F1
  HOR/WEW KT19 ....219 P9
  LHD/OX KT22 ....218 C10
  RSEV TN14 ....228 A9
  RYNPK SW20 ....200 F4
  STA TW18 ....173 K10
  STHGT/OAK N14 ....98 E3
  WARL CR6 ....242 B2

Meadway Cl GLDGN NW11 ....117 L4
  PIN HA5 ....94 A7
  STA TW18 ....173 J10
Meadway Dr ADL/WDHM KT15 ....215 M4
  WOKN/KNAP GU21 ....231 P2
Meadway Gdns RSLP HA4 ....112 E2
Meadway Pk CFSP/GDCR SL9 ....110 A6
The Meadway BKHH IG9 ....102 A2
  BKHTH/KID SE3 ....161 J8
  HORL RH6 ....280 D4
  ORP BR6 ....227 L2
  POTB/CUF EN6 ....60 G4
  SEV TN13 ....246 G8
Meaford Wy PGE/AN SE20 ....182 A10
Meanley Rd MNPK E12 ....122 B10
Meard St SOHO/CST W1F 11 J6
Meare Cl KWD/TDW/WH KT20 ....238 F10
Meath Cl STMC/STPC BR5 ....207 L5
Meath Crs BTSEA SW11 ....158 C7
Meath Green Av HORL RH6 ....280 A2
Meath Green La REDH RH1 ....275 P9
Meath Rd IL IG1 ....122 F8
  SRTFD E15 ....141 L4
Meath St BTSEA SW11 ....158 C7
Meautys STALW/RED AL3 ....37 N8
Mecklenburgh Pl BMSBY WC1N 11 N1
Mecklenburgh Sq BMSBY WC1N 11 N1
Mecklenburgh St BMSBY WC1N 11 N1
Medburn St CAMTN NW1 ....5 J7
Medbury Rd GVE DA12 ....191 J6
Medcalf Rd PEND EN3 ....80 E3
Medcroft Gdns
  MORT/ESHN SW14 ....155 P10
Medebourne Cl BKHTH/KID SE3 ....161 M9
Medebridge Rd CDH/CHF RM16 ....147 L8
Mede Fld PUT/ROE SW15 ....178 D3
Medesenge Wy PLMGR N13 ....99 J5
Medfield St PUT/ROE SW15 ....178 D3
  CHOB/PIR GU24 ....213 L5
Medhurst Crs GVE DA12 ....191 J6
Medhurst Gdns GVE DA12 ....191 J6
Median Rd CLPT E5 ....120 B10
Medick Ct GRAYS RM17 ....168 B5
Medina Av ESH/CLAY KT10 ....198 D10
Medina Rd GRAYS RM17 ....168 A4
  HOLWY N7 ....119 H8
Medlake Rd EGH TW20 ....172 F9
Medland Cl MTCM CR4 ....202 B8
Medlar Cl CRAWW RH11 ....283 M4
  GU GU1 ....249 P8
  NTHLT UB5 ....133 L4
Medlar Dr SOCK/AV RM15 ....147 K6
Medlar Rd GRAYS RM17 ....168 A5
Medlar St CMBW SE5 ....159 K7
Medley Rd KIL/WHAMP NW6 ....2 E2
Medman Cl UX/CGN UB8 ....131 M4
Medora Rd BRXS/STRHM SW2 ....180 G2
  ROMW/RG RM7 ....124 E2
Medow Md RAD WD7 ....56 F9
Medusa Rd LEW SE13 ....182 G2
Medway Cl CROY/NA CRO 204 B6
  GSTN WD25 ....55 K10
  IL IG1 ....122 F10
Medway Dr GFD/PVL UB6 ....134 E4
Medway Gdns ALP/SUD HA0 ....114 F9
Medway Pde GFD/PVL UB6 ....134 E4
Medway Rd BOW E3 ....140 D4
  CRAWW RH11 ....283 J8
  DART DA1 ....165 H9
  HHNE HP2 ....36 A1
Medway St WEST SW1P 17 J4
Medwick Ms HHNE HP2 ....36 C1
Medwin St BRXS/STRHM SW2 ....158 G10
Meerbrook Rd ELTH/MOT SE9 ....161 P9
Meeson Rd SRTFD E15 ....141 L4
Meesons La GRAYS RM17 ....167 L3
Meeson St CLPT E5 ....120 D9
Meeting Field Pth HOM E9 ....140 B1
Meeting House Aly WAP E1W 140 A10
Meeting House La PECK SE15 ....160 A7
Megg La KGLGY WD4 ....53 L5
Mehetabel Rd HACK E8 ....140 B1
Meister Cl IL IG1 ....122 D10
Melanda Cl CHST BR7 ....184 C8
Melanie Cl BXLYHN DA7 ....163 P7
Melaris Ms KIL/WHAMP NW6 ....117 K10
Melba Gdns TIL RM18 ....168 D6
Melbourne Av PLMGR N13 ....98 G7
  RYLN/HDSTN HA2 ....114 A1
  SL SL1 ....129 H8
  WEA W13 ....134 F10
Melbourne Cl ORP BR6 ....207 H7
  STALW/RED AL3 ....38 C2
  WLGTN SM6 ....222 D2
Melbourne Ct WGCW AL8 ....23 M7
Melbourne Gdns CHDH RM6 ....123 P5
Melbourne Gv EDUL SE22 ....159 N10
Melbourne Ms BRXN/ST SW9 ....159 H7
  CAT SE6 ....183 H1
Melbourne Pl HOL/ALD WC2B 11 N7
Melbourne Rd BUSH WD23 ....74 A9
  EHAM E6 ....142 C4
  IL IG1 ....122 E6
  LEY E10 ....120 E6
  TEDD TW11 ....177 H9
  TIL RM18 ....171 L8
  WALTH E17 ....120 D2
  WIM/MER SW19 ....201 K1
  WLGTN SM6 ....222 B4
Melbourne Sq BRXN/ST SW9 ....159 H7
Melbourne Wy EN EN1 ....79 N10
Melbury Av NWDGN UB2 ....154 A2
Melbury Cl BF/WBF KT14 ....215 K10
  CHERT KT16 ....195 K7
  CHST BR7 ....184 C6
  ESH/CLAY KT10 ....218 D1
Melbury Ct WKENS W14 ....14 C3
Melbury Dr CMBW SE5 ....159 M6
Melbury Gdns RYNPK SW20 ....200 E1
Melbury Rd KTN/HRWW/W HA3 ....115 C3
  WKENS W14 ....14 C3
The Melings HHNE HP2 ....36 C1
Melior Pl STHWK SE1 ....19 H1
Melior St STHWK SE1 ....19 H1
Meliot Rd CAT SE6 ....183 J5
Melksham Cl HARH RM3 ....105 N8
Melksham Dr HARH RM3 ....105 M8
Melksham Gdns HARH RM3 ....105 M8
Meller Cl WLGTN SM6 ....202 F10

Melling Dr EN EN1 ....79 P5
Melling Gdns WFD IG8 ....101 M6
Mellish Cl WOOL/PLUM SE18 ....163 N5
Mellish Gdns WFD IG8 ....101 M6
Mellison Rd TOOT SW17 ....179 P8
Mellitus St SHB W12 ....136 C8
Mellor Cl WOT/HER KT12 ....197 N7
Mellow Cl BNSTD SM7 ....221 M10
Mellow La East YEAD UB4 ....132 D6
Mellows Rd CLAY IG5 ....122 C1
  WLGTN SM6 ....222 E2
Mells Crs ELTH/MOT SE9 ....184 C7
Mell St GNWCH SE10 ....161 K4
Melody Rd BH/WHM TN16 ....243 P4
  WAND/EARL SW18 ....160 A6
Melon Pl KENS W8 ....14 E2
Melon Rd PECK SE15 ....159 P7
  WAN E11 ....121 N3
Melrose Av BORE WD6 ....75 N9
  CRICK NW2 ....116 F10
  GFD/PVL UB6 ....134 A4
  MTCM CR4 ....180 C10
  POTB/CUF EN6 ....59 P4
  STRHM/NOR SW16 ....202 G3
  WDGN N22 ....99 J9
  WHTN TW2 ....176 A3
  WIM/MER SW19 ....179 J5
Melrose Cl GFD/PVL UB6 ....134 A4
  LEE/GVPK SE12 ....183 M4
  YEAD UB4 ....133 H7
Melrose Crs ORP BR6 ....226 G1
Melrose Dr STHL UB1 ....133 P10
Melrose Gdns EDGW HA8 ....115 N1
  HMSMTH W6 ....156 F2
  NWMAL KT3 ....200 A3
  WOT/HER KT12 ....217 K2
Melrose Pl WAT WD17 ....72 C4
Melrose Rd BARN SW13 ....156 C8
  BH/WHM TN16 ....243 P2
  COUL/CHIP CR5 ....240 C1
  RYLN/HDSTN HA2 ....113 N2
  WAND/EARL SW18 ....179 J2
  WEY KT13 ....216 B2
  WIM/MER SW19 ....201 K2
Melrose Ter HMSMTH W6 ....156 F1
Melsa Rd MRDN SM4 ....201 M6
Melsted Rd HHW HP1 ....35 L6
Melstock Av UPMR RM14 ....126 B9
Melthorne Dr RSLP HA4 ....113 K8
Melthorpe Gdns
  WOOL/PLUM SE18 ....162 A7
Melton Cl RSLP HA4 ....113 K6
Melton Flds HOR/WEW KT19 ....220 A5
Melton Gdns ROM RM1 ....124 G4
Melton Pl HOR/WEW KT19 ....220 A5
Melton Rd REDH RH1 ....258 D6
Melton St CAMTN NW1 ....5 H10
Melville Av GFD/PVL UB6 ....114 E10
  RYNPK SW20 ....178 D10
  SAND/SEL CR2 ....223 N2
Melville Gdns PLMGR N13 ....99 H2
  RAIN RM13 ....145 H6
Melville Rd BARN SW13 ....156 D7
  ROMW/RG RM7 ....104 C9
  SCUP DA14 ....185 M5
  WALTH E17 ....120 E2
  WLSDN NW10 ....99 H10
Melville Villas Rd ACT W3 ....135 P10
Melvin Rd PGE/AN SE20 ....204 B1
Melvinshaw LHD/OX KT22 ....237 H7
Melvyn Cl CHESW EN7 ....61 J4
Memel St STLK EC1Y 12 E1
Memorial Av SRTFD E15 ....141 K5
Memorial Cl HEST TW5 ....153 N5
Memorial Wy WAT WD17 ....73 H7
Mendip Cl DTCH/LGLY SL3 ....150 D4
  HYS/HAR UB3 ....152 E6
  STALW/WH AL4 ....39 H1
  SYD SE26 ....182 B7
  WPK KT4 ....200 F9
Mendip Dr GLDGN NW11 ....117 H7
Mendip Rd BTSEA SW11 ....158 C5
  BUSH WD23 ....74 B10
  BXLYHN DA7 ....164 F7
  EMPK RM11 ....125 H5
  GNTH/NBYPK IG2 ....123 J5
Mendip Wy HHNE HP2 ....35 P3
Mendlesham WGCE AL7 ....23 P7
Mendora Rd FUL/PGN SW6 ....157 H6
Mendoza Cl EMPK RM11 ....125 M3
Menelik Rd CRICK NW2 ....117 M1
Menlo Gdns NRWD SE19 ....181 L10
Menotti St BETH E2 ....13 P1
Mentmore Cl KTN/HRWW/W HA3 ....115 N1
Mentmore Rd STAL AL1 ....38 C8
Mentmore Ter HACK E8 ....140 A2
Meon Cl KWD/TDW/WH KT20 ....238 E8
Meon Rd ACT W3 ....135 J1
Meopham Rd MTCM CR4 ....202 D1
Mepham Crs KTN/HRWW/W HA3 ....94 B8
Mepham Gdns KTN/HRWW/W HA3 ....94 B8
Mepham St STHWK SE1 ....12 A10
Mera Dr BXLYHN DA7 ....164 B10
Merantun Wy WIM/MER SW19 ....201 L1
Merbury Cl LEW SE13 ....183 H1
Merbury Rd THMD SE28 ....163 H1
Mercator Pl POP/IOD E14 ....160 F4
Mercator Rd LEW SE13 ....161 J10
Mercer Cl CRAWE RH10 ....284 D10
Merceron St WCHPL E1 ....140 A6
Mercer Pl PIN HA5 ....93 K10
Mercers HHNE HP2 ....35 P4
  HLWW/ROY CM19 ....46 D4
Mercers Cl GNWCH SE10 ....161 K3
Mercers Pl HMSMTH W6 ....156 F3
Mercers Rd ARCH N19 ....118 E8
Mercers Rw STAL AL1 ....38 B8
Merchant Dr HERT/BAY SG13 ....25 N4
Merchant St BOW E3 ....139 J2
Merchiston Rd CAT SE6 ....183 J5
Merchland Rd ELTH/MOT SE9 ....184 F4
Mercia Gv LEW SE13 ....161 H10
Mercian Wy SL SL1 ....128 D10
Mercier Rd PUT/ROE SW15 ....179 H1
Mercury Cl CRAWW RH11 ....283 H10
Mercury Gdns ROM RM1 ....124 G3
Mercury Wy NWCR SE14 ....160 G5
Mercy Ter LEW SE13 ....182 G1
Merebank La WLGTN SM6 ....222 G4
Mere Cl ORP BR6 ....206 E9
  PUT/ROE SW15 ....178 G3
Meredith Av CRICK NW2 ....117 L8
Meredith Cl PIN HA5 ....93 L4
Meredith Rd CDH/CHF RM16 ....148 A6
Merednith St CLKNW EC1R 6 C10
  PLSTW E13 ....141 M5
Meredyth Rd BARN SW13 ....156 D8
Mere End CROY/NA CRO 204 C7
Merefield SBW CM21 ....29 P2
Merefield Gdns
  KWD/TDW/WH KT20 ....238 G5
Mere Rd KWD/TDW/WH KT20 ....238 E10
  SHPTN TW17 ....196 C6
  SL SL1 ....149 J2
  WEY KT13 ....196 E10
Mereside ORP BR6 ....206 D9
Meretone Cl BROCKY SE4 ....160 D10
Merevale Crs MRDN SM4 ....201 N6
Mereway Rd WHTN TW2 ....176 C2
Merewood Cl BMLY BR1 ....206 D2
Merewood Rd BXLYHN DA7 ....164 D8
Mereworth Cl HAYES BR2 ....205 L5
Mereworth Dr CRAWE RH10 ....284 E5
  WOOL/PLUM SE18 ....162 E6
Meriden Cl BARK/HLT IG6 ....102 F9

BMLY BR1 ....184 A10
Meriden Gv HORL RH6 ....280 D3
Meridian Rd CHARL SE7 ....162 A6
Meridian Wy ED N9 ....100 B4
  UED N18 ....100 B5
  WARE SG12 ....26 G6
Merifield Rd ELTH/MOT SE9 ....161 P10
Merino Cl WAN E11 ....121 P2
Merivale Rd HRW HA1 ....114 B5
  PUT/ROE SW15 ....157 H10
Merland Cl KWD/TDW/WH KT20 ....238 F6
Merland Gn KWD/TDW/WH KT20 ....238 F6
Merle Av DEN/HRF UB9 ....91 M10
Merlewood Cl CTHM CR3 ....241 L6
Merlewood Dr CHST BR7 ....206 C1
Merley Ct CDALE/KGS NW9 ....115 P6
Merlin Cl CRAWW RH11 ....283 P7
  CROY/NA CRO 223 M1
  CRW RM5 ....104 E7
  DTCH/LGLY SL3 ....150 E5
  MTCM CR4 ....201 P3
  NTHLT UB5 ....133 K5
  WAB EN9 ....63 M10
Merlin Crs EDGW HA8 ....95 M8
Merlin Gdns CRW RM5 ....104 E7
Merling Cft BERK HP4 ....33 L4
Merlin Gv BARK/HLT IG6 ....102 E8
  BECK BR3 ....204 E4
Merlin Rd CRW RM5 ....104 E7
  MNPK E12 ....122 A7
  WELL DA16 ....163 K10
Merlin Rd North WELL DA16 ....163 K10
Merlins Av RYLN/HDSTN HA2 ....113 N8
Merlin St FSBYW WC1X 6 A10
Merlin Wy EPP CM16 ....66 B1
Mermagen Dr RAIN RM13 ....145 J2
Mermaid Ct STHWK SE1 ....18 G1
Mermerus Gdns GVE DA12 ....191 J7
Merredene St
  BRXS/STRHM SW2 ....180 C2
Merriam Cl CHING E4 ....101 H6
Merrick Rd NWDGN UB2 ....153 N3
Merrick Sq STHWK SE1 ....18 G2
Merridene WCHMH N21 ....79 J10
Merrielands Crs DAGW RM9 ....144 A4
Merrilands Rd WPK KT4 ....200 F8
Merrilees Rd BFN/LL DA15 ....185 H3
Merrilyn Cl ESH/CLAY KT10 ....218 F3
Merriman Rd BKHTH/KID SE3 ....161 P7
Merrington Rd FUL/PGN SW6 ....14 A7
Merrion Av STAN HA7 ....95 J6
Merritt Gdns CHSGTN KT9 ....219 J3
Merritt Rd BROCKY SE4 ....182 E1
Merrivale WCHMH N21 ....79 J10
Merrivale Av REDBR IG4 ....122 A2
Merrivale Gdns
  WOKN/KNAP GU21 ....231 P3
Merrow Cha GU GU1 ....250 F10
Merrow Common Rd RGUE GU4 ....250 G7
Merrow Copse GU GU1 ....250 F9
Merrow Cft GU GU1 ....250 F9
Merrow Dr HHW HP1 ....35 H5
Merrow La RGUE GU4 ....250 F5
Merrow Rd BELMT SM2 ....220 G5
Merrow St WALW SE17 ....18 G8
  WALW SE17 ....18 G8
Merrow Wy CROY/NA CRO 225 H3
Merrow Woods GU GU1 ....250 E8
Merrydown Wy CHST BR7 ....206 B1
Merryfield BKHTH/KID SE3 ....161 J8
Merryfield Gdns STAN HA7 ....95 H6
Merryfields STALE/WH AL4 ....39 K6
  UX/CGN UB8 ....131 N4
Merryfields Wy CAT SE6 ....182 E6
Merry Hill Mt BUSH WD23 ....94 A2
Merry Hill Rd BUSH WD23 ....93 P1
Merryhills Cl BH/WHM TN16 ....244 A2
Merryhills Dr ENC/FH EN2 ....78 F8
Merrylands STALE/WH AL4 ....39 K6
Merrylands Farm GT/LBKH KT23 ....235 N10
Merrylands Rd GT/LBKH KT23 ....235 N9
Merrymeet BNSTD SM7 ....222 A10
Merryweather Cl DART DA1 ....187 N2
Merrywood Gv
  KWD/TDW/WH KT20 ....256 G6
Merrywood Pk REIG RH2 ....257 L8
Mersey Av UPMR RM14 ....126 C4
Mersey Pl HHNE HP2 ....36 A1
Mersey Rd WALTH E17 ....120 E1
Mersham Dr CDALE/KGS NW9 ....115 M3
Mersham Pl PGE/AN SE20 ....204 A1
Mersham Rd THHTH CR7 ....203 L2
Merstham Rd REDH RH1 ....259 H6
Merten Rd CHDH RM6 ....123 P5
Merthyr Ter BARN SW13 ....156 E5
Merton Av CHSWK W4 ....156 D1
  HART DA3 ....211 K4
  HGDN/ICK UB10 ....132 C2
  NTHLT UB5 ....114 B10
Merton Gdns
  KWD/TDW/WH KT20 ....238 G5
  STMC/STPC BR5 ....206 A2
Merton Hall Gdns RYNPK SW20 ....201 H1
Merton Hall Rd WIM/MER SW19 ....201 H1
Merton High St WIM/MER SW19 ....179 M10
Merton La HGT N6 ....118 A7
Merton Pl CDH/CHF RM16 ....168 D5
Merton Ri HAMP NW3 ....3 N3
Merton Rd BARK IG11 ....143 J2
  ENC/FH EN2 ....79 L4
  GDMY/SEVK IG3 ....123 J5
  LEY E10 ....121 H5
  RYLN/HDSTN HA2 ....114 B6
  SL SL1 ....149 M2
  SNWD SE25 ....203 N5
  WAND/EARL SW18 ....179 K1
  WIM/MER SW19 ....179 L10
Merton Wy E/WMO/HCT KT8 ....198 B4
  HGDN/ICK UB10 ....132 C2
  LHD/OX KT22 ....236 F3
Merttins Rd PECK SE15 ....160 C10
Mervan Rd BRXS/STRHM SW2 ....159 N10
Mervyn Av ELTH/MOT SE9 ....184 F6
Mervyn Rd SHPTN TW17 ....196 F7
  WEA W13 ....154 F2
Merwin Wy WDSR SL4 ....148 B6
Mesne Wy RSEV TN14 ....245 C8
Messaline Av ACT W3 ....135 P8
Messant Cl GPK RM2 ....105 L2
Messent Rd ELTH/MOT SE9 ....183 P1
Messeter Pl ELTH/MOT SE9 ....184 D2
Messina Av KIL/WHAMP NW6 ....2 D4
Metcalf Rd ASHF TW15 ....174 C8
Metcalf Wy CRAWW RH11 ....283 H3
Meteor St BTSEA SW11 ....158 F3
Meteor Wy WLGTN SM6 ....222 F4
Metheringham Wy
  CDALE/KGS NW9 ....96 B9
Methley St LBTH SE11 ....18 B9
Methuen Cl EDGW HA8 ....95 M8
Methuen Pk MUSWH N10 ....98 C10
Methuen Rd BELV DA17 ....164 C3
  BXLYHS DA6 ....164 A1
  EDGW HA8 ....95 M8
Methwold Rd NKENS W10 ....136 G7
Metropolitan Station Ap
  WATW WD18 ....72 G7
Meux Cl CHESW EN7 ....61 P7
Mews Clare FUL/PGN SW6 ....157 L6
Mews North BGVA SW1W 16 E4

Mews Pl WFD IG8 ....101 M5
Mews South SW1V 17 H7
Mews St WAP E1W 13 M9
The Mews CEND/HSY/T N8 ....119 H2
  REDBR IG4 ....122 A3
  ROM RM1 ....124 F3
Mexfield Rd PUT/ROE SW15 ....179 J1
Meyer Gn EN EN1 ....79 P4
Meyer Rd ERITH DA8 ....164 D5
Meymott St STHWK SE1 ....12 C10
Meynell Crs HOM E9 ....140 C2
Meynell Gdns HOM E9 ....140 C2
Meynell Rd HARH RM3 ....105 J7
  HOM E9 ....140 C2
Meyrick Cl WOKN/KNAP GU21 ....231 K2
Meyrick Rd BTSEA SW11 ....157 N9
  WLSDN NW10 ....136 F1
Mezen Cl NTHWD HA6 ....92 E6
Micawber Av UX/CGN UB8 ....132 B6
Micawber St IS N1 ....6 G7
Michael Crs HORL RH6 ....280 B6
Michael Gdns EMPK RM11 ....125 L2
  GVE DA12 ....191 H9
Michael Gaynor Cl HNWL W7 ....134 E10
Michaelmas Cl RYNPK SW20 ....200 F3
Michael Rd FUL/PGN SW6 ....157 L7
  SNWD SE25 ....203 M3
  WAN E11 ....121 K6
Michaels Cl LEW SE13 ....161 K10
Michaels La HART DA3 ....210 G9
Micheldever Rd LEW SE13 ....183 K2
Michelet Cl LTWR GU18 ....212 A6
Michelham Gdns
  KWD/TDW/WH KT20 ....238 F6
  TWK TW1 ....176 E6
Michigan Av MNPK E12 ....122 C9

Michleham Down
  NFNCH/WDSP N12 ....97 J3
Nicholls Av CFSP/GDCR SL9 ....90 B6
Micklefield Rd HHNE HP2 ....36 D6
Micklefield Wy BORE WD6 ....75 K4
Mickleham Cl STMC/STPC BR5 ....207 J2
Mickleham Dr LHD/OX KT22 ....255 H2
Mickleham Gdns CHEAM SM3 ....221 H3
Mickleham Rd STMC/STPC BR5 ....207 J1
Mickleham Wy CROY/NA CRO 225 J4
Micklem Dr HHW HP1 ....35 J5
Micklethwaite Rd FUL/PGN SW6 ....14 F10
Midcot Wy BERK HP4 ....33 L3
Midcroft RSLP HA4 ....112 F6
  SLN SL2 ....128 G6
Mid Cross La CFSP/GDCR SL9 ....90 C6
Middle Boy ABR/ST RM4 ....85 L7
Middle Cl COUL/CHIP CR5 ....241 H6
  EW KT17 ....220 B8
Middle Dene MLHL NW7 ....96 A4
Middle Dr BEAC HP9 ....88 C6
Middle Farm Pl EHSLY KT24 ....253 L3
Middlefield HAT AL10 ....40 D3
  HORL RH6 ....280 D3
  STJWD NW8 ....3 L5
  WGCE AL7 ....23 H9
Middlefield Av HOD EN11 ....44 F1
Middlefield Cl HOD EN11 ....44 F1
  STALE/WH AL4 ....39 H3
Middlefield Gdns HOD EN11 ....44 F1
Middlefields WEA W13 ....134 G2
Middle Furlong BUSH WD23 ....74 A8
Middle Gn BRWN CM15 ....87 H3
  DTCH/LGLY SL3 ....130 B9
Middle Green Cl BRYLDS KT5 ....199 L6
Middlegreen Rd DTCH/LGLY SL3 ....130 A10
Middleham Gdns UED N18 ....99 P7
Middleham Rd UED N18 ....99 P7
Middle Hl EGH TW20 ....171 P8
Middleknights HHW HP1 ....35 K4
Middle La BGR/WK TN15 ....247 N7
  CEND/HSY/T N8 ....118 F4
  EW KT17 ....220 B8
  HHS/BOV HP3 ....52 D5
  TEDD TW11 ....176 E9
Middle Lane Ms CEND/HSY/T N8 ....118 F3
Middlemead Cl GT/LBKH KT23 ....253 P1
Middle Meadow CSTG HP8 ....89 P4
Middlemead Rd GT/LBKH KT23 ....253 N1
Middle Ope WATN WD24 ....73 J3
Middle Park Av ELTH/MOT SE9 ....184 A2
  ELTH/MOT SE9 ....184 A3
Middle Rd BERK HP4 ....33 N5
  DEN/HRF UB9 ....110 F9
  EBAR EN4 ....77 P10
  LHD/OX KT22 ....236 C7
  PLSTW E13 ....141 M4
  RBRW/HUT CM13 ....107 P5
  RYLN/HDSTN HA2 ....114 C7
  STRHM/NOR SW16 ....202 D2
  WAB EN9 ....8 G2
Middle Rw NKENS W10 ....136 B1
Middlesborough Rd UED N18 ....99 P6
Middlesex Pl HOM E9 ....140 B1
Middlesex Rd MTCM CR4 ....202 F5
Middlesex St WCHPL E1 ....13 K4
Middle St BRKHM/BTCW RH3 ....273 N2
  CROY/NA CRO 203 K10
  SHGR GU5 ....270 B5
  STBT EC1A 12 E3
  WAB EN9 ....45 L9
Middle Temple La TPL/STR WC2R 12 A6
Middleton Av CHING E4 ....100 E4
  GFD/PVL UB6 ....134 C4
  SCUP DA14 ....185 M9
Middleton Buildings GTPST W1W 10 C4
Middleton Cl CHING E4 ....100 E4
Middleton Dr BERM/RHTH SE16 ....160 C1
  PIN HA5 ....113 H1
Middleton Gdns
  GNTH/NBYPK IG2 ....122 E4
Middleton Gv HOLWY N7 ....118 F10
Middleton Hall La BRWN CM15 ....107 K3
Middleton Ms HOLWY N7 ....118 F10
Middleton Rd BRWN CM15 ....107 K3
  CAR SM5 ....201 N7
  COB KT11 ....235 J5
  GLDGN NW11 ....117 K5
  HACK E8 ....7 L4
  HOR/WEW KT19 ....220 A6
  HYS/HAR UB3 ....132 E7
  MRDN SM4 ....201 N6
  NWMAL KT3 ....199 P3
  RKW/CH/CXG WD3 ....91 K2
Middleton St BETH E2 ....140 A3
Middleton Wy CRAWW RH11 ....283 H8
  LEW SE13 ....161 J10
Middle Wk WOKN/KNAP GU21 ....231 P8
Middleway GLDGN NW11 ....117 L3
Middle Wy STRHM/NOR SW16 ....202 D2
  WATN WD24 ....73 J3
The Middle Wy
  KTN/HRWW/W HA3 ....94 E10
The Middlings SEV TN13 ....264 G5
Middlings Wd SEV TN13 ....264 G5
Midfield Av BXLYHN DA7 ....164 D9
  SWLY BR8 ....187 H3
Midfield Wy STMC/STPC BR5 ....207 L1
Midford Pl FITZ W1T 11 H2
Midgley Rd CRAWE RH10 ....284 A5
Midholm GLDGN NW11 ....117 L2
  WBLY HA9 ....115 M6
Midholm Cl CROY/NA CRO 204 D10
Midholm Rd CROY/NA CRO 204 D10
Mid Holmwood La RDKG RH5 ....272 C8
Midhope Cl WOKS/MYFD GU22 ....232 B5
Midhope Gdns
  WOKS/MYFD GU22 ....232 A5
Midhope Rd WOKS/MYFD GU22 ....232 A5
Midhope St STPAN WC1H 5 M10
Midhurst Av CROY/NA CRO 203 H7
  MUSWH N10 ....118 B5

348 Mid - Mon

Midhurst Cl CRAWW RH11 283 K6 1
HCH RM12 125 H9 2
Midhurst Gdns HGDN/ICK UB10 132 D2
Midhurst Hl BXLYHS DA6 186 B1
Midhurst Rd HNWL W7 154 F1
Midland Rd CAMTN NW1 5 K8
HHNE HP2 35 N6
LEY E10 121 H5
Midland Ter WLSDN NW10 136 B6 1
Midleton Industrial Estate Rd
GUW GU2 249 N9
Midleton Rd GUW GU2 249 N9
Midlothian Rd BOW E3 140 E6 4
Midmoor Rd BAL SW12 180 D4
WIM/MER SW19 200 G1
Midship Cl BERM/RHTH SE16 140 C10 10
Midstrath Rd WLSDN NW10 116 B9 4
Mid St REDH RH1 258 G10
Midsummer Av HSLWW TW4 153 N10
Midsummer Wk
WOKN/KNAP GU21 232 A2
Midway CHEAM SM3 201 J7
STALW/RED AL3 38 A9
WOT/HER KT12 197 J9
Midway Av CHERT KT16 195 L3
EGH TW20 194 E3
Midway Cl STA TW18 173 L6
Midwinter Cl WELL DA16 163 K9 1
Miena Wy ASHTD KT21 237 J3
Mighell Av REDBR IG4 122 A3
Milan Rd STHL UB1 153 N1
Milborne Gv WBPTN SW10 15 K8
Milborne St HOM E9 140 B1 7
Milborough Crs LEE/GVPK SE12 183 K2
Milbourne La ESH/CLAY KT10 218 B3
Milbrook ESH/CLAY KT10 218 B3
Milburn Dr WDR/YW UB7 131 P9 4
Milburn Wk EPSOM KT18 238 B1
Milcote St STHWK SE1 18 C2
Mildenhall Rd CLPT E5 120 B9
SL SL1 129 K8
Mildmay Av IS N1 7 H1
Mildmay Gv IS N1 119 L10
Mildmay Pk IS N1 119 L10
Mildmay Pl RSEV TN14 228 G7
Mildmay Rd IL IG1 122 E8
IS N1 119 L10
ROMW/RG RM7 124 D3
Mildmay St IS N1 7 H1
Mildred Av BORE WD6 75 M8
HYS/HAR UB3 152 E3
NTHLT UB5 114 A10
WATW WD18 73 H8
Mildred Cl DART DA1 187 P2
Mildred Rd ERITH DA8 164 F4
Mile Cl WAB EN9 63 H9 4
Mile End Pl WCHPL E1 140 C6
Mile End Rd BOW E3 140 E5
WCHPL E1 140 B7
The Mile End WALTH E17 100 C9
Mile House Cl STAL AL1 38 F9
Mile House La STAL AL1 38 E10
Mile Pth WOKS/MYFD GU22 231 N6
Mile Rd WLGTN SM6 202 B8
Miles Cl HLWW/ROY CM19 46 E2
Miles La COB KT11 217 M9
Milespit Hl MLHL NW7 96 E6
Miles Rd CEND/HSY/T N8 118 F1
HOR/WEW KT19 220 A8
MTCM CR4 201 P3
Miles St VX/NE SW8 17 L10
Milestone Cl BELMT SM2 221 N3
ED N9 99 P3
RPLY/SEND GU23 233 K8
Milestone Rd NRWD SE19 181 N9
Mile Stone Rd RDART DA2 188 A2
Miles Wy TRDG/WHET N20 97 P3
Milfoil St SHB W12 136 D9
Milford Cl ABYW SE2 163 P5
STALE/WH AL4 39 J2
Milford Ct SL SL1 149 M1 1
Milford Gdns ALP/SUD HA0 115 J10
EDGW HA8 95 M8
Milford Gv SUT SM1 221 M1
Milford La TPL/STR WC2R 12 A7
Milford Ms STRHM/NOR SW16 180 G6
Milford Rd STHL UB1 133 P9
WEA W13 134 G10 5
Milking La ORP BR6 226 B8
Milk St BMLY BR1 183 N8
CAN/RD E16 142 E10
CITYW EC2V 12 F5 5
Milkwell Gdns WFD IG8 101 N8
Milkwell Yd CMBW SE5 159 L7 8
Milkwood Rd HNHL SE24 181 J1
Milk Yd WAP E1W 140 B9
Millais Av MNPK E12 122 D10
Millais Gdns EDGW HA8 95 M10
Millais Pl TIL RM18 168 D6
Millais Rd EN EN1 79 N9
NWMAL KT3 200 B7
WAN E11 121 H9
Millais Wy HOR/WEW KT19 219 P1
Millan Cl ADL/WDHM KT15 215 L6 1
Milland Ct BORE WD6 76 A5 1
Mill Av UX/CGN UB8 131 M4 5
Millbank HHS/BOV HP3 35 N10 5
WEST SW1P 17 L5
Millbank Av CHONG CM5 67 N5
The Millbank CRAWW RH11 283 J7
Millbank Wy LEE/GVPK SE12 183 M1
Millbourne Rd FELT TW13 175 M7
Mill Br HERT/WAS SG14 25 K5 5
Millbro SWLY BR8 209 H1 1
Millbrook GUW GU2 268 A2
WEY KT13 216 F1 3
Millbrook Av WELL DA16 162 G10
Millbrook Gdns CHDH RM6 123 P4
GPK RM2 104 F10
Millbrook Rd BRXN/ST SW9 159 J9
BUSH WD23 73 N5
ED N9 100 A2
Mill Brook Rd STMC/STPC BR5 207 M4
Millbrook Wy DTCH/LGLY SL3 151 H8
Mill Cl CAR SM5 202 B9 2
CSHM HP5 51 K10
GT/LBKH KT23 235 P10
HHS/BOV HP3 54 B1
HHW HP1 35 L2
HORL RH6 279 P3
WARE SG12 26 C2
WDR/YW UB7 151 N2
WGCW AL8 22 D6
Millcombe Cl WOKN/KNAP GU21 231 N4 1
Mill Cnr BAR EN5 77 J5
Millcrest Rd CHESW EN7 61 J4
Millennium Br BLKFR EC4V 12 E8
Millennium Whf POP/IOD E14 161 J3
Miller Cl MTCM CR4 202 A7
Miller Pl CFSP/GDCR SL9 110 A3
Miller Rd CROY/NA CR0 202 G8 1
GVE DA12 191 K5
RGUE GU4 250 F7
WIM/MER SW19 179 N9
Miller's Av HACK E8 119 N10 5
Millers Cl CHIG IG7 103 L3
MLHL NW7 96 D5
STA TW18 173 L8
Millers Copse EPSOM KT18 238 A5
REDH RH1 277 J10
Miller's Ct CHSWK W4 156 C4
Millersdale HLWW/ROY CM19 46 E5
Millers Green Cl ENC/FH EN2 79 J7
Miller's La CHIG IG7 103 L2
REDH RH1 277 J10
WARE SG12 27 H7
Millers Ri STAL AL1 38 D7
Miller's Ter STNW/STAM N16 119 N10 6
Miller St CAMTN NW1 4 G7
Miller's Wy HMSMTH W6 156 F1
Millers Yd HERT/WAS SG14 25 L5 10
Millet Rd GFD/PVL UB6 134 A5
Mill Farm Av SUN TW16 174 F10
Mill Farm Cl PIN HA5 93 K10
Mill Farm Crs HSLWW TW4 175 M4
Millfield BERK HP4 34 A4
HART DA3 211 K9
Mill Fld HLWE CM17 29 M7
Millfield SUN TW16 196 E1
WGCE AL7 23 M4
Millfield Av WALTH E17 100 D9
Millfield Dr GVW DA11 190 B5
Millfield La HART DA3 211 K9
HGT N6 118 A7
KWD/TDW/WH KT20 257 K1
Millfield Rd EDGW HA8 95 P10
HSLWW TW4 175 M4
Millfields CSHM HP5 51 H9
Millfields Cl STMC/STPC BR5 207 L4
Millfields Rd CLPT E5 120 B9
Millfield Wk HHS/BOV HP3 36 B9
Millford WOKN/KNAP GU21 231 N3 2
Mill Gdns SYD SE26 182 A7
Mill Green La BRKMPK AL9 23 H10
Mill Green Rd MTCM CR4 202 B7
WGCE AL7 23 H6
Millgrove St BTSEA SW11 158 B8 4
Millharbour POP/IOD E14 160 G2
Millhaven Cl CHDH RM6 123 L4
Millhedge Cl COB KT11 235 M2
Mill Hl BARN SW13 156 D9
BRKHM/BTCW RH3 273 N1
BRWN CM15 107 K1
Mill Hill Gv ACT W3 135 N10 2
Mill Hill La BRKHM/BTCW RH3 255 N10
GVE DA12 191 N8
Mill Hill Rd ACT W3 155 N1
BARN SW13 156 E9
Mill Hill Ter ACT W3 135 N10
Millhouse La ABLGY WD5 55 H3
Mill House La CHERT KT16 194 E4
Millhouse Pl WNWD SE27 181 J7 4
Millhurst Ms HLWE CM17 29 P7
Millicent Rd LEY E10 120 E6 2
Milligan St POP/IOD E14 140 E9
Milling Rd EDGW HA8 96 A8
Millington Rd HYS/HAR UB3 152 F2
Mill La ABR/ST RM4 85 K6
AMSS HP7 68 F5
ASC SL5 192 G2
BF/WBF KT14 216 B9
BH/WHM TN16 262 F3
BROX EN10 44 E7
BRWN CM15 86 D3
BRWN CM15 87 J1
CAR SM5 222 B1
CFSP/GDCR SL9 110 C3
CHDH RM6 123 P4
CHES/WCR EN8 62 D4
CHING E4 80 G7
CHOB/PIR GU24 230 C10
CHONG CM5 49 K4
CHONG CM5 66 F5
CRAWE RH10 285 M2
CRAWW RH11 283 K5
CRICK NW2 117 H10
CROY/NA CR0 203 H10
CSTG HP8 89 M3
DORK RH4 272 G1
DTCH/LGLY SL3 150 E9
EGH TW20 194 F4
EW KT17 220 C5
EYN DA4 209 M8
GUW GU2 268 A2
HLWE CM17 29 P7
HORL RH6 279 N4
KGLGY WD4 54 B5
LHD/OX KT22 236 F8
ORP BR6 226 D6
OXTED RH8 261 L8
OXTED RH8 262 C7
RDKG RH5 278 A2
REDH RH1 258 D7
RGUE GU4 269 J5
RGUW GU3 267 P8
RPLY/SEND GU23 233 N5
RSEV TN14 228 G6
RSEV TN14 247 K7
WDSR SL4 148 F6
WFD IG8 101 L6
WOOL/PLUM SE18 162 D4
WTHK RM20 167 J4
Mill Lane Cl BROX EN10 44 E7
Millman Ms BMSBY WC1N 11 N2 1
Millman St BMSBY WC1N 11 N2
Millmark Gv NWCR SE14 160 D8
Millmarsh La PEND EN3 80 D6
Millmead BF/WBF KT14 216 A8
GUW GU2 267 P2
Mill Md STA TW18 173 J7
Mill Mead Rd TOTM N17 120 A1
Millmead Ter GUW GU2 267 P2
Mill Park Av HCH RM12 125 M7
Mill Pl CHST BR7 206 D1
DART DA1 165 H10
DTCH/LGLY SL3 150 A8
KUT KT1 199 L3
POP/IOD E14 140 D8 8
Mill Plat ISLW TW7 154 F8
Mill Plat Av ISLW TW7 154 F8
Mill Pond Cl SEV TN13 247 L7
Millpond Ct ADL/WDHM KT15 215 P2
Mill Pond Rd BFOR GU20 212 A1
DART DA1 187 M2
Mill Race WARE SG12 27 J7
Mill Rdg EDGW HA8 95 L6
Mill Rd CAN/RD E16 141 N10
COB KT11 235 K1
CRAWE RH10 284 C6
ERITH DA8 164 D6
ESH/CLAY KT10 197 P9
EW KT17 220 C8
GVW DA11 190 B3
HERT/BAY SG13 25 L4
HERT/WAS SG14 25 L4
IL IG1 122 D8
KWD/TDW/WH KT20 238 G9
PUR RM19 166 A5
RDART DA2 187 N7
RDKG RH5 273 H10
SEV TN13 246 F7
SOCK/AV RM15 146 B9
WDR/YW UB7 151 N2
WHTN TW2 176 B5
WIM/MER SW19 179 M10
Mill Rw IS N1 7 K6
Mills Cl HGDN/ICK UB10 132 B4
Mills Crs BGR/WK TN15 247 N6
Mills Gv HDN NW4 116 G1
POP/IOD E14 141 H8 7
Mill Shaw OXTED RH8 261 L8
Millshot Cl FUL/PGN SW6 156 F7
Millside CAR SM5 202 A9
Millside Pl ISLW TW7 154 G8
Millsmead Wy LOU IG10 82 C6
Millson Cl TRDG/WHET N20 97 N3
Mills Rd WOT/HER KT12 217 K2
Mills Rw CHSWK W4 156 A3
Mills Sp WDSR SL4 171 N3
Millstead Cl KWD/TDW/WH KT20 238 E9
Mill Stone Cl EYN DA4 210 B2 2
Millstone Ms EYN DA4 210 B1
Millstream Cl HERT/WAS SG14 25 J5 5
PLMGR N13 99 H6 1
Millstream La SL SL1 128 D10
Millstream Rd STHWK SE1 19 L2
Mill St BERK HP4 33 P5
BH/WHM TN16 262 G3
CONDST W1S 10 F7
DTCH/LGLY SL3 150 G6
HHS/BOV HP3 35 N10
HLWE CM17 47 P4
KUT KT1 199 K3
REDH RH1 275 P1
SLN SL2 129 L10
STHWK SE1 19 M2
Mills Wy RBRW/HUT CM13 107 P2
Millthorne Cl RKW/CH/CXG WD3 72 A9 2
Mill V HAYES BR2 205 M3
Mill View Cl EW KT17 220 C4
Millview Cl REDH RH1 257 N8
Mill View Gdns CROY/NA CR0 204 C10
Millwall Dock Rd POP/IOD E14 160 F2 2
Millwards HAT AL10 40 E7
Mill Wy BUSH WD23 73 M6
EBED/NFELT TW14 175 J1
LHD/OX KT22 255 L1
MLHL NW7 96 B6
RKW/CH/CXG WD3 91 J2
Millway REIG RH2 257 N10
Millway Gdns NTHLT UB5 133 N1
Millwell Crs CHIG IG7 102 G6
Millwood Rd HSLW TW3 176 B1
STMC/STPC BR5 207 M3
Milman Cl PIN HA5 113 L1
Milman Rd KIL/WHAMP NW6 136 G4
Milman's St WBPTN SW10 15 L10
Milne Cl CRAWW RH11 283 H10 3
Milne Fld PIN HA5 93 P8
Milne Gdns ELTH/MOT SE9 184 B1
Milne Pk East CROY/NA CR0 225 J7
Milne Pk West CROY/NA CR0 225 J7
Milner Ap CTHM CR3 241 P7
Milner Cl CTHM CR3 241 P8
GSTN WD25 55 J10 1
Milner Ct BUSH WD23 74 A10
Milner Dr COB KT11 217 N8
WHTN TW2 176 C3
Milner Pl IS N1 6 B5
Milner Rd BCTR RM8 123 M7
CTHM CR3 241 P8
KUT KT1 199 J3
MRDN SM4 201 N5
SRTFD E15 141 K5
THHTH CR7 203 L3
WIM/MER SW19 201 L1
Milner Sq IS N1 6 C4
Milner St CHEL SW3 16 A5
Milneway DEN/HRF UB9 91 L9
Milnthorpe Rd CHSWK W4 156 A5
Milo Rd EDUL SE22 181 N2
Milroy Av GVW DA11 190 B5
Milton Av BAR EN5 77 J9
CDALE/KGS NW9 115 N1
CFSP/GDCR SL9 110 A2
CROY/NA CR0 203 L7
DORK RH4 272 C3
EHAM E6 142 A2
GVE DA12 190 G4
HCH RM12 124 G7
HGT N6 118 D5
RSEV TN14 228 C6
SUT SM1 201 N10
WLSDN NW10 136 A3
Milton Cl DTCH/LGLY SL3 150 D9
EFNCH N2 117 M4 2
STHWK SE1 19 L6
SUT SM1 201 N10
YEAD UB4 133 H8
Milton Ct HGDN/ICK UB10 112 C8
WAB EN9 63 H10 3
Miltoncourt La DORK RH4 272 D2
Milton Court Rd NWCR SE14 160 D5
Milton Crs CHONG CM5 67 N2
GNTH/NBYPK IG2 122 F5
Milton Dene HHNE HP2 36 C1
Milton Dr BORE WD6 75 N9 1
SHPTN TW17 195 P4
Milton Flds CSTG HP8 89 N4
Milton Gdns EPSOM KT18 220 B10
STWL/WRAY TW19 174 A4 3
TIL RM18 168 E7
Milton Gv FBAR/BDGN N11 98 D6
STNW/STAM N16 119 L9
Milton Hall Rd GVE DA12 190 G4
Milton Hl CSTG HP8 89 N4 2
Milton Lawns AMS HP6 69 J2
Milton Mount Av CRAWE RH10 284 E4 6
CRAWE RH10 284 D5 3
Milton Pk HGT N6 118 D5
Milton Pl GVE DA12 190 F2
Milton Rd ACT W3 136 A10
ADL/WDHM KT15 215 K3
BELV DA17 164 B3
BRW CM14 106 G4
CDALE/KGS NW9 116 D4 3
CRAWE RH10 284 D6
CROY/NA CR0 203 L7
CSHM HP5 50 G5
CTHM CR3 241 L7
EGH TW20 172 C8
GRAYS RM17 167 N3
GVE DA12 190 F2 2
HARP AL5 20 A2
HGDN/ICK UB10 112 C9
HGT N6 118 D5
HNHL SE24 181 J1
HNWL W7 134 E9
HPTN TW12 175 P10
HRW HA1 114 D2
MLHL NW7 96 D6
MORT/ESHN SW14 156 A9
MTCM CR4 180 B10
ROM RM1 125 H4
SEV TN13 246 F7
SEVS/STOTM N15 119 J1
SLN SL2 129 J6
SUT SM1 201 K10
SWCM DA10 189 K2
WALTH E17 120 F2
WARE SG12 26 C1
WELL DA16 163 J7
WIM/MER SW19 179 M9
WLGTN SM6 222 D3
WOT/HER KT12 197 L10
Milton St BARB EC2Y 12 G3
DORK RH4 272 C3
SWCM DA10 189 J2
WATN WD24 73 J5
Milton Wy GT/LBKH KT23 254 B1
WDR/YW UB7 152 A3
Milverton Dr HGDN/ICK UB10 112 D9
Milverton Gdns GDMY/SEVK IG3 123 J7
Milverton Rd KIL/WHAMP NW6 136 F2
Milverton St LBTH SE11 18 B8
Milverton Wy ELTH/MOT SE9 184 D7
Milwards HLWW/ROY CM19 46 E5 1
Milward St WCHPL E1 140 A7
Mimms Hall Rd POTB/CUF EN6 58 G7
Mimms La BORE WD6 58 A9
RAD WD7 57 M9
Mimosa Cl BRWN CM15 86 G9 2
HARH RM3 105 K8
ORP BR6 207 M9 2
Mimosa Rd YEAD UB4 133 K7
Mimosa St FUL/PGN SW6 157 J7
Mimram Rd HERT/WAS SG14 25 J6
Mina Av DTCH/LGLY SL3 150 A1
Mina Rd WALW SE17 19 K8
WIM/MER SW19 201 K1
Minchenden Crs STHGT/OAK N14 98 E4
Minchen Rd HLW CM20 29 K10
Minchin Cl LHD/OX KT22 236 F8
Mincing La CHOB/PIR GU24 213 L5
MON EC3R 13 J7
Minden Rd CHEAM SM3 201 H9
PGE/AN SE20 204 A1 7
Minehead Rd RYLN/HDSTN HA2 113 P8
STRHM/NOR SW16 180 G8
Mineral La CSHM HP5 51 H8
Mineral St WOOL/PLUM SE18 163 H3
Minera Ms BGVA SW1W 16 D5
Minerva Cl BRXN/ST SW9 159 H6 4
SCUP DA14 185 H7 1
Minerva Dr WAT WD17 72 F2
Minerva Rd CHING E4 100 G8 1
KUT KT1 199 L2
WLSDN NW10 135 P6
Minerva St BETH E2 140 A4 8
Minerva Wy BEAC HP9 88 F10
Minet Av WLSDN NW10 136 B4
Minet Dr HYS/HAR UB3 133 H10
Minet Gdns HYS/HAR UB3 133 J10
WLSDN NW10 136 B4 2
Minet Rd CMBW SE5 159 J8
Minford Gdns WKENS W14 156 G1
Ming St POP/IOD E14 140 F9 5
Minimax Cl EBED/NFELT TW14 175 H2
The Minims HAT AL10 40 D3
Ministry Wy ELTH/MOT SE9 184 C5
Mink Ct HSLWW TW4 153 K8
Minniecroft Rd SL SL1 128 A5
Minniedale BRYLDS KT5 199 L5
Minorca Rd WEY KT13 216 B1 5
Minories TWRH EC3N 13 L6
Minshull St VX/NE SW8 158 E7 3
Minson Rd HOM E9 140 C3 3
Minstead Gdns PUT/ROE SW15 178 C3
Minstead Wy NWMAL KT3 200 B6
Minster Av SUT SM1 201 K9 2
Minster Cl HAT AL10 40 D6
Minster Dr CROY/NA CR0 223 M1
Minster Gdns E/WMO/HCT KT8 197 N4 3
Minsterley Av SHPTN TW17 196 F4
Minster Rd BMLY BR1 183 N10
CRICK NW2 117 H10
Minster Wy DTCH/LGLY SL3 150 C1
EMPK RM11 125 N6
Minstrel Cl HHW HP1 35 L5 3
Minstrel Gdns BRYLDS KT5 199 L4 3
Mint Cl HGDN/ICK UB10 132 C5
Mintern Cl PLMGR N13 99 J4 2
Minterne Av NWDGN UB2 153 P3
Minterne Rd KTN/HRWW/W HA3 115 L3 2
Minterne Waye YEAD UB4 133 K8
Mintern St IS N1 7 H7
Mint Gdns DORK RH4 272 F1
Mint La KWD/TDW/WH KT20 257 K5
Minton La HLWE CM17 47 M1
Minton Ms HAMP NW3 3 H1 4
Minton Ri MDHD SL6 128 A8
Mint Rd BNSTD SM7 239 M2
WLGTN SM6 222 C2
Mint St STHWK SE1 18 E1
Mint Wk CROY/NA CR0 203 K10
WARL CR6 242 C3
WOKN/KNAP GU21 231 K3
Mirabel Rd FUL/PGN SW6 157 J6
Mirador Crs SLN SL2 129 N9
Miramar Wy HCH RM12 125 L10 6
Miranda Cl WCHPL E1 140 B7 2
Miranda Rd ARCH N19 118 D6
Mirfield St CHARL SE7 162 A2 2
Miriam Rd WOOL/PLUM SE18 163 H4
Mirren Cl RYLN/HDSTN HA2 113 N9
Mirrie La DEN/HRF UB9 110 F3
Misbourne Av CFSP/GDCR SL9 90 B6
Misbourne Cl CFSP/GDCR SL9 90 B6 2
Misbourne Mdw DEN/HRF UB9 110 F6
Misbourne Rd HGDN/ICK UB10 132 B4
Miskin Rd DART DA1 187 K3
Miskin Wy GVE DA12 190 G9
Missden Dr HHS/BOV HP3 36 D8
Missenden Cl
EBED/NFELT TW14 174 G4 11
Missenden Gdns MRDN SM4 201 M6 6
SL SL1 128 A8
Missenden Rd CSHM HP5 50 E8
Mission Gv WALTH E17 120 E3 6
Mission Pl PECK SE15 159 P7 3
Mistletoe Cl CROY/NA CR0 204 C8 12
Mistley Rd HLW CM20 29 K9
Misty's Fld WOT/HER KT12 197 K8
Mitcham La STRHM/NOR SW16 180 D8
Mitcham Pk MTCM CR4 201 P4
Mitcham Rd CROY/NA CR0 202 E6
EHAM E6 142 B5
GDMY/SEVK IG3 123 J5
TOOT SW17 180 A8
Mitchell Av GVW DA11 190 A5
Mitchellbrook Wy WLSDN NW10 136 A1
Mitchell Cl ABLGY WD5 55 H8 6
ABYW SE2 163 M4
BELV DA17 164 D2
DART DA1 187 M5
HHW HP1 52 C3
RAIN RM13 145 K4
SL SL1 148 F1
STAL AL1 38 C10
WGCE AL7 23 M5 8
Mitchell Rd ORP BR6 227 J1
PLMGR N13 99 J6
Mitchells Cl RGUE GU4 268 B6 4
Mitchells Rd CRAWE RH10 284 A7
Mitchell St FSBYE EC1V 12 E1
Mitchell Wk AMS HP6 69 K4
Mitchell Wy BMLY BR1 205 M1 2
WLSDN NW10 135 P1
Mitchison Rd IS N1 6 G2
Mitchley Av PUR/KEN CR8 223 L9
Mitchley Gv SAND/SEL CR2 223 P9
Mitchley Hl SAND/SEL CR2 223 N9
Mitchley Rd TOTM N17 119 P1
Mitchley Vw SAND/SEL CR2 223 P9
Mitford Rd ARCH N19 118 F7
Mitre Cl BELMT SM2 221 M4
HAYES BR2 205 L2
SHPTN TW17 196 E6
Mitre Rd SRTFD E15 141 K4
STHWK SE1 18 B1
Mitre Sq HDTCH EC3A 13 K6
Mitre St HDTCH EC3A 13 K6
The Mitre POP/IOD E14 140 E9 4
Mitre Wy WLSDN NW10 136 E7
Mixbury Gv WEY KT13 216 E3 2
Mixnams La CHERT KT16 195 K3
Mizen Cl COB KT11 217 L10
Mizen Wy COB KT11 235 K1 2
Moat Cl BUSH WD23 74 A9 2
ORP BR6 227 J3
Moat Ct ASHTD KT21 237 K3
Moat Crs EFNCH N2 117 L1
Moat Cft WELL DA16 163 M9
Moat Dr HRW HA1 114 B2
RSLP HA4 112 F5 1
SLN SL2 129 P7
Moated Farm Dr
ADL/WDHM KT15 215 M4
Moat Farm Rd NTHLT UB5 133 N1
Moatfield Rd BUSH WD23 74 A9
Moat La ERITH DA8 165 H7
Moat Pl ACT W3 135 N8
BRXN/ST SW9 158 G9
DEN/HRF UB9 111 L9
Moat Side FELT TW13 175 K7
PEND EN3 80 B8
Moats La REDH RH1 276 F6
The Moat NWMAL KT3 200 B1
Moat Wk CRAWE RH10 284 D6
Moatwood Gn WGCE AL7 23 H6 3
Moberly Rd CLAP SW4 180 E3
Modbury Gdns HAMP NW3 4 B2
Model Farm Cl ELTH/MOT SE9 184 B6 1
Moelyn Ms HRW HA1 114 F3
Moffat Rd PLMGR N13 98 F7
THHTH CR7 203 K2
TOOT SW17 179 P7
Moffats Cl BRKMPK AL9 59 K2
Moffats La BRKMPK AL9 59 H3
Mogador Rd KWD/TDW/WH KT20 257 H4
Mogden La ISLW TW7 176 E1
Mohmmad Khan Rd WAN E11 121 L6 3
Moiety Rd POP/IOD E14 160 F1
Moira Cl TOTM N17 99 M10
Moira Rd ELTH/MOT SE9 162 C10
Moir Cl SAND/SEL CR2 223 P5
Molash Rd STMC/STPC BR5 207 N4
Mole Abbey Gdns
E/WMO/HCT KT8 197 P3
Mole Cl CRAWW RH11 283 L5 4
Mole Ct HOR/WEW KT19 219 P1
Molember Rd E/WMO/HCT KT8 198 D5
Mole Rd LHD/OX KT22 236 C7
WOT/HER KT12 217 L2
Molescroft ELTH/MOT SE9 184 F6
Molesey Av E/WMO/HCT KT8 197 N4
Molesey Cl WOT/HER KT12 217 L1
Molesey Dr CHEAM SM3 201 H9
Molesey Park Av
E/WMO/HCT KT8 198 A5
Molesey Park Cl E/WMO/HCT KT8 198 B5
Molesey Park Rd
E/WMO/HCT KT8 198 C5 2
Molesey Rd WOT/HER KT12 197 M5
WOT/HER KT12 217 L2
Molesford Rd FUL/PGN SW6 157 K8 1
Molesham Cl E/WMO/HCT KT8 198 A3 3
Molesham Wy E/WMO/HCT KT8 198 A4
Moles Hl LHD/OX KT22 218 C7
Molesworth HOD EN11 26 F9
Molesworth St LEW SE13 161 H9
Mole Valley Pl ASHTD KT21 237 J5
Molewood Rd HERT/WAS SG14 25 J4
Mollands Ct SOCK/AV RM15 147 K6
Mollands La SOCK/AV RM15 147 H6
Mollison Av PEND EN3 80 D1
PEND EN3 80 D6
Mollison Dr WLGTN SM6 222 F4
Mollison Ri GVE DA12 191 H8
Mollison Wy EDGW HA8 95 L10
Molly Huggins Cl BAL SW12 180 D3
Molteno Rd WAT WD17 73 H5
Molyneux Dr TOOT SW17 180 C7 1
Molyneux Rd BFOR GU20 212 C3 4
RGODL GU7 267 L10
WEY KT13 216 B1
Molyneux St MBLAR W1H 9 P4
Molyns Ms SL SL1 128 D10 4
Momples Rd HLW CM20 29 K10
Monahan Av PUR/KEN CR8 222 G8
Monarch Cl CRAWW RH11 283 K10
EBED/NFELT TW14 174 F3
TIL RM18 168 E8
WWKM BR4 225 L1
Monarch Dr CAN/RD E16 142 A7
Monarch Ms WNWD SE27 181 H8 1
Monarch Pl BKHH IG9 101 P3
Monarch Rd BELV DA17 164 B2
Monarch's Wy CHES/WCR EN8 62 C9 3
RSLP HA4 112 F6 1
Mona Rd PECK SE15 160 B8
Monastery Cl STALW/RED AL3 38 B6 2
Monastery Gdns ENC/FH EN2 79 L6
Mona St CAN/RD E16 141 L7
Monaveen Gdns
E/WMO/HCT KT8 198 A3 4
Monck St WEST SW1P 17 K4
Monclar Rd CMBW SE5 159 L10
Moncorvo Cl SKENS SW7 15 N2
Moncrieff St PECK SE15 159 P8 2
Mondial Wy WDR/YW UB7 152 D6
Monega Rd FSTGT E7 141 P1
Money Av CTHM CR3 241 L8
Money Hill Rd RKW/CH/CXG WD3 91 M2
Money Hole La WLYN AL6 23 P4
Money La WDR/YW UB7 151 N2
Money Rd CTHM CR3 241 L8
Mongers La EW KT17 220 D6 2
Monica Cl WATN WD24 73 L6
Monier Rd BOW E3 140 F2
Monivea Rd BECK BR3 182 E10
Monkchester Cl LOU IG10 82 D5 2
Monk Dr CAN/RD E16 141 M9
Monkfrith Av STHGT/OAK N14 78 C10 1
Monkfrith Wy STHGT/OAK N14 98 C1
Monkham's Av WFD IG8 101 N6
Monkham's Dr WFD IG8 101 N6
Monkham's La WFD IG8 101 N5
Monkleigh Rd MRDN SM4 201 H3
Monks Av BAR EN5 77 M10
E/WMO/HCT KT8 197 N5
Monksbury HLWS CM18 47 K4
Monks Cha RBRW/HUT CM13 107 P6
Monks Cl ABYW SE2 163 N3
ASC SL5 192 A6
BROX EN10 44 F6
ENC/FH EN2 79 K6
RSLP HA4 113 L9 1
RYLN/HDSTN HA2 114 A7 3
STAL AL1 38 D8
Monks Crs ADL/WDHM KT15 215 L2
WOT/HER KT12 197 J8
Monksdene Gdns SUT SM1 201 L10 1
Monks Dr ACT W3 135 M7
ASC SL5 192 A6
Monksfield CRAWE RH10 284 A7
Monksfield Wy SLN SL2 128 F6
Monks Gn LHD/OX KT22 236 B7
Monksgrove LOU IG10 82 D9
Monks Horton Wy STAL AL1 38 F4
Monksmead BORE WD6 75 P8
Monks Orch DART DA1 187 K5
Monks Orchard Rd BECK BR3 204 F8
Monks Pk WBLY HA9 135 P1
Monks Park Gdns WBLY HA9 135 N1
Monks Ri WGCW AL8 22 G1
Monks Rd BNSTD SM7 239 K3
ENC/FH EN2 79 J6
VW GU25 194 A4
WDSR SL4 148 C8
Monk St WOOL/PLUM SE18 162 D3
Monks Wk ASC SL5 192 A6
MEO DA13 189 M9
REIG RH2 257 L10
Monks Wy BECK BR3 204 F6
STA TW18 173 N10
STMC/STPC BR5 206 F8
Monkswell La COUL/CHIP CR5 239 L10
Monkswick Rd HLW CM20 29 J9
Monkswood WGCW AL8 22 F1
Monkswood Av WAB EN9 63 J9
Monkswood Gdns BORE WD6 76 A9
CLAY IG5 122 D1
Monkton Rd WELL DA16 163 J8
Monkton St LBTH SE11 18 B5
Monkville Av GLDGN NW11 117 J2
Monkwell Sq BARB EC2Y 12 F4 2
Monkwood Cl ROM RM1 125 H3
Monmouth Av KUT KT1 177 H10
SWFD E18 121 N2
Monmouth Cl CHSWK W4 156 A2 6
MTCM CR4 202 F4 6
WELL DA16 163 K10
Monmouth Gv BTFD TW8 155 K3 1
Monmouth Pl BAY/PAD W2 8 F6

Monmouth Rd *BAY/PAD* W2 ... 8 F6
 DAGW RM9 ... 124 A10
 ED N9 ... 100 A3
 EHAM E6 ... 142 C5
 HYS/HAR UB3 ... 152 A1
 WAT WD17 ... 23 J7
Monmouth St *LSO/SEVD* WC2H ... 11 L6
Monnery Rd *ARCH* N19 ... 118 D8
Monnow Rd *SOCK/AV* RM15 ... 146 B9
 STHWK SE1 ... 19 N6
Monoux Gv *WALTH* E17 ... 100 F9
Monro Dr *GUW* GU2 ... 249 N7
Monroe Crs *EN* EN1 ... 80 A5
Monroe Dr *MORT/ESHN* SW14 ... 177 N1
Monro Gdns *KTN/HRWW/W* HA3 ... 94 D8
Mons Cl *HARP* AL5 ... 20 C5
Monsell Rd *FSBYPK* N4 ... 119 H8
Monson Rd *BROX* EN10 ... 44 E6
 NWCR SE14 ... 160 C6
 REDH RH1 ... 258 A7
 WLSDN NW10 ... 136 H4
Mons Wk *EGH* TW20 ... 172 F8
Mons Wy *HAYES* BR2 ... 206 B6
Montacute Rd *BUSH* WD23 ... 94 D1
 CAT SE6 ... 182 A3
 CROY/NA CR0 ... 225 H5
 MRDN SM4 ... 201 N6
Montagu Crs *UED* N18 ... 100 A5
Montague Av *BROCKY* SE4 ... 160 L10
 HNWL W7 ... 134 E10
 SAND/SEL CR2 ... 223 M8
Montague St *STHWK* SE1 ... 12 G9
 SWLY BR8 ... 208 G4
 WOT/HER KT12 ... 197 H7
Montague Dr *CTHM* CR3 ... 241 K8
Montague Gdns *ACT* W3 ... 135 M9
Montague Hall Pl *BUSH* WD23 ... 73 P10
Montague Rd *BERK* HP4 ... 33 L5
 CEND/HSY/T N8 ... 118 G3
 CROY/NA CR0 ... 203 J8
 HACK E8 ... 119 P10
 HNWL W7 ... 154 E1
 HSLW TW3 ... 154 A9
 NWDGN UB2 ... 153 M3
 RCHPK/HAM TW10 ... 177 K2
 SEVS/STOTM N15 ... 119 P2
 SL SL1 ... 129 L9
 UX/CGN UB8 ... 131 N2
 WAN E11 ... 121 L7
 WEA W13 ... 134 G8
 WIM/MER SW19 ... 179 L10
Montague Sq *NWCR* SE14 ... 160 B6
 STBT EC1A ... 12 E4
Montagu Gdns *UED* N18 ... 100 A5
 WLGTN SM6 ... 222 D1
Montagu Man *MHST* W1U ... 10 B1
Montagu Ms North *MBLAR* W1H ... 10 B3
Montagu Ms South *MBLAR* W1H ... 10 B5
Montagu Ms West *MBLAR* W1H... ... 10 B5
Montagu Pl *DTCH/LGLY* SL3 ... 149 N7
 HDN NW4 ... 116 D10
 UED N18 ... 100 B5
Montagu Rw *MHST* W1U ... 10 B5
Montagu Sq *MBLAR* W1H ... 10 B5
Montagu St *MBLAR* W1H ... 10 B5
Montalt Rd *WFD* IG8 ... 101 L6
Montana Cl *SAND/SEL* CR2 ... 223 L6
Montana Gdns *CAT* SE6 ... 182 E8
 SUT SM1 ... 221 M2
Montana Rd *RYNPK* SW20 ... 200 F1
 TOOT SW17 ... 180 B6
Montbelle Rd *ELTH/MOT* SE9 ... 184 C1
Montbretia Cl *STMC/STPC* BR5 ... 207 M4
Montcalm Cl *HAYES* BR2 ... 205 M6
 YEAD UB4 ... 133 J5
Montcalm Rd *CHARL* SE7 ... 162 A6
Montclare St *BETH* E2 ... 7 L10
Monteagle Av *BARK* IG11 ... 142 F1
Monteagle Wy *PECK* SE15 ... 160 B9
Montefiore St *VX/NE* SW8 ... 158 C8
Monteith Rd *BOW* E3 ... 140 E1
Montem La *SL* SL1 ... 149 J1
Montem Rd *FSTH* SE23 ... 182 B3
 NWMAL KT3 ... 200 B4
Montem St *FSBYPK* N4 ... 118 G6
Montenotte Rd *CEND/HSY/T* N8 ... 118 C1
Monterey Cl *BXLY* DA5 ... 186 D5
Montford Pl *LBTH* SE11 ... 18 A9
Montford Rd *SUN* TW16 ... 197 H4
Montfort Gdns *BARK/HLT* IG6 ... 102 F7
Montfort Pl *WIM/MER* SW19 ... 178 G3
Montfort Ri *REDH* RH1 ... 276 A8
Montfort Rd *RSEV* TN14 ... 247 N3
Montgomerie Cl *BERK* HP4 ... 33 M3
Montgomerie Dr *GUW* GU2 ... 249 M5
Montgomery Av *ESH/CLAY* KT10 ... 198 C3
 HHNE HP2 ... 36 B5
Montgomery Cl *BFN/LL* DA15 ... 185 H1
 MTCM CR4 ... 202 F4
Montgomery Crs *HARH* RM3 ... 105 L6
Montgomery Dr *CHES/WCR* EN8 ... 62 D4
Montgomery Pl *SLN* SL2 ... 129 P8
Montgomery Rd *CHSWK* W4 ... 155 P3
 EDGW HA8 ... 95 L7
 EYN DA4 ... 210 C1
 WOKS/MYFD GU22 ... 232 B4
Montholme Rd *BTSEA* SW11 ... 180 A2
Montolieu Gdns *PUT/ROE* SW15 ... 178 L1
Montpelier Av *BXLY* DA5 ... 185 N3
 EA W5 ... 135 H7
Montpelier Cl *HGDN/ICK* UB10 ... 132 B3
Montpelier Gdns *CHDH* RM6 ... 123 M5
 EHAM E6 ... 142 A5
Montpelier Gv *KTTN* NW5 ... 118 D10
Montpelier Ms *SKENS* SW7 ... 15 P3
Montpelier Pl *SKENS* SW7 ... 15 P3
 WCHPL E1 ... 140 B8
Montpelier Ri *GLDGN* NW11 ... 117 H5
 WBLY HA9 ... 115 J6
Montpelier Rd *EA* W5 ... 135 J7
 FNCH N3 ... 97 M9
 PECK SE15 ... 160 A7
 PUR/KEN CR8 ... 223 J6
 SUT SM1 ... 221 M1
Montpelier Rw *BKHTH/KID* SE3 ... 161 J2
 TWK TW1 ... 176 G3
Montpelier Sq *SKENS* SW7 ... 15 P3
Montpelier St *SKENS* SW7 ... 15 P2
Montpelier Ter *SKENS* SW7 ... 15 P2
Montpelier V *BKHTH/KID* SE3 ... 161 L8
Montpelier Wk *SKENS* SW7 ... 15 P2
Montpelier Wy *GLDGN* NW11 ... 117 H5
Montrave Rd *PGE/AN* SE20 ... 182 B10
Montreal Pl *HOL/ALD* WC2B ... 11 N7
Montreal Rd *IL* IG1 ... 122 F5
 SEV TN13 ... 246 F2
 TIL RM18 ... 168 D9
Montrell Rd *BRXS/STRHM* SW2 ... 180 A4
Montrose Av *BFN/LL* DA15 ... 185 K3
 DTCH/LGLY SL3 ... 149 P6
 EDGW HA8 ... 96 A10
 GPK RM2 ... 105 K10
 KIL/WHAMP NW6 ... 2 B7
 SL SL1 ... 128 G3
 WELL DA16 ... 162 G9
 WHTN TW2 ... 176 A3
Montrose Cl *ASHF* TW15 ... 174 D9
 WELL DA16 ... 163 J9
 WFD IG8 ... 101 M5
Montrose Crs *ALP/SUD* HA0 ... 135 K1
 NFNCH/WDSP N12 ... 97 L7

Montrose Gdns *LHD/OX* KT22 ... 218 C8
 MTCM CR4 ... 202 A2
 SUT SM1 ... 201 M2
Montrose Pl *KTBR* SW1X ... 16 C2
Montrose Rd *EBED/NFELT* TW14 ... 174 B1
 KTN/HRWW/W HA3 ... 94 D10
 FSTH SE23 ... 182 C4
Montrose Wk *WEY* KT13 ... 196 C10
Montrose Crs *EW* KT17 ... 238 F2
Montserrat Av *WFD* IG8 ... 101 J8
Montserrat Cl *NRWD* SE19 ... 181 J8
Montserrat Rd *PUT/ROE* SW15 ... 157 H10
Monument Hl *WEY* KT13 ... 216 C1
Monument La *CFSP/GDCR* SL9 ... 90 B7
Monument Rd *WEY* KT13 ... 216 C1
 WOKN/KNAP GU21 ... 232 E1
Monument St *MON* EC3R ... 13 H5
Monument Wy East
 WOKN/KNAP GU21 ... 232 E1
Monument Wy West
 WOKN/KNAP GU21 ... 232 D1
Monza St *WAP* E1W ... 140 B9
Moodkee St *BERM/RHTH* SE16 ... 160 B2
Moody Rd *PECK* SE15 ... 159 H7
Moody St *WCHPL* E1 ... 140 C5
Moon La *BAR* EN5 ... 77 J7
Moon St *IS* N1 ... 6 C1
Moorcroft Rd *CRAWW* RH11 ... 283 C6
Moorcroft Gdns *HAYES* BR2 ... 206 B5
Moorcroft La *UX/CGN* UB8 ... 132 B7
Moorcroft Rd
 STRHM/NOR SW16 ... 180 F6
Moorcroft Wy *PIN* HA5 ... 113 M5
Moordown *WOOL/PLUM* SE18 ... 162 F9
Moore Av *TIL* RM18 ... 168 B8
Moore Cl *ADL/WDHM* KT15 ... 215 L2
 MORT/ESHN SW14 ... 155 P9
 MTCM CR4 ... 202 C2
 SL SL1 ... 148 C1
 WLGTN SM6 ... 222 F4
Moore Crs *DAGW* RM9 ... 143 J4
Moorefield Rd *TOTM* N17 ... 119 N1
Moore Grove Crs *EGH* TW20 ... 172 B10
Moore Park Rd *FUL/PGN* SW6 ... 157 L6
Moore Rd *BERK* HP4 ... 33 L3
 CHOB/PIR GU24 ... 230 A7
 NRWD SE19 ... 181 K9
 SWCM DA10 ... 189 K2
Morescroft *BRWN* CM15 ... 86 D3
Moores La *WDSR* SL4 ... 148 B3
Moore's Rd *DORK* RH4 ... 272 G1
Moore St *CHEL* SW3 ... 16 A5
Moore Wy *BELMT* SM2 ... 221 L6
Moorey Cl *SRTFD* E15 ... 141 L3
Moorfield Rd *CHSGTN* KT9 ... 219 K2
 DEN/HRF UB9 ... 111 K4
 GU GU1 ... 250 A6
 ORP BR6 ... 207 K7
 PEND EN3 ... 80 B5
 UX/CGN UB8 ... 131 N8
Moorfields *HLWS* CM18 ... 46 F6
 LVPST EC2M ... 12 G4
Moorfields Cl *STA* TW18 ... 195 H1
Moor Furlong *SL* SL1 ... 128 D10
Moorgate *LOTH* EC2R ... 12 G5
 LVPST EC2M ... 12 G4
Moorgate Pl *LOTH* EC2R ... 12 G5
Moorhall Rd *DEN/HRF* UB9 ... 111 L3
Moor Hall Rd *HLWE* CM17 ... 30 A7
Moorhayes Dr *STA* TW18 ... 195 M3
Moorhead Wy *BKHTH/KID* SE3 ... 161 N4
Moorhen Cl *ERITH* DA8 ... 165 J6
Moorhouse Rd *BAY/PAD* W2 ... 8 E5
 KTN/HRWW/W HA3 ... 115 J1
 OXTED RH8 ... 262 C6
Moorhurst Av *CHESW* EN7 ... 61 J5
The Moorings *BF/WBF* KT14 ... 215 M8
 STWL/WRAY TW19 ... 171 P3
Moorland Cl *HSLWW* TW4 ... 175 P3
 ROMW/RG RM7 ... 104 C9
Moorland Rd *BRXN/ST* SW9 ... 159 J10
 CRAWE RH10 ... 284 D10
 HHW HP1 ... 35 J8
 WDR/YW UB7 ... 151 M6
Moorlands *LCOL/BKTW* AL2 ... 56 D4
Moorlands Av *MLHL* NW7 ... 96 C4
The Moorlands
 WOKS/MYFD GU22 ... 232 C7
Moor La *BARB* EC2Y ... 12 G4
 CHSGTN KT9 ... 219 L2
 RKW/CH/CXG WD3 ... 71 H2
 RKW/CH/CXG WD3 ... 91 P3
 STWL/WRAY TW19 ... 172 F4
 WDR/YW UB7 ... 151 M5
 WOKS/MYFD GU22 ... 232 C7
Moor Lane Crossing *WATW* WD18 ... 92 D1
Moormead Dr *HOR/WEW* KT19 ... 220 B2
Moor Mead Rd *TWK* TW1 ... 176 B2
Moormede Crs *STA* TW18 ... 173 J7
Moor Mill La *LCOL/BKTW* AL2 ... 56 D6
Moor Park Crs *CRAWW* RH11 ... 282 C8
Moor Park Gdns *KUTN/CMB* KT2 ... 178 B10
Moor Park Rd *NTHWD* HA6 ... 92 B7
Moor Pl *BFOR* GU20 ... 212 A2
Moor Rd *CHIN* HP5 ... 51 H9
The Moor *RSEV* TN14 ... 247 J6
Moorside *WGCE* AL7 ... 23 K4
Moorside Rd *BMLY* BR1 ... 183 K7
Moorsom Wy *COUL/CHIP* CR5 ... 240 E3
The Moors *WGCE* AL7 ... 23 K4
Moorstown Ct *SL* SL1 ... 149 K1
Moor St *SOHO/SHAV* W1D ... 11 J5
Moortown Rd *OXHEY* WD19 ... 93 H5
Moor Vw *WATW* WD18 ... 93 H1
Morant Gdns *CRW* RM5 ... 104 C6
Morant Pl *CDH/CHF* RM16 ... 168 C2
Morants Court Rd *RSEV* TN14 ... 246 D4
Morant St *POP/IOD* E14 ... 140 F9
Mora Rd *CRICK* NW2 ... 116 F9
Mora St *FSBYE* EC1V ... 6 F10
Morat St *BRXN/ST* SW9 ... 158 G7
Moravian Pl *WBPTN* SW10 ... 15 M10
Moravian St *BETH* E2 ... 140 B5
Moray Av *HYS/HAR* UB3 ... 132 G10
Moray Cl *EDGW* HA8 ... 95 N3
 ROM RM1 ... 104 F8
Moray Ms *HOLWY* N7 ... 118 G7
Moray Rd *HOLWY* N7 ... 118 G7
Moray Wy *ROM* RM1 ... 104 F8
Mordaunt Gdns *DAGW* RM9 ... 143 P2
Mordaunt Rd *WLSDN* NW10 ... 136 A3
Mordaunt St *BRXN/ST* SW9 ... 158 G9
Morden Ct *MRDN* SM4 ... 201 L4
Morden Gdns *GFD/PVL* UB6 ... 114 E10
 MTCM CR4 ... 201 N4
Morden Hall Rd *MRDN* SM4 ... 201 L3
Morden Hl *LEW* SE13 ... 161 H8
Morden La *LEW* SE13 ... 161 H7
Morden Rd *BKHTH/KID* SE3 ... 161 J2
 CHDH RM6 ... 123 P5
 MRDN SM4 ... 201 M5
 WIM/MER SW19 ... 201 M1
Morden Road Ms *BKHTH/KID* SE3 ... 161 J2
Morden St *LEW* SE13 ... 161 L6
Morden Wy *CHEAM* SM3 ... 201 K1
Morden Wharf Rd *GNWCH* SE10 ... 161 H2
Mordred Rd *CAT* SE6 ... 183 K5

Moreau Wk *DTCH/LGLY* SL3 ... 130 B8
Morecambe Cl *CRAWW* RH11 ... 283 J10
 HCH RM12 ... 125 J10
 WCHPL E1 ... 140 C7
Morecambe Gdns *STAN* HA7 ... 95 J5
Morecambe St *WALW* SE17 ... 18 F7
More Cir *RGODL* GU7 ... 267 K10
More Cl *CAN/RD* E16 ... 141 J8
 PUR/KEN CR8 ... 222 G7
 WKENS W14 ... 156 G3
Morecoombe Cl
 KUTN/CMB KT2 ... 177 N10
Morecote Cl *RGUE* GU4 ... 268 D7
Moree Wy *UED* N18 ... 99 P5
Moreland Cl *DTCH/LGLY* SL3 ... 150 F6
Moreland Dr *CFSP/GDCR* SL9 ... 110 C5
Morelands Av *CDH/CHF* RM16 ... 167 P7
Moreland St *FSBYE* EC1V ... 6 D7
Moreland Wy *CHING* E4 ... 100 A4
More La *ESH/CLAY* KT10 ... 198 A10
Morel Ct *SEV* TN13 ... 247 J8
Morella Cl *VW* GU25 ... 193 P4
Morella Rd *BAL* SW12 ... 180 A3
Morello Av *UX/CGN* UB8 ... 132 C5
Morello Cl *SWLY* BR8 ... 208 E4
Morello Dr *DTCH/LGLY* SL3 ... 130 C10
Moremead Rd *CAT* SE6 ... 182 E7
Morena St *CAT* SE6 ... 182 C3
More Rd *RGODL* GU7 ... 267 K10
Moreton Av *ISLW* TW7 ... 154 D7
Moreton Br *CHONG* CM5 ... 49 K7
Moreton Cl *CHESW* EN7 ... 62 A3
 CLPT E5 ... 120 B6
 MLHL NW7 ... 96 F7
 SEVS/STOTM N15 ... 119 L4
Moreton Ct *DART* DA1 ... 164 F9
Moreton Gdns *WFD* IG8 ... 102 F6
Moreton Pl *PIM* SW1V ... 17 H7
Moreton Rd *CHONG* CM5 ... 49 K7
 SAND/SEL CR2 ... 223 L2
 SEVS/STOTM N15 ... 119 L4
 WPK KT4 ... 200 D9
Moreton St *PIM* SW1V ... 17 J7
Moreton Ter *PIM* SW1V ... 17 H7
Moreton Wy *SL* SL1 ... 128 C10
Morewood Cl *SEV* TN13 ... 246 C9
Morford Cl *RSLP* HA4 ... 113 J5
Morford Wy *RSLP* HA4 ... 113 J5
Morgan Av *WALTH* E17 ... 121 J2
Morgan Cl *DAGE* RM10 ... 144 B2
Morgan Crs *EPP* CM16 ... 83 J2
Morgan Dr *RDART* DA2 ... 188 D3
Morgan Gdns *GSTN* WD25 ... 74 A4
Morgan Rd *BMLY* BR1 ... 183 M10
 HOLWY N7 ... 119 H10
 NKENS W10 ... 139 L2
Morgans Cl *HERT/BAY* SG13 ... 25 L7
Morgan's La *HYS/HAR* UB3 ... 132 E7
 STHWK SE1 ... 13 J10
Morgan's Rd *HERT/BAY* SG13 ... 25 L8
Morgan St *BOW* E3 ... 140 D5
 CAN/RD E16 ... 141 L7
Morgan's Wk *HERT/BAY* SG13 ... 25 L8
Morgan Wy *RAIN* RM13 ... 145 K5
 WFD IG8 ... 102 B7
Moriatry Cl *HOLWY* N7 ... 118 F9
Morice Rd *HOD* EN11 ... 44 E1
Morie St *WAND/EARL* SW18 ... 157 L10
Morieux Rd *LEY* E10 ... 120 E6
Moring Rd *TOOT* SW17 ... 180 B7
Morland Av *CROY/NA* CR0 ... 203 M8
 DART DA1 ... 187 J3
Morland Cl *GLDGN* NW11 ... 117 J8
 HPTN TW12 ... 175 N8
 MTCM CR4 ... 201 P3
Morland Gdns *STHL* UB1 ... 134 A10
 WLSDN NW10 ... 136 A2
Morland Ms *IS* N1 ... 6 A2
Morland Rd *CROY/NA* CR0 ... 203 N7
 DAGE RM10 ... 144 B2
 IL IG1 ... 122 C7
 KTN/HRWW/W HA3 ... 115 K3
 PGE/AN SE20 ... 182 C10
 SUT SM1 ... 221 M2
 WALTH E17 ... 120 C3
Morland Wy *CHES/WCR* EN8 ... 62 D4
Morley Av *CHING* E4 ... 101 J8
 UED N18 ... 99 P5
 WDGN N22 ... 99 J9
Morley Cl *DTCH/LGLY* SL3 ... 150 C9
 ORP BR6 ... 206 E9
Morley Crs *EDGW* HA8 ... 95 P3
 RSLP HA4 ... 113 H1
Morley Crs East *STAN* HA7 ... 115 H1
Morley Crs West *STAN* HA7 ... 115 H1
Morley Gv *HLWW* CM20 ... 28 F10
Morley Hl *ENC/FH* EN2 ... 79 L4
Morley Rd *BARK* IG11 ... 142 G3
 CHDH RM6 ... 123 P5
 CHEAM SM3 ... 201 J8
 CHST BR7 ... 206 F1
 LEW SE13 ... 161 H10
 LEY E10 ... 121 H6
 SAND/SEL CR2 ... 223 N6
 SRTFD E15 ... 141 K2
 TWK TW1 ... 177 J2
Morley Sq *CDH/CHF* RM16 ... 168 D3
Morley's Rd *RSEV* TN14 ... 265 L9
Morley St *STHWK* SE1 ... 18 B2
Morna Rd *CMBW* SE5 ... 159 K8
Morning La *HOM* E9 ... 140 B1
Morningside Rd *WPK* KT4 ... 200 E9
Mornington Av *BMLY* BR1 ... 184 B1
 IL IG1 ... 122 D5
 WKENS W14 ... 14 C6
Mornington Crs *CAMTN* NW1 ... 4 D2
Mornington Ct *BXLY* DA5 ... 186 E4
Mornington Crs *HEST* TW5 ... 153 J7
Mornington Gv *BOW* E3 ... 140 F5
Mornington Ms *CMBW* SE5 ... 159 K7
Mornington Pl *CAMTN* NW1 ... 4 D1
Mornington Rd *ASHF* TW15 ... 174 D8
 CHING E4 ... 101 J1
 DEPT SE8 ... 160 E6
 GFD/PVL UB6 ... 133 P5
 RAD WD7 ... 56 F10
 WAN E11 ... 121 M4
Mornington St *CAMTN* NW1 ... 4 F6
Mornington Wk
 RCHPK/HAM TW10 ... 177 H7
Morocco St *STHWK* SE1 ... 19 J2
Morped St *BORE* WD6 ... 75 L4
Morpeth Gv *HOM* E9 ... 140 C3
Morpeth Rd *HOM* E9 ... 140 B3
Morpeth St *BETH* E2 ... 140 C2
Morpeth Ter *WEST* SW1P ... 16 G4
Morrab Gdns *GDMY/SEVK* IG3 ... 123 J8
Morrice Cl *DTCH/LGLY* SL3 ... 150 C3
Morris Av *MNPK* E12 ... 122 C10
Morris Cl *CFSP/GDCR* SL9 ... 90 C5
 CROY/NA CR0 ... 204 D6
 ORP BR6 ... 207 H10
Morris Ct *CHING* E4 ... 100 G4
 WAB EN9 ... 63 L10
Morris Gdns *DART* DA1 ... 187 P1
 WAND/EARL SW18 ... 179 K5
Morrish Rd *BRXS/STRHM* SW2 ... 180 F3
Morrison Av *TOTM* N17 ... 119 M1

Morrison Rd *BARK* IG11 ... 143 P4
 YEAD UB4 ... 133 J5
Morrison St *BTSEA* SW11 ... 158 B9
Morris Pl *FSBYPK* N4 ... 119 H7
 HARH RM3 ... 105 J8
 ISLW TW7 ... 154 E9
 POP/IOD E14 ... 140 C7
 REDH RH1 ... 258 G1
 WKENS W14 ... 14 A10
Morris St *WCHPL* E1 ... 140 A8
Morriston Cl *OXHEY* WD19 ... 93 K6
Morris Wy *LCOL/BKTW* AL2 ... 57 J2
Morse Cl *DEN/HRF* UB9 ... 91 M10
 PLSTW E13 ... 141 M5
Morshead Rd *MV/WKIL* W9 ... 2 F10
Morson Rd *PEND* EN3 ... 80 D10
Morston Cl *KWD/TDW/WH* KT20 ... 238 E6
Mortain Dr *BERK* HP4 ... 33 L3
Mortaine Rd *ASHF* TW15 ... 173 N6
Morten Gdns *DEN/HRF* UB9 ... 111 K5
Mortens Wd *AMSS* HP7 ... 69 J4
Morteyne Rd *TOTM* N17 ... 99 L9
Mortham St *SRTFD* E15 ... 141 K3
Mortimer Cl *BAL* SW12 ... 180 E5
 BUSH WD23 ... 74 A10
 CRICK NW2 ... 117 J8
Mortimer Crs *STJWD* NW8 ... 2 G6
 WPK KT4 ... 200 A10
Mortimer Dr *WCHMH* N21 ... 79 L9
Mortimer Ga *CHES/WCR* EN8 ... 62 E5
Mortimer Pl *KIL/WHAMP* NW6 ... 2 G6
Mortimer Rd *BH/WHM* TN16 ... 225 P8
 DTCH/LGLY SL3 ... 150 A2
 EHAM E6 ... 142 C4
 ERITH DA8 ... 164 E5
 IS N1 ... 7 K4
 MTCM CR4 ... 202 A1
 ORP BR6 ... 207 K8
 WEA W13 ... 135 H8
 WLSDN NW10 ... 136 F5
Mortimer Sq *NTGHL* W11 ... 136 G9
Mortimer St *REGST* W1B ... 10 E7
Mortimer Ter *KTTN* NW5 ... 118 C9
Mortlake Cl *CROY/NA* CR0 ... 202 G10
Mortlake Dr *MTCM* CR4 ... 201 P1
Mortlake High St
 MORT/ESHN SW14 ... 156 A9
Mortlake Rd *CAN/RD* E16 ... 141 N8
 IL IG1 ... 122 F9
Mortlock Cl *PECK* SE15 ... 159 J7
Morton *SM4* ... 201 N5
Morton Cl *WOKN/KNAP* GU21 ... 231 P1
 WCHPL E1 ... 140 C4
Morton Crs *STHGT/OAK* N14 ... 98 E9
Morton Dr *SLN* SL2 ... 108 D10
Morton Gdns *WLGTN* SM6 ... 222 D2
Morton Ms *ECT* SW5 ... 14 C6
Morton Pl *STHWK* SE1 ... 18 A4
Morton Rd *IS* N1 ... 6 F4
 MRDN SM4 ... 201 N5
 SRTFD E15 ... 141 L2
 WOKN/KNAP GU21 ... 231 P1
Morton Wy *STHGT/OAK* N14 ... 98 D4
Morvale Cl *BELV* DA17 ... 164 A3
Morval Rd *BRXS/STRHM* SW2 ... 181 H1
Morven Cl *POTB/CUF* EN6 ... 59 M7
Morven Rd *TOOT* SW17 ... 180 A6
Morville St *BOW* E3 ... 140 F4
Morwell St *FITZ* W1T ... 11 J4
Mosbach Gdns *RBRW/HUT* CM13 ... 107 N3
Moscow Pl *BAY/PAD* W2 ... 8 G7
Moscow Rd *BAY/PAD* W2 ... 8 F7
Moselle Cl *CEND/HSY/T* N8 ... 118 C1
Moselle Rd *BH/WHM* TN16 ... 244 B4
Moselle St *TOTM* N17 ... 99 N8
Mosford Cl *HORL* RH6 ... 280 A2
Mospey Crs *EW* KT17 ... 238 C1
Moss Bank *GRAYS* RM17 ... 167 L3
Mossborough Cl
 NFNCH/WDSP N12 ... 97 L2
Mossbury Rd *BTSEA* SW11 ... 157 P9
Moss Cl *PIN* HA5 ... 93 N10
 RKW/CH/CXG WD3 ... 91 N10
 WCHPL E1 ... 13 P3
Mossdown Cl *BELV* DA17 ... 164 B3
Mossendew Cl *DEN/HRF* UB9 ... 91 N9
Mossfield *COB* KT11 ... 217 H9
Mossford Gn *BARK/HLT* IG6 ... 122 E1
Mossford La *BARK/HLT* IG6 ... 102 F10
Mossford St *BOW* E3 ... 140 E6
Moss Gdns *SAND/SEL* CR2 ... 224 D4
Moss Gn *WGCE* AL7 ... 23 J1
Moss Hall Crs *NFNCH/WDSP* N12 ... 97 L7
Moss Hall Gv *FNCH* N3 ... 97 L1
Moss La *PIN* HA5 ... 113 N1
 ROM RM1 ... 124 G4
Mosslea Rd *CTHM* CR3 ... 241 N2
 HAYES BR2 ... 206 A5
 ORP BR6 ... 206 F10
 PGE/AN SE20 ... 182 B10
Mossop St *CHEL* SW3 ... 15 P5
Moss Rd *DAGE* RM10 ... 144 B2
 GSTN WD25 ... 55 J10
 SOCK/AV RM15 ... 147 H7
Moss Side *LCOL/BKTW* AL2 ... 55 N6
Mossville Gdns *MRDN* SM4 ... 201 J3
Moss Wy *RDART* DA2 ... 188 C3
Moston Cl *HYS/HAR* UB3 ... 152 G4
Mostyn Av *WBLY* HA9 ... 115 L10
Mostyn Gdns *WLSDN* NW10 ... 136 G5
Mostyn Gv *BOW* E3 ... 140 E4
Mostyn Rd *BRXN/ST* SW9 ... 159 H7
 EDGW HA8 ... 96 A8
 WIM/MER SW19 ... 201 J1
Mostyn Ter *REDH* RH1 ... 276 B1
Mosul Wy *HAYES* BR2 ... 206 B6
Mosyer Dr *STMC/STPC* BR5 ... 207 N9
Motcomb St *KTBR* SW1X ... 16 B3
The Mothers Sq *CLPT* E5 ... 120 A9
Motherwell Wy *WTHK* RM20 ... 166 F6
Motley Av *VX/NE* SW8 ... 158 D8
Motley St *VX/NE* SW8 ... 158 D8
Motspur Pk *NWMAL* KT3 ... 200 C6
Mottingham Gdns
 ELTH/MOT SE9 ... 184 A4
Mottingham La *ELTH/MOT* SE9 ... 183 P4
 ELTH/MOT SE9 ... 184 A4
Mottingham Rd *ED* N9 ... 80 C10
 ELTH/MOT SE9 ... 184 C6
Mottisfont Rd *ABYW* SE2 ... 163 K2
Motts Hill La *KWD/TDW/WH* KT20 ... 238 D9
Mott St *CHING* E4 ... 81 K5
Mouchotte Cl *BH/WHM* TN16 ... 204 E4
Moulins Rd *HOM* E9 ... 140 B2
Mountain Hl *SWLY* BR8 ... 209 H4
Moultrie Wy *UPMR* RM14 ... 126 D5
Moundfield Rd *STNW/STAM* N16 ... 119 P4
Mountacre Cl *SYD* SE26 ... 181 N7
Mount Adon Pk *EDUL* SE22 ... 181 P3
Mount Angelus Rd
 PUT/ROE SW15 ... 178 C3
Mount Ararat Rd
 RCHPK/HAM TW10 ... 177 K1
Mount Ash Rd *SYD* SE26 ... 182 A6
Mount Av *CHING* E4 ... 100 F4
 CTHM CR3 ... 241 K10
 EA W5 ... 135 J4
 HARH RM3 ... 105 K4
 RBRW/HUT CM13 ... 107 N1
 STHL UB1 ... 133 P6
Mountbatten Cl *NRWD* SE19 ... 181 M8
 WOOL/PLUM SE18 ... 163 H10
Mountbatten Ct *BKHH* IG9 ... 102 A3
Mountbel Rd *STAN* HA7 ... 94 F9

Mount Cl *BMLY* BR1 ... 206 B1
 CAR SM5 ... 222 B6
 CRAWE RH10 ... 284 D6
 EBAR EN4 ... 78 B8
 HHW HP1 ... 35 J6
 LHD/OX KT22 ... 236 E9
 PUR/KEN CR8 ... 241 K2
 SEV TN13 ... 246 G9
 SLN SL2 ... 109 N7
The Mount Cl *VW* GU25 ... 194 A6
Mountcombe Cl *SURB* KT6 ... 199 K7
Mount Ct *WWKM* BR4 ... 199 L9
Mount Crs *BRW* CM14 ... 107 J5
Mount Culver Av *SCUP* DA14 ... 185 N9
Mount Dr *LCOL/BKTW* AL2 ... 56 C1
 RYLN/HDSTN HA2 ... 113 N3
 WBLY HA9 ... 115 P7
The Mount Dr *REIG* RH2 ... 257 N8
Mountearl Gdns
 STRHM/NOR SW16 ... 180 G6
Mount Echo Av *CHING* E4 ... 100 G3
Mount Echo Dr *CHING* E4 ... 100 G2
Mount Ephraim La
 STRHM/NOR SW16 ... 180 E6
Mount Ephraim Rd
 STRHM/NOR SW16 ... 180 E6
Mount Felix *WOT/HER* KT12 ... 196 G8
Mountfield Cl *LEW* SE13 ... 183 J3
Mountfield Rd *EA* W5 ... 135 J4
 EHAM E6 ... 142 C4
 FNCH N3 ... 97 J3
 HHNE HP2 ... 35 P6
Mountfield Wy *STMC/STPC* BR5 ... 207 M4
Mountford St *WCHPL* E1 ... 13 N5
Mountfort Ter *IS* N1 ... 6 A4
Mount Gdns *SYD* SE26 ... 182 A6
Mount Grace Rd *POTB/CUF* EN6 ... 59 K6
Mount Gv *EDGW* HA8 ... 95 P4
Mountgrove Rd *FSBYPK* N4 ... 119 K8
Mount Harry Rd *SEV* TN13 ... 247 J9
Mount Hermon Rd
 WOKS/MYFD GU22 ... 232 A5
Mount Hill La *CFSP/GDCR* SL9 ... 109 N6
Mounthurst Rd *HAYES* BR2 ... 205 M7
Mountington Park Cl
 KTN/HRWW/W HA3 ... 115 J4
Mountjoy Cl *THMD* SE28 ... 163 J1
Mount La *CRAWE* RH10 ... 285 P9
 DEN/HRF UB9 ... 110 G7
Mount Lee *EGH* TW20 ... 172 B8
Mount Mills *FSBYE* EC1V ... 6 D10
Mount Nod Rd
 STRHM/NOR SW16 ... 180 G6
Mount Nugent *CSHM* HP5 ... 50 F3
Mount Pk *CAR* SM5 ... 222 B8
Mount Park Av *RYLN/HDSTN* HA2 ... 114 C7
 SAND/SEL CR2 ... 223 J5
Mount Park Crs *EA* W5 ... 135 J8
Mount Park Rd *EA* W5 ... 135 J7
 PIN HA5 ... 113 H3
 RYLN/HDSTN HA2 ... 114 C7
Mount Pl *ACT* W3 ... 135 N10
Mount Pleasant *ALP/SUD* HA0 ... 135 K3
 BH/WHM TN16 ... 244 A3
 DEN/HRF UB9 ... 91 K9
 EBAR EN4 ... 78 A8
 EHSLY KT24 ... 252 C5
 EHSLY KT24 ... 253 M4
 EW KT17 ... 220 C5
 FSBYW WC1X ... 11 P3
 RSLP HA4 ... 113 K8
 STALW/RED AL3 ... 38 B5
 WEY KT13 ... 196 B10
 WNWD SE27 ... 181 K7
Mount Pleasant *BRKMPK* AL9 ... 40 F1
Mount Pleasant Crs *FSBYPK* N4 ... 118 G5
Mount Pleasant Hl *CLPT* E5 ... 120 A6
Mount Pleasant La *BRKMPK* AL9 ... 40 F1
 CLPT E5 ... 120 A6
 LCOL/BKTW AL2 ... 55 L6
Mount Pleasant Pl
 WOOL/PLUM SE18 ... 162 G3
Mount Pleasant Rd *CHIG* IG7 ... 102 G5
 CRW RM5 ... 104 E7
 CTHM CR3 ... 241 P9
 DART DA1 ... 187 N2
 EA W5 ... 135 H6
 LEW SE13 ... 183 H2
 NWMAL KT3 ... 199 P3
 RSEV TN14 ... 235 J2
 TOTM N17 ... 99 M10
 WALTH E17 ... 100 D10
 WLSDN NW10 ... 136 F2
Mount Pleasant Vls *FSBYPK* N4 ... 118 F5
Mount Ri *FSTH* SE23 ... 182 B5
 REDH RH1 ... 275 N2
Mount Rd *BCTR* RM8 ... 124 A6
 BXLYHS DA6 ... 185 P1
 CHOB/PIR GU24 ... 213 N6
 CHSGTN KT9 ... 219 L2
 CRICK NW2 ... 116 E8
 DART DA1 ... 186 G2
 EBAR EN4 ... 77 P9
 EPP CM16 ... 65 P8
 FELT TW13 ... 175 M6
 HDN NW4 ... 116 D4
 HERT/WAS SG14 ... 25 H6
 HYS/HAR UB3 ... 153 H1
 IL IG1 ... 122 E10
 MTCM CR4 ... 201 N2
 NRWD SE19 ... 181 L9
 NWMAL KT3 ... 200 A3
 STALE/WH AL4 ... 21 H5
 WAND/EARL SW18 ... 179 K5
 WOKS/MYFD GU22 ... 231 N7
Mount Rw *MYFR/PKLN* W1K ... 10 E8
Mountsfield Cl
 STWL/WRAY TW19 ... 173 K1
Mounts Hl *ASC* SL5 ... 170 B8
 WDSR SL4 ... 170 B8
Mountside *GUW* GU2 ... 267 N3
 KTN/HRWW/W HA3 ... 94 D3
Mountsorrel *HERT/BAY* SG13 ... 25 N5
Mounts Pond Rd *BKHTH/KID* SE3 ... 161 J2
Mounts Rd *GRH* DA9 ... 188 G2
Mount Stewart Av
 KTN/HRWW/W HA3 ... 115 J4
Mount St *DORK* RH4 ... 272 F2
 MYFR/PKLN W1K ... 10 C7
Mount Ter *WCHPL* E1 ... 140 A7
The Mount *BRW* CM14 ... 107 H4
 CHESW EN7 ... 61 L2
 COUL/CHIP CR5 ... 240 F1
 ESH/CLAY KT10 ... 220 C6
 EW KT17 ... 220 C6
 GUW GU2 ... 267 N3
 HAMP NW3 ... 117 M9
 HARH RM3 ... 105 K4
 HORS RH12 ... 282 C4
 KWD/TDW/WH KT20 ... 257 J2
 LHD/OX KT22 ... 236 D9
 NWMAL KT3 ... 200 C3
 POTB/CUF EN6 ... 59 L6
 RKW/CH/CXG WD3 ... 71 M10
 TRDG/WHET N20 ... 97 M3
 VW GU25 ... 194 A6
 WARL CR6 ... 241 P5
 WBLY HA9 ... 115 P7
 WEY KT13 ... 196 F6
 WOKN/KNAP GU21 ... 232 A4
 WPK KT4 ... 220 E1
Mount Vw *ENC/FH* EN2 ... 78 G4
 LCOL/BKTW AL2 ... 57 K3
 RKW/CH/CXG WD3 ... 91 L2

Mountview *MLHL* NW7 96 A4 1
NTHWD HA6 93 H7
Mountview Cl *REDH* RH1 275 P2 2
Mountview Dr *REDH* RH1 275 P2
Mount View Rd *CDALE/KGS* NW9 116 A2
Mountview Rd *CHESW* EN7 61 M2
Mount View Rd *CHING* E4 101 H1
ESH/CLAY KT10 218 G4
FSBYPK N4 118 G5
Mountview Rd *ORP* BR6 207 K7
Mount Vls *WNWD* SE27 181 J6
Mount Wy *CAR* SM5 222 B5
Mountway *POTB/CUF* EN6 59 K6
Mount Wy *WGCE* AL7 23 J8
Mountway Cl *WGCE* AL7 23 J8
Mountwood *E/WMO/HCT* KT8 198 A3
Mountwood Cl *SAND/SEL* CR2 224 A6
Movers La *BARK* IG11 142 G3
Mowatt Cl *ARCH* N19 118 E7
Mowbray Av *BF/WBF* KT14 215 P9
Mowbray Crs *EGH* TW20 172 D8
Mowbray Dr *CRAWW* RH11 283 J9
Mowbray Gdns *DORK* RH4 254 G10
Mowbray Rd *BAR* EN5 77 M8
EDGW HA8 95 M5
HLW CM20 29 J9
KIL/WHAMP NW6 2 A3
NRWD SE19 203 N1
RCHPK/HAM TW10 177 H6
Mowbrays Cl *CRW* RM5 104 D9
Mowbrays Rd *CRW* RM5 104 D10
Mowbrey Gdns *LOU* IG10 82 F5 2
Mowlem St *BETH* E2 140 A3 7
Mowll St *BRXN/ST* SW9 159 H6
Moxom Av *CHES/WCR* EN8 62 D6
Moxon Cl *PLSTW* E13 141 L4 2
Moxon St *BAR* EN5 77 J7
MHST W1U 10 C4
Moyers Rd *WAN* E11 121 H5 5
Moylan Rd *HMSMTH* W6 14 B10
Moyne Pl *WLSDN* NW10 135 M5
Moynihan Dr *STHGT/OAK* N14 78 F9 4
Moys Cl *CROY/NA* CR0 202 F6
Moyser Rd *TOOT* SW17 180 C8
Mozart St *MV/WKIL* W9 2 C10
Muchelney Rd *MRDN* SM4 201 M6
Muckhatch La *EGH* TW20 194 E3
Muckingford Rd *TIL* RM18 169 J3
Muggeridge Cl *SAND/SEL* CR2 223 L2
Muggeridge Rd *DAGE* RM10 124 C9 2
Muirdown Av *MORT/ESHN* SW14 155 P10
Muirfield *ACT* W3 136 B8 2
Muirfield Cl *CRAWW* RH11 282 G8
OXHEY WD19 93 K6 3
OXHEY WD19 93 K6 5
Muirfield Crs *POP/IOD* E14 160 G2
Muirfield Gn *OXHEY* WD19 93 K5 1
Muirfield Rd *OXHEY* WD19 93 J5
WOKN/KNAP GU21 231 M4
Muirkirk Rd *CAT* SE6 183 H4
Muir Rd *CLPT* E5 119 P9
Muir St *CAN/RD* E16 142 C10 2
Mulberry Av *STWL/WRAY* TW19 173 P4
WDSR SL4 149 L9
Mulberry Cl *BROX* EN10 44 E10
CHING E4 100 F3
EBAR EN4 77 N8
GPK RM2 125 J2
HDN NW4 116 F1
LCOL/BKTW AL2 56 A4 1
NTHLT UB5 133 M4 1
STRHM/NOR SW16 180 D7
WEY KT13 196 C10
WOKN/KNAP GU21 214 B10 2
Mulberry Crs *BTFD* TW8 154 G6
WDR/YW UB7 152 B1
Mulberry Dr *DTCH/LGLY* SL3 150 B4
PUR RM19 165 N3
Mulberry Gdns *RAD* WD7 57 K9
Mulberry Gn *HLWE* CM17 29 N7
Mulberry Hl *BRWN* CM15 107 L1
Mulberry La *CROY/NA* CR0 203 N8
Mulberry Ms *NWCR* SE14 160 E7
Mulberry Pde *WDR/YW* UB7 152 B2
Mulberry Pl *HMSMTH* W6 156 D4 2
Mulberry Rd *CRAWW* RH11 283 L4 2
GVW DA11 190 B7
HACK E8 7 L4
Mulberry St *WCHPL* E1 13 N5
Mulberry Trees *SHPTN* TW17 196 E7 1
Mulberry Wk *CHEL* SW3 15 M9
Mulberry Wy *BARK/HLT* IG6 122 F2
BELV DA17 164 D1
SWFD E18 101 N10
Mulgrave Rd *BELMT* SM2 221 J4
CROY/NA CR0 203 L10
EA W5 135 J5
HRW HA1 114 F7
WKENS W14 14 C9
WLSDN NW10 116 C9
Mulgrave Wy *WOKN/KNAP* GU21 231 K4
Mulholland Cl *MTCM* CR4 202 C2
Mulkern Rd *ARCH* N19 118 E6
Mullards Cl *MTCM* CR4 202 A8
Mullein Ct *GRAYS* RM17 168 A5
Mullens Rd *EGH* TW20 172 F8
Mullet Gdns *BETH* E2 7 P9
Mullins Pth *MORT/ESHN* SW14 156 A9
Mullion Cl *KTN/HRWW/W* HA3 94 A9
Mullion Wk *OXHEY* WD19 93 L5 5
Mulready St *STJWD* NW8 9 N2
Multi Wy *ACT* W3 156 B1
Multon Rd *WAND/EARL* SW18 179 N3
Mumford Ct *CITYW* EC2V 12 F5
Mumford Rd *HNHL* SE24 181 J1 3
Mumfords La *CFSP/GDCR* SL9 109 M1
Muncaster Cl *ASHF* TW15 174 B7
Muncaster Rd *ASHF* TW15 174 C8
BTSEA SW11 158 A10
Muncies Ms *CAT* SE6 183 H5 1
Mundania Rd *EDUL* SE22 182 A2
Munday Rd *CAN/RD* E16 141 M8
Mundells *CHESW* EN7 61 P3
WGCE AL7 23 J4
Munden Gv *WATN* WD24 73 K4
Munden St *WKENS* W14 14 A5
Mundesley Sp *SL* SL1 129 K8
Mundesly Cl *OXHEY* WD19 93 K5 2
Mundford Rd *CLPT* E5 120 B7 2
Mundon Gdns *IL* IG1 122 G6
Mund St *WKENS* W14 14 D8
Mundy St *IS* N1 7 J9
Munford Dr *SWCM* DA10 189 L3
Mungo-park Cl *BUSH* WD23 94 B3 3
Mungo Park Rd *GVE* DA12 190 G8
RAIN RM13 145 J2 7
Mungo Park Wy *STMC/STPC* BR5 207 M7
Munnery Wy *ORP* BR6 206 D10
Munnings Gdns *ISLW* TW7 176 C1
Munro Ms *NKENS* W10 8 B3
Munro Rd *BUSH* WD23 74 A9
Munstead Vw *RGUW* GU3 267 N5
Munster Av *HSLWW* TW4 153 M10
Munster Gdns *PLMGR* N13 99 K5
Munster Rd *FUL/PGN* SW6 157 H6
TEDD TW11 177 H9
Munster Sq *CAMTN* NW1 4 F10
Munton Rd *WALW* SE17 18 F5
Murchison Av *BXLY* DA5 185 N4
Murchison Rd *HOD* EN11 44 G1
LEY E10 121 H7
Murdoch Cl *STA* TW18 173 K8
Murdock Cl *CAN/RD* E16 141 L8 7
Murdock St *PECK* SE15 160 A5 2
Murfett Cl *WIM/MER* SW19 179 H5
Murfitt Wy *UPMR* RM14 125 P9 1
Muriel Av *WATW* WD18 73 K9
Muriel St *IS* N1 5 P7
Murillo Rd *LEW* SE13 161 J10
Murphy St *STHWK* SE1 18 A2
Murray Av *BMLY* BR1 205 N3
HSLW TW3 176 A1
Murray Ct *ASC* SL5 192 B6
Murray Crs *PIN* HA5 93 L9
Murray Gv *IS* N1 6 G8
Murray Ms *CAMTN* NW1 5 J3
Murray Rd *BERK* HP4 33 P4
CHERT KT16 214 G3
EA W5 155 H3
NTHWD HA6 92 F9
RCHPK/HAM TW10 176 G5
STMC/STPC BR5 207 L3
WIM/MER SW19 178 G9
Murray's La *BF/WBF* KT14 215 N10
Murray Sq *CAN/RD* E16 141 M8
Murray St *CAMTN* NW1 5 H3
Murray Ter *HAMP* NW3 117 M9 6
Murrells Wk *GT/LBKH* KT23 235 P9
The Murreys *ASHTD* KT21 237 J4
Murthering La *ABR/ST* RM4 85 H8
Murton Ct *STAL* AL1 38 D5
Murtwell Dr *CHIG* IG7 102 F7
Musard Rd *HMSMTH* W6 14 B9
Musbury St *WCHPL* E1 140 B8
Muscatel Pl *CMBW* SE5 159 M7 2
Muschamp Rd *CAR* SM5 201 P9
PECK SE15 159 N9
Muscovy St *TWRH* EC3N 13 K8
Museum St *NOXST/BSQ* WC1A 11 L4 3
Musgrave Cl *CHESW* EN7 61 N3 5
EBAR EN4 77 M5
Musgrave Crs *FUL/PGN* SW6 157 K6
Musgrave Rd *ISLW* TW7 154 E7
Musgrove Rd *NWCR* SE14 160 C7
Musjid Rd *BTSEA* SW11 157 N8 1
Muskalls Cl *CHESW* EN7 61 P3 1
Muskham Rd *HLW* CM20 29 K8
Musk Hl *HHW* HP1 35 H7
Musleigh Mnr *WARE* SG12 26 E2 3
Musley Hl *WARE* SG12 26 D1
Musley La *WARE* SG12 26 D1
Musquash Wy *HSLWW* TW4 153 K8 4
Mussenden La *EYN* DA4 210 C6
Mustard Mill Rd *STA* TW18 173 J7
Muston Rd *CLPT* E5 120 A7
Muswell Av *MUSWH* N10 98 C10 1
Muswell Hl *MUSWH* N10 118 C1
Muswell Hill Broadway
MUSWH N10 118 C1 2
Muswell Hill Pl *MUSWH* N10 118 C2
Muswell Hill Rd *HGT* N6 118 B4
MUSWH N10 118 B2
Muswell Ms *MUSWH* N10 118 C1
Muswell Rd *MUSWH* N10 98 C10
Mutchetts Cl *GSTN* WD25 55 M9
Mutrix Rd *KIL/WHAMP* NW6 2 F5
Mutton La *POTB/CUF* EN6 58 G7
POTB/CUF EN6 59 L9
Mutton Rw *CHONG* CM5 67 K6
Muybridge Rd *NWMAL* KT3 199 P2
Myatt Rd *BRXN/ST* SW9 159 J7
Mycenae Rd *BKHTH/KID* SE3 161 M5
Myddelton Av *EN* EN1 79 M4
Myddelton Gdns *WCHMH* N21 99 K1
Myddelton Pk *TRDG/WHET* N20 97 N4
Myddelton Pas *CLKNW* EC1R 6 B9
Myddelton Rd *CEND/HSY/T* N8 118 F1
Myddelton Sq *CLKNW* EC1R 6 B9
Myddelton St *CLKNW* EC1R 6 B10
Myddleton Av *FSBYPK* N4 119 K7
Myddleton Rd *UX/CGN* UB8 131 M3
WARE SG12 26 C3
WDGN N22 98 F8
Myers Cl *RAD* WD7 57 K8 3
Myers La *NWCR* SE14 160 C5
Mygrove Cl *RAIN* RM13 145 L4 2
Mygrove Gdns *RAIN* RM13 145 L4
Mygrove Rd *RAIN* RM13 145 L4
Myles Ct *CHESW* EN7 61 K5
Mylis Cl *SYD* SE26 182 A7
Mylne Cl *CHES/WCR* EN8 62 E1
Mylne St *CLKNW* EC1R 6 A8
Mylor Cl *WOKN/KNAP* GU21 214 B10
Mymms Dr *BRKMPK* AL9 59 K3
Mynchen End *BEAC* HP9 88 C5 1
Mynn's Cl *EPSOM* KT18 219 N10 1
Myra St *ABYW* SE2 163 K4
Myrdle St *WCHPL* E1 13 P4
The Myrke *DTCH/LGLY* SL3 149 L3
Myrna Cl *WIM/MER* SW19 179 P10
Myron Pl *LEW* SE13 161 H9 3
Myrtle Aly *WOOL/PLUM* SE18 162 D2
Myrtle Av *EBED/NFELT* TW14 152 F10
RSLP HA4 113 H5
Myrtle Cl *DTCH/LGLY* SL3 151 H7 1
EBAR EN4 98 A2
ERITH DA8 164 F6
LTWR GU18 212 A7
UX/CGN UB8 132 A7 1
WDR/YW UB7 152 A3
Myrtle Crs *SLN* SL2 129 L9
Myrtledene Rd *ABYW* SE2 163 K4
Myrtle Gdns *HNWL* W7 134 D10
Myrtle Gv *ENC/FH* EN2 79 L4
NWMAL KT3 199 P2
SOCK/AV RM15 166 B1
Myrtle Pl *RDART* DA2 188 C4
Myrtle Rd *ACT* W3 135 P10
BRW CM14 107 H5
CROY/NA CR0 204 F10
DART DA1 187 L5
DORK RH4 272 F1
EHAM E6 142 B3
HARH RM3 105 K7
HPTN TW12 176 B9
HSLW TW3 154 B8
PLMGR N13 99 K4
SUT SM1 221 M2
WALTH E17 120 D4
Myrtleside Cl *NTHWD* HA6 92 E8
Mysore Rd *BTSEA* SW11 158 A10
Myton Rd *DUL* SE21 181 L6

N

Nadine St *CHARL* SE7 161 P4
Naffenton Ri *LOU* IG10 82 A9 1
Nagle Cl *WALTH* E17 101 J10
Nag's Head La *UPMR* RM14 106 B9
WELL DA16 163 L9 1
Nags Head Rd *PEND* EN3 80 B8
Nailsworth Crs *REDH* RH1 258 E5
Nailzee Cl *CFSP/GDCR* SL9 110 B5
Nairn Cl *HARP* AL5 20 C5
Nairne Gv *HNHL* SE24 181 L1
Nairn Gn *OXHEY* WD19 93 H4
Nairn Rd *RSLP* HA4 133 K1
Nairn St *POP/IOD* E14 141 H7
Nalders Rd *CSHM* HP5 51 K5
Nallhead Rd *FELT* TW13 175 K8
Namba Roy Cl *STRHM/NOR* SW16 180 G7
Namton Dr *STRHM/NOR* SW16 202 G4 2
Nan Clark's La *MLHL* NW7 96 C3
Nancy Downs *OXHEY* WD19 93 K1
Nankin St *POP/IOD* E14 140 F8 1
Nansen Rd *BTSEA* SW11 158 B10
GVE DA12 190 G7
Nantes Cl *WAND/EARL* SW18 157 M10
Nant Rd *CRICK* NW2 117 J7
Nant St *BETH* E2 140 A5 11
Naoroji St *FSBYW* WC1X 6 A10
Napier Av *FUL/PGN* SW6 157 J9
POP/IOD E14 160 F4
Napier Cl *DEPT* SE8 160 E6
HCH RM12 125 J6 8
LCOL/BKTW AL2 57 J1
WDR/YW UB7 152 A2
WKENS W14 14 C3
Napier Ct *CTHM* CR3 241 M8
LEE/GVPK SE12 183 N5
Napier Dr *BUSH* WD23 73 M8
Napier Gdns *GU* GU1 250 E9
Napier Gv *IS* N1 6 F8
Napier Pl *WKENS* W14 14 C4
Napier Rd *ALP/SUD* HA0 115 J10
ASHF TW15 174 E10
BELV DA17 164 A3
EHAM E6 142 D3
GVW DA11 190 C4
HAYES BR2 205 N4
ISLW TW7 154 F10
PEND EN3 80 C9
SAND/SEL CR2 223 L4
SNWD SE25 204 A4 4
SRTFD E15 141 K4
TOTM N17 119 M1
WAN E11 121 K8
WDR/YW UB7 151 N7
WKENS W14 14 B4
WLSDN NW10 136 E5
Napier Ter *IS* N1 6 C4
Napier Wk *ASHF* TW15 174 E10
Napier Wy *CRAWE* RH10 284 A4
Napoleon Rd *CLPT* E5 120 A8
TWK TW1 176 G3 5
Napsbury Av *LCOL/BKTW* AL2 57 H2
Napsbury La *LCOL/BKTW* AL2 56 F1
STAL AL1 38 F9
The Nap *KGLGY* WD4 54 B5
Napton Cl *YEAD* UB4 133 M6 3
Narbonne Av *CLAP* SW4 180 D1
Narboro Ct *ROM* RM1 125 H4 4
Narborough Cl *HGDN/ICK* UB10 112 D7 1
Narborough St *FUL/PGN* SW6 157 L8 5
Narcissus Rd *KIL/WHAMP* NW6 117 K10 4
Narcot Rd *CSTG* HP8 89 M4
Narcot Wy *CSTG* HP8 89 M5
Nare Rd *SOCK/AV* RM15 146 B9
Narford Rd *CLPT* E5 119 P8
Narrow La *WARL* CR6 242 A5
Narrow St *ACT* W3 135 N10 4
POP/IOD E14 140 D9
Narrow Wy *HAYES* BR2 206 B6
Nascot Pl *WAT* WD17 73 J6
Nascot Rd *WAT* WD17 73 J6
Nascot St *SHB* W12 136 F8 4
WAT WD17 73 J6
Nascot Wood Rd *WAT* WD17 72 G3
Naseby Cl *ISLW* TW7 154 D7
KIL/WHAMP NW6 3 K3
Naseby Rd *CLAY* IG5 102 C9
DAGE RM10 124 B8
NRWD SE19 181 L9
Nash Cl *BORE* WD6 75 L8
BRKMPK AL9 40 G9
Nash Cft *MEO* DA13 190 B7
Nash Gdns *REDH* RH1 258 A8
Nash Gn *BMLY* BR1 183 M10
Nash La *HAYES* BR2 225 M3
Nashleigh Hl *CSHM* HP5 51 J5
Nash Mills La *HHS/BOV* HP3 54 A2
Nash Rd *BROCKY* SE4 160 D10
CHDH RM6 123 N2
CRAWE RH10 283 P10
DTCH/LGLY SL3 150 C4
ED N9 100 B3
Nash St *CAMTN* NW1 4 F9
Nash Wy *KTN/HRWW/W* HA3 114 G4
Nasmyth St *HMSMTH* W6 156 E2
Nassau Rd *BARN* SW13 156 C7
Nassau St *GTPST* W1W 10 F4
Nassington Rd *HAMP* NW3 117 P9
Nasturtium Dr *CHOB/PIR* GU24 230 F1 4
Natalie Cl *EBED/NFELT* TW14 174 E3
Natal Rd *FBAR/BDGN* N11 98 F7
IL IG1 122 E9
STRHM/NOR SW16 180 E9
THHTH CR7 203 L3
Nathan Cl *UPMR* RM14 126 D6
Nathaniel Cl *WCHPL* E1 13 M4 3
Nathans Rd *ALP/SUD* HA0 115 H7
Nathan Wy *THMD* SE28 163 J2
Nation Wy *CHING* E4 101 H2 1
Natwoke Cl *BEAC* HP9 88 C6
Naunton Wy *HCH* RM12 125 L8 1
Naval Rw *POP/IOD* E14 141 H9
Navarino Gv *HACK* E8 7 P1
Navarino Rd *HACK* E8 7 P1
Navarre Gdns *CRW* RM5 104 C7
Navarre Rd *EHAM* E6 142 B4
Navarre St *BETH* E2 13 L1
Navestock Cl *CHING* E4 101 H4 5
Navestock Crs *WFD* IG8 101 P9
Navestock Rd *WFD* IG8 101 P8
Navestock Side *BRW* CM14 86 B6
Navestock Ter *WFD* IG8 101 P8
Navigator Dr *STHL* UB1 154 B1
Navy St *CLAP* SW4 158 E9
Naylor Gv *PEND* EN3 80 C9 1
Naylor Rd *PECK* SE15 160 A6
TRDG/WHET N20 97 M3
Nazareth Cl *PECK* SE15 160 A8 6
Nazeingbury Cl *WAB* EN9 45 J8 1
Nazeing Common *WAB* EN9 45 P9
Neal Av *STHL* UB1 133 N6
Neal Cl *CFSP/GDCR* SL9 110 E6
NTHWD HA6 93 H9
Neal Ct *HERT/WAS* SG14 25 K5
Nealden St *BRXN/ST* SW9 158 G9 3
Neale Cl *EFNCH* N2 117 M1
Neal St *LSQ/SEVD* WC2H 11 L6
WATW WD18 73 K9
Neaole Cl *BORE* WD6 75 P5 2
Near Acre *CDALE/KGS* NW9 96 C9
Neasden Cl *WLSDN* NW10 116 B10 2
Neasden La North *WLSDN* NW10 116 B8
Neasham Rd *BCTR* RM8 123 L10
Neate St *CMBW* SE5 19 J10
Neath Gdns *MRDN* SM4 201 M6 3
Neathouse Pl *PIM* SW1V 16 G5 3
Neats Acre *RSLP* HA4 112 E5
Neatscourt Rd *EHAM* E6 142 A7
Neave Crs *HARH* RM3 105 K9
Neb La *OXTED* RH8 261 H7
Nebraska St *STHWK* SE1 18 G2
Neckinger *STHWK* SE1 19 M3
Neckinger St *STHWK* SE1 19 M2
Nectarine Wy *LEW* SE13 160 G8 2
Necton Rd *STALE/WH* AL4 21 K3
Needham Cl *WDSR* SL4 148 D7
Needham Rd *NTGHL* W11 8 E6
Needleman St *BERM/RHTH* SE16 160 C1
Needles Bank *GDST* RH9 260 A7
Neela Cl *HGDN/ICK* UB10 112 C9
Neeld Crs *HDN* NW4 116 E3
WBLY HA9 115 M10
Neil Cl *ASHF* TW15 174 D8
Neild Wy *RKW/CH/CXG* WD3 91 J1
Nelgarde Rd *CAT* SE6 182 F3
Nella Rd *HMSMTH* W6 156 G5
Nelldale Rd *BERM/RHTH* SE16 160 B3 5
Nellgrove Rd *UX/CGN* UB8 132 C6
Nell Gwynn Av *SHPTN* TW17 196 E6
Nell Gwynn Cl *RAD* WD7 57 K8
Nell Gwynne Av *ASC* SL5 192 C4
Nell Gwynne Cl *HOR/WEW* KT19 219 M7 2
Nello James Gdns *WNWD* SE27 181 L7
Nelmes Cl *EMPK* RM11 125 N3
Nelmes Crs *EMPK* RM11 125 N3
Nelmes Rd *EMPK* RM11 125 M5
Nelmes Wy *EMPK* RM11 125 M2
Nelson Av *STAL* AL1 38 G9
Nelson Cl *AMSS* HP7 68 B10
BH/WHM TN16 244 B3
BRW CM14 107 J6
CRAWE RH10 284 D8
DTCH/LGLY SL3 150 A3
EBED/NFELT TW14 174 G4 12
HGDN/ICK UB10 132 C5
ROMW/RG RM7 104 C9
WOT/HER KT12 197 J8
Nelson Gdns *BETH* E2 7 P9
GU GU1 250 D9
HSLWW TW4 175 P2
Nelson Grove Rd
WIM/MER SW19 201 L1
Nelson La *HGDN/ICK* UB10 132 C5 3
Nelson Mandela Cl *MUSWH* N10 98 A10
Nelson Mandela Rd
BKHTH/KID SE3 161 P9
Nelson Pl *IS* N1 6 D8
SCUP DA14 185 K7
Nelson Rd *ASHF* TW15 173 P8
BELV DA17 164 A4
CEND/HSY/T N8 118 G3
CHING E4 100 G7
CTHM CR3 241 L9
DART DA1 187 K2
ED N9 100 A4
GNWCH SE10 161 H5 7
GVW DA11 190 C5
HAYES BR2 205 P4
HGDN/ICK UB10 132 C5
HSLWW TW4 175 P2
NWMAL KT3 200 A5
PEND EN3 80 C10
RAIN RM13 144 G4
RYLN/HDSTN HA2 114 C6
SCUP DA14 185 K7 2
SEVS/STOTM N15 119 M2 2
SOCK/AV RM15 147 H4
STAN HA7 95 H7
WAN E11 121 M2
WDR/YW UB7 152 A7
WDSR SL4 148 E9
WHTN TW2 176 A3
WIM/MER SW19 179 L10
Nelson Sq *STHWK* SE1 18 C1
Nelsons Rw *CLAP* SW4 158 E10
Nelson St *CAN/RD* E16 141 L9 4
EHAM E6 142 D3
HERT/WAS SG14 25 J4 1
WCHPL E1 140 A8
Nelson Ter *FSBYE* EC1V 6 D8
Nelwyn Av *EMPK* RM11 125 N3
Nemoure Rd *ACT* W3 135 P9
Nene Gdns *FELT* TW13 175 N5
Nene Rd *HTHAIR* TW6 152 C7
Nepaul Rd *BTSEA* SW11 157 P8 6
Nepean St *PUT/ROE* SW15 178 D2
Neptune Cl *CRAWW* RH11 283 H9 3
Neptune Dr *HHNE* HP2 35 P4
Neptune Rd *HRW* HA1 114 C4
HTHAIR TW6 152 D7 1
Neptune St *BERM/RHTH* SE16 160 B2
Nesbit Cl *BKHTH/KID* SE3 161 K9 2
Nesbit Rd *ELTH/MOT* SE9 162 A10
Nesham St *WAP* E1W 13 N9
Ness St *BERM/RHTH* SE16 19 N3
Nesta Rd *WFD* IG8 101 L7
Nestle's Av *HYS/HAR* UB3 152 G2
Neston Rd *WATN* WD24 73 K3
Nestor Av *WCHMH* N21 79 J10
Nethan Dr *SOCK/AV* RM15 146 B9
Netheravon Rd *CHSWK* W4 156 C4
HNWL W7 134 E10
Netheravon Rd South
CHSWK W4 156 C5
Netherbury Rd *EA* W5 155 J2
Netherby Gdns *ENC/FH* EN2 78 F8
Netherby Pk *WEY* KT13 216 F2
Netherby Rd *FSTH* SE23 182 B3
Nether Cl *FNCH* N3 97 K8
Nethercote Av
WOKN/KNAP GU21 231 L3
Nethercourt Av *FNCH* N3 97 K7
Netherfield Gdns *BARK* IG11 142 G1
Netherfield La *WARE* SG12 27 J8
Netherfield Rd *HARP* AL5 20 A7
NFNCH/WDSP N12 97 L6
TOOT SW17 180 B6 1
Netherford Rd *CLAP* SW4 158 D8
Netherhall Rd *HLW/ROY* CM19 45 L3
Netherhall Wy *HAMP* NW3 3 J1
HAMP NW3 117 M10 2
Netherlands Rd *BAR* EN5 77 N10
The Netherlands *COUL/CHIP* CR5 240 D5
Netherleigh Pk *REDH* RH1 276 F3
Nether Mt *GUW* GU2 267 N2
Nethern Court Rd *CTHM* CR3 242 F9
Netherne La *COUL/CHIP* CR5 240 E8
Netherpark Dr *GPK* RM2 104 G10
Nether St *NFNCH/WDSP* N12 97 M6 3
Netherton Gv *WBPTN* SW10 15 K10
Netherton Rd *SEVS/STOTM* N15 119 L4 5
TWK TW1 176 F1
Netherway *STALW/RED* AL3 37 P9
Netherwood *CRAWW* RH11 283 K10
Netherwood Rd *BEAC* HP9 88 C6
HMSMTH W6 156 G2
Netherwood St *KIL/WHAMP* NW6 2 D3
Netley Cl *CHEAM* SM3 220 G2
CROY/NA CR0 225 H4
Netley Dr *WOT/HER* KT12 197 N7
Netley Gdns *MRDN* SM4 201 M7 2
Netley Rd *BTFD* TW8 155 K5
GNTH/NBYPK IG2 122 G3
MRDN SM4 201 M7
WALTH E17 120 E3
Netley St *CAMTN* NW1 4 G10 1
Netteswellbury Farm
HLWS CM18 47 J2 1
Netteswell Orch *HLW* CM20 28 G10
Netteswell Rd *HLW* CM20 29 H9
Nettlecombe Cl *BELMT* SM2 221 L5 5
Nettlecroft *HHW* HP1 35 L7
WGCE AL7 23 L4 4
Nettleden Av *WBLY* HA9 135 M1
Nettleden Rd *BERK* HP4 34 D2
Nettlefold Pl *WNWD* SE27 181 J6 6
Nettlestead Cl *BECK* BR3 182 E10 2
Nettles Ter *GU* GU1 250 A10 4
Nettleton Rd *HGDN/ICK* UB10 112 A9
HTHAIR TW6 152 C7
NWCR SE14 160 C6
Nettlewood Rd
STRHM/NOR SW16 180 E10 3
Neuchatel Rd *CAT* SE6 182 E5
Nevada Cl *NWMAL* KT3 199 P4 1
Nevada St *GNWCH* SE10 161 H6
Nevell Rd *CDH/CHF* RM16 168 E2 5
Nevern Pl *ECT* SW5 14 F6
Nevern Rd *ECT* SW5 14 E6 1
Nevern Sq *ECT* SW5 14 F7
Nevil Cl *NTHWD* HA6 92 E6
Nevile Cl *CRAWW* RH11 283 K10
Neville Av *NWMAL* KT3 200 A1
Neville Cl *ACT* W3 155 P1 3
BFN/LL DA15 185 J7
BNSTD SM7 221 L10
ESH/CLAY KT10 217 N3
HSLW TW3 153 P8
KIL/WHAMP NW6 2 D8
PECK SE15 159 P6
POTB/CUF EN6 59 J7
SLN SL2 129 L1
WAN E11 121 L8
Neville Dr *EFNCH* N2 117 M4
Neville Gdns *BCTR* RM8 123 N8
Neville Gill Cl *WAND/EARL* SW18 179 K2
Neville Pl *WDGN* N22 98 G9
Neville Rd *BARK/HLT* IG6 102 F9
BCTR RM8 123 N7
CROY/NA CR0 203 L7
EA W5 135 J6
FSTGT E7 141 M2
KIL/WHAMP NW6 2 D8
KUT KT1 199 M2
RCHPK/HAM TW10 177 H6
Neville St *SKENS* SW7 15 L7
Neville Wk *CAR* SM5 201 P7 2
Nevill Gv *WATN* WD24 73 J5
Nevill Rd *STNW/STAM* N16 119 M9
Nevill Wy *LOU* IG10 82 B10
Nevil Wk *CAR* SM5 201 P7 3
Nevin Dr *CHING* E4 100 G2
Nevinson Cl *WAND/EARL* SW18 179 N2
Nevis Cl *ROM* RM1 104 F7
Nevis Rd *TOOT* SW17 180 B5
Newall Rd *HTHAIR* TW6 152 D7
Newark Cl *RGUE* GU4 250 E5 2
RPLY/SEND GU23 233 J7
Newark Ct *WOT/HER* KT12 197 K8 6
Newark Crs *WLSDN* NW10 136 A5
Newark Gn *BORE* WD6 76 B7
Newark Knok *EHAM* E6 142 D8
Newark La *RPLY/SEND* GU23 233 J6
Newark Rd *BFOR* GU20 212 A1
CRAWE RH10 284 A5
SAND/SEL CR2 223 L3
Newark St *WCHPL* E1 140 A7
Newark Wy *HDN* NW4 116 D2 4
New Ash Cl *EFNCH* N2 117 N1 5
New Barnes Av *STAL* AL1 38 F9
Newbarn La *BEAC* HP9 89 K5
New Barn La *CTHM* CR3 241 M3
RSEV TN14 244 G2
New Barn Rd *HART* DA3 211 N3
MEO DA13 189 P8
SWLY BR8 208 F1
New Barns Av *MTCM* CR4 202 E4
New Barn St *PLSTW* E13 141 M6
New Barns Wy *CHIG* IG7 102 E4 1
New Battlebridge La *REDH* RH1 258 C6
Newberries Av *RAD* WD7 74 G1
Newberry Crs *WDSR* SL4 148 B7
New Berry La *WOT/HER* KT12 217 L3
Newbery Rd *ERITH* DA8 164 G7
Newbery Wy *SL* SL1 149 J1 1
Newbiggin Pth *OXHEY* WD19 93 K5 3
Newbolt Av *CHEAM* SM3 220 F2
Newbolt Rd *STAN* HA7 94 E7 5
New Bond St *MYFR/PICC* W1J 10 F8 1
MYFR/PKLN W1K 10 F6
Newborough Gn *NWMAL* KT3 200 A4
New Brent St *HDN* NW4 116 F3
New Bridge St *STP* EC4M 12 C6
New Broad St *LVPST* EC2M 13 H4
New Broadway *EA* W5 135 J9
Newburgh Rd *ACT* W3 135 P10
Newburgh St *SOHO/CST* W1F 10 G6 3
New Burlington Ms *CONDST* W1S 10 G7
New Burlington Pl *CONDST* W1S 10 G7
New Burlington St *CONDST* W1S 10 G7 2
Newburn St *LBTH* SE11 17 P7
Newbury Av *PEND* EN3 80 E3
Newbury Cl *HARH* RM3 105 K7
NTHLT UB5 133 N1
Newbury Gdns *HARH* RM3 105 L7
HOR/WEW KT19 220 C1
UPMR RM14 125 N8
Newbury Ms *KTTN* NW5 4 D2
Newbury Rd *CHING* E4 101 H7
CRAWE RH10 284 E7
GNTH/NBYPK IG2 122 G4
HARH RM3 105 K6
HAYES BR2 205 M3
WDR/YW UB7 152 A7
Newbury St *STBT* EC1A 12 E4
Newbury Wk *HARH* RM3 105 L6 3
Newbury Wy *NTHLT* UB5 133 M1
New Butt La *DEPT* SE8 160 F6 5
Newby Cl *EN* EN1 79 M6
Newby Pl *POP/IOD* E14 141 H9 6
Newby St *VX/NE* SW8 158 C9 4
Newcastle Av *BARK/HLT* IG6 103 K7
Newcastle Cl *STP* EC4M 12 C5 4
Newcastle Pl *BAY/PAD* W2 9 M4
New Cswy *REIG* RH2 275 L3
New Cavendish St *MHST* W1U 10 D4
New Change *STP* EC4M 12 E6 3
New Charles St *FSBYE* EC1V 6 D9
New Church Rd *CMBW* SE5 159 K6 1
Newchurch Rd *SL* SL1 128 E7
New City Rd *PLSTW* E13 141 P5
New Cl *FELT* TW13 175 M8
WIM/MER SW19 201 M3
Newcombe Pk *ALP/SUD* HA0 135 L3 1
MLHL NW7 96 B6
Newcombe Ri *WDR/YW* UB7 131 P8 3
WDR/YW UB7 131 P8 5
Newcombe St *KENS* W8 8 F9 2
Newcome Gdns
STRHM/NOR SW16 180 F7 2
Newcomen Rd *BTSEA* SW11 157 N9
WAN E11 121 L8 4
Newcomen St *STHWK* SE1 18 G1
Newcome Rd *RAD* WD7 57 M10
New Compton St
LSQ/SEVD WC2H 11 K6 2
New Coppice *WOKN/KNAP* GU21 231 K5
New Cottages *BRKMPK* AL9 58 G4
New Ct *NTHLT* UB5 114 A10 1
Newcourt *UX/CGN* UB8 131 M7 2
Newcourt St *STJWD* NW8 3 N8
Newcroft Cl *UX/CGN* UB8 132 A7
New Cross Rd *GUW* GU2 249 M8
Newdales Cl *ED* N9 89 P3
Newdene Av *NTHLT* UB5 133 L4
Newdigate Gn *DEN/HRF* UB9 111 M9
Newdigate Rd *DEN/HRF* UB9 91 M9
HORS RH12 282 A5
Newdigate Rd East *DEN/HRF* UB9 91 N9
Newell Ri *HHS/BOV* HP3 35 P9
Newell Rd *HHS/BOV* HP3 35 P9
Newell St *POP/IOD* E14 140 E9
New End *HAMP* NW3 117 M9
New End Sq *HAMP* NW3 117 N9
New England St *STALW/RED* AL3 38 B6
Newenham Rd *GT/LBKH* KT23 253 P2
Newent Cl *CAR* SM5 202 A8
PECK SE15 159 M6
New Farm Av *HAYES* BR2 205 M4
New Farm Dr *ABR/ST* RM4 83 M7
New Farm La *NTHWD* HA6 92 F9
New Ferry Ap *WOOL/PLUM* SE18 162 D2
New Fetter La *FLST/FETLN* EC4A 12 B5
Newfield Cl *HPTN* TW12 197 P1 5
Newfield La *HHNE* HP2 36 A6
Newfield Ri *CRICK* NW2 116 D8
Newfields *WGCW* AL8 22 E6
Newfield Wy *STALE/WH* AL4 39 J8 1
Newford Cl *HHNE* HP2 36 C5
New Ford Rd *CHES/WCR* EN8 62 E10
New Forest La *CHIG* IG7 102 D7
Newgale Gdns *EDGW* HA8 95 L9 1
New Garden Dr *WDR/YW* UB7 151 P1 3
Newgate *CROY/NA* CR0 203 K7 3
Newgate Cl *FELT* TW13 175 M5 1
STALE/WH AL4 39 J3
Newgate St *CHING* E4 101 K4 2
HERT/BAY SG13 42 E9
STBT EC1A 12 D5
Newgatestreet Rd *CHESW* EN7 61 J2

New - Nor 351

Newgate Street Village
HERT/BAY SG13 60 F1
New Goulston St WCHPL E1 13 L5 1
New Green Pl NRWD SE19 181 M9 2
New Greens Av STALW/RED AL3 38 C1
Newhall Cl HHS/BOV HP3 52 D3 2
New Hall Dr HARH RM3 105 M9
Newhall Gdns WOT/HER KT12 197 K9
Newham's Rw STHWK SE1 19 K2
Newham Wy CAN/RD E16 141 L7
Newhaven Cl HYS/HAR UB3 152 G3 3
Newhaven Crs ASHF TW15 174 E8
Newhaven Gdns ELTH/MOT SE9 162 A10
Newhaven La CAN/RD E16 141 M7
PLSTW E13 141 L7
Newhaven Rd SNWD SE25 203 L5
Newhaven Sp SLN SL2 128 G6 2
New Haw Rd ADL/WDHM KT15 215 M3
New Heston Rd HEST TW5 153 N6
Newhouse Av CHDH RM6 123 N1
Newhouse Cl NWMAL KT3 200 B7
Newhouse Crs GSTN WD25 55 J9
New House Farm La RGUW GU3 249 H9
Newhouse La CHONG CM5 49 K8
New House La GVW DA11 190 C6
REDH RH1 276 E8
New House Pk STAL AL1 38 F9
Newhouse Rd HHW HP1 52 D2
Newhouse Wk MRDN SM4 201 M7 5
Newick Cl BXLY DA5 186 C2
Newick Rd CLPT E5 120 A8
Newing Gn BMLY BR1 184 A10
Newington Barrow Wy
HOLWY N7 118 G8 5
Newington Butts LBTH SE11 18 D6
Newington Cswy STHWK SE1 18 E3
Newington Gn
STNW/STAM N16 119 L10 5
Newington Green Rd IS N1 6 G1
New Inn Broadway SDTCH EC2A 13 K1 1
New Inn La RGUE GU4 250 E7
New Inn Sq SDTCH EC2A 13 K1 2
New Inn St SDTCH EC2A 13 K1 3
New Inn Yd SDTCH EC2A 13 K1
New Kelvin Av TEDD TW11 176 D9
New Kent Rd STAL AL1 38 C6 5
STHWK SE1 18 E5
New King's Rd FUL/PGN SW6 157 K8
FUL/PGN SW6 157 J8
New King St DEPT SE8 160 F5
Newland Cl PIN HA5 93 M7
STAL AL1 38 F9
Newland Dr EN EN1 80 A5
Newland Gdns HNWL W7 154 F1 2
Newland Rd CEND/HSY/T N8 118 F1
Newlands Av RAD WD7 56 E10
THDIT KT7 198 D8
WOKS/MYFD GU22 232 C7
Newlands Cl ALP/SUD HA0 135 H1
EDGW HA8 95 K4
HORL RH6 280 A2
NWDGN UB2 153 M4 2
WOT/HER KT12 217 M1 1
Newlands Ct WBLY HA9 115 M7
Newlands Dr DTCH/LGLY SL3 151 H9
Newlands Pk CRAWE RH10 285 M2
SYD SE26 182 B9
Newlands Pl BAR EN5 76 G9
Newlands Rd CRAWW RH11 283 M8
HHW HP1 35 H5
STRHM/NOR SW16 202 F2
WFD IG8 101 L3
The Newlands WLGTN SM6 222 D4
Newland St CAN/RD E16 142 C10
Newlands Wk GSTN WD25 55 L9
Newlands Wy CHSGTN KT9 219 H2
POTB/CUF EN6 59 L6 1
New La RGUE GU4 232 C10
Newling Cl EHAM E6 142 C8
New Lodge Dr OXTED RH8 261 L4
New London St MON EC3R 13 K7 5
New Lydenburg St CHARL SE7 161 P2
Newlyn Cl LCOL/BKTW AL2 55 M6
UX/CGN UB8 132 B7
Newlyn Gdns RYLN/HDSTN HA2 113 N5 2
Newlyn Rd BAR EN5 77 J8 1
TOTM N17 99 N9
WELL DA16 163 J8
Newman Cl CRAWE RH10 284 D9 2
EMPK RM11 125 M3
Newman Rd BMLY BR1 205 M1 2
CROY/NA CR0 202 G7 3
HYS/HAR UB3 133 J9 1
PLSTW E13 141 N5
WALTH E17 120 C3 3
Newmans Dr RBRW/HUT CM13 107 P1
Newmans La LOU IG10 82 D7
Newman's Rd GVW DA11 190 C5
Newman's Rw LINN WC2A 11 P4
Newman St FITZ W1T 11 H4
Newman's Wy EBAR EN4 77 M6
Newmarket Av NTHLT UB5 113 P10
Newmarket Rd CRAWE RH10 284 B10
Newmarket Wy HCH RM12 125 M9
New Mile Rd ASC SL5 192 A2
New Mill Rd STMC/STPC BR5 207 M1
Newminster Rd MRDN SM4 201 M6
New Mount St SRTFD E15 141 J2 5
Newnham Av RSLP HA4 113 K6
Newnham Cl LOU IG10 82 A10
NTHLT UB5 134 B1
THHTH CR7 203 K2 1
Newnham Gdns NTHLT UB5 134 B1
Newnham Pl CDH/CHF RM16 168 D3 2
Newnham Rd WDGN N22 98 G9
Newnhams Cl BMLY BR1 206 C3
Newnham Ter STHWK SE1 18 A3
Newnham Wy
KTN/HRWW/W HA3 115 K3
New North Pl SDTCH EC2A 13 J1
New North Rd BARK/HLT IG6 102 G8
IS N1 7 H8 1
REIG RH2 275 J3
New North St BMSBY WC1N 11 N3
Newnton Cl FSBYPK N4 119 L5
New Oak Rd EFNCH N2 97 M10
New Oxford St NOXST/BSQ WC1A 11 L5
New Park Av PLMGR N13 99 M4
New Park Cl NTHLT UB5 133 M1
New Park Dr HHNE HP2 36 C5
New Park Est UED N18 100 B6 1
New Park Rd ASHF TW15 174 D8
BAL SW12 180 F4
BRXS/STRHM SW2 180 F3
DEN/HRF UB9 91 M9
HERT/BAY SG13 42 D10
New Peachey La UX/CGN UB8 131 N8
Newpiece LOU IG10 82 E7
New Place Gdns UPMR RM14 126 C7
New Plaistow Rd SRTFD E15 141 K3
New Pond Rd RGUW GU3 267 K8
RGUW GU3 267 N9
Newport Av POP/IOD E14 141 J9
Newport Cl PEND EN3 80 D3 2
Newport Md OXHEY WD19 93 L5 5
Newport Pl SOHO/SHAV W1D 11 K7 5
Newport Rd BARN SW13 156 D7
HTHAIR TW6 152 B7 1
SLN SL2 128 D6
WALTH E17 120 D2 5
WAN E11 121 J7
YEAD UB4 132 E7
Newports SBW CM21 29 M2
SWLY BR8 208 E7
Newport St LBTH SE11 17 N6
Newquay Crs RYLN/HDSTN HA2 113 M7
Newquay Gdns OXHEY WD19 93 J3
Newquay Rd CAT SE6 182 G5
New Quebec St MBLAR W1H 10 B6
New River Av WARE SG12 26 G7
New River Cl HOD EN11 44 G2
New River Crs PLMGR N13 99 J5
New River Wy FSBYPK N4 119 L5 1
New Rd ABR/ST RM4 83 N10
ABYW SE2 163 N3
ALP/SUD HA0 114 E9
AMS HP6 69 K3
AMSS HP7 68 E8
BERK HP4 33 L2
BERK HP4 34 A4
BROX EN10 44 E5
BRW CM14 107 J3
BTFD TW8 155 J4 5
CEND/HSY/T N8 118 E3
CHING E4 100 G5
CSTG HP8 70 B7
DAGW RM9 144 B3
DTCH/LGLY SL3 150 A7
DTCH/LGLY SL3 150 D2
E/WMO/HCT KT8 197 P3
EBED/NFELT TW14 174 E2
EBED/NFELT TW14 175 J4
ED N9 99 P4
ESH/CLAY KT10 218 B1
EYN DA4 210 B2
FELT TW13 175 M8
GDMY/SEVK IG3 123 H7
GRAYS RM17 167 M5
GSTN WD25 74 D5
GVW DA11 190 D2 5
HERT/WAS SG14 25 L3
HLWE CM17 29 N7
HORL RH6 281 J4
HSLW TW3 154 A10
HYS/HAR UB3 152 D6
KGLGY WD4 53 J6
KUTN/CMB KT2 177 M10
KWD/TDW/WH KT20 238 F9
MLHL NW7 97 H8
MTCM CR4 202 B8
ORP BR6 207 K7
OXTED RH8 261 N6
POTB/CUF EN6 58 D9
RAD WD7 57 M10
RAD WD7 74 D2
RAIN RM13 144 D5
RCHPK/HAM TW10 177 H7
RGUE GU4 251 P7
RGUE GU4 268 E7
RKW/CH/CXG WD3 71 J5
RKW/CH/CXG WD3 72 B9
RSEV TN14 245 N10
SHGR GU5 268 E9
SHGR GU5 269 N5
SHGR GU5 270 D5
SHPTN TW17 196 B3
STA TW18 172 F8
SWLY BR8 208 G3
UX/CGN UB8 132 D6
WARE SG12 26 D2
WAT WD17 73 K8
WCHPL E1 140 A7
WDGN N22 99 K9
WELL DA16 163 L8
WEY KT13 216 D2
WGCW AL8 22 D8
New Road Hl HAYES BR2 226 B5
New Rw CHCR WC2N 11 L7
Newry Rd TWK TW1 154 F10
Newsam Av SEVS/STOTM N15 119 L3
Newsham Rd WOKN/KNAP GU21 231 L3
Newsholme Dr WCHMH N21 78 G9
New Spring Gardens Wk
LBTH SE11 17 M8 1
New Sq LINN WC2A 11 P5
SL SL1 149 L1 3
Newstead HAT AL10 40 C7
Newstead Av ORP BR6 206 G10
Newstead Cl NFNCH/WDSP N12 97 P7 3
Newstead Hall HORL RH6 280 E5
Newstead Ri CTHM CR3 260 A2
Newstead Rd LEE/GVPK SE12 183 L3
Newstead Wk MRDN SM4 201 M7
Newstead Wy WIM/MER SW19 178 G7
New St BERK HP4 34 A5
BH/WHM TN16 262 F3
CRAWE RH10 284 B6
LVPST EC2M 13 K4
STA TW18 173 K7
WATW WD18 73 K8 10
New Street Hl BMLY BR1 183 N8
New Street Rd BGR/WK TN15 211 P10
New Street Sq FLST/FETLN EC4A 12 B5 5
FLST/FETLN EC4A 12 B5 3
FLST/FETLN EC4A 12 B5 5
New Swan Yd GVE DA12 190 E2 1
Newteswell Dr WAB EN9 63 J8
Newton Abbot Rd GVW DA11 190 C5
Newton Av ACT W3 155 P1
MUSWH N10 98 B9
Newton Cl DTCH/LGLY SL3 150 C1
HARP AL5 20 C5 5
HOD EN11 26 G9
RYLN/HDSTN HA2 113 N5
WALTH E17 120 D4 4
Newton Ct WDSR SL4 171 M2
Newton Crs BORE WD6 75 P8 2
Newton Dr SBW CM21 29 N2
Newton Gv CHSWK W4 156 B2
Newton La WDSR SL4 171 N2
Newton Rd ALP/SUD HA0 135 L2
BAY/PAD W2 8 F6
CRAWE RH10 284 A3
CRICK NW2 116 F9
ISLW TW7 154 E8
KTN/HRWW/W HA3 94 D9
PUR/KEN CR8 222 D8
SEVS/STOTM N15 119 N3
SRTFD E15 121 J10 5
TIL RM18 168 D8
WDR/YW UB7 151 P7
WELL DA16 163 K9
WIM/MER SW19 179 H10
Newtons Cl RAIN RM13 144 F2
Newton's Ct GRH DA9 166 C10
Newton St HOL/ALD WC2B 11 M5
Newton's Yd WAND/EARL SW18 179 K1 5
Newton Ter HAYES BR2 206 A6
Newton Wy UED N18 99 K6
Newton Wood Rd ASHTD KT21 237 L2
New Town CRAWE RH10 285 J2
Newtown Rd DEN/HRF UB9 131 L1
Newtown St BTSEA SW11 158 C7 5
New Trinity Rd EFNCH N2 117 M1
New Union Cl POP/IOD E14 161 H2
New Union St BARB EC2Y 12 G4
New Wanstead WAN E11 121 M4
New Way La HLWE CM17 30 E10
HLWE CM17 48 C2
New Way Rd CDALE/KGS NW9 116 B2
New Wharf Rd IS N1 5 M7
New Wickham La EGH TW20 172 D10
New Wd WGCE AL7 23 M4
Newyears Green La
DEN/HRF UB9 112 A4
New Years La RSEV TN14 227 K10
New Zealand Av WOT/HER KT12 196 G8
New Zealand Wy RAIN RM13 144 G5
Niagara Av EA W5 155 H3
Niagara Cl CHES/WCR EN8 62 C5 1
IS N1 6 F7
Nibthwaite Rd HRW HA1 114 D3
Nicholas Cl GFD/PVL UB6 134 A4 2
SOCK/AV RM15 147 H5
STALW/RED AL3 38 C3
WATN WD24 73 J3
Nicholas Gdns EA W5 135 J10
SL SL1 128 D10 5
WOKS/MYFD GU22 233 H2
Nicholas La HERT/WAS SG14 25 L5 11
MANHO EC4N 13 H7
Nicholas Rd BCTR RM8 124 A7
BORE WD6 75 L10
CROY/NA CR0 222 F1
WCHPL E1 140 B6
Nicholas Wy HHNE HP2 36 A4 1
NTHWD HA6 92 D9
Nicholay Rd ARCH N19 118 E6
Nicholes Rd HSLW TW3 153 P10 1
Nicholl La BMLY BR1 183 M10
Nicholl Rd EPP CM16 65 J7
Nicholls WDSR SL4 148 B9
Nicholls Av UX/CGN UB8 132 B6
Nicholls Fld HLWS CM18 47 L2
Nicholl St BETH E2 7 N6
Nichols Gn EA W5 135 K7
Nicholson Dr BUSH WD23 94 B2
Nicholson Rd CROY/NA CR0 203 N8
Nicholson St STHWK SE1 12 C10
Nicholson Wk EGH TW20 172 D8 5
Nickelby Cl THMD SE28 143 M8
Nickleby Cl UX/CGN UB8 132 C8 2
Nickleby Rd GVE DA12 191 K4
Nicky Line HHNE HP2 35 P6
Nicola Cl KTN/HRWW/W HA3 94 C10
SAND/SEL CR2 223 K3
Nicola Ms BARK/HLT IG6 102 E7 1
Nicoll Pl HDN NW4 116 E4 1
Nicoll Rd WLSDN NW10 136 B3
Nicoll Wy BORE WD6 76 A9
Nicol Rd CFSP/GDCR SL9 89 P9
Nicolson Rd STMC/STPC BR5 207 M7
Nicosia Rd WAND/EARL SW18 179 P3
Niederwald Rd SYD SE26 182 D7 2
Nield Rd HYS/HAR UB3 152 G1
Nigel Cl NTHLT UB5 133 M3 2
Nigel Fisher Wy CHSGTN KT9 219 J4
Nigel Ms IL IG1 122 E9
Nigel Playfair Av HMSMTH W6 156 E4
Nigel Rd FSTGT E7 121 P10
PECK SE15 159 P9
Nigeria Rd CHARL SE7 161 P6
Nightingale Av CHING E4 101 K6
EHSLY KT24 252 E1
UPMR RM14 126 E6
Nightingale Cl ABLGY WD5 55 H7 2
BH/WHM TN16 243 P1
CAR SM5 201 P10 5
CHING E4 101 K5 4
CHSWK W4 155 P5 2
COB KT11 217 L7
CRAWW RH11 283 M5
GVW DA11 190 B7 4
HOR/WEW KT19 219 M8 1
PIN HA5 113 K3
RAD WD7 74 E2
Nightingale Crs EHSLY KT24 252 E1
Nightingale Dr HOR/WEW KT19 219 N3
Nightingale Gv LEW SE13 183 J1
Nightingale La BAL SW12 180 A3
BMLY BR1 205 P2
CEND/HSY/T N8 118 F2
RCHPK/HAM TW10 177 K3
RSEV TN14 264 C6
STAL AL1 39 H10
STALE/WH AL4 39 H9
WAN E11 121 N3
Nightingale Pk SLN SL2 128 E2
Nightingale Pl
RKW/CH/CXG WD3 91 N1 2
WBPTN SW10 15 K9
WOOL/PLUM SE18 162 E5
Nightingale Rd BUSH WD23 73 P9
CAR SM5 202 A10
CHESW EN7 61 K1
CLPT E5 120 A8
CSHM HP5 50 G5 5
E/WMO/HCT KT8 198 A5
ED N9 100 B1
EHSLY KT24 252 G1
ESH/CLAY KT10 217 N2
GU GU1 250 A10
HNWL W7 134 E10
HPTN TW12 175 P9
RKW/CH/CXG WD3 91 M1
RSEV TN14 247 L3
SAND/SEL CR2 224 C7
STMC/STPC BR5 206 F6
WDGN N22 98 F9
WLSDN NW10 136 C4 4
WOT/HER KT12 197 K7 1
Nightingale Shott EGH TW20 172 C9
Nightingales La CSTG HP8 70 A9
Nightingale Sq BAL SW12 180 B3
The Nightingales
STWL/WRAY TW19 174 A4 4
Nightingale V WOOL/PLUM SE18 162 D5
Nightingale Wk BAL SW12 180 C2
Nightingale Wy DEN/HRF UB9 111 J4
EHAM E6 142 B7
REDH RH1 259 M10
SWLY BR8 208 F3
Nile Cl STNW/STAM N16 119 N8
Nile Rd PLSTW E13 141 P4 1
Nile St IS N1 6 G9
Nile Ter PECK SE15 19 M8
Nimbus Rd HOR/WEW KT19 220 A6
Nimrod Cl NTHLT UB5 133 L5 5
STALE/WH AL4 39 H4
Nimrod Pas HACK E8 7 K2 1
Nimrod Rd STRHM/NOR SW16 180 C9
Nina Mackay Cl SRTFD E15 141 K3 5
Nine Acres SL SL1 128 E10
Nine Acres Cl MNPK E12 122 B10
Nineacres Wy COUL/CHIP CR5 240 F2
Nine Elms Cl
EBED/NFELT TW14 174 G4 13
UX/CGN UB8 131 N7
Nine Elms Gv GVW DA11 190 D3
Nine Elms La VX/NE SW8 17 J10
Ninefields WAB EN9 63 L9
Ninehams Cl CTHM CR3 241 L6
Ninehams Gdns CTHM CR3 241 L6
Ninehams Rd BH/WHM TN16 244 A7
CTHM CR3 241 L7
Nine Stiles Cl DEN/HRF UB9 131 L1 1
Nineteenth Rd MTCM CR4 202 F4
Ninhams Wd ORP BR6 226 D1
Ninian Rd HHNE HP2 35 P1
Ninnings Rd CFSP/GDCR SL9 90 C8
Ninnings Wy CFSP/GDCR SL9 90 C8 5
Ninth Av HYS/HAR UB3 133 H9
Nita Rd BRW CM14 107 H6
Nithdale Rd WOOL/PLUM SE18 162 E6
Nithsdale Gv HGDN/ICK UB10 112 D8 4
Niton Cl BAR EN5 76 G10
Niton Rd RCH/KEW TW9 155 M9 5
Niton St FUL/PGN SW6 156 G6
Niven Cl BORE WD6 75 P5 5
CRAWE RH10 284 E8 6
Nixey Cl SL SL1 149 M1
Nizels La RTON TN11 265 N10
Noak Hill Rd HARH RM3 105 L4
Nobel Dr HYS/HAR UB3 152 F6
Nobel Rd UED N18 100 B5
Noble St CITYW EC2V 12 E5
Nobles Wy EGH TW20 172 B10
Noel Park Rd WDGN N22 99 H10 5
Noel Rd ACT W3 135 M8
EHAM E6 142 B6
IS N1 6 D7
Noel St SOHO/CST W1F 11 H6 5
Noke Dr REDH RH1 258 B9
Noke La LCOL/BKTW AL2 55 M2
Noke Side LCOL/BKTW AL2 55 P3 1
The Nokes HHW HP1 35 K4 5
Nolan Wy CLPT E5 119 P9
Nolton Pl EDGW HA8 95 L9
Nonsuch Cl CHIG IG7 102 E7
Nonsuch Court Av EW KT17 220 E6
Nonsuch Wk BELMT SM2 220 G6
The Nook WARE SG12 26 G7 2
Noons Corner Rd RDKG RH5 271 N9
Norbiton Av KUT KT1 199 M2
Norbiton Common Rd
NWMAL KT3 199 N3 1
Norbiton Rd POP/IOD E14 140 E8
Norbroke St ACT W3 136 C9
Norburn St NKENS W10 8 A4
Norbury Av HSLW TW3 176 C1
STRHM/NOR SW16 202 G1
WATN WD24 73 K5
Norbury Cl STRHM/NOR SW16 203 H1
Norbury Court Rd
STRHM/NOR SW16 202 F2
Norbury Crs STRHM/NOR SW16 203 H2
Norbury Cross
STRHM/NOR SW16 202 F3
Norbury Gdns CHDH RM6 123 N3
Norbury Gv MLHL NW7 96 B4
Norbury Hl STRHM/NOR SW16 181 H10
Norbury Ri STRHM/NOR SW16 202 F3
Norbury Rd CHING E4 100 F6
REIG RH2 257 J10
THHTH CR7 203 K2
Norbury Wy GT/LBKH KT23 254 B1
Norcombe Gdns
KTN/HRWW/W HA3 115 H4
Norcott Cl YEAD UB4 133 K6
Norcott Rd STNW/STAM N16 119 P7
Norcroft Gdns EDUL SE22 181 P3
Norcutt Rd WHTN TW2 176 D4
Nordenfeldt Rd ERITH DA8 164 E4 1
Nordmann Pl SOCK/AV RM15 147 J6 4
Norelands Dr SL SL1 128 B4
Norfield Rd RDART DA2 186 D7
Norfolk Av PLMGR N13 99 J7
SAND/SEL CR2 223 P6
SEVS/STOTM N15 119 N4
SL SL1 129 H7
WATN WD24 73 K4
Norfolk Cl DART DA1 187 P2
EBAR EN4 78 B8
EFNCH N2 117 P1 1
HORL RH6 280 B5
PLMGR N13 99 J7
TWK TW1 176 G2 5
Norfolk Crs BAY/PAD W2 9 N5
BFN/LL DA15 185 H3
Norfolk Farm Cl
WOKS/MYFD GU22 232 F1
Norfolk Farm Rd
WOKS/MYFD GU22 232 G1
Norfolk Gdns BORE WD6 76 A8
BXLYHN DA7 164 A7
Norfolk House Rd
STRHM/NOR SW16 180 E6
Norfolk La RDKG RH5 272 G8
Norfolk Pl BAY/PAD W2 9 M5
WELL DA16 163 K8
Norfolk Rd BAR EN5 77 K7
BARK IG11 143 H2
DAGE RM10 124 C10
DORK RH4 272 F2
EHAM E6 142 C3
ESH/CLAY KT10 218 D2 2
FELT TW13 175 K4
GDMY/SEVK IG3 123 H6
GVE DA12 190 G2
HRW HA1 114 A3
RKW/CH/CXG WD3 91 P2
ROMW/RG RM7 124 D4
STJWD NW8 3 M6
THHTH CR7 203 K3
UPMR RM14 125 P8
UX/CGN UB8 131 N1
WALTH E17 100 D9
WIM/MER SW19 179 P10
WLSDN NW10 136 B2 5
Norfolk Rw STHWK SE1 17 N5
Norfolk Sq BAY/PAD W2 9 M6
Norfolk Square Ms BAY/PAD W2 9 M6
Norfolk St FSTGT E7 121 M10 2
Norgrove Pk CFSP/GDCR SL9 110 B2
Norgrove St BAL SW12 180 B4
Norheads La BH/WHM TN16 243 P2
Norhyrst Av SNWD SE25 203 N3
Nork Gdns BNSTD SM7 221 H10
Nork Ri BNSTD SM7 238 G2
Nork Wy BNSTD SM7 238 E1
Norland Pl NTGHL W11 8 B10
Norland Rd NTGHL W11 136 G10
Norlands Crs CHST BR7 206 E1 1
Norlands La EGH TW20 195 H2
Norland Sq NTGHL W11 8 A10
Norley V PUT/ROE SW15 178 D4 4
Norlington Rd LEY E10 121 H6
Norman Av EW KT17 220 C8
FELT TW13 175 M5
SAND/SEL CR2 223 K6
STHL UB1 133 M9
TWK TW1 176 G3
WDGN N22 99 K9
Normanby Cl PUT/ROE SW15 179 J1
Normanby Rd WLSDN NW10 116 C10
Norman Cl ORP BR6 206 F10
ROMW/RG RM7 104 C10
RSEV TN14 247 L3
WAB EN9 63 J9
Norman Ct POTB/CUF EN6 59 N6
Norman Crs HEST TW5 153 L6
PIN HA5 93 K9
RBRW/HUT CM13 107 M4 5
Normand Ms WKENS W14 14 B9
Normand Rd WKENS W14 14 C9
Normandy Av BAR EN5 77 J9
Normandy Cl CRAWE RH10 284 C9 5
SYD SE26 182 D6 2
Normandy Ct HHNE HP2 36 A6
Normandy Dr BERK HP4 33 M4
HYS/HAR UB3 132 D8
Normandy Rd BRXN/ST SW9 159 H7
STALW/RED AL3 38 C5
Normandy Ter CAN/RD E16 141 N8
Normandy Wy ERITH DA8 164 F7
Norman Gv BOW E3 140 D4
Normanhurst RBRW/HUT CM13 87 P10 5
Normanhurst Av WELL DA16 163 N7
Normanhurst Cl CRAWE RH10 284 A7
Normanhurst Dr TWK TW1 176 G1 1
Normanhurst Rd
BRXS/STRHM SW2 180 C5 1
STMC/STPC BR5 207 L2
WOT/HER KT12 197 L9
Norman Rd ASHF TW15 174 E9
BELV DA17 144 C10
DART DA1 187 M4
EHAM E6 142 C6
EMPK RM11 125 H5
GNWCH SE10 160 G6
IL IG1 122 E10
SEVS/STOTM N15 119 N3 5
SUT SM1 221 K3
THHTH CR7 203 J5
WAN E11 121 K7
WIM/MER SW19 179 M10 1
Normans Cl GVW DA11 190 D3
UX/CGN UB8 131 P7
WLSDN NW10 136 A1
Normansfield Av
E/WMO/HCT KT8 177 H10
Normansfield Cl BUSH WD23 94 A1 1
Normanshire Dr CHING E4 100 F5
Normans Md WLSDN NW10 136 A1
Norman's Rd HORL RH6 281 K2
The Normans SLN SL2 129 N8
Norman St FSBYE EC1V 6 E10
RSEV TN14 263 P6
Normanton Av WIM/MER SW19 179 K5
Normanton Pk CHING E4 101 K4
Normanton Rd SAND/SEL CR2 223 M3
Normanton St FSTH SE23 182 C5
Norman Wy ACT W3 135 N7
STHGT/OAK N14 98 F3
Normington Cl
STRHM/NOR SW16 181 H8 2
Norrels Dr EHSLY KT24 252 G2
Norrels Ride EHSLY KT24 252 G2
Norrice Lea EFNCH N2 117 N3
Norris Gv BROX EN10 44 D6
Norris La HOD EN11 44 F2
Norris Ri HOD EN11 44 E2
Norris Rd HOD EN11 44 F3
STA TW18 173 J7 2
Norris St STJS SW1Y 11 J8 5
Norris Wy DART DA1 164 G9
Norroy Rd PUT/ROE SW15 156 G10
Norrys Cl EBAR EN4 78 A9
Norrys Rd EBAR EN4 78 A8
Norseman Cl GDMY/SEVK IG3 123 L6 2
Norseman Wy GFD/PVL UB6 134 A3 1
Norstead Pl PUT/ROE SW15 178 D5
Norsted La ORP BR6 227 L7
North Access Rd WALTH E17 120 C4
North Acre BNSTD SM7 239 J2
CDALE/KGS NW9 96 B9 5
North Acton Rd WLSDN NW10 136 A4
Northallerton Wy HARH RM3 105 L6
Northall Rd BXLYHN DA7 164 D8
Northampton Avevue SL SL1 129 H8
Northampton Gv IS N1 119 K10
Northampton Pk IS N1 6 F1
Northampton Rd CLKNW EC1R 12 B1
CROY/NA CR0 203 P9
PEND EN3 80 D8 2
Northampton Sq FSBYE EC1V 6 C10
Northampton St IS N1 6 E3
Northanger Rd
STRHM/NOR SW16 180 F9
North Ap GSTN WD25 55 H10
RKW/CH/CXG WD3 92 D3
North Ash Rd HART DA3 211 L10
North Audley St MYFR/PKLN W1K 10 C6
North Av CAR SM5 222 B4 1
HYS/HAR UB3 133 H9
RAD WD7 57 K8
RCH/KEW TW9 155 M7 2
RYLN/HDSTN HA2 114 A4
STHL UB1 133 N9
UED N18 99 P5 7
WEA W13 134 G8
WOT/HER KT12 216 F5
Northaw Cl HHNE HP2 36 C1
Northaw Rd West POTB/CUF EN6 60 B6
North Bank STJWD NW8 3 N10
Northbank Rd WALTH E17 101 H10
North Barn BROX EN10 44 G8
North Birkbeck Rd WAN E11 121 J8
Northborough Rd SLN SL2 128 F6
STRHM/NOR SW16 202 F2
Northbourne HAYES BR2 205 M7
RGODL GU7 267 L9
Northbourne Rd CLAP SW4 158 E10
North Bridge Rd BERK HP4 33 L3
Northbrook Dr NTHWD HA6 92 F9
Northbrook Rd BAR EN5 77 H10
CROY/NA CR0 203 L5
IL IG1 122 D7
LEW SE13 183 J1
WDGN N22 98 F7
Northbrooks HLWW/ROY CM19 46 E2
Northburgh St FSBYE EC1V 12 D2
North Burnham Cl SL SL1 128 A4 2
North Carriage Dr BAY/PAD W2 9 P7
Northchurch La CSHM HP5 33 H7
Northchurch Rd IS N1 6 G3
WBLY HA9 135 M1 1
North Circular Rd CHING E4 100 D7 1
CRICK NW2 116 B8
EFNCH N2 97 M10
GLDGN NW11 117 H2
PLMGR N13 99 H6
SWFD E18 121 P1
WALTH E17 100 G9
WLSDN NW10 116 A10
Northcliffe Cl WPK KT4 200 B10
Northcliffe Dr TRDG/WHET N20 97 J2
North Cl BAR EN5 76 F9
BXLYHS DA6 163 N10
CHIG IG7 103 K6
CRAWE RH10 284 A6
DAGE RM10 144 B3
EBED/NFELT TW14 174 E2
LCOL/BKTW AL2 56 A1
MRDN SM4 201 H4
RDKG RH5 273 H6
WDSR SL4 148 E7
North Colonnade POP/IOD E14 140 F10 1
North Common WEY KT13 216 D1 3
North Common Rd EA W5 135 K9
UX/CGN UB8 111 N10
Northcote ADL/WDHM KT15 215 N1
Northcote Av BRYLDS KT5 199 M7
EA W5 135 K9
ISLW TW7 176 F1
STHL UB1 133 M9
Northcote Crs EHSLY KT24 252 D1
Northcote Rd BTSEA SW11 157 P10
CROY/NA CR0 203 L6
EHSLY KT24 252 D1
GVW DA11 190 C4
NWMAL KT3 199 P3
SCUP DA14 185 H7
TWK TW1 176 F1
WALTH E17 120 D2
WLSDN NW10 136 B2 4
Northcott Av WDGN N22 98 F9
North Countess Rd WALTH E17 100 E10
Northcourt RKW/CH/CXG WD3 91 K2 4
North Cray Rd BXLY DA5 186 B5
SCUP DA14 185 P9
North Crs CAN/RD E16 141 J6
FITZ W1T 11 J3
FNCH N3 97 J10
Northcroft SLN SL2 128 G6
Northcroft Cl EGH TW20 171 N8
Northcroft Gdns EGH TW20 171 N8
Northcroft Rd EGH TW20 171 N8
HOR/WEW KT19 220 B4
WEA W13 154 G1
Northcroft Vls EGH TW20 171 N8
North Cross Rd BARK/HLT IG6 122 F2
EDUL SE22 181 N1
Northdene CHIG IG7 102 G6
North Dene HEST TW5 154 A7
MLHL NW7 96 A4
Northdene Gdns
SEVS/STOTM N15 119 N4
North Down SAND/SEL CR2 223 M7
Northdown Cl RSLP HA4 112 G8
Northdown Gdns
GNTH/NBYPK IG2 123 H3
Northdown La GU GU1 268 B3
Northdown Rd BELMT SM2 221 K6 4
CFSP/GDCR SL9 90 B7

EMPK RM11 125 J5
GDST RH9 260 F1
HART DA3 211 K2
HAT HL10 40 D7
RSEV TN14 247 M3
WELL DA16 163 L8
North Downs Crs CROY/NA CR0 224 G6
North Downs Rd CROY/NA CR0 224 G6
Northdown St IS N1 5 M7 □
North Downs Wy
  BRKHM/BTCW RH3 256 B6
  OXTED RH8 243 M9
  RDKG RH5 253 P10
  REDH RH1 258 E4
  RGUE GU4 268 D4
  SEV TN13 246 E4
North End CHOB/PIR GU24 230 B7
  GPK RM2 125 K1
  HSLW TW3 154 B8
  ORP BR6 227 H1
  RSLP HA4 112 C5
  STRHM/NOR SW16 180 D7
  VW GU25 193 K5
North End BKHH IG9 101 P1
  CROY/NA CR0 203 K9
  GLDGN NW11 117 K3
Northend HHS/BOV HP3 36 J5
  RBRW/HUT CM13 117 M7
North End Av HAMP NW3 117 M7
North End Crs WKENS W14 14 C6
North End La ASC SL5 192 F5
  ORP BR6 226 E5
North End Rd ERITH DA8 164 G7
North End Rd FUL/PGN SW6 157 K6 □
  GLDGN NW11 117 K6
  WBLY HA9 115 M8
  WKENS W14 14 C5
North End Wy HAMP NW3 117 M7
Northern Av ED N9 99 N3
Northernhay Wk MRDN SM4 201 H4 □
Northern Perimeter Road (West)
  HTHAIR TW6 151 P7
Northern Relief Rd BARK IG11 142 C2
Northern Rd SLN SL2 129 J6
Northey Av BELMT SM2 220 G6
North Eyot Gdns HMSMTH W6 156 C4 □
North Farm LOU IG10 81 P10
Northfield HART DA3 211 L3
  LTWR GU18 212 A7 □
  RGUE GU4 268 B8
Northfield Av PIN HA5 113 L2
  STMC/STPC BR5 207 M6
  WEA W13 134 C10
Northfield Cl BMLY BR1 206 B1 □
  HYS/HAR UB3 152 G2 □
Northfield Ct STA TW18 195 L1
Northfield Crs CHEAM SM3 221 H1 □
Northfield Gdns WATN WD24 73 K3
Northfield Pk HYS/HAR UB3 152 G2 □
Northfield Pl WEY KT13 216 C4 □
Northfield Rd BORE WD6 75 N5
  CHES/WCR EN8 62 D6
  COB KT11 217 H9
  DAGW RM9 124 A9
  EBAR EN4 77 P7
  EHAM E6 142 C1
North Field Rd HEST TW5 153 L5
Northfield Rd PEND EN3 80 A9 □
  STA TW18 195 L1
  STNW/STAM N16 115 M5
  WDSR SL4 148 B5
  WEA W13 134 C1
Northfields ASHTD KT21 237 K5 □
  EW KT17 220 B7
  GRAYS RM17 167 P3
  WAND/EARL SW18 157 K10
Northfields Rd ACT W3 135 P7
North Gdns WIM/MER SW19 179 N10
North Ga HLW CM20 28 F10 □
Northgate NTHWD HA6 92 D8
Northgate Av CRAWE RH10 284 A6
Northgate Dr CDALE/KGS NW9 116 B4 □
Northgate Pth BORE WD6 75 L4 □
Northgate Pl CRAWE RH10 283 P6 □
Northgate Rd CRAWW RH11 283 N7 □
North Gower St CAMTN NW1 4 C10
North Gn SL SL1 129 K9
North Gv CHERT KT16 195 J6
  HGT N6 118 B5
  HLWS CM18 47 K2
  SEVS/STOTM N15 119 L3
North Hatton Rd HTHAIR TW6 152 E7
North Hl HGT N6 118 A4
  RKW/CH/CXG WD3 71 H4
North Hill Av HGT N6 118 B4 □
North Hill Dr HARH RM3 105 L5
North Hyde Gdns HYS/HAR UB3 153 H3
North Hyde La NWDGN UB2 153 M4
North Hyde Rd HYS/HAR UB3 152 F3
Northiam NFNCH/WDSP N12 97 K5 □
Northiam St HACK E8 140 A3
Northington St
  WAND/EARL SW18 179 M1 □
Northspur Rd SUT SM1 201 K10
North Sq GLDGN NW11 117 K3 □
North Station Ap REDH RH1 276 G2 □
Northstead Rd
  BRXS/STRHM SW2 181 H5
North St BARK IG11 142 H1
  BMLY BR1 205 M1
  BXLYHN DA7 164 B10
  CAR SM5 222 A1
  CRAWE RH10 285 P9
  DART DA1 187 L3
  DORK RH4 272 F2
  EGH TW20 172 C8
  EMPK RM11 128 L5
  CU GU1 268 A2
  GVE DA12 190 E5 □
  HDN NW4 116 F3
  ISLW TW7 154 F9
  LHD/OX KT22 236 F3
  PLSTW E13 141 N4
  REDH RH1 258 A4
  RGODL GU7 267 K10
  ROMW/RG RM7 124 C3
  VX/NE SW8 158 C9
  WAB EN9 45 J3
North Tenter St WCHPL E1 13 M6
North Ter CHEL SW3 15 N5
Northumberland Aly TWRH EC3N 13 K6 □
Northumberland Av CHCR WC2N 11 J1
  EMPK RM11 125 K3
  EN EN1 80 A7
  ISLW TW7 154 E7
  MNPK E12 121 P6
  WELL DA16 163 H10
Northumberland Cl ERITH DA8 164 D6 □
  STWL/WRAY TW19 173 J2
Northumberland Crs
  EBED/NFELT TW14 174 F2
Northumberland Gdns
  BMLY BR1 206 D4
  ED N9 99 N4 □
  MTCM CR4 202 E5 □
Northumberland Gv TOTM N17 100 A8
Northumberland Pk TOTM N17 99 P8
Northumberland Pl BAY/PAD W2 8 F1
Northumberland Rd BAR EN5 77 M10
  EHAM E6 142 B8
  MEO DA13 190 C10
  RYLN/HDSTN HA2 113 J3
  SLH/COR SS17 169 J1
  WALTH E17 120 F5
Northumberland Wy BXLYHN DA7 164 D10
Northumbria St POP/IOD E14 140 F8
North Verbena Gdns
  HMSMTH W6 156 D4 □
North Vw EA W5 135 H6
  PIN HA5 113 K5
Northview SWLY BR8 208 F2
North Vw WIM/MER SW19 178 E8
North View Av TIL RM18 168 D7
North View Crs EPSOM KT18 238 F5
Northview Crs WLSDN NW10 116 C9 □
Northview Dr WFD IG8 102 A10
North View Rd CEND/HSY/T N8 118 L1
  SEV TN13 247 K7
North Vis CAMTN NW1 5 J2
North Wy CDALE/KGS NW9 115 N1
  ED N9 100 B3
  FBAR/BDGN N11 98 B3
  HGDN/ICK UB10 131 P2
  PIN HA5 113 K1
Northway GLDGN NW11 117 L3 □
  GUW GU2 249 M8
  RGODL GU7 266 G10
  RKW/CH/CXG WD3 91 N1
  RYNPK SW20 201 H3
  WGCE AL7 23 J2 □
  WLGTN SM6 222 D1
Northway Crs MLHL NW7 96 C10 □
Northway Rd CMBW SE5 158 K9
  CROY/NA CR0 203 N6
North Weald La KUTN/CMB KT2 177 H8
  WATN WD24 72 C1
North Western Av GSTN WD25 73 H1
  WATN WD24 72 C1
North Western Avenue Colne Wy
  WATN WD24 73 K2 □
North Western Avenue Elton Wy
  GSTN WD25 74 A6
North Western Avenue Gade Side
  KGLGY WD4 72 D1
  WAT WD17 72 E1
North Western Avenue
  Otterspool Wy GSTN WD25 73 N1
North Western Avenue
  (Tylers Way) BUSH WD23 74 B3
North Western Avenue
  (Watford By-pass) STAN HA7 74 F10
North Wharf Rd BAY/PAD W2 9 L4
Northwick Av HRW HA1 114 F4
Northwick Cir
  KTN/HRWW/W HA3 115 H4
Northwick Cl STJWD NW8 9 L1 □
Northwick Park Rd HRW HA1 114 F4
Northwick Rd ALP/SUD HA0 135 J2 □
  OXHEY WD19 93 K5
Northwick Ter STJWD NW8 9 L1
Northwold Dr PIN HA5 113 K1 □
Northwold Rd STNW/STAM N16 119 N7
Northwood CDH/CHF RM16 168 E3 □
  WGCE AL7 23 N5 □
Northwood Av HCH RM12 125 J9
  PUR/KEN CR8 223 H9
  WOKN/KNAP GU21 231 J5
Northwood Cl CHESW EN7 61 N3 □
Northwood Gdns CLAY IG5 122 G3
  GFD/PVL UB6 114 E10
  NFNCH/WDSP N12 97 N6
Northwood Pl ERITH DA18 164 A2 □
Northwood Rd CAR SM5 222 D4
  DEN/HRF UB9 91 P9

EA W5 155 J2
EBED/NFELT TW14 174 F2
ED N9 100 A2
EDGW HA8 95 N9
EFNCH N2 97 P9
GDMY/SEVK IG3 123 N7
HERT/WAS SG14 25 K5
HEST TW5 153 K5
HGT N6 118 B5
HOD EN11 44 F2
HOLWY N7 5 L1
HYS/HAR UB3 132 E7
PUR RM19 166 B3
RCH/KEW TW9 155 M8
REIG RH2 275 J3
RKW/CH/CXG WD3 70 G3
SOCK/AV RM15 147 J2
STHL UB1 133 P9
SURB KT6 199 J6
TOOT SW17 179 N9 □
WDR/YW UB7 152 A2
WIM/MER SW19 179 M9
WOKN/KNAP GU21 232 B1
WOOL/PLUM SE18 163 H5
WOT/HER KT12 217 K2
WWKM BR4 204 G8 □
North Worple Wy
  MORT/ESHN SW14 156 A7
Nortoft Rd CFSP/GDCR SL9 90 C7
Norton Av BRYLDS KT5 199 N7
Norton Cl BORE WD6 75 M5
  CHING E4 101 N6
  RGUW GU3 249 J2
Norton Gdns STRHM/NOR SW16 202 F2
Norton Pk ASC SL5 192 B5
Norton Rd ALP/SUD HA0 135 J1
  DAGE RM10 144 E1
  LEY E10 120 E6
  UX/CGN UB8 131 N5
Norval Rd ALP/SUD HA0 114 G7
Norway Dr SLN SL2 129 N7
Norway Ga BERM/RHTH SE16 160 D2
Norway Pl POP/IOD E14 140 E8 □
Norway St GNWCH SE10 160 G5 □
Norwich Pl BXLYHS DA6 164 B10
Norwich Rd CRAWE RH10 284 B9
  FSTGT E7 121 M10
  GFD/PVL UB6 134 A3
  PIN HA5 112 G1
  THHTH CR7 203 K3
Norwich St FLST/FETLN EC4A 12 A1
Norwich Wk EDGW HA8 96 P8
Norwich Wy RKW/CH/CXG WD3 72 C7
Norwood Av ALP/SUD HA0 135 L3
  ROMW/RG RM7 124 C5
Norwood Cl EHSLY KT24 253 M4
  HERT/WAS SG14 24 G4
  NWDGN UB2 153 P3
  WHTN TW2 176 C5
Norwood Crs HTHAIR TW6 152 E7
Norwood Dr RYLN/HDSTN HA2 113 N4
Norwood Farm La COB KT11 217 H5
Norwood Gdns NWDGN UB2 153 N3 □
  YEAD UB4 133 H3
Norwood Green Rd NWDGN UB2 153 P3
Norwood Hl HORL RH6 278 C4
Norwoodhill Rd HORL RH6 279 H3
Norwood La IVER SL0 130 G2
Norwood Park Rd WNWD SE27 181 K8
Norwood Rd CHES/WCR EN8 62 D6
  EHSLY KT24 253 M4
  HNHL SE24 181 J4
  NWDGN UB2 153 M2
Notley End EDUL SE22 171 P10 □
Notley St CMBW SE5 159 L6 □
Notson Rd SNWD SE25 204 A4
Notting Barn Rd NKENS W10 136 G4
Nottingham Av CAN/RD E16 141 P7
Nottingham Cl GSTN WD25 55 H9 □
  WOKN/KNAP GU21 231 L4
Nottingham Pl MHST W1U 10 L2
Nottingham Rd ISLW TW7 154 E8 □
  LEY E10 121 H4
  RKW/CH/CXG WD3 90 F2
  SAND/SEL CR2 223 J5
  TOOT SW17 180 A4
Nottingham St MHST W1U 10 C3
Nova Ms MRDN SM4 201 H7 □
Novar Cl ORP BR6 207 J2
Nova Rd CROY/NA CR0 203 J8
Novar Rd ELTH/MOT SE9 184 F4
Novello St FUL/PGN SW6 157 K6
Novello Wy BORE WD6 76 A5
Nowell Rd BARN SW13 156 D5
Nower Hl PIN HA5 113 N2
Nower Rd DORK RH4 272 F2
The Nower RSEV TN14 245 J6
Noyna Rd TOOT SW17 180 A6
Nuding Cl LEW SE13 160 F9
Nuffield Rd SWLY BR8 187 H9
Nugent Rd ARCH N19 118 F6 □
  SNWD SE25 203 N3
Nugent's Pk PIN HA5 93 N9
Nugent Ter STJWD NW8 2 F3
Nunappleton Wy OXTED RH8 261 M8 □
Nuneaton Rd DAGW RM9 143 N2
Nunhead Gv PECK SE15 160 A9
Nunhead La PECK SE15 160 A10
Nunnery Cl STAL AL1 38 D8
Nunnery Stables STAL AL1 38 C8 □
Nunnington Cl ELTH/MOT SE9 184 H6
Nunn's Rd ENC/FH EN2 79 K6
Nuns Wy GRAYS RM17 168 A3
Nunsbury Dr BROX EN10 62 D1 □
Nuns La STAL AL1 38 D10
Nuns Wk VW GU25 194 A5
Nupton Dr BAR EN5 76 H10
Nurseries Rd STALE/WH AL4 21 K4
Nursery Av BXLYHN DA7 164 A10
  CROY/NA CR0 204 C9
  FNCH N3 97 L10
Nursery Cl ADL/WDHM KT15 215 J6
  AMSS HP7 69 K5
  BROCKY SE4 160 B8
  CHDH RM6 123 N4
  CROY/NA CR0 204 C9
  EBED/NFELT TW14 175 J3 □
  EW KT17 220 B6
  KWD/TDW/WH KT20 256 E1
  ORP BR6 207 J2
  PEND EN3 80 C5
  RDART DA2 188 B3
  SEV TN13 247 K8
  SOCK/AV RM15 147 N6
  SWLY BR8 208 D2 □
  WFD IG8 101 N6
  WOKN/KNAP GU21 231 L2
Nursery Flds SBW CM21 23 N1
Nursery Gdns CHST BR7 184 C6
  HSLWW TW4 175 N1 □
  PEND EN3 80 C5
  RGUE GU4 268 G6
  STA TW18 173 L10
  SUN TW16 196 C2
  WGCE AL7 23 H7 □
Nursery Hl WGCE AL7 23 J2 □
Nurserylands CRAWW RH11 283 K7
Nursery La BETH E2 7 L6 □
  DTCH/LGLY SL3 129 P10
  FSTGT E7 141 M1
  HORL RH6 279 N5
  NKENS W10 135 P6 □
Nurserymans Rd FBAR/BDGN N11 98 B3
Nursery Pl SEV TN13 247 J8 □
Nursery Rd BROX EN10 62 D1 □
  BRXN/ST SW9 158 C10 □
  EFNCH N2 97 H5
  HOD EN11 26 C10
  HOM E9 140 B1 □
  KWD/TDW/WH KT20 256 E1
  LOU IG10 82 A2
  MDHD SL6 128 A3 □
  MTCM CR4 201 P4
  PIN HA5 113 K1
  RGODL GU7 267 L10
  STHGT/OAK N14 98 C2
  SUN TW16 196 C2
  SUT SM1 221 M1 □
  THHTH CR7 203 L4
  WAB EN9 45 J4
  WIM/MER SW19 179 H10
  WOKN/KNAP GU21 231 J3
Nursery Rw BAR EN5 76 C3 □
  WALW SE17 19 K6
Nursery St TOTM N17 100 B5
The Nursery ERITH DA8 164 G6 □
Nursery Wk HDN NW4 116 E3

FSTH SE23 182 E4
HGT N6 118 C5
HTHAIR TW6 151 N7 □
THHTH CR7 203 K2
North Woolwich Rd CAN/RD E16 141 N10
Nursery Wy STWL/WRAY TW19 172 A2
Nursery Waye UX/CGN UB8 131 N3
Nurstead Rd ERITH DA8 164 B6
Nutberry Av CDH/CHF RM16 167 M1
Nutberry Cl CDH/CHF RM16 167 M1 □
Nutbourne St NKENS W10 2 A9
Nutbrook St PECK SE15 159 N9
Nutbrowne Rd DAGW RM9 144 A3
Nutcombe La DORK RH4 272 E1
Nutcroft Gv LHD/OX KT22 236 D5
Nutcroft Rd PECK SE15 160 A6
Nutfield WGCE AL7 23 K2
Nutfield Cl CAR SM5 201 P10
  UED N18 99 P7
Nutfield Gdns GDMY/SEVK IG3 123 N1
  NTHLT UB5 133 K4
Nutfield Marsh Rd REDH RH1 258 E7
Nutfield Rd COUL/CHIP CR5 240 C3
  CRICK NW2 116 D7
  EDUL SE22 181 N1
  REDH RH1 258 C10
  SRTFD E15 121 H9
  THHTH CR7 203 J4
Nutfield Wy ORP BR6 206 D9
Nutford Pl BAY/PAD W2 9 P5
Nut Gv WGCW AL8 22 G2
Nuthatch HART DA3 211 N3
Nuthatch Gdns REIG RH2 275 M4
  THMD SE28 162 G1
Nuthurst Av BRXS/STRHM SW2 180 C5
Nuthurst Cl CRAWW RH11 283 K6
Nutkins Wy CSHM HP5 51 K5
Nutley Cl SWLY BR8 208 C1
Nutley La REIG RH2 275 H3
Nutley Ter HAMP NW3 3 K1
Nutmead Cl BXLY DA5 186 D4
Nutmeg Cl CAN/RD E16 141 K6 □
Nutmeg La POP/IOD E14 141 J8
Nuttall St IS N1 7 K7
Nutter La WAN E11 121 P3
Nuttfield Cl RKW/CH/CXG WD3 72 C10 □
Nutt Gv EDGW HA8 95 J3
Nut Tree Cl ORP BR6 207 N10
Nutt St PECK SE15 159 N6
Nutty La SHPTN TW17 196 C2
Nutwell St TOOT SW17 179 P8
Nutwood Av BRKHM/BTCW RH3 273 P1
Nutwood Cl BRKHM/BTCW RH3 273 P1
Nuxley Rd BELV DA17 164 A5
Nyanza St WOOL/PLUM SE18 162 G5
Nyefield Pk KWD/TDW/WH KT20 256 D2
Nye Wy HHS/BOV HP3 52 D4
Nylands Av RCH/KEW TW9 155 M8
Nymans Ct CRAWE RH10 284 C10 □
Nymans Gdns RYNPK SW20 200 E3 □
Nynehead St NWCR SE14 160 D6
Nyon Gv FSTH SE23 182 C1
Nyssa Cl WFD IG8 102 C7 □
Nyth Cl UPMR RM14 126 C4

O

Oakapple Cl SAND/SEL CR2 224 A10 □
Oak Av CEND/HSY/T N8 118 F2
  CHOB/PIR GU24 230 F7
  CROY/NA CR0 204 F9
  EGH TW20 172 F10
  ENC/FH EN2 78 G5
  HEST TW5 153 L6
  HGDN/ICK UB10 112 C7
  HPTN TW12 175 M8
  LCOL/BKTW AL2 55 P6
  MUSWH N10 98 C8
  SEV TN13 265 J4
  TOTM N17 99 L8
  UPMR RM14 126 A8
  WDR/YW UB7 152 B2
Oakbank LHD/OX KT22 236 B9
  WOKS/MYFD GU22 232 B5
Oakbank Av WOT/HER KT12 197 N7
Oakbank Gv HNHL SE24 159 K10
Oakbrook Cl BMLY BR1 183 N7
Oakbury Rd FUL/PGN SW6 157 L8 □
Oak Cl CRAWE RH10 284 C2
  DART DA1 164 F10
  HHS/BOV HP3 36 A10
  KWD/TDW/WH KT20 255 N6
  RGODL GU7 267 K9
  STHGT/OAK N14 98 C1
  WAB EN9 63 J10
Oakcombe Cl NWMAL KT3 200 B1 □
Oak Cottage Cl CAT SE6 183 L4 □
Oak Crs CAN/RD E16 141 K7
Oakcroft Cl BF/WBF KT14 215 J10 □
  PIN HA5 93 J10 □
Oakcroft Rd BF/WBF KT14 215 J10
  BKHTH/KID SE3 161 L2
  CHSGTN KT9 219 L1
Oakcroft Vis CHSGTN KT9 219 L1 □
Oakdale STHGT/OAK N14 98 C2
  WGCW AL8 22 G2
Oakdale Av KTN/HRWW/W HA3 115 K3
  NTHWD HA6 93 H10
Oakdale Cl OXHEY WD19 93 K5
Oakdale Gdns CHING E4 101 H6
Oakdale La EDEN TN8 262 G5
Oakdale Rd FSBYPK N4 119 K4
  FSTGT E7 141 N2
  HOR/WEW KT19 220 A5
  OXHEY WD19 93 K4
  PECK SE15 160 B9
  STRHM/NOR SW16 180 F8
  SWFD E18 101 N10
  WAN E11 121 J5
  WEY KT13 196 B10 □
Oakdene ASC SL5 192 E6
  CHES/WCR EN8 62 D6
  CHOB/PIR GU24 213 L6
  KWD/TDW/WH KT20 239 H6
Oakdene Av CHST BR7 184 D8
  ERITH DA8 164 D5
  THDIT KT7 198 B8 □
Oakdene Cl BRKHM/BTCW RH3 273 P2
  GT/LBKH KT23 254 B5
  PIN HA5 93 N8
Oak Dene Cl ROM RM1 125 J4 □
Oakdene Dr BRYLDS KT5 199 P8
Oakdene Ms CHEAM SM3 201 J8
Oakdene Pk FNCH N3 97 J8
Oakdene Rd BRKHM/BTCW RH3 273 P1
  COB KT11 217 J10
  GT/LBKH KT23 235 N10 □
  HGDN/ICK UB10 132 C4
  HHS/BOV HP3 36 A10
  REDH RH1 258 A10
  RGUE GU4 267 P3
  SEV TN13 247 N8
  STMC/STPC BR5 207 K6
  WATN WD24 73 J2
Oakdene Wy STAL AL1 39 N6
Oakden St LBTH SE11 18 E6
Oak Dr BERK HP4 34 A6
  KWD/TDW/WH KT20 255 N6
  SBW CM21 29 M3
Oaken Coppice ASHTD KT21 237 M5 □
Oak End HLWS CM18 47 J3
Oak End Dr IVER SL0 130 G3
Oaken Dr ESH/CLAY KT10 218 C3
Oak End La ADL/WDHM KT15 215 H4
  CFSP/GDCR SL9 110 C3
Oaken Gv WGCE AL7 23 H8 □
Oaken La ESH/CLAY KT10 218 A3

Oakenshaw Cl SURB KT6 199 K7 □
Oakeshott Av HGT N6 118 B7
Oak Farm BORE WD6 75 N9
Oakfield CHING E4 100 C6 □
  WOKN/KNAP GU21 231 K1
Oakfield Av KTN/HRWW/W HA3 114 E2
  SL SL1 128 G10 □
Oakfield Cl NWMAL KT3 200 C5
  POTB/CUF EN6 59 J7
  WEY KT13 216 D1
Oakfield Dr REIG RH2 257 K8
Oakfield Gdns BECK BR3 204 F5
  CAR SM5 201 P8 □
  GFD/PVL UB6 134 C6
  UED N18 99 K6
Oakfield Gld WEY KT13 216 D1 □
Oakfield La DART DA1 187 L5
  HAYES BR2 225 P1
  RDART DA2 187 L5
Oakfield Pl DART DA1 187 L5
Oakfield Rd ASHF TW15 174 C8
  ASHTD KT21 237 K4
  COB KT11 217 J9
  CROY/NA CR0 203 K3
  EHAM E6 142 B3
  FNCH N3 97 L9
  FSBYPK N4 119 H4
  IL IG1 122 E8
  PGE/AN SE20 182 A10
  STHGT/OAK N14 98 F3
  WALTH E17 100 C10 □
  WIM/MER SW19 178 G6
Oakfields BF/WBF KT14 215 L10
  CRAWE RH10 286 C2
  GUW GU2 249 K8
  SEV TN13 265 J2
  WOT/HER KT12 197 H8
Oakfields Rd GLDGN NW11 117 H4
Oakfield St WBPTN SW10 15 J9
Oakford Rd KTTN NW5 118 D9
Oak Gdns CROY/NA CR0 204 F9
  EDGW HA8 95 P10 □
Oak Gld EPP CM16 65 N5
  NTHWD HA6 92 C9
Oak Gln EMPK RM11 125 M1
Oak Grange Rd RGUE GU4 251 L5
Oak Gv CRICK NW2 116 C9
  HAT AL10 40 C4
  HERT/BAY SG13 25 M7
  RSLP HA4 113 J6
  SUN TW16 175 J10
  WWKM BR4 205 H9
Oak Grove Rd PGE/AN SE20 204 B1
Oakhall Dr SUN TW16 176 C6
Oak Hall Rd WAN E11 121 H4
Oakham Cl CAT SE6 182 E5 □
Oakham Dr HAYES BR2 205 M4
Oakhampton Rd MLHL NW7 96 E7
Oakhaven CRAWE RH10 285 N9 □
Oak HI EPSOM KT18 238 A2
Oakhill ESH/CLAY KT10 218 F3
Oak HI RGUE GU4 250 F6
  RGUW GU3 248 F8
  SURB KT6 199 K7
  WFD IG8 101 J8
Oakhill Av HAMP NW3 117 L9
  PIN HA5 93 M1
Oakhill Cl ASHTD KT21 237 H4
  RKW/CH/CXG WD3 91 H5
Oak Hill Crs SURB KT6 199 K7 □
  WFD IG8 101 J8
Oak Hill Gdns WALTH E17 101 K9
Oakhill Gdns WEY KT13 196 C6
Oak Hill Gv SURB KT6 199 K7
Oak Hill Pk HAMP NW3 117 L9
Oak Hill Park Ms HAMP NW3 117 M9
Oakhill Pl PUT/ROE SW15 179 K1 □
Oakhill Rd ADL/WDHM KT15 215 J3
  ASHTD KT21 237 H4
  BECK BR3 205 H2
  ORP BR6 207 K6
  PUR RM19 166 A4
  PUT/ROE SW15 179 J1
  REIG RH2 275 L1
  RKW/CH/CXG WD3 90 C5
Oak Hill Rd SEV TN13 265 H1
  STRHM/NOR SW16 202 F1
Oak Hill Rd SURB KT6 199 K6 □
  SUT SM1 201 L10
Oak Hill Wy HAMP NW3 117 L9
Oakhouse Rd BXLYHS DA6 186 B1
Oakhurst CHOB/PIR GU24 213 K5
Oakhurst Av BXLYHN DA7 163 P6
  EBAR EN4 97 P1
Oakhurst Cl BARK/HLT IG6 102 F9
  TEDD TW11 176 B8 □
  WALTH E17 121 K2
Oakhurst Gdns BXLYHN DA7 163 P6
  CHING E4 101 L2
  WALTH E17 121 K2
Oakhurst Gv EDUL SE22 159 P10
Oakhurst Pl CHST BR7 206 C1 □
Oakhurst Ri CAR SM5 221 P6
Oakhurst Rd HOR/WEW KT19 219 P5
  PEND EN3 80 C2
Oakington WGCE AL7 23 N5 □
Oakington Av AMS HP6 70 B5
  HYS/HAR UB3 152 E3
  RYLN/HDSTN HA2 113 P5
  WBLY HA9 115 L8
Oakington Dr SUN TW16 197 K2
Oakington Manor Dr WBLY HA9 115 M10
Oakington Rd MV/WKIL W9 8 F1
Oakington Wy CEND/HSY/T N8 118 F5 □
Oakland Gdns RBRW/HUT CM13 87 P9
Oakland Pl BKHH IG9 102 G6
Oakland Rd SRTFD E15 121 K9
Oaklands BERK HP4 33 M5
  HORL RH6 280 D4
  LHD/OX KT22 236 C10
  NTHGT N13 98 G3
  PUR/KEN CR8 223 K10
Oaklands Av BFN/LL DA15 185 J3
  BRKMPK AL9 59 H3
  ED N9 80 A1
  ESH/CLAY KT10 198 C5
  ISLW TW7 154 E5
  OXHEY WD19 93 J2
  ROM RM1 124 F1
  THHTH CR7 203 H4
  WWKM BR4 204 G10
Oaklands Cl ALP/SUD HA0 115 J10
  BXLYHS DA6 186 A1
  CHSGTN KT9 219 H1
  RGUE GU4 268 B1
  STMC/STPC BR5 206 F1
Oaklands Ct ADL/WDHM KT15 195 H10
  WAT WD17 75 H5 □
Oaklands Dr HLWE CM17 47 M2
  REDH RH1 276 C2
  SOCK/AV RM15 147 P8
Oaklands Gdns PUR/KEN CR8 223 K10 □
Oaklands Ga NTHWD HA6 92 F7 □
Oaklands Gv BROX EN10 44 D10
  SHB W12 136 D10
Oaklands La BAR EN5 76 H7
  BH/WHM TN16 243 P1
  STALE/WH AL4 39 L4
Oaklands Ms CRICK NW2 116 C9 □
Oaklands Park Av IL IG1 122 F7
Oaklands Pl CLAP SW4 158 E10 □
Oaklands Rd BMLY BR1 183 K10
  BXLYHS DA6 164 A10

CHESW EN7 61 M2
CRICK NW2 116 G9
GVW DA11 190 C7
HNWL W7 154 E1
MORT/ESHN SW14 156 A9
RDART DA2 188 A4
TRDG/WHET N20 97 J1
Oaklands Wy
KWD/TDW/WH KT20 238 F8
WLGTN SM6 222 D4
Oakland Wy HOR/WEW KT19 220 A3
Oak La EFNCH N2 97 N10
EGH TW20 171 P6
FBAR/BDGN N11 98 E7
ISLW TW7 154 D10
POP/IOD E14 140 E9
POTB/CUF EN6 60 G4
SEV TN13 264 G5
TWK TW1 176 F3 5
WDSR SL4 148 F7
WFD IG8 101 L5
WOKS/MYFD GU22 232 E5
Oaklawn Rd LHD/OX KT22 236 E2
Oak Leaf Cl HOR/WEW KT19 219 P8 1
Oakleafe Gdns CLAY IG5 122 E1
Oakleigh Av EDGW HA8 95 N10
SURB KT6 199 M8
TRDG/WHET N20 97 N2
Oakleigh Cl SWLY BR8 208 F3
TRDG/WHET N20 98 A4
Oakleigh Ct EDGW HA8 95 P10 2
Oakleigh Crs TRDG/WHET N20 97 P4
Oakleigh Dr RKW/CH/CXG WD3 72 D10
Oakleigh Gdns EDGW HA8 95 L6
ORP BR6 227 H1
TRDG/WHET N20 97 M2
Oakleigh Park Av CHST BR7 206 D2
Oakleigh Pk North
TRDG/WHET N20 97 N2
Oakleigh Pk South
TRDG/WHET N20 97 P2
Oakleigh Rd HGDN/ICK UB10 132 D2
PIN HA5 93 N7
Oakleigh Rd North
TRDG/WHET N20 97 N3
Oakleigh Rd South
FBAR/BDGN N11 98 B5
Oakleigh Wy MTCM CR4 202 C1
SURB KT6 199 N8 2
Oakley Av ACT W3 135 M9
BARK IG11 143 J1
CROY/NA CR0 222 F1
Oakley Cl ADL/WDHM KT15 215 N1
CHING E4 101 H4 5
HNWL W7 134 D9
ISLW TW7 154 C7
WTHK RM20 167 H5
Oakley Crs FSBYE EC1V 6 D8 1
SL SL1 129 K9
Oakley Dell RGUE GU4 250 F8
Oakley Dr BFN/LL DA15 184 G5
ELTH/MOT SE9 184 G4
HARH RM3 105 P6
HAYES BR2 206 B10
LEW SE13 183 J2
Oakley Gdns BNSTD SM7 239 L1
CEND/HSY/T N8 118 G3 2
CHEL SW3 15 P9
Oakley Green Rd WDSR SL4 148 A6 1
Oakley Pk BFN/LL DA15 185 M3
Oakley Pl STHWK SE1 19 L8
Oakley Rd HARP AL5 20 C4
HAYES BR2 206 B10
HRW HA1 114 D4
IS N1 6 G3
SNWD SE25 204 A5
WARL CR6 241 P4
Oakley Sq CAMTN NW1 5 H7
Oakley St CHEL SW3 15 N9
Oak Lodge Av CHIG IG7 102 G6
Oak Lodge Cl STAN HA7 95 H6 5
WOT/HER KT12 217 K2
Oak Lodge Dr REDH RH1 276 B8
WWKM BR4 204 G7
Oak Lodge La BH/WHM TN16 262 G1
Oak Md RGODL GU7 267 J9
Oakmead Av HAYES BR2 205 M6
Oakmeade PIN HA5 93 P7
Oakmead Gdns EDGW HA8 96 A5
Oakmead Gn EPSOM KT18 237 P1
Oakmead Pl MTCM CR4 201 P1
Oakmead Rd BAL SW12 180 C4
CROY/NA CR0 202 E6
Oakmere Av POTB/CUF EN6 59 M9
Oakmere Cl POTB/CUF EN6 59 N7
Oakmere La POTB/CUF EN6 59 M8
Oakmere Rd ABYW SE2 163 K5
Oakmoor Wy CHIG IG7 103 H6
Oakmore Gdns STMC/STPC BR5 207 M4
Oak Pk BF/WBF KT14 215 H9
Oak Park Gdns WIM/MER SW19 178 G4
Oak Piece EPP CM16 66 D1
Oakridge CHOB/PIR GU24 212 E9
Oak Rdg DORK RH4 272 G5
Oakridge LCOL/BKTW AL2 55 N5
Oakridge Av RAD WD7 56 E9
Oakridge Dr EFNCH N2 117 N1
Oakridge La GSTN WD25 56 D10
Oakridge Rd BMLY BR1 183 K7
Oak Ri BKHH IG9 102 A4
Oak Rd BH/WHM TN16 262 G1
COB KT11 235 L1
CRAWW RH11 283 M8
CTHM CR3 241 M8
EA W5 135 J9
EPP CM16 65 J6
ERITH DA8 164 D6
GRAYS RM17 167 P5
GRH DA9 188 D2
GVE DA12 190 E6
HARH RM3 105 N9
LHD/OX KT22 236 F5
NWMAL KT3 200 A2
ORP BR6 227 K4
REIG RH2 257 L9
Oak Rw MTCM CR4 202 D2
Oakroyd Av POTB/CUF EN6 59 J9
Oakroyd Cl POTB/CUF EN6 59 J10
Oaks Av CRW RM5 104 D10
FELT TW13 175 M5
NRWD SE19 181 M8
WPK KT4 220 E1
Oaks Cl LHD/OX KT22 236 F7
RAD WD7 74 E1
Oaksford Av SYD SE26 182 A6
Oaks Gv CHING E4 101 K3
Oakshade Rd BMLY BR1 183 J7
LHD/OX KT22 218 B10
Oakshaw OXTED RH8 261 J3
Oakshaw Rd WAND/EARL SW18 179 L3
Oakside DEN/HRF UB9 131 L1
Oakside Ct HORL RH6 280 D3 10
Oakside La HORL RH6 280 D3
Oaks La CROY/NA CR0 204 B10
GNTH/NBYPK IG2 123 H2
RDKG RH5 272 G8
Oaks Rd CROY/NA CR0 224 A2
PUR/KEN CR8 223 J10
REIG RH2 257 N9
STWL/WRAY TW19 173 N1
WOKN/KNAP GU21 232 B3
The Oaks BERK HP4 33 M5
BF/WBF KT14 215 K10
EPSOM KT18 220 B10
NFNCH/WDSP N12 97 L5
OXHEY WD19 93 K2
RSLP HA4 112 E5
SURB KT6 199 H10 1
SWLY BR8 208 F2
WFD IG8 101 K8
WOOL/PLUM SE18 162 F4
YEAD UB4 132 D4 2
Oaks Tr CAR SM5 222 B6
Oak St HHS/BOV HP3 36 A10
ROMW/RG RM7 124 D3
Oaks Wy CAR SM5 222 A4
EPSOM KT18 238 E5
PUR/KEN CR8 223 K10
SURB KT6 199 J9
Oakthorpe Rd PLMGR N13 99 H6
Oak Tree Avenue GRH DA9 188 E3
Oaktree Av PLMGR N13 99 H4
Oak Tree Cl ABLGY WD5 54 E8
HAT AL10 40 D3
HERT/BAY SG13 26 B8
LOU IG10 82 F5
Oaktree Cl RBRW/HUT CM13 107 L4 5
Oak Tree Cl RGUE GU4 249 P4
RGUE GU4 250 F5
STAN HA7 95 H8 2
VW GU25 194 A6
WEA W13 135 H8 3
WOKN/KNAP GU21 230 G4
Oak Tree Ct BORE WD6 75 J10 4
Oak Tree Dell CDALE/KGS NW9 115 P3
Oak Tree Dr EGH TW20 171 P8
GU GU1 249 P6
TRDG/WHET N20 97 L2
Oak Tree Gdns BMLY BR1 183 N8
Oaktree Garth WGCE AL7 23 H6 4
Oaktree Gv IL IG1 122 G10
Oak Tree Rd STJWD NW8 3 M10
WOKN/KNAP GU21 230 G4
Oakview Cl CHESW EN7 62 A4
Oakview Gdns EFNCH N2 117 N2 1
Oakview Gv CROY/NA CR0 204 D8
Oakview Rd CAT SE6 182 G8
Oak Village HAMP NW3 118 B9 4
HAMP NW3 118 B9 4
KTTN NW5 118 B9
Oak Wy ACT W3 136 B10
REIG RH2 275 N1
ASHTD KT21 237 M2
STHGT/OAK N14 98 B1
CRAWE RH10 283 P5
CROY/NA CR0 204 C6
EBED/NFELT TW14 174 F4
Oakway AMS HP6 68 G1
CDH/CHF RM16 147 N10
HAYES BR2 205 J2
RYNPK SW20 200 F4
WOKN/KNAP GU21 231 K5
Oakway Cl BXLY DA5 185 P2
Oakways ELTH/MOT SE9 184 E2
Oakwell Dr POTB/CUF EN6 60 C9
Oak Wd BERK HP4 33 L6
Oakwood GUW GU2 249 M5 4
WLGTN SM6 222 C5
Oakwood Av BECK BR3 205 H2
BORE WD6 75 N8
HAYES BR2 205 N3 1
MTCM CR4 201 N2
PUR/KEN CR8 223 J8
STHGT/OAK N14 98 E1
STHL UB1 133 P9
Oakwood Cha EMPK RM11 125 N5
Oakwood Cl CHST BR7 184 C9
DART DA1 188 A4
EHSLY KT24 252 F3
REDH RH1 258 B10
REDH RH1 276 G2 2
STHGT/OAK N14 78 D10
WFD IG8 102 B7 5
Oakwood Ct CHOB/PIR GU24 230 F2
WKENS W14 14 C3
Oakwood Crs GFD/PVL UB6 134 F1
WCHMH N21 78 F10
Oakwood Dr BXLYHN DA7 164 D10
EDGW HA8 95 P7
EHSLY KT24 252 F3
NRWD SE19 181 L9
STALE/WH AL4 39 H5
Oakwood Gdns GDMY/SEVK IG3 123 J7
ORP BR6 206 F9
SUT SM1 201 K9 3
WOKN/KNAP GU21 230 F4
Oakwood Hl LOU IG10 82 D10
Oakwood Hill Industrial Est
LOU IG10 82 E9
Oakwood La WKENS W14 14 C3
Oakwood Park Rd
STHGT/OAK N14 78 F10
Oakwood Pl CROY/NA CR0 203 H6
Oakwood Ri CTHM CR3 259 M1
HART DA3 211 K3
Oakwood Rd BFOR GU20 212 D3
CROY/NA CR0 203 H6 4
GLDGN NW11 117 K3
HORL RH6 280 B3
LCOL/BKTW AL2 55 N5
ORP BR6 206 F9
PIN HA5 93 J10
REDH RH1 259 H5
RYNPK SW20 200 D1
VW GU25 193 P5
WOKN/KNAP GU21 231 K5
Oakworth Rd NKENS W10 136 F7
Oarsman Pl E/WMO/HCT KT8 198 D4 1
Oast House Cl STWL/WRAY TW19 172 B3
Oast House Wy STMC/STPC BR5 207 L4
Oast Rd OXTED RH8 261 L7
Oast Wy HART DA3 211 K6
Oates Cl HAYES BR2 205 J3
Oates Rd CRW RM5 104 C6
Oatfield Rd KWD/TDW/WH KT20 238 E7
ORP BR6 207 J8
Oatland Ri WALTH E17 100 D10
Oatlands CRAWW RH11 283 N3
HORL RH6 280 C3 15
Oatlands Av WEY KT13 216 E2
Oatlands Cha WEY KT13 196 F10
Oatlands Cl WEY KT13 216 D1
Oatlands Dr SL SL1 129 J8
WEY KT13 196 E10
Oatlands Gn WEY KT13 196 E10 5
Oatlands Mere WEY KT13 196 E10
Oatlands Rd KWD/TDW/WH KT20 239 H5
PEND EN3 80 B5
Oat La CITYW EC2V 12 E5
Oban Cl PLSTW E13 141 P6
Oban Ct SL SL1 149 J1
Oban Rd PLSTW E13 141 P5 2
SNWD SE25 203 L4 3
Oban St POP/IOD E14 141 J8
Oberon Cl BORE WD6 75 P5
Oberon Wy CRAWW RH11 283 H10 4
SHPTN TW17 195 P3
Oberstein Rd BTSEA SW11 157 N10 3
Oborne Cl HNHL SE24 181 J1 4
Observatory Gdns KENS W8 14 E1
Observatory Rd
MORT/ESHN SW14 155 P10
Occam Rd GUW GU2 249 J10
Occupation La EA W5 155 J3
WOOL/PLUM SE18 162 E7
Occupation Rd WALW SE17 18 E7
WATW WD18 73 J9
WEA W13 154 G1 4
Ocean St WCHPL E1 140 C7 2
Ockenden Cl WOKS/MYFD GU22 232 C4 5
Ockenden Gdns
WOKS/MYFD GU22 232 C5
Ockenden Rd WOKS/MYFD GU22 232 C4
Ockendon Rd IS N1 6 G2
UPMR RM14 146 C1
Ockham Dr EHSLY KT24 234 E10
STMC/STPC BR5 185 K10 1
Ockham La COB KT11 235 H4
RPLY/SEND GU23 234 D6
Ockham Rd North
RPLY/SEND GU23 234 C8
Ockham Rd South EHSLY KT24 252 F5 2
Ockley Ct RGUE GU4 250 E5 3
Ockley Rd CROY/NA CR0 202 G7
STRHM/NOR SW16 180 F6
Ockleys Md GDST RH9 260 B5
Octagon Rd WOT/HER KT12 216 F6
Octavia Cl MTCM CR4 201 P5
Octavia Ct WATN WD24 73 K6 1
Octavia Rd ISLW TW7 154 E9
Octavia St BTSEA SW11 157 P7
Octavia Wy STA TW18 173 K9
Octavius St DEPT SE8 160 F6 4
Odard Rd E/WMO/HCT KT8 197 P4
Odencroft Rd SLN SL2 128 F5
Odessa Rd FSTGT E7 121 L9
WLSDN NW10 136 D4
Odessa St BERM/RHTH SE16 160 E2
Odessey Rd BORE WD6 75 N5
Odger St BTSEA SW11 158 A8
Offa Rd STALW/RED AL3 38 B6
Offa's Md HOM E9 120 E9 1
Offas Wy STALE/WH AL4 21 J3
Offenham Rd ELTH/MOT SE9 184 C7
Offerton Rd CLAP SW4 158 D9
Offham Slope NFNCH/WDSP N12 97 J6
Offley Rd BRXN/ST SW9 159 H6
Offord Cl TOTM N17 99 P8
Offord Rd IS N1 5 P3
Offord St HOLWY N7 5 N3
Off Upper Manor Rd RGODL GU7 267 K10
Ogard Rd HOD EN11 45 H1
Ogilby St WOOL/PLUM SE18 162 C3
Oglander Rd PECK SE15 159 N10
Ogle St GTPST W1W 10 G3
Oglethorpe Rd DAGE RM10 124 B8 2
Ohio Rd PLSTW E13 141 L6
Oil Mill La HMSMTH W6 156 D4 4
Okeburn Rd TOOT SW17 180 B8 3
Okehampton Crs WELL DA16 163 L7
Okehampton Rd WLSDN NW10 136 F3
Okehampton Sq HARH RM3 105 K7 2
Olaf St NTGHL W11 136 G9
Old Acre BF/WBF KT14 215 K10
Oldacre CHOB/PIR GU24 212 E8
Old Amersham Rd
CFSP/GDCR SL9 110 E6
Old Av BF/WBF KT14 215 H10
WEY KT13 216 D4
Old Avenue Cl WOKN/KNAP GU21 215 H9
Old Bailey STP EC4M 12 D6
Old Barn Cl BELMT SM2 221 H4
BGR/WK TN15 247 P3
Old Barn La CTHM CR3 241 N2
RKW/CH/CXG WD3 72 A9
Old Barn Rd EPSOM KT18 237 P3
Old Barn Wy BXLYHN DA7 164 E10
Old Barrack Yd KTBR SW1X 16 C1
Oldberry Rd EDGW HA8 96 A7
Old Bethnal Green Rd BETH E2 7 P9
Old Bexley La BXLY DA5 186 E5
Old Bond St CONDST W1S 10 G8
Oldborough Rd ALP/SUD HA0 115 H7
Old Brewery Ms HAMP NW3 117 N9 5
Old Bridge Cl NTHLT UB5 133 P4
Old Bridge St KUT KT1 199 J2
Old Brighton Rd South
CRAWE RH10 283 P1
Old Broad St LVPST EC2M 13 J5
Old Bromley Rd BMLY BR1 183 J8
Old Brompton Rd ECT SW5 14 F8
Old Buildings LINN WC2A 12 A5
Old Burlington St CONDST W1S 10 G7
Oldbury Cl STMC/STPC BR5 207 N4
Oldbury Gv BEAC HP9 88 C6
Oldbury Pl MHST W1U 10 D2
Oldbury Rd CHERT KT16 195 H7
EN EN1 79 P6
The Old Carriageway SEV TN13 246 D9
Old Castle St WCHPL E1 13 L5
Old Cavendish St CAVSQ/HST W1G 10 E5
Old Chapel Rd SWLY BR8 208 D7
Old Charlton Rd SHPTN TW17 196 D5
Old Chertsey Rd CHOB/PIR GU24 213 N6
Old Chestnut Av ESH/CLAY KT10 217 P3
Old Church La CDALE/KGS NW9 115 P7
GFD/PVL UB6 134 F5 1
STAN HA7 94 G7
Old Church Pth ESH/CLAY KT10 218 A1 2
Oldchurch Ri ROMW/RG RM7 124 F5 1
Old Church Rd CHING E4 100 F4
Oldchurch Rd ROMW/RG RM7 124 F4
Old Church Rd WCHPL E1 140 C8 12
Old Church St CHEL SW3 15 M9
Old Claygate La ESH/CLAY KT10 218 F3
The Old Coach Rd HERT/WAS SG14 24 A8
Old Common Rd COB KT11 217 J8
Old Compton St SOHO/SHAV W1D 11 J7 5
Old Cote Dr HEST TW5 153 P5
Old Ct ASHTD KT21 237 K5
Old Court Pl KENS W8 14 G1
Old Court Rd GUW GU2 267 M1
The Old Ctyd BMLY BR1 205 N1 1
Old Crabtree La HHS/BOV HP3 35 P7
Old Cross HERT/WAS SG14 25 K5 6
Old Cross B158 HERT/WAS SG14 25 K5 7
Old Crown La BRW CM14 86 C6
Old Dartford Rd EYN DA4 209 N6
Old Dean HHS/BOV HP3 52 D4
Old Deer Park Gdns
RCH/KEW TW9 155 K9
Old Devonshire Rd BAL SW12 180 C3
Old Dock Cl RCH/KEW TW9 155 M5 1
Old Dover Rd BKHTH/KID SE3 161 M6
Old Downs HART DA3 211 K5
The Old Dr WGCW AL8 22 E6
Olden La PUR/KEN CR8 223 H8
Old Esher Cl WOT/HER KT12 217 L2 1
Old Esher Rd WOT/HER KT12 217 L2 2
Old Farleigh Rd SAND/SEL CR2 224 B6
WARL CR6 242 E1
Old Farm Av BFN/LL DA15 184 G4
STHGT/OAK N14 98 D1
Old Farm Cl BEAC HP9 88 B6
HSLWW TW4 153 N10
Old Farm Gdns SWLY BR8 208 G3 3
Old Farmhouse Dr LHD/OX KT22 236 C1
Old Farm Rd EFNCH N2 97 N9
GU GU1 250 A7
HPTN TW12 175 N9
WDR/YW UB7 151 N1
Old Farm Rd East BFN/LL DA15 185 K5
Old Farm Rd West BFN/LL DA15 185 J5
Old Ferry Dr STWL/WRAY TW19 171 P2
Old Field Cl AMS HP6 70 B5
Oldfield Cl BMLY BR1 206 C4
NTHLT UB5 114 D10 1
STAN HA7 94 F6
Oldfield Farm Gdns
GFD/PVL UB6 134 C3
Oldfield Gdns ASHTD KT21 237 J5
Oldfield Gv DEPT SE8 160 C3
Oldfield La GFD/PVL UB6 114 D10 2
Oldfield La North GFD/PVL UB6 134 C1
Oldfield La South GFD/PVL UB6 134 B5
Oldfield Ms HGT N6 118 D5 1
Oldfield Rd BMLY BR1 206 C4
BXLYHN DA7 163 P8
HHW HP1 35 H7
HORL RH6 280 A6
HPTN TW12 197 P1
LCOL/BKTW AL2 57 J1
SHB W12 156 C1 4
STNW/STAM N16 119 M8
WIM/MER SW19 179 H9
WLSDN NW10 136 C2
Oldfields Circ NTHLT UB5 134 B1 1
Oldfields Rd CHEAM SM3 201 K9
Oldfieldwood WOKS/MYFD GU22 232 E3
Old Fishery La HHW HP1 35 J8
Old Fish Street Hl BLKFR EC4V 12 E7 2
Old Fives Ct SL SL1 128 B5 4
Old Fleet La STP EC4M 12 C5
Old Fold Cl BAR EN5 77 J5 2
Old Fold La BAR EN5 77 J5
Old Fold Vw BAR EN5 76 F7
Old Ford Rd BETH E2 140 B4
BOW E3 140 E3
Old Forge Cl GSTN WD25 55 H9
STAN HA7 94 F5
WGCE AL7 23 J1
Old Forge Crs SHPTN TW17 196 C6 3
Old Forge Rd EN EN1 79 N4
Old Forge Wy SCUP DA14 185 L7
Old Fox Cl CTHM CR3 241 J7
Old French Horn La HAT AL10 40 E3
Old Gannon Cl NTHWD HA6 92 D5
The Old Gdn SEV TN13 246 E9
Old Gloucester St BMSBY WC1N 11 M3
Old Hall Cl PIN HA5 93 M9
Old Hall Dr PIN HA5 93 M9
Old Hall Ri HLWE CM17 47 P1
Oldhall St HERT/WAS SG14 25 L5 12
Oldham Ter ACT W3 135 P10
Old Harpenden Rd
STALW/RED AL3 38 D2
Old Herns La WGCE AL7 23 M3
Old Hertford Rd BRKMPK AL9 40 F2
Old Hwy HOD EN11 44 C1
Old Hl CHST BR7 206 D1
ORP BR6 227 H3
WOKS/MYFD GU22 232 A6
Oldhill St STNW/STAM N16 119 P6
Old Hollow CRAWE RH10 284 G5
Old Homesdale Rd HAYES BR2 205 P4 2
Old Horsham Rd CRAWW RH11 283 L9
Old Hospital Cl TOOT SW17 180 A4 1
Old House Cl EW KT17 220 C6
WIM/MER SW19 179 H8 2
Oldhouse Cft HLW CM20 29 H9
Oldhouse La CHOB/PIR GU24 212 F10
CHOB/PIR GU24 212 B5
Old House La HLWW/ROY CM19 46 A4
KGLGY WD4 72 B1
Old House Rd HHNE HP2 36 A6
Old Howlett's La RSLP HA4 112 E4 2
Oldings Cnr HAT AL10 22 E10
Old Jamaica Rd BERM/RHTH SE16 19 N3
Old James St PECK SE15 160 A9
Old Jewry LOTH EC2R 12 G5 3
Old Kenton La CDALE/KGS NW9 115 N3
Old Kent Rd PECK SE15 160 A5
STHWK SE1 19 P9
Old Kiln La BRKHM/BTCW RH3 255 P10
Old Kingston Rd WPK KT4 199 P10
Old La BH/WHM TN16 244 A7
COB KT11 234 E5
OXTED RH8 261 L6
Old Lane Gdns COB KT11 234 G8
Old Leys HAT AL10 40 D8
Old Lodge Dr BEAC HP9 88 C10
Old Lodge La PUR/KEN CR8 222 G9
Old Lodge Wy STAN HA7 94 F6
Old London Rd EPSOM KT18 238 D4
HERT/BAY SG13 25 M5
RDKG RH5 255 H4
RSEV TN14 228 B6
RSEV TN14 245 P1
STAL AL1 38 D7
Old Maidstone Rd SCUP DA14 186 A10
Old Malden La WPK KT4 200 B9
Old Malt Wy WOKN/KNAP GU21 232 A3
Old Manor Cl CRAWW RH11 283 K5
Old Manor Dr ISLW TW7 176 B2
Old Manor Gdns RGUE GU4 268 F6
Old Manor Wy BXLYHN DA7 164 E8
ELTH/MOT SE9 184 C8
Old Martyrs CRAWW RH11 283 N4 6
Old Marylebone Rd CAMTN NW1 9 P4
Old Md CFSP/GDCR SL9 90 B7
Old Merrow St RGUE GU4 250 F7
Old Mill Cl EYN DA4 209 M8
Old Mill Ct SWFD E18 121 P1
Old Mill Gdns BERK HP4 34 A5
Old Mill La REDH RH1 258 C4
UX/CGN UB8 131 L7
Old Mill Rd DEN/HRF UB9 111 K8
KGLGY WD4 54 D10
WOOL/PLUM SE18 162 C5
Old Montague St WCHPL E1 13 N4
Old Nazeing Rd BROX EN10 44 F7
WAB EN9 45 H8
Old Nichol St BETH E2 13 L1
Old North St FSBYW WC1X 11 N3 1
Old Nursery Ct SLN SL2 109 H7
Old Nursery Pl ASHF TW15 174 C8
Old Oak STAL AL1 38 D9
Old Oak Av COUL/CHIP CR5 239 P5
Old Oak Common La ACT W3 136 C8 2
ACT W3 136 C9 2
WLSDN NW10 136 B6
Old Oak La WLSDN NW10 136 C5
Old Oak Rd ACT W3 136 C9
Old Oaks WAB EN9 63 K8 3
Old Orch BF/WBF KT14 216 A8
HLWS CM18 46 G3
LCOL/BKTW AL2 56 C2
SUN TW16 197 K2
Old Orchard Cl UX/CGN UB8 132 B8
Old Orchard Ms BERK HP4 33 P6 1
Old Orchards CRAWE RH10 284 F7
The Old Orch HAMP NW3 118 A9 3
Old Otford Rd RSEV TN14 247 J4
Old Palace Rd CROY/NA CR0 203 K10
GUW GU2 267 M1
WEY KT13 196 C10
Old Palace Yd RCH/KEW TW9 177 H1
Old Paradise St LBTH SE11 17 N5
Old Park Av BAL SW12 180 B2
ENC/FH EN2 79 K8
Old Parkbury La LCOL/BKTW AL2 56 E5
Old Park Gv WCHMH N21 79 K8
Old Park La MYFR/PICC W1J 10 D10
Old Park Ms HEST TW5 153 N6
Oldpark Ride CHESW EN7 61 L8
Old Park Ridings WCHMH N21 79 J10
Old Park Rd ABYW SE2 163 K4
ENC/FH EN2 79 J7
PLMGR N13 98 G5
Old Park Rd South ENC/FH EN2 79 J8
Old Park Vw ENC/FH EN2 79 H7
Old Parvis Rd BF/WBF KT14 215 N8
Old Perry St CHST BR7 185 H10
GVW DA11 190 B5
Old Portsmouth Rd RGUW GU3 267 P6
Old Pottery Cl REIG RH2 275 L2
Old Pound Cl ISLW TW7 154 F7
Old Priory DEN/HRF UB9 112 C5
Old Pye St WEST SW1P 17 J3
Old Quebec St MBLAR W1H 10 B6
Old Queen St STJSPK SW1H 17 K2
Old Rectory Cl
KWD/TDW/WH KT20 238 D10
Old Rectory Dr HAT AL10 40 E4 1
Old Rectory Gdns EDGW HA8 95 M7
STALE/WH AL4 21 J2
Old Rectory La DEN/HRF UB9 111 H5
EHSLY KT24 252 F2
Old Rectory Rd CHONG CM5 67 J9
Old Redding KTN/HRWW/W HA3 94 A6
Old Redstone Dr REDH RH1 276 B1 1
Old Reigate Rd
BRKHM/BTCW RH3 255 P10
DORK RH4 255 K10
Oldridge Rd BAL SW12 180 B3
Old Rd ABR/ST RM4 85 L6
ADL/WDHM KT15 215 J4
BRKHM/BTCW RH3 256 C9
DART DA1 164 E10
HLWE CM17 29 M5
LEW SE13 161 K10
PEND EN3 80 B5
Old Rd East GVE DA12 190 G4
Old Rd West GVW DA11 190 C4
Old Royal Free Sq IS N1 6 B6
Old Ruislip Rd NTHLT UB5 133 L4 5
Old's Ap WATW WD18 92 D2
Old Sax La CSHM HP5 50 C3
Old School Cl BECK BR3 204 C2
Old School Ct STWL/WRAY TW19 172 B3
Old School Crs FSTGT E7 141 M1 1
Old School La BRKHM/BTCW RH3 273 M3
Old School Ms WEY KT13 216 E1
Old School Pl WOKS/MYFD GU22 232 B7
Old Schools La EW KT17 220 C5
Old's Cl WATW WD18 92 C2
Old Seacoal La STP EC4M 12 C6 5
Old Shire La CFSP/GDCR SL9 90 E4
RKW/CH/CXG WD3 70 D10
WAB EN9 63 M10
Old Shire Lane Circular Wk
RKW/CH/CXG WD3 90 F1
Old Slade La IVER SL0 151 J3
Old Sopwell Gdns STAL AL1 38 D8
Old South Cl PIN HA5 93 L9
Old Sq LINN WC2A 11 P5
Old Station Ap LHD/OX KT22 236 F7
Old Station La STWL/WRAY TW19 172 C2
Old Station Rd HYS/HAR UB3 152 G2 3
LOU IG10 82 B9
Oldstead Rd BMLY BR1 183 J7
Old St FSBYE EC1V 12 E1
IS N1 7 K10
PLSTW E13 141 P4
Old Swan Yd CAR SM5 222 A1
Old Town CLAP SW4 158 D9
CROY/NA CR0 203 J10
Old Tramyard WOOL/PLUM SE18 163 H3 4
Old Tye Av BH/WHM TN16 244 B2
Old Uxbridge Rd
RKW/CH/CXG WD3 91 J10
The Old Wk RSEV TN14 247 J3
Old Watford Rd LCOL/BKTW AL2 55 M6
Oldway La SL SL1 128 C10
Old Westhall Cl WARL CR6 242 B5
Old Woking Rd BF/WBF KT14 215 K9
WOKS/MYFD GU22 215 J10
WOKS/MYFD GU22 232 E4
Old Woolwich Rd GNWCH SE10 161 J5 2
The Old Yews HART DA3 211 N3
Old York Rd WAND/EARL SW18 179 L1 5
Oleander Cl ORP BR6 226 G2
Olga St BOW E3 140 D4
Olinda Rd STNW/STAM N16 119 N4
Oliphant St NKENS W10 2 A9
Oliver Av SNWD SE25 203 N3
Oliver Cl ADL/WDHM KT15 215 L1
CHSWK W4 155 N5
HHS/BOV HP3 35 P10
LCOL/BKTW AL2 56 C3
WTHK RM20 166 E6
Oliver Crs EYN DA4 209 N7
Oliver Gdns EHAM E6 142 B7
Oliver Gv SNWD SE25 203 N4
Olive Rd CRICK NW2 116 F9
DART DA1 187 L4
EA W5 155 J2
PLSTW E13 141 P5
WIM/MER SW19 179 M10 2
Oliver Ri HHS/BOV HP3 35 P10
Oliver Rd ASC SL5 192 A4
BRWN CM15 87 M9
HHS/BOV HP3 36 A10
LEY E10 120 G7
NWMAL KT3 199 P2
RAIN RM13 144 G3
SUT SM1 221 N1
SWLY BR8 208 E3
WALTH E17 121 H3
WTHK RM20 166 E7
Olivers Cl BERK HP4 34 F2
Oliver's Yd STLK EC1Y 13 H1
Olive St ROMW/RG RM7 124 E3
Olivia Gdns DEN/HRF UB9 91 M9
Olivier Rd CRAWE RH10 284 E8
Ollard's Gv LOU IG10 82 A8
Olleberrie La RKW/CH/CXG WD3 53 H8
Ollerton Gn BOW E3 140 E3
Ollerton Rd FBAR/BDGN N11 98 E6
Olley Cl WLGTN SM6 222 F4
Ollgar Cl ACT W3 136 C10
Olliffe St POP/IOD E14 161 H2 5
Olmar St STHWK SE1 19 N9
Olney Rd WALW SE17 18 D10
Olron Crs BXLYHS DA6 185 N1
Olven Rd WOOL/PLUM SE18 162 F6
Olveston Wk MRDN SM4 201 N6 3
Olwen Ms PIN HA5 93 L10
Olyffe Av WELL DA16 163 K8
Olyffe Dr BECK BR3 205 H1
Olympia Wy WKENS W14 14 B4
Olympic Wy GFD/PVL UB6 134 A3
WBLY HA9 115 M9
Oman Av CRICK NW2 116 F10
O'meara St STHWK SE1 12 F10 1
Omega Pl IS N1 5 M8
Omega Rd WOKN/KNAP GU21 232 D1
Omega St DEPT SE8 160 F7 5
Omega Wy EGH TW20 194 F1
Ommaney Rd NWCR SE14 160 C7
Omnibus Wy WALTH E17 100 F10
Ondine Rd EDUL SE22 159 N10
Onega Ga BERM/RHTH SE16 160 D2
One Pin La SLN SL2 109 H9
One Tree Cl FSTH SE23 182 B2
One Tree Hill Rd RGUE GU4 268 E2
One Tree La BEAC HP9 88 D8
Ongar Cl ADL/WDHM KT15 215 J3
CHDH RM6 123 M3
Ongar Hl ADL/WDHM KT15 215 K3
Ongar Pl ADL/WDHM KT15 215 J3
BRW CM14 107 J3
Ongar Rd ABR/ST RM4 83 M6
ADL/WDHM KT15 215 K2
BRWN CM15 86 F10
FUL/PGN SW6 14 F9
Ongar Wy RAIN RM13 144 F3
Onra Rd LEY E10 120 F5
Onslow Av BELMT SM2 221 J6
RCHPK/HAM TW10 177 K1
Onslow Cl CHING E4 101 J3 3
HAT AL10 40 E4
Onslow Crs CHST BR7 206 E1
WOKS/MYFD GU22 232 D3
Onslow Dr SCUP DA14 185 N6
Onslow Gdns CHONG CM5 67 P3
MUSWH N10 118 C3
SAND/SEL CR2 223 P8
SKENS SW7 15 L7
SWFD E18 121 N1
THDIT KT7 198 D8 2
WCHMH N21 79 H9
WLGTN SM6 222 D4
Onslow Ms CHERT KT16 195 J6
Onslow Ms East SKENS SW7 15 L6

Onslow Ms West SKENS SW7 ... 15 L6
Onslow Rd ASC SL5 ... 192 C10
  CROY/NA CR0 ... 203 H7
  GU GU1 ... 250 A10
  NWMAL KT3 ... 200 D4
  RCHPK/HAM TW10 ... 177 K2
  WOT/HER KT12 ... 217 H1
Onslow Sq SKENS SW7 ... 15 M6
Onslow St GU GU1 ... 267 J2
  HCIRC EC1N ... 12 B2
Onslow Wy THDIT KT7 ... 198 D8
  WOKS/MYFD GU22 ... 233 J1
Ontario CI HORL RH6 ... 281 H5
Ontario St STHWK SE1 ... 18 D4
Ontario Wy POP/IOD E14 ... 140 F9
On the HI OXHEY WD19 ... 93 M3
Opal CI CAN/RD E16 ... 142 A8
Opal Ct DTCH/LGLY SL3 ... 129 P6
Opal St LBTH SE11 ... 18 C7
Opendale Rd SL SL1 ... 128 A7
Openshaw Rd ABYW SE2 ... 163 L4
Openview WAND/EARL SW18 ... 179 M4
Ophir Ter PECK SE15 ... 159 P7
Oppenheim Rd LEW SE13 ... 161 H8
Oram PI HHS/BOV HP3 ... 35 N9
Orange Court La ORP BR6 ... 226 D5
Orange Gv CHIG IG7 ... 121 F2
  WAN E11 ... 121 K8
Orange PI BERM/RHTH SE16 ... 160 B2
Orangery La ELTH/MOT SE9 ... 184 C1
The Orangery RCHPK/HAM TW10 ... 177 H5
Orange St LSQ/SEVD WC2H ... 11 H8
Orange Tree HI ROM RM1 ... 104 E6
Oratory La CHEL SW3 ... 15 M7
Orbain Rd FUL/PGN SW6 ... 157 H6
Orbel St BTSEA SW11 ... 157 P7
Orbital Crs GSTN WD25 ... 72 C1
Orb St WALW SE17 ... 18 G6
Orchard Bush WD23 ... 94 C2
Orchard Av ADL/WDHM KT15 ... 215 P3
  ASHF TW15 ... 174 D9
  BELV DA17 ... 163 P5
  BERK HP4 ... 33 M5
  CROY/NA CR0 ... 204 D9
  DART DA1 ... 187 J3
  EBED/NFELT TW14 ... 174 E1
  FNCH N3 ... 117 K1
  GSTN WD25 ... 55 J7
  GVW DA11 ... 190 B4
  HEST TW5 ... 153 M6
  MTCM CR4 ... 202 B8
  NWMAL KT3 ... 200 D4
  RAIN RM13 ... 145 K6
  RBRW/HUT CM13 ... 107 L4
  SL SL1 ... 128 C7
  STHGT/OAK N14 ... 78 D10
  STHL UB1 ... 133 M10
  THDIT KT7 ... 198 F8
  TRDG/WHET N20 ... 97 N3
  WDSR SL4 ... 148 F7
Orchard CI ALP/SUD HA0 ... 135 K3
  ASHF TW15 ... 174 D9
  ASHTD KT21 ... 237 J6
  BNSTD SM7 ... 221 L10
  BORE WD6 ... 75 L7
  BXLYHN DA7 ... 163 P7
  CHING E4 ... 100 F5
  CHOB/PIR GU24 ... 212 C9
  CRICK NW2 ... 116 D8
  DEN/HRF UB9 ... 131 L1
  EDGW HA8 ... 95 K7
  EHSLY KT24 ... 234 C10
  FSTH SE23 ... 161 K2
  GU GU1 ... 250 E10
  HART DA3 ... 211 N2
  HHNE HP2 ... 36 A4
  HOR/WEW KT19 ... 219 N3
  HORL RH6 ... 280 A3
  LHD/OX KT22 ... 236 C8
  NKENS W10 ... 8 C3
  POTB/CUF EN6 ... 60 F4
  RAD WD7 ... 74 D3
  RBSF CM22 ... 30 D3
  RGUW GU3 ... 248 A10
  RKW/CH/CXG WD3 ... 70 G2
  RSEV TN14 ... 247 K2
  RSLP HA4 ... 112 C1
  RYNPK SW20 ... 200 F4
  SOCK/AV RM15 ... 147 H6
  STAL AL1 ... 38 E7
  WARE SG12 ... 26 C1
  WAT WD17 ... 72 C6
  WOKS/MYFD GU22 ... 232 G7
  WOT/HER KT12 ... 197 J7
Orchard Crs EDGW HA8 ... 95 P6
  EN EN1 ... 79 N5
Orchard Cft HLW CM20 ... 29 K9
Orchard Dr BKHTH/KID SE3 ... 161 K8
  EDGW HA8 ... 95 L6
  EPP CM16 ... 83 H2
  GRAYS RM17 ... 167 M4
  LCOL/BKTW AL2 ... 56 A2
  RKW/CH/CXG WD3 ... 70 F7
  SHPTN TW17 ... 196 F5
  UX/CGN UB8 ... 131 N6
  WAT WD17 ... 72 G1
  WOKN/KNAP GU21 ... 232 B1
Orchard End CTHM CR3 ... 241 M8
  GT/LBKH KT23 ... 236 B10
  WEY KT15 ... 196 F9
Orchard End Av AMSS HP7 ... 69 L5
Orchardfield Rd RCODL GU7 ... 267 L10
Orchard Gdns CHSGTN KT9 ... 219 K11
  EHSLY KT24 ... 234 C10
  EPSOM KT18 ... 237 P1
  WAB EN9 ... 62 C10
Orchard Ga CDALE/KGS NW9 ... 116 B2
  ESH/CLAY KT10 ... 198 C8
  GFD/PVL UB6 ... 134 C1
  SLN SL2 ... 109 H10
Orchard Gn ORP BR6 ... 207 N5
Orchard Gv CFSP/GDCR SL9 ... 89 P9
  CROY/NA CR0 ... 204 D7
  EDGW HA8 ... 95 M9
  KTN/HRWW/W HA3 ... 115 L3
  ORP BR6 ... 207 J9
  PGE/AN SE20 ... 181 P10
Orchard HI BFOR GU20 ... 212 C4
  DART DA1 ... 186 F1
  LEW SE13 ... 160 C8
Orchard House La STAL AL1 ... 38 C7
Orchard La AMS HP6 ... 69 J4
  BRWN CM15 ... 86 E9
  E/WMO/HCT KT8 ... 198 C6
  RYNPK SW20 ... 200 E1
  WFD IG8 ... 101 P5
Orchard Lea CI
  WOKS/MYFD GU22 ... 233 H1
Orchardleigh LHD/OX KT22 ... 236 C8
Orchardleigh Av PEND EN3 ... 80 B6
Orchard Mains
  WOKS/MYFD GU22 ... 231 P9
Orchard Md HAT AL10 ... 40 C4
Orchardmede WCHMH N21 ... 79 L10
The Orchard on the Gn
  RKW/CH/CXG WD3 ... 72 G4
Orchard PI POP/IOD E14 ... 141 K9
  TOTM N17 ... 99 N8
Orchard Ri CROY/NA CR0 ... 204 D8
  KUTN/CMB KT2 ... 199 P1
  RCHPK/HAM TW10 ... 155 N10
  RSLP HA4 ... 112 C1

Orchard Ri East BFN/LL DA15 ... 185 H1
Orchard Ri West BFN/LL DA15 ... 185 H1
Orchard Rd BAR EN5 ... 77 H8
  BEAC HP9 ... 88 C10
  BELV DA17 ... 164 B3
  BMLY BR1 ... 205 P1
  BTFD TW8 ... 155 H5
  CHSGTN KT9 ... 219 K11
  DAGE RM10 ... 144 B3
  DORK RH4 ... 272 G3
  GUW GU2 ... 267 L2
  GVW DA11 ... 189 P5
  HGT N6 ... 118 C6
  HORL RH6 ... 281 J4
  HPTN TW12 ... 175 N10
  HSLWW TW4 ... 175 N1
  HYS/HAR UB3 ... 133 M9
  KUT KT1 ... 199 K2
  ORP BR6 ... 226 E2
  ORP BR6 ... 227 M5
  PEND EN3 ... 80 B9
  RCH/KEW TW9 ... 155 M9
  REIG RH2 ... 257 L10
  RGUE GU4 ... 250 E6
  RGUE GU4 ... 268 C4
  ROMW/RG RM7 ... 104 C10
  RSEV TN14 ... 246 C2
  SAND/SEL CR2 ... 224 A10
  SCUP DA14 ... 185 H7
  SEV TN13 ... 246 F8
  SHGR GU5 ... 270 B5
  SOCK/AV RM15 ... 147 H7
  SUT SM1 ... 221 L2
  SUT SM1 ... 180 K1
  SWCM DA10 ... 190 K1
  TWK TW1 ... 176 F1
  WDSR SL4 ... 171 N3
  WELL DA16 ... 163 L9
Orchards CI BF/WBF KT14 ... 215 K10
Orchardson St STJWD NW8 ... 9 J2
The Orchards CRAWW RH11 ... 282 C8
  EPP CM16 ... 65 K8
  SBW CM21 ... 29 F1
Orchard St CRAWW RH11 ... 285 N7
  DART DA1 ... 187 M2
  HHS/BOV HP3 ... 35 N9
  MBLAR W1H ... 10 C1
  STALW/RED AL3 ... 38 B7
  THDIT KT7 ... 198 C8
  WALTH E17 ... 120 D2
The Orchard BKHTH/KID SE3 ... 161 J8
  CHSWK W4 ... 156 M5
  EW EN1 ... 220 C4
  EWKT N11 ... 97 K5
  HERT/WAS SG14 ... 25 J3
  KGLGY WD4 ... 54 B5
  LTWR GU18 ... 212 A7
  RDKG RH5 ... 273 H6
  SEV TN13 ... 246 F7
  SWLY BR8 ... 208 E2
  VW GU25 ... 194 B5
  WCHMH N21 ... 79 L10
  WGCW AL8 ... 22 G3
  WOKS/MYFD GU22 ... 232 B8
Orchard Wy ADL/WDHM KT15 ... 215 L2
  ASHF TW15 ... 174 A5
  BGR/WK TN15 ... 247 P3
  CHESW EN7 ... 61 M3
  CHIG IG7 ... 103 K4
  CROY/NA CR0 ... 204 D7
  DORK RH4 ... 272 G3
  DTCH/LGLY SL3 ... 130 B10
  ESH/CLAY KT10 ... 198 F6
  HHS/BOV HP3 ... 52 D4
  KWD/TDW/WH KT20 ... 257 H2
  OXTED RH8 ... 261 M9
  POTB/CUF EN6 ... 59 L4
  RDART DA2 ... 187 L6
  REIG RH2 ... 275 L3
  RGUW GU3 ... 248 A10
  RKW/CH/CXG WD3 ... 91 K1
  RPLY/SEND GU23 ... 250 F1
  SUT SM1 ... 221 N1

Ormiston Gv SHB W12 ... 136 E10
Ormiston Rd GNWCH SE10 ... 161 M4
Ormond Av HPTN TW12 ... 198 A1
  ORP BR6 ... 206 F9
Ormond CI BMSBY WC1N ... 11 M3
Ormond Crs HPTN TW12 ... 176 A10
Ormond Dr HPTN TW12 ... 176 A10
Ormonde Av HOR/WEW KT19 ... 220 A5
Ormonde Ga CHEL SW3 ... 16 A8
Ormonde PI BGVA SW1W ... 16 D6
Ormonde Ri BKHH IG9 ... 101 P2
Ormonde Rd MORT/ESHN SW14 ... 155 N9
  NTHWD HA6 ... 92 A3
  WOKN/KNAP GU21 ... 231 P7
Ormonde Ter STJWD NW8 ... 4 A4
  RCHPK/HAM TW10 ... 177 J1
Ormond Rd ARCH N19 ... 118 F4
  RCHPK/HAM TW10 ... 177 H1
Ormond Yd STJS SW1Y ... 11 H9
Ormrod Rd BMSBY WC1N ... 11 H8
Ormsby Gdns GFD/PVL UB6 ... 134 B4
Ormsby PI STNW/STAM N16 ... 119 N8
Ormsby St BETH E2 ... 12 L7
Ormside St PECK SE15 ... 160 B5
Ormside Wy REDH RH1 ... 258 C6
Ormskirk Rd OXHEY WD19 ... 93 L5
Ormston Av NWMAL KT3 ... 117 N10
Oronsay HHS/BOV HP3 ... 36 C3
Orphanage Rd WAT WD17 ... 154 G1
Orpheus St CMBW SE5 ... 159 L7
Orpington By-pass RSEV TN14 ... 228 B5
Orpington Gdns UED N18 ... 99 M4
Orpington Rd CHST BR7 ... 207 H3
  WCHMH N21 ... 99 H1
Orpin Rd REDH RH1 ... 258 D6
Orpwood CI HPTN TW12 ... 175 N10
Orsett Heath Crs RDH/CHF RM16 ... 168 D2
Orsett Ms BAY/PAD W2 ... 9 J5
Orsett Rd GRAYS RM17 ... 167 N4
Orsett St LBTH SE11 ... 17 P7
Orsett Ter BAY/PAD W2 ... 9 J5
Orsman Rd IS N1 ... 7 J6
Orton CI STAL/WH AL4 ... 38 F1
Orton St WAP E1W ... 13 N10
Orville Rd BTSEA SW11 ... 157 N8
Orwell CI HYS/HAR UB3 ... 132 F3
  WDSR SL4 ... 149 J9
Orwell Ct WATN SW24 ... 73 L6
Orwell Gdns REIG RH2 ... 275 L2
Orwell Rd PLSTW E13 ... 141 P4
Osbaldeston Rd STNW/STAM N16 ... 119 P7
Osbert St WEST SW1P ... 17 J6
Osborn CI HACK E8 ... 7 N1
Osborne Av STWL/WRAY TW19 ... 175 J4
Osborne CI BECK BR3 ... 204 D4
  EBAR EN4 ... 78 A7
  EMPK RM11 ... 125 J4
  FELT TW13 ... 175 J8
Osborne Gdns MLHL NW7 ... 96 G8
  POTB/CUF EN6 ... 59 L6
  THHTH CR7 ... 203 K2
Osborne Gv WALTH E17 ... 120 E2
Osborne Ms WDSR SL4 ... 149 H8
Osborne Rd ACT W3 ... 155 N1
  BELV DA17 ... 164 A4
  BKHH IG9 ... 101 P1
  BROX EN10 ... 62 D3
  BRWN CM15 ... 87 H1
  CHES/WCR EN8 ... 62 D3
  CRICK NW2 ... 136 E1
  ECH TW20 ... 172 C9
  EMPK RM11 ... 125 J4
  FSBYPK N4 ... 119 H6
  HSLWW TW4 ... 154 G9
  KGLGY WD4 ... 54 A3
  KUTN/CMB KT2 ... 177 K10
  LEY E10 ... 120 G8
  PEND EN3 ... 80 D6
  PLMGR N13 ... 99 H4
  POTB/CUF EN6 ... 59 L6
  REDH RH1 ... 258 B7
  THHTH CR7 ... 203 K2
  WATN SW24 ... 73 K4
  WDSR SL4 ... 149 J9
  WOT/HER KT12 ... 197 H8
Osborne Sq DAGW RM9 ... 124 A9
Osborne St SL SL1 ... 149 L1
Osborn La FSTH SE23 ... 161 L2
Osborn Rd UX/CGN UB8 ... 131 M2
Osborn St WCHPL E1 ... 13 M1
Osborn Ter BKHTH/KID SE3 ... 161 L10
Osbourne Av RAIN RM13 ... 111 J8
Osbourne Wy WGCW AL8 ... 22 C4
Osbourne Av KGLGY WD4 ... 54 A3
Osbourne Rd RDART DA2 ... 188 A2
Oscar St DEPT SE8 ... 160 F1
Oseney Crs KTTN NW5 ... 5 H1
Osgood Av ORP BR6 ... 227 M5
Osgood Gdns ORP BR6 ... 227 M5
O'shea Gv BOW E3 ... 139 L1
Osidge La STHGT/OAK N14 ... 98 A2
Osier PI EGH TW20 ... 172 F9
Osiers Rd WAND/EARL SW18 ... 157 K10
Osier St WCHPL E1 ... 139 M1
  LEY E10 ... 120 F8
Oslac Rd CAT SE6 ... 182 C6
Osman Rd ED N9 ... 99 J8
  HMSMTH W6 ... 137 J7
Osmond Gdns WLGTN SM6 ... 222 D3
Osmond CI RYLN/HDSTN HA2 ... 114 A7
Osmund St SHB W12 ... 136 C7
Osnaburgh St CAMTN NW1 ... 10 E2
  GTPST W1W ... 10 F1
Osnaburgh Ter CAMTN NW1 ... 10 F1
Osney CI CRAWW RH11 ... 283 M6
Osney Wk MRDN SM4 ... 201 N6
Osney Wy GVE DA12 ... 191 P6
Osprey CI EHAM E6 ... 142 B7
  SWFD E18 ... 121 M2
  WALTH E17 ... 100 D10
  WDR/YW UB7 ... 151 N1
Osprey Gdns SAND/SEL CR2 ... 224 C6
Osprey Ms PEND EN3 ... 80 B9
Osprey Rd WAB EN9 ... 63 M10
Ospringe CI PGE/AN SE20 ... 182 B10
Ospringe Rd KTTN NW5 ... 118 C9
Ossian Rd FSBYPK N4 ... 118 G5
Ossington Buildings MHST W1U ... 10 C3
Ossington CI BAY/PAD W2 ... 8 F8
Ossington St BAY/PAD W2 ... 8 E8
Ossory Rd STHWK SE1 ... 19 N8
Ossulston St CAMTN NW1 ... 5 J6
Ossulton PI EFNCH N2 ... 117 M2
Ostade Rd BRXS/STRHM SW2 ... 180 A1
Osten Ms SKENS SW7 ... 15 H4
Osterberg Rd DART DA1 ... 165 N10
Osterley Av ISLW TW7 ... 154 C6
Osterley Crs ISLW TW7 ... 154 D7
Osterley Gdns THHTH CR7 ... 203 K2
Osterley La ISLW TW7 ... 133 L10
Osterley Park Rd NWDGN UB2 ... 153 N2
Osterley Park View Rd HNWL W7 ... 154 C2
Osterley Rd ISLW TW7 ... 154 C5
  STNW/STAM N16 ... 119 N9
Oster St STALW/RED AL3 ... 38 A5
Ostliffe Rd PLMGR N13 ... 99 P5
Oswald CI LHD/OX KT22 ... 236 A5
Oswald Rd LHD/OX KT22 ... 236 A6
  STAL AL1 ... 38 D7
  STHL UB1 ... 133 M10
Oswald St CLPT E5 ... 120 C9
Oswald's Md CLPT E5 ... 120 D7
Oswald Ter CRICK NW2 ... 116 B10

Osward PI ED N9 ... 99 P3
Osward Rd BAL SW12 ... 180 A5
Oswin St LBTH SE11 ... 18 C7
Oswyth Rd CMBW SE5 ... 159 M8
Otford CI BMLY BR1 ... 206 D3
  BXLY DA5 ... 186 C2
  PGE/AN SE20 ... 204 B3
Otford Crs BROCKY SE4 ... 182 C2
Otford La RSEV TN14 ... 228 A9
Otford Rd RSEV TN14 ... 247 J2
Othello CI LBTH SE11 ... 18 C7
Otis St BOW E3 ... 141 H5
Otley Dr GNTH/NBYPK IG2 ... 123 M1
Otley Rd CAN/RD E16 ... 141 P8
Otley Ter CLPT E5 ... 120 E2
Otley Wy OXHEY WD19 ... 93 J3
Otlinge CI STMC/STPC BR5 ... 207 N4
Ottawa Gdns DAGE RM10 ... 144 C2
Ottawa Rd TIL RM18 ... 153 P8
Ottaway St CLPT E5 ... 119 P8
Otterbourne Rd CHING E4 ... 101 J4
  CROY/NA CR0 ... 203 K9
Otterburn Gdns ISLW TW7 ... 154 F5
Otterburn St TOOT SW17 ... 180 A9
Otter CI CHERT KT16 ... 214 E3
Otterden St CAT SE6 ... 182 F7
Otterfield Rd WDR/YW UB7 ... 131 P9
Otterham Wy DART DA1 ... 188 A1
Otterham DA1 HAT AL10 ... 40 C5
Ottermead La CHERT KT16 ... 214 F9
Otter Rd GFD/PVL UB6 ... 134 B6
Otters CI STMC/STPC BR5 ... 207 N4
Otterspool La GSTN WD25 ... 73 M4
Otterspool Wy GSTN WD25 ... 73 K7
Ottoman Ter WAT WD17 ... 72 D3
Otto St WALW SE17 ... 18 C10
Ottways Av ASHTD KT21 ... 237 J5
Ottways La ASHTD KT21 ... 237 K5
Otway CI CRAWW RH11 ... 283 J9
Otway Gdns BUSH WD23 ... 94 D1
Otways CI POTB/CUF EN6 ... 59 L9
Oulton Crs BARK IG11 ... 143 J1
  POTB/CUF EN6 ... 58 G2
Oulton Rd SEVS/STOTM N15 ... 119 L3
Oulton Wy OXHEY WD19 ... 93 N3
Oundle Av BUSH WD23 ... 74 B10
Ousden CI CHES/WCR EN8 ... 62 D4
Ousden Dr CHES/WCR EN8 ... 62 D4
Ouseley Rd BAL SW12 ... 180 A4
  STWL/WRAY TW19 ... 171 P3
Outdowns EHSLY KT24 ... 253 N9
Outer Cir CAMTN NW1 ... 10 A1
Outfield Rd CFSP/GDCR SL9 ... 90 A8
Outgate Rd WLSDN NW10 ... 136 C2
Outing's La BRWN CM15 ... 86 C2
Outlook Dr CSTG HP8 ... 90 A4
Outram PI WEY KT13 ... 216 D2
Outram Rd CROY/NA CR0 ... 203 N9
  EHAM E6 ... 142 B3
  WDGN N22 ... 98 E9
Outwich St HDTCH EC3A ... 13 K5
Outwood La KWD/TDW/WH KT20 ... 239 L8
  REDH RH1 ... 259 L10
  REDH RH1 ... 277 H5
Oval Gdns GRAYS RM17 ... 167 P4
Oval PI VX/NE SW8 ... 158 G6
Oval Rd CAMTN NW1 ... 4 E1
  CROY/NA CR0 ... 204 A10
Oval Rd North DAGE RM10 ... 144 C3
Oval Rd South DAGE RM10 ... 144 C4
The Oval BETH E2 ... 140 A4
  BFN/LL DA15 ... 185 K3
  BNSTD SM7 ... 221 K10
  BROX EN10 ... 62 D1
  GUW GU2 ... 267 N4
  HART DA3 ... 211 P3
  RGODL GU7 ... 267 L10
  RGUW GU3 ... 248 G9
Oval Wy CFSP/GDCR SL9 ... 110 B2
  LBTH SE11 ... 17 P8
Ovenden Rd RSEV TN14 ... 245 N1
Overbrae BECK BR3 ... 182 F9
Overbrook Wk EDGW HA8 ... 95 M8
Overbury Av BECK BR3 ... 204 C3
Overbury Crs CROY/NA CR0 ... 225 H6
Overbury Rd FSBYPK N4 ... 119 L4
Overbury St CLPT E5 ... 120 E3
Overcliff GVW DA11 ... 190 D2
Overcliff Rd GRAYS RM17 ... 168 A4
  LEW SE13 ... 160 E10
Overcourt CI BFN/LL DA15 ... 185 L2
Overdale ASHTD KT21 ... 237 K2
  RDKG RH5 ... 273 H1
  REDH RH1 ... 259 K9
  RSEV TN14 ... 265 J9
Overdale Av NWMAL KT3 ... 199 P2
Overdale Rd CSHM HP5 ... 50 C4
  EA W5 ... 155 J2
Overdene Dr CRAWW RH11 ... 283 P9
Overdown Rd CAT SE6 ... 182 F7
Overhill WARL CR6 ... 242 A9
Overhill Rd EDUL SE22 ... 181 P7
  PUR/KEN CR8 ... 223 H6
Overlea Rd CLPT E5 ... 119 P5
Overlord Cl BROX EN10 ... 44 D6
Overmead BFN/LL DA15 ... 184 C3
  SWLY BR8 ... 208 F5

Owlets Hall CI HARH RM3 ... 125 N1
Owletts CRAWE RH10 ... 284 E6
Ownstead Gdns SAND/SEL CR2 ... 223 N7
Ownsted HI CROY/NA CR0 ... 225 N6
Oxberry Av FUL/PGN SW6 ... 157 H8
Oxdowne CI COB KT11 ... 218 A10
Oxenden Wood Rd ORP BR6 ... 227 L3
Oxendon St STJS SW1Y ... 11 J8
Oxenford St PECK SE15 ... 159 N9
Oxenhill Rd RSEV TN14 ... 247 N1
Oxenpark Av WBLY HA9 ... 115 K5
Oxestalls Rd DEPT SE8 ... 160 D4
Oxfield CI BERK HP4 ... 33 M6
Oxford Av CDH/CHF RM16 ... 168 D3
  EMPK RM11 ... 125 P2
  HEST TW5 ... 153 P4
  HYS/HAR UB3 ... 152 G6
  RYNPK SW20 ... 201 H2
  SL SL1 ... 128 E7
  STAL AL1 ... 39 H1
Oxford CI ASHF TW15 ... 174 D10
  CHES/WCR EN8 ... 62 B5
  ED N9 ... 99 J2
  GVE DA12 ... 191 J5
  MTCM CR4 ... 202 D3
  NTHWD HA6 ... 92 D5
Oxford Crs NWMAL KT3 ... 200 A6
Oxford Dr RSLP HA4 ... 113 K7
Oxford Gdns CHSWK W4 ... 155 M4
  DEN/HRF UB9 ... 111 K8
  NKENS W10 ... 136 G8
  TRDG/WHET N20 ... 97 N2
  WCHMH N21 ... 99 K1
Oxford Ms BXLY DA5 ... 186 B4
Oxford Rd CAR SM5 ... 221 P3
  CFSP/GDCR SL9 ... 109 M2
  CFSP/GDCR SL9 ... 110 C7
  DEN/HRF UB9 ... 110 G7
  EA W5 ... 135 H6
  ED N9 ... 100 A3
  FSBYPK N4 ... 119 H6
  GU GU1 ... 268 A2
  HARH RM3 ... 105 N7
  HPTN TW12 ... 176 C8
  HRW HA1 ... 114 B4
  IL IG1 ... 122 F9
  KIL/WHAMP NW6 ... 2 F7
  KTN/HRWW/W HA3 ... 114 C1
  NRWD SE19 ... 181 L9
  PEND EN3 ... 80 E6
  PUT/ROE SW15 ... 157 H10
  REDH RH1 ... 257 P9
  SCUP DA14 ... 185 L8
  SRTFD E15 ... 141 J1
  WDSR SL4 ... 149 H7
  WFD IG8 ... 102 A6
  WLGTN SM6 ... 222 D2
Oxford Rd East WDSR SL4 ... 149 H7
Oxford Rd North CHSWK W4 ... 155 N4
Oxford Rd South CHSWK W4 ... 155 K4
Oxford Sq BAY/PAD W2 ... 9 M6
Oxford St MYFR/PKLN W1K ... 10 C6
  WATW WD18 ... 73 J9
Oxford Ter GU GU1 ... 268 A2
Oxford Wk STHL UB1 ... 133 N10
Oxford Wy FELT TW13 ... 175 J7
Oxgate Gdns CRICK NW2 ... 116 B8
Oxgate La CRICK NW2 ... 116 E7
Oxhawth Crs HAYES BR2 ... 206 D5
Oxhey Av OXHEY WD19 ... 93 L3
Oxhey Dr OXHEY WD19 ... 93 L1
Oxhey La OXHEY WD19 ... 93 K5
  PIN HA5 ... 94 A7
Oxhey Ridge CI OXHEY WD19 ... 93 H6
Oxhey Rd OXHEY WD19 ... 93 K1
Oxleas EHAM E6 ... 142 E8
Oxleas CI WELL DA16 ... 162 G8
Oxlease Dr HAT AL10 ... 40 E5
Oxleay Rd RYLN/HDSTN HA2 ... 113 P5
Oxleigh CI NWMAL KT3 ... 200 D5
Oxley CI GPK RM2 ... 105 K3
  STHWK SE1 ... 19 M7
Oxleys Rd CRICK NW2 ... 116 E6
  WAB EN9 ... 63 H9
The Oxleys HLWE CM17 ... 29 N7
Oxlow La DAGE RM10 ... 124 B9
  DAGW RM9 ... 124 A9
Oxonian St EDUL SE22 ... 159 N10
Oxshott Ri COB KT11 ... 217 M10
Oxshott Rd LHD/OX KT22 ... 236 F4
Oxshott Wy COB KT11 ... 235 M1
Oxted CI MTCM CR4 ... 201 N3
Oxted Rd GDST RH9 ... 260 E7
Oxtoby Wy STRHM/NOR SW16 ... 202 E7
Oyster Catchers CI CAN/RD E16 ... 141 N2
Oysterfields STALW/RED AL3 ... 38 A5
Oyster La BF/WBF KT14 ... 215 P8
Oyster Rw WCHPL E1 ... 140 B8
Ozolins Wy CAN/RD E16 ... 141 L8

P

Paceheath CI CRW RM5 ... 104 E7
Pace PI WCHPL E1 ... 140 A8
Pacific CI EBED/NFELT TW14 ... 174 G4
Pacific Rd CAN/RD E16 ... 141 M8
Packet Boat La UX/CGN UB8 ... 131 L8
Packham Rd GVW DA11 ... 190 C6
Packhorse CI STALE/WH AL4 ... 39 H3
Packhorse La RAD WD7 ... 58 A7
Packhorse La CFSP/GDCR SL9 ... 110 B4
  SEV TN13 ... 246 D9
Packington Sq IS N1 ... 6 F4
Packington St IS N1 ... 6 F4
Packmores Rd ELTH/MOT SE9 ... 184 G1
Padbrook OXTED RH8 ... 261 M1
Padbury CI EBED/NFELT TW14 ... 174 E4
Padbury Ct BETH E2 ... 7 M10
Padcroft Rd WDR/YW UB7 ... 131 N10
Paddenswick Rd HMSMTH W6 ... 156 D2
Paddick CI HOD EN11 ... 44 G1
Paddington Gn YEAD UB4 ... 133 L6
Paddington St MHST W1U ... 10 C3
Paddock CI BKHTH/KID SE3 ... 161 M9
  EYN DA4 ... 210 B1
  NTHLT UB5 ... 133 P4
  ORP BR6 ... 226 E1
  OXHEY WD19 ... 73 M10
  OXTED RH8 ... 261 L7
  SYD SE26 ... 181 L8
  WARE SG12 ... 28 A2
  WPK KT4 ... 200 C8
Paddock Gdns NRWD SE19 ... 181 M9
Paddock La BAR EN5 ... 76 B8
Paddock Md HLWS CM18 ... 46 F6
  CRICK NW2 ... 116 D8
  RSLP HA4 ... 113 L8
Paddocks CI COB KT11 ... 217 K10
  RYLN/HDSTN HA2 ... 113 P5
  STMC/STPC BR5 ... 207 N9
Paddocks Rd WOKN/KNAP GU21 ... 231 N2
Paddocks Wy CHERT KT16 ... 250 D6
The Paddocks ABR/ST RM4 ... 84 C10
  EBAR EN4 ... 78 A7
  GT/LBKH KT23 ... 254 A2
  HERT/BAY SG13 ... 26 A8
  RGUW GU3 ... 248 B10
  RKW/CH/CXG WD3 ... 71 J8

WBLY HA9 ... 115 N7
WEY KT13 ... 196 F10
WGCE AL7 ... 23 L5
Paddocks Wy ASHTD KT21 ... 237 K4
CHERT KT16 ... 195 L8
The Paddock BH/WHM TN16 ... 262 F2
BROX EN10 ... 44 H6
CFSP/GDCR SL9 ... 90 B6
CRAWE RH10 ... 284 E6
DORK RH4 ... 272 A3
DTCH/LGLY SL3 ... 149 N7
GU GU1 ... 250 G9
HAT AL10 ... 40 D3
HGDN/ICK UB10 ... 112 C9
Paddock Wk WARL CR6 ... 242 A5
Paddock Wy CHST BR7 ... 184 G10
OXTED RH8 ... 261 L7
WOKN/KNAP GU21 ... 214 E10
Paddock Wd HARP AL5 ... 20 D4
Padfield Rd CMBW SE5 ... 159 K9
Padnall Rd CHDH RM6 ... 123 P2
Padstow Cl DTCH/LGLY SL3 ... 150 B2
Padstow Rd ENC/FH EN2 ... 79 J6
Padstow Wk EBED/NFELT TW14 ... 174 G5
Padua Rd PGE/AN SE20 ... 204 B1
Pagden St VX/NE SW8 ... 158 C7
Pageant Cl TIL RM18 ... 168 F7
Pageant Crs BERM/RHTH SE16 ... 140 E1
Pageant St STAL AL1 ... 38 C7
Pageant Wk CROY/NA CR0 ... 203 M10
Page Cl DAGW RM9 ... 123 P10
FELT TW13 ... 175 M9
KTN/HRWW/W HA3 ... 115 L4
RDART DA2 ... 189 H6
Page Crs CROY/NA CR0 ... 223 J2
ERITH DA8 ... 164 G6

Page Green Rd SEVS/STOTM N15 ... 119 P3
Page Heath La BMLY BR1 ... 206 A3
Page Heath Vls BMLY BR1 ... 206 A3
Page Hl WARE SG12 ... 26 A1
Pagehurst Rd CROY/NA CR0 ... 203 P7
Page Meadow MLHL NW7 ... 96 D8
Page Rd EBED/NFELT TW14 ... 174 E2
HERT/BAY SG13 ... 25 P5
Page's Hl MUSWH N10 ... 98 B10
Page's La MUSWH N10 ... 98 B10
UX/CGN UB8 ... 131 M1
Page St MLHL NW7 ... 96 D9
WEST SW1P ... 17 K5
Page's Wk STHWK SE1 ... 19 J5
Paget Av SUT SM1 ... 201 N10
Paget Cl HPTN TW12 ... 176 C7
Paget Gdns CHST BR7 ... 206 E1
Paget La ISLW TW7 ... 154 C9
Paget Pl THDIT KT7 ... 198 E8
Paget Ri WOOL/PLUM SE18 ... 162 D6
Paget Rd DTCH/LGLY SL3 ... 150 C3
HGDN/ICK UB10 ... 132 D6
IL IG1 ... 122 F9
STNW/STAM N16 ... 119 L6
Paget St FSBYE EC1V ... 6 C9
Paget Ter WOOL/PLUM SE18 ... 162 L7
Pagette Wy GRAYS RM17 ... 167 M4
Pagewood Cl CRAWE RH10 ... 284 E9
Pagitts Gv EBAR EN4 ... 77 L5
Paglesfield Rd RBRW/HUT CM13 ... 87 P10
Pagnell St NWCR SE14 ... 160 E6
Pagoda Av RCH/KEW TW9 ... 155 L9
Pagoda Gdns BKHTH/KID SE3 ... 161 J8
Paiges Farm Cl RSEV TN14 ... 265 K9
Paignton Rd RSLP HA4 ... 113 H8
SEVS/STOTM N15 ... 119 M4
Paines Brook Wy HARH RM3 ... 105 N7
Paines Cl PIN HA5 ... 113 M1
Paine's La PIN HA5 ... 93 M10
Pain's Cl MTCM CR4 ... 202 C2
Pains Hl OXTED RH8 ... 261 P8
Painsthorpe Rd STNW/STAM N16 ... 119 M8
Painters Ash La CVW DA11 ... 190 A6
Painters La PEND EN3 ... 80 D1
Painters Rd GNTH/NBYPK IG2 ... 123 K1
Paisley Rd CAR SM5 ... 201 N8
WDGN N22 ... 99 J9
Pakeman St HOLWY N7 ... 118 C8
Pakenham Cl BAL SW12 ... 180 B4
Pakenham St FSBYW WC1X ... 5 K8
Pakes Wy EPP CM16 ... 83 H3
Palace Av KENS W8 ... 9 H10
Palace Cl KGLGY WD4 ... 54 C4
SL SL1 ... 128 E10
Palace Ct BAY/PAD W2 ... 8 G7
KTN/HRWW/W HA3 ... 115 K4
Palace Court Gdns MUSWH N10 ... 118 D1
Palace Dr WEY KT13 ... 196 C10
Palace Garden Ms KENS W8 ... 8 F9
Palace Gdns BKHTH IG9 ... 102 A2
Palace Gardens Ter KENS W8 ... 8 F9
Palace Gardens West WEY KT13 ... 196 C10
Palace Ga KENS W8 ... 15 J2
Palace Gates Rd WDGN N22 ... 98 F9
Palace Gn CROY/NA CR0 ... 224 E4
Palace Gv BMLY BR1 ... 205 N1
NRWD SE19 ... 181 N10
Palace Pl WESTW SW1E ... 16 E3
Palace Rd ADL/WDHM KT15 ... 215 L6
BH/WHM TN16 ... 244 D7
BMLY BR1 ... 205 N1
BRXS/STRHM SW2 ... 180 A6
CEND/HSY/T N8 ... 118 E3
E/WMO/HCT KT8 ... 198 B3
FBAR/BDGN N11 ... 98 F8
KUT KT1 ... 199 J4
NRWD SE19 ... 181 N10
RSLP HA4 ... 113 M9
Palace Sq NRWD SE19 ... 181 N10
Palace St WESTW SW1E ... 16 G3
Palace Vw BMLY BR1 ... 205 N3
CROY/NA CR0 ... 224 E1
LEE/GVPK SE12 ... 185 M5
Palace View Rd CHING E4 ... 100 G6
Palamos Rd LEY E10 ... 120 F6
Palatine Av STNW/STAM N16 ... 119 M9
Palatine Rd STNW/STAM N16 ... 119 M9
Palermo Rd WLSDN NW10 ... 136 D4
Palestine Gv WIM/MER SW19 ... 201 N1
Palewell Cl STMC/STPC BR5 ... 207 L2
Palewell Common Dr MORT/ESHN SW14 ... 178 A1
Palewell Pk MORT/ESHN SW14 ... 178 A1
Paley Gdns LOU IG10 ... 82 E7
Palfrey Cl STALW/RED AL3 ... 38 A1
Palfrey Pl BRXN/ST SW9 ... 158 G6
VX/NE SW8 ... 158 G6
Palgrave Av STHL UB1 ... 133 P9
Palgrave Rd SHB W12 ... 156 C5
Palins Wy CDH/CHF RM16 ... 147 M10
Palissy St BETH E2 ... 7 L10
Pallant Wy ORP BR6 ... 206 D10
Pallas Rd HHNE HP2 ... 36 A4
Pallet Wy WOOL/PLUM SE18 ... 162 B3
Pallingham Dr CRAWE RH10 ... 284 D10
Palliser Dr RAIN RM13 ... 145 H7
Palliser Rd CSTC HP8 ... 87 P10
HMSMTH W6 ... 14 A7
Pall MI STJS SW1Y ... 11 J10
Pall MI East STJS SW1Y ... 11 K9
Pall Mall Pl STJS SW1Y ... 11 H10
Palmar Crs BXLYHN DA7 ... 164 B2
Palmar Rd BXLYHN DA7 ... 164 B2
Palmarsh Cl STMC/STPC BR5 ... 207 N4
Palm Av SCUP DA14 ... 185 N3
Palm Cl LEY E10 ... 120 C7
Palmeira Rd WELL DA16 ... 163 N9
Palmer Av BUSH WD23 ... 74 A10

CHEAM SM3 ... 220 F1
GVE DA12 ... 190 G7
Palmer Cl HERT/WAS SG14 ... 25 K3
HEST TW5 ... 153 P7
HORL RH6 ... 280 A2
REDH RH1 ... 276 B1
WWKM BR4 ... 205 J9
Palmer Crs CHERT KT16 ... 214 G3
KUT KT1 ... 199 K3
Palmer Gdns BAR EN5 ... 76 C9
Palmer Pl HOLWY N7 ... 119 N10
Palmer Rd BCTR RM8 ... 123 N6
CRAWE RH10 ... 284 D10
HERT/WAS SG14 ... 25 L3
PLSTW E13 ... 141 N6
Palmer's Av GRAYS RM17 ... 167 P3
Palmers Dr GRAYS RM17 ... 167 P3
Palmers Gv E/WMO/HCT KT8 ... 197 P4
WAB EN9 ... 45 L8
Palmers Hl EPP CM16 ... 65 K5
Palmers La PEND EN3 ... 80 B5
Palmers Orch RSEV TN14 ... 228 C7
Palmers Rd BETH E2 ... 140 C4
BORE WD6 ... 75 P5
FBAR/BDGN N16 ... 98 D6
MORT/ESHN SW14 ... 155 P9
STRHM/NOR SW16 ... 202 C2
Palmerston Av DTCH/LGLY SL3 ... 149 N2
Palmerston Centre KTN/HRWW/W HA3 ... 114 E1
Palmerston Crs PLMGR N13 ... 98 G6
WOOL/PLUM SE18 ... 162 F5
Palmerston Gdns RAIN RM13 ... 145 K4
Palmerston Gv WIM/MER SW19 ... 179 K10
Palmerston Rd ACT W3 ... 155 P2
BKHH IG9 ... 101 P3
CAR SM5 ... 222 A1
CROY/NA CR0 ... 203 L5
FSTGT E7 ... 121 N10
HSLW TW3 ... 154 B7
KIL/WHAMP NW6 ... 2 D3
KTN/HRWW/W HA3 ... 114 D1
MORT/ESHN SW14 ... 155 P10
ORP BR6 ... 226 F1
SUT SM1 ... 221 M2
WALTH E17 ... 120 E2
WDGN N22 ... 98 G8
WHTN TW2 ... 176 D2
WHTN TW2 ... 176 E2
WIM/MER SW19 ... 179 K10
WTHK RM20 ... 167 J4
Palmerston St STJSPK SW1H ... 17 J3
Palmers Wy CHES/WCR EN8 ... 62 D5
GU GU1 ... 249 P5
Palm Rd ROMW/RG RM7 ... 124 D3
Pamela Av HHNE HP2 ... 36 A9
Pamela Gdns PIN HA5 ... 113 J5
Pampisford Rd PUR/KEN CR8 ... 223 H7
Pams Wy HOR/WEW KT19 ... 220 A2
Pancake La HHS/BOV HP3 ... 36 E7
Pancras La MANHO EC4N ... 12 F6
Pancras Rd CAMTN NW1 ... 5 K7
Pancroft ABR/ST RM4 ... 83 L7
Panfield Ms GNTH/NBYPK IG2 ... 122 D4
Panfield Rd ABYW SE2 ... 163 K1
Pangbourne Av NKENS W10 ... 136 F7
Pangbourne Dr STAN HA7 ... 95 J6
Panhard Pl GFD/PVL UB6 ... 134 A9
Pank Av BAR EN5 ... 77 N9
Pankhurst Cl ISLW TW7 ... 154 E10
Pankhurst Pl WATN WD24 ... 73 L7
Pankhurst Rd WOT/HER KT12 ... 197 K7
Panmuir Rd RYNPK SW20 ... 200 E1
Panmure Cl HBRY N5 ... 119 J9
Panmure Rd SYD SE26 ... 182 A6
Pannells Cl CHERT KT16 ... 195 J8
Panshanger Dr WGCE AL7 ... 23 L5
Pansy Gdns SHB W12 ... 136 D9
Panter's SWLY BR8 ... 186 A10
Panther Dr WLSDN NW10 ... 116 A10
Pantile Rd WEY KT13 ... 216 E1
Pantile Rw DTCH/LGLY SL3 ... 150 D3
Pantiles Cl PLMGR N13 ... 99 J6
WOKN/KNAP GU21 ... 231 N4
The Pantiles BMLY BR1 ... 206 B3
BUSH WD23 ... 94 C1
BXLYHN DA7 ... 164 A6
Panton St LSQ/SEVD WC2H ... 11 K8
STJS SW1Y ... 11 J8
Panxworth Rd HHS/BOV HP3 ... 35 N8
Papercourt La RPLY/SEND GU23 ... 233 J8
Paper Ms DORK RH4 ... 272 G1
Papermill Cl CAR SM5 ... 222 B1
Papillons Wk BKHTH/KID SE3 ... 161 M8
Papworth Wy BRXS/STRHM SW2 ... 181 J3
Parade Cl RPLY/SEND GU23 ... 232 F9
Parade Gv BRXS/STRHM SW2 ... 181 J3
The Parade CRAWE RH10 ... 285 P6
EPSOM KT18 ... 220 A9
ESH/CLAY KT10 ... 218 D3
SUN TW16 ... 174 C10
Paradise HHNE HP2 ... 35 N7
Paradise Cl CHESW EN7 ... 62 A4
Paradise Rd CLAP SW4 ... 158 F8
RCHPK/HAM TW10 ... 177 K1
WAB EN9 ... 63 L4
Paradise Rw BETH E2 ... 140 A5
Paradise St BERM/RHTH SE16 ... 160 A1
Paradise Wk CHEL SW3 ... 16 A9
Paragon Cl CAN/RD E16 ... 141 M8
Paragon Gv BRYLDS KT5 ... 199 J6
Paragon Ms WALW SE17 ... 19 H5
Paragon Pl BKHTH/KID SE3 ... 161 J8
Paragon Rd HACK E8 ... 140 A1
The Paragon BKHTH/KID SE3 ... 161 M8
Parbury Ri CHSGTN KT9 ... 219 K3
Parbury Rd FSTH SE23 ... 182 D2
Parchmore Rd THHTH CR7 ... 203 J6
Parchmore Wy THHTH CR7 ... 203 J2
Pardoner St STHWK SE1 ... 19 H3
Pardon St FSBYE EC1V ... 12 D1
Pares Cl WOKN/KNAP GU21 ... 232 A2
Parfett St WCHPL E1 ... 13 P4
Parfour Dr PUR/KEN CR8 ... 241 K2
Parfrey St HMSMTH W6 ... 156 F5
Parham Dr GNTH/NBYPK IG2 ... 122 A4
Parham Rd CRAWW RH11 ... 283 J6
Paringdon Rd HLWW/ROY CM19 ... 45 K8
Paris Gdn STHWK SE1 ... 12 C9
Parish Cl GSTN WD25 ... 55 L10
HCH RM12 ... 125 J7
Parish Gate Dr BFN/LL DA15 ... 185 H2
Parish La PGE/AN SE20 ... 182 C10
SLN SL2 ... 109 H8
Parish Whf WOOL/PLUM SE18 ... 162 B3
Park Ap WELL DA16 ... 163 L10
WBLY HA9 ... 135 M9
Park Ar BARK IG11 ... 142 F1
BMLY BR1 ... 183 L6
BUSH WD23 ... 75 L6
CAR SM5 ... 222 B5
CRICK NW2 ... 136 F1
CTHM CR3 ... 241 P1
EGH TW20 ... 172 A10
EHAM E6 ... 142 D3
EN EN1 ... 79 M10
FNCH N3 ... 97 J3
GLDGN NW11 ... 117 H4
GVE DA12 ... 190 F4

GVW DA11 ... 190 B4
HLWE CM17 ... 47 M4
HSLW TW3 ... 176 A2
IL IG1 ... 122 D7
MORT/ESHN SW14 ... 156 A10
MTCM CR4 ... 180 C10
ORP BR6 ... 206 C9
PLMGR N13 ... 99 H4
POTB/CUF EN6 ... 59 M9
RAD WD7 ... 56 C9
RBRW/HUT CM13 ... 107 P2
REDH RH1 ... 276 A8
RKW/CH/CXG WD3 ... 71 K9
RSLP HA4 ... 112 F4
SHPTN TW17 ... 196 F3
STA TW18 ... 173 J9
STAL AL1 ... 38 F5
STHL UB1 ... 153 N1
STWL/WRAY TW19 ... 172 A1
UED N18 ... 99 P5
UPMR RM14 ... 126 D5
WATW WD18 ... 73 H7
WCHMH N21 ... 98 E1
WDGN N22 ... 98 F10
WFD IG8 ... 101 N6
WLSDN NW10 ... 135 L5
WTHK RM20 ... 166 F5
WWKM BR4 ... 205 H9
Park Av East EW KT17 ... 220 D3
Park Av North CEND/HSY/T N8 ... 118 E2
WLSDN NW10 ... 116 E10
Park Avenue Rd TOTM N17 ... 100 A8
Park Av South CEND/HSY/T N8 ... 118 E2
Park Av West EW KT17 ... 220 D3
Park Barn Dr GUW GU2 ... 249 K9
Park Barn East GUW GU2 ... 249 L9
Park Bvd GPK RM2 ... 104 G9
Park Cha GU GU1 ... 250 B10
WBLY HA9 ... 115 L9
Park Cl ADL/WDHM KT15 ... 215 L6
BRKHM/BTCW RH3 ... 273 N5
BRKMPK AL9 ... 40 F5
BRKMPK AL9 ... 101 H1
BUSH WD23 ... 73 L7
CAR SM5 ... 222 A3
CRICK NW2 ... 136 D8
EPP CM16 ... 66 B3
ESH/CLAY KT10 ... 217 N3
HOM E9 ... 140 B3
HPTN TW12 ... 198 B1
ISLW TW7 ... 176 B1
KTN/HRWW/W HA3 ... 94 D9
KUTN/CMB KT2 ... 199 M1
LHD/OX KT22 ... 236 C10
RKW/CH/CXG WD3 ... 92 C5
WEY KT13 ... 196 C5
WKENS W14 ... 14 D3
WLSDN NW10 ... 135 L5
Park Copse RDKG RH5 ... 273 J2
Park Cnr WDSR SL4 ... 148 D9
Park Corner Dr EHSLY KT24 ... 252 F4
Park Corner Rd MEO DA13 ... 189 L7
Park Ct HLW CM20 ... 28 C9
HSLWW TW4 ... 175 H6
WBLY HA9 ... 115 K10
WOKS/MYFD GU22 ... 232 C4
Park Crs CRICK NW2 ... 192 E5
BORE WD6 ... 75 L7
EMPK RM11 ... 125 H5
ENC/FH EN2 ... 79 L8
ERITH DA8 ... 164 B5
FNCH N3 ... 97 L8
KTN/HRWW/W HA3 ... 94 D9
REGST W1B ... 10 D2
WHTN TW2 ... 176 C4
Park Crescent Ms East REGST W1B ... 10 F2
Park Crescent Ms West CAVSQ/HST W1G ... 10 E2
Park Cft EDGW HA8 ... 96 D5
Parkcroft Rd LEE/GVPK SE12 ... 183 L3
Parkdale Crs WPK KT4 ... 200 A10
Parkdale Rd WOOL/PLUM SE18 ... 163 H4
Park Dr ACT W3 ... 155 M2
ASC SL5 ... 192 E6
CHARL SE7 ... 162 B4
DAGE RM10 ... 124 D8
GLDGN NW11 ... 117 L6
HART DA3 ... 211 K3
KTN/HRWW/W HA3 ... 94 C7
MORT/ESHN SW14 ... 178 A1
POTB/CUF EN6 ... 59 L7
RBSF CM22 ... 31 J1
ROM RM1 ... 124 E2
RYLN/HDSTN HA2 ... 113 P5
UPMR RM14 ... 126 B9
WCHMH N21 ... 79 K10
WEY KT13 ... 216 C2
WOKS/MYFD GU22 ... 232 C4
Park End BMLY BR1 ... 205 L1
HAMP NW3 ... 117 P9
Park End Rd ROM RM1 ... 124 F2
Parker Av HERT/WAS SG14 ... 25 N4
TIL RM18 ... 168 F7
Parker Cl CAN/RD E16 ... 142 B10
CRAWE RH10 ... 284 E9
Parker Ms HOL/ALD WC2B ... 11 M5
Parke Rd BARN SW13 ... 156 D7
SUN TW16 ... 197 H4
Parker Rd CROY/NA CR0 ... 223 K1
GRAYS RM17 ... 167 L4
Parker's Cl ASHTD KT21 ... 237 K5
Parker's Hl ASHTD KT21 ... 237 K5
Parker's La ASHTD KT21 ... 237 L5
Parker's Rw STHWK SE1 ... 19 M2
Parker St CAN/RD E16 ... 142 B10
HOL/ALD WC2B ... 11 M5
WATN WD24 ... 73 J5
Parkes Rd CHIG IG7 ... 103 J6
Park Farm Cl EFNCH N2 ... 117 M1
Park Farm Cl BMLY BR1 ... 206 A1
KUTN/CMB KT2 ... 177 K10
UPMR RM14 ... 125 K10
Parkfield BGR/WK TN15 ... 247 N9
RKW/CH/CXG WD3 ... 71 J8
Parkfield Av AMS HP6 ... 69 K3
FELT TW13 ... 175 H6
HGDN/ICK UB10 ... 132 C5
MORT/ESHN SW14 ... 156 B10
NTHLT UB5 ... 133 L4
RYLN/HDSTN HA2 ... 114 A8
Parkfield Cl EDGW HA8 ... 96 B3
NTHLT UB5 ... 133 M4
Parkfield Crs FELT TW13 ... 175 H6
RSLP HA4 ... 113 P4
RYLN/HDSTN HA2 ... 114 A8
Parkfield Dr NTHLT UB5 ... 133 L4
Parkfield Gdns RYLN/HDSTN HA2 ... 114 A7
Parkfield Pde FELT TW13 ... 175 H6
Parkfield Rd IS N1 ... 6 B7
NTHLT UB5 ... 133 M4
RYLN/HDSTN HA2 ... 114 A9
Parkfields CROY/NA CR0 ... 204 B8
Park Fids HLWW/ROY CM19 ... 45 M1
Parkfields LHD/OX KT22 ... 218 A11
PUT/ROE SW15 ... 156 F10
WCCW AL8 ... 22 A1
Parkfields Av CDALE/KGS NW9 ... 116 A6
RYNPK SW20 ... 200 E1
Parkfields Cl CAR SM5 ... 222 B1
Parkfields Rd KUTN/CMB KT2 ... 177 H6
Park Gdns CDH/CHF RM16 ... 168 A2
ERITH DA8 ... 164 E3
KUTN/CMB KT2 ... 177 L8

Parkgate BKHTH/KID SE3 ... 161 L9
EFNCH N2 ... 117 N1
Park Ga EA W5 ... 135 J7
Park Ga WCHMH N21 ... 98 G1
Parkgate SL SL1 ... 128 B6
Parkgate Cl KUTN/CMB KT2 ... 177 N9
Parkgate Crs EBAR EN4 ... 77 M5
Parkgate Gdns MORT/ESHN SW14 ... 178 A1
Parkgate Rd BTSEA SW11 ... 157 P6
CAR SM5 ... 222 A4
ORP BR6 ... 228 D1
REIG RH2 ... 275 L1
WATN WD24 ... 73 K3
Park Gn BMLY BR1 ... 205 N1
Park Gv BMLY BR1 ... 205 N1
Park Grove Rd WAN E11 ... 121 F3
Park Hall Rd DUL SE21 ... 181 L5
EFNCH N2 ... 117 P2
REIG RH2 ... 257 K8
Parkham St BTSEA SW11 ... 157 P2
Park Hl BMLY BR1 ... 206 B4
CAR SM5 ... 222 A3
CLAP SW4 ... 180 L1
EA W5 ... 135 J7
FSTH SE23 ... 182 A5
HLWE CM17 ... 29 L8
LOU IG10 ... 82 A9
RCHPK/HAM TW10 ... 177 L2
Park Hill Cl CAR SM5 ... 221 P2
Parkhill Cl HCH RM12 ... 125 J7
Park Hill Ri CROY/NA CR0 ... 203 M9
Parkhill Rd BFN/LL DA15 ... 185 H6
BXLY DA5 ... 186 A3
CHING E4 ... 101 H1
Park Hill Rd CROY/NA CR0 ... 203 N9
EW KT17 ... 220 C7
Parkhill Rd HAMP NW3 ... 118 A10
HAYES BR2 ... 205 K2
HHW HP1 ... 35 L6
RSEV TN14 ... 247 N3
WLGTN SM6 ... 222 C4
Parkholme Rd HACK E8 ... 7 N2
Park Horsley EHSLY KT24 ... 253 H2
Park House Dr REIG RH2 ... 275 J2
Park House Gdns TWK TW1 ... 177 H1
Parkhouse St CMBW SE5 ... 159 L6
Parkhurst HOR/WEW KT19 ... 219 P6
Parkhurst Gdns BXLY DA5 ... 186 B3
Parkhurst Gv HORL RH6 ... 279 P5
Parkhurst Rd BXLY DA5 ... 186 B3
FBAR/BDGN N11 ... 98 B5
GUW GU2 ... 249 M9
HERT/WAS SG14 ... 25 N4
HOLWY N7 ... 118 F9
HORL RH6 ... 279 P5
MNPK E12 ... 122 D9
SUT SM1 ... 221 N1
TOTM N17 ... 99 P10
WALTH E17 ... 120 D2
WDGN N22 ... 98 G8
Parkinson Cl STALE/WH AL4 ... 21 J3
Parkland Av DTCH/LGLY SL3 ... 150 A4
ROM RM1 ... 104 F10
UPMR RM14 ... 126 A10
Parkland Cl HOD EN11 ... 26 C10
SEV TN13 ... 265 K5
Parkland Gv ASHF TW15 ... 174 B7
Parkland Rd ASHF TW15 ... 174 B7
WDGN N22 ... 98 G10
WFD IG8 ... 101 N8
Parklands ADL/WDHM KT15 ... 215 M2
BRYLDS KT5 ... 199 L5
CHIG IG7 ... 102 F4
GT/LBKH KT23 ... 235 P9
HGT N6 ... 118 C5
HHW HP1 ... 35 K1
OXTED RH8 ... 261 K7
RDKG RH5 ... 272 G6
WAB EN9 ... 63 K8
Parklands Cl EBAR EN4 ... 77 N4
MORT/ESHN SW14 ... 177 P1
STALW/RED AL3 ... 37 P7
Parklands Dr FNCH N3 ... 117 H1
Parklands Pl GU GU1 ... 250 E10
Parklands Rd TOOT SW17 ... 180 C8
Parklands Wy WPK KT4 ... 200 B3
Parkland Wy CHONG CM5 ... 67 N6
Park La ASHTD KT21 ... 237 L4
BEAC HP9 ... 88 E10
BGR/WK TN15 ... 247 N4
BROX EN10 ... 44 D5
CAR SM5 ... 222 B5
CHDH RM6 ... 123 N4
CHEAM SM3 ... 221 H5
CHES/WCR EN8 ... 62 D10
CHSWK W4 ... 156 A5
COUL/CHIP CR5 ... 240 F7
DEN/HRF UB9 ... 91 K9
DTCH/LGLY SL3 ... 149 N2
DTCH/LGLY SL3 ... 150 A3
EMPK RM11 ... 125 H5
HHNE HP2 ... 35 N7
HLW CM20 ... 28 C9
HYS/HAR UB3 ... 153 H6
MBLAR W1H ... 10 B7
MYFR/PICC W1J ... 16 C1
MYFR/PKLN W1K ... 10 B7
RAIN RM13 ... 145 J1
RCH/KEW TW9 ... 155 J10
REIG RH2 ... 257 J10
RGUE GU4 ... 250 C7
RYLN/HDSTN HA2 ... 114 A8
SEV TN13 ... 247 K10
SL SL1 ... 108 D10
SOCK/AV RM15 ... 143 K3
SRTFD E15 ... 141 J3
STALE/WH AL4 ... 39 P4
SWLY BR8 ... 209 N2
TEDD TW11 ... 176 E9
TOTM N17 ... 99 N8
UED N18 ... 99 N4
WBLY HA9 ... 115 N4
WDSR SL4 ... 170 A4
YEAD UB4 ... 132 F6
Park La East REIG RH2 ... 275 J3
Park Lane Paradise BROX EN10 ... 43 P10
Parklawn Av EPSOM KT18 ... 219 N9
HORL RH6 ... 280 A2
Park Lawn Rd WEY KT13 ... 216 D1
Parklea Cl CDALE/KGS NW9 ... 96 B9
Parkleigh Rd WIM/MER SW19 ... 201 L2
Park Ley Rd CTHM CR3 ... 242 C6
Parkleys RCHPK/HAM TW10 ... 177 H4
Park Md BFN/LL DA15 ... 185 K1
RYLN/HDSTN HA2 ... 114 A8
Parkmead LOU IG10 ... 82 D9
Park Mead Rd BRKHM/BTCW RH3 ... 273 M5
Parkmead Gdns MLHL NW7 ... 96 F5
Park Meadow BRKMPK AL9 ... 40 F3
BRWN CM15 ... 87 J4
Park Ms CHST BR7 ... 184 C3
NKENS W10 ... 2 A3
STWL/WRAY TW19 ... 174 A3
Park Nook Gdns ENC/FH EN2 ... 79 L3
Park Pde ACT W3 ... 155 J5

Park Pde WLSDN NW10 ... 136 C4
ACT W3 ... 155 M3
AMS HP6 ... 69 J4
BEAC HP9 ... 89 J6
EA W5 ... 135 J10
GVE DA12 ... 190 F2
HPTN TW12 ... 176 B9
LCOL/BKTW AL2 ... 56 C3
POP/IOD E14 ... 140 F10
SEV TN13 ... 246 E9
WBLY HA9 ... 115 L9
WHALL SW1A ... 10 G10
Park Place Vls BAY/PAD W2 ... 9 G3
Park Ridings CEND/HSY/T N8 ... 119 H1
Park Ri BERK HP4 ... 33 K3
KTN/HRWW/W HA3 ... 94 D9
LHD/OX KT22 ... 236 F7
Park Rise Cl LHD/OX KT22 ... 236 G7
Park Rise Rd FSTH SE23 ... 182 C4
Park Rd ALP/SUD HA0 ... 135 K1
AMS HP6 ... 69 L3
ASHF TW15 ... 174 C8
ASHTD KT21 ... 237 K6
BAR EN5 ... 76 C6
BECK BR3 ... 182 E10
BMLY BR1 ... 205 N1
BNSTD SM7 ... 239 M2
BRW CM14 ... 106 C2
BRYLDS KT5 ... 199 L6
BUSH WD23 ... 73 P10
CAMTN NW1 ... 10 B2
CDALE/KGS NW9 ... 116 A5
CEND/HSY/T N8 ... 118 E3
CHEAM SM3 ... 221 H3
CHES/WCR EN8 ... 62 C9
CHST BR7 ... 184 E9
CHSWK W4 ... 156 A5
CSHM HP5 ... 50 C7
CTHM CR3 ... 241 M9
DART DA1 ... 187 P3
E/WMO/HCT KT8 ... 198 A4
E/WMO/HCT KT8 ... 199 H1
EBAR EN4 ... 77 N8
EFNCH N2 ... 117 N1
EGH TW20 ... 172 D7
EHAM E6 ... 141 P7
ESH/CLAY KT10 ... 218 A1
FBAR/BDGN N11 ... 98 E8
FELT TW13 ... 175 L7
GU GU1 ... 250 A10
GVW DA11 ... 190 E5
HDN NW4 ... 116 E4
HERT/BAY SG13 ... 25 M5
HGDN/ICK UB10 ... 131 P7
HHW HP1 ... 35 M8
HNWL W7 ... 134 E9
HOD EN11 ... 44 F3
HORL RH6 ... 281 K6
HPTN TW12 ... 176 B8
HSLW TW3 ... 176 B1
IL IG1 ... 122 G8
ISLW TW7 ... 154 C7
KUT KT1 ... 199 H1
KUTN/CMB KT2 ... 199 M1
LEY E10 ... 120 F6
MNPK E12 ... 121 N7
MNPK E12 ... 122 A9
NWMAL KT3 ... 200 A4
OXTED RH8 ... 261 L4
PEND EN3 ... 80 D2
POTB/CUF EN6 ... 60 B6
PUR/KEN CR8 ... 241 K1
RAD WD7 ... 74 F1
RCHPK/HAM TW10 ... 177 L2
REDH RH1 ... 258 A8
RKW/CH/CXG WD3 ... 91 P1
SEVS/STOTM N15 ... 119 J2
SHGR GU5 ... 269 P7
SHPTN TW17 ... 196 F3
SLN SL2 ... 129 J4
SNWD SE25 ... 203 M4
SRTFD E15 ... 141 M3
STHCT/OAK N14 ... 98 E1
STJWD NW8 ... 3 P10
STMC/STPC BR5 ... 207 N6
STWL/WRAY TW19 ... 173 L2
SUN TW16 ... 175 J10
SWCM DA10 ... 189 K2
SWLY BR8 ... 208 C4
TEDD TW11 ... 176 E10
TWK TW1 ... 177 H2
UED N18 ... 99 N5
UPMR RM14 ... 125 P9
UX/CGN UB8 ... 131 N2
WALTH E17 ... 120 E3
WAN E11 ... 121 N6
WARE SG12 ... 26 A2
WARL CR6 ... 225 K10
WAT WD17 ... 73 H5
WIM/MER SW19 ... 179 N10
WLGTN SM6 ... 222 C2
WLSDN NW10 ... 136 B3
WOKS/MYFD GU22 ... 232 E3
WOKS/MYFD GU22 ... 232 C5
Park Rd East ACT W3 ... 155 P1
UX/CGN UB8 ... 131 N7
Park Rd North ACT W3 ... 155 N1
CHSWK W4 ... 156 A5
Park Rw GNWCH SE10 ... 161 J5
Park Royal Rd WLSDN NW10 ... 135 P5
Parkshot RCH/KEW TW9 ... 155 J10
Park Side ADL/WDHM KT15 ... 215 L6
BKHH IG9 ... 101 N3
CRICK NW2 ... 116 D8
Parkside CDH/CHF RM16 ... 168 A2
CFSP/GDCR SL9 ... 110 C3
CHEAM SM3 ... 221 H3
CHES/WCR EN8 ... 62 D10
CRAWE RH10 ... 283 P7
FNCH N3 ... 97 L9
HPTN TW12 ... 176 D7
MLHL NW7 ... 96 D7
RSEV TN14 ... 227 P9
SCUP DA14 ... 185 L5
Parkside Av BMLY BR1 ... 206 B4
BXLYHN DA7 ... 164 F1
ROM RM1 ... 104 E10
TIL RM18 ... 168 E8
WIM/MER SW19 ... 178 G8
Parkside Cl EHSLY KT24 ... 252 C1
PGE/AN SE20 ... 182 B10
Parkside Crs BRYLDS KT5 ... 199 P6
HOLWY N7 ... 119 H8
Parkside Cross BXLYHN DA7 ... 164 F1
Parkside Dr EDGW HA8 ... 95 M4
WAT WD17 ... 72 F6
Parkside Gdns COUL/CHIP CR5 ... 240 C5
EBAR EN4 ... 98 A2
WIM/MER SW19 ... 178 G7
Parkside Pl EHSLY KT24 ... 252 F1
Park Side Rd ASC SL5 ... 192 F6
BELV DA17 ... 164 C3
HSLW TW3 ... 176 C6
NTHWD HA6 ... 92 C6
Parkside St BTSEA SW11 ... 158 D7
Parkside Wk SL SL1 ... 149 M2
Parkside Wy RYLN/HDSTN HA2 ... 114 A2
Park Sq East CAMTN NW1 ... 10 E1
Park Square Ms CAMTN NW1 ... 10 E2
Parkstead Rd PUT/ROE SW15 ... 178 D1
Parkstone Av EMPK RM11 ... 125 M4
UED N18 ... 99 N6
Parkstone Rd PECK SE15 ... 159 P8
Park St BERK HP4 ... 33 N4
BRKMPK AL9 ... 40 F3
CROY/NA CR0 ... 203 K10

DTCH/LGLY SL3 .... 150 G7
GU GU1 .... 267 P2
LCOL/BKTW AL2 .... 56 C3
MYFR/PKLN W1K 10 C8
SL SL1 .... 149 L2
STHWK SE1 .... 12 E9
TEDD TW11 .... 176 D9
WDSR SL4 .... 149 J7
Park Street La LCOL/BKTW AL2 ... 56 A5
Park Ter GRH DA9 .... 188 G1
WPK KT4 .... 200 D8
The Park CAR SM5 .... 222 A2
EA W5 .... 135 J10
GLDGN NW11 .... 117 L6
GT/LBKH KT23 .... 235 P10
HGT N6 .... 118 B5
SCUP DA14 .... 185 J8
STAL AL1 .... 38 F4
Parkthorne CI RYLN/HDSTN HA2 .. 114 A4
Parkthorne Dr RYLN/HDSTN HA2 .. 113 P4
Parkthorne Rd BAL SW12 .... 180 E3
Park Vw ACT W3 .... 135 P7
BRKMPK AL9 .... 40 E9
CRAWW RH11 .... 283 N6
GT/LBKH KT23 .... 253 P1
HOD EN11 .... 44 F4
HORL RH6 .... 280 B4
NWMAL KT3 .... 200 C3
PIN HA5 .... 93 N9
POTB/CUF EN6 .... 59 M9
SOCK/AV RM15 .... 146 C10
WBLY HA9 .... 115 N10
WCHMH N21 .... 98 G1
Parkview Cha SL SL1 .... 128 C8
Park View Rd STAL AL1 .... 38 D7
Park View La FBAR/BDGN N11 .... 98 C5
Park View Gdns GRAYS RM17 ..... 167 N4
HDN NW4 .... 116 F3
Park View Rd BERK HP4 .... 33 N5
CRICK NW2 ....
Parkview Rd CROY/NA CR0 .... 203 P8
Park View Rd CTHM CR3 .... 242 E8
EA W5 .... 135 K7
ELTH/MOT SE9 .... 184 E4
FNCH N3 .... 97 L9
PIN HA5 .... 93 J7
REDH RH1 .... 276 B7
STHL UB1 .... 133 P10
TOTM N17 .... 99 P10
UX/CGN UB8 .... 132 B8
WDR/YW UB7 .... 132 A8
WELL DA16 .... 163 M9
Parkview V RGUE GU4 .... 250 E3
Park Village East CAMTN NW1 ... 4 E7
Park Village West CAMTN NW1 ... 4 E7
Parkville Rd FUL/PGN SW6 ...... 157 L6
Park Vis GNWCH SE10 .... 161 J5
Park Wk WBPTN SW10 .... 15 N9
Park Wy BRWN CM15 .... 107 L2
BXLY DA5 .... 186 G6
CRAWE RH10 .... 284 D5
E/WMO/HCT KT8 .... 198 A3
EBED/NFELT TW14 .... 175 J5
EDGW HA8 .... 95 N9
ENC/FH EN2 .... 79 N3
GLDGN NW11 .... 117 K3
GT/LBKH KT23 .... 235 P9
RKW/CH/CXG WD3 .... 91 M2
RSLP HA4 .... 113 H6
TRDG/WHET N20 .... 98 A5
Parkway CAMTN NW1 .... 4 F5
CROY/NA CR0 .... 225 H5
DORK RH4 .... 272 F1
ERITHM DA18 .... 163 P2
GDMY/SEVK IG3 .... 123 J8
GPK RM2 .... 104 C10
GU GU1 .... 250 B9
HGDN/ICK UB10 .... 132 B2
HLWW/ROY CM19 .... 46 B1
RAIN RM13 .... 145 H6
RYNPK SW20 .... 200 G4
SBW CM21 .... 29 P2
STHGT/OAK N14 .... 98 F3
WEY KT13 .... 216 E11
WFD IG8 .... 101 P6
WGCW AL8 .... 22 C5
Parkway Ct STAL AL1 .... 38 C9
Parkway Gdns WGCW AL8 .... 22 C5
The Parkway IVER SL0 .... 130 F3
NTHLT UB5 .... 133 L5
Park West BAY/PAD W2 .... 9 P5
Park West Pl BAY/PAD W2 .... 9 P5
Parkwood BECK BR3 .... 182 F10
Parkwood Av ESH/CLAY KT10 ..... 198 D4
Parkwood Cl HOD EN11 .... 44 D5
Parkwood Dr HHW HP1 .... 35 J6
Parkwood Gv SUN TW16 .... 197 H5
Parkwood Ms HGT N6 .... 118 C4
Parkwood Rd BH/WHM TN16 .... 244 B7
Park Wood Rd BNSTD SM7 .... 238 G1
Parkwood Rd BXLY DA5 .... 186 A3
ISLW TW7 .... 136 A3
REDH RH1 .... 258 F7
WIM/MER SW19 .... 179 J8
Park Wood Vw BNSTD SM7 .... 238 F2
Park Works Rd REDH RH1 .... 258 G9
Parlaunt Rd DTCH/LGLY SL3 ..... 150 E3
IVER SL0 .... 150 G2
Parley Dr WOKN/KNAP GU21 ...... 231 P4
Parliament HI HAMP NW3 .... 117 P9
Parliament Sq HERT/WAS SG14 ... 25 L5
Parliament St WHALL SW1A 17 L1
Parma Crs BTSEA SW11 .... 158 A10
Parmiter St BETH E2 .... 140 A4
Parnall Rd HLWS CM18 .... 46 G5
Parndon Mill La HLW CM20 ...... 28 E8
Parndon Wood Rd
HLWW/ROY CM19 .... 46 F6
EDGW HA8 .... 95 P5
Parnell Cl ABLGY WD5 .... 54 G6
EDGW HA8 .... 95 P5
Parnell Gdns WEY KT13 .... 216 A7
Parnell Rd BOW E3 .... 140 E3
HOM E9 ....
Parnel Rd WARE SG12 .... 26 E1
Parnham Av LTWR GU18 .... 212 C7
Parnham St POP/IOD E14 .... 140 D8
Parolles Rd ARCH N19 .... 118 D6
Paroma Rd BELV DA17 .... 164 D2
Parr Av EW KT17 .... 220 E5
Parr Cl ED N9 .... 100 A5
LHD/OX KT22 .... 236 C6
Parr Crs HHNE HP2 .... 36 C1
Parris Cft RDKG RH5 .... 273 H5
Parrock Av GVE DA12 .... 190 G4
Parrock Rd GVE DA12 .... 190 F3
Parrotts Cl RKW/CH/CXG WD3 .... 72 B8
Parrotts Fld HOD EN11 .... 44 F4
Parr Rd EHAM E6 .... 142 A3
STAN HA7 .... 95 J5
Parrs Cl SAND/SEL CR2 .... 223 L5
Parr's Pl HPTN TW12 .... 175 P10
Parr St IS N1 .... 6 C1
Parry Av EHAM E6 .... 142 C4
Parry Cl EW KT17 .... 220 D4
Parry Dr WEY KT13 .... 216 B6
Parry Gn North DTCH/LGLY SL3 .. 150 C3
Parry Gn South DTCH/LGLY SL3 .. 150 D3
Parry Pl WOOL/PLUM SE18 .... 162 G4
Parry Rd NKENS W10 .... 2 E9
SNWD SE25 .... 203 M3
Parry St VX/NE SW8 .... 17 L9
Parsifal Rd KIL/WHAMP NW6 ..... 117 K10

Parsloe Rd EPP CM16 .... 46 D7
Parsloes Av DAGW RM9 .... 123 P10
Parsonage Av ABLGY WD5 .... 54 F6
HYS/HAR UB3 .... 132 G8
WARL CR6 .... 242 G2
Parsonage Fld BRWN CM15 .... 87 J3
Parsonage Gdns ENC/FH EN2 ..... 79 K6
Parsonage La BRKMPK AL9 .... 40 E9
DORK RH4 .... 272 A3
ENC/FH EN2 .... 79 L6
EYN DA4 .... 188 A9
SCUP DA14 .... 186 A7
SLN SL2 .... 129 H1
WDSR SL4 .... 148 F1
Parsonage Leys HLW CM20 .... 47 J1
Parsonage Manorway
ERITH DA8 .... 164 B5
Parsonage Rd BRKMPK AL9 .... 40 E9
CSTG HP8 .... 89 N4
EGH TW20 .... 172 A8
RAIN RM13 .... 145 K4
RKW/CH/CXG WD3 .... 91 H1
WTHK RM20 .... 167 H5
Parsonage Sq DORK RH4 .... 272 F1
Parsonage St POP/IOD E14 ...... 161 H3
Parsons CI HORL RH6 .... 279 P3
Parsonsfield CI BNSTD SM7 ..... 238 G1
Parsonsfield Rd BNSTD SM7 ..... 238 G2
Parsons Gn FUL/PGN SW6 .... 157 K7
Parsons Green La FUL/PGN SW6 .. 157 K7
Parsons Gv EDGW HA8 .... 95 M4
Parsons La RDART DA2 .... 187 J6
Parson's Md CROY/NA CR0 .... 203 J8
E/WMO/HCT KT8 .... 198 A3
Parson St EDGW HA8 .... 95 M4
Parson St HDN NW4 .... 116 F1
Parson's Wood La SLN SL2 ...... 129 J2
Parthenia Rd FUL/PGN SW6 ...... 157 K7
Parthia CI KWD/TDW/WH KT20 .... 238 E5
Partingdale La MLHL NW7 .... 96 G6
Partington CI ARCH N19 .... 76 F10
BUSH WD23 .... 94 E2
CAN/RD E16 .... 142 A7
CSHM HP5 .... 51 K4
STAN HA7 .... 95 K5
Partridge Ct HLWS CM18 .... 47 H3
Partridge Dr ORP BR6 .... 206 F10
Partridge Gn ELTH/MOT SE9 ..... 184 D6
Partridge Knoll PUR/KEN CR8 ... 223 J8
Partridge La HORS RH12 .... 282 B3
RDKG RH5 .... 278 A3
Partridge Md BNSTD SM7 .... 238 F1
Partridge Rd HLWS CM18 .... 46 G3
HPTN TW12 .... 175 N9
SCUP DA14 .... 185 H6
STALW/RED AL3 .... 38 C2
Partridge Wy RGUE GU4 .... 250 G8
WDGN N22 .... 98 F9
Parva CI ALP/SUD HA0 .... 20 C5
Parvills WAB EN9 .... 63 J8
Parvis Rd BF/WBF KT14 .... 215 P8
Pasadena CI HYS/HAR UB3 .... 153 H1
Pascal St VX/NE SW8 .... 158 A6
Pascoe Rd LEW SE13 .... 161 N4
Pasfield WAB EN9 .... 63 J9
Pasley CI WALW SE17 .... 18 D8
Pasquier Rd WALTH E17 .... 120 D1
Passey PI ELTH/MOT SE9 .... 184 C2
Passfield Dr POP/IOD E14 ...... 140 G7
Passmore Gdns FBAR/BDGN N11 ... 98 E7
Passmore St BGVA SW1W 16 C6
Pastens Rd OXTED RH8 .... 261 P7
Pastern CI ELTH/MOT SE9 .... 184 C5
The Pastures HAT AL10 .... 40 E5
HHW HP1 .... 35 H5
LCOL/BKTW AL2 .... 37 P10
OXHEY WD19 .... 93 K1
TRDG/WHET N20 .... 97 J2
WGCE AL7 .... 23 K7
The Pasture CRAWE RH10 .... 284 D5
Patcham Ter VX/NE SW8 .... 158 C7
Patching CI CRAWW RH11 .... 283 J6
Patching Wy YEAD UB4 .... 133 M7
The Patch SEV TN13 .... 246 F8
Paternoster CI WAB EN9 .... 63 L9
Paternoster HI WAB EN9 .... 63 L9
Paternoster Rw ABR/ST RM4 ..... 105 K2
STP EC4M 12 D6
Pater St KENS W8 .... 14 E4
Pates Manor Dr
EBED/NFELT TW14 .... 174 E3
Patricia CI SL SL1 .... 128 D9
Patricia Ct WELL DA16 .... 163 L6
Patricia Dr EMPK RM11 .... 105 L3
Patrick Rd PLSTW E13 .... 141 P5
Patrington CI CRAWW RH11 ...... 283 K10
UX/CGN UB8 .... 131 M5
Patriot Sq BETH E2 .... 140 A4
Patrol PI CAT SE6 .... 182 G2
Patshull Cl KTTN NW5 .... 4 C2
Patshull Rd KTTN NW5 .... 4 C2
Pattenden Rd FSTH SE23 .... 182 E1
Patten Rd WAND/EARL SW18 ...... 179 P3
Patterdale Rd BMLY BR1 .... 183 K9
CRAWW RH11 .... 283 H9
Patterdale Rd PECK SE15 .... 160 B6
RDART DA2 .... 188 B4
Patterson Rd CSHM HP5 .... 50 G4
NRWD SE19 .... 181 N9
Pattina Wk BERM/RHTH SE16 ..... 140 D10
Pattison Rd CRICK NW2 .... 117 K6
Paul CI SRTFD E15 .... 141 K1
Paulet Rd CMBW SE5 .... 159 J8
Paul Gdns CROY/NA CR0 .... 205 N9
Paul Julius CI POP/IOD E14 .... 141 J9
Paul Robeson CI EHAM E6 .... 142 D5
Pauls La HOD EN11 .... 44 D4
Paul's PI ASHTD KT21 .... 237 N4
Paul St SDTCH EC2A 13 J1
SRTFD E15 .... 141 K3
Paultons Sq CHEL SW3 .... 15 M9
Paultons St CHEL SW3 .... 15 M10
Pauntley St ARCH N19 .... 118 D6

Paveley Dr BTSEA SW11 .... 157 P6
Paveley St STJWD NW8 .... 3 P10
The Pavement CLAP SW4 .... 158 D10
Pavet CI DAGE RM10 .... 144 C1
Pavilion Gdns STA TW18 .... 173 L10
Pavilion Rd IL IG1 .... 122 C5
KTBR SW1X 16 B2
The Pavilions EPP CM16 .... 66 D1
Pavilion St KTBR SW1X 16 B3
Pavilion Wy AMS HP6 .... 69 P5
EDGW HA8 .... 95 P8
RSLP HA4 .... 113 K7
Pawleyne CI PGE/AN SE20 .... 182 B10
Pawsey CI PLSTW E13 .... 141 M10
Pawson's Rd CROY/NA CR0 .... 203 K6
Pax CI CRAWW RH11 .... 283 H9
Paxford Rd ALP/SUD HA0 .... 114 C7
Paxton Av SL SL1 .... 149 H2
Paxton CI RCH/KEW TW9 .... 155 L8
WOT/HER KT12 .... 197 K7
Paxton PI WNWD SE27 .... 181 M7
Paxton Rd BERK HP4 .... 34 B5
BMLY BR1 .... 183 M10
FSTH SE23 .... 182 B5
STAL AL1 .... 38 D7
TOTM N17 .... 99 P8
Paxton Ter PIM SW1V 16 F9
Paycock Rd HLWW/ROY CM19 ...... 46 B3
Payne CI CRAWE RH10 .... 284 C5
Payne Rd BOW E3 .... 140 C4
Paynell Ct BKHTH/KID SE3 ...... 161 K9
Payne Rd BOW E3 .... 140 C4
Paynesfield Av
MORT/ESHN SW14 .... 156 A9
BUSH WD23 .... 94 E1
Paynesfield Rd BH/WHM TN16 .... 243 P6
Paynes La WAB EN9 .... 45 H10
Payne St DEPT SE8 .... 160 E5
Peabody Cl CROY/NA CR0 .... 204 B8
Peabody Est HNHL SE24 .... 181 J3
Peabody Hi DUL SE21 .... 181 J4
Peabody Sq STHWK SE1 .... 18 B1
Peace CI SNWD SE25 .... 203 M4
STHGT/OAK N14 .... 85 P4
Peace Wy WBLY HA9 .... 115 N8
Peacemaker CI CRAWW RH11 ...... 283 H9
Peace Prospect WAT WD17 .... 73 H7
Peace Rd DTCH/LGLY SL3 .... 130 C5
Peace St WOOL/PLUM SE18 .... 162 D5
Peaches CI BELMT SM2 .... 221 H4
Peachey CI UX/CGN UB8 .... 131 N8
Peachey La UX/CGN UB8 .... 131 N7
Peach Rd NKENS W10 .... 136 G5
Peachum Rd BKHTH/KID SE3 ...... 161 L5
Peacock Av EBED/NFELT TW14 .... 174 E4
Peacock Gdns CROY/NA CR0 ...... 224 D6
Peacocks CI BERK HP4 .... 33 L3
Peacock St GVE DA12 .... 190 F3
WALW SE17 .... 18 D6
Peacock Yd WALW SE17 .... 18 D6
Peakes La CHESW EN7 .... 61 N3
Peakes Wy CHESW EN7 .... 61 N3
Peaketon Av REDBR IG4 .... 122 A3
Peak HI SYD SE26 .... 182 B7
Peak Hill Av SYD SE26 .... 182 B7
Peak Hill Gdns SYD SE26 .... 182 B7
Peak Rd GUW GU2 .... 249 M7
Peaks HI PUR/KEN CR8 .... 222 F6
Peaks Hill Ri PUR/KEN CR8 ..... 222 F6
The Peak SYD SE26 .... 182 B6
Pea La BERK HP4 .... 33 J3
UPMR RM14 .... 146 F1
Peal Gdns WEA W13 .... 134 F1
Peall Rd CROY/NA CR0 .... 202 G6
Pear Av SHPTN TW17 .... 196 F5
Pearce CI MTCM CR4 .... 202 B2
Pearcefield Av FSTH SE23 ...... 182 B4
Peareswood Gdns STAN HA7 ...... 95 J9
Peareswood Rd ERITH DA8 .... 164 C7
Pearfield Rd FSTH SE23 .... 182 B6
Pearl CI CRICK NW2 .... 116 G5
EHAM E6 .... 142 D8
Pearl Ct WOKN/KNAP GU21 .... 231 K2
Pearl Gdns SL SL1 .... 128 C10
Pearl Rd WALTH E17 .... 120 F1
Pearl St WAP E1W 140 B10
Pearmain CI SHPTN TW17 .... 196 C5
Pearman St STHWK SE1 .... 18 B3
Pear PI STHWK SE1 .... 18 A1
Pearscroft Ct FUL/PGN SW6 ..... 157 L7
Pearscroft Rd FUL/PGN SW6 ..... 157 L7
Pearson Av HERT/BAY SG13 ...... 25 K7
Pearson Rd CRAWE RH10 .... 284 C5
Pearson's Av DEPT SE8 .... 160 F7
Pearsons CI HERT/BAY SG13 ..... 25 K7
Pearson St BETH E2 .... 7 L7
Pearson Wy DART DA1 .... 187 N5
Pear St HSLW TW3 .... 154 C9
Pear Tree Av WDR/YW UB7 .... 132 A8
Pear Tree CI ADL/WDHM KT15 .... 215 K2
AMSS HP7 .... 69 L5
BEAC HP9 .... 89 H7
Peartree CI BROX EN10 .... 43 N7
Pear Tree CI BXLYHN DA7 .... 164 E7
Peartree CI ERITH DA8 .... 164 C7
Pear Tree CI MTCM CR4 .... 202 A3
Peartree CI SAND/SEL CR2 ...... 224 A10
SL SL1 .... 128 E10
SOCK/AV RM15 .... 147 H4
Peartree CI SWLY BR8 .... 208 F3
Peartree Ct WCCE AL7 .... 23 H5
Peartree Gdns BCTR RM8 .... 123 L10
ROMW/RG RM7 .... 104 C10
Peartree La BRWN CM15 .... 87 H3
WAP E1W 140 B9
WGCE AL7 .... 23 H6
Pear Tree Md HLWS CM18 .... 47 K3
Pear Tree Rd ADL/WDHM KT15 .... 215 K2
ASHF TW15 .... 174 D8
HHW HP1 .... 35 K5
Peartree Rd EN EN1 .... 79 M7
Peartree St FSBYE EC1V 12 D1
Pear Tree Wk CHESW EN7 .... 61 J5
Peary PI BETH E2 .... 140 B5
Peascod St WDSR SL4 .... 149 J7
Peascroft Rd HHS/BOV HP3 ...... 36 B9
Pease CI HCH RM12 .... 145 J2
Peatfield CI BFN/LL DA15 ...... 185 H6
Peatmore Av WOKS/MYFD GU22 .... 233 K2
Peatmore CI WOKS/MYFD GU22 .... 233 K1
Peatmore Dr CHOB/PIR GU24 ..... 230 D7
Pebble HI KWD/TDW/WH KT20 ..... 256 F6
Pebble La EPSOM KT18 .... 237 M8
Pebblehill Rd BRKHM/BTCW RH3 . 256 F6
Pebble La EPSOM KT18 .... 237 M8
Pebworth Rd HRW HA1 .... 114 F7
Peckarmans Wd DUL SE21 .... 181 P6
Peckett Sq HBRY N5 .... 6 G1
Peckford PI BRXN/ST SW9 .... 159 H8
Peckham Gv PECK SE15 .... 159 M6
Peckham High St PECK SE15 ..... 159 P6
Peckham Hill St PECK SE15 ..... 159 P6
Peckham Park Rd PECK SE15 ..... 159 P6
Peckham Rye EDUL SE22 .... 159 P9
PECK SE15 .... 159 P9
Peck's HI WAB EN9 .... 45 K7
Peckwater St KTTN NW5 .... 118 D10

Pedlars End CHONG CM5 .... 49 J7
Pedley Rd BCTR RM8 .... 123 M6
Pedley St WCHPL E1 .... 13 M2
Pednor Bottom CSHM HP5 .... 50 A4
Pednormead End CSHM HP5 .... 50 G8
Pednor Rd CSHM HP5 .... 50 B5
Pedro St CLPT E5 .... 120 C8
Pedro St CLPT E5 .... 120 C8
Peek Crs WIM/MER SW19 .... 178 G8
Peeks Brook La HORL RH6 .... 280 G5
Peel CI CHING E4 .... 100 C3
ED N9 .... 99 P4
WDSR SL4 .... 148 G9
Peel Crs HERT/WAS SG14 .... 25 J2
Peel Dr CDALE/KGS NW9 .... 116 C1
CLAY IG5 .... 122 B1
Peel Gv BETH E2 .... 140 B4
Peel Pas KENS W8 .... 8 E10
Peel PI CLAY IG5 .... 102 B10
Peel Rd ALP/SUD HA0 .... 115 H8
KIL/WHAMP NW6 .... 2 A6
KTN/HRWW/W HA3 .... 114 D1
ORP BR6 .... 226 F1
SWFD E18 .... 101 L9
Peel St KENS W8 .... 8 E10
Peel Wy HARH RM3 .... 105 N10
UX/CGN UB8 .... 131 P6
Peerage Wy EMPK RM11 .... 125 N5
Peerless Dr DEN/HRF UB9 .... 111 M3
Peerless St FSBYE EC1V 6 G10
Pegamoid Rd UED N18 .... 100 A3
Pegasus Ct BTFD TW8 .... 155 L4
GVE DA12 .... 190 G1
Pegasus Rd CROY/NA CR0 .... 223 H3
Pegasus Wy FBAR/BDGN N11 ...... 98 C3
Pegelm Gdns EMPK RM11 .... 125 N5
Peggotty Wy UX/CGN UB8 .... 132 C8
Pegg Rd HEST TW5 .... 153 L6
Pegler Wy CRAWW RH11 .... 283 N7
Pegley Gdns LEE/GVPK SE12 ..... 183 M5
Pegmire La GSTN WD25 .... 74 D5
Pegrams Rd HLWS CM18 .... 46 G3
Peg's La HERT/BAY SG13 .... 25 L6
Pegwell CI CRAWW RH11 .... 283 J9
Pegwell St WOOL/PLUM SE18 ..... 163 J9
Peket CI STA TW18 .... 195 H1
Pekin St POP/IOD E14 .... 140 F9
Peldon Rd HLWW/ROY CM19 .... 46 D3
Pelham Av BARK IG11 .... 143 J3
Pelham CI CMBW SE5 .... 159 M9
Pelham Ct HHNE HP2 .... 36 D6
WGCE AL7 .... 23 M6
Pelham Crs SKENS SW7 .... 15 M5
Pelham PI SKENS SW7 .... 15 M5
Pelham Rd BXLYHN DA7 .... 164 B9
GVW DA11 .... 190 C3
IL IG1 .... 122 G7
PGE/AN SE20 .... 204 B2
SEVS/STOTM N15 .... 119 N1
SWFD E18 .... 101 N1
WDGN N22 .... 98 G7
WIM/MER SW19 .... 179 K10
Pelham Rd South GVW DA11 ...... 190 C4
Pelhams CI ESH/CLAY KT10 ...... 197 P6
Pelhams Wk ESH/CLAY KT10 ...... 197 P6
Pelham Wy GT/LBKH KT23 .... 254 A10
Pelier St WALW SE17 .... 18 F9
Pelinore Rd CAT SE6 .... 183 K5
Pellant Rd FUL/PGN SW6 .... 14 B10
Pellatt Gv WDGN N22 .... 99 H9
Pellatt Rd EDUL SE22 .... 181 N1
Pellerin Rd STNW/STAM N16 ..... 119 M10
Pelling HI WDSR SL4 .... 171 N3
Pelling St POP/IOD E14 .... 140 F9
Pellipar CI PLMGR N13 .... 99 H4
Pellipar Rd WOOL/PLUM SE18 .... 162 C4
Pelly Ct EPP CM16 .... 65 J7
Pelly Rd PLSTW E13 .... 141 M3
Pelter St BETH E2 .... 7 L7
Pelton Av BELMT SM2 .... 221 L6
Pelton Rd GNWCH SE10 .... 161 K4
Pembar Av WALTH E17 .... 120 D1
Pemberley Cl HOR/WEW KT19 ..... 219 N2
Pemberley CI HOR/WEW KT19 ..... 219 N2
Pemberton Av GPK RM2 .... 125 J1
Pemberton Gdns ARCH N19 .... 118 C8
CHDH RM6 .... 123 P3
SWLY BR8 .... 208 F3
Pemberton PI ESH/CLAY KT10 .... 198 B10
HACK E8 .... 140 A2
Pemberton Rd E/WMO/HCT KT8 .... 198 A1
FSBYPK N4 .... 119 H3
SLN SL2 .... 128 D6
Pemberton Rw FLST/FETLN EC4A . 12 B5
Pemberton Ter ARCH N19 .... 118 D8
Pembley Gn CRAWE RH10 .... 285 M2
Pembrey Wy HCH RM12 .... 145 K1
Pembridge Av HSLWW TW4 .... 175 N4
Pembridge CI HHS/BOV HP3 ...... 52 C4
Pembridge Crs NTGHL W11 .... 8 D7
Pembridge Gdns BAY/PAD W2 ..... 8 E7
Pembridge La BROX EN10 .... 43 N7
NTGHL W11 .... 8 E8
Pembridge Ms NTGHL W11 .... 8 E7
Pembridge PI BAY/PAD W2 .... 8 E7
Pembridge Rd HHS/BOV HP3 ...... 52 D4
NTGHL W11 .... 8 E8
Pembridge Sq BAY/PAD W2 .... 8 E8
Pembridge Vls NTGHL W11 .... 8 E7
Pembroke Av ASC SL5 .... 192 C5
BNSTD SM7 .... 239 L3
BROX EN10 .... 44 D10
EMPK RM11 .... 125 P2
ERITH DA8 .... 164 E3
KTBR SW1X 16 D2
Pembroke Dr CHESW EN7 .... 61 J5
Pembroke Gdns DAGE RM10 .... 124 C8
KENS W8 .... 14 C5
WKENS W14 .... 14 D5
WOKS/MYFD GU22 .... 232 N1
Pembroke Gardens CI KENS W8 .. 14 C4
MUSWH N10 .... 98 B9
Pembroke PI EDGW HA8 .... 95 M8
EYN DA4 .... 210 A1
ISLW TW7 .... 154 D1
Pembroke Rd BMLY BR1 .... 205 P2
CEND/HSY/T N8 .... 118 F2
CRAWE RH10 .... 284 D4
ECT SW5 .... 14 C5
EHAM E6 .... 142 C1
ERITH DA8 .... 164 D3
GDMY/SEVK IG3 .... 123 J6
GFD/PVL UB6 .... 134 A6
MTCM CR4 .... 202 B2
MUSWH N10 .... 98 B9
NTHWD HA6 .... 94 A5
PLMGR N13 .... 99 K4
RSLP HA4 .... 112 F6
SEV TN13 .... 265 J1
SEVS/STOTM N15 .... 119 L3
SNWD SE25 .... 203 M4
WALTH E17 .... 120 G3
WBLY HA9 .... 115 N3
WKENS W14 .... 14 D5
WOKS/MYFD GU22 .... 232 D5
Pembroke Sq KENS W8 .... 14 C4
Pembroke St IS N1 .... 5 M4

Pembroke Vls KENS W8 .... 14 C5
Pembroke Wk KENS W8 .... 14 C5
Pembury Av WPK KT4 .... 200 D8
Pembury CI COUL/CHIP CR5 ...... 222 B10
HAYES BR2 .... 205 L7
Pembury Crs HYS/HAR UB3 .... 152 E5
Pembury Crs SCUP DA14 .... 185 P5
Pembury Rd BXLYHN DA7 .... 163 P6
CLPT E5 .... 120 A10
SNWD SE25 .... 203 P4
TOTM N17 .... 99 N9
Pemdevon Rd CROY/NA CR0 .... 203 H10
Pemell CI WCHPL E1 .... 140 F6
Pemerich CI HYS/HAR UB3 .... 152 G4
Pempath PI WBLY HA9 .... 115 J7
Pemsel Ct HHS/BOV HP3 .... 35 P7
Penally PI IS N1 .... 7 H1
Penang St WAP E1W 140 A10
Penarth St PECK SE15 .... 160 B5
Penates ESH/CLAY KT10 .... 198 E3
Penberth Rd CAT SE6 .... 183 H5
Penbury Rd NWDGN UB2 .... 153 N4
Pencombe Ms NTGHL W11 .... 8 D7
Pencroft Dr DART DA1 .... 187 K3
Pendall CI EBAR EN4 .... 77 M3
Penda Rd ERITH DA8 .... 164 C6
Pendarves Rd RYNPK SW20 .... 200 F1
Penda's Md HOM E9 .... 120 D9
Pendell Av HYS/HAR UB3 .... 152 E6
Pendell Rd REDH RH1 .... 259 J7
Pendennis CI BF/WBF KT14 ...... 215 K10
Pendennis Ct HARP AL5 .... 20 C4
Pendennis Rd ORP BR6 .... 207 N4
SEV TN13 .... 247 J9
STRHM/NOR SW16 .... 180 F7
TOTM N17 .... 119 L1
Penderel Rd HSLW TW3 .... 175 P5
Penderry Ri CAT SE6 .... 183 J5
Penderyn Wy HOLWY N7 .... 118 E9
Pendle Rd STRHM/NOR SW16 ...... 180 E10
Pendlestone Rd LEY E10 .... 120 C3
Pendleton CI REDH RH1 .... 276 A2
Pendleton Rd REDH RH1 .... 275 N3
Pendragon Rd BMLY BR1 .... 183 H10
Pendrell Rd BROCKY SE4 .... 160 D9
Pendrell St WOOL/PLUM SE18 .... 162 G5
Pendula Dr YEAD UB4 .... 133 L6
Penenden HART DA3 .... 211 L9
Penerley Rd CAT SE6 .... 182 G4
RAIN RM13 .... 145 J2
Penfold CI CROY/NA CR0 .... 203 H10
Penfold PI BAY/PAD W2 .... 9 L2
Penfold Rd ED N9 .... 100 C2
Penfold St STJWD NW8 .... 9 M1
Penford Gdns ELTH/MOT SE9 ..... 162 A10
Penford St CMBW SE5 .... 159 J8
Pengarth Rd BXLY DA5 .... 185 N1
Penge La PGE/AN SE20 .... 182 B10
Pengelly CI CHESW EN7 .... 62 A6
Penge Rd PLSTW E13 .... 141 P2
SNWD SE25 .... 203 P3
Penhall Rd CHARL SE7 .... 161 M8
Penhill Rd BXLY DA5 .... 185 M3
Penhurst WOKN/KNAP GU21 .... 214 C10
Penhurst Rd BARK/HLT IG6 ...... 102 E8
Penifather La GFD/PVL UB6 ..... 134 C5
Penington Rd BEAC HP9 .... 108 A1
Peninsular CI EBED/NFELT TW14 . 174 E2
Peninsular Park Rd CHARL SE7 . 161 M4
Penistone Rd STRHM/NOR SW16 .. 180 F10
Penlow Rd HLWS CM18 .... 46 F4
Penman CI LCOL/BKTW AL2 .... 55 P3
Penman's Gn KGLGY WD4 .... 52 G2
Penmon Rd ABYW SE2 .... 163 K2
Pennack Rd PECK SE15 .... 19 M10
Pennant Ms KENS W8 .... 14 C5
Pennant Ter WALTH E17 .... 100 E10
Pennard Rd SHB W12 .... 156 F1
The Pennards SUN TW16 .... 197 K3
Penn Av CSHM HP5 .... 50 F4
Penn CI CRAWW RH11 .... 283 N4
GFD/PVL UB6 .... 134 A4
KTN/HRWW/W HA3 .... 115 H2
RKW/CH/CXG WD3 .... 70 C10
UX/CGN UB8 .... 131 N6
Penne Cl RAD WD7 .... 56 F10
Penner CI WIM/MER SW19 .... 179 H5
Penners Gdns SURB KT6 .... 199 J7
Pennethorne CI HOM E9 .... 140 B3
Pennethorne Rd PECK SE15 ...... 160 B6
Penney CI DART DA1 .... 187 L3
Penn Gdns CHST BR7 .... 206 B2
CRW RM5 .... 104 B8
Penn Gaskell La CFSP/GDCR SL9 . 90 A8
Pennine CI CRAWW RH11 .... 283 L7
Pennine Dr CRICK NW2 .... 116 C7
Pennine La CRICK NW2 .... 117 N7
Pennine Rd SLN SL2 .... 128 F7
Pennine Wy BXLYHN DA7 .... 164 F7
GVW DA11 .... 190 B6
HHNE HP2 .... 36 A3
HYS/HAR UB3 .... 152 E6
Pennings Av GUW GU2 .... 249 L7
Pennington CI CRW RM5 .... 104 B7
Pennington Dr STHGT/OAK N14 .. 78 F7
WEY KT13 .... 196 F10
Pennington Rd CFSP/GDCR SL9 .. 90 A8
The Penningtons AMS HP6 .... 69 K3
Pennington St WAP E1W 140 A9
Pennington Wy LEE/GVPK SE12 .. 183 N5
Penniston CI WDGN N22 .... 99 K10
Penn La BXLY DA5 .... 185 N2
RSEV TN14 .... 263 J3
Penn Meadow SLN SL2 .... 129 L3
Penn Rd BEAC HP9 .... 88 B6
DTCH/LGLY SL3 .... 150 A7
HOLWY N7 .... 118 F10
LCOL/BKTW AL2 .... 56 B3
RKW/CH/CXG WD3 .... 91 J3
SLN SL2 .... 129 J6
Penn St IS N1 .... 7 H6
Penn Wy RKW/CH/CXG WD3 .... 70 C10
Penny CI RAIN RM13 .... 145 J9
Pennyfield COB KT11 .... 217 H9
Penny Flds BRW CM14 .... 107 H5
Pennyfields POP/IOD E14 .... 140 F9
Penny La SHPTN TW17 .... 196 F7
Pennylets Gn SLN SL2 .... 129 L2
Pennymead HLW CM20 .... 47 K1
Pennymead Dr EHSLY KT24 .... 252 G3
Pennypot La CHOB/PIR GU24 ..... 212 G9
Pennyroyal Av EHAM E6 .... 142 A1
Penpoll Rd HACK E8 .... 140 A1
Penpool La WELL DA16 .... 163 L6
Penrhyn Av WALTH E17 .... 100 F9
Penrhyn Crs
MORT/ESHN SW14 .... 155 P10
WALTH E17 .... 100 F9
Penrhyn Gv WALTH E17 .... 100 F9
Penrith CI BECK BR3 .... 204 A10
PUT/ROE SW15 .... 179 H1
REDH RH1 .... 275 P6
Penrith Crs RAIN RM13 .... 125 H10
Penrith PI WNWD SE27 .... 181 J5
Penrith Rd BARK/HLT IG6 .... 103 J7
HARH RM3 .... 105 N4
NWMAL KT3 .... 200 A4
SEVS/STOTM N15 .... 119 L3
THHTH CR7 .... 203 K7
Penrith St STRHM/NOR SW16 .... 180 D9
Penrose Av OXHEY WD19 .... 93 M3
Penrose Ct EGH TW20 .... 171 P9
HHNE HP2 .... 35 P7
Penrose Gv WALW SE17 .... 18 E8
Penrose Rd LHD/OX KT22 .... 236 B6

Penrose St *WALW* SE17 .... 18 E8
Penryn St *CAMTN* NW1 .... 5 J7
Penry St *STHWK* SE1 .... 19 K6 ⬚
Pensbury Pl *VX/NE* SW8 .... 158 D8
Pensbury St *VX/NE* SW8 .... 158 D8
Penscroft Gdns *BORE* WD6 .... 76 A8
Pensford Av *RCH/KEW* TW9 .... 155 M8
Penshurst *HLWE* EM7 .... 29 L8
Penshurst Av *BFN/LL* DA15 .... 185 K2
Penshurst Cl *CFSP/GDCR* SL9 .... 90 A10
  CRAWE RH10 .... 284 E6 ⬚
Penshurst Gdns *EDGW* HA8 .... 36 D3
Penshurst Gn *HAYES* BR2 .... 205 L5
Penshurst Rd *BXLYHN* DA7 .... 164 A7
  HOM E9 .... 140 C2
  POTB/CUF EN6 .... 59 N7
  THHTH CR7 .... 203 J8
  TOTM N17 .... 99 N8
Penshurst Wy *BELMT* SM2 .... 221 K4 ⬚
  STMC/STPC BR5 .... 207 M4 ⬚
Pensilver Cl *EBAR* EN4 .... 77 P8 ⬚
Penson's La *CHONG* CM5 .... 67 H4
Penstemon Cl *FNCH* N3 .... 97 K3
Pentelow Gdns
  EBED/NFELT TW14 .... 175 H2
Pentire Cl *UPMR* RM14 .... 126 D4
Pentire Rd *WALTH* E17 .... 101 N3
Pentland Av *EDGW* HA8 .... 95 N3
  SHPTN TW17 .... 196 B5
Pentland Cl *CRICK* NW2 .... 117 H7 ⬚
  NTHLT UB5 .... 133 M3
Pentland Rd *BUSH* WD23 .... 128 E10
  SLN SL2 .... 128 F7
Pentlands Cl *MTCM* CR4 .... 202 C3
Pentland St *WAND/EARL* SW18 .... 179 M2
Pentley Pk *WGCW* AL8 .... 22 G3 ⬚
Pentlow Cl *PUT/ROE* SW15 .... 156 F8
Pentlow Wy *BKHH* IG9 .... 102 B1
Pentney Rd *BAL* SW12 .... 180 D4
  CHING E4 .... 101 J2 ⬚
  RYNPK SW20 .... 201 H1 ⬚
Penton Av *STA* TW18 .... 173 M8
Penton Dr *CHES/WCR* EN8 .... 62 C5
Penton Gv *IS* N1 .... 6 A8
Penton Hall Dr *STA* TW18 .... 195 K1
Penton Hook Rd *STA* TW18 .... 173 K10
Penton Ri *FSBYW* WC1X 5 P9
Penton Rd *STA* TW18 .... 173 J10
Penton St *IS* N1 .... 6 A7
Pentonville Rd *IS* N1 .... 5 N8
Pentreath Av *GUW* GU2 .... 267 L1
Pentrich Av *EN* EN1 .... 79 L6
Pentridge St *PECK* SE15 .... 159 N6
Pentyre Av *UED* N18 .... 99 L6
Penwerris Av *ISLW* TW7 .... 154 B6
Penwith Rd *WAND/EARL* SW18 .... 179 L5
Penwortham Rd *SAND/SEL* CR2 .... 224 B3
  STRHM/NOR SW16 .... 180 C9
Penylan Pl *EDGW* HA8 .... 95 M8 ⬚
Penywern Rd *ECT* SW5 .... 14 C7
Penzance Cl *DEN/HRF* UB9 .... 91 N10 ⬚
Penzance Gdns *HARH* RM3 .... 105 P7 ⬚
Penzance Pl *NTGHL* W11 .... 8 A9
Penzance Rd *HARH* RM3 .... 105 P7
Penzance Sp *SLN* SL2 .... 128 G6
Penzance St *NTGHL* W11 .... 8 A9
Peony Gdns *SHB* W12 .... 136 D9
Peplins Cl *BRKMPK* AL9 .... 59 H1
Peplins Wy *BRKMPK* AL9 .... 59 H1
Peploe Rd *KIL/WHAMP* NW6 .... 136 C4
Peplow Cl *WDR/YW* UB7 .... 131 N10 ⬚
Peppard Rd *CRAWE* RH10 .... 284 D10
Pepper Cl *CTHM* CR3 .... 259 M1
  EHAM E6 .... 142 C7
Pepper Hl *GVW* DA11 .... 189 P6
  WARE 26 E6
Peppermint Cl *CROY/NA* CR0 .... 202 F7 ⬚
Pepper St *POP/IOD* E14 .... 160 G2
  STHWK SE1 .... 18 E1
Peppett's Cl *GSHM* HP5 .... 32 C9
Peppie Cl *STNW/STAM* N16 .... 119 M7
Pepys Cl *ASHTD* KT21 .... 237 L2
  DTCH/LGLY SL3 .... 150 E5
  GVW DA11 .... 190 A6
  HGDN/ICK UB10 .... 112 C10
  TIL RM18 .... 168 F7
Pepys Crs *BAR* EN5 .... 76 F9
Pepys Ri *ORP* BR6 .... 207 J8
Pepys Rd *NWCR* SE14 .... 160 C8
  RYNPK SW20 .... 200 F1
Pepys St *TWRH* EC3N 13 K3
Perceval Av *HAMP* NW3 .... 117 P10
Percheron Dr *WOKN/KNAP* GU21 .... 230 C5
Percheron Rd *BORE* WD6 .... 76 A10
Perch St *HACK* E8 .... 119 N9
Percival Gdns *CHDH* RM6 .... 123 N4
Percival Rd *EMPK* RM11 .... 125 K4
  EN EN1 .... 79 N8
  FELT TW13 .... 174 G5
  MORT/ESHN SW14 .... 177 J1
  ORP BR6 .... 206 E9
Percival St *FSBYE* EC1V 6 D10
Percival Wy *HOR/WEW* KT19 .... 219 N1
Percy Av *ASHF* TW15 .... 174 B8
Percy Bryant Rd *SUN* TW16 .... 174 F10 ⬚
Percy Bush Rd *WDR/YW* UB7 .... 152 A2
Percy Gdns *PEND* EN3 .... 80 C9
  WPK KT4 .... 200 A8
  YEAD UB4 .... 132 F5
Percy Ms *FITZ* W1T .... 11 J4 ⬚
Percy Pl *BXLYHN* DA7 .... 163 P8
Percy Rd *BXLYHN* DA7 .... 163 P8
  CAN/RD E16 .... 141 K7
  GDMY/SEVK IG3 .... 123 K5
  GUW GU2 .... 249 J1
  HPTN TW12 .... 175 P10
  ISLW TW7 .... 154 F10
  MTCM CR4 .... 202 B7
  NFNCH/WDSP N12 .... 97 M6
  PGE/AN SE20 .... 204 C1
  ROMW/RG RM7 .... 124 D1
  SHB W12 .... 156 D1
  SNWD SE25 .... 203 P5 ⬚
  WAN E11 .... 121 K5
  WATW WD18 .... 73 J8 ⬚
  WCHMH N21 .... 99 K1
  WHTN TW2 .... 176 A4
Percy St *FITZ* W1T 11 J3
  GRAYS RM17 .... 167 P5
Percy Ter *CSTG* HP8 .... 89 M4 ⬚
Percy Wy *WHTN* TW2 .... 176 A6
Peregrine Cl *WDR/YW* WD25 .... 55 N10 ⬚
  WLSDN NW10 .... 116 A10 ⬚
Peregrine Ct *WELL* DA16 .... 163 J7
Peregrine Gdns *CROY/NA* CR0 .... 204 D9 ⬚
Peregrine Rd *BARK/HLT* IG6 .... 103 L6
  SUN TW16 .... 196 F2
Peregrine Wy *WAB* EN9 .... 63 M10
Peregrine Wy *WIM/MER* SW19 .... 178 F10 ⬚
Perham Rd *WKENS* W14 .... 14 C4
Perham Wy *LCOL/BKTW* AL2 .... 57 J2
Peridot St *EHAM* E6 .... 142 B7
Perifield *DUL* SE21 .... 181 K4
Perimeade Rd *GFD/PVL* UB6 .... 135 H4
Perimeter Rd *HAT* AL10 .... 40 B1
Perimeter Rd East *HORL* RH6 .... 280 C8
Perimeter Rd North *HORL* RH6 .... 279 P6
Perimeter Rd South *HORL* RH6 .... 280 A10
Periton Rd *ELTH/MOT* SE9 .... 162 A10
Perivale Gdns *CSTN* WD25 .... 55 J10
  WEA W13 .... 134 G5
Perivale La *CFD/PVL* UB6 .... 134 F5
Perkin Cl *ALP/SUD* HA0 .... 114 C10

Perkins Cl *GRH* DA9 .... 188 E1
Perkin's Rents *WEST* SW1P 17 J3
Perkins Rd *BARK/HLT* IG2 .... 122 G3
Perkins Sq *STHWK* SE1 .... 12 F9
Perks Cl *BKHTH/KID* SE3 .... 161 K8
Perleybrooke La
  WOKN/KNAP GU21 .... 231 M3
Permain Cl *RAD* WD7 .... 57 N9
Perpins Rd *ELTH/MOT* SE9 .... 185 H2
Perran Cl *HART* DA3 .... 211 L4 ⬚
Perran Rd *BRXS/STRHM* SW2 .... 181 J5
Perren St *KTTN* NW5 .... 4 E1 ⬚
Perrers Rd *HMSMTH* W6 .... 156 F2
Perrin Cl *ASHF* TW15 .... 174 A8 ⬚
Perrin Rd *ALP/SUD* HA0 .... 114 F9
Perrin's Ct *HAMP* NW3 .... 117 M9 ⬚
Perrin's La *HAMP* NW3 .... 117 M9
Perrin's Wk *HAMP* NW3 .... 117 M9
Perrior Rd *RGODL* GU7 .... 267 K10
Perriors Cl *CHESW* EN7 .... 61 P3
Perry Av *ACT* W3 .... 136 A3
Perry Cl *RAIN* RM13 .... 144 E4 ⬚
  UX/CGN UB8 .... 132 C8
Perry Ct *SEVS/STOTM* N15 .... 119 M4 ⬚
Perrycroft *WDSR* SL4 .... 148 B3
Perryfield *HLWE* CM17 .... 31 K9
Perryfield Rd *CRAWW* RH11 .... 283 N8
Perryfields Wy *SLN* SL2 .... 128 B6 ⬚
  RCHPK/HAM TW10 .... 176 G5
Perry Gdns *ED* N9 .... 99 M6
Perry Garth *NTHLT* UB5 .... 133 K3
Perry Gv *DART* DA1 .... 165 P10
Perry Hall Cl *ORP* BR6 .... 207 K7
Perry Hall Rd *ORP* BR6 .... 207 J6
Perry Hl *CAT* SE6 .... 182 E5
  WAB EN9 .... 45 L9
Perry How *WPK* KT4 .... 200 D9
Perrylands La *HORL* RH6 .... 279 J8
Perrylands La *HORL* RH6 .... 280 G5
Perry Mnr *CHST* BR7 .... 185 H9
Perrymans Farm Rd
  GNTH/NBYPK IG2 .... 122 G4
Perryman Wy *SLN* SL2 .... 128 B6 ⬚
Perry Md *BUSH* WD23 .... 74 B10
  ENC/FH EN2 .... 79 H4
Perrymead St *FUL/PGN* SW6 .... 157 K7
Perryn Rd *ACT* W3 .... 136 A3
  BERM/RHTH SE16 .... 160 A2
Perry Oak Dr *HTHAIR* TW6 .... 151 N8
Perry Oaks Dr *WDR/YW* UB7 .... 151 L8
Perry Ri *FSTH* SE23 .... 182 D6
Perry Rd *HLWS* CM18 .... 46 F4
Perrysfield Rd *CHES/WCR* EN8 .... 62 D3
Perrys La *ORP* BR6 .... 227 L9
Perry Spring *HLWE* CM17 .... 47 M3
Perry St *CHST* BR7 .... 185 H9
  DART DA1 .... 164 F9
  GVW DA11 .... 190 B4
Perry V *FSTH* SE23 .... 182 C5 ⬚
Perry Wy *SOCK/AV* RM15 .... 146 B9
Persant Rd *CAT* SE6 .... 183 K6
Perseverance Pl *BRXN/ST* SW9 .... 159 H6 ⬚
Persfield Rd *EW* KT17 .... 220 D6 ⬚
Pershore Cl *FUL/PGN* SW6 .... 157 K8 ⬚
Pershore Gv *CAR* SM5 .... 201 N6
Pert Cl *MUSWH* N10 .... 98 C8
Perth Av *CDALE/KGS* NW9 .... 116 A5
  SL SL1 .... 128 C8
  YEAD UB4 .... 133 K6
Perth Cl *CRAWW* RH11 .... 283 N4
  RYNPK SW20 .... 200 C2
Perth Rd *BARK* IG11 .... 142 G4
  BECK BR3 .... 205 H2
  FSBYPK N4 .... 119 H6
  GNTH/NBYPK IG2 .... 122 A4
  LEY E10 .... 120 D6
  PLSTW E13 .... 141 M1
  WDGN N22 .... 99 J9
Perth Ter *GNTH/NBYPK* IG2 .... 122 F5
Perwell Av *RYLN/HDSTN* HA2 .... 113 N6
Pescot Hl *HHW* HP1 .... 35 L4
Petauel Rd *TEDD* TW11 .... 176 D9
Petavel Rd *TEDD* TW11 .... 176 D9
Peter Av *OXTED* RH8 .... 261 J5
  WLSDN NW10 .... 136 C2
Peterboat Cl *GNWCH* SE10 .... 161 K3
Peterborough Ms *FUL/PGN* SW6 .... 157 K8 ⬚
Peterborough Rd *CAR* SM5 .... 201 P6
  FUL/PGN SW6 .... 157 K9
  GUW GU2 .... 249 L8 ⬚
  HRW HA1 .... 114 G1
  LEY E10 .... 121 H3
Peterborough Vls *FUL/PGN* SW6 .... 157 L7 ⬚
Petergate *BTSEA* SW11 .... 157 N7 ⬚
Peterhead Ms *DTCH/LGLY* SL3 .... 150 D4
Peterhill Cl *CFSP/GDCR* SL9 .... 90 B6
Peterlee Ct *HHNE* HP2 .... 36 A2 ⬚
Peters Av *LCOL/BKTW* AL2 .... 57 H2
Peters Cl *BCTR* RM8 .... 123 N6
  EDGW HA8 .... 95 J7
  STAN HA7 .... 95 J7
  WELL DA16 .... 163 H8
Petersfield Av *HARH* RM3 .... 105 M7
  SLN SL2 .... 129 M10
  STA TW18 .... 173 M8
Petersfield Crs *COUL/CHIP* CR5 .... 240 F1
  UED N18 .... 99 K6
Petersfield Ri *PUT/ROE* SW15 .... 178 E4
Petersfield Rd *ACT* W3 .... 155 P1
  STA TW18 .... 173 M8
Petersham Av *BF/WBF* KT14 .... 215 P8
Petersham Cl *BF/WBF* KT14 .... 215 P8 ⬚
  RCHPK/HAM TW10 .... 177 J5 ⬚
  SUT SM1 .... 221 J2
Petersham Dr *STMC/STPC* BR5 .... 207 J2
Petersham Gdns *STMC/STPC* BR5 .... 207 J2
Petersham La *SKENS* SW7 .... 15 J3
Petersham Ms *SKENS* SW7 .... 15 J4
Petersham Pl *SKENS* SW7 .... 15 J3
Petersham Rd *RCHPK/HAM* TW10 .... 177 J5
Petersmead Cl
  KWD/TDW/WH KT20 .... 238 F9 ⬚
Peter's Pl *BERK* HP4 .... 33 K3
Peterstone Rd *ABYW* SE2 .... 163 L1
Peterstow Cl *WIM/MER* SW19 .... 179 H3
Peter St *SOHO/CST* W1F 11 J6
Peters Wood Hl *WARE* SG12 .... 26 C4
Petherton Rd *HBRY* N5 .... 119 K10
Petley Rd *HMSMTH* W6 .... 156 G4
Peto Pl *CAMTN* NW1 .... 10 F1
Peto St North *CAN/RD* E16 .... 141 L9
Petre Cl *CRAWW* RH11 .... 283 N4
Petresfield Wy *RBRW/HUT* CM13 .... 127 P4
Petridge Rd *REDH* RH1 .... 276 A5 ⬚
Pett Cl *HCH* RM12 .... 124 C3
Petten Cl *STMC/STPC* BR5 .... 207 P4
Petten Gv *STMC/STPC* BR5 .... 207 P5
Petters Rd *ASHTD* KT21 .... 237 L2
Pettits Bvd *ROM* RM1 .... 104 F10
Pettits Cl *ROM* RM1 .... 104 F10
Pettits La *BRWN* CM15 .... 87 K3
Pettits La North *ROM* RM1 .... 104 E9
Pettit's Pl *DAGE* RM10 .... 124 B10
Pettit's Rd *DAGE* RM10 .... 124 B10
Pettiward Cl *PUT/ROE* SW15 .... 156 F10 ⬚
Pettley Gdns *ROMW/RG* RM7 .... 124 E3 ⬚
Pettman Crs *THMD* SE28 .... 162 G3
Pettsgrove Av *ALP/SUD* HA0 .... 115 P1

Pett's Hl *RYLN/HDSTN* HA2 .... 114 A9
Petts La *SHPTN* TW17 .... 196 B4
Pett St *CHARL* SE7 .... 162 B3
Petts Wood Rd *STMC/STPC* BR5 .... 206 C5
Petty France *STJSPK* SW1H 17 H3
Pettys Cl *CHES/WCR* EN8 .... 62 C5
Petworth Cl *COUL/CHIP* CR5 .... 240 D5 ⬚
  NTHLT UB5 .... 133 N2 ⬚
Petworth Ct *CRAWW* RH11 .... 283 J10 ⬚
Petworth Gdns *HGDN/ICK* UB10 .... 132 D3
  RYNPK SW20 .... 200 E3 ⬚
Petworth Rd *BXLYHS* DA6 .... 186 B1
  NFNCH/WDSP N12 .... 97 P6
Petworth St *BTSEA* SW11 .... 157 P7
Petworth Wy *HCH* RM12 .... 124 C9
Petyt Pl *CHEL* SW3 .... 15 N10
Petyward *CHEL* SW3 .... 15 N6
Pevensey Av *EN* EN1 .... 79 L6
  FBAR/BDGN N11 .... 98 E5
Pevensey Cl *CRAWE* RH10 .... 284 D8 ⬚
  ISLW TW7 .... 154 B6
Pevensey Rd *FELT* TW13 .... 175 M4
  FSTGT E7 .... 121 N9
  SLN SL2 .... 128 F7
  TOOT SW17 .... 179 N7
Peverel *EHAM* E6 .... 142 C1
Peverel Rd *CRAWW* RH11 .... 283 H8
Peveril Dr *TEDD* TW11 .... 176 C7
Pewley Bank *GU* GU1 .... 268 B2
Pewley Hl *GU* GU1 .... 268 A2
Pewley Point *GU* GU1 .... 268 B2
Pewley Wy *GU* GU1 .... 268 B2
Peyton Pl *GNWCH* SE10 .... 161 H6 ⬚
Pharaoh Cl *MTCM* CR4 .... 202 A7 ⬚
Pheasant Cl *BERK* HP4 .... 33 P6 ⬚
  CAN/RD E16 .... 141 M8 ⬚
  PUR/KEN CR8 .... 223 J9
Pheasant Hl *CSTG* HP8 .... 89 P3
Pheasant Ri *CSHM* HP5 .... 51 J6
Pheasants Cl *CFSP/GDCR* SL9 .... 90 A7
Phelips Rd *HARL* CM19 .... 46 D6
Phelp St *WALW* SE17 .... 18 G8
Phelps Cl *HYS/HAR* UB3 .... 152 G3
Phene St *CHEL* SW3 .... 15 P9
Philanthropic Rd *REDH* RH1 .... 276 C1
Philan Wy *CRW* RM5 .... 104 E7
Philbeach Gdns *ECT* SW5 .... 14 C6
Philchurch Pl *WCHPL* E1 .... 13 P6 ⬚
Philimore Cl *WOOL/PLUM* SE18 .... 163 M4
Philip Av *ROM/RG* RM7 .... 124 C6
Philip Cl *BRWN* CM15 .... 86 G10
Philip Gdns *CROY/NA* CR0 .... 204 E9
Philip La *SEVS/STOTM* N15 .... 119 L2
Philippa Gdns *ELTH/MOT* SE9 .... 184 A1
Philip Rd *PECK* SE15 .... 159 P9
  RAIN RM13 .... 144 F1
  STA TW18 .... 173 N9
Philips Cl *MTCM* CR4 .... 202 B8
Philip St *PLSTW* E13 .... 141 M6
Phillida Rd *HARH* RM3 .... 105 P10
Phillimore Gardens Cl *KENS* W8 .... 14 E3 ⬚
Phillimore Gdns *KENS* W8 .... 14 E2 ⬚
  RAD WD7 .... 74 D2
Phillimore Wk *KENS* W8 .... 14 E3
Phillip Av *SWLY* BR8 .... 208 E4
Phillipp St *IS* N1 .... 7 K1
Phillippers *GSTN* WD25 .... 73 M1 ⬚
Phillips Cl *DART* DA1 .... 187 J2
Phillips Hatch *SHGR* GU5 .... 268 F7
Philpot La *CHOB/PIR* GU24 .... 213 P6
  FENCHST EC3M 13 J2
Philpots Cl *WDR/YW* UB7 .... 131 N9 ⬚
Phineas Pett Road Rd
  ELTH/MOT SE9 .... 162 B9
Phipp's Bridge Rd *MTCM* CR4 .... 201 N3 ⬚
  WIM/MER SW19 .... 179 N9
Phipps Bd *SL* SL1 .... 128 C7
Phipps Hatch La *ENC/FH* EN2 .... 79 K4
Phipp St *SDTCH* EC2A 13 J1
Phoebeth Rd *LEW* SE13 .... 182 F1
Phoenix Cl *NTHWD* HA6 .... 92 G5
  WWKM BR4 .... 205 J9
Phoenix Dr *HAYES* BR2 .... 226 A1
Phoenix Pk *BORE* WD6 .... 76 B1
Phoenix Pl *DART* DA1 .... 187 L1
  FSBYW WC1X 5 P1
Phoenix Rd *CAMTN* NW1 .... 5 J7
  PGE/AN SE20 .... 182 B9
Phoenix St *LSO/SEVD* WC2H 11 K6
Phoenix Wy *HEST* TW5 .... 153 L5
  NWMAL KT3 .... 200 A8
The Phygtle *CFSP/GDCR* SL9 .... 90 B7
Phyllis Av *NWMAL* KT3 .... 200 G3
Picardy Manorway *BELV* DA17 .... 164 C1
Picardy Rd *BELV* DA17 .... 164 B2
Picardy St *BELV* DA17 .... 164 B1
Piccadilly *MYFR/PICC* W1J 16 D1
Piccotts End La *HHNE* HP2 .... 35 M3
Piccotts End Rd *HHNE* HP2 .... 35 M3
Pickard Av *EHAM* E6 .... 142 C4 ⬚
Pickering Av *EHAM* E6 .... 142 C1
Pickering Cl *HOM* E9 .... 139 J3
Pickering Gdns *SNWD* SE25 .... 203 N6
Pickering St *IS* N1 .... 6 D5
Pickets Cl *BUSH* WD23 .... 94 B3
Pickets St *BAL* SW12 .... 180 B3
Pickett Cft *STAN* HA7 .... 95 N3
Picketts Av *AL* SW11 .... 22 G5
Picketts La *REDH* RH1 .... 276 D9
Pickett's Lock La *ED* N9 .... 100 D3
Pickford Cl *BXLYHN* DA7 .... 163 P8
Pickford Dr *DTCH/LGLY* SL3 .... 130 B10
Pickford La *BXLYHN* DA7 .... 163 P8
Pickford Rd *BXLYHN* DA7 .... 163 P9
  WOKS/MYFD GU22 .... 229 N6
Pick Hl *WAB* EN9 .... 45 N8
Pickhurst Gn *HAYES* BR2 .... 205 K6
Pickhurst La *WWKM* BR4 .... 205 L6
Pickhurst Md *HAYES* BR2 .... 205 K6
Pickhurst Pk *HAYES* BR2 .... 205 J5
Pickhurst Ri *WWKM* BR4 .... 205 K5
Pickins Piece *DTCH/LGLY* SL3 .... 150 D9
Pickwick Cl *HSLWW* TW4 .... 175 M1 ⬚
Pickwick Gdns *GVW* DA11 .... 190 A6
Pickwick Ms *UED* N18 .... 99 M6
Pickwick Pl *HRW* HA1 .... 114 E6
Pickwick Rd *DUL* SE21 .... 181 L3
Pickwick St *STHWK* SE1 .... 18 F2
Pickwick Wy *CHST* BR7 .... 184 F9
Picquets Wy *BNSTD* SM7 .... 239 H7
Picton Pl *MBLAR* W1H 10 B5
Picton St *CMBW* SE5 .... 159 K6
Piedmont Rd *WOOL/PLUM* SE18 .... 162 G4
Pield Heath Av *UX/CGN* UB8 .... 132 B6
Pield Heath Rd *UX/CGN* UB8 .... 132 A6
Pier Head *WAP* E1W .... 140 D10 ⬚
Pierian Spring *HHW* HP1 .... 35 L4 ⬚
Piermont Pl *BMLY* BR1 .... 206 A2
Piermont Rd *EDUL* SE22 .... 182 A1
Pierpoint Al *ACT* W3 .... 135 N7
Pierpoint Rd *CAR* SM5 .... 201 M4
Pier Rd *CAN/RD* E16 .... 160 C1
  EBED/NFELT TW14 .... 175 J1
  ERITH DA8 .... 166 C1
  GRH DA9 .... 166 G10
  GVW DA11 .... 190 C5
Pierson Rd *WDSR* SL4 .... 148 B3
Pier St *POP/IOD* E14 .... 161 N3
Pier Ter *WAND/EARL* SW18 .... 157 L10
Pier Wy *WOOL/PLUM* SE18 .... 162 G3
Pigeonhouse La *COUL/CHIP* CR5 .... 257 M1
Pigeon La *HPTN* TW12 .... 175 P7
Piggottshill La *HARP* AL5 .... 20 D1
Piggotts Orch *AMSS* HP7 .... 48 E5
Pigott St *POP/IOD* E14 .... 140 N9
Pike Cl *BMLY* BR1 .... 183 N4
  UX/CGN UB8 .... 132 A3
Pike La *UPMR* RM14 .... 126 E10
Pike Rd *MLHL* NW7 .... 96 A5

Pike's End *PIN* HA5 .... 113 J2
Pikes Hl *EPSOM* KT18 .... 220 B10 ⬚
Pike Wy *EPP* CM16 .... 66 B3
Pilgrimage St *STHWK* SE1 .... 18 G2
Pilgrim Cl *GSTN* WD25 .... 55 L9 ⬚
  LCOL/BKTW AL2 .... 56 B3
  MRDN SM4 .... 201 L10
Pilgrim Hl *WNWD* SE27 .... 181 K7
Pilgrims Cl *BRWN* CM15 .... 86 B9
  NTHLT UB5 .... 114 B10 ⬚
  PLMGR N13 .... 98 G5
  RDKG RH5 .... 273 K9
  SHGR GU5 .... 270 B5
Pilgrims Ct *DART* DA1 .... 187 J1
Pilgrim's La *BRW* CM14 .... 86 D8
  CDH/CHF RM16 .... 147 N10
  CDH/CHF RM16 .... 167 J3
  CTHM CR3 .... 258 C2
  HAMP NW3 .... 117 N9
  OXTED RH8 .... 243 P10
Pilgrims Ms *POP/IOD* E14 .... 141 P3 ⬚
Pilgrims Pl *REIG* RH2 .... 257 K8 ⬚
Pilgrim's Ri *EBAR* EN4 .... 77 P9
Pilgrim St *BLKFR* EC4V .... 12 C6 ⬚
Pilgrims Vw *SWCM* DA10 .... 167 K10
Pilgrims Wy *ARCH* N19 .... 118 E6
  CHOB/PIR GU24 .... 230 F2
  DART DA1 .... 188 A4
  RDKG RH5 .... 254 C7
  REIG RH2 .... 257 J8
  RGUE GU4 .... 268 A4
  RSEV TN14 .... 246 A4
  SAND/SEL CR2 .... 223 N3
  SHGR GU5 .... 270 B5
  WBLY HA9 .... 115 N6
Pilgrims Wy East *RSEV* TN14 .... 247 K2
Pilgrims Wy West *RSEV* TN14 .... 246 D2
Pilkington Rd *ORP* BR6 .... 206 F10
  PECK SE15 .... 160 A8
Pilkingtons *HLWE* CM17 .... 47 N1
Pilot Cl *DEPT* SE8 .... 160 A8 ⬚
Pilots Pl *GVE* DA12 .... 190 F2
Pilsden Cl *WIM/MER* SW19 .... 178 G4 ⬚
Piltdown Rd *OXHEY* WD19 .... 93 L5 ⬚
  OXHEY WD19 .... 93 L5 ⬚
Pimlico Rd *BGVA* SW1W 16 C7
Pimms Cl *RGUE* GU4 .... 250 C7
Pinceybrook Rd *HLWS* CM18 .... 46 F5
Pinchbeck Rd *ORP* BR6 .... 227 J3
Pinchin St *WCHPL* E1 .... 13 P7
Pincott La *EHSLY* KT24 .... 252 C5
Pincott Pl *BROCKY* SE4 .... 160 C9 ⬚
Pincott Rd *BXLYHS* DA6 .... 186 B1
  WIM/MER SW19 .... 179 M10 ⬚
Pindar St *SDTCH* EC2A 13 J3
Pindock Ms *MV/WKIL* W9 .... 9 H2
Pine Apple Ct *WESTW* SW1E .... 16 G3 ⬚
Pineapple Rd *AMSS* HP7 .... 69 L5
Pine Av *GVE* DA12 .... 190 G4
  SRTFD E15 .... 121 J10
  WWKM BR4 .... 204 A8
Pine Cl *ADL/WDHM* KT15 .... 215 K3
  BERK HP4 .... 33 N5
  CHES/WCR EN8 .... 62 B4
  CRAWW RH11 .... 283 M4
  NTHWD HA6 .... 92 F7
  PGE/AN SE20 .... 204 B3 ⬚
  STAN HA7 .... 95 H2
  STHGT/OAK N14 .... 98 D1
  SWLY BR8 .... 208 G4 ⬚
  WOKN/KNAP GU21 .... 231 P3
Pine Coombe *CROY/NA* CR0 .... 224 C1
Pinecote Dr *ASC* SL5 .... 192 E7
Pine Ct *UPMR* RM14 .... 125 P9
Pine Crs *CAR* SM5 .... 221 P7
Pinecrest Gdns *ORP* BR6 .... 226 E1
Pinecroft *GPK* RM2 .... 125 K2
  HHS/BOV HP3 .... 36 A10
  KTN/HRWW/W HA3 .... 115 L3
  RBRW/HUT CM13 .... 107 N1
  WELL DA16 .... 163 K6
Pinecroft Crs *BAR* EN5 .... 77 H8
Pine Dean *GT/LBKH* KT23 .... 254 A1
Pinefield Cl *POP/IOD* E14 .... 140 F9
Pine Gdns *BRYLDS* KT5 .... 199 M6
  HORL RH6 .... 280 B5 ⬚
  RSLP HA4 .... 113 J6
Pine Gld *ORP* BR6 .... 226 C2
Pine Gv *ARCH* N19 .... 118 F7 ⬚
  BFOR GU20 .... 212 C3
  BRKMPK AL9 .... 59 L1
  BUSH WD23 .... 73 N5
  LCOL/BKTW AL2 .... 55 N6
  TRDG/WHET N20 .... 97 J2
  WEY KT13 .... 216 C2
  WIM/MER SW19 .... 179 K3
Pine Hl *EPSOM* KT18 .... 238 C7
Pinehurst *ASC* SL5 .... 192 C5 ⬚
  RSEV TN14 .... 247 M7
Pinehurst Cl *ABLGY* WD5 .... 54 F8
  KWD/TDW/WH KT20 .... 239 K8
Pinehurst Wk *ORP* BR6 .... 207 H1
Pinel Cl *VW* GU25 .... 194 B4 ⬚
Pinemartin Cl *CRICK* NW2 .... 116 F7 ⬚
Pineneedle La *SEV* TN13 .... 247 N3
Pine Pl *HYS/HAR* UB4 .... 133 J2
  BNSTD SM7 .... 238 G7
Pine Rdg *CAR* SM5 .... 222 C7
Pine Rd *CRICK* NW2 .... 116 F9
  FBAR/BDGN N11 .... 98 B3
  WOKS/MYFD GU22 .... 229 P6
Pines Av *EN* EN1 .... 80 B2
Pines Cl *AMS* HP6 .... 68 G3
Pine Shaw *CRAWE* RH10 .... 284 D6
Pines Rd *BMLY* BR1 .... 206 B2
The Pines *BORE* WD6 .... 75 L6 ⬚
  CDH/CHF RM16 .... 147 N10 ⬚
  HHW HP1 .... 35 J10
  PUR/KEN CR8 .... 223 J9
  SUN TW16 .... 197 H3
  WFD IG8 .... 101 J8
  WOKN/KNAP GU21 .... 214 C10
Pine St *CLKNW* EC1R 12 A1
Pinetree Cl *CFSP/GDCR* SL9 .... 89 P8
Pine Tree Cl *HEST* TW5 .... 153 P7 ⬚
Pine Tree Hl *WOKS/MYFD* GU22 .... 232 B3
Pinetrees Cl *CRAWE* RH10 .... 285 J2
Pine Trees Dr *HGDN/ICK* UB10 .... 111 P9
Pine Vw Cl *RGUE* GU4 .... 269 J6
Pine Vw *BELMT* SM2 .... 221 N6 ⬚
  BERK HP4 .... 33 J2
  BNSTD SM7 .... 239 N6
  BRYLDS KT5 .... 199 N6
  CAR SM5 .... 221 N6
  COB KT11 .... 217 L10
  CTHM CR3 .... 241 M8
  EHSLY KT24 .... 252 A1
  GT/LBKH KT23 .... 254 A1
Pine Wy *EGH* TW20 .... 171 N9
Pinewood *WGCE* AL7 .... 23 H7 ⬚
Pinewood Av *ADL/WDHM* KT15 .... 215 K3
  BFN/LL DA15 .... 185 H4
  PIN HA5 .... 94 C5 ⬚
  RAIN RM13 .... 145 J6 ⬚
  SEV TN13 .... 247 L2
  UX/CGN UB8 .... 132 C4

ORP BR6 .... 206 G8 ⬚
  PIN HA5 .... 94 A7
  STAL AL1 .... 39 H6
  TIL RM18 .... 169 L2 ⬚
  WAT WD17 .... 73 H5 ⬚
  WOKN/KNAP GU21 .... 232 D1
Pinewood Dr *ORP* BR6 .... 227 L1
  POTB/CUF EN6 .... 59 J7
  STA TW18 .... 173 K8 ⬚
  HHW HP1 .... 35 L6
Pinewood Gdns *HHS/BOV* HP3 .... 35 P7 ⬚
Pinewood Gv *IVER* SL0 .... 130 F2
Pinewood Gv *ADL/WDHM* KT15 .... 215 K3 ⬚
  WEA W13 .... 135 H8
Pinewood Ms
  STWL/WRAY TW19 .... 173 N2 ⬚
Pinewood Pk *ADL/WDHM* KT15 .... 215 L2
Pinewood Rd *ABR/ST* RM4 .... 104 D5
  ABYW SE2 .... 163 N5
  FELT TW13 .... 175 J6
  HAYES BR2 .... 205 M4
  IVER SL0 .... 130 F3
  VW GU25 .... 193 L4
Pinfold Rd *BUSH* WD23 .... 73 N6
  STRHM/NOR SW16 .... 180 F7
Pinglestone Cl *WDR/YW* UB7 .... 151 P6
Pinkcoat Cl *FELT* TW13 .... 175 J6 ⬚
Pinkham Way North Circular Rd
  MUSWH N10 .... 98 A8
Pink La *SL* SL1 .... 128 A4
Pinks Hl *SWLY* BR8 .... 208 F5
Pinkwell Av *HYS/HAR* UB3 .... 152 E3
Pinkwell La *HYS/HAR* UB3 .... 152 D3
Pinley Gdns *DAGW* RM9 .... 143 L3
Pinnacle Hl *BXLYHN* DA7 .... 164 C10
Pinnacle Hl North *BXLYHN* DA7 .... 164 C9
Pinnacles *WAB* EN9 .... 63 K10
Pinnate Pl *WGCE* AL7 .... 23 H9
Pinn Cl *UX/CGN* UB8 .... 131 N8 ⬚
Pinnell Rd *ELTH/MOT* SE9 .... 162 A10
Pinner Ct *PIN* HA5 .... 113 P2
Pinner Gn *PIN* HA5 .... 93 K10
Pinner Gv *PIN* HA5 .... 113 M2
Pinner Hl *PIN* HA5 .... 93 J8
Pinner Hill Rd *PIN* HA5 .... 93 K9
Pinner Park Av *RYLN/HDSTN* HA2 .... 94 B10
Pinner Park Gdns
  RYLN/HDSTN HA2 .... 94 B10
Pinner Rd *HRW* HA1 .... 114 A3
  NTHWD HA6 .... 92 G9
  OXHEY WD19 .... 73 L10
  PIN HA5 .... 113 N2
Pinner Vw *RYLN/HDSTN* HA2 .... 114 B2
Pinnock's Av *CAR* SM5 .... 190 E4
Pinn Wy *RSLP* HA4 .... 113 J6
Pinstone Wy *CFSP/GDCR* SL9 .... 110 F2
Pintail Cl *EHAM* E6 .... 142 B7 ⬚
Pintail Rd *WFD* IG8 .... 101 N8
Pintail Wy *YEAD* UB4 .... 133 L7
Pinto Cl *BORE* WD6 .... 76 A10 ⬚
Pinto Wy *BKHTH/KID* SE3 .... 161 N10
Pioneer Cl *SHB* W12 .... 136 E8 ⬚
Pioneer St *PECK* SE15 .... 159 P7
Pioneer Wy *SHB* W12 .... 136 E8 ⬚
  SWLY BR8 .... 208 F3
  WATW WD18 .... 72 G10
Piper Cl *HOLWY* N7 .... 118 F1
Piper Rd *KUT* KT1 .... 199 M3 ⬚
Pipers Av *HARP* AL5 .... 20 C4
Pipers Cl *COB* KT11 .... 235 L1
  SL SL1 .... 128 B5
Piper's End *VW* GU25 .... 194 A3
Pipers Gdns *CROY/NA* CR0 .... 204 B8
Pipers Gn *CDALE/KGS* NW9 .... 115 P3
Pipers Green La *EDGW* HA8 .... 95 K4
Piper's Green Rd *BH/WHM* TN16 .... 263 K4
Pipers La *BH/WHM* TN16 .... 263 L3
  HARP AL5 .... 20 D4
Pipewell Rd *CAR* SM5 .... 201 N6
Pippbrook Gdns *DORK* RH4 .... 272 G3 ⬚
Pippens *WGCW* AL8 .... 23 H2
Pippin Cl *CRICK* NW2 .... 116 D8
  CROY/NA CR0 .... 204 E8
  RAD WD7 .... 57 K9
Pippins Cl *WDR/YW* UB7 .... 151 N2
Pippins Ct *ASHF* TW15 .... 174 C9
The Pippins *DTCH/LGLY* SL3 .... 130 C10
Piquet Rd *PGE/AN* SE20 .... 204 B2
Pirbright Crs *CROY/NA* CR0 .... 225 N1
Pirbright Rd *RGUW* GU3 .... 248 B5
  WAND/EARL SW18 .... 179 J3
Pirie Cl *CMBW* SE5 .... 159 H6 ⬚
Pirrip Cl *GVE* DA12 .... 191 J4
Pirton Cl *STALE/WH* AL4 .... 39 H1
Pishiobury Dr *SBW* CM21 .... 29 N3
Pitcairn Cl *ROMW/RG* RM7 .... 124 B2
Pitcairn Rd *MTCM* CR4 .... 180 A10
Pitchfont La *OXTED* RH8 .... 261 M2
Pitchford St *SRTFD* E15 .... 141 J2
Pit Farm Rd *GU* GU1 .... 250 D10
Pitfield Cl *HDNE* HP2 .... 211 L4
Pitfield Crs *THMD* SE28 .... 143 K10
Pitfield St *IS* N1 .... 7 J1 ⬚
Pitfield Wy *PEND* EN3 .... 80 B5 ⬚
  WLSDN NW10 .... 135 P1
Pitfold Rd *LEE/GVPK* SE12 .... 183 M3
Pitlake *CROY/NA* CR0 .... 203 J9
Pitman St *CMBW* SE5 .... 159 K6
Pitsea Pl *WCHPL* E1 .... 140 C8 ⬚
Pitsea St *WCHPL* E1 .... 140 C8 ⬚
Pitsfield *WGCW* AL8 .... 22 G2
Pitshanger La *W5* 134 G2
Pitson Cl *ADL/WDHM* KT15 .... 215 N1 ⬚
Pitstone Cl *STALE/WH* AL4 .... 39 H1 ⬚
Pitt Cr *WIM/MER* SW19 .... 179 L7
Pitt Dr *STALE/WH* AL4 .... 39 H1
Pittman Cl *RBRW/HUT* CM13 .... 107 P5
Pittman Gdns *IL* IG1 .... 122 F10
Pittman's Fld *HLW* CM20 .... 29 J10
Pitt Rd *EW* KT17 .... 220 B10
  ORP BR6 .... 226 F1
  RYLN/HDSTN HA2 .... 114 B7 ⬚
  THHTH CR7 .... 203 L2
Pitt's Head Ms *MYFR/PICC* W1J .... 10 E10 ⬚
Pittsmead Av *HAYES* BR2 .... 205 M7
Pitt St *KENS* W8 .... 14 F1
Pittville Gdns *SNWD* SE25 .... 203 P8
Pix Farm La *HHW* HP1 .... 34 E7
Pixham La *DORK* RH4 .... 255 H7
Pixholme Gv *DORK* RH4 .... 255 H10
Pixies Hill Crs *HHW* HP1 .... 35 J3
Pixies Hill Rd *HHW* HP1 .... 35 J3
Pixley St *POP/IOD* E14 .... 140 G8
Pixton Wy *CROY/NA* CR0 .... 224 C8
Place Farm Av *ORP* BR6 .... 206 G8
Place Farm La *BRWN* CM15 .... 86 D3
Place Farm Rd *REDH* RH1 .... 259 L6
Placehouse La *COUL/CHIP* CR5 .... 240 G5
Plackett Wy *SL* SL1 .... 148 B5
Plaines Cl *SL* SL1 .... 128 E10 ⬚
The Plain *EPP* CM16 .... 65 L5
Plaistow Gv *BMLY* BR1 .... 183 N10
  SRTFD E15 .... 141 L3
Plaistow La *BMLY* BR1 .... 183 N10
Plaistow Park Rd *PLSTW* E13 .... 141 N4
Plaistow Rd *PLSTW* E13 .... 141 L4
  SRTFD E15 .... 141 L3
Plaitford Cl *RKW/CH/CXG* WD3 .... 91 P3
Plane Av *GVW* DA11 .... 190 A4
The Planes *CHERT* KT16 .... 195 M7
Plane St *SYD* SE26 .... 182 A6 ⬚
Plane Tree Crs *FELT* TW13 .... 175 J6
Plantagenet Cl *WAB* EN9 .... 62 C9 ⬚
Plantagenet Pl *HOR/WEW* KT19 .... 220 L1 ⬚
Plantagenet Gdns *CHDH* RM6 .... 123 N5 ⬚

Plantagenet Pl CHDH RM6 ...... 123 N5 4
Plantagenet Pl BAR EN5 ...... 77 M8
Plantain Pl STHWK SE1 ...... 18 G1
Plantation Dr STMC/STPC BR5 ...... 207 N8
Plantation La WARL CR6 ...... 242 D5
Plantation Rd AMS HP6 ...... 69 K3
  ERITH DA8 ...... 165 H7
  SWLY BR8 ...... 187 H10
The Plantation BKHTH/KID SE3 ...... 161 M8
Plantation Wk HHW HP1 ...... 35 K3 2
  HHW HP1 ...... 35 K4 2
Plantation Wy AMS HP6 ...... 69 K3
Plashet Gdns RBRW/HUT CM13 ...... 117 M1
Plashet Gv EHAM E6 ...... 141 P3
Plashet Rd PLSTW E13 ...... 141 M3
Plashets RBSF CM22 ...... 30 D2
Plassy Rd CAT SE6 ...... 182 G3
Platford Gn EMPK RM11 ...... 125 M2
Platina St SDTCH EC2A 13 H1
Plato Rd CLAP SW4 ...... 158 F10
Platt Meadow RGUE GU4 ...... 250 C8 2
Platt's La HAMP NW3 ...... 117 K8
Platts Rd PEND EN3 ...... 80 B5
Platt St CAMTN NW1 ...... 5 J7
The Platt AMSS HP7 ...... 68 C6
Plawsfield Rd BECK BR3 ...... 204 C1 1
Plaxtol Cl BMLY BR1 ...... 205 P1
Plaxtol Rd ERITH DA8 ...... 164 B6
Playfair St HMSMTH W6 ...... 156 F4 3
Playfield Av CRW RM5 ...... 104 D9
Playfield Crs EDUL SE22 ...... 181 M1
Playfield Rd EDGW HA8 ...... 95 F10
Playford Rd FSBYPK N4 ...... 119 H7 3
Playgreen Wy CAT SE6 ...... 182 F7 1
Playground Cl BECK BR3 ...... 204 D4
Playhouse Sq CROY/NA CR0 ...... 46 F1 3
Playhouse Yd BLKFR EC4V 12 C1
Pleasance Rd PUT/ROE SW15 ...... 178 E1 1
  STMC/STPC BR5 ...... 207 L2
The Pleasance PUT/ROE SW15 ...... 156 E10 3
Pleasant Gv CROY/NA CR0 ...... 204 E10
Pleasant Mt GUW GU2 ...... 267 P2 1
  HERT/BAY SG13 ...... 26 B7
Pleasant Pl IS N1 ...... 6 D4
  WOT/HER KT12 ...... 217 L3
Pleasant Ri BRKMPK AL9 ...... 40 F1
  ORP BR6 ...... 226 F2
Pleasant Vw ERITH DA8 ...... 164 F4 1
Pleasure Pit Rd ASHTD KT21 ...... 237 N4
Plender St CAMTN NW1 ...... 4 C6
Pleshey Rd HOLWY N7 ...... 118 E9
Plessman Wy WLGTN SM6 ...... 222 F5 1
Plevna Cl POP/IOD E14 ...... 161 H2
  HPTN TW12 ...... 198 A1
Plevna Crs SEVS/STOTM N15 ...... 119 M4
Plevna Rd ED N9 ...... 90 B2
  HPTN TW12 ...... 198 A1
Plevna St POP/IOD E14 ...... 161 H2
Pleydell Av HMSMTH W6 ...... 156 F4 5
  NRWD SE19 ...... 181 N10
Pleydell St EMB EC4Y 12 B6 1
Plimsoll Cl POP/IOD E14 ...... 140 G8
Plimsoll Rd FSBYPK N4 ...... 119 J8
Plough Cl CRAWW RH11 ...... 283 J5 1
Plough Farm Cl RSLP HA4 ...... 112 E4 3
Plough Hl POTB/CUF EN6 ...... 60 F5
Plough La BERK 34 E1
  COB KT11 ...... 235 J2
  CROY/NA CR0 ...... 222 F1 2
  DEN/HRF UB9 ...... 91 M7
  EDUL SE22 ...... 181 N2
  PUR/KEN CR8 ...... 222 C6
  RKW/CH/CXG WD3 ...... 53 J9
  SLN SL2 ...... 129 N3
  WIM/MER SW19 ...... 179 L8
  WLGTN SM6 ...... 222 F5
Plough Lane Cl WLGTN SM6 ...... 222 F12
Ploughlees La SL1 ...... 129 K9
Ploughmans Cl CAMTN NW1 ...... 5 J5
Ploughmans End ISLW TW7 ...... 176 L12 3
  WGCE AL7 ...... 23 M6 2
Plough Pl FLST/FETLN EC4A 12 B5 1
Plough Ri UPMR RM14 ...... 126 D5
  HOR/WEW KT19 ...... 220 A4
  HORL RH6 ...... 281 K4
Plough St WCHPL E1 ...... 13 L5 1
Plough Ter BTSEA SW11 ...... 157 N10 1
Plough Yd SDTCH EC2A 13 K2
Plover Cl BERK HP4 ...... 33 P6 3
  CRAWW RH11 ...... 283 N6
  STA TW18 ...... 173 J6 2
Plover Gdns UPMR RM14 ...... 126 E6 1
Plovers Md BRWN CM15 ...... 87 J2
Plovers Ri CHOB/PIR GU24 ...... 230 D6
Plover Wy BERM/RHTH SE16 ...... 160 D2 1
  YEAD UB4 ...... 133 L8
Plowman Cl UED N18 ...... 99 L6
Plowman Wy BCTR RM8 ...... 123 M6
Ployters Rd HLWW/ROY CM19 ...... 46 F5 1
Plumbers Rw WCHPL E1 ...... 13 N4
Plumbridge St GNWCH SE10 ...... 161 H7 2
Plum Cl FELT TW13 ...... 155 J5 3
Plum Garth BTFD TW8 ...... 155 J3 3
Plum La WOOL/PLUM SE18 ...... 162 E6
Plummer La MTCM CR4 ...... 202 A1
Plummer Rd CLAP SW4 ...... 180 L3
Plumpton Av HCH RM12 ...... 125 N8
Plumpton Cl NTHLT UB5 ...... 133 P1
Plumpton Rd HOD EN11 ...... 45 H1
Plumpton Wy CAR SM5 ...... 201 P10
Plumstead Common Rd
  WOOL/PLUM SE18 ...... 162 G5
Plumstead High St
  WOOL/PLUM SE18 ...... 162 G3
Plumstead Rd WOOL/PLUM SE18 ...... 162 F3
Plumtree Cl DAGE RM10 ...... 144 D1 1
Plumtree Ct FLST/FETLN EC4A 12 B5
Pluto Ri HHNE HP2 ...... 35 P4
Plymouth Dr BGR/WK TN15 ...... 247 K10
Plymouth Rd BGR/WK TN15 ...... 247 K10
Plymouth Rd BMLY BR1 ...... 205 N1
  CAN/RD E16 ...... 141 M7
  SL1 ...... 128 D8
Plymouth Whf POP/IOD E14 ...... 161 J3
Plympton Av KIL/WHAMP NW6 ...... 2 C4
Plympton Cl BELV DA17 ...... 163 P2 3
Plympton Pl STJWD NW8 ...... 9 N2 2
Plympton Rd KIL/WHAMP NW6 ...... 2 C4
Plympton St STJWD NW8 ...... 9 N2
Plymstock Rd WELL DA16 ...... 163 M6
Pocklington Cl CDALE/KGS NW9 ...... 96 B10
Pocock Av WDR/YW UB7 ...... 152 A2 3
Pococks La WDSR SL4 ...... 149 K4
Pocock St STHWK SE1 ...... 18 C1
Podmore Rd WAND/EARL SW18 ...... 157 M10
Poets Cha HHW HP1 ...... 35 L5
Poets Ct HHW HP1 ...... 35 L5
Poets Ct HARP AL5 ...... 20 C2 1
Poets Ga CHESW EN7 ...... 61 L4
Poet's Rd HBRY N5 ...... 119 L10
Poets Wy HRW HA1 ...... 114 D2 2
Pointalls Cl FNCH N3 ...... 97 M10 2
Point Cl GNWCH SE10 ...... 161 H7
Pointer Cl THMD SE28 ...... 143 N8
Pointers Hl DORK RH4 ...... 272 E4 3
Pointers Rd COB KT11 ...... 234 E3
The Pointers ASHTD KT21 ...... 237 K6
Point Hl GNWCH SE10 ...... 161 H7
Point Pl WBLY HA9 ...... 135 N2
Point Pleasant
  WAND/EARL SW18 ...... 157 K10 3
Poland Rd SOHO/CST W1F 11 H5 3
Polayn Garth WGCW AL8 ...... 22 F4
Polebrook Rd BKHTH/KID SE3 ...... 161 P9
Polecroft La CAT SE6 ...... 182 G5
Polehanger La HHW HP1 ...... 35 H4
Pole Hill Rd CHING E4 ...... 101 H1

HGDN/ICK UB10 ...... 132 C6
Polesden Gdns RYNPK SW20 ...... 200 D6 3
Polesden Rd RPLY/SEND GU23 ...... 233 J9
Polesden Vw GT/LBKH KT23 ...... 254 A5
Polesden Vw GT/LBKH KT23 ...... 254 A3
Poles Hl CSHM HP5 ...... 50 F5
  RKW/CH/CXG WD3 ...... 53 H9
Poles La CRAWW RH11 ...... 283 M4 1
Polesteeple Hl BH/WHM TN16 ...... 244 A3
Polesworth Rd DAGW RM9 ...... 143 N2
Polhill RSEV TN14 ...... 246 D1
Police Station Rd WOT/HER KT12 ...... 217 K3
Pollard Av DEN/HRF UB9 ...... 111 J4
Pollard Cl CAN/RD E16 ...... 141 M9
  CHIG IG7 ...... 103 K6
  HOLWY N7 ...... 118 G10 3
  WDSR SL4 ...... 171 N1
Pollard Hatch HLWW/ROY CM19 ...... 46 E3 2
Pollard Rd MRDN SM4 ...... 201 N5
  TRDG/WHET N20 ...... 97 J3
  WOKS/MYFD GU22 ...... 232 E2
Pollards CRAWW RH11 ...... 283 M8 6
  RKW/CH/CXG WD3 ...... 90 G6
Pollards Cl CHESW EN7 ...... 61 K5
  LOU IG10 ...... 81 P2
Pollards Crs STRHM/NOR SW16 ...... 202 F3
Pollards Hl East
  STRHM/NOR SW16 ...... 202 G3
Pollards Hl North
  STRHM/NOR SW16 ...... 202 G3
Pollards Hl South
  STRHM/NOR SW16 ...... 202 F3
Pollards Hl West
  STRHM/NOR SW16 ...... 202 F3
Pollards Oak Crs OXTED RH8 ...... 261 M8 2
Pollards Oak Rd OXTED RH8 ...... 261 M8 1
Pollard St BETH E2 ...... 7 P9
Pollards Wood Hl OXTED RH8 ...... 261 M6
Pollards Wood Rd OXTED RH8 ...... 261 N7
  STRHM/NOR SW16 ...... 202 F2
Pollen St CONDST W1S 10 F6
Pollitt Dr STJWD NW8 ...... 9 L1
Pollyhaugh EYN DA4 ...... 209 M10
Polperro Cl ORP BR6 ...... 207 J6
Polsted La RGUW GU3 ...... 267 J6
Polsted Rd CAT SE6 ...... 182 E3
Polthorne Gv WOOL/PLUM SE18 ...... 162 F3
Poltimore Rd GUW GU2 ...... 267 M2
Polworth Rd STRHM/NOR SW16 ...... 180 F8
Polygon Rd CAMTN NW1 ...... 5 J9
The Polygon CLAP SW4 ...... 158 D10 3
Polytechnic St
  WOOL/PLUM SE18 ...... 162 D3 5
Pomell Wy WCHPL E1 ...... 13 M5 3
Pomeroy Av WATN WD25 ...... 73 J2 1
Pomeroy Crs WATN WD24 ...... 73 J2 1
Pomeroy St NWCR SE14 ...... 160 J9 3
Pomfret Rd CMBW SE5 ...... 159 J9 3
Pomoja La ARCH N19 ...... 118 F7 2
Pompadour Cl BRW CM14 ...... 107 H6 2
Pond Cl AMSS HP7 ...... 68 B10
  BKHTH/KID SE3 ...... 161 M8
  DEN/HRF UB9 ...... 91 M10
  NFNCH/WDSPK N12 ...... 97 P7
  WOT/HER KT12 ...... 217 P7
Pond Cottage La BECK BR3 ...... 204 F8
Pond Cft HAT AL10 ...... 40 C3
  WGCE AL7 ...... 23 H6
Ponder St HOLWY N7 ...... 5 N3 3
Pond Farm Cl
  KWD/TDW/WH KT20 ...... 238 E10 1
Pondfield Crs STALE/WH AL4 ...... 38 C3 3
Pondfield La GVE DA12 ...... 191 P10
  RBRW/HUT CM13 ...... 107 M5
Pondfield Rd DAGE RM10 ...... 124 C10
  HAYES BR2 ...... 205 K8
  ORP BR6 ...... 206 E10
  PUR/KEN CR8 ...... 241 J2
Pond Gn RSLP HA4 ...... 112 F7
Pond Hill Gdns CHEAM SM3 ...... 221 H3 1
Pond La CFSP/GDCR SL9 ...... 89 N9
  SHGR GU5 ...... 270 D10
Pond Md DUL SE21 ...... 181 L2
Pond Meadow GUW GU2 ...... 249 N10 1
Pond Park Rd CSHM HP5 ...... 50 C5
Pond Piece LHD/OX KT22 ...... 218 A10 3
Pond Pl CHEL SW3 ...... 15 N6
Pond Rd BKHTH/KID SE3 ...... 161 L8
  ECH TW20 ...... 172 F9
  HHS/BOV HP3 ...... 54 B1
  SRTFD E15 ...... 141 K4
  WOKS/MYFD GU22 ...... 231 M6 3
Pondside Cl HYS/HAR UB3 ...... 152 E6 3
Ponds La SHGR GU5 ...... 269 P8
The Ponds WEY KT13 ...... 216 E3
Pond St HAMP NW3 ...... 117 P10
Pond Wk UPMR RM14 ...... 126 D7 3
Pond Wy TEDD TW11 ...... 177 H9 3
Pondwicks AMSS HP7 ...... 68 G5 1
Pondwicks Cl STALW/RED AL3 ...... 38 B7
Pondwood Ri ORP BR6 ...... 207 H7
Pond Wood Rd CRAWE RH10 ...... 284 E5
Ponler St WCHPL E1 ...... 140 A8 10
Ponsard Rd WLSDN NW10 ...... 136 E5
Ponsford St HOM E9 ...... 140 B1 3
Ponsonby Pl WEST SW1P 17 K7
Ponsonby Rd PUT/ROE SW15 ...... 178 E3 1
Ponsonby Ter WEST SW1P 17 K7
Pontefract Rd BMLY BR1 ...... 183 M8
Ponton Rd VX/NE SW8 ...... 158 E6
Pont Street Ms CHEL SW3 ...... 16 A4
Pony Cha COB KT11 ...... 217 N9
Pool Cl BECK BR3 ...... 182 F8
  E/WMO/HCT KT8 ...... 197 N5
Pool Ct CAT SE6 ...... 182 E5
Poole Cl RSLP HA4 ...... 113 M7
Poole Court Rd HEST TW5 ...... 153 M8 1
Pool End Cl SHPTN TW17 ...... 196 B5 3
Pooles Buildings FSBYW WC1X 12 A2 1
Pooles La WLSDN NW10 ...... 119 H7 3
  WBPTN SW10 ...... 157 M1
Poole St IS N1 ...... 6 C6
Poole Wy YEAD UB4 ...... 132 F5 3
Pooley Av ECH TW20 ...... 172 E8
Pooley Green Rd ECH TW20 ...... 172 E8
Pooleys La BRKMPK AL9 ...... 40 E9
Pool La SL SL1 ...... 129 K9
Poolmans St BERM/RHTH SE16 ...... 160 F6 1
Poolmans St WDSR SL4 ...... 148 C9
Poolmans Rd BERM/RHTH SE16 ...... 160 F6 1
  HRW HA1 ...... 114 C5
Poolsford Rd CDALE/KGS NW9 ...... 114 F8
Poonah St WCHPL E1 ...... 140 B8 10
Pope CI EBED/NFELT TW14 ...... 174 A4 1
  WIM/MER SW19 ...... 179 N9 3
Pope Rd HAYES BR2 ...... 206 A5
Pope's La CRW RM5 ...... 176 B5 3
Popes Cl DTCH/LGLY SL3 ...... 150 F5
Popes Dr FNCH N3 ...... 97 K9
Popes Gv CROY/NA CR0 ...... 204 E10 3
  WHTN TW2 ...... 176 B5 3
Pope's La EA W5 ...... 155 J2 3
  WATN WD24 ...... 73 J3 3
Pope's Rd ABLGY WD5 ...... 54 F7
  BRXN/ST SW9 ...... 159 H9 3
Pope St STHWK SE1 ...... 19 L2
Popham Cl FELT TW13 ...... 175 M6 3
Popham Rd IS N1 ...... 6 C1
Popham St IS N1 ...... 6 B1
Popis Gdns WARE SG12 ...... 26 D1
Poplar Av AMSS HP7 ...... 69 L5
  GVE DA12 ...... 190 D4

HAT AL10 ...... 40 A4
LHD/OX KT22 ...... 236 G5 3
MTCM CR4 ...... 202 A1
NWDGN UB2 ...... 154 A2
ORP BR6 ...... 206 E9
Poplar Bath St POP/IOD E14 ...... 140 C9 3
Poplar Cl CRAWW RH11 ...... 283 N4 2
  CSHM HP5 ...... 51 H4
  DTCH/LGLY SL3 ...... 150 B1 3
  HOM E9 ...... 120 E10 3
  PIN HA5 ...... 93 L9
  SOCK/AV RM15 ...... 147 J6
Poplar Crs HMSMTH W6 ...... 156 F1
  HOR/WEW KT19 ...... 220 A4
  RBRW/HUT CM13 ...... 87 P10
Poplar Dr BNSTD SM7 ...... 220 G10 3
Poplar Farm Cl HOR/WEW KT19 ...... 219 P4 3
Poplar Gdns NWMAL KT3 ...... 200 A2
Poplar Gv FBAR/BDGN N11 ...... 98 A7 3
  WBLY HA9 ...... 115 P8
Poplar High St POP/IOD E14 ...... 140 C9 3
Poplar Mt BELV DA17 ...... 164 C3
Poplar Pl BAY/PAD W2 ...... 8 C7
  HYS/HAR UB3 ...... 133 H9
  THMD SE28 ...... 143 M9
Poplar Rd ASHF TW15 ...... 174 D8
  CHEAM SM3 ...... 201 J8
  DEN/HRF UB9 ...... 151 M1
  HNHL SE24 ...... 158 K10 3
  LHD/OX KT22 ...... 236 G8
  RGUE GU4 ...... 268 B7
  WIM/MER SW19 ...... 201 K2
Poplar Rd South WIM/MER SW19 ...... 201 K3
Poplar Rw EPP CM16 ...... 83 H3
Poplars WCCE AL7 ...... 23 L4
Poplars Cl GSTN WD25 ...... 55 J8 3
  HART DA3 ...... 211 P3
  HAT AL10 ...... 40 A4
  RSLP HA4 ...... 112 F5 3
Poplar Shaw WAB EN9 ...... 63 L3 3
Poplars Rd LEY E10 ...... 120 C4
The Poplars ABR/ST RM4 ...... 83 L7 3
  CHESW EN7 ...... 61 M2
  HHW HP1 ...... 35 L7 3
  STAL AL1 ...... 38 G10 3
Poplar St ROMW/RG RM7 ...... 124 D2 3
Poplar Vw WBLY HA9 ...... 116 C5 3
Poplar Wk CROY/NA CR0 ...... 203 K9
  CTHM CR3 ...... 241 M9
  HNHL SE24 ...... 159 K10 3
Poplar Wy BARK/HLT IG6 ...... 122 E2 3
  FELT TW13 ...... 175 J6
Poppins Ct FLST/FETLN EC4A 12 C5 3
Poppleton Rd WAN E11 ...... 121 K4
Poppy Cl HHW HP1 ...... 35 H5
  MTCM CR4 ...... 202 B8
Poppyfields WCCE AL7 ...... 23 M6 3
Poppy La CROY/NA CR0 ...... 204 B7
Poppy Wk CHESW EN7 ...... 61 L4
Porchester Cl EMPK RM11 ...... 125 M4 3
  HART DA3 ...... 211 L4
Porchester Garden Ms
  BAY/PAD W2 ...... 9 H6 3
Porchester Gdns BAY/PAD W2 ...... 9 H7
Porchester Gdns BECK BR3 ...... 182 G9
Porchester Pl BAY/PAD W2 ...... 9 P6
Porchester Rd BAY/PAD W2 ...... 9 H5
  KUT KT1 ...... 199 N2
Porchester Sq BAY/PAD W2 ...... 9 H5
Porchester Ter BAY/PAD W2 ...... 9 J7
Porchester Ter North BAY/PAD W2 ...... 9 H5
Porchfield Cl BELMT SM2 ...... 221 L6 3
  GVE DA12 ...... 190 F5
Porch Wy TRDG/WHET N20 ...... 98 A4 3
Porcupine Cl ELTH/MOT SE9 ...... 184 H5
Porden Rd BRXN/ST SW9 ...... 158 G10 3
Poriock Av RYLN/HDSTN HA2 ...... 114 B6
Poriock Rd EN EN1 ...... 99 N1
Poriock St STHWK SE1 ...... 19 H1
Porridge Pot Aly GUW GU2 ...... 268 A2 3
Porrington Cl CHST BR7 ...... 206 C1
Portal Cl RSLP HA4 ...... 113 H9
  WNWD SE27 ...... 181 H6
Port Av GRH DA9 ...... 188 G2
Portbury Cl PECK SE15 ...... 159 P7 3
Portchester Cl CMBW SE5 ...... 159 K10 3
Portelet Rd WCHPL E1 ...... 140 C5 3
Porten Rd WKENS W14 ...... 14 A4
Porter Rd EHAM E6 ...... 142 C8
Porters Av DAGW RM9 ...... 143 L1
Porters Cl BRW CM14 ...... 106 C3 3
Porters Park Dr RAD WD7 ...... 57 K8
Porter St MHST W1U 10 B3 3
  STHWK SE1 ...... 12 F9
Porters Wy WDR/YW UB7 ...... 152 A2 3
Porters Wd STALW/RED AL3 ...... 38 E2 3
Porteus Rd BAY/PAD W2 ...... 9 K4
Portgate Cl MV/WKIL W9 ...... 8 D1 3
Porthcawe Rd SYD SE26 ...... 182 D7
Port HI HERT/WAS SG14 ...... 25 K5 3
  ORP BR6 ...... 227 L8
Portia Wy BOW E3 ...... 140 E6
Portinscale Rd PUT/ROE SW15 ...... 179 H1
Portland Av BFN/LL DA15 ...... 185 K2
  GVE DA12 ...... 190 E5
  NWMAL KT3 ...... 200 C7
  STNW/STAM N16 ...... 119 N6
Portland Cl CHDH RM6 ...... 123 P3
  SL1 ...... 128 C6
Portland Crs ASHF TW15 ...... 174 E7
  ELTH/MOT SE9 ...... 184 B5
  GFD/PVL UB6 ...... 134 A6
  STAN HA7 ...... 95 J10
Portland Dr CHESW EN7 ...... 61 P7
  ENC/FH EN2 ...... 79 M4 3
  REDH RH1 ...... 258 D5
Portland Gdns CHDH RM6 ...... 123 N3
  FSBYPK N4 ...... 119 J4 3
Portland Gv VX/NE SW8 ...... 158 C7
Portland Ms SOHO/CST W1F 11 H6 3
Portland Pl CAVSQ/HST W1G 10 F4 3
  EW KT17 ...... 220 B8 3
  HERT/BAY SG13 ...... 26 B7 3
  SNWD SE25 ...... 203 P4 3
Portland Ri FSBYPK N4 ...... 119 J6 3
Portland Rd ASHF TW15 ...... 173 N6 3
  BMLY BR1 ...... 183 P7
  DORK RH4 ...... 272 F1 3
  ELTH/MOT SE9 ...... 184 B5
  GVW DA11 ...... 190 E4
  KUT KT1 ...... 199 K3
  MTCM CR4 ...... 201 P2
  NTGHL W11 ...... 8 B7 3
  NWDGN UB2 ...... 153 N2 3
  SEVS/STOTM N15 ...... 119 M2
  SNWD SE25 ...... 204 A4
  YEAD UB4 ...... 132 F5
Portland St STALW/RED AL3 ...... 38 B6
  WALW SE17 ...... 18 G8 3
Portley La CTHM CR3 ...... 241 M7
Portley Wood Rd CTHM CR3 ...... 241 N7
Portman Av MORT/ESHN SW14 ...... 156 A7
Portman Cl BXLY DA5 ...... 186 F4
  BXLYHN DA7 ...... 163 P9 3
  MBLAR W1H 10 C5 3
  STALE/WH AL4 ...... 39 H1
Portman Dr WFD IG8 ...... 102 A10 3
Portman Gdns CDALE/KGS NW9 ...... 116 A1 3
  HGDN/ICK UB10 ...... 132 B2
Portman Ga CAMTN NW1 ...... 9 N2
Portman Ms South MBLAR W1H 10 C5 3
Portman Pl BETH E2 ...... 140 B5 3

Portman Rd KUT KT1 ...... 199 L2
Portman Sq MBLAR W1H 10 C5
Portman St MBLAR W1H 10 B5
Portman Towers MBLAR W1H 9 P5
Portmeers Cl WALTH E17 ...... 120 E4 3
Portmore Gdns CRW RM5 ...... 104 B6
Portmore Park Rd WEY KT13 ...... 216 A1 3
Portmore Quays WEY KT13 ...... 216 A1 3
Portnall Dr WEY KT13 ...... 196 E10 3
Portnall Dr VW GU25 ...... 193 K6
Portnall Ri MV/WKIL W9 ...... 2 C9
Portnall Rd MV/WKIL W9 ...... 2 C9
  VW GU25 ...... 193 L5
Portnalls Cl COUL/CHIP CR5 ...... 240 C2 3
Portnalls Rd COUL/CHIP CR5 ...... 240 D2
Portnalls Rd COUL/CHIP CR5 ...... 240 D2
Portnoi Cl ROM RM1 ...... 104 G10 3
Portobello Cl CSHM HP5 ...... 50 G5 3
Portobello Ms NTGHL W11 ...... 8 E8 3
Portobello Rd NKENS W10 ...... 8 A3
  NTGHL W11 ...... 8 C6
Portpool La FSBYW WC1X 12 A3
Portree Cl STNW/STAM N16 ...... 119 N6 3
Portree St POP/IOD E14 ...... 141 J8
Portsdown Av GLDGN NW11 ...... 117 J4
Portsdown Av GLDGN NW11 ...... 117 J4 3
Portsea Pl BAY/PAD W2 ...... 9 P6
Portsea Rd TIL RM18 ...... 168 F7
Portslade Rd VX/NE SW8 ...... 158 D8
Portsmouth Av THDIT KT7 ...... 198 B10
Portsmouth Rd COB KT11 ...... 216 G9
  ESH/CLAY KT10 ...... 198 B10
  KUT KT1 ...... 199 J3
  PUT/ROE SW15 ...... 178 E3
  RPLY/SEND GU23 ...... 232 D3
Portsmouth St LINN WC2A 11 N6 3
Portsoken St TWRH EC3N 19 L4
Portugal Gdns WHTN TW2 ...... 176 B5 3
Portugal Rd WOKN/KNAP GU21 ...... 232 C2
Portugal St LINN WC2A 11 P6
Port V HERT/WAS SG14 ...... 25 J4
Port Wy CHOB/PIR GU24 ...... 230 F3 3
Portway EW KT17 ...... 220 D6
  SRTFD E15 ...... 141 L4
Portway Crs EW KT17 ...... 220 D5
Portway Gdns WOOL/PLUM SE18 ...... 162 A7
Postern Gn ENC/FH EN2 ...... 79 H6
Postfield WCCE AL7 ...... 23 K2
Postmill Cl CROY/NA CR0 ...... 204 B10
Post Meadow IVER SL0 ...... 130 G5
Post Office Aly FSTGT E7 ...... 121 N10 3
Post Office La DTCH/LGLY SL3 ...... 130 A8 3
Post Office Rd HLW CM20 ...... 28 F10 3
Post Rd NWDGN UB2 ...... 154 A2
Postway Ms IL IG1 ...... 122 A2 3
Postwood Gn HERT/BAY SG13 ...... 26 B5 3
Potash Rd HLWE CM17 ...... 31 L8
Potier St STHWK SE1 ...... 19 H4
Potken La BEAC HP9 ...... 109 H1
Potter Cl MTCM CR4 ...... 202 C2 3
The Potteries CHERT KT16 ...... 215 H3 3
Potterne Cl WIM/MER SW19 ...... 178 C3 3
Potters Cl CROY/NA CR0 ...... 204 D8
  LOU IG10 ...... 82 B6
Potters Cross IVER SL0 ...... 131 H5
Pottescrouch La LCOL/BKTW AL2 ...... 37 L10 3
Potters Fld HLWE CM17 ...... 31 J7 3
  STALW/RED AL3 ...... 38 D2 3
Potters Flds STHWK SE1 ...... 13 K10
Potters Gv NWMAL KT3 ...... 199 P4
Potters Heights Cl PIN HA5 ...... 93 J8
Potter's La BAR EN5 ...... 77 L8
  BORE WD6 ...... 75 P5
  RPLY/SEND GU23 ...... 250 E1
Potter's Rd BAR EN5 ...... 77 L8
  FUL/PGN SW6 ...... 157 M8
Potter St HLWE CM17 ...... 47 M2
  NTHWD HA6 ...... 93 H9
Potter Street Hl NTHWD HA6 ...... 93 J7
Pottery Wy REIG RH2 ...... 275 N4
Pottery La NTGHL W11 ...... 8 A8
Pottery Rd BTFD TW8 ...... 155 K5
  BXLY DA5 ...... 186 D5
Pottery St BERM/RHTH SE16 ...... 160 A11 3
Pott St BETH E2 ...... 140 A5 3
Pouchen End La HHW HP1 ...... 34 G7
Poulcott STWL/WRAY TW19 ...... 172 B8 3
Poulett Gdns TWK TW1 ...... 176 B5 3
Poulett Rd EHAM E6 ...... 142 C4
Poulters Wd HAYES BR2 ...... 226 A3 3
Poultney Cl RAD WD7 ...... 57 K8 3
Poulton Av SUT SM1 ...... 201 N10 3
Poultry LOTH EC2R 12 G5 3
Pound Cl ORP BR6 ...... 206 C9 3
  SURB KT6 ...... 199 H8
  WAB EN9 ...... 45 K9
Pound Ct ASHTD KT21 ...... 237 L4
  RGUW GU3 ...... 248 D2
Pound Court Dr ORP BR6 ...... 206 G9
Pound Crs LHD/OX KT22 ...... 236 C7
Pound Fld GSTN WD25 ...... 72 G1 3
  GU GU1 ...... 250 A9
Poundfield Gdns
  WOKS/MYFD GU22 ...... 232 F6
Poundfield Rd LOU IG10 ...... 82 D9
Pound Hl RGUE GU3 ...... 248 D2
Pound Hill Pl CRAWE RH10 ...... 284 D7 3
Pound La BFOR GU20 ...... 193 K8
  HOR/WEW KT19 ...... 220 A7 3
  RAD WD7 ...... 57 L9
  RGUW GU3 ...... 248 C9
  RSEV TN13 ...... 245 N1
  SEV TN13 ...... 247 K10 3
  WLSDN NW10 ...... 136 D1 3
Pound Park Rd CHARL SE7 ...... 162 A7 3
Pound Pl ELTH/MOT SE9 ...... 184 D2 3
  RGUE GU4 ...... 268 C6 3
Pound Place Cl RGUE GU4 ...... 268 C6 3
Pound Rd BNSTD SM7 ...... 239 K3 3
  CHERT KT16 ...... 195 L7
Pound St CAR SM5 ...... 222 A4 3
Poundwell WGCE AL7 ...... 23 K6 3
Pounsley Rd SEV TN13 ...... 246 F7 3
Pountney Rd BTSEA SW11 ...... 158 B9 3
Poverest Rd STMC/STPC BR5 ...... 207 J3
Povey Cross Rd HORL RH6 ...... 279 P6 3
Powderham Ct
  WOKN/KNAP GU21 ...... 231 J4 3
Powder Mill La DART DA1 ...... 187 M5 3
Powdermill La WAB EN9 ...... 62 C9
Powdermill Ms WAB EN9 ...... 62 G9 3
Powell Cl DAGE RM10 ...... 124 B3 3
  EDGW HA8 ...... 95 L7
  GUW GU2 ...... 267 J2
  HORL RH6 ...... 279 P5
  WLGTN SM6 ...... 222 G7 3
Powell Gdns DAGE RM10 ...... 124 B3 3
Powell Rd BKHH IG9 ...... 101 P7 3
  CLPT E5 ...... 120 A8 3
Power Rd CHSWK W4 ...... 155 M3
Powerscroft Rd CLPT E5 ...... 120 B7 3
  SCUP DA14 ...... 186 G9 3
Powis Ct POTB/CUF EN6 ...... 59 M10 3
Powis Gdns GLDGN NW11 ...... 117 J5
  NTGHL W11 ...... 8 D5
Powis Ms NTGHL W11 ...... 8 D5
Powis Pl BMSBY WC1N 11 M2 3
Powis Rd BOW E3 ...... 140 G5 3
Powis Sq NTGHL W11 ...... 8 D5 3
Powis St WOOL/PLUM SE18 ...... 162 G2 3
Powis Ter NTGHL W11 ...... 8 D5 3
Powlett Pl CAMTN NW1 ...... 4 B1 3

Pownall Gdns HSLW TW3 ...... 154 A10
Pownall Rd HACK E8 ...... 7 N6
  HSLW TW3 ...... 154 A10
Pownsett Ter IL IG1 ...... 122 F10 3
Powster Rd BMLY BR1 ...... 183 N5
Powys Cl BXLYHN DA7 ...... 163 N5
Poyle La SL SL1 ...... 128 A3
Poyle Rd DTCH/LGLY SL3 ...... 151 H8
  GU GU1 ...... 268 B2
Poynder Rd TIL RM18 ...... 168 E7
Poynders HI HHNE HP2 ...... 36 D7 3
Poynders Rd CLAP SW4 ...... 180 D3
Poynes Rd HORL RH6 ...... 279 P2 3
Poynings CLAP SW4 ...... 180 D3 3
Poynings Cl HARP AL5 ...... 20 E3 3
  ORP BR6 ...... 207 M9 3
Poynings Rd ARCH N19 ...... 118 D8
  CRAWW RH11 ...... 282 C8
Poyntell Crs CHST BR7 ...... 206 C1 3
Poynter Rd EN EN1 ...... 79 N9
Poynton Rd TOTM N17 ...... 99 F10 3
Poyntz Rd BTSEA SW11 ...... 158 A8 3
Poyser St BETH E2 ...... 140 A4 3
Prae Cl STALW/RED AL3 ...... 38 A5
Praed Ms BAY/PAD W2 ...... 9 M5
Praed St BAY/PAD W2 ...... 9 M5
Praetorian Ct STAL AL1 ...... 38 B7 3
Pragel St PLSTW E13 ...... 141 N4
Pragnell Rd LEE/GVPK SE12 ...... 183 M5
Prague Pl BRXS/STRHM SW2 ...... 180 F1 3
Prah Rd FSBYPK N4 ...... 119 H7
Prairie Cl ADL/WDHM KT15 ...... 195 L10
Prairie Rd ADL/WDHM KT15 ...... 195 L10
Prairie St VX/NE SW8 ...... 158 B9 3
Pratt Ms CAMTN NW1 ...... 4 D4 3
Pratts La WOT/HER KT12 ...... 217 L11 3
Pratt St CAMTN NW1 ...... 5 H5
Pratt Wk LBTH SE11 ...... 17 P5 3
Prayle Gv CRICK NW2 ...... 116 C6
Prebend Gdns CHSWK W4 ...... 156 C3 3
Prebend St IS N1 ...... 6 E6
Precinct Rd HYS/HAR UB3 ...... 133 H9 3
The Precincts SL SL1 ...... 128 A6 3
Premier Av CDH/CHF RM16 ...... 167 P1 3
Premiere Pl POP/IOD E14 ...... 140 F9 3
Premier Park Rd WLSDN NW10 ...... 135 M7 3
Prentice Ct STRHM/NOR SW16 ...... 180 E7 3
Prentis Rd STRHM/NOR SW16 ...... 162 A3 3
Prentiss Ct CHARL SE7 ...... 142 C10 3
Presburg Rd NWMAL KT3 ...... 200 B5
Prescelly Pl EDGW HA8 ...... 95 J3 3
Prescot St WCHPL E1 ...... 13 M7
Prescott Cl HCH RM12 ...... 125 K6 3
Prescott Cl STMC/STPC BR5 ...... 206 C6 3
Prescott Gn LOU IG10 ...... 82 F7 3
Prescott Pl CLAP SW4 ...... 158 E9 3
Prescott Rd CHES/WCR EN8 ...... 62 D3 3
  DTCH/LGLY SL3 ...... 151 H8 3
Presdales Dr WARE SG12 ...... 26 C3 3
Presentation Ms
  BRXS/STRHM SW2 ...... 180 G4 3
Presidents Dr WAP E1W 140 A10 3
President St FSBYE EC1V 6 E9 3
Press Rd UX/CGN UB8 ...... 131 N2 3
  WLSDN NW10 ...... 116 A8
Prestage Wy POP/IOD E14 ...... 141 H9 3
Prestbury Crs BNSTD SM7 ...... 240 E2 3
Prestbury Rd FSTGT E7 ...... 141 P2 3
Prestbury Sq ELTH/MOT SE9 ...... 184 C1 3
Prested Rd BTSEA SW11 ...... 157 P10 3
Preston Av CHING E4 ...... 101 J3 3
Preston Cl STHWK SE1 ...... 19 J5 3
  WHTN TW2 ...... 176 D6
Preston Ct WOT/HER KT12 ...... 197 K8 3
Preston Dr HOR/WEW KT19 ...... 220 B3 3
  WAN E11 ...... 121 P3 3
  WELL DA16 ...... 163 N7
Preston Gdns IL IG1 ...... 122 B4 3
  PEND EN3 ...... 80 A4 3
  WLSDN NW10 ...... 136 B1 3
Preston Gv ASHTD KT21 ...... 237 H3 3
Preston HI CSHM HP5 ...... 51 J5 3
  KTN/HRWW/W HA3 ...... 115 K5
Preston La KWD/TDW/WH KT20 ...... 238 F6 3
Preston Pl RCHPK/HAM TW10 ...... 177 K1 3
  WLSDN NW10 ...... 136 D1 3
Preston Rd GVW DA11 ...... 190 B4
  HARH RM3 ...... 105 L5
  KTN/HRWW/W HA3 ...... 115 K5
  NRWD SE19 ...... 181 J3
  RYNPK SW20 ...... 178 D10 3
  SHPTN TW17 ...... 196 B5
  SLN SL2 ...... 129 P9
  WAN E11 ...... 121 K4
  WBLY HA9 ...... 115 K7
Prestons Rd HAYES BR2 ...... 205 M10 3
  POP/IOD E14 ...... 141 H9 3
Preston Waye WBLY HA9 ...... 115 K6 3
Prestwick Cl CRAWW RH11 ...... 282 C8 3
  NWDGN UB2 ...... 153 M4 3
Prestwick Rd OXHEY WD19 ...... 93 L4 3
Prestwood SLN SL2 ...... 129 N8 3
Prestwood Av
  KTN/HRWW/W HA3 ...... 114 G2 3
Prestwood Cl CRAWW RH11 ...... 283 L4 3
  KTN/HRWW/W HA3 ...... 114 G2 3
  WOOL/PLUM SE18 ...... 163 K5 3
Prestwood Dr CRW RM5 ...... 104 D6
Prestwood Gdns CROY/NA CR0 ...... 203 K7 3
Prestwood La CRAWW RH11 ...... 282 F5 3
Prestwood St IS N1 ...... 6 F5 3
Pretoria Av WALTH E17 ...... 120 D2 3
Pretoria Crs CHING E4 ...... 101 H2 3
Pretoria Rd CAN/RD E16 ...... 141 H4
  CHERT KT16 ...... 195 J8 3
  CHING E4 ...... 101 H2 3
  IL IG1 ...... 122 C9 3
  ROMW/RG RM7 ...... 124 D2 3
  STRHM/NOR SW16 ...... 180 C9 3
  TOTM N17 ...... 99 N7 3
  WAN E11 ...... 121 J2 3
  WATW WD18 ...... 73 H8 3
Pretoria Rd North UED N18 ...... 99 N7 3
Pretty La COUL/CHIP CR5 ...... 240 D7 3
Prevost Rd FBAR/BDGN N11 ...... 98 B3 3
Prey Heath Cl WOKS/MYFD GU22 ...... 231 P10 3
Prey Heath Rd
  WOKS/MYFD GU22 ...... 231 N10 3
Price Cl MLHL NW7 ...... 97 H7 3
  TOOT SW17 ...... 180 A6 3
Price Rd CROY/NA CR0 ...... 223 H5 3
Price's La REIG RH2 ...... 275 K3 3
Price's St STHWK SE1 ...... 12 D10 3
Pricklers HI BAR EN5 ...... 77 L8 3
Prickley Wd HAYES BR2 ...... 205 L8 3
Prideaux Pl ACT W3 ...... 136 A9 3
  FSBYW WC1X 5 P9 3
Prideaux Rd BRXN/ST SW9 ...... 158 F9 3
Pridham Rd THHTH CR7 ...... 203 L4 3
Priest Croft Cl CRAWW RH11 ...... 283 K7 3
Priestfield Rd FSTH SE23 ...... 182 D6 3
Priest HI ECH TW20 ...... 171 P5 3
  OXTED RH8 ...... 261 N6 3
Priestlands Park Rd
  BFN/LL DA15 ...... 185 J6 3
Priest La CHOB/PIR GU24 ...... 212 B10 3
Priestley Gdns CHDH RM6 ...... 123 L4 3
  WOKS/MYFD GU22 ...... 232 D6 3
Priestley Rd GUW GU2 ...... 267 J2 3
  MTCM CR4 ...... 202 B2 3
Priestley Wy CRAWE RH10 ...... 284 B2 3
  CRICK NW2 ...... 99 J7 3
  WALTH E17 ...... 120 C1 3
Priest Park Av RYLN/HDSTN HA2 ...... 113 P7 3
Priests Av ROM RM1 ...... 104 E10 3
Priests Br MORT/ESHN SW14 ...... 156 B9 3

Priests Fld RBRW/HUT CM13 ...... 107 P6
Priest's La BRWN CM15 ...... 107 K3
Prima Rd BRXN/ST SW9 ...... 159 H6
Primley La RBSF CM22 ...... 30 D2
Primrose Av ENC/FH EN2 ...... 79 L9
　GDMY/SEVK IG3 ...... 123 K5
　HORL RH6 ...... 280 C6
Primrose Cl CAT SE6 ...... 183 H8
　CRAWW RH11 ...... 283 L10
　HAT AL10 ...... 40 E5
　MTCM CR4 ...... 202 C8
　RYLN/HDSTN HA2 ...... 113 N8
Primrose Dr CHOB/PIR GU24 ... 230 F1
　HERT/BAY SG13 ...... 26 A5
Primrose Fld HLWS CM18 ...... 47 J4
Primrose Gdns BUSH WD23 ...... 94 A3
　HAMP NW3 ...... 3 J1
　RSLP HA4 ...... 113 K10
Primrose Gln EMPK RM11 ...... 125 M2
Primrose Hl BRW CM14 ...... 107 H8
　EMB EC4Y 12 B6
　KGLGY WD4 ...... 54 C4
Primrose Hill Rd HAMP NW3 ...... 4 C4
Primrose Hill Studios CAMTN NW1 ... 4 C5
Primrose La CROY/NA CR0 ...... 204 B8
Primrose Pth CHESW EN7 ...... 61 P7
Primrose Rd LEY E10 ...... 120 C6
　SWFD E18 ...... 101 N10
　WOT/HER KT12 ...... 217 K2
Primrose Sq HOM E9 ...... 140 B2
Primrose St SDTCH EC2A 13 J1
　NWCR SE14 ...... 160 D6
Primrose Wk EW KT17 ...... 220 L4
　ALP/SUD HA0 ...... 135 L4
Primula St SHB W12 ...... 136 D9
Prince Albert STJWD NW8 ...... 3 J7
　STJWD NW8 ...... 3 J7
Prince Albert Rd CAMTN NW1 ... 4 C6
　STJWD NW8 ...... 3 J7
Prince Albert Sq REDH RH1 ...... 276 A5
Prince Arthur Rd HAMP NW3 ... 117 N9
Prince Charles Av EYN DA4 ...... 210 C2
Prince Charles Dr HDN NW4 ...... 116 F5
Prince Charles Rd
　BKHTH/KID SE3 ...... 161 L7
Prince Charles Wy WLGTN SM6 ... 202 C10
Prince Consort Cottages
　WDSR SL4 ...... 149 J8
Prince Consort Dr CHST BR7 ...... 206 G1
Prince Consort Rd SKENS SW7 ... 15 L3
Prince Consort's Dr WDSR SL4 ... 170 E3
Princedale Rd NTGHL W11 ...... 8 E9
Prince Edward Rd HOM E9 ...... 140 E1
Prince Edward St BERK HP4 ...... 33 P5
Prince George Av
　STNW/STAM N16 ...... 119 M9
Prince George's Av RYNPK SW20 ... 200 F2
Prince Georges Rd
　WIM/MER SW19 ...... 201 N1
Prince Henry Rd
　WOOL/PLUM SE18 ...... 162 A6
Prince Imperial Rd CHST BR7 ... 184 E10
　WOOL/PLUM SE18 ...... 162 B7
Prince John Rd ELTH/MOT SE9 ... 184 B1
Princelet St WCHPL E1 ...... 13 M3
Prince of Orange La
　GNWCH SE10 ...... 161 H6
Prince of Wales Cl HDN NW4 ... 116 F2
Prince of Wales Dr BTSEA SW11 ... 158 C6
Prince of Wales Pas CAMTN NW1 ... 4 G10
Prince of Wales Rd
　BKHTH/KID SE3 ...... 161 L7
　CAN/RD E16 ...... 141 P8
　KTTN NW5 ...... 4 C2
　REDH RH1 ...... 277 H8
　SUT SM1 ...... 209 P6
Prince of Wales Ter CHSWK W4 ... 156 B4
　KENS W8 ...... 15 L2
Prince Pk HHW HP1 ...... 35 K7
Prince Philip Av CDH/CHF RM16 ... 147 N9
Prince Regent La CAN/RD E16 ... 141 P8
　PLSTW E13 ...... 141 P6
Prince Regent Rd HSLW TW3 ... 154 A8
Prince Rd SNWD SE25 ...... 203 M5
Prince Rupert Rd ELTH/MOT SE9 ... 162 C10
Princes Av ACT W3 ...... 155 M2
　CAR SM5 ...... 222 A4
　CDALE/KGS NW9 ...... 115 M2
　FNCH N3 ...... 97 L9
　MUSWH N10 ...... 118 B1
　PEND EN3 ...... 80 D2
　PLMGR N13 ...... 99 H6
　RDART DA2 ...... 188 A4
　SAND/SEL CR2 ...... 242 A1
　STMC/STPC BR5 ...... 207 H5
　SURB KT6 ...... 199 M8
　WDGN N22 ...... 98 E2
　WFD IG8 ...... 101 N5
Princes Cl BERK HP4 ...... 33 M3
　CDALE/KGS NW9 ...... 115 M2
　EDGW HA8 ...... 95 M6
　EPP CM16 ...... 66 D1
　HPTN TW12 ...... 176 C7
　SAND/SEL CR2 ...... 242 A1
　SCUP DA14 ...... 185 N6
　WDSR SL4 ...... 148 E4
Princes Ct WBLY HA9 ...... 115 K10
Princes Dr HRW HA1 ...... 114 D1
　LHD/OX KT22 ...... 218 D8
Princesfield Rd WAB EN9 ...... 63 N9
Princes Gdns ACT W5 ...... 135 H6
　EA W5 ...... 135 H6
　SKENS SW7 ...... 15 S3
Prince's Ga SKENS SW7 ...... 15 N2
Princes Gate Ms SKENS SW7 ... 15 M3
Prince's Ms BAY/PAD W2 ...... 8 F7
Princes Pk RAIN RM13 ...... 145 H2
Princes Park Av GLDGN NW11 ... 117 H4
　HYS/HAR UB3 ...... 132 E9
Princes Park Cir HYS/HAR UB3 ... 132 E9
Princes Park Cl HYS/HAR UB3 ... 132 E9
Princes Park La HYS/HAR UB3 ... 132 E9
Princes Park Pde HYS/HAR UB3 ... 132 E9
Princes Pl NTGHL W11 ...... 8 A9
Prince's Pln HAYES BR2 ...... 206 B7
Princes Ri LEW SE13 ...... 161 M9
Princes Riverside Rd
　BERM/RHTH SE16 ...... 140 C10
Princes Rd ASHF TW15 ...... 174 A8
　BARK/HLT IG6 ...... 73 K2
　BARK IG9 ...... 101 P3
　BRW CM14 ...... 85 P6
　DART DA1 ...... 187 J3
　EGH TW20 ...... 172 C9
　FELT TW13 ...... 174 G6
　GVE DA12 ...... 190 F2
　HPTN TW12 ...... 176 C7
　KUTN/CMB KT2 ...... 199 M1
　MORT/ESHN SW14 ...... 156 A9
　PGE/AN SE20 ...... 182 G7
　RCH/KEW TW9 ...... 155 L7
　RCHPK/HAM TW10 ...... 177 L1
　REDH RH1 ...... 276 A2
　ROM RM1 ...... 125 H3
　SWLY BR8 ...... 187 H4
　UED N18 ...... 100 B2
　WEA W13 ...... 134 G10
　WEY KT13 ...... 216 C2
　WIM/MER SW19 ...... 179 K9
Princess Av WBLY HA9 ...... 115 K7
　WDSR SL4 ...... 148 E3
Princess Crs FSBYPK N4 ...... 119 J7
Princess Diana Dr STALE/WH AL4 ... 39 H7

Princess Gdns WOKS/MYFD GU22 ... 232 E2
Princess La RSLP HA4 ...... 113 H8
Princess Margaret Rd TIL RM18 ... 169 L3
Princess Mary's Rd
　ADL/WDHM KT15 ...... 215 M1
Princess May Rd
　STNW/STAM N16 ...... 119 M9
Princess Ms HAMP NW3 3
　HAMP NW3 ...... 117 N10
Prince's Sq BAY/PAD W2 ...... 8 F7
Princess Rd CAMTN NW1 ...... 283 M7
　CROY/NA CR0 ...... 203 K6
　KIL/WHAMP NW6 ...... 2 C1
　WOKS/MYFD GU22 ...... 232 E2
Princess St BXLYHN DA7 ...... 164 A9
　STHWK SE1 ...... 18 D4
　GVW DA11 ...... 190 E2
　LOTH EC2R 12 G6
　RCHPK/HAM TW10 ...... 177 K1
　SL SL1 ...... 149 N1
　SUT SM1 ...... 221 N1
　TOTM N17 ...... 99 M7
　WARE SG12 ...... 26 C1
Princess Wy REDH RH1 ...... 258 B9
Prince's Ter PLSTW E13 ...... 141 N3
Prince St DEPT SE8 ...... 160 E5
　WAT WD17 ...... 73 K7
Princes Vw DART DA1 ...... 187 P4
　CROY/NA CR0 ...... 222 G2
　RBRW/HUT CM13 ...... 107 M3
　RSLP HA4 ...... 113 M9
　WIM/MER SW19 ...... 178 C3
　WWKM BR4 ...... 225 L1
Prince's Yd NTGHL W11 ...... 8 B10
Princethorpe Rd SYD SE26 ...... 182 C7
Princeton St GINN WC1R 11 N4
Pringle Gdns PUR/KEN CR8 ...... 222 G6
　STRHM/NOR SW16 ...... 180 D7
Printer St FLST/FETLN EC4A ... 12 B5
Printers Wy HLW CM20 ...... 29 K6
Printinghouse La HYS/HAR UB3 ... 152 F7
Printing House Yd BETH E2 ...... 7 K10
Priolo Rd CHARL SE7 ...... 161 P4
Prior Av BELMT SM2 ...... 221 P4
Prior Bolton St IS N1 ...... 6 D2
Prior Cha GRAYS RM17 ...... 167 L5
Prioress Rd WNWD SE27 ...... 181 J6
Prioress St STHWK SE1 ...... 19 H4
Prior Gv CSHM HP5 ...... 51 H6
Prior Rd IL IG1 ...... 122 D8
Priors Ct HERT/BAY SG13 ...... 26 A5
　SL SL1 ...... 149 N2
Priors Ct WOKN/KNAP GU21 ... 231 M4
Priors Cft WALTH E17 ...... 100 D10
　WOKS/MYFD GU22 ...... 232 D6
Priors Fld NTHLT UB5 ...... 133 M1
Priorsfield Rd RGODL GU7 ...... 266 C8
Priorsford Av STMC/STPC BR5 ... 207 K4
Priors Gdns RSLP HA4 ...... 113 K10
Priors Hatch La RGODL GU7 ... 266 E8
Priors Md EN EN1 ...... 79 M5
　GT/LBKH KT23 ...... 254 B1
Priors Pk HCH RM12 ...... 125 K8
Priors Rd WDSR SL4 ...... 148 C9
The Priors ASHTD KT21 ...... 237 J5
Prior St GNWCH SE10 ...... 161 H6
Priors Wd CHOB/PIR GU24 ... 284 A7
Priorswood RGUW GU3 ...... 266 C7
Priors Wood Rd HERT/BAY SG13 ... 26 B8
Priory Av ALP/SUD HA0 ...... 114 B7
　CEND/HSY/T N8 ...... 118 E2
　CHEAM SM3 ...... 220 G1
　CHING E4 ...... 100 E4
　CHSWK W4 ...... 156 B2
　HLWE CM17 ...... 29 M6
　STMC/STPC BR5 ...... 206 G4
　WALTH E17 ...... 120 F3
Priory Cl ALP/SUD HA0 ...... 114 B7
　ASC SL5 ...... 192 F7
　BECK BR3 ...... 204 D3
　BMLY BR1 ...... 206 C1
　BROX EN10 ...... 44 D10
　BRWN CM15 ...... 86 F9
　CHING E4 ...... 100 E4
　DART DA1 ...... 187 K1
　DEN/HRF UB9 ...... 111 M2
　DORK RH4 ...... 272 F4
　HOD EN11 ...... 44 F4
　HORL RH6 ...... 280 A3
　HPTN TW12 ...... 197 N1
　HYS/HAR UB3 ...... 133 J9
　RSLP HA4 ...... 112 G6
　STAN HA7 ...... 94 E4
　STHGT/OAK N14 ...... 78 C9
　SUN TW16 ...... 175 H10
　SWFD E18 ...... 101 M9
　TRDG/WHET N20 ...... 97 J1
　WOKN/KNAP GU21 ...... 214 C9
　WOT/HER KT12 ...... 197 H10
Priory Ct HLWS CM18 ...... 47 L4
　VX/NE SW8 ...... 158 E7
　WALTH E17 ...... 120 L1
Priory Crs ALP/SUD HA0 ...... 114 F8
　CHEAM SM3 ...... 220 G1
　NRWD SE19 ...... 181 K10
Priory Dr ABYW SE2 ...... 163 N4
　REIG RH2 ...... 275 K2
　STAN HA7 ...... 94 E4
Priory Field Dr EDGW HA8 ... 95 N5
Priory Flds EYN DA4 ...... 209 N9
Priory Gdns ALP/SUD HA0 ...... 114 F8
　ASHF TW15 ...... 174 A2
　BARN SW13 ...... 156 C9
　BERK HP4 ...... 33 P5
　CHSWK W4 ...... 156 B2
　DART DA1 ...... 187 L2
　DEN/HRF UB9 ...... 111 M4
　HGT N6 ...... 118 C4
　HPTN TW12 ...... 175 N10
　SNWD SE25 ...... 203 N4
Priory Ga CHES/WCR EN8 ... 62 E3
Priory Gn STA TW18 ...... 173 J6
Priory Gv CLAP SW4 ...... 158 F7
　HARH RM3 ...... 105 M5
Priory Hl ALP/SUD HA0 ...... 114 F9
　DART DA1 ...... 187 L2
Priory La E/WMO/HCT KT8 ... 197 P4
　EYN DA4 ...... 209 N8
　PUT/ROE SW15 ...... 156 D10
Priory Md BRWN CM15 ...... 87 H2
Priory Ms STA TW18 ...... 173 L8
Priory Pk BKHTH/KID SE3 ...... 161 J9
Priory Park Rd ALP/SUD HA0 ... 114 F9
　KIL/WHAMP NW6 ...... 2 D5
Priory Pth HARH RM3 ...... 105 M4
Priory Pl DART DA1 ...... 187 L2
Priory Rd ASC SL5 ...... 192 F7
　BARK IG11 ...... 142 C2
　CEND/HSY/T N8 ...... 118 E2
　CFSP/GDCR SL9 ...... 109 P1
　CHEAM SM3 ...... 220 G1
　CHSGTN KT9 ...... 199 K10
　CHSWK W4 ...... 156 A2
　CROY/NA CR0 ...... 203 H7
　DART DA1 ...... 165 L10
　EHAM E6 ...... 142 A3
　HAMP NW3 ...... 3 H1
　HPTN TW12 ...... 175 N10
　HSLW TW3 ...... 155 J3
　KIL/WHAMP NW6 ...... 2 F1
　LOU IG10 ...... 82 B2
　MUSWH N10 ...... 118 D2
　RCH/KEW TW9 ...... 155 M5

REIG RH2 ...... 275 K2
　SL SL1 ...... 128 B7
　WIM/MER SW19 ...... 179 N10
Priory St BOW E3 ...... 140 C5
　HERT/WAS SG14 ...... 25 L5
Priory Ter KIL/WHAMP NW6 ...... 2 C5
The Priory BKHTH/KID SE3 ... 161 L9
Priory Vw BUSH WD23 ...... 94 D1
Priory Wk STAL AL1 ...... 38 D9
　WBPTN SW10 ...... 15 K8
Priory Wy CFSP/GDCR SL9 ...... 110 A1
　DTCH/LGLY SL3 ...... 149 N6
　NWDGN UB2 ...... 153 L2
　RYLN/HDSTN HA2 ...... 114 A1
　WDR/YW UB7 ...... 151 P5
Pritchard's Rd BETH E2 ...... 7 P7
Priter Rd BERM/RHTH SE16 ...... 139 L8
Private Rd EN EN1 ...... 79 L9
Probert Rd BRXS/STRHM SW2 ... 181 H1
Probyn Rd BRXS/STRHM SW2 ... 181 H3
Procter St BMSBY WC1N 11 N4
Proctor Cl CRAWE RH10 ...... 284 D9
　MTCM CR4 ...... 202 B1
Proctor Gdns GT/LBKH KT23 ... 254 A1
Proctors Cl EBED/NFELT TW14 ... 175 H4
Profumo Rd WOT/HER KT12 ... 217 L2
Progress Wy CROY/NA CR0 ...... 202 G9
　EN EN1 ...... 79 P9
　WDGN N22 ...... 99 H9
Promenade Approach Rd
　CHSWK W4 ...... 156 B6
Promenade De Verdun
　PUR/KEN CR8 ...... 222 E7
The Promenade CHSWK W4 ...... 156 B7
Prospect Cl BELV DA17 ...... 164 B3
　HEST TW5 ...... 153 N7
　RSLP HA4 ...... 113 L5
　SYD SE26 ...... 182 A7
Prospect Cottages
　WAND/EARL SW18 ...... 157 K10
Prospect Crs WHTN TW2 ...... 176 B2
Prospect Gv GVE DA12 ...... 190 C3
Prospect Hl WALTH E17 ...... 120 G2
Prospect La EGH TW20 ...... 171 M8
Prospect Pl CHSWK W4 ...... 156 A4
　CRAWW RH11 ...... 283 M7
　CRW RM5 ...... 104 D10
　DART DA1 ...... 187 P4
　EFNCH N2 ...... 117 N2
　EW KT17 ...... 220 B9
　GRAYS RM17 ...... 167 N5
　HAYES BR2 ...... 205 S
　RYNPK SW20 ...... 178 E10
　STA TW18 ...... 173 J8
　WFD IG8 ...... 101 P6
Prospect Rd BAR EN5 ...... 77 K8
　CHES/WCR EN8 ...... 62 B5
　CRICK NW2 ...... 117 J8
　SEV TN13 ...... 247 K9
　STAL AL1 ...... 38 C8
　SURB KT6 ...... 199 H6
　WFD IG8 ...... 101 P6
Prospect St BERM/RHTH SE16 ... 160 A1
　FBAR/BDGN N11 ...... 98 C5
Prospect V CHARL SE7 ...... 162 B3
Prospero Rd ARCH N19 ...... 118 B6
Prossers KWD/TDW/WH KT20 ... 258 G7
Prothero Gdns HDN NW4 ...... 116 E3
Prothero Rd FUL/PGN SW6 ...... 157 H6
Prout Gv WLSDN NW10 ...... 116 B9
Prout Rd CLPT E5 ...... 139 N1
Providence Ct MYFR/PKLN W1K ... 10 D7
Providence La HYS/HAR UB3 ... 152 E6
Providence Pl ROMW/RG RM7 ... 104 A4
Providence Rd WDR/YW UB7 ... 131 P10
Providence St GRH DA9 ...... 188 F1
Provost Rd HAMP NW3 ...... 4 F2
Provost St FSBYE EC1V 6 G10
　IS N1 ...... 6 G8
Prowse Av BUSH WD23 ...... 94 B9
Prowse Pl CAMTN NW1 ...... 4 C3
Prune Hl EGH TW20 ...... 172 A10
Prunus Cl CHOB/PIR GU24 ...... 212 D9
Prusom St WAP E1W 140 C4
Pryor Cl ABLGY WD5 ...... 54 C8
Puckshill WOKN/KNAP GU21 ... 231 J3
Pudding La CHIG IG7 ...... 83 H10
　HHW HP1 ...... 35 K4
　HORL RH6 ...... 280 A3
　MON EC3R 13 H7
Pudding Mill La SRTFD E15 ... 140 C2
Puddle Dock BLKFR EC4V 12 D7
Puddledock La BH/WHM TN16 ... 263 K8
　RDART DA2 ...... 186 F8
Puers La BEAC HP9 ...... 89 K7
Puffin Cl BARK IG11 ...... 143 K2
　CROY/NA CR0 ...... 204 C5
Puffin Rd CRAWW RH11 ...... 282 C8
Pulborough Wy HSLWW TW4 ... 153 K10
Pulford Rd SEVS/STOTM N15... 119 L4
Pulham Av BROX EN10 ...... 44 D6
　EFNCH N2 ...... 117 M2
Puller Rd BAR EN5 ...... 76 C6
　HHW HP1 ...... 35 K7
Pulleyns Av EHAM E6 ...... 142 B5
Pulleys Cl HHW HP1 ...... 35 J5
Pulleys La HHW HP1 ...... 35 J5
Pullfields CSHM HP5 ...... 50 F6
Pullman Ct BRXS/STRHM SW2... 178 F2
Pullman Pl ELTH/MOT SE9 ...... 164 D10
Pullmans Pl STA TW18 ...... 173 K8
Pulpit Cl CSHM HP5 ...... 50 F5
Pulross Rd BRXN/ST SW9 ...... 158 D10
Pulteney Cl BOW E3 ...... 140 E3
Pulteney Rd SWFD E18 ...... 121 N1
Pulton Pl FUL/PGN SW6 ...... 157 K6
Pump Aly BTFD TW8 ...... 155 L8
Pump Cl NTHLT UB5 ...... 133 P4
Pump Hl LOU IG10 ...... 82 D2
Pumping Station Rd CHSWK W4... 156 B6
Pumpkin Hl SL SL1 ...... 128 D2
Pump La ASC SL5 ...... 192 B7
　CSHM HP5 ...... 51 K9
　EPP CM16 ...... 46 E10
　HYS/HAR UB3 ...... 153 H1
　NWCR SE14 ...... 160 B6
Punch Bowl La CSHM HP5 ... 51 H8
　HHNE HP2 ...... 36 E3
Punchbowl La RDKG RH5 ...... 273 J1
Punch Bowl La STALW/RED AL3 ... 37 H2
Punch Copse Rd CRAWE RH10... 284 A1
Punch Cft HART DA3 ...... 211 K10
Punderson's Gdns BETH E2 ... 140 A5
Purbeck Av NWMAL KT3 ...... 200 D4
Purbeck Cl REDH RH1 ...... 258 D5
Purbeck Dr CRICK NW2 ...... 116 D5
　WOKN/KNAP GU21 ...... 214 C10
Purbeck Rd EMPK RM11 ...... 125 H5
Purberry Gv EW KT17 ...... 220 C8
Purbrook Av GSTN WD25 ...... 73 K2
Purbrook St STHWK SE1 ...... 19 L2
Purcell Cl BORE WD6 ...... 75 M4
　PUR/KEN CR8 ...... 223 K10
Purcell Crs FUL/PGN SW6 ...... 156 G6
Purcell Rd CRAWW RH11 ...... 283 J10
　GFD/PVL UB6 ...... 134 A7
Purcells Av EDGW HA8 ...... 95 M6
Purcell St IS N1 ...... 7 J2
Purchese St CAMTN NW1 ...... 5 H4
Purdy St BOW E3 ...... 140 G6
Purfleet By-pass PUR RM19 ...... 166 G3
Purfleet Rd SOCK/AV RM15 ...... 147 M10
Purford Gn HLWS CM18 ...... 47 K2
Purkis Rd HERT/BAY SG13 ...... 25 K8
Purland Cl BCTR RM8 ...... 124 A6

Purland Rd THMD SE28 ...... 163 J1
Purleigh Av WFD IG8 ...... 102 B7
Purley Av CRICK NW2 ...... 117 K6
Purley Bury Av PUR/KEN CR8 ... 223 K7
Purley Bury Cl PUR/KEN CR8 ... 223 D10
Purley Cl CLAY IG5 ...... 123 K4
　CRAWE RH10 ...... 284 E10
Purley Downs Rd PUR/KEN CR8... 223 K6
Purley Hl PUR/KEN CR8 ...... 223 J6
Purley Knoll PUR/KEN CR8 ...... 222 G6
Purley Oaks Rd SAND/SEL CR2... 223 J6
Purley Park Rd PUR/KEN CR8 ... 223 J6
Purley Pl IS N1 ...... 6 C3
Purley Rd ED N9 ...... 99 L4
　SAND/SEL CR2 ...... 223 L4
Purley V PUR/KEN CR8 ...... 223 J6
Purley Vw CROY/NA CR0 ...... 202 C10
Purley Wy CROY/NA CR0 ...... 202 D7
　PUR/KEN CR8 ...... 223 H7
Purlieu Wy EPP CM16 ...... 83 H1
Purlings Rd BUSH WD23 ...... 74 A9
Purneys Rd ELTH/MOT SE9 ...... 162 A10
Purrett Rd WOOL/PLUM SE18 ... 144 A10
Pursley Rd MLHL NW7 ...... 96 E8
Purton Ct SLN SL2 ...... 129 H2
Purton La SLN SL2 ...... 129 H2
Purves Rd WLSDN NW10 ...... 136 E5
Putney Br PUT/ROE SW15 ...... 157 H9
Putney Bridge Ap
　PUT/ROE SW15 ...... 157 H9
Putney Bridge Rd
　PUT/ROE SW15 ...... 157 H10
Putney Common PUT/ROE SW15... 156 F9
Putney Heath PUT/ROE SW15 ... 178 F1
Putney Heath La PUT/ROE SW15... 157 H10
Putney High St PUT/ROE SW15... 157 H10
Putney Hl PUT/ROE SW15 ...... 178 F1
Putney Park Av PUT/ROE SW15... 156 D10
Putney Park La PUT/ROE SW15 ... 156 E10
Puttenham Cl OXHEY WD19 ... 93 K4
Puttenham Heath Rd RGUW GU3... 266 C5
Puttenham Hl RGUW GU3 ...... 266 B4
Puttenham La MFD/CHID GU8 ... 266 B5
Putters Cft HHNE HP2 ...... 36 A1
Puttocks Cl BRKMPK AL9 ...... 40 F9
Puttocks Dr BRKMPK AL9 ...... 40 F9
Pycombe Cnr NFNCH/WDSP N12... 97 J5
Pyebush La BEAC HP9 ...... 108 F2
Pye Cl CTHM CR3 ...... 241 L9
Pyecombe Cnr CRAWW RH11 ... 283 J10
Pyenest Rd HLWW/ROY CM19 ... 46 C4
Pylbrook Rd SUT SM1 ...... 201 K10
Pyle Hl WOKS/MYFD GU22 ...... 232 A10
Pym Cl EBAR EN4 ...... 77 N3
Pymers Md DUL SE21 ...... 181 K4
Pymmes Brook Trail EBAR EN4 ... 98 F5
　PLMGR N13 ...... 98 F5
Pymmes Cl PLMGR N13 ...... 98 G2
　TOTM N17 ...... 100 A9
Pymmes Gdns North ED N9 ... 99 N4
Pymmes Gdns South ED N9 ... 99 N4
Pymmes Green Rd
　FBAR/BDGN N11 ...... 98 C5
Pymms Brook Dr EBAR EN4 ... 77 P8
Pym Pl GRAYS RM17 ...... 167 M3
Pynchester Cl HGDN/ICK UB10... 112 F2
Pyne Rd SURB KT6 ...... 199 M8
Pynest Green La WAB EN9 ...... 81 M3
Pynham Cl ABYW SE2 ...... 163 K2
Pynnacles Cl STAN HA7 ...... 94 G6
Pyrcroft La WEY KT13 ...... 216 C2
Pyrcroft Rd CHERT KT16 ...... 195 J7
Pyrford Common Rd
　WOKS/MYFD GU22 ...... 233 H2
Pyrford Heath
　WOKS/MYFD GU22 ...... 233 J1
Pyrford Rd BF/WBF KT14 ...... 215 K10
　WOKS/MYFD GU22 ...... 233 L2
Pyrford Woods Cl
　WOKS/MYFD GU22 ...... 233 J1
Pyrford Woods Rd
　WOKS/MYFD GU22 ...... 233 J1
Pyrland Rd HBRY N5 ...... 119 L10
　RCHPK/HAM TW10 ...... 177 L2
Pyrles Gn LOU IG10 ...... 82 E5
Pyrles La LOU IG10 ...... 82 E6
Pyrmont Gv WNWD SE27 ...... 181 J6
Pyrmont Rd CHSWK W4 ...... 155 M5
Pytchley Crs NRWD SE19 ...... 181 K9
Pytchley Rd CMBW SE5 ...... 159 J9
Pytt Fld HLWE CM17 ...... 47 L2
The Quadrangle GUW GU2 ... 267 M1
　WGCW AL8 ...... 22 E1

Q

Quadrant Gv HAMP NW3 ...... 118 A10
Quadrant Rd RCH/KEW TW9 ... 155 J10
　THHTH CR7 ...... 203 J4
The Quadrant BELMT SM2 ...... 221 M3
　BXLYHN DA7 ...... 163 N6
　PUR RM19 ...... 166 B3
　RCH/KEW TW9 ...... 155 K10
　RYNPK SW20 ...... 201 H1
　STALE/WH AL4 ...... 38 G3
Quadrant Wy WEY KT13 ...... 216 A1
Quaggy Wk BKHTH/KID SE3 ... 161 M10
Quail Gdns CROY/NA CR0 ...... 224 D6
Quainton St WLSDN NW10 ...... 116 A8
Quaker Cl SEV TN13 ...... 247 L9
Quaker La NWDGN UB2 ...... 153 P2
　WAB EN9 ...... 63 H10
Quakers Cl HART DA3 ...... 211 L3
Quakers Course CDALE/KGS NW9... 96 H8
Quaker's Hall La SEV TN13 ...... 247 K8
Quakers La POTB/CUF EN6 ...... 59 L6
Quakers Pl FSTGT E7 ...... 122 A10
Quaker St WCHPL E1 ...... 13 L2
Quakers Wk WCHMH N21 ...... 79 L10
Quaker Wy RGUW GU3 ...... 249 H6
Quality St REDH RH1 ...... 258 C4
Quantock Cl CRAWW RH11 ...... 283 L7
　DTCH/LGLY SL3 ...... 150 A4
　HYS/HAR UB3 ...... 152 E6
　STALE/WH AL4 ...... 39 H2
Quantock Dr BXLYHN DA7 ...... 164 F8
Quantock Gdns CRICK NW2 ...... 116 B5
Quantocks HHNE HP2 ...... 36 A3
Quarles Cl CRW RM5 ...... 104 B8
Quarrendon St FUL/PGN SW6 ... 157 K7
Quarr Rd CAR SM5 ...... 201 N6
Quarry Cl LHD/OX KT22 ...... 218 G10
　OXTED RH8 ...... 261 K6
Quarry Hl BGR/WK TN15 ...... 247 N10
　GRAYS RM17 ...... 167 M4
Quarry Hill Pk REIG RH2 ...... 257 M7
Quarry Ms PUR RM19 ...... 165 P3
Quarry Park Rd SUT SM1 ...... 221 J4
Quarry Ri SUT SM1 ...... 221 J4
Quarry Rd GDST RH9 ...... 260 D3
　OXTED RH8 ...... 261 K6
　RGODL GU7 ...... 266 F10
　WAND/EARL SW18 ...... 178 A9
Quarry Springs HLW CM20 ...... 47 K1
Quarry St GU GU1 ...... 268 A2
The Quarry BRKHM/BTCW RH3... 256 A8
Quarry Wy WTHK RM20 ...... 166 E5

Quartermaine Av
　WOKS/MYFD GU22 ...... 232 C8
Quartermass Cl HHW HP1 ...... 35 K5
Quartermass Rd HHW HP1 ...... 35 K5
Quartermile La LEY E10 ...... 120 C9
Quaves Rd DTCH/LGLY SL3 ...... 149 N2
Quay La GRH DA9 ...... 169 G10
Quebec Av BH/WHM TN16 ...... 262 G4
Quebec Cl HORL RH6 ...... 281 H4
Quebec Ms MBLAR W1H 10 B6
Quebec Rd GNTH/NBYPK IG2 ... 122 F5
　TIL RM18 ...... 168 D8
　YEAD UB4 ...... 133 K9
Quebec Sq BH/WHM TN16 ...... 262 G4
Quebec Wy BERM/RHTH SE16... 140 G6
Queen Adelaide Rd PGE/AN SE20... 182 B9
Queen Anne Av HAYES BR2 ... 205 M8
Queen Anne Dr ESH/CLAY KT10... 218 D4
Queen Anne Ga BXLYHN DA7 ... 164 G1
Queen Anne Ms
　WHTN TW2 ...... 176 C6
Queen Anne's Cl WHTN TW2 ... 176 C6
　EA W5 ...... 155 K1
　EN EN1 ...... 79 M10
　ED N9 ...... 99 L1
　EN EN1 ...... 79 M10
Queen Anne's Pl EN EN1 ...... 79 M10
Queen Anne's Ride WDSR SL4... 171 H3
Queen Anne's Ter LHD/OX KT22... 218 D5
Queen Anne St CAVSQ/HST W1G... 10 E4
Queenborough Gdns CHST BR7... 184 G3
　GNTH/NBYPK IG2 ...... 122 D2
Queen Caroline St HMSMTH W6... 156 F4
Queendale Ct WOKN/KNAP GU21... 231 L2
Queen Eleanor's Rd GUW GU2 ... 267 L1
Queen Elizabeth Av TIL RM18... 169 M3
Queen Elizabeth Gdns
　MRDN SM4 ...... 201 K4
Queen Elizabeth Ii Br PUR RM19... 166 D8
Queen Elizabeth Rd
　KUTN/CMB KT2 ...... 199 L1
　WALTH E17 ...... 120 D1
Queen Elizabeth's Cl
　STNW/STAM N16 ...... 119 L7
Queen Elizabeth's Dr
　CROY/NA CR0 ...... 225 J2
　STHGT/OAK N14 ...... 98 F2
Queen Elizabeth St STHWK SE1... 19 L1
Queen Elizabeth's Wk
　STNW/STAM N16 ...... 119 L7
　WDSR SL4 ...... 149 L8
　WLGTN SM6 ...... 222 E4
Queen Elizabeth Wk BARN SW13... 156 D7
Queen Elizabeth Wy
　WOKS/MYFD GU22 ...... 232 C5
Queenhithe Rd RGUE GU4 ...... 250 A4
Queen Margaret's Gv IS N1 ... 119 M10
Queen Mary Av MRDN SM4 ... 200 G3
　TIL RM18 ...... 169 M3
Queen Mary Cl CHSGTN KT9 ... 199 M10
　ROM RM1 ...... 124 G4
　WOKS/MYFD GU22 ...... 232 F2
Queen Mary Rd NRWD SE19 ... 181 J9
　SHPTN W17 ...... 196 D2
Queen Mary's Av CAR SM5 ... 222 A4
　WATW WD18 ...... 72 F8
Queen Mary's Dr
　ADL/WDHM KT15 ...... 215 J2
Queens Acre CHEAM SM3 ...... 220 G4
　WDSR SL4 ...... 149 J10
Queens Av BF/WBF KT14 ...... 215 N8
　FELT TW13 ...... 175 K7
　FNCH N3 ...... 97 M8
　GFD/PVL UB6 ...... 134 A8
　KTN/HRWW/W HA3 ...... 114 G1
　MUSWH N10 ...... 118 B1
　TRDG/WHET N20 ...... 97 N3
　WATW WD18 ...... 72 G8
　WCHMH N21 ...... 99 J2
　WFD IG8 ...... 101 N6
Queensberry Ms West
　SKENS SW7 ...... 15 L5
Queensberry Pl SKENS SW7 ... 15 L5
Queensberry Wy SKENS SW7 ... 15 L5
Queensborough Ms BAY/PAD W2... 9 J7
Queensborough Pas BAY/PAD W2... 9 J7
Queensborough Ter BAY/PAD W2... 9 H7
Queensbridge Pk ISLW TW7 ... 176 C2
Queensbridge Rd HACK E8 ...... 7 M4
Queensbury Rd ALP/SUD HA0 ... 135 L4
　CDALE/KGS NW9 ...... 116 A3
　WLSDN NW10 ...... 135 L4
Queensbury Station Pde
　EDGW HA8 ...... 115 L1
Queensbury St IS N1 ...... 6 F4
Queens Cl CHOB/PIR GU24 ...... 230 F3
　EDGW HA8 ...... 95 M6
　KWD/TDW/WH KT20 ...... 238 D10
　WDSR SL4 ...... 171 M1
　WLGTN SM6 ...... 222 C4
Queen's Club Gdns HMSMTH W6... 14 B10
　WKENS W14 ...... 14 B9
Queenscourt WBLY HA9 ...... 115 K9
Queens Ct WEY KT13 ...... 216 F3
Queens Court Ride COB KT11 ... 217 H9
Queen's Crs KTTN NW5 ...... 4 C2
　RCHPK/HAM TW10 ...... 177 L1
　STALE/WH AL4 ...... 38 G3
Queenscroft Rd ELTH/MOT SE9... 184 A2
Queensdale Crs NTGHL W11 ... 136 G10
Queensdale Rd NTGHL W11 ...... 8 A10
Queensdale Wk NTGHL W11 ... 8 A10
Queens Down Rd CLPT E5 ...... 120 A9
Queens Dr ABLGY WD5 ...... 54 C8
　BRYLDS KT5 ...... 199 M7
　CHES/WCR EN8 ...... 62 F10
　DTCH/LGLY SL3 ...... 130 C3
　EA W5 ...... 135 L8
　FSBYPK N4 ...... 119 J7
　GUW GU2 ...... 249 N7
　LEY E10 ...... 120 F5
　LHD/OX KT22 ...... 218 B2
　RGODL GU7 ...... 266 C5
　RSEV TN14 ...... 247 K6
　THDIT KT7 ...... 197 P9
The Queen's Dr RKW/CH/CXG WD3... 71 J10
Queen's Elm Sq CHEL SW3 ...... 15 M8
Queen's Farm Rd GVE DA12 ... 191 P5
Queen's Gdns BAY/PAD W2 ...... 9 J7
　EA W5 ...... 135 H7
　HEST TW5 ...... 153 M7
　RAIN RM13 ...... 144 E4
　RDART DA2 ...... 188 A4
　UPMR RM14 ...... 126 E4
Queensgate COB KT11 ...... 217 L8
Queens Ga HORL RH6 ...... 280 C6
　SKENS SW7 ...... 15 K6
Queens Gate Gdns CHST BR7 ... 206 G1
Queensgate Gdns
　PUT/ROE SW15 ...... 156 E10
Queen's Gate Ms SKENS SW7 ... 15 L4
Queen's Gate Ms SKENS SW7 ... 15 J3
Queen's Gate Pl SKENS SW7 ... 15 J3
Queen's Gate Place Ms
　SKENS SW7 ...... 15 K4
Queen's Gate Ter SKENS SW7 ... 15 J3
Queen's Grove Rd CHING E4 ... 101 D6
Queen's Head St IS N1 ...... 6 D6

Rayners Gdns NTHLT UB5....133 J5
Rayners La PIN HA5....113 N4
Rayner's Rd PUT/ROE SW15....179 H1
RYLN/HDSTN HA2....113 N4
Raynes Av WAN E11....121 P5
Raynham Av UED N18....99 P7
Raynham Rd HMSMTH W6....156 E3
UED N18....99 P7
Raynham St HERT/BAY SG13....25 N4
Raynham Ter UED N18....99 P7
Raynor Cl STHL UB1....133 N10
Raynor Pl IS N1....6 F5
Raynsford Rd WARE SG12....26 C2
Raynton Cl RYLN/HDSTN HA2....113 M6
YEAD UB4....132 C2
Raynton Dr YEAD UB4....132 C5
Raynton Rd PEND EN3....80 C3
Ray Rd CRW RM5....104 C6
E/WMO/HCT KT8....198 A5
Rays Av UED N18....100 B5
WDSR SL4....148 E6
Ray's HI CSHM HP5....32 B7
EYN DA4....210 B4
Rays Rd UED N18....100 B5
WWKM BR4....205 H7
Ray St CLKNW EC1R....12 C3
Ray Street Br CLKNW EC1R....12 B3
Raywood Cl WDR/YW UB7....152 D6
Reachview Cl CAMTN NW1....5 H4
Read Ct WAB EN9....63 M9
The Readens BNSTD SM7....239 P7
Reading Arch Rd REDH RH1....258 A10
Reading La HACK E8....140 A1
Reading Rd NTHLT UB5....114 A10
SUT SM1....221 M2
The Readings HLWS CM18....47 L8
RKW/CH/CXG WD3....71 J7
Read Rd ASHTD KT21....237 J3
Reads Cl IL IG1....122 E8
Reads Rest La KWD/TDW/WH KT20....239 J5
Read Wy GVE DA12....190 C8
Reapers Cl CAMTN NW1....5 H1
Reapers Wy ISLW TW7....176 C1
Reardon Pth WAP E1W....140 A10
Reardon St WAP E1W....140 A10
Reaston St NWCR SE14....160 B6
Reckitt Rd CHSWK W4....156 A4
Record St PECK SE15....160 B5
Recovery St TOOT SW17....179 P8
Recreation Av HARH RM3....105 N10
ROMW/RG RM7....124 D3
Recreation Rd GU GU1....249 P10
HAYES BR2....205 L2
NWDGN UB2....153 M3
SYD SE26....182 C7
Recreation Wy MTCM CR4....202 F3
Rector St IS N1....6 F1
Rectory Cha BRWN CM15....87 H3
RBRW/HUT CM13....127 K2
Rectory Cl ASHTD KT21....237 L1
BF/WBF KT14....215 P9
BRKMPK AL9....41 P3
CHING E4....100 F4
DART DA1....164 F10
FNCH N3....97 J9
RGUE GU4....250 C8
RYNPK SW20....200 F2
SCUP DA14....185 L7
SHPTN TW17....196 B5
SLN SL2....129 H5
STAN HA7....94 G7
SURB KT6....199 H8
WARE SG12....26 A3
WDSR SL4....148 B7
Rectory Fld HLWW/ROY CM19....46 E3
Rectory Field Crs CHARL SE7....161 P4
Rectory Gdns CEND/HSY/T N8....40 E4
HAT AL10....133 N3
NTHLT UB5....114 A10
UPMR RM14....122 C10
Rectory Gn BECK BR3....204 E1
Rectory Gv CLAP SW4....158 D9
CROY/NA CR0....203 J7
FELT TW13....175 N7
Rectory HI AMSS HP7....69 H5
Rectory La AMSS HP7....68 G5
ASHTD KT21....237 L4
BERK HP4....35 P5
BF/WBF KT14....215 P9
BFOR GU20....232 A8
BH/WHM TN16....244 B9
BH/WHM TN16....245 M10
BNSTD SM7....240 A1
BRKHM/BTCW RH3....256 C8
CRAWW RH11....283 J5
EDGW HA8....95 M7
GT/LBKH KT23....253 L9
HLWW/ROY CM19....46 E3
HORL RH6....278 G8
KGLGY WD4....54 B4
LOU IG10....82 D6
RAD WD7....57 J2
RAD WD7....57 N2
RKW/CH/CXG WD3....91 N1
SCUP DA14....185 L7
SEV TN13....265 J3
SHGR GU5....270 C4
STAN HA7....94 G6
SURB KT6....199 H8
TOOT SW17....180 B8
WLGTN SM6....222 D1
Rectory Meadow MEO DA13....189 M9
Rectory Orch WIM/MER SW19....179 H7
Rectory Pk SAND/SEL CR2....223 N6
Rectory Park Av NTHLT UB5....133 N5
Rectory Pl WOOL/PLUM SE18....162 D3
Rectory Rd ACT W3....135 N10
BARN SW13....156 D8
BECK BR3....204 F2
COUL/CHIP CR5....257 N1
DAGE RM10....144 B1
GRAYS RM17....168 A2
HAYES BR2....226 A4
HEST TW5....153 J8
HYS/HAR UB3....133 H8
MNPK E12....122 C10
NWDGN UB2....153 N2
RKW/CH/CXG WD3....91 N1
SUT SM1....201 K10
SWCM DA10....189 K3
TIL RM18....168 G8
WALTH E17....120 C2
WGCW AL8....22 C2
Rectory Sq WCHPL E1....140 C7
Rectory Wd HLW CM20....28 F10
Reculver Ms UED N18....99 P5
Reculver Rd BERM/RHTH SE16....160 A4
Redan Pl BAY/PAD W2....8 C6
Redan St WKENS W14....156 C10
Redan Ter CMBW SE5....159 J8
Red Barracks Rd WOOL/PLUM SE18....162 C3
Redberry Gv SYD SE26....159 M7
Redbourn Av FNCH N3....97 K9
Redbourn Rd HHNE HP2....36 E2
STALW/RED AL3....37 M2
Redbridge La East REDBR IG4....122 A4
Redbridge La West WAN E11....121 N4
Redburn St CHEL SW3....16 A9
Redcar Cl NTHLT UB5....114 A10
Redcar Rd HARH RM3....105 N6

Redcar St CMBW SE5....159 K6
Redcastle Cl WCHPL E1....140 B9
Red Cedars Rd ORP BR6....207 H10
Redchurch St BETH E2....13 L1
Redcliffe Gdns IL IG1....122 C10
WBPTN SW10....15 H8
Redcliffe Ms WBPTN SW10....15 H8
Redcliffe Pl WBPTN SW10....15 H9
Redcliffe Rd WBPTN SW10....15 J8
Redcliffe Sq WBPTN SW10....15 H8
Redcliffe St WBPTN SW10....15 H9
Redclose Av MRDN SM4....201 K5
Redclyffe Rd EHAM E6....141 P4
Redcote Pl DORK RH4....255 J6
Red Cottage Ms DTCH/LGLY SL3....149 P2
Red Ct SL SL1....129 K10
Redcourt WOKS/MYFD GU22....232 C3
Redcroft Rd GFD/PVL UB6....134 B9
Redcross Wy STHWK SE1....18 F1
Redden Court Rd HARH RM3....125 N1
Redding Cl RDART DA2....188 D5
Redding Dr AMS HP6....68 C3
Reddings HHS/BOV HP3....36 A8
WGCW AL8....22 F4
Reddings Av BUSH WD23....74 A9
Reddings Cl MLHL NW7....96 C5
The Reddings BORE WD6....75 L7
MLHL NW7....96 C4
Reddington Dr DTCH/LGLY SL3....150 A3
Reddington Rd GFD/PVL UB6....55 P5
Reddins Rd PECK SE15....159 P6
Reddons Rd BECK BR3....182 D10
Reddown Rd COUL/CHIP CR5....240 G5
Reddy Rd ERITH DA8....164 C5
Redehall Rd HORL RH6....281 J5
Rede Pl BAY/PAD W2....8 F6
Redesdale Gdns ISLW TW7....154 F6
Redesdale St CHEL SW3....16 A9
Redfern Av HSLWW TW4....175 H6
Redfern Cl UX/CGN UB8....131 M3
Redfern Gdns CRK RM2....105 L10
Redfern Rd CAT SE6....183 H3
WLSDN NW10....136 B2
Redfield La ECT SW5....14 C5
Redford Av COUL/CHIP CR5....240 C1
WLGTN SM6....222 F3
Redford Cl FELT TW13....174 C1
Redford Rd WDSR SL4....148 C7
Redford Wy UX/CGN UB8....131 M2
Redgate Dr HAYES BR2....205 N9
Redgate Ter PUT/ROE SW15....178 C2
Redgrave Cl SAND/SEL SE25....203 N6
Redgrave Dr CRAWE RH10....284 E5
Redgrave Rd PUT/ROE SW15....156 G10
Redhall Cl HAT AL10....40 C7
Redhall Dr HAT AL10....40 C7
Redhall La RKW/CH/CXG WD3....71 P5
Redheath Cl GSTN WD25....72 C1
Red HI CHST BR7....184 D8
Redhill Dr EDGW HA8....95 P10
Redhill Rd COB KT11....216 C9
Redhill St CAMTN NW1....4 B1
Red House La BEAC HP9....88 A7
WARE SG12....26 A4
Red House La BXLYHS DA6....163 N10
WOT/HER KT12....197 H9
Redhouse Rd BH/WHM TN16....243 P7
Redington Gdns HAMP NW3....117 L8
Redington Rd HAMP NW3....117 L8
Redland Gdns E/WMO/HCT KT8....197 N4
Redlands COUL/CHIP CR5....240 F2
Redlands La RDKG RH5....272 F8
Redlands Rd PEND EN3....80 D5
SEV TN13....265 G10
Redlands Wy BRXS/STRHM SW2....180 A5
Red La ESH/CLAY KT10....218 F3
OXTED RH8....261 N9
RDKG RH5....273 M7
Redleaf Cl BELV DA17....164 B5
Redleaves Av ASHF TW15....174 C9
Redlees Cl ISLW TW7....154 F10
Red Lion Cl CSTN WD25....74 A3
STMC/STPC BR5....207 N6
WALW SE17....18 G9
Red Lion Crs HLWE CM17....47 M3
Red Lion HI EFNCH N2....97 N10
Red Lion La CHOB/PIR GU24....213 K5
HHS/BOV HP3....54 A1
HLWE CM17....47 M3
RKW/CH/CXG WD3....71 K1
WOOL/PLUM SE18....162 D7
Red Lion Pl WOOL/PLUM SE18....162 D7
Red Lion Rd CHOB/PIR GU24....213 K5
SURB KT6....199 K5
Red Lion Rw WALW SE17....18 F10
Red Lion Sq BMSBY WC1N....11 K1
Red Lion St CSHM HP5....50 G8
GINN WC1R....11 N3
RCHPK/HAM TW10....177 H10
Red Lodge Crs BXLY DA5....186 E6
Red Lodge Gdns BERK HP4....33 N6
Red Lodge Rd BXLY DA5....186 E6
WWKM BR4....205 H8
Redman Cl NTHLT UB5....133 K4
Redmans Rd RSEV TN14....228 D3
Redman's Rd WCHPL E1....140 E7
Redmead La WAP E1W....13 N10
Redmead Rd HYS/HAR UB3....152 F3
Redmore Rd HMSMTH W6....156 E3
Red Oak Cl ORP BR6....206 E10
Red Pl MYFR/PKLN W1K....10 A1
Red Post HI HNHL SE24....181 L1
Redricks La HLW CM20....29 L3
Redriffe Rd PLSTW E13....141 L4
Redriff Rd BERM/RHTH SE16....160 E4
ROMW/RG RM7....104 C10
Red Rd BORE WD6....75 J1
BRW CM14....106 G5
Redroofs Cl BECK BR3....204 C1
Redruth Cl WDGN N22....98 G8
Redruth Rd HARH RM3....105 N6
HOM E9....139 G3
Redstart Cl CROY/NA CR0....225 J6
EHAM E6....142 B7
NWCR SE14....160 D6
Redstone HI REDH RH1....258 B10
Redstone Hollow REDH RH1....276 B1
Redstone Mnr REDH RH1....258 B10
Redstone Pk REDH RH1....276 B1
Redstone Rd REDH RH1....276 B1
Redston Rd CEND/HSY/T N8....118 G2
Red St MEO DA13....189 N9
Redvers Rd WARL CR6....242 C4
WDGN N22....99 H10
Redvers St IS N1....7 K8
Redwald Rd CLPT E5....120 C2
Redway Dr WHTN TW2....176 B3
Red Willow HLWW/ROY CM19....46 C4
Redwing Av RGODL GU7....267 J3
Redwing Cl SAND/SEL CR2....224 C7
Redwing Gdns BF/WBF KT14....215 H7
Redwing Rd WALL SM6....223 K6
Redwood ECH TW20....195 H2
Redwood Cha SOCK/AV RM15....147 J6
Redwood Cl BERM/RHTH SE16....140 D10
BFN/LL DA15....185 H4
HGDN/ICK UB10....132 C4
OXHEY WD19....93 K5
PUR/KEN CR8....223 K10
STHGT/OAK N14....98 E1
Redwood Dr ASC SL5....192 G6
HHS/BOV HP3....35 P8

SL SL1....129 J9
Redwood Gv RGUE GU4....268 G5
Redwood Mt REIG RH2....257 K7
Redwood Ri BORE WD6....75 M3
Redwoods ADL/WDHM KT15....215 A3
HERT/WAS SG14....25 K4
The Redwoods WDSR SL4....149 J9
Redwood Wy BAR EN5....76 C9
Reece Ms SKENS SW7....15 L5
Reed Av CAN/RD E16....141 H8
IVER SL0....131 H8
LCOL/BKTW AL2....57 J3
LEE/GVPK SE12....183 M1
Reede Rd DAGE RM10....144 B1
Reede Wy DAGE RM10....144 B1
Reedham Cl LCOL/BKTW AL2....55 P5
TOTM N17....120 A2
Reedham Dr PUR/KEN CR8....222 G9
Reedham Park Av PUR/KEN CR8....241 H2
Reedham St PECK SE15....159 P6
Reedholm Vis STNW/STAM N16....119 L9
Reed Pl WAND/EARL SW18....179 L1
Reed Pond Wk GPK RM2....104 G10
Reeds Crs WATN WD24....73 N6
Reeds Pl CAMTN NW1....4 C3
The Reeds WGCE AL7....22 G6
Reedworth St LBTH SE11....18 B6
Reenglass Rd STAN HA7....95 J5
Rees Dr STAN HA7....95 K5
Rees Gdns CROY/NA CR0....203 N6
Reesland Cl MNPK E12....122 D10
Rees St IS N1....6 G1
Reets Farm Cl CDALE/KGS NW9....116 B4
Reeve Rd REDH RH1....276 C1
Reeves Av CDALE/KGS NW9....116 A5
Reeves Cnr CROY/NA CR0....203 J9
Reeves La HLWW/ROY CM19....45 P5
Reeves Ms MYFR/PKLN W1K....10 A2
Reeves Rd BOW E3....139 M8
WOOL/PLUM SE18....162 E5
Reform Rw TOTM N17....99 N10
Reform St BTSEA SW11....158 A10
Regal Cl EA W5....135 J2
WCHPL E1....13 P3
Regal Crs WLGTN SM6....202 C10
UED N18....99 N6
Regal Dr FBAR/BDGN N11....98 A10
Regal La CAMTN NW1....4 D6
Regal Wy KTN/HRWW/W HA3....115 K4
WATN WD24....73 K4
Regan Cl GUW GU2....249 N5
Regan Wy IS N1....7 J8
Regarder Rd CHIG IG7....103 N5
Regarth Av ROM RM1....124 D3
Regency Cl CHIG IG7....102 F6
EA W5....135 K8
HPTN TW12....175 N8
Regency Ct BRW CM14....107 H3
EN EN1....79 J9
HLWS CM18....47 K4
Regency Dr BF/WBF KT14....215 J9
RSLP HA4....112 F6
Regency Gdns EMPK RM11....125 K5
WOT/HER KT12....197 K8
Regency Ms BECK BR3....205 H1
WLSDN NW10....136 D1
Regency St WEST SW1P....17 H6
Regency Wk CROY/NA CR0....204 D6
Regent Av BXLYHN DA7....163 N9
HGDN/ICK UB10....132 C2
Regent Cl ADL/WDHM KT15....215 M5
CTHM CR3....241 M4
HGDN/ICK UB10....132 C2
KTN/HRWW/W HA3....115 K4
NFNCH/WDSP N12....97 N6
REDH RH1....258 D4
STALE/WH AL4....39 H2
WGCE AL7....23 H6
Regent Crs REDH RH1....258 A8
Regent Gdns GDMY/SEVK IG3....123 K5
Regent Pl WIM/MER SW19....179 M5
Regent Rd BRYLDS KT5....199 L5
EPP CM16....65 J3
HNHL SE24....181 H2
SURB KT6....199 N2
Regents Av PLMGR N13....99 H6
Regents Cl CTHM CR3....241 M4
RAD WD7....56 F10
SAND/SEL CR2....223 M3
YEAD UB4....132 G7
Regent's Dr HAYES BR2....226 A2
Regents Ms STJWD NW8....3 K7
Regent's Park Rd CAMTN NW1....4 B5
FNCH N3....97 J10
Regents Pl LOU IG10....102 A1
Regent Sq BELV DA17....164 C3
STPAN WC1H....5 M10
Regent's Rw HACK E8....7 N6
Regents St CHSWK W4....155 M4
CONDST W1S....10 C6
STJS SW1Y....11 J8
WATN WD24....73 J4
WLSDN NW10....136 G2
Regents Wk ASC SL5....192 G6
Reginald Rd DEPT SE8....160 F6
FSTGT E7....141 M2
HARH RM3....105 P9
NTHWD HA6....92 C9
Reginald Sq DEPT SE8....160 F6
Regina Rd FSBYPK N4....118 G6
NWDGN UB2....153 M3
SNWD SE25....203 P5
WEA W13....134 F10
Regina Ter WEA W13....134 G10
Regis Rd KTTN NW5....118 C10
Regnart Buildings CAMTN NW1....5 H10
Reid Av CTHM CR3....241 J2
Reid Cl COUL/CHIP CR5....240 C2
PIN HA5....113 H1
Reidhaven Rd WOOL/PLUM SE18....163 H3
Reigate Av MRDN SM4....201 L1
Reigate Cl CRAWE RH10....284 E4
Reigate Hl REIG RH2....257 L8
Reigate Hill Cl REIG RH2....257 L7
Reigate Rd BMLY BR1....183 M5
BRKHM/BTCW RH3....255 K10
DORK RH4....255 K10
EPSOM KT18....238 G3
EW KT17....220 C6
GDMY/SEVK IG3....123 J7
HORL RH6....275 M10
HORL RH6....279 N5
LEE/GVPK SE12....183 M6
REIG RH2....257 M10
Reigate Wy WLGTN SM6....222 F2
Reighton Rd CLPT E5....120 C1
Reindorp Cl GUW GU2....267 M1
Relay Rd SHB W12....136 F7
Relf Rd PECK SE15....159 P9
Reliton Ms SKENS SW7....15 P3
Rembrandt Cl BGVA SW1W....16 C7
POP/IOD E14....160 A1
Rembrandt Dr GDW DA11....190 A6
Rembrandt Rd EDGW HA8....95 M10
LEW SE13....161 K10

Remington Rd EHAM E6....142 B8
SEVS/STOTM N15....119 L4
Remington St IS N1....6 D8
Remnant St HOL/ALD WC2B....11 N5
Remus Rd BOW E3....140 F2
Rendle Cl CROY/NA CR0....203 N5
Rendlesham Av RAD WD7....74 E3
Rendlesham Cl WARE SG12....26 A1
Rendlesham Rd CLPT E5....119 P9
ENC/FH EN2....79 L4
Rendlesham Wy RKW/CH/CXG WD3....70 F10
Renforth St BERM/RHTH SE16....160 B1
Renfree Wy SHPTN TW17....196 A7
Renfrew Cl EHAM E6....142 D9
Renfrew Rd HEST TW5....153 L8
KUTN/CMB KT2....177 P10
LBTH SE11....18 C5
The Renmans ASHTD KT21....237 L2
Renmuir St TOOT SW17....180 A9
Rennell St LEW SE13....161 H9
Renness Rd WALTH E17....120 D1
Rennets Cl ELTH/MOT SE9....184 G1
Rennets Wood Rd ELTH/MOT SE9....184 G1
Rennie Cl ASHF TW15....173 N6
Rennie St STHWK SE1....12 C9
Rennie Ter REDH RH1....276 B1
Rennison Cl WALTH E17....120 C3
Renown Cl CROY/NA CR0....203 J8
ROMW/RG RM7....104 C9
Rensburg Rd WALTH E17....120 C3
Renshaw Cl BELV DA17....164 A5
Renters Av HDN NW4....116 F4
Renton Dr STMC/STPC BR5....207 N7
Renwick Rd BARK IG11....143 L6
Repens Wy YEAD UB4....133 L6
Rephidim St STHWK SE1....19 H4
Replingham Rd WAND/EARL SW18....179 J4
Reporton Rd FUL/PGN SW6....157 H7
Repository Rd WOOL/PLUM SE18....162 C5
Repton Av ALP/SUD HA0....135 H1
GPK RM2....125 H1
HYS/HAR UB3....152 E3
Repton Cl SUT SM1....221 P2
Repton Ct BECK BR3....204 G1
Repton Dr GPK RM2....125 H2
Repton Gdns GPK RM2....125 H1
Repton Gn STALW/RED AL3....38 C3
Repton Gv IL IG5....102 C9
Repton Rd KTN/HRWW/W HA3....115 L2
ORP BR6....227 K1
Repton St POP/IOD E14....140 D8
Repton Wy RKW/CH/CXG WD3....72 B8
Repulse Cl ROMW/RG RM7....104 C9
Reservoir Rd BROCKY SE4....160 D8
RSLP HA4....112 D3
STHGT/OAK N14....78 D9
Resolon Wy HHW HP1....35 L7
Resory Wy WLGTN SM6....222 F5
Restell Cl BKHTH/KID SE3....161 K5
Restmor Wy WLGTN SM6....202 B9
Reston Cl BORE WD6....75 M4
Reston Pl SKENS SW7....14 G6
Restons Crs ELTH/MOT SE9....184 G3
Retford Cl BORE WD6....75 M4
HARH RM3....105 P7
Retford Pth HARH RM3....105 P8
Retford Rd HARH RM3....105 P8
Retford St BETH E2....7 K8
BETH E2....7 K8
Retingham Wy CHING E4....100 C3
Retreat Cl KTN/HRWW/W HA3....115 H3
Retreat Pl HOM E9....140 B1
Retreat Rd RCH/KEW TW9....177 J1
The Retreat AMS HP6....70 B5
BARN SW13....156 B9
BRW CM14....106 C2
BRYLDS KT5....199 L6
CDALE/KGS NW9....116 A3
EGH TW20....172 A9
GRAYS RM17....167 N5
ORP BR6....227 N4
RBRW/HUT CM13....87 N10
RYLN/HDSTN HA2....113 P5
THHTH CR7....203 L4
WPK KT4....200 E9
Retreat Wy CHIG IG7....103 L4
Reubens Rd RBRW/HUT CM13....87 N10
Revell Cl LHD/OX KT22....236 A8
Revell Dr LHD/OX KT22....236 A8
Revell Ri WOOL/PLUM SE18....163 J5
Revell Rd KUT KT1....199 N2
SUT SM1....221 J3
Revelon Rd BROCKY SE4....160 D10
Revels Cl HERT/WAS SG14....25 L3
Revels Rd HERT/WAS SG14....25 L3
Revelstoke Rd WIM/MER SW19....179 K5
Reventlow Rd ELTH/MOT SE9....184 F4
Reverdy Rd STHWK SE1....19 N6
Reverend Cl RYLN/HDSTN HA2....114 A8
Revesby Cl CHOB/PIR GU24....212 C9
Revesby Rd CAR SM5....201 P6
Review Rd CRICK NW2....116 C7
DAGE RM10....144 G7
Rewell St FUL/PGN SW6....157 M6
Rewley Rd CAR SM5....201 N6
Rex Av ASHF TW15....174 B9
Rex Pl MYFR/PKLN W1K....10 A1
Reydon Av WAN E11....121 P4
Reynard Cl BMLY BR1....206 C3
Reynard Dr NRWD SE19....181 N10
Reynard's Wy LCOL/BKTW AL2....55 N5
Reynard Wy HERT/BAY SG13....25 P5
Reynolds Av CHDH RM6....123 M5
CHSGTN KT9....219 K4
MNPK E12....122 D10
Reynolds Cl CAR SM5....202 A8
GLDGN NW11....117 L5
HHW HP1....35 K5
WIM/MER SW19....179 P4
Reynolds Crs STALE/WH AL4....38 G1
Reynolds Dr EDGW HA8....114 A6
Reynolds Pl BKHTH/KID SE3....161 N6
CRAWW RH11....283 N6
RCHPK/HAM TW10....177 L2
Reynolds Rd BEAC HP9....88 B8
CHSWK W4....155 P2
CRAWW RH11....283 M6
NWMAL KT3....200 A7
PECK SE15....182 B3
YEAD UB4....133 K6
Reynolds Wy CROY/NA CR0....223 M1
Rheidol Ms IS N1....6 E7
Rheidol Ter IS N1....6 D7
Rheingold Wy WLGTN SM6....222 F5
Rheola Cl TOTM N17....99 N9
Rhoda St BETH E2....13 M1
Rhodes Av WDGN N22....98 D9
Rhodes Cl EGH TW20....172 E8
Rhodesia Rd BRXN/ST SW9....158 F8
WAN E11....120 F3
Rhodes St HOLWY N7....118 G10
Rhodes Wy CRAWE RH10....284 G3
WATN WD24....73 L6
Rhodeswell Rd POP/IOD E14....139 M7
Rhodrons Av CHSGTN KT9....219 K2
Rhondda Gv BOW E3....139 L5
Rhyl Rd GFD/PVL UB6....135 H1
Rhyl St KTTN NW5....118 A2
Rhymes Hwy HAT AL10....39 N2
Rhys Av FBAR/BDGN N11....98 C6
Rialto Rd MTCM CR4....202 B1
Ribble Cl WFD IG8....101 P7
Ribblesdale LCOL/BKTW AL2....57 L3

Ribblesdale HHNE HP2....35 P3
Ribblesdale Av FBAR/BDGN N11....98 A7
NTHLT UB5....134 A1
Ribblesdale Rd CEND/HSY/T N8....118 E2
RDART DA2....188 B4
STRHM/NOR SW16....180 C8
Ribbon Dance Ms CMBW SE5....159 L1
Ribchester Av GFD/PVL UB6....134 E5
Ribston Cl HAYES BR2....206 C8
RAD WD7....57 J9
Rib V HERT/WAS SG14....25 L2
Ricardo Rd WDSR SL4....171 N2
Ricardo St POP/IOD E14....140 G8
Ricards Rd WIM/MER SW19....179 J8
Rice Cl HHNE HP2....36 A5
Richard Cl WOOL/PLUM SE18....162 B8
Richard House Dr CAN/RD E16....142 A8
Richard Rd ROMW/RG RM7....104 C5
Richards Cl BUSH WD23....94 C2
HGDN/ICK UB10....114 B3
HRW HA1....114 E3
HYS/HAR UB3....152 E5
Richards Fld HOR/WEW KT19....220 A5
Richardson Cl GRH DA9....188 E1
LCOL/BKTW AL2....57 K3
Richardson Crs CHESW EN7....61 J2
Richardson Pl STALW/RED AL4....39 M1
Richardson Rd SRTFD E15....141 K4
Richardson's Ms FITZ W1T....10 C2
Richard's Pl CHEL SW3....15 P5
WALTH E17....120 F1
Richards Rd COB KT11....218 A10
Richard Stagg Cl STAL AL1....38 F4
Richard St WCHPL E1....140 A8
WCHPL E1....140 A8
Richards Wy SL SL1....128 F10
Richbell Cl ASHTD KT21....237 J4
Richbell Pl BMSBY WC1N....11 N3
Richborne Ter VX/NE SW8....158 C6
Richborough Cl STMC/STPC BR5....207 N4
Richborough Rd CRICK NW2....116 C9
Richens Cl HSLW TW3....154 C8
Riches Rd IL IG1....122 F7
Richfield Rd BUSH WD23....94 C1
Richford Rd SRTFD E15....141 L3
Richford St HMSMTH W6....156 F1
Richings Wy IVER SL0....151 J2
Richland Av COUL/CHIP CR5....240 B1
Richlands Av EW KT17....220 D1
Richmond Av CHING E4....101 J6
CRICK NW2....136 F1
EBED/NFELT TW14....174 F2
HGDN/ICK UB10....132 C1
IS N1....6 A5
RYNPK SW20....201 H1
Richmond Buildings SOHO/CST W1F....11 J6
Richmond Cl BH/WHM TN16....243 N5
EPSOM KT18....236 B10
GT/LBKH KT23....236 B10
WALTH E17....120 E4
Richmond Ct BROX EN10....44 E6
CRAWE RH10....283 P8
HAT AL10....40 E7
POTB/CUF EN6....59 M7
Richmond Crs CHING E4....101 J6
ED N9....99 P2
IS N1....5 P5
SL SL1....149 M1
STA TW18....173 J8
Richmond Dr SHPTN TW17....196 D6
WAT WD17....72 F6
Richmond Gdns HDN NW4....116 D3
KTN/HRWW/W HA3....94 E8
Richmond Gn CROY/NA CR0....202 F10
Richmond Gv IS N1....6 A1
Richmond HI RCHPK/HAM TW10....177 K2
Richmond Ms SOHO/CST W1F....11 J6
Richmond Park Rd KUTN/CMB KT2....177 K10
MORT/ESHN SW14....156 C5
Richmond Pl WOOL/PLUM SE18....162 F3
Richmond Rd BAR EN5....77 L9
CHING E4....101 J2
COUL/CHIP CR5....240 C1
CROY/NA CR0....202 F10
EA W5....155 K1
EFNCH N2....97 M10
FBAR/BDGN N11....98 F7
FSTGT E7....121 N10
GRAYS RM17....167 P4
HACK E8....7 L3
IL IG1....122 F8
ISLW TW7....154 F9
KUTN/CMB KT2....199 K1
POTB/CUF EN6....59 M7
ROM RM1....124 G4
RYNPK SW20....200 E1
SEVS/STOTM N15....119 M4
STA TW18....173 J8
THHTH CR7....203 J4
TWK TW1....176 G2
WAN E11....121 J7
Richmond St PLSTW E13....141 M4
Richmond Ter WHALL SW1A....17 L1
Richmond Wy GT/LBKH KT23....236 A9
RKW/CH/CXG WD3....72 D8
SHB W12....156 G1
WAN E11....121 M7
Richmondwood ASC SL5....192 G8
Richmount Gdns BKHTH/KID SE3....161 M9
Rich St POP/IOD E14....140 D8
Rickard Cl BRXS/STRHM SW2....181 H4
HDN NW4....116 E2
WDR/YW UB7....151 N2
Rickards Cl SURB KT6....199 K9
Ricketts Hill Rd BH/WHM TN16....244 A4
Rickett St FUL/PGN SW6....14 D10
Rickfield CRAWW RH11....283 K8
Rickfield Cl HAT AL10....40 D6
Rickford HI RGUW GU3....249 J2
Rickman Crs ADL/WDHM KT15....195 L10
Rickman Hl COUL/CHIP CR5....240 C3
Rickman Hill Rd COUL/CHIP CR5....240 C4
Rickman's La SLN SL2....129 K1
Rickman St WCHPL E1....140 B6
Rickmansworth La CFSP/GDCR SL9....90 C6
Rickmansworth Rd AMS HP6....69 K4
DEN/HRF UB9....91 M9
NTHWD HA6....92 C3
PIN HA5....93 J10
RKW/CH/CXG WD3....71 H7
WATW WD18....72 E6
Rick Roberts Wy SRTFD E15....141 J3
Ricksons La EHSLY KT24....252 C3
Rickthorne Rd ARCH N19....118 F7
Rickwood REDH RH1....280 C3
Rickyard GUW GU2....249 J10
Ridding La GFD/PVL UB6....114 C5
Riddings La HLWS CM18....47 K5
The Riddings CTHM CR3....259 N1
Riddlesdown Av PUR/KEN CR8....223 K6
Riddons Rd LEE/GVPK SE12....183 P6
Ride La SHGR GU5....269 N10
Rideout St WOOL/PLUM SE18....162 C3
Rider Cl BFN/LL DA15....185 H2
Riders Wy GDST RH9....260 D3
The Ride BTFD TW8....154 G4
PEND EN3....80 B7
Ridgdale St BOW E3....140 B4
Ridge Av DART DA1....186 G2
WCHMH N21....99 K1
Ridgebank SL SL1....128 F9

Ridgebrook Rd ELTH/MOT SE9 161 P10
Ridge Cl BRKHM/BTCW RH3 273 N4
CDALE/KGS NW9 116 A2
HDN NW4 96 G10 1
THMD SE28 162 G1
WOKS/MYFD GU22 231 N7
Ridge Crest ENC/FH EN2 78 G5
Ridgecroft Cl BXLY DA5 186 D4
Ridgefield WAT WD17 72 F3
Ridgegate Cl REIG RH2 257 N8
Ridge Gn REDH RH1 276 F3
Ridge Green Cl REDH RH1 276 F3
Ridge Hl GLDGN NW11 117 H6
Ridgehurst Av GSTN WD25 54 G9
Ridgelands LHD/OX KT22 236 C10
Ridge La WAT WD17 72 F2
Ridge Langley SAND/SEL CR2 223 P6
Ridge Lea HHW HP1 35 J7
Ridgemead Rd EGH TW20 171 N6
Ridgemont Gdns EDGW HA8 95 P5 1
Ridgemount GUW GU2 267 N1
WEY KT13 196 F9
Ridgemount Av COUL/CHIP CR5 240 C3
CROY/NA CR0 204 C9
Ridgemount End CFSP/GDCR SL9 90 B6 3
Ridgemount Gdns ENC/FH EN2 79 J7
Ridge Mount Rd ASC SL5 192 F8
Ridgemount Wy REDH RH1 275 N2
Ridge Pk WLGTN SM6 222 E6
Ridge Rd CEND/HSY/T N8 118 G4
CHEAM SM3 201 J8
CRICK NW2 117 J8
MTCM CR4 180 C10
WCHMH N21 99 L2
Ridgeside CRAWE RH10 284 A7 2
The Ridges RGUW GU3 267 P5
Ridge St WATN WD24 73 J4
The Ridge BRYLDS KT5 199 M5
BXLY DA5 186 A3
COUL/CHIP CR5 222 F10
CTHM CR3 261 K1
EPSOM KT18 237 P4
LHD/OX KT22 236 C10
ORP BR6 206 G9
PUR/KEN CR8 222 E6
WHTN TW2 176 C3
WOKS/MYFD GU22 232 E3
Ridgeview LCOL/BKTW AL2 57 L4
Ridgeview Cl BAR EN5 76 G10
Ridgeview Rd NFNCH/WDSP N12 97 L4
Ridge Wy DART DA1 186 G2
FELT TW13 175 M6 1
IVER SL0 131 H9
RKW/CH/CXG WD3 91 L1
VW GU25 194 B5
Ridgeway BERK HP4 33 L5
GRAYS RM17 168 B3
HAYES BR2 205 M9
HOR/WEW KT19 219 P8
RBRW/HUT CM13 107 N2
RDART DA2 188 D8
TRING HP23 32 A1
WFD IG8 101 P5
WGCE AL7 23 L6
WOT/HER KT12 196 G8
Ridgeway Av EBAR EN4 78 A10
GVE DA12 190 E6
Ridgeway Cl CSHM HP5 50 G4
DORK RH4 272 F4
HHS/BOV HP3 54 A1
WOKN/KNAP GU21 232 A2
Ridgeway Ct REDH RH1 276 A1 2
Ridgeway Crs ORP BR6 207 H10
Ridgeway Crescent Gdns
ORP BR6 207 H10 2
Ridgeway Dr BMLY BR1 183 N7
DORK RH4 272 F5
Ridgeway East BFN/LL DA15 185 J1
Ridgeway Gdns REDBR IG4 122 B3
WOKN/KNAP GU21 232 A1
Ridgeway Rd CSHM HP5 50 G4
DORK RH4 272 F4
ISLW TW7 154 D6
REDH RH1 258 A10
Ridgeway Rd North ISLW TW7 154 D6
Ridgeways HLWE CM17 47 P1
The Ridge Wy SAND/SEL CR2 223 M6
The Ridgeway ACT W3 155 M2
AMSS HP7 69 K6
CDALE/KGS NW9 116 A2
CHING E4 101 H2
CHOB/PIR GU24 230 E6
CROY/NA CR0 202 G10
ENC/FH EN2 78 D2
FBAR/BDGN N11 98 A5
FNCH N3 97 L8
GLDGN NW11 117 J6
GPK RM2 125 H2
GVE DA12 191 P10
HARH RM3 105 M9
HERT/WAS SG14 24 G4
HORL RH6 280 B6
KTN/HRWW/W HA3 115 H4
LHD/OX KT22 218 B10
LHD/OX KT22 236 C9
LTWR GU18 212 A6
MLHL NW7 96 E5
POTB/CUF EN6 60 B3
POTB/CUF EN6 78 A1
RAD WD7 74 E3
RSLP HA4 113 H5
RYLN/HDSTN HA2 113 N3
STALE/WH AL4 38 F2
STAN HA7 95 H7
STHGT/OAK N14 98 F3
WAT WD17 72 F3
Ridgeway West BFN/LL DA15 185 H1
Ridgewell Cl DAGE RM10 144 C3
IS N1 6 F5
SYD SE26 182 E7
Ridgewood MEO DA13 211 P1
Ridgmont Rd STAL AL1 38 D7
Ridgmount Gdns GWRST WC1E 11 J3
Ridgmount Rd
WAND/EARL SW18 179 L1 5
Ridgmount St GWRST WC1E 11 J3
Ridgway WIM/MER SW19 178 F10
WOKS/MYFD GU22 233 J1
Ridgway Gdns WIM/MER SW19 178 G10
Ridgway Pl WIM/MER SW19 179 H9
Ridgway Rd BRXN/ST SW9 159 J9
WOKS/MYFD GU22 233 J1
The Ridgway BELMT SM2 221 N4
Ridgwell Rd CAN/RD E16 141 P7
Riding Court Rd DTCH/LGLY SL3 149 P6
Riding Hl SAND/SEL CR2 223 P9
Riding House St GTPST W1W 10 G4
REGST W1B 10 F4 5
Ridings Av WCHMH N21 79 J8
The Ridings ADL/WDHM KT15 215 H3
AMS HP6 69 J1
ASHTD KT21 237 J3
BH/WHM TN16 244 B3
BRYLDS KT5 199 M5
COB KT11 217 P8
CRAWE RH10 284 E6
CSHM HP5 70 A2
EA W5 135 L6
EHSLY KT24 252 F1
EPSOM KT18 238 B1
EW KT17 220 C5 2
HERT/WAS SG14 25 H6
IVER SL0 151 J3
KWD/TDW/WH KT20 239 J6
REDH RH1 257 N8
RPLY/SEND GU23 233 K9
SUN TW16 197 H1
The Riding GLDGN NW11 117 J5
WOKN/KNAP GU21 214 E10
Ridlands Gv OXTED RH8 262 B6
Ridlands La OXTED RH8 262 B6
Ridlands Ri OXTED RH8 262 B6
Ridler Rd EN EN1 79 M4
Ridley Av WEA W13 154 G2
Ridley Cl HARH RM3 105 J9
Ridley Rd FSTGT E7 121 P9
HACK E8 119 N10
HAYES BR2 205 L3
WARL CR6 242 B4
WELL DA16 163 L7
WIM/MER SW19 179 L10
WLSDN NW10 136 D4
Ridsdale Rd PGE/AN SE20 204 A1 8
WOKN/KNAP GU21 231 N3
Riefield Rd ELTH/MOT SE9 162 G10 1
Riesco Dr CROY/NA CR0 224 B3
Riffel Rd CRICK NW2 116 F10
Riffhams RBRW/HUT CM13 107 N4
Rifle Pl NTGHL W11 136 G10 3
Rifle Range La HRW HA1 114 E6
Rifle St POP/IOD E14 140 G7
Rigault Rd FUL/PGN SW6 157 H8
Rigby Cl CROY/NA CR0 203 H10
Rigby Gdns CDH/CHF RM16 168 E3
Rigby La STKPK UB11 152 D1
Rigby Ms IL IG1 122 D7
Rigden St POP/IOD E14 140 G8 6
Rigeley Rd WLSDN NW10 136 E5 5
Rigg Ap LEY E10 120 C6
Rigge Pl CLAP SW4 158 E10
Riggindale Rd STRHM/NOR SW16 180 E8
Riley Rd PEND EN3 80 B4
STHWK SE1 19 L3
Riley St WBPTN SW10 15 L10
Rillside CRAWE RH10 284 B10
Rinaldo Rd BAL SW12 180 C3
Ring Cl BMLY BR1 183 N10
Ringcroft St HOLWY N7 119 H10
Ringer's Rd BMLY BR1 205 M3
Ringford Rd WAND/EARL SW18 179 J1
Ringlet Cl CAN/RD E16 141 N7
Ringley Av HORL RH6 280 B5
Ringley Park Av REIG RH2 275 N1
Ringley Park Rd REIG RH2 257 M10
Ringmer Av FUL/PGN SW6 157 H7
Ringmer Pl WCHMH N21 79 L9
Ringmer Wy BMLY BR1 206 C5
Ringmore Dr RGUE GU4 250 F7
Ringmore Ri FSTH SE23 182 A3
Ringmore Rd WOT/HER KT12 197 K10
Ringshall Rd CHST BR7 207 K3
Ringslade Rd WDGN N22 98 G10 5
Ringstead Rd CAT SE6 182 G3
SUT SM1 221 N1
Ring Wy FBAR/BDGN N11 98 D7
Ringway NWDGN UB2 153 M4
Ringway Rd LCOL/BKTW AL2 56 A3
Ringwold Cl BECK BR3 182 D10
Ringwood Av CROY/NA CR0 202 F7
EFNCH N2 98 A10
HCH RM12 125 L7
ORP BR6 227 M6
REDH RH1 258 A7
Ringwood Cl ASC SL5 192 A4 1
CRAWE RH10 283 P9
PIN HA5 113 K1 3
Ringwood Gdns PUT/ROE SW15 178 D4 5
Ringwood Rd WALTH E17 120 E4
Ringwood Wy HPTN TW12 175 P7
WCHMH N21 99 J2 2
Ripley Av EGH TW20 172 B9
Ripley Cl BMLY BR1 206 C5
CROY/NA CR0 225 H3
DTCH/LGLY SL3 150 B3 1
Ripley Gdns MORT/ESHN SW14 156 A9
Ripley La RPLY/SEND GU23 234 A10
Ripley Rd BELV DA17 164 B3
CAN/RD E16 141 P8
ENC/FH EN2 79 K5
GDMY/SEVK IG3 123 J7
HPTN TW12 175 P10
RGUE GU4 251 N4
Ripley Vw LOU IG10 82 E4
Ripley Wy CHESW EN7 62 A6
HHW HP1 35 H5
Ripon Cl GUW GU2 249 L7
NTHLT UB5 113 P10
Ripon Gdns CHSGTN KT9 219 J2
IL IG1 122 B4
Ripon Rd ED N9 100 A1 4
TOTM N17 119 L1
WOOL/PLUM SE18 162 E5
Ripon Wy BORE WD6 75 P9
STALE/WH AL4 39 J2
Rippersley Rd WELL DA16 163 K7
Ripple Rd BARK IG11 142 F2
Ripplevale Gv IS N1 5 P4
Rippolson Rd WOOL/PLUM SE18 163 J4
Ripston Rd ASHF TW15 174 E8
Risborough Dr WPK KT4 200 D7
Risborough St STHWK SE1 18 D1 2
Risdens HLWS CM18 46 F4 1
Risdon St BERM/RHTH SE16 160 B1
Risebridge Cha ROM RM1 104 G8
Risebridge Rd GPK RM2 104 G10
Risedale Cl HHS/BOV HP3 35 P9 1
Risedale Hl HHS/BOV HP3 35 P9
Risedale Rd BXLYHN DA7 164 D9
HHS/BOV HP3 35 P9
Riseldine Rd FSTH SE23 182 D2
Rise Park Bvd GPK RM2 104 G9
Rise Park Pde ROM RM1 104 F10
Rise Rd ASC SL5 192 D6
The Rise AMSS HP7 69 H5
BKHH IG9 102 A2 1
BORE WD6 75 L9
BXLY DA5 185 M3
CRAWE RH10 284 D7
DART DA1 164 G10
EDGW HA8 95 N6
EHSLY KT24 252 F2
EW KT17 220 C6
GFD/PVL UB6 114 F10
GVE DA12 191 H7
HGDN/ICK UB10 132 A4
KWD/TDW/WH KT20 238 F7
LCOL/BKTW AL2 56 C1
MLHL NW7 96 C7
PLMGR N13 99 H5
SAND/SEL CR2 224 B5
SEV TN13 265 K4
WAN E11 121 M3
WLSDN NW10 116 A8
Riseway BRWN CM15 107 K4
Rising Gdns IL IG1 122 G6
Rising Hill Cl NTHWD HA6 92 D7 2
Risinghill St IS N1 6 A7
Risingholme Cl BUSH WD23 94 A1
KTN/HRWW/W HA3 94 D10 3
Risingholme Rd
KTN/HRWW/W HA3 94 D10
The Risings WALTH E17 121 J2
Risley Av TOTM N17 99 M9 2
Rita Rd VX/NE SW8 158 F6
Ritches Rd SEVS/STOTM N15 119 K3
Ritchie Rd CROY/NA CR0 204 A6
Ritchie St IS N1 6 B7
Ritchings Av WALTH E17 120 D2
Ritcroft Cl HHS/BOV HP3 36 C7
Ritcroft Dr HHS/BOV HP3 36 C7
Ritcroft St HHS/BOV HP3 36 C7
Ritherdon Rd TOOT SW17 180 B5
Ritson Rd HACK E8 7 M1
Ritter St WOOL/PLUM SE18 162 D5
Ritz Ct POTB/CUF EN6 59 K7 1
Rivaz Pl HOM E9 140 B1
Rivenhall End WGCE AL7 23 M5
Rivenhall Gdns SWFD E18 121 L2
River Av HOD EN11 44 G2
PLMGR N13 99 J4
THDIT KT7 198 F7
Riverbank E/WMO/HCT KT8 198 D3
River Bank THDIT KT7 198 E5
WCHMH N21 99 K1 1
Riverbank Rd BMLY BR1 183 M6
Riverbank Wy BTFD TW8 155 H5
River Barge Cl POP/IOD E14 161 H1
River Cl CHES/WCR EN8 62 F10
RAIN RM13 145 J7 2
RSLP HA4 112 G4
STHL UB1 154 B1 3
WAN E11 121 P4
River Ct WOKN/KNAP GU21 214 F10
Rivercourt Rd HMSMTH W6 156 E3
Riverdale Dr WAND/EARL SW18 179 L4
WOKS/MYFD GU22 232 C7
Riverdale Gdns TWK TW1 177 H1
Riverdale Rd BXLY DA5 186 A3
ERITH DA8 164 C4
FELT TW13 175 M7
TWK TW1 177 H2
WOOL/PLUM SE18 163 J4
Riverdene EDGW HA8 95 P5
Riverdene Rd IL IG1 122 D8
River Dr UPMR RM14 126 C4
Riverfield Rd STA TW18 173 J9
River Front EN EN1 79 L7
River Gdns CAR SM5 202 B9
EBED/NFELT TW14 175 J1
River Grove Pk BECK BR3 204 E1
Riverhead Cl WALTH E17 100 C10 1
Riverhead Dr BELMT SM2 221 L6 3
River Hl COB KT11 235 J1
Riverhill SEV TN13 265 M7
Riverholme Dr HOR/WEW KT19 220 A5
River La COB KT11 235 L2
LHD/OX KT22 236 C6
RCHPK/HAM TW10 177 J4
Rivermead BF/WBF KT14 216 A9
River Md CRAWW RH11 283 K4
Rivermead E/WMO/HCT KT8 198 B3
Rivermead Cl ADL/WDHM KT15 215 M4 2
TEDD TW11 176 G8
River Meads WARE SG12 27 H6
River Meads Av WHTN TW2 176 A6
Rivermill HLW CM20 28 F9
River Mt WOT/HER KT12 196 G7
River Mount Gdns GUW GU2 267 P3
Rivernook Cl WOT/HER KT12 197 K5
River Pk HHW HP1 35 K8
River Park Av STA TW18 172 G7
Riverpark Gdns HAYES BR2 183 J10
River Park Rd WDGN N22 98 G10
River Park Vw ORP BR6 207 L7
River Pl IS N1 6 E4
River Reach TEDD TW11 177 H9
River Rd BARK IG11 143 H4
BKHH IG9 102 B2
BRW CM14 106 D5
STA TW18 195 J1
Riversdale GVW DA11 190 B5
Riversdale Rd CRW RM5 104 C8
HBRY N5 119 J8
THDIT KT7 198 F5
Riversdell Cl CHERT KT16 195 J7
Riversend Rd HHS/BOV HP3 35 M9
Riversfield Rd EN EN1 79 M7
Riverside CHARL SE7 161 N2
DORK RH4 255 J10 1
EYN DA4 209 L9
GU GU1 250 A8
HDN NW4 116 E5
HORL RH6 280 B6
LCOL/BKTW AL2 57 K3 4
SHPTN TW17 196 F7
STWL/WRAY TW19 171 P3
TWK TW1 176 G4
Riverside Av BROX EN10 44 F8
E/WMO/HCT KT8 198 C5
LTWR GU18 212 B7
Riverside Cl CHOB/PIR GU24 230 E6
CLPT E5 120 B6
HNWL W7 134 D6
KGLGY WD4 54 C5
KUT KT1 199 J4
STA TW18 195 J1
STAL AL1 38 D8 1
STMC/STPC BR5 207 M2
WLGTN SM6 202 C10
Riverside Ct CHING E4 80 G10 4
HLW CM20 29 M5
Riverside Dr CHSWK W4 156 A6 2
ESH/CLAY KT10 217 P1
MTCM CR4 201 P5
RCHPK/HAM TW10 176 G6
RKW/CH/CXG WD3 91 N2
SHGR GU5 268 D10
STA TW18 195 J1
Riverside Gdns ALP/SUD HA0 135 K4 2
BERK HP4 33 M4
ENC/FH EN2 79 K6
HMSMTH W6 156 E4
WOKS/MYFD GU22 232 E7
Riverside Pl STWL/WRAY TW19 173 N2
Riverside Rd OXHEY WD19 73 J10
SCUP DA14 185 P6
SEVS/STOTM N15 119 P4 4
SRTFD E15 141 H4
STA TW18 173 J10
STAL AL1 38 D7
STWL/WRAY TW19 173 N1
TOOT SW17 179 L7
WOT/HER KT12 217 L1
Riverside Wk ISLW TW7 154 D9
WDSR SL4 149 J6
Riverside Wy DART DA1 187 M1
UX/CGN UB8 131 L3
Riversmead HOD EN11 44 F4 3
Riversmeet HERT/WAS SG14 25 J6
River St CLKNW EC1R 6 A9
WARE SG12 26 D2
WDSR SL4 149 J6
River Ter HMSMTH W6 156 F4 4
Riverton Cl MV/WKIL W9 2 D10 1
River Vw CDH/CHF RM16 168 D4
WGCE AL7 23 H1
Riverview Gdns BARN SW13 156 E5
COB KT11 217 H9 3
River View Gdns TWK TW1 176 E5
Riverview Pk CAT SE6 182 F5
Riverview Rd CHSWK W4 155 N6
GRH DA9 188 F1 3
HOR/WEW KT19 220 A2
River Wk DEN/HRF UB9 111 M10
SUN TW16 197 L2
WOT/HER KT12 197 H6
River Wy FELT TW13 176 A5
HLW CM20 29 K6
HOR/WEW KT19 220 A2
LOU IG10 82 D10
Riverway PLMGR N13 99 H6
STA TW18 195 L1
Riverwood La CHST BR7 206 G2
Rivett-drake Rd GUW GU2 249 M6
Rivey Cl BF/WBF KT14 215 J10
Rivington Av WFD IG8 102 A10
Rivington Crs CDALE/KGS NW9 96 B8
Rivington Pl IS N1 7 K10
Rivington St SDTCH EC2A 7 K10
Rivulet Rd TOTM N17 99 K8
Rixon Cl DTCH/LGLY SL3 130 B8
Rixon St HOLWY N7 119 H8
Rixsen Rd MNPK E12 122 B10
Roach Rd HOM E9 140 F2
Roads Pl ARCH N19 118 F7
Roakes Av ADL/WDHM KT15 195 L9
Roan St GNWCH SE10 161 H5
Robarts Cl PIN HA5 113 J3 2
Robb Rd STAN HA7 94 F7
Robbs Cl HHW HP1 35 K4 5
Robe End HHW HP1 35 J4
Robert Adam St MBLAR W1H 10 C5
Roberta St BETH E2 7 N9
Robert Av LCOL/BKTW AL2 38 B10
Robert Cl CHIG IG7 103 J6
MV/WKIL W9 9 K2
POTB/CUF EN6 59 H9
WOT/HER KT12 217 J2
Robert Keen Cl PECK SE15 159 P7 5
Robert Lowe Cl NWCR SE14 160 C6
Roberton Dr BMLY BR1 205 P1
Robert Rd SLN SL2 109 J7
Robertsbridge Rd CAR SM5 201 M7
Roberts Cl CHEAM SM3 220 G4 1
CHES/WCR EN8 62 D6 3
ELTH/MOT SE9 184 G4
HARH RM3 105 J9
STMC/STPC BR5 207 M5 3
STWL/WRAY TW19 173 M2
WDR/YW UB7 131 P10
Roberts Ct WLSDN NW10 136 B1 3
Roberts La CFSP/GDCR SL9 90 D6
Roberts Ms KTBR SW1X 16 C4 5
Robertson Cl BROX EN10 62 D2 3
Robertson Rd SRTFD E15 141 H3 3
Robertson St VX/NE SW8 158 C9
Robert's Pl CLKNW EC1R 12 B1 2
Roberts Rd BELV DA17 164 B4
MLHL NW7 97 H6
WALTH E17 100 G9
WATW WD18 73 K9 5
Robert St CAMTN NW1 4 F10
CHCR WC2N 11 M8 3
CROY/NA CR0 203 K10 5
WOOL/PLUM SE18 162 G3
Roberts Wy EGH TW20 171 P10
HAT AL10 40 C6
Roberts Wood Dr CFSP/GDCR SL9 90 D6
Robeson St BOW E3 140 E7 6
Robeson Wy BORE WD6 75 P5
Robina Cl BXLYHS DA6 163 N10
NTHWD HA6 92 G10
Robin Cl ADL/WDHM KT15 215 N2
CRAWW RH11 283 M5
CRW RM5 104 E8
HPTN TW12 175 M8
MLHL NW7 96 B4
WARE SG12 27 H8
Robin Gdns REDH RH1 258 B8 2
Robin Gv BTFD TW8 155 H5
HGT N6 118 B7
KTN/HRWW/W HA3 115 L4
Robin Hl BERK HP4 33 P6
RGODL GU7 267 J10
Robin Hill Dr CHST BR7 184 B9
Robinhood Cl MTCM CR4 202 D4
Robin Hood Cl SL SL1 128 D10
WOKN/KNAP GU21 231 L4
Robin Hood Crs
WOKN/KNAP GU21 231 K3
Robin Hood Dr BUSH WD23 73 N5
KTN/HRWW/W HA3 94 E8
Robin Hood Gn STMC/STPC BR5 207 K5
Robin Hood La BXLYHS DA6 185 P1
HAT AL10 40 D3
Robinhood La MTCM CR4 202 D3
Robin Hood La POP/IOD E14 141 H9
PUT/ROE SW15 178 B6
RGUE GU4 232 C10
SUT SM1 221 K2
Robin Hood Meadow HHNE HP2 36 A1 4
Robin Hood Rd BRWN CM15 106 G1
PUT/ROE SW15 178 B7
WOKN/KNAP GU21 231 L4
Robin Hood Wy GFD/PVL UB6 134 E1
Robin Hood Way (Kingston by Pass)
PUT/ROE SW15 178 B7
Robinia Av GVW DA11 190 A3
Robinia Cl BARK/HLT IG6 103 H7
Robinia Crs LEY E10 120 G7
Robin Md WGCE AL7 23 K2
Robins Cl LCOL/BKTW AL2 57 K3 5
UX/CGN UB8 131 M7
Robins Dl WOKN/KNAP GU21 231 H3
Robinsfield HHW HP1 35 K6
Robins Gv WWKM BR4 205 M10
Robins Nest Hl HERT/BAY SG13 42 D4
Robinson Av CHESW EN7 61 J4
Robinson Cl HCH RM12 145 J2 9
Robinson Crs BUSH WD23 94 B2
Robinson Rd BETH E2 140 B4
CRAWW RH11 283 N8
DAGE RM10 124 B9
WIM/MER SW19 179 P9
Robinson's Cl WEA W13 134 F7
Robinson St CHEL SW3 16 A9
Robins Orch CFSP/GDCR SL9 90 B7 3
Robins Rd HHS/BOV HP3 36 B8
The Robins BRWN CM15 87 J1
Robins Wy HAT AL10 40 C7
Robinsway WOT/HER KT12 217 K1
Robinswood Cl BEAC HP9 88 B6 1
Robin Wy GUW GU2 249 N6
POTB/CUF EN6 60 F4
STA TW18 173 J6
STMC/STPC BR5 207 L3
Robin Willis Wy WDSR SL4 171 M2
Robinwood Gv UX/CGN UB8 132 A6
Robinwood Pl RCHPK/HAM TW10 178 A7
Robsart St BRXN/ST SW9 158 G8
Robson Av WLSDN NW10 136 D3
Robson Cl CFSP/GDCR SL9 90 B6
EHAM E6 142 B8
ENC/FH EN2 79 J6
Robson Rd WNWD SE27 181 J6
Robsons Cl CHES/WCR EN8 62 B5 2
Robyns Cft GVW DA11 190 B6
Robyns Wy SEV TN13 246 G8
Roch Av EDGW HA8 95 L10
Rochdale Rd ABYW SE2 163 L4
Rochdale Wy DEPT SE8 160 F6 5
Rochelle Cl BTSEA SW11 157 N10
Rochelle St BETH E2 7 L10
Roche Rd STRHM/NOR SW16 202 G1 1
Rochester Av BMLY BR1 205 N2
FELT TW13 174 G5
PLSTW E13 141 P3
Rochester Cl BFN/LL DA15 185 L2 2
EN EN1 79 M5
STRHM/NOR SW16 180 F10 1
Rochester Dr BXLY DA5 186 B2
GSTN WD25 73 K1 3
PIN HA5 113 L3
Rochester Gdns CROY/NA CR0 203 M10 2
CTHM CR3 241 M8
IL IG1 122 C5
Rochester Ms CAMTN NW1 5 H3
Rochester Pl CAMTN NW1 4 G2
Rochester Rd CAMTN NW1 4 G2
CAR SM5 222 A1 4
DART DA1 187 P3
EGH TW20 172 G8
GVE DA12 191 J5
NTHWD HA6 112 G1
Rochester Rw WEST SW1P 17 H5
Rochester Sq CAMTN NW1 5 H3
Rochester St WEST SW1P 17 J4 3
Rochester Ter CAMTN NW1 4 G2
Rochester Wk STHWK SE1 12 G9 2
Rochester Wy BKHTH/KID SE3 161 P9 2
DART DA1 186 F3
ELTH/MOT SE9 162 B10 1
RKW/CH/CXG WD3 72 C8
Rochester Way Relief Rd
ELTH/MOT SE9 184 B1
Roche Wk MRDN SM4 201 N6
Rochford Av BRWN CM15 87 M9
CHDH RM6 123 M3
WAB EN9 63 J10
Rochford Cl BROX EN10 62 D2
EHAM E6 142 A4
HCH RM12 145 J1 5
Rochford Gn LOU IG10 82 F7
Rochfords Gdns SLN SL2 129 P10
Rochford Wy CROY/NA CR0 202 F6
Rockall Ct DTCH/LGLY SL3 150 E2
Rock Av MORT/ESHN SW14 156 A9
Rockbourne Rd FSTH SE23 182 C4
Rockchase Gdns EMPK RM11 125 M4 2
Rockcliffe Av KGLGY WD4 54 C6
Rockell's Pl EDUL SE22 182 A2
Rockfield Cl OXTED RH8 261 L7
Rockfield Rd OXTED RH8 261 L6
Rockford Av GFD/PVL UB6 134 G4
Rock Grove Wy BERM/RHTH SE16 19 P5
Rockhall Rd CRICK NW2 116 G9
Rockhampton Rd SAND/SEL CR2 223 M3
STRHM/NOR SW16 181 H7
Rock Hl NRWD SE19 181 N7
ORP BR6 228 C3
Rockingham Av EMPK RM11 125 J4
Rockingham Cl PUT/ROE SW15 156 C10 1
UX/CGN UB8 131 M3 3
Rockingham Pde UX/CGN UB8 131 M2
Rockingham Rd UX/CGN UB8 131 L3
Rockingham St STHWK SE1 18 E4
Rockland Rd PUT/ROE SW15 157 H10 2
Rocklands Dr KTN/HRWW/W HA3 94 G10
Rockleigh HERT/WAS SG14 25 J5
Rockleigh Ct BRWN CM15 107 M1
Rockley Rd SHB W12 156 G1
Rockmount Rd NRWD SE19 181 L9
WOOL/PLUM SE18 163 J4
Rockshaw Rd REDH RH1 258 D3
Rocks La BARN SW13 156 D9
Rock St FSBYPK N4 119 H7
Rockware Av GFD/PVL UB6 134 C3 1
Rockways BAR EN5 76 C10
Rockwell Gdns NRWD SE19 181 M7 4
Rockwell Rd DAGE RM10 124 C10
Rockwood Gdns LOU IG10 82 F7
Rocky La REIG RH2 258 B5
Rocliffe St IS N1 6 D8
Rocombe Crs FSTH SE23 182 B3 3
Rocque La BKHTH/KID SE3 161 L9
Rodborough Rd GLDGN NW11 117 K6
Roden Cl HLWE CM17 30 A7
Roden Gdns CROY/NA CR0 203 M6 2
Rodenhurst Rd CLAP SW4 180 D3
Roden St HOLWY N7 118 G8
IL IG1 122 D8
Rodeo Cl ERITH DA8 165 J7
Roderick Rd HAMP NW3 118 A9
Rodgers Cl BORE WD6 75 J10
Roding Dr BRWN CM15 86 E3
Roding Gdns LOU IG10 82 B10
Roding La BKHH IG9 102 B2
CHIG IG7 102 D2
Roding La North WFD IG8 102 B10
Roding La South REDBR IG4 122 A3
Roding Rd CLPT E5 120 C9
EHAM E6 142 E7
LOU IG10 82 C9
The Rodings UPMR RM14 126 C4
Roding Vw BKHH IG9 102 A2
Roding Wy RAIN RM13 145 L4 5
Rodmarton St MHST W1U 10 B4
Rodmell Cl YEAD UB4 133 M6
Rodmell Slope NFNCH/WDSP N12 97 J6
Rodmere St GNWCH SE10 161 K4
Rodmill La BRXS/STRHM SW2 180 F3 2
Rodney Av STAL AL1 38 F8
Rodney Cl NWMAL KT3 200 B5
PIN HA5 113 M5
WOT/HER KT12 197 K8 3
Rodney Crs HOD EN11 44 F1
Rodney Gdns PIN HA5 113 K3
WWKM BR4 225 M1
Rodney Pl STHWK SE1 18 F5
WALTH E17 100 D10
WIM/MER SW19 201 M1 1
Rodney Rd CHONG CM5 67 N5
HSLWW TW4 175 P2 1
HSLWW TW4 175 P3 6
MTCM CR4 201 P2
NWMAL KT3 200 B5
WALW SE17 18 F6
WAN E11 121 N2
WOT/HER KT12 197 J9
Rodney St IS N1 5 P7
Rodney Wy DTCH/LGLY SL3 151 H7
GU GU1 250 D9
ROMW/RG RM7 104 C9
Rodona Rd WEY KT13 216 E7
Rodway Rd BMLY BR1 205 N1
PUT/ROE SW15 178 D3
Rodwell Cl RSLP HA4 113 K6 4
Rodwell Rd EDUL SE22 181 N2
Roebuck Cl ASHTD KT21 237 K6
FELT TW13 175 J7
HERT/BAY SG13 25 P5
REIG RH2 257 K10
Roebuck Gn SL SL1 128 D10
Roebuck La BKHH IG9 101 P2
Roebuck Rd BARK/HLT IG6 103 L7
CHSGTN KT9 219 M2
Roedean Av PEND EN3 80 B5
Roedean Cl ORP BR6 227 L1
PEND EN3 80 B5
Roedean Crs PUT/ROE SW15 178 B2
Roe End CDALE/KGS NW9 115 P2
Roefields Cl HHS/BOV HP3 35 K10
Roe Gn CDALE/KGS NW9 115 P3
Roe Green Cl HAT AL10 40 B5
Roe Green La HAT AL10 40 C4
Roehampton Cl GVE DA12 191 H3
PUT/ROE SW15 156 D10 4
Roehampton Dr CHST BR7 184 F9
Roehampton Ga PUT/ROE SW15 178 B2
Roehampton High St
PUT/ROE SW15 178 D3
Roehampton La PUT/ROE SW15 178 D1
Roehampton V PUT/ROE SW15 178 C6
Roe Hill Cl HAT AL10 40 C5
Roehyde Wy HAT AL10 40 B6
Roe La CDALE/KGS NW9 115 N2
Roestock Gdns STALE/WH AL4 40 B8
Roestock La STALE/WH AL4 40 A9
Roe Wy WLGTN SM6 222 F3
Rofant Rd NTHWD HA6 92 F7
Roffes La CTHM CR3 259 L1
Roffey Cl HORL RH6 280 A4
PUR/KEN CR8 241 J2
Roffey's Cl CRAWE RH10 285 H1
Roffey St POP/IOD E14 161 H1
Roffords WOKN/KNAP GU21 231 N3
Rogers Cl COUL/CHIP CR5 241 J4
Rogers Ct SWLY BR8 209 H4 2
Rogers Gdns DAGE RM10 124 B10
Rogers La SLN SL2 129 L3
WARL CR6 242 E4
Rogers Md GDST RH9 260 A8
Rogers Rd CAN/RD E16 141 L8
DAGE RM10 124 B10
GRAYS RM17 167 P3

TOOT SW17 ... 179 N7
Rogers Ruff NTHWD HA6 ... 92 D9
Roger St BMSBY WC1N ... 11 F7
Rojack Rd FSTH SE23 ... 182 C4
Rokeby Gdns WFD IG8 ... 101 M9
Rokeby Rd BROCKY SE4 ... 160 E8
Rokeby Rd RYNPK SW20 ... 178 K10
Rokeby St SRTFD E15 ... 141 K3
Roke Cl PUR/KEN CR8 ... 223 K10
Roke Lodge Rd PUR/KEN CR8 ... 223 J9
Roke Rd PUR/KEN CR8 ... 241 K1
Roker Park Av HCDN/ICK UB10 ... 111 P4
Rokesby Cl WELL DA16 ... 162 G8
Rokesby Pl ALP/SUD HA0 ... 115 J10
Rokesby Rd SLN SL2 ... 128 E5
Rokesly Av CEND/HSY/T N8 ... 118 F3
Roland Gdns SKENS SW7 ... 15 K7
Roland Rd WALTH E17 ... 121 J2
Roland St STAL AL1 ... 38 F6
Roland Wy WALW SE17 ... 19 H8
  WBPTN SW10 ... 15 K7
  WPK KT4 ... 200 C9
Roles Gv CHDH RM6 ... 123 N2
Rolfe Cl EBEAC HP9 ... 88 D10
  EBAR EN4 ... 77 P8
Rolinsden Wy HAYES BR2 ... 226 A1
Rollesby Rd CHSGTN KT9 ... 219 M3
Rollesby Wy THMD SE28 ... 143 H9
Rolleston Av STMC/STPC BR5 ... 206 E6
Rolleston Cl STMC/STPC BR5 ... 206 E7
Rolleston Rd SAND/SEL CR2 ... 223 L4
Roll Gdns GNTH/NBYPK IG2 ... 122 D3
Rollins St PECK SE15 ... 160 D3
Rollit Crs HSLW TW3 ... 175 P1
Rollit St HOLWY N7 ... 119 H10
Rollo Rd SWLY BR8 ... 222 B10
Rolls Buildings FLST/FETLN EC4A ... 12 A5
Rollscourt Av HNHL SE24 ... 181 K1
Rolls Park Av CHING E4 ... 100 F7
Rolls Park Rd CHING E4 ... 100 C6
Rolls Rd STHWK SE1 ... 19 M7
Rollswood WGCE AL7 ... 23 H8
Rolt St DEPT SE8 ... 160 D5
Rolvenden Gdns BMLY BR1 ... 206 A1
Rolvenden Pl TOTM N17 ... 99 P3
Romanfield Rd
  BRXS/STRHM SW2 ... 180 G3
Roman Cl ACT W3 ... 155 N1
  EBED/NFELT TW14 ... 175 K1
  RAIN RM13 ... 144 E4
Romanhurst Av HAYES BR2 ... 205 K4
Romanhurst Gdns BECK BR3 ... 205 K4
Roman Ri NRWD SE19 ... 181 L9
  SBW CM21 ... 29 N1
Roman Rd BETH E2 ... 140 C2
  BOW E3 ... 140 E3
  CHSWK W4 ... 148 D5
  DORK RH4 ... 272 F4
  EHAM E6 ... 95 J4
  GVW DA11 ... 189 P6
  IL IG1 ... 142 E1
  MUSWH N10 ... 98 C8
  RAD WD7 ... 74 F1
  RDART DA2 ... 188 D7
Roman Sq THMD SE28 ... 143 K10
Roman St HOD EN11 ... 44 F2
Romans Wy WOKS/MYFD GU22 ... 233 L1
Roman V HLWE CM17 ... 29 M6
Roman Wy CROY/NA CR0 ... 203 J9
  DART DA1 ... 186 F1
  EN EN1 ... 79 N9
  HOLWY N7 ... 5 N1
Romany Ct HHNE HP2 ... 36 D5
Romany Gdns CHEAM SM3 ... 201 K4
Romany Ri STMC/STPC BR5 ... 206 F8
Roma Rd WALTH E17 ... 120 D1
Romberg Rd TOOT SW17 ... 180 B6
Romborough Gdns LEW SE13 ... 183 H1
Romborough Wy LEW SE13 ... 183 H1
Rom Crs ROMW/RG RM7 ... 124 F5
Romeland BORE WD6 ... 75 J10
  STALW/RED AL3 ... 38 B6
  WAB EN9 ... 63 H9
Romeland HI STALW/RED AL3 ... 38 B6
Romero Sq ELTH/MOT SE9 ... 185 P10
Romeyn Rd STRHM/NOR SW16 ... 180 A4
Romford Rd CHDH RM6 ... 103 N7
  CHIG IG7 ... 103 L5
  CHONG CM5 ... 59 P7
  CRW RM5 ... 103 P8
  FSTGT E7 ... 141 M1
  MNPK E12 ... 122 D8
  SOCK/AV RM15 ... 146 B5
  SRTFD E15 ... 141 K2
Romford St WCHPL E1 ... 13 P4
Romilly Dr OXHEY WD19 ... 93 M5
Romilly Rd FSBYPK N4 ... 119 J7
Romilly St SOHO/SHAV W1D ... 11 K7
Romney Av WNWD SE27 ... 181 L7
Romney Cha EMPK RM11 ... 125 P4
Romney Cl ASHF TW15 ... 174 D8
  CHSGTN KT9 ... 219 K1
  GLDGN NW11 ... 117 K6
  RYLN/HDSTN HA2 ... 113 P5
  TOTM N17 ... 100 A9
Romney Dr BMLY BR1 ... 184 A10
  RYLN/HDSTN HA2 ... 113 P5
Romney Gdns BXLYHN DA7 ... 164 A7
Romney Lock Rd WDSR SL4 ... 149 J2
Romney Rd GNWCH SE10 ... 161 H5
  GVW DA11 ... 190 A6
  NWMAL KT3 ... 200 A4
  YEAD UB4 ... 132 E4
Romola Rd BRXS/STRHM SW2 ... 181 J4
  ORP BR6 ... 226 F1
Romsey Cl DTCH/LGLY SL3 ... 150 J2
Romsey Dr SLN SL2 ... 109 J3
Romsey Rd DAGW RM9 ... 143 N3
  WEA W13 ... 134 F9
Ron Valley Wy ROMW/RG RM7 ... 124 F4
Rona Cl CRAWW RH11 ... 283 L10
Ronald Av SRTFD E15 ... 141 K5
Ronald Cl BECK BR3 ... 204 E5
Ronald Rd BEAC HP9 ... 88 D10
  HARH RM3 ... 105 P9
Ronaldsay Sp SL SL1 ... 129 K7
Ronalds Rd BMLY BR1 ... 205 M1
  HBRY N5 ... 119 H10
Ronaldstone Rd BFN/LL DA15 ... 185 H2
Ronald St WCHPL E1 ... 140 D10
Rona Rd HAMP NW3 ... 118 B9
Ronart St KTN/HRWW/W HA3 ... 114 E1
Rondu Rd CRICK NW2 ... 117 H10
Ronelean Rd SURB KT6 ... 199 L7
Roneo Cnr ROMW/RG RM7 ... 124 C6
Roneo Link HCH RM12 ... 124 C6
Ronfearn Av STMC/STPC BR5 ... 207 N10
Ronneby Cl WEY KT13 ... 196 F10
Ronsons Wy ST ALB AL3 ... 38 C2
Ronver Rd LEE/GVPK SE12 ... 183 M4
Roof La FENCH SE3M ... 13 J7
Rookby Ct WCHMH N21 ... 99 J3
Rookeries Cl FELT TW13 ... 175 J6
Rookery Cl LHD/OX KT22 ... 236 D10
  DORK RH4 ... 272 C1
Rookery Dr CHST BR7 ... 206 D1
Rookery Gdns STMC/STPC BR5 ... 207 M5
  REDH RH1 ... 281 J1
Rookery Hi ASHTD KT21 ... 237 N4
Rookery La HAYES BR2 ... 226 A6
  REDH RH1 ... 281 H5
  STA TW18 ... 173 L8
The Rookery WTHK RM20 ... 166 F5

Rookery Vw GRAYS RM17 ... 168 A4
Rookery Wy KWD/TDW/WH KT20 ... 257 J3
Rookesley Rd STMC/STPC BR5 ... 207 N7
Rookfield Av MUSWH N10 ... 118 D2
Rook La CTHM CR3 ... 241 H10
Rookley Cl BELMT SM2 ... 221 L5
  BELMT SM2 ... 221 L6
Rooks Hi RKW/CH/CXG WD3 ... 71 M8
  WGCW AL8 ... 22 F6
Rooksmead Rd SUN TW16 ... 196 G2
Rookstone Rd TOOT SW17 ... 180 A8
Rookwood Av LOU IG10 ... 82 F7
  NWMAL KT3 ... 200 D4
  WLGTN SM6 ... 222 E1
Rookwood Cl GRAYS RM17 ... 167 N3
  REDH RH1 ... 258 C5
Rookwood Ct GUW GU2 ... 268 D7
Rookwood Gdns CHING E4 ... 101 L8
Rookwood Rd STNW/STAM N16 ... 119 J4
Roosevelt Wy DAGE RM10 ... 144 E1
Rootes Dr NKENS W10 ... 136 C7
Roothill La BRKHM/BTCW RH3 ... 273 M6
Ropemaker Rd
  BERM/RHTH SE16 ... 160 D2
Ropemaker's Flds POP/IOD E14 ... 140 E9
Ropemaker St BARB EC2Y ... 12 G1
Roper La STHWK SE1 ... 19 K2
Ropers Av CHING E4 ... 101 H6
Roper St ELTH/MOT SE9 ... 184 C1
Ropery St BOW E3 ... 140 E6
Rope St BERM/RHTH SE16 ... 160 D2
Ropewalk Gdns WCHPL E1 ... 13 P5
Rope Yard Rails
  WOOL/PLUM SE18 ... 162 E2
Ropley St BETH E2 ... 7 N8
Rosa Alba Ms HBRY N5 ... 119 K9
Rosa Av ASHF TW15 ... 174 B7
Rosaline Rd FUL/PGN SW6 ... 157 H6
Rosamond St SYD SE26 ... 182 A6
Rosamund Cl SAND/SEL CR2 ... 223 L1
Rosamund Rd CRAWE RH10 ... 284 C9
Rosary Cl HSLW TW3 ... 153 M8
Rosary Ct POTB/CUF EN6 ... 59 L6
Rosary Gdns ASHF TW15 ... 174 C7
  BUSH WD23 ... 94 D1
  SKENS SW7 ... 15 K6
Rosaville Rd FUL/PGN SW6 ... 157 J6
Roscoe St STLK EC1Y ... 12 F2
Roscoff Cl EDGW HA8 ... 95 N9
Roseacre OXTED RH8 ... 261 M9
Roseacre Cl EMPK RM11 ... 125 N6
  SHPTN TW17 ... 196 B5
  WEA W13 ... 134 C7
Roseacre Gdns RGUE GU4 ... 269 J2
  WGCE AL7 ... 23 N5
Rose Aly STHWK SE1 ... 13 H8
Rose And Crown Yd STJS SW1Y ... 11 H10
Rose Av CWDR/WG UB7 ... 191 N4
Rose Av GVE DA12 ... 191 N4
  MRDN SM4 ... 201 M5
  MTCM CR4 ... 202 A1
  SWFD E18 ... 101 N10
Rose Bank BRW CM14 ... 107 J4
Rosebank ALP/SUD HA0 ... 114 E9
  HCH RM12 ... 125 K10
Rose Bank Cl NFNCH/WDSP N12 ... 97 P6
Rosebank Cl TEDD TW11 ... 176 F9
Rosebank Gdns BOW E3 ... 140 E4
  GVW DA11 ... 190 B4
Rosebank Gv WALTH E17 ... 120 E1
Rosebank Rd HNWL W7 ... 154 D1
  LEY E10 ... 120 C4
Rosebank Wy ACT W3 ... 136 A8
Rose Bates Dr CDALE/KGS NW9 ... 115 M2
Roseberry Av UPMR RM14 ... 126 A4
Roseberry Ct WAT WD17 ... 73 H5
Roseberry Gdns DART DA1 ... 187 K3
  FSBYPK N4 ... 119 J4
  ORP BR6 ... 207 H10
  UPMR RM14 ... 126 E5
Roseberry Pl HACK E8 ... 7 L2
Roseberry Rd EPSOM KT18 ... 238 B5
Roseberry St BERM/RHTH SE16 ... 160 A3
Rosebery Av BFN/LL DA15 ... 185 H3
  CLKNW EC1R ... 12 A1
  EW KT17 ... 220 B10
  MNPK E12 ... 142 B1
  NWMAL KT3 ... 200 C2
  RYLN/HDSTN HA2 ... 113 M9
  THHTH CR7 ... 203 K2
  TOTM N17 ... 99 P10
Rosebery Cl MRDN SM4 ... 200 G6
Rosebery Ct GVW DA11 ... 190 C4
Rosebery Gdns CEND/HSY/T N8 ... 118 F2
  SUT SM1 ... 221 L1
  WEA W13 ... 134 F8
Rosebery Rd BUSH WD23 ... 94 A2
  CLAP SW4 ... 180 F2
  ED N9 ... 90 D4
  GRAYS RM17 ... 167 K5
  ISLW TW7 ... 135 P4
  KUT KT1 ... 199 N2
  MUSWH N10 ... 98 C10
  SUT SM1 ... 221 J10
Rosebine Av WHTN TW2 ... 176 C3
Rosebriar Cl WOKS/MYFD GU22 ... 233 K2
Rosebriars CTHM CR3 ... 241 M6
  ESH/CLAY KT10 ... 218 B2
Rosebriar Wk WATN WD24 ... 72 C2
Rosebury Dr CHOB/PIR GU24 ... 230 F1
Rosebury Rd FUL/PGN SW6 ... 157 L8
Rosebury V RSLP HA4 ... 113 H7
Rose Bushes EW KT17 ... 238 F2
Rose Ct CHEW EN7 ... 61 P3
Rosecourt Rd CROY/NA CR0 ... 202 C6
Rose Wd WOKS/MYFD GU22 ... 232 D5
Rosecroft Av HAMP NW3 ... 117 K8
Rosecroft Dr WAT WD17 ... 72 F3
Rosecroft Gdns CRICK NW2 ... 117 H8
  WHTN TW2 ... 176 C4
Rosecroft Rd STHL UB1 ... 133 P6
Rosecroft Wk ALP/SUD HA0 ... 115 J10
  PIN HA5 ... 113 L3
Rosedale ASHTD KT21 ... 237 H4
Rose Di ORP BR6 ... 207 K5
Rosedale WGCE AL7 ... 23 J1
Rosedale Av CHESW EN7 ... 61 N5
  HYS/HAR UB3 ... 132 B7
Rosedale Cl ABYW SE2 ... 163 L2
  CRAWW RH11 ... 283 K9
  HNWL W7 ... 154 E1
  LCOL/BKTW AL2 ... 55 M6
  RDART DA2 ... 188 A3
  STAN HA7 ... 94 G7
Rosedale Gdns DAGW RM9 ... 143 L2
  DAGW RM9 ... 143 L2
Rosedale Pl CROY/NA CR0 ... 203 G10
Rosedale Rd DAGW RM9 ... 143 L2
  EW KT17 ... 220 D10
  FSTGT E7 ... 121 P10
  GRAYS RM17 ... 168 A4
  RCH/KEW TW9 ... 155 K10
Rosedale Wy CHESW EN7 ... 61 P5
Rosedene Av CROY/NA CR0 ... 202 G7
  GFD/PVL UB6 ... 133 P5
  MRDN SM4 ... 201 N5
  STRHM/NOR SW16 ... 180 A5
Rosedene Gdns GNTH/NBYPK IG2 ... 122 C7
Rosedene Ter LEY E10 ... 120 C7
Rosedew Rd HMSMTH W6 ... 156 G5

Rose Dr CSHM HP5 ... 51 J8
Rose End WPK KT4 ... 200 C8
Rosefield POP/IOD E14 ... 140 F9
  SEV TN13 ... 247 H10
Rosefield Cl CAR SM5 ... 221 P2
  POP/IOD E14 ... 140 F9
Rosefield Gdns CHERT KT16 ... 214 C3
Rosefield Rd STA TW18 ... 173 K7
Rose Garden Cl EDGW HA8 ... 95 K7
Rose Gdns EA W5 ... 155 J2
  FELT TW13 ... 175 H5
  STHL UB1 ... 133 P6
  STWL/WRAY TW19 ... 173 N3
  WATW WD18 ... 73 H7
Rose Gln CDALE/KGS NW9 ... 116 A2
  ROMW/RG RM7 ... 124 F6
Rosehart Ms NTGHL W11 ... 8 E6
Rosehatch Av CHDH RM6 ... 123 N1
Roseheath HHW HP1 ... 35 H5
Rosehill HSLWW TW4 ... 175 N1
Rosehill BERK HP4 ... 32 E7
Rosehill ESH/CLAY KT10 ... 218 F3
  HPTN TW12 ... 197 H1
Rose Hi SUT SM1 ... 201 L9
  WOKN/KNAP GU21 ... 231 P2
Rosehill Cl HOD EN11 ... 44 E3
Rosehill Farm Meadow
  BNSTD SM7 ... 239 L1
Rosehill Gdns ABLGY WD5 ... 54 D8
  GFD/PVL UB6 ... 114 E10
  SUT SM1 ... 201 L9
Rose Hill Pk West SUT SM1 ... 201 M8
Rosehill Rd BH/WHM TN16 ... 243 P5
  WAND/EARL SW18 ... 179 M2
Roseland Cl TOTM N17 ... 99 L8
Roselands Av HOD EN11 ... 44 E1
Rose La CHDH RM6 ... 123 P2
  RPLY/SEND GU23 ... 253 N8
  STALE/WH AL4 ... 21 H1
Roselare Cl BH/WHM TN16 ... 243 P8
Rose Lawn BUSH WD23 ... 94 B2
Roseleigh Av HBRY N5 ... 119 J9
Roseleigh Cl TWK TW1 ... 177 J2
Rosemary Av E/WMO/HCT KT8 ... 197 P3
  ED N9 ... 100 A2
  ENC/FH N2 ... 79 L5
  FNCH N3 ... 97 L10
  HSLWW TW4 ... 153 L8
  ROM RM1 ... 124 G1
Rosemary Cl CROY/NA CR0 ... 202 F7
  OXTED RH8 ... 261 M9
  SOCK/AV RM15 ... 147 H5
  UX/CGN UB8 ... 132 B7
Rosemary Crs RGUW GU3 ... 249 L6
Rosemary Dr POP/IOD E14 ... 141 J8
  REDBR IG4 ... 122 A3
Rosemary Gdns BCTR RM8 ... 124 A6
  CHSGTN KT9 ... 219 K10
  MORT/ESHN SW14 ... 156 A9
Rosemary La EGH TW20 ... 194 E3
  HORL RH6 ... 279 H8
  HORL RH6 ... 280 C5
  MORT/ESHN SW14 ... 156 A9
Rosemary Rd PECK SE15 ... 159 N6
  TOOT SW17 ... 179 M6
  WELL DA16 ... 163 J7
Rosemead CDALE/KGS NW9 ... 116 C5
  CHERT KT16 ... 195 L7
Rose Md POTB/CUF EN6 ... 59 M6
Rosemead Av FELT TW13 ... 174 C5
  MTCM CR4 ... 202 D3
  WBLY HA9 ... 115 K10
Rosemead Cl REDH RH1 ... 259 J7
Rosemont Av NFNCH/WDSP N12 ... 97 M7
Rosemont Rd ACT W3 ... 135 N9
  ALP/SUD HA0 ... 135 K3
  HAMP NW3 ... 3 J1
  NWMAL KT3 ... 199 P3
  RCHPK/HAM TW10 ... 177 K2
Rosemoor St CHEL SW3 ... 16 A6
Rosemount Av HLWW/ROY CM19 ... 46 C4
Rosemount Av BF/WBF KT14 ... 215 K9
Rosemount Cl WFD IG8 ... 102 F7
Rosemount Dr BMLY BR1 ... 206 C4
Rosemount Rd WEA W13 ... 134 F8
Rosenau Crs BTSEA SW11 ... 158 A7
Rosenau Rd BTSEA SW11 ... 157 P7
Rosendale Rd DUL SE21 ... 181 K5
  HNHL SE24 ... 181 K5
Roseneath Av WCHMH N21 ... 99 J2
Roseneath Ct CTHM CR3 ... 259 P1
Roseneath Rd BTSEA SW11 ... 180 B2
Roseneath Wk EN EN1 ... 79 M8
Rosenheath Cl ORP BR6 ... 227 L4
Rosens Wk EDGW HA8 ... 95 N4
Rosenthal Rd CAT SE6 ... 182 C2
Rosenthorpe Rd PECK SE15 ... 182 C1
Roserton St POP/IOD E14 ... 161 H1
The Rosery CROY/NA CR0 ... 204 C6
Roses La WDSR SL4 ... 148 C8
Rose St COV GN DA11 ... 189 N2
Rosethorn Cl BAL SW12 ... 180 D3
Rosetrees GU GU1 ... 268 D1
Rose V HOD EN11 ... 44 F1
Rose Va BRW CM14 ... 107 H4
Roseveare Rd LEE/GVPK SE12 ... 183 P7
Roseville Av HSLWW TW4 ... 175 K1
Roseville Rd HYS/HAR UB3 ... 153 H4
Rosevine Rd RYNPK SW20 ... 200 F1
Rose Wk BRYLDS KT5 ... 199 N5
  PUR/KEN CR8 ... 222 E7
  STALE/WH AL4 ... 38 C4
  WWKM BR4 ... 205 J9
The Rose Wk RAD WD7 ... 74 G2
Rosewarne Cl WOKN/KNAP GU21 ... 231 M4
Roseway DUL SE21 ... 181 L2
  EDGW HA8 ... 95 P3
Rose Wy LEE/GVPK SE12 ... 183 M1
Rosewell Cl PGE/AN SE20 ... 182 A10
Rosewood GFD/PVL UB6 ... 114 F10
  HCH RM12 ... 125 H10
Rosewood Cl SCUP DA14 ... 186 M6
  SOCK/AV RM15 ... 147 K5
Rosewood Ct HHW HP1 ... 35 H5
  KUTN/CMB KT2 ... 177 M10
Rosewood Dr ENC/FH EN2 ... 79 H1
  SHPTN TW17 ... 196 A5
Rosewood Gv SUT SM1 ... 201 M9
Rosewood Wy CHOB/PIR GU24 ... 212 D9
  SLN SL2 ... 109 L2
Rosher Cl SRTFD E15 ... 141 J2
Rosherville Wy GVW DA11 ... 190 B3
Rosina St HOM E9 ... 120 C10
Roskell Rd PUT/ROE SW15 ... 157 H9
Rosken Gv SLN SL2 ... 128 C3
Roslin Rd ACT W3 ... 155 N2
Roslin Wy BMLY BR1 ... 183 N8
Roslyn Cl BROX EN10 ... 44 D7
  MTCM CR4 ... 201 N2
Roslyn Gdns GPK RM2 ... 104 G10
Roslyn Rd SEVS/STOTM N15 ... 119 L3
Rosmead Rd NTGHL W11 ... 8 B7
Rosoman PL CLKNW EC1R ... 12 A1
Rosoman St CLKNW EC1R ... 6 A10
Rossall Cl EMPK RM11 ... 125 H4
Rossall Crs WLSDN NW10 ... 135 L1
Ross Av BCTR RM8 ... 124 A7
  MHLN NW7 ... 96 E5
Ross Cl CRAWE RH10 ... 284 A10
  HYS/HAR UB3 ... 153 G4
  KTN/HRWW/W HA3 ... 94 B10
Ross Crs GSTN WD25 ... 72 B3
Rossdale SUT SM1 ... 221 P2
Rossdale Dr CDALE/KGS NW9 ... 115 P8
  ED N9 ... 80 B10
Rossdale Rd PUT/ROE SW15 ... 156 F10

Rossell Rd TIL RM18 ... 168 C8
Rosse Ms BKHTH/KID SE3 ... 161 N1
Rossendale Cl CLPT E5 ... 120 A7
Rossendale St CLPT E5 ... 120 A7
Rossendale Wy CAMTN NW1 ... 5 H4
Rossetti Gdns COUL/CHIP CR5 ... 240 G5
Rossetti Rd BERM/RHTH SE16 ... 160 A4
Rossignol Gdns CAR SM5 ... 202 B9
Rossindel Rd HSLW TW3 ... 175 P1
Rossington Av BORE WD6 ... 75 K4
Rossington Cl EN EN1 ... 80 A1
Rossington St CLPT E5 ... 120 A7
Rossiter Cl DTCH/LGLY SL3 ... 150 B3
Rossiter Flds BAR EN5 ... 77 H10
Rossiter Rd BAL SW12 ... 180 C3
Rossland Cl BXLYHS DA6 ... 186 B5
Rosslare Cl BH/WHM TN16 ... 243 P8
Rosslyn Av BARN SW13 ... 156 A9
  BCTR RM8 ... 124 A5
  CHING E4 ... 101 L3
  EBAR EN4 ... 77 P10
  EBED/NFELT TW14 ... 175 H2
  HARH RM3 ... 105 M10
Rosslyn Cl HYS/HAR UB3 ... 132 E7
  SUN TW16 ... 174 F1
  WWKM BR4 ... 205 L10
Rosslyn Crs HRW HA1 ... 114 E2
  WBLY HA9 ... 115 K8
Rosslyn Hl HAMP NW3 ... 117 K10
Rosslyn Pk WEY KT13 ... 216 E1
Rosslyn Park Ms HAMP NW3 ... 117 N10
Rosslyn Rd BARK IG11 ... 142 G2
  TWK TW1 ... 177 H2
  WALTH E17 ... 121 H2
  WATW WD18 ... 73 J7
Rossmore Cl CRAWE RH10 ... 284 E3
Rossmore Rd CAMTN NW1 ... 9 P2
Ross Pde WLGTN SM6 ... 222 C3
Ross Rd COB KT11 ... 217 K9
  DART DA1 ... 187 H2
  SNWD SE25 ... 203 M3
  WHTN TW2 ... 176 B4
  WLGTN SM6 ... 222 D3
Ross Wy ELTH/MOT SE9 ... 162 B9
  NTHWD HA6 ... 92 G5
Rossway Dr BUSH WD23 ... 74 B9
Rossway La TRING HP23 ... 32 F1
Rosswood Gdns WLGTN SM6 ... 222 D3
Rostella Rd TOOT SW17 ... 179 N7
Rostrevor Av SEVS/STOTM N15 ... 119 N4
Rostrevor Gdns IVER SL0 ... 130 C4
  NWDGN UB2 ... 153 M4
Rostrevor Rd FUL/PGN SW6 ... 157 J7
  WIM/MER SW19 ... 179 K3
Roswell Cl CHES/WCR EN8 ... 62 D6
Rotary St STHWK SE1 ... 18 C3
Rothbury Av RAIN RM13 ... 145 J2
Rothbury Gdns ISLW TW7 ... 154 F6
Rothbury Rd HOM E9 ... 140 F2
Roth Dr RBRW/HUT CM13 ... 107 N3
Rother Av GSTN WD25 ... 55 K10
Rother Crs CRAWW RH11 ... 283 H9
Rotherfield Rd CAR SM5 ... 222 B1
  PEND EN3 ... 80 C3
Rotherfield St IS N1 ... 6 F1
Rotherham Wk STHWK SE1 ... 18 D2
Rotherhill Av STRHM/NOR SW16 ... 180 E9
Rotherhithe New Rd
  BERM/RHTH SE16 ... 160 A4
Rotherhithe Old Rd
  BERM/RHTH SE16 ... 160 D3
Rotherhithe St
  BERM/RHTH SE16 ... 140 D10
  BERM/RHTH SE16 ... 140 D10
  BERM/RHTH SE16 ... 160 A1
Rotherhithe Tnl
  BERM/RHTH SE16 ... 160 B1
Rothermere CROY/NA CR0 ... 222 C2
Rothervale HORL RH6 ... 280 A2
Rotherwick HI EA W5 ... 135 L6
Rotherwick Rd GLDGN NW11 ... 117 K5
Rotherwood Cl RYNPK SW20 ... 201 H1
Rotherwood Rd PUT/ROE SW15 ... 156 C9
Rothery St IS N1 ... 6 D5
Rothesay Av RCHPK/HAM TW10 ... 155 N10
  RYNPK SW20 ... 201 H2
Rothesay Rd SNWD SE25 ... 203 L4
Rothes Rd DORK RH4 ... 272 G1
Rothsay Av GVW DA11 ... 191 P2
Rothsay Rd FSTGT E7 ... 141 P2
Rothsay St STHWK SE1 ... 19 J3
Rothschild Rd CHSWK W4 ... 147 P3
Rothschild St WNWD SE27 ... 181 L9
Rothwell Gdns DAGW RM9 ... 143 M5
Rothwell Rd DAGW RM9 ... 143 M5
Rothwell St CAMTN NW1 ... 4 B5
Rotterdam Dr POP/IOD E14 ... 161 J2
Rouel Rd BERM/RHTH SE16 ... 19 N5
Rouge La GVE DA12 ... 190 E4
Rougemont Av MRDN SM4 ... 201 K6
Roughdown Av HHS/BOV HP3 ... 35 L9
Roughdown Rd HHS/BOV HP3 ... 35 L9
Roughdown Villas Rd
  HHS/BOV HP3 ... 35 K9
Roughets La REDH RH1 ... 259 N5
Roughlands WOKS/MYFD GU22 ... 233 H1
Rough Rew RDKG RH5 ... 272 G8
Rough Rd WOKS/MYFD GU22 ... 231 H8
The Roughs NTHWD HA6 ... 92 F4
Roughtallys EPP CM16 ... 66 A3
Roughwood La CSTG HP8 ... 70 B10
Rounce La CHOB/PIR GU24 ... 212 C9
Round Ash Wy HART DA3 ... 211 K6
Roundaway Rd CLAY IG5 ... 102 C10
Roundcroft CHESW EN7 ... 61 N3
Roundel Cl BROCKY SE4 ... 160 E10
Round Gv CROY/NA CR0 ... 204 C7
Roundhay Cl FSTH SE23 ... 182 C5
Roundheads End BEAC HP9 ... 88 A7
Roundhedge Wy ENC/FH EN2 ... 78 G4
Round Hi FSTH SE23 ... 182 A5
Roundhill Dr ENC/FH EN2 ... 78 G8
Roundhill Wy COB KT11 ... 218 A7
  GUW GU2 ... 249 L10
Roundhills WAB EN9 ... 63 K10
Roundhill Wy COB KT11 ... 218 A7
The Roundings HERT/BAY SG13 ... 26 B9
Roundmead Av LOU IG10 ... 82 D7
Roundmead Cl LOU IG10 ... 82 D7
Roundmoor Dr CHES/WCR EN8 ... 62 C1
Round Oak Rd WEY KT13 ... 216 A1
Roundtable Rd BMLY BR1 ... 183 L6
Roundthorn Wy
  WOKN/KNAP GU21 ... 231 L2
Roundtree Cl ALP/SUD HA0 ... 114 C10
Roundway EGH TW20 ... 172 F8
Roundways RSLP HA4 ... 112 C8
The Roundway ESH/CLAY KT10 ... 218 G3
  TOTM N17 ... 99 K9
  WATW WD18 ... 72 G10
Roundwood CHST BR7 ... 206 B5
  HHS/BOV HP3 ... 53 H8
Roundwood Av
  RBRW/HUT CM13 ... 107 N2
  STKPK UB11 ... 132 D10
Roundwood Cl RSLP HA4 ... 112 E5
Roundwood Gv
  RBRW/HUT CM13 ... 107 N1
Roundwood Rd AMS HP6 ... 69 N1
  WLSDN NW10 ... 136 D1
Roundwood Vw BNSTD SM7 ... 238 G7
Roundwood Wy BNSTD SM7 ... 238 G7
Rounton Rd BOW E3 ... 140 F6
  WAB EN9 ... 63 N2
Roupell Rd BRXS/STRHM SW2 ... 180 G4
Roupell St STHWK SE1 ... 12 B10

Rousden St CAMTN NW1 ... 4 G3
Rousebarn La RKW/CH/CXG WD3 ... 71 J7
Rouse Ct CFSP/GDCR SL9 ... 110 C3
Rouse Gdns DUL SE21 ... 181 M7
Rous Rd BKHH IG9 ... 102 B2
Routemaster Cl PLSTW E13 ... 141 N5
Routh Rd WAND/EARL SW18 ... 179 P3
Routh St EHAM E6 ... 142 C7
Rover Av BARK/HLT IG6 ... 103 J7
Rowallan Rd FUL/PGN SW6 ... 157 H6
Rowan Av CHING E4 ... 100 E7
  EGH TW20 ... 172 F8
Rowan Cl ALP/SUD HA0 ... 114 F8
  CRAWE RH10 ... 284 A1
  EA W5 ... 155 K1
  GU GU1 ... 249 N7
  IL IG1 ... 124 E9
  KTN/HRWW/W HA3 ... 94 E7
  LCOL/BKTW AL2 ... 55 P7
  NWMAL KT3 ... 200 B2
  REIG RH2 ... 275 M2
  STALE/WH AL4 ... 39 K6
  STRHM/NOR SW16 ... 202 D1
Rowan Crs DART DA1 ... 187 K4
  STRHM/NOR SW16 ... 202 D1
Rowan Dr BROX EN10 ... 44 E10
  CDALE/KGS NW9 ... 116 D1
Rowan Gdns CROY/NA CR0 ... 203 N10
  IVER SL0 ... 130 F4
Rowan Gn East
  RBRW/HUT CM13 ... 107 L4
Rowan Gn West
  RBRW/HUT CM13 ... 107 L4
Rowan Gv COUL/CHIP CR5 ... 240 C7
  SOCK/AV RM15 ... 146 B9
Rowanhurst Dr SLN SL2 ... 128 E5
Rowan Ms KWD/TDW/WH KT20 ... 238 E5
Rowan PI AMS HP6 ... 69 J4
  HYS/HAR UB3 ... 132 C9
Rowan Rd BTFD TW8 ... 154 G6
  BXLYHN DA7 ... 163 P9
  HMSMTH W6 ... 156 G3
  STRHM/NOR SW16 ... 202 D2
  SWLY BR8 ... 208 B3
  WDR/YW UB7 ... 151 N3
Rowans WGCE AL7 ... 23 J2
Rowans Cl HART DA3 ... 211 J2
The Rowans BROX EN10 ... 44 D5
  CFSP/GDCR SL9 ... 109 P1
  HHW HP1 ... 35 K5
  PLMGR N13 ... 99 K4
  SOCK/AV RM15 ... 147 J6
  SUN TW16 ... 174 G8
Rowans Wy LOU IG10 ... 82 C8
Rowan Tree Cl WCHMH N21 ... 99 L2
Rowantree Rd ENC/FH EN2 ... 79 J6
  WCHMH N21 ... 99 L2
Rowan Wk EFNCH N2 ... 117 M4
  EMPK RM11 ... 125 L2
  HAYES BR2 ... 206 C10
  NKENS W10 ... 8 A1
  SBW CM21 ... 29 P1
Rowan Wy CHDH RM6 ... 123 M1
  HARP AL5 ... 20 B3
  SL SL1 ... 128 C7
  SOCK/AV RM15 ... 147 J6
Rowanwood Av BFN/LL DA15 ... 185 K4
Rowbarns Wy EHSLY KT24 ... 252 G6
Rowben Cl TRDG/WHET N20 ... 97 L2
Rowberry Cl FUL/PGN SW6 ... 156 F6
Rowbury RGODL GU7 ... 267 L9
Rowcroft HHW HP1 ... 35 H7
Rowcross St STHWK SE1 ... 19 L7
Rowdell Rd NTHLT UB5 ... 133 P3
Rowden Rd BECK BR3 ... 204 D1
  CHING E4 ... 100 G7
  HOR/WEW KT19 ... 219 P1
Rowditch La BTSEA SW11 ... 158 B8
Rowdon Av WLSDN NW10 ... 136 E2
Rowdow La RSEV TN14 ... 247 L2
Rowdown Crs CROY/NA CR0 ... 225 J5
Rowdowns Rd DAGW RM9 ... 144 A3
Rowe Gdns BARK IG11 ... 143 J4
Rowe La CHOB/PIR GU24 ... 230 B10
  HOM E9 ... 120 B10
Rowena Crs BTSEA SW11 ... 157 P8
Rowe Wk RYLN/HDSTN HA2 ... 113 P8
Rowfant Cl CRAWE RH10 ... 284 F7
Rowfant Rd TOOT SW17 ... 180 B5
Rowhedge BRW CM14 ... 107 M4
Row Hi ADL/WDHM KT15 ... 215 J3
Rowhill Rd CLPT E5 ... 120 A9
  RDART DA2 ... 187 L9
Rowhurst Av ADL/WDHM KT15 ... 215 L3
Rowington Cl BAY/PAD W2 ... 8 C3
Rowland Av KTN/HRWW/W HA3 ... 115 J1
Rowland Crs CHIG IG7 ... 103 H5
Rowland Gv SYD SE26 ... 182 A6
Rowland Hill Av TOTM N17 ... 99 K8
Rowland Hill St HAMP NW3 ... 117 P10
Rowlands Av PIN HA5 ... 93 P7
Rowlands Cl CHES/WCR EN8 ... 62 C6
  MHLN NW7 ... 96 D8
Rowlands Rd BCTR RM8 ... 124 A7
Rowland Wy ASHF TW15 ... 174 E10
  WIM/MER SW19 ... 201 L1
Rowlatt Cl RDART DA2 ... 187 K4
Rowlatt Dr STALW/RED AL3 ... 37 P8
Rowley Av BFN/LL DA15 ... 185 L3
Rowley Cl ALP/SUD HA0 ... 135 M10
  OXHEY WD19 ... 93 M10
  WOKS/MYFD GU22 ... 233 K2
Rowley Ct CTHM CR3 ... 241 K8
Rowley Gdns FSBYPK N4 ... 119 K5
Rowley Green Rd BAR EN5 ... 76 A5
Rowley La BAR EN5 ... 76 B8
  BORE WD6 ... 75 L1
  DTCH/LGLY SL3 ... 130 B4
Rowley Md EPP CM16 ... 65 M1
Rowley Rd SEVS/STOTM N15 ... 119 K3
Rowley's Rd HERT/BAY SG13 ... 25 N4
Rowley Wk STJWD NW8 ... 3 K5
Rowleys Pl WDR/YW UB7 ... 151 J2
Rowlls Rd KUT KT1 ... 199 L3
Rowmarsh Cl GVW DA11 ... 190 A6
Rowney Gdns DAGW RM9 ... 143 M5
  SBW CM21 ... 29 M5
Rowney Rd DAGW RM9 ... 143 L5
Rowney Wd SBW CM21 ... 29 M2
Rowntree Cl KIL/WHAMP NW6 ... 2 F2
  PLSTW E13 ... 141 N6
Rowntree Path THMD SE28 ... 143 L10
Rowntree Rd WHTN TW2 ... 176 D3
Rowse Cl SRTFD E15 ... 141 H3
Rowsley Av HDN NW4 ... 116 A7
Rowstock Gdns HOLWY N7 ... 118 E10
Rowton Rd WOOL/PLUM SE18 ... 162 G4
Row Town ADL/WDHM KT15 ... 215 J4
Roxborough Av HRW HA1 ... 114 C5
  ISLW TW7 ... 154 E6
Roxborough Pk HRW HA1 ... 114 D5
Roxborough Rd HRW HA1 ... 114 C4
Roxbourne Cl NTHLT UB5 ... 133 L1
Roxburgh Av UPMR RM14 ... 126 B8
Roxburgh Rd WNWD SE27 ... 181 J8
Roxburn Wy RSLP HA4 ... 112 G8
Roxby Pl FUL/PGN SW6 ... 14 F7
Roxeth Green Av
  RYLN/HDSTN HA2 ... 114 A8
Roxeth Gv RYLN/HDSTN HA2 ... 114 A9
Roxeth Hl RYLN/HDSTN HA2 ... 114 C7
Roxford Cl SHPTN TW17 ... 196 B5
Roxley Rd LEW SE13 ... 182 G5

Roxton Gdns CROY/NA CR0 ...... 224 E3
Roxwell Cl SL1 ...... 128 D10
Roxwell Gdns RBRW/HUT CM13 ... 87 P9
Roxwell Rd BARK IG11 ... 143 K4
  SHB W12 ... 156 D1
Roxwell Wy WFD IG8 ... 101 P8
Roxy Av CHDH RM6 ... 123 M5
Royal Albert Rd EHAM E6 ... 142 D9
Royal Albert Wy CAN/RD E16 ... 142 A9
Royal Av CHEL SW3 ... 16 A7
  CHES/WCR EN8 ... 62 D9
  WPK KT4 ... 200 B9
Royal Circ WNWD SE27 ... 181 H6
Royal Cl GDMY/SEVK IG3 ... 123 K5
  WDR/YW UB7 ... 132 A4
  WPK KT4 ... 200 B9
Royal College St CAMTN NW1 ... 5 H4
Royal Ct HHS/BOV HP3 ... 35 P9
Royal Crs NTGHL W11 ... 156 G1
  RSLP HA4 ... 113 M9
Royal Crescent Ms NTGHL W11 ... 156 G1
Royal Docks Rd EHAM E6 ... 142 C7
Royal Dr EPSOM KT18 ... 238 E4
Royal HI GNWCH SE10 ... 161 H6
Royal Hospital Rd CHEL SW3 ... 16 A9
Royal La WDR/YW UB7 ... 132 A8
Royal Ms BAL SW12 ... 180 C3
The Royal Ms WHALL SW1A ... 16 A1
Royal Mint St TWRH EC3N ... 13 M7
Royal Naval Pl NWCR SE14 ... 160 E6
Royal Oak Rd BXLYHS DA6 ... 186 A1
  HACK E8 ... 140 A1
  WOKN/KNAP GU21 ... 231 P4
Royal Orchard Cl
  WAND/EARL SW18 ... 179 H3
Royal Pde BKHTH/KID SE3 ... 161 L8
  CHST BR7 ... 184 F10
Royal Pier Rd GVE DA12 ... 190 E22
Royal Pl GNWCH SE10 ... 161 H6
Royal Rd CAN/RD E16 ... 141 P8
  RDART DA2 ... 187 P8
  SCUP DA14 ... 185 N6
  STAL AL1 ... 38 C6
  TEDD TW11 ... 176 C8
  WALW SE17 ... 18 C9
Royal Route WBLY HA9 ... 115 L9
Royal St STHWK SE1 ... 17 P3
Royal Victor Pl BOW E3 ... 140 C4
Royce Cl BROX EN10 ... 44 E7
Royce Rd CRAWE RH10 ... 284 B5
Roycraft Av BARK IG11 ... 143 J4
Roycroft Cl SWFD E18 ... 101 N9
Roydene Rd WOOL/PLUM SE18 ... 163 N5
Roydon Cl LOU IG10 ... 102 B1
Roydon Ct WOT/HER KT12 ... 217 H1
  WARE SG12 ... 27 J7
Roydon Rd HLWW/ROY CM19 ... 28 B10
Roy Gdns GNTH/NBYPK IG2 ... 123 N2
Roy Gv HPTN TW12 ... 176 A9
Royle Cl CFSP/GDCR SL9 ... 90 C8
  GPK RM2 ... 125 J3
Royle Crs WEA W13 ... 134 F6
Roy Rd NTHWD HA6 ... 92 G8
Royston Av BF/WBF KT14 ... 215 P8
  CHING E4 ... 100 F6
  SUT SM1 ... 201 N10
  WLGTN SM6 ... 222 E1
Royston Cl CRAWE RH10 ... 284 B5
  HERT/WAS SG14 ... 25 J5
  HEST TW5 ... 153 J7
  WOT/HER KT12 ... 197 H8
Royston Gdns IL IG1 ... 122 A4
Royston Gv PIN HA5 ... 93 N7
Royston Park Rd PIN HA5 ... 93 N7
Royston Rd BF/WBF KT14 ... 215 P8
  DART DA1 ... 186 G2
  HARH RM3 ... 105 P8
  PGE/AN SE20 ... 204 C1
  RCHPK/HAM TW10 ... 177 K1
  STAL AL1 ... 38 C7
The Roystons BRYLDS KT5 ... 199 N5
Royston St BETH E2 ... 140 B4
Royston Wy SL SL1 ... 128 C7
Rozel Rd CLAP SW4 ... 158 D8
Rubastic Rd NWDGN UB2 ... 153 K2
Rubens Rd NTHLT UB5 ... 133 K4
Rubens St CAT SE6 ... 182 E5
Rubus Cl CHOB/PIR GU24 ... 212 D9
Ruby Cl SL SL1 ... 148 F1
Ruby Rd WALTH E17 ... 120 F1
Ruby St PECK SE15 ... 160 A5
Ruby Triangle PECK SE15 ... 160 A5
Ruckholt Cl LEY E10 ... 120 G8
Ruckholt Rd LEY E10 ... 121 H8
Rucklers La KGLGY WD4 ... 53 K4
Ruckles Wy AMSS NP7 ... 69 H6
Rucklidge Av WLSDN NW10 ... 136 C4
Ruddlesway WDSR SL4 ... 148 C7
Ruddington Cl CLPT E5 ... 120 D9
Ruddstreet Cl WOOL/PLUM SE18 ... 162 E5
Ruden Wy EW KT17 ... 238 E1
Rudge Ri ADL/WDHM KT15 ... 215 J2
Rudgwick Rd CRAWW RH11 ... 283 J6
Rudland Rd BXLYHN DA7 ... 164 C9
Rudloe Rd BAL SW12 ... 180 D3
Rudolph Rd BUSH WD23 ... 73 P10
  KIL/WHAMP NW6 ... 2 F8
  PLSTW E13 ... 141 L4
  PLSTW E13 ... 141 M4
Rudsworth Cl DTCH/LGLY SL3 ... 150 G7
Rudyard Gv EDGW HA8 ... 95 P7
Rue De St Lawrence WAB EN9 ... 63 H10
Ruffetts Cl SAND/SEL CR2 ... 224 A4
The Ruffetts SAND/SEL CR2 ... 224 A4
Rufford Cl HRW HA1 ... 114 F4
Rufford St IS N1 ... 5 M5
Rufus Cl RSLP HA4 ... 113 L8
Rufus St IS N1 ... 7 J10
Rufwood CRAWE RH10 ... 285 N5
Rugby Av ALP/SUD HA0 ... 115 H9
  ED N9 ... 99 N2
  NTHLT UB5 ... 134 C1
Rugby Cl HRW HA1 ... 114 D2
Rugby Gdns DAGW RM9 ... 143 M1
Rugby La BELMT SM2 ... 220 C5
Rugby Rd CDALE/KGS NW9 ... 115 M2
  CHSWK W4 ... 156 B1
  DAGW RM9 ... 143 L2
  WHTN TW2 ... 176 D2
Rugby St BMSBY WC1N ... 11 N2
Rugby Wy RKW/CH/CXG WD3 ... 72 C9
Ruggles-brise Rd ASHF TW15 ... 173 N8
Rugg St POP/IOD E14 ... 140 F9
Ruislip Cl GFD/PVL UB6 ... 134 A6
Ruislip Rd GFD/PVL UB6 ... 134 A5
  NTHLT UB5 ... 133 K3
Ruislip Rd East GFD/PVL UB6 ... 134 B6
  HNWL W7 ... 134 C6
Ruislip St TOOT SW17 ... 180 A7
Rumballs Rd HHS/BOV HP3 ... 36 B9
Rumbold Rd FUL/PGN SW6 ... 157 L6
  HOD EN11 ... 45 H1
Rum Cl WAP E1W ... 140 B9
Rumsey Cl HPTN TW12 ... 175 N9
Rumsey Rd BRXN/ST SW9 ... 158 C9
Rumsley CHESW EN7 ... 61 P3
Runbury Cir CDALE/KGS NW9 ... 116 A7
Runcie Cl STALE/WH AL4 ... 38 C1
Runciman Cl ORP BR6 ... 227 N6
Runcorn Cl WALTH E17 ... 120 A2
Runcorn Pl NTGHL W11 ... 8 A8
Rundell Crs HDN NW4 ... 116 E3

Rundells HLWS CM18 ... 47 K5
Runes Cl MTCM CR4 ... 201 N4
Runham Rd HHS/BOV HP3 ... 35 M9
Runnelfield HRW HA1 ... 114 D8
Runnemede Rd EGH TW20 ... 172 D8
Running Waters
  RBRW/HUT CM13 ... 107 M5
Runnymede WIM/MER SW19 ... 201 N1
Runnymede Ct EGH TW20 ... 172 D7
Runnymede Crs
  STRHM/NOR SW16 ... 202 E1
  WHTN TW2 ... 176 A2
Runnymede Gdns GFD/PVL UB6 ... 134 C4
  WHTN TW2 ... 176 A2
Runnymede Rd WHTN TW2 ... 176 A2
Runrig Rd AMS HP6 ... 69 K1
Runsley WGCE AL7 ... 23 K1
Runtley Wood La RGUE GU4 ... 250 C1
The Runway RSLP HA4 ... 113 J10
Rupack St BERM/RHTH SE16 ... 140 B10
Rupert Av WBLY HA9 ... 115 K10
Rupert Gdns BRXN/ST SW9 ... 158 C8
Rupert Rd ARCH N19 ... 118 E8
  CHSWK W4 ... 156 B2
  GUW GU2 ... 267 N1
  KIL/WHAMP NW6 ... 2 D8
Rupert St SOHO/SHAV W1D ... 11 J7
Rural Cl HCH RM12 ... 125 J6
Rural V GVW DA11 ... 190 B3
Rural Wy REDH RH1 ... 258 B10
  STRHM/NOR SW16 ... 180 C10
Ruscoe Dr WOKS/MYFD GU22 ... 232 D3
Ruscoe Rd CAN/RD E16 ... 141 L8
Ruscombe Dr LCOL/BKTW AL2 ... 56 B2
Ruscombe Gdns DTCH/LGLY SL3 ... 149 M6
Ruscombe Wy
  EBED/NFELT TW14 ... 174 G3
Rusham Park Av EGH TW20 ... 172 C9
Rusham Rd BAL SW12 ... 180 A2
  EGH TW20 ... 172 C9
Rushbrook Crs WALTH E17 ... 100 E9
Rushbrook Rd ELTH/MOT SE9 ... 184 F5
Rush Cl WARE SG12 ... 27 H2
Rush Cft RGDDL GU7 ... 207 M9
Rushcroft Rd BRXS/STRHM SW2 ... 159 H10
  CHING E4 ... 100 C8
Rushden Cl NRWD SE19 ... 181 L10
Rushdene ABYW SE2 ... 163 M2
Rushdene Av EBAR EN4 ... 97 J3
Rushdene Cl NTHLT UB5 ... 133 K4
Rushdene Crs NTHLT UB5 ... 133 J4
Rushdene Rd BRWN CM15 ... 107 H1
  PIN HA5 ... 113 K4
Rushdene Wk BH/WHM TN16 ... 244 A3
Rushden Gdns CLAY IG5 ... 122 D1
  MLHL NW7 ... 96 F7
Rushdon Cl CDH/CHF RM16 ... 167 M2
  ROM RM1 ... 125 H3
Rushen Dr HERT/BAY SG13 ... 26 B8
Rushent Rd CDH/CHF RM16 ... 167 M2
  UX/CGN UB8 ... 131 M3
Rushet Rd STMC/STPC BR5 ... 207 K2
Rushett Cl THDIT KT7 ... 198 C8
Rushett Dr DORK RH4 ... 117 C5
Rushett La CHSGTN KT9 ... 219 J8
Rushett Rd THDIT KT7 ... 198 C7
Rushetts Pl CRAWW RH11 ... 283 M4
Rushetts Rd CRAWW RH11 ... 283 L4
  REIG RH2 ... 275 M4
Rushey Cl NWMAL KT3 ... 200 A4
Rushey Gn CAT SE6 ... 182 C3
Rushey HI ENC/FH EN2 ... 78 G3
Rushey Md BROCKY SE4 ... 182 F1
Rushfield POTB/CUF EN6 ... 58 C3
  SBW CM21 ... 29 P1
Rushford Rd BROCKY SE4 ... 182 A2
Rush Green Gdns ROMW/RG RM7 ... 124 D6
Rush Green Rd ROMW/RG RM7 ... 124 D6
Rushgrove Av CDALE/KGS NW9 ... 116 C2
Rush Hill Ms BTSEA SW11 ... 158 B9
Rush Hill Rd BTSEA SW11 ... 158 B9
Rushleigh Av CHES/WCR EN8 ... 62 C6
Rushley Cl HAYES BR2 ... 226 A1
Rushmead BETH E2 ... 140 A5
  RCHPK/HAM TW10 ... 176 G6
Rushmere Av UPMR RM14 ... 126 B8
Rushmere Ct WPK KT4 ... 200 D9
Rushmere La CSHM HP5 ... 51 M4
Rushmere Pl EGH TW20 ... 172 B8
  WIM/MER SW19 ... 178 G3
Rushmoor Cl GUW GU2 ... 249 L7
  PIN HA5 ... 113 J2
  RKW/CH/CXG WD3 ... 91 N3
Rushmore Cl BMLY BR1 ... 206 B3
Rushmore HI ORP BR6 ... 227 M6
  RSEV TN14 ... 227 N10
Rushmore Rd CLPT E5 ... 120 B9
Rusholme Av DAGE RM10 ... 124 B8
Rusholme Gv NRWD SE19 ... 181 M8
Rusholme Rd PUT/ROE SW15 ... 178 G2
Rushout Av KTN/HRWW/W HA3 ... 114 C4
Rushton Av GSTN WD25 ... 73 H1
Rushton Gv HLWE CM17 ... 47 N1
Rushton St IS N1 ... 7 H7
Rushworth Rd REIG RH2 ... 257 K9
Rushworth St STHWK SE1 ... 18 D1
Rushymead BGR/WK TN15 ... 247 P4
Rushy Meadow La CAR SM5 ... 201 P10
Ruskin Av EBED/NFELT TW14 ... 174 C3
  MNPK E12 ... 142 C1
  RCH/KEW TW9 ... 155 M6
  UPMR RM14 ... 126 B5
  WAB EN9 ... 63 K10
  WELL DA16 ... 163 K9
Ruskin Cl CHESW EN7 ... 61 N1
  CRAWE RH10 ... 284 D4
  GLDGN NW11 ... 117 L4
Ruskin Dr ORP BR6 ... 207 H10
  WELL DA16 ... 163 K9
  WPK KT4 ... 200 E9
Ruskin Gdns EA W5 ... 135 J6
  HARH RM3 ... 105 J9
  KTN/HRWW/W HA3 ... 115 L3
Ruskin Gv DART DA1 ... 167 P1
  WELL DA16 ... 163 K9
Ruskin Pk House CMBW SE5 ... 181 L1
Ruskin Rd BELV DA17 ... 164 B3
  CAR SM5 ... 222 B2
  CDH/CHF RM16 ... 168 D3
  CROY/NA CR0 ... 203 J9
  ISLW TW7 ... 154 E9
  STA TW18 ... 173 J9
  STHL UB1 ... 133 M9
  TOTM N17 ... 99 N9
Ruskin Wk ED N9 ... 99 P5
  HAYES BR2 ... 206 B5
  HNHL SE24 ... 181 K1
Ruskin Wy WIM/MER SW19 ... 201 N1
Rusland Av ORP BR6 ... 206 C10
Rusland Park Rd HRW HA1 ... 114 D2
Rusper Cl CRICK NW2 ... 116 B5
  STAN HA7 ... 95 H5
Rusper Rd CRAWW RH11 ... 283 J7
  DAGW RM9 ... 143 M1
  WDGN N22 ... 99 J10
Ruspers Keep CRAWW RH11 ... 283 J6
Russel Cl BECK BR3 ... 204 C3
Russell Av STALW/RED AL3 ... 38 C5
  WDGN N22 ... 99 J10
Russell Cl AMS HP6 ... 70 A1
  BRWN CM15 ... 106 C1
  BXLYHN DA7 ... 164 B1
  CHARL SE7 ... 161 P6
  DART DA1 ... 165 P6
  CHSWK W4 ... 156 D5
  NTHWD HA6 ... 92 D6
  RSLP HA4 ... 113 K7
  WLSDN NW10 ... 135 H2
Russell Ct CSHM HP5 ... 51 H5
  LCOL/BKTW AL2 ... 55 P5
  LHD/OX KT22 ... 236 C3
  WHALL SW1A ... 11 H10
Russell Crs GSTN WD25 ... 72 C1
Russellcroft Rd WGCW AL8 ... 22 F4
Russell Dr STWL/WRAY TW19 ... 173 N2
Russell Gdns GLDGN NW11 ... 117 H4
  RCHPK/HAM TW10 ... 177 H5
  TRDG/WHET N20 ... 97 P3
  WDR/YW UB7 ... 152 B4
  WKENS W14 ... 14 A3
Russell Gardens Ms WKENS W14 ... 14 A3
Russell Green Cl PUR/KEN CR8 ... 242 C6
Russell Gv BRXN/ST SW9 ... 159 H6
  MLHL NW7 ... 96 B6
Russell Hill PUR/KEN CR8 ... 222 D6
Russell Hill Pl PUR/KEN CR8 ... 223 H7
Russell Hill Rd PUR/KEN CR8 ... 223 H6
Russell Kerr Cl CHSWK W4 ... 155 P6
Russell La TRDG/WHET N20 ... 98 A3
  WAT WD17 ... 72 C2
Russell Pl EYN DA4 ... 209 P1
  HAMP NW3 ... 117 P10
  HHS/BOV HP3 ... 35 L9
Russell Rd BKHH IG9 ... 101 P2
  CAN/RD E16 ... 141 M8
  CDALE/KGS NW9 ... 116 C4
  CEND/HSY/T N8 ... 118 C4
  CHING E4 ... 100 C5
  EN EN1 ... 79 N4
  GVE DA12 ... 190 G2
  LEY E10 ... 120 C4
  MTCM CR4 ... 201 P3
  NTHLT UB5 ... 114 D10
  NTHWD HA6 ... 92 D4
  SEVS/STOTM N15 ... 119 M3
  SHPTN TW17 ... 196 D7
  TIL RM18 ... 116 D2
  TRDG/WHET N20 ... 97 P3
  WALTH E17 ... 120 E1
  WDGN N22 ... 99 J10
  WHTN TW2 ... 176 E2
  WIM/MER SW19 ... 179 K10
  WKENS W14 ... 14 A3
  WOKN/KNAP GU21 ... 231 P7
  WOT/HER KT12 ... 197 H6
Russells KWD/TDW/WH KT20 ... 238 G8
Russell's Crs HORL RH6 ... 280 B5
Russell's Dr CHES/WCR EN8 ... 62 D7
Russell Sq GWRST WC1E ... 11 K3
Russell's Ride CHES/WCR EN8 ... 62 C7
Russell St HERT/WAS SG14 ... 25 K5
  HOL/ALD WC2B ... 11 N6
  WDSR SL4 ... 149 J3
Russell Wy CRAWE RH10 ... 284 B8
  OXHEY WD19 ... 93 J1
  SUT SM1 ... 221 L2
Russel Rd GRAYS RM17 ... 167 N3
Russet Av SUN TW16 ... 196 F5
Russet Cl CHESW EN7 ... 61 M2
  HORL RH6 ... 280 D4
  STWL/WRAY TW19 ... 173 J2
  UX/CGN UB8 ... 132 D6
  WOT/HER KT12 ... 197 L10
Russet Dr CROY/NA CR0 ... 204 D8
  RAD WD7 ... 57 K8
  STALE/WH AL4 ... 39 H7
Russets EMPK RM11 ... 125 M2
Russets Cl CHING E4 ... 101 J4
The Russets CFSP/GDCR SL9 ... 90 A10
Russett Cl ORP BR6 ... 227 L2
Russett Ct CFSP/GDCR SL9 ... 90 B5
Russetts Cl WOKN/KNAP GU21 ... 232 C1
Russet Wy SWLY BR8 ... 208 E2
Russett Wd WGCE AL7 ... 23 N6
Russia Ct CV RDKG RH5 ... 273 J5
Russia Dock Rd
  BERM/RHTH SE16 ... 140 D10
Russia La BETH E2 ... 140 B4
Russia Rw CITYW EC2V ... 12 F6
Russington Rd SHPTN TW17 ... 196 E6
Rusthall Av CHSWK W4 ... 156 A2
Rusthall Cl CROY/NA CR0 ... 204 B6
Rustic Av STRHM/NOR SW16 ... 180 C10
Rustic Cl UPMR RM14 ... 126 D6
Rustic Pl ALP/SUD HA0 ... 115 J9
Rustington Wk MRDN SM4 ... 201 J7
Ruston Av BRYLDS KT5 ... 199 N5
Ruston Cl CRAWE RH10 ... 284 D10
Ruston Ms NTGHL W11 ... 8 A1
Ruston Rd WOOL/PLUM SE18 ... 162 B2
Ruston St BOW E3 ... 140 E4
Rust Sq CMBW SE5 ... 159 L6
Rustwick Rd STRHM/NOR SW16 ... 180 D7
Ruth Cl KTN/HRWW/W HA3 ... 114 C5
Rutherford Cl BELMT SM2 ... 221 N3
  BORE WD6 ... 76 P5
  WDSR SL4 ... 148 C7
Rutherford St WEST SW1P ... 17 J5
Rutherford Wy BUSH WD23 ... 94 C2
  CRAWE RH10 ... 284 B2
  WBLY HA9 ... 115 M8
Rutherglen Rd ABYW SE2 ... 163 K5
Rutherwick Cl HORL RH6 ... 280 A4
Rutherwick Ri COUL/CHIP CR5 ... 240 F3
Rutherwyke Cl EW KT17 ... 220 D5
Rutherwyke Rd CHERT KT16 ... 195 H7
Ruthin Cl CDALE/KGS NW9 ... 116 B4
Ruthin Rd BKHTH/KID SE3 ... 161 M5
Ruthven Av WAB EN9 ... 63 K10
Ruthven St HOM E9 ... 140 C3
Rutland Ap EMPK RM11 ... 125 M2
Rutland Av BFN/LL DA15 ... 185 K3
  SL SL1 ... 129 H7
Rutland Cl ASHTD KT21 ... 237 K3
  BXLY DA5 ... 185 N4
  DART DA1 ... 187 L3
  HOR/WEW KT19 ... 220 B6
  MORT/ESHN SW14 ... 155 N9
  REDH RH1 ... 258 A9
Rutland Ct CHST BR7 ... 206 D1
Rutland Dr EMPK RM11 ... 125 P3
  MRDN SM4 ... 201 K7
  RCHPK/HAM TW10 ... 177 J4
Rutland Gdns BCTR RM8 ... 123 M10
  CROY/NA CR0 ... 223 M1
  FSBYPK N4 ... 119 J4
  SKENS SW7 ... 16 E2
  WEA W13 ... 134 F7
Rutland Gate BELV DA17 ... 164 C4
  HAYES BR2 ... 205 L6
  SKENS SW7 ... 15 N2
Rutland Gate Ms SKENS SW7 ... 15 N2
Rutland Gv HMSMTH W6 ... 156 F4
Rutland Ms STJWD NW8 ... 3 H1
Rutland Ms South SKENS SW7 ... 15 N3
Rutland Pk CAT SE6 ... 182 E5
  CRICK NW2 ... 136 B3
Rutland Pl BUSH WD23 ... 76 B8
  FARR EC1M ... 12 D3
Rutland Rd FSTGT E7 ... 142 A4
  HOM E9 ... 140 C3
  HRW HA1 ... 114 B4
  HYS/HAR UB3 ... 152 E3
  IL IG1 ... 122 C4
  STHL UB1 ... 133 P6
  WALTH E17 ... 120 F4
  WAN E11 ... 121 N3
  WHTN TW2 ... 176 C5
  WIM/MER SW19 ... 179 P10
Rutland St SKENS SW7 ... 15 P3
Rutland Wk CAT SE6 ... 182 C5
Rutland Wy STMC/STPC BR5 ... 207 M6
Rutley Cl WIM/MER SW19 ... 201 K1
Rutlish Rd WIM/MER SW19 ... 201 K1
Rutson Rd BF/WBF KT14 ... 216 A10
Rutter Gdns MTCM CR4 ... 201 N4
Rutters Cl WDR/YW UB7 ... 152 B3
Rutt's Ter NWCR SE14 ... 160 C7
The Rutts BUSH WD23 ... 94 C2
Ruvigny Gdns PUT/ROE SW15 ... 156 G9
Ruxbury Rd CHERT KT16 ... 194 G6
Ruxley Cl HOR/WEW KT19 ... 219 N2
  SCUP DA14 ... 185 N9
Ruxley Crs ESH/CLAY KT10 ... 218 G4
Ruxley La HOR/WEW KT19 ... 219 N3
Ruxley Ms HOR/WEW KT19 ... 219 N2
Ruxley Rdg ESH/CLAY KT10 ... 218 F3
Ruxton Cl SWLY BR8 ... 208 F3
Ruxton Ct SWLY BR8 ... 208 F3
Ryall Cl LCOL/BKTW AL2 ... 55 M5
Ryan Cl ELTH/MOT SE9 ... 161 N10
  RSLP HA4 ... 113 J6
Ryan Dr BTFD TW8 ... 154 F5
Ryan Wy WATN WD24 ... 73 K3
Ryarsh Crs ORP BR6 ... 227 H1
Rycroft WDSR SL4 ... 148 E9
Rycroft La RSEV TN14 ... 264 F6
Rycroft Wy TOTM N17 ... 119 N1
Ryculff Sq BKHTH/KID SE3 ... 161 L8
Rydal Cl CRAWW RH11 ... 282 C9
  HDN NW4 ... 97 H3
  PUR/KEN CR8 ... 223 L9
Rydal Crs GFD/PVL UB6 ... 134 C5
Rydal Dr BXLYHN DA7 ... 164 B2
  WWKM BR4 ... 205 K9
Rydal Gdns CDALE/KGS NW9 ... 116 C2
  HSLW TW3 ... 176 A2
  PUT/ROE SW15 ... 178 B8
  WBLY HA9 ... 115 H6
Rydal Pl LTWR GU18 ... 212 A7
Rydal Rd STRHM/NOR SW16 ... 180 E8
Rydal Wy EGH TW20 ... 172 E10
  PEND EN3 ... 79 J9
  RSLP HA4 ... 113 K9
Ryde Cl RPLY/SEND GU23 ... 233 M7
Ryde Heron WOKN/KNAP GU21 ... 231 K3
Rydens Av WOT/HER KT12 ... 197 K9
Rydens Cl WOT/HER KT12 ... 197 K9
Rydens Gv WOT/HER KT12 ... 217 L1
Rydens Pk WOT/HER KT12 ... 197 L9
Rydens Rd WOT/HER KT12 ... 197 J10
Rydens Wy WOKS/MYFD GU22 ... 232 D6
Ryde Pl TWK TW1 ... 177 H2
Ryder Cl BUSH WD23 ... 74 A10
  HERT/BAY SG13 ... 26 A4
  HHS/BOV HP3 ... 52 D4
Ryder Dr BERM/RHTH SE16 ... 160 A4
Ryder Gdns RAIN RM13 ... 144 C1
Ryders Av STALE/WH AL4 ... 40 B6
Ryder's Ter STJWD NW8 ... 3 J7
Ryder St STJS SW1Y ... 10 G7
Ryders Yd GUW GU2 ... 249 L7
Ryde's Hill Crs RGUW GU3 ... 249 L6
Ryde's Hill Rd GUW GU2 ... 249 L8
The Ryde BRKMPK AL9 ... 40 F2
  STA TW18 ... 195 L4
Ryde Vale Rd BAL SW12 ... 180 C5
Rydings WDSR SL4 ... 148 C5
Rydon's La COUL/CHIP CR5 ... 241 K6
Rydon St IS N1 ... 6 F1
Rydon's Wood Cl COUL/CHIP CR5 ... 241 K6
Rydston Cl HOLWY N7 ... 5 M3
Rye Ash CRAWE RH10 ... 284 B6
Rye Brook Rd LHD/OX KT22 ... 236 F4
Rye Cl BXLY DA5 ... 186 C2
  GUW GU2 ... 249 K9
  HCH RM12 ... 125 K10
Ryecotes Md DUL SE21 ... 181 M4
Ryecroft Av CLAY IG5 ... 102 F10
  WHTN TW2 ... 176 A4
Ryecroft Cl HHNE HP2 ... 36 D7
Ryecroft Crs BAR EN5 ... 76 B7
Ryecroft Rd CSHM HP5 ... 50 F9
  LEW SE13 ... 183 H1
  RSEV TN14 ... 247 H3
  STMC/STPC BR5 ... 206 G6
  STRHM/NOR SW16 ... 181 H9
Ryecroft St FUL/PGN SW6 ... 157 L7
Ryedale EDUL SE22 ... 182 A2
Ryedale Ct SEV TN13 ... 246 F7
Ryefeld Cl HOD EN11 ... 26 C9
Ryefield Av HGDN/ICK UB10 ... 132 D3
Ryefield Crs NTHWD HA6 ... 93 H10
Ryefield Rd NRWD SE19 ... 181 K9
Rye Gv CHOB/PIR GU24 ... 212 D6
Rye Hill Pk PECK SE15 ... 160 B10
Rye Hill Rd HLWS CM18 ... 46 G6
Ryeland Cl WDR/YW UB7 ... 131 P8
Ryelands CRAWW RH11 ... 283 K6
  HORL RH6 ... 280 D3
  WGCE AL7 ... 23 J6
Ryelands Cl CTHM CR3 ... 241 M7
Ryelands Ct LHD/OX KT22 ... 236 F4
Ryelands Crs LEE/GVPK SE12 ... 183 P2
Rye La PECK SE15 ... 159 P7
  RSEV TN14 ... 246 C5
Rye Rd HOD EN11 ... 27 J10
  HOD EN11 ... 44 D2
  PECK SE15 ... 160 C10
The Rye STHGT/OAK N14 ... 98 D7
Rye Wk PUT/ROE SW15 ... 178 C10
Rye Wy EDGW HA8 ... 95 L7
Ryfold Rd WIM/MER SW19 ... 179 K6
Rykhill CDH/CHF RM16 ... 168 A2
Ryland Cl FELT TW13 ... 174 G7
Rylandes Rd CRICK NW2 ... 116 D8
  SAND/SEL CR2 ... 224 A5
Ryland Rd KTTN NW5 ... 4 E1
Rylett Crs SHB W12 ... 156 C2
Rylett Rd SHB W12 ... 156 C1
Rylston Rd FUL/PGN SW6 ... 14 C10
  PLMGR N13 ... 99 L4
Rymer Rd CROY/NA CR0 ... 203 M7
Rymer St HNHL SE24 ... 181 J2
Rymill Cl HHS/BOV HP3 ... 52 D4
Rymill St CAN/RD E16 ... 142 D10
Rysbrack St CHEL SW3 ... 16 A5
Rysted La BH/WHM TN16 ... 262 F6
Rythe Cl THDIT KT7 ... 198 C7
Rythe Ct THDIT KT7 ... 198 C7
Rythe Rd ESH/CLAY KT10 ... 218 C2
The Rythe LHD/OX KT22 ... 218 A6
Ryvers End DTCH/LGLY SL3 ... 150 C2
Ryvers Rd DTCH/LGLY SL3 ... 150 C2

S

Sabbarton St CAN/RD E16 ... 141 L8
Sabina Rd CDH/CHF RM16 ... 168 C3
Sabine Rd BTSEA SW11 ... 158 A3
Sabines Gdn ABR/ST RM4 ... 85 N7
Sable Cl HSLWW TW4 ... 153 K9
Sable St IS N1 ... 6 D1
Sach Rd CLPT E5 ... 120 A7
Sackville Av HAYES BR2 ... 205 M8
Sackville Cl HRW HA1 ... 114 D6
  SEV TN13 ... 247 J8
Sackville Crs HARH RM3 ... 105 M9
Sackville Gdns IL IG1 ... 122 C6
Sackville Rd BELMT SM2 ... 221 K4

DART DA1 ... 187 L5
Sackville St MYFR/PICC W1J ... 11 H8
Sacombe Rd HERT/WAS SG14 ... 25 K2
  HHW HP1 ... 35 J4
Saddington St GVE DA12 ... 190 E5
Saddlebrook Pk SUN TW16 ... 174 F10
Saddle Rw CRAWE RH10 ... 283 N10
Saddlers Cl BORE WD6 ... 76 A9
  PIN HA5 ... 93 P6
Saddler's Pk EYN DA4 ... 209 L10
Saddlers Wy EPSOM KT18 ... 238 A5
Saddlescombe Wy
  NFNCH/WDSP N12 ... 97 K6
Saddleworth Sq HARH RM3 ... 105 K7
Sadleir Rd STAL AL1 ... 38 D9
Sadler Cl MTCM CR4 ... 202 A2
Sadlers Cl RGUE GU4 ... 250 C9
Sadlers Md HLWS CM18 ... 47 K2
Sadlers Ride E/WMO/HCT KT8 ... 198 A3
Saffron Cl CRAWW RH11 ... 283 K10
  CROY/NA CR0 ... 202 F6
  DTCH/LGLY SL3 ... 149 N7
  HOD EN11 ... 44 E2
Saffron HI HCIRC EC1N ... 12 B3
Saffron La HHW HP1 ... 35 L5
Saffron Platt GUW GU2 ... 249 M6
Saffron Rd CDH/CHF RM16 ... 167 H3
  CRW RM5 ... 104 E10
Saffron St HCIRC EC1N ... 12 B3
Saffron Wy SURB KT6 ... 199 J8
Sage Cl EHAM E6 ... 142 C7
Sage St WCHPL E1 ... 140 B9
Saigasso Cl CAN/RD E16 ... 142 A8
Sail St LBTH SE11 ... 17 P5
Sainfoin End HHNE HP2 ... 36 B4
Sainfoin Rd TOOT SW17 ... 180 B5
Sainsbury Rd NRWD SE19 ... 181 M8
St Agatha's Dr KUTN/CMB KT2 ... 177 L5
St Agatha's Gv CAR SM5 ... 202 A8
St Agnels La HHNE HP2 ... 36 B1
St Agnells La HHNE HP2 ... 36 B1
St Agnes Cl HOM E9 ... 140 E5
St Agnes Pl CMBW SE5 ... 18 D3
St Aidan's Rd EDUL SE22 ... 182 A2
  WEA W13 ... 154 C1
St Aidan's Wy GVE DA12 ... 191 H6
St Albans Av CHSWK W4 ... 156 A4
  EHAM E6 ... 142 C5
  FELT TW13 ... 175 L8
  UPMR RM14 ... 126 D6
  WEY KT13 ... 196 B10
St Alban's Cl GVE DA12 ... 190 G6
  RGUW GU3 ... 248 G9
St Albans Crs WDGN N22 ... 99 H9
St Alban's Gdns GVE DA12 ... 190 G6
  TEDD TW11 ... 176 F8
St Alban's Gv CAR SM5 ... 201 P7
  KENS W8 ... 15 H3
St Albans HI HHS/BOV HP3 ... 35 P9
St Albans La ABLGY WD5 ... 54 C2
  GLDGN NW11 ... 117 K6
St Alban's Ms BAY/PAD W2 ... 9 M3
St Alban's Pl IS N1 ... 6 C1
St Albans Rd BAR EN5 ... 77 H5
  DART DA1 ... 187 N2
  EPP CM16 ... 65 N5
  GDMY/SEVK IG3 ... 123 J6
  GSTN WD25 ... 55 L10
  HARP AL5 ... 20 A3
  HHNE HP2 ... 36 A7
  HHS/BOV HP3 ... 35 N7
  KTTN NW5 ... 118 B8
  KUTN/CMB KT2 ... 177 K9
  POTB/CUF EN6 ... 58 D8
  REIG RH2 ... 257 K8
  STALE/WH AL4 ... 38 F2
  SUT SM1 ... 221 J1
  WAT WD17 ... 73 J1
  WATN WD24 ... 73 J1
  WFD IG8 ... 101 M8
  WLSDN NW10 ... 136 E1
St Albans Rd East HAT AL10 ... 40 E3
St Albans Rd West HAT AL10 ... 39 P4
St Alban's St STJS SW1Y ... 11 J8
  WDSR SL4 ... 149 J7
St Alfege Rd CHARL SE7 ... 162 A5
St Alphage Gdn BARB EC2Y ... 12 F4
St Alphage Wk EDGW HA8 ... 95 P10
St Alphege Rd ED N9 ... 100 B1
St Alphonsus Rd CLAP SW4 ... 158 D10
St Amunds Cl CAT SE6 ... 182 F7
St Andrew Av CHOB/PIR GU24 ... 230 C7
St Andrews Av ALP/SUD HA0 ... 114 F9
  HCH RM12 ... 124 C10
St Andrew's Cl CRICK NW2 ... 116 E8
  EPP CM16 ... 48 D10
  NFNCH/WDSP N12 ... 97 M5
  REIG RH2 ... 275 L1
  RSLP HA4 ... 113 L7
  SHPTN TW17 ... 196 E4
  STAN HA7 ... 95 H10
  STWL/WRAY TW19 ... 172 B2
  WDSR SL4 ... 147 M2
  WOKN/KNAP GU21 ... 231 P3
St Andrew's Ct
  WAND/EARL SW18 ... 179 M5
St Andrew's Crs WDSR SL4 ... 148 E8
St Andrews Dr ORP BR6 ... 207 L6
  STAN HA7 ... 95 J9
St Andrews Gdns COB KT11 ... 217 K9
St Andrew's Gv STNW/STAM N16 ... 119 L6
St Andrew's HI BLKFR EC4V ... 12 D7
St Andrew's Ms
  STNW/STAM N16 ... 119 M6
St Andrews Pl BRWN CM15 ... 107 L3
  CAMTN NW1 ... 10 E1
St Andrew's Rd ACT W3 ... 136 B8
  CAR SM5 ... 201 P10
  CDALE/KGS NW9 ... 116 A6
  COUL/CHIP CR5 ... 240 C2
  CRAWW RH11 ... 282 G8
  CROY/NA CR0 ... 223 K1
  ED N9 ... 100 B1
  EN EN1 ... 79 J1
  GLDGN NW11 ... 117 J4
  GVE DA12 ... 190 E3
  HGDN/ICK UB10 ... 131 P3
  HHS/BOV HP3 ... 35 N10
  HNWL W7 ... 154 D1
  IL IG1 ... 122 C5
  PLSTW E13 ... 141 M1
  ROMW/RG RM7 ... 124 E4
  SCUP DA14 ... 185 N6
  SURB KT6 ... 199 H5
  TIL RM18 ... 168 B8
  WALTH E17 ... 121 K4
  WAN E11 ... 121 K4
  WKENS W14 ... 14 B9
  WLSDN NW10 ... 136 E1
St Andrew St HCIRC EC1N ... 12 B4
  HERT/WAS SG14 ... 25 K5
St Andrew's Wk COB KT11 ... 235 J1
St Andrews Wy BOW E3 ... 141 J2
  OXTED RH8 ... 262 B7
  SL SL1 ... 128 C9
St Anna Rd BAR EN5 ... 76 C9
St Anne's Av STWL/WRAY TW19 ... 173 N1
St Annes Cl CDH/CHF RM16 ... 147 N10
  CHESW EN7 ... 61 P4
  HGT N6 ... 118 B8
  OXHEY WD19 ... 93 K5
St Anne's Dr REDH RH1 ... 258 B9
St Anne's Dr North REDH RH1 ... 258 B9
St Annes Mt REDH RH1 ... 258 B9

St Anne's Pk BROX EN10 44 F6
St Annes Pas POP/IOD E14 140 E8 4
St Annes Ri REDH RH1 258 B9 4
St Anne's Rd ALP/SUD HA0 115 J10
BRWN CM15 87 P5
CRAWE RH10 284 D3
DEN/HRF UB9 111 M1
LCOL/BKTW AL2 57 J3
WAN E11 121 J7
St Anne's Rw POP/IOD E14 140 E8 4
St Anne St POP/IOD E14 140 E8 4
St Annes Wy REDH RH1 258 B9 4
St Ann's BARK IG11 142 F3
St Ann's Cl CHERT KT16 195 J5
St Ann's Crs WAND/EARL SW18 179 L2
St Ann's Gdns HAMP NW3 4 B1
St Ann's Hl WAND/EARL SW18 179 L1
St Ann's Hill Rd CHERT KT16 194 F6
St Ann's Park Rd
WAND/EARL SW18 179 M2 5
St Ann's Rd BARK IG11 142 F3 1
BARN SW13 156 C7 2
CHERT KT16 195 J6
ED N9 99 N3
HRW HA1 114 D4
NTGHL W11 136 G9
St Ann's St WEST SW1P 17 K3
St Ann's Ter STJWD NW8 3 M7
St Ann's Vls NTGHL W11 136 G10
St Ann's Wy CROY/NA CR0 223 J3
St Anselm's Pl MYFR/PKLN W1K 10 E7 2
St Anselms Rd HYS/HAR UB3 152 G1
St Anthonys Av HHS/BOV HP3 36 C8
WFD IG8 101 P7
St Anthonys Cl TOOT SW17 179 P5 1
St Anthony's Ct HAYES BR2 206 E8
St Anthony's Wy
EBED/NFELT TW14 152 G10
St Antony's Rd FSTGT E7 141 N2
St Arvans Cl CROY/NA CR0 203 M10
St Asaph Rd PECK SE15 160 C9
St Aubyn's Av HSLWW TW4 175 P1
WIM/MER SW19 179 J8
St Aubyns Cl ORP BR6 207 J10
St Aubyns Gdns ORP BR6 207 J9
St Aubyn's Rd NRWD SE19 181 N9 3
St Audrey Av BXLYHN DA7 164 B8
St Audreys Cl HAT AL10 40 E7
St Audreys Gn WGCE AL7 23 J6
St Augusta Ct STALW/RED AL3 38 C4 1
St Augustine Rd CDH/CHF RM16 168 E3
St Augustine's Av BMLY BR1 206 B5
EA W5 135 K4
SAND/SEL CR2 223 K4
WBLY HA9 115 K8
St Augustines Cl BROX EN10 44 E6 4
St Augustines Dr BROX EN10 44 E6
St Augustine's Rd BELV DA17 164 A3
CAMTN NW1 5 J3
St Austell Cl EDGW HA8 95 L10
St Austell Rd LEW SE13 161 H8
St Awdry's Rd BARK IG11 142 G2
St Barnabas Av CHOB/PIR GU24 230 F8
St Barnabas Cl BECK BR3 205 H2 2
St Barnabas Gdns E/WMO/HCT KT8 197 M5
St Barnabas Rd MTCM CR4 180 B10
SUT SM1 221 N2
SWFD E18 101 N9
Saint Barnabas Rd WALTH E17 120 F4
St Barnabas Ter HOM E9 120 C10 3
St Barnabas Vls VX/NE SW8 158 F7 1
St Barnabus St BGVA SW1W 16 D7
St Bartholomew's Cl SYD SE26 182 B7
St Bartholomew's Ct GU GU1 268 C2 2
St Bartholomew's Rd EHAM E6 142 B3 3
St Benedict's Av GVE DA12 191 H6
St Benedict's Cl TOOT SW17 180 B8 4
St Benets Cl TOOT SW17 179 P5 2
St Benet's Gv MRDN SM4 201 M7 4
St Benjamins Dr ORP BR6 227 M5
St Bernards CROY/NA CR0 203 M10 5
St Bernards Cl WNWD SE27 181 L7 2
St Bernards Rd DTCH/LGLY SL3 149 P2
EHAM E6 142 A3
STALW/RED AL3 38 C5
St Blaise Av BMLY BR1 205 N2
St Botolph Rd GVW DA11 190 A6
St Botolph's Av SEV TN13 247 H10
St Botolph's Rd SEV TN13 247 J10
St Botolph St HDTCH EC3A 13 L5 2
St Brelades Cl DORK RH4 272 F4
St Bride's Av EDGW HA8 95 L9
St Brides Cl ERITHM DA18 163 N1
St Bride St FLST/FETLN EC4A 12 C5
St Catharine's Rd BROX EN10 44 F5
St Catherines WOKS/MYFD GU22 231 P5
St Catherines Cl TOOT SW17 179 P5 3
St Catherines Ct FELT TW13 175 H4 3
St Catherine's Cross REDH RH1 259 M10
St Catherine's Dr GUW GU2 267 N4
NWCR SE14 160 C8
St Catherine's Pk GU GU1 268 C1
St Catherines Rd CHING E4 100 F3
CRAWE RH10 284 D4
St Cecilia Rd CDH/CHF RM16 168 E3
St Chad Av WOKS/MYFD GU22 231 H8
St Chads Cl SURB KT6 199 H7
St Chad's Dr GVE DA12 191 H6
St Chad's Gdns CHDH RM6 123 P5
St Chad's Pl FSBYW WC1X 5 M9
St Chad's Rd CHDH RM6 123 P5 2
TIL RM18 168 D7
St Chad's St STPAN WC1H 5 M8
St Charles Pl NKENS W10 8 A4
WEY KT13 216 B2
St Charles Rd BRW CM14 106 G3
St Charles Sq NKENS W10 8 A3
NKENS W10 136 G7 5
St Christopher Rd UX/CGN UB8 131 N8
St Christopher's Cl ISLW TW7 154 D7 5
St Christophers Dr
HYS/HAR UB3 133 J9 2
St Christopher's Ms WLGTN SM6 222 D2 3
St Clair Cl CLAY IG5 102 C10
OXTED RH8 261 H6
REIG RH2 257 M10
St Clair Dr WPK KT4 200 E10
St Clair Rd PLSTW E13 141 N5
St Clair's Rd CROY/NA CR0 203 M9
St Clare St TWRH EC3N 13 L6
St Clement Cl UX/CGN UB8 131 N8
St Clement's Av WTHK RM20 166 F5
St Clements Cl GVW DA11 190 C6 2
St Clements Ct PUR RM19 165 P3 1
St Clement's La LINN WC2A 11 P6
St Clement's Rd WTHK RM20 166 E5
St Clements St IS N1 6 A3 1
St Cloud Rd WNWD SE27 181 K7
St Columba's Cl GVE DA12 191 H6
St Crispins Cl HAMP NW3 117 P9 4
STHL UB1 133 N8
St Crispins Wy CHERT KT16 214 F5
St Cross Ct HOD EN11 44 F5 2
St Cross St HCIRC EC1N 12 B3
St Cuthbert's Cl EGH TW20 172 A9
St Cuthberts Gdns PIN HA5 93 N8 3
St Cuthbert's Rd CRICK NW2 2 C1
HOD EN11 27 H10
PLMGR N13 99 H7
St Cyprian's St TOOT SW17 180 A7 1
St David Cl UX/CGN UB8 131 N7
St David's COUL/CHIP CR5 240 G3
St David's Cl HHS/BOV HP3 36 E8
IVER SL0 130 G3
REIG RH2 257 M9
WBLY HA9 115 P8
WWKM BR4 204 G7
St David's Crs GVE DA12 190 G7
St David's Dr BROX EN10 44 E5
EDGW HA8 95 L9
EGH TW20 171 P10
St David's Rd SWLY BR8 186 G9
St Denis Rd WNWD SE27 181 L7
St Deny's Cl WOKN/KNAP GU21 231 J4 5
St Dionis Rd FUL/PGN SW6 157 J8
St Donatt's Rd NWCR SE14 160 E7
St Dunstan's Av ACT W3 136 A9
St Dunstans Cl HYS/HAR UB3 152 G3
St Dunstan's Dr GVE DA12 191 H6
St Dunstan's Gdns ACT W3 136 A9 2
St Dunstan's Hl MON EC3R 13 J8 2
SUT SM1 221 H1
St Dunstan's La BECK BR3 205 H6
MON EC3R 13 J8 3
St Dunstan's Rd FELT TW13 174 G6
FSTGT E7 141 N1
HEST TW5 153 K8 5
HMSMTH W6 156 G4
HNWL W7 154 D1
HSLWW TW4 153 J8 1
SNWD SE25 203 N4
WARE SG12 28 A3 1
St Edith's Rd BGR/WK TN15 247 P4
St Edmund Cl CRAWW RH11 283 N4 6
St Edmunds BERK HP4 33 P6
St Edmunds Av RSLP HA4 112 E4
St Edmunds Cl ABYW SE2 163 N1
STJWD NW8 4 A6
TOOT SW17 179 P5 4
St Edmunds Dr STAN HA7 94 F9
St Edmund's La WHTN TW2 176 A3 1
St Edmunds Rd DART DA1 165 N10
ED N9 99 P1
IL IG1 122 C4
St Edmund's Ter STJWD NW8 3 P6
St Edmunds Wk STALE/WH AL4 39 J7 1
St Edmund's Wy HLWE CM17 29 M7 2
St Edwards Cl CROY/NA CR0 225 J7
GLDGN NW11 117 K4 2
St Edwards Wy ROM RM1 124 F2
St Egberts Wy CHING E4 101 H2
St Elizabeth Dr EPSOM KT18 219 P10
St Elmo Crs SLN SL2 129 J6
St Elmo Rd ACT W3 156 C1
St Elmos Rd BERM/RHTH SE16 160 D1
St Erkenwald Ms BARK IG11 142 G3
St Erkenwald Rd BARK IG11 142 G3
St Ervans Rd NKENS W10 8 B3
St Etheldreda's Dr HAT AL10 40 F4 1
St Faith's Cl ENC/FH EN2 79 K5 2
St Faith's Rd HNHL SE24 181 J4
St Fidelis' Rd ERITH DA8 164 E3
St Fillans Rd CAT SE6 183 H4
St Francis Av GVE DA12 191 H7
St Francis Cl ORP BR6 207 H6
OXHEY WD19 93 J2
POTB/CUF EN6 59 M9
St Francis Gdns CRAWE RH10 285 K1
St Francis Rd DEN/HRF UB9 111 J4
EDUL SE22 159 M10
Saint Francis Wy CDH/CHF RM16 168 F3
St Francis Wy IL IG1 122 G9
St Gabriel's Cl WAN E11 121 N6
St Gabriel's Rd CRICK NW2 116 G10
St George Av CHOB/PIR GU24 230 C8
St George's Av CDALE/KGS NW9 115 P2
EA W5 155 J1 4
Saint George's Av EMPK RM11 125 N5
St George's Av FSTGT E7 141 N2
GRAYS RM17 167 P3
HOLWY N7 118 E9
STHL UB1 133 N9
WEY KT13 216 D3
St Georges Cl ALP/SUD HA0 114 F8
BRWN CM15 86 G1
GLDGN NW11 117 J4 4
HORL RH6 280 C4
WDSR SL4 148 D7
WEY KT13 216 D2 3
St Georges Ct CRAWW RH11 283 N6
St George's Crs GVE DA12 190 G7
SL SL1 128 C9
St George's Dr BGVA SW1W 16 E6
HGDN/ICK UB10 112 A8
OXHEY WD19 93 M4
PIM SW1V 16 G7
St George's Gdns EW KT17 220 C10
SURB KT6 199 N9 2
St George's Gv TOOT SW17 179 N6
St George's La ASC SL5 192 A3
MON EC3R 13 H7 3
St George's Ms HAMP NW3 4 B4
St Georges Rd ADL/WDHM KT15 215 M1
BECK BR3 204 G1
BMLY BR1 206 C2
CHSWK W4 156 A1 4
DAGW RM9 123 P10
ED N9 99 P4 6
EN EN1 79 N4
FELT TW13 175 L7
FSTGT E7 141 N2
HHS/BOV HP3 35 M10 1
HNWL W7 134 E10
IL IG1 122 C5
KUTN/CMB KT2 177 M10
LEY E10 121 H8
MTCM CR4 202 C3
PLMGR N13 98 G4
RCH/KEW TW9 155 L9
REDH RH1 276 E8
SCUP DA14 185 N9
SEV TN13 247 J8
STHWK SE1 18 C4
STMC/STPC BR5 206 G6
SWLY BR8 208 G4 3
TWK TW1 176 G1
WATN WD24 73 J4 4
WATN WD24 73 J3 2
WEY KT13 216 E3
WIM/MER SW19 179 J9
WLGTN SM6 222 C2
St Georges Rd West BMLY BR1 206 B2
St George's St STP EC4M 12 C5 5
St George's Sq FSTGT E7 141 N2
PIM SW1V 17 J8
St George's Square Ms PIM SW1V 17 J8
St George's Ter HAMP NW3 4 B4
St George St CONDST W1S 10 F7
St George's Wk CROY/NA CR0 203 K10 5
St George's Wy PECK SE15 19 K10
St Gerards Cl CLAP SW4 180 D1
St German's Pl BKHTH/KID SE3 161 M7
St German's Rd FSTH SE23 182 D4
St Giles Av DAGE RM10 144 C2
HGDN/ICK UB10 112 D9
POTB/CUF EN6 58 D9
St Giles Cl DAGE RM10 144 C2 2
ORP BR6 226 G2
St Giles High St LSQ/SEVD WC2H 11 K5
St Gothard Rd WNWD SE27 181 L6
St Gregory Cl RSLP HA4 113 K9 1
St Gregory's Crs GVE DA12 191 H5
St Helena Rd BERM/RHTH SE16 160 C3
St Helena St FSBYW WC1X 6 A10 1
St Helen Cl UX/CGN UB8 131 N8
St Helen's Cl STALE/WH AL4 21 J3 2
St Helen's Crs STRHM/NOR SW16 202 G1 2
St Helen's Gdns NKENS W10 136 G7 4
NKENS W10 136 G8 3
St Helen's Pl OBST EC2N 13 J5
St Helens Rd ERITHM DA18 163 N1
IL IG1 122 C4
STRHM/NOR SW16 202 G2
WEA W13 135 H10 2
St Helier Av MRDN SM4 201 M7
St Heliers Av HSLWW TW4 175 P1
St Helier's Rd LEY E10 121 H4 1
STALE/WH AL4 38 G1
St Hilda's Av ASHF TW15 173 P8
St Hilda's Cl CRAWE RH10 284 D4 4
HORL RH6 280 C4
TOOT SW17 179 P5
WOKN/KNAP GU21 231 J3
St Hilda's Rd BARN SW13 156 E5
St Hilda's Wy GVE DA12 190 G7
St Huberts Cl CFSP/GDCR SL9 110 B7
St Huberts La CFSP/GDCR SL9 110 C7
St Hughes Cl TOOT SW17 179 P5 5
St Hugh's Cl CRAWE RH10 284 D4
St Hugh's Rd PGE/AN SE20 182 A10 4
St Ives Cl HARH RM3 105 N8
St Ivians Dr GPK RM2 125 H1
St James' Av CHONG CM5 67 N6
EW KT17 220 C7
SUT SM1 221 K2
TRDG/WHET N20 97 P4
WEA W13 134 F10
St James Cl EPSOM KT18 220 B10
NWMAL KT3 200 C5
RSLP HA4 113 K7
TRDG/WHET N20 97 P4
WOKN/KNAP GU21 231 M4
St James' Ct WESTW SW1E 17 H3 1
St James' Gdns ALP/SUD HA0 135 J2
St James Ga CTHM CR3 241 P8 1
St James' La RDART DA2 188 D3
St James Ms POP/IOD E14 161 H2 6
WEY KT13 216 C1
St James Pl DART DA1 187 L2 2
SL SL1 128 B8 3
St James Rd CAR SM5 201 P10
EBAR EN4 77 N7
ED N9 100 A3
FSTGT E7 121 L10
MTCM CR4 180 B10
PUR/KEN CR8 223 J9
SURB KT6 199 J6
SUT SM1 221 K3
WATW WD18 73 J9
St James's NWCR SE14 160 D7
St James's Av BECK BR3 204 D3
BETH E2 140 B4
GVW DA11 190 D3
HPTN TW12 176 B8
St James's Cl TOOT SW17 180 A5 5
WOOL/PLUM SE18 162 F4
St James's Cottages
RCHPK/HAM TW10 177 J1 7
St James's Crs BRXN/ST SW9 159 H9
St James's Dr BAL SW12 180 A4
TOOT SW17 180 A4
St James's Gdns NTGHL W11 8 A9
St James's Gv BTSEA SW11 158 A8 5
St James's La MUSWH N10 118 C2
St James's Market STJS SW1Y 11 J8 7
St James's Ms WALTH E17 120 D3 5
St James's Pk CROY/NA CR0 203 K7
St James's Pl WHALL SW1A 10 G10
St James Sq SURB KT6 199 H7
St James's Rd BERM/RHTH SE16 19 P9 1
BERM/RHTH SE16 19 P3
BRW CM14 107 H4
CHESW EN7 61 K4
CROY/NA CR0 203 K7
GVW DA11 190 D3
HPTN TW12 176 A8
KUT KT1 199 J2 4
SEV TN13 247 J8
STHWK SE1 19 P8
St James's Sq STJS SW1Y 11 J9 1
St James's St GVW DA11 190 D2 4
WALTH E17 120 D3
WHALL SW1A 10 G9
St James's Ter STJWD NW8 4 A6 1
St James's Terrace Ms STJWD NW8 4 A6
St James St HMSMTH W6 156 F4 5
St James Wk CLKNW EC1R 12 B1 3
IVER SL0 151 H1
St James Wy SCUP DA14 185 P8
St Jerome's Gv UX/CGN UB8 132 D8
St Joan Cl CRAWW RH11 283 N4
St Joan's Rd ED N9 99 N3
St John Cl FUL/PGN SW6 157 K6 6
St John's RDKG RH5 273 H6
St John's Av BRW CM14 107 J5
EW KT17 220 C8
FBAR/BDGN N11 98 A6
HLWE CM17 29 M7
LHD/OX KT22 236 G7
PUT/ROE SW15 178 G1
St John's Church Rd HOM E9 120 B10 4
St John's Cl LHD/OX KT22 237 H7
POTB/CUF EN6 59 M9
RAIN RM13 145 H2 5
STHGT/OAK N14 78 D10 1
UX/CGN UB8 131 L3 2
WBLY HA9 115 K10
St John's Ct BKHH IG9 101 N2
EGH TW20 172 D8 7
HARP AL5 20 B4 6
ISLW TW7 154 E8 3
STAL AL1 38 G5
St John's Crs BRXN/ST SW9 159 H9
St John's Dr WAND/EARL SW18 179 L4
WDSR SL4 148 E8
WOT/HER KT12 197 K8
St John's Gdns NTGHL W11 8 C8
St John's Gv ARCH N19 118 D7
BARN SW13 156 C8 3
RCH/KEW TW9 155 K10 7
St John's Hl BTSEA SW11 157 P10
PUR/KEN CR8 241 H3
SEV TN13 247 K9
St John's Hill Gv BTSEA SW11 157 N10
St John's Hill Rd
WOKN/KNAP GU21 231 M5
St John's La FARR EC1M 12 C2
HART DA3 211 L6
WARE SG12 26 F5
St John's Lye WOKN/KNAP GU21 231 L5
St John's Lye (Festival Path)
WOKN/KNAP GU21 231 L5
St Johns Ms WOKN/KNAP GU21 231 M4
St John's Pk BKHTH/KID SE3 161 M6
St John's Pl FARR EC1M 12 C2
St Johns Ri WOKN/KNAP GU21 231 N5
St John's Rd BARK IG11 143 H3
BTSEA SW11 157 P10 6
CAN/RD E16 141 M8
CAR SM5 201 P10
CDH/CHF RM16 168 E4
CHING E4 100 G4
CRAWW RH11 283 M7 4
CROY/NA CR0 203 J10 5
CRW RM5 104 D6
DORK RH4 272 B3
E/WMO/HCT KT8 198 C4
EHAM E6 142 B3
EPP CM16 65 J6
ERITH DA8 164 E4
FELT TW13 175 N7
GLDGN NW11 117 J4
GNTH/NBYPK IG2 123 H5
GUW GU2 267 L1
GVE DA12 190 G3
HARP AL5 20 B4
HHW HP1 35 L8
HRW HA1 114 E4
ISLW TW7 154 E8
KUT KT1 199 H2
LHD/OX KT22 237 H7
LOU IG10 82 C6
NWDGN UB2 153 M2 4
NWMAL KT3 199 P3
PGE/AN SE20 182 B10
RCH/KEW TW9 155 K10 8
RDART DA2 188 B3
REDH RH1 276 A2
SCUP DA14 185 L7
SEV TN13 247 J8
SEVS/STOTM N15 119 M4
SLN SL2 129 M9
STMC/STPC BR5 206 G6
SUT SM1 201 L9 2
UX/CGN UB8 131 L3 3
WALTH E17 100 G10
WAT WD17 73 J6
WBLY HA9 115 J9
WDSR SL4 148 F8
WELL DA16 163 L9
WIM/MER SW19 179 H10
WOKN/KNAP GU21 231 M5
St John's Road Rd
WOKN/KNAP GU21 231 N4
St John's Sq FARR EC1M 12 C2 4
FSBYE EC1V 12 C2
St John's St HERT/WAS SG14 25 L5 14
St John's Ter ENC/FH EN2 79 L3 1
FSTGT E7 141 N1
NKENS W10 136 G6 7
WOOL/PLUM SE18 162 F5
St John's Terrace Rd REDH RH1 276 A2
St John St FSBYE EC1V 6 B8
St John's V BROCKY SE4 160 F8
St John's Vls ARCH N19 118 E7
KENS W8 15 H4 2
St Johns Wk HLWE CM17 29 M7 3
St John's Wy ADL/WDHM KT15 195 K9
St John's Well Ct BERK HP4 33 N4 1
St John's Well La BERK HP4 33 N4
St John's Wood High St
STJWD NW8 3 M8
St John's Wood Pk STJWD NW8 3 L6
St John's Wood Rd STJWD NW8 9 L1
St John's Wood Ter STJWD NW8 3 N7
St Josephs Cl ORP BR6 227 J1 1
St Joseph's Dr STHL UB1 133 M10
St Josephs Gv HDN NW4 116 E2 4
St Joseph's Rd ED N9 100 A1
St Joseph's St VX/NE SW8 158 C7 2
St Jude's Cl EGH TW20 171 P8
St Jude's Rd BETH E2 140 A4 10
EGH TW20 171 P7
St Jude St STNW/STAM N16 119 M10 5
St Julian's Cl STRHM/NOR SW16 181 H7 2
St Julian's Farm Rd WNWD SE27 181 H7
St Julian's Rd KIL/WHAMP NW6 2 D4
STAL AL1 38 C8
St Justin Cl STMC/STPC BR5 207 N3
St Katharine's Prec CAMTN NW1 4 E7 7
St Katharines Rd CTHM CR3 259 P1
St Katharine's Wy TWRH EC3N 13 M9
St Katherines Rd ERITHM DA18 163 N1
St Katherine's Wy BERK HP4 33 L2
St Keverne Rd ELTH/MOT SE9 184 B7
St Kilda Rd ORP BR6 207 J8
WEA W13 154 F1
St Kilda's Rd BRWN CM15 106 G1
HRW HA1 114 D4
STNW/STAM N16 119 L6
St Kitts Ter NRWD SE19 181 M8
St Laurence Cl STMC/STPC BR5 207 N3
UX/CGN UB8 131 M7
St Laurence Dr BROX EN10 44 D9
St Laurence's Cl
KIL/WHAMP NW6 136 G3 1
St Laurence Wy SL SL1 149 M2
St Lawrence Cl ABLGY WD5 54 F6
EDGW HA8 95 L8
HHS/BOV HP3 52 D3
St Lawrence Dr PIN HA5 113 J3
St Lawrence Rd UPMR RM14 126 B7
St Lawrence St POP/IOD E14 141 H10 5
St Lawrences Wy REIG RH2 257 K10
St Lawrence Ter NKENS W10 8 A4
St Lawrence Wy BRXN/ST SW9 159 H8 4
CTHM CR3 241 L9
LCOL/BKTW AL2 55 N6
St Leonard's Av CHING E4 101 J7
KTN/HRWW/W HA3 115 H3
WDSR SL4 149 H8
St Leonards Cl BUSH WD23 73 M8
HERT/WAS SG14 25 M3
WELL DA16 163 K9
St Leonard's Ct STALE/WH AL4 21 H10 1
St Leonards Crs STALE/WH AL4 21 H10
St Leonards Dr CRAWE RH10 284 B10
St Leonards Gdns HEST TW5 153 M6
Saint Leonards Gdns IL IG1 122 F10 2
St Leonard's Hl WDSR SL4 148 C10
St Leonards Ri ORP BR6 227 H1
St Leonards Rd AMS HP6 69 K2
CROY/NA CR0 203 J10 6
ESH/CLAY KT10 218 E3
HERT/WAS SG14 25 L3
KWD/TDW/WH KT20 238 F5
MORT/ESHN SW14 155 P9
POP/IOD E14 141 H7
SURB KT6 199 J5
THDIT KT7 198 F6
WAB EN9 45 J10
WDSR SL4 148 G10
WEA W13 135 H9
WLSDN NW10 136 A6 2
St Leonard's St BOW E3 140 G5 5
St Leonard's Ter CHEL SW3 16 A8
St Leonards Wk IVER SL0 151 J2
STRHM/NOR SW16 180 G10
St Leonards Wy HCH RM12 125 J6
St Loo Av CHEL SW3 15 P9
St Louis Rd WNWD SE27 181 K7
St Loy's Rd TOTM N17 99 M10
St Lucia Dr SRTFD E15 141 L3
St Luke Cl UX/CGN UB8 131 N8
St Luke's Av CLAP SW4 158 E10
ENC/FH EN2 79 L4
IL IG1 122 E10
St Lukes Cl RDART DA2 188 D8
SNWD SE25 204 A6
SWLY BR8 208 E2 4
St Lukes Ct WOKN/KNAP GU21 214 F10 1
St Luke's Ms NTGHL W11 8 D5
St Luke's Rd CTHM CR3 241 N4
HGDN/ICK UB10 131 P2 3
NTGHL W11 8 D4
WDSR SL4 171 M2
St Lukes's Cl FSBYE EC1V 12 F1
St Luke's Sq CAN/RD E16 141 L8 3
GU GU1 268 C1 4
St Luke's St CHEL SW3 15 N7
St Malo Av ED N9 100 B4
St Margarets BARK IG11 142 G3
GU GU1 250 C9
St Margarets Av ASHF TW15 174 B8
BFN/LL DA15 184 G6
CHEAM SM3 201 H10
RYLN/HDSTN HA2 114 B8
SEVS/STOTM N15 119 J2 5
TRDG/WHET N20 97 M2
UX/CGN UB8 132 A8
St Margaret's Cl BERK HP4 34 A6
IVER SL0 130 G4
ORP BR6 227 L1 1
RDART DA2 188 C5
St Margaret's Crs GVE DA12 191 H6
PUT/ROE SW15 178 E1 6
St Margarets Dr EPSOM KT18 220 A10 2
TWK TW1 176 G1
St Margaret's Gv TWK TW1 176 F2
WAN E11 121 L8 5
WOOL/PLUM SE18 162 F5
St Margaret's Rd BROCKY SE4 160 E10
COUL/CHIP CR5 240 C7
EDGW HA8 95 N6
EYN DA4 188 D10
HNWL W7 154 D1
MNPK E12 121 P7
RSLP HA4 112 E4
TOTM N17 99 M10
TWK TW1 154 G10
WARE SG12 26 F9
WLSDN NW10 136 F5
St Margaret's Ter
WOOL/PLUM SE18 162 F4 2
St Margaret St WEST SW1P 17 L2
St Margarets Wy HHNE HP2 36 E6 1
St Mark Av CHOB/PIR GU24 230 G9
St Mark's Av GVW DA11 190 B3
St Mark's Cl BAR EN5 77 L7
STALE/WH AL4 39 N8
St Mark's Crs CAMTN NW1 4 D5
St Marks Ga HOM E9 140 E2 2
St Mark's Gv WBPTN SW10 157 L6 6
St Mark's Hl SURB KT6 199 K6
St Mark's Pl NTGHL W11 8 B6
WDSR SL4 149 H8
WIM/MER SW19 179 J9 3
St Mark's Ri HACK E8 119 N10 7
HACK E8 119 N10 7
St Mark's Rd EA W5 135 K10
EN EN1 79 N10
EPSOM KT18 238 F4
HAYES BR2 205 N3 4
HNWL W7 154 D1
MTCM CR4 202 A2
NKENS W10 136 G7
NTGHL W11 8 A6
SNWD SE25 203 P4 5
TEDD TW11 176 G10
WDSR SL4 149 H8
St Mark's Sq CAMTN NW1 4 C5
St Mark St WCHPL E1 13 M6
St Martha's Av
WOKS/MYFD GU22 232 C7
St Martin Cl UX/CGN UB8 131 N8 3
St Martin's Ap RSLP HA4 112 F5
St Martin's Av EHAM E6 142 A4
EPSOM KT18 220 B10
St Martin's Cl CAMTN NW1 4 G5
EHSLY KT24 252 F5
EN EN1 80 A5
ERITHM DA18 163 N1
EW KT17 220 C9 1
OXHEY WD19 93 K5 4
WDR/YW UB7 151 M2
St Martin's Ct ASHF TW15 173 M8
St Martins Dr EYN DA4 209 L10
WOT/HER KT12 197 K10
St Martin's La CHCR WC2N 11 L7
St Martin's Le Grand STBT EC1A 12 E5
St Martins Meadow
BH/WHM TN16 245 M9
St Martins Ms DORK RH4 272 F2 4
WOKS/MYFD GU22 233 K2
St Martin's Pl CHCR WC2N 11 L8 6
St Martin's Rd BRXN/ST SW9 158 G8
DART DA1 187 N2
ED N9 100 A3
St Martin's St LSQ/SEVD WC2H 11 K8 2
St Martin's Wy TOOT SW17 179 M6
St Mary Abbot's Pl KENS W8 14 D4
St Mary Abbots Ter WKENS W14 14 D4 1
WKENS W14 14 D4 1
St Mary At Hl MON EC3R 13 J8
St Mary Av WLGTN SM6 202 B10
St Mary Axe HDTCH EC3A 13 J6
St Marychurch St
BERM/RHTH SE16 160 B1
St Mary Rd WALTH E17 120 F2
St Marys BARK IG11 142 G4
St Mary's Ap MNPK E12 122 C10 1
St Mary's Av BERK HP4 33 J3
BRWN CM15 87 M9
FNCH N3 97 H10
HAYES BR2 205 K3
NTHWD HA6 92 F6
NWDGN UB2 154 A3
STWL/WRAY TW19 173 N3
TEDD TW11 176 E9 3
WAN E11 121 N5
St Mary's Church Rd RSEV TN14 263 P1
St Mary's Cl CHSGTN KT9 219 L4
DEN/HRF UB9 111 L1
EW KT17 220 C4
GRAYS RM17 168 A5 1
GVE DA12 190 F5
LHD/OX KT22 236 C9
OXTED RH8 261 K5
STMC/STPC BR5 207 L2
SUN TW16 197 H4 1
TOTM N17 99 P9 4
St Mary's Ct BH/WHM TN16 262 C2
POTB/CUF EN6 59 L8
St Mary's Crs HDN NW4 116 E1
HYS/HAR UB3 132 G9
ISLW TW7 154 C6
STWL/WRAY TW19 173 N3
St Mary's Dr CRAWE RH10 284 C5
EBED/NFELT TW14 174 D3
SEV TN13 246 F9
St Mary's Gdns LBTH SE11 18 B5
St Mary's Gn BH/WHM TN16 243 P4
EFNCH N2 117 M1
St Mary's Gv BARN SW13 156 E9
BH/WHM TN16 243 P4
CHSWK W4 155 N5
IS N1 6 D2
RCH/KEW TW9 155 L10
St Mary's Hl ASC SL5 192 B6
St Mary's La HERT/WAS SG14 24 G7
UPMR RM14 125 P7
St Mary's Man BAY/PAD W2 9 K3
St Mary's Ms KIL/WHAMP NW6 2 G4
St Mary's Mt CTHM CR3 241 N10
St Mary's Pth IS N1 6 D5
St Mary's Pl EA W5 155 J1 5
KENS W8 15 H4 3
St Mary's Rd ASC SL5 192 A7
BXLY DA5 186 D4
CDH/CHF RM16 168 E3
CEND/HSY/T N8 118 F2 4
CHES/WCR EN8 62 B5
DEN/HRF UB9 111 L1
DTCH/LGLY SL3 150 B1
E/WMO/HCT KT8 198 C5
EA W5 155 J1
EBAR EN4 98 A1 1
ED N9 100 B2
GLDGN NW11 117 H5
GRH DA9 188 D1
HHNE HP2 35 N5
HYS/HAR UB3 132 G9
IL IG1 122 F7
LEY E10 121 H8
LHD/OX KT22 236 G8
PECK SE15 160 B8
PLSTW E13 141 N4
REIG RH2 275 L1
SAND/SEL CR2 223 L6
SNWD SE25 203 M3
SURB KT6 199 H7
SWLY BR8 208 E4
WATW WD18 73 J8
WEY KT13 216 E1
WIM/MER SW19 179 H8

WLSDN NW10 136 B3
WOKN/KNAP GU21 231 P3
WPK KT4 200 B9 4
St Mary's Sq BAY/PAD W2 9 L3
EA W5 155 J1 6
St Mary's Ter BAY/PAD W2 9 L3
St Mary St WOOL/PLUM SE18 162 C3
St Marys Vw KTN/HRWW/W HA3 115 H3
St Mary's Wk HYS/HAR UB3 132 G9
LBTH SE11 18 B5
STALE/WH AL4 38 G2
St Mary's Wy CFSP/GDCR SL9 90 A10
CHIG IG7 102 D6
CSHM HP5 50 G7
HART DA3 211 K3
St Matthew Cl UX/CGN UB8 131 N8
St Matthew's Av SURB KT6 199 K8
St Matthews Cl OXHEY WD19 73 L10 1
RAIN RM13 145 H2 6
St Matthews Dr BMLY BR1 206 C3
St Matthew's Rd
BRXS/STRHM SW2 180 G1
EA W5 135 K10
REDH RH1 258 A9 4
St Matthew's Rw BETH E2 7 N10
St Matthew St WEST SW1P 17 J3
St Matthias Cl CDALE/KGS NW9 116 C3 1
St Maur Rd FUL/PGN SW6 157 J7
St Merryn Cl WOOL/PLUM SE18 162 G5 1
St Michaels Av ED N9 100 B1
HHS/BOV HP3 36 C8 2
HHS/BOV HP3 36 C7
RGUW GU3 249 H5
WBLY HA9 135 M1
St Michaels Cl BMLY BR1 206 B3
CAN/RD E16 142 A7 10
ERITHM DA18 163 N1 1
FNCH N3 97 J10 2
HLW CM20 29 H10
NFNCH/WDSP N12 97 P6
SOCK/AV RM15 146 B9
WOT/HER KT12 197 K9 2
WPK KT4 200 C9
St Michael's Ct SLN SL2 128 C6 2
St Michael's Crs PIN HA5 113 M4
St Michaels Dr GSTN WD25 55 J9
RSEV TN14 247 L2
St Michael's Gdns NKENS W10 136 G7
St Michael's Gn BEAC HP9 88 D8
St Michaels Rd ASHF TW15 174 B8
BROX EN10 44 E6
BRXN/ST SW9 158 G8
CDH/CHF RM16 168 E4
CRICK NW2 116 F9
CROY/NA CR0 203 K8 2
CTHM CR3 241 L8
WELL DA16 163 L9 2
WLGTN SM6 222 D3
WOKN/KNAP GU21 214 G10
St Michael's St BAY/PAD W2 9 M5
STALW/RED AL3 38 A6
St Michael's Ter WDGN N22 98 F9 2
St Michaels Wy POTB/CUF EN6 59 L6 4
St Mildred's Ct LOTH EC2R 12 G6 6
St Mildreds Rd CAT SE6 183 K3
GU GU1 250 C9
St Monica's Rd
KWD/TDW/WH KT20 239 J7
St Nazaire Cl EGH TW20 172 F8 5
St Neots Cl BORE WD6 75 M4 3
St Neot's Rd HARH RM3 105 N8
St Nicholas Av GT/LBKH KT23 254 A1
HCH RM12 125 H8
St Nicholas Cl AMSS HP7 69 N5
BORE WD6 75 J10
UX/CGN UB8 131 N8
St Nicholas Crs
WOKS/MYFD GU22 233 K2
St Nicholas Dr SHPTN TW17 196 B7
St Nicholas Glebe TOOT SW17 180 B9 3
St Nicholas Gv RBRW/HUT CM13 107 P6
St Nicholas Hl LHD/OX KT22 236 G8
St Nicholas Mt HHW HP1 35 J6
St Nicholas Rd SUT SM1 221 L2 5
THDIT KT7 198 E6
WOOL/PLUM SE18 163 J4
St Nicholas St DEPT SE8 160 F7 7
St Nicholas Wy SUT SM1 221 L1
St Nicolas La CHST BR7 206 B1
St Ninian's Ct TRDG/WHET N20 98 A4
St Norbert Rd BROCKY SE4 160 D10
St Normans Wy EW KT17 220 D6
St Olaf's Rd FUL/PGN SW6 157 H6
St Olave's Cl STA TW18 173 J10
St Olave's Rd EHAM E6 142 D3
St Olave's Wk STRHM/NOR SW16 202 D2
St Omer Rdg GU GU1 268 D1
St Omer Rd GU GU1 268 D1
St Oswald's Pl LBTH SE11 17 N7
St Oswald's Rd
STRHM/NOR SW16 203 J1
St Oswulf St WEST SW1P 17 K6 1
St Pancras Wy CAMTN NW1 5 H3 1
St Patrick's Gdns GVE DA12 190 G7
St Patrick's Pl CDH/CHF RM16 168 E3
St Paul Cl UX/CGN UB8 131 N7
St Paul's Av BERM/RHTH SE16 140 C10 12
CRICK NW2 136 E1
KTN/HRWW/W HA3 115 L3
SLN SL2 129 L9
St Paul's Church Yd BLKFR EC4V 12 D6 7
St Paul's Cl ADL/WDHM KT15 215 K1
ASHF TW15 174 D8 2
CAR SM5 201 P7
CHARL SE7 162 A4 1
CHSGTN KT9 219 J1 3
EA W5 155 L1
EA W5 155 L1
HSLW TW3 153 M8 2
HYS/HAR UB3 152 E4
SOCK/AV RM15 146 B9 1
SWCM DA10 189 K3
St Paul's Cray Rd CHST BR7 206 G1
St Pauls Crs CAMTN NW1 5 K3
CAMTN NW1 5 K3
St Paul's Dr SRTFD E15 121 J10
St Pauls Ms CAMTN NW1 5 K3
St Paul's Pl IS N1 6 G1
SOCK/AV RM15 146 B9 2
STAL AL1 38 F6
St Pauls Ri PLMGR N13 99 J7
St Pauls Rd BARK IG11 142 F3
BTFD TW8 155 J5
ERITH DA8 164 D6
HHNE HP2 35 P5
IS N1 6 F1
RCH/KEW TW9 155 L9
STA TW18 172 G8
THHTH CR7 203 K3
TOTM N17 99 P8
WOKS/MYFD GU22 232 D3
St Paul's Rd East DORK RH4 272 G3
St Paul's Rd West DORK RH4 272 F3
St Pauls Ter WALW SE17 18 D9
St Paul St IS N1 6 E6
St Paul's Wy FNCH N3 97 L8
POP/IOD E14 140 E7
WAB EN9 63 J9 3
WATN WD24 73 K6 6
St Paul's Wood Hl
STMC/STPC BR5 207 H2
St Peter's Av CHONG CM5 67 N2
UED N18 99 P5
St Petersburgh Ms BAY/PAD W2 8 G7
St Petersburgh Pl BAY/PAD W2 8 G8 1
St Peter's Cl BAR EN5 76 E9
BETH E2 7 P8
BUSH WD23 94 C2
CHST BR7 184 G10
GNTH/NBYPK IG2 123 H2
HAT AL10 40 D3 2
RKW/CH/CXG WD3 91 L3
RSLP HA4 113 L7 2
SL SL1 128 A6
STA TW18 173 J9 1
STALW/RED AL3 38 C5
SWCM DA10 189 L3
TOOT SW17 179 P5 6
WDSR SL4 171 M1
WOKS/MYFD GU22 232 F6
St Peters Ct E/WMO/HCT KT8 197 P4 2
HDN NW4 116 F3 3
LEE/GVPK SE12 183 L1 2
St Peter's Gdns WNWD SE27 181 H6 3
St Peter's Gv HMSMTH W6 156 D3
St Peter's Pth WALTH E17 121 K2
St Peter's Rd BRW CM14 106 G5 1
CDH/CHF RM16 168 E3
CRAWW RH11 283 M7 5
CROY/NA CR0 223 L1
E/WMO/HCT KT8 197 P4
ED N9 100 A2
HMSMTH W6 156 D4 5
KUT KT1 199 M2 5
STAL AL1 38 D6
STHL UB1 133 P7
TWK TW1 176 G1
UX/CGN UB8 131 N7
WOKS/MYFD GU22 232 E7
St Peter's Sq BETH E2 7 P8
St Peter's St IS N1 6 D6
SAND/SEL CR2 223 L2
STAL AL1 38 C5
St Peter's Ter FUL/PGN SW6 157 J6 7
St Peter's Vls HMSMTH W6 156 D3 4
St Peter's Wy CHERT KT16 215 H1
EA W5 135 J7
HYS/HAR UB3 152 E4
IS N1 7 K4 1
RKW/CH/CXG WD3 70 E8
St Philip's Av WPK KT4 200 E9
St Philip Sq VX/NE SW8 158 C8 7
St Philip's Rd HACK E8 7 N2
SURB KT6 199 J6
St Philip St VX/NE SW8 158 C8
St Philip's Wy IS N1 6 F6
St Pinnock Av STA TW18 195 K1
St Quentin Rd WELL DA16 163 J9 1
St Quintin Av NKENS W10 136 F7
St Quintin Rd PLSTW E13 141 N5 5
St Raphael's Wy WLSDN NW10 115 P10
St Regis Cl MUSWH N10 98 C10
St Ronans Cl EBAR EN4 77 N4
St Ronans Crs WFD IG8 101 M8
St Rule St VX/NE SW8 158 D8
St Saviour Av CHOB/PIR GU24 230 G7
St Saviour's Rd
BRXS/STRHM SW2 180 G1
CROY/NA CR0 203 K6
Saints Cl WNWD SE27 181 J7 5
Saints Dr FSTGT E7 122 A10
St Silas Pl KTTN NW5 4 C2
St Simon's Av PUT/ROE SW15 178 F1
St Stephens Av ASHTD KT21 237 K3
SHB W12 136 E10
STALW/RED AL3 38 A8
WALTH E17 121 H3 3
WEA W13 134 G8
St Stephen's Cl STALW/RED AL3 38 A9 2
STHL UB1 133 P7
WALTH E17 120 G3 3
St Stephen's Crs BAY/PAD W2 8 F5 2
RBRW/HUT CM13 107 M5
THHTH CR7 203 H3 1
St Stephen's Gdns BAY/PAD W2 8 F5
TWK TW1 177 H2 2
St Stephen's Gv LEW SE13 161 H9 4
St Stephen's Hl STAL AL1 38 B8
St Stephen's Ms BAY/PAD W2 8 F4
St Stephens Rd BAR EN5 76 G9
BOW E3 140 D3
EHAM E6 141 P2
HSLW TW3 175 P2
LEY E10 120 G3 4
PEND EN3 80 C3
WDR/YW UB7 131 N10
WEA W13 134 G8
St Stephen's Ter VX/NE SW8 158 G6 3
Saint's Wk CDH/CHF RM16 168 F3
St Swithin's La MANHO EC4N 12 G7
St Swithun's Rd LEW SE13 183 J2 3
St Teresa Wk CDH/CHF RM16 168 E3
St Theresa Cl EPSOM KT18 219 P10 1
St Theresa's Rd
EBED/NFELT TW14 152 G10
St Thomas Cl SURB KT6 199 L8 2
WOKN/KNAP GU21 231 P3
St Thomas Ct BXLY DA5 186 B3
St Thomas' Dr PIN HA5 93 M9
STMC/STPC BR5 206 F8
St Thomas Gdns IL IG1 142 F1
St Thomas Pl STALE/WH AL4 21 J3
St Thomas Rd BELV DA17 164 D1
CAN/RD E16 141 M8
CHSWK W4 155 P6
GVW DA11 190 B4 2
STHGT/OAK N14 98 E1
St Thomas's Av GVW DA11 190 E5
St Thomas's Cl WAB EN9 63 N9
St Thomas's Dr RGUE GU4 251 P7 1
St Thomas's Gdns HAMP NW3 4 C1
St Thomas's Pl GRAYS RM17 167 P5 4
Saint Thomas's Rd FSBYPK N4 119 H7
St Thomas's Rd WLSDN NW10 136 B3
St Thomas's Sq HOM E9 140 B2 4
St Thomas St STHWK SE1 13 H10
St Thomas's Wy FUL/PGN SW6 157 J6
St Thomas Wk DTCH/LGLY SL3 150 G6 1
St Ursula Gv PIN HA5 113 L3
St Ursula Rd STHL UB1 133 P8
St Vincent Cl CRAWE RH10 284 E8 7
WNWD SE27 181 J8 2
St Vincent Dr STAL AL1 38 F8
St Vincent Rd WHTN TW2 176 B2
WOT/HER KT12 197 J10
St Vincents Rd DART DA1 187 P2
St Vincent St MHST W1U 10 D4
St Vincent's Wy POTB/CUF EN6 59 M9 4
St Wilfrid's Cl EBAR EN4 77 P9 2
St Wilfrid's Rd EBAR EN4 77 N9
St Winefride's Av MNPK E12 122 C10
St Winifred's Cl CHIG IG7 102 F6
St Winifred's Rd BH/WHM TN16 244 C4
TEDD TW11 176 G9
St Yon Ct STALE/WH AL4 39 J6
Sakins Cft HLWS CM18 47 J4
Saladin Dr PUR RM19 165 P3
Salamanca Pl LBTH SE11 17 N6
Salamanca St LBTH SE11 17 N6
Salamander Cl KUTN/CMB KT2 177 H8 1
Salamons Wy RAIN RM13 144 F8
Salcombe Dr CHDH RM6 124 A4
MRDN SM4 200 G8
Salcombe Gdns MLHL NW7 96 F7
Salcombe Rd ASHF TW15 173 P7
STNW/STAM N16 119 M10 6
WALTH E17 120 E5
Salcombe Wy RSLP HA4 113 H7
Salcot Crs CROY/NA CR0 225 H6
Salcote Rd GVE DA12 191 H8 2
Salcott Rd BTSEA SW11 179 P1
CROY/NA CR0 202 F10
Salehurst Cl KTN/HRWW/W HA3 115 K3
Salehurst Rd BROCKY SE4 182 E2
CRAWE RH10 284 F7
Salem Pl CROY/NA CR0 203 K10
GVW DA11 190 A3 3
Salem Rd BAY/PAD W2 9 H7
Sale Pl BAY/PAD W2 9 N5
Sale St BETH E2 13 N1
Salford Rd BAL SW12 180 E4
Salisbury Av BARK IG11 142 G2
BELMT SM2 221 J3
FNCH N3 97 J10
SLN SL2 129 H6
STAL AL1 38 G6
SWLY BR8 209 H4
Salisbury Cl AMSS HP7 69 K5 1
POTB/CUF EN6 59 M8
WALW SE17 18 G5
WPK KT4 200 C10 1
Salisbury Ct EMB EC4Y 12 B6 2
EMB EC4Y 12 C6 7
Salisbury Crs CHES/WCR EN8 62 C8
Salisbury Gdns WGCE AL7 23 J6
WIM/MER SW19 179 H10 1
Salisbury Pl BF/WBF KT14 215 M7 2
MBLAR W1H 10 A3
Salisbury Rd BAR EN5 77 H7
BNSTD SM7 239 L1
BXLY DA5 186 B4
CAR SM5 222 A3
CHING E4 100 F4
CROY/NA CR0 203 P6
DAGE RM10 144 C1
ED N9 99 P4
FELT TW13 175 K4
FSBYPK N4 119 J3
FSTGT E7 141 M1
GDMY/SEVK IG3 123 H7
GDST RH9 260 B7
GPK RM2 125 J3
GRAYS RM17 167 P5
GVW DA11 190 C4
HAYES BR2 206 B5
HOD EN11 45 H2
HOR/WEW KT19 220 A1
HRW HA1 114 C3
HSLWW TW4 153 K9
LEY E10 121 H7
MNPK E12 122 A10
NWDGN UB2 153 M3 3
NWMAL KT3 200 A3
PEND EN3 80 E3
PIN HA5 113 H2
RCH/KEW TW9 155 K10 9
RDART DA2 188 B4
UX/CGN UB8 131 L4
WALTH E17 121 H3
WATN WD24 73 J4
WDGN N22 99 J10
WEA W13 154 G1
WGCE AL7 23 J6
WIM/MER SW19 179 H10
WOKS/MYFD GU22 232 B5
Salisbury Sq HERT/WAS SG14 25 L5 15
Salisbury St ACT W3 155 P1 5
STJWD NW8 9 N2
Salisbury Ter PECK SE15 160 B9 5
Salix Cl SUN TW16 175 J10 2
Salix Rd GRAYS RM17 168 A5
Salmen Rd PLSTW E13 141 L4
Salmon Cl WGCE AL7 23 K2
Salmond's Gv RBRW/HUT CM13 107 P6
Salmon La POP/IOD E14 140 D8
Salmon Rd BELV DA17 164 B4
DART DA1 165 N9
Salmons La CTHM CR3 241 M6
Salmons La West CTHM CR3 241 M6
Salmons Rd CHSGTN KT9 219 K3
ED N9 99 P2
EHSLY KT24 253 K5
Salmon St CDALE/KGS NW9 115 P4 4
POP/IOD E14 140 E8 6
WBLY HA9 115 P7
Salomons Rd PLSTW E13 141 P7 1
Salop Rd WALTH E17 120 C4
Saltash Cl SUT SM1 221 J1
Saltash Rd BARK/HLT IG6 102 G8
WELL DA16 163 M7
Saltbox Hl BH/WHM TN16 225 N9
Salt Box Rd RGUW GU3 249 M5
Saltcoats Rd CHSWK W4 156 B1
Saltcroft Cl WBLY HA9 115 N6
Saltdean Cl CRAWW RH11 283 N10
Salter Cl RYLN/HDSTN HA2 113 N9 1
Salterford Rd TOOT SW17 180 B9
Salterns Rd CRAWE RH10 284 D10
Salter Rd BERM/RHTH SE16 140 D10
Salter's Cl BERK HP4 33 L3 4
RKW/CH/CXG WD3 91 P2
Salters' Hall Ct MANHO EC4N 12 G7 4
Salter's Hl NRWD SE19 181 L8
Salters Rd NKENS W10 136 G6
WALTH E17 121 J2
Salter St POP/IOD E14 140 F9
WLSDN NW10 136 D5
Salterton Rd HOLWY N7 118 F8
Saltford Cl ERITH DA8 164 F4
Salt Hill Av SL SL1 129 H10
Salt Hill Cl UX/CGN UB8 111 N10
Salt Hill Dr SL SL1 129 H10
Salt Hill Wy SL SL1 129 H10
Saltley Cl EHAM E6 142 B8
Saltram Crs MV/WKIL W9 2 D9
Saltwell St POP/IOD E14 140 F9
Saltwood Cl ORP BR6 227 M1
Salusbury Rd KIL/WHAMP NW6 2 B5
Salvador TOOT SW17 179 P8
Salvation Pl LHD/OX KT22 236 F10
Salvia Gdns GFD/PVL UB6 134 F4 1
Salvington Rd CRAWW RH11 283 J10
Salvin Rd PUT/ROE SW15 156 G9
Salway Cl WFD IG8 101 M8 1
Salway Pl SRTFD E15 141 J1 5
Salway Rd SRTFD E15 141 J1
Salwey Crs BROX EN10 44 E6
Samantha Cl WALTH E17 120 E5 5
Samaritan Cl CRAWW RH11 283 H9 7
Sam Bartram Cl CHARL SE7 161 P4
Samels Ct HMSMTH W6 156 D4
Samford St STJWD NW8 9 N2
Samian Ga STALW/RED AL3 37 N8
Samos Rd PGE/AN SE20 204 A2
Samphire Cl CRAWW RH11 283 K10 5
Samphire Ct GRAYS RM17 168 B5
Sampleoak La RGUE GU4 269 H7
Sampson Av BAR EN5 76 G9
Sampson Cl BELV DA17 163 N3 2
Sampsons Gn SLN SL2 128 E5 3
Sampsons Hl AMSS HP7 88 D1
Sampson St WAP E1W 13 P10
Samson St PLSTW E13 141 P4
Samuel Cl HACK E8 7 M5
NWCR SE14 160 C5
WOOL/PLUM SE18 162 B3
Samuel St WOOL/PLUM SE18 162 C3
Sancroft Cl CRICK NW2 116 E8
Sancroft Rd KTN/HRWW/W HA3 94 E10
Sancroft St LBTH SE11 17 P7
Sanctuary Cl DART DA1 187 K2
DEN/HRF UB9 91 M8
Sanctuary Rd STWL/WRAY TW19 174 B2
Sanctuary St STHWK SE1 18 F2
The Sanctuary BXLY DA5 185 N2
WEST SW1P 17 K3
Sandall Cl EA W5 135 K6
Sandall Rd EA W5 135 K6
KTTN NW5 5 H2
Sandalls Spring HHW HP1 35 J4
Sandal Rd NWMAL KT3 200 B4
UED N18 99 P6
Sandal St SRTFD E15 141 K3
Sandalwood GUW GU2 267 N1 2
Sandalwood Av CHERT KT16 194 G10
Sandalwood Cl WCHPL E1 140 D6 1
Sandalwood Dr RSLP HA4 112 D5 2
Sandalwood Rd FELT TW13 175 J6
Sanday Cl HHS/BOV HP3 36 C8
Sandbach Pl WOOL/PLUM SE18 162 F4
Sandbanks Hl RDART DA2 189 H9
Sandbourne Av WIM/MER SW19 201 L3
Sandbourne Rd BROCKY SE4 160 D8
Sandbrook Cl MLHL NW7 96 A7 3
Sandbrook Rd STNW/STAM N16 119 M8
Sandby Gn ELTH/MOT SE9 162 B9 1
Sandcliff Rd ERITH DA8 164 E3
Sandcroft Cl PLMGR N13 99 J7 2
Sandcross La REIG RH2 275 J3
Sandell's Av ASHF TW15 174 D7
Sandell St STHWK SE1 18 A1
Sandelswood End BEAC HP9 88 C6
Sanders Cl HPTN TW12 176 B8 6
LCOL/BKTW AL2 57 J3
Sandersfield Rd BNSTD SM7 239 K1
Sanders La MLHL NW7 96 F8
Sanderson Cl KTTN NW5 118 C9 5
RBRW/HUT CM13 127 P4 1
Sanderson Rd UX/CGN UB8 131 M1
Sandersons Av RSEV TN14 228 B6 1
Sanders Rd HHS/BOV HP3 36 A9
Sanderstead Av CRICK NW2 117 H7
Sanderstead Cl BAL SW12 180 D3
Sanderstead Court Av
SAND/SEL CR2 223 P9
Sanderstead Hl SAND/SEL CR2 223 M7
Sanderstead Rd LEY E10 120 D6
SAND/SEL CR2 223 L4
STMC/STPC BR5 207 L6 1
Sandes Pl LHD/OX KT22 236 F4
Sandfield Gdns THHTH CR7 203 J3
Sandfield Pl THHTH CR7 203 K3 1
Sandfield Rd STAL AL1 38 F6
THHTH CR7 203 J3
Sandfields RPLY/SEND GU23 232 G10
Sandfield Ter GU GU1 268 A1 2
Sandford Av LOU IG10 82 F7
WDGN N22 99 J9
Sandford Rd BXLYHS DA6 163 P10
EHAM E6 142 C5
HAYES BR2 205 M4
Sandford Rw WALW SE17 18 G7
Sandford St FUL/PGN SW6 157 L6 7
Sandgate Cl ROMW/RG RM7 124 D5
Sandgate La WAND/EARL SW18 179 P4
Sandgate Rd WELL DA16 163 M6
Sandgate St PECK SE15 160 A5
Sandhills WLGTN SM6 222 E1
Sandhills Ct VW GU25 194 B5
Sandhills La VW GU25 194 B5
Sandhills Rd REIG RH2 275 K2
Sandhurst Av BRYLDS KT5 199 N7
RYLN/HDSTN HA2 114 A4
Sandhurst Cl CDALE/KGS NW9 115 M1 2
SAND/SEL CR2 223 M5
Sandhurst Ct HARP AL5 20 C5 7
Sandhurst Dr GDMY/SEVK IG3 123 J9
Sandhurst Rd BFN/LL DA15 185 J6
BXLY DA5 185 N1
CAT SE6 183 J4
CDALE/KGS NW9 115 M1
ED N9 80 B10
ORP BR6 207 K10
TIL RM18 168 F8
Sandhurst Wy SAND/SEL CR2 223 M4
Sandifield HAT AL10 40 E7
Sandiford Rd CHEAM SM3 201 J9
Sandiland Crs HAYES BR2 205 L9
Sandilands CROY/NA CR0 203 P10
SEV TN13 246 E8
Sandilands Rd FUL/PGN SW6 157 L7
Sandison St PECK SE15 159 P9 2
Sandlands Gv
KWD/TDW/WH KT20 238 D9
Sandlands Rd
KWD/TDW/WH KT20 238 D9
Sandland St GINN WC1R 11 P4
Sandlers End SLN SL2 128 G6
Sandling Ri ELTH/MOT SE9 184 D6
Sandlings Cl PECK SE15 160 A8 7
Sandmere Cl HHNE HP2 36 B7 5
Sandmere Rd CLAP SW4 158 F10
Sandon Cl ESH/CLAY KT10 198 C7
Sandon Pl CHONG CM5 67 P6
Sandon Rd CHES/WCR EN8 62 B6
Sandow Crs HYS/HAR UB3 152 G2 4
Sandown Av DAGE RM10 144 D1
ESH/CLAY KT10 218 B2
HCH RM12 125 L7
Sandown Cl HEST TW5 153 H7
Sandown Ct DAGE RM10 144 D1 3
Sandown Dr CAR SM5 222 B5 2
Sandown Ga ESH/CLAY KT10 198 C9
Sandown Rd COUL/CHIP CR5 240 B2
ESH/CLAY KT10 218 B1
GVE DA12 190 F9
SL SL1 128 E7 1
SNWD SE25 204 A5
WATN WD24 73 K4
Sandown Wy NTHLT UB5 133 M1
Sandpiper Cl BERM/RHTH SE16 160 E1 3
CRAWW RH11 282 G9 4
WALTH E17 100 C8 1
Sandpiper Dr ERITH DA8 165 J6
Sandpiper Rd SAND/SEL CR2 224 C7
The Sandpipers GVE DA12 190 G5
Sandpiper Wy STMC/STPC BR5 207 N4
Sandpit Hall Rd CHOB/PIR GU24 213 M8
Sandpit Heath RGUW GU3 249 J6
Sandpit La BRW CM14 86 E10
STAL AL1 38 E5
Sandpit Pl CHARL SE7 162 B4
Sandpit Rd BMLY BR1 183 K8
REDH RH1 275 P1
WGCE AL7 23 H7
Sandpits Rd CROY/NA CR0 224 C1
RCHPK/HAM TW10 177 J5
Sandra Cl HSLW TW3 176 A1 4
WDGN N22 99 K9 1
Sandridgebury La STALW/RED AL3 20 G9
STALW/RED AL3 38 D2
Sandridge Cl HRW HA1 114 D2
Sandridge Rd STAL AL1 38 D4
Sandringham Av
HLWW/ROY CM19 46 B1
RYNPK SW20 201 H1
Sandringham Cl EN EN1 79 M6
WIM/MER SW19 178 G4 4
WOKS/MYFD GU22 233 K2
Sandringham Ct SL SL1 128 C8
Sandringham Crs
RYLN/HDSTN HA2 113 P8
STALE/WH AL4 38 G1
Sandringham Dr ASHF TW15 173 N7
WELL DA16 163 H8
Sandringham Gdns
BARK/HLT IG6 122 F1
CEND/HSY/T N8 118 F4 4
HEST TW5 153 H7 2
NFNCH/WDSP N12 97 N7
Sandringham Pk COB KT11 217 N8
Sandringham Rd BARK IG11 143 J1
BMLY BR1 183 M8
BRWN CM15 86 G9
CRICK NW2 116 E10
CROY/NA CR0 203 K5
FSTGT E7 121 P10
GLDGN NW11 117 H5
HACK E8 119 N10
LEY E10 121 J5
NTHLT UB5 133 P2
POTB/CUF EN6 59 L6 5
WATN WD24 73 J3
WDGN N22 119 K1
WPK KT4 200 D10
Sandringham Wy CHES/WCR EN8 62 B10
Sandrock Pl CROY/NA CR0 224 C1
Sandrock Rd DORK RH4 272 A4
LEW SE13 160 F9
Sandroyd Wy COB KT11 217 P9 1
Sands End La FUL/PGN SW6 157 L7
Sands Farm Dr SL SL1 128 B6
Sandstone Rd LEE/GVPK SE12 183 N5
Sands Wy WFD IG8 102 C7 7
Sandtoft Rd CHARL SE7 161 N5
Sandway Rd STMC/STPC BR5 207 M4
Sandwell Crs KIL/WHAMP NW6 2 F1
Sandwich St STPAN WC1H 5 L10
Sandwick Cl MLHL NW7 96 D8
Sandy Bank Rd GVE DA12 190 E4
Sandy Bury ORP BR6 206 G10
Sandy Cl HERT/WAS SG14 25 J5
WOKS/MYFD GU22 232 F3
Sandycombe Rd
EBED/NFELT TW14 175 H4
RCH/KEW TW9 155 M8
Sandycoombe Rd TWK TW1 177 H2
Sandy Ct COB KT11 217 N9
Sandycroft ABYW SE2 163 K5
Sandy Cft EW KT17 220 F6
Sandycroft Rd AMS HP6 69 N5
Sandy Dr COB KT11 217 P7
EBED/NFELT TW14 174 F4
Sandy Hill Av WOOL/PLUM SE18 162 E4 2
Sandy Hill La WOOL/PLUM SE18 162 E3
Sandyhill Rd IL IG1 122 E9
Sandy Hill Rd WLGTN SM6 222 D5 3
WOOL/PLUM SE18 162 E4
Sandy Holt COB KT11 217 N9
Sandy La ASC SL5 192 F5
BELMT SM2 221 H5
BH/WHM TN16 262 G1
BRKHM/BTCW RH3 256 B10
BUSH WD23 74 B7
CDH/CHF RM16 168 E5
CHOB/PIR GU24 213 K5
COB KT11 217 N8
CRAWE RH10 285 P5
E/WMO/HCT KT8 198 G1
KTN/HRWW/W HA3 115 L4
KWD/TDW/WH KT20 239 J10
MEO DA13 189 K7
MTCM CR4 202 B1
NTHWD HA6 92 G3
ORP BR6 207 K7
OXTED RH8 261 H5
OXTED RH8 261 N3
RCHPK/HAM TW10 177 H5
RDART DA2 189 J6
REDH RH1 258 F10
REDH RH1 259 J8
REIG RH2 274 E1
RGUW GU3 248 C7
RGUW GU3 267 M5
RPLY/SEND GU23 232 F9
SEV TN13 247 K9
SHGR GU5 269 N7
SHGR GU5 270 B6
SOCK/AV RM15 145 P9
STMC/STPC BR5 185 N10
TEDD TW11 176 F10
VW GU25 194 B5
WOKS/MYFD GU22 232 E4
WOKS/MYFD GU22 233 K2
WOT/HER KT12 197 J6
WTHK RM20 166 G5
Sandy La North WLGTN SM6 222 E2
Sandy Lodge La NTHWD HA6 92 E3
Sandy Lodge Rd
RKW/CH/CXG WD3 92 C3
Sandy Lodge Wy NTHWD HA6 92 F6
Sandymount Av STAN HA7 95 H6
Sandy Rdg CHST BR7 184 D9
Sandy Ri CFSP/GDCR SL9 90 B9
Sandy Rd ADL/WDHM KT15 215 K3
GLDGN NW11 117 L7
HAMP NW3 117 L7
Sandy's Rw WCHPL E1 13 K4
Sandy Wy COB KT11 217 P8
CROY/NA CR0 204 E10
WOKS/MYFD GU22 232 F3
WOT/HER KT12 196 G8
Sanford La STNW/STAM N16 119 N7 5
STNW/STAM N16 119 N7 5
Sanford St NWCR SE14 160 D5
Sanford Ter STNW/STAM N16 119 N8
Sanger Av CHSGTN KT9 219 L2
Sanger Dr RPLY/SEND GU23 232 F8
Sangers Dr HORL RH6 280 A5
Sangley Rd SNWD SE25 203 M4
Sangora Rd BTSEA SW11 157 N10 4
Sansom Rd WAN E11 121 L7 1
Sansom St CMBW SE5 159 L6
Sans Wk CLKNW EC1R 12 C1
Santers La POTB/CUF EN6 59 H9
Santley St BRXS/STRHM SW2 158 F10
Santos Rd PUT/ROE SW15 179 K1
Sanway Cl BF/WBF KT14 215 P10
Sanway Rd BF/WBF KT14 215 P10
Sapho Pk GVE DA12 191 J7
Saphora Cl ORP BR6 226 G2 1
Sappers Cl SBW CM21 30 A1
Sapphire Cl BCTR RM8 123 M6 5
Sapphire Rd DEPT SE8 160 D3
Sappho Ct WOKN/KNAP GU21 231 K2 2
Saracen Cl CROY/NA CR0 203 L6
Saracens Head HHNE HP2 36 B5 1
Saracen St POP/IOD E14 140 F8
Sara Crs GRH DA9 166 F10
Sarah St BETH E2 7 K9
Sara Pk GVE DA12 191 H7 1
Saratoga Rd CLPT E5 120 B9
Sardinia St HOL/ALD WC2B 11 N6
Sarel Wy HORL RH6 280 C2
Sargeants Cl UX/CGN UB8 131 N5 1
Sarita Cl KTN/HRWW/W HA3 94 C10
Sark Cl HEST TW5 153 P6
Sarnesfield Rd ENC/FH EN2 79 L7 2
Sarratt Av HHNE HP2 36 B1
Sarratt La RKW/CH/CXG WD3 71 L6
Sarratt Rd RKW/CH/CXG WD3 71 L3
Sarre Av HCH RM12 145 K1 6
Sarre Rd CRICK NW2 117 J10
Sarsby Dr STWL/WRAY TW19 172 D5
Sarsen Av HSLW TW3 153 N8
Sarsfeld Rd BAL SW12 180 A4
Sarsfield Rd GFD/PVL UB6 134 G4
Sartor Rd PECK SE15 160 C10
Sarum Gn WEY KT13 196 F10
Sarum Pl HHNE HP2 35 P2
Satanita Cl CAN/RD E16 142 A8
Satchell Md CDALE/KGS NW9 96 C9
Satchwell Rd BETH E2 7 N10 1
Satinwood Ct HHS/BOV HP3 35 P8 1
Saturn Cl CRAWW RH11 283 H9 8
Saturn Wy HHNE HP2 36 A3
Sauls Gn WAN E11 121 K8 8
Sauncey Av HARP AL5 20 A1
Saunders Cl CHES/WCR EN8 62 B4
CRAWE RH10 284 C7
GVW DA11 190 B5
Saunders Copse
WOKS/MYFD GU22 231 N8
Saunders End AMS HP6 50 B10
Saunders La WOKS/MYFD GU22 231 L8

Saunders Ness Rd POP/IOD E14 .... 161 J3
Saunders Rd HGDN/ICK UB10 ... 132 A2
Saunders St LBTH SE11 .... 18 A5
Saunders Wy DART DA1 .... 187 N5
  THMD SE28 .... 143 L9
Saunton Av ALP/SUD HA0 .... 114 G10
Saunton Rd HYS/HAR UB3 ... 152 C6
Saunton Rd HCM RM12 .... 125 H7
Savage Gdns EHAM E6 .... 142 G8
  TWRH EC3N 13 K7
Savay La DEN/HRF UB9 .... 111 K3
Savay La DEN/HRF UB9 .... 111 K5
Savernake Rd ED N9 .... 79 P10
  HAMP NW3 .... 118 A3
Savernake Wk CRAWE RH10 ... 284 A10
Savile CI NWMAL KT3 .... 200 B5
Savile CI THHTH CR7 .... 198 E1
Savile Rw CONDST W1S 10 G7
Savill CI CHESW EN7 .... 61 K1
Saville Crs ASHF TW15 ...... 174 E9
Saville Rd CAN/RD E16 ...... 142 B10
  CHDH RM6 .... 124 A4
  CHSWK W4 .... 156 A2
  TWK TW1 .... 176 E4
Saville Rw HAYES BR2 .... 205 L8
Savill Gdns RYNPK SW20 .... 200 D3
Savill Rw WFD IG8 .... 101 L7
Savona St VX/NE SW8 .... 158 D6
Savoy Av HYES UB3 .... 152 C6
Savoy CI DEN/HRF UB9 ...... 91 N10
  EDGW HA8 .... 95 M6
  SRTFD E15 .... 141 K3
Savoy Ct TPL/STR WC2R 11 M8
Savoy HI TPL/STR WC2R 11 M8
Savoy PI CHCR WC2N 11 M8
Savoy Rd DART DA1 .... 187 L3
Savoy Rw TPL/STR WC2R 11 N7
Savoy St TPL/STR WC2R 11 N7
Savoy Wy TPL/STR WC2R 11 N7
Savoy Wd EPP CM16 .... 46 E7
Sawbill CI YEAD UB4 .... 133 L7
Sawells BROX EN10 .... 44 E7
Sawkins CI WIM/MER SW19 ... 178 G5
Sawley Rd SHB W12 .... 139 J6
Sawtry CI CAR SM5 .... 201 N7
Sawtry Wy BORE WD6 .... 75 M4
Sawyer CI ED N9 .... 99 P5
Sawyer's CI WDSR SL4 ...... 148 D6
Sawyer's Hall La BRWN CM15 . 117 F1
Sawyers La POTB/CUF EN6 ... 58 G10
Sawyers Lawn WEA W13 ..... 134 E8
Sawyer St STHWK SE1 .... 18 F1
Sawyers Wy HHNE HP2 ...... 36 A6
Saxby Rd BRXS/STRHM SW2 .. 180 D7
Saxham Rd BARK IG11 .... 143 H3
Saxley HORL RH6 .... 280 C3
Saxlingham Rd CHING E4 .... 101 J4
Saxon Av FELT TW13 .... 175 N6
Saxonbury Av SUN TW16 .... 197 J3
Saxonbury CI MTCM CR4 .... 201 N3
Saxonbury Gdns SURB KT6 ... 199 H8
Saxon CI AMS HP6 .... 69 J3
  DTCH/LGLY SL3 .... 150 C1
  GVW DA11 .... 189 P6
  HARH RM3 .... 105 N10
  RBRW/HUT CM13 .... 107 M4
  RSEV TN14 .... 246 G3
  SURB KT6 .... 199 J6
  UX/CGN UB8 .... 131 P7
  WALTH E17 .... 120 F5
Saxon Ct BORE WD6 .... 75 K5
Saxon Dr ACT W3 .... 115 N8
Saxonfield CI BRXS/STRHM SW2 180 G3
Saxon PI EYN DA4 .... 210 B5
Saxon Rd ASHF TW15 .... 174 A5
  BMLY BR1 .... 183 L10
  BOW E3 .... 140 E4
  CRAWE RH10 .... 284 F8
  CROY/NA CR0 .... 203 L6
  EHAM E6 .... 142 C6
  IL IG1 .... 142 A3
  RDART DA2 .... 187 M7
  STALE/WH AL4 .... 21 J4
  STHL UB1 .... 133 M9
  WBLY HA9 .... 115 P8
  WOT/HER KT12 .... 197 L10
Saxons KWD/TDW/WH KT20 .. 238 G7
Saxon Shore Wy GVE DA12 .. 190 F2
Saxon Wy REIG RH2 .... 257 J9
  STHGT/OAK N14 .... 78 E10
  WDR/YW UB7 .... 151 M5
  WDSR SL4 .... 171 N2
Saxony Pde HYS/HAR UB3 ... 132 D7
Saxton CI LEW SE13 .... 161 J9
Saxville Rd STMC/STPC BR5 . 207 L3
Sayer CI GRH DA9 .... 188 F1
Sayers CI LHD/OX KT22 ..... 236 B10
Sayers La RAIN RM13 .... 144 C9
Sayesbury Rd SBW CM21 .... 29 P1
Sayes Ct ADL/WDHM KT15 ... 215 L2
Sayes Court Farm Dr
  ADL/WDHM KT15 .... 215 L2
Sayes Court Rd STMC/STPC BR5 207 K3
Sayes Court St DEPT SE8 ... 160 K4
Sayes Gdns SBW CM21 ...... 30 A1
Sayward CI CSHM HP5 ...... 51 J5
Scabharbour Rd RSEV TN14 .. 265 K9
Scadbury Gdns STMC/STPC BR5 207 K2
Scads Hill CI ORP BR6 ...... 207 J2
Scafell Rd SL SL1 .... 128 E7
Scala St FITZ W1T 11 H3
Scales Rd TOTM N17 .... 119 N1
Scallows CI CRAWE RH10 .... 284 B6
Scallows Rd CRAWE RH10 .... 284 B6
Scammell Wy WATW WD18 ... 72 G10
Scandrett St WAP E1W 140 A10
Scarborough CI BELMT SM2 .. 221 J6
  BH/WHM TN16 .... 243 P4
Scarborough Rd ED N9 ..... 100 B1
  FSBYPK N4 .... 119 H5
  WAN E11 .... 121 J6
Scarborough St WCHPL E1 .. 13 M6
Scarborough Wy SL SL1 ..... 148 G10
Scarbrook Rd CROY/NA CR0 . 203 K10
Scarle Rd ALP/SUD HA0 ..... 135 J1
Scarlet CI STMC/STPC BR5 .. 207 L4
Scarlet Rd CAT SE6 .... 183 K6
Scarlett CI WOKN/KNAP GU21 231 L4
Scarsbrook Rd BKHTH/KID SE3 162 A9
Scarsdale PI KENS W8 ...... 14 C5
Scarsdale Rd RYLN/HDSTN HA2 114 B10
Scarsdale Vls KENS W8 ..... 14 A4
Scarth Rd BARN SW13 ...... 156 C9
Scatterdells La KGLGY WD4 . 53 J6
Scawen CI CAR SM5 .... 222 B1
Scawen Rd DEPT SE8 .... 160 A4
Scawfell St BETH E2 .... 7 M8
Scaynes Link NFNCH/WDSP N12 97 K5
Sceptre Rd BETH E2 .... 140 F2
Scholars Ms WGCW AL8 ..... 22 G4
Scholars Rd BAL SW12 ...... 180 C4
  CHING E4 .... 101 J2
Scholars Wk AMS HP6 ...... 69 L4
Scholefield Rd ARCH N19 ... 118 D9
Schonfeld Sq STNW/STAM N16 119 L6
School CI BRKMPK AL9 ...... 42 D1
  CHOB/PIR GU24 .... 230 E1
  DART DA1 .... 168 G10
  GU GU1 .... 250 A9
Schoolfield Rd WTHK RM20 . 166 F5
School Green La EPP CM16 .. 66 D1

School HI REDH RH1 .... 258 D4
School House La TEDD TW11 . 176 G10
Schoolhouse La WAP E1W 140 C9
School La ADL/WDHM KT15 .. 215 L6
  AMSS HP7 .... 68 F5
  AMSS HP7 .... 68 A9
  BEAC HP9 .... 89 J7
  BFOR GU20 .... 212 C3
  BGR/WK TN15 .... 247 N7
  BRKMPK AL9 .... 42 A3
  BUSH WD23 .... 94 A1
  CFSP/GDCR SL9 .... 90 A10
  CHIG IG7 .... 103 J5
  CHOB/PIR GU24 .... 230 D8
  CHONG SM5 .... 48 E3
  DORK RH4 .... 272 C3
  EGH TW20 .... 172 D8
  EHSLY KT24 .... 252 F1
  EYN DA4 .... 210 E6
  HAT AL10 .... 40 E3
  HLW CM20 .... 29 H9
  KUT KT1 .... 199 H1
  LCOL/BKTW AL2 .... 55 N10
  LHD/OX KT22 .... 236 C3
  PIN HA5 .... 113 M2
  RBRW/HUT CM13 .... 107 P7
  RDART DA2 .... 189 H6
  RDKG RH5 .... 255 H5
  RGUE GU4 .... 251 P7
  RGUW GU3 .... 266 B5
  RPLY/SEND GU23 .... 234 C8
  SHPTN TW17 .... 196 C6
  SLN SL2 .... 129 N2
  SURB KT6 .... 199 L8
  SWLY BR8 .... 187 J10
  WELL DA16 .... 163 L9
  WLYN AL6 .... 23 J7
School Md ABLGY WD5 ...... 54 E8
School Pas KUT KT1 .... 199 L2
  STHL UB1 .... 133 N10
School Rd ASC SL5 .... 192 C5
  ASHF TW15 .... 174 C9
  BRWN CM15 .... 86 D3
  CHONG SM5 .... 66 G6
  CHST BR7 .... 206 F1
  DAGE RM10 .... 144 B3
  E/WMO/HCT KT8 .... 198 C4
  GVE DA12 .... 190 F6
  HPTN TW12 .... 176 B9
  HSLW TW3 .... 154 F9
  KUT KT1 .... 199 H1
  POTB/CUF EN6 .... 59 H4
  WDR/YW UB7 .... 151 N5
  WLSDN NW10 .... 136 A6
School Rw HHW HP1 .... 35 J7
School Wy BCTR RM8 .... 123 L8
Schoolway NFNCH/WDSP N12 . 97 N7
Schooner Ct GRH DA9 ...... 166 B10
Schroder Ct EGH TW20 ...... 171 N9
Schubert Rd BORE WD6 ..... 75 J10
  PUT/ROE SW15 .... 179 J1
Scillonian Rd GUW GU2 .... 267 M2
Sclater St WCHPL E1 .... 13 L1
Scoles Crs BRXS/STRHM SW2 . 181 H4
Scords La BH/WHM TN16 .... 263 M8
Scoresby St STHWK SE1 ..... 12 C10
Scorton Av GFD/PVL UB6 ... 134 F4
Scory CI CRAWW RH11 ...... 283 K10
Scotch Common WEA W13 ... 134 F7
Scot Gv PIN HA5 .... 93 L8
Scotia Rd BRXS/STRHM SW2 . 181 H3
Scotland Bridge Rd
  ADL/WDHM KT15 .... 215 N7
Scotland Gn TOTM N17 ..... 99 N10
Scotland Green Rd PEND EN3 80 C9
Scotland Green Rd North
  PEND EN3 .... 80 C8
Scotland La BKHH IG9 ...... 101 J7
Scotlands Dr SLN SL2 ...... 128 G1
Scots CI STWL/WRAY TW19 .. 173 N4
Scotscraig RAD WD7 .... 74 E1
Scotsdale Rd BELMT SM2 ... 221 H4
  CHST BR7 .... 207 H4
Scotsdale Rd LEE/GVPK SE12 183 N1
Scotshall La WARL CR6 ..... 243 H1
Scots HI RKW/CH/CXG WD3 .. 72 A10
Scots Hill CI RKW/CH/CXG WD3 72 A10
Scots Mill La RKW/CH/CXG WD3 72 A10
Scotswood CI BEAC HP9 .... 88 C6
Scotswood St CLKNW EC1R .. 12 B1
Scott Av WARE SG12 .... 26 C7
Scott CI GUW GU2 .... 249 M8
  HOR/WEW KT19 .... 219 P2
  SLN SL2 .... 109 H10
  STRHM/NOR SW16 .... 202 A3
  WDR/YW UB7 .... 152 A3
Scott Crs ERITH DA8 .... 164 C10
  RYLN/HDSTN HA2 .... 114 A6
Scott Ellis Gdns STJWD NW8 . 3 L10
Scottes La BCTR RM8 ...... 123 N6
Scott Farm CI THDIT KT7 ... 198 C8
Scott Gdns HEST TW5 ...... 153 L6
Scott Lidgett Crs
  BERM/RHTH SE16 .... 19 N2
Scott Rd CDH/CHF RM16 .... 168 D5
  CRAWE RH10 .... 284 A10
  GVE DA12 .... 190 G8
  SUN TW16 .... 174 F10
Scotts Av HAYES BR2 ...... 205 J2
  SUN TW16 .... 174 F10
Scotts CI HCH RM12 .... 125 K10
  WARE SG12 .... 26 C3
Scotts Dr HPTN TW12 ...... 176 A10
Scotts Farm Rd HOR/WEW KT19 219 P3
Scott's Grove CI CHOB/PIR GU24 212 E10
Scott's Grove Rd CHOB/PIR GU24 212 G10
Scott's HI HORL RH6 .... 281 L5
Scott's La HAYES BR2 ...... 205 J3
Scotts Rd BMLY BR1 .... 183 M10
  LEY E10 .... 121 H6
  NWDGN UB2 .... 153 M2
  SHB W12 .... 157 J1
  WARE SG12 .... 26 E1
Scott St WCHPL E1 .... 140 C1
Scotts Vw WGCW AL8 ...... 22 F6
Scotts Wy SEV TN13 .... 246 F8
  SUN TW16 .... 174 F10
Scottswood Rd BUSH WD23 . 73 M6
Scott Trimmer Wy HEST TW5 153 M8
Scottwell Dr CDALE/KGS NW9 116 C3
Scoulding Rd CAN/RD E16 .. 141 L8
Scouler St POP/IOD E14 .... 161 N3
Scout La CLAP SW4 .... 158 D9
Scout Wy MLHL NW7 .... 96 A5
Scovell Rd STHWK SE1 ..... 18 E2
Scratchers La EYN DA4 .... 210 C10
Scriveners CI HHNE HP2 .... 35 P6
Scrivenrs Ct HACK E8 ...... 7 M5
Scrooby St CAT SE6 .... 182 G2
Scrubbits Sq RAD WD7 ..... 74 F1
Scrubbits Park Rd RAD WD7 . 74 F1
Scrutton CI SDTCH SE2A 13 L1
Scudders HI HART SG14 .... 211 H6
Scutari Rd EDUL SE22 ..... 182 A1
Scylla Crs HTHAIR TW6 .... 174 C3
Scylla Rd HTHAIR TW6 ..... 174 C2
  PECK SE15 .... 160 A9
Seabourne Rd CDH/CHF RM16 168 F2
Seabright St BETH E2 ...... 140 D2
Seabrook Dr WWKM BR4 .... 205 H3
Seabrook Gdns ROMW/RG RM7 123 N6
Seabrook Rd BCTR RM8 ..... 123 N6
  KGLGY WD4 .... 54 C4
Seaburn Rd RAIN RM13 .... 144 F5
Seacole CI ACT W3 .... 136 A8

Seacourt Rd ABYW SE2 ..... 163 N1
  DTCH/LGLY SL3 .... 150 A3
Seacroft Gdns OXHEY WD19 . 93 L4
Seafield Rd FBAR/BDGN N11 98 E5
Seaford CI RSLP HA4 .... 112 E6
Seaford Rd EN EN1 .... 79 M8
  SEVS/STOTM N15 .... 119 L3
  WALTH E17 .... 120 E1
  WEA W13 .... 134 G10
Seaforth Av NWMAL KT3 ... 200 F5
Seaforth Crs HBRY N5 ..... 119 K10
Seaforth Dr CHES/WCR EN8 . 62 C10
Seaforth Gdns HOR/WEW KT19 220 C1
  WCHMH N21 .... 98 G3
  WFD IG8 .... 101 P6
Seager PI BOW E3 .... 140 E7
Seagrave Rd FUL/PGN SW6 . 14 B9
Seagry Rd WAN E11 .... 121 M4
Sealand Rd HTHW TW6 ..... 174 B2
Seal Dr BGR/WK TN15 ...... 247 N7
Seal Hollow Rd SEV TN13 .. 247 K10
Seal Rd SEV TN13 .... 247 L7
Seal St HACK E8 .... 119 N9
  HACK E8 .... 7 L1
Seaman CI LCOL/BKTW AL2 . 56 C1
Searches La ABLGY WD5 .... 55 J3
  HHS/BOV HP3 .... 55 J3
Searchwood Rd WARL CR6 . 242 A4
Searle HI REIG RH2 .... 275 K2
Searles CI BTSEA SW11 .... 157 P6
Searles Rd STHWK SE1 ..... 19 L5
Sears St CMBW SE5 .... 159 L6
Seasprite CI NTHLT UB5 .... 133 L5
Seaton Av ASHF TW15 ..... 173 P5
Seaton Dr ASHF TW15 ..... 173 P5
Seaton Gdns RSLP HA4 .... 113 H8
Seaton Rd ALP/SUD HA0 ... 135 K4
  DART DA1 .... 187 H3
  HHS/BOV HP3 .... 35 N9
  HYS/HAR UB3 .... 152 E3
  LCOL/BKTW AL2 .... 57 J3
  MTCM CR4 .... 201 P2
  WELL DA16 .... 163 N6
  WHTN TW2 .... 176 B2
Seaton St UED N18 .... 99 P6
Sebastian Av BRWN CM15 .. 87 M10
Sebastian St FSBYE EC1V .. 6 D10
Sebastopol Rd ED N9 ...... 99 P7
Sebbon St IS N1 .... 6 D1
Sebergham Gv MLHL NW7 .. 96 D3
Sebert Rd FSTGT E7 .... 121 N10
Sebright Rd BAR EN5 ...... 76 C6
  HHW HP1 .... 35 K8
Secker Crs KTN/HRWW/W HA3 94 B9
Secker St STHWK SE1 ...... 12 A11
Second Av ACT W3 .... 136 C10
  ADL/WDHM KT15 .... 215 J8
  CHDH RM6 .... 123 N3
  DAGE RM10 .... 144 C4
  EN EN1 .... 79 N9
  GSTN WD25 .... 73 L1
  HDN NW4 .... 116 G2
  HLWE CM17 .... 47 L2
  HLWS CM18 .... 47 J1
  HYS/HAR UB3 .... 132 G10
  MNPK E12 .... 122 E9
  MORT/ESHN SW14 .... 156 B9
  NKENS W10 .... 8 B1
  PLSTW E13 .... 141 M5
  UED N18 .... 100 F3
  WALTH E17 .... 120 F3
  WBLY HA9 .... 115 J4
  WOT/HER KT12 .... 197 M6
  WTHK RM20 .... 166 F5
Sedan Wy WALW SE17 ...... 19 J7
Sedcombe CI SCUP DA14 ... 185 M7
Sedcote Rd PEND EN3 ..... 80 B9
Sedding St KTBR SW1X 16 C5
Seddon Rd MRDN SM4 ..... 201 N5
Seddon St FSBYW WC1X 5 N10
Sedgebrook Rd BKHTH/KID SE3 162 A3
Sedgecombe Av
  KTN/HRWW/W HA3 .... 115 H3
Sedgefield CI CRAWE RH10 . 285 P10
  HARH RM3 .... 105 N5
Sedgefield Crs HARH RM3 .. 105 N5
Sedgeford Rd SHB W12 .... 136 C10
Sedge Gn HLWW/ROY CM19 . 45 L5
  WAB EN9 .... 45 K6
Sedgehill Rd CAT SE6 ..... 182 F6
Sedgemere Av EFNCH N2 .. 117 M2
Sedgemere Rd ABYW SE2 .. 163 M2
Sedgemoor Dr DAGE RM10 . 124 B1
Sedge Rd TOTM N17 .... 100 B8
Sedgeway CAT SE6 .... 183 J5
Sedgewick CI CRAWE RH10 . 284 D7
Sedgmoor PI CMBW SE5 .... 159 M6
Sedgwick Av HGDN/ICK UB10 132 C2
Sedgwick Rd LEY E10 ...... 121 P6
Sedgwick St HOM E9 ...... 120 C10
Sedleigh Rd WAND/EARL SW18 179 J2
Sedlescombe Rd FUL/PGN SW6 14 C10
Sedley MEO DA13 .... 189 M8
Sedley Gv DEN/HRF UB9 ... 111 M2
Sedley Ri LOU IG10 .... 82 C6
Sedum CI CDALE/KGS NW9 .. 115 P3
Seeley Dr DUL SE21 .... 181 M7
Seeleys HLWE CM17 .... 29 M7
Seeleys Rd BEAC HP9 ..... 88 B7
Seelig Av CDALE/KGS NW9 . 116 D5
Seely Rd TOOT SW17 ...... 180 C1
Seer Green La BEAC HP9 ... 89 K8
Seer Md BEAC HP9 .... 89 J7
Seething La TWRH EC3N 13 K7
Seething Wells La SURB KT6 199 H6
Sefton Av KTN/HRWW/W HA3 94 C10
  MLHL NW7 .... 96 A4
Sefton CI CHOB/PIR GU24 .. 212 D9
  SLN SL2 .... 129 L3
  STAL/AL1 .... 38 E5
  STMC/STPC BR5 .... 207 J4
Sefton Paddock SLN SL2 ... 129 M2
Sefton Rd CROY/NA CR0 .... 203 P8
  HOR/WEW KT19 .... 220 A6
  STMC/STPC BR5 .... 207 J4
Sefton St PUT/ROE SW15 .. 156 F8
Segal CI FSTH SE23 .... 162 A1
Segrave CI KTT KT13 ...... 216 A9
Sekforde St CLKNW EC1R ... 6 C12
Sekhon Ter FELT TW13 .... 175 P6
Selah Dr SWLY BR8 .... 208 D1
Selan Gdns YEAD UB4 ..... 133 J4
Selbie Av WLSDN NW10 .... 116 C10
Selborne Av BXLY DA5 ..... 185 M4
  MNPK E12 .... 122 G6
Selborne Gdns GFD/PVL UB6 134 F4
  HDN NW4 .... 116 A1
Selborne Rd CMBW SE5 .... 159 L8
  CROY/NA CR0 .... 203 M10
  IL IG1 .... 122 D10
  NWMAL KT3 .... 200 B10
  SCUP DA14 .... 185 L7
  STHGT/OAK N14 .... 98 F4
  WALTH E17 .... 119 P4
  WDGN N22 .... 98 G9
Selbourne Av ADL/WDHM KT15 215 L6
  SURB KT6 .... 199 L9

Selbourne CI ADL/WDHM KT15 215 L6
  CRAWE RH10 .... 284 C2
Selbourne Rd GU GU1 ...... 250 D7
Selbourne Sq GDST RH9 ... 280 B6
Selby Av STAL/WH/RED AL3 . 38 C6
Selby Cha RSLP HA4 .... 113 J7
Selby CI CHSGTN KT9 ...... 219 K4
  CHST BR7 .... 184 D9
Selby Gdns UT STHL UB1 ... 133 P6
Selby Gn CAR SM5 .... 201 P7
Selby Rd ASHF TW15 ...... 174 D9
  CAR SM5 .... 201 P7
  EA W5 .... 134 G6
  PGE/AN SE20 .... 203 P2
  PLSTW E13 .... 141 N7
  TOTM N17 .... 99 M7
  WAN E11 .... 121 K8
  WCHPL E1 .... 13 P2
Selby Wk WOKN/KNAP GU21 231 N4
Selcroft Rd PUR/KEN CR8 .. 223 J8
Selden HI HEMS HP2 ...... 35 P5
Selden Rd PECK SE15 ..... 160 B8
Sele MI HERT/WAS SG14 ... 25 J5
Sele Rd HERT/WAS SG14 ... 25 J6
Selham CI CRAWW RH11 ... 283 K6
Selhurst CI WIM/MER SW19 . 178 C4
  WOKN/KNAP GU21 .... 232 C1
Selhurst New Rd SNWD SE25 203 M6
Selhurst PI CROY/NA CR0 .. 203 M6
Selhurst Rd ED N9 .... 99 L4
  SNWD SE25 .... 203 M6
Selinas La BCTR RM8 ...... 123 P5
Selkirk Dr ERITH DA8 ..... 164 F7
Selkirk Rd TOOT SW17 .... 179 P7
  WHTN TW2 .... 176 B5
Sellar's Hall CI FNCH N3 ... 97 K8
Sellers Hall CI FNCH N3 ... 97 K8
Sellincourt Rd TOOT SW17 . 179 P8
Sellindge CI BECK BR3 .... 182 E10
Sellons Av WLSDN NW10 ... 136 C3
Sells Rd WARE SG12 ...... 26 E1
Sellwood Dr BAR EN5 ..... 76 C9
Selsdon Av SAND/SEL CR2 . 223 L3
Selsdon CI CRW RM5 ...... 104 D9
  SURB KT6 .... 199 K5
Selsdon Crs SAND/SEL CR2 . 224 B6
Selsdon Park Rd SAND/SEL CR2 224 D5
Selsdon Rd ADL/WDHM KT15 215 K7
  CRICK NW2 .... 117 J1
  PLSTW E13 .... 141 P3
  SAND/SEL CR2 .... 223 M4
  WAN E11 .... 121 M5
  WNWD SE27 .... 181 J6
Selsea PI STNW/STAM N16 . 119 M10
Selsey Crs WELL DA16 ..... 163 N7
Selsey St POP/IOD E14 .... 140 F7
Selsfield Rd CRAWE RH10 .. 285 P10
Selvage La MLHL NW7 ..... 96 A8
Selway CI PIN HA5 .... 113 J2
Selwood CI STWL/WRAY TW19 173 M2
Selwood Gdns STWL/WRAY TW19 173 M2
Selwood PI SKENS SW7 .... 15 L7
Selwood Rd BRW CM14 .... 106 C4
  CHEAM SM3 .... 201 J8
  CHSGTN KT9 .... 219 J1
  CROY/NA CR0 .... 204 A9
  WOKS/MYFD GU22 .... 232 E6
Selwood Ter SKENS SW7 ... 15 L7
Selworthy CI WAN E11 ..... 121 M3
Selworthy Rd CAT SE6 .... 182 C6
Selwyn Av HSLW TW3 ...... 154 F8
  CHING E4 .... 101 H7
  GDMY/SEVK IG3 .... 123 J4
  HAT AL10 .... 40 C1
  RCH/KEW TW9 .... 155 L9
Selwyn CI CRAWE RH10 .... 284 C4
  HSLWW TW4 .... 153 M10
  WDSR SL4 .... 146 C1
Selwyn Crs HAT AL10 ..... 40 D1
  WELL DA16 .... 163 L9
Selwyn Dr HAT AL10 ...... 40 C1
Selwyn Rd BOW E3 .... 140 E4
  NWMAL KT3 .... 200 A5
  PLSTW E13 .... 141 N3
  TIL RM18 .... 168 C8
  WLSDN NW10 .... 136 B2
Semaphore Rd GU GU1 ..... 7 G6
Semley PI BGVA SW1W 16 D6
Semley Rd STRHM/NOR SW16 202 F2
Semper CI WOKN/KNAP GU21 231 K3
Semper Rd CDH/CHF RM16 . 168 F1
Semphill Rd HHS/BOV HP3 . 35 N6
Senate St PECK SE15 ..... 160 B2
Send Barns La RPLY/SEND GU23 233 H10
Send CI RPLY/SEND GU23 .. 232 F10
Send HI RPLY/SEND GU23 .. 232 F10
Send Marsh Rd RPLY/SEND GU23 233 H1
Send Rd RPLY/SEND GU23 .. 232 F9
Seneca Rd THHTH CR7 ..... 202 D3
Senga Rd MTCM CR4 ...... 202 B8
Senhouse Rd CHEAM SM3 .. 200 G10
Senior St BAY/PAD W2 .... 8 D1
Senlac Rd LEE/GVPK SE12 . 183 N4
Sennen Rd EN EN1 .... 99 N1
Senrab St WCHPL E1 ...... 140 C8
Sentinel CI NTHLT UB5 .... 133 J9
September Wy STAN HA7 ... 94 G7
Sequoia CI BUSH WD23 .... 94 C2
Sequoia Gdns ORP BR6 .... 207 J7
Sequoia PK PIN HA5 ...... 94 A7
Serbin CI WAN E11 .... 121 N5
Sergehill La ABLGY WD5 ... 55 H1
Serle St LINN WC2A 11 P5
Sermon Dr SWLY BR8 ..... 208 D3
Serpentine Rd BAY/PAD W2 . 9 P10
  SEV TN13 .... 247 K9
Service Rd HORL RH6 ..... 280 A7
The Service Rd POTB/CUF EN6 59 K8
Service Route No 1 SRTFD E15 141 J2
Service Route No 3 SRTFD E15 141 J1
Serviden Dr BMLY BR1 .... 184 B5
Setchell Rd STHWK SE1 .... 19 L5
Seth St BERM/RHTH SE16 .. 160 A7
Seton Gdns DAGW RM9 .... 143 M2
Settle Rd HARH RM3 ...... 105 P3
Settles St WCHPL E1 ...... 13 N4
Settrington Rd FUL/PGN SW6 157 L8
Seven Acres CAR SM5 ..... 201 P9
  NTHWD HA6 .... 93 H7
Seven Arches Ap WEY KT13 216 A6
Seven Arches Rd BRW CM14 107 K4
Seven Hills CI WOT/HER KT12 216 F1
Sevenhills Rd IVER SL0 ... 110 E10
Seven Kings Rd GDMY/SEVK IG3 123 H6
Sevenoaks By-pass SEV TN13 246 F2
Sevenoaks CI BELMT SM2 .. 221 K6
  HARH RM3 .... 105 K5
Sevenoaks Rd BROCKY SE4 . 182 C2
  ORP BR6 .... 227 H6
  RSEV TN14 .... 228 A5
  RSEV TN14 .... 265 M1
Sevenoaks Wy STMC/STPC BR5 207 M2
Seven Sisters Rd FSBYPK N4 119 H10
  HOLWY N7 .... 118 C9
  SEVS/STOTM N15 .... 119 L4
Seventh Av HYS/HAR UB3 .. 133 H10
  MNPK E12 .... 122 G9
Severalls Av CSHM HP5 .... 51 L5
Severn TIL RM18 .... 169 L2
Severnake CI POP/IOD E14 . 160 E7
Severn Av GPK RM2 .... 125 J3
Severn Crs DTCH/LGLY SL3 . 150 C4
Severn Dr EN EN1 .... 79 P4

  ESH/CLAY KT10 .... 198 F9
  UPMR RM14 .... 126 C4
  WOT/HER KT12 .... 197 L10
Severn HI HHNE HP2 ...... 35 P3
Severn Rd CRAWE RH10 .... 284 D8
  SOCK/AV RM15 .... 146 B8
Severns Fld EPP CM16 .... 66 E1
Severn Wy GSTN WD25 .... 55 K10
  WLSDN NW10 .... 116 C10
Severus Rd BTSEA SW11 ... 157 P10
Seville Ms IS N1 .... 7 J4
Seville St KTBR SW1X 16 B2
Sevington Rd HDN NW4 ... 116 E4
Sevington St MV/WKIL W9 . 8 G2
Seward Rd BECK BR3 ...... 204 C2
  HNWL W7 .... 154 F1
Sewardstone Rd BETH E2 .. 140 B4
  CHING E4 .... 80 G8
  WAB EN9 .... 63 H10
Sewardstone St WAB EN9 .. 63 H10
Sewardstone Wy WAB EN9 . 81 H2
Seward St FSTGT E7 ...... 12 D1
Sewdley St CLPT E5 ...... 120 C8
Sewell CI STALE/WH AL4 ... 39 K10
Sewell Harris CI HLW CM20 . 29 K8
Sewell Rd ABYW SE2 ..... 163 K1
  THMD SE28 .... 143 M10
Sewells WGCW AL8 .... 23 H2
Sewell St PLSTW E13 ..... 141 M5
Sewill CI HORL RH6 ...... 279 J8
Sextant Av POP/IOD E14 .. 161 J3
Sexton CI CHESW EN7 ..... 61 J1
  RAIN RM13 .... 144 C3
Sexton Rd TIL RM18 ...... 168 C7
Seymer Rd ROM RM1 ...... 124 E1
Seymour Av CTHM CR3 .... 241 K9
  EW KT17 .... 220 E5
  MRDN SM4 .... 200 G7
  TOTM N17 .... 99 P10
Seymour CI E/WMO/HCT KT8 198 B5
  PIN HA5 .... 93 N9
Seymour Crs HHNE HP2 ... 35 P5
Seymour Dr HAYES BR2 .... 206 C8
Seymour Gdns BROCKY SE4 . 160 C9
  BRYLDS KT5 .... 199 L5
  FELT TW13 .... 175 J7
  IL IG1 .... 122 C4
  RSLP HA4 .... 113 L6
  TWK TW1 .... 176 C3
Seymour Ms WEW KT17 .... 220 D6
  MBLAR W1H 10 C3
Seymour PI MBLAR W1H 9 P4
  SNWD SE25 .... 204 A4
  WOKS/MYFD GU22 .... 231 N6
Seymour Rd BERK HP4 .... 33 K3
  CAR SM5 .... 222 B2
  CDH/CHF RM16 .... 167 H2
  CEND/HSY/T N8 .... 119 J3
  CHING E4 .... 100 G2
  CHSWK W4 .... 155 P3
  CSTG HP8 .... 89 P5
  E/WMO/HCT KT8 .... 198 B5
  ED N9 .... 100 A3
  EHAM E6 .... 142 A3
  FNCH N3 .... 97 L8
  GVW DA11 .... 190 C4
  HPTN TW12 .... 176 B8
  KUT KT1 .... 199 J1
  LEY E10 .... 120 E6
  MTCM CR4 .... 202 B7
  SL SL1 .... 149 H1
  STALW/RED AL3 .... 38 D3
  TIL RM18 .... 168 C7
  WAND/EARL SW18 .... 179 J3
  WIM/MER SW19 .... 178 G6
Seymours HLWW/ROY CM19 . 46 C4
Seymour St BAY/PAD W2 .. 9 P6
  CMBW SE5 .... 204 A1
Seymour Ter PGE/AN SE20 . 204 A1
Seymour Vls PGE/AN SE20 . 204 A1
Seymour Wk SWCM DA10 .. 189 K3
  WBPTN SW10 .... 15 J9
Seymour Wy SUN TW16 .... 174 F9
Seyssel St POP/IOD E14 ... 161 J3
Shaa Rd ACT W3 .... 136 D9
Shacklands Rd RSEV TN14 . 228 D7
Shackleford Rd MFD/CHID GU8 250 C10
  WOKS/MYFD GU22 .... 232 D6
Shacklegate La TEDD TW11 . 176 A5
Shackleton CI FSTH SE23 .. 182 A5
Shackleton Rd CRAWE RH10 283 P10
  SL SL1 .... 129 L9
  STHL UB1 .... 133 N9
Shackleton Wy ABLGY WD5 . 55 H8
  WGCE AL7 .... 23 N5
Shacklewell La HACK E8 ... 119 N5
Shacklewell Rd STNW/STAM N16 119 N5
Shacklewell St BETH E2 ... 13 M1
Shackleton Rw HACK E8 .. 119 N5
Shadbolt CI WPK KT4 ..... 200 C1
Shad Thames TWRH EC3N .. 13 L10
Shadwell Dr NTHLT UB5 ... 133 N5
Shadwell Gdns WCHPL E1 .. 140 B9
Shadwell Pierhead WAP E1W 140 B9
Shady Bush CI BUSH WD23 . 94 B1
Shady La WAT WD17 ...... 94 J6
Shaef Wy TEDD TW11 ..... 176 F10
Shafter Rd DAGE RM10 .... 144 D1
Shaftesbury LOU IG10 .... 82 A7
Shaftesbury Av BAR EN5 .. 77 M8
  EBED/NFELT TW14 .... 175 H2
  KTN/HRWW/W HA3 .... 115 J4
  LSQ/SEVD WC2H 11 L5
  MYFR/PICC W1J 10 G8
  NWDGN UB2 .... 153 P3
  PEND EN3 .... 80 C6
  RYLN/HDSTN HA2 .... 114 A6
Shaftesbury Cir
  RYLN/HDSTN HA2 .... 114 B6
Shaftesbury Crs STA TW18 . 173 N10
Shaftesbury Gdns
  WLSDN NW10 .... 136 D9
Shaftesbury La DART DA1 .. 166 A10
Shaftesbury Ms KENS W8 .. 14 A4
Shaftesbury Rd ARCH N19 . 118 F6
  BECK BR3 .... 204 E2
  CAR SM5 .... 201 N7
  CHING E4 .... 101 J2
  CHOB/PIR GU24 .... 230 E2
  CRAWE RH10 .... 284 E9
  EPP CM16 .... 66 E5
  FSTGT E7 .... 141 P2
  LEY E10 .... 120 C4
  LEY E10 .... 120 F6
  RCH/KEW TW9 .... 155 N9
  ROM RM1 .... 124 G4
  UED N18 .... 99 M7
  WAT WD17 .... 73 K7
  WOKS/MYFD GU22 .... 232 E5
The Shaftesburys BARK IG11 142 F4
Shaftesbury St IS N1 ..... 6 F8
Shaftesbury Wy WHTN TW2 176 C6
Shaftesbury Waye YEAD UB4 133 J7
Shafto Ms KTBR SW1X 16 A4
Shafton Rd HOM E9 ...... 129 M9
Shaggy Calf La SLN SL2 ... 129 M9
Shakespeare Av
  EBED/NFELT TW14 .... 175 H2
  FBAR/BDGN N11 .... 98 B8
  TIL RM18 .... 168 E8
  WLSDN NW10 .... 135 P3
  YEAD UB4 .... 133 H3
Shakespeare Crs MNPK E12 142 G2
  WLSDN NW10 .... 136 A3
Shakespeare Dr
  KTN/HRWW/W HA3 .... 115 J4
Shakespeare Gdns EFNCH N2 118 A2

Shakespeare Rd ACT W3 ... 135 P10
  ADL/WDHM KT15 ... 215 N1
  BXLYHN DA7 ... 163 P7
  DART DA1 ... 165 P10
  FNCH N3 ... 97 K9
  HARP AL5 ... 20 C1
  HNHL SE24 ... 181 J1
  HNWL W7 ... 134 E9
  MLHL NW7 ... 96 D5
  ROM RM1 ... 124 G4
  WALTH E17 ... 100 C10
Shakespeare Sq BARK/HLT IG6 ... 102 C10
Shakespeare St WATN WD24 ... 73 J4
Shakespeare Wy FELT TW13 ... 175 K7
Shakletons CHONG CM5 ... 67 P4
Shakspeare Ms
  STNW/STAM N16 ... 119 M9
Shalcombe St WBPTN SW10 ... 15 K10
Shalcross Dr CHES/WCR EN8 ... 62 E6
Shaldon Dr MRDN SM4 ... 201 H5
  RSLP HA4 ... 113 K8
Shaldon Rd EDGW HA8 ... 95 L10
Shaldon Wy WOT/HER KT12 ... 197 K10
Shalfleet Dr NKENS W10 ... 136 C9
Shalford Cl ORP BR6 ... 226 F1
Shalford Ct IS N1 ... 6 C7
Shalford La RGUE GU4 ... 268 B5
Shalford Rd GU GU1 ... 268 A5
Shalimar Gdns ACT W3 ... 135 P9
Shallons Rd ELTH/MOT SE9 ... 184 E7
Shallcross Crs HAT AL10 ... 40 C7
Shallstone Rd MORT/ESHN SW14 ... 155 N9
Shalston Vls SURB KT6 ... 199 L6
The Shambles GU ... 268 A2
Shambrook Rd CHESW EN7 ... 61 J1
Shamrock Cl LHD/OX KT22 ... 236 C7
Shamrock Rd CROY/NA CR0 ... 202 G6
  GVE DA12 ... 191 H3
Shamrock St CLAP SW4 ... 158 E3
Shamrock Wy STHGT/OAK N14 ... 98 C2
Shandon Rd CLAP SW4 ... 180 D2
Shand St STHWK SE1 ... 19 K1
Shandy St WCHPL E1 ... 140 C7
Shanklin Cl CHESW EN7 ... 61 N5
Shanklin Gdns OXHEY WD19 ... 93 K5
Shanklin Rd CEND/HSY/T N8 ... 118 E3
  SEVS/STOTM N15 ... 119 P2
Shannon Cl CRICK NW2 ... 116 C8
  HEST TW5 ... 153 L4
Shannon Gv BRXN/ST SW9 ... 158 G10
Shannon Pl STJWD NW8 ... 3 P7
Shannon Wy BECK BR3 ... 182 C9
  SOCK/AV RM15 ... 146 B8
Shantock Hall La HHS/BOV HP3 ... 52 B5
Shantock La HHS/BOV HP3 ... 52 B6
Shap Crs CAR SM5 ... 202 A8
Shardcroft Av HNHL SE24 ... 181 J1
Shardeloes Rd BROCKY SE4 ... 160 E8
Shard's Sq PECK SE15 ... 19 P10
Sharland Cl THHTH CR7 ... 203 H6
Sharman Ct SCUP DA14 ... 185 K7
Sharnbrooke Cl WELL DA16 ... 163 M9
Sharney Av DTCH/LGLY SL3 ... 150 E2
Sharon Cl CRAWE RH10 ... 284 B10
  GT/LBKH KT23 ... 235 P10
  HOR/WEW KT19 ... 19 P9
  SURB KT6 ... 199 H8
Sharon Gdns HOM E9 ... 140 B3
Sharon Rd CHSWK W4 ... 156 A4
  PEND EN3 ... 80 D6
Sharpcroft HHNE HP2 ... 35 N4
Sharpecroft HLWW/ROY CM19 ... 46 F1
Sharpes La HHW HP1 ... 34 E1
Sharples Hall St CAMTN NW1 ... 4 B4
Sharpthorne Cl CRAWW RH11 ... 283 J7
Sharp Wy DART DA1 ... 165 N9
Sharratt St PECK SE15 ... 160 B5
Sharsted St WALW SE17 ... 18 C4
Sharvel La NTHLT UB5 ... 133 H3
Shaw Av BARK IG11 ... 143 P4
Shawbridge HLWW/ROY CM19 ... 46 F4
Shawbrooke Rd ELTH/MOT SE9 ... 162 A10
Shawbury Rd EDUL SE22 ... 181 N1
Shaw Cl BUSH WD23 ... 94 D3
  CHERT KT16 ... 214 F3
  CHES/WCR EN8 ... 62 B5
  EW KT17 ... 220 C7
  HCH RM12 ... 125 J6
  SAND/SEL CR2 ... 223 N8
  THMD SE28 ... 143 L10
Shaw Crs SAND/SEL CR2 ... 223 M8
  TIL RM18 ... 168 E2
Shaw Dr WOT/HER KT12 ... 197 K7
Shawfield Pk BMLY BR1 ... 206 A2
Shawfield St CHEL SW3 ... 15 P8
Shawford Rd HOR/WEW KT19 ... 220 A3
Shaw Gdns BARK IG11 ... 143 P4
Shawley Crs EPSOM KT18 ... 238 E4
Shawley Wy EPSOM KT18 ... 238 F4
Shaw Rd BH/WHM TN16 ... 243 P6
  BMLY BR1 ... 183 L6
  EDUL SE22 ... 159 M10
  PEND EN3 ... 80 C5
Shaw's Cottages FSTH SE23 ... 182 B6
Shaw Sq WALTH E17 ... 100 D9
The Shaws WGCW AL7 ... 23 M6
Shaws Rd CRAWE RH10 ... 283 P6
Shaw Wy WLGTN SM6 ... 222 F4
Shaxton Crs CROY/NA CR0 ... 225 H5
Sheares Hoppit WARE SG12 ... 28 A1
Shearing Dr MRDN SM4 ... 201 M7
Shearling Wy HOLWY N7 ... 5 M1
Shearman Rd BKHTH/KID SE3 ... 161 L10
Shearwater HART DA3 ... 211 N3
Shearwater Rd SUT SM1 ... 221 J2
Shearwater Wy YEAD UB4 ... 133 L8
Shearwood Cresent DART DA1 ... 164 G9
Sheath La LHD/OX KT22 ... 218 A9
Sheehy Wy SLN SL2 ... 129 N9
Sheen Common Dr
  RCHPK/HAM TW10 ... 155 M10
Sheen Court Rd
  RCHPK/HAM TW10 ... 155 M10
Sheendale Rd RCH/KEW TW9 ... 155 L10
Sheenewood SYD SE26 ... 182 A8
Sheen Gate Gdns
  MORT/ESHN SW14 ... 155 P10
Sheen Gv IS N1 ... 6 A5
Sheen La MORT/ESHN SW14 ... 155 N10
Sheen Pk RCH/KEW TW9 ... 155 K10
Sheen Rd RCHPK/HAM TW10 ... 155 K10
  STMC/STPC BR5 ... 207 J4
Sheen Wy WLGTN SM6 ... 222 G4
Sheen Wd MORT/ESHN SW14 ... 177 P1
Sheepbarn La WARL CR6 ... 225 M8
Sheepcot Dr GSTN WD25 ... 55 N10
Sheepcote WGCE AL7 ... 23 K8
Sheepcote Cl BEAC HP9 ... 88 B7
  HEST TW5 ... 153 H6
Sheepcote Gdns DEN/HRF UB9 ... 111 K4
Sheepcote La BTSEA SW11 ... 158 A4
  STALE/WH AL4 ... 21 K3
  STMC/STPC BR5 ... 208 B4
Sheepcote Rd HHNE HP2 ... 36 A6
  HRW HA1 ... 114 C4
  WALTH E17 ... 148 C8
Sheepcotes Rd CHDH RM6 ... 123 N2
Sheepcot La GSTN WD25 ... 55 J9
Sheepfold La AMS HP7 ... 29 J5
Sheepfold Rd GUW GU2 ... 249 L2
Sheephouse Gn RDKG RH5 ... 271 N6
Sheephouse La RDKG RH5 ... 271 P10
  RDKG RH5 ... 271 N5
Sheephouse Rd HHS/BOV HP3 ... 36 A8

Sheephouse Wy NWMAL KT3 ... 200 A8
Sheeplands Av GU GU1 ... 250 A6
Sheep La HACK E8 ... 140 A3
Sheep St REIG RH2 ... 297 J7
Sheepwalk WOTTON ... 196 A6
Sheep Walk Ms WIM/MER SW19 ... 178 A4
Sheering Dr HLWE CM17 ... 29 P8
Sheering Lower Rd SBW CM21 ... 30 A3
Sheering Mill La SBW CM21 ... 30 A1
Sheering Rd HLWE CM17 ... 29 P7
Sheerwater Av ADL/WDHM KT15 ... 215 H8
  CAN/RD E16 ... 142 A7
  WOKN/KNAP GU21 ... 215 H8
Sheethanger La HHS/BOV HP3 ... 35 K10
Sheet's Heath La CHOB/PIR GU24 ... 230 F5
Sheet St WDSR SL4 ... 149 J8
Sheet Street Rd WDSR SL4 ... 170 A10
Sheffield Cl CRAWE RH10 ... 284 D7
  HARH RM3 ... 105 P6
Sheffield Rd EBED/NFELT TW14 ... 174 D2
  SL SL1 ... 129 H8
Sheffield St LINN WC2A ... 11 N6
Sheffield Ter KENS W8 ... 14 E1
Sheffield Wy HTHAIR TW6 ... 174 E1
Shefton Ri NTHWD HA6 ... 32 E7
Sheila Rd CRW RM5 ... 104 C8
The Sheilings BGR/WK TN15 ... 247 N6
  EMPK RM11 ... 125 N3
Shelbourne Cl PIN HA5 ... 113 N1
Shelbourne Rd TOTM N17 ... 100 A9
Shelburne Rd HOLWY N7 ... 118 O9
Shelbury Cl SCUP DA14 ... 185 K6
Shelbury Rd EDUL SE22 ... 182 A1
Sheldon Av CLAY IG5 ... 102 E10
  HGT N6 ... 118 A5
Sheldon Cl CHESW EN7 ... 61 L2
  CRAWE RH10 ... 284 E8
  HLWE CM17 ... 47 N1
  LEE/GVPK SE12 ... 183 N1
  PGE/AN SE20 ... 204 A1
  REIG RH2 ... 275 L1
Sheldon Ct GU GU1 ... 268 C1
Sheldon Rd BXLYHN DA7 ... 164 A7
  CRICK NW2 ... 116 G9
  DAGW RM9 ... 143 P2
  UED N18 ... 99 M5
Sheldon St CROY/NA CR0 ... 203 K10
Sheldrake Cl CAN/RD E16 ... 142 C10
Sheldrake Pl KENS W8 ... 14 D1
Sheldrick Cl MTCM CR4 ... 201 N2
Shelduck Cl FSTGT E7 ... 121 L10
Shelford Pl STNW/STAM N16 ... 119 L8
Shelford Ri NRWD SE19 ... 181 M10
Shelford Rd BAR EN5 ... 76 F10
Shelgate Rd BTSEA SW11 ... 180 A1
Shellbank La RDART DA2 ... 188 C8
Shell Cl HAYES BR2 ... 206 B6
Shelley Av GFD/PVL UB6 ... 134 C5
  HCH RM12 ... 124 G7
  MNPK E12 ... 142 B1
Shelley Cl CHONG CM5 ... 67 N2
  COUL/CHIP CR5 ... 240 G3
  CRAWE RH10 ... 284 D5
  DTCH/LGLY SL3 ... 150 D4
  EDGW HA8 ... 95 M5
  GFD/PVL UB6 ... 134 C5
  NTHWD HA6 ... 32 C6
  ORP BR6 ... 207 H10
  YEAD UB4 ... 133 H7
Shelley Crs HEST TW5 ... 153 L7
  STHL UB1 ... 133 N8
Shelley Dr WELL DA16 ... 163 M1
Shelley Gdns ALP/SUD HA0 ... 115 M7
Shelley Gv LOU IG10 ... 82 C8
Shelley La DEN/HRF UB9 ... 91 K8
Shelley Pl TIL RM18 ... 168 E7
Shelley Rd CSHM HP5 ... 50 C5
Shelleys La RSEV TN14 ... 245 K2
Shelley Wy WIM/MER SW19 ... 201 K1
Shellfield Cl STWL/WRAY TW19 ... 152 A8
Shellgrove Rd
  STNW/STAM N16 ... 119 M10
Shellness Rd CLPT E5 ... 120 A10
Shell Rd LEW SE13 ... 160 G9
Shellwood Dr RDKG RH5 ... 273 H6
Shellwood Rd BTSEA SW11 ... 158 A4
  REIG RH2 ... 274 A7
Shelly Cl BNSTD SM7 ... 238 G11
Shelmerdine Cl BOW E3 ... 140 F7
Shelson Av FELT TW13 ... 174 G6
Shelton Av WARL CR6 ... 242 B3
Shelton Cl GUW GU2 ... 249 M5
  WARL CR6 ... 242 B3
Shelton Rd WIM/MER SW19 ... 201 K1
Shelton St LSQ/SEVD WC2H ... 11 L6
Shelvers Gn KWD/TDW/WH KT20 ... 238 F7
Shelvers Hl KWD/TDW/WH KT20 ... 238 F7
Shelvers Sp KWD/TDW/WH KT20 ... 238 F7
Shelvers Wy KWD/TDW/WH KT20 ... 238 F7
Shenden Cl SEV TN13 ... 265 K4
Shenden Wy SEV TN13 ... 265 K4
Shenfield Cl COUL/CHIP CR5 ... 240 C5
Shenfield Ct HLWS CM18 ... 46 F4
Shenfield Crs BRWN CM15 ... 107 K3
Shenfield Gdns RBRW/HUT CM13 ... 87 N10
Shenfield Pl BRWN CM15 ... 107 M1
Shenfield Pl BRWN CM15 ... 107 K1
Shenfield Rd BRWN CM15 ... 107 K2
  WFD IG8 ... 101 N8
Shenfield St IS N1 ... 7 K4
Shenley Av RSLP HA4 ... 112 G7
Shenleybury RAD WD7 ... 57 K6
Shenleybury Cottages RAD WD7 ... 57 K7
Shenley Hl RAD WD7 ... 56 G10
Shenley La LCOL/BKTW AL2 ... 56 G10
Shenley Rd BORE WD6 ... 75 M7
  CMBW SE5 ... 159 M7
  DART DA1 ... 187 P2
  HEST TW5 ... 153 M7
  HHNE HP2 ... 36 C1
  RAD WD7 ... 75 J1
Shenstone Dr SL SL1 ... 128 C6
Shenstone Gdns HARH RM3 ... 105 K9
Shenstone Hl BERK HP4 ... 34 B4
Shenstone Pk ASC SL5 ... 192 D4
Shenwood Ct BORE WD6 ... 75 N3
  BORE WD6 ... 75 M3
Shepherd Cl CRAWE RH10 ... 283 N10
Shepherdess Pl FSBYE EC1V ... 6 F7
Shepherdess Wk IS N1 ... 6 F4
Shepherd Market
  MYFR/PICC W1J ... 10 E10
Shepherd's Bush Gn SHB W12 ... 156 F1
Shepherd's Bush Market
  SHB W12 ... 156 G1
Shepherd's Bush Pl SHB W12 ... 156 G1
Shepherd's Bush Rd
  HMSMTH W6 ... 156 F2
Shepherds Cl CHDH RM6 ... 123 N3
  HGT N6 ... 118 C4
  ORP BR6 ... 207 J10
  SHPTN TW17 ... 196 C6
  UX/CGN UB8 ... 131 M6
Shepherds Ct HERT/WAS SG14 ... 25 K2
Shepherds Gn CHST BR7 ... 184 C10
  HHW HP1 ... 35 F7
Shepherd's Hl GUW GU2 ... 249 M8
  HARH RM3 ... 105 P10
  HGT N6 ... 118 C4
  REDH RH1 ... 258 D2
Shepherds La BEAC HP9 ... 88 E10
  BFOR GU20 ... 212 F2
  DART DA1 ... 187 H4
  GUW GU2 ... 249 L7
  HOM E9 ... 140 C1
  RKW/CH/CXG WD3 ... 70 G10

Shepherds Pl MYFR/PKLN W1K ... 10 C7
Shepherds Rd WATW WD18 ... 72 C7
Shepherd St GVW DA11 ... 190 A3
  MYFR/PICC W1J ... 10 E10
Shepherds Wk BUSH WD23 ... 94 C3
  CRICK NW2 ... 116 D7
  EPSOM KT18 ... 237 N7
  HAMP NW3 ... 117 N10
Shepherds Wy BRKMPK AL9 ... 59 M3
  CSHM HP5 ... 51 J9
  RGUE GU4 ... 268 B4
  RKW/CH/CXG WD3 ... 91 L1
  SAND/SEL CR2 ... 224 C4
Shepiston La WDR/YW UB7 ... 152 C3
Shepley Cl CAR SM5 ... 202 B10
  HCH RM12 ... 125 L10
Shepley Dr ASC SL5 ... 193 H3
Shepley End ASC SL5 ... 193 H5
Sheppard Cl BERM/RHTH SE16 ... 160 A4
  EN EN1 ... 80 F7
Sheppard Dr BERM/RHTH SE16 ... 160 A4
Sheppards HLWW/ROY CM19 ... 46 C4
Sheppards Cl STALW/RED AL3 ... 38 D3
Sheppard St CAN/RD E16 ... 141 L6
Sheppards La BORE WD6 ... 76 A3
Shepperton Cl BORE WD6 ... 75 N2
Shepperton Court Dr
  SHPTN TW17 ... 196 C5
Shepperton Rd IS N1 ... 6 F5
  STA TW18 ... 195 N4
  STMC/STPC BR5 ... 206 F6
Sheppey Cl CRAWW RH11 ... 283 L10
  ERITH DA8 ... 165 J6
Sheppey Gdns DAGW RM9 ... 143 M2
Sheppey Rd DAGW RM9 ... 143 L2
Sheppey's Vls KGLGY WD4 ... 54 F4
Sheppy Pl GVE DA12 ... 190 E3
Sherard Rd ELTH/MOT SE9 ... 184 B1
Sheraton Dr HOR/WEW KT19 ... 219 P9
Sheraton Dr BORE WD6 ... 75 L9
Sheraton St SOHO/CST W1F ... 11 J2
Sherborne Av NWDGN UB2 ... 153 J2
  PEND EN3 ... 80 B6
Sherborne Cl DTCH/LGLY SL3 ... 151 H7
  EPSOM KT18 ... 238 F3
  YEAD UB4 ... 133 K8
Sherborne Crs CAR SM5 ... 201 P7
Sherborne Gdns CDALE/KGS NW9 ... 115 M1
  WEA W13 ... 134 G8
Sherborne La MANHO EC4N ... 12 G7
Sherborne Pl NTHWD HA6 ... 92 F7
Sherborne Rd CHEAM SM3 ... 201 K9
  CHSGTN KT9 ... 219 K2
  EBED/NFELT TW14 ... 174 E3
  STMC/STPC BR5 ... 207 J5
Sherborne St IS N1 ... 6 G5
Sherborne Wy RKW/CH/CXG WD3 ... 72 C3
Sherboro Rd SEVS/STOTM N15 ... 119 N4
Sherbourne SHGR GU5 ... 269 N5
Sherbourne Cl HHS/BOV HP3 ... 35 P7
Sherbourne Dr VW GU25 ... 193 J5
Sherbourne Gdns SHPTN TW17 ... 196 F7
Sherbourne Wk SLN SL2 ... 109 H9
Sherbrooke Cl BXLYHN DA7 ... 164 B10
Sherbrooke Rd FUL/PGN SW6 ... 157 H6
Sherbrook Gdns WCHMH N21 ... 99 J1
Shere Av BELMT SM2 ... 220 F6
Shere Cl CHSGTN KT9 ... 219 K3
  RDKG RH5 ... 273 H6
Sheredan Rd CHING E4 ... 101 J3
Sheredes Dr HOD EN11 ... 44 E4
Shere La SHGR GU5 ... 270 B5
Shere Rd EHSLY KT24 ... 252 D10
  GNTH/NBYPK IG2 ... 122 D3
  RGUE GU4 ... 269 L2
  SHGR GU5 ... 270 A4
Sherfield Av RKW/CH/CXG WD3 ... 91 N4
Sherfield Gdns PUT/ROE SW15 ... 178 C2
Sherfield Rd GRAYS RM17 ... 167 N5
Sheridan Cl HARH RM3 ... 105 J8
  HGDN/ICK UB10 ... 132 D6
  HHW HP1 ... 35 L7
Sheridan Ct DART DA1 ... 165 P10
  HSLWW TW4 ... 175 M1
Sheridan Crs CHST BR7 ... 206 E2
Sheridan Dr REIG RH2 ... 257 L8
Sheridan Gdns
  KTN/HRWW/WS HA3 ... 115 J4
Sheridan Pl HPTN TW12 ... 198 A1
Sheridan Rd BELV DA17 ... 164 B3
  BXLYHN DA7 ... 163 P9
  FSTGT E7 ... 121 L3
  MNPK E12 ... 122 B10
  OXHEY WD19 ... 93 L1
  RCHPK/HAM TW10 ... 177 H6
  WIM/MER SW19 ... 201 J1
Sheridans Rd GT/LBKH KT23 ... 254 B2
Sheridan St WCHPL E1 ... 140 A8
Sheridan Wk CAR SM5 ... 202 C3
Sheridan Wy BECK BR3 ... 204 E3
Sheringham Av MNPK E12 ... 122 C9
  ROMW/RG RM7 ... 124 D4
  STHGT/OAK N14 ... 78 E9
  WHTN TW2 ... 175 N4
Sheringham Dr BARK IG11 ... 123 J10
Sheringham Rd HOLWY N7 ... 5 P1
  PGE/AN SE20 ... 204 A2
Sherington Av PIN HA5 ... 93 P8
Sherington Rd CHARL SE7 ... 161 N5
Sherland Rd TWK TW1 ... 176 A4
Sherlies Av ORP BR6 ... 207 H9
Sherlock Ms MHST W1U ... 10 C3
Sherman Rd BMLY BR1 ... 205 M1
  SL SL1 ... 129 K7
Shernbroke Rd WAB EN9 ... 63 L10
Shernhall St LEY E10 ... 121 H3
  WALTH E17 ... 121 H3
Sherrard Rd FSTGT E7 ... 141 P1
Sherrards Av FELT TW13 ... 175 H6
  TOTM N17 ... 99 P10
Sherrardspark Rd WGCW AL8 ... 22 G3
Sherrards Wy BAR EN5 ... 77 K9
Sherrick Green Rd WLSDN NW10 ... 116 E10
Sherriff Rd KIL/WHAMP NW6 ... 2 F7
Sherringham Av FELT TW13 ... 175 H6
  TOTM N17 ... 99 P10
Sherrock Gdns HDN NW4 ... 116 D2
Sherry Ms BARK IG11 ... 142 G2
Sherwin Rd NWCR SE14 ... 160 F9
Sherwood SURB KT6 ... 199 J9
Sherwood Av GFD/PVL UB6 ... 134 D1
  POTB/CUF EN6 ... 160 F3
  RSLP HA4 ... 112 F4
  STALE/WH AL4 ... 38 C5
  STRHM/NOR SW16 ... 202 F1
  SWFD E18 ... 121 N1
Sherwood Cl BXLY DA5 ... 185 M2
  DTCH/LGLY SL3 ... 150 B2
  LHD/OX KT22 ... 236 B9
  WEA W13 ... 134 G10
  WOKN/KNAP GU21 ... 231 K3
Sherwood Crs REIG RH2 ... 275 L4
Sherwood Gdns BARK IG11 ... 142 G2
  BERM/RHTH SE16 ... 19 J8
  POP/IOD E14 ... 160 F3
Sherwood Park Av BFN/LL DA15 ... 185 K3
Sherwood Park Rd MTCM CR4 ... 202 B4
  SUT SM1 ... 221 K2
Sherwood Pk HHNE HP2 ... 36 C1
Sherwood Rd BARK/HLT IG6 ... 122 E2
  COUL/CHIP CR5 ... 240 G2
  CROY/NA CR0 ... 204 A7
  HDN NW4 ... 96 F10
  HPTN TW12 ... 176 B8
  RYLN/HDSTN HA2 ... 114 B7

  WELL DA16 ... 163 H9
  WIM/MER SW19 ... 179 J10
Sherwoods Ri HARP AL5 ... 20 C3
Sherwoods Rd OXHEY WD19 ... 93 M1
Sherwood St REGST W1B ... 11 H7
  TRDG/WHET N20 ... 97 N4
Sherwood Ter TRDG/WHET N20 ... 97 N4
Sherwood Wy WWKM BR4 ... 205 H9
Shetland Cl BORE WD6 ... 76 A10
  CRAWE RH10 ... 284 A10
  RGUE GU4 ... 250 F6
Shetland Rd BOW E3 ... 140 E4
Shevon Wy BRW CM14 ... 106 E5
Shewens Rd WEY KT13 ... 216 E1
Shey Copse WOKS/MYFD GU22 ... 232 F3
Shield Dr BTFD TW8 ... 154 G5
Shield Rd ASHF TW15 ... 174 D7
Shilburn Wy WOKN/KNAP GU21 ... 231 M4
Shillibeer Pl MBLAR W1H ... 9 F1
Shillibeer Wk CHIG IG7 ... 103 J1
Shillingford Cl MLHL NW7 ... 96 E7
Shillingford St IS N1 ... 6 D5
Shillitoe Av POTB/CUF EN6 ... 58 G5
Shimmings Gv GU GU1 ... 250 D9
Shinfield St SHB W12 ... 136 C6
Shingle Ct WAB EN9 ... 63 M9
Shinglewell Rd ERITH DA8 ... 164 B6
Shinners Cl SNWD SE25 ... 203 P3
Ship And Mermaid Rw
  STHWK SE1 ... 19 H1
Ship Field Dr BH/WHM TN16 ... 243 P7
  ERITH DA8 ... 165 J6
  SL SL1 ... 108 D6
Shipka Rd BAL SW12 ... 180 C4
Ship La EYN DA4 ... 209 M1
  MORT/ESHN SW14 ... 155 P9
  SOCK/AV RM15 ... 166 C1
  SWLY BR8 ... 209 L1
Shipleybridge La HORL RH6 ... 280 G10
Shipley Rd CRAWW RH11 ... 283 K7
Shipman Rd CAN/RD E16 ... 141 M8
  FSTH SE23 ... 182 C3
Ship St DEPT SE8 ... 160 F7
Shipton Cl BCTR RM8 ... 123 N8
Shipton Rd HGDN/ICK UB10 ... 112 A9
Shipton St BETH E2 ... 7 M2
Shipwright Rd BERM/RHTH SE16 ... 160 D1
Shipwright Yd STHWK SE1 ... 13 J10
Ship Yd WEY KT13 ... 196 B10
Shirburn Cl FSTH SE23 ... 182 B3
Shirbutt St POP/IOD E14 ... 140 G9
Shirebrook Rd BKHTH/KID SE3 ... 162 A8
Shire Cl BROX EN10 ... 62 E3
Shire Ct EW KT17 ... 220 C4
Shirehall HDN NW4 ... 116 G4
Shirehall Gdns HDN NW4 ... 116 G4
Shirehall La HDN NW4 ... 116 G4
Shirehall Pk HDN NW4 ... 116 G4
Shirehall Rd RDART DA2 ... 187 P3
Shire Horse Wy ISLW TW7 ... 154 E9
Shire La CFSP/GDCR SL9 ... 90 E6
  ORP BR6 ... 227 K2
  RKW/CH/CXG WD3 ... 70 E7
Shiremeade BORE WD6 ... 75 N4
Shire Pde CRAWE RH10 ... 284 E6
The Shires RCHPK/HAM TW10 ... 177 K7
Shirland Ms MV/WKIL W9 ... 2 D10
Shirland Rd MV/WKIL W9 ... 2 C10
Shirley Av BELMT SM2 ... 221 J6
  BXLY DA5 ... 185 N3
  COUL/CHIP CR5 ... 241 J5
  CROY/NA CR0 ... 204 B8
  REDH RH1 ... 276 A5
  SUT SM1 ... 221 P1
  WDSR SL4 ... 148 E7
Shirley Church Rd CROY/NA CR0 ... 204 C10
Shirley Cl BROX EN10 ... 44 E10
  CHES/WCR EN8 ... 62 B5
  DART DA1 ... 166 B4
  GVE DA12 ... 191 L5
  HSLW TW3 ... 176 B1
Shirley Crs BECK BR3 ... 204 B3
Shirley Dr HSLW TW3 ... 176 B1
Shirley Gdns BARK IG11 ... 143 H1
  HCH RM12 ... 125 K7
  HNWL W7 ... 134 E10
Shirley Gv BTSEA SW11 ... 159 K9
  N19 ... 100 D1
Shirley Hills Rd CROY/NA CR0 ... 224 C2
Shirley Oaks Rd CROY/NA CR0 ... 204 C8
Shirley Park Rd CROY/NA CR0 ... 204 A8
Shirley Pl WOKN/KNAP GU21 ... 231 H3
Shirley Rd ABLGY WD5 ... 54 C8
  BFN/LL DA15 ... 185 H6
  CHSWK W4 ... 156 A1
  CROY/NA CR0 ... 204 A8
  ENC/FH EN2 ... 79 K7
  SRTFD E15 ... 141 K2
  STAL AL1 ... 38 C7
  SWNLY BR8 ... 222 D5
Shirley St CAN/RD E16 ... 141 D5
Shirley Wy CROY/NA CR0 ... 204 E10
Shirlock Rd HAMP NW3 ... 118 A9
Shobden Rd TOTM N17 ... 99 P1
Shobroke Rd CRICK NW2 ... 116 F8
Shoebury Rd EHAM E6 ... 142 C2
Shoe La FLST/FETLN EC4A ... 12 C4
Sholden Gdns STMC/STPC BR5 ... 207 M5
Sholto Rd HTHAIR TW6 ... 153 K10
Shonks Mill Rd ABR/ST RM4 ... 86 F4
Shooters Av KTN/HRWW/WS HA3 ... 115 H2
Shooters Dr WAB EN9 ... 45 K9
Shooters Hill WOOL/PLUM SE18 ... 162 C1
  CHARL SE7 ... 161 P6
Shooters Hill Rd BKHTH/KID SE3 ... 161 H6
  CHARL SE7 ... 161 P6
Shootersway BERK HP4 ... 32 G3
Shootersway La BERK HP4 ... 33 G5
Shootersway Pk BERK HP4 ... 33 L5
Shoot-up Hl CRICK NW2 ... 2 C1
Shophouse La SHGR GU5 ... 269 N10
Shoplands WGCW AL8 ... 22 G2
Shord Hl PUR/KEN CR8 ... 241 L2
Shore Cl EBED/NFELT TW14 ... 174 A3
  HPTN TW12 ... 175 M8
Shorediche Cl HGDN/ICK UB10 ... 112 A9
Shoreditch High St BETH E2 ... 7 K10
  WCHPL E1 ... 13 K3
Shoreham Cl BXLY DA5 ... 184 G7
  CROY/NA CR0 ... 189 L10
  WAND/EARL SW18 ... 179 L10
Shoreham La ORP BR6 ... 228 B3
  RSEV TN14 ... 228 D4
  SEV TN14 ... 246 G5
Shoreham Pl RSEV TN14 ... 229 H7
Shoreham Ri SLN SL2 ... 128 C3
Shoreham Rd CRAWE RH10 ... 284 D10
  RSEV TN14 ... 247 H1
  STMC/STPC BR5 ... 207 N1
Shoreham Rd (East) HTHAIR TW6 ... 174 A1
Shoreham Rd (West) HTHAIR TW6 ... 173 P1
Shoreham Wy HAYES BR2 ... 205 M6
Shorndean St CAT SE6 ... 183 H4
Shorne Cl BFN/LL DA15 ... 185 H4
  STMC/STPC BR5 ... 207 N4
Shornefield Cl BMLY BR1 ... 206 B3
Shornells Rd FUL/PGN SW6 ... 157 N6
Shortacres REDH RH1 ... 258 G6
Short Cl CRAWW RH11 ... 283 N5
Short Cft BRWN CM15 ... 86 E3

Shortcroft Rd EW KT17 ... 220 C4
Shorter Av BRWN CM15 ... 87 L10
Shorter St WCHPL E1 ... 13 L7
Short Gallop CRAWE RH10 ... 284 E6
Short La STL SL2 ... 129 P8
Shortgate NFNCH/WDSP N12 ... 97 J3
Shortlands HMSMTH W6 ... 156 G3
  HYS/HAR UB3 ... 152 E5
Shortlands Av CHONG CM5 ... 67 N2
  UED N18 ... 99 L4
Shortlands Cl BELV DA17 ... 164 A2
  UED N18 ... 99 L4
Shortlands Gdns HAYES BR2 ... 205 K2
Shortlands Gv WGCE AL7 ... 23 J6
Shortlands Rd HAYES BR2 ... 205 J2
  KUTN/CMB KT2 ... 177 L10
  LEY E10 ... 120 C5
Short La LCOL/BKTW AL2 ... 55 N5
  OXTED RH8 ... 261 N8
  STWL/WRAY TW19 ... 174 A3
Shortmead Dr CHES/WCR EN8 ... 62 D7
Short Rd CHSWK W4 ... 156 B5
  WAN E11 ... 121 J2
Shorts Cft CDALE/KGS NW9 ... 115 N2
Shorts Gdns LSQ/SEVD WC2H ... 11 M5
Shorts Rd CAR SM5 ... 221 P1
Short St STHWK SE1 ... 18 E1
Shortway CSHM HP5 ... 50 C5
  ELTH/MOT SE9 ... 162 B9
Short Wy NFNCH/WDSP N12 ... 97 P7
  WHTN TW2 ... 176 B3
Shortwood Av STA TW18 ... 173 L6
Shotfield WLGTN SM6 ... 222 C5
Shothanger Wy HHS/BOV HP3 ... 35 J5
Shott Cl SUT SM1 ... 221 M2
Shottendane Rd FUL/PGN SW6 ... 157 K7
Shottery Cl ELTH/MOT SE9 ... 184 B6
Shottfield Av MORT/ESHN SW14 ... 156 B10
Shottfield Cl STALE/WH AL4 ... 21 H9
Shott Lower CHESW EN7 ... 61 N2
Shoulder of Mutton Aly
  POP/IOD E14 ... 140 D9
Shouldham St MBLAR W1H ... 9 P4
Showers Wy HYS/HAR UB3 ... 133 H10
Shrapnel Cl WOOL/PLUM SE18 ... 162 G4
Shrapnel Rd ELTH/MOT SE9 ... 162 G4
Shrewsbury Av
  KTN/HRWW/WS HA3 ... 115 K2
  MORT/ESHN SW14 ... 155 P10
Shrewsbury Cl SURB KT6 ... 199 K9
Shrewsbury Crs WLSDN NW10 ... 136 A3
Shrewsbury La
  WOOL/PLUM SE18 ... 162 E7
Shrewsbury Ms BAY/PAD W2 ... 8 E4
Shrewsbury Rd BAY/PAD W2 ... 8 E4
  BECK BR3 ... 204 C3
  CAR SM5 ... 201 P7
  EBED/NFELT TW14 ... 174 D2
  FBAR/BDGN N11 ... 98 E7
  HTHAIR TW6 ... 174 D2
  MNPK E12 ... 142 A1
  REDH RH1 ... 257 P10
Shrewsbury St NKENS W10 ... 136 F6
Shrewton Rd TOOT SW17 ... 180 A10
Shrimpton Cl BEAC HP9 ... 88 C5
Shrimpton Rd BEAC HP9 ... 88 C5
Shroffold Rd BMLY BR1 ... 183 K7
Shropshire Cl MTCM CR4 ... 202 F4
Shropshire Rd WDGN N22 ... 98 G8
Shroton St CAMTN NW1 ... 9 N3
The Shrubberies CHIG IG7 ... 102 F6
  SWFD E18 ... 101 M10
Shrubbery Gdns WCHMH N21 ... 99 J1
Shrubbery Rd EYN DA4 ... 210 C1
  GVE DA12 ... 190 E4
  STHL UB1 ... 133 P10
  STRHM/NOR SW16 ... 180 F7
The Shrubbery HHW HP1 ... 35 H5
  UPMR RM14 ... 126 B8
Shrubbs Hl CHOB/PIR GU24 ... 213 H5
Shrubbs Hill La ASC SL5 ... 193 H6
Shrub Hill Rd HHW HP1 ... 35 J7
Shrubland Gv WPK KT4 ... 200 F10
Shrubland Rd BNSTD SM7 ... 239 J2
  HACK E8 ... 7 N5
  LEY E10 ... 120 F5
  WALTH E17 ... 120 F5
Shrublands BRKMPK AL9 ... 59 L2
Shrublands Av BERK HP4 ... 33 L5
  CROY/NA CR0 ... 224 F1
Shrublands Cl CHIG IG7 ... 103 F1
  SYD SE26 ... 182 B6
Shrublands Dr LTWR GU18 ... 212 A7
The Shrublands POTB/CUF EN6 ... 59 H9
Shrubsall Cl ELTH/MOT SE9 ... 184 B4
Shurland Av EBAR EN4 ... 77 N10
Shurlock Av SWLY BR8 ... 208 E2
Shurlock Dr ORP BR6 ... 226 F1
Shuttle Cl BFN/LL DA15 ... 185 H5
Shuttlemead BXLY DA5 ... 185 J6
Shuttle Rd DART DA1 ... 165 H9
Shuttle St WCHPL E1 ... 13 N2
Shuttleworth Rd BTSEA SW11 ... 157 N8
Sibella Rd CLAP SW4 ... 158 E8
Sibley Av HARP AL5 ... 20 C4
Sibley Cl BXLYHS DA6 ... 185 P1
Sibley Ct UX/CGN UB8 ... 132 D7
Sibley Gv MNPK E12 ... 142 B2
Sibneys Gn HLWS CM18 ... 47 J4
Sibthorpe Rd BRKMPK AL9 ... 40 G10
  LEE/GVPK SE12 ... 183 P3
Sibthorp Rd MTCM CR4 ... 202 A2
Sibton Rd CAR SM5 ... 202 B7
Sicklefield Cl CHESW EN7 ... 61 N2
Sidbury Cl ASC SL5 ... 192 F5
Sidbury St FUL/PGN SW6 ... 157 H7
Sidcup By-pass Rd SCUP DA14 ... 185 H7
Sidcup Hl SCUP DA14 ... 186 B8
Sidcup Pl SCUP DA14 ... 186 B8
Sidcup Rd ELTH/MOT SE9 ... 184 B4
  LEE/GVPK SE12 ... 183 N1
Siddeley Dr HSLWW TW4 ... 175 H4
Siddons La CAMTN NW1 ... 10 B2
Siddons Rd CROY/NA CR0 ... 203 H10
  FSTH SE23 ... 182 D5
  TOTM N17 ... 99 P9
Side Rd DEN/HRF UB9 ... 110 G5
  WALTH E17 ... 120 E3
Sideways La HORL RH6 ... 279 M6
Sidewood Rd ELTH/MOT SE9 ... 184 G4
Sidford Cl HHW HP1 ... 35 H5
Sidford Pl STHWK SE1 ... 17 P4
The Sidings BROX EN10 ... 44 E8
  HAT AL10 ... 40 B5
  HHNE HP2 ... 35 N1
  STA TW18 ... 173 L7
  WAN E11 ... 121 H6
Sidmouth Av ISLW TW7 ... 154 D8
Sidmouth Cl OXHEY WD19 ... 93 J3
Sidmouth Dr RSLP HA4 ... 113 H8
Sidmouth Rd LEY E10 ... 121 H2
  PECK SE15 ... 159 J2
  STMC/STPC BR5 ... 207 L5
  WELL DA16 ... 163 M6
  WLSDN NW10 ... 136 B2
Sidmouth St STPAN WC1H ... 5 M10
Sidney Av PLMGR N13 ... 98 G2
Sidney Elson Wy EHAM E6 ... 142 D4
Sidney Gdns BTFD TW8 ... 155 J5
  RSEV TN14 ... 247 K2
Sidney Gv FSBYE EC1V ... 6 C4
Sidney Rd BECK BR3 ... 203 J2
  BRXN/ST SW9 ... 158 G8
  EPP CM16 ... 82 G2
  FSTGT E7 ... 121 M1
  RYLN/HDSTN HA2 ... 114 B7

SNWD SE25 203 P5
STA TW18 173 K7
TWK TW1 176 F2
WDGN N22 98 G8
WDSR SL4 148 B9
WOT/HER KT12 197 J10
Sidney Sq WCHPL E1 140 B7
Sidworth St HACK E8 140 A2
Siebert Rd BKHTH/KID SE3 181 M5
Siemens Rd WOOL/PLUM SE18 162 A2
Sierra Dr DAGW RM9 144 C4
Sigdon Rd HACK E8 119 P10
The Sigers RSLP HA4 113 J4
Signmakers Yd CAMTN NW1 4 F6
Silbury Av MTCM CR4 201 P1
Silbury St IS N1 6 C9
Silchester Dr CRAWW RH11 283 K10
Silchester Rd NKENS W10 136 G8
Silecroft Rd BXLYHN DA7 164 B7
Silesia Buildings HACK E8 140 A2
Silex St STHWK SE1 18 D2
Silk Cl LEE/GVPK SE12 183 M4
Silkfield Rd CDALE/KGS NW9 116 B3
Silkham Rd OXTED RH8 261 J3
Silk Mill Rd OXHEY WD19 93 J1
Silk Mills Cl RSEV TN14 247 K7
Silk Mills Pth LEW SE13 161 H9
Silkmore La EHSLY KT24 252 A3
RPLY/SEND GU23 252 A2
Silkstream Rd EDGW HA8 95 P9
Silk St BARB EC2Y 12 F3
Silo Cl RGODL GU7 267 L9
Silo Dr RGODL GU7 267 L9
Silo Rd RGODL GU7 267 L9
Silsoe Rd WDGN N22 98 G10
Silver Birch Av CHING E4 100 E6
EPP CM16 65 P3
Silver Birch Cl ADL/WDHM KT15 215 H8
FBAR/BDGN N11 98 B7
HGDN/ICK UB10 111 P9
RDART DA2 186 F7
THMD SE28 143 K10
Silver Birches RBRW/HUT CM13 107 M2
Silver Birch Ms BARK/HLT IG6 102 F7
Silvercliffe Gdns EBAR EN4 77 P8
Silver Cl KTN/HRWW/W HA3 94 C8
KWD/TDW/WH KT20 239 H10
NWCR SE14 160 D6
Silver Crs CHSWK W4 155 N5
Silverdale CAMTN NW1 4 G3
ENC/FH EN2 78 F8
HART DA3 211 L4
SYD SE26 182 B7
Silverdale Av LHD/OX KT22 218 B10
WEY KT13 196 G9
Silverdale Cl BRKHM/BTCW RH3 273 N3
HNWL W7 134 D10
NTHLT UB5 113 N10
SUT SM1 221 J1
Silverdale Dr ELTH/MOT SE9 184 B5
HCH RM12 125 J10
SUN TW16 197 J2
Silverdale Gdns HYS/HAR UB3 114 A3
Silverdale Rd BUSH WD23 73 M9
BXLYHN DA7 164 C8
CHING E4 101 J7
HYS/HAR UB3 153 H1
STMC/STPC BR5 207 K3
Silver Dell WATN WD24 72 G1
Silverfield BROX EN10 41 K3
Silverglade CHSGTN KT9 219 H8
Silverhall St ISLW TW7 156 B9
Silver HI BORE WD6 75 P2
CSTG HP8 89 N3
Silverholme Cl KTN/HRWW/W HA3 115 K5
Silverlands Cl CHERT KT16 194 G10
Silver La PUR/KEN CR8 222 E8
WWKM BR4 205 J9
Silverlea Gdns HORL RH6 280 D5
Silverleigh Rd THHTH CR7 202 A2
Silverlocke Rd GRAYS RM17 168 A5
Silvermere Av CRW RM5 104 C7
Silvermere Rd LEW SE13 182 F2
Silver Rd GVE DA12 191 H5
Silversmiths Wy WOKN/KNAP GU21 231 P4
Silver Spring Cl ERITH DA8 164 C5
Silversted La BH/WHM TN16 244 G7
Silverstone Cl REDH RH1 258 A6
Silverston Wy STAN HA7 95 H7
Silver St ABR/ST RM4 83 L7
CHESW EN7 61 L6
ENC/FH EN2 79 L7
UED N18 99 L5
WAB EN9 63 H10
Silverthorn Dr HHS/BOV HP3 36 C10
Silverthorne Rd VX/NE SW8 158 C8
Silverthorn Gdns CHING E4 100 F3
Silverton Rd HMSMTH W6 156 H6
Silvertown Wy CAN/RD E16 141 K8
Silvertree La GFD/PVL UB6 134 C5
Silver Trees LCOL/BKTW AL2 55 N6
Silver Wk BERM/RHTH SE16 140 E10
ROMW/RG RM7 124 C1
Silverwood Cl BECK BR3 182 F10
CDH/CHF RM16 147 M9
CROY/NA CR0 224 E5
NTHWD HA6 92 D9
Silvester Rd EDUL SE22 181 N1
Silvester St STHWK SE1 18 G1
Silwood Cl ASC SL5 192 C2
Silwood Rd ASC SL5 192 K4
Silwood St BERM/RHTH SE16 160 C4
Simmil Rd ESH/CLAY KT10 218 D2
Simmonds Ri RHS/BOV HP3 35 N8
Simmons La CHING E4 101 J2
Simmons Pl CDH/CHF RM16 147 M10
TRDG/WHET N20 97 P2
STA TW18 173 H8
Simmons Wy WOOL/PLUM SE18 162 L4
Simms Cl CAR SM5 201 P9
Simms Rd STHWK SE1 19 P6
Simnel Rd LEE/GVPK SE12 183 N5
Simon Cl NTGHL W11 8 D7
Simon Dean HHS/BOV HP3 52 D3
Simonds Rd LEY E10 120 F7
Simone Cl BMLY BR1 206 A1
Simone Dr PUR/KEN CR8 241 K2
Simon Gray Gdns KUTN/CMB KT2 199 K1
Simons Cl CHERT KT16 214 F3
Simons Dr BELMT SM2 221 L5
Simons Wk EGH TW20 171 P10
SRTFD E15 121 J10
SRTFD E15 141 J1
Simplemarsh Rd ADL/WDHM KT15 215 K1
Simpson Cl WCHMH N21 78 F9
Simpson Dr ACT W3 136 A10
Simpson Rd HSLWW TW4 175 N2
RAIN RM13 144 G1
RCHPK/HAM TW10 177 H7
Simpson's Cl HAYES BR2 205 M3
POP/IOD E14 140 C9
Simpson St BTSEA SW11 157 N8
Simpson Wy SURB KT6 199 H6
Simrose Ct IS ROM RM1 124 F3
Sinclair Cl CRAWE RH10 284 D9
Sinclair Dr BELMT SM2 221 L5
Sinclair Gdns WKENS W14 14 A3
Sinclair Gv GLDGN NW11 116 G4
Sinclair Rd CHING E4 100 E6
WKENS W14 14 A3
Sinclair Wy RDART DA2 188 C7

Sinclare Cl EN EN1 79 N5
Sincots Rd REDH RH1 258 A10
Sinderby La BORE WD6 75 K5
Singapore Rd HNWL W7 134 F10
Singer St FSBYE EC1V 7 H10
Single's Cross La RSEV TN14 245 M1
Single St BH/WHM TN16 244 E1
Singleton Cl CROY/NA CR0 203 K7
HCH RM12 124 C9
WIM/MER SW19 180 A10
Singleton Rd DAGW RM9 124 A10
Singleton Scarp NFNCH/WDSP N12 97 K6
Singlewell Rd GVW DA11 190 E6
Sinnott Rd WALTH E17 100 C9
Sion Rd TWK TW1 176 C4
Sipson Cl WDR/YW UB7 152 B5
Sipson La WDR/YW UB7 152 C5
Sipson Rd WDR/YW UB7 152 A3
Sipson Wy WDR/YW UB7 152 B6
Sir Alexander Cl ACT W3 136 C10
Sir Cyril Black Wy WIM/MER SW19 179 K10
Sir Francis Wy BRW CM14 106 C3
Sir Henry Peeks Dr SLN SL2 128 F1
Sirus La MANHO EC4N 12 G6
Sise La MANHO EC4N 12 G6
Siskin Cl BORE WD6 75 M8
BUSH WD23 73 M8
Sisley Rd BARK IG11 143 H3
Sispara Gdns WAND/EARL SW18 179 J2
Sissinghurst Cl BMLY BR1 184 A8
Sissinghurst Cl CRAWE RH10 284 E6
Sissinghurst Rd CROY/NA CR0 203 P7
Sister Mabel's Wy PECK SE15 159 P6
Sisters Av BTSEA SW11 158 A10
Sistova Rd BAL SW12 180 C4
Sisulu Pl BRXN/ST SW9 159 H9
Sittingbourne Av WCHMH N21 79 L10
Sitwell Gv STAN HA7 94 E6
Siverst Cl NTHLT UB5 134 A1
Siviter Wy DAGE RM10 144 C2
Siward Rd HAYES BR2 205 N3
TOOT SW17 179 N6
TOTM N17 99 L9
Six Acres HHS/BOV HP3 36 B9
Sixth Av HYS/HAR UB3 133 G10
MNPK E12 122 C9
NKENS W10 2 A10
Sixth Cross Rd WHTN TW2 176 B6
Skardu Rd CRICK NW2 117 H10
Skarnings Ct WAB EN9 63 M9
Skeena HI WIM/MER SW19 179 H3
Skeet Hill La STMC/STPC BR5 208 A4
Skeffington Rd EHAM E6 142 C3
Skelbrook St WAND/EARL SW18 179 N6
Skelgill Rd PUT/ROE SW15 157 J10
Skelley Rd SRTFD E15 141 L2
Skelton Rd FSTGT E7 141 M1
Skelton's La LEY E10 120 C5
Skelwith Rd HMSMTH W6 156 F5
Skerne Rd KUTN/CMB KT2 191 J1
Sketchley Gdns BERM/RHTH SE16 160 C4
Sketty Rd EN EN1 79 N7
Skibbs La ORP BR6 207 P10
Skid Hill La WARL CR6 243 L1
Skidmore Wy RKW/CH/CXG WD3 91 P7
Skiers St SRTFD E15 141 K3
Skiffington Cl BRXS/STRHM SW2 181 H4
Skimpans Cl BRKMPK AL9 40 C1
Skinner Pl BGVA SW1W 16 C6
Skinners La ASHTD KT21 237 J4
HEST TW5 154 A7
Skinner St FSBYE EC1V 6 C10
Skinney La EYN DA4 210 C3
Skippers Cl GRH DA9 188 C1
Skipsey Av EHAM E6 142 D6
Skipton Cl FBAR/BDGN N11 98 B7
Skipton Dr HYS/HAR UB3 152 D2
Skipton Wy HORL RH6 280 C2
Skipworth Rd HOM E9 140 B5
Skyes Dr STA TW18 173 L8
Skylark Rd DEN/HRF UB9 110 F6
Sky Peals Rd WFD IG8 101 J3
Skyport Dr WDR/YW UB7 151 N6
Skys Wood Rd STALE/WH AL4 38 G2
Sladebrook Rd BKHTH/KID SE3 162 A9
Slade Ct CHERT KT16 214 D5
RAD WD7 74 C2
Sladedale Rd WOOL/PLUM SE18 163 H4
Slade End EPP CM16 83 J7
Slade Gdns ERITH DA8 164 G7
Slade Green Rd ERITH DA8 164 G7
Sladen Pl CLPT E5 120 A9
Slade Oak La DEN/HRF UB9 110 B6
CHOB/PIR GU24 230 C6
Slades Cl ENC/FH EN2 79 H7
Slades Dr CHST BR7 184 F7
Slades Gdns ENC/FH EN2 79 H6
Slades Hi ENC/FH EN2 79 H7
Slades Ri ENC/FH EN2 79 H7
The Slade WOOL/PLUM SE18 163 H1
Slagrove Pl BROCKY SE4 182 F1
Slaidburn St WBPTN SW10 15 L10
Slaithwaite Rd LEW SE13 161 H10
Slaney Pl HOLWY N7 119 H10
Slaney Rd ROM RM1 124 F3
Slattery Rd FELT TW13 175 K4
Slaugham Ct CRAWW RH11 283 J10
Sleaford Gn OXHEY WD19 93 J1
Sleaford St VX/NE SW8 158 D6
Sleapcross Gdns STALE/WH AL4 39 P1
Sleapshyde La STALE/WH AL4 39 P1
Sleddale HHNE HP2 35 P3
Sleepers Farm Rd CDH/CHF RM16 168 E1
Sleets End HHW HP1 35 L4
Slewins Cl EMPK RM11 125 K3
Slewins La EMPK RM11 125 K3
Slievemore Dr STALE/WH AL4 158 F2
Slines New Rd CTHM CR3 242 C6
Slines Oak Rd CTHM CR3 242 F9
Slinfold Wk CRAWW RH11 283 K6
Slingsby Pl COVGDN WC2E 11 L6
Slipe La BROX EN10 44 E10
Slippers Hi HHNE HP2 35 N5
Slippers Pl BERM/RHTH SE16 160 A8
Slipshatch Rd REIG RH2 275 J4
Slipshoe St REIG RH2 257 J10
The Slip BH/WHM TN16 262 F6
Sloane Av CHEL SW3 15 P6
Sloane Ct East CHEL SW3 16 C7
Sloane Ct West CHEL SW3 16 C7
Sloane Gdns BCVA SW1W 16 B6
ORP BR6 206 F10
Sloane St KTBR SW1X 16 B4
Sloane Ter KTBR SW1X 16 B5
Sloane Wk CROY/NA CR0 204 E6
Sloansway WCCE AL7 23 J8
Slocock Hi WOKN/KNAP GU21 231 P3
Slocum Cl THMD SE28 143 H9
Slough La BRKHM/BTCW RH3 256 D9
CDALE/KGS NW9 115 P5
EPSOM KT18 255 J5
IVER SL0 130 C5
Slyfield Gn GU GU1 140 A8
Sly St WCHPL E1 140 A8

Smaldon Cl WDR/YW UB7 152 B2
Small Acre HHW HP1 35 J6
Smallberry Av ISLW TW7 154 E8
Smallbrook Ms BAY/PAD W2 9 L6
Smallcroft WGCE AL7 23 N5
Smalley Cl STNW/STAM N16 119 N8
Smallfield Rd HORL RH6 280 G10
Small Grains HART DA3 210 G10
Smallmead HORL RH6 280 C4
Smalls Hill Rd REIG RH2 274 F10
Smalls Md CRAWW RH11 283 M7
Smallwood Cl STALE/WH AL4 21 K4
Smallwood Rd TOOT SW17 179 N7
Smarden Cl BELV DA17 164 B4
Smart Cl HARH RM3 105 L4
Smarts Gn CHESW EN7 61 N2
Smart's Heath La WOKS/MYFD GU22 231 M9
Smart's Heath Rd WOKS/MYFD GU22 231 M9
Smart's La LOU IG10 32 B8
Smart's Pl HHOL WC1V 11 M5
UED N18 99 P6
Smart St BETH E2 140 C5
Smeaton Cl CHSGTN KT9 219 J4
WAB EN9 63 K8
Smeaton Rd WAB EN9 80 F4
WAND/EARL SW18 179 K3
WFD IG8 102 C6
Smedley St VX/NE SW8 158 F8
Smeed Rd BOW E3 140 F2
Smiles Pl LEW SE13 161 H8
Smitham Bottom La PUR/KEN CR8 222 E8
Smitham Downs Rd COUL/CHIP CR5 222 F9
Smithbarn Cl HORL RH6 280 C3
Smithbarn CRAWE RH10 283 N10
Smith Cl BERM/RHTH SE16 140 C10
The Smithers BRKHM/BTCW RH3 273 N2
Smithfield HHNE HP2 35 N4
Smithfield St STBT EC1A 12 C4
Smithies Rd ABYW SE2 163 L5
Smith Rd REIG RH2 275 J3
Smith's Ct SOHO/SHAV W1D 11 J7
Smiths La CHESW EN7 61 L2
EDEN TN8 262 F9
WDSR SL4 148 D3
Smithson Rd TOTM N17 99 L9
Smith St BRYLDS KT5 199 L6
CHEL SW3 16 A7
WATW WD18 73 K8
Smith Ter CHEL SW3 16 A8
Smithwood Cl WIM/MER SW19 179 H3
Smithy Cl KWD/TDW/WH KT20 257 J2
Smithy La KWD/TDW/WH KT20 257 J2
Smithy's Gn BFOR GU20 212 C3
Smithy St WCHPL E1 140 E7
Smoke La REIG RH2 275 J2
Smugglers Wy WAND/EARL SW18 157 L10
Smugglers Whf GRH DA9 188 C1
Smug Oak La LCOL/BKTW AL2 56 A6
Smyrks Rd WALW SE17 19 K8
Smyrna Rd KIL/WHAMP NW6 2 E2
Smythe Rd EYN DA4 209 P1
Smythe St POP/IOD E14 140 C9
Snag La RSEV TN14 226 F1
Snakes Hi BRW CM14 86 B7
Snakes La East WFD IG8 101 P7
Snakes La West WFD IG8 101 M7
Snape Sp SL SL1 129 K8
Snaresbrook Dr STAN HA7 95 J5
Snaresbrook Rd WAN E11 121 K2
Snarsgate St NKENS W10 136 F7
Snatts HI OXTED RH8 261 L5
Sneath Av GLDGN NW11 117 J5
Snell Hatch CRAWW RH11 283 L7
Snelling Av GVW DA11 190 C5
Snellings Rd WOT/HER KT12 217 K2
Snells La AMSS HP7 36 B1
Snell's Pk UED N18 99 N1
Snells Wood Ct CSTG HP8 69 P6
Sneyd Rd CRICK NW2 116 F10
Snipe Cl ERITH DA8 165 J6
Snowbury Rd FUL/PGN SW6 157 L8
Snowden Av HGDN/ICK UB10 132 C4
Snowden Cl WDSR SL4 148 C10
Snowdon Cl CDALE/KGS NW9 116 B4
Snowdon Crs HYS/HAR UB3 152 D2
Snowdon Rd West HTHAIR TW6 174 D2
Snowdon Wy PGE/AN SE20 204 B1
Snowdrop Cl HPTN TW12 175 P9
Snowdrop Wy CHOB/PIR GU24 230 F3
Snowerhill Rd BRKHM/BTCW RH3 274 A1
Snow HI CRAWE RH10 281 N10
STBT EC1A 12 C4
Snowhill Cottages CSHM HP5 33 L10
Snowhill La CRAWE RH10 281 N10
Snowsfields STHWK SE1 19 H1
Snowshill Rd MNPK E12 122 B10
Snows Paddock BFOR GU20 192 A10
Snows Ride BFOR GU20 192 A10
Snowy Fielder Waye ISLW TW7 154 G8
Soames St PECK SE15 159 N9
Soames Wk NWMAL KT3 200 B1
Soane Cl CRAWW RH11 283 H9
Soham Rd PEND EN3 80 E3
Soho Sq SOHO/SHAV W1D 11 J5
Soho St SOHO/SHAV W1D 11 J5
Solebay St WCHPL E1 140 G5
Solecote GT/LBKH KT23 253 P1
Sole Farm Av GT/LBKH KT23 235 N10
Sole Farm Cl GT/LBKH KT23 253 N1
Sole Farm Rd GT/LBKH KT23 253 N1
Solefields Rd SEV TN13 265 J5
Solent Ri PLSTW E13 141 M5
Solent Rd KIL/WHAMP NW6 117 K10
HTHAIR TW6 174 A2
Soleoak Dr SEV TN13 265 J3
Solesbridge Cl RKW/CH/CXG WD3 71 J7
Solesbridge La RKW/CH/CXG WD3 71 J6
Solid La BRWN CM15 86 E5
Solna Av PUT/ROE SW15 178 F1
Solna Rd WCHMH N21 98 C3
Solomon Av UED N18 99 P5
Solomons Court RD BNSTD SM7 240 A3
COUL/CHIP CR5 240 A3
Solomon's HI RKW/CH/CXG WD3 91 N1
Solomon's Pas PECK SE15 160 A10
Solon New Rd CLAP SW4 158 F10
Solon Rd CLAP SW4 158 F10
Solway HHNE HP2 36 A1
Solway Cl HSLWW TW4 153 M2
HACK E8 119 M2
Solway Rd EDUL SE22 159 P10
WDGN N22 99 H9
Somaford Dr EBAR EN4 77 N10
Somali Rd CRICK NW2 117 J2
Somerby Cl BROX EN10 44 F7
Somerby Rd BARK IG11 142 G2
Somercoates Cl EBAR EN4 77 P7
Somerden Rd STMC/STPC BR5 207 N7
Somerfield Cl KWD/TDW/WH KT20 239 H5
Somerfield Rd FSBYPK N4 119 J7
Somerford Cl PIN HA5 113 H4
Somerford Gv STNW/STAM N16 119 N9
TOTM N17 99 P8
Somerford St WCHPL E1 140 C6
Somerford Wy BERM/RHTH SE16 141 J7
Somerhill Av WELL DA16 164 E8
Somerhill Rd WELL DA16 164 E8
Someries Rd HHW HP1 35 J4
Somerleyton Pas BRXN/ST SW9 159 H10

Somersby Gdns REDBR IG4 122 C3
Somers Cl CAMTN NW1 5 J7
REIG RH2 257 K9
Somers Crs BAY/PAD W2 9 N6
Somerset Av CHSGTN KT9 219 J1
RYNPK SW20 200 E2
WELL DA16 185 J1
Somerset Cl HOR/WEW KT19 220 B5
NWMAL KT3 200 B6
TOTM N17 99 L10
WFD IG8 101 N9
Somerset Gdns EMPK RM11 125 P6
HGT N6 118 B5
LEW SE13 160 G8
STRHM/NOR SW16 202 C3
TEDD TW11 176 D8
Somerset Rd BAR EN5 77 L9
BTFD TW8 155 H5
CHSWK W4 156 A2
DART DA1 187 J2
HDN NW4 116 F2
HRW HA1 114 B4
KUT KT1 199 L2
ORP BR6 207 K7
PEND EN3 80 F4
REIG RH2 257 K9
SLH/COR SS17 169 K1
STHL UB1 133 P7
TEDD TW11 176 D8
TOTM N17 119 N1
UED N18 99 N6
WALTH E17 120 F5
WEA W13 134 G10
WIM/MER SW19 178 G6
Somerset Sq WKENS W14 14 B2
Somerset Street Little TWRH EC3N 13 L6
Somerset Wy IVER SL0 151 J1
Somerset Waye HEST TW5 153 M5
Somersham WCCE AL7 23 N5
Somersham Rd BXLYHN DA7 165 P8
Somers Pl BRXS/STRHM SW2 181 P2
Somers Rd BRKMPK AL9 40 F10
BRXS/STRHM SW2 181 P2
REIG RH2 257 K9
WALTH E17 120 C2
Somers Wy BUSH WD23 94 B1
Somerswey RGUE GU4 268 B8
Somerton Av RCH/KEW TW9 155 N9
Somerton Cl PUR/KEN CR8 241 K2
Somerton Rd CRICK NW2 116 G8
PECK SE15 160 A10
Somertons Cl GUW GU2 249 M6
Somertrees Av LEE/GVPK SE12 183 N5
Somervell Rd RYLN/HDSTN HA2 113 N10
Somerville Av BARN SW13 156 E5
Somerville Dr CRAWE RH10 284 D4
Somerville Rd CHDH RM6 123 M3
COB KT11 217 P10
DART DA1 187 N2
PGE/AN SE20 182 C10
WDSR SL4 149 H4
Sonderburg Rd HOLWY N7 118 C3
Sondes Place Dr DORK RH4 272 E2
Sondes St WALW SE17 18 G10
Sonia Cl OXHEY WD19 93 K1
Sonia Gdns CRICK NW2 116 C9
HEST TW5 153 P6
NFNCH/WDSP N12 97 M5
Sonning Gdns HPTN TW12 175 M9
Sonning Rd CROY/NA CR0 203 P6
Soothouse Spring STALW/RED AL3 38 E2
Soper Cl CHING E4 100 E6
FSTH SE23 182 F4
Soper Dr CTHM CR3 241 L9
Soper Ms PEND EN3 80 F4
Sopers Rd POTB/CUF EN6 60 G5
Sophia Rd CAN/RD E16 141 N8
LEY E10 120 C6
Sophia Sq POP/IOD E14 140 D9
Sopwell La STAL AL1 38 C7
Sopwith Av CHSGTN KT9 219 K2
Sopwith Cl BH/WHM TN16 244 A2
RCHPK/HAM TW10 177 L8
Sopwith Rd HEST TW5 153 K6
Sopwith Wy KUTN/CMB KT2 199 K1
VX/NE SW8 158 C6
Sorbie Cl WEY KT13 216 D3
Sorrel Cl THMD SE28 143 K10
Sorrel Gdns EHAM E6 142 B7
Sorrel La POP/IOD E14 141 J8
Sorrell Cl NWCR SE14 160 D6
BRXN/ST SW9 159 K4
Sorrel Wk ROM RM1 124 G1
Sorrento Rd SUT SM1 201 L10
Sospel Ct SLN SL2 129 H4
Sotheby Rd HBRY N5 119 K9
Sotheran Cl HACK E8 7 P5
Sotheron Rd WAT WD17 73 K6
FUL/PGN SW6 158 B6
Soudan Rd BTSEA SW11 158 G2
Souldern Rd WKENS W14 14 A2
Souldern St WATW WD18 73 J9
Sounds Ldge SWLY BR8 208 D6
South Access Rd WALTH E17 120 D5
South Acre CDALE/KGS NW9 96 C10
Southacre Wy PIN HA5 93 K9
South Africa Rd SHB W12 136 E9
South Albert Rd REIG RH2 257 K9
Southall Cl WARE SG12 26 C1
Southall La HEST TW5 153 H7
Southall Pl STHWK SE1 18 G2
Southam St NKENS W10 136 C9
South Ap NTHWD HA6 92 E4
South Audley St MYFR/PKLN W1K 10 D8
South Av CAR SM5 222 B4
CHING E4 101 M2
EGH TW20 172 G9
RCH/KEW TW9 155 N8
WOT/HER KT12 216 F6
South Avenue Gdns STHL UB1 133 N9
South Bank SURB KT6 199 G7
THDIT KT7 198 C7
South Bank Rd REDBR IG4 122 C2
South Bank Ter SURB KT6 199 K6
South Birkbeck Rd WAN E11 121 J6
South Black Lion La HMSMTH W6 156 D4
South Bolton Gdns WBPTN SW10 15 H7
The South Border PUR/KEN CR8 222 E7
Southborough Cl SURB KT6 199 J8
HAYES BR2 206 C5
Southborough La BMLY BR1 206 C5
HOM E9 140 B5
Southborough Rd BMLY BR1 206 D5
HOM E9 140 B5
SURB KT6 199 K8
Southborough Road (The Lane) SURB KT6 199 K8
Southbourne HAYES BR2 205 M9
Southbourne Av CDALE/KGS NW9 95 P6
Southbourne Cl PIN HA5 113 M5
Southbourne Crs HDN NW4 116 B2
Southbourne Gdns IL IG1 122 F10
LEE/GVPK SE12 183 N5
RSLP HA4 113 J6

Southbridge Rd CROY/NA CR0 223 K1
Southbridge Wy NWDGN UB2 153 M1
Southbrook SBW CM21 22 G2
Southbrook Dr CHES/WCR EN8 62 C4
Southbrook Rd LEW SE13 183 K2
STRHM/NOR SW16 202 F1
South Bucks Wy CFSP/GDCR SL9 90 B6
DEN/HRF UB9 111 K6
Southbury Av EN EN1 79 P8
Southbury Cl HCH RM12 125 L10
South Carriage Dr KTBR SW1X 16 B1
SKENS SW7 15 N2
South Charlton Mead La HOD EN11 45 J4
Southchurch Ct PLMGR N13 98 C6
Southchurch Rd EHAM E6 142 C4
Southcliffe Dr CFSP/GDCR SL9 90 B6
South Cl BAR EN5 76 C3
BXLYHS DA6 163 N10
CRAWE RH10 284 A6
DAGE RM10 144 B3
HGT N6 118 C4
LCOL/BKTW AL2 56 A1
PIN HA5 113 N5
SL SL1 128 C9
WDR/YW UB7 152 A2
WOKN/KNAP GU21 231 P2
South Close Gn REIG RH2 258 C5
South Colonnade POP/IOD E14 140 F10
Southcombe St WKENS W14 14 A5
Southcote WOKN/KNAP GU21 232 A2
Southcote Av BRYLDS KT5 199 N7
FELT TW13 175 H5
Southcote Ri RSLP HA4 112 E5
Southcote Rd ARCH N19 118 D9
REDH RH1 258 D6
SAND/SEL CR2 223 M6
SNWD SE25 204 A5
WALTH E17 120 C3
South Cottage Dr RKW/CH/CXG WD3 71 J9
South Cottage Gdns RKW/CH/CXG WD3 71 J9
South Countess Rd WALTH E17 120 E1
South Cres CAN/RD E16 141 J6
GWRST WC1E 11 J3
South Croft EGH TW20 171 N8
SLN SL2 128 G6
South Cross Rd BARK/HLT IG6 122 F3
South Croxted Rd DUL SE21 181 L6
Southdale CHIG IG7 102 G7
South Dean MLHL NW7 96 A4
Southdean Gdns WIM/MER SW19 179 J7
Southdown RSEV TN14 228 A9
Southdown Av HNWL W7 154 F2
Southdown Ct HAT AL10 40 D7
Southdown Crs GNTH/NBYPK IG2 123 H3
RYLN/HDSTN HA2 114 A3
Southdown Dr RYNPK SW20 178 G10
Southdown Rd CAR SM5 222 B5
CTHM CR3 242 E8
EMPK RM11 125 J5
HARP AL5 20 A3
HAT AL10 40 D7
RYNPK SW20 200 G1
WOT/HER KT12 217 M1
South Downs Wy BRKHM/BTCW RH3 256 C6
DORK RH4 255 H6
KWD/TDW/WH KT20 255 L8
South Dr BEAC HP9 108 A1
BELMT SM2 221 H6
BNSTD SM7 221 P9
BRW CM14 107 J5
CHOB/PIR GU24 230 B7
COUL/CHIP CR5 240 E1
GPK RM2 124 E2
ORP BR6 227 H2
POTB/CUF EN6 60 G5
RDKG RH5 273 H2
RSLP HA4 112 F6
STALE/WH AL4 39 K5
VW GU25 193 M7
South Ealing Rd EA W5 155 H1
South Eastern Av ED N9 99 N4
South Eaton Pl BGVA SW1W 16 C5
South Eden Park Rd BECK BR3 206 A1
South Edwardes Sq KENS W8 14 D4
South End CROY/NA CR0 223 K1
GT/LBKH KT23 254 A2
KENS W8 15 H1
Southend Arterial Rd EMPK RM11 125 M1
RBRW/HUT CM13 126 G3
Southend Cl ELTH/MOT SE9 184 E2
Southend Crs ELTH/MOT SE9 184 D2
Southend La CAT SE6 182 G10
WAB EN9 63 N10
Southend Rd BECK BR3 182 F10
GRAYS RM17 167 P3
South End Rd HAMP NW3 117 P3
HAMP NW3 117 P3
RAIN RM13 145 H3
REDBR IG4 122 A4
Southend Road (North Circular Road) SWFD E18 101 L1
WALTH E17 101 J9
South End Rw KENS W8 15 H3
Southerland Cl WEY KT13 216 D1
Southern Av EBED/NFELT TW14 175 H4
REDH RH1 276 B7
SNWD SE25 204 B7
Southern Dr LOU IG10 32 C10
Southerngate Wy NWCR SE14 160 G6
Southern Gv BOW E3 140 E5
Southernhay LOU IG10 32 A9
Southern Pl SWLY BR8 208 E4
Southern Rd EFNCH N2 118 A2
PLSTW E13 141 N4
Southern Row NKENS W10 136 B8
Southern St IS N1 5 N7
Southern Wy CHDH RM6 124 B4
Southernwood Cl HEMP HP2 36 B5
Southerton Rd HMSMTH W6 156 F3
Southey Rd BRXN/ST SW9 159 J7
SEVS/STOTM N15 119 M3
WIM/MER SW19 178 B4
Southey St PGE/AN SE20 182 C10
Southey Wk TIL RM18 168 E7
Southfield BAR EN5 76 G10
WGCE AL7 22 C7
Southfield Cl UX/CGN UB8 132 B4
South Field WDSR SL4 148 B2
Southfield Gdns SL SL1 128 A7
TWK TW1 176 E7
Southfield Pk RYLN/HDSTN HA2 114 A3
Southfield Pl WEY KT13 216 E5
Southfield Rd CHES/WCR EN8 62 D8
CHST BR7 207 J3
CHSWK W4 156 A1
HOD EN11 46 E1
PEND EN3 80 A10
Southfields E/WMO/HCT KT8 198 B7
HDN NW4 116 B2
Southfields Av ASHF TW15 174 C9
Southfields Ct CTHM CR3 242 C9

WBLY HA9 ... 115 L9
Staffa Rd LEY E10 ... 120 D6
Stafford Av EMPK RM11 ... 125 L1
  SLN SL2 ... 129 H6
Stafford Cl CDH/CHF RM16 ... 167 H1
  CHEAM SM3 ... 221 H3
  CHES/WCR EN8 ... 62 A5
  CTHM CR3 ... 241 N9
  KIL/WHAMP NW6 ... 188 E3 1
  MDHD SL6 ... 128 A8 2
  SLH/COR SS17 ... 169 K2
  STHGT/OAK N14 ... 78 D9
  WALTH E17 ... 120 E4 2
Stafford Dr BROX ... 44 F6 2
Stafford Gdns CROY/NA CR0 ... 222 G2 2
Stafford Lake CHOB/PIR GU24 ... 230 F4
Stafford Pl RCHPK/HAM TW10 ... 177 L3
Stafford Rd BOW E3 ... 140 E4
  CRAWW RH11 ... 283 K4
  CROY/NA CR0 ... 223 H1
  CTHM CR3 ... 241 N9
  FSTGT E7 ... 141 P2
  KIL/WHAMP NW6 ... 2 E9
  KTN/HRWW/W HA3 ... 94 B8
  NWMAL KT3 ... 199 P3
  RSLP HA4 ... 112 C9
  SCUP DA14 ... 185 H7
  WLGTN SM6 ... 222 D5
Staffords HLWE CM17 ... 159 P7 2
Staffordshire St PECK SE15 ... 159 P7 2
  PECK SE15 ... 160 A7 2
Stafford Ter KENS W8 ... 14 E5 3
Stafford Wy SEV TN13 ... 265 K3
Stagbury Av COUL/CHIP CR5 ... 239 P4
Stagbury Cl COUL/CHIP CR5 ... 239 P7
Stag Cl EDGW HA8 ... 95 N10
Stagelands CRAWW RH11 ... 283 L5
Staggart Gn BARK/HLT IG6 ... 103 K7 2
Stagg Hl POTB/CUF EN6 ... 77 N1
Stag Green Av BRKMPK AL9 ... 40 F2
Stag Hl GUW GU2 ... 267 M1
Stag La BERK HP4 ... 33 M4
  BKHH IG9 ... 101 L4
  EDGW HA8 ... 95 N10
  PUT/ROE SW15 ... 178 D10
  RKW/CH/CXG WD3 ... 70 F10
Stag Leys ASHTD KT21 ... 237 K6
Stag Leys Cl BNSTD SM7 ... 239 P1
Stag Pl WESTW SW1E ... 16 C3
Stags Wy ISLW TW7 ... 154 E5
Stainash Crs STA TW18 ... 173 L8
Stainbank Rd MTCM CR4 ... 202 C3
Stainby Cl WDR/YW UB7 ... 151 P2
Stainby Rd SEVS/STOTM N15 ... 119 N10
Stainer Rd BORE WD6 ... 75 J3
Staines Av CHEAM SM3 ... 200 G9
Staines By-pass
  STWL/WRAY TW19 ... 173 H6
Staines La CHERT KT16 ... 195 K6
Staines Lane Cl CHERT KT16 ... 195 J5 2
  EBED/NFELT TW14 ... 174 E3
  HSLWW TW4 ... 175 L1
  IL IG1 ... 122 C9
  STA TW18 ... 195 L1
  STWL/WRAY TW19 ... 172 C4
  WHTN TW2 ... 176 B6
Staines Rd East SUN TW16 ... 197 K1
Staines Rd West ASHF TW15 ... 174 D10
Stainford Cl ASHF TW15 ... 174 E8
Stainforth Rd GNTH/NBYPK IG2 ... 122 G5
  WALTH E17 ... 120 F2
Staining La CITYW EC2V ... 12 F5
Stainmore Cl CHST BR7 ... 206 G1 2
Stainsbury St BETH E2 ... 140 B4
Stainsby Cl POP/IOD E14 ... 140 F8
Stainsby Pl POP/IOD E14 ... 140 F8 2
Stainsby Rd POP/IOD E14 ... 140 F8
Stainton Rd LEW SE13 ... 183 J3
  PEND EN3 ... 80 B5
Stairfoot La SEV TN13 ... 246 D4
Staithes Wy KWD/TDW/WH KT20 ... 238 E6
Stakers Ct HARP AL5 ... 20 A2
Stakescorner Rd RGUW GU3 ... 267 M9
Stalbridge St CAMTN NW1 ... 9 P5
Stalham St BERM/RHTH SE16 ... 160 A8
Stambourne Wy NRWD SE19 ... 181 M10
  WWKM BR4 ... 205 H10
Stamford Brook Av HMSMTH W6 ... 156 C2
Stamford Brook Gdns
  HMSMTH W6 ... 156 C2 2
Stamford Brook Rd HMSMTH W6 ... 156 C2
Stamford Cl KTN/HRWW/W HA3 ... 94 D8
  POTB/CUF EN6 ... 59 P1
  SEVS/STOTM N15 ... 119 P2 2
  STHL UB1 ... 133 P6 2
Stamford Dr HAYES BR2 ... 205 L4
Stamford Gdns DAGW RM9 ... 143 M2
Stamford Green Rd EPSOM KT18 ... 219 N9
Stamford Gv East
  STNW/STAM N16 ... 119 P6 2
Stamford Gv West
  STNW/STAM N16 ... 119 P6 2
Stamford Hl STNW/STAM N16 ... 119 N6
Stamford Rd DAGW RM9 ... 143 L2
  EHAM E6 ... 142 B3
  IS N1 ... 7 K3
  SEVS/STOTM N15 ... 119 P2 2
  WAT WD17 ... 73 J6
  WOT/HER KT12 ... 197 L10 2
Stamp Pl BETH E2 ... 7 L9
Stanborough Cl BORE WD6 ... 7 L9 2
  HPTN TW12 ... 175 N9 2
  WGCW AL8 ... 22 F6 2
Stanborough Gn WGCW AL8 ... 22 F7 2
Stanborough La ISLW TW7 ... 154 C7 2
  WGCW AL8 ... 22 F7 3
Stanborough Rd ISLW TW7 ... 154 C7
  WGCW AL8 ... 22 B8
Stanbridge Pl CRAWW RH11 ... 283 H7 2
Stanbridge Pl WCHMH N21 ... 99 J3 2
Stanbridge Rd PUT/ROE SW15 ... 156 F9 2
Stanbrook Rd ABYW SE2 ... 163 L1
  GVW DA11 ... 190 C4
Stanbury Av WAT WD17 ... 72 F3
Stanbury Ct HAMP NW3 ... 4 A2
Stanbury Rd PECK SE15 ... 160 B4
Stancroft CDALE/KGS NW9 ... 112 G1
Standale Gv RSLP HA4 ... 112 C9
Standard Rd BELV DA17 ... 164 B4
  BXLYHS DA6 ... 163 F10
  HSLWW TW4 ... 153 M9
  ORP BR6 ... 226 D6
  PEND EN3 ... 80 D4
  WLSDN NW10 ... 135 P6
Standen Av HCH RM12 ... 125 L8
Standen Rd WAND/EARL SW18 ... 179 K3
Standfield ABLGY WD5 ... 54 C7
Standfield Rd DAGE RM10 ... 124 B1
Standinghall La CRAWE RH10 ... 285 H9
Standish Rd HMSMTH W6 ... 156 D3
Standring Ri HHS/BOV HP3 ... 56 B4
Stane Cl WIM/MER SW19 ... 179 L10 3
Stane Wy EW KT17 ... 220 D6
  WOOL/PLUM SE18 ... 162 A6
Stanfield Rd BOW E3 ... 140 D4 10
Stanford Cl HPTN TW12 ... 175 N9 2
  ROMW/RG RM7 ... 124 C4
  RSLP HA4 ... 112 D4
  WAB EN9 ... 65 N4
Stanford Ct WAB EN9 ... 63 M9 2
Stanford Gdns SOCK/AV RM15 ... 146 D10

Stanford Pl STHWK SE1 ... 19 J6
Stanford Rivers Rd CHONG CM5 ... 57 P7
Stanford Rd CDH/CHF RM16 ... 168 D3 2
  FBAR/BDGN N11 ... 98 A6
  KENS W8 ... 15 A6
  STRHM/NOR SW16 ... 202 F2 2
The Stanfords EW KT17 ... 220 C8 2
Stanford St WEST SW1P ... 17 J6
Stanford Wy STRHM/NOR SW16 ... 202 E2 2
Stangate CRORE VW6 ... 76 B9 2
Stangate Gdns STAN HA7 ... 94 G5
Stanger Rd SNWD SE25 ... 203 P4
Stanham Pl DART DA1 ... 165 H10 2
Stanham Rd DART DA1 ... 187 K1
Stan Hl HORL RH6 ... 278 F7
Stanhope Av FNCH N3 ... 117 J1
  HAYES BR2 ... 205 N8
  KTN/HRWW/W HA3 ... 94 C9
Stanhope Cl BERM/RHTH SE16 ... 160 C1 2
Stanhope Gdns FSBYPK N4 ... 119 J4
  HGT N6 ... 118 C4
  IL IG1 ... 122 C4
  MLHL NW7 ... 96 C6 2
  SKENS SW7 ... 15 K3
Stanhope Ga MYFR/PKLN W1K ... 10 D10
Stanhope Gv BECK BR3 ... 204 D5
Stanhope Heath
  STWL/WRAY TW19 ... 173 M2 2
Stanhope Ms East SKENS SW7 ... 15 K4
Stanhope Ms South SKENS SW7 ... 15 K4
Stanhope Ms West SKENS SW7 ... 15 K4
Stanhope Park Rd
  GFD/PVL UB6 ... 134 B6 2
Stanhope Pl BAY/PAD W2 ... 10 A1
Stanhope Rd BAR EN5 ... 76 G10
  BCTR RM8 ... 124 A7
  BFN/LL DA15 ... 185 K7
  BXLYHN DA7 ... 163 P8
  CAR SM5 ... 222 B4
  CHES/WCR EN8 ... 62 D9
  CROY/NA CR0 ... 203 M10
  GFD/PVL UB6 ... 134 B7
  HGT N6 ... 118 D4
  NFNCH/WDSP N12 ... 97 M6
  RAIN RM13 ... 145 H4
  SL SL1 ... 128 C3
  STAL AL1 ... 38 E7
  SWCM DA10 ... 189 L1
  WALTH E17 ... 120 E1
Stanhope Rw MYFR/PICC W1J ... 10 E10 2
Stanhopes OXTED RH8 ... 261 N4
Stanhope St CAMTN NW1 ... 4 C9
Stanhope Ter BAY/PAD W2 ... 9 N1
Stanhope Wy SEV TN13 ... 246 E1
  STWL/WRAY TW19 ... 173 M2 2
Stanier Cl WKENS W14 ... 19 L2 2
Stanier Ri BERK HP4 ... 33 L2
Staniland Dr WEY KT13 ... 216 A7
Stanlake Ms SHB W12 ... 136 F10 2
Stanlake Rd SHB W12 ... 136 F10
Stanlake VIs SHB W12 ... 136 F10
Stanley Av ALP/SUD HA0 ... 135 K2
  BARK IG11 ... 143 L5
  BCTR RM8 ... 124 A6
  BECK BR3 ... 185 L3
  CSHM HP5 ... 50 C7
  GFD/PVL UB6 ... 134 B3
  GPK RM2 ... 125 H2
  LCOL/BKTW AL2 ... 55 P1
  NWMAL KT3 ... 200 D5
Stanley Cl ALP/SUD HA0 ... 135 K2 2
  COUL/CHIP CR5 ... 240 G3
  CRAWE RH10 ... 283 P9
  GPK RM2 ... 125 H2
  GRH DA9 ... 188 D1
  HCH RM12 ... 125 L8
  UX/CGN UB8 ... 131 N4 2
Stanley Cottages SLN SL2 ... 129 L10
Stanley Crs GVE DA12 ... 190 G8
  NTGHL W11 ... 8 C1
Stanley Dr HAT AL10 ... 40 E6
Stanleycroft Cl ISLW TW7 ... 154 D7 2
Stanley Gardens Rd TEDD TW11 ... 176 D6
Stanley Gdns ACT W3 ... 156 A1
  BORE WD6 ... 75 K5
  CRICK NW2 ... 116 F4 2
  MTCM CR4 ... 180 B9 2
  NTGHL W11 ... 8 C1
  SAND/SEL CR2 ... 223 P8 1
  WLGTN SM6 ... 222 D5
  WOT/HER KT12 ... 217 K2
Stanley Gardens Ms AMSS HP7 ... 69 K6
Stanley Hill Av AMSS HP7 ... 69 J5
Stanley Park Dr ALP/SUD HA0 ... 135 L6
Stanley Park Rd CAR SM5 ... 222 A4
  WLGTN SM6 ... 222 B5
Stanley Rd ACT W3 ... 155 N2
  ASHF TW15 ... 173 P8
  BELMT SM2 ... 221 L8
  CAR SM5 ... 222 B4
  CHING E4 ... 101 P2
  CROY/NA CR0 ... 203 H7
  ED N9 ... 99 P2
  EFNCH N2 ... 117 N2
  EN EN1 ... 79 N7
  FBAR/BDGN N11 ... 98 E7
  GRAYS RM17 ... 167 N4
  HAYES BR2 ... 205 P3
  HCH RM12 ... 125 K7
  HRT/BAY SG13 ... 25 M6
  HSLW TW3 ... 154 B10
  IL IG1 ... 122 G4
  LEY E10 ... 120 C4
  MNPK E12 ... 122 B10
  MORT/ESHN SW14 ... 155 N10
  MRDN SM4 ... 201 K4
  MTCM CR4 ... 180 B10
  MUSWH N10 ... 98 B1
  NTHWD HA6 ... 93 H9
  ORP BR6 ... 207 J8
  PEND EN3 ... 80 D4
  RYLN/HDSTN HA2 ... 114 B7
  SCUP DA14 ... 185 K6
  SEVS/STOTM N15 ... 119 J2
  SRTFD E15 ... 141 J5 1
  STHL UB1 ... 133 J6
  SWCM DA10 ... 189 L2
  SWFD E18 ... 102 D6
  TEDD TW11 ... 176 D6 2
  WAT WD17 ... 73 K7 2
  WBLY HA9 ... 135 L1
  WHTN TW2 ... 176 B7
  WIM/MER SW19 ... 179 K10
  WOKN/KNAP GU21 ... 232 C2
Stanley Rd North RAIN RM13 ... 144 H3
Stanley Rd South RAIN RM13 ... 144 H4
Stanley Sq CAR SM5 ... 222 A5
Stanley St CTHM CR3 ... 241 K8
  DEPT SE8 ... 140 F2
Stanley Ter ARCH N19 ... 118 F7 2
Stanmer St BTSEA SW11 ... 157 P7
Stanmore Gdns RCH/KEW TW9 ... 155 L9 2
  SUT SM1 ... 201 M10 2
Stanmore Hl STAN HA7 ... 94 G6 1
Stanmore Rd BELV DA17 ... 164 D3
  RCH/KEW TW9 ... 155 L9
  SEVS/STOTM N15 ... 119 J2
  WAN E11 ... 121 L5
  WATN WD24 ... 73 J1
Stanmore St IS N1 ... 5 N5
Stanmore Ter BECK BR3 ... 204 F2 1
Stanmore Wy LOU IG10 ... 82 D5

Stanmount Rd LCOL/BKTW AL2 ... 55 P1
Stannard Rd HACK E8 ... 7 N1
Stannary St LBTH SE11 ... 18 B9
Stansfeld Rd CAN/RD E16 ... 142 A9
Stansfield Rd BRXN/ST SW9 ... 158 C9
  HSLWW TW4 ... 153 H9
Stansgate Rd DAGE RM10 ... 124 B9
Stanstead Cl HAYES BR2 ... 205 L6 2
Stanstead Dr HOD EN11 ... 44 G1
Stanstead Gv CTHM CR3 ... 241 M10
Stanstead Gdns STAN HA7 ... 182 E4 2
Stanstead Rd CTHM CR3 ... 241 M10
  FSTH SE23 ... 182 C4
  HERT/BAY SG13 ... 25 P4
  HOD EN11 ... 26 G10
  WAN E11 ... 121 N1
  WARE SG12 ... 26 C5
Stansted Cl HCH RM12 ... 145 K1 2
Stansted Crs BXLY DA5 ... 185 N4
Stanswood Gdns CMBW SE5 ... 159 N6
Stanthorpe Rd
  STRHM/NOR SW16 ... 180 F1 2
Stanton Av TEDD TW11 ... 176 D9
Stanton Cl HOR/WEW KT19 ... 219 N2
  STALE/WH AL4 ... 39 J7
  STMC/STPC BR5 ... 207 M4
  WPK KT4 ... 200 G8 2
Stanton Rd BARN SW13 ... 156 D8
  CROY/NA CR0 ... 205 M2
  RYNPK SW20 ... 200 C3
Stantons Whf SHGR GU5 ... 268 D10
Stanton Wy DTCH/LGLY SL3 ... 150 B3
  SYD SE26 ... 182 F7
Stanway Cl CHIG IG7 ... 103 H6
Stanway Gdns ACT W3 ... 135 M10
  EDGW HA8 ... 95 P7
Stanway St IS N1 ... 7 J3
Stanwell Cl STWL/WRAY TW19 ... 173 N2 2
Stanwell Gdns STWL/WRAY TW19 ... 173 N2
Stanwell Moor Rd
  STWL/WRAY TW19 ... 173 H2 2
  WDR/YW UB7 ... 151 J7
Stanwell New Rd STA TW18 ... 173 L7
Stanwell Rd ASHF TW15 ... 173 P6
  DTCH/LGLY SL3 ... 150 B9
  EBED/NFELT TW14 ... 174 C3
Stanwick Rd WKENS W14 ... 14 A4
Stanworth St STHWK SE1 ... 19 L2 2
Stanwyck Gdns HARH RM3 ... 105 J6
Stapenhill Rd ALP/SUD HA0 ... 114 C8
Staple Cl BXLY DA5 ... 186 E6
Staplefield Cl PIN HA5 ... 94 H9
  REDH RH1 ... 275 M4
Stapleford Av GNTH/NBYPK IG2 ... 123 H4
  HAYES BR2 ... 205 M9
Stapleford Cl CHING E4 ... 101 H4 2
  KUT KT1 ... 199 M3 2
  WIM/MER SW19 ... 179 J1
Stapleford Gdns CRW RM5 ... 104 B7
Stapleford Rd ABR/ST RM4 ... 84 C8
  ALP/SUD HA0 ... 135 J2
Stapleford Wy BARK IG11 ... 143 L5 1
Staplehurst Cl REDH RH1 ... 275 M4
Staplehurst Rd CAR SM5 ... 221 P4
  LEW SE13 ... 183 J1
  REDH RH1 ... 275 M4
Staple La RGUE GU4 ... 270 A1
Staples Cl BERM/RHTH SE16 ... 140 D10 2
Staples Rd LOU IG10 ... 82 B7
Staple St STHWK SE1 ... 19 J2 2
Stapleton Cl POTB/CUF EN6 ... 59 N7
Stapleton Crs RAIN RM13 ... 145 J1
Stapleton Gdns CROY/NA CR0 ... 223 H2
Stapleton Hall Rd FSBYPK N4 ... 118 G5
Stapleton Rd BORE WD6 ... 75 M4
  BXLYHN DA7 ... 164 A6
  ORP BR6 ... 207 J10
  TOOT SW17 ... 180 B5
Stapley Rd BELV DA17 ... 164 B4
  STALW/RED AL3 ... 38 C5
Staplyton Rd BAR EN5 ... 77 H7
Star And Garter Hl
  RCHPK/HAM TW10 ... 177 K4
Starboard Av GRH DA9 ... 188 G2
Starboard Wy POP/IOD E14 ... 160 F2
Starch House La BARK/HLT IG6 ... 102 G10
Starcross St CAMTN NW1 ... 5 H9
Starfield Rd SHB W12 ... 156 D1
Star Hl DART DA1 ... 186 F1
  WOKS/MYFD GU22 ... 231 P5
Star Hill Rd RSEV TN14 ... 246 A7
Star Holme Ct WARE SG12 ... 26 D2
Starkey Cl CHESW EN7 ... 61 K1 2
Star La CAN/RD E16 ... 141 K6
  COUL/CHIP CR5 ... 240 B8
  EPP CM16 ... 65 K6
  PLSTW E13 ... 141 L6 5
  STMC/STPC BR5 ... 207 N4
Starling Cl BKHH IG9 ... 101 M2
  HART DA3 ... 211 L6
  PIN HA5 ... 113 K1
Starmans Cl DAGW RM9 ... 143 N3
Star Rd HGDN/ICK UB10 ... 132 D6
  ISLW TW7 ... 154 C8
  WKENS W14 ... 14 C9
Starrock La COUL/CHIP CR5 ... 240 B9
Starrock Rd COUL/CHIP CR5 ... 240 G5
Star St BAY/PAD W2 ... 9 M5
  WARE SG12 ... 26 D2
Starts Cl ORP BR6 ... 206 D10
Starts Hill Av ORP BR6 ... 226 E2
Starts Hill Rd ORP BR6 ... 206 E10
Starveall WDR/YW UB7 ... 152 A2
Starwood Cl WDR/YW UB7 ... 217 M5
Starwood Ct DTCH/LGLY SL3 ... 149 P2 2
State Farm Av ORP BR6 ... 226 E1
Staten Gdns TWK TW1 ... 176 A4
Statham Gv STNW/STAM N16 ... 119 M6 2
  UED N18 ... 99 M6 2
Station Ap ALP/SUD HA0 ... 174 A7
  ASHF TW15 ... 77 M8
  BAR EN5 ... 77 M8
  BECK BR3 ... 182 D10
  BELMT SM2 ... 221 H4 3
  BELMT SM2 ... 221 L6 2
  BF/WBF KT14 ... 211 M5
  BKHTH/KID SE3 ... 161 N9 2
  BXLYHN DA7 ... 163 P9
  BXLYHN DA7 ... 164 D3
  CAT SE6 ... 182 B8
  CFSP/GDCR SL9 ... 32 B1
  CHES/WCR EN8 ... 62 D10 2
  CHST BR7 ... 206 D1
  COUL/CHIP CR5 ... 240 C6
  COUL/CHIP CR5 ... 240 G4
  CTHM CR3 ... 241 P3
  DART DA1 ... 187 M2
  DEN/HRF UB9 ... 110 D5
  DORK RH4 ... 272 A1
  EHSLY KT24 ... 252 F2
  ESH/CLAY KT10 ... 217 K10
  EW KT17 ... 220 E6 1
  FBAR/BDGN N11 ... 98 C2 2
  FUL/PGN SW6 ... 157 K7
  GFD/PVL UB6 ... 134 D2
  HAYES BR2 ... 205 K8 2
  HAYES BR2 ... 220 C10 2
  HOR/WEW KT19 ... 220 D2 2
  HORL RH6 ... 280 C1 2
  HPTN TW12 ... 197 J1
  HYS/HAR UB3 ... 152 F3 2
  IL IG1 ... 122 A3 2
  KGLGY WD4 ... 54 C4
  KUT KT1 ... 199 J1 2
  KUTN/CMB KT2 ... 199 M1 2
  LCOL/BKTW AL2 ... 55 L3
  LHD/OX KT22 ... 236 H9
  LOU IG10 ... 82 B9
  MEO DA13 ... 189 M7
  MLHL NW7 ... 96 B7
  MNPK E12 ... 122 B10 2
  NRWD SE19 ... 181 P3 2
  NWMAL KT3 ... 200 A1
  ORP BR6 ... 207 M3
  PGE/AN SE20 ... 182 F6 2
  POTB/CUF EN6 ... 60 C2
  PUR/KEN CR8 ... 223 K1 2
  RAD WD7 ... 74 F1 2
  REDH RH1 ... 258 B7 1
  RGDL GU7 ... 267 J10 2
  RGUE GU4 ... 268 B6
  RKW/CH/CXG WD3 ... 91 N1 2
  RSEV TN14 ... 228 A7

ORP BR6 ... 207 J3
  BR6 ... 227 L2
OXHEY WD19 ... 93 L4 2
OXTED RH8 ... 261 K5
PIN HA5 ... 113 N1
PUR/KEN CR8 ... 223 H7 2
RAD WD7 ... 74 F1
RCH/KEW TW9 ... 155 M7 2
RKW/CH/CXG WD3 ... 70 F3
RSEV TN14 ... 247 K2
RSLP HA4 ... 112 F6
RSLP HA4 ... 113 J10
SAND/SEL CR2 ... 223 L2 2
SHPTN TW17 ... 196 D5 2
STA TW18 ... 173 K7
STMC/STPC BR5 ... 207 L4
STRHM/NOR SW16 ... 180 E8
SUN TW16 ... 197 H1
SURB KT6 ... 199 K6 2
SWLY BR8 ... 208 F4 3
VW GU25 ... 194 A4
WAN E11 ... 121 M3
WDR/YW UB7 ... 131 P10
WEA W13 ... 135 J8
WEY KT13 ... 216 B5
WLSDN NW10 ... 136 C5 2
WOKS/MYFD GU22 ... 232 C3
WPK KT4 ... 200 D8 2
Station Ap East REDH RH1 ... 276 A2 2
Station Approach Rd CHSWK W4 ... 155 P6 2
  COUL/CHIP CR5 ... 240 C7
  HORL RH6 ... 280 C7 1
  KWD/TDW/WH KT20 ... 238 F8
  TIL RM18 ... 168 D10
Station Ap West REDH RH1 ... 276 A2 3
Station Av CTHM CR3 ... 241 P10
  HOR/WEW KT19 ... 220 B5
  NWMAL KT3 ... 200 B3 2
  WOT/HER KT12 ... 216 C1 2
Station Cl BRKMPK AL9 ... 59 N2 1
  HPTN TW12 ... 198 A1
  POTB/CUF EN6 ... 59 J7
Station Crs ALP/SUD HA0 ... 134 C1
  ASHF TW15 ... 173 N7
  BKHTH/KID SE3 ... 161 M4
  SEVS/STOTM N15 ... 119 J2
Station Est BECK BR3 ... 204 C4 2
Station Estate Rd
  EBED/NFELT TW14 ... 175 J4
Station Footpath KGLGY WD4 ... 54 C6
Station Gdns CHSWK W4 ... 155 P6 2
Station Gv ALP/SUD HA0 ... 135 K1
Station Hl CRAWE RH10 ... 284 C6 2
  HAYES BR2 ... 205 M9
Station House Ms UED N18 ... 99 P5 2
Station La HCH RM12 ... 125 K8
Station Pde BARK IG11 ... 142 E7
  CRICK NW2 ... 136 F1
  DEN/HRF UB9 ... 111 K5
  HCH RM12 ... 125 J9 2
  RCH/KEW TW9 ... 155 N6
  STHGT/OAK N14 ... 98 E7 2
Station Pas PECK SE15 ... 160 B2 2
  SWFD E18 ... 101 N10 2
Station Pl FSBYPK N4 ... 119 H7 2
Station Ri WNWD SE27 ... 181 J5 2
Station Rd ADL/WDHM KT15 ... 215 N1 2
  AMSS HP7 ... 69 H5
  ARCH N19 ... 118 D8
  ASC SL5 ... 192 F6
  ASHF TW15 ... 77 M8
  BAR EN5 ... 77 N6
  BARK/HLT IG6 ... 122 F2 2
  BCTR RM8 ... 123 N6
  BEAC HP9 ... 88 D2
  BELMT SM2 ... 221 K6
  BELV DA17 ... 164 B2
  BERK HP4 ... 34 A4
  BF/WBF KT14 ... 215 K8
  BFN/LL DA15 ... 185 K5
  BH/WHM TN16 ... 245 L2
  BMLY BR1 ... 205 M1
  BORE WD6 ... 75 M8
  BRKHM/BTCW RH3 ... 256 B7
  BRKMPK AL9 ... 58 C1
  BROX EN10 ... 44 E6
  BXLYHN DA7 ... 163 P9
  CAR SM5 ... 222 A1
  CFSP/GDCR SL9 ... 110 B3
  CHERT KT16 ... 195 J8
  CHES/WCR EN8 ... 62 F10
  CHIG IG7 ... 103 J2
  CHING E4 ... 101 P2
  CHOB/PIR GU24 ... 213 L8
  CHSGTN KT9 ... 219 K2
  COB KT11 ... 235 M3
  CRAWE RH10 ... 283 N8 2
  CROY/NA CR0 ... 205 K8
  CSHM HP5 ... 50 C7
  CTHM CR3 ... 241 N4
  CTHM CR3 ... 242 D8
  DART DA1 ... 186 C2
  DORK RH4 ... 272 A1
  DTCH/LGLY SL3 ... 150 D1
  EA W5 ... 135 L8 2
  EDGW HA8 ... 95 M7
  EGH TW20 ... 172 D8
  EPP CM16 ... 65 N7
  EPP CM16 ... 66 C3
  ESH/CLAY KT10 ... 218 C2 2
  EYN DA4 ... 209 L10
  EYN DA4 ... 210 A2
  EYN DA4 ... 229 L1 2
  FNCH N3 ... 97 K9
  FBAR/BDGN N11 ... 98 C2
  GPK RM2 ... 125 J2
  GRH DA9 ... 188 G2
  GVW DA11 ... 189 N7
  HARH RM3 ... 105 N9 2
  HARP AL5 ... 20 C7
  HAYES BR2 ... 205 M9
  HERT/WAS SG14 ... 24 C1
  HHS/BOV HP3 ... 39 L8
  HLWE CM17 ... 29 M7
  HPTN TW12 ... 197 J2
  HWL W7 ... 134 D10
  HORL RH6 ... 280 C6 1
  HPTN TW12 ... 198 A1
  HRW HA1 ... 114 E4
  HSLW TW3 ... 154 A10
  HYS/HAR UB3 ... 152 F3 2
  IL IG1 ... 122 C4
  KGLGY WD4 ... 54 C6
  KUT KT1 ... 199 J1 2
  KUTN/CMB KT2 ... 199 M1 2
  LCOL/BKTW AL2 ... 55 L3 2
  LEW SE13 ... 161 H9
  LHD/OX KT22 ... 236 H9
  LOU IG10 ... 82 B9
  MEO DA13 ... 189 L7
  MLHL NW7 ... 96 B7
  MNPK E12 ... 122 B10
  NRWD SE19 ... 181 P3 2
  NWMAL KT3 ... 200 A1
  ORP BR6 ... 207 K4
  PGE/AN SE20 ... 182 F6 2
  POTB/CUF EN6 ... 60 C2
  PUR/KEN CR8 ... 223 H7 2
  RAD WD7 ... 74 F1
  REDH RH1 ... 258 B7
  RGDL GU7 ... 267 J10 2
  RGUE GU4 ... 268 B6
  RKW/CH/CXG WD3 ... 91 N1 2
  RSEV TN14 ... 228 A7

RSEV TN14 ... 229 H7
  TN14 ... 247 J2
RYLN/HDSTN HA2 ... 114 A3
SCUP DA14 ... 185 K6
SEV TN13 ... 246 F6
SEVS/STOTM N15 ... 119 P1 2
SHGR GU5 ... 268 C10 3
  GU5 ... 270 E5
SHPTN TW17 ... 196 D5
SL SL1 ... 128 D8
SNWD SE25 ... 203 N4
STALE/WH AL4 ... 21 J2
  AL4 ... 39 N5
STMC/STPC BR5 ... 207 M4 2
STWL/WRAY TW19 ... 175 H10 3
SUN TW16 ... 197 H1
SWLY BR8 ... 208 F4 3
TEDD TW11 ... 176 F9
THDIT KT7 ... 198 C7
TIL RM18 ... 168 C7
TWK TW1 ... 176 E4
UX/CGN UB8 ... 131 N6 2
WAB EN9 ... 65 K3
WALTH E17 ... 120 D4
WARE SG12 ... 26 C5
  SG12 ... 27 H7
WAT WD17 ... 73 J3
WCHMH N21 ... 99 J2
WDGN N22 ... 98 F10 2
WDR/YW UB7 ... 151 P1
WIM/MER SW19 ... 201 M1 2
WLSDN NW10 ... 136 C4
WWKM BR4 ... 205 H8
Station Rd East OXTED RH8 ... 261 K5
  BELV DA17 ... 164 C2 2
Station Rd North BELV DA17 ... 164 C2
  REDH RH1 ... 258 C2
Station Rd South REDH RH1 ... 258 D4
Station Rd West OXTED RH8 ... 261 K5
Station Rw RGUE GU4 ... 268 B6
Station Sq STMC/STPC BR5 ... 206 F5 2
Station St SRTFD E15 ... 141 J2
  SRTFD E15 ... 159 K7 2
Station Ter CMBW SE5 ... 159 K7
  WLSDN NW10 ... 136 F4 2
Station Vw GFD/PVL UB6 ... 134 C3 2
  GU UB6 ... 267 J7 2
Station Wy BKHH IG9 ... 102 A5 2
  CHEAM SM3 ... 221 H3
  CRAWE RH10 ... 283 N8
Station Yd TWK TW1 ... 176 F3 2
Staunton Rd KUTN/CMB KT2 ... 177 L10
  SLN SL2 ... 129 L7
Staunton St DEPT SE8 ... 160 E5
Staveley Cl HOLWY N7 ... 118 F9 2
  PECK SE15 ... 160 B7 2
Staveley Gdns CHSWK W4 ... 156 A7
Staveley Rd ASHF TW15 ... 174 B1
  CHSWK W4 ... 156 A6
Staveley Wy WOKN/KNAP GU21 ... 231 K3
Staverton Rd CRICK NW2 ... 136 F2
  EMPK RM11 ... 125 L4 2
Stave Yard Rd
  BERM/RHTH SE16 ... 140 D10
Stavordale Rd CAR SM5 ... 201 M7
  HBRY N5 ... 119 H9
Stayne End VW GU25 ... 193 M4
Stayner's Rd WCHPL E1 ... 140 C6
Stayton Rd SUT SM1 ... 201 K10
St Catherines Rd RSLP HA4 ... 112 D3
Steadfast Rd KUT KT1 ... 199 J3
Stead St WALW SE17 ... 18 G6 2
Steam Farm La
  EBED/NFELT TW14 ... 152 G10 2
Stean St HACK E8 ... 7 L5
Stebbing Wy BARK IG11 ... 143 K4
Stebondale St POP/IOD E14 ... 161 H4
Stedman Cl BXLY DA5 ... 186 F6
  HGDN/ICK UB10 ... 112 B8
Steed Cl HCH RM12 ... 125 J7 2
Steedman St WALW SE17 ... 18 E6 1
Steeds Rd MUSWH N10 ... 98 A9
Steeds Wy LOU IG10 ... 82 B7
Steel Ap BARK IG11 ... 143 L4
Steele Av GRH DA9 ... 188 F1
Steele Rd CHSWK W4 ... 155 P2 3
  ISLW TW7 ... 154 F10
  TOTM N17 ... 119 M1
  WAN E11 ... 121 K9 2
  WLSDN NW10 ... 135 M4
Steele's Ms South HAMP NW3 ... 4 B2
Steele's Ms North HAMP NW3 ... 4 B2
Steele's Rd HAMP NW3 ... 4 A2
Steel's La LHD/OX KT22 ... 218 A10
  WCHPL E1 ... 140 B8
Steelyard Pas CANST EC4R ... 12 G8
Steep Cl ORP BR6 ... 227 J3
Steep Hl CHOB/PIR GU24 ... 213 H4
  CROY/NA CR0 ... 223 N1
  STRHM/NOR SW16 ... 180 E6
Steeplands BUSH WD23 ... 94 A1
Steeple Cl FUL/PGN SW6 ... 157 H9
  WIM/MER SW19 ... 179 H7
Steeple Heights Dr
  BH/WHM TN16 ... 244 A3
Steeplestone Cl UED N18 ... 99 K6
Steeple Wy BRWN CM15 ... 86 G3 2
Steerforth St WAND/EARL SW18 ... 179 L5
Steers La CRAWE RH10 ... 284 D1
Steers Md MTCM CR4 ... 202 A1
Steers Wy BERM/RHTH SE16 ... 160 D1 2
Stella Rd TOOT SW17 ... 180 A4
Stelling Rd ERITH DA8 ... 164 E9
Stellman Cl CLPT E5 ... 119 P8
Stembridge Rd PGE/AN SE20 ... 204 A2
Stenning Av TIL RM18 ... 169 L1 2
Stenton Av TIL RM18 ... 169 L1 2
Stepgates CHERT KT16 ... 195 L7 2
Stepgates Cl CHERT KT16 ... 195 L7 2
Stephan Cl HACK E8 ... 7 P5
Stephen Av RAIN RM13 ... 145 H1
Stephen Cl CRAWW RH11 ... 283 N4 2
  EGH TW20 ... 172 B9
  ORP BR6 ... 227 L2
Stephendale Rd FUL/PGN SW6 ... 157 L7 2
Stephen Ms FITZ W1T ... 11 J2 2
Stephen Pl CLAP SW4 ... 158 D9 3
Stephen Rd BXLYHN DA7 ... 164 D9
Stephens Cl HARH RM3 ... 105 K6
Stephenson Av TIL RM18 ... 169 L1 2
Stephenson Dr WDSR SL4 ... 148 C7
Stephenson Pl CRAWE RH10 ... 284 C7
Stephenson Rd HNWL W7 ... 134 D10
  HSLWW TW4 ... 175 P3 2
  WALTH E17 ... 120 D3 2
  WLSDN NW10 ... 136 C4
Stephenson Wy BUSH WD23 ... 73 L5
  CAMTN NW1 ... 11 H1
  CRAWE RH10 ... 284 C7
Stephen's Rd SRTFD E15 ... 141 L3 2
Stephen St FITZ W1T ... 11 J2 2
Stepney Cswy WCHPL E1 ... 140 C8 10
Stepney Gn WCHPL E1 ... 140 C7
Stepney High St WCHPL E1 ... 140 D7
Stepney Wy WCHPL E1 ... 140 C7
Sterling Av CHES/WCR EN8 ... 62 C10
  EDGW HA8 ... 95 L5
  SHPTN TW17 ... 196 F5
Sterling Cl WLSDN NW10 ... 136 D2 2
Sterling Gdns NWCR SE14 ... 160 D5
Sterling Pl BTFD TW8 ... 155 H5
  EA W5 ... 155 L5
Sterling Rd ENC/FH EN2 ... 79 L3
Sterling St SKENS SW7 ... 15 N2 2
Sterling Way
  (North Circular Road) UED N18 ... 99 M6
Stern Cl BARK IG11 ... 143 N4
Sterndale Rd DART DA1 ... 187 N3 2
  WKENS W14 ... 156 G2

Sterne St *SHB* W12 ... 156 G1
Sternhall La *PECK* SE15 ... 159 P9
Sternhold Av *BRXS/STRHM* SW2 ... 180 F5
Sterry Crs *DAGE* RM10 ... 124 B10
Sterry Dr *HOR/WEW* KT19 ... 220 B1
  THDIT KT7 ... 198 D6
Sterry Gdns *DAGE* RM10 ... 144 B2
Sterry Rd *BARK* IG11 ... 143 J3
  DAGE RM10 ... 124 B9
Sterry St *STHWK* SE1 ... 18 G2
Steucers La *FSTH* SE23 ... 182 D4 2
Steve Biko La *CAT* SE6 ... 182 F7
Steve Biko Rd *HOLWY* N7 ... 119 H8
Steve Biko Wy *TWS* TW3 ... 153 H8
Stevedale Rd *WELL* DA16 ... 148 C4
Stevedore St *WAP* E1W ... 140 A10 8
Stevenage Crs *BORE* WD6 ... 75 K5
Stevenage Ri *HHNE* HP2 ... 36 A2
Stevenage Rd *EHAM* E6 ... 142 D1
  FUL/PGN SW6 ... 156 D7
Stevens Av *HOM* E9 ... 140 B1
Stevens Cl *BECK* BR3 ... 182 F19 5
  BXLY DA5 ... 186 E7
  EW KT17 ... 220 B8 7
  HPTN TW12 ... 175 N9
  PIN HA5 ... 113 K3 2
  RDART DA2 ... 188 D8
Stevens Gn *BUSH* WD23 ... 94 B2 3
Stevens La *ESH/CLAY* KT10 ... 218 F4
Stevenson Cl *BAR* EN5 ... 77 N10
  ERITH DA8 ... 165 J6 2
Stevenson Crs *BERM/RHTH* SE16 ... 19 P7
Stevens Pl *PUR/KEN* CR8 ... 223 J9 8
Stevens St *STHWK* SE1 ... 19 K3
Steventon Rd *SHB* W12 ... 136 C9
Steward Cl *CHES/WCR* EN8 ... 62 D6
Stewards Cl *EPP* CM16 ... 65 K9
Stewards Green Rd *EPP* CM16 ... 65 L8
Steward St *WCHPL* E1 ... 13 L3
Stewart *KWD/TDW/WH* KT20 ... 238 C7
Stewart Cl *ABLGY* WD5 ... 55 H8
  CDALE/KGS NW9 ... 115 P4 8
  CHST BR7 ... 184 E7 2
  HPTN TW12 ... 175 M9
  WOKN/KNAP GU21 ... 231 L3 8
Stewart Rd *HARP* AL5 ... 20 A1
  WAN E11 ... 121 J9
Stewart's Cl *UED* N18 ... 99 K6 6
Stewarts Dr *SLN* SL2 ... 108 C10
Stewart's Gv *CHEL* SW3 ... 15 M7
Stewart's La *VX/NE* SW8 ... 158 C6 8
Stewart St *POP/IOD* E14 ... 161 H1
Stew La *BLKFR* EC4V ... 12 E7
Stew Rd *ACT* W3 ... 135 P10 8
Steyning Cl *CRAWE* RH10 ... 285 J3
  PUR/KEN CR8 ... 241 J2
Steyning Gv *ELTH/MOT* SE9 ... 184 C7 2
Steynings Wy *NFNCH/WDSP* N12 ... 97 K6
Steyning Wy *HSLWW* TW4 ... 153 K10
Steynton Av *BXLY* DA5 ... 185 P5
Sthrathbrook Rd *STRHM/NOR* SW16 ... 180 G10
Stickland Rd *BELV* DA17 ... 164 B5 3
Stickleton Cl *GFD/PVL* UB6 ... 134 A5
Stifford Clays Rd *CDH/CHF* RM16 ... 147 M9 2
Stifford Hl *CDH/CHF* RM16 ... 147 J10
Stifford Rd *SOCK/AV* RM15 ... 146 C9
  SOCK/AV RM15 ... 147 H9 2
Stile Cft *HLWS* CM18 ... 47 K3
Stilecroft Gdns *ALP/SUD* HA0 ... 114 C8
Stile Hall Gdns *CHSWK* W4 ... 155 M4
Stile Pth *SUN* TW16 ... 197 H3 5
Stiles Cl *ERITH* DA8 ... 164 C4 1
  HAYES BR2 ... 206 C6
Stillingfleet Rd *BARN* SW13 ... 156 D6
Stillington St *WEST* SW1P ... 17 N5
Stillness Rd *FSTH* SE23 ... 182 D2
Stilton Crs *WLSDN* NW10 ... 135 P12
Stilton Pth *BORE* WD6 ... 75 M4 6
Stipularis Dr *YEAD* UB4 ... 133 L6
Stirling Cl *BNSTD* SM7 ... 239 J3
  CRAWE RH10 ... 284 D6
  RAIN RM13 ... 145 J5
  STRHM/NOR SW16 ... 202 D9
  UX/CGN UB8 ... 131 M5 4
  WDSR SL4 ... 148 E8
Stirling Gv *HSLW* TW3 ... 154 E8
Stirling Rd *ACT* W3 ... 155 N2
  BRXN/ST SW9 ... 158 F8
  HYS/HAR UB3 ... 133 J9
  KTN/HRWW/W HA3 ... 114 A1
  PLSTW E13 ... 141 N4
  SL SL1 ... 128 F7
  TOTM N17 ... 99 P9
  WALTH E17 ... 120 D1
  WDGN N22 ... 99 J9
  WHTN TW2 ... 175 P3
Stirling Wy *ABLGY* WD5 ... 55 H8
  BORE WD6 ... 76 A10
  WCCE AL7 ... 23 G5
Stirrup Ms *CRAWE* RH10 ... 284 E6
Stites Hill Rd *CTHM* CR3 ... 241 J6
Stiven Crs *RYLN/HDSTN* HA2 ... 113 N8
Stoat Cl *HERT/BAY* SG13 ... 25 P7
Stoats Nest Rd *COUL/CHIP* CR5 ... 240 F1
Stockbreach Cl *HAT* AL10 ... 40 D3
Stockbreach Rd *HAT* AL10 ... 40 D3
Stockbury Rd *CROY/NA* CR0 ... 204 D5
Stockdale Rd *BCTR* RM8 ... 124 A7
Stockdove Wy *GFD/PVL* UB6 ... 134 C5
Stockers Farm Rd
  RKW/CH/CXG WD3 ... 91 M4
Stockfield RH6 ... 280 C3 17
Stockfield Av *HOD* EN11 ... 44 F1
Stockfield Rd *ESH/CLAY* KT10 ... 218 D2 1
  STRHM/NOR SW16 ... 180 G6
Stockhams Cl *SAND/SEL* CR2 ... 223 L6 2
Stock Hl *BH/WHM* TN16 ... 244 A2
Stockholm Rd *BERM/RHTH* SE16 ... 160 B4
Stockhurst Cl *PUT/ROE* SW15 ... 156 F8 1
  STRHM/NOR SW16 ... 202 E1
Stockingswater La *PEND* EN3 ... 130 D7
Stockings La *HERT/BAY* SG13 ... 42 N4
Stock La *RDART* DA2 ... 187 K7
Stockley Cl *WDR/YW* UB7 ... 152 C1
Stockley Farm Rd *WDR/YW* UB7 ... 152 C2
Stockley Rd *UX/CGN* UB8 ... 132 B8
Stock Orchard Crs *HOLWY* N7 ... 118 G10 3
Stock Orchard St *HOLWY* N7 ... 118 G10 3
Stockport Rd *RKW/CH/CXG* WD3 ... 90 F1
  STRHM/NOR SW16 ... 202 E1
Stocksfield Rd *WALTH* E17 ... 121 J1 1
Stocks La *BRWN* SE5 ... 86 E3
Stocks Meadow *HHNE* HP2 ... 36 A1
Stocks Pl *POP/IOD* E14 ... 140 E9 7
Stockton Cl *BAR* EN5 ... 77 N4
  TOTM N17 ... 99 M8
  UED N18 ... 99 L8
Stockton Gdns *MLHL* NW7 ... 96 A4
  TOTM N17 ... 99 M8
Stockton Rd *REIG* RH2 ... 275 K3
  UED N18 ... 99 P7
Stockwell Av *BRXN/ST* SW9 ... 158 F8
Stockwell Cl *BMLY* BR1 ... 205 N2
  CHESW EN7 ... 61 P4

Stockwell Gdns *BRXN/ST* SW9 ... 158 G7
Stockwell Gn *BRXN/ST* SW9 ... 158 G8
Stockwell La *CHES/WCR* EN8 ... 158 G8 2
Stockwell Park Crs *BRXN/ST* SW9 ... 158 G8
Stockwell Park Rd *BRXN/ST* SW9 ... 158 G7
Stockwell Park Wk *BRXN/ST* SW9 ... 158 G9
Stockwell Rd *BRXN/ST* SW9 ... 158 G8
Stockwell St *GNWCH* SE10 ... 161 H5
Stockwell Ter *BRXN/ST* SW9 ... 158 G7 2
Stocton Cl *GU* GU1 ... 249 P9
Stocton Rd *GU* GU1 ... 249 P9
Stodart Rd *PGE/AN* SE20 ... 204 B1
Stoford Cl *WIM/MER* SW19 ... 179 H4 6
Stoke Av *BARK/HLT* IG6 ... 105 K2
Stoke Cl *COB* KT11 ... 235 N2
Stoke Common Rd *SLN* SL2 ... 109 M9
Stoke Court Dr *SLN* SL2 ... 129 K3
Stoke Flds *GU* GU1 ... 250 A10
Stoke Gdns *SL* SL1 ... 129 K10
Stoke Gn *SLN* SL2 ... 129 M6
Stoke Gv *GU* GU1 ... 250 A10
Stoke Ms *GU* GU1 ... 250 A10
Stokenchurch St *FUL/PGN* SW6 ... 157 L7
Stoke Newington Church St
  STNW/STAM N16 ... 119 M7 5
Stoke Newington Common
  STNW/STAM N16 ... 119 N7 5
Stoke Newington High St
  STNW/STAM N16 ... 119 N8
Stoke Newington Rd
  STNW/STAM N16 ... 119 N10
Stoke Park Av *SLN* SL2 ... 129 H5
Stoke Pl *WLSDN* NW10 ... 136 C5
Stoke Poges La *SL* SL1 ... 129 K10
Stoke Rd *COB* KT11 ... 235 M2
  GU GU1 ... 250 A9
  KUTN/CMB KT2 ... 177 P10
  RAIN RM13 ... 145 L5 6
  SLN SL2 ... 129 M7
  WOT/HER KT12 ... 197 K6 2
Stokesay *SL* SL1 ... 129 L9
Stokesby Rd *CHSGTN* KT9 ... 219 L3
Stokes Cl *CRAWE* RH10 ... 284 D9 11
Stokesheath Rd *LHD/OX* KT22 ... 218 C1
Stokesley St *SHB* W12 ... 136 C7 8
Stokes Ridings
  KWD/TDW/WH KT20 ... 238 C9 1
Stokes Rd *CROY/NA* CR0 ... 204 C6 4
  EHAM E6 ... 142 B6
Stoll Cl *CRICK* NW2 ... 116 F8
Stompond La *WOT/HER* KT12 ... 197 H9
Stomp Rd *SL* SL1 ... 128 A7
Stonard Rd *BCTR* RM8 ... 123 L10
  PLMGR N13 ... 99 H4
Stonards Hl *LOU* IG10 ... 82 C10
Stondon Pk *FSTH* SE23 ... 182 D3
Stonebanks *WOT/HER* KT12 ... 197 H7
Stonebridge Fld *WDSR* SL4 ... 148 C4
Stonebridge Flds *RGUE* GU4 ... 268 A7
Stonebridge Pk *WLSDN* NW10 ... 136 A2
Stonebridge Rd *GVW* DA11 ... 189 M11
  SEVS/STOTM N15 ... 119 M3
Stonebridge Wy *HA9* ... 135 N1 1
Stonebridge Whf *RGUE* GU4 ... 268 A7
Stone Buildings *LINN* WC2A ... 11 P4
  CLAP SW4 ... 158 D8 2
  WDR/YW UB7 ... 132 A10
Stonecot Cl *MRDN* SM4 ... 201 H8
Stonecot Hl *CHEAM* SM3 ... 201 H8 1
  MRDN SM4 ... 201 J7 2
Stonecourt Cl *HORL* RH6 ... 280 C4
Stone Crs *EBED/NFELT* TW14 ... 174 C3
Stonecroft Av *IVER* SL0 ... 131 H8
Stonecroft Cl *BAR* EN5 ... 76 B8
Stonecroft Rd *ERITH* DA8 ... 164 D6
Stonecroft Wy *CROY/NA* CR0 ... 202 F7
Stonecrop Cl *CRAWW* RH11 ... 283 L10 6
Stonecrop Rd *GU* GU1 ... 250 D3
Stonecross *STAL* AL1 ... 38 D5
  STALW/RED AL3 ... 38 D5
Stonecross Rd *HAT* AL10 ... 40 E2
Stonecutter St *FLST/FETLN* EC4A ... 12 C5 8
Stonefield Cl *BXLYHN* DA7 ... 164 B9
  CRAWE RH10 ... 283 N8
  RSLP HA4 ... 113 M10
Stonefield St *IS* N1 ... 6 B5
Stonefield Wy *CHARL* SE7 ... 162 A6 1
  RSLP HA4 ... 113 L10
Stonegate Cl *STMC/STPC* BR5 ... 207 M3 2
Stone Gv *EDGW* HA8 ... 95 L6
  STAN HA7 ... 95 L6
Stonegrove Gdns *EDGW* HA8 ... 95 L6
Stonehall Av *IL* IG1 ... 122 B4
Stone Hall Rd *WCHMH* N21 ... 98 C1
Stoneham Rd *FBAR/BDGN* N11 ... 98 B6
Stonehill Cl *GT/LBKH* KT23 ... 253 P1
  MORT/ESHN SW14 ... 178 A1
Stonehill Crs *CHERT* KT16 ... 214 B3
Stonehill Rd *CHERT* KT16 ... 214 B3
  CHOB/PIR GU24 ... 155 M4 6
  CHSWK W4 ... 177 N7
  MORT/ESHN SW14 ... 177 N7 3
Stonehills *WCCW* AL8 ... 22 C5
Stonehills Ct *DUL* SE21 ... 181 M6
Stonehorse Rd *PEND* EN3 ... 130 B9
Stonehouse Gdns *CTHM* CR3 ... 259 H1
Stonehouse La *ORP* BR6 ... 227 N5
  PUR RM19 ... 166 D4
Stonehouse Rd *ORP* BR6 ... 227 N5
Stoneings La *RSEV* TN14 ... 245 J2
Stoneland Av *HHS/BOV* HP3 ... 36 A9
Stoneleigh Av *EN* EN1 ... 80 A4
  WPK KT4 ... 200 E3
Stoneleigh Broadway *EW* KT17 ... 220 D2 8
Stoneleigh Cl *CHES/WCR* EN8 ... 62 C9 8
Stoneleigh Crs *HOR/WEW* KT19 ... 220 D2
Stoneleigh Dr *HOD* EN11 ... 26 C10
Stoneleigh Pk *WEY* KT13 ... 216 D3 2
Stoneleigh Park Av
  CROY/NA CR0 ... 204 C6
Stoneleigh Park Rd
  HOR/WEW KT19 ... 220 C3
Stoneleigh Pl *NTGHL* W11 ... 136 C5
Stoneleigh Rd *CAR* SM5 ... 201 P7
  CLAY IG5 ... 122 B1
  OXTED RH8 ... 262 B6
  TOTM N17 ... 99 N1
Stoneleigh St *NTGHL* W11 ... 136 C5
Stonemasons Cl
  SEVS/STOTM N15 ... 119 L2 8
Stoneness Rd *WTHK* RM20 ... 166 G6 2
Stonenest St *FSBYPK* N4 ... 118 G6
Stone Park Av *BECK* BR3 ... 204 D2
Stone Pl *WPK* KT4 ... 200 D9
Stone Place Rd *GRH* DA9 ... 188 D1
Stone Rd *HAYES* BR2 ... 205 M4
Stones Cross Rd *SWLY* BR8 ... 208 D5
Stones End St *STHWK* SE1 ... 18 E2
Stone's Rd *EW* KT17 ... 220 B7
Stone St *CROY/NA* CR0 ... 223 J4
  GVE DA12 ... 190 C2
Stonewood *OXTED* RH8 ... 261 N5
Stonewall *EHAM* E6 ... 142 D1
Stonewood Rd *ERITH* DA8 ... 164 F4 2
Stoney Aly *WOOL/PLUM* SE18 ... 162 G9
Stoneyard La *POP/IOD* E14 ... 140 G9 2
Stoney Brook *GUW* GU2 ... 249 L9
Stoney Cl *BERK* HP4 ... 33 L3
Stoneycroft Cl *LEE/GVPK* SE12 ... 183 L3
Stoneycroft Rd *WFD* IG8 ... 102 G2

Stoneydown *WALTH* E17 ... 120 D2
Stoneydown Av *WALTH* E17 ... 120 D2 8
Stoneyfields Gdns *EDGW* HA8 ... 95 P5
Stoneyfields La *EDGW* HA8 ... 95 P6 1
Stoneyland Ct *EGH* TW20 ... 172 C8
Stoneylands Rd *EGH* TW20 ... 172 C8
Stoney La *HDTCH* EC3A ... 13 K5
  HHS/BOV HP3 ... 35 N10
  HHW HP1 ... 34 E9
  KGLGY WD4 ... 53 H6
Stoneyshotts *WAB* EN9 ... 63 K10
Stony Cft *ASHTD* KT21 ... 237 L3
Stonor Rd *WKENS* W14 ... 14 C6
Stony Hl *ESH/CLAY* KT10 ... 217 N4
Stony La *CHONG* CM5 ... 49 J9
Stony Pth *LOU* IG10 ... 82 C5
Stopes St *PECK* SE15 ... 159 N6
Stopford Rd *PLSTW* E13 ... 141 M3
  WALW SE17 ... 18 B7
Stopham Rd *CRAWE* RH10 ... 284 D10
Store Rd *CAN/RD* E16 ... 162 D1
Storers Quay *POP/IOD* E14 ... 161 N4
Store St *GWRST* WC1E ... 11 J4
  RSTFD E15 ... 121 J10
Storey Rd *HGT* N6 ... 118 A4
  WALTH E17 ... 120 E2 3
Storey's Ga *WEST* SW1P ... 17 K2
Storey St *HHS/BOV* HP5 ... 35 N10
Stories Ms *CMBW* SE5 ... 159 M9
Stork Rd *FSTGT* E7 ... 141 L1
Storksmead Rd *EDGW* HA8 ... 96 B8
Storks Rd *BERM/RHTH* SE16 ... 19 P4
Stormont Rd *BTSEA* SW11 ... 158 B10
  HGT N6 ... 118 A5
Stormont Wy *CHSGTN* KT9 ... 219 H2
Stornaway Rd *DTCH/LGLY* SL3 ... 150 F3
Stornaway Strd *GVE* DA12 ... 191 J7
Stornoway *HHS/BOV* HP3 ... 36 C8 8
Storrington Rd *CROY/NA* CR0 ... 203 N8
Storr's La *RGUW* GU3 ... 231 H10
Stortford Rd *HOD* EN11 ... 44 C2
Stort Mill *HLW* CM20 ... 29 N4
Stort Valley Wy *HLW* CM20 ... 29 N4
  HLWE CM17 ... 48 D9
  HLWE CM17 ... 48 D8
  HLWW/ROY CM19 ... 47 M4
  SBW CM21 ... 30 D1
Story Rd *IS* N1 ... 5 N4 8
Stothard St *WCHPL* E1 ... 140 B6 9
Stoughton Av *CHEAM* SM3 ... 220 G2
Stoughton Cl *PUT/ROE* SW15 ... 178 D4
Stoughton Rd *GUW* GU2 ... 249 M7
Stour Av *NWDGN* UB2 ... 153 P2
Stourcliffe St *MBLAR* W1H ... 10 A6 3
Stourhead Cl *WIM/MER* SW19 ... 178 G3 8
Stourhead Gdns *RYNPK* SW20 ... 200 D3 1
Stour Rd *BOW* E3 ... 140 F2
  DAGE RM10 ... 124 B7
  DART DA1 ... 165 H9
Stourton Av *FELT* TW13 ... 175 N7
Stour Wy *UPMR* RM14 ... 126 D4
Stovell Rd *WDSR* SL4 ... 148 G6
Stowage *DEPT* SE8 ... 160 F5
Stow Crs *WALTH* E17 ... 101 M10
Stowe Crs *RSLP* HA4 ... 112 C4 1
Stowe Gdns *ED* N9 ... 99 N2
Stowell Av *CROY/NA* CR0 ... 225 J4
Stowe Pl *WLSDN* NW10 ... 119 M1 5
Stowe Rd *ORP* BR6 ... 227 L1
  SHB W12 ... 156 E1
  SL SL1 ... 128 D9
The Stow *HLW* CM20 ... 29 J9
Stowting Rd *ORP* BR6 ... 227 H1
Stox Md *KTN/HRWW/W* HA3 ... 94 C9
Stracey Rd *WLSDN* NW10 ... 136 A3
Strachan Pl *RYNPK* SW20 ... 178 F9
Stradbroke Dr *CHIG* IG7 ... 102 E7
Stradbroke Gv *BKHH* IG9 ... 102 A2
  CLAY IG5 ... 122 B1
Stradbroke Pk *BARK/HLT* IG6 ... 102 E7
Stradbroke Rd *HBRY* N5 ... 119 K9 3
Stradbrook Cl *RYLN/HDSTN* HA2 ... 113 N8 2
Stradella Rd *HNHL* SE24 ... 181 A2
Strafford Av *CLAY* IG5 ... 102 D10
Strafford Cl *POTB/CUF* EN6 ... 59 K8 2
Strafford Ga *POTB/CUF* EN6 ... 59 K8
Strafford Pl *ACT* W3 ... 155 P7 2
  BAR EN5 ... 77 H7
  HSLW TW3 ... 153 N9
  TWK TW1 ... 176 F3
Strafford St *POP/IOD* E14 ... 160 F1
Strahan Rd *BOW* E3 ... 140 D5
Straight Rd *HARH* RM3 ... 105 J6
  WDSR SL4 ... 171 N2
Straightsmouth *GNWCH* SE10 ... 161 H6
The Straight *NWDGN* UB2 ... 153 L1
Strait Rd *EHAM* E6 ... 142 B9
The Straits *WAB* EN9 ... 62 G8
Straker's Rd *EDUL* SE22 ... 160 A10
Strand *CHCR* WC2N ... 11 L6
Strand *DCH* WC2R ... 11 P6
  TPL/STR WC2E ... 11 L6
Strand Cl *CRAWE* RH10 ... 284 E9
  EPSOM KT18 ... 238 A5
Strandfield Cl *WOOL/PLUM* SE18 ... 163 H4
Strand-on-the-green *CHSWK* W4 ... 155 M5
Strand Pl *UED* N18 ... 99 M5
Strangeways *WAT* WD17 ... 72 F2
Strangways Ter *WKENS* W14 ... 14 C1
Stranraer Gdns *SL* SL1 ... 129 K10
Stranraer Wy *IS* N1 ... 5 N4
Strasbourg Rd *BTSEA* SW11 ... 158 A9
Stratfield Dr *BROX* EN10 ... 44 D5
Stratfield Park Cl *WCHMH* N21 ... 98 G3
Stratfield Rd *BORE* WD6 ... 75 K3
  SL SL1 ... 149 N1
Stratford Av *HGDN/ICK* UB10 ... 132 A4 1
  KENS W8 ... 14 B3
Stratford Cl *BARK* IG11 ... 143 L6
  DAGE RM10 ... 144 D2
  SLN SL2 ...
Stratford Ct *NWMAL* KT3 ... 200 A4 8
Stratford Dr *WOT/HER* KT12 ... 156 C10
Stratford Gv *PUT/ROE* SW15 ... 157 H10
Stratford House Av *BMLY* BR1 ... 206 B3
Stratford Pl *MHST* W1U ... 10 C6
Stratford Rd *KENS* W8 ... 14 A4
  NWDGN UB2 ... 153 M3
  PLSTW E13 ... 141 M1
  THHTH CR7 ... 203 H1
  WAT WD17 ... 73 M4
  YEAD UB4 ... 133 J4
Stratford Vls *CAMTN* NW1 ... 5 H1
Strath Av *HHS/BOV* HP3 ... 35 N7
Strathan Cl *WAND/EARL* SW18 ... 179 J4
Strathaven Rd *LEE/GVPK* SE12 ... 183 J7
Strathblaine Rd *BTSEA* SW11 ... 158 C4
Strathbrook Rd *STRHM/NOR* SW16 ... 180 G10 1
Strathcona Gdns
  WOKN/KNAP GU21 ... 231 J3
Strathcona Rd *WBLY* HA9 ... 114 D9

Strathdale *STRHM/NOR* SW16 ... 180 G8
Strathdon Dr *TOOT* SW17 ... 179 N6
Strathearn Av *HYS/HAR* UB3 ... 152 G10 1
  WHTN TW2 ... 176 B4
Strathearn Pl *BAY/PAD* W2 ... 9 N7
Strathearn Rd *SUT* SM1 ... 221 L2
  WIM/MER SW19 ... 179 M3
Stratheden Rd *BKHTH/KID* SE3 ... 161 M7
Strathfield Gdns *BARK* IG11 ... 142 G1
Strathleven Rd
  BRXS/STRHM SW2 ... 180 F1
Strathmore *Tl* MLHR UB3 ... 169 M3
Strathmore Gdns *EDGW* HA8 ... 95 N10 3
  EMPK RM11 ... 124 G6
  FNCH N3 ... 97 L9
  HCH RM12 ... 124 G6
  KENS W8 ... 2 B1
Strathmore Cl *CTHM* CR3 ... 241 N10
Strathmore Rd *CRAWW* RH11 ... 283 K4
  CROY/NA CR0 ... 203 L7 8
  TEDD TW11 ... 176 D2
  WIM/MER SW19 ... 179 K6 7
Strathnairn St *STHWK* SE1 ... 19 P6 8
Strathray Gdns *HAMP* NW3 ... 3 L2 2
Strath Ter *BTSEA* SW11 ... 157 P10
Strathville Rd *WAND/EARL* SW18 ... 179 L7
Strathyre Av *STRHM/NOR* SW16 ... 203 H3
Stratton Av *ENC/FH* EN2 ... 79 L3
  WLGTN SM6 ... 222 E5
Stratton Chase Dr *CSTG* HP8 ... 89 M5
Stratton Cl *BXLYHN* DA7 ... 165 P9
  EDGW HA8 ... 95 L7
  HEST TW5 ... 153 N7
  WIM/MER SW19 ... 201 J2
  WOT/HER KT12 ... 197 K8 8
Strattondale St *POP/IOD* E14 ... 161 N2
Stratton Dr *BARK* IG11 ... 123 H10
Stratton Gdns *STHL* UB1 ... 133 N8
Stratton Rd *BXLYHN* DA7 ... 163 P9
  HARH RM3 ... 105 P6
  SUN TW16 ... 196 G2
  WIM/MER SW19 ... 201 J2
Stratton St *MYFR/PICC* W1J ... 10 F9
Stratton Ter *BH/WHM* TN16 ... 262 F3 8
Stratton Wk *HARH* RM3 ... 105 P6 8
Strauss Rd *CHSWK* W4 ... 156 A1 5
Strawberry Cl *CHOB/PIR* GU24 ... 230 C7
Strawberry Fieds *WARE* SG12 ... 26 A1
Strawberry Flds *CHOB/PIR* GU24 ... 230 F1
  SWLY BR8 ... 208 F2 8
Strawberry Hill Rd *TWK* TW1 ... 176 E6
Strawberry Ri *CAR* SM5 ... 202 A10
Strawberry Ri *CHOB/PIR* GU24 ... 230 F1
Strawberry V *EFNCH* N2 ... 97 H6
  TWK TW1 ... 176 E6
Straw Cl *CTHM* CR3 ... 241 K9
Strawfields *WGCE* AL7 ... 23 L4 2
Strawmead *HAT* AL10 ... 40 E2 2
Strayfield Rd *ENC/FH* EN2 ... 79 H2
Streakes Field Rd *CRICK* NW2 ... 116 D7
Stream Cl *BF/WBF* KT14 ... 215 P8
Streamdale *ABYW* SE2 ... 163 L5
Streamside Cl *ED* N9 ... 99 N2
  HAYES BR2 ... 205 M4
Stream Wy *BELV* DA17 ... 164 B5
Streatfeild Av *EHAM* E6 ... 142 C3
Streatfield Rd
  KTN/HRWW/W HA3 ... 115 H1
Streatham Common North
  STRHM/NOR SW16 ... 180 G8
Streatham Common South
  STRHM/NOR SW16 ... 180 F9
Streatham Ct *STRHM/NOR* SW16 ... 180 F6
Streatham High Rd
  STRHM/NOR SW16 ... 180 F7
Streatham Hill *BRXS/STRHM* SW2 ... 180 F3
Streatham Pl *BRXS/STRHM* SW2 ... 180 F1
Streatham Rd *MTCM* CR4 ... 202 A1
Streatham St *NOXST/BSQ* WC1A ... 11 L5 8
Streatham V *STRHM/NOR* SW16 ... 180 D5
Streathbourne Rd *TOOT* SW17 ... 180 G5
Streatley Pl *HAMP* NW3 ... 117 N9 8
Streatley Rd *KIL/WHAMP* NW6 ... 2 C4
Streeters La *WLGTN* SM6 ... 202 E10
Streetfield Ms *BKHTH/KID* SE3 ... 161 M8
Street Hl *CRAWE* RH10 ... 284 F8
Streets Heath *CHOB/PIR* GU24 ... 212 E7
The Street *ASHTD* KT21 ... 237 L4
  BRKHM/BTCW RH3 ... 256 A10
  EHSLX KT24 ... 252 C4
  EHSLX KT24 ... 253 L4
  EYN DA4 ... 191 P8
  GVE DA12 ... 210 A4
  HORL RH6 ... 280 A8
  KGLGY WD4 ... 53 K7
  LHD/OX KT22 ... 236 C10
  MFD/CHID GU8 ... 250 C10
  RBSF CM22 ... 30 E3
  RGUE GU4 ... 251 K6
  RGUE GU4 ... 251 K6
  RGUW GU3 ... 266 A5
  RGUW GU3 ... 266 C3
  SHGR GU5 ... 268 D10
Streimer Rd *SRTFD* E15 ... 141 H3 8
Strelley Wy *ACT* W3 ... 136 A9
Stretton Rd *CROY/NA* CR0 ... 203 M7
  RCHPK/HAM TW10 ... 177 H5
Stretton Wy *BORE* WD6 ... 75 K4
Strickland Av *DART* DA1 ... 165 N3
Strickland Cl *CRAWW* RH11 ... 283 H8 2
Strickland Rw *WAND/EARL* SW18 ... 179 N3
Strickland St *DEPT* SE8 ... 160 F7
Strickland Wy *ORP* BR6 ... 227 J1 2
Stride Rd *PLSTW* E13 ... 141 L1
Stringer's Rd *RGUE* GU4 ... 250 A4
Stringhams Copse
  RPLY/SEND GU23 ... 233 J10
Stripling Wy *WATW* WD18 ... 73 H10
Strode Cl *MUSWH* N10 ... 98 B8
Strode Rd *FSTGT* E7 ... 121 N9
  FUL/PGN SW6 ... 157 H6
  TOTM N17 ... 99 M10
  WLSDN NW10 ... 119 N4
Strodes College La *EGH* TW20 ... 172 C8
Strode St *EGH* TW20 ... 172 D7
Stroma Cl *HHS/BOV* HP3 ... 36 D8 8
Stroma Ct *SL* SL1 ... 128 C9
Strone Rd *FSTGT* E7 ... 141 P1
Strongbow Crs *ELTH/MOT* SE9 ... 184 C1
Strongbow Rd *ELTH/MOT* SE9 ... 184 C1
Strongbridge Cl
  RYLN/HDSTN HA2 ... 113 P6
Stronsa Rd *SHB* W12 ... 156 C3 2
Stronsay Cl *HHS/BOV* HP3 ... 36 D8 8
Strood Av *ROMW/RG* RM7 ... 124 E6
Strood La *ASC* SL5 ... 170 A9
Strood La *WDSR* SL4 ... 148 C9
Stroud Crs *PUT/ROE* SW15 ... 178 C9
Stroude Rd *EGH* TW20 ... 172 D9
  VW GU25 ... 194 B3
Stroudes Cl *WPK* KT4 ... 200 C7 8
Stroud Fld *NTHLT* UB5 ... 133 H4
Stroud Ga *RYLN/HDSTN* HA2 ... 114 A9
Stroud Green Rd *FSBYPK* N4 ... 118 G6
Stroud Green Wy *CROY/NA* CR0 ... 204 B6 8
Stroudley Cl *CRAWE* RH10 ... 284 C10 8
Stroud Rd *SNWD* SE25 ... 203 P5
  WIM/MER SW19 ... 179 K6
Strouds Cl *CHDH* RM6 ... 123 M1
Stroudwater Pk *WEY* KT13 ... 216 C3 8
Stroud Wy *ASHF* TW15 ... 174 C9
Stroughton Cl *LBTH* SE11 ... 17 P6 8
Strout's Pl *BETH* E2 ... 13 L1
Strudgate Cl *CRAWE* RH10 ... 284 G9 8
Strutton Gnd *WEST* SW1P ... 17 J3
Struttons Av *GVW* DA11 ... 190 C5

Strype St *WCHPL* E1 ... 13 L4 8
Stuart Av *CDALE/KGS* NW9 ... 116 D5
  EA W5 ... 155 L1
  HAYES BR2 ... 205 M8
  RYLN/HDSTN HA2 ... 113 N8
  WOT/HER KT12 ... 197 K8
Stuart Cl *BORE* WD6 ... 75 J10 8
  CRAWE RH10 ... 284 E8
  HGDN/ICK UB10 ... 132 B1
  SWLY BR8 ... 186 G10
  WDSR SL4 ... 148 E8
Stuart Ct *BORE* WD6 ... 75 J10 8
Stuart Crs *CROY/NA* CR0 ... 204 E10
  HYS/HAR UB3 ... 132 D8
  REIG RH2 ... 275 K3
  WDGN N22 ... 98 G9
Stuart Evans Cl *WELL* DA16 ... 163 M9
Stuart Gv *TEDD* TW11 ... 176 D8
Stuart Mantle Wy *ERITH* DA8 ... 164 E6
Stuart Pl *MTCM* CR4 ... 202 A1
Stuart Rd *ACT* W3 ... 135 P10 8
  BARK IG11 ... 143 J3
  EBAR EN4 ... 97 P1
  GRAYS RM17 ... 167 N4 8
  GVW DA11 ... 190 D2
  KIL/WHAMP NW6 ... 2 A4
  KTN/HRWW/W HA3 ... 114 E1
  PECK SE15 ... 160 B10
  RCHPK/HAM TW10 ... 176 G5
  REIG RH2 ... 275 K3
  THHTH CR7 ... 203 K4
  WARL CR6 ... 242 A6
  WELL DA16 ... 163 L7
  WIM/MER SW19 ... 179 K6
Stuarts Cl *HHS/BOV* HP3 ... 35 N8 8
Stuart Wy *CHESW* EN7 ... 62 A1 6
  STA TW18 ... 173 L9
  VW GU25 ... 193 M4
  WDSR SL4 ... 148 D8
Stubbers La *UPMR* RM14 ... 146 D1
Stubbs Dr *BERM/RHTH* SE16 ... 160 A14 2
Stubbs End Cl *AMS* HP6 ... 69 K3
Stubbs Hl *ORP* BR6 ... 227 M9
Stubbs Wy *WIM/MER* SW19 ... 201 N1 8
Stubbs Wd *AMS* HP6 ... 69 K2
Stubs Cl *DORK* RH4 ... 273 H4
Stubs Hl *DORK* RH4 ... 273 H4
Stucley Pl *CAMTN* NW1 ... 4 F4
Stucley Rd *ISLW* TW7 ... 154 B6
Studdridge St *FUL/PGN* SW6 ... 157 K8
Studd St *IS* N1 ... 6 C5
Stud Gn *GSTN* WD25 ... 55 H8
Studholme St *PECK* SE15 ... 160 A6
Studios Rd *SHPTN* TW17 ... 196 A3
The Studios *BUSH* WD23 ... 73 P10 8
Studio Wy *BORE* WD6 ... 75 P8
Studland Cl *BFN/LL* DA15 ... 185 J6 8
Studland Rd *BF/WBF* KT14 ... 216 A9 8
  HNWL W7 ... 134 C8
  KUTN/CMB KT2 ... 177 K9
  SYD SE26 ... 182 C8
Studland St *HMSMTH* W6 ... 156 E3
Studley Av *CHING* E4 ... 101 J8
Studley Cl *CLPT* E5 ... 120 D10 1
Studley Ct *SDUP* DA14 ... 185 L8
Studley Crs *HART* DA3 ... 211 P1
Studley Dr *REDBR* IG4 ... 122 A4
Studley Grange Rd *HNWL* W7 ... 154 D2
Studley Rd *CLAP* SW4 ... 158 F7
  DAGE RM9 ... 144 A5
  FSTGT E7 ... 141 N1 8
Stukeley Rd *FSTGT* E7 ... 141 N1
Stukeley St *HOL/ALD* WC2B ... 11 M5
Stumbles *CRAWE* RH10 ... 284 D6 2
Stumps Hill La *BECK* BR3 ... 182 F3
Sturdy Rd *PECK* SE15 ... 160 A8
Sturge Av *WALTH* E17 ... 100 G9
Sturgeon Rd *WALW* SE17 ... 18 E9
Sturges Fld *CHST* BR7 ... 184 G3
Sturgess Av *HDN* NW4 ... 116 E5
Sturge St *STHWK* SE1 ... 18 E2
Sturlas Wy *CHES/WCR* EN8 ... 62 C9
Sturmer Wy *HOLWY* N7 ... 118 C10 8
Sturminster Cl *YEAD* UB4 ... 133 K8 8
Sturrock Cl *SEVS/STOTM* N15 ... 119 L2
Sturry St *POP/IOD* E14 ... 140 G8
Sturt Ct *GU* GU1 ... 250 E8
Sturt's La *KWD/TDW/WH* KT20 ... 256 C5
Sturt St *IS* N1 ... 6 F1
Stutfield St *WCHPL* E1 ... 13 P6 8
Stychens Cl *REDH* RH1 ... 259 K9
Stychens La *REDH* RH1 ... 259 K9
Styles End *GT/LBKH* KT23 ... 254 A3 8
Styles Gdns *BRXN/ST* SW9 ... 159 J9
Styles Wy *BECK* BR3 ... 205 H4
Styventon Pl *CHERT* KT16 ... 195 J7 2
Succomb's Hl *CTHM* CR3 ... 242 A6
Succombs Pl *WARL* CR6 ... 242 A6
Sudbourne Rd *BRXS/STRHM* SW2 ... 180 F1
Sudbrook Gdns *RCHPK/HAM* TW10 ... 177 K6
Sudbrook La *RCHPK/HAM* TW10 ... 177 K4
Sudbury *EHAM* E6 ... 142 D8 2
Sudbury Av *ALP/SUD* HA0 ... 114 F8
Sudbury Court Dr *HRW* HA1 ... 114 F8
Sudbury Court Rd *ALP/SUD* HA0 ... 114 F8
Sudbury Crs *ALP/SUD* HA0 ... 114 C10 1
  BMLY BR1 ... 183 M8
Sudbury Cft *ALP/SUD* HA0 ... 114 L9
Sudbury Gdns *CROY/NA* CR0 ... 223 M1 8
Sudbury Heights Av
  GFD/PVL UB6 ... 114 E10
Sudbury Hl *HRW* HA1 ... 114 D8
Sudbury Hill Cl *ALP/SUD* HA0 ... 114 E8
Sudbury Rd *BARK* IG11 ... 123 J10
Sudeley St *IS* N1 ... 6 D1
Sudicamps Ct *WAB* EN9 ... 63 M9 8
Sudlow Rd *WAND/EARL* SW18 ... 157 K10
Sudrey St *STHWK* SE1 ... 18 E2
Suez Av *GFD/PVL* UB6 ... 134 E4 2
Suez Rd *PEND* EN3 ... 130 D2
Suffield Cl *SAND/SEL* CR2 ... 224 C8
  PGE/AN SE20 ... 204 B2
  SEVS/STOTM N15 ... 119 N3 2
Suffolk Cl *BORE* WD6 ... 76 A9 3
  HORL RH6 ... 280 B5 8
  LCOL/BKTW AL2 ... 57 H1
  SL SL1 ... 128 C8
Suffolk Dr *RGUE* GU4 ... 250 E5
Suffolk La *CANST* EC4R ... 12 G7
Suffolk Park Rd *WALTH* E17 ... 120 D2
Suffolk Rd *BARK* IG11 ... 142 F1
  DAGE RM10 ... 124 C10
  DART DA1 ... 187 K4
  GDMY/SEVK IG3 ... 123 H4
  GVE DA12 ... 190 C2
  PEND EN3 ... 83 A9
  PLSTW E13 ... 141 L2
  POTB/CUF EN6 ... 59 H8
  RYLN/HDSTN HA2 ... 113 N4
  SCUP DA14 ... 186 D4
  SEVS/STOTM N15 ... 119 L4
  SNWD SE25 ... 203 N3
  WLSDN NW10 ... 136 B2 8
  WPK KT4 ... 200 C9
Suffolk St *FSTGT* E7 ... 121 H10 2
  STJS SW1Y ... 11 J8
Suffolk Wy *BCR/WK* TN15 ... 265 K1
  EMPK RM11 ... 125 P2 8
Sugar House La *SRTFD* E15 ... 141 H4
Sugar La *HHW* HP1 ... 34 E8
Sugden Rd *BTSEA* SW11 ... 158 B9

THDIT KT7 198 G8
Sugden Wy BARK IG11 143 J4
Sulgrave Gdns HMSMTH W6 156 F1 4
Sulgrave Rd HMSMTH W6 156 F1
Sulina Rd BRXS/STRHM SW2 180 F3
Sulivan Ct FUL/PGN SW6 157 K8
Sulivan Rd FUL/PGN SW6 157 K9
Sullington Hl CRAWW RH11 283 N9 4
Sullivan Av CAN/RD E16 142 A7
Sullivan Cl BTSEA SW11 157 P9
DART DA1 187 J2
E/WMO/HCT KT8 197 P3
Sullivan Crs DEN/HRF UB9 91 N10
Sullivan Dr CRAWW RH11 283 H10
Sullivan Rd LBTH SE11 18 B5
TIL RM18 168 D7
Sullivans Reach WOT/HER KT12 196 G7 1
WOT/HER KT12 197 H7 3
Sullivan Wy BORE WD6 75 H10
Sultan Rd WAN E11 121 N2 1
Sultan St BECK BR3 204 C2
CMBW SE5 159 K6
Sumatra Rd KIL/WHAMP NW6 2 E1
Sumburgh Rd BAL SW12 180 B2
Sumburgh Wy SL SL1 129 J7
Summer Av E/WMO/HCT KT8 198 D5
Summercourt Rd WCHPL E1 140 B8
Summer Dl WGCW AL8 22 G1
Summerene Cl
STRHM/NOR SW16 180 D10 2
Summerfield ASHTD KT21 237 J5 1
HAT AL10 40 D7
Summerfield Av KIL/WHAMP NW6 2 B7
NFNCH/WDSP N12 97 P7
Summerfield Cl LCOL/BKTW AL2 57 H2
Summerfield La SURB KT6 199 J9
Summerfield Rd GSTN WD25 73 H1
LOU IG10 82 A10
WEA W13 134 G6
Summerfields Cl
ADL/WDHM KT15 215 K2 5
Summerfield St LEE/GVPK SE12 183 L3
Summer Gdns E/WMO/HCT KT8 198 D5
Summer Gv BORE WD6 75 J10
Summerhayes Cl
WOKN/KNAP GU21 214 B10
Summerhays COB KT11 217 L9
Summer Hl BORE WD6 75 M9
CHST BR7 206 D2
Summerhill Cl ORP BR6 227 H1
Summerhill Gv EN EN1 79 M10
Summerhill Rd DART DA1 187 L3
SEVS/STOTM N15 119 L2
Summerhill Wy MTCM CR4 202 B1 5
Summerhouse Av HEST TW5 153 M7
Summerhouse Dr RDART DA2 186 E8
Summerhouse La DEN/HRF UB9 91 K8
GSTN WD25 74 B5
WDR/YW UB7 151 N5
Summerhouse Rd
STNW/STAM N16 119 M7 6
Summerhouse Wy ABLGY WD5 54 G6 1
Summerland Gdns MUSWH N10 118 C1 4
Summerlands Av ACT W3 135 P9
Summerlay Cl
KWD/TDW/WH KT20 239 H7
Summerlea SL SL1 128 G10 5
Summerlee Av EFNCH N2 118 A2
Summerlee Gdns EFNCH N2 118 A2
Summerley St WAND/EARL SW18 179 L5
Summerly Av REIG RH2 257 K9
Summer Rd E/WMO/HCT KT8 198 C5 3
THDIT KT7 198 E5
Summersbury Dr RGUE GU4 268 B8
Summersby Rd HGT N6 118 C4
Summers Cl BELMT SM2 221 K4
WBLY HA9 115 N6 1
WEY KT13 216 B7
Summersland Rd STALE/WH AL4 39 H2 3
Summers La NFNCH/WDSP N12 97 N8
RGODL GU7 266 F9
Summer's Rd RGODL GU7 267 L10 1
SL SL1 128 B5
Summers Rw NFNCH/WDSP N12 97 P7 4
Summerstown TOOT SW17 179 M6
Summersvere Cl CRAWE RH10 284 B4
Summerswood Cl PUR/KEN CR8 241 L2
Summerswood La BORE WD6 76 B1
Summerton Wy THMD SE28 143 N9
Summer Trees SUN TW16 197 J1 3
Summerville Gdns SUT SM1 221 J3
Summerwood Rd TWK TW1 176 E2
Summit Av CDALE/KGS NW9 116 A3
Summit Cl CDALE/KGS NW9 116 A2
EDGW HA8 95 M8
STHGT/OAK N14 98 D3
Summit Dr WFD IG8 102 A10
Summit Rd NTHLT UB5 133 P2
POTB/CUF EN6 59 H6
WALTH E17 120 G2
The Summit LOU IG10 82 C5
Summit Wy NRWD SE19 181 M10
STHGT/OAK N14 98 C3
Sumner Av PECK SE15 159 N7 6
Sumner Cl LHD/OX KT22 236 C10
ORP BR6 226 F1 7
Sumner Gdns CROY/NA CR0 203 H8
Sumner Pl ADL/WDHM KT15 215 K2
SKENS SW7 15 M6
Sumner Place Ms SKENS SW7 15 M6
Sumner Rd CROY/NA CR0 203 J8
HRW HA1 114 B5
PECK SE15 159 N7 7
Sumner Rd South CROY/NA CR0 203 H8
Sumners Farm Cl EPP CM16 46 D6 1
Sumner St STHWK SE1 12 E9
Sumnmit Pl WEY KT13 216 B4 6
Sumpter Yd STAL AL1 38 C7 1
Sunbeam Crs NKENS W10 136 F6
Sunbeam Rd WLSDN NW10 135 P6
Sunbury Av MLHL NW7 96 A6
MORT/ESHN SW14 156 A10
Sunbury Ct SUN TW16 197 L2
Sunbury Court Rd SUN TW16 197 K2
Sunbury Gdns MLHL NW7 96 A6
Sunbury La BTSEA SW11 157 N7
WOT/HER KT12 197 H6
Sunbury Rd CHEAM SM3 200 G10
FELT TW13 174 G6
WDSR SL4 149 J5 1
Sunbury St WOOL/PLUM SE18 162 C2
Sunbury Wy FELT TW13 175 K8
Sun Cl WDSR SL4 149 J5
Sun Ct ERITH DA8 164 G8
Suncroft Pl SYD SE26 182 B6
Sundale Av SAND/SEL CR2 224 B6
Sunderland Av STAL AL1 38 F5
Sunderland Rd EA W5 155 J2 2
FSTH SE23 182 C5
Sunderland Ter BAY/PAD W2 8 G5
Sunderland Wy MNPK E12 122 A7
Sundew Av SHB W12 136 D9
Sundew Cl LTWR GU18 212 C7
Sundew Rd HHW HP1 35 H7 6
Sundial Av SNWD SE25 203 N2
Sundon Crs VW GU25 193 N5
Sundorne Rd CHARL SE7 161 N4
Sundown Av SAND/SEL CR2 223 N7
Sundown Rd ASHF TW15 174 D8 3
Sundridge Av BMLY BR1 184 A10
WELL DA16 162 G8
Sundridge Cl DART DA1 187 P2
Sundridge Hl RSEV TN14 245 M4
Sundridge La RSEV TN14 245 L3
Sundridge Rd CROY/NA CR0 203 N8
RSEV TN14 246 B6
WOKS/MYFD GU22 232 D5
Sunfields Pl BKHTH/KID SE3 161 N6 3
Sunflower Wy HARH RM3 105 L9
Sun Hl HART DA3 210 F9
WOKS/MYFD GU22 231 N7
Sunkist Wy WLGTN SM6 222 F5
Sunland Av BXLYHS DA6 163 P10
Sun La GVE DA12 190 F5
Sunleigh Rd ALP/SUD HA0 135 K3
Sunley Gdns GFD/PVL UB6 134 F4
Sunlight Cl WIM/MER SW19 179 M9 4
Sunmead Cl LHD/OX KT22 236 E8
Sunmead Rd HHNE HP2 35 N4
SUN TW16 197 H3
Sunna Gdns SUN TW16 197 J2
Sunning Av ASC SL5 192 D7
Sunningdale STHGT/OAK N14 98 E6
Sunningdale Av ACT W3 136 B9
BARK IG11 142 G3
FELT TW13 175 M5
RAIN RM13 145 J6 3
RSLP HA4 113 K6
Sunningdale Cl STAN HA7 94 F8
SURB KT6 199 K9 2
THMD SE28 143 P8 1
Sunningdale Ct CRAWW RH11 283 N9 5
Sunningdale Gdns
CDALE/KGS NW9 115 P3 2
Sunningdale Ms WGCE AL7 23 J1 1
Sunningdale Rd HAYES BR2 206 B4
RAIN RM13 145 H2
SUT SM1 201 J10
Sunningfield Rd HDN NW4 116 E1
Sunningfields Crs HDN NW4 96 E10
Sunningfields Rd HDN NW4 96 E10
Sunninghill GVW DA11 190 B5 2
Sunninghill Cl ASC SL5 192 C4
Sunninghill Rd ASC SL5 170 C8
ASC SL5 192 C5
LEW SE13 160 G8 6
Sunnings La UPMR RM14 146 C1
Sunningvale Av BH/WHM TN16 243 P3
Sunningvale Cl BH/WHM TN16 244 A2
Sunny Av CRAWE RH10 285 P5
Sunny Bank EPSOM KT18 237 P2
SNWD SE25 203 P3 2
WARL CR6 242 D3
Sunnybank Rd POTB/CUF EN6 59 K9
Sunny Crs WLSDN NW10 135 P2
Sunny Cft HLWS CM18 47 J4 1
Sunnycroft Gdns UPMR RM14 126 E5
Sunnycroft Rd HSLW TW3 154 A8
SNWD SE25 203 P3
STHL UB1 133 P7
Sunnydale ORP BR6 206 D9
Sunnydale Gdns MLHL NW7 96 A7
Sunnydale Rd LEE/GVPK SE12 183 N1
Sunnydell LCOL/BKTW AL2 56 A2
Sunnydene Av CHING E4 101 J6
RSLP HA4 113 H6 1
Sunnydene Cl HARH RM3 105 N8
Sunnydene Gdns ALP/SUD HA0 135 H1 4
Sunnydene Rd PUR/KEN CR8 223 J9
Sunnydene St SYD SE26 182 D7
Sunnyfield BRKMPK AL9 40 G1
MLHL NW7 96 C5
Sunny Gardens Rd HDN NW4 96 F10
Sunny Hl HDN NW4 116 E1
Sunnyhill Cl CLPT E5 120 D9 6
CRAWE RH10 285 P5 1
Sunnyhill Rd HHW HP1 35 L6
RKW/CH/CXG WD3 90 G7
STRHM/NOR SW16 180 F7
Sunnyhurst Cl SUT SM1 201 K10 2
Sunnymead CRAWW RH11 283 N7
Sunnymead Av MTCM CR4 202 E3 1
Sunnymead Rd CDALE/KGS NW9 116 A5
PUT/ROE SW15 178 E1
Sunnymede CHIG IG7 103 L4
Sunnymede Av CAR SM5 221 N7
CSHM HP5 51 K4
HOR/WEW KT19 220 B5
Sunnymede Dr BARK/HLT IG6 122 E2
Sunny Nook Gdns
SAND/SEL CR2 223 L3 3
Sunny Pl HDN NW4 116 F2 7
Sunny Ri CTHM CR3 241 L10
The Sunny Rd PEND EN3 80 C5
Sunnyside CRICK NW2 117 J8 3
WAB EN9 45 L8
WIM/MER SW19 179 H9
WOT/HER KT12 197 K5
Sunnyside Dr CHING E4 101 H1
Sunnyside Gdns UPMR RM14 126 B8
Sunnyside Rd ARCH N19 118 E5
CSHM HP5 50 G6
EA W5 135 J10
EPP CM16 65 J8
IL IG1 122 F8
LEY E10 120 F6
TEDD TW11 176 C7
Sunnyside Rd East ED N9 99 P4
Sunnyside Rd North ED N9 99 P4 7
Sunnyside Rd South ED N9 99 P4 8
Sunny Vw CDALE/KGS NW9 116 A3 3
Sunny Wy NFNCH/WDSP N12 97 P8
Sun Pas BERM/RHTH SE16 19 N3
Sunray Av BRYLDS KT5 199 N9
CMBW SE5 159 L10
HAYES BR2 206 B6
HNHL SE24 159 L10 4
WDR/YW UB7 151 N1
Sunrise Av HCH RM12 125 K8 2
Sunrise Cl FELT TW13 175 N6 1
Sunrise Crs HHS/BOV HP3 36 A9 1
Sun Rd SWCM DA10 189 L2
WKENS W14 14 C8
Sunset Av CHING E4 100 G2
WFD IG8 101 M6
Sunset Cl ERITH DA8 165 J6 5
Sunset Gdns SNWD SE25 203 N2 1
Sunset Rd CMBW SE5 159 K10
THMD SE28 143 K10
Sunset Vw BAR EN5 77 H6
Sunshine Wy MTCM CR4 202 A2
Sun St SBW CM21 30 A2
SDTCH EC2A 13 H3
WAB EN9 63 H9
Superior Dr ORP BR6 227 J3 4
Surbiton Crs SURB KT6 199 K4
Surbiton Hall Cl KUT KT1 199 K4 4
Surbiton Hill Pk BRYLDS KT5 199 L5
Surbiton Hill Rd SURB KT6 199 K4
Surbiton Rd KUT KT1 199 J4
Surlingham Cl THMD SE28 143 N9 5
Surly Hall Wk WDSR SL4 148 E7
Surma Cl WCHPL E1 13 P2
Surman Crs RBRW/HUT CM13 107 P1
Surrendale Pl MV/WKIL W9 8 F2
Surrey Av SLN SL2 129 H7
Surrey Canal Rd
BERM/RHTH SE16 160 B5
Surrey Crs CHSWK W4 155 M4 5
Surrey Dr EMPK RM11 125 P3
Surrey Gdns COB KT11 234 G9
FSBYPK N4 119 K4 3
Surrey Gv SUT SM1 201 N10
WALW SE17 19 J8
Surrey Hills Av
KWD/TDW/WH KT20 255 P7 2
Surrey Hills Wy
KWD/TDW/WH KT20 255 P6
Surrey La BTSEA SW11 157 P7
Surrey Ms WNWD SE27 181 M7 5
Surrey Quays Rd
BERM/RHTH SE16 160 B2
Surrey Rd BARK IG11 143 H2
DAGE RM10 124 C10
HRW HA1 114 B4
PECK SE15 182 C1
WWKM BR4 204 G8
Surrey Rw STHWK SE1 18 C1
Surrey Sq WALW SE17 19 J7
Surrey St CROY/NA CR0 203 K10
PLSTW E13 141 N5
TPL/STR WC2R 11 P7
Surrey Ter WALW SE17 19 K6
Surrey Water Rd
BERM/RHTH SE16 140 C10
Surridge Cl RAIN RM13 145 K5
Surridge Gdns NRWD SE19 181 L9 4
Surr St HOLWY N7 118 F10
Susan Cl ROMW/RG RM7 124 D1
Susannah St POP/IOD E14 141 H8 8
Susan Rd BKHTH/KID SE3 161 N8
Susan Wd CHST BR7 206 D1
Sussex Av HARH RM3 105 N8
ISLW TW7 154 D9
Sussex Border Pth CRAWE RH10 285 L3
HORL RH6 279 M7
Sussex Cl CSTG HP8 89 N3 1
HOD EN11 44 F2 4
NWMAL KT3 200 B4
REDBR IG4 122 C4
REIG RH2 275 N1
SL SL1 149 N1
TWK TW1 176 G2 10
WOKN/KNAP GU21 231 H4 1
Sussex Ct WOKN/KNAP GU21 231 H3
Sussex Crs NTHLT UB5 133 P1
Sussex Gdns BAY/PAD W2 9 M6
CHSGTN KT9 219 J3
EFNCH N2 118 A3
FSBYPK N4 119 K3 3
Sussex Ms East BAY/PAD W2 9 M7 1
Sussex Ms West BAY/PAD W2 9 M7
Sussex Pl BAY/PAD W2 9 M6
CAMTN NW1 10 A1
DTCH/LGLY SL3 149 N1
HMSMTH W6 156 F4
NWMAL KT3 200 B4
SL SL1 149 M1
Sussex Rd BRW CM14 106 G5
CAR SM5 222 A3
DART DA1 187 P3
EHAM E6 142 D4
ERITH DA8 164 C6
HGDN/ICK UB10 112 D9
HRW HA1 114 B3
MTCM CR4 202 F5 4
NWDGN UB2 153 L2
NWMAL KT3 200 B4 5
SAND/SEL CR2 223 L3
SCUP DA14 185 L8
STMC/STPC BR5 207 M6
WATN WD24 73 H4
WOKN/KNAP GU21 231 H4
WWKM BR4 204 G8 2
Sussex Sq BAY/PAD W2 9 M7
Sussex St PIM SW1V 16 F8
PLSTW E13 141 N5
Sussex Wy ARCH N19 118 E6
EBAR EN4 78 C9
Sutcliffe Cl BUSH WD23 74 B8
GLDGN NW11 117 L3 1
Sutcliffe Rd WELL DA16 163 M8
WOOL/PLUM SE18 163 H5
Sutherland Av BH/WHM TN16 244 A3
HYS/HAR UB3 153 H3 1
MV/WKIL W9 8 F2
POTB/CUF EN6 60 E4
RGUE GU4 250 A4
STMC/STPC BR5 207 J6
SUN TW16 196 G2
WEA W13 134 G8
WELL DA16 162 G10
Sutherland Cl BAR EN5 77 H8
GVE DA12 191 L5 4
Sutherland Ct CDALE/KGS NW9 115 N2
WGCE AL7 23 J4 4
Sutherland Dr GU GU1 250 D7
WIM/MER SW19 201 N1
Sutherland Gdns
MORT/ESHN SW14 156 B9 5
SUN TW16 196 G2 1
WPK KT4 200 E8 2
Sutherland Gv TEDD TW11 176 D8
WAND/EARL SW18 179 J3
Sutherland Pl BAY/PAD W2 8 E5
Sutherland Rd BELV DA17 164 B2
BOW E3 140 E4
CHSWK W4 156 B5
CROY/NA CR0 203 H7
ED N9 99 P2
PEND EN3 80 C10
STHL UB1 133 N8 4
TOTM N17 99 P8
WALTH E17 120 D1
WEA W13 134 F8
Sutherland Rw PIM SW1V 16 F7 1
Sutherland Sq WALW SE17 18 E8
Sutherland St PIM SW1V 16 F7
Sutherland Wk WALW SE17 18 F8
Sutherland Wy POTB/CUF EN6 60 E4
Sutlej Rd CHARL SE7 161 P6
Sutterton St HOLWY N7 5 N2
Sutton Av DTCH/LGLY SL3 149 P1
WOKN/KNAP GU21 231 K5
Sutton Cl BECK BR3 204 G1 5
BROX EN10 44 D6
LOU IG10 102 B1
PIN HA5 113 H3
Sutton Common Rd CHEAM SM3 201 J7
Sutton Ct BELMT SM2 221 M4
Sutton Court Rd BELMT SM2 221 M3
CHSWK W4 155 P5
HGDN/ICK UB10 132 C3
PLSTW E13 141 P5
SUT SM1 221 M3 3
Sutton Crs BAR EN5 76 G9
Sutton Dene HSLW TW3 154 A7
Sutton Gdns CROY/NA CR0 203 N5 1
REDH RH1 258 E5
Sutton Green Rd RGUE GU4 250 B2
Sutton Gv SUT SM1 221 N2
Sutton Hall HEST TW5 153 P6
Sutton La BELMT SM2 221 L8
BNSTD SM7 239 L1
CHSWK W4 155 P4
DTCH/LGLY SL3 150 E5
HSLW TW3 153 N8
RDKG RH5 271 J9
Sutton La South CHSWK W4 155 P5
Sutton Park Rd SUT SM1 221 L3
Sutton Pl DTCH/LGLY SL3 150 E5
HOM E9 120 B10 5
SHGR GU5 270 G9
Sutton Rd BARK IG11 143 H4
HEST TW5 153 P7
MUSWH N10 98 B9
PLSTW E13 141 L6
STAL AL1 38 G7
WALTH E17 100 C9
WAT WD17 73 K7
Sutton Rw SOHO/SHAV W1D 11 K5 5
Suttons Av HCH RM12 125 K8
Suttons Gdns HCH RM12 125 L8
Suttons La HCH RM12 125 L10
Sutton Sq HACK E8 120 B10 6
HEST TW5 153 N7
Sutton St WCHPL E1 140 B8
Sutton Wy HEST TW5 153 N7
NKENS W10 136 F7
Swabey Rd DTCH/LGLY SL3 150 D3
Swaby Rd WAND/EARL SW18 179 M5
Swaffield Rd SEV TN13 247 K8
WAND/EARL SW18 179 M3
Swain Cl TOOT SW17 180 C9
Swain Rd THHTH CR7 203 K5
Swains Cl WDR/YW UB7 151 P1 2
Swain's La HGT N6 118 B6
Swainson Rd ACT W3 156 C1 5
Swains Rd MTCM CR4 180 A10
Swaisland Rd DART DA1 187 J1
Swaislands Dr DART DA1 186 G1
Swakeleys Dr HGDN/ICK UB10 112 B9
Swakeleys Rd HGDN/ICK UB10 112 C8
HGDN/ICK UB10 112 A8 1
Swale Cl SOCK/AV RM15 146 B8 2
Swaledale Cl CRAWW RH11 283 M10 1
FBAR/BDGN N11 98 B7 4
Swaledale Rd RDART DA2 188 B4
Swale Rd DART DA1 165 H9
Swallands Rd CAT SE6 182 F6
Swallow Cl BUSH WD23 94 A2
BXLYHN DA7 164 F7
CDH/CHF RM16 167 H3
GRH DA9 188 E1
NWCR SE14 160 C7 3
RKW/CH/CXG WD3 91 M1 1
STA TW18 173 J7
Swallowdale IVER SL0 130 G5
SAND/SEL CR2 224 C5
Swallowdale La HHNE HP2 36 B3
Swallow Dr NTHLT UB5 133 P4
WLSDN NW10 136 A1 4
Swallow End WGCE AL7 23 J5
Swallowfield EGH TW20 171 N9 6
Swallowfield Rd CHARL SE7 161 N4
Swallowfields WGCE AL7 23 J5 2
Swallowfield Wy HYS/HAR UB3 152 E1
Swallow Gdns HAT AL10 40 D6 3
STRHM/NOR SW16 180 E8 4
Swallow La RDKG RH5 272 G8
STAL AL1 38 G9
Swallow Oaks ABLGY WD5 54 G8 3
Swallow Pl CONDST W1S 10 F6 4
Swallow Ri WOKN/KNAP GU21 231 H3
Swallow Rd CRAWW RH11 283 M5
Swallows HLWE CM17 29 M7
The Swallows WGCE AL7 23 J1 2
Swallow St CONDST W1S 11 H8
EHAM E6 142 B7
IVER SL0 130 G5
Swallowtail Cl STMC/STPC BR5 207 N4 9
Swanage Rd CHING E4 101 H8
WAND/EARL SW18 179 M2
Swanage Waye YEAD UB4 133 K8
Swan And Pike Rd PEND EN3 80 F4
Swan Ap EHAM E6 142 B7
Swan Av UPMR RM14 126 E6
Swanbourne Dr HCH RM12 125 L9
Swanbridge Rd BXLYHN DA7 164 B7
Swan Cl CSHM HP5 50 G3
FELT TW13 175 M7
RKW/CH/CXG WD3 91 N1
STMC/STPC BR5 207 K3
WALTH E17 100 D9 3
Swan Ct GU GU1 250 A8
Swandon Wy WAND/EARL SW18 157 L10
Swan Dr CDALE/KGS NW9 96 B10
Swanfield Rd CHES/WCR EN8 62 D9
Swanfield St BETH E2 7 L10
Swanhill WGCE AL7 23 K2
Swanland Rd BRKMPK AL9 58 E3
POTB/CUF EN6 58 E10
Swan La BRWN CM15 86 D3
CANST EC4R 13 H8
DART DA1 186 G3
GU GU1 268 A1
HORL RH6 279 J8
LOU IG10 101 P1
TRDG/WHET N20 97 M4
Swanley Bar La POTB/CUF EN6 59 L4
Swanley Crs POTB/CUF EN6 59 L5
Swanley La SWLY BR8 208 G3
Swanley Rd WELL DA16 163 M7
Swanley Village Rd SWLY BR8 209 J1
Swan Md HHS/BOV HP3 54 A1
STHWK SE1 19 J4
Swan Ms BRXN/ST SW9 158 G8 5
Swan Mill Gdns DORK RH4 255 H10
Swanns Meadow GT/LBKH KT23 253 P2
Swan Pl BARN SW13 156 C8 4
Swan Rd BERM/RHTH SE16 160 B1
FELT TW13 175 M7
GFD/PVL UB6 134 A8
IVER SL0 131 J8
WDR/YW UB7 151 N1
Swans Cl STALE/WH AL4 39 K7
Swanscombe Rd CHSWK W4 156 B4 4
NTGHL W11 136 G10 4
Swanscombe St SWCM DA10 189 L2
Swansea Rd HTHAIR TW6 174 D2
PEND EN3 80 B8 3
Swanshope LOU IG10 82 E6 2
Swans Rd CHES/WCR EN8 62 C10
Swanston Pth OXHEY WD19 93 K4 4
Swan St ISLW TW7 154 G9
STHWK SE1 18 F2
Swanton Gdns WIM/MER SW19 178 G4 5
Swanton Rd ERITH DA8 164 B6
Swan Wk CHEL SW3 16 A9
SHPTN TW17 196 F7
Swan Wy PEND EN3 80 C6
Swanwick Cl PUT/ROE SW15 178 C3
Swanworth La RDKG RH5 254 G4
Swan Yd IS N1 6 C2
Swanzy Rd RSEV TN14 247 K6
Sward Rd STMC/STPC BR5 207 K6
Swaton Rd BOW E3 140 F6
Swaylands Rd BELV DA17 164 B5
Swaynesland Rd OXTED RH8 262 C10
Swayne's La GU GU1 251 H10
Swaythling Cl UED N18 100 A5
Sweden Ga BERM/RHTH SE16 160 D3 1
Sweeney Crs STHWK SE1 19 M2
Sweeps Ditch Cl STA TW18 195 K1
Sweeps La EGH TW20 172 C8
STMC/STPC BR5 207 N5
Sweet Briar WGCE AL7 23 K7
Sweetbriar Cl HHW HP1 35 K3
Sweet Briar Gn UED N18 99 N4
Sweet Briar Gv ED N9 99 N4
Sweet Briar Wk UED N18 99 N5
Sweetcroft La HGDN/ICK UB10 132 A2
Sweet La SHGR GU5 270 E9
Sweetmans Av PIN HA5 113 L1
Sweets Wy TRDG/WHET N20 97 N3
Swete St PLSTW E13 141 M4
Sweyne HLWE CM17 47 M4
Sweyne Rd SWCM DA10 189 K2
Sweyn Pl BKHTH/KID SE3 161 M8
Swievelands Rd BH/WHM TN16 243 N5
Swift Cl HYS/HAR UB3 132 G8
RYLN/HDSTN HA2 114 A7
UPMR RM14 126 D6 3
WALTH E17 100 D8
WARE SG12 27 H8
Swiftfields WGCE AL7 23 J4
Swift La CRAWW RH11 283 N5
Swift Rd FELT TW13 175 L7
NWDGN UB2 153 N2
Swiftsden Wy BMLY BR1 183 K9
Swift St FUL/PGN SW6 157 H7
Swiftsure Rd CDH/CHF RM16 167 H3
Swiller's La GVE DA12 191 P8
Swinbrook Rd NKENS W10 8 B3
Swinburne Crs CROY/NA CR0 204 B6
Swinburne Gdns TIL RM18 168 E8
Swinburne Rd PUT/ROE SW15 156 D10
Swinderby Rd ALP/SUD HA0 135 K1
Swindon Cl GDMY/SEVK IG3 123 H7
Swindon Gdns HARH RM3 105 N6 1
Swindon La HARH RM3 105 N6
Swindon Rd HTHAIR TW6 174 D2 1
Swindon St SHB W12 136 F10 3
Swinfield Cl FELT TW13 175 M7 6
Swinford Gdns BRXN/ST SW9 159 J9 3
Swingate La WOOL/PLUM SE18 163 H6
Swing Gate La BERK HP4 34 A6
Swinnerton St HOM E9 120 D10 4
Swinton Cl WBLY HA9 115 N6
Swinton Pl FSBYW WC1X 5 N9 1
Swinton St FSBYW WC1X 5 N9
Swires Shaw HAYES BR2 226 A1
Swiss Av WATW WD18 72 F8
Swiss Cl WATW WD18 72 F7
Swithland Gdns ELTH/MOT SE9 184 C7
Swyncombe Av BTFD TW8 154 G3
Swynford Gdns HDN NW4 116 D2 5
Sybil Phoenix Cl DEPT SE8 160 C4 1
Sybourn St WALTH E17 120 E5 6
Sycamore Ap RKW/CH/CXG WD3 72 D9
Sycamore Av BFN/LL DA15 185 J2
EA W5 155 J2 3
HAT AL10 40 D5
HYS/HAR UB3 132 F9
UPMR RM14 125 P8
Sycamore Cl ACT W3 136 B10
AMS HP6 69 J3
BUSH WD23 73 M6 2
CAN/RD E16 141 K6 3
CAR SM5 222 A1
CHESW EN7 61 N3 3
CRAWW RH11 283 M4
EBAR EN4 77 N10
FELT TW13 175 H6
GSTN WD25 73 J1
GVE DA12 190 G3 2
LHD/OX KT22 236 E8
NTHLT UB5 133 M3 3
TIL RM18 168 C7
UED N18 99 P5
WDR/YW UB7 132 A9 2
Sycamore Ct WEY KT13 196 G10 1
Sycamore Dene CSHM HP5 51 J4
Sycamore Dr BRW CM14 107 H2
LCOL/BKTW AL2 56 C3 2
SWLY BR8 208 F3
Sycamore Fld HLWW/ROY CM19 46 D5
Sycamore Gdns MTCM CR4 201 N2 2
SHB W12 156 E1
Sycamore Gv CAT SE6 183 H2
CDALE/KGS NW9 115 P5
NWMAL KT3 200 B3
PGE/AN SE20 203 P1 1
Sycamore Hl FBAR/BDGN N11 98 B7
Sycamore Ms CLAP SW4 158 D9 5
Sycamore Ri BERK HP4 34 A6
BNSTD SM7 220 G10 6
CSTG HP8 89 M4
Sycamore Rd AMS HP6 69 J3
CSTG HP8 89 M4
DART DA1 187 L3
GU GU1 250 A10
RKW/CH/CXG WD3 72 D9
WIM/MER SW19 178 F9
The Sycamores HHS/BOV HP3 35 J9
RAD WD7 56 G10
Sycamore St FSBYE EC1V 12 E2 2
Sycamore Wk DTCH/LGLY SL3 130 B8 5
EGH TW20 171 N9
NKENS W10 8 A1 3
REIG RH2 275 M3
Sycamore Wy SOCK/AV RM15 147 J6
TEDD TW11 177 H9
Sydenham Av SYD SE26 182 A8
WCHMH N21 78 G9
Sydenham Cl ROM RM1 124 G2 2
Sydenham Hl EDUL SE22 182 A5
SYD SE26 181 P6
Sydenham Pk SYD SE26 182 B6
Sydenham Park Rd SYD SE26 182 B6
Sydenham Ri FSTH SE23 182 A5
Sydenham Rd CROY/NA CR0 203 K9
GU GU1 268 A2
SYD SE26 182 C8
Sydenham Station Ap SYD SE26 182 B7 3
Sydner Rd STNW/STAM N16 119 N9
Sydney Av PUR/KEN CR8 222 G8 1
Sydney Cl SKENS SW7 15 M6
Sydney Crs ASHF TW15 174 C9
Sydney Gv HDN NW4 116 F3
SL SL1 129 H8
Sydney Ms SKENS SW7 15 M6
Sydney Pl GU GU1 268 C1 5
SKENS SW7 15 M6
Sydney Rd ABYW SE2 163 N2
BARK/HLT IG6 102 F10
BXLYHS DA6 163 N10
CEND/HSY/T N8 119 H2
EBED/NFELT TW14 175 H4 4
ENC/FH EN2 79 L8
GU GU1 268 C1
MUSWH N10 98 C9
RCH/KEW TW9 155 K10 10
RYNPK SW20 200 G2
SCUP DA14 185 H7
SUT SM1 221 K1
TEDD TW11 176 E8 6
TIL RM18 168 D8
WAN E11 121 N4 2
WATW WD18 72 F9
WEA W13 134 F10
Sydney St CHEL SW3 15 N7
Syke Cluan IVER SL0 151 H1
Syke Ings IVER SL0 151 H2
Sykes Rd SL SL1 128 G8
Sylvana Cl HGDN/ICK UB10 132 A3
Sylvan Av CHDH RM6 124 A4
EMPK RM11 125 N4
FNCH N3 97 K10
MLHL NW7 96 B7
WDGN N22 99 H8
Sylvan Cl CDH/CHF RM16 167 K3
HHS/BOV HP3 36 B7
OXTED RH8 261 N5
SAND/SEL CR2 224 A6
WOKS/MYFD GU22 232 E4
Sylvandale WGCE AL7 23 M6
Sylvan Gdns SURB KT6 199 J7
Sylvan Gv CRICK NW2 116 G9 4
PECK SE15 160 A6
Sylvan Hl NRWD SE19 203 M1
Sylvan Rd CRAWE RH10 284 B9
FSTGT E7 141 M1
IL IG1 122 F7
NRWD SE19 203 N1
WALTH E17 120 F3 6
WAN E11 121 M3
Sylvan Wy BCTR RM8 123 L9 1
CHIG IG7 103 L4
REDH RH1 276 C1
WGCE AL7 23 N5 7
WWKM BR4 225 K1
Sylverdale Rd CROY/NA CR0 203 J10
PUR/KEN CR8 223 J9
Sylvester Av CHST BR7 184 C9
Sylvester Rd ALP/SUD HA0 115 H10
EFNCH N2 97 M10
HACK E8 140 A1 7
WALTH E17 120 E5 7
Sylvesters HLWW/ROY CM19 46 C3
Sylvia Av PIN HA5 93 N7
RBRW/HUT CM13 107 P3
Sylvia Cl CHOB/PIR GU24 230 F1
Sylvia Gdns WBLY HA9 135 N2
Symes Ms CAMTN NW1 4 G7 2

Symonds Ct CHES/WCR EN8 ... 62 C4
Syon Gate Wy BTFD TW8 ... 154 F6
Syon La BTFD TW8 ... 154 C6
  ISLW TW7 ... 154 E5
Syon Park Gdns ISLW TW7 ... 154 E6
Syracuse Av RAIN RM13 ... 145 L5
Sythwood WOKN/KNAP GU21 ... 231 N5
Szabo Crs RGUW GU3 ... 248 A10

T

Tabard St STHWK SE1 ... 18 G3
Tabarin Wy EW KT17 ... 238 F2
Tabernacle Av PLSTW E13 ... 141 M6
Tabernacle St SDTCH EC2A ... 13 H2
Tabley Rd HOLWY N7 ... 118 F9
Tabor Gdns CHEAM SM3 ... 221 J6
Tabor Gv WIM/MER SW19 ... 179 H10
Tabor Rd HMSMTH W6 ... 156 C6
Tabrums Wy UPMR RM14 ... 126 D5
Tachbrook Rd EBED/NFELT TW14 ... 174 D2
  NWDGN UB2 ... 153 L3
  UX/CGN UB8 ... 131 M4
Tachbrook St PIM SW1V ... 17 H6
Tack Ms BROCKY SE4 ... 160 F9
Tadema Rd WBPTN SW10 ... 185 M6
Tadlows Cl UPMR RM14 ... 126 A10
Tadmor Cl SUN TW16 ... 196 G4
Tadmor St SHB W12 ... 136 C10
Tadorne Rd KWD/TDW/WH KT20 ... 238 F7
Tadworth Av NWMAL KT3 ... 200 C5
Tadworth Cl KWD/TDW/WH KT20 ... 238 G8
Tadworth Pde HCH RM12 ... 125 J9
Tadworth Rd CRICK NW2 ... 116 D7
Tadworth St KWD/TDW/WH KT20 ... 238 F9
Taeping St POP/IOD E14 ... 160 G3
Taffy's How MTCM CR4 ... 201 J9
Tait Rd CROY/NA CR0 ... 203 M7
  WAB/Ing N9 ... 63 J9
Takeley Cl CRW RM5 ... 104 C8
Talacre Rd KTTN NW5 ... 4 D1
Talbot Av EW KT17 ... 238 C6
  EFNCH N2 ... 117 N1
  OXHEY WD19 ... 93 M1
Talbot Cl REIG RH2 ... 275 L1
  SEVS/STOTM N15 ... 119 N2
Talbot Ct BANK EC3V ... 13 H7
  HHS/BOV HP3 ... 35 H8
Talbot Crs HDN NW4 ... 116 C9
Talbot Gdns GDMY/SEVK IG3 ... 123 K7
Talbot Pl BKHTH/KID SE3 ... 161 K8
  DTCH/LGLY SL3 ... 149 K7
Talbot Rd ALP/SUD HA0 ... 115 J10
  ASHF TW15 ... 173 N8
  BAY/PAD W2 ... 8 C5
  CAR SM5 ... 222 D2
  DAGW RM9 ... 144 A2
  EDUL SE22 ... 159 M10
  EHAM E6 ... 142 C4
  FSTGT E7 ... 121 M9
  HAT AL10 ... 40 D1
  HGT N6 ... 118 B4
  ISLW TW7 ... 154 F10
  KTN/HRWW/W HA3 ... 94 E10
  NTGHL W11 ... 8 C6
  NWDGN UB2 ... 153 M5
  RKW/CH/CXG WD3 ... 91 P2
  SEVS/STOTM N15 ... 119 N2
  WEA W13 ... 134 F10
  WHTN TW2 ... 176 E2
Talbot Sq BAY/PAD W2 ... 9 M6
Talbot St HERT/BAY SG13 ... 25 M5
Talbrook BRW CM14 ... 106 E4
Taleworth Cl ASHTD KT21 ... 237 J6
Taleworth Pk ASHTD KT21 ... 237 J6
Taleworth Rd ASHTD KT21 ... 237 J5
Talfourd Pl PECK SE15 ... 159 N7
Talfourd Rd PECK SE15 ... 159 N7
Talgarth Rd HMSMTH W6 ... 14 A7
Talisman Cl GDMY/SEVK IG3 ... 123 L6
Talisman Sq SYD SE26 ... 181 P7
Talisman Wy EW KT17 ... 238 F2
  WBLY HA9 ... 115 L8
Tallack Rd LEY E10 ... 120 E6
Tall Elms Cl HAYES BR2 ... 205 L5
Tallents Cl EYN DA4 ... 188 A10
Tallis Cl CAN/RD E16 ... 141 N8
  CRAWW RH11 ... 283 J10
Tallis Gv CHARL SE7 ... 161 N5
Tallis St EMB EC4Y ... 12 B7
Tallis Vw WLSDN NW10 ... 136 A1
Tallis Wy BORE WD6 ... 75 J3
Tall Oaks AMS HP6 ... 69 J3
Tall Trees DTCH/LGLY SL3 ... 151 L4
  STRHM/NOR SW16 ... 202 G3
Tall Trees Cl EMPK RM11 ... 125 L4
Tally Rd OXTED RH8 ... 262 B7
Talma Gdns WHTN TW2 ... 176 D3
Talmage Cl FSTH SE23 ... 182 B3
Talman Cl CRAWW RH11 ... 283 H8
Talman Gv STAN HA7 ... 95 J7
Talma Rd BRXS/STRHM SW2 ... 159 H10
Talus Cl PUR RM19 ... 166 C3
Talwin St BOW E3 ... 140 G5
Tamar Cl BOW E3 ... 140 E3
  CRAWE RH10 ... 284 D8
  UPMR RM14 ... 126 D4
Tamar Dr SOCK/AV RM15 ... 146 B8
Tamar Gn HNHE HP2 ... 36 A1
Tamarind Cl GUW GU2 ... 249 M5
Tamarisk Cl STALW/RED AL3 ... 38 D2
Tamarisk Rd SOCK/AV RM15 ... 147 N5
  SOCK/AV RM15 ... 147 N6
Tamarisk Sq SHB W12 ... 136 C9
Tamarisk Wy SL1 ... 128 F10
Tamar St CHARL SE7 ... 162 B3
Tamar Wy DTCH/LGLY SL3 ... 150 L4
Tamerton Sq WOKS/MYFD GU22 ... 232 B5
Tamesis Gdns WPK KT4 ... 200 B9
Tamesis Strd GVE DA12 ... 191 H8
Tamian Wy HSLWW TW4 ... 153 K10
Tamworth Av WFD IG8 ... 101 K7
Tamworth La MTCM CR4 ... 202 C3
Tamworth Pk MTCM CR4 ... 202 C4
Tamworth Pl CROY/NA CR0 ... 203 K9
Tamworth Rd CROY/NA CR0 ... 203 K9
  HERT/BAY SG13 ... 25 N4
Tancred Rd FSBYPK N4 ... 119 L2
Tandridge Dr ORP BR6 ... 206 G8
Tandridge Gdns SAND/SEL CR2 ... 223 N9
Tandridgehill La GDST RH9 ... 260 E4
Tandridge La OXTED RH8 ... 260 B10
Tandridge Rd WARL CR6 ... 242 C6
Tanfield Av CRICK NW2 ... 116 C9
Tanfield Cl CHESW EN7 ... 61 P7
Tanfield Rd CROY/NA CR0 ... 223 K1
Tangier Rd GU GU1 ... 268 C5
  RCHPK/HAM TW10 ... 155 N9
Tangier Wy KWD/TDW/WH KT20 ... 239 H3
Tangier Wd KWD/TDW/WH KT20 ... 239 H4
Tangleberry Cl BMLY BR1 ... 184 F6
Tangle Tree Cl EFNCH N2 ... 97 L10
Tanglewood Cl CHERT KT16 ... 193 N10
  CROY/NA CR0 ... 204 B10
  STAN HA7 ... 94 D3
  UX/CGN UB8 ... 132 B5

  WOKS/MYFD GU22 ... 232 G2
Tanglewood Ride CHOB/PIR GU24 ... 212 C8
Tanglewood Wy FELT TW13 ... 175 J6
Tangley Gv PUT/ROE SW15 ... 178 C3
Tangley La RGUW GU3 ... 249 L6
Tangley Park Rd HPTN TW12 ... 175 M8
Tanglyn Av SHPTN TW17 ... 196 B5
Tangmere Crs HCH RM12 ... 145 J1
Tangmere Gdns NTHLT UB5 ... 133 K4
Tangmere Gv KUTN/CMB KT2 ... 177 J3
Tangmere Rd CRAWW RH11 ... 283 J7
Tangmere Wy CDALE/KGS NW9 ... 96 B10
Tan House La BRW CM14 ... 85 P7
Tanhouse Rd OXTED RH8 ... 261 J8
Tankerton Rd SURB KT6 ... 199 L9
Tankerton St STPAN WC1H ... 5 M10
Tankerville Rd STRHM/NOR SW16 ... 180 E10
Tank Hill Rd PUR RM19 ... 165 P3
Tankridge Rd CRICK NW2 ... 116 E7
Tanners Cl STALW/RED AL3 ... 38 B5
  WOT/HER KT12 ... 197 J6
Tanners Ct HERT/BAY SG13 ... 25 K7
Tanners Dean LHD/OX KT22 ... 237 J3
Tanners End La UED N18 ... 99 M5
Tannersfield SHGR GU5 ... 268 B8
Tanners Hi ABLGY WD5 ... 54 C7
  BRKHM/BTCW RH3 ... 273 N2
  DEPT SE8 ... 160 F7
Tanners La BARK/HLT IG6 ... 122 F1
Tanners Meadow BRKHM/BTCW RH3 ... 273 N4
Tanner St BARK IG11 ... 142 F1
  STHWK SE1 ... 19 K2
Tanners Wy WARE SG12 ... 27 P2
Tanners Wood La ABLGY WD5 ... 54 C10
Tannery Cl CROY/NA CR0 ... 204 C5
  DAGE RM10 ... 124 C8
Tannery La RPLY/SEND GU23 ... 233 H8
The Tannery REIG RH1 ... 257 P10
Tannsfeld Rd SYD SE26 ... 182 C8
Tannsfield Dr HHNE HP2 ... 36 A4
Tannsmore Cl HHNE HP2 ... 36 A3
Tanswell St STHWK SE1 ... 18 A2
Tansy Cl EHAM E6 ... 142 D8
  HARH RM3 ... 105 M7
  RGUE GU4 ... 250 F3
Tansycroft WGCE AL7 ... 23 L4
Tantallon Rd BAL SW12 ... 180 L4
Tant Av CAN/RD E16 ... 141 L8
Tantony Gv CHDH RM6 ... 123 J3
Tanworth Gdns PIN HA5 ... 93 J10
Tanyard Crs RAEW RH10 ... 284 D10
Tanyard Hi GVE DA12 ... 191 P9
Tan Yard La BXLY DA5 ... 186 B3
Tanyard La SHGR GU5 ... 268 C10
Tapestry Cl BELMT SM2 ... 221 L4
Taplow Ct MITC CR4 ... 201 P4
Taplow St IS N1 ... 6 E5
Tapner's Rd REIG RH2 ... 274 C6
Tappesfield Rd PECK SE15 ... 160 B3
Tapping Cl KUTN/CMB KT2 ... 177 M10
Tapp St WCHPL E1 ... 140 A6
Tapster St BAR EN5 ... 77 J7
Taransay Rd HHS/BOV HP3 ... 36 C8
Tara Pk COUL/CHIP CR5 ... 240 A6
Tarbay La WDSR SL4 ... 148 A8
Target Cl EBED/NFELT TW14 ... 174 F2
Tarham Cl HORL RH6 ... 279 P2
Tariff Rd UED N18 ... 99 P8
Tarleton Gdns FSTH SE23 ... 182 A4
Tarling Cl SCUP DA14 ... 185 L6
Tarling Rd CAN/RD E16 ... 141 L8
  EFNCH N2 ... 97 N10
Tarmac Wy WDR/YW UB7 ... 151 L6
Tarnbank STHGT/OAK N14 ... 78 F9
Tarn St STHWK SE1 ... 18 F4
Tarnwood Pk ELTH/MOT SE9 ... 184 C4
Tarnworth Rd HARH RM3 ... 105 P6
Tarpan Wy BROX EN10 ... 62 A2
Tarragon Cl NWCR SE14 ... 160 D6
Tarragon Dr GUW GU2 ... 249 M5
Tarragon Gv SYD SE26 ... 182 C9
Tarrant St HARP AL5 ... 20 B4
Tarriff Crs DEPT SE8 ... 160 E3
Tarrington Cl STRHM/NOR SW16 ... 180 E6
Tartar Hi COB KT11 ... 217 J9
Tartar Rd COB KT11 ... 217 K9
Tarver Rd WALW SE17 ... 18 D8
Tarves Wy GNWCH SE10 ... 160 G6
Tash Pl FBAR/BDGN N11 ... 98 C5
Tasker Cl HYS/HAR UB3 ... 152 D6
Tasker Rd CDH/CHF RM16 ... 168 E2
  HAMP NW3 ... 118 A10
Tasmania Ter UED N18 ... 99 K7
Tasman Rd BRXN/ST SW9 ... 158 F9
Tasso Rd HMSMTH W6 ... 14 A9
Tate Cl LHD/OX KT22 ... 237 H9
Tate Rd CAN/RD E16 ... 142 C10
  CFSP/GDCR SL9 ... 90 C6
  SUT SM1 ... 221 K2
Tates Orch HART DA3 ... 211 L6
Tatnell Rd FSTH SE23 ... 182 D2
Tatsfield La BH/WHM TN16 ... 244 C7
Tattenham Corner Rd EPSOM KT18 ... 238 D4
Tattenham Crs EPSOM KT18 ... 238 D4
Tattenham Gv EPSOM KT18 ... 238 E4
  KWD/TDW/WH KT20 ... 238 E4
Tattenham Wy KWD/TDW/WH KT20 ... 239 H3
Tattersall Cl ELTH/MOT SE9 ... 184 B1
Tattle Hi HERT/WAS SG14 ... 24 A1
Tatton Crs STNW/STAM N16 ... 119 N5
Tatum St WALW SE17 ... 19 H6
Tauber Cl BORE WD6 ... 75 L8
Tauheed Cl FSBYPK N4 ... 119 K7
Taunton Av CTHM CR3 ... 241 N9
  HSLW TW3 ... 154 B8
  RYNPK SW20 ... 200 E3
Taunton Cl BARK/HLT IG6 ... 103 J7
  BXLYHN DA7 ... 167 N7
  CHEAM SM3 ... 201 K8
Taunton Dr EFNCH N2 ... 97 M10
  ENC/FH EN2 ... 79 N7
Taunton La COUL/CHIP CR5 ... 241 H5
Taunton Ms CAMTN NW1 ... 10 A2
Taunton Pl CAMTN NW1 ... 10 A1
Taunton Rd GFD/PVL UB6 ... 134 A3
  GVW DA11 ... 189 N4
  HARH RM3 ... 105 K5
  LEW SE13 ... 183 K1
Taunton V GVE DA12 ... 190 C6
Taunton Wy STAN HA7 ... 113 N1
Tavern Cl CAR SM5 ... 201 P7
Taverners HHNE HP2 ... 35 P4
Taverners Wy CHING E4 ... 101 K2
  HOD EN11 ... 44 F3
Tavistock Av GFD/PVL UB6 ... 134 F4
  STAL AL1 ... 38 B3
  WALTH E17 ... 120 C1
Tavistock Cl HARH RM3 ... 105 J9
  POTB/CUF EN6 ... 59 N7
  STA TW18 ... 173 N10
  STAL AL1 ... 38 C1
Tavistock Crs MTCM CR4 ... 202 F4
  NTGHL W11 ... 8 C1

Tavistock Gdns GDMY/SEVK IG3 ... 123 H9
Tavistock Gv CROY/NA CR0 ... 203 L7
Tavistock Ms NTGHL W11 ... 8 C5
Tavistock Pl STHGT/OAK N14 ... 78 C10
  STPAN WC1H ... 11 K1
Tavistock Rd CAR SM5 ... 201 N8
  CROY/NA CR0 ... 203 L8
  EDGW HA8 ... 95 J4
  FSBYPK N4 ... 119 L4
  FSTGT E7 ... 121 J2
  HAYES BR2 ... 205 M4
  HGDN/ICK UB10 ... 112 E10
  NTGHL W11 ... 8 C4
  SRTFD E15 ... 141 L1
  SWFD E18 ... 121 M1
  WATN WD24 ... 73 L1
  WDR/YW UB7 ... 131 N10
  WELL DA16 ... 163 M7
  WLSDN NW10 ... 136 C4
Tavistock Sq STPAN WC1H ... 11 K1
Tavistock St COVGDN WC2E ... 11 M7
Taviton St STPAN WC1H ... 11 J1
Tawney Common EPP CM16 ... 66 B8
Tawney La ABR/ST RM4 ... 84 D5
  EPP CM16 ... 66 D8
Tawny Cl FELT TW13 ... 175 H6
  WEA W13 ... 134 G10
Tawny Wy BERM/RHTH SE16 ... 160 C3
Tawneys Rd HLWS CM18 ... 47 J3
Tawny Av UPMR RM14 ... 126 A10
Taybridge Rd BTSEA SW11 ... 158 B9
Tayburn Cl POP/IOD E14 ... 141 N8
Tayfield Cl HGDN/ICK UB10 ... 112 D8
Tayles Hill Dr EW KT17 ... 220 C6
Taylor Av RCH/KEW TW9 ... 155 N8
Taylor Cl CRW RM5 ... 104 B8
  HPTN TW12 ... 175 M8
  HSLW TW3 ... 154 B7
  ORP BR6 ... 227 J1
  STALE/WH AL4 ... 38 F1
  TOTM N17 ... 99 P8
Taylor Rd ASHTD KT21 ... 237 J3
  WIM/MER SW19 ... 179 P10
  WLGTN SM6 ... 222 C2
Taylor Rw RDART DA2 ... 187 K6
Taylors Cl SCUP DA14 ... 185 J7
Taylors Ct FELT TW13 ... 175 H5
Taylor's Gn ACT W3 ... 136 B6
Taylor's La BAR EN5 ... 77 J3
  SYD SE26 ... 182 A7
  WLSDN NW10 ... 136 B2
Taylors Rd CSHM HP5 ... 51 J5
Taymount Ri FSTH SE23 ... 182 B5
Taynton Dr REDH RH1 ... 258 E6
Tayport Cl IS N1 ... 5 N4
Tayside Dr EDGW HA8 ... 95 N4
Tay Wy ROM RM1 ... 104 D9
Taywood Rd NTHLT UB5 ... 133 N5
Teak Cl BERM/RHTH SE16 ... 140 D10
Teal Av STMC/STPC BR5 ... 207 N4
Teal Cl CAN/RD E16 ... 142 A7
  SAND/SEL CR2 ... 224 C7
Teal Dr NTHWD HA6 ... 92 D8
Teale St BETH E2 ... 7 P2
Tealing Dr HOR/WEW KT19 ... 220 A1
Teasel Cl CRAWW RH11 ... 283 L10
  CROY/NA CR0 ... 204 C3
Teasel Wy SRTFD E15 ... 141 K5
Teazlewood Pk LHD/OX KT22 ... 236 F3
Tebworth Rd TOTM N17 ... 99 N8
Teck Cl ISLW TW7 ... 154 F8
Tedder Cl CHSGTN KT9 ... 219 H2
  HGDN/ICK UB10 ... 132 A2
Tedder Rd HHNE HP2 ... 36 B5
  SAND/SEL CR2 ... 224 C4
Teddington Cl HOR/WEW KT19 ... 220 A6
Teddington Pk TEDD TW11 ... 176 E8
Teddington Park Rd TEDD TW11 ... 176 F7
Tedworth Gdns CHEL SW3 ... 16 A8
Tedworth Sq CHEL SW3 ... 16 A8
Tees Av GFD/PVL UB6 ... 134 D4
Tees Cl UPMR RM14 ... 126 D4
Teesdale Av ISLW TW7 ... 154 F7
Teesdale Cl BETH E2 ... 7 N1
Teesdale Gdns ISLW TW7 ... 154 F7
  SNWD SE25 ... 203 M2
Teesdale Rd RDART DA2 ... 188 B4
  WAN E11 ... 121 E7
Teesdale St BETH E2 ... 7 N1
Tees Dr HARH RM3 ... 105 L4
The Tee ACT W3 ... 136 B8
Teevan Cl CROY/NA CR0 ... 203 P7
Teevan Rd CROY/NA CR0 ... 203 P7
Tegg's La WOKS/MYFD GU22 ... 233 J2
Teignmouth Cl CLAP SW4 ... 158 E10
  EDGW HA8 ... 95 L10
Teignmouth Rd CRICK NW2 ... 116 C10
  WELL DA16 ... 163 M8
Telcote Wy RSLP HA4 ... 113 K5
Telegraph Hi HAMP NW3 ... 117 L8
Telegraph La ESH/CLAY KT10 ... 218 L1
Telegraph Pl POP/IOD E14 ... 160 G8
Telegraph Rd PUT/ROE SW15 ... 178 F3
Telegraph St LOTH EC2R ... 12 G5
Telegraph Tr WLGTN SM6 ... 222 B7
Telferscot Rd BAL SW12 ... 180 E3
Telford Av BAL SW12 ... 180 E4
  BRXS/STRHM SW2 ... 180 E4
Telford Cl GSTN WD25 ... 73 L1
  NRWD SE19 ... 181 N9
  WALTH E17 ... 120 D5
Telford Dr SL SL1 ... 128 F10
  WOT/HER KT12 ... 197 K7
Telford Pl CRAWE RH10 ... 283 P8
Telford Rd CDALE/KGS NW9 ... 116 D4
  CHST BR7 ... 184 G5
  GFD/PVL UB6 ... 134 A9
  HSLW TW4 ... 175 P5
  LCOL/BKTW AL2 ... 57 K3
  NKENS W10 ... 8 A3
Telford Road North Circular Rd FBAR/BDGN N11 ... 98 D2
Telford Wy ACT W3 ... 136 D7
  YEAD UB4 ... 133 H7
Telham Ct CRAWW RH11 ... 283 J10
Telham Rd EHAM E6 ... 142 D4
Tell Gv EDUL SE22 ... 159 N10
Tellisford ESH/CLAY KT10 ... 218 A1
Tellson Av WOOL/PLUM SE18 ... 162 B7
Telscombe Cl ORP BR6 ... 207 H9
Telston La RSEV TN14 ... 246 F1
  SEV TN13 ... 246 F2
Temeraire St BERM/RHTH SE16 ... 160 B1
Tempelhof Av HDN NW4 ... 116 B5
Temperance St STALW/RED AL3 ... 38 B6
Temperley Rd BAL SW12 ... 180 B3
Tempest Av POTB/CUF EN6 ... 59 M8
Tempest Rd EGH TW20 ... 172 F9
Tempest Wy RAIN RM13 ... 145 L1
Templar Dr GVW DA11 ... 190 D8
  THMD SE28 ... 143 N8
Templar Pl HPTN TW12 ... 175 P10
Templars Crs FNCH N3 ... 97 K10

Templars Dr KTN/HRWW/W HA3 ... 94 C7
Templar St CMBW SE5 ... 159 J8
Temple Av BCTR RM8 ... 124 B6
  CROY/NA CR0 ... 204 E10
  EMB EC4Y ... 12 B7
  TRDG/WHET N20 ... 97 N1
Temple Bank WOKN/KNAP GU21 ... 231 L5
Temple Bar Rd WOKN/KNAP GU21 ... 231 L5
Temple Cl CHESW EN7 ... 61 P7
  CRAWE RH10 ... 284 E8
  FNCH N3 ... 97 J10
  WAN E11 ... 121 K5
  WAT WD17 ... 72 G6
  WOOL/PLUM SE18 ... 162 F2
Templecombe Ms WOKS/MYFD GU22 ... 232 E2
Templecombe Rd HOM E9 ... 140 B3
Templecombe Wy MRDN SM4 ... 201 H6
Templecroft ASHF TW15 ... 174 E9
Templedene Av STA TW18 ... 173 L10
Temple Field Cl ADL/WDHM KT15 ... 215 L3
Temple Flds HERT/WAS SG14 ... 25 K2
Temple Fortune Hi GLDGN NW11 ... 117 K3
Temple Fortune La GLDGN NW11 ... 117 K3
Temple Gdns BCTR RM8 ... 123 N8
  GLDGN NW11 ... 117 J4
  RKW/CH/CXG WD3 ... 92 C4
  STA TW18 ... 195 J1
Temple Gv ENC/FH EN2 ... 79 J7
  GLDGN NW11 ... 117 K4
Temple Hi DART DA1 ... 187 N1
Temple Hill Sq DART DA1 ... 187 N1
Temple La EMB EC4Y ... 12 B6
Temple Md HLWW/ROY CM19 ... 45 N1
Templemead Cl ACT W3 ... 136 E8
Temple Mead Cl STAN HA7 ... 94 G7
Temple Mills La SRTFD E15 ... 121 K10
Temple Mills Rd LEY E10 ... 120 F9
Templepan La RKW/CH/CXG WD3 ... 71 P3
Temple Pk UX/CGN UB8 ... 132 B5
Temple Rd CEND/HSY/T N8 ... 118 G2
  CHSWK W4 ... 155 P2
  CRICK NW2 ... 116 F9
  EA W5 ... 155 J2
  EHAM E6 ... 142 B3
  HOR/WEW KT19 ... 220 A8
  HSLW TW3 ... 154 A10
  RCH/KEW TW9 ... 155 L8
  WDSR SL4 ... 149 M8
Temple Sheen Rd MORT/ESHN SW14 ... 155 P10
Temple St BETH E2 ... 140 A4
Templeton Av CHING E4 ... 100 F5
Templeton Cl NRWD SE19 ... 203 L1
Templeton Pl ECT SW5 ... 14 C6
Templeton Rd SEVS/STOTM N15 ... 119 L4
Temple Vw STALW/RED AL3 ... 38 B4
Temple Vw WEA W13 ... 134 G7
Temple Wy SLN SL2 ... 109 H10
  SUT SM1 ... 201 N10
Templewood WEA W13 ... 134 G7
  WGCW AL8 ... 22 G2
Templewood Av HAMP NW3 ... 117 L8
Templewood Gdns HAMP NW3 ... 117 L8
Templewood La SLN SL2 ... 109 L9
Tempsford WGCE AL7 ... 23 N5
Tempsford Av BORE WD6 ... 76 A8
Tempsford Cl ENC/FH EN2 ... 79 M8
Temsford Cl RYLN/HDSTN HA2 ... 94 C10
Ten Acre WOKN/KNAP GU21 ... 231 M4
Ten Acre La EGH TW20 ... 194 F2
Ten Acres Cl LHD/OX KT22 ... 236 C10
Tenbury Cl FSTGT E7 ... 122 A10
Tenbury Ct BAL SW12 ... 180 E4
Tenby Av KTN/HRWW/W HA3 ... 94 C10
Tenby Cl CHDH RM6 ... 123 P4
  SEVS/STOTM N15 ... 119 L4
Tenby Dr ASC SL5 ... 192 C5
Tenby Gdns NTHLT UB5 ... 133 P1
Tenby Rd CHDH RM6 ... 123 P4
  EDGW HA8 ... 95 L9
  ENC/FH EN2 ... 79 N7
  WALTH E17 ... 120 D5
  WELL DA16 ... 163 N7
Tenchleys La OXTED RH8 ... 262 A9
Tench St WAP E1W ... 140 A10
Tenda Rd BERM/RHTH SE16 ... 160 A3
Tendring Rd HLWS CM18 ... 46 F3
Tendring Wy CHDH RM6 ... 123 M3
Tenham Av BRXS/STRHM SW2 ... 180 A3
Tennand Cl CHESW EN7 ... 61 N2
Tenniel Cl BAY/PAD W2 ... 9 J7
  GUW GU2 ... 249 N6
Tennison Av BORE WD6 ... 75 N9
Tennison Cl COUL/CHIP CR5 ... 241 H9
Tennison Rd SNWD SE25 ... 203 N4
Tennis St STHWK SE1 ... 18 G1
Tenniswood Rd EN EN1 ... 79 M5
Tennyson Av CDALE/KGS NW9 ... 115 M9
  GRAYS RM17 ... 167 N2
  MNPK E12 ... 142 B2
  NWMAL KT3 ... 200 G4
  TWK TW1 ... 176 E4
  WAB/Ing N9 ... 63 K10
  WAN E11 ... 121 M5
Tennyson Cl CRAWE RH10 ... 284 C5
  EBED/NFELT TW14 ... 175 H2
  PEND EN3 ... 80 C7
  WELL DA16 ... 163 J7
Tennyson Rd ADL/WDHM KT15 ... 215 P1
  ASHF TW15 ... 173 J8
  DART DA1 ... 187 P1
  HARH RM3 ... 105 K8
  HNWL W7 ... 135 P5
  HSLW TW3 ... 154 C8
  KIL/WHAMP NW6 ... 2 B1
  LCOL/BKTW AL2 ... 55 P2
  LEY E10 ... 120 F6
  MLHL NW7 ... 96 C6
  PGE/AN SE20 ... 182 C10
  RBRW/HUT CM13 ... 107 P1
  SRTFD E15 ... 141 K2
  WALTH E17 ... 120 D6
  WIM/MER SW19 ... 179 M9
Tennyson St VX/NE SW8 ... 158 C8
Tennyson Wk GVW DA11 ... 190 A6
  TIL RM18 ... 168 D7
Tennyson Wy HCH RM12 ... 128 D6
Tensing Av GVW DA11 ... 190 B6
Tensing Rd NWDGN UB2 ... 153 P2
Tentelow La NWDGN UB2 ... 154 A1
Tenterden Cl ELTH/MOT SE9 ... 184 D7
  HDN NW4 ... 116 B2
Tenterden Dr HDN NW4 ... 116 B2
Tenterden Gdns CROY/NA CR0 ... 203 P7
  HDN NW4 ... 116 B2
Tenterden Gv HDN NW4 ... 116 B1
Tenterden Rd BCTR RM8 ... 124 A6
  CROY/NA CR0 ... 203 P7
  TOTM N17 ... 99 N6
Tenterden St CONDST W1S ... 10 D6
Tenter Gnd WCHPL E1 ... 13 L4
Tent St WCHPL E1 ... 140 A6
Tenzing Rd HHNE HP2 ... 36 A4
Tercel Pth CHIG IG7 ... 103 L3
Terence Ct GVE DA12 ... 191 J5
Teresa Gdns CHES/WCR EN8 ... 62 B10
Terling Cl WAN E11 ... 121 L5
Terling Rd BCTR RM8 ... 124 B1
The Terlings BRW CM14 ... 106 F4
Terminus Pl PIM SW1V ... 16 F3
Terminus St HLW CM20 ... 28 C10

Tern Rd CRAWW RH11 ... 282 G8
Tern Wy BRW CM14 ... 106 C5
Terrace Gdns BARN SW13 ... 156 C8
Terrace La RCHPK/HAM TW10 ... 177 K2
Terrace Rd HOM E9 ... 140 B2
  PLSTW E13 ... 141 M8
  WOT/HER KT12 ... 197 J7
The Terraces RDART DA2 ... 188 B3
Terrace St GVE DA12 ... 190 C2
The Terrace ADL/WDHM KT15 ... 192 C5
  ASC SL5 ... 192 C5
  BARN SW13 ... 156 B8
  GVE DA12 ... 190 C2
  KIL/WHAMP NW6 ... 2 E5
  SEV TN13 ... 246 E8
Terrace Wk DAGW RM9 ... 123 P9
Terrapin Rd TOOT SW17 ... 180 C6
Terrick Rd WDGN N22 ... 98 F9
Terrilands PIN HA5 ... 93 N1
Terront Rd SEVS/STOTM N15 ... 119 K3
Tessa Sanderson Wy NTHLT UB5 ... 114 C10
Testard Rd GUW GU2 ... 267 P2
Testers Cl OXTED RH8 ... 261 N7
Testwood Rd WDSR SL4 ... 148 C3
Tetcott Rd WBPTN SW10 ... 157 M6
Tetherdown MUSWH N10 ... 118 B3
Tethys Rd HHNE HP2 ... 36 A3
Tetty Wy HAYES BR2 ... 205 M2
Teversham La VX/NE SW8 ... 158 F7
Teviot Av SOCK/AV RM15 ... 146 B8
Teviot Cl GUW GU2 ... 249 M7
  WELL DA16 ... 163 L7
Teviot St POP/IOD E14 ... 141 N7
Tewin Cl STALE/WH AL4 ... 39 H7
Tewin Ct WGCE AL7 ... 23 J4
Tewin Rd HHNE HP2 ... 36 D6
  WGCE AL7 ... 23 J4
Tewkesbury Av FSTH SE23 ... 182 A4
  PIN HA5 ... 113 M3
Tewkesbury Cl BF/WBF KT14 ... 215 N7
Tewkesbury Gdns CDALE/KGS NW9 ... 115 N1
Tewkesbury Rd CAR SM5 ... 201 N8
  SEVS/STOTM N15 ... 119 L5
  WEA W13 ... 134 F10
Tewkesbury Ter FBAR/BDGN N11 ... 98 D7
Tewsham Pl WOOL/PLUM SE18 ... 163 H4
Teynham Av WCHMH N21 ... 79 H5
Teynham Gn HAYES BR2 ... 205 M5
Teynton Ter TOTM N17 ... 99 K9
Thackeray Av TIL RM18 ... 168 E7
  TOTM N17 ... 99 P8
Thackeray Cl ISLW TW7 ... 154 F8
  RYLN/HDSTN HA2 ... 113 P6
  UX/CGN UB8 ... 132 C3
  WIM/MER SW19 ... 178 G10
Thackeray Dr CHDH RM6 ... 123 K5
Thackeray Rd EHAM E6 ... 142 A4
  VX/NE SW8 ... 158 C8
Thakeham Cl SYD SE26 ... 182 A8
Thalia Cl GNWCH SE10 ... 161 J5
That Massing Cl RBRW/HUT CM13 ... 107 H4
Thame Rd BERM/RHTH SE16 ... 160 C1
Thames Av CHERT KT16 ... 195 K3
  DAGW RM9 ... 144 C6
  GFD/PVL UB6 ... 134 E4
  HHNE HP2 ... 36 A1
  WBPTN SW10 ... 157 M7
Thames Bank MORT/ESHN SW14 ... 155 P10
Thamesbank Pl THMD SE28 ... 143 M8
Thames Cir POP/IOD E14 ... 160 G8
Thames Cl CHERT KT16 ... 195 L7
  HPTN TW12 ... 196 A5
  RAIN RM13 ... 145 J8
Thamesdale LCOL/BKTW AL2 ... 57 L3
Thames Down Link ASHTD KT21 ... 237 M2
  CHSGTN KT9 ... 219 P1
  EPSOM KT18 ... 219 L10
  WPK KT4 ... 200 A10
Thamesfield Ct SHPTN TW17 ... 196 D7
Thames Ga DART DA1 ... 187 P1
Thamesgate Cl RCHPK/HAM TW10 ... 176 L10
Thameside TEDD TW11 ... 177 J10
Thames Md WDSR SL4 ... 148 D7
  WOT/HER KT12 ... 197 H7
Thames Meadow E/WMO/HCT KT8 ... 197 P2
  SHPTN TW17 ... 196 E8
Thamesmere Dr THMD SE28 ... 143 K9
Thames Pth BERM/RHTH SE16 ... 19 P1
  BOW E3 ... 141 H4
  BTSEA SW11 ... 16 D10
  CHSWK W4 ... 156 C7
  CLPT E5 ... 120 D8
  LBTH SE11 ... 17 M7
  POP/IOD E14 ... 160 F2
  RCH/KEW TW9 ... 155 J8
  STA TW18 ... 173 J8
  SUN TW16 ... 197 J3
  WDSR SL4 ... 146 C1
  WEY KT13 ... 196 C10
Thamesvale Cl HSLW TW3 ... 153 N8
Thames Vw GRAYS RM17 ... 168 C4
Thames Village CHSWK W4 ... 155 P7
Thamley PUR RM19 ... 165 P3
Thanescroft Gdns CROY/NA CR0 ... 203 M10
Thanet Dr HAYES BR2 ... 206 A10
Thanet Pl CROY/NA CR0 ... 223 K1
Thanet Rd BXLY DA5 ... 164 F6
  ERITH DA8 ... 164 F6
Thanet St STPAN WC1H ... 5 L10
Thane Vis HOLWY N7 ... 118 G8
Thane Vs HOLWY N7 ... 118 G8
Thant Cl LEY E10 ... 120 C9
Tharp Rd WLGTN SM6 ... 222 E3
Thatcham Gdns TRDG/WHET N20 ... 97 M1
Thatcher Cl CRAWE RH10 ... 283 N10
Thatchers Cl HORL RH6 ... 280 C2
  LOU IG10 ... 82 F6
Thatchers Cft HHNE HP2 ... 35 P2
Thatchers La RGUW GU3 ... 249 J3
Thatchers Wy ISLW TW7 ... 176 C1
Thatches Gv CHDH RM6 ... 123 P2
Thaxted Pl RYNPK SW20 ... 178 G10
Thaxted Rd BKHH IG9 ... 102 B1
  ELTH/MOT SE9 ... 184 F1

Thaxted Wy WAB EN9.... 63 J9
Thaxton Rd WKENS W14.... 14 D1
Thayers Farm Rd BECK BR3.... 204 D1
Thayer St MHST W1U.... 10 D4
Thaynesfield POTB/CUF EN6.... 59 N7
Theatre St BTSEA SW11.... 158 A9
Theberton St IS N1.... 6 F1
Theed St STHWK SE1.... 12 A10
Thele Av WARE SG12.... 27 J7
Theleway Ct HOD EN11.... 26 G10
Thellusson Wy RKW/CH/CXG WD3.... 91 K1
Thelma Cl GVE DA12.... 191 J8
Thelma Gv TEDD TW11.... 176 F9
Thelusson Rd WD7.... 74 F1
Thorn Av BUSH WD23.... 94 B2
Theobald Crs KTN/HRWW/W HA3.... 94 A9
Theobald Rd CROY/NA CRO.... 203 J9
  WALTH E17.... 120 E5
Theobalds Av GRAYS RM17.... 167 P4
Theobald's Cl POTB/CUF EN6.... 60 G6
Theobald's Gv CHES/WCR EN8.... 62 C8
Theobalds La CHES/WCR EN8.... 62 A8
Theobalds Pk ENC/FH EN2.... 79 J1
Theobald's Rd BMSBY WC1N.... 11 M4
  FSBYW WC1X.... 11 N3
  POTB/CUF EN6.... 60 F6
Theobald St RAD WD7.... 74 C2
  STHWK SE1.... 18 G4
Theodora Wy PIN HA5.... 112 G1
Theodore Rd LEW SE13.... 183 J2
Thepps Cl REDH RH1.... 276 E3
Therapia La CROY/NA CRO.... 202 E7
Therapia Rd EDUL SE22.... 182 B2
Theresa Rd HMSMTH W6.... 156 D4
Theresa's Wk SAND/SEL CR2.... 223 L5
Therfield Ct FSBYPK N4.... 38 C3
Thermopylae Ga POP/IOD E14.... 160 G3
Thesiger Rd PGE/AN SE20.... 182 C10
Thetford Cl PLMGR N13.... 99 J7
  WDGN N22.... 99 J7
Thetford Gdns DAGW RM9.... 143 N2
  NWMALL KT3.... 200 A6
Theydon Cl CRAWE RH10.... 284 B9
Theydon Ct WAB EN9.... 63 J9
Theydon Gdns RAIN RM13.... 144 G2
Theydon Ga EPP CM16.... 83 H2
Theydon Gv EPP CM16.... 65 K6
  WFD IG8.... 101 P7
Theydon Park Rd EPP CM16.... 83 H5
Theydon Pl EPP CM16.... 65 J7
Theydon Rd CLPT E5.... 120 B7
  EPP CM16.... 64 G10
Theydon St WALTH E17.... 119 N5
Thicket Crs SUT SM1.... 221 N1
Thicket Gv DAGW RM9.... 143 M1
  PGE/AN SE20.... 181 P10
  SUT SM1.... 221 M1
The Thicket WDR/YW UB7.... 131 P8
Thickthorne La STA TW18.... 173 N10
Thieves La HERT/WAS SG14.... 24 G5
  HERT/WAS SG14.... 24 G5
Third Av ACT W3.... 136 C10
  CHDH RM6.... 123 M4
  DAGE RM10.... 144 C3
  EN EN1.... 79 N9
  GSTN WD25.... 75 L1
  HLWS CM18.... 46 G1
  HLWW/ROY CM19.... 46 E2
  HYS/HAR UB3.... 132 G10
  MNPK E12.... 122 B9
  NKENS W10.... 8 B1
  PLSTW E13.... 141 M5
  WALTH E17.... 120 E1
  WBLY HA9.... 115 J7
  WTHK RM20.... 166 F5
Third Cl E/WMO/HCT KT8.... 198 A4
Third Crs SL SL1.... 129 H7
Third Cross Rd WHTN TW2.... 176 C5
Third Wy WBLY HA9.... 115 N9
Thirkleby Cl SL SL1.... 129 H10
  WEST SW1P.... 17 H4
Thirleby Rd EDGW HA8.... 96 A9
Thirlestane STAL AL1.... 11 D5
Thirlmere Av GFD/PVL UB6.... 135 H5
  SL SL1.... 128 B7
Thirlmere Cl EGH TW20.... 172 G10
Thirlmere Dr STAL AL1.... 38 C1
Thirlmere Gdns NTHWD HA6.... 92 C6
  WBLY HA9.... 115 H6
Thirlmere Ri BMLY BR1.... 183 L9
Thirlmere Rd BXLYHN DA7.... 164 D8
  CRAWW RH11.... 282 C6
  MUSWH N10.... 98 C9
  STRHM/NOR SW16.... 180 D9
Thirsk Cl NTHLT UB5.... 133 P1
Thirsk Rd BORE WD6.... 75 M4
  BTSEA SW11.... 158 B9
  MTCM CR4.... 180 B10
  SNWD SE25.... 203 L4
Thirza Rd DART DA1.... 187 N2
Thistlebrook ABYW SE2.... 163 M2
Thistle Cl HHW HP1.... 35 H7
Thistlecroft HHW HP1.... 35 L5
Thistlecroft Gdns STAN HA7.... 95 J9
Thistlecroft Rd WOT/HER KT12.... 215 J9
  THDIT KT7.... 198 D6
Thistledene BF/WBF KT14.... 215 J9
  RYLN/HDSTN HA2.... 113 M8
Thistle Gv WCCE AL7.... 23 K5
Thistlemead CHST BR7.... 206 E2
Thistle Md LOU IG10.... 82 D7
The Thistles HHW HP1.... 35 L5
Thistlewaite Rd CLPT E5.... 120 A8
Thistle Wy HORL RH6.... 281 K4
Thistlewood Cl HOLWY N7.... 118 C9
Thistlewood Crs CROY/NA CRO.... 225 J8
Thistleworth Cl ISLW TW7.... 154 C6
Thistley Cl NFNCH/WDSP N12.... 97 P7
Thoby La BRWN CM15.... 87 P3
Thomas A'beckett Cl ALP/SUD HA0.... 114 E9
Thomas Av CTHM CR3.... 241 K7
Thomas Baines Rd BTSEA SW11.... 157 N9
Thomas Bata Av TIL RM18.... 169 L3
Thomas Cl BRWN CM15.... 107 K5
Thomas Cribb Ms EHAM E6.... 142 D8
Thomas Dean Rd SYD SE26.... 182 E7
Thomas Dinwiddy Rd LEE/GVPK SE12.... 183 N1
Thomas Doyle St STHWK SE1.... 18 C3
Thomas Dr GVE DA12.... 190 G5
Thomas' La CAT SE6.... 182 G3
Thomas Moore Wy EFNCH N2.... 117 N1
Thomas More St WAP E1W.... 13 N4
Thomas Rd POP/IOD E14.... 140 E8
Thomas Rochford Wy CHES/WCR EN8.... 62 E3
Thomas St WOOL/PLUM SE18.... 162 G3
Thomas Wall Cl SUT SM1.... 221 L2
Tompkins La SLN SG3.... 128 L2
Thompson Av RCH/KEW TW9.... 155 N9
Thompson Cl DTCH/LGLY SL3.... 150 D3
  IL IG1.... 122 F7
Thompson Rd DAGW RM9.... 124 A3
  EDUL SE22.... 181 N2
  HGDN/ICK UB10.... 131 P2
Thompson's Av CMBW SE5.... 159 K6
Thompsons Cl CHESW EN7.... 61 M5
  CHOB/PIR GU24.... 250 C9
Thompson's La CHOB/PIR GU24.... 213 J5
Thompson Wy RKW/CH/CXG WD3.... 91 K1
Thomson Crs CROY/NA CRO.... 203 H8

Thomson Rd KTN/HRWW/W HA3.... 114 D1
Thong La GVE DA12.... 191 K10
Thoresby St IS N1.... 6 F9
Thorkhill Gdns THDIT KT7.... 198 F8
Thorkhill Rd THDIT KT7.... 198 F7
Thorley Cl BF/WBF KT14.... 215 K10
Thorley Gdns BF/WBF KT14.... 215 K10
Thorley Rd CDH/CHF RM16.... 147 M10
Thornaby Gdns UED N18.... 99 P7
Thornash Cl WOKN/KNAP GU21.... 231 P1
Thornash Rd WOKN/KNAP GU21.... 231 P1
Thornash Wy WOKN/KNAP GU21.... 231 P1
Thorn Av BUSH WD23.... 94 B2
Thornbank Cl STWL/WRAY TW19.... 173 K1
Thornbridge Rd IVER SL0.... 130 F3
Thornbury HARP AL5.... 20 C2
Thornbury Av ISLW TW7.... 154 C6
Thornbury Cl HOD EN11.... 26 C9
  STNW/STAM N16.... 7 J1
Thornbury Gdns BORE WD6.... 75 P3
Thornbury Rd CLAP SW4.... 180 F2
  ISLW TW7.... 154 C6
Thornby Rd CLPT E5.... 120 E2
Thorncliffe Rd CLAP SW4.... 180 E2
  NWDGN UB2.... 153 N4
  NTHLT UB5.... 133 N5
Thorncombe Rd EDUL SE22.... 181 M1
Thorncroft EGH TW20.... 171 P10
  EMPK RM11.... 125 J4
  HHS/BOV HP3.... 36 C8
Thorncroft Cl COUL/CHIP CR5.... 241 H5
Thorncroft Rd SUT SM1.... 221 L1
Thorncroft St VX/NE SW8.... 158 F6
Thorndales BRW CM14.... 107 J5
Thorndean St WAND/EARL SW18.... 179 M5
Thorndene Av TRDG/WHET N20.... 98 B2
Thorndike SLN SG3.... 128 F7
Thorndike Cl WBPTN SW10.... 157 M6
Thorndike Rd IS N1.... 6 F1
Thorndike St PIM SW1V.... 17 J6
Thorndon Av RBRW/HUT CM13.... 127 P3
Thorndon Cl STMC/STPC BR5.... 207 J2
Thorndon Gdns HOR/WEW KT19.... 220 B1
Thorndon Rd STMC/STPC BR5.... 207 J2
Thorn Dr DTCH/LGLY SL3.... 130 B8
Thorndyke Ct PIN HA5.... 93 N8
Thorne Cl ASHF TW15.... 174 D10
  CAN/RD E16.... 141 M8
  ERITH DA8.... 164 C5
  HHW HP1.... 35 L8
  WAN E11.... 121 K9
Thorneloe Gdns CROY/NA CRO.... 223 J2
Thorne Rd VX/NE SW8.... 158 F6
Thorne's Cl BECK BR3.... 203 H5
Thornes Cl BARN SW13.... 156 B9
Thornet Wood Rd BMLY BR1.... 206 D3
Thorney La BTSEA SW11.... 157 N6
Thorneycroft Cl WOT/HER KT12.... 197 K6
Thorney Hedge Rd CHSWK W4.... 155 P1
Thorney La North IVER SL0.... 131 J8
Thorney La South IVER SL0.... 151 J1
Thorney Mill Rd IVER SL0.... 151 L2
Thorney St WEST SW1P.... 17 L5
Thornfield Rd BNSTD SM7.... 239 K3
  SHB W12.... 156 E1
Thornford Rd LEW SE13.... 183 H1
Thorngate Rd MV/WKIL W9.... 8 F1
Thorngrove Rd PLSTW E13.... 141 N3
Thornham Gv SRTFD E15.... 121 J10
Thornham St GNWCH SE10.... 160 G5
Thornhaugh St STPAN WC1H.... 11 K2
Thornhill Av SURB KT6.... 199 K9
  WOOL/PLUM SE18.... 163 H6
Thornhill Bridge Whf IS N1.... 5 N6
Thornhill Cres IS N1.... 5 P4
Thornhill Gdns BARK IG11.... 143 H7
  LEY E10.... 120 C7
Thornhill Gv IS N1.... 6 A4
Thornhill Rd CROY/NA CRO.... 205 K7
  HGDN/ICK UB10.... 112 B9
  IS N1.... 6 A3
  LEY E10.... 120 C7
  NTHWD HA6.... 92 D5
  SURB KT6.... 199 K9
Thornhill Sq IS N1.... 5 P4
Thornhill Wy SHPTN TW17.... 196 B5
Thorn La RAIN RM13.... 145 L4
Thornlaw Rd WNWD SE27.... 181 H7
Thornleas Pl EHSLY KT24.... 252 F7
Thornley Cl TOTM N17.... 100 C6
Thornley Dr RYLN/HDSTN HA2.... 114 A7
Thornridge BRW CM14.... 106 G2
Thornsbeach Rd CAT SE6.... 183 H4
Thornsett Pl PGE/AN SE20.... 204 A4
Thornsett Rd PGE/AN SE20.... 204 A4
  WAND/EARL SW18.... 179 L4
Thornton Av BAL SW12.... 180 B2
  CHSWK W4.... 156 B3
  CROY/NA CRO.... 202 G6
  WDR/YW UB7.... 132 B1
Thornton Cl GUW GU2.... 249 M7
  HORL RH6.... 279 P4
  WDR/YW UB7.... 152 A2
Thornton Crs COUL/CHIP CR5.... 241 H5
Thornton Dene BECK BR3.... 204 D4
Thornton Gdns BAL SW12.... 180 E4
Thornton Gv PIN HA5.... 93 P7
Thornton Hl WIM/MER SW19.... 178 F8
Thornton Pl HORL RH6.... 280 A4
  MBLAR W1H.... 10 A3
Thornton Rd BAL SW12.... 180 E3
  BAR EN5.... 76 A4
  BELV DA17.... 164 C3
  BMLY BR1.... 183 M8
  CAR SM5.... 202 B1
  IL IG1.... 122 E9
  MORT/ESHN SW14.... 156 A9
  POTB/CUF EN6.... 59 H6
  THHTH CR7.... 203 H5
Thornton Rw THHTH CR7.... 203 H5
Thorntons Farm Av ROMW/RG RM7.... 124 D7
Thornton St BRXN/ST SW9.... 159 H8
  HERT/WAS SG14.... 25 L5
  STALW/RED AL3.... 38 B5
Thorntree Rd CHARL SE7.... 162 A4
Thornville Gv MTCM CR4.... 201 M2
Thornville Rd DEPT SE8.... 160 F7
Thornwood Cl SWFD E18.... 101 N10
Thornwood Rd EPP CM16.... 65 J4
  LEW SE13.... 183 K1
Thorogood Gdns SRTFD E15.... 121 K1
Thorogood Wy RAIN RM13.... 144 F3
Thorold Cl SAND/SEL CR2.... 224 C6
Thorold Rd IL IG1.... 122 C7
  WDGN N22.... 98 F8
Thorparch Rd VX/NE SW8.... 158 E7
Thorpebank Rd SHB W12.... 136 D10
Thorpe By-pass EGH TW20.... 194 B3
Thorpe Cl CROY/NA CRO.... 225 H7
  NKENS W10.... 8 B5
  ORP BR6.... 207 H9
Thorpe Crs OXHEY WD19.... 93 J1

WALTH E17.... 100 E10
Thorpedale Gdns GNTH/NBYPK IG2.... 122 E2
Thorpedale Rd FSBYPK N4.... 118 F6
Thorpefield Cl STALE/WH AL4.... 39 J3
Thorpe Hall Rd WALTH E17.... 101 H9
Thorpe Lea Rd EGH TW20.... 172 E10
Thorpe Rd BARK IG11.... 142 E2
  CHERT KT16.... 194 C5
  EGH TW20.... 172 G9
  EHAM E6.... 142 C3
  FSTGT E7.... 121 M8
  KUTN/CMB KT2.... 177 K10
  SEVS/STOTM N15.... 119 M4
  STAL AL1.... 38 C7
  WALTH E17.... 101 H10
Thorpes Cl GUW GU2.... 249 M7
Thorpeside Cl EGH TW20.... 195 H4
Thorpewood Av FSTH SE23.... 182 A5
Thorpland Av HGDN/ICK UB10.... 112 D8
Thorsden Cl WOKS/MYFD GU22.... 232 B5
Thorsden Wy NRWD SE19.... 181 M8
Thorverton Rd CRICK NW2.... 117 H8
Thoydon Rd BOW E3.... 140 D4
Thrale Rd STRHM/NOR SW16.... 180 D8
Thrale St STHWK SE1.... 12 F10
Thrawl St WCHPL E1.... 13 M4
Threadneedle St LOTH EC2R.... 13 H6
Three Arch Rd REDH RH1.... 276 D4
Three Bridges Rd CRAWE RH10.... 284 C7
Three Castles Pth ASC SL5.... 170 D7
  WDSR SL4.... 149 N10
Three Cherrytrees La HHNE HP2.... 36 C2
Three Close La BERK HP4.... 33 P6
Three Colts La BETH E2.... 140 A6
Three Colts St POP/IOD E14.... 140 E9
Three Corners BXLYHN DA7.... 164 G1
  HHS/BOV HP3.... 36 B3
Three Forests Wy ABR/ST RM4.... 84 A3
  HLWW/ROY CM19.... 45 L1
  LOU IG10.... 82 A5
  SBW CM21.... 29 P2
  WAB EN9.... 46 A7
Three Gates GU GU1.... 250 F9
Three Gates Rd HART DA3.... 210 F7
Three Horseshoes Rd HLWW/ROY CM19.... 46 E3
Three Households CSTG HP8.... 89 L9
Three Oak La STHWK SE1.... 19 L1
Three Oaks Cl HGDN/ICK UB10.... 112 A8
Three Pears Rd GU GU1.... 250 D10
Three Valleys Wy BUSH WD23.... 73 L9
Threshers Pl NTGHL W11.... 8 A7
Thriftwood FSTH SE23.... 182 B6
Thrift Farm La BORE WD6.... 75 N4
Thrifts Md EPP CM16.... 83 H3
The Thrift RDART DA2.... 189 H6
Thrift V RGUE GU4.... 250 G3
Thrigby Rd CHSGTN KT9.... 219 L3
Throckmorton Rd CAN/RD E16.... 141 N8
Throgmorton Av OBST EC2N.... 13 H4
Throgmorton St LOTH EC2R.... 13 H4
Throwley Cl ABYW SE2.... 163 M2
Throwley Rd SUT SM1.... 221 L2
Throwley Wy SUT SM1.... 221 L1
Thrums WATN WD24.... 73 J5
Thrupp Cl MTCM CR4.... 202 C2
Thrupps Av WOT/HER KT12.... 217 J2
Thrupps La WOT/HER KT12.... 217 J2
Thrush Av HAT AL10.... 40 C5
Thrush Gn RYLN/HDSTN HA2.... 91 M1
Thrush La POTB/CUF EN6.... 60 F4
Thrush St WALW SE17.... 18 E7
Thumbswood WGCE AL7.... 23 K8
Thumpers HHNE HP2.... 35 P4
Thundercourt WARE SG12.... 26 C1
Thunderer Rd DAGW RM9.... 143 P6
Thundridge Cl WGCE AL7.... 23 L6
Thurbarn Rd CAT SE6.... 182 G8
Thurgood Rd HOD EN11.... 44 F1
Thurland Rd BERM/RHTH SE16.... 19 N3
Thurlby Cl WFD IG8.... 102 C6
Thurlby Rd ALP/SUD HA0.... 135 J1
  WNWD SE27.... 181 H7
Thurleigh Av BAL SW12.... 180 B2
Thurleigh Rd BAL SW12.... 180 A2
Thurleston Av MRDN SM4.... 201 H5
Thurlestone Av GDMY/SEVK IG3.... 123 J4
  NFNCH/WDSP N12.... 98 A7
Thurlestone Cl SHPTN TW17.... 196 C6
Thurlestone Rd WNWD SE27.... 181 H6
Thurloe Gdns ROM RM1.... 124 F4
Thurloe Pl SKENS SW7.... 15 M5
Thurloe Place Ms SKENS SW7.... 15 M5
Thurloe Sq SKENS SW7.... 15 M5
Thurloe St SKENS SW7.... 15 M5
Thurloe Wk GRAYS RM17.... 167 M2
Thurlow Gdns ALP/SUD HA0.... 115 J10
  CHIG IG7.... 102 C2
Thurlow Hl DUL SE21.... 181 P1
Thurlow Park Rd DUL SE21.... 181 J5
Thurlow Rd HAMP NW3.... 117 H1
  HNWL W7.... 135 L4
Thurlow St WALW SE17.... 19 J8
  WALW SE17.... 19 J7
Thurlston Rd RSLP HA4.... 113 H6
Thurlton Ct WOKN/KNAP GU21.... 232 B2
Thurnby Ct WHTN TW2.... 176 C5
Thurnham Wy KWD/TDW/WH KT20.... 238 G6
Thurrock Park Wy GRAYS RM17.... 168 A6
Thursby Rd WOKN/KNAP GU21.... 231 M4
Thursland Rd SCUP DA14.... 185 P8
Thursley Crs CROY/NA CRO.... 225 J4
Thursley Gdns WIM/MER SW19.... 178 G5
Thursley La CRAWE RH10.... 284 B5
Thursley Rd ELTH/MOT SE9.... 184 C6
Thurso Cl HARH RM3.... 106 A7
Thurso St TOOT SW17.... 179 N7
Thurstan Rd RYNPK SW20.... 178 E10
Thurstans HLWW/ROY CM19.... 46 B6
Thurston Rd DEPT SE8.... 160 G8
  SL SL1.... 129 N8
  STHL UB1.... 133 N8
Thurtle Rd BETH E2.... 7 N7
Thwaite Cl ERITH DA8.... 164 D5
Thyer Ct ORP BR6.... 226 F1
Thyme Ct GU GU1.... 250 E7
Thyra Gv NFNCH/WDSP N12.... 97 L7
Tibbat's Rd BOW E3.... 140 D6
Tibbets Cl WIM/MER SW19.... 178 E3
Tibbet's Ride PUT/ROE SW15.... 178 G3
Tibbles Cl GSTN WD25.... 75 M1
Tibbs Hill Rd ABLGY WD5.... 56 E2
Ticehurst Cl CRAWE RH10.... 284 F7
  STMC/STPC BR5.... 185 K10
Ticehurst Rd FSTH SE23.... 182 C6
Tichborne RKW/CH/CXG WD3.... 71 M8
Tichmarsh HOR/WEW KT19.... 219 P6
Tickenhall Dr HLWE CM17.... 47 N1
Tickford Cl ABYW SE2.... 163 M1
Tidal Basin Rd CAN/RD E16.... 141 J9
Tidenham Gdns CROY/NA CRO.... 203 M10
Tideswell Rd CROY/NA CRO.... 204 F10
  PUT/ROE SW15.... 156 F10
Tideway Cl RCHPK/HAM TW10.... 176 D6
Tidey St BOW E3.... 140 F7
Tidford Rd WELL DA16.... 163 P3
Tidworth Rd BOW E3.... 140 F2
Tidy's La EPP CM16.... 65 N5
Tiepigs La WWKM BR4.... 205 M3
Tierney Rd BRXS/STRHM SW2.... 180 F4
Tiger La HAYES BR2.... 205 N4
Tiger Wy CLPT E5.... 120 A3
Tilbrook Rd BKHTH/KID SE3.... 161 P9
Tilburstow Hill Rd GDST RH9.... 260 B8

Tilbury Cl PECK SE15.... 159 N6
  STMC/STPC BR5.... 207 L2
Tilbury Gdns TIL RM18.... 168 D10
Tilbury Md HLWS CM18.... 47 N3
Tilbury Rd EHAM E6.... 142 C4
  LEY E10.... 121 H5
Tilbury Wk DTCH/LGLY SL3.... 150 E2
Tildesley Rd PUT/ROE SW15.... 178 F2
Tilecroft WGCW AL8.... 22 C2
Tile Farm Rd ORP BR6.... 206 G10
Tilegate Rd CHM CM5.... 48 D5
  HLWS CM18.... 47 J5
Tilehouse Cl BORE WD6.... 75 L7
Tilehouse La DEN/HRF UB9.... 111 H3
  RKW/CH/CXG WD3.... 91 H9
Tilehouse Rd RGUE GU4.... 268 C3
Tilehouse Wy DEN/HRF UB9.... 111 J5
Tilehurst La RDKG RH5.... 273 K3
Tilehurst Rd CHEAM SM3.... 221 H2
  WAND/EARL SW18.... 179 N4
Tile Kiln Cl HHS/BOV HP3.... 36 C7
Tile Kiln La BXLY DA5.... 186 E5
  DEN/HRF UB9.... 112 C5
  HGT N6.... 118 C6
  HHS/BOV HP3.... 36 C7
Tiler's Wy REDH RH1.... 275 M4
Tileyard Rd HOLWY N7.... 5 L3
Tilford Av CROY/NA CRO.... 225 H4
Tilford Gdns WIM/MER SW19.... 178 C4
Tilgate Common REDH RH1.... 259 K9
Tilgate Dr CRAWE RH10.... 283 P10
Tilgate Pl CRAWE RH10.... 283 P10
Tilgate Wy CRAWE RH10.... 283 P10
Tilia Rd CLPT E5.... 120 A9
Till Av EYN DA4.... 209 N7
Tiller Rd POP/IOD E14.... 160 F2
Tillett Cl WLSDN NW10.... 135 P1
Tillet Wy BETH E2.... 7 N9
Tilley La EPSOM KT18.... 257 P9
Tilley Rd FELT TW13.... 153 K5
Tillingbourne Gdns FNCH N3.... 117 J1
Tillingbourne Rd RGUE GU4.... 268 D4
Tillingbourne Wy FNCH N3.... 117 J2
Tillingdown Hl CTHM CR3.... 242 A4
Tillingdown La CTHM CR3.... 242 A10
Tillingham Ct WAB EN9.... 63 M9
Tillingham Wy NFNCH/WDSP N12.... 97 K3
Tilling Rd CRICK NW2.... 99 K6
Tilman Rd WCHPL E1.... 140 A8
Tilloch St IS N1.... 5 N4
Tillotson Cl CRAWE RH10.... 284 F8
Tillotson Rd ED N9.... 99 N3
  IL IG1.... 122 D5
  KTN/HRWW/W HA3.... 94 A8
Tillwicks Rd HLWS CM18.... 47 J3
Tilmans Md EYN DA4.... 209 N7
Tilney Gdns IS N1.... 6 G2
Tilney Rd DAGW RM9.... 144 A1
  NWDGN UB2.... 153 K5
Tilney St MYFR/PKLN W1K.... 10 D9
Tilson Gdns CLAP SW4.... 180 F3
Tilson Rd TOTM N17.... 100 E8
Tilstone Av WDSR SL4.... 148 D4
Tilstone Cl WDSR SL4.... 148 D4
Tilsworth Rd BEAC HP9.... 108 B1
Tilt Cl COB KT11.... 235 M2
Tilthams Corner Rd RGODL GU7.... 267 N9
Tilthams Gn RGODL GU7.... 267 N10
Tilt Meadow COB KT11.... 235 M2
Tilton St FUL/PGN SW6.... 14 B10
Tilt Rd COB KT11.... 235 L2
The Tiltwood ACT W3.... 135 P9
Tilt Yard Ap ELTH/MOT SE9.... 184 C2
Timber Cl CHST BR7.... 206 D2
  GT/LBKH KT23.... 254 B3
  WOKS/MYFD GU22.... 233 J1
Timbercroft HOR/WEW KT19.... 220 B1
  WGCE AL7.... 23 J2
Timbercroft La WOOL/PLUM SE18.... 163 H5
Timberdene HDN NW4.... 96 G10
Timberdene Av BARK/HLT IG6.... 102 F9
Timberham Farm Rd HORL RH6.... 279 N7
Timber Hill Rd CTHM CR3.... 241 P10
Timberling Gdns SAND/SEL CR2.... 223 L6
Timber Mill Wy CLAP SW4.... 158 F10
Timber Orch HERT/WAS SG14.... 25 H1
Timber Pond Rd BERM/RHTH SE16.... 160 C1
Timber Rdg RKW/CH/CXG WD3.... 71 M8
Timberslip Dr WLGTN SM6.... 222 E5
Timber St STLK EC1Y.... 12 E1
Timbertop Rd BH/WHM TN16.... 243 P4
Timberwharf Rd SEVS/STOTM N15.... 119 P4
Timothy Cl BXLYHS DA6.... 185 P4
Timothy Rd POP/IOD E14.... 140 E7
Timperley Gdns REDH RH1.... 257 P8
Timplings Rw HHW HP1.... 35 L4
Timsway STA TW18.... 173 J8
Tindale Cl SAND/SEL CR2.... 223 L7
Tindall St BRXN/ST SW9.... 159 J7
Tine Rd CHIG IG7.... 103 H6
Tinkers La TRING HP23.... 32 F3
Tinsey Cl EGH TW20.... 172 G9
Tinsley Gn CRAWE RH10.... 284 G1
Tinsley La CRAWE RH10.... 284 G2
Tinsley La North CRAWE RH10.... 284 G2
Tinsley La South CRAWE RH10.... 284 B5
Tintagel Cl EW KT17.... 220 C10
  HHNE HP2.... 35 N1
Tintagel Crs EDUL SE22.... 159 N10
Tintagel Dr STAN HA7.... 95 J6
Tintagel Gdns STMC/STPC BR5.... 207 M9
Tintagel Wy WOKS/MYFD GU22.... 232 C2
Tintells La EHSLY KT24.... 252 C4
Tintern Av CDALE/KGS NW9.... 95 N9
Tintern Cl PUT/ROE SW15.... 179 H1
  WIM/MER SW19.... 179 M1
Tintern Gdns WCHMH N21.... 98 F1
Tintern Rd CAR SM5.... 201 N8
  WDGN N22.... 99 K8
Tintern St CLAP SW4.... 158 F10
Tintern Wy RYLN/HDSTN HA2.... 114 A6
Tinto Rd CAN/RD E16.... 141 M7
Tinwell Ms BORE WD6.... 75 N4
Tinworth St LBTH SE11.... 17 M7
Tippendell La LCOL/BKTW AL2.... 56 G1
Tippetts Cl ENC/FH EN2.... 79 K5
Tips Cross Md BRWN CM15.... 86 G1
Tipthorpe Rd BTSEA SW11.... 158 B9
Tipton Dr CROY/NA CRO.... 223 M1
Tiptree Cl CHING E4.... 101 H4
  EMPK RM11.... 125 P6
Tiptree Crs CLAY IG5.... 102 D10
Tiptree Dr ENC/FH EN2.... 79 L8
Tiptree Rd RSLP HA4.... 113 J9
Tirlemont Rd SAND/SEL CR2.... 223 K6
Tirrell Rd CROY/NA CRO.... 203 K6
Tisbury Rd STRHM/NOR SW16.... 202 F2
Tisdall Pl WALW SE17.... 19 H6
Titan Cl BTFD TW8.... 155 L6
Titan Rd GRAYS RM17.... 167 M4
Titchborne Rw BAY/PAD W2.... 9 P6
Titchfield Rd CAR SM5.... 201 N8

PEND EN3.... 80 D3
  STJWD NW8.... 3 P6
Titchwell Rd WAND/EARL SW18.... 179 N3
Tite Hl EGH TW20.... 172 A8
Tite St CHEL SW3.... 16 A9
Tithe Barn Cl KUTN/CMB KT2.... 199 L1
  STAL AL1.... 38 B9
Tithe Barn Wy NTHLT UB5.... 133 J4
Tithe Cl MLHL NW7.... 96 D9
  VW GU25.... 194 A6
  WOT/HER KT12.... 197 J6
  YEAD UB4.... 132 C2
Tithe Ct DTCH/LGLY SL3.... 150 D3
Tithe Farm Av RYLN/HDSTN HA2.... 113 P8
Tithe Farm Cl RYLN/HDSTN HA2.... 113 P8
Tithelands HLWW/ROY CM19.... 46 C4
Tithe La STWL/WRAY TW19.... 172 C2
Tithepit Shaw La SAND/SEL CR2.... 242 A1
  WARL CR6.... 242 A3
Titian Av BUSH WD23.... 94 D1
Titlarks Hill Rd ASC SL5.... 192 C8
Titley Cl CHING E4.... 100 F6
Titmus Dr CRAWE RH10.... 284 A10
Titmuss Av THMD SE28.... 143 L9
Titmuss St SHB W12.... 156 E1
Titsey Hl OXTED RH8.... 243 N10
  WARL CR6.... 243 L10
Titsey Rd OXTED RH8.... 261 N3
Tiverton Av CLAY IG5.... 122 D1
Tiverton Ct HARP AL5.... 20 D5
Tiverton Dr ELTH/MOT SE9.... 184 F4
Tiverton Gv HARH RM3.... 105 P6
Tiverton Rd ALP/SUD HA0.... 135 K4
  EDGW HA8.... 95 L10
  HSLW TW3.... 154 A8
  POTB/CUF EN6.... 59 N7
  RSLP HA4.... 113 H8
  SEVS/STOTM N15.... 119 L4
  UED N18.... 99 M6
  WLSDN NW10.... 136 G3
Tiverton St STHWK SE1.... 18 E3
Tiverton Wy CHSGTN KT9.... 219 H2
Tivoli Gdns CHARL SE7.... 162 B3
Tivoli Rd CEND/HSY/T N8.... 118 C3
  HSLWW TW4.... 153 M10
  WNWD SE27.... 181 K8
Toad La HSLWW TW4.... 153 N10
Tobago St POP/IOD E14.... 160 F1
Tobin Cl HAMP NW3.... 3 P3
Toby Wy SURB KT6.... 199 N9
Tockley Rd SL SL1.... 128 A5
Toddbrook HLWW/ROY CM19.... 46 E2
Todd Cl RAIN RM13.... 145 L6
Todds Cl HORL RH6.... 279 P2
Toft Av GRAYS RM17.... 168 A3
Toftwood Cl CRAWE RH10.... 284 D8
Tokenhouse Yd LOTH EC2R.... 12 G5
Tokyngton Av WBLY HA9.... 135 M1
Toland Sq PUT/ROE SW15.... 178 D1
Tolcarne Dr PIN HA5.... 93 H10
Toley Av WBLY HA9.... 115 K5
Toll GRH.... 166 B10
Tollbridge Cl NKENS W10.... 8 C2
Tolldene Cl WOKN/KNAP GU21.... 231 K3
Tollers La COUL/CHIP CR5.... 240 F6
Tollesbury Gdns BARK/HLT IG6.... 122 C1
Tollet St WCHPL E1.... 140 C6
Tollgate GU GU1.... 250 C6
Tollgate Av REDH RH1.... 276 A5
Tollgate Cl RKW/CH/CXG WD3.... 71 J8
Tollgate Dr DUL SE21.... 181 M5
  YEAD UB4.... 133 L2
Tollgate Rd BRKMPK AL9.... 57 P1
  CHES/WCR EN8.... 80 C1
  DORK RH4.... 272 G5
  EHAM E6.... 142 B7
  RDART DA2.... 188 C3
  STALE/WH AL4.... 40 B10
Tollhouse La WLGTN SM6.... 222 E8
Tollington Pk HOLWY N7.... 118 G2
Tollington Pl FSBYPK N4.... 118 C2
Tollington Rd HOLWY N7.... 118 F1
Tollington Wy HOLWY N7.... 118 D1
Tollpit End HHW HP1.... 35 K3
Tolmers Av POTB/CUF EN6.... 60 F1
Tolmers Gdns POTB/CUF EN6.... 60 F1
Tolmers Ms POTB/CUF EN6.... 60 F1
Tolmers Rd POTB/CUF EN6.... 60 F1
Tolmers Sq CAMTN NW1.... 11 H1
Tolpits Cl WATW WD18.... 72 C2
Tolpits La WATW WD18.... 72 G5
Tolpuddle Av PLSTW E13.... 141 P3
Tolpuddle St IS N1.... 6 A7
Tolsford Rd CLPT E5.... 120 A10
Tolson Rd ISLW TW7.... 154 F9
Tolvaddon WOKN/KNAP GU21.... 231 M3
Tolverne Rd RYNPK SW20.... 200 F1
Tolworth Cl SURB KT6.... 199 N8
Tolworth Gdns CHDH RM6.... 123 N3
Tolworth Park Rd SURB KT6.... 199 N9
Tolworth Ri North BRYLDS KT5.... 199 P7
Tolworth Ri South BRYLDS KT5.... 199 P8
Tolworth Rd SURB KT6.... 199 L9
Tom Coombs Cl ELTH/MOT SE9.... 162 B10
Tom Cribb Rd WOOL/PLUM SE18.... 162 G2
Tom Jenkinson Rd CAN/RD E16.... 141 M10
Tomkins Cl BORE WD6.... 75 K5
Tomkyns La UPMR RM14.... 126 C3
Tomlin Cl HOR/WEW KT19.... 220 A7
Tomlin Rd SLN SG3.... 128 D6
Tomlin's Gv BOW E3.... 140 F5
Tomlinson Cl BETH E2.... 7 M10
  CHSWK W4.... 155 N4
Tomlins Orch BARK IG11.... 142 F3
Tomlin's Ter POP/IOD E14.... 140 D8
Tom Mann Cl BARK IG11.... 143 H3
Tom Nolan Cl SRTFD E15.... 141 K4
Tomswood Ct IL IG6.... 102 C3
Tomswood Hl BARK/HLT IG6.... 102 C3
Tomswood Rd CHIG IG7.... 102 G1
Tonbridge By-pass RSEV TN14.... 265 M9
Tonbridge Crs KTN/HRWW/W HA3.... 94 C10
Tonbridge Rd E/WMO/HCT KT8.... 197 N4
  HARH RM3.... 105 J2
  SEV TN13.... 265 K9
Tonbridge St STPAN WC1H.... 5 J8
Tonfield Rd CHEAM SM3.... 201 J8
Tonsley Hl WAND/EARL SW18.... 179 L1
Tonsley Pl WAND/EARL SW18.... 179 L1
Tonsley Rd WAND/EARL SW18.... 179 L1
Tonsley St WAND/EARL SW18.... 179 L1
Tonstall Rd HOR/WEW KT19.... 220 A6
  MTCM CR4.... 202 B2
Tooke Cl PIN HA5.... 93 M9
Tooke's Ct FLST/FETLN EC4A.... 11 P4
Toorack Rd KTN/HRWW/W HA3.... 94 C10
Toot Hill Rd CHONG CM5.... 66 G5
Tooting Bec Gdns STRHM/NOR SW16.... 180 E7
Tooting Bec Rd TOOT SW17.... 180 B6
Tooting Gv TOOT SW17.... 179 H8
Tooting High St TOOT SW17.... 179 H7
Tootswood Rd HAYES BR2.... 205 K5
Tooveys Mill Cl KGLGY WD4.... 54 B5
Topaz Cl SL SL1.... 128 C10
Topcliffe Dr ORP BR6.... 226 G1

Top Dartford Rd *SWLY* BR8 ... 187 H9
Topham Sq *TOTM* N17 ... 99 K9
Topham St *CLKNW* EC1R ... 12 A1
Top House B Ri *CHING* E4 ... 101 J1
Topiary Sq *RCH/KEW* TW9 ... 155 P7
The Topiary *ASHTD* KT21 ... 237 K6
Topland Rd *CFSP/GDCR* SL9 ... 90 A8
Toplands Av *SOCK/AV* RM15 ... 146 A9
Topley St *ELTH/MOT* SE9 ... 162 A10
Top Pk *BECK* BR3 ... 205 K5
　CFSP/GDCR SL9 ... 109 P4
Topping La *UX/CGN* UB8 ... 131 N5
Topsfield Rd *CEND/HSY/T* N8 ... 118 F3
Topsham Rd *TOOT* SW17 ... 180 A5
Topstreet Wy *HARP* AL5 ... 20 B3
Torbay Rd *KIL/WHAMP* NW6 ... 2 C4
　RYLN/HDSTN HA2 ... 113 M7
Torbay St *CAMTN* NW1 ... 4 F4
Torbridge Cl *EDGW* HA8 ... 95 K8
Torcross Dr *FSTH* SE23 ... 182 K8
Torcross Rd *RSLP* HA4 ... 113 C8
Tor Gdns *KENS* W8 ... 14 E1
Torin Ct *ECH* TW20 ... 171 P8
Torland Dr *LHD/OX* KT22 ... 216 E7
Tor La *WEY* KT13 ... 216 E7
Tormead Cl *SUT* SM1 ... 221 K3
Tormount Rd *WOOL/PLUM* SE18 ... 163 H5
Toronto Av *MNPK* E12 ... 122 C9
Toronto Dr *HORL* RH6 ... 281 H5
Toronto Rd *IL* IG1 ... 122 E6
　TIL RM18 ... 168 D8
　WAN E11 ... 121 J9
Torquay Gdns *REDBR* IG4 ... 122 A2
Torquay Sp *SLN* SL2 ... 128 G5
Torquay St *BAY/PAD* W2 ... 8 C4
Torrance Cl *HCH* RM12 ... 125 K6
Torrens Rd *BRXS/STRHM* SW2 ... 180 C1
　SRTFD E15 ... 141 L1
Torrens St *EC1V* ... 6 C8
Torrens Wk *GVE* DA12 ... 191 P8
Torriano Av *KTTN* NW5 ... 118 E10
Torridge Gdns *PECK* SE15 ... 160 B10
Torridge Rd *DTCH/LGLY* SL3 ... 150 E5
Torridon Cl *WOKN/KNAP* GU21 ... 231 N5
　THHTH CR7 ... 205 J3
Torridon Rd *CAT* SE6 ... 183 J4
　LEW SE13 ... 183 J5
Torrington Av *NFNCH/WDSP* N12 ... 97 N6
Torrington Cl *ESH/CLAY* KT10 ... 218 D3
　LOU IG10 ... 82 F8
　POTB/CUF EN6 ... 59 H4
　RYLN/HDSTN HA2 ... 114 A8
Torrington Gdns *FBAR/BDGN* N11 ... 98 D7
　GFD/PVL UB6 ... 135 H3
　LOU IG10 ... 82 F8
Torrington Gv *NFNCH/WDSP* N12 ... 97 P6
Torrington Pk *NFNCH/WDSP* N12 ... 97 N5
Torrington Pl *FITZ* W1T ... 11 H3
　WAP E1W ... 13 P10
Torrington Rd *BCTR* RM8 ... 124 A6
　BERK HP4 ... 33 N5
　ESH/CLAY KT10 ... 218 D3
　GFD/PVL UB6 ... 135 H3
　RSLP HA4 ... 113 H8
Torrington Sq *GWRST* WC1E ... 11 K7
Torrington Wy *MRDN* SM4 ... 201 K7
Tor Rd *WELL* DA16 ... 163 M7
Torr Rd *PGE/AN* SE20 ... 182 C10
Tortoiseshell Wy *BERK* HP4 ... 33 L5
Torver Rd *HRW* HA1 ... 114 D2
Torver Wy *ORP* BR6 ... 206 G10
Torwood Cl *BERK* HP4 ... 33 L5
Torwood La *CTHM* CR3 ... 241 N6
Torwood Rd *PUT/ROE* SW15 ... 178 D1
Torworth Rd *BORE* WD6 ... 75 L5
Tothill St *STJSPK* SW1H ... 17 J2
Totnes Rd *WELL* DA16 ... 163 L6
Totnes Wk *EFNCH* N2 ... 117 N2
Tottenhall Rd *PLMGR* N13 ... 99 H7
Tottenham Court Rd
　CAMTN NW1 ... 11 H1
　FITZ W1T ... 11 H2
Tottenham Gn East
　SEVS/STOTM N15 ... 119 N2
Tottenham La *CEND/HSY/T* N8 ... 118 F3
Tottenham Ms *FITZ* W1T ... 11 H3
Tottenham Rd *IS* N1 ... 7 J2
Tottenham South Side
　SEVS/STOTM N15 ... 119 N2
Tottenham St *FITZ* W1T ... 11 H3
Totteridge Common
　TRDG/WHET N20 ... 96 D3
Totteridge La *TRDG/WHET* N20 ... 97 E3
Totteridge Rd *PEND* EN3 ... 80 C7
Totteridge Village
　TRDG/WHET N20 ... 97 J2
Totternhoe Cl
　KTN/HRWW/W HA3 ... 115 H3
Totton Rd *THHTH* CR7 ... 203 H3
Toulmin Dr *STALW/RED* AL3 ... 38 B2
Toulmin St *STHWK* SE1 ... 18 E2
Toulon St *CMBW* SE5 ... 159 K6
Tournay Rd *FUL/PGN* SW6 ... 157 J6
Tovey Av *HOD* EN11 ... 44 F1
Tovey Cl *LCOL/BKTW* AL2 ... 57 J7
　WAB EN9 ... 45 K9
Tovil Cl *PGE/AN* SE20 ... 203 P2
Towcester Rd *BOW* E3 ... 140 C6
Tower Br *TWRH* EC3N ... 13 L9
Tower Bridge Ap *TWRH* EC3N ... 13 L9
Tower Bridge Rd *STHWK* SE1 ... 19 L1
Tower Cl *BERK* HP4 ... 33 M6
　CHIG IG7 ... 102 F7
　EPP CM16 ... 48 E10
　GVE DA12 ... 191 H8
　HORL RH6 ... 280 A4
　ORP BR6 ... 207 J9
　PGE/AN SE20 ... 182 A10
　WOKN/KNAP GU21 ... 232 A3
Tower Ct *BRW* CM14 ... 106 G3
Tower Cft *EYN* DA4 ... 209 M9
Tower Gdns *ESH/CLAY* KT10 ... 218 F4
　ESH/CLAY KT10 ... 218 G4
Tower Gardens Rd *TOTM* N17 ... 99 K9
Tower Gv *WEY* KT13 ... 196 F9
Tower Hamlets Rd *FSTGT* E7 ... 121 L10
　WALTH E17 ... 120 F1
Tower Hl *BRW* CM14 ... 106 F4
　DORK RH4 ... 272 G4
　KGLGY WD4 ... 53 H5
Towerhill *SHGR* GU5 ... 270 D8
Tower Hl *TWRH* EC3N ... 13 L8
Tower Hill La *STALE/WH* AL4 ... 21 L6
Tower Hill Ri *SHGR* GU5 ... 270 D6
Tower Hill Rd *DORK* RH4 ... 272 G4
Tower Ri *RCH/KEW* TW9 ... 155 N8
Tower Rd *AMSS* HP7 ... 68 F9
　BELV DA17 ... 164 D3
　BXLYHN DA7 ... 164 B10
　DART DA1 ... 187 K3
　EPP CM16 ... 65 H4
　KWD/TDW/WH KT20 ... 238 F9
　ORP BR6 ... 207 J9
　WARE SG12 ... 26 D1
　WHTN TW2 ... 176 D6
　WLSDN NW10 ... 136 G2
Tower Royal *MANHO* EC4N ... 12 F7
Towers Av *HCDN/ICK* UB10 ... 152 C6
Towers Pl *RCH/PK/HAM* TW10 ... 177 K1
Towers Rd *GRAYS* RM17 ... 192 F7
　HHNE HP2 ... 35 P5
　PIN HA5 ... 93 M3
　STHL UB1 ... 133 P6
The Towers *PUR/KEN* CR8 ... 241 K1
Tower St *HERT/WAS* SG14 ... 25 M1
　LSQ/SEVD WC2H ... 11 K6

Towers Wk *WEY* KT13 ... 216 C3
Towers Wd *EYN* DA4 ... 210 C1
Tower Ter *WDGN* N22 ... 98 G10
Tower Vw *CROY/NA* CR0 ... 204 C8
Towfield Rd *FELT* TW13 ... 175 N5
Town Barn Rd *CRAWW* RH11 ... 283 M7
Town Bridge Ct *CSHM* HP5 ... 52 G8
Towncourt Crs *STMC/STPC* BR5 ... 206 F3
Towncourt La *STMC/STPC* BR5 ... 206 G6
Towncourt Pth *FSBYPK* N4 ... 119 K6
Townend *CHST* BR7 ... 241 M8
Town End Cl *CTHM* CR3 ... 241 M8
Towney Farm Wy
　STWL/WRAY TW19 ... 173 N3
Townfield *CSHM* HP5 ... 51 H8
　RKW/CH/CXG WD3 ... 91 M1
Townfield Cnr *GVE* DA12 ... 190 F4
Townfield Rd *DORK* RH4 ... 272 F3
　HYS/HAR UB3 ... 132 G10
Town Flds *HAT* AL10 ... 40 D3
Townfield Sq *HYS/HAR* UB3 ... 132 G10
Town Field Wy *ISLW* TW7 ... 154 F8
Towngate *COB* KT11 ... 235 M1
Town Hall Approach Rd
　SEVS/STOTM N15 ... 119 N2
Townhall Av *CHSWK* W4 ... 156 A4
Town Hall Rd *BTSEA* SW11 ... 158 A9
Townholm Crs *HNWL* W7 ... 154 E2
Town La *STWL/WRAY* TW19 ... 173 N3
　DUL SE21 ... 181 M1
Townley St *WALW* SE17 ... 18 G7
Town Md *CRAWW* RH11 ... 283 N6
　REDH RH1 ... 259 L9
Town Meadow *BTFD* TW8 ... 155 J6
Townmead Rd *FUL/PGN* SW6 ... 157 M8
　RCH/KEW TW9 ... 155 N8
Town Mead Rd *WAB* EN9 ... 63 H10
Town Quay *BARK* IG11 ... 142 E3
　STA TW18 ... 195 M3
Town Rd *ED* N9 ... 100 A3
Townsend *HHNE* HP2 ... 35 N4
Townsend Av *STAL* AL1 ... 38 D5
　STHGT/OAK N14 ... 98 E5
Townsend Dr *STALW/RED* AL3 ... 38 C3
Townsend La *CDALE/KGS* NW9 ... 116 A5
　WOKS/MYFD GU22 ... 232 E7
Townsend Rd *ASHF* TW15 ... 173 P8
　CSHM HP5 ... 50 G6
　SEVS/STOTM N15 ... 119 N3
　STHL UB1 ... 133 M10
Townsend St *WALW* SE17 ... 19 H5
Townsend Wy *NTHWD* HA6 ... 92 C8
Townsend Yd *HGT* N6 ... 118 C6
Townshead Cl *SCUP* DA14 ... 185 L9
Townshend Cl *CHST* BR7 ... 184 B8
　RCH/KEW TW9 ... 155 L10
　STJWD NW8 ... 3 N6
Townshend Rd *HERT/WAS* SG14 ... 25 M5
Townshend St *GNWCH* SE10 ... 161 J4
Townshend Ter *RCH/KEW* TW9 ... 155 L10
Townsott Cl *LBTH/LBKH* KT23 ... 253 P2
Townson Av *NTHLT* UB5 ... 133 H4
Townson Wy *NTHLT* UB5 ... 133 H4
Town Tree Rd *ASHF* TW15 ... 174 B8
Towpath *SHPTN* TW17 ... 196 A8
Towpath Wy *CROY/NA* CR0 ... 203 N6
Towton Rd *WNWD* SE27 ... 181 K5
Toynbec Cl *CHST* BR7 ... 184 E7
Toynbee Rd *RYNPK* SW20 ... 201 H1
Toyne St *WCHPL* E1 ... 13 L4
Toyne Wy *HGT* N6 ... 118 A4
Toy's Hl *BH/WHM* TN16 ... 263 M7
The Tracery *BNSTD* SM7 ... 239 L1
Tracey Av *CRICK* NW2 ... 116 F10
Tracious Cl *WOKN/KNAP* GU21 ... 231 N2
Tracyes Rd *HLWS* CM18 ... 47 L3
Trade Cl *PLMGR* N13 ... 99 H5
Trader Rd *EHAM* E6 ... 142 E8
Tradescant Rd *VX/NE* SW8 ... 158 F6
Trading Estate Rd *WLSDN* NW10 ... 135 P6
Trafalgar Av *BROX* EN10 ... 44 E7
　STHWK SE1 ... 19 M8
　TOTM N17 ... 99 M7
　WPK KT4 ... 200 G8
Trafalgar Cl *EBED/NFELT* TW14 ... 174 A4
Trafalgar Dr *WOT/HER* KT12 ... 197 J10
Trafalgar Gdns *WCHPL* E1 ... 140 C7
　KENS W8 ... 14 G2
Trafalgar Gv *GNWCH* SE10 ... 161 J5
Trafalgar Pl *UED* N18 ... 99 P6
　WAN E11 ... 121 M2
Trafalgar Rd *DART* DA1 ... 187 M5
　GNWCH SE10 ... 161 K4
　GVW DA11 ... 190 D3
　RAIN RM13 ... 144 G4
　WHTN TW2 ... 176 C5
　WIM/MER SW19 ... 179 L10
Trafalgar Sq *CHCR* WC2N ... 11 K9
Trafalgar St *WALW* SE17 ... 18 G7
Trafalgar Wy *CROY/NA* CR0 ... 202 G9
　POP/IOD E14 ... 141 H10
Trafford Cl *RAD* WD7 ... 57 K8
　SRTFD E15 ... 120 G10
Trafford Rd *THHTH* CR7 ... 202 C5
Tramway Av *ED* N9 ... 100 A1
　SRTFD E15 ... 141 K2
Tramway Pth *MTCM* CR4 ... 201 P4
Tranmere Rd *ED* N9 ... 99 N1
　WAND/EARL SW18 ... 179 M5
　WHTN TW2 ... 176 A3
Tranquil Dl *BRKHM/BTCW* RH3 ... 256 C8
Tranquil Ri *ERITH* DA8 ... 164 F4
Tranquil V *BKHTH/KID* SE3 ... 161 L3
Tansept St *CAMTN* NW1 ... 9 P4
Transmere Rd *STMC/STPC* BR5 ... 206 F6
Transom Sq *POP/IOD* E14 ... 160 A4
Transport Av *BTFD* TW8 ... 154 G5
Tranton Rd *BERM/RHTH* SE16 ... 160 A2
Trapp's La *CSHM* HP5 ... 51 H9
Trapstyle Rd *WARE* SG12 ... 25 P1
Trasher Md *RDKG* RH5 ... 273 H5
Travellers Cl *BRKMPK* AL9 ... 40 F1
Travellers La *BRKMPK* AL9 ... 40 D6
　HAT AL10 ... 40 D6
Travellers Wy *HEST* TW5 ... 153 K8
Travers Cl *WALTH* E17 ... 100 C9
Travers Rd *HOLWY* N7 ... 119 H8
Travic Rd *SLN* SL2 ... 128 C5
Travis Ct *SLN* SL2 ... 128 C5
Treacher's Cl *CSHM* HP5 ... 50 G7
Treacy Cl *BUSH* WD23 ... 94 B3
Treadgold St *NTGHL* W11 ... 136 G9
Treadway St *BETH* E2 ... 140 A12
Treadwell Rd *EPSOM* KT18 ... 238 C1
Treaty St *IS* N1 ... 5 N6
Trebble Rd *SWDM* DA10 ... 189 G2
Trebellan Dr *HHNE* HP2 ... 36 A5
Trebovir Rd *ECT* SW5 ... 14 C6
Treby St *BOW* E3 ... 140 E3
Tredegar Rd *BOW* E3 ... 140 L4
　FBAR/BDGN N11 ... 98 E4
　RDART DA2 ... 187 H6
Tredegar Sq *BOW* E3 ... 140 E6
Tredennick Rd *HACK* E8 ... 7 G2
Tredown Rd *SYD* SE26 ... 182 B8
Tredwell Cl *HAYES* BR2 ... 206 A4
Tredwell Rd *WNWD* SE27 ... 181 J7
Treebourne Rd *BH/WHM* TN16 ... 248 J7
Treebys Av *RGUE* GU4 ... 250 A4
Tree Cl *HHS/BMSF* HP3 ... 36 C8
　RCHPK/HAM TW10 ... 177 J4
Treelands *RDKG* RH5 ... 273 H5
Treen Av *BARN* SW13 ... 156 N9
Tree Rd *CAN/RD* E16 ... 141 P8

Treeside Cl *WDR/YW* UB7 ... 151 N3
Treetops *BGR/WK* TN15 ... 247 P3
Tree Tops *BRWN* CM15 ... 107 H2
Treetops *GVE* DA12 ... 190 E8
Tree Tops *WARL* CR6 ... 241 P4
Treetops Cl *ABYW* SE2 ... 163 P4
　NTHWD HA6 ... 92 A4
Tree View Cl *NRWD* SE19 ... 203 M1
Treewall Gdns *BMLY* BR1 ... 183 N1
Treeway *REIG* RH2 ... 257 L7
Trefgarne Rd *DAGE* RM10 ... 124 B7
Trefoil Rd *WAND/EARL* SW18 ... 179 M1
Trefusis Wk *WAT* WD17 ... 72 F5
Tregaron Av *CEND/HSY/T* N8 ... 118 F4
Tregaron Gdns *NWMAL* KT3 ... 200 B8
Tregarthen Pl *LHD/OX* KT22 ... 237 H7
Tregarth Pl *WOKN/KNAP* GU21 ... 231 L3
Tregarvon Rd *BTSEA* SW11 ... 158 B10
Tregelles Rd *HOD* EN11 ... 44 F1
Tregenna Av *RYLN/HDSTN* HA2 ... 113 P9
Tregenna Cl *STHGT/OAK* N14 ... 78 D2
Trego Rd *HOM* E9 ... 140 F2
Tregothnan Rd *BRXN/ST* SW9 ... 158 F9
Tregunter Rd *WBPTN* SW10 ... 15 J9
Trehaven Pde *REIG* RH2 ... 275 L3
Treherne Rd *BARK/HLT* IG6 ... 102 C8
　MORT/ESHN SW14 ... 156 A9
Trehurst St *CLPT* E5 ... 120 D10
Trelawn Cl *CHERT* KT16 ... 214 F4
Trelawney Av *DTCH/LGLY* SL3 ... 150 A2
Trelawney Gv *WEY* KT13 ... 216 B3
Trelawney Rd *BARK/HLT* IG6 ... 102 C8
　LEY E10 ... 120 B1
Trelawny Cl *WALTH* E17 ... 120 C2
Treloar Gdns *NRWD* SE19 ... 181 L9
Tremadoc Rd *CLAP* SW4 ... 158 E10
Tremaine Gv *HHNE* HP2 ... 35 P2
Tremaine Rd *PGE/AN* SE20 ... 204 A2
Tremlett Gv *ARCH* N19 ... 118 C5
Tremlett Ms *ARCH* N19 ... 118 D5
Trenance *WOKN/KNAP* GU21 ... 231 M3
Trenance Gdns *GDMY/SEVK* IG3 ... 123 K8
Trenchard Cl *CDALE/KGS* NW9 ... 96 B9
　STAN HA7 ... 94 C7
　WOT/HER KT12 ... 217 K2
Trenchard St *GNWCH* SE10 ... 161 J4
Trenches La *DTCH/LGLY* SL3 ... 150 D10
Trenham Dr *WARL* CR6 ... 242 B2
Trenholme Rd *PGE/AN* SE20 ... 182 A10
Trenholme Ter *PGE/AN* SE20 ... 182 A10
Trenmar Gdns *WLSDN* NW10 ... 136 E5
Trent Av *EA* W5 ... 155 H2
　UPMR RM14 ... 126 C4
Trentbridge Cl *BARK/HLT* IG6 ... 103 J7
　DTCH/LGLY SL3 ... 150 D10
Trent Cl *CRAWW* RH11 ... 283 J9
　RAD WD7 ... 57 K8
Trent Gdns *STHGT/OAK* N14 ... 78 C10
Trentham Crs *WOKS/MYFD* GU22 ... 232 D7
Trentham Dr *STMC/STPC* BR5 ... 207 K4
Trentham Rd *REDH* RH1 ... 276 A2
Trentham St *WAND/EARL* SW18 ... 179 K4
Trent Rd *BKHH* IG9 ... 101 N2
　BRXS/STRHM SW2 ... 180 C1
　DTCH/LGLY SL3 ... 150 F5
Trent Wy *WPK* KT4 ... 200 G8
　YEAD UB4 ... 132 F5
Trentwood Side *ENC/FH* EN2 ... 78 G7
Treport St *WAND/EARL* SW18 ... 179 L3
Tresco Cl *BMLY* BR1 ... 183 K9
Trescoe Gdns *CRW* RM5 ... 104 D6
　PIN HA5 ... 113 M5
Tresco Gdns *GDMY/SEVK* IG3 ... 123 J7
Tresco Rd *BERK* HP4 ... 33 L7
　PECK SE15 ... 160 A10
Tresham Crs *STJWD* NW8 ... 9 N1
Tresham Rd *BARK* IG11 ... 143 J2
Tresilian Av *WCHMH* N21 ... 78 G9
Tressillian Crs *BROCKY* SE4 ... 160 F9
Tressillian Rd *BROCKY* SE4 ... 160 F9
Tresta Wk *WOKN/KNAP* GU21 ... 231 M3
Trestis Cl *YEAD* UB4 ... 133 L6
Treswell Rd *DAGW* RM9 ... 143 P3
Tretawn Gdns *MLHL* NW7 ... 96 F5
Tretawn Pk *MLHL* NW7 ... 96 B5
Trevalga Ws *HHNE* HP2 ... 35 N1
Trevanion Rd *NKENS* W14 ... 14 B7
Trevanne Plat *CRAWE* RH10 ... 284 E6
Treve Av *HRW* HA1 ... 114 B5
Trevellance Wy *GSTN* WD25 ... 55 L9
Trevelyan Av *MNPK* E12 ... 122 C9
Trevelyan Cl *DART* DA1 ... 165 N10
Trevelyan Crs *KTN/HRWW/W* HA3 ... 115 J5
Trevelyan Gdns *WLSDN* NW10 ... 136 F3
Trevelyan Rd *FSTGT* E7 ... 121 K9
　TOOT SW17 ... 179 P9
Trevelyan Wy *BERK* HP4 ... 33 N3
Trevereux HI *OXTED* RH8 ... 262 D8
Treveris St *STHWK* SE1 ... 12 D10
Treverton St *NKENS* W10 ... 136 G6
Treves Cl *WCHMH* N21 ... 78 C9
Trevithick Cl *EBED/NFELT* TW14 ... 174 A4
Trevithick Dr *DART* DA1 ... 165 N10
Trevithick St *DEPT* SE8 ... 160 F5
Trevone Gdns *PIN* HA5 ... 113 M4
Trevor Cl *EBAR* EN4 ... 77 N10
　HAYES BR2 ... 205 L7
　ISLW TW7 ... 176 E1
　KTN/HRWW/W HA3 ... 94 E8
　NTHLT UB5 ... 133 K4
Trevor Crs *RSLP* HA4 ... 112 C9
Trevor Gdns *EDGW* HA8 ... 96 A9
　NTHLT UB5 ... 133 K4
Trevor Pl *SKENS* SW7 ... 15 P2
Trevor Rd *EDGW* HA8 ... 96 A9
　HYS/HAR UB3 ... 152 F1
　WFD IG8 ... 101 M8
　WIM/MER SW19 ... 179 H10
Trevor Sq *SKENS* SW7 ... 15 P2
Trevor St *SKENS* SW7 ... 15 P2
Trevose Av *BF/WBF* KT14 ... 215 J10
Trevose Rd *WALTH* E17 ... 101 J9
Trewarden Av *IVER* SL0 ... 130 G4
Trewenna Dr *CHSGTN* KT9 ... 219 J2
　POTB/CUF EN6 ... 59 N8
Trewince Rd *RYNPK* SW20 ... 200 F1
Trewint St *WAND/EARL* SW18 ... 179 M5
Trewsbury Rd *SYD* SE26 ... 182 C8
Treyford Cl *CRAWW* RH11 ... 283 J7
Triandra Wy *YEAD* UB4 ... 133 L7
Triangle Pl *CLAP* SW4 ... 158 A10
Triangle Rd *HACK* E8 ... 140 A3
The Triangle *NWMAL* KT3 ... 199 P2
　WOKN/KNAP GU21 ... 231 P4
Trident Rd *GSTN* WD25 ... 54 G10
Trident Rd *BERM/RHTH* SE16 ... 160 C3
Trident Wy *NWDGN* UB2 ... 153 J2
Trigg's Cl *WOKS/MYFD* GU22 ... 232 A5
Trigg's La *WOKN/KNAP* GU21 ... 231 P5
Trigon Rd *VX/NE* SW8 ... 158 G6
Trilby Rd *FSTH* SE23 ... 182 A4
Trim St *NWCR* SE14 ... 160 E5
Trinder Rd *ARCH* N19 ... 118 F6
　BAR EN5 ... 76 A7
Trindles Rd *REDH* RH1 ... 277 M1
Tring Av *EA* W5 ... 155 N1
　STHL UB1 ... 133 N8
　WBLY HA9 ... 135 M1
Tring Cl *BARK/HLT* IG6 ... 122 F1
　HARH RM3 ... 105 N3
Tring Gdns *HARH* RM3 ... 105 M3

Tringham Cl *CHERT* KT16 ... 214 E2
Tring Rd *BERK* HP4 ... 33 H2
Trinidad Gdns *DAGE* RM10 ... 144 C2
Trinidad St *POP/IOD* E14 ... 140 E9
Trinity Av *EFNCH* N2 ... 117 N1
　EN W1 ... 79 N10
Trinity Church Rd *BARN* SW13 ... 156 E5
Trinity Church Sq *STHWK* SE1 ... 18 F3
Trinity Cl *CRAWE* RH10 ... 284 D5
　HAYES BR2 ... 206 B8
　HSLWW TW4 ... 153 M9
　LEW SE13 ... 161 J10
　NTHWD HA6 ... 92 F7
　SAND/SEL CR2 ... 223 M5
　STWL/WRAY TW19 ... 173 M2
　WAN E11 ... 121 K7
Trinity Crs *ASC* SL5 ... 192 F5
　TOOT SW17 ... 180 A5
Trinity Gdns *BRXN/ST* SW9 ... 158 C10
　CAN/RD E16 ... 141 J7
　DART DA1 ... 187 L2
Trinity Gv *GNWCH* SE10 ... 161 H7
　HERT/WAS SG14 ... 25 K4
Trinity La *CHES/WCR* EN8 ... 62 D8
　HGS/MBV HP3 ... 36 E7
Trinity Pl *BXLYHS* DA6 ... 164 A10
　WDSR SL4 ... 148 H7
Trinity Ri *HNHL* SE24 ... 181 J3
Trinity Rd *BARK/HLT* IG6 ... 122 F1
　EFNCH N2 ... 117 N1
　GVE DA12 ... 190 F3
　HERT/BAY SG13 ... 26 B8
　RCH/KEW TW9 ... 155 L9
　STHL UB1 ... 133 M10
　TOOT SW17 ... 180 A5
　WAND/EARL SW18 ... 179 N2
　WARE SG12 ... 26 D1
　WDGN N22 ... 98 G9
　WIM/MER SW19 ... 179 K9
　WOKN/KNAP GU21 ... 230 G4
Trinity Sq *TWRH* EC3N ... 13 K8
Trinity St *CAN/RD* E16 ... 141 J7
　ENC/FH EN2 ... 79 K6
　STHWK SE1 ... 18 F2
　WOT/HER KT12 ... 217 K2
Trinity Wk *HERT/BAY* SG13 ... 26 B8
Trinity Wy *ACT* W3 ... 136 B9
　CHING E4 ... 100 F7
Trio Pl *STHWK* SE1 ... 18 F2
Tripton Rd *HLWS* CM18 ... 47 H2
Tristan Sq *BKHTH/KID* SE3 ... 161 H9
Tristram Cl *WALTH* E17 ... 121 J1
Tristram Rd *BMLY* BR1 ... 183 L1
Triton Wy *HHNE* HP2 ... 36 A4
Tritton Av *CROY/NA* CR0 ... 222 F1
Tritton Rd *WNWD* SE27 ... 181 L6
Trittons *KWD/TDW/WH* KT20 ... 238 F7
Triumph Cl *CDH/CHF* RM16 ... 167 H3
Triumph Rd *EHAM* E6 ... 142 C8
Trivett Cl *GRH* ... 188 F1
Trodd's La *RGUE* GU4 ... 269 J1
Trojan Wy *CROY/NA* CR0 ... 202 G10
Trolling Down HI *RDART* DA2 ... 188 A5
Troon Cl *CRAWW* RH11 ... 282 G8
　BERM/RHTH SE16 ... 160 B5
Troon St *WCHPL* E1 ... 140 D8
Tropers Dr *HARH* RM3 ... 105 L5
Trosley Av *GVW* DA11 ... 190 E5
Trosley Rd *BELV* DA17 ... 164 B5
Trossachs Rd *EDUL* SE22 ... 181 M1
Trothy Rd *STHWK* SE1 ... 19 P6
Trotsworth Av *VW* GU25 ... 194 A4
Trotters Bottom *BAR* EN5 ... 76 D3
Trotter's Gap *WARE* SG12 ... 27 K7
Trotters La *CHOB/PIR* GU24 ... 213 N8
Trott Rd *MUSWH* N10 ... 98 B8
Trotton Cl *CRAWE* RH10 ... 284 D10
Trott St *BTSEA* SW11 ... 157 N7
Trotwood *CHIG* IG7 ... 102 G6
Troughton Rd *CHARL* SE7 ... 161 N4
Troutbeck Cl *SLN* SL2 ... 129 M9
Troutbeck Rd *NWCR* SE14 ... 160 D7
Trout La *WDR/YW* UB7 ... 131 M9
Trout Ri *RKW/CH/CXG* WD3 ... 71 L7
Trout Rd *WDR/YW* UB7 ... 131 N10
Troutstream Wy
　RKW/CH/CXG WD3 ... 71 L3
Trouvere Pk *HHW* HP1 ... 35 L4
Trouville Rd *BAL* SW12 ... 180 D2
Trowbridge Rd *HARH* RM3 ... 105 L2
　HOM E9 ... 140 E1
Trowers Wy *REDH* RH1 ... 258 F7
Trowley Ri *ABLGY* WD5 ... 54 F7
Trowlock Av *TEDD* TW11 ... 177 H9
Trowlock Wy *TEDD* TW11 ... 177 H9
Troy Ct *KENS* W8 ... 14 E3
Troy Rd *NRWD* SE19 ... 181 L9
Troy Town *PECK* SE15 ... 159 P9
Trueman Cl *EDGW* HA8 ... 95 M1
Truesdale Dr *DEN/HRF* UB9 ... 111 M2
Trulock Rd *TOTM* N17 ... 99 P8
Trumpers Wy *HNWL* W7 ... 154 C2
Trumpetshill Rd *REIG* RH2 ... 274 D1
Trumper Wy *SL* SL1 ... 128 E10
Trumpington Dr *STAL* AL1 ... 38 C9
Trumpington Rd *FSTGT* E7 ... 121 L9
Trumpsgreen Av *VW* GU25 ... 194 A6
Trumps Green Cl *VW* GU25 ... 194 B5
Trumpsgreen Rd *VW* GU25 ... 193 P8
Trumps Mill La *VW* GU25 ... 194 C6
Trump St *CITYW* EC2V ... 12 F6
Trundlers Wy *BUSH* WD23 ... 94 D2
Trundle St *STHWK* SE1 ... 18 E1
Trundleys Rd *DEPT* SE8 ... 160 C5
Trundley's Ter *DEPT* SE8 ... 160 C3
Trunley Heath Rd *SHGR* GU5 ... 267 P8
Truro Gdns *IL* IG1 ... 122 B5
Truro Rd *GVE* DA12 ... 190 G6
　WALTH E17 ... 120 E2
　WDGN N22 ... 98 F7
Truro St *KTTN* NW5 ... 4 C2
Truro Wy *YEAD* UB4 ... 132 F5
Trusedale Rd *EHAM* E6 ... 142 C8
Truslove Rd *WNWD* SE27 ... 181 H6
Truss Hill Rd *ASC* SL5 ... 192 B5
Trussley Rd *HMSMTH* W6 ... 157 H6
Trustons Gdns *EMPK* RM11 ... 125 H5
Trust Rd *CHES/WCR* EN8 ... 62 D10
Trystings Cl *ESH/CLAY* KT10 ... 218 F5
Tuam Rd *WOOL/PLUM* SE18 ... 162 G9
Tubbenden Cl *ORP* BR6 ... 226 F6
Tubbenden Dr *ORP* BR6 ... 226 E7
Tubbenden La *ORP* BR6 ... 226 G6
Tubbenden La South *ORP* BR6 ... 226 G7
Tubbs Hl *SEV* TN13 ... 247 N4
Tubbs Rd *WLSDN* NW10 ... 136 C4
Tubwell Rd *SLN* SL2 ... 129 N3
Tucker Rd *CHERT* KT16 ... 214 C8
Tucker St *WATW* WD18 ... 73 K9
Tuckey Gv *RPLY/SEND* GU23 ... 233 J10
Tuck Rd *RAIN* RM13 ... 145 H1
Tudor Av *CHESW* EN7 ... 62 A7
　GPK RM2 ... 125 M8
　HPTN TW12 ... 175 P9
　WATN WD24 ... 73 L3
　WPK KT4 ... 200 G8
Tudor Cir *GDODL* GU7 ... 267 K10

Tudor Cl *ASHF* TW15 ... 173 P7
　BNSTD SM7 ... 239 H1
　BRWN CM15 ... 87 L10
　CDALE/KGS NW9 ... 115 P7
　CHEAM SM3 ... 220 G2
　CHESW EN7 ... 62 A7
　CHIG IG7 ... 102 G5
　CHSGTN KT9 ... 219 K2
　CHST BR7 ... 206 C1
　COB KT11 ... 217 N10
　COUL/CHIP CR5 ... 241 H4
　CRAWE RH10 ... 284 E8
　DART DA1 ... 187 J2
　GT/LBKH KT23 ... 235 N10
　GVW DA11 ... 190 B4
　HAT AL10 ... 40 B7
　HGT N6 ... 118 D5
　HORL RH6 ... 281 J4
　HPTN TW12 ... 176 B8
　MLHL NW7 ... 96 G7
　PIN HA5 ... 113 H3
　SAND/SEL CR2 ... 242 A1
　WARE SG12 ... 28 A3
　WFD IG8 ... 101 N6
　WLGTN SM6 ... 222 D4
　WOKS/MYFD GU22 ... 232 D5
Tudor Ct *BORE* WD6 ... 75 K6
　SWLY BR8 ... 187 M4
　WALTH E17 ... 120 E2
Tudor Ct North *WBLY* HA9 ... 115 M10
Tudor Ct South *WBLY* HA9 ... 115 M10
Tudor Crs *BARK/HLT* IG6 ... 102 F7
　ENC/FH EN2 ... 79 K5
　RSEV TN14 ... 247 K3
Tudor Dr *GPK* RM2 ... 125 M8
　KUTN/CMB KT2 ... 177 K8
　MRDN SM4 ... 201 J7
　RSEV TN14 ... 247 K2
　WATN WD24 ... 73 L4
　WOT/HER KT12 ... 197 L8
Tudor Gdns *ACT* W3 ... 135 M8
　BARN SW13 ... 156 B9
　CDALE/KGS NW9 ... 115 P7
　GPK RM2 ... 125 H2
　SL SL1 ... 128 B7
　TWK TW1 ... 176 E4
　UPMR RM14 ... 126 B7
　WWKM BR4 ... 205 H10
Tudor Gv *HOM* E9 ... 140 B2
Tudor La *WDSR* SL4 ... 171 P3
Tudor Manor Gdns *GSTN* WD25 ... 55 L8
Tudor Pk *AMS* HP6 ... 69 H3
Tudor Pl *WIM/MER* SW19 ... 179 Q10
　SWLY BR8 ... 187 M4
Tudor Ri *BROX* EN10 ... 44 D7
Tudor Rd *ASHF* TW15 ... 174 E9
　BAR EN5 ... 77 K7
　BARK IG11 ... 143 J2
　BECK BR3 ... 205 H3
　CHING E4 ... 100 G7
　ED N9 ... 100 A1
　EHAM E6 ... 141 P3
　HACK E8 ... 140 A3
　HPTN TW12 ... 175 P10
　HSLW TW3 ... 154 D10
　HYS/HAR UB3 ... 132 E8
　KUTN/CMB KT2 ... 177 L10
　NRWD SE19 ... 181 N10
　PIN HA5 ... 93 G10
　SNWD SE25 ... 204 A3
　STALE/WH AL4 ... 38 D2
　STALW/RED AL3 ... 21 K3
　STHL UB1 ... 133 M9
Tudor St *EMB* EC4Y ... 12 B7
Tudor Wk *LHD/OX* KT22 ... 236 F6
　BEX DA5 ... 73 L3
Tudor Wy *ACT* W3 ... 155 M1
　HERT/WAS SG14 ... 25 H5
　HGDN/ICK UB10 ... 132 B1
　RKW/CH/CXG WD3 ... 91 K2
　STHGT/OAK N14 ... 98 E2
　WAB EN9 ... 63 J9
　WDSR SL4 ... 148 D7
Tudor Well Cl *STAN* HA7 ... 94 C4
Tudway Rd *ELTH/MOT* SE9 ... 161 P10
Tufnail Rd *DART* DA1 ... 187 N2
Tufnell Park Rd *HOLWY* N7 ... 118 C2
Tufter Rd *CHIG* IG7 ... 103 J6
Tufton Gdns *E/WMO/HCT* KT8 ... 198 A5
Tufton Rd *CHING* E4 ... 100 F5
Tufton St *WEST* SW1P ... 17 L4
Tugboat St *THMD* SE28 ... 163 H1
Tugela Rd *CROY/NA* CR0 ... 203 L6
Tugela St *CAT* SE6 ... 182 E3
Tugmutton Cl *ORP* BR6 ... 226 E1
Tulip Cl *BRWN* CM15 ... 86 G9
　CROY/NA CR0 ... 204 C8
　EHAM E6 ... 142 C7
　HARH RM3 ... 105 K7
　HPTN TW12 ... 175 N9
　STHL UB1 ... 154 B1
Tulip Gdns *IL* IG1 ... 142 C1
Tull St *MTCM* CR4 ... 202 A7
Tulse Cl *BECK* BR3 ... 205 H3
Tulse HI *BRXS/STRHM* SW2 ... 181 H5
Tulsemere Rd *WNWD* SE27 ... 181 K5
Tulyar Cl *KWD/TDW/WH* KT20 ... 238 C5
Tumber St *EPSOM* KT18 ... 255 P7
Tumbler Rd *HLWS* CM18 ... 47 L2
Tumblewood Rd *BNSTD* SM7 ... 239 H2
Tumbling Bay *WOT/HER* KT12 ... 197 N6
Tummons Gdns *SNWD* SE25 ... 203 N2
Tuncombe Rd *UED* N18 ... 99 M5
Tunfield Rd *HOD* EN11 ... 26 C10
Tunis Rd *SHB* W12 ... 136 F10
Tunley Rd *BAL* SW12 ... 180 B3
　WLSDN NW10 ... 136 B3
Tunmarsh La *PLSTW* E13 ... 141 L2
Tunman Leys *EHAM* E6 ... 142 D2
Tunmead *CRAWW* RH11 ... 283 H8
Tunnan Leys *EHAM* E6 ... 29 M10
Tunsgate *GU* GU1 ... 268 G2
Tunstall Av *BARK/HLT* IG6 ... 103 K7
Tunstall Cl *ORP* BR6 ... 227 H1
Tunstall Rd *BRXN/ST* SW9 ... 158 C10
　CROY/NA CR0 ... 203 M8
Tunstock Wy *BELV* DA17 ... 163 M3
Tunworth Crs *PUT/ROE* SW15 ... 178 C2
Tupelo Rd *LEY* E10 ... 120 C7
Tupwood Cl *CTHM* CR3 ... 259 P4
Tupwood Scrubbs Rd *GDST* RH9 ... 259 P6
Turene Cl *BTSEA* SW11 ... 157 M10
Turfhouse La *CHOB/PIR* GU24 ... 213 K5
Turin Rd *ED* N9 ... 100 B1
Turin St *BETH* E2 ... 20 M1
Turkey Oak La *NRWD* SE19 ... 203 M1
Turkey St *EN* N1 ... 80 A3
Turks Cl *UX/CGN* UB8 ... 132 A3
Turks Rw *CHEL* SW3 ... 16 G8
Turle Rd *FSBYPK* N4 ... 118 G7
　STRHM/NOR SW16 ... 202 F2
Turlewray Cl *FSBYPK* N4 ... 118 G6
Turley Cl *SRTFD* E15 ... 141 K3

Turmore DI WCCW AL8 .... 22 H8
Turnagain La STP EC4M 12 C5
Turnage Rd BCTR RM8 .... 123 P6
Turnant Rd TOTM N17 .... 99 K9
Turnberry Ct OXHEY WD19 .... 93 K4
Turnberry Dr RDART DA2 .... 188 C3
Turnberry Wy ORP BR6 .... 206 G8
Turnbull CI RDART DA2 .... 188 D1
Turnbury CI THMD SE28 .... 143 N8
Turner Av MTCM CR4 .... 202 A1
SEVS/STOTM N15 .... 119 M2
WHTN TW2 .... 176 B6
Turner CI BH/WHM TN16 .... 225 J5
CMBW SE5 .... 159 J2
GLDGN NW11 .... 117 L4
GU GU1 .... 250 C7
Turner Ct DART DA1 .... 187 K1
BUSH WD23 .... 74 B8
DTCH/LGLY SL3 .... 149 P1
EDGW HA8 .... 95 K10
NWMAL KT3 .... 200 A7
RDART DA2 .... 188 C6
WALTH E17 .... 121 H2
Turners CI CHONG CM5 .... 67 N5
STA TW18 .... 173 L8
Turners Gdns SEV TN13 .... 265 K4
Turner's HI CHES/WCR EN8 .... 62 C6
HHNE HP2 .... 35 P7
Turners Hill Rd CRAWE RH10 .... 284 F7
CRAWE RH10 .... 285 N2
Turners La WOT/HER KT12 .... 217 J3
Turners Meadow Wy BECK BR3 .... 204 E1
Turner's Oak Shaw HART DA3 .... 211 K9
Turner's Rd POP/IOD E14 .... 140 E2
Turner St CAN/RD E16 .... 141 L8
WCHPL E1 .... 140 C1
Turners Wy CROY/NA CR0 .... 203 H9
Turners Wd GLDGN NW11 .... 117 M6
Turners Wood Dr CSTG HP8 .... 96 A4
Turneville Rd WKENS W14 .... 14 C9
Turney Rd DUL SE21 .... 181 K3
Turneys Orch RKW/CH/CXG WD3 .... 70 C3
Turnham CI GUW GU2 .... 267 P4
Turnham Green Ter CHSWK W4 .... 156 B3
Turnham Rd BROCKY SE4 .... 182 D1
Turnmill St FARR EC1M 12 B2
Turnoak Av WOKS/MYFD GU22 .... 232 B6
Turnoak La WOKS/MYFD GU22 .... 232 B6
Turnoak Pk WDSR SL4 .... 148 D10
Turnors HLWW/ROY CM19 .... 46 F1
Turnpike CI DEPT SE8 .... 160 E6
Turnpike Dr ORP BR6 .... 227 M5
Turnpike Gn HHNE HP2 .... 36 A1
Turnpike La CDH/CHF RM16 .... 168 C4
CEND/HSY/T N8 .... 119 H2
SUT SM1 .... 221 M2
UX/CGN UB8 .... 131 P5
Turnpike Link CROY/NA CR0 .... 203 M9
Turnpike PI CRAWW RH11 .... 283 N6
Turnpike Wy ISLW TW7 .... 154 F7
Turnstone HART DA3 .... 211 M3
Turnstone CI CDALE/KGS NW9 .... 96 B10
HGDN/ICK UB10 .... 112 C10
PLSTW E13 .... 141 N5
SAND/SEL CR2 .... 224 D6
The Turnstones GSTN WD25 .... 75 N2
GVE DA12 .... 190 G5
Turp Av CDH/CHF RM16 .... 167 P1
Turpentine La PIM SW1V 16 F7
Turpington CI HAYES BR2 .... 206 B6
Turpington La HAYES BR2 .... 206 B6
Turpin La ERITH DA8 .... 165 H5
Turpin Rd EBED/NFELT TW14 .... 174 G2
Turpins La HERT/WAS SG14 .... 24 C5
Turpin's La WFD IG8 .... 102 C1
Turpins Ri BFOR GU20 .... 212 A1
Turpin Wy WLGTN SM6 .... 222 B7
Turquand St WALW SE17 .... 18 F6
Turret Gv CLAP SW4 .... 158 F3
Turton Rd ALP/SUD HA0 .... 115 K10
Turton Wy SL SL1 .... 149 J2
Turville St BETH E2 .... 13 L1
Tuscan CI WOOL/PLUM SE18 .... 162 G4
Tuscany Gdns CRAWE RH10 .... 283 P4
Tushmore Av CRAWW RH11 .... 283 P2
Tushmore Crs CRAWW RH11 .... 283 P2
Tushmore La CRAWE RH10 .... 285 P3
Tuskar St GNWCH SE10 .... 161 K4
Tussock CI CRAWW RH11 .... 283 N9
Tuxford CI BORE WD6 .... 75 K4
CRAWE RH10 .... 284 D9
Tweed TIL RM18 .... 169 M3
Tweed CI BERK HP4 .... 33 N4
Tweeddale Gv HGDN/ICK UB10 .... 112 D9
Tweeddale Rd CAR SM5 .... 201 N8
Tweed La BRKHM/BTCW RH3 .... 273 N6
CRAWW RH11 .... 283 J3
Tweedmouth Rd PLSTW E13 .... 141 L1
Tweed Rd DTCH/LGLY SL3 .... 150 E5
Tweedy Rd BMLY BR1 .... 205 M1
Tweenways CSHM HP5 .... 51 M1
Twelve Acre CI GT/LBKH KT23 .... 235 N10
Twelve Acres WCCE AL7 .... 23 H7
Twelvetrees Crs BOW E3 .... 141 H6
Twentyman CI WFD IG8 .... 101 M6
Twickenham CI CROY/NA CR0 .... 202 G10
Twickenham Gdns CRO/PVL UB6 .... 114 F10
KTN/HRWW/W HA3 .... 94 D9
Twickenham Rd FELT TW13 .... 175 N6
ISLW TW7 .... 154 F10
RCH/KEW TW9 .... 177 H1
WAN E11 .... 102 G7
Twig Folly CI BOW E3 .... 140 C4
Twigg CI ERITH DA8 .... 164 F6
Twilley St WAND/EARL SW18 .... 179 J2
Twinches La SL SL1 .... 128 G10
Twine CI BARK IG11 .... 143 L5
Twine Ct WCHPL E1 .... 140 B9
Twineham Gn NFNCH/WDSP N12 .... 97 K5
Twining Av WHTN TW2 .... 176 B6
Twinn Rd MLHL NW7 .... 97 H7
Twinoaks COB KT11 .... 217 N9
Twisleton Ct DART DA1 .... 187 L2
Twitton La RSEV TN14 .... 246 F1
Twitton Mdw RSEV TN14 .... 246 F2
Two Acres WCCE AL7 .... 23 J8
Two Dells La CSHM HP5 .... 51 J2
Two Gates La CSHM HP5 .... 32 C10
Two Waters Rd HHS/BOV HP3 .... 35 M10
Twybridge Wy WLSDN NW10 .... 135 P2
Twycross Rd RGODL GU7 .... 267 L7
Twyford Abbey Rd WLSDN NW10 .... 135 L5
EFNCH N2 .... 118 A1
Twyford Crs ACT W3 .... 135 M10
IL IG1 .... 122 F10
RYLN/HDSTN HA2 .... 113 P3
STALE/WH AL4 .... 39 H2
Twyford St IS N1 .... 5 N5
Twyne CI CRAWW RH11 .... 283 H9
Twyner CI HORL RH6 .... 280 D3
Twynersh Av CHERT KT16 .... 195 L2
Tyas Rd CAN/RD E16 .... 141 H5
Tyberry Rd EN EN1 .... 80 A7
Tyburn La HRW HA1 .... 114 D5
The Tyburns RBRW/HUT CM13 .... 107 P3
Tycehurst HI LOU IG10 .... 82 C8
Tychbourne Dr RGUE GU4 .... 250 F2
Tydcombe Rd WARL CR6 .... 241 J8
Tye Green Village HLWS CM18 .... 47 J4
Tye La ORP BR6 .... 226 F2
Tyers Ga STHWK SE1 .... 19 J2

Tyers St LBTH SE11 .... 17 N7
Tyers Ter LBTH SE11 .... 17 N8
Tyeshurst CI ABYW SE2 .... 163 P4
Tyfield CI CHES/WCR EN8 .... 62 B6
Tylecroft Rd STRHM/NOR SW16 .... 202 F2
Tyle Gn EMPK RM11 .... 125 M3
Tylehost GUW GU2 .... 249 M6
Tyle PI WDSR SL4 .... 171 M1
Tyler CI BETH E2 .... 7 L7
Tyler Gdns ADL/WDHM KT15 .... 215 M1
Tyler Rd CRAWE RH10 .... 283 N10
Tylers HARP AL5 .... 20 C2
Tylers Cswy HERT/BAY SG13 .... 42 D8
Tylers CI GDST RH9 .... 260 A6
KGLGY WD4 .... 54 A5
Tylers Crs HCH RM12 .... 125 K10
Tylersfield ABLGY WD5 .... 54 G7
Tylers Gn MTHVW/W HA3 .... 115 K4
Tylers Green Rd SWLY BR8 .... 208 D6
Tylers Hill Rd CSHM HP5 .... 51 L6
Tylers Rd HLWW/ROY CM19 .... 46 A6
Tyler St GNWCH SE10 .... 161 K4
Tyler Wy BRW CM14 .... 106 C2
Tylney Av NRWD SE19 .... 181 N8
Tylney Cft HLWW/ROY CM19 .... 46 E3
Tylney Rd BMLY BR1 .... 206 A2
FSTGT E7 .... 121 P9
Tynan CI EBED/NFELT TW14 .... 175 H4
Tyndale La IS N1 .... 6 C3
Tyndale Ter IS N1 .... 6 C3
Tyndall Rd LEY E10 .... 121 H7
WELL DA16 .... 163 J3
Tyne CI CRAWE RH10 .... 284 D8
UPMR RM14 .... 126 C4
Tynedale LCOL/BKTW AL2 .... 57 L3
Tynedale Rd RDART DA2 .... 188 C4
Tynedale Rd BRKHM/BTCW RH3 .... 273 N4
Tyne Gdns SOCK/AV RM15 .... 146 B3
Tyneham Rd BTSEA SW11 .... 158 B3
Tynemouth CI EHAM E6 .... 142 E8
Tynemouth Dr EN EN1 .... 79 P4
Tynemouth Rd MTCM CR4 .... 180 B10
SEVS/STOTM N15 .... 119 N2
WOOL/PLUM SE18 .... 163 H4
Tynemouth St FUL/PGN SW6 .... 157 N8
Tyne St WCHPL E1 .... 13 M5
Tynley Gv RGUE GU4 .... 250 A4
Type St BETH E2 .... 140 C4
Typleden CI HHNE HP2 .... 35 N4
Tyrawley Rd FUL/PGN SW6 .... 157 L7
Tyrell CI HRW HA1 .... 114 D9
Tyrell Gdns WDSR SL4 .... 148 B7
Tyrells CI UPMR RM14 .... 126 A7
Tyrone Rd EHAM E6 .... 142 C4
Tyron Wy SCUP DA14 .... 185 L5
Tyrrell Av WELL DA16 .... 185 L1
Tyrrell Rd EDUL SE22 .... 159 P10
Tyrrells Hall CI GRAYS RM17 .... 168 A5
Tyrrel Wy CDALE/KGS NW9 .... 116 C5
Tyrwhitt Av GUW GU2 .... 249 N6
Tyrwhitt Rd BROCKY SE4 .... 160 F9
Tysea CI HLWS CM18 .... 47 J4
Tysea HI ABR/ST RM4 .... 104 C2
Tysea Rd HLWS CM18 .... 47 J4
Tysoe Av PEND EN3 .... 80 F9
Tysoe St CLKNW EC1R 6 A10
Tyson Rd FSTH SE23 .... 181 B3
Tyssen PI SOCK/AV RM15 .... 147 H5
Tyssen Rd STNW/STAM N16 .... 119 N10
Tyssen St HACK E8 .... 7 M1
Tythebarn CI RGUE GU4 .... 250 E5
Tythebarns La RPLY/SEND GU23 .... 251 K2
Tytherton Rd ARCH N19 .... 118 E8
Tyttenhanger Gn STALE/WH AL4 .... 39 J9

U

Uamvar St POP/IOD E14 .... 140 G7
Uckfield Gv MTCM CR4 .... 202 B1
Uckfield Rd PEND EN3 .... 80 B1
Udall Gdns CRW RM5 .... 104 B7
Udall St WEST SW1P 17 L7
Udney Park Rd TEDD TW11 .... 176 F8
Uffington Rd WLSDN NW10 .... 136 D3
WNWD SE27 .... 181 H1
Ufford CI KTN/HRWW/W HA3 .... 94 A7
Ufford Rd KTN/HRWW/W HA3 .... 94 A8
Ufford St STHWK SE1 .... 18 B1
Ufton Gv IS N1 .... 7 J3
Ufton Rd IS N1 .... 7 J4
Ullathorne Rd STRHM/NOR SW16 .... 180 D7
Ulleswater Rd PLMGR N13 .... 98 F5
Ullin St POP/IOD E14 .... 141 H7
Ullswater CI BMLY BR1 .... 183 K9
LTWR GU18 .... 212 A6
PUT/ROE SW15 .... 178 A7
SL SL1 .... 128 B7
YEAD UB4 .... 132 F4
Ullswater Crs COUL/CHIP CR5 .... 240 G1
PUT/ROE SW15 .... 178 A7
Ullswater Rd BARN SW13 .... 156 D6
HHS/BOV HP3 .... 36 B8
LTWR GU18 .... 212 A6
WNWD SE27 .... 181 J3
Ullswater Wy HCH RM12 .... 125 H10
Ulstan CI CTHM CR3 .... 242 F9
Ulster Gdns PLMGR N13 .... 99 K5
Ulster PI CAMTN NW1 .... 10 E2
Ulundi Rd BKHTH/KID SE3 .... 161 K5
Ulva Rd PUT/ROE SW15 .... 156 G10
Ulverscroft Rd EDUL SE22 .... 181 H1
Ulverston Rd WALTH E17 .... 101 J10
Ulwin Av BF/WBF KT14 .... 215 M5
Ulysses Rd KIL/WHAMP NW6 .... 117 J10
Umberston St WCHPL E1 .... 140 A8
Umberville Wy SLN SL2 .... 128 B6
Umbria St PUT/ROE SW15 .... 178 D2
Umfreville Rd FSBYPK N4 .... 119 J4
Underacres CI HHNE HP2 .... 36 B5
Undercliff Rd LEW SE13 .... 160 F9
Underhill Park Rd REIG RH2 .... 257 K7
Underhill Rd EDUL SE22 .... 181 P1
Underhill St CAMTN NW1 .... 4 J1
Underne Av STHGT/OAK N14 .... 98 C3
Undershaft HDTCH EC3A 13 J6
Undershaw Rd BMLY BR1 .... 183 K6
Underwood Ct CTHM CR3 .... 241 N10
Underwood Rd CHING E4 .... 101 M1
CTHM CR3 .... 259 M1
WCHPL E1 .... 13 M2
WFD IG8 .... 102 A8
Underwood Rw IS N1 .... 6 F9
The Underwood ELTH/MOT SE9 .... 184 E7
Undine Rd POP/IOD E14 .... 160 G5
Undine St TOOT SW17 .... 180 A8
Uneeda Dr GFD/PVL UB6 .... 134 C3
Unicorn Wk GRH DA9 .... 188 E1
Union CI CLAP SW4 .... 158 B3
Union Dr WCHPL E1 .... 140 D6
Union Gn HHNE HP2 .... 35 N5
Union Gv VX/NE SW8 .... 158 B3
Union Rd ALP/SUD HA0 .... 135 K1
CLAP SW4 .... 158 C3
CROY/NA CR0 .... 203 K7
NWMAL KT3 .... 200 D2
HAYES BR2 .... 204 A1
NTHLT UB5 .... 133 P2
Union Sq IS N1 .... 6 G1
Union St BAR EN5 .... 77 H4
KUT KT1 .... 199 J2
SRTFD E15 .... 141 J3
STHWK SE1 .... 12 D10

Union Wk BETH E2 .... 7 L9
Unity CI CROY/NA CR0 .... 224 G5
WLSDN NW10 .... 136 D1
WNWD SE27 .... 181 K8
Unity Ms CAMTN NW1 .... 5 J7
Unity Rd PEND EN3 .... 80 B1
Unity Wy WOOL/PLUM SE18 .... 162 A2
University Gdns BXLY DA5 .... 186 A3
University Gdns WIM/MER SW19 .... 179 N9
University St FITZ W1T 11 L1
Unstead La SHGR GU5 .... 267 P10
Unwin Av EBED/NFELT TW14 .... 174 A1
Unwin CI PECK SE15 .... 19 N10
Unwin Rd ISLW TW7 .... 154 D9
Upbrook Ms BAY/PAD W2 .... 9 K6
Upcerne Rd WBPTN SW10 .... 157 M6
Upcroft WDSR SL4 .... 148 C9
Upcroft Av EDGW HA8 .... 95 P6
Updale CI POTB/CUF EN6 .... 59 H9
Updale Rd SCUP DA14 .... 185 J7
Updown HI BFOR GU20 .... 212 C3
Upfield CROY/NA CR0 .... 204 A9
HORL RH6 .... 280 B6
Upfield Rd HNWL W7 .... 134 E6
Upfolds Gn RGUE GU4 .... 250 F6
Uphall Rd IL IG1 .... 122 E10
Upham Park Rd CHSWK W4 .... 156 B3
Uphill Dr CDALE/KGS NW9 .... 115 P3
MLHL NW7 .... 96 B6
Uphill Gv MLHL NW7 .... 96 B5
Uphill Rd MLHL NW7 .... 96 B5
Upland Av CSHM HP5 .... 50 G4
Upland Court Rd HARH RM3 .... 105 N10
Upland Dr BRKMPK AL9 .... 59 L1
Upland Rd BELMT SM2 .... 221 N6
BXLYHN DA7 .... 164 A9
CTHM CR3 .... 242 F6
EPP CM16 .... 64 C4
PLSTW E13 .... 141 M6
SAND/SEL CR2 .... 223 L2
Uplands ASHTD KT21 .... 237 J6
BECK BR3 .... 204 F2
RKW/CH/CXG WD3 .... 72 A10
WARE SG12 .... 26 E1
WGCW AL8 .... 22 F1
Uplands Av WALTH E17 .... 120 C1
Uplands CI CFSP/GDCR SL9 .... 110 B6
MORT/ESHN SW14 .... 177 N1
Uplands Dr LHD/OX KT22 .... 218 C10
Uplands Park Rd CEND/HSY/T N8 .... 118 C3
CHDH RM6 .... 123 N1
EBAR EN4 .... 98 B2
ORP BR6 .... 227 L8
PUR/KEN CR8 .... 241 K3
WFD IG8 .... 103 H3
The Uplands CFSP/GDCR SL9 .... 110 B7
LCOL/BKTW AL2 .... 55 N6
LOU IG10 .... 82 C7
RSLP HA4 .... 94 B8
Uplands Wy SEV TN13 .... 246 G9
WCHMH N21 .... 79 H9
Upland Wy EPSOM KT18 .... 238 F4
Upminster Rd HCH RM12 .... 125 N7
Upminster Rd North RAIN RM13 .... 145 K5
Upminster Rd South RAIN RM13 .... 145 H6
Upney CI HCH RM12 .... 125 L10
Upney La BARK IG11 .... 143 J1
Upnor Wy WALW SE17 .... 19 K7
Uppark Dr GNTH/NBYPK IG2 .... 122 F4
Upper Abbey Rd BELV DA17 .... 164 A3
Upper Addison Gdns WKENS W14 .... 14 A1
Upper Ashlyns Rd BERK HP4 .... 33 N6
Upper Austin Lodge Rd EYN DA4 .... 229 L2
Upper Barn HHS/BOV HP3 .... 36 A9
Upper Belgrave St KTBR SW1X 16 B3
Upper Belmont Rd CSHM HP5 .... 50 G4
Upper Bourne End La HHW HP1 .... 34 D10
Upper Brentwood Rd GPK RM2 .... 125 K1
Upper Bridge Rd REDH RH1 .... 257 P10
Upper Brighton Rd SURB KT6 .... 199 J6
Upper Brook St MYFR/PKLN W1K 10 C7
Upper Butts BTFD TW8 .... 155 H5
Upper Cheyne Rw CHEL SW3 .... 15 N10
Upper Clabdens WARE SG12 .... 26 E2
Upper Clapton Rd CLPT E5 .... 120 A7
Upper Cornsland BRW CM14 .... 107 J2
Upper Court Rd CTHM CR3 .... 242 F9
HOR/WEW KT19 .... 219 P7
Upper Culver St STAL AL1 .... 38 C4
Upper Dagnall St
STALW/RED AL3 .... 38 C6
Upper Dr BEAC HP9 .... 88 C3
BH/WHM TN16 .... 225 J7
Upper Dunnymans BNSTD SM7 .... 221 J10
Upper Edgeborough Rd GU GU1 .... 268 C1
Upper Elmers End Rd BECK BR3 .... 204 D3
BECK BR3 .... 204 F6
Upper Fairfield Rd LHD/OX KT22 .... 236 C7
Upper Farm Rd E/WMO/HCT KT8 .... 197 N4
Upperfield Rd WGCE AL7 .... 23 J6
Upper George St CSHM HP5 .... 51 H6
Upper Gladstone Rd CSHM HP5 .... 51 H6
Upper Gn East MTCM CR4 .... 202 A2
Upper Gn West MTCM CR4 .... 202 A2
Upper Grosvenor St
MYFR/PKLN W1K 10 C8
Upper Grotto Rd TWK TW1 .... 176 B6
Upper Gnd STHWK SE1 .... 12 A9
Upper Gv SNWD SE25 .... 203 M9
Upper Grove Rd BELV DA17 .... 164 A5
Upper Guildown Rd GUW GU2 .... 267 N5
Upper Halliford Rd SHPTN TW17 .... 196 F2
Upper Hall Pk BERK HP4 .... 34 B7
Upper Ham Rd
RCHPK/HAM TW10 .... 177 J7
Upper Harestone CTHM CR3 .... 259 P3
Upper Harley St CAMTN NW1 .... 10 D2
Upper Heath Rd STAL AL1 .... 38 E4
Upper High St EW KT17 .... 220 B9
Upper Highway ABLGY WD5 .... 54 C6
Upper Hill Ri RKW/CH/CXG WD3 .... 71 L10
Upper Holly Hill Rd BELV DA17 .... 164 C4
Upper Hook HLWS CM18 .... 47 J3
Upper Hitch OXHEY WD19 .... 93 M2
Upper John St REGST W1F 11 H7
Upper Lattimore Rd STAL AL1 .... 38 D3
Upper Lees Rd SLN SL2 .... 128 F5
Upper Manor Rd RGODL GU7 .... 267 K10
Upper Marlborough Rd STAL AL1 .... 38 D6
Upper Marsh STHWK SE1 .... 17 N3
Upper Marsh La HOD EN11 .... 44 F4
Upper Meadow CSHM HP5 .... 50 G6
Upper Mealines HLWS CM18 .... 47 K4
Upper Montagu St MBLAR W1H 10 A3
Upper Mulgrave Rd BELMT SM2 .... 221 H6
Upper Paddock Rd OXHEY WD19 .... 73 M10
Upper Pk LOU IG10 .... 82 A9
Upper Pk HLW CM20 .... 28 C10
Upper Park Rd BELV DA17 .... 164 C5
BMLY BR1 .... 205 L1
FBAR/BDGN N11 .... 98 C6
HAMP NW3 .... 4 A1
KTN/HRWW/W HA3 .... 115 K3
Upper Phillimore Gdns KENS W8 .... 14 C1
Upper Pillory Down CAR SM5 .... 222 B9
Upper Pines BNSTD SM7 .... 240 A3
Upper Rainham Rd HCH RM12 .... 124 G9
Upper Richmond Rd
PUT/ROE SW15 .... 156 E10

Upper Richmond Rd West
RCHPK/HAM TW10 .... 155 M10
Upper Rd DEN/HRF UB9 .... 110 C5
PLSTW E13 .... 141 M5
WLGTN SM6 .... 222 E2
Upper Rose HI DORK RH4 .... 272 G3
Upper Ryle BRW CM14 .... 106 C1
Upper Sales HHW HP1 .... 35 J7
Upper Sawleywood
BNSTD SM7 .... 221 J10
Upper Selsdon Rd SAND/SEL CR2 .... 221 N5
Upper Sheridan Rd BELV DA17 .... 164 B3
Upper Shirley Rd CROY/NA CR0 .... 204 B10
Upper Shot WGCE AL7 .... 23 K4
Upper Shott CHESW EN7 .... 61 N2
Upper Sq ISLW TW7 .... 154 F9
Upper Stanford Rd
CHOB/PIR GU24 .... 248 E1
Upper Station Rd RAD WD7 .... 74 F1
Upper Stonyfield
HLWW/ROY CM19 .... 46 E1
Upper St IS N1 .... 6 D2
SHGR GU5 .... 270 A4
Upper Sunbury Rd HPTN TW12 .... 197 N1
Upper Sutton La HEST TW5 .... 153 P7
Upper Swaines EPP CM16 .... 65 J6
Upper Tachbrook St PIM SW1V 17 H5
Upper Tail OXHEY WD19 .... 93 M4
Upper Teddington Rd KUT KT1 .... 199 H1
Upper Ter HAMP NW3 .... 117 M8
Upper Thames St BLKFR EC4V 12 E7
Upper Tollington Pk FSBYPK N4 .... 119 H6
SCUP DA14 .... 185 J8
Upperton Rd GUW GU2 .... 267 P1
Upperton Rd East PLSTW E13 .... 141 P5
Upperton Rd West PLSTW E13 .... 141 N5
Upper Tooting Pk TOOT SW17 .... 180 A5
Upper Tooting Rd TOOT SW17 .... 180 A7
Upper Tuise HI BRXS/STRHM SW2 .... 181 J2
Upper Vernon Rd SUT SM1 .... 221 N2
Upper Village Rd ASC SL5 .... 192 B4
Upper Wk VNY GU25 .... 194 B4
Upper Walthamstow Rd
WALTH E17 .... 121 J2
Upper West St REIG RH2 .... 257 J10
Upper Wickham La WELL DA16 .... 163 L6
Upper Wimpole St
CAVSQ/HST W1G 10 D3
Upper Woburn PI CAMTN NW1 .... 5 K10
Upper Woodcote Village
PUR/KEN CR8 .... 222 E9
Uppingham Av STAN HA7 .... 115 H1
Upsdell Av PLMGR N13 .... 99 H7
Upshire Rd WAB EN9 .... 63 L8
Upshott La WOKS/MYFD GU22 .... 233 J3
Upstall St CMBW SE5 .... 159 J7
Upton Av FSTGT E7 .... 141 M2
STALW/RED AL3 .... 38 C5
Upton CI BXLY DA5 .... 186 A2
LCOL/BKTW AL2 .... 56 C1
Upton Court Rd DTCH/LGLY SL3 .... 149 M2
Upton Dene BELMT SM2 .... 221 L8
Upton Gdns KTN/HRWW/W HA3 .... 115 H4
Upton La FSTGT E7 .... 141 M3
Upton Lodge CI BUSH WD23 .... 94 B1
Upton Pk SL SL1 .... 149 J2
Upton Park Rd FSTGT E7 .... 141 N2
Upton Rd BXLYHS DA6 .... 165 P10
DTCH/LGLY SL3 .... 149 M2
HSLW TW3 .... 153 P9
THHTH CR7 .... 203 L2
UED N18 .... 99 P6
WATW WD18 .... 73 P6
WOOL/PLUM SE18 .... 162 F5
Upton Rd South BXLY DA5 .... 186 A2
Upway CFSP/GDCR SL9 .... 90 C9
NFNCH/WDSP N12 .... 97 M3
Upwood Rd LEE/GVPK SE12 .... 183 L2
STRHM/NOR SW16 .... 202 F1
Uranus Rd HHNE HP2 .... 35 K8
Urban Av HCH RM12 .... 125 K8
Urlwin St CMBW SE5 .... 18 E10
Urlwin Wk BRXN/ST SW9 .... 159 H7
Urmston Dr WIM/MER SW19 .... 179 H4
Ursula Ms FSBYPK N4 .... 119 J3
Ursula St BTSEA SW11 .... 157 P7
Urswick Rd CLPT E5 .... 120 B10
DAGW RM9 .... 143 P7
Usher Rd BOW E3 .... 140 E3
Usherwood CI
KWD/TDW/WH KT20 .... 277 J8
Usk Rd BTSEA SW11 .... 157 M10
SOCK/AV RM15 .... 147 H5
Usk St BETH E2 .... 140 C5
Uvedale CI CROY/NA CR0 .... 225 J7
Uvedale Crs CROY/NA CR0 .... 225 J7
Uvedale Rd DAGE RM10 .... 124 B8
ENC/FH EN2 .... 79 L9
OXTED RH8 .... 260 A6
Uverdale Rd WBPTN SW10 .... 157 M6
Uxbridge Rd DTCH/LGLY SL3 .... 130 B7
FELT TW13 .... 175 H5
HGDN/ICK UB10 .... 132 C6
HNWL W7 .... 134 D10
HPTN TW12 .... 175 P7
RKW/CH/CXG WD3 .... 91 L2
SL SL1 .... 149 N1
SLN SL2 .... 133 P10
STHL UB1 .... 133 P10
SURB KT6 .... 199 J4
WEA W13 .... 134 G10
WHTN TW2 .... 176 B6
Uxbridge Road
(Hatch End) PIN HA5 .... 93 N8
Uxbridge Road High St STHL UB1 .... 133 N10
Uxbridge Road (Pinner) PIN HA5 .... 93 L10
Uxbridge Road
(Stanmore) STAN HA7 .... 94 E7
Uxbridge Road the Broadway
YEAD UB4 .... 133 L2
Uxbridge St KENS W8 .... 8 F9
Uxendon Crs WBLY HA9 .... 115 L6
Uxendon HI WBLY HA9 .... 115 L6

V

Vache La CSTG HP8 .... 89 P3
Vaillant Rd WEY KT13 .... 216 D1
Valance Av CHING E4 .... 101 J2
Valan Leas HAYES BR2 .... 205 K3
Vale Av BORE WD6 .... 75 N4
Vale CI BRWN CM15 .... 86 A9
CFSP/GDCR SL9 .... 90 A3
COUL/CHIP CR5 .... 222 F10
EFNCH N2 .... 118 A1
MV/WKIL W9 .... 3 J10
ORP BR6 .... 226 C1
WEY KT13 .... 196 E10
WOKN/KNAP GU21 .... 231 M3
Vale Ct STALE/WH AL4 .... 21 J4
WEY KT13 .... 196 E10
Vale Cft ESH/CLAY KT10 .... 218 C4
PIN HA5 .... 113 M3
Vale Dr BAR EN5 .... 77 J3
Vale End EDUL SE22 .... 159 N10
Vale Farm Rd WOKN/KNAP GU21 .... 231 J4
Vale Gv ACT W3 .... 136 A10
FSBYPK N4 .... 119 K3
SL SL1 .... 149 N2
Vale La ACT W3 .... 135 M7
Vale Ri BRWN CM15 .... 90 A10
Valence Av BCTR RM8 .... 123 N6
Valence Circ BCTR RM8 .... 123 N6

Valence Dr CHESW EN7 .... 61 P4
Valence Rd ERITH DA8 .... 164 E6
Valence Wood Rd BCTR RM8 .... 123 N6
Valencia Rd STAN HA7 .... 95 H5
Valency CI NTHWD HA6 .... 92 G5
Valentia PI BRXN/ST SW9 .... 159 H10
Valentine Av BXLY DA5 .... 185 P5
Valentine PI STHWK SE1 .... 18 C1
Valentine Rd HOM E9 .... 140 C1
RYLN/HDSTN HA2 .... 114 A8
Valentines Rd IL IG1 .... 122 E6
Valentines Wy DAGE RM10 .... 124 F7
Valentyne CI CROY/NA CR0 .... 225 K7
Vale of Health HAMP NW3 .... 117 M8
Valerian Wy SRTFD E15 .... 141 K5
Valerie CI STAL AL1 .... 38 G2
Vale Ri CSHM HP5 .... 51 H4
GLDGN NW11 .... 117 J6
Vale Rd BMLY BR1 .... 206 D2
BUSH WD23 .... 73 M9
CSHM HP5 .... 51 H3
DART DA1 .... 187 J4
ESH/CLAY KT10 .... 218 C5
FSBYPK N4 .... 119 K5
FSTGT E7 .... 141 N1
GVW SW13 .... 190 B4
HOR/WEW KT19 .... 220 C1
MTCM CR4 .... 202 E3
SUT SM1 .... 221 L1
WDSR SL4 .... 148 E7
WEY KT13 .... 196 E10
WPK KT4 .... 200 C10
Vale Rd North SURB KT6 .... 199 K9
Vale Royal HOLWY N7 .... 5 L4
Valeside HERT/WAS SG14 .... 25 H6
Valeswood Rd BMLY BR1 .... 183 L8
Vale Ter FSBYPK N4 .... 119 K4
The Vale ACT W3 .... 136 A10
BH/WHM TN16 .... 207 H2
CFSP/GDCR SL9 .... 90 A3
CHEL SW3 .... 15 N10
COUL/CHIP CR5 .... 222 F10
CRICK NW2 .... 116 C8
CROY/NA CR0 .... 204 C9
EBED/NFELT TW14 .... 175 J2
GLDGN NW11 .... 117 J6
HEST TW5 .... 153 M5
MUSWH N10 .... 98 B9
RSLP HA4 .... 113 K9
STHGT/OAK N14 .... 98 F1
SUN TW16 .... 175 H9
WFD IG8 .... 101 M8
Valetta Gv PLSTW E13 .... 141 M4
Valetta Rd ACT W3 .... 156 B1
Valette St HACK E8 .... 140 A1
Valiant CI NTHLT UB5 .... 133 L5
ROMW/RG RM7 .... 104 C10
Valiant Wy EHAM E6 .... 142 C7
Vallance Rd BETH E2 .... 7 P10
WDGN N22 .... 98 D10
Vallentin Rd WALTH E17 .... 121 H2
Valley Av NFNCH/WDSP N12 .... 97 N5
Valley CI DART DA1 .... 186 G2
HERT/BAY SG13 .... 82 C10
LOU IG10 .... 82 C10
PIN HA5 .... 93 J10
WAB EN9 .... 63 H8
WARE SG12 .... 26 A1
Valley Dr CDALE/KGS NW9 .... 115 N3
GVE DA12 .... 190 G7
SEV TN13 .... 265 J1
Valley End DTCH/LGLY SL3 .... 129 P6
Valley End Rd CHOB/PIR GU24 .... 212 G3
Valleyfield Rd STRHM/NOR SW16 .... 180 G8
Valley Fields Crs ENC/FH EN2 .... 79 H6
Valley Gdns ALP/SUD HA0 .... 135 L2
GRH DA9 .... 188 G2
WIM/MER SW19 .... 179 N10
The Valley Gn WGCW AL8 .... 22 F4
Valley Gv CHARL SE7 .... 161 P4
Valley HI LOU IG10 .... 102 B1
Valley Ms TWK TW1 .... 176 A6
Valley Ri GSTN WD25 .... 55 J9
STALE/WH AL4 .... 38 G1
Valley Rd BERK HP4 .... 33 L3
DART DA1 .... 186 D3
ERITH DA8 .... 164 D3
HART DA3 .... 210 G8
HAYES BR2 .... 205 K2
HGDN/ICK UB10 .... 131 P4
PUR/KEN CR8 .... 241 L5
RKW/CH/CXG WD3 .... 71 K9
STALW/RED AL3 .... 38 C5
STMC/STPC BR5 .... 207 L1
STRHM/NOR SW16 .... 180 G7
WGCW AL8 .... 22 F3
Valley Side CHING E4 .... 100 F7
Valleyside HHW HP1 .... 35 J6
Valley Vw BAR EN5 .... 77 H10
BH/WHM TN16 .... 243 P4
CHESW EN7 .... 61 K4
CSHM HP5 .... 50 F5
GRH DA9 .... 188 G2
Valley View Gdns PUR/KEN CR8 .... 241 M1
Valley Wk CROY/NA CR0 .... 204 B9
RKW/CH/CXG WD3 .... 72 D9
Valliere Rd WLSDN NW10 .... 136 D5
Valliers Wood Rd BFN/LL DA15 .... 184 C4
Vallis Wy CHSGTN KT9 .... 219 J3
WEA W13 .... 135 L8
Valmar Rd CMBW SE5 .... 159 K7
Valnay St TOOT SW17 .... 180 A8
Valognes Av WALTH E17 .... 100 G9
Valonia Gdns WAND/EARL SW18 .... 179 J2
Vambery Rd WOOL/PLUM SE18 .... 162 F5
Vanbrough Crs NTHLT UB5 .... 133 K4
Vanbrugh CI CRAWW RH11 .... 283 H10
Vanbrugh Dr WOT/HER KT12 .... 197 K7
Vanbrugh Flds BKHTH/KID SE3 .... 161 K5
Vanbrugh Gn BKHTH/KID SE3 .... 161 L6
Vanbrugh Park Rd
BKHTH/KID SE3 .... 161 L6
Vanbrugh Park Rd West
BKHTH/KID SE3 .... 161 L6
Vanbrugh Rd CHSWK W4 .... 156 A2
Vanbrugh Ter BKHTH/KID SE3 .... 161 L6
Vanburgh CI CAN/RD E16 .... 142 A7
ORP BR6 .... 207 H8
Vancouver CI HOR/WEW KT19 .... 219 P7
Vancouver Ct HORL RH6 .... 281 H4
Vancouver Dr CRAWW RH11 .... 283 N4
Vancouver Rd EDGW HA8 .... 95 N9
FSTH SE23 .... 182 D5
RCHPK/HAM TW10 .... 177 H7
YEAD UB4 .... 133 J2
Vanda Crs STAL AL1 .... 38 D4
Vandome CI CAN/RD E16 .... 141 L9
Vandon St STJSPK SW1H 17 H3
Van Dyck Av NWMAL KT3 .... 200 A7
Vandyke CI PUT/ROE SW15 .... 178 G2
REDH RH1 .... 258 A8
Vandyke Crs EDUL/MOT SE9 .... 184 B11
Vandy St SDTCH EC2A 13 J2
Vane CI HAMP NW3 .... 117 N9
KTN/HRWW/W HA3 .... 115 L4
Vanessa CI BELV DA17 .... 164 B3
Vanessa Wk GVE DA12 .... 191 L4
Vanessa Wy BXLY DA5 .... 186 E6
Vanguard CI CAN/RD E16 .... 141 N7
CROY/NA CR0 .... 2 E3
ROMW/RG RM7 .... 104 C10
Vanguard St DEPT SE8 .... 160 F7
Vanguard Wy CROY/NA CR0 .... 223 J7
EDEN TN8 .... 262 D10
OXTED RH8 .... 261 L1

WARL CR6 224 E9
WLGTN SM6 222 F4
Vanneck Sq PUT/ROE SW15 178 D1
Vannes CRAWE RH10 283 P6
Vanoc Gdns BMLY BR1 183 M7
Vanquisher Wk GVE DA12 191 U6
WDSR SL4 148 C6
Vansittart St NWCR SE14 160 D6
Vanston Pl FUL/PGN SW6 157 K6
Vantorts Cl SBW CM21 29 P1
Vantorts Rd SBW CM21 29 P1
Vant Rd TOOT SW17 180 A8
Vapery La CHOB/PIR GU24 230 C7
Varcoe Rd BERM/RHTH SE16 160 A4
Vardens Rd BTSEA SW11 157 N10
Varden St WCHPL E1 140 A8
Varley Rd CAN/RD E16 141 N8
Varley Wy MTCM CR4 201 N2
Varna Rd FUL/PGN SW6 157 H6
HPTN TW12 198 A1
Varndell St CAMTN NW1 4 G9
Varney Cl CHESW EN7 61 P3
HHW HP1 35 J6
Varney Rd HHW HP1 35 J6
Varsity Dr ISLW TW7 176 E1
Varsity Rw MORT/ESHN SW14 155 P8
Vartry Rd SEVS/STOTM N15 119 M4
Vassall Rd BRXN/ST SW9 159 H6
Vauban St BERM/RHTH SE16 19 M4
Vaughan Av HCH RM12 125 L9
HDN NW4 116 D3
HMSMTH W6 156 C3
Vaughan Gdns IL IG1 122 C5
Vaughan Rd CMBW SE5 159 K9
HARP AL5 20 A2
HRW HA1 114 B5
SRTFD E15 141 L1
THDIT KT7 198 G7
WELL DA16 163 J8
Vaughan Wy BERM/RHTH SE16 160 E1
Vaughan Wy DORK RH4 272 F2
SLN SL2 128 D6
WAP E1W 13 P8
Vaughan Williams Cl DEPT SE8 160 F6
Vaux Crs WOT/HER KT12 217 J3
Vauxhall Br LBTH SE11 17 L8
Vauxhall Bridge Rd PIM SW1V 16 C4
Vauxhall Cl GVW DA11 190 C3
Vauxhall Gdns SAND/SEL CR2 223 K3
Vauxhall Gv VX/NE SW8 17 M3
Vauxhall Pl DART DA1 187 M3
Vauxhall Rd HHNE HP2 36 B6
Vauxhall St LBTH SE11 17 P8
Vauxhall Wk LBTH SE11 17 M8
Vawdrey Cl WCHPL E1 140 B6
Veals Md MTCM CR4 201 P1
Vectis Gdns TOOT SW17 180 D1
Vectis Rd TOOT SW17 180 C9
Veda Rd LEW SE13 160 F10
Vega Crs NTHWD HA6 92 C6
Vega Rd BUSH WD23 94 B1
Veldene Wy RYLN/HDSTN HA2 113 N8
Velizy Av HLW CM20 28 C10
Vellum Dr CAR SM5 202 B10
Venables Cl DAGE RM10 124 C9
Venables St STJWD NW8 9 M2
Vencourt Pl HMSMTH W6 156 D4
Venetian Rd EA W5 159 K8
Venetia Rd EA W5 155 J1
FSBYPK N4 119 J4
Venette Cl RAIN RM13 145 J7
Venner Rd SYD SE26 182 B9
Venners Cl BXLYHN DA7 164 F8
Venn St CLAP SW4 158 D10
Ventnor Av STAN HA7 94 C9
Ventnor Dr NFNCH/WDSP N12 97 L4
Ventnor Gdns BARK IG11 143 H1
Ventnor Rd BELMT SM2 221 L4
NWCR SE14 160 C6
Venton Cl WOKN/KNAP GU21 231 N3
Ventura Pk LCOL/BKTW AL2 56 E3
Venture Cl BXLY DA5 185 J6
Venue St POP/IOD E14 141 H7
Venus Hl HHS/BOV HP3 52 D7
Venus Rd WOOL/PLUM SE18 162 C2
Veny Crs HCH RM12 125 L10
Vera Av WCHMH N21 99 H9
Vera Ct OXHEY WD19 93 L1
Vera Lynn Cl FSTGT E7 121 M9
Vera Rd FUL/PGN SW6 157 H7
Verbena Cl CAN/RD E16 141 K6
SOCK/AV RM15 147 H8
WDR/YW UB7 151 N4
Verbena Gdns HMSMTH W6 156 D4
Ver-colne Valley Wk BUSH WD23 73 L7
HHS/BOV HP3 52 A1
STAL AL1 38 D7
Verdant La CROY/NA CR0 204 C8
Verdayne Av CROY/NA CR0 204 C8
Verdayne Gdns WARL CR6 242 B2
Verderers Rd CHIG IG7 103 K6
Verdun Rd BARN SW13 156 D5
WOOL/PLUM SE18 163 K6
Verdure Cl GSTN WD25 55 M8
Vereker Dr SUN TW16 197 H3
Vereker Rd WKENS W14 157 H3
Vere Rd LOU IG10 82 F8
Vere St MHST W1U 10 E6
Verity Cl NTGHL W11 8 A7
Verlum Cl WGCE AL7 23 J5
Vermont Cl ENC/FH EN2 79 J3
Vermont Rd NRWD SE19 181 L9
SLN SL2 128 D6
SUT SM1 201 L10
WAND/EARL SW18 179 L2
Verney Cl BERK HP4 33 L4
Verney Gdns DAGW RM9 123 P9
Verney Rd BERM/RHTH SE16 160 A4
DAGW RM9 123 P9
DTCH/LGLY SL3 150 D3
Verney St LEW SE13 160 G9
Verney Wy WLSDN NW10 116 A8
Verney Wy BERM/RHTH SE16 160 A4
Vernham Rd WOOL/PLUM SE18 162 F5
Vernon Av MNPK E12 122 C2
PEND EN3 80 D2
RYNPK SW20 200 G2
WFD IG8 102 B8
Vernon Ri FSBYW WC1X 5 P9
NTHLT UB5 114 C10
Vernon Rd BOW E3 140 E4
BUSH WD23 73 M9
CEND/HSY/T N8 119 H1
CRW RM5 104 D6
FELT TW13 174 A5
GDMY/SEVK IG3 123 J8
MORT/ESHN SW14 156 A9
SRTFD E15 141 K2
SUT SM1 221 M2
SWCM DA10 189 L2
WALTH E17 120 E3
WAN E11 121 K6
Vernon's Cl STAL AL1 38 D7
Vernon Sq FSBYW WC1X 5 P9
Vernon St WKENS W14 14 A6
Vernon Wk KWD/TDW/WH KT20 238 G7

Vernon Wy GUW GU2 249 L9
Veronica Wy NTGHL W11 8 C7
Veroan Rd BXLYHN DA7 163 P8
Verona Dr SURB KT6 199 K9
Verona Gdns GVE DA12 191 K7
Veronica Cl HARH RM3 105 K8
Veronica Rd TOOT SW17 180 C6
Veronique Gdns
  GNTH/NBYPK IG2 122 F3
Verralls WOKS/MYFD GU22 232 E3
Verran Rd BAL SW12 180 C3
Ver Rd STALW/RED AL3 38 B6
Verulam Av PUR/KEN CR8 222 D8
  WALTH E17 120 E5
Verulam Rd GFD/PVL UB6 133 P6
  STALW/RED AL3 38 A5
Verulam St FSBYW WC1X 12 A3
Verwood Dr EBAR EN4 78 A7
Verwood Rd RYLN/HDSTN HA2 94 B10
Veryan WOKN/KNAP GU21 231 M3
Veryan Cl STMC/STPC BR5 207 M4
Vespan Rd SHB W12 156 C1
Vesta Av STAL AL1 38 B9
Vesta Rd BROCKY SE4 160 B10
Vestris Rd FSTH SE23 182 C5
Vestry Rd CMBW SE5 159 M7
  RSEV TN14 247 K5
  WALTH E17 120 G3
Vestry St IS N1 6 G3
Vevers Rd REIG RH2 275 L3
Vevey St FSTH SE23 182 E5
Vexil Cl PUR RM19 166 C3
Veysey Cl HHW HP1 35 L8
Viaduct Pl BETH E2 140 A10
Viaduct Rd EFNCH N2 97 N10
  WARE SG12 26 D3
Viaduct St BETH E2 140 A5
The Viaduct SWFD E18 101 M10
Viaduct Wy WGCE AL7 23 J2
Vian Av PEND EN3 80 D1
Via Romana GVE DA12 191 L4
Vibart Gdns BRXS/STRHM SW2 180 A2
Vibia Cl STWL/WRAY TW19 173 N3
Viburnum Ct CHOB/PIR GU24 212 D9
Vicarage Av EGH TW20 172 E9
Vicarage Cl BEAC HP9 89 H7
  BRW CM14 106 D5
  ERITH DA8 164 D5
  GT/LBKH KT23 253 P1
  HHW HP1 35 M8
  HHW HP1 35 M7
  KWD/TDW/WH KT20 239 H10
  NTHLT UB5 133 N3
  POTB/CUF EN6 60 A6
  RSLP HA4 112 E5
  STAL AL1 38 B9
  WPK KT4 200 B8
Vicarage Ct EGH TW20 172 E9
Vicarage Crs BTSEA SW11 157 N7
  EGH TW20 172 E8
Vicarage Dr BARK IG11 142 F2
  BECK BR3 204 F1
  GVW DA11 189 P2
  MORT/ESHN SW14 179 P10
Vicarage Farm Rd HEST TW5 153 M7
  HSLWW TW4 153 M8
Vicarage Flds WOT/HER KT12 197 K6
Vicarage Gdns BH/WHM TN16 262 G5
  CHIG IG7 102 G4
  EHAM E6 142 C5
  EPP CM16 48 C10
  GVE DA12 191 K5
  HHS/BOV HP3 52 E2
  HORL RH6 280 A3
  IL IG1 122 G6
  KGLGY WD4 54 A5
  LHD/OX KT22 236 G8
  RPLY/SEND GU23 250 F2
  SRTFD E15 141 K1
  STA TW18 195 L3
  STWL/WRAY TW19 172 A3
Vicarage Pk WOOL/PLUM SE18 162 F4
Vicarage Rd BERK HP4 34 D2
  BXLY DA5 186 C4
  CHOB/PIR GU24 213 J6
  CRAWE RH11 285 P6
  CROY/NA CR0 203 H10
  DAGE RM10 144 C2
  E/WMO/HCT KT8 199 H1
  EGH TW20 172 E8
  EPP CM16 65 M5
  HCH RM12 125 H6
  HDN NW4 116 D4
  KUT KT1 199 J2
  LEY E10 120 G5
  MORT/ESHN SW14 177 P1
  SRTFD E15 141 L2
  STA TW18 172 G6
  SUN TW16 174 G8
  SUT SM1 221 K1
  TEDD TW11 176 F8
  TOTM N17 99 P8
  WARE SG12 26 D2
  WATW WD18 73 J8
  WFD IG8 102 B8
  WHTN TW2 176 B2
  WOKS/MYFD GU22 232 C7
  WOOL/PLUM SE18 162 F4
Vicarage Sq GRAYS RM17 167 M5
Vicarage Wk BTSEA SW11 157 N7
Vicarage Wy CFSP/GDCR SL9 110 C4
  DTCH/LGLY SL3 150 C6
  RYLN/HDSTN HA2 113 P5
  WLSDN NW10 116 A8
Vicarage Wd HLW CM20 29 J10
Vicars Bridge Cl ALP/SUD HA0 135 K4
Vicar's Cl EN EN1 79 M6
  HACK E8 140 B3
  SRTFD E15 141 M3
Vicars Hl LEW SE13 160 G10
Vicar's Moor La WCHMH N21 99 H1
Vicars Oak Rd NRWD SE19 181 M9
Vicar's Rd KTTN NW5 118 B10
Viceroy Rd VX/NE SW8 158 F7
Vickers Dr North WEY KT13 215 P5
Vickers Dr South WEY KT13 215 P7
Vickers Rd ERITH DA8 164 E4
Victor Ap HCH RM12 125 L6
Victor Cl HCH RM12 125 L6
Victor Gdns HCH RM12 125 L6
Victor Gv ALP/SUD HA0 135 K2
Victoria Av CAR SM5 202 B10
  CDH/CHF RM16 167 P1
  CRW RM5 104 C1
  E/WMO/HCT KT8 198 A3
  EHAM E6 142 A3
  FNCH N3 97 K2
  HGDN/ICK UB10 132 C2
  HSLWW TW4 175 P1
  SAND/SEL CR2 223 H8
  SURB KT6 199 J6
  WBLY HA9 135 N1
Victoria Cl CDH/CHF RM16 167 P1
  E/WMO/HCT KT8 197 P3
  EBAR EN4 77 N4
  HORL RH6 280 B4

HYS/HAR UB3 132 E8
RKW/CH/CXG WD3 91 N1
WEY KT13 196 E10
Victoria Cottages RCH/KEW TW9 155 L7
Victoria Ct WBLY HA9 135 M1
Victoria Crs IVER SL0 131 K9
  NRWD SE19 181 M8
  RBRW/HUT CM13 107 N3
  SEVS/STOTM N15 119 M3
  WIM/MER SW19 179 J10
Victoria Dock Rd CAN/RD E16 141 K8
Victoria Dr EYN DA4 210 C2
  SLN SL2 128 C1
  WIM/MER SW19 178 G3
Victoria Emb EMB EC4Y 12 B7
  TPL/STR WC2R 11 N8
  WHALL SW1A 17 M2
Victoria Gdns BH/WHM TN16 243 P1
  HEST TW5 153 M7
  NTGHL W11 8 D9
Victoria Ga HLWE CM17 47 L1
Victoria Gv KENS W8 15 J3
  NFNCH/WDSP N12 97 N6
Victoria Grove Ms NTGHL W11 8 G8
Victoria Hill Rd SWLY BR8 208 G1
Victoria La HYS/HAR UB3 152 E4
Victoria Ms KIL/WHAMP NW6 2 E6
  WAND/EARL SW18 179 M4
Victorian Gv STNW/STAM N16 119 M8
Victorian Rd STNW/STAM N16 119 M8
Victoria Park Sq BETH E2 140 B5
Victoria Pl EW KT17 220 B8
  RCHPK/HAM TW10 177 J1
Victoria Ri CLAP SW4 158 C9
Victoria Rd ACT W3 136 A7
  ADL/WDHM KT15 215 N1
  ASC SL5 192 A5
  BARK IG11 142 E1
  BERK HP4 33 P6
  BFN/LL DA15 185 J6
  BKHH IG9 102 A3
  BRW CM14 107 H5
  BUSH WD23 94 A2
  BXLYHS DA6 186 B1
  CHING E4 101 K2
  CHST BR7 184 D8
  COUL/CHIP CR5 240 C1
  CRAWW RH11 283 M7
  CSHM HP5 91 K2
  DAGE RM10 124 D10
  DART DA1 187 L1
  EBAR EN4 77 N8
  ED N9 99 N4
  ERITH DA8 164 F5
  ESH/CLAY KT10 198 A10
  GT/LBKH KT23 236 A9
  HAYES BR2 205 N4
  HARP AL5 20 A2
  HAYES BR2 206 A5
  HDN NW4 116 D4
  HORL RH6 280 B4
  KENS W8 15 J4
  KIL/WHAMP NW6 2 C7
  KUT KT1 199 J2
  MLHL NW7 96 C6
  MORT/ESHN SW14 156 A9
  MTCM CR4 179 P10
  NWDGN UB2 153 N2
  PLSTW E13 141 M4
  REDH RH1 276 H1
  ROM RM1 124 G3
  RSLP HA4 113 H7
  SEVS/STOTM N15 119 P2
  SLN SL2 129 H1
  SLN SL2 129 N10
  STA TW18 173 H6
  SURB KT6 199 J6
  SUT SM1 221 N2
  SWFD E18 121 N1
  TEDD TW11 176 F9
  TWK TW1 176 G3
  UED N18 99 N5
  UX/CGN UB8 131 M2
  WAB EN9 63 H10
  WALTH E17 101 H10
  WAN E11 121 J9
  WATN WD24 73 J4
  WDGN N22 98 D9
  WDSR SL4 148 K4
  WEA W13 134 G7
  WEY KT13 196 E10
  WLSDN NW10 136 B6
  WOKN/KNAP GU21 231 J5
Victoria Sq BCVA SW1W 16 F3
Victoria St BELV DA17 164 A4
  EGH TW20 171 P9
  SL SL1 149 L1
  SRTFD E15 141 K1
  STAL AL1 38 D6
  WCHPL E1 13 P4
  WEST SW1P 16 G4
  WESTW SW1E 16 F4
Victoria Ter DORK RH4 272 F2
  FSBYPK N4 119 H6
  RYLN/HDSTN HA2 114 D6
Victoria Vls RCH/KEW TW9 155 L9
Victoria Wy CHARL SE7 161 N4
  WEY KT13 196 E10
  WOKN/KNAP GU21 232 B3
Victor Rd PGE/AN SE20 182 C10
  RYLN/HDSTN HA2 114 B1
  TEDD TW11 176 D8
  WDSR SL4 149 H9
  WLSDN NW10 136 E5
Victors Dr HPTN TW12 175 M9
Victors Wy BAR EN5 77 N3
Victory Av MRDN SM4 201 M5
Victory Park Rd ADL/WDHM KT15 195 M10
  WALW SE17 19 H6
Victory Pl NRWD SE19 181 M9
  POP/IOD E14 13 M3
  WALW SE17 19 H6
Victory Rd BERM/RHTH SE16 160 D1
  WIM/MER SW19 178 G3
Victory Wy BERM/RHTH SE16 160 D1
  DEPT SE8 160 F8
  MTCM CR4 202 B8
Vienna Cl CLAY IG5 102 A10
Viewfield Cl KTN/HRWW/W HA3 115 K5
Viewfield Rd BFN/LL DA15 185 M4
  WAND/EARL SW18 179 J2
Viewland Rd WOOL/PLUM SE18 163 N5
Viewlands Av BH/WHM TN16 245 H6
View Rd HGT N6 118 A5
  POTB/CUF EN6 59 M8
The View ABYW SE2 163 P4
Viga Rd WCHMH N21 99 H10
Vigerons Wy CDH/CHF RM16 168 F3
Viggory La WOKN/KNAP GU21 231 N1
Vigilant Cl SYD SE26 181 P7
Vigilant Wy GVE DA12 191 M8
Vignoles Rd ROMW/RG RM7 124 B6
Vigors Cft HAT AL10 40 C5
Vigo St MYFR/PICC W1J 10 C2
Viking Gdns EHAM E6 141 P8
Viking Pl LEY E10 120 B6
Viking Rd GVW DA11 189 P6
  NWDGN UB2 133 M7
Viking Wy BELV DA17 164 D2

BRWN CM15 86 G10
Villa Cl GVE DA12 191 L5
Villacourt Rd ABYW SE2 163 K5
Village Cl CHING E4 101 H6
  WEY KT13 196 E10
Village Gdns EW KT17 220 C6
Village Green Av BH/WHM TN16 244 B5
Village Green Rd DART DA1 187 H10
Village Gv BH/WHM TN16 244 B5
Village La SLN SL2 109 J6
Village Park Cl EN EN1 79 M10
Village Rd AMSS HP7 68 E10
  DEN/HRF UB9 111 K6
  EGH TW20 194 F3
  EN EN1 79 L10
  FNCH N3 97 H10
Village Rw BELMT SM2 221 K4
The Village CHARL SE7 161 P5
Village Wy AMSS HP7 70 A6
  ASHF TW15 174 A7
  BECK BR3 204 A7
  HNHL SE24 181 L2
  PIN HA5 113 M5
  SAND/SEL CR2 223 P9
  WLSDN NW10 116 A9
Village East RYLN/HDSTN HA2 113 N5
Village Wy East RYLN/HDSTN HA2 113 N5
Villa Rd BRXN/ST SW9 159 H6
Villas Rd WOOL/PLUM SE18 162 F3
Villa St WALW SE17 19 H8
Villiers Av BRYLDS KT5 199 L5
  WHTN TW2 175 N4
Villiers Cl BRYLDS KT5 199 L4
  LEY E10 120 A5
Villiers Crs STALE/WH AL4 39 J3
Villiers Gv BELMT SM2 220 G5
Villiers Rd BECK BR3 204 C2
  CRICK NW2 136 D1
  ISLW TW7 154 D8
  KUT KT1 199 L3
  OXHEY WD19 73 M10
  SLN SL2 129 J7
  STHL UB1 133 N10
Villiers St CHCR WC2N 11 M9
  HERT/WAS SG14 25 M5
Villier St UX/CGN UB8 131 N5
Vincam Cl WHTN TW2 175 P3
Vince Av BRYLDS KT5 199 N8
  CAR SM5 221 N7
Vincent Cl BAR EN5 77 K7
  BARK/HLT IG6 102 F7
  BFN/LL DA15 185 H4
  CHERT KT16 195 H7
  CHES/WCR EN8 62 D4
  ESH/CLAY KT10 198 A10
  GT/LBKH KT23 236 A9
  HAYES BR2 205 N4
  WDR/YW UB7 152 B5
Vincent Dr DORK RH4 272 F3
  SHPTN TW17 196 F3
Vincent Gdns CRICK NW2 116 C8
Vincent La DORK RH4 272 F2
Vincent Rd ACT W3 155 P2
  ALP/SUD HA0 135 L2
  CHERT KT16 195 H7
  CHING E4 101 J7
  COB KT11 235 M2
  COUL/CHIP CR5 240 D2
  CROY/NA CR0 203 M7
  DAGW RM9 143 P2
  DORK RH4 272 F2
  HSLWW TW4 153 L9
  ISLW TW7 154 C7
  KUT KT1 199 M3
  RAIN RM13 145 K6
  SEVS/STOTM N15 119 K2
  WDGN N22 99 H10
  WOOL/PLUM SE18 162 E3
Vincent Rw HPTN TW12 176 B8
Vincents Cl BERM/RHTH SE16 160 D1
  COUL/CHIP CR5 240 A6
Vincent Sq BH/WHM TN16 225 P9
  WEST SW1P 17 H5
Vincent St CAN/RD E16 141 M7
  WEST SW1P 17 J5
Vincent Ter IS N1 6 C4
Vincenzo Cl BRKMPK AL9 40 F9
Vince St FSBYE EC1V 7 H10
Vine Av SEV TN13 247 J10
Vine Cl BRYLDS KT5 199 L6
  RGUW GU3 249 J2
  STWL/WRAY TW19 173 K1
  SUT SM1 201 M10
  WDR/YW UB7 152 B3
  WGCW AL8 23 H3
Vine Ct KTN/HRWW/W HA3 115 K4
  WCHPL E1 13 P4
Vine Court Rd SEV TN13 247 K10
Vinegar Aly WALTH E17 120 F10
Vinegar Yd STHWK SE1 19 L3
Vine Gv HLW CM20 28 G2
Vine Hl CLKNW EC1R 12 A2
Vine La HGDN/ICK UB10 132 A3
  STHWK SE1 13 K10
Vine Pl HSLW TW3 154 A8
Vineries Bank MLHL NW7 96 C2
Vineries Cl WDR/YW UB7 152 B5
The Vineries EN EN1 79 M7
  STHGT/OAK N14 78 D10
Vine Rd BARN SW13 156 C9
  E/WMO/HCT KT8 198 B4
  ORP BR6 227 J3
  SLN SL2 129 L1
  SRTFD E15 141 L2
Viners Cl WOT/HER KT12 197 K6
Vines Av FNCH N3 97 L9
Vine St CONDST W1S 11 H2
  ROMW/RG RM7 104 C10
  UX/CGN UB8 131 N3
  WCHPL E1 13 P4
Vine Street Br FARR EC1M 12 B2
Vine Street Crs TWRH EC3N 13 L7
The Vine SEV TN13 247 K10
Vineway BRW CM14 107 H2
Vine Yd STHWK SE1 18 F1
Vineyard Av MLHL NW7 97 H6
Vineyard Cl CAT SE6 182 F4
  KUT KT1 199 L3
Vineyard Gv FNCH N3 97 L9
Vineyard Hill Rd WIM/MER SW19 179 J4
Vineyard Pas RCH/KEW TW9 177 J1
Vineyard Pth MORT/ESHN SW14 156 A9
Vineyard Rd FELT TW13 175 H6
Vineyard Rw KUT KT1 199 H1
Vineyards Rd POTB/CUF EN6 60 C5
The Vineyard RCHPK/HAM TW10 177 J1
  WARE SG12 26 E1
  WGCW AL8 22 G3
Vineyard Wk CLKNW EC1R 12 A1
Viney Rd LEW SE13 160 G9
Vining St BRXS/STRHM SW2 159 H10
Vinlake Av HGDN/ICK UB10 112 A9
Vinson Cl ORP BR6 227 K8
Vintry Ms WALTH E17 120 F2
Viola Av ABYW SE2 163 L3
  EBED/NFELT TW14 175 J4
  STWL/WRAY TW19 173 P1
Viola Cl SOCK/AV RM15 147 L5
Viola Sq SHB W12 136 C9
Violet Av ENC/FH EN2 79 L4
  UX/CGN UB8 132 A7
Violet Cl CAN/RD E16 141 K6
  DEPT SE8 160 E8
  MTCM CR4 202 B8
Violet Gdns CROY/NA CR0 223 J5

Violet Hl STJWD NW8 3 J8
Violet La CROY/NA CR0 223 J2
Violet Rd BOW E3 140 G6
  LEY E10 120 F4
  SWFD E18 101 N10
Violet St BETH E2 140 A5
Violet Wy RKW/CH/CXG WD3 71 M8
Virgil Dr BROX EN10 44 E5
Virgil St STHWK SE1 17 M4
Virginia Av VW GU25 193 P5
Virginia Cl ASHTD KT21 257 J4
  CRW RM5 104 D8
  NWMAL KT3 199 P4
  STA TW18 195 M3
  WEY KT13 216 D3
Virginia Dr VW GU25 193 P4
Virginia Gdns BARK/HLT IG6 102 G10
Virginia Rd BETH E2 7 L10
  THHTH CR7 181 P8
Virginia St WAP E1W 13 P8
Viscount Cl FBAR/BDGN N11 98 B6
Viscount Dr EHAM E6 142 C7
Viscount Gdns BF/WBF KT14 215 P8
Viscount Gv YEAD UB4 133 L5
Viscount Rd STWL/WRAY TW19 173 N3
Viscount St STLK EC1Y 12 E2
Viscount Wy HTHAIR TW6 152 F10
Vista Av ENF EN3 80 C6
Vista Dr REDBR IG4 122 A1
The Vista ELTH/MOT SE9 184 A3
Vista Wy KTN/HRWW/W HA3 115 K4
Viveash Cl HYS/HAR UB3 152 G2
Vivian Av HDN NW4 116 C3
  WBLY HA9 135 M1
Vivian Cl OXHEY WD19 93 H3
Vivian Gdns OXHEY WD19 93 H2
  WBLY HA9 115 M10
Vivian Rd BOW E3 140 D4
Vivian Sq PECK SE15 160 A9
Vivian Wy EFNCH N2 117 N3
Vivienne Cl CHSGTN KT9 219 K4
Vivienne Cl CRAWW RH11 283 N4
  TWK TW1 177 J2
Vixen Dr HERT/BAY SG13 25 P5
Voce Rd WOOL/PLUM SE18 162 G6
Voewood Cl NWMAL KT3 200 C6
Vogan Cl REIG RH2 275 L3
Volante Wy GVE DA12 191 H7
Voltaire Rd CLAP SW4 158 E9
Voltaire Wy CROY/NA CR0 202 F2
Voluntary Pl WAN E11 121 M4
Vorley Rd ARCH N19 118 D7
Voss Ct STRHM/NOR SW16 180 F9
Voss St BETH E2 7 P10
Voyagers Cl THMD SE28 143 M8
Vulcan Ga ENC/FH EN2 79 H6
Vulcan Rd BROCKY SE4 160 E8
Vulcan Ter BROCKY SE4 160 E8
Vulcan Wy CROY/NA CR0 225 K6
  HOLWY N7 118 F4
Vyner Rd ACT W3 136 A9
Vyner St BETH E2 140 A4
Vyners Wy HGDN/ICK UB10 112 B10
The Vyne BXLYHN DA7 164 C9
Vyse Cl BAR EN5 76 F8

W

Wacketts CHESW EN7 61 P3
Wadding St WALW SE17 18 G6
Waddington Av COUL/CHIP CR5 241 H5
Waddington Cl COUL/CHIP CR5 241 J5
  CRAWW RH11 283 K10
  EN EN1 79 M8
Waddington Rd SRTFD E15 121 J10
  STAL AL1 38 C6
Waddington St SRTFD E15 141 J1
Waddington Wy NRWD SE19 203 K1
Waddon Cl CROY/NA CR0 203 H10
Waddon Court Rd CROY/NA CR0 223 H1
Waddon Marsh Wy CROY/NA CR0 202 G8
Waddon New Rd CROY/NA CR0 203 J10
Waddon Park Av CROY/NA CR0 223 H3
Waddon Rd CROY/NA CR0 203 J10
Waddon Wy CROY/NA CR0 223 H3
Wade Av STMC/STPC BR5 207 N7
Wade Dr SL SL1 128 F10
Wade Rd CAN/RD E16 141 P8
Wade's Gv WCHMH N21 99 H1
Wade's Hl WCHMH N21 79 H10
Wade's La TEDD TW11 176 F8
Wadesmill Rd HERT/WAS SG14 25 L2
Wadeson St BETH E2 140 A1
Wade's Pl POP/IOD E14 140 G9
The Wades HAT AL10 40 D7
The Wade WGCE AL7 23 J8
Wadeville Av CHDH RM6 123 P6
Wadeville Cl BELV DA17 164 B4
Wadham Av CHING E4 100 C3
  SHPTN TW17 196 D7
Wadham Gdns CRAWE RH10 284 D4
  HAMP NW3 3 N4
  NTHLT UB5 134 C1
Wadham Rd ABLGY WD5 54 G7
  CHING E4 100 C3
  PUT/ROE SW15 157 H10
Wadhurst Cl PGE/AN SE20 204 A2
Wadhurst Rd CHSWK W4 156 A2
  VX/NE SW8 36 A7
Wadley Cl HHNE HP2 36 A7
Wadley Rd WAN E11 121 K5
Wadsworth Cl GFD/PVL UB6 135 H4
  PEND EN3 80 C2
Wadsworth Rd GFD/PVL UB6 134 G4
Wager St BOW E3 140 G3
Waggon Cl GUW GU2 249 K9
Waghorn Rd KTN/HRWW/W HA3 115 J3
  PLSTW E13 141 P3
Waghorn St PECK SE15 159 P3
Wagner St PECK SE15 160 B6
Wagon Rd BAR EN5 77 L3
Wagon Wy RKW/CH/CXG WD3 71 M8
Wagstaff Gdns DAGW RM9 143 M9
Wagtail Cl SAND/SEL CR2 224 C6
Wagtail Wy STMC/STPC BR5 207 N4
Waid Cl DART DA1 187 N2
Waights Ct KUTN/CMB KT2 199 K1
Wain Cl POTB/CUF EN6 59 L5
Wainfleet Av CRW RM5 104 D10
Wainford Cl WIM/MER SW19 178 G4
Wainwright Gv ISLW TW7 154 C10
Wainwrights CRAWW RH11 283 H10
Waite Davies Rd LEE/GVPK SE12 183 M3
Waite St PECK SE15 159 M5
Wakefield Cl BF/WBF KT14 215 P8
Wakefield Gdns IL IG1 122 B4
  NRWD SE19 181 M10
Wakefield Rd FBAR/BDGN N11 98 E6
  GRH DA9 189 H1
  RCHPK/HAM TW10 177 J1
  SEVS/STOTM N15 119 N5
Wakefield St BMSBY WC1N 11 M1
  EHAM E6 142 A2
  UED N18 99 P6
Wakehams Green Dr CRAWE RH10 284 E1
Wakehams Hl PIN HA5 113 N1
Wakeham St IS N1 6 G2
Wakehurst Dr CRAWE RH10 283 N10
Wakehurst Rd BTSEA SW11 178 E7
Wakeling Rd HNWL W7 134 F7
Wakeling St WCHPL E1 140 D8
Wakelin Rd SRTFD E15 141 K4
Wakely Cl BH/WHM TN16 243 P4

Wakeman Rd WLSDN NW10 .... 136 F5
Wakemans Hill Av
  CDALE/KGS NW9 .... 116 A3
Wakering Rd BARK IG11 ...... 142 F2
Wakerly Cl EHAM E6 .... 142 C8
Wakley St FSBYE EC1V 6 C9
Walberswick St VX/NE SW8 .. 158 F16
Walbrook MANHO EC4N 12 C7
Walburton Rd PUR/KEN CR8 .. 222 D9
Walcorde Av WALW SE17 ..... 18 F6
Walcot Rd PEND EN3 .... 80 E6
Walcot Sq LBTH SE11 .... 18 B5
Walcott St WEST SW1P 17 H5
Waldeck Gv WNWD SE27 ..... 181 J6
Waldeck Rd CHSWK W4 ...... 155 M5
  DART DA1 .... 187 H3
  MORT/ESHN SW14 .... 155 P9
  SEVS/STOTM N15 .... 119 J1
  WEA W13 .... 134 C8
Waldegrave Av TWK TW1 ..... 176 E5
  UPMR RM14 .... 126 A7
Waldegrave Pk HARP AL5 .... 20 C2
  TWK TW1 .... 176 E7
Waldegrave Rd BMLY BR1 .... 206 B5
  CEND/HSY/T N8 .... 119 H1
  EA W5 .... 135 L9
  NRWD SE19 .... 181 N10
  TWK TW1 .... 176 E7
Waldegrove CROY/NA CR0 .... 203 N10
Waldemar Av FUL/PGN SW6 .. 157 H7
  WEA W13 .... 135 H7
Waldemar Rd WIM/MER SW19 . 179 K8
Walden Av CHST BR7 .... 184 C7
  PLMGR N13 .... 99 K5
  RAIN RM13 .... 144 E4
Walden Cl BELV DA17 .... 164 A4
Walden Gdns THHTH CR7 .... 202 G4
Waldenhurst Rd STMC/STPC BR5 .. 207 N7
Walden Pl WGCW AL8 .... 22 C3
Walden Rd CHST BR7 .... 184 C9
  EMPK RM11 .... 125 L4
  TOTM N17 .... 99 L9
  WCCW AL8 .... 22 G3
Waldens Cl STMC/STPC BR5 .. 207 N7
Waldenshaw Rd FSTH SE23 .. 182 B4
Waldens Park Rd
  WOKN/KNAP GU21 ...... 231 P9
Waldens Rd STMC/STPC BR5 . 207 P6
  WOKN/KNAP GU21 ...... 232 A3
Walden St WCHPL E1 .... 140 A8
Walden Wy BARK/HLT IG6 ... 103 H8
  EMPK RM11 .... 125 L4
  MLHL NW7 .... 96 C7
Waldo Cl CLAP SW4 .... 180 D1
Waldon Til RM18 .... 169 L3
Waldo Pl WIM/MER SW19 .... 179 P10
Waldorf Cl SAND/SEL CR2 ... 223 J5
Waldo Rd BMLY BR1 .... 205 P3
  WLSDN NW10 .... 136 F5
Waldram Crs FSTH SE23 .... 182 B4
Waldram Park Rd FSTH SE23 . 182 C4
Waldrist Wy ERITHM DA18 ... 164 A1
Waldron Gdns HAYES BR2 ... 205 J3
Waldronhyrst CROY/NA CR0 .. 223 J1
Waldron Rd RYLN/HDSTN HA2 . 114 D6
  WAND/EARL SW18 .... 179 M6
The Waldrons CROY/NA CR0 .. 223 K1
  OXTED RH8 .... 261 L7
Waldron's Yd RYLN/HDSTN HA2 .. 114 C7
Waldstock Rd THMD SE28 ... 143 K9
Waleran Cl STAN HA7 ...... 94 E7
Walerand Rd LEW SE13 ..... 161 H8
Wales Av CAR SM5 .... 222 A4
Walesbeech CRAWE RH10 ... 284 B8
Wales Farm Rd ACT W3 ..... 136 A4
Waley St WCHPL E1 .... 140 C7
Walfield Av TRDG/WHET N20 . 97 L1
Walford Rd RDKG RH5 ...... 272 G6
  STNW/STAM N16 .... 119 N9
  UX/CGN UB8 .... 131 N8
Walfords Cl HLWE CM17 .... 29 M4
Walfrey Gdns DAGW RM9 ... 143 P2
Walham Gv FUL/PGN SW6 ... 157 K6
Walham Ri WIM/MER SW19 .. 179 H3
Walham Yd FUL/PGN SW6 ... 157 K6
Walkden Rd CHST BR7 ...... 184 D7
Walker Cl DART DA1 .... 164 G9
  EBED/NFELT TW14 ...... 174 A3
  FBAR/BDGN N11 .... 98 D5
  HNWL W7 .... 134 D10
  HPTN TW12 .... 175 N9
  WOOL/PLUM SE18 .... 162 F5
Walker Rd CRAWE RH10 .... 284 C9
Walkers Cl HARP AL5 ...... 20 B4
Walkerscroft Md DUL SE21 .. 181 K4
Walker's Pl PUT/ROE SW15 . 157 H10
Walkers Rd HARP AL5 ...... 20 A4
Walkfield Dr EPSOM KT18 ... 238 E9
Walkley Rd DART DA1 ...... 187 J1
The Walks EFNCH N2 .... 117 N1
The Walk EMPK RM11 ...... 125 N7
  OXTED RH8 .... 260 F9
  POTB/CUF EN6 .... 59 K8
Walk Wood Ri BEAC HP9 .... 108 B1
Wallace Cl HGDN/ICK UB10 . 131 P4
  RGUW GU3 .... 266 G5
  SHPTN TW17 .... 196 E4
  THMD SE28 .... 143 N9
Wallace Crs CAR SM5 ...... 222 A2
Wallace Flds EW KT17 ..... 220 C8
Wallace Gdns SWCM DA10 .. 189 K2
Wallace Rd GRAYS RM17 ... 167 M3
  IS N1 .... 6 F1
Wallace Wk ADL/WDHM KT15 . 215 M1
  DTCH/LGLY SL3 .... 149 L4
Wallage La CRAWW RH11 ... 285 L7
Wallasey Crs HGDN/ICK UB10 . 112 B7
Wallbutton Rd BROCKY SE4 . 160 D8
Wallcote Av CRICK NW2 .... 116 G6
The Walled Gdn
  BRKHM/BTCW RH3 ...... 274 A1
Wall End Rd EHAM E6 ...... 142 D2
Wallenger Av GPK RM2 ..... 125 J1
Waller Dr NTHWD HA6 ...... 93 H10
Waller La CTHM CR3 .... 241 N9
Waller Rd BEAC HP9 .... 88 E4
  NWCR SE14 .... 160 C8
Wallers Cl DAGW RM9 ..... 143 P3
  WFD IG8 .... 102 C7
Waller's Hoppet LOU IG10 . 82 C6
Wallers Wy HOD EN11 ..... 26 G10
Wallflower St SHB W12 .... 136 G5
Wallgrave Rd ECT SW5 .... 14 C5
Wallhouse Rd ERITH DA8 .. 165 N4
Wallingford Av NKENS W10 . 136 G7
Wallingford Rd UX/CGN UB8 . 131 L4
Wallingford Wk STAL AL1 .. 38 G3
Wallington Cl RSLP HA4 ... 112 C4
Wallington Rd CSHM HP5 .. 50 C6
  GDMY/SEVK IG3 .... 123 J3
Wallis Cl BTSEA SW11 ..... 157 N1
  HCH RM12 .... 125 J6
  RDART DA2 .... 187 H6
Wallis Rd GFD/PVL UB6 .... 134 A8
  HOM E9 .... 140 C1
Wallorton Gdns
  MORT/ESHN SW14 ...... 156 A10
Wall St IS N1 .... 7 H2
Wallwood Rd WAN E11 .... 121 J3
Wallwood St POP/IOD E14 . 140 E7
Walmar Cl EBAR EN4 ...... 77 N5
Walmer Cl CHING E4 ...... 100 G3
  ORP BR6 .... 226 G1
  ROMW/RG RM7 .... 104 C10
Walmer Gdns HNWL W7 .... 154 F1

Walmer Rd NTGHL W11 ...... 8 A8
Walmer Ter WOOL/PLUM SE18 . 162 F3
Walmgate Rd GFD/PVL UB6 .. 134 G3
Walmington Fold
  NFNCH/WDSP N12 ...... 97 K7
Walm La CRICK NW2 .... 116 G10
Walnut Av WDR/YW UB7 .... 152 B2
Walnut Cl BARK/HLT IG6 ... 122 F2
  CAR SM5 .... 222 B3
  DEPT SE8 .... 160 E5
  EPSOM KT18 .... 238 C11
  HYS/HAR UB3 .... 132 F9
  LCOL/BKTW AL2 .... 56 A3
Walnut Ct WCCE AL7 ...... 23 H8
Walnut Dr KWD/TDW/WH KT20 . 239 H10
Walnut Gdns SRTFD E15 .... 121 K10
Walnut Gv BNSTD SM7 ..... 220 G10
  HHNE HP2 .... 35 N6
  WCHMH N21 .... 79 J9
  WGCE AL7 .... 23 H8
Walnut La CRAWW RH11 ... 283 L4
Walnut Ms BELMT SM2 .... 221 M4
Walnut Rd LEY E10 .... 120 F7
Walnut Tree Av DART DA1 .. 187 M5
  MTCM CR4 .... 201 P3
Walnut Tree Cl BARN SW13 . 156 C7
  BNSTD SM7 .... 221 H8
  CHES/WCR EN8 .... 62 C7
  CHST BR7 .... 206 F1
  GU GU1 .... 249 P10
  HOD EN11 .... 44 F5
Walnut Tree Gdns RGODL GU7 . 267 K10
Walnut Tree La BF/WBF KT14 . 215 N8
Walnut Tree Rd BCTR RM8 . 123 N7
  BTFD TW8 .... 155 K5
  ERITH DA8 .... 164 F4
  GNWCH SE10 .... 161 K4
  HEST TW5 .... 153 N5
  SHPTN TW17 .... 196 D3
Walnut Tree Wk LBTH SE11 . 18 C6
  WARE SG12 .... 26 C3
Walnut Wy AMS HP6 ...... 68 B1
  BKHH IG9 .... 102 A4
  RSLP HA4 .... 133 K1
  SWLY BR8 .... 208 E2
Walpole Av COUL/CHIP CR5 . 240 A5
  RCH/KEW TW9 .... 155 L8
Walpole Cl GRAYS RM17 ... 167 P3
  PIN HA5 .... 93 P8
  WEA W13 .... 155 H1
Walpole Crs TEDD TW11 .... 176 B8
Walpole Gdns CHSWK W4 .. 155 P4
  WHTN TW2 .... 176 D5
Walpole Pl TEDD TW11 ..... 176 E8
Walpole Rd CROY/NA CR0 .. 203 L9
  EHAM E6 .... 141 P2
  HAYES BR2 .... 206 A5
  SL SL1 .... 128 C8
  SURB KT6 .... 199 K7
  SWFD E18 .... 101 L9
  TEDD TW11 .... 176 E8
  TOTM N17 .... 99 K10
  WALTH E17 .... 120 D2
  WDSR SL4 .... 171 K3
  WHTN TW2 .... 176 D5
  WIM/MER SW19 .... 179 N9
Walpole St CHEL SW3 ..... 16 A7
Walrond Av WBLY HA9 ..... 115 K10
Walsham Cl STNW/STAM N16 . 119 P6
  THMD SE28 .... 143 N9
Walsham Rd EBED/NFELT TW14 . 175 J3
  NWCR SE14 .... 160 C8
Walsh Crs CROY/NA CR0 ... 225 K8
Walshford Wy BORE WD6 .. 75 M4
Walsingham Cl HAT AL10 .. 40 C7
Walsingham Gdns
  HOR/WEW KT19 .... 220 B1
Walsingham Pk CHST BR7 .. 206 G2
Walsingham Rd BTSEA SW11 . 180 B2
  CLPT E5 .... 119 P8
  CROY/NA CR0 .... 225 H6
  ENC/FH EN2 .... 79 L8
  MTCM CR4 .... 202 A5
  STMC/STPC BR5 .... 207 L1
  WEA W13 .... 134 F10
Walsingham Wk BELV DA17 . 164 B5
Walsingham Wy LCOL/BKTW AL2 . 57 H3
Walter's Md ASHTD KT21 ... 237 K3
Walters Rd PEND EN3 ...... 80 B9
  SNWD SE25 .... 203 M4
Walter St BETH E2 .... 140 C5
  KUTN/CMB KT2 .... 199 K1
Walters Wy FSTH SE23 ..... 182 C2
Walters Yd BMLY BR1 ..... 205 M4
Walter Ter WCHPL E1 ...... 140 C8
Walterton Rd MV/WKIL W9 . 8 D2
Walter Wk EDGW HA8 ..... 95 P7
Waltham Av CDALE/KGS NW9 . 115 M4
  GUW GU2 .... 249 N10
  HYS/HAR UB3 .... 152 D2
Waltham Cl DART DA1 ..... 187 H2
  RBRW/HUT CM13 .... 87 P10
  STMC/STPC BR5 .... 207 N8
Waltham Dr EDGW HA8 .... 95 M10
Waltham Gdns PEND EN3 .. 80 B3
Waltham Ga CHES/WCR EN8 . 62 D2
Waltham Pk WALTH E17 ... 102 B1
Waltham Rd CAR SM5 ..... 201 N8
  CTHM CR3 .... 242 A8
  NWDGN UB2 .... 153 M2
  WAB EN9 .... 63 K2
  WFD IG8 .... 102 B7
Walthamstow Av CHING E4 . 100 D7
Walthamstow Avenue
  (North Circular Road)
  CHING E4 .... 100 D6
Waltham Wy CHING E4 .... 100 E4
Waltheof Av TOTM N17 ... 99 L9
Waltheof Gdns TOTM N17 . 99 L9
Walton Av CHEAM SM3 .... 201 J10
  NWMAL KT3 .... 200 C4
  RYLN/HDSTN HA2 .... 113 N10
Walton Bridge Rd SHPTN TW17 . 196 F7
Walton Cl CRICK NW2 ..... 116 C2
  HRW HA1 .... 114 C2
  VX/NE SW8 .... 158 F6
Walton Dr HRW HA1 ...... 114 C2
  WLSDN NW10 .... 136 A1
Walton Gdns ACT W3 ..... 135 N2
  FELT TW13 .... 174 A2
  RBRW/HUT CM13 .... 87 P9
  WAB EN9 .... 62 G9
  WBLY HA9 .... 115 K7
Walton Gn CROY/NA CR0 .. 224 D9
Walton Heath CRAWE RH10 . 284 E5
Walton La SHPTN TW17 ... 196 E6
  SLN SL2 .... 128 E4
  WEY KT13 .... 196 D9
  WOT/HER KT12 .... 196 D8
Walton Pk WOT/HER KT12 . 197 L9
Walton Park La WOT/HER KT12 . 197 M9
Walton Pl CHEL SW3 ...... 16 A3
Walton Rd BUSH WD23 .... 73 L8
  CRW RM5 .... 104 A8
  EPSOM KT18 .... 237 P7
  HOD EN11 .... 44 C1
  HRW HA1 .... 114 C2
  MNPK E12 .... 122 D9
  PLSTW E13 .... 141 P4
  SCUP DA14 .... 185 L6
  SEVS/STOTM N15 .... 119 N2
  WARE SG12 .... 26 C3
  WOKN/KNAP GU21 ...... 232 D2
  WOT/HER KT12 .... 197 L5
Walton St CHEL SW3 ...... 15 P5

  ENC/FH EN2 .... 79 L5
  KWD/TDW/WH KT20 ..... 238 D10
  STAL AL1 .... 38 E5
Walton Ter WOKN/KNAP GU21 . 232 E1
Walton Wy ACT W3 .... 135 N1
  MTCM CR4 .... 202 D4
Walt Whitman Cl HNHL SE24 . 159 J10
Walverns Cl OXHEY WD19 .. 73 K10
Walworth Pl WALW SE17 ... 18 F8
Walworth Rd WALW SE17 .. 18 E5
Walwyn Av BMLY BR1 ..... 206 A3
Wambrook Cl RBRW/HUT CM13 . 107 P3
Wanborough Dr PUT/ROE SW15 . 178 E4
Wanborough Hl RGUW GU3 . 266 B3
Wanderer Dr BARK IG11 ... 143 L5
Wandle Bank CROY/NA CR0 . 202 F10
  WIM/MER SW19 .... 179 N9
Wandle Cl CRAWE RH10 ... 284 D8
Wandle Ct KWD/TDW/WH KT19 . 219 P1
Wandle Court Gdns
  CROY/NA CR0 .... 202 F10
Wandle Rd CROY/NA CR0 .. 202 F10
  MRDN SM4 .... 201 N5
  TOOT SW17 .... 179 P5
  WLGTN SM6 .... 202 C10
Wandle Side CROY/NA CR0 . 202 C10
  WLGTN SM6 .... 202 C9
Wandle Wy MTCM CR4 .... 202 A5
  WAND/EARL SW18 ...... 179 L4
Wandon Rd FUL/PGN SW6 . 157 L6
Wandsworth Br
  WAND/EARL SW18 ...... 157 N10
Wandsworth Bridge Rd
  FUL/PGN SW6 .... 157 L7
Wandsworth Common West Side
  WAND/EARL SW18 ...... 179 M1
Wandsworth High St
  WAND/EARL SW18 ...... 179 K3
Wandsworth Rd CLAP SW4 . 158 C9
  VX/NE SW8 .... 158 C9
  VX/NE SW8 .... 158 E8
Wangey Rd CHDH RM6 .... 123 N5
Wanless Rd HNHL SE24 ... 159 K9
Wanley Rd CMBW SE5 ..... 159 L10
Wanlip Rd PLSTW E13 ..... 141 N6
Wannions Cl CSHM HP5 ... 51 M6
Wannock Gdns BARK/HLT IG6 . 102 E8
Wansbeck Rd HOM E9 ..... 140 E2
Wansbury Wy SWLY BR8 ... 209 H5
Wansdown Pl FUL/PGN SW6 . 157 L6
Wansey St WALW SE17 .... 18 F6
Wansford Cl BRW CM14 ... 106 E4
Wansford Pk BORE WD6 ... 76 A8
Wansford Rd WFD IG8 .... 101 P9
Wanstead Cl BMLY BR1 ... 205 P2
Wanstead La IL IG1 ...... 122 B4
Wanstead Park Av MNPK E12 . 122 A7
Wanstead Park Rd IL IG1 . 122 B6
Wanstead Pl WAN E11 .... 121 M4
Wanstead Rd BMLY BR1 ... 205 P2
Wansunt Rd BXLY DA5 .... 186 E4
Wantage Cl CRAWE RH10 .. 284 D10
Wantage Rd LEE/GVPK SE12 . 183 L1
Wantz La RAIN RM13 ...... 145 J6
Wantz Rd DAGE RM10 .... 124 C9
Wapping Dock St WAP E1W . 140 A10
Wapping High St WAP E1W . 13 H10
Wapping Wall WAP E1W ... 140 B10
Wapseys Rd SLN SL2 ..... 109 K4
Wapshott Rd STA TW18 ... 173 H9
Warbank Cl CROY/NA CR0 . 225 K6
Warbank Crs CROY/NA CR0 . 225 K6
Warbank La KUTN/CMB KT2 . 178 C10
Warbeck Rd SHB W12 ..... 136 G10
Warberry Rd WDGN N22 .. 98 G10
Warboys Ap KUTN/CMB KT2 . 177 N9
Warboys Crs CHING E4 .... 101 H6
Warboys Rd KUTN/CMB KT2 . 177 N9
Warburton Cl KTN/HRWW/W HA3 . 94 C7
  WHTN TW2 .... 176 A4
Warburton Rd HACK E8 ... 140 A3
Warburton Ter WALTH E17 . 102 B10
Warburton Wy WOKN/KNAP GU21 . 231 H1
War Coppice Rd REDH RH1 . 259 L3
Ward Av GRAYS RM17 .... 167 N3
Ward Cl CHESW EN7 ...... 61 P3
  ERITH DA8 .... 164 E5
  IVER SL0 .... 131 J9
  SAND/SEL CR2 .... 223 M2
  WARE SG12 .... 26 B1
Wardell Cl CDALE/KGS NW9 . 96 B8
Warden Av CRW RM5 ..... 104 D6
  RYLN/HDSTN HA2 .... 113 M6
Warden Rd KTTN NW5 .... 4 D1
Wardens Gv STHWK SE1 .. 12 C10
Ward Gdns SL SL1 .... 128 D9
Ward Hatch HLW CM20 ... 29 L8
Ward La WARL CR6 .... 242 F1
Wardle St HOM E9 .... 121 H9
Wardley St WAND/EARL SW18 . 179 L3
Wardo Av FUL/PGN SW6 ... 157 H7
Wardour Ms SOHO/CST W1F . 11 H5
Wardour St SOHO/CST W1F . 11 H3
Ward Rd ARCH N19 .... 118 D9
  SRTFD E15 .... 141 J5
The Wardrobe RCH/KEW TW9 . 177 J11
Wards Hl EGH TW20 ...... 172 F9
Wards Rd GNTH/NBYPK IG2 . 122 G5
Ward St GU GU1 .... 268 A1
Wareham Cl HSLW TW3 ... 154 E10
Waremead Rd GNTH/NBYPK IG2 . 122 E3
Warenford Wy BORE WD6 . 75 M5
Warenne Hts REDH RH1 ... 275 N2
Warenne Rd LHD/OX KT22 . 236 B8
Warepoint Dr THMD SE28 . 162 G1
Ware Rd HERT/BAY SG13 .. 25 P4
  HOD EN11 .... 44 F1
  WARE SG12 .... 26 F8
Warescot Cl BRWN CM15 .. 106 G1
Warescot Rd BRWN CM15 . 106 G1
Wareside Cl WGCE AL7 ... 23 L6
Warfield Rd EBED/NFELT TW14 . 174 F3
  HPTN TW12 .... 198 A1
  WLSDN NW10 .... 136 G5
Wargrave Av SEVS/STOTM N15 . 119 N4
Wargrave Rd RYLN/HDSTN HA2 . 114 B8
Warham Rd FSBYPK N4 ... 119 H5
  KTN/HRWW/W HA3 ...... 94 E10
  RSEV TN14 .... 247 J2
  SAND/SEL CR2 .... 223 K2
Warham St CMBW SE5 .... 159 J6
Waring Cl ORP BR6 .... 227 J9
Waring Dr ORP BR6 ...... 227 J9
Waring Rd SCUP DA14 ... 185 M9
Waring St WNWD SE27 ... 181 K7
Warkworth Gdns ISLW TW7 . 154 F5
Warkworth Rd TOTM N17 . 99 H6
Warland Rd WOOL/PLUM SE18 . 162 G6
Warley Av ROMW/RG RM7 . 124 A5
  YEAD UB4 .... 133 H8
Warley Cl LEY E10 .... 121 J6
Warley Gap RBRW/HUT CM13 . 106 C3
Warley Hl RBRW/HUT CM13 . 107 H6
Warley Mt BRW CM14 .... 106 H5
Warley Rd CLAY IG5 ...... 102 D9
  ED N9 .... 100 G3
  RBRW/HUT CM13 .... 106 C10
  WFD IG8 .... 101 N8
  YEAD UB4 .... 133 H8
Warley St BETH E2 .... 140 C4
  UPMR RM14 .... 127 J5
Warlingham Rd THHTH CR7 . 203 J4
Warlock Rd MV/WKIL W9 .. 8 D1

Warlters Cl HOLWY N7 .... 118 F9
Warlters Rd HOLWY N7 ... 118 F9
Warltersville Wy HORL RH6 . 280 C6
Warmark Rd HHW HP1 .... 35 H4
Warming Cl CLPT E5 ...... 120 C8
Warmington Rd HNHL SE24 . 181 K2
Warmington St PLSTW E13 . 141 M6
Warminster Sq SNWD SE25 . 203 P2
Warminster Wy MTCM CR4 . 202 C1
Warndon St BERM/RHTH SE16 . 160 B3
Warneford Pl OXHEY WD19 . 73 M10
Warneford Rd
  KTN/HRWW/W HA3 ...... 115 J1
Warneford St HOM E9 .... 140 A3
Warne Pl BFN/LL DA15 ... 185 L2
Warner Av CHEAM SM3 ... 201 H9
Warner Cl CDALE/KGS NW9 . 116 C5
  HPTN TW12 .... 175 N8
  HYS/HAR UB3 .... 152 E6
  SL SL1 .... 128 D10
  SRTFD E15 .... 121 K10
Warner Pl BETH E2 .... 7 P8
Warner Rd BMLY BR1 ..... 183 L10
  CEND/HSY/T N8 .... 118 E2
  CMBW SE5 .... 159 K7
  WALTH E17 .... 120 D2
  WARE SG12 .... 26 C3
Warners Av HOD EN11 .... 44 E5
Warners End Rd HHW HP1 . 35 K6
Warners La KUTN/CMB KT2 . 177 K10
Warner St CLKNW EC1R ... 12 A1
Warnford Rd ORP BR6 .... 227 J2
Warnham Court Rd CAR SM5 . 222 A4
Warnham Rd CRAWE RH10 . 284 D9
  NFNCH/WDSP N12 ...... 97 N6
Warple Wy ACT W3 .... 156 B1
Warren Av BELMT SM2 ... 221 J6
  BMLY BR1 .... 183 K10
  ORP BR6 .... 227 J2
  RCHPK/HAM TW10 ...... 155 N10
  SAND/SEL CR2 .... 224 C4
  WAN E11 .... 121 J8
Warren Cl BXLYHS DA6 ... 186 B1
  DTCH/LGLY SL3 .... 150 B2
  ED N9 .... 100 C1
  ESH/CLAY KT10 .... 218 A1
  HAT AL10 .... 40 C4
  WBLY HA9 .... 115 J7
  YEAD UB4 .... 133 K7
Warren Ct BGR/WK TN15 . 265 K11
  CHIG IG7 .... 102 G5
Warren Crs ED N9 .... 99 N1
Warren Cutting KUTN/CMB KT2 . 178 A10
Warren Di WGCW AL8 .... 22 G2
  CSHM HP5 .... 51 K5
Warrender Rd ARCH N19 . 118 B9
Warrender Wy RSLP HA4 . 113 H6
Warren Dr CRAWW RH11 . 283 K6
  GFD/PVL UB6 .... 134 A6
  HCH RM12 .... 125 H8
  KWD/TDW/WH KT20 ..... 239 J6
  ORP BR6 .... 227 L2
  RSLP HA4 .... 113 L5
The Warren Dr WAN E11 . 121 P5
Warren Dr North SURB KT6 . 199 N8
Warren Dr South SURB KT6 . 199 P8
The Warren Dr WAN E11 . 121 P5
Warreners La WEY KT13 . 216 E5
Warren Fld EPP CM16 .... 65 K3
  IVER SL0 .... 130 F4
Warrenfield Cl CHESW EN7 . 61 P7
Warren Gdns ORP BR6 ... 227 K2
Warren Hl EPSOM KT18 .. 238 C12
  LOU IG10 .... 81 P9
Warren La BRWN CM15 ... 86 D5
  CDH/CHF RH4 .... 167 J3
  LHD/OX KT22 .... 218 A10
  OXTED RH8 .... 261 M10
  STAN HA7 .... 94 F3
  WOKS/MYFD GU22 ..... 233 K4
  WOOL/PLUM SE18 ...... 162 E2
Warren Lodge Dr
  KWD/TDW/WH KT20 .... 239 H10
Warren Md BNSTD SM7 .. 238 F1
Warren Ms GTPST W1W .. 10 C2
Warren Pk KUTN/CMB KT2 . 177 P9
  WARL CR6 .... 242 C4
Warren Park Rd HERT/WAS SG14 . 25 K4
  SUT SM1 .... 222 D3
Warren Pond Rd CHING E4 . 101 L1
Warren Ri NWMAL KT3 ... 200 A1
Warren Rd ADL/WDHM KT15 . 215 K6
  ASHF TW15 .... 174 F10
  BARK/HLT IG6 .... 122 C5
  BNSTD SM7 .... 238 C1
  BUSH WD23 .... 94 B2
  BXLYHS DA6 .... 186 B1
  CHING E4 .... 101 H3
  CRICK NW2 .... 116 C2
  CROY/NA CR0 .... 203 M8
  DART DA1 .... 187 N6
  GU GU1 .... 268 D1
  HAYES BR2 .... 205 M9
  HDN/ICK UB10 .... 111 P9
  KUTN/CMB KT2 .... 177 P9
  LCOL/BKTW AL2 .... 38 B10
  LEY E10 .... 121 H8
  MEO DA13 .... 189 N8
  ORP BR6 .... 227 J3
  PUR/KEN CR8 .... 223 J1
  REIG RH2 .... 257 J2
  RGODL GU7 .... 267 N3
  SCUP DA14 .... 185 M6
  WAN E11 .... 121 N1
  WHTN TW2 .... 176 C2
  WIM/MER SW19 .... 179 H3
Warren Rw ASHTD KT21 .. 237 L6
Warren St FITZ W1T 10 C2
The Warren ASHTD KT21 . 237 L6
  CAR SM5 .... 221 N6
  CFSP/GDCR SL9 .... 90 C2
  CSHM HP5 .... 50 C4
  EHSLY KT24 .... 252 D11
  GVE DA12 .... 190 G7
  HEST TW5 .... 153 N5
  HOR/WEW KT19 .... 220 A1
  KGLGY WD4 .... 54 A5
  KWD/TDW/WH KT20 .... 239 H10
  LHD/OX KT22 .... 218 B2
  RAD WD7 .... 56 F9
  YEAD UB4 .... 133 H8
Warren Wood Cl HAYES BR2 . 205 M9
Warriner Av HCH RM12 .. 125 L7
Warriner Dr ED N9 ...... 99 P4
Warriner Gdns BTSEA SW11 . 158 A7
Warrington Av SL SL1 .... 131 H8
Warrington Crs MV/WKIL W9 . 9 H1
Warrington Gdns EMPK RM11 . 125 K4
  MV/WKIL W9 .... 9 G3
Warrington Pl POP/IOD E14 . 141 H10
Warrington Rd BCTR RM8 . 123 N7
  CROY/NA CR0 .... 203 J10
  HRW HA1 .... 114 D3
  RCHPK/HAM TW10 ...... 177 J11

Warrington Sp WDSR SL4 .. 171 N3
Warrington Sq BCTR RM8 . 123 N7
Warrior Av GVE DA12 .... 190 F7
Warrior Sq MNPK E12 .... 122 D9
Warsaw Cl RSLP HA4 ..... 133 J1
Warspite Rd WOOL/PLUM SE18 . 162 E2
Warton Rd SRTFD E15 .... 141 H3
Warwall EHAM E6 .... 142 E8
Warwick Av EDGW HA8 ... 95 N4
  EGH TW20 .... 194 C1
  MV/WKIL W9 .... 9 H2
  POTB/CUF EN6 .... 60 F3
  RYLN/HDSTN HA2 ...... 113 N9
  SLN SL2 .... 129 H6
  STA TW18 .... 173 M9
Warwick Cl BUSH WD23 .. 94 D1
  BXLY DA5 .... 186 A3
  EBAR EN4 .... 77 N5
  HERT/BAY SG13 .... 25 K7
  HPTN TW12 .... 176 B3
  ORP BR6 .... 207 K10
  POTB/CUF EN6 .... 60 E3
  RDKG RH5 .... 272 G10
Warwick Ct RKW/CH/CXG WD3 . 71 J7
  SURB KT6 .... 199 K7
  YEAD UB4 .... 132 G6
Warwick Deeping CHERT KT16 . 214 F2
Warwick Dene EA W5 .... 135 K10
Warwick Dr BARN SW13 .. 156 E9
  CHES/WCR EN8 .... 62 C4
Warwick Gdns ASHTD KT21 . 237 H3
  FSBYPK N4 .... 119 K3
  GPK RM2 .... 125 K1
  IL IG1 .... 122 E6
  THDIT KT7 .... 198 B5
  WKENS W14 .... 14 D5
Warwick Gv BRYLDS KT5 . 199 L7
  CLPT E5 .... 120 A6
Warwick House St STJS SW1Y . 11 K9
Warwick La RAIN RM13 .. 145 N4
  STP EC4M 12 D5
  WOKN/KNAP GU21 ...... 231 M5
Warwick Pl BRW CM14 ... 86 B5
  EA W5 .... 155 J1
  CVW DA11 .... 189 N1
  MV/WKIL W9 .... 9 J3
  UX/CGN UB8 .... 131 M2
Warwick Pl North PIM SW1V . 16 G5
Warwick Rd ASHF TW15 .. 173 P8
  BAR EN5 .... 77 L8
  BEAC HP9 .... 88 C8
  BORE WD6 .... 76 A7
  CHING E4 .... 100 F6
  COUL/CHIP CR5 .... 222 D11
  EA W5 .... 135 K10
  FBAR/BDGN N11 .... 98 F3
  FSTGT E7 .... 141 L1
  HSLWW TW4 .... 153 J9
  KUT KT1 .... 199 H1
  MNPK E12 .... 122 B10
  NWDGN UB2 .... 153 N2
  NWMAL KT3 .... 199 P3
  PEND EN3 .... 80 E3
  PGE/AN SE20 .... 204 A3
  RAIN RM13 .... 145 K6
  REDH RH1 .... 258 A9
  SCUP DA14 .... 185 L8
  STAL AL1 .... 38 E4
  SUT SM1 .... 221 M2
  THDIT KT7 .... 198 B5
  THHTH CR7 .... 203 H3
  UED N18 .... 99 M5
  WALTH E17 .... 100 E9
  WAN E11 .... 121 N3
  WDR/YW UB7 .... 131 P10
  WELL DA16 .... 165 M9
  WHTN TW2 .... 176 D4
  WKENS W14 .... 14 D6
Warwick Rw WESTW SW1E . 16 G3
Warwicks Bench GU GU1 . 268 B3
Warwicks Bench La GU GU1 . 268 B3
Warwick Sq PIM SW1V ... 16 G7
  STP EC4M 12 D5
Warwick Square Ms PIM SW1V . 16 G6
Warwick St REGST W1B .. 11 H7
Warwick Ter WOOL/PLUM SE18 . 162 G5
  WALTH E17 .... 101 N1
Warwick Wy PIM SW1V ... 16 F6
  RKW/CH/CXG WD3 ...... 72 D8
Warwick Wold Rd REDH RH1 . 259 H5
Warwick Yd STLK EC1Y ... 12 F2
Washington Av HHNE HP2 . 35 P1
  MNPK E12 .... 122 B7
Washington Cl BOW E3 .. 140 C5
  REIG RH2 .... 257 K8
Washington Dr SL SL1 ... 128 C9
  WDSR SL4 .... 148 D9
Washington Rd BARN SW13 . 156 D6
  CRAWW RH11 .... 283 H10
  EHAM E6 .... 141 P2
  KUT KT1 .... 199 M2
  SWFD E18 .... 101 L10
  WPK KT4 .... 200 F9
Wash La BAR EN5 .... 76 F1
  POTB/CUF EN6 .... 58 F9
Washneys Rd ORP BR6 ... 227 K9
Washpond La WARL CR6 .. 243 H4
The Wash HERT/WAS SG14 . 25 L5
Wasp Green La REDH RH1 . 277 P9
Wassand Cl CRAWE RH10 . 284 B7
Wastdale Rd FSTH SE23 .. 182 C4
Watchlytes WGCE AL7 ... 23 M5
Watchmead WGCE AL7 ... 23 K5
Watcombe Rd SNWD SE25 . 204 A3
Waterbank Rd CAT SE6 .. 182 C6
Waterbeach Cl SL SL1 ... 129 J8
Waterbeach Rd DAGW RM9 . 143 M1
  SL SL1 .... 129 J8
Watercress Dr RSEV TN14 . 247 K6
Watercress Wy
  WOKN/KNAP GU21 ...... 231 N5
Watercroft Rd RSEV TN14 . 228 A6
Waterdale HERT/BAY SG13 . 25 K7
Waterdale Rd ABYW SE2 . 163 K9
Waterdales GVW DA11 ... 190 A4
Waterden La STALE/WH AL4 . 21 P3
Water End Rd BERK HP4 . 34 E3
Waterer Gdns
  KWD/TDW/WH KT20 .... 239 H4
Waterer Ri WLGTN SM6 .. 222 G4
Waterers Ri WOKN/KNAP GU21 . 231 J3
Waterfall Cl VW GU25 ... 193 L3
Waterfall Cottages
  WIM/MER SW19 .... 179 N9
Waterfall Rd STHGT/OAK N14 . 98 D4
  WIM/MER SW19 .... 179 N9
Waterfall Ter TOOT SW17 . 179 P9
Waterfield KWD/TDW/WH KT20 . 238 E6
  WGCE AL7 .... 23 L4
Waterfield Cl BELV DA17 . 164 B2
  THMD SE28 .... 143 L10
Waterfield Dr WARL CR6 . 242 A5
Waterfield Gdns CRAWW RH11 . 283 H10
  SNWD SE25 .... 203 M4
Waterfield Gn
  KWD/TDW/WH KT20 .... 238 E6
Waterfields LHD/OX KT22 . 236 C5
Waterfields Wy WAT WD17 . 73 L6
Waterford Cl COB KT11 .. 217 M7
Waterford Common
  HERT/WAS SG14 .... 25 J1
Waterford Gn WGCE AL7 . 23 L5
Waterford Rd FUL/PGN SW6 . 157 L6

Water Gdns STAN HA7 94 G7
Watergate St DEPT SE8 160 F5
The Watergate OXHEY WD19 93 L3 1
Waterhall Av CHING E4 101 K5 5
Waterhall Cl WALTH E17 100 C9
Waterhead Cl ERITH DA8 164 F6
Waterhoose Moor HLWS CM18 47 H2
Waterhouse Cl HAMP NW3 117 N10
Waterhouse La
KWD/TDW/WH KT20 239 J7
PUR/KEN CR8 241 K5
REDH RH1 259 N8
Waterhouse St HHW HP1 35 M6
Wateringbury Cl STMC/STPC BR5 207 L3
Water La BERK HP4 33 P5
CHOB/PIR GU24 230 D5
COB KT11 217 N10
ED N9 100 A2
GDMY/SEVK IG3 123 J8
GT/LBKH KT23 253 M2
HHS/BOV HP3 52 E5
HLWW/ROY CM19 46 B5
KGLGY WD4 54 C5
KUT KT1 199 J1
OXTED RH8 261 M2
PECK SE15 160 B6
PUR RM19 165 P3
RCH/KEW TW9 177 J1
RDKG RH5 271 J9
RSEV TN14 228 G8
SCUP DA14 186 A6
SHGR GU5 269 L4
SRTFD E15 141 K1
TWK TW1 176 F4
WAT WD17 73 K8 12
Water Lea CRAWE RH10 284 B8
Water Lily Cl STHL UB1 154 B1 5
Waterloo Cl EBED/NFELT TW14 174 G4
Waterloo Gdns BETH E2 140 B4 9
ROMW/RG RM7 124 E4
Waterloo Pl RCH/KEW TW9 155 M5 2
STJS SW1Y 11 J9
Waterloo Rd BARK/HLT IG6 102 F10
BRW CM14 107 H2
CRICK NW2 116 D7
EHAM E6 141 P2 4
FSTGT E7 121 L10 4
HOR/WEW KT19 220 A8
LEY E10 120 F5
ROMW/RG RM7 124 E3
STHWK SE1 11 P9
SUT SM1 221 N2
UX/CGN UB8 131 M3
Waterloo St GVE DA12 190 F3 5
Waterloo Ter IS N1 6 C4
Waterlow Rd ARCH N19 118 D6
REIG RH2 275 M1
Waterman Cl OXHEY WD19 73 J10
Waterman Ct SL SL1 128 D10 7
Waterman St PUT/ROE SW15 156 G9
Watermans Wy EPP CM16 66 B3
Waterman Wy WAP E1W 140 A10 20
Watermark Wy HERT/BAY SG13 25 N5 7
Watermead EBED/NFELT TW14 174 F4
KWD/TDW/WH KT20 238 E7
WOKN/KNAP GU21 231 L2
Watermead La MTCM CR4 202 A6
Water Meadow CSHM HP5 50 G8 3
Watermeadow Cl ERITH DA8 165 J7 1
Watermeadow La
FUL/PGN SW6 157 M8 3
Watermead Rd CAT SE6 183 H7
Watermead Wy TOTM N17 100 B9
Water Ms PECK SE15 160 B10
Watermill Cl RCHPK/HAM TW10 177 H6
Watermill La HERT/WAS SG14 25 L2
UED N18 99 M6
Water Mill Wy EYN DA4 210 A2
FELT TW13 175 N5
Watermill Wy WIM/MER SW19 201 M1
Watermint Cl STMC/STPC BR5 207 N4 10
Watermint Quay CLPT E5 119 P5
Waterperry La CHOB/PIR GU24 213 L6
Water Rd ALP/SUD HA0 135 L3
Waters Dr RKW/CH/CXG WD3 91 P2 1
STA TW18 173 J7
Watersedge HOR/WEW KT19 219 P1
Watersfield Wy EDGW HA8 95 J8
Waterside CSHM HP5 51 H8
DART DA1 186 F1
HORL RH6 280 B2 3
KGLGY WD4 54 B5
LCOL/BKTW AL2 57 K3
RAD WD7 56 G10 1
UX/CGN UB8 131 M7 2
WALTH E17 120 B4
WGCE AL7 23 K3
Waterside Cl BARK IG11 123 K9
BERM/RHTH SE16 19 P2 2
CRAWW RH11 283 H9
HARH RM3 105 P8
HOM E9 140 E3
NTHLT UB5 133 N5 5
SURB KT6 199 K9 3
Waterside Ct KGLGY WD4 54 C5 1
Waterside Dr DTCH/LGLY SL3 150 C1
WOT/HER KT12 197 J5
Waterside Ms GU GU1 249 P8
Waterside Pl CAMTN NW1 4 D5 1
Waterside Rd GU GU1 250 A7
NWDGN UB2 153 P2
Waterside Wy TOOT SW17 179 M7
WOKN/KNAP GU21 231 N4
Waterslade REDH RH1 257 P10
Watersmeet HLWW/ROY CM19 46 E5
Watersmeet Cl RGUE GU4 250 D5 3
Watersmeet Wy THMD SE28 143 N8
Waterson Rd CDH/CHF RM16 168 E3
Waterson St BETH E2 7 K9
Watersplash Cl KUT KT1 199 K3 3
Water Splash La ASC SL5 192 D1
Watersplash La HEST TW5 153 J4
HYS/HAR UB3 153 H3
Watersplash Rd SHPTN TW17 196 B4
Waters Rd CAT SE6 183 K6
KUT KT1 199 N2
Waters Sq KUT KT1 199 N3
Water St TPL/STR WC2R 12 A7
Waterton Av GVE DA12 191 H3
Water Tower Cl UX/CGN UB8 111 P10
Water Tower Hl CROY/NA CR0 223 L1
Water Tower Pl IS N1 6 B6
Waterway Rd LHD/OX KT22 236 F8
Waterworks La CLPT E5 120 C7
Waterworks Rd
BRXS/STRHM SW2 180 F2
Watery La CHOB/PIR GU24 213 J6
CHONG CM5 49 L1
HAT AL10 40 B5
HYS/HAR UB3 152 E4 1
NTHLT UB5 133 K4
RYNPK SW20 201 J2
SCUP DA14 185 L9
Wates Wy BRWN CM15 107 J2
MTCM CR4 202 A6
Wateville Rd TOTM N17 99 K9
Watford Cl BTSEA SW11 157 P7
GU GU1 250 C10
Watford Field Rd WAT WD17 73 K8 13
WATW WD18 73 K9
Watford Heath OXHEY WD19 93 L1
Watford Rd BORE WD6 75 H10
CAN/RD E16 141 M7
HRW HA1 114 F7
KGLGY WD4 54 B6
LCOL/BKTW AL2 55 P3
NTHWD HA6 92 G8
RAD WD7 74 D2
RKW/CH/CXG WD3 72 E9
STAL AL1 38 A9
Watford Wy HDN NW4 116 D2
Watford Way (Barnet By-pass)
MLHL NW7 96 B5
Wathen Rd DORK RH4 272 G1
Watkin Rd WBLY HA9 115 N8
Watkinson Rd HOLWY N7 5 N1
Watling Av EDGW HA8 95 P9
Watling Cl HHNE HP2 35 P3 1
Watling Knoll RAD WD7 56 E9
Watlings Cl CROY/NA CR0 204 D6
Watling St BXLYHS DA6 164 C10
DART DA1 188 A3
GVW DA11 190 E8
LCOL/BKTW AL2 56 C1
MEO DA13 189 N6
STAL AL1 38 B9
STP EC4M 12 E6
Watlington Gv SYD SE26 182 D8 1
Watlington Rd HLWE CM17 29 N7
Watling Vw STAL AL1 38 B9
Watney Rd MORT/ESHN SW14 155 P9
Watneys Rd MTCM CR4 202 E5
Watney St WCHPL E1 140 A8 23
Watson Av CHEAM SM3 201 H9
EHAM E6 142 D2
STALW/RED AL3 38 E3
Watson Cl CRAWE RH10 284 D10
STNW/STAM N16 119 L10 4
WIM/MER SW19 179 P9 5
WTHK RM20 166 F7
Watson Rd DORK RH4 272 B3
Watson's Ms MBLAR W1H 9 P4
Watsons Rd WDGN N22 98 G9
Watson's St DEPT SE8 160 F6
Watson's Wk STAL AL1 38 D7
Wattendon Rd PUR/KEN CR8 241 J2
Wattisfield Rd CLPT E5 120 B8
Wattleton Rd BEAC HP9 88 C10
Watton Rd WARE SG12 26 B1
Watts Cl SEVS/STOTM N15 119 M3 8
Watts Crs PUR RM19 166 B3
Watts Gv BOW E3 140 F7
Watt's La CHST BR7 206 E1
KWD/TDW/WH KT20 238 G8
TEDD TW11 176 F8
Watts Lea WOKN/KNAP GU21 231 M2
Watt's Md KWD/TDW/WH KT20 238 G8
Watts Rd THDIT KT7 198 F7
Watts St WAP E1W 140 A10
Wat Tyler Rd BKHTH/KID SE3 161 H8
Wauthier Cl PLMGR N13 99 J6
Wavell Cl CHES/WCR EN8 62 D3
Wavell Dr BFN/LL DA15 185 H2
Wavell Gdns SLN SL2 128 E5
Wavell Rd BEAC HP9 88 G10
Wavel Ms KIL/WHAMP NW6 2 G4
Wavel Pl NRWD SE19 181 N7
Wavendene Av EGH TW20 172 F10
Wavendon Av CHSWK W4 156 A4
Waveney HHNE HP2 36 A1
Waveney Av PECK SE15 160 A10
Waverley Av BRYLDS KT5 199 N6
CHING E4 100 E5
PUR/KEN CR8 241 M2
SUT SM1 201 L9
WALTH E17 121 J1 5
WBLY HA9 115 L10
WHTN TW2 175 N4
Waverley Cl E/WMO/HCT KT8 197 P5
HAYES BR2 206 A5
HYS/HAR UB3 152 E3 2
Waverley Crs HARH RM3 105 K7
WOOL/PLUM SE18 162 G5
Waverley Dr CHERT KT16 194 G10
VW GU25 193 M4
Waverley Gdns BARK IG11 143 H4
BARK/HLT IG6 102 F10
CDH/CHF RM16 167 M1
EHAM E6 142 B7 6
NTHWD HA6 93 H9 2
Waverley Gv HDN NW4 116 G1
Waverley Pl FSBYPK N4 119 J6 2
LHD/OX KT22 236 G8 5
STJWD NW8 3 L7 2
Waverley Rd CEND/HSY/T N8 118 E4
COB KT11 218 A10
ENC/FH EN2 79 J8
EW KT17 220 E2
RAIN RM13 145 J5
SL SL1 129 H7
SNWD SE25 204 A4
STALW/RED AL3 38 B4
STHL UB1 133 P9 2
SWFD E18 101 P9 1
TOTM N17 100 A8
WALTH E17 121 H1
WEY KT13 216 B2
WOOL/PLUM SE18 162 F4
Waverley Wy CAR SM5 221 P3
Waverton Rd WAND/EARL SW18 179 M3
Waverton St MYFR/PICC W1J 10 D9
MYFR/PKLN W1K 10 D9
Wavertree Rd BRXS/STRHM SW2 180 G4
SWFD E18 101 M10 3
Waxlow Crs STHL UB1 133 P8
Waxlow Rd WLSDN NW10 135 P4
Waxwell La PIN HA5 93 L10
Wayborne Gv RSLP HA4 112 D4
Waycross Rd UPMR RM14 126 D4
Waye Av HEST TW5 153 H7
Wayfarer Rd NTHLT UB5 133 M5
Wayfaring Gn GRAYS RM17 167 L4 1
Wayford St BTSEA SW11 157 P8
Wayland Av HACK E8 119 P10
Waylands HYS/HAR UB3 132 E7
STWL/WRAY TW19 172 B2
SWLY BR8 208 G4
Waylands Cl RSEV TN14 245 P1
Waylett Pl ALP/SUD HA0 115 J9 3
WNWD SE27 181 J6
Wayne Cl ORP BR6 207 J10
Wayneflete Tower Av
ESH/CLAY KT10 197 P10
Waynflete Av CROY/NA CR0 203 J10 7
Waynflete Sq NKENS W10 136 G9 5
Waynflete St WAND/EARL SW18 179 M5
Wayre St HLWE CM17 29 M7
Wayside CRAWW RH11 283 H9
CRICK NW2 117 H6
KGLGY WD4 53 L6
MORT/ESHN SW14 155 P10
POTB/CUF EN6 59 N9 2
RAD WD7 57 J9
Wayside Av BUSH WD23 74 C10
HCH RM12 125 L7
Wayside Cl ROM RM1 124 G1
STHGT/OAK N14 78 D10
Wayside Ct TWK TW1 177 H2 3
Wayside Gdns CFSP/GDCR SL9 110 A5
DAGE RM10 124 B10
Wayside Gv CHST BR7 184 C7
Wayside Ms GNTH/NBYPK IG2 122 D4
The Wayside HHS/BOV HP3 36 D7
The Way REIG RH2 257 N9
Wayville Rd DART DA1 188 A3
Weald Br EPP CM16 48 F8
Weald Bridge Rd EPP CM16 48 F8
Weald Cl BERM/RHTH SE16 160 A4 2
BRW CM14 106 F4
HAYES BR2 206 B9
MEO DA13 190 B10
RGUE GU4 268 B6 5
RSEV TN14 265 J9
Weald Dr CRAWE RH10 284 B10
Weald Hall La EPP CM16 65 M1
Weald La KTN/HRWW/W HA3 94 C10
Weald Park Wy BRW CM14 106 D4
Weald Ri KTN/HRWW/W HA3 94 E8
Weald Rd BRW CM14 105 P2
HGDN/ICK UB10 132 B4
SEV TN13 265 J4
Wealdstone Rd CHEAM SM3 201 J9
The Weald CHST BR7 184 C9
Wealdway MEO DA13 190 E9
Weald Wy REDH RH1 259 M4
REIG RH2 275 M4
ROMW/RG RM7 124 C4
YEAD UB4 132 F5
Wealdwood Gdns PIN HA5 94 A7 2
Weale Rd CHING E4 101 J4
Weall Gn GSTN WD25 55 J8
Weardale Av RDART DA2 188 B5
Weardale Gdns ENC/FH EN2 79 L5
Weardale Rd LEW SE13 183 J1
Wear Pl BETH E2 140 A5 17
Wearside Rd LEW SE13 160 G10
Weasdale Ct WOKN/KNAP GU21 231 L2
Weatherall Cl ADL/WDHM KT15 215 L2
Weatherhill Cl HORL RH6 280 G4
Weatherhill Rd HORL RH6 281 H4
Weaver Cl CRAWW RH11 283 H8 15
EHAM E6 142 E9 3
Weavers Cl GVW DA11 190 D4 1
ISLW TW7 154 E10 1
Weavers La RSEV TN14 247 K7
STHWK SE1 13 K10
Weaver St WCHPL E1 13 N2
Weavers Wy CAMTN NW1 5 J5
Weaver Wk WNWD SE27 181 J7 7
Webb Cl CSHM HP5 50 G6
DTCH/LGLY SL3 150 A3
Webber Cl BORE WD6 75 J10 7
ERITH DA8 165 J6 6
Webber Rw STHWK SE1 18 B3 1
Webber St STHWK SE1 18 B1
Webb Pl WLSDN NW10 136 C5
Webb Rd BKHTH/KID SE3 161 L5
Webbscroft Rd DAGE RM10 124 C9
Webb's Rd BTSEA SW11 180 A1
YEAD UB4 133 H5
Webb St STHWK SE1 19 J4
Webster Cl COB KT11 218 A10
HCH RM12 125 L8 2
WAB EN9 63 M9 5
Webster Gdns EA W5 135 J10
Webster Rd BERM/RHTH SE16 19 P4
WAN E11 121 H8 3
Websters Cl WOKS/MYFD GU22 231 M6
Weddell Rd CRAWE RH10 284 A10
Wedderburn Rd BARK IG11 142 G3
HAMP NW3 117 N10
Wedgewood Cl EPP CM16 65 K6
NTHWD HA6 92 D7 4
Wedgewood Dr HLWE CM17 47 N2
Wedgwoods BH/WHM TN16 243 P7 1
Wedgwood Wy NRWD SE19 181 K9 1
Wedhey HLWW/ROY CM19 46 F1
Wedlake Cl EMPK RM11 125 M6 5
Wedlake St NKENS W10 8 B1 2
Wedmore Av CLAY IG5 102 D9 2
Wedmore Gdns ARCH N19 118 E8
Wedmore Rd GFD/PVL UB6 134 C5
Wedmore St ARCH N19 118 E8
Wednesbury Gdns HARH RM3 105 N8
Wednesbury Gn HARH RM3 105 N8 5
Wednesbury Rd HARH RM3 105 N8
Weech Rd KIL/WHAMP NW6 117 K9
Weedington Rd KTTN NW5 118 B10 5
Weedon Cl CFSP/GDCR SL9 89 N9
Weedon Hl AMS HP6 68 C1
Weedon La AMS HP6 68 F2
Weekes Dr SL SL1 128 G10
Weekley Sq BTSEA SW11 157 N9 11
Weigall Rd LEE/GVPK SE12 161 M10
Weighbridge Rd
ADL/WDHM KT15 215 L5
Weighhouse St MYFR/PKLN W1K 10 D7
Weighton Rd KTN/HRWW/W HA3 94 C9
PGE/AN SE20 204 A2
Weihurst Gdns SUT SM1 221 N2
Weimar St PUT/ROE SW15 157 H9
Weirbrook CRAWE RH10 284 B10
Weirdale Av TRDG/WHET N20 98 A3
Weird Wd HART DA3 211 P3
Weir Hall Av UED N18 99 L7
Weir Hall Gdns UED N18 99 L6
Weir Hall Rd UED N18 99 L6
Weir Pl STA TW18 195 H1
Weir Rd BAL SW12 180 D4
BXLY DA5 186 C3
CHERT KT16 195 L7
WIM/MER SW19 179 L6
WOT/HER KT12 197 H6
Weiss Rd PUT/ROE SW15 156 G9
Welbeck Av BFN/LL DA15 185 K4
BMLY BR1 183 M7
YEAD UB4 133 J6
Welbeck Cl BORE WD6 75 M7 4
EW KT17 220 D4
NWMAL KT3 200 C5 5
Welbeck Ri HARP AL5 20 C5
Welbeck Rd CAR SM5 201 P7 5
CAR SM5 201 P8 1
EBAR EN4 77 N10
EHAM E6 142 A5
RYLN/HDSTN HA2 114 A6
SUT SM1 201 N9
Welbeck St MHST W1U 10 D4
Welbeck Wy MHST W1U 10 E5 1
Welby St CMBW SE5 159 J7
Welch Pl PIN HA5 93 K9 1
Welclose St STALW/RED AL3 38 B6
Welcomes Rd PUR/KEN CR8 241 K1
Welden SLN SL2 129 P8 3
Weldon Cl RSLP HA4 133 J1
Weldon Dr E/WMO/HCT KT8 197 N4 7
Weldon Wy REDH RH1 258 E5
Weld Pl FBAR/BDGN N11 98 C6 5
Welfare Rd SRTFD E15 141 K2 8
Welford Cl CLPT E5 120 C8 4
Welford Pl WIM/MER SW19 179 H7
Welham Cl BRKMPK AL9 40 F10
Welham Mnr BRKMPK AL9 40 F10
Welham Rd TOOT SW17 180 B8
Welhouse Rd CAR SM5 201 P8
Welkin Gn HHNE HP2 36 D5 3
Wellacre Rd KTN/HRWW/W HA3 114 G4
Wellan Cl BFN/LL DA15 185 L1
Welland Cl DTCH/LGLY SL3 150 D5
Welland Gdns GFD/PVL UB6 134 E4
Wellands HAT AL10 40 D2 3
Wellands Cl BMLY BR1 206 C2
Welland St GNWCH SE10 161 H5 9
Well Ap BAR EN5 76 F9 2
Wellbrook Rd ORP BR6 226 D1
Well Cl RSLP HA4 113 M8
STRHM/NOR SW16 180 G7
WOKN/KNAP GU21 231 P3
Wellclose Sq WAP E1W 13 P7
WCHPL E1 13 P7
Wellclose St WAP E1W 13 P8 3
Wellcome Av DART DA1 165 M10
Well Cottage Cl WAN E11 121 P5 1
Well Cft HHW HP1 35 L5
Wellcroft Cl WGCE AL7 23 K7
Wellcroft Rd SL SL1 128 G10
WGCE AL7 23 K6
Welldon Crs HRW HA1 114 D4
Well End Rd BORE WD6 75 P3
Wellen Ri HHS/BOV HP3 35 P9
Weller Cl AMS HP6 69 K3
CRAWE RH10 284 E8
Weller Rd AMS HP6 69 K3
Wellers Cl BH/WHM TN16 262 F3
Wellers Ct CAMTN NW1 5 L8
Wellers Gv CHESW EN7 61 P4 3
Weller St STHWK SE1 18 E1
Wellesford Cl BNSTD SM7 239 J3
Wellesley EPP CM16 46 D6
Wellesley Av HMSMTH W6 156 E2 4
IVER SL0 151 J2
NTHWD HA6 92 G6
Wellesley Ct MV/WKIL W9 3 J9
Wellesley Court Rd
CROY/NA CR0 203 L9 1
Wellesley Crs POTB/CUF EN6 59 H9
WHTN TW2 176 D5
Wellesley Gv CROY/NA CR0 203 L9
Wellesley Park Ms ENC/FH EN2 79 J6 4
Wellesley Pl CAMTN NW1 5 J10 1
KTTN NW5 118 B10 6
Wellesley Rd BELMT SM2 221 M3
BRW CM14 107 H2
CHSWK W4 155 M4
CROY/NA CR0 203 K8
HRW HA1 114 D3
IL IG1 122 E7
KTTN NW5 118 B10
SL SL1 149 M1
WALTH E17 120 F4
WAN E11 121 M3
WHTN TW2 176 C6
Wellesley St WCHPL E1 140 C7 10
Wellesley Ter IS N1 6 F9
Welley Av STWL/WRAY TW19 150 B10
Welley Rd STWL/WRAY TW19 172 B1
Well Farm Rd CTHM CR3 241 P5
Well Fld HART DA3 211 L4
Wellfield Av MUSWH N10 118 C1
Wellfield Cl HAT AL10 40 D3
Wellfield Gdns CAR SM5 221 P5
Wellfield Rd HAT AL10 40 E3 5
STRHM/NOR SW16 180 F7
Wellfields LOU IG10 82 D7
Wellfit St HNHL SE24 159 J9 4
Wellgarth GFD/PVL UB6 134 G1
Well Garth WGCE AL7 23 H6
Wellgarth Rd GLDGN NW11 117 L6
Well Gv TRDG/WHET N20 97 M2
Well Hall Pde ELTH/MOT SE9 162 C10 1
Well Hall Rd ELTH/MOT SE9 162 C9
Well Hl ORP BR6 228 C3
Well Hill La ORP BR6 228 C4
Wellhouse La BAR EN5 76 F8
Wellhouse Rd BECK BR3 204 E4
BRKHM/BTCW RH3 274 A3
Welling High St WELL DA16 163 L9
Wellington Av BFN/LL DA15 185 K2
CHING E4 100 F3
ED N9 100 A4
HSLWW TW4 175 P1
PIN HA5 93 N9 2
SEVS/STOTM N15 119 P4
VW GU25 193 N6
WPK KT4 200 F10
Wellington Cl CRAWE RH10 284 F4 3
DAGE RM10 144 D2 7
NTGHL W11 8 E6
NWCR SE14 160 C7 4
OXHEY WD19 93 M4
WOT/HER KT12 196 G8
Wellington Crs NWMAL KT3 199 P3
Wellington Dr DAGE RM10 144 D2
PUR/KEN CR8 222 G6
WGCE AL7 23 M5
Wellington Gdns CHARL SE7 161 P4
HPTN TW12 176 C7
Wellington Gv GNWCH SE10 161 J6 2
Wellington Hl LOU IG10 81 N4
Wellingtonia Av ABR/ST RM4 104 F4
Wellington Pl BRW CM14 107 H6
COB KT11 217 P8
RGODL GU7 267 K10 4
STJWD NW8 3 M9
Wellington Rd ASHF TW15 173 P8
BELV DA17 164 A4
BXLY DA5 185 N2
CROY/NA CR0 203 J7 2
CTHM CR3 241 K8
DART DA1 187 K2
EA W5 155 H3
EBED/NFELT TW14 174 F1
EHAM E6 142 C3
EN EN1 79 M9
EPP CM16 66 B3
FSTGT E7 121 M10
HAYES BR2 205 P4
HPTN TW12 176 C7
KTN/HRWW/W HA3 114 D1
LCOL/BKTW AL2 57 J2
LEY E10 120 D6
PIN HA5 93 N9
STAL AL1 38 G7
STJWD NW8 3 M8
STMC/STPC BR5 207 L6
TIL RM18 168 D9
UX/CGN UB8 131 M3
WALTH E17 120 D1
WAN E11 121 M3
WAT WD17 73 J6 6
WIM/MER SW19 179 K5
WLSDN NW10 136 G5 4
Wellington Rd North
HSLWW TW4 153 N9
Wellington Rd South
HSLWW TW4 153 N10
Wellington Rw BETH E2 7 M9
Wellington Sq CHEL SW3 16 A7 2
Wellington St BARK IG11 142 F3
COVGDN WC2E 11 M7
GVE DA12 190 F3
HERT/WAS SG14 25 J4
SL SL1 149 L1
WOOL/PLUM SE18 162 D3
Wellington Ter
RYLN/HDSTN HA2 114 C6 2
Wellington Wy BOW E3 140 F5
HORL RH6 280 A2
WEY KT13 216 A6
Welling Wy ELTH/MOT SE9 162 G9
Well La BRWN CM15 86 E7
CDH/CHF RM16 147 K10
HLW CM20 46 D1
HLWW/ROY CM19 28 D10
MORT/ESHN SW14 177 P1
WOKN/KNAP GU21 231 P3
Wellmeade Dr SEV TN13 265 J3
Wellmeadow Rd HNWL W7 154 F3
LEW SE13 183 K2
Well Pth WOKN/KNAP GU21 231 P3
Well Rd BAR EN5 76 F9
HAMP NW3 117 N8
POTB/CUF EN6 59 P5
RSEV TN14 247 K3
Well-row HERT/BAY SG13 42 G3
Wells Cl CHESW EN7 61 K1
GT/LBKH KT23 236 A10
NTHLT UB5 133 K5 3
STALW/RED AL3 38 B5
WDSR SL4 148 F6
Wells Dr CDALE/KGS NW9 116 A6
Wells Gdns IL IG1 122 B5
RAIN RM13 144 G1
Wells House Rd WLSDN NW10 136 B7
Wellside Cl BAR EN5 76 F8
Wellside Gdns
MORT/ESHN SW14 155 P10 3
Wells La ASC SL5 192 A4
Wells Ms FITZ W1T 11 H4 1
Wellsmoor Gdns BMLY BR1 206 D3
Wells Park Rd SYD SE26 181 P6
Wells Pl REDH RH1 258 C6
Wellsprings Crs WBLY HA9 115 N8
Wells Ri STJWD NW8 4 A6
Wells Rd BMLY BR1 206 C2
EPSOM KT18 237 N1
HMSMTH W6 156 F1
RGUE GU4 250 F7
Wells St GTPST W1W 10 G4
Wellstead Av ED N9 100 B1
Wellstead Rd EHAM E6 142 D4
Wells Ter FSBYPK N4 119 H7 7
The Wells STHGT/OAK N14 98 E2 4
Wellstones WAT WD17 73 J8 4
Well St SRTFD E15 141 K1
Wells Wy CMBW SE5 19 H10
Wellswood Cl HHNE HP2 36 C5 2
Well Wk HAMP NW3 117 N8
Well Wy EPSOM KT18 219 M10
Wellwood Cl COUL/CHIP CR5 222 F10
Wellwood Rd GDMY/SEVK IG3 123 K6
Welsford St STHWK SE1 19 N7
Welsh Cl PLSTW E13 141 M5
Welstead Wy CHSWK W4 156 C2
Welsummer Wy CHES/WCR EN8 62 C3
Weltje Rd HMSMTH W6 156 D4
Welton Rd WOOL/PLUM SE18 163 H6
Welwyn Av EBED/NFELT TW14 174 G2 2
Welwyn Cl CRAWW RH11 283 H10
Welwyn Ct HHNE HP2 36 A2 5
Welwyn Rd HERT/WAS SG14 24 F4
Welwyn St BETH E2 140 B5 16
Welwyn Wy YEAD UB4 132 F6 2
Wembley Hill Rd WBLY HA9 115 L10
Wembley Park Dr WBLY HA9 115 L9
Wembley Rd HPTN TW12 197 P1 4
Wembley Wy WBLY HA9 135 N1
Wemborough Rd STAN HA7 94 G9
Wembury Rd HGT N6 118 C5 2
Wemyss Rd BKHTH/KID SE3 161 L8
Wendela Cl WOKS/MYFD GU22 232 C4
Wendela Ct HRW HA1 114 D8
Wendell Rd SHB W12 156 C1
Wendley Dr ADL/WDHM KT15 215 J6
Wendling Rd CAR SM5 201 N8
Wendon St BOW E3 140 E3 9
Wendover Cl HARP AL5 20 C2 4
STALE/WH AL4 39 H1
YEAD UB4 133 L6 9
Wendover Dr NWMAL KT3 200 C6
Wendover Gdns
RBRW/HUT CM13 107 N3
Wendover Pl STA TW18 172 G8 2
Wendover Rd ELTH/MOT SE9 162 A9
HAYES BR2 205 N4
SL SL1 128 A7
STA TW18 172 G8
WLSDN NW10 136 C4
Wendover Wy BUSH WD23 74 B10
HCH RM12 125 K10 8
ORP BR6 207 K6 2
WELL DA16 185 K1
Wendron Cl WOKN/KNAP GU21 231 M4 6
The Wend COUL/CHIP CR5 222 E10
Wendy Cl EN EN1 79 N10
Wendy Crs GUW GU2 249 M8
Wendy Wy ALP/SUD HA0 135 K3
Wengeo La WARE SG12 26 A1
Wenlak Cl DEN/HRF UB9 111 K8 4
Wenlock Cl CRAWW RH11 283 K9
Wenlock Gdns HDN NW4 116 D2 6
Wenlock Rd EDGW HA8 95 P7
IS N1 6 E8
Wenlock St IS N1 6 F8
Wennington Gn RAIN RM13 145 M9
Wennington Rd BOW E3 140 C4 5
RAIN RM13 145 J7
Wensley Av WFD IG8 101 M8
Wensley Cl CRW RM5 104 B6
ELTH/MOT SE9 184 C2
HARP AL5 20 C5
Wensleydale CRAWW RH11 283 M10
HHNE HP2 35 P3
Wensleydale Av CLAY IG5 102 B10
Wensleydale Gdns HPTN TW12 176 A10
Wensleydale Rd HPTN TW12 175 P10
Wensley Rd UED N18 100 A7
Wensum Wy RKW/CH/CXG WD3 91 N2
Wentbridge Pth BORE WD6 75 M4 6
Wentland Cl CAT SE6 183 J5 1
Wentland Rd CAT SE6 183 J5
Wentworth Av BORE WD6 75 L9
FNCH N3 97 K8
SLN SL2 128 F5
Wentworth Cl ASHF TW15 174 C7 3
FNCH N3 97 L8 2
GVW DA11 190 D8 2
HAYES BR2 205 M9 2
MRDN SM4 201 K7 2
ORP BR6 227 H2 2
POTB/CUF EN6 59 K7 2
RPLY/SEND GU23 233 L7
SURB KT6 199 J9
THMD SE28 143 N8 2
WAT WD17 72 G4
Wentworth Crs HYS/HAR UB3 152 E2
PECK SE15 159 P6 4
Wentworth Dr CRAWE RH10 284 E6
DART DA1 187 H3
PIN HA5 113 H3
VW GU25 193 L4
Wentworth Gdns PLMGR N13 99 J4
Wentworth Hl WBLY HA9 115 L6
Wentworth Ms BOW E3 140 D6 3
Wentworth Pk FNCH N3 97 L8 3
Wentworth Pl CDH/CHF RM16 168 A2 1
STAN HA7 94 G7 2
Wentworth Rd BAR EN5 76 G6
CROY/NA CR0 203 H7
GLDGN NW11 117 J4
HERT/BAY SG13 25 K8
MNPK E12 122 A9 4
NWDGN UB2 153 K3
Wentworth St WCHPL E1 13 L5
Wentworth Wy PIN HA5 113 L2
RAIN RM13 145 J5
SAND/SEL CR2 241 P1
Wenvoe Av BXLYHN DA7 164 C8
Wernbrook St WOOL/PLUM SE18 162 F5
Werndee Rd SNWD SE25 203 P4
Werneth Hall Rd CLAY IG5 122 C1
Werrington St CAMTN NW1 5 H8
Werter Rd PUT/ROE SW15 157 H10
Wescott Wy UX/CGN UB8 131 M4
Wesleyan Pl KTTN NW5 118 C9 6
Wesley Av CAN/RD E16 141 M10
HSLW TW3 153 M8
WLSDN NW10 136 A5
Wesley Cl CHESW EN7 61 K4
CRAWW RH11 283 H10
HOLWY N7 118 G7 4
HORL RH6 280 B2
REIG RH2 275 J1
RYLN/HDSTN HA2 114 B7
STMC/STPC BR5 207 M3
Wesley Dr EGH TW20 172 D9
Wesley Hl CSHM HP5 50 G6 4
Wesley Rd EFNCH N2 97 P10
HYS/HAR UB3 133 H9
LEY E10 121 H5
WLSDN NW10 135 P3
Wesley St CAVSQ/HST W1G 10 D4 4
Wessels KWD/TDW/WH KT20 238 G7
Wessex Av WIM/MER SW19 201 K2
Wessex Cl GDMY/SEVK IG3 123 H4

KUT KT1 199 N1 2
Wessex Dr ERITH DA8 164 F8
PIN HA5 93 M8
Wessex Gdns CRICK NW2 117 H6
Wessex La GFD/PVL UB6 134 C4
Wessex Rd HTHAIR TW6 151 M10
Wessex St BETH E2 140 B5 17
Wessex Wy GLDGN NW11 117 H5
Westacott YEAD UB4 132 F7
West Acres AMSS HP7 69 J6
Westacres ESH/CLAY KT10 217 N4 1
Westall Cl HERT/WAS SG14 25 K6
Westall Rd LOU IG10 82 E7
Westanley Av AMSS HP7 69 J5
West Ap STMC/STPC BR5 206 F5
West Arbour St WCHPL E1 140 C8
West Av CRAWE RH10 284 A5
FNCH N3 97 K7
HDN NW4 116 G3
HYS/HAR UB3 132 G9
LCOL/BKTW AL2 56 A1
PIN HA5 113 N5
REDH RH1 276 A6
STHL UB1 133 N9
WALTH E17 120 G3
WLGTN SM6 222 F2
WOT/HER KT12 216 F6
West Avenue Rd WALTH E17 120 F2
West Bank BARK IG11 142 E3
DORK RH4 272 E3
ENC/FH EN2 79 K7
STNW/STAM N16 119 M5
Westbank Rd HPTN TW12 176 B9
West Barnes La NWMAL KT3 200 D5
RYNPK SW20 200 E3
Westbeech Rd WDGN N22 119 H1
Westbere Dr STAN HA7 95 J6
Westbere Rd CRICK NW2 117 H9
Westbourne Av ACT W3 136 A8
CHEAM SM3 201 H9 2
Westbourne Cl YEAD UB4 133 K6 1
Westbourne Crs BAY/PAD W2 9 L7
Westbourne Dr BRW CM14 106 E5
FSTH SE23 182 C4
Westbourne Gdns BAY/PAD W2 8 G5 1
Westbourne Gv BAY/PAD W2 8 F6
NTGHL W11 8 C7
Westbourne Grove Ms
NTGHL W11 8 E6 2
Westbourne Grove Ter
BAY/PAD W2 8 G5
Westbourne Park Rd BAY/PAD W2 8 F5
NTGHL W11 8 C5
Westbourne Park Vls BAY/PAD W2 8 F4
Westbourne Pl ED N9 100 A4 1
Westbourne Rd BXLYHN DA7 163 N6
CROY/NA CR0 203 N6
FELT TW13 174 G6
HOLWY N7 5 P1
STA TW18 173 L10 1
SYD SE26 182 C9
UX/CGN UB8 132 C6
Westbourne St BAY/PAD W2 9 L7
Westbourne Ter BAY/PAD W2 9 J4
Westbourne Terrace Rd
BAY/PAD W2 9 J4
Westbridge Cl SHB W12 136 D10 2
Westbridge Rd BTSEA SW11 157 N7
Westbrook Av HPTN TW12 175 N10
Westbrook Cl EBAR EN4 77 N7
Westbrook Crs EBAR EN4 77 N7
Westbrook Dr STMC/STPC BR5 207 N8
Westbrooke Crs WELL DA16 163 M9
Westbrooke Rd BFN/LL DA15 184 G5
WELL DA16 163 M9
Westbrook Rd BKHTH/KID SE3 161 N7
HEST TW5 153 N6
STA TW18 173 J8 7
THHTH CR7 203 L1
West Burrowfield WGCE AL7 22 G7 1
Westbury CHES/WCR EN8 62 C6 2
Westbury Av ALP/SUD HA0 135 K2
ESH/CLAY KT10 218 E3 3
STHL UB1 133 P6
WDGN N22 99 J10
Westbury Cl CTHM CR3 241 N4 1
RSLP HA4 113 H5
SHPTN TW17 196 C6 5
Westbury Dr BRW CM14 106 G4
Westbury Gv FNCH N3 97 K7
Westbury La BKHH IG9 101 P3
Westbury Lodge Cl PIN HA5 113 L1
Westbury Pl BTFD TW8 155 J5 9
Westbury Ri HLWE CM17 47 N2
Westbury Rd ALP/SUD HA0 135 K2
BARK IG11 142 G3
BECK BR3 204 D3
BKHH IG9 101 P2
BMLY BR1 206 A1
BRW CM14 107 H3
CROY/NA CR0 203 L6
EA W5 135 K8
FBAR/BDGN N11 98 F7
FELT TW13 175 L4
FSTGT E7 121 N10
NFNCH/WDSP N12 97 K7
NTHWD HA6 92 F5
NWMAL KT3 200 A4
PGE/AN SE20 204 C1
WALTH E17 120 F2
WATW WD18 73 J9 4
Westbury Ter BH/WHM TN16 262 F2
FSTGT E7 141 N1 2
UPMR RM14 126 D7
Westbush Cl HOD EN11 26 E10
Westcar La WOT/HER KT12 217 J3
West Carriage Dr BAY/PAD W2 9 M8
West Central St NOXST/BSQ WC1A 11 L5
West Chantry RYLN/HDSTN HA2 94 A9 1
Westchester Dr HDN NW4 116 G1
West Cl ASHF TW15 173 P7
BAR EN5 76 E9
EBAR EN4 78 B8
ED N9 99 N4
GFD/PVL UB6 134 B4 3
HOD EN11 44 F1
RAIN RM13 145 J6
WBLY HA9 115 L6
Westcombe Av CROY/NA CR0 202 F6
Westcombe Dr BAR EN5 77 K9
Westcombe Hl BKHTH/KID SE3 161 M5
Westcombe Park Rd
BKHTH/KID SE3 161 M6
West Common CFSP/GDCR SL9 110 A3 1
HARP AL5 20 A5
West Common Cl HARP AL5 20 A6 1
West Common Gv HARP AL5 20 A5
West Common Rd HAYES BR2 205 M9
UX/CGN UB8 111 N10
Westcoombe Av RYNPK SW20 200 C1
Westcote Ri RSLP HA4 112 D5
Westcote Rd STRHM/NOR SW16 180 D8
Westcott WGCE AL7 23 N4
Westcott Av GVW DA11 190 D6
Westcott Cl BMLY BR1 206 B5 2
CROY/NA CR0 224 C5 2
SEVS/STOTM N15 119 N4 5
Westcott Crs HNWL W7 134 D7
Westcott Rd DORK RH4 272 E2
WALW SE17 18 D9
Westcott St DORK RH4 272 A3
Westcott Wy BELMT SM2 220 F6
West Ct ALP/SUD HA0 115 H7
West Crs WDSR SL4 148 E8
West Crescent Rd GVE DA12 190 E2
Westcroft SLN SL2 128 G6 4
Westcroft Cl CRICK NW2 117 H9
PEND EN3 80 B4 2
Westcroft Ct BROX EN10 44 F5 3
Westcroft Gdns MRDN SM4 201 J3
Westcroft Rd CAR SM5 222 B1
Westcroft Sq HMSMTH W6 156 D3 5
Westcroft Wy CRICK NW2 117 H9
West Cromwell Rd WKENS W14 14 D7
West Cross Route SHB W12 136 G9
West Cross Wy BTFD TW8 154 G5
Westdale Rd WOOL/PLUM SE18 162 E5
Westdean Av LEE/GVPK SE12 183 N4
Westdean Cl WAND/EARL SW18 179 L2 3
Westdean La CSHM HP5 50 B4
West Dene Dr HARH RM3 105 L6
Westdene Wy WEY KT13 196 F10
West Down GT/LBKH KT23 254 A3
Westdown Rd CAT SE6 182 F3
SRTFD E15 121 H9
West Drayton Park Av
WDR/YW UB7 151 P2
West Drayton Rd UX/CGN UB8 132 D7
UX/CGN UB8 132 D7
West Dr ADL/WDHM KT15 215 L6 3
ASC SL5 193 J5
BELMT SM2 220 G5
CAR SM5 221 N6
GSTN WD25 73 J2
KTN/HRWW/W HA3 94 C7
KWD/TDW/WH KT20 238 G4
TOOT SW17 180 C7
VW GU25 193 J6
West Drive Gdns
KTN/HRWW/W HA3 94 C7
West Eaton Pl KTBR SW1X 16 C5
West Eaton Place Ms KTBR SW1X 16 C5 3
Wested La SWLY BR8 209 H7
West Ella Rd WLSDN NW10 136 B2
West End BGR/WK TN15 247 N3
BH/WHM TN16 263 L1
West End Av LEY E10 121 H3
PIN HA5 113 L2
West End Gdns ESH/CLAY KT10 217 N2
NTHLT UB5 133 K4
West End La BAR EN5 76 G8
BRKMPK AL9 41 M4
ESH/CLAY KT10 217 N4
HYS/HAR UB3 152 D6
KIL/WHAMP NW6 2 F6
KIL/WHAMP NW6 117 K10 7
PIN HA5 113 L1
SLN SL2 129 K3
West End Rd BROX EN10 43 N9
NTHLT UB5 133 K2
RSLP HA4 113 J10 2
STHL UB1 133 M10
Westerdale HHNE HP2 35 P3
Westerdale Rd GNWCH SE10 161 M4 2
Westerfield Rd
SEVS/STOTM N15 119 N3 10
Westerfolds Cl
WOKS/MYFD GU22 232 F3
Westergate Rd ABYW SE2 163 P5
Westerham Av UED N18 99 L4
Westerham Cl ADL/WDHM KT15 215 M3
BELMT SM2 221 K6 5
Westerham Dr BFN/LL DA15 185 M2
Westerham Hl BH/WHM TN16 244 E8
Westerham Rd BH/WHM TN16 263 K1
HAYES BR2 226 A3
LEY E10 120 G4
OXTED RH8 261 M5
RSEV TN14 246 B9
SEV TN13 246 D9
Westerley Crs SYD SE26 182 E8 2
Westermain ADL/WDHM KT15 215 M6 1
Western Av ACT W3 135 P6
BRW CM14 107 H2
CHERT KT16 195 K3
CHOB/PIR GU24 230 F7
DAGE RM10 144 D1
DEN/HRF UB9 111 M9
EA W5 135 K5
EGH TW20 194 E3
EPP CM16 65 J8
GFD/PVL UB6 134 E5
GLDGN NW11 116 G4
GPK RM2 105 K10
HGDN/ICK UB10 132 C1
RSLP HA4 133 J2
Western Ct FNCH N3 97 K7 3
Western Cross Cl GRH DA9 189 H2
Western Dr SHPTN TW17 196 E5
Western Gdns ACT W3 135 M9
Western Gtwy CAN/RD E16 141 N9 2
Western La BAL SW12 180 B3
Western Ms MV/WKIL W9 8 D2
Western Pde BAR EN5 77 K9
Western Perimeter Rd
STWL/WRAY TW19 151 L10
Western Rd BRW CM14 107 H3
BRXN/ST SW9 159 H9
EA W5 135 J9
EFNCH N2 118 A1
MTCM CR4 201 P1
NWDGN UB2 153 K3
PLSTW E13 141 N3
ROM RM1 124 G3
SUT SM1 221 K2
WAB EN9 45 K8
WALTH E17 121 H3
WDGN N22 98 G10 3
WLSDN NW10 135 P6
Western Vw HYS/HAR UB3 152 G1 2
Westernville Gdns
GNTH/NBYPK IG2 122 F5
Western Wy BAR EN5 77 K10
THMD SE28 163 J1
West Farm Av ASHTD KT21 237 H4
West Farm Cl ASHTD KT21 237 H5
West Farm Dr ASHTD KT21 237 J5
Westfield AMS HP6 68 B1
BRKMPK AL9 41 K9
HLWS CM18 47 H2
REIG RH2 257 L7
SEV TN13 247 K8
SHGR GU5 270 F9
WGCE AL7 23 K4
Westfield Av SAND/SEL CR2 223 L9
WATN WD24 73 L4
WOKS/MYFD GU22 232 B7
Westfield Cl CDALE/KGS NW9 115 P1
CHES/WCR EN8 62 E7
GVE DA12 190 F9
PEND EN3 80 D7
SUT SM1 221 J1 5
Westfield Common
WOKS/MYFD GU22 232 B8
Westfield Ct STALE/WH AL4 39 J3 4
Westfield Dr GT/LBKH KT23 236 A8
KTN/HRWW/W HA3 115 J3
Westfield Gdns
KTN/HRWW/W HA3 115 J2
Westfield Gv WOKS/MYFD GU22 232 B6 1
Westfield La KTN/HRWW/W HA3 115 J2
Westfield Pk PIN HA5 93 N8
Westfield Park Dr WFD IG8 102 B7
Westfield Rd BEAC HP9 88 B10
BECK BR3 204 E2
BERK HP4 33 K3
BXLYHN DA7 164 D9
CRAWW RH11 283 L7
CROY/NA CR0 203 J9
DAGW RM9 123 P9
GU GU1 250 B6
HERT/WAS SG14 25 K3
HOD EN11 44 E2
MLHL NW7 96 A4
MTCM CR4 201 P2
SLN SL2 128 G6
SURB KT6 199 J5
SUT SM1 221 J1
WEA W13 154 G1
WOKS/MYFD GU22 232 A9
WOT/HER KT12 197 M7
Westfields BARN SW13 156 C9
STALW/RED AL3 37 P8
Westfields Av BARN SW13 156 B9
Westfields Rd ACT W3 135 N7
Westfield St WOOL/PLUM SE18 162 A2
Westfield Wy RSLP HA4 112 F8
WCHPL E1 140 D5
WOKS/MYFD GU22 232 B8
West Flexford La RGUW GU3 266 D1
West Gdns EW KT17 220 B6
WAP E1W 140 A9 8
WIM/MER SW19 179 P9
West Ga EA W5 135 K5
HLW CM20 46 F1
Westgate Crs SL SL1 128 E9
Westgate Rd BECK BR3 205 H1
DART DA1 187 L2
SNWD SE25 204 A4
Westgate St HACK E8 140 A3 12
Westgate Ter WBPTN SW10 15 H8
Westglade Ct
KTN/HRWW/W HA3 115 J3 1
West Green Dr CRAWW RH11 283 M7
West Green Pl GFD/PVL UB6 134 C3 3
West Green Rd SEVS/STOTM N15 119 L2
West Gv GNWCH SE10 161 H7
WFD IG8 101 P7
WOT/HER KT12 217 J1
Westgrove La GNWCH SE10 161 H7
West Halkin St KTBR SW1X 16 C3
West Hallowes ELTH/MOT SE9 184 A4
Westhall Pk WARL CR6 242 B5
West Hall Rd RCH/KEW TW9 155 N7
Westhall Rd WARL CR6 241 P4
West Ham La SRTFD E15 141 J2 8
West Hampstead Ms
KIL/WHAMP NW6 2 G2
West Harding St
FLST/FETLN EC4A 12 B5 9
Westharold SWLY BR8 208 E3 1
West Hatch Mnr RSLP HA4 112 G6
Westhay Gdns MORT/ESHN SW14 177 N1
West Heath CHOB/PIR GU24 230 C9 1
West Heath Av GLDGN NW11 117 K6
West Heath Cl DART DA1 186 G2 1
HAMP NW3 117 K8
West Heath Dr GLDGN NW11 117 K6
West Heath Gdns HAMP NW3 117 K7
West Heath La SEV TN13 265 J4
West Heath Rd BXLYHN DA7 163 N5
DART DA1 186 G2
HAMP NW3 117 K8
West Hl DART DA1 187 L2
HGT N6 118 B6
HOR/WEW KT19 219 P9
ORP BR6 226 C8
OXTED RH8 261 J6
PUT/ROE SW15 178 G3
RYLN/HDSTN HA2 114 D7
SAND/SEL CR2 223 M5
WAND/EARL SW18 179 K1
WBLY HA9 115 L6
West Hill Av HOR/WEW KT19 219 P8
West Hill Bank OXTED RH8 261 J6
West Hill Cl CHOB/PIR GU24 230 G6
Westhill Cl GVE DA12 190 E4
West Hill Dr DART DA1 187 K2
Westhill Pk HGT N6 118 A7
West Hill Ri DART DA1 187 L2
West Hill Rd HOD EN11 44 E1
WAND/EARL SW18 179 J2
WOKS/MYFD GU22 232 A5
West Hill Wy TRDG/WHET N20 97 L2
Westholm GLDGN NW11 117 L2 4
West Holme ERITH DA8 164 D7
Westholme ORP BR6 207 H7
Westholme Gdns RSLP HA4 113 H6
Westhorne Av ELTH/MOT SE9 183 P2
Westhorpe Gdns HDN NW4 116 F1
Westhorpe Rd PUT/ROE SW15 156 F9
West House Cl WIM/MER SW19 179 H4
Westhumble St RDKG RH5 254 G7
Westhurst Dr CHST BR7 184 E8
West Hyde La CFSP/GDCR SL9 90 C8
West India Av POP/IOD E14 140 F10
West India Dock Rd
POP/IOD E14 140 E8
West Kent Av GVW DA11 189 P2
Westlake Cl PLMGR N13 99 H4 1
YEAD UB4 133 M6
Westland Av EMPK RM11 125 M6
Westland Cl STWL/WRAY TW19 173 P2 5
Westland Dr BRKMPK AL9 59 H3
HAYES BR2 205 L9
Westland Pl FSBYE EC1V 6 G10
Westland Rd WAT WD17 73 J6 7
Westlands Av SL SL1 128 B8
Westlands Cl HYS/HAR UB3 153 H3 2
SL SL1 128 B8 4
Westlands Ct EPSOM KT18 237 P1
Westlands Ter BAL SW12 180 D2 5
Westlands Wy OXTED RH8 261 J3
Westland Vw CDH/CHF RM16 147 M10 5
West La BERM/RHTH SE16 160 A1
RDKG RH5 271 L5
Westlea Av GSTN WD25 73 M3
Westlea Cl BROX EN10 44 E10 3
Westlea Rd BROX EN10 44 E9
HNWL W7 154 F2 1
Westleas HORL RH6 279 P2
Westlees Cl RDKG RH5 273 H5
Westleigh Av COUL/CHIP CR5 240 B2
PUT/ROE SW15 178 F1
Westleigh Dr BMLY BR1 206 B2
Westleigh Gdns EDGW HA8 95 M9
West Links ALP/SUD HA0 135 J5
Westlinton Cl MLHL NW7 97 H7
West Lodge Av ACT W3 135 M10
Westlyn Cl RAIN RM13 145 K6 4
Westly Wd WGCE AL7 23 K4
Westmacott Dr
EBED/NFELT TW14 175 H4 6
West Ml KENS W8 8 F9 6
West Malling Wy HCH RM12 125 J10
West Md HOR/WEW KT19 220 B3
Westmead PUT/ROE SW15 178 E3
West Md RSLP HA4 113 K9
Westmead WDSR SL4 148 G9
West Md WGCE AL7 23 L8
Westmead WOKN/KNAP GU21 231 N4
Westmead Dr REDH RH1 276 B8
Westmeade Cl CHESW EN7 62 A5
Westmead Rd SUT SM1 221 N1
West Meads GUW GU2 267 L1
Westmede BARK/HLT IG6 102 F7
Westmere Dr MLHL NW7 96 A4
West Ms PIM SW1V 16 F6
Westminster Av THHTH CR7 203 J2
Westminster Br WEST SW1P 17 M2
Westminster Bridge Rd
STHWK SE1 17 N2
Westminster Cl
EBED/NFELT TW14 175 H4
TEDD TW11 176 F8 5
Westminster Ct STALW/RED AL3 38 B8 1
Westminster Dr PLMGR N13 98 F6
Westminster Gdns BARK IG11 143 H4
BARK/HLT IG6 102 G10
CHING E4 101 K2
Westminster Rd CRAWE RH10 284 D8
ED N9 100 A2
HNWL W7 134 D10
SUT SM1 201 N9
Westmoat Cl BECK BR3 183 H10 1
Westmont Rd ESH/CLAY KT10 198 D9
Westmoor Gdns PEND EN3 80 C6
Westmoor Rd PEND EN3 80 C6
Westmoor St CHARL SE7 162 A3
Westmoreland Av EMPK RM11 125 K3 2
WELL DA16 163 H9
Westmoreland Dr BELMT SM2 221 L4 7
Westmoreland Pl EA W5 135 J7 2
PIM SW1V 16 F8
Westmoreland Rd BARN SW13 156 C7
CDALE/KGS NW9 115 L2
HAYES BR2 205 K5 2
WALW SE17 18 G9
Westmoreland St CAVSQ/HST W1G 10 D4
Westmoreland Ter PIM SW1V 16 F7
Westmore Rd BH/WHM TN16 243 P7
Westmorland Cl
HOR/WEW KT19 220 B5 3
MNPK E12 122 A7
TWK TW1 176 G2 11
Westmorland Rd HRW HA1 114 A3
LEY E10 120 F4 6
Westmorland Wy MTCM CR4 202 E4
Westmount Rd ELTH/MOT SE9 162 C8
West Oak BECK BR3 205 J1
Westoe Rd ED N9 100 A3
Weston Av ADL/WDHM KT15 215 K1
E/WMO/HCT KT8 197 M4
ESH/CLAY KT10 198 D7
WTHK RM20 166 E3
Weston Cl COUL/CHIP CR5 240 G6
POTB/CUF EN6 59 J8 2
RBRW/HUT CM13 107 P1
Weston Dr KTN/HRWW/W HA3 94 C9
Weston Flds SHGR GU5 269 M5
Weston Gdns ISLW TW7 154 D7 5
WOKS/MYFD GU22 233 H2
Weston Gn DAGW RM9 123 P9
THDIT KT7 198 D9
Weston Green Rd ESH/CLAY KT10 198 C8
THDIT KT7 198 D8
Weston Gv BMLY BR1 205 L1
Weston Lea EHSLY KT24 252 E1
Weston Pk CEND/HSY/T N8 118 F4
KUT KT1 199 K2 4
THDIT KT7 198 D8
Weston Park Cl THDIT KT7 198 D8 3
Weston Ri FSBYW WC1X 5 P9
Weston Rd BMLY BR1 205 L1
CHSWK W4 155 P2
DAGW RM9 123 P9
ENC/FH EN2 79 L6 2
EW KT17 220 B7
GUW GU2 249 M9
SL SL1 128 E7
THDIT KT7 198 D8
Weston St STHWK SE1 19 H2
Weston Wk HACK E8 140 A2 9
Weston Wy WOKS/MYFD GU22 233 H2
Westover Cl BELMT SM2 221 L5 7
Westover Hl HAMP NW3 117 K7
Westover Rd WAND/EARL SW18 179 M2
Westow Hl NRWD SE19 181 M9
Westow St NRWD SE19 181 M9
West Pk ELTH/MOT SE9 184 B5
West Park Av RCH/KEW TW9 155 M7
West Park Cl CHDH RM6 123 N3
HEST TW5 153 N5
West Park Hl BRW CM14 106 F4
West Park Rd CRAWE RH10 285 N2
HOR/WEW KT19 219 L8
LING RH7 281 P9
RCH/KEW TW9 155 M7
STHL UB1 134 B10
West Pl WIM/MER SW19 178 F8
West Point WDSR SL4 128 C10
Westpole Av EBAR EN4 78 C8
Westport Rd PLSTW E13 141 N6
Westport St WCHPL E1 140 C8
West Poultry Av FARR EC1M 12 C4
West Quarters SHB W12 136 D8
West Quay YEAD UB4 133 M7 5
West Quay Dr YEAD UB4 133 M7
West Rp HTHAIR TW6 152 B7
Westray HHS/BOV HP3 36 D8 5
Westridge Cl HHW HP1 35 J6 4
West Ridge Gdns GFD/PVL UB6 134 B4 4
West Riding LCOL/BKTW AL2 55 N6
West Rd BERK HP4 33 M4
CHDH RM6 123 P4
CHSGTN KT9 219 H7
CLAP SW4 180 E1
EA W5 135 K7
EBAR EN4 98 B2
EBED/NFELT TW14 174 E3
EFNCH N2 97 N10
GU GU1 268 B1
HLW CM20 29 K7
KUTN/CMB KT2 199 P1
REIG RH2 275 L1
ROMW/RG RM7 124 E5
SOCK/AV RM15 146 G5
SRTFD E15 141 L3
TOTM N17 100 A7
WDR/YW UB7 152 A2
WEY KT13 216 C5
West Rw NKENS W10 136 G6
Westrow Dr BARK IG11 143 J1
Westrow Gdns GDMY/SEVK IG3 123 J7
West Shaw HART DA3 211 J2
West Sheen V RCH/KEW TW9 155 L10
West Side BROX EN10 62 D1
Westside HDN NW4 96 E10
West Side Common
WIM/MER SW19 178 F8
West Smithfield STBT EC1A 12 D4 2
West Sq LBTH SE11 18 C4
West St BETH E2 140 A4 13
BMLY BR1 205 M1
BXLYHN DA7 164 A10
CAR SM5 202 A10
CRAWW RH11 283 N8
CROY/NA CR0 223 K1
DORK RH4 272 F2
EPSOM KT18 219 P9
ERITH DA8 164 E3
EW KT17 220 B6
GRAYS RM17 167 M5
GVW DA11 190 D2
HERT/BAY SG13 25 K6
HOR/WEW KT19 219 P9
LEY E10 120 G3 5
REIG RH2 257 J10
RYLN/HDSTN HA2 114 C6
SUT SM1 221 L2
WAN E11 121 K8 9
WARE SG12 26 C2
WAT WD17 73 J6 8
WOKN/KNAP GU21 232 C3
West Street La CAR SM5 222 A1
West Street Pl CROY/NA CR0 223 K1 6
West Temple Sheen
MORT/ESHN SW14 177 N1
West Tenter St WCHPL E1 13 M6
West Thurrock Wy WTHK RM20 166 F3
West Towers PIN HA5 113 L4
West Valley Rd HHS/BOV HP3 35 M10
West Vw CSHM HP5 51 J5
EBED/NFELT TW14 174 D4
HAT AL10 40 D2
LOU IG10 82 C7
Westview HNWL W7 134 D8
West View Av CTHM CR3 241 N4
Westview Cl NKENS W10 136 F8 6
West View Cl RAIN RM13 145 K5 3
Westview Cl REDH RH1 275 P3
WLSDN NW10 116 C10
Westview Ct BORE WD6 75 J10 3
Westview Crs ED N9 99 M1
Westview Dr WFD IG8 102 A10
West View Gdns BORE WD6 75 J10
Westview Ri HHNE HP2 35 N5
West View Rd DART DA1 187 N2
STALW/RED AL3 38 C5
SWLY BR8 208 E6 1
WARL CR6 242 A5
Westville Rd SHB W12 156 D1
THDIT KT7 198 F7
West Wk EBAR EN4 98 B2
HYS/HAR UB3 133 H10
Westward Ho GU GU1 250 C8
Westward Rd CHING E4 100 E6
Westward Wy
KTN/HRWW/W HA3 115 K4
West Warwick Pl PIM SW1V 16 G6 3
West Wy BRW CM14 106 F4
CAR SM5 221 N6
CRAWE RH10 284 B6
CROY/NA CR0 204 D9
EDGW HA8 95 P7
HARP AL5 20 B1
HEST TW5 153 N7
PIN HA5 113 L2
RKW/CH/CXG WD3 91 L2
RSLP HA4 112 G6
SHPTN TW17 196 E6
STMC/STPC BR5 206 G5
UED N18 99 L5
WAB EN9 80 G3
WLSDN NW10 116 A9
WWKM BR4 205 J6
Westway CRAWE RH10 285 H2
CTHM CR3 241 L8
GUW GU2 249 L8
RYNPK SW20 200 E4
Westway Cl RYNPK SW20 200 E3
West Way Gdns CROY/NA CR0 204 C9
Westway Gdns REDH RH1 258 B7
Westways BH/WHM TN16 262 F2
HOR/WEW KT19 220 C1
Westwell Cl STMC/STPC BR5 207 N8
Westwell Rd STRHM/NOR SW16 180 F9
Westwell Road Ap
STRHM/NOR SW16 180 F9 1
Westwick Cl HHNE HP2 36 E7
Westwick Gdns HEST TW5 153 J8
HMSMTH W6 156 G1
Westwick Pl GSTN WD25 55 K10
Westwick Rw HHNE HP2 36 E7
Westwood Av ADL/WDHM KT15 215 J8
BRW CM14 106 F5
NRWD SE19 203 K1 2
RYLN/HDSTN HA2 114 A9
Westwood Cl AMS HP6 70 A5
BMLY BR1 206 A3 2
ESH/CLAY KT10 198 B10 2
POTB/CUF EN6 59 K6
RSLP HA4 112 C4
Westwood Dr AMS HP6 70 A5
Westwood Gdns BARN SW13 156 C9 4
Westwood Hl SYD SE26 181 P8
Westwood La RGUW GU3 266 A2
WELL DA16 163 K10
Westwood Pk FSTH SE23 182 A3
Westwood Rd BARN SW13 156 C9
BFOR GU20 192 D9
CAN/RD E16 141 N10 5
COUL/CHIP CR5 240 E4
GDMY/SEVK IG3 123 J6
MEO DA13 189 K8
West Woodside BXLY DA5 185 P4 2
Wetheral Dr STAN HA7 94 G9
Wetherby Cl NTHLT UB5 134 A1
Wetherby Gdns ECT SW5 15 J6
Wetherby Ms ECT SW5 15 H7 1
Wetherby Pl ECT SW5 15 J6
Wetherby Rd BORE WD6 75 K5
ENC/FH EN2 79 K5
Wetherby Wy CHSGTN KT9 219 K4 3
Wetherden St WALTH E17 120 E5 9
Wethered Rd SL SL1 128 A8
Wetherell Rd HOM E9 140 C3
Wetherill Rd MUSWH N10 98 B9
Wetherly Cl HLWE CM17 29 M8
Wettern Cl SAND/SEL CR2 223 M6 1
Wetton Pl EGH TW20 172 C8 6
Wexfenne Gdns
WOKS/MYFD GU22 233 L2
Wexford Rd BAL SW12 180 A3
Wexham Park La DTCH/LGLY SL3 129 P6
Wexham Rd SL SL1 149 M1
SLN SL2 129 N7
Wexham St SLN SL2 129 N5
Wexham Woods DTCH/LGLY SL3 129 P7
Wey Av CHERT KT16 195 K3
Weybank RPLY/SEND GU23 233 P2
Weybarton BF/WBF KT14 216 A9
Weybourne Cl HARP AL5 20 C1
Weybourne Pl SAND/SEL CR2 223 L6
Weybourne St WAND/EARL SW18 179 M5
Weybridge Pk WEY KT13 216 C2 3
Weybridge Rd ADL/WDHM KT15 215 P1
THHTH CR7 203 H4
Weybrook Dr RGUE GU4 250 E5
Wey Cl BF/WBF KT14 215 L9
Wey Ct ADL/WDHM KT15 215 N5
HOR/WEW KT19 219 P1
Weydown Cl GUW GU2 249 L5
WIM/MER SW19 179 H4
Weydown La GUW GU2 249 M5
Weyhill Rd WCHPL E1 13 P5 3
Weylands Pk WEY KT13 216 E3
Wey La CSHM HP5 50 G8
Weylea Av RGUE GU4 250 D7
Weylond Rd BCTR RM8 124 A8
Wey Manor Rd ADL/WDHM KT15 215 N5
Weyman Rd BKHTH/KID SE3 161 P7
Weymead Cl CHERT KT16 195 M8
Weymouth Av EA W5 155 H2
MLHL NW7 96 B6
Weymouth Cl EHAM E6 142 E8 2
Weymouth Ms CAVSQ/HST W1G 10 E4 3
Weymouth Rd YEAD UB4 132 F5
Weymouth St CAVSQ/HST W1G 10 D3
HHS/BOV HP3 35 N10
Weymouth Ter BETH E2 7 M7
Weymouth Wk STAN HA7 94 F7
Wey Rd WEY KT13 196 A10
Weyside Cl BF/WBF KT14 216 A8
Weyside Gdns GU GU1 249 N8
Weyside Rd GU GU1 249 N9
Wey - South Pth GUW GU2 267 P2
RGUE GU4 268 B8
Weyview Cl GU GU1 249 P8
Wey View Ct GU GU1 267 P1 2
Whadcoat St FSBYPK N4 119 H7 8
Whalebone Av CHDH RM6 124 A4
Whalebone Gv CHDH RM6 124 A4 2
Whalebone La North CHDH RM6 123 P2
Whalebone La South BCTR RM8 124 A5
Whaley Rd POTB/CUF EN6 59 M9
Wharf Bridge Rd ISLW TW7 154 G9
Wharfdale Rd IS N1 5 M7
Wharfedale HHNE HP2 35 P3
Wharfedale Gdns
STRHM/NOR SW16 202 G4
Wharfedale Rd RDART DA2 188 B4 3
Wharfedale St WBPTN SW10 14 G8
Wharf La RKW/CH/CXG WD3 91 P1
RPLY/SEND GU23 232 F9

TWK TW1 176 F4
Wharf Pl BETH E2 7 P6
Wharf Rd BROX EN10 44 E10
BRW CM14 107 H4
GRAYS RM17 167 L5
GU GU1 249 P10
GVE DA12 191 H2
HHW HP1 35 L8
IS N1 6 E8
PEND EN3 80 D10
SRTFD E15 141 J3
STWL/WRAY TW19 171 P3
Wharfside Rd CAN/RD E16 141 K8
Wharf St CAN/RD E16 141 K7
Wharley Hook HLWS CM18 47 J4
Wharncliffe Dr STHL UB1 134 C10 1
Wharncliffe Gdns SNWD SE25 203 M2
Wharncliffe Rd SNWD SE25 203 L2
Wharton Cl WLSDN NW10 136 B1
Wharton Rd BMLY BR1 205 N1
Wharton St FSBYW WC1X 5 P10
Whateley Rd EDUL SE22 181 N1
GUW GU2 249 M5
PGE/AN SE20 182 C10
Whatley Av RYNPK SW20 200 G3
Whatman Rd FSTH SE23 182 C3
Whatmore Cl STWL/WRAY TW19 173 K2 1
Wheastone Rd NKENS W10 8 B3 2
Wheatash Rd ADL/WDHM KT15 195 L9
Wheatbarn WGCE AL7 23 L4 5
The Wheatbutts WDSR SL4 148 E3 2
Wheat Cl STALE/WH AL4 38 F2
Wheatfield HAT AL10 40 E3 5
HHNE HP2 35 N4
Wheatfields HLWE CM17 29 N5 1
PEND EN3 80 D5
Wheatfield Wy HORL RH6 280 C3
KUT KT1 199 K3
Wheathampstead Rd HARP AL5 20 C3
Wheathill Rd PGE/AN SE20 204 A2
Wheat Knoll PUR/KEN CR8 241 K2
Wheatlands HEST TW5 153 P5
Wheatlands Rd DTCH/LGLY SL3 149 N2
TOOT SW17 180 B6 2
Wheatley Cl EMPK RM11 125 L3
GRH DA9 188 F1 4
HDN NW4 96 D10
SBW CM21 29 M2
WGCE AL7 23 K7
Wheatley Gdns ED N9 99 M3
Wheatley Rd ISLW TW7 154 E9
WGCE AL7 23 J6
Wheatleys STALE/WH AL4 39 H4 1
Wheatley St CAVSQ/HST W1G 10 D4 5
Wheatley Terrace Rd ERITH DA8 164 G5
Wheatley Wy CFSP/GDCR SL9 90 B7
Wheatly Crs HYS/HAR UB3 133 H9 5
Wheatsheaf Cl CHERT KT16 214 G3
WOKN/KNAP GU21 232 C1
Wheatsheaf Hl RSEV TN14 228 A5
RSEV TN14 264 A7
Wheatsheaf La FUL/PGN SW6 156 F6 2
STA TW18 173 J10
VX/NE SW8 158 F6 5
Wheatsheaf Rd ROM RM1 124 G4 6
WARE SG12 28 A1
Wheatsheaf Ter FUL/PGN SW6 157 J6 5
Wheatstone Cl CRAWE RH10 284 C2
WIM/MER SW19 201 N1
Wheeler Av OXTED RH8 261 J5
Wheeler La WCHPL E1 13 L3 2
Wheeler Rd CRAWE RH10 284 C9
Wheelers EPP CM16 65 K5 5
Wheelers Cl WAB EN9 45 K8
Wheelers Cross BARK IG11 142 G4
Wheelers Dr RSLP HA4 112 D4 2
Wheelers Farm Gdns EPP CM16 66 C2 2
Wheelers La BRKHM/BTCW RH3 273 N2
BRW CM14 86 A8
EPSOM KT18 219 P10
HHS/BOV HP3 35 P8
HORL RH6 281 H5
Wheelers Orch CFSP/GDCR SL9 90 B7
Wheel Farm Dr DAGE RM10 124 D8
Wheelright Cl BUSH WD23 74 A10 5
Wheelwright St HOLWY N7 5 N3
Whelan Wy WLGTN SM6 202 E10
Wheler St WCHPL E1 13 L2
Whellock Rd CHSWK W4 156 B2
Whenman Av BXLY DA5 186 D5
Wherwell Rd GUW GU2 267 P2
Whetstone Cl TRDG/WHET N20 97 N3 1
Whetstone Pk LINN WC2A 11 N5
Whetstone Rd BKHTH/KID SE3 161 P8
Whewell Rd ARCH N19 118 F7 5
Whichcote St STHWK SE1 12 A10 2
Whidborne Cl LEW SE13 160 F8 2
Whielden La AMSS HP7 68 F7
AMSS HP7 68 C9
Whielden St AMSS HP7 68 G7
Whimbrel Cl PUR/KEN CR8 223 L7
Whimbrel Wy YEAD UB4 133 L8
Whinchat Rd THMD SE28 162 G2
Whinfell Cl STRHM/NOR SW16 180 E8
Whinfell Wy GVE DA12 191 J7
Whinshill Ct ASC SL5 192 F8
Whinyates Rd ELTH/MOT SE9 162 B9
Whipley Cl RGUE GU4 250 E5 5
Whippendell Cl STMC/STPC BR5 207 L1
Whippendell Hl KGLGY WD4 53 M6
Whippendell Rd WATW WD18 72 F9
Whippendell Wy STMC/STPC BR5 207 L1
Whipps Cross Rd WAN E11 121 K3
Whiskin St CLKNW EC1R 6 C10
Whisper Wd RKW/CH/CXG WD3 71 L7
Whistler Cl CRAWE RH10 284 A10
Whistler Gdns EDGW HA8 95 L10
Whistlers Av BTSEA SW11 157 N6 5
Whistler St HBRY N5 119 J9
Whiston Rd BETH E2 7 L7
Whitakers Wy LOU IG10 82 C5
Whitbread Cl TOTM N17 99 P9 5
Whitbread Rd BROCKY SE4 160 D10
Whitburn Rd LEW SE13 182 G1
Whitby Av WLSDN NW10 135 N5
Whitby Cl BH/WHM TN16 243 N5
GRH DA9 188 F1
Whitby Gdns CDALE/KGS NW9 115 M1
SUT SM1 201 N9 2
Whitby Rd RSLP HA4 113 J8
RYLN/HDSTN HA2 114 B8
SL SL1 129 H9
SUT SM1 201 N9
WOOL/PLUM SE18 162 C3
Whitby St WCHPL E1 13 L1 2
Whitcher Cl NWCR SE14 160 D5 5
Whitcher Pl CAMTN NW1 4 G2
Whitchurch Av EDGW HA8 95 L8
Whitchurch Cl EDGW HA8 95 L7 5
Whitchurch Gdns EDGW HA8 95 L8 5
Whitchurch La EDGW HA8 95 K8
STAN HA7 95 K8
Whitchurch Rd HARH RM3 105 M5 1
NKENS W10 136 G9
Whitcomb St SOHO/SHAV W1D 11 J7
White Acre CDALE/KGS NW9 96 B10
Whitear Wk SRTFD E15 141 J1 5
SRTFD E15 141 J1 5
White Av GVW DA11 190 C6
Whitebarn La DAGE RM10 144 B4
Whitebeam Av HAYES BR2 206 D7
Whitebeam Cl CHESW EN7 61 M2 5
Whitebeam Dr REIG RH2 275 M3
SOCK/AV RM15 147 H5 5
Whitebeams HAT AL10 40 D7 4
LCOL/BKTW AL2 56 A4
White Beam Wy
KWD/TDW/WH KT20 238 D7
White Bear Yd CLKNW EC1R 12 A2 5
Whiteberry Rd RDKG RH5 272 A10
White Bridge Av MTCM CR4 201 N4
White Bridge Cl
EBED/NFELT TW14 174 G2
Whitebroom Rd HHW HP1 35 H4 2
White Bushes REDH RH1 276 B4
White Butts Rd RSLP HA4 113 L8
Whitechapel High St WCHPL E1 13 M5
Whitechapel Rd WCHPL E1 13 N4
White Church La WCHPL E1 13 N5
White City Cl SHB W12 136 F9
White City Rd SHB W12 136 E9
White Cl SL SL1 129 J10
White Conduit St IS N1 6 B7
Whitecote Rd GFD/PVL UB6 134 A8
White Craig Cl PIN HA5 93 P6
Whitecroft STAL AL1 38 G9
SWLY BR8 208 F2 5
Whitecroft Cl BECK BR3 205 J4
Whitecroft Wy BECK BR3 205 H4
Whitecross St STLK EC1Y 12 F1
Whitefield Av CRICK NW2 116 F5
PUR/KEN CR8 241 H2
Whitefield Cl STMC/STPC BR5 207 M3 5
WAND/EARL SW18 179 H2
Whitefields Rd CHES/WCR EN8 62 B4
Whitefoot La BMLY BR1 183 H7
Whitefoot Ter BMLY BR1 183 L6
Whiteford Rd SLN SL2 129 K7
White Friars SEV TN13 265 H3
Whitefriars Dr KTN/HRWW/W HA3 94 D10
Whitefriars St EMB EC4Y 12 B6
White Gate Gdns
KTN/HRWW/W HA3 94 D8
White Gates HCH RM12 125 K7 1
Whitegates WOKS/MYFD GU22 232 C6 5
Whitegates Cl RKW/CH/CXG WD3 72 B8
Whitegate Wy
KWD/TDW/WH KT20 238 E6
Whitehall LSQ/SEVD WC2H 11 K8
WHALL SW1A 11 L10
Whitehall Cl CHIG IG7 103 K4 1
WAB EN9 45 K8 2
Whitehall Ct WHALL SW1A 11 L10
Whitehall Crs CHSGTN KT9 219 J2
Whitehall Dr CRAWW RH11 283 H7
Whitehall Farm La VW GU25 194 B3
Whitehall Gdns ACT W3 135 M10
CHING E4 101 J2
CHSWK W4 155 N5
WHALL SW1A 11 L10
Whitehall La BKHH IG9 101 M3
EGH TW20 172 C10
ERITH DA8 164 G8
GRAYS RM17 167 P5
REIG RH2 275 J4
STWL/WRAY TW19 172 D2
Whitehall Pk ARCH N19 118 D6
Whitehall Park Rd CHSWK W4 155 N5
Whitehall Pl CAR SM5 222 C1 2
WHALL SW1A 11 L10
Whitehall Rd CHING E4 101 K3
GRAYS RM17 167 P3
HAYES BR2 206 A5
HNWL W7 154 F1
HRW HA1 114 D5 1
THHTH CR7 203 H5
UX/CGN UB8 131 N3
Whitehall St TOTM N17 99 N8
Whitehands Cl HOD EN11 44 E3 1
White Hart Cl CSTG HP8 89 M4
SEV TN13 265 K4
White Hart Dr HHNE HP2 36 A7
White Hart La BARN SW13 156 B8
RGUW GU3 248 F9
ROMW/RG RM7 104 B9
WDGN N22 99 H9
White Hart Meadow BEAC HP9 88 D9
White Hart Mdw RPLY/SEND GU23 233 M7
White Hart Rd HHNE HP2 36 B7
ORP BR6 207 K7
WDSR SL4 149 J2
WOOL/PLUM SE18 163 H3
White Hart Rw CHERT KT16 195 K7 1
White Hart St LBTH SE11 18 B7
White Hart Wd SEV TN13 265 K5
Whitehaven Cl HAYES BR2 205 M4
Whitehaven St STJWD NW8 9 N2 5
Whitehead Cl RDART DA2 187 K6
UED N18 99 L6
WAND/EARL SW18 179 M3 2
Whitehead's Gv CHEL SW3 15 P7
White Heart Av UX/CGN UB8 132 D7
Whiteheath Av RSLP HA4 112 D5
White Hedge Dr STALW/RED AL3 38 B4
White Heron Ms TEDD TW11 176 E9 5
White Hl BERK HP4 33 P10
Whitehill BERK HP4 34 A4
White Hl BFOR GU20 212 A1
COUL/CHIP CR5 239 N9
CSHM HP5 51 H7
HHW HP1 51 J1
NTHWD HA6 92 B7
SAND/SEL CR2 223 L6 5
WLYN AL6 22 D1
White Hill Cl CSHM HP5 51 H6
Whitehill Ct BERK HP4 34 A4
Whitehill La GVE DA12 190 G6
REDH RH1 259 L3
RPLY/SEND GU23 234 D9
Whitehill Pde GVE DA12 190 F6
Whitehill Pl VW GU25 194 B5
Whitehill Rd DART DA1 187 H1
GVE DA12 190 F5
HART DA3 211 J2
MEO DA13 189 J10
Whitehills Rd LOU IG10 82 D7
Whitehorn Pl WDR/YW UB7 132 A10
White Horse Dr EPSOM KT18 237 P1 2
White Horse Hl CHST BR7 184 D7
White Horse La LCOL/BKTW AL2 57 K2
RPLY/SEND GU23 233 M7
Whitehorse La SNWD SE25 203 M4
White Horse La WCHPL E1 140 C6
Whitehorse Rd EHAM E6 142 C5
White Horse Rd WCHPL E1 140 D7 2
Whitehorse Rd WDSR SL4 148 C8
White Horse St MYFR/PICC W1J 10 F10 2
Whitehouse Av BORE WD6 75 N8
White House Cl CFSP/GDCR SL9 90 B8
Whitehouse Dr GU GU1 250 E10 1
White House Dr STAN HA7 95 H5 2
Whitehouse La ABLGY WD5 55 J2
White House La ENC/FH EN2 79 K5
RGUE GU4 250 A5
White House Rd RSEV TN14 264 G6
Whitehouse Wy IVER SL0 130 G5 2
STHGT/OAK N14 98 C3
White Kennett St WCHPL E1 13 K5
White Knights Rd WEY KT13 216 D4
White Knobs Wy CTHM CR3 259 P1
Whitelands BRWN CM15 87 J1
Whitelands Av RKW/CH/CXG WD3 70 E7
Whitelands Wy HARH RM3 105 L9
White La BH/WHM TN16 243 N9
RGUE GU4 268 F2
Whiteleaf Rd HHS/BOV HP3 35 M9
White Ledges WEA W13 135 H8
Whitelegg Rd PLSTW E13 141 L4
Whiteley WDSR SL4 148 D6
Whiteley Rd NRWD SE19 181 L8
Whiteleys Wy FELT TW13 175 P6
White Lilies Island WDSR SL4 148 F6
White Lion Rd AMSS HP7 69 M5
White Lion St HHS/BOV HP3 35 N10 2
IS N1 6 A8
White Ldg NRWD SE19 181 J10
White Lodge Cl BELMT SM2 221 M4
EFNCH N2 117 N4
SEV TN13 247 J9
White Lodge Gdns REDH RH1 276 B8 1
White Lyons Rd BRW CM14 107 H4 4
Whitemore Rd GU GU1 250 A6
White Oak Dr BECK BR3 205 H2
White Oak Gdns BFN/LL DA15 185 J3
Whiteoaks BNSTD SM7 221 L9
Whiteoaks La GFD/PVL UB6 134 C4 2
White Orchards STAN HA7 94 F6
TRDG/WHET N20 97 J1
White Post Fld SBW CM21 29 N1
White Post Hl EYN DA4 209 P7
Whitepost Hl REDH RH1 257 P10
White Post La HOM E9 140 E2
White Post St PECK SE15 160 B6 5
White Rd SRTFD E15 141 K2 5
White Rose La WOKS/MYFD GU22 232 C3
Whites Av GNTH/NBYPK IG2 123 H4
Whites Cl GRH DA9 189 H2
Whites Dr HAYES BR2 205 L7 1
White's Grounds STHWK SE1 19 K1 1
White Shack La RKW/CH/CXG WD3 72 A3
Whites La DTCH/LGLY SL3 149 N5
White's Rw WCHPL E1 13 L4
White's Sq CLAP SW4 158 E10 5
Whitestile Rd BTFD TW8 155 H4
Whitestone La HAMP NW3 117 M8
Whitestone Wk HAMP NW3 117 M8 5
HHW HP1 35 K3 5
White St NWDGN UB2 153 L1
White Stubbs La BROX EN10 43 N7
Whitethorn WGCE AL7 23 K6
Whitethorn Av COUL/CHIP CR5 240 B1
WDR/YW UB7 131 P9
Whitethorn Gdns CROY/NA CR0 204 A9
EMPK RM11 125 K4 5
ENC/FH EN2 79 L9
Whitethorn St BOW E3 140 F6
Whitewaits HLW CM20 29 H10
White Wy GT/LBKH KT23 254 A2
Whitewebbs La ENC/FH EN2 79 N1
Whitewebbs Rd ENC/FH EN2 79 J1
Whitewebbs Wy STMC/STPC BR5 207 J1
Whitewood Cottages
BH/WHM TN16 243 P6
Whitewood Rd BERK HP4 33 M5 1
Whitfield Cl GUW GU2 249 M7
Whitfield Pl FITZ W1T 10 G2
Whitfield Rd BXLYHN DA7 164 A6
EHAM E6 141 P2
GNWCH SE10 161 J7
Whitfield St FITZ W1T 11 H3
Whitfield Wy RKW/CH/CXG WD3 91 J2
Whitford Gdns MTCM CR4 202 A3
Whitgift Av SAND/SEL CR2 223 K2
Whitgift St CROY/NA CR0 203 K10
LBTH SE11 17 N5
Whit Hern Ct CHES/WCR EN8 62 B6
Whitings Rd BAR EN5 76 F9
Whitings Wy EHAM E6 142 D7
Whitland Rd CAR SM5 201 N8
Whitlars Dr KGLGY WD4 54 B4 1
Whitley Cl ABLGY WD5 55 H8
STWL/WRAY TW19 173 P2
Whitley Rd HOD EN11 44 G1
TOTM N17 99 M10
Whitlock Dr WIM/MER SW19 179 H3
Whitman Rd WCHPL E1 140 D6 2
Whitmead Cl SAND/SEL CR2 223 L3
Whitmoor La RGUE GU4 250 A2
Whitmore Av CDH/CHF RM16 147 N9
HARH RM3 105 M10
Whitmore Cl FBAR/BDGN N11 98 C6
Whitmore Gdns WLSDN NW10 136 F4
Whitmore La ASC SL5 192 F5
Whitmore Rd BECK BR3 204 E3
HRW HA1 114 B5
IS N1 7 J6
Whitmores Cl EPSOM KT18 237 P1 5
Whitmores Wd HHNE HP2 36 C5
Whitmore Wy HORL RH6 279 N3
Whitnell Wy PUT/ROE SW15 178 F1 1
Whitney Av REDBR IG4 122 A2
Whitney Rd LEY E10 120 F5
Whitney Wk SCUP DA14 185 P9
Whitstable Cl BECK BR3 204 E1 5
Whitstable Pl CROY/NA CR0 223 K1
Whittaker Av RCH/KEW TW9 177 J1 12
Whittaker Rd CHEAM SM3 201 J10
EHAM E6 142 A2 1
SLN SL2 128 D6
Whittaker St BGVA SW1W 16 A6
Whitta Rd MNPK E12 122 A9
Whittell Gdns SYD SE26 182 B6
Whittenham Cl SLN SL2 129 M10
Whittingstall Rd FUL/PGN SW6 157 J7
HOD EN11 44 G1
Whittington Av BANK EC3V 13 J6 5
YEAD UB4 132 G7
Whittington Ms
NFNCH/WDSP N12 97 M5
Whittington Rd CRAWE RH10 283 N10
WDGN N22 98 G7
Whittington Wy PIN HA5 113 M3
Whittlebury Cl CAR SM5 222 A4 1
Whittle Cl GFD/PVL UB6 134 A8
WALTH E17 120 D4
Whittle Pkwy SL SL1 128 C8
Whittle Rd HEST TW5 153 K6
NWDGN UB2 154 A1 1
Whittlesea Rd KTN/HRWW/W HA3 94 B8
Whittlesey St STHWK SE1 12 B10
White Wy CRAWE RH10 284 B1
Whitton Av East GFD/PVL UB6 114 E10
Whitton Av West NTHLT UB5 114 A10
Whitton Cl GFD/PVL UB6 134 G1
Whitton Dene HSLW TW3 176 A1
WHTN TW2 176 C2
Whitton Dr GFD/PVL UB6 134 F1
Whitton Manor Rd ISLW TW7 176 B2
Whitton Rd HSLW TW3 154 A10
WHTN TW2 176 D2
Whitton Waye HSLW TW3 175 P2
Whitwell Rd GSTN WD25 73 L1
PLSTW E13 141 M5
Whitworth Rd CRAWW RH11 283 N2
SNWD SE25 203 M3
WOOL/PLUM SE18 162 D6
Whitworth St GNWCH SE10 161 K4
Whopshott Av WOKN/KNAP GU21 231 P2
Whopshott Cl WOKN/KNAP GU21 231 N2
Whopshott Dr
WOKN/KNAP GU21 231 P2 1
Whorlton Rd PECK SE15 159 P9
Whybridge Cl RAIN RM13 144 F3
Whymark Av WDGN N22 119 H1
Whytebeam Vw CTHM CR3 241 N4
Whytecliffe Rd North
PUR/KEN CR8 223 J7
Whytecliffe Rd South
PUR/KEN CR8 223 J7 5
Whytecroft HEST TW5 153 L6
Whyteleafe Hl CTHM CR3 241 M5
Whyteleafe Rd CTHM CR3 241 M7
Whyteville Rd FSTGT E7 141 N1
Wichling Cl STMC/STPC BR5 207 N8 5
Wick Av STALE/WH AL4 21 J3
Wickenden Rd SEV TN13 247 K8
Wickersley Rd BTSEA SW11 158 B9 5
Wicket Rd GFD/PVL UB6 134 F5
The Wickets ASHF TW15 173 P7
Wickets Wy BARK/HLT IG6 103 J7
The Wicket CROY/NA CR0 224 F2
Wickford Dr HARH RM3 105 N6
Wickford St WCHPL E1 140 B6
Wickford Wy WALTH E17 120 C2
Wickham Av CHEAM SM3 220 F2
CROY/NA CR0 204 D9
Wickham Cha WWKM BR4 205 J7
Wickham Cl DEN/HRF UB9 91 N9
EN EN1 80 A7
HORL RH6 280 A3
NWMAL KT3 200 C5 5
Wickham Court Rd WWKM BR4 205 H9
Wickham Crs WWKM BR4 205 H9
Wickham Gdns BROCKY SE4 160 E9
Wickham La ABYW SE2 163 K5
EGH TW20 172 D10
Wickham Rd BECK BR3 204 G3
BROCKY SE4 160 E9
CDH/CHF RM16 168 F1
CHING E4 101 H8
CROY/NA CR0 204 B9
KTN/HRWW/W HA3 94 C10 1
Wickham St LBTH SE11 17 N7
WELL DA16 163 H8
Wickhams Wy HART DA3 211 L5 1
Wickhams Whf WARE SG12 26 D2 2
Wickham Wy BECK BR3 205 H4
Wickhurst Rd RSEV TN14 264 G8
Wicklands Rd WARE SG12 28 A3
Wick La BOW E3 140 F4 2
EGH TW20 171 L9
Wickliffe Av FNCH N3 97 H10
Wickliffe Gdns WBLY HA9 115 M7
Wicklow St FSBYW WC1X 5 N9
Wick Rd EGH TW20 171 N10
HOM E9 140 C1
TEDD TW11 176 G10
TRING HP23 32 B1
Wicks Cl LEE/GVPK SE12 184 A7
Wicksteed Cl BXLY DA5 186 E6
The Wick HERT/WAS SG14 25 J2
Wickwood St CMBW SE5 159 J8 2
Widbrook BRWN CM15 87 H2
Widbury Gdns WARE SG12 26 E2 4
Widbury Hl WARE SG12 26 F2
Widdenham Rd HOLWY N7 118 G9
Widdicombe Av
RYLN/HDSTN HA2 113 M7
Widdin St SRTFD E15 141 K2 10
Widecombe Cl HARH RM3 105 L9 5
Widecombe Gdns REDBR IG4 122 B2
Widecombe Rd ELTH/MOT SE9 184 B6
Widecombe Wy EFNCH N2 117 N3
Widecroft Rd IVER SL0 131 H8
Widegate St WCHPL E1 13 K4 2
Widenham Cl PIN HA5 113 K3 5
Wide Wy STRHM/NOR SW16 202 E3
Widford Rd WARE SG12 28 A1
WGCE AL7 23 L5
Widgeon Cl CAN/RD E16 141 N8
Widgeon Rd ERITH DA8 165 J6
Widgeon Wy GSTN WD25 73 M2 2
Widley Rd MV/WKIL W9 2 F10
Widmore Cl CSHM HP5 50 D2
Widmore Dr HHNE HP2 36 B4
Widmore Lodge Rd BMLY BR1 206 A2
Widmore Rd BMLY BR1 205 N2
UX/CGN UB8 132 C6
Widworthy Hayes
RBRW/HUT CM13 107 N2
Wieland Rd NTHWD HA6 93 H8
Wigeon Wy YEAD UB4 133 L8
Wiggenhall Rd WATW WD18 73 J9
Wiggie La REDH RH1 258 B8
Wiggington Bottom TRING HP23 32 C1
Wiggins Md CDALE/KGS NW9 96 C8
Wigginton Av WBLY HA9 135 M1
Wightman Rd CEND/HSY/T N8 119 H2
Wigley Bush La BRW CM14 106 D3
Wigley Rd FELT TW13 175 L5
Wigmore Pl CAVSQ/HST W1G 10 E5 5
Wigmore Rd CAR SM5 201 N9
Wigmores North WGCW AL8 22 G4 2
Wigmore St MBLAR W1H 10 D5
Wigram Rd WAN E11 121 P4
Wigram Sq WALTH E17 101 H10
Wigston Cl UED N18 99 M6
Wigston Rd PLSTW E13 141 N6
Wigton Gdns STAN HA7 95 K9
Wigton Pl LBTH SE11 18 B8 1
Wigton Rd HARH RM3 105 M5
WALTH E17 100 E9
Wigton Wy HARH RM3 105 M5
Wilberforce Rd CDALE/KGS NW9 116 C3
FSBYPK N4 119 K8 2
FSBYPK N4 119 J7 5
Wilberforce Wy GVE DA12 190 G8
WIM/MER SW19 178 G9 2
Wilbraham Pl KTBR SW1X 16 B5
Wilbury Av BELMT SM2 221 J6
Wilbury Wy UED N18 99 L6
Wilby Ms NTGHL W11 8 D8
Wilcot Av OXHEY WD19 93 M1
Wilcot Cl CHOB/PIR GU24 230 F2
OXHEY WD19 93 M1
Wilcot Gdns CHOB/PIR GU24 230 E2
Wilcox Cl BORE WD6 75 P5
Wilcox Gdns SHPTN TW17 196 A3 2
Wilcox Rd SUT SM1 221 L1 5
TEDD TW11 176 C7
VX/NE SW8 158 F6
Wild Acres BF/WBF KT14 215 M7
Wild Ct HOL/ALD WC2B 11 N5 1
Wildcroft Dr RDKG RH5 273 J5
Wildcroft Gdns STAN HA7 95 J7 1
Wildcroft Rd PUT/ROE SW15 178 F3
Wilde Cl HACK E8 7 N5
TIL RM18 168 E8
Wilde Pl PLMGR N13 99 J7
Wilder Cl RSLP HA4 113 J6
Wilderness Av BGR/WK TN15 247 N8
Wilderness Mt SEV TN13 247 L8
Wilderness Rd CHST BR7 184 E10
GUW GU2 267 L2
OXTED RH8 261 K6
The Wilderness BERK HP4 33 P5 5
E/WMO/HCT KT8 198 B5
HPTN TW12 176 A7 2
Wilde Rd ERITH DA8 164 C6
Wilders Cl WOKN/KNAP GU21 231 P4
Wilderton Rd STNW/STAM N16 119 M5
Wildfell Rd CAT SE6 182 G3
Wildfield Cl RGUW GU3 248 G9
Wild Goose Dr NWCR SE14 160 B7 5
Wildgreen North
DTCH/LGLY SL3 150 D3 7
Wildgreen South
DTCH/LGLY SL3 150 D3 5
Wild Hatch GLDGN NW11 117 K4
Wildhill Rd BRKMPK AL9 41 J7
Wild Oaks Cl NTHWD HA6 92 G7
Wild's Rents STHWK SE1 19 J3
Wild St HOL/ALD WC2B 11 M6
Wildwood NTHWD HA6 92 E7
Wildwood Av LCOL/BKTW AL2 55 N6
Wildwood Cl EHSLY KT24 252 G1
LEE/GVPK SE12 183 L3
WOKS/MYFD GU22 233 J1
Wildwood Ct PUR/KEN CR8 241 L1
Wildwood Gv GLDGN NW11 117 M6
Wildwood Ri GLDGN NW11 117 M6
Wildwood Rd GLDGN NW11 117 M5
Wilford Cl ENC/FH EN2 79 L7 5
NTHWD HA6 92 E8
Wilford Rd CROY/NA CR0 203 K7 5
DTCH/LGLY SL3 150 B3
Wilfred Av RAIN RM13 145 H7
Wilfred St GVE DA12 190 E2 14
WESTW SW1E 16 G3
WOKN/KNAP GU21 232 A4 1
Wilfrid Gdns ACT W3 135 P7
Wilhelmina Av COUL/CHIP CR5 240 D5
Wilkes Rd BTFD TW8 155 K5 4
Wilkes St WCHPL E1 13 M3
Wilkins Cl HYS/HAR UB3 152 G4
MTCM CR4 201 P1
Wilkin's Green La HAT AL10 39 P5
STALE/WH AL4 39 P6
Wilkins Gv WGCW AL8 22 G6
Wilkinson Rd CAN/RD E16 141 P8
Wilkinson St VX/NE SW8 158 G6
Wilkinson Wy CHSWK W4 156 A1
HHS/BOV HP3 36 A10
Wilkin St KTTN NW5 4 D1
Wilks Av DART DA1 187 N5
Wilks Gdns CROY/NA CR0 204 D8
Wilks Pl IS N1 7 K8
Willan Rd TOTM N17 99 L10
Willan Wall CAN/RD E16 141 L9 5
Willard St VX/NE SW8 158 C9 5
Willats Cl CHERT KT16 195 J6 2
Willcocks Cl CHSGTN KT9 199 K10
Willcott Rd ACT W3 135 N10
Will Crooks Gdns ELTH/MOT SE9 161 P10
Willenhall Av BAR EN5 77 M10
Willenhall Dr HYS/HAR UB3 132 F9
Willenhall Rd WOOL/PLUM SE18 162 E4
Willersley Av BFN/LL DA15 185 J4
ORP BR6 206 G10
Willersley Cl BFN/LL DA15 185 J4
Willesden La KIL/WHAMP NW6 136 G2
Willes Rd KTTN NW5 4 E1
Willet Cl NTHLT UB5 133 K5 4
Willett Cl STMC/STPC BR5 207 H6
Willett Rd THHTH CR7 203 H5
Willetts La DEN/HRF UB9 111 J9
Willett Wy STMC/STPC BR5 206 G5
Willey Broom La CTHM CR3 259 H1
Willey Farm La CTHM CR3 259 K2
Willey La CTHM CR3 259 L1
William Barefoot Dr
ELTH/MOT SE9 184 D5
William Booth Rd PGE/AN SE20 203 P1
William Carey Wy HRW HA1 114 D4 5
William Cl CRW RM5 104 D9
EFNCH N2 117 N1
LEW SE13 161 H9 5
STHL UB1 154 B1 6
William Ct HHS/BOV HP3 35 N10 6
William Covell Cl ENC/FH EN2 78 G4 5
William Ellis Cl WDSR SL4 171 M1
William Gdns PUT/ROE SW15 178 E1
William Guy Gdns BOW E3 140 G5 7
William Iv St CHCR WC2N 11 L8
William Margrie Cl PECK SE15 159 P8 5
William Ms KTBR SW1X 16 B2
William Morley Cl EHAM E6 142 A3
William Morris Cl WALTH E17 120 E1
William Morris Wy FUL/PGN SW6 157 M9
William Moulder Ct CSHM HP5 50 G4 2
William Rd CAMTN NW1 4 G10
CTHM CR3 241 L8
GU GU1 249 P10
SUT SM1 221 M2
WIM/MER SW19 179 H10
Williams Av WALTH E17 100 E9
William's Buildings BETH E2 140 B6 12
Williams Gv WDGN N22 99 H9 2
Williams La MORT/ESHN SW14 155 P9
MRDN SM4 201 M6
Williamson Cl GNWCH SE10 161 L4 6
Williamson Rd FSBYPK N4 119 J4 5
Williamson St HOLWY N7 118 F9 5
Williamson Wy MLHL NW7 97 H7 1
RKW/CH/CXG WD3 91 K2
William Sq POP/IOD E14 140 D9 5
Williams Rd NWDGN UB2 153 M3
WEA W13 134 F10 5
Williams Ter CROY/NA CR0 223 H3
William St BARK IG11 142 F2
BERK HP4 34 A5
BUSH WD23 73 L7
CAR SM5 201 P10
GRAYS RM17 167 P5 5
GVE DA12 190 E3
KTBR SW1X 16 B2
LEY E10 121 H4
SL SL1 129 L10
TOTM N17 99 N8
WDSR SL4 149 J7
Williams Wy CRAWE RH10 284 C7 5
RAD WD7 75 H1
Willifield Wy GLDGN NW11 117 K3
Willingale Rd LOU IG10 82 F5
Willingdon Rd WDGN N22 99 J10
Willinghall Cl WAB EN9 63 J8 1
Willingham Ter KTTN NW5 118 D10 5
Willingham Wy KUT KT1 199 M2
Willington Rd BRXN/ST SW9 158 F9
Willis Av BELMT SM2 221 P3
Willis Cl EPSOM KT18 219 N9
Willis Rd CROY/NA CR0 203 K7
ERITH DA8 164 D3
SRTFD E15 141 L4
Willis St POP/IOD E14 140 G8
Willmore End WIM/MER SW19 201 L1
Willoners SLN SL2 128 F6 1
Willoughby Av CROY/NA CR0 222 G1
Willoughby Cl BROX EN10 44 D7 2
Willoughby Dr RAIN RM13 144 F2 1
Willoughby Gv TOTM N17 100 A8 4
Willoughby La TOTM N17 100 A8
UED N18 100 A7 1
Willoughby Ms TOTM N17 100 A8 5
Willoughby Park Rd TOTM N17 100 A8
Willoughby Rd CEND/HSY/T N8 119 H1
DTCH/LGLY SL3 150 E2
HAMP NW3 117 N9
KUTN/CMB KT2 199 L1
TWK TW1 177 H1 2
Willoughby Wy CHARL SE7 161 N3
Willow Av BARN SW13 156 C8
BFN/LL DA15 185 K2
DEN/HRF UB9 131 M1
SWLY BR8 208 G4
WDR/YW UB7 132 A9
Willow Bank WOKS/MYFD GU22 232 B8
Willowbank Gdns
KWD/TDW/WH KT20 238 E8
Willow Brean HORL RH6 279 P3
Willow Bridge Rd IS N1 6 E2
Willowbrook WDSR SL4 149 J3
Willowbrook Rd NWDGN UB2 153 N2
PECK SE15 19 M10
STWL/WRAY TW19 173 P4
Willowby Ct LCOL/BKTW AL2 57 J2
The Willow Centre MTCM CR4 202 A5
Willow Cl ADL/WDHM KT15 215 J7
BKHH IG9 102 A4
BRWN CM15 87 J4
BTFD TW8 155 H5
BXLY DA5 186 A2
CHESW EN7 61 M2
CRAWE RH10 283 P5
DTCH/LGLY SL3 150 F6 5
HAYES BR2 206 C5
HCH RM12 125 J8 4
RBRW/HUT CM13 87 N10 1
STMC/STPC BR5 207 L6
Willow Cnr HORL RH6 279 J8
Willowcourt Av
KTN/HRWW/W HA3 114 G3
Willow Crs STAL AL1 39 H6
Willow Crs East DEN/HRF UB9 111 M10

Willow Crs West DEN/HRF UB9 ...... 111 M10
Willow Dean PIN HA5 ...... 93 L10
Willowdene BRWN CM15 ...... 86 E9
Willow Dene BUSH WD23 ...... 94 D1
Willowdene CHES/WCR EN8 ...... 62 D3
Willow Dene PIN HA5 ...... 93 L10
Willowdene Cl CBRW CM14 ...... 107 H5
Willow Dr BAR EN5 ...... 77 H8
  RGUW GU3 ...... 248 B10
  RPLY/SEND GU23 ...... 233 K10
Willow Edge KGLGY WD4 ...... 54 B5
Willow End NTHWD HA6 ...... 93 H7
  TRDG/WHET N20 ...... 97 K3
Willowfield HLWS CM18 ...... 46 G2
Willow Gdns HEST TW5 ...... 153 P7
  RSLP HA4 ...... 112 G7
Willow Gn CHOB/PIR GU24 ...... 212 P9
Willow Gv CHST BR7 ...... 184 D9
  RSLP HA4 ...... 112 G7
Willowhayne Dr WOT/HER KT12 ...... 197 J7
Willowhayne Gdns WPK KT4 ...... 220 F1
Willow La AMSS HP7 ...... 69 L7
  GU GU1 ...... 250 D9
  MTCM CR4 ...... 202 A5
  WATW WD18 ...... 73 H9
Willowmead CHIG IG7 ...... 103 K4
Willowmead HERT/BAY SG14 ...... 25 H6
Willow Md DORK RH4 ...... 272 F1
Willowmead SBW CM21 ...... 29 J8
Willowmead STA TW18 ...... 195 L1
  WOKN/KNAP GU21 ...... 231 M2
Willowmere ESH/CLAY KT10 ...... 218 A1
Willow Mt CROY/NA CR0 ...... 203 M10
Willow Pk RSEV TN14 ...... 246 C3
  SLN SL2 ...... 129 N2
Willow Pl HLWE CM17 ...... 48 A5
  WDSR SL4 ...... 149 H5
  WEST SW1P 17 H5
Willow Rdg CRAWE RH10 ...... 285 P10
Willow Rd CHDH RM6 ...... 123 P4
  DART DA1 ...... 187 H4
  DTCH/LGLY SL3 ...... 151 M9
  EA W5 ...... 155 K1
  EN N1 ...... 79 M6
  ERITH DA8 ...... 165 H7
  HAMP NW3 ...... 117 N9
  NWMAL KT3 ...... 199 P4
  REIG RH2 ...... 275 M2
  RGODL GU7 ...... 267 G4
  WLGTN SM6 ...... 222 C4
Willows Av MRDN SM4 ...... 201 L5
Willows Cl PIN HA5 ...... 93 K10
Willowside LCOL/BKTW AL2 ...... 57 K3
Willows Pth EPSOM KT18 ...... 219 N10
The Willows AMS HP6 ...... 68 C1
  BF/WBF KT14 ...... 215 P9
  ESH/CLAY KT10 ...... 218 D3
  GRAYS RM17 ...... 168 A5
  LTWR GU18 ...... 212 B7
  OXHEY WD19 ...... 93 J1
  RKW/CH/CXG WD3 ...... 91 K3
  STAL AL1 ...... 38 C10
  WEY KT13 ...... 196 B10
Willow St CHING E4 ...... 101 J1
  ROMW RM7 ...... 124 D2
  SDTCH EC2A 13 J1
Willowtree Cl HGDN/ICK UB10 ...... 112 D8
  WAND/EARL SW18 ...... 179 L4
  YEAD UB4 ...... 133 K6
Willow Tree La YEAD UB4 ...... 133 K6
Willow Tree Wk BMLY BR1 ...... 205 N1
Willowtree Wy
  STRHM/NOR SW16 ...... 203 H1
Willow V CHST BR7 ...... 184 D9
  GT/LBKH KT23 ...... 236 A9
  SHB W12 ...... 136 D10
Willow Vw WIM/MER SW19 ...... 201 N1
Willow Wk CHEAM SM3 ...... 201 J10
  EGH TW20 ...... 171 P8
  KWD/TDW/WH KT20 ...... 255 N6
  ORP BR6 ...... 206 E10
  REDH RH1 ...... 276 C2
  SEVS/STOTM N15 ...... 119 J2
  SHGR GU5 ...... 270 B5
  STHWK SE1 ...... 19 K5
  UPMR RM14 ...... 126 B6
  WALTH E17 ...... 120 E3
  WCHMH N21 ...... 78 G10
Willow Wy ALP/SUD HA0 ...... 114 F8
  BF/WBF KT14 ...... 215 M7
  FNCH N3 ...... 97 L8
  GDST RH9 ...... 260 A8
  GU GU1 ...... 249 N6
  HARH RM3 ...... 106 A7
  HAT AL10 ...... 40 C7
  HHW HP1 ...... 35 L4
  HOR/WEW KT19 ...... 220 A3
  LCOL/BKTW AL2 ...... 55 P3
  POTB/CUF EN6 ...... 59 L9
  RAD WD7 ...... 74 D2
  SUN TW16 ...... 197 H4
  SYD SE26 ...... 182 A6
  WHTN TW2 ...... 176 A5
  WOKS/MYFD GU22 ...... 232 B6
Willow Wood Crs SNWD SE25 ...... 203 M6
Willrose Crs ABYW SE2 ...... 163 L4
Wills Crs HSLW TW3 ...... 176 A4
Wills Gv MLHL NW7 ...... 96 D6
Willshaw St NWCR SE14 ...... 160 F7
Wilson Rd EGH TW20 ...... 171 N4
Wilman Gv HACK E8 ...... 7 J3
Wilmar Cl UX/CGN UB8 ...... 131 N2
  YEAD UB4 ...... 132 F3
Wilmar Gdns WWKM BR4 ...... 204 G8
Wilmar Wy BGR/WK TN15 ...... 247 N6
Wilmer Cl RCHPK/HAM TW10 ...... 177 L8
Wilmer Crs KUTN/CMB KT2 ...... 177 L8
Wilmer Gdns IS N1 ...... 7 J6
Wilmerhatch La EPSOM KT18 ...... 237 N3
Wilmer Lea Cl SRTFD E15 ...... 141 J2
Wilmer Pl STNW/STAM N16 ...... 119 N7
Wilmer Wy STHGT/OAK N14 ...... 98 E6
Wilmington Av CHSWK W4 ...... 156 M9
  ORP BR6 ...... 207 M9
Wilmington Court Rd
  RDART DA2 ...... 187 H6
Wilmington Gdns BARK IG11 ...... 142 G2
Wilmington Sq FSBYW WC1X 6 A10
Wilmington St FSBYW WC1X 6 A10
Wilmot Cl REIG RH2 ...... 257 N9
Wilmot's La HORL RH6 ...... 281 M3
  REDH RH1 ...... 277 L10
Wilmot St BETH E2 ...... 140 A6
Wilmot Wy BNSTD SM7 ...... 221 K10
Wilmount St
  WOOL/PLUM SE18 ...... 162 E3
Wilna Rd WAND/EARL SW18 ...... 179 N3
Wilsham St NTGHL W11 ...... 136 G10
Wilshere Av STAL AL1 ...... 38 B9
Wilsman Rd SOCK/AV RM15 ...... 147 H4
Wilson Av MTCM CR4 ...... 179 P10
  SAND/SEL CR2 ...... 223 L2

WBLY HA9 ...... 115 L5
Wilson Dr CHERT KT16 ...... 214 E2
  WBLY HA9 ...... 115 L5
Wilson Gdns HRW HA1 ...... 114 D5
Wilson Gv BERM/RHTH SE16 ...... 160 A1
Wilson La EYN DA4 ...... 210 G2
Wilson Rd CHSGTN KT9 ...... 219 L3
  CMBW SE5 ...... 159 L7
  IL IG1 ...... 122 C5
  PLSTW E13 ...... 142 A5
Wilsons KWD/TDW/WH KT20 ...... 238 G7
Wilson's Av TOTM N17 ...... 99 N10
Wilson's Pl POP/IOD E14 ...... 140 E8
Wilson's Rd HMSMTH W6 ...... 156 C4
Wilson St SDTCH EC2A 13 H3
  WALTH E17 ...... 121 H3
  WCHMH N21 ...... 77 L1
Wilstone Cl YEAD UB4 ...... 133 M6
Wilstone Dr STALE/WH AL4 ...... 39 H1
Wilthorne Gdns DAGE RM10 ...... 144 C2
Wilton Av CHSWK W4 ...... 156 B4
Wilton Cl WDR/YW UB7 ...... 151 N5
Wilton Crs HERT/BAY SG13 ...... 25 J3
  KTBR SW1X 16 C2
  WDSR SL4 ...... 148 C10
  WIM/MER SW19 ...... 201 J1
Wilton Dr CRW RM5 ...... 104 D3
Wilton Gdns E/WMO/HCT KT8 ...... 197 P5
  WOT/HER KT12 ...... 197 L8
Wilton Gv NWMAL KT3 ...... 200 C6
  WIM/MER SW19 ...... 179 J10
Wilton La ABLY HA9 ...... 89 J8
Wilton Ms KTBR SW1X 16 C1
Wilton Pl ADL/WDHM KT15 ...... 215 N5
  KTBR SW1X 16 C1
Wilton Rd ABYW SE2 ...... 163 M2
  BEAC HP9 ...... 88 D7
  EBAR EN4 ...... 78 A8
  HSLWW TW4 ...... 153 H4
  MUSWH N10 ...... 98 B10
  PIM SW1V 16 E4
  REDH RH1 ...... 276 C4
  WIM/MER SW19 ...... 179 P9
Wilton Rw KTBR SW1X 16 C2
Wilton Sq IS N1 ...... 6 G5
Wilton St KTBR SW1X 16 D3
Wilton Ter KTBR SW1X 16 C2
Wilton Vls IS N1 ...... 6 G6
Wilton Wy HACK E8 ...... 7 N2
  HERT/BAY SG13 ...... 25 K7
Wiltshire Av EMPK RM11 ...... 125 N2
  SLN SL2 ...... 129 N6
Wiltshire Cl MLHL NW7 ...... 96 C6
  RDART DA2 ...... 188 C3
Wiltshire Gdns FSBYPK N4 ...... 119 K4
  WHTN TW2 ...... 176 B4
Wiltshire La PIN HA5 ...... 113 J1
  RSLP HA4 ...... 112 G1
Wiltshire Rd BRXN/ST SW9 ...... 159 H9
  ORP BR6 ...... 207 K7
  THHTH CR7 ...... 203 H3
Wiltshire Rw IS N1 ...... 6 G6
Wilverley Crs NWMAL KT3 ...... 200 B6
Wimbart Rd BRXS/STRHM SW2 ...... 130 A6
Wimbledon Br WIM/MER SW19 ...... 179 J9
Wimbledon Hill Rd
  WIM/MER SW19 ...... 179 H9
Wimbledon Park Rd
  WIM/MER SW19 ...... 179 H6
Wimbledon Park Side
  WIM/MER SW19 ...... 178 G5
Wimbledon Rd TOOT SW17 ...... 179 M7
Wimbolt St BETH E2 ...... 7 N9
Wimborne Av NWDGN UB2 ...... 153 P3
  REDH RH1 ...... 276 A5
  STMC/STPC BR5 ...... 207 J3
  YEAD UB4 ...... 133 J8
Wimborne Cl BKHH IG9 ...... 101 P5
  EW KT17 ...... 220 B9
  LEE/GVPK SE12 ...... 183 L1
  SBW CM21 ...... 29 J1
  WPK KT4 ...... 200 F8
Wimborne Dr CDALE/KGS NW9 ...... 115 M1
  PIN HA5 ...... 113 M1
Wimborne Gdns WEA W13 ...... 134 G4
Wimborne Gv WAT WD17 ...... 72 F3
Wimborne Rd ED N9 ...... 99 P3
  TOTM N17 ...... 99 M10
Wimborne Wy BECK BR3 ...... 184 E2
Wimbourne St IS N1 ...... 6 G4
Wimlands La HORS RH12 ...... 282 A10
Wimpole Cl HAYES BR2 ...... 205 P5
  KUT KT1 ...... 199 M2
Wimpole Ms CAVSQ/HST W1G 10 D2
Wimpole Rd WDR/YW UB7 ...... 131 N10
Wimpole St CAVSQ/HST W1G 10 E5
Wimshurst Cl CROY/NA CR0 ...... 202 F8
Winans Wk BRXN/ST SW9 ...... 159 H8
Wincanton Cl CRAWE RH10 ...... 284 E7
Wincanton Crs NTHLT UB5 ...... 113 P10
Wincanton Gdns BARK/HLT IG6 ...... 122 E1
Wincanton Rd HARH RM3 ...... 105 L4
  WAND/EARL SW18 ...... 179 J3
Winchcombe Rd CAR SM5 ...... 201 N7
Winchcomb Gdns
  ELTH/MOT SE9 ...... 162 B9
Winchdells HHS/BOV HP3 ...... 36 B9
Winchelsea Av BXLYHN DA7 ...... 146 A8
Winchelsea Cl PUT/ROE SW15 ...... 178 G1
Winchelsea Rd TOTM N17 ...... 119 M1
  WLSDN NW10 ...... 136 A3
Winchelsey Ri SAND/SEL CR2 ...... 223 N3
Winchendon Rd FUL/PGN SW6 ...... 157 J6
  TEDD TW11 ...... 176 C7
Winchester Av CDALE/KGS NW9 ...... 115 L1
  HEST TW5 ...... 153 N5
  KIL/WHAMP NW6 ...... 2 B5
  UPMR RM14 ...... 126 E6
Winchester Cl AMSS HP7 ...... 69 K5
  DTCH/LGLY SL3 ...... 151 H7
  EN EN1 ...... 79 M10
  ESH/CLAY KT10 ...... 217 P1
  HAYES BR2 ...... 205 L3
  KUTN/CMB KT2 ...... 177 N10
Winchester Crs GVE DA12 ...... 190 G6
Winchester Dr PIN HA5 ...... 113 J3
Winchester Pk HAYES BR2 ...... 205 L3
Winchester Pl HACK E8 ...... 119 N10
  HGT N6 ...... 118 C6
Winchester Rd CHING E4 ...... 101 K1
  ED N9 ...... 99 N2
  FELT TW13 ...... 175 N6
  HAMP NW3 ...... 3 M3
  HAYES BR2 ...... 205 L3
  HYS/HAR UB3 ...... 152 C6
  IL IG1 ...... 122 G8
  KTN/HRWW/W HA3 ...... 115 K2
  ORP BR6 ...... 227 N1
  TWK TW1 ...... 176 C2
  WELL DA16 ...... 163 N8
  WOT/HER KT12 ...... 197 M5
Winchester Sq STHWK SE1 ...... 12 G9
Winchester St ACT W3 ...... 135 P10
  PIM SW1V 16 F7
Winchester Wy RKW/CH/CXG WD3 ...... 72 C9
Winchfield Cl KTN/HRWW/W HA3 ...... 115 H4
Winchfield Rd SYD SE26 ...... 182 A10
Winchfield Wy RKW/CH/CXG WD3 ...... 91 M1
Winchilsea Crs E/WMO/HCT KT8 ...... 198 B2
Winchmore Hill Rd
  STHGT/OAK N14 ...... 98 F1
Winchstone Cl SHPTN TW17 ...... 196 A4
Winch Vw EPP CM16 ...... 65 L5
Winckley Cl KTN/HRWW/W HA3 ...... 115 L3

Wincott St LBTH SE11 ...... 18 B5
Wincrofts Dr ELTH/MOT SE9 ...... 162 G10
Windall Cl NRWD SE19 ...... 203 P1
Windborough Rd CAR SM5 ...... 222 B4
Windermere Av FNCH N3 ...... 97 K10
  HCH RM12 ...... 125 H10
  KIL/WHAMP NW6 2
  RSLP HA4 ...... 113 K5
  STAL AL1 ...... 38 D7
  WBLY HA9 ...... 115 H5
  WIM/MER SW19 ...... 201 L1
Windermere Gdns REDBR IG4 ...... 122 B3
Windermere Rd ARCH N19 ...... 118 D7
  BXLYHN DA7 ...... 164 D3
  COUL/CHIP CR5 ...... 240 F1
  CROY/NA CR0 ...... 203 P1
  EA W5 ...... 155 J3
  LTWR GU18 ...... 212 A6
  MUSWH N10 ...... 98 C9
  PUT/ROE SW15 ...... 178 C9
  STHL UB1 ...... 133 N7
  STRHM/NOR SW16 ...... 202 D1
  WWKM BR4 ...... 205 K4
Windermere Wy REDH RH1 ...... 257 P9
  WDR/YW UB7 ...... 131 P10
Winders Rd BTSEA SW11 ...... 158 D8
Windfield LHD/OX KT22 ...... 237 H7
Windfield Cl SYD SE26 ...... 182 C7
Windgates RGUE GU4 ...... 250 F7
Windham Av CROY/NA CR0 ...... 225 P7
Windham Rd RCH/KEW TW9 ...... 155 L9
Wind Hl CHONG CM5 ...... 49 H5
Windhill WGCE AL7 ...... 23 K4
Windhover Wy GVE DA12 ...... 191 K7
Winding Shot HHW HP1 ...... 35 K5
Winding Wy BCTR RM8 ...... 123 M8
  DAGE RM10 ...... 144 G1
Windlass Pl DEPT SE8 ...... 160 G8
Windle Cl BFOR GU20 ...... 212 C3
Windlesham Ct BFOR GU20 ...... 212 A6
Windlesham Gv WIM/MER SW19 ...... 178 G4
Windlesham Rd CHOB/PIR GU24 ...... 212 F4
Windley Cl FSTH SE23 ...... 182 B5
Windmill Av EW KT17 ...... 220 F7
  STALE/WH AL4 ...... 39 H2
Windmill Cl CTHM CR3 ...... 241 K7
  EW KT17 ...... 220 C8
  HORL RH6 ...... 259 P3
  LEW SE13 ...... 161 H8
  SUN TW16 ...... 174 F10
  SURB KT6 ...... 199 H8
  UPMR RM14 ...... 125 P7
  WAB EN9 ...... 63 K10
  WARE SG12 ...... 148 G8
Windmill Ct CRAWW RH11 ...... 283 N5
Windmill Dr CLAP SW4 ...... 180 C1
  HAYES BR2 ...... 225 P1
  LHD/OX KT22 ...... 236 C9
  REDH RH1 ...... 257 N8
  RKW/CH/CXG WD3 ...... 72 A10
Windmill End EW KT17 ...... 220 C8
Windmill Fld BFOR GU20 ...... 212 C3
  WARE SG12 ...... 26 C3
Windmill Flds HLWE CM17 ...... 30 A7
Windmill Gdns ENC/FH EN2 ...... 79 M4
Windmill Gv CROY/NA CR0 ...... 203 K7
Windmill Hl AMSS HP7 ...... 88 E1
  ENC/FH EN2 ...... 79 M4
  KGLGY WD4 ...... 53 J8
  RSLP HA4 ...... 112 C5
Windmill La BAR EN5 ...... 76 C10
  BUSH WD23 ...... 94 D2
  CHES/WCR EN8 ...... 62 D6
  EW KT17 ...... 220 B8
  GFD/PVL UB6 ...... 134 B7
  NWDGN UB2 ...... 154 C2
  SRTFD E15 ...... 141 J1
  STHL UB1 ...... 134 B10
  THDIT KT7 ...... 198 B9
Windmill Pas CHSWK W4 ...... 156 B3
Windmill Ri KUTN/CMB KT2 ...... 177 N10
Windmill Rd CFSP/GDCR SL9 ...... 90 A8
  CHSWK W4 ...... 156 B3
  CROY/NA CR0 ...... 203 K7
  DTCH/LGLY SL3 ...... 110 A10
  EA W5 ...... 155 H3
  HHNE HP2 ...... 35 P6
  HPTN TW12 ...... 176 A8
  MTCM CR4 ...... 202 D5
  SEV TN13 ...... 265 J6
  SL SL1 ...... 129 J10
  SUN TW16 ...... 196 F1
  UED N18 ...... 99 L5
  WAND/EARL SW18 ...... 179 N2
  WIM/MER SW19 ...... 178 E8
Windmill Rd West SUN TW16 ...... 196 F1
Windmill Rw LBTH SE11 ...... 18 A3
Windmill Shott WTFD E20 ...... 172 C9
Windmill St BUSH WD23 ...... 94 D2
  FITZ W1T 11 J4
  GVE DA12 ...... 190 C7
Windmill Wk STHWK SE1 ...... 12 B10
Windmill Wy BRWN CM15 ...... 86 D5
  REDH RH1 ...... 257 N8
  RSLP HA4 ...... 112 C6
Windmore Av POTB/CUF EN6 ...... 58 F7
Windridge Cl STALW/RED AL3 ...... 37 P8
Windrose Cl BERM/RHTH SE16 ...... 160 F7
Windrush Av DTCH/LGLY SL3 ...... 151 P3
Windrush Cl BTSEA SW11 ...... 157 N10
  CHSWK W4 ...... 155 P6
  CRAWW RH11 ...... 283 H7
  HGDN/ICK UB10 ...... 112 A9
Windrush La FSTH SE23 ...... 182 A10
Winds End Cl HHNE HP2 ...... 36 B4
Windsor Av CDH/CHF RM16 ...... 171 N7
  CHEAM SM3 ...... 201 H10
  E/WMO/HCT KT8 ...... 197 P3
  EDGW HA8 ...... 95 N5
  HGDN/ICK UB10 ...... 132 C2
  NWMAL KT3 ...... 199 P5
  WALTH E17 ...... 100 D10
  WIM/MER SW19 ...... 201 M1
Windsor Br WDSR SL4 ...... 149 H1
Windsor Cl CHESW EN7 ...... 61 N6
  CHST BR7 ...... 184 G8
  FNCH N3 ...... 97 H10
  GUW GU2 ...... 267 G4
  HHS/BOV HP3 ...... 35 P8
  NTHWD HA6 ...... 93 H10
  RYLN/HDSTN HA2 ...... 113 P8
  WNWD SE27 ...... 181 K7
Windsor Ct STHGT/OAK N14 ...... 98 D1
Windsor Court Rd
  CHOB/PIR GU24 ...... 213 K5
Windsor Crs RYLN/HDSTN HA2 ...... 113 P8
  WBLY HA9 ...... 115 K5
Windsor Dr ASHF TW15 ...... 157 N7
  DART DA1 ...... 187 K5
  EBAR EN4 ...... 78 A5
  HERT/WAS SG14 ...... 24 C4
  ORP BR6 ...... 227 K3
Windsor End BEAC HP9 ...... 108 A1
Windsor Gdns CROY/NA CR0 ...... 202 F10
  HYS/HAR UB3 ...... 152 A2
  MV/WKIL W9 ...... 8 E2

Windsor Gv WNWD SE27 ...... 181 K7
Windsor La SL SL1 ...... 128 B6
Windsor Ms CAT SE6 ...... 183 H4
Windsor Park Rd HYS/HAR UB3 ...... 152 G6
Windsor Rd ASC SL5 ...... 170 A10
  BAR EN5 ...... 76 C10
  BCTR RM8 ...... 123 P8
  BRWN CM15 ...... 86 G10
  BXLYHS DA6 ...... 163 P10
  CFSP/GDCR SL9 ...... 109 P6
  CHING E4 ...... 100 C9
  CHOB/PIR GU24 ...... 213 K5
  CRICK NW2 ...... 136 B3
  CSHM HP5 ...... 50 C4
  DTCH/LGLY SL3 ...... 149 M6
  EA W5 ...... 135 J5
  ECH TW20 ...... 171 M4
  EMPK RM11 ...... 125 K5
  FNCH N3 ...... 97 H10
  FSTGT E7 ...... 121 N10
  GVE DA12 ...... 190 E7
  HOLWY N7 ...... 118 F8
  HSLWW TW4 ...... 153 J8
  IL IG1 ...... 122 F9
  KTN/HRWW/W HA3 ...... 94 B9
  KUTN/CMB KT2 ...... 177 K10
  LEY E10 ...... 120 C7
  NWDGN UB2 ...... 153 N2
  PEND EN3 ...... 80 C2
  PLMGR N13 ...... 99 H1
  RCH/KEW TW9 ...... 155 L8
  SL SL1 ...... 149 K2
  STWL/WRAY TW19 ...... 172 A4
  SUN TW16 ...... 176 C8
  TEDD TW11 ...... 176 C8
  THHTH CR7 ...... 203 J2
  TOTM N17 ...... 99 P10
  WAN E11 ...... 121 M6
  WATN WD24 ...... 73 H4
  WDSR SL4 ...... 171 P3
  WPK KT4 ...... 200 D9
The Windsors BKHH IG9 ...... 102 B3
Windsor St CHERT KT16 ...... 195 K6
  IS N1 ...... 6 C1
  UX/CGN UB8 ...... 131 M3
Windsor Ter IS N1 ...... 6 F9
Windsor Wk CMBW SE5 ...... 159 L8
  WEY KT13 ...... 216 C2
Windsor Wy HMSMTH W6 ...... 156 C3
  RKW/CH/CXG WD3 ...... 91 K2
  WOKS/MYFD GU22 ...... 232 F2
Windsor Wd WAB EN9 ...... 63 K9
Winds Rdg RPLY/SEND GU23 ...... 250 F1
Windus Rd STNW/STAM N16 ...... 119 N6
Windward Cl PEND EN3 ...... 80 C1
Windycroft Cl PUR/KEN CR8 ...... 222 E9
Windy Hl RERW/HUT CM13 ...... 107 P2
Windy Rdg BMLY BR1 ...... 206 B2
Windyridge CRAWW RH11 ...... 283 K8
Windy Ridge Cl WIM/MER SW19 ...... 178 G8
Wine Cl WAP E1W 140 E9
Winern Glebe BF/WBF KT14 ...... 215 N4
Winery La KUT KT1 ...... 199 L3
Winford Dr BROX EN10 ...... 44 E8
Winforton St GNWCH SE10 ...... 161 H7
Winfrith Rd WAND/EARL SW18 ...... 179 M3
Wingate Crs CROY/NA CR0 ...... 202 F6
Wingate Rd HMSMTH W6 ...... 156 E2
  IL IG1 ...... 122 C10
  SCUP DA14 ...... 185 M8
Wingfield Ms PECK SE15 ...... 159 P9
Wingfield Rd KUTN/CMB KT2 ...... 177 N10
  SRTFD E15 ...... 121 K10
  WALTH E17 ...... 120 C3
Wingfield St PECK SE15 ...... 159 P9
Wingfield Wy RSLP HA4 ...... 133 J1
Wingford Rd CLAP SW4 ...... 180 F2
Wingletye La EMPK RM11 ...... 125 N6
Wingmore Rd HNHL SE24 ...... 159 K9
Wingrave Crs BRW CM14 ...... 106 D5
Wingrave Rd HMSMTH W6 ...... 156 F5
Wingrove Rd CAT SE6 ...... 183 K5
Wings Cl SUT SM1 ...... 221 K1
Wingway BRWN CM15 ...... 107 H2
Winifred Av HCH RM12 ...... 125 H5
Winifred Pl NFNCH/WDSP N12 ...... 97 M6
Winifred Rd BCTR RM8 ...... 123 P7
  COUL/CHIP CR5 ...... 240 C5
  DART DA1 ...... 187 J1
  ERITH DA8 ...... 164 F4
  HHS/BOV HP3 ...... 35 N10
  HPTN TW12 ...... 175 P7
  WIM/MER SW19 ...... 201 K1
Winifred St CAN/RD E16 ...... 142 C10
Winifred Ter ED N9 ...... 99 N1
  EN EN1 ...... 79 M5
Winkers Cl CFSP/GDCR SL9 ...... 90 C9
Winkers La CFSP/GDCR SL9 ...... 90 C9
Winkfield Pln WDSR SL4 ...... 170 A3
Winkfield Rd WDGN N22 ...... 99 H9
  SRTFD E15 ...... 141 L1
  WDSR SL4 ...... 170 A3
Winkley St BETH E2 ...... 140 A4
Winkworth Rd BNSTD SM7 ...... 221 K10
Winlaton Rd BMLY BR1 ...... 183 J7
Winmill Rd BCTR RM8 ...... 124 A8
Winn Bridge Cl WFD IG8 ...... 102 A9
Winn Common Rd
  WOOL/PLUM SE18 ...... 163 H5
Winnett St SOHO/SHAV W1D 11 H7
Winnington Cl EFNCH N2 ...... 117 H4
Winnington Rd EFNCH N2 ...... 117 N5
  PEND EN3 ...... 80 E2
Winnington Wy
  WOKN/KNAP GU21 ...... 231 N4
Winnipeg Dr ORP BR6 ...... 227 J3
Winnock Rd WDR/YW UB7 ...... 131 N10
Winn Rd LEE/GVPK SE12 ...... 183 M4
Winns Av WALTH E17 ...... 101 H10
Winns Ms SEVS/STOTM N15 ...... 119 N2
Winns Ter WALTH E17 ...... 101 J10
Winsbeach WALTH E17 ...... 101 N10
Winscombe Crs EA W5 ...... 135 J6
Winscombe St KTTN NW5 ...... 118 C3
Winscombe Wy STAN HA7 ...... 95 G3
Winsford Rd CAT SE6 ...... 182 A6
Winsham Gv BTSEA SW11 ...... 180 F1
Winslade Rd BRXS/STRHM SW2 ...... 180 B1
Winsland Ms BAY/PAD W2 ...... 9 J1
Winsland St BAY/PAD W2 ...... 9 J1
Winsley St GTPST W1W 10 G5
Winslow Cl PIN HA5 ...... 113 J4
  WLSDN NW10 ...... 116 B8
Winslow Gv CHING E4 ...... 101 K1
Winslow Wy FELT TW13 ...... 155 P6
  WOT/HER KT12 ...... 197 K6
Winstanley Cl COB KT11 ...... 217 J10
Winstanley Rd BTSEA SW11 ...... 157 N9
Winstead Gdns DAGE RM10 ...... 124 D10
Winston Av CDALE/KGS NW9 ...... 116 C4
Winston Churchill Wy
  CHES/WCR EN8 ...... 62 B9
Winston Cl GRH DA9 ...... 188 C2
  KTN/HRWW/W HA3 ...... 94 B7
  ROMW/RG RM7 ...... 124 A3
Winston Ct PIN HA5 ...... 94 A8
Winston Dr COB KT11 ...... 235 M2
Winston Gdns BERK HP4 ...... 33 L5
Winston Rd STNW/STAM N16 ...... 119 M8
Winston Wy IL IG1 ...... 122 C10
  POTB/CUF EN6 ...... 59 K9

WOKS/MYFD GU22 ...... 232 E6
Winstre Rd BORE WD6 ...... 75 M5
Winter Av EHAM E6 ...... 142 B3
Winterborne Av ORP BR6 ...... 206 G10
Winterbourne Rd BCTR RM8 ...... 123 M7
  FSTH SE23 ...... 182 E4
  THHTH CR7 ...... 203 H4
Winter Box Wk
  RCHPK/HAM TW10 ...... 177 L1
Winterbrook Rd HNHL SE24 ...... 181 M7
Winterfold CRAWE RH10 ...... 285 N8
Winterfold Cl WIM/MER SW19 ...... 179 H5
Winterhill Wy RGUE GU4 ...... 250 E6
Winterscroft Rd HOD EN11 ...... 44 E2
Wintersells Rd BF/WBF KT14 ...... 215 N6
Winters Rd THDIT KT7 ...... 198 C7
Winterstoke Rd FSTH SE23 ...... 182 E4
Winters Wy WAB EN9 ...... 63 M9
Winterton Pl WBPTN SW10 ...... 15 K9
Winterwell Rd BRXS/STRHM SW2 ...... 180 F1
Winterthorpe Rd PUT/ROE SW15 ...... 157 H10
Winthrop St WCHPL E1 ...... 140 A7
Winton Ap RKW/CH/CXG WD3 ...... 72 D9
Winton Av FBAR/BDGN N11 ...... 98 D3
Winton Cl ED N9 ...... 100 G1
Winton Crs RKW/CH/CXG WD3 ...... 72 C9
Winton Dr CHES/WCR EN8 ...... 62 D5
  RKW/CH/CXG WD3 ...... 72 D9
Winton Gdns EDGW HA8 ...... 95 L8
Winton Rd ORP BR6 ...... 226 E1
  WARE SG12 ...... 26 E2
Winton Wy STRHM/NOR SW16 ...... 181 H8
Winvale SL SL1 ...... 149 K2
Winwood SLN SL2 ...... 129 P8
Wireless Rd BH/WHM TN16 ...... 244 A13
Wirral Wood Cl CHST BR7 ...... 184 D9
Wisbeach Rd CROY/NA CR0 ...... 203 L5
Wisborough Ct CRAWW RH11 ...... 283 J10
Wisborough Rd SAND/SEL CR2 ...... 223 N5
Wisdons Cl DAGE RM10 ...... 124 C6
Wise La MLHL NW7 ...... 96 D7
  WDR/YW UB7 ...... 151 N3
Wiseman Rd LEY E10 ...... 120 F7
Wisemans Gdns SBW CM21 ...... 29 M2
Wise Rd SRTFD E15 ...... 141 H3
Wiseton Rd TOOT SW17 ...... 179 A4
Wishart Rd BKHTH/KID SE3 ...... 162 A7
Wishbone Wy WOKN/KNAP GU21 ...... 231 L2
Wisley Cl RPLY/SEND GU23 ...... 233 P2
Wisley Rd BTSEA SW11 ...... 180 A1
  STMC/STPC BR5 ...... 185 K10
Wistaria Cl BRWN CM15 ...... 85 K10
  ORP BR6 ...... 206 G9
Wisteria Cl IL IG1 ...... 122 C10
Wisteria Gdns SWLY BR8 ...... 208 E2
Wisteria Rd LEW SE13 ...... 161 J10
Wistlea Crs STALE/WH AL4 ...... 39 N8
Wiston Ct CRAWW RH11 ...... 283 J10
Witan St BETH E2 ...... 140 A13
Witches La SEV TN13 ...... 246 E9
Witchford WGCE AL7 ...... 23 N5
Witham Cl LOU IG10 ...... 82 B10
Witham Rd DAGE RM10 ...... 124 B10
  GPK RM2 ...... 125 J3
  ISLW TW7 ...... 154 C7
  PGE/AN SE20 ...... 204 B3
  WEA W13 ...... 134 F10
Withens Cl STMC/STPC BR5 ...... 207 M4
Witherby Cl SAND/SEL CR2 ...... 223 M2
Wither Dl HORL RH6 ...... 279 P3
The Witherings EMPK RM11 ...... 125 M3
Witherington Rd HBRY N5 ...... 119 H10
Withers Md CDALE/KGS NW9 ...... 96 C9
Witherston Wy ELTH/MOT SE9 ...... 184 D5
Withey Brook HORL RH6 ...... 279 N6
Withey Cl WDSR SL4 ...... 148 D7
Witheygate Av STA TW18 ...... 173 L9
Withey Mdw HORL RH6 ...... 279 N6
Withies La RGUW GU3 ...... 267 H7
The Withies LHD/OX KT22 ...... 236 G6
  WOKN/KNAP GU21 ...... 231 K3
Withybed Cnr
  KWD/TDW/WH KT20 ...... 238 G9
Withy Cl LTWR GU18 ...... 212 B6
Withy Cft DTCH/LGLY SL3 ...... 130 B8
Withy La RSLP HA4 ...... 112 D3
Withy Md CHING E4 ...... 101 J4
Withypitts CRAWE RH10 ...... 285 P10
Withypitts East CRAWE RH10 ...... 285 P10
Withy Pl LCOL/BKTW AL2 ...... 56 B4
Witley Crs CROY/NA CR0 ...... 225 H3
Witley Gdns NWDGN UB2 ...... 153 N3
Witley Rd ARCH N19 ...... 118 D7
Witney Cl HGDN/ICK UB10 ...... 112 A9
  PIN HA5 ...... 93 N7
Wittenham Wy CHING E4 ...... 101 J4
Wittering Cl KUTN/CMB KT2 ...... 177 J8
Wittersham Rd BMLY BR1 ...... 183 L8
Wivenhoe Cl PECK SE15 ...... 159 P9
Wivenhoe Ct HSLWW TW4 ...... 153 N10
Wivenhoe Rd BARK IG11 ...... 143 K4
Wiverton Rd SYD SE26 ...... 182 B9
Wix Hl EHSLY KT24 ...... 252 C6
Wix Rd DAGW RM9 ...... 143 N5
Wix's La BTSEA SW11 ...... 158 C10
Woburn Av EPP CM16 ...... 83 H3
  HCH RM12 ...... 125 H9
  PUR/KEN CR8 ...... 223 H7
Woburn Cl BUSH WD23 ...... 74 B10
  WIM/MER SW19 ...... 179 M9
Woburn Pl ADL/WDHM KT15 ...... 195 M9
  STPAN WC1H 11 K1
Woburn Rd BAR SM5 ...... 201 P8
  CRAWW RH11 ...... 283 K9
  CROY/NA CR0 ...... 203 K8
Woburn Sq STPAN WC1H 11 K2
Wodehouse Av CMBW SE5 ...... 159 P6
Wodehouse Rd DART DA1 ...... 165 P10
Wodeland Av GUW GU2 ...... 267 H7
Woffington Cl E/WMO/HCT KT8 ...... 199 H1
Wokindon Rd CDH/CHF RM16 ...... 168 E2
Woking Cl PUT/ROE SW15 ...... 156 C10
Woking Rd GU GU1 ...... 250 A6
  RGUE GU4 ...... 249 P3
Wold Cl CRAWW RH11 ...... 283 J9
Woldham Pl HAYES BR2 ...... 205 P4
Woldham Rd HAYES BR2 ...... 205 P4
Woldhurstlea Cl CRAWW RH11 ...... 283 K9
Woldingham Rd CTHM CR3 ...... 242 A6
Wolds Dr ORP BR6 ...... 226 D7
The Wold CTHM CR3 ...... 242 F8
Wolfe Cl HAYES BR2 ...... 205 M6
  YEAD UB4 ...... 133 J5
Wolfe Crs CHARL SE7 ...... 162 A4
Wolferton Rd MNPK E12 ...... 122 C9
Wolfington Rd WNWD SE27 ...... 181 J7
Wolf La WDSR SL4 ...... 148 C9
Wolfram Cl LEW SE13 ...... 183 K1
Wolf's Hl OXTED RH8 ...... 261 M7
Wolf's Rd OXTED RH8 ...... 261 N7
Wolfs Wd OXTED RH8 ...... 261 M8
Wolftencroft Cl BTSEA SW11 ...... 157 P9
Wolmer Gdns EDGW HA8 ...... 95 M4
Wolseley Av WAND/EARL SW18 ...... 179 L5
Wolseley Gdns CHSWK W4 ...... 155 N5
Wolseley Rd CEND/HSY/T N8 ...... 118 C4
  CHSWK W4 ...... 155 P3
  FSTGT E7 ...... 141 N2
  KTN/HRWW/W HA3 ...... 114 D1
  MTCM CR4 ...... 202 B7
  ROMW/RG RM7 ...... 124 C5
  WDGN N22 ...... 98 D9

Wolseley St STHWK SE1 19 M2
Wolsey Av CHESW EN7 61 N5 4
EHAM E6 142 D5
WALTH E17 120 E1 6
Wolsey Cl HSLW TW3 154 B10
KUTN/CMB KT2 199 N1
NWDGN UB2 154 B2
RYNPK SW20 178 E10
WPK KT4 220 D1
Wolsey Crs CROY/NA CR0 225 H5
MRDN SM4 201 J7
Wolsey Dr KUTN/CMB KT2 177 K8
WOT/HER KT12 197 L8
Wolsey Gdns BARK/HLT IG6 102 F7 5
Wolsey Gv EDGW HA8 96 A8
ESH/CLAY KT10 218 A1 3
Wolsey Ms KTTN NW5 4 G1
ORP BR6 227 J2
Wolsey Rd ASHF TW15 173 P7
E/WMO/HCT KT8 198 C4
EN EN1 80 A6
ESH/CLAY KT10 218 A1
HHNE HP2 35 N7
HPTN TW12 176 A9
IS N1 119 L10
RKW/CH/CXG WD3 92 D3
SUN TW16 174 G10
Wolsey St WCHPL E1 140 B7
Wolsey Wy CHSGTN KT9 219 M2
Wolsley Cl DART DA1 186 F1
Wolstan Cl DEN/HRF UB9 111 K8 5
Wolstonbury NFNCH/WDSP N12 97 K6
Wolstonbury Cl CRAWW RH11 283 M9
Wolvens La DORK RH4 271 P6
Wolvercote Rd ABYW SE2 163 N1
Wolverley St BETH E2 140 A5 19
Wolverton Av KUTN/CMB KT2 199 M1
Wolverton Cl HORL RH6 280 A6
Wolverton Gdns EA W5 135 L9
HMSMTH W6 156 G3
HORL RH6 280 A5
Wolverton Rd STAN HA7 94 G7
Wolverton Wy STHGT/OAK N14 78 D9
Wolves La WDGN N22 99 H8
Wombwell Gdns GVW DA11 190 A5
Womersley Rd CEND/HSY/T N8 118 G4
Wonersh Wy BELMT SM2 220 G5
Wonford Cl KWD/TDW/WH KT20 256 D2
NWMAL KT3 200 B1
Wonham La BRKHM/BTCW RH3 274 C1
Wonham Wy SHGR GU5 270 E8
Wontford Rd PUR/KEN CR8 241 H1
Wontner Rd BAL SW12 180 A5
Wooburn Cl UX/CGN UB8 132 C6 4
Wooburn Common Rd
FLKWH HP10 108 A7
Woodall Rd PEND EN3 80 C10
Wood Av PUR RM19 166 B3
Woodbank Av CFSP/GDCR SL9 110 A4
Woodbank Dr CSTG HP8 90 A4
Woodbank Rd BMLY BR1 183 L6
Woodbastwick Rd SYD SE26 182 C9
Woodberry Av RYLN/HDSTN HA2 114 B2
WCHMH N21 99 H3
Woodberry Cl SUN TW16 175 H9
Woodberry Crs MUSWH N10 118 C1 5
Woodberry Down EPP CM16 65 K5
FSBYPK N4 119 K6
Woodberry Gdns
NFNCH/WDSP N12 97 M7 3
Woodberry Gv BXLY DA5 186 E6
FSBYPK N4 119 K5 4
NFNCH/WDSP N12 97 M7
Woodberry Wy CHING E4 101 H1
NFNCH/WDSP N12 97 M7
Woodbine Cl HLWW/ROY CM19 46 F3
WHTN TW2 176 C5 1
Woodbine Gv ENC/FH EN2 79 L4
PGE/AN SE20 182 A10
Woodbine La WPK KT4 200 E10
Woodbine Pl WAN E11 121 M4
Woodbine Rd BFN/LL DA15 185 H4
Woodbines Av KUT KT1 199 J3
Woodbine Ter HOM E9 140 B1 10
Woodborough Rd
PUT/ROE SW15 156 E10
Woodbourne Av
STRHM/NOR SW16 180 E6
Woodbourne Dr ESH/CLAY KT10 218 E3
Woodbourne Gdns WLGTN SM6 222 C4 1
Woodbridge Av LHD/OX KT22 236 F4
Woodbridge Cl HARH RM3 105 L5 1
HOLWY N7 118 G7 5
Woodbridge Gv LHD/OX KT22 236 F4
Woodbridge Hl GUW GU2 249 N9
Woodbridge Hill Gdns
GUW GU2 249 M9 1
Woodbridge La HARH RM3 105 L4
Woodbridge Mdw GU GU1 249 P9
Woodbridge Rd BARK IG11 123 J10
GU GU1 249 P9
GU GU1 268 A1
Woodbridge St CLKNW EC1R 12 C1 1
Woodbrook Gdns WAB EN9 63 K9
Woodbrook Rd ABYW SE2 163 K5
Woodburn Cl HDN NW4 116 G3 6
Woodbury Cl BH/WHM TN16 244 C4
CROY/NA CR0 203 N9
WAN E11 121 N2 2
Woodbury Dr BELMT SM2 221 M6
Woodbury Hl LOU IG10 82 B6
Woodbury Park Rd WEA W13 134 G6
Woodbury Rd WALTH E17 120 G2
Woodbury St TOOT SW17 179 P8
Woodby Dr ASC SL5 192 E7
Woodchester Pk BEAC HP9 88 B5
Woodchester Sq BAY/PAD W2 8 G3
Woodchurch Cl BFN/LL DA15 184 G6
Woodchurch Dr BMLY BR1 184 A10 1
Woodchurch Rd KIL/WHAMP NW6 2 F4
Wood Cl BETH E2 13 N1
BXLY DA5 186 F6
CDALE/KGS NW9 116 A5
HAT AL10 40 E4
HRW HA1 114 C5
REDH RH1 276 B9
WDSR SL4 149 H10
Woodclyffe Dr CHST BR7 206 D2
Woodcock Ct KTN/HRWW/W HA3 115 K5
Woodcock Dell Av
KTN/HRWW/W HA3 115 H5
Woodcock Dr CHOB/PIR GU24 213 H4
Woodcock Hl KTN/HRWW/W HA3 115 H3
RKW/CH/CXG WD3 91 P6
Woodcockhill STALE/WH AL4 21 J10
Woodcock La CHOB/PIR GU24 212 G4
Woodcocks CAN/RD E16 141 P7
Woodcombe Crs FSTH SE23 182 B4
Wood Common HAT AL10 40 E1
Woodcot Cl ED N9 80 B10
Woodcote HORL RH6 280 C3
RGUW GU3 267 N4
Woodcote Av HCH RM12 125 H9
MLHL NW7 96 F7
THHTH CR7 203 J4
WLGTN SM6 222 C5
Woodcote Cl CHES/WCR EN8 62 B6
EPSOM KT18 220 A10
KUTN/CMB KT2 177 L8
Woodcote Dr ORP BR6 206 G7
Woodcote End EPSOM KT18 238 A1
Woodcote Gn WLGTN SM6 222 D5
Woodcote Green Rd
EPSOM KT18 237 P2
Woodcote Grove Rd
COUL/CHIP CR5 240 E1
Woodcote Hurst EPSOM KT18 237 P2
Woodcote La PUR/KEN CR8 222 E7
Woodcote Ms LOU IG10 102 A1
WLGTN SM6 222 C3
Woodcote Park Av PUR/KEN CR8 222 D7
Woodcote Park Rd EPSOM KT18 237 P2
Woodcote Pl WNWD SE27 181 J8 3
Woodcote Rd WAN E11 121 M5
WLGTN SM6 222 C3
Woodcote Side EPSOM KT18 237 N1
Woodcote Valley Rd
PUR/KEN CR8 222 E9
Wood Crs HHS/BOV HP3 35 N7
Woodcrest Rd PUR/KEN CR8 222 F9
Woodcrest Wk REDH RH1 257 P8
Woodcroft ELTH/MOT SE9 184 C6
GFD/PVL UB6 134 F1 1
HLWS CM18 46 F3
WCHMH N21 98 G2
Woodcroft Av MLHL NW7 96 B8
STAN HA7 94 F9
WARE SG12 27 J7
Woodcroft Crs HGDN/ICK UB10 132 C3
Woodcroft Ms DEPT SE8 160 D3
Woodcroft Rd CRAWW RH11 282 G9 5
CSHM HP5 51 J4
THHTH CR7 203 J5
Woodcutters Av CDH/CHF RM16 167 P1 3
Wood Dr CHST BR7 184 B9
SEV TN13 264 G2
Woodedge Cl CHING E4 101 L2
Wood End HYS/HAR UB3 132 F8
LCOL/BKTW AL2 56 B4
SWLY BR8 208 D4 1
Woodend ESH/CLAY KT10 198 B9
LHD/OX KT22 255 H1
NRWD SE19 181 K9
SUT SM1 201 M9
Wood End Av RYLN/HDSTN HA2 114 A9
Woodend Cl CRAWE RH10 284 B5 3
Wood End Cl HHNE HP2 36 D5 4
NTHLT UB5 114 C10 8
SLN SL2 109 J8
Woodend Cl WOKN/KNAP GU21 231 M5
Wood End Cl WOKS/MYFD GU22 233 J2
Woodend Dr ASC SL5 192 A5
Woodend Gdns ENC/FH EN2 78 F8 4
Wood End Gdns NTHLT UB5 114 B10
Wood End Green Rd
HYS/HAR UB3 132 E7
UX/CGN UB8 132 D8 2
Wood End La NTHLT UB5 134 A1
Woodend Pk COB KT11 235 L1
Wood End Rd NTHLT UB5 114 C9
Woodend Rd WALTH E17 101 H10
The Wood End WLGTN SM6 222 C5 1
Wood End Wy NTHLT UB5 114 B10
Wooder Gdns FSTGT E7 121 L9
Wooderson Cl SNWD SE25 203 M4
Woodfall Av BAR EN5 77 J9
Woodfall Dr DART DA1 164 G10
Woodfall Rd FSBYPK N4 119 H6
Woodfall St CHEL SW3 16 A8
Wood Farm Rd HHNE HP2 35 P6
Woodfarrs CMBW SE5 159 L10
Woodfield ASHTD KT21 237 J3
Woodfield Av ALP/SUD HA0 115 H8
CAR SM5 222 B3
CDALE/KGS NW9 116 B2
EA W5 135 H6
GVW DA11 190 E5
NTHWD HA6 92 F5
STRHM/NOR SW16 180 E6
Woodfield Cl ASHTD KT21 237 J3
COUL/CHIP CR5 240 D5
CRAWE RH10 283 P6
EN EN1 79 M8 3
NRWD SE19 181 K10
REDH RH1 257 P9
Woodfield Crs EA W5 135 J6
Woodfield Dr EBAR EN4 98 B2
GPK RM2 125 H2
HHS/BOV HP3 36 E8
Woodfield Gdns HHS/BOV HP3 36 E8 1
NWMAL KT3 200 C5
Woodfield Gv
STRHM/NOR SW16 180 E6 3
Woodfield Hl COUL/CHIP CR5 240 C5
Woodfield La ASHTD KT21 237 K3
BRKMPK AL9 41 P9
Woodfield Pk AMS HP6 68 G3
Woodfield Ri BUSH WD23 94 C1
Woodfield Rd ASHTD KT21 237 J3
CRAWE RH10 284 A5
EA W5 135 H6
ESH/CLAY KT10 198 E9 1
HSLWW TW4 153 J7 6
MV/WKIL W9 8 D3
RAD WD7 74 F2
WGCE AL7 23 J5
Woodfields SEV TN13 246 E9
The Woodfields SAND/SEL CR2 223 N7
Woodfield Wy FBAR/BDGN N11 98 E8
HCH RM12 125 L6 1
REDH RH1 257 P9
STALE/WH AL4 39 H3
The Woodfines EMPK RM11 125 L4
Woodford Av GNTH/NBYPK IG2 122 C3
Woodford Bridge Rd REDBR IG4 122 A1
Woodford Ct WAB EN9 63 M9
Woodford Crs PIN HA5 93 J10
Woodford New Rd WFD IG8 101 L8
Woodford Pl WBLY HA9 115 K6
Woodford Rd FSTGT E7 121 N9
SWFD E18 121 M2
WAT WD17 73 J6
Woodford Wy SLN SL2 128 F5
Woodgate GSTN WD25 55 J9
Woodgate Av CHSGTN KT9 219 J2
POTB/CUF EN6 60 C9
Woodgate Crs NTHWD HA6 93 H7
Woodgate Dr STRHM/NOR SW16 180 E10
Woodgavil BNSTD SM7 239 J2
Woodger Cl GU GU1 250 F8
Woodger Rd SHB W12 156 F1 5
Woodgers Gv SWLY BR8 208 G2 1
Woodget Cl EHAM E6 142 B8 4
Woodgrange Av ACT W3 135 L10
EN EN1 79 P10
KTN/HRWW/W HA3 115 H3
NFNCH/WDSP N12 97 N7
Woodgrange Cl
KTN/HRWW/W HA3 115 J3
Woodgrange Gdns EN EN1 79 P10
Woodgreen Rd WAB EN9 63 P9
Woodhall Av DUL SE21 181 N6
PIN HA5 93 M9
Woodhall Cl HERT/WAS SG14 25 K3 3
UX/CGN UB8 111 N10
Woodhall Ct WGCE AL7 23 H6
Woodhall Crs EMPK RM11 125 N5
Woodhall Dr DUL SE21 181 N6
PIN HA5 93 L9
Woodhall Ga PIN HA5 93 L8
Woodhall La BFOR GU20 192 D9
HHNE HP2 35 P5
OXHEY WD19 93 L4
RAD WD7 57 M10 1
WGCE AL7 23 H7
Woodham Ct SWFD E18 121 L2 5
Woodham La ADL/WDHM KT15 215 L6
ADL/WDHM KT15 215 H8
WOKN/KNAP GU21 214 E9
Woodham Park Rd
ADL/WDHM KT15 215 J6
Woodham Park Wy
ADL/WDHM KT15 215 J7
Woodham Ri WOKN/KNAP GU21 232 D1
Woodham Rd CAT SE6 183 H6
WOKN/KNAP GU21 214 C10
Woodham Wy WARE SG12 27 H7 2
Woodham Waye
WOKN/KNAP GU21 214 E9
Woodhatch Cl EHAM E6 142 B7 7
Woodhatch Rd REDH RH1 276 A5 2
Woodhatch Spinney
COUL/CHIP CR5 240 F2
Woodhaw EGH TW20 172 E7
Woodhayes HORL RH6 280 C3 18
Woodhayes Rd RYNPK SW20 178 F10
WIM/MER SW19 178 F9 1
Woodhead Dr ORP BR6 207 H10
Woodheyes Rd WLSDN NW10 116 B10
Woodhill CHARL SE7 162 B3
HLWS CM18 47 H4
RPLY/SEND GU23 250 G1
Woodhill Av CFSP/GDCR SL9 110 C4
Woodhill Crs KTN/HRWW/W HA3 115 J4
Woodhouse Av GFD/PVL UB6 134 E4
Woodhouse Cl GFD/PVL UB6 134 E4
HYS/HAR UB3 152 F2
Woodhouse Eaves NTHWD HA6 93 H6 1
Woodhouse Gv MNPK E12 142 B1
Wood House La BROX EN10 43 N7
Woodhouse La SHGR GU5 271 H9
Woodhouse Rd NFNCH/WDSP N12 97 P7
WAN E11 121 L8
Woodhurst Av GSTN WD25 73 L1
STMC/STPC BR5 206 F6
Woodhurst Dr DEN/HRF UB9 111 J3
Woodhurst La OXTED RH8 261 K7
Woodhurst Pk OXTED RH8 261 K6
Woodhurst Rd ABYW SE2 163 K4
ACT W3 135 P10
Woodhyrst Gdns PUR/KEN CR8 241 J1
Wooding Gv HLWW/ROY CM19 46 E1
Woodington Cl ELTH/MOT SE9 184 D2
Woodison St BOW E3 140 D6 5
Woodknoll Dr CHST BR7 206 C1
Woodland Ap GFD/PVL UB6 134 F1 2
Woodland Av HART DA3 211 L5
HHW HP1 35 L7
RBRW/HUT CM13 87 P9
SL SL1 129 J9
WDSR SL4 148 E10
Woodland Cl CDALE/KGS NW9 115 P4
EHSLY KT24 252 G3 1
HART DA3 211 P3
HGDN/ICK UB10 112 C7
HHW HP1 35 L7 4
HOR/WEW KT19 220 B3 2
NRWD SE19 181 M9 5
RBRW/HUT CM13 87 P9
WFD IG8 101 N4
Woodland Ct OXTED RH8 261 J4
Woodland Crs GNWCH SE10 161 K5 3
Woodland Dr EHSLY KT24 252 G3
STALE/WH AL4 39 H5
WAT WD17 72 G5
Woodland Gdns ISLW TW7 154 D9
MUSWH N10 118 C3
SAND/SEL CR2 224 B7
Woodland Gld SLN SL2 109 J8
Woodland Gv WEY KT13 216 E1
Woodland Hl NRWD SE19 181 M9
Woodland La RKW/CH/CXG WD3 70 G7
Woodland Mt HERT/BAY SG13 25 N5
Woodland Pl HHW HP1 35 L7 5
Woodland Ri BGR/WK TN15 247 N8
GFD/PVL UB6 134 F1
MUSWH N10 118 C2
OXTED RH8 261 K6
WGCW AL8 22 F3
Woodland Rd CHING E4 101 H2
FBAR/BDGN N11 98 C6
HERT/BAY SG13 26 B8
LOU IG10 82 B7 2
NRWD SE19 181 M8
RKW/CH/CXG WD3 90 G6
THHTH CR7 203 H4
Woodlands ADL/WDHM KT15 195 P10
BRKMPK AL9 59 L3
CFSP/GDCR SL9 110 C4
CRAWE RH10 284 E5
GLDGN NW11 117 H3
LCOL/BKTW AL2 56 B3
RAD WD7 56 F10 2
RPLY/SEND GU23 251 J1 2
RYLN/HDSTN HA2 113 P2
RYNPK SW20 200 G4 1
WOKS/MYFD GU22 232 B4
Woodlands Av ACT W3 135 N10 5
BERK HP4 34 A6
BF/WBF KT14 215 J9
BFN/LL DA15 185 H4
CHDH RM6 123 P4
EMPK RM11 125 L3
FNCH N3 97 M8
NWMAL KT3 200 A1
REDH RH1 276 A1
RSLP HA4 113 K6
WAN E11 121 N6
WPK KT4 200 C9
Woodlands Cl BMLY BR1 206 C2
BORE WD6 75 N8
CDH/CHF RM16 168 B2
CFSP/GDCR SL9 110 D4
CHERT KT16 214 E6
ESH/CLAY KT10 218 E4 1
HOD EN11 44 F4 4
SWLY BR8 208 G2 2
Woodlands Dr BEAC HP9 88 B7
HOD EN11 44 F5
STAN HA7 94 E7
SUN TW16 197 K2
Woodlands Gld BEAC HP9 88 B7
Woodlands Gv COUL/CHIP CR5 240 C3
GNWCH SE10 161 K4 7
ISLW TW7 154 D8
Woodlands Hl BEAC HP9 108 D4
Woodlands La CHOB/PIR GU24 212 E4
COB KT11 235 P3
GVE DA12 191 N10
Woodlands Pde ASHF TW15 174 D9 1
Woodlands Pk ADL/WDHM KT15 215 J2
BXLY DA5 186 E7
GU GU1 250 E9
KWD/TDW/WH KT20 255 N7
WOKN/KNAP GU21 214 F9
Woodlands Park Rd
BKHTH/KID SE3 161 K5 4
GNWCH SE10 161 K5
SEVS/STOTM N15 119 K3
Woodlands Ri SWLY BR8 208 G2 3
Woodlands Rd BARN SW13 156 C9
BF/WBF KT14 215 J10
BMLY BR1 206 C2
BUSH WD23 73 M8
BXLYHN DA7 163 P9
ED N9 100 B2
EHSLY KT24 253 N4
ENC/FH EN2 79 L4
EPSOM KT18 237 M1
GU GU1 250 A6
HARH RM3 105 P9
HERT/BAY SG13 25 N5
HRW HA1 114 E3
IL IG1 122 F8
ISLW TW7 154 D9
KGLGY WD4 54 B3
LHD/OX KT22 236 C4
ORP BR6 227 K3
REDH RH1 276 A2
ROM RM1 124 G1
STHL UB1 133 L10
SURB KT6 199 J7
VW GU25 193 P4
WALTH E17 121 H1
WAN E11 121 K7 2
Woodlands Rd East VW GU25 193 P4
Woodlands Rd West VW GU25 193 P3
Woodlands St LEW SE13 183 J3
The Woodlands AMS HP6 69 H1
ESH/CLAY KT10 198 B9
HORL RH6 281 J4
ISLW TW7 154 E8
LEW SE13 183 J3
NRWD SE19 181 K10
ORP BR6 227 L3
STHGT/OAK N14 98 C2
WLGTN SM6 222 C5 2
Woodland St HACK E8 7 L1 4
Woodlands Wy ASHTD KT21 237 M2
KWD/TDW/WH KT20 255 P6
PUT/ROE SW15 179 J1 3
Woodland Ter CHARL SE7 162 B3
Woodland Vw CSHM HP5 51 J9
RGODL GU7 267 K8
Woodland Wk HAMP NW3 117 P10 5
HOR/WEW KT19 219 M3
Woodland Wy ABYW SE2 163 N3
BRYLDS KT5 199 N9 3
CHESW EN7 61 J4
CHONG CM5 67 N6
CROY/NA CR0 204 D8
EPP CM16 83 H1
GRH DA9 188 F1
KWD/TDW/WH KT20 239 H8
MLHL NW7 96 B7
MRDN SM4 201 J4
MTCM CR4 180 B10
PUR/KEN CR8 223 H9
REDH RH1 259 M4
STMC/STPC BR5 206 F4
WCHMH N21 99 H3
WEY KT13 216 E2
WFD IG8 101 N4
WWKM BR4 205 H10
Wood La CDALE/KGS NW9 116 A5
CTHM CR3 241 L10
DAGE RM10 124 B7
HCH RM12 125 H10
HGT N6 118 C4
HHNE HP2 35 N7
ISLW TW7 154 D5
IVER SL0 130 F6
KWD/TDW/WH KT20 239 J3
RDART DA2 188 E6
RSLP HA4 112 E7
SHB W12 136 F8
SL SL1 148 E2
STAN HA7 94 G4
WEY KT13 216 D5
WFD IG8 101 L6
WOKN/KNAP GU21 231 J4
Wood Lane End HHNE HP2 36 C5
Woodlawn Cl PUT/ROE SW15 179 J1 4
Woodlawn Crs WHTN TW2 176 A5
Woodlawn Dr FELT TW13 175 L5
Woodlawn Gv WOKN/KNAP GU21 232 C1
Woodlawn Rd FUL/PGN SW6 156 G6
Woodlea HART DA3 211 P3
LCOL/BKTW AL2 55 P1
Woodlea Dr HAYES BR2 205 K5
Woodlea Gv NTHWD HA6 92 D7
Woodlea Rd STNW/STAM N16 119 M8
Woodleigh Av NFNCH/WDSP N12 97 P7
Woodleigh Gdns
STRHM/NOR SW16 180 F6
Woodley Cl TOOT SW17 180 A10 5
Woodley Hl CSHM HP5 51 J10
Woodley La SUT SM1 201 P10
Woodley Rd ORP BR6 207 M9
WARE SG12 26 E1
Wood Lodge Gdns BMLY BR1 184 B10
Wood Lodge La WWKM BR4 205 H10
Woodmancote Gdns
BF/WBF KT14 215 K9
Woodmancourt RGODL GU7 267 H9
Woodman La CHING E4 81 J9
Woodman Pth BARK/HLT IG6 103 H6
Woodman Rd BRW CM14 107 H6
COUL/CHIP CR5 240 D2
HHS/BOV HP3 35 P8
Woodmans Gv WLSDN NW10 116 C10 1
Woodmansterne La BNSTD SM7 239 L1
CAR SM5 222 A8
WLGTN SM6 222 C7
Woodmansterne Rd CAR SM5 221 P6
COUL/CHIP CR5 240 D1
STRHM/NOR SW16 202 F1
Woodmansterne St BNSTD SM7 239 P1
Woodman St CAN/RD E16 142 D10
Woodmans Yd WAT WD17 73 K8 14
Wood Meads EPP CM16 65 K5
Woodmere ELTH/MOT SE9 184 C3
Woodmere Av CROY/NA CR0 204 C7
WATN WD24 73 L4
Woodmere Cl CROY/NA CR0 204 C7
Woodmere Gdns CROY/NA CR0 204 C7
Woodmere Wy BECK BR3 205 J5
Woodmount SWLY BR8 208 E7
Woodnook Rd
STRHM/NOR SW16 180 C8
Wood Peckarmans DUL SE21 181 P6
Woodpecker Cl BUSH WD23 94 B2
COB KT11 217 M8
ED N9 80 A10
HAT AL10 40 C7 3
KTN/HRWW/W HA3 94 E9 2
Woodpecker Rd THMD SE28 143 M9 3
Woodpecker Wy
WOKS/MYFD GU22 232 A9
Woodplace Cl COUL/CHIP CR5 240 D5
Woodplace La COUL/CHIP CR5 240 D6
Wood Pond Cl BEAC HP9 89 H7
Woodquest Av HNHL SE24 181 J1
Woodredon Cl HLWW/ROY CM19 45 N2 1
Woodridden Hl WAB EN9 82 A1
Wood Ride EBAR EN4 77 N5
STMC/STPC BR5 206 G4
Woodridge Cl ENC/FH EN2 79 H5 1
Woodridge Wy NTHWD HA6 92 F7
Wood Riding WOKS/MYFD GU22 233 H1
Woodridings Av PIN HA5 93 N9
Woodridings Cl PIN HA5 93 N8
Woodriffe Rd WAN E11 121 J5
Wood Ri GUW GU2 249 K8
PIN HA5 113 H3
Wood Rd BH/WHM TN16 243 P4
RGODL GU7 267 L10
SHPTN TW17 196 B4
Woodrow WOOL/PLUM SE18 162 B3
Woodrow Av YEAD UB4 132 G7
Woodrow Cl GFD/PVL UB6 134 G2
Woodrow Ct TOTM N17 100 A8 6
Woodroyd Av HORL RH6 280 A5
Woodroyd Gdns HORL RH6 280 A6
Woodruff Av GU GU1 250 D7
Woodrush Cl NWCR SE14 160 D6 9
Woodrush Wy CHDH RM6 123 N2
Woods Av HAT AL10 40 D5
Woodseer St WCHPL E1 13 M3
Woodshire Rd DAGE RM10 124 C8
Woodshore Cl VW GU25 193 N6
Woodshots Meadow WATW WD18 72 E9
Woodside BKHH IG9 101 P3
BORE WD6 75 L8 2
CHESW EN7 61 P7
EHSLY KT24 252 D2
EPP CM16 65 N3
GLDGN NW11 117 K3
HERT/BAY SG13 26 B8
KWD/TDW/WH KT20 257 J4
LHD/OX KT22 236 A8
ORP BR6 227 K2
WATN WD24 73 H3
WIM/MER SW19 179 J8
WOT/HER KT12 197 H8
Woodside Av ALP/SUD HA0 135 K3
AMS HP6 69 J2
BEAC HP9 88 B8
CHST BR7 184 F8
ESH/CLAY KT10 198 D7
HGT N6 118 A3
NFNCH/WDSP N12 97 M5
SNWD SE25 204 A6
WOT/HER KT12 217 J1
Woodside Cl ALP/SUD HA0 135 K3
BEAC HP9 88 B8
BRYLDS KT5 199 P7
BXLYHN DA7 164 E10
CFSP/GDCR SL9 90 B10 2
CTHM CR3 241 M10
RAIN RM13 145 K6
RSLP HA4 112 E4 4
STAN HA7 94 F6
WOKN/KNAP GU21 231 J3
Woodside Court Rd
CROY/NA CR0 203 P7
Woodside Crs BFN/LL DA15 185 H6
HORL RH6 281 H4
Woodside Dr RDART DA2 186 F7
Woodside End ALP/SUD HA0 135 K3
Woodside Gdns CHING E4 100 G6
TOTM N17 99 N10
Woodside Grange Rd
NFNCH/WDSP N12 97 L5
Woodside Gn CROY/NA CR0 203 P7
SNWD SE25 203 P6
Woodside Gv NFNCH/WDSP N12 97 M4
Woodside Hl CFSP/GDCR SL9 90 B10
Woodside La ASC SL5 170 B8
BRKMPK AL9 41 K8
BXLY DA5 185 N2
NFNCH/WDSP N12 97 L4
WDSR SL4 170 B7
Woodside Pk SNWD SE25 203 P6
Woodside Park Av WALTH E17 121 J2
Woodside Park Rd
NFNCH/WDSP N12 97 L5
Woodside Pl ALP/SUD HA0 135 K3 4
Woodside Rd AMS HP6 69 J3
ASC SL5 170 A8
BEAC HP9 88 B8
BFN/LL DA15 185 H6
BMLY BR1 206 B5
BXLYHN DA7 164 E10
COB KT11 217 P9
CRAWE RH10 284 A5
GSTN WD25 55 J7
GUW GU2 249 L9
KUTN/CMB KT2 177 K10
LCOL/BKTW AL2 55 N6
NTHWD HA6 92 G8
NWMAL KT3 200 A2
PLSTW E13 141 P6
PUR/KEN CR8 222 F9
RSEV TN14 245 N10
SEV TN13 247 J9
SNWD SE25 204 A6
SUT SM1 201 M10
WDGN N22 99 H8
WFD IG8 101 M5
Woodside Wy CROY/NA CR0 204 B6 6
MTCM CR4 202 D1 3
REDH RH1 276 B1
VW GU25 193 N3
Woodslands HORL RH6 280 E3
Woods Ms MYFR/PKLN W1K 10 B7
Woodsome Rd KTTN NW5 118 B8
Wood's Pl STHWK SE1 19 K4
Woodspring Rd WIM/MER SW19 179 H5
Wood's Rd PECK SE15 160 A7
Woodstead Gv EDGW HA8 95 K7
The Woods HGDN/ICK UB10 112 C9
NTHWD HA6 93 H6
RAD WD7 56 G10
Woodstock RGUE GU4 251 L4
Woodstock Av CHEAM SM3 201 J7
DTCH/LGLY SL3 150 A3
GLDGN NW11 117 H5
HARH RM3 106 A6
HNWL W7 154 F2
ISLW TW7 176 F1
STHL UB1 133 N5 6
Woodstock Cl BXLY DA5 186 A4
HERT/BAY SG13 26 A7 1
STAN HA7 95 K10
WOKN/KNAP GU21 232 B2
Woodstock Crs ED N9 80 A10
Woodstock Dr HGDN/ICK UB10 111 P9
Woodstock Gdns BECK BR3 204 G1
GDMY/SEVK IG3 123 K7
YEAD UB4 132 G7
Woodstock Gv RGODL GU7 267 K10 5
SHB W12 156 G1
Woodstock La North SURB KT6 199 H9
Woodstock La South
ESH/CLAY KT10 218 G2
Woodstock Ms CAVSQ/HST W1G 10 D4 6
Woodstock Ri CHEAM SM3 201 J8
Woodstock Rd ALP/SUD HA0 135 L2
BROX EN10 44 D5
BUSH WD23 94 D1
CAR SM5 222 B2
CHSWK W4 156 B3
COUL/CHIP CR5 240 C2 1
CROY/NA CR0 203 L10
FSBYPK N4 119 H6
FSTGT E7 141 P2
GLDGN NW11 117 J5
WALTH E17 101 J10
Woodstock Rd North STAL AL1 38 G4
Woodstock Rd South STAL AL1 38 G6
Woodstock St CAN/RD E16 141 L8 11
MYFR/PKLN W1K 10 E6 3
Woodstock Ter POP/IOD E14 140 G9
Woodstock Wy MTCM CR4 202 D2
Wood Stoke SLN SL2 109 L9
Woodstone Av EW KT17 220 D2
Wood St BAR EN5 76 F8
BARB EC2Y 12 F4
CAN/RD E16 141 N9 3
CHSWK W4 156 B4
CITYW EC2V 12 F5 7
GRAYS RM17 167 P5
KUT KT1 199 J2
MTCM CR4 202 B7
REDH RH1 258 D5
SWLY BR8 209 K1
WALTH E17 121 H1
Woodsway LHD/OX KT22 218 D10
Woodsyre NRWD SE19 181 N7
Woodthorpe Rd ASHF TW15 173 N8
PUT/ROE SW15 156 E10
Woodtree Cl HDN NW4 96 F10
Wood V EDUL SE22 182 A4
HAT AL10 40 E4
MUSWH N10 118 D3
Woodvale Av SNWD SE25 203 N3
Woodvale Wy CRICK NW2 116 G8
Woodview CHSGTN KT9 219 H8
Wood Vw GRAYS RM17 168 B3
HHW HP1 35 L4
POTB/CUF EN6 60 F3
Woodview Av CHING E4 101 H5 1
Woodview Cl KUTN/CMB KT2 178 A7
SAND/SEL CR2 224 A10

Woodview Rd SWLY BR8 .... 208 D2
Woodville Cl LEE/GVPK SE12 .... 183 M1 ⁴
  TEDD TW11 .... 176 F7 ²
Woodville Court Ms WAT WD17 .. 73 H6 ⁵
Woodville Gdns BARK/HLT IG6 .. 122 E1
  EA W5 .... 135 K8
  RSLP HA4 .... 112 D5
Woodville Pl GVE DA12 .... 190 E3 ⁴
Woodville Rd BAR EN5 .... 77 ⁴
  EA W5 .... 135 K8
  GLDGN NW11 .... 117 H5
  KIL/WHAMP NW6 .... 2 D7
  LHD/OX KT22 .... 236 C6
  MRDN SM4 .... 201 K4
  RCHPK/HAM TW10 .... 176 C6
  STNW/STAM N16 .... 119 M10
  SWFD E18 .... 101 N10
  THHTH CR7 .... 203 K4 ⁴
  WALTH E17 .... 120 D2
  WAN E11 .... 121 L6
Woodville St CHARL SE7 .... 162 B5 ⁴
Woodward Av HDN NW4 .... 116 D3
Woodward Cl ESH/CLAY KT10 ... 218 C3
  GRAYS RM17 .... 167 N3
Woodwarde Rd EDUL SE22 .... 181 M2
Woodward Gdns DAGW RM9 ...... 143 M2
  STAN HA7 .... 94 E8
Woodward Hts GRAYS RM17 ...... 167 N3
Woodward Rd DAGW RM9 .... 143 L2
  WALTH/WROY CM19 .... 46 F3
Woodward Ter GRH DA9 .... 188 D2
Wood Wy ORP BR6 .... 206 D9
Woodway RBRW/HUT CM13 .... 107 N2
  GU GU1 .... 250 E9
Woodway Crs HRW HA1 .... 114 F4
Woodwaye OXHEY WD19 .... 93 K1
Woodwell St WAND/EARL SW18 . 179 N1
Wood Whf GNWCH SE10 .... 160 C5
Woodwicks RKW/CH/CXG WD3 ... 90 C6 ²
Woodyard Cl KTTN NW5 .... 118 C10 ³
Woodyard La DUL SE21 .... 181 M3
Woodyates Rd LEE/GVPK SE12 . 183 M2
Woodyers Cl SHGR GU5 .... 268 E10
Woolacombe Cl CRAWE RH10 .... 283 P6 ⁵
  REDH RH1 .... 276 C9
Woolborough Rd CRAWE RH10 .. 283 M9 ⁵
Wooler St WALW SE17 .... 18 G8
Woolf Cl THMD SE28 .... 143 L10 ⁶
Woolf Ms STPAN WC1H 11 L1
Woolhampton Wy CHIG IC7 ...... 103 L4 ⁶
Woolhams CTHM CR3 .... 259 N2 ⁶
Woollam Crs STALW/RED AL3 .... 38 B2
Woollard St WAB EN9 .... 63 H10
Woollaston Rd FSBYPK N4 .... 119 J4 ⁶
Woollett Cl DART DA1 .... 165 H10 ⁴
Woolmans Cl BROX EN10 .... 44 E4
Woolmead Av CDALE/KGS NW9 . 116 D5
Woolmer Cl BORE WD6 .... 75 M4
Woolmerdine Ct BUSH WD23 ..... 73 L7
Woolmer Dr HHNE HP2 .... 36 D6
Woolmer Gdns UED N18 .... 99 P7
Woolmer Rd UED N18 .... 99 P6
Woolmers La HERT/WAS SG14 .. 24 C9
Woolmore St POP/IOD E14 .... 141 N9
Woolneigh St FUL/PGN SW6 ..... 157 L9
Wool Rd RYNPK SW20 .... 178 E9
Woolstaplers Wy
  BERM/RHTH SE16 .... 19 N4
Woolston Cl WALTH E17 .... 100 C10 ²
Woolstone Rd FSTH SE23 .... 182 D5
Woolwich Church St CHARL SE7 . 162 A3
Woolwich Common
  WOOL/PLUM SE18 .... 162 D5
Woolwich High St
  WOOL/PLUM SE18 .... 162 D2
Woolwich Manor Wy
  CAN/RD E16 .... 142 E10
Woolwich Manorway
  CAN/RD E16 .... 162 E1
Woolwich Manor Wy EHAM E6 .. 142 C6
Woolwich New Rd
  WOOL/PLUM SE18 .... 162 D4 ⁴
Woolwich Rd ABYW SE2 .... 163 P5
  BELV DA17 .... 164 A4 ⁴
  BXLYHN DA7 .... 164 B9
  CHARL SE7 .... 161 P3
  GNWCH SE10 .... 161 M4
Wooster Gdns POP/IOD E14 ..... 141 J8 ⁶
Wooster Rd BEAC HP9 .... 88 B7
Wootton Cl EMPK RM11 .... 125 L3
  EPSOM KT18 .... 238 E2
Wootton Dr HHNE HP2 .... 36 A1
Wootton Gv FNCH N3 .... 97 K9 ⁶
Wootton St STHWK SE1 .... 18 B1
Worbeck Rd PGE/AN SE20 .... 204 A2
Worcester Av TOTM N17 .... 99 P8
  UPMR RM14 .... 126 E6
Worcester Cl CRICK NW2 .... 116 D8
  CROY/NA CR0 .... 204 D9
  GRH DA9 .... 188 C1
  MEO DA13 .... 190 C10
  MTCM CR4 .... 202 B2
Worcester Ct ASHF TW15 .... 174 C8 ⁴
Worcester Crs MLHL NW7 .... 96 B4
  WFD IG8 .... 101 N6
Worcester Gdns IL IG1 .... 122 B5
  NTHLT UB5 .... 134 B1
  SL SL1 .... 149 L1
  WPK KT4 .... 200 B10
Worcester Ms HAMP NW3 .... 3 H1 ⁵
Worcester Park Rd WPK KT4 ..... 199 P10
Worcester Rd BELMT SM2 .... 221 K4
  GUW GU2 .... 249 L8
  HAT AL10 .... 40 C3
  MNPK E12 .... 122 C8
  REIG RH2 .... 257 K9 ⁵
  UX/CGN UB8 .... 131 M7
  WALTH E17 .... 100 C10
  WIM/MER SW19 .... 179 J8
Worcesters Av EN EN1 .... 79 P4
Wordsworth Av GFD/PVL UB6 ... 134 C4
  MNPK E12 .... 142 B2
  PUR/KEN CR8 .... 241 L1
  SWFD E18 .... 121 L1
Wordsworth Cl CRAWE RH10 .... 284 C5 ⁵
  HARH RM3 .... 105 K9 ⁴
  TIL RM18 .... 168 F8 ⁶
Wordsworth Dr CHEAM SM3 ..... 220 F1
Wordsworth Md REDH RH1 .... 258 C8
Wordsworth Rd
  ADL/WDHM KT15 .... 215 N1
  FELT TW13 .... 175 N7
  HPTN TW12 .... 175 N7
  PGE/AN SE20 .... 182 C10
  SLN SL2 .... 128 C6
  STHWK SE1 .... 19 M6 ²
  STNW/STAM N16 .... 119 M9 ²
  WELL DA16 .... 163 H7
  WLCTN SM6 .... 222 D3
Wordsworth Wk GLDGN NW11 .. 117 J2
Wordsworth Wy DART DA1 .... 165 P10

WDR/YW UB7 .... 151 P3
Worfield St BTSEA SW11 .... 157 P6
Worgan St BERM/RHTH SE16 .... 160 C2
  LBTH SE11 .... 17 N7
Works Rd ADL/WDHM KT15 ...... 215 L5
  WCHMH N21 .... 78 G9
Worland Rd SRTFD E15 .... 141 K2 ⁵
Worlds End La ORP BR6 .... 227 K4
  WCHMH N21 .... 78 G9
Worley Rd STALW/RED AL3 ...... 38 C5
Worlidge St HMSMTH W6 .... 156 F14
Worlingham Rd EDUL SE22 .... 159 N10
Wormholt Rd SHB W12 .... 136 D10
Wormley Ct WAB EN9 .... 63 M9 ⁶
Wormley Lodge Cl BROX EN10 .. 44 E9 ⁴
Wormwood St LVPST EC2M 13 L3
Wornington Rd NKENS W10 ...... 8 A2
Woronzow Rd STJWD NW8 .... 3 M6
Worple Av ISLW TW7 .... 176 F1
  STA TW18 .... 173 L9
  WIM/MER SW19 .... 178 G10
Worple Cl RYLN/HDSTN HA2 ..... 113 N6 ⁶
Worple Rd EPSOM KT18 .... 238 A1
  ISLW TW7 .... 154 F10
  LHD/OX KT22 .... 236 C9
  PUT/ROE SW15 .... 179 H1
  RYNPK SW20 .... 200 C1
  STA TW18 .... 173 L10
  WIM/MER SW19 .... 179 H10
Worple Road Ms
  WIM/MER SW19 .... 179 J9 ⁶
Worplesdon Hill Heath House Rd
  WOKS/MYFD GU22 .... 231 H8
Worplesdon Rd GUW GU2 .... 249 N9
  RGUW GU3 .... 249 N8
Worple St MORT/ESHN SW14 .... 156 A9
Worple Wy RCHPK/HAM TW10 .. 177 K1
  RYLN/HDSTN HA2 .... 113 N6
Worrin Cl BRWN CM15 .... 107 L2
Worrin Rd BRWN CM15 .... 107 L3
Worships HI SEV TN13 .... 246 F9
Worship St SDTCH EC2A 13 H2
Worslade Rd TOOT SW17 .... 179 N7
Worsley Bridge Rd CAT SE6 ...... 182 E8
Worsley Rd WAN E11 .... 121 K9
Worsopp Dr CLAP SW4 .... 180 D1
Worsted Gn REDH RH1 .... 258 E5
Worth Cl ORP BR6 .... 227 H1
Worthfield Cl HOR/WEW KT19 .. 220 A4
Worthing Cl SRTFD E15 .... 141 K3 ⁵
Worthing Rd HEST TW5 .... 153 N5
Worthington Cl MTCM CR4 .... 202 C4
Worth Park Av CRAWE RH10 .... 284 D6
Worthington Rd SURB KT6 .... 199 L8
Worth Wy CRAWE RH10 .... 284 E8 ⁵
Wortley Rd CROY/NA CR0 .... 203 H7
  EHAM E6 .... 142 A2
Worton Gdns ISLW TW7 .... 154 C8
Worton Rd ISLW TW7 .... 154 C9
Worton Wy ISLW TW7 .... 154 C8
Wotton Dr RDKG RH5 .... 271 M6
Wotton Gn STMC/STPC BR5 ..... 207 N4
Wotton Rd CRICK NW2 .... 116 F9
Wotton Wy BELMT SM2 .... 220 F6
Wouldham Rd CAN/RD E16 .... 141 L8 ⁵
  WTHK RM20 .... 167 K5
Wrabness Wy STA TW18 .... 195 P1
Wragby Rd WAN E11 .... 121 K8 ⁶
Wrampling Pl ED N9 .... 99 P2 ⁶
Wrampley Ct WAB EN9 .... 63 M9 ⁶
Wray Av CLAY IG5 .... 122 D1
Wray Cl EMPK RM11 .... 125 L5
Wray Common Rd REIG RH2 ..... 257 M9
Wray Crs FSBYPK N4 .... 118 F7
Wrayfield Av REIG RH2 .... 257 M9
Wrayfield Rd CHEAM SM3 .... 200 G10
Wraylands Dr REIG RH2 .... 257 N8
Wray La REIG RH2 .... 257 M6
Wray Mill Pk REDH RH1 .... 257 N9
Wray Park Rd REIG RH2 .... 257 L9
Wray Rd BELMT SM2 .... 221 J5
Wraysbury Cl HSLWW TW4 ...... 175 L1
Wraysbury Rd STWL/WRAY TW19 172 F6
Wrays Wy YEAD UB4 .... 132 F7
Wrekin Rd WOOL/PLUM SE18 ... 162 F6
Wren Av CRICK NW2 .... 116 F9
  NWDGN UB2 .... 153 N3 ⁶
Wren Cl CAN/RD E16 .... 141 L8 ⁶
  ED N9 .... 100 C2 ⁵
  SAND/SEL CR2 .... 224 C5 ⁵
  STMC/STPC BR5 .... 207 N3
Wren Crs ADL/WDHM KT15 ...... 215 N2
  BUSH WD23 .... 94 B2
Wren Dr WAB EN9 .... 63 M10
  WDR/YW UB7 .... 151 N2 ⁴
Wren Gdns DAGW RM9 .... 123 N10
  HCH RM12 .... 124 C6
Wren Pl BRW CM14 .... 107 J4
Wren Rd CMBW SE5 .... 159 L7
  DAGW RM9 .... 123 N10
  SCUP DA14 .... 185 M6
Wren's Av ASHF TW15 .... 174 D8
Wrens Cft GVW DA11 .... 190 B7 ⁵
Wrensfield HHW HP1 .... 35 K6
Wren's HI LHD/OX KT22 .... 236 B1
The Wrens HLWW/ROY CM19 ... 46 E1 ⁶
Wren St FSBYW WC1X 11 P1
Wrentham Av WLSDN NW10 ..... 136 G4
Wrenthorpe Rd BMLY BR1 .... 183 K7
Wren Wk TIL RM18 .... 168 F6
Wren Wd WCCE AL7 .... 23 L4
Wrenwood Wy PIN HA5 .... 113 J2
Wrexham Rd BOW E3 .... 140 F4
  HARH RM3 .... 105 L5
Wricklemarsh Rd BKHTH/KID SE3 .. 161 N5
Wrigglesworth St NWCR SE14 .. 160 C6 ⁶
Wright Cl LEW SE13 .... 161 J10
  STALE/WH AL4 .... 21 J4
Wright Gdns SHPTN TW17 .... 196 B5
Wright Rd HEST TW5 .... 153 K6
Wrightsbridge Rd BRW CM14 .. 105 N2
Wrights Cl DAGE RM10 .... 124 C9
Wrights La KENS W8 .... 14 C3
Wrights Pl WLSDN NW10 .... 135 P1 ⁶
Wright's Rd BOW E3 .... 140 E4 ⁴
  BOW E3 .... 140 E4 ⁴
  SNWD SE25 .... 203 M3
Wright's Rw CAR SM5 .... 222 C1
Wrotham Rd BAR EN5 .... 77 H6
  CAMTN NW1 .... 5 H4 ⁶
  GVW DA11 .... 190 D7
  MEO DA13 .... 190 F10
  WEA W13 .... 135 H10 ⁵
  WELL DA16 .... 163 M7
Wroths Pth LOU IG10 .... 82 C5
Wrottesley Rd WLSDN NW10 ... 136 E4 ⁶
  WOOL/PLUM SE18 .... 162 F5
Wroughton Rd BTSEA SW11 ..... 180 A2
Wroughton Ter HDN NW4 .... 116 E2 ⁶
Wroxall Rd DAGW RM9 .... 143 M1

Wroxham Av HHS/BOV HP3 ...... 35 N8
Wroxham Gdns ENC/FH EN2 ..... 79 H1
  FBAR/BDGN N11 .... 98 D8
  POTB/CUF EN6 .... 58 G7
Wroxham Rd THMD SE28 .... 143 N9
Wroxton Rd PECK SE15 .... 160 B8 ⁶
Wrythe Gn CAR SM5 .... 202 A10 ⁴
Wrythe Green Rd CAR SM5 .... 202 A10 ⁴
Wrythe La CAR SM5 .... 202 A7
Wyatt Cl BUSH WD23 .... 94 D1
  FELT TW13 .... 175 L4
  YEAD UB4 .... 133 H7
Wyatt Park Rd
  BRXS/STRHM SW2 .... 180 G5
Wyatt Rd DART DA1 .... 164 G9
  FSBYPK N4 .... 119 K8
  FSTGT E7 .... 141 M1
  STA TW18 .... 173 K8
  WDSR SL4 .... 146 C4
Wyatt's Cl RKW/CH/CXG WD3 ... 71 K7
Watts Green La BRWN CM15 ..... 87 J2
Wyatt's Green Rd BRWN CM15 . 87 J2
Wyatt's La WALTH E17 .... 121 H1
Wyatt's Rd RKW/CH/CXG WD3 . 71 J8
Wybert St CAMTN NW1 .... 10 F1 ⁵
Wyborne Wy WLSDN NW10 ...... 135 P2
Wyburn Av BAR EN5 .... 77 J7
Wyche Gv SAND/SEL CR2 .... 223 M6
Wych Elm HLW CM20 .... 28 F10
Wych Elm Cl EMPK RM11 .... 125 P4 ⁴
Wych Elm Ri GU GU1 .... 268 E5
Wych Elm Rd EMPK RM11 .... 125 P4
Wychelm Rd LTWR GU18 .... 212 A1
Wychelms LCOL/BKTW AL2 ..... 56 A4
Wycherley Cl BKHTH/KID SE3 ... 161 L6
Wycherley Crs BAR EN5 .... 77 L10
Wychford Dr SBW CM21 .... 29 M2
Wych Hl WOKS/MYFD GU22 ..... 231 P5
Wych Hill La WOKS/MYFD GU22 232 A5
Wych Hill Wk WOKS/MYFD GU22 232 A6
Wych Hill Ri WOKS/MYFD GU22 231 P5
Wychwood Av EDGW HA8 .... 95 J7
  THHTH CR7 .... 203 J3
Wychwood Cl EDGW HA8 .... 95 J7
  SUN TW16 .... 175 H9
Wychwood End HGT N6 .... 118 D5
Wychwood Gdns CLAY IG5 .... 122 C8 ⁵
Wychwood Wy NTHWD HA6 ..... 92 C8 ⁴
Wycliffe Cl WELL DA16 .... 163 J7
Wycliffe Rd BTSEA SW11 .... 158 B9 ⁴
  WIM/MER SW19 .... 179 L9
Wycliffe Rw GVW DA11 .... 190 C4
Wycliff St FSBYE EC1V 6 C10
Wycombe End BEAC HP9 .... 108 C1
Wycombe Gdns CRICK NW2 ...... 117 J7
Wycombe Pl WAND/EARL SW18 . 179 M2 ⁶
Wycombe Rd ALP/SUD HA0 ...... 135 M3 ⁵
  GNTH/NBYPK IG2 .... 122 C3
  TOTM N17 .... 99 P9
Wycombe Wy STALE/WH AL4 ... 38 C9 ⁴
Wyddial Cl MRDN SM4 .... 200 C5
Wydehurst Rd CROY/NA CR0 .... 203 P7
Wydell Cl MRDN SM4 .... 200 B5
Wydeville Manor Rd
  LEE/GVPK SE12 .... 183 N7
Wyecliffe Gdns REDH RH1 .... 258 D6
Wye Cl ASHF TW15 .... 174 C7
  ORP BR6 .... 207 J2
  RSLP HA4 .... 112 D4 ⁵
Wyedale LCOL/BKTW AL2 .... 57 L3
Wyemead Crs CHING E4 .... 101 K3
Wye Rd GVE DA12 .... 190 G4
Wye St BTSEA SW11 .... 157 N9 ⁵
Wyeth's Rd EW KT17 .... 220 C9
Wyevale Cl PIN HA5 .... 113 H1
Wyfields CLAY IG5 .... 102 E9 ⁵
Wyfold Rd FUL/PGN SW6 .... 157 H7
Wyke Cl ISLW TW7 .... 154 E5
Wyke Gdns HNWL W7 .... 154 E2
Wykeham Av DAGW RM9 .... 143 M1
  EMPK RM11 .... 125 L4
Wykeham Cl GVE DA12 .... 191 H9
  WDR/YW UB7 .... 152 B5 ⁵
Wykeham Gn DAGW RM9 .... 143 M1
Wykeham HI WBLY HA9 .... 115 L6
Wykeham Ri TRDG/WHET N20 . 97 H2
Wykeham Rd GU GU1 .... 116 F3
  HDN NW4 .... 116 E3
  KTN/HRWW/W HA3 .... 114 E2
Wyke Rd BOW E3 .... 140 F2
  RYNPK SW20 .... 200 F2
Wylands Rd DTCH/LGLY SL3 .... 150 D4
Wylchin Cl PIN HA5 .... 112 C2
Wyldes Cl GLDGN NW11 .... 117 M6
Wyldfield Gdns ED N9 .... 99 N3
Wyld Wy WBLY HA9 .... 136 D4
Wyldwood Cl HLWE CM17 .... 29 M5
Wyleu St FSTH SE23 .... 182 D3
Wylie Rd NWDGN UB2 .... 153 P2
Wyllen Cl WCHPL E1 .... 140 B6 ⁵
Wylo Dr BAR EN5 .... 76 D10
Wymering Rd MV/WKIL W9 ...... 2 F10
Wymers Cl SL SL1 .... 128 A4
Wymond St PUT/ROE SW15 ..... 156 F9
Wynan Rd POP/IOD E14 .... 160 G4
Wynaud Ct WDGN N22 .... 98 G7 ²
Wyncham Av BFN/LL DA15 ...... 165 J6
Wynches Farm Dr STALE/WH AL4 39 J6 ⁶
Wynchgate KTN/HRWW/W HA3 94 D8
  STHGT/OAK N14 .... 98 F1
Wynchlands Crs STALE/WH AL4 39 J6
Wyncote Wy SAND/SEL CR2 .... 224 C5
Wyncroft Cl BMLY BR1 .... 206 C1
Wyndale Av CDALE/KGS NW9 ... 115 M4
Wyndcliff Rd CHARL SE7 .... 161 N5
Wyndcroft Cl ENC/FH EN2 .... 79 J7
Wyndham Av COB KT11 .... 217 N1
Wyndham Cl BELMT SM2 .... 221 K5
  ORP BR6 .... 206 F8
Wyndham Crs HSLWW TW4 ..... 175 J8
  KTTN NW5 .... 118 D8
  SL SL1 .... 128 A4
Wyndham Ms MBLAR W1H ...... 10 A4 ⁴
Wyndham Pl MBLAR W1H .... 10 A4 ⁴
  MBLAR W1H .... 10 A4 ⁵
  MBLAR W1H .... 10 A4 ⁶
Wyndham Rd CMBW SE5 .... 159 K6
  EBAR EN4 .... 98 A2
  KUTN/CMB KT2 .... 177 L10
  WEA W13 .... 154 G2
  WOKN/KNAP GU21 .... 231 N10
Wyndhams End WELGE AL9 ..... 23 J9 ⁴
Wyndham St MBLAR W1H 10 A3
Wyneham Rd HNHL SE24 .... 181 L1
Wynell Rd FSTH SE23 .... 182 B4
Wynford Gv STMC/STPC BR5 ... 207 L3
Wynford Pl BELV DA17 .... 164 B5 ⁴
Wynford Rd IS N1 .... 5 N7
Wynford Wy ELTH/MOT SE9 .... 184 C6

Wynlea Cl CRAWE RH10 .... 285 P5
Wynlie Gdns PIN HA5 .... 93 J10
Wynndale Rd SWFD E18 .... 101 N9
Wynne Rd BRXN/ST SW9 .... 159 N8
Wynns Av BFN/LL DA15 .... 185 K1 ⁴
Wynn's Av BFN/LL DA15 .... 185 K1
Wynnstay Gdns KENS W8 .... 14 F3
Wynnswick Rd BEAC HP9 .... 89 H6
Wynsham Wy BFOR GU20 .... 212 A2
Wynter St BTSEA SW11 .... 157 M10
Wynton Gdns SNWD SE25 .... 203 M5
Wynton Gv WOT/HER KT12 ...... 197 H10
Wynton Pl ACT W3 .... 135 N8
Wynyard Ter LBTH SE11 .... 17 P7 ⁵
Wynyatt St FSBYE EC1V 6 C9
Wyre Gv EDGW HA8 .... 95 P4 ²
  HYS/HAR UB3 .... 153 H3
Wyresdale Crs GFD/PVL UB6 .... 134 E5
Wysemead HORL RH6 .... 280 D3
Wyteleaf Cl RSLP HA4 .... 112 D4
Wythburn Pl MBLAR W1H 10 A6
Wythenshawe Rd DAGE RM10 .. 124 B8
Wythes Cl BMLY BR1 .... 206 C2
Wythes Rd CAN/RD E16 .... 142 B10
Wythfield Rd ELTH/MOT SE9 .... 184 C2
Wyton WGCE AL7 .... 23 N5
Wyvenhoe Rd RYLN/HDSTN HA2 114 B8 ⁵
Wyvern Cl DART DA1 .... 187 K5
  ORP BR6 .... 207 L10
Wyvern Rd PUR/KEN CR8 .... 223 H6
Wyvern Wy UX/CGN UB8 .... 131 L2
Wyvil Rd VX/NE SW8 .... 158 F6
Wyvis St POP/IOD E14 .... 140 D7

Y

Yabsley St POP/IOD E14 .... 141 H10
Yaffle Rd WEY KT13 .... 216 D6
Yalding Cl STMC/STPC BR5 ...... 207 N4 ⁴
Yalding Rd BERM/RHTH SE16 ... 19 N4
Yale Cl HSLWW TW4 .... 175 N1
Yale Wy HCH RM12 .... 125 H9
Yarborough Rd
  WIM/MER SW19 .... 201 N1 ⁶
Yarbridge Cl BELMT SM2 .... 221 L6 ⁶
Yardley Cl CHING E4 .... 80 C9 ⁴
  REIG RH2 .... 257 L8
Yardley La CHING E4 .... 80 C9
Yardley St FSBYW WC1X .... 6 A10 ⁴
  FSBYW WC1X .... 12 A1 ⁵
Yard Md EGH TW20 .... 172 D6
Yarm Cl LHD/OX KT22 .... 237 H9
Yarm Court Rd LHD/OX KT22 ... 237 H9
Yarmouth Cl CRAWE RH10 ...... 284 B9
Yarmouth Crs WALTH E17 .... 120 A3
Yarmouth Rd SL SL1 .... 129 H8
  WATN WD24 .... 73 J4
Yarm Wy LHD/OX KT22 .... 237 H9
Yarnton Wy ERITHM DA18 .... 164 A2
Yarrow Crs EHAM E6 .... 142 B7
Yarrowside AMSS HP7 .... 69 N6
Yateley St WOOL/PLUM SE18 ... 162 A2
Yattendon Rd HORL RH6 .... 280 C4
Yeading Av RSLP HA4 .... 113 M7
Yeading Fk YEAD UB4 .... 133 K7
Yeading Gdns YEAD UB4 .... 133 J7
Yeading La YEAD UB4 .... 133 J8
Yeames Cl WEA W13 .... 134 F8
Yearling Cl WARE SG12 .... 26 E4
Yeate St IS N1 .... 6 G4
Yeatman Rd HGT N6 .... 118 A4
Yeats Cl REDH RH1 .... 275 M3
  WLSDN NW10 .... 136 B1
Yeend Cl E/WMO/HCT KT8 ...... 197 P4
Yeldham Rd HMSMTH W6 .... 156 G4
Yellowcress Dr CHOB/PIR GU24 . 230 F2 ⁵
Yellowpine Wy CHIG IG7 .... 103 L5
Yelverton Cl HARH RM3 .... 105 K9
Yelverton Rd BTSEA SW11 ...... 157 N8
Yenston Cl MRDN SM4 .... 201 K6
Yeoman Cl EHAM E6 .... 142 E9 ⁵
Yeoman Rd NTHLT UB5 .... 133 M2
Yeomanry Cl EW KT17 .... 220 C8 ⁶
Yeomans Acre RSLP HA4 .... 113 H4
Yeomans Mdw SEV TN13 .... 265 H2
Yeoman's Rw CHEL SW3 .... 15 P4
Yeoman St BERM/RHTH SE16 ... 160 D3
Yeomans Wy EN EN1 .... 80 A6 ⁵
Yeoman Wy REDH RH1 .... 276 A5
Yeomen Wy BARK/HLT IG6 ..... 102 F7
Yeo St BOW E3 .... 140 G7
Yeoveney Cl STWL/WRAY TW19 172 G5
Yeovil Cl ORP BR6 .... 207 H9
Yeovil Rd SL SL1 .... 128 D7
Yeovilton Pl KUTN/CMB KT2 .... 177 J8
Yerbury Rd ARCH N19 .... 118 E8
Yester Dr CHST BR7 .... 184 B10
Yester Pk CHST BR7 .... 184 C10
Yester Rd CHST BR7 .... 184 C10
Yeveley Wy EMPK RM11 .... 125 M5
Yew Av WDR/YW UB7 .... 131 P9
Yewbank Cl PUR/KEN CR8 .... 241 L1
Yew Cl BKHH IG9 .... 102 A3 ⁵
  CHESW EN7 .... 61 M3 ⁴
Yewdale Cl BMLY BR1 .... 183 K9 ⁴
Yewfield Rd WLSDN NW10 .... 136 C2
Yew Gv CRICK NW2 .... 116 C9 ⁵
  WGCE AL7 .... 23 M6
Yewlands HOD EN11 .... 44 F4
  SBW CM21 .... 29 P2 ⁵
Yewlands Cl BNSTD SM7 .... 239 L1
Yewlands Dr HOD EN11 .... 44 F4
Yews Av EN EN1 .... 80 A2
The Yews GVE DA12 .... 190 G5
Yew Tree Bottom Rd EW KT17 .. 238 E3
Yewtree Cl RYLN/HDSTN HA2 .. 114 A2
Yew Tree Cl BEAC HP9 .... 88 C10
  COUL/CHIP CR5 .... 240 A5
  CSHM HP5 .... 51 M6
  HORL RH6 .... 280 B8
  RBRW/HUT CM13 .... 87 N10
  SEV TN13 .... 246 E9
  WCHMH N21 .... 99 H1 ⁶
  WELL DA16 .... 163 K7
  WPK KT4 .... 200 B8 ⁴
Yew Tree Ct BORE WD6 .... 75 J10 ⁶
Yew Tree Dr CTHM CR3 .... 259 N1
  GU GU1 .... 249 N5
  HHS/BOV HP3 .... 52 F5
Yew Tree Gdns CHDH RM6 ...... 123 P3
  EPSOM KT18 .... 237 P1
  ROMW/RG RM7 .... 124 C3
Yew Tree La REIG RH2 .... 257 L7
Yewtree Rd BECK BR3 .... 204 E3 ⁴
Yew Tree Rd DORK RH4 .... 254 F10
  HGDN/ICK UB10 .... 132 A3
  HORL RH6 .... 279 H8
  SHB W12 .... 136 C9 ⁴
  SL SL1 .... 149 M2
Yewtrees EGH TW20 .... 194 H3 ⁴
Yew Tree Wk EHSLY KT24 .... 253 L3

HSLWW TW4 .... 175 N1
PUR/KEN CR8 .... 223 K6
Yew Wk HOD EN11 .... 44 F4
  HRW HA1 .... 114 D6
Yoakley Rd STNW/STAM N16 ... 119 M7
Yoke Cl HOLWY N7 .... 5 M1 ⁴
Yolande Gdns ELTH/MOT SE9 ... 184 B1
York Av BFN/LL DA15 .... 184 G3
  HNWL W7 .... 135 H5
  KTN/HRWW/W HA3 .... 94 C9 ⁴
  MORT/ESHN SW14 .... 177 P1
  SL SL1 .... 129 J8
  UX/CGN UB8 .... 132 C8
  WDSR SL4 .... 148 G8
York Br CAMTN NW1 .... 10 C1
York Buildings CHCR WC2N ...... 11 M8 ⁵
York Cl BF/WBF KT14 .... 215 P8
  BRWN CM15 .... 107 L1
  EHAM E6 .... 142 C8
  HNWL W7 .... 134 D10 ⁶
  KGLGY WD4 .... 54 B5 ⁶
  MRDN SM4 .... 201 L4
York Crs BORE WD6 .... 76 A6
  LOU IG10 .... 82 B7
Yorke Gdns REIG RH2 .... 257 K9
Yorke Ga WAT WD17 .... 73 H6 ⁶
Yorke Gate Rd CTHM CR3 .... 241 L8
York Ga CAMTN NW1 .... 10 C2
  RKW/CH/CXG WD3 .... 72 E9 ⁵
Yorkes HLWS CM18 .... 47 J3
York Gdns WOT/HER KT12 .... 197 L9
York Ga CAMTN NW1 .... 10 D2
  STHGT/OAK N14 .... 98 F1
York Gv PECK SE15 .... 160 B7
York HI LOU IG10 .... 82 B7
  STRHM/NOR SW16 .... 181 J6
Yorkland Av WELL DA16 .... 163 J10
York Ms IL IG1 .... 122 D7
  KTTN NW5 .... 118 C10 ²
York Pl BTSEA SW11 .... 157 M9
  GRAYS RM17 .... 167 M5 ⁶
  IL IG1 .... 122 D7
York Ri KTTN NW5 .... 118 C9
  ORP BR6 .... 207 H8
York Rd ACT W3 .... 135 P8
  BAR EN5 .... 77 M9
  BELMT SM2 .... 221 K3
  BF/WBF KT14 .... 215 P8
  BH/WHM TN16 .... 243 N5
  BRWN CM15 .... 107 L1
  BTFD TW8 .... 155 J4
  CHES/WCR EN8 .... 62 D10
  CHING E4 .... 100 F4
  CROY/NA CR0 .... 203 H7
  DART DA1 .... 187 N3
  EA W5 .... 155 H2
  EPP CM16 .... 66 B3
  FBAR/BDGN N11 .... 98 E7
  FSTGT E7 .... 141 M1
  GU GU1 .... 268 A1
  GVE DA12 .... 190 F6
  GVW DA11 .... 190 A3
  HSLW TW3 .... 154 A9
  IL IG1 .... 122 D8
  KUTN/CMB KT2 .... 177 L10
  LEY E10 .... 121 H9 ⁵
  NTHWD HA6 .... 93 H10
  RAIN RM13 .... 144 J2 ⁵
  RCHPK/HAM TW10 .... 177 L1 ⁵
  SAND/SEL CR2 .... 224 C6
  STAL AL1 .... 38 E5
  STHWK SE1 .... 17 P1
  TEDD TW11 .... 176 D7
  UED N18 .... 100 A6
  UX/CGN UB8 .... 131 N2
  WALTH E17 .... 120 C3
  WATW WD18 .... 73 K9
  WCHMH N21 .... 99 L1
  WDSR SL4 .... 148 G8
  WEY KT13 .... 216 D2
  WIM/MER SW19 .... 179 L9
  WOKS/MYFD GU22 .... 232 A5
Yorkshire Cl STNW/STAM N16 .. 119 M8
Yorkshire Gdns UED N18 .... 100 A6
Yorkshire Grey Yd HHOL WC1V . 11 M4 ⁶
Yorkshire Rd MTCM CR4 .... 202 F5
  POP/IOD E14 .... 140 D8
York Sq POP/IOD E14 .... 140 D8 ⁴
York St BARK IG11 .... 142 E3
  MBLAR W1H 10 B3
  MHST W1U 10 B3
  MTCM CR4 .... 202 B7
  TWK TW1 .... 176 F4
York Ter ENC/FH EN2 .... 79 K4 ⁴
  ERITH DA8 .... 164 D7
York Ter East CAMTN NW1 ...... 10 D2
York Ter West CAMTN NW1 ...... 10 C2
Yorkton St BETH E2 .... 7 N7
York Wy CHSGTN KT9 .... 219 J4 ⁵
  FELT TW13 .... 175 N6
  GSTN WD25 .... 73 L2
  HHS/BOV HP3 .... 35 P7
  HOLWY N7 .... 5 L2
  IS N1 .... 4 A4
  TRDG/WHET N20 .... 98 A4
Youngfield Rd HHW HP1 .... 35 J5
Youngmans Cl ENC/FH EN2 ..... 79 K5
Young Rd CAN/RD E16 .... 141 P8
Youngs Rd GNTH/NBYPK IG2 ... 122 G3
Young St KENS W8 .... 14 C2
  LHD/OX KT22 .... 236 E10
Youngstroat La CHOB/PIR GU24 214 B6
Yoxley Ap GNTH/NBYPK IG2 .... 122 F4
Yoxley Dr GNTH/NBYPK IG2 .... 122 F4
Yukon Rd BAL SW12 .... 180 C3
Yule Cl LCOL/BKTW AL2 .... 55 N6
Yuletide Cl WLSDN NW10 .... 136 B1
Yunus Khan Cl WALTH E17 ...... 120 F3

Z

Zambra Wy BGR/WK TN15 .... 247 N6
Zampa Rd BERM/RHTH SE16 .... 160 B4
Zander Ct BETH E2 .... 7 P9
Zangwill Rd BKHTH/KID SE3 ..... 162 A7
Zealand Av WDR/YW UB7 .... 151 N6
Zealand Rd BOW E3 .... 140 D4
Zelah Rd STMC/STPC BR5 .... 207 L7
Zennor Rd BAL SW12 .... 180 D4 ⁵
Zenoria St EDUL SE22 .... 159 N10 ⁵
Zermatt Rd THHTH CR7 .... 203 K4
Zetland St POP/IOD E14 .... 141 H7
Zig Zag Rd PUR/KEN CR8 .... 241 K2
  RDKG RH5 .... 255 H6
Zinnia Dr CHOB/PIR GU24 .... 230 F2 ⁴
Zion Pl GVE DA12 .... 190 E3 ⁶
  THHTH CR7 .... 203 L4 ⁴
Zion Rd THHTH CR7 .... 203 L4
Zoar St STHWK SE1 .... 12 E1 ⁵
Zoffany St ARCH N19 .... 118 E7

20th Century Gallery
FUL/PGN SW6 .... 157 H7
Aarotya Medical Centre
TOTM N17 .... 119 K2
Abbey Business Centre
VX/NE SW8 .... 158 D7
The Abbey Clinic
BELV DA17 .... 164 A4
Abbey C of E JMI School
STALW/RED AL3 .... 38 B7
Abbey Industrial Estate
ALP HA0 .... 135 L3
Abbey Industrial Estate
MTCM CR4 .... 202 A5
Abbeylands School
ADL/WDHM KT15 .... 215 K2
Abbey Mead Industrial Park
WAB EN9 .... 62 C10
Abbey Medical Centre
STJWD NW8 .... 3 H6
Abbey Park Industrial Estate
BARK IG11 .... 142 E4
Abbey Primary School
ABYW SE2 .... 163 M2
Abbey Road Health Centre
SRTFD E15 .... 141 K3
Abbey Road Surgery
CHES/WCR EN8 .... 62 D10
Abbey Trading Estate
SYD SE26 .... 182 D8
Abbey Wharf Industrial Estate
BARK IG11 .... 142 G5
Abbey Wood Podiatry Clinic
ABYW SE2 .... 163 L3
Abbey Wood Secondary School
ABYW SE2 .... 163 K2
Abbotsbury Primary First School
MRDN SM4 .... 201 K5
Abbotsfield School
HGDN/ICK UB10 .... 132 C4
Abbot's Hill School
HHS/BOV HP3 .... 54 C1
Abbots Hospital
GU GU1 .... 268 A1
Abbots Langley Parish Council
ABLGY WD5 .... 54 C7
Abbots School
ABLGY WD5 .... 54 C6
Abbotsweld Primary School
HLWS CM18 .... 46 G3
Abbotswood Medical Centre
ABLGY WD5 .... 55 H8
A B C Cinema
BECK BR3 .... 204 F2
A B C Cinema
CAT SE6 .... 182 G4
A B C Cinema
ESH/CLAY KT10 .... 198 A10
A B C Cinema
FITZ W1T 11 J4
A B C Cinema
GVE DA12 .... 190 E2
A B C Cinema
PUT/ROE SW15 .... 157 H9
A B C Cinema
STA TW18 .... 173 H8
A B C Cinema
STRHM/NOR SW16 .... 180 F5
Abercorn Place School
STJWD NW8 .... 3 K8
Aberdour School
KWD/TDW/WH KT20 .... 239 J4
Aberglen Industrial Estate
HYS/HAR UB3 .... 152 E1
Abinger Common Primary School
RDKG RH5 .... 271 L8
Abinger Hammer School
RDKG RH5 .... 270 G5
Aboyne Lodge School
STALW/RED AL3 .... 38 C5
Acacia Business Centre
WAN E11 .... 121 K8
Aches & Pains Osteopathic Clinic
HOR/WEW KT19 .... 220 A2
Acland Burghley School
KTTN NW5 .... 118 C9
The Acorn Group Practise
TWK TW1 .... 176 F3
Acorn Industrial Park
DART DA1 .... 187 H1
Acorn Medical Centre
HGDN/ICK UB10 .... 132 B3
The Acorn Surgery
PECK SE15 .... 160 A6
Acorn Trading Centre
WTHK RM20 .... 167 J5
Acre Road Health Clinic
KUTN/CMB KT2 .... 177 L10
Acton Business Centre
WLSDN NW10 .... 136 A6
Acton Central Industrial Estate
ACT W3 .... 135 N9
Acton Health Centre
ACT W3 .... 135 P10
Acton High School
ACT W3 .... 155 M1
Acton Hospital
ACT W3 .... 155 M1
Acton Lane Medical Centre
CHSWK W4 .... 156 A1
Acton Park Industrial Estate
ACT W3 .... 136 C10
Acton Park Industrial Estate
CHSWK W4 .... 156 A1
Acton Superbowl
ACT W3 .... 135 M6
Acton Swimming Baths
ACT W3 .... 135 P10
Adams Bridge Business Centre
WBLY HA9 .... 115 N10
Adamsrill Primary School
SYD SE26 .... 182 D6
Addey & Stanhope School
NWCR SE14 .... 160 E7
Addington Business Centre
CROY/NA CR0 .... 225 K6
Addiscombe Cricket Club
CROY/NA CR0 .... 203 N10
Addison Primary School
WKENS W14 .... 156 G2
Adeyfield School
HHNE HP2 .... 36 B6
Adler Industrial Estate
HYS/HAR UB3 .... 152 E1
Admiral Hyson Industrial Estate
BERM/RHTH SE16 .... 160 A3
The Adrian Ross Gallery
REIG RH2 .... 257 K9
A D T College
PUT/ROE SW15 .... 179 J1
The Adult College of Barking
& Dagenham
BARK IG11 .... 143 H1

Adult Education Centre
GU GU1 .... 268 B2
Adult Education Centre
POP/IOD E14 .... 161 H2
Africa Centre
COVGDN WC2E 11 M7
Ailsa Gallery
TWK TW1 .... 176 G2
Ainslie Wood Primary School
CHING E4 .... 100 G6
Airbase Unity Elementary School
RSLP HA4 .... 112 D7
Airedale Physiotherapy Clinic
CHSWK W4 .... 156 C4
Air Links Industrial Estate
HEST TW5 .... 153 K4
Airport Industrial Estate
BH/WHM TN16 .... 244 A1
Aksaray Sports Club
STNW/STAM N16 .... 119 L9
Akshaya Dance Theatre
GNWCH SE10 .... 161 H6
Alan Carter Gallery
OXTED RH8 .... 261 K5
Alban Wood Infant School
GSTN WD25 .... 55 J8
Albanwood School
GSTN WD25 .... 55 J8
Albany Centre & Theatre
DEPT SE8 .... 160 E6
Albany Clinic
BFN/LL DA15 .... 185 K7
Albany Clinic
WIM/MER SW19 .... 179 L10
The Albany College
HDN NW4 .... 116 F3
Albany School Grant Maintained
PEND EN3 .... 80 C4
The Albany School
HCH RM12 .... 125 J7
Albemarle College
BAY/PAD W2 .... 9 H7
Albemarle Gallery
FUL/PGN SW6 .... 157 L9
Albemarle Primary School
WIM/MER SW19 .... 179 H5
Albion Health Centre
WCHPL E1 .... 140 A7
Albion Junior & Infant School
BERM/RHTH SE16 .... 160 B1
Albion Street Health Centre
BERM/RHTH SE16 .... 160 B1
Albion Surgery
BXLYHS DA6 .... 164 B10
Albright Industrial Estate
RAIN RM13 .... 144 G7
The Alchemy Gallery
CLKNW EC1R 12 A1
Aldenham Parish Council
RAD WD7 .... 74 F2
Aldenham School
BORE WD6 .... 74 E6
Alderbrook Primary School
BAL SW12 .... 180 C3
Aldersbrook County
Secondary School
MNPK E12 .... 121 P6
Aldersbrook Primary School
WAN E11 .... 121 P6
Alderton County Junior
& Infant School
LOU IG10 .... 82 D9
Alderwood Primary School
ELTH/MOT SE9 .... 184 G2
Aldgate Gallery
WCHPL E1 .... 13 L4
Aldro School
MFD/CHID GU8 .... 266 B10
Aldwickbury Park Golf Club
HARP AL5 .... 20 D2
Aldwych Theatre
HOL/ALD WC2B 11 N6
Alexander Barracks
WDSR SL4 .... 148 B8
Alexander First School
WDSR SL4 .... 148 B8
Alexander Mcleod Junior School
ABYW SE2 .... 163 L4
Alexandra Avenue Clinic
RYLN/HDSTN HA2 .... 113 P7
Alexandra Avenue School
RYLN/HDSTN HA2 .... 113 P7
Alexandra Infant School
PGE/AN SE20 .... 182 C10
Alexandra Junior & Infant School
WDGN N22 .... 98 G10
Alexandra Junior School
HSLW TW3 .... 154 A8
Alexandra Junior School
SYD SE26 .... 182 C9
Alfred Mizen First School
MTCM CR4 .... 202 E3
Alfred Salter Primary School
BERM/RHTH SE16 .... 160 C1
Alfreds Way Industrial Estate
BARK IG11 .... 143 K3
Alfriston School
BEAC HP9 .... 88 B5
Algerian Embassy
NTGHL W11 .... 8 B10
Allegery Clinic
CAVSQ/HST W1G 10 E5
Allenby Road School
GFD/PVL UB6 .... 134 A8
Allen Edwards Primary School
CLAP SW4 .... 158 F7
The All England Lawn Tennis
& Croquet Club
WIM/MER SW19 .... 179 H6
Allerton Road Surgery
FSBYPK N4 .... 119 K7
Alleyns School
EDUL SE22 .... 181 M1
Allfarthing Junior School
WAND/EARL SW18 .... 179 M2
All Nations Christian College
WARE SG12 .... 26 G3
All Saints Benhilton School
SUT SM1 .... 201 L10
All Saints C of E First School
WIM/MER SW19 .... 179 M10
All Saints C of E Primary School
BKHTH/KID SE3 .... 161 K8
All Saints C of E School
CRICK NW2 .... 117 J8
All Saints C of E School
LHD/OX KT22 .... 236 F5
All Saints C of E School
PUT/ROE SW15 .... 156 F9
All Saints Primary School
TRDG/WHET N20 .... 97 N3
All Saints School
BCTR RM8 .... 124 B6

All Saints School
FUL/PGN SW6 .... 157 H8
All Saints School
NRWD SE19 .... 203 M1
Allum Medical Centre
WAN E11 .... 121 J5
Alma Junior & Infant School
BERM/RHTH SE16 .... 19 N5
The Almanac Gallery Christmas
Collection
BAY/PAD W2 .... 9 K7
The Almanac Gallery
FUL/PGN SW6 .... 157 J8
Alma Road Junior & Infant School
PEND EN3 .... 80 C9
Almeida Theatre
IS N1 .... 6 C4
Al Muntada Islamic School
FUL/PGN SW6 .... 157 J7
Alperton Community School
ALP/SUD HA0 .... 135 K2
Alperton High School
ALP/SUD HA0 .... 135 J3
Alperton Sports Ground
ALP/SUD HA0 .... 135 J4
Alpha Business Centre
WALTH E17 .... 120 E3
Alpha Business Park
BRKMPK AL9 .... 40 F9
Alternative Health Practice
HAMP NW3 .... 117 K8
Altmore Infant School
EHAM E6 .... 142 C2
Alton Medical Practice
PUT/ROE SW15 .... 178 D3
The Alton School
PUT/ROE SW15 .... 178 C3
Ambassadors Theatre
LSQ/SEVD WC2H 11 K7
Ambler School
FSBYPK N4 .... 119 J8
Ambleside Junior School
WOT/HER KT12 .... 197 K8
Ambresbury Banks Fort
EPP CM16 .... 64 E10
A M C Business Centre
WLSDN NW10 .... 135 N5
American Community School
HGDN/ICK UB10 .... 132 A3
The American
Community School
COB KT11 .... 217 L6
Amersham & Chiltern Rugby Club
AMS HP6 .... 68 F2
Amersham Hill Cricket Club
AMS HP6 .... 69 K4
The Amersham School
AMSS HP7 .... 69 K6
Amersham Town Football Club
AMS HP6 .... 68 F5
Amersham & Wycombe College
AMSS HP7 .... 69 L5
A M F Bowling
CRAWW RH11 .... 283 N7
A M F Bowling
HHNE HP2 .... 36 C4
A M F Bowling
LEW SE13 .... 161 H9
Amherst County Junior School
SEV TN13 .... 246 E9
Amherst Primary School
HACK E8 .... 119 P10
Ampthill Square Medical Centre
CAMTN NW1 .... 4 G8
Amwell View School
WARE SG12 .... 26 G7
Amy Johnson Primary School
WLGTN SM6 .... 222 F4
Andover Medical Centre
HOLWY N7 .... 118 C9
Andrew Ewing Junior
& Infant School
HEST TW5 .... 153 N6
Andrew Sketchley Theatre
WCHPL E1 .... 13 P3
Andrews Lane Junior
& Infant School
CHESW EN7 .... 61 P4
Anerley Primary School
PGE/AN SE20 .... 203 P1
Anerley Secondary
Boarding School
NRWD SE19 .... 203 P1
Anerley Surgery
PGE/AN SE20 .... 204 A1
Angel Natural Health Practice
IS N1 .... 6 B2
Anglia Polytechnic University
BRWN CM15 .... 107 J2
Annandale Primary School
GNWCH SE10 .... 161 L4
The Anna Scher Theatre
IS N1 .... 6 A6
Anne Mount School
EFNCH N2 .... 117 N4
Annunciation RC School
EDGE HA8 .... 96 A9
Anson Primary School
CRICK NW2 .... 116 G10
Ante Natal Clinic
MUSWH N10 .... 118 B1
Anthony Roper County
Primary School
EYN DA4 .... 209 M9
Antigua & Barbuda High Comm
MHST W1U 10 D5
The Antiques Gallery
BELMT SM2 .... 221 K6
Apex Industrial Estate
WLSDN NW10 .... 136 C4
Apex Retail Park
FELT TW13 .... 175 N6
Apollo Business Centre
DEPT SE8 .... 160 C4
Apollo Theatre
SOHO/SHAV W1D 11 J7
Apollo Victoria Theatre
PIM SW1V 16 G4
Apostolic Nuncio
WIM/MER SW19 .... 178 F6
Applecroft Junior Middle
& Infant School
WGCW AL8 .... 22 E6
Applegarth Infant School
CROY/NA CR0 .... 224 G3
Apsley House
BAY/PAD W2 .... 16 C1
Apsley Mills Retail Park
HHS/BOV HP3 .... 35 P10
Aquarelles Gallery
NTGHL W11 .... 8 C9
Aquarius Business Park
CRICK NW2 .... 116 D6

Arbormar Tree Surgery
ADL/WDHM KT15 .... 215 H6
Arbour Vale School
SLN SL2 .... 129 M8
Arbras Gallery
NTGHL W11 .... 8 D7
The Archbishop Michael
Ramsey School
CMBW SE5 .... 159 J6
Archbishop Sumners
C of E Primary School
LBTH SE11 .... 18 B6
Archbishop Tenisons
C of E School
CROY/NA CR0 .... 203 N10
Archbishop Tenison's School
VX/NE SW8 .... 17 N10
Archdale Business Centre
RYLN/HDSTN HA2 .... 114 B7
Archdeacon Cambridges School
WHTN TW2 .... 176 D5
Arches Business Centre
NWDGN UB2 .... 153 N1
Arches Leisure Centre
GNWCH SE10 .... 161 J5
Archgate Business Centre
NFNCH/WDSP N12 .... 97 M6
Architon Group Practice
EPSOM KT18 .... 219 P9
Archway Surgery
HHS/BOV HP3 .... 52 D3
Archway Theatre
HORL RH6 .... 280 C5
Ardleigh Green Junior School
EMPK RM11 .... 125 L1
Arena Estate
FSBYPK N4 .... 119 J4
Argentine Embassy
MYFR/PKLN W1K 10 E7
Argile Gallery
NTGHL W11 .... 8 C6
Argyle Primary School
STPAN WC1H 5 L9
Argyle Surgery
WEA W13 .... 134 F8
Ark College
LBTH SE11 .... 18 C8
Arklow Trading Estate
NWCR SE14 .... 160 D5
Armchair Theatre
LBTH SE11 .... 18 B9
Armourers & Braziers' Hall
CITYW EC2V 12 G4
Army
SKENS SW7 .... 15 K4
Army Training Regiment
CHOB/PIR GU24 .... 230 B7
Arndale Health Centre
WAND/EARL SW18 .... 179 L1
Arnethill School
RKW/CH/CXG WD3 .... 71 K10
Arnhem Wharf Primary School
POP/IOD E14 .... 160 E2
Arnold House School
STJWD NW8 .... 3 L7
Arnott Abbey
FARR EC1M 12 C3
Arsenal Football Club
HBRY N5 .... 119 J8
Artbank Gallery
FARR EC1M 12 C2
Art Gallery
LOTH EC2R 13 H6
Art Gallery
RSLP HA4 .... 113 H6
Art Gallery
WLSDN NW10 .... 136 E1
The Art Gallery
CMBW SE5 .... 159 K6
The Art Gallery
RCH/KEW TW9 .... 155 K10
The Artisan Gallery
GRH DA9 .... 188 E3
The Artisan Gallery
WFD IG8 .... 101 N7
Art School
BECK BR3 .... 204 D5
The Art Space Gallery
IS N1 .... 6 E7
Ashbourne Independent
Sixth Form College
KENS W8 .... 15 H1
Ashburnham Primary School
WBPTN SW10 .... 157 N6
Ashburton Primary School
CROY/NA CR0 .... 204 A6
Ashby Mill School
CLAP SW4 .... 180 F1
The Ashcombe School
DORK RH4 .... 254 G10
Asheridge Road Industrial Estate
CSHM HP5 .... 50 F5
Ashfield Junior School
BUSH WD23 .... 94 A1
Ashford Clinic
ASHF TW15 .... 173 P6
Ashford C of E School
ASHF TW15 .... 174 C9
Ashford High School
ASHF TW15 .... 173 P6
Ashford Hospital A & E
STWL/WRAY TW19 .... 173 P5
The Ashford & St Peters
Hospitals NHS Trust
CHERT KT16 .... 194 G10
Ashford Sports Club
ASHF TW15 .... 173 N7
Ashford Sports Club
STWL/WRAY TW19 .... 174 A4
Ashgrove College
WALTH E17 .... 120 F1
Ashgrove Estate
BMLY BR1 .... 183 J9
Ashgrove School
BMLY BR1 .... 205 N2
Ash Industrial Estate
HLWW/ROY CM19 .... 46 C2
Ashleigh Commercial Estate
CHARL SE7 .... 161 P3
Ashley Centre Surgery
EPSOM KT18 .... 220 A9
Ashley Gallery
HPTN TW12 .... 197 P1
Ashley Infant School
WOT/HER KT12 .... 197 H8
Ashlyns School
BERK HP4 .... 33 P7
Ashmead Primary School
BROCKY SE4 .... 160 F8
Ashmead Primary School
DEPT SE8 .... 160 F8
Ashmole Primary School
VX/NE SW8 .... 17 P10

Ashmole School
STHGT/OAK N14 .... 98 D2
Ashmount Junior
& Infant School
ARCH N19 .... 118 D5
Ashtead Clinic
ASHTD KT21 .... 237 K3
Ashtead Cricket Club
ASHTD KT21 .... 237 K3
Ashtead Hospital
ASHTD KT21 .... 237 K6
Ashton House School
ISLW TW7 .... 154 C7
Ashvale Medical Centre
TOOT SW17 .... 180 A8
Ashville Surgery
FUL/PGN SW6 .... 157 J7
The Ashworth Practice
ORP BR6 .... 207 L7
Aspen House School
CMBW SE5 .... 18 C10
Aspen House Secondary
& Primary School
BRXS/STRHM SW2 .... 180 F3
Asquith Court School
KTN/HRWW/W HA3 .... 114 G4
Asquith School
PEND EN3 .... 80 B8
Associated Newspapers
BERM/RHTH SE16 .... 160 C2
Astley Cooper School
HHNE HP2 .... 36 B1
Aston Clinic
NWMAL KT3 .... 200 B4
Aston House School
EA W5 .... 135 J8
Astoria Theatre
SOHO/SHAV W1D 11 K5
Astra Business Centre
REDH RH1 .... 276 B10
Asylum Medical Centre
CEND/HSY/T N8 .... 119 H1
Athelney Primary School
CAT SE6 .... 182 F6
Athelstan House School
HPTN TW12 .... 197 P1
Athelstone Road Industrial Estate
CLPT E5 .... 120 B9
Athena Theatre
CLPT E5 .... 120 B9
Atherton Leisure Centre
FSTGT E7 .... 141 L1
Athlone House Hospital
HGT N6 .... 118 A6
Athlon Industrial Estate
ALP/SUD HA0 .... 135 J4
Atkinson Morley Hospital
RYNPK SW20 .... 178 E10
Atlas Business Centre
CRICK NW2 .... 116 E7
Atlas Medical Centre
HORL RH6 .... 280 B8
Atlas Transport Estate
BTSEA SW11 .... 157 M8
Atwood Primary School
SAND/SEL CR2 .... 223 P9
Audley CP School
CTHM CR3 .... 241 M6
Aultone Yard
CAR SM5 .... 202 A10
Auriol Junior School
HOR/WEW KT19 .... 220 C1
Australian High Commission
HOL/ALD WC2B 11 P6
Austrian Embassy
KTBR SW1X 16 C3
Avalon Chinese Medicine Clinic
CHSWK W4 .... 155 P6
Aveley Football Club
SOCK/AV RM15 .... 146 F5
Aveley Medical Centre
SOCK/AV RM15 .... 147 H6
Aveley Primary School
SOCK/AV RM15 .... 146 D10
The Aveley School
SOCK/AV RM15 .... 146 C9
Aveling Park School
WALTH E17 .... 100 F10
Avenue Industrial Estate
CHING E4 .... 100 E7
Avenue Industrial Estate
GPK RM2 .... 105 L10
Avenue Medical Centre
SLN SL2 .... 128 F5
Avenue Primary School
KIL/WHAMP NW6 .... 2 A4
Avenue Primary School
MNPK E12 .... 122 B9
The Avenue Primary School
BELMT SM2 .... 221 K6
Avenue Road Surgery
BRW CM14 .... 107 H5
Avicenna Medical Practice
REIG RH2 .... 275 L3
Avigdor High School
STNW/STAM N16 .... 119 L7
Avondale Park Primary School
NTGHL W11 .... 8 A8
Avondale Park Primary School
NTGHL W11 .... 136 C9
Avon House School
WFD IG8 .... 101 M5
Avril Noble Gallery
TPL/STR WC2R 11 M7
Axton Chase School
HART DA3 .... 211 L3
Aycliffe Drive Primary School
HHNE HP2 .... 35 P2
Aylands School
PEND EN3 .... 80 B2
Ayloff Primary School
HCH RM12 .... 125 J9
Aylward First & Middle Schools
STAN HA7 .... 95 J6
Aylward School
UED N18 .... 99 L5
Aylwin Secondary School
BERM/RHTH SE16 .... 19 M5
Aysgarth Medical Centre
IVER SL0 .... 130 G4
Baa Visitor Centre
HTHAIR TW6 .... 152 D7
Babington House School
CHST BR7 .... 184 C9
Back Care Clinic
WPK KT4 .... 200 D8
Bacon's College
BERM/RHTH SE16 .... 140 D10
Bacons College
BERM/RHTH SE16 .... 160 C1
Baden Powell County
Primary School
CLPT E5 .... 120 A8
Baden Powell House
SKENS SW7 .... 15 K5

Bahamas High Comm
  MYFR/PICC W1J 10 D9
Bahram Gallery
  IS N1 .... 6 C6
Balaam Leisure Centre
  PLSTW E13 .... 141 M6
Balfour Business Centre
  NWDGN UB2 .... 153 L2
Balfour Medical Centre
  GRAYS RM17 .... 167 P3
Balgowan Primary School
  BECK BR3 .... 204 D2
Balham Health Centre
  BAL SW12 .... 180 C5
Balham Mosque
  BAL SW12 .... 180 C3
Ballater Surgery
  ORP BR6 .... 207 J7
Baltic Exchange
  HDTCH EC3A 13 K5
Bancrofts School
  WFD IG8 .... 101 M4
Bandon Hill School
  WLGTN SM6 .... 222 E3
Bangabandhu Primary School
  BETH E2 .... 140 B5
Bangladesh High Comm
  SKENS SW7 .... 15 K3
Bank Gallery
  CHOB/PIR GU24 .... 213 K7
Bank of England Extension
  STP EC4M 12 E6
Bank of England
  LOTH EC2R 12 C6
Bankside Gallery
  STHWK SE1 .... 12 D8
Bankside Industrial Estate
  BARK IG11 .... 143 K5
Bankside Park Industrial Estate
  BARK IG11 .... 143 K5
The Bank Street Gallery
  BGR/WK TN15 .... 265 K1
Bannockburn CP School
  WOOL/PLUM SE18 .... 163 J3
Banqueting House
  WHALL SW1A 11 L10
Banstead Athletic Football Club
  KWD/TDW/WH KT20 .... 238 F6
Banstead Clinic
  BNSTD SM7 .... 239 K1
Banstead County Infants School
  BNSTD SM7 .... 239 J1
Banstead Sports Centre
  KWD/TDW/WH KT20 .... 238 F6
Banstead Village Clinic
  BNSTD SM7 .... 239 L1
Barbados High Comm
  FITZ W1T 11 K5
Barbara Castle Health Centre
  HLWW/ROY CM19 .... 46 D5
Barber Surgeons' Hall
  BARB EC2Y 12 F4
The Barbican
  STBT EC1A 12 E3
Barbican Theatre
  BARB EC2Y 12 F3
Barclay Junior & Infant School
  LEY E10 .... 121 J4
Barham Primary School
  ALP/SUD HA0 .... 135 H1
Baring Primary School
  LEE/GVPK SE12 .... 183 M3
Baring Road Medical Centre
  LEE/GVPK SE12 .... 183 M5
Barkantine Clinic
  POP/IOD E14 .... 160 F1
Barking Abbey
  Comprehensive School
  BARK IG11 .... 122 G10
Barking Abbey Industrial Estate
  BARK IG11 .... 142 E3
Barking College
  ROMW/RG RM7 .... 124 E7
Barking & Dagenham Council
  DAGW RM9 .... 144 A1
Barking Football Club
  BCTR RM8 .... 123 L10
Barking Hospital
  BARK IG11 .... 143 J2
Barking Industrial Park
  BARK IG11 .... 143 J3
Barking Rugby Union
  Football Club
  DAGW RM9 .... 143 N3
Barkingside Football Club
  BARK/HLT IG6 .... 122 G2
Barlby Primary School
  NKENS W10 .... 136 C6
Barley Lane Primary School
  CDHH RM6 .... 123 L5
Barnabas Medical Centre
  NTHLT UB5 .... 134 B1
Barncroft JMI School
  HHNE HP2 .... 35 N1
Barncroft Primary School
  WALTH E17 .... 120 D4
Barnehurst Junior School
  BXLYHN DA7 .... 164 D7
Barn Elms Water Sports Centre
  BARN SW13 .... 156 F8
Barnes Cray Primary School
  DART DA1 .... 165 H10
Barnes Hospital
  MORT/ESHN SW14 .... 156 B9
Barnes Sports Club
  BARN SW13 .... 156 C7
Barnet College
  NFNCH/WDSP N12 .... 97 M6
Barnet College
  of Further Education
  BAR EN5 .... 77 J8
Barnet County Court
  BAR EN5 .... 77 M8
Barnet County Court
  FNCH N3 .... 97 K9
Barnet Football Club
  BAR EN5 .... 77 K9
Barnet General Hospital
  BAR EN5 .... 76 C8
Barnet Health Centre
  BAR EN5 .... 77 K9
Barnet Hill Primary School
  BAR EN5 .... 77 J9
Barnet Hospital Chest Clinic
  BAR EN5 .... 76 C8
Barnet Magistrates Court
  BAR EN5 .... 77 J8
Barnet Synagogue
  BAR EN5 .... 77 M9
Barnett Wood County School
  ASHTD KT21 .... 237 J3
Barnfield Road School
  EDGE HA8 .... 95 P9

Barnhill Community High School
  YEAD UB4 .... 133 J5
Barnsbury County Infant School
  WOKS/MYFD GU22 .... 232 A7
Barnsbury Gallery
  IS N1 .... 6 A4
Barnsbury School for Girls
  IS N1 .... 6 A3
Barn Theatre
  WGCW AL8 .... 22 F5
The Barn Theatre Club
  WOT/HER KT12 .... 217 J1
Barnwood County First School
  GUW GU1 .... 249 J9
Barons Court Theatre
  WKENS W14 .... 14 B7
Barracuda Swimming Club
  POTB/CUF EN6 .... 59 N9
Barratt Industrial Park
  BOW E3 .... 141 H6
Barrett Industrial Park
  STHL UB1 .... 133 P10
Barrett Way Industrial Estate
  HRW HA1 .... 114 C1
Barrington Primary School
  WELL DA16 .... 163 N8
Barron Ingrid Gallery
  HAMP NW3 .... 117 P9
Barrow Hedges School
  CAR SM5 .... 221 P4
Barry Jackson Practice
  RPLY/SEND GU23 .... 232 F10
Barton House Health Centre
  STNW/STAM N16 .... 119 L8
Barwell Business Park
  CHSGTN KT9 .... 219 J4
Bashir Gallery
  MBLAR W1H 10 B4
Bata Medical Centre
  TIL RM18 .... 169 M3
Batchwood Golf Club
  STALW/RED AL3 .... 38 A3
Batchwood School
  STALW/RED AL3 .... 38 C3
Bates Industrial Estate
  HARH RM3 .... 105 P8
Bath Factory Estate
  HNHL SE24 .... 181 K2
Battersea Business Centre
  BTSEA SW11 .... 158 B9
Battersea Fields Practice
  VX/NE SW8 .... 158 D7
Battersea Sports Centre
  BTSEA SW11 .... 157 N9
Battersea Technology College
  BTSEA SW11 .... 158 A7
Battersea Tutorial College
  TOOT SW17 .... 180 B5
Baumkotter Gallery
  KENS W8 .... 14 F1
Bayfordbury College
  of Hertfordshire
  HERT/BAY SG13 .... 25 J10
Bayford Junior Middle
  & Infant School
  HERT/BAY SG13 .... 42 G4
Baylis Court School for Girls
  SL SL1 .... 129 J7
BBC
  REGST W1B 10 F4
BBC Studios
  MV/WKIL W9 .... 8 G1
BBC Television Centre
  SHB W12 .... 136 F9
B Day Hospital
  BCTR RM8 .... 123 P7
Beacon Hill Industrial Estate
  PUR RM19 .... 166 A3
Beacon House School
  EA W5 .... 135 L10
Beacon School
  BNSTD SM7 .... 239 H3
The Beacon School
  AMS HP6 .... 68 G1
Beaconsfield Cricket Club
  BEAC HP9 .... 88 F10
Beaconsfield High School
  BEAC HP9 .... 88 C10
Beaconsfield Road First School
  STHL UB1 .... 133 M10
Beaconsfield Rugby
  Football Club
  BEAC HP9 .... 108 E1
Beaconsfield School
  BEAC HP9 .... 88 D10
Beagle Gallery
  NTGHL W11 .... 8 C7
Beal High School
  REDBR IG4 .... 122 B1
Beam Primary School
  DACE RM10 .... 144 D4
Bean Primary School
  RDART DA2 .... 189 H7
Beatrix Potter Primary School
  WAND/EARL SW18 .... 179 M4
Beauclerc County Infant School
  SUN TW16 .... 197 K3
Beaufort County Primary School
  WOKN/KNAP GU21 .... 231 L2
Beaumont Primary School
  LEY E10 .... 120 G5
Beaumont Primary School
  PUR/KEN CR8 .... 222 G10
Beaumont School
  STALE/WH AL4 .... 39 J5
Beavers Primary School
  HSLWW TW4 .... 153 K9
Beaverwood School for Girls
  CHST BR7 .... 185 H9
Beckenham Business Centre
  BECK BR3 .... 182 D9
Beckenham Cricket Club
  BECK BR3 .... 182 G10
Beckenham Hospital
  BECK BR3 .... 204 E2
Beckenham Leisure Centre
  BECK BR3 .... 204 D1
Beckenham Rugby Football Club
  BECK BR5 .... 204 D4
Beckenham Town Football Club
  BECK BR3 .... 204 F5
Beckford Primary School
  KIL/WHAMP NW6 .... 117 J10
Beckmead School
  BECK BR3 .... 204 F8
The Beck Theatre
  HYS/HAR UB3 .... 132 C8
Beckton Ski Centre
  EHAM E6 .... 142 D6
Beckton Special School
  CAN/RD E16 .... 93 A7
Becontree School
  BCTR RM8 .... 123 L8

Bective House Clinic
  PUT/ROE SW15 .... 157 J10
Beddington Infant School
  WLGTN SM6 .... 222 D1
Beddington Infants School
  WLGTN SM6 .... 202 D10
Beddington Medical Centre
  CROY/NA CR0 .... 222 F1
Beddington Park Primary School
  WLGTN SM6 .... 202 F10
Beddington Trading Estate
  CROY/NA CR0 .... 202 F8
Bedelsford School
  KUT KT1 .... 199 K3
Bedensfield Clinic
  SCUP DA14 .... 185 P8
Bedfont Health Clinic
  EBED/NFELT TW14 .... 174 F3
Bedfont Junior & Infant School
  EBED/NFELT TW14 .... 174 F2
The Bedford Park Surgery
  CHSWK W4 .... 156 A3
Bedmond JMI School
  ABLGY WD5 .... 54 G4
Bedonwell Clinic
  ABYW SE2 .... 163 P5
Bedonwell Medical Centre
  BELV DA17 .... 164 A4
Bedonwell Primary Junior
  & Infant School
  BELV DA17 .... 163 P5
Beech Avenue Surgery
  UPMR RM14 .... 126 A9
Beechcroft Farm
  Industrial Estate
  BGR/WK TN15 .... 211 J10
Beechfield Junior Middle
  & Infant School
  WATN WD24 .... 73 H3
Beech House School
  SAND/SEL CR2 .... 223 N6
Beech Hyde Junior Middle
  & Infant School
  STALE/WH AL4 .... 21 J4
Beecholme Primary School
  MTCM CR4 .... 202 C1
Beechwood Secondary School
  SLN SL2 .... 128 C5
Beis Rochel D'satmar Girls School
  STNW/STAM N16 .... 119 M5
Beis Yaakov Primary School
  CDALE/KGS NW9 .... 116 A2
Belcon Industrial Estate
  HOD EN11 .... 45 H3
Belhus Golf Club & Leisure Centre
  SOCK/AV RM15 .... 146 D8
Belize High Comm
  CAVSO/HST W1G 10 E5
Bellegrove Surgery
  WELL DA16 .... 163 J8
Bellenden Junior & Infant School
  PECK SE15 .... 159 P9
Bellenden Road Business Centre
  PECK SE15 .... 159 N8
Bellenden Road Group Practice
  PECK SE15 .... 159 N8
Bellerbyth
  GU GU1 .... 268 A1
Belleville School
  BTSEA SW11 .... 180 A1
Bell Farm County Middle School
  WOT/HER KT12 .... 217 K1
Bellgate JMI School
  HHNE HP2 .... 35 P4
Bell Industrial Estate
  CHSWK W4 .... 155 P3
Bellingham Trading Estate
  CAT SE6 .... 182 C6
Bell Lane County
  Combined School
  AMS HP6 .... 69 N4
Bell Lane JMI School
  HDN NW4 .... 116 G2
Belmont First & Middle School
  KTN/HRWW/W HA3 .... 94 E10
Belmont Junior & Infant School
  WDGN N22 .... 119 K1
Belmont Medical Centre
  UX/CGN UB8 .... 131 N2
Belmont Mill Hill Junior School
  MLHL NW7 .... 96 D4
Belmont Primary School
  BXLYHN DA7 .... 164 B6
Belmont Road Primary School
  CHSWK W4 .... 156 A3
Belmore Primary School
  YEAD UB4 .... 133 K5
Belsize Square Synagogue
  HAMP NW3 .... 3 M1
Belswains Infant School
  HHS/BOV HP3 .... 36 A10
Belvedere C of E Trinity School
  BELV DA17 .... 164 C3
Belvedere Day Hospital
  WLSDN NW10 .... 136 D3
Belvedere Industrial Estate
  BELV DA17 .... 144 E10
Belvue Business Centre
  NTHLT UB5 .... 134 A2
Belvue School
  NTHLT UB5 .... 133 P3
Bengeo Junior & Infant School
  HERT/WAS SG14 .... 25 K2
Benhurst JMI School
  HCH RM12 .... 125 J8
Ben Jonson Primary School
  WCHPL E1 .... 140 D6
Bennetts End Surgery
  HHS/BOV HP3 .... 36 B9
Bensham Manor School
  THHTH CR7 .... 203 K5
Benson Primary School
  CROY/NA CR0 .... 204 D10
Bentalls Shopping Centre
  KUT KT1 .... 199 J1
Benthal Primary School
  STNW/STAM N16 .... 119 P8
Bentley Street Industrial Estate
  GVE DA12 .... 190 F2
Bentley Wood High School
  STAN HA7 .... 94 E6
Bentworth Primary School
  SHB W12 .... 136 E8
Benyon CP School
  SOCK/AV RM15 .... 147 H4
Beormund Primary School
  STHWK SE1 .... 18 G2
Berger Junior & Infant Schools
  HOM E9 .... 140 C1
Berkeley Clinic
  RKW/CH/CXG WD3 .... 91 M2
Berkeley School
  HEST TW5 .... 153 L5

Berkhamsted Football Club
  BERK HP4 .... 33 N4
Berkhamsted Golf Club
  BERK HP4 .... 34 B2
Berkhamsted Health Centre
  BERK HP4 .... 33 M4
Berkhamsted School
  BERK HP4 .... 33 P5
Berkhamsted School for Girls
  BERK HP4 .... 33 N5
Berkhamsted School House
  BERK HP4 .... 33 P5
Berkhamsted Tennis Club
  BERK HP4 .... 33 P4
Berkley Gallery
  BERK HP4 .... 33 N5
Berkshire County Council
  SL SL1 .... 149 K1
Bermondsey Town Hall
  STHWK SE1 .... 19 M4
Bermondsey Trading Estate
  BERM/RHTH SE16 .... 160 B4
Bernards Heath Infant School
  STAL AL1 .... 38 E4
Berrymede First & Junior School
  ACT W3 .... 155 N1
Bertrum House
  & Little Wandsworth School
  TOOT SW17 .... 180 B5
Bessemer Grange Junior
  & Infant School
  CMBW SE5 .... 159 M10
Beta Health Clinic
  HHW HP1 .... 35 N6
Betchworth Park Golf Club
  RDKG RH5 .... 273 K1
Bethams C of E School
  GFD/PVL UB6 .... 134 C5
Bethel Temple
  STRHM/NOR SW16 .... 180 C7
Beth Hamedrash
  Skver Synagogue
  STNW/STAM N16 .... 119 N5
The Bethlem & Maudsley
  NHS Trust
  CMBW SE5 .... 159 L8
Bethlem Royal Hospital
  BECK BR3 .... 204 F7
Bethnal Green High School
  BETH E2 .... 7 M10
Bethnal Green Museum
  of Childhood
  BETH E2 .... 140 A5
Beulah Junior & Infant School
  THHTH CR7 .... 203 K2
Beverley County Secondary
  School for Boys
  NWMAL KT3 .... 200 C5
Beverley Primary School
  GNWCH SE10 .... 160 G6
Beverley Trading Estate
  MRDN SM4 .... 200 G7
Bevington Primary School
  NKENS W10 .... 8 B3
Bewbush Community
  Middle School
  CRAWW RH11 .... 283 H10
Bewbush Medical Centre
  CRAWW RH11 .... 283 H10
Bewhurst County First School
  CRAWW RH11 .... 283 J10
Bexley College
  ABYW SE2 .... 163 N5
Bexley College
  BELV DA17 .... 164 D3
Bexley College
  ERITH DA8 .... 164 D3
Bexley Cricket Club
  BXLY DA5 .... 186 B4
Bexley Erith Technical
  Boys School
  BXLY DA5 .... 186 B2
Bexley Grammar Mixed School
  WELL DA16 .... 163 L10
Bexleyheath Centre
  BXLYHS DA6 .... 163 P10
Bexleyheath School
  BXLYHN DA7 .... 164 B9
Bexley Hospital
  BXLY DA5 .... 186 F5
Bexley Rugby Club
  BXLY DA5 .... 186 B3
The Bharani Medical Centre
  SL SL1 .... 128 C8
Bickley Park Cricket Club
  BMLY BR1 .... 206 B2
Bickley Park School
  BMLY BR1 .... 206 B3
Bickley Parva School
  BMLY BR1 .... 206 A3
Biggin Hill Business Park
  BH/WHM TN16 .... 244 A1
Biggin Hill Junior School
  BH/WHM TN16 .... 244 B2
Billingsgate Fish Market
  POP/IOD E14 .... 140 G10
Binscombe Medical Centre
  RGODL GU7 .... 267 J9
Birbeck College
  STPAN WC1H 11 J1
Birch Court Colindale Hospital
  CDALE/KGS NW9 .... 96 B10
Birchwood County
  Primary School
  SWLY BR8 .... 208 E1
Birchwood Leisure Centre
  HAT AL10 .... 40 E1
Birkbeck Primary School
  SCUP DA14 .... 185 L6
Bishop Challoner RC
  Secondary School
  WCHPL E1 .... 140 B8
Bishop Challoner School
  HAYES BR2 .... 205 J2
Bishop David Brown School
  WOKN/KNAP GU21 .... 214 C9
Bishop Douglass RC High School
  EFNCH N2 .... 117 M1
Bishop Gilpin Primary School
  WIM/MER SW19 .... 179 J8
Bishophalt School
  UX/CGN UB8 .... 132 A5
Bishop John Robinson
  Primary School
  THMD SE28 .... 143 M9
Bishop Perrin School
  WHTN TW2 .... 176 A3
Bishop Ramsay C of E School
  RSLP HA4 .... 113 H5
Bishop Ramsey C of E School
  RSLP HA4 .... 112 C5
Bishop Reindorp C of E School
  GU GU1 .... 249 P7

Bishopsgate Institute
  WCHPL E1 .... 13 K4
Bishopsgate School
  EGH TW20 .... 171 M6
Bishops Hatfield Girls School
  HAT AL10 .... 40 D4
Bishop Stopford School
  EN EN1 .... 80 A6
Bishops Wood Hospital
  RKW/CH/CXG WD3 .... 92 B6
Bishop Thomas Grant RC School
  STRHM/NOR SW16 .... 180 C8
Bishop Wand C of E School
  SUN TW16 .... 196 C2
Bittacy Business Centre
  MLHL NW7 .... 97 H7
Blackburn Trading Estate
  STWL/WRAY TW19 .... 174 A2
Blackfen School for Girls
  BFN/LL DA15 .... 185 L2
Blackfriars Medical Practice
  STHWK SE1 .... 12 B10
The Blackheath Clinic
  BKHTH/KID SE3 .... 161 M10
Blackheath High School
  BKHTH/KID SE3 .... 161 M6
Blackheath High School Gpdst
  BKHTH/KID SE3 .... 161 L8
Blackheath Hospital
  BKHTH/KID SE3 .... 161 L9
The Blackheath Practice
  BKHTH/KID SE3 .... 162 A7
Blackshots Leisure Centre
  CDH/CHF RM16 .... 168 A1
Blackthorn Junior School
  WGCE AL7 .... 23 K6
Blackwall Trading Estate
  POP/IOD E14 .... 141 H9
Blaire Peach School
  STHL UB1 .... 133 L10
Blanche Neville School
  WDGN N22 .... 99 H9
Blenheim Business Centre
  MTCM CR4 .... 202 A1
Blenheim High School
  HOR/WEW KT19 .... 220 A6
Blenheim Junior & Infant School
  ORP BR6 .... 207 M9
Blenheim Shopping Centre
  PGE/AN SE20 .... 182 B10
Blessed Cuthbert Mayne
  RC School
  HHW HP1 .... 35 L5
Blessed Dominic RC
  Primary School
  CDALE/KGS NW9 .... 96 B10
Blessed John Roche
  Secondary School
  POP/IOD E14 .... 140 F8
Blessed Sacrament School
  IS N1 .... 5 M6
Bletchingley Golf Club
  REDH RH1 .... 259 L9
Bloomfield Clinic Guys
  STHWK SE1 .... 19 H1
Bloomsbury College
  FUL/PGN SW6 .... 157 K6
Bloomsbury Health Authority
  CAMTN NW1 .... 5 H9
Bloomsbury Theatre
  STPAN WC1H 11 J1
Blossoms Inn Medical Centre
  BLKFR EC4V 12 F7
Bluecoat School
  STJSPK SW1H 17 J3
The Blue C of E School
  ISLW TW7 .... 154 F9
Blue Gate Fields Primary School
  WCHPL E1 .... 140 B9
Bnois Jerusalem School
  STNW/STAM N16 .... 119 L5
Boathouse Gallery
  SHPTN TW17 .... 196 G7
The Bob Hope Theatre
  ELTH/MOT SE9 .... 184 B2
Bob Lawrence Gallery
  CHEL SW3 .... 15 N8
Bobs Park Surgery
  BOW E3 .... 140 C5
Bodywise Natural Health Centre
  BETH E2 .... 140 B5
Bolingbroke Hospital
  BTSEA SW11 .... 179 P1
Bolingbroke Primary School
  BTSEA SW11 .... 157 N7
Bond First School
  MTCM CR4 .... 202 A2
Bond Road School
  MTCM CR4 .... 202 A2
Bonner Primary School
  BETH E2 .... 140 C4
Bonneville Primary School
  CLAP SW4 .... 180 D2
Bonneygrove Junior
  & Infant School
  CHESW EN7 .... 61 P6
Bonnygate CP School
  SOCK/AV RM15 .... 146 G7
Bon Secours Hospital
  BEAC HP9 .... 88 D9
Bonus Pastor Roman
  Catholic School
  BMLY BR1 .... 183 K7
Bookham Galleries
  GT/LBKH KT23 .... 254 B1
Boomes Industrial Estate
  RAIN RM13 .... 144 C6
Booster Cushion Theatre
  WDGN N22 .... 98 G10
Borehamwood Football Club
  BORE WD6 .... 75 N6
Borehamwood Industrial Park
  BORE WD6 .... 76 A6
Borers Business Park
  CRAWE RH10 .... 285 K2
Borough Market
  STHWK SE1 .... 12 G9
Borough of Broxbourne
  CHES/WCR EN8 .... 62 A6
Bosnia Embassy
  CAVSO/HST W1G 10 F5
Boston Business Park
  NWDGN UB2 .... 154 D2
Boston University
  SKENS SW7 .... 15 J6
Botany Bay Cricket Club
  ENC/FH EN2 .... 78 E2
Botswana High Comm
  OXSTW W1C 10 E6
Botwell House Primary School
  HYS/HAR UB3 .... 152 G1
Boundary Business Centre
  WOKN/KNAP GU21 .... 232 D1

Bounds Green Health Centre
FBAR/BDGN N11................ 98 E8
Bounds Green Industrial Estate
FBAR/BDGN N11................ 98 D7
Bounds Green Junior
& Infant School
FBAR/BDGN N11................ 98 F8
Bourne CP School
RSLP HA4........................ 113 K10
Bourne Gallery
REIG RH2........................ 275 L1
Bourne Hall Health Centre
EW KT17......................... 220 C5
Bournehall Junior & Infant School
BUSH WD23...................... 73 P9
Bourneside Sports Club
STHGT/OAK N14................. 98 F2
Bournewood Community
& Mental Health NHS Trust
WOKN/KNAP GU21.............. 231 M3
Bournewood Community
& Mental NHS Trust
ECH TW20........................ 172 D8
Bousfield Primary School
WBPTN SW10..................... 15 J7
Boutcher C of E Primary School
STHWK SE1....................... 19 L5
Bovingdon Junior Mixed School
HHS/BOV HP3.................... 52 E3
Bovingdon Parish Council
HHS/BOV HP3.................... 52 D3
Bovingdon Primary School
HHS/BOV HP3.................... 52 E3
Bowater House
SKENS SW7....................... 16 A2
Bow County Court
SRTFD E15....................... 141 L1
Bowden House Clinic
HRW HA1......................... 114 D7
Bower Park School
ROM RM1......................... 104 F7
Bowes Primary School
FBAR/BDGN N11................ 98 E6
Bowes Road Clinic
FBAR/BDGN N11................ 98 D6
Bow Industrial Park
SRTFD E15....................... 140 F2
Bowling Alley
BERM/RHTH SE16................ 160 C2
Bowman Trading Estate
CDALE/KGS NW9................. 115 M1
Bow Road Surgery
BOW E3........................... 140 E5
Bow Surgery
BOW E3........................... 140 G5
Bow Triangle Business Centre
BOW E3........................... 140 F6
Boxgrove Primary School
ABYW SE2......................... 163 M2
Box Hill School
RDKG RH5........................ 254 G3
Boxmoor Golf Club
HHW HP1......................... 35 H10
Boxmoor House School
HHS/BOV HP3.................... 35 J9
Boxwell Road Surgery
BERK HP4......................... 33 N5
Boyd School
UPMR RM14...................... 126 D7
Brackenbury Health Centre
HMSMTH W6...................... 156 E2
Brackenbury Primary School
HMSMTH W6...................... 156 E2
Bradbourne School
RSEV TN14....................... 247 H7
Brady Primary School
RAIN RM13....................... 145 K7
Brady Recreation Centre
WCHPL E1........................ 13 N3
Braeside Surgery
EYN DA4.......................... 209 P7
Braincroft Primary School
CRICK NW2....................... 116 C8
Braintree Road Industrial Estate
RSLP HA4......................... 113 J9
Bramah Tea & Coffee Museum
STHWK SE1....................... 19 M1
Brambletye County
Middle School
REDH RH1......................... 276 B2
Bramley Golf Club
SHGR GU5........................ 268 B10
Brampton Manor
Comprehensive School
PLSTW E13....................... 142 A6
Brampton Primary School
EHAM E6.......................... 142 B5
Brampton Primary School
WELL DA16....................... 163 N8
Brandlehow Primary School
PUT/ROE SW15................... 157 J10
Brandler Galleries
BRW CM14........................ 107 J3
Branfil Junior & Infant School
UPMR RM14...................... 125 P9
Branollys Health Centre
PLSTW E13....................... 141 M6
Brasted Surgery
BH/WHM TN16................... 263 M1
Brays Grove
Comprehensive School
HLWS CM18....................... 47 L3
Breakspeare School
ABLGY WD5....................... 54 F7
Breakspear Junior School
HGDN/ICK UB10.................. 112 B7
Breaside Preparatory School
BMLY BR1......................... 206 A1
Brecknock Primary School
HOLWY N7........................ 5 K1
Bredinghurst School
PECK SE15........................ 160 B10
Brent Adult College
WLSDN NW10..................... 136 A3
Brent Arts Council
CRICK NW2........................ 116 D8
Brent Child & Family Clinic
WLSDN NW10..................... 116 C10
Brent Council
WBLY HA9........................ 115 J8
Brent CP School
RDART DA2....................... 188 B3
Brent Cross Shopping Centre
HDN NW4......................... 116 F5
Brentfield Medical Centre
WLSDN NW10..................... 136 A1
Brentfield Primary School
WLSDN NW10..................... 136 A1
Brentford Business Centre
BTFD TW8......................... 155 H6
The Brentford Clinic
BTFD TW8......................... 155 K5

Brentford County Court
BTFD TW8......................... 155 J6
Brentford Fountain
Leisure Centre
CHSWK W4........................ 155 M4
Brentford Health Centre
BTFD TW8......................... 155 H5
Brentford Medical Centre
BTFD TW8......................... 155 J5
Brentford School for Girls
BTFD TW8......................... 155 J5
Brent & Harrow Health Authority
HRW HA1......................... 114 C5
Brent & Harrow Health NHS Trust
HRW HA1......................... 114 D5
Brent Knoll School
SYD SE26......................... 182 C6
Brent Magistrates Court House
WLSDN NW10..................... 136 B1
Brentmead Gardens Surgery
WLSDN NW10..................... 135 L5
Brentside First School
HNWL W7......................... 134 D7
Brentside High School
HNWL W7......................... 134 D6
Brentside Primary School
HNWL W7......................... 134 D6
Brentwaters Business Park
BTFD TW8......................... 155 H6
Brentwood Borough Council
BRW CM14........................ 107 H3
Brentwood Borough Council
RBRW/HUT CM13................. 107 J7
Brentwood Chiropody Surgery
BRW CM14........................ 107 H3
The Brentwood Clinic
BRW CM14........................ 107 J2
Brentwood Community Hospital
BRWN CM15...................... 107 K2
Brentwood County High School
BRW CM14........................ 107 J4
Brentwood Preparatory School
BRWN CM15...................... 107 K2
Brentwood Rugby Football Club
BRW CM14........................ 107 K5
Brentwood School
BRWN CM15...................... 107 J3
Brentwood Sports Ground
BRWN CM15...................... 107 J2
Brentwood Ursuline High School
BRW CM14........................ 107 J4
Brewers' Hall
CITYW EC2V....................... 12 F4
Brickendon Grange Golf
& Country Club
HERT/BAY SG13................... 43 J5
Brickfields Industrial Estate
HHNE HP2......................... 36 C2
The Bridewell Theatre
EMB EC4Y......................... 12 C6
The Bridge Business Centre
NWDGN UB2....................... 153 P1
Bridge Industrial Estate
HORL RH6......................... 280 C4
Bridge Lane Theatre
BTSEA SW11...................... 157 P7
Bridge Medical Centre
CRAWE RH10..................... 284 B6
Bridge View Industrial Estate
WTHK RM20....................... 166 F5
Bridgewater School
BERK HP4......................... 33 M3
The Brigidine School
WDSR SL4......................... 149 J9
Brigstock Medical Centre
THHTH CR7........................ 203 J5
Brimsdown Junior
& Infant School
PEND EN3......................... 80 C7
Brindishe Primary School
LEE/GVPK SE12................... 183 L1
Brinkleys Wine Gallery
WBPTN SW10..................... 15 J9
Briset Corner Surgery
ELTH/MOT SE9.................... 162 B10
Britannia Business Centre
CHES/WCR EN8................... 62 E10
Britannia Business Centre
CRICK NW2........................ 116 G9
Britannia Industrial Estate
DTCH/LGLY SL3................... 151 H8
Britannia Sports Ground
WALTH E17........................ 100 F8
British Dental Ass
CAVSQ/HST W1G.................. 10 E4
The British Editorial Society
of Bone & Joint Surgery
CHCR WC2N....................... 11 M8
British Library
CAMTN NW1....................... 5 K9
British Medical Association
STPAN WC1H...................... 11 K1
British Museum
MYFR/PICC W1J................... 10 G8
British Museum
RSQ WC1B......................... 11 L4
British Telecom Tower
GTPST W1W....................... 10 G3
Brit Performing Arts
& Technology School
SNWD SE25........................ 203 L6
Brittania Business Park
CHES/WCR EN8................... 62 E10
Brittons School
RAIN RM13....................... 144 G2
Britwell Health Clinic
SLN SL2........................... 128 F5
Brixton Art Gallery
BRXN/ST SW9.................... 159 H9
Brixton College
for Further Education
BRXS/STRHM SW2................ 180 G1
Brixton Hill Group Practice
BRXS/STRHM SW2................ 180 G2
Brixton Mosque
BRXN/ST SW9.................... 159 H9
Brixton Recreation Centre
BRXN/ST SW9.................... 159 H9
Broadfield Infant School
HHNE HP2......................... 36 A6
Broadfield Junior School
HHNE HP2......................... 36 A6
Broadfield School
HLW WD20........................ 29 H10
Broadfields Infant School
EDGE HA8......................... 23 M3
Broadfields Junior School
EDGE HA8......................... 95 N3
Bradford Park Business Centre
RGUE GU4......................... 268 A7
Bradford Primary School
HARH RM3......................... 105 L7

Broadgate
LVPST EC2M....................... 13 H3
Broadhurst School
HOD NW6.......................... 3 J3
Broadmead Junior School
CROY/NA CR0..................... 203 L6
Broadmere County
Middle School
WOKN/KNAP GU21............... 214 D3
Broadwalk Shopping Centre
EDGE HA8......................... 95 M3
Broadwater Farm Junior School
TOTM N17......................... 99 L10
Broadwater Farm Primary School
TOTM N17......................... 99 L10
Broadwater Junior
& Infant School
TOOT SW17....................... 179 P7
Broadwater Park Golf Club
RGODL GU7....................... 267 N9
Broadwater School
RGODL GU7....................... 267 M9
Broadway Clinic
EDGE HA8......................... 95 N9
Broadway Retail Park
CRICK NW2........................ 116 G9
Broadway Shopping Centre
HMSMTH W6...................... 156 F4
Brockham School
BRKHM/BTCW RH3................ 273 N2
Brocklebank Health Centre
WAND/EARL SW18................ 179 L3
Brocklebank Industrial Estate
GNWCH SE10...................... 161 M3
Brockley Cross Business Centre
BROCKY SE4....................... 160 D9
Brockley Primary School
BROCKY SE4....................... 182 E1
Brockwell Primary School
BRXS/STRHM SW2................ 181 H7
Bromet School
OXHEY WD19...................... 93 L1
Bromley City Council
BMLY BR1......................... 205 L1
Bromley College of Further
& Higher Education
HAYES BR2......................... 206 A6
Bromley County Court
BMLY BR1......................... 205 M1
Bromley Health Authority
HAYES BR2......................... 205 M8
Bromley High School for Girls
BMLY BR1......................... 206 D4
Bromley Hospital
HAYES BR2......................... 205 N4
Bromley Hospitals NHS Trust
ORP BR6........................... 226 D1
Bromley Hospitals NHS Trust
ORP BR6........................... 227 J1
Bromley Industrial Centre
BMLY BR1......................... 206 A3
Bromley Mall Indoor Market
BMLY BR1......................... 205 M2
Bromley Museum
ORP BR6........................... 207 L7
Bromley Road Infant School
BECK BR3......................... 204 C1
Brompton Medical Centre
WBPTN SW10..................... 15 H7
Bromyard Leisure Centre
ACT W3........................... 136 B10
Brondesbury College for Boys
KIL/WHAMP NW6.................. 136 G2
Brook Business Centre
IVER SL0.......................... 131 K4
Brooke Trading Estate
ROM RM1......................... 124 C5
Brook Farm Industrial Estate
ABR/ST RM4...................... 104 E1
Brookfield House School
WFD IG8........................... 101 K7
Brookfield Primary School
ARCH N19......................... 118 C7
Brookfield Primary School
CHEAM SM3....................... 201 H8
Brook Gallery
CHIG IG7.......................... 102 C4
Brook General Hospital
WOOL/PLUM SE18................ 162 B7
Brook House Football Club
YEAD UB4......................... 132 G5
Brookhurst Surgery
ORP BR6........................... 207 K9
Brook Industrial Estate
YEAD UB4......................... 133 L10
Brookland Junior & Infant School
CHES/WCR EN8................... 62 C6
Brookland Primary School
GLDGN NW11...................... 117 L2
Brooklands College
WEY KT13......................... 216 A3
Brooklands Museum
WEY KT13......................... 216 B5
Brooklands School
BKHTH/KID SE3................... 161 M9
Brooklands School
REIG RH2......................... 257 L8
Brook Lane Business Centre
BTFD TW8......................... 155 J4
Brook Lane Mission Practice
BMLY BR1......................... 183 M9
Brook Lane Mission Practice
ELTH/MOT SE9.................... 184 A7
Brookmans Park Gm
Primary School
BRKMPK AL9...................... 59 H2
Brookmarsh Trading Estate
DEPT SE8......................... 160 G6
Brookmead Industrial Estate
MTCM CR4........................ 202 D6
Brookside Junior & Infant School
HARH RM3......................... 105 M6
Brookside School
YEAD UB4......................... 133 K5
Brookweald Cricket Club
BRW CM14........................ 106 D2
Brookwood County
Primary School
CHOB/PIR GU24.................. 230 F6
Broomfield House School
RCH/KEW TW9.................... 155 H4
Broomfield School
STHGT/OAK N14.................. 98 D10
Broomleigh Business Park
CAT SE6........................... 182 G8
Broomwood Hall School
BAL SW12........................ 180 B3
Brownlow Medical Centre
FBAR/BDGN N11................ 98 F6
Broxbourne Borough Council
CHES/WCR EN8................... 62 C2
Broxbourne Business Centre
CHES/WCR EN8................... 62 C2

Broxbourne C of E JMI School
BROX EN10........................ 44 C1
Broxbourne Sailing Club
HOD EN11......................... 45 J6
The Broxbourne School
BROX EN10........................ 44 D8
Broxbourne Sports Club
BROX EN10........................ 44 E7
Bruce Castle Museum
TOTM N17......................... 99 M9
Bruce Grove Junior School
TOTM N17......................... 99 M10
Brunei Darrusalam High Comm
KTBR SW1X........................ 16 C3
Brunel Engine House
BERM/RHTH SE16................ 160 B1
Brunel University
ISLW TW7......................... 154 D6
Brunel University
TWK TW1.......................... 154 C10
Brunel University
UX/CGN UB8...................... 131 P5
Brunswick Health Centre
FBAR/BDGN N11................ 98 B3
Brunswick Housing
and Shopping Centre
BMSBY WC1N..................... 11 M1
Brunswick Industrial Park
FBAR/BDGN N11................ 98 C5
Brunswick Medical Centre
BMSBY WC1N..................... 11 L1
Brunswick Park JMI School
FBAR/BDGN N11................ 98 B2
Brunswick Park Junior
& Infant School
CMBW SE5........................ 159 L6
Brushwood Middle School
CSHM HP5......................... 51 K5
BT Centre
STBT EC1A........................ 12 E5
Buckhurst Hill CP School
BKHH IG9......................... 102 A6
Buckhurst Hill Football Club
BKHH IG9......................... 102 B2
Buckhurst Hill Reform Synagogue
LOU IG10.......................... 82 A9
Buckingham College School
HRW HA1......................... 114 D3
Buckingham Palace
WHALL SW1A...................... 16 E2
Buckingham Primary School
HPTN TW12....................... 175 N8
Buckinghamshire Chilterns
University College
CSTG HP8......................... 90 D3
Buckinghamshire County Council
AMS HP6.......................... 69 J4
Buckinghamshire County Council
CSHM HP5......................... 50 G7
Buckinghamshire County Council
DTCH/LGLY SL3................... 130 D10
Buckinghamshire Golf Club
DEN/HRF UB9..................... 111 M7
Buckland County Junior
& Infant School
STA TW18......................... 173 M10
Buckland Infant School
CHSGTN KT9...................... 219 L2
Buddhapadipa Temple
WIM/MER SW19................... 178 G7
Building Centre
GWRST WC1E...................... 11 J4
The Bulgarian Embassy
SKENS SW7....................... 15 K3
Bullers Wood School for Girls
CHST BR7......................... 206 C1
Bullsbridge Industrial Estate
NWDGN UB2....................... 153 J3
The Bull Theatre
BAR EN5.......................... 77 J8
Bupa Roding Hospital
REDBR IG4........................ 122 A1
Burbage Junior & Infant School
IS N1.............................. 7 J7
Burdett Coutts School
WEST SW1P....................... 17 J4
Burgess Industrial Park
CMBW SE5........................ 159 L6
Burghwood Clinic
BNSTD SM7....................... 239 J2
Burhill County Infant School
WOT/HER KT12................... 217 L2
Burhill Golf Club
WOT/HER KT12................... 217 L1
Burleigh Primary School
CHES/WCR EN8................... 62 C6
Burlington Danes School
SHB W12.......................... 136 E8
Burlington Road School
NWMAL KT3....................... 200 C4
Burnham Beeches Golf Club
SL SL1............................ 128 C3
Burnham Football Club
SL SL1............................ 128 A4
Burnham Grammar School
SL SL1............................ 128 C6
Burnham Health Centre
SL SL1............................ 128 A5
Burnham Trading Estate
DART DA1.......................... 165 L10
Burnham Upper School
SL SL1............................ 128 A6
Burnhill Business Centre
BECK BR3......................... 204 F2
Burnley Road Clinic
WLSDN NW10..................... 116 D10
Burnside Industrial Estate
BARK/HLT IG6.................... 103 L6
Burnt Ash Infant School
BMLY BR1......................... 183 M8
Burnt Ash School
BMLY BR1......................... 183 L8
Burnt Mill Comprehensive School
HLW CM20........................ 29 H9
Burntmill Industrial Estate
HLW CM20........................ 28 F8
Burnt Oak Primary School
BFN/LL DA15...................... 185 K4
Burntwood School
TOOT SW17....................... 179 N5
Burpham Primary School
RGUE GU4......................... 250 D6
Bursted Woodprimary School
BXLYHN DA7...................... 164 C8
Bursted Wood Surgery
BXLYHN DA7...................... 164 C8
Burstow Business Centre
HORL RH6......................... 281 J2
Burstow First & Middle School
HORL RH6......................... 281 J4
Burvill House Surgery
HAT AL10......................... 40 D4

Burwell Industrial Estate
LEY E10........................... 120 D6
Burwood Park School & College
WOT/HER KT12................... 216 G3
Burwood School
ORP BR6.......................... 207 N9
Burys Court School
REIG RH2......................... 274 G6
Business College
CONDST W1S..................... 10 F6
Bushey & District Synagogue
BUSH WD23...................... 94 B1
Bushey Hall School
BUSH WD23...................... 73 N10
Bushey Hall Swimming Pool
BUSH WD23...................... 73 N9
Bushey Health Centre
BUSH WD23...................... 73 N10
Bushey Heath Primary School
BUSH WD23...................... 94 C2
Bushey Manor School
BUSH WD23...................... 73 M9
Bushey Meads School
BUSH WD23...................... 74 B9
Bushey Middle School
RYNPK SW20...................... 200 E3
Bushey Museum & Art Gallery
BUSH WD23...................... 73 P10
Bush Hill Park Junior
& Infant School
EN EN1............................ 79 P9
Bush Hill Park Medical Centre
EN EN1............................ 79 N10
Bush House
HOL/ALD WC2B.................... 11 N6
Bush Industrial Estate
ARCH N19......................... 118 D8
Bush Industrial Estate
WLSDN NW10..................... 136 A5
Bush Theatre
SHB W12.......................... 156 F1
Bushy Hill Junior School
GU GU1........................... 250 G8
Business Centre
CHEL SW3......................... 15 P3
Business Centre
BAY/PAD W2...................... 9 N4
Business Centre
HAMP NW3........................ 117 K7
Business Centre
LOU IG10.......................... 82 G8
Business Centre
RAD WD7.......................... 56 G10
The Business Centre
IL IG1............................. 122 E7
The Business Centre
HARH RM3......................... 105 L8
The Business Centre
IS N1.............................. 6 B6
The Business Centre
WDGN N22......................... 98 F10
Business Park
BERM/RHTH SE16................ 19 P4
Business Park
ELTH/MOT SE9.................... 184 D5
Business Park 5
LHD/OX KT22..................... 236 F6
Bute House Preparatory
School for Girls
HMSMTH W6...................... 156 F3
Butlers Court County First
& Middle School
BEAC HP9......................... 88 C10
Butterfly Sports Club
ELTH/MOT SE9.................... 184 C4
Buxlow Preparatory School
WBLY HA9........................ 115 K8
Buzzard Creek Industrial Estate
BARK IG11........................ 143 J5
Byam Shaw School of Art
ARCH N19......................... 118 D7
Byfleet Business Centre
BF/WBF KT14..................... 215 N4
Byfleet CP School
BF/WBF KT14..................... 215 N4
Byfleet Industrial Estate
WATW WD18...................... 92 D2
Bygrove Primary School
POP/IOD E14..................... 140 G8
Byron Court Primary School
ALP/SUD HA0..................... 115 H7
Byron Junior School
COUL/CHIP CR5................... 240 F3
Cabinet Gallery
FSBYE EC1V........................ 12 C1
Cabinet War Rooms
WHALL SW1A...................... 17 K1
Cable House School
WOKN/KNAP GU21............... 232 B1
Cab Mech Theatre
COVGDN WC2E.................... 11 M7
Caelt Gallery
NTCHL W11....................... 8 D6
Cake Gallery
AMSS HP7......................... 69 H4
Calcot Medical Centre
CFSP/GDCR SL9................... 90 A9
Caledonian Market
STHWK SE1....................... 19 K3
Calvary Temple
CMBW SE5........................ 159 K6
Calverton Primary School
CAN/RD E16...................... 142 A8
Cambell Infant School
DAGW RM9....................... 143 N2
Camberwell Business Centre
CMBW SE5........................ 159 L6
Camberwell College of Arts
CMBW SE5........................ 159 M7
The Camberwell Green Surgery
CMBW SE5........................ 159 K7
Camberwell Trading Estate
CMBW SE5........................ 159 J8
Cambridge Park Bowling
& Sports Club
TWK TW1.......................... 177 H2
Cambridge Park Convent School
WAN E11.......................... 121 M4
Cambridge School
HMSMTH W6...................... 156 F6
Camb Theatre
LSQ/SEVD WC2H.................. 11 L6
Camden House Clinic
BKHTH/KID SE3................... 161 K8
Camden Junior School
CAR SM5.......................... 221 P1
Camden Peoples Theatre
CAMTN NW1....................... 4 G10
Camden Road Surgery
CAMTN NW1....................... 4 G3
Camden School for Girls
CAMTN NW1....................... 5 H2

Camden Theatre
  CAMTN NW1 .... 4 G7
Camden Town Hall
  CAMTN NW1 .... 5 L9
Camelot Primary School
  PECK SE15 .... 160 A6
Cameron House School
  CHEL SW3 .... 15 M9
Camperdown House
  WCHPL E1 .... 13 M6
Camphill Industrial Estate
  ADL/WDHM KT15 .... 215 L7
Camphill Road First School
  BF/WBF KT14 .... 215 L8
Campion House College
  ISLW TW7 .... 154 C6
The Campion School
  EMPK RM11 .... 125 N2
Camp Junior Middle
  & Infant School
  STAL AL1 .... 38 G7
Campsmere Junior School
  CEND/HSY/T N8 .... 118 F1
Campshill Surgery
  LEW SE13 .... 183 H1
Canada House Business Centre
  RSLP HA4 .... 113 K6
Canada Water Retail Park
  BERM/RHTH SE16 .... 160 C2
Canadian High Comm
  MYFR/PKLN W1K 10 D7
Canal Cafe Theatre
  BAY/PAD W2 .... 9 H3
Canal Industrial Park
  GVE DA12 .... 190 G2
Canary Wharf Tower
  POP/IOD E14 .... 140 G10
Canberra Primary School
  SHB W12 .... 136 B9
Canbury Business Centre
  KUTN/CMB KT2 .... 199 K1
Canbury 2000 Business Park
  KUTN/CMB KT2 .... 199 K1
Canbury Medical Centre
  KUTN/CMB KT2 .... 199 L1
Canbury School
  RCHPK/HAM TW10 .... 177 N9
Cann Hall Primary School
  WAN E11 .... 121 L8
The Canning School
  KENS W8 .... 14 E1
Cannock House School
  ORP BR6 .... 228 A2
Cannon Hill Clinic
  STHGT/OAK N14 .... 98 F4
Cannon Lane School
  PIN HA5 .... 113 L4
Cannon Sports Club
  CANST EC4R 12 F7
Cannon Trading Estate
  WBLY HA9 .... 115 N9
Cannon Wharf Business Centre
  DEPT SE8 .... 160 D3
Cannon Workshops
  POP/IOD E14 .... 140 F9
Canonbury JMI School
  IS N1 .... 6 C2
Canon Palmer Catholic School
  GDMY/SEVK IG3 .... 123 H6
Canons Brook Golf Club
  HLW CM20 .... 28 D10
Canons High School
  EDGE HA8 .... 95 L10
Capelfield Surgery
  ESH/CLAY KT10 .... 218 E3
Capel Manor Primary School
  EN EN1 .... 79 P1
Capital Business Centre
  ALP/SUD HA0 .... 135 J4
Capital Business Centre
  MTCM CR4 .... 202 A5
Capital Business Centre
  WATN WD24 .... 73 L2
Capital Industrial Estate
  BELV DA17 .... 164 C3
Capital Radio
  LSQ/SEVD WC2H 11 K8
Capitol Industrial Park
  CDALE/KGS NW9 .... 116 A1
Caplan Estate
  MTCM CR4 .... 202 D1
Capswood Business Centre
  CFSP/GDCR SL9 .... 110 F6
Cardiff Road Industrial Estate
  WATW WD18 .... 73 J10
Cardinal Hinsley High RC
  School Gm
  WLSDN NW10 .... 136 D3
Cardinal Newman RC School
  WOT/HER KT12 .... 197 L10
Cardinal Pole RC
  Secondary Lower School
  HOM E9 .... 140 C2
Cardinal Pole RC
  Secondary School Upper
  HOM E9 .... 120 D10
Cardinal Road School
  FELT TW13 .... 175 J4
Cardinal Vaughan School
  WKENS W14 .... 14 A1
Cardinal Wiseman
  Secondary School
  GFD/PVL UB6 .... 134 B7
Cardwell School
  WOOL/PLUM SE18 .... 162 C3
Carew Manor Special School
  WLGTN SM6 .... 202 E10
Carlisle Primary School
  HPTN TW12 .... 176 A9
Carlton Gate Development
  MV/WKIL W9 .... 8 F3
Carlton House
  STJS SW1Y 11 J10
Carlton House Surgery
  ENC/FH EN2 .... 79 M5
Carlton Primary School
  KTTN NW5 .... 118 B10
Carlton Vale Infant School
  MV/WKIL W9 .... 2 D9
Carlyle Business Centre
  CHERT KT16 .... 195 K7
Carlyle's House
  CHEL SW3 .... 15 N10
Carnwath Road Industrial Estate
  FUL/PGN SW6 .... 157 L9
Carolyn School Shop
  PIN HA5 .... 113 M2
Carpenters' Hall
  LVPST EC2M 13 H4
Carpenters Primary School
  SRTFD E15 .... 141 H3
The Carpet Gallery
  BTSEA SW11 .... 157 P8

The Carpet Gallery
  HAMP NW3 .... 117 M9
The Carpet Gallery
  HCH RM12 .... 125 J6
The Carpet Gallery
  STJWD NW8 .... 9 M2
Carshalton College
  CAR SM5 .... 202 A10
Carshalton High School for Boys
  CAR SM5 .... 201 N9
Carshalton High School for Girls
  CAR SM5 .... 201 P10
Carshalton War
  Memorial Hospital
  CAR SM5 .... 222 A2
Carterhatch School
  EN EN1 .... 80 A5
Caryl Thomas Clinic
  HRW HA1 .... 114 D2
Cascades Leisure Centre
  GVE DA12 .... 191 K7
Cashmere Gallery
  SKENS SW7 .... 16 A1
Castle (Remains)
  BERK HP4 .... 34 A1
The Cassel Hospital
  RCHPK/HAM TW10 .... 177 J7
Cassidy Medical Centre
  FUL/PGN SW6 .... 157 K6
Cassio Surgery
  WATW WD18 .... 73 J8
Castilion Primary School
  THMD SE28 .... 143 M8
Castlebar Special School
  WEA W13 .... 134 F7
Castlecombe Primary School
  ELTH/MOT SE9 .... 184 B4
The Castlegate Surgery
  HERT/BAY SG13 .... 25 L6
Castle Industrial Estate
  WALW SE17 .... 18 C5
Castle Montessore School
  BERK HP4 .... 34 A5
Castle Road Practice
  CAMTN NW1 .... 4 E2
Castleview School
  DTCH/LGLY SL3 .... 150 A3
The Caterham Dene Hospital
  CTHM CR3 .... 241 N9
Caterham High School
  CLAY IG5 .... 102 C10
Caterham Preparatory School
  CTHM CR3 .... 259 N2
Caterham School
  CTHM CR3 .... 259 N2
Catford & Bromley Synagogue
  CAT SE6 .... 182 C5
Catford County Girls School
  CAT SE6 .... 183 J6
Catford Cricket & Sports Club
  CAT SE6 .... 182 G4
Catford Cyphers Cricket Club
  CAT SE6 .... 182 E5
Catford Synagogue
  CAT SE6 .... 182 C5
Catford Trading Estate
  CAT SE6 .... 182 G5
Catford Wanderers Sports Club
  CAT SE6 .... 183 H7
Cathall Leisure Centre
  WAN E11 .... 121 L8
Cathedral of St Mary & St Helen
  BRWN CM15 .... 107 J3
Cathedral School of St Saviour
  & St. Mary Overie
  STHWK SE1 .... 18 F1
Catherington School
  CRAWW RH11 .... 283 N3
Cator Park School for Girls
  BECK BR3 .... 182 D10
Cavendish College
  FITZ W1T 11 J4
Cavendish Primary School
  CHSWK W4 .... 156 A6
The Cavendish School
  CAMTN NW1 .... 4 E5
The Cavendish School
  HHW HP1 .... 35 L5
Cavendish Special School
  HNWL W7 .... 134 E8
Caxton Hall
  STJSPK SW1H 17 J3
Caxton Trading Estate
  HYS/HAR UB3 .... 152 F1
Cayley Primary School
  POP/IOD E14 .... 140 D7
Cecil Avenue Surgery
  EMPK RM11 .... 125 M1
Cecil Park Clinic
  PIN HA5 .... 113 M2
Cecil Road County Primary School
  CVW DA11 .... 190 C4
The Cedar House Gallery
  RPLY/SEND GU23 .... 233 M7
The Cedar School
  FSTGT E7 .... 141 P1
Cedars First School
  KTN/HRWW/W HA3 .... 94 B9
Cedars Middle School
  KTN/HRWW/W HA3 .... 94 B9
The Cedars Primary School
  HEST TW5 .... 153 H6
Cedar Way Industrial Estate
  CAMTN NW1 .... 5 J4
Centaur Gallery
  ARCH N19 .... 118 F5
Centaurs Business Centre
  ISLW TW7 .... 154 F5
Centaurs Rugby Football Club
  ISLW TW7 .... 154 E5
Central Business Centre
  WLSDN NW10 .... 116 B10
Central Criminal Court
  STP EC4M 12 C5
Central Estate
  E/WMO/HCT KT8 .... 197 N5
Central Foundation Boys School
  SDTCH EC2A 13 H1
Central Foundation Girls School
  BOW E3 .... 140 E5
Central Foundation Girls School
  BOW E3 .... 140 D5
Central Hall
  STJSPK SW1H 17 K2
Central Hendon Clinic
  HDN NW4 .... 116 E2
Central London County Court
  CAVSQ/HST W1G 10 E2
Central London Markets
  STBT EC1A 12 C4
Central Medical Centre
  MRDN SM4 .... 201 M4

Central Middlesex Hospital
  WLSDN NW10 .... 135 P5
Central Park Primary School
  EHAM E6 .... 142 A4
Central Park Swimming Pool
  HARH RM3 .... 105 M6
Central Primary School
  WAT WD17 .... 73 K8
Central Road Surgery
  MRDN SM4 .... 201 M4
Central St Martins College of Art
  & Design
  COVGDN WC2E 11 L7
Central School of Speech & Drama
  HAMP NW3 .... 3 L3
Central School Speech & Drama
  CAMTN NW1 .... 5 J6
Central Surgery
  SBW CM21 .... 29 P1
Central Synagogue
  REGST W1B 10 F3
Central YMCA
  ELTH/MOT SE9 .... 184 A5
Centre Point
  LSQ/SEVD WC2H 11 K5
Century Gallery
  DTCH/LGLY SL3 .... 149 N6
Cen Uni of Iowa
  RSQ WC1B 11 M1
The Chadwell Heath
  Foundation School
  CHDH RM6 .... 123 L4
Chadwell Heath Hospital
  CHDH RM6 .... 123 L3
Chadwell Heath Industrial Park
  BCTR RM8 .... 123 P6
Chadwell Heath Luncheon
  & Leisure Centre
  CHDH RM6 .... 123 N4
Chadwell St Mary Primary School
  CDH/CHF RM16 .... 168 D3
The Chafford Hundred
  Medical Centre
  CDH/CHF RM16 .... 167 K7
Chafford School
  RAIN RM13 .... 145 K7
Chailey House Chailey
  Industrial Estate
  HYS/HAR UB3 .... 153 H1
Chailey Industrial Estate
  HYS/HAR UB3 .... 153 H1
Chalcot School
  CAMTN NW1 .... 4 E3
Chalfont Leisure Centre
  CFSP/GDCR SL9 .... 89 P9
Chalfont St Giles County
  Middle School
  CSTG HP8 .... 89 N4
Chalfont St Giles Infant School
  CSTG HP8 .... 89 N4
Chalfont St Peter C of E
  Middle School
  CFSP/GDCR SL9 .... 90 A9
Chalfont St Peter Football Club
  CFSP/GDCR SL9 .... 90 A8
The Chalfonts Community College
  CFSP/GDCR SL9 .... 89 P8
Chalfonts & Gerrards Cross
  Health Clinic
  CFSP/GDCR SL9 .... 90 A9
Chalgrove Primary School
  FNCH N3 .... 117 H1
Chalk Farm Gallery
  CAMTN NW1 .... 4 D4
Chalkhill Infant School
  WBLY HA9 .... 115 N8
Chalvey County Infant School
  SL SL1 .... 149 H1
Chambersbury JMI School
  HHS/BOV HP3 .... 36 C9
Chambers Business Park
  WDR/YW UB7 .... 152 B5
Chancellors School
  BRKMPK AL9 .... 59 L1
Chandlers Field Primary School
  E/WMO/HCT KT8 .... 197 P5
Chandos Business Centre
  WLGTN SM6 .... 222 D3
Channing School
  HGT N6 .... 118 C6
Chantry Medical Practice
  SEV TN13 .... 265 J1
Chantry Special School
  WDR/YW UB7 .... 131 P8
Chapel End Infant School
  WALTH E17 .... 100 G10
Chapel End Junior School
  WALTH E17 .... 100 H10
Chapman Park Industrial Estate
  WLSDN NW10 .... 136 C1
Charing Cross Hospital
  HMSMTH W6 .... 156 G5
Charles Darwin School
  BH/WHM TN16 .... 244 C1
Charles Edward Brooke
  Girls School
  CMBW SE5 .... 159 J7
Charles Edward Brooke School
  for Girls
  CMBW SE5 .... 159 J7
Charles Lamb Primary School
  IS N1 .... 6 E5
Charlton Athletic Fc
  CHARL SE7 .... 161 P4
Charlton House
  CHARL SE7 .... 162 A5
Charlton Mosque
  CHARL SE7 .... 161 P4
Charlton Park School
  CHARL SE7 .... 162 B5
Charlton Rugby Club
  ELTH/MOT SE9 .... 184 E3
Charlwood Village School
  HORL RH6 .... 279 J8
Charrington Bowl
  SURB KT6 .... 199 N9
Charville Primary School
  YEAD UB4 .... 132 F4
Charter Clinic
  CHEL SW3 .... 16 A8
Charterhouse School
  FARR EC1M 12 D3
Charterhouse School
  RGODL GU7 .... 267 H10
Charterhouse School Students
  Residences
  RGODL GU7 .... 266 G10
Charterhouse Sutton's School
  FARR EC1M 12 D3
Charters Comprehensive School
  ASC SL5 .... 192 C7
Chartfield School
  PUT/ROE SW15 .... 178 E1

Chartridge County
  Combined School
  CSHM HP5 .... 50 B3
Chartridge Park Golf Club
  CSHM HP5 .... 50 C4
Chartwell Business Centre
  BMLY BR1 .... 206 A3
Chase Bridge School
  WHTN TW2 .... 176 D2
Chase Community School
  EN EN1 .... 79 N1
Chase Farm Hospitals NHS Trust
  ENC/FH EN2 .... 79 N1
Chase Lane Infant School
  CHING E4 .... 100 E5
Chase Road Trading Estate
  WLSDN NW10 .... 136 A6
Chase Side Junior & Infant School
  ENC/FH EN2 .... 79 K6
Chater Infant School
  WATW WD18 .... 73 H8
Chater Junior School
  WATW WD18 .... 73 H8
Chatsworth Infant School
  BFN/LL DA15 .... 185 K4
Chatsworth Junior
  & Infant School
  HSLW TW3 .... 154 B10
Chaucer Clinic
  STHL UB1 .... 154 C1
Chaulden Junior & Infant School
  HHW HP1 .... 35 J7
The Chauncy School
  WARE SG12 .... 26 A1
Cheam Common County
  Junior School
  WPK KT4 .... 200 E9
Cheam Common Infant School
  WPK KT4 .... 200 E9
Cheam Family Practice
  CHEAM SM3 .... 221 J10
Cheam Family Practice
  SUT SM1 .... 201 J10
Cheam High School
  CHEAM SM3 .... 221 J6
Cheam Leisure Centre
  CHEAM SM3 .... 220 G1
Cheam Park Farm Junior School
  CHEAM SM3 .... 201 H10
Cheam Sports Club
  BELMT SM2 .... 220 G4
Cheapside C of E School
  ASC SL5 .... 192 D1
Chelsea Barracks
  BGVA SW1W 16 D8
Chelsea Bridge Business Centre
  BTSEA SW11 .... 158 B6
Chelsea College of Art & Design
  CHEL SW3 .... 15 M8
Chelsea College of Art & Design
  FUL/PGN SW6 .... 157 M8
Chelsea Fields Industrial Estate
  WIM/MER SW19 .... 201 N1
Chelsea Fire Station
  CHEL SW3 .... 15 N8
Chelsea Football Club
  FUL/PGN SW6 .... 157 L6
Chelsea Galleries
  WBPTN SW10 .... 157 M6
Chelsea Gallery
  WBPTN SW10 .... 157 M6
Chelsea Old Town Hall
  CHEL SW3 .... 15 P8
The Chelsea Practice
  WBPTN SW10 .... 15 K9
Chelsea Sports Centre
  CHEL SW3 .... 15 P8
Chelsea Synagogue
  CHEL SW3 .... 15 P8
Chelsea & Westminster Hospital
  WBPTN SW10 .... 15 K10
Chelsfield Park Hospital
  ORP BR6 .... 228 A2
Chelsfield Primary School
  ORP BR6 .... 227 P2
Chenies Cricket Club
  RKW/CH/CXG WD3 .... 70 F5
Chenies School
  RKW/CH/CXG WD3 .... 70 D4
Chenil Galleries
  CHEL SW3 .... 15 N8
Chennestone County
  Middle School
  SUN TW16 .... 197 J2
Cherington House Health Centre
  HNWL W7 .... 134 E10
Cherry Garden School
  BERM/RHTH SE16 .... 19 P5
Cherry Lane Junior School
  WDR/YW UB7 .... 152 A3
Cherry Orchard School
  CHARL SE7 .... 161 P6
Cherry Tree JMI School
  WATN WD24 .... 73 J2
Chertsey Business Centre
  CHERT KT16 .... 195 K7
Chertsey Museum
  CHERT KT16 .... 195 K7
Chertsey Recreation Centre
  CHERT KT16 .... 195 J8
Chertsey Town Football Club
  CHERT KT16 .... 195 J6
Chesham Bois C E
  Combined School
  AMS HP6 .... 69 K1
Chesham Community Hospital
  CSHM HP5 .... 51 H8
Chesham Health Centre
  CSHM HP5 .... 50 G8
Chesham High School
  CSHM HP5 .... 51 J6
Chesham Leisure Centre
  CSHM HP5 .... 51 J7
Chesham Park Community College
  CSHM HP5 .... 50 F6
Chesham Preparatory School
  CSHM HP5 .... 51 M3
Chesham United Football Club
  CSHM HP5 .... 50 C9
Cheshunt Community Hospital
  CHES/WCR EN8 .... 62 B10
Cheshunt Football Club
  CHES/WCR EN8 .... 62 B8
Cheshunt School
  CHES/WCR EN8 .... 62 B6
Cheshunt & Waltham
  Cross Council
  CHES/WCR EN8 .... 62 D10
Chessington Community College
  CHSGTN KT9 .... 219 J4
Chessington Cricket Club
  CHSGTN KT9 .... 219 H4

Chesterfield Junior
  & Infant School
  PEND EN3 .... 80 D3
Chesterton Junior Mixed School
  BTSEA SW11 .... 158 B7
Chestnut Lane First School
  AMS HP6 .... 69 K2
Chevening Primary School
  RSEV TN14 .... 246 C8
Cheyne Centre
  CHEL SW3 .... 15 N10
Cheyne Galleries
  TWK TW1 .... 176 G2
Chigwell County Primary School
  CHIG IG7 .... 102 F3
Chigwell & Hainault Synagogue
  CHIG IG7 .... 102 F6
Chigwell Row County
  First School
  CHIG IG7 .... 103 M3
Chigwell School
  CHIG IG7 .... 102 F3
Childerditch Industrial Park
  RBRW/HUT CM13 .... 127 L1
Childeric Junior School
  NWCR SE14 .... 160 D6
Childrens Hospital Trust Fund
  WIM/MER SW19 .... 179 J7
Childs Hill Clinic
  CRICK NW2 .... 117 H7
Childs Hill School
  CRICK NW2 .... 117 H8
Childs Welfare Clinic
  DAGW RM9 .... 123 M10
Chiltern District Council
  CSTG HP8 .... 69 M9
Chiltern House Surgery
  SLN SL2 .... 129 M3
Chiltern Open Air Museum
  CSTG HP8 .... 90 C3
Chiltonian Industrial Estate
  LEE/GVPK SE12 .... 183 L2
Chilworth C of E School
  RGUE GU4 .... 268 G4
Chinese Health Centre
  BECK BR3 .... 204 D3
Chinese Health Centre
  LEW SE13 .... 161 J10
Chinese Health Centre
  NWCR SE14 .... 160 C6
Chinese Health Centre
  PGE/AN SE20 .... 182 C10
Chinese Medical Centre
  BAR EN5 .... 77 H7
Chinese Medical Centre
  DART DA1 .... 187 M2
Chinese Medical Centre
  ED N9 .... 100 A4
Chinese Medical Centre
  HCH RM12 .... 125 M8
Chinese Medical Centre
  MHST W1U 10 C4
Chinese Medical Centre
  REGST W1B 10 G6
Chinese Medical Centre
  ROM RM1 .... 124 F4
Chinese Medical Centre
  STNW/STAM N16 .... 119 M7
Chinese Medical Centre
  WAND/EARL SW18 .... 179 K1
Chinese Medical Centre Watford
  WAT WD17 .... 73 K8
Chinese Medicine Clinic
  STRHM/NOR SW16 .... 180 F7
Chingford C of E Infant School
  CHING E4 .... 101 J2
Chingford C of E Junior School
  CHING E4 .... 101 J2
Chingford Hall Primary School
  CHING E4 .... 100 E7
Chingford Health Centre
  CHING E4 .... 100 E5
Chingford Industrial Centre
  CHING E4 .... 100 D6
Chingford Rugby Football Club
  CHING E4 .... 100 F2
Chingford School
  CHING E4 .... 100 G2
Chinthurst School
  KWD/TDW/WH KT20 .... 238 F9
Chipperfield Junior
  & Infant School
  KGLGY WD4 .... 53 K7
Chipping Ongar Primary School
  CHONG CM5 .... 67 N6
Chipstead Rugby Football Club
  COUL/CHIP CR5 .... 240 A7
Chipstead Valley Schools
  COUL/CHIP CR5 .... 240 B2
Chipstead Vp School
  COUL/CHIP CR5 .... 240 B2
Chiropodist Podiatrist Surgery
  WPK KT4 .... 200 D8
Chiropody Surgery
  WBLY HA9 .... 135 M1
Chiropractic Surgery
  COUL/CHIP CR5 .... 222 D10
Chisenhale Primary School
  BOW E3 .... 140 D4
Chislehurst Natural Health Centre
  CHST BR7 .... 184 E9
Chislehurst & Sidcup
  Grammar School
  BFN/LL DA15 .... 185 K5
Chiswick Community School
  CHSWK W4 .... 156 A6
Chiswick House
  CHSWK W4 .... 156 A5
Chobham Football Club
  CHOB/PIR GU24 .... 213 L7
Chobham Parish Council
  CHOB/PIR GU24 .... 213 K7
Chobham St Lawrence C of E
  First & Middle School
  CHOB/PIR GU24 .... 213 K7
Choir School
  WEST SW1P 17 H5
Chorleywood Golf Club
  RKW/CH/CXG WD3 .... 70 C8
Chorleywood Health Centre
  RKW/CH/CXG WD3 .... 70 F8
Chorleywood Parish Council
  RKW/CH/CXG WD3 .... 71 H7
Chorleywood Primary
  RKW/CH/CXG WD3 .... 70 F10
Chrisp Street Health Centre
  POP/IOD E14 .... 140 C8
Christchurch Bentinck C of E
  School
  CAMTN NW1 .... 9 N3
Christ Church C of E Primary
  School
  KIL/WHAMP NW6 .... 2 C4

Christ Church C E Primary School
 CAMTN NW1 .... 4 F9
Christchurch C of E Infant School
 VW GU25 .... 193 M3
Christ Church C of E
 Junior School
 NWMAL KT3 .... 200 A3
Christ Church C of E
 Middle School
 EA W5 .... 135 J9
Christ Church C of E
 Primary School
 BAR EN5 .... 76 G6
Christ Church C of E
 Primary School
 BRXN/ST SW9 .... 159 H7
Christ Church C of E
 Primary School
 BRXS/STRHM SW2 .... 180 G4
Christ Church C of E
 Primary School
 BRYLDS KT5 .... 199 M6
Christ Church C of E
 Primary School
 CHEL SW3 .... 16 A9
Christ Church C of E School
 CHERT KT16 .... 214 G3
Christ Church C of E School
 FSTH SE23 .... 182 C5
Christchurch C of E
 Secondary School
 NFNCH/WDSP N12 .... 97 N6
Christchurch Junior
 & Infant School
 IL IG1 .... 122 F6
Christ Church Junior
 Middle & Infant School
 WARE SG12 .... 26 D2
Christ Church Primary School
 BTSEA SW11 .... 157 P9
Christ Church Primary School
 NWMAL KT3 .... 200 B3
Christ Church Primary School
 PUR/KEN CR8 .... 223 J6
Christchurch Primary School
 WCHPL E1 .... 13 M3
Christchurch School
 FSTH SE23 .... 182 C5
Christ Church School
 RKW/CH/CXG WD3 .... 71 J8
Christchurch Shooters Hill
 C of E Primary School
 WOOL/PLUM SE18 .... 162 D7
Christopher Wren School
 for Boys
 SHB W12 .... 136 D9
Christs College
 BKHTH/KID SE3 .... 161 M7
Christs College School
 EFNCH N2 .... 117 L1
Christs School
 RCHPK/HAM TW10 .... 177 L1
Christ Temple
 Ministry International
 HACK E8 .... 120 A10
Christ the King RC First School
 STWL/WRAY TW19 .... 173 N2
Christ the King School
 FSBYPK N4 .... 118 G6
Chrysalis Theatre
 BAL SW12 .... 180 B4
Chrysanthemum Clinic
 CHSWK W4 .... 155 P6
Church Down Adult School
 LEE/GVPK SE12 .... 183 M5
Church End Medical Centre
 WLSDN NW10 .... 136 B1
Church Farm House Museum
 HDN NW4 .... 116 E1
Churchfield Primary School
 ED N9 .... 99 N2
Churchfield School
 WOOL/PLUM SE18 .... 163 J3
Churchfields Junior
 & Infant School
 SWFD E18 .... 101 M9
Churchfields Primary School
 BECK BR3 .... 204 C3
Churchgate C of E
 Primary School
 HLWE CM17 .... 30 A8
Church Hill Junior Middle
 & Infant School
 EBAR EN4 .... 98 A1
Churchill Business Park
 BH/WHM TN16 .... 262 G2
Churchill Clinic
 STHWK SE1 .... 18 B3
Churchill College
 RYNPK SW20 .... 200 F2
Churchill College
 TOOT SW17 .... 180 A5
Churchill Gallery
 BH/WHM TN16 .... 262 F3
Churchill Gardens
 Primary School
 PIM SW1V 16 G8
Churchill School
 BH/WHM TN16 .... 262 F1
Churchill Theatre
 BMLY BR1 .... 205 M2
Church Lane Practice
 WIM/MER SW19 .... 201 J1
Church Lane School
 UPMR RM14 .... 126 C10
Church Langley Primary School
 HLWE CM17 .... 47 M1
Church Mead Infant School
 LEY E10 .... 120 F6
Church Mead Junior School
 LEY E10 .... 120 F6
Churchmead School
 DTCH/LGLY SL3 .... 149 N6
Church of England School
 COUL/CHIP CR5 .... 240 C1
The Church School
 BTFD TW8 .... 155 K5
Church Street Surgery
 WARE SG12 .... 26 C1
Church Trading Estate
 ERITH DA8 .... 165 H6
The Cinema Museum
 LBTH SE11 .... 18 C5
Cippenham County First School
 SL SL1 .... 128 C9
Cippenham Medical Centre
 SL SL1 .... 128 C10
Cippenham Middle School
 SL SL1 .... 128 C9
City Business Centre
 BERM/RHTH SE16 .... 160 B1
The City Business Centre
 CRAWW RH11 .... 283 N3

City Business College
 FSBYE EC1V 6 D10
City Central Estate
 FSBYE EC1V 6 E10
City Gallery
 LOTH EC2R 13 H5
City & Guilds of London
 Art School
 LBTH SE11 .... 18 C8
City & Hackney Community
 Health Council
 BETH E2 .... 7 L6
City & Islington College
 FSBYPK N4 .... 119 J7
City & Islington College
 HOLWY N7 .... 118 F9
City & Islington College
 IS N1 .... 6 G5
City of London Club
 OBST EC2N 13 J5
City of London College
 WCHPL E1 .... 13 N4
City of London Freemans School
 ASHTD KT21 .... 237 N5
City of London
 Magistrates Court
 MANHO EC4N 12 G6
City of London Polytechnic
 Sports Ground
 ELTH/MOT SE9 .... 183 P5
City of London School
 BLKFR EC4V 12 D7
City of London School for Girls
 BARB EC2Y 12 E3
City of London Schools
 Sports Ground
 ELTH/MOT SE9 .... 183 P6
City of Westminster College
 BAY/PAD W2 .... 9 L3
City of Westminster Vehicle Pound
 BAY/PAD W2 .... 9 K4
City Temple
 STBT EC1A 12 C4
City University
 FSBYE EC1V 6 D10
City University
 FSBYE EC1V 12 D1
City University Business School
 BARB EC2Y 12 F3
The City University
 FSBYE EC1V 6 C10
Civic Centre & Dacorum
 Borough Council
 HHW HP1 .... 35 M6
Civic Hall
 GU GU1 .... 268 B1
Civic Medical Centre
 HRW HA1 .... 114 D3
Civil Service College
 ASC SL5 .... 192 E5
Civil Service Recreation Centre
 WEST SW1P 17 K4
Civil Service Sports Ground
 ELTH/MOT SE9 .... 183 P2
Clair Gallery
 BRWN CM15 .... 87 M10
Clandon C of E First School
 RGUE GU4 .... 251 K7
Clandon Regis Golf Club
 RGUE GU4 .... 251 L7
Clapham Common Clinic
 CLAP SW4 .... 158 E10
Clapham Family Practice
 CLAP SW4 .... 158 E10
Clapham Manor Primary School
 CLAP SW4 .... 158 D9
Clapham Manor Street
 Public Baths
 CLAP SW4 .... 158 E9
Clapham North Business Centre
 CLAP SW4 .... 158 E9
Clapham Park School
 CLAP SW4 .... 180 E1
Clapham Park Surgery
 CLAP SW4 .... 180 E2
Clapham Picture House
 CLAP SW4 .... 158 D10
Clapton Central Surgery
 CLPT E5 .... 120 A8
Clapton County
 Secondary School
 CLPT E5 .... 120 B9
Clapton Jewish Boys School
 STNW/STAM N16 .... 119 N5
Clapton Synagogue
 CLPT E5 .... 120 B8
Clara Grant Primary School
 BOW E3 .... 140 F6
Clare House Primary School
 BECK BR3 .... 205 H2
Claremont Clinic
 FSTGT E7 .... 121 N10
Claremont Fan Court School
 ESH/CLAY KT10 .... 218 A3
Claremont High School
 KTN/HRWW/W HA3 .... 115 K3
Claremont Way Industrial Estate
 CRICK NW2 .... 116 F6
Clarence House
 WHALL SW1A 17 H1
Clarendon County
 Primary School
 ASHF TW15 .... 174 A6
Clarendon School
 HPTN TW12 .... 176 A9
Claycots Middle School
 SLN SL2 .... 128 F6
Claygate Junior School
 ESH/CLAY KT10 .... 218 D4
Clayhall Clinic
 IL IG5 .... 122 B1
Clayponds Hospital
 BTFD TW8 .... 155 K3
Cleeve Park School
 SCUP DA14 .... 185 M6
Clementine Churchill Hospital
 HRW HA1 .... 114 E8
Clerkenwell County Court
 IS N1 .... 6 C7
Clerkenwell Heritage Centre
 FARR EC1M 12 C2
Clerkenwell Parochial
 C of E Primary School
 FSBYW WC1X 6 A10
Clerklands Surgery
 HORL RH6 .... 280 A4
Cleveland Junior & Infant School
 IL IG1 .... 122 E9
Cleves County Junior School
 WEY KT13 .... 216 G1
Cleves Primary School
 EHAM E6 .... 142 A3

Cliff Road Medical Practice
 HOLWY N7 .... 5 J1
Clifton JMI School
 NWDGN UB2 .... 153 M3
Clifton Lodge Preparatory
 School for Boys
 EA W5 .... 135 J9
Clifton School
 CTHM CR3 .... 241 L10
Clink Exhibition
 STHWK SE1 .... 12 G9
Clissold Park Natural
 Health Centre
 STNW/STAM N16 .... 119 M7
Clitterhouse Junior School
 CRICK NW2 .... 116 G7
C & L Leisure Centre
 NTHLT UB5 .... 133 J2
Clockhouse Industrial Estate
 EBED/NFELT TW14 .... 174 C4
Clockhouse Junior School
 CRW RM5 .... 104 C7
Clock Museum
 CITYW EC2V 12 F5
The Clocktower Practice
 CEND/HSY/T N8 .... 118 E3
Cloisters Business Centre
 VX/NE SW8 .... 158 C6
Clore Gallery
 WEST SW1P 17 L6
Clothworkers' Hall
 FENCHST EC3M 13 K7
Clouster's Green
 WAP E1W 13 N9
Coach House Surgery
 WATW WD18 .... 73 H8
Coach Museum
 WDSR SL4 .... 149 K7
Coates Way School
 GSTN WD25 .... 55 M9
Cobbold Estate
 WLSDN NW10 .... 136 C1
Cobden Hill Infant School
 RAD WD7 .... 74 G2
Cobham Bus Museum
 COB KT11 .... 216 D8
Cobham Galleries Antiques
 & Fines Arts
 COB KT11 .... 217 H10
The Cobham Health Centre
 COB KT11 .... 217 J9
Cobourg Primary School
 CMBW SE5 .... 19 L9
Cochrane Theatre
 GINN WC1R 11 N4
Cockfosters & N Southgate
 Synagogue
 STHGT/OAK N14 .... 98 D1
Cockfosters Sports Ground
 EBAR EN4 .... 78 A7
The Cockpit Theatre
 STJWD NW8 .... 9 M2
The Coffee Gallery
 RSQ WC1B 11 L4
Coldharbour Sports Ground
 ELTH/MOT SE9 .... 184 D5
Colebrooke Primary School
 IS N1 .... 6 C7
Colegrave Primary School
 SRTFD E15 .... 121 J10
Colehill Cricket Club
 AMSS HP7 .... 68 G9
Coleraine Park Junior
 & Infant School
 TOTM N17 .... 100 A9
Coleridge Primary School
 HGT N6 .... 118 E5
Coleshill C of E First School
 AMSS HP7 .... 68 E10
Colfes School
 LEE/GVPK SE12 .... 183 N2
Colham Manor Junior
 & Infant School
 UX/CGN UB8 .... 132 A8
Colindale Business Park
 CDALE/KGS NW9 .... 115 P1
Colindale Hospital
 CDALE/KGS NW9 .... 116 B1
Colindale Primary School
 CDALE/KGS NW9 .... 116 C2
The Colin Dove Practice
 ROM RM1 .... 124 G3
Coliseum
 CHCR WC2N 11 L8
College
 LBTH SE11 .... 18 B8
College
 STLK EC1Y 12 G2
College Fields Business Centre
 WIM/MER SW19 .... 201 P1
College of Arms
 BLKFR EC4V 12 E6
College of Fuel Technology
 HGT N6 .... 118 B4
The College of Law
 GWRST WC1E 11 J3
The College of Law
 LINN WC2A 12 A5
College of North East London
 CEND/HSY/T N8 .... 119 H2
College of North East London
 FBAR/BDGN N11 .... 98 D9
College of North East London
 SEVS/STOTM N15 .... 119 N2
College of North West London
 KIL/WHAMP NW6 .... 2 E5
College of North West London
 WBLY HA9 .... 115 M8
College of North West London
 WLSDN NW10 .... 116 C10
College of Teachers
 EPP CM16 .... 82 G2
College Park School
 BAY/PAD W2 .... 8 F6
College Road Clinic
 WBLY HA9 .... 115 J6
The Collett School
 HHW HP1 .... 35 L5
Collier Row Clinic
 ROMW/RG RM7 .... 104 C9
Collier Row Health Club
 ROMW/RG RM7 .... 104 A9
Colliers Wood Surgery
 WIM/MER SW19 .... 179 P9
Collingham Sixth Form College
 ECT SW5 .... 15 H6
Collingwood Business Centre
 ARCH N19 .... 118 F8
Collingwood School
 WLGTN SM6 .... 222 C2
Collins Method School
 CRICK NW2 .... 136 F1

Collis Primary School
 TEDD TW11 .... 176 G9
College of Art & Design
 NOXST/BSQ WC1A 11 M4
College of Law
 GWRST WC1E 11 J3
College of Organists
 FLST/FETLN EC4A 12 B5
College of Surgical Sci
 LINN WC2A 11 P5
Colnbrook C of E
 Combined School
 DTCH/LGLY SL3 .... 150 F6
Colnbrook School
 OXHEY WD19 .... 93 K3
Colnbrook Sports Club
 DTCH/LGLY SL3 .... 151 J7
Colne Bridge Retail Park
 WAT WD17 .... 73 L9
Colney Heath JMI School
 STALE/WH AL4 .... 39 P8
Coln Industrial Estate
 DTCH/LGLY SL3 .... 151 J6
Colombian Consulate
 CTYW EC2V 12 F5
Colonial Business Park
 WATN WD24 .... 73 K5
The Colonnades Shopping Centre
 BCVA SW1W 16 E5
Colours Sports Club
 SUT SM1 .... 221 M2
Columbia Primary School
 BETH E2 .... 7 M9
Colville Primary School
 NTGHL W11 .... 8 C6
Colyers Lane Medical Centre
 BXLYHN DA7 .... 164 E7
Combe Bank School
 RSEV TN14 .... 245 P9
Comber Grove Junior
 & Infant School
 CMBW SE5 .... 159 K6
Combermere Barracks
 WDSR SL4 .... 148 G9
Comelle House Trading Estate
 DEPT SE8 .... 160 D4
Comm for the Rep of Sth Africa
 CHCR WC2N 11 K9
Comm for the Rep of Sth Africa
 STJS SW1Y 11 K9
Commonside School
 HLWS CM18 .... 47 J5
Commonswood JMI School
 WGCE AL7 .... 23 L8
Commonwealth Lodge School
 PUR/KEN CR8 .... 222 E8
Community Clinic
 HLWS CM18 .... 47 J4
Community Mental Health Cen
 BRXN/ST SW9 .... 159 H6
Community Mental Health Centre
 GSTN WD25 .... 55 K10
Community Mental Health Centre
 HHNE HP2 .... 35 N5
Compass Theatre
 HGDN/ICK UB10 .... 112 D8
Complementary Health Centre
 LEW SE13 .... 183 K2
The Compton School
 NFNCH/WDSP N12 .... 97 P7
Concord Business Centre
 ACT W3 .... 135 N7
Concord Shopping Centre
 SHB W12 .... 156 G1
Coney Hill School
 HAYES BR2 .... 205 L9
Con General of Chile
 CAVSQ/HST W1G 10 E2
Congress House (TUC)
 RSQ WC1B 11 K4
Connaught Business Centre
 CDALE/KGS NW9 .... 116 C3
Connaught Business Centre
 CROY/NA CR0 .... 222 G3
Connaught Girls School
 WAN E11 .... 121 K6
Connections Business Park
 RSEV TN14 .... 247 J6
Consort Clinic
 PECK SE15 .... 160 A9
Consulate General of Monaco
 SKENS SW7 .... 15 L5
Consulate General of
 the Republic of Guinea Bissau
 KENS W8 .... 15 J3
The Consulate of the State
 of Eritrea
 IS N1 .... 6 B7
Contemporary Applied Arts
 LSQ/SEVD WC2H 11 L6
Contemporary Fine Art Gallery
 WDSR SL4 .... 149 J5
Convent of Jesus & Mary Gm
 High School
 WLSDN NW10 .... 136 C3
Convent of Jesus
 & Mary Infant School
 CRICK NW2 .... 136 F1
Conway Hall
 FSBYW WC1X 11 N3
Conway Junior School
 WOOL/PLUM SE18 .... 163 H3
Conway Medical Centre
 WOOL/PLUM SE18 .... 162 G4
Coombe Girls School
 NWMAL KT3 .... 200 A2
Coombe Hill Junior
 & Infant School
 NWMAL KT3 .... 200 A1
Coopersale Hall School
 EPP CM16 .... 65 L9
Coopersale & Theydon Garnon
 C of E Primary School
 EPP CM16 .... 65 N5
Coopers' Hall
 LVPST EC2M 13 K4
Coopers Lane Primary School
 LEE/GVPK SE12 .... 183 M5
Coopers School
 CHST BR7 .... 206 F1
Copenhagen Primary School
 IS N1 .... 5 M6
Copland Community School &
 Technology Centre Gms
 WBLY HA9 .... 115 L10
Copperfields Shopping Centre
 DART DA1 .... 187 M2
Coppermill Primary School
 WALTH E17 .... 120 C3
Coppetts Wood Hospital
 MUSWH N10 .... 98 A9
Coppetts Wood School
 MUSWH N10 .... 98 B8

Coppice Primary School
 CHIG IG7 .... 103 K6
Copthall School
 MLHL NW7 .... 96 D7
The Copthorne Business Centre
 CRAWE RH10 .... 285 J2
Copthorne Fairway
 Infant School
 CRAWE RH10 .... 285 J2
Copthorne Golf Club
 CRAWE RH10 .... 285 K2
Copthorne Junior School
 CRAWE RH10 .... 285 J2
Copthorne Squash Club
 CRAWE RH10 .... 285 H3
Coram Gallery
 BMSBY WC1N 11 N1
Corbets Tey School
 UPMR RM14 .... 126 A10
Cordwainers College
 HOM E9 .... 140 B2
Corelli Surgery
 WOOL/PLUM SE18 .... 162 A7
Corinium Industrial Estate
 AMS HP6 .... 69 L4
Corinthian Casuals Football Club
 CHSGTN KT9 .... 199 M10
Corinthian Sports Club
 HART DA3 .... 211 J6
Corn Exchange
 HERT/WAS SG14 .... 25 L5
Cornhill Sports Club
 BECK BR3 .... 182 F8
Coroners Court
 HACK E8 .... 120 B10
Coroners Court
 WALTH E17 .... 120 E4
Cosmopolitan College
 IS N1 .... 5 N8
Costa Rican Embassy
 BAY/PAD W2 .... 9 K7
Coston Secondary Modern
 Girls School
 GFD/PVL UB6 .... 134 B5
Coteford Infant School
 RSLP HA4 .... 113 H3
Cottenham Park C of E
 Primary School
 RYNPK SW20 .... 200 D1
Coulsdon College
 COUL/CHIP CR5 .... 241 H5
The Coulsdon Eye Clinic
 COUL/CHIP CR5 .... 240 D1
Coulsdon High School
 COUL/CHIP CR5 .... 241 J6
Coultauld Institute Galleries
 HOL/ALD WC2B 11 N7
Council Offices
 OXHEY WD19 .... 93 L4
Council Offices
 SEV TN13 .... 265 J1
Council Offices
 WCHPL E1 .... 140 A9
Council Offices
 WDSR SL4 .... 149 J8
Council of Mosques
 FITZ W1T 11 H4
Counterpoint Theatre
 STPAN WC1H 5 M9
Countess Anne C of E
 Primary School
 HAT AL10 .... 40 F3
Country Gardens Estate
 BFOR GU20 .... 192 G3
County Council
 Community Services
 RYLN/HDSTN HA2 .... 114 C7
County Court at the Borough
 STHWK SE1 .... 18 D1
County Junior & Infant School
 BRWN CM15 .... 86 F10
County Oak Retail Park
 CRAWW RH11 .... 283 N3
Courtfield Medical Centre
 ECT SW5 .... 15 H6
Courtland JMI School
 MLHL NW7 .... 96 B3
Court Lodge First School
 HORL RH6 .... 280 A4
Courtwood Primary School
 CROY/NA CR0 .... 224 E6
The Courtyard Gallery
 IS N1 .... 5 M8
Covent Garden Flower Market
 VX/NE SW8 .... 17 K10
The Coventry Gallery
 SDTCH EC2A 13 J1
Coward Industrial Estate
 CDH/PUR RM16 .... 168 E4
Cowarth Park School
 CHOB/PIR GU24 .... 212 G1
Cowley Business Park
 UX/CGN UB8 .... 131 M5
Cowley Hill First School
 BORE WD6 .... 75 N5
Cowley Mill Industrial Estate
 IVER SL0 .... 131 K4
Cowley Mill Trading Estate
 IVER SL0 .... 131 K4
The Coworth Gallery
 ASC SL5 .... 192 E5
CPfc Soccer & Sports Centre
 BRXN/ST SW9 .... 158 G9
CP House Business Centre
 GSTN WD25 .... 73 N5
Crabtree Junior Mixed School
 HARP AL5 .... 20 C2
Crabtree Lane Infant School
 HARP AL5 .... 20 B2
Crafts Council
 IS N1 .... 6 B8
Crampton Junior & Infant School
 WALW SE17 .... 18 D7
Cranborne Industrial Estate
 POTB/CUF EN6 .... 59 H5
Cranborne Primary School
 POTB/CUF EN6 .... 59 H7
Cranbourne School
 HOD EN11 .... 26 C10
Cranbrook College
 IL IG1 .... 122 D7
Crane School
 FELT TW13 .... 175 N5
Cranford Business Park
 HYS/HAR UB3 .... 152 G1
Cranford Community School
 HEST TW5 .... 153 J5
Cranford Infant School
 HSLWW TW4 .... 153 H8
Cranford Park Junior School
 HYS/HAR UB3 .... 152 G2
Cranford School
 HSLWW TW4 .... 153 J8

Cranham Health Centre
UPMR RM14 .... **126** D5
Cranmer Middle School
MTCM CR4 .... **202** A5
Cranmore School
EHSLY KT24 .... **252** D5
Crauford Business Park
HYS/HAR UB3 .... **152** G2
The Craven Clinic
HMSMTH W6 .... **156** E3
Craven Park Health Centre
WLSDN NW10 .... **136** A3
Craven Park Junior School
SEVS/STOTM N15 .... **119** P4
Craven Park Medical Centre
WLSDN NW10 .... **136** A3
Crawford Primary School
CMBW SE5 .... **159** K7
Crawley College
CRAWE RH10 .... **283** P7
Crawley College Annexe
CRAWW RH11 .... **283** M6
Crawley Down Health Centre
CRAWE RH10 .... **285** P5
Crawley Health Clinic
CRAWE RH10 .... **283** P7
Crawley Hospital
CRAWW RH11 .... **283** M7
The Crawley Lawn Tennis Club
CRAWE RH10 .... **284** C6
Crawley Leisure Centre
CRAWE RH10 .... **284** A8
Crawley Rugby Club
CRAWW RH11 .... **283** K3
Crayfield Industrial Park
STMC/STPC BR5 .... **207** M2
Crayfields Business Park
STMC/STPC BR5 .... **207** M5
Crayford Industrial Estate
DART DA1 .... **186** G1
Crayford Leisure Centre
& Greyhound Stadium
DART DA1 .... **186** F2
Crayford Medical Centre
DART DA1 .... **186** G1
Crayside Industrial Estate
DART DA1 .... **165** H9
Creek Road Health Centre
DEPT SE8 .... **160** F5
Creek Road Industrial Estate
DEPT SE8 .... **160** C5
Crescent Surgery
STMC/STPC BR5 .... **207** L5
Creswick Primary School
WGCE AL7 .... **22** C8
Crewe House
MYFR/PICC W1J **10** E9
Crews Hill Golf Club
ENC/FH EN2 .... **60** G10
Cricket Club
EPP CM16 .... **83** H3
The Cricket Club
SLN SL2 .... **129** M6
The Cricket Club
SLN SL2 .... **129** H5
Cricket School Caretaker
FNCH N3 .... **117** L1
Cricklewood Synagogue
CRICK NW2 .... **116** G10
Cricklewood Trading Estate
CRICK NW2 .... **117** H8
Crispin Industrial Centre
UED N18 .... **100** B6
Criterion Theatre
STJS SW1Y **11** J8
Crockenhill CP School
SWLY BR8 .... **208** D6
Crockham Hill C of E
Primary School
EDEN TN8 .... **262** F9
Crofton Leisure Centre
BROCKY SE4 .... **182** F2
Crofton School
BROCKY SE4 .... **182** F2
Croham Hurst School
SAND/SEL CR2 .... **223** N2
Cromer Road JMI School
BAR EN5 .... **77** L7
Cromwell Business Centre
BARK IG11 .... **143** H5
Cromwell Hospital
KENS W8 .... **14** C5
Cromwell Industrial Estate
LEY E10 .... **120** D5
Crook Log Baths
BXLYHS DA6 .... **163** N10
Crook Log Primary School
BXLYHS DA6 .... **163** N10
Crook Log Sports Centre
WELL DA16 .... **163** N9
Crosby House Surgery
SL SL1 .... **129** K9
Cross Deep Surgery
TWK TW1 .... **176** F4
Crosshall Surgery
STMC/STPC BR5 .... **207** M4
Cross Street Gallery
IS N1 .... **6** C4
Crouch End Art School
CEND/HSY/T N8 .... **118** F3
Crouch End Health Centre
CEND/HSY/T N8 .... **118** F3
Crouch Hall Road Surgery
CEND/HSY/T N8 .... **118** E4
Crouch Hill Recreation Centre
ARCH N19 .... **118** F5
Crouch Industrial Estate
LHD/OX KT22 .... **236** F5
Crowland Primary School
SEVS/STOTM N15 .... **119** N3
Crowlands Junior
& Infant School
ROMW/RG RM7 .... **124** D4
Crown Business Centre
WDR/YW UB7 .... **132** A10
Crown Business Estate
CSHM HP5 .... **51** H6
Crown Close Business Centre
BOW E3 .... **140** F3
Crown Court
GU GU1 .... **267** P1
Crown Court
ISLW TW7 .... **154** D7
Crown Court
STAL AL1 .... **38** D6
Crowndale Health Centre
CAMTN NW1 .... **5** H7
Crownfield School
ROMW/RG RM7 .... **104** B10
Crown Lane Clinic
STHGT/OAK N14 .... **98** D2
Crown Lane CP School
WNWD SE27 .... **181** J8

Crown Plaza Hotel
WDR/YW UB7 .... **152** B2
Crown Prosecution Service
HRW HA1 .... **114** D4
Crown Prosecution Service
SRTFD E15 .... **141** K1
Crown Prosecution Service
STAL AL1 .... **38** C6
Crown Road Doctors Surgery
TWK TW1 .... **176** C3
Crown Trading Centre
HYS/HAR UB3 .... **152** F1
Crown Woods Secondary School
ELTH/MOT SE9 .... **184** F1
Crow Place Doctors Surgery
CRAWW RH11 .... **283** N8
Croydon Council
CROY/NA CR0 .... **204** A7
Croydon Football Club
SNWD SE25 .... **204** B5
Croydon Health Authority
CROY/NA CR0 .... **203** J8
Croydon Health Authority
CROY/NA CR0 .... **223** P1
Croydon High School for Girls
SAND/SEL CR2 .... **224** B7
Croydon Mosque
& Islamic Centre
THHTH CR7 .... **203** H6
Croydon Road Industrial Estate
SNWD SE25 .... **204** B4
Crusader Industrial Estate
FSBYPK N4 .... **119** K4
Crusoe House School
IS N1 .... **6** C9
Crystal Palace Football Club
SNWD SE25 .... **203** M4
Crystal Palace Museum
NRWD SE19 .... **181** N9
Crystal Palace National
Sports Centre
NRWD SE19 .... **181** P9
Cuaco Sports Ground
BECK BR3 .... **182** F9
Cubitt Town Primary School
POP/IOD E14 .... **161** H2
Cuckoo Hall Lane Junior
& Primary School
ED N9 .... **100** B1
Cuddington CP School
HOR/WEW KT19 .... **200** C10
Cudham School
BH/WHM TN16 .... **244** D2
Cuffley School
POTB/CUF EN6 .... **60** G6
Culloden Primary School
POP/IOD E14 .... **141** J8
Culvers House Primary School
MTCM CR4 .... **202** B8
Cumberland Business Park
WLSDN NW10 .... **135** N5
Cumberland Comprehensive
School
CAN/RD E16 .... **141** L7
Cumnor House School
SAND/SEL CR2 .... **223** J5
Cunningham Hill Junior
Middle & Infant School
STAL AL1 .... **38** F8
Curwen Primary School
PLSTW E13 .... **141** M4
Curzon Avenue Surgery
PEND EN3 .... **80** C9
Curzon C of E Primary School
AMSS HP7 .... **68** A8
Curzon Phoenix Theatre
SOHO/SHAV W1D **11** K6
Custom House
MON EC3R **13** J8
Cutlers' Hall
STP EC4M **12** D5
The Cycle Surgery
HBRY N5 .... **119** H10
Cygnet Clinic Beckton
EHAM E6 .... **142** E8
Cygnet Leisure Centre
GVW DA11 .... **190** B5
Cygnets Galleries
WOKN/KNAP GU21 .... **232** B3
Cygnus Business Centre
WLSDN NW10 .... **116** C10
Cypress Infant School
SNWD SE25 .... **203** M2
Cypress Junior School
SNWD SE25 .... **203** M2
Cyprus College of Art
WNWD SE27 .... **181** J7
Cyprus High Comm
MYFR/PKLN W1K **10** C7
Cyprus High Comm Trade Centre
CONDST W1S **10** F6
Cyril Jackson Primary School
POP/IOD E14 .... **140** E9
Dacorum Athletics Track
HHS/BOV HP3 .... **36** A8
Dacorum District Sports Centre
HHW HP1 .... **35** M8
Dacre Industrial Estate
CHES/WCR EN8 .... **62** D5
Dagenham Chest Clinic
BCTR RM8 .... **124** A8
Dagenham Civic Centre
DAGE RM10 .... **124** C7
Dagenham Priory School
DAGE RM10 .... **144** C2
Dagenham & Redbridge
Football Club
DAGE RM10 .... **124** C10
Dagenham Superbowl
DAGE RM10 .... **144** C4
Dagenham Swimming Pool
BCTR RM8 .... **124** A7
Daggett Gallery & Old Frames
NTGHL W11 .... **8** C6
Daily Mirror Offices
FLST/FETLN EC4A **12** B4
Daily Telegraph
POP/IOD E14 .... **160** F2
Dalmain Primary School
FSTH SE23 .... **182** D4
Dame Alice Owens School
POTB/CUF EN6 .... **59** H9
Dame Tipping School
ABR/ST RM4 .... **104** E4
Danegrove Primary School
EBAR EN4 .... **77** P10
Dane Junior High School
IL IG1 .... **122** F6
Danesfield Preparatory School
WOT/HER KT12 .... **197** J9
Danes Hill Preparatory School
LHD/OX KT22 .... **218** B10

Danetree School
HOR/WEW KT19 .... **219** P4
Danson Gallery
STMC/STPC BR5 .... **206** F5
Danson Primary School
WELL DA16 .... **163** K10
Darell Junior & Infant School
RCH/KEW TW9 .... **155** M9
Darenth CP School
RDART DA2 .... **188** E9
Dargent Gallery
STHWK SE1 .... **12** B8
Darley Dene CP School
ADL/WDHM KT15 .... **215** M2
Darrick Wood Junior
& Primary School
ORP BR6 .... **226** E1
Darrick Wood Swimming Pool
ORP BR6 .... **206** E10
Dartford Borough Council
DART DA1 .... **187** L4
Dartford County Court
DART DA1 .... **187** M2
Dartford F C
EYN DA4 .... **209** P1
Dartford F C
RDART DA2 .... **188** A4
Dartford Golf Club
DART DA1 .... **187** J5
Dartford Grammar School
DART DA1 .... **187** K2
Dartford Grammar School
for Girls
DART DA1 .... **187** K3
Dartford Hospital School
HART DA3 .... **211** M3
Dartford Magistrates Court
DART DA1 .... **187** L2
Dartford Natural Health Centre
DART DA1 .... **187** M3
Dartford West Boys School
DART DA1 .... **187** L3
Dartford West Health Centre
DART DA1 .... **187** K2
Dartford West High School
for Girls
DART DA1 .... **187** K3
Dashmesh Darbar Sikh Temple
MNPK E12 .... **142** C1
Datapoint Business Centre
CAN/RD E16 .... **141** J6
Datchet C of E School
DTCH/LGLY SL3 .... **149** N6
Datchet Sports Club
DTCH/LGLY SL3 .... **149** N6
Daubeney Primary School
CLPT E5 .... **120** D9
Davenant Foundation School
LOU IG10 .... **82** F4
Davenies Boys
Preparatory School
BEAC HP9 .... **88** D9
David Curzon Gallery
WIM/MER SW19 .... **179** H8
David Game Tuitorial College
SKENS SW7 .... **15** L6
David Livingstone School
THHTH CR7 .... **203** K1
David Lloyd Leisure Centre
SKENS SW7 .... **15** H5
Davidson Infant & Junior School
CROY/NA CR0 .... **203** N7
Davies Infant School
WAN E11 .... **121** L7
Davies's College
STHWK SE1 .... **18** F1
Dawlish Primary School
LEY E10 .... **121** H7
Day Hospital
CAMTN NW1 .... **5** H3
Day Hospital
PUR/KEN CR8 .... **223** H7
Days Lane Primary School
BFN/LL DA15 .... **185** J2
Deanesfield Primary School
RSLP HA4 .... **113** L9
Deansbrook Junior
& Infant School
MLHL NW7 .... **95** P7
Debden Sports Club
LOU IG10 .... **82** F9
De Beauvoir Primary School
IS N1 .... **7** K2
De Beauvoir Surgery
IS N1 .... **7** H7
De Bohun School
STHGT/OAK N14 .... **78** C9
Decima Gallery
WALW SE17 .... **18** D8
Dedworth Clinic
WDSR SL4 .... **148** D7
Dedworth County Middle School
WDSR SL4 .... **148** D7
Dedworth Green County
First School
WDSR SL4 .... **148** D8
Deerswood School
CRAWW RH11 .... **283** K5
Delrow School
GSTN WD25 .... **74** B5
Deneholm CP School
CDH/CHF RM16 .... **167** P1
Dene House Hospital
WDSR SL4 .... **149** H9
Denham County Infant School
DEN/HRF UB9 .... **111** J7
Denham Parish Council Office
DEN/HRF UB9 .... **111** J7
Denmead School
HPTN TW12 .... **175** P10
Dental Health Centre
CAMTN NW1 .... **4** G2
The Dental Health Centre
TWK TW1 .... **177** J2
Dentist Surgery
LEE/GVPK SE12 .... **183** N4
The Dentist Surgery
OXHEY WD19 .... **93** J6
Department of Health
WHALL SW1A **17** L1
Department of Trade
and Industry
STJSPK SW1H **17** K3
Dep of Clinical Haematology
GWRST WC1E **11** J2
Deptford Green School
NWCR SE14 .... **160** E6
Deptford Park Business Centre
DEPT SE8 .... **160** D4
Deptford Park Primary School
DEPT SE8 .... **160** D4
Deptford Trading Estate
DEPT SE8 .... **160** D4

Dersingham Infant School
MNPK E12 .... **122** C10
Derwent Water Primary School
ACT W3 .... **135** P10
Design Museum
STHWK SE1 .... **19** M1
De Stafford School
CTHM CR3 .... **241** N7
Deutsche Schule
RCHPK/HAM TW10 .... **177** J4
Devonshire Hill Junior
& Infant School
TOTM N17 .... **99** L7
Devonshire Hospital
MHST W1U **10** D3
Devonshire House
Preparatory School
HAMP NW3 .... **117** M10
Devonshire House School
HAMP NW3 .... **117** M10
Devonshire School
BELMT SM2 .... **221** M4
Devons Road Surgery
BOW E3 .... **140** C5
Dewhurst St Mary Junior
Middle & Infant School
CHESW EN7 .... **62** A5
Diakonos Physical Theatre
PECK SE15 .... **159** N9
Diamond College
FITZ W1T **11** K5
Diane Matthews Clinic
ROMW/RG RM7 .... **124** E2
Diaspora Museum
KTTN NW5 .... **4** C2
Dilkes CP School
SOCK/AV RM15 .... **146** E8
Dilloway Industrial Estate
NWDGN UB2 .... **153** M1
Discover Bible School
GSTN WD25 .... **73** K1
Divine Saviour RC JMI School
ABLGY WD5 .... **54** E8
Docklands Medical Centre
POP/IOD E14 .... **160** F3
Docklands Sailing Centre
POP/IOD E14 .... **160** F2
Docklands Sailing
& Watersports Centre
POP/IOD E14 .... **160** F2
Dockley Road Industrial Estate
BERM/RHTH SE16 .... **19** N4
Dockmaster's House
POP/IOD E14 .... **140** F9
Dock Offices
BERM/RHTH SE16 .... **160** B2
Dockyard Industrial Estate
WOOL/PLUM SE18 .... **162** B2
Doctors Chakrabarti Surgery
CRW RM5 .... **104** C8
Doctors Group Practice
BELMT SM2 .... **221** L6
The Doctors Practice
SKENS SW7 .... **15** H4
Doddinghurst C of E
Junior School
BRWN CM15 .... **86** G3
Doddinghurst County
Infant School
BRWN CM15 .... **86** G3
D of Y Theatre
CHCR WC2N **11** L8
Dog Kennel Hill Primary School
CMBW SE5 .... **159** M9
Dokal Industrial Estate
NWDGN UB2 .... **153** M1
Dollis County Infant School
MLHL NW7 .... **96** E8
Dollis Hill Synagogue
CRICK NW2 .... **116** E9
Dollis Junior School
MLHL NW7 .... **96** F8
Dolphin School
BTSEA SW11 .... **180** A1
Dominica High Comm
ECT SW5 .... **15** H6
The Dominican Rep Embassy
BAY/PAD W2 .... **9** H6
Dominion Business Park
ED N9 .... **100** C3
Dominoes Health Centre
GRAYS RM17 .... **167** M5
Donmar Warehouse Theatre
LSQ/SEVD WC2H **11** L6
Donnington Primary School
WLSDN NW10 .... **136** E2
Donyngs Recreation Centre
REDH RH1 .... **257** P9
Doods Brow School
REDH RH1 .... **258** C9
Dorchester Primary School
WPK KT4 .... **200** F8
The Dorking Business Park
DORK RH4 .... **272** F1
Dorking Football Club
RDKG RH5 .... **255** H5
Dorking General Hospital
DORK RH4 .... **272** F3
Dorking Golf Club
RDKG RH5 .... **273** H3
Dorking Lawn Tennis
& Squash Club
DORK RH4 .... **272** F2
Dorking Museum
DORK RH4 .... **272** F2
Dorking Rugby Football Club
BRKHM/BTCW RH3 .... **255** N10
Dorking Swimming
& Sports Centre
DORK RH4 .... **273** H1
Dormers Wells High School
GFD/PVL UB6 .... **133** P8
Dormers Wells JMI School
STHL UB1 .... **134** A9
Dormers Wells Medical Centre
GFD/PVL UB6 .... **133** P8
Dorney Court
WDSR SL4 .... **148** A2
Dorothy Barley Infant School
BCTR RM8 .... **123** L10
Dorset Road Infant School
ELTH/MOT SE9 .... **184** B5
Dorton College of Further
Education
BGR/WK TN15 .... **247** M8
The Douay Martyrs RC School
HGDN/ICK UB10 .... **112** C9
Douglas Bader Foundation
PUT/ROE SW15 .... **178** D2
The Dover House Surgery
UED N18 .... **99** N6
Dover Road Primary School
GVW DA11 .... **190** D4

Dovers Corner Industrial Estate
RAIN RM13 .... **144** C5
Dovers Green First School
REIG RH2 .... **275** M4
Downderry Primary School
BMLY BR1 .... **183** K7
Downe Primary School
ORP BR6 .... **226** D7
Downfield School
CHES/WCR EN8 .... **62** D7
Downham Health Centre
BMLY BR1 .... **183** K7
Downhill Junior School
TOTM N17 .... **119** L2
Down Ho
ORP BR6 .... **226** D8
Downland Surgery
COUL/CHIP CR5 .... **240** C5
Down Lane Junior School
TOTM N17 .... **99** N10
Down Manor Combined
First & Middle School
NTHLT UB5 .... **133** J5
The Downs CP School
HLW CM20 .... **46** G1
Downsell Primary School
WAN E11 .... **121** J9
Downside Primary School
CLPT E5 .... **119** P9
Downsview Junior School
SWLY BR8 .... **209** H3
Downsview School
CLPT E5 .... **120** A9
Downs Way School
OXTED RH8 .... **261** K3
Drapers Sports Ground
SRTFD E15 .... **121** H9
Drayton Gardens Surgery
WBPTN SW10 .... **15** J7
Drayton Green Primary School
WEA W13 .... **134** F9
Drayton Manor High School
HNWL W7 .... **134** E9
Drayton Park School
HBRY N5 .... **119** H10
Drca Business Centre
BTSEA SW11 .... **158** B7
Dr Challoners Grammar School
AMS HP6 .... **69** H4
Dr Challoners High School
for Girls
AMSS HP7 .... **69** N6
Drew Primary School
CAN/RD E16 .... **142** B10
Dr Ghosh's Surgery
SEVS/STOTM N15 .... **119** L4
Drill Hall
GWRST WC1E **11** J3
Dr Johnson's House
FLST/FETLN EC4A **12** B5
Dropmore County First School
SL SL1 .... **108** B8
Dr Samuels Surgery
HNWL W7 .... **121** K8
Dr Shafiq Surgery
SL SL1 .... **128** E9
Dr Sherriff & Partners
PECK SE15 .... **159** N7
Dr Tripletts School
HYS/HAR UB3 .... **132** C8
Drury Way Industrial Estate
WLSDN NW10 .... **116** A9
Dry Ski Slope
HGDN/ICK UB10 .... **112** A10
Dry Ski Slope
RBRW/HUT CM13 .... **107** H8
Duch Theatre
COVGDN WC2E **11** L7
Duke of York Column
STJS SW1Y **11** K10
Duke of York's HQ
CHEL SW3 .... **16** B6
Duke of Yorks Theatre
SOHO/SHAV W1D **11** H7
Dukes Avenue Practice
MUSWH N10 .... **118** C1
Dulverton School
BFN/LL DA15 .... **184** C5
Dulwich College
DUL SE21 .... **181** M4
Dulwich College Picture Gallery
DUL SE21 .... **181** L3
Dulwich College
Preparatory School
DUL SE21 .... **181** M6
Dulwich Hamlet Football Club
CMBW SE5 .... **159** M10
Dulwich Hamlet Junior School
HNHL SE24 .... **181** L2
Dulwich High School for Boys
HNHL SE24 .... **181** L1
Dulwich Medical Centre
EDUL SE22 .... **181** P1
Dulwich Village C of E
Infant School
DUL SE21 .... **181** M2
Dunbar Wharf
POP/IOD E14 .... **140** E9
Duncombe Primary School
ARCH N19 .... **118** F6
Duncombe School
HERT/WAS SG14 .... **25** K4
Dun Cow Surgery
STHWK SE1 .... **19** L7
Dundee Wharf
POP/IOD E14 .... **140** E9
Dundonald Primary School
WIM/MER SW19 .... **179** J10
Dunningford Primary School
HCH RM12 .... **124** G10
Dunottar School
REIG RH2 .... **275** N1
Dunraven Lower School
STRHM/NOR SW16 .... **180** C6
Dunraven Upper School
STRHM/NOR SW16 .... **180** C6
Dunton Green County
Primary School
SEV TN13 .... **246** F6
Duppas Primary School
CROY/NA CR0 .... **223** J2
Durand Primary School
BRXN/ST SW9 .... **158** C7
Durants School
EN EN3 .... **80** D7
Durdans Park School
STHL UB1 .... **133** N7
Durrant CP School
CSHM HP5 .... **50** G4
Durston House School
EA W5 .... **135** J8
Dycorts School
HARH RM3 .... **105** P5

Dysart School
KUTN/CMB KT2 ...... 177 J7

Eagle House Surgery
PEND EN3 ...... 80 B8

Eaglesfield Secondary School
WOOL/PLUM SE18 ...... 162 D7

Eagle Trading Estate
MTCM CR4 ...... 202 A6

Ealdham Primary School
ELTH/MOT SE9 ...... 161 P10

Ealing Abbey
EA W5 ...... 135 H8

Ealing Abbey Scriptorium
WEA W13 ...... 135 H8

Ealing & Acton Synagogue
EA W5 ...... 135 J10

Ealing Central Sports Ground
GFD/PVL UB6 ...... 134 F4

Ealing College Upper School
WEA W13 ...... 134 G8

Ealing Cricket Club
EA W5 ...... 135 K8

Ealing Gallery
EA W5 ...... 155 J1

Ealing Hospital NHS Trust
STHL UB1 ...... 154 C1

Ealing Liberal Synagogue
WEA W13 ...... 134 F8

Ealing Northern Sports Centre
NTHLT UB5 ...... 114 C10

Ealing Park Health Centre
EA W5 ...... 155 J3

Ealing Road Trading Estate
BTFD TW8 ...... 155 J4

Ealing Sports Centre
EA W5 ...... 135 K9

Ealing Tertiary College
EA W5 ...... 135 J10

Ealing Tutorial College
EA W5 ...... 135 H9

Eardley Primary School
STRHM/NOR SW16 ...... 180 D9

The Earl Gallery
POTB/CUF EN6 ...... 59 J4

Earlham Junior & Infant School
WDGN N22 ...... 99 H8

Earlham Primary School
FSTGT E7 ...... 121 L10

Earls Court Exhibition Centre
ECT SW5 ...... 14 E8

Earlsfield Primary School
WAND/EARL SW18 ...... 179 M4

Earlsmead Junior & Infant School
SEVS/STOTM N15 ...... 119 N3

Earlsmead School
RYLN/HDSTN HA2 ...... 113 N9

Earlswood First School
REDH RH1 ...... 276 A1

Earlswood Mosque
REDH RH1 ...... 276 A2

Earth Gallery
SKENS SW7 ...... 15 M4

Earthworks Gallery
HCH RM12 ...... 125 M6

East Acton Primary School
ACT W3 ...... 136 B9

East Barking Luncheon & Leisure Centre
BCTR RM8 ...... 123 M10

East Barnet Grammar School
EBAR EN4 ...... 78 A10

East Barnet Health Centre
EBAR EN4 ...... 77 N9

East Barnet School
EBAR EN4 ...... 77 N7

East Berkshire College
DTCH/LGLY SL3 ...... 150 D1

East Berkshire College
WDSR SL4 ...... 149 H8

East Berkshire Health Authority
SL SL1 ...... 149 L2

Eastbrook Junior School
HHNE HP2 ...... 36 A1

Eastbrook Secondary School
DAGE RM10 ...... 124 D9

Eastbury Comprehensive School
BARK IG11 ...... 142 G2

Eastbury Infant School
BARK IG11 ...... 143 J2

Eastbury Infant School
NTHWD HA6 ...... 92 G5

Eastcote Cricket Club
PIN HA5 ...... 113 J3

Eastcote Health Centre
PIN HA5 ...... 113 K5

Eastcote Industrial Estate
RSLP HA4 ...... 113 K5

Eastcote Primary School
ELTH/MOT SE9 ...... 162 G8

Eastcote Surgery
RSLP HA4 ...... 113 J4

Eastcourt Independent School
GDMY/SEVK IG3 ...... 123 K6

East Dulwich Baths
EDUL SE22 ...... 159 N10

Eastern Art Gallery
NOXST/BSQ WC1A 11 L5

Eastfield Primary & Infant School
PEND EN3 ...... 80 C4

Eastfields Secondary Modern Boys School
MTCM CR4 ...... 202 C2

East Finchley Medical Centre
EFNCH N2 ...... 117 P2

East Greenwich Christ Church C of E Primary School
GNWCH SE10 ...... 161 K3

East Ham Industrial Estate
CAN/RD E16 ...... 142 A6

East Ham Memorial Hospital
FSTGT E7 ...... 142 A2

East Herts District Council
HERT/BAY SG13 ...... 25 K6

East Herts District Council
HERT/WAS SG14 ...... 24 G4

East Herts District Council
SBW CM21 ...... 29 P1

East Herts Golf Clubhouse
WARE SG12 ...... 26 B3

Eastlea Community School
CAN/RD E16 ...... 141 K6

East London Business College
WAN E11 ...... 121 K6

East London Central Synagogue
WCHPL E1 ...... 140 A8

East London & City Health Authority
BOW E3 ...... 140 F4

East London & City Health Authority
PLSTW E13 ...... 141 N6

East London & City Health Authority
WCHPL E1 ...... 13 P5

East London Markazi Mosque
WCHPL E1 ...... 13 P6

East London Mosque
WCHPL E1 ...... 13 P4

East London Rugby Club
EHAM E6 ...... 142 C7

East Molesey Cricket Club
E/WMO/HCT KT8 ...... 198 B3

East Molesey Infants School
E/WMO/HCT KT8 ...... 198 C5

East Sheen CP Junior School
MORT/ESHN SW14 ...... 156 B10

East Surrey College
REDH RH1 ...... 258 B6

East Surrey Hospital
REDH RH1 ...... 276 C4

East Surrey Museum
CTHM CR3 ...... 241 N10

East Tilbury Surgery
TIL RM18 ...... 169 L3

Eastwick County Junior School
GT/LBKH KT23 ...... 236 A10

East Wickham Primary School
WELL DA16 ...... 163 K7

Eaton Manor Rugby Club
WAN E11 ...... 121 P3

Eaton Square Preparatory School
BGVA SW1W 16 E5

Eaton Square School
PIM SW1V 16 G6

Ebbisham County Infants School
EPSOM KT18 ...... 219 P10

Ebbisham Sports Club
HOR/WEW KT19 ...... 219 P8

Ebury Galleries
BGVA SW1W 16 D6

Ecclesbourne Junior & Infants School
THHTH CR7 ...... 203 K5

Ecclesbourne Primary School
IS N1 ...... 6 G3

Echelford Primary School
ASHF TW15 ...... 174 C8

Eckerd College
GWRST WC1E 11 J3

Eclipse Estate
HOR/WEW KT19 ...... 219 P9

Ecole De Mime Corporel Theatre De Lange Fou
ARCH N19 ...... 118 F7

Eden College
STHWK SE1 ...... 18 D3

Edenham High School
CROY/NA CR0 ...... 204 E7

Eden Medical Centre
WKENS W14 ...... 14 D6

Edenvale Child Health Clinic
TOOT SW17 ...... 180 B10

Edes Business Park
WLGTN SM6 ...... 202 B9

Edgebury Primary School
CHST BR7 ...... 184 F7

Edge Business Centre
CRICK NW2 ...... 116 E7

Edgware Clinic
EDGW HA8 ...... 95 M7

Edgware College
HAMP NW3 ...... 3 K2

Edgware Infant School
EDGW HA8 ...... 95 M7

Edgware Junior School
EDGW HA8 ...... 95 N7

Edgware Reform Synagogue
EDGW HA8 ...... 95 L5

Edgware Secondary School
EDGW HA8 ...... 95 L5

Edgware Town Football Club
EDGW HA8 ...... 95 M8

Edgware United Synagogue
EDGW HA8 ...... 95 N5

Edinburgh Primary School
WALTH E17 ...... 120 E3

Edith Grove Gallery
WBPTN SW10 ...... 15 J10

Edith Neville Primary School
CAMTN NW1 ...... 5 J8

Edmonton County Court
UED N18 ...... 99 N6

Edmonton Leisure Centre
ED N9 ...... 99 P4

Edmonton School
EN EN1 ...... 99 N1

Edmund Waller School
NWCR SE14 ...... 160 C8

Edward Ash Gallery
ORP BR6 ...... 206 D10

Edward Cross Gallery
WEY KT13 ...... 196 E10

Edward Pauling School
FELT TW13 ...... 174 F5

Edward Wilson Primary School
BAY/PAD W2 ...... 8 G3

Edwin Lambert Schooll
EMPK RM11 ...... 125 H4

Effingham Cricket Club
EHSLY KT24 ...... 235 J10

Effingham Golf Club
EHSLY KT24 ...... 253 L4

Effingham Park Golf Club
CRAWE RH10 ...... 285 N1

Effra Primary School
BRXS/STRHM SW2 ...... 181 H1

Egerton Rothesay School
BERK HP4 ...... 33 L5

Egham Cricket Club
EGH TW20 ...... 172 B6

Egham Sports Centre
EGH TW20 ...... 172 C9

Egham Town Football Club
EGH TW20 ...... 172 B7

Eglinton Infant School
WOOL/PLUM SE18 ...... 162 D5

Eglinton Junior School
WOOL/PLUM SE18 ...... 162 D6

Elangeni County Middle School
AMS HP6 ...... 69 K2

Elbourne Trading Estate
BELV DA17 ...... 164 C2

Eldenwall Industrial Estate
BCTR RM8 ...... 124 A6

Eldon JMI School
ED N9 ...... 100 B2

Eleanor Estate
CHES/WCR EN8 ...... 62 E10

Eleanor Palmer Primary School
KTTN NW5 ...... 118 D9

Eleanor Smith Special School
PLSTW E13 ...... 141 M4

Electrical Trades Union College
ESH/CLAY KT10 ...... 217 P1

The Electric Theatre
GU GU1 ...... 267 P1

The Electrolysis Clinic
BCTR RM8 ...... 123 L6

Elephant & Castle Shopping Centre
STHWK SE1 ...... 18 D4

Elers Clinic
HYS/HAR UB3 ...... 152 E3

Elfrida Primary School
CAT SE6 ...... 182 G7

Elica Gallery
NRWD SE19 ...... 181 M9

Eliot Bank Primary School
FSTH SE23 ...... 182 A5

Elizabeth Avenue Group Practice
IS N1 ...... 6 F5

Elizabeth Garrett Anderson School
IS N1 ...... 5 P7

Elizabeth Page Gallery
FARR EC1M 12 D3

Elizabeth Selby Infant School
BETH E2 ...... 7 P9

Elizabeth Trading Estate
NWCR SE14 ...... 160 C5

Ellen Wilkinson High School
EA W5 ...... 135 L8

Ellen Wilkinson Primary School
EHAM E6 ...... 142 A7

Ellerslie Square Industrial Estate
CLAP SW4 ...... 158 F10

Ellingham Primary School
CHSGTN KT9 ...... 219 J4

Elliott Gm School
PUT/ROE SW15 ...... 178 F2

Ellisslea Lawn Tennis Club
HARP AL5 ...... 20 A1

Elmbridge Borough Council
COB KT11 ...... 235 M2

Elmbridge Borough Council
WOT/HER KT12 ...... 197 H7

Elmbridge Leisure Centre
WOT/HER KT12 ...... 197 J5

Elmbridge Museum
WEY KT13 ...... 216 B1

Elmcourt School
WNWD SE27 ...... 181 J9

Elmgrove First & Middle School
KTN/HRWW/W HA3 ...... 114 F2

Elm Row Surgery
BECK BR3 ...... 204 E2

Elmhurst Preparatory School
BGVA SW1W 16 F4

Elmhurst Primary School
FSTGT E7 ...... 141 N2

Elmhurst School
CROY/NA CR0 ...... 223 L1

Elm Lea Trading Estate
TOTM N17 ...... 99 P8

Elmlodge Surgery
HNHL SE24 ...... 181 K2

The Elms Health Centre
POTB/CUF EN6 ...... 59 M7

The Elms Medical Practice
HARP AL5 ...... 20 A1

Elmtree County Infant School
CSHM HP5 ...... 50 F6

Elmwood Junior & Infant School
CROY/NA CR0 ...... 203 J7

Elm Wood Primary School
WNWD SE27 ...... 181 L6

Elsdale Street Health Centre
HOM E9 ...... 140 B2

Elsley Primary School
BTSEA SW11 ...... 158 B9

Elsley Primary School
WBLY HA9 ...... 135 L1

Elstree & Borehamwood Town Council
BORE WD6 ...... 75 N7

Elstree Studios
BORE WD6 ...... 75 M7

Elstree Way Clinic
BORE WD6 ...... 75 N6

Eltham Baths
ELTH/MOT SE9 ...... 184 B1

Eltham C of E Primary School
ELTH/MOT SE9 ...... 184 C1

Eltham College
ELTH/MOT SE9 ...... 184 A5

Eltham College Junior School
ELTH/MOT SE9 ...... 184 A4

Eltham Green School
ELTH/MOT SE9 ...... 184 A2

Eltham Health Clinic
ELTH/MOT SE9 ...... 184 B1

Eltham Hill School
ELTH/MOT SE9 ...... 184 B2

Eltham Palace
ELTH/MOT SE9 ...... 184 B3

Elthorne High School
HNWL W7 ...... 154 E2

Elthorne Park Surgery
HNWL W7 ...... 154 F1

Elystan Business Centre
HYS/HAR UB3 ...... 133 K3

Emanuel School
WAND/EARL SW18 ...... 179 N1

Embassy of Afghanistan
SKENS SW7 ...... 15 L2

Embassy of Angola
MYFR/PKLN W1K 10 C7

Embassy of Bahrain
SKENS SW7 ...... 15 J4

Embassy of Belarus
KENS W8 ...... 15 J1

Embassy of Belgium
KTBR SW1X 16 D4

Embassy of Bolivia
KTBR SW1X 16 D4

Embassy of Brazil
MYFR/PKLN W1K 10 C7

Embassy of Cote d'ivoire
KTBR SW1X 16 D3

Embassy of Cuba
HHOL WC1V 11 L5

Embassy of Ecuador
KTBR SW1X 16 A3

Embassy of Ethiopia
SKENS SW7 ...... 15 M2

Embassy of Finland
KTBR SW1X 16 C3

Embassy of France
KTBR SW1X 16 B1

Embassy of Greece
KENS W8 ...... 8 C10

Embassy of Guatemala
WBPTN SW10 ...... 15 J9

Embassy of Honduras
MBLAR W1H 10 B3

Embassy of Iceland
KTBR SW1X 16 C5

Embassy of Iraq
SKENS SW7 ...... 15 K3

Embassy of Israel
KENS W8 ...... 14 G1

Embassy of Japan
MYFR/PICC W1J 10 F10

Embassy of LaTvia
CAMTN NW1 ...... 10 C2

Embassy of Lebanon
KENS W8 ...... 8 G9

Embassy of Liberia
BAY/PAD W2 ...... 8 F7

Embassy of Mexico
MYFR/PICC W1J 10 E10

Embassy of Mongolia
KENS W8 ...... 15 H2

Embassy of Morocco
SKENS SW7 ...... 15 J5

Embassy of Nepal
KENS W8 ...... 8 G9

Embassy of Netherlands
SKENS SW7 ...... 15 K2

Embassy of Paraguay
SKENS SW7 ...... 15 H4

Embassy of Portugal
KTBR SW1X 16 C2

Embassy of Romania
KENS W8 ...... 14 G1

Embassy of Sudan
WHALL SW1A 10 G10

Embassy of Sweden
MBLAR W1H 10 A4

Embassy of Switzerland
MBLAR W1H 10 A4

Embassy of the Arab Rep of Egypt
MYFR/PICC W1J 10 E9

Embassy of the Democratic Rep of the Congo
KTBR SW1X 16 B4

Embassy of the Federal Rep of Germany
KTBR SW1X 16 B1

Embassy of the Hashemite Kingdom of Jordan
KENS W8 ...... 14 D2

Embassy of the Islamic Rep of Iran
SKENS SW7 ...... 15 M2

Embassy of the Peoples Rep of China
CAVSQ/HST W1G 10 E3

Embassy of the Rep of Albania
BGVA SW1W 16 F4

Embassy of the Rep of Croatia
GTPST W1W 10 F2

Embassy of the Rep of Gabon
SKENS SW7 ...... 15 K4

Embassy of the Rep of Krygyz
MBLAR W1H 10 A4

Embassy of the Rep of Mozambique
FITZ W1T 10 G2

Embassy of the Rep of Poland
CAVSQ/HST W1G 10 E3

Embassy of the Rep of Slovenia
MHST W1U 10 E5

Embassy of the Republic of Armenia
KENS W8 ...... 14 C2

Embassy of the Republic of Korea
WESTW SW1E 17 H3

Embassy of the Republic of Senegal
CRICK NW2 ...... 136 F2

Embassy of the Russian Federation
KENS W8 ...... 8 G10

Embassy of the Slovak Republic
KENS W8 ...... 8 G10

Embassy of the Socialist Republic of South Vietnam
KENS W8 ...... 15 H3

Embassy of the State of Qatar
MYFR/PKLN W1K 10 D10

Embassy of the Syrian Arab Rep
KTBR SW1X 16 C2

Embassy of the Union of Myanmar
MYFR/PICC W1J 10 E9

Embassy of the United Arab Emirates
SKENS SW7 ...... 15 M1

Embassy of Tunisia
SKENS SW7 ...... 15 M2

Embassy of Turkmeistan
GTPST W1W 11 H4

Embassy of Ukraine
NTGHL W11 ...... 8 B10

Embassy of United Republic of Cameroon
WKENS W14 ...... 8 B10

Embassy of Uruguay
SKENS SW7 ...... 15 P3

Embassy of Venezuela
SKENS SW7 ...... 15 M4

Ember Sports Club
ESH/CLAY KT10 ...... 198 B8

Embroidery World Business Centre
WFD IG8 ...... 102 A10

Emerson Park School
EMPK RM11 ...... 126 A5

Emmanuel C of E School
NTHWD HA6 ...... 92 G8

Empson & Ewell Bo Co
EW KT17 ...... 220 A9

Endeavour School
BRWN CM15 ...... 107 L4

Endsleigh Industrial Estate
NWDGN UB2 ...... 153 M3

Enfield Business Centre
PEND EN3 ...... 80 B7

Enfield Chace Lower School
ENC/FH EN2 ...... 79 M4

Enfield College
PEND EN3 ...... 80 B7

Enfield Cricket Club
EN EN1 ...... 79 M9

Enfield Football Club
ED N9 ...... 100 B3

Enfield Football Club
EN EN1 ...... 79 P8

Enfield Grammar School
ENC/FH EN2 ...... 79 L7

Enfield & Haringey Health Authority
EBAR EN4 ...... 78 D4

Enfield Lower Grammar School
ENC/FH EN2 ...... 79 L6

Enfield School of Swimming
FBAR/BDGN N11 ...... 98 E6

Engayne Junior School
UPMR RM14 ...... 126 D4

Englefield Green School
EGH TW20 ...... 171 P8

English College
SOHO/SHAV W1D 11 J5

English Martyrs RC Primary School
WALW SE17 ...... 18 G6

English Martyrs RC Primary School
WCHPL E1 ...... 13 M6

The English Teaching Theatre
IS N1 ...... 7 K4

Enid Lawson Gallery
KENS W8 ...... 14 G1

Ennersdale Primary School
LEW SE13 ...... 183 J1

Ensham Secondary School
TOOT SW17 ...... 180 A8

Enterprise Business Park
POP/IOD E14 ...... 160 G1

Enterprise Industrial Estate
BERM/RHTH SE16 ...... 160 B4

Epping County Infant School
EPP CM16 ...... 65 H5

Epping County Junior School
EPP CM16 ...... 65 J6

Epping Forest District Council
CHIG IG7 ...... 102 G6

Epping Forest District Council
EPP CM16 ...... 65 K6

Epping Forest District Council
EPP CM16 ...... 65 J3

Epping Forest District Council
LOU IG10 ...... 82 F9

Epping Forest District Council
LOU IG10 ...... 82 F8

Epping House School
HERT/BAY SG13 ...... 42 D7

Epping & Ongar Rural District Council
EPP CM16 ...... 65 N10

Epping Sports Centre
EPP CM16 ...... 64 G10

Epping Sports Centre
EPP CM16 ...... 65 J7

Epping Town Council
EPP CM16 ...... 65 J7

Epping Upland Cofe Primary School
EPP CM16 ...... 64 E1

Epsom Business Park
EW KT17 ...... 220 B7

Epsom College
EW KT17 ...... 220 D10

Epsom County Court
EPSOM KT18 ...... 220 A9

Epsom CP School
HOR/WEW KT19 ...... 220 A7

Epsom Downs County Infant School
EPSOM KT18 ...... 238 A5

Epsom & Ewell Borough Council
EPSOM KT18 ...... 238 B2

Epsom & Ewell High School
HOR/WEW KT19 ...... 219 P2

Epsom Ewell & St Hellier NHS Trust
EPSOM KT18 ...... 237 P1

Epsom Ewell & St Helliers NHS Trust
HOR/WEW KT19 ...... 219 L8

Epsom Golf Club
EW KT17 ...... 238 D1

Epsom Health Clinic
EPSOM KT18 ...... 220 A8

Epsom School of Art & Design
EW KT17 ...... 220 B8

Epsom Sports Club
EPSOM KT18 ...... 237 P1

Erdos Chinese Medical Centre
RSLP HA4 ...... 112 F6

Erith & Belvedere Football Club
BELV DA17 ...... 164 C2

Erith & District Hospital
ERITH DA8 ...... 164 E5

Erith Health Centre
ERITH DA8 ...... 164 F5

Erith Library & Museum
ERITH DA8 ...... 164 F4

Erith School
ERITH DA8 ...... 164 D6

Erith Small Business Centre
ERITH DA8 ...... 164 G5

Erith Theatre Guild
ERITH DA8 ...... 164 G4

Ernest Bevin School
TOOT SW17 ...... 179 P6

Esher Church School
ESH/CLAY KT10 ...... 218 B3

Esher College
THDIT KT7 ...... 198 D7

Esher Green Surgery
ESH/CLAY KT10 ...... 197 P10

Esher Rugby Club
WOT/HER KT12 ...... 197 M3

Essendon Primary School
BRKMPK AL9 ...... 42 A3

Essex County Council
BKHH IG9 ...... 102 A4

Essex County Council
BRW CM14 ...... 106 C2

Essex County Council
BRW CM14 ...... 107 J3

Essex County Council
CHIG IG7 ...... 102 F2

Essex County Council
CHONG CM5 ...... 67 J2

Essex County Council
EPP CM16 ...... 65 N4

Essex County Council
GRAYS RM17 ...... 167 N4

Essex County Council
LOU IG10 ...... 82 D6

Essex County Council
LOU IG10 ...... 82 E7

Essex County Council
RBRW/HUT CM13 ...... 106 G7

Essex County Council
TIL RM18 ...... 168 D8

Essex County Council
WAB EN9 ...... 63 H9

Essex Galleries
IL IG1 ...... 122 D7

Essex House Surgery
BARN SW13 ...... 156 C8

The Essex Nuffield Hospital
BRWN CM15 ...... 107 K2

Essex Primary School
MNPK E12 ...... 142 B1

Estonian Embassy
SKENS SW7................ 15 K2
Ethelburga Gm School
BTSEA SW11................ 157 P7
Ethel Davis School
CHDH RM6................ 123 L3
Eton College
WDSR SL4................ 149 J4
Eton Porny C of E
Combined School
WDSR SL4................ 149 J5
Eton Town Council
WDSR SL4................ 149 J6
Eton Wick C of E
Combined School
WDSR SL4................ 148 F4
Eton Wick Football & Social Club
WDSR SL4................ 148 E4
Eurolink Business Centre
BRXS/STRHM SW2................ 159 H10
Euro Link Business Centre
BRXS/STRHM SW2................ 181 H1
Europa Trading Estate
ERITH DA8................ 164 E4
Europa Trading Estate
WTHK RM20................ 167 J4
European School of Economics
KTBR SW1X................ 16 D2
European Vocational College
HDTCH EC3A................ 13 K5
Euro Temple
SOHO/CST W1F................ 11 H6
Euro Way School
CEND/HSY/T N8................ 119 H1
Euro Way School London
FSBYPK N4................ 119 J5
Euston Centre
CAMTN NW1................ 10 G1
Euston Tower
CAMTN NW1................ 10 G1
Eveline Lowe Primary School
STHWK SE1................ 19 N8
Evelyns Secondary School
WDR/YW UB7................ 132 A8
Evendine College
SOHO/SHAV W1D................ 11 J5
Evendine College
WIM/MER SW19................ 179 H9
Everest House Surgery
HHNE HP2................ 36 F1
Everest Sports Club
CHES/WCR EN8................ 62 A5
Eversley College
SBW SW20................ 29 N1
Eversley Medical Centre
THHTH CR7................ 203 H6
Eversley Primary School
WCHMH N21................ 78 F9
Ewell Castle School
EW KT17................ 220 D5
Ewell Grove Infant School
EW KT17................ 220 C5
Exhibition Halls
STLK EC1Y................ 12 F3
Eye Clinic
LSQ/SEVD WC2H................ 11 L5
The Eye Clinic
IL IG1................ 122 E9
Eye Clinic
CAVSQ/HST W1G................ 10 E4
The Eye Practice
HAMP NW3................ 117 N9
Eynsford Castle
EYN DA4................ 209 M9
Eynsford Cricket Club
EYN DA4................ 209 M9
Fairacres Industrial Estate
WDSR SL4................ 148 B8
Fairbrook Medical Centre
BORE WD6................ 75 N6
Faircharm Trading Estate
DEPT SE8................ 160 G6
Faircharm Trading Estate
IS N1................ 6 E7
The Faircross Complementary
Medical Centre
BARK IG11................ 143 H1
Fairfield Clinic
BKHH IG9................ 101 N2
Fairfield Industrial Estate
KUT KT1................ 199 L3
Fairfield Medical Centre
GT/LBKH KT23................ 254 A2
Fairfield Pool & Leisure Centre
DART DA1................ 187 M3
Fairfield Primary School
RAD WD7................ 74 D2
Fairfields Junior Middle
& Infant School
CHESW EN7................ 61 P3
Fairhill Medical Practice
KUTN/CMB KT2................ 177 M10
Fairholme Junior & Infant School
EBED/NFELT TW14................ 174 E4
Fairlands Practice
RGUW GU3................ 249 H6
Fairlawn Primary School
FSTH SE23................ 182 B3
Fairley House School
WEST SW1P................ 17 J6
Fairlop Primary School
BARK/HLT IG6................ 102 F9
Fairview Industrial Centre
DAGW RM9................ 144 E8
Fairview Industrial Estate
AMS HP6................ 69 L4
Fairview Industrial Estate
HYS/HAR UB3................ 152 G1
Fairview Industrial Estate
OXTED RH8................ 261 M9
Fairview Medical Centre
STRHM/NOR SW16................ 202 F1
Fairway JMI School
MLHL NW7................ 96 A3
Fairway Primary School
MLHL NW7................ 96 A3
Fairways Business Park
LEY E10................ 120 D7
The Fairways
CHES/WCR EN8................ 62 C2
Falconbrook School
BTSEA SW11................ 157 N8
Falcon Business Centre
BTSEA SW11................ 157 P10
Falconer School
BUSH WD23................ 73 N9
Falkland Road Practice
KTTN NW5................ 118 D10
Family Doctor Unit Surgery
HSLW TW3................ 153 P9
Fanmakers' Hall
LVPST EC2M................ 13 J4

Fan Museum
GNWCH SE10................ 161 H6
Faraday Building
BLKFR EC4V................ 12 D6
Farleigh Rovers F C
WARL CR6................ 242 E1
Farley Road Surgery
SAND/SEL CR2................ 224 A5
Farm Lane Trading Estate
FUL/PGN SW6................ 14 E10
Farnborough Primary School
ORP BR6................ 226 G2
Farncombe C of E Infant School
RGODL GU7................ 267 K10
Farncombe Cricket Club
RGODL GU7................ 267 L10
Farnell House Medical Centre
HSLW TW3................ 154 A7
Farnham Common County
First School
SLN SL2................ 108 G9
Farnham Common County
Middle School
SLN SL2................ 109 H9
Farnham Common Sports Club
SLN SL2................ 109 H9
Farnham Green Primary School
GDMY/SEVK IG3................ 123 K4
Farnham Road Hospital
GUW GU2................ 267 N2
Farnham Road Surgery
SLN SL2................ 128 G6
Farnham Royal
Combined School
SLN SL2................ 129 H5
Farrington School
CHST BR7................ 185 H10
Farringtons Girls School
CHST BR7................ 184 G10
Fashion Gallery
MORT/ESHN SW14................ 155 P9
Fawbert & Barnards
Primary School
HLWE CM17................ 29 M8
Fawkham Manor Hospital
HART DA3................ 211 H8
Fawkham Primary School
HART DA3................ 210 F8
Feathers Gallery
HMSMTH W6................ 156 F2
Featherstone High School
NWDGN UB2................ 153 L3
Featherstone Industrial Estate
NWDGN UB2................ 153 M1
Featherstone Infant School
NWDGN UB2................ 153 M2
Featherstone Junior
Mixed School
NWDGN UB2................ 153 M2
Featherstone Road Health Clinic
NWDGN UB2................ 153 M2
Felnex Trading Estate
WLGTN SM6................ 202 B9
Feltham Airparcs Leisure Centre
FELT TW13................ 175 L5
Feltham Hill Junior School
FELT TW13................ 174 G6
Feltham & Hounslow Boro
Football Club
EBED/NFELT TW14................ 175 H3
The Feltham School
FELT TW13................ 175 K5
Feltham Superbowl
FELT TW13................ 175 J5
Fenstanton Junior
& Infant School
BRXS/STRHM SW2................ 181 H4
Ferndale Surgery
WFD IG8................ 101 P7
Fern Hill Primary School
KUTN/CMB KT2................ 177 K9
Fernville Surgery
HHNE HP2................ 35 N6
Ferrier Industrial Estate
WAND/EARL SW18................ 157 L10
Ferry Lane Industrial Estate
RAIN RM13................ 145 H7
Ferry Lane Industrial Estate
WALTH E17................ 120 B1
Ferry Lane Primary School
WALTH E17................ 120 A2
Fetcham County First School
LHD/OX KT22................ 236 C8
Fetcham Village Surgery
GT/LBKH KT23................ 254 A1
Ficino Gallery
RYLN/HDSTN HA2................ 114 C6
Fiddlebridge Industrial Centre
HAT AL10................ 40 D3
Field End Junior School
RSLP HA4................ 113 L7
Fielding First & Middle School
WEA W13................ 154 G2
Field Junior School
WATW WD18................ 73 K9
Fiji High Comm
SKENS SW7................ 15 J2
Financial Times
STHWK SE1................ 12 F9
Finborough Theatre Club
WBPTN SW10................ 14 G9
Finchley Catholic High School
NFNCH/WDSP N12................ 97 M4
Finchley Central Synagogue
FNCH N3................ 97 K9
Finchley Cricket Club
FNCH N3................ 97 L10
The Finchley Industrial Centre
NFNCH/WDSP N12................ 97 M5
Finchley Memorial Hospital
FNCH N3................ 97 M8
Finchley Osteopathic Surgery
FNCH N3................ 97 K8
Finchley Progressive Synagogue
NFNCH/WDSP N12................ 97 L6
Finchley Reform Synagogue
FNCH N3................ 97 L8
Finchley Synagogue
FNCH N3................ 117 J1
Finchley Youth Theatre
EFNCH N2................ 117 P1
Fine Arts College
HAMP NW3................ 3 P2
Finsbury Circus Medical Centre
LOTH EC2R................ 12 C5
Finsbury Health Centre
CLKNW EC1R................ 12 A1
Finsbury Leisure Complex
FSBYE EC1V................ 12 E1
Finsbury Park District Synagogue
FSBYPK N4................ 119 L2
Finton House School
TOOT SW17................ 180 A5

Fircroft Primary School
WOT SW17................ 180 A5
Fire Brigade Museum
STHWK SE1................ 18 E1
Fir Road Surgery
FELT TW13................ 175 M8
Firs Farm Primary School
PLMGR N13................ 99 L4
First School
CFSP/GDCR SL9................ 89 P8
Fisher Athletic Football Club
BERM/RHTH SE16................ 140 C10
Fisher Industrial Estate
WATW WD18................ 73 K9
Fishmonger's Hall
CANST EC4R................ 12 G8
Fitness Unlimited Leisure Centre
BOW E3................ 140 F4
Fitzjohns Primary School
HAMP NW3................ 117 N10
Fitznells Manor Surgery
EW KT17................ 220 C5
Five Elms School
DAGW RM9................ 124 A8
Five Ways Business Centre
FELT TW13................ 175 J6
Flamstead End Junior School
CHESW EN7................ 61 P3
Flaxman Sports Centre
CMBW SE5................ 159 K8
Fleecefield Primary School
ED N9................ 99 P5
Fleetdown Infants School
RDART DA2................ 188 B4
Fleetdown Junior School
RDART DA2................ 188 B5
Fleet Primary School
HAMP NW3................ 118 A10
FleeTVille Infant School
STAL AL1................ 38 F6
FleeTVille Jm School
STAL AL1................ 38 F6
Fleetway Business Park
GFD/PVL UB6................ 134 C4
Fleetway Sports Club
GVE DA12................ 190 F4
Fleur De Lys Gallery
NTGHL W11................ 8 D6
Flora Gardens Primary School
HMSMTH W6................ 156 E3
Floral Gallery
CTHM CR3................ 241 P10
Florance Nightingale
Health Centre
HLWE CM17................ 47 N2
Florence Nightingale Museum
STHWK SE1................ 17 N2
Florence Road Surgery
EA W5................ 135 K9
The Flower Gallery
KIL/WHAMP NW6................ 2 F2
Flutters Leisure Centre
FUL/PGN SW6................ 157 N6
Flying Colours Gallery
CHEL SW3................ 15 P7
Focus Gallery
NOXST/BSQ WC1A................ 11 L4
The Focus Gallery
GLDGN NW11................ 117 J3
Follys End Christian High School
SNWD SE25................ 203 M6
Fondu Sports Club
PUR RM19................ 166 B3
Fontigarry Farm Business Park
REIG RH2................ 275 M9
Football & Social Club
WCCE KT2................ 23 L3
The Foot Clinic
WIM/MER SW19................ 179 H8
The Foot Health Centre
COUL/CHIP CR5................ 240 E1
Fordbridge Medical Centre
ASHF TW15................ 174 A7
The Ford College
CONDST W1S................ 10 F7
Fordview Estate
RAIN RM13................ 144 E5
Fordwater Trading Estate
ADL/WDHM KT15................ 195 M8
Foreign and Commonwealth
Office
WHALL SW1A................ 17 K1
Foreland Medical Centre
NTGHL W11................ 8 A7
Forest Business Park
WALTH E17................ 120 C5
Forestdale Primary School
CROY/NA CR0................ 224 D5
Foresters Primary School
WLGTN SM6................ 222 E3
Forest Gate Community School
FSTGT E7................ 121 M10
Forest Girls School
WALTH E17................ 121 K2
Forest Healthcare NHS Trust
WALTH E17................ 121 H1
Forest Healthcare Trust
WALTH E17................ 120 D3
Forest Healthcare Trust
WAN E11................ 121 J4
Forest Hill Business Centre
FSTH SE23................ 182 B5
Forest Hill Industrial Estate
FSTH SE23................ 182 B5
Forest Hill Secondary School
FSTH SE23................ 182 C6
Forest House Business Centre
WAN E11................ 121 L5
Forest Industrial Park
BARK/HLT IG6................ 103 H8
Forest Medical Centre
LOU IG10................ 82 B9
Forest Road Medical Centre
WALTH E17................ 120 E1
Forest Surgery
WALTH E17................ 101 H10
Forest Trading Estate
WALTH E17................ 120 C1
Forge Close Clinic
HAYES BR2................ 205 M8
Forge Lane Junior School
FELT TW13................ 175 M8
Forge Wood Industrial Estate
CRAWE RH10................ 284 C3
The Former Health Centre
CHARL SE7................ 162 A3
Forres CP School
HOD EN11................ 26 G10
Forster Park Primary School
CAT SE6................ 183 K6
Forte Crest Hotel
WDR/YW UB7................ 152 B4

The Fort House Surgery
WOT/HER KT12................ 197 H9
Fortismere School North Wing
MUSWH N10................ 98 A10
Fortismere Secondary School
MUSWH N10................ 118 B1
Fortune Theatre
HOL/ALD WC2B................ 11 M6
Forty Hill C of E School
EN EN1................ 79 P3
Fossdene Primary School
CHARL SE7................ 161 N4
Fosters Primary School
WELL DA16................ 163 M8
Foulds Primary School
BAR EN5................ 76 G7
The Foundling Museum
BMSBY WC1N................ 11 M1
Fountayne Road Health Centre
CLPT E5................ 119 P7
The Four Swanns JMI School
CHES/WCR EN8................ 62 D9
Foxborough School
DTCH/LGLY SL3................ 150 D4
Fox Primary School
KENS W8................ 8 E10
Framing Gallery
LVPST EC2M................ 13 K4
Frances Bardsley School
for Girls
ROM RM1................ 125 H4
Francis Bacon School
STAL AL1................ 38 C9
Franciscan Primary School
TOOT SW17................ 180 B7
The Franciscan Surgery
TOOT SW17................ 180 A7
Francis Combe
Secondary School
GSTN WD25................ 55 K8
Francis Graham Dixon Gallery
STNW/STAM N16................ 119 M8
Francis Holland School
BGVA SW1W................ 16 C6
Frank Barnes School
STJWD NW8................ 3 M4
Franklin Industrial Estate
PGE/AN SE20................ 204 B1
Frays College
UX/CGN UB8................ 131 M1
Freehold Industrial Estate
HSLWW TW4................ 175 K1
Freemantles School
CHERT KT16................ 195 H7
Free Trade Wharf
WAP E1W................ 140 C9
Fresh Wharf Estate
BARK IG11................ 142 E3
Freuchen Medical Centre
WLSDN NW10................ 136 C4
Freud Cafe Bar Gallery
LSQ/SEVD WC2H................ 11 K6
Freud Museum
HAMP NW3................ 3 K1
Friars Primary School
STHWK SE1................ 18 C1
Friends House
CAMTN NW1................ 5 J10
Friends of Bar Ilan University
GLDGN NW11................ 117 K6
Friends of Orpington Hospital
ORP BR6................ 227 H3
Friends of the Hebrew
University
CAMTN NW1................ 4 E6
Friern Barnet County School
FBAR/BDGN N11................ 98 A6
Friern Bridge Retail Park
FBAR/BDGN N11................ 98 C7
Frithwood Primary School
NTHWD HA6................ 92 G7
Froebel College
PUT/ROE SW15................ 178 D2
Frogmore House
WDSR SL4................ 149 M7
Frogmore Industrial Estate
HYS/HAR UB3................ 152 F1
Frogmore Industrial Estate
WLSDN NW10................ 135 P5
Frogmore Road Industrial Estate
HHS/BOV HP3................ 35 N9
Fryent Medical Centre
CDALE/KGS NW9................ 115 P5
Fryent Primary School
CDALE/KGS NW9................ 115 P5
Fulham Clinic
FUL/PGN SW6................ 14 D9
Fulham Cross Secondary School
FUL/PGN SW6................ 156 G6
Fulham Football Club
FUL/PGN SW6................ 156 C7
Fulham Medical Centre
FUL/PGN SW6................ 157 L6
Fulham Palace Chiropractic
& Health Centre
HMSMTH W6................ 156 G5
Fulham Preparatory School
FUL/PGN SW6................ 157 H8
Fulham Prep School
FUL/PGN SW6................ 157 H8
Fulham Primary School
FUL/PGN SW6................ 14 E10
Fullbrook County
Secondary School
ADL/WDHM KT15................ 215 K7
Fuller Smith & Turner Sports Club
CHSWK W4................ 156 B7
Fullwell Cross Health Centre
BARK/HLT IG6................ 102 F10
Fullwood Primary School
BARK/HLT IG6................ 122 F2
Fulmer County First School
DTCH/LGLY SL3................ 110 B9
Furnace Green Surgery
CRAWE RH10................ 284 A9
Furness School
SWLY BR8................ 186 G9
Furness Swanley Football Club
SWLY BR8................ 208 E4
The Furniture Gallery
HDN NW4................ 116 E2
The Furniture Gallery
STHGT/OAK N14................ 98 D2
Furzedown Primary School
TOOT SW17................ 180 C9
Furzefield Primary School
REDH RH1................ 258 E4
Furzehill School
BORE WD6................ 75 M8
Furze Infant School
CHDH RM6................ 123 P4

Gade Valley JMI School
HHW HP1................ 35 L5
Gaflac Sports Ground Pavilion
SUN TW16................ 197 H1
Gagliardi Gallery
WBPTN SW10................ 157 M6
Gainsborough Junior
& Infant School
HOM E9................ 140 E1
Gainsborouh Clinic
PLMGR N13................ 98 G4
Galleries
BAY/PAD W2................ 9 N6
Galleries
MYFR/PKLN W1K................ 10 D8
Gallery
KENS W8................ 15 J3
Gallery
MYFR/PKLN W1K................ 10 D8
The Gallery
NTGHL W11................ 8 D5
The Gallery at Lakeside
WTHK RM20................ 166 C3
The Gallery Cafe
NTGHL W11................ 8 C5
The Gallery House
MYFR/PICC W1J................ 10 F7
Gallery on the Heath
BKHTH/KID SE3................ 161 K8
The Gallery
BEAC HP9................ 88 D10
The Gallery
CAMTN NW1................ 5 H4
The Gallery
HNHL SE24................ 181 J2
The Gallery
IS N1................ 5 N8
The Gallery
IS N1................ 6 A8
The Gallery
IS N1................ 119 M10
The Gallery
ORP BR6................ 207 K7
The Gallery
SNWD SE25................ 203 N4
The Gallery
STP EC4M................ 12 D6
The Gallery
VX/NE SW8................ 17 M9
The Gallery
WDGN N22................ 98 G10
The Gallery
WOKN/KNAP GU21................ 231 H3
Galley Hill Industrial Estate
SWCM DA10................ 189 K1
Galleywall Primary School
BERM/RHTH SE16................ 160 A3
Galliard Primary School
ED N9................ 79 P10
Gallions Mount Primary School
WOOL/PLUM SE18................ 163 J4
The Gambia High Comm
KENS W8................ 15 H2
Gants Hill Medical Centre
GNTH/NBYPK IG2................ 122 D4
The Garden City Practice
WGCW AL8................ 22 G4
Garden Court Business Centre
WGCE AL7................ 23 J5
Gardener Industrial Estate
BECK BR3................ 182 D8
Garden Fields Junior Middle
& Infant School
STALW/RED AL3................ 38 C3
Garden Suburb Infant School
GLDGN NW11................ 117 J3
Garden Vets Surgery
EFNCH N2................ 117 M1
Garfield First School
WIM/MER SW19................ 179 M9
Garfield Primary School
FBAR/BDCN N11................ 98 C6
The Garratt Lane Surgery
WIM/MER SW19................ 179 L6
Garratt Park School
WAND/EARL SW18................ 179 M6
Garrick Industrial Centre
CDALE/KGS NW9................ 116 C3
Garston Clinic
WATN WD24................ 73 J2
Garston JMI School
GSTN WD25................ 73 L1
Garston Manor School
GSTN WD25................ 55 K8
Garston Medical Centre
GSTN WD25................ 73 K2
Garth Primary School
MRDN SM4................ 201 N5
Gascoigne Junior
& Infant School
BARK IG11................ 142 F3
Gascoyne Cecil Primary School
HAT AL10................ 40 E2
Gatehouse Surgery
BETH E2................ 140 C4
Gate House Surgery
BRXN/ST SW9................ 158 G9
The Gatehouse Theatre
HGT N6................ 118 B5
Gateway Industrial Estate
WLSDN NW10................ 136 C5
Gateway Primary School
STJWD NW8................ 9 M1
Gatton Park Business Centre
REDH RH1................ 258 C6
Gatwick Medical Centre
HORL RH6................ 280 C8
Gatwick Park Hospital
HORL RH6................ 279 P5
Gavin Graham Gallery
NTGHL W11................ 8 E7
Gayhurst Primary School
HACK E8................ 7 P3
Gayhurst School
CFSP/GDCR SL9................ 109 P2
Gaynes School
UPMR RM14................ 126 B10
Gazelda Industrial Estate
WAT WD17................ 73 K9
Gearies Infant School
GNTH/NBYPK IG2................ 122 D3
Gearies Junior School
GNTH/NBYPK IG2................ 122 E3
Geffrye Museum
BETH E2................ 7 L8
General Medical Clinics
WCHPL E1................ 13 L3
General Medical Practice
PECK SE15................ 160 A7
General Practice
WOOL/PLUM SE18................ 162 F3
Genesis Business Park
WOKS/MYFD GU22................ 232 F1

Genevieve the Gallery
EGH TW20 ...... 171 P8
Geoffrey Chaucer
Secondary School
STHWK SE1 ...... 18 G4
The Geoffrey Lloyd
Foulkes Clinic
IL IG1 ...... 122 D7
Geoffrey Whitworth Theatre
DART DA1 ...... 164 G10
George Abbot School
GU GU1 ...... 250 D8
George Eliot Junior
& Infant School
STJWD NW8 ...... 3 L5
George Green School
POP/IOD E14 ...... 161 H3
George Lowe Court
BAY/PAD W2 ...... 8 C3
George Mitchell
Comprehensive School
LEY E10 ...... 120 G6
George Mitchell School Annexe
LEY E10 ...... 120 G6
George Spicer Primary School
EN EN1 ...... 79 N7
George Tomlinson
Primary School
WAN E11 ...... 121 K6
Georgian Embassy
KENS W8 ...... 14 C2
Gerrards Cross C of E
Combined School
CFSP/GDCR SL9 ...... 110 B5
Gerrards Cross Golf Course
CFSP/GDCR SL9 ...... 110 D1
Gerrards Cross Sports Centre
CFSP/GDCR SL9 ...... 110 A5
The Ghana Embassy
HGT N6 ...... 118 C6
Gibson Business Centre
TOTM N17 ...... 99 N7
The Gibson Business Centre
TOTM N17 ...... 99 N8
Gidea Park College
GPK RM2 ...... 125 H1
Gidea Park Primary School
GPK RM2 ...... 124 C2
Gidea Park Sports Ground
GPK RM2 ...... 105 K10
The Gielgud Theatre
SOHO/CST W1F 11 J7
Giffin Business Centre
DEPT SE8 ...... 160 F6
Gifford Junior & Infant School
NTHLT UB5 ...... 133 N4
Giggs Hill Surgery
THDIT KT7 ...... 198 E7
Gilbert Colvin School
CLAY IG5 ...... 102 D9
Gilbert Scotts Primary School
SAND/SEL CR2 ...... 224 D4
Gillespie Primary School
FSBYPK N4 ...... 119 J8
Gillian House Surgery
PLMGR N13 ...... 99 H4
Gillmark Gallery
HERT/BAY SG13 ...... 25 K6
Girdlers' Hall
CITYW EC2V 12 F4
Girls School
WCHPL E1 ...... 13 H7
The Glade Business Centre
WTHK RM20 ...... 166 E4
Glade Primary School
CLAY IG5 ...... 102 C9
Gladesmore Community
Secondary School
SEVS/STOTM N15 ...... 119 P3
Gladstone Court Business Centre
VX/NE SW8 ...... 158 D7
Gladstone Medical Centre
CRICK NW2 ...... 116 C9
Gladstone Park Primary School
WLSDN NW10 ...... 116 E10
Glaziers/scientific Instrument
Makers Hall
STHWK SE1 ...... 12 G9
Glebe First & Middle School
KTN/HRWW/W HA3 ...... 115 J2
Glebe Primary School
HGDN/ICK UB10 ...... 112 E9
Glebe School
WWKM BR4 ...... 205 J8
Gleen Lecky Health Centre
PUT/ROE SW15 ...... 156 G10
Glenbrook Junior
& Infant School
CLAP SW4 ...... 180 E2
Glencairn Sports Club
FBAR/BDGN N11 ...... 98 D8
Glendower School
SKENS SW7 ...... 15 K5
Glenesk House
Preparatory School
EHSLY KT24 ...... 252 E1
Glenham College
IL IG1 ...... 122 D7
Glenlyn Medical Centre
E/WMO/HCT KT8 ...... 198 B5
Glenthorne High School
CHEAM SM3 ...... 201 K8
Globe Industrial Estate
GRAYS RM17 ...... 167 P5
Globe Theatre
STHWK SE1 ...... 12 D8
Globe Town Surgery
BETH E2 ...... 140 B5
Globe Wharf
BERM/RHTH SE16 ...... 140 C10
Globe Works Industrial Estate
GRAYS RM17 ...... 168 A4
Gloucester Primary School
PECK SE15 ...... 159 M6
Glyn A D T Technology School
EW KT17 ...... 220 C7
Goal Farm Golf Club
CHOB/PIR GU24 ...... 230 C7
Gobions JMI School
CRW RM5 ...... 104 E7
Godalming Leisure Centre
RGODL GU7 ...... 267 M10
Godolphin County First School
SL SL1 ...... 129 J7
Godolphin County Middle School
SL SL1 ...... 129 J8
Godolphin & Latymer School
HMSMTH W6 ...... 156 E3
Godwin Junior School
FSTGT E7 ...... 121 N9
Godwin Primary School
DAGW RM9 ...... 143 P2

Goffs Oak JMI School
CHESW EN7 ...... 61 J4
Goffs School
CHESW EN7 ...... 61 P5
Goldbeaters School
EDGE HA8 ...... 96 A9
Golden Hinde
STHWK SE1 ...... 12 G9
Golders Green Beth Hamedrash
Synagogue
GLDGN NW11 ...... 117 H5
Golders Green College
of Business Studies
GLDGN NW11 ...... 117 K6
Golders Green Health Centre
GLDGN NW11 ...... 117 L6
Golders Hill Health Centre
EFNCH N2 ...... 117 M4
Goldhawk Industrial Estate
SHB W12 ...... 156 E2
Goldings Hill Clinic
LOU IG10 ...... 82 D7
Goldsmiths College
BROCKY SE4 ...... 160 E9
Goldsmiths College
DEPT SE8 ...... 160 F5
Goldsmiths College
LEW SE13 ...... 161 K10
Goldsmiths College
NWCR SE14 ...... 160 E7
Goldsmiths College
Sports Ground
SCUP DA14 ...... 186 A6
Goldsmiths College University
of London
NWCR SE14 ...... 160 D7
Goldsmiths Hall
STBT EC1A 12 E5
Goldsworth CP School
WOKN/KNAP GU21 ...... 231 P3
Goldsworth Park Trading Estate
WOKN/KNAP GU21 ...... 231 M2
Goldsworth Rd Industrial Estate
WOKN/KNAP GU21 ...... 232 A3
Golf Centre
STMC/STPC BR5 ...... 207 N2
Golf Club Club House
BF/WBF KT14 ...... 215 J9
Golf Club Flat
NTHWD HA6 ...... 92 E8
Golf Club House
REIG RH2 ...... 256 F10
Golf Course
DEN/HRF UB9 ...... 110 G4
Golf Course
RKW/CH/CXG WD3 ...... 72 D6
Golf School
KTBR SW1X 16 B2
The Gomshall Gallery
SHGR GU5 ...... 270 E5
Gonville School
THHTH CR7 ...... 202 C5
The Gooday Gallery
RCHPK/HAM TW10 ...... 177 J2
Goodinge Health Centre
HOLWY N7 ...... 5 L1
Goodrich Junior & Infant School
EDUL SE22 ...... 181 P2
The Good Shepherd
RC Primary School
SHB W12 ...... 156 C1
Good Shepherd RC School
BMLY BR1 ...... 183 L7
Goodwyn School
MLHL NW7 ...... 96 D6
Goose Green Trading Estate
EDUL SE22 ...... 159 P10
Gordonbrook Primary School
BROCKY SE4 ...... 182 F1
Gordon Hospital
WEST SW1P 17 J6
Gordon House Health Centre
WEA W13 ...... 135 H10
Gordon Infant School
IL IG1 ...... 122 G8
Gordon Primary School
ELTH/MOT SE9 ...... 162 C10
Goresbrook Leisure Centre
DAGW RM9 ...... 143 N3
Gorhambury
STALW/RED AL3 ...... 37 J3
Gorringe Park Middle School
MTCM CR4 ...... 202 B1
Gosbury Hill Health Centre
CHSGTN KT9 ...... 219 K1
Gosden House Special School
SHGR GU5 ...... 268 B9
Gospel Oak Primary School
HAMP NW3 ...... 118 B9
Gossops Green Clinic
CRAWW RH11 ...... 283 J10
Gossops Green First
& Middle School
CRAWW RH11 ...... 283 K8
Government Offices
WHALL SW1A 11 L9
The Gowan Gallery
SBW CM21 ...... 29 P7
Grace Business Centre
MTCM CR4 ...... 202 A6
Grace Theatre at the Latchmere
BTSEA SW11 ...... 158 A10
Graduate School
of Management
TOTM N17 ...... 99 N9
Grafton Primary School
BCTR RM8 ...... 123 P7
Grafton Primary School
HOLWY N7 ...... 118 F8
Grahame Park Health Centre
CDALE/KGS NW9 ...... 96 B9
Grahame Park Junior
& Infant School
CDALE/KGS NW9 ...... 96 B9
Graham Gallery
IS N1 ...... 6 C7
Granard Business Centre
EDGE HA8 ...... 96 B7
Granard Primary School
PUT/ROE SW15 ...... 178 E2
Granby Sports Club
ELTH/MOT SE9 ...... 184 B8
Grand Avenue Infant
& Primary School
BRYLDS KT5 ...... 199 P6
Grand Drive Surgery
RYNPK SW20 ...... 200 F3
Grande Vitesse Industrial Centre
STHWK SE1 ...... 12 D10
Grand Union Industrial Estate
WLSDN NW10 ...... 135 N4
Grange CP School
ADL/WDHM KT15 ...... 215 K6

Grange First & Middle School
EA W5 ...... 155 J1
Grange First & Middle School
RYLN/HDSTN HA2 ...... 114 A6
Grange Infant School
CAN/RD E16 ...... 141 L5
The Grange Museum
CRICK NW2 ...... 116 C9
Grange Park Clinic
YEAD UB4 ...... 132 G6
Grange Park Junior School
YEAD UB4 ...... 132 G6
Grange Park Preparatory School
WCHMH N21 ...... 79 J10
Grange Park Primary School
ENC/FH EN2 ...... 79 H8
Grange Park Surgery
LEY E10 ...... 121 H7
Grange Primary School
STHWK SE1 ...... 19 J4
Grange Street Doctors Surgery
STALW/RED AL3 ...... 38 C5
Grangewood
Independent School
FSTGT E7 ...... 141 P2
Grangewood Junior School
RSLP HA4 ...... 113 H3
Granton Primary School
STRHM/NOR SW16 ...... 180 D10
Granville House Practice
REDH RH1 ...... 257 P9
Granville Road Industrial Estate
CRICK NW2 ...... 117 J7
The Granville School
SEV TN13 ...... 247 H9
The Grapevine Gallery
REDH RH1 ...... 258 A9
Grasmere Primary School
STNW/STAM N16 ...... 119 M9
Grasshoppers Rugby
Football Club
ISLW TW7 ...... 154 E5
Grasvenor Avenue Infant School
BAR EN5 ...... 77 K10
Gravel Hill Primary School
BXLYHS DA6 ...... 186 C1
Graveney School
TOOT SW17 ...... 180 C9
Gravesend County Court
GVE DA12 ...... 190 E2
Gravesend Cricket Club
GVW DA11 ...... 190 D3
Gravesend Grammar
School for Boys
GVE DA12 ...... 190 G3
Gravesend Grammar
School for Girls
GVW DA11 ...... 190 D4
Gravesend Museum
GVW DA11 ...... 190 E2
Gravesend & Northfleet
Football Club
GVW DA11 ...... 189 P2
Gravesend & North Kent Hospital
GVW DA11 ...... 190 D2
Gravesend Rowing Club
GVE DA12 ...... 190 F2
Gravesend Yacht Club
GVE DA12 ...... 190 G2
Gravesham Borough Council
GVW DA11 ...... 189 P4
Gravesham Borough Council
GVW DA11 ...... 190 D8
Graves Yard Industrial Estate
WELL DA16 ...... 163 K8
Grays Athletic Football Club
GRAYS RM17 ...... 167 N5
Grays Business Centre
GRAYS RM17 ...... 167 P2
Grays Convent High School
GRAYS RM17 ...... 167 N5
Grays County Court
GRAYS RM17 ...... 167 M5
Grays Farm Primary School
STMC/STPC BR5 ...... 207 L1
The Grays Gm School
GRAYS RM17 ...... 167 N2
Grays Health Centre
GRAYS RM17 ...... 167 M4
Grays Inn Medical Practice
FSBYW WC1X 11 P2
Grazebrook Primary School
STNW/STAM N16 ...... 119 M7
Great Bookham County
Infant School
GT/LBKH KT23 ...... 253 P2
Great Bookham Middle School
GT/LBKH KT23 ...... 253 P2
Greater London Council
CLAP SW4 ...... 180 C1
Greater London Council
HOM E9 ...... 120 D9
Great Jubilee Wharf
WAP E1W 140 B10
Great Ormond Street
Childrens Hospital
BMSBY WC1N 11 M2
Great Stony School
CHONG CM5 ...... 67 P3
Great Synagogue
WCHPL E1 ...... 13 P4
Greenacres Primary School
ELTH/MOT SE9 ...... 184 D5
Green Business Centre
EGH TW20 ...... 172 V7
The Green C of E Primary School
TOTM N17 ...... 119 N1
Green Dragon School
BTFD TW8 ...... 155 K4
Green End Business Centre
RKW/CH/CXG WD3 ...... 71 K3
Greenfield Medical Centre
CRICK NW2 ...... 117 H8
Greenfield Primary School
OXHEY WD19 ...... 93 K6
Greenfield School
WOKS/MYFD GU22 ...... 232 B5
Greenfields Junior School
SHB W12 ...... 136 C9
Greenfields Special School
MUSWH N10 ...... 98 A3
Greenford Avenue
Medical Centre
HNWL W7 ...... 134 D7
Greenford Green Clinic
NTHLT UB5 ...... 114 D10
Greenford High School
STHL UB1 ...... 133 P5
Greenford Road Medical Centre
GFD/PVL UB6 ...... 134 C4
Greenford Synagogue
GFD/PVL UB6 ...... 134 B5

Greengate Medical Centre
PLSTW E13 ...... 141 N5
Greengrove College
STHGT/OAK N14 ...... 98 F3
Green Haven Surgery
ELTH/MOT SE9 ...... 185 H3
Greenheath Business Centre
BETH E2 ...... 140 A5
Greenhill College
HRW HA1 ...... 114 D5
Greenhill Park Medical Centre
WLSDN NW10 ...... 136 B3
Greenhithe Health Clinic
GRH DA9 ...... 188 C1
Green Lane Primary School
WPK KT4 ...... 200 E7
Green Lanes School
HAT AL10 ...... 22 C10
Greenleaf Primary School
WALTH E17 ...... 120 E1
Greenmead Primary School
PUT/ROE SW15 ...... 178 E1
Greens Antique Galleries
KENS W8 ...... 8 F10
The Green School for Girls
ISLW TW7 ...... 154 F6
Greenshaw High School
SUT SM1 ...... 201 M9
Greenshield Industrial Estate
CAN/RD E16 ...... 141 M10
Greenside Primary School
SHB W12 ...... 156 D1
Greenslade Primary School
WOOL/PLUM SE18 ...... 162 G5
Green Street Primary School
ORP BR6 ...... 227 J3
The Green Surgery
WHTN TW2 ...... 176 D5
Greenvale Primary School
SAND/SEL CR2 ...... 224 C7
Green Waters Surgery
STAN HA7 ...... 94 G5
Greenway County First School
BERK HP4 ...... 33 M5
Greenway CP School
CSHM HP5 ...... 50 C3
Greenway School
UX/CGN UB8 ...... 131 N4
Greenwich Borough Council
GNWCH SE10 ...... 161 H5
Greenwich Borough Museum
WOOL/PLUM SE18 ...... 163 J4
Greenwich Centre Business Park
DEPT SE8 ...... 160 G6
Greenwich College
GNWCH SE10 ...... 161 H6
Greenwich Community College
WOOL/PLUM SE18 ...... 162 G5
Greenwich Community College
WOOL/PLUM SE18 ...... 162 E3
Greenwich Coroners Office
GNWCH SE10 ...... 160 G6
Greenwich Council
ELTH/MOT SE9 ...... 184 C2
Greenwich District Hospital
BKHTH/KID SE3 ...... 161 K5
Greenwich Gallery
GNWCH SE10 ...... 161 H5
Greenwich Health Authority
THMD SE28 ...... 143 K9
Greenwich Health Authority
WOOL/PLUM SE18 ...... 162 D8
Greenwich Healthcare NHS Trust
CHARL SE7 ...... 162 B6
Greenwich Healthcare NHS Trust
WOOL/PLUM SE18 ...... 162 E8
Greenwich Healthcare NHS Trust
WOOL/PLUM SE18 ...... 163 H4
Greenwich Industrial Estate
CHARL SE7 ...... 161 N3
Greenwich Natural Health Centre
GNWCH SE10 ...... 161 H6
Greenwich Park School
GNWCH SE10 ...... 161 H6
Greenwich Theatre & Art Gallery
GNWCH SE10 ...... 161 J5
Greenwood First School
MTCM CR4 ...... 202 E3
Greenwood Park Leisure Centre
LCOL/BKTW AL2 ...... 56 A1
Greenwood Primary School
NTHLT UB5 ...... 114 B10
Greenwood School
WOOL/PLUM SE18 ...... 163 H7
Greenwood Theatre
STHWK SE1 ...... 19 H1
Green Wrythe Primary School
CAR SM5 ...... 201 N6
Grenfell Primary School
WCHPL E1 ...... 140 A8
Gresham College
FLST/FETLN EC4A 12 A4
Gresham School
SAND/SEL CR2 ...... 223 N8
Gresham Way Industrial Estate
WIM/MER SW19 ...... 179 L6
Gresswell Street School
FUL/PGN SW6 ...... 156 G7
The Greville CP School
ASHTD KT21 ...... 237 L3
Grey Coat Hosp
WESTW SW1E 16 G7
The Greycoat Hospital
WEST SW1P 17 J7
Grey Coat Hospital Upper School
WEST SW1P 17 J4
Grey Court School
RCHPK/HAM TW10 ...... 177 H6
Greystone House Practice
REDH RH1 ...... 257 P9
Griffen Manor School
WOOL/PLUM SE18 ...... 163 H7
Griffin Galleries
PIN HA5 ...... 93 K10
Grimsdyke First & Middle School
PIN HA5 ...... 93 N7
Grimsdyke Golf Club
PIN HA5 ...... 93 P6
Grinling Gibbons Primary School
DEPT SE8 ...... 160 E5
Grist Memorial Sports Club
E/WMO/HCT KT8 ...... 198 D5
Grocers' Hall
CITYW EC2V 12 G6
Grosvenor Gallery
NTHWD HA6 ...... 92 F7
Grosvenor Hospitals
MLHL NW7 ...... 116 E3
Grosvenor House Surgery
HNWL W7 ...... 134 F10
Group Medical Practice
HAMP NW3 ...... 4 B4

Grove Health Centre
KENS W8 ...... 8 F9
The Grove Health Centre
HMSMTH W6 ...... 156 E1
Grovehill Medical Centre
HHNE HP2 ...... 36 A2
Grove House Primary School
WNWD SE27 ...... 181 J5
The Grove Infant School
HARP AL5 ...... 20 C3
The Grove JMI School
HARP AL5 ...... 20 C3
Grovelands Business Centre
HHNE HP2 ...... 36 D4
Grovelands Priory Hospital
STHGT/OAK N14 ...... 98 F2
Grovelands School
WOT/HER KT12 ...... 197 J6
Grove Medical Centre
DEPT SE8 ...... 160 D3
The Grove Medical Centre
ARCH N19 ...... 118 C2
Grove Medical Practice
HMSMTH W6 ...... 156 F2
The Grove Medical Practice
NTHLT UB5 ...... 114 A10
Grove Park Primary School
CHSWK W4 ...... 155 P5
Grove Park School
CDALE/KGS NW9 ...... 115 P2
Grove Road Primary School
HSLW TW3 ...... 153 P10
The Groves Medical Centre
NWMAL KT3 ...... 200 B3
Grove Vale Primary School
EDUL SE22 ...... 159 N10
Grove Village Medical Centre
EBED/NFELT TW14 ...... 174 F4
Grrck Theatre
LSQ/SEVD WC2H 11 K8
Grundy Park Leisure Centre
CHES/WCR EN8 ...... 62 D6
Guardian Angels RC
Primary School
BOW E3 ...... 140 D6
Guardian Business Centre
HARH RM3 ...... 105 L8
Guardian Newspapers
POP/IOD E14 ...... 160 G1
Guards' Chapel and Museum
WHALL SW1A 17 J2
Guildford Borough Council
GU GU1 ...... 250 B6
Guildford Borough Council
GUW GU2 ...... 267 P3
Guildford Castle
GU GU1 ...... 268 A2
Guildford County College of
Further & Higher Education
GU GU1 ...... 250 A9
Guildford County School
GUW GU2 ...... 267 N2
Guildford Golf Club
GU GU1 ...... 250 F10
Guildford High School for Girls
GU GU1 ...... 250 B10
Guildford Hockey & Cricket Club
GUW GU2 ...... 249 P10
Guildford Industrial Estate
GUW GU2 ...... 249 M9
The Guildford Nuffield Hospital
GUW GU2 ...... 249 K10
Guildford Rowing Club
GU GU1 ...... 268 A3
Guildhall School of Music & Drama
BARB EC2Y 12 F3
Guildhall University
WCHPL E1 ...... 13 P5
Guinea Consulate
MYFR/PKLN W1K 10 C7
Gumley House Convent School
for Girls
ISLW TW7 ...... 154 F9
Gunnersbury Catholic School
for Boys
BTFD TW8 ...... 155 J5
Gunnersbury Park Museum
ACT W3 ...... 155 M2
Gurnell Leisure Centre
WEA W13 ...... 134 E5
Gurnell Middle School
WEA W13 ...... 134 E7
Guru Gobind Singh
Khalsa College
CHIG IG7 ...... 102 C2
Guru Nanak Medical Centre
STHL UB1 ...... 133 M10
Guru Nanak Sports Club
GVE DA12 ...... 190 F3
Guyana High Commission
NTCHL W11 ...... 8 G9
Guys Hospital
STHWK SE1 ...... 13 H10
Guys & St Thomas Hospital Trust
LBTH SE11 ...... 18 C5
Guys & St Thomas Hospital Trust
PECK SE15 ...... 160 B6
Gwyn Jones Primary School
WAN E11 ...... 121 J5
G X Superbowl
EHAM E6 ...... 142 D7
Haberdashers Askes
Hatcham Boys School
NWCR SE14 ...... 160 C8
Haberdashers Askes
Hatcham Girls School
NWCR SE14 ...... 160 D7
Haberdashers Askes School
for Girls
BORE WD6 ...... 74 C7
Haberdashers' Hall
CITYW EC2V 12 F5
Haberdashers Rugby Club
BORE WD6 ...... 75 L6
Hackbridge Junior School
WLGTN SM6 ...... 202 B8
Hackney African Caribbean
Disability Association
HOM E9 ...... 120 C10
Hackney Borough Council
CLPT E5 ...... 119 P7
Hackney Borough Council
HOM E9 ...... 140 B1
Hackney Business Centre
HACK E8 ...... 140 A1
Hackney Community College
CLPT E5 ...... 120 A8
Hackney Community College
IS N1 ...... 7 J4
Hackney Council
BETH E2 ...... 7 L8

Hackney Council
for Voluntary Service
HACK E8 .... 7 L1
Hackney Empire Theatre Variety
HACK E8 .... 140 A1
Hackney Hospital
HOM E9 .... 120 D10
The Hackney Museum
HOM E9 .... 140 B3
Hackney Racial Equality Council
HACK E8 .... 7 L1
Hackney Sports Centre
HOM E9 .... 120 F9
Hacton Infant School
HCH RM12 .... 125 M9
Hadley Wood School
EBAR EN4 .... 77 M4
The Haelan Clinic
CEND/HSY/T N8 .... 118 E4
Haggerston School
BETH E2 .... 7 M7
Haggerston Swimming Pool
BETH E2 .... 7 M6
Hague Primary School
BETH E2 .... 140 A6
Haileybury College
HERT/BAY SG13 .... 26 C9
Hailey Hall School
HOD EN11 .... 26 E9
Haimo Primary School
ELTH/MOT SE9 .... 184 A1
Hainault Forest High School
CHIG IG7 .... 103 K6
Hainault Industrial Estate
BARK/HLT IG6 .... 103 M6
Hakim Qureshi Clinic
NWDGN UB2 .... 153 N1
Hales Gallery
DEPT SE8 .... 160 F6
Haling Manor High School
CROY/NA CR0 .... 223 J4
Halley Primary School
POP/IOD E14 .... 140 D7
Hallfield Clinic NHS
BAY/PAD W2 .... 9 J6
Hallfield Estate
BAY/PAD W2 .... 9 H6
Hallfield Junior & Infant School
BAY/PAD W2 .... 9 H6
Halliford Health Clinic
SHPTN TW17 .... 196 F4
Halliford School
SHPTN TW17 .... 196 D7
The Hall Junior School
HAMP NW3 .... 3 M2
Hallmark Trading Estate
WBLY HA9 .... 115 P9
Hall Mead School
UPMR RM14 .... 126 C5
Halls
CANST EC4R 12 C7
Halls Business Centre
HYS/HAR UB3 .... 153 H2
Hall School Wimbledon
PUT/ROE SW15 .... 178 D6
The Hall Senior School
HAMP NW3 .... 3 M2
Hallsville Primary School
CAN/RD E16 .... 141 M8
Halstead Place School
RSEV TN14 .... 227 P8
Halstead Preparatory School
WOKN/KNAP GU21 .... 232 C1
Halstead Primary School
RSEV TN14 .... 228 A8
Halstow Primary School
GNWCH SE10 .... 161 L4
Hambrough First School
STHL UB1 .... 133 M10
Hamer Indoor Market
BOW E3 .... 140 E4
Ham Health Clinic
RCHPK/HAM TW10 .... 177 H6
Hamlet International
Industrial Estate
ERITH DA8 .... 164 E4
Hammel House Surgery
TOOT SW17 .... 179 P7
The Hammersmith Hospitals
NHS Trust
SHB W12 .... 136 D8
Hammersmith Industrial Estate
HMSMTH W6 .... 156 F5
Hammersmith Physio
& Sportsinjury Clinic
HMSMTH W6 .... 156 F3
Hammersmith & West Kensington
Synagogue
HMSMTH W6 .... 156 G2
Hammersmith & West London
College
WKENS W14 .... 14 B5
The Hammond Junior Mixed
Infant School
HHNE HP2 .... 36 A2
Ham & Petersham Cricket Club
RCHPK/HAM TW10 .... 177 J7
Hampstead Cricket Club
KIL/WHAMP NW6 .... 117 L10
Hampstead Garden
Suburb Synagogue
EFNCH N2 .... 117 M3
The Hampstead Group Practice
HAMP NW3 .... 117 P10
Hampstead Medical Centre
HAMP NW3 .... 117 M9
Hampstead School
CRICK NW2 .... 117 H9
Hampstead Synagogue
KIL/WHAMP NW6 .... 2 F1
Hampton Community College
HPTN TW12 .... 175 P8
Hampton Court Palace
E/WMO/HCT KT8 .... 198 E3
Hampton Farm Industrial Estate
FELT TW13 .... 175 M6
Hampton Football Club
HPTN TW12 .... 198 A1
The Hampton Hill Gallery
HPTN TW12 .... 176 B8
Hampton Hill Junior
Mixed School
HPTN TW12 .... 176 B8
Hampton Infants School
HPTN TW12 .... 175 N10
Hampton Junior School
HPTN TW12 .... 197 P1
The Hampton Medical Centre
HPTN TW12 .... 175 P10
Hampton School
HPTN TW12 .... 175 P8
Hampton Swimming Baths
HPTN TW12 .... 176 B10

Hampton Wick Infants School
KUT KT1 .... 177 H10
Hampton Wick Surgery
KUT KT1 .... 199 H1
Hamshere Gallery
BARN SW13 .... 156 C8
Ham Surgery
RCHPK/HAM TW10 .... 177 H6
Handsworth Health Clinic
CHING E4 .... 101 J7
Handsworth Primary School
CHING E4 .... 101 J7
Hanover Primary School
IS N1 .... 6 D7
Hanover Trading Estate
HOLWY N7 .... 118 F10
Hanover West Industrial Estate
WLSDN NW10 .... 135 P5
Hanworth Trading Estate
FELT TW13 .... 175 M6
Happy Valley Industrial Estate
KGLGY WD4 .... 54 C4
Harbinger County
Primary School
POP/IOD E14 .... 160 F3
Harborough School
ARCH N19 .... 118 D7
Hardware Gallery
HGT N6 .... 118 D5
Harefield Cricket Club
DEN/HRF UB9 .... 91 N10
Harefield Health Centre
DEN/HRF UB9 .... 91 M9
Harefield Hospital
DEN/HRF UB9 .... 91 M9
Harefield Infant School
DEN/HRF UB9 .... 91 L9
Harefield Junior School
DEN/HRF UB9 .... 91 M9
Harenc School
SCUP DA14 .... 185 M8
Haresfoot Prep School
BERK HP4 .... 33 N8
Haresfoot Senior School
BERK HP4 .... 34 D3
Hare Street County Junior
& Infant School
HLWW/ROY CM19 .... 46 F1
Harewood Down Golf Club
CSTG HP8 .... 69 N8
Hargrave Park Primary School
ARCH N19 .... 118 D7
Haringey Arts Council
ED N9 .... 100 A3
Haringey Community
Health Clinic
SEVS/STOTM N15 .... 119 N1
Haringey Council
SEVS/STOTM N15 .... 119 N1
Haringey Health Care NHS Trust
SEVS/STOTM N15 .... 119 N2
Haringey Magistrate Court
HGT N6 .... 118 B4
Harkness Industrial Estate
BORE WD6 .... 75 M8
Harland First School
WIM/MER SW19 .... 201 M2
Harlequin Football Club
WHTN TW2 .... 176 D3
Harlequin Gallery
GNWCH SE10 .... 160 C6
Harlequin Shopping Centre
WAT WD17 .... 73 K8
Harlequin Theatre & Cinema
REDH RH1 .... 258 B9
Harlesden Primary School
WLSDN NW10 .... 136 B4
Harley Medical Centre
CAVSQ/HST W1G 10 E5
The Harley Medical Centre
CANST EC4R 12 F7
The Harley Street Clinic
CAVSQ/HST W1G 10 E3
Harlington Upper School
HYS/HAR UB3 .... 152 E3
Harlowbury School
HLWE CM17 .... 29 N7
Harlow Business Park
HLWW/ROY CM19 .... 46 B1
Harlow College
HLW CM20 .... 29 H10
Harlow College
HLW CM20 .... 46 F1
Harlow Museum
HLWS CM18 .... 46 F2
Harlow Rugby Football Club
HLW CM20 .... 28 E9
Harlow Sports Centre
HLW CM20 .... 28 F9
Harlow Sports Centre
HLW CM20 .... 28 C9
Harlow Urban District
Swimming Pool
HLW CM20 .... 29 H9
Harlyn School
PIN HA5 .... 113 J1
Harold Court School
HARH RM3 .... 105 P8
The Harold Macmillan
Medical Centre
HRW HA1 .... 114 C5
Harold Wood Clinic
HARH RM3 .... 105 N10
Harold Wood JMI School
HARH RM3 .... 125 P1
Harp Business Centre
CRICK NW2 .... 116 D7
Harpenden Common Golf Club
HARP AL5 .... 20 A5
Harpenden Memorial Hospital
HARP AL5 .... 20 A1
Harperbury Hospital
RAD WD7 .... 57 H7
Harpley Special School
WCHPL E1 .... 140 B6
Harrington Hill Primary School
CLPT E5 .... 120 A6
Harris City Technology College
NRWD SE19 .... 203 N1
Harrodian School
BARN SW13 .... 156 C6
Harrods Store
CHEL SW3 .... 16 A3
Harrow Borough Football Club
RYLN/HDSTN HA2 .... 113 P9
Harrow Central Mosque
HRW HA1 .... 114 E2
Harrow Cricket Club
HRW HA1 .... 114 D9
Harrow Crown Courts
HRW HA1 .... 114 C1
Harrow Health Authority
RYLN/HDSTN HA2 .... 114 D7

Harrow Heritage Museum
RYLN/HDSTN HA2 .... 114 B1
Harrow High School
HRW HA1 .... 114 F4
Harrow & Hillingdon
Health Authority
STAN HA7 .... 95 J9
Harrow & Hillingdon Healthcare
NHS Trust
KTN/HRWW/W HA3 .... 94 F9
Harrow & Hillingdon Healthcare
NHS Trust
UX/CGN UB8 .... 131 N5
Harrow Leisure Centre
KTN/HRWW/W HA3 .... 114 E1
Harrow Magistrates Court
HRW HA1 .... 114 E2
Harrow Road Health Centre
BAY/PAD W2 .... 8 F3
Harrow Rugby Football Club
STAN HA7 .... 94 G4
Harrow School
HRW HA1 .... 114 D5
Harrow School
RYLN/HDSTN HA2 .... 114 D7
Harrow Superbowl
RYLN/HDSTN HA2 .... 114 A3
Harrow Town Cricket Club
RYLN/HDSTN HA2 .... 113 P6
Harry Gosling Primary School
WCHPL E1 .... 13 P6
Hart Gallery
IS N1 .... 6 C5
Hartley CP School
HART DA3 .... 211 K6
Hartley Primary School
EHAM E6 .... 142 B3
Hartsbourne JMI School
BUSH WD23 .... 94 C3
Hartspring Industrial Park
GSTN WD25 .... 73 P6
Hartspring Sports Centre
BUSH WD23 .... 73 P6
The Hartswood Clinic
RBRW/HUT CM13 .... 106 G7
Harven School
WOKS/MYFD GU22 .... 232 D3
Harvey Centre
HLW CM20 .... 46 F1
Harvington School
EA W5 .... 135 H8
Haselbury Junior & Infant School
ED N9 .... 99 M4
Haselrigge School
CLAP SW4 .... 158 E10
Haslemere Business Centre
EN EN1 .... 80 A8
Haslemere Industrial Estate
HLWW/ROY CM19 .... 46 D2
Haslemere Industrial Estate
WAND/EARL SW18 .... 179 L5
Haslewood Junior School
HOD EN11 .... 44 F2
Hasmonean Boys High School
HDN NW4 .... 96 G10
Hasmonean High School
Girls Section
MLHL NW7 .... 96 D9
Hasmonean Primary School
HDN NW4 .... 116 G3
Hastings Clinic
BRXS/STRHM SW2 .... 180 G1
Hastingwood Trading Estate
UED N18 .... 100 D7
Hatcham Mews Business Centre
NWCR SE14 .... 160 C6
Hatch End High School
KTN/HRWW/W HA3 .... 94 A8
Hatfield House
BRKMPK AL9 .... 40 G4
Hatfield London County Club
BRKMPK AL9 .... 42 A5
The Hat Gallery
HACK E8 .... 7 P6
Hatton Medical Practice
EBED/NFELT TW14 .... 174 F2
Hatton School
REDBR IG4 .... 122 A1
Havelock First School
NWDGN UB2 .... 153 N2
Haven Green Clinic
EA W5 .... 135 J8
Haverfield Surgery
KGLGY WD4 .... 54 B5
Havering College of Further
& Higher Education
EMPK RM11 .... 125 M2
Havering College of Further
& Higher Education
EMPK RM11 .... 125 J5
Havering College of Further
& Higher Education
HARH RM3 .... 105 N5
Havering Court Nursing Home
ROM RM1 .... 104 F6
Havering Cricket Club
ABR/ST RM4 .... 84 C7
Havering Hospitals NHS Trust
HARH RM3 .... 105 M9
Havering Magistrates Court
ROM RM1 .... 124 F2
Havering Sixth Form College
EMPK RM11 .... 125 N6
Haverstock School
CAMTN NW1 .... 4 C2
Hawes Down Clinic
WWKM BR4 .... 205 J9
Hawes Down Junior
& Infant School
WWKM BR4 .... 205 J8
Hawkedale GM School
SUN TW16 .... 196 G3
Hawker Galleries
AMSS HP7 .... 68 F5
Hawkins Clinic
EW KT17 .... 238 F1
Hawkins Clinic
PUT/ROE SW15 .... 156 G10
Hawkins Clinic
RYNPK SW20 .... 200 G1
Hawksmoor Gm Primary School
THMD SE28 .... 143 L9
Hawkswood School & Centre
CHING E4 .... 81 H9
Hawridge & Cholesbury
C of E Primary School
CSHM HP5 .... 32 C7
The Hawth Theatre & Conference
Complex
CRAWE RH10 .... 284 A8
Haydon School
PIN HA5 .... 112 G1

Haydons Medical Practice
WIM/MER SW19 .... 179 L9
Hayes Bridge Middle School
STHL UB1 .... 133 M10
Hayes Bridge Retail Park
HYS/HAR UB3 .... 133 K9
Hayes Cricket Club
HYS/HAR UB3 .... 132 G8
Hayes Football Club
HYS/HAR UB3 .... 132 G9
Hayes Grove Priory Hospital
HAYES BR2 .... 205 M9
Hayes Manor Secondary School
HYS/HAR UB3 .... 132 E8
Hayes Park Junior
& Infant School
YEAD UB4 .... 132 G6
Hayes Primary School
HAYES BR2 .... 205 N8
The Hayes Primary School
PUR/KEN CR8 .... 241 J2
Hayes School
HAYES BR2 .... 205 N9
Hayes Social and Sports Club
HYS/HAR UB3 .... 132 G9
Haymerle School
PECK SE15 .... 19 N10
Hays Galleria
STHWK SE1 .... 13 J9
Hayward Gallery
STHWK SE1 .... 11 P10
Hazeldene Medical Centre
WBLY HA9 .... 135 N1
Hazel Grove JMI School
HAT AL10 .... 40 C7
Hazelhurst School
RYNPK SW20 .... 200 G1
Hazelwick School
CRAWE RH10 .... 284 B5
Hazelwood Infant School
PLMGR N13 .... 99 J5
Hazelwood School
OXTED RH8 .... 261 M7
Healy Medical Centre
CLPT E5 .... 120 A6
The Healy Practice
EFNCH N2 .... 118 A2
Hearnville Primary School
BAL SW12 .... 180 B4
The Heart Hospital
CAVSQ/HST W1G 10 D4
Heathbrook Primary School
VX/NE SW8 .... 158 D8
Heath Business Centre
HSLW TW3 .... 154 B10
Heath Business Centre
REDH RH1 .... 276 B9
Heathcote Medical Centre
KWD/TDW/WH KT20 .... 238 G8
Heathcote School
CHING E4 .... 101 K3
Heatherley School of Fine Art
WBPTN SW10 .... 157 M6
Heathermount School
ASC SL5 .... 192 C6
Heathfield College
HAYES BR2 .... 225 P3
Heathfield Junior School
WHTN TW2 .... 175 P4
Heathfield School
PIN HA5 .... 113 L4
Heath House Preparatory School
BKHTH/KID SE3 .... 161 L8
Heathland School
HSLWW TW4 .... 175 N2
Heathlands School
for Deaf Children
STALW/RED AL3 .... 38 D3
Heathmere Primary School
PUT/ROE SW15 .... 178 D4
Heathrow Airport
WDR/YW UB7 .... 151 M7
Heathrow International
Trading Estate
HSLWW TW4 .... 153 J9
Heathrow Medical Centre
HYS/HAR UB3 .... 152 E4
Heathrow School
WDR/YW UB7 .... 152 A5
Heathside School
WEY KT13 .... 216 A2
Heathway Medical Centre
DAGW RM9 .... 124 A9
Heavers Farm Primary School
SNWD SE25 .... 203 N5
Heber School
EDUL SE22 .... 181 N2
Heckford Street Business Centre
WAP E1W 140 C9
Hedges & Butler Estate
SRTFD E15 .... 141 H4
Hedgewood School
YEAD UB4 .... 132 F5
Hedley Walter High School
BRWN CM15 .... 107 H1
Helena Road Clinic NHS
WLSDN NW10 .... 116 E9
Heliport Industrial Estate
BTSEA SW11 .... 157 N8
Hellenic College of London
KTBR SW1X 16 A4
Hemel Hempstead Rugby Club
HHW HP1 .... 35 J8
Hemel Hempstead
General Hospital
HHNE HP2 .... 35 N7
Hemel Hempstead Rugby
League Club
HHNE HP2 .... 36 A3
Hemel Hempstead School
HHW HP1 .... 35 M7
Hemel Hempstead
Town Cricket Club
HHS/BOV HP3 .... 35 M8
Hemel Hempstead
United Football Club
HHNE HP2 .... 36 C6
Henderson Hospital
BELMT SM2 .... 221 K5
Hendon College
CDALE/KGS NW9 .... 96 C9
Hendon Football Club
CRICK NW2 .... 116 G7
Hendon Golf Club
HDN NW4 .... 96 F8
Hendon Preparatory School
HDN NW4 .... 116 G1
Hendon Reform Synagogue
HDN NW4 .... 116 G3
Hendon School
HDN NW4 .... 116 G3
Hendon Secretarial College
HDN NW4 .... 116 E3

Hendon United Synagogue
HDN NW4 .... 116 F3
Hendon Youth Sports Centre
CRICK NW2 .... 116 C5
Hengrove CP School
WATW WD15 .... 173 N7
Henrietta Barnett School
GLDGN NW11 .... 117 L3
Henry Cavendish Junior School
BAL SW12 .... 180 D4
Henry Compton School
FUL/PGN SW6 .... 156 C7
Henry Fawcett Junior School
LBTH SE11 .... 18 A9
Henry Green Primary School
BCTR RM8 .... 123 N6
Henry Maynard Infant School
WALTH E17 .... 121 H3
Henry Maynard Junior School
WALTH E17 .... 121 H3
Henwick Primary School
ELTH/MOT SE9 .... 162 A9
Herbert Morrison Primary School
VX/NE SW8 .... 158 F6
The Hereward County School
LOU IG10 .... 82 C5
Hereward House School
HAMP NW3 .... 3 N3
Herington House
Preparatory School
BRWN CM15 .... 87 M10
Heritage House School
CSHM HP5 .... 51 J6
Hermitage County First School
WOKN/KNAP GU21 .... 231 K5
Hermitage County
Primary School
WOKN/KNAP GU21 .... 231 K5
Hermitage Primary School
UX/CGN UB8 .... 131 N2
Hermitage Primary School
WAP E1W 13 N9
Herne Hill Group Practice
HNHL SE24 .... 181 K1
Herne Hill Road Medical Practice
CMBW SE5 .... 159 K9
Herne Hill School
HNHL SE24 .... 181 K1
Heron Industrial Estate
SRTFD E15 .... 140 G4
Heronsgate Primary School
THMD SE28 .... 162 G2
Heron Trading Estate
ACT W3 .... 135 N7
Herringham County
Infant School
CDH/CHF RM16 .... 168 E3
Herschel Grammar School
SL SL1 .... 129 H8
The Herschel Medical Centre
SL SL1 .... 149 L2
Hersham Surgery
WOT/HER KT12 .... 217 L3
Hertford County Hospital
HERT/WAS SG14 .... 25 J5
Hertford Police Station
HERT/BAY SG13 .... 25 L6
Hertford Regional College
WARE SG12 .... 26 C3
Hertfordshire Business Centre
LCOL/BKTW AL2 .... 57 J2
Hertfordshire Country Club
WGCE AL7 .... 22 F8
Hertfordshire
County Constabulary
HHW HP1 .... 35 M6
Hertfordshire County Council
BUSH WD23 .... 94 C1
Hertfordshire County Council
GSTN WD25 .... 73 K2
Hertfordshire County Council
HERT/BAY SG13 .... 25 L6
Hertfordshire County Council
OXHEY WD19 .... 93 J4
Hertfordshire County Council
POTB/CUF EN6 .... 59 M8
Hertfordshire County Council
RKW/CH/CXG WD3 .... 91 G4
Hertfordshire County Council
WAT WD17 .... 73 H6
Hertfordshire Family
Health Authority Services
WGCW AL8 .... 22 G4
Hertford Town Football Club
HERT/WAS SG14 .... 25 J6
Herton Court School
SCUP DA14 .... 185 M7
Hertsmere Borough Council
BORE WD6 .... 75 P6
Hertsmere Council
BORE WD6 .... 75 M6
Hertsmere Jewish
Primary School
RAD WD7 .... 75 H4
Hertsmere Progressive
Synagogue
BORE WD6 .... 75 J10
Heston Community School
HEST TW5 .... 153 P6
Heston Infants School
HEST TW5 .... 153 P5
Heston Junior School
HEST TW5 .... 153 P5
Heston Park Cricket Club
HEST TW5 .... 153 N5
Heston Swimming Baths
HEST TW5 .... 153 N5
Hextable Comprehensive School
SWLY BR8 .... 208 C1
Hextable CP School
SWLY BR8 .... 186 C9
Hibernia House Surgery
HSLW TW3 .... 153 P10
Higgs Industrial Estate
BRXN/ST SW9 .... 159 J9
Highams Lodge Business Centre
WALTH E17 .... 120 C1
Highams Park Gm School
CHING E4 .... 101 J7
High Beech C of E
Primary School
LOU IG10 .... 81 M7
High Beeches JMI School
HARP AL5 .... 20 C3
Highbridge Industrial Estate
DEN/HRF UB9 .... 131 M1
Highbury Corner
Magistrates Court
HBRY N5 .... 6 B1
Highbury Fields School
HBRY N5 .... 119 J10
Highbury Grove School
HBRY N5 .... 119 K10

Highbury Park Clinic
HBRY N5 .... 119 J8
Highbury Quadrant
Primary School
HBRY N5 .... 119 K9
High Comm for Pakistan
KTBR SW1X 16 B3
High Commission of the Federal
Republic of Nigeria
CHCR WC2N 11 L9
High Comm of Brunei
BAY/PAD W2 .... 9 J4
High Comm of the Republic
of Maldives
MHST W1U 10 C3
High Comm of the Republic
of Namibia
CAVSQ/HST W1G 10 F3
High Elms Golf Course
ORP BR6 .... 226 A3
Highfield Infants School
HAYES BR2 .... 205 K4
Highfield Junior & Infant School
WCHMH N21 .... 99 J2
Highfield Junior School
HAYES BR2 .... 205 K4
Highfield School
HGDN/ICK UB10 .... 132 C5
Highfield Surgery
HHNE HP2 .... 36 A4
High Firs CP School
SWLY BR8 .... 208 G4
Highgate Group Practice
HGT N6 .... 118 A4
Highgate Junior School
HGT N6 .... 118 A5
Highgate Primary School
HGT N6 .... 118 A4
Highgate Private Hospital
HGT N6 .... 118 A4
Highgate School
HGT N6 .... 118 A5
Highgate Synagogue
HGT N6 .... 118 B5
Highgate Wood
Secondary School
CEND/HSY/T N8 .... 118 D3
Highgrove Swimming Pool
RSLP HA4 .... 113 H4
Highlands Junior & Infant School
IL IG1 .... 122 C6
High March School
BEAC HP9 .... 88 C7
The High Road Surgery
WDGN N22 .... 98 G8
High Road Swimming Baths
IL IG1 .... 122 G7
Highshore School
PECK SE15 .... 159 N7
High Street Surgery
& Medical Centre
EPP CM16 .... 65 K6
High View Primary School
BTSEA SW11 .... 157 N10
Highview Primary School
WLGTN SM6 .... 222 F1
Highview Surgery
POTB/CUF EN6 .... 59 M9
The Highways Primary School
ORP BR6 .... 227 M2
The Highway Trading Centre
WAP E1W 140 C9
Highwood Hospital
BRWN CM15 .... 106 G2
Highwood Primary School
BUSH WD23 .... 73 M5
Hillbrook Primary School
TOOT SW17 .... 180 A7
Hillcrest Surgery
ACT W3 .... 135 N10
Hillcroft College
SURB KT6 .... 199 K6
Hillcroft Primary School
CTHM CR3 .... 241 M9
Hilldene Junior School
HARH RM3 .... 105 K7
Hille Business Centre
WATN WD24 .... 73 J5
Hillel School
STHGT/OAK N14 .... 78 E10
Hill Farm Industrial Estate
GSTN WD25 .... 54 C9
Hillgate Hill Murugan Temple
HGT N6 .... 118 C5
Hillgrove Business Park
WAB EN9 .... 45 H8
Hillingdon Area Health Authority
RSLP HA4 .... 112 F5
Hillingdon Borough
Football Club
RSLP HA4 .... 112 C3
Hillingdon Health Authority
NTHWD HA6 .... 93 H9
Hillingdon Health Authority
WDR/YW UB7 .... 131 P9
Hillingdon Hospital
UX/CGN UB8 .... 132 A6
Hillingdon Junior
& Infant School
UX/CGN UB8 .... 132 B6
Hill Mead Infant School
HNHL SE24 .... 159 J10
Hill School
BH/WHM TN16 .... 244 F8
Hillside Primary School
WELL DA16 .... 163 M6
Hillside Junior & Infant School
NTHWD HA6 .... 93 H8
Hillside School
BORE WD6 .... 75 P8
Hilltop First School
WDSR SL4 .... 148 C7
Hilly Fields Medical Centre
BROCKY SE4 .... 182 F1
The Hiltongrove Business Centre
WALTH E17 .... 120 F2
Hinchley Wood Practice
NWMAL KT3 .... 200 C6
Hinchley Wood
Secondary School
ESH/CLAY KT10 .... 198 F9
Hindu Temple
SL SL1 .... 149 H1
Hindu Temple
STHL UB1 .... 133 N10
Hindu Temple
WLSDN NW10 .... 136 A1
Hippodrm
LSQ/SEVD WC2H 11 K7
Hitherfield Junior School
STRHM/NOR SW16 .... 181 H5
Hither Green Primary School
LEW SE13 .... 183 J2

HM Prison
CLAP SW4 .... 180 F2
HM Prison
CSHM HP5 .... 52 C2
HM Prison
HOLWY N7 .... 5 N2
HM Prison
WAND/EARL SW18 .... 179 N2
HM Prison Wormwood Scrubs
SHB W12 .... 136 D8
HMS President
EMB EC4Y 12 B7
HM Young Offender Institution
FELT TW13 .... 174 E6
Hobbayne First & Middle School
HNWL W7 .... 134 E8
Hobbs Hill Wood Primary School
HHS/BOV HP3 .... 36 A4
Hoblets Manor Junior School
HHNE HP2 .... 36 A4
Hoddesdon Health Centre
HOD EN11 .... 44 F4
Hoddesdon Industrial Estate
HOD EN11 .... 45 H4
Hoddesdon Lawn Tennis Club
HOD EN11 .... 44 F4
Hoddesdon St Pauls
Infant School
HOD EN11 .... 44 G3
Hoe Bridge School
WOKS/MYFD GU22 .... 232 E5
Hogan Business Centre
WOKN/KNAP GU21 .... 232 B3
Hogarth Business Park
CHSWK W4 .... 156 B5
Hogarth Industrial Estate
WLSDN NW10 .... 136 D6
Hogarth Primary School
BRWN CM15 .... 107 L4
Hogarth Primary School
CHSWK W4 .... 156 A5
Hogarth's House
CHSWK W4 .... 156 A5
Holbeach Primary School
CAT SE6 .... 182 F3
Holborn College
WKENS W14 .... 14 B9
Holborn Galleries
HHOL WC1V 11 P4
Holborn Town Hall
HHOL WC1V 11 M5
Holdbrook Junior Middle
& Infant School
CHES/WCR EN8 .... 62 E10
Holland & Holland
Shooting School
DEN/HRF UB9 .... 92 B10
Holland House School
EDGE HA8 .... 95 M5
Holland Park Secondary School
KENS W8 .... 14 D1
Holland Park Theatre
KENS W8 .... 14 D2
Holland Street Clinic
KENS W8 .... 14 F2
Hollick Wood Primary School
MUSWH N10 .... 98 C8
Holloway School
HOLWY N7 .... 118 E10
Hollybush Centre
HERT/WAS SG14 .... 25 H5
Hollydale Primary School
PECK SE15 .... 160 B8
Hollyfield Secondary School
SURB KT6 .... 199 K5
Holly House Private Hospital
BKHH IG9 .... 101 N3
Holly Industrial Park
WATN WD24 .... 73 K5
Hollymount Primary School
RYNPK SW20 .... 200 F1
Holly Park School
FBAR/BDGN N11 .... 98 B5
The Holly Trees County
Infant School
BRW CM14 .... 106 G5
Hollytrees Junior School
BRW CM14 .... 106 G5
Hollywood Bowl
BMLY BR1 .... 205 M1
Hollywood Bowl
CRAWW RH11 .... 283 N6
Hollywood Road Gallery
WBPTN SW10 .... 15 J9
Holmers First School
WDSR SL4 .... 148 C7
Holmesdale Cf School
REIG RH2 .... 257 L8
Holmesdale Picture Galleries
HAYES BR2 .... 205 P4
The Holme
CAMTN NW1 .... 4 B10
Holmleigh Primary School
STNW/STAM N16 .... 119 N6
Holmshill School
BORE WD6 .... 75 P8
Holmwood Corner Surgery
NWMAL KT3 .... 200 B5
Holtsmere End Junior
& Infant School
HHNE HP2 .... 36 C1
Holwell Junior & Infant School
WGCE AL7 .... 23 J6
Holy Cross Boarding
& Day School
CFSP/GDCR SL9 .... 90 A9
Holy Cross Convent School
NWMAL KT3 .... 200 A4
Holy Cross Preparatory School
KUTN/CMB KT2 .... 177 P10
Holy Cross RC Primary School
HLWS CM18 .... 47 K3
Holy Cross RC School
CAT SE6 .... 183 H4
Holy Cross RC School
SOCK/AV RM15 .... 146 G9
Holy Family College
WALTH E17 .... 120 C1
Holy Family RC Primary School
ADL/WDHM KT15 .... 215 K2
Holy Family RC School
DTCH/LGLY SL3 .... 150 C4
Holy Ghost RC Primary School
BAL SW12 .... 180 A3
Holy Innocents RC
Primary School
ORP BR6 .... 207 J10
Holyrood Infant School
WAT WD17 .... 72 E2
Holy Rood Junior School
WAT WD17 .... 72 E2
Holy Trinity C of E First School
WIM/MER SW19 .... 179 K9

Holy Trinity C of E Junior
& Infant School
HACK E8 .... 7 L2
Holy Trinity C of E Middle School
GU GU1 .... 268 C3
Holy Trinity C of E
Primary School
BRXS/STRHM SW2 .... 180 G3
Holy Trinity C of E
Primary School
CHES/WCR EN8 .... 62 C8
Holy Trinity C of E
Primary School
DART DA1 .... 187 K1
Holy Trinity C of E
Primary School
EFNCH N2 .... 117 N1
Holy Trinity C of E
Primary School
KTBR SW1X 16 C5
Holy Trinity C of E School
CRAWW RH11 .... 283 K9
Holy Trinity C of E School
GVE DA12 .... 190 F3
Holy Trinity C of E School
RCHPK/HAM TW10 .... 155 M10
Holy Trinity College & Convent
Preparatory School
BMLY BR1 .... 205 P1
Holy Trinity Primary School
CAMTN NW1 .... 4 E3
Holy Trinity Primary School
HAMP NW3 .... 3 K2
Holy Trinity School
CHEL SW3 .... 16 B5
Holy Trinity School
CHOB/PIR GU24 .... 212 F8
Holy Trinity School
FSTH SE23 .... 182 B5
Holy Trinity School
NTHWD HA6 .... 92 D7
Holy Trinity School
WLGTN SM6 .... 222 D1
Holywell School
WATW WD18 .... 72 G10
Home Farm Industrial Estate
WARE SG12 .... 27 L6
Home Office
STJSPK SW1H 17 H2
Homeopathic Hosp
BMSBY WC1N 11 M3
Home Park Industrial Estate
KGLGY WD4 .... 54 C6
Homerswood Junior
& Infant School
WGCW AL8 .... 22 G1
Homerton Hospital Social Services
CLPT E5 .... 120 C10
Homerton House Secondary
Boys School
HOM E9 .... 120 B10
Homewood School
LCOL/BKTW AL2 .... 56 A4
Homoeopathic Health Centre
PLSTW E13 .... 141 M6
The Homoeopathic Health Centre
MLHL NW7 .... 96 C6
Honeypot Business Centre
STAN HA7 .... 95 K9
Honeypot Medical Centre
STAN HA7 .... 95 K10
Honeywell Junior & Infant School
BTSEA SW11 .... 180 A2
Hong Kong & Shanghai
Sports Club
BECK BR3 .... 182 D9
Honilands Junior & Infant School
EN EN1 .... 80 A2
Honorary Consulate
of Burkina Faso
FUL/PGN SW6 .... 157 M9
Honor Oak Gallery
FSTH SE23 .... 182 C2
Honor Oak Health Centre
BROCKY SE4 .... 160 D10
Honourable Artillery
Company H.q.
STLK EC1Y 12 G2
Hook Lane Primary School
WELL DA16 .... 163 K9
Hook Rise South Industrial Park
CHSGTN KT9 .... 199 M10
Hook Road Surgery
SURB KT6 .... 199 K10
Horizon Business Centre
ED N9 .... 100 C3
Horizon Industrial Estate
PECK SE15 .... 19 N10
Horizon School
STNW/STAM N16 .... 119 M9
Horley Health Centre
HORL RH6 .... 280 B4
Hornchurch Clinic
EMPK RM11 .... 125 M6
Hornchurch Sports Centre
HCH RM12 .... 125 K7
Horndon Industrial Park
RBRW/HUT CM13 .... 127 P4
Horniman Museum
GNWCH SE10 .... 161 K2
The Horniman Museum
& Gardens
FSTH SE23 .... 182 A4
Horniman School
FSTH SE23 .... 182 A4
Horn Lane Surgery
ACT W3 .... 135 P9
Hornsey Central Hospital
CEND/HSY/T N8 .... 118 E3
Hornsey Coroners Court
& Public Mortuary
CEND/HSY/T N8 .... 118 F2
Hornsey County School
FSBYPK N4 .... 119 J3
Hornsey Rise Health Centre
ARCH N19 .... 118 E5
Hornsey School for Girls
CEND/HSY/T N8 .... 118 G3
Horseferry Road
Magistrates Court
WEST SW1P 17 K4
Horse Guards Parade
WHALL SW1A 11 K10
Horsell C of E School
WOKN/KNAP GU21 .... 231 P2
Horsell High School
WOKN/KNAP GU21 .... 232 A1
Horsell Village County
Infants School
WOKN/KNAP GU21 .... 232 A2
Horsenden Primary School
GFD/PVL UB6 .... 134 D1

Horseshoe Business Park
LCOL/BKTW AL2 .... 56 A6
Horsley Sports Club
EHSLY KT24 .... 252 G3
Horton Hospital
HOR/WEW KT19 .... 219 P7
Horton Industrial Park
WDR/YW UB7 .... 132 A10
Horton Kirby C of E
Primary School
EYN DA4 .... 210 B3
Horton Kirby & South
Darenth Parish Council
EYN DA4 .... 210 B2
Horton Kirby Trading Estate
EYN DA4 .... 210 B2
Horton Trading Estate
DTCH/LGLY SL3 .... 150 E9
Hospital
BETH E2 .... 7 L10
Hospital
FITZ W1T 10 G2
Hospital
LSQ/SEVD WC2H 11 L6
Hospital
MBLAR W1H 10 A5
Hospital
MHST W1U 10 D3
Hospital
MHST W1U 10 D2
Hospital
MYFR/PKLN W1K 10 C7
Hospital
REGST W1B 10 F2
Hospital Annexe
DEN/HRF UB9 .... 91 M8
Hospital & Counselling Centre
CAMTN NW1 .... 9 P3
Hospital of St John & St. Elizabeth
STJWD NW8 .... 3 L8
Hotham Primary School
PUT/ROE SW15 .... 156 G10
Hotham Primary School
PUT/ROE SW15 .... 156 F10
Hot Shots Ten Pin Bowling
HHS/BOV HP3 .... 36 A7
Hotspur Industrial Estate
TOTM N17 .... 100 A7
Houndsfield Primary School
ED N9 .... 100 A1
Hounslow Business Park
HSLW TW3 .... 153 P10
Hounslow College
Independent School
FELT TW13 .... 175 L7
Hounslow Cricket Club
HSLW TW3 .... 153 N8
Hounslow Heath Junior School
HSLWW TW4 .... 153 M9
Hounslow Manor School
HSLW TW3 .... 154 A9
Hounslow & Spelthorne
Community & Mental
Health NHS Trust
STA TW18 .... 173 K8
Hounslow Town Primary School
HSLW TW3 .... 154 B9
House of Detention
CLKNW EC1R 12 B1
Houses of Parliament
WEST SW1P 17 M2
Houston Business Park
YEAD UB4 .... 133 K10
Howard Business Park
WAB EN9 .... 63 J10
Howard Industrial Estate
CSHM HP5 .... 51 H5
Howard of Effingham School
EHSLY KT24 .... 253 M3
Howard School
CROY/NA CR0 .... 223 K1
Howe Dell School
HAT AL10 .... 40 E4
How Wood Junior & Infant School
LCOL/BKTW AL2 .... 56 B3
Hoxton Hall Theatre
IS N1 .... 7 K8
Hqs Wellington
TPL/STR WC2R 12 A7
H R Chinese Medical Centre
WLSDN NW10 .... 136 C4
H R H Princess Christians Hospital
WDSR SL4 .... 149 H7
H & S Community & NHS Trust
STWL/WRAY TW19 .... 173 P5
Hse of St Barnabus
SOHO/SHAV W1D 11 J6
Hughes Fields School
DEPT SE8 .... 160 F5
Hugh Myddelton Primary School
CLKNW EC1R 6 B10
The Humana Wellington Hospital
STJWD NW8 .... 3 M9
Humber Trading Estate
CRICK NW2 .... 116 E7
Hungarian Embassy
KTBR SW1X 16 C4
Hungerford Primary School
HOLWY N7 .... 5 K1
Huntercombe Manor Hospital
WDSR SL4 .... 128 B9
Hunters Hall School
DAGE RM10 .... 124 C10
Huntsman Sports Club
BKHTH/KID SE3 .... 161 M10
Hurley Clinic
LBTH SE11 .... 18 C6
Hurlingham Business Park
FUL/PGN SW6 .... 157 K9
Hurlingham & Chelsea School
FUL/PGN SW6 .... 157 K9
Huron University
SKENS SW7 .... 15 K5
Huron University
SKENS SW7 .... 15 M3
Hurricane Trading Centre
CDALE/KGS NW9 .... 96 C9
Hurst Drive JMI School
CHES/WCR EN8 .... 62 C10
Hurst Lodge School
ASC SL5 .... 192 A8
Hurstmere Secondary School
BFN/LL DA15 .... 185 L4
Hurst Park Primary School
HPTN TW12 .... 197 P2
Hurst Place Surgery
BXLY DA5 .... 185 N4
Hurst Primary School
BXLY DA5 .... 185 N4
Hurtmore Golf Club
RGODL GU7 .... 266 E10
Hydeburn School
BAL SW12 .... 180 B4

Hyde Heath County First School
AMS HP6 .... 50 B10
The Hyde Industrial Estate
CDALE/KGS NW9 .... 116 C3
The Hyde School
CDALE/KGS NW9 .... 116 C3
Hyland Business Centre
REDH RH1 .... 258 A10
Hyland House School
WALTH E17 .... 101 J10
Hyleford Leavers Unit School
BARK/HLT IG6 .... 102 G10
Hyleford Special School
IL IG1 .... 122 G10
The Hythe School
STA TW18 .... 172 G8
Ibstock Place School
PUT/ROE SW15 .... 178 B2
Ichthus Primary School
CMBW SE5 .... 159 L6
Ickburgh School
CLPT E5 .... 120 A8
Ickenham Clinic
HGDN/ICK UB10 .... 112 D8
Ide Hill School
RSEV TN14 .... 263 P7
Ifield Community College
CRAWW RH11 .... 283 K6
Ifield First School
CRAWW RH11 .... 283 J5
Ifield Gallery
WBPTN SW10 .... 15 H9
Ifield Golf & Country Club
CRAWW RH11 .... 283 H7
Ifield Middle School
CRAWW RH11 .... 283 K6
Ifield School
GVE DA12 .... 190 F4
Ihlara Sport F C
HBRY N5 .... 119 K9
Ikra Primary School
STNW/STAM N16 .... 119 M9
Ilderton Primary School
BERM/RHTH SE16 .... 160 B5
Ilford County Court
IL IG1 .... 122 G7
Ilford County High School
for Boys
BARK/HLT IG6 .... 102 F10
Ilford Jewish Primary School
BARK/HLT IG6 .... 122 G1
Ilford Medical Centre
IL IG1 .... 122 E8
Ilford Preparatory School
GDMY/SEVK IG3 .... 123 J6
Ilford Synagogue
IL IG1 .... 122 D4
Imber Court Trading Estate
E/WMO/HCT KT8 .... 198 C6
Immanuel College
BUSH WD23 .... 94 D1
Immanuel & St Andrew
C of E Primary School
STRHM/NOR SW16 .... 180 F9
Immanuel School
ROM RM1 .... 104 F7
Imperial College
PUT/ROE SW15 .... 156 G8
Imperial College
SKENS SW7 .... 15 L3
Imperial College
SKENS SW7 .... 15 L8
Imperial College Athletic Ground
HYS/HAR UB3 .... 152 D5
Imperial College of Science
FUL/PGN SW6 .... 14 G3
Imperial College of Science
& Technology
SKENS SW7 .... 15 M2
Imperial College of Science
Technology & Medicine
ASC SL5 .... 192 E3
Imperial College of Science
Technology & Medicine
SKENS SW7 .... 15 K3
Imperial College School
of Medicine
HMSMTH W6 .... 156 G7
Imperial Retail Park
GVW DA11 .... 190 D2
Imperial Trading Estate
RAIN RM13 .... 145 K6
Imperial War Museum
STHWK SE1 .... 18 B4
Independent Industrial Estate
WDR/YW UB7 .... 132 A10
India High Commission
HOL/ALD WC2B 11 N7
Indonesian Embassy
MYFR/PKLN W1K 10 D8
Indoor Market
DEPT SE8 .... 160 F7
Indoor Market
WAT WD17 .... 73 K7
Industrial Cen
STHWK SE1 .... 12 E9
Industrial Estate
CMBW SE5 .... 159 K8
Industrial Estate
DEN/HRF UB9 .... 91 K7
Industrial Estate
EPP CM16 .... 65 M1
Industrial Estate
GNWCH SE10 .... 160 G6
Industrial Estate
NWCR SE14 .... 160 C5
Industrial Estate
POP/IOD E14 .... 140 F4
Industrial Estate Annexe
RAIN RM13 .... 144 F8
Industrial Health Clinic
UX/CGN UB8 .... 131 P7
Industrial Park
CHES/WCR EN8 .... 62 C4
Infant College
IL IG1 .... 122 D7
The Infirmary Royal Hospital
CHEL SW3 .... 16 C8
Ingrave Johnstone C of E School
RBRW/HUT CM13 .... 107 P7
Ingrebourne CP School
HARH RM3 .... 105 K5
In House Gallery
KENS W8 .... 8 G10
Inner London Sessions House
STHWK SE1 .... 18 E3
Inner Temple
EMB EC4Y 12 A7
Innholders Hall
CANST EC4R 12 F7
Inns of Court School of Law
GINN WC1R 11 P3

Institut Francais
SKENS SW7 .... 15 L5
The Instructor College
HRW HA1 .... 114 D4
International Financial Centre
OBST EC2N 13 J5
International Medical Centre
ECT SW5 .... 14 F6
International School of London
ACT W3 .... 155 M3
International Trading Estate
NWDGN UB2 .... 153 K2
International University
BUSH WD23 .... 73 N8
Invicta Industrial Estate
SRTFD E15 .... 141 H5
Invicta Primary School
BKHTH/KID SE3 .... 161 M5
Invicta Sports Club
DART DA1 .... 187 L1
Inwood Business Centre
HSLW TW3 .... 154 A10
Irish Embassy
KTBR SW1X 16 E2
Ironmongers Hall
STBT EC1A 12 E4
Islamic College
WCHPL E1 .... 13 P5
Islamic College
for Advanced Studies
WLSDN NW10 .... 136 E2
Islamic Cultural Centre
& London Central Mosque
CAMTN NW1 .... 3 P10
The Islamic Grammar School
WAND/EARL SW18 .... 179 J3
Island Clinic
POP/IOD E14 .... 161 H1
Isleworth Baths
ISLW TW7 .... 154 E10
Isleworth Centre Practice
ISLW TW7 .... 154 F9
Isleworth & Syon School
for Boys
ISLW TW7 .... 154 D6
Isleworth Town Primary School
ISLW TW7 .... 154 E8
Islington Business Centre
IS N1 .... 6 B1
Islington Council
HBRY N5 .... 6 C1
Islington Council
IS N1 .... 6 C5
Islington Green Medical Centre
IS N1 .... 6 C5
Islington Green School
IS N1 .... 6 D6
Islington Health Authority
ARCH N19 .... 118 C7
Islington Town Hall
IS N1 .... 6 C3
Ismaili Centre
SKENS SW7 .... 15 M5
Italia Conti Academy
of Theatre Arts
BRXN/ST SW9 .... 158 F9
Italia Conti Academy
of Theatre Arts
FARR EC1M 12 E2
Italian Embassy
MYFR/PKLN W1K 10 D7
Italian Hospital
WEST SW1P 16 G5
Ithaca College
SKENS SW7 .... 15 J6
Iver Doctors Surgery
IVER SL0 .... 131 H8
Iver Golf & Leisure Centre
IVER SL0 .... 130 E10
Iver Heath First School
IVER SL0 .... 130 C5
Iver Heath Health Centre
IVER SL0 .... 130 G4
Iver Heath Middle School
IVER SL0 .... 130 G4
Iver Village Infant School
IVER SL0 .... 131 J8
Iver Village Junior School
IVER SL0 .... 131 H8
Ivy Bower Surgery
GRH DA9 .... 188 G1
Ivybridge Primary School
TWK TW1 .... 176 E2
Ivy Chimneys Primary School
EPP CM16 .... 65 J8
Ivydale Primary School
PECK SE15 .... 160 C10
Jack & Jill School
HPTN TW12 .... 175 P9
Jack Taylor School
STJWD NW8 .... 3 J5
Jaina House Surgery
STHGT/OAK N14 .... 98 E4
Jamahiriya School
CHEL SW15 .... 15 N9
Jamaican High Comm
SKENS SW7 .... 15 L2
James Allens Girls School
HNHL SE24 .... 181 L1
James Dixon Primary School
PGE/AN SE20 .... 181 P10
James Elliman School
SL SL1 .... 129 K8
Jamestown Mental
Health Centre
HAMP NW3 .... 4 A3
Janet Adegoke Leisure Centre
SHB W12 .... 136 D9
Japanese Gallery
IS N1 .... 6 C6
Japanese Gallery
KENS W8 .... 8 F10
Japan Green Medical Centre
ACT W3 .... 135 N10
Jayram Surgery
BGR/WK TN15 .... 160 F7
Jenner Health Centre
FSTH SE23 .... 182 D4
The Jerdan Gallery
FUL/PGN SW6 .... 157 K6
Jermyn Street Theatre
STJS SW1Y 11 H8
Jerounds Junior & Infant School
HLWW/ROY CM19 .... 46 E4
Jessop Primary School
HNHL SE24 .... 159 J10

Jewel Tower
WEST SW1P 17 L3
Jewish Community Theatre
CMBW SE5 .... 159 L9
The Jewish Museum
CAMTN NW1 .... 4 E6
The Jewish Preparatory School
KIL/WHAMP NW6 .... 2 G7
Jews College London
HDN NW4 .... 116 C2
JMI School
SURB KT6 .... 199 J5
Johanna Primary School
STHWK SE1 .... 18 A2
John Ball Primary School
BKHTH/KID SE3 .... 161 K8
John Betts Primary School
HMSMTH W6 .... 156 D2
John Bramston Infant School
HDN NW4 .... 103 K7
John Busch School
ISLW TW7 .... 154 C7
John Chilton School
NTHLT UB5 .... 133 M2
The John Deal Practice
RPLY/SEND GU23 .... 233 M7
The John Denham Gallery
CRICK NW2 .... 117 J10
John Dixon Clinic
BERM/RHTH SE16 .... 160 A2
John Donne Primary School
PECK SE15 .... 160 A7
John Fisher School
PUR/KEN CR8 .... 222 F6
John Fisher School
RYLN/HDSTN HA2 .... 113 P2
John Fisher Sports Club
WARL CR6 .... 242 D4
John F Kennedy School
HHW HP1 .... 35 H5
John F Kennedy Special School
SRTFD E15 .... 141 J3
John Kelly Boys & Girls
Technology College
CRICK NW2 .... 116 C8
John Lyon School
RYLN/HDSTN HA2 .... 114 C6
John Milton Primary School
VX/NE SW8 .... 158 D6
John Nightingale School
E/WMO/HCT KT8 .... 197 N3
John Paul Ii School
WIM/MER SW19 .... 178 G3
John Penrose School
DEN/HRF UB9 .... 91 N9
John Perryn Primary School
ACT W3 .... 136 B7
John Perry School
DAGE RM10 .... 144 E1
John Roan Lower School
BKHTH/KID SE3 .... 161 L5
John Roan Secondary School
GNWCH SE10 .... 161 K6
John Ruskin Junior
& Infant School
CMBW SE5 .... 18 E10
John Ruskin Sixth Form College
SAND/SEL CR2 .... 224 D4
John Scott Health Centre
FSBYPK N4 .... 119 K6
John Scurr Primary School
WCHPL E1 .... 140 B6
John Smith House
WALW SE17 .... 18 E6
Johnsons Industrial Estate
HYS/HAR UB3 .... 153 H2
John Stainer Primary School
BROCKY SE4 .... 160 D9
John the Baptist C of E
Junior School
KUT KT1 .... 177 J10
John Vickers Theatre Collection
FUL/PGN SW6 .... 157 J6
The John Warner School
HOD EN11 .... 26 G10
Jordans CP School
BEAC HP9 .... 89 K7
Joseph Clarke Special School
CHING E4 .... 101 J7
Joseph Hood Primary
& Middle School
RYNPK SW20 .... 201 H2
Joseph Lancaster Primary School
STHWK SE1 .... 18 F4
Joseph Tritton Primary School
BTSEA SW11 .... 157 M9
Joyce Green Hospital
DART DA1 .... 165 N8
Joydens Wood CP School
BXLY DA5 .... 186 F7
Jubilee Hall Clinic
CRAWE RH10 .... 284 B7
Jubilee Market
COVGDN WC2E 11 M7
Jubilee Primary School
STNW/STAM N16 .... 119 P6
Jubilee School
THMD SE28 .... 143 M9
Jubilee Sports Ground
CHING E4 .... 101 J5
Judd Street Gallery
STPAN WC1H 5 L10
Julians Primary School
STRHM/NOR SW16 .... 181 H7
Junior School
KIL/WHAMP NW6 .... 2 E4
Junior School
KWD/TDW/WH KT20 .... 238 F5
Junior School
SAND/SEL CR2 .... 223 L5
Junior & Youth Centre
POP/IOD E14 .... 140 E7
Jupiter Drive JMI School
HHNE HP2 .... 36 A4
J V C Business Park
CRICK NW2 .... 116 D6
Kangley Business Centre
SYD SE26 .... 182 E3
Karizma Frame Gallery
PLMGR N13 .... 98 C6
Katella Trading Estate
BARK IG11 .... 143 H5
Katherine Road Medical Centre
FSTGT E7 .... 141 P1
Katherines Primary School
HLWW/ROY CM19 .... 46 C3
The Keats Group Practice
HAMP NW3 .... 117 N9
Keats House Museum
HAMP NW3 .... 117 P9
Keats Surgery
ED N9 .... 99 M3

Keble Preparatory School
for Boys
WCHMH N21 .... 99 H1
Keen Students
Supplementary School
WCHPL E1 .... 13 N3
The Keet Clinic
COVGDN WC2E 11 L7
Keir Hardy Primary School
CAN/RD E16 .... 141 M7
Keith Davis Cue Sports Club
DAGW RM9 .... 143 N2
Kelmscott Leisure Centre
WALTH E17 .... 120 E4
Kelmscott School
WALTH E17 .... 120 E4
Kelrose Swimming Pool Centre
RBRW/HUT CM13 .... 127 K3
Kelsey Park School
BECK BR3 .... 204 F3
Kelvedon Hatch CP School
BRWN CM15 .... 86 D2
Kelvin Business Centre
CRAWE RH10 .... 284 A4
Kemsing CP School
BGR/WK TN15 .... 247 P3
Kemsing Parish Council
BGR/WK TN15 .... 247 P3
Ken Barrington Centre
LBTH SE11 .... 17 P10
Kender Primary School
NWCR SE14 .... 160 B7
Kenilworth Primary School
BORE WD6 .... 76 A7
Kenley Primary School
PUR/KEN CR8 .... 241 M2
Kenley Sports Club
PUR/KEN CR8 .... 223 K10
Kenmont Primary School
WLSDN NW10 .... 136 D5
Kenmore Park School
KTN/HRWW/W HA3 .... 115 J1
Kenneth More Theatre
IL IG1 .... 122 F8
Kenningtons Primary School
SOCK/AV RM15 .... 146 B8
Kensal Rise Primary School
WLSDN NW10 .... 136 G4
Kensington and Chelsea
Town Hall
KENS W8 .... 14 C4
Kensington Avenue Junior
& Infant School
THHTH CR7 .... 203 H1
Kensington & Chelsea College
NKENS W10 .... 8 A3
Kensington & Chelsea College
WBPTN SW10 .... 157 M6
Kensington & Chelsea
Health Authority
BAY/PAD W2 .... 9 K6
The Kensington Clinic
KENS W8 .... 14 C4
Kensington Market
KENS W8 .... 14 C2
Kensington Palace
KENS W8 .... 15 H1
Kensington Park School
CAVSQ/HST W1G 10 F3
Kensington Preparatory School
FUL/PGN SW6 .... 157 J7
Kensington Primary School
MNPK E12 .... 142 C1
Kensington School of Business
HCIRC EC1N 12 B3
Kensington Sports Centre
NTGHL W11 .... 136 C9
Kensit Memorial College
FNCH N3 .... 97 H10
Kent County Council
DART DA1 .... 187 L3
Kent County Council
DART DA1 .... 187 L2
Kent County Council
DART DA1 .... 187 L2
Kent County Council
GVW DA11 .... 190 D2
Kent County Council
GVW DA11 .... 190 D3
Kent County Council
GVW DA11 .... 190 B6
Kent County Council
RDART DA2 .... 187 K7
Kentish Town Health Centre
KTTN NW5 .... 4 C1
Kentish Town Industrial Estate
KTTN NW5 .... 118 C10
Kentish Town Primary School
KTTN NW5 .... 118 D10
Kent Kraft Industrial Estate
GVW DA11 .... 167 L10
Kent Kraft Industrial Estate
SWCM DA10 .... 189 L1
Kenton Clinic
KTN/HRWW/W HA3 .... 115 K3
Kenton Cricket Club
KTN/HRWW/W HA3 .... 115 H2
Kenton Synagogue
KTN/HRWW/W HA3 .... 115 J3
Kent Park Industrial Estate
PECK SE15 .... 160 A5
Kenwood House
HGT N6 .... 117 P6
Kenya High Comm
CAVSQ/HST W1G 10 E3
Kenynngton Manor CP School
SUN TW16 .... 175 H9
The Kerem School
EFNCH N2 .... 117 N3
Kestner Industrial Estate
GRH DA9 .... 166 F10
Keston Ave Infant
Primary School
COUL/CHIP CR5 .... 241 H5
Keston C of E Primary School
HAYES BR2 .... 226 A2
Keston County Junior School
COUL/CHIP CR5 .... 241 H5
Keston House Medical Practice
PUR/KEN CR8 .... 222 G8
Kevington CP School
STMC/STPC BR5 .... 207 N5
Kevin Hinds Practice
WARE SG12 .... 26 C2
Kew Bridge Steam Museum
BTFD TW8 .... 155 L4
Kew College
RCH/KEW TW9 .... 155 M6
Kew Palace
RCH/KEW TW9 .... 155 K6
Keyworth Junior & Infant School
WALW SE17 .... 18 C8
Khalsa College London
HRW HA1 .... 114 E4

Kidbrooke Park Primary School
BKHTH/KID SE3 .... 161 P8
Kidbrooke School
BKHTH/KID SE3 .... 162 A8
Killick Street Medical Centre
IS N1 .... 5 N7
Killigrew Junior Middle
& Infant School
LCOL/BKTW AL2 .... 56 A1
Kilmorie Primary School
FSTH SE23 .... 182 D5
Kimberley Industrial Estate
WALTH E17 .... 100 E9
Kincade Gallery
GRH DA9 .... 188 E3
King Alfred School
GLDGN NW11 .... 117 L6
King Athelstan Primary School
KUT KT1 .... 199 L3
King Edwards Road Clinic
RSLP HA4 .... 112 E6
King Edward Vii Hospital
WDSR SL4 .... 149 H9
King Edward Vii Hospital
for Officers
MHST W1U 10 D3
Kingfield School
WOKS/MYFD GU22 .... 232 D6
The Kingfisher Medical Centre
DEPT SE8 .... 160 E5
King George Hospital
GDMY/SEVK IG3 .... 123 K3
Kingham Industrial Estate
WLSDN NW10 .... 136 A5
King Harold Comprehensive
School
WAB EN9 .... 63 K9
King & Queen Wharf
WAP E1W 140 C9
Kings Acre Primary School
CLAP SW4 .... 180 F1
Kings Avenue Medical Centre
GFD/PVL UB6 .... 134 B8
Kingsbury Green Primary School
CDALE/KGS NW9 .... 115 N3
Kingsbury High School
CDALE/KGS NW9 .... 115 N2
Kingsbury Hospital
CDALE/KGS NW9 .... 115 M2
Kingsbury Synagogue
CDALE/KGS NW9 .... 115 P3
Kingsbury Tamil School
CDALE/KGS NW9 .... 115 N1
Kingsbury Trading Estate
CDALE/KGS NW9 .... 115 P4
Kingsbury Watermill Museum
& Waffle House
STALW/RED AL3 .... 38 A6
Kings College
LSQ/SEVD WC2H 11 M6
Kings College
GUW GU2 .... 249 K10
Kings College
TPL/STR WC2R 11 P7
Kings College Hospital
EDUL SE22 .... 159 M10
Kings College London
CHEL SW3 .... 15 N8
Kings College London
CMBW SE5 .... 159 L8
Kings College London
HAMP NW3 .... 117 K9
Kings College London
KENS W8 .... 14 E1
Kings College London
STHWK SE1 .... 12 D9
Kings College London
STHWK SE1 .... 12 F9
Kings College London
STHWK SE1 .... 17 P1
King's College School
WIM/MER SW19 .... 178 F9
Kings College School
of Medicine & Dentistry
HNHL SE24 .... 181 L2
Kings College Sports Ground
RSLP HA4 .... 112 F4
Kings Corner Surgery
ASC SL5 .... 192 D5
Kingscote School
CFSP/GDCR SL9 .... 110 B1
Kings Court Gallery
FUL/PGN SW6 .... 157 H8
Kings Court Primary School
WDSR SL4 .... 171 M3
Kingscroft School
STA TW18 .... 173 K9
Kings Cross Practice
STPAN WC1H 5 L10
Kingsdale Secondary School
DUL SE21 .... 181 M6
Kingsdowne Surgery
SURB KT6 .... 199 L8
Kings Estate
HCH RM12 .... 125 H9
Kings Farm Infant School
GVE DA12 .... 190 F8
Kings Farm Junior School
GVE DA12 .... 190 F7
Kingsfield Business Centre
REDH RH1 .... 276 B1
Kingsgate Business Centre
KUTN/CMB KT2 .... 199 K1
Kingsgate Infant School
KIL/WHAMP NW6 .... 2 E3
Kings Head Theatre
IS N1 .... 6 C5
Kings House School
RCHPK/HAM TW10 .... 177 L1
Kingsland Health Centre
IS N1 .... 7 K3
Kingsland Secondary School
HACK E8 .... 119 N10
Kingsland Surgery
IS N1 .... 7 K7
Kings Langley Parish Council
KGLGY WD4 .... 54 B5
Kings Langley Primary School
KGLGY WD4 .... 54 A4
Kingsley Primary School
CROY/NA CR0 .... 202 C8
Kingsmead Junior
& Infant School
CLPT E5 .... 120 D9
Kingsmead Medical Centre
CLPT E5 .... 120 D10
Kingsmead School
EN EN1 .... 79 P8
Kingsmoor Junior & Infant School
HLWW/ROY CM19 .... 46 F5
Kingsmoor Recreation Centre
HLWW/ROY CM19 .... 46 E5

The Kings Oak Private Hospital
ENC/FH EN2 .... 79 H4
King Solomon High School
BARK/HLT IG6 .... 102 G10
Kings Park Industrial Estate
KGLGY WD4 .... 54 C5
Kings Private Clinic
GDMY/SEVK IG3 .... 123 J6
Kingston Business Centre
CHSGTN KT9 .... 199 K10
Kingston College
KUT KT1 .... 199 J3
Kingston Council
for Voluntary Service
KUT KT1 .... 199 K2
Kingston Crown Court
KUT KT1 .... 199 J3
Kingston & District Community
NHS Trust
SURB KT6 .... 199 M9
Kingston Grammar School
KUT KT1 .... 199 L2
Kingston Hospital NHS Trust
KUTN/CMB KT2 .... 199 N1
Kingston Hospital NHS Trust
KUTN/CMB KT2 .... 199 M1
Kingstonian Football Club
KUT KT1 .... 199 N3
Kingston Liberal Synagogue
THDIT KT7 .... 198 G7
Kingston Magistrates Court
KUT KT1 .... 199 J2
Kingston Museum
& Heritage Service
KUTN/CMB KT2 .... 177 J9
Kingston & Richmond
Health Authority
BRYLDS KT5 .... 199 J3
Kingston Sport
& Recreation Centre
NWMAL KT3 .... 200 C4
Kingston University
KUT KT1 .... 199 L3
Kingston University
KUT KT1 .... 199 K3
Kingston University
KUTN/CMB KT2 .... 178 A8
Kingston University
KUTN/CMB KT2 .... 178 A10
Kingston University
KUTN/CMB KT2 .... 200 A1
King Street College
HMSMTH W6 .... 156 F3
Kingsway Business Park
HPTN TW12 .... 197 N1
Kingsway College
CLKNW EC1R 12 B1
Kingsway College
FSBYW WC1X 5 P9
Kingsway College
KTTN NW5 .... 4 E1
Kingsway Junior School
GSTN WD25 .... 55 H10
Kingswey Business Park
WOKN/KNAP GU21 .... 214 F10
Kingswey Business Park
WOKN/KNAP GU21 .... 232 F1
Kingswood CP School
KWD/TDW/WH KT20 .... 257 J4
Kingswood House School
HOR/WEW KT19 .... 219 N9
Kingswood Primary School
WNWD SE27 .... 181 L7
Kings Wood School
HARH RM3 .... 105 P5
Kisharon Day School
GLDGN NW11 .... 117 J4
Klc School of Design
WBPTN SW10 .... 157 M7
Knaphill County Junior School
WOKN/KNAP GU21 .... 231 H4
Knaphill Lower School
WOKN/KNAP GU21 .... 230 G4
Knaphill Surgery
WOKN/KNAP GU21 .... 231 H4
Knightland Road Synagogue
CLPT E5 .... 120 A7
Knightsbridge Barracks
SKENS SW7 .... 15 P2
Knightsmead School
SOCK/AV RM15 .... 146 F9
Knockholt School
RSEV TN14 .... 245 L3
Knollmead Primary School
WPK KT4 .... 199 P9
Knowledge Point School
HOLWY N7 .... 5 N2
Knowle Park County School
STA TW18 .... 173 K8
Knowl Hill School
CHOB/PIR GU24 .... 230 D8
Knutsford Junior
& Infant School
WATN WD24 .... 73 L4
Kp Estate
RAIN RM13 .... 144 F9
K S Medical Centre
STHL UB1 .... 134 A9
Kufa Gallery
BAY/PAD W2 .... 8 C6
Kuwait Embassy
KTBR SW1X 16 B1
Laburnum Health Centre
DAGE RM10 .... 124 B7
Laburnum Junior & Infant School
HACK E8 .... 7 L6
Ladbroke School
POTB/CUF EN6 .... 59 L8
Lady Banks Primary School
RSLP HA4 .... 113 H7
Lady Boswell C of E School
BGR/WK TN15 .... 265 K1
Lady Edens School
KENS W8 .... 15 J3
The Lady Eleanor Holles School
HPTN TW12 .... 176 A8
Lady Margaret Junior Middle
& Infant School
STHL UB1 .... 133 N7
Lady Margaret Secondary
School for Girls
FUL/PGN SW6 .... 157 K7
Lady of Holy Rosary School
BFN/LL DA15 .... 185 H2
Laharna Trading Estate
WATN WD24 .... 73 K4
Laine Theatre Arts
EW KT17 .... 220 B9
Laings Sports Ground
BAR EN5 .... 76 B8

Lake Business Centre
TOTM N17 ...99 P7
Laker Industrial Estate
BECK BR3 ...182 D8
Lakeside Industrial Estate
DTCH/LGLY SL3 ...151 K5
Lakeside Industrial Estate
DTCH/LGLY SL3 ...151 H6
Lakeside School
WGCW AL8 ...22 E7
Lakeside Shopping Centre
WTHK RM20 ...166 G2
Laleham C of E Primary School
STA TW18 ...195 M2
Lambeth College
CLAP SW4 ...180 D1
Lambeth College
STHWK SE1 ...13 K10
Lambeth Palace
STHWK SE1 ...17 M1
Lambeth Southwark and Lewisham
Health Authority
LEW SE13 ...182 G2
Lambeth Walk Group Practice
LBTH SE11 ...18 A4
Lambourne CP School
ABR/ST RM4 ...83 L8
Lambourne Golf Club
SL SL1 ...128 A1
Lambs Court
POP/IOD E14 ...140 D9
Lamont Business Centre
CROY/NA CR0 ...202 F7
Lamont Gallery
BETH E2 ...140 B5
Lamorbey Swimming Centre
BFN/LL DA15 ...185 K5
Lampton School
HEST TW5 ...153 P7
The Lanark Medical Centre
MV/WKIL W9 ...3 H9
Lancaster House
WHALL SW1A ...16 G1
Lancasterian Junior
& Infant School
TOTM N17 ...99 N9
Lancelot Medical Centre
ALP/SUD HA0 ...115 J10
Lanford Obesity Clinic
ED N9 ...100 A1
Lanfranc Secondary School
for Boys
CROY/NA CR0 ...202 F6
Langafel C of E Primary School
HART DA3 ...211 M3
Langbourne Primary School
DUL SE21 ...181 M6
Langdon Comprehensive School
EHAM E6 ...142 E4
Langdon Park Secondary School
POP/IOD E14 ...140 G8
Langford Primary School
FUL/PGN SW6 ...157 L8
The Langham School
SEVS/STOTM N15 ...119 K2
Langhedge Lane
Industrial Estate
UED N18 ...99 N7
Langley Business Centre
DTCH/LGLY SL3 ...150 D1
Langley Corner Surgery
CRAWW RH11 ...283 J5
Langley Grammar School
DTCH/LGLY SL3 ...150 C3
Langley Green First School
CRAWW RH11 ...283 N3
Langley Health Centre
DTCH/LGLY SL3 ...150 D4
Langley Manor School
DTCH/LGLY SL3 ...130 B10
Langley Park School for Boys
BECK BR3 ...204 G6
Langley Park School for Girls
BECK BR3 ...204 G6
Langleywood Secondary School
DTCH/LGLY SL3 ...150 B2
Langshott County Infant School
HORL RH6 ...280 C4
Langthorne Health Centre
WAN E11 ...121 J8
Langthorne Hospital
WAN E11 ...121 J9
Langton Galleries
WBPTN SW10 ...157 M6
Langtons Junior
& Infant School
EMPK RM11 ...125 M6
The Lansbury Estate
WOKN/KNAP GU21 ...231 J4
Lansdowne County
Primary School
TIL RM18 ...168 C8
Lansdowne School
BRXN/ST SW9 ...158 G9
La Retraite RC Girls School
BAL SW12 ...180 D3
Lark Hall Infants School
CLAP SW4 ...158 E8
Lark Hall Junior School
CLAP SW4 ...158 E8
Larkswood Junior & Infant School
CHING E4 ...100 G5
Larmenier Infant School
HMSMTH W6 ...156 H1
La Sainte Union Convent School
KTTN NW5 ...118 C8
La Salette RC Primary School
RAIN RM13 ...145 H5
Laser Clinic
CHESW EN7 ...62 A6
Latchmere Junior School
KUTN/CMB KT2 ...177 L9
Latchmere Leisure Centre
BTSEA SW11 ...158 A8
Lathom Junior School
EHAM E6 ...142 B2
Latimer Industrial Estate
SHB W12 ...136 F6
Latton Bush Business Centre
HLWS CM18 ...47 J4
Latton Bush Recreation Centre
HLWS CM18 ...47 H4
Latymer All Saints C of E
Primary School
ED N9 ...99 N3
The Latymer School
ED N9 ...99 M3
Latymer Upper School for Boys
HMSMTH W6 ...156 D3
Launcelot Primary School
BMLY BR1 ...183 M7
Laurel Clinic
EA W5 ...155 H3

Laurence Haines School
WATW WD18 ...73 H10
Lauriston Junior & Infant School
HOM E9 ...140 C3
Lavender Hill Group Practice
BTSEA SW11 ...158 B9
Lavender Junior
& Infant School
ENC/FH EN2 ...79 M4
Lavenders Fields Surgery
MTCM CR4 ...201 P1
Lawdale Junior School
BETH E2 ...7 P9
Lawn CP School
GVW DA11 ...189 P2
Lawn Tennis Club
HORL RH6 ...280 A4
Lawn Tennis Club
REDH RH1 ...258 A8
Lawrence Trading Estate
GNWCH SE10 ...161 K3
Lawrence University
SKENS SW7 ...15 K6
Lawrence Wharf
BERM/RHTH SE16 ...140 E10
The Lawson Practice
IS N1 ...7 K7
Laycock Primary School
IS N1 ...6 B2
Lazards Sports Club
SUN TW16 ...197 J1
L B H Hayes Swimming Baths
HYS/HAR UB3 ...132 G10
Lea Bridge Industrial Estate
LEY E10 ...120 D6
Lea County First School
SLN SL2 ...129 M9
Lea County Middle School
SLN SL2 ...129 M9
Leacroft Medical Practice
CRAWW RH11 ...283 M5
Leacroft Medical Practice
CRAWW RH11 ...283 L7
Leadenhall Market
BANK EC3V ...13 J6
Lea Farm Junior School
GSTN WD25 ...73 L2
Lea Gallery
IS N1 ...7 J10
Lea Green Special School
LEY E10 ...120 G4
Lea Park Trading Estate
LEY E10 ...120 E5
Leather Gallery
KENS W8 ...14 G1
Leatherhead Clinic
LHD/OX KT22 ...237 H7
Leatherhead Cricket Club
LHD/OX KT22 ...236 F9
Leatherhead Football Club
LHD/OX KT22 ...236 F8
Leatherhead Hospital
LHD/OX KT22 ...237 H8
Leatherhead Industrial Estate
LHD/OX KT22 ...236 F7
Leatherhead Leisure Centre
& Water Park
LHD/OX KT22 ...236 F9
Leathersellers Sports Ground
ELTH/MOT SE9 ...183 P3
Leathers Hall
HDTCH EC3A ...13 J5
Lea Valley High School
PEND EN3 ...80 B1
Lea Valley Ice Centre
LEY E10 ...120 C7
Lea Valley Junior & Infant School
TOTM N17 ...99 P8
Lea Valley Trading Estate
UED N18 ...100 B5
Leavesden Green Junior Middle
& Infant School
GSTN WD25 ...55 H10
Leavesden Hospital
ABLGY WD5 ...55 H7
Lee C of E Primary School
LEW SE13 ...161 K10
Lee Manor Primary School
LEW SE13 ...183 K2
Leeside Court
BERM/RHTH SE16 ...140 C10
Leeside Trading Estate
TOTM N17 ...100 B8
Leesons Infant School
STMC/STPC BR5 ...207 K3
Lee Valley Leisure Centre
ED N9 ...100 D2
Lee Valley Watersports Centre
CHING E4 ...100 D7
Leicester Galleries
IS N1 ...6 D7
Leigh City Technology College
DART DA1 ...187 P4
Leigh Close Industrial Estate
NWMAL KT3 ...200 A4
Leigh Gallery
STPAN WC1H ...5 L10
Leigh Primary School
REIG RH2 ...274 D6
Leighton House Museum
& Art Gallery
WKENS W14 ...14 D3
Leisure Centre
FUL/PGN SW6 ...14 G10
Leisure Centre
KUT KT1 ...199 K2
Leisure Centre
WDSR SL4 ...148 G6
Lena Gardens Primary School
HMSMTH W6 ...156 F2
Lent Rise County
Combined School
SL SL1 ...128 A7
Leopold Primary School
WLSDN NW10 ...136 C2
Leopold Street Clinic
BOW E3 ...140 C8
Lesney Park Primary School
ERITH DA8 ...164 E5
Lesotho High Comm
KTBR SW1X ...16 C3
Lessness Heath CP School
BELV DA17 ...164 B4
Leverstock Green JMI School
HHNE HP2 ...36 E7
Leverstock Green Lawn
Tennis Club
HHS/BOV HP3 ...36 C8
Lewin Mead Community
Mental Health Centre
STRHM/NOR SW16 ...180 E9
Lewis Clinic
CAR SM5 ...222 B1

Lewisham Bridge Primary School
LEW SE13 ...160 G9
Lewisham Business Centre
NWCR SE14 ...160 C5
Lewisham College
BROCKY SE4 ...160 F8
Lewisham College
DEPT SE8 ...160 F7
Lewisham Coroners Office
LEW SE13 ...182 G1
Lewisham Council
CAT SE6 ...182 G6
Lewisham Council
DEPT SE8 ...160 G5
Lewisham Council
DEPT SE8 ...160 G5
Lewisham Council
DEPT SE8 ...160 F6
Lewisham & Guys Mental
Health NHS Trust
STHWK SE1 ...18 C2
Lewisham Hospital NHS Trust
LEW SE13 ...182 G1
Lewisham Hospital NHS Trust
LEW SE13 ...183 J1
Lewisham & North
Southwark Health Authority
GNWCH SE10 ...161 H7
Lewisham & North
Southwark Health Authority
LEE/GVPK SE12 ...183 N5
Lewisham Triangle Surgery
LEW SE13 ...161 H10
Lewisham Way Practice
BROCKY SE4 ...160 F8
Ley Hill CP School
CSHM HP5 ...51 N6
Ley Hill Cricket Club
CSHM HP5 ...51 P7
Ley Park CP School
BROX EN10 ...44 E8
Leys Infant School
DAGE RM10 ...144 D2
Leyton Business Centre
LEY E10 ...120 F7
Leyton Football Club
LEY E10 ...120 E6
Leyton Foot Clinic
SRTFD E15 ...121 H9
Leyton Orient Football Club
LEY E10 ...120 G8
Leyton Sixth Form College
LEY E10 ...121 J4
Leytonstone Mosque
WAN E11 ...121 L6
Leytonstone School
WAN E11 ...121 K4
Leyton Youth Sports Ground
LEY E10 ...120 G6
Liberal Jewish Synagogue
STJWD NW8 ...3 M10
The Liberty City Clinic
SDTCH EC2A ...13 J1
Liberty Middle School
MTCM CR4 ...201 P2
Lifecare NHS Trust
CTHM CR3 ...241 M9
Lilian Baylis School
VX/NE SW8 ...17 N10
Lilian Baylis Theatre
CLKNW EC1R ...6 B9
Lillan Baylis School
LBTH SE11 ...17 P6
Lilyville Surgery
FUL/PGN SW6 ...157 J7
Limehouse Town Hall
POP/IOD E14 ...140 E8
Limes Business Centre
HORL RH6 ...279 J9
Limes Farm County Primary
& Infant School
CHIG IG7 ...102 G7
The Limes Medical Centre
EPP CM16 ...65 L5
The Limes Medical Centre
EPP CM16 ...66 C2
Limestone Gallery
VX/NE SW8 ...17 L10
Lime Tree Surgery
SRTFD E15 ...121 K9
Lime Walk JMI School
HHS/BOV HP3 ...36 A8
Limpsfield Chart Golf Club
OXTED RH8 ...261 P5
Limpsfield C of E School
OXTED RH8 ...261 N5
Limpsfield Grange School
OXTED RH8 ...261 M3
Limpsfield Lawn Tennis Club
OXTED RH8 ...261 M4
Lincoln Health Surgery
HHNE HP2 ...35 N7
Lincoln Road Clinic
EN EN1 ...79 P9
Linda Blackstone Gallery
PIN HA5 ...113 M1
Linden Bridge School
WPK KT4 ...200 B10
Linden Lodge School
WIM/MER SW19 ...179 H4
Lindon Bennett School
FELT TW13 ...175 L8
The Link Primary School
CROY/NA CR0 ...222 F1
Links Primary School
TOOT SW17 ...180 B9
Linley Sambourne House
KENS W8 ...14 E2
Linnet House Clinic
STJWD NW8 ...3 N8
Linton Mead Primary School
THMD SE28 ...143 L9
Lionel Road School
BTFD TW8 ...155 N3
Lion House School
PUT/ROE SW15 ...156 G10
Lismarine Industrial Estate
BORE WD6 ...74 G10
Lisson Grove Health Centre
STJWD NW8 ...9 N1
Lister Community
Secondary School
PLSTW E13 ...141 N4
The Lister Hospital
BGVA SW1W ...16 E8
Lister House Clinic
CAVSQ/HST W1G ...10 E5
Lister House Surgery
HAT AL10 ...40 D3
Lister Medical Centre
HLWS CM18 ...46 F4
Little Angel Theatre
IS N1 ...6 D5
Littlebrook Business Centre
DART DA1 ...166 B9

Little Chalfont CP School
AMS HP6 ...70 B5
Little Chalfont Surgery
AMSS HP7 ...69 P6
Little Danson Welfare Clinic
WELL DA16 ...163 K10
Littledown School
SL SL1 ...129 L9
Little Ealing Primary School
EA W5 ...155 H2
Little Furze School
OXHEY WD19 ...93 J4
Little Green CP School
RKW/CH/CXG WD3 ...72 C7
Little Hands Theatre Co
HDN NW4 ...116 F2
Little Heath Junior Mixed School
POTB/CUF EN6 ...59 M6
Little Ilford
Comprehensive School
MNPK E12 ...122 C10
Little Reddings Primary School
BUSH WD23 ...74 A9
Little St Helens School
NTHWD HA6 ...92 G8
Little Stanmore First
& Middle School
EDGE HA8 ...95 L9
Little Thurrock County
Primary School
GRAYS RM17 ...168 A2
Littleton C of E Infant School
SHPTN TW17 ...196 B3
Livesey Museum
PECK SE15 ...160 A5
Livingstone Hospital
DART DA1 ...187 N3
Livingstone Primary School
EBAR EN4 ...77 N7
Llewelyn Surgery
WAB EN9 ...63 H9
Lloyd's
FENCHST EC3M ...13 J6
Lloyds Register Cricket Club
DUL SE21 ...181 L4
Lochinver House School
POTB/CUF EN6 ...59 L6
Lockers Park School
HHW HP1 ...35 L6
Locks View Court
POP/IOD E14 ...140 D9
Lockwood Industrial Park
TOTM N17 ...120 A1
Lodge Sun Sports Club
WAT WD17 ...72 F5
Lodge Surgery
STALW/RED AL3 ...38 C4
Loggia Gallery
WESTW SW1E ...16 G2
Lombard Business Centre
BTSEA SW11 ...157 N8
Lombard Business Park
CROY/NA CR0 ...202 G7
Lombard Business Park
WAND/EARL SW18 ...179 N2
Lombard Business Park
WIM/MER SW19 ...201 M2
Lombard Trading Estate
CHARL SE7 ...161 N3
Lombardy Retail Park
HYS/HAR UB3 ...133 J9
Lon Brgh of Sthwark
STHWK SE1 ...19 L5
London Aquarium
STHWK SE1 ...17 M1
London Ballet Theatre
HAMP NW3 ...3 M3
London Bible College
NTHWD HA6 ...92 E7
London Borough of Bromley
BMLY BR1 ...205 N2
London Borough of Camden
KTTN NW5 ...118 B10
London Borough
of Croydon Council
CROY/NA CR0 ...203 K6
London Borough of Hillingdon
HYS/HAR UB3 ...132 E8
London Borough
of Waltham Forest
WALTH E17 ...120 C1
London Bridge City Pier
STHWK SE1 ...13 J9
London Bridge Hospital
STHWK SE1 ...13 H9
London Bridge Sports Centre
CANST EC4R ...12 G8
London Bubble Theatre
BERM/RHTH SE16 ...160 A1
London Canal Museum
IS N1 ...5 M7
London Capital College
CAMTN NW1 ...4 F5
London City Mission
STHWK SE1 ...19 K1
The London Clinic
MHST W1U ...10 D2
London College of Business
& Computing
BETH E2 ...140 A4
London College of Fashion
MHST W1U ...10 D6
London College of Fashion
SDTCH EC2A ...13 K1
London College
of Further Education
LBTH SE11 ...18 C6
London College
of Higher Education
CLAP SW4 ...158 C9
London College of International
Business Studies
NOXST/BSQ WC1A ...11 M4
London College of Printing
STHWK SE1 ...18 D4
London Colney JMI School
LCOL/BKTW AL2 ...57 J1
London Commodity Exchange
WAP E1W ...13 M8
London County Courts
LINN WC2A ...12 A1
London Day Surgery Clinic
NFNCH/WDSP N12 ...97 M4
London Dungeon
STHWK SE1 ...13 H9
London Electronics College
ECT SW5 ...14 G7
The London Executive College
TOOT SW17 ...180 B6
London Fields Primary School
HACK E8 ...140 A3
London Foot Hospital
FITZ W1T ...10 G2

London Fo Temple
GTPST W1W ...10 G5
London Gatwick Airport
HORL RH6 ...279 N8
London Gatwick Airport
HORL RH6 ...280 D8
London Gatwick Airport
HORL RH6 ...280 B8
London Gender Clinic
HDN NW4 ...116 F4
London Group Business Park
CRICK NW2 ...116 C6
London Guildhall University
LVPST EC2M ...13 H4
London Guildhall University
TWRH EC3N ...13 L6
London Guildhall
University Sports Ground
LEE/GVPK SE12 ...183 P5
London Guildhall
University Sports Ground
LEE/GVPK SE12 ...183 P5
London International Festival
of Theatre
FSBYE EC1V ...12 D2
The London & International
School of Acting
MV/WKIL W9 ...8 D2
London Irish Rugby
Football Club
SUN TW16 ...197 H1
The London Irish Youth Theatre
HGT N6 ...118 C6
London Ladies
& Girls Football Club
CAT SE6 ...182 G6
London Lane Clinic
BMLY BR1 ...183 L10
London Lei Zang Si Temple
WOOL/PLUM SE18 ...162 G3
London Living Theatre
SYD SE26 ...182 C7
London Nautical School
STHWK SE1 ...12 B9
London Open College
FSBYE EC1V ...6 D9
London Oratory School
FUL/PGN SW6 ...157 L6
London Pavilion
REGST W1B ...11 J8
London Road Clinic
ALP/SUD HA0 ...115 K10
London Road Medical Centre
THHTH CR7 ...203 H6
London School of Economics
LSQ/SEVD WC2H ...11 L5
London School of Economics
STHWK SE1 ...12 E9
London School of Hygiene
& Tropical Medicine
RSQ WC1B ...11 K4
London Silver Vaults
LINN WC2A ...12 A4
London Sri Murugan Temple
MNPK E12 ...122 C10
The London Television Centre
STHWK SE1 ...12 A9
London Toy & Model Museum
BAY/PAD W2 ...9 J7
London Toy & Model Museum
SHB W12 ...136 F8
London Underwriting Centre
MON EC3R ...13 K7
London University
CMBW SE5 ...159 L8
London Welsh Football Club
RCH/KEW TW9 ...155 K9
London Welsh School
CRICK NW2 ...136 F1
London Zendo
CAMTN NW1 ...4 D3
London Zoo
CAMTN NW1 ...4 C1
Lonesome First School
MTCM CR4 ...202 C2
Long Close School
DTCH/LGLY SL3 ...149 M3
The Longcroft Clinic
BNSTD SM7 ...239 M1
Longdean School
HHS/BOV HP3 ...36 C9
Long Ditton County
Infant School
SURB KT6 ...199 H8
Longfield School
RYLN/HDSTN HA2 ...113 P4
Longford School
EBED/NFELT TW14 ...174 G3
Longlands Junior Middle
& Infant School
BROX EN10 ...62 D1
Longlands Primary School
BFN/LL DA15 ...185 H6
Long Lane A F C
BKHTH/KID SE3 ...161 P8
Longley Trading Estate
CRAWE RH10 ...283 P8
Longmead Business Centre
HOR/WEW KT19 ...220 A7
Longmead Industrial Estate
HOR/WEW KT19 ...220 A7
Longmead Junior
& Infant School
WDR/YW UB7 ...151 N2
Long Ridings Junior
& Infant School
RBRW/HUT CM13 ...87 N9
Longrove Surgery
BAR EN5 ...77 H7
Longshaw Primary School
CHING E4 ...101 J4
Lord Chancellors Dep
RSQ WC1B ...11 K4
Lord Chancellors Dep
WEST SW1P ...17 K4
Lord Chancellors Dep
WESTW SW1E ...17 H3
Lord Chancellors Department
HOL/ALD WC2B ...11 N6
Lord Chancellors Department
LINN WC2A ...12 A5
Lord Chancellors Department
TPL/STR WC2R ...11 P7
Lord Lister Health Centre
FSTGT E7 ...121 M9
Lords Cricket Museum
STJWD NW8 ...3 L10
Lordship Lane Clinic
TOTM N17 ...99 M10
Lordship Lane Primary School
WDGN N22 ...99 K9
Lord Snootys Gallery
KIL/WHAMP NW6 ...117 J10

Loreto College *STAL* AL1 ... 38 D6
Loseley House *RGUW* GU3 ... 267 L6
Loughborough Junior & Infant School *BRXN/ST* SW9 ... 159 J8
Loughton Cricket Club *LOU* IG10 ... 82 C7
Loughton Hall Clinic *LOU* IG10 ... 82 E7
Loughton Health Centre *LOU* IG10 ... 82 B7
Loughton Mental Health Centre *LOU* IG10 ... 82 B9
Lovelace Primary School *CHSGTN* KT9 ... 219 H2
Lower Clapton Health Centre *CLPT* E5 ... 120 B10
Lower Place Business Centre *WLSDN* NW10 ... 135 P4
Lower Sydenham Industrial Estate *CAT* SE6 ... 182 E8
Lowewood Museum *HOD* EN11 ... 44 F4
Lowfield Medical Centre *DART* DA1 ... 187 M3
Lowfield Sports Ground *HOD* EN11 ... 44 E3
Low Hall Sports Ground *WALTH* E17 ... 120 C4
Lowther CP School *BARN* SW13 ... 156 D6
Loxford High School *IL* IG1 ... 122 G10
Loyola Preparatory School *BKHH* IG9 ... 101 P2
L P R Sports Club *BARK/HLT* IG6 ... 103 J9
L S E Sports Club *NWMAL* KT3 ... 199 P6
LT Lost Property *CAMTN* NW1 ... 10 B2
Lucas Vale Junior School *DEPT* SE8 ... 160 F7
Lullingstone Castle *EYN* DA4 ... 229 J2
Lutomer House Business Centre *POP/IOD* E14 ... 140 G10
Luxembourg Embassy *KTBR* SW1X ... 16 C2
The Lyceum Theatre *TPL/STR* WC2R ... 11 N7
Lynch Hill Combined School *SLN* SL2 ... 128 E5
Lyndean Industrial Estate *ABYW* SE2 ... 163 M2
Lyndhurst Middle School *BORE* WD6 ... 75 L5
Lyndhurst Primary School *CMBW* SE5 ... 159 L8
Lyne & Longcross C of E School *CHERT* KT16 ... 194 E9
Lynton Preparatory School *EW* KT17 ... 220 C7
Lyon Business Park *BARK* IG11 ... 143 H4
Lyon Park Junior & Infant School *ALP/SUD* HA0 ... 135 L2
Lyons Industrial Estate *UX/CGN* UB8 ... 131 N8
Lyons Industrial Estate *WDR/YW* UB7 ... 131 M8
Lyric Theatre *SOHO/SHAV* W1D ... 11 J7
Lyric Theatre Hammersmith *HMSMTH* W6 ... 156 F3
Mabwin Supplementary School *ED* N9 ... 100 A3
Macaulay Primary School *CLAP* SW4 ... 158 C10
Madame Tussaud's *CAMTN* NW1 ... 10 C2
Madeira Grove Clinic *WFD* IG8 ... 101 N7
Madison Bowl *NTHWD* HA6 ... 92 F8
Magna Carta Secondary School *EGH* TW20 ... 172 C9
Magnet Estate *WTHK* RM20 ... 167 H4
Magnolia House Surgery *ASC* SL5 ... 192 E5
Mahatma Gandhi Industrial Estate *BRXN/ST* SW9 ... 159 J9
The Maheswaran Practice *CRICK* NW2 ... 117 J8
Mahieu Osteopathic Surgery *KENS* W8 ... 14 F3
Maida Vale Hospital *MV/WKIL* W9 ... 9 K1
Maida Vale Medical Centre *MV/WKIL* W9 ... 2 G10
Maidenbower First School *CRAWE* RH10 ... 284 D9
Malawi High Comm *MYFR/PKLN* W1K ... 10 E7
Malayan High Comm *MBLAR* W1H ... 10 A5
Malaysia High Comm *KTBR* SW1X ... 16 D2
Malcolm Primary School *PGE/AN* SE20 ... 182 B10
Malden Manor Junior School *NWMAL* KT3 ... 200 B7
Malden Parochial School *WPK* KT4 ... 200 B8
Malden Road Baths *CHEAM* SM3 ... 220 G1
Malham Road Industrial Estate *FSTH* SE23 ... 182 C4
Mall Galleries *STJS* SW1Y ... 11 K9
The Mall School *WHTN* TW2 ... 176 C6
Malmesbury Middle School *MRDN* SM4 ... 201 M6
Malmesbury Primary School *BOW* E3 ... 140 E5
Malmesbury Primary School *MRDN* SM4 ... 201 M7
Malorees Gm Junior & Infant School *KIL/WHAMP* NW6 ... 136 C2
Malory School *BMLY* BR1 ... 183 M7
Maita High Comm *MYFR/PICC* W1J ... 11 H8
Maltings Arts Theatre *STAL* AL1 ... 38 C6

The Maltings Industrial Estate *SBW* CM21 ... 30 A1
The Maltings Surgery *STAL* AL1 ... 38 C6
Maltmans Green Preparatory School *CFSP/GDCR* SL9 ... 109 P1
Malvern Way School *RKW/CH/CXG* WD3 ... 72 D9
Manby Lodge Infant School *WEY* KT13 ... 216 D2
Mandeville Health Centre *STAL* AL1 ... 38 C9
Mandeville Primary School *CLPT* E5 ... 120 D8
Mandeville Primary School *STAL* AL1 ... 38 C9
Mandeville Special School *NTHLT* UB5 ... 133 N1
Manford Industrial Estate *ERITH* DA8 ... 165 J5
Manford Way Health Centre *BARK/HLT* IG6 ... 103 J7
Manor Brook Medical Centre *BKHTH/KID* SE3 ... 161 N8
Manorcroft School *EGH* TW20 ... 172 D9
Manor Drive Health Centre *WPK* KT4 ... 200 C8
Manorfield Primary School *POP/IOD* E14 ... 140 G7
Manor Gallery *GVE* DA12 ... 190 E3
Manor House Hospital *GLDGN* NW11 ... 117 L6
Manor House School *EHSLY* KT24 ... 253 M3
Manor Junior & Infant School *BARK* IG11 ... 143 J1
Manor Lodge School *RAD* WD7 ... 57 P6
Manor Mead School *SHPTN* TW17 ... 196 C5
The Manor of Groves *SBW* CM21 ... 29 J1
Manor Park Medical Centre *SL* SL1 ... 129 J7
Manor Park Methodist School *MNPK* E12 ... 122 B9
Manor Park Primary School *SUT* SM1 ... 221 M2
Manor Practice *WLGTN* SM6 ... 222 F4
Manor Practice *WLGTN* SM6 ... 222 C2
Manor Primary School *SRTFD* E15 ... 141 K4
Manor Primary School *WLSDN* NW10 ... 136 F4
The Manor Primary School *ROM* RM1 ... 124 G3
Manor Road Surgery *DAGE* RM10 ... 144 E1
The Manor School *BF/WBF* KT14 ... 215 P10
Manorside Primary School *FNCH* N3 ... 97 L9
Manor Street Surgery *BERK* HP4 ... 33 P5
Manor Way Business Centre *DAGW* RM9 ... 144 E7
Manor Way Industrial Estate *GRAYS* RM17 ... 167 P6
Mansion House *MANHO* EC4N ... 12 G6
Manzoori Clinic *SWLY* BR8 ... 186 G10
Maple Cross Industrial Estate *RKW/CH/CXG* WD3 ... 91 H5
Maple Cross Junior Middle & Infant School *RKW/CH/CXG* WD3 ... 90 C6
Mapledown School *CRICK* NW2 ... 116 F5
Maple Grove Business Centre *HSLWW* TW4 ... 153 K10
Maple Industrial Estate *FELT* TW13 ... 175 H5
Maple Junior & Infant School *STAL* AL1 ... 38 D5
Maple River Industrial Estate *HLW* CM20 ... 29 L5
Maples Business Centre *IS* N1 ... 6 B5
Marble Arch *BAY/PAD* W2 ... 10 B7
Marden Lodge School *CTHM* CR3 ... 242 A7
Mardyke Surgery *PUR* RM19 ... 165 P3
Margaret Roper RC Primary School *PUR/KEN* CR8 ... 222 G6
Margaret Wix Junior & Infant School *STALW/RED* AL3 ... 38 B2
Maria Fidelis Convent Lower School *CAMTN* NW1 ... 5 H10
Maria Fidelis Convent Upper School *CAMTN* NW1 ... 5 J9
Marillac Hospital *RBRW/HUT* CM13 ... 107 J3
Marion Vian Primary School *BECK* BR3 ... 204 C5
Marish County Middle School *DTCH/LGLY* SL3 ... 150 C2
Marist RC Primary School *BF/WBF* KT14 ... 215 J10
Marist Senior School *ASC* SL5 ... 192 C4
Maritime Industrial Estate *CHARL* SE7 ... 161 N3
Maritime Museum *GNWCH* SE10 ... 161 K3
The Marjory Kinnon School *EBED/NFELT* TW14 ... 174 F1
The Market *COVGDN* WC2E ... 11 M7
Market Trading Estate *NWDGN* UB2 ... 153 J3
Mark Hall Comprehensive School *HLWE* CM17 ... 29 M8
Mark Hall Cycle Museum *HLW* CM20 ... 29 L8
Marks Gate Junior School *CHDH* RM6 ... 123 P1
Marlborough Cricket Club *DUL* SE21 ... 181 P4
Marlborough Day Hospital *STJWD* NW8 ... 3 K7

Marlborough Park School *BFN/LL* DA15 ... 185 K4
Marlborough Primary School *CHEL* SW3 ... 15 P6
Marlborough School *HRW* HA1 ... 114 D2
Marlborough School *ISLW* TW7 ... 154 F7
Marlborough School *STAL* AL1 ... 38 B9
Marlowe Business Centre *NWCR* SE14 ... 160 D6
Marlowes Health Centre *HHW* HP1 ... 35 M6
Marner Primary School *BOW* E3 ... 140 G6
Marshall Gallery *WKENS* W14 ... 156 C2
Marshalls Park School *ROM* RM1 ... 104 F10
Marshalls Park Upper School *ROM* RM1 ... 124 F2
Marshfield C of E School *ADL/WDHM* KT15 ... 215 H3
Marshgate Trading Estate *SRTFD* E15 ... 140 C2
Marsh Green School *DAGE* RM10 ... 144 B4
Marston Fine Arts Gallery *MLHL* NW7 ... 96 C5
Martan College *HOL/ALD* WC2B ... 11 M5
Martin Baker Sports Ground *DEN/HRF* UB9 ... 111 J5
Martinbridge Industrial Estate *EN* EN1 ... 79 P9
Martindale JMI School *HHW* HP1 ... 35 J5
Martinfield Business Centre *WGCE* AL7 ... 23 J4
Martin Hewitt Practice *TOOT* SW17 ... 179 P4
Martin Primary School *EFNCH* N2 ... 97 P10
Marvels Lane Primary School *LEE/GVPK* SE12 ... 183 P7
Mary Boone School *WKENS* W14 ... 14 B5
Maryland Industrial Estate *SRTFD* E15 ... 121 K10
Maryland Primary School *SRTFD* E15 ... 121 K10
Marylebone Cricket Club *STJWD* NW8 ... 3 M10
Marylebone Mag Ct *CAMTN* NW1 ... 9 P3
Marymount International School *KUTN/CMB* KT2 ... 177 P10
Mary Wallace Theatre *TWK* TW1 ... 176 F4
Masorti Synagogue *EDGE* HA8 ... 95 N6
Maswell Park Health Centre *HSLW* TW3 ... 176 B1
Matching Green C of E Primary School *HLWE* CM17 ... 31 L9
Matilda Marks School *MLHL* NW7 ... 96 A6
Matrix Business Centre *DART* DA1 ... 187 M1
Matthew Arnold County Secondary School *STA* TW18 ... 173 M9
Matts Gallery *WCHPL* E1 ... 140 D7
Maudesley Hospital Day Programme *CMBW* SE5 ... 159 L8
Maudlin's Green *WAP* E1W ... 13 N9
Maudsley Hospital Annexe *EDUL* SE22 ... 159 N10
The Maudsley Hospital *CMBW* SE5 ... 159 K9
Maunds Wood CP School *HLWS* CM18 ... 46 C5
Mauritius High Comm *SKENS* SW7 ... 15 K4
Mawbrey Brough Health Centre *VX/NE* SW8 ... 158 F6
Mawney Infant School *ROMW/RG* RM7 ... 124 E3
May Avenue Industrial Estate *GVW* DA11 ... 190 C4
Maybury County First School *WOKN/KNAP* GU21 ... 232 C2
The Maybury Surgery *WOKS/MYFD* GU22 ... 232 E2
Mayday Healthcare NHS Trust *THHTH* CR7 ... 203 J6
Mayespark Primary School *GDMY/SEVK* IG3 ... 123 K8
Mayfair Gallery *KTTN* NW5 ... 118 C10
Mayfield County Infant School *CHES/WCR* EN8 ... 62 D3
Mayfield High School *BCTR* RM8 ... 123 M6
Mayfield Primary School *GFD/PVL* UB6 ... 134 C8
Mayfield School *PIN* HA5 ... 113 M1
Mayfield Surgery *PUT/ROE* SW15 ... 178 E3
Mayflower Junior & Infant School *POP/IOD* E14 ... 140 F8
Maylands Golf Club *HARH* RM3 ... 106 A6
Mayplace Primary School *BXLYHN* DA7 ... 164 E10
Maypole Community School *BXLY* DA5 ... 186 F5
Maytime School *IL* IG1 ... 122 D8
Mayville Infant School *WAN* E11 ... 121 K8
Mayville Junior School *WAN* E11 ... 121 K7
Maze Hill School *GNWCH* SE10 ... 161 K5
Mazenod RC Primary School *KIL/WHAMP* NW6 ... 2 F4
Mcentee School *WALTH* E17 ... 100 E9
Mckay Trading Estate *DTCH/LGLY* SL3 ... 151 H8
Mckay Trading Estate *NKENS* W10 ... 8 A1
Mcmillan Clinic *HYS/HAR* UB3 ... 132 D9

The Mead Business Centre *HERT/BAY* SG13 ... 25 M4
The Mead County First School *HOR/WEW* KT19 ... 220 C1
Mead Industrial Park *HLW* CM20 ... 29 J7
Mead Infant School *HARH* RM3 ... 105 N7
Meadlands School *RCHPK/HAM* TW10 ... 177 H7
Meadowcroft County First School *CHERT* KT16 ... 195 J10
Meadowgate School *PECK* SE15 ... 160 C9
Meadow School *UX/CGN* UB8 ... 131 P7
Meadow Wood School *BUSH* WD23 ... 74 B9
Mead Road Infant School *CHST* BR7 ... 184 F9
The Mead School *HLWS* CM18 ... 47 H3
Meath Green County Junior School *HORL* RH6 ... 280 A2
Meath Green First School *HORL* RH6 ... 280 A2
Meath School *CHERT* KT16 ... 214 C4
Medical Express Clinic *CAVSQ/HST* W1G ... 10 E3
The 157 Medical Practice *FSBYPK* N4 ... 118 C3
Medical Sch *GTPST* W1W ... 10 C3
Medical School *BAY/PAD* W2 ... 9 M5
Mednurs Clinic *SEVS/STOTM* N15 ... 119 L4
Medwyn Doctors Surgery *DORK* RH4 ... 272 C1
Megabowl *BRXS/STRHM* SW2 ... 180 F5
Melcombe Primary School *HMSMTH* W6 ... 156 C5
Mellow Lane School *HGDN/ICK* UB10 ... 132 D6
Melrose School *MTCM* CR4 ... 201 P3
Memorial Hospital *WOOL/PLUM* SE18 ... 162 D8
Menorah Foundation School *EDGE* HA8 ... 95 P8
Menorah Grammar School *GLDGN* NW11 ... 117 H5
Mental Health Trust *STHWK* SE1 ... 13 H10
Mercers College *WARE* SG12 ... 26 C2
Mercers' Hall *CITYW* EC2V ... 12 F6
The Merchant Taylors Hall *BANK* EC3V ... 13 H6
Merchant Taylors School *NTHWD* HA6 ... 92 F3
Mercury Theatre *LSQ/SEVD* WC2H ... 11 L6
The Mercury Theatre *NTGHL* W11 ... 8 E8
Meriden Primary School *GSTN* WD25 ... 73 L2
Meridian Clinic *BRXN/ST* SW9 ... 159 H9
Meridian Locality Mental Health Centre *CHARL* SE7 ... 161 P5
Meridian School *GNWCH* SE10 ... 161 J4
Meridian Sports Club *CHARL* SE7 ... 162 B5
Meridian Trading Estate *CHARL* SE7 ... 161 N3
Merland Rise County First School *KWD/TDW/WH* KT20 ... 238 F5
Merlin Primary School *BMLY* BR1 ... 183 M6
Merlin School *PUT/ROE* SW15 ... 178 G1
Mermaid Theatre *BLKFR* EC4V ... 12 D7
Merrist Wood College *RGUW* GU3 ... 249 H4
Merrow Clinic *GU* GU1 ... 250 E9
Merrow C of E First School *RGUE* GU4 ... 250 G8
Merrow Park Surgery *RGUE* GU4 ... 250 G8
Merryhills Clinic *ENC/FH* EN2 ... 78 G7
Merryhills Primary School *ENC/FH* EN2 ... 78 G7
Merstham County Primary School *REDH* RH1 ... 258 D4
Merton Abbey Primary School *WIM/MER* SW19 ... 201 L1
Merton Adult College *RYNPK* SW20 ... 201 H3
Merton College *MRDN* SM4 ... 201 J5
Merton Industrial Park *WIM/MER* SW19 ... 201 M1
Merton Park Primary School *WIM/MER* SW19 ... 201 J2
Merton Surgery *WIM/MER* SW19 ... 179 L10
Merton Sutton & Wandsworth Health Authority *MTCM* CR4 ... 202 A4
Merton Sutton & Wandsworth Health Authority *SUT* SM1 ... 201 M8
Meryfield School *BORE* WD6 ... 75 L5
Metro Business Centre *SYD* SE26 ... 182 E9
Metropolitan Business Centre *HACK* E8 ... 7 K4
Metropolitan Hospital *STHWK* SE1 ... 18 B3
Metropolitan Police *STJWD* NW8 ... 3 N8
Metropolitan Police Football Club *E/WMO/HCT* KT8 ... 198 C6
Metropolitan Police Hayes Sports Club *HAYES* BR2 ... 205 L10
Metropolitan Tabernacle *LBTH* SE11 ... 18 D4

Metro Trading Centre *WBLY* HA9 ... 115 N9
Meyer Vet Surgery *FUL/PGN* SW6 ... 157 J6
Michael Faraday Primary School *WALW* SE17 ... 19 H9
Michael Manley Industrial Estate *VX/NE* SW8 ... 158 D8
Micklem JMI School *HHW* HP1 ... 35 J5
Midas Business Centre *DAGE* RM10 ... 124 B9
Midas Industrial Estate *DAGE* RM10 ... 124 B9
Midas Industrial Estate *UX/CGN* UB8 ... 131 L4
Middlegreen Trading Estate *DTCH/LGLY* SL3 ... 150 A1
Middle Park Primary School *ELTH/MOT* SE9 ... 184 A3
Middle Row Primary School *NKENS* W10 ... 8 A1
Middlesex Business Centre *NWDGN* UB2 ... 153 P1
Middlesex Guildhall *WEST* SW1P ... 17 K2
Middlesex Hospital *GTPST* W1W ... 11 H4
Middlesex Hospital Sports Ground *CHST* BR7 ... 185 J8
Middlesex New Synagogue *HRW* HA1 ... 114 C5
Middlesex University *GLDGN* NW11 ... 117 L6
Middlesex University *TOTM* N17 ... 99 M7
Middlesex University *WDGN* N22 ... 98 F10
Middlesex University Business School *HDN* NW4 ... 116 E2
Middle Temple *EMB* EC4Y ... 12 A7
Middleton School *WARE* SG12 ... 26 C4
Mid Essex Adult Community College *RBRW/HUT* CM13 ... 87 N10
Midfield Primary School *CHST* BR7 ... 185 K10
Mildmay Medical Practice *HBRY* N5 ... 119 L10
Mile End & Bow Business Centre *WCHPL* E1 ... 140 A7
Mile End Hospital *WCHPL* E1 ... 140 C5
Milehams Industrial Estate *PUR* RM19 ... 165 P2
Miles Coverdale Primary School *SHB* W12 ... 156 F1
Milestone School *HART* DA3 ... 211 L8
Millbank School *WEST* SW1P ... 17 K6
Millbank Tower *WEST* SW1P ... 17 L6
Millbarn Medical Centre *BEAC* HP9 ... 88 E10
Millbourne Lodge Junior School *ESH/CLAY* KT10 ... 218 B2
Millbourne Lodge Senior School *ESH/CLAY* KT10 ... 218 C3
Millbrook Junior Middle & Infant School *CHES/WCR* EN8 ... 62 D5
Millenium Experience *GNWCH* SE10 ... 141 K10
Millenium Harbour Development *BERM/RHTH* SE16 ... 160 E1
Millenium Wharf Development *POP/IOD* E14 ... 161 J2
Millennium Balloon *STHWK* SE1 ... 13 K10
The Miller Practice *HBRY* N5 ... 119 K10
Mill Farm Business Park *HSLWW* TW4 ... 175 M3
Millfields Junior & Infant School *CLPT* E5 ... 120 B9
Millfield Theatre *UED* N18 ... 99 L5
Mill Green Business Park *MTCM* CR4 ... 202 A7
Mill Hill County High School *MLHL* NW7 ... 96 B3
The Mill Hill Cricket Club *MLHL* NW7 ... 96 F4
Mill Hill Industrial Estate *MLHL* NW7 ... 96 C7
Mill Hill School *MLHL* NW7 ... 96 E5
Mill Hill Synagogue *MLHL* NW7 ... 96 B7
Mill Lane Medical Centre *KIL/WHAMP* NW6 ... 117 K10
Mill Lane Trading Estate *CROY/NA* CR0 ... 202 G10
Millmead Junior & Infant School *HERT/WAS* SG14 ... 25 K5
Millside Industrial Estate *DART* DA1 ... 165 L10
Mill Street Clinic *STHWK* SE1 ... 19 M1
Mill Studio Business Centre *WARE* SG12 ... 26 D2
Millwall Football Club *BERM/RHTH* SE16 ... 160 B4
Millwards CP School *HLWW/ROY* CM19 ... 46 E5
Millway Medical Practice *MLHL* NW7 ... 96 C6
Milmead Industrial Centre *TOTM* N17 ... 100 A10
Milton House Surgery *BERK* HP4 ... 33 N5
Milton Mount School *CRAWE* RH10 ... 284 D5
Milton Natural Health Centre *HGT* N6 ... 118 D5
Milton Road Business Park *GVE* DA12 ... 190 F3
Minet Clinic *HYS/HAR* UB3 ... 133 H10
Minet Junior & Infant School *HYS/HAR* UB3 ... 133 J10
Ministry of Agriculture *WHALL* SW1A ... 11 L10
Ministry of Defence *WHALL* SW1A ... 11 L10
Mini Town Hall *WOOL/PLUM* SE18 ... 163 J4

Mint Business Park
CAN/RD E16 .... 141 M7
Mirravale Trading Estate
BCTR RM8 .... 123 P5
The Misbourne Practice
CFSP/GDCR SL9 .... 90 A9
Mitcham Cricket Club
MTCM CR4 .... 201 P4
Mitcham Industrial Estate
MTCM CR4 .... 202 B1
**Mitcham Parochial
Church Council**
MTCM CR4 .... 201 P3
Mitcham Road Surgery
TOOT SW17 .... 180 B9
Mitchell Brook Primary School
WLSDN NW10 .... 136 A1
Mitchell Junior School
HCH RM12 .... 145 J1
Mitre Bridge Industrial Park
WLSDN NW10 .... 136 E6
Moat Bridge School
ELTH/MOT SE9 .... 184 A2
Mocha Museums
CAMTN NW1 .... 5 H6
Modern Gallery
GTPST W1W 11 H4
Modern Tutorial College
NKENS W10 .... 136 C5
Mole Business Park
LHD/OX KT22 .... 236 F7
Molesey Hospital
E/WMO/HCT KT8 .... 197 P5
Mole Valley District Council
LHD/OX KT22 .... 236 G5
Mole Valley District Council
LHD/OX KT22 .... 236 F7
Mollison Drive Health Centre
WLGTN SM6 .... 222 F4
Monega Primary School
MNPK E12 .... 122 A10
**Monken Hadley C of E
Primary School**
EBAR EN4 .... 77 K5
Monkfrith Primary School
EBAR EN4 .... 98 B1
Monksmead School
BORE WD6 .... 75 P7
Monks Orchard School
CROY/NA CR0 .... 204 C5
Monro Industrial Estate
CHES/WCR EN8 .... 62 D10
Monson Primary School
NWCR SE14 .... 160 C6
Montbelle Primary School
ELTH/MOT SE9 .... 184 E6
Monteagle School
DAGW RM9 .... 143 L3
Montem County Middle School
SL SL1 .... 148 C1
Montem Junior & Infant School
HOLWY N7 .... 118 G8
Montem Sports Centre
SL SL1 .... 149 J1
Montessore School
BERK HP4 .... 33 N5
Montpelier Primary School
EA W5 .... 135 J7
**Monument Hill County
Primary School**
WOKS/MYFD GU22 .... 232 F1
Moorcroft School
UX/CGN UB8 .... 132 C7
Moorfields Eye Hospital
FSBYE EC1V 6 C10
Moorfields Primary School
STLK EC1Y 12 G1
Moor House School
OXTED RH8 .... 261 L8
Moor Lane Junior School
CHSGTN KT9 .... 219 L2
Moor Park Industrial Estate
WATW WD18 .... 92 C1
Mora Primary School
CRICK NW2 .... 116 F9
Morden College Homes
BKHTH/KID SE3 .... 161 M8
Morden First School
MRDN SM4 .... 201 K5
Morden Hall Medical Centre
WIM/MER SW19 .... 201 L3
Morden Hill Surgery
LEW SE13 .... 161 H8
Morden Mount School
LEW SE13 .... 160 G8
Morden Road Clinic
WIM/MER SW19 .... 201 L3
Morehouse School
ISLW TW7 .... 154 D7
**Moreland Junior Middle
& Infant Primary School**
FSBYE EC1V 6 D10
Moreton Bay Industrial Estate
GPK RM2 .... 105 L10
Moreton C of E Primary School
CHONG CM5 .... 49 K6
Moreton Industrial Estate
SWLY BR8 .... 209 J4
Moreton Street Gallery
PIM SW1V 17 H7
Morgans Junior School
HERT/BAY SG13 .... 25 L7
**Morgans Walk Junior
Mixed School**
HERT/BAY SG13 .... 25 L7
**Morgans Walk Junior
Mixed School**
HERT/WAS SG14 .... 25 H7
Morningside Primary School
HOM E9 .... 140 B1
Mornington Leisure Centre
CAMTN NW1 .... 4 F7
Morpeth Secondary School
BETH E2 .... 140 B8
Morris House Surgery
TOTM N17 .... 99 L8
Mortimer Road Clinic
WLSDN NW10 .... 136 F5
Mortimer School
STRHM/NOR SW16 .... 180 E5
Moselle School
TOTM N17 .... 99 L10
**Mosiah Foundation
Supplementary School**
STNW/STAM N16 .... 119 M6
Mosque
BETH E2 .... 7 L6
Mosque
BETH E2 .... 140 A4
Mosque
FSTGT E7 .... 141 M1

**The Mosque & Islamic Centre
of Brent**
CRICK NW2 .... 116 G9
The Mosque
NWDGN UB2 .... 153 M2
Mosquito Aircraft
LCOL/BKTW AL2 .... 57 N5
Mosquito Aircraft Museum
LCOL/BKTW AL2 .... 57 J2
Mossford Green Primary School
BARK/HLT IG6 .... 102 F10
Moss Hall Infant School
FNCH N3 .... 97 L7
Moss Hall Junior School
FNCH N3 .... 97 L7
The Mother & Baby Clinic
HOM E9 .... 140 B1
Motley Thtr
HOL/ALD WC2B 11 N6
**Mottingham Community
Health Clinic**
ELTH/MOT SE9 .... 184 B7
Mount Alvernia Hospital
GU GU1 .... 268 B2
The Mountfield Surgery
FNCH N3 .... 117 K1
Mount Grace Gm School
POTB/CUF EN6 .... 59 L6
The Mount Infant School
NWMAL KT3 .... 199 N3
Mount Medical Centre
FELT TW13 .... 175 M5
Mount Pleasant School
LCOL/BKTW AL2 .... 55 M6
Mount School
MLHL NW7 .... 96 E6
Mount Stewart School
KTN/HRWW/W HA3 .... 115 J4
Mount Vernon Hospital
RKW/CH/CXG WD3 .... 92 C6
MountView Theatre School
CEND/HSY/T N8 .... 118 F4
MountView Theatre School
WDGN N22 .... 98 G10
The Moving Gallery
CHSWK W4 .... 156 B2
Mowat Industrial Estate
WATN WD24 .... 73 K4
Mowlem Junior & Infant School
BETH E2 .... 140 B4
Mowlem Trading Estate
TOTM N17 .... 100 B8
Mr Youngs Preview Theatre
SOHO/CST W1F 11 H6
M S Business Centre
PIN HA5 .... 113 L1
M S P Business Centre
WBLY HA9 .... 115 N9
Mudchute City Farm
POP/IOD E14 .... 161 H3
Mudlands Estate
RAIN RM13 .... 144 F5
Muhammads Mosque
SHB W12 .... 156 F1
Mulberry Business Centre
BERM/RHTH SE16 .... 160 C1
Mulberry House School
CRICK NW2 .... 117 H10
Mulberry School
WCHPL E1 .... 140 A8
Mulgrave Jm and I School
WOOL/PLUM SE18 .... 162 C4
The Multilingual Gallery
IS N1 .... 6 D1
**Murky Puddle Theatre Co/magic
Fox/panic**
NWMAL KT3 .... 200 C3
Murray Business Centre
STMC/STPC BR5 .... 207 L3
Museum Ass
CLKNW EC1R 12 B2
**Muschamp Junior
& Infant School**
CAR SM5 .... 201 P9
Museum
BERM/RHTH SE16 .... 140 E10
Museum
BLKFR EC4V 12 E7
Museum
BMSBY WC1N 11 P2
Museum
CHEL SW3 .... 16 C8
Museum
COVGDN WC2E 11 M7
Museum
LSQ/SEVD WC2H 11 K5
Museum
SRTFD E15 .... 141 K1
Museum
WAB EN9 .... 63 H10
Museum
WALW SE17 .... 18 E6
Museum Gallery
RSQ WC1B 11 L4
Museum in Docklands
POP/IOD E14 .... 140 F9
Museum & Library
WALW SE17 .... 18 E6
Museum of Artillery
WOOL/PLUM SE18 .... 162 C4
Museum of Fulham Palace
FUL/PGN SW6 .... 156 C8
Museum of Garden History
STHWK SE1 .... 17 M4
Museum of Installation
LBTH SE11 .... 18 A4
Museum of London
IS N1 .... 6 F6
Museum of London
STBT EC1A 12 C4
Museum of Mankind
CONDST W1S 10 G8
Museum of the Order of St John
FARR EC1M 12 D2
Museum of Womens Art
FSBYE EC1V 12 D2
The Museum Practice
RSQ WC1B 11 K4
The Musical Museum
BTFD TW8 .... 155 K5
Musley Infant School
WARE SG12 .... 26 D1
Museum Service
BARB EC2Y 12 E4
Muswell Hill Bowling Club
MUSWH N10 .... 118 B1
Muswell Hill Synagogue
MUSWH N10 .... 118 B1
Myatt Garden Primary School
BROCKY SE4 .... 160 E8
Myatts Field Clinic
BRXN/ST SW9 .... 159 J7

Nagi Business Centre
ALP/SUD HA0 .... 135 J4
Nanjuwany Eye Practice
FUL/PGN SW6 .... 157 H8
Napsbury Hospital
LCOL/BKTW AL2 .... 56 G3
**Nascot Wood Junior
& Infant School**
WAT WD17 .... 73 H4
Nash Mills C of E Primary School
HHS/BOV HP3 .... 54 A1
National Army Museum
CHEL SW3 .... 16 B9
**National Association for Gallery
Education**
CLKNW EC1R 12 B2
National Film Theatre
STHWK SE1 .... 11 P9
National Hospital
RSQ WC1B 11 L3
**National Hospital for Neurology
& Neurosurgery**
RSQ WC1B 11 L2
National Maritime Museum
GNWCH SE10 .... 161 J5
National Portrait Gallery
LSQ/SEVD WC2H 11 K8
National Postal Museum
STBT EC1A 12 D5
**National Temperance
Hospital NHS Trust**
CAMTN NW1 .... 4 C9
National Youth Theatre of Gb
HOLWY N7 .... 118 F8
The Natural Health Practice
IS N1 .... 5 N5
Natural History Museum
SKENS SW7 .... 15 L4
Natural Therapy Clinic
TOOT SW17 .... 180 C8
Natwest Sports Club
BECK BR3 .... 182 E9
Navigation College
MANHO EC4N 12 F7
Nazeing CP School
WAB EN9 .... 45 K9
Nazeing Golf Club
WAB EN9 .... 45 P10
Nazeing Parish Council
WAB EN9 .... 63 N1
Nazeing Park (School)
WAB EN9 .... 45 P8
The Nd Theatre
NOXST/BSQ WC1A 11 K5
Neil Graham Gallery
BRWN CM15 .... 107 J3
**Nelmes Primary
& Junior Schooll**
EMPK RM11 .... 125 N2
Nelson Dock Museum
BERM/RHTH SE16 .... 140 E10
Nelson Hospital
WIM/MER SW19 .... 201 J2
Nelson Primary School
EHAM E6 .... 142 D4
Nelson Primary School
WHTN TW2 .... 176 A2
Nelson's Colmn
CHCR WC2N 11 L9
Nelson Trading Estate
WIM/MER SW19 .... 201 L1
Neo Clinic
PIM SW1V 16 G6
Netley Primary School
CAMTN NW1 .... 4 C10
**New Addington
Swimming Pools**
CROY/NA CR0 .... 225 H6
New Amb Theatre
LSQ/SEVD WC2H 11 K6
**New Ash Green County
Primary School**
HART DA3 .... 211 L9
**The New Aylesbury
Medical Centre**
WALW SE17 .... 19 H7
New Beacon School
SEV TN13 .... 264 C3
New Briars School
HAT AL10 .... 40 D4
Newbury Park Health Centre
GNTH/NBYPK IG2 .... 122 G4
Newbury Park Primary School
GNTH/NBYPK IG2 .... 122 G4
Newbury Park Synagogue
GDMY/SEVK IG3 .... 123 J4
New Caledonian Wharf
BERM/RHTH SE16 .... 160 E2
New Chiswick Swimming Pool
CHSWK W4 .... 156 B6
New City Gallery
STHWK SE1 .... 12 C10
New City Primary School
PLSTW E13 .... 141 P5
The New College
WDSR SL4 .... 149 J6
New Connaught Rooms
HOL/ALD WC2B 11 M5
New Court Business Park
HLWW/ROY CM19 .... 46 F5
New Crane Wharf
WAP E1W 140 B10
New Elgiva Theatre
CSHM HP5 .... 51 J8
New Eltham Galleries
ELTH/MOT SE9 .... 184 F4
New End Theatre
HAMP NW3 .... 117 M8
New England Industrial Estate
BARK IG11 .... 142 F4
New England Industrial Estate
HOD EN11 .... 45 H2
Newfield Primary School
WLSDN NW10 .... 136 C2
The New Furness Primary School
WLSDN NW10 .... 136 D4
New Grafton Gallery
BARN SW13 .... 156 C8
**Newham College
of Further Education**
EHAM E6 .... 142 C4
**Newham College
of Further Education**
SRTFD E15 .... 141 K2
Newham Community College
CAN/RD E16 .... 141 K6
Newham General Hospital
PLSTW E13 .... 141 P6
Newham Leisure Centre
PLSTW E13 .... 141 P7
Newham Medical Centre
PLSTW E13 .... 141 P4

Newham Museum Service
SRTFD E15 .... 141 J2
Newham Sixth Form College
PLSTW E13 .... 141 N6
New Haw Therapy Clinic
ADL/WDHM KT15 .... 215 L6
New Health Centre
TOTM N17 .... 99 M9
New House Surgery
DORK RH4 .... 272 F3
**Newington Court
Business Centre**
STHWK SE1 .... 18 E4
Newington Green Infant School
STNW/STAM N16 .... 119 M10
Newington Industrial Estate
WALW SE17 .... 18 D6
New Inn Surgery
GU GU1 .... 250 E7
New Kings Primary School
FUL/PGN SW6 .... 157 J8
Newland House School
TWK TW1 .... 176 E7
New London Synagogue
STJWD NW8 .... 3 J7
New London Theatre
LSQ/SEVD WC2H 11 M5
Newnham Junior & Infant School
RSLP HA4 .... 113 K6
New Peckham Mosque
CMBW SE5 .... 19 L9
New Pennyfarthing Galleries
HNHL SE24 .... 181 J2
Newport Junior & Infant School
WAN E11 .... 121 H7
New Rush Hall School
IL IG1 .... 122 F7
New School
FUL/PGN SW6 .... 157 J7
New Scotland Yard
STJSPK SW1H 17 J3
News International
WAP E1W 13 P8
News International
WAP E1W 140 A9
New Southgate Industrial Estate
FBAR/BDGN N11 .... 98 D6
**New Southgate Pain Clinic
& Medical Centre**
FBAR/BDGN N11 .... 98 D6
Newstead Wood School for Girls
ORP BR6 .... 206 G10
New Surgery
BH/WHM TN16 .... 243 P7
The New Surgery
CLAP SW4 .... 158 F10
The New Surgery
CSHM HP5 .... 50 G6
The New Surgery
KGLGY WD4 .... 54 B5
**New Swan Valley
Community School**
SWCM DA10 .... 189 L3
**Newton Farm First
& Middle School**
RYLN/HDSTN HA2 .... 113 N7
Newton Medical Centre
BAY/PAD W2 .... 8 F5
Newton Preparatory School
VX/NE SW8 .... 158 C6
Newtons Primary School
RAIN RM13 .... 144 E4
New Victoria Hospital
KUTN/CMB KT2 .... 178 B10
New West End Synagogue
BAY/PAD W2 .... 8 G8
New Woodlands School
BMLY BR1 .... 183 K7
New Zealand Comm
STJS SW1Y 11 K9
New Zealand Golf Club House
WOKN/KNAP GU21 .... 215 H8
Nicholas Breakspear RC School
STALE/WH AL4 .... 39 K7
Nicholas Hawksmoor School
BORE WD6 .... 75 N5
Nigeria High Commission
EMB EC4Y 12 B6
Nightingale Clinic
PLSTW E13 .... 141 P4
Nightingale House Surgery
ED N9 .... 80 B10
Nightingale Practice
CLPT E5 .... 119 P8
Nightingale Primary School
SWFD E18 .... 121 P2
Nightingale Primary School
WDGN N22 .... 98 F9
Nightingale Primary School
WOOL/PLUM SE18 .... 162 E4
Nightingale School
TOOT SW17 .... 179 P5
The Nightingale School
STHWK SE1 .... 17 N2
Nineacres School
WOOL/PLUM SE18 .... 162 G4
Nizels Hotel Golf & Leisure Club
RTON TN11 .... 265 M10
Noel Park Junior & Infant School
WDGN N22 .... 99 H10
Nomad Theatre
EHSLY KT24 .... 252 N2
Nonsuch High School for Girls
EW KT17 .... 220 C10
Nonsuch Industrial Estate
EW KT17 .... 220 B7
Nonsuch Primary School
EW KT17 .... 220 E2
**Norbury Complementary
Therapy Clinic**
STRHM/NOR SW16 .... 202 G1
Norbury First & Middle School
HRW HA1 .... 114 D3
Norbury Health Centre
STRHM/NOR SW16 .... 202 G2
Norbury Manor Primary School
STRHM/NOR SW16 .... 202 F1
**Norbury Manor Secondary
Girls School**
STRHM/NOR SW16 .... 202 C1
Norbury Trading Estate
STRHM/NOR SW16 .... 202 G2
**Norfolk House
Preparatory School**
MUSWH N10 .... 98 C10
Norlington School
LEY E10 .... 121 J2
Normand Park Primary School
FUL/PGN SW6 .... 14 C9
Normandy Primary School
BXLYHN DA7 .... 164 E7
Normanhurst School
CHING E4 .... 101 J1

Norman Shaw Building
WHALL SW1A 17 L1
Northaw C of E School
POTB/CUF EN6 .... 60 B5
North Beckton Primary School
EHAM E6 .... 142 C7
North Bridge House School
CAMTN NW1 .... 4 E6
**Northbrook C of E
Secondary School**
LEW SE13 .... 183 K1
Northbury Junior & Infant School
BARK IG11 .... 142 E1
Northchurch Cricket Club
BERK HP4 .... 33 J2
**Northchurch St Marys C of E
First School**
BERK HP4 .... 33 K3
North Clinic
BMLY BR1 .... 205 M1
Northcote Lodge School
BTSEA SW11 .... 179 P2
**Northcourt County
Primary School**
GVE DA12 .... 191 H4
North Cray Primary School
SCUP DA14 .... 185 P9
North Croydon Medical Centre
THHTH CR7 .... 203 J6
North Downs Business Park
RSEV TN14 .... 246 D2
North Downs Golf Club
GDST RH9 .... 260 F1
North Ealing Primary School
WEA W13 .... 134 G6
**North East Surrey College
of Technology**
EW KT17 .... 220 D7
Northend CP School
ERITH DA8 .... 164 G7
Northfields Industrial Estate
ALP/SUD HA0 .... 135 M3
**Northfields Prospect
Business Centre**
WAND/EARL SW18 .... 157 J10
Northfleet Boys School
GVW DA11 .... 190 A4
Northfleet Industrial Estate
GVW DA11 .... 167 M10
Northfleet School for Girls
GVW DA11 .... 190 A5
Northgate Business Centre
EN EN1 .... 80 A7
Northgate Clinic
CDALE/KGS NW9 .... 116 B4
Northgate First & Middle School
CRAWE RH10 .... 283 P5
Northgate Industrial Park
CHDH RM6 .... 104 A9
Northgate Surgery
CRAWE RH10 .... 283 P6
**North Harringay Junior
& Infant School**
CEND/HSY/T N8 .... 119 H2
**North Havering College of Adult
Education**
ROM RM1 .... 124 F2
North Holmwood Cricket Club
RDKG RH5 .... 273 H7
North Lodge Queens School
BUSH WD23 .... 73 N7
North London Collegiate School
EDGE HA8 .... 95 K7
**North London Progressive
Synagogue**
FSBYPK N4 .... 119 K4
**North London School
of Physiotherapy**
ARCH N19 .... 118 D6
North London Tutorial College
HDN NW4 .... 116 F4
**North Middlesex Hospital
NHS Trust**
UED N18 .... 99 M6
North Mymms Cricket Club
BRKMPK AL9 .... 58 D2
Northolt First & Middle School
NTHLT UB5 .... 133 L2
Northolt High School
NTHLT UB5 .... 133 N1
Northolt Park Infant School
NTHLT UB5 .... 114 A10
Northolt Road Clinic
RYLN/HDSTN HA2 .... 114 B8
North Orbital Trading Estate
STAL AL1 .... 38 F10
North School
STHL UB1 .... 133 N9
Northside Primary School
NFNCH/WDSP N12 .... 97 M6
The North Street Health Centre
CLAP SW4 .... 158 D9
**Northumberland Heath
Medical Centre**
ERITH DA8 .... 164 E6
**Northumberland Heath
Primary School**
ERITH DA8 .... 164 C6
Northumberland Park School
TOTM N17 .... 99 P8
**Northumbland Park
Industrial Estate**
TOTM N17 .... 100 A7
Northview Primary School
WLSDN NW10 .... 116 B10
North Watford Health Clinic
GSTN WD25 .... 55 K10
Northway School
MLHL NW7 .... 95 P4
North Weald Golf Club
EPP CM16 .... 48 B9
**North & West Essex Adult
Community College**
HLW CM20 .... 28 E7
North West Kent College
GVE DA12 .... 191 J4
**North West Kent College
of Technology**
DART DA1 .... 187 L3
**North West London Jewish
Day Gm Primary School**
KIL/WHAMP NW6 .... 2 A3
**North West London
Medical Centre**
STJWD NW8 .... 3 J9
**North Westminster
Community School**
BAY/PAD W2 .... 9 M4
**North Westminster Community
Secondary School**
MV/WKIL W9 .... 8 F1
North Westminster School
STJWD NW8 .... 9 N3

North Weylands Industrial Estate
  WOT/HER KT12 .... 197 M9
Northwick Park Hospital
& Clinical Research Centre
  HRW HA1 .... 114 C5
Northwold Junior
& Infant School
  CLPT E5 .... 119 P7
Northwood College Educational
Foundation
  NTHWD HA6 .... 92 E8
Northwood Football Club
  NTHWD HA6 .... 92 G10
Northwood & Pinner Community
Hospital
  NTHWD HA6 .... 93 H9
Northwood Pinner
Liberal Synagogue
  NTHWD HA6 .... 92 F7
Northwood Preparatory School
  RKW/CH/CXG WD3 .... 92 D3
Northwood School
  NTHWD HA6 .... 93 J9
Northwood Sports Centre
  PIN HA5 .... 93 J9
Northwood United Synagogue
  NTHWD HA6 .... 92 F8
Norwegien/british Monument
  BAY/PAD W2 .... 9 P10
Norwood Green Junior
& Infant School
  NWDGN UB2 .... 153 N4
Norwood Park Primary School
  WNWD SE27 .... 181 K7
Norwood School
  WNWD SE27 .... 181 K8
Norwood Surgery
  WNWD SE27 .... 181 J6
Notre Dame RC Girls School
  STHWK SE1 .... 18 C3
Notre Dame Senior School
  WOT/HER KT12 .... 216 C7
Notting Hill & Ealing High School
  WEA W13 .... 134 C7
Novello Theatre
  ASC SL5 .... 192 C5
Novotel Hotel
  WDR/YW UB7 .... 152 B3
Nower Hill High School
  PIN HA5 .... 113 P2
Nower Lodge School
  DORK RH4 .... 272 F3
Now Showing Art Gallery
  NTGHL W11 .... 8 E9
N T G B Sports Ground
  EHAM E6 .... 142 D1
Nucleus Gallery
  CFSP/GDCR SL9 .... 90 A4
Nuffield Hospital Midland
Regional Office
  SURB KT6 .... 199 J5
Nugent Industrial Park
  STMC/STPC BR5 .... 207 M4
The Nunhead Surgery
  PECK SE15 .... 160 A9
Nutfield Church Primary School
  REDH RH1 .... 276 C1
Nutley Dean Business Park
  HORL RH6 .... 279 H1
N W 5 Theatre School
  KTTN NW5 .... 118 D10
Oakdale Infant School
  SWFD E18 .... 101 N10
Oakdale Junior School
  SWFD E18 .... 101 P10
Oak Farm Clinic
  HGDN/ICK UB10 .... 132 C2
Oak Farm Junior & Infant School
  HGDN/ICK UB10 .... 132 C3
Oakfield CP Junior School
  DART DA1 .... 187 L5
Oakfield First School
  WDSR SL4 .... 148 C8
Oakfield Junior School
  LHD/OX KT22 .... 236 B9
Oakfield Preparatory School
  DUL SE21 .... 181 L5
Oakfield School
  WOKS/MYFD GU22 .... 233 J1
Oak Hill College
  EBAR EN4 .... 78 B10
Oak Hill Health Centre
  SURB KT6 .... 199 K6
Oakhurst Grange School
  CTHM CR3 .... 259 L2
Oakington Manor Gm
Primary School
  WBLY HA9 .... 115 N10
Oakland CP School
  EBAR EN4 .... 78 A10
Oakland Primary School
  BH/WHM TN16 .... 243 P2
Oakland School
  BNSTD SM7 .... 221 K10
Oaklands College
  BORE WD6 .... 75 P6
Oaklands College
  HARP AL5 .... 20 A2
Oaklands College
  STAL AL1 .... 38 D6
Oaklands College
  STALE/WH AL4 .... 39 K5
Oaklands College
  WGCW AL8 .... 22 C4
Oaklands First & Middle School
  HNWL W7 .... 154 E1
Oaklands Junior School
  BH/WHM TN16 .... 243 P2
Oaklands School
  ISLW TW7 .... 154 C9
Oaklands School
  LOU IG10 .... 82 A9
Oak Lane Medical Centre
  TWK TW1 .... 176 C3
Oakleigh School
  TRDG/WHET N20 .... 97 P4
Oak Lodge JMI School
  WWKM BR4 .... 204 G7
Oak Lodge Medical Centre
  EDGE HA8 .... 95 N8
Oak Lodge School
  EFNCH N2 .... 117 M1
Oakmere School
  POTB/CUF EN6 .... 59 N8
The Oaks First & Middle School
  CRAWE RH10 .... 284 A10
The Oaks Industrial Estate
  HLW CM20 .... 29 J8
Oaks Sports Centre
  CAR SM5 .... 222 A7
Oakthorpe Junior Mixed School
  PLMGR N13 .... 99 K6

Oak Tree Clinic
  WOKN/KNAP GU21 .... 231 J4
Oak Tree Medical Centre
  GDMY/SEVK IG3 .... 123 H7
Oakwood Business Park
  WLSDN NW10 .... 136 A5
Oakwood Estate
  HLW CM20 .... 29 K8
Oakwood Hill Industrial Estate
  LOU IG10 .... 82 E9
Oakwood Independent School
  PUR/KEN CR0 .... 223 J9
Oakwood Industrial Park
  CRAWE RH10 .... 284 B4
Oakwood JMI School
  STALE/WH AL4 .... 39 H5
Oakwood Medical Centre
  STHGT/OAK N14 .... 78 D9
Oasis Sports Centre
  LSQ/SEVD WC2H 11 L5
Oatlands Infant School
  WEY KT13 .... 216 E1
Objectives Museum Design
  KIL/WHAMP NW6 .... 117 J10
Obstetrics Hospital
  GWRST WC1E 11 H2
Occupational Health Centre
  CROY/NA CR0 .... 203 L10
Ockendon School
  SOCK/AV RM15 .... 146 F7
October Gallery
  RSQ WC1B 11 M3
Odeon Cinema
  BAR EN5 .... 77 K9
Odeon Cinema
  CAMTN NW1 .... 4 F5
Odeon Cinema
  ELTH/MOT SE9 .... 162 B10
Odeon Cinema
  CNTH/NBYPK IG2 .... 122 D4
Odeon Cinema
  HAYES BR2 .... 205 M2
Odeon Cinema
  HHS/BOV HP3 .... 36 A7
Odeon Cinema
  HLW CM20 .... 28 F10
Odeon Cinema
  HOLWY N7 .... 118 F8
Odeon Cinema
  KENS W8 .... 14 E3
Odeon Cinema
  KIL/WHAMP NW6 .... 3 L4
Odeon Cinema
  LSQ/SEVD WC2H 11 K8
Odeon Cinema
  MUSWH N10 .... 118 B2
Odeon Cinema
  RCH/KEW TW9 .... 177 J1
Odeon Cinema
  ROM RM1 .... 124 G3
Odeon Cinema
  STRHM/NOR SW16 .... 180 F6
Odeon Cinema
  UX/CGN UB8 .... 131 M2
Odeon Cinema
  WIM/MER SW19 .... 179 K10
Odeon Multiplex
  GU GU1 .... 267 P1
Odessa Infant School
  FSTGT E7 .... 121 M10
Odhams Industrial Estate
  WATN WD24 .... 73 K3
Odhams Trading Estate
  WATN WD24 .... 73 H2
Odyssey Business Park
  RSLP HA4 .... 113 J10
Oglethorpe County Junior
& Infant School
  UPMR RM14 .... 126 E7
Old Actonians Sports Club
  EA W5 .... 155 L1
Old Admiralty
  WHALL SW1A 11 K10
Old Bancroftians F C
  BKHH IG9 .... 102 A5
Old Bank Gallery
  DTCH/LGLY SL3 .... 149 N6
Old Barn Theatre
  CRAWW RH11 .... 283 J5
Old Beckehamian Rugby
Football Club
  WWKM BR4 .... 205 J10
Old Bellgate Wharf Development
  POP/IOD E14 .... 160 E14
Old Bexley Business Park
  BXLY DA5 .... 186 C3
Old Bexley C of E Primary School
  BXLY DA5 .... 186 A4
Old Brockleians Sports Ground
  ELTH/MOT SE9 .... 183 P2
Old Bromlians Cricket Club
  HAYES BR2 .... 205 N5
Old Chigwellians Sports Club
  CHIG IG7 .... 102 E2
Old Church Galleries
  CHEL SW3 .... 15 M9
Oldchurch Hospital
  ROMW/RG RM7 .... 124 E4
Old Club House
  CRAWE RH10 .... 285 N9
Old Colfeian Sports Club
  LEE/GVPK SE12 .... 183 M1
The Old Cottage Hospital
  EW KT17 .... 220 C9
Old Curiosity Shop
  LINN WC2A 11 N5
Old Elthamians Sports Club
  CHST BR7 .... 185 H9
Oldfield Family Practice
  GFD/PVL UB6 .... 134 B5
Oldfield House School
  HPTN TW12 .... 197 N1
Oldfield Infants School
  GFD/PVL UB6 .... 134 C4
Old Fold Manor Golf Club
  BAR EN5 .... 77 H5
Old Ford Primary School
  BOW E3 .... 140 E4
The Old Guild Theatre
  GVW DA11 .... 190 A4
Old Hall
  WEST SW1P 17 J5
Old Harlow Health Centre
  HLWE CM17 .... 29 M7
Oldhill Medical Centre
  STNW/STAM N16 .... 119 N6
Old Lyonian Sports Ground
  RYLN/HDSTN HA2 .... 114 B3
Old Merchant Taylors Sports Club
  RKW/CH/CXG WD3 .... 72 C8
Old Millhillians Sports Ground
  PIN HA5 .... 93 P9

Old Oak Primary School
  SHB W12 .... 136 C8
Old Operating Theatre Museum
  STHWK SE1 .... 12 G10
Old Owens Sports Ground
  TRDG/WHET N20 .... 97 N2
Old Palace Primary School
  BOW E3 .... 140 G5
Old Palace School
  CROY/NA CR0 .... 203 J10
Old Royel Obsevatory Greenwich
  GNWCH SE10 .... 161 J6
Old St Patricks School
  WCHPL E1 .... 13 N2
Old Station Museum
  CAN/RD E16 .... 162 C6
Old Sun Wharf
  POP/IOD E14 .... 140 D9
Old Tiffinians Sports Ground
  E/WMO/HCT KT8 .... 198 D5
Old Treasury
  WHALL SW1A 17 L1
Old Verulamians Rugby
Football Club
  LCOL/BKTW AL2 .... 57 H1
Old Vic Theatre
  STHWK SE1 .... 18 B1
Old War Office
  WHALL SW1A 11 L10
Old Wilsonians Sports Club
  WWKM BR4 .... 205 K8
Oliver Business Park
  WLSDN NW10 .... 135 P4
Oliver Goldsmith Infant
& Junior Schools
  CMBW SE5 .... 159 M7
Oliver Goldsmith Primary School
  CDALE/KGS NW9 .... 116 A3
Olympia Industrial Estate
  WDGN N22 .... 98 G10
Olympic Industrial Estate
  WBLY HA9 .... 115 N9
Olympic Retail Park
  WBLY HA9 .... 115 M9
Olympic Trading Estate
  WBLY HA9 .... 115 N9
Omnibus Business Centre
  HOLWY N7 .... 118 F10
Omnibus Business Centre
  HOLWY N7 .... 118 F10
The One Stanley Medical Centre
  ALP/SUD HA0 .... 135 K2
Ongar & District Sports Club
  CHONG CM5 .... 67 P4
Ongar Health Centre
  CHONG CM5 .... 67 P4
Ongar Leisure Centre
  CHONG CM5 .... 67 P2
Ongar Parish Council
  CHONG CM5 .... 67 P4
Ongar Place Infant School
  ADL/WDHM KT15 .... 215 K3
Ongar War Memorial Hospital
  CHONG CM5 .... 67 P2
On Sai Clinic
  ECT SW5 .... 14 C6
Onslow County Infant School
  GUW GU2 .... 267 L2
On the Road Tours C C
  WAND/EARL SW18 .... 179 M2
Open Air Theatre
  CAMTN NW1 .... 4 C10
The Open University
  FSBYW WC1X 5 N9
The Open University
  KIL/WHAMP NW6 .... 117 K9
Ophaboom Theatre
  WLSDN NW10 .... 136 E5
Ophthalmic Hospital
  MBLAR W1H 9 P3
The Optical Gallery
  CHSGTN KT9 .... 219 J2
The Optical Gallery
  TWK TW1 .... 176 F4
Optimax Laser Eye Clinic
  HAMP NW3 .... 3 K1
Optimum Health Services
NHS Trust
  CMBW SE5 .... 159 M7
Optimum Health Services
NHS Trust
  FSTH SE23 .... 182 D4
Optimum Health Services
NHS Trust
  LEE/GVPK SE12 .... 183 L1
Optimum Health Services
NHS Trust
  NWCR SE14 .... 160 E6
Optimum Health Services
NHS Trust
  STHWK SE1 .... 19 L5
Orange House Action Clinic
  BOW E3 .... 140 E4
Orange Tree Theatre
  RCH/KEW TW9 .... 155 K10
Oratory School
  CHEL SW3 .... 15 N7
Orchard Business Centre
  REDH RH1 .... 276 B9
Orchard Business Centre
  SYD SE26 .... 182 E8
Orchard County Primary School
  WATN WD24 .... 72 G2
The Orchard Health Centre
  BARK IG11 .... 142 F4
Orchard House Industrial Estate
  CSHM HP5 .... 51 H8
Orchard Infant School
  REIG RH2 .... 275 K3
Orchard Junior & Infant School
  HOM E9 .... 140 B2
Orchard School
  HSLW TW3 .... 153 P10
The Orchard Theatre
  DART DA1 .... 187 M2
Orchard Way Primary School
  CROY/NA CR0 .... 204 D7
Oriel Junior & Infant School
  FELT TW13 .... 175 M6
Oriental Medical Centre
  ECT SW5 .... 14 C6
Oriental Rug Gallery
  WDSR SL4 .... 149 H5
Orient Industrial Park
  LEY E10 .... 120 F7
Orion Business Centre
  BERM/RHTH SE16 .... 160 C4
Orleans House Gallery
  TWK TW1 .... 176 G4
Orleans Infant School
  TWK TW1 .... 176 G3
Orleans Park School
  TWK TW1 .... 176 G3

Orley Farm School
  HRW HA1 .... 114 C8
Orpington College
of Further Education
  ORP BR6 .... 207 K8
Orpington Mental Health Centre
  ORP BR6 .... 207 J10
Orpington Retail Park
  STMC/STPC BR5 .... 207 M4
Orpington Sports Centre
  ORP BR6 .... 207 K8
Orpington Superbowl
  ORP BR6 .... 207 K8
Osbourne Studio Gallery
  KTBR SW1X 16 B3
Osidge JMI School
  STHGT/OAK N14 .... 98 D2
Osidge Medical Practice
  FBAR/BDGN N11 .... 98 B2
Osmani Primary School
  WCHPL E1 .... 13 P2
Osterley Rugby Football Club
  NWDGN UB2 .... 154 A2
Otford County Primary School
  RSEV TN14 .... 247 H2
Otford Medical Practice
  RSEV TN14 .... 247 J1
Our Lady Immaculate
RC Primary School
  SURB KT6 .... 199 M8
Our Lady of Grace RC JMI School
  CHARL SE7 .... 161 N5
Our Lady of Grace
RC Junior School
  CRICK NW2 .... 116 E8
Our Lady of Hartley RC School
  HART DA3 .... 211 L5
Our Lady of Lourdes RC
Primary School
  LEW SE13 .... 161 J9
Our Lady of Lourdes RC
Primary School
  WAN E11 .... 121 L4
Our Lady of Lourdes RC
Primary School
  WLSDN NW10 .... 135 P3
Our Lady of Muswell RC
Infants & Junior School
  MUSWH N10 .... 98 B10
Our Lady of Peace R C
Middle School
  SL SL1 .... 128 B7
Our Lady of the Rosary School
  STA TW18 .... 173 K9
Our Lady of the Sacred
Heart School
  HOLWY N7 .... 5 P1
Our Lady Queen of Heaven
RC Primary School
  WIM/MER SW19 .... 178 G3
Our Lady RC Primary School
  POP/IOD E14 .... 140 E8
Our Lady & St John RC
Primary School
  BTFD TW8 .... 155 H4
Our Lady & St Joseph RC
Primary School
  IS N1 .... 7 J2
Our Lady & St Philip Neri
RC Primary School
  FSTH SE23 .... 182 C6
Our Ladys Catholic
Primary School
  WCCE AL7 .... 23 H7
Our Ladys Convent High School
  STNW/STAM N16 .... 119 M5
Our Ladys RC Primary School
  CAMTN NW1 .... 5 H5
Our Ladys RC Primary School
  DART DA1 .... 187 K2
Our Ladys School
  AMS HP6 .... 68 G1
Oval Business Centre
  LBTH SE11 .... 17 P8
Oval House Theatre
  LBTH SE11 .... 17 P10
Oval Primary School
  CROY/NA CR0 .... 203 M8
The Oval
  LBTH SE11 .... 17 P9
Overton Grange School
  BELMT SM2 .... 221 L4
Oxford Gardens Primary School
  NKENS W10 .... 136 C8
Oxford House College
  SOHO/SHAV W1D 11 J5
Oxhey Infant School
  BUSH WD23 .... 73 M9
Oxheywood Junior
& Infant School
  OXHEY WD19 .... 93 K5
Oxleas NHS Trust
  BXLY DA5 .... 186 F5
Oxleas NHS Trust
  ORP BR6 .... 207 L7
Oxleas NHS Trust
  WOOL/PLUM SE18 .... 163 H4
Oxo Tower Wharf
  STHWK SE1 .... 12 B8
Oxshott Medical Practice
  LHD/OX KT22 .... 218 B9
Oxted County School
  OXTED RH8 .... 261 L4
Oxted Gallery
  OXTED RH8 .... 261 K5
Oxted Health Centre
  OXTED RH8 .... 261 L5
Oxted & Limpsfield Hospital
  OXTED RH8 .... 261 J3
Ozten Zeki Gallery
  SKENS SW7 .... 15 N5
Paddington Bowling
& Sports Club
  MV/WKIL W9 .... 8 G1
Paddington Green
Primary School
  BAY/PAD W2 .... 9 L2
Paddock School
  PUT/ROE SW15 .... 156 C10
Pain Relief Clinic
  HDN NW4 .... 116 E4
Painters Ash Primary School
  GVW DA11 .... 190 A6
Pakeman Junior School
  HOLWY N7 .... 118 C8
Palace Road Surgery
  BRXS/STRHM SW2 .... 180 G4
Palace Theatre
  WAT WD17 .... 73 J7
Palladium Theatre
  REGST W1B 10 C6

Palmer Galleries
  RCH/KEW TW9 .... 177 J1
Palmers College
  GRAYS RM17 .... 168 C3
Palmers Green High School
  WCHMH N21 .... 99 H3
Palmers Green
& Southgate Synagogue
  FBAR/BDGN N11 .... 98 E6
Palmerston Business Centre
  SUT SM1 .... 221 M2
Panama Consulate
  MYFR/PKLN W1J 10 D10
Panshanger Golf Club
  WGCE AL7 .... 23 M3
Panshanger JMI School
  WGCE AL7 .... 23 K4
Papua New Guinea High Comm
  STJS SW1Y 11 J9
Paradise Road Practice
  RCHPK/HAM TW10 .... 177 K1
Paradise Swimming Pools
  MLHL NW7 .... 96 B6
Paramount Industrial Estate
  WATN WD24 .... 73 K4
Parayhouse School
  WBPTN SW10 .... 157 M6
Parchmore Medical Centre
  THHTH CR7 .... 203 K3
Pardes House School
  FNCH N3 .... 97 J10
Parent Infant Clinic
  HAMP NW3 .... 117 M10
Parish C of E Primary School
  BMLY BR1 .... 183 M9
Park Avenue Clinic
  WAT WD17 .... 73 H6
Parkbury House Surgery
  STAL AL1 .... 38 D5
Park Business Centre
  KIL/WHAMP NW6 .... 2 E10
Parkend Surgery
  HAMP NW3 .... 117 P9
The Parker Gallery
  BGVA SW1W 16 D6
Parker Industrial Centre
  RDART DA2 .... 188 B3
Parkers Row Family Practice
  STHWK SE1 .... 19 M2
Parkfield Industrial Estate
  BTSEA SW11 .... 158 B8
Parkfield JMI School
  HDN NW4 .... 116 E5
Parkfield Medical Centre
  POTB/CUF EN6 .... 59 L8
Park Gallery
  KUTN/CMB KT2 .... 199 M1
Parkgate Infant School
  WATN WD24 .... 73 K3
Parkgate Junior School
  WATN WD24 .... 73 K3
Parkgate School
  CLAP SW4 .... 158 B10
Park Hall Trading Estate
  WNWD SE27 .... 181 K6
Park High School
  STAN HA7 .... 95 J10
Parkhill Junior School
  CLAY IG5 .... 122 D1
Park Hill Junior School
  CROY/NA CR0 .... 203 L10
Park House Medical Centre
  KIL/WHAMP NW6 .... 2 B7
Parkhouse Middle School
  WIM/MER SW19 .... 179 J7
Park House Rugby Football Club
  HAYES BR2 .... 205 P9
Park Industrial Estate
  LCOL/BKTW AL2 .... 56 D3
Parklands School
  ROM RM1 .... 124 E1
Park Lane Primary School
  WBLY HA9 .... 115 K9
Park Lane Surgery
  BROX EN10 .... 44 E6
Park Medical Centre
  BERM/RHTH SE16 .... 160 C3
Park Mews Small
Business Centre
  HNHL SE24 .... 181 K2
The Park Practice
  PGE/AN SE20 .... 181 P10
Park Primary School
  SRTFD E15 .... 141 L2
Park Road Clinic
  CEND/HSY/T N8 .... 118 E3
Park Road Industrial Estate
  SWLY BR8 .... 208 G3
Park Road Surgery
  WLGTN SM6 .... 222 C2
Park Royal Business Centre
  WLSDN NW10 .... 135 P6
Park School
  WOKS/MYFD GU22 .... 232 D3
Parks Golf Courses
& Sports Grounds
  STA TW18 .... 173 L6
Parkside Clinic
  NTGHL W11 .... 8 B5
Parkside First School
  BORE WD6 .... 75 L4
Parkside Group Practice
  SAND/SEL CR2 .... 223 L5
Parkside Health
  NTGHL W11 .... 8 B6
Parkside Health NHS Trust
  ALP/SUD HA0 .... 135 J1
Parkside Health NHS Trust
  WBLY HA9 .... 115 N7
Parkside Hospital
  WIM/MER SW19 .... 178 C6
Parkside School
  COB KT11 .... 235 P4
Park Street C of E
Primary School
  LCOL/BKTW AL2 .... 56 C3
Park Surgery
  WAND/EARL SW18 .... 179 K2
Park Walk Gallery
  WBPTN SW10 .... 15 K9
Park Walk Primary School
  WBPTN SW10 .... 15 L10
Parkway Primary School
  ERITHM DA18 .... 163 P2
Parkway Trading Estate
  HEST TW5 .... 153 K5
Parkwood Hall School
  SWLY BR8 .... 209 J3
Parkwood Primary School
  FSBYPK N4 .... 119 J7
Parlaunt Park County
Combined School
  DTCH/LGLY SL3 .... 150 E2

Parliament Hill School
KTTN NW5 .... 118 B9
Parmiter Industrial Centre
BETH E2 .... 140 A4
Parmiters School
GSTN WD25 .... 55 K7
Parndoni Mill Gallery
HLW CM20 .... 28 E8
Parnells Sports Ground
KTN/HRWW/W HA3 .... 115 L4
The Parochial Church Council
of Goffs Oak St James
CHESW EN7 .... 61 L4
Parrock Street Surgery
GVE DA12 .... 190 E2
Parsloes School
DAGW RM9 .... 144 A1
Parsonage Farm Infant School
RAIN RM13 .... 145 K5
Parsons Green Health Clinic
FUL/PGN SW6 .... 157 K7
Parsons Mead School
ASHTD KT21 .... 237 K5
Passmores
Comprehensive School
HLWS CM18 .... 46 G3
Patent Office
HHOL WC1V 12 A4
Paton Gallery
HACK E8 .... 140 A2
The Patrick Doody Clinic
& Health Centre
WIM/MER SW19 .... 179 K10
Pattinson Clinic
RCHPK/HAM TW10 .... 177 J1
Paul Mason Gallery
CHEL SW3 .... 16 B5
The Paul Robeson Theatre
HSLW TW3 .... 154 A9
Paultons Square Practice
CHEL SW3 .... 15 M10
Pavilion Barclays Sports Ground
EA W5 .... 135 K7
Paxton Green Group Practice
DUL SE21 .... 181 M7
Paxton Primary School
NRWD SE19 .... 181 N9
Payne Clinic
EW KT17 .... 220 D9
Peacock Estate
TOTM N17 .... 99 N7
Peacock Industrial Estate
TOTM N17 .... 99 N8
The Peacock Theatre
HOL/ALD WC2B 11 N6
Peak Practice
GINN WC1R 11 N4
Peall Road Industrial Estate
CROY/NA CRO 202 G6
Pearl Galleries of Windsor
WDSR SL4 .... 149 H7
Peartree Surgery
SOCK/AV RM15 .... 147 J4
Peaslake School
SHGR GU5 .... 270 F10
Peckham Park Junior School
PECK SE15 .... 159 P6
The Peckham Pulse Health
& Leisure Centre
PECK SE15 .... 159 P7
Peckham Rye Junior
& Infant School
PECK SE15 .... 160 A9
Pedham Place Industrial Estate
SWLY BR8 .... 209 H5
Peerglow Industrial Estate
WATW WD18 .... 92 C1
Pegasus Gallery
SEV TN13 .... 265 J1
Pelham CP School
WIM/MER SW19 .... 179 K10
Pelham Primary School
BXLYHN DA7 .... 164 B9
Pendragon Secondary School
BMLY BR1 .... 183 M6
Penrhyn Avenue Surgery
WALTH E17 .... 100 E9
Pentavia Retail Park
MLHL NW7 .... 96 C8
Penton Primary School
IS N1 .... 6 B7
Penwortham Primary School
STRHM/NOR SW16 .... 180 C9
Perivale Industrial Park
GFD/PVL UB6 .... 134 F3
Perivale New Business Centre
GFD/PVL UB6 .... 135 H4
Perivale Primary School
GFD/PVL UB6 .... 135 H4
Perrin Road Clinic
ALP/SUD HA0 .... 114 C9
Perrins Art Gallery
HAMP NW3 .... 117 M9
Perry Hall School
ORP BR6 .... 207 J6
Perrymount Primary School
FSTH SE23 .... 182 C5
Perrywood Business Park
REDH RH1 .... 276 C8
Perth Trading Estate
SL SL1 .... 128 G7
Peruvian Embassy
KTBR SW1X 16 B3
Peterborough
& Queensmill School
FUL/PGN SW6 .... 157 K8
Peterborough
& St Margarets School for Girls
STAN HA7 .... 94 D2
Peter Hills C of E Primary School
BERM/RHTH SE16 .... 140 C10
Peter James Business Centre
HYS/HAR UB3 .... 153 H1
Peterley Business Centre
BETH E2 .... 140 A4
Peter Pan Statue
BAY/PAD W2 .... 9 L9
Peterswood Junior
& Infant School
HLWS CM18 .... 46 G5
Pewley Down Infant School
GU GU1 .... 268 B2
Pewterers' Hall
CITYW EC2V 12 F4
Pheonix Court
POP/IOD E14 .... 160 F3
Pheonix Theatre
LSQ/SEVD WC2H 11 K6
Philippine Embassy
KENS W8 .... 8 G10
Phoenix Business Centre
CSHM HP5 .... 50 F4

Phoenix College
MRDN SM4 .... 201 L5
Phoenix College
TOOT SW17 .... 179 P5
Phoenix Industrial Estate
HRW HA1 .... 114 C3
Phoenix Leisure Centre
CAT SE6 .... 182 G5
Phoenix School
HAMP NW3 .... 3 L2
Phoenix Special School
BOW E3 .... 140 E5
Phoenix Trading Estate
GFD/PVL UB6 .... 135 H3
The Photographers Gallery
LSQ/SEVD WC2H 11 L7
Physical Energy Statue
BAY/PAD W2 .... 9 L10
Piccadilly Theatre
REGST W1B 11 H8
Pickford Lane Medical Centre
BXLYHN DA7 .... 163 P7
Pickhurst Junior
& Infant School
HAYES BR2 .... 205 L6
Pictorem Gallery
LEY E10 .... 120 G4
The Picture Frame Gallery
ROM RM1 .... 124 E3
Picture Gallery
PUT/ROE SW15 .... 156 G10
The Picture House
HLW CM20 .... 28 F10
Picture Perfect Gallery
CLAY IG5 .... 122 E1
Picture Perfect Gallery
WAN E11 .... 121 N3
Pield Heath House RC School
UX/CGN UB8 .... 131 P6
Piers Feetham Gallery
FUL/PGN SW6 .... 157 L6
Pike Practice
WAND/EARL SW18 .... 157 N10
Pilgrims Way Junior
& Infant School
PECK SE15 .... 160 B5
Pilton Estate
CROY/NA CR0 .... 203 J9
Pimlico Area Secondary School
PIM SW1V 17 H8
The Pines Trading Estate
RGUW GU3 .... 249 L8
Pinewood Primary School
CRW RM5 .... 104 C3
Pine Wood School
WARE SG12 .... 26 C4
Pinkwell Junior & Infant School
WDR/YW UB7 .... 152 D3
Pinner & District Synagogue
PIN HA5 .... 113 M2
Pinner Park First School
RYLN/HDSTN HA2 .... 114 A1
Pinner View Medical Centre
HRW HA1 .... 114 B3
Pinner Wood School
PIN HA5 .... 93 K9
Pinn Medical Centre
PIN HA5 .... 113 M2
Pioneers Industrial Park
CROY/NA CR0 .... 202 F8
Pippins School
DTCH/LGLY SL3 .... 151 H7
Pirbright Camp
CHOB/PIR GU24 .... 230 A6
Pirbright County First
& Middle School
CHOB/PIR GU24 .... 230 D8
Pitfarm Lawn Tennis Club
GU GU1 .... 250 C10
Pitfield Street Surgery
IS N1 .... 7 H9
Pitmans College
CAVSQ/HST W1G 10 F5
Pitshanger Manor Museum
EA W5 .... 135 H10
Pitwood Park Industrial Estate
KWD/TDW/WH KT20 .... 238 G6
Pixham School
DORK RH4 .... 255 H10
Pixies Hill JMI School
HHW HP1 .... 35 J7
The Place Theatre
CAMTN NW1 .... 5 K10
Plaistow Hospital
PLSTW E13 .... 141 N4
Planetarium
CAMTN NW1 .... 10 C2
Plantation House Medical Centre
LOTH EC2R 13 H5
Plashet Comprehensive School
EHAM E6 .... 142 B2
Plashet Road Medical Centre
FSTGT E7 .... 141 N2
Players Theatre
CHCR WC2N 11 L9
Plaza Business Centre
PEND EN3 .... 80 E6
Plough Industrial Estate
LHD/OX KT22 .... 236 F6
Plumcroft Primary School
WOOL/PLUM SE18 .... 162 F5
Plumstead Manor
Secondary School
WOOL/PLUM SE18 .... 162 G4
The Pointer School
BKHTH/KID SE3 .... 161 M7
Police Cadet School
WAN E11 .... 121 M6
The Polish Institute
& Sikorski Museum
SKENS SW7 .... 15 M7
Polka Theatre for Children
WIM/MER SW19 .... 179 L9
Pollard Row Surgery
BETH E2 .... 7 P9
Polygon Business Centre
DTCH/LGLY SL3 .... 151 J8
The Pompadour Gallery
GPK RM2 .... 125 H2
Ponders End Industrial Estate
PEND EN3 .... 80 E8
Ponsbourne St Marys JMI School
HERT/BAY SG13 .... 42 F10
Pooles Park Junior School
HOLWY N7 .... 118 G7
Pope John School
SHB W12 .... 136 E9
Pope Paul RC Primary School
POTB/CUF EN6 .... 59 J9
Poplar Business Park
POP/IOD E14 .... 141 H9
Poplar Central Mosque
POP/IOD E14 .... 141 H8

Poplar Coroners Court
POP/IOD E14 .... 140 G9
Poplar First School
WIM/MER SW19 .... 201 K3
Pop Up Theatre
FSBYE EC1V 6 C8
Porchester Leisure Centre
BAY/PAD W2 .... 8 G5
Portland Business Centre
DTCH/LGLY SL3 .... 149 N7
Portland House Medical Centre
GFD/PVL UB6 .... 134 A6
Portland Medical Centre
SNWD SE25 .... 204 A5
The Portman Clinic
HAMP NW3 .... 3 L1
Portobello Gallery
NKENS W10 .... 8 A3
Portobello Medical Centre
NTGHL W11 .... 8 B6
The Portrait Gallery
CTHM CR3 .... 241 P10
Portway Primary School
SRTFD E15 .... 141 M3
Potten End School
BERK HP4 .... 34 E3
Potterells Medical Centre
BRKMPK AL9 .... 58 G1
Potters Bar Cricket Club
POTB/CUF EN6 .... 59 L8
Potters Bar Golf Club
SKENS SW7 .... 15 J6
Potter Street Primary School
HLWE CM17 .... 47 L3
Pound Hill First & Middle School
CRAWE RH10 .... 284 D6
Pound Hill Surgery
CRAWE RH10 .... 284 D6
The Pountney Clinic
HSLW TW3 .... 153 P9
Poverest Primary School
STMC/STPC BR5 .... 207 K5
Powell Corderoy CP School
DORK RH4 .... 272 E3
Power Industrial Estate
ERITH DA8 .... 165 H7
Prae Wood JMI School
STALW/RED AL3 .... 37 P7
Prassard Surgery
WDGN N22 .... 98 G8
Pratts Bottom Primary School
ORP BR6 .... 227 M7
Prendergast School
BROCKY SE4 .... 160 F10
Preparatory School
HAMP NW3 .... 3 M3
Presdales School
WARE SG12 .... 26 C3
Preston Cross Hotel
& Country Club
GT/LBKH KT23 .... 253 N2
Preston Hill Surgery
KTN/HRWW/W HA3 .... 115 L4
Preston Manor Senior
High School
WBLY HA9 .... 115 L7
Preston Medical Centre
WBLY HA9 .... 115 K8
P R for Schools
SYD SE26 .... 182 B6
Priestmead First
& Middle Schools
KTN/HRWW/W HA3 .... 114 G1
Primrose Hill Gallery
HAMP NW3 .... 4 A4
Primrose Hill Primary School
CAMTN NW1 .... 4 D5
Prince Charles
SOHO/SHAV W1D 11 K7
Prince Edward Theatre
SOHO/SHAV W1D 11 J6
Prince Hotel
STALW/RED AL3 .... 37 P4
Prince of Wales Junior
& Infant School
PEND EN3 .... 80 E4
Prince of Wales Road
Group Practice
KTTN NW5 .... 4 D2
Prince of Wales Theatre
STJS SW1Y 11 J8
Princes Avenue School
MUSWH N10 .... 118 C1
Princes Court Business Centre
WAP E1W 140 A9
Princess Alexandra Hospital
HLW CM20 .... 28 E10
Princess Frederica C of E
Primary School
WLSDN NW10 .... 136 F7
Princess Louise Hospital
NKENS W10 .... 136 F7
Princess Margaret Hospital
WDSR SL4 .... 149 J8
Princess Margaret Royal Free
C of E School
WDSR SL4 .... 149 H10
Prins Willem-alexander School
WOKS/MYFD GU22 .... 232 F7
The Print Room/museum
Books & Prints
BAR EN5 .... 77 H9
Priory Boys & Infant School
ACT W3 .... 155 P1
Priory C of E Middle School
WIM/MER SW19 .... 179 L8
Priory Hospital Group
KWD/TDW/WH KT20 .... 257 K4
Priory House School
CAT SE6 .... 182 G4
Priory School
BNSTD SM7 .... 239 J1
Priory School
SL SL1 .... 128 C7
Priory School
SNWD SE25 .... 203 N4
Priory School
STMC/STPC BR5 .... 207 M8
The Priory School
DORK RH4 .... 272 E3
Private Health Centre
FSTGT E7 .... 141 N1
Privy Council
STJS SW1Y 11 H10
Privy Council Office
WHALL SW1A 17 L1
Progress Business Centre
SL SL1 .... 128 C8
Progress Business Park
CROY/NA CR0 .... 202 D9
Prospect Business Park
LOU IG10 .... 82 G8

Prospect House School
PUT/ROE SW15 .... 178 G3
Prospect Industrial Estate
CSHM HP5 .... 51 H8
Prospect of Whitby
WAP E1W 140 B10
Providence Road School
WDR/YW UB7 .... 131 P10
Provident Industrial Estate
HYS/HAR UB3 .... 153 H1
Pruskin Gallery
KENS W8 .... 14 F1
Public Baths
FSTH SE23 .... 182 B5
Public Swimming Pool
OXHEY WD19 .... 93 M6
Pump House
BERM/RHTH SE16 .... 140 D10
Pump House Theatre
WAT WD17 .... 73 K9
Pumping Station
POP/IOD E14 .... 161 H1
Pump Lane Industrial Estate
HYS/HAR UB3 .... 153 J1
Puppet Theatre Barge
MV/WKIL W9 .... 9 J7
The Purcell School
BUSH WD23 .... 73 N6
The Purcell School
HRW HA1 .... 114 C8
Purdy Hicks Gallery
STHWK SE1 .... 12 C9
Purdy Hicks Gallery
STHWK SE1 .... 12 C9
Purfleet Primary School
PUR RM19 .... 165 P3
Purford Green School
HLWS CM18 .... 47 K3
Purley Community Health Clinic
PUR/KEN CR8 .... 223 H7
Purley & District War
Memorial Hospital
PUR/KEN CR8 .... 223 H6
Purley Gallery
PUR/KEN CR8 .... 223 H7
Purley Oaks Primary School
SAND/SEL CR2 .... 223 L4
Purley Sports Club
WLGTN SM6 .... 223 E6
Purley Swimming Pool
& Recreation Centre
PUR/KEN CR8 .... 223 J7
Pursuit Centre
WAP E1W 140 B9
Putney High School
PUT/ROE SW15 .... 178 G1
Putney Hospital
PUT/ROE SW15 .... 156 F9
Putney Leisure Centre
PUT/ROE SW15 .... 156 F10
Putneymead Medical Centre
PUT/ROE SW15 .... 156 F10
Putney School of Art
PUT/ROE SW15 .... 157 H10
Putney Surgery
PUT/ROE SW15 .... 157 H10
Puttenham C of E School
RGUW GU3 .... 266 A5
Puttenham Golf Club
RGUW GU3 .... 266 C5
Pylon Trading Estate
CAN/RD E16 .... 141 J6
Pyrcroft Grange Primary School
CHERT KT16 .... 195 H7
Pyrford County Middle School
WOKS/MYFD GU22 .... 233 J2
Qatar Embassy
MYFR/PKLN W1K 10 D9
Q E Conf Centre
WEST SW1P 17 K2
Quainton Hall School
HRW HA1 .... 114 D3
Quaker Gallery
CHCR WC2N 11 L8
Quarry Hill County Junior School
GRAYS RM17 .... 167 N4
Quarryside Business Park
REDH RH1 .... 258 C6
Queen Anne First School
WDSR SL4 .... 149 J9
Queen Charlottes
& Chelsea Hospital
HMSMTH W6 .... 156 D2
Queen Eleanors C of E
Junior School
GUW GU2 .... 267 L1
Queen Elizabeth Hall
STHWK SE1 .... 11 N9
Queen Elizabeth Hospital
BNSTD SM7 .... 239 M4
Queen Elizabeth Ii Hospital
BRKMPK AL9 .... 23 K9
Queen Elizabeth Ii Jubilee School
MV/WKIL W9 .... 8 C2
Queen Elizabethmilitary Hospital
CHARL SE7 .... 162 C5
Queen Elizabeth Museum
CHING E4 .... 101 K1
Queen Elizabeths Girls School
BAR EN5 .... 77 J8
Queen Elizabeths School
BAR EN5 .... 76 G7
Queen Marys Hospital
SCUP DA14 .... 185 K8
Queen Marys Hospital
for Children
CAR SM5 .... 222 A5
Queen Marys Sidcup NHS Trust
ABYW SE2 .... 163 N1
Queen Mary & Westfield College
SWFD E18 .... 101 M9
Queen Mary & Westfield College
WCHPL E1 .... 140 C6
Queen Mother Sports Centre
PIM SW1V 16 G5
Queensbridge Group Practice
HACK E8 .... 7 M3
Queensbridge Infant School
HACK E8 .... 7 M4
The Priory School
DORK RH4 .... 272 E3
Private Health Centre
FSTGT E7 .... 141 N1
Queens College
CAVSQ/HST W1G 10 E4
Queens Ice Skating Club
BAY/PAD W2 .... 8 F7
Queens Manor Primary School
FUL/PGN SW6 .... 156 D6
Queensmead
Comprehensive School
RSLP HA4 .... 113 L9
Queensmead Sports Centre
RSLP HA4 .... 113 H7

Queens Medical Centre
RCHPK/HAM TW10 .... 177 L1
Queens Park Community School
WLSDN NW10 .... 136 F3
Queens Park Health Centre
NKENS W10 .... 2 B9
Queens Park Primary School
NKENS W10 .... 8 B1
Queens Park Rangers
Football Club
SHB W12 .... 136 E10
Queens Road Practice
NWCR SE14 .... 160 C7
Queens Road Practice
NWCR SE14 .... 160 C7
Queens Road Surgery
WIM/MER SW19 .... 179 K9
Queens Schools
WDSR SL4 .... 149 G8
Queens Sports Centre
RGODL GU7 .... 266 G10
Queens Theatre
EMPK RM11 .... 125 L5
Queens Theatre
SOHO/SHAV W1D 11 J7
Queensway Business Centre
PEND EN3 .... 80 B8
Queensway Health Centre
HAT AL10 .... 40 E3
Queenswell Infant School
TRDG/WHET N20 .... 97 L3
Queenswood School
BRKMPK AL9 .... 59 N4
The Questors Theatre
EA W5 .... 135 K9
Quicksilver Theatre
IS N1 .... 7 K4
Quintin Kynaston School
STJWD NW8 .... 3 L6
Rabbs Farm Primary School
WDR/YW UB7 .... 131 N9
Rachor House Surgery
ASC SL5 .... 192 A3
RADA
GWRST WC1E 11 K2
Radcliffe College
SOHO/CST W1F 10 G6
Radha Krishna Temple
BAL SW12 .... 180 C3
Radlett & Bushey
Reform Synagogue
RAD WD7 .... 74 F1
Radlett Cricket Club
RAD WD7 .... 74 G3
Radlett Lodge School
RAD WD7 .... 56 F8
Radlett Parochial Church Council
RAD WD7 .... 74 F2
Radlett Preparatory School
RAD WD7 .... 75 H4
The Rae-smith Gallery
LSQ/SEVD WC2H 11 L8
Ragged School Museum Trust
BOW E3 .... 140 D7
Raglan Infant School
EN EN1 .... 79 M10
Raglan Junior School
EN EN1 .... 99 M1
Raglan Primary School
HAYES BR2 .... 205 P4
Railton Road Clinic
HNHL SE24 .... 181 J1
Rainbow Industrial Estate
RYNPK SW20 .... 200 E2
Rainbow Industrial Estate
WDR/YW UB7 .... 131 N9
Rainbow Natural Health Centre
REDH RH1 .... 276 A1
Rainbow Quay
BERM/RHTH SE16 .... 160 D2
Rainham Primary School
RAIN RM13 .... 145 H6
Rainham Trading Estate
RAIN RM13 .... 144 G6
The Raleigh School
EHSLY KT24 .... 252 D1
Ramgarhia Sikh
Gurdwara Temple
SRTFD E15 .... 141 H10
Rams Episcopal Primary School
HACK E8 .... 120 B10
Randal Cremer Primary School
BETH E2 .... 7 L7
Randolph Medical Centre
DTCH/LGLY SL3 .... 149 N6
Randolph Surgery
MV/WKIL W9 .... 3 H9
Ranelagh Primary School
SRTFD E15 .... 141 K4
Rangefield Primary School
BMLY BR1 .... 183 K8
Ransomes Dock Business Centre
BTSEA SW11 .... 157 P6
Raphael School
EMPK RM11 .... 125 H4
Rathfern Primary School
FSTH SE23 .... 182 E4
Ravandos Sikh Temple
MNPK E12 .... 122 B9
Ravenor Primary School
GFD/PVL UB6 .... 133 P5
Ravensbourne College
of Design & Communication
CHST BR7 .... 184 D3
Ravensbourne College
of Design & Communication
CHST BR7 .... 184 C8
Ravensbourne Galleries
BECK BR3 .... 205 H3
Ravensbourne NHS Trust
HAYES BR2 .... 205 N4
Ravensbourne School
HARH RM3 .... 105 L3
The Ravensbourne School
HAYES BR2 .... 205 N4
Ravensbourne Trust
COUL/CHIP CR5 .... 240 E3
Ravenscourt Park
Preparatory School
HMSMTH W6 .... 156 D3
Ravenscourt Theatre School
HMSMTH W6 .... 156 E3
Ravenscroft Medical Centre
GLDGN NW11 .... 117 J5
Ravenscroft Primary School
PLSTW E13 .... 141 M4
Ravenscroft School
TRDG/WHET N20 .... 97 J1
Ravenside Retail Park
UED N18 .... 100 C6
Ravensquay Business Centre
STMC/STPC BR5 .... 207 L5

Ravenstone Primary School
BAL SW12 .... 180 B4
Ravenswood Industrial Estate
WALTH E17 .... 121 H2
Ravenswood School for Boys
HAYES BR2 .... 206 A10
Ravin Galleries
FSTH SE23 .... 182 B5
Raw Gallery
WCHPL E1 .... 140 A8
**Ray Lodge Junior
& Infant School**
WFD IG8 .... 102 A7
Raynehurst CP School
GVE DA12 .... 191 J6
Raynes Park High School
NWMAL KT3 .... 200 E3
Raynes Park Sports Ground
RYNPK SW20 .... 200 D2
Raynes Park Vale Football Club
RYNPK SW20 .... 200 C5
Raynham Primary School
UED N18 .... 99 P6
R C A Sculpture School
BTSEA SW11 .... 157 N6
Real Tennis Club
BRKMPK AL9 .... 40 G4
Reay Primary School
BRXN/ST SW9 .... 158 C6
Records Office
CLKNW EC1R 12 B1
Recreation Centre
LBTH SE11 .... 18 D5
Rectory Business Centre
SCUP DA14 .... 185 L7
Rectory Paddock School
STMC/STPC BR5 .... 207 M2
Redbridge College
CHDH RM6 .... 123 L3
Redbridge Health Authority
GDMY/SEVK IG3 .... 123 K3
**Redbridge Junior
& Infant School**
REDBR IG4 .... 122 B3
Redbridge Museum Service
IL IG1 .... 122 F7
Redbridge Sports Centre Trust
BARK/HLT IG6 .... 102 C9
**Redbridge & Waltham
Forest Health Authority**
MNPK E12 .... 122 D8
Redburn Industrial Estate
PEND EN3 .... 80 C10
Redcliffe School
WBPTN SW10 .... 15 H9
Redcliffe Surgery
WBPTN SW10 .... 15 H9
Redden Court School
HARH RM3 .... 125 N1
Reddiford School
PIN HA5 .... 113 M2
Reddings JMI School
HHS/BOV HP3 .... 36 A8
**Redford Lodge
Psychiatric Hospital**
ED N9 .... 99 P3
Redhill Business Centre
REDH RH1 .... 258 A9
Redhill Football Club
REDH RH1 .... 276 A4
Redhill Junior School
CHST BR7 .... 184 E8
Redhill & Reigate Golf Club
REDH RH1 .... 275 N3
Red Hill Surgery
CHST BR7 .... 184 E8
Red House Surgery
RAD WD7 .... 74 F1
Redlands Junior School
RDKG RH5 .... 272 G5
Redlands Primary School
WCHPL E1 .... 140 B7
Red Lion Business Park
SURB KT6 .... 199 L9
Redriff Junior & Infants School
BERM/RHTH SE16 .... 160 D1
Red Rose Trading Estate
BAR EN5 .... 77 N9
Reedham Park School
PUR/KEN CR8 .... 223 H10
Reeds School
COB KT11 .... 217 P8
Reed's Wharf Gallery
CLKNW EC1R 12 A2
Refuge Temple
STRHM/NOR SW16 .... 180 F7
Regal Gallery
EGH TW20 .... 172 C8
Regent Business Centre
HYS/HAR UB3 .... 153 J1
Regent Clinic
CAVSQ/HST W1G 10 E4
Regent's College
CAMTN NW1 .... 4 C1
Regent's College
CAMTN NW1 .... 10 C1
Regent's Park Barracks
CAMTN NW1 .... 4 E7
The Regina Codi School
CROY/NA CR0 .... 223 J4
Regional Sports Centre
TIL RM18 .... 168 E8
**Reigate & Banstead
Borough Council**
BNSTD SM7 .... 239 J3
Reigate College
REIG RH2 .... 257 L9
Reigate Day Hospital
REIG RH2 .... 257 N10
Reigate Grammar School
REIG RH2 .... 257 M10
Reigate Priory Middle School
REIG RH2 .... 257 K10
**Reigate St Marys Preparatory
& Choir School**
REIG RH2 .... 257 L10
Reigate School
REIG RH2 .... 275 M3
Renwick House Surgery
ACT W3 .... 135 M10
Renwick Industrial Estate
BARK IG11 .... 143 L4
Replingham Clinic
WAND/EARL SW18 .... 179 K4
Restaurant and Cafe
BAY/PAD W2 .... 15 N1
The Retail Business Centre
EW KT17 .... 220 D6
Reynolds Health Centre
DART DA1 .... 187 L2
R H M Medical Centre
WDSR SL4 .... 149 J7

Rhodes Avenue Primary School
FBAR/BDGN N11 .... 98 D9
Rhodes Farm Clinic
MLHL NW7 .... 96 F5
Rhyl Primary School
KTTN NW5 .... 4 C1
RIBA
REGST W1B 10 F3
**RIBA Drawings Collection
& Heinz Gallery**
MBLAR W1H 10 B5
Ricards Lodge High School
WIM/MER SW19 .... 179 J8
Richard Alibon Infant School
DAGE RM10 .... 124 B10
Richard Atkins School
BRXS/STRHM SW2 .... 180 F3
Richard Cloudesley School
STLK EC1Y 12 E2
Richard Cobden Primary School
CAMTN NW1 .... 5 H6
**Richards Osteopathic Clinic
& Natural Health Centre**
CRAWE RH10 .... 283 P7
Richard Tudor Gallery
CHING E4 .... 101 K1
Rich Industrial Estate
PECK SE15 .... 160 A5
Rich Industrial Estate
STHWK SE1 .... 19 M7
Rich Industrial Estate
STHWK SE1 .... 19 K4
Richings Park Sports Club
IVER SL0 .... 151 J2
**Richmond Adult
& Community College**
RCH/KEW TW9 .... 155 J10
**Richmond Adult
& Community College**
TWK TW1 .... 176 E4
The Richmond Clinic
RCHPK/HAM TW10 .... 155 L10
Richmond College
KENS W8 .... 14 G3
Richmond College
RCHPK/HAM TW10 .... 177 K2
Richmond Football Club
RCH/KEW TW9 .... 155 J10
**The Richmond Green
Medical Centre**
RCH/KEW TW9 .... 177 J1
**Richmond House
Doctors Surgery**
WALW SE17 .... 18 G7
Richmond House School
HPTN TW12 .... 175 N8
Richmond Magistrates Court
RCH/KEW TW9 .... 155 J10
Richmond Road Medical Centre
KUTN/CMB KT2 .... 177 K10
Richmond Synagogue
RCH/KEW TW9 .... 155 K10
Richmond Theatre
RCH/KEW TW9 .... 155 J10
**Richmond Twickenham
& Roehampton NHS Trust**
HPTN TW12 .... 175 N9
Richmond-upon-thames College
WHTN TW2 .... 176 D3
**Rickmansworth Public
Golf Course**
RKW/CH/CXG WD3 .... 92 A3
Rickmansworth School
RKW/CH/CXG WD3 .... 72 A10
Rickmansworth Sports Club
RKW/CH/CXG WD3 .... 71 P10
Riddlesdown School
SAND/SEL CR2 .... 223 M10
Ridge House Clinic
WCHMH N21 .... 99 L1
Ridgeway Infant School
SAND/SEL CR2 .... 223 M5
The Ridgeway Surgery
RYLN/HDSTN HA2 .... 113 P4
Ripley C of E School
RPLY/SEND GU23 .... 233 L7
Ripley Court School
RPLY/SEND GU23 .... 233 M7
Ripley Cricket Club
RPLY/SEND GU23 .... 233 M6
Ripple Junior & Infant School
BARK IG11 .... 142 C3
Rise Park Infant School
ROM RM1 .... 104 E9
Risley Avenue School
TOTM N17 .... 99 M9
River Brent Business Park
NWDGN UB2 .... 154 D2
Riverdene Industrial Estate
WOT/HER KT12 .... 217 L2
River Gardens Business Centre
EBED/NFELT TW14 .... 153 J10
Riverhead County Infant School
SEV TN13 .... 246 J1
River Place Health Centre
IS N1 .... 6 A1
River Road Business Park
BARK IG11 .... 143 H5
River Road Practice
BKHH IG9 .... 102 B2
Riversdale Primary School
WAND/EARL SW18 .... 179 K4
Riverside Business Centre
WAND/EARL SW18 .... 179 L4
The Riverside Business Centre
GU GU1 .... 249 P10
Riverside Business Park
WIM/MER SW19 .... 201 M1
**Riverside Community
Health Care**
WKENS W14 .... 156 C7
Riverside Health Authority
ECT SW5 .... 15 H6
Riverside Health Authority
PIM SW1V 17 J7
Riverside Health Authority
WBPTN SW10 .... 157 H8
Riverside Industrial Estate
BARK IG11 .... 143 K5
Riverside Industrial Estate
DART DA1 .... 187 M1
Riverside Industrial Estate
ED N9 .... 80 D10
Riverside Industrial Estate
LCOL/BKTW AL2 .... 57 K3
Riverside Primary School
BERM/RHTH SE16 .... 19 P7
Riverside Retail Park
RSEV TN16 .... 247 K5
Riverside Swimming Centre
ERITH DA8 .... 164 F4
Riverside Wandle Trading Estate
MTCM CR4 .... 202 A7

Riverston School
LEE/GVPK SE12 .... 183 M1
Riverview Clinic
GVE DA12 .... 191 J8
Riverview CP School
HOR/WEW KT19 .... 219 P1
Riverview Park Surgery
GVE DA12 .... 191 H7
Riverview Primary School
GVE DA12 .... 191 H7
Riverway Industrial Estate
RGODL GU7 .... 267 P9
R N I B Sunshine House School
NTHWD HA6 .... 92 E7
Robert Blair Primary School
HOLWY N7 .... 5 M2
**Robert Browning Junior
& Infant School**
WALW SE17 .... 18 F7
Robert Clack School
BCTR RM8 .... 124 A6
**Robertswood County
Combined School**
CFSP/GDCR SL9 .... 90 C8
Robin Hood Junior School
SUT SM1 .... 221 L2
Robin Hood Lane Health Centre
SUT SM1 .... 221 K2
Robin Hood Primary School
KUTN/CMB KT2 .... 178 A8
Robinsfield Infant School
STJWD NW8 .... 3 M7
Rochdale Surgery
PLMGR N13 .... 98 C5
The Roche School
WAND/EARL SW18 .... 179 K1
Rockliffe Manor School
WOOL/PLUM SE18 .... 163 J5
Rockmount School
NRWD SE19 .... 181 K9
Rockware Business Centre
GFD/PVL UB6 .... 134 C3
Rodd Estate
SHPTN TW17 .... 196 D5
Roding Primary School
BCTR RM8 .... 123 M9
Roding Primary School
WFD IG8 .... 102 B8
Roding Valley High School
LOU IG10 .... 82 E8
Roding Valley High School
LOU IG10 .... 82 B9
Roebuck Road Trading Estate
BARK/HLT IG6 .... 103 L7
Roe Green Junior & Infant School
CDALE/KGS NW9 .... 115 N2
Roehampton Church School
PUT/ROE SW15 .... 178 E3
Roehampton Community Council
PUT/ROE SW15 .... 178 C2
Roehampton Institute
PUT/ROE SW15 .... 178 D1
Roehampton Institute
WAND/EARL SW18 .... 179 H2
The Roehampton Priory Hospital
PUT/ROE SW15 .... 156 C10
Roehampton Recreation Centre
PUT/ROE SW15 .... 178 D3
The Roehampton Surgery
PUT/ROE SW15 .... 178 D3
Roger Ascham Primary School
WALTH E17 .... 100 E9
Roger Bannister Sports Ground
KTN/HRWW/W HA3 .... 94 B7
Roger Black Gallery
CROY/NA CR0 .... 203 K9
Rokeby Secondary School
SRTFD E15 .... 141 J2
Roke Primary School
PUR/KEN CR8 .... 223 K10
Rokesly Primary & Junior School
CEND/HSY/T N8 .... 118 F3
Roman Bath
TPL/STR WC2R 11 P7
Roman Industrial Estate
CROY/NA CR0 .... 203 M7
Roman Road Primary School
EHAM E6 .... 142 A6
Roman Theatre
STALW/RED AL3 .... 37 P6
Roman Wall Remains
BARB EC2Y 12 E4
Romford Clinic
ROM RM1 .... 124 G2
Romford County Court
ROM RM1 .... 124 G2
Romford Ice Rink
ROMW/RG RM7 .... 124 F5
Ronald Rose Primary School
WIM/MER SW19 .... 178 G3
Rood Lane Medical Centre
FENCHST EC3M 13 J7
Rooks Heath High School
RYLN/HDSTN HA2 .... 113 P8
Roosevelt Memorial
MYFR/PKLN W1K 10 D7
Ropery Business Park
CHARL SE7 .... 161 P3
Rosary Priory High School
BUSH WD23 .... 74 D10
Rosary RC Junior School
HEST TW5 .... 153 N5
Rosebery Industrial Park
TOTM N17 .... 100 A10
Rosebery School
EPSOM KT18 .... 219 P10
Rose Bruford College
DEPT SE8 .... 160 F5
**Rose Bruford College of Speech
& Drama**
BFN/LL DA15 .... 185 L4
Rosedale Clinic
CHESW EN7 .... 61 P3
**Roseland Junior Middle
& Infant School**
HOD EN11 .... 26 E10
Roselands Clinic
NWMAL KT3 .... 199 P4
Rosemary School
CLKNW EC1R 12 C1
Rosemary Surgery
FNCH N3 .... 97 L10
Rose Mcandrew Clinic
BRXN/ST SW9 .... 158 C8
Rosemead Preparatory School
DUL SE21 .... 181 K5
Rosendale Junior & Infant School
DUL SE21 .... 181 K3
The Rose Street School
LSQ/SEVD WC2H 11 L7
Rose Theatre Exhibition
STHWK SE1 .... 12 F9

Rosetta Primary School
CAN/RD E16 .... 141 N7
Rosewood Medical Centre
HCH RM12 .... 125 J10
Rosherville C of E School
GVW DA11 .... 190 B2
Rosh Pinah School
EDGW HA8 .... 95 N3
Rossgate JMI School
HHW HP1 .... 35 K4
**Rosslyn Park
Rugbyfootball Club**
PUT/ROE SW15 .... 156 C10
Rotherhithe Civic Centre
BERM/RHTH SE16 .... 160 B1
**Rotherhithe Junior
& Infant School**
BERM/RHTH SE16 .... 160 B3
Rotunda Museum
CHARL SE7 .... 162 C4
The Roundhouse Theatre
CAMTN NW1 .... 4 C3
Roundwood Park Medical Centre
WLSDN NW10 .... 136 D2
Rowan High School
CLAP SW4 .... 180 E2
Rowan High School
MTCM CR4 .... 202 D2
**Rowans Junior Mixed
Infant School**
WCCE AL7 .... 23 K2
Rowans School
RYNPK SW20 .... 178 D10
The Rowans Surgery
STRHM/NOR SW16 .... 202 D1
Rowfant Business Centre
CRAWE RH10 .... 285 M7
Rowhill School
RDART DA2 .... 187 K7
Rowley Industrial Park
ACT W3 .... 155 N2
Roxbourne First School
RSLP HA4 .... 113 M7
Roxbourne Medical Centre
RYLN/HDSTN HA2 .... 114 A7
Roxeth First & Middle School
RYLN/HDSTN HA2 .... 114 C7
Roxeth Mead School
RYLN/HDSTN HA2 .... 114 C7
Royal Academy of Arts
CONDST W1S 10 G8
Royal Air Force Museum
CDALE/KGS NW9 .... 96 D10
Royal Albert Hall
SKENS SW7 .... 15 L2
**The Royal Alexandra
& Albert School**
REIG RH2 .... 257 P5
Royal Army Medical College
WEST SW1P 17 K7
Royal Artillery Museums
WOOL/PLUM SE18 .... 162 D6
**Royal Borough of Kingston Upon
Thames Health Clinic**
NWMAL KT3 .... 199 P3
**Royal Brompton
& National Heart Hospitals**
CHEL SW3 .... 15 N7
Royal College of Anaesthetists
RSQ WC1B 11 L3
Royal College of Art
SKENS SW7 .... 15 K2
Royal College of Music
SHB W12 .... 156 D2
Royal College of Music
SKENS SW7 .... 15 L3
Royal College of Nursing
CAMTN NW1 .... 11 H1
Royal College of Nursing
IS N1 .... 6 C6
**Royal College of Obstetricians &
Gynaecologists**
CAMTN NW1 .... 10 A1
**Royal College
of Ophthalmologists**
CAMTN NW1 .... 10 C2
**Royal College of Paediatrics
& Child Health**
GTPST W1W 10 F3
The Royal College of Pathology
STJS SW1Y 11 H10
Royal College of Physicians
CAMTN NW1 .... 10 E1
Royal Courts of Justice
LINN WC2A 11 P6
Royal Court Theatre
BCVA SW1W 16 C6
Royal Court Young Peoples Theatre
NKENS W10 .... 8 B4
Royal Danish Embassy
KTBR SW1X 16 A3
Royal Docks Medical Centre
EHAM E6 .... 142 D8
Royal Embassy of Saudi Arabia
MYFR/PICC W1J 10 E9
Royal Festival Hall
STHWK SE1 .... 11 N10
Royal Free Hampstead NHS Trust
HAMP NW3 .... 117 P10
**Royal Free Hospital
& School of Medicine**
HAMP NW3 .... 117 P10
Royal Gallery
CHST BR7 .... 184 F10
Royal Geographical Soc
SKENS SW7 .... 15 L2
Royal Grammar School
GU GU1 .... 268 A1
Royal Holloway College
EGH TW20 .... 172 A9
Royal Holloway College
EGH TW20 .... 194 A1
**Royal Holloway University
of London**
EGH TW20 .... 172 B10
**Royal Holloway University
of London**
EGH TW20 .... 172 A9
**Royal Horticultural
Society New Hall**
WEST SW1P 17 J4
**Royal Horticultural
Society's Gardens**
RPLY/SEND GU23 .... 233 P4
Royal Hospital
RCH/KEW TW9 .... 155 J9
Royal Hospital Chelsea
CHEL SW3 .... 16 C9
**Royal Hospital
for Neuro-disability**
PUT/ROE SW15 .... 178 D4

**Royal Hospital
for Neuro-disability**
PUT/ROE SW15 .... 179 H2
Royal Hospital & Home
PUT/ROE SW15 .... 178 E3
The Royal Hospitals NHS Trust
STBC EC1A 12 D5
Royal Institute
MYFR/PICC W1J 10 F8
Royal Kent First & Middle School
LHD/OX KT22 .... 218 B10
Royal Liberty School
GPK RM2 .... 125 K1
The Royal London Estate
TOTM N17 .... 100 A8
Royal London Hospital NHS Trust
BETH E2 .... 140 B4
The Royal London Hospital
BOW E3 .... 140 E5
The Royal London Hospital A & E
WCHPL E1 .... 140 A7
Royal Marsden Hospital
BELMT SM2 .... 221 M6
Royal Marsden Hospital
CHEL SW3 .... 15 M7
Royal Marsden Hospital
SKENS SW7 .... 15 M7
The Royal Masonic School
RKW/CH/CXG WD3 .... 71 N10
The Royal Mews
WHALL SW1A 16 F3
Royal Mint Court
TWRH EC3N 13 M8
Royal National Orthopaedic
STAN HA7 .... 95 H3
**Royal National Orthopaedic
Hospital Trust**
GTPST W1W 10 F2
Royal National Theatre
BRXN/ST SW9 .... 159 H6
Royal National Theatre
STHWK SE1 .... 12 C9
Royal National Theatre Studio
STHWK SE1 .... 18 B1
**Royal National Throat
Nose & Ear Hospital**
FSBYW WC1X 5 N9
Royal Naval College
GNWCH SE10 .... 161 J5
Royal Navy
POP/IOD E14 .... 140 D8
Royal Navy & Royal Marines
CHCR WC2N 11 L8
Royal Norwegian Embassy
KTBR SW1X 16 D3
Royal Opera House
COVGDN WC2E 11 M6
Royal Park Primary School
SCUP DA14 .... 185 P9
The Royal School Hampstead
HAMP NW3 .... 117 N9
Royal Society of Arts
CHCR WC2N 11 M8
Royal Society of Medicine
CAVSQ/HST W1G 10 E5
Royal Surrey County Hospital
GUW GU2 .... 249 K10
Royal Thai Embassy
SKENS SW7 .... 15 K4
Royal Veterinary College
BRKMPK AL9 .... 58 G4
**Royal Victoria Docks
Watersports Centre**
CAN/RD E16 .... 141 M5
Roydonbury Industrial Estate
HLWW/ROY CM19 .... 46 C1
Roydon CP School
HLWW/ROY CM19 .... 45 N1
Roydon Leisure Park
HLWW/ROY CM19 .... 27 M10
Royston Primary School
BECK BR3 .... 204 C1
R T R Healthcare NHS Trust
PUT/ROE SW15 .... 178 D2
Rudolf Steiner School
KGLGY WD4 .... 53 P5
Rudolph Steiner Hall
CAMTN NW1 .... 10 A1
Rufus Business Centre
WAND/EARL SW18 .... 179 L5
Rugby Club
COB KT11 .... 217 L8
Rugby Club
COUL/CHIP CR5 .... 241 H6
The Rugby Club
CHOB/PIR GU24 .... 213 K6
Ruislip Manor Football Club
RSLP HA4 .... 112 G7
Ruislip Rugby Football Club
RSLP HA4 .... 112 F7
Runnymede Borough Council
CHERT KT16 .... 195 L8
Runnymede Borough Council
CHERT KT16 .... 195 K7
Runnymede Hospital
CHERT KT16 .... 194 G10
Runnymede Medical Practice
WDSR SL4 .... 171 M3
Rushcroft Secondary School
CHING E4 .... 100 C8
Rushey Green Group Practice
CAT SE6 .... 182 F4
Rush Green School
ROMW/RG RM7 .... 124 E6
Rush Green Surgery
ROMW/RG RM7 .... 124 E7
Rushmore Junior School
CLPT E5 .... 120 C2
Ruskin House School
HNHL SE24 .... 181 K1
Russell Clinic
STALW/RED AL3 .... 38 C6
Russell County Primary School
RKW/CH/CXG WD3 .... 70 A8
The Russell JMI School
RCHPK/HAM TW10 .... 177 J5
The Russell School
RCHPK/HAM TW10 .... 177 J4
Russet House School
EN EN1 .... 80 A5
Russian Arts Gallery
ACT W3 .... 135 N10
Rutland House Surgery
MUSWH N10 .... 98 C10
Rutlish School
RYNPK SW20 .... 201 J2
Ruxley Corner Industrial Estate
SCUP DA14 .... 185 N9
Ruxley Manor School
ELTH/MOT SE9 .... 184 D7
Ryde College
WATW WD18 .... 72 F10

Ryde Junior Mixed Infant School
BRKMPK AL9 .... 40 F1
Rydens County Senior School
WOT/HER KT12 .... 217 K1
Rydes Hill Preparatory School
GUW GU2 .... 249 L8
Ryefield Primary School
HGDN/ICK UB10 .... 132 E3
Rye House Stadium
HOD EN11 .... 45 J1
Ryelands JMI School
HOD EN11 .... 44 G2
Ryelands Primary School
SNWD SE25 .... 204 A5
Rylett Road Surgery
SHB W12 .... 156 C2
Ryvers County First
& Middle School
DTCH/LGLY SL3 .... 150 A2
Saatchi Gallery
KIL/WHAMP NW6 .... 3 H6
Saatchi Synagogue
KIL/WHAMP NW6 .... 2 G7
Sackville Galleries
SAND/SEL CR2 .... 223 K5
Sacred Heart High School
HMSMTH W6 .... 156 F3
Sacred Heart Junior Middle
& Infant School
OXHEY WD19 .... 73 N10
Sacred Heart Junior School
HMSMTH W6 .... 156 G3
The Sacred Heart of Mary
RC School
UPMR RM14 .... 126 A7
Sacred Heart RC Junior
& Infant School
RSLP HA4 .... 112 F7
Sacred Heart RC Junior
& Middle School
BTSEA SW11 .... 157 P9
Sacred Heart RC Primary School
NWMAL KT3 .... 200 D4
Sacred Heart RC School
BTSEA SW11 .... 157 P7
Sacred Heart RC School
KTN/HRWW/W HA3 .... 94 D10
Sacred Heart RC School
TEDD TW11 .... 176 G10
Sacred Heart RC School
WARE SG12 .... 26 C2
Sacred Heart RC
Secondary School
CMBW SE5 .... 159 K7
Sacred Heart School
HOLWY N7 .... 118 G10
Saddlers Hall
CITYW EC2V 12 E6
Sadlers Wells Thtr
CLKNW EC1R 6 B9
Saffron Green First School
BORE WD6 .... 76 A8
Sai Medical Centre
POP/IOD E14 .... 141 H10
St Adrians RC JMI School
STAL AL1 .... 38 E6
St Agathas RC Primary School
KUTN/CMB KT2 .... 177 L9
St Agnes Primary School
BOW E3 .... 140 F5
St Agnes RC Primary School
CRICK NW2 .... 116 G8
St Aidans Primary School
FSBYPK N4 .... 119 H5
St Aidans RC Primary School
IL IG1 .... 122 G6
St Albans City Football Club
STAL AL1 .... 38 E6
St Albans City Hospital
STALW/RED AL3 .... 38 B4
St Albans CP School
DART DA1 .... 187 N2
St Albans Girls School
STALW/RED AL3 .... 38 D2
St Albans Health Clinic
KTTN NW5 .... 118 B8
St Albans High School for Girls
STAL AL1 .... 38 D5
St Albans Junior
& Infant RC School
PECK SE15 .... 159 N7
St Albans Lawn Tennis Club
STALE/WH AL10 .... 39 H4
St Albans Museum
STAL AL1 .... 38 C5
St Albans Musical Museum
LCOL/BKTW AL2 .... 56 A4
St Albans Music School
STALW/RED AL3 .... 38 C3
St Albans Organ Museum
STAL AL1 .... 38 G7
St Albans Primary School
E/WMO/HCT KT8 .... 198 A5
St Albans Principal Health Centre
STAL AL1 .... 38 C6
St Albans RC Church
& School Presbytery
HCH RM12 .... 125 H10
St Albans RC Primary School
HLW CM20 .... 29 J9
St Albans RC School
RAIN RM13 .... 145 J2
St Albans Retail Park
STAL AL1 .... 38 C8
St Albans School
FSBYW WC1X 12 A3
St Albans Synagogue
STALW/RED AL3 .... 38 B6
St Albans & Stephen RC
JMI School
STAL AL1 .... 38 F6
St Albans Synagogue
STAL AL1 .... 38 D7
St Alban & Stephen Junior
& Middle School
STAL AL1 .... 38 E7
St Albert the Great RC
Primary School
HHS/BOV HP3 .... 36 B8
St Aloysius College
HGT N6 .... 118 D6
St Aloysius RC Infant School
CAMTN NW1 .... 5 J9
St Andrews C of E (gm)
Primary School
EPP CM16 .... 48 D10
St Andrews C of E
Primary School
BRXN/ST SW9 .... 158 G8
St Andrews C of E
Primary School
BRXN/ST SW9 .... 159 H7

St Andrews C of E
Primary School
HERT/WAS SG14 .... 24 L8
St Andrews C of E
Primary School
TRDG/WHET N20 .... 97 J3
St Andrews C of E
Primary School
UX/CGN UB8 .... 131 N3
St Andrews C of E School
EN EN1 .... 79 L6
St Andrews C of E
Secondary School
COB KT11 .... 217 K9
St Andrews Greek School
CAMTN NW1 .... 4 F7
St Andrews Hospital
BOW E3 .... 140 G6
St Andrews Primary School
CRAWE RH10 .... 284 B9
St Andrews Primary School
STHGT/OAK N14 .... 98 E2
St Andrews RC School
LHD/OX KT22 .... 237 H6
St Andrews RC School
STRHM/NOR SW16 .... 180 F8
St Andrews School
CROY/NA CR0 .... 203 J10
St Andrews School
IS N1 .... 5 P5
St Andrews School
RYLN/HDSTN HA2 .... 114 A3
St Andrews School
WARE SG12 .... 27 J7
St Andrews School
WLSDN NW10 .... 136 E2
St Andrews School
WOKN/KNAP GU21 .... 232 A2
St Angelas RC Secondary School
FSTGT E7 .... 141 N1
St Angelo Preparatory School
EA W5 .... 135 J7
St Annes Catholic School
for Girls
PLMGR N13 .... 99 H5
St Annes Convent School
EN EN1 .... 79 L8
St Annes Primary School
CHERT KT16 .... 195 K8
St Annes Primary School
STWL/WRAY TW19 .... 173 P3
St Annes Primary School
WCHPL E1 .... 13 N1
St Annes RC Primary School
BNSTD SM7 .... 239 K2
St Annes RC Primary School
LBTH SE11 .... 17 N9
St Annes School
MRDN SM4 .... 201 L5
St Anns C of E Primary School
WAND/EARL SW18 .... 179 L1
St Ann's General Hospital
SEVS/STOTM N15 .... 119 K3
St Anns Heath County
Junior School
VW GU25 .... 194 C5
St Anns Primary School
SEVS/STOTM N15 .... 119 L3
St Anns School
HNWL W7 .... 134 D10
St Ann's Shopping Centre
HRW HA1 .... 114 D4
St Anselms RC Primary School
DART DA1 .... 187 P1
St Anselms RC School
NWDGN UB2 .... 153 L1
St Anselms School
HRW HA1 .... 114 D5
St Anslems RC School
TOOT SW17 .... 180 B6
St Anthony RC School
PGE/AN SE20 .... 204 A1
St Anthonys Hospital
WPK KT4 .... 200 G8
St Anthonys RC
Combined School
SLN SL2 .... 129 H5
St Anthonys RC First School
SLN SL2 .... 129 H5
St Anthonys RC Junior School
WATW WD18 .... 72 F9
St Antonys RC Primary School
FSTGT E7 .... 141 M2
St Antonys RC Primary School
WFD IG8 .... 101 M5
St Aubyns School
WFD IG8 .... 101 L8
St Augustine Junior School
BELV DA17 .... 164 A3
St Augustine Primary School
BELV DA17 .... 164 A2
St Augustines C of E School
KIL/WHAMP NW6 .... 2 F8
St Augustines Primary School
FUL/PGN SW6 .... 14 B10
St Augustines RC Junior School
GNTH/NBYPK IG2 .... 122 E3
St Augustines R C Primary School
CAT SE6 .... 182 G8
St Barnabas C of E School
BCVA SW1W 16 D7
St Barnabas & St Philips
C of E Primary School
KENS W8 .... 14 E4
St Bartholomews Hospital
STBT EC1A 12 D4
St Bartholomews Hospital
SWLY BR8 .... 208 G3
St Bartholomew's Medical School
FARR EC1M 12 D2
St Bartholomews
Primary School
SYD SE26 .... 182 B7
St Bartholomews RC
Primary School
SWLY BR8 .... 208 F3
St Bartholomew's the Great
STBT EC1A 12 D4
St Barts Hospital Sports Ground
CHST BR7 .... 185 H9
St Bedes C of E Junior School
RPLY/SEND GU23 .... 232 C10
St Bedes Primary School
BAL SW12 .... 180 E4
St Bedes RC School
CHDH RM6 .... 123 M3
St Benedicts Junior RC School
EA W5 .... 135 H7
St Benedicts School
EA W5 .... 135 J7
St Bernadette JMI School
LCOL/BKTW AL2 .... 57 H3

St Bernadettes RC First
& Middle School
KTN/HRWW/W HA3 .... 115 L2
St Bernadettes RC School
HGDN/ICK UB10 .... 132 C3
St Bernards Convent School
DTCH/LGLY SL3 .... 149 N1
St Bonaventures RC
Secondary School
FSTGT E7 .... 141 M7
St Boniface RC School
TOOT SW17 .... 179 P8
St Botolphs C of E
Primary School
GVW DA11 .... 190 A3
St Brelades Surgery
DORK RH4 .... 272 F4
St Catherine of Siena RC School
GSTN WD25 .... 55 L8
St Catherines RC Girls School
BXLYHS DA6 .... 186 C1
St Catherines RC Middle School
NWMAL KT3 .... 200 F5
St Catherines RC Primary School
WDR/YW UB7 .... 151 N1
St Catherines School
SHGR GU5 .... 268 C10
St Catherines School
TWK TW1 .... 176 E5
St Cecilias RC School
WPK KT4 .... 200 G9
St Chads RC Primary School
SNWD SE25 .... 203 M5
St Chads School
TIL RM18 .... 168 D7
St Charles Catholic Sixth
Form College
NKENS W10 .... 136 G7
St Charles Hospital
NKENS W10 .... 136 G7
St Charles RC Primary School
WEY KT13 .... 196 B10
St Christophers School
BECK BR3 .... 205 H2
St Christophers School
EPSOM KT18 .... 220 B10
St Christophers School
WBLY HA9 .... 115 L8
St Christophor House
STHWK SE1 .... 12 E9
St Clare Business Park
HPTN TW12 .... 176 B9
St Clement Danes School
RKW/CH/CXG WD3 .... 70 G6
St Clements Mixed Junior School
CHES/WCR EN8 .... 62 D3
St Clements & St James
C of E Primary School
NTGHL W11 .... 8 A9
St Clements School
EW KT17 .... 220 C5
St Columbas College
Preparatory School
STALW/RED AL3 .... 38 B8
St Columbas RC Boys School
BXLYHS DA6 .... 186 C1
St Cross RC Primary School
HOD EN11 .... 44 F5
St Cuthberts RC Primary School
EGH TW20 .... 171 P10
St Cuthbert with
St. Mattias School
ECT SW5 .... 14 F7
St Davids College
WWKM BR4 .... 204 G7
St Davids Group Practise
FELT TW13 .... 175 H5
St Davids Health Centre
STWL/WRAY TW19 .... 173 N3
St Davids School
ASHF TW15 .... 174 A6
St Davids School
PUR/KEN CR8 .... 222 G7
St Dominic RC School
HARP AL5 .... 20 A3
St Dominics Primary School
HAMP NW3 .... 118 A10
St Dominics RC Junior
& Infant School
HOM E9 .... 140 C1
St Dominics Sixth Form College
HRW HA1 .... 114 D7
St Dunstans C of E
Primary School
CHEAM SM3 .... 220 G4
St Dunstans College
CAT SE6 .... 182 E3
St Dunstans RC Primary School
WOKS/MYFD GU22 .... 232 D3
St Edmunds RC Primary School
POP/IOD E14 .... 160 F3
St Edmunds RC Primary School
WHTN TW2 .... 176 A3
St Edmunds RC School
ED N9 .... 100 A2
St Edwards C of E
Comprehensive School
CHDH RM6 .... 124 B4
St Edwards C of E Primary School
ROM RM1 .... 124 E1
St Edwards RC First School
WDSR SL4 .... 148 F7
St Edwards RC JMI School
STJWD NW8 .... 9 N2
St Edwards Royal Free
Ecumenical Middle School
WDSR SL4 .... 148 F7
St Elizabeths RC School
RCHPK/HAM TW10 .... 177 L1
St Elpheges RC School
WLGTN SM6 .... 222 F3
St Ethelberts RC First
& Middle School
SLN SL3 .... 129 M8
St Faiths C of E School
WAND/EARL SW18 .... 179 M1
St Fidelis RC Primary School
ERITH DA8 .... 164 D5
St Francesca Cabrini
Primary School
FSTH SE23 .... 182 B2
St Francis Middle School
CRAWE RH10 .... 283 P8
St Francis RC Primary School
CTHM CR3 .... 241 N7
St Francis RC Primary School
PECK SE15 .... 19 P10
St Francis Xavier
Sixth Form College
BAL SW12 .... 180 C2
St Georges Business Park
WEY KT13 .... 216 B5

St George's Cathedral
STHWK SE1 .... 18 B3
St Georges C of E Primary School
AMSS HP7 .... 69 K5
St Georges C of E Primary School
CMBW SE5 .... 19 J10
St Georges C of E Primary School
VX/NE SW8 .... 158 D6
St Georges College
GVW DA11 .... 190 D5
St Georges College
ADL/WDHM KT15 .... 195 N10
St Georges College
HOLWY N7 .... 119 H8
St Georges Elizabethan Theatre
HOLWY N7 .... 118 E9
St Georges Hospital
HCH RM12 .... 125 M9
St Georges Hospital
TOOT SW17 .... 179 P8
St Georges Hospital
TOOT SW17 .... 179 N7
St Georges Industrial Estate
AMSS HP7 .... 69 L5
St Georges Industrial Estate
KUTN/CMB KT2 .... 177 J8
St Georges Industrial Estate
WDGN N22 .... 99 J8
St Georges Medical Centre
HDN NW4 .... 116 E1
St Georges RC First
& Middle School
HRW HA1 .... 114 E8
St Georges RC Primary School
ENC/FH EN2 .... 79 L6
St Georges RC Primary School
STHWK SE1 .... 18 C3
St Georges RC Secondary School
KIL/WHAMP NW6 .... 3 H8
St Georges School
ASC SL5 .... 192 A4
St Georges School
BMLY BR1 .... 205 P2
St Georges School
WDSR SL4 .... 149 J6
St Gildas RC Junior School
CEND/HSY/T N8 .... 118 F5
St Giles C of E School
ASHTD KT21 .... 237 L4
St Giles C of E Primary School
POTB/CUF EN6 .... 58 D8
St Giles C of E Primary School
POTB/CUF EN6 .... 58 E9
St Giles College London Central
RSQ WC1B 11 L3
St Giles School
CROY/NA CR0 .... 223 J3
St Giles Surgery
CSTG HP8 .... 89 P4
St Gregorys RC First
& Middle School
EA W5 .... 135 J6
St Gregorys RC High School
KTN/HRWW/W HA3 .... 115 J3
St Helens College
HGDN/ICK UB10 .... 132 B2
St Helens Junior School
BRWN CM15 .... 107 J1
St Helens RC Infant School
BRW CM14 .... 107 J3
St Helens RC Primary School
PLSTW E13 .... 141 L6
St Helens RC School
BRXN/ST SW9 .... 159 H9
St Helens School
NTHWD HA6 .... 92 F7
St Helens School
STALE/WH AL4 .... 21 J3
St Hilarys School
SEV TN13 .... 247 J8
St Hugh of Lincoln RC
First School
WOKN/KNAP GU21 .... 231 J5
St Ignatius College
EN EN1 .... 79 P3
St Ignatius Primary School
SEVS/STOTM N15 .... 119 N4
St Ignatius RC Primary School
SUN TW16 .... 197 H1
St James Church School
HLWS CM18 .... 46 G5
St James C of E Junior School
FSTGT E7 .... 121 L10
St James C of E Primary School
BERM/RHTH SE16 .... 19 N3
St James C of E Primary School
PEND EN3 .... 80 B6
St James C of E Primary School
WEY KT13 .... 196 D10
St James Hatcham C of E School
NWCR SE14 .... 160 D7
St James Medical Centre
CROY/NA CR0 .... 203 L7
St James RC Primary School
HAYES BR2 .... 206 E5
St James School
MUSWH N10 .... 118 B2
St James's Health Centre
WALTH E17 .... 120 D3
St James's Palace
WHALL SW1A 11 H10
St James's School
WHTN TW2 .... 176 D6
St James the Great School
THHTH CR7 .... 203 J2
St Joan of Arc RC School
RKW/CH/CXG WD3 .... 91 P1
St John Baptist School
BMLY BR1 .... 183 H7
St John Baptist School
WARE SG12 .... 26 F6
St John Fisher RC JMI School
STALE/WH AL4 .... 39 H3
St John Fisher RC Junior School
LOU IG10 .... 82 F6
St John Fisher RC Primary School
ERITHM DA18 .... 163 P2
St John Fisher RC Primary School
NWMAL KT3 .... 200 F5
St John Fisher School
CFD/PVL UB6 .... 135 H5
St John of Jerusalem C of E
Primary School
HOM E9 .... 140 B2
St John Rigby School
WWKM BR4 .... 225 J1
St John & St James School
UED N18 .... 99 N6
St Johns C of E First School
STAN HA7 .... 94 F5
St Johns C of E Infant School
HDN NW4 .... 116 E3

St Johns C of E Junior
& Infant School
ENC/FH EN2 .... 79 J2
St Johns C of E Middle School
STAN HA7 .... 94 B7
St Johns C of E Primary School
ARCH N19 .... 118 E8
St Johns C of E Primary School
BETH E2 .... 140 A4
St Johns C of E Primary School
BKHH IG9 .... 101 N2
St Johns C of E Primary School
FBAR/BDGN N11 .... 98 A5
St John's C of E Primary School
FUL/PGN SW6 .... 157 H7
St Johns C of E Primary School
TRDG/WHET N20 .... 97 M3
St Johns C of E Primary School
WGCW AL8 .... 22 C6
St Johns C of E Primary School
WLYN AL6 .... 23 J1
St Johns C of E School
CDALE/KGS NW9 .... 116 B3
St Johns C of E School
EPP CM16 .... 65 H6
St John's Concert Hall
WEST SW1P 17 L4
St Johns CP School
WOKN/KNAP GU21 .... 231 K4
St Johns Hill Surgery
SEV TN13 .... 247 K8
St John's Hospital
SOHO/SHAV W1D 11 J7
St John's Hospital Day Centre
BTSEA SW11 .... 157 N10
St Johns Infant School
CTHM CR3 .... 260 A1
St Johns Infant School
RAD WD7 .... 74 E1
St Johns Junior School
CTHM CR3 .... 260 A2
St Johns Primary School
IS N1 .... 7 J8
St Johns Primary School
KUT KT1 .... 199 K3
St Johns Primary School
REDH RH1 .... 275 P2
St Johns RC
Comprehensive School
GVE DA12 .... 190 G4
St Johns RC Junior Middle
& Infant School
RKW/CH/CXG WD3 .... 91 L2
St Johns RC Primary School
BERM/RHTH SE16 .... 160 D1
St Johns RC Primary School
GVE DA12 .... 190 G4
St Johns School
BRXN/ST SW9 .... 159 H8
St Johns School
ENC/FH EN2 .... 79 H6
St Johns School
HBRY N5 .... 119 J8
St Johns School
LHD/OX KT22 .... 236 G7
St Johns School
NTHWD HA6 .... 93 J7
St Johns Special School
WFD IG8 .... 102 D6
St Johns Way Medical Centre
ARCH N19 .... 118 E6
St Johns Wood Synagogue
STJWD NW8 .... 3 K8
St John the Baptist RC
Comprehensive School
WOKS/MYFD GU22 .... 232 D5
St John the Divine
Primary School
CMBW SE5 .... 159 J6
St John Vianney RC School
SEVS/STOTM N15 .... 119 J2
St Joseph RC School
DART DA1 .... 164 F10
St Josephs Catholic
Primary School
EPSOM KT18 .... 219 P10
St Joseph School
DACW RM9 .... 124 A9
St Josephs College
STRHM/NOR SW16 .... 181 J9
St Josephs Infant School
CMBW SE5 .... 159 K6
St Josephs Infant School
HDN NW4 .... 116 E2
St Josephs Infant School
NRWD SE19 .... 181 K9
St Josephs Junior School
HDN NW4 .... 116 E2
St Josephs Junior School
WBLY HA9 .... 115 L10
St Josephs Preparatory School
GVE DA12 .... 190 F5
St Josephs Primary School
ARCH N19 .... 118 C6
St Josephs Primary School
BARK IG11 .... 142 F3
St Joseph's Primary School
PUT/ROE SW15 .... 179 K1
St Josephs RC Combined School
CFSP/GDCR SL9 .... 109 P1
St Josephs RC Infant
& Junior School
BERM/RHTH SE16 .... 19 N2
St Josephs RC JMI School
CHES/WCR EN8 .... 62 D9
St Josephs RC Junior School
LEY E10 .... 120 C6
St Josephs RC Junior School
NRWD SE19 .... 181 K9
St Josephs RC Primary School
BERM/RHTH SE16 .... 160 B2
St Josephs RC Primary School
BMLY BR1 .... 183 P10
St Josephs RC Primary School
DORK RH4 .... 272 F2
St Josephs RC Primary School
GNWCH SE10 .... 161 K4
St Josephs RC Primary School
HNWL W7 .... 134 D10
St Josephs RC Primary School
HOL/ALD WC2B 11 M5
St Josephs RC Primary School
KUT KT1 .... 199 K2
St Josephs RC Primary School
MV/WKIL W9 .... 3 J10
St Josephs RC Primary School
STHWK SE1 .... 18 F1
St Josephs RC School
DEPT SE8 .... 160 F6
St Josephs RC School
GVW DA11 .... 190 A4
St Josephs RC School
OXHEY WD19 .... 93 J4

St Josephs RC School
WBLY HA9 .... 115 L10
St Josephs RC Secondary School
SLN SL2 .... 129 M8
St Josephs School
KTN/HRWW/W HA3 .... 94 F10
St Josephs School
REDH RH1 .... 257 P9
St Josephs School
UPMR RM14 .... 126 A7
St Joseph the Worker RC
Primary School
RBRW/HUT CM13 .... 87 P10
St Judes C of E School
EGH TW20 .... 171 P9
St Judes & St Pauls C of E
Primary School
IS N1 .... 7 J1
St Lawrence Business Centre
FELT TW13 .... 175 J5
St Lawrence Catholic School
FELT TW13 .... 175 J4
St Lawrence C of E Junior School
E/WMO/HCT KT8 .... 198 C3
St Lawrence C of E Junior School
UX/CGN UB8 .... 131 M7
St Lawrence C of E School
WAB EN9 .... 63 L9
St Lawrence CP School
EHSLY KT24 .... 253 L3
St Leonards C of E Primary
School
STRHM/NOR SW16 .... 180 E8
St Leonards Hospital
IS N1 .... 7 K7
St Lukes C of E Primary School
CAN/RD E16 .... 141 L8
St Lukes C of E Primary School
KIL/WHAMP NW6 .... 2 C8
St Lukes C of E Primary School
KUTN/CMB KT2 .... 199 L1
St Luke's Health Centre
CAN/RD E16 .... 141 L8
St Lukes Primary School
FSBYE EC1V 6 F10
St Lukes Primary School
POP/IOD E14 .... 161 J3
St Lukes RC Primary School
HLWW/ROY CM19 .... 46 F3
St Lukes School
THHTH CR7 .... 203 H4
St Lukes Special School
LOU IG10 .... 82 D8
St Lukes Surgery
GU GU1 .... 268 C1
St Lukes Woodside Hospital
MUSWH N10 .... 118 B2
St Margaret Clitherow RC
Primary School
THMD SE28 .... 143 L10
St Margaret Clitherow RC
Primary School
WLSDN NW10 .... 116 A8
St Margarets C of E
Primary School
BARK IG11 .... 142 F3
St Margarets C of E
Primary School
CRAWW RH11 .... 283 L6
St Margarets Hospital
EPP CM16 .... 65 L5
St Margarets Medical Practice
TWK TW1 .... 176 C1
St Margarets School
BUSH WD23 .... 93 P1
St Margarets School
HAMP NW3 .... 117 J3
St Marks C of E School
LBTH SE11 .... 17 P9
St Marks C of E School
SNWD SE25 .... 203 P4
St Marks Medical Centre
WOOL/PLUM SE18 .... 162 E5
St Marks Primary School
ARCH N19 .... 118 F7
St Marks Primary School
HAYES BR2 .... 205 M3
St Marks Primary School
MTCM CR4 .... 202 A2
St Marks Primary School
STHL UB1 .... 154 D1
St Marks RC Comprehensive
School
HLWS CM18 .... 47 H2
St Marks RC School
HSLW TW3 .... 153 N9
St Marthas Convent
Senior School
EBAR EN4 .... 77 K5
St Martin in the Fields
High School
BRXS/STRHM SW2 .... 181 J4
St Martin of Porres RC
Primary School
FBAR/BDGN N11 .... 98 D7
St Martins C of E Junior School
EPSOM KT18 .... 238 A1
St Martins C of E School
DORK RH4 .... 272 E1
St Martins House
Business Centre
EHSLY KT24 .... 252 F5
St Martins Medical Centre
RSLP HA4 .... 112 F5
St Martins RC Junior School
EDGE HA8 .... 95 P7
St Martins School
MLHL NW7 .... 96 B6
St Martins School
NTHWD HA6 .... 92 E6
St Martins School
RBRW/HUT CM13 .... 107 P2
St Martins School of Art
SOHO/SHAV W1D 11 K6
St Martins Theatre
LSQ/SEVD WC2H 11 K7
St Mary Abbots C of E
Primary School
KENS W8 .... 14 F2
St Mary & All Saints C of E Primary
School
BEAC HP9 .... 88 D9
St Mary Magdalene
C of E Primary School
PECK SE15 .... 160 A8
St Mary Magdalene C of E School
HOLWY N7 .... 6 A1
St Mary Magdalenes School
BROCKY SE4 .... 160 D10
St Mary Magdalens RC
Junior School
CRICK NW2 .... 136 E1

St Mary Magdalines
Primary School
MV/WKIL W9 .... 8 C2
St Mary Magdelens
Primary School
MORT/ESHN SW14 .... 156 A9
St Mary of the Angels RC
Primary School
BAY/PAD W2 .... 8 E5
St Marys Abbey
MLHL NW7 .... 96 D4
St Mary & St. Josephs RC School
SCUP DA14 .... 185 J8
St Mary & St. Pancras
Primary School
CAMTN NW1 .... 5 J8
St Marys Church
of England High School
HDN NW4 .... 116 F1
St Marys C of E Infant School
LHD/OX KT22 .... 237 H8
St Marys C of E JMI School
EBAR EN4 .... 77 P10
St Marys C of E Junior School
CEND/HSY/T N8 .... 118 F2
St Marys C of E Primary School
AMSS HP7 .... 68 G5
St Marys C of E Primary School
BF/WBF KT14 .... 215 P9
St Marys C of E Primary School
BRWN CM15 .... 87 L10
St Marys C of E Primary School
CHSGTN KT9 .... 219 K3
St Marys C of E Primary School
IS N1 .... 6 D4
St Marys C of E Primary School
SWLY BR8 .... 208 F4
St Marys C of E Primary School
THDIT KT7 .... 198 G8
St Marys C of E Primary School
WLSDN NW10 .... 136 B1
St Marys C of E School
LEW SE13 .... 182 C1
St Marys C of E School
PUT/ROE SW15 .... 156 C9
St Marys C of E School
TWK TW1 .... 176 F3
St Marys Greek Cathedral
WDGN N22 .... 98 C9
St Marys Hare Park School
GPK RM2 .... 125 K1
St Marys High School
CHESW EN7 .... 62 A6
St Marys Hospital
BAY/PAD W2 .... 9 M5
St Marys Infant School
CAR SM5 .... 221 P1
St Mary's Infant School
SEVS/STOTM N15 .... 119 L3
St Marys Junior School
CFSP/GDCR SL9 .... 110 B2
St Marys Middle School
OXTED RH8 .... 261 K4
St Marys Primary School
BECK BR3 .... 183 H10
St Marys Primary School
FNCH N3 .... 97 J9
St Marys Primary School
WKENS W14 .... 156 C3
St Marys Primary School
WOOL/PLUM SE18 .... 162 D3
St Marys RC Church & School
HCH RM12 .... 125 H6
St Marys RC County
Primary School
TIL RM18 .... 168 C8
St Marys RC Infant School
CROY/NA CR0 .... 203 L8
St Marys RC Junior School
CAR SM5 .... 222 A1
St Marys RC Junior School
SEVS/STOTM N15 .... 119 L4
St Marys RC Junior School
WALTH E17 .... 121 H1
St Marys RC Primary School
CHING E4 .... 101 J2
St Marys RC Primary School
CLAP SW4 .... 180 D1
St Marys RC Primary School
KIL/WHAMP NW6 .... 2 E7
St Marys RC Primary School
PEND EN3 .... 80 C8
St Mary's RC Primary School
VX/NE SW8 .... 158 C7
St Marys RC Primary School
WIM/MER SW19 .... 179 K10
St Marys RC School
ELTH/MOT SE9 .... 184 D1
St Marys & St Peters
C of E Primary School
TEDD TW11 .... 176 E8
St Marys School
ASC SL5 .... 192 A7
St Marys School
CEND/HSY/T N8 .... 118 G3
St Marys School
HAMP NW3 .... 117 M10
St Mary's School
STNW/STAM N16 .... 119 M7
St Marys School
UX/CGN UB8 .... 131 M3
St Marys Tutorial College
GUW GU2 .... 267 P3
St Marys University College
TWK TW1 .... 176 E6
St Matthews C of E First School
COB KT11 .... 235 J4
St Matthews C of E
Primary School
PEND EN3 .... 80 B9
St Matthews C of E
Primary School
REDH RH1 .... 258 A8
St Matthews C of E
Primary School
SURB KT6 .... 199 K7
St Matthews C of E
Primary School
WDR/YW UB7 .... 131 N10
St Matthews School
WEST SW1P 17 K4
St Matthias C of E School
STNW/STAM N16 .... 119 M10
St Matthias Primary School
BETH E2 .... 13 M1
St Maurs School
WEY KT13 .... 196 C10
St Meryl Junior Middle
& Infant School
OXHEY WD19 .... 93 M4
St Michael at Bowes C of E
Junior Mixed School
PLMGR N13 .... 99 H7

St Michaels C of E Aided
Primary School Hall
WELL DA16 .... 163 M7
St Michaels C of E JMI School
STALW/RED AL3 .... 38 A6
St Michaels C of E Junior
& Infant School
WDGN N22 .... 98 G9
St Michael's C of E School
SYD SE26 .... 182 D7
St Michaels Grammar School
NFNCH/WDSP N12 .... 97 L6
St Michaels Junior
& Infant School
ENC/FH EN2 .... 79 K5
St Michaels RC School
ASHF TW15 .... 174 B8
St Michaels RC School
BERM/RHTH SE16 .... 19 N2
St Michaels RC School
GSTN WD25 .... 55 L8
St Michaels School
HGT N6 .... 118 B5
St Michaels School
HSLWW TW4 .... 153 N9
St Michael's School
WAND/EARL SW18 .... 179 J3
St Monicas RC Primary School
STHGT/OAK N14 .... 98 F4
St Nicholas C of E First School
GUW GU2 .... 267 P2
St Nicholas C of E JMI School
SHPTN TW17 .... 196 C6
St Nicholas House School
HHS/BOV HP3 .... 54 C1
St Nicholas School
CHST BR7 .... 184 F10
St Nicholas School
HLWE CM17 .... 30 A8
St Nicholas School
PUR/KEN CR8 .... 222 G9
St Nicholas Special School
REDH RH1 .... 258 E5
St Nicks Art Gallery
SUT SM1 .... 221 L2
St Olaves Grammar School
ORP BR6 .... 207 L10
St Olaves Preparatory School
ELTH/MOT SE9 .... 184 C3
St Osmunds RC Primary School
BARN SW13 .... 156 C7
St Pancras Hospital
CAMTN NW1 .... 5 J6
St Pancras International
Youth Hostel
CAMTN NW1 .... 5 K9
St Patricks Church School
STHWK SE1 .... 12 A10
St Patricks Infants School
WAP E1W 140 A10
St Patricks RC Junior
& Infant School
WALTH E17 .... 120 D2
St Patricks RC Junior School
WAP E1W 140 A10
St Patricks RC School
WOOL/PLUM SE18 .... 162 G3
St Patricks School
ROMW/RG RM7 .... 104 C9
St Paulinus C of E
Primary School
DART DA1 .... 164 F10
St Pauls Cathedral
STP EC4M 12 E6
St Pauls Catholic School
SUN TW16 .... 197 H1
St Pauls Choir School
STP EC4M 12 E6
St Pauls C of E (aided)
Primary School
DORK RH4 .... 272 G2
St Pauls C of E Junior School
KUTN/CMB KT2 .... 177 M10
St Pauls C of E Primary School
BRW CM14 .... 86 C7
St Pauls C of E Primary School
BTFD TW8 .... 155 J5
St Pauls C of E Primary School
FBAR/BDGN N11 .... 98 B6
St Pauls C of E Primary School
HAMP NW3 .... 3 P4
St Pauls C of E Primary School
WALW SE17 .... 18 E8
St Pauls C of E Primary School
WCHMH N21 .... 99 J1
St Pauls C of E Primary School
WCHPL E1 .... 13 P7
St Pauls C of E School
SWLY BR8 .... 208 F4
St Pauls Cray C of E
Primary School
STMC/STPC BR5 .... 207 M3
St Pauls Cray Health Clinic
STMC/STPC BR5 .... 207 K2
St Pauls Girls School
HMSMTH W6 .... 156 C3
St Pauls Middle School
ADL/WDHM KT15 .... 215 K1
St Pauls Primary School
HMSMTH W6 .... 156 F4
St Pauls Primary School
KGLGY WD4 .... 54 D10
St Pauls Primary School
MLHL NW7 .... 96 E5
St Pauls RC Primary School
ESH/CLAY KT10 .... 198 D7
St Pauls RC Primary School
WDGN N22 .... 98 G10
St Pauls RC Secondary School
WOOL/PLUM SE18 .... 163 J5
St Pauls Road Medical Centre
IS N1 .... 6 D1
St Pauls Roman Catholic
JMI School
CHESW EN7 .... 62 A3
St Pauls School
BARN SW13 .... 156 D4
St Pauls School
CHSGTN KT9 .... 219 K1
St Pauls Way Community School
BOW E3 .... 140 F7
St Pauls Westminster Cathedral
WEST SW1P 16 G4
St Pauls with St Michaels
C of E Primary School
HACK E8 .... 7 P5
St Paul with St Luke
C of E Primary School
BOW E3 .... 140 E7
St Peter Chanel RC School
SCUP DA14 .... 185 M8

St Peter & Paul RC
Primary School
IL IG1 .... 122 G8
St Peter & St Paul RC
Primary School
MTCM CR4 .... 202 A4
St Peters Catholic
Comprehensive School
GU GU1 .... 250 F9
St Peter's Church
of England Primary School
HMSMTH W6 .... 156 D4
St Peters C of E
Combined School
SL SL1 .... 128 A5
St Peters C of E Primary School
BRW CM14 .... 106 D3
St Peters C of E Primary School
MV/WKIL W9 .... 8 E2
St Peters C of E Primary School
WALW SE17 .... 18 C8
St Peters C of E School
WDSR SL4 .... 171 L2
St Peter's Hospital
COVGDN WC2E 11 M7
St Peters JMI School
STAL AL1 .... 38 D7
St Peters Junior Middle
& Infant School
RKW/CH/CXG WD3 .... 91 L2
St Peters Primary School
WAP E1W 140 B10
St Peters RC Primary School
LHD/OX KT22 .... 237 H6
St Peters RC Primary School
ROM RM1 .... 124 E1
St Peters RC Primary School
WOOL/PLUM SE18 .... 162 E4
St Peters RC School
DAGW RM9 .... 144 A3
St Peters & St Paul C of E
Primary School
CTHM CR5 .... 259 H1
St Peters School
SAND/SEL CR2 .... 223 L3
St Peters Street Medical Practice
IS N1 .... 6 C1
The St Philip Howard
Catholic Primary School
HAT AL10 .... 40 E4
St Philips School
CHSGTN KT9 .... 219 J3
St Philips School
SKENS SW7 .... 15 K6
St Phillips Infant School
SYD SE26 .... 182 A7
St Philomenas RC Primary School
STMC/STPC BR5 .... 207 M3
St Philomenas School
CAR SM5 .... 221 P2
St Quintins Health Centre
NKENS W10 .... 136 F7
St Raphaels Hospice
WPK KT4 .... 200 C9
St Raphaels School
NTHLT UB5 .... 133 J4
St Raphaels Way Medical Centre
WBLY HA9 .... 115 P10
St Richards with St. Andrews
C of E Primary School
RCHPK/HAM TW10 .... 176 C6
St Robert Southwell RC
Primary School
CDALE/KGS NW9 .... 115 P4
St Roses Infants School
HHW HP1 .... 35 K8
St Saviours Catholic
Primary School
LEW SE13 .... 161 H10
St Saviours C of E Infant School
EA W5 .... 135 J9
St Saviours C of E Primary School
HNHL SE24 .... 159 K9
St Saviours C of E Primary School
MV/WKIL W9 .... 9 H2
St Saviours C of E Primary School
POP/IOD E14 .... 140 G7
St Scholasticas RC Junior Middle
& Infant School
STNW/STAM N16 .... 119 P8
St Stephens C of E Junior School
TWK TW1 .... 176 F2
St Stephens C of E
Primary School
BAY/PAD W2 .... 8 F4
St Stephens C of E
Primary School
SHB W12 .... 136 E10
St Stephens RC Primary School
WELL DA16 .... 163 K8
St Swithun Wells RC
Primary School
RSLP HA4 .... 113 L8
St Teresa RC Primary School
BCTR RM8 .... 123 M9
St Teresas Preparatory School
EHSLY KT24 .... 253 L4
St Teresas RC School
KTN/HRWW/W HA3 .... 94 B9
St Teresas School
RDKG RH5 .... 255 L8
St Theresas Primary School
FNCH N3 .... 117 K1
St Thomas Childrens
Day Hospital
LBTH SE11 .... 17 P7
St Thomas C of E Primary School
NKENS W10 .... 8 A2
St Thomas C of E Primary School
STNW/STAM N16 .... 119 N6
St Thomas Hospital
Operation Theatre
STHWK SE1 .... 13 H10
St Thomas Moore RC JMI School
BERK HP4 .... 33 M5
St Thomas More RC Primary School
BXLYHN DA7 .... 164 A8
St Thomas More RC Primary School
ELTH/MOT SE9 .... 162 B9
St Thomas More RC School
ELTH/MOT SE9 .... 184 D2
St Thomas More School
WDGN N22 .... 98 G8
St Thomas of Canterbury
Junior & Infant School
BRWN CM15 .... 107 J1
St Thomas of Canterbury
RC Middle School
MTCM CR4 .... 202 B3
St Thomas of Canterbury
RC Primary School
FUL/PGN SW6 .... 157 J6

St Thomas RC Primary School
GRAYS RM17 .... 167 N3
St Thomas's Hospital
STHWK SE1 .... 17 N3
St Thomas the Apostle College
PECK SE15 .... 160 B7
St Ursulas Convent School
GNWCH SE10 .... 161 J6
St Ursulas Junior School
HARH RM3 .... 105 J3
St Vincents Hospital
RSLP HA4 .... 112 F1
St Vincents Primary School
ELTH/MOT SE9 .... 184 B7
St Vincents RC Primary School
ACT W3 .... 135 N3
St Vincents RC Primary School
BCTR RM8 .... 123 M7
St Vincents RC Primary School
MHST W1U 10 C4
St Vincents RC Primary School
MLHL NW7 .... 96 F5
St Vincent & the Grenadines
High Comm
KENS W8 .... 15 H2
St Walter
& St John Sports Ground
TOOT SW17 .... 179 P4
St Wilfrids RC School
CRAWW RH11 .... 283 L11
St William of York School
FSTH SE23 .... 182 D4
St Winifreds Junior School
LEE/GVPK SE12 .... 183 L1
St Winifreds RC School
LEW SE13 .... 183 K1
Salamanca Chenil Galleries
CHEL SW3 .... 15 N8
Salcombe Preparatory School
STHGT/OAK N14 .... 98 E1
Salesian College
BTSEA SW11 .... 157 P7
Salesian College
CHERT KT16 .... 195 K8
Salesian College
CHERT KT16 .... 195 H9
Salfords First School
REDH RH1 .... 276 B6
Salfords Industrial Estate
REDH RH1 .... 276 B8
Salisbury Hall
LCOL/BKTW AL2 .... 57 N5
Salisbury Infant School
HAT AL10 .... 40 E2
Salisbury Lawn Tennis Club
STAL AL1 .... 38 G5
Salisbury Primary School
MNPK E12 .... 122 A10
Salisbury School
ED N9 .... 100 B2
Salisbury Surgery
FUL/PGN SW6 .... 157 H6
Salters' Hall
BARB EC2Y 12 G4
Salusbury Primary School
KIL/WHAMP NW6 .... 2 C6
Salvatorian College
KTN/HRWW/W HA3 .... 94 D10
Samuel Jones Industrial Estate
PECK SE15 .... 159 M6
Samuel Rhodes School
IS N1 .... 6 A5
Sandcross School
REIG RH2 .... 275 J3
The Sanders Draper
Secondary School
HCH RM12 .... 125 K9
Sandfield CP School
GU GU1 .... 268 A1
Sandgate Trading Estate
BERM/RHTH SE16 .... 160 A4
Sandhurst Junior School
CAT SE6 .... 183 K3
Sandiford Industrial Estate
CHEAM SM3 .... 201 J9
Sandown Industrial Park
ESH/CLAY KT10 .... 197 P9
Sandridge Gate Business Centre
STALW/RED AL3 .... 38 E2
Sandridge JMI School
STALE/WH AL4 .... 21 J9
Sandridge Youth Club
& Sports Centre
STALW/RED AL3 .... 20 G10
Sandringham Practice
HACK E8 .... 119 P10
Sandringham Primary School
FSTGT E7 .... 141 P1
Sandringham School
STALE/WH AL4 .... 38 G2
Sandys Row Synagogue
WCHPL E1 .... 13 K4
Sangers County Middle School
HORL RH6 .... 280 A4
Saracens Rugby Football Club
STHGT/OAK N14 .... 78 B10
Sarah Bonnell
Comprehensive School
SRTFD E15 .... 141 K1
Sarah Devonport Gallery
SKENS SW7 .... 15 N5
Sarbir Industrial Park
HLW CM20 .... 29 M6
Sarratt Junior Middle
& Infant School
RKW/CH/CXG WD3 .... 71 K2
Sarum Hall School
HAMP NW3 .... 3 P3
Satay Gallery Restaurant
BRXN/ST SW9 .... 159 H10
Satmer Trust School
STNW/STAM N16 .... 119 P7
Savoy Theatre
TPL/STR WC2R 11 N8
Sawbridge Health Clinic
SBW CM21 .... 29 P1
Saxeway Business Centre
CSHM HP5 .... 50 D4
Saxon Business Centre
WIM/MER SW19 .... 201 M2
Saxon CP School
SHPTN TW17 .... 196 A5
Sayer Clinic
CROY/NA CR0 .... 222 G1
Sayer Clinics
MBLAR W1H 10 B6
Sayes Court Junior School
ADL/WDHM KT15 .... 215 L2
Scarsdale Place Medical Centre
KENS W8 .... 14 C3
S C C Clinic
REDH RH1 .... 258 D5

Schiller International University
   STHWK SE1...................... 12 A10
Sch of Econ & Pol Sci
   LINN WC2A...................... 11 P6
Sch of Fine Art
   STPAN WC1H...................... 5 K10
Sch of Hygiene
   & Tropical Medicine
   STPAN WC1H...................... 11 J1
Sch of Medicine
   FARR EC1M...................... 12 E3
Sch of Medicine
   PIM SW1V...................... 17 J10
Sch of Music & Drama
   BARB EC2Y...................... 12 F4
Sch of Physiotherapy
   FITZ W1H...................... 11 H3
Schoolhouse
   ABR/ST RM4...................... 105 L3
School House Aveley School
   SOCK/AV RM15...................... 146 D10
School House Grammar School
   BFN/LL DA15...................... 185 L5
Schooling Licensed
   Conveyancers
   GRAYS RM17...................... 167 N4
School of Art College
   REIG RH2...................... 257 N10
School of Health
   RDART DA2...................... 188 A2
The School of St David
   & St Katharine
   CEND/HSY/T N8...................... 118 F2
School of the Good Shepherd
   CROY/NA CR0...................... 224 G4
Schopwick Surgery
   BORE WD6...................... 75 J10
Science Museum
   SKENS SW7...................... 15 L4
The Science Museum Library
   SKENS SW7...................... 15 L3
The Scott Gallery
   HORL RH6...................... 280 B5
The Scott Gallery
   REDH RH1...................... 276 B1
The Scottish Hospital
   COVGDN WC2E...................... 11 L7
Scotts Park Primary School
   BMLY BR1...................... 205 P1
Scotts Primary School
   HCH RM12...................... 125 K10
Scott Wilkie Primary School
   CAN/RD E16...................... 141 P8
Screen on Baker Street
   MHST W1U...................... 10 B3
Seaton House School
   BELMT SM2...................... 221 N6
Sebright Primary School
   BETH E2...................... 7 N7
Secombe Theatre
   SUT SM1...................... 221 K2
Secretarial College
   BECK BR3...................... 204 D1
Sedgehill School
   CAT SE6...................... 182 L3
Sedgewick Centre
   WCHPL E1...................... 13 M5
Sedleys C of E Primary School
   MEO DA13...................... 189 M8
Seer Green C of E
   Primary School
   BEAC HP9...................... 89 H7
S E H A Hindu Temple
   WOOL/PLUM SE18...................... 162 E3
Selborne School
   GFD/PVL UB6...................... 134 E4
The Sele School
   HERT/WAS SG14...................... 24 G5
The Selhurst Medical Centre
   SNWD SE25...................... 203 L6
Sellincourt School
   TOOT SW17...................... 180 A9
Selsdon CP School
   SAND/SEL CR2...................... 224 B5
Selsdon High School
   SAND/SEL CR2...................... 224 C4
The Selsdon Park
   Medical Practice
   SAND/SEL CR2...................... 224 A6
Selwyn Infant School
   CHING E4...................... 100 G7
Selwyn Junior School
   CHING E4...................... 101 H7
Selwyn Primary School
   PLSTW E13...................... 141 M3
Send C of E First School
   RPLY/SEND GU23...................... 232 G10
Send Cricket Club
   RPLY/SEND GU23...................... 232 E10
Send Surgery
   RPLY/SEND GU23...................... 232 F9
Sergeant Industrial Estate
   WAND/EARL SW18...................... 179 L2
Serpentine Galleries
   BAY/PAD W2...................... 9 M10
Service Practice
   BERK HP4...................... 33 P5
Servite RC Primary School
   WBPTN SW10...................... 15 J9
Seven Islands Leisure Centre
   BERM/RHTH SE16...................... 160 B2
Seven Kings Health Centre
   GDMY/SEVK IG3...................... 123 H6
Seven Kings High School
   GNTH/NBYPK IG2...................... 122 G5
Seven Mills Primary School
   POP/IOD E14...................... 160 F1
Sevenoaks Business Centre
   RSEV TN14...................... 247 J6
Sevenoaks CP School
   SEV TN13...................... 247 J8
Sevenoaks Hospital
   SEV TN13...................... 247 K7
Sevenoaks School
   BGR/WK TN15...................... 265 K2
Sevenoaks Swimming Centre
   BGR/WK TN15...................... 265 K1
Sevenoaks Town Council
   SEV TN13...................... 247 J8
Sevenoaks Way Industrial Estate
   STMC/STPC BR5...................... 207 M3
Seychelles High Comm
   MHST W1U...................... 10 B3
Seymour Gardens Medical Centre
   IL IG1...................... 122 C6
Seymour Leasure Centre
   MBLAR W1H...................... 10 A4
Shaare Zedek Medical Centre
   GLDGN NW11...................... 117 J4
Shaftesbury Medical Centre
   RYLN/HDSTN HA2...................... 114 B6
Shaftesbury Park School
   BTSEA SW11...................... 158 A8

Shaftesbury Primary School
   FSTGT E7...................... 141 P2
Shaftesbury School
   KTN/HRWW/W HA3...................... 94 A9
Shahjalal Medical Centre
   WCHPL E1...................... 13 P6
Shakespeare Business Centre
   BRXN/ST SW9...................... 159 J3
Shakespeare Globe Exhibition
   STHWK SE1...................... 12 E8
Shakespeare Industrial Estate
   WATN W24...................... 73 H4
Shalford County First School
   RGUE GU4...................... 268 B6
The Shamrock Sports Club
   ACT W5...................... 135 P8
Shanghai Traditional
   Chinese Medical Centre
   TWK TW1...................... 177 J2
Shannon Corner Retail Park
   NWMAL KT3...................... 200 C4
Shapla Junior & Infant School
   WCHPL E1...................... 13 N7
Sharp Sports Centre
   EDGE HA8...................... 95 M7
Shaw County Junior
   & Infant School
   SOCK/AV RM15...................... 146 A6
Shawcroft School
   STMC/STPC BR5...................... 207 P5
Shawley County First
   & Middle School
   EPSOM KT18...................... 238 F4
Shears Green CP School
   GVW DA11...................... 190 C6
Shears Green Infant School
   GVW DA11...................... 190 C6
Sheeji Medical Centre
   SL SL1...................... 129 J9
Sheen Lane Health Centre
   MORT/ESHN SW14...................... 155 P9
Sheen Mount Primary School
   RCHPK/HAM TW10...................... 177 N1
Sheen Sports Centre
   MORT/ESHN SW14...................... 156 B10
Sheepcot Medical Centre
   GSTN WD25...................... 55 K10
Sheering C of E Primary School
   RBSF CM22...................... 30 E2
Shell Centre
   STHWK SE1...................... 11 P10
Shelley County Primary School
   CHONG CM5...................... 67 M2
Shelley School
   CLAP SW4...................... 158 D9
Shelley School
   LBTH SE11...................... 18 B6
Shene School
   MORT/ESHN SW14...................... 156 A10
Shenfield Cricket Club
   BRWN CM15...................... 87 L10
Shenfield High School
   BRWN CM15...................... 87 M9
Shenfield Sports Centre
   BRWN CM15...................... 87 M9
Shenley JMI School
   RAD WD7...................... 57 L10
Shen Nong Chinese
   Medical Centre
   STAL AL1...................... 38 C6
Shenstone School
   DART DA1...................... 186 E1
Shenval Industrial Estate
   HLW CM20...................... 29 K7
Shepherds Bush Cricket Club
   ACT W3...................... 136 B9
Shepherds Bush Market
   MBLAR W1H...................... 10 B5
Shepherds Community
   School Y W A M
   BROCKY SE4...................... 160 F9
Shepperton Business Park
   SHPTN TW17...................... 196 D5
Shepperton Health Centre
   SHPTN TW17...................... 196 C5
Sheraton Business Centre
   GFD/PVL UB6...................... 135 H4
Shere C of E Primary School
   SHGR GU5...................... 270 B5
Sheredes School
   HOD EN11...................... 44 D1
Shere Surgery & Dispensary
   SHGR GU5...................... 270 C5
Sheringdale Primary School
   WAND/EARL SW18...................... 179 J4
Sheringham Junior School
   MNPK E12...................... 122 H3
Sherington School
   CHARL SE7...................... 161 N5
Sherlock Holmes Museum
   CAMTN NW1...................... 10 B2
Sherwood First School
   MTCM CR4...................... 202 D4
Sherwood Park School
   WLGTN SM6...................... 202 W2
Shimmi Shake Dance School
   STMC/STPC BR5...................... 206 G6
Shirley Clinic
   CROY/NA CR0...................... 204 B8
Shirley High School
   CROY/NA CR0...................... 204 C10
Shirley Medical Centre
   CROY/NA CR0...................... 204 D9
Shirley Wanderers
   Rugby Football Club
   WWKM BR4...................... 225 H1
Shomrei Hadath Synagogue
   KIL/WHAMP NW6...................... 117 K9
Shooters Hill Golf Club
   WOOL/PLUM SE18...................... 162 F7
Shopping Trolley Gallery
   BECK BR3...................... 182 E10
Shoreditch
   Comprehensive School
   IS N1...................... 7 K8
Shoreditch County Court
   STLK EC1Y...................... 13 H1
Shoreham County
   Primary School
   RSEV TN14...................... 228 G7
Shorne C of E Primary School
   GVE DA12...................... 191 P8
Shortlands Golf Club
   HAYES BR2...................... 205 K1
Shortwood County
   Infant School
   STA TW18...................... 173 L6
Shotfield Health Clinic
   WLGTN SM6...................... 222 C3
Shree Ghanapathy Temple
   WIM/MER SW19...................... 179 M9
Shree K S Swaminarayan Temple
   WOOL/PLUM SE18...................... 162 F4

Shree Swaminarayan Temple
   STRHM/NOR SW16...................... 202 F1
Shrewsbury Road Health Centre
   FSTGT E7...................... 142 A2
Sidcup Health Centre
   SCUP DA14...................... 185 K6
Sidcup Hill Primary School
   SCUP DA14...................... 185 L8
Sidcup Sports Club
   SCUP DA14...................... 185 J7
Sidney Russell School
   DAGW RM9...................... 123 P9
Sierra Leone High Comm
   OXSTW W1C...................... 10 C1
Sikh Temple
   BELV DA17...................... 164 D2
Sikh Temple
   DART DA1...................... 187 L3
Sikh Temple
   GVE DA12...................... 190 E4
Sikh Temple
   HYS/HAR UB3...................... 132 F10
Sikh Temple
   SL SL1...................... 129 J3
Sikh Temple
   SLN SL2...................... 129 N9
Silicon Business Centre
   GFD/PVL UB6...................... 135 H4
Silverdale Industrial Estate
   HYS/HAR UB3...................... 153 H1
Silver Fox Gallery
   NTGHL W11...................... 8 C6
Silverglade Business Park
   CHSGTN KT9...................... 219 H8
Silver Street Medical Centre
   UED N18...................... 99 M5
Silver Wing Industrial Estate
   CROY/NA CR0...................... 222 C2
Simmons Gallery
   BMSBY WC1N...................... 11 N3
Simon Balle School
   HERT/BAY SG13...................... 25 M6
Simon Marks Primary School
   STNW/STAM N16...................... 119 N6
Simpson Health Centre
   BEAC HP9...................... 88 B8
Sinai Primary School
   KTN/HRWW/W HA3...................... 115 M4
Sinai Synagogue
   GLDGN NW11...................... 117 H5
Singapore High Comm
   KTBR SW1X...................... 16 B2
Singapore High Comm
   STJS SW1Y...................... 11 J9
Singapore High Comm
   WEST SW1P...................... 17 H5
Singh Sabha Temple
   BARK IG11...................... 142 E2
Singlegate First School
   WIM/MER SW19...................... 179 N10
Singlewell CP School
   GVE DA12...................... 190 C9
Sion College
   EMB EC4Y...................... 12 B7
Sion Manning RC
   Secondary School
   NKENS W10...................... 136 V7
Sir Francis Drake School
   DEPT SE8...................... 160 D4
Sir Frederic Osborn School
   WGCE AL7...................... 23 L4
Sir George Monoux
   Sixth Form College
   WALTH E17...................... 100 G10
Sir James Barrie School
   VX/NE SW8...................... 158 D7
Sir John Cass College of Art
   WCHPL E1...................... 13 N5
Sir John Lillie Primary School
   FUL/PGN SW6...................... 14 B10
Sir John Newsom School
   WGCE AL7...................... 23 H8
Sir John Soanes Museum
   LINN WC2A...................... 11 N5
Sir Thomas Abney Junior School
   STNW/STAM N16...................... 119 L5
Sir Thomas Lipton
   Memorial Hospital
   STHGT/OAK N14...................... 98 C1
Sir William Burrough
   Primary School
   POP/IOD E14...................... 140 D8
Sir William Perkins School
   CHERT KT16...................... 195 J8
Six Bridges Trading Estate
   STHWK SE1...................... 19 P8
Ski Centre
   HHS/BOV HP3...................... 35 P8
Skidmore Clinic
   RKW/CH/CXG WD3...................... 91 P2
Skillion Business Park
   BARK IG11...................... 143 J5
Skinners Co Lower Girls School
   CLPT E5...................... 120 A6
Skinners Co School for Girls
   STNW/STAM N16...................... 119 N5
Ski Slope
   STMC/STPC BR5...................... 207 N1
Sky Business Park
   EGH TW20...................... 194 F2
Skyswood JMI School
   STALE/WH AL4...................... 39 H3
Slade Green Football Club
   ERITH DA8...................... 165 J7
Slade Green Infant School
   ERITH DA8...................... 165 H6
Slaughter House Art Gallery
   FARR EC1M...................... 12 C3
Sleaford Industrial Estate
   VX/NE SW8...................... 158 D6
Sloane Hospital
   BECK BR3...................... 205 J1
Slough Borough Council
   SL SL1...................... 129 J10
Slough Borough Council
   SL SL1...................... 149 M1
Slough Borough Council
   SLN SL2...................... 129 N9
Slough Community
   Mental Health Centre
   DTCH/LGLY SL3...................... 150 D3
Slough & Eton C of E School
   SL SL1...................... 149 J2
Slough Grammar School
   DTCH/LGLY SL3...................... 149 N2
Slough Museum
   SL SL1...................... 129 J10
Slough Rugby Club
   DTCH/LGLY SL3...................... 149 N4
Slough Sports Club
   SL SL1...................... 149 K2
Slough Town Football Club
   SLN SL2...................... 129 M7

Slough Trading Estate
   SL SL1...................... 128 F7
Smallberry Green School
   ISLW TW7...................... 154 F8
Smallwood Primary School
   TOOT SW17...................... 179 N7
S M A Medical Centre
   LEY E10...................... 120 G5
Smitham Primary School
   COUL/CHIP CR5...................... 240 D2
The Smith Gallery
   TEDD TW11...................... 176 F8
Smith Village Gallery
   STNW/STAM N16...................... 119 L7
Smug Oak Green
   Business Centre
   LCOL/BKTW AL2...................... 56 A5
Snaresbrook College
   SWFD E18...................... 101 M10
Snaresbrook Crown Court
   WAN E11...................... 121 L3
Snaresbrook Primary School
   SWFD E18...................... 121 M2
Snowhill Business Centre
   CRAWE RH10...................... 285 P1
Snowsfields Primary School
   STHWK SE1...................... 19 J1
Sobell Leisure Centre
   HOLWY N7...................... 118 G8
Sobel Medical Centre
   HOLWY N7...................... 119 H9
The Soho Practice
   SOHO/SHAV W1D...................... 11 J7
Soho Theatre
   SOHO/SHAV W1D...................... 11 J7
Solefield School House
   SEV TN13...................... 265 J3
Solefields School
   SEV TN13...................... 265 K3
Somerford Grove Health Centre
   STNW/STAM N16...................... 119 N9
Somerford Grove Practice
   STNW/STAM N16...................... 119 N9
Somerset House
   COVGDN WC2E...................... 11 N7
Somers Heath School
   SOCK/AV RM15...................... 146 F9
Somers Town Community
   Sports Centre
   CAMTN NW1...................... 5 H8
Sonic Surgery
   IS N1...................... 7 H5
Sophie Hanna Flower School
   VX/NE SW8...................... 158 E6
Sopwell House Hotel
   & Country Club
   STAL AL1...................... 38 E10
Sorsby Health Centre
   CLPT E5...................... 120 C9
Southbank Business Centre
   VX/NE SW8...................... 17 K10
Southbank International School
   NTGHL W11...................... 8 E8
South Bank University
   STHWK SE1...................... 18 F4
South Bank University
   STHWK SE1...................... 18 D3
Southbank University
   STHWK SE1...................... 18 E3
Southbank University
   STHWK SE1...................... 18 C2
Southbank University
   VX/NE SW8...................... 158 E7
South Bookham School
   GT/LBKH KT23...................... 254 B3
Southborough Primary School
   HAYES BR2...................... 206 D5
Southborough School
   SURB KT6...................... 199 K10
South Buckinghamshire
   NHS Trust
   AMS HP6...................... 69 H4
South Buckinghamshire
   NHS Trust
   AMSS HP7...................... 68 F7
South Bucks District Council
   SL SL1...................... 149 K1
Southbury Primary
   & Infant School
   PEND EN3...................... 80 B8
Southbury Primary School
   PEND EN3...................... 80 A8
South Camden
   Community School
   CAMTN NW1...................... 5 H7
South Croydon Medical Centre
   SAND/SEL CR2...................... 223 K4
South Croydon Medical Practice
   SAND/SEL CR2...................... 223 K3
South Croydon Sports Club
   SAND/SEL CR2...................... 223 M2
South Dene Surgery
   SWFD E18...................... 101 M10
Southdown Industrial Estate
   HARP AL5...................... 20 B3
South Eastern University
   HOLWY N7...................... 118 G8
Southern Clinic
   REIG RH2...................... 275 M1
Southern Road Infant School
   PLSTW E13...................... 141 N4
Southern Road Primary School
   PLSTW E13...................... 141 N4
South Essex Health Authority
   RBRW/HUT CM13...................... 107 H6
Southfield First & Middle School
   CHSWK W4...................... 156 B1
Southfield Medical Centre
   CHSWK W4...................... 156 A1
The Southfields Clinic
   WAND/EARL SW18...................... 179 K2
Southfields Community College
   WAND/EARL SW18...................... 179 K4
Southfields Group Practice
   WAND/EARL SW18...................... 179 K5
Southfields School
   GVE DA12...................... 190 F8
Southgate College
   STHGT/OAK N14...................... 98 D3
Southgate Compton Cricket Club
   EBAR EN4...................... 78 A3
Southgate First School
   CRAWE RH10...................... 283 N10
Southgate Leisure Centre
   STHGT/OAK N14...................... 98 E1
Southgate Middle School
   CRAWE RH10...................... 283 N9
Southgate Road Medical Centre
   IS N1...................... 7 H3
Southgate School
   CRAWW RH10...................... 283 M9
Southgate School
   EBAR EN4...................... 78 C9

Southgate Surgery
   STHGT/OAK N14...................... 78 C10
South Grove Primary School
   WALTH E17...................... 120 D4
South Hampstead Cricket Club
   CRICK NW2...................... 136 F2
South Hampstead High School
   HAMP NW3...................... 3 L2
South Hampstead Synagogue
   HAMP NW3...................... 4 A2
South Harringay Junior School
   FSBYPK N4...................... 119 H3
South Hill JMI School
   HHW HP1...................... 35 M7
South Lambeth Road Practice
   VX/NE SW8...................... 158 F7
Southlands College
   PUT/ROE SW15...................... 156 C10
Southlands Surgery
   ORP BR6...................... 207 H10
South Lewisham Health Centre
   CAT SE6...................... 183 H7
South Lodge Queens School
   BUSH WD23...................... 73 P7
South London Art Gallery
   CMBW SE5...................... 159 M7
South London Liberal Synagogue
   STRHM/NOR SW16...................... 180 E6
The South London Natural
   Health Centre
   CLAP SW4...................... 158 D10
South London Tamil School
   CROY/NA CR0...................... 203 K7
South London Temple
   PECK SE15...................... 159 P8
South London Theatre Centre
   WNWD SE27...................... 181 J6
South Meadow Surgery
   WDSR SL4...................... 149 H5
Southmead Primary School
   WIM/MER SW19...................... 179 H4
Southmead Surgery
   SLN SL2...................... 128 G1
South Norwood Hill
   Medical Centre
   SNWD SE25...................... 203 M2
South Norwood Medical Centre
   SNWD SE25...................... 203 M4
South Norwood Primary School
   SNWD SE25...................... 203 P4
South Nutfield Cricket Club
   REDH RH1...................... 276 G2
South Park Business Centre
   IL IG1...................... 123 H7
South Park Clinic
   IL IG1...................... 123 H9
South Park Junior
   & Infant School
   GDMY/SEVK IG3...................... 123 H8
South Quay Plaza
   POP/IOD E14...................... 160 G1
South Rise Junior School
   WOOL/PLUM SE18...................... 162 G4
Southside Industrial Estate
   VX/NE SW8...................... 158 D6
South Thames College
   PUT/ROE SW15...................... 178 G1
South Thames College /
   Wandsworth Adult College
   PUT/ROE SW15...................... 178 C2
South Tottenham
   District Synagogue
   SEVS/STOTM N15...................... 119 N3
Southview Surgery
   WOKS/MYFD GU22...................... 232 B4
Southville Junior School
   EBED/NFELT TW14...................... 174 G4
Southwark Cathedral
   STHWK SE1...................... 12 G9
Southwark College
   BERM/RHTH SE16...................... 160 A2
Southwark College
   CMBW SE5...................... 159 M6
Southwark College
   STHWK SE1...................... 18 C1
Southwark College
   STHWK SE1...................... 19 K3
Southwark Coroners Court
   STHWK SE1...................... 18 C1
Southwark Council
   PECK SE15...................... 159 N6
Southwark Council
   STHWK SE1...................... 18 B4
Southwark Council
   STHWK SE1...................... 19 H2
Southwark Council
   STHWK SE1...................... 19 P9
Southwark Council
   for Community Relations
   PECK SE15...................... 159 P8
Southwark Crown Court
   STHWK SE1...................... 13 J9
Southwark Park Primary School
   BERM/RHTH SE16...................... 160 A2
Southwark Sports Ground
   DUL SE21...................... 181 N4
South Western
   Magistrates Court
   BTSEA SW11...................... 158 A9
South West Essex
   Reform Synagogue
   GNTH/NBYPK IG2...................... 123 H3
Southwold Primary School
   CLPT E5...................... 120 B7
South Woodford Health Centre
   SWFD E18...................... 101 M9
Southwood Hospital
   HGT N6...................... 118 B5
Sovereign Business Centre
   PEND EN3...................... 80 E7
Spanish Embassy
   KTBR SW1X...................... 16 C3
Spanish & Portuguese Synagogue
   MV/WKIL W9...................... 3 H10
Spanish & Portuguese Synagogue
   NTGHL W11...................... 8 A10
The Spare Tyre Theatre Co
   KTTN NW5...................... 4 D1
Sparrow Farm County
   Junior School
   EW KT17...................... 220 E2
Sparrow Farm Infant School
   EBED/NFELT TW14...................... 175 K3
Sparrow Farm Junior School
   EBED/NFELT TW14...................... 175 K3
Speakers Corner
   BAY/PAD W2...................... 10 B7
Spectrum Leisure Centre
   GU GU1...................... 250 C9
Speedway Industrial Estate
   HYS/HAR UB3...................... 152 L1
Speke's Monument
   BAY/PAD W2...................... 9 K9

Spelthorne Borough Council
  STA TW18 .... 173 K9
Spelthorne Borough Council
  STA TW18 .... 173 K8
Spelthorne Clinic
  ASHF TW15 .... 174 F9
Spelthorne College
  ASHF TW15 .... 174 A7
Spelthorne Council for Voluntary
  Services
  STA TW18 .... 173 H7
Spelthorne County School
  ASHF TW15 .... 174 E9
Spelthorne Leisure Centre
  STA TW18 .... 173 K8
Spelthorne Museum
  STA TW18 .... 173 H8
Spelthorne Sports Club
  ASHF TW15 .... 174 E10
Spencer House
  WHALL SW1A 10 G10
Spencer Primary Jm School
  STALW/RED AL3 .... 38 D3
Sphere Industrial Estate
  STAL AL1 .... 38 F7
The Sphinx Theatre Co
  STHWK SE1 .... 18 C1
The Spinney Junior School
  HLW CM20 .... 29 K10
The Spires Shopping Centre
  BAR EN5 .... 77 H7
Spiritualist Temple
  CAMTN NW1 .... 5 H3
Spitalfields Health Centre
  WCHPL E1 .... 13 M4
Spitalfields Market
  LEY E10 .... 120 F8
Spitalfields Market
  WCHPL E1 .... 13 L3
Sports Centre
  BORE WD6 .... 75 P5
Sports Centre
  DAGW RM9 .... 143 P3
Sports Centre
  ERITH DA8 .... 164 F5
Sports Centre
  HHS/BOV HP3 .... 36 A7
Sports Centre
  LCOL/BKTW AL2 .... 56 B7
Sports Centre
  TOTM N17 .... 99 N9
Sports Club
  ESH/CLAY KT10 .... 217 N3
Sports Club
  LHD/OX KT22 .... 218 B10
Sports Club
  LHD/OX KT22 .... 236 D7
Sports Ground
  BAR EN5 .... 76 B10
Sports Ground
  THHTH CR7 .... 203 J2
Sports Ground
  TOOT SW17 .... 179 P6
Sports Ground
  WDSR SL4 .... 148 G8
Sports Ground Pavilion
  HGDN/ICK UB10 .... 132 E4
Springfield Hospital
  TOOT SW17 .... 179 P6
Springfield Primary School
  SUN TW16 .... 196 C1
Springfield Primary School
  VX/NE SW8 .... 158 E6
Springfield Surgery
  CFSP/GDCR SL9 .... 110 B3
Spring Grove Primary School
  ISLW TW7 .... 154 C8
Springmead JMI School
  WGCE AL7 .... 23 M4
Spring Park School
  CROY/NA CR0 .... 204 F10
Springwell Junior School
  HEST TW5 .... 153 M6
Sprint Industrial Estate
  BF/WBF KT14 .... 215 N7
Spurgeons College
  SNWD SE25 .... 203 M2
Squires Lane Medical Practice
  FNCH N3 .... 97 M9
Squirrels Heath Junior School
  GPK RM2 .... 125 J3
Squirrels Heath Junior School
  ROM RM1 .... 125 H3
Squirrels Trading Estate
  HYS/HAR UB3 .... 152 C2
Sri Lanka High Commission
  BAY/PAD W2 .... 9 M7
Sri Saddhatissa International
  Buddhist Temple
  CDALE/KGS NW9 .... 115 P3
The Stables Gallery & Art Centre
  CRICK NW2 .... 116 D9
Stadium Business Centre
  WBLY HA9 .... 115 N8
Stadium Retail Park
  WBLY HA9 .... 115 M8
Stafford Cross Business Park
  CROY/NA CR0 .... 222 C2
Stafford Industrial Estate
  EMPK RM11 .... 125 L1
Staffords Gallery
  SOHO/SHAV W1D 11 K7
Stag Lane Medical Centre
  CDALE/KGS NW9 .... 115 P1
Stag Lane School
  EDGE HA8 .... 95 M10
Stags School
  STALW/RED AL3 .... 38 D2
Stag Theatre
  SEV TN13 .... 265 J1
Staines County Court
  STA TW18 .... 173 K8
Staines & District Synagogue
  STA TW18 .... 173 J8
Staines Preparatory School
  STA TW18 .... 173 K8
Staines Rugby Football Club
  FELT TW13 .... 175 H7
Staines Town Football Club
  STA TW18 .... 173 K10
Staines Youth Sports Centre
  STA TW18 .... 173 K7
Stamford Clinic
  HMSMTH W6 .... 156 D3
Stamford Green Primary School
  HOR/WEW KT19 .... 219 N8
Stamford Hill Group Practice
  CLPT E5 .... 119 N5
Stamford Hill Primary School
  SEVS/STOTM N15 .... 119 L4
Stanborough School
  GSTN WD25 .... 73 J1

Stanborough School
  WGCW AL8 .... 22 E7
Stanburn First School
  STAN HA7 .... 95 H8
Standard Industrial Estate
  CAN/RD E16 .... 162 C1
Standard Industrial Estate
  CAN/RD E16 .... 162 A1
Stanford Middle School
  STRHM/NOR SW16 .... 202 E1
Stanhope Junior Mixed School
  GFD/PVL UB6 .... 134 B6
The Stanlake Practice
  SHB W12 .... 136 F10
Stanley Infant School
  TEDD TW11 .... 176 D7
Stanley Junior School
  WHTN TW2 .... 176 D7
Stanley Park High School
  CAR SM5 .... 222 B3
Stanley Park Infant School
  CAR SM5 .... 222 A4
Stanley Technical High School
  SNWD SE25 .... 203 N3
Stanmore College
  STAN HA7 .... 94 G7
Stanmore Synagogue
  STAN HA7 .... 95 J5
Stanton Square Industrial Estate
  CAT SE6 .... 182 E7
Stanway School
  DORK RH4 .... 254 C9
Stapleford Abbotts
  County Primary School
  ABR/ST RM4 .... 84 C9
Staple Inn Buildings
  HHOL WC1V 12 A4
Staples Corner Business Park
  CRICK NW2 .... 116 E6
Staples Road Junior
  & Infant School
  LOU IG10 .... 82 B7
Staple Tye Shopping Centre
  HLWS CM18 .... 46 G4
Star Business Centre
  DAGW RM9 .... 144 E7
Starhurst School
  RDKG RH5 .... 273 H4
Stark Gallery
  LEE/GVPK SE12 .... 161 L10
Star Primary School
  CAN/RD E16 .... 141 K6
The Start Gallery
  FUL/PGN SW6 .... 157 H8
State Registered
  Chiropody Practice
  CRICK NW2 .... 136 D1
Statham Grove Surgery
  STNW/STAM N16 .... 119 L9
Station Approach
  WAN E11 .... 121 J9
Stationary Office
  GINN WC1R 11 P4
Stationers Hall
  STP EC4M 12 C6
Station Road Surgery
  HDN NW4 .... 116 D4
Station Yard
  KWD/TDW/WH KT20 .... 239 J7
Staunton Group Practice
  WDGN N22 .... 98 C9
Staverton Surgery
  WLSDN NW10 .... 136 F2
Stepgates Primary School
  CHERT KT16 .... 195 L7
Stepney Day Hospital
  WCHPL E1 .... 140 B8
Stepney Greencoats
  Primary School
  POP/IOD E14 .... 140 E8
Stepney Green Secondary School
  WCHPL E1 .... 140 C7
Stepping Stone School
  HAMP NW3 .... 3 K1
Sterling Industrial Estate
  DAGE RM10 .... 124 C9
Sterling Way Clinic
  UED N18 .... 99 N6
Stewards Comprehensive School
  HLWS CM18 .... 46 F5
Stewart Fleming School
  SNWD SE25 .... 204 B3
Stewart Headlam Primary School
  WCHPL E1 .... 140 A6
Stifford Clays County
  Junior School
  CDH/CHF RM16 .... 147 N10
Stifford Clays Health Centre
  CDH/CHF RM16 .... 147 N10
Stifford County Primary School
  GRAYS RM17 .... 167 K4
Stillness Junior & Infant School
  BROCKY SE4 .... 182 D2
Stirling Industrial Centre
  BORE WD6 .... 76 A9
Stirling Way Industrial Estates
  CROY/NA CR0 .... 202 F7
Stockwell Group Practice
  BRXN/ST SW9 .... 158 C8
Stockwell Lodge Medical Centre
  CHESW EN7 .... 61 P4
Stockwell Park
  Secondary School
  BRXN/ST SW9 .... 158 G7
Stoke Hill CP School
  GU GU1 .... 249 P7
Stoke Newington School
  STNW/STAM N16 .... 119 L8
Stoke Poges City First School
  SLN SL2 .... 129 N3
Stoke Poges County
  Middle School
  SLN SL2 .... 129 L2
The Stonebridge Primary School
  WLSDN NW10 .... 135 P3
Stonebridge Shopping Centre
  WLSDN NW10 .... 136 A3
Stonecot Surgery
  MRDN SM4 .... 201 J7
Stonehill Business Centre
  UED N18 .... 100 C7
Stonehill Business Park
  UED N18 .... 100 C6
Stoneleigh Galleries
  EW KT17 .... 220 D2
Stoney Dean School
  AMSS HP7 .... 69 L5
Storey Primary School
  CAN/RD E16 .... 142 D10
Stormont House School
  CLPT E5 .... 120 A9
Stormont School
  POTB/CUF EN6 .... 59 M7

Stoughton County Junior School
  GUW GU2 .... 249 N7
Stowford College
  BELMT SM2 .... 221 M4
Strand on the Green Junior
  & Infant School
  CHSWK W4 .... 155 M5
Strand Theatre
  HOL/ALD WC2B 11 N7
Stratford Gm School
  FSTGT E7 .... 141 M2
Stratford Magistrates Court
  SRTFD E15 .... 141 J2
Strathmore School
  RCHPK/HAM TW10 .... 177 J4
Stream Woods School
  HAT AL10 .... 40 E5
Streatham & Croydon
  Rugby Football Club
  THHTH CR7 .... 203 H5
Streatham Hill & Clapham
  High School
  BRXS/STRHM SW2 .... 180 G4
Streatham Hill & Clapham
  High School
  STRHM/NOR SW16 .... 180 D6
Streatham Ice Rink
  STRHM/NOR SW16 .... 180 F8
Streatham Modern School
  STRHM/NOR SW16 .... 180 F9
Streatham Park Surgery
  STRHM/NOR SW16 .... 180 D8
Streatham Swimming Pool
  STRHM/NOR SW16 .... 180 F8
Streatham Vale Sports Club
  STRHM/NOR SW16 .... 180 D10
Streatham Wells Primary School
  BRXS/STRHM SW2 .... 180 G5
Streete Court School
  GDST RH9 .... 260 D6
Strodes College
  EGH TW20 .... 172 C8
Stroud Green Primary School
  FSBYPK N4 .... 119 H6
Stroud Wood Business Centre
  LCOL/BKTW AL2 .... 56 D3
Students Gallery
  RYNPK SW20 .... 201 J1
Studholme Medical Centre
  ASHF TW15 .... 174 A7
Studio Sienko Gallery
  STHWK SE1 .... 18 F2
Study Preparatory School
  WIM/MER SW19 .... 178 C8
The Study School
  NWMAL KT3 .... 200 B5
Sturt Priory Hospital
  KWD/TDW/WH KT20 .... 256 D2
Sudbourne Primary School
  BRXS/STRHM SW2 .... 180 C1
Sudbury Court Sports Club
  ALP/SUD HA0 .... 115 H8
Sudbury Infant School
  ALP/SUD HA0 .... 114 G9
Suffolks Junior & Infant School
  EN EN1 .... 80 A6
Sulivan Primary School
  FUL/PGN SW6 .... 157 K8
Summerside JMI School
  NFNCH/WDSP N12 .... 97 N7
Summerswood Primary School
  BORE WD6 .... 75 N8
Summit Business Park
  SUN TW16 .... 175 H10
Sumners Community
  Recreation Centre
  HLWW/ROY CM19 .... 46 D5
Sunbury Business Centre
  SUN TW16 .... 196 F1
Sunbury Health Centre
  SUN TW16 .... 197 H2
Sunbury Leisure Centre
  SUN TW16 .... 196 C1
Sunbury Manor School
  SUN TW16 .... 196 C1
Sunderland Estate
  KGLGY WD4 .... 54 C5
Sundridge Medical Practice
  BMLY BR1 .... 183 M10
Sundridge Primary School
  RSEV TN14 .... 263 P1
Sunningdale Golf Course
  ASC SL5 .... 192 F9
Sunningdale School
  ASC SL5 .... 192 D6
Sunnydown School
  CTHM CR3 .... 241 N7
Sunnyfield School
  HDN NW4 .... 116 F1
Sunnyfields Primary School
  HDN NW4 .... 116 E1
Sunnyhill Primary School
  STRHM/NOR SW16 .... 180 G7
Sunny Meed Surgery
  WOKS/MYFD GU22 .... 232 C4
Sun Strp Thtr
  SOHO/CST W1F 11 J6
Super Bowl
  BXLYHS DA6 .... 164 A10
Supreme Court Taxing Office
  FLST/FETLN EC4A 12 B6
Surbiton Business Centre
  SURB KT6 .... 199 J6
Surbiton High School for Girls
  KUT KT1 .... 199 K4
Surbiton Hospital
  SURB KT6 .... 199 K6
Surbiton Natural Health Centre
  SURB KT6 .... 199 K6
Surex Swimming Pools
  BH/WHM TN16 .... 244 A1
Surrey County Council
  ADL/WDHM KT15 .... 195 M9
Surrey County Council
  BNSTD SM7 .... 239 J1
Surrey County Council
  E/WMO/HCT KT8 .... 197 P4
Surrey County Council
  EW KT17 .... 220 B8
Surrey County Council
  EW KT17 .... 220 D5
Surrey County Council
  HOR/WEW KT19 .... 220 B5
Surrey County Council
  HOR/WEW KT19 .... 220 A7
Surrey County Council
  KUT KT1 .... 199 K3
Surrey County Council
  LHD/OX KT22 .... 236 F8
Surrey County Council
  LHD/OX KT22 .... 236 F6
Surrey County Council
  THDIT KT7 .... 198 F6

Surrey County Council
  WEY KT13 .... 216 A1
Surrey County Council
  WEY KT13 .... 216 C1
Surrey County Council
  WOKN/KNAP GU21 .... 231 L5
Surrey County Council
  WOKN/KNAP GU21 .... 232 C2
Surrey County Council
  WOT/HER KT12 .... 197 J9
Surrey County Cricket Club
  LBTH SE11 .... 17 P9
Surrey Docks Farm
  BERM/RHTH SE16 .... 160 E1
Surrey Docks Health Centre
  BERM/RHTH SE16 .... 160 D1
Surrey Heartlands NHS Trust
  HOR/WEW KT19 .... 219 P5
Surrey Quays Leisure Park
  BERM/RHTH SE16 .... 160 C2
Surrey Quays Shopping Centre
  BERM/RHTH SE16 .... 160 C2
Surrey Square Junior
  & Infant School
  WALW SE17 .... 19 J7
Susan Lawrence Primary School
  POP/IOD E14 .... 140 C8
Sussex House School
  KTBR SW1X 16 A5
Sussex Manor Business Park
  CRAWE RH10 .... 284 B3
The Sussex Place Surgery
  SL SL1 .... 149 M1
Sutton Alternative Health Centre
  SUT SM1 .... 221 M2
Sutton at Hone C of E
  Primary School
  EYN DA4 .... 187 P10
Sutton at Hone
  & Hawley Parish Council
  EYN DA4 .... 188 A9
Sutton Bowling Club
  BELMT SM2 .... 221 K5
Sutton General Hospital
  BELMT SM2 .... 221 L6
Sutton Grammar School for Boys
  SUT SM1 .... 221 M2
Sutton High School for Girls
  SUT SM1 .... 221 L3
Suttons Business Park
  RAIN RM13 .... 144 E5
Suttons JMI School
  HCH RM12 .... 125 L9
Suttons Manor Clinic
  ABR/ST RM4 .... 84 F4
Sutton Station Chiropractic
  Health Centre
  BELMT SM2 .... 221 L3
Sutton Superbowl
  SUT SM1 .... 221 L2
Sutton United Football Club
  SUT SM1 .... 221 K1
Swaffield Primary School
  WAND/EARL SW18 .... 179 M2
Swakeleys School
  HGDN/ICK UB10 .... 132 D4
Swaminarayan School
  WLSDN NW10 .... 136 A1
Swan Business Centre
  CHSWK W4 .... 156 A3
Swan Business Park
  DART DA1 .... 165 L10
Swanlea Secondary School
  WCHPL E1 .... 140 A6
Swanley School
  SWLY BR8 .... 208 E3
Swanley Town Council
  SWLY BR8 .... 208 F3
Swanley White Oak
  County Primary School
  SWLY BR8 .... 208 F2
Swanscombe Business Centre
  SWCM DA10 .... 189 K1
Swansea City A F C
  BAY/PAD W2 .... 9 N4
Swansmere School
  WOT/HER KT12 .... 197 K8
Swan Wharf Business Centre
  UX/CGN UB8 .... 131 L4
Swaziland High Comm
  WESTW SW1E 16 G3
Swedish School
  CRAWE RH10 .... 284 A9
Sweyne CP Junior School
  SWCM DA10 .... 189 L3
Swimming Pool
  AMS HP6 .... 69 J4
Swimming Pool
  HERT/WAS SG14 .... 25 L3
Sybil Elgar School
  EA W5 .... 135 K9
Sybil Elgar School
  NWDGN UB2 .... 153 N2
Sybourn Infant School
  LEY E10 .... 120 D6
Sybourn Infant School
  WALTH E17 .... 120 E5
Sybourn Junior School
  WALTH E17 .... 120 E5
Sydenham High School
  SYD SE26 .... 182 A8
Sydenham High School
  SYD SE26 .... 182 A7
Sydenham Pre-school
  FSTH SE23 .... 182 A5
Sydenham Secondary School
  SYD SE26 .... 182 A6
Sydney Russell School
  DAGW RM9 .... 123 N10
Synagogue
  EHAM E6 .... 142 B5
Synagogue
  HDN NW4 .... 116 G3
Synagogue
  HDTCH EC3A 13 K5
Synagogue
  MV/WKIL W9 .... 2 G10
Synagogue
  NTCHL W11 .... 8 C6
Synagogue
  SURB KT6 .... 199 J5
The Synagogue
  E/WMO/HCT KT8 .... 199 J5
The Synagogue
  RSLP HA4 .... 113 H6
The Synagogue
  SWFD E18 .... 101 M9
The Synagogue
  TPL/STR WC2R 12 A7
Syon House
  BTFD TW8 .... 155 H7

Syracuse University
  London Centre
  NTCHL W11 .... 8 C8
S Y Thtr Sch
  STJWD NW8 .... 9 N2
Sythwood County
  Primary School
  WOKN/KNAP GU21 .... 231 N2
Tabard Rugby Club
  RAD WD7 .... 74 C3
Tabard Theatre
  CHSWK W4 .... 156 B3
Tadema Gallery
  IS N1 .... 6 C7
Tadworth County
  Primary School
  KWD/TDW/WH KT20 .... 238 D3
Tadworth Farm Surgery
  KWD/TDW/WH KT20 .... 238 E6
Tait Road Industrial Estate
  CROY/NA CR0 .... 203 L7
Talisman Gallery
  WKENS W14 .... 14 C4
Tamworth Manor High School
  STRHM/NOR SW16 .... 202 E3
Tandridge Golf Club
  OXTED RH8 .... 261 H7
Tandridge Primary School
  GDST RH9 .... 260 F9
Tanners Wood Junior
  & Infant School
  ABLGY WD5 .... 54 F8
Tanys Dell Junior School
  HLW CM20 .... 29 K8
Tapling Trading Estate
  WDR/YW UB7 .... 131 N9
Taplow Health Centre
  MDHD SL6 .... 128 A8
Tate Gallery
  STHWK SE1 .... 19 K6
Tate Gallery of British Art
  WEST SW1P 17 L6
Tate Gallery of Modern Art
  STHWK SE1 .... 12 D9
Tatsfield Primary School
  BH/WHM TN16 .... 244 A7
Tattenham Health Centre
  EPSOM KT18 .... 238 E4
Tavistock Clinic
  HAMP NW3 .... 3 L2
Tavy Clinic
  ABYW SE2 .... 163 M1
Teardrop Industrial Park
  SWLY BR8 .... 209 K5
Teddington Business Park
  TEDD TW11 .... 176 E8
Teddington Clinic
  TEDD TW11 .... 176 D9
Teddington Memorial Hospital
  TEDD TW11 .... 176 D9
Teddington School
  TEDD TW11 .... 177 J9
Teddington Swimming Pool
  TEDD TW11 .... 176 F8
The Teddington Theatre Club
  E/WMO/HCT KT8 .... 198 C5
The Teddington Theatre Club
  HPTN TW12 .... 176 A10
Teikyo School
  DTCH/LGLY SL3 .... 130 A2
Telegraph Hill School
  BROCKY SE4 .... 160 D8
Telephone Exchange
  WATW WD18 .... 73 J8
Temple
  IL IG1 .... 122 E10
Temple
  TPL/STR WC2R 12 A7
Temple Hill County Infant
  & Primary School
  DART DA1 .... 187 P1
Temple of Bacchus
  CMBW SE5 .... 159 K4
Temple of Mithras
  MANHO EC4N 12 G6
The Temple
  KENS W8 .... 14 D4
Templewood School
  WGCW AL8 .... 22 F5
Templewood Surgery
  IVER SL0 .... 130 F4
Tenby Road Clinic
  EDGE HA8 .... 95 L10
Tennis Lawn Club
  WDSR SL4 .... 148 A3
Tenterden Sports Ground
  KTN/HRWW/W HA3 .... 115 K5
Tewin Road Business Centre
  WGCE AL7 .... 23 H4
Tewin School
  WLYN AL6 .... 23 P1
Tewin Water School
  WLYN AL6 .... 23 L1
Thackeray Gallery
  KENS W8 .... 14 C2
Thames Ditton County
  First School
  THDIT KT7 .... 198 E6
Thames Ditton Junior School
  THDIT KT7 .... 198 E7
Thames Galleries
  EDUL SE22 .... 159 P10
Thames Gateway NHS Trust
  RDART DA2 .... 188 B3
Thames House
  WEST SW1P 17 L1
Thameside County
  Infant School
  GRAYS RM17 .... 167 P5
Thameside Industrial Estate
  CAN/RD E16 .... 142 A10
Thameside Industrial Estate
  CAN/RD E16 .... 162 B1
Thameside Theatre
  GRAYS RM17 .... 167 M4
Thameslink Healthcare
  Services NHS Trust
  RDART DA2 .... 188 B2
Thames Magistrates Court
  BOW E3 .... 140 F5
Thamesmead
  Community College
  ERITHM DA18 .... 163 P1
Thamesmead County
  Secondary School
  SHPTN TW17 .... 196 E6
Thames Police Station
  TPL/STR WC2R 11 P8
The Thames Valley
  Nuffield Hospital
  DTCH/LGLY SL3 .... 129 P3
Thames Valley University
  EA W5 .... 135 J10

Thames Valley University
EA W5 .... 155 J1
Thames Valley University
SL SL1 .... 129 K10
Thames View Business Centre
RAIN RM13 .... 144 F7
Thames View Clinic
BARK IG11 .... 143 J4
Thames View Junior
& Infant School
BARK IG11 .... 143 K4
Thamesview School
GVE DA12 .... 191 J6
Theatre
CHCR WC2N 11 L7
Theatre
COVGDN WC2E 11 M8
Theatre
LSQ/SEVD WC2H 11 L5
Theatre
LSQ/SEVD WC2H 11 K8
Theatre De Complicite
HOLWY N7 .... 118 G10
Theatre for Mankind
FSBYPK N4 .... 118 G6
Theatre Magenta
LHD/OX KT22 .... 236 F6
Theatre Museum
COVGDN WC2E 11 M7
The Theatre Nightclub
WAND/EARL SW18 .... 179 L1
Theatre of the Dispossessed
WIM/MER SW19 .... 178 G4
The Theatre on the Hill
CTHM CR3 .... 241 M8
Theatre Royal
HOL/ALD WC2B 11 N6
Theatre Royal
SRTFD E15 .... 141 J2
Theatre Royal
WDSR SL4 .... 149 J6
Therapia Trading Estate
CROY/NA CR0 .... 202 E7
Therfield County
Secondary School
LHD/OX KT22 .... 236 E5
Theydon Bois CP School
EPP CM16 .... 83 H2
Theydon Gallery
EPP CM16 .... 82 G3
Thomas Becket RC
Primary School
SNWD SE25 .... 203 P6
Thomas Bennett
Community College
CRAWW RH11 .... 283 N10
Thomas Buxton Primary School
WCHPL E1 .... 13 N2
The Thomas Coram Middle School
BERK HP4 .... 34 A7
Thomas Fairchild Primary School
IS N1 .... 6 G7
Thomas Gamuel Primary School
WALTH E17 .... 120 F4
Thomas Harding County
Middle School
CSHM HP5 .... 50 G8
The Thomas Rivers Medical Centre
HLW CM20 .... 29 M4
The Thomas Rivers
Medical Centre
SBW CM21 .... 29 M2
Thomas's Preparatory School
BTSEA SW11 .... 157 N7
Thomas Tallis School
BKHTH/KID SE3 .... 161 N9
Thomas Tallis School
WAB EN9 .... 63 L9
The Thomas Willingale Gm School
LOU IG10 .... 82 F7
Thorkhill Surgery
THDIT KT7 .... 198 G8
Thorn Chase & Grove School
GU GU1 .... 250 F10
Thornhill Primary School
IS N1 .... 6 A4
Thornton Heath Baths
THHTH CR7 .... 203 L4
Thornton Heath Health Centre
THHTH CR7 .... 203 K4
Thornton Road Industrial Estate
CROY/NA CR0 .... 202 G6
Thornton Road Surgery
CROY/NA CR0 .... 202 G6
Thorntree School
CHARL SE7 .... 162 A4
Thorpe C of E Infant School
EGH TW20 .... 194 F3
Thorpe Cricket Club
EGH TW20 .... 194 C4
Thorpe Hall Primary School
WALTH E17 .... 101 H9
Thorpe Lea Primary School
EGH TW20 .... 172 G9
Three Bridge County
Middle School
CRAWE RH10 .... 284 A7
Three Bridges Cricket Club
CRAWE RH10 .... 284 B7
Three Bridges First School
CRAWE RH10 .... 284 B6
Three Bridges Football Club
CRAWE RH10 .... 284 B7
Three Bridges Primary School
NWDGN UB2 .... 153 L3
Three Bridges Primary School
NWDGN UB2 .... 154 A2
Three Lions Gallery
STJWD NW8 .... 3 N8
Three Rivers District Council
OXHEY WD19 .... 93 K4
Three Rivers District Council
RKW/CH/CXG WD3 .... 91 P1
Three Way Surgery
SLN SL2 .... 129 L3
Theatre Mus Lib & Arc
COVGDN WC2E 11 M7
Thumbswood Infant School
WGCE AL7 .... 23 K6
Thurlow Park School
WNWD SE27 .... 181 J5
Thurrock Borough Council
GRAYS RM17 .... 167 P6
Thurrock Borough Council
GRAYS RM17 .... 167 N5
Thurrock Borough Council
SOCK/AV RM15 .... 146 F8
Thurrock Business Centre
WTHK RM20 .... 166 E5
Thurrock College
CDH/CHF RM16 .... 168 C3
Thurrock Council
PUR RM19 .... 165 N3

Thurrock Council
for Voluntary Services
GRAYS RM17 .... 167 N4
Thurrock Council Office
GRAYS RM17 .... 167 N4
Thurston Industrial Estate
LEW SE13 .... 160 G9
Tidemill Primary School
DEPT SE8 .... 160 F6
Tideway Industrial Estate
VX/NE SW8 .... 17 H10
Tiffin Girls School
KUTN/CMB KT2 .... 177 K8
Tiffin School
KUTN/CMB KT2 .... 199 L2
Tilbury Fort
TIL RM18 .... 168 F10
Tilbury Manor Infant School
TIL RM18 .... 168 E6
Tilbury Surgery
TIL RM18 .... 168 D8
Tilehouse County School
DEN/HRF UB9 .... 111 J4
Tile House Surgery
BRWN CM15 .... 107 J2
Tiller Centre
POP/IOD E14 .... 160 F2
Tiller Leisure Centre
POP/IOD E14 .... 160 F2
Tillingbourne County
Secondary School
RGUE GU4 .... 268 E7
Timbercroft Primary School
WOOL/PLUM SE18 .... 163 H6
Timbers Clinic
KTN/HRWW/W HA3 .... 94 C7
Titan Industrial Estate
GRAYS RM17 .... 167 M3
Tiverton Road School
SEVS/STOTM N15 .... 119 L4
Tobacco Dock
WAP E1W 140 A9
Toldos School
STNW/STAM N16 .... 119 M6
Tolgate School
CROY/NA CR0 .... 204 A6
Tollgate Primary School
PLSTW E13 .... 141 P6
Tolworth CP School
SURB KT6 .... 199 L8
Tolworth Recreation Centre
CHSGTN KT9 .... 199 L10
Tolworth Secondary Girls School
SURB KT6 .... 199 L10
Tom Hood School
WAN E11 .... 121 L8
Tomo Industrial Estate
UX/CGN UB8 .... 131 M8
Tonga High Comm
MBLAR W1H 9 P4
Tonybee Hall & Curtain Theatre
WCHPL E1 .... 13 M4
Toot Hill Golf Club
CHONG CM5 .... 66 G7
Tooting Bec Surgery
TOOT SW17 .... 180 B6
Tooting & Mitcham
United Football Club
MTCM CR4 .... 202 B1
Topcukoy F C
HACK E8 .... 7 L3
Torells County Secondary
School for Girls
CDH/CHF RM16 .... 168 C1
Tormead School
GU GU1 .... 250 C10
Torriano Junior & Infant School
KTTN NW5 .... 118 D10
Torridon Junior & Infant School
CAT SE6 .... 183 J5
Torrington Clinic
NFNCH/WDSP N12 .... 97 M6
Torrington Park Health Centre
NFNCH/WDSP N12 .... 97 M5
Total Health Clinic
SHB W12 .... 156 E1
Tottenhall Infants School
PLMGR N13 .... 99 H6
Tottenham Hale Retail Park
SEVS/STOTM N15 .... 119 P2
Tottenham Hotspur
Football Club
TOTM N17 .... 99 N8
Totteridge Cricket Club
TRDG/WHET N20 .... 97 K3
The Totteridge Gallery
TRDG/WHET N20 .... 97 M3
Touch Wood Gallery
EN EN1 .... 79 M9
Tourist Board
BGVA SW1W 16 E3
Tower Bridge Museum
STHWK SE1 .... 13 K10
Tower Hamlets College
BETH E2 .... 7 N10
Tower Hamlets College
POP/IOD E14 .... 140 G9
Tower Hamlets College
WCHPL E1 .... 140 B7
Tower House Preparatory
School for Boys
MORT/ESHN SW14 .... 155 P10
Tower Industrial Estate
SNWD SE25 .... 203 P4
Tower of London
TWRH EC3N 13 L8
Towers Business Park
WBLY HA9 .... 115 N9
Towers Infant School
EMPK RM11 .... 125 K5
Towers Junior School
EMPK RM11 .... 125 K5
Tower Theatre
IS N1 .... 6 D2
The Tower Theatre Shop
IS N1 .... 6 D2
Town Council
HAT AL10 .... 40 D3
Town Farm County
Primary School
STWL/WRAY TW19 .... 173 N3
Townley Grammar School
for Girls
BXLYHS DA6 .... 186 A2
Townmead Business Centre
FUL/PGN SW6 .... 157 M9
Town Medical Centre
SEV TN13 .... 265 J1
Townsend C of E School
STALW/RED AL3 .... 38 B1
Townsend Industrial Estate
WLSDN NW10 .... 135 P3

Townsend Primary School
STHWK SE1 .... 19 J5
Toy Museum
FITZ W1T 11 H3
Trabzon Spor F C
STNW/STAM N16 .... 119 L9
Trading Estate
BERM/RHTH SE16 .... 160 A3
Trading Estate
HYS/HAR UB3 .... 153 J1
Trading Estate
WTHK RM20 .... 166 F4
Trafalgar Business Centre
BARK IG11 .... 143 J6
Trafalgar Galleries
WHALL SW1A 10 G9
Trafalgar Junior School
WHTN TW2 .... 176 C5
Trafalgar Trading Estate
PEND EN3 .... 80 E8
Training School
IS N1 .... 6 E5
Tramshed Theatre
WOOL/PLUM SE18 .... 162 S13
Trans Atlantic College
BETH E2 .... 7 L7
Transport House
WEST SW1P 17 L4
Treasury
WHALL SW1A 17 K2
The Tredegar Practice
BOW E3 .... 140 E4
Treetops School
GRAYS RM17 .... 167 N3
Trent C of E Primary School
EBAR EN4 .... 78 A8
Trestle Theatre Co
STALE/WH AL4 .... 39 H7
Trevelyan Middle School
WDSR SL4 .... 148 F8
Triangle Surgery
WAND/EARL SW18 .... 179 K1
Tricor Business Park
CHES/WCR EN8 .... 62 D10
Tricor Trading Estate
CHES/WCR EN8 .... 62 D10
Tricycle Theatre
KIL/WHAMP NW6 .... 2 D3
Trident Business Centre
TOOT SW17 .... 180 A8
Trident Industrial Estate
DTCH/LGLY SL3 .... 151 H9
Trident Industrial Estate
HOD EN11 .... 45 H3
Trinidad & Tobago High Comm
KTBR SW1X 16 C3
Trinity Business Centre
BERM/RHTH SE16 .... 160 E1
Trinity Catholic Lower
High School
WFD IG8 .... 101 M5
Trinity Catholic Upper
High School
WFD IG8 .... 101 M5
Trinity College Centre
CMBW SE5 .... 159 M6
Trinity College of Music
MHST W1U 10 D4
Trinity Hospital
GNWCH SE10 .... 161 J4
Trinity House
TWRH EC3N 13 K7
Trinity St Marys C of E
Primary School
BAL SW12 .... 180 B4
Trinity St Stephen First School
WDSR SL4 .... 149 H7
Trinity School
DAGE RM10 .... 124 B8
The Trinity Surgery
WAND/EARL SW18 .... 179 N3
Trinity Trading Estate
HYS/HAR UB3 .... 153 H2
Triumph Trading Estate
TOTM N17 .... 99 P7
Trocadero Centre
MYFR/PICC W1J 11 J8
Trojan Business Centre
WLSDN NW10 .... 136 C1
Trowbridge Gallery
FUL/PGN SW6 .... 157 M6
Troy Industrial Estate
HRW HA1 .... 114 E3
True Buddha School
IS N1 .... 5 N6
Trumps Green County
First School
VW GU25 .... 194 A6
The T Shirt Gallery
HAMP NW3 .... 3 N1
Tudor Court CP School
CDH/CHF RM16 .... 167 L1
Tudor Junior Mixed School
STHL UB1 .... 133 M9
Tudor Lodge Health Centre
WIM/MER SW19 .... 178 G3
Tudor Primary School
FNCH N3 .... 97 M9
Tudor School
HHS/BOV HP3 .... 35 P8
Tufnell Park Primary School
HOLWY N7 .... 118 E9
Tuke School
PECK SE15 .... 160 A7
Tulloch Clinic
SHB W12 .... 136 G10
Tunnel Avenue Trading Estate
GNWCH SE10 .... 161 J1
Tunnel Industrial Estate
WTHK RM20 .... 166 E3
Turkish Embassy
KTBR SW1X 16 D2
Turners Hill C of E School
CRAWE RH10 .... 285 P10
Turney School
DUL SE21 .... 181 K3
Turnford School
CHES/WCR EN8 .... 62 D4
Turnham Primary School
BROCKY SE4 .... 160 D10
Tweedale Infant School
CAR SM5 .... 201 N7
Tweedale Junior School
CAR SM5 .... 201 N7
Twickenham Park Health Centre
TWK TW1 .... 177 H2
Twickenham Rugby
Football Ground
WHTN TW2 .... 176 D2
Twickenham Trading Estate
TWK TW1 .... 176 E2
Twin Bridges Business Park
SAND/SEL CR2 .... 223 L3

Two Rivers Retail Park
STA TW18 .... 173 H7
Two Waters JMI School
HHS/BOV HP3 .... 53 N1
Twyford C of E High School
ACT W3 .... 135 N10
Tyburn Infant School
STJWD NW8 .... 9 M1
The Type Museum
Operation Hannibal
BRXN/ST SW9 .... 158 G7
U C I Cinema
BAY/PAD W2 .... 9 H6
U C I Cinema
BERM/RHTH SE16 .... 160 C2
U C I Cinema
ED N9 .... 100 C1
U C I Cinema
WTHK RM20 .... 166 E3
UCL
FITZ W1T 11 H3
UCL Hospitals NHS Trust
FITZ W1T 11 H2
Uganda High Commission
STJS SW1Y 11 K9
Ullswater Business Park
COUL/CHIP CR5 .... 240 C1
The Ullswater Business Park
COUL/CHIP CR5 .... 240 C1
Ullswater Trading Estate
COUL/CHIP CR5 .... 240 C1
Underhill Junior & Infant School
BAR EN5 .... 77 H9
Unicorn School
RCH/KEW TW9 .... 155 L7
University of Notre Dame
LSQ/SEVD WC2H 11 K8
Union of Liberal & Progressive
Synagogues
FITZ W1T 11 H2
United Elizabeth Garrett Anderson
Hospital for Women
CAMTN NW1 .... 5 K9
United Services Sports Ground
CHSWK W4 .... 156 B7
United States Embassy
CAVSQ/HST W1G 10 E5
United Synagogue
CHING E4 .... 100 G7
United Synagogue
CLPT E5 .... 119 P5
Unity College
KTTN NW5 .... 118 C9
Unity Trading Estate
WFD IG8 .... 122 A1
University College
STPAN WC1H 5 K10
University College
STPAN WC1H 11 J1
University College Hospital
HAMP NW3 .... 3 M2
University College London
GWRST WC1E 11 J2
University College London
STPAN WC1H 11 K2
University College School
HAMP NW3 .... 117 M9
University College School
HAMP NW3 .... 117 M10
University of East London
BCTR RM8 .... 123 L9
University of East London
PLSTW E13 .... 141 N5
University of Greenwich
DART DA1 .... 187 N5
University of Greenwich
DART DA1 .... 187 K5
University of Greenwich
ELTH/MOT SE9 .... 184 F3
University of Greenwich
ELTH/MOT SE9 .... 184 F2
University of Greenwich
GNWCH SE10 .... 161 J4
University of Greenwich
WOOL/PLUM SE18 .... 162 D3
University of Greenwich
WOOL/PLUM SE18 .... 162 D2
University of Hertfordshire
GSTN WD25 .... 74 A2
University of Hertfordshire
HAT AL10 .... 40 A1
University of Hertfordshire
HAT AL10 .... 40 C5
University of Hertfordshire
HERT/BAY SG13 .... 25 N7
University of Hertfordshire
STAL AL1 .... 38 D7
University of London
BAY/PAD W2 .... 9 L6
University of London
BMSBY WC1N 11 M2
University of London
ENC/FH EN2 .... 79 P2
University of London
GWRST WC1E 11 K3
University of London
NWCR SE14 .... 160 D7
University of London
STPAN WC1H 11 K1
University of London
TPL/STR WC2R 11 N7
University of Middlesex
EBAR EN4 .... 78 D6
University of Middlesex
PEND EN3 .... 80 A9
University of North London
HOLWY N7 .... 118 G10
University of Surrey
GUW GU2 .... 249 N10
University of Westminster
CAMTN NW1 .... 10 G1
University of Westminster
CHSWK W4 .... 155 P7
University of Westminster
GTPST W1W 10 F3
University of Westminster
GTPST W1W 10 G3
University of Westminster
HGT N6 .... 118 C6
University of Westminster
HRW HA1 .... 114 F5
University Vandals
Rugby Football Club
WOT/HER KT12 .... 196 E8
Uphall Primary School
IL IG1 .... 122 E10
Upland Junior School
BXLYHN DA7 .... 164 A9
Uplands Business Park
WALTH E17 .... 100 C10
Uplands Business Park
WALTH E17 .... 120 C1

Upminster Infant School
UPMR RM14 .... 126 A8
Upminster Primary School
UPMR RM14 .... 126 B8
Upper Clapton
Rugby Football Club
EPP CM16 .... 47 L10
Upper Selsdon Road Surgery
SAND/SEL CR2 .... 224 A6
Upper Tooting Independent
High School
TOOT SW17 .... 179 P5
Upshire CP School
WAB EN9 .... 63 N8
Upton Cross Primary School
PLSTW E13 .... 141 N3
Upton Day Hospital
BXLYHS DA6 .... 163 P10
Upton House School
WDSR SL4 .... 149 H8
Upton Lane Medical Centre
FSTGT E7 .... 141 N1
Upton Primary School
BXLY DA5 .... 185 P1
Upton Road School
BXLYHS DA6 .... 185 P1
Ursuline High School
IL IG1 .... 122 E7
Ursuline High School
RYNPK SW20 .... 178 G10
US Embassy
MYFR/PKLN W1K 10 C7
US Navy Comm In Chief
MYFR/PKLN W1K 10 D7
Uxbridge College
HGDN/ICK UB10 .... 131 P1
Uxbridge College
HYS/HAR UB3 .... 133 H9
Uxbridge County Court
HYS/HAR UB3 .... 132 F7
Uxbridge County Court
UX/CGN UB8 .... 131 M2
Uxbridge Cricket Club
HGDN/ICK UB10 .... 131 P1
Uxbridge Football Club
WDR/YW UB7 .... 132 B9
Uxbridge Health Centre
UX/CGN UB8 .... 131 N1
Uxbridge Swimming Pool
HGDN/ICK UB10 .... 131 P1
Uxendon Manor School
KTN/HRWW/W HA3 .... 115 K3
Uzbekistan Embassy
NTGHL W11 .... 8 C10
Vale Industrial Estate
WATW WD18 .... 92 D2
The Vale Medical Centre
FSTH SE23 .... 182 D5
Valence House Museum
& Library
BCTR RM8 .... 123 N7
Valence School
BH/WHM TN16 .... 263 J2
Valentine High School
IL IG1 .... 122 D4
Valentines High Lower School
GNTH/NBYPK IG2 .... 122 E3
Vale Primary School
EPSOM KT18 .... 238 A5
The Vale School
SKENS SW7 .... 15 J4
Vallance Road School
WCHPL E1 .... 13 P3
Valley End C of E Infant School
CHOB/PIR GU24 .... 212 F3
Valley End Cricket Club
CHOB/PIR GU24 .... 212 F4
Valley Primary School
HAYES BR2 .... 205 L2
Valmar Trading Estate
CMBW SE5 .... 159 K7
The Vanbrugh Group Practice
GNWCH SE10 .... 161 L4
Vanbrugh Theatre
GWRST WC1E 11 J2
Van & Car Surgery
PEND EN3 .... 80 C8
Vanguard Trading Estate
SRTFD E15 .... 141 H3
Vaughan Middle School
RYLN/HDSTN HA2 .... 114 B4
Vauxhall Primary School
LBTH SE11 .... 17 N7
Vernon House School
WLSDN NW10 .... 115 P10
Verulam Golf Club
STAL AL1 .... 38 E8
Verulam Industrial Estate
STAL AL1 .... 38 E8
Verulamium Museum
STALW/RED AL3 .... 38 A6
Verulam School
STAL AL1 .... 38 F5
Vestry House Museum
WALTH E17 .... 120 G2
Vestry Industrial Estate
RSEV TN14 .... 247 J5
Vestry Medical Practice
CMBW SE5 .... 159 M8
Vicarage Fields Health Clinic
BARK IG11 .... 142 F7
The Vicarage Field
Shopping Centre
BARK IG11 .... 142 F2
Vicarage Primary School
EHAM E6 .... 142 C5
Vicarage School
RCHPK/HAM TW10 .... 177 J2
Vicars Green Primary School
GFD/PVL UB6 .... 135 H4
Victoria & Albert Museum
SKENS SW7 .... 15 M4
Victoria Barracks
WDSR SL4 .... 149 J7
Victoria Chiropractic Clinic
CHEL SW3 .... 16 A2
Victoria Clinic
WOKN/KNAP GU21 .... 232 C2
The Victoria Clinic
for Sexual Health
WEST SW1P 17 J5
Victoria C of E Primary School
BERK HP4 .... 33 P5
Victoria Industrial Estate
ACT W3 .... 136 A7
Victoria Junior School
FELT TW13 .... 175 J4
Victoria Medical Centre
PIM SW1V 16 G6
Victoria Palace
WESTW SW1E 16 F4
Victoria Park Industrial Centre
HOM E9 .... 140 E2

Victoria Place Shopping Centre
 PIM SW1V............................ 16 F5
Victoria Retail Park
 RSLP HA4............................ 113 L10
Victoria Wharf
 POP/IOD E14........................ 140 D9
Victoria Wharf Industrial Estate
 DEPT SE8............................ 160 E4
Victor Seymour School
 CAR SM5............................. 202 A10
Victory Business Centre
 ISLW TW7............................ 154 E10
Victory Junior & Infant School
 WALW SE17........................... 18 F5
Video Gallery
 ARCH N19............................ 118 F6
Vigo Sternberg Galleries
 GLDGN NW11.......................... 117 J3
Viking Business Centre
 ROMW/RG RM7......................... 124 D5
Viking First & Middle School
 NTHLT UB5........................... 133 L5
The Village Family Dental
 Health Centre
 CFSP/GDCR SL9....................... 110 C3
Village Gallery
 KENS W8............................. 8 E9
The Village Gallery
 PIN HA5............................. 113 M1
The Village Medical Centre
 SL SL1.............................. 128 C10
Village School
 HAMP NW3............................ 4 B1
Village Shopping Centre
 SL SL1.............................. 149 L1
Village Surgery
 NWMAL KT3........................... 200 B4
The Village Surgery
 PIN HA5............................. 93 M10
Villiers High School
 STHL UB1............................ 133 P10
The Vine Clinic
 KUTN/CMB KT2........................ 177 K9
Vine Medical Centre
 E/WMO/HCT KT8....................... 198 B3
The Vines School
 BTSEA SW11.......................... 158 B10
Vineyard Hill Road Surgery
 WIM/MER SW19........................ 179 K6
Vinopolis
 STHWK SE1........................... 12 F9
Vinters' Hall
 BLKFR EC4V.......................... 12 F7
V I P Trading Estate
 CHARL SE7........................... 161 P3
Virgin Cinema
 EA W5.............................. 135 J9
Virgin Cinema
 WBPTN SW10.......................... 15 K8
Virgin Cinemas
 CHEL SW3............................ 15 M9
Virgin Cinemas
 CRICK NW2........................... 116 E6
Virgin Cinemas
 HLW CM20............................ 29 J7
Virgin Cinemas
 SL SL1.............................. 149 L1
Virginia Primary School
 BETH E2............................. 7 L10
Virgin Multiplex Cinema
 CRAWW RH11.......................... 283 N6
Virgo Fidelis Convent Schools
 NRWD SE19........................... 181 K9
Viscount Industrial Estate
 DTCH/LGLY SL3....................... 151 H9
Visitor Cen
 STJS SW1Y........................... 11 J9
Vndvl Theatre
 COVGDN WC2E......................... 11 M7
The Vogue Gallery
 EA W5.............................. 135 J9
Vulcan Business Centre
 CROY/NA CRO......................... 225 K5
Vyners School
 HGDN/ICK UB10....................... 112 A9
Waddon Clinic
 CROY/NA CRO......................... 223 H2
Waddon Infant School
 CROY/NA CRO......................... 223 H2
Wadham Lodge Sports Centre
 WALTH E17........................... 100 C9
Wadsworth Business Centre
 GFD/PVL UB6......................... 135 H4
The Waldegrave Clinic
 TEDD TW11........................... 176 E8
Waldegrave School
 WHTN TW2............................ 176 C6
Waldorf School of S W London
 STRHM/NOR SW16...................... 180 D5
Waldorf Steiner School
 of S W London
 STRHM/NOR SW16...................... 180 E7
Walford Road Synagogue
 STNW/STAM N16....................... 119 M9
Walford Secondary School
 NTHLT UB5........................... 133 M3
Walker Primary School
 STHGT/OAK N14....................... 98 E3
Wallace Collection
 MHST W1U............................ 10 C5
Wallace Fields County
 First School
 EW KT17............................ 220 D8
Wallace Fields CP School
 EW KT17............................ 220 D8
Wallbrook Business Centre
 HSLWW TW4........................... 153 J9
Wallington County
 Grammar School
 WLGTN SM6........................... 202 C10
Wallington High
 School for Girls
 WLGTN SM6........................... 222 C5
Walmer Road Clinic
 NTGHL W11........................... 8 A7
Walm Lane Clinic
 CRICK NW2........................... 116 G10
Walm Lane Surgery
 CRICK NW2........................... 136 C1
Walnuts Leisure Centre
 ORP BR6............................. 207 K8
Walnut Tree Walk Primary School
 LBTH SE11........................... 18 A5
Waltham Abbey Swimming Pool
 WAB EN9............................. 81 J1
Waltham Forest Black People
 Mental Health Authority
 WALTH E17........................... 120 F3
Waltham Forest College
 WALTH E17........................... 100 C10
Waltham Forest College
 WALTH E17........................... 120 C1

Waltham Forest College
 WALTH E17........................... 120 C1
Waltham Forest
 Magistrates Court
 WALTH E17........................... 120 C1
Waltham Forest Theatre
 WALTH E17........................... 120 E1
Waltham Holy Cross Council
 WAB EN9............................. 62 C9
Waltham Holy Cross
 Junior School
 WAB EN9............................. 63 J9
Walthamstow Business Centre
 WALTH E17........................... 101 H10
Walthamstow School for Girls
 WALTH E17........................... 120 C2
Walton Business Centre
 WOT/HER KT12........................ 197 J7
Walton Casuals Football Club
 WOT/HER KT12........................ 197 J4
Walton Community Hospital
 WOT/HER KT12........................ 197 J9
Walton Heath Golf Club Shop
 KWD/TDW/WH KT20..................... 256 E1
Walton & Hersham
 Football Club
 WOT/HER KT12........................ 197 H9
Walton Leigh School
 WEY KT13............................ 216 C1
Walton-on-Thames Cricket Club
 WOT/HER KT12........................ 196 G8
Walton-on-the-hill C of E
 Junior School
 KWD/TDW/WH KT20..................... 256 D1
Walton-on-the-hill CP School
 KWD/TDW/WH KT20..................... 238 E8
Walton Swimming Pool
 WOT/HER KT12........................ 197 J8
Walton & Weybridge
 Urban District Council
 WEY KT13............................ 216 B1
Walworth Lower School
 WALW SE17........................... 19 H7
Walworth Town Hall
 WALW SE17........................... 18 E6
Walworth Upper
 Secondary School
 WALW SE17........................... 19 K8
Wandle Primary School
 WAND/EARL SW18...................... 179 L4
Wandle Recreation Centre
 WAND/EARL SW18...................... 179 L2
Wandsworth Adult College
 TOOT SW17........................... 179 P7
Wandsworth Adult College
 TOOT SW17........................... 179 P5
Wandsworth Borough Council
 TOOT SW17........................... 180 A8
Wandsworth Borough Council
 WAND/EARL SW18...................... 179 L3
Wandsworth Borough Council
 WAND/EARL SW18...................... 179 L1
Wandsworth Community
 Health Trust
 TOOT SW17........................... 180 B8
Wandsworth County Court
 PUT/ROE SW15........................ 179 H1
Wandsworth Public Baths
 TOOT SW17........................... 180 B5
Wandsworth Trading Estate
 WAND/EARL SW18...................... 179 L3
Wansfell College
 EPP CM16............................ 82 G1
Wanstead Church School
 WAN E11............................. 121 M3
Wanstead Cricket Club
 WAN E11............................. 121 N5
Wanstead High School
 WAN E11............................. 121 P4
Wanstead Hospital
 WAN E11............................. 121 N2
Wanstead Place Surgery
 WAN E11............................. 121 M3
Wapping
 WAP E1W............................. 140 B10
Wapping Sports Centre
 WAP E1W............................. 140 A10
Warden Lodge Surgery
 CHES/WCR EN8........................ 62 C1
Warehouse Theatre
 CROY/NA CRO......................... 203 L9
Warley County Junior School
 BRW CM14............................ 107 H6
Warley Hill Business Park
 RBRW/HUT CM13....................... 107 H7
Warley Hospital
 BRW CM14............................ 106 C6
Warley Lodge Hospital
 RBRW/HUT CM13....................... 107 J9
Warlingham County
 Junior School
 WARL CR6............................ 242 C3
Warlingham County
 Secondary School
 WARL CR6............................ 242 A2
Warlingham Park Hospital
 WARL CR6............................ 242 F2
Warlingham Park School
 WARL CR6............................ 242 F2
Warlingham Rugby
 Football Club
 WARL CR6............................ 242 E3
Warlingham Sports Club
 WARL CR6............................ 242 C3
War Memorial Sports Ground
 SUT SM1............................. 221 P1
War Museum
 STHWK SE1........................... 13 J10
Warner Bros Cinema
 ACT W3.............................. 135 M6
Warner Bros Cinema
 CROY/NA CRO......................... 202 C9
Warner Brothers Cinema
 WTHK RM20........................... 166 F7
Warnford Industrial Estate
 HYS/HAR UB3......................... 152 F1
Warrendell School
 OXHEY WD19.......................... 93 K4
Warrender School
 RSLP HA4............................ 112 C5
Warren Junior School
 CHDH RM6............................ 124 A3
Warren Mead Infant School
 BNSTD SM7........................... 238 F1
Warren Mead Junior School
 BNSTD SM7........................... 238 G1
The Warren Medical Centre
 YEAD UB4............................ 133 J8
Warren Primary School
 CDH/CHF RM16........................ 167 H2
Warren Road Primary School
 ORP BR6............................. 227 J1

Warren School
 CHDH RM6............................ 124 A3
Warwick Estate
 BAY/PAD W2.......................... 9 H4
Warwick Leadlay Gallery
 GNWCH SE10.......................... 161 H5
Warwick Park
 Secondary School
 PECK SE15........................... 159 N7
Warwick School for Boys
 WALTH E17........................... 121 H2
The Warwick School
 REDH RH1............................ 258 B9
Wasps Rugby Football Club
 ALP/SUD HA0......................... 115 H9
The Watch Gallery
 CHEL SW3............................ 15 N6
Watchlytes JMI School
 WGCE AL7............................ 23 L5
Waterden Road Private
 Medical Clinic
 GU GU1.............................. 268 B1
Waterfield School
 CRAWW RH11.......................... 283 H9
Watergate School
 LEW SE13............................ 160 G10
Waterloo Health Centre
 STHWK SE1........................... 18 A2
Watermans Business Park
 STA TW18............................ 173 H7
The Watermans Hall
 MON EC3R............................ 13 J8
Water Meadow Surgery
 CSHM HP5............................ 50 C10
Watermeads High School
 MRDN SM4............................ 201 N6
Watermill Business Centre
 PEND EN3............................ 80 E6
Water Rats Theatre
 STPAN WC1H.......................... 5 M9
Waterside Business Centre
 ISLW TW7............................ 154 G10
Waterside County
 Combined School
 CSHM HP5............................ 51 J9
Waterside Industrial Estate
 HOD EN11............................ 45 J4
The Waterside Trading Centre
 NWDGN UB2........................... 154 D2
Water Sports Centre
 BERM/RHTH SE16...................... 160 D2
Waterways Heritage Museum
 RKW/CH/CXG WD3...................... 91 P2
Watford Arches Retail Park
 WATW WD17........................... 73 K9
Watford Borough Council
 WAT WD17............................ 73 H7
Watford Business Centre
 WATW WD17........................... 73 J7
Watford Central Swimming Bath
 WAT WD17............................ 73 H6
Watford County Court
 WAT WD17............................ 73 J6
Watford Eye Clinic
 WATN WD24........................... 73 J4
Watford Football Club
 WATW WD18........................... 73 J9
Watford General Hospital
 WATW WD18........................... 73 J9
Watford Grammar School
 for Boys
 WATW WD18........................... 72 G8
Watford Grammar School
 for Girls
 WATW WD18........................... 73 H9
Watford Museum
 WAT WD17............................ 73 K9
Watford Sports & Leisure Centre
 GSTN WD25........................... 55 K9
Watford Springs Pool
 WATW WD18........................... 73 K9
Watford United Synagogue
 WAT WD17............................ 73 J5
Watling Clinic
 EDGE HA8............................ 96 A8
Watling Medical Centre
 EDGE HA8............................ 95 P9
Watling View School
 STAL AL1............................ 38 C10
Wattenden Primary School
 PUR/KEN CR8......................... 241 H2
Watts Gallery
 RGUW GU3............................ 266 C5
Waverley Industrial Estate
 HRW HA1............................. 114 C1
Waverley Lower
 Secondary School
 EDUL SE22........................... 182 A1
Waverley School
 PEND EN3............................ 80 B8
Waverley Upper
 Secondary School
 EDUL SE22........................... 182 B1
Waxchandlers' Hall
 CITYW EC2V.......................... 12 F5
Weald College
 KTN/HRWW/W HA3...................... 94 D7
Weald CP School
 RSEV TN14........................... 265 J9
Weald First & Middle School
 KTN/HRWW/W HA3...................... 94 E8
Weald Gallery
 RSEV TN14........................... 263 N2
Websters Art Gallery
 LHD/OX KT22......................... 218 B9
Weekend Arts College
 KTTN NW5............................ 4 E1
Welbeck Clinic
 CRICK NW2........................... 117 K8
Welbourne Junior School
 SEVS/STOTM N15...................... 119 N2
Wellcome Institute
 CAMTN NW1........................... 11 J1
Weldon Park Middle School
 RYLN/HDSTN HA2...................... 114 A9
Wellhouse NHS Trust
 EDGE HA8............................ 95 N4
The Welling Clinic
 WELL DA16........................... 163 K8
Welling Medical Centre
 WELL DA16........................... 163 J10
Welling School
 WELL DA16........................... 163 L7
Welling Secondary Girls School
 WELL DA16........................... 163 L7
Wellington Barracks
 STJSPK SW1H......................... 17 L1
Wellington Primary School
 BOW E3.............................. 140 F5

Wellington Primary School
 HSLW TW3............................ 153 N8
Welling United Football Club
 WELL DA16........................... 163 M9
The Wells Park Practice
 SYD SE26............................ 182 A6
Wells Park School
 CHIG IG7............................ 103 J5
Wells Primary School
 WFD IG8............................. 103 N5
The Well Street Surgery
 HOM E9.............................. 140 B2
Welwyn Garden City Cricket Club
 WGCW AL8............................ 22 F1
Welwyn Garden City Golf Club
 WGCW AL8............................ 22 E4
Welwyn Garden Hebrew
 Congregation Synagogue
 WGCW AL8............................ 22 E5
Welwyn Hatfield District Council
 HAT AL10............................ 40 E3
Welwyn Hatfield Museum Service
 BRKMPK AL9.......................... 41 H1
Welwyn Rugby Football Club
 WGCW AL8............................ 22 E6
Wembley Business Centre
 WBLY HA9............................ 115 P8
Wembley Football Club
 ALP/SUD HA0......................... 114 C9
Wembley High School
 ALP/SUD HA0......................... 115 H8
Wembley Manor Junior School
 WBLY HA9............................ 115 K8
Wembley Park Business Centre
 WBLY HA9............................ 115 N8
Wembley Station
 WBLY HA9............................ 115 M10
Wembley Synagogue
 WBLY HA9............................ 115 L8
Wendell Park Primary School
 SHB W12............................. 156 C1
Wennington Hall Farm
 Business Centre
 RAIN RM13........................... 145 M8
The Wenta Business Centre
 WATN WD24........................... 73 L3
Wentworth County Infant School
 DART DA1............................ 186 G3
Wentworth CP Junior School
 DART DA1............................ 187 H3
Wentworth Tutorial College
 GLDGN NW11.......................... 116 G4
Wesley's House & Chapel
 STLK EC1Y........................... 12 G1
Wessex Gardens Infant School
 CRICK NW2........................... 117 H6
West Acton Primary School
 ACT W3.............................. 135 N8
West Ashtead CP School
 ASHTD KT21.......................... 237 K6
West Becton Health Centre
 CAN/RD E16.......................... 142 A8
Westbourne Green Sports Complex
 BAY/PAD W2.......................... 8 F3
Westbourne Primary School
 SUT SM1............................. 201 K10
Westbridge College
 BTSEA SW11.......................... 157 P7
Westbrooke School
 WELL DA16........................... 163 N9
Westbrook Hay
 Preparatory School
 HHW HP1............................. 34 C9
Westbury Medical Centre
 WDGN N22............................ 99 K10
West Byfleet County
 Infant School
 BF/WBF KT14......................... 215 L8
West Byfleet Health Centre
 BF/WBF KT14......................... 215 N9
West Byfleet
 Physiotherapy Clinic
 BF/WBF KT14......................... 215 K8
Westcott School
 DORK RH4............................ 272 B3
Westcourt County
 Primary School
 GVE DA12............................ 191 H5
The Westcroft Leisure Centre
 CAR SM5............................. 222 B1
West Dene School
 PUR/KEN CR8......................... 222 G9
West Drayton Cricket Club
 WDR/YW UB7.......................... 151 M3
West Drayton Primary School
 WDR/YW UB7.......................... 151 P1
West Ealing Business Centre
 WEA W13............................. 134 F9
West End Great Synagogue
 MBLAR W1H........................... 10 A6
Western Hospitality
 NWDGN UB2........................... 153 J3
Western House City First School
 SL SL1.............................. 128 E9
Western House Hospital
 WARE SG12........................... 26 C1
Western Trading Estate
 WLSDN NW10.......................... 135 P6
West Ewell County Infant School
 HOR/WEW KT19........................ 220 A4
Westfield JMI School
 HOD EN11............................ 44 E2
Westfield Primary School
 WOKS/MYFD GU22...................... 232 B7
Westfield School
 WATW WD18........................... 72 G10
Westfields School
 BARN SW13........................... 156 C9
Westfield Surgery
 WOKS/MYFD GU22...................... 232 B7
Westgate CP School
 DART DA1............................ 187 L3
Westgate Retail Park
 SL SL1.............................. 128 F9
Westgate School
 SL SL1.............................. 128 F10
West Green County First School
 CRAWW RH11.......................... 283 M6
West Grove Primary School
 STHGT/OAK N14....................... 98 E1
West Hackney Synagogue
 HACK E8............................. 119 P9
West Hackney Synagogue
 STNW/STAM N16....................... 119 N8
West Ham Church
 Primary School
 SRTFD E15........................... 141 L3
West Ham Lane Clinic
 SRTFD E15........................... 141 K3
West Hampstead Clinic
 KIL/WHAMP NW6....................... 2 F3
West Ham United Football Club
 CHDH RM6............................ 124 A5

West Ham United Football Club
 PLSTW E13........................... 141 P4
West Hatch High School
 CHIG IG7............................ 102 C6
West Heath School
 SEV TN13............................ 265 J5
West Hendon Clinic
 CDALE/KGS NW9....................... 116 C4
West Hertfordshire College
 WAT WD17............................ 73 H4
West Herts College
 BUSH WD23........................... 73 L7
West Herts College
 HHW HP1............................. 35 M5
West Hill County Primary School
 DART DA1............................ 187 J2
West Hill Hospital
 DART DA1............................ 187 L2
West Hill Primary School
 WAND/EARL SW18...................... 179 K1
West Hill School
 LHD/OX KT22......................... 236 F4
West Lambeth Community
 Care NHS Trust
 BRXN/ST SW9......................... 158 F9
West Lambeth Health Authority
 STRHM/NOR SW16...................... 180 F9
West Lea School
 ED N9............................... 99 M4
West Lodge School
 BFN/LL DA15......................... 185 K6
West Lodge School
 PIN HA5............................. 113 L2
West London Healthcare
 NHS Trust
 NWDGN UB2........................... 153 M2
West London Healthcare
 NHS Trust
 NWDGN UB2........................... 153 N1
West London Magistrates Court
 HMSMTH W6........................... 156 C4
West London Synagogue
 of British Jews
 BAY/PAD W2.......................... 9 P6
West London Tamil School
 WLSDN NW10.......................... 136 C4
West Mead Clinic
 RSLP HA4............................ 113 K8
West Middlesex Hospital
 ISLW TW7............................ 154 F8
Westminster Abbey Choir School
 WEST SW1P........................... 17 J1
Westminster Cathedral
 Primary School
 PIM SW1V............................ 17 K7
Westminster City Council
 BAY/PAD W2.......................... 8 G4
Westminster City Council
 BAY/PAD W2.......................... 9 L4
Westminster City Council
 BGVA SW1W........................... 16 E8
Westminster City Council
 BGVA SW1W........................... 16 D7
Westminster City Council
 MBLAR W1H........................... 10 A3
Westminster City Council
 NKENS W10........................... 2 A9
Westminster City Council
 NKENS W10........................... 136 C6
Westminster City Council
 PIM SW1V............................ 16 F8
Westminster City Council
 SOHO/CST W1F........................ 11 H6
Westminster City Council
 SOHO/SHAV W1D....................... 11 K7
Westminster City Council
 STJWD NW8........................... 3 P1
Westminster City Council
 STJWD NW8........................... 9 M2
Westminster City Council
 STJWD NW8........................... 9 M1
Westminster City Council
 WEST SW1P........................... 17 J4
Westminster City Hall
 WESTW SW1E.......................... 17 H3
Westminster College
 BTSEA SW11.......................... 158 B7
Westminster Coroners Court
 WEST SW1P........................... 17 K5
Westminster Gallery
 STJSPK SW1H......................... 17 K2
Westminster Lodge
 Sports Centre
 STALW/RED AL3....................... 38 B8
Westminster School
 WEST SW1P........................... 17 J5
Westminster Synagogue
 SKENS SW7........................... 15 P2
Westminster Technical College
 WEST SW1P........................... 17 H5
Westminster Theatre
 WESTW SW1E.......................... 16 G3
Westmoor Community Clinic
 PUT/ROE SW15........................ 178 D3
West Norwood Clinic
 WNWD SE27........................... 181 K5
Weston Park Clinic
 CEND/HSY/T N8....................... 118 F3
Weston Park Primary School
 CEND/HSY/T N8....................... 118 G3
Westpoint Trading Estate
 ACT W3.............................. 135 N7
West Ruislip Elementary School
 HGDN/ICK UB10....................... 112 D8
West Thames College
 ISLW TW7............................ 154 D8
West Thornton Primary School
 CROY/NA CRO......................... 202 G7
West Thurrock CP School
 WTHK RM20........................... 166 F5
West Twyford Primary School
 WLSDN NW10.......................... 135 M4
Westway Business Centre
 BAY/PAD W2.......................... 8 G3
The Westway Clinic
 REDH RH1............................ 257 P9
Westway Sports Centre
 NKENS W10........................... 136 G8
West Wickham Swimming Baths
 WWKM BR4............................ 205 H8
Westwood High School for Girls
 NRWD SE19........................... 181 K10
Westwood Primary I
 nfant School
 WELL DA16........................... 163 H10
Westwood Primary School
 WELL DA16........................... 162 G10
Westwood Technology College
 WELL DA16........................... 163 H10
Wexham Court County
 First School
 SLN SL2............................. 129 P7

Wexham School
SLN SL2 .... 129 N7
Weybridge Business Park
ADL/WDHM KT15 .... 215 P1
Weybridge Cricket Club
WEY KT13 .... 196 F9
Weybridge Hospital
& Primary Care Centre
WEY KT13 .... 216 B1
Weyfield Primary School
GU GU1 .... 250 A7
Wey House School
SHGR GU5 .... 268 B9
Whaddon House Clinic
CMBW SE5 .... 159 M9
Wheatcroft JMI School
HERT/BAY SG13 .... 25 P4
Wheatfields Junior
& Infant School
STALE/WH AL4 .... 38 G2
Whipps Cross Hospital
WAN E11 .... 121 K3
Whiston Road School
BETH E2 .... 7 L6
The White Bridge County
Infant & Junior School
LOU IG10 .... 102 B1
Whitechapel Art Gallery
WCHPL E1 .... 13 M5
White City Child Guidance Unit
SHB W12 .... 136 E9
Whitefield School
CRICK NW2 .... 116 G5
Whitefield Schools & Centre
WALTH E17 .... 101 H10
Whitefriars School
KTN/HRWW/W HA3 .... 94 D10
Whitefriars Trading Estate
KTN/HRWW/W HA3 .... 94 C10
Whitefriars Trading Estate
KTN/HRWW/W HA3 .... 114 C1
Whitehall Estate
HLWW/ROY CM19 .... 46 B2
Whitehall Primary School
CHING E4 .... 101 K3
White Hall Primary School
UX/CGN UB8 .... 131 M3
White Hart Lane School
WDGN N22 .... 99 J8
Whiteheath Infant School
RSLP HA4 .... 112 C4
Whiteheath Primary School
RSLP HA4 .... 112 D4
Whitehill House Surgery
DART DA1 .... 187 H1
Whitehill Junior School
GVE DA12 .... 190 F6
Whitehorse Manor Junior School
THHTH CR7 .... 203 L4
White House Gallery
WAND/EARL SW18 .... 179 L4
The White House Gallery
BH/WHM TN16 .... 262 G2
The White House Surgery
CRICK NW2 .... 117 J9
Whitelodge Medical Practice
ENC/FH EN2 .... 79 L7
The Whitewebbs Museum
of Transport & Industry
ENC/FH EN2 .... 79 J1
The Whitgift Galleries
CROY/NA CR0 .... 223 K1
Whitgift School
SAND/SEL CR2 .... 223 K2
Whitmore High School
RYLN/HDSTN HA2 .... 114 B6
Whitmore Junior & Infant School
IS N1 .... 7 H6
Whittingham Community
Primary School
WALTH E17 .... 100 C9
Whittings Hill School
BAR EN5 .... 76 F9
Whittington Hospital
ARCH N19 .... 118 D7
Whittington Hospital
ARCH N19 .... 118 C7
Whittle Business Centre
SL SL1 .... 128 C8
Whittlesea School
KTN/HRWW/W HA3 .... 94 B8
Whitton Health Centre
WHTN TW2 .... 176 B4
Whitton Health Clinic
WHTN TW2 .... 176 A4
Whitton School
WHTN TW2 .... 176 A5
Wholist Health Centre
SAND/SEL CR2 .... 223 K2
Whybridge Infant School
RAIN RM13 .... 145 H3
Whybridge Junior School
RAIN RM13 .... 144 G3
Whyllotts Council Offices
POTB/CUF EN6 .... 59 J8
Whyteleafe Football Club
CTHM CR3 .... 241 N5
Whyteleafe School
CTHM CR3 .... 241 N4
Wickham Theatre
WWKM BR4 .... 205 J10
Wide Way Health Clinic
MTCM CR4 .... 202 E3
Wigfall Group Practice
STHWK SE1 .... 12 B10
Wigmore Hall
MHST W1U 10 E5
Wilberforce Primary School
NKENS W10 .... 2 B9
Wilbury Primary School
UED N18 .... 99 L6

Wildernesse Golf Club
BGR/WK TN15 .... 247 P8
Wildernesse School
BGR/WK TN15 .... 247 M7
Wilderness Sports Centre
BGR/WK TN15 .... 247 M7
Willesden & Brondesbury
Synagogue
CRICK NW2 .... 136 F1
Willesden Community Hospital
WLSDN NW10 .... 136 D2
Willesden County Court
WLSDN NW10 .... 136 B4
Willesden Green Surgery
WLSDN NW10 .... 136 E1
Willesden High School
WLSDN NW10 .... 136 E3
Willesden Medical Centre
CRICK NW2 .... 136 E1
William Bellamy Junior
& Infant School
DAGE RM10 .... 124 B7
William Byrd School
HYS/HAR UB3 .... 152 D5
William Edwards Gm School
CDH/CHF RM16 .... 147 P9
William Ellis School
KTTN NW5 .... 118 B8
William Ellis Sports Ground
EDGE HA8 .... 95 M9
William Ford School
DAGE RM10 .... 144 B2
William Morris Gallery
WALTH E17 .... 120 F1
William Morris Middle School
MTCM CR4 .... 202 E3
William Morris School
WALTH E17 .... 100 D9
William Penn County
Middle School
SLN SL2 .... 129 J6
William Penn Leisure Centre
RKW/CH/CXG WD3 .... 91 J2
William Torbitt Junior
& Infant School
GNTH/NBYPK IG2 .... 123 H3
William Tyndale School
IS N1 .... 6 D3
Willington School
WIM/MER SW19 .... 179 J9
Willow Business Centre
MTCM CR4 .... 202 A5
Willow Business Park
SYD SE26 .... 182 B6
Willow Court Colindale Hospital
CDALE/KGS NW9 .... 96 A10
Willowfield Adult
Education Centre
WALTH E17 .... 120 C1
Willowfield School
HNHL SE24 .... 159 K10
Willowfield Secondary School
WALTH E17 .... 120 D1
Willow House Surgery
EN EN1 .... 79 M7
The Willow School
YEAD UB4 .... 133 L6
The Willows Clinic
CHST BR7 .... 184 E8
Willow Tree Primary School
NTHLT UB5 .... 133 M1
Willow Tree Surgery
CDALE/KGS NW9 .... 115 P3
Willow Tree Surgery
YEAD UB4 .... 133 M7
Wilmington Grange Grammar
School for Girls
RDART DA2 .... 187 J5
Wilmington High School
RDART DA2 .... 187 J6
Wilmington Parish Council
DART DA1 .... 187 L5
Wilmington Primary School
RDART DA2 .... 187 J6
Wilsons Grammar School
WLGTN SM6 .... 222 F3
Wimbledon Chase Middle School
RYNPK SW20 .... 201 H1
Wimbledon College for Boys
WIM/MER SW19 .... 178 G10
Wimbledon Common
Preparatory School for Boys
WIM/MER SW19 .... 178 F10
Wimbledon Football Club
SNWD SE25 .... 203 M4
Wimbledon High School for Girls
WIM/MER SW19 .... 179 H9
Wimbledon House School
WIM/MER SW19 .... 201 K1
Wimbledon Magistrates Court
WIM/MER SW19 .... 179 K9
Wimbledon Park First School
WIM/MER SW19 .... 179 L5
Wimbledon Rugby Club
RYNPK SW20 .... 178 C10
Wimbledon School of Art
WIM/MER SW19 .... 179 K10
Wimbledon School of Art
WIM/MER SW19 .... 201 H1
Wimbledon Stadium
Business Centre
WIM/MER SW19 .... 179 L6
Wimbledon Synagogue
WIM/MER SW19 .... 178 G5
Wimbledon Theatre
WIM/MER SW19 .... 179 L10
Winchcombe Business Centre
PECK SE15 .... 19 K10
Winchmore Hill Clinic
WCHMH N21 .... 99 J2

Winchmore Hill Cricket Club
AMSS HP7 .... 68 A10
Winchmore Hill Cricket Club
WCHMH N21 .... 99 K2
Winchmore Secondary School
WCHMH N21 .... 99 K3
Windermere JMI Primary School
STAL AL1 .... 38 G8
Windmill Medical Practice
CRICK NW2 .... 117 H10
Windmill School
BRXS/STRHM SW2 .... 180 F1
Windmill Trading Estate
MTCM CR4 .... 202 D5
Windsor Boys School
WDSR SL4 .... 148 G7
Windsor Business Centre
WDSR SL4 .... 149 H6
Windsor Castle
WDSR SL4 .... 149 K6
Windsor & Eton Cricket Club
WDSR SL4 .... 149 K5
Windsor & Eton Football Club
WDSR SL4 .... 148 G10
Windsor Girls School
WDSR SL4 .... 148 F9
Windsor Rugby Football Club
WDSR SL4 .... 149 K5
Windsor Victoria Cricket Club
WDSR SL4 .... 149 K5
Wine Gallery
NTGHL W11 .... 8 C7
Winfield House
CAMTN NW1 .... 3 P9
Wingate & Finchley Football Club
NFNCH/WDSP N12 .... 97 N8
Wingate Trading Estate
TOTM N17 .... 99 N8
Wingfield Primary School
BKHTH/KID SE3 .... 161 M9
Winnington Ingram School
RSLP HA4 .... 112 E5
Winns Primary School
WALTH E17 .... 100 E10
Winsor Primary School
EHAM E6 .... 142 C8
The Winston Churchill School
WOKN/KNAP GU21 .... 231 K4
Winston Galleries
RYLN/HDSTN HA2 .... 114 D6
Winterton Surgery
BH/WHM TN16 .... 262 G3
Winton Primary School
IS N1 .... 5 N8
Wishmore Cross School
CHOB/PIR GU24 .... 213 K6
Witley Industrial Estate
NWDGN UB2 .... 153 N3
Witnitz School
STNW/STAM N16 .... 119 N6
Wix School
BTSEA SW11 .... 158 C9
Woking Borough Council
WOKN/KNAP GU21 .... 214 C10
Woking Borough Council
WOKN/KNAP GU21 .... 232 B2
Woking Business Park
WOKN/KNAP GU21 .... 232 E1
Woking College
WOKS/MYFD GU22 .... 232 D6
Woking Community Hospital
WOKS/MYFD GU22 .... 232 B4
Woking Football Club
WOKS/MYFD GU22 .... 232 C6
Woking Leisure Centre
WOKS/MYFD GU22 .... 232 C5
Woking Nuffield Hospital
WOKN/KNAP GU21 .... 214 B10
Woldingham School
GDST RH9 .... 260 D1
Wolf Fields First School
NWDGN UB2 .... 153 N3
Wolfson Medical Centre
RYNPK SW20 .... 178 D10
Wolfs Wood Primary School
OXTED RH8 .... 261 M8
Wolsey Business Park
WATW WD18 .... 92 E1
Women & Medical Practice
CEND/HSY/T N8 .... 119 H1
Women's Theatre Workshop
CONDST W1S 11 H8
Wonersh Surgery
SHGR GU5 .... 268 E10
Woodacre
SOCK/AV RM15 .... 146 F7
The Woodberry Clinic
MUSWH N10 .... 118 C1
Woodbridge Business Park
GU GU1 .... 249 P9
Woodbridge High School
WFD IG8 .... 101 N8
Woodbridge Surgery
STHL UB1 .... 133 L10
Woodbrook School
BECK BR3 .... 204 E1
Woodcote Group Practice
PUR/KEN CR8 .... 222 G7
Woodcote High School
COUL/CHIP CR5 .... 222 E9
Woodcote House School
BFOR GU20 .... 212 A2
Woodcote Junior & Infant School
COUL/CHIP CR5 .... 222 D10
Woodcroft Junior School
EDGE HA8 .... 96 A8
Wood End Infant School
NTHLT UB5 .... 114 C10
Wood End Park Junior School
UX/CGN UB8 .... 132 D9

Woodfield School
CDALE/KGS NW9 .... 116 B6
Woodfield School
HHS/BOV HP3 .... 36 D8
Woodfield School
REDH RH1 .... 258 F5
Woodford County High School
for Girls
WFD IG8 .... 101 L7
Woodford Progressive
Synagogue
SWFD E18 .... 121 M1
Woodford Trading Estate
WFD IG8 .... 101 P10
Woodgrange Infant School
FSTGT E7 .... 121 N9
Woodgrange Medical Practice
FSTGT E7 .... 121 N10
Wood Green Crown Court
WDGN N22 .... 99 H9
Wood Green Health Centre
WDGN N22 .... 98 G9
Wood Green Old Boys
Football Club
WDGN N22 .... 99 H8
Woodhill Primary School
CHARL SE7 .... 162 B3
Woodhouse Sixth Form College
NFNCH/WDSP N12 .... 97 N6
Woodlands Infant
& Junior School
IL IG1 .... 122 G10
Woodlands Infant School
BORE WD6 .... 75 M5
Woodlands Park Infant School
SEVS/STOTM N15 .... 119 K3
Woodlands Preparatory School
RBRW/HUT CM13 .... 127 J2
Woodlands Surgery
LHD/OX KT22 .... 237 H8
Woodlands Surgery
BFN/LL DA15 .... 185 H4
Woodlands Surgery
CRAWE RH10 .... 283 P10
Woodland Surgery
GNWCH SE10 .... 161 K4
Wood Lane Medical Centre
RSLP HA4 .... 112 F6
Wood Lane School
FUL/PGN SW6 .... 157 M7
Wood Lane School
SHB W12 .... 136 E8
Wood Lane Sports Centre
BCTR RM8 .... 124 C6
Wood Lane Surgery
HCH RM12 .... 125 H10
Woodlea Primary School
CTHM CR3 .... 242 E8
Woodmansterne CP School
BNSTD SM7 .... 222 A10
Woodmansterne Primary School
STRHM/NOR SW16 .... 202 E1
Woodmansterne Sports Club
BNSTD SM7 .... 239 P1
Woodridge Primary School
NFNCH/WDSP N12 .... 97 J4
Woodside Community School
PLSTW E13 .... 141 P6
Woodside County Primary School
CDH/CHF RM16 .... 168 C2
Woodside Health Centre
SNWD SE25 .... 204 A5
Woodside JMI School
CHESW EN7 .... 61 K5
Woodside Junior School
CROY/NA CR0 .... 203 P7
Woodside Park School
FBAR/BDGN N11 .... 98 A6
Woodside Park School
NFNCH/WDSP N12 .... 97 L5
Woodside Park Synagogue
NFNCH/WDSP N12 .... 97 L6
Woodside School
BELV DA17 .... 164 C3
Wood Street County
Infant School
RGUW GU3 .... 249 H8
Wood Street Medical Centre
WALTH E17 .... 121 H1
The Woodvill School
LHD/OX KT22 .... 236 G6
Wood Wharf
POP/IOD E14 .... 140 G10
Woolmore Primary School
POP/IOD E14 .... 141 H9
Woolwich College
WOOL/PLUM SE18 .... 162 A3
Woolwich County Court
WOOL/PLUM SE18 .... 162 D2
Woolwich Crown Court
THMD SE28 .... 163 H1
Woolwich Polytechnic School
THMD SE28 .... 143 K10
Worcesters Infant
& Primary School
EN EN1 .... 79 N4
Workers Gallery
SOHO/CST W1F 11 J6
World Business Centre Heathrow
HTHAIR TW6 .... 152 D7
World of Football Hall of Fame
STHWK SE1 .... 17 N2
World Trade Centre
TWRH EC3N 13 M8
World University Service
STLK EC1Y 12 G2
Worsley Bridge Junior
Mixed School
BECK BR3 .... 182 F10

Wormholt Park Primary School
SHB W12 .... 136 D9
Wormley JMI School
BROX EN10 .... 44 D9
Worple Primary School
ISLW TW7 .... 154 F10
Worplesdon CP School
RGUW GU3 .... 249 J6
Worton Hall Industrial Estate
ISLW TW7 .... 154 D10
Wray Common County
Middle School
REIG RH2 .... 257 N9
Wray Common County
Primary School
REDH RH1 .... 257 N9
Wraysbury Combined School
STWL/WRAY TW19 .... 172 B2
Wraysbury Medical Centre
STWL/WRAY TW19 .... 172 C2
Wrexham Park Hospital
SLN SL2 .... 129 P6
Wrotham Road CP School
GVW DA11 .... 190 E3
Wrotham Road Health Clinic
GVW DA11 .... 190 E4
Wroxham JMI School
POTB/CUF EN6 .... 58 G7
The Wrythe Green Surgery
SUT SM1 .... 201 P10
Wyborne Primary Mixed School
ELTH/MOT SE9 .... 184 E4
Wycliffe School
BTSEA SW11 .... 158 B8
Wykeham Junior School
HCH RM12 .... 125 H6
Wykeham Primary School
WLSDN NW10 .... 116 A8
Wyllie Gallery
SKENS SW7 .... 15 J4
Wyvil Primary School
VX/NE SW8 .... 158 F6
Xanadu Theatres
WEY KT13 .... 215 P6
Yacob Gallery
KENS W8 .... 8 F9
Yale University Press
HAMP NW3 .... 117 P9
Yardley Primary School
CHING E4 .... 80 G9
Yattenden Middle School
HORL RH6 .... 280 B3
Yeading Football Club
HYS/HAR UB3 .... 133 K10
Yeading JMI School
YEAD UB4 .... 133 K7
Yeading Medical Centre
NTHLT UB5 .... 133 K5
Yehudi Gordons Practice
STJWD NW8 .... 3 L7
Yehudi Menuhin School
COB KT11 .... 235 P5
Yemen Embassy
SKENS SW7 .... 15 L5
Yerbury Primary School
ARCH N19 .... 118 E8
Yeshivo Horomo
Talmudical College
STNW/STAM N16 .... 119 L6
Yeshurun Synagogue
EDGE HA8 .... 95 M7
Yiewsley Health Centre
WDR/YW UB7 .... 131 P10
Yin Yang Chinese Medical Centre
GDMY/SEVK IG3 .... 123 K6
YMCA
ECT SW5 .... 14 G7
York Clinic
STHWK SE1 .... 12 C10
York Clinic
WOKN/KNAP GU21 .... 232 B3
York Galleries
TWK TW1 .... 176 F4
York House Medical Centre
WOKS/MYFD GU22 .... 232 C4
York House Surgery
RKW/CH/CXG WD3 .... 72 A6
York Road Surgery
DART DA1 .... 187 N3
York Water Gate
CHCR WC2N 11 M9
Young England Rugby Club
VX/NE SW8 .... 17 M10
Young Victoria Theatre
STHWK SE1 .... 18 B1
Youth Hostel
BERM/RHTH SE16 .... 140 C10
Youth Hostel
BLKFR EC4V 12 D6
Yvonne Arnaud Theatre
GU GU1 .... 268 A2
Zambia High Comm
SKENS SW7 .... 15 J2
Zebra Two Gallery
HAMP NW3 .... 117 M9
Zella Gallery
WBPTN SW10 .... 15 K9
Zenith Gallery
BAL SW12 .... 180 C3
Zennor Road Industrial Estate
BAL SW12 .... 180 D4
Zimbabwe High Commission
CHCR WC2N 11 L8
Zobel College
SEV TN13 .... 247 J10
Zoo
IL IG1 .... 122 F7

Page 6
C8
1 Owen St

Page 9
H7
1 Inverness Ms
J2
1 Warrington Gdns

Page 8
F9
1 Lucerne Ms
2 Newcombe St
3 Palace Gardens Ter
4 Rabbit Rw
5 Uxbridge St
6 West Mall
F10
1 Vicarage Gdns
G10
1 Inverness Gdns

Page 10
A6
1 Great Cumberland Ms
2 Hampden Gurney St
3 Stourcliffe St
C5
1 Ashland Pl
2 Ossington Buildings
3 Sherlock Ms
D4
1 Bulstrode Pl
2 Cross Keys Cl
3 De Walden St
4 Wesley St
5 Wheatley St
6 Woodstock Av
D6
1 Gray's Yd
F4
1 Cavendish Ms South
2 Duchess Ms
3 Langham St
4 Portland Pl
5 Riding House St
F6
1 Harewood Pl
2 Mason's Arms Ms
3 Princes St
4 Swallow Pl
F10
1 Half Moon St
2 White Horse St

Page 11
H6
1 Berwick St
2 D'arblay St
3 Dufour's Pl
4 Canton St
5 Livonia St
6 Noel St
7 Portland Ms
8 Wardour St
J8
1 Carlton St
2 Great Windmill St
3 Norris St
4 Oxendon St
5 Panton St
6 St Alban's St
7 St James's Market
K5
1 Andrew Borde St
2 Bainbridge St
3 Earnshaw St
4 Great Russell St
5 Sutton Rw
K7
1 Gerrard Pl
2 Leicester Pl
3 Lisle St
4 Macclesfield St
5 Newport Pl
L5
1 Bloomsbury St
2 Bucknall St
3 Dyott St
4 Grape St
5 Shaftesbury Av
6 Streatham St
L9
1 Charing Cross
M7
1 Burleigh St
2 Henrietta St
3 James St
4 Southampton St
M9
1 Craven St
N2
1 Millman Ms
N3
1 Old North St
2 Orde Hall St
3 Red Lion St
N5
1 Wild Ct
2 Wild Ct
N6
1 Kemble St
2 Portsmouth St
3 Russell St
4 Sheffield St
N7
1 Catherine St
2 Montreal Pl
3 Savoy Rw
4 Tavistock St
N8
1 Savoy Steps
P6
1 Houghton St
P7
1 Melbourne Pl

Page 12
A2
1 Baker's Rw
2 Pooles Buildings
3 White Bear Yd
B3
1 Saffron Hill
B5
1 Bartlett Ct
2 East Harding St
3 Great New St
4 Little New St
5 New Street Sq
6 Pemberton Rw
7 Plough Pl
8 Printer St
9 West Harding St
C6
1 Apothecary St
2 Bridewell Pl
3 Dorset Buildings
4 Hutton St
5 Old Seacoal La
6 Pilgrim St
7 Salisbury Ct
D6
1 Amen Cnr
2 Amen Ct
3 Creed La
4 Dean's Ct
5 Ludgate Broadway
6 Ludgate Sq
7 St Paul's Church Yd
E4
1 Albion Wy
2 Bartholomew Cl
3 Kinghorn St
4 Little Britain
5 Montague St

Page 13
F1
1 Anchor Yd
H5
1 Austin Friars
2 Austin Friars Sq
3 Copthall Av
4 Langthorn Cl
5 Throgmorton St
J5
1 Camomile St
2 Great St Helen's
K6
1 Aldgate
2 Billiter Sq
3 Bury St
4 Creechurch La
5 Heneage La
6 Northumberland Alley
N5
1 Manningtree St
2 Mountford St
3 Plough St
N10
1 Orton St
2 Redmead La

Page 16
C5
1 Belgrave Ms West
2 Chesham Ms
3 Chesham Pl
4 Halkin Ms
5 Halkin St
C7
1 Denbigh Pl

Page 18
F6
1 Asolando Dr
2 Colworth Gv
3 Ethel St
4 Turquand St
5 Walcorde Av
G7
1 Townley St

Page 23
H7
1 Raymonds Cl
2 Raymonds Pln
H8
1 Harebell
2 Hunters Wy
3 Little Ley
4 Oaken Gv
5 Walnut Ct
J5
1 Home Meadow
2 Swallowfields
3 Verlum St
L4
1 Buddcroft
2 Claycroft
3 Kingscroft
4 Nettlecroft
5 Smallcroft
6 Strawfields
7 Waterfield
8 Wheatbarn
L6
1 Amwell Common
2 Batford Cl
3 Bushey Cl
4 Bushey Gn
5 Graveley Dell
6 Thundridge Cl
7 Wareside Cl
M5
1 Andrewsfield
2 Bericot Wy
3 Beverley Gdns
4 Douglas Wy
5 Elizabeth Cl
6 Jacklaws
7 Lindbergh
8 Mitchell Cl
M7
1 Aspen Wy
2 Birchall Wd
3 Copperfields
4 Forresters Dr
5 Glenwood
6 High Wickfield
7 Holwell Hyde
8 Pelham Ct
9 Ploughmans End
10 Poppyfields

Page 25
L5
1 Bell La
2 Bircherley Ct
3 Bluecoats Av
4 Church St
5 The Gulphs
6 Maidenhead St
7 Maidenhead Yd
8 Market Pl
9 Millers Yd
10 Nicholas La
11 Oldhall St
12 Parliament Sq
13 St John's St
14 St John's Sq
15 Salisbury Sq
16 The Wash

Page 33
L3
1 Bulbourne Cl
2 Bulbourne Ct
3 Midcot Wy
4 Midcot Wy
5 Peacocks Cl
6 Peacocks Cl
7 Salter's Cl
8 Salter's Ct
9 Stoney Cl
10 Stoney Ct

Page 35
H7
1 Bluebell Cl
2 Damask Gn
3 Hazeldell Link
4 Huntsmill Rd
5 Shepherds Gn
6 Wellingford Rd
7 Westland Rd
8 West St
J6
1 Canterbury Rd
2 Franklin Rd
3 Keston Ms
4 Shady La
5 Wellington Rd
K3
1 Plantation Wk
2 Spencer Wy
3 Whitestone Wk
K4
1 Galley Hl
2 Marnham Rd
3 The Nokes
4 Plantation Ms
5 Robbs Ct
K7
1 The Broadway
2 Earl St
3 Lord St
4 Ottoman Ter
5 Queen's Pl
6 Queen's Rd
7 Shady La
8 Trinity Hall Cl
N9
1 Manor Av
2 Orchard St
N10
1 Edward St
2 Frogmore Rd
3 Henry St
4 Kents Av
5 Millbank
6 St Andrew's Rd
7 White Lion St
8 William St
P7
1 Corfe Cl
2 Denbigh Cl
3 Furtherground
4 Pinewood Gdns
5 Sherbourne Cl
P8
1 Satinwood Ct

Page 36
A10
1 Anelle Ri
2 Hatfield
3 Gunnery Gv
B10
1 Chaffinches Gn
B8
1 Three Corners
C1
1 Catherine Cl
2 Chenies Cl
3 Crackley Meadow
4 Medwick Ms
5 The Melings
D8
1 Birch Leys
2 Half Moon Meadow
3 Lower Emms
4 Rowley Wk
D8
1 Crossett Gn
2 Manan Cl
3 Stroma Cl
4 Stronsay
5 Westray
D9
1 Cloister Garth
2 Lectern La
C10
1 The Poplars

Page 38
C6
1 Bowes Lyon Ms
2 Britton Av
3 French Rw
4 The Maltings
5 New Kent Rd
6 Selby Rd
7 Upper Dagnall St
8 Waddington Rd
C10
1 Deacon Cl
2 Martyr Cl
D7
1 Approach Rd
2 Black Cut
3 Devon Ct
4 Henrys Grant
5 Hopkins Yd
6 Lime Tree Pl
7 Lower Paxton Rd
8 Vernon's Cl
D10
1 Howards Cl
2 Oakcroft Cl

Page 40
F10
1 Alderman Cl
2 Grove Pl
G10
1 Coningsby Cl
2 Silbthorpe Rd

Page 44
D10
1 Priory Cl
E10
1 Orchard Sq
2 Shirley Cl
3 Westlea Rd

Page 46
E10
1 Chestnut Wk

Page 62
C5
1 Niagara Ct
C9
1 Lambton Av
2 Leven Ct
3 Monarch's Wy
4 Park Rd
5 Stoneleigh Cl
C10
1 Dumbarton Av
D9
1 Annette Cl
2 Green Way Gdns
3 Risingholme Cl
D6
1 Foster Ct
2 Guinevere Gdns
3 Roberts Cl
4 Roswell Ct
D10
1 Abbey Rd
2 Lodge Crs
3 Station Ap
4 Trust Rd
E10
1 Fowley Cl
2 Queens Wy

Page 73
H5
1 Langwood Gdns
2 Maple Gv
3 Pinewood Cl
4 Roseberry Ct
H7
1 Hyde Rd
2 Memorial Wy
3 Peace Prospect
H10
1 Barclay Cl
K10
1 The Coppice
2 Rainbow Ct
3 Walverns Cl
L1
1 St Matthews Cl
L10
1 Brownswell Rd
2 King St
3 Red Lion Rd

Page 75
J10
1 The Bartons
2 Fox Cl
3 Georges Mead
4 Oak Tree Cl
5 Romeland
6 Stuart Ct
7 Webber Cl
8 Westview St
9 Yew Tree Wk
L6
1 Badgers Cl
2 Chiltern Cl
3 Holmdale Cl
4 Holme Pk
5 The Pines
P5
1 Cygnet Cl
2 Neaole Cl
3 Niven Cl
4 Palmers Rd
P8
1 Kimbolton Gn
2 Newton Crs

Page 79
J10
1 Homewillow Cl
L8
1 Bentley Ms
2 Sittingbourne Av
3 Teynham Rd
N10
1 Harrow Av

Page 80
B7
1 Broadlands Cl
D10
1 Boundary Rd
J10
1 Abridge Cl
2 Dewgrass Gv
3 The Greenway
4 Hawksmead Cl
5 Kingsfield Wy
D3
1 Coldham Gv
2 Cornhill Dr
3 The Generals Wk
4 Johnby Cl
5 Newport Cl
D10
1 Hamilton Av
2 Hamilton Rd
P1
1 Burbridge Wy

Page 93
H10
1 Colchester Rd
2 Ryefield Cl
3 Waller Dr
G10
1 The Poplars

Page 94
A7
1 Willoughby La
A9
1 Ferriman Ct
2 Pymmes Cl
3 Romney Cl
C10
1 Riverhead Cl
2 Woolston Cl
B10
1 Almond Wy
2 Temsford Cl
C10
1 Wickham Rd
D10
1 Annette Cl
2 Green Way Gdns
3 Risingholme Cl
E7
1 Berwick Cl
2 Coppice Cl
3 Fortnums Acre
4 Jellicoe Gdns
5 Newbolt Rd
6 Rowan Cl
7 Uxbridge Rd (Stanmore)
8 Waleran Cl
E10
1 Harkett Cl

Page 95
H10
1 St Andrews Cl
M10
1 Rembrandt Rd
N10
1 Argyll Gdns
2 Kenmore Gdns
3 Strathmore Gdns
P8
1 Botham Cl
2 Brearley Cl
3 Compton Cl
4 Deanstrook Cl
5 Gatting Cl
6 Grace Cl
7 Hutton Rw
P10
1 Oak Gdns
2 Oakleigh Cl
3 St Alphage Wk

Page 96
B10
1 Kestrel Cl
2 Ludford Cl
3 Spilsby Cl
4 Turnstone Cl
D10
1 Barford Cl

Page 97
H10
1 Cumberland Gdns
2 Freeland Pk
3 Queenswood Pk
4 Windsor Cl
J10
1 College Ter
2 St Michael's La
3 Temple Cl

Page 98
B7
1 Hornbeams Ri
2 Kensington Cl
3 Kettlewell Cl
4 Swaledale Cl
5 Teynham Rd
C6
1 The Avenue
2 Colebrook Wy
3 Massey Cl
4 Westview Ct
5 Yew Tree Ct
C10
1 Muswell Av
E3
1 The Green
F10
1 Station Rd

Page 99
H10
1 Ashley Crs
2 Coombe Rd
3 Gladstone Ms
4 Glynne Rd
5 Noel Park Rd
J5
1 Connaught Wy
2 Handsworth Av
3 Lawrence Av
N4
1 Briary La
2 Dunholme La
3 Northumberland Gdns
N7
1 Bennetts Cl
2 Bradford Cl
3 Castleford Cl
4 Cooperage Cl
5 Langhedge Cl
N10
1 Honeysett Rd
2 Wilson's Av
P1
1 Hamilton Av
2 Hamilton Rd
P10
1 Burbridge Wy
2 Cromer Rd

Page 100
A7
1 Willoughby La
A9
1 Ferriman Ct
2 Pymmes Cl
3 Romney Cl
C10
1 Riverhead Cl
2 Woolston Cl
D10
1 Church Rd
2 Cumberland Rd
3 Oakfield Rd
G7
1 Beaufort Cl
2 Field Ct
3 Thurlow Cl
G8
1 Minerva Rd
2 Wadham Rd
G9
1 Cheshire St

Page 101
H3
1 Berrybank Cl
2 Conference Cl
3 Goldsborough Crs
H5
1 Woodview Av
J2
1 Cambridge Rd
2 Carbis Cl
3 Cranworth Crs
4 Glendower Rd
5 The Green Wk
6 Pentney Rd
7 Queens Wk
8 Richmond Rd
9 Shaftesbury Rd
J10
1 Fernhill Ct
K7
1 Brook Meadow Cl
L10
1 Crediton Hl
2 Honeybourne Rd
M10
1 Frognal Cl
2 Netherhall Wy
N1
1 Claybrook Cl
2 Eagans Cl
3 Elmhurst Av
4 Market Pl
5 New Ash Cl
6 The Walks
N10
1 Beechcroft Rd
2 Cowslip Rd
3 Station Pas
4 Thornwood Cl
P8
1 Ewanrigg Ter
2 Frankland Cl
3 Hillside Cl
4 Manorway
5 Meadway
6 Parkway
P10
1 Norfolk Cl

Page 102
B7
1 Gainsborough Rd
2 Green Wk
3 Latchingdon Gdns
4 Morgan Wy
5 Oakwood Cl

Page 112
C10
1 Turnstone Cl

Page 113
A10
1 Acol Crs
2 West End Rd
C10
1 Doncaster Gdns
1 The Link
P6
1 Thackeray Cl

Page 114
A7
1 Drinkwater Rd
2 Lodgehill Park Cl
3 Monks Ct
4 Thornley Dr
A10
1 New Ct
C9
1 Grainger Cl
2 Pilgrims Cl
C9
1 Cassandra Cl
C10
1 Brasher Cl
2 Hammond Cl
3 Hemery Rd
4 Hutton Cl
5 Matthews Rd
6 Ramsey Cl
7 Tessa Sanderson Wy
8 Wood End Cl
C10
1 Oldfield Cl
2 Oldfield Rd
G4
1 Draycott Av
G10
1 Chestnut Gv

Page 115
H10
1 Beaumont Ct
J10
1 Rokesby Pl
2 Rosecroft Wk
3 Thurlow Gdns
K10
1 Ecclestone Ct
2 Ecclestone Ms
3 Rupert Av
L10
1 Dennis Av
2 Ecclestone Pl
N4
1 Hawthorne Cl
P8
1 Buddings Cir
2 Chalklands
3 Demeta Cl
4 Gervase Cl

Page 116
A10
1 Cygnet Cl
2 Hardie Cl
3 Herne Cl
4 Kestrel Cl
5 Kingfisher Wy
6 Peregrine Cl
C10
1 Iron Bridge Cl
2 Neasden Cl
E10
1 Chapter Rd
F2
1 Brampton La
2 Foster Wk
3 Glebe Crs
4 Harmony Wy
5 Prince Of Wales Cl
6 Somerset Rd
7 Sunny Pl
F10
1 Gardiner Cl
2 Henson Av
3 Kenneth Crs
4 Tracey Av
G3
1 Dairyman Cl
2 Oaklands Ms
3 Sheldon Rd
4 Sylvan Gv
5 Yew Gv

Page 117
H10
1 Rondu Rd
J4
1 Hendon Park Rw
2 Highcroft Gdns
3 Portsdown Ms
4 St George's Cl
J10
1 Broomsleigh St
2 Dornfell St
3 Glastonbury St
4 Hillfield Rd
K10
1 Glenbrook Rd
2 Inglewood Rd
3 Melaris Ms
4 Narcissus Rd
5 Parsifal Rd
6 Solent Rd
7 West End La
L10
1 Crediton Hl
2 Honeybourne Rd

Page 118
A10
1 Belsize Court Garages
2 Belsize Pl
3 Lyndhurst Gdns
4 Hillside Cl
5 Princess Ms
6 Rosslyn Park Ms
J10
1 Fergus Rd
2 Gallia Rd
K10
1 Ashdown Crs
2 Dale Rd
3 Dengil Crs
4 Maiden Pl
5 Weedington Rd
6 Wellesley Pl
P6
1 Feldman Cl
2 Stamford Gv East
3 Stamford Gv West

Page 119
C1
1 Athenaeum Rd
2 Muswell Hill Broadway
3 Queens La
4 Summerland Gdns
5 Woodberry Crs
C9
1 Carrol Cl
2 Evangelist Rd
3 Little Green St
4 Mortimer Ter
5 Sanderson Cl
6 Wesleyan Pl
C10
1 Arctic St
2 Fortess Wk
3 Woodward Cl
4 York Ms
A10
1 Ascham St
2 Countess Rd
3 Dunollie Pl
4 Fortess Gv
5 Frideswide Pl
6 Leighton Pl
7 Leverton St
8 Peckwater St
9 Willingham Ter
C4
1 Charlton King's Rd
2 Hampshire St
F3
1 Aubrey Rd
2 Back La
3 Elder Av
4 Fairfield Gdns
5 Greig Cl
6 Lightfoot Rd
7 Middle Lane Ms
8 Nicholas Gdns
9 Topsfield Cl
F5
1 Oakington Wy
F7
1 Bracey St
2 Pine Gv
3 Rickthorne Rd
4 Stanley Ter
5 Whewell Rd
F8
1 Bowman's Ms
2 Bowman's Pl
3 Hercules Pl
4 Hercules St
F9
1 Bardolph Rd
2 Cardwell Rd
3 Chambers Rd
4 Holbrooke Cl
5 Keighley Cl
6 Staveley Cl
7 Warlters Cl
8 Williamson St
F10
1 Cardozo Rd
2 Hartham Cl
3 Hungerford Rd
4 Middleton Gv
C1
1 Moselle Cl
C2
1 Ferrestone Rd
2 Hillfield Av
3 Temple Rd
E10
1 Chapter Rd
F2
1 Brampton La
2 Foster Wk
3 Glebe Crs
4 Harmony Wy
5 Prince Of Wales Cl
6 Somerset Rd
7 Sunny Pl
G5
1 Holly Pk
2 Mount Pleasant Crs
C6
1 Almington St
2 Dulas St
3 Everleigh St
4 Japan Crs
5 Lorne Rd
6 Stonenest St
7 Turlewray Cl
C7
1 Briset Wy
2 Thistlewood Cl
3 Turle Rd
4 Wesley Cl
5 Woodbridge Cl
G8
1 Annette Rd
2 Kinloch St
3 Newington Barrow Wy
4 Pakeman St
5 Sonderburg Rd
G9
1 Annette Rd
2 Caedmon Rd
3 Quemerford Rd
4 Shelburne Rd
G10
1 Eden Gv
2 Hartnoll St
3 Heddington Gv
4 Hornsey Gv
5 Lough Rd
6 Pollard Cl
7 Rhodes St
8 Stock Orchard Crs
9 Stock Orchard St
10 Sturmer Wy
H10
1 Chillingworth Rd
2 Courtney Rd
3 Horsell Rd
4 Lowther Rd
5 Palmer Pl
6 Rollit St
N10
1 Birkbeck Ms
2 Chester Crs
3 Gateway Ms
4 Gillett Pl
5 Ronalds Rd
6 Sigdon Rd
7 Slaney Pl
8 Witherington Rd
J1
1 Crescent Rd
2 Hawke Park Rd
3 Langham Rd
4 Winchester Rd
J2
1 Alfoxton Av
2 Hallam Rd
3 Harringay Gdns
4 St Margaret's Av
5 Willow Wk
J5
1 Coningsby Rd
J9
1 Coach House La
2 Elphinstone St
3 Highbury Pk
4 Jack Walker Ct
5 Martineau Rd
6 Roseleigh Av
J10
1 Community Rd
2 Falmouth St
3 Major Rd
4 Newton Rd
5 Simons Wk
K9
1 Belton Rd
2 Borthwick Ms
3 Morris Rd
4 Steele Rd
5 Thorne Cl
K10
1 Carolina Cl
2 Cherry Tree Rd
3 Hazel Rd
4 Janson Cl
5 Walnut Gdns
L2
1 Althorne Gdns
2 Audley Cl
3 Bradwell Cl
4 Rayne Ct
5 Woodham Ct
L4
1 Berkeley Rd
2 Fladbury Rd
3 Manchester Rd
4 Moreton Cl
5 Netherton Rd
6 Remington Rd
L10
1 Auriga Ms
2 Hedley Rw
3 Newington Gn
4 Watson Cl
M2
1 Brunswick Rd
2 Clyde Circ
3 Elizabeth Clyde Cl
4 Grove Park Rd
5 Lawrence Yd
6 Lomond Cl
7 Nelson Rd
8 Winns Ms
M3
1 Birstall Rd
2 Brunswick Rd
3 Durnford St
4 Elizabeth Rd
5 Gourley Pl
6 Gourley St
7 Maynard Cl
8 Watts Cl
M4
1 Candler St
2 Chisley Rd
3 Frinton Rd
4 Holmdale Ter
5 Howard Rd
6 Langford Cl
7 Latimer Rd
8 Paignton Rd
9 Perry Ct
10 Thorpe Rd
M5
1 Bergholt Crs
2 Colberg Pl
3 Hillside Rd
M6
1 St Andrew's Ms
M7
1 Barn St
2 Bouverie Ms
3 Fleetwood St
4 Lancell St
5 Stoke Newington Church St
6 Summerhouse Rd
M8
1 Ayrsome Rd
2 Hawksley Rd
3 Marton Rd
4 Painsthorpe Rd
5 Victorian Rd
M10
1 Bradbury St
2 Cressington Cl
3 John Campbell Rd
4 Kingsbury Rd
5 St Jude St
6 Salcombe Rd
7 Selsea Pl
8 Shellgrove Rd
N1
1 Chaplin Cl
2 Chesnut Gv
3 Drapers Rd
4 Felixstowe Rd
5 Holcombe Rd
6 Rycroft Wy
7 Wedmore St
N2
1 Bushmead Cl
2 Colsterworth Rd
3 Copperfield Dr
4 Houghton Rd
5 Talbot Cl
6 Tottenham Gn East
7 Tottenham South Side
8 Walton Rd
N3
1 Ashmount Rd
2 Bernard Rd
3 Earlsmead Rd
4 Enterprise Rw
5 Harold Rd
6 Norman Rd
7 Pembroke Rd
8 Suffield Rd
9 Townsend Rd
10 Westerfield Rd
N5
1 Annette Rd
2 Kinloch St
3 Newington Barrow Wy
4 Pakeman St
5 Sonderburg Rd
N6
1 Margaret Rd
N7
1 Belfast Rd
2 Garnham St
3 Gibson Gdns
4 Martaban Rd
5 Sanford La
6 Stoke Newington Common
7 Wilmer Pl
P4
1 Ashley Rd
2 Burdock Rd
3 Cape Rd
4 Chesnut Gv
5 Fairbanks Rd
6 The Hale
7 High Cross Rd
8 Malvern Rd
9 Station Rd
P7
1 Briggeford Cl
2 Geldeston Rd
P8
1 Elmton Wy
2 Ottaway St
P10
1 Langford Cl
2 Lushington Ter

Page 120
A7
1 Brampton Cl
2 Charnwood Cl
3 Comberton Rd
4 Rossington St
5 Southwold Rd
A9
1 Apprentice Wy
2 Downs La
3 Downs Rd
4 Lower Clapton Rd
5 The Mothers Sq
6 Sladen Pl
A10
1 Athlone Cl
2 Brett Pas
3 Gould Ter
4 Institute Pl
5 Kenmure Rd
6 Spurstowe Ter
B10
1 Furrow La
2 Isabella Rd
3 Rowe La
4 St John's Church Rd
5 Sutton Pl
6 Sutton Sq
C10
1 Crozier Ter
2 Mackintosh La
3 St Barnabas Ter
D3
1 Carisbrooke Rd
2 Courtenay Rd
3 The Crescent
4 Frederic St
5 Grange Rd
6 Manning Rd
7 Maude Rd
8 St James's Av
9 St James's St
10 Stephenson St
D9
1 Durrington Rd
2 Kenworthy Rd
3 Kingsmead Wy
4 Penda's Mead
5 Ruddington Cl
6 Sunnyhill Cl
D10
1 Kemey's St
2 Lyneham Wk
3 Studley Cl
4 Swinnerton St
E3
1 Ansar Gdns
2 Arkley Crs
3 Arkley Rd
4 Brunner Rd
5 Glen Rd
6 Mission Gv
7 Side Rd
8 Vernon Rd
E5
1 Boundary Av
2 Broomfield
3 Harris St
4 Herbert Rd
5 Samantha Cl
6 Sybourn St
7 Sylvester Rd
8 Verulam Av
9 Wetherden St
E10
1 Crowfoot Cl
2 Lee Conservancy Rd
3 Lockgate Cl
4 Poplar Ct
F3
1 Connaught Rd
2 Exeter Rd
3 First Av
4 Leamington Av
5 Second Av
6 Sylvan Rd
F5
1 Larch Rd
2 Magnolia St
3 Meadows Cl
4 Simonds Rd
5 Wiseman Rd
F7
1 Allan Barclay Cl
2 Barry Av
3 Hillside Rd
4 Sherboro Rd
5 Westcott Cl
G3
1 Grosvenor Ri East
2 Randolph Rd
3 St Stephen's Rd
4 St Stephen's Rd
5 West St
G5
1 Eden Gv
2 Hartnoll St
3 Heddington Gv
4 Hornsey Gv
5 Lough Rd
6 Pollard Cl
7 Rhodes St
8 Stock Orchard Crs
9 Stock Orchard St
10 Sturmer Wy
H4
1 Chillingworth Rd
2 Courtney Rd
3 Horsell Rd
4 Lowther Rd
5 Palmer Pl
6 Rollit St
H9
1 Etchingham Rd
J2
1 Chesnut Av North
2 Upper Walthamstow Rd
J8
1 Anglian Rd
2 Claremont Rd
3 Francis Rd
4 Holloway Rd
5 Warren Rd
J10
1 Cheshire Cl
M7
1 Binstead Cl
2 Cambus Cl
3 Fossdyke Cl
4 Kilpatrick Wy
5 West Quay

Page 121
H2
1 Brookfield Av
2 Browning Cl
3 Evelyn Rd
4 Leyburn Cl
5 Ravenswood Rd
6 Rosslyn Rd
N5
1 Channing Cl
N6
1 Dury Falls Cl
P3
1 Belmont Av

Page 122
B10
1 Cranbourne Cl
C10
1 St Mary's Ap
D10
1 Reesland Cl
F10
1 Pownsett Ter
2 Saint Leonards Gdns

Page 123
J10
1 Brockdish Av
L10
1 Constable Ms
2 Davington Gdns
3 Hogarth Rd
M10
1 Kirklees Rd
N10
1 Christopher Gdns
2 Durell Gdns

Page 124
E3
1 Cherry St
2 Pettley Gdns
G10
1 Dunningford Cl

Page 125
N7
1 Aldwych Cl
2 Broadstone Rd
N10
1 Cumbrae Cl

Page 128
B5
1 Baldwin Rd
2 Bay Tree Ct
3 Green Lane Ct
4 Old Fives Ct

Page 126
H10
1 Hall Park Rd
2 Londons Cl
A10
1 Tadlows Cl
B5
1 Murfitt Cl

Page 128
B10
1 Biddles Cl
2 Chapels Cl
3 Duchess St
4 Molyns Ms
5 Roxwell Cl
6 Waterman Wy
E10
1 Cobham Cl
2 Manor Ct
3 Marcia Ct
4 Palace Ct
5 Plaines Cl
6 Streamside
7 Trumper Wy
F8
1 Bradford Rd
2 Durham Av
3 Eastbourne Rd
4 Falmouth Rd
5 Glasgow Rd
6 Gresham Rd
F9
1 Corfe Gdns
2 Dunster Gdns
3 Fotheringay Rd
F10
1 Adam Cl
2 Egremont Rd
3 Raleigh Cl
4 Tamarisk Wy
G9
1 Bunten Meade
2 Corse Meade
3 Oakfield Av
4 Stoney Meade
5 Summerlea

Page 129
H10
1 Bath Rd
2 Cranbourne Cl
3 Farnham Rd
4 Grace Ct
5 Hadlow Ct
J10
1 Hartland Cl
K10
1 Conegar Ct
2 Gatewick Cl
3 Lansdowne Ct
4 Red Ct
L10
1 Littledown Rd
H10
1 Heathcote Av
2 Peplow Cl
P9
1 Cousins Cl
2 Elder Cl
3 Maple Av
4 Milburn Dr
5 Spinney Cl
P10
1 Windermere Wy

Page 131
H10
1 Eastholme
J4
1 Butts Piece
J10
1 Halsend
L6
1 Brentford Cl
2 Cosgrove Cl
3 Dove Cl
4 Dunsmore Cl
5 Fellowes Cl
6 Hobart Dr
7 Homefield Cl
8 Repens Wy
9 Wendover Cl
L8
1 Grebe Av
2 Ibis Wy
3 Lapwing Wy
4 Shearwater Wy
M7
1 Binstead Cl
2 Cambus Cl
3 Fossdyke Cl
4 Kilpatrick Wy
5 West Quay

Page 132
A10
1 Cedar Av
C10
1 Bennetsfield Cl
D6
1 De Salis Rd
2 Fulham Cl
3 Paget Rd
4 Russet Cl
5 Sheridan Cl
6 Towers Av
E10
1 Archdale Ct
F2
1 Brondesbury Pk
F3
1 Chelmsford Cl
2 Egerton Gdns
3 Trevelyan Gdns
F4
1 Station Ter
F5
1 Hiley Rd
F7
1 Pangbourne Dr
2 Snarsgate St
F8
1 Caverswall St
2 Glenroy St
3 Latimer Pl
4 Nascot St
5 Stable Wy
6 Westview Cl
F9
1 Batman Cl
F10
1 Hopgood St
2 Poplar Ms
3 Swindon St

Page 133
H10
1 Eastholme
J4
1 Butts Piece
J10
1 Halsend
L6
1 Brentford Cl
2 Cosgrove Cl
3 Dove Cl
4 Dunsmore Cl
5 Fellowes Cl
6 Hobart Dr
7 Homefield Cl
8 Repens Wy
9 Wendover Cl
L8
1 Grebe Av
2 Ibis Wy
3 Lapwing Wy
4 Shearwater Wy

Page 134
A10
1 Lyndhurst Av
C3
1 St Laurence's Cl
C5
1 Bayford Rd
2 Regent St
3 Warfield Rd
4 Wellington Rd
C6
1 Admiral Ms
2 Barlby Gdns
3 Canal Cl
4 Humber Dr
5 Maple Wk
6 Matthews Cl
7 St John's Ter
8 Treverton St
C7
1 Archway Cl
2 Rootes Dr
3 St Charles Sq
4 St Helen's Gdns
C8
1 Bridge Cl
2 Charlotte Ms
3 St Helen's Gdns
G9
1 Blechynden St
2 Evesham St
3 Mortimer Sq
4 Stoneleigh St
5 Waynflete St

Page 135
H10
1 Purslewardens Cl
2 St Helen's Rd
3 Wrotham Rd
J10
1 Kerrison Pl
D10
1 Denehurst Gdns
2 Mill Hill Gv
3 Mount Av
4 Narrow St
5 Woodlands Av
P10
1 Cromwell Rd
2 Edgecote Cl
3 Hooper's Ms
4 Locarno Rd
5 Melville Villas Rd
6 Steyne Rd

Page 136
A10
1 Barrs Rd
2 Kingthorpe Rd
A6
1 Gorst Rd
2 St Leonard's Ter
J10
1 Anderson Cl
2 Curtis Dr
3 Ferguson Dr
4 Friars Gdns
5 Simpson Dr
L10
1 Littledown Rd
B2
1 Bishop Wy
2 Guilsborough Cl
3 Norfolk Rd
4 Northcote Rd
5 Suffolk Rd
6 Taylor's La
B3
1 Bolton Rd
2 Charlton Rd
3 Connaught Rd
4 Craven Pk
5 Greenhill Pk
6 Greenhill Rd
7 Langdon Ct
8 Park Rd
B9
1 Beechwood Gv
2 East Acton La
3 Kingsdown Av
4 Trinity Wy
B10
1 Cubitt Sq
1 Curricle St
C10
1 Wharncliffe Dr
1 Caple Rd
2 High Street Harlesden
3 Honeywood Rd
4 Nightingale Rd
5 Ranelagh Rd
6 Tavistock Rd
7 Tubbs Rd
1 Clairville Gdns
2 Maudesville Cottages
3 Silverdale Ct
4 Warwick Cl
5 York Cl
D10
1 Coningham Ms
2 Westbridge Rd
E8
1 Maurice Ct
2 Moneyer St
3 Terrick St
E9
1 Bennelong Cl
2 Canada Wy
3 Commonwealth Av
4 Dicando Gv
5 India Wy
E10
1 Burdett Cl
2 Cheringford Rd
3 Maunder Rd
1 Archdale Ct
F2
1 Brondesbury Pk
F3
1 Chelmsford Cl
2 Egerton Gdns
3 Trevelyan Gdns
F4
1 Station Ter
F5
1 Hiley Rd
F7
1 Pangbourne Dr
2 Snarsgate St
F8
1 Caverswall St
2 Glenroy St
3 Latimer Pl
4 Nascot St
5 Stable Wy
6 Westview Cl
1 Bonchurch Rd
2 Bowmans Cl
3 Broomfield Rd
4 Kirkfield Cl
5 Milford Rd
6 Princes Rd
7 Regina Ter
F9
1 Batman Cl
F10
1 Hopgood St
2 Poplar Ms
3 Swindon St
1 Brownlow Cl
2 Chignell Pl
3 Hatfield Rd
4 Leeland Rd
5 Melbourne Av
6 Talbot Rd
7 Walsingham Rd
8 William's Rd

C8
1 Albert Gdns
2 Arbour St
3 Boulcott St
4 Bower St
5 Caroline St
6 Chudleigh St
7 Devonport St
8 Dunelm St
9 Havering St
10 Head St
11 Lighterman Ms
12 Old Church Rd
13 Pitsea Pl
14 Pitsea St
15 Ratcliffe Cross St
16 Ronald St
17 Senrab St
18 Stepney Cswy

C10
1 Abbotshade Rd
2 Burnside Cl
3 Bury Cl
4 Byelands Cl
5 Deck Cl
6 Gunwhale Cl
7 Hull Cl
8 Katherine Cl
9 Keel Cl
10 Midship Cl
11 Princes Riverside Rd
12 St Paul's Av

D5
1 Longfellow Rd

D7
1 Dupont St
2 Durham Rw
3 Elsa St
4 Halley St
5 Maroon St
6 Rhodeswell Rd
7 Whitehorse Rd

D8
1 Bekesbourne St
2 Blount St
3 Branch Rd
4 Brenton St
5 Brunton Pl
6 Chaseley St
7 Conder St
8 Mill Pl
9 Parnham St
10 Raby St
11 Troon St
12 Wakeling St
13 York St

D9
1 Branch Rd
2 Elizabeth St
3 Frederick Sq
4 Helena Sq
5 Shoulder Of Mutton Alley
6 Sophia Sq
7 Spert St
8 William St

D10
1 Bevin Cl
2 Farrins Rents
3 Foundry Cl
4 Globe Pond Rd
5 Rotherhithe St
6 Russia Dock Rd
7 Staples Cl
8 Stave Yard La

E1
1 Southmoor Wy

E2
1 Cadogan St
2 St Marks Ga

E3
1 Alma Ter
2 Annie Besant Cl
3 O'shea Gv
4 Pulteney Cl
5 Ranwell Cl
6 Roman Rd
7 Tamar Cl
8 Usher Rd
9 Wendon St
10 Wright's Rd

E5
1 Merchant St

E6
1 Hamlets Wy
2 Lockhart St
3 Maritime St
4 Midlothian Rd
5 Mossford St

E7
1 Baythorne St
2 Callingham Cl
3 Huddart St
4 Kirk's Pl
5 Leopold St
6 Robeson St
7 Seager Pl

E8
1 Island Rw
2 Norway Pl
3 St Anne's Pas
4 St Anne's Rw
5 St Anne St
6 Salmon St
7 Wilson's Pl

E9
1 Bate St
2 Brightlingsea Pl
3 Limehouse Cswy
4 The Mitre
5 Rich St
6 Ropemaker's Flds
7 Stocks Pl
8 Three Colt St
9 Trinidad St

E10
1 Silver Wk

F1
1 Felstead Rd
2 Leabank Sq

F2
1 Hepscott Rd
2 Remus Rd
3 Rothbury Rd

F3
1 Maverton Rd

F4
1 Hartfield Ter
2 Wick La

F5
1 Dimson Crs
2 Mornington Gv

F6
1 Fairfoot Rd
2 Ireton St

F7
1 Celandine Cl
2 Furze St
3 Hawgood St

F8
1 Nankin St
2 Stainsby Pl

F9
1 Dingle Gdns
2 Garford St
3 Kemp Dr
4 Limehouse
5 Ming St
6 Morant St
7 Pinefield Cl
8 Premiere Pl
9 Rosefield
10 Rugg St

F10
1 North Colonnade

G5
1 Bromley High St
2 Franklin St
3 Glebe Ter
4 Powis Rd
5 St Leonard's St
6 Washington Cl
7 William Guy Gdns

G6
1 Broxbourne House
2 Devas St
3 Tibbatt's Rd

G7
1 Balladier Wk
2 Barchester St
3 Chadbourn St
4 Clutton St
5 Daniel Bolt Cl
6 Godalming Rd
7 Passfield Dr

G10
1 Churchill Pl

Page 141

H8
1 Aberfeldy St
2 Adderley St
3 Athol Sq
4 Byron St
5 Culloden St
6 Kirkmichael Rd
7 Mills Gv
8 Susannah St
9 Tayburn Cl

H10
1 Bridge House Quay
2 Managers St
3 St Lawrence St
4 Warrington Pl

J1
1 Alma St
2 Amber St
3 Grove Crescent Rd
4 Oxford Rd
5 Salway Pl
6 Service Route No 3
7 Simons Wk
8 Waddington St
9 Whitear Wk

J5
1 Dell Cl
2 Mcewan Wy
3 Park La
4 Stanley Rd
5 Union St
6 Ward Rd

J8
1 Ada Gdns
2 Benledi St
3 Ettrick St
4 Goodway Gdns
5 Lansbury Gdns
6 Rosemary Dr
7 Sorrel La
8 Wooster Gdns

K2
1 Covier Cl
2 Hyderabad Wy
3 Mandrake Wy
4 Mantle Wy
5 Mark St
6 Shirley Rd
7 Tramway Av
8 Welfare Rd
9 White Rd
10 Widdin St
11 Worland Rd

K7
1 Birch Cl

L7
1 Bernard Cassidy St
2 Cooper St
3 Formunt Cl
4 Lawrence St
5 Malmesbury Rd
6 Mary St
7 Trinity Gdns

L8
1 Burke St
2 Caxton St North
3 Emily St
4 Fendt Cl
5 George St
6 Hoy St
7 Murdock Cl
8 Sabbarton St
9 St Luke's St
10 Turner St
11 Woodstock Av
12 Wouldham Rd

M3
1 Crescent Ms

M6
1 Beatrice Cl
2 Boyce Wy
3 Braemar Rd
4 Clove St
5 Edward St
6 Graham Rd
7 Ingal Rd
8 Seaton Cl
9 Upland Rd
10 Warmington St

M10
1 Badminton Ms
2 Britannia Ga
3 Charles Flemwell Ms
4 Tom Jenkinson Rd

N3
1 Bishops Av
2 Lawrence Rd
3 Prince's Ter

N5
1 Augurs La
2 Clifford Cl
3 Dongola Rd West
4 Dragonfly Cl
5 St Quintin Rd

N6
1 Jones Rd
2 Rowntree Rd

N7
1 Cranley Rd
2 Denmark St
3 Vanguard St

N8
1 Hartington Rd
2 Oyster Catchers Cl
3 Pheasant Cl
4 Throckmorten Rd

N9
1 Chaundler Rd
2 Western Gateway
3 Wood St

N10
1 Beaulieu Av
2 Hanameel St
3 Pier St
4 Rayleigh Rd
5 Westwood Rd

P1
1 Ashley Rd
2 Walpole Rd
3 Washington Rd
4 Waterloo Rd

P3
1 Florence Rd
2 Greenleaf Rd
3 Tolpuddle Av

P4
1 Nile Rd

P5
1 Angus Rd
2 Oban St

P7
1 Salomons Rd

P8
1 Lawson Cl
2 Randolph Ap

Page 142

A5
1 Alfred St
2 Belmont Gv
3 Clement Cl
4 Clifton Gdns
5 Essex Place Sq
6 Holly Rd
7 Kirton Cl
8 South Pde

A10
1 Larches Av

B1
1 Bradford Rd
2 Hawkshead Rd
3 Rugby Rd
4 Vanburgh St

B4
1 Alkerden Rd
2 Ingress St
3 Prince Of Wales Rd
4 Swanscombe Rd

C4
1 Dovehouse Mead

Page 143

L10
1 Booth Cl
2 Campion Cl
3 Galsworthy Cl
4 Waterfield Cl
5 Woolf Cl

Page 152

G8
1 Ely Rd
2 Epsom Sq

G10
1 The Hermitage
2 St Anns Rd

C10
1 Steam Farm La

Page 153

J8
1 St Dunstan's Rd

K8
1 Aston Gn
2 Badger Cl
3 Ermine Cl
4 Musquash Wy

1 Selwyn Cl

Page 154

A10
1 Carlton Ter
2 Ivy Rd
3 Wareham St

B10
1 Atcham Rd

C10
1 Dalmeny Crs
2 Leigh Rd

D10
1 Leigham Dr

E10
1 Weavers Cl

F5
1 Rowberry Cl
2 Wheatsheaf La

F8
1 Stockhurst Cl

F9
1 Abbotstone Rd
2 Stanbridge Rd

F10
1 Pettiward Cl

G9
1 Manor House Wy

Page 155

J5
1 Albany Pl
2 Albany Rd
3 Alexandra Rd
4 Brockshot Cl
5 Brook La North
6 Half Acre Ms
7 Hamilton Rd
8 Sidney Gdns
9 Westbury Pl

J10
1 Park La
2 Quadrant Rd

K10
1 Catherine Cl
2 Clarence St
3 Drummonds Av
4 Duncan Rd
5 Larkfield Rd
6 The Quadrant
7 St John's Gv
8 St John's Rd
9 Salisbury Rd
10 Sydney Rd

L10
1 Adelaide Rd
2 Crown Rd

M2
1 Gunnersbury Av

M5
1 Old Dock Cl
2 Waterloo Pl

M7
1 Lonsdale Ms
2 North Av
3 Station Ap

N10
1 Coval Gdns
2 Langdale Cl

P10
1 Medcroft Gdns
2 Penrhyn Crs
3 Wellside Gdns

P2
1 Beaulieu Rd
2 Cleveland Rd
3 Reynolds Rd
4 Steele Rd
5 Vincent Rd

P3
1 Colonial Dr
2 Ravenscroft Rd
3 Seymour Rd
4 Wolseley Rd

P9
1 Beechcroft Rd
2 Cromwell Rd
3 Eastbourne Gdns
4 Hanson Cl
5 Langdon Pl
6 Moore Cl
7 Waldeck Rd

Page 156

A7
1 Firbank Pl
2 Fleetwood Cl
3 Glencairne Cl
4 Goldcrest Cl
5 Heathfield Cl
6 Hickman Cl
7 Hogarth Cl
8 Meadowsweet Cl
9 Partridge Cl
10 Rigden St

B10
1 Constance St

C4
1 Ben Tillet St
2 Muir St
3 Rawsthorne Cl
4 Sheldrake Cl

C10
1 Dolphin La
2 Lawless St
3 Malam Gdns
4 Poplar Bath St
5 Shirbutt St
6 Smythe St
7 Stoneyard La

Page 157

H3
1 Avonmore Pl
2 Avonmore Rd
3 Bishop King's Rd
4 Earsby St
5 Fitz-george Av
6 Fitzjames Av
7 Glazbury Rd
8 Gliddon Rd
9 Gunterstone Rd
10 Perham Rd

N2
1 Imperial College Rd

N3
1 Barnaby Pl
2 Bute St
3 Cromwell Ms
4 Cromwell Pl
5 Exhibition Rd
6 Glendower Pl
7 Kendrick Ms
8 Kendrick Pl
9 Manson Ms
10 Onslow Ms East
11 Onslow Ms West
12 Queensberry Ms West
13 Queensberry Pl
14 Queensberry Way
15 Reece Ms
16 Sumner Place Ms
17 Sydney Cl
18 Thurloe Place Ms

K1
1 Argyll Rd
2 Campden Gv
3 Campden House Cl
4 Drayson Ms
5 Gloucester Wk
6 Gordon Pl
7 Holland St
8 Hornton Pl
9 Melon Pl
10 Observatory Gdns
11 Phillimore Pl
12 St Tor Gdns
13 Upper Phillimore Gdns

K2
1 Adam & Eve Ms
2 Earls Ter
3 Eden Cl
4 Iverna Ct
5 Leonard Ct
6 Pater St
7 Pembroke Ms
8 Pembroke Gardens Cl
9 Scarsdale Vls
10 Troy Ct
11 Wynnstay Gdns

K4
1 Empress Pl
2 Kramer Ms

K7
1 Delvino Rd
2 Harbledown Rd
3 Heathman's Rd
4 Pursers Cross Rd
5 Shottendane Rd

K10
1 Prospect Cottages

L1
1 Cambridge Pl
2 Carmel Ct
3 Derry St
4 Gregory Pl
5 Holland St
6 Kensington Church Wk
7 Kensington Ct
8 Kensington Ct Pl
9 Kensington Court Ms
10 Prince Of Wales Ter
11 Vicarage Ga
12 Young St

L2
1 Ansdell St
2 Ansdell Ter
3 Beatrice Pl
4 Blithfield St
5 Cheniston Gdns
6 Cornwall Gardens Wk
7 Cornwall Ms West
8 Devonshire Cl
9 Kensington Court Ms
10 Kensington Court Pl
11 Lexham Gdns
12 Radley Ms
13 St John's Vls
14 St Margarets La
15 St Mary's Ga
16 St Mary's Pl
17 Scarsdale Pl

L5
1 Cathcart Rd
2 Redcliffe St
3 Tregunter Rd

L7
1 Edith Rw
2 Emden St
3 Fulmead St
4 Hyde La

P5
1 Bellamy Cl
2 Challoner Crs
3 Franklin Cl
4 May St
5 Stanier Cl

Page 158

A3
1 Blacklands Ter
2 Lennox Gardens Ms
3 Lincoln St
4 Rosemoor St
5 Sprimont Pl

A6
1 Anderson St
2 Bywater St
3 Cheltenham Ter
4 Coulson St
5 Durham Pl
6 Markham St
7 Ormonde Ga
8 Ralston St
9 Redesdale St
10 Tedworth Sq
11 Wellington Sq
12 Woodfall St

A8
1 Atherton St
2 Latchmere St
3 Matthews St
4 Poyntz Rd
5 Sleivemore Cl

A10
1 Hafer Rd

B1
1 Belgrave Ms North
2 Capener's Cl
3 Duke Of Wellington Pl
4 Kinnerton Yd
5 Old Barrack Yd
6 Pembroke Cl

B2
1 Belgrave Ms South
2 Chesham Cl
3 Chesham Ms
4 Chesham Pl
5 Groom Pl
6 Halkin Ms
7 Halkin Pl
8 Lowndes Cl
9 Lyall Ms
10 Lyall Ms West
11 Lyall St

B3
1 Boscobel Pl
2 Burton Ms
3 Cundy St
4 Eaton Ms
5 Eaton Ms West
6 Eaton Terrace Ms
7 Gerald Rd
8 Grosvenor Cottages
9 Ormonde Pl
10 Sedding St
11 Skinner Pl
12 Sloane Ter Ms
13 Symons St
14 West Eaton Pl
15 West Eaton Place Ms
16 Whittaker St

B4
1 Bloomfield Ter
2 Bunhouse Ms
3 Passmore St
4 Ranelagh Gv
5 Rembrandt Cl
6 Sloane Ct East
7 Sloane Ct West

M4
1 The Boltons
2 Boltons Pl
3 Cavaye Pl
4 Eagle Pl
5 Harley Gdns
6 Milborne Gv
7 Priory Wk

M5
1 Hollywood Ms
2 Oakfield St
3 Redcliffe Pl
4 Wintertons Pl

M6
1 Ashburnham Rd
2 Cremorne Rd
3 Damer Ter
4 Edith Ter
5 Meek St
6 Rewell St
7 Tadema Rd
8 Thornlike Cl
9 Upcerne Rd
10 Uverdale Rd

N4
1 Cranley Gdns
2 Hugh Gaitskell Cl
3 Margaret Ingram Cl
4 Mulgrave Rd
5 Tilton St

J7
1 Beaconsfield Wk
2 Epple Rd

P2
1 Banbury St
2 Colestown St
3 Coppock Cl
4 Crombie Ms
5 Frere St
6 Nepaul Rd
7 Winders Rd

P9
1 Albert Ms
2 Bremner Rd
3 Canning Pl
4 Canning Place Ms
5 Elvaston Ms
6 Elvaston Pl
7 Gore St
8 Grenville Pl
9 Hyde Park Ga
10 Kensington Ga
11 Kynance Pl
12 Petersham La
13 Queen's Gate Gdns
14 Queen's Gate Ms
15 Queen's Gate Place Ms
16 Queen's Gate Ter

N5
1 Camera Pl
2 Henniker Ms
3 Hobury St
4 Lavender Cl
5 Moravian Pl

N6
1 Apollo Pl
2 Thorney Crs
3 Whistlers Av

N7
1 Bolingbroke Rd
2 Granfield St
3 Vicarage Wk

N8
1 Musjid Rd
2 Orville Rd

N9
1 Benham Cl
2 Fenner Sq
3 Fowler Cl
4 Heaver Rd
5 John Parker Sq
6 Kambala Rd
7 Mantua St
8 Weekley Sq
9 Winstanley Rd
10 Wye St

N10
1 Beverley Cl
2 Kennet Cl
3 Oberstein Rd
4 Sangora Rd
5 Windrush Cl

P1
1 Gate Ms
2 Moncorvo Cl
3 Montpelier Ter
4 Rutland Gate Ms

P2
1 Egerton Gdns
2 Egerton Gardens Ms
3 Egerton Pl
4 Egerton Ter
5 Ennismore Ms
6 Fairholt St
7 Glynde Ms
8 Montpelier Ms
9 Montpelier Sq
10 Ovington Ms
11 Ovington Sq
12 Relton Ms
13 Rutland Ms South
14 Rutland St
15 Sterling St
16 Trevor Sq
17 Trevor St

P3
1 Alexander Sq
2 Crescent Pl
3 Leverett St
4 Marlborough St
5 Pelham Pl

P4
1 Danube St
2 Flood Wk
3 Guthrie St

P5
1 Chelsea Manor Gdns
2 Justice Wk
3 Lawrence St
4 Lordship Pl
5 Petyt Pl
6 Phene St

P6
1 Kingswater Pl
2 Paveley Dr
3 Radstock St

P7
1 Ethelburga St
2 Henty Cl
3 Hyde La

P9
1 Bramlands Cl
2 Falcon Ter
3 Fownes St
4 Grant Rd
5 Lavender Ter
6 Marney Rd
7 Mossbury Rd
8 Wolfencroft Cl

P10
1 Abyssinia Cl
2 Abyssinia Rd
3 Barnard Ms
4 Buckmaster Rd
5 Prested Rd
6 St John's Rd

Page 159

B7
1 Alexandra Av
2 Charlotte Despard Av
3 Chesney St
4 Cupar Rd
5 Francis Chichester Wy
6 Harpsden St
7 Parkside St
8 Rawson St

B9
1 Basnett Rd
2 Brassey Sq
3 Craven Ms
4 Evesham Wy
5 Marmion Ms
6 Rush Hill Ms
7 Tipthorpe Rd
8 Tyneham Rd
9 Wickersley Rd
10 Wycliffe Rd

C2
1 Beeston Pl
2 Chester Ms
3 Chester Square Ms
4 Dorset Ms
5 Eaton La
6 Grosvenor Gardens
7 Grosvenor Gardens Ms South
8 Little Chester St
9 Lygon Pl
10 Ms North
11 Victoria Sq
12 Warwick Rw
13 Wilton Ms

C8
1 Broughton St
2 Coleridge Cl
3 Froude St
4 Gambetta St
5 Montefiore St
6 Peardon St
7 St Philip Sq

C9
1 Cedars Ms

D1
1 Ambassadors' Ct
2 Marlborough Rd

D2
1 Bressenden Pl
2 Buckingham Ms
3 Catherine Pl
4 Emery Hill St
5 Greencoat Pl
6 Palace Pl
7 Pine Apple Ct
8 Stag Pl
9 Vandon St

D3
1 Bloomburg St
2 Charlwood Pl
3 Churton Pl
4 Coburg Cl
5 Denbigh Ms
6 Denbigh St
7 Eccleston Square Ms
8 Gillingham Ms
9 Gillingham Rw
10 Gillingham St
11 Hatherley St
12 Neathouse Pl
13 Neathouse Ms
14 Tachbrook Ms
15 Udall St
16 Upper Tachbrook St
17 Vane St
18 Walcott St
19 Warwick Pl North
20 Warwick Square Ms
21 West Ms

D6
1 Bradmead

D10
1 Downer's Cottages
2 The Polygon

E2
1 Abbey Orchard Street Est
2 Arneway St
3 Artillery Rw
4 Chadwick St
5 Dacre St
6 Dean Farrar St
7 Greycoat Pl
8 Greycoat St
9 Little Smith St
10 Perkin's Rents
11 Rochester St
12 St Ermin's Hl
13 St Matthew St
14 The Sanctuary

E3
1 Bulinca St
2 Esterbrooke St
3 Fynes St
4 Greycoat La
5 Hugh Pl
6 Osbert St
7 Rutherford St
8 St Oswulf St
9 Stanford St
10 Thorndike St

E8
1 Wandsworth Rd

E9
1 Gauden Cl
2 Littlebury Rd
3 Shamrock St
4 Sudbourne Rd

E10
1 Abbeville Ms
2 Carfax Pl
3 Clement Av
4 Cresset St
5 Gavel St
6 Halpin Pl
7 Hearn's Buildings
8 John Maurice Cl
9 Larissa St
10 Paragon Ms
11 Salisbury Cl

F2
1 Canon Rw
2 Little George St
3 Little Sanctuary

F3
1 Barton St
2 Cowley St
3 Dean Bradley St
4 Dean Stanley St
5 Dean Trench St
6 Little College St
7 Lord North St
8 Smith Sq

F4
1 Dean Ryle St

F5
1 New Spring Gardens Wk
2 South Lambeth Pl
3 Trenchold St

F6
1 Walberswick St
2 Walton Cl
3 Wheatsheaf La

F7
1 St Barnabas Vls

F8
1 Clarence Wk

F9
1 Cottage Gv
2 Fenwick Cl
3 Lendal Ter

F10
1 Ashmere Gv
2 Felmersham Rd
3 Hetherington Rd
4 Linom Rd
5 Tintern St

G1
1 Addington St
2 Chicheley St

G3
1 Ingram Ct
2 Lilac Pl
3 Randall Rw

G4
1 Auckland St
2 Brangton Rd
3 Dolland St
4 Gasholder St
5 Loughborough St
6 Wynyard Ter

G5
1 Kennington Gv
2 Meadow Rd

G7
1 Johnston Cl
2 Stockwell Ter

G8
1 Broomgrove Rd
2 Eastcote St
3 Fenton Cl
4 Stockwell La
5 Wordsworth Rd

G9
1 Bellefields Rd
2 Burgoyne Rd
3 Bythorn St
4 Nealden St

G10
1 Glendall St
2 Shannon Gv

H3
1 Hornbeam Sq
2 Kempsford Rd
3 St Mary's Gdns
4 St Mary's Wk
5 Saunders St

H5
1 Brixton Rd
2 Hanover Gdns
3 Pegasus Pl

H7
1 Melbourne Ms
2 Melbourne Sq

H8
1 Burton Rd
2 Ingleborough St
3 Peckford Pl
4 St Lawrence Wy

H9
1 Astoria Wk
2 Beehive Pl
3 Knowle Cl
4 Pope's Rd

H10
1 Brixton Ov
2 Oxonian St
3 Spurling Rd
4 Zenoria St

M6
1 Cottage Gn
2 Dowlas St
3 Lynbrook Cl
4 Marchwood Cl
5 Melbury Dr

M7
1 Brunswick Vls
2 Muscatel Pl
3 Redbridge Gdns

N1
1 Ainsworth Cl
2 Cactus Cl
3 Canning Cross

N2
1 Bridewain St
2 Canon Murnane Rd
3 Gedling Pl
4 Neckinger St

N3
1 Alscot Wy
2 Burnham Cl
3 Buttermere Cl
4 Keats Cl
5 Longfellow Wy
6 Setchell Rd
7 Wordsworth Rd

N4
1 Mercator Pl

N5
1 Pennack Rd
2 Sumner Rd

N6
1 Boathouse Wk
2 Branch Pl
3 Chandler Wy
4 Hordle Prom North
5 Lidgate Rd
6 Mattingly Wy
7 Tilbury Cl

N7
1 Charles Coveney Rd
2 Crane St
3 Finch Ms
4 Grummant Rd
5 Lyndhurst Sq
6 Sumner Av
7 Sumner Rd

N8
1 Azenby Rd
2 Highshore Rd

N9
1 Everthorpe Rd

N10
1 Frogley Rd
2 Oxonian St
3 Spurling Rd
4 Zenoria St

P1
1 Bevington St
2 Damsel Ct
3 East La
4 Leeson Rd
5 Marcus Garvey Wy
6 Farthing Alley
7 Flockton St
8 John Felton Rd
9 Loxford St
10 Waterside Cl

P2
1 Linsey St
2 Major Rd
3 Ness St
4 Pritter Rd
5 Storks Rd
6 Sun Pas
7 Woolstaplers Wy

P3
1 Strathnairn St

P4
1 Acanthus Dr
2 Ainslade Dr
3 Cordelia Cl
4 Culloden St

P5
1 Lovegrove St
2 Maismore St
3 Shard's Sq

P6
1 Freda Corbett Cl
2 Hereford Retreat
3 Sister Mabel's Wy
4 Wentworth Cres

P7
1 Clayton Rd
2 Collyer Pl
3 Mission Pl
4 Porthbury Cl
5 Robert Keen Cl
6 Staffordshire St

P8
1 Atwell Rd
2 Moncrieff St
3 Parkstone Rd
4 Reedham St
5 William Margrie Cl

P9
1 Fenwick Gv
2 Sandison St
3 St Stephen's Gv
4 William Cl

Page 160

A8
1 Claude Rd
2 Firbank Rd
3 Godman Rd
4 Harders Rd
5 Lulworth Rd
6 Nazareth Cl
7 Sandlings Cl

K10
1 Bankwell Rd
2 Belmont Park Cl
3 John Wooley Cl
4 Kingswood Rd
5 Michaels Cl

L10
1 Osborn Ter

L5
1 Lyndale Cl
2 Peachum Rd

M9
1 Guy Barnett Gv
2 Medebourne Cl
3 Richmount Gdns

J10
1 Freshfield Cl

N1
1 Bramley Wy
2 Brompton Cl
3 Crestwood Wy
4 Nursery Gdns

N9
1 Bramble La
2 Chichester Cl
3 Hawley Cl
4 Homewood Cl
5 Langridge Ms
6 Orpwood Cl
7 Stanborough Cl
8 Stanford Cl
9 Tulip Cl
10 Walker Cl

N10
1 Markhole Cl

P9
1 Begonia Cl
2 Cyclamen Cl
3 Daffodil Cl
4 Gladioli Cl
5 Hyacinth Cl
6 Marlborough Rd
7 Woodstock Cl

Page 161

J7
1 Douglas Pl
2 Horseshoe Cl

H4
1 Gloucester Circ
2 Peyton Pl
3 Prince Of Orange La
4 Royal Pl
5 Straightsmouth

H9
1 Kings Hall Ms
2 Myron Pl
3 Rennell St
4 St Stephen's Gv
5 William Cl

H10
1 Station Rd

J10
1 Barnard Cl
2 Salix Cl

Page 162

A10
1 Bland St
2 Ealdham Sq

D10
1 Bragg Rd

Page 163

D6
1 Alexandra Ms
2 Batavia Rd
3 Clifton Rd
4 Cottesbrook St
5 Redstart Cl
6 Silver Cl
7 Tarragon Cl
8 Vansittart St
9 Woodrush Cl

D10
1 Meretone Cl

E3
1 Deptford Whf
2 Enterprize Wy
3 Kempthorne Rd
4 Tarriff Cl

E6
1 Douglas Wy
2 Exeter Wy
3 Hereford Pl
4 Railway Gv
5 Royal Naval Pl
6 Turnpike Cl

F1
1 Chandlers Av
2 Hutching's St
3 Tobago St

F2
1 Kingsbridge Ct
2 Millwall Dock Rd

F3
1 Britannia Cl
2 Copeland Dr
3 Crews St
4 Dartmoor Wk
5 Dockers Tanner Rd
6 Mast House Ter
7 Sherwood Gdns
8 Thames Cir

F4
1 Mercator Pl

F5
1 Armada St
2 Bawdale Rd
3 Caravel Ms
4 Carrick Ms
5 Frigate Ms
6 Grinling Pl
7 Lamerton St
8 Mcmillan St
9 Trevithick St

F6
1 Crossfield St
2 Ffinch St
3 New Butt La
4 Octavius St
5 Rochdale Wy
6 Speedwell St
7 Vaughan Williams Cl

F7
1 Cranbrook Rd
2 Deloraine St
3 Deptford Br
4 Deptford Broadway
5 Omega St
6 Pearson's Av
7 St Nicholas St
8 Strickland St
9 Willshaw St

F8
1 Clandon St
2 Whidborne Cl

F10
1 Greatfield Cl

G1
1 Indescon Ct

G3
1 Ambassador Sq
2 Marsh St

G5
1 Conson St
2 Haddo St
3 Norway St
4 Thornham St

G6
1 Ashburnham Retreat
2 Devonshire Dr
3 Invicta Cl
4 Kendal Cl
5 Missenden Cl
6 Nelson Cl
7 Nine Elms Cl
8 Oxford Cl
9 Radley Ct

G7
1 Burgos Gv
2 Friendly Pl
3 Orchard Hl

G8
1 Bracken Cl
2 Camilla Cl
3 Cavendish Cl
4 Chestnut Cl
5 Green Leas Cl

G9
1 Branscombe St
2 Horton St

G10
1 Dale Rd

Page 164

A10
1 Arnsberg Wy
2 Hawthorn Av

B10
1 Highland Rd
2 Mayplace Rd West
3 Sherbrooke Cl

Page 173

A3
1 Augur Cl
2 The Cygnets
3 Elmsleigh Rd
4 Eton Ct
5 Richmond Crs
6 Thames St
7 Westbrook Rd

P9
1 Ashview Cl

Page 174

A4
1 Chesterton Dr
2 Laburnum Wy
3 Milton Gdns
4 The Nightingales

G8
1 Cloister Cl

Page 175

A4
1 Brassey Cl
2 Eastleigh Wy
3 St Catherines Ct
4 Sydney Rd
5 Tyvan Cl
6 Westmacott Dr

H6
1 Charleston Ct
2 Chervil Cl
3 Heathfield Av
4 Sherringham Av

H10
1 Station Rd

J10
1 Barnard Cl
2 Salix Cl

Page 176

B8
1 Albert Rd
2 Deernurst Crs
3 Edward Cl
4 Fitz Wygram Cl
5 Radcliff Ms
6 Tudor Cl
7 Vincent Rw

E8
1 Alice Ms
2 Boucher Cl
3 Bychurch End
4 Hall Ct
5 Latimer Rd
6 Sydney Rd
7 Walpole Crs
8 Walpole Pl

E3
1 Anglesea Ms
2 Anglesea Rd
3 Ashlar Pl
4 General Gordon Pl
5 Greens End
6 Helen St
7 Masons Hl
8 Ruddstreet Cl
9 Taylor's Buildings
10 Vincent Rd
11 Willmount St

F3
1 Cheltenham Av
2 Devoncroft Gdns
3 Marsh Rd
4 Mary's Ter
5 Oak La
6 Railway Av
7 Station Yd
8 Strafford Rd

F7
1 Chatsworth Pl
2 Clavering Pl
3 Hawkesley Ct
4 Woodville St

G1
1 Normanhurst Gv

G6
1 Acland Cl

G10
1 Riefield Rd

G7
1 Birch Cl
2 Cambridge Crs
3 Christchurch Av
4 Springfield Rd
5 Westminster Cl

H3
1 Bebbington Rd
2 Gunning St
3 Hector St
4 Old Tramyard

P5
1 Adams Sq
2 Portman Cl

Page 177

A4
1 Amyand Cottages
2 Baronsfield Rd
3 Bridge Rd
4 Bridle La
5 Cumberland Cl
6 Downes Ct
7 King's Rd
8 Norfolk Cl
9 South Western Rd
10 Sussex Cl
11 Westmorland Cl

A9
1 Amyand Park Gdns
2 Chapel Rd
3 Hartington Rd
4 Marble Hl
5 Napoleon Rd

G4
1 Little Ferry Rd

G7
1 Ferrymoor
2 Rushmead

G9
1 Thamesgate Cl

G8
1 Cloister Cl

G9
1 Elmer's Dr
2 Hawkins Rd
3 Kingston La

G10
1 Bushy Park Rd
2 Harlequin Rd
3 School House La

Page 178

A4
1 Coombe La West

D4
1 Breamore Cl
2 Horndean Cl
3 Hyacinth Rd
4 Norlex V
5 Ringwood Gdns
6 Stoughton Cl

E10
1 Cottenham Cl
2 Hillview

F10
1 Durrington Av
2 Hampton Cl
3 Peregrine Wy

G5
1 Chobham Gdns
2 Queensmere Cl

G9
1 Homefield Rd
2 Wilberforce Wy

G10
1 Cumberland Cl
2 Lansdowne Cl
3 Southridge Dr
4 Thackeray Cl
5 Thaxted Pl

Page 179

H4
1 Burghley Hall Cl
2 Claudia Pl
3 Galgate Cl
4 King Charles Wk
5 Levana Cl
6 Stoford Cl

J1
1 Cavalry Gdns

J6
1 Ashdale Cl
2 Woodlands Wy
3 Woodlawn Cl

J10
1 Sherwood Rd
2 Victoria Crs

K1
1 Adelaide Rd
2 All Saints Rd
3 Cush Cottages
4 Carter's Yd
5 Chesterton Ct
6 Church Rw
7 Dutch Yd
8 Merton Rd
9 Newton's Yd
10 North Pas
11 Oakhill Pl

K10
1 Ashbourne Ter
2 Derby Rd
3 Gladstone Rd
4 Granville Rd
5 Harcourt Rd
6 Palmerston Gv
7 Palmerston Rd
8 Sir Cyril Black Wy

L1
1 Barchard St
2 Cricketers Ms
3 Lancaster Ms
4 Old York Rd
5 Ridgmount Rd
6 Shoreham Cl
7 Tonsley Pl
8 Tonsley Rd

L10
1 Dowman Cl
2 Hamilton Road Ms
3 Stane Cl

M9
1 Abingdon Cl
2 Ashbury Pl
3 Battle Cl
4 Sunlight Cl
5 Tintern Cl
6 Woburn Cl

M10
1 Norman Rd
2 Olive Rd
3 Pincott Rd

N6
1 Glentanner Wy

N7
1 Thurso St

N9
1 Burns Cl
2 Keats Cl
3 North Rd
4 Pope Cl
5 Shelley Wy
6 Waterfall Rd

P1
1 Arundel Cl

P2
1 Cobham Cl

P4
1 Burntwood Cl
2 Lyminge Gdns
3 Marham Gdns

P5
1 St Anthonys Cl
2 St Benets Cl
3 St Catherines Cl
4 St Edmunds Cl
5 St Hughes Cl
6 St Peters Cl

P8
1 Aldis Ms
2 Ivy Rd
3 Recovery St

P9
1 Daniel Cl
2 Defoe Cl
3 Marlborough Cl
4 Waterfall Ter
5 Watson Cl

P10
1 Alphea Cl
2 Holmbury Ct
3 Rutland Rd
4 Tudor Pl

Page 180

A10
1 Dovedale Ri
2 Kenmare Dr
3 North Pl
4 Shrewton Rd
5 Woodley Cl

B9
1 Freshwater Cl
2 Knapton Ms
3 St Nicholas Glebe
4 Sirdar Rd
5 Stanley Grn

C10
1 The Bungalows

D10
1 Bencroft Rd
2 Summerene Cl

E7
1 Babington Rd
2 Campbell Cl

E8
1 Gleneagle Ms
2 Gleneagle Rd
3 Keens Cl
4 Swallow Gdns

E9
1 Brunswick Ms
2 Edgington Rd
3 Potter's La
4 Rotherhill Av

E10
1 Broadview Rd
2 Drakewood Rd
3 Nettlewood Rd

F1
1 Magnolia Pl

F2
1 Bowater Cl

F3
1 Brixton Hill Pl
2 Rodmill La

F5
1 Barrhill Rd
2 Broadlands Cl
3 Goodman Crs

F6
1 Blakemore Rd
2 Brancaster Rd
3 Cherry Tree Dr
4 Moorcroft Rd

F7
1 Gleneldon Ms
2 Newcome Gdns

F9
1 Westwell Road Ap

F10
1 Rochester Cl

G2
1 Merredene St

G3
1 Saxonfield Cl
2 Wimbart Rd

G4
1 Claremont Cl
2 Huggins Pl
3 Limetree Cl
4 Presentation Ms

G5
1 Normanhurst Cl

G6
1 Leigh Orchard Cl

G7
1 Francis Barber Cl

G8
1 Beechcroft Cl

G10
1 Courtland Av
2 Hermitage La

Page 181

J4
1 Jarrett Cl

J6
1 Bloom Gv
2 Chartham Gv
3 Manor Ms
4 Hamen Rd
5 Lansdowne Wood Cl
6 Nettlefold Pl
7 Pyrmont Gv

J8
1 Holderness Wy
2 St Vincent Cl
3 Swadcote Pl

J10
1 Covington Wy

K7
1 Advance Rd
2 Currick's La
3 Dunkirk St
4 Hobbs Rd
5 Langmead St
6 Waring St
7 Windsor St
8 Windsor Gv

K10
1 Downsview Gdns
2 Founders Gdns
3 Hermitage Gdns

L10
1 Elizabeth Wy
2 Rushden Cl

M9
1 Childs La
2 New Green Pl
3 Paddock Gdns
4 Victory Pl
5 Woodland Cl

M10
1 Fox Hill Gdns

N10
1 Buckleigh Wy
2 Dargate Cl
3 Reynard Dr

P9
1 Crystal Palace
2 Station Rd

P10
1 Bargrove Cl
2 Beaver Cl
3 Brunswick Pl
4 Thicket Gv

Page 182

A6
1 Brickwood Cl
2 Hassocks Cl
3 Plane St
4 Rowland Gv

A8
1 Charleville Circ
2 The Martins
3 Thakeham Cl

A10
1 Bridgewood Cl
2 Chakenden Cl
3 Limes Av
4 St Hugh's Rd
5 Tower Cl
6 Trenholme Ter

B3
1 Bowmans Lea
2 Greystead Rd
3 Rocombe Cs
4 Talmage Cl

B6
1 Carlton Ter
2 Shrublands Cl
3 Thriftwood

B10
1 Blenheim Rd
2 Gladstone Ms
3 Heath Gv
4 Montrave Rd
5 Ospringe Cl

C10
1 Bycroft St
2 Kingsdale Rd

D10
1 Station Ap

E10
1 Bethersden Cl
2 Nettlestead Cl
3 Sellindge Cl

C10
1 Chislet Cl
2 Gainsborough Cl

G1
1 Mercy Ter

G2
1 Scrooby St

G9
1 Hanson Cl

Page 183

H10
1 Westmoat Cl

J2
1 Lullingstone La
2 Maythorne Cottages
3 St Swithun's Rd

L1
1 Falmouth Cl
2 St Peters Ct

L10
1 Belcroft Cl

M10
1 Cambridge Rd
2 Paxton Rd

N10
1 Dairy Cl

P6
1 Charlesfield
2 Chinbrook Rd
3 Dyneley Rd

Page 184

A10
1 Woodchurch Cl

C10
1 Squires Wood Dr

D10
1 Bonchester Cl

F10
1 Church Row Ms

G10
1 Bull La
2 Hollybrake Cl

Page 185

K10
1 Ockham Dr
2 Ticehurst Cl

L10
1 Dorchester Cl
2 Lullingstone Cl

P9
1 Calvert Cl

Page 190

C10
1 Bramley Cl

E2
1 Bank St
2 Bath St
3 Berkley Rd
4 Bernard St
5 Brewhouse Yd
6 Chase Sq
7 Garrick St
8 Horn Yd
9 Jury St
10 Manor Rd
11 New Swan Yd
12 Parrock St
13 Railway St
14 Wilfred St

F10
1 Codrington Gdns

Page 195

J10
1 Inglewood
2 Jersey Cl

L10
1 Douglas Rd

P10
1 Jay Av

Page 196

B10
1 Glencoe Rd
2 Oakdale St
3 Portmore Wy

C7
1 Cemetery La

C10
1 Darnley Pk
2 Dovecote Cl
3 Gascoigne Rd
4 Palace Gdns West
5 Thames St

D10
1 Meadows Leigh Cl

E10
1 Anderson Rd
2 Cross Rd
3 Grosvenor Pl
4 Mere Rd
5 Oatlands Gn
6 Victoria Cl
7 Village Cl

F10
1 Charlton Kings

C7
1 Sullivans Reach

G10
1 Sycamore Ct

Page 197

H7
1 Harvey Rd
2 Montague Cl
3 Sullivans Reach
4 Thames Mead

J1
1 The Chase
2 Laburnum Crs
3 Summer Trees

J10
1 Copenhagen Wy

K7
1 Nightingale Rd
2 Paxton Cl

L10
1 Carrow Rd
2 Marlborough Cl
3 Stamford Rd

N3
1 Augusta Cl
2 Lytcott Cl

N6
1 Brockenhurst

P4
1 Churchfields
2 St Peters Ct

Page 199

H10
1 The Oaks

J2
1 Bath Pas
2 Bishop's Hall
3 Clarence St
4 St James's Rd

K1
1 Cowleaze Rd
2 David Twigg Cl
3 Dolphin St
4 Waights Ct
5 Walter St

K6
1 Firebell Ms
2 Hazelwood Ct
3 Oak Hill Rd
4 South Bank Ter
5 Station Ap

K8
1 Dunton Cl
2 Southborough Rd (The Lane)

K10
1 Elmcroft Cl
2 Kent Wy

L1
1 Cromwell Rd
2 Elm Rd
3 Harding Cl
4 John Austin Cl
5 Queen Elizabeth Rd

L7
1 Birchington Rd
2 Iris Cl
3 Mayberry Pl
4 South Pl

L10
1 Beechcroft Rd

M10
1 Queen Mary Cl

M3
1 Franklin Cl
2 Piper Rd
3 Stapleford Cl

N8
1 Austyn Gdns
2 Oakleigh Wy

N9
1 Lansdowne Cl
2 St George's Gdns
3 Woodland Wy

P1
1 Lord Chancellor Wk

P2
1 Dickerage Rd
2 The Triangle

P3
1 Ashcombe Sq
2 Lincoln Rd
3 Rosemont Rd
4 Warwick Rd

P4
1 Nevada Cl
2 Oregon Cl
3 Virginia Cl

Page 200

B5
1 Coombefield Cl
2 Oxleigh Cl
3 Ranelagh Pl

B9
1 Barrow Hill Cl
2 The Denningtons
3 Parklands Wy
4 St Mary's Rd
5 Tamesis Gdns

C6
1 Field Pl
2 Kingswood Cl
3 Voewood Cl

C10
1 Salisbury Cl

D10
1 Dewsbury Gdns
2 Haymer Gdns

F10
1 Huntingdon Gdns
2 Shrubland Gv

G8
1 Handside Cl
2 Stanton Cl

G9
1 Andrews Cl
2 Dorking Cl
3 Edwards Cl
4 Gareth Cl

Page 201

H4
1 Cherry Cl
2 Hillside Cl
3 Northenhay Wk

H7
1 Cleveland Ri
2 Nova Ms

H8
1 Stonecot Hl

H9
1 Egham Wy
2 Westbourne Av

J10
1 Aldrich Gdns

K1
1 Charles Rd

K4
1 Goodwood Cl
2 Hatherleigh Cl
3 Queen Elizabeth Gdns
4 Queen's Pl
5 Queens Rd

K9
1 Arlington Cl
2 Minster Wy
3 Oakwood Gdns

K10
1 Bishops Cl
2 Sunnyhurst Cl

L3
1 Harland Cl

L7
1 Dore Gdns
2 Carendon Gdns

L9
1 Conifer Gdns
2 St John's Rd

L10
1 Monksdene Gdns

M5
1 Calder Rd
2 Cartmel Gdns
3 Chester Gdns
4 Langdon Wk

M6
1 Croxden Wk
2 Darley Gdns
3 Leominster Wk
4 Malling Gdns
5 Marham Gdns
6 Missenden Gdns
7 Neath Gdns

M7
1 Lovett Dr
2 Netley Gdns
3 Newhouse Wk
4 St Benet's Gv

M10
1 Chilworth Gdns
2 Stanmore Gdns

N2
1 Horner La
2 Sycamore Ms
3 Varley Wy

N4
1 Deer Park Gdns
2 Hatfield Cl
3 Rawnsley Av

N9
1 Connaught Cl
2 Whitby Gdns

P3
1 Benedict Whf
2 Blake Rd
3 Morland Rd
4 Taffy's How
5 Walnut Tree Av

P7
1 Assembly Wk
2 Neville Wk
3 Nevil Wk
4 Thornton Rd
5 Welbeck Rd

P8
1 Welbeck Rd

P9
1 Brooklyn Cl
2 Marfleet Cl
3 Seven Acres
4 Simms Cl

P10
1 Laburnum Av
2 Rushy Meadow La

Page 202

A3
1 Chatsworth Rd
2 Pear Tree Cl
3 Queen Anne's Gdns
4 Regal Cl

A5
1 Burghley Pl

A8
1 Chestnut Cl

A10
1 Highgrove Ms
2 Kynersley Cl
3 Langcroft Cl
4 Wrythe Gn

B1
1 Beaulieu Cl
2 The Driftway
3 Kennedy Cl
4 Proctor Cl
5 Summerhill Wy

B9
1 Hackbridge Park Gdns
2 Mill Cl
3 Nightingale Cl
4 Rossignol Gdns

B10
1 Elm Grove Pde
2 Vellum Dr

C10
1 Bowman's Meadow
2 Caraway Pl
3 Regal Crs
4 Wandle Side

D10
1 Berkeley Ct

E10
1 Croydon Rd
2 Gisbourne Cl

F3
1 Caernarvon Cl
2 Cranbourne Cl
3 Glamorgan Cl
4 Huntingdon Cl

F5
1 Buckingham Rd
2 Lincoln Rd
3 Southampton Gdns
4 Sussex Rd

F10
1 Archway Cl
2 Blandford Cl
3 Wandle Court Gdns
4 Windsor Gdns

G1
1 Roche Rd
2 St Helen's Crs

G2
1 Palmers Rd

G4
1 Dorset Gdns
2 Namton Dr

G7
1 Drake Rd
2 Fairmead Rd
3 Newman Rd
4 Rosedene Av

G8
1 Miller Rd

G10
1 Twickenham Cl
2 Wandle Side

Page 203

H6
1 Dunheved Cl
2 Furtherfield Cl
3 Kenmare Rd
4 Oakwood Rd
5 Sharland Cl

H10
1 Penfold Cl

J9
1 Ainsworth Rd
2 Booth Rd
3 Cairo New Rd
4 Lower Church St
5 Reeves Cnr

J10
1 Arundel Cl
2 Hanover St
3 Latimer Rd
4 Ravenswood Rd
5 St John's Rd
6 St Leonard's Rd
7 Waynflete Av

K3
1 Sandfield Pl

K7
1 Hogarth Crs
2 Hughes Wk
3 Newgate
4 Singleton Cl
5 Wilford Rd

K10
1 Halstead Cl
2 Innes Yd
3 Meadow Stile
4 Middle St
5 Robert St
6 St George's Wk

L10
1 Fairfield Pth

M4
1 Clifton Ms
2 Walter's Rd
3 Waterfield Gdns

M6
1 Bullrush Cl
2 Roden Gdns

M8
1 Alexandra Pl
2 Heron Rd
3 Jackson's Pl
4 John's Ter

M10
1 Crusader Gdns
2 Rochester Gdns
3 St Bernards
4 Willow Mt

N2
1 Sunset Gdns

N3
1 Hambledon Gdns
2 Holmesdale Cl

N5
1 Sutton Gdns

N6
1 Grindley Gdns
2 Redgrave Cl

N7
1 Amberley Gv
2 Burnham Gdns

N10
1 Anselm Cl
2 Bracewood Gdns
3 Coverdale Gdns
4 Delmey Cl
5 Lyndhurst Cl
6 Rowan Gdns

P1
1 Sycamore Gv
2 Windall Cl

P2
1 Haysleigh Gdns
2 Lakeside Cl
3 Warminster Sq

P3
1 Bradshaws Cl
2 Sunny Bank

P4
1 Brierley Cl
2 Gresham Rd
3 Grosvenor Rd
4 Portland Pl
5 St Mark's Rd

P5
1 Greenmead Cl
2 Percy Rd
3 Sidney Rd

P6
1 Akabusi Cl
2 Dickenson's Pl
3 Hardcastle Cl

P7
1 Sissinghurst Rd
2 Teevan Cl
3 Tenterden Gdns

P9
1 Ashburton Cl
2 Ashburton Gdns

Page 204

C1
1 Plawsfield Rd

C8
1 Alison Cl
2 Angelica Gdns
3 Basil Gdns
4 Betony Cl
5 Cottongrass Cl
6 Crocus Cl
7 Daffodil Cl
8 Fennel Cl
9 Kingcup Cl
10 Lupin Cl
11 Mallow Cl
12 Mistletoe Cl

F10
1 Broom Gdns
2 Douglas Dr

Page 205

L10
1 Rosslyn Cl

N1
1 Denmark Rd
2 Haxted Rd
3 Horsley Rd
4 The Old Ctyd
5 Willow Tree Wk

N10
1 Barnet Wood Rd

P4
1 Carisbrooke Rd
2 Old Homesdale Rd

Page 206

G8
1 Eccleston Cl
2 Ferndown Av
3 Pinewood Cl
4 Turnberry Wy

A10
1 Haverthwaite Rd

Page 207

C10
1 Ambrose Cl
2 Bishop Butt Cl
3 Shepherds Cl

K8
1 Mortimer Cl

M5
1 Burwash Cl
2 Copper Beech Cl
3 Roberts Cl

N4
1 Admiral Cl
2 Buttermere Rd
3 Kingfisher Cl
4 Mayfly Cl
5 Otinge Cl
6 Otters Cl
7 Palmarsh Cl
8 Richborough Cl
9 Swallowtail Cl
10 Watermint Cl
11 Yalding Cl

N10
1 Hawfield Bank

Page 215

J9
1 Grafton Cl
2 Knowle Gdns
3 Madeira Crs
4 Regency Dr
5 Thistledene

J10
1 Longridge Gv
2 Oakcroft Cl

K2
1 High Tree Cl
2 Pear Tree Cl
3 Pear Tree Rd
4 Summerfields Cl

M2
1 Bush Cl
2 Caselden Cl
3 Frenchaye
4 Garfield Rd
5 Hazeldene

Page 216

B1
1 Churchfield Rd
2 Church La
3 Curzon Cl
4 Devonshire Cl
5 Minorca Rd

Page 218

A10
1 Arnewood Cl

C10
1 Uplands Dr

Page 219

N10
1 Mynn's Cl
2 Ruthen Cl

P9
1 Hunters Cl
2 Manor House Ct
3 Mathias Cl
4 Meadow Ct

P10
1 St Theresa Cl

Page 220

A10
1 Caithness Dr
2 St Margarets Dr

B9
1 Ash Ms
2 Clayton Rd
3 Prospect Pl

B10
1 Little Orchards
2 Richmond Cl

C8
1 Dirdene Cl
2 Dirdene Gdns
3 Dirdene Gv
4 The Stanfords
5 Windmill End
6 Yeomanry Cl

C10
1 Acacia Dr
2 Aspen Wy
3 Maple Pl
4 Pine Pl
5 Poplar Dr
6 Sycamore Ri

Page 221

H10
1 Hawthorn Cl

H5
1 Church Farm La
2 Church Rd
3 Dallas Rd
4 Pond Hill Gdns
5 Springclose La

J1
1 Dale Rd
2 Elizabeth Cl
3 Ennerdale Cl
4 Frederick Cl
5 Westfield Cl

J10
1 Lower Dunnymans
2 Lower Northfield
3 Lower Sawleywood
4 Upper Dunnymans
5 Upper Sawleywood

K10
1 Ashley Dr

L4
1 Abbotsleigh Cl
2 Bonchurch Cl
3 Chanctonbury Gdns
4 Eastleigh Cl
5 Grange V
6 Upton Dene
7 Westmoreland Dr

L6
1 Bicknoller Cl
2 Porchfield Cl
3 Riverhead Dr
4 Rookley Cl
5 Station Ap
6 Yarbridge Cl

L10
1 Barn Fld
2 Orchard Cl

M2
1 Chalk Pit Rd
2 Clowser Cl
3 Goossens Cl
4 Hope Cl
5 Marlins Cl
6 Montana Gdns
7 Palmerston Rd
8 Shott Cl
9 Turnpike La
10 Warwick Rd

P2
1 Corrib Dr
2 Park Hill Cl
3 Rosefield Cl

Page 222

A4
1 Whittlebury Cl

A10
1 Tonbridge Cl

B1
1 Arcadia Cl
2 Caledon Rd
3 Devonshire Rd
4 Parkfields Cl

C10
1 June Cl

D2
1 Melbourne Rd
2 Oxford Rd
3 St Christopher's Ms
4 Spring Gdns

F10
1 Bouverie Gdns
2 Mead Dr
3 Vale Cl

Page 223

J8
1 Friends Rd
2 Hamilton Cl

J10
1 Frensham Rd

K1
1 Brafferton Rd
2 Dering Rd
3 St Andrew's Rd
4 Thanet Pl
5 West Street Pl

K10
1 Oaklands Cl
2 Purcell Cl
3 Redwood Cl

L2
1 Baines Cl
2 Bartlett St
3 Blunt Rd
4 Cliffe Rd
5 Doveton Rd
6 Heathfield Rd
7 Wilson Cl

M1
1 Caroline Cl
2 Chichele Gdns
3 Dittoncroft Cl
4 Hunters Wy
5 Spindlewood Gdns
6 Sudbury Gdns
7 Tipton Dr

Page 231

K3
1 Chipstead Ct
2 Randolph Cl
3 Tolldene Cl
4 The Withies

Page 239

H10
1 Silver Cl
2 Walnut Dr

J10
1 Acorn Gv
2 Birch Gv

Page 250

D10
1 Fielders Gn

E10
1 Whitehouse Dr

Page 257

J10
1 Duncroft Cl
2 Slipshoe St

L10
1 Church Ct
2 Church Wk

Page 280

C5
1 Albury Keep
2 Birchwood Cl
3 Brookwood
4 Cartersmead Cl
5 Collingwood Cl
6 Fairstone Cl
7 Fallowfield Wy
8 Fieldview
9 Greatlake Ct
10 Harrowsley Ct
11 Herons Wood Cl
12 Homefield Cl
13 Larksfield
14 Meadowside
15 Oatlands
16 Smithbarn Cl
17 Stockfield
18 Woodhayes

D3
1 Broadlands
2 Broadmead
3 Hayfields
4 Heatherlands
5 Hedingham Cl
6 Lambyn Cft
7 Maizecroft
8 Meridian Gv
9 Oakside Ct
10 Rylands

Page 283

H7
1 Galahad Rd
2 Guinevere Rd
3 Lancelot Cl
4 Merlin Cl
5 Stanbridge Cl

H8
1 Arnfield Cl
2 Beaumont Cl
3 Behenna Cl
4 Bitmead Cl
5 Compassion Cl
6 Dewar Cl
7 Dobbins Pl
8 Excalibur Cl
9 Garton Cl
10 Gorling Cl
11 Grier Cl
12 Strickland Cl
13 Talman Cl
14 Tunnmeade
15 Weaver Cl

H9
1 Comper Cl
2 Harmony Cl
3 Hyperion Ct
4 Lutyens Cl
5 Neptune Cl
6 Peacemaker Cl
7 Samaritan Cl
8 Saturn Cl
9 Soane Cl

H10
1 Brettingham Cl
2 Ivory Wk
3 Milne Cl
4 Oberon Wy
5 Vanbrugh Cl

J5
1 Plough Cl

K8
1 Almond Cl
2 Dairyfields
3 Rickfield
4 Ryelands
5 Windyridge

K10
1 Brideake Cl
2 Chailey Cl
3 Lulworth Cl
4 Saffron Cl
5 Samphire Cl

L7
1 Cotswold Cl
2 Ginhams Rd
3 Pennine Cl
4 Quantock Cl
5 Snell Hatch

L10
1 Bilberry Cl
2 Bluebell Cl
3 Burbeach Cl
4 Harris Cl
5 Primrose Cl
6 Stonecrop Cl

M9
1 Biggin Cl
2 Blackcap Cl
3 Crockham Cl
4 Grisedale Cl
5 Hindhead Cl
6 Patterdale Cl

M10
1 Swaledale Cl

N10
1 Caxton Cl
2 Loriners
3 Saddler Rw
4 Smith Cl
5 Wainwrights

P10
1 Gresham Wk

P6
1 Covert Cl
2 Northgate Pl
3 The Parade
4 Vanners
5 Woolborough Cl

P7
1 Parkside

Page 284

A10
1 Sherwood Wk

B8
1 Beverley Ms
2 Blackfold Rd
3 Brambletye Rd
4 Burwash Rd
5 Dedisham Cl
6 Freshfield Cl
7 Gosden Cl
8 Walesbeech

B10
1 Fontwell Rd
2 Goodwood Cl
3 Winterfold

C10
1 Charleston Ct
2 Holder Rd
3 Leonardslee Ct
4 Nymans Ct

D9
1 Atkinson Rd
2 Aveling Cl
3 Ellison Cl
4 Garrett Cl
5 Maidenbower La
6 Maidenbower Cl
7 Newman Cl
8 Raworth Cl
9 Sinclair Cl
10 Stepney Cl
11 Stokes Cl

D10
1 Baldwin Cl
2 Birchwood Cl
3 Bosham Rd
4 Emsworth Cl
5 Gibbons Cl
6 Houghton Rd
7 Ladymead Cl
8 Ruston Cl
9 Trotton Cl

E6
1 The Cackstones
2 Denmans
3 Greyhound Slip
4 Knole Cl
5 Owletts
6 The Paddock
7 Penshurst Cl
8 Shire Pde
9 Short Gallop
10 Trevanne Plat

E8
1 Albion Cl
2 Bethune Cl
3 Burdett Cl
4 Collingwood Rd
5 Mayflower Cl
6 Niven Cl
7 St Vincent Cl
8 Stuart Cl
9 Thorndyke Cl
10 Worth Wy

E10
1 Bisham Cl
2 Purley Cl
3 Wilson Cl

F4
1 Binney Ct
2 Hampden Cl
3 Wellington Cl